Contemporary Literary Criticism

Contemporary Literary Criticism

Excerpts from Criticism
of the Works of Today's
Novelists, Poets, Playwrights,
and Other Creative Writers

Dedria Bryfonski
Editor

Gale Research Company
Book Tower
Detroit, Michigan 48226

STAFF

Dedria Bryfonski, *Editor*

Laurie Lanzen Harris, *Associate Editor*
Laura A. Buch, Dennis Poupard, Jean C. Stine,
Carolyn Voldrich, *Assistant Editors*

Phyllis Carmel Mendelson, *Contributing Editor*

Sharon R. Gunton, *Production Editor*

Linda M. Pugliese, *Manuscript Coordinator*
Thomas E. Gunton, *Research Coordinator*
Emily W. Barrett, Anna H. Crabtree, Catherine E. Daligga,
Jeanne A. Gough, Tom Ligotti, Marsha R. Mackenzie,
Nancy C. Mazzara, James E. Person, Jr., *Editorial Assistants*

L. Elizabeth Hardin, *Permissions Coordinator*
Dawn L. McGinty, *Permissions Assistant*

Contents

Preface vii   **Appendix** 623

Authors Forthcoming in *CLC* ix   **Cumulative Index to Critics** 631

Cumulative Index to Authors 697

Authors in this volume:

Alice Adams 1	Roch Carrier 140	Doris Grumbach 257
Edward Albee 3	Camilo José Cela 144	Donald Hall 259
A. Alvarez 8	Arthur C. Clarke 148	James Hanley 260
Jorge Amado 10	Laurie Colwin 156	Kenneth O. Hanson 263
Kingsley Amis 12	Julio Cortázar 157	Elizabeth Hardwick 264
Jean Anouilh 16	Donald Davidson 166	Anne Hébert 266
John Arden 23	Robertson Davies 171	Anthony Hecht 269
John Ashbery 30	Nicholas Delbanco 174	Ernest Hemingway 270
Miguel Ángel Asturias 37	Don DeLillo 175	William Heyen 281
Margaret Atwood 41	W. E. B. Du Bois 180	Mary Hocking 284
James Baldwin 48	Andre Dubus 182	Daniel Hoffman 286
Donald Barthelme 54	Lawrence Durrell 184	Bohumil Hrabal 290
Ann Beattie 64	Russell Edson 190	John Irving 292
Saul Bellow 66	T. S. Eliot 191	Randall Jarrell 298
John Berryman 75	Harlan Ellison 202	Paulette Jiles 304
Adolfo Bioy Casares 83	Gavin Ewart 208	Diane Johnson 304
Elizabeth Bishop 88	Leslie A. Fiedler 211	David Jones 307
Marie-Claire Blais 96	E. M. Forster 215	Margaríta Karapánou 314
Edward Bond 98	Robert Frost 222	Anna Kavan 315
Martin Booth 103	Carlos Fuentes 231	Galway Kinnell 318
Jorge Luis Borges 104	Hugh Garner 234	Pavel Kohout 323
Joseph Brodsky 113	Penelope Gilliatt 237	Maxine Kumin 326
Ernest Buckler 118	Allen Ginsberg 239	Pär Lagerkvist 330
Anthony Burgess 123	Caroline Gordon 241	Philip Larkin 335
Stanley Burnshaw 128	Mary Gordon 249	Margaret Laurence 341
Vincent Canby 131	Henry Green 251	Ursula K. Le Guin 345
Truman Capote 132	Trevor Griffiths 255	Mario Luzi 352

Cynthia Macdonald   355

Gwendolyn MacEwen   357

Alistair MacLean   359

André Malraux   364

Ian McEwan   369

William Meredith   372

James Merrill   376

W. S. Merwin   382

Christopher Middleton   387

John Montague   390

Marianne Moore   392

Sławomir Mrożek   398

Lisel Mueller   399

Susan Musgrave   400

V. S. Naipaul   402

P. H. Newby   407

Robert Nye   412

Edna O'Brien   415

Flannery O'Connor   416

Frank O'Hara   423

Tillie Olsen   431

George Oppen   433

Joe Orton   435

Robert Pack   438

Lucio Piccolo   440

Robert Pinget   441

Bernard Pomerance   444

Katherine Anne Porter   446

Peter Porter   451

Ezra Pound   453

Reynolds Price   463

V. S. Pritchett   465

Barbara Pym   469

James Reaney   472

Ishmael Reed   476

Mordecai Richler   481

Yannis Ritsos   486

Sinclair Ross   490

Jean-Paul Sartre   498

Robin Skelton   506

C. P. Snow   508

Susan Sontag   514

Muriel Spark   519

Mickey Spillane   525

John Steinbeck   529

Emma Tennant   536

Audrey Thomas   537

D. M. Thomas   541

R. S. Thomas   542

Charles Tomlinson   545

Jean Toomer   550

John Updike   557

Ted Walker   565

Irving Wallace   567

Robert Penn Warren   570

Ngugi Wa Thiong'o   583

Evelyn Waugh   584

Glenway Wescott   590

John A. Williams   598

Jonathan Williams   600

William Carlos Williams   601

Ethel Davis Wilson   606

Charles Wright   612

Abraham B. Yehoshua   616

Yevgeni Yevtushenko   619

Preface

Literary criticism is indispensable to the layman or scholar attempting to evaluate and understand creative writing—whether his subject is one poem, one writer, one idea, one school, or a general trend in contemporary writing. Literary criticism is itself a collective term for several kinds of critical writing: criticism may be normative, descriptive, interpretive, textual, appreciative, generic. Conscientious students must consult numerous sources in order to become familiar with the criticism pertinent to their subjects.

Until now, there has been nothing resembling an ongoing encyclopedia of current literary criticism, bringing together in one series criticism of all the various kinds from widely diverse sources. *Contemporary Literary Criticism* is intended to be such a comprehensive reference work.

The Plan of the Work

Contemporary Literary Criticism presents significant passages from the published criticism of work by well-known creative writers—novelists and short story writers, poets and playwrights. Some creative writers, like James Baldwin and Paul Goodman, are probably better known for their expository work than for their fiction, and so discussion of their nonfiction is included.

Contemporary Literary Criticism is not limited to material concerning long-established authors like Eliot, Faulkner, Hemingway, and Auden, although these and other writers of similar stature are included. Attention is also given to two other groups of writers—writers of considerable public interest—about whose work criticism is hard to locate. These are the newest writers (like Bernard Pomerance, John Irving, and Fran Lebowitz) and the contributors to the well-loved but nonscholarly genres of mystery and science fiction (like Georges Simenon, Agatha Christie, Robert Heinlein, and Arthur C. Clarke).

The definition of *contemporary* is necessarily arbitrary. For purposes of selection for *CLC*, contemporary writers are those who are either now living or who have died since January 1, 1960. Contemporary criticism is more loosely defined as that written any time during the past twenty-five years or so and currently relevant to the evaluation of the writer under discussion.

Each volume of *CLC* lists about 150 authors, with an average of about five excerpts from critical articles or reviews being given for the works of each author. Altogether, there are about 750 individual excerpts in each volume taken from about 100 books and several hundred issues of some one hundred general magazines, literary reviews, and scholarly journals. Each excerpt is fully identified for the convenience of readers who may wish to consult the entire chapter, article, or review excerpted. Each volume covers writers not previously included and also provides significant new criticism pertaining to authors included in earlier volumes.

Beginning with Volume 10, *CLC* contains an appendix which lists the sources from which material has been reprinted in that volume. It does not, however, list books or periodicals merely consulted during the preparation of the volume.

A Note on Bio-Bibliographical References and Page Citations

Notes in many entries directing the user to consult *Contemporary Authors* for detailed biographical and bibliographical information refer to a series of biographical reference books published by the

Gale Research Company since 1962, which now includes detailed biographical sketches of more than 57,000 authors who have lived since 1960, many of whose careers began during the post-World War II period, or earlier.

Beginning with *CLC*, Volume 5, the method for referring to pages in the original sources has been standardized. Page numbers appear after each fragment (unless the entire essay was contained on one page). Page numbers appear in citations as well only when the editors wish to indicate, with an essay or chapter title and its *inclusive* page numbers, the scope of the original treatment.

Acknowledgments

The editors wish to thank the copyright holders of the excerpts included in this volume for their permission to use the material, and the staffs of the Detroit Public Library, Wayne State University Library, and the libraries of the University of Michigan for making their resources available to us.

Authors Forthcoming in *CLC*

With the publication of *Contemporary Literary Criticism*, Volume 12, the series has expanded its scope to encompass songwriters, filmmakers, cartoonists, screenwriters, producers, and other creative writers whose work is often evaluated from a literary perspective. These writers take their place with the novelists, poets, dramatists, and short story writers who will continue to be the primary focus of *CLC*. Volume 14 will include criticism on a number of authors not previously listed, and will also feature criticism of newer works of authors included in earlier volumes. Volume 15 will focus on filmmakers and their works.

To be Included in Volume 14

W. H. Auden (Anglo-American poet, essayist, and dramatist)

Beryl Bainbridge (British novelist, poet, and essayist) Will feature criticism on new novel, *Young Adolf*

Peter Benchley (American novelist) Will feature criticism on new work, *The Island*

Morley Callaghan (Canadian novelist) Will feature criticism on new novel, *Close to the Sun Again*

René Char (French poet)

Joan Didion (American novelist and essayist) Will feature criticism on new collection of essays, *The White Album*

Stanley Elkin (American short story writer and novelist) Will feature criticism on new novel, *The Living End*

Buchi Emecheta (Nigerian novelist) Will feature criticism on new novel, *The Joys of Motherhood*

Shusaku Endo (Japanese dramatist and novelist) Will feature criticism on new novel, *When I Whistle*

Jean Genet (French novelist, dramatist, and poet)

Robert Heinlein (American science fiction novelist and short story writer) Will feature criticism on new book, *The Notebooks of Lazarus Long*

Ted Hughes (British poet and dramatist) Will feature criticism on new collection of poetry, *Cave Birds*

David Ignatow (American poet) Will feature criticism on new collection of poetry, *Tread the Dark*

Thomas Keneally (Australian novelist) Will feature criticism on new novel, *Passenger*

Denise Levertov (American poet) Will feature criticism on new collection of poetry, *Life in the Forest*

László Nagy (Hungarian poet)

Frank O'Connor (Irish short story writer)

John Sayles (American novelist and short story writer) Will feature criticism on new collection of short stories, *The Anarchists' Convention*

Gilbert Sorrentino (American poet and novelist) Will feature criticism on new novel, *Mulligan's Stew*

May Swenson (American poet) Will feature criticism on new collection of poetry, *New and Selected Things Taking Place*

Derek Walcott (West Indian poet and dramatist) Will feature criticism on new collection of poetry, *The Star-Apple Kingdom*

Lanford Wilson (American dramatist) Will feature criticism on new play, *Talley's Folly*

Richard Wright (American short story writer and novelist)

To Be Included in Volume 15

Woody Allen (American Academy Award-winning filmmaker)

Bernardo Bertolucci (Italian poet and filmmaker) Best known for the controversial film, *Last Tango in Paris*

Tod Browning (American filmmaker) His credits include both silent and sound films, most notably horror films such as *Dracula* and *Freaks*

Luis Buñuel (Spanish filmmaker of surrealistic films)

Michael Cimino (American filmmaker) Established himself as a director with the Academy Award-winning film, *The Deer Hunter*

Jean Cocteau (French filmmaker) His technical expertise with special effects is evident in *Orphée*

Maya Deren (American filmmaker) An important figure in the avant-garde cinema

Carl Dreyer (Danish filmmaker) Emotional impact and visual beauty characterize films such as *La Passion de Jeanne d'Arc*

Federico Fellini (Italian filmmaker) Blends elements of fantasy and autobiography in his films, most notably, *8 1/2*

John Ford (American filmmaker) Has made several classic westerns, including *Stagecoach* and *The Searchers.*

Alfred Hitchcock (British-born filmmaker) Director of many classic thrillers

Elia Kazan (Turkish-born American filmmaker) Director of *East of Eden* and the Academy Award-winning *On the Waterfront*

Stanley Kubrick (American filmmaker) A pioneer in spectacular special effects

Akira Kurosawa (Japanese filmmaker) When his *Rashomon* won the Grand Prix in Venice in 1951, the West first became aware of the Japanese film industry

George Lucas (American filmmaker) Director of the immensely popular films *Star Wars* and *American Graffiti*

David and Albert Maysles (American documentary filmmakers) Their credits include clear examples of cinéma verité, such as *Grey Gardens* and *Salesman*

Ken Russell (British filmmaker) His films are flamboyant spectaculars; *Tommy* is an example

François Truffaut (French filmmaker) A leading New Wave filmmaker, Truffaut has become the prototype of the auteur by writing, directing, and sometimes acting in his own films.

Lina Wertmuller (Italian filmmaker) Her films, for example, *Swept Away,* often involve themes of sexual stereotyping and struggles for supremacy

A

ADAMS, Alice 1926-

Adams is an American novelist and short story writer. Her fiction is characterized by its spare, clean prose and its focus on the emotional life of her protagonists. (See also *CLC*, Vol. 6.)

JANE LARKIN CRAIN

[Alice Adams's] widely acclaimed "Families and Survivors" succeeded chiefly as high soap opera that chronicled an avalanche of marital castastrophe overtaking its upper-middle-class cast of characters as the hidebound 50's gave way to the "liberated" decade that followed. . . .

[In] "Listening to Billie," the author, still pretty much preoccupied with moneyed cosmopolitan types, narrows her cultural perspective somewhat, to focus on two women, half-sisters, whose separate fates are meant to embody specific contemporary ordeals and options of their sex. (p. 15)

Powered by the author's cool, spare prose, this novel creates beautiful surfaces—tableaux composed of sleek creatures perfectly arranged in elegant rooms, romantic, exquisitely detailed landscapes—that have an almost tactile appeal for the reader, like fine wood and fabric. The seedier side is reproduced with equal vividness: the neurotic intimacy of women thrown together in dull, workaday routines, tawdry city scapes in rundown neighborhoods, the suffocating vacuity that sometimes masquerades as the good life behind impeccable suburban facades.

But even as one is drawn into these various and well-wrought surroundings, a curious lifelessness abounds; despite the passionate dramas one is *told* are everywhere unfolding—the plot involves suicide, divorce, the making of fortunes, heartbreak, travail of every sort—"Listening to Billie," is an emotionally unevocative book.

Is this, one wonders, because the narrator is running away from the dangers of melodrama? No, as it turns out, more than excessive narrative control is involved in the great distance the reader feels from the novel's action. Only rarely do any of the characters' reactions seem rooted in the scene at hand and not in a schematic sense of things fixed in the mind of the author. Eventually, it becomes clear that a falsification of reality is under way here, a falsification that ostensibly hails and champions brave new turning points in the life of the contemporary woman, but which actually winds up minimizing and trivializing her.

Thus Daria, whom Eliza is pleased to call at the novel's close "a kind of heroine," is in fact from beginning to end a bizarrely motiveless creation, and one must have reference to categories altogether outside the novel in an effort to fathom her. Really, what is one to make of a character who is granted heroic stature for giving her (despised) husband's money away to the United Farm Workers? Or of a financially independent Eliza, who wins a pat on the head from the narrator when she is at last able to hug herself for being a writer? Is woman no more than this?

Although the profusion of "mad housewife" novels spawned by women's-liberation rhetoric seems, blessedly, to be waning, a new genre of woman's novel appears to be emerging. Like Eliza, the heroines of such novels eventually find "fulfillment" in a kind of sanctified selfishness, with a total devotion to the self and its "needs" held up as salvatory. Not surprisingly, such arid and circumscribed notions result in less than resonant fiction. One feels that ideology is doing its dirty work throughout Miss Adams's novel and that it ultimately succeeds in banishing genuine feeling from its pages.

Ironically, the author alludes in her title to a woman who, at certain boozy 3-o'clock-in-the-mornings, seems unmistakably to be singing of women's timeless sorrows and joys. How odd that Miss Adams should have chosen Billie Holiday, the real thing, as an emblem of this book's bloodless ups and downs. (pp. 15, 37)

> Jane Larkin Crain, "Sanctified Selfishness," in
> The New York Times Book Review (© 1978 by
> The New York Times Company; reprinted by permission), February 26, 1978, pp. 15, 37.

KATHA POLLITT

Alice Adams's clean, spare prose and subtle choice of details make *Listening to Billie* a pleasure to read. She has, moreover, a rare sympathy for almost all her characters: Even Daria's sexist, Nixonite husband is generously portrayed. At the center of the novel, though, Eliza herself is curiously unfocused. Although we are told that she "pursued intensity with lemminglike directness," she seems on the contrary a woman of considerable emotional guardedness. Although she sleeps with many men, she falls in love with only two, and then only briefly; and when one of these men is unfaithful, she throws him out with admirable pres-

1

ence of mind (no lemminglike self-destructive urges there!) and lets what seem to me rather fancy hesitations keep her from marrying the other. Eliza is likable and mature but as self-contained as a cat—the antithesis of the passionate, reckless singer she so deeply admires. (p. 31)

Katha Pollitt, in Saturday Review (© 1978 by Saturday Review Magazine Corp.; reprinted with permission), March 4, 1978.

KATHA POLLITT

The typical Alice Adams short story [in "Beautiful Girl"] announces itself in the very first sentence as a thing of edgy wit and compressed narrative power. . . .

What blossoms from such packed beginnings can be a marvel of delicacy. . . .

[Admirers of Miss Adams's novels] will feel at home in her first collections of stories, for all but two of the stories are set on familiar Adams turf: the South with its aging good ole boys and fading belles, San Francisco with its wistful hippies and well-heeled sophisticates. Familiar, too, is the tenderness that Miss Adams bestows on the worlds she evokes. . . . (p. 14)

Miss Adams writes with a seductive grace that burnishes even a slight tale such as "Winter Rain," a reminiscence of a student year in Paris and the formidable, quintessentially French widow in whose luxurious flat the narrator boarded for an outrageous sum. She is a consummately pleasing writer. Is it churlish of me to wish that she had given her gifts more of a workout, strained more against her limits? Too many of these stories are about a certain type of woman: She is married to someone prosperous, a little stolid, and not much in evidence; she has an independent income or a little part-time job, and no serious interests; she is romantic, prone to love at first sight, and she establishes her claim to sensitivity to rereading Jane Austen every summer, up at her place in the country. I kept waiting for Miss Adams to flash an ironic smile toward these supremely sheltered, idle, unexamined people, like the narrator of "Attrition," who sees portents of doom for Western civilization in the prospect of another middle-aged couple moving to Israel, in a few weeks of drought, in the theft of her purse at a dinner party. She never does.

Perhaps because she is used to the larger scope of the novel, Miss Adams seems sometimes to underestimate the possibilities of the short-story form. While deft and careful . . . her stories do not always dig deep enough into their subject to satisfy the interest their craftsmanship arouses. In "Gift of Grass" we see teen-age Cathy at a session with her unsympathetic and mercenary psychiatrist, then we follow her to Golden Gate Park, where she stretches out on the grass with a joint and waits "for the melting of her despair." Now, we think, we'll find out what goes on inside her head —what is she thinking, fantasizing, remembering, wishing? Instead of telling us, Miss Adams just has her fall asleep. Of course, we know in a general sort of way what's bothering Cathy, but that's not because she's a vivid fictional character, it's because she's a recognizable type. (pp. 14, 27)

What Miss Adams can do when she sets herself a real imaginative challenge is brilliantly demonstrated in "Verlie I Say Unto You," the first of three stories about a Southern family, the Todds. Verlie is the Todd's maid, in the 1930's, and her story is both a moving narrative of her difficult life

and a sharp-eyed depiction of her employers. There is plenty of real grist for Miss Adams's powers of observation in the Todd's leisurely, "enlightened" racism.

The everyday unhappiness of the Todds—he philanders in a kind of awful, technically chaste Fugitive-poet sort of a way; she is lonely and puzzled by the meagerness of her life —stands in stark contrast to Verlie's passionate and tragic love affair with the gardener, which takes place before the Todds' unseeing eyes. Of the many sorrows produced by racism, Miss Adams seems to be saying, the most profound is the mutual loneliness it creates between black and white: Jessica Todd and Verlie, who should be able to comfort each other, are unable to acknowledge their griefs to each other. Theirs is a story that gathers meaning with each reading, and one that makes me hope Miss Adams's next collection will contain many stories as ambitious and as hard-won. (p. 27)

Katha Pollitt, "Good Ole Boys and Wistful Hippies," in The New York Times Book Review (© 1979 by The New York Times Company; reprinted by permission), January 14, 1979, pp. 14, 27.

SUSAN WOOD

No other writer in recent memory has called to mind quite so clearly the work of F. Scott Fitzgerald, both in style and subject matter, as Alice Adams does in [the short stories in *Beautiful Girl*]. But to say that her work resembles Fitzgerald's—a resemblance that was apparent in her novels, *Careless Love, Families and Survivors* and *Listening to Billie*—is not to suggest that Adams is some sort of second-rate imitator. Like all writers of any significance, she knows her past, her inheritance, and has learned how to use it in her own time and place; it is a matter of carrying on and extending a particular tradition. . . .

Like Fitzgerald, [Alice Adams] has a fine satiric eye softened by a tenderness toward human desire and frailty. The first three stories in the book introduce us to the Todds, carrying us through a period of 35 years in their lives. "Verlie I Say Unto You," surely one of the finest of these fine stories, shows both the inadequacy of the Todds' response to their black housekeeper's grief at the death of her lover and Jessica Todd's dim awareness of her feeling of kinship with sorrowing Verlie. All three of the Todd stories, in fact, satirize the family . . . while at the same time gently reminding us how we are all caught in the human predicament of loss. Part of their power to move us lies in Adams' ability to sustain a delicate tension between ideas of free will and circumstance, of how we choose and are chosen.

A great deal of a writer's success is related to the strength of his "voice"; it is a difficult factor to define, impossible to identify by quotation because its essence is continuous and cumulative. In Alice Adams' case the voice of her prose gives a certain tone and pitch to her sentences, a certain richness and fullness of style that has to do with the warmth she feels toward the people she writes about.

It is refreshing and hopeful to find a writer in this day and time who, although recognizing love's possibilities for destruction, can still write about the ways in which love, both sexual and platonic, is akin to salvation.

Susan Wood, "Stories of Loss and Love," in Book World—The Washington Post (© 1979, The Washington Post), January 21, 1979, p. G3.

JANET DOMOWITZ

If [Edna] O'Brien is the bold red heart of the Valentine, then Adams is the lacy edging. Distance and time help these characters [in *Beautiful Girl*] sort out the delicate significance of love's mysterious hold on them. These are very private dramas: a jealous husband, a girl confused by her parents' marriages, or a woman insecure after an apartment break-in—all keep silent about it.

Adams concentrates on emotions so poignant they are almost beyond words of expression. (p. B6)

> *Janet Domowitz, in* The Christian Science Monitor *(reprinted by permission from* The Christian Science Monitor; © 1979 by The Christian Science Publishing Society; all rights reserved), February 12, 1979.*

*   *   *

ALBEE, Edward   1928-

Albee is an American dramatist whose best plays rank among the finest in contemporary theater. The problem of human communication in a world of increasing callousness is a recurrent concern in his works, notably *The Zoo Story, The American Dream,* and *Who's Afraid of Virginia Woolf?* Albee's plays are noted for their powerful language and reveal a fine sense of dramatic tension. He was twice the recipient of the Pulitzer Prize in Drama and has also written fiction and poetry. (See also *CLC,* Vols. 1, 2, 3, 5, 9, 11, and *Contemporary Authors,* Vols. 5-8, rev. ed.)

ROSE A. ZIMBARDO

Somewhat startling is the realization that Albee's are traditional Christian symbols which, despite their modern dress, retain their original significance—or, more precisely, express their original significance in modern terms. The relationship between traditional symbol and naturalistic dialogue, situation and setting is, however, never forced, as it so often is in, say, a Williams' play. (p. 45)

What Albee has written in *The Zoo Story* is a modern Morality play. The theme is the centuries old one of human isolation and salvation through sacrifice. Man in his natural state is alone, a prisoner of Self. If he succumbs to fear he enforces his isolation in denying it. Pretending that he is not alone, he surrounds himself with things and ideas that bolster the barrier between himself and all other creatures. The good man first takes stock of himself. Once he has understood his condition, realized his animality and the limitations imposed upon him by Self, he is driven to prove his kinship with all other things and creatures, "with a bed, with a cockroach, with a mirror. . . ." (The progression that Jerry describes is Platonic.) In proving this kinship he is extending his boundaries, defying Self, proving his humanity, since the kinship of all nature can be recognized only by the animal who has within him a spark of divinity. He finds at last, if he has been completely truthful in his search, that the only way in which he can smash the walls of his isolation and reach his fellow creatures is by an act of love, a sacrifice, so great that it altogether destroys the self that imprisons him, that it kills him. Albee, in recreating this theme, has used a pattern of symbolism that is an immensely expanded allusion to the story of Christ's sacrifice. But the symbolism is not outside of the story which he has to tell, which is the story of *modern* man and *his* isolation and hope for salvation. He uses the allusion to support his

own story. He has chosen traditional Christian symbols, I think, not because they are tricky attention-getters, but because the sacrifice of Christ is perhaps the most effective way that the story has been told in the past. (p. 53)

> *Rose A. Zimbardo, "Symbolism and Naturalism in Edward Albee's 'The Zoo Story'," in* Twentieth Century Literature *(copyright 1962, Hofstra University Press), April, 1962 (and reprinted in* Edward Albee: A Collection of Critical Essays, *edited by C.W.E. Bigsby, Prentice-Hall, Inc., 1975, pp. 45-53).*

HENRY HEWES

Just as Mr. Albee used the name Nick in *Who's Afraid of Virginia Woolf?* to suggest that the character was related to Nikita Khrushchev and was therefore an exponent of a totalitarian society, so he occasionally enriches moments in *Tiny Alice* with verbal puzzles. For instance, Julian will paraphrase the words of Jesus, but to interpret Julian as Jesus would be carrying the analogy further than the author intended. On a more realistic level, the playwright reminds us that most religious people relate themselves to Christ in their hallucinations. And he also believes that Julian is like many religiously dedicated people in being subconsciously motivated by sexual repression. (pp. 100-01)

[The] ending may seem more negative than was intended. . . . [The] sound of heartbeats and heavy breathing as the doors open have been widely misinterpreted as being those of an increasingly terrified Julian, whereas they are meant to belong to whatever comes through the door. . . . While the author intended the ending to be terrifying, he also wished to leave the audience with two possibilities for Julian: total hallucination or the personification of the abstraction. (pp. 101-02)

[The] playwright wishes the audience would come to *Tiny Alice* with fewer preconceptions, to experience the play as we experience music. "If you are not a trained musician," he says, "you intuit the structure of the piece by osmosis." Thus, as an author, he is most concerned with construction and with getting the play's musical rhythms right, and he is convinced that if he does this honestly and well, people will respond to the play even if they are confused about it or dislike what they think it says. "What matters is not whether the play coincides with how a critic thinks it should be written, or what a critic thinks of what it says," argues Mr. Albee. "What a critic should tell his reader is how effectively he thinks the play has said whatever it chooses to say." . . .

[I wonder] if Mr. Albee would have been pleased if someone had called *Tiny Alice* "a play that unfolds with great skill, whatever the hell it is choosing to say." (p. 105)

> *Henry Hewes, "The 'Tiny Alice' Caper," in* Saturday Review *(© 1965 by Saturday Review Inc.; reprinted with permission), January 30, 1965 (and reprinted in* Edward Albee: A Collection of Critical Essays, *edited by C.W.E. Bigsby, Prentice-Hall, Inc., 1975, pp. 99-104).*

JOHN SIMON

Albee is progressing. *Who's Afraid of Virginia Woolf?* was about the emptiness that surrounds and threatens to swallow our relationships; *Tiny Alice* was about the void lurking behind our deepest beliefs; now, *A Delicate Balance* is about the nothingness, the bare nothingness of it all—it is a play about nothing. . . . [The] nothingness—perhaps more accurately *nothingness*—of Albee's play is petty, self-indulgent, stationary. Albee's nothing is as dull as anything. (p. 96)

I am tired of this mythical "meaningless world" when the playwright fails to create or suggest any outer world (one isolated reference to income taxes might as well have been to Chinese calligraphy), and when he neglects to indicate what meaningfulness might have been before it got mislaid. This posturing play abounds in the cocktail-party profundities and family-reunion soundings that bloated up Eliot's drama, but at least Eliot was, however flatfootedly, after some sort of myth or metaphysic. (pp. 97-8)

Albee is in love with language, which sets him above your average playwright who does not even realize that language exists, but, for all that, Albee's love affair is sadly one-sided. . . .

But there is a much more profound insensitivity to language at work here, and the more painful since Albee (as he did in *Tiny Alice*) has one of his characters apologize for his alleged articulateness. But Albee's "articulateness" is either self-conscious poeticism, "When the daylight comes, comes order with it," or long, syntactically overburdened sentences and paragraphs, or putative shockers. . . . (p. 98)

What, one wonders, was the real motive behind *A Delicate Balance?* I, for one, still believe in Albee's perceptiveness and even in his talent (he did, after all, write *The Zoo Story* and *Virginia Woolf*); why would he hurtle into such utter pointlessness? It occurs to me that, at least since *Virginia Woolf*, Albee's plays and adaptations have been viewed by many as dealing overtly or covertly with homosexual matters; Albee may have resolved here to write a play reeking with heterosexuality. (p. 99)

John Simon, "'A Delicate Balance'" (1966-67), in his Uneasy Stages: A Chronicle of the New York Theater, 1963-1973 *(copyright © 1975 by John Simon; reprinted by permission of Random House, Inc.), Random House, 1975, pp. 96-9.*

JOHN SIMON

Edward Albee's *All Over* is about the dying of some unnamed and unclassified great man behind a screen in his living room, while in front of the screen his wife, mistress, son, daughter, lawyer, doctor and nurse talk, wrangle, and have an occasional tantrum. The play is so eventless, pointless, and, above all, lifeless that it could actually have been improved by being turned around on its axis. Then, at least, we could have witnessed some hemorrhages, bladder discharges, oscultations, injections, perhaps a death rattle—none of them my idea of drama, but all positively enlivening compared to what we do get.

The anonymous characters this side of the screen, i.e., the supposedly living, have, with the possible exception of the mistress, no more personality than they have names. (pp. 323-24)

The play, I repeat, is about nothing. There is no plot, no problem, no conflict, no character. The dramatis personae are a set of attitudes, and their talk is made up mostly of digressions: about parents and grandparents, gardens and travels, dreams and childhood recollections. And when one of these humanoid nebulae launches on yet another irrele-

vant reminiscence of an even hazier ancestor, it is like watching a gas being superseded by a vacuum. That leaves language. But language (as opposed to snide or lacerating repartee) is what Albee has always been deficient in—and I don't mean anything as simple as incorrect usage, though there is that too, as when "verbal" is used in the sense of "oral." I mean that this language huffs and puffs and bloats itself up to be poetic, doubles up and contorts itself out of any resemblance to human syntax in order to be distinctive, and sounds in one character's mouth almost exactly as in another's. (p. 324)

Having in his last few plays thoroughly de-dramatized life, Albee now succeeds in taking the dramatic sting out of death. If *All Over* is anything, it is an argument for euthanasia: had the unseen hero been put to sleep before the writing of the play, the audience would not have been put to sleep—or to the torture—for two hours. (p. 325)

John Simon, "'All Over'" (1971), in his: Uneasy Stages: A Chronicle of the New York Theater, 1963-1973 *(copyright © 1975 by John Simon; reprinted by permission of Random House, Inc.), Random House, 1975, pp. 323-26.*

C.W.E. BIGSBY

Few playwrights can have been so frequently and mischievously misunderstood, misrepresented, overpraised, denigrated, and precipitately dismissed [as Edward Albee]. Canonized after the performance of his first play, *The Zoo Story* [produced Off-Broadway], he found himself in swift succession billed as America's most promising playwright, leading dramatist, and then, with astonishing suddenness, a "one-hit" writer with nothing to his credit but an ersatz masterpiece patched together from the achievements of other writers. The progression was essentially that suggested by George in *Who's Afraid of Virginia Woolf?*, "better, best, bested." (p. 1)

To read the bulk of criticism that Albee's work has inspired is to discover the depths to which abstruse pedantry and the Ph.D. industry can go. And, worse still, a number of sizable red-herrings have been dragged across the path of audience and reader alike by those who wish to see his work as an expression of a particular dramatic movement or pathological condition. (p. 2)

There is no doubt that the Broadway production of *Who's Afraid of Virginia Woolf?* provided the basis for Albee's amazing popular reputation; less obviously, but equally certainly, it was also the primary reason for the suspicion with which some reviewers and critics approached his work. For there was a sense in which the move to Broadway seemed a betrayal of the nascent values of Off-Broadway—a confession that he was a mere entertainer with a talent for simulating seriousness. . . . Yet *Who's Afraid of Virginia Woolf?* is by no means conventional Broadway fare. The single claustrophobic set, the excoriating language, the disconcerting emotional and theatrical power, were remote from the usually bland products of the Great White Way. And Albee's decision to use some of the profits from the production to encourage new American dramatists merely underlined his continuing concern with experiment.

The success of *Who's Afraid of Virginia Woolf?* established Albee's reputation around the world, and the curious assaults on the play as epitomizing some presumed decadence either in the state of the American theatre or in his personal sensibility only served to promote considerable interest in him by the media. He became a public figure, . . . in other words, the Famous American Playwright, whom he had satirized in an early sketch. And now, public and reviewers alike expected him to repeat his early success. His failure to do so lead to a curious sense of betrayal in the minds of some people, as the man singled out to take on the burden formerly carried by O'Neill, Miller, and Williams began an apparently eccentric series of experiments which seemed ill-adapted to one now widely regarded as a Broadway writer. The truth was that Albee has remained at heart a product of Off-Broadway, claiming the same freedom to experiment and, indeed, fail, which is the special strength of that theatre. The difficulty is that he continues to offer his plays to a Broadway audience who, even given their tolerance for anything which can be officially ratified as "art," find his refusal to repeat the formula of *Who's Afraid of Virginia Woolf?* increasingly perverse. The animus directed at Albee in recent years thus comes, at least in part, from his failure to realize expectations formed by his first Broadway success as well as, partly, from genuine failures of craft and slackness of artistic control.

What he in fact chose to do was to alternate new works of his own with adaptations of the work of Carson McCullers, James Purdy, and Giles Cooper respectively. But while the choice of these particular works (*The Ballad of the Sad Café, Malcolm, Everything in the Garden*) was entirely explicable in terms of his own thematic concerns, the decision to lend his talents to such a project was not. He had early voiced a suspicion of the whole process of adaptation which has, unfortunately, proved more than justified by his own efforts in that direction. (pp. 4-6)

His original plays tell a different story. Though all of them are, I think, flawed in some important respect, they offer clear evidence of Albee's commitment to extending his range as a writer. They stand as proof of his fascination with the nature of theatricality and of his determination to trace those social and psychological concerns which have provided the focus for so much American drama to their root in metaphysical anguish. . . . If he is to be regarded as a social critic, as a number of writers have suggested, then he is what he himself has described as "a demonic social critic," intent on establishing the connection between a collapse of social structure and the failure of nerve on an individual level. And though his work has revealed a considerable stylistic diversity, it is legitimate to talk of his central concerns in this way, for thematically there is a unity to his work which links his first Off-Broadway play to his latest Broadway offering.

His heroes have all failed in some fundamental way. They have betrayed the values to which, even now, they are capable of pledging a belated allegiance. They are liberal humanists who have allowed themselves to become detached from a reality which disturbs them and hence from those individuals who are the expression of their commitment to a vision of private and public responsibility. They have sold out; not for wealth or success, but for an untroubled existence—to preserve their own innocence. Unwilling to recognize that pain is a natural corollary of a free existence, they have blunted their moral convictions with alcohol and a sterile intellectualism, as George has done in *Who's Afraid of Virginia Woolf?;* or they have embraced the spurious consolation offered by religious determinism,

as Julian has done in *Tiny Alice;* or they have simply permitted the slow disintegration of human responsibilities, as Tobias has done in *A Delicate Balance*. The consequence of such a drift toward moral extinction is clear enough in the apocalyptic imagery of *Who's Afraid of Virginia Woolf?, Box, Quotations from Chairman Mao Tse-Tung,* and *All Over*. The action of the first of these takes place in a town which is pointedly called New Carthage and which is likened to two other cities destroyed by their hedonism and capitalist frenzy, Penguin Island and Gomorrah. The action of the last is concerned with the final collapse of structure in the moment of death.

Albee's work is characterized by an overwhelming sense of loss which, though doubtless rooted in the details of his own painful childhood, becomes an image, firstly, of the loss by America of the principles which had been invoked by its founders, and, secondly, of the inevitable process of deprivation which is the basis of individual existence. The problem which he sets himself is that of formulating a response to this sense of loss which involves neither a self-pitying despair nor capitulation to those facile illusions endorsed by Madison Avenue, the Church, or simply the conventional wisdom of contemporary society. The solution which he advances is essentially a New Testament compassion, a liberal commitment to the Other. That is to say, he attacks a social system which fails in its primary duty of creating a communal responsibility and presents characters who must strip themselves of all pretense if they are to survive as autonomous individuals and accept their responsibility toward other people.

Albee's work is a prophecy and a warning. Nor should the splendid articulateness of the dialogue or the brilliant wit, which is a mark of so many of his plays, be seen as detracting from the seriousness of his diagnosis. For they are themselves a part of the evidence—the means deployed by a sophisticated society to evade the pain of real communication and the menace of a world slipping towards dissolution. (pp. 6-8)

Albee has brought to the theatre not merely a magnificent command of language, a control of rhythm and tone which has never been rivaled in America, but also a sensitivity to dramatic tradition and particularly to the achievements of European dramatists, which gives his work a dimension all too often lacking in American writers. . . . [Though] one can indeed detect in his work elements of Ionesco's style, Strindberg's obsessive misogyny, Eliot's suburban metaphysics, and Miller's liberal *angst,* this is to say no more than that Albee has shown an awareness of the achievement of other writers and a commitment to examining the nature of theatrical experiment. It is surely as much a mistake to regard *Who's Afraid of Virginia Woolf?* as simply a modern version of Strindberg's *A Dance of Death* as it is to see *Tiny Alice* as only a transcribed version of *The Cocktail Party*. The Influence is there; the voice is Albee's. The gulf between eclecticism and impersonation is the gulf between honesty and fraud, a receptive imagination and an impoverished sensibility. The Byzantine complexity of *Tiny Alice,* the fascinating blend of strict structure and free form in *Quotations from Chairman Mao Tse-Tung,* and even the misguided attempt to adapt the "surreal" imagination of James Purdy all provide evidence of his refusal to limit his talent or to accept conventional notions of theatrical propriety. If Albee is not what he seemed when he first burst upon the scene at the beginning of the sixties, if he was never the absurdist he was taken to be nor the man summoned to redeem Broadway, he was in some ways much more. He was a serious artist with the courage to refuse the blandishments of the commercial theatre. He was a writer who offered genuine gifts, including a mastery of words, a musician's sense of rhythmic structure, an undeniable ability to create dramatic metaphors of compelling power, and, most important of all, a stunning integrity which permits no compromise with his artistic objectives. If this latter has at times led him into misjudgments on a considerable scale, it is also the guarantee that Albee will remain, not merely a dramatist of international reputation, but also, and in ways which early reviewers could not really appreciate, one of the mainstays of American drama over the next decade. (pp. 8-9)

> *C.W.E. Bigsby, in his introduction to* Edward Albee: A Collection of Critical Essays, *edited by C.W.E. Bigsby (copyright © 1975 by Prentice-Hall, Inc.; reprinted by permission of Prentice-Hall, Inc., Englewood Cliffs, New Jersey), Prentice-Hall, 1975, pp. 1-9.*

RACHEL BLAU DUPLESSIS

Albee transforms social "problems" for which no solution is offered into sexual and family strife, problems for which he has readily available solutions. . . .

Two prominent problems resolved by the ending of *Virginia Woolf* concern the bitch goddess, who is tamed, and the non-existent child, who is "killed." Martha is a brilliantly constructed and dramatically sufficient portrait of the stereotypical emasculating woman. The missing male child is doubly non-existent, for he is first imaginary and at the end of the play he is also dead. It is no secret that parent-child and husband-wife relationships figure importantly in Albee's world, although Albee is squeamish about recognizing this. In fact, many relationships in his plays that do not specifically conform to family models can be assimilated to them. (p. 134)

Who's Afraid of Virginia Woolf ends with a now familiar tableau of an American first family and an Albeean primal family, a tableau which reveals Martha's essential insecurity and dependence on George, and George's control and dominance of their relationship and her needs. The problems in the play are the failure of the man and the bitchiness of the woman. The problems—henpecked man, nagging wife—are constructed in stereotypes; the solutions too are envisaged in stereotypes, when George is shown to be basically stronger, smarter and more resiliant than the promiscuous and pugnacious Martha. George is returned to his position of mastery and dominance over the newly subordinate, dependent woman by "exocising" (Albee's word) all challengers and rivals to this central couple: Martha's Daddy, the college president; the couple's son, who exists by and for the *coup de theatre* built around him; and Nick, who functions as a rival in university workplace and as a substitute Oedipal son in Martha's dramatic affections.

The men's social function, according to the stereotypes which function at the play's end, is to be a "success," which really means to be emotionally alert and sexually potent. The woman's social function is to engage in reproduction and/or non-productive work. Both Honey and Martha had distorted these terms, by engaging in non-produc-

tive reproduction—that is, by not having children or by having a false child. The women are also supposed to help husbands be "successes" and to remain tempting and non-threatening subordinate partners in marriage. The re-establishment of these norms, banal but potent in their familiarity, is the play's object. (pp. 134-35)

[Given George's] wit and intelligence, why is he a failure? Why must we assume that wit and intelligence are associated with failure? What stopped George from "playing the game" of success—considering that he loves to play other games with Martha? . . . No answer is worked out within the play. We are faced with a full-blown and definitive problem, George's failure, for which there is no explanation, and whose source lies entirely out of the actions of the play. The lack of fit between problem and explanation is one place to insert a critical wedge, pry open, and see what is revealed.

Albee accounts for George's failure by noting, once, his "high moral sense" which "would even let him *try* to better himself." . . . For the weight the play puts on George's failure, this is a meager explanation, which itself hides an unexamined social law: that only low and unprincipled people win. More importantly, this "high moral sense" is not entirely ratified by the exhibition of George's malice, bitterness and nastiness in the course of the play.

A second reason Albee offers for George's failure is more promising. Daddy had prevented George from publishing an autobiographical account of a family trauma about a boy who accidentally kills both his parents. . . . We must accept that George's major scholarship *as a historian* lies in autobiography, as if the killing of parents were a historical issue. . . . It is striking that the man's major *work* in career terms is about family relations. This is, of course, deeply and hurtfully comic, but it reveals a significant pattern in Albee's world view. Nick's major work in biology is likewise "about" sex and children. This transposition from the professional world to sex and the family is further repeated in the dialogue between George and Nick, in which there is a constant shift of topic *from* science, technology, the university, genetic regulation—topics of public and career import *to* sex, women, children, and Daddy—topics of private and personal import. As we will see, throughout the play Albee takes questions of power, work, failure and success and privatizes them—giving them status and value exclusively as family issues.

Albee's women conform to the stereotypical notions of women's place: that women take care of home and children (imaginary or not) while the men take care of the rest of the world. . . . Mother, courtesan, consumer, sex object, wife, cook, volunteer, semi-professional, hostess—these are the dependent social roles Albee's women play. Why then are they accused of emasculating Albee's men?

Because none of his women ever tries to enter the "male" worlds outside the home . . . one cannot say they are emasculating because they intrude. However, they do consider whether or not the men succeed in their proper sphere. They notice and comment on the men's failure to hold up their half of the bargain, insistently remarking that the men are flops. The women are verbally abusive to the men precisely because the men do not succeed in the same stereotypical terms as do the women. So the women fail to conform to the sex role stereotypes only in their refusal to be silent about the already on-going failures of their men. They do not cause these failures; they accentuate them. (pp. 135-37)

Yet at the end of *Who's Afraid of Virginia Woolf?* the humiliated, weak, unsuccessful man is shown to be stronger than the brutal, emasculating woman. The family problems are solved, not by investigating their ultimate source, which lies outside the home, but by regulating family relations in a highly normative manner. George gains control over Martha by ridding the central family of all intruders and rivals to his power. . . .

[The] male child is killed because he is too tempting to his mother—imaginatively tempting in *Virginia Woolf* and sexually tempting in *American Dream.* A powerful mother-son team disrupts the proper order of the family. . . . The reasons that would lead to the murder or multilation of the younger male rival are not investigated. Rather, Albee assumes them. (p. 137)

In the conclusion, George replaces the Daddy above him, subordinates the wife-child, and successfully fights a rearguard action against his own replacement by the son(s) below. This reversal is constructed by Albee's taking questions of power, work, failure or success and privatizing them, making social issues appear exclusively *as* family issues, and solving them *as if they were* family issues. For this, the woman functions as a scapegoat.

What then is the fundamental contradiction in Albee's family plays? On one side, there is the idea that problems and clashes found in the family actually originate in the family and can be solved in the family. On the opposing side is the idea that problems and clashes expressed by the family originate outside the family and can be solved only by turning to these origins. Albee wants to put forward the first idea: his resolution and the audience's admiration alike are based on it. Yet strong indications of the second idea can be found in his work. (p. 138)

[Outside problems in *Virginia Woolf*] are work, careerism, science, the fall of the West; even—and Albee *is* reasonably serious—the problem of power politics which he feels is personified by Nikita Khrushchev. ("Nick is very much like the gentleman who used to run the Soviet Union": Albee.) The problems cited in the play are a mixed bag of undigested bits, but their very confusion is significant. . . . Albee is not clear where the problems lie, what to call them, or how to organize them, but Nick as a character does *represent* them. And there is no dialogue between George and the problems Nick represents. The scenes between them consist of sportly monologues by George. Albee gives Nick no rebuttals.

As a problem from the outside, Nick resembles the friends, Edna and Harry, in *A Delicate Balance* . . . , who have a vague terror and creep into the play's major family, accentuating its dislocations. The play asks what is to be done with them. The beginning of the resolution in *Delicate Balance,* as in *Virginia Woolf,* requires masculine dominance. (pp. 138-39)

At the climax of the play, Tobias performs a difficult aria that perfectly expresses the contradictory position of the family in Albee: either as the source of, and the cure for problems, or, because not the source of problems, not ultimately their cure. He states that the family did not ask for

this invasion, acknowledging that it was not born inside the family. . . . However, the vague, troubling "plague" must stay within the family, because in Albee's world, it is only in the bosom of the family that the problems can be transformed and solved. "BY CHRIST, YOU'RE GOING TO STAY HERE. YOU'VE GOT THE RIGHT". . . . Why the *right*? Again, because the family is the place where social problems are transformed to family relationships and resolved by Albee's one characteristic solution—a strong man placed unchallenged as the head, aided by a subordinate, his wife. All problems must be privatized in order to be solved.

But despite Tobias' pleading to preserve this function of the family, . . . the problems decide to go home anyway. If on one hand the "delicate balance" of the family has been restored by Tobias' taking—or exhibiting good faith by trying to take—a manly position, on the other hand, the delicate balance also gets restored, concurrently and necessarily, by letting the problems depart, having them slip away from the family which could not solve them. Because the family cannot solve or resolve Edna and Harry's terror, it cannot restore a "delicate balance" to society. . . . So the family ultimately fails, and in this play nothing takes its place.

According to Albee these existential or "outside" problems are solved only if they can be made over on the model of relationships within the family: Nick as son; Nick and Honey as children . . . ; Edna and Harry as children; the menacing Van Man in *American Dream* as son . . . ; death as an Oedipal grandson in *The Sandbox.* Although in *Virginia Woolf* there is an apparent finality about the solution that implies that the problems entering with Nick have been solved, George does not actually meet the challenge Nick poses. The problem simply understands and vanishes. However cooperative the problems are as they leave, their unmotivated exit is a clear indication that the family cannot and does not provide a real solution. Although the plays overtly state the opposite, in fact not all the problems evoked by the plays can be transposed to family relationships.

So the fundamental contradiction in Albee has to do with opposing ideas about the function and centrality of the family. Overtly the plays propose that problems and conflicts seen in the family originate in distortions of family relationships and can be solved by righting these relationships in stereotypical—even heavy-handed—ways. Covertly within the plays the opposing issue is also posed: that problems and conflicts seen in the family originate outside the family (in work, politics, society, and existence, all quite vaguely presented by Albee), and that the family is incapable of solving them. (pp. 139-40)

The resolution therefore turns on two necessarily linked evasions. Order is restored by assimilating all problems to family relationships, and curing them by re-establishing sexual stereotypes and killing (or mutilating) the rival. This solution never traces the sources of the man's failure, but rather confuses the cause of the man's failure with its effect—the dominance of the woman. This is the first evasion. Then, problems raised in the play which cannot be assimilated or transformed into family issues simply decamp, unsolved and unaccounted for at the end. This is the second evasion, which logically follows from the first. (p. 140)

Losing power over men, over career, over rivals, an Albee

character will seek to gain power over women and children. The injured pride of semi-displaced persons seems to be at stake, since those people would need the almost self-congratulatory messages that their failure is not a real failure after all, and that their powerlessness can magically resurface as power in normative sexual and family relations.

The role of the middle group in modern capitalist society is very possibly reflected in the play's almost impotent angers, which are saved by the transformation of failure to "choice" and powerlessness to power, all elements of the larger solution: privatization. . . . [Albee] makes available a set of explanations and transformations appropriate to the needs of this group: their failure is a more heroic kind of success, involving choice or will. And the private world of family and sexual relations is still controllable. Further, Albee's play makes available a stylized matrix of vicious ripostes which gives the audience the cathartic satisfaction of total malice, without laws or norms, all at the service of a restoration of order. . . . The anger and nastiness of the play's dialogue is therefore an expression of the actual powerlessness and apparent power of the social group in the audience whose belligerent malaise Albee so piercingly, and even prophetically, expresses. (pp. 141-42)

The issue by the plays is who or what will control the future. Control of the future is implied in everything Nick represents: technology and science, genetic research, world political alignments, the "decline of the west." George stands with his embattled values and fights against Nick, the "dry run for the wave of the future." . . . Eventually, Nick leaves, chastened by George's display of mastery over Martha. Presumably, George's setting his house in order according to strict principles of family dominance will enable him to have authority in the outside world. However, it is unclear that this is so. We know that Nick-as-Oedipalson has been thwarted, but has Nick-as-career-rival really given up? So George's achievement of dominance at home may have to simply substitute for his dominance in the outside world. In any event, it is clear that Albee favors re-establishing traditional order, even without implying the larger curative effect which this restoration may have.

Following this interpretation, we can appreciate the otherwise random political and social remarks in the play. Albee's association of Nick with Nikita Krushchev, the racial slur of the "yellow bastards" who will one day take over, the alleged decline of the West, the danger which "technology" poses to George's asserted "humanism" all imply a preoccupation with threats to the existing structure of domination. The hero, as a member of the ruling sex, a citizen of the ruling country, and a professor of a ruling discipline, is not unchallenged within the play; therefore the West is declining, and civilization, which the hero claims to represent, is in danger. (p. 142)

From the "decline of the West" to the failure of the man in the workplace, social problems are evoked in Albee, and are transposed on to the family and sexual plane. By making these questions of power and work, failure and success appear exclusively as family and sexual issues, Albee can then resolve them by "righting" the relationship between Martha and George in a highly normative and conservative way: the taming of the erstwhile shrew into a docile, frightened child-woman. . . .

[Critics] who follow Albee say that at the end of his plays

illusions have been broken and "reality" recognized. In this specific case, "reality" is the conservative ideology of sex roles in the family. . . . (p. 144)

> *Rachel Blau Duplessis, "In the Bosom of the Family: Contradition and Resolution in Edward Albee," in* The Minnesota Review *(© 1977 The Minnesota Review), Spring, 1977, pp. 133-45.*

*   *   *

ALVAREZ, A(lfred) 1929-

Alvarez is an influential British literary critic, poet, essayist, editor, and novelist. Throughout his vigorous, idiosyncratic, and firmly subjective criticism, Alvarez examines and endorses the "extremist" artists, those like Sylvia Plath and Robert Lowell who will pursue their insights to the edge of breakdown—and beyond. He is best known for his highly subjective study of suicide, *The Savage God. Hunt* **is his most recent work, a psychological thriller that has been compared to the early works of Graham Greene. (See also** *CLC,* **Vol. 5, and** *Contemporary Authors,* **Vols. 1-4, rev. ed.)**

STUART SUTHERLAND

A. Alvarez is best known as a successful literary critic and poet and as a failed suicide. He has protested against the gentlemanly tradition in English letters: he derides its bland and superficial emotional response and has called for confrontation with the darker forces within ourselves and within society. Unusually for someone adopting this standpoint, his writing has always been lucid, spare and witty.

A psychologist who set out to discover what internal evil most worried the ordinary man found that people worry most about inner emptiness and their inability to match the exigencies of life with appropriately deep emotions. [*Hunt*] is the story of just such a man. Conrad's feelings have been blunted by his stale marriage, his tedious children, his monotonous office job and the obligatory blue jokes made by his colleagues in the pub: the greyness of his life is reflected in the grey light of London. . . .

[The] emptiness lies within and is not to be filled by the bizarre external events into which Conrad is thrown. He is so dead to feeling that he cannot even feel deeply about not feeling deeply. . . .

Hunt is a very good novel, fast-moving and compulsive. The different scenes—the dreary terrace household, the office with the blowzy but kind-hearted secretary, the police station, Hampstead Heath and the recurrent poker games— are convincingly described. The prosaic is used to offset the sinister. The dialogue is accurate and witty. There is only one caveat to be made. Although Alvarez navigates his reader with skill through the shoals of psychology and conducts him to enthralling ports of call, we have surely visited these shores before. The terse sentences, the laconic presentation without comment from the author, the hollow heart of the ordinary man, his embroilment with mysterious forces of evil, and his redemption through an unexpected touch of sentimentality—what have we here but a whiff of Graham Greene. Indeed, it is more than a whiff: Alvarez achieves his effects with more economy and precision than Greene himself. Had *Hunt* been written in the 1930s, it would have been a superb novel in an original genre: as it is, it remains a splendid entertainment in the best sense of the word.

Stuart Sutherland, "Going through the Emotions," in The Times Literary Supplement *(© Times Newspapers Ltd. (London) 1978; reproduced from* The Times Literary Supplement *by permission), April 21, 1978, p. 433.*

JOHN NAUGHTON

[It seems as if we in Britain are acquiring a] taste for grey heroes in our fiction. A. Alvarez's thriller [*Hunt*] echoes this trend, by concerning itself with the affairs of one Conrad Hunt, sales manager unextraordinary, who tries to mix a boring business and family life with a bit of painting and a lot of gambling. . . . Conrad is harassed, assaulted, intimidated. So is the reader, who finally begins to suspect that there is Something Really Big behind all the gloomy paranoia. But there isn't really, and Mr Alvarez has the last laugh in a well-written, atmospheric and sophisticated thriller which demonstrates that even conspiracies these days are neither black nor white, but that inevitable intermediate shade. (p. 651)

John Naughton, in The Listener *(© British Broadcasting Corp. 1978; reprinted by permission of John Naughton), May 18, 1978.*

DEREK STANFORD

Hunt [is] a psychological thriller of a completely riveting nature and with some undertones of a deeper nature.

Among other things, it is a tale of addiction, and here Dostoyevsky (himself a convulsive, sometimes self-destructive player) has the edge on [A Alvarez] in *The Gambler*. Mr Alvarez's professionalism as a poker player is at war with his professionalism as an artist. The games he describes are mostly dramatic, but they sometimes fail in communicating, being too full of the terminology which only the long-hardened card player knows. This apart, I find no flaw in a brilliantly succinct story (the author gauges perfectly the length of each chapter—some long, some very short—according to the episode to be highlighted). It is also a splendidly evocative portrait of Dante's narrator in the person of Conrad Hunt, half-way through his life and with his sense of direction confused. (p. 44)

The novel ends with . . . Conrad going off on his own—to squander his last remaining thousands, we imagine. One thing only he has learnt: there is no such thing as luck—only skill or lack of it and the web of circumstances we do not understand.

In this sense, it is a disillusioning book (if we grant the author's conclusion which I myself do not); but its pace, its weird verve and its tough cynical relish give it an obsessive compulsive quality. Shades of the early Graham Greene (*It's a Battlefield* and *A Gun for Sale*), a touch of Dashiel Hammett (whom Mr Alvarez much admires), plus just the minutest sprinkling of Kafka (feeling persecuted by forces unknown) might serve as an approximate formula for a novel which has its own special flavour, its own elegant, independent economic life.

Our author, who is not the most modest of men . . . is said to have told Atticus of *The Sunday Times* that while *Hunt* was a 'good novel', his poems were 'bloody good'. I certainly have deeply enjoyed most of the thirty seven pieces which make up his volume of verse *Autumn to Autumn and Selected Poems 1953-1976*. . . . It has the same elegiac near-nihilistic tone which the later poetry of MacNeice evinced, though without the latter's variety and range. Age, autumn, love's sickness and decay, the poignant (pointless?) beauty of nature—quite a touch of Gottfried Benn about these poems—and the sense, the scent of death upon the air—these are the impressions we draw from his poetry. '*Timor mortis conturbat me*' (the fear of death disturbs and shakes me): this is what Mr Alvarez seems to say—William Dunbar in a minor key. (pp. 44-5)

There is a mortal sadness about many of these urban pastoral poems with Hampstead Heath playing the role of Stoke Poges in Gray's *Elegy*—an elegy without the didactic note; an elegy strained, so to speak, through *The Waste Land*: good, very good, strictly minor poetry, much of which poets with bigger names might justifiably be proud of. . . . (p. 45)

Derek Stanford, "Poetry and Poker," in Books and Bookmen *(© copyright Derek Stanford 1978; reprinted with permission), June, 1978, pp. 44-5.*

FRANCIS LANDY

From the painful, meticulous 1950s efforts to the brilliant shimmer of the eponymous sequence, Alfred Alvarez's poems are always interesting, subtle and wonderfully sensuous. In other words, he is fun, and free of the ghastly inhibitions or smalltype garrulity that British poets have made their own. . . . Yet it is only in the latest cycle of poems, *Autumn to Autumn*, that his voice sounds clear and no longer afraid of what others may think or guess. These are poems that one can, and I did, read over and over. At last a poet is willing to repeat words for the sheer pleasure of hearing them twice, to allow himself luxury and richness. So once again poetry can be beautiful.

The difference between these and the earlier poems is not in the texture of the language, always skilful and pliable. It is thematic inadequacy that dates them. The familiar subjects of the sixties—madness, savagery, Lawrentian landscapes—so safe to hide behind. Genuine poems interspersed, like the anxious *Waking*, at dawn (1959) . . .

> The birds began
> Before the humans the birds were harshly twittering,
> Crying on all sides, rustling and peopling the air
> With outcry, like a river suddenly heard,
> A heavy, persistent down-calling. So the birds
> Were shaking their song out, wrenching and spilling it
> Out of the roots of the heart painfully singing.

But in *Autumn to Autumn* the themes vanish. What could they be about? Weather, landscape, dreams, people separate and wishing, harrowing and simple. A wistful middle age, the nostalgia of autumn, of a total recall of the scents and surprise of childhood and love. So that through dream and reminiscence all seasons come together in the autumn. It works partly through penetrating observation, precise and patient, partly through the fullness of the music accepted without self-consciousness. . . . The poems are fully personal—family poems with the sharp tremor of listening to children, matrimonial poems where the accumulated hurts and longings are too inextricable for resolution—yet the lyrical energy, the regret and anticipation, is carried by the seasons, the rain hissing under cars, the dead whiteness of snow, brilliant promise of Christmas, heavy heads of summer, and so to another autumn, the trees, "the last big spenders". (pp. 119-20)

[*Hunt* is] a strange novel, in that it breaks the rules and refuses to answer questions; it is also very very funny. . . .

The hunt takes us through London, familiar and cosy as a nursery, and as full of obscure terrors. As a cry against the oppression and waste of life in offices, clubs and suburbs, impersonal even in love, deceptive and drab even in adventure, the novel works, surprisingly, partly because of its acute and witty observation; partly because of a foil, its only truly trusting, three-dimensional character, Conrad's sheepdog, Kim. Kim, inevitably, is the only one to die, because of his loyalty. But equally the novel is destructive of Conrad's search through or for himself. In the end, all he can think of to say is "Fuck you". For the real fear is that there is nothing to discover, nowhere to escape, that the hunt is a terrible farce. For this reason all the people in the novel are flattened, whether caught in the trap, like Conrad and Olivia, or cops and robbers, playing the game. In his critical work on Beckett, Mr. Alvarez defines two forms of the Absurd: outrageous farce, the theatre of Ionesco; and the empty, appalled vision of Beckett and Ecclesiastes. At the end of *Hunt* this is what we are left with. Instead of the little boy of Beckett, a large sheepdog. (p. 121)

> *Francis Landy, "A Poet's Harvest," in* The Jewish Quarterly *(© The Jewish Quarterly 1979), Autumn-Winter, 1978-79, pp. 119-21.*

RICHARD FREEDMAN

Walking his dog in Hampstead Heath late one hot summer night, Conrad Jessup [name given to protagonist Conrad Hunt in the U.S. edition of "Hunt"]—failed artist, husband, father and gambler—comes upon the nearly dead body of a spiffily turned-out young lady.

He makes the mistake of phoning the police without volunteering his name. From there on his life is made a paranoid nightmare in this grimly absorbing novel by the English poet and critic A. Alvarez. . . .

Mr. Alvarez [in "Hunt"] is ambitiously out to make a statement about the dismal state of contemporary English society through a loser hero. . . .

But as a parable of England's decline, "Hunt" is rather too murky, schematic and arbitrary. The harder Mr. Alvarez tries to compare sagging London with Kafka's Prague, the less convincing he is to an American reader, who is likely to feel the novelist is jolly lucky to be living in what may be the last relatively civilized country on earth.

The police who give Jessup a hard time are model detectives by American standards. His disaffected wife, who sits all day glued to the telly, at least has the option of watching the BBC. The Big Statement the novel is laboring to make turns out to be little more than the self-pitying whine of a not very likable hero whose best trait is his love for his dog.

Yet on the less exalted level of psychological suspense thriller, "Hunt" is reasonably successful. Mr. Alvarez is every bit as adept as Greene and Theroux in evoking private angst against a seedy background of failed marriages, posh gambling halls, grungy Soho digs and trendy Knightsbridge boutiques. . . .

"Hunt" vertiginously keeps crossing the border between genuine paranoia and justified terror.

The only trouble is that in his efforts to come up with an anti-hero sufficiently mediocre and doomed to be sympto-

matic of our time, Mr. Alvarez has failed to give him enough redeeming qualities for us to get very worked up about his fate. We don't want a James Bond, particularly, but through three-quarters of "Hunt" Conrad Jessup is so spineless and formless that he can barely carry the narrative and symbolic weight that Mr. Alvarez has placed on his drooping shoulders.

> *Richard Freedman, "England as a Loser Hero," in* The New York Times Book Review *(© 1979 by The New York Times Company; reprinted by permission), February 11, 1979, p. 14.*

ROGER SALE

[*Hunt* bears a] kind of eerie connection to Graham Greene's *Brighton Rock.* . . . It is not an imitation in the usual sense yet never seems able to stop imitating and be itself. Alvarez . . . assembles a cast of disagreeable characters and then traps them in a strong plot. Isn't that what Graham Greene does? But it isn't that simple. . . . Jessup is facing middle age, he is destroying himself, and he spends a lot of this long novel not taking things in. . . . The only being he can care for is his dog, and the only activity that brings him to life is playing poker—and it is not surprising that the moments with the dog and the poker scenes are much the best things in the book. . . .

Alvarez wants Jessup himself to be a drifting, unlikable man bent on something; he surrounds him with shadowy and unlikable characters· out of whose actions he can construct a plot. But he seems not to see that the stronger he makes the plot the more Jessup is dragged into it and the less clear he becomes. Or to see that the plot itself is unworkable, strong enough to dominate the novel, but pointless at every turn. . . . In the final maneuvers to capture the villains, Jessup's dog is killed, and this allows him to storm off into the night, claiming some kind of disgust or superiority that is unearned. But we see all too clearly that the dog must be killed; for if he weren't, Alvarez would be trapped, his novel having reached its climax and gotten absolutely nowhere. Which is a way of saying that for a novel that is somber and pretentious, *Hunt* is too full of the unlikely, the unexplained, and the unimportant to come even close to justifying itself. (p. 19)

> *Roger Sale, in* The New York Review of Books *(reprinted with permission from* The New York Review of Books; *copyright © 1979 Nyrev, Inc.), February 22, 1979.*

["Hunt"] is a fiercely contemporary thriller. That is to say, much of the action is arbitrary or irrelevant, the motivations are muted, the characters are assemblages of mannerisms, and there is an aura of calculated squalor. . . . (p. 128)

> The New Yorker *(© 1979 by The New Yorker Magazine, Inc.), March 5, 1979.*

*   *   *

AMADO, Jorge   1912-

Amado, a renowned Brazilian novelist, playwright, scriptwriter, and editor, writes about the people of his native region, Bahia. He portrays them as impoverished and socially repressed but not without hope, and his concern for their future is evident throughout his work. Marxist ideology pervades his early work and critics agree that structure and characterization often seem less important than the promo-

tion of his political theories. His early work was often censored and Amado has frequently been imprisoned or exiled because of his views. His later work, characterized by more emphasis on the individual and on stylistic techniques, is referred to as lyrical and precise in detail. Always active politically, Amado helped draft the current Brazilian constitution. (See also *Contemporary Authors*, Vols. 77-80.)

NANCY FLAGG

["The Violent Land" should be successful] with the many readers who like their adventure, romance, crime, seduction and social injustice in exotic fancy dress, peeping through veils of literary language.

It isn't likely that this book has lost very much in translation. Too much is left: too much style for style's sake, too much indignation with the powerful and pity for the poor, too many excited, shadowy characters, too much love and lust and greed and arson and killing. (p. 8)

> *Nancy Flagg, in* The New York Times Book Review *(© 1945 by The New York Times Company; reprinted by permission), June 24, 1945.*

ANTHONY WEST

["Home Is the Sailor" is] a deftly written, lighthearted, and genuinely funny comic novel. Its hero is an old gentleman who enjoys years of tranquil happiness late in life by masquerading as a retired sea captain and telling the most outrageous lies.... Amado's humor is fresh, innocent, and inventive, and his altogether delightful comedy ... has some profound things to say, in passing, about the human desire for importance.... (pp. 89-90)

> *Anthony West, in* The New Yorker *(© 1964 by The New Yorker Magazine, Inc.), August 8, 1964.*

DONALD A. YATES

Brazilian novelist Jorge Amado has returned to his beloved Bahia, that tropical coastal city of whites, mulattos, and blacks, to lay the scene for another adventure of the human spirit. And his message, presented more vehemently [in *Tent of Miracles*] than in his two most successful earlier novels, *Gabriela, Clove and Cinnamon* (1962) and *Dona Flor and Her Two Husbands* (1969), is again the need to love and have tolerance towards one's fellow man.

Buttressed by delightful ribaldry and exotic trimmings, along with detailed observations of black culture and religion, *Tent of Miracles* is basically a propagandistic work that advocates miscegenation.... For a novel with such didactic purpose, *Tent of Miracles* reads exceptionally well.... (pp. 26-7)

Bahia surely has no greater poet than Jorge Amado. (p. 27)

> *Donald A. Yates in* Saturday Review *(© 1971 by Saturday Review Inc., reprinted with permission), August 28, 1971.*

North American readers have precious few chances to look at the dynamic giant of the New World's southern half through the eyes of a gifted novelist. "Gabriela, Clove and Cinnamon" ... offers one of the most precious. Jorge Amado builds his long "chronicle of a city of the interior" around two superbly alive characters: Gabriela, the mulatto girl with the cinnamon thighs and clove in her hair, and Mundinho Falcao.... The other characters and the back-

ground reveal the tensions that developed during the 1920's as a new bourgeois society cropped up where great landowners were once all-powerful. An "exciting and enjoyable romp of a book," Juan de Onis called it, in an "elegant and ingenious translation." ... (p. 34)

> *The New York Times Book Review (© 1974 by The New York Times Company; reprinted by permission), May 12, 1974.*

WILLIAM KENNEDY

If we were back in the 1940s [*Tereza Batista: Home From The Wars*] would be a great vehicle for Dorothy Dandridge, or maybe Rita Hayworth in brownface. [Amado's] heroine, Tereza Batista, is a lithe and loving, copper-colored saint, a glorious nonesuch from the subcontinent, a fantastic beauty with a bod of bods, a prism of strength, a champion prostitute, a magnificent concubine, the personification of selflessness, a martyr to charity, a paradigm of virtue and fidelity, a cop-kicker and leper-licker, but also, sad to say, rather a bore, and a literary joke.

Amado has written a sensual, comic work this time out, again about Bahia in Brazil, again with all the lavish detail of life as it is lived in the torrential spew of his imagination....

Perhaps also, in his own language, the book is different from the product at hand. The translation ... is fine English. Yet it has the same quality to be found in the translations of Isaac Babel, another regionalist whose dialect and slang are not entirely lost in translation but arrive here like a package that has been too long at the bottom of the parcel post truck. It's not the same as it started out. Babel is a masterful writer, a giant of concision and meaning. Amado is logerrheic, repititious and in quite another literary dimension from the Russian maestro. Yet their language comes at us from the funhouse mirror, and that distortion—once the art is missing—may be at the heart of why Amado makes it in Portuguese but not English.

Or is it simply that the art is clearly missing, even in Portuguese? Amado believes not only in repeating himself four, five, six times, but also in summarizing each of Tereza's adventures in advance, so that we not only drown in verbosity but we are also denied the surprise that even rotten fiction usually dangles before us. (p. 26)

Amado has made his book dense with superficiality, and in doughty Tereza he has created an affectionate, affronting literary icon for these times of multi-angular sexuality: a composite of Wonder Woman, Mary Magdalene, Lola Montes, Lupe Velez, Melina Mercouri, Clara Barton, Foxy Brown and Little Annie Fanny. *Ms.* magazine will probably not print an excerpt. (p. 27)

> *William Kennedy, in* The New Republic *(reprinted by permission of* The New Republic; *© 1975 by The New Republic, Inc.), June 28, 1975.*

MALCOLM SILVERMAN

Although Jorge Amado is undisputably Brazil's greatest living writer, his sixteen previous novels are of varying quality. Perhaps best remembered from Amado's earlier years are *Jubiabá* (1935), *Mar Morto* (1936) and *Terras do Sem Fim* (1942), while *Gabriela, Cravo e Canela* (1958) and *Dona Flor e Seus Dois Maridos* (1966) highlight his more recent successes. In *Tieta do Agreste*, as in all his post-1958 works, the author continues with his brand of humorous satire, lambasting bourgeois shortcomings in an atmosphere of picaresque adventures and contagious optimism.

Happily, his present narrative has none of the excesses common to his previous two novels; and the development of both plot an content seems to signal a reactivated desire to consolidate rather than experiment—a tendency also echoed in the work's theme. (p. 573)

Amado presents his tragicomic story through the eyes of an obtrusive narrator whose humorous interjections serve to enhance further the light-hearted tone evident throughout the narrative. Long, chronicled headings, which precede both the book's six sections as well as its endless chapters, inform as well as entertain, summarizing what immediately follows. Amid almost continuous action, tongue in cheek suspense and profuse dialogue, Tieta and Agreste's colorful personae get to know each other on several fronts. Subplots center around the usual gamut of small town sexual mores, which Amado realistically portrays with appropriate (and often comical) language. While colloquialisms abound, however, the infusion of cosmopolitan Paulista ways into Agreste's provincialism clearly makes for a story of national appeal—and universal undercurrents.

Jorge Amado has always been at his novelistic best in re-creating Bahian life with its mixture of poetry, mystery and telluric regionalism. For almost half a century, this focus has been evolving from one of violent conflict to increasing if imperfect harmony; and *Tieta do Agreste,* a sort of updated *Gabriela, Cravo e Canela* (the present heroine is neither innocent nor naive), follows nobly in this tradition. (pp. 573-74)

Malcolm Silverman, in Hispania (© 1978 The American Association of Teachers of Spanish and Portuguese, Inc.), September, 1978.

JOHN STURROCK

Mr. Amado is Brazil's most illustrious and venerable novelist, and a veteran rhapsodist of its native assets. He has also taken a radical line politically, and spoken up emotively for the poor and disfavored. In "Tieta" he has gone soft, celebrating the goodness and vitality of his home province of Bahia, more from memory than conviction, and at crushing length. This is a slow, explicit, sentimental novel with a theme that might have made a short, sharp fable. . . .

[Tieta herself] is, as they say, a catalyst, an agent of change who herself knows of only one way to behave, warmly and openly; she is the original golden-hearted whore. Her goings-on would be more entertaining if they didn't go on so. Mr. Amado spells everything out and tells us again and again what sort of people his very simple characters are, as if there were some danger of our forgetting. In short chapters of commentary he interrupts the story to make ironical or dismissive remarks about it, calling it "a threepenny novel" and a "soap opera," and complaining about its length. Well, "Tieta" is too long, and it does have a lot of the blandness and cheap contrasts in character of the soap opera. It is as if Mr. Amado had one eye on the film or television rights and another on his more sophisticated readers, who need to be reassured that he knows just what sort of book he is writing. (p. 11)

Corruption and industrialization are presumably urgent

matters in Brazil, but they are less than urgent matters in "Tieta." Mr. Amado's businessmen are absurd, inadequate even as caricatures, graduates from the fantasies of Harold Robbins, never the Harvard Business School, and more likely to titillate (with their immoralities) than to appall. Indeed, the satire as a whole, when it comes, is stale and discounted by the oppressive benignity of the rest of the novel. The people whom Mr. Amado would protect, in Sant'Ana do Agreste, may seem worth protecting to their creator, but few of them will seem so to his readers. His Rousseauesque trust in the survival and benevolence of human instinct strikes one as horribly insufficient to cope with the genuine moral and economic dilemmas raised here in fun. (p. 25)

John Sturrock, "Brazilian Soap Opera," in The New York Times Book Review (© 1979 by The New York Times Company; reprinted by permission), July 1, 1979, pp. 11, 25.

* * *

AMIS, Kingsley 1922-

A distinguished English novelist, short story writer, poet, editor, and essayist, Amis won critical acclaim in 1954 with the publication of his first novel, *Lucky Jim*. He is a skillful satirist whose subject, in his own words, is the "relations between people." Amis's interest in science fiction has been sustained throughout his career: he was coeditor of the *Spectrum* science fiction anthologies and was the author of the first English full-length critical survey of the genre in *New Maps of Hell*. He has also written under the pseudonym Robert Markham. (See also *CLC*, Vols. 1, 2, 3, 5, 8, and *Contemporary Authors*, Vols. 9-12, rev. ed.)

W. HUTCHINGS

Disconcerting his readers has long been a speciality of Amis. Since *Lucky Jim* (1954) announced a talent for inventively comic writing, he has seldom been content to stay still. Even in that early novel, the memorable and splendid farce of the burnt bed-clothes and drunken lecture has to take its place alongside the developing relationship between Jim Dixon and the neurotic Margaret, where the writing is less assured and more tentative as the material is less scathing and more weighty. A disturbing co-existence of two distinct types of writing is often to be found in an Amis novel. In *I Want It Now* (1968), for example, satire of the trendy and corrupt world of chat-show television celebrities goes along with celebration of one such man's triumph over the predatory upper-class world. The character of Ronnie Appleyard is not strong enough to support writing which is now appropriately incisive and now rather pretentious.

Amis, however, is a game enough novelist to keep experimenting with ways of confounding the reader who hopes for a single focus. Accidental death and voluntary therapy for the male of the species loosely hold together the characters and theme of *The Anti-Death League* (1966). Maurice Allington, a whisky addict and ageing, but imaginative, lover, becomes involved in a ghost-story which oscillates between farce and seriousness; between the Reverend Tom Rodney Sonnenschein . . . and God (*The Green Man*, 1969). Most recently, a detailed analysis of the way of 'life' of a household of geriatrics is flauntingly and surprisingly ended with the almost simultaneous deaths of all the characters. This is narrated in six paragraphs: the sudden switch from intricate detail to authorial arrogance is extraordinary (*Ending Up*, 1974).

What, then, are we to make of Amis's insistence on such perversity? . . . [Jim] Dixon is the first of a line of Amis heroes who stand for common sense rather than anger; for the belief that life is there to be made happy now; for the notion that, as Bradbury puts it, nice things are nicer than nasty things. Patrick Standish, for example, in *Take a Girl Like You* (1960) finally achieves his goal of destroying Jenny Bunn's provincial 'Bible-class ideas'. Such destruction, he says, was inevitable, and Jenny can only reply that, even so, it seems rather a pity: nostalgia isn't much of an opponent for easy-going morality. Ronnie Appleyard similarly gets his girl despite the machinations of snobbish and arrogant Mummy (not to mention the efforts of the American police); and they walk off, if not into the sunset, then into a life where they hope to help each other to be not as bad as they would be without each other. Again, the victory goes to common sense and easy-going morality. (pp. 71-2)

It could be claimed that Amis's presentation of a liberal morality within a novel form which alternates the farcical and the serious, refusing to be tied down to a single focus, sets him in one line of English novel-writing. Henry Fielding may serve as an example: Tom Jones, like many of Amis's heroes, finally gets the girl in a triumph of good-heartedness over hypocrisy and meanness. But we are really in a different mode of writing with Amis: what has he to substitute for Fielding's exact relation to past values and literary norms in his use of picaresque and mock-epic? Amis's points of reference are uncompromisingly modern: hence the ghost story of *The Green Man* or (loosely) the science fiction of *The Alteration*. . . .

[For Amis] the novel presents ways of making sense of a world both absurd and threatening. Death, which dominates much of his fiction (for example, *The Anti-Death League*, *The Green Man* and *Ending Up*), may be meaningless, but it cannot be viewed dispassionately. If death is horrible and God, should he exist, is either cruel or teasing, life has all the more to be lived for its present values. If we don't want it now, we'll never get it.

This is the nub of Amis's problem as a novelist. To like it now means to be superbly comic about the world's absurdity *and* to be serious about what makes the world worth living in; conversely, death has to be put in perspective as the end of a life worth living *and* has to be seen in all its meaningless horror. Hence the novels present a love of farce and satire *and* a belief in common-sense values; an insistence on life *and* a hatred of death. This may explain the presence of different kinds of writing within one book; but does not tell us how a satisfying work of art may be produced. (p. 73)

It is here that *The Alteration* represents a fascinating new step in Amis's career. If art is to have any value in such a world, then it must be part of the reason for wanting it now. The structure of the novel and its use of a musically talented main character bring a consciousness of the importance of art directly into its presentation of some problems of life. The alteration is not just what the [*The Alteration*] itself defines as 'Counterfeit World, a class of tale set more or less at the present date, but portraying the results of some momentous change in historical fact'. Hubert Anvil is a boy soprano at Coverley Abbey whose voice has achieved such renown that news has reached the unartistic but acquisitive pope. Two ambassadors, themselves 'altered' to preserve their voices, are sent to check up, with the resultant decision to operate on Hubert and bring him to Rome. Much of the book amounts to a debate on the justice of this decision. The strongest forces against are represented by Hubert's mother, Margaret, and her newly-found lover, the family chaplain, Father Lyall. Hubert decides to try to escape, and is helped by the kindly ambassador of New England (a schismatic country), Cornelius van den Haag. Irony, though, strikes: as Hubert is about to be flown to safety, he is found to need immediate castration on medical grounds, and consequently ends up in Rome after all. Meanwhile, Father Lyall is visited by human, not providential, agency: his sin is bruatally punished by the Secular Arm. Tyranny and fate conspire, each in its own way, to thwart the impulse to live.

The need to experience the joy of life is at the centre of the novel. Hubert's situation forces him into an attempt to comprehend the consequences of adulthood and of his possible failure ever to experience adulthood in the sexual sense. In a novel of ironies, a fundamental one is that Hubert has to be altered before he has achieved maturity: he is to be denied experience before he can discover what it is. (pp. 73-4)

[A] problem over language occurs when Hubert asks his older brother, Anthony, to explain what sex is like. That this is impossible is the point: explanation is no substitute for experience. To express this, Amis's language oscillates between the bathetic and the conventionally vague. . . . Since description is impossible, any attempt is going to be uneasy; but I wonder if we can accecpt the idea that language is an unsatisfactory expression of experience when that idea is conveyed simply by unsatisfactory language.

This conversation quickly gets round to another important issue, one which is handled more certainly. Lovers, says Anthony, are 'closer to each other than they can ever be to God'. This idea is at the centre of the relationship between Margaret and Lyall. The affair begins when Lyall, having refused to give his permission for the alteration, comforts Margaret's grief at the prospect of the church getting its way. Thus the belief that Hubert should be allowed to grow to adulthood coincides with Margaret's discovery of love, and with her statement of the opposition between theological and human values: God, she says, will take care of their sin, but what Lyall thinks of her is also of importance. His reaction to her beauty acts as an expression of the value of human relations. (pp. 74-5)

The freedom to choose, necessary if man is to experience life for himself, is denied by the human agency which puts God's will into operation. Hubert points out to the Abbot of Coverley that a monk chooses of his own free will to be a monk, whereas his own celibacy is to be enforced. He silently adds the further point that a monk can break his vow as easily as he takes it. . . . The choice, then, is to accept one's limited freedom within an established pattern, or to follow the dangerous path of putting personal values before that pattern. Lyall and Hubert attempt to do the latter: Lyall is destroyed by the church, Hubert suffers the irony of chance.

The novel's conclusion is pretty sour, like that of *The Anti-Death League*, where a series of meaningless deaths is concluded by the accidental killing of a dog. At the time of this accident the owner of the dog, a keen amateur musician, is giving the first performance of a newly-discovered work. In *The Alteration,* music is brought fully into the central issue: it, after all, is an important area of human experience. The theme of choice is bound up with Hubert's musical talent. Not only is that talent the cause of the alteration, but it is open to development in two ways. Hubert's gift can be used, as the abbot expresses it, 'directly to the greater glory of God'. Ironically, such a view seems to depend on man's disruption of the natural course of events; but, to complicate the irony, nature then seems to step in to save man the bother. Furthermore, the view that one's duty to art is one's duty to God involves uncertainty: the abbot himself expresses concern that, in spite of the alteration, Hubert's powers may decline. They cannot know for certain, just as the love of God cannot be immediately tested by experience. (pp. 75-6)

Despite Amis's struggle with unsatisfactory language, and despite a niggling feeling that he still likes to do the simple things because they *are* simple for him, *The Alteration* is shaped into a nicely-judged analysis of the problems and values of human experience. The world of the novel is a counterfeit one, so that the analysis takes place within an artificially-imposed pattern. But, as the arrogant conclusion of *Ending Up* demonstrated, Amis seems to be moving towards the view that the necessarily artificial form of a novel (as of all art) should be used deliberately, rather than unsatisfactorily obscured. As a novel, *The Alteration* is itself a counterfeit world formed by the novelist. It begins with Hubert's voice rising above the choir and orchestra in Coverley; it ends with Hubert singing 'Che è migliore?' in Rome. This pattern demonstrates that the church has had its way, so that the two altered ambassadors can give final thanks to God. But the question of that final aria ('What is better?') breaks out of that pattern: art and life continue to exist in a suggestive, if uneasy, relationship. (pp. 76-7)

> *W. Hutchings, "Kingsley Amis's Counterfeit World," in* Critical Quarterly (© *Manchester University Press 1977), Summer, 1977, pp. 71-7.*

KARL MILLER

The writing in [*Jake's Thing*] is determined throughout by Jake's manner of speaking, and it has all the virtuosity of Amis at his comic best, though there are those who will be offended by its strain of hostility and contempt. The prose is ultra-conversational, abusive, and yet allusive, too, and elegantly syntactic. . . .

The description of [Jake's neighbor] Geoffrey has a . . . significance which relates to the underlying tensions of the present book. Here is a backward-looking chap forwardly using oaths which would not have been printed before the Second World War. The oaths used by the recent young, and the spirit of an age whose student activists mail him a plastic phallus, don't appeal to Jake, but the old oaths do. His swearing and womanizing form part of a liberation, in other words, but it has been overtaken by another that he can't abide. . . . The main question that emerges here, for a consideration of the book, is how far its attack on the new, 1970s permissiveness is also an attack on the freedoms which have made Jake what he is.

Mr Amis fastens reproaches on a character who will not always wear them, being, if you like, too likable, and some are reproaches which the novel tries to discredit. When Jake calls himself a male chauvinist, we might wonder whether this is another of its attacks on the kind of people who use that expression, which is one of the new oaths. . . . The novel could be read as that of a writer who is saying (later in life) that promiscuity is bad, after all, that male lust conceals indifference or dislike, and that desire and affection, desire and knowledge, are very different. But [Jake's wife's] argument that people's sex-drives keep them steady is important to the book, and it is not an argument that supports such a reading, since it implies that sex-drives can work with other sorts of drive, and that men and women have a good deal in common. Nor does Jake himself wholly support such a reading. So little has he resembled someone who is unable to feel affection for women, so easy is it to see him, at the same time, as a character in a licentious book, that only the politically motivated will be quite happy to treat his confession as a snub to the licentious behaviour in Mr Amis's earlier fiction, as the permissive society's *mea culpa.*

> *Karl Miller, "The Post-Sexual Revolution," in* The Times Literary Supplement (© *by Times Newspapers Ltd. (London) 1978; reproduced from* The Times Literary Supplement *by permission), September 22, 1978, p. 1043.*

PAUL LEVY

[*Jake's Thing*] is anti the Women's Movement. It's anti-Women's Lib, anti-feminist and anti-female. I can see nothing whatever sinister about being anti all those things, providing one doesn't hide these sentiments by dressing them up in a tatty little plot about what we all know are the lunacies of the sillier disciples of Masters and Johnson. When the scene shifts from Harley Street consulting rooms and the sleazy North London 'workshop' to Comyns College, Oxford . . . the plot improves slightly, for co-education seems to be a topic better suited to Kingley Amis's barbed pen than is coitus. And the real comic *tour de force* of the book is the scene where Jake puts on academical dress and raises a glass of sherry in his hand in front of the windows of his college rooms: he is posing for his photograph to be taken by the foreign tourists who have been in hot pursuit of a genuine don. That rings a great deal truer than all that Amisian waffle about 'genital sensate focusing', which sounds anyway like it has come straight from a clinical guide, and would be quite funny enough on its own—funnier than when it's endowed by Amis with indignity.

There is, in *Jake's Thing,* something that is new though; a gritty, tough and *difficult* style of writing, that is sustained through the whole book. A refined stream-of-consciousness manner informs the whole of the narrative, and Amis has got it very nearly perfectly right, so that Jake's Army obscenities—the genuine contents of his thoughts—contrast comically with the conventionally polite words he actually utters. Technically very well done—I wish it had been more worth doing. (p. 8)

> *Paul Levy, in* Books and Bookmen (© *copyright Paul Levy 1978; reprinted with permission), October, 1978.*

MELVYN BRAGG

Jake is an Oxford don, approaching 60, which he finds almost impossible to believe and, equally incredibly, out of libido. His "thing" isn't up to it and his other "thing" is to be prepared to find out why. What he is left with is the thing itself which makes him live. The course of [*Jake's Thing*] follows Jake's quest. . . .

Jake ends up with a view of women such as might have been held by Thor and might nowadays be most commonly expressed by a drunken Celtic supporter whose wife has left him because of his addiction to football. Jake's view of life—particularly of life in London today—is scarcely less despairing. His only real pleasure is in finding his expectations of dirt, decay, inefficiency, boringness and stupid behaviour by brain damaged citizens fulfilled. If this novel offers us a picture of our own times then what we see rising to the top of society is—according to the perception of Jake —scum.

Then there's the race issue which has to be faced up to in this novel. People are muttering about it and I'm sure that Amis intended that they should. Amis does not deny the feelings of prejudice which his protagonist might have. And he too as an author has his rights and can curse whomsoever he chooses to. Amis insists on variety, he insists on the differences in society. He also refuses to patronize or to deny what he observes are genuine feelings. . . .

The very tight style of the book owes an enormous amount to the care and devotion with which Amis takes everyday sayings—cliches, turns of phrase, figures of speech—and presses them into the service of a resonant English prose. . . . He makes determined, even pedagogic efforts to distil and employ the language used in society today.

This is one of the things which gives the novel its excitement. Another is the general feeling . . . that somehow we have Lucky Jim one generation on. The book is indeed 25 years after Lucky Jim and in some ways Jake resembles him. . . . But Jake is a much less definite character than Jim. He will be much harder to make representative and that cannot displease Amis who has an acute sense of what a novel should be.

Amis has a talent for flicking minor characters into life with a couple of sentences. Here they are scattered generously through the book but I could have wished for even more and for more of those already invented. The strongest character—in her way stronger even than Jake although she has much less of the attention of the author—is Brenda, Jake's wife. We tend to believe in her more than we believe in Jake and that leads to an enriching of the novel in an area where you would have expected Amis to have been entirely unambiguous. For Jake—as you would expect—quite soon finds the whole sexual therapy business to be a total sham and says as much. Brenda, however, won't have this. . . .

Jake's scorn is what one feels most after putting the book down. It is a cover for his despair. As he moves towards old age and death—and remember Amis's *Anti-Death League*—there is a reflective and impotent wondering at the existence he has. At the thing he has that makes him live.

This novel—widely and rightly given the highest acclaim— shows us that Mr Amis will not go gentle into that good night. For which, many thanks. (p. 564)

Melvyn Bragg, in Punch (© *1978 by Punch Publications Ltd.; all rights reserved; may not be reprinted without permission), October 4, 1978.*

TOM PAULIN

Traditionally John Bull is a bloody-minded, insular, beer-swilling, xenophobic philistine with a thick neck and a truculent manner. He hates wogs, he hates the young, and he wishes women would disappear as soon as it's over. This choleric figure has been lying low of late, and I'm sorry to report that he has dictated a novel to a battered amanuensis called Kingsley Amis. His novel [*Jake's Thing*] has half-a-dozen good jokes, a brilliant title, but it is often tedious and sometimes insolently stupid. (p. 52)

As Amis—or John Bull—charts [his] banal hell of rancid grievances and utterly average sensuality he has the cheek to suggest that undergraduates today are a poor lot who are vandalising the English language. . . . More of Amis's prose emphatically means worse. Take this sentence:

> Jake stood at the window in thought, though not of any very purposeful description, for a couple of minutes.

This desecration of a once-noble language is evident throughout the novel. The sentences are often jammed with infinitives:

> Jake took him on to dessert and gave him port; to help to seem to be giving rather than plying with he took a small glass himself.

No undergraduate in my experience has ever written as badly as this. Reading Amis's prose is like getting kicked in the stomach—I found myself virtually retching at its sheer awfulness. And what does he mean by "an O'Casey peasant"? Someone Irish, I suppose. . . . (pp. 52-3)

However, some of his targets are well-chosen: academic laziness, waterlogged Brussels sprouts, the more lunatic extremes of the Women's Movement, and a certain Oxford don who writes plays. But throughout there is a huge imaginative slackness and a heavy obviousness. And behind the brusquely average cynicism there is a tone of plaintive self-pity and puzzled misogyny. (p. 53)

Tom Paulin, in Encounter (© *1979 by Encounter Ltd.), January, 1979.*

V. S. PRITCHETT

As a comic novelist Kingsley Amis still practices the revival of the robust masculine tradition of English farce with its special taste for the sententious that skids into the vernacular and the joke of the flat tire. Not for the dramatic flat, but for the rising paranoia of the slow puncture. He is the connoisseur, even the pedant, of the air going out and things running vulgarly down. One looks at the thing at first with the healthy impulse to give it a kick and then have a drink. The object may have started its life as a gleaming example of contemporary ersatz, but the rapid onset of repairs shows it to be on the way out just as it came in, and a deceiver of hopes. Then a doubt enters the owner's mind: is the flat "one of those things" or is it oneself? All comic writers are serious in their grudges. . . .

Jake's Thing is a very funny book, less for its action or its talk than in its prose. . . . Mr. Amis is a master of laconic mimicry and of the vernacular drift. (p. 12)

Jake's Thing has its comic Oxford side, the panic-stricken dons conducting ingeniously dishonest arguments about letting women into Colleges. There is a thundering account of a lamentable hangover. Jake's kind of mind is amusing but doesn't allow others to have much of an inning, indeed for him there is something fatally wrong or ridiculous about everyone. The novel is really a comic diatribe and is less about sex than about paranoia. (pp. 12-13)

V. S. Pritchett, "Upmanship," in The New York Review of Books *(reprinted with permission from* The New York Review of Books; *copyright* © *1979 Nyrev, Inc.), May 17, 1979, pp. 12-13.*

*   *   *

ANOUILH, Jean   1910-

A French dramatist, screenwriter, editor, and translator, Anouilh has written plays ranging from tragedy (*pièces noires*), to sophisticated comedy (*pièces roses*), to art for art's sake (*pièces brillantes*), to black humor (*pièces grinçantes*). He often uses idealistic heroes and heroines whose romantic dreams are contrasted with harsh reality. Several of his plays have been drawn from history for the modern theater; most notably *L'alouette*, based on Joan of Arc's life, and *Becket*. His satiric *Pauvre Bitos* mocks a Liberation magistrate as the revolutionary Robespierre. *Antigone*, his most popular play, is based on classical mythology. (See also *CLC*, Vols. 1, 3, 8, and *Contemporary Authors*, Vols. 17-20, rev. ed.)

LEONARD CABELL PRONKO

Anouilh's view of life and man's place in the universe has remained essentially unchanged throughout his career. The later plays clarify and elaborate upon ideas presented in the early ones. To be sure, there is a certain development and a shift in focus as the author matures. But it is noteworthy that Anouilh's basic concepts are present from the beginning and have not changed fundamentally in the course of almost thirty years. If this has led to some degree of repetition, it is to be regretted, but that very repetition tends to give a certain unity to Anouilh's theater. He has developed what we might call a personal mythology, composed of characters, situations, and language which are peculiar to his world and reflect effectively his view of life.

The development of Anouilh's themes makes it possible to divide the plays into several periods, based upon fundamental similarities among the plays of the various groups. (pp. 3-4)

The plays of the first group—those written during the thirties—stress the plight of man trying to escape from his past, sometimes succeeding but more often than not, failing. (p. 4)

The real drama of *L'hermine*, as in every one of Anouilh's serious plays, lies in the conflict between the hero's inner world and the exterior world he faces. The latter imposes upon him certain conditions that he feels are diametrically opposed to the person he considers himself to be. (p. 6)

In *Le bal des voleurs* (1932), *Le rendez-vous de Senlis* (1937), and *Léocadia* (1939), all *Pièces roses*, we see one or more of the protagonists escaping, to some degree at least, from the past and also from the present. But their only means of escape is flight into a world of fancy created in each instance by the characters involved, or made possible by the circumstances. The *Pièces roses* in themselves neither assure us that one can successfully escape from reality for any length of time, nor do they tell us the contrary: that man cannot escape. However, when placed beside the *Pièces noires*, with which they are contemporaneous, the

fugacity of such a solution becomes apparent, for we can see that the dreams in which the characters lose themselves are not a valid answer to the problems with which we have seen them confronted in the *Pièces noires*. One might even wonder whether Anouilh has not sought to satirize in these "rosy" plays those facile writers of entertainment who treat the problems of life in a superficial way. (p. 14)

If the characters of the *Pièces roses* are unheroic in their compromise with happiness and their refusal to accept life as it is, they at least possess the noble desire for the purity of life that dares to be what it is without excuses. But they are satisfied with a happiness that Anouilh later satirizes as illusory and unworthwhile. (pp. 16-17)

The dramatic conflict in these plays of the first period, from *L'hermine* to *Léocadia*, is between the hero's inner image of what he most believes himself to be, and the environment and past that impose upon him a character that is at variance with his imagined "true self." The struggle for freedom ensues, and the hero inevitably returns to his former misery, or at any rate, does not deny it or forget it, for to do so would be to become untrue to a part of himself. The power of one's environment and past is so strong that it pulls apart those who under other circumstances might have had some chance for happiness together. The opposition between environments is usually made in terms of wealth and poverty. In all these plays, wealth means happiness, but a happiness at the expense of insensitivity to the suffering of others, for the wealthy have been protected from real life, and know nothing but the surfaces. (p. 17)

Although the hero is not clearly defined yet in the plays of the first period, he is established as the person who is opposed to the compromises of life; whose first purpose is the quest for purity through fidelity to what he considers his truest self. This purity is usually expressed in terms of childhood—that period of freedom and spontaneity before we learned the games of pretense and hypocrisy. It is another version of the Garden of Eden, Baudelaire's green paradise which represents a positive value of the past. The hero would like to cling tenaciously to the purity represented by such a vision, and consequently he tends to reject the adult world. Throughout the plays of Anouilh we hear of the hero refusing to grow up, or regretting his lost childhood. Unfortunately, this innocent paradise is not our only past. Superimposed upon it is the miserable past of man afflicted with sin, represented in most instances by the intolerable world of the poor. The hero attempts to escape from the latter and to return to the former. (pp. 18-19)

When the protagonist goes beyond the limits of his role, forgetting his past, as do Gaston and the characters of the *Pièces roses*, we feel he is not being true to all the aspects of his being, which includes his past as well as his aspirations in the present. The protagonists of the *Pièces roses* are not of a heroic stature. They are not like those who, refusing to escape into a world of dreams, face reality as it is, at the same time denouncing it and remaining aware of its limitations. (pp. 19-20)

[Anouilh's next four plays] lay more stress upon the author's fundamental ideas than had his previous plays. *Eurydice* (1941), *Antigone* (1942), *Roméo et Jeannette* (1945), and *Médée* (1946) place the heroic individual in the center of the stage as he faces reality and says no to it. The feeling of death is ever-present, and every one of the heroines goes down morally victorious. The central struggle is no longer between the protagonist's past and his aspirations. It has shifted to something more universal: the inner world versus the entire outer world, which is the only one recognized by society. The revolt against the past is only part of a larger revolt, and in *Antigone* there is no past against which to revolt, for Antigone creates herself only in the present. (p. 21)

Eurydice (1941) still shows some preoccupation with the escape from a sordid past, and in this respect it belongs to Anouilh's first period. But insofar as this escape is only part of a larger refusal of the compromises of life, and insofar as *Eurydice* treats with greater emphasis and clarity the essential notions only suggested in the first group of plays—enlarging upon them and imbuing them with a new universality—it belongs to the second period. (p. 22)

Eurydice shows, as does *La sauvage,* that man cannot successfully escape from his past. This theme is expressed much more clearly and forcefully in the later play. The past includes not only the persons and circumstances with which man has had dealings, but all past events—even those that seemed alien. The stranger that one happened to look at from a distance leaves an indelible imprint, because one cannot help reacting to even the most objective stimuli. (p. 23)

In *Antigone* (1942) there is no past weighing upon the heroine: she has chosen her role. As she tells her sister Ismène: "You chose life, and I death." . . . And, indeed, Antigone goes to her death, thinking it is the only answer that one can give to life if one is to remain true to oneself. She represents the universe of childhood—the kingdom of the ideal judged through subjectively chosen values. Her revolt is gratuitous; without direction; unmotivated in terms of a past. Her action arises only from a deep-felt necessity to become what she believes to be her truest self. (pp. 24-5)

Antigone's refusal of happiness is also her refusal of life, for the two terms are equated. "I want to know how I'll go about it, to be happy also," she cries out to Créon. "You say that life is so beautiful. I want to know how I'll go about it, to live." This is no refusal of reality: it is a refusal of life itself. If such a refusal is negative, with no positive values implied, it is because Antigone sees life in such terms that a positive stand has no meaning. If life is a compromise and the evil is to wish to live, then Antigone may assert her freedom by choosing death. . . . All those who make the compromise are no longer free in Anouilh's world, despite the strength of their will or the power of their intellect. (pp. 27-8)

The conflict in *Roméo et Jeannette* is between the concepts of the virtuous bourgeois, who believe one must grow up one day and accept the fact that life is not so beautiful as one had thought as a child, and the absolute refusal of Jeannette to accept life on such terms. "I don't want to grow up. I don't want to learn to say yes. Everything is too ugly," she says—reminding us of Antigone. (p. 29)

Antigone, Roméo et Jeannette, and *Médée* show the same conflict between the hero's or the heroine's aspirations and the world of compromise that they must face and in contact with which they would become sullied. Antigone, Jeannette, and Médée, like Orphée, say no to life and realize themselves victoriously in death. Their morality is one of completeness, and they must remain faithful to the inner

self by answering spontaneously the imperious demands of the "savage" individual. Contrasted to them are the mediocre who consent to play the game, and who seek happiness by hiding the truth of life's absurdity from themselves. Lacking the necessary intelligence to perceive any facet of the truth, they simply vegetate, saying, like Monsieur Delachaume in *Le rendez-vous de Senlis:* "Money and love: what else can you ask for? Life is simple after all, for God's sake!" In varying degrees this simple, pleasant picture of life is opposed to the nothingness that the hero sees behind the illusion.

L'alouette, written in 1953, actually belongs to this central period of Anouilh's theater, for in it we see again the intransigent heroine who refuses to say yes to life. Unlike the other plays written during the third period, *L'alouette* shows us the unconquered heroine who remains true to herself. This play is thus linked in a very tangible way with the preceding group of plays; but at the same time it seems to foreshadow Anouilh's later works. (pp. 36-7)

The third group of plays includes all those written since *Médée,* with the exception of *L'alouette* (1953) and Anouilh's last play, *Becket ou L'honneur de Dieu* (1959). The volume ironically entitled *Pièces brillantes* contains *L'invitation au château* (1947), *Cécile ou L'école des pères* (1949), *La répétition ou L'amour puni* (1950), and *Colombe* (1950). Four other plays—*Ardèle ou La marguerite* (1948), *La valse des toréadors* (1951), *Ornifle ou Le courant d'air* (1955), and *Pauvre Bitos ou Le dîner de têtes* (1956)—have been gathered together under the title *Pièces grincantes.* *L'hurluberlu* is published separately but belongs in spirit to the last collection. The only brilliance in these plays is the superficial one given by the witty dialogue, the colorful or gaudy costumes, and the hollow histrionics of the frivolous characters who take the stage; but beneath this superficial brightness we feel the grating disillusion that is fundamental to Anouilh.

The playwright's interest is no longer centered on the heroic personage as he encounters life with its compromises. He now directs his attention to the mediocre people who have accepted life. Sometimes, as in *La répétition,* he shows what a change is effected in the life of a member of the lower race when the real world is revealed to him by a member of the heroic race. Most often, however, the unheroic claims the center of the stage. Rather than contrasting those who accept life with those who refuse it, these "brilliant" plays and "grating" plays oppose the innocent and sincere to the, sometimes unwittingly, wicked and cruel. The pathetic struggles of the few good characters, almost lost midst the others, give rise to a deep feeling of despair in their behalf, for we realize that the cards are stacked against them. This pessimistic attitude constitutes a profound criticism of the adult characters who have lost the purity of childhood. (pp. 40-1)

In the plays of the first and second periods, Anouilh's heroes gave some semblance of meaning to life by making it the means through which they realized themselves, by their very refusal of it. In the plays of the third period, however, the picture is one of compromise, and the outlook seems more pessimistic than ever. We can find no hole in the fabric of an absurd universe through which to bring in some meaning. (p. 55)

One is justified in suspecting Anouilh's heroes of "arrogant nihilism,'' and in asking whether they have not attempted to make of their lack of faith in humanity a system that overlooks those elements of man's constitution which are capable of saving him from himself. In the last group of plays especially, the weakness and immorality of the characters seems to point to the conclusion that man is not worth saving. . . .

In *Becket ou L'honneur de Dieu* (1959) Anouilh returns to the intransigent characters of his first and second periods, but presents a more mature and positive hero than any of the earlier ones. (p. 56)

Although Becket recalls Antigone in his intractable attitude before the King, he strikes us at once as being more mature and more logical. For Becket is not revolting in a vacuum, and he is not reduced to admitting that he is acting for himself. He is defending a positive value—the honor of God— and he stands for ''the unwritten law which always bends the heads of kings at last.'' (p. 57)

We begin to suspect that Becket is more like Antigone than is at first apparent. Although he may lack her childish arrogance, he may very well share her ''nihilism,'' for God's honor turns out to be another way of expressing the heroic desire for an impossible absolute.

But Becket's ''no'' is not spoken against life; unlike Antigone's, it does not represent the will to refuse. It has a more positive side: it is spoken against compromise, and in favor of a value (God, the Church) which, however incomprehensible it may be as an absolute, does have a meaning in human terms. In this sense, Becket is more profoundly human than Antigone or Jeannette. He does not go toward death with that eagerness, scorning ''filthy hope'' and happiness. He accepts death because it is a necessary part of his role. (p. 60)

Several years earlier Anouilh had paused in his portrait of the world empty of heroes to tell the story of Jeanne d'Arc. *Becket* may be another momentary reversion to this heroic world. It is interesting to note, however, that both *Becket* and *L'alouette* indicate a more positive outlook than the earlier heroic dramas. Whether Anouilh is on the threshold of a new period we cannot say on the evidence of a single play. As yet he has not suggested any practical solution to the problems posed by life as it is revealed in his theater. But it is not the function of the dramatist to supply us with answers. It is enough if he presents his picture of the human predicament in a dramatically effective way. Philosophers and prophets may propose solutions. Anouilh has been content to show us the various roles man is condemned to play in his unfriendly universe. (pp. 60-1)

Although both Anouilh and the existentialists are ultimately optimistic in their placing of man at the center of the universe and in their conception of man as a free being, their understanding of that freedom differs. For the existentialists, man is not a creature, for he has not been created; God is dead, and man is an existent who is constantly creating himself by his own free choice. His birth and death were willed by no one and governed by no law save that of absurdity. The heroic race of Anouilh is free to choose also, but only within the bounds of their parts, for they are creatures and owe their beings to a God or destiny, however vaguely that force may be conceived. In the chaos of the universe there is at least sufficient plan for us to realize that each man has his place, whether that place has any meaning

or not. And ultimately it cannot have meaning unless the creature asserts his liberty by living to the very depths of his being. It is a kind of liberty through self-realization, akin to the liberty attained by realizing the will of God and resigning one's self to acting within that will. But Anouilh's heroic liberty is not a resignation. On the contrary, it is a revolt against human standards and a refusal to take a place in a solidified universe; a refusal to lose one's plasticity and become caught in the *viscosité*, to use Sartre's word, of the bourgeois ideals. Here . . . Anouilh and existentialists join hands. (p. 73)

Despite the obvious parallels between Anouilh's outlook and that of the existentialists, we cannot conclude that Anouilh is a member of that group, or has even been influenced by them. All the ideas that the two outlooks have in common were expressed by Anouilh before Sartre had developed and popularized his brand of existentialism: man's solitude; the hero's refusal to accept any standards other than those he creates for himself; the hell created by the realization that we are what others believe us to be as well as what we desire to be; and the ''dreadful freedom'' of heroic man who realizes that he must choose his own being or dominate his role.

We must resist the temptation to impose any particular philosophical frame upon Anouilh's concepts, remembering that he is a dramatist first of all, or even exclusively, and any philosophy expressed through his plays must be considered an indication of the dramatist's sensitivity to and awareness of the tragic sense of life which is so much a part of our time. He has founded no system, and has established no school. But his ideas are significant because, although sometimes contradictory, they reveal Anouilh as a writer who is bound to the cause of man's freedom, and an author whose work is valid first of all for his contemporaries. He shows us the difficulties and the anguish in store for the man who will accept his responsibilities, and the dignity of man true to himself. (pp. 74-5)

Anouilh continues to reflect a profound awareness of our anxious era when man, insecure in a universe that seems devoid of reason, has come to doubt the authenticity of those values he had always accepted. Anouilh has revealed to him more clearly his predicament. If this is scant consolation, it offers at any rate a heroic inspiration (be it valid or not) for man's facing of his destiny. And because man must always face his destiny, such a theater will always be of value and interest, for it helps make him aware, not only of those forces with which he must contend, but of those qualities within himself which may give him strength for the struggle. (p. 214)

Leonard Cabell Pronko, in his The World of Jean Anouilh *(copyright © 1961 by The Regents of the University of California; reprinted by permission of the University of California Press), University of California Press, 1961.*

MARGUERITE ARCHER

The controversies which arise about [Jean Anouilh's] plays stem from the fact that he escapes clear-cut identification. This is due not to obscurity in his *oeuvre* or deviousness on his part but simply to the Protean aspect of his plays. They are variations on given themes, and as such they give the impression that they constitute contradictions. This apparent inconsistency may originate in the ambiguous behavior of the protagonists. But it is simply a fact of life that ambiguity is an integral component of man's plight in relation to himself and others; thus to ask that an image of man be in clear and unambiguous focus is to ask for comforting falsehood. Besides, if man is a "disconsolate but gay animal," as Anouilh asserts, won't he be a paradox to himself?

The isolated works of some authors give evidence of those authors' characteristics, but a particular play of Anouilh reveals at best only a few elements of his work, never his total make-up. Any one of his plays can only be judged as one hue in the spectrum of his *oeuvre*. It is interesting to discover that a reading of all of Anouilh's plays reveals a yearning on the author's part to treat each piece as a step in a progression. This interpretation is supported by the presence in newer plays of lines quoted from preceding plays. And as one notes in novels of Balzac or Faulkner, mere names in earlier parts of Anouilh's work appear as full-fledged characters in later plots. (pp. 4-5)

Anouilh has said that his grouping of plays under the headings of *pièces noires, nouvelles pièces noires, pièces roses, pièces brillantes, pièces grinçantes,* and *pièces costumées* (that is: black plays, new black plays, rosy plays, polished plays, grating plays, and costume plays) aims to satisfy the public's need for classifications. As he indicates, we must consider such divisions somewhat arbitrary, since he did not write all the plays included in a collection at one time. But the groups nevertheless represent the different phases of his evolution.

Pièces noires (black plays) are not tragedies in the classical sense of the word but dramas in the sense that they display the defeat of individuals in their quest to live within the framework of society and humanity, while at the same time preserving the self. The term "tragedy" would seem overly formal to the unpretentious Anouilh, who at the onset of his vocation aspired to nothing more than the role of a man of the theatre in the image of Molière, the writer capable of distracting men from their cares. (pp. 8-9)

As we look at [the *pièces noires*] as a whole, it is clear that the same yearning for complete freedom and integrity drives all the protagonists to despair, although the circumstances vary. In Anouilh's vision, every sight, every touch, every experience, every moment of time, leave their imprint on man's soul and preclude any rebirth of interior freshness, of innocence. Man seems to resemble a sheet of blotting paper which can never be cleansed of its spots, even though he wishes to regain his purity.

In addition, according to their heredity, their past history of poverty or wealth, pain or pleasure, men are divided into two races which cannot communicate: as Baudelaire expressed it, the race of Cain and the race of Abel. When the protagonists could be saved by redeemerlike characters who would graciously give of themselves to prevent their beloved's fate, they respond with a sardonic but melancholy refusal. (p. 12)

As he developed the cycle of the *pièces noires,* Anouilh was accused of treating only one subject. Actually, these four plays constitute variations on the dilemma of life. As such, they tend to show the pride, the yearnings, the frustrations of certain characters rather than to expose the definitive philosophy of the dramatist. At this point in his career the young playwright was primarily concerned with the creation of characters, not with the growth of plot, hence the enigmatic quality of the characters' rejection. From the debates the characters engage in, however, general trends of thought can be deduced, which Anouilh elaborates more fully in later plays. What mainly stands out in his early work is an interest in the complexity of man's motives and the difficulties of making a lucid choice in the chaotic modern world which pulls a man in opposite directions. (pp. 12-13)

Once the case of each hero in the *pièces noires* is examined, one realizes that the premise given at the very beginning of the play, involving only the way in which he will find serenity or happiness, becomes the academic question: Does the order of life, the make-up of man, the nature of the world, allow any man to achieve happiness or peace within himself? In Anouilh's kaleidoscope, at this point, the answer is negative. For life transforms and erodes the subject and the object of happiness to different degrees; it may be impossible for man to subscribe to serenity within himself, although he keeps thinking that he desires it above all things; at the same time, society nullifies man's effort toward his own fulfillment by enslaving him with mass-produced rules. In *Antigone,* Anouilh will go so far as to advance the theory that happiness is only a human fabrication. (pp. 13-14)

As the generic title indicates, the *nouvelles pièces noires* stand closely linked to the *pièces noires;* all the plays together form a progression, with each gaining a larger degree of impact. In *L'Hermine, La Sauvage,* and *Le Voyageur sans bagage,* the prime origin of fate rests in the inflexibility of the characters, in their polarization. Though they represent extremes, they do deserve understanding, even sympathy, for we share a thin affinity with them. . . . Each play mixes the elements of choice and alienation: each plot develops within the narrow social confines of a couple or a family, except *Antigone,* which widens to include the political circle. Generally (*Jézabel* being the exception), the *nouvelles pièces noires* offer an ennobling picture of man's courage. (pp. 15-16)

[*Antigone*] ends with a disturbing lack of hope for the discovery of a rational meaning to our constant strife; yet it consoles us through its existence as a moving work of art. A brilliant handling of dramatic elements gives it a satisfying homogeneity which never falls into dullness. The character development and the organization of the plot impart complete plausibility to the action. The play maintains a smooth dynamic rhythm, thanks to the perfect balance of moods. The moments of intense emotion and those of banter or trivial discussion fit carefully together with the help of the classical restraint of the language. Whereas Sophocles' play is forbidding, Anouilh's work touches the whimsical at times, allowing the modern spectator necessary respite from its strong emotional content. . . . [The] playwright not only aims at the comic relief often encountered in Shakespeare but satirizes contemporary society. . . . Anouilh is irrepressible at heart, and he admits he plays such tricks to amuse himself.

He remains a master of dialogue by skillfully mixing humor with the poetic lines of Antigone. . . . Anouilh presents a very human though heroic Antigone who elicits curiosity, fear, pity, compassion, amusement, sorrow, and reflection; she provokes not only admiration but attachment, as if she were a real person. (pp. 23-4)

[*Roméo et Jeannette*] offers a good occasion to examine Anouilh's ideas on love. He has yet to present love as a salutary tie between man and woman; it can be sublime for a while and then it leads to death; sometimes it appears to be a grotesque masquerade among caricatures, at other times it is what people talk about in make-believe, a kind of fairy tale resembling the *pièces roses;* in *Cher Antoine,* Anouilh presents it as a miracle, blessing very few chosen people. (p. 24)

The [former] play, meant by its title to remind us of *Romeo and Juliet,* recalls more *Tristan and Isolde,* or better still *Pelléas et Mélisande,* simply because its rhythm plunges the spectator into the sort of mystic wasteland one finds in the Maeterlinck play. Inasmuch as the central characters keep groping for a way to express their predicament, they seem far removed from Romeo and Juliet, who can elucidate so well their situation.

While the style in *Antigone* showed the firmness befitting a grandiose subject, *Roméo et Jeannette* reveals a controlled poetic fluidity which testifies to Anouilh's amazing versatility. He has explained that he first visualizes a play before he captures it on paper. This play has been transposed with its aura of unreality, as *Léocadia* will be. It offers the charms of an elegy, for the dialogue possesses a contemplative tone that puts one in a mood of gentle mourning. (pp. 24-5)

[*Médée*] marks an important step in Anouilh's development: for the first time in his *oeuvre,* the author paints in Jason a character who, having first rejected men's rules for the sake of an absolute, comes to terms with the imperfections inherent in man's condition. (p. 26)

During the early part of his career, Anouilh alternated between writing *pièces noires* and *pièces roses.* Then, after effecting a kind of personal catharsis through the creation of three *nouvelles pièces noires* in a row, he immersed himself in art for art's sake with the *pièces brillantes,* and in black humor with the *pièces grinçantes.* (p. 29)

In the *pièces grinçantes* he no longer divides the world between idealists and realists, but fills it with ludicrous puppets and cynical hypocrites. He once praised Molière for having written the blackest form of theatre in a manner which made men laugh at their own misery and hideousness. As the use of the term "grinçantes" shows, Anouilh intends to do something similar in this new collection of plays. The word "grinçantes" implies, first, the interrupted motion of something which hits a snag. As such it can be applied to laughter interrupted by the awareness that one should probably cry. Secondly, it refers to the unpleasant sound of something which crushes or grinds, thus recalling the sound of things one does. (p. 31)

There is no obvious tie between *Ardèle* and *La Valse des Toréadors,* other than the reappearance of General Saint-Pé. He emerges from both plays as an especially well-defined anti-hero who deserves close scrutiny. He represents especially the confused modern individual desperately trying to keep from drowning in the maze of contradictory forces which rule the world. He is made dizzy by the sweep of changing values in modern society, so he waits for a miraculous inspiration to move him in one direction or another. Since none materializes, he freezes into inaction. Face to face with evil, he does not recognize it or does not dare to acknowledge it. He struggles to find an ethic, al-

though he is fallible enough to expect it to be easy to follow. A little cowardly, incredibly patient, he has been put on earth to be a victim, not a victor. He survives by sinking into sexual gratification, and by wearing a uniform which becomes his crutch. When he has the uniform on, others think that he is strong and brave. He knows that deep inside he is a lonely, frightened man, but appearances are good enough for him. He is Anouilh's image of today's man. (pp. 34-5)

[*Ornifle ou le courant d'air*] succeeds in offering an interesting modern version of Molière's *Don Juan.* But Anouilh's motives when he created it were less innocent than Molière's. Whereas the action remains forbidding in both plays, Anouilh lends a more airy, flippant tone to his hero so as better to allow him to flaunt his views. Furthermore, when Ornifle collapses of a heart attack as he is about to engage in the betrayal of another weakling, the suddenness of his death does not imply punishment as it does in the Molière play, for Anouilh does not show that his death is inflicted by a mystic supernatural power stronger than he, as is the case with Don Juan. In this instance, Ornifle falls dead as if struck by lightning; thus Anouilh bestows on him an almost painless death, such as we think only innocent creatures deserve. Anouilh is saying that Ornifle was an innocent creature, for he did not hide his wickedness. (p. 35)

[Anouilh] distinguished two kinds of opportunists: the Don Juan type, who openly join the forces of evil but who can be recognized, and the more dangerous variety, who wrap up their wickedness in all sorts of beautiful trappings. In *Pauvre Bitos,* the latter are the ones he pursues, while in *Ornifle* he shows how harmless openly wicked individuals actually may be. (p. 36)

[An apparent sequel to *Ornifle,*] his first brilliant satire [was] *Pauvre Bitos.*

As might be expected, the play's strong impact derives from Anouilh's daring frankness and the clever device he chooses to denounce the true character of the *Epuration* (the Purge). By allowing the participants in the debate between Bitos and his tormentors to wear the headdress of French Revolutionary leaders, he makes them express their motives more forcefully, for they can act safely behind what amounts to a mask. Since Anouilh wants to show the French their unfortunate tendency to repeat mistakes, the parallelism with the Terror initiated by Robespierre during the Revolution serves to concretize and reinforce his theory.

The indictment is a very severe one, for Anouilh lashes out not only at Bitos, the righteous self-appointed "defender of the people," but also at his tormentors. (p. 37)

Strangely enough, many critics reacted to *Pauvre Bitos* by lamenting that Anouilh was a man who hated humanity. But the play is precisely an indictment addressed to those who treat humanity with cold, mechanized methods instead of indulgence, compassion, and love. (p. 38)

When asked in August, 1969, what his favorite play was, Anouilh replied that it was *Pauvre Bitos:* first, because he had created a new character, which is always a "rosy" event in his life, and second, because he had dared to tell the French, at a time when it was unthinkable to do so, the things they needed to hear. What must be added is that satire is his natural medium of expression. The sweep of the discussion in *Pauvre Bitos* attests to that; so does the fact that in this form of drama his targets have no way of escaping his unrelenting scrutiny. Since he has the eye of Strindberg, the tongue of Shaw, and the aspirations of Molière, it has been hard for him not to choose exclusively to mock men for their weaknesses. There are signs that he may have come to acknowledge his talents in that field, for his widely acclaimed recent plays, *Cher Antoine* and *Les Poissons rouges,* are primarily satires.

Anouilh's propensity for lampooning does not mean that he necessarily looks for objects to blame. If possible, he would just as soon encounter moral beauty of the quality seen in *L'Alouette* . . . or *Becket ou l'honneur de Dieu.* . . . These two *pièces costumées* are, to date, his only serious yet optimistic plays. (The third *pièce costumée* is *La Foire d'empoigne* [1962].) (pp. 38-9)

It would seem that at last, in these two plays, Anouilh found the pure idealism he had searched for in his earlier plays. By contrast with the heroes of the *pièces noires,* the heroine and hero of *L'Alouette* and *Becket,* respectively, give their lives for a cause which goes far beyond the self. They refuse the ways of materialism for definite reasons instead of ambiguous ones, as was the case with [his earlier characters]. (p. 39)

At the same time, these champions of idealism remain human and accessible instead of becoming alienated from humanity, as did the protagonists of the *pièces noires.* (pp. 39-40)

As a result of this careful characterization, we feel that, although the characters do not share the ideals of their opponents, they still belong to the same "race." There is no need for two groups, one, the elected, and the other the damned, as there was in the *pièces noires.* The protagonists' plight in the *pièces costumées* seems the more pathetic, since there should be a way for at least the men of the same group to live in harmony.

Although the two plays are similar so far as meaning is concerned, any resemblance stops there. Each one does far more than conform to the patterned discussion of idealism which Anouilh started in his early plays. *Becket* unfurls the gripping history of a friendship which was meant to bring each partner lifelong comfort; it is the story of a mutual affection which lasts even through adversity. *L'Alouette* illustrates Anouilh's image of the lark that still sings in the sky while being shot at. It depicts the combination of strength and vulnerability that characterizes mankind. It is proof of the moral indestructibility of the man or the woman who is truly good. (pp. 40-1)

The dialogue in the case of each is a masterpiece of nuances. In *Becket* the strong, earthy language of the King and the barons is played against the measured, restrained language which Becket uses to seek understanding. In *L'Alouette,* Jeanne uses a language which seems rudimentary, but which translates her acute common sense in such a way that what she says becomes irrefutable. At the same time, Cauchon uses expressions filled with double meaning, while the short exclamations of the *promoteur* betray his lewdness in a hilarious manner. The pageantry one expects in a historical play is smoothly fitted into the plot so that one has the impression of witnessing an authentic yet modernized version of the story. (p. 41)

It was inevitable that Anouilh, indefatigable observer of men, would reach a point where he could not remain impassive at the sight of the excesses they commit, and would create a sort of spokesman. He did so in *Cher Antoine ou l'amour raté* (Dear Antoine; or, Lost Love), his first play of the 1969-70 season, where he introduced the playwright Antoine de Saint-Flour. . . . [He] presented a second play that season, *Les Poissons rouges ou mon père ce Héros* (The Goldfish; or, My Father, That Hero), where the same protagonist, seen at an earlier time, takes stock of himself. (pp. 45-6)

Permeated with the good-natured reactions of Antoine, opposed to the sourness and self-righteousness of others, the play greatly amuses by its wealth of impish repartee. In the exchange lies many a truth about the privileged and the not-so-privileged of our society. "Refreshing" is the epithet critics have used to qualify this comedy both *rose* and *noire.* Actually, Anouilh has never been anything else. (p. 46)

> *Marguerite Archer, in her* Jean Anouilh *(Columbia Essays on Modern Writers Pamphlet No. 55; copyright © 1971 Columbia University Press; reprinted by permission of the publisher),* Columbia University Press, 1971.

GAËTAN PICON

A mainspring of Jean Anouilh's work has been a savage indictment of society, despite his belonging to the political right (although there is, to be sure, the phenomenon of right-wing anarchism). His work has had an abundance and diversity that puts it in the first rank. Anouilh was famous before the war for *L'hermine* (1931, The Ermine), *Le voyageur sans bagage* (1936, Traveler without Luggage), and *La sauvage* (1934, The Savage). In these, the Anouilh hero, obsessed by youthful idealism and rejecting the compromises of ordinary life, appeared in various guises. *Antigone* gave the Anouilh hero (or heroine, in this case) the prestige of an ancient myth. Creon, who accepts the demands society makes on the individual, is not an entirely contemptible figure, but the play is naturally dominated by Antigone herself, whose unreasonable behavior is seen as reasonable.

This conflict (close to the one we find in Montherlant) between personal purity and the demands of society tended, after the war, to disappear in Anouilh's work in favor of a savage pessimism that rejected any alternative. His early division of his plays into the *pièces noires* and the *pièces roses* gave way to a uniform atmosphere of sourness and asperity. *Ardèle, ou la marguerite* (1948, Ardèle, or the Daisy) was a pitiless debunking of all respectability and all enthusiasm. A sexuality of resentment, not unlike that found in Sartre's novels, was expressed in the harrowing scene in which two children parody their parents' dissolute behavior. In *La valse des toréadors* (1952, The Waltz of the Toreadors) and *Le boulanger, la boulangère et le petit mitron* (1968, The Baker, the Baker's Wife, and the Little Baker's Boy) Anouilh continued this picture of incurable degradation and disgust. This exaggerated pessimism seems to have been caused largely by the events of the Liberation of France, which Anouilh felt had involved excess and injustice, proving that evil inevitably results from the illusion of good.

Anouilh's attitude toward current events perhaps explains the temporal distancing he sought through his historical plays. (Did the break with the present drive Anouilh, like Giono, back toward the past? Or did the past serve Anouilh merely as a prudent disguise?) *Becket, ou l'honneur de Dieu* (1959, Becket, or the Honor of God) reasserted the absurdity of the noblest conflicts, and *La foire d'empoigne* (1960, Catch as Catch Can) put Louis XVIII in a better light than Napoleon. In *L'alouette* (1953, The Lark) the trial of Joan of Arc offered many analogies to the contemporary world. And in *Pauvre Bitos* (1958, Poor Bitos) a magistrate who has terrorized his town just after the Liberation is persuaded to adopt the role of Robespierre at a fancy dress party.

In his most recent plays—*Cher Antoine* (1969, Dear Antoine) and *Les poissons rouges* (1970, The Goldfish)—Anouilh adopted a more confidential, autobiographical form; but he obsessively continued to attack social hypocrisy, above all the vacillations of progress and progressivist optimism. Anouilh has experimented ingeniously, sometimes daringly, in almost all of his plays: plays within plays, liberties taken with time, and so forth. But he has remained traditional in that he links a quite explicit content, based usually upon a central problem, to a form that primarily seeks to effect a convincing illusion of reality. (pp. 173-75)

> *Gaëtan Picon, in his* Contemporary French Literature: 1945 and After *(copyright © 1974 by Frederick Ungar Publishing Co., Inc.), Ungar, 1974.*

JOHN SIMON

[*Ring Round the Moon*] is a typical bittersweet Anouilh confection: a dizzy farandole laced with bitterness, sarcasm, despair, capriciously manipulated into a deliberately preposterous happy ending. It is the precise fairy-tale method: after monstrous cruelties, a magically blissful forever-after. But as Anouilh handles them, the lacerating ironies and heart-splintering witticisms are meant to remind us how painful, indeed deadly, this game would be if it were real; how grateful we must be to the theater for being merely theater. Life in this comedy is present by its absence: we are allowed to luxuriate in an elegant distaste for living that goes up in epigrammatic fireworks, in outrageous plot twists turned as anodyne as wild beasts domesticated by art. (p. 62)

> *John Simon, in* New York Magazine *(copyright © 1975 by News Group Publications, Inc.; reprinted with the permission of* New York *Magazine), July 21, 1975.*

JOHN H. STROUPE

There is now general critical agreement about Anouilh's *Becket*. Formerly docile to the random quality of life, willing to play whatever role is offered him, without an honor of his own to value, agnostic if not atheistic, Becket determines finally to consummate his life in the role of Archbishop of Canterbury. His heightened sense of aesthetics tells him that the role he embraces to give meaning to his existence must finally protect the honor of God at all costs. . . . [His] is not a death which draws on adamant convictions about the truth of the church's position in the conflict. His criterion is an aesthetic view of human morality, and what gives his role authenticity, what makes its artificial behavior timelessly Becket's own behavior is his selection of death as the means to unadulterated selfhood. What has not been examined critically within the play, however, is one of the central methods by which Anouilh

links the many aspects of the quarrel between church and state, between Becket and Henry: the use of continuing familial imagery. For enemies refer to each other as father, son, or brother. Members of the church deny kinship, and the parental nature of societal structures is emphasized throughout the play.

The familial strand is at its most determinate in the form of the genealogy of the two central protagonists, for it initially sets each in his place in the world. Henry, hedged around by rank, race, and ancestry, is the Norman king by right of conquest and the law of primogeniture. Becket, on the other hand, says he is a "double bâtard." His admission describes not only his natal and political illegitimacy, but the transgressions of his parents which are the real source of the shame he has in his Saxon ancestry. . . . An implicit thought in Becket's mind must be that he is following too faithfully in his parents' footsteps.

A further irony is that his parents' love story has become a song which is a constant reminder of Becket's shame. . . . Yet, when the abstract principle of his parents' love for each other is set against Henry's concrete image of his own "augustes père et mère" [distinguished mother and father] and his revulsion, "je tremble en pensant à ce qui a dû se passer" [I tremble at the thought of what must have come to pass], who would deny that Becket's heritage is the better one?

Familial imagery also depicts the fragmented nature of England under Henry's reign. A Saxon peasant's inability to protect his daughter and her willing cooperation in her own shame become a vignette that exemplifies the breakdown of a central unit of society. In a broader sense each rape of a Saxon girl by a Norman overlord is a replay of the rape of England at Hastings one hundred years before. Finally, Becket himself is the center of a scene that emblematizes the incoherent nature of life in an England whose father does not recognize half his children. (pp. 16-19)

The most important illustration of familial metaphor occurs when Henry appoints Becket Archbishop of Canterbury, and it signals a major change in Becket's character. For the dispossessed Saxon Becket, the Primacy of England becomes the source of both ancestry and heritage. . . . Here, as well as acquiring spiritual parents—for he has exchanged mother England for mother church—he is also given what he calls the "l'honneur de Dieu" to protect. . . . Thus Becket as Archbishop becomes a potent father-figure, secure in ancestry and issue, and endowed with patriarchal dignity. Henry, who only a few days before had jokingly called Becket "Père," does not understand the significance of the change. He still thinks of Becket as the mock-father, mock-brother, and the mock-son of their old relationship. But—as the insistent family analogy hammers home—by exchanging the seal of England for the See of Canterbury, Becket has become the King's spiritual father, and they no longer share the same mother.

Just as Becket attains stature in his role of spiritual father of England, the spoilt-child quality which is a focal point of Henry's character gains ascendence in the last two acts of the play. . . . The fight with Becket, which in political terms involves complicated patterns of the rival hegemonies of church and state, is for Henry a direct threat to his manhood. (pp. 19-20)

In the end, of course, whatever else the rivalry between

church and state holds for the future, Becket's own final gift to Henry is a united English family, for Becket's death is the means whereby England achieves "sa victoire finale sur le chaos" [its final victory over chaos]. His death and the King's subsequent penance join Henry and Becket for the last time. And for the first time the Saxon populace recognizes a link between their dead spiritual father and national hero, and the King. They flock to his side against his own usurping son. (p. 21)

> *John H. Stroupe, "Familial Imagery in Anouilh's 'Becket'," in* Romance Notes, *Fall, 1978, pp. 16-21.*

*   *   *

ARDEN, John   1930-

Arden is a British dramatist and screenwriter noted for his satirical treatment of social and political themes. His work is often compared to that of Harold Pinter, which it resembles for its subtle, comic presentation of confrontations between nonconformity and convention. (See also *CLC*, Vol. 6, and *Contemporary Authors*, Vols. 13-16, rev. ed.)

G. W. BRANDT

[*Serjeant Musgrave's Dance*] had the great virtue of crystallising and sharply dividing critical opinions; the one thing with which it did not meet was indifference. Some of the reactions to the play make an interesting study. They were, incidentally, comments on the parable as a dramatic form. (p. 49)

[We] have three distinct attitudes: hostile, mixed, and friendly.... We may feel that the argument is loaded: Musgrave is too peculiar, indeed pathological, a character to give any general validity to the parable. What cannot be said is that the play is impenetrably obscure. Could it be that some of the hostile critics found the message not so much obscure as unpalatable? (pp. 50-1)

We are only shown a *wrong* reaction to an iniquitous state of affairs [in *Serjeant Musgrave's Dance*]. But why should a playwright dot all his I's and cross all his T's?

He must of course expect to run into trouble if he demands of the spectator that he do his own brainwork in the theatre. A well-told parable stirs up questions and then refuses to give all the answers. This is hardly the proverbial tired businessman's idea of after-dinner fun, and somebody has to give in—the would-be passive spectator or the thrustful playwright. In the case of *Serjeant Musgrave's Dance* the anti-parable faction won the day. (p. 51)

[It] would make for an easier acceptance of *Serjeant Musgrave's Dance* if the fanatical sergeant were to be either wholly condemned or wholly approved of. But is it not disturbing to see a morally sensitive man trying to start a public massacre? It is. Does his fanaticism invalidate his moral protest as such? It does not. The contradiction between laudable indignation and reprehensible conclusions drawn from it may either alienate the spectators out of all sympathy with the play (as happened to some critics), or else it may jolt them into stirring moral speculations (as was the experience of some other critics).

It is only fair to say that Arden does not guide the spectators' response with any regimental firmness. The play is diffident in putting forward its moral—a diffidence in curious contrast with the violence of its action....

Perhaps a structural flaw in the play is the division in its dramatic purpose between the demands of suspense and surprise. Musgrave and the three Soldiers under his command are under great mental pressure, thinking about the impending day of reckoning, the recruiting-meeting in the town square. The study of this strain builds up suspense and constitutes the main psychological interest of the first two acts. Then, in Act III, the surprise is sprung: the hoisting up of the skeleton, and the training of the Gatling gun on the crowd. As a surprise it works powerfully. But the more genuine the surprise, the less the audience were in a position to understand the causes and the significance of the strain under which the Soldiers had been labouring before.

Arden's language in *Serjeant Musgrave's Dance* is earthy, with a rich north-country flavour; but it is not naturalistic for all that. It is a highly charged prose that at times abruptly rises into verse. There is no need to seek for the roots of Arden's dramatic poetry in Brecht, although the analogy is obvious enough. (p. 52)

The essentially poetic conception of *Serjeant Musgrave's Dance* is reinforced by recurrent colour imagery—particularly black (the blackness of the night, of the coal-fields, of the haunted mind of Black Jack Musgrave himself); white (the snow of the winter scene, the white skeleton of Billy Hicks); and red (the colour of blood, of the Mayor's gown and the Soldiers' coats). Visually as well as verbally, these colours are firmly established in the very first scene, with references to the darkness of the night, the snow, the red and black of the Soldiers' pack of cards, and the Bargee's taunting of the Soldiers as 'blood-red roses'. (p. 53)

In its protest against the folly and beastliness of war, *Serjeant Musgrave's Dance* does not use the all-out expressionism of *The Silver Tassie*. But like O'Casey's play it uses elements of realism in order to build up an image going beyond realism. The parable has been made to yield poetry-of-the-theatre. (p. 54)

> *G. W. Brandt, in* Contemporary Theatre, *Stratford-upon-Avon Studies 4, edited by John Russell Brown and Bernard Harris (© Edward Arnold (Publishers) Ltd 1962), Edward Arnold (Publishers) Ltd, 1962.*

CHARLES MAROWITZ

The curse of John Arden is that he simply won't play ball. After creating a picture of Welfare State slovenliness in the farcical *Live Like Pigs*, he switched gears and gave us the spare and chilling *Serjeant Musgrave's Dance*. Then, all set for more thought-provoking austerity, he trots out *The Happy Haven*, a Commedia dell' Arte zanni on old age....

Along comes the much-heralded, long-awaited *Workhouse Donkey* and again Arden pulls a volte-face. The play turns out to be an ornery comedy of humours which is as opposed to quick sense as it is to pat conclusions, and the critics, now out of patience, smother it with indifference and cultivate their peevishness. (p. 238)

But putting to one side the reactions of our erudite ... drama critics, let us (with full recognition of our biases) examine the virtues of John Arden's [*The Workhouse Donkey*].

—It is intelligent. There is a skill in the writing which breezily creates outside characters and craftily develops a fanciful language to suit their dimensions.

—It is funny (not hilarious) and creates the sort of thoughtful laughter we expect from plays that do not set out to simply tickle our ribs.

—It is a generous play. It proliferates incidents; it tangles plot and sub-plot and, as it turns out, is generous to a fault. The play was conceived as a three-acter, and divided in two, the material does not properly resolve itself. One should either have scaled it down to the given time, or insisted on its natural full length.

—It is meaningfully complex. Beneath a bouncy exterior lies a maze of meaning. Municipal corruption is its amusing façade, but the play winds downward to connect with hard-boned ideas concerning law, justice and developments in social history. For me, the historical aspects are the most pertinent.

Councillor Butterthwaite, who runs a feather-bedded Yorkshire town like a family business, is a relic of a 1920s socialist idealism; the same idealism that spawned the English trade-union movement and turned labour solidarity into narrow-minded factionalism. He contains the ruins of pioneer Socialist principles and the contradictions of present-day Labour Party. He is a glib and aggressive anachronism and stands as a valid symbol for what early twentieth-century idealism turned into.

With that inbred and relentless objectivity which makes Arden the writer least committed to sects and most committed to truth, he sketches in the other dominant forces.... No villains, no heroes, only varying degrees of grayness which in one light appear black, and in another, white. (pp. 239-40)

Arden has given us a richness and a fulsomeness and I, for one, prefer a well-stocked buffet to a predictable round of fish and chips. (p. 241)

> *Charles Marowitz, "'The Workhouse Donkey'" (1963), in* The Encore Reader: A Chronicle of the New Drama, *edited by Charles Marowitz, Tom Milne and Owen Hale (copyright © 1965 Encore Publishing Company), Methuen & Co Ltd, 1965, pp. 238-41.*

J. D. HAINSWORTH

Arden is very much more than just a provincial playwright. Though he often draws on his northern background, he writes plays which should be of interest to playgoers anywhere. One of the difficulties—it is also one of the strengths—of Arden's plays, is that he doesn't create characters who are simply black or white.... Nor does Arden create characters who are simply mouthpieces for his own point of view. Musgrave, in *Serjeant Musgrave's dance,* is a soldier so revolted by the bloodshed of a colonial war, that he wants to get over the horror of it to the civilian population back home, and convince them of their responsibility for what has happened. So far, both playwright and audience must be on his side. But this is no longer so when Musgrave, through the very strength of his convictions, himself resorts to violence and bloodshed.

Failed idealists like Musgrave are fairly common in Arden's plays.... Set against them are more cynical characters like Crooked Joe Bludgeon, the Bargee in *Serjeant Musgrave's dance,* and Dr Blomax in *The workhouse donkey.* Blomax and Crooked Joe are the ones who triumph in the end, when Musgrave is waiting to be hanged, and Colonel Feng

has been forced to resign. These cynics, especially in Arden's later plays, are treated just as sympathetically as the idealists. We learn to understand their cynicism and even to wonder whether "cynicism" is a fair description.... Arden's plays are all plays about society. This is true in a more superficial sense—he writes about the colour question, about "problem" families, about the state of local politics, etc.—but equally true at a deeper level of his drama. Whatever their starting point, the impression his plays finally leave us with is of the basic anarchy of our society. The intricate entanglements of his plots—at a time when many dramatists are trying to make do with as little plot as possible—help to get over this anarchy to the audience.

Arden's plays offer no solutions either to the surface problems of local politics, etc. or to the underlying anarchy of our society. This is not a weakness in them but a strength. For it would be very silly to imagine that questions of such importance can be solved inside a theatre. (pp. 25-6)

Paradoxically, Arden's concern with present reality sometimes leads him to set his plays in the past. *Serjeant Musgrave's dance* reminds us of the Cyprus situation of the 1950s, and *Armstrong's last goodnight* of the recent civil war in the Congo, but the first is set in Victorian England and the second in sixteenth century Scotland. If Arden had written directly of Cyprus or the Congo, his plays would have had to take a more documentary form, and he would have had to concentrate on being objective and accurate in his facts. The historical settings allow him much greater liberty in shaping his material and dramatising the issues which seem to him important.

You can get some understanding of Arden's plays from reading the scripts of them, but nothing like their full impact. A reading will give a sense of what he is trying to say and some indication of his powers of language—he can create as convincing an impression of the speech of sixteenth century Scotsmen as of a "problem" family on a northern council estate (*Live like pigs,* 1958) and his vernacular dialogue is heightened, in the appropriate places, by poetry and haunting song. But you miss, in a reading, his visual qualities.... Arden is a playwright who compels his audience to thought, he is also, first and foremost, a playwright. (pp. 26-7)

> *J. D. Hainsworth, in* The Hibbert Journal, *Autumn, 1966.*

LAURENCE KITCHIN

The action of [*Armstrong's Last Goodnight*] is framed by the diplomat Lindsay who introduces it and signs it off. He and Armstrong are the main structural pillars. (p. 86)

[The play] registers equally as action drama with the basic appeal of a Western movie, or—given a nodding acquaintance with Middle English and the Border ballads—as recited epic. Beyond that it has [a] coherent political structure.... Lindsay's position in Armstrong's domain is like that of Machiavelli on his mission to Cesare Borgia and Armstrong meets the same fate as the rivals enticed by Borgia to a peace conference.... I'm not sure what's gained except entertainment by having Lindsay and Armstrong share the same mistress. But the infusion of evangelical religion, as in *Musgrave,* has Arden's signature on it. Perhaps the lack of it pulls down the temperature of his Magna Carta play a little; though not as much as King

John's late and disastrous address to the audience, which takes one back to the early pseudo-Brechtian days of the Royal Court on a Sunday night. (pp. 87-8)

What epic can't do is to accommodate private, esoteric states of feeling or complex analysis of character. From Virgil to screen Westerns, the characters act out the *type* of a Roman, a barbarian, an outlaw or whatever. The generic terms gun-man or law-man are of crucial importance. In this play, we ought to be thinking of political man, clansman, and man of God. . . . The language barrier is another matter; it depends on how far an audience should be made to work. If instant comprehension is the aim, then Arden is taking a risk. . . . Rather than question Arden's wisdom in choosing this idiom, we ought to thank him for reminding us of its directness and power. (p. 88)

> *Laurence Kitchin, in his* Drama in the Sixties: Form and Interpretation *(© 1966 by Laurence Kitchin; reprinted by permission of the author), Faber and Faber, 1966.*

MALCOLM PAGE

John Arden is, as Jack Richardson noted, "considered by many close to the theater to be England's best contemporary playwright." Yet his most-discussed play, *Serjeant Musgrave's Dance*, continues to puzzle or anger many critics. . . . Clearly there are grounds for uncertainty about the import of the play; difficulties in comprehension arose mainly because neither method nor subject was what the critics expected.

Arden has frequently explained his objectives in articles and interviews. He wishes to comment on the contemporary scene, and at the same time to express what is permanently important, to criticize "a sludgy uninterested nation, married to its telly and its fish and chips" through "the framework of the traditional poetic truths." Social relevance should be expressed through "a proper moral concern and a constant hatred of injustice and meanness." However, his morality is an unorthodox one, as it shows the values of freedom and spontaneity in the gypsies of *Live Like Pigs* (1958) and of Armstrong in *Armstrong's Last Goodnight* (1964) and then suggests that their outrageous behavior cannot be tolerated in an ordered, civilized society. Arden wants to be fair to both sides. . . . Conclusions may also be obscured because Arden evolves his judgments only as he writes. . . . Further, he approves the play that is provocative because action and argument contradict each other. . . . In *Serjeant Musgrave's Dance* what is right emotionally (Musgrave's generously-motivated fury) is wrong rationally (more killing is evil). There is thus abundant explanation for the absence of clear messages in Arden's work: his comments will not be confined to contemporary issues; he wants to be fair to the other side; his own view may be unresolved; he welcomes provocative contradictions within a play. The keynote of these remarks is caution and openness of mind.

Ultimately, however, he finds it possible both to be fair and to support one side . . . , though he considers also that "it would be presumptuous to make this sort of positive statement within the terms of an individual play." He hopes, instead, that his work "has suggested, play by play, that the existing social structure is entirely inadequate." Arden's political activities show that he is as involved with society as Arnold Wesker, though Arden's perspectives are

longer and he finds artistic considerations more important in his plays. . . . *Serjeant Musgrave's Dance* is sub-titled "an unhistorical *parable*" and Arden has explained that this play originated in a moment of anger at British violence in Famagusta. . . . The description of the atrocity given by the three soldiers towards the climax of the market-place scene of the play is very similar to the Cyprus episode. Apart from this, as in the other plays, the particular topical inspiration of the plays is concealed, though in some cases, the subjects—gypsies, violence and pacifism—might suggest that the author held radical views. Arden . . . is one of the writers who supports Left-wing ideas, but whose work shows this more by subject than by 'moral.' Arden finds it hard to reconcile his political views, his ability to see both sides of a question, and the kind of play he actually finds himself writing. (pp. 66-8)

[Arden himself thematically associated his play with the Viet Nam war conflicts, and] is desperately anxious that audiences should look for continued topical significance in *Musgrave*, and not dismiss it because the nature of the Cyprus dispute has changed. (p. 69)

[In his Introduction to the published text] Arden first emphasizes the topic of how easy it is to want to respond to the evil of violence with further and greater violence, then adds that this reaction is very wrong. Although this is the most common response at the level of power politics, Arden presents it in such a way in the market-place scene that the spectator is horrified. . . . There are five acts of violence in the play. . . . Each is presented to make clear Arden's disapproval. But he goes on to enrich the theme in a less usual way, by looking at the difficulties of the alternative. . . . [It] is precisely because the anti-war document is a hackneyed one in the theatre that Arden has done something much more unusual and controversial: he asks why pacifist ideas have not had more influence.

The play suggests that pacifists are not sure enough about what they are trying to do, and have not understood the complexities of the world. Musgrave's band have not worked out exactly what they are trying to do in the market-place, as Musgrave kept his plans to himself. His faith in Logic does not fit the facts of the world. . . . It is the strike, however, that is the unforseen complication for Musgrave's group. The strike could be a kind of non-violent action beyond the range of Musgrave's imagination, but the strikers do not put all their trust in this, and attempt to steal the soldiers' Gatling gun. . . . Most important, the strike exposes class conflict: the Mayor and Parson want an army since it removes and disciplines potential trouble-makers, a question hinting at the problem of who benefits from wars.

The limitations of the men themselves are more responsible for their failure than such circumstances as the strike. Attercliffe is a complete pacifist, asserting "all wars is sin," and "they've got to turn against all wars." . . . Yet even he can be aggressive toward Hurst near the end of the inn scene. . . . (pp. 70-1)

Ultimately it is Attercliffe, not their oratorical leader, who understands non-violence and puts himself in front of Musgrave's gun. Hurst is not a convert to pacifism, but a deserter . . . eager to kill in revenge for his suffering in the army. Sparky, too, has joined Musgrave in a moment of anger, at the useless death of his friend Billy. . . . Musgrave is limited by putting his faith in "good order and the discipline: it's the only road I know." . . . His religious fanaticism leads him in the end to see his actions as the work of God. . . . (p. 71)

The motives of pacifists are thus questioned. Repressed hostility is prominent in both Musgrave and Hurst, while his wife's unfaithfulness was a decisive experience in Attercliffe's life. Sparky's views are an unthinking and emotional reaction. Hurst's shortcomings suggest that pacifists are sometimes unwise in those they accept as allies. None of the privates is sufficiently dedicated and singleminded: drink and lust lead to the fight in the stable and Sparky's death. Though this is accidental, these confused and angry men are too feeble to lead the world to new and worthier standards. Arden suggests the virtues pacifists need, especially self-knowledge of the violence that may underlie pacifist principles. (pp. 71-2)

There are several other ideas in the play, perhaps too many. Musgrave and his followers are obsessed with guilt at the evil in which they joined, raising the issue of how to expiate it. . . . *Musgrave* touches, too, on the question of what principle is: where and how can one begin to apply principles in an imperfect world; does the quest of absolute principle lead to madness? *Armstrong's Last Goodnight* and *Left-Handed Liberty* (1965) develop the theme of principle versus expediency. The play refers specifically to the difficulty of attending both to immediate domestic problems, like the strike, and to foreign involvements. . . . The implication is that Britain becomes involved in situations like that in Cyprus because the public does not care about such issues.

Musgrave's venture, which will cost the lives of all four, has apparently changed nothing. . . . [Neither] the colliers nor Annie show any sign that they are going to be influenced by the action so that the soldier's protest will be continued. (p. 72)

Malcolm Page, "The Motives of Pacifists: John Arden's 'Serjeant Musgrave's Dance'" (copyright by Malcolm Page), in Drama Survey, *Spring-Summer, 1967, pp. 66-72.*

JOAN TINDALE BLINDHEIM

It is a common feature of criticism that the work of dramatists is explored from every conceivable literary angle, while its stage functions are usually neglected. This is particularly unfortunate in the case of John Arden, a writer who . . . displays acute awareness in his work of the demands and potentialities of the stage. (p. 306)

In his first published work for the stage, "The Waters of Babylon," Arden already shows in his brief note on the sets, not only that he has been aware of the problems involved in staging the play, but also that his knowledge of stage history has suggested solutions to him. The largely realistic form of the play, broken however by the frequent use of verse, might well tempt a director to give it a succession of realistic sets, but this would create scene-shifting problems on the practical level, and would also, I think, reduce the general application of the themes of the play. To avoid this, Arden directs that any localization of scenes should be suggested rather than illustrated, and in order to manage quick scene-changes which at the same time will constantly remind the audience that they are in a theatre, watching a play (Arden's recurring alienation effect), he proposes the use of sliding flats or drop curtains while the actors are on stage, as in eighteenth- or early nineteenth-century theatre. This is a neat device in "The Waters of Babylon," where Krank is "discovered" by the opening curtain, and the transfer to the next scene, a street, is achieved by the closing of the scene, which subsequently opens and closes continually. The furniture and other properties disclosed then indicate the locality—an architect's office, Speakers' Corner, and so on. It may be noted that in this first stage play Arden already uses the device of direct address to the audience, to extend the scope of the stage and reduce the barrier between actor and audience, which is a repeated feature of his later work. (pp. 306-07)

[Arden emerges] as a conscious and imaginative exploiter of visual effects and stage resources. His knowledge of stage history and his trained eye add dimensions to his work that are often absent from that of more "literary" writers. These are aspects that must not be ignored when his contribution to the drama is considered, and it is through them that he is likely to make a lasting contribution to the theatre too, in helping to break down theatre conventions and in striving towards a richer and more active relationship between actors and audience. (p. 316)

Joan Tindale Blindheim, "John Arden's Use of the Stage," in Modern Drama *(copyright © 1968, University of Toronto, Graduate Centre for Study of Drama; with the permission of* Modern Drama), *December, 1968, pp. 306-16.*

JOHN MILLS

Malcolm Page, in a recent article [see excerpt above], suggests that in *Sergeant Musgrave's Dance* John Arden is asking the question "why pacifist ideas have not had more influence" and that the answer, or moral, that the play expresses lies in the uncertain motives of the pacifists themselves. Since the play ends with a defeat of the four soldiers and a triumphal dance celebrating the continuity of the *status quo* (however uneasy and factional it may be) it would appear that Arden's ultimate position is one of pessimism. Though I agree with much of Dr. Page's commentary, I think that the play is a little more hopeful than he indicates. For one thing, it seems to me that *Musgrave* is less about pacifism than it is about anarchism, a doctrine which the play tentatively (as Arden himself might put it) urges.

To start with, the key event in the play is not the atrocity which takes place before the action starts and which motivates the desertion of the four soldiers, nor is it Act 3, Scene 1 wherein Musgrave's band confronts the population of the Northern mining town, although the latter scene, of course, is the play's climax in terms of narrative. Instead, the meaning of this very tightly constructed drama is developed in the pub scene, Act 2, Scene 3, and the key event is Annie's attempt to offer her love to each of the soldiers in turn.

Arden suggests that "a study of the roles of the women, and of Private Attercliffe, should be sufficient to remove any doubts as to where the 'moral' of the play lies." (p. 45)

[The] major threat to the performance of [the soldiers'] "duty" is the "life or love" that Annie has to offer.

Let us admit that Annie is scarcely an embodiment of the Life Force! Her "life" in this bleak town is harsh and sour. . . . Yet despite her bitterness and the sardonic quality of her speech she represents "all there is" in the bleak landscape of the play. (p. 46)

But Hurst rejects her, and it seems to me important to understand why.

Arden tells us in his introduction that he visualizes Hurst as "bloody-minded, quick tempered, handsome, cynical, tough, but not quite as intelligent as he thinks he is." Yet he emerges in the play in a somewhat different light. For one thing he is an obeyer of orders, a man who respects power, who cowers before the power invested in others, and who yearns to exert power of his own. Musgrave has little difficulty with him. . . . His rebelliousness, or at least the period during which he questions Musgrave's authority, is short lived. Musgrave can even make him accept the notion of God, or at least, pretend to accept it. . . . (pp. 46-7)

But Musgrave's talk of God seems, to Hurst, a fundamental weakening of the Sergeant's position. God is for parsons, old women, and other sentimentalists and in no sense can organized religion be made to correspond to the world as Hurst understands it. Life, to such a man, is tough, raw, brutal. Justice is a matter of power, and power is a combination of will, strategy, and brute strength. So Hurst's submission to Musgrave is only temporary and remains a surface matter with him until he overhears the Sergeant translating "God's plan" into secular terms. . . . "A clear plan, drawn out straight and black" means more to Hurst than vague talk about God. Particularly can he understand Musgrave's warning to Annie not to "stand between [these men] and their strength." . . .

Love equals desertion, or at least a dereliction of duty, as far as Hurst is concerned. (p. 47)

If there is little place for Annie in Hurst's violent world of discipline, authority, and good order, there is none at all in Attercliffe's. Attercliffe, Arden suggests, is "aged about fifty, grey-haired, melancholy, a little embittered." He seems to represent the position of complete non-violence in the play. . . . Attercliffe is dominated by an impulse to modify the behavior of others—by a desire to police the world. He interrupts the fight between the collier and the constable and it is he who puts his own body in the line of fire of the Gatling gun which Hurst has trained onto the crowd in the town square. He is, in other words, a non-violent man whose desire to reform human beings, i.e. to make them accept *his* point of view, involves him in violent events. He is a hollow man whose somewhat empty obsession renders him incapable of accepting the life and love that Annie offers him. He rejects her, just as Hurst does, and becomes, instead, a victim of other people's savagery. The fight in the stable, during which Sparky is killed, is at the same time an ironic manifestation of Attercliffe's own role in the events of the play, and a little parable about war: the impetus to kill comes from the savage Hurst, but the man who actually wields the bayonet, and does the killing, is Attercliffe, the man of decent and generous impulses.

Arden tells us that a study of Attercliffe's role should help us see where the "moral" of the play lies. He later suggests that the play may be advocating, "with some timidity," the doctrine of complete pacifism. If, however, the moral *is* complete pacifism and if this doctrine is embodied in the character of Attercliffe, then the play seems to me to fail. Attercliffe, as I have tried to show, is too much of a hollow man, too much of a "loser" to exemplify any set of values one could describe as "positive." In addition, there seems little to choose between Hurst's programmatic violence and Attercliffe's equally programmatic non-violence. Both attitudes imply authoritarian superstructures—Hurst's implies discipline, obedience, and therefore power over others, while Attercliffe's implies *prevention, police work,* etc.—in other words *power over others.* The play does not seem to me to fail, however, because there is an effective alternative to Attercliffe's position and it is expressed through the character of Sparky.

Sparky, Arden says, is "easily led, easily driven, inclined to hide from himself behind a screen of silly stories and irritating clownishness." . . . He appears stupid and incoherent—frivolous, even, throughout most of the play, but his emotion regarding the loss of his friend is genuine to the point of overpowering him. Coupled with this emotion is fear—chiefly of Musgrave whom he refers to, half ironically, as God. . . . When Annie, who has failed with Hurst and Attercliffe, breaks down and begins to weep, Sparky attempts, somewhat fearfully, to comfort her, and, in doing so, himself. When the light goes out in Musgrave's room Sparky gradually gains confidence. . . . And, no longer in God's eye or what amounts to the same thing, Musgrave's "good order," Sparky can offer himself to the girl. . . . This, he discovers, is what payment means—although Billy Hicks cannot be avenged it may be that he can be "replaced." The concept begins to take shape and Sparky, "following his thought in great disturbance of mind," expresses it "with a sudden access of resolution," and "with a switch to hard seriousness." (pp. 48-50)

At this point, then, and just before he is killed, Sparky attains a genuinely anarchic point of view which (in terms of the play) runs something like this: the problem is not one of violence or nonviolence, pacifism or hostility, rather the question is how, and with what, does a man survive? The soldiers' life is basically little different from the life of a civilian—in fact life in this bleak, wintry, coal town as a "free" man is probably worse than life in some sunlit colony. In the Army there are Musgraves, Hursts, and Attercliffes—but their counterparts in civilian life, mayors, constables, and parsons, disguise themselves a little more and are thus probably a good deal more dangerous. The point is that a man is free neither as a soldier, nor as a deserter, nor as a civilian and, in any walk of life, he encounters those who wish him to conform to their point of view and use authority, discipline, or brutality to achieve their ends. So that a man who values his freedom is everywhere on the run. But just as the Army is like civilian life in this negative respect, so is it as a means of pursuing "life and love." In the Army there is a Billy Hicks; in civilian life, an Annie. One survives by refusing to be used and the most, and the best, that one can do is to seek out love—not for mankind, or for institutions, but for individuals. One dies in the end, of course, as Sparky dies, for there is no final escape from the forces that are trying to kill. But "life and love" before this happens is an escape from authority and a refusal to allow oneself to be used—either as victim or as executioner.

This, then, seems to me to be the message of the play. If Arden were to have allowed Sparky to survive after he has, at last, ceased to "hide from himself" the play would not have been any the less pessimistic (if the message is, in fact, pessimistic) and his action would have been weakened structurally. For it is the knowledge that Sparky has been killed that causes the colliers to refuse to join in Musgrave's insane dance. (pp. 50-1)

John Mills, "Love and Anarchy in 'Sergeant Musgrave's Dance'," in Drama Survey (copyright 1969 by The Bolingbroke Society, Inc.), Winter, 1968-69, pp. 45-51.

ARNOLD P. HINCHLIFFE

[John Arden is not] lacking in personal anger but he is the dramatist *par excellence* who translates that anger into situations of a strictly impersonal nature. Arden's characters are primarily used as representatives, and his plots bring about conflicts between social groups. His characters, of course, exist as very colourful individuals, but their personality is shaped at all times to suggest what they stand for . . . and add to the picture of the community as a whole. Thus, the isolated town or national politics reflected in local government is observed with an accurate social eye and a strong historical sense which combine to 'translate the concrete life of today into terms of poetry that shall at the one time illustrate that life and set it within the historical and legendary tradition of our culture'. (p. 76)

Like Brecht, Arden is a political playwright but only in the sense that he feels it is impossible to avoid being political since man is a political animal. Everything that man does is a political act. For Arden politics means the art of living together and if the actual technical aspects are the province of the politician everyone should be concerned and recognise that any play about people is political. But where Brecht, as a practising communist, is didactic, Arden sees the Marxist analysis as only one of many sources and solutions. It can be used, as in *Sjt. Musgrave's Dance,* but not to the extent of making the play Marxist. Arden discovered Brecht the theatre technician only after writing plays and believes that both Brecht and himself had been inspired by the same things: the Middle Ages, the Elizabethans and various styles, such as the Chinese and Japanese theatres. Arden does invite us to watch and judge the action of the play (like Brecht) but like his contemporary dramatists on a human rather than an ideological level. [Brecht] achieves alienation through the use of blatantly theatrical devices, like song and dance, but for Arden such devices must be integral rather than interrupt the performance.

The Waters of Babylon (1957) showed the Arden method albeit in confused shape. Starting as a satire on Macmillan's Premium Bond scheme it deals with the career of Sigismanfred Krankiewiecz—a pimp, an unscrupulous landlord and at work during the day in an architect's office. The play shows a use of plot, a large amount of incident and a large number of characters—all three necessary to exhibit the triple life of the central character. . . . The dialogue is written in too many styles, and the private lives of the characters are too lively for them to be submerged in the public events which are Arden's main interest. But the play is always interesting and presents, if one looks at it closely, the embryonic shape of that opposition between vitality and order which is the basis of most of Arden's work.

This opposition emerged in his next play *Soldier, Soldier* (1960). . . . Here most of the characters speak in prose but the central character uses a rough type of blank verse. Arden intended this to suggest values: the strident, disorderly soldier (verse) and the respectable, quiet townsfolk (prose). The soldier enjoys the kind of life which invites trouble while the townsfolk sacrifice everything, including pleasure, to avoid trouble. . . . Arden intends this soldier to be seen as representative of every soldier and likeable: as the

poetry in life. But he also insists that we do not think of the victims as contemptible, a balance explored dramatically in [*Live Like Pigs* (1958)]. . . . It is written almost entirely in prose and looks at the results of putting a gypsy family on a housing estate somewhere in the West Riding of Yorkshire. Many critics felt . . . that it needed pruning; but they also noted the racy, turbulent vitality of the play. Most critics also seem to feel that our sympathy was intended for the intruders and that at the end, as with the town in *Soldier, Soldier,* order may be restored but life is none the better for that. If sympathy on Arden's part is limited for restored order his dispassionate presentation scarcely makes the gypsies likeable as neighbours. (pp. 77-8)

Arden broke with naturalism fairly decisively in *Sjt. Musgrave's Dance* (1959) and has since been moving towards simplicity, extreme formalism and a bold use of primary colours. . . . [The] complex plot is hardly susceptible to précis and confusing in the theatre. Is Arden supporting pacifism in his play, as he certainly does in life, or is he pointing out the complex roots of violence with a pessimistic conclusion? Arden himself confesses that he had problems; he started with the climax of the play and was then left with the task of making that climax credible in a number of scenes which would allow both the soldiers and the townsfolk to reveal their attitudes. . . . The play owes something to Brecht's version of *The Recruiting Officer—Drums and Trumpets*—and took hints from an American film called *The Raid.* It is Arden's first excursion into a historical setting. But where dramatists like Osborne and Bolt concentrate on an individual, isolated and therefore modern, and using language in a heroic manner, Arden is interested in groups and his historical setting deliberately suggests no particular period while evoking many. . . . Some of the characters are still far from convincing even as representatives (*e.g.* the mayor and the parson) but Arden has described them as caricatures by omission rather than exaggeration. Some of the situations are clearly decided by the plot rather than by character—for example the reaction of the soldiers to Annie in the stable. The colliers, who are to look like figures in a Lowry painting, do not need to stand out but when one has to speak as an individual the dialogue is not strong enough. Possibly this weakness stems from the ballad tradition espoused by Arden. (pp. 79-80)

Arden sees the ballad as the bedrock of English poetry and the method by which he could become a poet of the theatre. He recognised that he must not become too private or his plays would be valuable only for reading, or, like Yeats's, actable only in a drawing-room theatre before an inevitably élitist audience. The ballad, with its sense of season, the passing of time, strong primary colours and strong narrative line was suitable for a theatre where costumes, movement, verbal patterns and music must all be strong and hard. If verse is to be used it must be obviously verse as opposed to the surrounding prose and never allowed to droop into what Arden calls 'casual flaccidities'. Arden, therefore, sought simple but basic situations and themes to express social criticism and a framework of traditional poetic truths to give weight to what might otherwise be only contemporary documentary facility. Such a technique can be misunderstood since audiences find it difficult to give a simple response to the story. In the ballad, as in the fable, we draw our own conclusions. Arden chose verse though he recognised that other forms are available and has remarked, for example, on the effects gained by Pinter whose dialogue *becomes* poetic. His choice of the ballad is political. It reaches back into history and works in a moral atmosphere of multiple standards which he prefers and demonstrates in *Sjt. Musgrave's Dance*. There we meet the dilemma of war and violence in which pacifism (his own instinctive choice) is shown to be not self-sufficiently right. . . . The issue of war and violence, of order versus anarchy, has . . . shifted into terms of good government and the clash between principle and expediency. (pp. 80-2)

The commedia dell'arte mask obviously appealed to Arden for [*The Happy Haven* (1959-60)]. He wanted a style of theatre which used types [as he] was using young people to play old characters. The masks were appropriate, for age is seen as a mask which has hardened over the years and can be ripped off by rejuvenation. Possibly, too, the circumstances of the play led Arden to award the victory to anarchy in this play as the old people refuse to be made young (albeit for very childish reasons) and turn the doctor into a child.

Arden returned to the subject of good government in 1960 with his nativity play. . . . *The Business of Good Government* is an odd title for a Nativity play but Arden's version is scarcely orthodox. Its central character is really Herod, a man pushed into a corner from which the only escape is by massacring the innocents. Arden admits that his Herod is blatantly unhistorical. Critics have complained that the end of the play is inconclusive and that Arden should have kept his initial focus on Herod. However fascinating that exercise would have been the play is restored to its proper direction and ends with the miracle of the field of corn that shields the Holy Family on its flight into Egypt. Arden is noticeably trying to simplify the dramatic action aware that people have no time to watch *and* listen. But he still uses language contrasts. The Angel [for example] speaks with Biblical grandeur. . . . Herod on the other hand uses colloquial prose although at the end of the play when he discusses the business of good government this rises to something nearer the poetic. (pp. 82-3)

[*The Workhouse Donkey* (1963)] is an apparently domestic play, a comedy or as he called it a 'vulgar melodrama' in an idiom close to that of 'low music-hall and seaside picture postcards'. In this he revived a favourite character Alderman Charlie Butterthwaite. . . . It is a full picture of the local borough as a modern city state (and hence not domestic in scope) derived from Arden's observation of how councils still ran the boroughs of the West Riding in the grand nineteenth-century manner. Its subject is the business of good government dealt with through groups which cover all the social elements (except, curiously, the working class) attached to a story which centres, as in *Ironhand* [a translation and rewriting he did of Goethe's *Goetz von Berlichingen*], on two men, Butterthwaite and Feng. . . . In the end both men lose their positions and Arden pointed out that if his personal preference was for Butterthwaite he does not want to convert anyone. There are many people who would have integrity at any price rather than corruption. But the only conclusion, as in *Ironhand,* is that the ones who survive are the compromisers, the little men. (p. 84)

Arden reaches his clearest statement of the basic theme in his work with *Armstrong's Last Goodnight* (1964). . . . After reading Conor Cruise O'Brien's *To Katanga and Back* he fused the desire to write a play about the Congo

with this incident in Scottish history making O'Brien into Lindsay and Tshombe/Lumumba into Armstrong. Through these characters he shows the inadequacy of political expediency and yet deliberately avoids suggesting whether there is an alternative. As before, the characters fall into groups and the plot resolves itself into the familiar conflict between two principles: anarchy (the robber baron Armstrong) and order (the mature, but devious, Lindsay). (pp. 84-5)

As in his Nativity play Arden shifts the centre [in *Left-Handed Liberty* (1965)] to the character usually thought to be the villain of the piece: King John. The conflict here lacks epic scope but it also lacks the linguistic difficulties encountered in *Armstrong's Last Goodnight* where Arden had deliberately invented his own version of Middle Scottish. The themes are liberty, the value of treaties and the irony of history. There is clarity of argument but also the sense that texture and individuality are lost beneath historical research. . . . The play sustains the idea that 'an agreement on paper is worth nothing to nobody unless it has taken place in their minds as well'. (pp. 85-6)

If the central attitudes to naturalism have not been seriously challenged, Arden has added ambiguity to identification and illusion as a theatrical method. This is more than lip service to Brecht whom Arden places with dramatists like Euripides, Jonson and Ibsen as makers of a new idiom in the theatre. Since Brecht is closest in time he is probably the strongest influence. But Arden's dramatised attitudes are seldom absolutes—right or wrong—and his personal preferences never obtrude and are, as he continues to insist, irrelevant. These attitudes he tries to strengthen and make universal by the use of historical parallels which challenge an easy judgement and require, as it seems to him, that mixture of prose and verse he has worked at with such earnestness. (pp. 86-7)

It is the plays themselves [and not the staging] that create a sense of strangeness—by incident and language—revealing a vision of the world which is essentially pessimistic, and shows life as senseless, absurd. But it is more than Brechtian devices that separates Arden from the theatre of the Absurd. His plays are acted out in the real world not dream or fantasy, and the vision is not subjective. Absurd Drama reaches social problems through individuals whereas for Arden individuals are representative, and however vigorous and lively as individuals, their failure or success is first and foremost a tragic comment on the state of society. It is always the *social* predicament that faces us at the end of the play. Moreover, Arden needs plot to create the network of social inter-relationships from which this judgement proceeds, whereas the theatre of the Absurd must positively discourage plot to convey its sense of futility.

Arden appears to be sitting on a fence; and he pleases few. As he ruefully recognises, from *Live Like Pigs* onwards, his plays have resisted the propagandist and the poetic: not programmatic enough for the former and too documentary for the latter. The only absolute to emerge from Arden's work is that absolutes—even in good causes and for better reasons—only drive their followers into a simplistic attitude. This attitude overlooks the complex nature of human beings and society and finally serves only itself rather than human ends and desires. By *Armstrong's Last Goodnight* Arden can show sympathy towards both Lindsay and Armstrong but he curtails warmth towards either; the audience probably expects warmth. More than any other contemporary dramatist Arden seems to find the lack of forms and conventions frustrating. He continues to be worried by the fact that people find his plays incomprehensible. Theatre, after all, is a public art and a dramatist who is out of touch is failing to practise his art properly. On the other hand, if theatre is not to atrophy, a dramatist must get out of touch to step forward. Perhaps a lapse of time is needed to show whether Arden took one step too many and resolve the paradox of this twentieth-century poetic dramatist. (pp. 88-9)

> *Arnold P. Hinchliffe, in his* British Theatre 1950-70 *(© Basil Blackwell 1974), Rowman and Littlefield, 1974.*

* * *

ASHBERY, John   1927-

Ashbery is an American poet, dramatist, novelist, editor, and critic. He has sustained an active interest in art and art criticism throughout his career and acknowledges the influence of abstract painting on his verse. Ashbery's poetry has often been criticized for what seems to be intentional obscurity. He has collaborated with James Schuyler on the novel, *A Nest of Ninnies.* **(See also** *CLC,* **Vols. 2, 3, 4, 6, 9, and** *Contemporary Authors,* **Vols. 5-8, rev. ed.)**

HAROLD BLOOM

I cannot avoid the judgment that the year's best book of poems is Ashbery's *Houseboat Days.* . . . The modish eccentricities that once weakly defended this great poet against tradition are now all but gone. Instead, a subtle rhetoric, masking itself in images of transparency and as a style of amazing limpidity, evades and reinterprets poetic tradition as sinuously and persuasively as did the rhetoric of Frost and of Stevens. Four poems in particular are likely to impose themselves upon the canon: "Loving Mad Tom," "Wet Casements," the Orphic elegy, "Syringa," and the very ambitious and mellow longer poem, "Fantasia on 'The Nut-Brown Maid'," which sustains comparison with the magnificent "Fragment" of "The Double Dream of Spring." "Wet Casements," which is as powerful as "Soonest Mended" in that volume, is a short meditation that immediately establishes its inevitability. Ashbery has suffered both from the aura of his supposed "school" and from the incomprehension of readers who weary too quickly of authentic poetic difficulty. The difficulty that remains in Ashbery's poetry is inseparable from its glory. (pp. 24-5)

> *Harold Bloom, in* The New Republic *(reprinted by permission of* The New Republic; *© 1977 by The New Republic, Inc.), November 26, 1977.*

RICHARD HOWARD

Most of the poems in *Houseboat Days* which I can make out at all are . . . deliberations on the meaning of the present tense, its exactions and falsifications, its promises and reward. "There are no other questions than these, / half-squashed in mud, emerging out of the moment / we all live, learning to like it"—Ashbery is often painfully clear as to what he would wring from his evasive experience ("what I am probably trying to do is to illustrate opacity and how it can suddenly descend over us . . . it's a kind of mimesis of how experience comes to me"), and the pain is there in the tone, now goofy and insolent, then again tender and self-deprecating, vulnerable but not without its gnomic as-

sertions ("It is the nature of things to be seen only once"), various but not without a consistent grimace ("It's all bits and pieces, spangles, patches, really; nothing / stands alone").

The position from which these proceedings flow and flare is rather the converse of what I read in the [*Self-Portrait in a Convex Mirror*]; in that book, the problem was how to deal with the world—if it is all there, then how do I get into it, how do I find a place in what is already *given* and, if I am already there, how can there be room for all that besides? But in [*Houseboat Days*] there is a cool resolution about the dialectic of self and other; the poet seems more or less content (more or less sad) to be at grips with "this tangle of impossible resolutions and irresolutions," but only *for now.* The trouble, and his subject, is that the moment passes, that *now* becomes *then,* losing everything in the process. Whatever is easy-moving, free and pleasant tends to calcify, or to rot, leaving dust and ash on the mind's plate: "The songs decorate our notion of the world / and mark its limits, like a frieze of soap-bubbles."

Whence a prosody of intermittence and collage; no such conventional markings as rhyme or repetition—rather, *seamless verse,* jammed rather than enjambed, extended rather than intense; it must go on and on to keep the whole contraption from coming round again, and to work upon us its deepest effect, which is a kind of snake-charming. . . . [The title poem] refers specifically, I believe, to living in the present, one's domicile upon an inconstant element, one's time at the mercy and the rigor of the stream: "The mind / is so hospitable, taking in everything / like boarders, and you don't see until / it's all over how little there was to learn / once the stench of knowledge has dissipated . . ." The misery in this poem, as in all the rest, is that of being deprived by the past and the future of the present; it is only now that the poet can see and seize the clutter as fertilizing, "not just the major events but the whole incredible / mass of everything happening simultaneously and pairing off, / channeling itself into history"; experience is wrenched away—is no longer "his"—by the suspect neatness of memory, as by the sacrificial omissions of art, and so these poems are not to record a life, they are not memorials, any more than they are to decorate a tradition, they are not monuments. "What I am writing to say is, the timing, not / the contents, is what matters"—hence almost anything will turn up inside these "parts of the same body," and almost anyone—any pronoun—will become someone else. . . . Ashbery twitches the text away from personality: "I don't think my poetry is inaccessible . . . I think it's about the privacy of everyone." And perhaps that is why they present such brutal clarifications: the privacy of everyone is a hard thing to acknowledge, especially when it is staring you from the page, hysterically open to distraction, eager to grab the language of packaging and put it into the *perpetuum mobile* of poetry. The texts include everything, they leave out only the necessary transitions and gearshifts which we call narrative and which have traditionally governed the decorum of our attention. In such a world, "things overheard in cafes assume an importance previously reserved for letters from the front"—and indeed, the front itself shifts to the back room, the view from the kitchen window, the voices overheard in the next bedroom. Of course no poem can keep pace with "eventuality," with the character and quality of existence as it becomes event—not even Ashbery's poem can satisfy him as to the scope and focus of "the present"—but the zany failures mount up as the only important enterprise, undertaking, over-drive. . . . (p. 25)

So Ashbery's poems will be meditations on how to write his poems, where to begin in order always to be beginning, without that dying fall of classical recital, instead inscribed upon the evanescence of eternity: "a final flourish / that melts as it stays." Painting and music too will help—take the string quartet:

> The different parts are always meddling with each
>   other,
> Pestering each other, getting in each other's ways
> So as to withdraw skillfully at the end, leaving—what?
> A new kind of emptiness, maybe bathed in freshness,
> Maybe not. Maybe just a new kind of emptiness.

That is the risk this poetry takes, of course: by jettisoning the traditional baggage of the art and assimilating instead the methods and "morality" of the other arts . . . , the poet incurs the possibility of "maybe just a new kind of empti-ness." But the risk is worth it to Ashbery, who has never dismissed the religious possibility of emptiness—affectless-ness, abjection—as *the* condition of fulfillment. . . . It is worth what I call the risk and what he would call the neces-sity of emptiness—boredom, confusion, irritation, even torment—to reach what he undoubtedly and diligently *does* reach, a world whose terms are refreshed to the point, to the pinnacle, where experience is without anxiety because it is *delivered,* in both senses of that word: presented and released. A world without anxiety, without repression, without the scandal and the labor of the negative. Or as Ashbery puts it:

> Something
> Ought to be written about how this affects
> You when you write poetry:
> The extreme austerity of an almost empty mind
> Colliding with the lush, Rousseau-like foliage of its
>   desire to communicate
> Something between breaths, if only for the sake
> Of others and their desire to understand you
>   and desert you
> For other centers of communication, so that
>   understanding
> May begin, and in doing so be undone.
>
>   (p. 26)

> *Richard Howard, "New Ashbery," in* New York Arts Journal *(copyright © 1977 by Richard W. Burgin), #7, November-December, 1977, pp. 25-6.*

DAVID KALSTONE

Familiar notions about a poet's development won't quite apply to Ashbery's work. He doesn't return to objects, fig-ures and key incidents which, as the career unfolds, gather increasing symbolic resonance. Nor do his poems refer to one another in any obvious way. Ashbery writes autobiog-raphy only inasmuch as he writes about the widening sense of what it is like to gain—or to try to gain—access to his experience. The present is the poem. "I think that any one of my poems might be considered to be a snapshot of what-ever is going on in my mind at the time. . . ." (p. 171)

In his images of thwarted nature, of discontinuity between present and past, Ashbery has turned his agitation into a principle of composition. From the start he has looked for

sentences, diction, a syntax which would make these feel-ings fully and fluidly available. When he used strict verse forms, as he did in much of his first book, *Some Trees,* it was always with a sense of their power to explore rather than to certify that he was a poet. (pp. 171-72)

The long title poem of [*Self-Portrait in a Convex Mirror*] is in every sense a major work, a strong and beautiful resolu-tion of besetting and important problems. Ashbery had al-ready broached these problems in *The Double Dream of Spring,* in which he characteristically approached the world as a foreigner, sometimes in the role of explorer, sometimes as a pilgrim, and almost always as someone bewildered by the clutter of a situation which, wryly phrased, "could not be better." The world of that book is often divided, out of bristling necessity, between inside and outside, between *we* and a dimly identified *they*. . . . (p. 173)

A lot could be said about Ashbery's entrance into poems and his habit of tentative anchorage: "As on a festal day in early spring," "As One Put Drunk into the Packet Boat" (title: first line of Marvell's "Tom May's Death"). Such openings are reticent, similes taking on the identity of an-other occasion, another person—a sideways address to their subject or, in the case of "Self-Portrait," a way of dealing with temptation. The speaker in "Self-Portrait" appears to "happen" upon Parmigianino's painting as a solution to a problem pondered before the poem begins. At first glimpse the glass of art and the face in the portrait offer him just the right degree of self-disclosure and self-asser-tion, the right balance of living spirit and the haunting con-centrated maneuvers of art. The judicious give-and-take appeals to him: thrust and swerve; toward and away; pro-tect and advertise. (This is, by the way, one of the best descriptive impressions of a painting I know.) That bal-anced satisfaction never returns. What at first comforts him, the face "in repose," prompts an unsettling fear: "It is what is / Sequestered." This is the first full sentence of the poem—brief, shocked and considered, after the glancing descriptive phrases. An earlier draft of the lines was weaker: "protected" rather than "sequestered" and the word placed unemphatically at the end of the line, as if some of the menace to be sensed in the finished portrait hadn't yet surfaced.

From then on the poem becomes, as Ashbery explains it in a crucial pun, "speculation / (From the Latin *speculum,* mirror)," Ashbery's glass rather than Francesco's. All questions of scientific reflection, capturing a real presence, turn instantly into the other kind of reflection: changeable, even fickle thought. The whole poem is a series of revisions prepared for in the opening lines, where in Parmigianino's receding portrait he imagines first that "the soul establishes itself," then that "the soul is a captive." (pp. 176-77)

"The soul is not a soul." Acting on an earlier hint that Parmigianino's mirror chose to show an image "glazed, embalmed," Ashbery sees it in its hollow (overtones of bur-ial) rather than in the neutral "space intended." "Our moment of attention" draws sparks between the glazed sur-face of the portrait and the poet's transient interest which awakens it, and places notions like the *soul* irredeemably in the eye of the beholder. When the poet looks at this ghostly double, alive in its mirroring appeal, the emerging fear comes across. . . . (pp. 177-78)

Throughout "Self-Portrait in a Convex Mirror" the poet

speaks to the portrait as in easy consultation with a familiar, but with an ever changing sense of whether he is addressing the image, trapped on its wooden globe, or addressing the free painter standing outside his creation, straining to capture a real presence, restraining the power to shatter what may become a prison. . . . Philosophic questions mount, but always apprehended through gestures, new expressions glimpsed as one stares at the painting—here a glint of self-mockery, as the painter absorbed with prowess finds himself trapped by his medium after all. "But your eyes proclaim / That everything is surface. . . . / There are no recesses in the room, only alcoves." The window admits light, but all sense of change is excluded, even "the weather, which in French is / *Le temps,* the word for time." (pp. 178-79)

[There is] a series of struggles with the past, with "art," with the notion of "surface," with the random demands of the present—struggles which are not only at the heart of this poem but a paradigm of Ashbery's work. Parmigianino's portrait has to compete with the furniture of the mind confronting it: the poet's day, memories, surroundings, ambitions, distractions. . . . There is a rhythm to reading this poem, however wandering it may seem. We experience it as a series of contractions and expansions of interest in the painting, depending upon how much the poet is drawn to its powers of foreshortening and concentration, and alternately how cramped he feels breathing its air. The transitions between sections are marked as easy shifts in inner weather, opposed to the weatherless chamber of Parmigianino's portrait. . . . (pp. 179-80)

[What happens] when we start to imagine the life of cities behind the surface of a work of art, in this case the sack of Rome which was going on where Francesco was at work; Vienna where Ashbery saw the painting in 1959; New York where he is writing his poem? These are ways Ashbery has of summoning up the countless events which nourished the painting and his response to it. That outside life, again imagined in terms of risk, adventure, voyages, can be profoundly disturbing—a life not palpable in a "finished" work.

>   a chill, a blight
> Moving outward along the capes and peninsulas
> Of your nervures and so to the archipelagoes
> And to the bathed, aired secrecy of the open sea. . . .

Such images focus the problem of how much life is lived in and outside a work of art. There is no point in disentangling what is hopelessly intertwined. The images flow toward and counter one another, and the reader accumulates a bewildering sense of what it is to be both fulfilled and thwarted by his own grasped moments of vision (all attempts at order, not just artistic creation, Ashbery tries to remind us). Francesco's portrait has the capacity to make us feel at home; we "can live in it as in fact we have done." Or "we linger, receiving / Dreams and inspirations on an unassigned / Frequency." But at another moment the portrait seems like a vacuum drawing upon *our* plenty, "fed by our dreams." If at one point the mind straying from the conical painting is like a balloon bursting, not much later the straying thoughts are imagined as wayward, even sinister progeny of the painting: the balloon has not burst at all. "Actually / The skin of the bubble-chamber's as tough as / Reptile eggs."

Struggling with the past, with art and its completeness, Ashbery is also struggling with the impulses behind his own writing at the very moment of writing. (pp. 181-82)

By the closing pages of the poem two irreconcilable views of "living" have proposed themselves. Parmigianino's appears to be a "Life-obstructing task." ("You can't live there.") More than that, the portrait exposes the poet's own efforts in the present:

> Our time gets to be veiled, compromised
> By the portrait's will to endure. It hints at
> Our own, which we were hoping to keep hidden. . . .

When "will to endure" and "life-obstructing" are identified with one another, as they are here in describing our daily fiction-making activities, the psychological contradictions are themselves almost unendurable. Imagining is as alien and miraculous as the ambivalent image he finds for it: "A ship / Flying unknown colors has entered the harbor." Our creations, torn out of our hands, seem installed "on some monstrous, near / Peak, too close to ignore, too far / For one to intervene." Another way of looking at it: "the way of telling" intrudes "as in the game where / A whispered phrase passed around the room / Ends up as something completely different."

An alternative? Though the poem is always pressing us out of the past, it has no unmediated language for the present, which is as hard to locate as other poets' Edens. . . . There is no comfort in the provisional, in being open to the rush of things. In fact, one of the most devastating contemporary critiques of randomness in poetry comes in the final moments of Ashbery's poem. Yet it is a critique from within, in a poem open to the vagaries of mind—and from a writer deeply committed to describing the struggles we undergo in describing our lives. This is his unique and special place among contemporary poets. The blurring of personal pronouns, their often indeterminate reference, the clouding of landscapes and crystal balls, are all ways of trying to be true not only to the mind's confusions but also to its resistance of stiffening formulations.

In the distorting self-portrait of Parmigianino, Ashbery found the perfect mirror and the perfect antagonist—a totem of art and the past caught in the act of trying to escape from itself. . . . Francesco is the indispensable partner in a continuing conversation; yet Ashbery's final reading of the painterly hand in the self-portrait is the boldest stroke of all:

> Therefore I beseech you, withdraw that hand,
> Offer it no longer as shield or greeting,
> The shield of a greeting, Francesco:
> There is room for one bullet in the chamber:
> Our looking through the wrong end
> Of the telescope as you fall back at a speed
> Faster than that of light to flatten ultimately
> Among the features of the room, . . .
>
>   (pp. 182-84)

The pun on *chamber,* the dizzying transformations of rounded room into telescope and gun barrel, are triumphant tributes to all the contradictions of this poem and the hard-won struggle to be free of them. It would be a shallow reading which sees this poem as a modernist's dismissal of the past. Ashbery translates that *topos* into radical and embracing human terms. The elation we feel comes from the writer's own unwillingness to take permanent shelter in his work. Any work of art—not just those of the distant past—has designs on us, exposes for what it is our "will to endure." Ashbery builds the awareness of death and change into the very form of his work. . . . Ashbery admits into the interstices of his poem a great deal of experience—confusion, comedy, befuddlement, preoccupation—in which he takes as much joy as in the "cold pockets / Of remembrance, whispers out of time," which he also celebrates. His withdrawal from the privileged moments is never as regretful or as final as Keats's from his "cold pastoral." Nor is it as rueful as Ashbery's own sense of desertion in "Definition of Blue" where "you, in this nether world that could not be better / Waken each morning to the exact value of what you did and said, which remains." In that earlier poem Ashbery feels diminished and powerless before a "portrait, smooth as glass, . . . built up out of multiple corrections," which "has no relation to the space or time in which it was lived." In the spaciousness of "Self-Portrait in a Convex Mirror" Ashbery radiates a new confidence in his ability to accommodate what is in the poet's mind: the concentrated poem and its teeming surroundings. In its achieved generosity and fluidity, in its stops and starts and turns, Ashbery's long poem dispels some of the frustrations of language and form, or assimilates them more closely into the anxieties and frustrations of living. (pp. 184-85)

[With] *Three Poems* Ashbery rounded a critical corner. Its *perpetuum mobile* style prepared him, when he returned to verse, for a new fluidity, a way to re-admit the self to his poetry. Alive in its present, and determined as a Jack-in-the-Box, that self pops up when any moment of poetic concision threatens to falsify or obliterate it. The discovery comes as a relief, not so much a calculation as a necessity. Leaving things out, "forget as we will, something soon comes to stand in their place. Not the truth, perhaps, but—yourself."

I am talking, then, about complementary gifts or voices in Ashbery's poetry. He has his own deadpan way of putting it: "In the last few years I have been attempting to keep meaningfulness up to the pace of randomness . . . but I really think that meaningfulness can't get along without randomness and that they somehow have to be brought together." No wonder that the long "Self-Portrait in a Convex Mirror" stands as a centerpiece to his work in the early 1970s; no single short poem could handle such a copious problem. It would be a mistake to see this merely as an aesthetic question, a poet talking about poetry, about the relative virtues of condensed vision and expansive randomness. The emotional coloring that Ashbery gives this conflict, especially in his long poem, suggests psychological dimensions and stresses. Art "leaving things out" involves a sense of melancholy and sacrifice, a restlessness, a threat to vitality.

The Double Dream of Spring is shadowed by such feelings; the short poems of *Self-Portrait in a Convex Mirror* often counter them. Together these two books, five years apart, with their different moods, give a sense of the range and playfulness and boldness of Ashbery's emerging work. (pp. 187-88)

In *The Double Dream of Spring* Ashbery seems absorbed in the forms that lie just behind an experience; the day's events, in "Years of Indiscretion," are "Fables that time invents / To explain its passing." Common phrases are chal-

lenged; buried meanings are coaxed out of them so that they surprise us with a life of their own, or chastise us for a sleepy acceptance of the "phraseology we become." Ashbery wants to push past the hardening of life into habit, the way it congeals into patterned phrases. . . . (p. 188)

I am struck by the frequency with which Ashbery returns in *Double Dream* to myths of the seasons, as to photographic negatives, for the true contours governing experience—and what's more important, he is looking not for myths of rebirth but for myths of diminution. . . .

Ashbery takes his title *The Double Dream of Spring* from de Chirico and so puts us on warning that we are stepping through the looking glass into those deep perspectives and receding landscapes of the mind. He leads us, once we are prepared to follow, to yearned-for, difficult states, free of casual distraction. . . .

Does the present exist principally "To release the importance / Of what will always remain invisible?" he asks, with some urgency, in "Fragment." *The Double Dream of Spring* seems to answer that question in the affirmative. It is Ashbery's most successfully visionary book, however sad its tone. Unlike *Self-Portrait in a Convex Mirror,* which struggles to include and authenticate the present, *Double Dream* finds the most striking images in its glimpses of the fables behind our lives, and it most yearns for the state which is both free and deathlike, diminished. (p. 191)

"Soonest Mended"—so goes the title of one of the best of these poems, illustrating a point we can scarcely grasp until we supply the first half of a proverb which has been mimetically suppressed: "least said; soonest mended." *Double Dream* calls for tight-lipped irony as well as yearning for visionary release. In "Soonest Mended" comic self-awareness and proverbial wisdom are the ways Ashbery finds to deal with the deposits of history and hazard which determine the course of life:

> They were the players, and we who had struggled at
> the game
> Were merely spectators, though subject to its
> vicissitudes
> And moving with it out of the tearful stadium, borne on
> shoulders, at last.

It is entirely in keeping with the tone of this poem that we are left uncertain as to whether we are borne out of the stadium triumphant or dead. Or both. Just as, at the end of "Soonest Mended," action is described as

> this careless
> Preparing, sowing the seeds crooked in the furrow,
> Making ready to forget, and always coming back
> To the mooring of starting out, that day so long ago.

The brave carelessness here is licensed by some certainty that no matter how many mistakes we make, no matter what happens, we *do* return to the "mooring of starting out." We can also read this as helplessness. The tone is partly elegiac, owning up to the futility of our efforts, with "mooring" sounding as much like death as a new life. The entire poem has this doubleness of feeling. Its long breathy lines shift quickly from one historical hazard to another; it doesn't take long to get from the endangered Angelica of Ariosto and Ingres to Happy Hooligan in his rusted green automobile. Caught up in a whirligig of historical process, the self has no chance to recover balance, and above all, no conceptual means, no language to do so. Still, the energetic lines breathe the *desire* to assert ego and vitality. The poem sees the world as so full of bright particulars that no rules of thumb can keep up with them; and so it is fairly bitter about standard patterns of history and learning, sees them only as shaky hypotheses. "Soonest Mended" doesn't yet pretend pleasure in the present, a pleasure Ashbery *does* experience in later poems; and yet the poem doesn't entirely fall back on dreams of another world. Falling back, not with too much conviction, on the proverbial wisdom of the title, Ashbery has found a middle diction: ready to improvise, yielding to but not swamped by randomness. (pp. 192-93)

[In "Self-Portrait" as well as earlier poems, Ashbery acknowledges] a constellation of dreams perhaps more "real" than "real life" ("the certainty that it / Wasn't a dream"). But the version in "Self-Portrait" is wistful, rather than driven: Ashbery seems open to the varieties of experience, registers more pleasurably the ache of the veiled and ineluctable dream. He makes his bow to an ironic view of the visionary self ("the 'it was all a dream' / Syndrome") before returning to a hidden truth behind colloquial language ("the 'all' tells tersely / Enough how it wasn't"). The present *disguises* the tempting dream behind Parmigianino's portrait, but disguises it in the "radiance" of the poet's room. No need to choose between the present and the unseen—and in the pressured light of the passing of time, no *way* to do so.

It is the jumble of everyday pleasures and frustrations that we hear most often in the fluid style of some of the shorter poems of *Self-Portrait in a Convex Mirror*. Even the longer poem "Grand Galop" is almost literally an attempt to keep the poem's accounting powers even with the pace of inner and outer events. Naturally it doesn't succeed. The mind moves in several directions at once, and the poem is partly about the exhaustions and comic waste carried along by the "stream of consciousness":

> The custard is setting; meanwhile
> I not only have my own history to worry about
> But am forced to fret over insufficient details related to
>   large
> Unfinished concepts that can never bring themselves to
>   the point
> Of being, with or without my help, if any were
>   forthcoming.

At the start of the poem, the mind moves on ahead of some lists of names (weigela, sloppy joe on bun—the end of the line for Whitman's famous catalogues) and then the poem says we must stop and "wait again." "Nothing takes up its fair share of time." Ashbery calls our attention repeatedly, and with frustration rather than exultation, to the fact that the poem's time is not actual time.

"Grand Galop" also laments the generalizing and pattern-making powers which intervene and block our experience of particulars. . . . Poetry can never be quite quick enough, however grand the "galop," however strong the desire to "communicate something between breaths." This explains some of the qualities of Ashbery's style which trouble readers. What seems strange is not so much *what* he says as the space between his sentences, the quickness of his transitions. "He" will become "you" or "I" without warning as experiences move close and then farther away, photographs and tapes of themselves. Tenses will shift while the poem

refers to itself as part of the past. We feel as if something were missing; we become anxious as if a step had been skipped. So does the poet who, in several of the shorter poems, describes himself as a dazed prologue to someone else's play. (pp. 194-95)

Ashbery, who was on speaking terms with both the formalism of the American 1950s and the unbuttoned verse of the 1960s, is now bold and beyond them. His three most recent books have explored apparently contradictory impulses—a melancholy withdrawal and a bewildered, beguiling openness—which stand in provocative tension with one another. Older readers have tended to find the poems "difficult"; younger readers either do not experience that difficulty or see past it, recognizing gestures and a voice that speak directly to them. Perhaps it is reassuring to them: a voice which is honest about its confusions; a voice which lays claim to ravishing visions but doesn't scorn distraction, is in fact prey to it. Ashbery does what all real poets do, and like all innovators his accents seem both too close and too far from the everyday, not quite what we imagine *art* to be. He mystifies and demystifies at once. (pp. 198-99)

David Kalstone, "John Ashbery: 'Self-Portrait in a Convex Mirror'," in his Five Temperaments: Elizabeth Bishop, Robert Lowell, James Merrill, Adrienne Rich, John Ashbery *(copyright © 1977 by David Kalstone; used by permission of Oxford University Press, Inc.), Oxford University Press, 1977, pp. 170-99.*

PETER STITT

Ashbery is generally viewed as such a radical innovator, so thoroughly *nouveau* a poet, that perhaps the most surprising thing is how little his methods have changed during the intervening years. He has become somewhat more consistently good, and his work is now more allusive (not more illusive) and resonant than it was; essentially, however, we may say that this poet was precociously born nearly fully formed.

Ashbery is most notable, perhaps, for his legendary obscurity—that feature of his work which has led so many critics into calling him a surrealist. That the poet has spent so much of his life living and working in Paris seems to lend credence to this identification. An elementary distinction is in order, however. There are at least three varieties of surrealism—French, which is arbitrary and antirational, funny, and sexy; Spanish, which is deep, serious, and dark, relying more upon emotional than intellectual logic; and American, which is primarily verbal rather than conceptual —and thus is not properly surrealism at all, but a technical device. . . . American "surrealism" is a homegrown hybrid which owes its birth to such verbal innovators as Wallace Stevens and Gertrude Stein. It is not concerned with subconscious or preconscious parts of the mind, but involves the intentional and experimental replacement of certain words in a given syntactical pattern with other words that have just as much grammatical rightness being there, but most likely far less logical rightness. (pp. 940-41)

[John Ashbery] performs such secret rites under cover of darkness, no doubt in a ruined garret somewhere on the upper East Side. To my mind the poems in *Some Trees* most revealing of Ashbery's ultimate technique are those several that are most obviously exercises in the verbally redundant French forms. Such poems as "Pantoum,"

"Canzone," "Poem," "A Pastoral," and "The Painter" involve repeating selected end words in a complexly-changing but predetermined pattern in every one of several stanzas. If there are six lines to a stanza then there will be six words to use in a different order, one at the end of each line, in each of six stanzas. The seventh stanza will then be three lines long and demand the use of two of these words per line, one in the middle and one at the end. Such poems tend towards arbitrariness and meaninglessness, as any dedicated reader knows; it is almost inevitable that the words take over direction of the poem from the poet. What we end up with is verbal trickiness, a boring pre-form of American surrealism.

That John Ashbery wrote so many of these poems at the beginning of his career is a sure tip-off that his chief preoccupation as poet is with words rather than with meaning. Given this fact, and given his long immersion in the art world, it would not be amiss to say that he is the equivalent in poetry of the abstract expressionists in painting. Among the many parallels between his work and theirs, two especially stand out—a shared devotion to texture and a preoccupation with the art process itself. The devotion to texture is present everywhere in his work, but is especially central in his narrative poems. These are the works most frustrating to most reviewers—one feels always on the verge of understanding the situation but never quite able to. The reason is that these poems exist primarily on the micro level—that is, the smallest details have the greatest accuracy and clarity—and are most baffling on the macro level —we are never sure of the overall situation, the pattern into which the details might fit. Consider the enticing second stanza of the opening poem in the volume:

A fine rain anoints the canal machinery.
This is perhaps a day of general honesty
Without example in the world's history
Though the fumes are not of a singular authority
And indeed are dry as poverty.
Terrific units are on an old man
In the blue shadow of some paint cans
As laughing cadets say, "In the evening
Everything has a schedule, if you can find out what it is."

If you worry about just what that means, what is happening, the stanza will make you furious—as it obviously did many of the book's early reviewers. I would suggest instead that we devote our attention not to the larger question of plot but to the smaller one of detail—prefer the micro, that is, over the macro. When this is done, the stanza becomes thoroughly funny and enjoyable. Of course this process does not give the poem any greater meaning—no matter how we read it, it really doesn't *mean* anything, in the usual sense of the word. The poem's necessity is textural and verbal rather than expository.

Sometimes, of course, these poems do have meaning in the ordinary sense of the word. When this is so we are likely to be astonished at how little they mean, how small the fire turns out to be given the vast profusion of smoke encountered elsewhere. (pp. 941-42)

The preoccupation with the art process itself, which I have said Ashbery shares with the abstract expressionists, is a chief feature of *Houseboat Days*. Ashbery has come to write, in the poet's most implicitly ironic gesture, almost exclusively about his own poems, the ones he is writing as

he writes about them. The artist becomes his own theoretical critic, caught in the critical lens even at the moment of conception.

Interviewers of poets often ask the question: what gets you started on a poem—is it an idea, a theme, an image, a rhythm, or what? In "Variant," Ashbery not only answers this question—"Sometimes a word will start it," he says— but goes on to exemplify his doctrine. The unseen interlocutor observes that "The way / Is fraught with danger"; Ashbery gratefully accepts the word "fraught" as the text for the rest of his poem, and composes an imagistic and narrative definition of it. Such a poem, and the example was chosen because typical, is highly ironic and self-conscious, and shows the poet's preoccupation with his art.

Poetry can be whatever Ashbery wants it to be, and this freedom or control is applied not just to language, as we have seen in *Some Trees,* but to the raw material of reality itself. Ashbery agrees with Stevens that the imagination can do whatever it wants with reality, once it is taken into the poem: "You can have whatever you want. / . . . In the sense / Of twisting it to you, through long, spiralling afternoons." It is true that Ashbery occasionally claims to be a realist, a poet of the everyday: "The orchestra is starting to tune up. / The tone-row of a dripping faucet is batted back and forth / Among the kitchen, the confusion outside, the pale bluster / Of the sky, the correct but insidious grass." But this is just a pose; Ashbery is even less of a realist, literalist, than Stevens, as he makes abundantly clear in yet another poem on poetry:

It is argued that these structures address themselves
To exclusively aesthetic concerns, like windmills
On a vast plain. To which it is answered
That there are no other questions than these,
Half squashed in mud, emerging out of the moment
We all live, learning to like it.

The first two-and-a-half lines echo a criticism often directed against Ashbery's poetry. The answer self-consciously reiterates the poet's artistic credo just as it exemplifies it. In working these questions out, Ashbery of course continues to use the real world, its accouterments, its details and texture, as pawns in his game, and so we are still tempted to look for a kind of sense that simply is not there. Oh, sometimes it is—as in the lovely, haunting, and funny poem "Melodic Trains"—but mostly not.

Ashbery's most conspicuous failures come when his typical methods are applied seriously rather than with offhanded charm and wit. The longest poem in *Houseboat Days*, "Fantasia on 'The Nut-Brown Maid,'" is also the worst. Besides being impenetrable, it is vague, diffuse, vapid, abstract, and boring. What a shame! At his best Ashbery operates very much in the ironic mode as described by Northrop Frye; he is among the first of our poets to arrive there. The fiction writer he most resembles is probably Donald Barthelme, who has the same love of texture and nuance, the same arbitrary sense of humor, the same decadent love of the trivial and the enchanting. (p. 944)

Peter Stitt, in The Georgia Review *(copyright, 1978, by the University of Georgia), Winter, 1978.*

ROSEMARY JOHNSON

John Ashbery offers the reader a sort of *Pilgrim's Progress* [in *Houseboat Days*]: one may indulge with him in the frivolities of Vanity Fair, or one may follow his very rigorous trains of thought about the nature of modern poetry itself. (p. 118)

This reader prefers the Roman side of Ashbery to the Rococo, for when he tries his hand at political bread and circuses, there is about it something sinister and arrogant. He nabokovs us, with a wild goose chase after the likes of Daffy Duck or a glut of the sugary confections of "Valentine." The gyrations of "Pyrography" grate less, but it's still a pastiche of Americana—a *papier-mâché* carousel. Ashbery takes his busman's holiday—it would seem—as a necessary escape from the stern task he has set himself.

To the persistent reader John Ashbery reveals himself as a poet of high moral seriousness, an epistemological poet no less, whose work explores the modes, limits, and grounds of true knowledge, and if he can help it, he really doesn't budge from this stance. It's hard work for him to clear away the tangles of language and root out old habits, so that the wood can be seen for the trees, and it's hard work for us, but rewarding, to read this sort of cultivated verse. It hones the mind. Ashbery discloses a moral stance similar to that of a Stoic.... With stringent logic he accents the given: "What is, is what happens." We are condemned to live in the present and also in mutability.... He purifies his verse with this cold fact, chews it over, and achieves his clear flow of thought by means of and around the impediment. Demosthenes-in-training stopping his mouth up with pebbles could do no better.... It's a difficult thing for him, letting the past go. He will despite himself keep trying to warm the past up, trifling with its leftovers, waffling through "Drame Bourgeoise."... In "Collective Dawns" he finds the known-now infinitely preferable to either the Wordsworthian "mill-pond of chill doubt" or the glacier fraught with the loud notes of the cuckoo. (pp. 118-19)

Sometimes his "long spiralling afternoons" barley-sugar into Wallace Stevens' forget-me-not time and the poetry melts into a mush of allusions.... Better Ashbery should fight his own battle with modern means and square up to the twentieth-century embarrassment of being awash in time's flux yet stuck inexorably in the present.... A secure foothold in the ooze, an ethical stance eludes him. He has the planks—the means of saying things—but no platform.... This bailing out of the present, rescuing the known, channeling the flood, salvaging the language, and refusing to bog down in the slough of despond—in sum his poetical labors—makes the experiencing of his work worthwhile. Ashbery is a poet, not a philosopher. No original thinker, he builds his edifices out of philosophical driftwood: "A handful of things we know for sure." Moreover he tub-thumps. The dogged craftsmanship makes his poetry watertight, feasible—yare. Afloat. Without self-advertisement yet ambitiously, he reconstructs a great variety of new forms from the old timber, offering us a Pindaric ode in the elegiac mode ("Two Deaths"), occasion poems, fifteen-line sonnets, a Romantic ballad based on the "Nut-Brown Maid," a Horatian pastoral, and a mock epic ("Melodic Trains").

Generally speaking, poems could be said to beg to be dissected, their choice bits set aside to be savored later. These poems are built to repel critical evaluation. It's boring to mull over their separate parts most of which are readymades, *trouvaille*, casual remarks, cliché—that sort of thing. Furthermore, if the would-be critic pulls out one unit

of thought the rest of the stack threatens collapse. Again most poetry, unlike prose, while it may not necessarily invite it almost always admits paraphrase. These poems seek to explain *themselves,* to argue from initial premises about the uses and abuses of poetry itself. Criticism uncomfortably housed next door is all but reduced to finding analogies among the neighboring arts.

The syntactical use of long lines of interlacing preformed phrases like chords of music rather than single notes does lead one to make musical analogies. The idea of a movement that catches one up, sweeps one along, and ends in the abandonment of the project to silence is also very similar.... "Syringa" for all its wit is a poem in a minor key. It's a pastoral tragicomedy starring Orpheus with the great Apollo making a guest appearance, Eurydice in a cameo role, and a chorus line of scholars. The word-music on this occasion plaits threads of thought, strings of words, strands of comments into a raveling and unraveling argument for a revival of the occasion poem. This happens but with the Ashberyian addition of a disclaimer: one cannot isolate a single occasion.... "Syringa" is a poem-picture of "flowing, scenery," the latter being how it must be written now, as a kind of film script perhaps? Anyway "Syringa" is very much a Restoration piece suitably witty, droll, and stylish. Orpheus apotheosized as a "bluish cloud with white contours" hovers above it all. No pedagogical centaurs appear, but out of the horse's mouth we learn about the nature of its reality.... Along the way in this book Ashbery jettisons a deal of poetic ballast. Emblems remain, some alliteration and similes are suffered because of their satiric uses. Metaphor, which doubles the mind back into itself and its recollections of other times, things, etc., and synaesthesia, which does this in triplicate, are discouraged. The manufacture of the text itself becomes very important.

These poems celebrate things man-made, the artificial. Nature barely appears and then only in pastoral or theatrical garb. Tissue-paper clouds are at hand and their artificiality has more substance and is longer lasting and more reassuring than the hot-air cumulonimbus variety that one infers hover above us out of reach.... Not only can Ashbery never leave Plato's cave in search of anything, let alone the ineffable, but the shadows on the cavern promise to be more rewarding and more real and readily available than whatever might lie outside. The most grubby dubious artifice offers us more, unashamedly, than all of Mother Nature's elusive offerings. (pp. 119-23)

The aesthetics of this seem to be mannerist eighteenth-century stuff. We make art and it styles things for us. As far as the politics of it goes, Ashbery nurses the Romantic hope that in a man-made or man-defined world everything and anything is possible: "what continues / Does so with our participation and consent." In this, Ashbery's houseboat chugs along in Shelley's splendid wake. Ashbery lines his more ascetic poems with this roseate insulation as wadding however temporary against the gathering chill outside.

The idea nests well in that stylistic box of necessary tricks, the theater: an edifice and an occasion which traps time within itself.... Theatrical time encapsulates one in an ever-present now.... The dry spots in *Houseboat Days* tend to be little theaters in [this] sense. Rooms, trains, boats, barrels going over Niagara provide not only a carapace against time's corrosions but a cocoon as well where there is room enough and time to gather one's wits and to reflect on events speeded up outside in an Einsteinian-tram-in-Zurich sense. The way time moves his Show Boats along makes Ashbery a modern. It also relates him to the English Romantics, who were ever conscious of the passage and the ways of time. The manner in which he erects facades as poetical shoring against outside realities seems to indicate neo-Augustan as a label. Style bars its door against time. It hobnobs with tradition—a very different thing. The Romantics undertook one-way journeys but not shielded from the elements. Ashbery prefers to take day excursions as a tourist. At heart, one feels, he is urbane, cultivated, a gentleman poet writing for gentlemen—a Restoration man. (pp. 123-24)

Rosemary Johnson, "Paper Boats: Notes on 'Houseboat Days'," in Parnassus: Poetry in Review *(copyright © Poetry in Review Foundation), Spring/Summer, 1978, pp. 118-24.*

*   *   *

ASTURIAS, Miguel Ángel   1899-1974

Asturias, a Guatemalan novelist, poet, journalist, playwright, and translator, won the Nobel Prize for Literature in 1967. Seeking to give "a universal consciousness to the problems of Latin America," Asturias fused native legends, folklore, and myths with harsh reality. In his "banana trilogy" he examined U.S. imperialism, and in *The President*, he attacked a Guatemalan political dictatorship. (See also *CLC*, Vols. 3, 8, and *Contemporary Authors*, Vols. 25-28; obituary, Vols. 49-52; *Contemporary Authors Permanent Series*, Vol. 2.)

GERALD MARTIN

Miguel Ángel Asturias' *Mulata de tal* (1963) is what Spanish-speaking critics are given to calling a *novela–hipérbole*, and it must be treated as such. No respectable critical approach to this novel has yet been found, which is partly why so little has been written about it, and yet its intrinsic interest and its importance for an understanding of Asturias' literary development are unmistakable. (p. 397)

[As] far as *Mulata de tal* is concerned, there can be no question that influences are largely pre-Columbian and wholly American. There are innumerable elements on almost every page which are familiar to anyone who has read the *Popol Vuh*, the *Anales de los Xahil*, or *El libro de los libros de Chilam Balam*. The real problem is to decide exactly where each element comes from, what it represented to the Mayas (or, in the case of contemporary material, what it represents to their descendants), and what it now represents in the novel, that is, how it has been adapted to the requirements of the author's fictional form. . . . [Of] *Mulata de tal* we can say quite categorically that [this problem] is insurmountable, for four main reasons: (1) There was considerable confusion among the Maya themselves, and much deliberate mystification on the part of their priests which was facilitated by the overlapping and often contradictory significance of even their central symbols. (2) There is little consensus of opinion among Maya scholars as to the broad outlines of Maya culture, still less its details. (3) Even when an evident reference to an identifiable cultural phenomenon is isolated, we can still not be sure, from a reading of the various authorities, that Asturias is using the material in any given way, especially as he is known to mistrust the findings of many of the experts in the field. (4) Finally, there are simply too many elements in the novel.

Asturias has worked in most of what he has learned about his native land, both before and since the Conquest, and the finished product is a formidable tissue of incident and detail. All of which, though a considerable aid to his conception and execution of *Mulata de tal*, makes interpretation an extremely hazardous business, and a single, static perspective is virtually impossible to attain. Instead, we should shift our attention away from meaning and concentrate on method. (pp. 397-99)

I hope to show that the real identity of *Mulata de tal* is hidden not in its subject matter, but, in so far as the two can be separated, in its language, which is also its method. The attempt to find one comprehensive interpretation would mean, irremediably, the abandonment of any attempt to delve into the real workings of a highly original experiment in fiction.

The subject of *Mulata de tal*, if it has one, is that of cultural conflict. To some extent this is an extension of the clash between Indian and Ladino in *Hombres de maíz* (1949), but in the later novel the conflict is viewed simultaneously through all periods of Guatemalan history and at many levels of human experience. This requires a new narrative technique, and a move away from the method which had proved so successful artistically in *El Señor Presidente* (1946) and *Hombres de maíz*. In those novels Asturias examines what he calls an *hecho central*, a situation whose point of reference outside the novel, however fragmented it might become inside it, is a single one and a real one, whose examination is carried out through a literary technique which converts the materials of fiction—plot, characters, scenes—into patterns of imagery. For *Mulata de tal* he now required to unite, on one literary plane, elements from a multitude of temporal, cultural and geographical realities. The continuous switching of these different realities onto one single screen completely annuls historical perspective and all sense of reality as we know it. *Mulata de tal* becomes a fantasy, a wildly peripatetic fairy tale whose elements are the myths, legends and folk tales which have danced accompaniment to the development of culture in Guatemala since the Conquest. (pp. 399-400)

The function of metaphor in the two earlier works I have mentioned was to assume the role traditionally allotted to plot and character by acting as the true vehicle for the development of the novel and unifying an otherwise fragmentary narrative as it was unfolded, until a complete and meaningful pattern emerged. In *Mulata de tal* metaphor and other linguistic devices are used to give dynamic motion to the action, to fuse the heterogeneous elements indicated above into a homogeneous literary whole. Fragments now become a story, a series of dynamic situations, whereas in *El Señor Presidente* and *Hombres de maíz* a central situation was fragmented into its suggestive nuclei and then expanded into a wider pattern. *Mulata de tal* has no plot or even chapters as such, only a motion. It is this motion that is all-important.

The novel is composed of a series of *cuentos*, each with its own title. It represents the culmination of Asturias' increasing stylization over the last forty years. It gives a deformed picture of reality, as all Asturias' work does, but here the deformation is integrated and unified, and there is no single reality as a point of departure. . . . Although *Mulata de tal* rests on the assumption of a series of different implicit realities, there is no one reality from which all the others derive, and so there are no determinable norms. . . . Asturias in *Mulata de tal* is emphasizing the dynamic nature of cultural development through the ages. It is the difference between a strip cartoon in a newspaper and an animated cartoon film in full color. . . . The result of the heterogeneity and the dynamism I have mentioned is a narrative of extraordinary flexibility. *Mulata de tal* is cellular: it seems to grow out of itself, rather than out of reality. It is the possible links between fictional elements, forged according to a kind of caricature of the laws of structural possibility that Lévi-Strauss detects in cultural development, which determine the selection and ordering of events in the novel. It is the only work in which Asturias' innate tendency to rely on the suggestiveness of his elements alone reaches an extreme form.

The intention behind the conflict of culture traits reproduced in this novel is not to present us with a merely static vision of the Guatemalan version of Latin American *mestizo* culture, but to show us how it evolved, to somehow simulate the process of acculturation in a dynamic and concentrated form. The mutual attraction and rejection between cultures takes form early in the novel, where it is dramatized in the strange Yumí–Catalina–Mulata triangle, itself a re-enactment of the ancient sexual struggle between sun and moon which is a constant of Middle American myth. This intersexual struggle becomes superimposed upon the religious conflict of the later parts, as the novel gains in complexity, and the continuation of the sexual motif is a constant reminder that cultural change is not an abstract or isolated movement, but one carried on through human agents and in an organic fashion. This is why the novel seems to be cellular. (pp. 400-02)

[Sex] and religion were the most direct points of contact between conquerors and conquered in the sixteenth century, and sexual and religious attitudes still provide the most interesting examples of syncretism in Guatemala today. Asturias implicitly suggests that only too often the European innovations were by no means an improvement upon their native equivalents, and many of the themes of the novel derive from a union of Asturias' own professed dismay at the direction of much of modern life, and the pathetic Indian protests against Spanish sexual and religious violence which are to be found in *El libro de los libros de Chilam Balam* and other sacred books of the Maya. . . . [The Maya] saw their deities in human terms, and this is the significance of the battle of the sexes which dominates the first part [of the novel], and pervades the second. (p. 404)

Vulgarity and eroticism, together with violence, set the tenor of the novel, but any offensiveness fades before the overpowering force of the language itself. Asturias' fundamental asset is still his primitive strength, which turns force of imagination into force of expression with the most natural ease. The combination . . . of crude naturalism and exotic fantasy is reminiscent of the wonders of a childhood visit to the zoo. (p. 405)

The advantage of the animated cartoon film is that it can use every kind of visual style . . . , and can actualize anything that the human mind can visualize. . . . [Asturias, with his novel], has almost prepared what cartoonists call a storyboard, for he has already adapted his subject matter to the demands of animation by dynamizing it, and it is here that his originality lies. . . . Though obviously limited by language in a way that animators are not, Asturias manages to inject an extraordinary motion into his narrative by ani-

mating myths and legends into a swiftly flowing fairy tale. In the process his language becomes almost as plastic as the episodes themselves. . . . (pp. 406-07)

Almost all Asturias' characters are *muñecos,* but those in *Mulata de tal* are not caricatures of real people. When they speak it is the *pueblo* or even the language itself, abstracted, stylized, that seems to be speaking, but not the characters. They perform human actions (though not all their actions are humanly possible), without being human. They are, in short, cartoon characters, which become simply elements in a seething turmoil of other elements, all of which have their own existence. . . . (p. 407)

This was foreshadowed in the 1930's, when Asturias' literary activities were otherwise more or less at a standstill, by his creation of the *fantomimas* (the pun is typical), poem-dramas where words themselves are the ghostly actors in a weird, often chilling world of language. Similarly, in *Mulata de tal,* the characters are autonomous, episodes grow, swell and merge into one another in a primitive, cellular world where the missing link is repeatedly provided by the author's own unfailing ingenuity with language. The whole novel is a turmoil of warring elements struggling for survival, and may be viewed as a battle for the soul of the Guatemalan people over the centuries. . . .

The unspoken identification of creatures appearing in the narrative with the background is a frequent device which adds to the air of magic which pervades the novel. Laws of nature are ignored or misapplied, and the fusion of foreground and backcloth produces an impression of dense possibility. (p. 408)

Condensation has always been a part of Asturias' art. Cartoons rely on immediacy of impact for their visual jokes (what animators call "takes"), or on a rapid juxtaposition of incongruities. . . . [Most] of Asturias' writing in this novel presents the reader with a definite scenic vantage point. (p. 410)

Asturias is "seeing" his subject matter in a special way, and in terms of scenes. Usually, the action itself is ideally suited to cartoon treatment: a bear licking at flames; a cat licking itself clean with the light from open windows; blackened trees, all eyes, jeering at a woodcutter; a little devil skating on centipedes; or a fight between the same baby demon and a monkey which disperses into a swarm of flies whenever it is struck at. What Asturias is adding to the basic cartoon situation, however, is a new and fluid motion which will animate it. . . . (p. 411)

It is sufficiently obvious that the whole art of this novel rests upon its language. In general, Asturias matches the visual freedom of the cartoon by using every resource the Spanish language offers him. His use of color is striking and immeasurably more liberal than in earlier novels, and alliteration . . . is used frequently and cunningly, as in the vision of the mule on which the old priest flees from Tierra-paulita: "una mula prieta de ojos rojos como rábanos." The diabolical contrast wherein the mule's red eyes blaze out from its black body jolts first into the *ojos-rojos* (*-como*) rhyme, and then into the *rojos-rábanos* alliteration, creating a unified picture which reproduces the spasmodic motion of the animated process.

Sounds are reproduced by the constant use of onomatopoeia, which Asturias has always exploited. None of his novels is considered right until he has read it through to himself and approved its sounds and rhythms. There is also a constant flow of Joycean word-games and puns, many of them extremely vulgar, which accompany the flexible and rapid action with an equally rapid display of popular humor. . . . At sentence level the writer's personal imprint is equally striking. . . . Many of the sentences are extremely long, uniting different scenes and characters in the same fluid way that the narrative as a whole contrives to do, and thereby achieving the homogeneity of the cartoon in every cell of the novel.

Asturias' long sentences first complicate and then unravel highly rhythmical and elastic coils of language. He tends toward a systematic frustration of normal syntactical patterns, replacing these by a new pattern dependent upon seemingly endless sentences with clauses either intricately dove-tailed into one another to produce a jerking effect . . . or strung out in looping chains to give a sense of effortless fluidity. Thus the pronounced emphasis on action and movement—the number of incidents on each page, and of verbs in even short sentences, is remarkable—is reinforced by the powerful ebb and flow of the language itself.

Language itself, in short, is the real hero of *Mulata de tal*, where recurrent references to the power of the word remind us of the sacred role attributed to it in all primitive cultures. . . . Despite such mystification, however, and despite his repeated attacks upon science and "progress," [Asturias'] effects are more directly produced by carefully prepared, purely linguistic devices than those of any other Latin American writer, whether he knows it or not. (pp. 413-14)

I believe that Asturias has provided us with a new literary experience, and that all that is needed to appreciate it is the right lens. It is not a work that can be emulated, for Asturias' gifts are not such as schools are built upon, and yet it is a good deal more sophisticated than most critics have been prepared to admit. Throughout his fiction Asturias' problem has been to remain true to his time and country, to remain loyal to his unschooled and illiterate fellow countrymen whilst writing a modern literature. Much of his subject matter apparently leaves him outside of the most recent literature from Latin America, which is why many people questioned the justice of his receiving the Nobel Prize; but where such critics should look for his true innovating genius is to his language. Although his subject matter is unfailingly simple in appearance (it could not be otherwise without his abandoning Guatemala), his thematic networks and technical resources, built only on his extraordinary facility with language, are extremely complex and yet at the same time astonishingly coherent. True and more lasting recognition is still to come. (p. 415)

> *Gerald Martin, "'Mulata de tal': The Novel As Animated Cartoon," in* Hispanic Review, *Vol. 4, No. 2, Spring, 1973, pp. 397-415.*

JOSEPH SOMMERS

As Richard Callan indicates in his brief introduction [to Asturias' *América, fábula de fábulas, y Otros ensayos*], many essays, because of their personal, subjective tone afford special insights into the personality of Asturias. What comes through, particularly in the post-Nobel pieces, is the image of a wry observer of modern man's foibles, who notes ironically how modernization and technological

change come into frequently abrasive confrontation with humanistic tradition and regional culture. While rarely failing to entertain, the essays would not stand comparison with those of a distinguished antecedent, José Marti. Similarly, the selections treating Latin American literature, its history, its themes and its idiosyncrasies lack the grounding in history and in concepts of literary and art criticism that characterize the articles of Asturias' contemporary, Alejo Carpentier.

On the other hand, Asturias is at his best when detailing the artistic and sculptural achievements of the Mayas at Copan and Bonampak, blending a solid knowledge of cultural anthropology with an eye for form and theme and a deep sensibility to the Mayan world view.

Finally, in the most interesting (and the longest) essay, Asturias records the genesis of *El Señor Presidente*, conjures up a dramatic scene in which he jousts verbally with the resurrected characters who question his efficacy as creator, and then proceeds to discuss the mythic under-pinnings of the novel. This is high Asturias tradition, wedding the personal, the imaginative and the conceptual to create, in the mold of his great novels, a literary product of genuine originality. (pp. 405-06)

> *Joseph Sommers, in* Hispania *(© 1975 The American Association of Teachers of Spanish and Portuguese, Inc.), May, 1975.*

ARIEL DORFMAN

[*Men of Maize*], both the fountainhead and the backbone of all that is being written on our continent today, has suffered a strange fate, like so many works which close a period and open up a new epoch.

Many essayists have judged the novel deficient, pointing to its lack of unity, its ungainly and evasive segmentation and its vacillation between genres, in contrast to that solid cathedral of dynamic coherence, that satanic church, *El Señor Presidente*, the most famous of Asturias' novels. . . . Many critics dispose of *Men of Maize* in a couple of lines or ignore it altogether, irritated by this confusing, explosive offshoot which cannot be comfortably fit into the orderly evolution of the author toward the political themes of his banana trilogy. (p. 12)

A few critics have recognized the extraordinary quality of the novel, although they have not succeeded in refuting the arguments of its detractors, and they find themselves on the defensive, affirming its greatness in spite of its defects. . . . [Some], in support of the novel's singular structure, have excused it as "poetic," as a "symphonic poem," or have called attention to its fusion of the social and the mythic. The use of these vague and ineffectual terms symptomizes a basic misunderstanding of the text, for they are inadequate to describe a work which has contributed to founding a new dynasty of the real, a new way of seeing our America. (pp. 12-13)

[The] events must be decoded by the reader who plunges into the buzzing stream of words flowing dreamily between the real and the fictitious, into an atmosphere which develops and thickens, raining lights and shadows that struggle in thunderheads of words. He must interpret, undo the linguistic spells, unearth from this shifting cave the outline of a meaning. This narrative mode serves to indicate that we are confronted by a moment at the start of the book in which dream and reality cohabit, in which the mythological is still wholly embodied in man, in which the human and the natural are still conjugated together, still fused even to the extent of being designated by the same interchangeable terms. (p. 13)

Everything related to Gaspar [the novel's protagonist] is seen through myth, through clouds of smoke from an apparent chaos where all things vibrate with the secret form of ritual. The exacerbated language; the baroque, serpentine syntax; the slithering advance of a world; the merging of dissimilar elements; their transfiguration through words that are sacred, solemn, and distant; brief glimpses of the action: everything recreates in the mind of the reader the encircling primitivism lived by the characters, forcibly equalizes dream and reality and mixes fiction and *factum* until the reader is not able to—does not wish to—separate them. The central theme of the novel, the relation between myth and reality, finds its narrative and linguistic correlative in this fusion, only fully realized in the first chapter, in which myth covers everything like a skin. The fact that legend and reality, word and event, are here the same experience for reader and character will contrast with the other chapters, in which the nearness and distance of these dimensions become problematic, preventing a manifestation of their union. . . .

[The] repetition of events, once in a dream and again in reality without defining which is which, blurs our habitual way of seeing occurrences in the outside world. The reader must absorb and interpret what happens by himself; suddenly he has become, in his turn, a magician. That which is dreamed and that which is lived are inextricable and this means that any effort by the reader to order the world of the book will falsify it and end in failure. Just as his characters make war on civilization and everyday reality, so, in the rest of the book, Asturias will attempt to destroy the rational mentality, using, although less outrageously, any method he can to set the language seething: letting disorders slip into his chronology; weaving together personal and impersonal points of view; confounding popular rumors and the thoughts of the characters with the supposedly objective narration of events; silencing men and animating the world of plants and animals; dislocating points of reference; shattering the molds of academic conventions—so he carried out a great experiment, the birth of the future. Fire, one of the protagonists of the novel, is also its formal principle: its words are flames, they spark, they leap, they cannot be classified, they are like shining yellow rabbits, they rise and fall with the irrepressible rhythm of vengeance, the vengeance of fire, grandfather and son. (p. 14)

It has been said that Asturias' basic theme is liberty. On the contrary, it seems to me that what preoccupies him most is tyranny, alienation, the monstrous threat of retribution in a fallen world. The political dictatorship of *El Señor Presidente* has become, in this book, a dictatorship of fire and words but both are tyrannies which man himself invokes, helps to construct and worships. As the Señor Presidente can rule because he is sustained by the fear and the conscious or involuntary support of others, so legend can impose itself on reality because man consents to live it out as a way of ransoming his humanity. . . . Although it could be argued that political tyranny is anti-natural and anti-human, while the tyranny of language and of the earth is essential to cosmic harmony, in any case there is no doubt that the

spectre of inhuman powers ensnaring man runs through all of Asturias' work, from *The Bejeweled Boy* to [*Mulata de tal*], where man suffers victimization in the magical and Pantagruelish land of Tierrapaulita. Asturias leaves man with the consolation that he is responsible for his own condition. (pp. 15-16)

[*Men of Maize*] is filled with dialogues in which characters dispute a past event, ritualizing it until it achieves a permanent linguistic form. At times this event, already witnessed by the reader, is retold word for word. At other times, the dialogue begins to deform the original event, to transform its meaning. In either case, the significance of these interchanges is clear: the legend is not entirely created in its first moment, the moment of human action but continues to be formed in the process of transmission, in the rise and fall of that original instant, unforgettable and forgotten. . . . [The] myth is reduced to its essentials; it picks up momentum for the present and the future, it remakes itself, and it slips into the future along with man. (p. 17)

[The first four chapters] show an obvious unity, developing around the death of Gaspar Ilóm and the vengeance wreaked on his executioners, a punishment carried out by human hands for superhuman reasons, a destruction which is reality and, at the same time, legend. The passage of time will allow each episode to be consolidated into a story, further mythified by each succeeding generation. The fifth chapter, however, seems to escape this unity. It has been called a jewel in itself, but it is repeatedly declared an episode independent from the others, without organic relation to the rest of the book.

At first glance, it would seem that the critics are right. What relation could the preceding chapters have to the story of Goyo Yic, the blind man who recovers his sight in order to search for María Tecún, the wife who has abandoned him? Only tenuous threads of plot unite this episode to the first four, which seem to unfold in another time-period, almost in another geographic space.

Nevertheless, this story is essential to the subterranean development of the book. In essence, the chapter narrates the process of forgetting, the gradual disappearance of a woman down the roads of memory, due to the invisible passage of time. (p. 18)

Goyo Yic experiences the same process of the distancing and loss of a primary event which forms the theme of the rest of the novel, except that here the process is encarnated in an individual man, and the narration seeks out the psychological roots of what had appeared to be a purely social phenomenon. Goyo Yic lives out a specific process of forgetting, his subjectivity absorbed by the tricks of time. The same process unfolds in the other chapters of *Men of Maize;* throughout the novel things are done or suffered so that afterwards they may survive in the words of the future. Like a trick mirror, these words distance the original event as they reflect it but they capture its palpitating essence as legend, transcending the dismal truth of everyday life. . . .

By individualizing the mythical phenomenon in the [story of Goyo Yic], by making it coincide with the life-cycle of every man, the irremediable weakening and loss of the self, Asturias has explored the creation of legend from another angle, the angle of the minute hand which hacks away at our life, with destroys its original once it has molded the myth into a series of events that stretches beyond us and allows us to touch others through mouths that reproduce us and tongues that repeat us. (p. 19)

In speaking of the past, the characters always give the impression that they are looking back over a vast, unbridgeable abyss created by the irreversible march of time. Because of the unresolvable confusion of its chronology and the distance of its points of reference, the transformation of the past into myth thrusts its characters into an eternal time. Normal duration is either unknown or nonexistent; limitless man cannot be measured with a clock. The story of Machojón, for example, not only passes from mouth to mouth, altered and autonomous but it also becomes part of the vocabulary used by the people to interpret reality, a *cliché* that appears automatically whenever it is needed, a mental structure which men apply unconsciously. The events which the readers have witnessed survive only as folk sayings, as part of the dictionary of daily conversation: for example, something is said to become "a Machojón of hail-stones."

This incorporation of the past into the mythology of the present is underlined by the many dialogues in which a legend takes form in the midst of men's words. What had seemed past is relived and altered in order to escape from the prison of measurable time. This is the transformation of the impersonal by the individual human voice: the event, which before had existed only in the words of the narrator, now takes its being from the words of a character. The "objective" knowledge which the reader enjoyed while the characters suffered from the tyranny of facts, reintegrates itself into the world, digested by a thousand anonymous stomachs and sent out again so that it can continue its journey. It has become independent of its factual origin and lives only in its linguistic context; it has entered an atemporal world.

But in order that this other dimension, this communicative context which transcends the clock, may exist, time is necessary. In this sense, Asturias takes his place in the line of Proust, Mann, and Joyce, who demonstrated the presence of the eternal, of the mythical, in the corrosion of every moment, in the miniscule death of every object.

For this reason, it is no paradox that confronting this vague atemporality, this chaos of dates, there should also appear concrete references to measurable, regular time; just as we find, mixed with magical, associative language, the prosaic phrases of ordinary speech. It is in this great mosaic of growth and decay, among these unfolding lives, that the legend can appear and develop. Between the first and the last page of the novel stretch no more than fifty years but those pages are also separated by an eternity. . . . This contrast between the two types of time, this living in both dimensions, can also be observed in *El Señor Presidente* and in the rest of Asturias' work. The tension between eternity and subjection to time pulls the bonds between fiction and reality even tighter and duplicates on a temporal plane the fundamental structure of the novel. (pp. 19-20)

[This] deformation of the world in language, these vertiginous metaphors which twist objects until they are unrecognizable, this kingdom of the grotesque, this mirror in which time and the word sweat in monstrous copulation, is much more than a literary technique or an echo of European surrealism. It is an expression of horror at the loss of the magical, an attempt to expose the decadence of a world by using

a baroque imagery of rotting flesh, to project a demonic reality through the twisted lens of the bestial. Perhaps, at bottom, it deals with the problem of that mysterious force which controls us and which we seek to exorcize with a spell that reproduces the image of the hell that it would banish. (p. 20)

For Asturias, truth does not consist in the correspondence which can be established between a story and the factual events which gave rise to it; but a story becomes real when it transmutes these events profoundly, until they become unforgettable, when it rescues the myth from its circumstantial origin, although to do this it must obliterate part of what seemed to have happened. Human beings, blind and lost in a fallen world, have only their myths to help them find their way in the darkness, to gather up their essence, scattered through time. Reality begins to imitate legend, man becomes the instrument that plays for other ears, that perpetuates other beings. Thus, in the poetic acts of Asturias and of his characters, the individual merges with his social being, the real and the imaginary touch, time is eternalized and eternity becomes mortal, and the two types of men of maize make peace, for their struggle has finally been shown to be an intense solidarity, the two dimensions of one irreducible man. Myth and movement support each other, they need each other in order to survive: eternity feeds on the mobility of vagabond men, imperfect crosscurrents in the veins of time; and man's endless motion sustains itself with the eternal company of his imagination.

The union of the men of corn finds its correlative in the unification of the text itself: what had seemed chaos is a deeper order, what was scorned as irregular narrative is the creation of a new cosmic vision, what had seemed disjointed expresses the temporal form of realities turning into words. Asturias narrated this experience (time, myth, reality, language, the internalization of social forces, America, our America) in the only way it could be narrated. Old woman Moncha never spoke so truly (and she was speaking to Asturias, who invented her . . .) as when she said: "If it had not been you, it would have been another, but someone would have told it so it wouldn't be all lost and forgotten, because its existence, fictitious or real, is part of the life, of the landscape of these places, and life cannot be lost; it is an eternal risk, but it is never lost eternally." (p. 22)

> *Ariel Dorfman, "Myth As Time and Word,"*
> *translated by Paula Speck, in* Review *(copyright*
> *© 1975 by the Center for Inter-American Relations, Inc.), Fall, 1975, pp. 12-22.*

*   *   *

ATWOOD, Margaret   1939-

Atwood is a Canadian poet, novelist, critic, and scriptwriter. At times nearly confessional in nature, hers is intensely personal poetry, praised for its imaginative imagery and striking detail. Elements of fantasy pervade her fiction and poetry alike. Atwood's tightly controlled, deceptively simple style allows her work an impact which Melvin Maddocks calls "the kick of a perfume bottle converted into a Molotov cocktail." (See also *CLC*, Vols. 2, 3, 4, 8, and *Contemporary Authors*, Vols. 49-52.)

PATRICIA MORLEY

You could call it an adventure thriller set in the wilds of northern Quebec. You could call it a detective story centering on the search for the main character's missing father. You could call it a psychological novel, a study of madness both individual and social. You could call it a religious novel which examines the origin and nature of the human lust to kill and destroy. You could call it any of these and I wouldn't quarrel. But you'd better call it a novel to be reckoned with, a step in the direction of that mythic creature, the Great Canadian Novel, whose siren song echoes mockingly in the ears of our writers. (p. 99)

[Margaret Atwood] said that it took a stay in Boston to make her realize she was a Canadian. This is interesting, in connection with a motif in [*Surfacing*] which might appear as anti-American until one examines it more closely. Americans tend to destroy what they can't eat or take home. Americans prefer powerboats to canoes, and build dams at the cost of flooding and killing the land. Come now, murmurs the voice of reason and fair play, Americans aren't the only ones who do these things. But it's okay, Atwood knows this too.

In *Surfacing,* the American is a metaphor of modern man in his most unlovable state: "It doesn't matter what country they're from, my head said, they're still Americans, they're what's in store for us, what we are turning into". Eyes blank behind dark glasses, they spread like a virus: if you look and think and talk like them, then you are them. We're all Americans now, evolving, "halfway to machine, the leftover flesh atrophied and diseased". Atwood's American is a fictional version of Jacques Ellul's technological man who has let his mechanical means come to dominate and determine his ends, his values, his goals. (pp. 99-100)

The narrator, like so many of the characters in the novels of Hugh MacLennan, is an orphan figure, a female Odysseus, a disturbed and frightened individual in search of a lost father and a lost way of life. She is in search of roots. . . .

We find we can't believe everything the narrator tells us. She can't believe herself. A modified stream-of-consciousness technique is effective here. The last half-dozen chapters become increasingly surreal and fantastic. After some literal deep-diving, where the drowned body of her father merges in her mind with her aborted child, the narrator accepts the mistakes of her earlier life. She returns, like a time-traveller home from a prehistoric junket, to present realities. Withdrawal, secrecy, non-feeling is no longer possible. To 'surface' is to choose love, defined by its failures, over the safety of death: "To trust is to let go". (p. 100)

> *Patricia Morley, "Multiple Surfaces," in* Journal of Canadian Fiction *(reprinted by permission from* Journal of Canadian Fiction, *2050 Mackay St., Montreal, Quebec H3G 2J1, Canada), Vol. I, No. 4, 1972, pp. 99-100.*

GLORIA ONLEY

In *Survival: A Thematic Guide to Canadian Literature* . . . Margaret Atwood argues that every country or culture has a single unifying and informing symbol at its core: for America, the Frontier; for England, the Island; for Canada, Survival, *la Survivance.* In her Afterword to *The Journals of Susanna Moodie* (1970) she had previously diagnosed the national mental illness as paranoid schizophrenia . . . ; here she develops the idea that most Canadian writers must be neurotic because, "given a choice of the negative or positive aspects of any symbol—sea as life-giving Mother, sea as what your ship goes down in; tree as symbol of growth,

tree as what falls on your head—Canadians show a marked preference for the negative." . . . This general immersion in the turgid depths of what Northrop Frye calls "the world of experience," where tragedy darkens into irony, she attributes to Canada's colonial status. The very function of a colony and of a colonial person is to be exploited; politics are always *Power Politics* (Atwood, 1971), whether the area of experience is sexual love or finance and international relations.

The poet who earlier wrote of modern woman's anguish at finding herself isolated and exploited (although also exploiting) by the imposition of a sex role power structure . . . now perceives a strong sado-masochistic patterning in Canadian literature as a whole. She believes that there is a national fictional tendency to participate, usually at some level as Victim, in a Victor/Victim basic pattern. Only rarely, in Atwood's view, which has no patience with old-fashioned concepts of spiritual or ethical victory, do Canadian characters move from ignorance to self-knowledge, from projection to creative interaction with other characters. . . . She sees earlier Canadian writers preoccupied with external obstacles to survival, such as the land or climate, and later writers concerned with "harder to identify and more internal" obstacles to "spiritual survival, to life as anything more than a minimally human being." . . . She begins with "capsule Canadian plots" as examples of what she means, some displaying outright "failures", others, "crippled successes". . . . Her satirical style, here at its crudest, relentlessly drives home her sense of a basic difficulty in human relations that seems to emerge with particular acuteness in what she briskly refers to as "Canlit." From her human relations point of view, the name of the game is to move forward into Position Four, that of creative non-victim. By definition, an author is in Position Four at the moment of writing.

To me, the structure of Atwood's thematic analysis is reminiscent of the psychology of R. D. Laing who talks about violence disguised as love, about people imposing psychological power structures or value structures on one another and on themselves, and about people in bondage to these structures. In fact, I feel that Atwood's four Basic Victim Positions (and the fifth mystical one which she postulates but leaves undefined), are almost a non-symmetrical "mapping" of Laing's psychology onto Northrop Frye's theory of fictional modes in which fictions are classified by the hero's power of action, ranging from the frustration and bondage of the ironic mode to the mythic creativity of the divine hero. For Atwood, power of action is directly related to degree of enlightenment. Atwood states that she has not read Laing, but the general idea of psychological power structures is now very much with us and has been linked, in various ways, with Laing's psychology. . . . These ideas have been, we might say, *Surfacing* all over the place for some time now, and especially in Margaret Atwood's own work, beginning with *The Edible Woman* (1969). To me, her most exciting contemporary significance as poet, novelist, and observer of her country's literature, lies in the fact that she is so clearly in tune with the radical spirit of her times.

In her early poetry, such as *The Circle Game* (1966), where she first enunciates the theme "Talking is difficult," . . . she is acutely aware of the problem of alienation, the need for real human communication and the establishment of genuine human community—real as opposed to mechanical or manipulative; genuine as opposed to the counterfeit community of the body politic.... A persistent strain in her imagery, appearing in the poetry as well as in *Surfacing* ..., is the head as disconnected from or floating above the body. Sometimes the neck is sealed over; always the intellectual part of the psyche is felt to be a fragment, dissociated from the whole. (pp. 51-2)

As Atwood notes in the Introduction to *Survival,* Northrop Frye suggests that in Canada "Who am I?" at least partly equals "Where is here?" Here, in *Surfacing,* is the liberated naked consciousness, its doors of perception symbolically cleansed; the "place" is the Canadian wilderness, which becomes the new body or rediscovered original body of the psychosomatic human Canadian man/woman in contradistinction to American schizophrenic man/woman, exiled from the biosphere and from himself/herself.

Surfacing, is, for Canadians, an anatomy of the "deluge of values and artifacts flowing in from outside" which "render invisible the values and artifacts that actually exist 'here'." ... A fusion of many literary forms, Menippean satire, diary, wilderness venture, even the Canadian animal story, *Surfacing* is mainly concerned with indicating what must be removed so that a true sense of self may be uncovered and a movement begun in the direction of communication and community. The suggestion is implanted at the end of the psychological quest, when the surfaced female self decides to rejoin the "half-formed" father of her recently conceived child and attempt to have a human as opposed to mechanical relationship with him, that the often unsatisfactory nature of male-female relationships in modern urban society is a function of a general human failure to communicate, to use language as a tool instead of a weapon. Exile from the biosphere is related, almost metaphysically, to the exploitative use of language to impose psychological power structures. (pp. 52-3)

Atwood's wit ranges in *Survival* from a running put down of all power structures embodied and exposed in "Canlit" to the scathing dismissal of fictional characters as if they were one's neurotic neighbors for whom self-destruction is a kind of busy work.... This somewhat one-dimensional interpretation of "Canlit" as if it were a series of case histories of human failure can be both funny and, one hopes, enlightening to potential victims. It can also, of course, be considered an oversimplification unless one keeps firmly in mind that the basic premise of the book is to "articulate the skeleton of Canadian literature," and, as it were, let others (critics, teachers, the students themselves) put the flesh back on the bones....

Chapter Ten, "Ice Women versus Earth Mothers," ... translates women's liberation insights into fairytale symbolism and mythic terms. Canadian women, to Margaret Atwood, suffer from the "Rapunzel syndrome"; in fact, in Canada Rapunzel and the tower are the same, for Canadian heroines "have internalized the values of their culture to such an extent that they have become their own prisons." Moreover, the struggle of Canadian women in the Canadian novel is the attempt of buried Venuses and Dianas to free themselves from the Hecate-Ice-Goddess stereotype. These depth charges should clear out a lot of murky underwater territory: if reading *A Jest of God* discourages spinsterhood, surely reading *The Fire Dwellers* equally discourages matrimony. The net result for the Canadian girl observing these unsatisfactory patterns of womanly fulfilment might

be to make her less idealistic and romantic, less the Sensuous Woman manqué, and rather more pragmatic and realistic in her approach to love and human relationships. In fact, for the Canadian student, Atwood's guide to "Canlit" is a map of dangerous territories to study vicariously and avoid as much as possible in one's own life. As Atwood points out in the Introduction: "Much of our literature is a diagram of what is *not* desired. Knowing what you don't want isn't the same as knowing what you want, but it helps." ...

What if it is not a national neurosis after all, but part of what might be called the civilized human condition to create/become a victim? The victor/victim patterning may have become a risk inherent in any use of language whatsoever, since, depending on the experiential and interpretative context, and the circumstances and psychological background of the persons involved, even a single word can be used as/become a power structure implying superiority/inferiority, aggression/destruction, and many other polarities. The need for communication in *Power Politics* is paralleled by the realization that language tends to warp in the hand from tool to weapon ..., and there is a corresponding recognition of the value of silence.... (p. 53)

To use language at all is to risk participation in its induction structure; to define is to risk committing or inciting violence in the name of love.

In her poetry Atwood implicitly recognizes that the new frontier is the language barrier and the new pioneers are those who can help us avoid what Laing calls "the mystification of experience," that is the use of language to cultivate a false consciousness in ourselves and others. Obviously the highly literate, articulate self is more sensitive to the distortions imposed by the language barrier than is the average person, although the average person is, if anything, more subject to it because less aware of what's going on.

Survival is a first step towards awareness, the basic realization that there is a victor/victim patterning inherent in life, that it may be traced in the relationships of characters in a novel, in external action, in psychological movement, in image patterns, in symbolism. (pp. 53-4)

If it were not for the inherent tendency to use language for the "mystification of experience" or, as Atwood would say, for "mythologizing", we might venture forth more confidently with the verbal diagram of *Survival* in our hands. As the wilderness guide in *Surfacing* discovers, imaginary maps may lead to real discoveries but only if we can be flexible enough in our approaches. (p. 54)

> *Gloria Onley, "Margaret Atwood: Surfacing in the Interests of Survival," in* West Coast Review *(copyright © January, 1973 West Coast Review Publishing Society), January, 1973, pp. 51-4.*

VALERIE TRUEBLOOD

It is the life-impulse [Atwood] uncovers and venerates [in *Surfacing*] alone on the island peeling off her civilized skins. This is the impulse [she] uncovers in her poetry, honoring the claim-to-life of whatever lives.

The narrator of *Surfacing* sees a heron killed for sport hanging in a tree and is as powerfully converted as Saint Eustace coming upon the stag with the cross between its antlers. . . . Her magnified understanding is not occupied with what the heron might stand for, or mean to humans, but with the mutilated bird itself, the violation of its life. Atwood's birds and beasts aren't symbols. She hails in each thing its own life, and its own physique: for her these are enough to express its sacredness. (p. 19)

A new poetry of love and death has been taking shape since the outrush of feminist energy in the 60's. Some of its elements are that the speaker is (usually) a woman, revoked love is seen as a public act which deflects the secure progression of life, a grave, reciting, schoolgirl voice may announce intention to do violent harm, and the poet's quarrel is less with an individual than with a modern temperament unsuccessful at keeping love going or assenting to Yeats' idea of love as a discipline. In [the poems in *You Are Happy*] Atwood avoids the litigious, civic-minded mood of the bereft that has colored much of this poetry. Her misdoers are just as hapless as their victims. . . . The thrill of the carnal, when it is allowed at all, is a sad thrill. (pp. 19-20)

In this book, and each of her others, what is at the root of the sorrow? While it feeds the feminism and anger that show aboveground, the root seems to tap something much purer and colder, two things really: a disaffection from people, the mishandlers of all that is sacred, and a female sense of kinship with the natural world that waits to be plundered. People are the unhungry consumers, killers of animals, disrupters of old rhythms, living in a time they have appropriated for themselves and for whose wretchedness they are responsible. . . . The same sense is present everywhere in her work, most notably in *The Animals in that Country* and in the fine *Procedures for Underground,* where poem after poem celebrates the patience of the landscape under the human spur. . . .

[Unlike Annie Dillard, who works in the same area and] can become rhapsodic, Margaret Atwood is not a poet susceptible to happiness. Flushing out the harm-doers she keeps encountering herself. Her personae at various times repudiate food, love, which is predatory, Americans (this belongs elsewhere than in a parenthesis: Atwood is a Canadian with a deep fear of usurpation by the consumerism of the United States), and civilization. Her poetry has the steady unrelenting pace of conscience. But out of the same mouth proceedeth blessing and cursing, and Atwood makes blessings of her exquisite cold landscapes and the animals watching from them, and of the struggle of some of her characters to be humane.

Many of the earlier poems were baleful, a quality that persists in the first section of *You Are Happy,* where the subject is loss, and occasionally in Part Two, "Songs of the Transformed", where animals and a corpse speak as revolutionaries. "Pig Song" is a good example of what [D. B.] Wyndham Lewis called the Enumerative-Vituperative. But Part One closes with "You Are Happy" and an ordinary but somehow miraculous "Bird / running across the glaring / road against the low pink sun", and in the final Song of the Transformed a corpse asks the living for prayers and warns them "Sing now / . . . or you will drift as I do / . . . swollen with hoarded love". Part Three, "Circe/Mud Poems", has a chastened Circe alternating benevolence with a child's fitful rancor reminiscent of Plath, but trying to keep the wanderer—his protective *moly* here simply masculinity—near her.

Occasionally, too, we can hear Plath in the pathologist's dissecting-describing cadence (here is . . . , this is . . . , it is . . .) and directions to an infuriating lover or to the reader (see, take) as if to a slow-witted assistant. "Tricks with Mirrors", the mordant, unenamoured poem that most brings Plath to mind, seems to lack the tone of clemency that is Atwood's own. The only other poem I felt belied her gifts, "Is/Not", is an odd combination: sharp disclaimer of interest in curability (of a love affair or marriage) and concession to the California-transactional vocabulary. But it contains the dry, lively "Permit me the present tense" and the author's reverential feeling for words as the only totems left, needing "to be said and said".

"A language is everything you do," she says in *Surfacing.* Her sense of words as things, as having properties, permeates these poems. . . . She has pared her language to what proves, what alerts the senses and then the imagination to rightness, and she creates a world of ice and burned forest and deer tracks, and the reprieve of this world by the wet spring that makes her "dream of reconciliations". The lavish "Spring Poem" is full of the names of rebirths: "dandelions / whirl their blades upwards", a snake "sidewinds" in its "chained hide", "the hens / roll in the dust, squinting with bliss". For Atwood, to name a thing is to make a gesture towards it, to propitiate it. Words are the repositories of spirit; their sway is strict; it is the *words* of the sirens that lure sailors. . . . Atwood's dictum "There Is Only One of Everything" is expressed in the lovely poem by that name, in which the speaker tells us she can say the incantation "I want this" only once, it is so powerful (a rare glimpse, in a poem, of the droll Atwood we saw in the novel *Edible Woman:* she then says it twice). . . .

The poem that seems to me the strongest in the book (though the hushed "Late August" rivals it) is one of the most accessible and the most pervaded by the mysticism Atwood everywhere resists and makes ironic: "First Prayer", a hymn to the human body. . . . This poem will be anthologized; it is passionate and wistful by turns, its ending "O body, descend / from the wall where I have nailed you / . . . give me this day" inverts the profane by its humility and leads to the final poem "Book of Ancestors" in which the task of being alive is a sacred one: "to take / that risk, to offer life and remain / alive, open yourself like this and become whole."

Delmore Schwartz says "Every living poet would like to be direct, lucid and immediately intelligible" but the poet's immersion in the powers and reaches of language cut him off from people not so preoccupied. Atwood's gift is to make us share her extravagant interest in what exists and discover a language inhabited, as the world she recreates is inhabited, by spirit. (p. 20)

Valerie Trueblood, "Conscience and Spirit," in The American Poetry Review *(copyright © 1977 by World Poetry, Inc.; reprinted by permission of Valerie Trueblood), March/April, 1977, pp. 19-20.*

ELSPETH CAMERON

Atwood's central theme in [*Lady Oracle* and *Dancing Girls*] is the "self," . . . a complex and fascinating mixture of reality and fantasy. Playing a part, or, as Atwood would put it, dancing a role, involves difficult decisions. Mainly it means choosing between a private and a public life. . . . Both in *Lady Oracle* and *Dancing Girls* the "self" competes with one or more "roles" for center stage.

With characteristic wit, Atwood explores the tensions involved in the fractured identity of the artist in *Lady Oracle.* The first overlay of Joan's real self occurs as a result of her mother's determined imposition of two mutually inconsistent roles on her daughter. . . . Responding early in life to what others need her to be, she becomes devious in her efforts to preserve the real self within from annihilation. Recognition of this real self comes only from her Aunt Lou. . . . Through Aunt Lou's support, moral and financial, Joan is able to fly by the nets her mother casts, reducing to normal size, moving to London and changing her name to that of her Aunt Lou—Louisa K. Delacourt. Through this new name, Joan adopts another identity, not one inflicted upon her, but one, as her surname suggests, "fostered" by identification with the Aunt she has idealized. And, like Aunt Lou, she writes; not editorial letters *to* girls in distress, but tales *of* girls in distress in Costume Gothic novels. . . . (pp. 36-7)

For a time in London, Joan (now Louisa), indulges in the role of "mistress" to a Polish Count whose romantic patter and writing career insulate her from the banality of Canada House and the tawdriness of London. In a short time, however, another identity takes over in the form of an affair with a young fringe radical named Arthur whom she eventually marries in Toronto. At this point, Joan "fosters" yet another identity, that of the Automatic Writer who produces a book of poems called *Lady Oracle,* "a combination of Rod McKuen and Kahlil Gibran," which catapult her into instant fame. Meanwhile, behind Arthur's back, she launches an intense affair with the Royal Porcupine, Concreate Artist, whose frozen animal carcasses have wowed the Toronto art scene. The tension of keeping all these selves separate and functional is finally too much for her, so she "kills" Joan Foster by faking her drowning in Lake Ontario. Free again to begin yet another life, Louisa K. Delacourt, appearance transformed, boards the plane for Italy where she plans to continue writing her Costume Gothics in a small Italian village, the scene of the novel's brilliant denouement.

For Joan/Louisa, this plethora of roles is the fate of the artist: "I might as well face it," she thinks after her flight to Italy, "I was an artist, an escape artist. I'd sometimes talked about love and commitment, but the real romance of my life was that between Houdini and his ropes and locked trunk; entering the embrace of bondage, slithering out again." "Hooked on plots" in life and in art, Joan uses her ingenious imagination to survive—economically through her writing and emotionally through her series of lives she invents and lives.

Though Joan Foster is the main example of this view of life, the other artists or pseudo-artists in *Lady Oracle* also inhabit more than one self. . . . Without exception, the real self behind the mask is more ordinary, less dramatic than the projected persona. The real self, Atwood seems to say, is too dull to be valued, must be dressed up and dramatized to attract attention. The problem is that the attention so gained is for the "role" and not for the "self" who, consequently, feels unloved, insignificant and angry.

Much is made of the significance of clothes, not only in Louisa's Costume Gothics, but in life's roles as well. As the narrator of "Hair Jewellery" in *Dancing Girls* says:

 I resurrect myself through clothes. In fact

it's impossible for me to remember what I did, what happened to me, unless I can remember what I was wearing, and every time I discard a sweater or a dress I am discarding part of my life. I shed identities like a snake, leaving them pale and shrivelled behind me, a trail of them, and if I want any memories at all I have to collect, one by one, those cotton and wool fragments, piece them together, achieving at last a patchwork self.

Seen in this way, life is nothing more than a series of roles tenuously "pieced together" into "a patchwork self" by a central consciousness. And the Costume Gothics which Louisa writes are not, as one might suppose, sheer fantasy, unrelated to real life; they are elaborate dramatizations of the issues of Joan Foster's life, which is itself, in turn, an elaborate combination of the roles others devise for her and those she devises for herself.

Bizarre and whimsical as Joan's world is, tensions as sinister as those in the Costume Gothic novels lurk beneath the surface. The real self is always in danger of being annihilated if the persona takes over. And personae as unalike as the Stone and Bronze Ages must be kept separate in space and time lest they neutralize each other. How, Atwood asks, can one patch together aspects of the self which threaten to pull apart the identity? The novel's story line involves the reader in this question with a suspense reminiscent of the detective novels Joan reads in her father's library. . . . As Joan confesses, "If I brought the separate parts of my life together . . . , surely there would be an explosion." (pp. 37-9)

In "Lives of the Poets," from *Dancing Girls,* Atwood treats the same theme of the split within the artist who has a public "role" and a private "self." Mocking Samuel Johnson's title, she describes an evening in the life of a Canadian poet which is a far cry from the eminent lives of Pope, Milton and others that Johnson described. Just prior to giving a reading in the bleak industrial town of Sudbury, Ontario, she develops a nosebleed—one of the several minor symptoms that often plague her before the readings she gives to keep herself and her man solvent. His inaccessibility by phone may or may not be evidence of infidelity—an anxiety which jolts her from the concerns of the "self" into the "role" she must play. Sending out her "dancing girl" persona to read onstage, she feels a powerful hostility to the docile audience who cannot possibly appreciate how her dedication to art has jeopardized her personal life. . . . (p. 39)

Especially when it comes to relationships between men and women is the conflict of "role" and "self" a deadly one. Though Atwood focuses on the artist as a complex example of the creation of roles, fantasies and fictions, hers is no esoteric portrait of the artist which excludes ordinary people. In both these books, she shows the ways in which all people create "roles" for themselves and others, especially when they fall in love. . . .

Only relationships between the real "selves" of men and women bring fulfillment; interaction between the "roles" they play is hollow and unsatisfying.

Several of the stories in *Dancing Girls* are based on this theme; that of the romantic persona sent out to love who has no chance of succeeding because the real self remains hidden. (p. 40)

The institution of marriage with its continuous intimacy is bound to result in profound disillusionment for romantic men and women. In "The Resplendent Quetzal," the married couple, Sarah and Edward, are trapped in a hideous relationship in which neither is free to be authentic. The images each has had of the other at first have faded into incompatible reality. "It was almost as if he'd had an affair with another woman, she had been so different. He'd treated her body then as something holy, a white and gold chalice, to be touched with care and tenderness." As for Sarah, "At first Edward's obsessions had fascinated her, since she didn't understand them, but now they merely made her tired." To confront their many deceptions "would be the end, all the pretences would come crashing down and they would be left standing in the middle, staring at each other." Atwood shows here the pain and true heroism involved in loving another human being once the masks are removed.

Atwood at her most extreme shows, in some of the stories in *Dancing Girls,* how the stress of real relationships can lead to insanity. Her treatment of madness is best understood by considering psychiatrist R. D. Laing's well-known theories on the subject. For Laing, "normality" in a culture like ours that suppresses both the instincts and any form of transcendence, is nothing more than a collective "pervasive madness." . . . Those who have transcendent experiences, like the heroine of *Surfacing,* even those who simply refuse to adjust to society's standards of "normal," like Marian in *The Edible Woman,* may be viewed as mad by "normal" people. If "normal" means only the way in which things are done in a given society, people from other societies are likely to seem mad; as one character puts it in "The Man From Mars," "the thing about people from another culture was that you could never tell whether they were insane or not because their ways were so different." Atwood plays with the ambiguity of such frames of reference by using first person narration to let us see the cogency of people who, observed objectively, would be to a greater or lesser degree, certifiable. She is most effective when she presents madness and sanity as shades of gray, indistinguishable one from the other. She strikes this ambivalence in "Polarities" where the heroine, Louise, seeks for completeness in a fragmentary world and ends up in a mental institution. Seen from society's point of view, she is insane, but compared to her lover, Morrison and their friends, her utterances and notes indicate another level of reality the reader is inclined to accept. The story's title suggests not only the "polar" landscape and the "polar" opposites, Louise and Morrison, but also the "polarities" within Louise and, by extension, other individuals. As Louise, in what is taken for mad raving, confides, "I *am* the circle. I have the poles within myself. What I have to do is keep myself in one piece." As her room, with its "air of pastiche," suggests, Louise struggles grimly to hold a "patchwork self" together. (pp. 41-2)

[Atwood's] techniques for the dissection of the human personality—the detached point of view, the clinical precision of language, the scientific imagery—all are reminiscent of the scientist or medical expert. . . . Frequently, the effectiveness of her narrator's point of view comes from the tension that arises when highly charged emotional situations are observed with the cool detachment of someone looking

through a microscope. This detachment is especially suitable when the narrator is insane, as in "When it Happens"— a device Atwood may have gleaned from Agatha Christie's most famous mystery, *The Murder of Roger Ackroyd.* Other techniques which Atwood uses related to this scientific point of view are the journal form, the splitting of point of view and scientific analogy. In "The War in the Bathroom," for example, the journal form is used to give a day-by-day record of precise observations which eventually enable the narrator to retaliate effectively. The same technique, in a more subtle way, is used in both Atwood's previous novels, as well as in several of the other stories in *Dancing Girls.* Atwood's narrators are often seen to keep a close watch on everything around them as if, like people stranded in the bush, their very lives depended on it. In cases where a real self, such as we have seen in *Lady Oracle,* hides behind one or more personae, Atwood frequently splits the point of view, using first person for the real self, third person for the persona. This device is the organizing principle in *The Edible Woman,* as it is in such stories as "Giving Birth" and "The War in the Bathroom." . . . Finally, analogy with scientific situations, especially those drawn from biology, provide Atwood with symbols suitable for her subjects. "Under Glass," as the title suggests, views the breakdown of a relationship in much the same way as the narrator herself watches the animals in the Moonlight Pavilion of the zoo. . . . (pp. 42-3)

Atwood's prose is filled with images and descriptions taken from the world of science. (p. 43)

This adaptation of the scientific for literary purposes, gives Atwood's prose its characteristic cool, tense tone. For her, it is a way of seeing clearly, of getting close to the truth, since it allows a rational penetration through superficial appearance to an underlying truth. Though some readers will feel that the "expert surgeon" Atwood murders to dissect, there is no denying the powerful impact of the tension between her emotional subject matter and her emotionless tone. "Natural," then, in Atwood's view, is true or authentic; "artificial" is misleading or distorted. This view of life inevitably gives rise to biting satire when such "artificial" aspects of contemporary life as dress, customs, even language, are examined carefully. Atwood often seems like an anthropologist from another world, accurately recording the things people do in our society as if she herself had never done them. . . . Atwood shows that through the "artifice" of social behavior which represses real feelings and hides or distorts the real self, man has created for himself dense and chaotic mazes which are surely hideous, were they not so funny. (p. 44)

Atwood shows men and women at their best, their truest, when social masks are stripped away so that man can be viewed as a species in nature. The real issues, she shows, are those which mankind hold in common with all living creatures—survival of the fittest (*Lady Oracle*), territorial aggression ("The War in the Bathroom"), the finding of a mate ("The Man From Mars"), anger and jealousy ("Lives of the Poets") and reproduction ("Giving Birth"). Man's "creativity" through which he imagines and then lives roles with values other than these simple basic truths, interferes with and threatens his potential for happiness and for spiritual fulfillment. "For true happiness," Eunice P. Revele advises Arthur and Joan in *Lady Oracle,* "you must approach life with a feeling of reverence. . . . Avoid deception and falsehood. . . . Above all, you should love each other for what you are and forgive each other for what you are not." Coming from a woman who has herself adopted a persona, these words indicate ironically both what is best for man and the impossibility for man of living out this truth. Since art itself is a kind of falsehood, Atwood often gives the impression, like the Russian novelist Nabokov, that the very forms with which she works are a distortion, even to the point in *Surfacing* and "Giving Birth," of suggesting that language itself is an "artifice" that interferes with the singleness of emotion, thought and action that animals experience. Atwood views character as a series of transformations in the form of imagined personae who, chameleon-like, enable the inner "self" to survive. Holding together all these phases of the identity in some sort of "patchwork self" may be the most difficult task man faces in contemporary society. (pp. 44-5)

Elspeth Cameron, "Margaret Atwood: A Patchwork Self," in Book Forum *(copyright © 1978 by The Hudson River Press), Vol. IV, No. 1, 1978, pp. 35-45.*

B

BALDWIN, James   1924-

Baldwin is a black American essayist, novelist, short story writer, and playwright. His work consistently reveals a moral purpose: to make art reflect a sense of reality and clarity, rather than the falsehood of illusion. (See also *CLC*, Vols. 1, 2, 3, 4, 5, 8, and *Contemporary Authors*, Vols. 1-4, rev. ed.)

CHARLES NEWMAN

James Baldwin has made a reputation by exploiting social paradoxes, so it should not be surprising to trace his literary antecedents to neither Richard Wright nor Harriet B. Stowe, but to that Brahmin, Henry James. . . . The amphibian elegance of [Baldwin's] syntax comes naturally to an artist obsessed by dualities, paradox. The Atlantic Ocean separated James's mind into opposed hemispheres, and the gulf of color so cleaves Baldwin. The antipodes of their worlds propose a dialectical art. (p. 52)

Baldwin's characters suffer no more from their color than James's suffer from their money—these are only the peculiar conditions of their suffering. The problem for both is more universal—the opacity of their culture and the question of their identity within it. For Baldwin assumes, in the consequences of his culture, the crisis of his identity, the reflective burden of Western Man. His color is his metaphor, his vantage. But in his despair, he is closer to Henry Adams than John Henry.

Both Baldwin and James were victims of a "mysterious childhood accident." Only their society's different reaction to puberty sets them apart. It is not so much a question of how it happened, but the consequences. "I'm the reaction against the mistake," says Lambert Strether in *The Ambassadors,* and Baldwin certifies this most finally for his contemporaries. "They were so other," James elaborates in *A Small Boy and Others,* "that was what I felt; and to be other, *other almost anyhow,* seemed as good as the probable taste of the bright compound wistfully watched in the confectioner's window" (emphasis mine).

Their hurts are obscure only because such wounds are generally ignored by those enamored of the big candy in the window. The pose necessitated is that of the *powerless, feeling young man.* The psychological consequence is self-imposed exile; to be "other almost anyhow." The literary consequence is the novel of "manners" (read prejudice); this being the drama of how personal histories conflict with the public history of the time. Personal action can only be understood in terms of its public consequences. Morality, in this sense, may not be relative, but it is always comparative. (pp. 52-3)

Baldwin's first paradox is that he uses the Negro, uses him ruthlessly, to show the White Man what the White Man is. Repeatedly in his work, he returns to that image of a Negro hung from a fine Southern tree with his sex cut out. We confront the Negro, we cannot miss him. But we know little about him except that he suffered. We know more, implicitly, about the White Man who left him there. The insights and blind spots of such a technique are illustrated in Baldwin's most ambitious work, *Another Country.*

This novel is populated by a series of characters, or rather couples, as geometrically entangled as Far Eastern erotic sculpture, the only undocumented relationship being that unlovely norm—monogamous, heterosexual marriage. . . . [In the novel the attempt of the characters Rufus and Leona] to confront, transcend, their past results in her madness and his suicide. This couple is removed from the action relatively early. Subsequent relationships embellish this dazzling affair from other sexual and moral perspectives, through the use of *ficelles*—James's word for characters who, while not self-sustaining, provide *relief* or depth by their juxtaposition to the primary figures of the work. . . .

Tempered, perhaps, by the knowledge that their respective talents may gain them escape from the ghetto, Ida and Vivaldo seem one generation removed from the heat of Rufus and Leona. They are reincarnations; history is personalized for them through the primary disastrous affair. (p. 54)

What Cass comes to resent in her husband [Richard] is not clear—he is disciplined rather than talented perhaps—he does not indulge in the other's frenetic search for a large identity—he actually finishes a book and gets it published. In any case, Cass has an affair with Eric, ex-Alabama actor, formerly a lover of Rufus and later involved with Vivaldo, then in an interlude awaiting the arrival of his present lover, Yves, French, ex-male prostitute. . . . Cass and Eric arrange their *Te Deum* in the Museum of Modern Art. The scene is crucial and among the best in the book. . . . [They] move through the unending anterooms of the modern world —all glass and steel, no texture there—rooms emblazoned with incomprehensible abstractions, cold walls ogled by triumphant myopics, ". . . like tourists in a foreign grave-yard." Before an enormous red canvas, stand a boy and girl holding hands, American Gothic against the Apocalypse.

Here, in one scene, is all that distance between Christopher Newman, James's *American,* and more contemporary stuff. For despite Newman's inability to accept his own culture or to fathom a foreign atmosphere no less stifling, he could find solace in the red doors of Notre Dame, as James did in the *Galerie d'Appallon.* . . . Newman could construe the nature of his rebuff; that it was his part to pay his absentee rent and return home.

That is the nostalgic quality of James's characters—they divine their atmosphere, their responses are equal to the situation. They make their peace with a precise if unhappy destiny. But the atmosphere is more opaque for Baldwin's characters, it elicits no response, they simply suffer from it. . . . [Their] sensitivity, their culture, their very cosmopolitanism is turned against them. (pp. 54-5)

Cass is pithy as any Jamesian interlocutor. "He can suffer, after all," she says of Richard. "I told him because . . . that if we were going to—continue together—we could begin on a new basis with everything clear between us. But I was wrong—some things cannot be clear . . . or perhaps some things *are* clear, only one won't face those things."

In that parallelism hangs the book. Tolstoy would have used those last sentences as his first. The story would have unfolded from their dichotomy. It is characteristic of modern art that the thesis is not hung until we have been dragged kicking through every conceivable blind alley—the self being the sum of the destruction of all false selves.

Echoes of these three relationships [Rufus and Leona, Ida and Vivaldo, and Cass and Richard] reverberate through another series of *ficelles.* . . . Baldwin once accused Richard Wright of substituting violence for sex. He has come full circle.

In the end, things are magnificently unresolved, save for Rufus's death and Leona's madness. (p. 56)

The irresolution of these destinies . . . has brought some critics down hard on Baldwin. The charge is formlessness. But if *Another Country* is formless, it has that in common with this nation's greatest literature. . . .

[The language of the novel's final scene] is not the language of Henry James, the understated snippet of dialogue or restrained image which brings things to a close. It is the language of Gatsby and the Green Light, Huck Finn, "striking out for the territory," Ishmael, picked up, alone, to tell the tale—the picaresque open-end of American Literature. . . .

[In] this ecstatic scene, no one is fleeing injustice with high hopes . . . ; this is no rendezvous with destiny, but a discomforting liaison. The visionary rhetoric is utterly undercut.

So the legend of America as refuge for the oppressed, opportunity for the pure in heart, is invoked only to be exposed. From the very first, he is saying, our vision has been parochial. We have not accounted for the variety of man's motives, the underside of our settlers, the cost of a new life. The plague has come over as part of the baggage, and we will be sick until we isolate that cargo and deal with it. . . . If *Another Country* is formless, it is so because it rejects the theories of history available to it. (p. 57)

[What about the] characters that set *Another Country* in motion, Leona and Rufus? It is what Baldwin does not know, or say, about them which is interesting, for they must bear the primary burden, they are the myth which the other couples mime. As myths, Baldwin tends to monumentalize them, give them stature by arresting their development. Like Greek royalty, their personality is gradually subsumed by the enormity of the crime which killed them.

But who are they? Rufus Scott has that ethereal sensitivity of the modern hero, half-adolescent, half-prophet, that *powerless, feeling young man* celebrated, apparently, because he rejects a success already denied him—the man who in Norman Mailer's words would "affect history by the sheer force of his sentiments." Or so the logic goes. But really, he is a monument from the very first, he is that Negro hanging from the tree with his sex cut out.

The fact is, that Rufus is nothing but his own potential, and the world is simply what thwarts it. He is a brilliantly rendered testament. But he is not a character. What *he* can't do and why *they* won't let him, is more vague than mysterious. He is, if you will, the Seymour Glass of his class, his virtue postulated by his lesser apostles. It is significant that although Rufus is a musician, we never hear him play. As with Seymour's alleged poetry, we await the aria that never comes.

And Leona? Poor white trash Isolde? Significantly, the only character in the book not devoted in some way to the arts. Symbols, representation, mean nothing to her. It is commerce, communication in the most direct sense, that she lives. "Do you love me?" everyman's saxophone asks. Leona says, "Don't hurt me." The pale white liberal; impotent (I ain't gonna have no more babies), platitudinous (it don't matter what two people's color is so long as they love each other), ineradicably guilty. She tries to love Rufus because she needs him, and he won't let her because it smacks of retribution. Her effort, pathetic, styleless, is for nothing. She is committed to an institution. But that is only the legal acknowledgment. If Baldwin does not see what Rufus might become, he does not see what Leona *is.* She does not go crazy; she has been mad from the beginning. As characters, they *go* nowhere; they die of nothing more than their own abstraction.

"What they (Negroes) hold in common is their precarious, their unutterably painful relation to the white world," Baldwin says. What the characters of *Another Country* hold in common is their precarious relation to a world which is defined by little more than its victims' resentment. One by one, we come upon them, hung from their respective trees, but the executioner never appears; like *Godot,* his name is simply invoked to "explain things." What is explicitly absent in Baldwin's politics—the differentiation between enemies, the priorities and strategies of rebellion—is implicitly absent in his literature.

To structure the dialogue in this way has its dramatic usefulness. The conflicts are elucidated in all their hopeless solipsism. But the consequence is also to make development, in terms of plot, psychology, or character, impossible. He is overwhelmed by the eloquence of his own dialectic. He has reached that moment which defines much of modern fiction—when the characters start to repeat themselves endlessly. Recapitulation of this sort has its irony—upon which the theatre of the absurd had capitalized—but artistically, it is also a dead end.

To understand how an artist can get into this situation, *Another Country* must be considered the result of a long and certainly uplifting process. Baldwin's progress as an artist has been his ability to articulate, confront, his central problems as a man and a writer. . . . What began as a crippling disgust with both his race and country, as an *American*, a *Negro*, becomes a subtle distinctive pride in each as *americanegro*. (pp. 59-60)

[Baldwin's] progress is apparent in *Another Country*, but it is a work of a different order [from the other works]. It is less explicitly therapeutic, more ambitious. It is the very repetition, the surface perversity of the encounters, that gradually makes perversity irrelevant. For this is not at all a book about interracial affairs, homosexual affairs, adulterous affairs, but about *affairs*—it evolves in the same way that *Portrait of a Lady*, say, unfolds upon the loom of marriage. The various approaches, styles, perspectives are secondary. They all need the same thing if they face different obstacles, they all pay the same dues. Everyone hits bottom in his own way and that is that. Yves and Eric's liaison is significant on one level of irony, but ultimately it is of no peculiar issue. Their final significance is that they simply carry on the central burden of the book, the frantic attempt to know something of one another. Perversion is no single act; but rather, *any* unaffecting love.

Baldwin has constructed his terrible dialectic; he has drawn up the battle lines so that we may never be safe again. But what he has done, in scrupulously avoiding everybody's social protest novel, is to write everybody's existential novel. (p. 60)

James's characters have an extraordinary freedom based on money—and it is no accident that Baldwin's characters are similarly unaffected by conventional economic problems. This is not because they are more spiritual, but simply because this is as accurate an index of modern affluent society as James's analysis of the international aristocracy. In short, the economics of both situations are only manifestations of more significant and complex problems. Rufus did not kill himself because he did not have enough to eat when he was a child, but because he understood the dimensions of ignorance and fear, one consequence of which was to affect his diet. Unhampered by the obvious, Baldwin has cut through the pop-sociology of his time to the roots of contemporary frustration—the curse not of slavery, but leisure; not of organization, but alienation; not of social evil, but of individual love. Baldwin's assertion that we are all second-class citizens in our existential dilemma, that the terms of our exclusion are similar, is his greatest achievement. In the end, his protagonists are not black anymore than we are white. (pp. 60-1)

The message of this existentialism is the equality of guilt, the equality of men before no law—but when the rebellion has been justified, then what happens? Experience under these assumptions is predictable, sensibility has but one consequence. To say that the self is not what we commonly thought, even to say it again and again, is not to say what the self is. . . .

Another Country is our country, real, repressed, and envisioned, and Baldwin's return to it does not break down the parallel with James in the least. His point of view remains that of the exile. Under existential assumptions, self-exile, to paraphrase a politician, is not a choice, but a condition.

It is the condition of that *powerless, feeling young man*, an echo of that "reaction against a mistake," that dangling emasculate Negro, that rage to be "other almost anyhow."

But how do you differentiate when everybody is "other" anyway? Why do Rufus and Richard give up? Why do Ida and Vivaldo persevere? These are ambiguities in the work that cannot be justified by saying that life is ambiguous as well. The underground man is pretty thin fare by this time. Too many of us live there now to be celebrated as either indicative or unique. "There is no structure," Baldwin says, "that he [the artist] can build to keep out self-knowledge." But he has not yet demonstrated, except in his essays, that the artist can build a structure to *use* self-knowledge. (p. 61)

James refused to be satisfied by the type of the *powerless, feeling young man,* for he knew how easy it was for him to uphold such a one, and how graciously his audience would accept him. He was too involved in his own cultural adventure to settle for the drama of limited character and obvious dichotomy. His concern can be seen in his notebooks— "the web of consciousness," his own metaphor, replaces the dialectic as a structural principle. Whatever the argument over the convolutions of the later style, the consequences of his continued exile, it is apparent that the later heroes of sensibility are transfigured, and again I use his own words, into "personalities of transcendent value." He is not satisfied simply to doom his characters in his later work, not because they ought not to go down, but because that story was written—those conflicts were charted—and now the problem was to develop the internal relations between the sides he had so artfully chosen. It was a question of creating characters sufficiently complex to sustain them beyond the dialectical conflict which created them. (pp. 62-3)

The remarkable thing about [James's] later characters is that they refuse to draw conclusions that would preclude further investigation on their part, and for that matter, further involvement for the reader. The galling thing about Baldwin's characters—and most "existential" heroes—is that they are so susceptible to conclusions which define them immediately. It is not that their truth is bitter, it is that their truth comes so easily—however hard it may be to shake it. In fact, they are all *ficelles.*

The quality of the later James lies in the tension between characters. Who is guilty? Who is innocent? Our final knowledge is that Paris, France, and Wollett, Mass., are not knowable without the other, that the categories with which we began the book no longer can apply. Radical innocence and guileless evil are neither opposed nor reconciled—they are intermeshed in a genuine mystery. Baldwin is shocking; not yet terrifying. What he has shown us is that everyone is guilty. This is the true paradox of the existential hero, for in all his hefty insistence that rebellion is justified, he seems to end up lacking the energy to achieve the *engagement* to which he pays his coffee-house lip-service.

Henry James was able to achieve what his notebooks anticipated: the reclamation of large areas of social experience, the transformation of these abstractions into material for the imagination. Baldwin has yet to progress beyond the initial encounter. He has, most powerfully, given us an opportunity to test our preconceptions, but that ultimately is social science, not literature.

The question remains, why pick on Baldwin when these are questions to be applied to modern fiction generally? Why does he take the burden of the breakthrough?

For one thing, Baldwin has progressed in each of his works, his dialectic has become progressively more refined. He has shown a flexibility and perseverance equal to our most influential artists. Further, and almost alone, he has continued to confront the unmanageable questions of modern society, rather than creating a nuclear family in which semantic fantasies may be enacted with no reference to the larger world except that it stinks. There can be no escape into technique or historiography. It will not do for him to remember something else. He must continue to find out about himself. It is his actual experience, perhaps, even more than the shaping of it, which will be crucial. To bring us to the door in Rufus's name will not be enough next time.

Baldwin's experience is unique among our artists in that his artistic achievements mesh so precisely with his historical circumstances. He is that nostalgic type—an artist speaking for a genuinely visible revolution. He is first in line for that Nirvana of American liberals, a Ministry of Culture. As with James, his problem is to give artistic life to the critical insights of his prefaces, his notebooks, in short, to develop characters which have a subtle and various consciousness equal to the omniscient, cranky narrator of the essays. This particular problem accounts for the failure of both artists as playwrights. Theatrical success depends upon rendering the particulars of a character through bald dialogue. Only rarely can a narrator amplify a character through abstract description; no disembodied voice can bridge the gap between an idea and its personification as in an essay or narrative literature. For those obsessed with the dialectic, for those whose characters are forever battling their own abstraction, the proscenium marks a treacherous zone. (pp. 63-4)

> *Charles Newman, "The Lesson of the Master: Henry James and James Baldwin," in* The Yale Review *(© 1966 by Yale University; reprinted by permission of the editors), October, 1966 (and reprinted in* James Baldwin: A Collection of Critical Essays, *edited by Keneth Kinnamon, Prentice-Hall, Inc., 1974, pp. 52-65).*

C.W.E. BIGSBY

Go Tell it on the Mountain is concerned with the initiation of John Grimes, a fourteen year-old Negro boy. He is exposed to the bitter realities of ghetto life and sees at first hand the consequences of the resulting tensions in terms of individual lives. In the course of the book he undergoes what is apparently a profound religious conversion—a conversion which seems to reconcile him with his situation. . . .

But his conversion does not represent an acknowledgment of religious truth or an acceptance of his father's bitterness or his mother's passivity. It is a desperate expression of his own need for love and his desire for a sense of identity and common brotherhood. Yet his own mixed motives create a difficulty for the reader which is reflected throughout Baldwin's work. The central ambiguity of the book arises from the confusion between Eros and Agape. John's conversion is not the result of spiritual revelation but of a homosexual attraction which he feels for Elisha, a young Negro convert. . . . While setting out to establish the desirability and

viability of compassion, Baldwin can only visualize this love in terms of sexual alliances, more particularly in terms of homosexual relationships. The physical is made to stand for the metaphysical but the intensity of the sexual relationship subverts its symbolic effectiveness. Throughout his work it is the homosexual, virtually alone, who can offer a selfless and genuine love because he alone has a real sense of himself, having accepted his own nature. Yet while Baldwin is clearly suggesting that the acknowledgment of one's true identity is the key to a constructive life his overly sentimental approach to the homosexual relationship destroys its utility as an image.

The real core of the book is the struggle between hatred and love which Baldwin sees as the major battle to be fought by Black and White alike. The fight in essence is that between the Old and New Testaments; between retribution and love, the father and the son, servitude and freedom. (p. 236)

The most bitter characters, Gabriel, his son Roy and Elizabeth's lover, Richard, are all destroyed by hatred, as are similar characters throughout his work. Salvation it seems lies only through suffering and compassion. . . . (pp. 236-37)

Baldwin's central theme is the need to accept reality as a necessary foundation for individual identity and thus a logical prerequisite for the kind of saving love in which he places his whole faith. For some this reality is one's racial or sexual nature, for others it is the ineluctable fact of death. Like Edward Albee, Baldwin sees this simple progression as an urgent formula not only for the redemption of individual men but for the survival of mankind. In this at least black and white are as one and the Negro's much-vaunted search for identity can be seen as part and parcel of the American's long-standing need for self-definition. It is a theme which runs through Baldwin's work but nowhere is it stated more directly than in the much misunderstood *Giovanni's Room.*

Baldwin has said that "a writer who is bi-sexual is probably but not surely going to identify himself with other minorities," and in many ways this gives us some clue as to his intention in his second novel. *Giovanni's Room* is ostensibly about a homosexual relationship and yet we have Baldwin's somewhat baffling assurance that the novel is "not about homosexuality." The book is concerned with the protagonist's refusal to confront his own bi-sexuality. Having had a brief affair with a young Italian boy, David, an expatriate American, tries to return to the 'normality' of a relationship with his fiancée. In the name of some intangible standard of respectability and in retreat from that element of his nature which seems to make him the victim of his own irrational desires and the equally irrational contempt of others, he callously sacrifices a genuine relationship to one which has the sanction of society. In evading the truth he succeeds only in destroying himself and those he loves. The relevance of this to Baldwin's racial as well as sexual predicament hardly needs underlining. Both were aspects of a personal reality which he had struggled to avoid, but which he had finally come to accept as the substance of his own identity. Thus the predicament of the homosexual, on the fringe of society, regarded with suspicion and prejudice by others, becomes in Baldwin's mind, an appropriate image of those similarly estranged. Therefore, when Baldwin says of homosexuality in America that "if people were not so *frightened* of it . . . it really would cease in effect . . . to exist. I mean in the same way the Negro problem would disappear," it is no accident that the two ideas should appear so closely related. Similarly, when the protagonist of the novel remarks that "I had decided to allow no room in the universe for something which shamed and frightened me" and admits that he has "succeeded very well—by not looking at the universe, by not looking at myself, by remaining, in effect, in constant motion" we are reminded of the author who fled to Paris in order to escape his racial identity and the consequences of that identity. (pp. 237-38)

Baldwin's is an uneven talent. For all the measured articulateness of the essays his rhetoric can get hopelessly out of control in the novels. . . . But in spite of this and his unconquerable sentimentality he remains a writer of considerable power and surely one of the most significant American writers to emerge during the 50s. (pp. 239-40)

> *C.W.E. Bigsby, in* The Fifties: Fiction, Poetry, Drama, *edited by Warren French (copyright ©*
> *1970 by Warren French), Everett/Edwards, Inc.,*
> *1970.*

ALFRED KAZIN

As a writer Baldwin is as obsessed by sex and family as Strindberg was, but instead of using situations for their dramatic value, Baldwin likes to pile up all possible emotional conflicts as assertions. But for the same reason that in *Giovanni's Room* Baldwin made everybody white just to show that he could, and in *Tell Me How Long the Train's Been Gone* transferred the son-father quarrel to a quarrel with a brother, so one feels about *Another Country* that Baldwin writes fiction in order to use up his private difficulties; even his fiction piles up the atmosphere of raw emotion that is his literary standby. Why does so powerful a writer as Baldwin make himself look simpleminded by merely asserting an inconsequential succession of emotions? (p. 222)

[In] *Notes of a Native Son, Nobody Knows My Name, The Fire Next Time,* Baldwin dropped the complicated code for love difficulties he uses in his novels and simplified himself into an "angry Black" very powerfully indeed—and this just before Black nationalists were to turn on writers like him. The character who calls himself "James Baldwin" in *his* nonfiction novel is more professionally enraged, more doubtfully an evangelist for his people, than the actual James Baldwin, a very literary mind indeed. But there is in *Notes of a Native Son* a genius for bringing many symbols together, an instinctive association with the 1943 Harlem riot, the streets of smashed plate glass, that stems from the all too understandable fascination of the Negro with the public sources of his fate. The emphasis is on heat, fire, anger, the sense of being hemmed in and suffocated; the words are tensed into images that lacerate and burn. Reading Baldwin's essays, we are suddenly past the discordancy that has plagued his fiction—a literal problem of conflict, for Baldwin's fiction shows him trying to transpose facts into fiction without sacrificing the emotional capital that has been his life. (pp. 223-24)

> *Alfred Kazin, in his* Bright Book of Life: American Novelists & Storytellers from Hemingway to Mailer *(copyright © 1971, 1973 by Alfred Kazin; reprinted by permission of Little, Brown and Co. in association with The Atlantic Monthly Press), Atlantic-Little, Brown, 1973.*

KENETH KINNAMON

A decade ago James Baldwin, more than any other author, seemed to liberal white Americans to personify as well as to articulate the outrage and anguish of black Americans struggling to put an end to racial oppression and to achieve their civil and human rights. . . . Though as Northern as Martin Luther King was Southern, James Baldwin preached a more secular and apocalyptic but not really dissimilar sermon: the redemptive force of the love of a prophetic, interracial few could, even at that late date, yet prevail over the bigotry of the white majority, and so "end the racial nightmare, and achieve our country, and change the history of the world." If these brave words today seem both naïve and anachronistic, the reason is partly the nation's recent habit of giving more publicity than credence to its seers, of lavishing attention while withholding belief. (p. 1)

A proper understanding of Baldwin and his work must take into account a complicated amalgam of psychological and social elements sometimes thought to be antithetical. If, like most major black writers, Baldwin has extracted from his private ordeal the symbolic outline of his race's suffering, he has done so without obscuring the uniqueness of his personal experience. (p. 2)

However much he may revile the historical role of Christianity in the enslavement of black people, *The Fire Next Time* attests that [Baldwin] has never forgotten the compensatory values of his [adolescent] religious experience: "In spite of everything, there was in the life I fled a zest and a joy and a capacity for facing and surviving disaster that are very moving and very rare." And for good or ill, Baldwin's work is of a kind in which the didactic—even homiletic—element is of the essence. (p. 3)

Out of Baldwin's experience have emerged certain recurring themes in his writing, the most important of which is the quest for love. On a personal level, the search is for the emotional security of a love of which the protagonist has always been deprived. In his brilliant first novel, *Go Tell It on the Mountain,* the theme develops with autobiographical clarity, as is also the case in the related short story "The Outing" or such essays as "Notes of a Native Son," "The Black Boy Looks at the White Boy," "Down at the Cross," and "No Name in the Street." But elsewhere the search for love is equally imperative. David finds it in *Giovanni's Room* but loses it again because of his failure to commit himself totally. The interracial and bisexual bedhopping of *Another Country* constitutes a frenzied effort to realize love in the loveless city of New York. It falls to Leo Proudhammer of *Tell Me How Long the Train's Been Gone* to articulate the poignant paradox of Baldwin's love theme: "Everyone wishes to be loved, but, in the event, nearly no one can bear it. Everyone desires love but also finds it impossible to believe that he deserves it." If the search for love has its origin in the desire of a child for emotional security, its arena is an adult world which involves it in struggle and pain. Stasis must yield to motion, innocence to experience, security to risk. This is the lesson that the black Ida inculcates in her white lover Vivaldo in *Another Country,* and it saves Baldwin's central fictional theme from sentimentality.

Similarly, love as an agent of racial reconciliation and national survival is not for Baldwin a vague yearning for an innocuous brotherhood, but an agonized confrontation with reality, leading to the struggle to transform it. It is a quest for truth through a recognition of the primacy of suffering and injustice in the American past. In racial terms, the black man as victim of this past is in a moral position to induce the white man, the oppressor, to end his self-delusion and begin the process of regeneration. . . . Baldwin wrote in 1962 in "My Dungeon Shook," ["This] is what [integration] means: that we, with love, shall force our brothers to see themselves as they are, to cease fleeing from reality and begin to change it." By 1972, the year of *No Name in the Street,* the redemptive possibilities of love seemed exhausted in that terrible decade of assassination, riot, and repression, of the Black Panthers and Attica. Social love had now become for Baldwin more a rueful memory than an alternative to disaster. Violence, he now believes, is the arbiter of history, and in its matrix the white world is dying and the third world is struggling to be born. In his fiction, too, this shift in emphasis is apparent. Though love may still be a sustaining personal force, its social utility is dubious. (pp. 5-6)

Whether through the agency of love or violence, Baldwin is almost obsessively concerned with the writer's responsibility to save the world. As an essayist, he assumes the burden not only of reporting with eloquent sensitivity his observations of reality, but also of tirelessly reminding us of the need to transform that reality if Armageddon is to be averted. Over and over he concludes an essay by enlarging the perspective to a global scale. . . . Introducing the theme of self-examination in *Nobody Knows My Name,* he asserts that "one can only face in others what one can face in oneself. On this confrontation depends the measure of our wisdom and compassion. This energy is all that one finds in the rubble of vanished civilizations, and the only hope for ours." . . . Two of the simplest expressions of his faith in the possibility of change are the concluding challenges of the speeches entitled "In Search of a Majority" and "Notes for a Hypothetical Novel": "The world is before you and you need not take it or leave it as it was when you came in" and "We made the world we're living in and we have to make it over." *Nobody Knows My Name* concludes with an account of Baldwin's friendship with Norman Mailer, another writer who emphasizes the social value of the literary perspective: "For, though it clearly needs to be brought into focus, he has a real vision of ourselves as we are, and it cannot be too often repeated in this country now, that, where there is no vision, the people perish." The possibility of just such a perishing is pursued further in *The Fire Next Time,* and the possibility has become a probability in *No Name in the Street,* where Baldwin speaks of "the shape of the wrath to come" and the setting of the white man's sun. (pp. 6-7)

James Baldwin has always been concerned with the most personal and intimate areas of experience and also with the broadest questions of national and global destiny—and with the intricate interrelationships between the two. Whatever the final assessment of his literary achievement, it is clear that his voice—simultaneously that of victim, witness, and prophet—has been among the most urgent of our time. (p. 7)

> *Keneth Kinnamon, in his introduction to* James Baldwin: A Collection of Critical Essays, *edited by Keneth Kinnamon (copyright © 1974 by Prentice-Hall, Inc.; reprinted by permission of Prentice-Hall, Inc., Englewood Cliffs, New Jersey), Prentice-Hall, 1974, pp. 1-8.*

DONALD C. MURRAY

In the world of "Sonny's Blues," the short story by James Baldwin, the author deals with man's need to find his identity in a hostile society and, in a social situation which invites fatalistic compliance, his ability to understand himself through artistic creation which is both individual and communal. "Sonny's Blues" is the story of a boy's growth to adulthood at a place, the Harlem ghetto, where it's easier to remain a "cunning child," and at a time when black is not beautiful because it's simpler to submerge oneself in middle-class conformity, the modish antics of the hipster set, or else, at the most dismal level, the limbo of drug addiction, rather than to truly find oneself. Sonny's brother, the narrator of the story, opts for the comforts of a respectable profession and his specialty, the teaching of algebra, suggests his desire for standard procedures and elegant, clear-cut solutions. On the other hand, Sonny at first trafficks with the hipster world. . . . Eventually, however, as if no longer able to hold his own through all those other sounds of enticement and derision, Sonny is sentenced to a government institution due to his selling and using heroin. (p. 353)

Playing upon the homonym of Sonny, Baldwin writes that, for the narrator's brother, "all the light in [Sonny's] face" had gone out.

Images of light and darkness are used by Baldwin to illustrate his theme of man's painful quest for an identity. Light can represent the harsh glare of reality, the bitter conditions of ghetto existence which harden and brutalize the young. . . .

Another kind of light is that of the movie theater, the light which casts celluloid illusions on the screen. It is this light, shrouded in darkness, which allows the ghetto-dwellers' temporary relief from their condition. "All they really knew were two darknesses," Baldwin writes, "the darkness of their lives, which was now closing in on them, and the darkness of the movies, which had blinded them to that other darkness." . . . (p. 354)

There is no escape from the darkness for Sonny and his family. Dreams and aspirations are always dispelled, the narrator comments, because someone will always "get up and turn on the light." "And when light fills the room," he continues, "the child is filled with darkness." . . . Grieved by the death of his child, fortuitously named Grace, and aware of the age difference between himself and Sonny, the narrator seems unconsciously to seek out the childlike qualities of everyone he meets. He is not quite the self-satisfied conformist which some critics have made him out to be. . . . To the extent that he is given to this psychological penchant, the narrator is close in age to Sonny and "Sonny's Blues" is the story of the narrator's dawning self-awareness. The revelation of his father's brother's murder and the fact of Grace's death make Sonny's troubles real for the narrator and prompt the latter's growth in awareness. (pp. 354-55)

The age difference between the narrator and Sonny, like that between the narrator and his uncle and that between Sonny and his fellow musician Creole, all suggest that the fates of the generations are similar, linked by influences and effects. "The same things happen," the narrator reflects, "[our children will] have the same things to remember." . . .

So, too, the story is cyclical. . . . Similarities in characters and events link the various sections of the story. (p. 355)

The narrator's apprehension [when Sonny comes to live with him] is justified in that he is about to witness Sonny's torturous rebirth as a creative artist. . . . Because of the enormous energy and dedication involved in his role as Blues musician, Sonny is virtually described as a sacrificial victim as well as an initiate into the mysteries of creativity. . . . As the pressure mounts within Sonny, the author sets the scene for the final episode of the story.

Befitting the special evening which ends "Sonny's Blues," the locale shifts to the "only night club" on a dark downtown street. . . . The imagery of light now blends with that of water as the narrator, describing the light which "spilled" from the bandstand and the way in which Sonny seems to be "riding" the waves of applause, relates how Sonny and the other musicians prepare to play. It is as if Sonny were about to undergo another stage in his initiation into mature musicianship, this time a trial by fire. "I had the feeling that they, nevertheless, were being most careful not to step into that circle of light too suddenly," the narrator continues, "that if they moved into the light too suddenly, without thinking, they would perish in flame." . . . Next the imagery suggests that Sonny is embarking upon a sacred and perilous voyage, an approach to the wholly other in the biblical sense of the phrase; for the man who creates music, the narrator observes, is "hearing something else, is dealing with the roar rising from the void and imposing order on it as it hits the air." . . . The roaring darkness of the subway is transformed into something luminous. Appropriately, the lighting turns to indigo and Sonny is transfigured. (pp. 356-57)

Creole now takes on the dimensions of the traditional father-figure. He is a better teacher than the narrator because he has been in the deep water of life; he is a better witness than Sonny's father because he has not been "burned out" by his experiences in life. Creole's function in the story, to put it prosaically, is to show that only through determination and perseverance, through the taking of a risk, can one find a proper role in life. To fail does not mean to be lost irretrievably, for one can always start again. To go forward, as Sonny did when Creole "let out the reins," is to escape the cycle which, in the ghetto of the mind, stifles so many lives, resulting in mean expectations and stunted aspirations. The narrator makes the point that the essence of Sonny's blues is not new; rather, it's the age-old story of triumph, suffering, and failure. But there is no other tale to tell, he adds, "it's the only light we've got in all this darkness." . . .

Baldwin is no facile optimist. The meaning of "Sonny's Blues" is not, to use the glib phrase, the transcendence of the human condition through art. Baldwin is talking about love and joy, tears of joy because of love. As the narrator listens to his brother's blues, he recalls his mother, the moonlit road on which his uncle died, his wife Isabel's tears, and he again sees the face of his dead child, Grace. Love is what life should be about, he realizes; love which is all the more poignant because involved with pain, separation, and death. Nor is the meaning of "Sonny's Blues" the belief that music touches the heart without words; or at least the meaning of the story is not just that. His brother responds deeply to Sonny's music because he knows that he is with his black brothers and is watching his own broth-

er, grinning and "soaking wet." . . . The final point of the story is that the narrator, through his own suffering and the example of Sonny, is at last able to find himself in the brotherhood of man. Such an identification is an act of communion and "Sonny's Blues" ends, significantly, with the image of the homely Scotch-and-milk glass transformed into "the very cup of trembling," the Grail, the goal of the quest and the emblem of initiation. (p. 357)

Donald C. Murray, "James Baldwin's 'Sonny's Blues': Complicated and Simple," in Studies in Short Fiction *(copyright 1977 by Newberry College), Fall, 1977, pp. 353-57.*

*   *   *

BARTHELME, Donald   1931-

Barthelme is an American short story writer, novelist, and writer of children's fiction. His fictional world is surreal and often despairing. Barthelme explores and satirizes the possibilities of narrative form in his fiction, offering on one occasion a questionnaire to his readers with ideas for alternative endings to a story; on another presenting a "story" consisting of a series of numbered sentences. These are perhaps presented in concurrence with Barthelme's philosophy that "the only forms I trust are fragments." (See also *CLC*, Vols. 1, 2, 3, 5, 6, 8, and *Contemporary Authors*, Vols. 21-24, rev. ed.)

ALFRED KAZIN

[Barthelme] is one of the few authentic examples of the "antinovelist"—that is, he operates by countermeasures only, and the system that is his own joy to attack permits him what an authoritarian system always permits its lonely dissenters: the sense of their own weakness. The almighty state is always in view. So Barthelme sentences us to the complicity with the system that he suffers from more than anyone. He is wearingly attentive to every detail of the sophistication, the lingo, the massively stultifying second-handedness of everything "we" say. Barthelme is outside everything he writes about in a way that a humorist like Perelman could never be. He is under the terrible discipline that the System inflicts on those who are most fascinated with its relentlessness. He is so smart, so biting, himself so unrelenting in finding far-flung material for his ridicule that his finished product comes out a joke about Hell. We go up sentence, down sentence, up and down. What severity we are sentenced to by this necessary satire! That is because Barthelme the antinovelist is based on the perfect inversion of all current practice, and keeps too many records. This is the way Salinger's characters would write *if* they were writers, for it is all based on books.

Barthelme is funniest and even touching in *Snow White*, where the multifaceted plenty of sex (as opposed to the old economy of scarcity) does not bring happiness to our raven-haired heroine and her seven boyfriends. Parodying fairy tales, anti-fairy tales, the captions in Godard movies, market research questionnaires, Barthelme makes it clear that everyone is now so mired in cultured explanations of his and her plight that it is hard to get to bed. . . . We have been cut off by the words hanging over our heads; our poor little word-riddled souls are distributed all over the landscape. (pp. 273-74)

Alfred Kazin, in his Bright Book of Life: American Novelists & Storytellers from Hemingway to Mailer *(copyright © 1971, 1973 by Alfred Kazin;*

reprinted by permission of Little, Brown, and Co. in association with The Atlantic Monthly Press), Atlantic-Little, Brown, 1973.

ALAN WILDE

[The] obstinate triviality of life increasingly impinges on the literary consciousness.... The modernist sensibility, haunted by a vision of pervasive grayness and (as in *Howards End*) of a creeping red rust, finds ultimate expression in one of Forster's comments in *A Passage to India:* "Most of life is so dull that there is nothing to be said about it . . . and a perfectly adjusted organism would be silent." But for all its flat and bitter finality, the remark heralds not silence but a dramatic exploration of metaphysical extremes . . . ; and if Forster fails in his quest for a redeeming order, it is not because of complacence or a willingness to accede to the dailiness of life. Barthelme's ["Critique de la Vie Quotidienne,"] on the other hand . . . , accommodates itself more easily to the banal horrors of *la vie quotidienne*. Not that the story is without incident (there is, notably, the moment when the narrator's former wife tries to "ventilate" him with a horse pistol . . . , but if it is true, as Philip Stevick notes in his introduction to *Anti-Story,* that "to allow the middle range of experience to co-exist, in a single work, with the extremities of contemporary experience is to do strange things to that ordinariness, to deny it its solidity," it is equally the case that that coexistence may, as it does in Barthelme's fiction, serve to render extremity more ordinary—to deny *it,* and not the middle range of experience, a solidity of specification and response.

In any case, the "Critique," though it manages, characteristically, to combine the hilarious and the dismal, provides a rather too facile treatment of its subject, and its value is more representative than particular, supplying as it does a pattern for more successful examples (the Edward and Pia stories of *Unspeakable Practices,* among others) of Barthelme's relentless investigation of the humdrum. Of these, the best is probably the title story of *City Life.* More eccentric in incident and development, it expresses in a number of ways Barthelme's relation to *la vie quotidienne*. Speculating in the final section of the tale on "the most exquisite mysterious muck," which is the city she lives in and "which is itself the creation of that muck of mucks, human consciousness" . . . , Ramona goes on to contemplate the possible explanation of the virgin birth of her child: "Upon me, their glance has fallen," she thinks, reflecting on various of the men in her life. "The engendering force was, perhaps, the fused glance of all of them. From the millions of units crawling about on the surface of the city, their wavering desirous eye selected me. . . . *I accepted. What was the alternative?*" (. . . my italics). Ramona's last words sum up, *mutatis mutandis,* that is, allowing for a different level of awareness and for the artist's privileged sense of control, Barthelme's attitude as well. Implicated in the world he describes, Barthelme accepts—at least in this group of stories—not only the material that world offers him but the ironically suspensive mood resignation entails. How else to react to "brain damage," when, as the narrator of the story by that name admits: "*I could describe it better if I weren't afflicted with it . . .*" . . . ? Or, as Dan announces, in a much quoted passage from *Snow White,* apropos of the linguistic "trash phenomenon": "I hazard that we may very well soon reach a point where it's 100 percent. Now at such a point, you will agree, the question turns from a question of disposing of this 'trash' to a question of appreciating its qualities, because, after all, it's 100 percent, right?" (pp. 48-9)

There is a danger, however, of equating appreciation or even acceptance with the presence in these stories of a significative void—especially if one attempts to bring to bear on them the same analytic techniques regularly applied to the classics of modern literature. But [despite various critical arguments] the lack of an easily paraphrasable theme or an extractable moral or, on the other hand, of a pattern of search and, if not resolution, then closure doesn't necessarily imply the absence of human reference of one kind or another. (pp. 49-50)

[The] stories of daily life do "refer," . . . they refer most directly to the kind of inner life Barthelme (or his narrators) frequently deny their "characters." In other words, . . . the knowledge they provide is of the forms of feeling. Not to recognize this fact is to miss what may be most distinctive about Barthelme's work—the articulation not of the larger, more dramatic emotions to which modernist fiction is keyed but of an extraordinary range of minor, banal dissatisfactions. "Yours is not a modern problem," one character tells another in "City Life." "The problem today is not angst but lack of angst." . . . Barthelme's stories express not anomie or accidie or dread but a muted series of irritations, frustrations, and bafflements. The title of his fifth volume is exactly right. Even at its most funny or absurd, Barthelme's is a world of *Sadness,* sadness occasionally moderated by snatches after sexual satisfaction, by a persistent intellectual curiosity, and by the inventive pleasures of art—but never, especially in the stories of acceptance, cancelled by any of them. (p. 51)

"The Balloon" can be seen as a parable of reactions to reality as an irreducibly mysterious, varied, and changing surface; and as such, the story serves as prototype for those of Barthelme's fictions in which he and his narrators perceive the world as a kind of haphazard, endlessly organizable and reorganizable playground. Thus, whereas the presentational stories [concerning feelings] take as their recurrent starting point the inevitable flaws of human relations, the ludic ones (to borrow a word from Barthelme out of Huizinga) deal with the odd relationship between the individual mind and the humanized world of things and objects on which that mind has, collectively and precariously, left its imprint.

Predictably, the ludic fictions most obviously inspire Barthelme's technical innovations. The use of collage, of fragments, of pictures and black spaces; the sudden irruption of large, capitalized remarks, which may or may not comment on the surrounding text; the reliance on what one critic (referring to his own "rhythms") calls "interval (with abrupt interface) & repeat/repeat of cliché (with slight variation)"; the constant experimentation with styles, ranging from the severely paratactic to the most involutedly subordinative: all function, of course, to call attention to the fact of writing (or *écriture,* as we are learning to say), to the medium in which Barthelme and his perceptual field intersect. . . . The emphasis on surface has, of course, spatial, moral, and psychological implications, but the force . . . of Barthelme's practice suggests that the question is, in the first instance, an aesthetic one. . . . (p. 52)

Like the Pop artists, Barthelme puts aside the central modernist preoccupation with epistemology, and it may well be the absence of questions about how we know that has operated most strongly to "defamiliarize" his (and their) work. Barthelme's concerns are, rather, ontological in their acceptance of a world that is, willy-nilly, a given of experience. Here, one can speak legitimately of surface in that there is not for Barthelme, as there is for Clive Bell, a potential awareness of . . . "that which lies behind the appearance of all things—that which gives to all things their individual significance, the thing in itself, the ultimate reality." But the absence of depth implies the lack not of meaning but of certainties. Life has become, for better or for worse, less mysterious but more puzzling, and beside Bell's cadenced, assured phrases one needs to juxtapose Ramona's laconic "I accepted. What was the alternative?" Not for Ramona—and not for Barthelme—"the ultimate reality." Over the past several decades the quest has become a futile, indeed an unreal, one. "We must not . . . wonder," Merleau-Ponty writes, "whether we really perceive a world, we must instead say: the world is what we perceive." . . . The question, then, is how exactly to live in that world (a largely humanized world in Barthelme's fiction), and Ramona's answer—a kind of grim-lipped hilarity in the face of the provisional—is emblematic of her author's in many ways as well. "The world in the evening seems fraught with the absence of promise," . . . the narrator of "Critique de la Vie Quotidienne" remarks; and so too do the days. . . . Wisdom, so it seems, lies in a stoicism of sorts. . . . To be conscious and even to value, as he obviously does, that "muck of mucks" called consciousness and at the same time to acquiesce completely in an attitude of suspensiveness toward things as they are, exacts a difficult balance. So it is hardly surprising that from time to time and increasingly, Barthelme's acceptance moves beyond Ramona's resignation to explore alternatives both more affirmative and more complex, creating in the process a more comprehensive and flexible irony as well. (pp. 54-5)

The point [of "Games Are the Enemies of Beauty, Truth, and Sleep, Amanda Said"] is simply that in [Amanda's] refusal of life as a game and of games as an adequate representation of life she gestures toward a more conceptual mode of apprehending and defining her situation; and this generalizing, reflective response to the experiential, to the immediately perceived, works better in some ways for Barthelme also, whose most successful, if not always his most obviously and dramatically innovative, fictions are of this kind. Furthermore, if Amanda's gesture is, despite its vocabulary, essentially negative, the same can be said of the force behind much of Barthelme's conceptual work. So much then for Amanda. Barthelme's rejections are the more interesting, and they are very much of a piece. Except in some of the more feeble parodies, however, they are *not,* as one might expect, rejections of the daily (though they do in fact lead ultimately to a reassessment of attitudes toward it) but of those who seek to stabilize and rationalize that world. In other words, Barthelme is, at his best, an anti-conceptual conceptualizer, working inductively toward an understanding of the necessity but also of the limits of acceptance.

In a general way, what Barthelme takes his stand against are pretensions to certainty and the insistence on perfection; large demands and great expectations; dogmatisms and theories of all kinds. (pp. 55-6)

[Barthelme is] less seriously attracted by an escape into the realm of total otherness than by the temptation to find *within* the ordinary possibilities of a more dynamic response. The distinction is important. Modernist irony, seeking in its opposite (in the anironic) some release from its own vision of fragmentation, characteristically imagines . . . an image of total order. . . . Postmodern ironists are less sanguine; and rightly so, for the anironic has come to suggest in recent times not resolution but annihilation. Through the looking-glass of contemporary chaos, one glimpses death or the death of consciousness—which may explain the concern with the apocalyptic in much recent fiction or with the self-abnegations of the minimalist and the aleatory in painting and music.

Still, if the present surrounds the ironist with a different and less hopeful context and offers him fewer possibilities of reconstruction or escape, his problems are, nevertheless, in some sense the same as his predecessors'. The change in irony over the past two hundred years from technique to vision, its development from the chief instrumentality of satire into an autonomous sensibility, has had as probably its most interesting result the transformation of distance (then and still one of the main aesthetic conditions for the successful functioning of irony) into a metaphor for a series of psychological and moral problems. . . . [It] is the figure of the outsider, the uncommitted spectator, longing to overcome his self-consciousness and make contact with the world outside his limited and limiting ego, that dominates the literary landscape of writers such as Eliot, Joyce, and Forster, to mention only the most obvious. If Barthelme differs from these authors, it is not because he perceives the tension between distance and involvement any less intensely. Indeed, he is in many ways far more conscious of the nature and implications of his irony. His originality lies, rather, . . . in his treatment of the problem and in his solution to it.

But first the problem itself, which undergoes its most extended and ingenious exploration in "Kierkegaard Unfair to Schlegel." Against the background of a dialogue about the ineffectiveness of his political activities, "A," the transparently authorial respondent, gradually begins a defense of his own irony in terms of the power and control it confers on him. The introduction of Kierkegaard's *The Concept of Irony,* however, with its familiar but brilliantly summarized arguments about the ironist's subjective freedom, his alienation of existence, and his infinite absolute negativity, leads finally to A's admission that "mostly I am trying to annihilate Kierkegaard in order to deal with his disapproval." . . . The ultimate failure to do so becomes apparent. . . . If the story charts A's loss of his freedom and particularity, it confirms, in its construction (the abrupt and apparently illogical cuts from one section to another, the absurdist elements, the narrative and tonal shifts), the power that Barthelme as author and ironist retains. The fundamental tension of "Kierkegaard Unfair to Schlegel" inheres, then, not in A's unwilling fall from ironic grace but in the disparity between that internal drama and the authorial techniques used to articulate it. . . . To a degree at least, structure becomes a window not a frame. I don't want to exaggerate this point: a good deal of modern literature, as [well as postmodern] uses technique as discovery . . . , not to mention the *nouveau* and the *nouveau nouveau roman.* A number of Barthelme's pieces too verge on the precious and the contrived, but what one senses in the best of his work is an effort to use art to overcome art (as the moderns characteristically employ consciousness to move beyond consciousness)—or, better still, an attempt, parallel to that in "The Glass Mountain," to disenchant the aesthetic, to make of it something not less special but less extraordinary.

The desire to tame the extraordinary relates back, in turn, to the question of irony and distance. Unlike the classic modernists attempting to annex the world to the self or to lose the self in the world . . . Barthelme has more modest aims. If, indeed, he is, as ironist, already part of the world around him and not its distant observer, if that world is, furthermore, perceived not as object but as field, and if, finally, the phenomenal presents itself not as the veil of appearance but as multiform, irreducible reality, then the notion of involving himself with, or of encompassing, all of life is in any case an impossibility. But the suspensive no less than the equivocal involves its psychological and moral distances, and Barthelme seems of late less willing or able to abide them. (pp. 59-61)

[How], exactly, does Barthelme go about narrowing the [distance between activity and awareness]? In two ways. First, by a further series of rejections, which come, interestingly, among his several portraits of the artist. (p. 61)

"The Temptation of St. Anthony," although it is by no means an encomium to conformity, asserts, in its sympathetically critical portrait, the need for the extraordinary to find its place amidst the quotidian. And the retreat back to the desert, marking a failure to do just that, indicates another stage in Barthelme's questioning of the distance, the suspensiveness that Anthony—parabolically the saint as artist or the artist as saint—represents.

But if escape is unacceptable and if acceptance, in the sense of . . . acquiescence, is not enough, what then? The fact is that increasingly in Barthelme's work, if not consistently, acceptance is modified by a more positive, more affirmative attitude of *assent*. . . . [The] objects of Barthelme's or his characters' assent are remarkable not by virtue of being outside or substantially different from common life. It is not a question of discovering Bell's "ultimate reality" but of agreeing with Wilde that "the true mystery of the world is the visible, not the invisible." The extraordinary exists as part of the phenomenal world or it doesn't, effectively, exist at all. . . . What is at issue is not an essentialist but an existential quest: a subjective, though not for that reason a random or arbitrary, conferring of value, based on a continuing sense of the nature of *la vie quotidienne*. (pp. 63-4)

Assent, then, is dynamic, exploratory, on-going, experiential. . . . In some sense, of course, Barthelme's fictions are themselves the best examples of his own particular form of assent—the prevalence of short stories itself, perhaps, the sign of a preference or an affinity for mixed and modest pleasures, as opposed to the larger and more final satisfactions sought by an earlier time. . . . Barthelme suggests the nature of assent in "Engineer-Private Paul Klee Misplaces an Aircraft between Milbertshofen and Cambrai, March 1916," one of the most amusing and successful of his works. . . . [If] Klee is inexplicably thrown into an absurd world, he manages nonetheless to enjoy thoroughly the openness and fecundity he also finds (or creates) in it, agreeing apparently with Heidegger that "the ordinary is basically not ordinary; it is extra-ordinary." Neither a rebel nor an accomplice, he accepts what he must and assents to

what he can: a totally ingratiating model of *Dasein,* the contingency of being-in-the-world.

As one of the most attractive and attractively rendered figures in the stories, Klee offers himself as an obvious antithesis to Barthelme's Kierkegaard, the two suggesting in some ways the oppositional archetypes of their author's fictional universe. Humanistic, tolerant, non-directive, Klee intimates the possibility of irony as a graceful, even integrative gesture toward the world. Kierkegaard, on the other hand, religious and prescriptive, presents irony, disapprovingly, . . . as an infinite absolute negativity. However, as one traces Barthelme's movement (admittedly a serpentine and by no means consistent movement) from acceptance, through the rejection of dogmatisms and certainties, to assent, Kierkegaard gradually takes on a less monolithic typological significance. Leaving aside the religious question —and that is a large omission, of course—one can see that, in fact, Kierkegaard pronounces what Klee, less magisterially, to be sure, enacts: "What is wanted, Kierkegaard says, is not a victory over the world but a reconciliation with the world." . . . To put it another way, as the self-viewed antagonist of Barthelme's ironic distance, his defensiveness, his infinite absolute negativity, Kierkegaard (or, more accurately, I suppose, the tradition he in part initiates) supplies precisely that existential-phenomenological background out of which Barthelme operates, even as he, not infrequently, parodies it. (pp. 64-5)

[The] modification of Barthelme's suspensive irony is precipitated by exactly that current of thought which has supplied twentieth-century artists with their visions of dailiness, absurdity, and drift. And inevitably so. For the postmodern writer, at least for those who refuse the lure of a new, ultra-formalism, there is no consolation in the thought of other, more perfect worlds—those heterocosms that haunt the modernist imagination. There is only the open, temporal field of the phenomenal, with which, in Barthelme's case, "reconciliation" is achieved through the homeopathic agency of his critiques of *la vie quotidienne* and *la vie extraordinaire*. Not, it needs to be stressed again, that assent (still sporadic, in any case) *replaces* acceptance in Barthelme's more recent work. . . . [He denies] that what Forster calls "the smaller pleasures of life" constitute the whole of it. For Barthelme, assent is added to without cancelling the more generalized attitude of acceptance, as stories like "The Sandman" and, of course, "Engineer-Private Paul Klee" make clear. (pp. 65-6)

It is just possible that with figures such as Klee, Barthelme helps to define still another stage in the development of irony—one in which the gaps and discontinuities of twentieth-century literature, heretofore the mark of absence or negation, become instead the sign of a not yet constituted presence. Thus, no longer the familiar cause of horror or paralysis or suspensiveness, they are transformed rather . . . into the source of a continuing activity predicated on the need to choose, to confer meaning: to add to the humility of acceptance (even, or especially, of those gaps in which future meaning lies latent) the irreducibly human function of assent. (p. 66)

Barthelme's work [demonstrates] that a writer can, rejecting illusionist and psychological depth in fiction, nonetheless avoid the all too frequent banality of flatness, not by reimposing a metaphysical perspective or a theologically schematic worldview but by recognizing in what ways the dynamics of surface (of moral as well as aesthetic surface) are determined by an acknowledgment of the "horizons of the flesh." Surface, in other words, may generate a particular, complex dimensionality of its own—or a depth of a kind different from that of classical perspective. . . . [The] horizon of the phenomenal world is not an objective thing or place "out there"; it is the subjective, but no less real, result of being in the world: the shifting boundary of *human* depth, the pledge of man's necessary interaction with a world of which he is not only part but partner.

Barthelme's assumption of that partnership is manifest precisely in the movement from the relative passivity of acquiescence to the activity of decision and judgment (however tentative or qualified), which is implied in the transvalued irony of his assent. . . . (pp. 66-7)

Ramona, Amanda, and Klee, though in different degrees at different times, all populate the Barthelmean landscape, suggesting the varied, overlapping impulses to accept, to reject, and to affirm. The ludic strain in his work persists, not as a denial of meaning, of referentiality, but as an assertion of the artist's privilege to create meaning. And so too does the suspensiveness, at least in the sense that his work refuses the epistemological quest for ultimates and absolutes. Barthelme remains part of the world he perceives, approaching it through a process of interrogation to which he opens himself as well. Furthermore, life, as he sees it, not only refuses to offer up assurances and answers; it continues to be in large part, for human beings trying to make their way through it, frustrating, disjointed, and drab. . . . In the final analysis, the alternative presents itself, however malapropos or offensive the word sounds to many today, as a humanism of sorts—less anthropocentric, less hopeful, to be sure, than that of the modernists; based instead, like Sartre's or Merleau-Ponty's, on an ethic of subjectivity and risk. Thus, if the necessary incompleteness of Barthelme's world is in one sense the definition of its persisting sadness, it is, in another, the source of its pleasures. Still, no doubt, as the title of his latest collection suggests, guilty pleasures —but the signs too of a normative presence forging, tentatively, a morality and an irony for postmodern (or, possibly, post-postmodern?) man. (p. 68)

> *Alan Wilde, "Barthelme Unfair to Kierkegaard: Some Thoughts on Modern and Postmodern Irony," in* boundary 2 *(copyright © boundary 2, 1976), Fall, 1976, pp. 45-70.*

ERIC S. RABKIN

Donald Barthelme shows us, again and again, that he has a way with words: the way of a stone-cutter. With a deft and dangerous whack at the raw language he suddenly reveals a new facet of the inner mineral. When he has done with his chopping, a gem lies before us—hard and immutable and with the appearance of warmth that light gives, but brilliant for all that. Surely of Barthelme it is true that "Le style est l'homme même" [the style is the man himself]. And what is that style? A despairing playfulness whereby the reading punishes us into understanding. The quote, of course, is from Le Comte de Buffon. In Barthelme's style, that pun itself would fit. The gem may be rhinestone, his detractors would say, but, his admirers respond, in that case the clown is Pagliacci. (p. 232)

Snow White and *The Dead Father* are both "novels" by virtue of structure, structures that, like *Ulysses*, recall other structures: the standard fairy tale in the first case, the myth of the Fisher King in the second. But they aren't tight novels at all: their intellectually clear structures organize and justify the placement of parts but do not lend the movement from part to part a dramatic or emotional unity. The burial of the Dead Father, for instance, corroborates the notion that "Repetition is reality" but does not make it *feel* true. The feelings, in reading Barthelme, accompany the discrete flashes of language. But for me this is quite enough. Although the "novels" may not be novels as we usually understand them, they are certainly more than the pieces of worthwhile wit within them. And those pieces themselves, in Barthelme's fashion, are assaults on language that rape it and reveal through it new insights for his readers. (pp. 234-35)

> *Eric S. Rabkin, "What Was That, Again?" in* Michigan Quarterly Review *(copyright © The University of Michigan, 1977), Spring, 1977, pp. 232-35.*

BETTY CATHERINE DOBSON FARMER

[The human-god-mechanical Dead Father character of Barthelme's *Dead Father*] offers a multi-faceted study in ambiguity. The Dead Father is "dead but still with us, still with us, but dead. . . . a sleeper in troubled sleep, the whole great expanse of him running from the Avenue Pommard to the Boulevard Grist. Overall length, 3,200 cubits." The Dead Father is a part of the landscape "from the Avenue Pommard to the Boulevard Grist," just as the Irish giant Finn MacCool is a part of Joyce's Irish landscape in *Finnegans Wake.* . . .

The close relationship of *The Dead Father* to *Finnegans Wake* is obvious from an overt parody of Barthelme's main source for this novel, *Finnegans Wake.* . . .

Just as Joyce's abbreviation for his mythical Earwicker hero, HCE, is an acronym for Here Comes Everybody or Everyman, Barthelme makes the Dead Father the all-inclusive embodiment of Everybody's idols. (p. 40)

Barthelme achieves an effective "cosmopolitanization" or world application of the Dead Father figure by taking him from the narrow confines of the Avenue Pommard and the Boulevard Grist and making him the embodiment of world idols through the use of a wealth of [mythological, biblical, and literary allusions]. . . . (p. 41)

In addition to the worldwide mythological, Biblical, and literary allusions that Barthelme used, he "globalized" the Dead Father by using, inconspicuously throughout the novel, words that have foreign (other than English) origin: *pemmican,* North American Cree Indian; *ukase,* Russian; *piroque,* French, especially Cajun French. (p. 47)

[Mythological], Biblical, and literary allusions have the effect of making the Dead Father character a world symbol. At the conclusion of the novel when Barthelme calls for "Bulldozers" to fill in the Dead Father's crater-sized grave, he is (in the mythological-Biblical-literary framework that he has established) calling for the interment of all world idols, huddled together at the bottom of the grave, awaiting the final clodthunder, a true "Ragnarok" of *total darkness* for the gods rather than just a "Twilight of the Gods." (p. 48)

> *Betty Catherine Dobson Farmer, "Mythological, Biblical, and Literary Allusions in Donald Bar-*

thelme's 'The Dead Father'," in The International Fiction Review (© copyright International Fiction Association), Winter, 1979, pp. 40-8.

ROBERT TOWERS

I doubt that Donald Barthelme's new collection [*Great Days*] will alter significantly anyone's perception of this accomplished miniaturist. His admirers can again enjoy the delicacy with which he picks his way through the detritus of our civilization, marvel at the many voices he commands, and renew their appetites for the surreal morsels he serves up. Those who have been less impressed in the past will find yet another occasion to shrug. The one really innovative feature of *Great Days* is Barthelme's use, in seven of the pieces, of a staccato dialogue form in which two speakers bounce phrases off one another at high speed; sometimes the phrases answer each other, often they do not. Uninterrupted by narrative or description, the dialogues vibrate at high intensity, achieving a strobe-lit effect that can be pleasurably nerve-wracking. Fortunately, the pieces stop short of a sensory overload.

In "The Crisis," the dialogue really consists of the juxtaposition of two monologues—one that comments on the progress of a rebellion, another that rambles on inanely, frequently mouthing platitudes. . . . Toward the end of "The Crisis," the monologues converge slightly. Meanwhile, their incongruities have reflected that quality of twitchy contemporaneity to which Barthelme is so perfectly attuned.

The most ambitious of the dialogues is "The New Music," in which riffs and flights of language create an extraordinary medley of sound effects that evoke nearly a century of ragtime, blues, and jazz. The two speakers shift voices frequently, but the voice that throbs most insistently is lowdown Southern, as in the exchange which summons the image of a powerful, pistol-packing Momma. . . . But Momma is also "lost in the Eleusinian mysteries and the art of love"; while in her rocking chair she is given to pondering "The goddess Demeter's anguish for all her children's mortality." There is a reference to "The chanting in the darkened telesterion," to the appearance of Persephone herself . . . , and to "Hallucinatory dancing. All the women drunk." Here—and in other places—Barthelme seems to be alluding to, as well as employing, the technique of startling cultural juxtapositions we associate with T. S. Eliot, the Eliot of the Sweeney poems and *The Waste Land*. . . . But whereas Eliot opposes the "meaningful" past to the trivialized present in a mood of despairing irony, I do not get the impression that Barthelme is concerned with shoring up fragments against his ruin; instead, he appears perfectly content to play with the fragments of past and present alike, to rattle them in a can, to make a little music. As one of the speakers says at the end of the piece, "The new music burns things together, like a welder. The new music says, life becomes more and more exciting as there is less and less time." To which the other replies, "Momma wouldn't have 'lowed it. But Momma's gone."

A quasi-musical organization is evident in almost all the pieces. . . . A phrase is typically introduced, repeated, varied, placed in surprising contexts, sounded for one last time. Sometimes the motif is a visual image, which also undergoes modifications. In the tiny, fragile, and often beautiful historical fantasy called "Cortés and Montezuma," the repeated phrase is "walking down by the docks."

. . . The recurrent image, variously linked with the strollers, is of little green flies, sometimes brushed away by a fly whisk made of golden wires.

One other piece—"Concerning the Bodyguard"—is admirable. Constructed of short paragraphs which consist almost entirely of unanswered questions, it introduces a series of images which, though innocent enough in themselves, create an ominous atmosphere of political assassination when assembled. . . .

Having for the most part denied himself the sustaining props of narrative fiction, Barthelme must make his impact immediately, and within a small compass. The longer works —the so-called novels—become quickly mired in tedium, a tedium that is not dispelled or transcended, as in the case of "difficult" great books, by an intelligent reader's perseverance. Even with his successful short pieces, Barthelme is surely the most ephemeral of the gifted writers of our time. . . .

When all his talents are engaged—his wit, his stylistic precision, his powers of mimicry—in the pursuit of one of those bizarre possibilities that excite his imagination, Barthelme is indeed a verbal wondermaker, providing not only a succession of gaily wrapped surprises but moments of sharp sensory pleasure and sometimes the fleeting illusion of profundity; when they are not so engaged, the results are little more than a kind of clever doodling. I think Barthelme scores very well in five or six of the sixteen items that make up *Great Days;* the experience of reading the others seemed to me like the blowing of dandelion fluff: an inconsequential but not unpleasant way of passing the time. (p. 15)

Robert Towers, in The New York Review of Books (reprinted with permission from The New York Review of Books; copyright © 1979 Nyrev, Inc.), January 25, 1979.

DIANE JOHNSON

["Great Days"] is bare Barthelme at his best, quite inimitable, with a new kind of calm confidence, a new depth of subject, and no pictures. And, one hopes, his imitators in disarray; for it should now be clear to everybody that nobody can write a Barthelme story as well as he can.

What are the present stories about and what are they like? . . . Two pieces—the one about Cortés and "The Death of Edward Lear,"—have historical referents. One piece, the author says, is an *objet trouvé* from "Godey's Lady's Book," 1850, slightly altered by him. One, "Tales of the Swedish Army," seems like an earlier, wackier Barthelme. A number of stories impressively challenge formal problems—for example, "Concerning the Bodyguard."

The bodyguard: new fact of modern life, therefore typical Barthelme subject. An ordinary writer of fiction, imagining a bodyguard, would give him a name, a past, would follow his life, report his conversations and thoughts, invent a little disturbing event or two to dramatize his spiritual condition, and end with a climax of triumph or failure, some moment of bodyguard truth. Barthelme instead writes six pages of questions. . . . (pp. 1, 36)

Readers will read for profit; they will also read for prophecy. So uncannily tuned is Barthelme's sense of what's happening in our times, in our world, he even picks up eerily on what will happen, as in one dialogue, "Morning," one of the seven dialogues that form the substance and principal distinction of this volume. . . .

These dialogues reflect a solemn mood in Barthelme, and his eye on Great Subjects (fear, faith, hope, sexual contention). They are naturally different from the work of two other writers in this form that come to mind, Pinter and Beckett, but like them remind us of how curiously well adapted the dialogue is for displaying a writer's particularity. In Pinter, who comes from a society in which people still converse, the voices engage, contend. Here the voices are dreamy, parallel, each probing personal memory, and the contents of memory have not the fiercely egotistical humanity of Beckett but instead comprise the things of our society. . . .

You wonder if these dialogues were spoken aloud would the dynamics of the conversations be easier to follow than they are on the plain page without "he saids" and names. (p. 36)

The voices, male and female, hopeful or reflective, are funny, sad, smart. They fit together. It's possible that all of Barthelme's stories fit together, like a wardrobe of well-chosen basics; but they provide in combination something more than a sum of the parts. By denying himself the full-dress trappings of the conventional novel, with its resources (plot, characters) for self-concealment, the author, bare, scuttles speedily across a stage empty except for these austere pillars, marked "The Leap," "Morning" and so on, hiding behind first one, then another, yet seen—funny, sad, smart. His sensibility is the game, and to mark him as a banner-carrier in some new legion has been rather to belittle his accomplishment. It's also unfair to construe a writer's phrase in another context as a comment on his own work, but in this volume he has one character say, "I'm some kind of an artist, but I'm conservative. Mine is the art of the possible, plus two." It seems apposite. (pp. 36-7)

> *Diane Johnson, in* The New York Times Book Review *(© 1979 by The New York Times Company; reprinted by permission), February 4, 1979.*

JEROME KLINKOWITZ

Barthelme's new collection of short fiction, aptly titled "Great Days," is built on [the] notion of routines and how to play them. . . .

In all cases, the emphasis is on doing a routine, playing out situations as if they were vaudeville acts. In their least pretentious form, bits like these need only the two voices of straight man and comic, and in "Great Days" Barthelme tries his hand at keeping everything else out of the way.

When the technique works, Barthelme's sentences bounce off each other like overpacked dodgem cars, but only because they are strong enough to run on their own, unhampered even by quotation marks (he uses the European style of dashes instead). Seven of the 16 stories in "Great Days" are written this way, and their effect is to underline the purely verbal comedy of Barthelme's art, which now reads like the swiftly bantered exchange in a high-toned knock-knock joke.

Three of these new dash-dialog stories lead off the volume. From there, Barthelme moves through nine pieces written in the various styles of his six previous collections: dramatized cliches, comic exaggerations, wacky anachronisms, and even traditional storytelling with just a few elements deliberately askew.

But from these nine more familiar fictions, neatly framed in

the book's center, it's easy to see that their most important element is voice, whether in expressed or implied dialog. . . . [The volume's construction makes it] carefully expand and contract in its method. Reading "Great Days" is like breathing in and breathing out. Challenging, innovative fiction can be that natural.

As he has done again and again, since his first collection was published in 1964, Donald Barthelme is teaching readers how to read his stories. When voiced by humans, Barthelme's clever plays with language seem to mean much more, and "Great Days" will speak in the reader's hands. By keeping himself out of the story—even by his apparent silence—the writer has found a new way to talk with us.

> *Jerome Klinkowitz, "Barthelme at Play in Comic Routines," in* Book Week *(copyright © 1979 by The Chicago Sun-Times; reprinted by permission from The Chicago Sun-Times), February 4, 1979, p. 12.*

JOE DAVID BELLAMY

When we look back on this period, will the work of Donald Barthelme seem the forerunner of a whole new variety of consciousness or merely a particularly skilled and elegant example of decadence? *Great Days* . . . is another emotional and linguistic demolition derby in the characteristic manner: whimsical, elusive, and miraculously inventive.

Barthelme's aesthetic elevates the liberation of pure imagination above all other notions. Bringing novelties into being is his primary objective, and he faces the task with the sure-footedness of a tightrope walker and the precision of a clock-maker. He believes utterly in the delights of mind-travel and in the healing powers of dreams. Art, as it embodies these modes, is one of the new human activities, he seems to be saying, to save us from despair.

Despair has become one of his favorite subjects for jest. "At dusk medals are awarded those who have made it through the day," someone quips in his story, "The New Music." "The New Music" is a collage of fractured dialogues, where the characters are seen "sighing and leaning against each other, holding their silver plates"—as if to say, "If we're so rich, how come we ain't happy?" Another, more consoling voice chimes in: "Luckily we have the new music now. To give us aid and comfort." The implication is that "the new music" will save us from despair, or "sadness," as Barthelme called it in another of his books; and "The New Music" is, after all, not simply music but also the title of his own literary concoction.

Characteristically, there is always something else going on in a Barthelme story, something other than the apparent subject or content. Metaphorical traps and tricks proliferate in an apparent effort to describe emotional conditions and human situations too obvious, personal, ridiculous, difficult, embarrassing, or full of pain to confront directly. The astute reader is stimulated to speculate at length over these hidden mountain ranges of feeling-content, or else to supply his own filler. Snatches of eavesdropped conversations as matter-of-fact and believable as those overheard in the local bus station may alternate with subconscious voices answering implied questions the reader must seek on his own. Meanwhile, on the surface of the narrative, the laws of nature are suspended as are the laws of human probability. The improbable is commonplace, and ironies abound. (pp. F1, F4)

There are repeated complaints and bitter jokes throughout *Great Days* about betrayal and the impermanence and difficulty of human relationships. Barthelme's characters evidently need someone to love them forever, but they are of the opinion that such love is a romantic delusion.

More than ever before, Barthelme begins to seem, in some ways, a classic satirist, obsessed by the predominance and multiplicity of human vanities. Yet, the typical Barthelme protagonist whistles along good-naturedly in the teeth of the boredom, despair, absurdity, betrayal, moral decay, and deplorable behavior surrounding him. He has access to all the best technical information from a gamut of fields, but he is simply swamped by it. He has little sense of which bits of endless data should prove useful to him. The promise of science and technology—to make the world ultimately knowable—has backfired by overwhelming him with unclassifiable facts.

Great Days is challenging and funny—further proof, if we needed it, that Donald Barthelme deserves his repuation as a major literary phenomenon of these great days. Whatever his standing in the year 2000, I predict that other writers and anthropologists of the imagination, when searching for creative folklore, will continue to peruse his pages, like so many interior decorators combing through books of wallpaper samples. (p. F4)

> Joe David Bellamy, "Barthelme and Delights of Mind-Travel," in Book World—The Washington Post (© 1979, The Washington Post), February 11, 1979, pp. F1, F4.

MARC GRANETZ

Barthelme's art is not static. He is an explorer of prose forms. He stays abreast of literary developments in America and elsewhere and his fiction constantly changes to reflect slight changes in the way we experience our lives. *Great Days* continues where *Amateurs*, the previous collection, left off; the stories are increasingly clipped, less visual, more difficult. The range of pleasure available upon a first reading has grown even narrower.

As usual, about half of these new stories are baubles, one-notion entertainments. . . . [They] are crankier, less funny than earlier *jeux d'esprit*. . . . The voices in these stories discourse on a variety of topics; non-specific references (her, it, that) allow the topics to be linked together grammatically, a kind of layering of meanings. The stories are open to all suggestions, and can stop on a dime and head in any direction. Even in "On the Steps of the Conservatory" and "The Leap," which read more like ordinary dialogues, the voices make numerous allusions and go off on all sorts of tangents.

It seems natural for Barthelme to be experimenting increasingly with aural forms. His ear for speech is impeccable. Repartee is amenable to his obsessive frivolity with language. His characters are usually cut-outs; this form allows him virtually to dispense with characterization. But most important is the freedom it permits from the strictures of the traditional short story form. Although opening and closing sequences are not haphazard, in these stories beginnings, middles and endings don't really exist. And plot, since nothing happens, is more a proliferation and blossoming than a procession of events.

Barthelme's fiction . . . has always demanded patience. The

trouble with *Great Days* is that it isn't as enjoyable to read as his earlier work. His fans may find in his technical innovations justification for the less rewarding, or at least less immediately rewarding, fiction; readers less smitten with him may have begun to give up on his work a while ago. "We feel only 25 percent of what we ought to feel, according to recent findings," a voice in the opening story claims. This might be a gloss on *Great Days:* it celebrates life less and less. One must hesitate to judge prematurely the progress of a writer as good as Barthelme, but one wonders about a growth that carries a writer away from the pains and elations of the heart toward fiction that is increasingly thin, enigmatic and obscure. (pp. 37-8)

> Marc Granetz, in The New Republic *(reprinted by permission of* The New Republic; © 1979 by The New Republic, Inc.), February 17, 1979.*

RICHARD HOWARD

In the polysynthetic languages, linguists tell us, a certain word will mean "to throw a slippery object far away," though no part of the word means "throw" or "slippery" or "far." This is how we feel about those literary works of our moment which we distance, if we do not domesticate, by calling them "original": We feel that they are something new and something entire, though we fail to perceive how that new entity is arrived at.

In fact, a better name for original writing might just be "polysynthetic language"—certainly that is how Donald Barthelme's six books of fictions (stories? texts? apostrophes? aporias? no one knows yet what to label them) strike me. I know they have a certain general effect (as of throwing a slippery object far away), but the way this operation is performed is so new to me that I cannot determine the elements, cannot detect the parts that make the cunning device function. The one thing I can tell so far—and this latest book of brief inventions confirms—is that the very brevity for which Barthelme is on the one hand so prized . . . and on the other hand so taxed . . . —this very brevity is a signal part of his form. . . .

Great Days, then, is a further installment of Barthelme's characteristic serial. And a particularly rewarding one, because seven of its 16 pieces enact, I believe, a distinct awareness on the writer's part of the responsibilities of his own form. . . .

The seven pieces are dialogues, or rather, intersecting monologues (Barthelme has always had a gift for the introspection of other people), with a great deal of what we usually expect of a "rendered" conversation cut away: We are not told *where* they speak, . . . or *when* the conversations were had, heard, overheard, transcribed. The speakers are never extrinsically identified as to class or circumstance, nor intrinsically located by quotation marks and the supposedly invisible convention of "she said," "he interrupted," the stage directions of literary manners. The conversations also begin very much in the middle of things, in situations we divine only in the most secular fashion, much as we suppose they end by divine fiat (the author's will), rather than by any internal dramatic necessity.

Of course, all these conventions are shown up quite fiercely by Barthelme's less-is-more-fun program; for example, by leaving out the dialogue attribution, he has made us listen much harder. We become a new kind of reader, shrewder in the perception of overtone and undercurrent, as well as of that middle voice which weaves *any* set of utterances together, the sense-making apparatus Sophocles calls, in one of his choruses, "the voice of the shuttle." By apparently taking so much away, Barthelme gives us back a great deal more; that is what I mean by the morality of his form, the ethics of his brevity.

Moreover, the seven dialogues, a stichomythia of astonishment, are balanced between the sexes so delicately . . . that I suspect Barthelme has a very recondite design upon our politics, sexual and otherwise. I believe he is telling us (dramatically) about the nearly incredible ignorance of each other the sexes live in—an ignorance that breeds mistrust and fantasy on the plains of id, and contempt and dismissal in the mountains of superego. That is why there is no dialogue here between a man and a woman.

Not that there is that much solidarity *within* the sexes. Rather, there is a muttering withdrawal when any two of a kind are together, to the prison of individual associations, of selfish memories and indeed mnemonics. And this is where Barthelme's earlier cuteness and hilarities—what Mr. [William] Gass, in the slyest of all Barthelme's many put-downs, called "the cutting edge of the trash phenomenon"—are now utilized in a new acceptation. All the old honing of our cultural detritus (". . . not so dumb as a lady I once knew who thought the Mark of Zorro was an N . . .") becomes part of the lyrical self-love of identity; not conversation, not communication, but antiphonal reassurance by what one leaps to in recollecting that one is there at all. (p. 15)

I recall when I read the first of them to appear in the *New Yorker*—the one called "Morning," the one that begins "Say you're frightened. Admit it."—I was convinced that Barthelme had gone too far, that his puppets were too crazy for me to enjoy reading their extravagances, and that he had become merely—merely!—a virtuoso of hysteria. Now that I see the seven pieces together, with the many other pieces that afford the brilliantly faceted matrix from which these triumphs are argued out, I am happy to discover how mistaken I was.

Barthelme has ennobled his art and advanced his enterprise. His new fictions—the seven dialogues, I mean—provide a basis for us to understand ourselves in a new way. Part of the news is the acknowledgment of failure, is an aporia; but that is after all nothing so new. The better part is the basis on which we delight ourselves, the pleasure we (here, for once) are permitted to take in our own narcissisms. Firbank begins to seep through the bandages, no longer Beckett, certainly not Kafka, as the psychopomp of these beautiful inventions: One begins to discern the lineaments of a new artist, one who can teach us to throw a slippery object far away, all in the one word, the one pleasure, touching, coherent, profound. (p. 17)

> *Richard Howard, "Polysynthetic Barthelme," in* The New Leader *(© 1979 by the American Labor Conference on International Affairs, Inc.), February 26, 1979, pp. 15, 17.*

DENIS DONAGHUE

Donald Barthelme is more attracted to the indisputable charm of brevity than to the disputable charm of narration. If he has a design upon us, it is that we will be rendered unable to resist the temptation of fondling his sentences. We are to read his 16 stories, collected in *Great Days*, as

we read Shakespeare's sonnets, attending to what they do while they pretend to do nothing more than say: "You, my beloved, have killed me." The stories are brief for the same reason that the sonnets have 14 lines—because that is enough. The discrepancy between the brevity of the event and the amount of verbal business negotiated is part of the appeal in both cases. But "appeal" is the wrong word. I take it back. These stories do not emit appeals. They do not ask to be believed, or even to have disbelief suspended for the duration of the narrative.

It is a shock to come upon a sentence of truth here and there in Barthelme's fiction. . . . The truth doesn't damage Barthelme's story, I admit, but it encourages a recidivist nostalgia for the conjunction of sentence and event, an emotion generally and firmly held at bay in Barthelme's fiction. If we are to fall back into the habit of believing things and crediting what we're told, there will be no end to our debauchery: In the twinkling of an I we shall be found longing for the old fleshpots of conviction, form, continuity, the priority of beginning over middle and of middle, in turn, over end. . . .

Barthelme could tell a truth if he wanted to: He could tell anything, even a story, given the same desire. If he does not tell truths or stories, it is not because the moon for such commitments is not in his sky. A more probable reason was given several years ago in Barthelme's *Snow White*, when in answer to someone who accused Henry of living in a world of his own, Henry retorted, "I can certainly improve on what was given." So can Barthelme. His work belongs to the history of rhetoric in one of the senses, as having to do with embellishing the given experience, decorating its margins, turning its capital letters into scrolls. With this difference: Normally the rhetorician tries to show the beauties of Creation by revealing them as inexhaustible, and emphasizes God's text by underlining it for the benefit of dim-witted readers. He would have nailed himself as a blasphemer if he had caught in his work the slightest implication that the text was discontinuous, separate from God's original and superior to it. Barthelme blasphemes from morn till dewy eve. He wants us to feel that the embellishments, his sentences, are so much more beautiful than God's version that we will repudiate the latter as a mere vulgate of experience, a first shot, at best a near-miss. Barthelme's sentences are shot with unerring nonchalance toward their mark: The arrow, having defined the circle by taking possession of the center, rustles its feathers to show that precision is not the whole story.

Barthelme's fiction, then, is written according to Henry's method, as an improvement on the original. There are signs in *Great Days* that Barthelme has a certain tenderness, recidivist again, for things "perfect and ordinary and perfect," but he makes his art by suppressing that emotion. Perfection resides in the sentence, since this is a literature appropriate of closing time in the gardens of the West. Barthelme's ideal reader would quietly disengage himself from objects, possessions, the Hippocrene of venereal life to turn to the comtemplation of one word's way with another. (p. 50)

Start with possessions and lusts if you like, Barthelme says, but be ready to convert them into syllables, an adjective followed by a noun, metrically perhaps a trochee followed by an iamb.

Without proposing to pluck out the heart of his mystery, I think I know what Barthelme is up to. He is trying to detach us from things, possessions, conventional urgencies. Trying to stuff our lives with equanimity, we stuff them with objects. We enforce our will upon the world and identify victory with our possessions. Barthelme wants to tease us out of rage and lust by offering us the superior accomplishment of appreciation; in this case, appreciation of art, word-play, the composition of sentences. Snow White was peevish one day. "Oh I wish there were some words in the world that were not the words I always hear!" God, Yes, wouldn't it be wonderful? But Barthelme doesn't waste much spirit on that mood. He knows that there are only the same old words in the world, but that an accomplished word-man can upset their complacency, set them free from their attachment to objects, convert them to a new music with runcible cadences. He uses English as a second language, hoping to release us from the preoccupations of the first. (pp. 50-1)

Barthelme's stories are related to the given world only in terms of rivalry. They rarely condescend to say anything about that world directly, their lines do not run to mockery or satire. Indeed, daily life plays about the same role in Barthelme's fiction as rapid transit systems play in the choreography of polkas. Barthelme balanchines his sentences with little regard for the merit of getting there fustest with the mostest; his decorum aspires rather to the condition of a perfectly adjudged minstrel show. Of the 16 stories in *Great Days,* four are fairly straightforward; they would be good stories in any class but they would not affront the criteria of theme and form deemed applicable to, say, John Cheever.... The remaining 12 had to be written by the Donald Barthelme whose work, whether he likes the fact or not, is continuous with the work of Samuel Beckett. If you're going to dispose your language in the form of two disembodied voices, rotten with experience transpiring as idioms, you can't help their recalling, with appropriately lyric ironies, Beckett's duet-makers. (p. 51)

I would hate Barthelme's fiction if he found relinquishment easy; if, like rich folk, he kept telling us that money isn't everything, isn't much, isn't anything, really, we're all brothers under the suntanned skin. Barthelme can destroy when he wants to. There must be thousands of Golden Treasury-lovers who will hold him forever unforgiven for reciting the first lines of a favorite poem as "I think that I shall never see slash a poem lovely as a tree." (pp. 51-2)

Barthelme's stories, lively and witty and, yes, yes, disturbing as they are, are practice shots at dispossession. For all I know, there may be objects he despises, and other objects dear to his venereal life, but internal evidence drawn from his fiction suggests that his main quarrel with objects is that they are too many.... Writers as diverse as Stanley Elkin, Susan Sontag, and Donald Barthelme are engaged with this matter: how to deal with a situation which has moved from plenitude, to proliferation, to plethora.... Wherefore Donald Barthelme and other writers of similar persuasion have given up the ambition of linking convictions to facts; instead, they transfer to sentences of their own scrupulous devising such talent for conviction as they retain. Love me, love my sentences, Barthelme demands. And I reply, I do, I do. (p. 52)

Denis Donaghue, "For Brevity's Sake," in Saturday Review *(© 1979 by Saturday Review Magazine Corp.; reprinted with permission), March 3, 1979, pp. 50-2.*

JAMES RAWLEY

[Donald Barthelme's] *Great Days,* is about success. "Yes, success is everything," says one of his characters, or rather one of his half embodied, half-unrealized voices. The voice goes on:

> Failure is more common. Most achieve a sort of middling thing, but fortunately one's situation is always blurred, you never know absolutely quite where you are. This allows, if not peace of mind, ongoing attention to other aspects of existence.

The paragraph illustrates Barthelme's much-praised ability to switch from style to style, from the professorial "absolutely quite" to the bureaucratic "ongoing attention," all within fifteen words, and all while holding things together with an unfaltering sense of rhythm. This is the kind of fingering people expect from a regular writer for *The New Yorker,* and Barthelme's surrealist intensity never distorts his civilized charm. Indeed, this charm serves as a reminder that surrealists, unlike some other members of the avant-garde, continue to respect the popular myth, the varnished surface and the ordinary human face, with or without skull peeping through the skin. . . .

The technique throughout gets away with calling attention to itself. The stories that are all in dialogue, like the ones in which almost every sentence ends with a question mark, succeed even when, as we are meant to do, we lose track of the characters and perceive nothing but verbal sparkles over a ground tone of lament. . . . "The Death of Edward Lear," a work of homage to an ancestor, ends with one of the most frightening and elaborately prepared puns in modern literature, and gives a history it seemed to lack to the theater of the absurd.

Yet even this, and the poignant title story, are mellower achievements than the author's previous works. Oedipal suffering, the anguish of divorce—themes he has handled in the past with startling power for so urbane a craftsman—have now given way to a sharply focused but distant look at age and loss. Horror and fun are both muted to melancholy. . . .

The mood recalls other *New Yorker* writers of the past: Thurber's ineffectuals, Benchley's occasional sorrow over being no more than a feuilletonist. E. B. White's controlled evocation of neurosis in "The Door." The world of literary surrealists is a small one, curiously curved in on itself, so that Barthelme's kinship with Borges. Buzzati or Calvino seems at first stronger than any relation he may have to other American authors. But just as Borges has his librarian's bibliomania and love for metaphysics, just as Calvino echoes Ariosto, and Buzzati collected and believed in Venetian ghost stories, so Barthelme preserves the diffident, whimsical, cultured tone that defined *The New Yorker* through so many decades. In fact, some of his works are less surreal than some of Perelman's, which they thoroughly resemble.

But Barthelme has liberated himself, for good or for ill, from mere funniness. Though his stories are often revue turns, and as much in need of a wow finish, the wow finish may not get a laugh, may succeed by plunging the reader into world-weariness and pain, as the last lines of *Great Days* do.

Blake said, "He who mocks the infant's faith/Shall be mocked in age and death." Nowadays it is we who, from childhood, mock our superheroes and the watered-down cultural values given us on television. We approach middle age with our own laughter ringing unpleasantly in our ears. Donald Barthelme, who has always seen something sad in our skits and parodies, has composed a set of serious burlesques as a tribute to the tragedy of life. It is a quiet achievement, a deliberately qualified success, and the most haunting book anyone ever chuckled over.

James Rawley, "The New Music," in The Nation *(copyright 1979 The Nation Associates, Inc.), April 7, 1979, p. 374.*

*　　*　　*

BEATTIE, Ann   1947-

American novelist and short story writer, Beattie is a frequent contributor to *The New Yorker*. Her fiction is concerned primarily with the fortunes of the Woodstock generation in the spiritless seventies. (See also *CLC*, Vol. 8.)

TERENCE WINCH

In this new book of stories, *Secrets and Surprises*, Beattie imagines a very real world of people trapped in relationships that don't work. Resignation is everybody's *modus operandi*, a spiritual routine that gets them from one day to the next. . . .

Secrets and Surprises represents a great leap forward for Beattie. This new collection recognizes that the more interesting distortions are those which blend inconspicuously into our lives so as to be almost invisible. But nonetheless powerful. (p. E1)

Her novel [*Chilly Scenes of Winter*] can be read as a story about people and what they do when they find themselves outside of a relationship, but living in the pull of its force. These new stories complement that vision. They represent the other side of things: what happens when people are attached, involved with each other. What happens, of course, is love.

But love, in Ann Beattie's new stories, comes in a wealth of shapes and sizes. And the varieties of love are not all wonderful. Some versions are horrible. And sometimes the horror is civilized, even sophisticated.

Her characters are most often intelligent, educated, white, middle-class Americans in their late twenties. They have survived the social turbulence of the '60s only to find themselves confused by the emotional turbulence of the '70s. "Normal" family life seems a hair's breadth away in Beattie's stories: couples (if they have been married at all) are divorced or on the verge of divorce. Marijuana and Bob Dylan help, but ultimately nothing dispels the emotional dislocation of those who inhabit Beattie's fictional world. At the end of "Colorado," Robert is stoned and "confused": "What state is this?" is all he can say. He has been permanently damaged by the psychic violence that colors Beattie's stories.

Beattie can convey that violence with the eye of a great painter: "The sky is pale blue, streaked with orange, which seems to be spreading through the blue sky from behind,

like liquid seeping through a napkin, blood through a bandage." Or she can transform the ordinary into something revealing and chilling: "Still at the kitchen table, he ran his thumb across a pea pod as though it were a knife."

If people are emotionally mistreated by others in Ann Beattie's stories, they are just as often collaborators in the process: victimization and self-victimization are everywhere. And frequently people's relationship to things runs parallel to their involvement with others. Karen's Thunderbird in "A Vintage Thunderbird," the finest story in the book, takes on a complexity of meaning and comes to symbolize the history of her affair with Nick. Nick "loved to go to her apartment and look at her things. He was excited by them. . . ." But it is her car that excites him most. When Karen is "conned" out of her car by a "New York architect" in what Nick knows is a "set up," he asks her if "the deal is final." Nick, who has been mugged twice and stood up once during the story, knows instinctively that the loss of the car spells the loss of love. It is a masterful story in which a vocabulary of money becomes the language of love.

And love is just another rip-off in a world gone wrong. . . . Predators, emotional and otherwise, stalk through every story.

But this stark world is qualified by the talent and sensitivity of the author who created it. Ann Beattie's intelligence is illuminating. Some of these stories are disappointing, but the five or six solid successes are works of vivid honesty and insight that confirm Beattie's reputation as one of our best young writers. (pp. E1, E4)

Terence Winch, "Love's Resignation," in Book World—The Washington Post *(© 1979, The Washington Post), January 7, 1979, pp. E1, E4.*

GAIL GODWIN

The characters who populate [*Secrets and Surprises*] came of age during the 1960's. They are, on the whole, a nice-looking bunch of people who have never suffered from any of the basic wants. Most of them, for reasons often unexplained, share a mistrust of passion and conversation. If a man and woman get together, it is because of a shared car or animal, or because each has a famous parent, or maybe simply because one of them has run out of other people to live with; and, even when they live together, they speak in cool little ironies or deadpan non sequiturs. They live in student apartments in Boston or New Haven, or young-married or young-career quarters in Philadelphia or Manhattan, or sometimes a group of them share a house in Vermont; but they exist mainly in a stateless realm of indecision and—all too often—rather smug despair. . . .

Frequently, in these stories, things are substitutes for the chancier commitment to people; things people buy or live with or give one another are asked to bear the responsibility of objective correlatives, but too often they become a mere catalogue of trends. The reader is left holding an armful of objects and wondering what emotional responses they were meant to connect him with.

Perhaps the best level on which to enjoy these stories is as a narrative form of social history. Miss Beattie has a cooly accurate eye for the *moeurs* of her generation. . . . But a sharp eye for *moeurs* doesn't add up to a full fiction any more than the attitude of irony can be said to represent a full human response.

The story that, to my taste, best weds feeling with artistic control is "Distant Music," in which an office girl and a graduate-school dropout are brought together by a mongrel puppy named Sam. They take the dog because they fear for its life. They order their lives around it and for a time, consequently, they protect and nourish each other, the thriving puppy their evidence that survival is possible even in huge cities. Each of them grows, but, as is frequently the case, in opposite directions. When Jack leaves for California, where his songs soon catch on (there is a good one about "a dog named Sam") the dog left behind turns vicious. A bad mix, says the veterinarian, and Sharon must put Sam away. But when we last see Sharon, she has taken a man "new to the city" over to New Jersey to show him that, from the proper perspective, New York can be scaled to human possibility. The form of the story and the experiences of its characters have added up to something meaningful.

> Gail Godwin, "Sufferers from Smug Despair," in The New York Times Book Review (© 1979 by The New York Times Company; reprinted by permission), January 14, 1979, p. 14.

DAPHNE MERKIN

The people in Ann Beattie's second book of stories, *Secrets and Surprises* . . . have gone beyond anger into numbness. As were the protagonists of her first collection, *Distortions,* they are generally in their mid-'30s; some of them are parents; all of them share disquietingly sophomoric tastes and desires. They listen to Bob Dylan or Keith Jarrett, display vaguely artistic interests and get stoned a lot. They are by and large unlikable, albeit not uninteresting, and even, on occasion, touching. The predominant mood, dire enervation, is oddly contagious.

Beattie has been polishing her style of mannered naturalism for some time now, and it is beginning to show signs of wear. One can discern in her work traces of the repressed poignancy of J. D. Salinger, to whom she has been compared. But Beattie's method—her painstakingly accurate rendition of the commonplace, her reliance upon the artifacts of popular culture (Perry Mason, *Newsweek, Notorious*)—reminds me not so much of other writers as of the sculptor Duane Hanson, who uses wax to capture grubby likenesses—waitresses, construction workers and museum guards. While seldom grubby, her characters are fixed by a similar eye for homely detail, and the deliberate flatness of her prose imparts an almost tactile quality to the narrative.

Most of these stories feature couples in various stages of mutual unrelatedness. . . . In one piece ("A Reasonable Man"), a woman going quietly crazy continues to prepare gourmet dinners for the man she is living with. They have a "civilized discussion" about her cooking techniques, notwithstanding the fact that "he does not know exactly what she is talking about." Their situation is a bit more extreme than the average one in this collection, if only because we are given hints that the woman's disturbance is recognized by others and is therefore not merely a heightened form of lethargy. But her emotional minimalism, the drastically reduced expectations that comprise her social outlook, could serve as a credo for the book: "If you have something to say about the weather, you will always be able to make conversation with people, and communicating is very important."

The author does have a few secrets up her sleeve, and at least one surprise. She is a veritable wizard at devising resonant last lines that cast retrospective significance over an entire story. . . . The surprise is "The Lawn Party," a delicate, Cheeveresque story that evokes the drenched, lyric atmosphere Beattie is usually careful to avoid.

A future social scientist who stumbled across the stories and wondered at their cultural implications could conclude that ours was a dazed, lost time. He would undoubtedly remark upon the consistent displacement of emotional affect on to nonpeople: cats, dogs, songs, cars. And his speculations might converge on the following hypothetical problem: If one of Beattie's characters were to murder another with a hammer, would anyone care? (p. 17)

> Daphne Merkin, in The New Leader (© 1979 by the American Labor Conference on International Affairs, Inc.), January 15, 1979.

ANN HULBERT

Secrets and surprises might seem like unexpected specialties for Ann Beattie. In the pages of *The New Yorker* and of her two previous books—*Distortions* . . . and *Chilly Scenes of Winter* . . .—she anatomizes the everyday lives of characters who are headed nowhere in particular and are unfamiliar with the usual literary kind of secrets and surprises—the kind associated with epiphanies. But as Beattie has hinted all along and emphasizes in [*Secrets and Surprises*], hidden knowledge and unexpected discoveries are also staples of ordinary, undramatic life. They don't just belong to rare moments, and they don't necessarily irradiate life with significance. Her characters are lonely and can't help having secrets; they are used to being taken aback by the unexpected because they foresee little and control less. Their lives don't really change after they acknowledge their secrets to themselves or partially reveal them to others. Instead, another disorderly day dawns. In the appropriately uninflected prose and loosely structured stories of *Secrets and Surprises* Beattie makes the days and characters come to life—almost paradoxically—more powerfully and poignantly than she has before. (p. 34)

Beattie's central theme is one that calls for variations; for the relationships she describes are distinguished by seeming —at least to those involved in them—*not* to follow any standard pattern. Commitments are unclear, expectations unformulated and communications faulty. Beattie imagines variations in all their minute particularity in her stories; and this collection of them conveys an often dispiriting sense of the common underlying muddle. (p. 35)

There is a lot of disquieting, empty space in these stories— in the characters' heads and hearts and in the holes between characters.

But Beattie sees more than blankness. The secret she shares with us in acutely captured moments and carefully recorded details is of the unobtrusive but crucial presence of generous impulses and good intentions in lives that are lonely and undirected, in friendships that are full of ignorance and confusion. And at a time when hopelessness and bleak isolation are assumed in much fiction—and are never very far from her own—that is a surprise. (p. 36)

> Ann Hulbert, in The New Republic (reprinted by permission of The New Republic; © 1979 by The New Republic, Inc.), January 20, 1979.

E. S. DUVALL

Beginning to read [*Secrets and Surprises*] is like going out alone into the night in the country: it's very dark, and the flashlight doesn't seem to illuminate much. Single objects— a car, a dog—loom up with uncanny significance. Familiar things look strange, one-dimensional. There are barely audible rustlings in the undergrowth which could mean anything, or nothing. It is very quiet.

But gradually one becomes accustomed to the faint light and realizes that there is more going on in these spare tales than first meets the eye. Although the men and women Ann Beattie writes about are well endowed with cars and dogs— and histories, and homes, and "relationships"—their most compelling feature is the profound anomie that darkens their lives. . . . Action is the result of chance; will is discomfiting; passion is terrifying.

The unrelieved passivity of these characters might seem repellent, but Beattie is skillful at provoking our interest in them. Personality glints off their most trivial actions, and a stubborn refusal to give in (to whom? to what?) lies behind their lethargy. A tightly controlled, monochromatic prose gives these portraits the revealing clarity of photographs. (pp. 132-33)

> *E. S. Duvall, in* The Atlantic Monthly *(copyright © 1979 by The Atlantic Monthly Company, Boston, Mass.; reprinted with permission), March, 1979.*

*   *   *

BELLOW, Saul   1915-

Bellow, a Canadian-born Jewish-American novelist, short story writer, essayist, playwright, editor, and translator, is regarded by many to be the most important spokesman of the post-war generation. The realization of selfhood in a time when the concept of individualism is degenerating has been the task of nearly all of his protagonists, of whom several— Herzog, Henderson, Augie March, Mr. Sammler—have come to stand for tooth-and-nail optimism in the face of chaos and despair. Augie's famous cry "I want! I want!" expresses the primal knowledge of Bellow men, those who *will* survive, who *will not* surrender. Chester E. Eisinger provides an excellent summary: Bellow "knows that man is less than what the Golden Age promised us, but he refuses to believe that man is nothing. He is something, Bellow says, and saying it he performs an act of faith." A recipient of three National Book Awards, he won both the Pulitzer Prize in Fiction and the Nobel Prize for Literature in 1976. (See also *CLC*, Vols. 1, 2, 3, 6, 8, 10, and *Contemporary Authors*, Vols. 5-8, rev. ed.)

PETER M. AXTHELM

Moses Herzog, the hero of Bellow's most brilliantly realized confessional novel, . . . arrives at a unique kind of perception—one which is in relation to nothing and, at the same time, to everything. An examination of this seemingly paradoxical state and of how it is achieved provides an understanding of what may be the ultimate possibility for the modern confessional hero.

Herzog's perception relates to nothing, in that it is a simple, quiet decision to stop his confession, a signal that his internal storm has at last been calmed; it simultaneously relates to everything, in that it indicates a profound understanding of his past and present existence. It contains nothing in the

form of a momentary vision or an affirmation of one special value, but its development includes glimpses of almost everything in man's intellectual repertory. Finally, it relates to nothing because, conceived in isolation, it affirms the joy of isolation; yet this isolation simultaneously connects Moses Herzog with everything—in his rare state, both his mind and the world are at peace. (pp. 129-30)

Before he arrives at this unprecedented level of peace and self-understanding in his hero, Bellow considers many traditional themes of the confessional genre. Two of these themes are developed to an extent which requires some discussion before we can turn to a specific treatment of Bellow's work. First, the intellectual hero who has been developing throughout the course of the confessional novel reaches a rich maturation in *Herzog;* second, Bellow approaches the problem of suffering with the sensitive insight of Jewish tradition.

"Your intelligence is so high," a friend tells Moses Herzog, "—way off the continuum." . . . Herzog employs his great mental capacities not only as a thinker or philosopher in the sense of the Sartrean hero, but also as a near-encyclopedic source of intellectual references and allusions. . . . It is one of the triumphs of *Herzog* that it is able to encompass such a wide range of facts and thoughts without becoming irrelevant or dull. The technique of having the hero write letters to many scholarly colleagues gives some degree of unity to his observations, but the manner in which they remain consistently vital to his personal problems is chiefly attributable to the remarkable use of irony.

In part, Bellow's irony resembles that satirical humor used so effectively by his modern Jewish counterparts, such as Salinger in "Franny" and Philip Roth in *Goodbye, Columbus*. It also includes an ironic view of the hero, undercutting his approaches to profundity in the manner of Dostoevsky and Sartre's use of the sharp letdown. (pp. 131-32)

The most distinctive aspect of the irony in *Herzog* is not that of the author, but of the hero. He, too, can satirize others. . . . This satirical ability frequently adds life to basically gloomy scenes. (p. 132)

More important than his satiric wit, however, is Herzog's capacity for self-directed irony. "There was a passionate satire in him," and this quality is one of the basic tools of his self-scrutiny. Just as the author undercuts the hero's own early attitude, Herzog gradually comes to revel in an irreverent treatment of the generalizations which he and other intellectual historians had long held dear. (p. 133)

Through his enduring irony, [Herzog] maintains control over his wide-ranging thoughts, never allowing his intellectualism to separate him from his most pressing problems. In fact, his intellectual comments become an integral part of his mind, reflecting its whims as well as its suffering. Eventually, they lead him, in a gradual and painful progression, toward a harmonious relation of his mind with the world. (p. 134)

The Jewish legacy of suffering is an important theme of *Herzog*, and it is interesting to note its special nature. The Jewish hero is not, like the Underground Man, "passionately in love with suffering"; he cannot share the malignant pleasure which Dostoevsky's hero finds in his humiliation and pain. However, he accepts suffering as his inevitable fate, and he takes a certain pride in knowing how to suffer.

The Jew doesn't "love" suffering, but in a sense he needs it to feel his identity. (p. 135)

Bellow qualifies the theme of his hero's Jewish heritage in two important ways. First, the same element of irony which directs Herzog's intellectual excursions has a similar effect on references to his race. Herzog speaks of his ancestors in short phrases which remind us that he is a member of a suffering race, without attempting to blame any of his personal suffering on that race. Perhaps the finest example of this rueful humor is his lament about Madeleine: "She's built a wall of Russian books around herself. Vladimir of Kiev, Tikhon Zadonsky. In my bed! It's not enough they persecuted my ancestors!" (p. 137)

Bellow's second modification of the Jewish theme occurs in its relation to the novel as a whole. . . . [For Bellow], suffering is not the "only certainty." Herzog's ultimate act is not one of submission to pain but one of transcendence. Suffering presses upon him, and he accepts it; yet he also refuses to become immersed in it. His Jewish background is intrinsically related to his suffering, but the two are not synonymous. (pp. 137-38)

The essential point is that, for Bellow, Jewish tradition is meant to define, not to determine; it is important only as long as it elucidates the nature of an individual's problem. . . . Bellow's heroes will not be placed on a stockpile. They never cease to affirm their individual natures, and they accept their suffering, as well as their joy, as an intensely personal fact.

The Jewish theme, as applied to Herzog, introduces two central aspects of his confession. He is, on the one hand, an outcast, a descendant of the Wandering Jew; at the same time, he is deprived of the cultural continuity which sustains the Jews—he cannot hope for his child to achieve the peace which he himself has been denied, because that child has been snatched from him. . . . The essential solution to his alienation must be sought far from the "oceanic" realm, in his own personal world. (pp. 138-39)

[Arthur Koestler's] *Darkness at Noon*, in which the hero frequently compares himself to Moses, and [William Golding's] *Free Fall*, with its relation to the Fall from Paradise, suggest that the confessional hero's quest for reconstructed values leads him toward mythic patterns. In *Herzog*, Bellow brings modern man even closer to myth. The hero's life is the quest of a modern Moses for his own Promised Land. Herzog seeks fulfillment by leading his wife Madeleine and his friends Valentine and Phoebe Gersbach to the peaceful country life of Ludeyville. His flock soon deserts him, and his quest proves disastrous. Left alone, he sees himself as "a broken-down monarch of some kind." His confession is a renewal of his search, a pilgrimage through his disintegrated life toward a state of true peace and perception. The theme of this mental journey remains linked to the story of Moses, but its structure of rambling meditations and memories is organized on the pattern of the *Odyssey*.

When he begins his first search, Moses Herzog is married to a woman named Daisy. "Stability, symmetry, order, containment were Daisy's strength," he recalls. "By my irregularity and turbulence of spirit I brought out the very worst in Daisy." . . . In seeking a life more attuned to his own spirit, Herzog is attracted to a woman even more unpredictable and passionate than himself. His relationship with Madeleine is described as a constant, raging battle, in which he proves hopelessly overmatched. The nature of their struggle is elucidated by the symbols which come to represent their battle standards. (p. 147)

Madeleine gradually destroys Moses' control over his life and reduces all its order to chaos. He has been drifting away from his Jewish heritage all his life, as he realized during his affair with the Japanese girl Sono; but Madeleine forces him to reject it outright in a painful ritual of surrender. He begins to feel this pain when she makes him accompany her to church: "He was a husband, a father. He was married, he was a Jew. Why was he in church?" He proceeds to give up his first wife and son, but she insists on extracting the final toll. (p. 149)

In a gesture of total renunciation of his past, Moses invests all his father's savings, "representing forty years of misery in America," in the Ludeyville house and spends a year rebuilding it as the site of his Promised Land. Madeleine reacts by keeping it in constant disorder. Herzog makes several attempts to reassert his own position with her. Before they marry, he takes some pleasure in the fact that "She had been a Catholic for only three months, and already because of Herzog she couldn't be confessed, not by Monsignor, anyway." . . . But this victory fades quickly, and, by making him feel like a corruptor, Madeleine humbles Herzog still more. At Ludeyville, he tries again to gain the upper hand by requiring her to make love on the bathroom floor; this desperate effort only feeds her constant interior rage. When Herzog, still possessing his powerful intellect, first clashes directly with Madeleine concerning his disordered house, the result is one of the most unforgettable scenes in the novel; it is . . . a brilliant example of Madeleine's terrifying power. . . . This exchange ends like a clap of doom, an ominous declaration that Madeleine will always be in control of both Herzog and the child, June, who is still within her. (pp. 150-51)

Moses Herzog's search for his Promised Land is a kind of mental epic, and Bellow, like Joyce, uses the *Odyssey* as the basis of his structure. Odyssean themes are neither as prominent nor as consciously invoked in *Herzog* as they are in *Ulysses*, and the hero's quest remains as close to that of Moses as it is to that of Odysseus. Nevertheless, this source provides an illuminating insight into the form and the overall significance of Herzog's vast and chaotic range of thoughts.

Herzog's confession can be divided into five movements, each distinguished by an external action. The first is a gesture of escape, an attempt to find meaning in exile; he takes a train from New York to Cape Cod for a vacation but returns the same night, unable to rest. His thoughts while he rides are a dirge of disintegration, an echo of another epic vision of modern man, Eliot's *The Waste Land*. The second phase is a night at home, during which Herzog listens to the song of the Sirens from his past. His glimpse at past romances brings a faint light into his world, but love is ultimately seen as elusive and destructive. In the third section, Herzog spends a night with Ramona—his Nausicaa—and considers her offer of peace and happiness. On the following day, the hero begins his journey through hell, which takes him to the New York criminal court and then to the origin of his sufferings in Chicago, outside the house occupied by Madeleine and Gersbach. Only after the purification of this episode can he proceed to the fifth stage of his confession, in which he returns to Ludeyville and finds true perception. (p. 152)

Moses Herzog's trip through hell is the longest of the five sections of his confession, a wandering adventure which takes him from New York to Chicago and forces his consciousness into the depths of his intellectual and spiritual existence. It begins with a call to the lawyer Simkin and the thought, "I should have phoned Simkin earlier." This casual phrase suggests that Herzog has been in need of some positive gesture for some time and reminds us that he had indeed attempted a kind of journey to hell before. That first effort was the trip to Europe which Moses took just before the beginning of his confession. *"This year I covered half the world,"* he writes to the Polish girl Zinka, *"and saw people in such numbers—it seems to me I saw everybody but the dead.* Whom perhaps I was looking for." . . . In Poland, "he went many times to visit the ruins of the ghetto." This effort to commune with the shades of his ancestors proves as unsuccessful as all his subsequent approaches to the past he has rejected. His search brings him nothing but a slight venereal infection—a parody of the purification which he had sought. This early failure indicates that real purification for Herzog cannot be achieved in a physical gesture or in the shades of his past. It lies instead in a *mental* reenactment of the *Nekuia,* an effort to communicate with the dark and hidden forces within the hero himself. It is this effort which becomes the crucial fourth movement of Herzog's confession and the prelude to perception.

The *Nekuia* of Moses Herzog can be seen as a gradual process of dispelling the illusions and preoccupations which have obscured true meaning in his life. His conversation with Simkin about suing Madeleine emphasizes his desire for revenge, as well as the thought that his daughter's presence would restore all order to his life. Another of his illusions is the hope, a vestige of his intellectual career, that a sound world-view can bring him peace; he also holds a vague belief that suffering itself is a redeeming factor in his life. On his journey, he comes to see that all these solutions are as limited as the sensual creed he has rejected in Ramona. (pp. 163-64)

[After he is] stripped of his visions of the world and his romantic notions of revenge, Herzog at last frees himself from the limitations imposed by his own confession and sees that truth lies beyond the scope of intellectual constructions, however elaborate they might be.

The self-awareness which has come to Herzog in stages is fully defined . . . on his disastrous outing with June. The end to all his abstractions comes after the accident, as he passes out. When he awakes, he looks at June: "Her face was tearless, clouded, and this was far worse. It hurt him. It tore his heart." He knows that, in her child's mind, "he was spattered forever with things that bled or stank." Despite his pain, however, Herzog sees another new light. His daughter, still wonderful and the object of his deepest love, somehow loses her quality as a savior; he sees that it is not June he needs, but something deeper for which she stands. . . . In the darkest recess of his personal hell, at the moment of his most dismal blunder, the hero has cast off the last illusion and found himself. For the first time, he is in harmony with his world. (pp. 169-70)

Herzog has abandoned the intellectual historian's attempt to fit all functions into a pattern, but he has not been lured to the opposite pole, where all functions are divided and destroyed. . . . Between these absolutes, Moses has confronted the ambiguity and complexity of the problem and

found in it a satisfying conception of the world—the first stage of his perception. This marks the beginning of the final movement of Herzog's confession, the return to Ludeyville and the realization of his true Promised Land. This initial step toward full perception begins to elucidate the dual definition of perception which was at the start of this chapter. Moses affirms a *division* of functions which cuts him off from those around him, yet it brings him a sense of peace and an ability to relate to others, which *unite* him to the world. The second aspect of his perception is similarly paradoxical; he finds the joy of freedom only in the denial of one part of it. (p. 171)

[When, in Ludeyville, he writes a letter to his dead mother repudiating his past wishes for death], Herzog is overcome by "a deep, dizzy eagerness to *begin.*"

This word leads us back to a fuller understanding of the structure of the novel and to a consideration of what confession has meant in the life of Moses Herzog. Herzog is in the country, strangely happy, writing the last of his letters; wondering what he should write, he thinks, "If I am out of my mind, it's all right with me." . . . This repetition of the opening line of the novel is not a thematic device. It does not *recall* that opening moment; it *is* that moment. Everything that has gone on since that first sentence has been a part of the hero's memory. During Herzog's confession, Bellow has suspended all temporal order and replaced it with mythic structure. At the end of his mental odyssey, even the hero himself is surprised at the temporal compression of the events he has recalled: "Was it only a week—five days? Unbelievable! How different he felt!" . . .

This subtle joining of the mythic and temporal dimensions of Herzog's quest points toward a fusion of the two basic legends which lie behind it. The hero, who began as Moses seeking his Promised Land, allowed his mind to journey through its own *Odyssey* of choices and purifications and has arrived back at his starting point—like Odysseus returning to Ithaca. (p. 174)

The crucial sundering of the hero's bond to Moses occurs early in the novel, when it becomes apparent that revelation is no longer possible in Herzog's world. He parodies a prayer: "O Lord! forgive all these trespasses. Lead me not into Penn Station." . . . More important, however, than the hero's attitude is the condition of the world itself, plunging onward toward its own disintegration at a pace too fast to be arrested by any heavenly emissary. . . . For Herzog, cut off from his Jewish heritage and incapable of accepting revelation, the archetype of Moses offers little; with his tremendous intellect, he is more attuned to emulation of Odysseus, the versatile, crafty, inventive Greek. Before he can develop that inventiveness beyond the constructions of his letters, he must proceed on his odyssey; at its conclusion, he has broken down his old constructions and created a new, coherent one—the fulfillment of his Promised Land.

Whether Ludeyville can best be described as an Ithaca or an Israel is basically irrelevant; the crucial fact is that the hero *constructs* it, rather than *finds* it. Among the weeds and the rats and the musty closets, Moses Herzog has arrived, stripped of illusion, free and self-aware. Out of the fusion of Moses and Odysseus within him, there arises a hero who is, like his confessional predecessors, a sufferer, a wanderer, even at times a destroyer; but Herzog has added a new dimension—that of the inventor or creator. (pp. 175-76)

Ultimately, Herzog's success goes beyond the knowledge and understanding that are traditional goals of the confessional hero. The hopeful conclusion which had seemed so contrived in *Crime and Punishment* and so far from realization in *Nausea* at last becomes an integral part of a confessional novel. The hero has gained a self-awareness so deep and a peace so profound that he can cease his letter writing and halt his mental journey. In contrast to every other confessional novel, *Herzog* does not stop short of complete perception for the hero; it leaves no feeling that more should be said. Indeed, Moses Herzog has reached an end to confession and an entrance into meaningful life. No longer challenged to *know,* he hastens forward to *begin.* (p. 177)

> *Peter M. Axthelm, "The Full Perception: Bellow," in his* The Modern Confessional Novel *(copyright © 1967 by Yale University), Yale University Press, 1967, pp. 128-77.*

DAVID R. JONES

Despite its initial success, [*The Adventures of Augie March*] has not worn well.... [Difficult] questions continue to disrupt considerations of the novel. Bellow's strategy ... is a reckless one, to fling an individual out across the surface of a very large work. Any such book depends for its success on the resiliency of that individual, on his ability to become, like a new coat, comfortable with time. There is also a problem of focus, for Bellow parades American types and deformities past the reader in considerable number, and we often have to peer over their heads to get a glimpse of Augie. As if to complicate matters, we must continually adjust our register to accommodate the two Augie Marchs, narrator and actor, an adjustment which is not always easy. And after we have resolved these problems, how are we to take this expatriate American, disenchanted Chicagoan, non-Jewish Jew, and unadventurous adventurer? Is he, unlike Bellow's earlier heroes, a proof that modern society can bring to maturity a man who affirms—by his words and his presence—the brutish, glorious, squalid, monumental, and petty life of men? Or is he an example of our society's ability to make all motion circular, to reduce men to demented jabbering in the face of its alternating demands and rejections? Finally, and more important for the reader approaching the book for the first time, does the style of Augie's reminiscences bear enduring? The pitch of the writing here is more extreme than anything else Bellow has attempted in his career. Augie's prose is either daringly successful or very aggravating, and more than one reader has put the novel aside because he could not tolerate its surface.

Augie tells us at the first that "a man's character is his fate," ... and if this is true, we need to know who and what Augie March is. He introduces himself with a naive bluster which is neither informative nor encouraging, and the initial words, "an American, Chicago born," are most helpful to the hunter of allegories. We find out a great many irrelevancies in the next pages (to be exact, in the first half of the book), but we still do not know the answer to this question.... Augie, a free soul, will not be defined by neighborhood. Neither can we place him by occupation.... Throughout, rich women are constantly present, and only his particular sense of himself saves Augie from becoming a gigolo. No, we will not find him out there.

We begin to discover Augie in the reactions he provokes in

others.... By his character rather than his will, he is thrust into the middle of a philosophic battlefield. (pp. 84-6)

Life is the swindling of the brutes by the managers, the trade of advantage for pain. In the middle stands Augie, the free agent, the "man of feeling." ... Urged to find a profession and become "a specialist" before the world closes up, he vacillates. Overpowered by his opponents, he wiggles away and strikes off on his own. Mired in inaction, he is called "fool," ... "mushhead," ... and "too dumb to live." ... His form of "opposition" is to duck a shoulder under the outreached arm and sidle off into another chapter, another adventure. He admits his own "larkiness," but knows that it is in the best cause, the search for a "worthwhile fate." ... (pp. 86-7)

In the middle of the book, while Augie is peacefully down-and-out, Thea Fenchel appears.... But when the affair with Thea begins, the novel, like the glue on its binding, cracks in half. First, the style alters considerably. Augie leaves Chicago for the first sustained period, and the bursting descriptive passages which had dominated the novel disappear entirely. So does Augie's basic preoccupation with others. From the opening battles of the book, we have a very difficult time learning anything about the young Augie March. The principles behind his actions are obscure.... Larger issues are explained with equal vagueness, for the older March, the writer of the memoirs, is usually as mystified as his readers.... What little we learn about Augie himself is drowned in the descriptions of his surroundings and recruiters. At the beginning of another new adventure, the narrator alludes to the difficulty which bothers his readers: "All the influences were lined up waiting for me. I was born, and there they were to form me, which is why I tell you more of them than of myself." ... The book, however, is about his submission and resistance to these influences, and we should know more about the character which determines his fate. A *bildungsroman* is usually about somebody, and Augie March seems suspiciously, at times, like nobody. But in the latter half of the novel, as if to reward us for our patience, he turns what was a trickle of self-reflection into a torrent. The collapse of the affair with Thea is the signal for his incessant gabbing to begin. By the end of the novel, when he meets an old friend in Paris and refuses to discuss his accumulated ideas, we gasp in relief.

More important, the disintegration of his love for Thea provides the emotional climax of the book and his first significant insight.... [He realizes that his] "simplicity" is an invention, and this "devising" costs him dearly in his "secret heart." He too is creating a "someone who can exist before" external life and is advertising, if only to himself, a "version of what's real." "Personality," he moans, "is unsafe in the first place. It's the types that are safe." ... (pp. 87-8)

This is an important and pertinent revelation, that even those who resist the "versions" of others do so by creating their own fictions. But it would have had more force if the novel had not lapsed back into another series of bouts with the Machiavellians. Augie returns to Chicago and is interrogated in turn by nearly all his acquaintances there. (p. 88)

The principal difficulty in approaching Bellow's third novel, then, is in getting to know Augie March. At first he tells us too little about himself as he piles up the remarkably detailed picture of Chicago. Later, by talking compulsively, he tells us nothing. And as a narrator, he becomes increasingly ponderous. . . .

Aggravations multiply. As he ages, Augie becomes surlier, and the negative facets of the poolroom wise-guy show more frequently. But nowhere is he more tiresome than in his prose. He describes his method of writing as "freestyle," and it is, in fact, as simple and repetitive as the freestyler's crawl. Augie's stroke is the simile, a device he almost invariably secures with the debris of his self-education. (p. 89)

Besides appearing on nearly every page, the similes become long, mixed, and wildly inappropriate. On the occasion of the Depression, Augie glosses Einhorn with a two-hundred word comparison to Croesus, and a later friend is compared at similar length to Clemenceau's statue in the Champs Elysées. . . . [In] contrast with the use Joyce makes of such parallels in *Ulysses,* Bellow's devices seem undirected, superficial, and wearying—in short, a self-indulgence.

In general, the prose is a child's wildest ice-cream sundae dream. Augie prefers verbs and adjectives six or eight in a row. The historical material shoulders its way among slang [, eminent people of the time and the familiar objects of life]. . . . At its best, the prose is like the city, a pile of objects and people. . . . When successful, this prose is among modern America's finest. We forget the "etceteras," the "whatnots," and the "who-else-nots" which dangle on the ends of clauses and the "kind of's" which are liberally sprinkled throughout. All too often, however, the prose is simply elephantine or uncomfortably limp and soggy. . . . (pp. 90-1)

These things said, the vital failure of *The Adventures of Augie March* is still not explained. If we dislike Augie himself (some readers find him "masochistic"), his occasionally bloated prose, and his speeches with their air of old theatrical rant, we can find convincing rationalizations. Structural flaws, of themselves, do not consign works to the categories of "interesting" and "little read." *Huckleberry Finn,* a book very like *Augie March* in obvious ways, is broken in the middle but still entrancing. There is something else wrong here. What? The question arises at many points in discussing the book, and the answer may lie not in its imperfections, but in a quality which it lacks.

The holiday nature of the book's composition is an attractive, if vexed, answer. (pp. 91-2)

[The] exuberance between the novel's lines often resembles the cry of a boy let out from school, and simple "liberation" (a word Bellow used for the writing of *Augie March*) is not necessarily a ticket to success. In his rejection of polish and tight, clear structure for episodic jaunting and steam-powered prose, Bellow obviously found this a delightful book to write. It has, in addition, many of the material ingredients of a great novel. But at that place in its creation where the imagination should have fired the material into life, a vagueness crept in.

If this vagueness is the problem, it surely must trouble our impressions of the novel's two central characters, Augie March and the city of Chicago. In the case of Augie, the borderline between his "opposition" and sheer passivity is too cloudy; his adventures all too clearly happen *to* him. The definition of character by negative action ("opposi-

tion" or passivity) leaves Augie uncertain about himself in very many ways and frustrates our search for that character among the details and behind the talk. The same can be said for Bellow's Chicago. He has said that, while writing the book, "Chicago itself had grown exotic to me," and the word "exotic" illuminates the difficulty we encounter. For all the portraits, caricatures, massive detail, and inside knowledge, his Chicago is not alive, like Dickens' London or Joyce's Dublin. The picture of the city is taken from a fascinated traveler's notebook.

Unfortunately—for the novel has many successes and spectacular potential—the man and his city have become their superficies. (p. 92)

> *David R. Jones, "The Disappointments of Maturity: Bellow's 'The Adventures of Augie March',"* in The Fifties: Fiction, Poetry, Drama, *edited by Warren French (copyright © 1970 by Warren French), Everett/Edwards, Inc., 1970, pp. 83-92.*

IRVING MALIN

In the stage directions [for *The Last Analysis*], Bellow indicates that the action of his play occurs in a "two-story loft in a warehouse. . . ." The setting seems perfectly ordinary. Is there, however, an additional meaning? Can we see the symbolism of the physical facts? The play, as we shall learn, deals with the various stories told (or retold) by the hero. These stories are "double" in effect because he needs in his present condition to create (or recreate) a new self— to shed his skin. He tells *certain* stories for his own mental well-being. "Loft." *Luftmensch* (remember Augie March). Left. I free-associate, but I think Bellow does the same. Surely, his play is about the "upper depths"—the phrase is his—and it ends, we should note, with a raising of the "arms in a great gesture." How can his hero *rise and fly?* What should he *leave* behind? These questions are at the heart of *The Last Analysis.* . . .

At curtain we discover Bummidge, the hero, "lying in the barber chair, completely covered by a sheet." Is he dead or alive? Will he be spruced up or embalmed? (Remember the endings of *Seize the Day* and *Mr. Sammler's Planet.*) We do not know right away. In this crazy environment, we cannot be certain of anything!

It is significant that the first words are spoken by an intruder, Winkleman, Bummidge's cousin. They are: "Imogen, where's my cousin?" Again, we sense symbolic meaning. This shrewd businessman (and keeper of the "law") does not know how to react to his location. It is, after all, loony. And, of course, Bummidge—called "Bummy" affectionately—does not really know where *he* is; he is looking for his true self.

Winkleman notes the television equipment, saying that it's "not the real thing." It is only "closed-circuit"—an interesting choice of words, which underlines the hero's sense of enclosure and his relative obscurity. (p. 116)

Bummy is comedian *and* analyst. When he looks at himself in the mirror—certainly, the entire proceedings are a kind of mirror: dream mirrors reality (and vice versa); the cousins mirror each other; the "action" mirrors the soliloquies —he shrewdly wonders: "Can people accept my message of sanity and health if I look like death or madness?" It is too early for decent answers. But he already reaches for "everyone" and "everything": "Heart, reason, comic spirit.'' He knows that he has to perform his own act despite the fact that the ''enterprise is bigger than me.'' (p. 117)

[Later] Bummy plays an even more difficult role. He is both patient and analyst; he wears glasses as analyst and removes them as patient. (The glasses suggest the distortions of the play itself.) As patient, he recounts dreams about swimming pools, old gentlemen; as analyst, he gives standard, trite readings of symbols. But these interpretations are limited because they fail to account for quirky differences. The point is clear: there must be more than ''breast castration, anxiety, fixation to the past.'' Bummy (as patient) screams: ''I am desperately bored with these things, sick of them.''

What can he do? He must recreate his ambivalences; he must *become his dreams*. Therefore, he again ''carries himself away''; he flies away from the present as he relives his childhood hostility toward his father. . . . He tries to get at the ''bottom'' of things. He is funny, of course, but he strangely echoes the heroic plights of Oedipus and, later, Christ—as well as Bellow's earlier and later protagonists. (p. 118)

Bummy moves beyond conventional role playing into a world of his own. He splits into fragments, but at least they are ''authentic'' (unlike the institutionalized ones of the business world). (pp. 118-19)

Bummy emerges as an artist. (Surely, there is a parallel between him and Bellow the playwright.) His art is crude—to say the least!—but it is in touch with realities. (p. 119)

Despite the desire of the [other characters] to use him—the parasite image is . . . underlined—Bummy exerts his sly strength and ''directs'' them. He ''ad libs'' their lines, not for materialist gain but for comic expression. He presents a play within the play. He has them perform roles that are, in a sense, more representative of their souls than their usual petty conspiracies. (pp. 119-20)

The ''Greek'' playlet they perform is *The Upper Depths, or the Birth of Philip Bomovitch*. It is trite and grand—as are all of our lives?—because it mixes language, characters, and events in a deliberately odd pattern. (pp. 120-21)

Bummy seems changed. When the playlet ends, he ''seems far removed from them all.'' He feels ''both old and new.'' He is Lazarus, Christ reborn—no wonder that his performance has ''wowed'' the supporting players and the audience, including the great impressario, Fiddelman!—but he must still live in *this world*. ''Something has happened.'' He floats.

Bellow could stop here, concluding his play on a *lofty* plane. But he is too serious to rescue his hero entirely. Thus, Bummy may tear up his new contract and toss out the others, but he lacks irony. He is ''over the edge'' as he hopes to build ''The Bummidge Institute of Nonsense.'' . . . Bummy is ''ready for the sublime'' as the play ends; we are not sure, however, that he can handle it (or that it is so easily available.)

We are ''double-crossed.'' We are sad because we recognize, even if Bummy doesn't, that there is no ''last analysis,'' no final moment of Truth. The comic work must continue! Bummy has somehow stopped—even though he talks about training programs for the Institute—and he lacks the ''mental comedy'' needed for higher elevation.

The final effect of *The Last Analysis* is mixed. We are uncertain whether or not to join Bummy as he ''saves the world''; we cannot merely laugh or cry. We dangle between different worlds—ours and his, Bellow's and his, Bellow's and ours. Surely, we do know one thing: we have been strangely touched by this powerful, shrewd, and funny play. (p. 121)

> Irving Malin, ''Bummy's Analysis,'' in *Saul Bellow: A Collection of Critical Essays, edited by Earl Rovit (copyright © 1975 by Irving Malin; reprinted by permission of Irving Malin), Prentice-Hall, Inc., 1975, pp. 115-21.*

EARL ROVIT

The problematic theme to which Bellow has been irresistibly drawn from *Dangling Man* to *Mr. Sammler's Planet* is that of trying to reconcile *virtue* with the fact of self-consciousness: can modern man attain ''dignity,'' can he live a ''good'' life when he must assume the traditional function of God, when he himself must judge his own frailties, cowardices, and ignoble motives? . . .

For Bellow, a story-line seems more than anything else a weblike scenario that he weaves more and more tightly around his captured protagonist; it is primarily a method of presenting the stifling power of the human predicament in order to measure his hero's ability to endure the harrowing weight of his own life. In effect, the typical Bellow plot is rarely more than a device to bring his protagonist and his reader into a heightened emotional awareness of the thin sliver of freedom that life permits to consciousness. In fact, one can readily imagine Bellow under different circumstances being perfectly comfortable as an eighteenth-century essayist—formidably intelligent, comprehensively ''liberal'' in a crisply satirical way, and slightly contemptuous of such errant frivolities as fiction. In Mailer's work, the story-line appears to be almost arbitrary and incidental to the sporadic pronouncements of ''truth'' that the continuity of events (usually encounters of violence and/or sex) provides for. . . . (p. 163)

[Although] Mailer can always be counted on for flights of verbal excitement . . . , and though Bellow conveys a brilliant stylistic exuberance in *The Adventures of Augie March* and in the first section of *Henderson the Rain King*, I think it fair to say that neither man has made any radical experimentation or exploration of the novel form itself. Perhaps both have been so vividly engrossed in *substance* —in the urgencies of the ideas that move them—that they have been tolerably satisfied to leave the conventional solutions of style and structure pretty much in the places where they found them. (p. 164)

Ultimately, and most concretely, the naturalistic tradition may help Bellow and Mailer to express their deepest sense of reality—to locate it, to strive to understand it, and to drive their total energies in an effort to articulate it. Here, I think, we may begin to discern the very different focuses of their work—here in their differing responses to a Dreiserian sense of reality. Both Bellow's and Mailer's earliest works (*Dangling Man, The Victim, The Naked and the Dead*) take for granted an objective reality that is essentially indifferent —if not actively hostile—to man; an utterly claustrophobic environment that can be adequately defined only in terms of interlocking power-relationships, within which Bellow's early heroes dangle as pathetic victims, and which Mailer's officers and infantrymen express in barely more than animal responses and as animated embodiments. From the beginning, Mailer's has been the harsher and more uncompromising point of view. . . . But Bellow (who has singled out *Jennie Gerhardt* as the novel that best illustrates Dreiser's power) never fully succumbed to the stark naturalistic view. Joseph, Leventhal, and Tommy Wilhelm are clearly victims, but they are victims who are intensely aware of themselves as victims. And it is precisely Bellow's commitment to the fact of their developed self-awareness that has led him to exploit the introspective space between history and personality—the precious human space in which morality, humor, grace, and creativity may conceivably exist. In fact, the steady current of development from Bellow's earliest work to his latest can be appreciated partially in terms of his painstakingly honest efforts to widen that space between—to present victim-man with valid opportunities to enlarge his human capacities. Augie, Henderson, Herzog, and Sammler are continually victimized, but they are not victims; for want of a better descriptive term, we could call them "survivors." (pp. 164-65)

Bellow's survivors pick their way gingerly through the detritus of their experience, straining to maintain a precarious balance between the irrevocabilities of the past and the dwindling possibilities of the future. . . .

Bellow's work has developed along relatively traditional lines. Composed in a period of some thirty years, his individual fictions have a strong family resemblance to one another, and his thematic concern with the ambiguities of morality and personality has grown suppler and more tensile with his increasing craftsmanship. Along with this mastery, his later novels seem to breathe an air of richer repose; Bellow gives the impression of moving with larger ease and freedom through the bleak foreground of his own world as he gains confidence in the reality and value of the creative self-consciousness. One consequence of this, apparent in *Mr. Sammler's Planet,* is a greater receptivity to the possibilities of religious experience; however, a less happy by-product is the tone of acerbic self-righteousness that tinges that novel. Nevertheless, the steady publication of serious, well-wrought novels over a long period of time augurs well for their survival and suggests that Bellow's art will continue to grow and unfold with slow richness and quiet surprise. (p. 167)

> *Earl Rovit, in* Saul Bellow: A Collection of Critical Essays, *edited by Earl Rovit (copyright © 1975 by Earl Rovit; reprinted by permission of Earl Rovit), Prentice-Hall, Inc., 1975.*

SEYMOUR EPSTEIN

The failures of Western civilization and the pleasures of it spin out the thematic thread that runs through the novels under discussion here. As a theme, it is as worthy as any being worked in contemporary fiction, and proof of this is in the unity and persuasiveness of Bellow's *oeuvre* as compared to any of his contemporaries who might be considered at the same level of seriousness. (p. 36)

Bellow's first three novels—*Dangling Man* (1944), *The Victim* (1947), and *The Adventures of Augie March* (1953)—are interesting, varied, but essentially diverse in theme. *Augie March,* that large, trumpeting announcement of Self, is in many ways a prototype of Bellow's subsequent use of character, and of those juxtapositions that make a novelist com-

fortable and fecund within the enclosure of his fictional world. In any event, the major theme, as perceived and discussed in this essay, does not yet make an unequivocal appearance. *Augie March* ends with the proclamation:

> Look at me, going everywhere! Why, I am a sort of Columbus of those near-at-hand and believe you can come to them in this immediate *terra incognita* that spreads out in every gaze. I may well be flop at this line of endeavor. Columbus too thought he was a flop, probably, when they sent him back in chains. Which didn't prove there was no America.

But it is Bellow's named and occupied America will be investigated here.

Dr. Tamkin, a Mephisphelean swinger, whose "bones were peculiarly formed, as though twisted twice where the ordinary human bones was turned only once" . . . , is one of Bellow's early "reality instructors". In *Seize the Day* . . . , Bellow has this charlatan play the role of one of man's legendary bedevilers. He is Puck, the Pied Piper, Loki, the Devil, and Baron Munchausen rolled into one. He is a swindler, a healer, and a mythomaniac. He is a creature who has mutated into his queer form in order to survive in a rapidly deteriorating culture. His client-victim, a *Lumpen*-Faust with as many names as failures (Tommy will do), is the single natural *schlemiel* in Bellow's entire cast of losers. (pp. 38-9)

The symbol of Tommy as a failure is in some respects crude, since he was so obviously doomed to fail; but his failure is instructive at least in its causes if not in its tragic implications. He is society's dupe. He is the quintessentially *modern* failure. The particular manner of his failure(s) would have been impossible for his historical counterpart fifty years previous, or indeed at any other previous time in human history. . . . Almost everything about him is synthetic. *Almost* everything. The only genuine thing in Tommy's life is his capacity to suffer—and this is what *Seize the Day* is about: the suffering of a totally alienated man. In all his subsequent novels, Bellow hasn't limned this much overdramatized and overpublicized condition as truly and poignantly as he did in this novella written in 1956. (pp. 39-40)

Almost to escape the realizations of *Seize the Day,* Bellow sends his next hero-failure off to Africa to see if some restorative mightn't be discovered by poking around in primitive origins.

Eugene Henderson of *Henderson the Rain King* is a large, lumbering man—a bigger, wiser, braver, gentile Tommy—but a man who also wears his suffering heart on his sleeve, whose desire to do good, to "burst the spirit's sleep", is no less than that of his pathetic, New York predecessor. Bellow suggests that Henderson has set out on his journey because he has been afflicted almost to destruction by the antilife forces present in technological America. Unlike Tommy, he is familiar with the Western world's art and philosophy, but this cranky millionaire's suffering takes the form of a huge hunger rather than a thwarted ambition. There is a voice in him that is always chanting, *"I want, I want, I want!"*

Among the Arnewi tribe. Henderson learns the expression *gruntu-molani*—man-wants-to-live—and this is precisely what he has come to Africa for: to learn how to live: to submit his volcanic energy to some natural imperative. His failure is neither personal nor small, but general and colossal. In attempting to rid the Arnewi watering place of a plague of frogs, he explodes both frogs and retaining wall, destroying the resource and the pollution in one blast. (p. 40)

Henderson's impulse was his society's impulse to subdue nature, and he brought this impulse to peoples whose religions and customs were all shaped around the accommodation and placation of nature rather than its conquest. Far from benefiting from his Rousseauian adventures, he has loused up the natural balance where it did exist, and confirmed his own hopeless addiction to Western civilization's drug of humanism.

Henderson was published in 1959, *Herzog* in 1964. Between those two dates (in November 1963, to be exact) there appeared in *Encounter* an article by Bellow entitled "Some Notes on Recent American Fiction". In his comments on J. F. Powers's novel, *Morte d'Urban* (1962), Bellow finds deficiency in Powers's view of Self, because "there is curiously little talk of souls in this book about a priest. Spiritually, its quality is very thin." A look at the dates makes it clear that Bellow must have been working on *Herzog* at the time he wrote the article, and, of course, the views of a novelist-in-progress must be looked at with adjusted lens. Not every detraction need be a defense, but the two have more than a casual connection. Bellow goes on to say in his critique of *Morte d'Urban:*

> A man might well be meek in his own interests, but furious at such abuses of the soul and eager to show what is positive and powerful in his faith. The lack of such power makes faith itself shadowy, more like obscure tenacity than spiritual conviction.

Whether or not Bellow personally holds any traditional theistic views is not to be determined from his novels, but that "spiritual conviction"—or the dread of its disappearance—is to become a growing part of his creative life is easily demonstrable. His advocacy of the individual, or the Self, as announced in his *Encounter* article, and reiterated with increasing thematic centrality in all subsequent works, is not a nineteenth-century, Romantic view of Self (Moses Herzog's studies in romanticism lay in a closet, "eight hundred pages of chaotic argument"), but rather a new individuality as conceived through social awareness and a deepening sense of responsibility. (pp. 40-1)

Most Bellow heroes are men in the middle—and no one is more in the middle than Moses Herzog. His middleness is his agony—or so Bellow would have us believe—but is it possible to believe in the agony of a man who has the wit and the locution to address himself to Presidents, philosophers, spiritual leaders, scientists, new frauds, and old lovers? A man who styles himself a "suffering joker"? A man who feels enormously sorry for himself but agrees with the saying, "Grief, sir, is a species of idleness"?

Herzog is an intellectual and a teacher. His major unfinished work, *Romanticism and Christianity,* stands as a sad analogue of his other sad defeats, particularly his marital defeats. In his book he had tried to trace those religious and political innovations that had aspired to bring man into a more advantageous relationship with himself and his fellow

mortals; but it is critically, almost hysterically, apparent to Herzog that man is no better off now than he was a thousand years ago. The poison of historical hope has precipitated into the petty realization that he has been a bad husband and a bad father. People of Herzog's generation measure their failures not in terms of broken faith but in broken marriages. The Miltonic council of fallen angels takes place in the marriage counselor's office.

In *Herzog* it is sometimes difficult to know whether what one is hearing is a comic note in the despair or a desperate note in the comedy, but the fact that they are mingled in no way diminishes the sincerity of either. There is both desperation and comedy, and it is to be noted that the mixture is most pungent where the narration is most personal. *Herzog* is written in the first person. So is *Henderson*. And *Augie March*. And *Humboldt*. *Seize the Day* and *Mr. Sammler's Planet* are third-person novels, and in both instances the desperation far outweighs the comedy. Which would seem to indicate a greater degree of authorial self-consciousness working in the more personal form. That is not surprising, since the true fictional function of the first-person form is to give the creating mind the instantaneous freedom to turn on itself and reveal the mockery in every posture. (pp. 42-3)

Bellow's women are among the most misunderstood and castrating in all of literature. Not all his women, but those who do take on the bitch-role fairly sizzle in it. Madeleine is one of the angriest. She turns on Herzog with such hatred that one is prompted to go back and pick up the overlooked reasons for all that venom. There are a few hints that Herzog may have been sexually inconsiderate (or incompetent), and that he may have been equally inconsiderate in meeting Madeleine's intellectual needs, but these are rather inconclusive hints. What we are given to see most clearly is a picture of Herzog trotting devotedly after beautiful, blazing Madeleine, with her mixed religions and mixed ambitions.

There is a deliberate ironic comedy in the whole business of Madeleine's Catholic conversion, and in Herzog's being persuaded to try some religiosity himself in order to get better adjusted to Madeleine's nature. It serves to bring the failure of the last few centuries and the predicament of the modern intellectual, as personified in Herzog, into painful relief. The late twentieth-century's modality is not religious (even Madeleine gave it up after a while), but the history of religion becomes one more item in the intellectual's inventory of ideas. The fact that traditional religions have lost their force has not obviated man's need to feel a passionate faith in some higher order, intelligence, or idea that will do as medium through which one can seek transcendence.

Herzog's search for such an absolute was conducted in places other than heaven. There was (in Herzog's historical time) the Marxist hope, and that, for many, failed. There was the hope that through self-understanding (the Freudian dispensation) man would come considerably closer to civilized behavior; and that, too, seems to have failed. These various failures have urged Herzog from idea to idea, as well as from woman to woman, and marriage to marriage. (pp. 43-4)

These personal mistakes are bad enough in themselves, but in Herzog's eyes they are also symptomatic of some kind of world disarrangement. Madeleine is not just another woman unhappy in her marriage, but an historical correction officer sent to teach him a lesson. Mind will not substitute for instinct, and the great thoughts of three centuries are not worth a damn in bed, or in the daily rub of domestic life. Beginning again over the wreckage of marriages, religions, and world systems is just too much for a man weighted down with daily responsibilities and a still-operative sex life. The young are fortunately free of the first, and the old are thankfully (or regretfully) free of the second, and what the young and old make of it is examined in Bellow's next novel, *Mr. Sammler's Planet*.

In *Mr. Sammler's Planet* (1970) we learn from the outset that Elya Gruner, Mr. Sammler's faulty but faithful nephew, has been hospitalized with a dangerous condition, a threatening aneurysm. This condition becomes the pervasive symbol of the novel. Civilization, too, is suffering a dangerous condition, but the difference between Elya Gruner and civilization is that Elya's death will be immediately ascertainable while civilization's death may be protracted and disguised through countless convulsions.

Bellow is here posing the imminent death of an attitude as well as a man. Elya is no saint. He has been corrupted by the times. He has connections with the underworld in his profession as gynecologist, performing illegal abortions for Mafia money. And he has spoiled his children to the point of imbecility, allowing his daughter too much money and license, and his son too much time and whimsy. (pp. 44-5)

The significant point about these two costly parasites is that their peculiar existences require very large subsidies. Centuries of scientific and artistic cultivation have produced such strange fruit. Removing all monetary and moral necessity from their lives, Elya Gruner has made his family a showcase of the final corruption of the Puritan ethic.

Artur Sammler himself is a survivor. He is from another country and another time. He is keenly aware of the anachronistic nature of his survival. He knows better than anyone else that his sense of values is rapidly disappearing from the world around him. More, he is that old and has been through so much that he has cast himself in the role of disinterested observer. He has absolutely no hope of changing anything, and the combination of his own experience and his living obsolescence gives him a special vantage point which has indissoluble links to the past and an apocalyptic view of the future. (p. 45)

Bellow places Mr. Sammler in New York City, where the stresses and contradictions of society are at their most severe. If there is something wrong with our civilization, it will find its most extravagant expression in this city; and what Mr. Sammler finds most seriously wrong is the almost total attrition of humanism. The people he comes into contact with seem to have lost all faith in the future. The incident of the princely Negro pickpocket who exhibits himself to Mr. Sammler in the lobby of an apartment house in Manhattan (one of the most vividly effective scenes in recent fiction) is illustrative of the condition Bellow is defining. The national sin of racial injustice has gone on for too long, and the victims of that injustice no longer have patience with the slow processes of history. (p. 46)

Civilization, Bellow would appear to be saying, maintains itself by a consensus of values and a desire to project those values into the future. Here is the principal area of breakdown. "The ideas of the last few centuries are used up." On one hand you have the pleasure-seekers like Angela; on the other hand you have cynics like Lionel Feffer, the young man who uses his brilliance and organizational abilities to practice every con game going in the intellectual and/or investment market. For Lionel, intellectuality is no longer tied to the ideal of improving mankind, but to mere cleverness and kicks. Idealism is not simply dead, it is ludicrous.

The novel ends with the death of Elya Gruner, and his death is indicative of Bellow's pessimism. (pp. 46-7)

The cry of all Bellow heroes: to do good. But they are all pleasure-seekers as well, striving, stumbling pleasure-seekers. Indeed, some of the most brilliant insights in Bellow's novels spring from the loss of love or money. Bellow characters declare their hunger for spiritual transcendence, and their author plays with as many means as past religions and philosophies can supply; but while there's a scintilla of pleasure to be wrung from the body, that's where the body is—in good restaurants, in expensive clothes, in the arms of dream-sexy lovers.

Having brought his theme of Western civilization's bankruptcy to near-ultimate definition in *Mr. Sammler's Planet*, Bellow has little choice other than reiteration or new ground. In *Humboldt's Gift* he went for reiteration, but a peculiar kind or reiteration. Enough has been said already about Von Humboldt Fleisher and Delmore Schwartz to avoid the point here, but it doesn't really matter whether the character of Humboldt was modeled on Delmore Schwartz or not. Another prototype could have been found who would have evoked the *Zeitgeist* equally as well. Bellow's shuffling between that bright beginning and the frayed present adds nothing to an understanding or appreciation of either. Charlie Citrine is an aging Augie March, still the Chicago boy sitting down to the feast of life; but now the exotic dishes are all familiar, and instead of the marvelous appetite that stimulated the early Bellow *fressers* there's a definite dyspepsia souring the many pages of *Humboldt's Gift*.

Perhaps a clue is to be taken from what Charlie has to say about the dead Humboldt:

> He blew his talent and his health and reached home, the grave, in a dusty slide. He plowed himself under. Okay. So did Edgar Allan Poe, picked out of the Baltimore gutter. And Hart Crane over the side of a ship. And Jarrell falling in front of a car. And poor John Berryman jumping from a bridge. For some reason this awfulness is peculiarly appreciated by business and technological America. The country is proud of its dead poets. It takes terrific satisfaction in the poets' testimony that the USA is too tough, too big, too much, too rugged, that American reality is overpowering.
>
> (p. 48)

The imperious, hot-eyed women are here, and the "reality instructors" who teach the hero the difference between idealism and reality, and the inventory of dead ideologies, and the onomastic fireworks (Proust and Charlus . . . Wheeler-Bennett, Chester Wilmot, Liddell Hart, Hitler's generals . . . Walter Winchell, Earl Wilson, General Rommel, John Donne, T. S. Eliot, and many more, all on a single page!), but somehow there is no plangency in the recitation of these names. They seem to be there for their own sake. The former wives and the present lovers are still as demanding and castrating as ever, but their connection to the hero doesn't seem as organic. It's as if Charlie Citrine and his retinue occupy separate stages where each works out separate disillusions and destinies. Indeed, the whole novel seems more a dramatic *theory* of a life than a dramatic presentation of one. The clownishness and cultural detritus has finally clogged the fictional pipeline, and it wouldn't be too unfair to assume that this has come about through a general debilitation of the theme's vitality. The push is no longer strong enough to wash it all through. (p. 49)

Bellow—or any novelist—owes us no answers. That's an old story. But the novelist who has raised important questions owes us the integrity not to trivialize those questions by repetitive improvisations on a theme, no matter how adroit. So adept is Bellow's hand that one can read *Humboldt's Gift* with almost all the pleasure that previous Bellow novels have given . . . but when the book is put away there is a curious lack of residue; there is the feeling that these ideas and these people can yield no more.

But what they have yeilded is great. No contemporary American author has made his theme yield more. Historians must surely suffer from the plethora of means and materials at their disposal, and the very profusion must make a manageable perspective almost impossible to obtain. But if they would wish to know how it was in the hearts of men (and the discrimination is deliberate; Bellow is no feminist) in post-World War II America, there is no better single source than the novels of Saul Bellow. (p. 50)

> *Seymour Epstein, "Bellow's Gift," in* The Denver Quarterly *(copyright © 1976 by The University of Denver), Winter, 1976, pp. 35-50.*

*　　　*　　　*

BERRYMAN, John　　1914-1972

Berryman was an American poet, biographer, and editor. Along with Robert Lowell and Sylvia Plath, he led the confessional movement in modern poetry and is considered one of the twentieth century's most important poets. A striking feature of his verse is the combination of a strict stanzaic pattern with idiosyncratic language, a lively poetic voice, and emotionally intense, highly personal themes. Berryman's Dream Songs, which he worked on from 1964 until his death, are generally considered his most outstanding poetic achievement. The poet took his own life in 1972. (See also *CLC*, Vols. 1, 2, 3, 4, 6, 8, 10, and *Contemporary Authors*, Vols. 15-16; obituary, Vols. 33-36, rev. ed.; *Contemporary Authors Permanent Series*, Vol. 1.)

RANDALL JARRELL

[John Berryman] is a complicated, nervous, and intelligent writer whose poetry has steadily improved. At first he was possessed by a slavishly Yeats-ish grandiloquence which at its best resulted in a sort of posed, planetary melodrama, and which at its worst resulted in monumental bathos. . . . (p. 80)

[His latest poetry, "The Dispossessed"], in spite of its occasional echoes, is as determinedly individual as one could wish. Doing things in a style all its own sometimes seems the primary object of the poem, and its subject gets a rather spasmodic and fragmentary treatment. The style—conscious, dissonant, darting; allusive, always over- or under-satisfying the expectations which it is intelligently exploiting—seems to fit Mr. Berryman's knowledge and sensibility surprisingly well, and ought in the end to produce poetry better than the best of the poems he has so far written in it, which have raw or overdone lines side by side with imaginative and satisfying ones. (p. 81)

> *Randall Jarrell, in* The Nation *(copyright 1948 The Nation Associates), July 17, 1948.*

WILLIAM DICKEY

[It is] the quality of voice that dominates John Berryman's *His Toy, His Dream, His Rest*, the . . . book which extends and completes the *77 Dream Songs* of 1964. The annex is a good deal larger than the original building: there are 308 poems here, most of them following the three-stanza, eighteen-line pattern the earlier book established. They rhyme with some regularity; their line lengths vary considerably; sometimes they do and sometimes they do not run on.

But the statistics are only evasions, and will not characterize what the organized sprawl of the book is like or about. Berryman himself has given his own answer to the second question: "The poem then, whatever its wide cast of characters, is essentially about an imaginary character (not the poet, not me) named Henry, a white American in early middle age sometimes in blackface, who has suffered an irreversible loss and talks about himself sometimes in the first person, sometimes in the third, sometimes even in the second; he has a friend, never named, who addresses him as Mr Bones and variants thereof." I would be happy to believe all that . . . , but I really don't. Unless the protagonist of the dream songs is very close to being Berryman, as man and as poet, there seems little reason for his extraordinary language to exist.

That language does two things that seem to me unusual. First, it attempts a formal diction of poetry, with the compression and heightening such a diction normally implies, while at the same time remaining open to the largest possible range of the idioms of American speech. Second, the language attempts, within one continuous identifiable kind of formal poetic voice, to deal with a range of experience that is otherwise ordered only by the fact that it has some relationship to a central figure. The book seems to combine many elements of the journal and of the novel: its effort is not only to refute a boundary between public and private, but also to subvert distinctions of formal and spontaneous, to have both at once and to have them with equal force.

Such a possibility can come about only by rejecting the tug of the convention and establishing a pattern of consistent arbitrary forms. This Berryman does by reversing syntactical patterns, using subjunctive forms, crossing the arcane with the colloquial. . . . The invention of so personal a language makes it very difficult to distinguish between the speaker and the subject of the poem, especially when the subject is both human and continuously present. The effort is in any event an unnecessary one. If we recognize that the "I" of even the most intimate journal cannot be the identical "I" who writes it, we will have made all the differentiation that is required of us.

But if the poem is exceptionally personal, it is also still a world, it is inclusive. It has the unevenness that a world has: it is selfish, self-pitying, trivial, exalted, funny. It moves by its own laws, but they can be communicated. It sets entirely, entirely its own terms, and if they are sometimes maudlin and sometimes infuriating, they have still the power of great concentration and great consistency, and for that reason they are finally impressive and successful. (pp. 360-62)

William Dickey, in The Hudson Review *(copyright © 1969 by The Hudson Review, Inc.; reprinted by permission), Vol. XXII, No. 2, Summer, 1969.*

ROBERT F. MOSS

Through his spokesman Henry, the central character of the *Dream Songs*, Berryman articulated his view of literary criticism unequivocally: "—I can't read any more of this Rich Critical Prose, / he growled, broke wind, and scratched himself and left / that fragrant area. / When the mind dies it exudes rich critical prose." But Berryman exuded enough of this despised substance throughout his own career to fill a sizeable volume, and that, plus a handful of short stories, is what makes up *The Freedom of the Poet*. Assembled posthumously from a schema he left behind, the book includes sections on Elizabethan writers, other Europeans from Cervantes to Anne Frank, American fiction, poetry from England and America, stories, and general essays.

Even Berryman's detractors will have to concede that *The Freedom of the Poet* demonstrates an exceptional range and depth in the poet's cultural interests. (pp. 707-08)

The critical essays in this collection, which occupy the bulk of the volume, also lead us in and out of Berryman's other work, though much more obliquely than the stories. The poet's lifelong fascination with Freud (he was in analysis himself for quite some time) resulted in a good deal of surrealistic verse (*e.g.*, "The Traveller"). Unhappily, the many psychoanalytic interpretations in this collection are surrealistic too; that is, they are best described as textual distortions which obey the logic of dreams rather than rational discourse. An unintentionally funny critique of *The Diary of Anne Frank* turns that classically simple work into a Freudian cryptogram in which the most straightforward episodes must be treated as dark messages from the unconscious. Freud is invoked again in "Conrad's Journey," a reading of *Heart of Darkness* which ignores the conscious level of Conrad's dense and difficult text in order to fish for sexual imagery, all of it supererogatory. The student of Berryman's work will recall that Freudian excesses were a shortcoming in the poet's *Stephen Crane* (1951), a sporadically impressive biography.

The mixture of admiration and dissatisfaction one feels toward the Crane study reminds us of another critical commonplace about Berryman's work: its unevenness. The present volume is no exception. Not only are the essays of varying quality, but individual pieces often rock wildly back and forth from insight to absurdity. Berryman's panoramic reflections on Thomas Nashe, including the full sweep of Elizabethan prose narrative, are perceptive and convincing; however, they are also ignorant (Swift's *A Tale of a Tub* is described as unread) and wrong-headed (topical feuds are ruled out as a proper subject for literature, thus annihilating the heart of 18th century letters). The poet's ruminations on Cervantes and Thomas Hardy are equally spotty. He is at his worst in the incoherent "Despondency and Madness:

On Lowell's 'Skunk Hour'"; he stumbles blindly through the Lowell poem, bumping into symbols and themes as he goes, explicating nothing.

Turning to the other side of the ledger, Berryman's gifts as a critic are best displayed in his commentaries on Shakespeare, Isaac Babel, and a number of American writers. Much of his strength lies in a combination of scholarly thoroughness, sensible, cant-free critical judgments, and an unusual catholicity of taste and mind. (pp. 709-10)

Although Berryman's observations about his own poetry are unilluminating, and even misleading, he has some discerning thoughts on his contemporaries. From the vantage point of the seventies, one can appreciate Berryman's astute complaints during the forties about the "Auden Climate," whose deadening effects he perceives in John Ciardi, Howard Nemerov, and others. In a more positive vein, we are astounded by his prescience in celebrating Henry Reed's newly published "Naming of Parts," destined to become one of the few post-war English poems that is widely read. (p. 710)

[The] tone of these essays, like most of the work in *The Freedom of the Poet*, is highly personalized—the loves and hates are set forth emphatically. Thus, Hemingway's "A Clean, Well-Lighted Place" emerges as a "short, almost desperate and beautiful story," while Ring Lardner's stories "convey a perpetual effect of going behind an appearance—perpetual, and cheap, because the appearance is not one that could have taken in an experienced man for five minutes: the revelation is to boobs." In fact, one senses that *The Freedom of the Poet* is constantly striving toward the status of art, embodying not only a distinctive voice (one is tempted to say a speaker or persona) but also flourishing the kind of prose that recalls Berryman's verse. As he cultivated a repertoire of poetic styles (flat and conversational, surreal, allusive and symbolic), here he shifts restlessly from the colloquial to the meditative to the lyrical. (pp. 710-11)

Surveying his own critical accomplishment just before his death, Berryman exulted, "Hurrah for me: my prose collection is going to be a beauty." If *The Freedom of the Poet* has more blemishes than Berryman realized, it nevertheless comes to us at a time when works of literary criticism, whether handsome or homely, are one of the more endangered species in the publishing world. The author has earned his hurrah. (p. 711)

Robert F. Moss, "Berryman's Last Hurrah," in Virginia Quarterly Review *(copyright, 1976, by Virginia Quarterly Review, The University of Virginia), Vol. 52, No. 4 (Autumn, 1976), pp. 707-11.*

JOEL CONARROE

I think what strikes any reader of Berryman is how very self-conscious an artist he is: he practices a self-conscious craft, he achieves a self-conscious and deliberate range, he is almost arrogantly self-conscious in his use of the personal. He knows precisely what he wants to accomplish and how to accomplish it. He also knows how very much of his material has to be shaped by the dark turbulence of the human psyche.... Out of the insecurities and disorders and disasters of his life, he constructs with mathematical care what may be the most mature poetry of the twentieth century. (pp. xi-xii)

Berryman, who was in love with form, recognized early on that form gains in power as it is tested. Form, order, harmony—the cohering principles—are attractive but in their purest states not necessarily characteristic of high art. The totally harmonious work, pleasant enough, can be and frequently is dull. On the other hand, out of the conflict between form and formlessness, order and disorder, harmony and the inharmonious can come work of extraordinary intensity. . . . [Study] taught him that the most effective forms are those that can be forced into flexibility, forms with perimeters elastic enough to provide maximum "stretch," maximum tension.

The job of the artist is to cram into such forms accurate representations of feeling. Under pressure, his works will seem almost—but not quite—to explode. The explosion, when it takes place, is within the consciousness of the audience. (p. xii)

Berryman tackles all the big subjects: the big emotions (love, friendship, hatred, fear, passion, anger), the big intellectual concerns (politics, race relations, the value of history, the nature of art), the big spiritual questions (the 'reality' of a God, the significance of good and evil, the function of sin and redemption). (p. xv)

Berryman inhabits his characters and—much more important—so do we. Precisely because they are so full of private stuff, they remind us of ourselves. Because Berryman accepts his own stubborn self and *uses* it, Berryman forces us to participate in and to share that self.

In recognizing this paradox—that the unique individual is in fact everyman—Berryman is freed to take liberties that in lesser writers lead to pointlessly 'confessional' writing. But confession—'exposure'—is the last thing Berryman is interested in. Truth, on the other hand, is something that means a great deal to him. By turning the events of his life into significant fictions—by being both himself and his 'other'—he is able to let us also discover truth, not truth about Berryman but truth—to hover on the edge of a dangerous phrase—about our own being and about the nature of being itself. (p. xix)

The Berryman selections [in *Five Young American Poets* (1940) are] ominous, flat, social, indistinctly allusive, exhausted. . . . [The twenty poems] give clear evidence of his literary debts (the collection is an echo chamber) as well as of his slavish adherence to conventional forms. A typical Berryman poem of the period organizes itself into stanzas, often of eight or nine lines, with a carefully worked out rhyme scheme. There is a pervasive, generally stultifying reliance on iambic pentameter; some of the work seems to have been composed by a well-programmed computer with Weltschmerz. The speaker, typically, is seated in a room at dusk, alone in thought, brooding about the dangerous reality beyond his walls, all the while making disturbing connections between this public world, with its nightmarish history and uncertain future, and his own private world, haunted by fears and spectres. Certain images appear over and over, invariably related to disease, darkness, fear, exhaustion, inaction, sleeplessness. (p. 25)

"Winter Landscape," the best known of the works in this selection, provides good examples of both the virtues and shortcomings of Berryman's early voice. A commentary on Peter Brueghel's "Hunters in the Snow," it is tightly organized into five-line stanzas, all in regular iambic pentameter,

with two seemingly random rhymes. It is actually in blank verse, with stanza breaks serving to reinforce the impression of parts making up a whole, appropriate in a poem modelled on a painting. Since the poem is composed in one flowing sentence (a colon near the middle separates the details of presentation from the philosophical speculations that emerge), one reads the lines as one might look at the painting, the eye moving rapidly from detail to detail and not coming to a complete rest until the composition has been seen in its entirety.

Although its general intentions are admirable (Berryman was responding to Yeats' seductive rhetoric and to the hysterical political atmosphere of the period) the work is flawed by a ponderous, sententious tone. . . .

The pamphlet [*Poems* (1942)] as a whole, which is very curious, serves to illustrate both the ways in which Berryman's poetry at this stage of his career is utterly unexceptional and the kinds of inhibitions he had to break through to discover an original style. *Poems* has practically no voice at all; it could have been written by any one of a score of post-Yeats-Eliot-Auden writers confronting the political realities of 1939. The reason for this absence of a unique presence, of a special language, is that the poet, dealing with ideas and politics, almost wholly ignores his feelings. (p. 29)

Certain characteristics that dominate the work help account for its sterility. One is the introduction of topical events that assumes a conditioned response from the politically sympathetic reader. . . . Another, borrowed from Yeats ("Did she put on his knowledge with his power / Before the indifferent beak could let her drop?") is the significant unanswered question that has as its principal function the resurrection of sagging lines. . . .

Another verbal mannerism, learned from Auden, is the capitalized abstraction: "Our Man of Fear," "the God Exaggeration," "The Hero." There are phrases throughout the book which, if not quite clichés, are flat, tired, ordinary. (p. 30)

[One] gets the impression of a sensibility that is blocked off from a sense of its personal needs, that speaks instead for a generation. For all his references to heartbreak, fear, sorrow, and hate the poem's speaker appears to be far more aware of civic woe than of his own. It is hard to believe that this voice would modulate into that of Henry Pussycat, a creature for whom nothing in the world is more important, newsworthy, or in an odd way, universal than his own private sorrows. Poetry of feeling, of course, is not necessarily more powerful than poetry of social awareness, but it is clearly more compatible with Berryman's gifts. It took him a great many years to realize this. He was in his early work as thoroughly the product of the Age of Anxiety as he was later on the product, and victim, of the Age of Catharsis. (pp. 31-2)

The sense of hopelessness about the state of the world comes through unambiguously in poem after poem [in *The Dispossessed*]. (p. 32)

Images of night run persistently through this gloomy book, and relate to the brooding sensibility at its center. He associates sunlight and daytime with art, the spirit, and the intellect. Night and darkness are related to the disturbances of man, be they political or sensual (though at this point in

Berryman's work the senses are still in harness). And there are so many occasions of night falling or of a night wind rising that these devices finally function as a sort of *deus ex nocturna*, a way of giving resonance and mystery to lines that otherwise might remain coldly intellectual. . . . (p. 33)

In addition to sharing repeated, ritualistic, lighting and sound effects, the lines are also indistinguishable rhythmically; any one stanza could be substituted for any other without causing the slightest structural disruption. This is revealing, since it points up just how conventional Berryman's rhythms are at this point, and since rhythm, more than anything else, is what distinguishes one poet from another, just how conventional a poet he was. . . . Nevertheless, the book is technically interesting and even shows flashes of originality. This is because of Berryman's versatility in the use of stanzaic patterns and because of his extraordinarily skillful use of complex rhyme schemes, many of which employ approximate rhymes to good effect. (p. 34)

Berryman at this stage was most comfortable . . . with the Yeatsian eight-line stanza. . . . This stanza, like the octave of a sonnet, affords both rigorous formal constraints and room for considerable flexibility, permitting the technically facile craftsman to create the illusion of freedom within a rigorously circumscribed space. . . . [It] is understandable that he chose it for *Homage to Mistress Bradstreet*. The work of *The Dispossessed*, moreover, looks ahead even further in time: the nine "Nervous Songs" (inevitably, for one especially responsive to the later Berryman, the most successful section of the book) introduce for the first time the extended sonnet that was to become the vehicle of the *Songs*, the eighteen-line lyric composed of three self-contained but fluid six-line stanzas. (pp. 34-5)

Reading straight through *The Dispossessed* one moves suddenly from language that is lucid, uncluttered, rather fluid, into passages that are clogged, wrenched, often tortured—a dizzying leap from diction that resembles sometimes Yeats and sometimes Auden to that suggesting, more than anyone else, Hopkins. The difference is largely one of compression (again looking toward *Mistress Bradstreet*), which, coupled with a jagged cacophony, sometimes makes for difficulties of interpretation. A few of the poems, notably "The Long Home" and "Narcissus Moving," are incomprehensible, largely because Berryman has not yet honed the complex new language to his purposes. Others ("A Winter-Piece" and "The Dispossessed" for example) are uneven, the shifting language occasionally working brilliantly, sometimes remaining private and unduly obscure. Since these strange poems help prepare the way for the later sequences, one welcomes them. Their value, however, is historical rather than aesthetic. (pp. 35-6)

Whatever their relative merit, [the poems of the second section of *The Dispossessed*] are important poems in the early Berryman canon; they represent a breakthrough of the most crucial sort, involving a willingness to let the senses play some part in his life as a poet. (p. 41)

[In the three love poems of Section IV of *The Dispossed*] Berryman demonstrates absolute control of terza rima, transcending its technical restrictions to create an effect that is fluid and open. The tone is consistently affectionate without ever lapsing into sentimentality, and the diction is sharp, interestingly quirky rather than strained. The image patterns of light and darkness, heat and cold, storm and

quiet, and of "new musics," are elegantly worked out and coalesce in a way that is engagingly solemn and luminously clear. (p. 43)

[In addition to the love poems] the other major achievement of *The Dispossessed* [is] the sequence of nervous songs [in which] Berryman for the first time adopts the dramatic mode. The nine soliloquies are spoken by an odd collection of men and women who seem on the surface to have little in common but who are actually variations on a single type. They are solitary figures, and all are slightly (or not so slightly) neurotic, agitated, living on the edge of breakdown, confused, tormented, obsessed. Their songs are "nervous" in that they express emotional tension, restlessness, agitation—a disordered state of the nerves. . . . Though some are more effective than others, the nine poems stand as a compelling series of psychological studies. In its form, the three six-line stanzas with flexible rhyme schemes, and in its mood of intense auto-revelation, the sequence is an important forerunner of *The Dream Songs*. (p. 45)

The 115 poems [in *Berryman's Sonnets,* published in 1967, twenty years after they were composed] are the record of a story "Knock-down-drag-out love," and as such they represent, in their confessional intensity and personal imagery, a major departure from the work of *The Dispossessed*. (pp. 51-2)

Since the sonnets contain patterns of recurring imagery, themes, characters, and settings, there is a temptation to find in the sequence a carefully worked out organizational plan. Any such strategy, however, would be in the mind of the reader rather than of the poet. The poems are diary entries (and love letters) chronicling events and emotions over which the poet has little control. They chart a love affair over a period of several months, and as such the highs and lows are determined by the course of the relationship rather than by the exigencies of literary form. There is a gently unobtrusive temporal framework, worth noticing but not, ultimately, terribly important. (p. 62)

Since the poems were, apparently, written in the order in which they appear, there are occasionally illuminating transitions and continuations, as one sonnet picks up an image, or carries forward a dialogue, or suggests a response to the poem that precedes it. (pp. 63-4)

The final four poems also form a small, unified section, serving, after the erotic intensities that make up most of the book, to bring the sequence to a gentle conclusion. . . . At the end of number 115 we see that the experience of the liaison is the source of creative energy, more important to the poet, perhaps, than is the relationship itself. . . . (pp. 64-5)

[The sequence] is important in the development of Berryman's craft because for the first time, in any really substantial way, he drops the mask of neutral objectivity, abandons the cool, slightly exhausted and more than slightly derivative voice, and emerges as a unique man who records his own sensibility in a voice that, at least in the strongest, truest sonnets, is recognizably his own. . . . It is the experiments with colloquial language, slangy, often inelegant, hot off the heart, going directly to a feeling without attempting to sublime it into formal art, that give this book of utterly conventional structures its unconventional power and importance. (pp. 65-6)

The seeds of the so-called confessional mode can clearly be discovered in [the sonnets]. Much of their quirky strength and odd appeal derive from the sort of vulnerability that makes it necessary for their creator to play games with himself, to adopt masks as a way of separating himself . . . from some of his darker, perhaps even weaker, personal qualities, though these are invariably revealed. . . . (p. 67)

So the voices—the formal and the vernacular—alternate, respond to each other [in the *Sonnets*] together suggesting the nature of the speaker in ways neither could do by itself. The careful, stately lines, grievous and sublime, would be impressive but ultimately dull without the nervous interruptions of the Groucho mode—the puns, bawdy jokes, word play, self-deflating epithets, outlandish diction, personal anecdotes. If the sequence suffers from this slightly schizophrenic behavior it is not because the voices interrupt each other too often, but because they do not do so often enough. *The Dream Songs* is an eccentric masterpiece precisely because the vernacular mode is given full play, the exuberant persona permitted totally to crowd out the more conventional aspects of his sensibility when there are reasons for this to happen. In the *Sonnets* the disreputable side of the lover is still held in check; it threatens on occasion to burst forth in all its inventive vitality, but Berryman was not yet quite prepared to run the risks of such public behavior. (p. 68)

His beautiful tribute [*Homage to Mistress Bradstreet*], long in the making (he accumulated details for nearly five years), was the result of a total immersion in the work of the Puritan poet [Anne Bradstreet] and of the history of Colonial America. It has about it, as a result, an authority and a degree of erudition that both attracted and puzzled readers at its first appearance in *Partisan Review* in 1953. . . . The poem was published without notes and with no introductory apparatus, and as a result the demands it made were very rigorous indeed. (p. 69)

With the publication of this book [Berryman] suddenly and spectacularly emerged as a major figure in contemporary letters. (p. 70)

The poem's stanza is composed of eight highly compressed lines filled with jagged rhythms, puns, repeated words, assonance, allusions, rhetorical climaxes, rhymes, and slant rhymes. The rhythms and the rhyme schemes vary subtly from stanza to stanza, but all the stanzas, or virtually all, share certain characteristics. In all but two (and in these the absence of closure is significant) the first and final lines rhyme, thus giving each small unit, even those eleven without end punctuation, a sense of self-containment. The first and last lines of the final stanza end with the word "loves," the repetition producing a sense of resolution even firmer than that created by rhyme. Each stanza is thus a small push forward, the momentum slowed briefly before the insistent advance begins again.

This overall sense of acceleration and retardation is reinforced by the measure of the individual lines and by frequent punctuation. In each stanza the first two lines, often fairly regular iambic but in any case containing five strong stresses, give way to the shorter third line, made up of three stresses, so that the initial motion is brought to a semi-halt. The momentum then increases gradually in the fourth line, of four stresses, accelerates in the fifth and sixth, which have five stresses each, and is then again

balked in the short seventh line, an echo of the third, with three stresses, often in as few as four words. The conclusion then resolves the sense of flow and stasis with a long line, six stresses, that moves slowly and deliberately, resembling nothing so much as an alexandrine, toward the final word, with its small resolution. What Berryman was seeking in this stanza was "something at once flexible and grave, intense and quiet, able to deal with matter both high and low." (pp. 71-2)

The measured, tentative quality of the language is suited to the drama it records, a dialogue taking place, out of time and out of space, between two poets, one living, the other, summoned from the past, shimmering for an intense duet and then disappearing. . . . The work is a variation on and at the same time a reversal of the sonnets, the one of celebration of art, of the power of the imagination to transcend the limitations of the flesh, the other a celebration, one meant to be private, of a physical relationship that could never achieve public sanction. The works are essentially products of the two Berrymans, the man and the artist; some of the intensities of his "respectable" seduction of the spirit of Anne Bradstreet derive from the experience, which he was unable to reveal explicitly, of his adulterous affair with Lise [the persona's love interest in the *Sonnets*]. (pp. 72-3)

The poem's final four stanzas make up a coda, or peroration, in which Berryman's voice reappears, bringing several of the work's images together in a beautifully cadenced conclusion.

The first four stanzas describe a resurrection, the final four a burial, and these related sections, narrated with high seriousness by a deeply moved poet, comprise an elegant frame for the poem. This pairing of parts is repeated in the long second and fourth sections, the halves of Bradstreet's monologue, which are separated by the passionate dialogue of section three. Thus the work as a whole is in the shape of an arch, the line of descent reversing the line of ascent (Berryman, Bradstreet, dialogue, Bradstreet, Berryman), giving the poem an overall form and sense of closure that help account for its aesthetic power. Were the two Bradstreet sections of equal length the sense of classical harmony would be even more pronounced, though it is right that the second monologue, concerned with decay and dissolution, should be shorter in duration than the first one, which creates a sense of the new world settled by the pilgrims. (pp. 73-4)

[Berryman] is clearly more interested in [Anne Bradstreet's] rebellion than in her extraordinarily dull work; she manifested in her life the sort of tough-minded independence that she never achieved in her poetry. He has shown her in a series of defiant moments, rebelling against youthful virtue, the new environment, an arranged marriage, her barrenness, her confinement to household duties, a life of illness and loss, and against God's will. The submission, or capitulation, that follows each of these brave moments establishes one of the basic rhythms of the poem, that is, a sequence of alternating assertions and defeats. (p. 81)

What is most impressive is the way he manages to create, out of shards, borrowed images, Hopkinsesque rhythms, and his own imagination, a language that so effectively evokes the atmosphere—social, religious, political—of her era. . . . [As Hyatt Waggoner says in *American Poets from the Puritans to the Present*] "In Berryman's poem we get the existential life that is generally buried under the theology and borrowed imagery of Mrs. Bradstreet's own verse writing." (p. 82)

The *77 Dream Songs,* published in 1964, were written before nearly all of the songs that appeared four years later in *His Toy, His Dream, His Rest;* some of the later work, in fact, comments on responses to the earlier book. The poems, however, are not for the most part placed in the order in which they were composed, nor are they organized around any clearly delimited period of time, such as a year in Berryman's life. . . . [Although] we know that Berryman wrote songs for eleven years we do not know how much "internal" time elapses between the first section and the last, nor is the question either very important or very interesting. (p. 87)

Each [section] suggests in microcosm the overall pattern of the work as a whole, moving from a prying open to a resolution, from imagery of arrival and spring to that of departure and autumn. Each ends with a sense of summing up, a moment of stasis, and it is this stasis, or suspension of process, that the beginning of each section disrupts in images of renewal. To be specific, section one, which begins with images of the sea (invariably associated with Berryman's parents), of an oyster (or coffin, or patient) "pried open," and of a bird in a sycamore, closes twenty-five poems later with a song that reintroduces the singing bird motif ("The glories of the world struck me, made me aria, once") and that then suggests, symbolically, an end of singing: "—I had a most marvellous piece of luck. I died." If the work is to continue there clearly must be some sort of resurrection or rebirth. The opening poem of the second section satisfies this necessity, bringing the work back to life with the lush line, "The greens of the Ganges delta foliate." "Green" appears in each of the three stanzas, accounting for the poem's vitality. To leave no doubt, moreover, about whether the sequence has been resurrected, the song ends "while good Spring / returns with a dance and a sigh." The new section, despite its promising beginning, is filled with images of loss and death, and by its final poem the dance of Spring has given way to "dwarfs' dead times" and to seas that, far from being fructuous and life-giving, are "remorseless." (pp. 87-8)

The final poem of *77 Dream Songs* (and thus of section three), though set "in a world of Fall," actually sounds like an opening song, and with good reason, since too strong a sense of closure at this point would block the poet's (and Henry's) options. And so Berryman indicates, in assertive images, that though this book is finished there is more to come. . . . He is barely getting started, a fact borne out by the publication, four years later, of *His Toy, His Dream, His Rest.*

Section four, the "Op. Posth." poems that introduce the new volume, continues this reversal of the ascent-descent scheme, its opening song, number 78, dealing not with renewal and spring but with physical and mental diminution, with castration and decay. . . . (pp. 89-9)

[Book five] documents a symbolic faring forth or resurrection—Henry, suffocating in his hospital room, yearning for oblivion, and still as his cadaver, nevertheless "waking to march." A new series is thus initiated. The book ends fifty-three songs later with a suicide. It is not

Henry who seeks the grave this time, however, but his father. . . . The song ends, like section three, with the assurance of more to come, but the detailed images of the successful suicide create a strong sense of finality. The placement of these opening and closing songs is always anything but arbitrary. (pp. 89-90)

The book ends, in the fall, with references to Henry's house and to the sea (bringing the work full cycle), and with the beautifully resonant final words, "my heavy daughter." . . . [It] is not possible to imagine a reopening of the *Songs* after number 385, so absolute is the sense of closure.

[Henry] has suffered an "irreversible loss," we learn in the note to *His Toy, His Dream, His Rest,* and though we never find out exactly what this is, the evidence suggests that it is related to his father's suicide, the loss that "wiped out" his childhood and filled his adult life with dread and rage. Henry himself is suicidal, often so anxious and depressed that he can barely make through the night. (p. 93)

Confronted with such loathing and suicidal despair, noteworthy even in a generation of depressives, it is possible to overlook the somewhat gentler sides of things. If one of Berryman's sources is Rilke, the great poet of death, he was also deeply affected by "Song of Myself," that great poem of life. Henry is a complex sensibility who at odd moments even sees himself as gentle, friendly, savage & thoughtful, happy & idle, imperishable. . . . His highs, like his lows, are extreme, not surprising in a performer addicted to self-dramatization, and, like all theatrical personalities, given to bursts of melodrama, hyperbole, and uninhibited self-revelation. He is, moreover, addicted to autotherapy, and the songs represent, as much as anything else, attempts to get his dreams, memories, and fears out in the open as a means of coming to grips with them, of escaping their tyranny. (I say Henry and mean Berryman. I think that anyone who reads the songs carefully will reject the assertion that they are about an imaginary character—some details, of course, are invented, but the sequence adheres closely to the facts of the poet's life and mind.) . . . [Many] of these songs, in their wit and high spirits, ward off the horror that is their source. (pp. 94-5)

The reader, willing or not, becomes a participant in [a] therapeutic process, sitting as silent auditor and monitoring the material in an effort to discover and understand its mysteries and patterns. . . . [The reader] may discover what it feels like to *be* Henry, how it feels, literally, to want to jump out of one's skin. It is because such a reader, secure in the quiet of his home, can get outside Henry by an act of spiritual migration (rather than by leaping from a bridge) that this dangerous book is ultimately liberating and even protective. Our lives are all potentially disastrous, and artists like Berryman and Lowell who live perilously close to the abyss make it possible for us to journey over threatening terrain, to experience its terror, and to return intact. Literature does not tell us anything; it permits us to participate in a life, to share an angle of vision, and often to make some crucial personal discoveries. In courting certain kinds of disaster, Henry spares us the necessity of doing so for ourselves, overpowering as the attractions sometimes are. (pp. 95-6)

A charge frequently levelled at Berryman is that many of his songs are . . . impenetrable, so that even the most rigorous analysis fails to yield up their secrets. . . . A poem is not a puzzle to be solved, and in any case no amount of footnoting or explication will communicate the power of an intricate song if one is not attentive, first of all, to its sound and shape. There are indeed many passages in Berryman (as there are in Pound and Joyce) that remain baffling, and perhaps impenetrable, even after numerous readings, but if one is responsive to the general spirit of Henry's language and if one listens attentively to the music these should not finally undermine significantly the delight to be derived from the work. (p. 96)

When Berryman errs on the side of easy generalizations his work invariably goes flat. He is much more effective when he requires his reader to be an imaginative collaborator, when he provides provocative hints and clues rather than bald declarations.

The extraordinary technical dexterity demonstrated over and over in the more successful songs reveals just how gifted and versatile a craftsman Berryman was. In moving from the sonnets to *Homage to Mistress Bradstreet* he had shifted from one rigidly inhibiting form to another. . . . For the dream songs he created a form which, while also quite regular (so that any variations are highlighted), permits even more flexibility, more of the sort of raffishness that he could never resist.

Resembling extended sonnets, the songs are composed of three sections of six lines each, the stanzas separated by white space. There are, within this regular pattern, endless possibilities for variation, and since Berryman has chosen not to close off his options (songs about dreams should, after all, have at least some of the freedom of dreams), virtually any assertion about formal characteristics can be challenged. . . . While the eighteen-line pattern is plainly the standard on which all structural variations are played, the norm for the work's measure, line by line, is more difficult to determine, the variety being greater, the repeated patterns less predictable. More often than not, however, the words fall into iambs, hundreds of lines being as regular as anything in Frost or Yeats. . . . (pp. 106-07)

What is especially absorbing about [Song 224, ''Eighty,'' for example], and what accounts for its beauty, is the series of elegant variations wrought within the regular framework. (p. 109)

If [Song 224] is quite representative of Berryman's rhythmical strategies, it is, in its elaborate formal organization, rather atypical, most of the poems giving the impression (though it is often just that) of a movement more spontaneous, more dreamlike, less deliberately plotted. (p. 111)

The flaws in the songs generally result either from a dormant imagination (so that the language sounds tired rather than newly minted) or from a reaching for an effect that doesn't quite come off. . . . [It] is not surprising to find in a work of nearly four hundred pages some lapses in intensity and invention. Particularly in the sequence in which Delmore Schwartz is eulogized inspiration seems to fail, and this suggests that Berryman was able to deal more eloquently with general sorrow, especially involving himself, than with a specific loss. The tone tends to be flat and petulant rather than deeply felt. . . . (p. 117)

Since the seven books that make up the work are at best occasionally flawed and at worst extremely uneven, every reader is likely to become his or her own godlike editor,

identifying those songs that should definitely be included in a slimmed-down version of the book. My own view is that a rather large number, particularly in Books V and VI, perhaps as many as fifty in all, could be dropped without any great loss to the overall work. *The Dream Songs* gets off to a stunning beginning, the first fifty songs being, line by line, richer, denser, and more complex than any other comparable section. Books III and IV, if not so consistently brilliant as the first two, maintain a high level. The fifth book, with some notable exceptions, shows a marked falling off. Things improve in VI, the longest of the sections, which contains a large number of superb pages as well as many that are relatively flat and loose, the density of imagery in the early sections replaced by an easier prosiness. Book VII is the most unified, the most novelistic, and in many ways, especially in its combination of lucidity and eloquence, the strongest of the sections. It completes the poem in a fashion worthy of its remarkable opening. (p. 118)

[Would not] deletions, however, interfere with the movement and thematic coherence of the individual sections, not to mention the organizational integrity of the work as a whole? I do not think so. Berryman did not have anyone to do for *The Dream Songs* what Pound did for (and to) *The Waste Land,* nor did he, like Whitman, continue to revise and edit his song of himself after its initial publication. (pp. 119-20)

It is not very surprising that [*Love & Fame*] was attacked and misunderstood. The first edition contains something to offend nearly everyone. The unprecedented exhibitionistic revelations of the first two sections, moreover, caused unsympathetic readers to overlook the later poems, which quietly but effectively undercut the hubris of the earlier parts. In the 7,000 lines of the *Songs* Berryman is able to say the most intimate and outrageous things. Since he is speaking through Henry, however, a reader, even if he makes little distinction between poet and persona, can attribute and especially shocking excesses to the imaginary character. (p. 151)

Whether the six poems [Berryman] deleted from the second edition are disgusting is a matter of taste, but that they are inferior to the other work in the book is indisputable. One is surprised not that they were deleted but that they were ever included in the first place. (p. 152)

The question of reinforced and undercut motifs is of particular importance in this book since the poems derive much of their point and all of their irony from a careful patterning of the sequence as a whole. . . . [The book] takes a dramatic turn at the beginning of section three, progressing from the poet's randy and confident young manhood to his depressed present, from ribald skirt-chasing and self-promotion to a humble series of prayers to God, who judges a man's merit not by his verses but by his virtue. (pp. 153-54)

With part three, however, we leave behind all the discoveries and pretensions, the hubris and awkwardness, the hope and energy. The poet now focuses exclusively on the present, and it is very grim indeed, any illusions of love and fame, as they exist in the earlier parts, disappearing completely. . . . [This] section, the richest and most moving of the four, has considerable thematic range, far more than any other. It is constructed as a descent into the dark night of the soul that is followed by a gradual recovery, or, to use a word that figures importantly in two of the later poems, by *survival*. (pp. 158-59)

Many of the poems [in *Love & Fame*], particularly in the first two parts, are prosy and free. One generally gets the sense of a voice talking naturally, informally, without embellishment, the phrases produced by the breath and by the details that make up the telling rather than by adherence to a rhythmical norm. (p. 168)

There are a few poems in the book that have fairly conventional rhythmical patterns—that is, they can be scanned— and these contrast dramatically with the work's more representative idiomatic passages. Some of the more regular poems are deceptive, seeming at first to strive for a sing-song regularity that doesn't quite fall into place, that sounds, in fact, more chaotic than harmonious. If the lines are read aloud several times, however, one begins to hear underlying rhythms which, anything but clumsy, are hauntingly beautiful. (pp. 168-69)

[However,] there are passages here and there in the book that are technically weak. These lapses are anything but unobtrusive, and yet they do not really account for the fact that *Love & Fame* has been almost universally reviled, regarded more often than not as a sequence of poetic mistakes that should never have been published. There are, I believe, two principal reasons for this low critical esteem. The work, first of all, unlike *Mistress Bradstreet* and *The Dream Songs,* is not a good seminar text, and a generation of teachers and critics responsive to the labyrinths of Nabokov, Robbe-Grillet, Pynchon, Lowell, Beckett, and others (including Berryman himself) find little here to unravel or to illuminate. There are so few mysteries, metaphysical and stylistic (the most engaging problems, as I have suggested, are structural) that the most one can do by way of explication in many cases is simply read a poem out loud. What is one to demonstrate, after all, about lines, however crafty, that sound so much like unembellished prose? Finding themselves with virtually nothing to say, critics have assumed that it is the poems themselves that lack inspiration.

The book has also been consistently misread, or worse, not read at all, by those who damn it most vigorously. . . . [If] a reader is so annoyed by the poet's supposed vanity that he fails to notice that love and fame finally sink to nothingness, then the capacity for misinterpretation is virtually limitless. (p. 170)

I regard *Love & Fame* as a finer book, by a good deal, than *Delusions, Etc.* It is not, however, either so brilliant or so startlingly eccentric as *Mistress Bradstreet* or *The Dream Songs.* There is, nevertheless, after the intricacies of these two superb sequences, much that can be said for a work that strives for direct, unambiguous communication, and that more often than not achieves its goal. Lacking this vulnerable book, whatever its shortcomings, the Berryman canon would be noticeably slighter. (pp. 171-72)

The poems in *Delusions, Etc.,* already in proof at the time of Berryman's death, were all composed during his final months, and as such this volume represents the real culmination of the poetic journey that took him from the restrained elegance of the early lyrics through the mannered confessions of the sonnets, to the compressed intensity of *Anne Bradstreet,* the eccentric drama of the dream songs, the lucid revelations of *Love & Fame,* and finally to these nervous, obscure religious musings.

The "Etc." of the title is deceptive, a casual gesture that suggests an informality that is utterly at odds with the puzzlingly dense character of the book. And what, after all, does "et cetera" encompass—fears? suspicions? guilt? renunciations? We never quite find out, for the title serves as an earnest of other obscurities to follow. What we do know is that like the latter *Songs* and like *Love & Fame,* this "final" book has as its central concerns questions of belief and doubt, reinforcing the view that the later Berryman is a religious poet par excellence, a man engaged in a strenuous, nearly obsessive dialogue with his God. (p. 174)

The book is divided into five sections, the first and last bearing directly on the poet's relationship with his God. Part one, "Opus Dei," opens with an epigraph on which variations are played throughout the book: "And he did evil, because he prepared not his heart to seek the Lord." This opening sequence of eleven poems is structured around the canonical hours, not, the poet tells us, through one day, but over many weeks. They reveal the poet at his prayers. . . . These lyrics are expressions of fear, shame, and suspicion. They communicate the poet's ambivalent yearnings in a language that is clotted and obscure, one that lacks completely the vernacular ingeniousness of *Love & Fame.* The transition from book to book could hardly be greater. . . .

The book's final section also consists of eleven poems, again all centered on the poet's relationship with his God, as indicated by such titles as "Somber Prayer," "A Usual Prayer," "The Prayer of the Middle-Aged Man." This series resembles canonical hours without any sequential pattern. The last two poems bring the section, and the book, to a rousing conclusion. In "The Facts & Issues" the poet experiences a profound sense of God's presence, but expresses, nevertheless, a feeling of intense self-loathing, concluding on a note of despair that is suicidal. . . . (p. 175)

[It] is clear that Henry's voice is far better suited to the expression of fears and struggles than is the more impersonal, less consistent mode that dominates most of this final collection.

The five sections, then, with their forty-three poems written in a variety of forms, in a number of voices, about a number of subjects, comprise a curious heterogeneous collection, a gathering together of random pieces, a congeries of notes sent to the world from a soul in a state of extreme agitation, a state that precludes, more often than not, the kind of control required if desperate emotion is to be translated into art. *Delusions, Etc.* lacks the structural coherence that characterizes all of Berryman's other work—especially *Love & Fame*—and it is obvious that the collection was not subjected to the rigorous self-editing and pruning that help give the other works their shape. The book is, in all, an honorable failure, one that raises questions about whether Berryman could have continued to produce had he lived on —though it is altogether possible, each of his books being so remarkably different from the ones that preceded it, that he would have surprised us with a new approach.

One of the stylistic peculiarities that makes this book distinctive, setting it apart in particular from the direct, prosy locutions of *Love & Fame,* is an odd juxtaposition of formal, academic language (relating to canonical hours, Latin phrases, and astronomy, to give but three examples) with breezy colloquialisms usually associated with adolescence. (pp. 178-79)

This fusing of disparate modes, combining the bookish with the colloquial, is related to the juxtaposition of language that is odd and muddled with that characterized by luminous directness and simplicity. The most effective (and affecting) lines in the book are those few, clear and deeply felt, that float to the surface from a murk of clotted rhetoric:

> I'm not a good man
>   • • •
> I am ashamed
>   •
> I've got to get as little as possible wrong.
>   • • •
> I still feel rotten about myself
>   • • •
> I have not done well

These spontaneous laments of a man in distress make much of the surrounding verbiage sound cluttered, cranked out by a nervous, tinkering imagination. Much of the book's complex religious poetry, in fact, seems to exist at several removes from the poet's deepest feelings, while the simpler statements emerge because of emotional necessity. After giving up Henry, Berryman was not able, consistently, to find a voice that would communicate, believably and consistently, his inner hell, his awful guilt, or his accidie, and the moments in *Delusions, Etc.* that are moving are those most reminiscent of the dream songs. Like so many of the extremist poets, as John Thompson writes [in "Last Testament," *The New York Review of Books*], "he found that on the far side of his breakthrough—or his breakdown—everything was flat. Henry, that blithe and desperate spirit, came no longer with his fractured dreamy songs, his softshoe shuffle, his baby-talk that frightened the grown-ups with its naked infantilism. Without him, the world was small and orderly like a room made of cement blocks."

The obvious contrasts in the work, between what is mannered and what is deeply felt, go far toward explaining the book's central problem. Berryman is primarily a poet of loss, and when he expresses his griefs, his guilt, his depressions, the language is credible, the poems affecting. In his noisy, disputatious poems, however, one senses that he protests too much, almost as if trying to convince himself, and his God, of his faith, both in individual prayers and in the placement of these prayers at the beginning and end of the book. As A. Alvarez observes, it is as though Berryman were attempting to defend himself against his own depression. . . . Alvarez (for whom the poet had great respect) holds the view that Berryman's was "a gift for grief," and that his masterpiece is the late *Dream Songs* [see *CLC*, Vol. 2], in which he mourns a generation of friends and artists, in the process mourning his own impending death. This tone is found in a few of the private poems in the final collection. . . . These intensely personal poems—"He Resigns," "No," "Henry by Night," "Henry's Understanding"—make up the radiant center of the book. Next to them the prayers seem strained and somewhat manic—again quoting Alvarez, "Berryman's religious verse seems like a willed, nervous defense against the appalling sadness which permeates the real poems at the heart of the book." (pp. 179-81)

[It is] somehow fitting that the other of his major posthumous books should be in prose, and that it should succeed where many of the final poems fail. *Recovery*, written during the same period as *Delusions, Etc.*, recounts more memorably than do the poems some of Berryman's struggles, principally to regain the faith of his childhood and to shake his dependence on alcohol. . . . Rough and incomplete as it is, however, it is a strong and moving work, one of the most important things the poet did, both for its own intrinsic merit and for the light it throws on Berryman and on his poetry, particularly on *The Dream Songs*. (pp. 183-84)

> *Joel Conarroe, in his* John Berryman: An Introduction to the Poetry *(copyright © 1977 Columbia University Press; reprinted by permission of the publisher), Columbia University Press, 1977.*

FLEUR ADCOCK

[The posthumous collection *Henry's Fate*] begins with 45 Dream Songs, not necessarily rejected by Berryman but uncollected; they followed on from *His Toy, His Dream, His Rest* in 1968 and were written "just out of habit", as he admitted. But a habit is not always a mere tic, a mannerism, and many of these are well worth having. They seem in fact to suffer less from mannerism (using the word now of style) than some of the earlier Songs; even allowing for the fact that familiarity has reduced the impression of obscurity in Berryman's work, his crabbed, knotted language and dislocated syntax are here less evident as a barrier to understanding. . . . Not all of these work; some are merely silly or self-obsessed. But there are some good pieces, including several on his tour of European cities ("my God what visible places".) Assuming that one can take the Dream Songs at all, with their first-person/third-person Henry and their relentless tricksiness, one can well take these.

The remainder of the book is in three sections: finished poems in forms other than that of the 18-line Dream Songs; a few fragments and unfinished poems (interesting to scholars and aficionados but not in themselves very satisfying); and finally a group of poems written at the end of the poet's life when he was once again receiving treatment for his alcoholism. These are agonised and agonising, full of pain; full also, inevitably, of self-pity. But why not? It was natural in the circumstances, and as it is an emotion to which so many of us are subject we may as well have it expressed for us in literature. (pp. 84-5)

> *Fleur Adcock, in* Encounter *(© 1978 by Encounter Ltd.), August, 1978.*

*   *   *

BIOY CASARES, Adolfo   1914-

Bioy Casares is an Argentinian novelist, short story writer, essayist, and screenwriter. He is an inventive, imaginative writer whose work is frequently compared with that of Jorge Luis Borges. Like his fellow Argentinian, Bioy Casares is preoccupied with labyrinths and metaphysical puzzles. He has also published under the pseudonyms Martin Sacastru and Javier Miranda, and has collaborated with Borges under the joint pseudonyms H(onorio) Bustos Domecq and B. Suarez Lynch. (See also *CLC*, Vols. 4, 8, and *Contemporary Authors*, Vols. 29-32, rev. ed.)

D. P. GALLAGHER

Bioy Casares's novels and short stories are comic masterpieces whose fundamental joke is the gap that separates what his characters know from what is going on. The most notorious victim of that gap is the narrator of *La invención de Morel,* who frequently attempts to declare his love for one Faustine without realizing that she is a sort of holographic image who cannot therefore perceive his presence. Yet even the most trite situations that occur in Bioy's work contain the same fundamental dilemma. Thus his sex comedies in *Guirnalda con amores* or *El gran serafin* depict situations in which a man is convinced he has achieved a spectacular success only to discover that the girl's motives were notoriously less flattering than he imagined them to be. (p. 247)

Bioy Casares imposes upon his characters an *adventure,* whether plausible or fantastic, in order to reveal their comic puniness.

Traditional adventure stories (those of say Stevenson, Defoe, Wells or Verne) have long been dear to Bioy as they have to Borges. . . . Bioy Casares's novels, and in particular *La invención de Morel* and *Plan de evasión* (1945), are to a large extent *readings* of earlier, less sophisticated adventure stories. They are novels which reveal the extent to which the adventure story furnishes a dynamic dramatic form to express the gap that separates what a man knows from what there is. (p. 248)

Bioy's adventure stories emphasize the suspense and mystery of the adventures without in the end resolving them. Sometimes, they *appear* to be resolved; the concluding 'explanation' seems to fit exactly. But usually the attentive reader will find that an alternative explanation fits equally well. . . . Always the effect is one of bringing to bear on the conventional adventure story a new perspective, a new reading, one in which we visualize what is implied, what is at stake in stories which we traditionally hurried through as a 'good read', unaware, perhaps, of how much our breathless longing to reach the explanatory end was telling us about our fundamental ignorance. (p. 249)

Bioy Casares is not a trendy man, and it would be wrong to see the plot [of *Diario de la guerra del cerdo*] as a reflection of the current generation gap. The 'pig's war' designation is, I think, a coincidence topically speaking. The point is rather that Bioy has deliberately devised a somewhat abstract plot in order to show up certain archetypal mechanisms pertaining to persecution in general which would probably be disguised if the plot were more recognizably familiar, if the novel were about the persecution of the Jews for instance. If you make the object of a persecution in a novel a fantastic one, you are probably in a better position to investigate the nature of persecution in general. And indeed the novel parades all the structural mechanisms that perhaps all persecutions share. (p. 260)

[The plot of *Diario de la guerra del cerdo* is] an abstract game designed to expose the structure of persecution in an undisguised form, just as the plot of *La invención de Morel* is designed to expose the structure both of investigation and of communication. The more abstract the game, the more the padding which conceals the basic structure will be dismantled.

Much of what I have written so far about Bioy Casares's novels could be applied also to Borges's work. Borges too confronts limited hypothesizers with contingent reality, and Borges too forces his reader into a similarly intimidating hypothesizing enterprise with respect to the fiction he is reading. Yet Borges and Bioy Casares are very different writers. For instance, though both present characters whose most notorious characteristic it is to be limited, Borges would appear to be interested mainly in the mere fact that they *are* limited, whereas Bioy Casares is concerned to depict the specific forms their limitations take. . . . The difference in the two writers may be the difference between a novelist and a writer of lapidary short stories. Bioy Casares at any rate investigates the limitations of his characters in depth, and is as keen to depict the specific form their limitations take as he is to state the fact that they are limitations. (pp. 260-61)

Bioy Casares has a Chekhovian skill in dissecting pathetic details in the behaviour of his characters: little quirks, mannerisms, or accidents of dress for instance, which again serve to circumscribe their limitations. The comedy and the pathos is of course enhanced when the ruthlessly dissected characters believe their absurd behaviour to be vastly important. The joke rests on the gap that separates what a character believes to be important from what is important, on the character's sublime confidence in his insular perspective. . . .

Language is the signature of Bioy Casares's characters. Their language tells us who they are, where they come from, what they are like—whether they are mad or in love or self-opinionated or timid and in particular what their values are. For Bioy Casares's characters are consistently attempting to impress each other, and his narrators to impress us, by imitating what they assume to be an impressive model of style. The language of each one is an unconscious parody of what they or the class or profession from which they come believe to be an impressive way of speaking or writing. (p. 262)

In Bioy Casares's books, . . . we have observed a use of language that is not only polysemantic in the Borgesian sense but also socially and psychologically polyphonous. And on the evidence of Bioy Casares's work, who could honestly deny that the books they have written together such as *Seis problemas para don Isidro Parodi* (1942) may well contain more of Bioy than of Borges? For only in Bioy's work is there anything comparable to that splendid gallery of parodied voices that Bioy and Borges have construed under the pseudonym of H. Bustos Domecq. (p. 265)

It would be absurd to claim that Bioy Casares was a 'better' writer than Borges through being, in a sense, a more 'complete' writer, one more deeply rooted in a given historical reality. As Borges once said, 'La literatura no es un certamen'. It is anyway churlish to divide two great friends by comparing their value. But there do seem to be healthy signs that Bioy is now beginning to be identified as something apart from Borges, and that is a different matter. (p. 266)

D. P. Gallagher, "The Novels and Short Stories of Adolfo Bioy Casares," in Bulletin of Hispanic Studies *(© copyright 1975 Liverpool University Press), Vol. 52 No. 3, July, 1975, pp. 247-66.*

EMIR RODRIGUEZ MONEGAL

The story told by Bordenave [the protagonist of *Dormir al sol* (Sleeping in the Sun)] is very strange but it takes place in the context of everyday trivia. He is a common man, who runs a watch-repair shop, is married to Diana, a beautiful and tyrannical woman. . . . One day his wife becomes a patient in Dr. Samaniego's clinic. Bordenave tries, very inefficiently, to bring about her release. He even buys a female dog which he immediately baptizes Diana, to give to his wife as soon as she comes home. At last, Diana (the wife) does come home; however, she is a different woman: she is still beautiful but now she is also gentle and pleasant. Bordenave recognizes her former self less in his wife than in the bitch, and the solution to this mysterious transformation takes him into labyrinths of confusion until Bordenave reaches the point where he is sent to the Clinic to suffer a decisive mutation.

As in Bioy Casares' former novels, there is in this latest one a baffling situation, the menace of God-knows-what sort of surgical operations, a solution which is not supernatural but still quite fantastic. Also as in his former novels, a different text (invisible but "quoted" in the present text's filigree) suggests false leads, parallel horrors and thrills. I am talking, of course, of H. G. Wells' *The Island of Dr. Moreau* (1896), a story which today is probably better known in its movie version: *The Island of Lost Souls*. . . . [In Wells' fiction, the sinister Dr. Moreau] changed animals into men by means of sadistic operations. The readers or spectators will probably remember that Dr. Moreau was not successful in maintaining the metamorphoses of the beasts intact and, little by little, they reverted to animality.

In three of his five novels to date, Bioy Casares makes some allusion to that novel. In *The Invention of Morel* (1940), it is the image of Moreau's tropical island and the name of the inventor (Moreau-Morel) which are "quoted"; in *A Plan for Escape* (1945), Dr. Castel's experiments to alter the vision of the prisoners of Devil's Island provide both the common location and the similarity in the operations. In *Dormir al sol*, Bioy Casares returns to Wells in a way at once more literal (Dr. Samaniego really manages to metamorphose men into beasts) but less scientific than the Wellsian prototype since Wells had placed his fiction very close to what the science of his time could believe possible while Bioy Casares displaces his tale to the realm of pure fantasy. Dr. Samaniego (a name that in Spanish brings echoes of a famous XVIIIth century writer of animal fables) is really less interested in the scientific side of his operations and more concerned with the permutation of souls between men and animals. From this point of view, Bioy Casares' latest novel is less indebted to Wells' fiction than to Bioy's own previous works.

What *Dormir al sol* is really about is the impossible possession of the loved one. Bordenave loves his wife but she runs away. When Dr. Samaniego sends her back home, changed for the better, Bordenave refuses to accept the change. Yes, the new Diana is better, she is more loving, she is more faithful, but she is another woman. Very soon Bordenave has to admit that one loves somebody even because of his/her defects. The new Diana won't do.

This subject traverses, like an invisible thread of fire, all Bioy Casares' novels. In *The Invention of Morel,* what really mattered was not the fantastic machinery which could project three-dimensional images on the air, but the impossible love between the narrator and the woman he used to meet in his walks on the island: a woman made of film images. When the protagonist finds the machine that projects the images and learns how to make it work, he changes himself into an image that can be projected alongside her image. Thus, he is able to walk with her, to talk to her, to create the fiction that she is also looking and talking to him. That is what love is, Bioy Casares seems to say: a

sustained fiction. The true invention of Morel is that one, and not the amusing but impossible "scientific" machinery. (pp. 41-2)

Bioy Casares has changed style. In his more recent books, adventure is no longer at the center of the text or is no longer so blatantly presented. In fact, adventure has been internalized and disguised. In choosing for his last two novels a deliberately gray part of Buenos Aires (the world of the poor middle-classes) and the ominous times of the first post-Peronist era, Bioy Casares has demythified the adventure story. If Diana is not a sophisticated woman, she is no less complicated than the Faustine of *The Invention of Morel*. . . . The body triumphs, the animal finally wins. But now he, like his "missis," is an animal and they can finally meet in this new dimension of flesh. That end, which is only suggested in the book, is really as horrid as Dr. Moreau's. As terrible as the (apparently) happy ending of *The Invention of Morel*. If the human body is a prison and one cannot possibly escape from it, what will become of the animal body in which Bordenave is finally imprisoned? (pp. 42-3)

[The changed] perception of reality [is] the theme which unifies Bioy Casares' five novels. In *The Invention of Morel*, the woman that the protagonist loved was only a cinematographic image in three dimensions, in *Diary of the War of the Pig*, a political fiction masks the allegory of the corruption of the body; in *Dormir al sol*, the "other" Diana is no longer the woman Dr. Samaniego sends back home but the bitch. In the three novels, a different perception of reality is the secret miracle performed by fiction.

The same thing happens in the other novels written by Bioy Casares. In *El sueño de los héroes* (The Dream of Heroes, 1954), Emilio Gauna relives the same carnival night twice. . . . [The same reality] produces two parallel and different versions of life. In *A Plan for Escape*, Bioy Casares advances a theory of perception. Dr. Castel, a rather literal disciple of William James, alters the perception of reality of the Devil's Island inmates by a series of delicate operations on their senses. . . . Once the perception is altered, the external world becomes another, we become another.

This is what Bordenave finally discovers: the body of a dog in which he is caught is still a prison, but all bodies are prisons, although bodies are our only means of salvation.

Bioy Casares' characters are not only imprisoned in their bodies. They are also imprisoned in another body, even more impossible to escape. It is the body of the novel. It is not casual that out of five novels, four consist of "reports" or "diaries" written by somebody to communicate the protagonist's adventures. (p. 43)

The only apparent exception is *El sueño de los héroes*, a third-person narrative. But even in this novel, the impersonal narrative is interrupted at least four times to identify an "I" who seems to be a witness to the adventure. In all cases, either using a first person account or a third person narrative, Bioy Casares attracts the attention of the reader to the fact that he is reading a text. There is a motive behind this decision.

Practically all Bioy Casares' characters write, although they are not professional writers. They are forced to write by a sort of compulsion created by the circumstances in which they are placed. . . .

Writing is another prison. . . . In the text, inside the text, or in the lines in between the texts, is the only reality these characters will ever have. They are made of words, and not of bodies and souls. Nevertheless, their words talk about the fire of love, the horror of being in prison, the despair of loneliness. . . .

Bioy Casares has developed in five novels and several volumes of short stories the infinite parable of man, imprisoned in a fiction, menaced by "adverse miracles," trying to escape from the circularity of a writing which, fatally, always refers to itself. In *Dormir al sol*, this writing reaches a sort of warm, luminous perfection. In maturing and mellowing, Bioy Casares has learned how to substitute for the most unbearable complexity of *A Plan for Escape* and the stories of *The Celestial Plot*, a fluid narrative style which is already evident in *El sueño de los héroes* and reaches a perfect balance in the stories of *Guirnalda con amores* (A Garland of Love, 1959). In his last two novels, this balance has reached a perfect, unassuming mastery.

But if Bioy Casares did learn how to hide the structural complexities of his former books in plain-looking, deceptive narratives, he has not renounced the basic quest which marks all his work: the quest for reality. Inscribed on the body or the soul of the woman they love (a real text which is decoded through desire) or written on paper, the code of reality is what Bioy Casares' characters are after. They are in search of an elusive gnoseology of reality which is a gnoseology of fiction: the fiction covered by the name of Adolfo Bioy Casares. There one can find the final unity of an extraordinary series of texts. . . . (p. 44)

> *Emir Rodriguez Monegal, "The Invention of Bioy-Casares," in* Review *(copyright © 1975 by the Center for Inter-American Relations, Inc.), Fall, 1975, pp. 41-4.*

DEBORAH WEINBERGER

[The] world of Bioy Casares is endless: a world of unlimited possibilities for new worlds which then will form part of it. Everything Bioy Casares writes offers a world or postulates the possibility of worlds different from the one we inhabit, or think we inhabit. Sometimes a character may be a world apart from others and from his surroundings. Frequently the worlds we discover in the works of Bioy Casares are fantastic, and consist of rearrangements of the elements of our own "real" world. Because of their departure from a natural order, these new worlds are at first not understood by those who stumble into them. Unaware that they have discovered new worlds, they only understand that they are faced with something strange and puzzling. Thus, Bioy Casares' fiction frequently involves a character's confrontation with an enigma.

Access to these enigmatic worlds is through perception and the character must consider his mental perception of his sensory perceptions. In his attempt to decipher the unknown then, the character is limited in two ways: he can only perceive what his senses permit him to perceive; he can only interpret his sensory data according to his ability to use his imagination. Accordingly, Bioy Casares demonstrates through the characters' reactions to these enigmatic worlds the inadequacy of perception, both sensory and mental.

A Plan for Escape is based on a theory of perception, although this theory and the importance of sensory percep-

tion and possible variants on it, are concealed throughout most of the novel, which is taken up with Henri Nevers' perception of the mystery and the evidence which might explain it. Nevers realizes that there is something odd happening on Devil's Island but since he is forbidden entry, he tries to explain the oddness by the evidence he gathers from observation, from what others tell him and from his own imagination. (p. 45)

Nevers is not an objective observer who can collect evidence without preconceived notions as to what the explanation may be. Because he wants to avoid any serious complications, he would rather see the mystery of Devil's Island explained by something quite innocent, Nevers often deliberately chooses what he will see with that end in mind. As a result of his physical state, his perspective, his emotional condition, his lack of objectivity, Nevers' perceptions—even the information on which he must base his conclusions—may not be accurate. His perceptions may be flawed, as may be his reasoning.

Throughout the novel, the reader follows Nevers' observations and conclusions, watching them change as Nevers obtains evidence to support or destroy his latest theory. (p. 46)

[When] he has discovered the true explanation, Henri rejects it because it is too fantastic to be acceptable. . . . He will not doubt that he sees what he sees, but since he cannot believe it, he must find an explanation which will not contradict what he can accept: he concludes that they must be mad, because four men slowly rotating in outrageously painted cells cannot be fit into a sane scheme. Hence, Castel is mad. (Ironically, Henri's conclusion is similar to Castel's plan for curing mental illness by changing the patient's sensory perception of the world to conform with the patient's mental view of it.)

In Nevers' rejection of a fantastic explanation there is another example of the inadequacy of perception. It is not sensory perception which is the problem here, but the mental perception: Nevers rejects what he considers an impossible explanation for the apparently inexplicable behavior of Castel because it does not conform to what one may normally expect. His lack of imagination, his thinking only in set patterns which allow him to accept only what he already knows, are further limitations on sensory perception. The perceptions themselves—no matter how accurate—are useless, except as an aid to gaining understanding or knowledge. Nevers neither perceives entirely accurately nor makes the most of his perceptions. (p. 48)

It is not necessary for there to be a change in the senses for the image to change: it is enough that the interpretation of the sensory perceptions change; in other words, that the mental perception or understanding of the information provided by the senses be different. For example, Nevers and Bernheim see the same thing but interpret it differently; Castel and Nevers make the same observations about the nature of things, but their mental perception of such ideas differs.

Of course Nevers is correct in maintaining that symbols are the only way man has for dealing with reality, but he does not realize the significance of his idea. For him, an object *is* that object, not a symbol of an object. In Castel's newly created world, there are no objects as we perceive them, merely symbols which are interpreted as objects because of the alteration in the prisoners' sensory perception. Thus, a yellow sheet of paper is a symbol of a lance, because with the altered perception, yellow is perceived as length. Thus, a cell, rather than imprisoning, is experienced as liberating because it is perceived as an island paradise. . . .

Through Castel with his experiments in perception, and Nevers with his problems in perception, Bioy Casares suggests that perception, both mental and sensory, is generally inadequate. The world is as we see (and hear and taste and smell and feel) it. Beyond that knowledge is impossible. Even within this world, though, our senses and perceptions are inadequate, and because they are, so is our imagination. Bioy Casares therefore calls some of the unknown worlds to our attention. Perhaps he considers us incapable of perceiving them on our own. (p. 49)

> *Deborah Weinberger, "Problems in Perception," in* Review *(copyright © 1975 by the Center for Inter-American Relations, Inc.), Fall, 1975, pp. 45-9.*

ROBERT M. ADAMS

Both *Morel* and *Escape* center on that favorite figure of our cultural fantasies, the mad scientist. To make him omnipotent, the scientist must be isolated, and since H. G. Wells' "The Island of Doctor Moreau" (lurking in the background of both Bioy stories), desert islands have been much in vogue for this purpose. Bioy attempts no untoward novelties. In both his tales, the story is narrated by an outsider who comes to the island, is baffled by some baffling appearances, and finally penetrates to the heart of them: they turn out to involve a series of experiments in systematically deranged perception. The movement of both stories is thus from the outside inward. But there is another dimension to the present novel, a movement from the inside out, which surrounds the other motion without negating it, and which renders the latest book a good deal more intricate than the earlier one.

The narration of *A Plan for Escape* is beset with complexities and ambiguities which render practically everything said in the book subject to question. (p. 50)

[The] structure of the world within which Lieutenant Nevers encounters his fantastic, but ultimately decipherable, enigma on Devil's Island is more enigmatic and less decipherable than the enigma itself. The very texture of unrelated life is absurd. . . . The book works in two ways; as Nevers penetrates to the heart of his problem, expounding its formal solution in an extended lecture, confusion, blur, and overlay spread outwards through the world surrounding the problem. (p. 51)

Allegories, phantasms, doublings, and parallels abound in the novel; they are not necessarily significant or insignificant. They may be the product of Nevers' peculiar mind; a possibility is scouted that in some particular matter he may be driven by a "diabolical need for symmetry." (p. 52)

[The book] strikes an unusual balance. By resolving an anomaly or ordering the fragments of a problem, the usual "mystery" book spreads the normal light of natural phenomena across an exceptional dark spot. Here, as the light of nature darkens, what seemed to be a mystery of iniquity turns out to be one area of life at least accessible to the mind, to explanation. The artificial paradise of Commandant Castel may be ghastly when seen from the outside—it

is a group of stoned, catatonic zombies wallowing slow-motion in the peristaltic waves of their own stunned nervous systems. But the outside from which it is seen is also ghastly, not so much physically, as in the painful, devious efforts of the characters to explain, to justify, to comprehend a reality that's as queasy and unpredictable as the English Channel on a choppy day. . . . "Escape," then, must be defined, not as an escape from the island, but from the hallucinations, half-intentions, and tantalizing equivocations that surround it, and from which the fiction itself offers no escape. "Plan" must surely be ironic as well.

Stylistically, the book is sparse, dry, and flat, after the fashion of Borges; there is little heightening or rendering. Characterization is of the stick type, familiar from science fiction. Lieutenant Nevers, for example, has no father, no mother, no schooling, no profession, no friends, practically no memories, and, apart from the quite specific problem in which he is involved, very few experiences. The tropics of the South American landscape, within which he is set, could be extrapolated from an *Encyclopedia Britannica* description of Madagascar. Metaphors, imagery, and flights of highly colored fancy are non-existent. Bioy has written, less a novel than an extended parable—complicated, unlike those of Kafka which otherwise it resembles so much, by a few specific bearings of time, place, and history. The reverberations that the book contains are literary, philosophical, social; on the psychological side, they do not go much beyond the constant sense of unrelieved anxiety; stylistically, they are deliberately flat. (pp. 53-4)

Even at their most evasive, [Bioy's dry] equivocations define, with the clarity of strong sunlight on wrinkled sand, the things they are not saying. . . . In the phantom world of Bioy's Iles du Salut, slack and casual conversations generally have to be read for what they are artfully *not* saying, quite as much as for what they are. (p. 54)

> *Robert M. Adams, "No Escaping Evasion," in* Review *(copyright © 1975 by the Center for Inter-American Relations, Inc.), Fall, 1975, pp. 50-4.*

F. JEANNERET

The esthetic roots of a work [like *Asleep In the Sun*]—self-contained, circular, non-referential, suicidal—are many, but the keystone may be found in that passage from the Bioy Casares-Borges collaboration, *The Chronicles of H. Bustos Domecq*, in which a literary critic, determined to perfectly assay *The Divine Comedy*, realizes that in order to do so he must reproduce the poem word for word—i.e., the only legitimate criticism of the text is the text itself. From this angle, *Asleep In the Sun* is private language masquerading as public language; a riddle that solves itself, asking only that the observer document the cycle.

This kind of puzzle often stumps the critic. . . . (p. 76)

It needn't be so. *Asleep In the Sun* is a text which through transparency of novelistic convention denies us direct access. The plot is comic book stuff, seasoned with no-tech science fiction, thematically related to *The Stepford Wives*, *Terminal Man*, perhaps even *Coma*. The prose is scruffy — a translation intentionally thick on the tongue, making, on the page, a rug of coarse hemp that prickles the intellect. The characters, carefully drawn, are near-simpletons; another aspect of the structure of exclusion, they allow no conventional handles—try to grab one, to "understand" one, and it evaporates or breaks away in your hand. The story might be allegory, but on inspection the fat that is rendered is commonplace: isolation, impossibility of communication, inevitable failure of psychiatry, hopeless struggle of the individual against the forces of something-or-other, and, be it ever so humble, there's no place like home.

Yet here, at home in the lethargic, caterwumpus world of the read, something *is* left—a residue, a powder flecked with black, warm in the palm. The work blocks both traditional and post-modern exegesis, but we are not paralyzed. We can notice that the fiction is quark-like, impenetrable; study the joints, the modulations of the surface, the size of the object, the shadow it throws; poke it with tools, not to lay it open, but to see if it bounces, slides, or rolls, or if it moves at all. It is slim critical purchase, but authentic, the experience of the reading act—a residue of mental nods, grimaces, hoots, of grins and groans and frowns, of thoughts-errant hand signals, acknowledgments of shared and unshared experience, a residue of patches of boredom and the pleasures of words. Like the food of a surprisingly good meal, these words are to be taken, savored, and swallowed; their taste is meaning, real meaning in the real world, *outside* the text. And if this is an unfashionable way to read compared with that which, *while not admitting as much,* focuses almost wholly on the critic, it seems immensely more productive and satisfying.

In *Asleep In the Sun* Bioy Casares offers a plan of escape—temporary, of course; he intends to re-boggle our minds by not boggling them in the first place, and he succeeds wonderfully. He comes at us with blood in his eye, a glistening blade glistening between his pearly teeth. For a moment we are frightened, but soon enough we learn that the knife is made of painted rubber, and that pressed into our sides it does not make pain, it tickles. Now we see that the teeth, too, are rubber, and we begin to laugh, desperately, because we have been forced to laugh with the author, to know that the text is only itself. In a flash, the use of our black-flecked powder comes suddenly clear: it is to dust into the nearest critic's eye, in the hope of opening it. (pp. 76-7)

F. Jeanneret, "A Self-Solving Riddle," in Review *(copyright © 1978 by the Center for Inter-American Relations, Inc.), No. 23, pp. 76-7.*

* * *

BISHOP, Elizabeth   1911-1979

Bishop was an American poet, short story writer, editor, translator, and critic who spent much of her life in Brazil. Her poetry and prose is noted for its attention to detail and masterful craftsmanship. She often employed elaborate rhyme schemes in poems marked by an ironic sense of humor and a subtle use of fantasy. Bishop has been the recipient of both the Pulitzer Prize and the National Book Award. (See also *CLC*, Vols. 1, 4, 9, and *Contemporary Authors*. Vols. 5-8, rev. ed.)

MARIE-CLAIRE BLAIS

The body of [Elizabeth Bishop's] work is relatively small, yet one cannot read a single line either of her poetry or prose without feeling that a real poet is speaking, one whose sense of life is as delicately and finely strung as a Stradivarius, whose eye is both an inner and an outer eye. The outer eye sees with marvelous objective precision, the vision is translated into quite simple language, and this language with the illuminated sharpness of an object under a microscope works an optical magic, slipping in and out of imagery, so that everything seen contains the vibration of meaning on meaning.

In "The Armadillo," for instance, there is the baby rabbit on whose peaceful world a fire balloon falls: "So soft!—a handful of intangible ash / with fixed, ignited eyes." Bishop makes such an image stand for a whole world of violence, vulnerability, helpless terror and protest. One cannot read the poem without quivering with a sense of the pain inherent in every form of beauty. Or she can say something that seems to mean exactly what it says, such as "we are driving to the interior," in "Arrival at Santos," although we have been prepared earlier by "Oh, tourist, / is this how this country is going to answer you" for the idea that every great personal change is a country waiting to be explored in its interior.

Yet Bishop is not personal as Lowell or Plath or Berryman is personal. Everything we know about her from her poetry comes through images that transform her particular suffering or loneliness or longing into archetypal states of being. "Four Poems," for example, is a sequence about the pain of the loss of love in which there is a flow of energy between the interior and exterior landscapes, the latter imitating the shape, color and anguish of the former. Somehow Bishop performs the miracle of fusion without ever altering her exterior truth. The fourth stanza makes one think of Donne in its mingling of physical and metaphysical, in the preciseness of the last lines: "a separate peace beneath / within if never with." No poet has ever spoken more concisely of the state of loving someone who is no longer there, of willing good to crystallize out of the pain.

Much of Bishop's poetry is the result of this struggle for accommodation with what is intolerable in life. Some poets turn their struggle to rage and hate, but she has arrived at a kind of pure nostalgia that is both past and present and at the peace "beneath" and "within" (but not necessarily "with") which I consider essential to great poetry.

Marie-Claire Blais, "Presentation of Elizabeth Bishop to the Jury," in World Literature Today *(copyright 1977 by the University of Oklahoma Press), Vol. 51, No. 1, Winter, 1977, p. 7.*

CANDACE SLATER

[The] Brazil in which Bishop so recently lived is already of another era. The early days which the poet spent in the emperor's old summer resort, Petropolis, represented a kind of latter-day Golden Age of Brazilian letters. Bishop was personally acquainted with a good number of the nation's most famous writers, many of whom had been active in the extremely important Modern Art Week of 1922, which sought to make Brazilian literature, painting and music more true to contemporary realities as well as native roots. . . .

By 1971, when she left the country to resume life in the US, Brazil had undergone a significant number of profound changes. Most of the great artists were dead, and so, in a sense, was Brazil's age of innocence. While authoritarianism and economic dependency coupled with severe poverty for a large percentage of the populace are problems which have plagued Brazil throughout its history, the nation of the 1950s and 60s appeared somehow freer. Even though much of what makes Brazil Brazilian has not changed, present realities are clearly different from those of five, and certainly twenty-five years ago. Therefore, while Bishop's poems remain fresh in their sense of discovery, they mirror a society which has changed and will change even more dramatically.

Questions of Travel contains two sections: "Brazil" and "Elsewhere." Both reveal the most characteristic traits of Bishop's poetry: rueful humor, exquisite images, a highly developed if unobtrusive control of metrical forms reinforcing a marked insistence on psychic as well as material limits. ("Continent, city, country, society," declares the poet, "the choice is never wide and never free.") . . . Elizabeth Bishop's poetry is wry, low-key and, above all, cumulative in effect. . . . [She] phrases universal "questions of travel" in a particularly Brazilian way.

Although the "Brazil" section of *Questions of Travel* contains a number of not surprising references to coffee beans and waterfalls, one is struck by allusions to Brazilian folklore as well as underlying Portuguese speech patterns and verse forms, as in the "Burglar of Babylon" ballad. Aside from these more obvious elements, there are also a number of recurring Brazil-linked themes. The nation's exorbitant beauty, its delightful illogic and the powerful cycles marking its tropical climate reappear throughout these eleven poems. (p. 34)

Naturally, the landscape which the poet paints with such brilliant hues in the "Januaries" poem can also be terrible, and an awareness of misery runs through the "Brazil" poems. In, "Squatter's Children," for instance, Bishop portrays a "specklike girl and boy" enveloped in "gigantic waves of light and shade." Creating an increasingly ominous atmosphere in which their mother's harsh voice competes with claps of thunder, the poet emphasizes the children's defenseless position. Like "The Armadillo" and "The Burglar of Babylon," the poem reveals a strong reaction to suffering. In her Brazilian pieces Bishop indicates a definite consciousness of injustices such as those described in her translation of João Cabral de Melo Neto's "The Death and Life of a Severino," a long protest poem based on Northeast Brazilian chants for the dead.

And yet, although there is no doubt that Bishop responds to wrongs, her poetry reveals more diffuse sympathy for the oppressed than definite anger at the oppressor. Stressing effect more than cause, the poet concentrates on manifestations rather than roots of social evils. For instance, instead of attacking the conditions which make them prisoners, she speaks directly to the boy and girl. . . . Although Bishop's reasons for leaving Brazil in 1971 were largely personal, she makes no secret of her discomfort with present political realities in that nation. It is possible, though not certain, that the indignation evident in poems such as the above might have sharpened into direct protest, were she to have remained in the country.

One must hasten to point out, however, that ragged children and bandits are not the only individuals in Bishop's poems. The black boy Balthazár carries his four-gallon can like a king. Asserting that the water spirit called The Dolphin has singled him out, the speaker in "The Riverman" decides to become a *sacaca* or witch doctor. . . . In "Manuelzinho" the writer reveals an exasperation whose profundity borders on love. Clearly this individual and this country, with their overwhelming and heartfelt disregard

for North American logic, have gotten well beneath the speaker's skin. (p. 35)

Rich in slightly barbed whimsy, ["Manuelzinho"] is comic but not condescending in its portrayal of a kind of once common relationship which is beginning to disappear. Paying tribute to the nonrigidity if not seeming illogic which has traditionally given life in Latin America much of its recognized warmth, the poet ends with an apology and an affirmation. . . .

Although the tongue-in-cheek humor as well as the real tenderness evident in "Manuelzinho" runs throughout the "Brazil" poems, not all of these focus on people. In "Song for the Rainy Season," for instance, the landscape once again dominates the poem. Unlike the "Januaries" piece, however, the natural setting is not all-powerful but remains subject in turn to elemental forces. Because the intense impact of both sun and rain is so evident in a tropical country, their presence in this poem represents a particularly Brazilian emphasis on Bishop's habitual theme of boundaries. . . .

By emphasizing the unavoidable presence of death within the most vigorous, ongoing cycle, Elizabeth Bishop reaffirms the limits upon which she insists throughout her poetry. This insistence is all the same joyous in its recognition that the maculate is also the cherished and that the wet air has the force to forgive. In a gentle but nonetheless radiant manner the poet calls the reader's attention to the rain and rainbows rather than to the imposing and permanent rock. While our life is small, shadowy and above all provisory, it is neither shabby nor futile. (p. 36)

Candace Slater, "Brazil in the Poetry of Elizabeth Bishop," in World Literature Today *(copyright 1977 by the University of Oklahoma Press), Vol. 51, No. 1, Winter, 1977, pp. 33-6.*

WILLIAM JAY SMITH

It is with the location, both factual and spiritual, of places that [Elizabeth Bishop's] poems often begin. It is with journeys, real and imaginary, to these places that they develop. Her definition and consideration of herself as a rational being, and her reaction as a sensitive instrument to her surroundings, to her place in the world and in the universe, have been, and continue to be, the central concerns of her poetry.

Geography III refers, I take it, to elementary geography at a grade-school level—but it must bear the added reference to the fact that this is Miss Bishop's third book of geographical exploration, the first two being *North & South* and *Questions of Travel*. (p. 3)

Geography III is a short book, slighter perhaps than Miss Bishop's previous volumes, but it contains at least three poems that rank among the best that she has written: "In the Waiting Room," "Crusoe in England," and "The Moose." "In the Waiting Room," which opens the volume, is extremely personal, but it is so controlled as to seem almost clinically impersonal. . . . Her work relies frequently on personal experiences, but like the great autobiographical work of Isak Dinesen, *Out of Africa*, it is as remarkable for what it omits as for what it reveals. Like Isak Dinesen she sets out to tell the truth, but in doing so, is reticent and highly selective. There is never a note of the self-pity that has become so often the badge of the confessional poet.

Indeed, in "Crusoe in England" she examines self-pity in Crusoe's words:

> I often gave way to self-pity.
> "Do I deserve this? I suppose I must.
> I wouldn't be here otherwise. Was there
> a moment when I actually chose this?
> I don't remember, but there could have been."
> What's wrong about self-pity, anyway?
> With my legs dangling down familiarly
> over a crater's edge, I told myself
> "Pity should begin at home." So the more
> pity I felt, the more I felt at home.

The irony here is that while describing the self-pity to which anyone in such a lonely situation would be reduced the speaker is able to joke about what was clearly no joke. The irony is all the greater when the reader realizes that the poem is concerned with home, with identity. Confined to his island, Crusoe dreamt of other islands. . . . [He] concludes:

> Now I live here, another island,
> that doesn't seem like one, but who decides?
> My blood was full of them; my brain
> bred islands. But that archipelago
> has petered out. I'm old.

It is in registering in both daylight and dream the flora, fauna, and geography of places both real and imaginary that Elizabeth Bishop establishes her relationship to the world and to the universe. It is fitting that the epigraph to this volume should be from an elementary textbook on geography, for there has always been in Elizabeth Bishop's work a kind of childlike, primitive discovery of relationship. Children ask, "Why? What? Where? How?" Their speech is filled with prepositions relating one thing or one person to another. Kornei Chukovsky has spoken of the young child as a linguistic explorer finding his place in the world through a conquest of language, which involves a careful establishment of relationships. He reports on a child asking, "What is a knife—the fork's husband?" thereby establishing their close kinship in human terms. Elizabeth Bishop asks a child's questions and gives mature, adult answers which in their very simplicity startle us by being in themselves so childlike. (pp. 4-5)

The child [in "In the Waiting Room" is] re-enacting the trauma of her own birth: outside the waiting room everything is black; the war is on and death is everywhere. Inside the waiting room is bright and hot and the people are sitting clothed as they are every day. Within the frame of the *National Geographic* everything echoes what is outside (we have the poem within the poem, the frame within the frame) but inside everyone is naked, out of the volcano's mouth pours fire, the women are literally light bulbs. From the dentist's office (from inside the inside which merges in the child's mind with the frame of the *National Geographic*) comes the cry of pain from her aunt's mouth, which, in turn, becomes her own cry as she falls through darkness and emerges into the white, hot world of the waiting room, where she will be clothed and made to look like those around her, and then move outside again on toward death. The child, in re-experiencing her birth, is experiencing at the same time the birth of consciousness; and the poet by creating herself as a child in the process of experiencing creation has triumphed consciously over her own subconscious. (p. 8)

No poem of Elizabeth Bishop's exemplifies more fully the "always-more-successful surrealism of everyday life" and the "perfectly useless concentration" that can by being "self-forgetful" create a new and memorable self than "In the Waiting Room." And nowhere, one might add, does the word "geography" and "geographic" take on greater resonance.

Another example in *Geography III* of Elizabeth Bishop's "self-forgetful, perfectly useless concentration"—and this is one of the finest poems that Miss Bishop has ever written —is "The Moose." (p. 9)

In this poem the poet travels out into wild, unformed nature, crossing (on a macadam highway, of course, constructed by man) into the dark "impenetrable" wood, which is "hairy, scratchy, splintery." Traveling westward, hearing around her the voices of the dead, she sees the very spirit of the wood appear in her path. The moose is a plain, enormous female, taking her time in a "grand, otherworldly" way; she is mother nature herself, homely, safe, and in her odd and towering manner, strangely protective—an emblem of unadulterated joy appearing suddenly to the group of drifting human beings. Like the dark peak that pursues the young Wordsworth across the lake, this creature towers over the poet. Unlike Wordsworth's peak, however, it does not represent a dark, tragically foreboding moral force of nature but rather a clumsy, comic, benevolent essence that comes curiously upon the travelers almost as a kind if accidental blessing. While Wordsworth's peak is, of course, phallic, the moose is female. The entire poem is filled with images of women and womanly things: the landscape itself with the bay, where the river "enters or retreats / in a wall of brown foam" is feminine. The houses themselves which the traveller watches show signs of feminine attention: sweet peas clinging to whitewashed fences, a woman shaking out a tablecloth after supper. In the midst of the "dreamy divagation" it is in an old featherbed that the grandmother would have fashioned that the poet hears the voices speaking of birth, marriage, and death.

The animals in the civilized world that the traveller leaves behind are domesticated creatures. . . . The undomesticated, otherwordly creature that emerges from impenetrable nature (and barbaric nature appears to be masculine— "Hairy, scratchy, splintery") is female, both productive and benevolent. While it is plain and homely, it is at the same time "high as a church;" and appears to take on a curious sacred quality. The poem seems to say that just as woman is the civilizing influence in society, so is she in the wild the Earth Mother protective of all living creatures on their way from the cradle to the grave. Years of evolution in nature have produced the strange creature that is the moose, and years of evolution in the poet's consciousness have produced the poet's comic acceptance of the world as it is. She is able in the poem to meet the emblematic creature in the middle of the dark wood like Dante in his *selva oscura,* and to say, with the grandparents, "Life's like that. / We know *it* (also death)."

Elizabeth Bishop's exploration of her place in the world, her search for home, leads her in this volume as it does so often back into herself. It leads her to a playful look at her own desk as if it were a country being visited for the first time by explorers. Here is her typewriter, as one of them reports it in the charming prose poem "12 O'Clock News":

The escarpment that rises abruptly from the central plain is in heavy shadow, but the elaborate terracing of its southern glacis gleams faintly in the dim light, like fish scales. What endless labor those small, peculiarly shaped terraces represent! And yet, on them the welfare of this tiny principality depends.

That tiny principality seems, on the basis of *Geography III*, to be in excellent shape. (pp. 10-11)

William Jay Smith, in The Hollins Critic *(copyright 1977 by Hollins College), February, 1977.*

HERBERT LEIBOWITZ

With its calmly circumscribed being and elegant finish, deploying space in formally perfect patterns, each small portfolio of [Elizabeth Bishop's] work resembled classical architecture.

Living in Brazil most of the time, Bishop was unaffected by the shifts in fashion, the catholicity of taste and often bitter factionalism that have marked American poetry since the end of World War II . . . yet she has appealed to poets as radically different as Frank O'Hara, Robert Lowell, Octavio Paz and John Ashbery. Lowell, for example, has praised her "tone of large, grave tenderness and sorrowful amusement," while Ashbery, citing her "quirkiness" and "rightness of vision," has singled out her grandeur, "which, because it remains rooted in everyday particulars, never sounds 'grand,' but is as quietly convincing as honest speech."

What accounts for such acclaim? Bishop's brilliant technique certainly. But her spare descriptive style is remote from the luxuriant randomness, the sleek verbal flourishes and longueurs of Ashbery's verse and the nervous eloquence of Lowell's struggle to understand and master the linked pathologies of self, family and history which invest his poems with their dramatic power. Even as a neo-classical poet she is miles away from Richard Wilbur's witty and amiable gregariousness; society doesn't interest her and love doesn't call her to the things of this world.

Whenever we grow weary of the self-regarding jostle, the coercive intimacy, of confessional poetry and the violence of our public life, we turn with pleasure to Bishop's poems as to a shelter. Bishop has simply pulled down all vanity: the reality of what or whom she sees is never extorted by the ego, just accepted in its unfathomable and equivocal otherness. A cool light bathes the objects that come before her eye, or her mind's eye—armadilloes, roosters, sandpipers, coves, monuments—which she registers with the imaginative exactitude of a mapmaker. Bishop has inherited the mantle of Marianne Moore, though without Miss Moore's lapidary wit. (p. 7)

"Geography III" is written in an austere meditative style. Quietly autumnal in mood, . . . the ten poems probe the themes of survival and home. The approach to autobiography is gingerly, oblique, through geography, that neutral science. In "The Moose" . . . what Bishop glimpses through the bus windows . . .—though transient, melancholy and solitary—takes on the aura of moral safety.

In the darkened bus itself, . . . she feels the security of intimacy: "things cleared up finally." For a timeless moment, she and the passengers, though strangers to each other, become the intact family of her weathered dreams. So when the moose comes out of the "impenetrable wood," "grand, otherworldly," "high as a church / homely as a house / (or safe as houses)," they all share in a mystical concord, a "sweet / sensation of joy," that hangs in the air long after the moose vanishes.

The other outstanding poem of "Geography III," "Crusoe in England," offers a gloomier resolution. Geography is here a synonym for blankness and desolation. Back in England, bored and old, Robinson Crusoe testily recalls his sojourn on the arid island ("a cloud dump") waiting for rescue. Bishop's Crusoe is not the exemplar of bourgeois ingenuity and piety Defoe gave us. (pp. 7, 20)

His recurring nightmare of being marooned on "infinities of islands," "registering their flora, / their fauna, their geography," is perhaps Bishop's self-mocking comment on the self-enclosure of her poems.

The style of "Geography III" has the serene detachment of plainsong. We feel we are listening to a solemn music. The best poems have a virtuoso simplicity like the structure of crystals. . . . A sort of reticent Yankee sensuousness underpins them. (p. 20)

Even in her first two books, "North and South" (1946) and "A Cold Spring" (1955), she was a mature poet, enacting the ceremonies of experience, not innocence; her curiosity about the world was not naïve wonder. "More delicate than the historians' are the map-makers' colors," she observes. That judgment may serve as a fitting emblem of her silvery, estimable art, but also of its limitations. By looking at objects close up, as through a microscope, she evokes their indwelling form and spirit; by scanning them with a wide lens, as if she were an aerial photographer, she brings out large contours, distant perspectives.

The danger, however, is that for Bishop—as for Emerson, Stevens and Marianne Moore before her—life is more an affair of places than of people. With one notable exception: "Questions of Travel" (1965), her most relaxed and inventive book. There, to the cartographer's refined beauty she adds the novelist's gifts. Amused and enchanted by their bravado, color and robustness, their customs and folklore, she draws near to the Brazilian people. Her affectionate vignettes . . . reward her faith in particulars: she is freed from self-enclosure into the "large, grave tenderness" Lowell noted.

"Geography III" reverts to the narrower sympathies of Bishop's early work. Its subtle inflections, its scrupulously carved forms, its lucid and caged grandeur are admirable. "The reflector of the inner eye / scatters the spectacle: / God all alone above an extinct world," she says of Cornell's magical boxes. This is the dilemma that has always absorbed Bishop. The artist, compelled to record the rich spectacle of the world as it passes before her eye, cannot shake off a doubt that the process is somehow futile and self-cancelling. But "The Moose" suggests a possible resolution: to climb down from her solitary perch and, by standing in the tricky currents of history, to bear witness to men and women like herself struggling to fulfill themselves in finite circumstances. Perhaps Elizabeth Bishop's next book will be called "History I." (pp. 20, 22)

Herbert Leibowitz, "The Elegant Maps of Elizabeth Bishop," in The New York Times Book Review (© 1977 by The New York Times Company; reprinted by permission), February 6, 1977, pp. 7, 20, 22.

DAVID KALSTONE

[From] the very start, there was something about [Elizabeth Bishop's] work for which elegantly standard literary analysis was not prepared. Readers have been puzzled, as when [Stephen Stepanchev] writes about "Florida": "the poet's exuberance provides a scattering of images whose relevance to the total structure is open to question. It is as though Miss Bishop stopped along the road home to examine every buttercup and asphodel she saw." [See *CLC*, Vol. 4.] First of all, Bishop writes about alligators, mangrove swamps, skeletons and shells—things exotic and wild, not prettified. More important, there is some notion of neat and total structure which the critic expects and imposes, but which the poem subverts. What makes the quoted critic nervous is a quality which becomes more and more prominent in Bishop's work—her apparent lack of insistence on meanings beyond the surface of the poem, the poem's seeming randomness and disintegration. There is something personal, even quirky, about her apparently straightforward descriptive poems which, on early readings, it is hard to identify. This is an offhand way of speaking which Bishop has come to trust and master, especially in her important book of 1965, *Questions of Travel,* and in the extraordinary poems she has published since then.

I am talking about matters of tone, the kind of authority a single voice will claim over the material included in a poem. Anyone who has heard Miss Bishop read will know how flat and modest her voice is, how devoid of flourish, how briefly she holds her final chords and cadences and allows a poem to resonate. (p. 14)

The opening line [of "Florida"] is so disarming, almost trivializing, that we are in danger of taking what follows for granted: the odd changes of scale that are among this poem's secrets.

> The state with the prettiest name,
> the state that floats in brackish water,
> held together by mangrove roots
> that bear while living oysters in clusters,
> and when dead strew white swamps with skeletons,
> dotted as if bombarded, with green hummocks
> like ancient cannon-balls sprouting grass.

The scale changes as rapidly as Gulliver's: first the whole state, afloat, intact with its boundaries, the mapmaker's or aerial photographer's vision; then an organism (held together by mangrove roots), the geologist's or botanist's fanciful X ray. Her Florida is a barnacled world refined to residues. Oysters dot the mangrove roots; dead mangroves strew the swamps with skeletons. Dead turtles leave their skulls and their shells, which are themselves hosts to other growths, barnacled. The coastline is looped with seashells painstakingly and exotically named. There is sediment in the water; solvents in wood-smoke; charring on stumps and dead trees. Yet the charring is "like black velvet." The residues studding this landscape are its principal ornaments as well: artistic and historical growths, like the "tide-looped strings of fading shells" turning the "monotonous . . . sagging coast-line" to something else.

At first the description occurs in a free-floating eternal present, a series of phrases which don't commit the observer to any main verb at all. They seem if anything to exclude her, re-awakening memories of geological change that stretch far before and beyond her in scale, habitually repeated historical action. The strange shifts of scale—of size and space—in a seemingly timeless, self-renewing present remind us constantly, by implication, of the frailty of our merely human observer. A descriptive poem, which in other hands, say Whitman's, appropriates landscapes and objects, here makes us aware just how, just why we are excluded from such appropriations.

Only when we get to the buzzards, two-thirds of the way through the poem, is there a form of the present tense (they "are drifting down, down, down") restricted to her particular moment of watching, a definite *now*. Here also, two strange mirrors in which we do not find ourselves. First:

> Thirty or more buzzards are drifting down, down, down,
> over something they have spotted in the swamp,
> in circles like stirred-up flakes of sediment
> sinking through water.
> Smoke from woods-fires filters fine blue solvents.

And then:

> After dark, the fireflies map the heavens in the marsh
> until the moon rises.

The four elements form a self-enclosed world. Creatures of the air mirror the earth's discards (are they really there?) floating through water; and fire, as if completing the cycle, exhales fine smoke into the blue. Then again with the fireflies, air and flickering fire are reflected in the marsh, earth and water together. In other words, alternate creations dwarf or frame the poet's own: the long scale of eroding nature with its fossils and predators (buzzards, mosquitoes with "ferocious obbligatos"), and then the daily repeating creation and fadings. When the moon comes up, the landscape pales. Its wonderful sounds and colors—the flashy tanagers, the pelicans gold-winged at sunset, the musical screeching—turn skeletal once more.

The world in its processes provides a delicate model for the poet's work, for art—its shells with beautiful names, its finely observed (and alliterative) oysters in clusters. But the poem continually stresses how such contrivance is made for fading and how nature's contrivances survive the artist's own. Building toward a phrase whose effect is worthy of what she admires in Darwin ("a sudden relaxation, a forgetful phrase"), Bishop sums up the impact of the scene, grasped for the fullness of her own understanding:

> Cold white, not bright, the moonlight is coarse-meshed,
> and the careless, corrupt state is all black specks
> too far apart, and ugly whites; the poorest
> post-card of itself.

At the end Florida contracts to the alligator's five primitive calls ("friendliness, love, mating, war, and a warning"), and with its whimper is restored to darkness and its mysterious identity as "the Indian Princess." (pp. 16-18)

At first [in "At the Fishhouses"], as in "Florida," a landscape seems almost without a spectator, the speaker comically unwelcome in an air which smacks of another element and which makes her eyes water and her nose run. She slowly exposes the scene, present tense, with a tempered willingness to let it speak for itself in declarative simplicity. Things *are;* things *have.* The lone fisherman, a Wordsworthian solitary, is worn into the scene, his net "almost invisible," his shuttle "worn and polished," his "black old knife" with a blade "almost worn away." The dense opening description—deliberately slow, close to fifty lines of the poem—is in all details of sight, sense and sound intended to subject us to the landscape, to draw us deeply into it. . . . The reader is meant to become what the speaker jokingly claims herself to be later in this poem: "a believer in total immersion."

In its fidelity to setting—to what is both jagged and strangely jewelled—["At the Fishhouses"] accumulates the sense of an artistry beyond the human, one that stretches over time, chiselling and decorating with its strange erosions. The human enterprise depends upon and is dwarfed by the sea, just as the fishhouse ramps lead out of, but back into the water. . . . (p. 19)

"At the Fishhouses" makes explicit what is usually implicit, invisible and vital in Miss Bishop's poems, like a pulse: a sense of the encircling and eroding powers in whose presence all minute observations are valuably made. She is, in fact, rather like a sandpiper she describes in ["Sandpiper"]: the bird pictured as subject to the water's roar, the earth's shaking—imagined in "a state of controlled panic, a student of Blake." He watches the sand, no detail too small . . . :

> The world is a mist. And then the world is
> minute and vast and clear. The tide
> is higher or lower. He couldn't tell you which.
> His beak is focussed; he is preoccupied,
>
> looking for something, something, something.
> Poor bird, he is obsessed!
> The millions of grains are black, white, tan, and gray,
> mixed with quartz grains, rose and amethyst.

Here again are those shifts of scale which, instead of unsettling, actually strengthen our perspective. The poem is a critique of Blake's auguries of innocence: his seeing the world in a grain of sand. "The world is a mist. And then the world is / minute and vast and clear." The adjectives appear to make a quiet claim. Yet what an odd collocation—minute and vast and clear. The scales are not really commensurable; one sees the world, one sees the grain of sand, and the clarity comes in making a primitive and definite distinction about what is and is not within our grasp. The bird, on the one hand, is battered and baffled . . . , is preoccupied, obsessed with the grains of sand, a litany of whose colors, minutely and beautifully distinguished, ends the poem. That is all it knows of the world.

These poems both describe and set themselves at the limits of description. Bishop lets us know that every detail is a boundary, not a Blakean microcosm. Because of the limits they suggest, details vibrate with a meaning beyond mere physical presence. Landscapes meant to sound detached are really inner landscapes. They show an effort at reconstituting the world as if it were in danger of being continually lost. (pp. 21-2)

What animates the scene [in "The Bight"] is the observer's deliberate activity, celebrating her birthday in an off-key way with an unrelenting and occasionally mischievous series of comparisons: pilings dry as matches; water turning to gas (and which Baudelaire might hear turning to marimba music); pelicans crashing like pickaxes; man-of-war birds opening tails like scissors; sharktails hanging like plow-

shares. The whole rundown world is domesticated by comparisons to our mechanical contrivances, our instruments of workaday survival, enabling, in turn, an outrageous simile (stove-boats "like torn-open, unanswered letters") and an equally outrageous pun ("The bight is littered with old correspondences"). The letters wickedly enough bring Baudelaire back into the poem, merge with his "correspondences." They are unanswered letters to boot, in a poem where the author has shot off one comparison after another, like firecrackers. . . .

It is no accident that much of Bishop's work is carried on at the mercy of or in the wake of the tides. There are divided and distinguished stages in her encounters: moments of civilized, provisional triumph; and then again, times when landscapes leave us behind—the northern seas of "At the Fishhouses," the abundant decay of "Florida" and later, of her adopted Brazil, magnetic poles sensed even in the title of her first volume, *North & South*. (p. 23)

"In the Village" is the vital center from which many of Bishop's poems radiate, the darker side of their serene need to reclaim "the elements speaking: earth, air, fire, water." She printed it among the poems of her 1965 volume, *Questions of Travel*, as if to make that point.

For a moment "In the Village" offers a radiant primal world, available to human energies. It is almost unique in Bishop's work for the way it resolves tensions between the remembered, inaccessible, inhuman call of the four elements and her affectionate grasp of the more precarious details of human life. In the glow of memory she is for once licensed to glide from the scream ("But surely it has gone away, forever") to the noise of the anvil, the two distantly merged like the bell buoy at sea, the elements speaking. For once, in the suffused light of childhood, she is allowed to hear those perfectly inhuman elements as if they were the voices of paradise, a fulfilled retreat from the intense inescapable world of change and loss. For once, losing hold of details is not an engulfment or a drowning, but a situation quietly accepted with a muted question. . . .

Exile and travel are at the heart of her poems from the very start—and sometimes as if they could reconstitute the vision of "In the Village," as if they led somewhere, a true counter to loss. (p. 26)

The volume *Questions of Travel* in effect constitutes a sequence of poems, its Brazilian landscapes not so much providing answers as initiating us into the mysteries of how questions are asked. It is important that the book also includes poems about her Nova Scotia childhood and the central story of the period, "In the Village." In the light of those memories, the Brazilian poems become a model of how, with difficulty and pleasure, pain and precision, we re-introduce ourselves into a world.

There are three important initiating poems: in order, "Arrival at Santos," "Brazil, January 1, 1502" and "Questions of Travel." The first is deliberately superficial, comic, sociable. We watch her straining from tourist into traveller. . . . The familiar and merely instrumental melt away and we know something more than geographical is meant by the last line: "We are driving to the interior."

We go there by means of one of Bishop's characteristic changes of scale. "Arrival at Santos"—it's not Bishop's usual practice—had been dated at the end, *January, 1952*.

The next poem is "Brazil, January 1, 1502," and its first word is the generalizing *Januaries*. No longer in the "here" and "now" of the uninstructed tourist, the poem fans out into the repeating present of the botanist and the anthropologist. Our drive to the interior is through the looking glass of natural history. There is a comforting epigraph from Lord Clark's *Landscape into Art,* "embroidered nature . . . tapestried landscape," that seems to familiarize the scene, appropriate it for European sensibilities. Yet this is a wild burgeoning tapestry, not "filled in" with foliage but "every square inch *filling in* with foliage," tirelessly self-renewing. Its distinctions of shade and color force her into relentless unflagging specificty: "big leaves, little leaves, and giant leaves, / blue, blue-green, and olive." A parade of shades: silver-gray, rust red, greenish white, blue-white. The powers of description are deliberately and delightfully taxed; it's hard for mere humans to keep up.

Then, with a bow to our desire for a familiar tapestry, Bishop draws our attention to something in the foreground. It is first identified as "Sin: / five sooty dragons near some massy rocks." The rocks are "worked with lichens" and "threatened from underneath by moss / in lovely hell-green flames." Then, in a deliberate change of scale, the little morality play turns to something wilder, more riveting, making fun of our tame exaggerations. Those dragons are, in fact, lizards in heat. . . . Then the most daring change of all:

> Just so the Christians, hard as nails,
> tiny as nails, and glinting,
> in creaking armor, came and found it all,
> not unfamiliar.

For a moment, until we unravel the syntax, "just so" identifies the invaders with the lizards in heat. Tiny in scale, dwarfed by the scene, the settlers, after Mass, are out hunting Indian women. . . . The tapestry—initially it seemed like a device to domesticate the landscape—instead excludes invaders from it. At the beginning we were identified with those settlers of 1502: "Nature greets our eyes // exactly as she must have greeted theirs." At the end that proves to be a dubious privilege. Nature's tapestry endures, renews itself. After our initial glimpse of order, we shrink like Alice or Gulliver—toy intruders, marvelling.

Bishop's book, then, imagines first the mere tourist, then the invader, and finally, in the title poem, faces what is actually available to the traveller. "Questions of Travel" anticipates a new submissive understanding, taking what comes on its own terms. . . . The key to this new openness and affection is in the movement of the title poem. It proceeds through a cautious syntax of questions, with tentative answers in negative clauses. The glutted, excluded observer of the two opening poems ("There are too many waterfalls here") hallucinates mountains into capsized hulls, her own sense that travel might turn into shipwreck. Her first questions are asked with a guilty air: "Should we have stayed at home and thought of here? . . . Is it right to be watching strangers in a play . . . ?"

> What childishness is it that while there's a breath of life
> in our bodies, we are determined to rush
> to see the sun the other way around?
> The tiniest green hummingbird in the world?
> To stare at some inexplicable old stonework,
> inexplicable and impenetrable,
> at any view,

instantly seen and always, always delightful?

You can hear Bishop's spirits rise to the bait of detail, the word "childishness" losing its air of self-accusation and turning before our eyes into something receptive, *childlike,* open to wonder. This is finally a less ambiguous approach than that of the traveller yearning to "look and look our infant sight away." "Questions of Travel" does not expect, as "Over 2000 Illustrations" did, that vision will add up, restore our ancient home. The yearning remains ("Oh, must we dream our dreams / and have them, too?"). But the observer is drawn very cautiously by accumulating detail, and questions themselves begin to satisfy the imagining mind. (pp. 28-31)

[Details] are also boundaries for Elizabeth Bishop, that whatever radiant glimpses they afford, they are also set at the vibrant limits of her descriptive powers. "In the Village" and "Questions of Travel" show us what generates this precarious state. . . . [Bishop is] aware of the smallness and dignity of human observation and contrivance. She sees with such a rooted, piercing vision, so realistically, because she has never taken our presence in the world as totally real. (p. 32)

Her "questions of travel" modulate [in *Geography III*] almost imperceptibly, into questions of memory and loss. Attentive still to landscapes where one can feel the sweep and violence of encircling and eroding geological powers, poems such as "Crusoe in England" and "The Moose" pose their problems retrospectively. Crusoe lives an exile's life in civilized England, lord in imagination only of his "un-rediscovered, un-renamable island." In "The Moose" we are city-bound, on a bus trip away from Nova Scotia, and the long lean poem reads like a thread the narrator is laying through a maze—to find her way back? . . .

The shock of birth, the secret joy of naming, of knowing a place "un-renamable"—these emotions shadow the surface [of "Crusoe in England"] as they do for the child of "In the Waiting Room." Crusoe's whole poem is pervaded by the play of curiosity. (p. 35)

[Note] Crusoe's joy in the homemade and under the pressure of having to re-invent the world: "the parasol that took me such a time / remembering the way the ribs should go"; the baby goat dyed red with the island's one kind of berry "just to see / something a little different"; a flute, "Homemade, homemade! But aren't we all?" The poem is crowded with fresh experience: hissing turtles, small volcanoes. Crusoe has his longings—one fulfilled when Friday appears. He also has his nightmares. When he is on the island, he dreams about being trapped on infinite numbers of islands, each of which he must in painful detail explore. Back in England the nightmare is just the opposite: that such stimulation, imaginative curiosity and energy will peter out. His old knife ("it reeked of meaning, like a crucifix") seems to have lost its numinous power. The whole poem poses a question about imagination when it is no longer felt to be intimately related to survival. Bishop seems involved with the figure of Crusoe because of the questions *after* travel, a kind of "Dejection Ode" countered by the force and energy that memory has mustered for the rest of the poem. It acts out ways of overcoming and then reexperiencing loss.

Elizabeth Bishop has always written poetry to locate herself—most obviously when she is challenged by the exotic landscapes of North and South. She now performs her acts of location in new ways—sometimes showing the pains and joys of domestication. . . . More important is the relocation in time, no longer seeing herself and her characters in long geological—Northern or tropical—perspectives, but in a landscape scaled down to memory and the inner bounds of a human life. What she finds are the pleasures and the fears of something like Crusoe's experience: the live memories of naming, the sudden lapse of formerly numinous figures. (pp. 36-7)

In another sense the past has its sustaining surprises. "Poem" is about the feelings awakened by a small painting passed down in her family, a landscape apparently by the great-uncle responsible for the "Large Bad Picture" which Bishop approached with diffidence and only submerged affection in *North & South*. In the new poem, the painter's work is welcomed as it brings alive, slowly, a scene from her childhood. . . . I hear in these guarded, modest, still radiant lines a new note in Bishop's work: a shared pleasure in imaginative intensity, almost as if this remarkable writer were being surprised (you *hear* the surprise in her voice) at the power over loss and change which memory has given her writing. What else is it that we hear in "The Moose," as the bus gets going through a lovingly remembered trip from salt Nova Scotia and New Brunswick, world of her childhood, toward Boston where she now lives? . . . The moose seems both to crystallize the silence, security and awe of the world being left behind and to guarantee a nourishing and haunting place for it in memory.

In "The End of March" Bishop follows a looped cord along a deserted beach to a snarl of string the size of a man, rising and falling on the waves, "sodden, giving up the ghost. . . . / A kite string?—But no kite." It might be an emblem for these recent poems which touch on lost or slender connections. Bishop seems more explicit about that than she used to be. Where loss was previously the unnamed object against which the poems ventured forth, it is now one of the named subjects. Her poems say out very naturally: "the little that we get for free, / the little of our earthly trust. Not much." Memory is her way of bringing to the surface and acknowledging as general the experience of losing which has always lain behind her work and which the work attempts to counter. (pp. 37-9)

If Bishop's writing since *Complete Poems* still displays her tough idiosyncratic powers of observation, it also makes a place for those observations in very natural surroundings of the mind. The title *Geography III* (and its epigraph from "First Lessons in Geography") is at once a bow to her real-life relocation and a deep acknowledgment of the roots of these poems in childhood memory and loss. The time and the space these poems lay claim to are more peculiarly Elizabeth Bishop's own—less geological, less historical, less vastly natural; her poems are more openly inner landscapes than ever before. (p. 40)

> *David Kalstone, "Elizabeth Bishop: Questions of Memory, 'Questions of Travel','" in his* Five Temperaments: Elizabeth Bishop, Robert Lowell, James Merrill, Adrienne Rich, John Ashbery *(copyright © 1977 by David Kalstone; used by permission of Oxford University Press, Inc.), Oxford University Press, 1977, pp. 12-40.*

DENIS DONOGHUE

Elizabeth Bishop's work issues from a disposition not even to consider the temptation [to be great]. For a long time she seemed content with the natural piety featured in observation, looking with care at things that happened to offer themselves to her attention. But her way of looking at things showed that her real subject is the mutuality of eye and mind in a world largely but not completely given. Since "Geography III," her readers have recognized that the brick-on-brick procedure has produced a building not at all grandiose but simply grand. "Crusoe in England" and "The Moose" are poems that could not have been written if their poet had allowed herself, even for a second, to luxuriate in a feeling of grand possibility: They are large in implication, but untainted, unvulgar. It is natural to be moved by those poems, especially by the feeling that Bishop was moved enough to write them but did not let herself be shaken from her native poise. (p. 88)

> *Denis Donoghue, in* The New York Times Book Review *(© 1978 by the New York Times Company; reprinted by permission), December 3, 1978.*

ROBERT HOLLAND

In *Geography III*, Elizabeth Bishop teaches us once again that cartography can, in the right hands, be an exact science. Asking again her inveterate traveler's questions—*What is in the East? In the West? In the South? In the North?*—she answers them with the same miraculous (though seemingly offhand) clarity, the same order in apparent disorder, the same alchemy which changes, without our noticing, the exterior into the interior landscape. Bishop seems more preoccupied, as she travels that way, with what lies in the West; and, as corollary, with her own past. She seems to be revisiting, as several commentators have noted, the scenes and subjects of her earlier poems—Nova Scotia, the tropics, the New England shore—bringing to them a new intimacy and directness, a domestication which is at the same time a deeper exploration of their significance.

There are three poems in this volume which stand with Bishop's very best work: "Crusoe in England," "The Moose," and "The End of March." They are all concerned with, for want of a better word, "retirement"—not in its narrow sense, but rather as a withdrawal from imaginative engagement with the world. For a poet with so intense a relationship with the real, the thought of such retirement must at times be seductive, and Bishop explores it at length, trying it on for size, but finally rejecting it as unsatisfactory, if not, in fact, impossible. (pp. 352-53)

For her, the temptation to surrender to sleep is always countered by the greater pressure of reality reasserting its persistent claims upon the mind. . . . [In] "The End of March," my favorite in this remarkable collection, the poet yearns for withdrawal as she walks the winter beach at Duxbury, this time in her "crypto-dream-house" . . . :

> I'd like to retire there and do *nothing*,
> or nothing much, forever, in two bare rooms:
> look through binoculars, read boring books,
> old, long, long books, and write down useless notes.

But this, too, is impossible, for the world persists, and beckons, lit by the play of the mind's light. . . . At home anywhere, everywhere an exile, Elizabeth Bishop fails again in this book to find a resting place in the world. Since it has given us the poems, it is a failure for which we must all be grateful. (pp. 353-54)

Robert Holland, in Poetry *(© 1979 by The Modern Poetry Association; reprinted by permission of the Editor of* Poetry*), March, 1979.*

*   *   *

BLAIS, Marie-Claire 1939-

Blais is a French-Canadian novelist and poet. *A Season in the Life of Emmanuel,* **which won the French Prix Medicis in 1966, is generally considered her best work. In it Blais explores with compassion and delicacy the life of an impoverished French-Canadian family. Her imagery is powerful and compelling, and her prose, even in the description of the misery and horror inherent in the lives of her characters, has a lyrical quality. (See also** *CLC,* **Vols. 2, 4, 6, and** *Contemporary Authors,* **Vols. 21-24, rev. ed.)**

ELLIOTT GOSE

Before finishing the first chapter of [*Mad Shadows*], I had that sinking feeling all composition teachers have experienced reading the intensely subjective outpourings of an adolescent mind. But by the time I had read half of the book, I was caught in the world created by the author's nineteen-year-old imagination. She had proved the validity of Conrad's stricture on the Romantic sensibility, that it must "in the destructive element immerse". Miss Blais has plunged into her nature and written a parable out of what she discovered there. Like other figurative narratives, this novel can be understood on more than one level. (pp. 72-3)

Freud, for instance, would appreciate the mother's love for her idiot son, and the daughter's hatred of both, not to mention her idealization of her dead father: "Far off in her childhood, she could see her father, the austere peasant, the maker of bread. When he tilled the virgin loins of the earth, he was penetrating to the heart of God." The daughter's concern with the farm and with making bread become in this light perhaps a little too obvious, as are many of the motifs that run through the novel. But like Emily Brontë, though Miss Blais may tell, she never explains. As a result *Mad Shadows* has the convincing irrationality and vivid detail of a dream (and dreams are frequently mentioned in it). Fortunately it also has an imagistic complexity and unity of purpose which elevate it to the realm of art. Its many striking scenes convince, not as having been re-created from observed outer reality, but as having been created for the first time from felt inner reality. (p. 73)

[The images used in the novel] interweave in patterns controlled by an imagination which the sympathetic reader must admire. Striking and readable, *Mad Shadows* is an impressive first novel. (p. 74)

Elliott Gose, "The Witch Within," in Canadian Literature, *Winter, 1961, pp. 72-4.*

GEORGE W. KNOWLES

As Alain Robbe-Grillet says in his *For a New Novel: Essays on Fiction,* the *nouveau roman* is an exploration and an evolution of the genre of the novel. While aiming at total subjectivity, the modern novel should not be a representation of anything but itself. Reality is sense perception and concerns only man in his situation in the world. Sequence of events and narrative are often eliminated, with the result

a plotless train of occurrences alternating without warning between present and past.

Such is the style of the extraordinary young French-Canadian, Marie-Claire Blais, the only writer in this hemisphere who has fully mastered the trend current in France. (p. 708)

Through the relationships of the possessed figures in [*The Day Is Dark* and *Three Travelers*], among whom the narrative shifts, Mlle. Blais creates a unique microcosm of her own wherein the characters, isolated from the conventional forms of time and space, are liberated to obey what seem to be the forces of predestination that drive them knowingly and almost willingly to their fates. The mood evoked by Marie-Claire Blais is that of suffering and gloom, yet the poetic imagery . . . is of such tender and delicate quality that the reader, like the characters, must follow the compelling forces to the end. To some, the characters may appear negative and weak, in that they take no positive measures to free themselves from their torments. But they are caught in a predetermined universe which they are powerless to change. This is Mlle. Blais's vehicle wherein she is free to mingle reality and the fantasy of the characters' thoughts. As each personage is gifted with exceptional powers to perceive the objects and happenings around him, the effect Mlle. Blais achieves is almost poetic. (pp. 708, 710)

George W. Knowles, in The American Scholar *(copyright © 1967 by the United Chapters of Phi Beta Kappa; reprinted by permission of the publishers), Vol. 36, No. 4, Autumn 1967.*

JOAN COLDWELL

When Marie-Claire Blais was asked which writers had influenced her work she named Virginia Woolf and Katherine Mansfield, authors who experimented boldly with forms of psychological fiction. In looking over the nine novels Mlle Blais has written up to now one can see signs of that influence in a variety of technical devices. Diaries and letters are used for psychological introspection and analysis in *Tête Blanche, A Season in the Life of Emmanuel* and *L'Insoumise,* while the stream of consciousness method is explored in the "novel-poems" and notably in *The Day Is Dark,* where the form appears to be markedly influenced by Virginia Woolf's *The Waves.* As well as being explorations of the nature of evil and its particular manifestations in Quebec society, these novels are technical experiments in conveying the inner life of the mind and especially of the adolescent mind.

It is in this context that one must approach Mlle. Blais' first novel, *Mad Shadows.* But whereas the psychological concerns of her later novels are apparent, those of *Mad Shadows* may be obscured by the unusual form and gothic content, with the result that critics have either written the novel off altogether, as many early reviewers did, or have been tempted to read into it a metaphor of "the world before birth" or an allegory of the Apocalypse of St. John. One simpler way of reading *Mad Shadows* is as a psychological novel whose method is, like that of Kafka's *America,* the projection of inner states through fantastic actions. The fantasies enacted here are those of an adolescent girl in her response to sexuality, sex being the turning point between innocence and bitter experience as it is also in the more conventionally structured *Tête Blanche.*

At first, *Mad Shadows* may also appear to be a conventional "realistic" novel. Features of a landscape are mentioned: fields, farms, lake, woods, railway, asylum, and the narrative develops in straightforward chronological order, the simplicity of its superficial framework marked by a style which is at key moments as elementary as that of a child's primer.... But these normal situations explode into sensational developments: the jealous sister starves and ravages the spoilt brother, disillusionment in marriage provokes instant separation, the son murders his stepfather, the daughter kills the mother, both children commit suicide. Only Greek and Elizabethan tragedies have exploited so much horror and violence in so confined a space; generally speaking, novelists work on a larger scale where the fearful actions do not hammer obsessively one upon another. It is the number of horrors within a very short novel that threatens credibility here and alerts one to the fact that this is not, after all, a novel of the realistic school.

The method of *Mad Shadows* consists of creating action out of normally sublimated emotional responses. Given Isabelle-Marie's jealousy of Patrice as a recognisable normal state, the nature of that passion is then explored, not by interior monologue nor by the author's analysis, but by projecting as external actions the extremes to which, in most people, only fantasy gives free play. The sense of nightmare in *Mad Shadows* arises from this surrealist technique. The landscape appears to be real, actions seem to be logical, but they are so only on the level of the subconscious mind. "It is all a picture," Marie-Claire Blais herself said, "it is all art while life goes on, it is a picture of the emotions of love or fear."...

The picture metaphor is enforced in the novel itself by references to film: in the first paragraph, Patrice's mental confusion is "like a billowing stormcloud on a screen" and, later, Louise and Lanz have the "artificial depravity of faces in the movies". Most insistently, theatre imagery suggests that this is not reality we observe but an artificial enactment: the characters are described as marionettes or as "grave performers" in a "vast tragedy" and Patrice uses make-up to turn his face into a devil's mask. The culmination of this pattern is the inclusion, late in the novel, of the character Faust, a retired actor who becomes Patrice's friend in the asylum where they are both confined. It is in the Faust episode that the technique of creating "art while life goes on" is most fully explored. Faust, like his legendary namesake, possesses the magical art of living and exerting power by illusions. (p. 65)

The Faust story is only one of several legends, myths or fairy tales evoked in the novel.... More obviously, the strange family relationships recall certain Greek myths: the Oedipus pattern is suggested in the almost incestuous obsession of Louise and Patrice for each other while the two filial murders recall the Orestes-Electra story. The Narcissus myth is introduced not only in Patrice's adoration of his own image in the lake and his death there but in Louise's worship of her own beauty reflected in her son. Metaphor enforces this link with Narcissus: "without him she was lost, shorn of both roots and flowers." (pp. 65-6)

The most obvious echo in the novel, clearly indicated by the French title *La Belle Bête*, is of the Beauty and the Beast tale, "la belle et la bête", where the beast is under a spell which can only be broken by the love of a princess. Here again illusion is important (the beast is really a handsome prince) but in *Mad Shadows* the image is turned so that the beauty and the beast are one. Patrice is beast be-

cause he lacks reason but his body is divinely beautiful, that of an Adonis. In its origins the Beauty and Beast tale no doubt enforces a moral lesson about sexuality, the physical in man being given sanction by pure spiritual love. The fact that Marie-Claire Blais fuses the two, making the beauty-love figure totally beast-physical; points to one of the dominant themes in this novel, namely the essential destructiveness of human love.

All of the legendary tales mentioned above have sexual connotations and within the novel the echoes of them reflect on a series of relationships which are all self-centered and superficial.... In this novel, love is literally only skin-deep and without physical attraction it does not exist. To provide a visual emblem of imperfection, each of the characters is made physically defective, Michael blind, Lanz lame, Isabelle weak-ankled, Louise hideously scarred and Patrice wholly beautiful but both empty-headed and finally rendered grotesquely ugly. The emblem is reflected in the animal kingdom, with the seemingly gratuitous, surrealistic detail of a one-winged bird flying near the lake. (p. 66)

Before she dies, Isabelle appears to have a momentary spiritual illumination: "She thought it was Louise's land that she was destroying but suddenly she realized it was God's land. Terror rose to her eyes. And shame."... Up to this point there has been very little religious reference in this man-centered novel: only an identification of Isabelle with Eve, a comparison of the asylum to a "cathedral with bars" and, most important, ... observations on the character of Isabelle's father in which we may find a clue to her final experience.

[We] are told that the daughter resembled the father, "that gallant dreamer and poet who used to speak of his land as though of a virgin consecrated to God."...

Marie-Claire Blais seems to suggest that only love for God and love for the land are non-destructive; all other human love is corrosive, especially in its sexual manifestations. The only release into humanity is by loss of concern for the body: when Patrice perceives his ugliness and destroys his body, he finds his soul. That pervasive theme of Quebec literature, the dichotomy of body and spirit, is here once more projected, not by allegory but by externalisation of inner impulses.

"My first and second novels are about passions, the emotions which are so dangerous to liberate," said Marie-Claire Blais. *Mad Shadows* shows the liberation not merely of passion into action but of concealed fantasies into external story. The novel is an experiment in fictional technique, one which is dangerously open to a literal interpretation and therefore close to the absurd and unintelligible. But if read as psychological fiction, an exploration of the dark recesses of the mind, then *Mad Shadows* may well appear to be, like Patrice's face, "so dazzling that it makes one think of genius." (p. 67)

Joan Coldwell, "'Mad Shadows' as Psychological Fiction," in Journal of Canadian Fiction *(reprinted by permission from* Journal of Canadian Fiction, *2050 Mackay St., Montreal, Quebec H3G 2J1, Canada), Vol. II, No. 4, 1973, pp. 65-7.*

D. NYREN

Le loup is the story of a lamb who is caught by or, more accurately, captures a series of wolves. It is a study of types of male homosexual love, a succession of character sketches rather than a developed plot or philosophical investigation; it grows by accretion rather than extension.

While Blais continues to write about the less ordinary passions, *Le loup* eschews the violence of her earlier books and is more suave and nuanced. She has become more perceptive of psychological differences as she has grown from child prodigy to professional writer; however, considerably more development will still be needed before she can be adjudged a novelist of any literary significance. (p. 80)

D. Nyren, in Books Abroad *(copyright 1975 by the University of Oklahoma Press), Vol. 49, No. 1, Winter, 1975.*

*   *   *

BOND, Edward   1934-

Bond, a Londoner from a working class background, is a controversial playwright whose brilliant plays filled with violence and cruelty were twice banned by the Lord Chamberlain. An intensely moral dramatist, he writes his plays, he maintains, as "an examination of what it means to be living at this time." (See also *CLC*, **Vols. 4, 6, and** *Contemporary Authors*, **Vols. 25-28, rev. ed.)**

MARTIN ESSLIN

What a brilliant play *Saved* is, how well it has stood the test of time! Bond has succeeded in making the inarticulate, in their very inability to express themselves, become transparent before our eyes: their speechlessness becomes communication, we can look right inside their narrow, confined, limited and pathetic emotional world. This is the final step and the ultimate consummation of the linguistic revolution on the British stage: what a distance we have come from the over-explicit clichés of the flat well-mannered banter, the dehumanized upper-class voices of an epoch which now appears positively antediluvian. . . . (p. 174)

Saved is a deeply moral play: the scene of the stoning of the baby which led to the first outcry about it, is one of the key points in its moral structure. (p. 175)

In his own note in the published version of the play, Bond himself calls it an optimistic piece, because of Len's loyalty to the girl who rejects him. It is true: Len is a touching character in his stubborn devotion to the girl. And yet I am not at all convinced that this is the main message of *Saved*. Why indeed is the play called *Saved*? As far as I can see the only direct reference to the title is in the scene when Pam is trying to win Fred, the murderer—and perhaps the father?—of her child, back to her after his release from prison. Len, who foresees that she will be rebuffed, has come with her to the café where the reunion is to take place. When Fred *does* reject her with contempt, Pam wants to believe that he is doing this because of Len's, a rival's, presence. She cries out: *'Somebody's got a save me from 'im.'* The irony of the title therefore seems to me to lie in the fact that Pam at the end has lost Fred and continues to live in the same home, the same household as Len, and that, although all speech has ceased in that house, she will inevitably go on living with him, in every sense of the word. So that, eventually, she has *not* been saved.

A thorough study of the text reveals many equally subtle and complex insights and ironies. . . . (pp. 175-76)

At first glance there could be no greater contrast than that between *Saved* and *Narrow Road to the Deep North*. Here the dialect of the speechless, there the clarity of stylized poetic speech; here deepest London, there the farthest, most exotic orient. Yet, a closer look reveals the common ground. Here, as there, the problem of the disastrous influence of a morality based on an intellectually bankrupt religion, here as there the horror of violence which expresses itself in images of violence. (p. 176)

[*Narrow Road to the Deep North*] is a beautiful parable play, very Brechtian in its mixture of orientalism (used as an 'alienation effect' to show familiar problems in an unexpected light) and moral didacticism. It is Brechtian also in the spareness and economy of its writing. (p. 177)

Is [*Early Morning*] a play about death? Is it about the court of Queen Victoria and Prince Albert? Or, if neither of these, what *is* it about? (p. 178)

'The events of this play are true,' states Bond's own note on the first page of the printed text. Now, clearly, of the real Queen Victoria, the real Prince Albert, the real Florence Nightingale there is nothing that is historically true in the play. Prince Arthur and Prince George were not Siamese twins, Florence Nightingale was not engaged to one of them, there was no civil war in England in which Disraeli captured the Queen after she had murdered her husband and wanted to have her shot, etc., etc. Yet, the events of the play *are* true. They are true insofar as they mirror establishment politics and history as they might appear to a child exposed to the history teaching practised in most of our schools, where stereotypes and idiotic clichés of history are paraded before working class children who are barely able to understand the vocabulary of battles, civil and external wars, dynasties, and the whole panoply of terms in which politics and power are discussed.

But the events of the play are also true, perhaps even more so, in the way in which they portray the process by which out of this half-understood, and therefore already mythical, fairy tale material, a child would build up its private mythology, using the strange mythical beings it has been told about to express its subconscious fears and desires. Then the child's anxiety about the quarrels between his parents—and whose parents don't quarrel?—could easily be transmuted into civil wars between giant figures of authority, a Queen and her Consort; the image of the Siamese twins who hate each other's guts but are condemned to stick together through thick and thin is clearly a child's nightmare about being stuck with his brother with whom he shares a room or perhaps even a bed. And finally the strong emphasis on cannibalism which pervades the whole play, from the incident in the cinema queue in Kilburn (where a man and his girl-friend killed the chap in front of them because he had tried to jump the queue and ate him out of boredom) to the whole of the third act in Heaven, where the whole cast are reassembled after death to orgies of mutual cannibalism, simply because there is no pain and no death in heaven and it does not hurt to have one's limbs torn out and eaten, and anyway they grow again instantly.

The world of the establishment, therefore, mirrored in a child's consciousness, and in turn mirroring its subconscious sexuality (the oral phase of sexuality is, according to Freud, the earliest phase of the sex drive and leads to dreams about eating people) is the true theme of *Early*

Morning. Hence, in my opinion also, the title, pointing to the fact that this is a picture of the world as it might appear in childhood, life's early morning. (pp. 178-79)

Martin Esslin, "Edward Bond's Three Plays," in his Brief Chronicles: Essays on Modern Theatre (copyright © 1961, 1962, 1963, 1966, 1967, 1968, 1969, 1970 by Martin Esslin), Temple Smith, 1970, pp. 174-80.

KATHARINE J. WORTH

[Bond] provides the most massive demonstration that a new theatre is forming round us, a theatre of acting out rather than analysis, a colloquial theatre that is also visionary and poetic. He constructs his plays poetically, around images: *Lear,* he says, grew out of the image of the Gravedigger's Boy, and others have begun from phrases or sentences 'which seem to have some sort of curious atmosphere about them that one wants to explore and open up.' (p. 168)

Bond is also a very conscious moralist and has much in common with the writers in epic mode.... There is a similar fascination with Victorian subjects, a similar feeling for big, episodic forms and for broad, pantomime techniques. Linguistically, however, he stands apart. His isn't a Babylonish dialect but something much more convincing, that can sound natural even in the act of defining some darkly fantastic, gargantuan event like the cannibalism in *Early Morning* or the ritualistic blinding of Lear.

His language has a peculiarly flat, deadpan quality and a rather unexpected range. It can be wonderfully comical and winning.... Bond gets the same sort of time blur that [Charles] Wood aims at but with much less sense of strain. His style is always open to this sort of knockabout but he can move easily into plain statement with a kind of highly charged simplicity about it.... And he can produce rhetoric of some grandeur when the feeling requires it.... (pp. 168-69)

It's the relation between this austere rhetoric and the coarse, gritty ground it grows out of that gives Bond's language so much of its special flavour. In his earliest plays the groundwork is almost everything. *The Pope's Wedding* might even be mistaken for a plain piece of faithful realism with its slow moving, day-to-day action and its choked dialect exchanges among the inarticulate teenagers who are its characters. Wesker doesn't seem too far off in scenes like [the] one between Scopey and the old hermit, Alen, for whom he and his wife have accepted a curious responsibility. (p. 169)

But the sense of some terrible incident looming up gives this close, dry accumulation of detail a peculiar, un-Wesker-like force. There is a feeling of mystery. The questions Scopey presses on Alen are tormenting; they may seem sadistic. But they are tormented too. We feel the frustration—partly caused by inarticulacy—of a mind groping to understand why things are as they are. Eventually something explodes and he murders the old man.

The handling of the murder is very distinctive. It happens between scenes: we're told nothing about it until the very end and yet we seem to be deeply involved in it.... The lack of any attempt at explanation makes a strange effect here. Partly, I think, it seems a little arbitrary and unsatisfactory—the technique is more tentative than in later plays—but partly too the bareness, the inarticulacy, the

withholding of meaning creates a mysterious sense of meaning; a poetic dimension starts to take shape.

These are unexpected notes in a play which like all Bond has so far written asks in a way simply to be taken as moral fable. Moral passion is certainly a great driving force behind his writing. He is very close in some ways to the moralist playwrights in the Shavian tradition, to Osborne and even to Shaw himself. He has written moral fables (*Black Mass, Passion*) for specific occasions of social protest and in all his plays characters are apt to moralize and talk in parables. Like Shaw, he uses prefaces and pamphlets to drive home prophetic warnings, calling on us to turn from our violent ways before Judgement falls.... (pp. 170-71)

For Bond, like Shaw, unjust social arrangements are a root cause of the evils we suffer from: 'People with unjust social privileges have an obvious emotional interest in social morality'; 'Social morality is a form of suicide'. Even the style often has as here, a touch of Shavian aphorism and paradox. And he allies himself with Shaw by continually drawing attention to the social optimism of his plays; *Saved* is 'almost irresponsibly optimistic', and *Early Morning* is 'easily the most optimistic of my plays'. People *can* be changed, there *is* free will. In both plays, as also in *Lear* (much less equivocally than in *King Lear*) the movement is towards redemption. *Saved* ends with restorative acts: Len mends a chair, a great proof of his resilience in that grim context, as Bond remarks, and the outline of a family group dimly appears. *Early Morning* ends—grotesquely and beautifully—with the resurrection of the suffering character, Prince Arthur, the one who chose to be consumed rather than join in consuming his fellows. And Lear dies in the act of working to undo the wall, symbol of all that he ought not to have done.

To speak of the images through which Bond expresses his passion is at once to feel his great distance from Shaw, however. Emotionally, he is closer to Osborne and in fact there are some rather striking affinities between them. Both put an un-Shavian emphasis on suffering, are taken up with characters who have unusual capacity for feeling the pain of others. Their phrases and ideas could often be interchangeable. (pp. 171-72)

There are similarities too in their feeling for metaphor. Osborne believes in the responsiveness of English audiences to violent and poetic metaphors and this is what he tries to give them. But here a gulf begins to open up as wide as the gulf between Osborne and Shaw. In fact the line from Shaw through Osborne to Bond could almost be taken as the characteristic movement towards a more violent, more poetic theatre which has been developing during the period. On Bond's stage metaphors are acted out in a stunningly direct way. His imagination for 'incidents' is one of the most impressive things in his art. He wants a metaphor for what society does when it is 'heavy with aggression' and he finds it in the horrific incident of some youths stoning a baby in its pram for no reason that any one of them could possibly give. He looks for a way of suggesting inner deadness—the feeling expressed by Osborne's Archie—'I'm dead behind the eyes, I'm dead, just like the whole inert, shoddy lot out there'—and gets it in the form of a monstrous heaven where dead people picnic on each others' bones and congratulate themselves on feeling no more pain.

Early Morning represents a great leap forward in technique. The focus is sharper than in *Saved*, where the stoning incident is rather too overwhelming, thrusting itself forward as a rather too believable and very particular event. No danger of that happening, one would think, in a play which renders the Victorian scene in such fantastic terms as *Early Morning*. It's a strange dream we're in, where Victoria rampages like the prison governess Prince Albert says she ought to have been, enjoying in her spare moments an affair with Florence Nightingale disguised as John Brown (a hilariously funny episode, this); where Disraeli and Gladstone are almost indistinguishable power-mad gangsters and at the centre is a mythical character, Prince Arthur, who drags round with him his Siamese twin attachment even after it has died and turned to a skeleton.

The danger here, one might suppose, would be of our refusing to take the action in real terms at all or possibly of our trying to turn it into a rather rigid allegory. In fact for some of the first audiences (including, presumably, the Lord Chamberlain, who banned the play) it came over in astonishingly real terms as a tremendous libel on eminent Victorians. This seems a great testimony to Bond's skill in clothing his fantasies with flesh. His ability to keep so many lines open, juggle with so many different sorts of reality is what makes *Early Morning* such a startling achievement, coming after one-level plays like *The Pope's Wedding* and *Saved*. (pp. 172-73)

And yet although the parabolic element is strong, the sense of it all somehow *really* happening is wonderfully preserved. We recognize ordinary human feelings, commonplace situations behind the fantastic forms and this can be both very funny and very disturbing. (p. 173)

The relation between his prefaces and the action of his plays is always clear, but there are such fantastic leaps of imagination between one process and the other that the plays seem to exist in a dimension entirely their own. . . .

Bond gets an enormous extension of control in [*Early Morning*] by the surrealistic pantomime techniques he uses (significantly, good effects can be got by directorial inventions like having Joyce played as a pantomime dame by a male actor in drag). These techniques from a children's entertainment—as English pantomime now is—are a deeply appropriate means of expressing a vision which has so much of a child's directness in it. This horrific, funny and upsetting world in which 'angry, gleeful ghosts' chase each other for their next meal is like a world of Blake's crossed with Lewis Carroll's, a child's view of a baffling and terrifying grown-up life. (p. 175)

Early Morning occasionally threatens to become repetitive. But the rush of invention in it is enormously exhilarating. In the next play, *Narrow Road to the Deep North*, similar techniques are applied with more austerity: perhaps the Japanese element—it is set in Japan 'about the seventeenth, eighteenth or nineteenth centuries'—disciplined the Gothic exuberance of *Early Morning*. The control is impressive (though one rather misses the wild zest of the earlier play) and certainly needed, for the atrocities here—the slaughter of the five children, Kiro's self-disembowelling—could easily become oppressive; they are more 'real', more easily imagined happening than the events of *Early Morning*. It's a painfully believable moment, for instance, when Georgina tries to save the children from the soldiers, calling them to

their prayers as though nothing threatened: 'It's nothing, children. The men are playing. On your knees. Eyes shut. Hands together.' But the horror is kept well in control by sharp distancing techniques, Noh-like devices such as the identical, paper cut-out look of the five children—their bodies were represented by Japanese rag dolls—and the absolute silence of the ritualistic disembowelling sequence. Attention isn't allowed to settle on physical torment but is directed to what the play is really about, different attempts to deal with the horror of life—by acquiring power or by withdrawing like Basho in search of enlightenment. *Narrow Road to the Deep North* is a particularly difficult play to appreciate without aid of production partly because the style is so especially dry and laconic and so much of the effect depends on these very austere visual stylizations.

This ability of his to create compelling and deeply meaningful stage pictures is an enormous help to Bond in his latest and richest play so far, *Lear*. For a start it makes it easier for him to cut free of Shakespeare. Bond's scene is so much his own that it immediately takes our full attention; we drop the comparing and measuring we must surely have started out with (it would be hard to come to a play called *Lear* leaving Shakespeare quite behind). There's a strange dream-like inconsistency in the costumes: Lear and his daughters in flowing robes (Fontanelle a dreadful schoolgirl with hair in bunches); the guards and soldiers in modern uniform with guns and hints of concentration camp equipment. A common-place business-like episode is taking place, it seems. Lear is behaving like a works supervisor, or, as Bill Gaskill suggested, he and his daughters are like the Royal Family visiting a shipyard, carrying umbrellas. He enquires into the trouble holding up the building of the off-stage wall; a man has been accidentally killed by someone dropping an axe. Suddenly the action lurches into nightmare. Lear calls the act sabotage, sentences the offender to death, not for manslaughter but for holding up the work; when his daughters object and countermand the order to the firing squad he takes a gun and shoots the man himself. As Bodice and Fontanelle express it, he has gone mad.

So the wall imposes itself from the first moment as a dark shadow over the action, the central symbol, and this at once takes us away from the familiar Shakespearean ambience and lures us to think in Bond's terms. We remain constantly aware of it but don't see it until the last scene when a tremendous physical shock is got by having it suddenly appear, filling the whole stage—horizontally, as Bond wanted it—looking like a cross between the Pyramids and the Great Wall of China; a great earthy monster threatening us as well as the characters. The effect brings home the terrible, sad irony of people in the play continuing to see this dreadful wall as their defence and protection. 'Pull it down', says Lear at the end. 'We'd be attacked by our enemies', says Cordelia. After all she has suffered because of the wall she still believes that good will be served by maintaining it.

The inconsistencies, or anachronisms, I first spoke of run through the action and are a vital part of the technique, 'desperate facts' Bond calls them. 'They are for the horrible moments in a dream when you know it's a dream but can't help being afraid.' Obvious signposts to time and place go; place names, topical allusions; even some of the Shakespearean place marks are taken out. Lear and Cordelia remain, but the rest change name in a way that usually points to something primitive or fundamental about them. (pp. 176-78)

It would be possible to take *Early Morning* as essentially a satire on Victorian history, though the kaleidoscopic technique includes plenty of pointers to our time, lines like Arthur's: 'Don't touch me. I've got Porton Plague.' That mistake couldn't be made about *Lear*. The action is kept astoundingly open, with lines leading back to antiquity (the Wall, the Sophoclean scenes at the end) to Tolstoy, to Shakespeare, and insistently and sadly to our own time.

If we can never for a moment forget that it's our time, this is very largely because of the idiom: the slang, the rough colloquialisms and above all the humour. The sombre incidents are continually being checked and measured against humour.... (pp. 178-79)

Even the cruelty is in a way humanized by the humour. The elements are very skilfully balanced. (p. 179)

[What] Bond is showing us has been 'real' in our time; this is really a much cleaned up version of the obscene events that took place in the Nazi concentration camps.

It's by that route that Bond came to Shakespeare; not that he set out to measure himself against him, but that in these areas of feeling all lines run to that point. He has said that he wanted to rewrite *King Lear* 'so that we now have to use the play for ourselves, for our society, for our time, for our problems . . .'.... (pp. 179-80)

It's a measure of Bond's power that he can impose his own vision and his own terms on the great, formidable material and take us away from Shakespeare in the act of using him. And it's a measure of his subtlety that he can risk venturing as close as he occasionally does to the Shakespearean version, most audaciously perhaps, in the scene of the autopsy. . . . The horror of the scene when Lear put his hands into Fontanelle and drew out her entrails is about as far in the direction of Grand Guignol as Bond has gone. It was a 'big gesture', as Bill Gaskill put it and obviously a risky one: it could so easily have been either ludicrous, or overpoweringly offensive. But it worked. There was no laughter of the wrong kind and indeed, unlike earlier episodes in the vein of horror, this one drew no laughter at all. We were too deep in feeling, too affected by the solemn and complex movement of events. (p. 180)

The echoes of Shakespeare called up here enriched without undermining—a remarkable achievement. It was as though at this level of suffering and imagination all Lears must inevitably echo and pick up from each other's words.

Some of Bond's divergences from the Shakespearean model make his play seem the more pessimistic of the two. He calls himself a pessimist by experience and an optimist by nature (another of his Shavian-sounding phrases) and it is the pessimism of experience that forces him to see Cordelia —not in his play Lear's natural daughter—as doomed to go the same way as the 'wicked' daughters, once she starts to use force to combat them. This is the great central theme of the play, the idea of violence as a vicious circle of chain reactions; the chain gang of prisoners, where tyrants end up shackled to their victims, Fontanelle fastened on to Lear, is the fierce visual image that expresses it. (p. 181)

In his handling of the blinding . . . , Bond's optimism as-

serts itself. The change he makes here—transferring Gloucester's blindness to Lear—allows him to push the Shakespearean action to the Sophoclean end he has designed for it. Blindness becomes an unequivocal symbol of insight. (pp. 181-82)

[It is] traumatic memories which are exorcised by blind Lear. Like Oedipus at Colonus, he becomes a sacred figure, both receiving and extending care, and attracting pilgrims to the place where he is. We are right out of Shakespeare and into Sophocles in the scene where the blind old man leaning on his stick relates to a devout chorus of villagers the parable of the bird in the cage; 'just as the bird had the man's voice, the man now had the bird's pain'. Our faith in Bond's optimism at this point is kept up, I think, by the reminders of human frailty behind the rhetorical eloquence. . . . It's because of [the] complexity, [the] recognition of shades of light and darkness in human character that Bond is able to bring off so triumphantly . . . the stunningly simple, parabolic ending (obviously fraught with theatrical hazards) when Lear in his Tolstoyan tunic crawls up the wall to dig it up with a peasant's spade and is shot and dies there.

Although it seemed to me this worked as Bond intended and one was able to accept the heroic gesture because of all that had gone before, there were moments in the humanly optimistic parts of the play where the didactic intention seemed rather too pushed, and one sometimes became uncomfortably aware of a flat, thematic quality in the characterization (of Thomas and Susan, for instance).

As so often with Bond, it's in the most grotesque areas of the play that his technique is seen at its most boldly inventive and—strange paradox—the mystery of human feeling is given most delicate expression. In this area the Fool or Ghost is a key figure; finally his relationship with Lear comes to seem the most interesting in the play.

Around him the action is kept exquisitely balanced between moral fable and mystery. From the start there is a fairy-tale quality about him; he is a man without a name, the Gravedigger's Boy who puts dead bodies into the ground and draws them up from deep wells. After his own death, when he reappears as the Ghost, a bizarre visual poetry begins to operate very strongly. It's pathetic and terrifying to see the gentle Boy dwindling and wasting until he has become one of the walking Auschwitz skeletons who haunt Bond's stage: at the end he is hardly more than a death's head, with a face 'like a seashell', Bond says, and eyes full of terror. Only Lear sees him and clearly in a way he represents something in Lear, something which has to die before he can find his true strength. This happens when he is able to tell Thomas and Susan that he has been 'lucky' in their affection, a totally new concept of good fortune for this passionate and violent man, and that his phase of withdrawal is over: 'Now I have only one more wish—to live till I'm much older and become as cunning as the fox, who knows how to live. Then I could teach you.' Then the old black memories well up again; the frenzied sound of pigs' squealing is heard and the Ghost stumbles in, covered with blood, to die finally and leave Lear free.

But although he has to be seen partly as an inner thing, he is also rather frighteningly separate and independent. (pp. 182-84)

And yet the Ghost is pathetic and childlike too, Lear's

'boy' whom he comforts and who comforts him. And he has too—it's such distinctions that deepen one's trust in Bond—a separate existence which he never quite loses as the husband of Cordelia, an identity which is movingly recalled in his final scene. (p. 184)

The symbolism is immensely powerful here and yet Bond finds room for small, human, one might almost say Chekhovian, touches: Lear asking Cordelia, 'You've been to the house? Did it upset you?'; the Ghost pathetically urging Lear, 'Tell her I'm here. Make her talk about me'. Such scenes make very clear what one means by speaking of Bond's art as poetic. It is a true dramatic poetry of structure and dynamic imagery in which brilliantly imagined visual elements play an essential part.

It seems appropriate to end my discussion of recent drama on this high note of audacious innovation by a playwright who seems almost certain to be foremost among the shapers of the modern English tradition. (p. 186)

> Katharine J. Worth, "Edward Bond," in her *Revolutions in Modern English Drama (copyright © Katharine J. Worth 1972; reprinted by permission of Bell & Hyman Ltd.), G. Bell & Sons, Ltd., 1973, pp. 168-87.*

JOHN PETER

[No] one would have guessed from the title or the sub-title [of Edward Bond's *Bingo: Scenes of Money and Death*] that its hero was William Shakespeare. This is entirely appropriate because in an important sense it is not about Shakespeare at all. . . .

[Essentially the play] is the continuation of an argument Bond had begun earlier . . . , in *Narrow Road to the Deep North,* his bitter parable about the seventeenth-century Japanese poet Basho. In the play, you will recollect, Basho helped to bring terrible suffering to his country by ignoring individual suffering as he travelled north in search of personal enlightenment.

The subject of *Bingo* is the same: the utter inadequacy, indeed the harmfulness, of the artist as a social animal. Bond's point is that writing is not enough: the artist is a man among men and must be a functioning part of the moral structure of society. . . .

[In an interview with *Gambit* Bond] said that 'art is the confrontation of justice with law and order'—a definition which might have made even Shelley uneasy. (I take it that Bond was using these much abused words in their modish false meaning of 'reaction and repression'.) This prepares you for the fact that the writer Bond would most despise is one who sides with 'law and order.' Such a writer, for him, is Shakespeare. (p. 28)

Like most of Bond's plays, *Bingo* is a play of conscience. The very structure shows its severe moral intention: the first three scenes relate Shakespeare's offence, the second three present his retribution. (p. 29)

[Bond] has always been a moralist; but a moral view of life means seeing it in terms of acts and their consequences. Morality demands the responsibility of logic; yet Bond often comes over as a dramatist of stark statement. Morality, in the theatre, also demands the responsibility of scrupulous characterisation; Bond likes to present states of mind which do not respond to our questioning. (pp. 29-30)

[Both] *Early Morning,* Bond's only really bad play, and *Lear* are fatally weakened by an almost total absence of moral reasoning. 'Souls live and bodies die,' says Prince Arthur, the suffering hero of *Early Morning;* and Bond's plays could be described as a world of soulless bodies and dead souls where the cause of death is almost impossible to identify. Always we are left with the conclusion that we live in an unspeakably cruel world: a rhetorical message that has the finality and the self-justification of a nightmare. This is why Bond's plays so often breed either indifference or unquestioning devotion. The most compassionate mind reels into dulled impotence if it is confronted with nothing but abrupt and unexplained examples of human monstrosity. On the other hand, temperamental pessimists and shallow anarchists respond to Bond's plays with the unquestioning gratitude that comes from reassurance.

The paradox is that both reactions are deeply contrary to the aims of a compassionate moralist which is the stance Bono takes. Time and again he creates the expectation of a moral argument made up of understanding, compassion and unsparing inquiry; all too often he ends up as the dramatist of narcosis.

One aspect of this, by the way, is his treatment of politicians and public men. For Bond representatives of power, indeed of organised society, are stereotyped monsters: vicious, or dotty, or both. . . .

Bond's best play is *The Sea,* the last one he wrote before *Bingo.* Here he has come to terms with his apostolic temperament and the practical problems of a moral view of the world. In other words he presents not unmotivated puppets but people. (p. 30)

The evil that people do to one another is put in the context of their own suffering: the aching flesh seeks to inflict pain on someone else. Yet Bond invites no facile pity. . . .

For in almost all Bond's plays there is a killing, and a great deal of their action takes place with a dead body on stage. I have said that his plays are plays of conscience; they are also, in yet another paradoxical sense, plays of pity. In every one of them (*Bingo* is no exception) someone asks for help and is refused. 'The man without pity is mad,' his Lear says, but it is remarkable how few of Bond's characters show any, and how often those who do, like Len in *Saved,* carry decency to the point of softness or feebleness. They do not raise a hand. They can prevent nothing, neither do they try. They have only a dogged, grim humanity; they endure, when they do, like stone.

Indeed, the real indictment of the violence in Bond's plays is not so much that it is often gratuitous (it is), or overdone (it is), but that it is unopposed. . . . Bond seems to say that humanity is made up of murderous beasts and helpless or feeble-minded victims; that the world is entirely predatory and almost devoid of human charity and kindness. In the face of that the spectator can only stand up and declare that it isn't, it isn't, it isn't.

Let me finally return to *Bingo.* It is filled with the same anger Bond had expressed about Basho and his poetry in the *Gambit* interview; and it is another of the great contradictions of his art that he, a careful craftsmen and a considerable master of language, can so summarily dismiss an artist. Shakespeare's works are simply not relevant to *Bingo,* just as Basho's were not to *Narrow Road,* except as the (by implication) useless products of wasted or pernicious lives. And yet the earlier play seems to have been inspired by something more than Bond's dislike of a self-regarding poet. Its language, like the language of Bond's few published poems, reminds you again and again of the Japanese *haiku* itself. At its best it is spare, concise, densely poetic; and the most memorable passages of Bond's plays all have just such a bony, allusive eloquence. This is why, in production, the plays need such carefully placed silences. And so it is no accident that many of Bond's characters are watchers and listeners. Sometimes indeed it is their silence that condemns them: Len, Basho, Lear and Shakespeare all have to pay, in the end, for being silent when they should have spoken. (p. 31)

[*Bingo*] fails in the end not only because of the improbability of Shakespeare's death [a suicide]; not only because Bond never explains, cannot explain, why Shakespeare had got into a state of moral checkmate in the first place; but also because of the formal, over-written language of his disintegration in the snow. The phrases are ponderous, turgid and hollow: they present the idea but not the suffering of human failure. This climactic scene carries intellectual force but no real feeling and conviction whatever. Bond the puritan moralist executes Shakespeare; Bond the poet, who wrote *The Sea* and the last scene of *Saved,* seems to cooperate without conviction. It is as if, in killing the other poet, he were killing a part of himself. (p. 32)

> *John Peter, "Edward Bond, Violence and Poetry," in* Drama, *Autumn, 1975, pp. 28-32.*

JOHN LAHR

A playwright's task is to stun an audience awake, to make it see what life forces it to forget. Edward Bond is one of the few English playwrights with the cunning and craft to meet this challenge. He is obsessed with man's death-dealing in a society whose myths of justice and fair play make it numb to its own brutality. Bond's sense of outrage has turned him, at times, into the Ancient Marineer of the English stage, buttonholing his audience and hectoring it with gruesome and generalised images of suffering (*Lear, Bingo*). But in his superb new play, *The Fool: Scenes of Bread and Love,* Bond attains a new theatrical maturity. Luring his audience into the robust and violent rural world of John Clare, the farm labourer turned poet, at the beginning of England's industrialisation in 1815, Bond creates a pageant of exploitation which demonstrates how imagination as well as manpower were victimised by the ruthless pursuit of profit.... *The Fool* follows Clare's sad career from his life on the land to literary celebrity and finally, estranged from both land and literature, into madness. (p. 23)

Bond, even more than most, has known the terrible frustration of writing well and being dismissed by those who have never dared journey as far as himself. He is a big talent.... (p. 25)

> *John Lahr, in* Plays and Players (© *copyright John Lahr 1976; reprinted with permission), January, 1976.*

*   *   *

BOOTH, Martin   1944-

Booth, a British poet, journalist, script writer, editor, novelist, and juvenile writer, writes about the relationship of past to present, drawing largely on mythological imagery and symbolism.

[Martin Booth in *Coronis* espresses a] fondness for the laconic fragment—a device which, enforced in his case by a trick of ritual repetition and a gravely hieratic tone, can become irritating; but otherwise he writes in a quite different vein. For the most part he eschews detailed observation for some attractively off-beat imaginings, where real things become significant in terms of the symbolic roles they play within some ceremony of the imagination. It is not always easy to discriminate in his work between the authentically original and the bizarrely fanciful: some of his images seem to float up fortuitously, others work out an impressively coherent logic of feeling. A mixed volume, in short, with some painfully false notes ... and some signs of genuine talent. (p. 1154)

> The Times Literary Supplement (© *Times Newspapers Ltd. (London) 1973; reproduced from* The Times Literary Supplement *by permission), October 5, 1973.*

ROGER GARFITT

[Martin Booth] is far too inclined to settle for easy answers, viz. his imitations of *Crow,* his intermittent sentimentality, and his rather easy recourse to the imagery of magic. He is one of those who hold the iatric view of poetry, that it exists to resolve the forces of the unconscious.... Booth's work is best when he focuses his style firmly onto the object in view, with certain personal ironies implicit underneath as in 'Whales off Sasketeewan' and 'Direption'. And when he combines his mythological interest with a sense of the present time, rooted both in history and in the galactic dimension, then the writing really does seem to promise something.... (pp. 111-12)

> *Roger Garfitt, in* London Magazine (© *London Magazine 1974), August-September, 1974.*

D. M. THOMAS

[*The Knotting Sequence* is] rooted in a landscape: the hamlet of Knotting, where [Mr. Booth] lives. The first half of the book explores his feelings towards this landscape through the persona of the hamlet's Anglo-Saxon founder, Cnot....

Cnot is too shadowy a figure, and too limited in metaphor and suggestiveness, to be able to sustain a fairly long sequence with undiminished energy, with the result that some of the poems seem slight affairs; one, for example, is built around a weak pun: "sorrow's / a marriage of / good and / sad he / said ...". I am not sorry when Cnot vanishes and Mr. Booth can turn to the living landscape and its seasons, its small births and deaths, and these he describes beautifully, in controlled, strong, *haiku*-like poems.... [*The Knotting Sequence*] is a stage in the development of a genuine poet. (p. 66)

> *D. M. Thomas, in* The Times Literary Supplement (© *Times Newspapers Ltd. (London) 1978; reproduced from* The Times Literary Supplement *by permission), January 20, 1978.*

VERNON SCANNELL

Charm is not a quality that Martin Booth's poetry offers nor, I imagine, would he be flattered by any suggestion of its presence there; but . . . *Extending Upon the Kingdom* is a vigorous, always interesting collection, and at least half-a-dozen of the poems carry a strong sense of real experience observed with clarity and expressed with force and unwavering truthfulness. (p. 160)

Vernon Scannell, in The Times Literary Supplement (© Times Newspapers Ltd. (London) 1978; reproduced from The Times Literary Supplement by permission), February 10, 1978.

ROBERT S. HALLER

The poems [in *The Knotting Sequence*] are made up of short lines, reminiscent of *haiku* . . . , but the spirit is distinctly Western. A spare diction expresses the mythic consciousness of present-day poets on both sides of the Atlantic, the attempt to find in landscape and daily activities signs of communion with a past still alive and determinate of the present. It would perhaps be more accurate to say that poetry creates the past and brings to life the roots in the ground. The "Guide to the Metaphysical Anatomy of Cnot, son of Kings, Lord and Worshipper" speaks of "winter elms' / shadows cast / by a / full November / moon / the lines / of Cnot's / palms upon / the roadway . . . no smell / or touch // these few / I'll lend / to you, // forefather Cnot." Such powers as the founder of the village can have are given him by those who see and feel the place as he did.

So brought to life, Cnot's relations with the poet are not always amicable: Booth apologizes (for plantings, trimmings and plowings) and complains (of a twisted lane which still follows a path to avoid Cnot's hovel). And neither Cnot nor his poet settle into a quiet pastoral life: there was bloodshed in Saxon times, and blood shed by hunters in the present. (p. 291)

This dialogue between Cnot and his poet even takes place over the Atlantic. Booth writes to Cnot from New York that he is in "the promised land" where "the houses pile / into the clouds // the cars are / gold and red." Even the sirens weep out sound, and the streets are known to breathe. "ah! says / Cnot, cynic // now tell / me you've / met / god." (p. 292)

Robert S. Haller, "Polishing the Sherds," in Prairie Schooner (© 1978 by University of Nebraska Press; reprinted by permission from Prairie Schooner), Fall, 1978, pp. 291-92.

*   *   *

BORGES, Jorge Luis   1899-

An Argentinian poet, essayist, short story writer, and translator, Borges is one of the world's most respected authors. Borges's writings present a surreal, labyrinthine world of dream-like parables where there are few solid cause and effect relationships. Obsessed with fantasy and the idea of literature as "fun," this blind author has been described by William Barnstone as "a clever metaphysician who has given us an enormous and varied literature, ranging from re-creations of an ancient Chinese 'Book Guardian' to the characteristics of imaginary beasts." Borges has collaborated with Adolfo Bioy Casares under the pseudonyms of H(onorio) Bustos Domecq and B. Suarez Lynch. (See also *CLC*, Vols. 1, 2, 3, 4, 6, 8, 9, and *Contemporary Authors*, Vols. 21-24, rev. ed.)

CARTER WHEELOCK

Borges's affinity for the "cult of courage" (a phrase he took from the poet Evaristo Carriego) stretches across four decades of fiction-writing to 1970, when he filled the stories of *Doctor Brodie's Report* with duels and death. These primeval battles take on, by accumulation, the look of legend or myth and seem to celebrate Argentina's heroic, violent past—her national glory and tragedy.

But Borges's fascination with bravery is much more than a preoccupation with national history, fighting, and physical bravado. In a duel to the death a man comes to grips with destiny, which sweeps aside all the moral and philosophical complexities of this confusion called life. . . .

Borges's preoccupations with bravery, then, is not based on admiration of combat nor on defense of the right. Alongside his cult of courage, moreover, we must put his cult of cowardice and treachery. In a number of stories he draws our attention to men who refuse to fight or whose loyalty is fickle. (p. 101)

When we come right down to it, it is not Borges who venerates physical courage; he merely writes about men who do. What fascinates him is that such men have made a religion of it. . . . (p. 102)

But although ["The Challenge" and] other tales of duels portray knife-fighting as [a] kind of impersonal, unemotional, even ceremonial obeisance to the iron gods of courage, in many of them the code is not idealized. Some (such as "Streetcorner Man" and "Rosendo's Tale") show dueling as the first and last resort of the bully and the coward. In the latter type, a man's true calling or destiny requires that he reject blind devotion to the tyrannical custom. What is significant here is that the gesture—the violence—is carried to a level above dueling and embodied in its opposite, a refusal to fight ("Rosendo's Tale") or a betrayal of some other sacrosanct idea of loyalty ("The Unworthy Friend," "History of the Warrior and the Captive," "The Life of Tadeo Isidoro Cruz"). The cult of courage is courageously repudiated.

It is no wonder that Borges, so famously bewildered by the inscrutable, labyrinthine universe, should dramatize the arbitrary knife that resolves all complexities in the same way that Omar's "whirlwind Sword" scatters the "black Horde of Fears and Sorrows that infest the Soul," or that he should finally extol the higher philosophical or religious act that the duel symbolizes. When he idealizes the duel, as in "The Challenge," he makes it a symbol of an apostasy that it takes courage to uphold—a religious or philosophical position which makes the individual human will the sole arbiter of what is correct or incorrect, right or wrong, saving or damning. The common denominator—the only thing finally given reverence in Borges's stories of the knife, or in his whole work for that matter—is the individual's obligation to live, move, and have his being without any kind of official sanction. Borges will not be bullied (this, of course, is well known) by hallowed ideas, sacred dogmas, or authoritarian truths, not to mention despotic men like Borges's favorite enemy, the late Juan Perón. Borges seems to declare in his stories of supposed cowards and turncoats that loyalty and treachery, courage and cowardice, are relative to one's personal and even momentary values; one man's marching music is another man's cacophony, and the only "right" drumbeat is the rhythm of one's own heart. Borges's "violence" is an arbitrary resistance to the arbitrary, a willful counterattack on the imperious and inflexible. It is not this or that unbending dogma he fights, but unbendingness itself when it expects human beings to sacrifice their integrity and identity to it.

The duel—whether fought with knives or with paint brushes—is an apt symbol of human self-affirmation unsupported by logic or any other authority than one's existence and will. We must not be fooled by Borges's continual implications that human personality is an illusion, that all men are the same man, and that he is "in a sense" or "more or less" Borges; he is very much concerned for his identity and integrity *vis-a-vis* the universe. Somewhere in his past he has been disturbed by the existential questions—guilt, fate, meaninglessness—but these have been answered in the man, and his work is built on his conclusions. In Borges's work suprahuman destiny is usually credited with determining the fate of the characters, but this is only a way of giving cosmic validity to their autocratic and often unconscious choices; what a person chooses is what he was destined to choose. This is not a denial of free will nor an affirmation of "official sanction" but a declaration that will and destiny are the same thing and that the will is the "God in any man."

Borges is steeped in the ideas of Schopenhauer, as well as in Spinoza's, Nietzsche's, and others'. Schopenhauer held that everything that happens to us is willed by us and that every man's destiny is his own choosing even when it seems accidental or Providential. He advocated getting rid of the will because it brings unhappiness, but Borges sees this as impossible although he uses the idea sometimes. What he takes from Schopenhauer with some seriousness is the notion of will as destiny. (pp. 102-03)

[When] Borges puts two hoodlums, scholars, painters, or theologians against each other, he is talking about courage and will which are exercised without appeal to argument, logic, doctrine, or right, although these may be the superficial trappings. Whether he romanticizes and idealizes physical conflict or whether he scorns it as foolish, there is always something in it which speaks of the faith of the doctrinal skeptic, the courage of the agnostic, the stoicism of the deep-dyed humanist, the courage-to-be of the confirmed freethinker. The knife puts an end to speculation, it ignores reason, it cares not for sacred beliefs; but the knife can be a cowardice, as Borges shows, when it becomes an end in itself. Borges is honest to the last; his gods denied him the epic destiny of his fathers and caused him to conclude, as he wrote in "The Life of Tadeo Isidoro Cruz" [from *The Aleph and Other Stories*], that "one destiny is no better than another, but that every man must obey what is within him." . . . (p. 104)

But what shall we do with those lady painters of "The Duel"? How does their charming story fit in? It, too, is violence. In several stories it is implied with emphasis that the duel is in the rivalry, not in the act of combat or killing. This is clear in "The End of the Duel," where the hapless gauchos have their throats cut and run a race; their deaths are the end of their competition of many years, which was the only thing that gave value to their "poor and monotonous lives." . . . It is also clear in "The End" (*Ficciones*), where a long enmity is closed with the death of Martin Fierro. But more important, in calling attention to duels as long-time rivalries which are ended, Borges combines the loser's death with the existential reduction of the winner.

The Black gaucho who kills Fierro loses his identity: "Now he was nobody; or rather, he was the other one." . . . When one of the rival painters of "The Duel" dies, the other's life as an artist loses its meaning; she paints her dead competitor's portrait and lays down the brush.

I conclude that the principle of "againstness" is fundamental. For Borges, the human personality exists only in relation to something opposite and challenging, because it consists in the will. The will cannot operate if it has nothing against which to assert itself. Again, a theological concept is involved; faith as courage or will exists only in the face of doubt and opposition. If the meaning of the world were clear, we would not have to think or to create our own meaning. We would be nothing, write nothing, paint nothing; the duel would be finished. If God were visible, we would become one with Him; we would be God. Borges's "God in any man" is the will-principle spread among all, and it alone survives. When the rival thinkers of "The Theologians" (*El Aleph*) die and go to God, the Creator is unable to tell them apart.

We should finally acknowledge, I suppose, that all of this can be taken out of the philosophical arena and put into the purely aesthetic. In the production of literature a la Borges, the arbitrary will of the writer is the creative force, and the writer creates ambiguously, not expressively, because if he is too clear he leaves the reader nothing to do. The reader has a will of his own, and his interpretation is a willful, creative act. Where there is perfect clarity there is no need for continued reading; the reader becomes the writer and the duel is finished. Borges's literature is an endless duel, he hopes, in which the reader goes on seeing "the imminence of a revelation which never comes." [The critic is quoting Borges's famous definition of the aesthetic event from his essay "The Wall and the Books."] (pp. 104-05)

> *Carter Wheelock, "Borges, Courage, and Will,"*
> *in* The International Fiction Review, *July, 1975,*
> *pp. 101-05.*

JOHN STURROCK

Borges enjoys metaphysics for what it offers him as a writer of fiction. He appreciates speculative styles of philosophy for the very reasons that most practising philosophers in the West despair of them, as offering unfounded, contradictory, and frequently incredible representations of the cosmos. Borges is not in the least sceptical of the human mind, only of its medium, language, whose co-ordination with reality, which is not verbal, he rightly finds unconvincing. (p. 21)

He values philosophy for something quite other than its likely truth or falsehood: for its power to attract or astonish, and there is all too little to attract or astonish in the work of contemporary logicians. Borges can deal aesthetically with metaphysics because he disbelieves the justifications traditionally made of it. He is the freest of all free thinkers in the sense that he sees no need to refer metaphysical thoughts to reality in order to establish some degree of correspondence with the facts. (p. 22)

Borges is an Idealist in philosophy only when he writes; his subscription to the ideas of Berkeley and Schopenhauer begins and ends with the making of his fictions. These are ideas to play with, not ones to live by. Their literary possibilities are straight-forward. The Idealism of Berkeley and Schopenhauer is seamless; it is a pure mentalism. (p. 23)

Idealism is, self-evidently, the one philosophy which helps to define the specific fictiveness of fiction. We are being asked to read all fiction, but especially Borges's own fiction, just as if we were Berkeley or Schopenhauer 'reading' the world. As readers we have the advantage, over even the most optimistic of Idealist philosophers, of knowing for a fact that the reality which confronts us is commensurate with our powers of comprehension, since it has been constructed by a mind no different in kind from our own. As an author, Borges gladly and logically affiliates himself to the Idealists because he wishes to demonstrate the true nature of fiction: the immateriality of fictional objects, the distinction between succession and causation, the juxtaposition on an equal footing of the possible with the impossible, and the provisional but complete authority of the fiction-maker over the fictions he makes. (pp. 23-4)

All Borges's fictions dramatize, in some measure, the life-cycle of a fiction: its birth, as a wilful departure from fact, its life, as a succession of choices made by its author, and its death, which is marked by a return to the world as it is, and no longer as we might like it to be. Borges has now and again asked to be taken as a realist, while knowing full well that it is very difficult for us to take him as anything of the kind. His realism, if it is realism, is of an etiolated kind: it is mimetic not of the happenings of the real world but of the activity of mimesis itself. Borges holds the mirror up to art, not to nature. Realism of this secondary sort I suspect contradicts rather than extends the realism we are used to. It involves, for Borges, fidelity not to the outside world but to the situation within that world of the maker of fictions; both his physical situation and his mental situation. The proper place to begin an analysis of Borges's fictions is with the special conditions which make fiction possible. (p. 33)

Physical isolation comes repeatedly into Borges's stories as the necessary condition of authorship. It comes into one of his earliest inventions, a brief tale loosely derived from the Arabic called 'El brujo postergado' ('The Sorcerer Postponed') in the *Historia universal de la infamia* (*Universal History of Infamy*). (pp. 34-5)

[This tale] embodies all the stages of a fiction. The magic art in which [the protagonist] Don Illán is so well versed is the art of fiction, of whose magical properties Borges has written in his essays. . . . Don Illán makes a habit of seclusion; he is first discovered in 'a room apart' and then takes his pupil to 'a place apart'. On the first occasion he is discovered reading, on the second he and the dean are interrupted as they examine his books. These symmetrical interruptions mark the points at which fiction intrudes on fact; the first interruption is followed by a meal and by a postponement of any instruction in magic, the second interruption (caused this time by two men instead of one) by the incredible, magical satisfaction of the dean's ambition and then by the refusal of a meal. There are thus two, symmetrical stories in 'El brujo postergado', the first taking us from the first interruption of Don Illán's solitary reading to the second, no longer solitary reading, the second story from that interruption to the end. The second story is the transformation of the first, with magic instead of a meal, or emotional instead of biological satisfaction. The form the second story takes, of the amazing *a*scent of the dean, is prefigured in the first story by his *de*scent into the underground room; the 'well-worked' staircase wrought by the magic of Don Illán naturally serves to carry people up as well as down.

That magic originates in the act of reading, and the 'magic instruments' to be found in Don Illán's hide-away surely include books—the realization of other men's magic. Borges, as I have said, wishes to show fictions at their point of departure from facts, but the facts he shows them as departing from are literary facts: the stock of existing fictions which the new maker of fictions takes as his models. (pp. 34-5)

The exploits of Don Isidro Parodi [the detective of *Seis problemas para don Isidro Parodi*] were invented . . . to display the conventionality of detective fiction and, by extension, all fiction. One of the nicest aspects of Parodi's immobility is that, although he never moves himself, he unfailingly discovers what makes other people move: he is skilled, that is to say, in the detection of motive. The establishment of a motive in the investigation of a crime is a paradigm of the causal process in narrative generally. (p. 38)

[Isolation and immobility] are the two conditions the imagination requires if it is to be preserved from the ruinous distractions or 'invasions' of reality. The author must not be importuned. (p. 41)

Borges, whose writing is all intelligence and rigour, likes to present himself, and his representative authors in his stories, as men inspired. Partly this is a game: there is nothing at all wild or dishevelled even in the lyric poetry which Borges has written, no evidence at all that he has ever been carried away. Partly, however, it is more serious: a justification, in conventional terms, of the fact that those who write must have a reason for writing. Inspiration, in this sense, does not replace work, it precedes it: it is the excuse the author has for subjecting himself to a considerable intellectual ordeal. Borges's pose is to imply that inspiration lasts and is even coextensive with composition. (pp. 47-8)

[In Borges, 'fever'] symbolizes the unnatural state of mind the author has to cultivate if he is to make satisfactory, rigorous fictions. Isolation from reality is not enough, he also needs an abnormal concentration of the mind which might well be experienced as a kind of excitement. Where Borges is most truly misleading is in employing a symbol for literary inspiration which makes that peculiar state of mind seem so undesirable, an imposition on the mind by a disordered body. Borges makes fictions, as anyone makes fictions, because the pleasure of making them outweighs whatever strain is entailed; he does not write them because he cannot help himself. Borges's 'fever' is far from being a pathological condition, as one sees the minute one turns from its aetiology to its effects. These effects, in their supreme ludicity, are not merely discrepant from their advertised cause, they are contradictory of it. (p. 60)

[The] hallucinations to which the maker of fictions is professionally liable are not of the usual random and disorganized kind. They are, as Borges puts it in his piece on Shakespeare in *El Hacedor* (*The Maker*), 'controlled hallucinations'. That definition, and the other, synonymous definition which Borges also uses of the 'controlled dream' or *sueño dirigido,* probably qualifies as oxymoron. Oxymoron appeals to Borges because it is a combinatory figure which brings into conjunction two terms we would normally think of as contradictory of each other; it thus flaunts the freedom which a speaker or writer enjoys of forming verbal combinations for which there is no logical justification and no referent in the real world. And so with the 'controlled hallucination', a perfectly comprehensible idea but one which makes apparent a dominant factor of mimesis: real hallucinations are not controlled but foisted on us by the malfunctioning of our bodies or minds; 'controlled' hallucinations can therefore only be the deliberate imitation of such involuntary states. (p. 61)

Once one has begun to see the somewhat deviant sense of the word 'dream' Borges is using, talk of 'controlled' dreams looks a good deal less like oxymoron and a good deal more like tautology. To Idealists, or to those who, like Borges, have hoisted philosophical Idealism as their flag of convenience, dreaming is the very specification of mental activity; all our thoughts are fictions, only a great many of them also correspond with particular states of affairs in the outside world. Authentic fictions are those thoughts and sequences of thoughts which do not so correspond.

To 'dream', then, is to idealize, and we idealize simply by turning the world into words. Borges's world is the sum of what can be said, not the sum of what there is, so that to equate thinking with dreaming, and thus abolish the distinction between the real and the hallucinatory, is to inflate the world quite monstrously. But this inflation is temporary because it is fictive. (p. 63)

[It] is not living which is a dream for Borges, only writing. . . . The dream, for him, is a passing distraction from reality; once the dream is over the dreamer must go back to living and to being the victim instead of the master of time. (p. 64)

Borges's 'controlled dreams', unlike life itself, are combinations of words or, as he likes to say, 'symbols'. They are combinations, therefore, of general terms. Idealization, or generalization, is the founding principle of Borges's fiction, as it is the founding principle of natural language. (pp. 64-5)

Borges keeps the necessary abstractness of language very much in view in his fictions; he is constantly challenging the realist illusion that general terms can be a full substitute for particular things. . . . Borges, like Schopenhauer, has very little time for history or, to be more precise, historiography, which is in so many ways a fraud, a hopelessly insufficient and therefore misleading verbal representation of the past.

The history which Borges prefers, and which he has dabbled in himself, is more abstract, more in tune with the nature of language. It is not the history of life itself but of what has been thought or written about life: the history of ideas. (p. 65)

Borges, in his fictions, conducts a platonic affair with language. It is an important part of his purpose to *show* that, in fiction, the old philosophical modalities of *de dicto* and *de re* are one, that the name of a thing is the essence of that thing. (p. 72)

[The tiger] is the creature from which [Borges] . . . has felt cut off; the dividing glass stands not between him and flesh-and-blood tigers exactly, but between fictive tigers and flesh-and-blood ones. In a short piece in *El Hacedor* called —the title is in English—'Dreamtigers', Borges claims that 'In infancy I practised with fervour the adoration of the tiger'; even if, later on, 'tigers and the passion for them fell into disuse, but they are still in my dreams'. Borges goes on, in 'Dreamtigers' and in a poem which overlaps with it, 'El otro tigre' ('The Other Tiger'), to enrich the archetype by making it ambivalent. The tiger of his dreams is desir-

able but not sufficient: it is not the real animal which stalks the living jungle. He knows he will never make the two coincide, and trap reality in his writing, but he will go on trying, he will keep after the other tiger, 'the one which is not in the line of poetry'.

The insufficiency of fictive tigers thus becomes Borges's explanation of his will to go on writing—and creating more and more insufficient tigers. . . . The tigers in Borges's life have been dream tigers from the start, and he was launched on their pursuit by his precocious adoration of them. . . . The tigers which dominated his imagination are the 'striped, asiatic, royal (*real*) tigers, which only men of war could confront, on a castle above an elephant'. These royal, or 'real' tigers, and the men of war who fought them, represent that side of Borges's and his archetypal author's, ancestry which flows together with and is domesticated by the other, more peaceable, sedentary side. . . . They symbolize whatever energy it is that keeps Borges writing, that obscure inspiration but for which he would never be able to practise his civilized skills in the making of rigorous, unemotional fictions. We do not believe, any more than he does, that his real inspiration is the superstitious belief that ultimately words will become the things themselves. The satisfactions of writing are the exact opposite: of making words suffice for the thing themselves. (pp. 74-5)

Fictions which, like Borges's, avow themselves openly to be the systematic deployment of symbols, do not come easily under the heading of Realism—literary Realism, that is, and no longer philosophical Realism. It is the condition of art, Borges believes, that it should be seen to be art; instead of *ars est celare artem,* his motto might be *ars est divulgare artem.* His stories divulge not only the conventions and procedures of his own art but of the art of narrative in general, and to that extent they rank among the criticism of literature at the same time as extending the possibilities of creative writing. (p. 79)

Borges, a writer for whom reality lies, by definition, outside literature—lies, indeed, outside language—is unconcerned with the mimesis of real life. He is concerned with the mimesis of convention. To the fundamental question of how one can reconcile the incompatible, the word with the thing, abstraction with reality, mind with matter, he gives a simple answer: one cannot, one backs out of that age-old illusionist game altogether and uses abstractions *as* the reality proper to literature. Borges is thus a realist of the absolute kind, in that the reality which he transcribes is the reality of his own mind. The verisimilitude of his fictions is unassailable, given that the private mental world of Borges is the only world to which they might legitimately be referred, and all we know of that world is what Borges has chosen to make public of it, in the composition of a particular story. (p. 84)

The maker of fictions is free to postulate a reality which observes the natural laws of the world we live in or one which infringes them. Borges, for whom reality is the reality of the mind—an ideality—infringes them so as to exploit fiction's independence. (p. 90)

[The] wise maker of fictions, suggests Borges, will deliberately *not* try to compete with reality. (p. 93)

Ultimately, the logic of Borges's provocative interpretation of Realism leads to a pleasantly fantastic result. If Realism entails a correspondence with reality and if reality happens to be, as in the case of 'El impostor inverosímil', an existing literary text, then it follows that the truest Realist of all would be an author whose narrative matched, circumstance for circumstance, the 'reality' which first provoked it. This remarkable hypothesis, of a total correspondence between model and representation is one, naturally, which Borges was quick to realize: in the story of 'Pierre Menard, autor del Quijote', Menard, in his twentieth-century reproduction of a Spanish Golden Age text, repostulates a small part at least of a reality already postulated by Cervantes. The reality which Cervantes postulates tends very strongly towards the Classical, and is short on local colour; the same reality, repostulated by Pierre Menard three centuries later, is more Classical still, since it is no longer to be confused, even by the gullible, with the contemporary state of Spain. By interposing a text between an author and reality Borges cuts the last links with conventional notions of Realism; in his own dispensation everything which appears in a work of literature—every last circumstance—is displayed for what it is: a concept. (pp. 94-5)

[In his essay 'El arte narrativo y la magia' ('Narrative Art and Magic')] Borges is not making the naïve claim that [William Morris in *Life and Death of Jason*] convinces us that centaurs are possible; he is demonstrating that centaurs may be successfully postulated as elements of a fictional reality, as words among other words: he is demonstrating the autonomy of language. (p. 97)

In Borges's own stories the incidental postulation of reality, which implies a reality more complex than the text has the time or inclination to describe, is used more deviously and more ambitiously than ever William Morris used it. It is used to smuggle in impossibilities: Borges's stories are full of 'centaurs' or incongruities, often so shyly introduced that their presence goes unnoticed. It is also used to exemplify the gross discrepancy in scale between the postulated and the postulatable, between the reality which a given fiction represents and the reality it might in principle represent: the universe. (pp. 97-8)

One of Borges's most engaging and persistent fantasies is of a total representation of Everything, of the world turned into words. This beautiful fancy is especially well suited to a writer of such extreme concision, a man too fastidious ever to have written a novel and who has suggested that the novels of other writers are too long and too random to be read with pleasure. It is right that an author who has stuck all his life to the shortest forms of prose writing, the story and the essay, should entertain the largest notions of literary possibilities. This is to turn the discrepancy of scale between life and literature into a joke.

But it is quite a serious joke. Borges may be pessimistic about the handicaps under which human systems of representation must labour but he does not deride them. (p. 98)

The problems of representation are ones of scale. Is there perhaps a point where the process of abstraction becomes, as it has become in painting, non-representational, leaving us with a fiction that is merely abstract? Or is there a continuum between, at one extreme, a complete representation of reality, and, at the other, a complete abstraction? In terms of language, the first extreme would be the unimaginable sum of whatever might be said, the second the equally unimaginable reduction of that sum to a single word. It is to these unimaginable extremes that Borges, as is his way, steers our imaginations. (pp. 98-9)

The many mirrors which appear in Borges's stories, or, to be more exact and loyal to his own beliefs, the one mirror which appears in them many times, are there as symbols of representation itself; they are real objects but they do not really duplicate the reality reflected in them. (p. 101)

'La biblioteca de Babel' is a very subversive story. It is subversive in the first place of the common, and Romantic, view that authors, when they write, make language do exactly as they order it to; which is to give the author the entire credit for what he writes and his native tongue no credit at all. Borges's story calls our attention to the claims of language as an agency in literary creation. There *is* an element of combination in writing, as there is in any use of language. . . .

Borges's story is subversive, secondly, of the idea that there are psychological, physiological, moral, or any other limits on what, as language-users, we can say. Those limits, according to 'La biblioteca de Babel', are in fact verbal: we can say anything that our language allows us to say. The combinations which the library contains are conspicuous by their total irresponsibility; they recognize no distinction between truth and falsehood, good and evil, sense and nonsense. The lesson is that anything, in theory and given sufficient time, may be said, however false, wicked, or nonsensical. Again, Borges is not saying that real authors are such paragons of irresponsibility, he is saying that we are too deterministic in thinking that they can but write what they do write, being the sort of people they are. . . . (p. 102)

The Library of Babel is not the real universe but the artificial universe of literature, the dystopia of a literary man envisaging the totality of literature, the moment when it has all been said. Borges's story becomes more alarming still when one realizes that the library is, like all representations, a huge simplification of the actual universe. (p. 103)

The Aleph [from the story 'El Aleph'] is a 'small, iridescent sphere of almost intolerable brilliance' to be found in the cellar of the house of Carlos Argentino Daneri, a comically stilted and ambitious poet who is at work on the poem to end all poems, a total representation of the known world to be entitled *La tierra* (*The Earth*). The inspiration for this vast literary undertaking has been the discovery of the Aleph. Daneri does not need to leave the house in order to document himself on the world he wishes to represent because it is all in the Aleph. This wonderful object is the pictorial equivalent of the Library of Babel, it is the sum of all the possible visual representations of the universe: all the possible snapshots from all the possible cameras. Reality, as ever, is excluded; Daneri, the fanatical Realist, works from representations of reality. (p. 106)

The narrator, Borges by name, makes a florid little speech to [the surviving image of Beatriz, the narrator's Muse]: 'Beatriz, Beatriz Elena, Beatriz Elena Viterbo, dear Beatriz, Beatriz lost for ever, I am I, I am Borges.' This odd invocation completes the process of idealization: Beatriz, first a girl, then the photographic image of a girl, is now only the name of a girl. Similarly, in 'El Aleph' reality as a whole is first itself, then a representation in the Aleph, and finally the very partial representation of that representation in Daneri's poetry. There is something elegiac about the story. Nor does the transformation of a person into a name quite end the process, because in time the name itself will be transformed: to start with it will be the name inseparable from that particular image, but once the image fades and vanishes it will be nothing more than a name. In the end is the Word. (p. 107)

The postulation, as in 'El Aleph' or 'La biblioteca de Babel', of a reality which exhausts the powers of representation of the camera or the alphabet, is one of Borges's most instructive hypotheses. The fantastic complexity of such a reality can, needless to say, be indicated but never reproduced. On these occasions Borges faces, in an extreme form, the problem that faces all writers of fiction all of the time: how to postulate a reality richer and more extensive than they have power to tell. (p. 108)

In his early days, as something of an *avant-garde* poet, Borges met with and adopted the modernist technique of abrupt juxtaposition, a technique that was meant to shock and frequently did shock. Borges soon abjured it, but he has never abjured a belief that the representation of reality, whether that reality be an existing narrative, a person, or a scene, should be *seen* to be less, and other, than its model, that the discontinuities on which representation depends should be blatant. This is not simply the capricious adaptation to prose of a technique he learnt as a poet, but a demonstration that the activity of the human mind, and the nature of human language, can never match the complexity or continuity of what they seek to represent. (p. 113)

For Borges the maker of a fiction stands in the same relation to his own small creation as God, seen as the author of the universe, stands to creation as a whole. (p. 144)

As Borges chooses to look at it, the present moment—if we allow that to be a simple, determinate event—is subtended by the whole of the past. . . . Were the history of the universe to be written it would therefore be a narrative of infinite ramifications. These ramifications enter the merely human fictions of Borges in the form of another favourite symbol, the labyrinth, which reduces the potential ramifications of any given event to the more manageable power of two. The labyrinth faces those who would penetrate it with a series of alternatives, but never more than two at any one time. It is a pity, where Borges is concerned, that the labyrinth should so readily be taken as the symbol of a hopeless confusion, a place into which we enter only to blunder this way or that without a hope of reaching the centre. But labyrinths are man-made and even if we fail to 'read' them properly we know their code can be cracked.

A Borges story is not itself labyrinthine; it does not face us with alternative continuations. It is the writer of a narrative, not its reader, who must tackle the labyrinth, because it is he who is confronted, at every turn of his story, by alternative ways of continuing it. (pp. 145-46)

The labyrinth is born of duplication, of the postulation of an alternative to a given reality, and founded on duplication thereafter. Labyrinthine man is one who lives and works by twos. (p. 146)

Borges never dreams the impossible dream of stopping time dead; he exploits, as all narrative is bound to do, the possibilities of postponing it. . . .

The mind is never wholly free of time and there is no ultimate salvation in Borges's eternity. Distraction must have a stop. We can postpone our reunion with reality but we cannot avoid it. (p. 209)

[In Borges's eternity we can pretend] that time is really space, and that we can play divisive games with it without growing any older ourselves as we do so. Borges, with his love of symmetrical compositions, of events arranged in series, and of narratives whose end is also in their beginning, exemplifies as few writers do what the Formalist Eichenbaum claims to be 'the general principle of verbal art's being structured step by step, with progress arrested.' He has every right repeatedly to symbolize his own constructions as edifices. We do not think of buildings as being extended in time, although, as we walk around them, they are. In just the same way, a fiction is an architectural structure which we extend in time by reading it.

The most grandiose architect to be found in Borges is the Chinese emperor Shih Huang Ti, celebrated for having inaugurated the Great Wall of China and for having burnt all the books published before his own time. This emperor, according to Borges, prohibited the mention of death and 'shut himself up in a figurative palace' with as many rooms as the year has days. These data, if they really are data, 'suggest that the wall in time and the fire in space were magical barriers intended to detain death'. Shih Huang Ti is a master of artifice, clearly, and a man after Borges's own heart. (pp. 212-14)

And one of his ideal constructions, the Great Wall, is still there. For the final paradox of such constructive Idealism is that it adds to the stock of real things. Borges, as a maker of fictions, has made material objects—books—out of his immaterial speculations. The mirror, which represents the objects in the world, is itself an object in the world. Once they have acquired this real, durable form, an author's 'intellectual exercises' become a factor in the intellectual experience of whoever reads them. They are, in a double sense, an imposition: a product of the printing-press and a make-believe. And as real objects they also enter into the unimaginably complex system of causes and effects of which history consists. We cannot know what effects a particular work of literature will cause, but we can be sure that it will not be without effect. It exists, in Borges's own terms, at the point of intersection between a past and a future. Behind it there extends the pyramid of causes of which it is itself the effect; ahead of it, as a speculation, the pyramid of effects of which it will be the cause. For better or for worse, the pyramid of effects which stretched ahead of Borges's exemplary fictions when they were first published included the present study. (pp. 213-14)

> *John Sturrock, in his* Paper Tigers: The Ideal Fictions of Jorge Luis Borges *(© Oxford University Press 1977; reprinted by permission of Oxford University Press), Oxford University Press, Oxford, 1977.*

ANTHONY KERRIGAN

Borges, we all know by now, is too good, and too "wrong" in his politics, ever to receive a Nobel Prize awarded in accord with Swedish *Realpolitik*. . . .

Any dealing with Borges as poet must necessarily begin by admitting that the Argentinian is first of all a master of succinct prose. (p. 11)

Borges writes with great compression, but what he writes is not necessarily verse. Some of the best pages in [*The Gold of the Tigers*] are lists of concepts/impressions/evocations.

In his Preface to [the collection], Borges had spoken of his [admiration for] Whitman, but he had qualified his admiration for the great American: ". . . his careful enumerations do not always rise above a kind of crude cataloguing." Perhaps Borges' lists are less prosy than Whitman's, but still they are based on the dubious spontaneity of an imagistic and over-comprehensive imagination. His earliest list in this book is called, accurately, "Things." (pp. 11-12)

But even mere lists will serve us. And even if we are only to dream, lists exist for our life-as-dream: "The dream which . . . was dreamed close to dawn one day in 1946 consisted . . . not of images but of slow specific words."

In Borges—as in Faulkner—there are a plethora of military allusions. In Borges—as in Faulkner—the military deeds are the stuff of epics. There are many allusions to bravery (even to "the scent of bravery"). Swords and knives are emblems of good death. "A vow of vengeance" moves many. His country's battles, commanded on both sides in Spanish (even in the mouths of the Wild Geese from Ireland), are as fascinating as dreams. Every deed is matter for myth and epic. . . .

Borges is resolutely anti-modern. In his own Preface to *The Unending Rose* he asserts "For *Muse,* we must read what the Hebrews and Milton called *Spirit,* and what our own woeful mythology refers to as the *Subconscious.*"

Borges "subconsciously" describes his own style (it is also a matter of "things"), which ascribing it to another poet, in a poem on Browning:

> I shall make ordinary words
> (The people's word-coinage,
> the marked cards of the sharper)
> yield up magic . . .
>
> . . . .
> In the dialect of today
> I will in my turn say the eternal things . . .
>
> (p. 13)

> Anthony Kerrigan, "The Other Horn of the Unicorn," in The University Bookman (copyright 1978 by The Educational Reviewer, Inc.), Autumn, 1978, pp. 11-14.

GRACE SCHULMAN

Two new works by Jorge Luis Borges, *The Gold of the Tigers: Selected Later Poems,* and *The Book of Sand,* a collection of prose tales, offer a deeper realization of the intriguing network of symbols in the Argentinian writer's artistic world. Primarily, though, they embody human insights: throughout his work, the most striking effects, as well as true meanings, are to be found not in his allegory, however fascinating, but in his construction of images and characters.

So, too, with the new collections. *The Gold of the Tigers* is pervaded with polarities of blindness and sight, those contrasts Borges has developed throughout his work. In his "Preface to *The Unending Rose,*" which appears in this book, he writes: "Blindness is a confinement, but it is also a liberation, a solitude propitious to invention, a key and an algebra." In Borges' poetic world, to be blind is to live with the reality of darkness, for to see in an illusory world is actually a delusion. . . .

At an extreme from those perceptions of darkness are the images of radiant light, presented as golden moments of awareness. Often they are generated by thoughts of great images in literature or by myths, which are, to Borges, the poet's touchstones, or "talismans" in a world without substance. In "The White Deer," that animal is perceived in "a moment's flash." The speaker dreams of "a lithe, illusory creature, half-remembered / and half-imagined," suspecting it has originated from an English ballad or "Persian etching." The speaker's identification with the deer is based on his conviction that both he and the animal are illusory in a gossamer world: "I too am dream, lasting a few days longer / than that bright dream of whiteness and green fields."

Often those luminous images occur in moments of passion, as in "Tankas":

> High on the summit
> the garden is all moonlight,
> the moon is golden.
> More precious is the contact
> of your lips in the shadow.

And in the beautiful title poem of this collection, the speaker imagines brilliant touchstones such as "the blazing tiger of Blake, burning bright" and "the amorous gold shower disguising Zeus." The poem ends in an excited outcry:

> O sunsets, O tigers, O wonders
> of myth and epic,
> O gold more dear to me, gold of your hair
> which these hands crave to touch.

Another of the striking antinomies in this book is that of solitude and unity. (p. 74)

In "You," many notable figures—Ulysses, Abel, Cain—are presented as one solitary man: "One man alone has looked on the enormity of dawn." In "Proteus," on the other hand, one figure becomes many: the god takes on "the substance of a lion or a bonfire / or a tree." The poet enjoins: "Do not take fright at Proteus the Egyptian, / you, who are one, and also many men."

In these remarkable poems, Borges creates an image of man alone in a universe filled with curious contradictions, having only his talismans, his brief glimpses of light, his loves, his memories of beauty. The truth is remote, and can be known only after he is dead, as we learn in the amazing poem, "The Unending Rose." . . .

The Book of Sand is a collection of fables that, like many literary ballads, contain precise information about irrelevant details, while the central situation is veiled in mystery. "Exact dates are of no account," he writes in "Congress," then proceeds to give exact dates, places and names. . . .

Despite their appearance of reality, however, the tales are filled with wonder. The title story concerns a bibliophile who exchanges a black-letter Wycliffe Bible for a Book of Sand, so-named because, like sand, the pages have no beginning or end. He acquires the book from a stranger "with nondescript features" that are, nevertheless, described in detail. Alone with the infinite book, the pedantic narrator is overcome by the nightmarish, terrifying object.

Unlike his poems, Borges' prose does not often turn on the theme of love. An exception is the beautiful story "Ulrike," in which the narrator, an aging bachelor, is loved by a young Norwegian woman. At the moment of their erotic union, the author suspends his detailed narrative, for love itself is the central mystery. . . .

More commonly, Borges' stories exhibit the theme of the double, and concern two people who, the author states in an "Afterword," are "sufficiently different to be two persons and alike enough to be one." An example of this use of the theme is found in "The Other," a tale in which Borges points unquestionably to himself by using his own name for the bemused speaker who meets a stranger of the same name. Appropriately, the stranger is writing a book on the brotherhood of man. In their meeting, the central character learns more about himself. And yet that very knowledge is illusory, since it is an insubstantial reflection of a person whose very existence is doubtful.

For me, the most haunting story in this collection is "The Mirror and the Mask," in which Ollan, the court poet of Ireland, is given a silver mirror for composing songs of war. Taking the mirror with him, the bard invents an ode that was "not a description of the battle—it was the battle." After the king gives him a mask, Ollan composes a single line that tells of Beauty. Then, for the sin of knowing Beauty, the poet kills himself and the king becomes a beggar in his own kingdom.

The mirror, the double, memory—all are symbols of knowing reality that may itself be unknowable. And yet at times we are closer to the truth, as when we perceive we are familiar with the darkness that rules our lives. That is the truth of Borges who, though resigned to darkness, loves the light. Although he knows that truth may be illusory, he pursues truth. And while he understands that solitude may be the law of life, he persists in seeking out the other. (p. 75)

> *Grace Schulman, "Gold and Sand," in* Review *(copyright © 1978 by the Center for Inter-American Relations, Inc.), No. 23, pp. 74-5.*

ROBIN LYDENBERG

The short stories of Jorge Luis Borges are representative of a major trend in twentieth-century fiction which concentrates on aesthetic rather than moral issues. Borges himself has stressed the essentially amoral and literary perspective which distinguishes his work from that of more ethically oriented writers: "I want to make it quite clear that I am not, nor have I ever been, what used to be called a preacher of parables . . . and is now known as a committed writer." The committed writer, for Borges, is one whose ethical preoccupations not only dominate, but dictate a creative style which invariably "declines into allegory." In contrast to such morally didactic literature, Borges presents his own stories as mere efforts to entertain or to move, but not to persuade. He expresses impatience not only with the aggressively didactic writer, but also with those readers who approach literature expecting symbols or lessons, and he often constructs his narratives deliberately to frustrate such allegorical interpretations. Borges would have his audience come to resemble himself, rich "in perplexities rather than in certainties." Fiercely antidogmatic, he perceives his stories as "tenuous and eternal crevices of unreason" in man's presumptuous architectural ordering of the universe.

Borges fosters this uncertainty in his audience by accumulating in his tales imagery rich in oxymorons, ideas based on paradoxes, and narrative structures of reversal. By writing in the suggestiveness of allusion rather than in the more fixed structures of symbol or allegory, Borges avoids the dogmatic singularity of purpose of the committed writer. These devices keep the reader of Borges's stories in a constant state of confusion which opens up new ways of perceiving both the word and the world in their infinite complexity and inexhaustibility.

Borges thus defines his work by the effect his narratives have on the reader. He recognizes in the reader's response to or participation in the dialogue of the text the power to determine and even to transform the nature of that text: "[If] I were granted the possibility of reading any present day page—this one, for example—as it will be read in the year two thousand, I would know what the literature of the year two thousand will be like." Despite his belief in the primacy and independence of reader response, however, Borges's effort to produce "perplexities" in his audience is certainly part of a deliberate attempt to undermine the reader's complacency of expectation and to persuade him into a more problematic vision of the universe. His allegedly innocent design to be "entertaining or moving, but not persuasive" should be examined more critically.

The ethically based literary tradition of parable from which Borges so explicitly disassociates himself bears a curious resemblance to the theory and practice of his short fiction. A concentration on audience participation rather than passive receptivity and an effort to break through dogma by creating uncertainty in the reader or listener are characteristics which distinguish the indirect and suggestive persuasion of parable from the more static and hierarchical didacticism of allegory. Parable "avert[s] the hearer by its vividness or strangeness and leave[s] him in sufficient doubt about its precise application to tease him into active thought" [according to John Donimic Crossan in *In Parables*]. When Biblical parable is examined as a morally neutral "language event" it may be defined by its utilization of the particular literary devices of paradox and structural reversal. It would appear, therefore, that despite his denial Borges is to some extent a writer of parables. (pp. 31-2)

Borges's parables most closely resemble . . . Biblical parables of reversal which focus on epistomological rather than moral contradiction; he consistently challenges the reader's assumptions about the distinction between dream and reality, literature and life, the particular one and the universal many. Like Biblical parable, the Borgesian parable renders the reversal of these categories convincing through an accumulation of a precise and implacable particularity of detail.

Borges's use of polar reversal and particularity is clearly represented in his short story "The Zahir," the narration of his chance acquisition of an ordinary coin which becomes an obsession. Borges proceeds directly from the wake of an elegant and aloof society woman, whom he worshipped, to have a drink in a common and vulgar wine shop, where he is given the Zahir as change. He considers the contradictory circumstances leading to this event as a "kind of oxymoron." The Zahir is not only paradoxical in its origins but in its effect, for it soon proliferates an infinite series of divergent associations in the narrator's mind, rendering its individual existence disturbingly multiple. . . . From the single coin of Borges's history the Zahir becomes every other coin, real and fictional, each with its own weighty and undeniable particularity. Conversely, the material reality of Borges's Zahir dissolves in his thoughts into the airy uncertainty and potentiality of "a repertory of possible futures" and "unforeseeable time, Bergsonian time." . . .

Despite these divine transformations of the one into the many, of the material into the abstract, Borges soon discovers that the Zahir is demonic as well. The dangerous power of this coin . . . is its resistance to the very transformations and allusions it implies. Even after accomplishing with "scrupulous lack of plan" . . . the random and accidental loss of the Zahir, the actual coin remains insistently and immutably unforgettable in Borges's consciousness. The resulting telescoping of all time, place and identity into a single obsessive object leaves Borges himself in a state of utter confusion in which dream and reality have been, or threaten to be, reversed. . . . (pp. 32-3)

Both reductively obsessive and limitlessly expandable, the Zahir is in itself an emblem of paradox or reversal. In his involuntary meditations on the coin, Borges visualizes both sides simultaneously, not by superimposition but "as though [his] eyesight were spherical, with the Zahir in the center." . . . Such properties of the Zahir suggest to Borges the divine vision of the inconceivable mind of God: "[In] the language of God every word would enunciate that infinite concatenation of facts, and not in an implicit but in an explicit manner, and not progressively but instantaneously." "Perhaps the [two contrary] stories I have related are one single story. The obverse and the reverse of this coin are, for God, the same." To the human mind, such a totality of particulars and simultaneity of opposites would be intolerable, causing a terrifying confusion with its vertiginous multiplicity. (pp. 33-4)

The effort to replace the world or to re-create it in its encyclopedic entirety is an impulse which appears in and behind many of Borges's stories, reflecting the artist's fearful aspiration to divine vision. In his effort to construct the entire world in a word, a poem, or a single map, every artist is continually thwarted by the limitations of the human mind which perceives successively rather than simultaneously. The plan of "ciphering the universe / in one book" is recognized by Borges as infinitely rash, its incomplete results merely monstrous. In the "Parable of the Palace" he relates the story of the creation of a poetic text consisting of a single word which reproduces in every minute detail and thus obliterates an emperor's infinite palace. Borges finally denounces this legend as mere literary fiction, perhaps recognizing his kinship with the executed and anonymous poet whose "descendants still seek, and will not find, the word for the universe."

Such a word could only be written in what Borges calls "God's Script," a language which is by its very nature indecipherable. Borgesian and Biblical parable both respond to the necessity of presenting the divine vision in human language by utilizing the familiar and the particular to express the extraordinary and impossible. Christ speaks in parables not as in a secret language to an elite, but to the uninitiated who must be approached through mediation. . . . Like Biblical parables, the modern parables of Borges are a medium of exchange which he compares to coins, "small material objects, hard and bright, tokens of something else." The ultimate aim of Christ's teaching through parable and Borges's writing of parable is to transcend the limits of the mediation itself—to get behind the token to that secret something else. Thus Borges voices a final desperate hope at the conclusion of "The Zahir": "In order to lose themselves in God, the Sufis recite their own names, or the 99 divine names, until they become meaningless. I long to

travel that path. Perhaps I shall conclude by wearing away the Zahir simply through thinking of it again and again. Perhaps behind the coin I shall find God." . . . (pp. 34-5)

Such divine revelation, however, always retreats just before the reader of parable, remaining always beyond his grasp. In Borges's parables, therefore, patterns of reversal evolve into patterns of infinite regression which he compares to a series of microcosmic labyrinths: "I thought of a labyrinth of labyrinths, of one sinuous spreading labyrinth that would encompass the past and the future and in some way involve the stars." Thus the complex aesthetic games which characterize his intricate tales retain to some extent the ultimately mystical or transcendent goals of traditional Christian parable. (p. 35)

[The] familiar literary device of the dream within the dream, the tale within the tale, is typical of both traditional and modern parable. Borges examines this device in his essay "Partial magic in the *Quixote*" in an attempt to discover why such patterns of infinite regression as the Don Quixote of Part II becoming a reader of *Don Quixote: Part I* tend to disturb readers: "I believe I have found the reason: these inversions suggest that if the characters of a fictional work can be readers or spectators, we, its readers or spectators, can be fictitious." The regressive or ascending uncertainty of Borges's fictions, then, unsettles not only the reader's expectations of the world or of literature, but also his very existence.

Seen as presenting the reader or listener with a language event rather than imposing an allegorical message, Biblical parable also lends itself to a critical focus in which "it is not ultimately the text which is interpreted and clarified, but the interpreter and his situation are illuminated." The external spectator becomes the internal subject of the parable. The experience of Borgesian parable is also a gradual assimilation of the audience, which is drawn into the uncertain spiral of each narrative The reader of "The Zahir," for example, is exposed to the same obsession from which Borges suffers. Once he encounters the coin in Borges's narrative, it contains not only all the encyclopedic associations catalogued by the author, but the additional reference to Borges's *own* story. For Borges, not only parable but all literary forms are thus a dialogue with the reader, a result of the "changing and durable images it leaves in his memory." (p. 36)

Borges perceives the reader as his partner in the potential but impossible goal of achieving "God's Script" in human language, of reaching the infinitely receding divine revelation: "If the plan does not fail, some reader of 'Kubla Khan' will dream, on a night centuries removed from us, of marble or of music. This man will not know that two others also dreamed. Perhaps the series of dreams has no end or the last one who dreams will have the key." As we have already seen, however, the single word, the key to the code, is never found, but perpetually eludes both writer and reader in the infinite regression of parable.

The silence of Biblical parable which withholds the certainty of salvation and the suspension of Borgesian parable on the permanent verge of discovery do not, surprisingly, produce a hopeless paralysis or frustration in the reader or listener. Their effect is instead to generate an intense sense of wonder and surprise at the continually shifting universe. Thus the very techniques of paradox, reversal, and regression which assimilate and enclose the readers in parable, also open up their world, exposing them to a "new way of understanding their situation in history."

Borges's most striking divergence from traditional parable in the disturbingly claustrophobic and self-enclosed quality which pervades his stories. Thus Borges's fiction simultaneously opens up the reader's world and closes in on itself; his expansive sense of mystical wonder at the universe turns back on himself in the narrow confines of his own mind and perhaps his blindness. While he laments the lack of awe and surprise in most people's perception of the world, his own astonishment arises from a very private perception of self: "I remember . . . when my father said to me, 'What a queer thing, he said, that I should be living, as they say, behind my eyes, inside my head, I wonder if that makes sense?' And then, it was the first time I felt that, and then instantly I pounced upon that because I knew what he was saying. But many people hardly understand that. And they say, 'Well, but where else could you live?'"

Borges's sense of wonder at himself or at the experiences in his life is thus peculiarly removed, almost alienated: "I am no longer the 'I' of that episode," or "my narration was a symbol of the man I was as I wrote it and . . . in order to compose that narration, I had to be that man." Since "that man" composed his story from the experience of what is now another "I," Borges in a sense becomes his own reader; he tells himself literary jokes in the lonely privacy of his composition: "That is a kind of stock joke. . . . For example, if I quote an apocryphal book, then the next book to be quoted is a real one, or perhaps an imaginary one by a real writer, no? When a man writes he feels rather lonely, and then he has to keep his spirits up, no?" Borges's confusion of fact and fantasy, of the real and the apocryphal, is directed as much towards himself as towards his readers.

The problem which confronts Borges in his activity as a writer is the basic challenge of traditional parable, [which Dan Otto Via, Jr. defines in *The Parables* as] "the gain or loss of existence, becoming authentic or inauthentic." While this challenge is directed at the audience of Biblical parable, in Borges's case it confronts the teller himself. Borges's loneliness is that of the artist who is not one but many, who is "Everything and Nothing" like the Shakespeare he dramatizes in that parable. He is composed of innumerable but ephemeral personae like his vision of George Bernard Shaw. Borges loses even his stories and his passions to some other official Borges, analogous to "that G.B.S. who represented the English playwright in public, and who lavished in the newspaper columns so many facile witticisms."

In "Borges and I" the voice of an "I" whispers to the reader behind Borges' back, telling of the gradual and continual assimilation into this public Borges of anything which might identify and characterize the nameless "I." "I live," he laments, "so that Borges may contrive his literature." But even this attempt at some intimate converse with a reader belongs to "Borges" or to oblivion, or at best to "language and tradition" . . . the anonymous repositories of all good literature. A deep sadness and isolation reverberate beneath the witty joke which ends the parable: "I do not know which of us has written this page." . . . Just as Christ was transformed in Biblical commentary from a teller of parables (a speaker in paradox) to a parable himself, the Parable (Paradox) of God, so Borges contemplates

with a mixture of amusement and horror this transformation of his self into literature or symbol.

Borges consents to this loss of self in the vain hope that part of him will survive and be justified in Borges. . . . It is with regret that Borges confronts the lonely subjectivity of his work, for he has set out to create a universe of "provinces, kingdoms, mountains, bays, ships, islands, fishes, rooms, instruments, stars, horses and people," only to discover finally that the "patient labyrinth of lines traces the image of his own face." Again the Borgesian parable turns back on itself and the mind of its creator instead of transcending the limits of artist and work.

This failed transcendence, however, forms in itself an open ended structure, for Borges never abandons the divine search. To see behind his own face, as behind the Zahir, the face of God, he keeps trying to reach through but beyond his literature to the more complex and divine creation which constitutes reality itself. (pp. 36-8)

This yearning towards the other, this impulse to break out of the self and the limits of its familiarity, characterize the experience of Biblical parable as dialogue and interaction. . . . The unexpected shattering surprise which makes religious illumination possible is also necessary for the success of the aesthetic experience. . . .

The essential uncertainty of the experience of Biblical parable is the mystery of the sublime and the holy which theologians define as that which "extends us beyond ourselves." Similarly the expansion of the reader's horizon through literature has been described as that which extends "Beyond my situation as reader, beyond the author's situation, to the possible ways of being-in-the-world which the text opens up and discovers for me." The self-enclosed and self-conscious privacy of the individual may be undermined by reversal and infinite regression—patterns of parable which serve both aesthetics and religion.

The permanent and progressive eschatology of Biblical parable, which points always to a mystery just beyond the listener's expectation or comprehension, mirrors Borges's repeated evocations of the "imminence of a revelation which does not occur." This imminence constitutes, for Borges, the essence of the aesthetic phenomenon. The many points of intersection of Borges's literary parables and traditional Christian parable necessitate some qualification of Borges's separation of his work from the tradition of moral narrative. We may find this qualification expressed by Borges himself, who recognizes in his writing the convergence of ethics and aesthetics, an examination of the "literary possibilities of metaphysics and religion." (p. 39)

Robin Lydenberg, "Borges as a Writer of Parables: Reversal and Infinite Regression," in The International Fiction Review *(© copyright International Fiction Association), Winter, 1979, pp. 31-9.*

*   *   *

BRODSKY, Joseph   1940-

A lyric poet and translator now living in the United States, Brodsky was expelled from his native Russia in 1972, despite defense by some of the most important cultural figures in the U.S.S.R., for his "parasitism" and "decadent" poetry. He is generally regarded as the most important living Russian poet. (See also *CLC*, Vols. 4, 6, and *Contemporary Authors*, Vols. 41-44.)

[Mr. Brodsky's] poetry is religious, intimate, depressed, sometimes confused, sometimes martyr-conscious, sometimes élitist in its views, but it does not constitute an attack on Soviet society or ideology unless withdrawal and isolation are deliberately construed as attack: of course they can be, and evidently were. . . .

Because of the distractions of the political background, it is not too easy to come to a clear judgment of Mr. Brodsky's poetry. In addition, the irrelevant novelty value of a young Soviet poet expressing himself in terms of God and the devil, angels and cherubim, paradise and hell has to be adjusted to an objective interpretation of how far this area of reference has been convincingly applied. At the moment, Mr. Brodsky's work appears genuine but limited. It may be that his sense of isolation has hindered his development, and while there is nothing inherently wrong in going back to the time of Blok or Mandelshtam or the early Akhmatova for influences, one feels that Mr. Brodsky could well have learnt more from contemporary poetic modes. . . .

Mr. Brodsky is good at evoking certain scenes and atmospheres: an autumn garden, a Christmas in Moscow, a suburban hill-slope with its strange mixture of natural wildness and human detritus, and above all the sleeping snowy London of John Donne in the title-poem ["Elegy for John Donne"]. This last poem, a long meditation on the soul in which the uneasily sleeping Donne becomes a meeting-place of struggling spiritual forces, moves with real power and interesting shifts of perspective. The other long poem translated [in *Elegy for John Donne*], "The Hills", tries to combine a wedding-party and a murder with an "I to the hills will lift mine eyes" theme, but the material is less well integrated, and this poem is not entirely successful. Some short poems, like "To the New Tenant", show a sensibility not unlike Mr. Philip Larkin's; others, such as "A Christmas Romance", have that almost paradoxical sort of vivid sensuous detail, at once rich and laconic, which is purely Russian.

Altogether this is a volume which is of considerable interest, and it will surprise many who have rigid ideas about the nature of Soviet poetry.

> *"Work-Shy Element," in* The Times Literary Supplement (© *Times Newspapers Ltd. (London), 1967; reproduced from* The Times Literary Supplement *by permission), July 20, 1967, p. 637.*

RICHARD LOURIE

In the poetry written in Russia since Stalin's death, Vinokurov's transparent simplicity and Voznesensky's near incantations define one set of extremes. When Vinokurov fails, his poetry loses a dimension, becoming flat, and too often Voznesensky produces fireworks that dazzle but leave no lasting impression. Only Joseph Brodsky, it would seem, has a reach great enough to span both extremes and a grip strong enough to hold onto both at once, as he does in his "Elegy for John Donne."

This collection consists of seventy-two poems written between 1961 and 1969. Four of Brodsky's translations of Donne are included, as well as a poem on the death of T. S. Eliot, written in imitation of Auden's poem on the death of Yeats. Brodsky's fascination with English poetry makes him especially interesting to us and probably somewhat unique among young Soviet poets. Brodsky can be slangy and toughly sentimental when he draws portraits of his school chums and is at home both with the *poema* and the lyric (One, "Verses in April," begins "Again this winter / I did not lose my mind."). Though his versatility and dexterity are extraordinary, what is most remarkable in Brodsky is a quality of consciousness which can only be termed religious. It can also be found in the works of Solzhenitsyn and Sinyavsky but, being so individual a matter, should not give rise to undue speculation on a resurgence of spirituality in Russia. (p. 202)

> *Richard Lourie, in* The Russian Review *(copyright 1971 by The Russian Review, Inc.), April, 1971.*

R. D. SYLVESTER

Joseph Brodsky, perhaps the most interesting of contemporary Russian poets, is a moralist and an ironist concerned with the false values men live by in an age which has thrown away the past, and with it the past's spiritual heritage. His work shows a persistent need for contact with poets outside the Russian tradition: Norwid, Eliot, Auden, Cavafy, Horace, and, above all, John Donne, are names that come to mind in a reading of his *Ostanovka v pustyne* (*Halt in the Wilderness*). He is, indeed, the first Russian poet I know of who has brought the English Metaphysicals into his poetic workshop, to learn from them and to grow under the influence of his kinship with them. At the same time his poetry has deep roots in the Russian tradition too. . . . Unlike the older generation, who were nurtured at a time when a great poetic culture was flourishing in Russia, Brodsky, who was born in 1940, grew up at a time when Russian poetry was in a state of chronic decline; as a result, he had to find his way largely on his own. His development has been exceptionally interesting. He began as a dropout from high school, and some of his earliest poems belong to Soviet underground literature of the late 1950s. He has retained the outsider's point of view, but he has given it much wider implications as he has grown. His work constitutes an outsider's critique, but it is a critique of the human condition rather than of political or social organization. Its polemical thrust is aimed at keeping possibilities open for the human psyche, whose need to reestablish spiritual bearings in the twentieth century is proof of the inadequacy of our official doctrines. (pp. 303-04)

[There are] two key images that run through his work. The first is *rodina*, birthland. It occurs without adjective or pronoun modifiers that would circumscribe its meaning, and this keeps open its potential for accumulating a weight of meaning that is something like "what one is born to" in every sense. In traditional Russian usage, *rodina* is a strongly positive image of one's native land, or even native region or city. Through overuse in patriotic slogans it has become a kind of icon. Brodsky never mocks nor rejects *rodina*, but he does use irony to chip away at its false, official halo. . . . For Brodsky *rodina* has a religious meaning in addition to its concrete meaning of "native land." In its spiritual sense *rodina* is the place where the last illusions and falsehoods are stripped away: where a man, or a people, stand naked before the Word of God. In connection with the theme of *rodina*, Brodsky has made extensive use of the Christian motif of *Rozhdestvo* (Nativity), a word which has the same root as *rodina*. It is, of course, the Christmas holiday, as celebrated in Moscow. . . . The themes of *rodina* and *Rozhdestvo* are always accompanied by pain, but it has to be understood that this is a salutary pain, which affirms more strongly than anything else in

Brodsky's poetry the reality of the divine, or sacred, order of life. *Rodina* is the setting in space, and *Rozhdestvo* the setting in time, of that central experience in which man most truly faces God—or feels his distance from Him.

The second key image that one needs to keep a bearing on in reading Brodsky is *razluka,* separation: the separation of lovers, but also separation in a wider sense, from others, from self, from God. It prefigures the final separation, which is death. Just as Brodsky uses the Christian motif of the Nativity in connection with *rodina,* so in connection with *razluka* he uses the Crucifixion. Here, too, there is always pain, but it is the pain of devastating loss; if there is anything salutary to it, it is only to be found in the paradox that separation *for* eternity constitutes a kind of faith *in* eternity. (pp. 304-06)

Brodsky's work continues the lyric tradition that has been associated since the eighteenth century with his native city of Leningrad, but its relation to the tradition is not quite what might be expected and has become much more complex as his art has developed. When he began to write in 1958 at the age of eighteen, it was stylistically outside the tradition altogether. The earliest poems were short fables and allegories like "*Khudozhnik,*" a statement of the artist's need to go his own way and his determination to believe in himself.... Brodsky, to his credit, did not try to hide this youthful pessimism, expressed in the images of martyrdom that appear in a great many of these early poems.... The short, brilliant "*Stikhi pod epigrafom,*" written in a style that recalls Tsvetaeva, transforms the martyrdom image into something positive by asserting the basic validity in this life of the religious ideas of suffering and immortality. (pp. 306-07)

Around 1960 Brodsky began to work with traditional meters, especially the iamb and the anapest.... Continuing these experiments over the next ten years, Brodsky has developed the iambic pentameter into a line that bears his own individual signature.... Out of these experiments grew the verse of two of his long poems, "Isaac and Abraham" and "Elegy for John Donne" (both 1963). What makes this verse-line so remarkable is that it achieves nearly the maximum possible density of stressed syllables.... This saturated line is difficult to sustain, because it requires the use of predominantly one- and two-syllable words. Yet Brodsky manages to do it, and in his hands it becomes a powerful rhythmic device that creates an iambic music with a sense of maximum fullness in the line.

At the other end of the spectrum are his experiments with mobile intonational breaks that lead to a very high frequency of enjambments, and his development of the long sentence with complex syntax, which spills over from line to line and even from one stanza to the next. (pp. 307-09)

Since 1960 Brodsky has done interesting work in the anapest too, using enjambment and a variable line length. A striking example is "*Fontan*" (1967).... (p. 311)

One way of looking at these innovations is that through them Brodsky has aimed at developing a style that would be independent of Pushkin, or at least stand apart from the most typical features of Pushkin's verse. Since 1962 he has looked primarily *outside* the native lyric tradition of the nineteenth and twentieth centuries for his inspiration.... He learned from Norwid (see "*Sadovnik v vatnike*") how to broach a subject indirectly, giving expression to his wit and

playfulness and at the same time allowing the subject to take on whatever serious implications it may. This dates from 1964 and is a turning point in his work.

In Donne's verse Brodsky discovered a poetry of *this* world, which contains, at the same time, angels and luminous objects, set in a form of discourse that is dramatic, richly metaphorical, and intellectually complex, in which no line of separation stands between the sacred and the profane. Brodsky has incorporated all this into his own style. Donne's influence can be felt in particular ways, as when he borrows an image or a conceit, or writes in a Donne genre. "*Otkazom*" (1967) and "*Strofy*" (1968) are valedictions modeled on Donne, but his presentation of the theme of *razluka* is very much his own. Just as important is the general influence felt in Brodsky's habit of ratiocination through metaphor, and in his syntax, especially his Donne-like manner of steering an argument through twists and turns by using subordinating conjunctions and other hypotactic connectors to create a series of continually changing logical relationships: *ibo, raz, to-est', vprochem, khot', posemu, kol',* and so on.

Brodsky's themes—or what is really a densely interwoven complex of themes—appeared early in his work. His subsequent stylistic development has been a growth in the means for taking up their various strands, and thus a widening of their implications. An important stage in that growth was his discovery of T. S. Eliot, in whose "spirit unappeased and peregrine" he perhaps recognized a tie of kinship. One very interesting strand in his work is the "imperial" theme, the theme of the state as empire. Eliot's use of the *persona* in *Journey of the Magi* and *Gerontion* lies behind Brodsky's recent treatment of that theme. In "*Anno Domini*" (1968) the speaker is a poet in exile.... The exiled poet meditates on the lives of the bureaucrats who serve the imperial will, far from the Metropolis at the center of the empire: men long ago compelled to compromise whatever standards of truth and loyalty to spiritual values they may once have known. They are left with an empty legacy, their lives devoid of meaning, eking out their days in trepidation in a remote corner of the empire. It is a moral and political theme; there is an air of blasphemy brooding over these images of a secular order that has gone wrong. Brodsky can at times convey a sense of disgust that reminds us of Swift. At other times the language recalls the summations of *Gerontion,* in which the irony works more quietly but has a devastating effect....

> —we are not the judges of the fatherland. The sword of
>   judgment shall sink deep in our own disgrace—
> . . .
> the holy nimbus is replaced by the halo of the lie,
>   and the immaculate conception—by gossip.
>
> (pp. 312-13)

The search for alternatives to Pushkin led Brodsky, within the Russian tradition, to the eighteenth century. He was drawn there by the work of particular poets like Derzhavin and Kantemir, and by the spirit of an age that believed in universal values but kept a skeptical eye on man and the world. He likes the remoteness and occasional obtuseness of its language, the heavy way it has of making a light point, and vice versa. He has used this to enrich the tonal range of his own poetic language. If Brodsky's early poems are in monotones, his later verse maintains a balance between light and serious, using puns of different kinds and making the most of the possibilities for ambiguity: double meanings abound. . . . But it is clear from the opening lines that ["Poslanie k stikham" ("Epistle to His Verses")] is] a sophisticated treatment of the theme of "writing for the desk drawer" (almost none of Brodsky's work has been published in the Soviet Union), and shows how Brodsky's poetry always contains the potential for commentary on contemporary themes. And this makes it very much a twentieth-century text. (pp. 314-15)

["Almost an Elegy"] gives a good insight into the nature of Brodsky's religious themes. Brodsky sees life as a gift from God. His early interest in yoga reflected an innate contemplative or mystical bent. Now it is his poetry that has become for him a mode of contemplative activity, though it is not only that. He deals with Old Testament motifs from the point of view of one who is on native ground; he identifies easily and naturally with an Isaac or a Jacob. So far, Brodsky's perception of what it is like to know God personally is rooted in an earth-centered, Old Testament outlook rather than in a Christian experience. The "Elegy for John Donne," despite the fact that its subject is replete with possibilities for meditation on Christian themes, nevertheless resolves the problem of death in terms of an eternal rest on the earth under the old dispensation. However, since the early 1960s, New Testament motifs occur in his verse with increasing frequency, especially the Nativity and the Crucifixion. It is natural that he should be drawn to the Christian mysteries of the birth and death of God, for in them there is both the pathos of mortality and a sign of victory over death. (p. 319)

"Almost an Elegy" is a poem about the memory of a miracle as seen after a fall from grace: the poet looks back on a time of former brightness from a perspective of encroaching darkness. The seasonal metaphor for this passage from brightness to darkness is the coming of fall. The next poem, "Verses in April," was written some six months later at the opposite point in the seasonal cycle. It is a poem about a time when brightness (spring) is arriving, and darkness (winter) is passing into memory. . . . (pp. 319-20)

"Verses in April" is a poem about the memory, not of miracle, but of evil, in a season when evil seems to be receding. *Pominanie* can be used to mean both the church prayers for one who has died, and the ritual feast celebrated by the mourners. In either case, *pominanie zla* means "laying evil to rest (now that it is dead)." This is one way of bringing about the ridding of evil. Brodsky chooses a different way. He defines his poetry as a "scapegoat for bearing away wrongs." This also is a ridding of evil, but in doing so it sets those evils down. Just as the memory of a miracle cannot be forgotten (for it is the greatest loneliness), so the memory of evil cannot be forgotten either. This is the motivation for the naming of Mnemosyne in the poem's final line: Mnemosyne, mother of the Muses, is the goddess of Memory.

The idea that the poem is a scapegoat provides a key to the meaning of the image of the desert, or wilderness (*pustynia*), in the title *Ostanotka v pustyne*. After Aaron has laid down his own sins and the sins of the people on the scapegoat, the goat is led into the wilderness. . . . (p. 323)

"Verses in April," like "Almost an Elegy," is a poem in which there is no "music," nor can there be in unruly spring when the Muses crowd and shove, quarreling among themselves. The need to admit wrongs in order to be rid of them is perhaps an unpleasant subject in a season when poems are supposed to be cheerful, and Brodsky wittily lays the blame on the Muses, who are squabbling instead of singing. But of course there *is* music here: the music of wit and seriousness together, a music something like that "tough reasonableness" beneath the lyric grace which Eliot so prized in Andrew Marvell and the other Metaphysicals. (pp. 324-25)

R. D. Sylvester, "The Poem as Scapegoat: An Introduction to Joseph Brodsky's 'Halt in the Wilderness'," in Texas Studies in Literature and Language: Special Russian Issue *(copyright © 1975 by the University of Texas Press), Vol. XVII, 1975, pp. 303-25.*

BYRON LINDSEY

[Brodsky] is no doubt the most important name in contemporary Russian poetry, both at home and in emigration. It is no new reputation, but stems from the 1960s, when the intensity and severity of his lyrics, read mainly in manuscript, awakened memories of dormant muses, of Annensky, Mandelstam, Tsvetaeva. His poems to John Donne and T. S. Eliot were striking, especially coming from a young Russian poet. (p. 129)

Konec prekrasnoj èpoxi (The End of a Fine Epoch) comprises poems written in the period 1964-71 and, for its time span and diversity of style and theme, is probably the best collection for making first acquaintance with Brodsky. The early poems seem inferior to those collected in *Ostanovka*, but Brodsky's own voice is more intimate, his view of the world more openly exposed. By placing a fine and characteristic lyric from 1971 first in the collection, it would seem that he wishes to make his own introduction. In clean and solid lines the poet-persona observes a second Christmas in Yalta: of the visible world, only the sea transports his doubts of gods and memories of love to another inaccessible but tangible shore. Trapped between existence and hope, the poet makes his way to that shore only through his own lines.

"Nature-morte," a tribute to Cesare Pavese in short, shining lines, and "Ljubov" (Love), one of his most melodic and forthright love lyrics, form an impressive end to the collection. In a world where color is present only through its very absence ("These last days I / sleep in the white of day") the poet walks between light and shadow, sustained at night by illuminated dreams. They speak not of memory as much as of birth and of his own responsibility for saving love's offspring from "the kingdom of shadows."

Cast' reci, a book of the poet's work since emigration (1972-76), is by comparison brighter, more mobile and more difficult. Brodsky seems to explore with simultaneous pleasure and trepidation the real sites of his ongoing imagination: the poems range from a musical divertissement in Mexico, to a sad December in Florence, to Chelsea. The past is as important as before: he writes twenty sonnets to Maria Stuart. The freedom of exploration is seen more significantly in his language itself, particularly in "A Part of Speech," the cycle of short lyrics which gives the book its title. Here there is perhaps greater tension and polish than earlier. In an especially light and graceful poem Brodsky recommends America to a fellow émigré, dancer Mikhail Baryshnikov, as a place to touch down. But the inner landscape seems unchanged: it is a place of myth, old empires and departures also not very new. Language itself, like the lovely, fragile wings of a perished butterfly, is the only embodiment, the only true measure between the poet and Nothing ("Babocka" [The Butterfly]). In American exile Brodsky seems still more distant, more elusive, philosophically perhaps more courageous.

In both volumes there is much more than meets the eye and ear. Brodsky is not a poet of easy statements or facile solutions, whether technical or thematic. He puts any reader interested in Russian poetry to a personal, linguistic and cultural challenge. That Brodsky is a good poet there is no doubt. Even a non-Russian reader can confirm this quickly. As a link to the tradition of the Russian poet who speaks either with his own free voice or with that of the prophet, he commands attention. But whether there is song in his music and purpose in his sometimes chilling distance, only time and his Russian readers—who for the moment can only be few—will be able to say. (p. 130)

> *Byron Lindsey, in* World Literature Today *(copyright 1978 by the University of Oklahoma Press), Vol. 52, No. 1, Winter, 1978.*

HENRY GIFFORD

Since 1972 Iosif Brodsky, the most talented Russian poet of his generation, has been living in the United States. When some forty years ago Auden (whom Brodsky knew and admired) made a similar choice, the implications for him were scarcely so grave as for a Russian poet today. . . . [Auden's] ears were not constantly assailed by a foreign language; he could not know the dread of being estranged from the native hearth, and of gradually losing touch with what Mandelstam once called "the formidable and boundless element of the Russian language", and with the creative processes at work in popular speech.

Mandelstam is particularly relevant here, because of all Brodsky's predecessors in that generation—and he has learnt much at various times from Tsvetaeva, Khlebnikov and Mayakovsky—none stands closer to him. . . . For Brodsky as for Mandelstam there can be no question of the poet's authority. He explains in one of the new poems here, "Conversation with a Celestial Being" (1970):

> . . . if my soul had a profile
>   you would see
>   that it too
> is merely a mould from my
>   sorrowful gift,
>   that it possessed nothing more,
> that together with this it is turned
>   towards you. . . .

The responsibility that lies on the present [Russian artistic] emigration is clearly understood, but the basic problem remains. Can a culture survive in dispersal? . . .

It is natural, then, that the later [volume *Chast' rechi: Stikhotvoreniya 1972-76*] by Brodsky should interest more [than the earlier]. There are excellent pieces in the earlier [*Konets prekrasnoy epokhi: Stikhotvoreniya 1964-1971*], which foreshadows the situation he must accept; and the period before his departure shows a mind preparing itself and devising the appropriate forms for the new experience.

The second volume closes with "A Cape Cod Lullaby" (1975), in twelve parts, followed by a shorter poem "De-cember in Florence" (1976). Brodsky is remarkably good at evoking the spirit of place. The other volume has an attractive set of poems about Lithuania, and here not only Cape Cod but also the Thames at Chelsea and Mexico make their appearance. These poems, too, are about empires in decay (London), or illusory (Maximilian in Mexico), or actual (the United States, forming the reverse side of the familiar coin). The theme of his "Lullaby" is the change of empires. (p. 902)

The man who leaves behind his native country to settle where his own language is not spoken brings with him as it were a thick wad of traveller's cheques which cannot be supplemented. Thus Brodsky, coming upon a statue of Mary Queen of Scots in the Luxembourg, writes twenty sonnets in her honour, and says in the first, "I spend what is left of Russian speech / on your likeness full face and lustreless shoulders". The group of poems that precedes "A Cape Cod Lullaby", like the second book itself, is entitled "A Part of Speech", and in the last but one of them he says:

> Life, which
> like a thing given you do not look
>   in the mouth,
> bares its teeth at every meeting.
> Of the whole man there is left to
>   you a part
> of speech. A part of speech
> in general. A part of speech.

Not the whole stretch of the language, a part only. Yet for the man to be made whole again there is only one resource: he must cling on to his participation in the language.

The poem that closes the second volume, "December in Florence", carries an epigraph from Anna Akhmatova: "This man, going away, did not look back . . .". (pp. 902-03)

The poem to which Brodsky alludes here is a tribute to Dante for refusing to end his exile by public penance: "With lighted candle he did not walk / Through his Florence, desired / Perfidious, base, long-awaited. . . ." Dante did not look back, as did Orpheus, and again Lot's wife, to their own ruin.

Eight of the nine stanzas in Brodsky's poem have Florence as their setting, but behind it there are hints of another scene. He notes a "decrepit goldfinch" caged in a café, and this recalls the bird with whom Mandelstam identified in his exile. The association is deepened as a ray of light comes through

> and the goldfinch overflows in the
>   centre of a wire Ravenna.

In the final stanza Brodsky speaks of "cities to which there is no return", and the scene has shifted to Leningrad:

> there the crowd speaks, as it
> besieges the corner of the tram,
> in the language of the man who has
>   gone away. . . .

[The] man in the poem has been diminished by his going. As, when Orpheus looked back, Eurydice faded away, so the true self of the poet, empowered by his full possession of the language, seems to shrink away at the poem's close.

> Yet look back he must—the Muses

were the children of Mnemosyne,
. . . and at the word "future" from
                    the Russian language
run out mice and a whole horde
they nibble away the sweet morsel
of memory like your cheese in
                              holes. . . .

That becomes the natural movement of his thought. . . .

Whatever Brodsky may fear, he is still marvellously at home in the language. At the same time, he is putting exile to good use, by seeking out affinities and extensions. . . .

An accident of the cruellest kind (and common enough in our century) has thrown Brodsky into the cosmopolitan world. The potential loss, to him and to Russian poetry, is plain enough. . . .

He is more fortunate, however, than his American contemporaries. The Russian language that has so recently answered the needs of Tsvetaeva, Pasternak, Mandelstam and Akhmatova must be a source of undying strength to a modern poet, even away from Russian soil and Russian voices. He has not been left with "shabby equipment always deteriorating", even in this "second-rate epoch". One may hope that the Russian language has momentum enough to carry it through the barren decades until a divided culture is brought together again. Meanwhile, by an irony characteristic of our time, it could be that the best poetry from America in recent years is the work of this Russian. (p. 903)

> Henry Gifford, "The Language of Loneliness," in The Times Literary Supplement (© Times Newspapers Ltd. (London) 1978; reproduced from The Times Literary Supplement by permission), August 11, 1978, pp. 902-03.

*   *   *

BUCKLER, Ernest   1908-

Buckler is a Canadian novelist, short story writer, essayist, and scriptwriter. He creates a fictive world rooted in his native Nova Scotian village; characters in this microcosm are intricately drawn and psychologically complex. Buckler's fiction is characterized by its contemplative tone and frequent use of allegory. While critics have found some of his work to be overly obscure or verbose, Buckler's first novel, *The Mountain and the Valley*, is generally regarded as a minor masterpiece. (See also *Contemporary Authors*, Vols. 11-12; *Contemporary Authors Permanent Series*, Vol. 1.)

WARREN TALLMAN

[In the severe isolation of David Canaan in *The Mountain and the Valley*, one encounters an] attempt to discover new ground upon which the withdrawn self might stand in its efforts to move into presence. During his childhood and youth David's vivid impulses fascinate his family and friends. . . . Throughout childhood and early youth David moves among others with the aura about him of the chosen person, the mysterious Nazarite who is motioned toward an unknowable destiny by unseen gods. But what is an advantage during his early years becomes a disadvantage later when the appealing mystery of his loneliness becomes the oppressive ordeal of his unbreakable solitude. More devastating still, at no point in his life is he capable of actions which might rescue him from the limbo in which he dwells. (p. 12)

That the male mountain and the female valley of the title loom up so prominently in the novel is surely a sign, here as with Wordsworth, that natural objects have been endowed with all the seeming numenousness of their inaccessible human equivalents. Conversely, other persons in the novel are invested with a deceptive glamour. The breath of life fans the nucleus of David's impulses into a glow, but because these impulses are checked they never achieve the release of communication, much less communion. Unable to know his family in their ordinariness, he must create his own knowledge in the image of his arrested, his childish and childlike psychic life. Consequently his parents are perceived as mythical, almost biblical beings and this appearance is sustained as long as David's response is intense enough, the glow white hot. Such intensities are . . . the hallmark of the novel. . . . (pp. 12-13)

David is trying to sustain an illusion. Whenever the hot impulse cools the glow goes out of the novel and we see David's family and friends for what they are, very unbiblical, unmythical, ordinary human beings. At no time does his friend Toby demonstrate those distinguished qualities with which David invests him. His sister Anna is represented as soul of David's soul, but it is only possible for David to sustain this sublimated conception by overlooking the almost overtly incestuous basis for their relationship. Only the looming mountain can provide adequate expression for the childlike awe with which he regards his father. In his relations with others David is much like one inside a house which he cannot leave looking out at persons he has never known because he has never actually moved among them. As one by one these persons depart, he begins to notice the emptiness, room leading silently to room. The novel is an account of David's attempt to ward off such knowledge. But fathers and mothers die, and brothers, friends and sisters—soul of his soul—depart. Until only the grandmother is left, calling out "Where is that child?", even as the child, unable to endure both an outer and an inner emptiness, goes at last up the snow covered mountain into the final dimension of his solitude. The emptiness, the silence and the snow into which he sinks down at the end of the novel figure forth the constant nothingness against which his bright intensities had beat, thinking it the high shores of this actual world. His life would be pathetic if it were not heroic.

The heroism is in his effort, in the extreme tenacity with which David clings to the sources of his suffering, and it is in the novel, in the record of that suffering. The very intensity which creates those illusions with which David tries to live also creates a distinctive lyric exaltation. Because perception is so consistently at fever pitch, the descriptive surfaces of the novel are exceptionally fine-grained, the communion with nature, with appearances, with actions, so close that many passages read like lyric poems. But paradoxes are endless, and if the unreleased intensity which is a tragedy for David becomes an advantage for the novelist it in turn becomes another kind of disadvantage for the reader. For Buckler has no compositional key except maximum intensity. Sentence after sentence is forced to a descriptive pitch which makes the novel exceptionally wearing to read. (pp. 13-14)

> Warren Tallman, in Canadian Literature, Summer, 1960.

ALAN R. YOUNG

Ernest Buckler's *The Mountain and the Valley* (1952) is a

118

fine example of the pastoral impulse, and its meaning is greatly illuminated when viewed within the framework of the pastoral tradition. When the novel is considered in these terms, one is able to perceive the profound manner in which Buckler transforms his geographically-, chronologically- and morally-defined pastoral world into a spiritual landscape itself symbolic of the mind of his semi-autobiographical protagonist, David Canaan. . . .

Like some special form of latter-day enclosed garden, Entremont [the novel's geographical setting] (as the name suggests) is bounded by North and South Mountains and for David Canaan, by a river to the north "cut wide by the Fundy tides" . . . and a stream to the south. These natural barriers, which are constantly referred to in the novel, offer David a choice between the world of the Valley and the world beyond, and, as the novel develops, it becomes clear that this choice symbolizes the spiritual dilemma that confronts him throughout the thirty years of his life described in the novel. (p. 220)

In chronological terms Buckler's pastoral is set in the recent past, presenting an image of rural Nova Scotia prior to the Second World War. It is a world that has now largely disappeared but, as so often in modern pastoral, its disappearance is recent enough for the reader's nostalgia (and even guilt if he shares the environmentalist's sense of responsibility) to be made especially acute. As such the externals of the choice that David faces are close to us. We may live in an urbanised environment by choice or necessity, but we remain aware of the garden that has so recently been desecrated. At the same time, Buckler presents his pastoral world as the childhood memory of his literary *persona* David. The Theocritean pastoral pattern, in typically post-Romantic fashion, is transformed into a journey from childhood to maturity and from innocence to experience. In these terms David's choice between Mountain and Valley is a choice between failure (or refusal) to accept himself and full self-recognition.

The moral pattern of life in Buckler's Valley derives from a fundamental sense of community, manifested in [communal rituals]. . . . Coupled with this is the reverence accorded to the family unit. . . . In the Valley, man lives in harmony with nature and feels himself part of an eternal historical process. (pp. 220-21)

The positive attributes of Buckler's pastoral world are relatively clear. The true complexity of the novel, however, rests with the manner in which Buckler invests his *persona* with the double vision one finds in almost all the more perceptive pastoralists. . . . David, sensitive and complex in his responses, a person of quick thoughts . . . , realizes that life in the Valley at times can be characterised by brutish sensibility, lack of communication between those who love each other most, and general self-perpetuating mindlessness. . . . (p. 221)

Throughout the novel we expect David to opt for some form of voluntary exile rather in the manner of Stephen Dedalus with whom he has so much in common. We expect too the familiar pattern of pastoral to assert itself by a final swing of the protagonist away from the pastoral world, which represents (like Eden) only a temporary domicile in life's larger pattern, towards the complexities and sophistication of life in an urban and technological culture. Howev-

er, David makes if anything a tougher decision: he elects to live in the Valley. Here more than anywhere else, Buckler (perhaps recreating his own experiences) makes a striking departure from the traditional formula of pastoral. David's choice represents a triumph, and his eventual climb to the summit of the Mountain provides the looked-for symbolic demonstration of his coming to terms with himself and his heritage. (p. 222)

As David begins to walk towards the Mountain, Buckler makes clear that what we are about to witness is a spiritual journey, the externals of landscape being a manifestation of the state of David's inner consciousness. . . . In something close to mystical trance, David loses consciousness of his own body . . . and feels himself to be in absolute isolation. . . . Now at last his sense of temporal progression, which has so distinguished his sensibility from that of his rural neighbours throughout the novel, is overcome in a transcendent fusion of past and present. . . . The brook symbolically behind him, David is transplanted to another time—a time which permits a new beginning, something which he has hitherto felt to be impossible. . . . Incidents and thoughts from the past flash through his mind and he climbs higher. What he describes as "voices" swarm about him, becoming increasingly insistent until they are unbearable and force David to scream for them to stop. . . . (pp. 223-24)

David's arrival at the top of the Mountain coincides with this climax and a further "translation" occurs as the voices are "soaked up at once. Not in a vanishing, but as the piercing clamor of nerves in fever is soaked up in sleep". . . . Like the epiphany experienced by Stephen Dedalus on the seashore in *Portrait of the Artist,* David's "translation" is accompanied by a sense of his destiny as a writer, and indeed we realize during these closing pages that the book David would have written has indeed been written, for it is the one just read. (p. 224)

David's experience is followed by his death. Snow falls and his body becomes indistinguishable from the log beside him. He becomes one with nature in a way that his father never perhaps achieved. . . . His death, startling as it may seem in the pattern of pastoral, is not in any sense representative of failure, like that, say, of Gerald Crich (also in the snow) in Lawrence's *Women in Love.* Instead it represents the paradoxical triumph of "ripeness is all". . . .

Buckler's novel is thus a pastoral in which the hero, in contradiction of all traditional patterns, never passes beyond the boundaries of the pastoral world in which he finds himself. The achievement of Buckler's hero is to unite within his own consciousness the double vision of the pastoralist and to testify in his life to the equal claims of the values of Mountain and Valley. (p. 225)

> Alan R. Young, "The Pastoral Vision of Ernest Buckler," in The Dalhousie Review, *Summer, 1973, pp. 219-25.*

ALAN R. YOUNG

[One must be grateful] that at last there is an available anthology of Buckler's stories. What they reveal collectively is that Buckler's gifts as a fiction writer are by no means restricted to his novels. Indeed, stories like "Penny in the Dust", "The Quarrel", or "The Dream and the Triumph" are equal to the very best in Buckler's longer works. Though [*The Rebellion of Young David and Other Stories*] confirms the impression one has from the novels that Buckler's narrative technique is limited to the conventional and that his themes and plot motifs are limited in their variety, the stories also confirm that at his best Buckler is a writer with a superlative degree of skill, perceptiveness, emotional power, and control, and a writer whose themes are the compelling universals of the inherent conflicts between past and present, city and country, family and outsider, man and woman, age and youth, and society and the individual. (p. 387)

Alan R. Young, in The Dalhousie Review, *Summer, 1975.*

ROBERT D. CHAMBERS

The particular interest of Buckler's early sketches and stories is in following themes and characters which would appear in more serious and mature form in the later fiction. In this sense, all his early work was a dress rehearsal for *The Mountain and the Valley.*

Buckler's first published story was "One Quiet Afternoon," which appeared in the April, 1940 issue of *Esquire* magazine. Here one senses Buckler struggling to find an appropriate form for his materials. The story lacks a central narrative interest; there is simply too much going on. Any signs of such weakness had disappeared utterly with his next effort, a story called "The First Born Son," published by *Esquire* in July, 1941. This masterful story combined two themes which were to become central to Buckler's mature work: the tension between fathers and sons, and the city/country conflict. (pp. 55-6)

[For a beginner] the differences between city and country were a useful way to define characterization. . . . Buckler leaves us with a strong sense of the country as a creative force. By contrast, the city, with its disfiguring drives toward sophistication and materialism, cuts one off from a meaningful flow of experience. (pp. 56-7)

Perhaps more important than the city/country theme in Buckler's early stories is the depiction of family life. . . . Buckler's best achievements adopt [the narrative voice of a young country boy]. (p. 57)

"Penny in the Dust" might well stand as a kind of archetype of Buckler's achievements in the story form. To begin with, it uses a retrospective framework, a technique of thinking-back which unexpectedly creates a warm glow of memory upon events long buried in the past. . . . (p. 58)

[In "Penny in the Dust" the] combination of retrospective framework, realistic reconstruction of past emotion, and clear symbolic meaning became the unique imprint of Buckler's short stories. (p. 59)

The essential problem with "A Present for Miss Merriam" is Buckler's handling of Miss Merriam's narration. One feels his uneasiness in adopting the woman's narrative voice—a stiffness not found in his better work. It is therefore useful to contrast the relatively weak "A Present for Miss Merriam" with the superbly successful "Last Delivery Before Christmas." Here the story of Ronnie's gaining a second father, in the person of Syd Weston, and Syd's heroic effort to overcome Ronnie's hostility, is narrated by the very convincing voice of Ronnie himself. . . . We instinctively respond to the immediacy of Ronnie's narration. . . . (p. 62)

Taken together, Buckler's early sketches, short stories, and first draft of a novel [*Excerpts from a Life*] reveal a writer seeking through endless experiment the full and mature expression of his unique vision. All his early writing points unerringly toward his major work, *The Mountain and the Valley* (1952). (p. 65)

[The] span of perhaps three-quarters of a century [in *The Mountain and the Valley*] allows Buckler to pursue one of his favourite concerns: the fall-out from one generation to the next of both physical and psychological characteristics—the ways in which habits and mannerisms, oddities of speech and gesture will move down through a family.

The structural device Buckler employs to convey this sense of movement within the Canaan family is Ellen's rug. As she sits, throughout the novel, rummaging in the rag-bag for bits of cloth to weave into her growing rug, her associations in memory with each piece of cloth draw together, like the rug itself, into a kind of family history. This device for widening out the span of time adds both depth and density to the foreground narrative, the story of David Canaan's life. Ellen's rug, moreover, is being worked circle by circle. We thus seem to be watching the growth of a pattern which is closed ring after ring, like the generations of the family, and which, by the end of the novel, is finally complete. (pp. 66-7)

The depiction of David's character is the major concern of "Part One—The Play," but Buckler must also establish the minor characters and sketch in the life of the valley community. He combines these purposes by narrating the events of a single day, with a subtle shifting of focus from David's youthful dreams to the communal tragedy of a double death. In this section, too, he forges the basic symbolic tension of the whole book, the pull between mountain and valley, which will ultimately shape the narrative and open out the book's full significance. (pp. 67-8)

[David's] capacity to invest the future with a dream-like perfection, to impose upon poor mundane reality a splendour it simply cannot sustain—these reactions mark David as different, a difference which Buckler develops by way of contrast with the characters of Joseph and Chris. (p. 68)

David's sense of self is rooted in his difference from others. He exists by reason of a distinct apartness—in this case, a gift with words which marks him off from the rest of the community. One of the strategies of the novel is David's inability to find, literally, a soul mate. Buckler thus confronts us with two basic, and widely contrasting, personalities: one fulfils himself by doing; the other by naming, seeing, and describing what is done. In broader terms, the novel investigates the place of the artist or writer in a communal context which by tradition values arms and muscles more than insight and brains. (p. 69)

It is astonishing how much Buckler accomplishes in these opening chapters. . . . The major characters have been given unique personalities, and this effect is achieved not by block descriptions or set pieces which, in effect, say to the reader, "This is what this character is like." Buckler's narrative and descriptive process is a finer weave, in which patterns of meaning are established through concrete images. (p. 71)

In addition to the ten characters already established in these opening chapters, Buckler creates a structural pattern which will be sustained throughout. He works his materials into sharply contrasting forces, as the title of the book suggests. . . . [The] contrasts also exist at an abstract level: fathers and sons, mothers and daughters; youth and age; people who do and people who think; life and death. (p. 72)

By the end of Part Three, Buckler has fully orchestrated [a] powerful but fateful rhythm—David's every act of assertion, however motivated, ironically leading to failure, guilt, and isolation. In the first half of the book, however, this process has been worked mainly with David's external relationships. . . . The function of Parts Four and Five is to take this destructive rhythm into the heart of the Canaan family.

As Part Four opens, we are aware, from the progress on Ellen's rug, that some time has passed. . . . David and Joseph are clearing rocks from the field, and David has changed ominously. . . . [His] dull and resentful mood intensifies in David as together he and his father work the field for rocks. In perhaps the most brilliant writing in the book . . . , Buckler builds a terrible tension, using a structure of alternating viewpoints, placing one interior monologue over against the other, creating dramatic irony through the mutual misconceptions of David and Joseph. (p. 77)

Part Five, entitled "The Scar," is not only the most physical section of the book, but also the one which seals David's fate. . . . It is a deeply impressive piece of writing, in which Buckler slowly works David—no match for the other men in physical strength—into a mood of desperate recklessness. His attempt to prove equality ends in a feat of daring which nearly kills him in a fall from the barn beam, and the resultant wound and scar symbolize henceforth his physical difference, which is only aggravated in David's mind by his family's constant solicitude. (p. 79)

In the early pages of [Part Six], Buckler conveys a strong feeling of claustrophobia, partly achieved by a conscious shift in style. As Buckler approaches the final stage of David's story, his prose increasingly takes on an abstract quality, as though the time had arrived for the full meaning of the narrative to unfold. . . . Buckler thus transforms into empathy that earlier tendency of David to project his own desires into the external world. But it is a development which brings no sense of serenity, no feeling of the mind calmed and the passion spent. Instead, Buckler finds again a rhythm—at once excited but enervating—for this feverish state of mind. . . . (pp. 79-80)

[Acceptance] is the dominant mood of the Epilogue. As David makes his way by stages up the mountain, Buckler allows us to see again the course of David's life. When he meets Steve on the road, we recall a dozen instances when, disguising his true nature, David acted out the crude idiom of the valley men. The David/Joseph conflict of character is before us again. Now, however, David feels no sense of isolation or guilt; like the actor on the stage, he plays the role that Steve expects, and passes on.

Higher up the mountain, his calm mind begins to stir with thoughts and memories, but this mental activity has about it a fluidity, a truly creative ease, which allows David to enter with complete empathy into both past and present. . . . Here Buckler celebrates the maturing of an artistic personality. David has always been stirred by the power of the printed word, but his own efforts to write have failed be-

cause his melodramatic imagination chose subjects beyond his realm of experience. . . . Now, however, David sees that he must recreate the world he knows—the one that he has loved so intensely and so often been hurt by. We sense that David is just beginning the process which Buckler as novelist is just completing.

In time, this flood of creative energy overwhelms David: Buckler finds the perfect external image in the tangled variety of trees growing up the mountain slope. In a final moment of stillness at the very top of the mountain, Buckler bestows upon David a vision of creative harmony which binds together and heals the conflicts of his life: the mountain *and* the valley. . . . [David's] acceptance of himself as one of [the valley people] is achieved without any sense of strain. . . . Within a page, David lies dead in the snow. At the same moment, Ellen completes her rug, by adding a final piece of delicate white lace just at the centre. It symbolizes the wedding of valley—the rug is meant for practical wear—and mountain, a complexly patterned thing of artifice such as the novelist David had begun to weave at the moment of his death. (pp. 82-3)

[Buckler's second novel, *The Cruelest Month* (1963)], everywhere gives evidence of immensely careful planning. Its four-part structure, gradual interweaving of themes and characters, and almost total neglect of action, in the conventional sense, all indicate that he wished his meaning to emerge slowly and brokenly, as it might in a great symphony. . . .

With the exception of the boy Peter, who dies early in the book, the novel is peopled with adults. *The Cruelest Month* thus tackles human relationships and problems which were largely precluded from *The Mountain and the Valley* because of David's inability to make, though not to imagine, meaningful adult ties. (p. 84)

Part I establishes not only the major characters but also the themes which Buckler wishes to explore. . . . Like Letty, Endlaw's housekeeper, Paul is a calm centre within the novel, a still eye around which rage the psychological tempests of the other characters. As such, he is more talked about than talking; Buckler seems content, much of the time, merely to describe Paul rather than to show him in action. (p. 85)

As the book develops, it becomes possible to see the characters in three distinct categories: Letty and Paul; Kate and Morse; Bruce, Rex and Sheila. While these groups are continually interacting against the backdrop of the Endlaw setting, it is clear from Part I that Buckler will use each group to work out a series of closely connected themes. . . . To pursue a musical analogy, Letty's questioning of her relationship with Paul functions as does a *leit-motiv* in a Wagner opera or Richard Strauss tone poem. We hear the theme from time to time throughout the book, now modulated or transposed to another key, but always recognizable, especially when it returns in full measure towards the close of Part IV. This is the basic structure of *The Cruelest Month*, a series of interwoven themes, all with an affinity of family resemblance, which the reader, like the concert goer, must hold in a creative tension as they develop and finally meld. (pp. 85-6)

[The curious trio of characters—Bruce, Rex, and Sheila]— two guilt-ridden men and a loveless woman caught between them—jostles with Paul, Kate and Morse for the reader's interest in Parts II and III of the book. Indeed this stretch of the novel attempts the mixture of memory and desire which characterizes T. S. Eliot's cruelest month in *The Waste Land*. The deeply buried guilts of the past (memory) are here in transition to idealized projections of future happiness and fulfilment (desire). . . . While it is true that the pseudo-intellectual word-juggling of Paul, Kate and Morse can grow tedious, one needs to recognize too that this bookish banter, despite its constant puns and allusions, often accompanied by mimicry, serves a thematic purpose within the book. Buckler is not striving to be light and clever, and somehow failing at both effects. (p. 90)

Buckler's real purpose is to reveal and dramatize his characters' basic selves. Faced with the alternative, in life or in art, between surface trivia and human essence, he has chosen the more difficult narrative path which lies through the "swamp of earnestness." . . . His preference for the deeper layers in human relationships explains the relative slowness of the book's development. . . . Buckler's method insists that the reader pay attention, not to what happens, but to what *is*. (p. 91)

The novel's end also brings the least expected alliance of all, between Paul and Letty. . . . It is a curious way to end a novel about the process of becoming, this unexpected coupling of master and housekeeper in an untouched oasis of burned out Annapolis Valley—especially since Letty has received so little attention in the middle sections of the book. Buckler's final vision rests, nonetheless, with Paul and Letty, a simple and natural relationship but one deeply rooted in the flesh's longing.

Buckler originally called this novel *The Cells of Love,* and indicated that it was a title which faced two ways, thus implying a paradox about the human condition. In one sense of the word, each of us forms a unique cell of life, each defining that prison of personality which Eliot describes so vividly in the final section of *The Waste Land*. But the other sense of the word, as in cell of blood, suggests the possibility of rich and vital union with the full stream of life. The April background of *The Cruelest Month,* again with Eliot in mind, symbolizes the harsh discrepancy between nature joyfully regenerating itself and human nature paralyzed by a terrible awareness of death-in-life. Thus each of the characters in *The Cruelest Month* seeks release from the prison cell into the exciting and constantly reforming dance of the blood cells. In the background of each character is the spectre of death, but each must find a way to go on with the business of living. It is the possibility of future love, and its growth from the immuring experiences of the past, that Buckler explores here so painstakingly. Yet our ultimate feeling about the book is one of dissatisfaction, for despite the traditional importance and modern relevance of its theme, one senses here that Buckler is really an alien on uncomfortable ground. (pp. 91-2)

Ox Bells and Fireflies (1968) belongs to no obvious literary genre. Rather, it is a series of loosely connected memories imaginatively recreated along fictional lines. (p. 93)

Ox Bells and Fireflies immediately calls to mind *The Mountain and the Valley,* since in both books Buckler has reached back for his materials into his store of childhood memories. Memory is here the major thread, and as such it carries with it a personal character which we allow Buckler to draw out at his own pace.

There is, too, about this book a sense of freedom from restraint. If we recall Morse's general criticism of the novel as a literary form in *The Cruelest Month,* the need of the novelist to create conventional modes of action, and to develop recognizable characters, had been a problem very much on Buckler's mind in the earlier book. The desire to write without the incessant demands of plot and character may have shaped Buckler's decision to try on the much looser clothing, and less encumbered stretch, of the style of *Ox Bells and Fireflies.* (pp. 93-4)

Indeed, if the book uses any major structural device, it is [the] constant shifting between the two worlds of boy and man, endless variations on a Then/Now theme. . . . From the time of his earliest writing, [Buckler] has tried to catch the perfect moment of experience, using what he has always regarded (irony of ironies!) as the very make-shift and inadequate net of words. (pp. 94-5)

The narrative voice of the boy Mark records only the very detailed and specific memories of childhood. When Buckler turns to the adult world, the Now of the book, this voice grows generalized, vague, imprecise. The wonderful names of the boy's world, with their exact shades of meaning and particular idioms, become distanced, as though the present somehow fails to yield the individualized accents of past experience.

This sense of time taking the edge off experience (no new phenomenon in the stages of poetic development) is rendered with especial power in the sequences which deal with human loneliness and isolation. . . . (p. 95)

The book is not, however, primarily an introspective affair. It is really Then which predominates, and all Buckler's youthful memories, even the sad ones, are touched with the glory of aliveness. It is a book, too, of much good humour, especially when found in the unique local idioms of the Valley people. . . . Indeed, the beauty of *Ox Bells and Fireflies* resides in [the] capacity to recreate not only such unique moments but whole segments of Valley life as Buckler knew it in his youth. . . . The book's real celebration is of another time and place which has been lovingly recreated and made to glow once again, especially for those who did not know that its beauty had ever existed. Perhaps few nets of words, dipped into memory's pool, have brought in such a harvest of lovely treasure. (pp. 97-8)

Buckler's *The Cruelest Month* affords [an] example of work which arises from materials that have not fully engaged the writer's imagination. What signifies its difference from *The Mountain and the Valley* is the loss of the family context, where relationships between characters have a natural basis. *The Cruelest Month,* on the contrary, seems artificial; the characters have to be brought together and then deployed like so many mathematical permutations. These characteristics also mar some of Buckler's later short stories, especially the long sequence, begun in 1956, for *The Atlantic Advocate.*

One measure of difference between [Buckler's] early and late works . . . is the changing emphasis from action to talk. . . . Possibly a novelist allows his characters merely to talk when he can no longer meaningfully dramatize their human situations, when the sense of a symbolically significant environment has permanently faded. (p. 100)

[What was clear to] Buckler, and to others of [his] generation, was that independent existence as a writer was not possible in Canada. It is thus all the more admirable that [he] went on writing, trying through experiment—and often through failure—to create literature for a country which didn't very much care. Perhaps here we may find a partial explanation for the power with which [his] most memorable characters are realized—. . . [for is not David Canaan an artist] without a public? . . . [Remember] David Canaan's longing to put it all down in words that would last forever. Surely in such characters . . . Buckler [has] given us a deep perception into what it was like to be born, and burdened, with an artistic personality in the first half of Canada's twentieth century. (pp. 101-02)

We acknowledge the regionalist aspect of [Buckler's] work, but the overall value of [his] books ensures a wider response. It is undeniably clear that [his] major creations . . . —Buckler's Canaan family and folk of the Annapolis Valley —take us into the heartland of both literature and life. The creative tensions so powerfully and dramatically rendered in [his] books, [his] sensitive awareness of beauty and of its inevitable passing, [his] compassion for the human condition—all these forge important links with the tradition of great imaginative writing. (p. 102)

> Robert D. Chambers, in his Sinclair Ross and Ernest Buckler (© Robert D. Chambers; reprinted by permission of the publishers; distributed by Douglas & McIntyre Ltd.), Copp Clark Publishing, 1975, McGill-Queen's University Press, 1975.

LINDA SANDLER

Buckler was not entirely certain that his readers shared his knowledge and assumptions about rural life. In 'The Wild Goose' . . . his account of the hunt is written with the voice of one conveying an intricate and esoteric religion to the uninitiated: 'Wild geese had something—well, sort of mystic—about them.'

The stories draw abundantly on the clichés of rural romance; they have a certain derivative charm. . . . Buckler's themes match well with the concerns of the neo-pastoral revisionists. (p. 86)

> Linda Sandler, in The Tamarack Review, Summer, 1976.

* * *

BURGESS, Anthony 1917-

Born John Anthony Burgess Wilson, Burgess is an English novelist, editor, translator, essayist, composer, and critic. A remarkably prolific writer with a wide range of subjects, he frequently uses his knowledge of music and linguistics in his fiction. Burgess's fascination with languages is evident in many of his novels, most notably *A Clockwork Orange*. Terming himself a "renegade Catholic," Burgess explores free will versus determinism in his novels. Admittedly influenced by James Joyce, Burgess has endeavored to explicate his genius in *Here Comes Everybody: An Introduction to James Joyce for the Ordinary Reader*. He has also published under the pseudonym of Joseph Kell. (See also *CLC*, Vols. 1, 2, 4, 5, 8, 10, and *Contemporary Authors*, Vols. 1-4, rev. ed.)

GEOFFREY AGGELER

In Burgess's view, the liberal's optimism, his belief in the

fundamental goodness and perfectability of man, derives from an ancient heresy—the Pelagian denial of Original Sin. And not surprisingly, he feels that the doctrinal bases of much of the pessimism pervading western conservative thinking can be traced to Augustine's well known refutations of Pelagian doctrine. In view of the frequency of clashes between 'Augustinians' and 'Pelagians' in Burgess's fiction, it may be worthwhile to review briefly the seminal debate.

Pelagius, a British monk who resided in Rome, Africa, and Palestine during the early decades of the fourth century, set forth doctrines concerning human potentiality which virtually denied the necessity of Divine Grace and made the Redemption a superfluous gesture. (p. 43)

It is not surprising that Grace, in its most widely accepted orthodox Christian sense, as an infusion of the Holy Spirit, did not occupy a very prominent place in his scheme of salvation. He likened it to a sail attached to a rowboat in which the only essential instruments of locomotion are the oars. The oars he likened to the human will, and while the sail may make rowing easier, the boat could move without it. (p. 44)

In Augustine's view, human nature had been vitiated and corrupted as a result of Adam's sin, and all of Adam's descendants are in a 'penal' condition wherein they are effectively prevented from choosing the path of righteousness by ignorance and the irresistible urgings of the flesh. Men may overcome this condition and lead virtuous lives only if they have been granted God's free gift of grace. . . . Whereas Pelagius had thought of sin as merely action, which had no permanent effect upon the sinner, Augustine saw sin as 'an abiding condition or state'. All men are spiritually enfeebled by Original Sin, but an actively sinful man increasingly paralyzes his moral nature by his deeds. (p. 45)

When the debate is viewed in broader terms, the nature of man himself emerges as the pivotal issue, and one can see that the diametrically opposed assumptions of Augustine and Pelagius could be taken as premises of diametrically opposed political philosophies as well as attitudes toward social progress as far removed as hope and despair. The Pelagian view of humanity justifies optimism and a Rousseauvian trust in *la volonté générale*. Indeed, if one could accept Pelagius's sanguine estimates of human potentiality, one might hope to see Heaven on earth. For surely, if men can achieve spiritual perfection and merit eternal salvation solely through the use of their natural gifts, then the solutions to all problems of relations within earthly society must be well within their grasp. They need only to be enlightened properly, and their fundamental goodness will inevitably incline them toward morally desirable social goals. The realization of a universally acceptable utopia would not depend upon the imposition of any particular social structure. Rather, humanity, if properly enlightened, could be trusted to impose upon itself a utopian social scheme. (pp. 45-6)

Burgess's view of the debate encompasses its broadest implications, and some awareness of these implications, especially within social and political spheres of western thinking, is essential to an appreciation of his social satire. In *The Wanting Seed*, for instance, we are shown a fascist police state of the future emerging from the ruins of a future socialist democracy, and emerging with it are eager entrepreneurs, 'rats of the Pelphase but Augustine's lions'. The full irony of this metaphor cannot be grasped simply with reference to Augustinian doctrine in its pre-Calvinist, pre-Gilded Age purity. Burgess intends to remind us of the ways in which Augustinian-Calvinist doctrines on grace, election and unregenerate human nature have molded the socio-economic ethics of Calvin's intellectual and spiritual heirs both in the Old World and the New. In this same novel and in his other proleptic nightmare, *A Clockwork Orange,* he also reveals some likely doctrinal developments of the future. The forces which contend for governmental mastery are labelled 'Pelagian' and 'Augustinian', but they are more obviously Rousseauvian and Hobbesian. And it is natural that their conflicting philosophies should seem to echo *Leviathan, De Cive, Du Contrat Social* and the *Discours sur l'inégalité,* rather than the treatises of Pelagius and Augustine, since both novels are set in a future in which the issue of Divine Grace and indeed theology itself are virtually forgotten matters. Augustinianism without theology becomes Hobbism, while Pelagianism even in its original form was not far removed from Romantic primitivism. In short, Burgess's satiric vision encompasses the entire debate—past, present, and future—and one may find, especially in his dystopian books, echoes of the writings of all the participants I have mentioned and a good many more. (pp. 46-7)

Clearly, [Burgess] views philosophical extremes—Pelagian, Augustinian or whatever—as avenues to moral blindness and collective insanity, but it is not merely the extremes he rejects. Any tendency to promote a generalized view of human nature is liable to be a butt of his merciless satire. His satiric implication seems to be that both Pelagius and Augustine, and their numerous philosophical heirs, have been hopelessly myopic in their analyses of the human condition. Their views of man have been determined and severely limited by preconceived notions about 'man', which leave little room for the uniqueness of individual men. True, many of Burgess's most sympathetically drawn protagonists, such as Victor Crabbe in the Malayan Trilogy, Richard Ennis in *A Vision of Battlements,* Paul Hussey in *Honey for the Bears* and the flatulent Mr. Enderby, are Pelagian liberals, but they are totally ineffectual human beings. They are believers in social progress through the liberation of beneficent human energies, but they themselves can accomplish little more than the utterance of stale leftist sentiments at inopportune moments. (p. 54)

In other words, by exalting human potentiality and discarding Divine Grace, Pelagius and his heirs have actually reduced individual human significance immeasurably. For when Divine Grace has no place, when sin in the Augustinian sense doesn't exist, when man is in need of nothing but a greater exertion of his will to improve his moral and spiritual condition, then the only significant distributors of 'grace' in any sense are the managers of the earthly communities wherein the effort must be made. And it is these managers—corporation heads, commissars, bureaucrats and others—who are most desirous of standardizing humanity, of bringing its affairs within the compass of their finite wisdoms.

The Augustinian tradition is of course even more inimical to the dignity of man, but at least it acknowledges a distinction between regenerate and unregenerate human nature. However, since present day Augustinian thinkers, like the Pelagians, have largely abandoned the traditional idea of grace, the categories 'regenerate' and 'unregenerate' have meaning only with reference to social stability. One must subordinate one's self to the social machinery, become functionally or economically significant as a part of it, in order to be of the Elect. The individual 'self', asserting its existence by purely self-determined actions is sand in the machinery of Augustinian society. In the Augustinian view, moral evil and self-assertion are so inextricably bound up with each other that they tend to be identified. (pp. 54-5)

In Burgess's view, then, the Pelagian-Augustinian debate, which manifests itself historically as a 'waltz', is symptomatic of western man's acceptance of a faulty dilemma. Presumably, sanity and vision could lead men to a rejection of both 'Pelagianism' and 'Augustinianism' and a creation of society based upon a realistic assessment of individual human potentiality. But since sanity and vision are lacking, and since the individual 'self' is viewed as a threat to social stability by both Pelagians and Augustinians, then man is left with the two bleak alternatives presented in *The Wanting Seed.* If he isn't, in one sense or another, 'eaten' by a military-industrial complex, he will be persuaded to castrate himself, in one way or another, for the sake of social stability. (p. 55)

Geoffrey Aggeler, "Pelagius and Augustine in the Novels of Anthony Burgess," in English Studies *(© 1974 by Swets & Zeitlinger B.V.), Vol. 55, No. 1, February, 1974, pp. 43-56.*

DAVID RIEFF

Burgess is a natural writer, if such an animal exists, but he is certainly no struggler. Throughout his career he has been all too content to let his undeniable talents as a wordsmith, and his not inconsiderable erudition, carry more than their fair share of the artistic burden. That is a great pity since Burgess, a Joyce scholar and a writer almost painfully attuned to the possibilities of language in modern fiction, is superbly equipped to undertake a really major work. His apparent unwillingness to do this—to take the time to do it —is the worst kind of arrogance. It is as if he feels he is so clever, so on top of things, he need not exert himself. He's wrong.

Burgess has written only one first-rate novel: *A Clockwork Orange.* In it, he succeeded in transforming his oft-expressed anxieties about the future into an inspired work. But it would be a mistake to attribute the artistic success of the book to its theme: It is possible to disagree totally with Burgess' assertions and still admire his achievement. *Clockwork* is a brilliant tour de force because, for once, the author marshaled all his linguistic inventiveness to the service of his art—rather than simply to make a point or to exhibit his cleverness. And the book sang.

Unfortunately, *1985* is merely the most recent confirmation that *A Clockwork Orange,* far from marking a turning point in Burgess' career, was one of those happy accidents where a writer who has been his own worst enemy succeeds briefly in giving full voice to his talent. . . .

As the title indicates, the book is in part Burgess' attempt to correct and amend the totalitarian prospect as put forward by George Orwell. . . . [The] book *in toto* is a kind of polemic that Burgess has chosen to express in a variety of different prose forms. The argument, it must be emphasized, is practically the same one made in *A Clockwork Orange,* but that book did not demand to be judged as an argument. . . .

Burgess believes that Orwell's vision of the future, as expressed in *1984*, does not even come near to being an accurate portrayal of what real totalitarianism might be like. . . . The future, he argues, will be both more anarchic and more repressive than Orwell would have imagined, since Orwell had no notion of what Burgess calls "the scientific takeover of the free mind." In short, Burgess faults Orwell for believing that the individual consciousness had the slightest chance of surviving the pressures brought against it by state-controlled technologies.

To illustrate, Burgess presents *1985*. In place of Orwell's Winston Smith we are given Bev Jones and taken on a revised tour of late 20th century Britain. It is a chaotic place, brimming with Arabs, and utterly dominated by the trade unions. . . .

Bev Jones rebels against this system after his wife dies in a fire (the firemen were, of course, on strike). His odyssey through the underworld of Tucland comprises the bulk of *1985*. Without a union card he is an unperson: The true totalitarian state will brook no resistance, nor will any be successful. (p. 16)

There is nothing particularly novel about all this. Science fiction writers have been cranking out similar narratives for a good many years now. . . . Moreover, Burgess' criticisms of Orwell for having extrapolated too much from his own historical situation make very curious reading when one realizes that the anarchic Britain painted so lovingly in *1985* is itself little more than an exaggerated rendering of a certain kind of Tory rhetoric. . . .

Not only is Burgess guilty of precisely what he attacks Orwell for, but in his case the offense is more serious. Orwell was not fundamentally concerned with the details of life under Big Brother; he was trying to depict the nature and danger of totalitarianism. In contrast to Burgess, he really knew something about politics, about the totalitarian impulse and the totalitarian temptation. Burgess, who understands almost nothing about politics, dismisses or distorts the real nature of Orwell's thrust and proposes instead a vision of the future that is little more than cranky union-baiting. . . .

Unlike sadness or horror or foreboding or despair, indignation—particularly in sclerotic form—is a rather callow emotion. And while *1985* is rich in indignation it is poor in everything else. Burgess' cleverness is not enough to carry him through what is, by any reckoning, a project demanding a great deal of thought, and enormous sophistication and, above all, sobriety. None of this would have been required to produce an interesting novel, as witness *A Clockwork Orange*. The artist can fulminate to his heart's content without endangering his enterprise; that is his special privilege. But in seeking to apply the artist's freedom outside of its realm, Burgess only serves to demonstrate how widely the laws and rights of art have diverged, in the modern period, from the laws and obligations of political and social discourse. (p. 17)

> *David Rieff, "Future Shock," in* The New Leader *(© 1978 by the American Labor Conference on International Affairs, Inc.), November 20, 1978, pp. 16-17.*

RICHARD KUCZKOWSKI

[What] are we to make of *1985*, Burgess' melodramatization of "certain tendencies" of the present? In the prefatory and epilogue material (whose length—almost equal to that of the novella around which it clusters—is the only Shavian thing about it), Burgess argues, rather obviously, that Orwell's *1984* was not a prophecy of a plausible or probable future, but a vision of an ideally evil state, a demonic satire (Burgess calls it, rather willfully, a comic novel) modelled on the Britain of the 40's. Burgess' project is to isolate the seeds of a probable future in the Britain of the present, reveal their perniciousness, and dramatize their stifling overgrowth seven years hence.

The pernicious seeds? There is violence and murder in the streets. The monuments and standards of the past are forgotten in favor of a perpetual present where quality and taste—in education, in food, in work, in entertainment, in language, in every area of life—are reduced to the lowest vulgarized denominator of mass consumption. (p. 27)

Along with such familiar indictments, we are given tedious learning: latin and greek etymologies (utopia, anarchy, martyr, etc.; it's like being in high school again) are insisted upon; a poor pun (*virginibus*, a transport vehicle for nymphets) and an unnecessary coinage (cacotopia) are made. Obviously Burgess regards the present as a bad place rapidly becoming the worst of all possible worlds; obviously he fears and distrusts liberalism and secularism; by equating them with the pelagian heresy and solipsism (history and etymology supplied), he intends to expose their satanic nature; by preaching the practice of Christian principles, he intends to counteract their poison. In short, the "ideas" served up in numerous courses by the essayistic portions of *1985* are the canned, cold staples of conservative Christian humanism, with the traditional bitter sauce of hatred for human institutions and for the present, garnished with pedantry—not a very appetizing feast, I'm afraid. (pp. 27-8)

[The novella] is less fiction than a continuation of the self-interviews, essays, indictments, and what-have-you that surround it. It's all the work of an author operating at half-steam, trivializing his ability by blowing up material suitable for one or two neat op-ed pieces into scads of repetitious, unconvincing blather, an author so enamored of his own ideas that he cannot achieve any intellectual or fictional distance from them. The present and the future are by no means rosy, but Burgess does them, us, and himself no service by taking us for a long ride on that special breed of pet hobby horse, the slipshod nightmare. (p. 28)

> *Richard Kuczkowski, "Burgessian Utopia," in* New York Arts Journal *(copyright © 1978 by Richard W. Burgin), #12, November-December, 1978, pp. 27-8.*

PAUL LUKACS

Anthony Burgess' *Ernest Hemingway and His World* is trying to be an attractive (there are over a hundred photographs) summary of Hemingway's life. Yet there is more to writing a biography, even one as short as this, than merely mixing facts and anecdotes with occasional off-hand interpretations. Burgess' central theme is that "Hemingway the man was as much a creation as his books, and a far inferior creation."

While this is an interesting thesis, Burgess never argues it. Even the crudest of amateur psychologists could make better sense of Hemingway's self-creation. I say psychologists because Burgess himself plays this role, his fundamental critical assumption being that a writer's work can be explained and understood through a knowledge of his life. This can be a valuable assumption, especially with a writer whose work is as autobiographical as Hemingway's. But instead of exploring the relationship between Hemingway's life and the lives of his characters, Burgess draws preposterous one-sentence conclusions, claiming, for example, that Hemingway's "obsession with death and killing" in *Death in the Afternoon* (which is, after all, about bullfighting) stems from guilt over his recent divorce.

Although he claims to want to separate man from myth, Burgess treats Hemingway's life unevenly, paying far more attention to the mature celebrity than to either the adolescent from Oak Park or the struggling writer in Paris. (p. 428)

Burgess virtually ignores Hemingway's literary achievements, devoting almost as much of this book to the movies made from Hemingway's fiction as to the fiction itself. His only real discussion of Hemingway's style comes in the middle of a passage about Hemingway's habit of boxing with his friends. This boxing, says Burgess, was "an outward expression of the big inner fight that was going on . . . a struggle to write a 'true simple declarative sentence.'" This kind of comment is both misleading and presumptuous. It is possible, after all, that Hemingway simply liked to box; but, more significantly, the inner struggle he waged throughout his life had to do not so much with writing as with coming to terms with his own inadequacies. How long has it been since Burgess has read "The Snows of Kilimanjaro"—where Harry, the dying writer, thinks of how "he had destroyed his talent by not using it, by betrayals of himself and what he believed in"?

Because he cannot, despite his claims to the contrary, distinguish the man from the legend, Burgess does not see that Hemingway's fiction reveals a side of the man that the legend obscures. This legend was partly of Hemingway's own making, and his creation of a living yet fictional self is a fascinating story. Burgess, however, because he is content merely to sketch the legend's growth and eventual self-destruction, does not tell it. There was a complex man beneath the mask. This sketch is so vague that it not only distorts but ignores that man. (pp. 428, 430)

Paul Lukacs, "A Fictional Self," in National Review (© National Review, Inc., 1979; 150 East 35th St., New York, N.Y. 10016), March 30, 1979, pp. 428, 430.

BENJAMIN DeMOTT

[There] is evidence of imaginative energy in "Man of Nazareth." If the book's portrait of Salome seems a shade lubricous and overelaborate, the portrait of Judas Iscariot (political innocent cynically used by the Establishment) is cunning and provocative. And genuine liveliness breathes in the disciples' often coarse talk among themselves. "I touched him," says Thomas after the Resurrection, "and then he gave me this mouthful about it being better to believe without seeing. . . . There was no doubt at all about it. Right, Matt?"

In the end, though, "Man of Nazareth" doesn't achieve for this reader its goal of lending solidity to Jesus' teachings. The reason is, I think, that the author is insufficiently concerned with the intellectual dimensions and power of the deeds at the center of the life of Christ. In recent decades

writers of many persuasions, not merely crisis theologians, have come to understand this life in contexts different from that of otherworldly salvation. They have seen it as charging Christendom with the obligation of reconceiving human freedom as a choice for or against self-transformation in the here and now. Re-examining the Gospels, novelistically, from such a perspective might have put readers in touch, at the minimum, with the still unexhausted capacity of this religious tradition for imaginative renewal. But "Man of Nazareth" misses the chance. It behaves throughout as though the secret of revitalization lay solely in lightness or off-handedness—in empty urbanity, breezy colloquialism and the rhetoric of skepticism and comical play.

"Your Jesus has wept; you may joke now," Auden said in "The Age of Anxiety," noting wryly the firmness with which the Passion, once understood even by unbelievers as bearing profoundly on the whole of daily human life, is now sealed off from seriousness. Anthony Burgess's grinning "Man of Nazareth" might have had more impact if, once or twice in its length, it had aspired to break that seal. (p. 20)

Benjamin DeMott, "According to Burgess," in The New York Times Book Review (© 1979 by The New York Times Company; reprinted by permission), April 15, 1979, pp. 1, 20.

S. J. EDELHEIT

1985 is neither feathery nor amusing; but it *is* a truly bad book. I'm afraid no amount of "plumping up" would save it; indeed, one wishes the prolific Mr. Burgess had thought better of it and left this one in the locked and darkened drawer.

That *1985* is so very bad is curious as well as disappointing. One would think Burgess the very man to take on Orwell. . . .

Finding the modern world so dangerous and inhospitable a place, it is not surprising that Burgess and Orwell cast quick, backward glances to seemingly safer, more sensible times. . . . Burgess and Orwell can only look stonily, warily ahead; and the shape they give us of things to come is distinctly unpleasant. Orwell left us with *1984*, that dark and looming prophecy of totalitarianism. And Burgess has churned out a series of what he chooses to call "cacotopian" (from GK *Kakos* bad + *topos* place) novels—*A Clockwork Orange*, *The Wanting Seed*, and, now, the unfortunate *1985*.

While Burgess's earlier utopian fictions are highly imaginative, they are also curiously limited. *The Wanting Seed* is set in a distant future of the Perpetual Peace. . . . [This] novel obviously affords Burgess room to be clever and amusing; but it is hardly thought-provoking. Ideas, as all too often in Burgess's books, are slippery, few, and far between.

A Clockwork Orange is better known and a better book. Some readers, overpowered by the Kubrick film version, may believe Burgess has written a flip testimonial on behalf of mindless, juvenile violence. But the novel is actually a quite serious setting out of the author's argument in favor of free will whatever the consequences. It is Burgess's fictional lashing of Skinnerism and the possibility of automatic virtue. . . . Far better, says Burgess, to tolerate senseless aggression than to deny individual choice and so make a mockery of morality. "Die with Beethoven's Ninth howling and crashing away or live in a safe world of silly clockwork music.'' That is the choice Burgess stakes out for us again and again in his fiction; he will return to it in *1985*.

The author himself admits that *Clockwork* is not a very good book—''too didactic, too linguistically exhibitionist,'' he has said of it. But whatever its limitations, it does at least grapple with the serious ideal of the ''free and fully human life.'' Orwell would have politely applauded. Given Burgess's sensitivities to, his temperamental affinities for, Orwell's real concerns, why has he gone so stubbornly wrong with *1985*? There seems little excuse for the klutzy treatment Orwell receives there. It is difficult to decide which half of the book, criticism or fiction, is the greater disaster. Let's swallow, and take on the critical portion first.

To be blunt, Burgess's critical discussion is a mess, a confused hodgepodge of essays, staged conversations, and ''self-interviews'' (a clumsy device perhaps best left to Norman Mailer). What emerges is an out-of-focus argument in which Burgess scores occasional points but in the process manages to misunderstand Orwell in a quite remarkable manner. Much of what he chooses to tell us about Orwell's novel is belabored and not particularly helpful. Burgess spends a good deal of energy rooting out the real-life sources of Orwell's fictional creation; his object is to convince us that *1984* is largely a ''melodramatization'' of the world of 1948.... Burgess concludes that *1984* is a ''comic transcription of the London at the end of World War Two,'' that what Orwell has given us is hardly a forecast of the future but really only ''an exaggerated picture of a bad time.''

Just as we are about to yell ''rot'' and ''nonsense,'' Burgess admits that, of course, there must be more to *1984* than mere exaggeration and transcription. But he has a difficult time telling us what that ''more'' is. Perhaps if he spent less space on the sources of minutiae and told us more about the sources of Orwell's ideas, his critique would be less tiresome and more enlightening.... It is Burgess's purpose to persuade us that *1984* is not prophecy but a ''testimony of despair.'' ... Burgess hasn't done his homework well enough to compel our agreement. What comes crashing is his own tottering critical enterprise. It will not stand. The case is simply not made.

We turn to the novel with hopes that Burgess can bring off there what he so notably fails to accomplish with his criticism. But in his fiction, Burgess is content to do what he mistakenly accuses Orwell of doing in *1984*, ''melodramatizing,'' giving us only an exaggerated picture of a bad time. (p. 9)

The novel is a bomb. It is badly conceived and pedestrianly executed. The familiar Burgess rant against the deplorable state of modern industrial life is all there. But what could be amusing in the *Enderby* novels seems only shrill and querulous here. But then Enderby was an engaging character; Bev Jones is hardly a ''character'' at all. Burgess has forsaken his fictional talents and turned his hero into a tiresome mouthpiece forever.... Burgess should know by now that for his didacticism to be effective, his fiction must minimally hold the reader. It does not.

But Orwell wasn't much of a novelist either. What then is the telling distinction between *1984* and *1985*? Put simply, it is that where Burgess gives us a catalogue of irritants, Or-

well offers us ideas. Not that Orwell couldn't turn cranky from time to time; he could and did. But Burgess all too often, and especially in this latest work, seems just a crank. ''Permissiveness,'' the closed shop, television, homosexuality, abortion, terrorism, women's lib, frisking at airports, all are grit in Burgess's eye. But behind the irritation there's little insight. As Bertrand Russell noted at the time of its publication, *1984* is that rare occurrence, a philosophical novel. *1985* proves how rare, for Burgess's book contains hardly any ideas at all. The difference is primarily one of political vision. Orwell has it; Burgess does not.

One can agree or disagree with Orwell's brand of socialist politics, think his fictional ''prophecy'' foolish or prescient. But the vision of *1984* is at least whole and terrifyingly clear. Burgess's version, however, is all a muddle. in *1985* Burgess labels himself a ''Hebreo-Helleno-Christian humanist.'' What does this mean? Your guess is as good as his. At times, Burgess sounds like an old-fashioned bully Tory; he's worried, he tells us, about the dangers of too much equality and forced ''levelling.'' And while it's good to have National Insurance, ''what happens,'' he wants to know, ''to the exercise of charity? We can't be kind to the poor when the state kills the very concept of poverty.'' If this is Christian humanism, spare us please.

Burgess's politics center around a confused mix that he identifies as half romantic, half reactionary. Unfortunately, neither strain, as revealed in *1985*, makes much sense. Burgess's chant, like that of the Savage in *Brave New World*, is for God, poetry, danger, freedom, sin. And any and all of these are liable to be lumped together to produce some peculiar statements.... This is certainly romantic, but it is also adolescent. And then there is his notion of the possibility of uniting culture and anarchy, a thought that also surfaced, you'll recall, in *A Clockwork Orange*, there in the form of Alex, the Beethoven-loving street thug. Here, in *1985*, the ideal, as one gang member puts it, is to ''Read Virgil and then rip some guy up.'' Is Burgess serious about any of this? Apparently, at least some of the time, he is. As a ''reactionary,'' he believes not only in denying progress and ''the engines of enforced improvement,'' but also in cherishing man's ''unregenerate nature.''

What does this ''romantic reaction,'' this idiosyncratic and fragmented mixture of Burgess's finally lead to? Sometimes to nice, even useful distinctions, more often to genuine nonsense.... What it does not lead to, evidently, is any clear or focused political sense.

Burgess's confused politics cause some disharmony between his novel and his criticism. Nowhere is this discordance more apparent than in his treatment of the workers. In the first half of *1985*, Burgess bitterly castigates Orwell for the very creation of the proles. It was Orwell's inherited class consciousness, he argues, that led him insultingly to compare the workers to sturdy animals, his guilt that caused him either to romanticize or sentimentalize the proles.... What Burgess and the others conveniently ignore is that, by design, there are *no* real or fully human characters in *1984*. There are only madmen, automatons, and a variety of half-persons like Winston Smith—whose struggle is, as he himself tells us, precisely to become more and more human. The proles, though far from whole, are at least endowed with privacy, with common sense, with compassion and decency. As such, they are more human than Winston, Julia, O'Brien, or any other figure in the novel. Orwell's choice of inhuman metaphors to describe them—he compares them to animals, birds, plants inexorably seeking the light, blocks of granite, etc.—is in no way demeaning. The metaphors carry the message (admittedly a romantic one) of endurance against all odds.

That Burgess should commit such a common critical error concerning the proles is perhaps surprising but not in itself alarming. The alarm comes after one has read the novel-half of *1985*. Burgess does without proletarian metaphors, but his own portrait of the workers is both demeaning and damning; amazingly, he seems not to realize it. In *1985* the workers are feckless, greedy, and stupid. For Burgess to vehemently protest Orwell's creation and then offer us his own slighting vision reveals an egregious blankness, an astounding obtuseness. Does the right hand know what the left is up to? Apparently not. (pp. 9-10)

The pity of all this confusion is that Burgess thinks, apparently, that he sees the workers steadily and fairly, without guilt and without class consciousness. There's really no difference between us and them, he democratically announces. But the only equality Burgess allows is an equality of baseness. "We are all, alas, much the same, i.e., pretty horrible." Alas, the reactionary in him seems to have nastily triumphed over the romantic.

It would do little good to dwell further on political blankness and bumbling in *1985*. The truth, of course, is that Burgess is not much interested in politics. . . . He is, as he himself admits, a "linguistic exhibitionist." He loves to play with language and flaunt his considerable expertise. It's all very clever and all very ostentatious. If you're a Nabokov, such showing off, such knowledgeable playfulness, can take you a long way. But Burgess is no Nabokov. His linguistic acrobatics can produce stumbles as well as delight. That the youth gangs of *1985* speak Latin is explained well enough as an arcane protest of the utilitarian education the state forces upon them. But their use of Swahili slang makes no more sense here than did the Russianized vocabulary of Alex and friends in *A Clockwork Orange*. More to the point, compare the appendices on Newspeak in *1984* and on WE (Workers' English) in *1985*. Orwell is interested in thought, in the use of language to control consciousness and enforce political orthodoxy. Newspeak is a clever invention, but we never forget that there is a point to the cleverness. Burgess is clever too; but, as the appendix makes clear, he is more interested in phonemes than in politics, in dazzling us with linguistic footwork than in throwing any hard or thoughtful punches.

1985 is an unfortunate book for Burgess. It necessitates a close comparison with Orwell, and the comparison is anything but flattering. In fact, it shows him at his worst. Orwell was a bad novelist, yet he managed to write a far better book than Burgess shows himself capable of here. Orwell was not the most original or powerful thinker; but next to him, Burgess appears a true lightweight. Despite Burgess's assault, *1984* still stands and will last; *1985* will get what it deserves—a merciless and quick remaindering. (p. 10)

S. J. Edelheit, "Does '1985' Follow '1984'?" in New Boston Review (copyright 1979 by Boston Critic, Inc.), April/May 1979, pp. 9-10.

*   *   *

BURNSHAW, Stanley   1906-

Burnshaw is an American poet, novelist, critic, and essayist.

The Seamless Web is his best known work, a critical manifesto which James Dickey termed "the most exciting, releasing book on the nature of poetry since *Biographia Literaria*." (See also *CLC*, Vol. 3, and *Contemporary Authors*, Vols. 9-12, rev. ed.)

GERMAINE BRÉE

"Although everyone knows that humanity is only one strand in the web of creation, one can rarely speak about man's condition as a creature without eliciting defensiveness and confusion." It is to man's condition as a creature, his need and indeed drive to regain his primary organic unity with the rest of creation, that Stanley Burnshaw's title [*The Seamless Web*] refers. It is to that particular drive that he connects the work of the artist—all artists, but more particularly the poet, whom Stanley Burnshaw considers to be the archetype of the artist. And it is to an elucidation of the nature of the poet's activity that *The Seamless Web* addresses itself. . . . In [Burnshaw's] investigation he considers a wide variety of approaches to art: Freud and the various brands of psychoanalysis; structuralism and the "new critics," exploring the limits of their approach with great clarity and intellectual precision. The discretion with which he uses his vast knowledge is a measure of his mastery over it. . . .

Besides being himself a poet, willing dispassionately to examine his own activity as poet, Burnshaw is a man with a wide knowledge of his fellow craftsmen, past and present, writing in different languages from within different cultures. . . . But, beyond the whole range of testimony concerning the creative act gathered from the artists themselves, the volume brings to the reader a wealth of examples, a rich harvest of verse in an analytic context that illuminates and appeals simultaneously to the reader's imagination and understanding. Stanley Burnshaw is a man who can range far and wide in the world of poetry itself, a critic with an acute sense of the precise techniques and the imponderables that make up the poet's craft and of the many traps his use of words will set a reader bent on some single explanation of a poet's meaning. He is as nondogmatic in his approach to poetry as he is unpedantic in the formulation of his ideas. (p. 522)

The book progresses with great honesty and thoughtfulness, opening up new avenues for speculation along the way. The poet is always present, throughout the book, which is most certainly, as Hiram Haydn has said, a "pivotal book," and a much needed book, which may well influence the general approach to literature, and perhaps, to some degree, the poets' own understanding of their art. It requires careful reading if one is to come to grips with the "common and uncommon" sense it makes, with Burnshaw's deep concern with the human sensibility and his unerring aesthetic sense. (p. 524)

Germaine Brée, "'The Poet Is Always Present'," in The American Scholar (copyright © 1970 by the United Chapters of Phi Beta Kappa; reprinted by permission of the publishers), Vol. 39, No. 3, Summer, 1970, pp. 522, 524.

PETER DALE

[In *The Seamless Web*, Mr. Burnshaw] tries to show how mankind, in replacing biological evolution which was imperceptibly slow with cultural progress which is massive and speedy, lost its at-oneness with nature, its seamlessness with living things, to suffer thereafter the dichotomy between the so-called "higher" centres of the brain and the "lower" areas of motor action and instinctive response. None of this sounds very new or greatly in need of further clarification, you might say. Yet much of the first part of Mr. Burnshaw's argument is to show how it is the cultural, linguistic structuring of the higher centres that compel us to trust in the truth of this split and to make so often the derogatory distinction between primitive qualities and those we call civilised. In fact, he spends a long section on showing that the split is not so certain, nor so complete as the cultured structuring of our thoughtways would have us believe. (p. 33)

The book now proceeds to investigate the creation of works of art. And here Mr. Burnshaw's experience as a poet helps him to give one of the clearest expositions of the creative trace that I have yet read. He intends to show how the "higher" centres which so often consider themselves in charge of the creative process are in fact nudged and directed almost without their knowledge and certainly without their consent all along the line even when it comes to revision, rightly called re-vision here. . . . (p. 34)

Mr. Burnshaw now turns his mind to consider the thing made by the creative process, concentrating again on poems. This section is the most directly useful to the reader or writer dismayed by the range of science in the first parts. It contains some of the wisest and clearest things ever said about prosody, syntax, language and sound as used in a poem. He does not, like an academic, come to poetry with his ideas over his eyes and select only those samples which suit his case but takes a wide range of works rather like the mythical general reader and considers what differences or samenesses they reveal.

The "poem" is then shown to consist of an amalgam of syntaxes from different levels of use, conscious, unconscious, rational, informative, questioning, common, unique and so on. What all the poets do is to blend such various strata of language into the union of a poem—each being unique in its blending. Rhythm and sound cannot be separated from syntax and meaning; unique beyond metrical naming, the rhythmic language-area of the poem cannot be distinguished from its meaning. The whole union acts on the reader as a respondent body.

Where so many previous theorists have concentrated on what a poem is or means and have sought sketchily embracing generalisations for their chosen samplings, Mr. Burnshaw concentrates on what a poem *does*. . . . (p. 36)

The importance of his book is manifold: it cuts through much of the oversophistication of the critics and gives the poem back as of right to readers; catholic itself, it encourages a greater openness in readers and critics to the way a poem works, the multiple unions of different types of meaning, resonance and response it can create. It states clearly some of the most overlooked truisms about the nature of writing and reading; while emphasising bodily wisdom it does not deny the mind, while emphasising individual responsiveness, it does not set aside the culture or tradition. It is a book that shows creation as a magnificent compromise; it is the best way to understand most and more of what Coleridge meant when he defined a poem, or described it, in his famous pairings.

But what makes it most valuable is that the book itself is a creative experience. It is written with considered passion and it reads with excitement, an excitement for me only paralleled by such books as Collingwood's *Principles*. (p. 38)

> *Peter Dale, in* Agenda, *Autumn, 1974.*

CHAD WALSH

[Stanley Burnshaw] calls *Mirages* a public poem, and thereby indirectly explains one reason why it is so enormously moving. The poetry-reading public has had its fill of the confessionals, who treat their psyches as though each were a complete universe. *Mirages* is about something vaster and deeper than one sensibility. It is a series of meditations and conversations about the fact and mystery of Israel —the modern nation, with all its hustle and bustle, interwoven with the external land of Canaan and the strong destiny of those who have inhabited it at various times. To read the book is like seeing one transparent slide superimposed upon another, and then another and another. . . .

The poem is written in a free verse that could easily slip into outright prose, but almost never does; Stanley Burnshaw's control is very exact. At times the verse rises to a biblical eloquence, at other times it is quiet and unobtrusive. Perhaps the main poem is the land of Canaan itself, and the verse is a series of footnotes on that reality, ancient and contemporary. In any case, this book makes much contemporary poetry seem—how can one express it?—trivial or self-indulgent. (p. E4)

> *Chad Walsh, in* Book World—The Washington Post *(© 1979, The Washington Post), May 22, 1977.*

PETER DALE

Mr. Burnshaw is a courageous man but even he, I imagine, would not have wanted the slogan "A Public Poem" printed so largely as his publisher seems to have decided. And yet he would be mistaken, for what makes [*Mirages*] so interesting and important is precisely that it is public in a way that poems have not been for decades. The poem concerns the Israeli-Arab problem in all its complexity. Mr. Burnshaw brings to it a complexity of his own which gives him the authority to speak. His own culture is deeply American-European as can be seen from his translation-work in *The Poem Itself* and his *The Seamless Web*, not to mention his earlier poems. But *The . . . Web* is underwritten with the Paradisal myth of man united with his natural world, and the poems return to the legend of Abraham sacrificing Isaac as does part of this work. In addition he has powerful biographical factors which enable him to feel deeply the confused issues of the middle East. . . . For this reason he has the right to speak publicly on these matters and he has the ear and the intelligence to do so in verse that is cumulatively compelling.

The poem stems from, and deals with, a visit that he made to the sacred and historical places in Israel and from his reaction to the people he met. And because it deals with an issue to which verse can provide no instant answer much of the tone is elegiac. (p. 142)

The poem concludes with a humanism that asks not "Who am I?" but "What am I?" and suggests the recognition of the body as our limit—an idea that underlies *The Seamless*

Web. It is, as the poet knows, an utopian idea and not likely to be tried by numbers, on any side, sufficient to solve any problems.

What is impressive about this poem is its general accessibility to the unliterary; its resolute desire not to call attention to itself as a poem. It is, in fact, a triumph of tone. Many of the ideas and attitudes contained in the poem will not command general assent from all parties but one can consider them because they are presented in such a convincing tone of passionate sincerity. I would myself have liked to have felt that I understood the versification with its strange line-ends and variable line-lengths but in the end, this is a small criticism of such a courageous piece of work. (p. 146)

Peter Dale, "Going Public," in Agenda, *Summer-Autumn, 1977, pp. 142-46.*

C

CANBY, Vincent 1924-

Although he is chiefly known as film critic for the *New York Times*, Canby has also written two novels and one play. (See also *Contemporary Authors*, Vols. 81-84.)

HOLLIS ALPERT

Film critics who write novels are often suspected of trying to enter the world of filmmaking through the back door. In Vincent Canby's case, let us dispose of the suspicion. His first novel, [*Living Quarters,*] although it begins with an act of violence, soon turns into a recounting of the life, loves, and schizophrenia of a madcap heiress from the Midwest. (p. 26)

Mr. Canby's prose is flat and dry, glinting now and then with satiric, disenchanted humor. The book's method is that of remembered gossip, told in monotone, but not monotonously. Little in the way of sympathy is allowed any of the characters—so careful is the author in keeping any sentiment or unseemly emotion from coloring the tale. All incidents of the past, he seems to be saying, have the same weight in memory, whether it be a failed movie actress who takes her life or a jaded Frenchman who suffers the embarrassment of a dog's suddenly urinating against his leg. The text might have been taken from Ecclesiastes: All is vanity. Yet Daisianna, caught in off-hand glimpses that add up to a portrait, emerges as memorable, as does an aspect of America that no longer knows where it is going. Mr. Canby doesn't reach for very much with his first novel, but what he gives us is done with professional care and an amused appreciation of the not always lovable quirkiness of his characters. (p. 27)

> *Hollis Alpert, in* Saturday Review *(© 1975 by Saturday Review/World, Inc.; reprinted with permission), March 8, 1975.*

WEBSTER SCHOTT

"Living Quarters" is the story of a charmingly psychotic woman in the deranged late 20th century. It's told in language that shimmers. It's a story that emerges from plots that explore human longing, suffering and pleasure among the civilized on three continents as though seeking a statement about a condition beyond articulation. . . .

If I understand "Living Quarters" correctly, it suggests, while offering champagne-and-acid entertainment, that the present environment requires a streak of madness if you want to live in it at all. Deception, betrayal, exploitation, faithlessness are bred into us by our surroundings, along with our drinking habits and a drive to be made whole through the uses of the flesh. We need not wonder why Daisianna gets off scot-free. Vincent Canby's society cultivates all kinds of nuts.

Meanwhile, despite his confirmation of what tolerant people have been thinking for some time, Canby gives us art, so that we can taste the truth and not find it unbearably bitter. His novel explodes with forms and techniques: pictures of places that look like paintings, intense short stories and strange yarns that surface briefly in the midst of other events, home movies and scenarios, vivid tableaux of families, characters moving as though documented on film.

Some of the pleasure of this novel lies in seeing Canby build this jeweled structure that goes backward and forward in time as it reports on society's mental health by watching the weather inside human heads. But most of the pleasure won't submit to scrupulous examination: it's inherent in the novel in a larger sense. Canby creates a world; he makes people live there, luxuriating in desire, waste, comic boredom. And he insists that we believe and understand them by almost *becoming* them—he has that power. . . .

Vincent Canby's film criticism in The Times shows that he was born to think and to write. This first novel says that he may have been born to write fiction. (pp. 4-5)

> *Webster Schott, in* The New York Times Book Review *(© 1975 by The New York Times Company; reprinted by permission), April 13, 1975.*

JULIAN BARNES

[There's] much generic ambiguity about Vincent Canby's [*Living Quarters*]: the crime, victim and culprit are swiftly identified, and the book sets off in a series of ever-retreating flashbacks to root out the social and psychological background to the event. Daisianna turns out to be an archetypal American whore/bitch/goddess, pill-slugging, schizophrenic, religioso, selfish and idle; her friends and family are scarcely less neurotically self-indulgent. Even straight Jimmy Barnes, Daisianna's lawyer, who actively seeks an exciting life, turns out to have a wrecky streak, and is laid low by alcohol, troilism and divorce. The flashbacks eventually (if bafflingly) reach flash-back-of-beyond with an ancestor's journal; and we wait for Mr. Canby to drop his tone of glazed detachment and lay a moral on us. Jimmy runs into it on an archaeological site. Pondering on a handy cross-section of the dig, he is told that there are 17 different periods of human habitation represented there. Some layers have been squashed down by later generations into a mere 15 inches of clay. It's quite a thought. (p. 285)

> *Julian Barnes, in* New Statesman *(© 1976 The Statesman & Nation Publishing Co. Ltd.), February 20, 1976.*

BENJAMIN DeMOTT

Can a chilly, misanthropic, half-crippled, middle-aged, twice-divorced, multimillionaire WASP whose hobby is researching the Albigensian heresies find happiness with a radical Jewish journalist who's 20 years younger than he, depressed by his money and resolved "never, *never* [to] marry a goy?"

Yes and no is the answer delivered in ["Unnatural Scenery"]. . . . Marshall Lewis Henderson, the WASP multimillionaire, and Jackie Gold, the Jewish journalist, commence living together at Caesars Palace in Las Vegas. . . . Their lovemaking is animated (Henderson is *half*-crippled, repeat) as is their talk, and over a period of nine years the culture gap narrows a bit. . . .

Finding happiness is one thing, though, and preserving it is another. Miss Gold shows up late for dinner one night, and objects when Marshall Henderson punishes her tardiness by pummeling her with lobster salad. She turns to an Esquire editor for comfort and, soon thereafter, splits for good.

Such personal disasters are an old story for the hero, a loser, despite his money, almost from birth. . . . Adding things up after the Jackie defeat, Henderson decides that "something has to be done, a gesture made." And the book culminates in his search for an ideal late-20th-century American gesture of protest against things as they are.

"Unnatural Scenery" is shrewdly paced, nimbly written and full of ingenious cross-cutting, fast forwards and the like. And, as Marshall Henderson's wit races through the early pages, indignantly slicing up mother, father, brother, in-laws, preppies, nostalgic Southerners, textbook publishers, liberals, the liberated and Florida retirement villages, many high-gloss Broadway gags are struck off. . . .

But there is a serious problem with the book: the hero's imperviousness. Marshall Lewis Henderson is ever on the attack, and comes across less as a vulnerable human being than as an ice-cold Spirit of Satire or Criticism, superior to all misfortunes and also to everybody on earth. . . .

If the author were content to let Henderson stand as a savage, or hardnose, the problem could be shrugged off. But instead, Vincent Canby asks the reader at the crisis to *care* about this hero, to treat him as though he could be hurt. . . .

The root of the trouble, clearly, is mistaken faith in the ease of commerce between literary opposites. . . . And great effort toward this end isn't expended here. In its absence we notice not just critical intelligence and humor in "Unnatural Scenery," but also, I'm afraid, a measure of tonal and moral confusion.

> *Benjamin DeMott, "Henderson the Loser," in* The New York Times Book Review *(© 1979 by*

The New York Times Company; reprinted by permission), January 28, 1979, p. 15.

DAPHNE MERKIN

[*Unnatural Scenery*] whirrs with rapid, centrifugal force, yet gives little indication of the generative impulse behind all the noise—other than possibly an interest in the geographical lore of the state of Virginia.

Marshall Lewis Henderson, the narrator, is one of those larger-than-life figures who is, at best, representative of the world around him and, at worst, an oafish presence. His childhood is depicted from a bewildering variety of angles, featuring elements of gentility and reclusiveness that usually characterize WASP boyhoods; alongside these are contrasting elements of dissipation and familial violence that typify novels dealing with the Southern gentry. . . .

Unnatural Scenery is "antic," which means that believability is sacrificed in the interests of diversity. Canby orchestrates his novel like a ringmaster at a three-ring circus, constantly sparking the flagging attention of his audience with new acts and daredevil performers. The book is admittedly entertaining in parts, yet only because it is so furiously *au courant*. The humor seldom penetrates. . . . [For] all its efforts *Unnatural Scenery* palls frequently, mainly because Canby supplies us with heaps of information in place of characterization. Marshall remains a distant curiosity rather than the touching survivor he is meant to be. The reader, meanwhile, remains very much on the outside, wondering what all the damned fuss is about. (p. 15)

> *Daphne Merkin, in* The New Leader *(© 1979 by the American Labor Conference on International Affairs, Inc.), January 29, 1979.*

*   *   *

CAPOTE, Truman   1924-

An American novelist, short story writer, playwright, and essayist, Capote achieved literary fame as a young man, and has remained a literary celebrity ever since. His early writings focus on the Deep South, where he was born, but his later works have varied tremendously in locale and style. His best known work, *In Cold Blood*, contributed to the formation of a new genre, the nonfiction novel. Capote is currently at work on *Answered Prayers*. The volume contains thinly veiled portraits of many of Capote's friends, and several have appeared as excerpts in periodicals, creating a minor sensation in literary and social circles and making the book notorious even before its publication. (See also *CLC*, Vols. 1, 3, 8, and *Contemporary Authors*, Vols. 5-8, rev. ed.)

ALBERTO MORAVIA

Other Voices, Other Rooms is a very good novel, with an extremely simple scheme and plot which the author slowly loads with baroque and decorative details, yet without complicating it. (p. 478)

Mention has been made of Poe in connection with this book of Capote's. It seems to me, however, that the points of resemblance are purely casual and are due to a similarity of subject matter rather than to conscious derivation. In certain of Poe's tales, *The Fall of the House of Usher, The Gold-Bug* and others, set in the American provinces, in decaying houses full of memories, it is easy to discern the forebears of the country house in Truman Capote. But there is a difference between Poe's and Capote's approach to reality. Poe, even at his most fantastic and unreal, is always extremely literal, accurate, and realistic in his aims and intentions. . . . [Poe] really believed in the existence of a reality outside of himself. And it matters little whether this reality was moral and psychological or . . . erotic and sexual.

For Truman Capote, instead, this process worked in reverse. The motive which encouraged Capote to accumulate details which build up a fantastic atmosphere, page after page, in a rich and crowded design, was instead a longing to evade reality by means of an impressionistic and imprecise transcription of actions, suspicions, tastes and feelings which are purely subjective. Capote, in particular, has a magpie's passion for household chattels: countless pieces of furniture, ornaments, knicknacks and trifles decorate his pages. And nature itself is seen with the same morbid passion, enlarging the details at the expense of the general picture. Obviously Capote is concerned not with the real properties of these objects but with the unhealthy feelings to which they give rise in [the central character] Joel's breast. We are, that is to say, faced with a genre of novel which in the last few years has become increasingly common, the novel of imaginary and fantastic distortions of reality seen through the eyes of a child or adolescent. It recalls the more charming fairy-tale atmosphere of *Le Grand Meaulnes* or even *A High Wind in Jamaica*. But Capote does not always succeed in leading us, via the grotesque and the baroque, back to normality. Sometimes the transition from fantasy to reality is arbitrary and gratuitous, sometimes the literariness, the taste for decoration for its own sake, makes itself felt. The book belongs to a class which is already adult both in America and elsewhere, and Capote does not ignore his immediate predecessors. He seems to belong rather to the tradition of a writer like Carson McCullers than to that of Poe. (pp. 479-81)

Alberto Moravia, in Sewanee Review *(reprinted by permission of the editor; © 1960 by The University of the South), Summer, 1960.*

WILLIAM L. NANCE

It is one of my intentions in this study to show that the changes in Capote's career have not been casual but are the result of a strong and highly conscious effort at growth. From the start he wrote stories which were among the best of their narrow kind, but even then he was trying to make his fiction both a source and an expression of deeper understanding, broader sympathy, greater fidelity to the reality outside his private childhood world. So far has he moved in twenty-three years of publishing that one is tempted to identify at least two distinct Truman Capotes. There is, of course, only one: *In Cold Blood* retains deep traces of the earliest stories, and the intellectual toughness so evident in the nonfiction novel was really there all the time. (p. 11)

Some knowledge of Capote's early life is essential to an understanding of his work, for that work, even through *In Cold Blood*, bears the clear marks of his childhood. It was, Capote has said, "the most insecure childhood I know of," and his early stories are psychological records of it. (pp. 11-12)

The early fiction of Truman Capote is dominated by fear. It descends into a subconscious ruled by the darker archetypes, a childhood haunted by bogeymen, a world of blurred realities whose inhabitants are trapped in unendurable isolation. The stories set in this dark world include "A Tree of Night" (1943), "Miriam" (1944), "The Headless Hawk" (1946), "Shut a Final Door" (1947), and "Master Misery" (1948). . . . Deep below the surface they are really one story, and they have one protagonist. This story will be continued, and its hero will achieve a peculiar liberation in Capote's first novel, *Other Voices, Other Rooms* (1948). The fear and sense of captivity that overshadow these stories result from the individual's inability to accept and respond properly to reality. On the social level this means inability to love other persons. More essentially, it means refusal to accept mysterious and frightening elements within the self, for the persons encountered by the protagonist are most properly viewed as projections of inner personae. One indication of the climate of the protagonist's inner world is the fact that nearly all of these persons are grotesques.

The stories are fundamentally psychic in orientation. In at least two cases—"Miriam" and "Shut a Final Door"—the line between realism and fantasy is definitely crossed: things happen that are literally impossible. Usually, however, the settings seem realistic; we are kept in a world that is conceivably real, though strange, and the effects are wrought through manipulations of the protagonist's consciousness. The characteristic style of the early work is intensely poetic, and the meaning of the stories rests heavily on intricate patterns of symbolism. The most prominent stylistic and symbolic motif in the fiction up to and including *Other Voices, Other Rooms* is that of descent into a state of intensified and distorted consciousness. This happens in each story, the differences being mostly in what might be termed focal length. Sometimes the setting remains normal and the character simply becomes sleepy or drunk, or has a dream. At other times the entire setting takes on dreamlike characteristics, often through weather imagery such as darkness or snow. In the most extreme cases the reader is pulled completely into the illusion by means of apparitions or mysterious voices presented as real. This scale of reader involvement is one of several ways of looking at the stories and not, incidentally, a simple measure of their total effectiveness: Capote handles his various effects always with considerable skill.

Perhaps the most obvious thing to be noted about Capote's early work is its highly personal quality. The stories take place in an inner world almost entirely devoid of social or political concern. Because of this subjective orientation, even the treatment of human relations has about it an air of isolation, of constriction. With this qualification in mind, one may go on to observe that love and the failure of love are of central concern in Capote's fiction. The meaning of love, as it emerges in the early work, would seem to be uncritical acceptance. In each story the protagonist is given an opportunity to accept someone and something strange and disturbing, to push back the frontier of darkness both in the surrounding world and in the soul. Not until Joel works his way through *Other Voices, Other Rooms* does one of them manage to do so. Their characteristic kind of failure appears in simplest form in the tendency to dismiss any challenging new presence as "crazy." Capote's impulse, from "A Tree of Night" to *In Cold Blood*, is to accept and understand the "abnormal" person; it has been, indeed, one of the main purposes of his writing to safeguard the unique individual's freedom from such slighting classifications as "abnormal." (pp. 16-17)

In the closing line of *Other Voices, Other Rooms*, its young hero turns to look back, symbolically, "at the boy he had left behind." . . . The novel is an account of Joel's growth from childhood to maturity. He achieves this growth by learning, with the help of a series of lessons and ordeals, to accept wholeheartedly—that is, to love—the life that awaits him, however disappointing and mysterious it may seem. He finds and accepts "his proper place" and in so doing gains the freedom that goes with the achievement of a sense of identity.

Described in these general terms, the novel might seem to depict the initiation of any young man into full stature in his society, but it does not. It might be better described as an initiation out of society; for in *Other Voices, Other Rooms*, as in the stories that preceded it, the world the hero is asked to accept is a world whose norm is abnormality. It is a world that begins where daylight merges into shadow—a refuge from society for the maimed in body and spirit. Though unconventional in this sense, it is nevertheless a place of trial where one achieves freedom by understanding and acceptance. Joel does what his older counterparts failed to do: he outfaces the monsters of his childhood, sees them in truer perspective and with proper detachment, and exposes them for what they are. (p. 41)

Other Voices, Other Rooms is an almost unbelievably intricate novel—a fact not surprising if one has read the earlier stories, particularly "The Headless Hawk" and "Master Misery." In all of them, the symbolic patterns lead toward an ultimate complex oneness, an overlapping and merging of symbols. *Other Voices, Other Rooms* in particular might be compared to a closed sphere of interwoven endless circles, or even of one endless strand. The novel's question is: Who is Joel? His answer—"I am me. . . . I am Joel, we are the same people"—completes a circle. Furthermore, his "we" includes almost everyone and everything in the book. His identity is his father, whom he came to find, but also Randolph, whom he found. His father is the sun, and also Little Sunshine, who is also the Cloud Hotel and Drownin Pond and the sinking Landing. The Landing is Skully's, or death's, and so is the snake, which is also Mr. Sansom, as well as Idabel's father and Zoo's grandfather and all fathers. And so on. It is a remarkable achievement, if somewhat like a maze with no exit. This maze entangles the reader in a poetic experience which has the irrational power of childhood itself: it must be grown out of, but, like childhood, it continues to haunt the memory. Capote was completely right when he remarked of the book, eight years after finishing it, "Despite awkwardness, it has an amazing intensity, a real voltage."

Viewed as a liberation, the story is markedly ambivalent. Its explicit meaning is that Joel has broken out of his childhood prison and achieved maturity, yet the way in which he does it, and the symbolic pattern surrounding the action, suggest a narcissistic confinement. This contradiction is presumably intended to function as a vital paradox; still, one feels uneasily that Joel and Capote have not made quite as clean a break with childhood as they think, though they are moving in the right direction. (pp. 63-4)

The year 1948 saw the publication not only of "Master Misery" and *Other Voices, Other Rooms*, but also of a story which seems at first glance to have little in common with them—"Children on Their Birthdays." If Capote's early stories are about captivity and *Other Voices, Other Rooms* is about liberation, the later stories—though some of their characters are quite literally imprisoned—have about them an air of limitless vistas. Among the other works of this later period are "A Diamond Guitar" (1950), "House of Flowers" (1951), "A Christmas Memory" (1956), and "Among the Paths to Eden" (1960). . . .

The typical protagonist of these stories—as of the two longer works written during the same years, *The Grass Harp* and *Breakfast at Tiffany's*—is an unattached, unconventional wanderer, usually a girl or a childlike woman, whose life is a pursuit of some ideal of happiness. (p. 65)

[The] Capote heroine first assumes her definitive shape and central position in Miss Bobbit [of "Children on Their Birthdays"]. The significance she has for Billy Bob gives a clue to her significance for Capote. She is the dreamer in him, the child, the delicate spirit wandering in search of ideal happiness. She is "the queer things in him," and also, perhaps, the things he has been too wise an artist to show anyone else. One of the most important results of the liberation he achieved at the time of *Other Voices, Other Rooms* was the ability to place his alter ego in perspective by somehow managing to find it embodied in real persons he has known, thus freeing himself from it while at the same time continuing to possess it lovingly. Though still narcissistic in its deeper levels, his later fiction has a new air of turning outward, of freshness and sunlight. There is a new sadness in it, too, for the break with childhood is not made without pain. Miss Bobbit and her later counterparts exist finally not as real persons but as bittersweet memories.

One sign of new vigor in Capote's grasp of reality, and evidence of the tougher side of his nature, is the very real strength these heroines possess during their brief hour. Their confident pursuit of an ideal gives them the power to beat society at its own game and to compel its grudging admiration. Like Capote himself, they know how to get what they want. This was not the case with their predecessors, all of whom were directionless and fated to destruction. (pp. 70-1)

In "House of Flowers" Capote moved in a very different direction. The romantic, tropical world . . . becomes the actual setting of this story, a product of Capote's 1948-49 vacation in Haiti. He published the story in 1951 and three years later collaborated with Harold Arlen in its production as a musical play. Unlike any of his other stories, it was apparently written as a preparatory exercise for a stage version. As this would suggest, it is the most exotic of all Capote's stories, told in a whimsical, playful tone that seems to place it even further from his personal world of experience and imagination than "A Diamond Guitar." It was, in fact, based on stories he heard, as Capote himself has explained. . . . Though remote from his other work in many ways, it is still about a girl who is a prisoner and a dreamer. This time, however, he decided to let the dream come true. (pp. 75-6)

In finding her dream come true, Ottilie moves into a world of romance in which nothing, not even death, need be taken seriously. Capote has sometimes been called a fantasist and has indignantly denied it. Taken as a charge of irresponsibility, the designation would be better applied to "House of

Flowers" than to the earlier, more apparently fantastic, stories, which, as Capote insists, are serious examinations of real states of mind. The story of Ottilie has a fundamental unseriousness which Capote has, fortunately, seldom put into his fiction. And, where it deviates from romantic cliché, the story has something rather chilling about it. Though Old Bonaparte somewhat resembles the archetypal bogeys of the dark fiction, the atmosphere of the story does not sustain that kind of reading, and Ottilie's murderous innocence seems an extreme case of the chill exclusiveness that tends to mar Capote's dreamers.

"A Christmas Memory" is Truman Capote's nonfiction short story. (p. 78)

[It is] a frank memoir which, while generally accepted as one of his finest and most charming short stories, has become his own avowed favorite among his shorter works because it is "true." . . .

The story is his idealized recollection of his relationship with [the elderly cousin with whom he spent much of his childhood]. As such it has a unique importance among his works, for it embodies the archetype of an emotional pattern which underlies all his later fiction and even exerts a subtle influence on *In Cold Blood*. Asexual admiration of a childlike dreamer-heroine is the usual attitude of the Capote narrator. The pastness of the experience is also essential; Capote's is a fiction of nostalgia. "A Christmas Memory" is one of his best and most satisfying works because it places the feelings he can dramatize most powerfully in the setting which is best suited to them—which, as Henry James would say, artistically does most for them. (p. 79)

"Among the Paths to Eden," published at about the time Capote began his Kansas research for *In Cold Blood*, shows signs of the new strength and freedom he feels he derived from his work on the nonfiction novel. One of his principal aims in that project was to enlarge the range of characters he could portray sympathetically. In this story he does precisely that.

"Among the Paths to Eden" resembles earlier works in depicting a non-sexual encounter between a male observer and a wistful dreamer-heroine, but its spirit is new. The story is told in the third person in a playful comic tone that places the author at a slight, good-natured distance from the hero, Mr. Ivor Belli—who in turn views his brief acquaintance, Miss Mary O'Meaghan, in much the same way. The setting is a very real, undreamlike New York, and the time —virtually the first instance of it in Capote's fiction—is the present. (pp. 83-4)

Three years after *Other Voices, Other Rooms*, Truman Capote published his next major work, the short novel *The Grass Harp* (1951). The story opens on a note of reminiscence: "When was it that first I heard of the grass harp? Long before the autumn we lived in the china tree; an earlier autumn, then; and of course it was Dolly who told me, no one else would have known to call it that, a grass harp." . . .

[The opening lines] establish much of the story's basic pattern: the first-person narrator recalls a past episode and a heroine who had a special meaning for him. (p. 88)

The grass harp is a field of Indian grass between River Woods and the hilltop cemetery outside a small Southern town. In autumn the wind turns it into a "harp of voices"

that tells the story of all the people buried on the hill, "of all the people who ever lived." . . . Dolly Talbo, who explains this to Joel, is his father's cousin. Since the age of eleven, when his mother died, he has lived with her and her sister Verena, both of them unmarried. (pp. 88-9)

The line of alienation separating Capote's chosen few from the rest of the world—a line first drawn in "Master Misery" and taken for granted in *Other Voices, Other Rooms*— is, in *The Grass Harp*, drawn more distinctly than ever. It is, in fact, the backbone of the story's plot.

Life in the Talbo house has some of the bizarre qualities that it had at Skully's Landing, but its isolation from the outer world is less complete. (p. 90)

The Grass Harp contains Capote's fullest expression of antagonism between his chosen dreamers and the rest of society. The Capote characters we have met don't fit in, and, since Joel Knox, they don't seem to want to. They are innocent pilgrims wandering in search of some better place. Society for its part considers them "crazy" and tries to put them into its prisons and its starchy straitjackets. But, as Miss Bobbit divined, beneath its hostility lies envy. On the present occasion the representatives of society stand below Dolly and her crew "like dogs gathered around a tree of trapped possums." (pp. 93-4)

Judge Cool embodies another kind of progression in the development of Capote's themes. Though his dreamers may easily be dismissed by society as of no value, the same cannot be said of Dolly's new recruit. In him, society is condemned by someone right out of its highest ranks, a man whose profession gives him a special claim to wisdom. A broadening of the social base has already been evident, of course, in the selection of Capote code heroes. (p. 94)

The judge announces that they must be prepared, and begins a systematic statement of their "position" that is more philosophical than military. . . .

> But here we are, identified: five fools in a tree. A great piece of luck provided we know how to use it; no longer any need to worry about the picture we present—free to find out who we truly are. If we know that no one can dislodge us; it's the uncertainty concerning themselves that makes our friends conspire to deny the differences. . . .
>
> (pp. 95-6)

Capote has made Judge Cool his foremost spokesman, and this passage is the author's fullest statement of the values that underlie his fiction and perhaps all his writing. The judge is describing the Capote hero, the dreamer-victim. Everyone we have met in his stories is included here. Here are the early sufferers, prisoners even in their hearts because even in their hearts they were afraid to accept the differences, to recognize the bogeymen who were part of themselves.

The fiction turned from dark to light when, in Joel Knox, they jumped to inner freedom by accepting their identity. Joel found his "one person in the world" in Randolph, and with him retreated into his private rooms, moving almost completely out of the social world. Most of his later counterparts are involved to some extent in that social world but with the full realization that even if they themselves accept the differences, the world of convention and law does not.

Consequently they remain victims, but defiant ones. What each of them longs for is a friend—someone who will accept him completely as he has accepted himself—someone who is, in fact, the self. Even a passing encounter with such a one may be all that can be hoped for. (pp. 96-7)

This kind of love obviously tends away from the personal, and above all from the sexual. (p. 97)

Breakfast at Tiffany's almost completes the movement in Truman Capote's fiction from the submerged world of childhood to the real world of people and events. It employs the same New York setting as "The Headless Hawk" and "Shut a Final Door," but there the resemblance ends. Between those stories and this one, Capote the writer has grown up. The early stories were inward-turning, conscious of the outside world only as a symbolic extension of inner fears. *Breakfast at Tiffany's,* on the other hand, is as topical as Winchell's column, as cool and sophisticated as the tough, eccentric society it talks about. Its unnamed narrator, an aspiring writer who might well be Capote himself during his first months in New York, is an older Collin Fenwick who has set his own affairs in order and begun to look around him at the world. He observes it more objectively than before, but once again his attention is focused on a dreamer-heroine whose prototype is the elderly friend of "A Christmas Memory." This story, too, is a memory. (p. 107)

Holly Golightly, a remote descendant of the heroine of "Master Misery," has not let the psychiatrists steal her dreams. She belongs to a later generation of Capote heroines who have learned to preserve their integrity by safeguarding their uniqueness. Society helplessly admires her and considers her crazy at the same time, but Capote and his narrator have only admiration for her. . . .

[She] joins the narrator [during a party], and stays long enough to give him a considerable new insight into her thinking. She explains that she didn't want to be a movie star because it requires the sacrifice of one's ego, and "I want to still be me when I wake up one fine morning and have breakfast at Tiffanys." . . . Holly's life of traveling is really a search for a home, a place "where me and things belong together." . . . She hasn't found the place yet, but she knows it will make her feel like Tiffany's does, with the sense of security, the "quietness and proud look of it." (p. 112)

Holly's ideal of love is simply not a sexual one, nor is it likely to be satisfied by any real human being she will meet. The ideal relationship she aspires to is approximated by the narrator's own relationship with her: tender but distant, and consisting largely of admiration for her brilliance and strength. That Holly makes honesty to self her guiding principle is not surprising when we remember that on the deepest level she is the Capote-narrator's alter ego, representing for him—as Miss Bobbit did for Billy Bob—the strange, unconventional side of himself. In admiring Holly he is being true to himself, making that act of acceptance that has been the dominant impulse in most of Capote's writing. (p. 119)

Breakfast at Tiffany's is a showcase for Holly Golightly. O. J. Berman introduced her as a "*real* phony" who honestly "believes all this crap she believes," and the remainder of the story is a gradual exposition of the content of this belief. We learn that her idea of love is a non-sexual focus-

ing of esthetically oriented feeling, just as it was for Randolph, Judge Cool, and Dolly Talbo. Honesty to oneself, or acceptance of one's identity, is as important to her as it came to be for Joel Knox. All her life she has known deprivation and death and fought a desperate battle against fear. It is, finally, the awareness of death that keeps her from feeling at home anywhere and impels her on a constant search for something better. Here at the end of *Breakfast at Tiffany's*—which is, except for the genial "Among the Paths to Eden," Capote's last fictional "word" on life up to the time of *In Cold Blood*—we learn what seems to be Holly's deepest motivating force. Her regret at losing her nameless, battered "slob" of a cat, far from being a sentimental excess on her part (and the narrator's), is an intensely serious expression of a profound fear of relinquishment. Just as the dominant willed movement in Capote's fiction is acceptance—of things, persons, life—so its deepest fear seems to be of the inner principle of rejection that leads one to throw away those few and tenuous possessions life does permit. The fight against death must be carried on even in the innermost recesses of the self.

Holly's values are those of the Capote-narrator: she is a part of himself set free like a broken-stringed kite to wander toward an ambiguous land of dreams and death. Her brief presence is his own breakfast at Tiffany's, his taste of the idyll which always vanishes, leaving pain. (pp. 122-23)

In Cold Blood might be called a remarkably successful attempt at an impossible job. Capote has professed surprise that no one else has done quite the same thing, but it is really not surprising at all. Critics have, for the most part, tended to classify *In Cold Blood* as simply an extreme form of a familiar class of writing, the documentary novel. (The definite sound of this term is rather illusory, since the documentary novel is a particularly ill-defined subtype of a large class, the novel—itself never strong on definition.) It is interesting to note, however, that Capote does not classify his book this way, but tends always to speak of it as something unique. (p. 177)

If the documentary novelist is doomed to wander between the fixed poles of journalistic factuality and imaginative power, Capote has tried to force the poles together. He has done this, he feels, by living his way so deeply into the real-life events that his eventual incorporation of them in a novel would have as much "poetic altitude" as any of his more purely imaginative works.

It is a fascinating ideal: to reach a point at which the inner reality coincides with the outer and the free use of the artist's shaping power results not in distortion but in heightened fidelity. (p. 178)

Capote's aim eluded his grasp, as it would have eluded anyone's. The book he finally wrote, failing to attain that charmed circle in which fact and fiction would blend, falls back into a category which may as well be labeled "documentary novel"—though it must be added that *In Cold Blood* is certainly one of the finest specimens of that "impure genre" and quite possibly the best piece of artistic journalism ever written.

There is a sense, however, in which Capote's achievement is not so important as his aim. Neither his literary career nor *In Cold Blood* itself can be adequately understood without some knowledge of what he hoped to achieve in the nonfiction novel. Capote himself seems, with the supreme self-confidence that artists must breathe like air, to feel that he *has* achieved it. His extravagant claims for the book are more than mere expressions of his natural flamboyance and high-pressure salesmanship. Confidence in his technical ability is not a new thing with Capote; what is new is his assurance that he has done an immense piece of social groundwork successfully, not only on the level of accurate reporting but on the deeper level of personal understanding. Stated simply, it is the conviction that his talent for writing and his talent for friendship have been fully and triumphantly integrated.

The foundation of *In Cold Blood* was to be "immaculate" factuality. (pp. 178-79)

Accuracy on the factual level is meant to undergird Capote's really important concern: objectivity with regard to the internal action.... Neither the undisputed factuality of the book nor the author's claims for it should be allowed to obscure the fact that what *In Cold Blood* presents is Truman Capote's view of the facts. Here, just as in *The Grass Harp* or *Breakfast at Tiffany's,* he had to decide what the book was to say, then direct every smallest part of it toward that end. (p. 180)

Capote's claims to objectivity can be resolved only by reference to his conviction that, through painstaking investigation and deep personal sympathy with those involved, he reached a correct judgment about the Clutter case. For the book to be a complete success on Capote's terms, the reader would have to share this conviction. (p. 181)

Within the book itself, granted Capote's fundamental control, he has succeeded in giving a strong impression of objectivity. The very subject he chose made possible an effective show of impartiality through sympathetic portrayal of both victims and killers. Capote says he answered questions about his motive for writing the book by ... [saying] that "it didn't have anything to do with changing the reader's opinion about anything, nor did I have any moral reasons worthy of calling them such—it was just that I had a strictly aesthetic theory about creating a book which could result in a work of art."

In terms of narrative technique, Capote kept himself out of the book.... (p. 182)

The limitations I have ascribed to *In Cold Blood* are inherent to the very concept of a nonfiction novel. Viewed as fictional art, any such work would be found lacking in that self-containedness which the artifact should possess; viewed as reportage, it would always seem to present spurious claims to truth. These flaws are pervasive, setting up disturbing vibrations all through the book. On the other hand, the ores refined in the heat of Capote's intention did turn, if not into pure gold, at least into a very high grade alloy. *In Cold Blood* is a remarkable blend of compassion and craftsmanship, of life and art, possessing large measures of the factual persuasiveness and poetic altitude its author sought. It is also ... the product of an amazing collaboration between design and chance and, for Capote, between the new and the old. (pp. 184-85)

The form Truman Capote gave his nonfiction novel was well chosen from both the journalistic and the artistic points of view. *In Cold Blood* is written in small sections.... Journalistically this gives, more effectively than a smoothly flowing account could do, the impression of a great multi-

plicity of events skillfully encompassed. The abrupt scene-shifting often has the effect of an up-to-the-minute news bulletin. (p. 186)

The most obvious advantage of the vignette structure, cinematic or not, is the way it enables Capote to reinforce the contrast between victims and killers by repeated jolts from one group to the other, especially in the section preceding the murders. (p. 188)

In Cold Blood is divided into four equal sections entitled "The Last To See Them Alive," "Persons Unknown," "Answer," and "The Corner." These headings, like the title of the book itself, have the journalistic flavor and are, indeed, taken from the verbal matrix of the case rather than from Capote's imagination. All, however, are rich with a multiple suggestiveness that is the result of his artistry. As Capote told Perry Smith, though without explaining fully, the book's title has a "double meaning," referring both to the murders and the executions, with the ironic emphasis falling heavily on the latter. Capote has always enjoyed disturbing the complacent. Here he shows us that the familiar phrase "in cold blood," if it means anything, doesn't mean quite what we thought it did. (pp. 188-89)

Though portrayed at some length and even permitted to speak on occasion, Dick emerges as an unsympathetic character—shrewd, mean, able to take care of himself. It is Perry who haunts the memory, overshadowing not only Dick but everyone else. (p. 203)

But our feeling for Perry does not, as in the case of Raskolnikov or even of Clyde Griffiths, derive principally from his commission of a gravely immoral act—from his "dynamic badness"—but rather from his amoral, pathetic blending of violence and aspiration. In addition to being a murderer by "psychological accident," Perry is a childlike dreamer, a romantic wanderer.

Perry's physical appearance is that of a grotesque child. (p. 204)

[His] aspiration to artistic success takes several forms. He says of himself, "I had this great natural musical ability.... I liked to read, too. Improve my vocabulary. Make up songs. And I could draw. But I never got any encouragement." ... Capote describes a portrait of Jesus he did in prison as "in no way technically naive." ... During his talks with Capote, when the latter insisted that his only intention in writing *In Cold Blood* was to create a work of art, Perry would remark, "What an irony, what an irony." Capote explains, "I'd ask what he meant, and he'd tell me that all he ever wanted to do in his life was to produce a work of art.... 'And now, what has happened? An incredible situation where I kill four people, and you're going to produce a work of art.'" (p. 205)

It is in the portrayal of Perry Smith that Capote's achievement comes closest to his ideal for the nonfiction novel: a perfect identification of the inner vision with the outer reality....

Capote succeeded best with Perry, not only because the latter resembled his fictional characters, but because in his similarity to these childlike dreamer-victims he resembled the author's imaginative projection of himself. Capote obviously thought of Perry as similar to himself even in physical appearance. In the book he makes much of Perry's small stature and speaks of his "changeling's face." ...

Capote does not stop at the superficial parallels between Perry's life and his own. When Perry, resentful of his questioning, challenged him to tell about his *own* sex life, Capote did. "I told him honestly in great detail all about myself—some of my own problems were very close to his. He could see I was very sincere." . . .

That Capote should find such a "congenial" character in the Clutter case might be explained in two ways: either he distorted Perry in the book, or he was remarkably lucky. (p. 211)

The evidence suggests, in fact, that chance plays an immensely important role in the writing of the nonfiction novel—another reason, no doubt, why the field is so thinly populated. Although Capote had tried other subjects, nothing had worked until the Clutter case, and even that choice depended finally on the presence of Perry. Moreover, without the help of Dick's photographic memory, Capote would have been hard put to reproduce in detail the career of the killers between the murder and the arrest. I would even suggest, without in the least intending to imply that Capote personally desired or neglected opportunities to avert the execution, that the book might very likely not have been completed without that particular conclusion. The extreme difficulty experienced in the writing of the last few pages may well reflect a profound conflict between human anguish and artistic necessity. (p. 212)

Capote's deep sympathy for Perry makes *In Cold Blood* a powerful work of art and a probing and admirable attempt to understand a human being. If it is less than completely successful, so are all such efforts. (p. 215)

[Capote's] stated purpose in attempting a nonfiction novel was to achieve an artistic and personal liberation—to escape from his private imaginative world into the larger world of reality. He believes that in writing *In Cold Blood* he achieved that purpose. Today he speaks of having come over the hump, of being able now to apply his artistic intelligence to a wide range of contemporary experience.

The reader who picks up Capote's factual account of a Kansas murder case hardly expects it to have much in common with his fictional accounts of haunted Southern childhoods. (pp. 216-17)

While Capote can take well-deserved pride in *In Cold Blood* as a genuine enlargement of his artistic scope, his deepest satisfaction probably derives from its being something even more important to him: a vindication of his imagination. In its portrayal of Perry Smith and in its pervasive theme of victimization, the book is a factual echo of Capote's earliest fiction.

That fiction began . . . with a series of "dark" stories in each of which the rather unattractive protagonist was trapped in a cage of childhood fears. Near the end of the dark period, in "Master Misery," there appeared a new tendency to see the protagonist (though doomed, like the others) as a somewhat admirable *dreamer,* together with a concomitant scorn for conventional society. (p. 218)

Perry Smith closely resembles the protagonists of these early stories, as do the other characters of *In Cold Blood* insofar as they are sufferers and dreamers. (p. 219)

The tendency toward acceptance that first appears in *Other Voices, Other Rooms* is part of a broad movement in the

author's work that expresses itself in several other recurrent motifs and has, at least implicitly, a rather coherent philosophical foundation. The kind of love Joel is initiated into finds its perfect object in Randolph, a completely dependent, completely receptive individual in whom sexual distinctions are virtually nonexistent. The desire to obliterate such distinctions, along with all the other classifications that society imposes on persons, is apparent in all of Capote's work. Closely related to it is a movement away from morality in the narrow sense toward a more spiritual standard. His heroines—Miriam, Sylvia, Idabel, Miss Bobbit, Dolly Talbo—are always shocking people, and they are always right; their way proves always to be the most practical or at least the most pleasant. When "morality" and convention enter the stories, they enter to be refuted by someone with a vision that transcends them.

There is, indeed, a strain of American transcendentalism in Capote, which reminds us that his "student" Perry Smith developed, in his last days, a strong admiration for Thoreau. Behind transcendentalism is Platonism. . . . (p. 221)

Randolph and Judge Cool, Capote's two principal lecturers on the nature of love, certainly reflect the Platonic side of the Western mentality; and Dolly Talbo and his other heroines seem to be both highly committed seekers for and actual representatives of the transcendent realm. The maturing of Joel Knox, which we have seen to be the turning point in Capote's fiction, assumes broad relevance when viewed—as [Frank] Baldanza views it—as a recapitulation of the "passage from the Heraclitan flux of constant change to the Platonic absolute of love, . . . a momentous achievement of Greek intellectual history."

The spiritual liberation that took place in Capote's work at the time of *Other Voices, Other Rooms* was bound up with another movement that was to reach its ultimate development in *In Cold Blood:* a turning outward to the world of social experience. . . . In style, the stories gradually become less poetic. Their tone becomes less subjective, their atmosphere less thickly crowded with a dreamlike profusion of symbols. Most important, there is a new protagonist at the center of the stories, and this person is usually a woman. Capote had always tended to use feminine protagonists, but in the early work gender did not matter especially, since all the main characters were mirror-images of a single isolated consciousness. The attitude taken toward this captive protagonist ranged from pity to a scorn that was really self-hatred.

Slowly, however, a polarity began to reveal itself. Implicit criticism began to be directed mostly at male characters (Vincent, Walter), and women became the objects of compassion and eventually even of admiration (D. J., Sylvia). Immediately after *Other Voices, Other Rooms,* this heroine achieved a major breakthrough to freedom. Still a sufferer at the hands of life, she was now predominantly a dreamer —an unconventional childlike wanderer whose integrity in the search for an ideal happiness gave her strength to resist the encroachments of society.

While this heroine had obviously been evolving in Capote's imagination, and in fact is, from beginning to end, a projection of himself, a crucial difference from this time on is that her portrayal begins to be based on real girls and women whom Capote has known. Thus the new heroine illustrates most clearly how Capote's liberation is related to a shift—at least partial—from inner to outer experience. *Other Voices, Other Rooms* is the first of his works that has the flavor of factual autobiography, though he describes it as a Gothic dream. While maintaining that the book is not literally true, he says that it is "made of all sorts of things from my childhood." Specifically, it deals with one of his first friendships, that with Harper Lee, and some of the experiences they shared. (pp. 221-23)

From the time of *Other Voices, Other Rooms*, most of Capote's stories are based on his "Platonic" relationships with real women.... Even in *In Cold Blood* Capote tends to favor the use of women observers. (p. 223)

It is Capote's highly objective narrative technique that most clearly distinguishes *In Cold Blood* from his fiction and even—as many have remarked—from much journalism. Even this, however, is the completion of a trend that may be observed throughout his work. The early stories portray a world of abnormal, trapped individuals viewed as though from within that world itself: its rules are the only rules; its dreams are realities. There is little or no use of narrative technique to gain an effect of objectivity. In *Other Voices, Other Rooms* we see a similar world, still without clear or consistent distancing through narrative technique or tone; there is, however, a distinction made between the abnormal world and the outside world of society, and, more important, there is the beginning of a division between the central consciousness and this abnormal world through the use of a protagonist who comes from the outside, sees Skully's Landing as distinct from himself, and accepts it freely.

In his later work—as though Capote were coming to identify narrative distance with maturity—the narrative consciousness is more carefully defined and progressively withdrawn from the center of action, which is now dominated by a gently eccentric protagonist wandering through an increasingly realistic world.... In *In Cold Blood* the narrator is in fact Mr. Capote, and he has virtually refined himself out of the book altogether.

Capote has done in his fiction what Billy Bob did in "Children on Their Birthdays," that first and most delightful expression of Capote's liberation. Having found a heroine who magically embodies the best, most private part of himself, he sadly but determinedly relinquishes her, allowing her to wander free and finally escape him by death.... The same relinquishment can be seen taking place near the end of *The Grass Harp*, in a scene that exemplifies Capote's literary strategy more clearly than any other. Collin is seated in the rain-soaked tree house, waiting with Verena and the Judge to hear Dolly's decision about whether to marry: "My impatience equaled theirs, yet I felt exiled from the scene, again a spy peering from the attic, and my sympathies, curiously, were nowhere; or rather, everywhere: a tenderness for all three ran together like raindrops, I could not separate them, they expanded into a human oneness." ... Objectivity of view blends with universality of sympathy: there could hardly be a better definition of Capote's aim in the nonfiction novel. (Self-effacing in one way, the stance is also godlike in its assumption of unlimited knowledge, power, and benevolence, and accords well with Capote's persistent drive toward a transcendental unity).

Collin's voluntary exile is attended with a strong reluctance to give up the narrower, more childlike identification with Dolly, and it is this reluctance that produces that nostalgic

sadness which repeatedly appears as Capote's last word on experience, be it fictional or nonfictional. Standing among graves, listening to a grass harp or gazing at autumn Kansas wheat, he knows that growth is a series of deaths. (pp. 224-26)

Perfect universal sympathy eluded Capote in *In Cold Blood* as surely as did perfect objectivity. Still, his account of the Clutter murders is deeply and broadly compassionate and thus marks a considerable advance along another of the lines Capote has been tracing in his career. Sympathy was almost completely absent in his earliest stories. (p. 226)

In Cold Blood, by bestowing its understanding in every quarter, emerges into a larger world. Here one feels that Capote attributes the sufferings of his victims not to stupid and malicious "other people" but to a more remote and mysterious principle—one closer to the source of genuine tragedy....

While Capote's vision of man's fate has grown larger and in that respect come closer to the stature of tragedy, it remains, even in *In Cold Blood*, essentially one of pathos. The tragic world view is an earth-centered one. But Capote's neoplatonists can be only exiles and victims in this world, for they have cast their lot in some other place. Even their power is eccentric, not geocentric. Speaking of the grotesque characters in the fiction of Capote, McCullers, and other Southern writers, Baldanza suggests that "on the philosophical level, the defects of the characters serve symbolically to represent the worthlessness of the material realm." Capote's portrayal of Perry Smith has, finally, the same effect as does the scene in which neighbors burn a pile of the Clutters' belongings and one of the men muses, "How was it possible that such effort, such plain virtue, could overnight be reduced to this—smoke, thinning as it rose and was received by the big, annihilating sky?" ... It is this strong current of evanescence tugging at a solid fabric of places, facts, and people that gives *In Cold Blood* its deepest intensity. (p. 227))

On its deepest level *In Cold Blood* is not a tragic drama but a meditation on reality. Its immediate dramatic interest lies primarily in the sensational quality of the murders and the pursuit of the criminals, but Capote's approach to the events is not, as has been claimed, voyeuristic. In a *tour de force* ..., Capote has transcended the *True Detective* genre story just as in "The Duke in His Domain" he transcended the *Photoplay*-type interview.

Truman Capote has not chosen to take the easy way. In the avowedly autobiographical *The Grass Harp*, Collin said, "I've read that past and future are a spiral, one coil containing the next and predicting its theme. Perhaps this is so; but my own life has seemed to me more a series of closed circles, rings that do not evolve with the freedom of a spiral: for me to get from one to the other has meant a leap, not a glide." ... With intelligence and determination, Capote the artist has tried to grow up. (p. 228)

William L. Nance, in his The Worlds of Truman Capote *(copyright © 1970 by William L. Nance; reprinted with permission of Stein and Day Publishers), Stein and Day, 1970.*

LEE ZACHARIAS

Called "daylight gothic" by Mark Shorer [in his introduction to Capote's *Selected Writings*, "Children on Their

Birthdays''] contains none of the dark gothic paraphernalia of such stories as "The Headless Hawk" or "Shut a Final Door." ... Shorer describes the mood of the story as "buoyant summer rain shot through with sun," but quotes out of context: "Since Monday it has been raining buoyant summer rain shot through with sun, but dark at night and full of sound, full of dripping leaves, watery chimneys, sleepless scuttlings." ... The mood of the story is a balance between sun and darkness, buoyant summer rain and sleepless scuttlings. It is gothic in the sense that *Lolita* is gothic; both have that delicate balance of nostalgia and terror, accuracy and imagination that Leslie Fiedler considers so important in *Huckleberry Finn*. What *Lolita* and "Children" share is a moving, affectionate comedy that is also brutal and shattering, a brilliant use of black humor that allows us to delight in that which should spin us into despair. Thus Capote places the wall that is art between man and the horror of life. ... (p. 343)

"Children" is less subjective than Capote's adolescent novel *Other Voices, Other Rooms;* the narrator includes himself "at least to some degree" among "the grownup persons of the house," hinting that he will be a reliable narrator who needs little initiating. Common to the adolescent novel (and *Lolita*) is an unwillingness to grow up, a wish to stop time. Though this episodic story has a definite duration of one year, the sense of being trapped by a small town suggests timelessness: "It was the summer that never rained; rusted dryness coated everything; sometimes when a car passed on the road, raised dust would hang in the still air an hour or more. Aunt El said if they didn't pave the highway soon she was going to move down to the seacoast; but she's said that for such a long time." ...

Time has stopped, but it hasn't; duality is the heart of the story. (p. 344)

Who [Miss Bobbit, a] combination Shirley Temple/Gypsy Rose Lee, really is, what happens to her as metaphor not as character is the key. ... (p. 345)

Miss Bobbit is [Billy Bob's] dreams. The wealth of American cultural details suggests that she may be all our dreams. ...

David Madden [in *American Dreams, American Nightmares*] correctly points out that in America there is an implicit responsibility to live dreams; the American Dream is supposed to be the American Reality, although there is no single definition for that dream. "Children" is about some forms of that dream. (p. 346)

Two phony dreams, those drilled into us as education and those sold to us as entertainment, make up Miss Bobbit's voice.

A duality in Miss Bobbit's character suggests a duality in our dreams. Both innocent and tainted, she is aloof, demanding chivalry that goes unrewarded; yet she is also seductress. ...

The paradox of her character makes clear the inconsistent absurdities of our dreams, which, because like Miss Bobbit dreams have a certain magic, gradually seem natural. (p. 347)

"Children" is scarcely soft humor, though so many of its characters are gentle. Holly, heroine of the novella, understands what Miss Bobbit does not, that "it's better to look

at the sky than live there. Such an empty place, so vague. Just a country where the thunder goes and things disappear." Miss Bobbit's dedication to the imaginative realm of experience has been inspiring to the town. Even the narrator wonders if she couldn't come back just as though she were really there, but he knows that for her to do so the shadows must be confused. By instinct he understands what Miss Bobbit does not. Miss Bobbit's failure is that she responds pragmatically to phenomena that require imaginative response. She fatally mingles the modes, trying to live an experience that is only to be dreamed.

Yes, she is more than being thirteen years old and crazy in love, and "Children on Their Birthdays" is after all a story of initiation, Billy Bob's and ours, to the sad truth that those things we are afraid to show are not to be shown, for they are dreams, worlds private to the imagination. If we do bring them out and they grow to seem natural and we think we might live them, our dreams become illusions, and what happens to illusions Capote makes brutally clear. ...

> You could see what was going to happen;
> and we called out, our voices like lightning
> in the rain, but Miss Bobbit, running toward
> those moons of roses, did not seem to hear.
> That is when the six o'clock bus ran over
> her. ...
>
> (p. 350)

Lee Zacharias, "Living the American Dream: 'Children on Their Birthdays'," in Studies in Short Fiction (copyright 1975 by Newberry College), Fall, 1975, pp. 343-50.

*   *   *

CARRIER, Roch   1937-

Carrier is a French-Canadian novelist and short story writer who interlaces personal and political themes in fiction that is richly symbolic. A recurrent subject in his work is the separatist movement in Quebec.

RONALD SUTHERLAND

Floralie, où es-tu, filled with boisterous, ribald humour and stylistic fireworks, is another impressive accomplishment—a genuine relief from the agonized, novel-escaped-from-the-confessional-booth trend in contemporary French-Canadian writing. In more ways than one, however, *Floralie* is a step backward. *La Guerre, yes sir* centres around the return of the body of a soldier killed in the war to his native village in rural Quebec. *Floralie* moves even farther into the past and describes the wedding night of the soldier's parents, Anthyme and Floralie Corriveau. But this chronological retrogression is attended by a curious retrogression in narrative technique. The book incorporates much of the paraphernalia of mediaeval literature, including dream allegory, monologue debate, sorcerer of a sort, enchanted forest and the seven deadly sins. Carrier seems to have taken the "Middle Ages" motif quite seriously.

Between fantastical realism and real fantasy, however, there is a very thin line. And it seems to me that the difference between Carrier's *La Guerre* and his *Floralie,* the difference which makes the former a more powerful and meaningful novel, is that *Floralie* crosses the thin line into fantasy. If the first book can be described as Faulknerian realism in its method of probing the motivating forces and special genius of a society through exploration of the more grotesque and bizarre means by which that society reveals itself, the same cannot be said of the second book. *Floralie* is funny, often hilariously funny, and Carrier's gift for engaging narrative and brilliant colloquial diction stands him in good stead. But the novel offers few insights into what makes Quebec tick, and that, for better or worse, is what I suspect many readers of *La Guerre, yes sir* may have come to expect of Carrier.

On the other hand, *Floralie* does have something to say about what makes people tick, and about the mental peregrinations which can occur when they are not ticking the way they should. . . . The reason for the anxieties of both Anthyme and Floralie on their wedding night, anxieties which resolve into quarrels, agitated soul-searching and troubled dreams, is that the young bride, having once rolled in a field of oats with an itinerant Italian railroad worker who played sweetly on the harmonica, does not come to the union complete with maidenhead. Anthyme is not an experienced lover and he is not sure what to think, but he does have the idea fixed in his head that somewhere along the line there ought to have been a little "mur" or "au moins un rideau à déchirer." And if there was one field of oats in Floralie's past, perhaps there were several fields of oats, and of hay and barley and wheat besides.

Floralie, où es-tu, like Carrier's first novel, is rich in amusing dialogue and incident. It is entertainment of a high order. There can be no doubt that here is a major talent, temporarily marking time in terms of psychological and social insight perhaps, but capable of producing a great deal more and very likely to do so. (pp. 88-9)

> Ronald Sutherland, "Crossing the Thin Line," in
> Canadian Literature, *Spring, 1970, pp. 88-9.*

JOAN HARCOURT

La Guerre, Yes Sir! and *Floralie, Where Are You?* are much more alike in mood than *Is It The Sun, Philibert?* . . . is to either of the others. The action of the first two covers, in each case, the span of a single rural night. *Philibert* takes us to the city and compresses months of misery into a brief hundred pages.

The first two books are a mordant mixture of desperate joy and surrealist horror, morality plays on the rampage. *La Guerre* revolves around the funeral and wake of a young soldier, whose union-jack draped body has been brought back to his home for burial. . . . The villagers are divided viciously each from the other, and as quickly united against any outside influence, so that, in the end, a grim communal front prevails. *Les maudits anglais* are frequently invoked but are not really seen as a tangible threat. . . . It is the Church that looms over all, dictatorial, resented, but an utterly binding force. As rough cider loosens tongues, the most sacred concepts become terms of invective and hate. Thus purged, the villagers wearily file into church the following morning, to hear their curé deliver a blood-chilling sermon on the evils of resisting the state in which God has seen fit to place them.

Floralie takes us back thirty years in time, to the wedding night of the parents of the dead boy in *La Guerre*. The setting is reminiscent of Bergman's "The Seventh Seal," with its symbolic overtones. There is a gruesome journey through a forest from the bride's home to the groom's, during which the marriage is "celebrated" in what must be one of the bleakest consummation scenes in literature. . . . The book ends on a tender note, with neither we nor they knowing whether the horrors of the night had actually taken place or had all been a dream born of generations of harsh conditioning. What we do know is that the devil is an ever-present reality, an image by means of which the Church reins in those who would break away, in fact or in fantasy. Again, it is the language of the Mass which provides the more colourful oaths. As in *La Guerre*, there is, on one level, no questioning of clerical authority. But in the dark regions of the unconscious, the characters are straining for freedom.

Philibert, in some ways, is light years beyond the medieval ethos of the first two books. Philibert, the son of the grave-digger in *La Guerre*, decides, the morning after the wake, to leave home, "and he wouldn't come back until he'd forgotten the kicks he had received." He arrives in Montreal to find the city ugly, dirty, and hostile. (pp. 568-69)

The first two books explore the events of a few hours in an explosion of fantasy. The same compressed approach brought to *Philibert*, which covers a much longer period of time, is less successful. Yet it may be the most significant of the three in that it not only opens out the world of *La Guerre* and *Floralie*, but suggests the casting-off of the old order. Philibert might be anyone come to the city. No longer dogged by village myths or bound by parish mores, he is also deprived of the warmth of familiarity. New social villains emerge. We might ask whether it is desperation or enlightenment that makes Philibert, caught between two worlds, shout: "God doesn't exist, but me, I exist. You haven't been born till you've said those words in the middle of the night, crossing Sainte-Catherine Street . . . God doesn't exist, but me, I exist."

This moment of liberation and self-discovery, Carrier may be telling us, had to occur before other changes could take place in the minds and hearts of that generation of French Canadians. "Après toi, Philibert, le déluge." (p. 569)

> Joan Harcourt, in Queen's Quarterly, *Winter,*
> *1972.*

ROBERT J. GREEN

La Guerre, Yes Sir! is a first novel of staggering sophistication and control, proving that there now exists in Montreal a major international writer. . . .

[In] the course of a few pages Roch Carrier has succeeded in portraying with memorable vividness all the frustrations the Quebec rural proletariat suffered at the hands of its two rulers: an incomprehensible Catholic God who dominated their spiritual lives, and the hated English ('maudits Anglais') who have forced French Canadians to fight a war that is not their concern. (p. 113)

The climax of the novel is the wake at which the villagers, well fortified with roast pig and local cider, gather to pray for the dead Corriveau. The result is a counterpointing of the peasant's naïve ribaldry and the stark terror of the Hell that they fear awaits them. Finally, the combination of succulent pork, vintage cider and earthy anecdote overcomes the threatening terror of purgatorial fires: the Quebec villagers, we sense, have reasserted their own humanity and independence in the face of God and the English soldiery, the twin enemies. Thus the scene that follows, in which the

Anglophone soldiers, offended by the raw vigour of the Francophone villagers, throw them out of the house of mourning takes on great symbolic weight as an acting out of French Canada's political and cultural deprivation.... All the novel's themes, of personal and social castration, are drawn close together in the last sentence: '... the war ... had dirtied the snow.'

The political undertones are always present but what makes Carrier's novel so impressive is his ability to weave serious political observations—about Quebec, past, present, and future—into a picture of a village in which political, sexual, and religious issues make up life's whole. (The reader is often reminded of Stendhal and Balzac.) One closes the book not with the sadness of having read another account of defeat at the hands of Anglo-Saxon imperialism, but with a feeling of joy in the demonstration of the energies of the defeated, who are so much more human than their English conquistadors. The breadth of Carrier's sympathies, in conjunction with a Kafkaesque economy in narration, signals the advent of a major new novelist. (pp. 114-15)

Robert J. Green, "Québec's Two Enemies," in Journal of Commonwealth Literature *(copyright by Robert J. Green 1972; by permission of Hans Zell (Publishers) Limited), June, 1972, pp. 113-15.*

NANCY I. BAILEY

[A closer look at *La Guerre, Yes Sir!*] suggests that its wide appeal may come less from a regional social realism than from the universal themes around which Carrier builds his fable, themes as true for Europeans and Americans as for Canadians. Carrier dedicates the novel (which he says he has "dreamed") "to those who have perhaps lived it." The vividness of his treatment of the lives of his Quebec villagers during World War II often resembles the grotesque, slightly enlarged scenes of dream and nightmare. But his themes, though mirrored in the concreteness of the French Canadian village, are concerned with the issues of our time: the hatred of war and the impossibility of being isolated from it; the failure of the Church to deal with problems of faith, or morality, and of alienation; the difficulty of relating to other cultures in the global village; and above all, the strange, stimulating presence of death as a means to authentic existence in life itself. These are not trivial themes, nor are they of concern only to French Canadians. (p. 43)

Throughout the novel we are kept aware of the villagers' religion—a popular form of Catholicism, to which the older people cling for comfort. The younger people are more inclined to use its sacred terms—*hostie, calice, tabernacle, crucifice,* etc.—in their blasphemies. The theological implications of prayers for the dead rise to the surface now and then: Corriveau was not bad enough to be burned in hellfire for ever, but he was bad enough to be burned in purgatory for quite a while, and God, who put him in the milder flames for his purification, will take him out sooner if they all keep repeating their garbled, nonsensical prayers. No wonder they need frequent draughts of cider to keep them at it. (p. 44)

The many parallels Carrier establishes between the war and the Church convey his criticism of this the dominant institution of the village. Through images too he links the Church to the life-diminishing forces of the community. The holy water freezes as the priest sprinkles Corriveau's grave. In the warped mind of Henri the Church and death are so

closely associated that Corriveau's coffin becomes the ark into which the whole world enters. The nun with her thin smile and sharp teeth appears like a vulture peering in through the open window from the dark cold winter night on to the mourners, "whose sweat turned to ice on their backs." (pp. 44-5)

The book is founded on a paradox and itself participates in the paradox which it discovers to us, namely, that it is death which teaches us to appreciate life, just as hunger makes us appreciate food, and absence makes the heart grow fonder. Carrier has observed that the villagers are never so enamoured of life as when they are celebrating a wake. He therefore makes his novel the story of a wake. But paradoxically, the book, like the wake, turns out to be a celebration of life. The characters, who may at first sight appear to be a bunch of warped individuals, full of frustrations and inhibitions, turn out, on better acquaintance, to have a healthy love of life—and more common sense than the Church.

The bilingual title of the novel reflects the division between Canadian cultures but also the more essential thematic conflict between the negative force of death and the positive affirmation of life. Through Carrier's mastery of the technique of the modern fable, the war of the title takes on the implications of the war of life itself, with its division between man and woman, man and his God, man and himself, father and son. But the pessimism of the novel does not stem from the recognition that this is a condition of life. The blackness of *La Guerre, Yes Sir!* arises from the inexorable advance of what man seeks most to avoid, namely death, through the very agencies which man has created, Church and State, agencies which he may hate but cannot entirely avoid....

In [the] last novel of Carrier's trilogy, *Is it the sun, Philibert?* there are many echoes of *La Guerre.* Molly, who faded against the snow, reappears in Philibert's nameless love, the English matron who gives him happiness along with food and sex, but whose home disappears as "streets ... stretched out, crossed one another, made knots, formed letters that could only be deciphered from the sky ..." and Philibert feels "the immense hand of the city ... closing up." Now instead of thinking the city should have been called Bonheur, he fears "he would be crushed between these streets that looked so much alike," for "he had no idea where to find the house of the woman who had changed his life." (p. 46)

The echoes make all the more striking the contrasts between the two novels. Gone is the warmth and vitality of the gatherings in *La Guerre,* which mitigated the claustrophobic atmosphere of the Corriveau home and the loneliness of the winter night. The movement of Henri and Arthur from the dark cold attic to the warmth of Amélie's bed while the roast is cooking is much different from Philibert's abortive trip to "Heaven", out of the dark, lightless cellar where he peels potatoes, into the bed in the cellar with Papatakos's wife, guided there by the husband. Philibert returns to his potato job hungry and sad because "when the woman was in his arms he had wept because he felt so little joy." In *Is it the sun, Philibert?* the gatherings in restaurants and fairs, not in homes, celebrate the unnatural. Violence for its own sake motivates the people who pay to assault the Ninth Wonder of the World, the Man with the Face of Steel, who will not hit back. Food, a major metaphor in *La Guerre,* is replaced by hunger in the city-world where in Philibert's room even "the water pipes rumbled like a hungry belly," while his memory of life in the village is like "the fragrance of fresh bread," and Philibert becomes "so drunk that he forgets his whole life." The joyful wake of *La Guerre* becomes the perverted veneration by Philibert's landlord and his wife of the skeleton of their dead child who they insist "lives."

The same themes of life and death unite the novels and their essential difference does not stem from the social realism, the dominance of the English so evident in *Is it the sun, Philibert?* but from the fact that in the society of the latter novel *thanatos* dominates. Death has become a way of life not just for those contaminated as in *La Guerre* by the war or the Church but for all the urban dwellers. Montreal is "like a funeral wreath placed on the ground" and Philibert's instinct for life, inherited from the village, cannot overcome the antagonist in this hostile urban environment. (pp. 46-7)

Philibert never becomes completely corrupted by this world of death, because he still has the desire to love, the *eros* that is man's last defense against *thanatos.* His last thought before his accident is of the woman whose "woman's heart would know that (he) was capable of love." Carrier reinforces this theme by ending the section immediately before the car overturns with the repetition, "Ah! To love . . . to love . . . to love. . . ." . . . But in a world where no one is living no one can love. . . .

In contrast to *La Guerre,* only Philibert fights the encroachment of death in his novel, and only he lives. The rest are automatons. But *thanatos* has triumphed not through inhibitions, poverty and fear that Philibert associates with the village, but through materialism and the technological society.

The daylight settings of the third novel are much darker than the nocturnal ones of the preceeding two. The village world of the past contained all of life including death. The sun that Carrier sees rising over the modern world is that of death, replacing the procreative and life-enhancing though often violent instincts and filling the vacuum left by the disappearance of warmth, kindness and love. Without these instincts there is no healthy struggle against death which then becomes the victor in the war that is life itself. (p. 47)

> *Nancy I. Bailey, "The Corriveau Wake: Carrier's Celebration of Life," in* Journal of Canadian Fiction *(reprinted by permission from* Journal of Canadian Fiction, *2050 Mackay St., Montreal, Quebec H3G 2J1, Canada), Vol. I, No. 3, 1972, pp.43-7.*

KENNETH GIBSON

Roch Carrier's trilogy, of which *Is It the Sun, Philibert?* is the last part and the newest Dark Age, drives on remorselessly from rural Quebec to the civilization of Montreal, where the real heart of darkness lies. The more leisurely tempo of the earlier novels, with their attenuated nights, slow drives, and long meditations between speech, is now abandoned for the newest rhythm. Those repeated images in *La Guerre, Yes Sir!* and *Floralie* are now the mental furniture of young Philibert; they haunt his speech and make him turn his most individual acts into threatening allegories.

With a ferocious irony Carrier thrusts the new world on us as he does on Philibert. The novel has not so much a plot as a conspiracy: if something *can* go wrong, it *will* go wrong. Freedom is death, but only so recognized at the moment of embrace. "A man alone," Philibert groans, "can do nothing." But he has fled the stifling family to be independent; to be alone. He reads a pamphlet that asserts "Life should be beautiful"; one of his employers, Papatakos (who also pimps for his own wife), shouts "Money! Work! That's the life!"; and a mad couple who pray to the "little white skeleton with minuscule bones" of their dead child, force Philibert to pray with them: "To die is to live." He cannot survive with these vicious paradoxes, nor can he abandon them: they mesh too well with his past.

The horror of that past is the true focus of Carrier's trilogy. Yet if nearly everything in these novels turns towards symbol, or allegorical action, nothing is wholly abstract or diffuse. These singular images of, and for, an unseen power, are invariably *human,* and part of a vision of history as a hopeless confusion; a stupid mime acted out in what Wyndham Lewis called "the white pestilence of the Canadian winter." As the books move towards the present the images rotate wildly, until they blur with the speed. In the car-crash that ends *Philibert* a spinning tire seen through eyes smeared with blood becomes the unreachable source of life.

To tally up the figurations of language is to discover a violent and suffocating zodiac. Snow provides the canvas backdrop. In *La Guerre, Yes Sir!* the snow is patched with human blood from a self-inflicted wound; yet by the end it is the civilization of war that has "dirtied the snow." Floralie herself is a kind of paradox, the Sullied Virgin; sledtracks over the snow form an unreadable message or a code; and in the silence of sleep "you should never dream," as Anthyme, Floralie's husband, commands. (pp. 43-4)

The monstrosities of rural Quebec and the garage-stink of Montreal begin to fuse; as civic sprawl and international warfare reach the towns, Philibert runs away to the city. In such a hallowed satirical situation, Carrier does not stop to pot-hunt. Although Philibert's situations are degrading, they are raucously funny, never more so than when he has become the manager of Boris Rataploffsky, "the Ninth Wonder of the World," whose specialty is withstanding, for a fee, the punches of outrage from a frustrated audience. . . .

The split-second of his death is drawn out to seven infernal pages; the slow crumpling and wadding of metal in its agony makes us connect the crash with the image of the Christmas toy car Philibert received when a boy.

In these Dark Ages life is a flimsy permit, usually issued by the *maudits Anglais*; and always nasty, British and short. Quebec awaits either Marat or Edison. Into this rotting cellar called *La Belle Province* Roch Carrier has forced us to stare compulsively; the measure of his art is in a hundred disturbing scenes that the imagination will not dare push aside. *Je me souviens* is threat as well as history. (p. 44)

> *Kenneth Gibson, "Not So Much a Plot As a Conspiracy," in* Saturday Night *(copyright © 1972 by* Saturday Night), *July, 1972, pp. 43-4.*

BRIAN VINTCENT

They Won't Demolish Me! is not only a fantastic farce full of the most extraordinary comic invention. It deals with more than the funny antics of a group of oddballs who seem to be living through a never ending naughty childhood. This comedy is just one of the many levels on which the book moves, and it is a level which is firmly rooted in the serious.

"They" of the title are the developers, of course, the big guys, the capitalists, the faceless bosses who never appear. Ever expanding, "they" are also the City Administration, the English, change, progress, even death and God himself. On the other side, the "me" who resists demolition is Dorval, his house, the little man, the French Canadian, the drones in a heartless society, the irrepressible forces of life which make a man wrestle to maintain himself and the small area of the world he has claimed as his refuge against all comers. At its broadest interpretation, the book pits whatever supports life against whatever embraces death.

In terms of Carrier's own development as a writer, *They Won't Demolish Me!* shows signs of a new maturity. The explosive violence of *La Guerre, Yes Sir!*, the fused world of dreams and reality of *Floralie, Where Are You?*, the exuberant characters and stirring disorder of *Is It the Sun, Philibert?* are all here. And certainly the protests against the "goddamn capitalists" and the "*maudits Anglais*" are no less strong. But for the first time in his work, there is a sense that whatever is wrong is not necessarily someone else's fault. For the first time, his characters find they can laugh at their own absurdities and weaknesses. They still shout their heads off, but that has become their way of saying "we are alive; we are bursting with pain and high spirits." Carrier's characters are coming to terms with themselves. They have entered the adult world.

They Won't Demolish Me! is the book English Canada has been waiting so long to come out of Quebec. The recent literary renaissance in Canada has been nowhere more impressive than in French Canada, but English Canadians, while admiring and applauding the liberating results of the "quiet revolution," have felt unease at the strange world turned up by the *Québécois* digging around in their past. We have not been comfortable with the cruel, repressive mothers, the sombre forests, the nihilists, the murderers and guilt-ridden suicides, the clergy whose public and private lives are at odds with each other. With *They Won't Demolish Me!*, we are offered a book more in line with our own comic tradition stretching from Leacock through such writers as Robertson Davies and W. O. Mitchell to Leo Simpson. These English-Canadian novelists, and Davies in particular, have recently been searching for a more serious base, a deeper meaning on which to build their comedies. The remarkable achievement of *They Won't Demolish Me!* is that Carrier has found that elusive key which can bind high farce and high seriousness together in a solid, convincing unity.

> Brian Vintcent, "The Innocent Guerillas of Roch Carrier," in Saturday Night (copyright © 1974), August, 1974, p. 31.

EMILE J. TALBOT

The point of view in Roch Carrier's brilliant sixth novel [*Il n'y a pas de pays sans grand-père*] is that of Vieux-Thomas, once a vigorous man, now in his seventies and restricted to a rocking chair by his own family. Refused all freedom in his own house, he is left to musing about his past. However poignant Vieux-Thomas's situation may be, it soon be-

comes clear that this is not only a perceptive novel about the pain of old age, but that it carries a powerful political message as well. For the rocking chair which Vieux-Thomas has built himself and on which he has carved fleurs-de-lis is, by its back-and-forth movement which never goes anywhere, clearly emblematic of Québec, just as Vieux-Thomas's situation is not without analogy to that of the Québécois people, who do not consider themselves free in the very land which they have built. (p. 249)

There is no sentimentality or heavy-handedness in this truly moving narrative, but Carrier's discreet sympathy for Vieux-Thomas ennobles this aging man, who in a surge of generosity commits the last free act of his life. (p. 250)

> Emile J. Talbot, in World Literature Today (copyright 1978 by the University of Oklahoma Press), Vol. 52, No. 2, Spring, 1978.

*   *   *

CELA, Camilo José   1916-

A novelist, poet, playwright, and travel writer, Cela is considered the most important voice in Spanish letters since the Civil War. His work ranges from the psychological to the surreal, often mirroring the tragedy his country has experienced with harsh realism and violence. Cela's prose style is experimental, frequently employing elements of fragmentation, repetition, and interior monologue within a shifting narrative perspective. It is a complex prose, praised for its powerful characterization and effective dialogue. *The Family of Pascual Duarte* is Cela's best known work. (See also CLC, Vol. 4, and *Contemporary Authors*, Vols. 21-24, rev. ed.)

SAUL BELLOW

It is not to be wondered that the Franco censorship disapproves of Cela's novels. Life in Madrid as he portrays it is brutal, hungry and senseless. Hypocrisy, fear and oppression are in command. Cela's political loyalties may be conservative or reactionary but his literary affiliations are of the most radical; they are with Camus and Sartre, with Moravia, with Zola and French naturalism. Only Cela has very little of the theoretician about him and has no existential, sexual or political message to deliver. It is in his directness and lack of squeamishness that he resembles Sartre and Moravia. . . .

Cela does not ramble so much as he jumps. Now we are with the powerful Dona Rosa, who tyrannizes over her waiters and customers; now with a cafe musician; now with a mediocre nonconformist poet; then with a tender-hearted money lender; then with the bookkeeper of a black-marketeer; with old maids and prostitutes, with singers and seducers. . . . All of this is rather abruptly and sketchily represented, it is forceful and it is bald.

One sympathizes with Cela in his impatience with literature. Probably he is attacking his conformist contemporaries within Spain. But there is a great deal to be said for his attitude. Literature is conservative; it is "behind the times," and it does not easily cope with certain familiar modern horrors. One asks one's self how Goethe would have described a concentration camp, or how Lope de Vega would have dignified a black-marketeer. Journalists and writers of memoirs rather than imaginative writers have told us most of what we know of these and other phenomena of contemporary life. Apparently, however, these reporters do not satisfy the highest demands of the imagination. Attacking literature and writing novels, the talented Señor Cela puts himself into a rather paradoxical position.

*Saul Bellow, "The Evil That Has Many Names,"
in* The New York Times Book Review *(© 1953 by
The New York Times Company; reprinted by permission), September 27, 1953, p. 5.*

MAXWELL GEISMAR

Camilo José Cela, whose new book, "The Hive," is one of the first important literary documents to reach us from inside the fascist state, is suffused with anger and bitterness at society in Madrid. "They lie," he says, "who want to disguise life with the crazy mask of literature. The evil that corrodes the soul, the evil that has as many names as we choose to give it, cannot be fought with poultices of conformism or the plasters of rhetorics and poetics. My novel sets out to be no more—yet no less either—than a slice of life, told step by step, without reticences, without external tragedies, without charity, exactly as life itself rambles on."

Wonderful words—which we have not often heard in this country since the first generation of native realists in the 1900's. It is interesting, too, that our own intellectual return to realism . . . is such a delayed sequel to the new generation of European novelists who have had to face the historical crisis directly and intimately. And "The Hive" itself, as a study of impoverished, frustrated lower-middle-class city people—less vicious, really, than ignoble and less ignoble maybe than starved—has undoubted power and a deliberately flat, acrid, angry style.

Cela's true position, however, is that of the aristocratic moralist who scourges the values of a corrupt and decaying urban society; the moments of warmth and affection in his narrative are few. (p. 404)

Maxwell Geismar, in The Nation *(copyright 1953
The Nation Associates), November 14, 1953.*

GEORGE WOODCOCK

Among the native novels [to emerge from Spain since the Civil War] the most significant, both in terms of their perception of contemporary Spanish life and also in sheer literary quality, have been José Cela's—*Pascual Duarte's Family,* his recently published *The Hive,* and a little volume of travel sketches in rural Spain, *Viaje a la Alcarria.* . . .

The first thing that strikes one on reading one of these recent Spanish novels is the chasm of feeling that separates them from that literary renaissance of the twenties and thirties which graced European literature with the works of Unamuno and Ortega y Gasset, of Galdos and Barojo and Sender, of Lorca and Machado. . . . [While] the writers now emerging have not forgotten this departed generation, they themselves are working in an atmosphere which is inevitably dominated and changed by the Civil War and its social aftermath.

One thing unites them with their predecessors. It is what Barea (a survivor in spirit from the pre-Civil-War Spain) has called "the note of hunger." . . . Where the moderns differ is in the scope they give to this "note of hunger." For them it is no longer a mere hunger of the body; it is rather a starvation of the spirit such as has never before appeared as a dominant factor in Spanish writing. . . .

In *The Hive* Cela deliberately presents the inconsequential moments of his hundred and sixty characters in a disjointed and episodic manner which emphasizes the atomization of city living, the breakup of a cohesive pattern of society and social feeling. His people are tragic not because they are poor, but because they have no longer the resources that in the past made poverty something a man could bear with dignity. (p. 16)

In Cela's work the contrast is clear, between the serenity he sees in the country people described in *Viaje a la Alcarria,* who can endure poverty and humiliation because of a view of life that makes these things less important than a man's sense of his own worth, and the rootless, shiftless people of *The Hive,* dissolving as individuals and as a social group in the great impersonal flux of urban living. (p. 17)

George Woodcock, in The New Republic *(reprinted by permission of* The New Republic; ©
1954 by The New Republic, Inc.), July 12, 1954.*

EMILE CAPOUYA

Spain has been forcibly exporting talented elements of its population for a millennium; the expulsion of the Arabs, then of the Jews, and in our own time of the artists and scholars opposed to fascism, represent only the most notorious examples of the endless attempt to purify the nation of its intellectual and moral vitality. And this historical observation is relevant in two ways to our appreciating *The Family of Pascual Duarte.* First, it helps to explain the fact that in post-Christian Western Europe, Spain is a stronghold of pre-Christian attitudes and values. Secondly, it provides the immediate context for the desperate apathy and desperate violence that are the substance of Cela's novel. . . .

Pascual Duarte speaks of suffering and ferocity so appalling as to be almost beyond the reach of our sympathy. They stun even more than they horrify—and that, incidentally, is the ground for differing with the common judgment that Camilo José Cela's novel is a literary classic. Powerful it is without a doubt. Archetypically portentous it seems to be, but what meaning can be attached to Pascual Duarte's mindless violence and mindless repentance eludes our power of conception. . . . As children of the Enlightenment, we are quite firm about wanting to change the conditions that produce a Pascual Duarte. But there is that in him that suggests a condition anterior to all "conditions," and evokes in us a superstitious terror that the humanization of man may be unrealizable.

*Emile Capouya, "To Die and Never Know Why,"
in* Saturday Review *(© 1964 by Saturday Review,
Inc.; reprinted with permission), November 23,
1964, p. 38.*

ANTHONY KERRIGAN

In his poetry—and Cela's overall intuition, and his conditioned use of language, too, is that of a poet—Cela expresses, even more directly, his "nothingism" (and sometimes his "uglyism" as well). His principal contribution to poetry, though [*The Family of Pascual Duarte*] is written in prose, is a work with the hybrid title *Mrs. Caldwell habla con su hijo.* In this book, the author sings the infinitude of hallucinations and fancies in the mind of an incestuous mother conversing wistfully with her dead son, drowned at sea in an ocean of memories and symbols. Certainly the book is one of the more remarkable poetic documents of modern Spain. (p. xii)

[Camilo José Cela] has created a world filled with the swooning of wills, wills kowtowing to a nearly mystic nothingness at the heart of the self. His characters never go towards their destiny through the social complex, via the paths of society at all, let alone the Body of Christ or the Church. They may writhe and struggle, but they always submit to themselves in the end. They may do so outside the law, like Pascual Duarte, or alienated from sanity, like Mrs. Caldwell, or beyond morality, like his wild-Western heroine La Catira, but neither do they struggle against themselves, nor do they strive towards anything beyond themselves. They are content to accept the full measure of their selfness. In Baroja this tendency to be true to one's nature was a vindication of extreme individuality, of man against society and other men, and not merely of an instinctive egotism. In Cela, it is an almost mystical belief in the rightness of unpremeditation. (pp. xiv-xv)

Cela's nihilism is not Yeats's; there is no News for the Delphic Oracle; no Caesar in his tent "That civilization may not sink," though his own "mind moves upon silence"; no comment on the fact that now "The best lack all conviction, while the worst / Are full of passionate intensity." In Cela, religious sentiment flags in the middle of a local pilgrimage because the children get rosin on their behinds and the old lady hoards all the Vichy water for herself on a hot day . . . ; marriage is slightly ridiculous, and even the sacrament is absurd, not because of disbelief—but because the bride's shoes pinch. . . . There is no Second Coming, either, foiled or frustrated, even. Only the *pícaro*'s everlasting war, more potent and deadly than the class war, for an individual can be more venomous than an army, and more tireless. Cela's Pascual Duarte is the most murderous *pícaro* in all of the picaresque in Spain, the continuing picaresque of Spain. (p. xv)

The Family of Pascual Duarte is a study in the psychology of fear, of the aggressiveness of fear. More fully: the aggressiveness of fear and timidity, and of guilt about both. Pascual is a toilless obsessive, albeit more sympathetic than most of his victims. His story is the history of a field worker to all intents withdrawn (the better to pursue his passions?) from orchard or field, from stream or woods. He smells no seasons' smells (but only carrion, a stream stinking like a troop of gypsies, and his own pants, the crotch thereof), sees no flora (the white sight of Lola's leg above the knee is the most memorable visual flash in the book), and hears—only the owl, the sound of a symbol. (pp. xvi-xvii)

All this is stark, as devoid of humanity as a rock, when it is not stage property, telling and appropriate as it may be. The strength of the work is in the bare-boned action of an annihilated will, or a will-to-annihilation. There is a master horror in the mother who had given suck biting off the useless male nipple of the son she had suckled, a son given over to the persuasion that a mother is for killing. There is a disturbing pathos in the deadened country when a hunting dog is meaninglessly killed in the throes of a killer's autonomic fixation, in the spasm of this fixation. And there is an epical violence, telluric and terrible, when a horse is killed for love-revenge, and the taste of bitter and senseless irony when the wife's betrayer is killed almost by mistake. There is enough, in short, to make *Pascual Duarte* a superior

modern novel in (to borrow a term from painting) the "figurative" tradition.

Camilo José Cela is undoubtedly the finest writer of fiction in post-Civil War Spain. Specifically, he is doubtless the finest writer of fiction remaining in Spain. Such distinction is sufficient without needlessly comparing him with the great Spaniards of the Spanish Exodus, the gifted Spaniards in exile, who remain Spanish with astonishing and single-minded intensity but whose existential world is totally different from Cela's.

All distinctions of existential worlds and place of residence aside, Cela is certainly the writer of the most redolent Spanish today: redolent of sounding, breathing spoken Spanish.

Cela's Spain, the Spain which begins as an epoch at the beginning of the Civil War, with the disruption of tradition by the two contending sides, is not eternal Spain. Cela's Spain is not legendary. And Cela's Spain is not traditionalist. But Cela's prose—whatever his anti-heroics and anti-legend—even his highly poetical later prose, is in the vein of the vernacular, the spoken speech of legendary and traditional Spain written down. However baroque the flourishes, the sound is as fresh as country speech. And it is always as rotund as the language of a Salamanca countryman, a Madrid city man, or, in short, of a Castilian gentleman-pauper with the gold toothpick in his pocket. His is the language of both Don Quixote and Sancho Panza. Most fortunately, its inventiveness is only as "baroque" as Sancho's, as he muddles old proverbs, and only as "sparse" as Quixote's, as the knight outlines his grandiose (truly baroque) aims. (pp. xvii-xviii)

Like Baroja and Solana—or all of Spain geographically—his center is Madrid. And he—and they—were propelled there by the peculiar centripetal force characteristic of Spain. . . . Camilo José Cela, the public scribe for the anti-hero from Castile, for the anti-*conquistador* from Extremadura on the Portuguese border, and for the Aragonese anti-saint, is at the very center of Spanish literary tradition. (p. xix)

Anthony Kerrigan, "Introduction" (introduction copyright © 1964 by Anthony Kerrigan; reprinted by permission of Little, Brown and Co. in association with The Atlantic Monthly Press), in The Family of Pascual Duarte, by Camilo José Cela, translated by Anthony Kerrigan, Atlantic-Little, Brown and Company, 1964, pp. vii-xx.

PAUL WEST

If we add Unamuno's concern for the Nietzschean, the violent, even the demonic, to Baroja's rejection of systematic assembly, we have something close to the essence of Camilo José Cela. . . . Cela prefers the weird, the apparently meaningless and the amorphous. The world of his novels has been likened to that of Hieronimus Bosch and Brueghel; he sees man as a prisoner in a forbidding universe where chaos and imperfection always defeat the idealist. His first novel, *La familia de Pascual Duarte* (1942), exemplifies his objective technique: Pascual Duarte, epitome of the unlucky and the lowly, tells his story from the prison cell to which he has been condemned. One thing follows another; there is no distinction made according to quality. In fact the evaluating mind is quite absent—a technique that we find in the rather more outlandish novels of Robbe-Grillet. Pascual is a kind of camera: no intentions, no prophecies, no hopes. He takes things as they come in much the same way as the traditional picaro of the Spanish novel always did. Just as the main characters of *La Vida de Lazarillo de Tormes* and *Gil Blas* allowed the current of life to take them where it would, so does the typical Cela character embody the qualities of the anti-hero, the man who just cannot be bothered to persist in the chase after any chimerical Good. (pp. 419-20)

Cela's second novel, *La colmena,* was published in Buenos Aires in 1952. Again the account of life, this time of proliferating Madrid, is amorphous, nihilistic and distorted. The dialogues are squalid exchanges between persons of whom the novelist has no expressed opinion. The novel reads like the fragmentation and recombination of several Zola documents: the scenes follow one another in meaningless succession. It is bitter honey that he crams into the combs. There is nothing here of Galdós's symmetrical, coherent, patiently expository image: instead the method is cinematic: it flickers, falters and bewilders. The whole kaleidoscope is based on one day in Madrid in 1943. There are plots but they are so intricately interwoven as to remind one of Dos Passos. There is no hero; rather, the intricacy and 'swarmingness' of life are shown to preclude heroism of any kind. But if there is no hero, there are at least objects of respect: the white-collar and manual classes, slaving away to no purpose beyond surviving to slave again tomorrow. This is a vision of disintegration, chastening to read and obviously indebted to the example of Baroja.

Cela's own view appears in the prologue to *Viaje a la Alcarria* (1948). He explains that he will deny himself the role of 'being meddlesome and so risking a setback for drawing conclusions philosophical, political or moral'. But his opinion of modern life is eloquent in every capricious transition. He not only takes considerable trouble with his style; he weights it heavily with popular idiom. Cela is the 'tramp' who wanders about, recording with a hard and experienced eye the landscape and other travellers in Alcarria, only about forty miles from Madrid. The absence of meditation and discussion is occasionally frustrating; it is just as tedious to read a brilliant catalogue as to wade through lengthy disquisitions that hold up the action. The main thing in this novel, however, is the traveller's frame of mind: not daring an opinion; noting the external world like a man who needs to cling to it in order to preserve a sense of his own reality. Cela is a prolific novelist. With over a score of books to his name he still pursues the bizarre and the sordid grotesque, almost as if he thinks that a heightening of the everyday will amount to an opinion expressed. It does, provided we can attune ourselves to his stylish garbling of an already garbled society. Cela is the Goya of Franco's Spain. (pp. 420-21)

> *Paul West, in his* The Modern Novel, Volume 2: The United States and Other Countries *(copyright © Paul West 1963), Hutchinson & Co. Ltd., 1965.*

JOAN CAIN

Readers familiar with *La familia de Pascual Duarte* and *La colmena* will find little in [*Oficia de tinieblas 5*] reminiscent of those works. There are no defined characters, no action, no plot development. Cela himself admits that this is not a novel; it serves more as a vehicle for expressing many ideas.

The book contains 1,194 monads, or philosophical units, three of which refer specifically to the tenebrae service of the title, a ritual which terminates at the work's conclusion. Monad 1,097 informs the reader that it is a rite from which no man can escape; in it, magic serves evil in a struggle against man.

The book contains no chapter divisions; each monad consists of a series of words without capital letters or punctuation. There is much repetition of word and thought, and often there is reference to another monad by specific number.

Cela alludes to some of our most pressing contemporary concerns: drugs, abortion, Vietnam, technology, homosexuality. In addition, he treats such themes as love, death and religion. His preoccupation with sex seems excessive; even the book's cover portrays this inordinate concern. It is one which seems incongruous when one considers the book's title plus a note at the very end stating that it was written between All Souls' Day, 1971 and Holy Week, 1973.

The variety of philosophical, historical and literary allusions is striking. Quotations are given, not only in Spanish, but in several other languages. The reader will be challenged to ask himself what the work means. He should also ask himself whether it is of value in itself or merely as part of a comparative study of its well-known author's works. (p. 92)

> *Joan Cain, in* Books Abroad *(copyright 1975 by the University of Oklahoma Press), Vol. 49, No. 1, Winter, 1975.*

FRANCIS DONAHUE

The social realist cast of the novel in the Gray Age [of Spanish Literature] was set in 1942 by twenty-six-year-old Camilo José Cela who, in his *La Familia de Pascual Duarte* ("The Family of Pascual Duarte"), produced Spain's first major novel of the postwar period. This novel is the supposed autobiography of a criminal awaiting execution. Crowding its pages are violence, cruelty, murder, even matricide, as the protagonist seems driven to act because of the influence of a harsh environment and his own violent nature. An account of man in his tragic human situation, *La Familia de Pascual Duarte* employs a vernacular prose and elicits from the reader not sympathy but a compassionate understanding.

This novel recalls the picaresque tradition in Spanish letters; once again an antihero points up obliquely the social sores of a flawed society. There is, too, a typically Spanish fondness for deformation of reality and for the monstrous, inasmuch as Cela, with his penchant for sardonic humor, bizarrely lights up the grotesque unreality of his sufferingly real characters. With his novel, Cela gave rise to a peculiarly Spanish version of social realism known as *Tremendismo,* a term used by one critic to describe the effect caused by Cela's work. *Tremendismo* pairs emphatic realism with literary techniques drawn from James Joyce, Marcel Proust, and John Dos Passos, and with a philosophical orientation vaguely related to existentialism.

In his second major novel, *La Colmena* ("The Hive," 1951), Cela moves to the mainstream of social realism, charting the misdirected lives of more than 160 characters as they move in and out of Doña Rosa's sleazy Madrid café. Procurers, waiters, prostitutes, homosexuals, mental defectives—all appear briefly, and are gone. There is no sequential plot, there are no heroes or heroines, but there is hunger, sex, alienation, all adding up to a depressing portrait of post-Civil War Madrid. Cela himself termed his novel "a pale reflection of the harsh, intimate, painful reality of everyday life . . . a slice of life told step by step, without reticence, without external tragedies, without charity, exactly as life itself rambles on." (pp. 408-09)

Francis Donahue, in Southwest Review *(© 1978 by Southern Methodist University Press), Autumn, 1978.*

* * *

CLARKE, Arthur C(harles) 1917-

An English science fiction novelist, short story writer, screenplay writer, and astronomer, Clarke is best known for his novel *Childhood's End* and for his screenplay for Stanley Kubrick's *2001: A Space Odyssey*. (See also *CLC*, Vols. 1, 4, and *Contemporary Authors*, Vols. 1-4, rev. ed.)

PETER BRIGG

Arthur C. Clarke's extensive *corpus* of science fiction writing is an expression of his varied interests in the limits of man's knowledge as it is approached through the scientific method. Three principal types of work can be traced in his writing. . . .

Clarke's best known approach is precise scientific extrapolation that depends upon detailed scientific knowledge carefully explained to the reader to communicate Clarke's fascination with the possibilities at the frontiers of scientific thinking. (p. 15)

Within [his] carefully chosen, clear, straightforward plots Clarke holds character development to an absolute minimum, employing melodramatic types to focus attention on the ideas. A number of the short stories have heroes whose principal emotion is sheer fear for their lives that can only be relieved by the scientific point upon which the story is premised. (pp. 17-18)

One of Clarke's most striking hard extrapolations is "A Meeting with Medusa" (1962), and here the intense concentration on Howard Falcon . . . could have provided a detailed characterization. But Clarke is concentrating upon the creations of technology and speculating on the possible life forms of Jupiter. . . . The starting point is the events of the story, the end point is character and motivation. This approach is the reverse of modern literary custom, but it is admirably suited to the hard extrapolations in which it is employed.

The concrete projections in this type of story are set forth in matter-of-fact narrative tone, and Clarke writes briskly in stories of this type, producing either very short stories or novels covering enormous amounts of material very quickly. (p. 19)

Verbal action moves as quickly as physical action in this type of factual story. . . . Clarke usually frames segments of dialogue so that the reader knows their importance and the feelings of the speakers. This makes for a quick, methodical dialogue without verbal frills or subtleties. (pp. 20-1)

In dialogue as in plot, characterization, and narrative tone, Clarke is moving quickly and efficiently to build the bones upon which the real flesh of the hard extrapolation can rest: the scientific explanation of the story and the vivid and haunting descriptions of strange futures and places.

The stratagems used to explain the scientific content of these stories involve variations in narrative voice. Clarke has tried a variety of methods, seeking to combine narrative ease with a clear statement of scientific premise. One direct form has a narrator who reasons out the story as it progresses, mixing narrative with explanation. . . . [Clarke's] tight mixture of narrative and explanation is most effective. It is modeled not only on detective fiction, with its sudden assembly of information into a complete picture, but on the scientific experiment, where an event is viewed and then explained in retrospect. (pp. 21-2)

The dominant way of presenting this type of story has always been the team of questioning listener and scientifically competent explainer. In its early form this type of narrative began with "Tell me, Professor" but of course Clarke works sophisticated variations on this. The reader is put at ease when the question he wants to ask is asked by the "straight man" and answered in terms of the events of the narrative. . . . This very practical form of exposition is extremely spare, for the characters are mouthpieces from a familiar mold.

Another easy and natural format for the hard extrapolations is the omniscient narrator who can tell the story and explain the scientific events at the same time. (p. 23)

On several occasions Clarke has gone beyond the omniscient narrator to speak as Arthur C. Clarke. This applies to the comic stories of *Tales from the 'White Hart'* but he stays very much in the background in these, making Harry Purvis the storyteller. However, in "I Remember Babylon" (1960) Clarke himself tells of an encounter in Ceylon [and creates a story that is strikingly solid and realistic]. . . . In many ways this story is representative of Clarke's direct approach to hard science materials, for he weaves together a number of known and practical scientific propositions in a brisk, efficient way. As in "Venture to the Moon" and "The Other Side of the Sky" sequences, he is examining the potentials of immediate science. The hard science stories depend for their excitement upon the efficiency with which precise scientific reasoning can be embodied and explained in narrative format and Clarke uses the full variety of means at his disposal.

The uncomplicated narratives of these stories are punctuated by some of the most positive "purple passages" in all of science fiction. Arthur Clarke's true sense of wonder is most vividly expressed in lyrical descriptions of the cosmos and man's present or future achievements. In story after story he draws from an imagination carefully tempered by scientific knowledge to create sweeping physical descriptions of the marvels of nature and of man. The descriptions of Saturn in "Saturn Rising" (1961), the pulsing coded hues of the squid in "The Shining Ones" (1962) . . . , and the images of the mighty being in "Out of the Sun" (1958) are all unforgettable moments in Clarke's writing. (pp. 24-5)

In his stories which are projections of hard science, whether presently proven or speculation based upon the limits of our knowledge Clarke works sharply and clearly, stating the bases of his speculations, explaining, reasoning and describing with energy. If there are weaknesses in this "first style of Clarke" they are inherent in the limited aims of such stories. This leads to mechanical plotting, a generally factual narration, and a lack of depth in characterization, but these traits reflect the style of the pulp magazines in which these stories were originally published, and the need to get on with the real excitement of the universe and man's ability to conquer it by bringing reason to bear in understanding its wonders. If these are weaknesses they are overridden by the skill with which the stories make scientific processes and man's observation of the cosmos an exciting adventure.

A second style of Clarke's work is the comic mode, stories that may contain and even conceal hard scientific ideas. Comedy in science fiction is best when rooted in the plot, executing an idea based on a quirk in scientific knowledge or illustrating a tiny fantasy suggested by some scientific fact. It works best in the short story where the idea does not have to be sustained, and it may work even better as an extended joke. As befits comic creations, the characters in these stories and anecdotes are often stereotypes of professions such as scientist, bureaucrat, militarist, or alien. Many of the stories have twist endings and Clarke takes particular pleasure in playing the conjurer who prepares a surprise and springs it upon the unsuspecting reader. Clarke's comic stories are colored by the British tone of his humor, featuring understatement, irony, and wit. This comedy is delicate and when these stories work they are fine, but they can also be dismal, flat failures if they do not hit their comic mark.

The plots of the extrapolations are "closed" in that they prove a point or illustrate a concept. The plots of comic writing are "closed" because they finish a joke or resolve the comic situation they have created. As comedy depends upon surprise there are often sudden reversals or changes of perspective at the finish. The suddenness is comic and may also be thought-provoking. . . . (p. 27)

The efficient plots of the comic stories serve to do several things. As with the hard science stories, they may expound a scientific concept, but they add a wry and comic angle. They may parody scientific logic and solutions. Some of the stories are logically impossible, and Clarke will often admit this and go on to tell them with humor and such a veneer of logic that the reader will be inclined to distrust the disclaimer. *Tales From the 'White Hart'* contains stories that serve as examples of both approaches. (p. 29)

Clarke can use science in the comic stories either to reveal scientific curiosities or to create a logical tone to conceal and explain fantastic flights of the imagination.

The characters in Clarke's comic stories, and who often put in brief appearances in some of his other work, are frequently comic stereotypes of professions or positions. Clarke is particularly good at describing scientists and the military, perhaps because he has had practical experience in both areas. But he is equally capable of picturing comic bureaucrats, aliens, or exceptional characters such as Buddhist monks or spinster aunts. The characters are often victims whom the reader wishes to see victimized or the meek who emerge victorious by guile or scientific trickery. (p. 31)

The general tone of the comic stories owes a great deal to the traditions of British humor. Clarke has much in common with the dry, ironic wit and techniques of understatement frequently associated with P. G. Wodehouse, Evelyn Waugh, and some of the writing of Aldous Huxley. His wit is low-keyed and is especially effective because it allows the reader to share with him the thought that none of this amazing stuff need be taken wholly seriously. (p. 32)

The strength of Clarke's comic writing is best seen when he combines a good scientific idea with effective caricature and his dry style to lead to a shockingly funny reversal. The best stories have simple comic plots involving jealousy and love, struggles for property and the dangers of curiosity, with the additional amusement of the puzzles presented by science and by human failures to take full account of physical reality. Often the characters in these stories become victims of their own Machiavellianism. Clarke is wryly cynical about human behavior, seeing it in the larger perspective of the universe at large.

Although Clarke has written a number of highly successful comic stories his efforts can fall flat if they do not hit just the right edge of wit. (pp. 33-4)

[At times] Clarke seems to be *striving* to be funny and these obvious efforts are awkward and uncertain.

However, Clarke's best comic stories are very successful indeed, blending the quirks of science and the quirks of human behavior with surprise twists. Comedy injects energy into tales with strict scientific antecedents and Clarke has developed it as a delightful adjunct to fantastic speculations. (p. 34)

[Many of Clarke's works] attempt to go beyond the limits of the hard extrapolations and the humorous entertainments. It is a serious mistake to think of Clarke as a writer whose imagination is bounded by the known, a scientist of the old school who is deeply reluctant to consider anything but emphatically proven data. . . . [There] is no doubt that he seeks to go beyond "known" and more "practical" extrapolations to metaphysics. His writings in this third style reflect a dissatisfaction with the concrete and a longing for the unknown. It is in these free and experimental works that Clarke moves his readers most effectively; yet it is here the limitations of his abilities as a writer are most glaringly obvious, for he is attempting to describe universes and creatures at the outer limits of the imagination.

Clarke's experiments with the unknown speculate in diverse directions and unlike the hard extrapolations and comic stories they end in suggestions of further expansion in many directions. A number of stories put man's evolution in perspective, placing human history as a tiny fragment of the past of the universe and suggesting what lies ahead. (p. 35)

The general direction of Clarke's metaphysical speculations owes a good deal to the work of Olaf Stapledon whose sprawling predictive prose fictions *Last and First Men* (1930) and *Star Maker* (1937) have a sweep unmatched in science fiction. . . .

Clarke echoes Stapledon's optimism toward man's expanding abilities to comprehend the wonder of the cosmos, but he also reflects the pessimism implicit in *Star Maker*. This is particularly fascinating in light of the optimism in short-run projections in Clarke's fiction. (p. 36)

The characteristics of Clarke's metaphysical speculations are dominated by this aspect of open-ended plotting. Whereas his other stories are symmetrical, offering solutions and conclusions to the experiment or comic situation they propose, the mystical stories provide opening terms of infinite series. (p. 37)

Clarke's clear, methodical style, perfected in the hard extrapolations, would not seem to be the natural vehicle for metaphysics, usually the region of mystical and symbolic writing. But on the whole the reverse seems the case, for Clarke's level-headed narrators communicate the sense of wonder that is felt when one travels far beyond the known, and Clarke's own quiet, factual voice as an omniscient narrator is equally effective. (p. 38)

All of the stories that end with a reach toward the unknown begin in the mundane. People bustle about preparing space shots; briefings take place; a conference is held on the Moon to discuss a mysterious artifact; or a young man dares to visit an ancient city to prove his love. The stories move outward while the calm tone keeps the sense of concrete reality. . . . It is not the unbelievable that Clarke specializes in. It is the "un-thought of," presented to expand the reader's range of possibilities. (p. 39)

Clarke's metaphysical stories are not parables or symbolic in nature, then, but attempts to carry the powers of physical description out to the indefinable. Like Stapledon, Clarke seeks to communicate a sense of the vastness of the cosmos and its possibilities through stories that move outward from a core to ever-enlarging perspectives. And it is precisely at the boundaries of this exploration that Clarke, like Stapledon, fails to consistently exhibit the imaginative powers necessary to carry the reader with him. (p. 40)

The thrust of most of Clarke's mystical fiction is sentimental in its optimistic view of human destiny. Although he is only charting possibilities Clarke consistently hints that the universe will be man's and that man, coming to grips with the physical universe through science, will emerge the final victor. . . . Yet there is a curious wavering in this confidence when Clarke catches, perhaps from Stapledon, the sense of the awesome objectivity of the cosmos, the lack of evidence in the stars for anything approaching a benign being. Clarke dismisses conventional religion as superstition on numerous occasions. . . . [He] seems to want a belief that is adequate for the scope of the universe, but that belief in turn is one in which human existence is infinitesimal. It is the crux of the dilemma that Clarke is both hazy in his writing and appealing, for he captures in a naive fashion that sense of distant things that has always haunted men who looked at the stars, and he does so in the context of the modern scientist and space adventurer. This enigmatic sentimentalism may deter the trained metaphysician, but it is the stuff of appealing fiction. . . . (pp. 40-1)

Although Arthur C. Clarke's work can be divided into three principal styles most of his stories and novels contain combinations of hard extrapolation, humorous vignettes, and some gesture in the direction of metaphysical possibilities. In his two recent novels, *Rendezvous with Rama* (1973) and *Imperial Earth* (1976), Clarke has achieved varying blends of these elements worth careful consideration, particularly to test arguments that he is an "old-fashioned" writer, uncomfortably bound to a corpus of work stretching from 1937 to the present. Clarke's most old-fashioned position is his commitment to telling a good story in an accurately conceived and described universe, traits that seem to this writer to be aspects of most good and enduring literature.

Rendezvous with Rama is the latest of Clarke's works in which hard science plays the dominant role. . . . It is built upon ideas that Clarke has toyed with in earlier works, but its synthesis is a distinctive distillation of the author's writing experience. (pp. 41-2)

In *Rendezvous with Rama* Clarke has achieved a most successful synthesis of the styles in which he characteristically works. The hard extrapolative element is immaculately detailed in a series of practical mysteries that are solved by experiment, investigation, and revelation in dramatic events. Rama is a tangible object to the reader of the story. One does not come away questioning its existence but rather questioning the unanswered final mysteries of its purpose and the destiny of its makers. There can be no greater proof of Clarke's ability to produce rational scientific extrapolation than the mass of carefully assembled factual detail that makes *Rama* real to the reader. At the same time the comic elements in Clarke's writing fit nicely into the work because they provide a human scale, like the figure of a man placed in the foreground of engineering drawings. In this context almost no comic note could be out of place. So despite tiny man striving in the foreground to explain its individual functioning areas, Rama as a whole cannot be understood. . . . It is like a mighty and carefully prepared stage set, and Clarke's judgment in withholding the principal actors means that the suspense will be maintained in future acts of the cosmic drama. This concrete evocation of the mystery of the universe is Clarke's finest blending of the elements of his fiction.

Imperial Earth is a different sort of endeavour on Clarke's part, and its component parts do not cohere as effectively as those of *Rendezvous with Rama*. Yet it contains strong elements of the best of Clarke's writing and a vigor of plotting that carries the reader over uncertain sections and makes the novel as a whole a qualified success. In contrast to the unity gained by absolute concentration on a single object in *Rendezvous with Rama*, *Imperial Earth* draws most of its strength from the sheer variety of topics and ideas that it touches upon and attempts to integrate. (pp. 44-5)

Clarke has always been master of expert touches such as toilet design or the method of walking in free fall in *2001*. In *Imperial Earth* he provides a great variety of adaptive trivia for Duncan when the latter lands on Earth. These details make the reading of the hard extrapolations like eating an unknown candy full of unexpected little delights. In this case he achieves this effect in a special new fashion, for the surprises are things that we already live with but which catch Duncan unawares. . . . These bits of information about the trivial problems of living in strange environments have always been one of Clarke's assets in creating lifelike, logical worlds. Their inevitable cumulative effect is heightened in *Imperial Earth* by the reader's immediate knowledge of the earthly context of the small problems and sudden shocks. (p. 47)

If the hard extrapolation of *Imperial Earth* is not so immediately impressive as that of *Rendezvous with Rama*, that is because it lacks the obvious coherence of the latter. Yet Clarke has created as effectively and perhaps in more detail in the later book, allowing his fascination with the logical extrapolation and the natural world to range from the depths of the sea to Titan and the Star Beasts who may lurk outside of the solar system.

The lighter elements of *Imperial Earth* are archetypical Clarke, combining some suitable wit and amusing observation with moments when undergraduate British humor mars the telling of the tale. (p. 48)

There can only be a reserved judgment on the mystical, open-ended aspect of *Imperial Earth* because on the one hand it appears to be tacked on to the novel without adequate preparation while careful examination of the book suggests that it was planned and that Clarke has created a substructure for the novel to justify its inclusion. (p. 49)

In partial defense of the way in which the mystical elements are incorporated in *Imperial Earth,* one can determine what appears to be Clarke's attempt to integrate many of the events in the book to give it cohesion. . . . [For example, all] of the images in the book are tied together in the Titanite cross that combines the mystery of hexagonal crystals with the puzzle of the pentominoes that links Duncan and Karl and which stands for the complex possible solutions to human dilemmas. . . .

Yet the links are not entirely adequate, because they are usually submerged beneath the surface of a picaresque novel wandering from place to place and idea to idea. In the judgment of this writer *Imperial Earth* is a successful Clarke novel because of its variety and sharply perceived and detailed extrapolation. Its weaknesses are the lack of a structure adequately articulated to hold it together and Clarke's characteristic insertions of humor and the metaphysical in slightly uneasy fashion. (p. 50)

[In conclusion, then, the] styles in which Clarke has worked are distinctive and have different purposes. They are not always comfortably integrated in the same story; when they are, it is in situations such as *Rendezvous with Rama* where the hard extrapolation has natural mystical implications without any need to pin them on from the outside and where humor serves to fit man into his tiny niche in the universal scheme. Clarke is perfectly capable of the variety of styles that have been suggested, but closest to his heart and, more importantly, to his head, is the commitment to the real universe as it is understood by the laws of the sciences or as it probably exists if those laws are extended to strange places or different times. When he approaches the metaphysical he does so best through the concrete and although a good deal of his writing contains an ill-suppressed desire to find the gods through science, his abilities as a writer weaken as he approaches the metaphysical. Sensing this, Clarke has evolved a story mode featuring hard science, sprinkled with wit and turning suddenly at its conclusion to its metaphysical speculation in a breathtaking leap from hard reality into the unknown. When this technique works smoothly, as it does in *Rendezvous with Rama* and to a lesser extent in the potpourri of *Imperial Earth,* Arthur C. Clarke gains the advantages inherent in the different styles he has evolved. (pp. 50-1)

> *Peter Brigg, "Three Styles of Arthur C. Clarke: The Projector, the Wit, and the Mystic," in Arthur C. Clarke, Writers of the 21st Century Series, edited by Joseph D. Olander and Martin Harry Greenberg (copyright © 1977 by Joseph D. Olander and Martin Harry Greenberg; published by Taplinger Publishing Co., Inc., New York; abridged and reprinted by permission), Taplinger, 1977, pp. 15-51.*

GEORGE EDGAR SLUSSER

In pursuing what I call the "Odyssey pattern," I seek to define a central organizing structure in Clarke's fiction, one which bears interesting and precise analogies to the writer's cultural and social situation and hence to ours. If all litera-ture possesses such significant structures, Clarke's work is of particular interest for its angle of vision—here is a scientist writing about the quandary of modern scientific man, drawing on deep and persistent currents of Western literature. This firm grounding in the "two cultures" alone would make Clarke worthy of our attention. As we shall discover, there is much more. (p. 3)

More than characters or wise pronouncements in Clarke (the first are usually flat, the second commonplace), the reader notices the insistence with which he returns to the same ambiguous pattern over and over. Ambiguity is not some anomaly to be excused or circumvented. On the contrary, it is the central "idea" in Clarke: an idea that is inseparable from formal configurations, one not "said" but expressed in the structural dynamics of the work itself. (p. 4)

Clarke's use of "myth" or cultural allusion might partially (or primarily) be [ironic]. . . . The name Bowman, for instance, might simply be an ironic reference to the hero of that earlier epic of voyage and return which serves as titular model here. In the epilogue to his *Lost Worlds of 2001,* Clarke makes this obvious parallel clear: "When Odysseus returned to Ithaca, and identified himself in the banqueting hall by stringing the great bow that he alone could wield, he slew the parasitical suitors who for years had been wasting his estate." Will the Star Child returning to Earth follow Homer's transfigured hero? Here is another resonance ironically imparted to an already ambiguous ending, and a valuable insight into the pattern of this novel and Clarke's sense of structure in general. It is reasonable to assume that Clarke would be fascinated with *The Odyssey,* for the very essence of its form is ambiguity. Moreover, that form shapes and controls exactly the same oppositions that [John] Huntington and [Michael] Thron isolate in Clarke's work: the alien and the mundane, the domestic and the transcendent. In the travels of Odysseus (as with those of Bowman), beginning and end are at one and the same time coincident (Phaeacia and Ithaca are adjacent lands) and antipodal. The narrative line itself is built on two opposing and contradictory strands—progress and stasis. In the act of going out the hero is simultaneously coming back; his voyage is simultaneously an exploration of the fabulous and a homecoming. In the same manner, the miraculous and the commonplace exist together in *The Odyssey.* Just as the posts of the hero's fabled symbolic bed are living trees rooted in his native soil, so the transcendent grows out of the most banal everyday objects and actions: Odysseus's baths, Athena's golden lamp amid the domestic torches. In *2001* this pattern merely emerges to a new degree of self-consciousness.

A closer look, however, reveals that a similar dynamic informs the scientific odysseys of almost all Clarke's heroes. To claim that Clarke here is consciously rewriting *The Odyssey*—even with irony—is absurd, of course. The famous epic does, however, embody an archetypal situation. The archetype is qualified, though: "eternal" human rhythms are shaped by cultural patterns firmly rooted in Western tradition. Clarke is simply a modern heir to this tradition; in his work the older pattern has undergone significant changes in answer to the new pressures of his society. Less than a myth, but more than a simple trick or literary device, Clarke's "Odyssey pattern" is what Lucien Goldmann calls a "cultural fact." I propose to study it in terms of Goldmann's structural sociology—a method which seeks homological relationships between just such a fundamental literary structure and the mental structures or "world view" of the social group that produces an author and his works. (pp. 5-7)

For Goldmann, social group is primarily social class—his bias is that of Marxist economics. Certainly Clarke's ambiguities can be "explicated" profitably in this light: here is a representative of the scientific middle class, with roots in nineteenth-century capitalism. Torn asunder by the inherent contradictions of his class's world view, he is doomed to chronicle progress, and to deny it at the same time. Clarke's pattern, however, is both less and more than this —it touches other problematic aspects of Western cultural tradition as well. On one hand, it is curiously limited, parochial even, grounded in a literary and scientific heritage that is specifically English. American SF, grappling with the same critical relationship between individual scientific man and his world, produces a different basic pattern, one with opposite emphasis. On the other hand, it (like its American counterpart) is nonetheless the mirror of a general crisis in Western humanist tradition, to which Marxism is no more than another proposed solution with its own roots in a specific social group. (p. 7)

[His] stories and novels reflect the anxieties of humanist science facing a future it is helping to bring about. The price man must pay for continued progress is the human form divine. Technology too bears the seeds of its own dissolution: man achieves rational control over his environment, only to relinquish it to some higher, inscrutable fatality. Clarke's response to this dilemma is interesting. Instead of opting for one or the other, man or progress, he chooses both. His characters invariably go out, and this invariably leads to suspension of the human: whether they are dwarfed by the alien, or themselves lifted to another, alien plane of existence, the result is the same. This going out is balanced by a coming back, progress by preservation. If man loses his humanity, he paradoxically reaffirms it at the same time. Levels are changed in the process. What stands in opposition both to utopia and transcendence is, in Northrop Frye's term, the "individual varieties of experience." In Clarke's world, clearly, the individual who abides is not the old action hero. On the contrary, he gradually loses his function, first in the utopian world of comfort and plenty, then finally and irrevocably in the mystical resignation of the end. But as "active" man is lost, a new man is retrieved—the hero has become lyrical observer. At the limits of human experience, Clarke's new voyager can no longer affirm man's essence by acts of defiance, but by lament. He discovers that among the alien there is no place for man in his present form. As he does so, however, he in turn "humanizes" the alien by infusing it with a lyrical sadness heightened by this sense of exclusion and loss. . . . [For Clarke] what "makes" man in the face of blank indifference is no longer reason or knowledge, but something far more solitary and passive. In his stories and novels, the lyric beauty that briefly transforms these infinite silences is that of elegy. (pp. 8-9)

Clarke's response to the dilemma of human progress as modern science conceives it is oddly ambiguous. The split between man and such inexorable, inhuman processes as evolution appears to be more radically accepted in our century. An example is the bitter prediction of Sir Charles

Darwin (a grandson of the great Darwin) in his book *The Next Million Years* (1952) that man can progress no farther: "to do better will require a brand new species." Clarke faces this prospect neither with the cosmic rapture of [an Olaf] Stapledon nor with a retreat to faith in man's eternity. Instead he embraces both man and his passing. His tone is rather the elegiac weariness of [H. G.] Wells's Time Traveller, who contemplates an end-of-the-world landscape barren of man, only to return to the mediocrities of his Edwardian drawing room. . . . [In Clarke] an individual lyrical voice is raised against inexorable, inhuman forces.

To evolution, in fact, Clarke seems to prefer entropy. . . . Everywhere in his fiction, man's world is literally running down—his "utopias" such as Diaspar or New Atlantis are in the final stages of heat-death. Collective man no longer struggles or resists. Pushed by "progress" or pulled by some alien overseer, he moves inexorably toward a point of stasis. But if this appears (as it most clearly does in *Childhood's End*) a moment of transcendence—thus of further progress—it is actually a moment of conservation of human energy as well, in a form different but abiding. As man ceases to act, his powers to observe and intuit are augmented and he rediscovers wonder in the drab existence of everyday life. Set against progress and evolutionary patterns is this closed system of human energy. Both pessimism and optimism are suspended here by what can only be called an alchemical humanism. As energy becomes unavailable in the heroic sphere, it is gradually transmuted into the gold of lyricism.

This lyrical voice reborn in Clarke is also a product of the nineteenth century. In the isolated singer of the Romantic we have what is perhaps the ultimate expression of individualism in Western literary tradition. Already in the Romantic poets there was radical rupture between the subjective "poetic" individual and the objective natural processes modern science was describing and formulating into laws. (pp. 9-10)

[The] true heir to the Romantics and their struggles with the method of science is Wells in his scientific romances. In Wells, emphases have drastically shifted. More significant here than differences, however, is the resiliency of a certain wider-lying pattern. *The Time Machine*, no more or less than Keats's "Ode to a Nightingale," qualifies as a modern version of *The Odyssey:* in both there is a voyage out and back, movement between poles of the wondrous and the commonplace. . . . There are two contending relationships, in fact—and here we are at the heart of Wellsian ambiguity. There is evolution and entropy. (p. 11)

Clarke's work is a perfect example of this. Invariably, there is an adventure of human "progress." In some way or other a man journeys to contact with the unknown, and comes face to face simultaneously with the possibility of transcendence and the limits of his humanity. Invariably too, the going out is balanced by some sort of coming back. In these "homecomings" the voyager's wonder and resignation before the mysteries of the universe are recaptured (if only momentarily) in a trivial incident, infused into the most mundane object. "Out there," man is absorbed in human vastness; "in here," he reawakens new meaning in the everyday world, "humanizing" some microcosmic part of that greater nature. This is not linear advancement but oscillation, a form of perpetual motion. As with Well's Time Traveler, homecoming leads to a new voyage:

progress/stasis/progress. Out of these interpenetrating opposites a new set of Odyssean transformations arises. The final passage from *The Time Machine* shows how clearly Wells set this pattern. . . . [Entropy] carries us to the brink —the heroic virtues have run down and are no more. Yet these ruins are shorn up by heightened poetic intuition— new insight into the gentler human qualities of "gratitude" and "tenderness." The poetry that ennobles these flowers is that of dying mankind. *In extremis,* the only balance struck is that of the elegaic voice brooding on shrivelled remains. Even in his farthest vision, Clarke will go no farther in the exercise of this elegaic humanism.

Over his long career Clarke has written short fiction, novellas, and novels of different lengths. . . . Whatever diversity there is in Clarke, however, exists only on the surface. Indeed, anyone who reads great doses of his writing is struck by just the opposite—in spite of variations in tone or length, it is all very similar. This is due mainly to the underlying persistence of the Odyssey pattern. . . . [The] various tones of Clarke's writing are better described as different modes of a same and unique verbal figure—the oxymoron, a surprising and transformatory juxtaposition of opposites. (pp. 13-14)

Clarke's reenactment of [a] pattern of contradictions and paradoxes in work after work seems almost a ritualistic act. Again and again his hero is painstakingly placed in his social setting, only to be yanked from it—the adventure is invariably a solitary one. More surprisingly, it is passive as well—the hero is less actor than a spectator to the drama of evolution. Clarke flaunts both evolution and relativity, for however much the protagonist may "move" in time, or see the most fearful changes, he remains firmly anchored in space. (pp. 22-3)

[Clarke's works] become tales of impotence and guilt in which the writer/scientist, through his narrative rhythms, seeks to reassert control over processes (physical and social) which he has discovered or formulated but been unable to direct, and which are now slipping entirely from his grasp. Once again the writer damns. Invariably, Clarke confronts short-term technological optimism with long-term evolutionary pessimism. Not only is human progress denied, but the efforts of man to advance are cruelly mocked in story after story: the moment chosen for revelation of man's cosmic insignificance is constantly his farthest point of technical success—a pioneering moon or space exploration. Behind such reductive processes we find the author playing god in his own creation, taking man to the brink of nothingness, only to snatch him back at the last moment unharmed. And yet, though he wields this double power of destructive scientific vision and redeeming mysticism, this author's dynamic proves sterile and self-cancelling in the end. What remains is only a helpless litany for worlds and values that are gone. . . . In this light, Clarke does not look forward to classless utopias or progress for the masses but backward to that contradiction in terms, the bourgeois aristocrat, the "exceptional" man of Romantic lore, the alienated artist as solitary nightingale. Clarke's golden dream is thus doubly displaced. (pp. 24-5)

Another stumbling block to Goldmann's Marxist-oriented structuralism is the fundamentally national and parochial nature of Clarke's Odyssean response. The dilemma of man in the increasingly alienating universes that modern science erects would seem a general one, arising naturally in all technologically advanced societies, and especially in those capitalist ones where such scientific visions have become enshrined as repressive myths. Yet it is interesting to note the relative absence of Wells's and Clarke's Odyssey pattern both in American SF and in the literary tradition that nourishes it. (p. 28)

To be useful in criticism, general patterns must pass the practical test: does the search for this "Odyssey pattern" in individual novels of Clarke impoverish them, or does it open their respective meaning structures to increasingly subtle and flexible analysis? The second part of this essay confronts the pattern with six novels chosen from all periods of Clarke's activity. These have been purposely selected at random in hopes that they will thus offer maximum resistance to any preconceived idea of order. They do, however, fall roughly into categories: early, middle, and later Clarke. Novels like *The Sands of Mars* (1951) and *Islands in the Sky* (1952), in spite of their dates of publication, actually plunge their roots into the '40s and the American magazine SF of that period. Less "primitive" is a work like *Childhood's End* (1953), where Clarke in one big step seems to have moved away from the manipulation of space opera conventions toward Odyssean adventure that is openly in the speculative manner of Wells. What appears evolutionary is actually parallel development: this strain too, with the early *Against the Fall of Night,* reaches back into the '40s. . . . If *Childhood's End* is Clarke's first major Odyssean adventure, *2001: A Space Odyssey* (1968)—whatever Kubrick's role in its creation—remains his most classic. Indeed, the fact that it is an omnibus work, composed consciously and laboriously out of various short pieces from this middle period, may account for its linear purity, its almost literal self-awareness of the pattern it develops. This self-conscious stance becomes more obvious in Clarke's two novels of the '70s: *Rendezvous with Rama* (1973) and *Imperial Earth* (1976). In spirit these works seem to turn away from the elegaic mysticism of Clarke's middle period back toward the creative vision of the earliest pulp-inspired novels. Both are aware of a set of conventions as manipulable counters; both weave increasingly intricate and personal figures out of them. This time, however, the raw material is more sophisticated—not the cliches of the juveniles but the Odyssey pattern itself. The goal of this fictional game seems far different in these latest novels—no longer neutral analysis of man's condition so much as pointed satire against his foibles and follies. (pp. 35-6)

However derivative novels like *The Sands of Mars* and *Islands in the Sky* may seem on the surface, they are surprisingly original creations, and in their structural dynamics already thoroughly Clarkean. Their originality does not lie in the larger narrative patterns—these are stock juvenile or "adult" space adventure—but rather in the way in which these conventional structures are subordinated to a persistent intellectual framework. Informing and reshaping the familiar cliches and themes everywhere in these two novels is an embryonic form of the Odyssey pattern. In both, a perfectly bland surface map is drawn—as readers of SF our conventional expectations would lead us blindfolded over its contours—only to be dotted with numerous and unexpected points of encounter with cosmic mystery. "Drama" lies less in resolution of plot than in a cumulation of these moments of tension between man and material limits. In these novels too—though in ways more often humorous than ponderous—man is constantly suspended at the crossroads between transcendent possibility and the pull of his lost home. What is really unique here is not so much the fact that Clarke uses "entertaining" genres—juvenile and space operas—to make more serious investigations, as the manner in which he proceeds and the inflection he gives these investigations. His attitude is essentially playful, analytical in a detached sense. In other, later novels the problem will not change—it is ever the human condition—but only the writer's stance: the mode of analysis passes from cerebral to elegiac, and finally to ironic. If Clarke's latest novels appear to come full circle to these stylized games with the convention of the beginning, it is with a different accent: the late Clarke shades toward the satirical, while these early tales are pure arabesque. (p. 37)

At first glance *Childhood's End* seems a very different novel in theme and form—evolutionary pretense has become transcendence, the individual adventure of boy or man a collective one of the human race itself. . . . In speculating about a "higher being" as far above man as man above Martian, Clarke presents a series of races not so much linked by evolution as separated by it: the only contact between such self-contained compartments is transcendental. In *Childhood,* however, this transcendent progress is nonetheless offset by the regressive rhythms of the old Odyssey pattern. Individual adventure does not disappear here; on the contrary, the novel is a series of such adventures—self-contained circles joined less by magical transitions than by ties of a basic human sort: those of family. (pp. 49-50)

In *Childhood* the familiar out-and-back rhythm continues to shape the narrative; its workings, however, have become much more subtle. What is more, this basic pattern has been transposed from the realm of space to that of time: progressive and regressive elements are incorporated in a larger interplay of sequency and simultaneity. (p. 50)

Next to the intricate clockwork of *Childhood's End, 2001: A Space Odyssey* seems sparsely linear, a manifesto more than a novel, the transformation of the Odyssey pattern into self-conscious formula. Drawing strongly on that tradition of elegiac response leading back through Wells to 19th century English poetry, the structure of *Childhood* is itself eminently lyrical in nature: through delicate interplay of repetitive and contrastive patterns, a tension that is not drama but lyrical poignancy is gradually developed around the situations leading to that final encounter between Last Man and Overmind. In contrast *2001* seems dry, intellectualized, stylized. In this later novel the Odyssean adventure of modern scientific man is transposed from the lyrical plane to one which is primarily symbolic in nature. As a result *2001* tends to develop twice removed from the materials of the adventure drama it transforms—on a level that should perhaps be called "metaphysical." The lyrical response of the heroes of *Childhood* is still a human response. Here, cut away from even this grounding, Clarke's symbols seem to become murky as "philosophy" or religious statement, empty as human experience.

2001 is classic only in the sense that it is the epitome of Clarkean space adventure—a restatement of the out and back pattern which not only resumes all the stock devices of the early works but seeks to reconcile them with the transcendent ending of *Childhood*. In more ways than one the novel betrays its composite nature—a work made of earlier bits and pieces, put together after the fact to explain

a film. It reads at times like a haphazard compendium of old themes and situations: there is the "Earthlight" epiphany—the familiar globe is suddenly alien, "a giant moon to the Moon"; there is the alienation of the spaceborn—the onlooker suspended "between hope and sadness" as Earth "like all mothers" bids farewell to her children. This in fact is primarily a novel of onlooking, of these maxim-like catch phrases which themselves epitomize the experience of excessively passive encounters. In long sections of *2001,* the voyager-man, as immobile as the moviegoer overwhelmed by the film's visual effects, confronts alien landscapes—Jupiter, Saturn, the Star Gate. Each confrontation is followed by its aphoristic resume: "The time had not yet come when Man could leave his mark upon the Solar System." . . . In skeletal form *2001* develops the same interplay of progressive and regressive elements as *Childhood*. Here again are a series of compartments—not only different adventures but different species as well—that are simultaneously self-contained and overlapping, evolving and not evolving. (pp. 56-7)

[The structure of *2001*] neatly suspends its representative hero between transcendence and return . . . , but in doing so bypasses the elegiac encounter altogether. Where such exist in the novel, they are transposed to a symbolic level—emphasis shifts from human brushes with cosmic mystery to external phenomena which themselves come to stand for such encounters. (p. 59)

Both going out and coming home in the world of *2001* are paths of violence and corruption: Moon-Watcher claws his way upward only to end in Bowman's hotel-haven where home has become a sloppily-built illusion; Star Child in turn goes back to an Earth so polluted that the only "cleaning" possible is destruction. Has the encounter with the alien become here, at the same time, an encounter with our own fallen selves—not so much suspended as trapped between ape and god? This doubt echoes through Clarke's latest two novels, where a clearly skeptical view of man's capacities in the face of cosmic mystery inflects the Odyssey pattern, mitigating both adventure and homecoming. In these novels lyrical dignity gives way to satire, elegiac nobility to something closer to foolish impotence.

The theme of *Rendezvous with Rama* is itself the compartmentalization of man: the novel not only depicts his helplessness before the mysteries of the universe, but seeks to deflect some of the blame for that helplessness back on man as well. The analytical, satirical thrust of this "rendezvous" is betrayed not only by the frivolous overtones of the designation itself but by the microscopic nature of the situation—the space odyssey structure of *2001* is literally turned inside out here, the mysteries of outer space bounded in this floating nutshell. Once again the inspiration for *Rama* is a composite one. . . . In *Rama*, however, Clarke has shaped these old themes to new satirical purposes.

The Odyssey pattern is not superseded here. On the contrary, it is made to function so that its bases can be examined: if there is for man a simultaneous voyage and homecoming, what is the nature of these eternal roots to which he returns? The satirical shift is already visible in *2001*, in the portrait of Floyd and the moon scientists before the slab: the lyrical encounter has become the source of wry jest at human vanity and folly; man has become the stupid tourist before the mysteries of the universe. The world of *Rama* is filled with such deflating moments. In its texture this is a book of empty discussions and wranglings, futile heroics, where the exhilaration of space walks has become the tasteless observation of female breasts in weightlessness. . . . The ending of the novel, in fact, is a piece of tongue-in-cheek transcendence. (pp. 60-1)

Imperial Earth, Clarke's latest novel, is a huge elaboration of this same reductive dynamic. As Clarke's most deeply pessimistic view of man's capacity before the infinite, of his evolutionary and transcendental inviability, it stands as a corrective to the elegaic humanism of *Childhood's End.* The voyage here exactly reverses that of the earlier novel— the hero goes back to Earth only to reveal human roots as shallow as space is deep. At a Pascalian middle between empty point and void of space, the accent falls less on man's lament than on his helplessness and its causes. For it seems, in *Earth,* that man is physically menaced on both extremes—by "Star Beasts" from without, and from within by the "fingers" of the asymptotic point drawing matter to its "death." Yet it is clear that man himself has created these menaces. . . . The source of flaws in this novel is man himself; throughout the book Clarke probes the blighted root with satirical fingers. (pp. 61-2)

The leisurely pace of the new novel may lead the reader to think Clarke has taken a step beyond philosophical parable or lyrical novel here, toward real men, their socioeconomic preoccupations, their lives and loves. This is not so. Economics and intrigue have served Clarke before (in the early *Earthlight* as well as the late *Rama*) as raw material to be worked into Odyssean correspondences and suspensions. If anything, Clarke's view of man in *Earth* is the opposite of sympathetic or tragic. Insofar as it functions on a human level at all, it is a scrupulous anatomy of man's labyrinthine attempts to escape from the physical and moral boundaries that hold him, and which may ultimately be of his own creation. (p. 62)

If the transcendent moment has any locus in *Earth,* however, it is in the family. On this level the novel clearly reads like a parody of *Childhood's End.* All the principal figures act out traditional relationships, yet there is no real blood bond between them. . . . The recipe is present here, not only for future triumph, but for Icarian fall. What is more, that Icarian past is a singularly banal one—his fall was a "brain burning" with a "joy machine." Nor is the look forward more reassuring—there lie the hollow voices of space. As dynasty has become a curse . . . , so the Odyssey pattern itself, instead of suspending man between cosmic beauty and vital past, has become a prison. . . . In *Earth* the Odyssean roots—alive still in the elegaic poetry of *Childhood's End*—are blasted. Man is contained in new limits no longer physically neutral or even traditionally humanist. Behind Clarke's growing satirical vision lies more than a hint of theology—the primal curse. (pp. 63-4)

> *George Edgar Slusser, in his* The Space Odysseys
> *of Arthur C. Clarke (copyright © 1978 by George
> Edgar Slusser), The Borgo Press, 1978.*

KINGSLEY AMIS

Mr Clarke has specialised in the exploration of space, and so enjoys an edge when he comes to write fiction concerned with it. A story set in the future is not thereby a prophecy, and he is too good a novelist to make the confusion; but an intimate knowledge of the possible and the plausible greatly

assists in that naturalising of the marvellous which is the characteristic achievement of the best science fiction.

With the heavy stuff out of the way, let it be said at once that Mr Clarke's new novel [*The Fountains of Paradise*] is no easier to put down than any of his others. It takes us to the 22nd century and the equatorial island of Taprobane. . . . (p. 119)

The book becomes an action story instead of a metaphysical romance, but the action is tense enough. . . . As I read I kept pushing myself further and further back in my chair, squealing with vertigo. This is not Arthur Clarke's best novel, though the blurb says he says it is; the most that can be said is that it's delightfully written, always interesting and at times almost unbearably exciting.

Two grumbles: the miles I have quoted are my own conversions; the author has gone metric. Must he? (Does he think it's more *scientific*?) The year of the story is 2142, and the changeover will almost certainly be complete by then, but my calendar only says 1979. And really, honestly, have we got to call it Sri Lanka? I dare says its inhabitants do call it that, but it's Ceylon in English, which is what I'm using. Next thing you know it'll be Deutschland, Ellas, Suomi and the bloody old CCCP. (p. 120)

> *Kingsley Amis, "Action Man," in* New Statesman
> *(© 1979 The Statesman & Nation Publishing Co.
> Ltd.), January 26, 1979, pp. 119-20.*

GERALD JONAS

In science-fiction terms, ["The Fountains of Paradise"] is hardly as daring as the galactic odysseys of some of [Mr. Clarke's] earlier books, but it is presented with sufficient technical detail to lend plausibility—and the more plausible it sounds, the more stupendous it becomes. . . .

Morgan's struggle to realize his dream is presented against a curious backdrop: A highly advanced galactic civilization has already communicated with the human race through a robot probe. After leaving behind some enigmatic messages, the probe has returned to its distant home; no one knows what the next contact will bring. One might imagine a period of cultural stagnation during this time; but Mr. Clarke, ever the optimist, shows us a world civilization expending enormous energies to erect its own "stairway to heaven."

This enterprise may sustain the spirit of the human race; unfortunately, it does not sustain the novel. What little plot there is concerns the efforts of a few reactionaries to abort the project—efforts easily suppressed by Morgan and his allies. (p. 13)

Like most of Arthur Clarke's fiction, this novel suffers from the absence of a true villain. Virtually everyone we meet is decent and rational, and those who are not seem merely misguided. Even the good, clean political infighting, of the sort that enlivened Mr. Clarke's last book, "Imperial Earth," seems merely *pro forma.*

There is one nice Clarkean touch: A device called CORA— for coronary alarm—continuously monitors the cardiac function of people whose hearts have begun to show signs of weakness. At the first hint of danger, CORA begins to talk. (pp. 13, 25)

As in "2001" when HAL the computer "dies," a mechanical voice utters the most affecting words we hear. (p. 25)

Gerald Jonas, "Bridge to the Stars," in The New York Times Book Review (© 1979 by The New York Times Company; reprinted by permission), March 18, 1979, pp. 13, 25.

*   *   *

COLWIN, Laurie   1945-

Colwin is an American short story writer and novelist. Her subject is the nature of human love, and her tone is one of abiding optimism. (See also *CLC*, Vol. 5.)

J. D. O'HARA

Last summer a handful of people who follow the whims of publishing were dining elegantly at the proper end of Long Island and speculating whimsically on coming trends in the novel biz. Recognizing that existential Angst, oppression of minority groups, uncloseting of homosexuals, feminism, s & m, and incest were beginning to pall, the group searched for a new thrill. Goodness! they exclaimed, and conjured up a novel at the climax of which a couple sat holding hands and beaming as their child graduated from an excellent college, with distinction.

Sure enough, the next Sunday's Times Book Review carried a two-page ad for a novel whose theme, hushedly announced, was Friendship. But the new movement didn't peak until Laurie Colwin's *Happy All the Time* appeared, shining cheerily even through the murk of the newspaper strike. The novel tells about two perfectly normal young men, friends but straight, who meet, woo, and wed perfectly normal young women, one of whom produces a perfectly perfect baby.... Everyone here really *is* happy all the time. Luckily for Colwin and the story, however, they don't realize it, and they spend most of the novel engaging in low-level kvetching. Colwin's skill at making this whining witty, her creation of young women whom—who?—most young women would want to be, and her clear, straightforward prose style make a comic success out of this unpromisingly uplifting material. (p. 231)

J. D. O'Hara, in New England Review *(copyright © 1978 by Kenyon Hill Publications, Inc.), Vol. I, No. 2, Winter, 1978.*

MARTHA SPAULDING

Two young men court and wed two young women in this breezy novel [*Happy All the Time*], and all comes right with the world. Though little else of note occurs, Laurie Colwin's characters are so fresh and likable, and she tells her story with such wit, that the reader, amused and disarmed, wouldn't think of accusing her of undue sentimentality.

Guido Morris and Vincent Cardworthy, cousins and best friends, are undeniably the stuff of which Wodehouse heroes were made. They are good-natured, generous, and old-fashioned in love; both work at rather silly jobs; both are held in willing enslavement and perpetual confusion by the strong-minded women they fancy....

But their difficulties are minor, quickly overcome, and the foursome exits drinking a toast to their happiness present and future. The author of *Passion and Affect* and *Shine On Bright and Dangerous Object* has delivered in her third book a lighthearted, genuinely funny treat for the romantically minded. (p. 114)

Martha Spaulding, in The Atlantic Monthly *(copy-*

right © 1978 by The Atlantic Monthly Company, Boston, Mass.; reprinted with permission), October, 1978.

ELIOT FREMONT-SMITH

[*Happy All the Time* is an] elegant, fresh, funny tale of four people in love.... Colwin is a wonderful, knowing writer; her sentences are quick with information and wit. Her book conjures up Manet's picnic painting as it might be reinterpreted by Koren. But gently: Comedy is the other face of High Romantic passion, but love and friendship count. There's electricity here—nothing dumb—pure delight. (p. 136)

Eliot Fremont-Smith, in The Village Voice *(reprinted by permission of* The Village Voice; *copyright © The Village Voice, Inc., 1978), October 9, 1978.*

ROSS FELD

Laurie Colwin's approach in *Happy All the Time* is to elbow right past the agonizing.... Her characters do not suffer their thirties; they *use* them, like people who've received a new, vaguely untrustworthy, but intriguing gift.... First as graduate students in Cambridge, Mass., then as professionals in New York, [Guido and Vincent] go looking for future wives in the refreshingly blithe belief that "one is always foolish until one is correct"—the carefully polished attitude we used to get from the high-spirited, tuxedoed boy/men of Forties movies. (p. 63)

It's bright, it's funny, and it's very very willful; Colwin is out to invent not only a Seventies comedy of manners but the manners themselves. What makes the book special fun are the tartly endearing reversals: The girls are close-to-the-vest and tentative, while the slightly boobish boys roll with the punches, secure in their eagerness to love, attend, and do their full duty. Colwin writes effervescently—if the book has a flaw, it's that there is a sludgy build-up of adorableness. But a thirtyish book it remains. The personal, dependent on quick wits, good will, and high hopes, is still the lifeboat. (p. 64)

Ross Feld, in Saturday Review *(© 1978 by Saturday Review Magazine Corp.; reprinted with permission), October 10, 1978.*

JOHN ROMANO

We've been waiting, haven't we, for a writer with *glad* gifts? By which I mean a writer with delicacy, affection and wit to sing for us the well-adjusted joys of the on-the-whole-quite-happy-thank-you life.... Well, Laurie Colwin's "Happy All the Time" is our chance; and I hereby wish my fellow fortunates joy of our collective self-image.

It's a lovely book: I mean it. The people in it are nice and better than nice. Laurie Colwin writes a sentence of porcelain-like clarity, to use an adjective she favors. Her book has the elegance called Mozartian—pretty themes, memorable melodies. The four people in it are a kind of quartet, a counterpoint of character-types, and their effect is harmony. If I found myself hoping, halfway through, that a busload of underprivileged kids with tommy-guns would disembark in the novel's sunny landscape, this should perhaps be chalked up to some morbid restlessness of my own.

Here are the details. Like all smiling social comedies since

"As You Like It," "Happy All the Time" features two couples, men and women deeply right for each other if only they would realize it; which they do, in plenty of time to toast each other's happiness in the last scene. There are Vincent and Misty, Guido and Holly. They all have been to good schools, wear clothes well and have enough money. They all have settled into a good career by age 30 or so, except Holly. . . . The crisis, such as it is, comes when Holly picks up and leaves on an unannounced, indefinite vacation the very day she tells Guido she's pregnant. Though he's not *very* disconcerted—no one is *very* anything here—he does at least threaten to become unhappy.

It's at such a pass as this that one feels that Laurie Colwin's china shop is badly in need of a bull. . . . None of [the male spouses of my acquaintances], I hope, would be satisfied, as Guido is, by the amiable lack of profundity he's offered by Misty, his best friend's wife, when he goes to her with his confusion. . . .

Misty herself is a self-styled "scourge of God," which means in context that, unlike the three others, she doubts (a little) that we're all having a swell time. She has an expression on her face that Vincent calls "the only Jew at the dinner table." As for Vincent, whereas Guido is too analytical, it's feared that Vincent isn't analytical enough. My own opinion is that no one in this dollhouse of a book has anything to worry his little head about. Laurie Colwin is not going to let bogeymen—erotic or fiscal or even psychological—move in next door.

So you're going to enjoy this book, because it's charming and funny, but I warn you that you may feel, from page to page, like "the only Jew at the dinner table." Nor is this mere grouchiness. Happiness itself, after all, is a complex and volatile state; it has less to do with brightness and neatness than with energy and desire. Laurie Colwin's art—and art it is, and a joy—gives the impression that it's just plain afraid of energy and desire. Without them, the happiness she can portray must ring, for the Analytical, a little thin. (p. 14)

> John Romano, in The New York Times Book Review (© 1978 by The New York Times Company; reprinted by permission), November 19, 1978.

FRANCES TALIAFERRO

Laurie Colwin's *Happy All the Time* miraculously, uncloyingly describes two happy couples who enjoy their lives; this delicious book has the sweetness of *Così Fan Tutte* without its shadows. . . .

Conditioned by literary experience, we read edgily at first, suspecting all the pleasantness, waiting for the terrible blow to fall. It doesn't. Gradually we relax and yield to the celebration of healthy relationships, benign pleasures, and creature comforts, for which it is possible to develop an agreeable and pleasing appetite. . . . Such pleasures would be objectionable if they were totally bland, but [Colwin] produces the literary equivalent of the anchovy—a prickly character, a threatening event—to relieve the sweetness.

Aristotle ennobled the digestive metaphor when he spoke of the *catharsis* of tragedy. Indeed the signal characteristic of great art may be its power to trouble the viscera, and our greatest artists may continue to be dyspeptic. Still, there is no intrinsic superiority in a bad digestion and a cranky tem-

per. Let a comfortable word be said for the artist of cheerful, eupeptic disposition. (p. 83)

> Frances Taliaferro, in Harper's (copyright © 1979 by Harper's Magazine; all rights reserved; excerpted from the April, 1979 issue by special permission), April, 1979.

*   *   *

CORTÁZAR, Julio   1914-

An Argentinian novelist, short story writer, translator, and poet, Cortázar is considered a master of fantastic literature. In his hands, the fabric of reality is woven almost imperceptibly with threads of fantasy, creating a unique fiction that often bears the influence of his fellow fantasist, Borges. Cortázar probes the subconscious of his characters, and often the reader is confounded in his attempt to decipher whether he is in the realm of the bizarre or is witness to the machinations of a deranged mind. Cortázar's work marks a departure from traditional Latin American literature, offering a dazzling display of language and structural openness. (See also *CLC*, Vols. 2, 3, 5, 10, and *Contemporary Authors*, Vols. 21-24, rev. ed.)

JOSÉ VÁSQUEZ AMARAL

The contemporary Argentinian . . . is suffering from a grave crisis of identity. The crisis is much more serious than the one that usually accompanies the individual who wishes that a certain man were his father but knows deep in his heart that he is not. All the *apparent* factors for a legitimate origin from the *gaucho* are present and it is only by a cruel twist of fate that the contemporary Argentinian is not even an illegitimate child of the *gaucho*. About all that he can claim is a literary or imaginary descent from that immensely seductive figure, unique in the history of the disappeared races of the Americas. With a great deal more complexity and morbidity than one would suspect from the non-existence of a particular much desired ancestor, the contemporary Argentine is suffering from a loss that he cannot possibly replace by any means at his disposal. It is this complexity and this morbid state of the Argentine people that is the very core of the novel by Julio Cortázar, *Hopscotch*.

Cortázar is one of the most accomplished craftsman in both the novel and the short story in the letters of his country and indeed, in the Spanish-speaking world. In the short story he has only one rival, the master of the short story in Spanish and one of the great masters of the genre, Jorge Luis Borges, his compatriot. Some of the short stories that are included in one of his early volumes (*End of the Game*) are masterpieces that bear comparison with any produced in any contemporary literature. One of these, "The Lines of the Hand," seemed to me to foreshadow the length and the style of the short story of the future. Another, "Flattening the Drops," seemed to indicate the type of short story that could be conveniently read by a passenger being shot into space in a rocket that would land him in any part of the world in a matter of minutes. Julio Cortázar has a decided genius and inclination towards the shorter narrative, beyond question. (pp. 160-61)

One may safely say that what holds [*Hopscotch*] together, in the last analysis, is the quest of the entire Argentine nation for a personal and a national identity. . . . *Hopscotch* is the inevitable return trip of the Spanish galleons that went back to Spain and Europe laden with the gold of the New World. Or, at least, *Hopscotch* is the tolling of the bell for the trips that the Latin American used to make in search of that sense of "belonging" that took him to the studios, universities, taverns, and fleshpots of the Old World.

In *Hopscotch* even the protagonists cease to be natives of the country to become an assortment of the flotsan and jetsam of the world cast upon the sand of ancient gay Paree. The novel, had James Joyce not preempted the title, could just as well have been called *Exiles*. The dramatis personae of the narrative are a group of displaced persons who have not been uprooted from their original homes by the wars but by the sense of no longer being able to feel that they are in the right place or locale. (p. 161)

Significantly, too, the two main characters of the novel, La Maga and Horacio Oliveira, are both Argentinians who have come to Paris in search of nothing in particular, of anything that comes along or of whatever they can find. . . .

Horacio Oliveira and La Maga are not irresistibly drawn to one another like the lovers of old. Theirs is not the *grand passion* that used to sear the pages and inflame the reading avidity of the generation that was brought up on Lawrence or Miller. (p. 162)

The two main characters were poor devils when they left their native country and city; they are perhaps even more impoverished devils when they return, or at least, when one of them returns.

The novel is filled to the bursting point with all the current and past philosophies and attitudes of man both East and West. It can be used as a compendium of what people have thought from the Bible, the Upanishads, the Golden Flower and the I Ching to Alejandro Korn and Creative Evolution. It is all there and it is made to appear, one must agree, in a rather plausible human context. Plausible because it is, in effect, a summation of all the disenchantment of Western man with what he has sought, thought, or loved, that has slowly but inexorably turned to ashes, even as he has thought and felt that it is secure and tightly felt in his very hands.

Reading the acrostic novel that this Argentinian has produced, many points of similarity and contact come to mind. . . . [*Hopscotch*] is like a threnody or a funeral dirge for all the golden dreams that the once pink and glowing man of the West had thought possible. In its succession of all kinds of defeatist and sad little stories one is also reminded of the circles in hell that Dante, the archetype of the man of the Middle Ages, saw. But there is a difference: Dante's inferno was located in a hereafter and as punishment for foul deeds performed on this sinful earth. *Hopscotch* is a compendium, rather complete, of the labyrinth adumbrating the ruins of the edifice of the West.

For this reason, the reason that always accompanies the prophets of doom, this novel mainly concerns itself not with the grandiose failure that *Paradise Lost* or Mann's *The Magic Mountain* tells about; its failure is the niggling, corrosive, everyday hacking away at the very core of contemporary man. Remember that Horacio Oliveira is an Argentinian, and that this means that he is one of the first Europeans to have witnessed the collapse of dreams of the grandiose which have never come true. . . . [Every] single instance of rebellion in the novel of Cortázar is a rebellion against a column of smoke. (pp. 163-64)

No one in contemporary Latin American letters is more successful in the acquarelle of minimal failure. The big failure is always a mural or an etching: Cortázar is a master of the watercolor. (p. 164)

In many respects this novel is a sort of carbon copy of *Ulysses* by James Joyce. Had it been written 50 years ago, it would have been considered as revolutionary as the Irish master's work. Unfortunately so much of what Cortázar does, technical and otherwise, has that ashen flavor of the *déja vù*. No matter how hard he tries, the reader always knows how and, sometimes, what is going to happen next. It is only as a piece of literary information for those who cannot read Joyce in the original, for the monolingual of Latin America, that *Hopscotch* is a decided and brilliant boon. Its ultimate value may lie in that it is a much more decadent production than the Irishman's. And it is much more decadent in the sense that it mirrors a national tragedy that is absent in the work of Joyce. Argentina and the Argentinian move on to the wide screen of the world and proclaim their frustration and total ennui with everything that the West has until now sold as the guiding light of the entire planet. (p. 165)

> *José Vásquez Amaral, "Julio Cortázar's 'Hopscotch' and Argentinian Spiritual Alienation," in his* The Contemporary Latin American Narrative *(copyright © 1970 by Las Americas Publishing Co.), Las Americas Publishing Co., 1970, pp. 157-65.*

ROBERTO GONZÁLEZ ECHEVARRIA

[Cortázar suggests] that there is no break between the 'real' and 'fantastic' in his stories but instead a mode of presenting the 'real' that transfers it to the level of the 'unusual' (*insólito*). . . .

As in many of his short stories, Cortázar builds "La autopista del sur" upon a single situation; a set of circumstances within which the action and the characters are framed (more on this later). In "La autopista del sur" the situation is a traffic jam on the outskirts of Paris that begins on a Sunday afternoon and lasts days, months, and perhaps even years. The people caught in the jam are forced to organize communes to pool their supplies, trade services and help one another until they can reach Paris. The story focuses on one of these communes. . . . (p. 133)

The technique of building a story upon a single situation is a device that Cortázar uses quite consciously. He has compared it to the photographer's technique. . . .

[The plot] is not the whole story; the story is encased within a situation that is charged with potential meaning in itself. . . . The situation, then, works as a sign, charged with multiple potential meanings that emerge in the telling of the story, the 'utterance' of that sign. This is obviously the case in "Blow-up," in which the protagonist, a photographer, explores the various possible meanings that arise from a situation he has captured on film; the story begins hesitantly, as if the narrator were uncertain of how to make of this 'situation-sign' an utterance, a *praxis*. . . . (p. 134)

The situation-sign that serves as point of departure for "La autopista del sur" is both a "slice of life" (*a recorte de la realidad* in the sense given this term by Cortázar) and a blatantly literary device [that of continuing heterogeneous characters in an inclosure of some kind]. (pp. 134-35)

The inclosure has several functions. It may serve to isolate a group of characters in order to observe their responses under unusual circumstances . . . where the emphasis lies upon the psychological and moral behavior of the characters. It may also . . . present a perfectly rounded microcosm that is a scaled down model of a macrocosm, or a model for a possible one. Here the emphasis lies not so heavily on individual responses as on the model institutions created to regulate them. . . . Finally, the inclosure may be an allegory. (p. 135)

In "La autopista del sur" Cortázar exploits all these traditional functions of the enclosure: the commune is a microcosm, an isolated society that depends only on itself for survival, institutions and customs are created to regulate the interaction of the characters and . . . it is also a sort of *theatrum mundi*.

But in Cortázar's story the nature of the device is particularly complex because there are, in fact, two inclosures—the traffic jam and the commune created by the characters. The aperture of which Cortázar speaks in his [essay] "Algunos aspectos del cuento" produces in "La autopista del sur" a double exposure—a picture where two distinct images are superimposed. . . . [In "La autopista del sur," however, the split worlds do not offer a direct commentary upon] general metaphysical problems. If the story does indeed refer to them, it does so only in a very devious way. (pp. 135-36)

It is quite obvious that Cortázar saw in *La rentrée* [the return to the city of Parisians after August vacations] a ready-made symbol for something that has been a major theme throughout his works—modern technological society and its very precarious balance. Confined in their useless metal cages, the people in the jam are obvious examples of alienated modern man. At the end, when the jam finally dissolves, each person returns to a mechanized existence controlled by machines. . . . The commune, on the other hand, is a primitive, tribal world of food-gathering, rituals and folklore. The people, deprived of all the trappings of modern civilization, return to a natural state where each depends on the other directly and where bonds of solidarity form; it is almost a perfect primitive Christian society.

It could very well be concluded then, particularly in view of the slightly melodramatic ending, that Cortázar offers in "La autopista del sur" an alternative to modern civilization; that the story is an indictment against modern life. In short, that the double exposure creates a dialectic between the modern and primitive worlds present in the two images. Yet, while this interpretation may be valid and justifiable, it seems to me that the 'topicality' of the story conceals a more profound reflection, not directly about man's condition, but about fiction.

The most salient characteristic of the traffic jam is its facility as metaphor. The commune, too, is not only a standard (and today standardized) alternative to technological society but consists of a series of literary *topoi*. . . . Implicit in the entire story is also the image of the highway of life, so dear to the writers of romances of chivalry and of picaresque novels. In addition, there is the suggestion that the commune is organized by a mysterious supernatural being that keeps all the cars in close formation. . . . And the characters of the commune form, as a group, a sort of *theatrum mundi* or medieval dance of dea : there is Youth—the two

boys in the Simca—; Old Age—the old couple in the ID Citroen—; the Clergy—the nuns in the 2HP—; a Soldier—the soldier in the Volkswagen; and a couple of lovers, the engineer and the girl in the Dauphine. The dance of death motif is accentuated when someone throws a sickle into the middle of the commune, another symbol of medieval vintage. Cortázar's symbols are nearly always trite and obvious. . . . This is not due to Cortázar's lack of imagination or subtlety. The triteness and the platitudinous meaning of his symbols and devices have a very specific purpose in his works: to focus attention not on the meaning of the literary sign but on the sign itself.

Some years ago—in 1947—Cortázar suggested in one of his first publications that the contrivance of an autonomous, self-sufficient fictional world was an absolute requirement in short-story writing. . . . (pp. 136-38)

The inclosure device is not merely one mode of short-story writing but an ontological characteristic of the genre; all fiction and short fiction in particular is a closed, autonomous world. Thus, the inclosures in "La autopista del sur," while projecting the obvious meanings indicated above, as well as being a 'recorte de la realidad', are ultimately symbols of fiction itself. This is the reason why Cortázar utilizes literary signs that are so blatantly literary and also the reason for the platitudinous meanings of those signs.

This interpretation of the inclosures becomes clearer if one notices the relationship between the traffic jam and the commune at a formal level. Cortázar creates the commune before the reader, as when in the modern theater the actors themselves bring the properties onto the stage and then proceed with the representation of the play. In this respect the relationship between the commune and the traffic jam could be said to be homologous to that between the play within the play and the play itself. . . . Cortázar gives a meticulous phenomenological description of a self-contained world, of a complete cosmos. But the important thing is that he creates that fictitious world openly and arbitrarily, as if he were inviting the reader to analyse the elements of his fiction, the props of the set and the grease paint on the actors' faces.

The arbitrariness by which Cortázar constructs his fictional microcosm alludes to the arbitrariness of the real world. His 'utopia' points to a macrocosm that may be just as arbitrary and perhaps just as fictional. . . . In Cortázar's utopia everything has a place because he has arbitrarily created a grammar that will contain it; everything, including the characters, has a name because he has wrought a grammar that will accept it. Toward the end of "La autopista del sur" snow covers the ground—winter has set in on the people who had left for Paris on an August afternoon. But this is not a break with the syntax of Cortázar's new world. . . . The two situation signs have become one; a fiction within a larger fiction, all fictions a fiction, all fires a fire. Cortázar's "La autopista del sur" falls within a very rich tradition of literature whose main preoccupation is literature. (pp. 138-40)

Roberto González Echevarria, "'La autopista del sur' and the Secret Weapons of Julio Cortázar's Short Narrative," in Studies in Short Fiction *(copyright 1971 by Newberry College), Winter, 1971, pp. 130-40.*

LANIN A. GYURKO

In "Las babas del diablo," one of the most challenging of

the short stories of . . . Cortázar, the protagonist Roberto Michel is confronted with and, finally, overwhelmed by the deceptions posed by visual perception, chronological time, and discursive language. His account is a desperate attempt to arrive at the nature of truth about the traumatic experience that has destroyed him—ironically, rendering him incapable of conveying it in a rational manner. The reality of the experience is so unsettling that Michel ends by doubting whether it is knowable, communicable, or even whether it really exists apart from his imaginative consciousness.

Michel is a split personality in several respects. His background is both French and Chilean. His life is composed primarily of his professional work as a translator and his avocation, amateur photography. As a translator he constantly deals with the problem of finding the exact form to transmit meaning between Spanish and French, two different modes of structuring reality. Michel is also split psychologically. His identity and his sanity are destroyed by the imaginative reliving of an experience that he initially has believed are the maneuvers toward the seduction of a young boy by a woman. When he re-creates the episode within his consciousness, he comes to the anguished realization that the woman is merely the bait, acting to lure the boy for a man who is waiting in the background, outside the frame of the photograph that Michel has taken of the encounter and subsequently blown up. Desperately wishing to intervene to save the boy from this new menace that for Michel represents the truth which he had initially failed to comprehend, the protagonist is driven to the limits of imaginative and emotional participation and cracks under the strain.

The protagonist finds that truth is difficult to arrive at because his senses are limited or faulty in their perception of external reality. In particular, he profoundly distrusts his visual sense. . . . Roberto sees photography as a means of complementing his visual sense. For him it is more than a mere hobby; it is a means of capturing truth. . . . For Michel photography is the means of discovering new, unexpected, and hidden meaning of a reality that is complex and multi-dimensional. For the protagonist, truth lies not in external appearance but in subjective apprehension. There is no absolute, exteriorized truth independent of the effect of experience upon the perceiving consciousness. The course of Michel's narrative demonstrates the danger of his solipsism, as he becomes entirely absorbed within the "truth" created by his own mind, a truth that may not only be a relative one but a self-delusion.

The camera wielded by Michel the photographer is analogous to the point of view expressed by Michel the writer. Photography becomes a means of expressing his own personality—his own unique way of viewing reality. . . . The concrete world thus becomes an external correlate of the mind, just as language becomes the symbol or metaphor of emotion. And just as Roberto rebels against the tyranny of the camera lens, that forces his subjectivity into a fixed mold, so also does he chafe at the restrictiveness of traditional grammar, syntax, and conceptual language, which bind his emotions into a prefabricated, rigid mold that dilutes or distorts them and thus falsifies his identity. (pp. 204-05)

Although Michel begins by focussing objectively upon the woman and the boy, describing their appearance and be-

havior, he quickly moves into a realm in which he feels much more comfortable, that of imaginative attribution and prediction. (p. 206)

As he watches the woman and the youth [engaging in what appears to be a seduction attempt on the part of the woman], Michel is like an imaginative author who supplies alternative endings to the encounter. . . . That Michel's imaginative world is much more the center of his attention than the more prosaic reality he is witnessing is indicated by his closing his eyes on the captivated boy and the predatory woman while he is in the very process of observing them, in order imaginatively to formulate a salacious outcome. . . . Michel himself unwittingly gives an indication of the romanticized, fantasy quality of his thought when he states that the persons would be acting "como en las novelas" [like in novels]. Roberto seems to be deliberately cutting himself off from what is actually happening in order to fictionalize the incident. Ironically, although he believes he is moving toward absolute truth, he may be manufacturing only fictional truth, i.e., writing a story.

Michel himself is at times aware of the impetuousness of his imagination. He originally believes that his snapping of the photograph will act as a means of placing the episode in a banal or innocuous perspective free of the menacing quality he may be only projecting onto the encounter. He thinks that the photograph will act to reduce the blowup of the incident that his febrile imagination already is making to its "tonta verdad" [silly reality]. . . . But just the opposite occurs. Michel later makes two enlargements of the photograph, increasing it to life-size. He thus acts to convert what may only be a pedestrian external reality into a physical form that coincides with his imaginative exaggeration of the incident. The result is an ironic equating of Michel and the blowup, and, finally, the dominance of photographic image over the helpless individual. (pp. 207-08)

It is ironic that the photograph which has served to foil the seduction attempt and to save the boy now turns on its creator. Michel sees the blowup as the means used by the frustrated man and irate woman to exact their vengeance on him. As Roberto becomes convinced of the full horror of the episode, he now wants desperately to rescue the boy again. The tension that he feels and his anguish and frustration become excruciating as his desire to intervene is seemingly rendered impossible by his entrapment within another time and space. . . . Michel's own weapon has been turned against him. Sure now that what he had originally perceived was a lie, he can only stand shocked and bewildered before the blowup, which now becomes a theatre of consciousness in which the inevitable victory of the woman and the man seems to be occurring.

Imagination for Michel is both a positive and negative force. It is his imagination that turns the blowup into a nightmare which Roberto responds to as a reality. Yet, at the same time, imagination becomes the means through which the protagonist transcends chronological time and physical space, projecting himself into the photograph, again diverting the attention of the woman and permitting the youth to escape. . . . Once Michel has imaginatively entered the frozen time and space of the photograph, he remains trapped there. The first time, on that Sunday in early November, when he opened his eyes after having shut them to speculate on the sordid outcome of the encounter, he came back to everyday reality. This time, however, upon opening his eyes that he has closed in terror, the danger has disappeared. The photograph is tranquil; the woman and the man have disappeared, and there is only the sky: "el cielo limpio, y después una nube que entraba por la izquierda, paseba lentamente su gracia y se perdía por la derecha" [a limpid sky, and then a cloud that entered from the left, passed slowly in its grace and disappeared to the right]. . . . Yet the quietness is eery and deceptive because it does not mark the return of Michel to normalcy but instead indicates that the protagonist is now so alienated from reality that instead of the blowup of the scene as literally taken he can see only the enlargement as it has been transformed by his imagination. The reader finally realizes that the mentionings of clouds and birds that Michel repeatedly made throughout his narrative are not references to real objects but only imaginary ones, racing across the sky of the blowup, i.e., within the dislocated psyche of the protagonist. It is extremely ironic that Michel, who has lamented the frequency with which his visual sense deceives him by misinterpreting the true nature of physical reality, is now the uncomprehending victim of a much severer deception—he is deluded in believing that he can still separate the external from the internal world. . . . Michel sits mesmerized before the photograph. As the blowup acquires a demonic life, the identity of Roberto is reduced, until at the end of his experience he no longer knows who he is. His mind has become blank. He has been dehumanized to an object, an inert camera lens, incapable of asserting his integrity or his will. He has been spiritually crushed by the experience. This is why he states at the beginning of his account "estoy muerto" [I am dead]. . . . (pp. 209-11)

Chronological time no longer has any meaning for Michel. Immersed in the past that he is experiencing as a present reality, he realizes the absurdity of the word *now:* "Ahora mismo (qué palabra, *ahora,* qué estúpida mentira)" [Right now (what a word, *now,* what a stupid lie)]. . . . He thus finds clock time to be deceptive; for him, true time is cyclic. (p. 211)

Michel moves from an interested but uninvolved contemplator of both the real-life experience and the photograph of it, to an ironic hero. It is only in retrospect, when he is back in his apartment reflecting on his intervention, that he congratulates himself on taking the photograph whose moral basis has come after the fact. . . . But the second time that Michel intervenes, his intent is totally moral. Even though he plays the part of the camera, it is without the aesthetic preoccupation that has marked his first shot on the scene, except perhaps in a symbolic sense, i.e., he now wishes imaginatively to remove the man as a threat to the boy just as he previously has deleted both man and car for their aesthetic irrelevance.

As a narrator, Michel struggles to capture with words a reality that seems to defy linguistic expression. Roberto feels himself constrained by the limitations of conventional language in the same way that he has previously felt himself to be imprisoned within chronological time and sequential space. His linguistic captivity also parallels his mental confinement within the hell of his own turbulent consciousness. Although he feels compelled to communicate his experience as a means of emotional catharsis, perhaps as a way of restoring his shattered identity, he is at the same time overwhelmed by the futility of attempting to understand and express the truth of the incident. . . . The protagonist finds the mold of rational expression inadequate to convey the bewilderment, horror, and absurdity of his experience and the corrosive effect it has had upon him. What he winds up with after rupturing established linguistic patterns is a deformed language that borders on gibberish and yet that does, ironically, reflect his mental derangement. . . . The unbalanced Michel has become like the impressionable but static lens of the camera, that records the image of anything it is focussed on. (pp. 212-13)

Michel's narrative is a mélange of three types of language. The associative language with which he begins his account captures the flux of his disoriented consciousness, in a form that seems to be going nowhere. . . . The second type is a smooth, direct, and coherent language that contrasts with Michel's muddled first-person account. It is employed by the third-person voice that may be either an author with limited omniscience who intervenes in the narrative of Michel, confining himself only to the personality of Roberto, or it may be the means used by Michel to exteriorize the self in order to obtain a clearer focus upon it, through a more objective stance that shores up and provides direction to his first-person rambling. An indication that this voice may be merely a disguised first-person is that the scattered impressions of clouds interrupt the third-person narrative as well. . . . The continual shifting between first and third persons provides another indication of the split in Michel's identity. The third-person voice, basically sympathetic, at times chides Michel for his imaginative exuberance through parenthetical asides . . . and yet at the same time concedes that Roberto's febrile speculation may hold the key to understanding the true intent of the woman, i.e., that truth can be revealed through the imagination. . . . (pp. 213-14)

Just as Michel has little confidence in his visual sense so also does he distrust language. He is sensitive to the way that the careless use of language can deceive. . . . The inadequacy of conventional language to convey the subtleties of truth parallels not only the limitations of reportorial photography but also the insufficiency of the aesthetic photograph that Michel makes of the woman and the boy, that records only a half-truth. Just as Roberto imaginatively transforms the blowup, inserting the figure that will complete the meaning, he also transforms language to conform to the subjective patterns of emotional experience. Just as Michel has made a visual blowup of the image of the woman, he now provides the reader with a verbal closeup of her. He does not wish merely to describe her appearance but to fashion a word-portrait that will reveal her soul.

He finds conventional adjectives inadequate, since they only approximate her true nature (a type of soft-focus). . . . He ends up by discarding this vague, abstract language and replacing it with one that is poetic—associative and evocative, concrete, sharp and vivid. This is the third type of language. . . . Symbol and metaphor dramatically convey Michel's emotional state. Green symbolizes the horror and revulsion that Roberto feels as he is confronted with what he believes are the preliminaries to sexual perversion. The delicate malevolence—the paradoxical combination of attractiveness and ominousness, softness and cruelty that the woman represents for Michel—is conveyed through the poetic devices of metaphor and hyperbole. . . . Michel gives language a wry twist to express the complex, ambivalent reality of the scene that juxtaposes innocence and perversion. Roberto begins by describing the boy as escaping swiftly and lyrically: "perdiéndose como un hilo de la Virgen en el aire de la mañana" [fleeing as the spit of the Virgin in the air of the morning] . . . , and then goes on to provide an ironic amplification to his simile: "Pero los hilos de la Virgen se llaman también babas del diablo" [But the spit of the Virgin is also called the spit of the devil]. . . . The same substance can be referred to by two names that have connotations which are diametrically opposed: angel spit and devil spit, just as Michel's photograph contains both the angelic and the demonic, and just as the process that results in the freedom and salvation of the boy will eventuate in Michel's own damnation. Although the boy escapes, Roberto is left to confront the monstrous underside of the situation, as the frustration of the man and woman at losing their prey is now directed toward the protagonist.

Michel's narrative is a paradoxical fusion of creation, recreation, and destruction. On the one hand, he attempts and at least partially succeeds in creating a new idiom to capture the trauma of his experience. He also replaces the incomplete truth that is the photograph with the fuller, imaginative creation that he accepts as the whole truth. Significantly, however, the climax to the narrative is only an imaginative one. Narrative tension increases at this point, as Michel's thoughts pile up on top of one another to convey his anguish and desperation. Now the third-person voice drops out of the narrative, and the perspective is intensified by being confined totally to Michel's stricken consciousness. . . . The movement of the narrative as a whole is from limited objectivity to total subjectivity, from nonengagement to overwhelming vicarious participation and from rational and controlled use of language to disassociated psychic flux. The main movement is also primarily a negative one, from initial misapprehension to final self-delusion. (pp. 214-16)

The truth about what actually occurred that Sunday morning is impossible to establish. Michel's imaginative intuition is extremely intriguing and quite plausible, yet it nevertheless remains unsubstantiated. (p. 216)

His attitude of not acting but always reacting, allowing himself to be determined by circumstance, event, and other personalities, is one that pervades his entire narrative and, even more, his whole life. As a translator he is linguistically passive, acted upon by the language of another person, whose thoughts and syntax he is subordinate to. As a photographer, instead of fixing unstable, elusive reality in his lens and forcing it to yield up its truth, it is Michel who becomes fixed by his photograph. Even the climax of his narrative, which on one level presents him as an intervening figure, is but his desperate reaction to the overwhelming power of his own imagination. . . .

The maximum irony of the narrative may lie in the distinct possibility that the horrible truth that Michel believes he has discovered about what was actually occurring between the man, woman, and boy, may be but another fabrication of his volatile consciousness. He thus may have destroyed his own self, becoming ironically, the victim of a mere self-delusion. Michel himself is aware of the relative nature of what he has accepted as truth. . . . Truth within "Las babas del diablo" is like the clouds that float across the blowup that is Michel's imagination, the clouds that constantly change in size and shape. Truth is protean, evanescent, and perhaps only imaginary—or nonexistent. The only truth for Michel, and one which, ironically, he is unaware of, is the

horrible reality of his own broken, obsessed, and deluded consciousness. (p. 217)

Lanin A. Gyurko, "Truth and Deception in Cortázar's 'Las Babas del Diablo'," in The Romanic Review *(copyright © by the Trustees of Columbia University of the City of New York; reprinted by permission), Vol. LXIV, No. 3 (May, 1973), pp. 204-17.*

ANA MARÍA HERNÁNDEZ

Cortázar has always shown a keen interest in the Gothic aspects of vampirism. He is thoroughly acquainted with the numerous *nosferati* preceding and following Bram Stoker's darkly illustrious Count and jokingly refers to himself as one of the "undead," since he is allergic to garlic and preserves an oddly youthful appearance at sixty-two years of age. (p. 570)

62 works with a very complex system of cross-references and allusions, functioning on different levels but with the central theme of vampirism as a common basis. The novel's major "keys" are presented in the first paragraph. The words spoken by the fat client ("Je voudrais un chateau saignant") refer to a raw Chateaubriand, but also to the "blood castle" at Csejthe (near the town of Fagaraş in Romanian Transylvania) where Erszebet Báthory (the "Blood Countess") performed the deeds that made her famous in the early seventeenth century. The restaurant Polidor alludes to Juan's namesake, Dr. John William Polidori (private physician to Lord Byron), who conceived his novel *The Vampyre* during the memorable soirée at the Villa Diodati in Switzerland (15 June 1816) at which Mary Shelley's *Frankenstein* was born. (p. 571)

Upon entering the restaurant Polidor, Juan decides to sit facing a mirror; immediately we are reminded that vampires, according to folklore, have no reflection. Even though we are not told whether Juan sees his reflection or not, his mental confusion at this point shows that he lacks mental "reflection." Loss of reflection or of the "shadow" is a rather common occurrence in tales of supernatural horror; in most cases, this phenomenon is associated with some kind of diabolical pact or ceremony performed in one of the magical vespers. . . . The loss of the shadow—Jungian symbol for the repressed, true self—implies a loss of the soul or a loss of virility. Most importantly, it implies the loss of the capacity to establish lasting human relations. A man without a "shadow" is [a wanderer]. . . . Juan performs his ritual (entering the restaurant Polidor, buying the book, sitting in front of the mirror) on a magical vesper, Christmas Eve. Christmas Eve marks the birth of a Divine Child, likewise a Jungian symbol for the true self. But this child will be condemned to death by men's spiritual "blindness." Similarly, the young patient who represents Juan's true self is condemned to death by Juan's own spiritual blindness and egoism. Juan deliberately looks for loneliness and degradation in the magical vesper associated with love and hope; and as a result of his diabolical rite, he will lose his soul at the end of the novel. The mirror also alludes to the incantatory spells celebrated by Countess Báthory in order to preserve her youthful appearance. She celebrated these rituals at dawn, facing a mirror.

Another "key" is provided by the bottle of Sylvaner that Juan orders. The first letters of its name contain a reference to . . . Transylvania, Cradle of Vampires. Throughout the novel Cortázar alludes to "the Countess" in connection with the Hotel of the King of Hungary but does not mention her by name. Countess Báthory, a native of Hungarian Transylvania, was walled in as a punishment for her crimes. However, neither the crimes nor the punishment took place in Vienna. Critics who have traced the allusions to the Blood Countess have skipped a second set of mirror images: those associating the Viennese Frau Marta with Erszebet Báthory's Aunt Klara, who initiated her niece in the sadistic practices that made her famous. . . . Significantly, Clara is the name of the heroine of Cortázar's first, unpublished novel, "El examen." She was married *to a character named Juan*. Does Cortázar include Klara Báthory (Frau Marta) in the novel because he sees her as his own sweet Clara twenty years later? Does he blame Juan for her metamorphosis?

A further key is provided by Tell, who reads a novel by Joseph Sheridan Le Fanu. The novel is, most probably, "Carmilla," reputedly the best vampire story ever written. In this novel, as in "Christabel," the vampire is a woman and a lesbian. . . . In the novel we find a play of mirrors involving an older, sinister vampiress (Countess Mircalla Karnstein) and a younger, seductive one (Carmilla) who captivates the young heroine with her fatal charms. The theme of lesbianism plays a central role in Cortázar's works. This aberration, openly admitted in the case of Hélène, is subtly suggested in most other feminine characters. Paula forms a strange liaison with the homosexual Raúl; Paula/Raúl, as their names indicate, seem to be two sides of the same personality. During Horacio's conversation with the *clocharde* the latter hints at a possible relationship between herself and La Maga. Ludmilla, Andrés Fava's mistress in *Libro de Manuel,* has a lesbian past as well. (pp. 571-73)

Homosexuality involves a failure to grow beyond the early narcissistic stage and come to terms with the "otherness" of the opposite sex. Cortázar's self-centered, narcissistic heroes are bound to look for women who resemble them as much as possible, so that in loving them they would still be loving themselves. Likewise, in possessing them they would really be possessing themselves. Juan and Hélène are two manifestations of the same personality. A relationship which originates in a failure to deal with "the Other" and in a desire to "recover oneself" must be, in essence, vampiristic.

By dealing with its psychological implications we discover the very essence of Cortázar's vampirism, which is—in spite of the many references to Gothic novels—essentially psychological, like Poe's. Rather than Sheridan Le Fanu's "locked room" situation (briefly parodied in the episode of Frau Marta and the English girl), what we have here is a set of relationships like those uniting Ligeia to her husband or Madeline Usher to her brother. Juan's obsession with the remote, cold and cruel Hélène is as metaphysical as that of the typical Poe hero. For Juan, as for Morella's or Ligeia's husband, "the fires were not of Eros." He really wants to possess Hélène's essence, not her body. He cannot even approach her, and when he does, he does not "see" her. He makes love to "Hélène Arp, Hélène Brancusi, Hélène dama de Elche." Nor does he "see" Tell, on whom he projects his ideal vision of Hélène, too. . . . Tell is indeed nothing more than a "thing" on which Juan "feeds." . . . The rest of the characters, too, are vampires or are vampir-

ized in their turn: Nicole and Marrast by each other, Celia and Austin by their respective parents, Austin by Nicole, Nicole by Calac (aspiring), "la gorda" by Polanco.

Hélène, the most evident vampiress, is branded by the pin she wears, which has the form of a basilisk: "The basilisk has such a dreadful stare that birds at which it merely glances fall down and are devoured." The vampire, likewise, fixes and petrifies its victim with its stare. "Vision" is Hélène's terrible attribute. Her vision, however, is no different from Juan's "blindness." Hélène does not look at the other in order to see him; she looks at him in order to immobilize and devour him. Neither she nor Juan will be able to break the spell that hangs over them, for they are incapable of understanding the symbolic events of which they are part. (p. 573)

Allen Tate and D. H. Lawrence agree that Poe's heroines are turned into vampires through a man's inability to awaken them to womanhood: "D. H. Lawrence was no doubt right in describing as vampires [Poe's] women characters; the men, soon to join them as 'undead,' have, by some defect of the moral will, made them so." The same can be said of Hélène. . . . [It has been said that] love for an ideal vision is a sin against the Moon Goddess, against life. . . . His inability to see Hélène makes Juan cling to her, vampire-fashion—or like a child to its mother—expecting her to satisfy his needs and conform to his ideal of her. (pp. 574-75)

Austin's meeting and falling in love with Celia stands out as one of the most idyllic love scenes in the whole of Cortázar's writings. In this scene Austin and Celia "look"—literally and symbolically—at one another. Open, honest love between man and woman breaks the spell of the vampire. Through their act of love Austin and Celia, now free, are cleansed from their former "perverse" entanglements; they take the "bath" Juan and Hélène were always unable to take in their nightmare. Juan and Hélène, on the other hand, experience a blind, negative and mutually destructive encounter. Imprisoned in their respective egos, they act out a grotesque parody of the act of love.

Austin, described as "Parsifal" and later as "Gallahad" and "Saint George," acts the part of the mythological hero, slaying the Dragon he has first "seen." . . . Nicole is, in reality, a mirror image of Hélène, just as Marrast and Calac are mirror images of Juan. The latter's spiritual impotence is reflected in Marrast's statue (sculpted on an "oilcloth stone" and, as such, "soft") and in Calac's "failure." Juan/Marrast/Calac fail Hélène/Nicole through their deliberate blindness and softness, and the latter retaliate by turning into vampires and haunting them. At the end of the novel Juan cannot participate in Feuille Morte's "rescue." He is a victim of his own monster. (pp. 575-76)

Ana María Hernández, "Vampires and Vampiresses: A Reading of '62'," in Books Abroad *(copyright 1976 by the University of Oklahoma Press), Vol. 50, No. 3, Summer, 1976, pp. 570-76.*

EVELYN PICON GARFIELD

In Cortázar's short stories we expect to encounter a multifaceted reality. By depicting a normal setting and conventional characters Cortázar gains our confidence and puts us at ease with his tales. Innocently reading on, we suddenly find ourselves trapped by a strange and sometimes unreal situation, an oneiric and even fantastic turn of events. In this way we are exposed to and at times threatened by another possible but illogical dimension of the apparently routine reality set forth in the stories. From "Casa tomada" (The House Taken Over) and "Lejana" (The Distances) in *Bestiario* (1951) to "El otro cielo" (The Other Heaven) in *Todos los fuegos el fuego* (1966) Cortázar has presented us with a view of reality riddled with holes, what I like to call a "Swiss cheese" reality. One of his most famous characters, Johnny of "El perseguidor" (The Pursuer) describes this reality:

> That made me jumpy, Bruno, *that they felt sure of themselves.* Sure of what, tell me what now, when a poor devil like me with more plagues than the devil under his skin had enough awareness to feel that everything was like a jelly, that everything was very shaky everywhere, you only had to concentrate a little, feel a little, be quiet for a little bit, to find the holes. In the door, in the bed: holes. In the hand, in the newspaper, in time, in the air: everything full of holes, everything spongy, like a colander straining itself. . . .
>
> (p. 577)

Ever since *Las armas secretas* (1958) the exceptional departures from routine life and the glimpses of an illogical and provocative facet of everyday reality seem to have become gradually suppressed by the heavy and relentless hand of custom. Routine seems to reestablish itself more and more in Cortázar's stories, despite the author's clear protests in his volumes of miscellaneous excerpts. Even in "El perseguidor" the jazz critic Bruno sought refuge in his customary life in order to protect himself from the provocative reality that Johnny perceived and described through his music. Neither did the protagonist of "El otro cielo" return to the mysterious galleries of Paris, but instead he remained in Buenos Aires, subjected to a conventional life.

Of all the stories published before *Octaedro,* "La autopista del sur" (The Southern Throughway) best exemplifies the definitive victory of routine over a desired and exceptional reality. In that story . . . some travelers find themselves immobilized in a traffic jam. This common situation achieves unrealistic proportions when the traffic jam lasts months. As the seasons rapidly progress, the people organize a societal nucleus among the stationary cars and eventually embrace a new routine as inhabitants of the highway, until suddenly the cars once again begin to move toward the capital. Even in the face of a fantastic and bizarre situation such as a traffic jam which lasts months, custom reestablishes its sovereignty. (p. 578)

Unlike the disquieting invasions found in the short stories of *Bestiario,* in "Verano" [in *Octaedro*] the unusual provocation to daily routine materializes in the form of a horse, a less oneiric danger than an inexplicable noise, a less fantastic threat than some fabulous *mancuspias* [the strange, menacing animals of "Cefalea" in *Bestiario*] and a more realistic intrusion than that of a tiger roaming through a house [as in "Bestiario"]. In addition, the ephemeral presence of the horse and child does not threaten to destroy permanently the couple's ordered daily coexistence. In fact, at the end of the story a long sentence rhythmically embodies the implacable return of routine:

> . . . if everything was in order, if the watch kept on measuring the morning and after Florencio came to get the little girl perhaps around 12 o'clock the mailman would arrive whistling from afar, leaving the letters on the garden table where he or Zulma would pick them up silently, just before deciding together what they felt like having for lunch.
>
> (pp. 579-80)

Perhaps it is the presence of death and tears that exasperates me as I read *Octaedro.* Nevertheless, death is constantly a part of almost all of Cortázar's works. As he himself pointed out, "death is a very important and omnipresent element in all I have written." Perhaps my reaction to these stories is influenced in part by Cortázar's last novel, *Libro de Manuel,* published a year before *Octaedro.* In that book, as before in *Rayuela,* the author juxtaposes playful and humorous situations with serious ones and adds a new political emphasis. I miss the homo ludens so apparent in Lonstein's language, in the scenes concerning the strange mushroom, the fantastic turquoise penguins or the absurd protests unleashed in the restaurant. By now, however, I should be quite accustomed to the obvious lack of humor in Cortázar's short stories. Since *Historias de cronopios y de famas,* perhaps his most surrealistic book from the perspective of a playful atmosphere reminiscent of paintings by Joan Miró, the short stories have continued to be devoid of the humor found in the novels. It was, in fact, Calac and Polanco's ridiculous adventures which at moments saved the novel *62* from its abysmal cynicism. Are there any such playful and humorous elements which deliver *Octaedro* from the weary despair and sadness which penetrate every page? (p. 586)

I should have believed Cortázar when he said that *Historias de cronopios y de famas* is a book which should only be written once. He categorized it as his most playful book, "really a game, a very fascinating game, lots of fun, almost like a tennis match, sort of like that." Then he cautioned me that it was necessary to distinguish between the ingenuous joy of that collection and the humor which he planned to conserve in the rest of his books. Nevertheless, in *Octaedro* he has hardly preserved humor in any form.

Traditionally humor had not played an important role in Cortázar's short stories, nor does it now. Instead, the primary characteristics of his short stories have been the constant threat of an illogical and mysterious force to man in his daily existence and the subsequent defeat of that apparent reality by the unknown. *Octaedro* continues the short story tradition established by Cortázar, for it, too, haunts us with nightmares, obsessions and disconcerting provocations which menace everyday existence. But there is a serious and sad divergence from previous tales. The strange zone which Cortázar continues to describe no longer implacably terrifies nor intrigues the protagonists, nor the reader nor even Cortázar himself, as much as it produces despair. The author tries to describe this other illogical facet of reality in more realistic terms than was done in previous stories. It seems that the terror once experienced in the face of the unknown has now given way to a compromise won over many years. As Cortázar himself says in "Las fases de Severo": "It is always surprising to see how sudden lapses into normalcy, so to speak, distract and even deceive us." . . .

The different atmospheres that prevail in Cortázar's novels and short stories have become more obvious in these last few years. In the short stories man is as impotent as ever when faced with the exceptional in life, although at times he still seeks it out and plays to discover it. He now more easily accepts fleeting chance encounters and momentary outbursts of terror, after which he almost always returns in despair to accept routine life or to face death. In the novels, on the other hand, the author's joyful imagination fights to survive by means of unusual adventures, ingeniously playful language and political optimism. For instance, despite the descriptions of political torture, *Libro de Manuel* saves Cortázar's fiction from wallowing in the cynicism of the previous novel, *62.* As with *Rayuela, Libro de Manuel* embodies possible searches; and in opposition to the pervasive and definitive presence of death at the end of *62,* death in the final scenes of *Libro de Manuel* promises regeneration.

It is important to note that love continues to fail completely in the last two novels, for Juan and his friends in *62* as well as for Andrés in *Libro de Manuel.* Nevertheless, in the latter novel the pessimism generated by the absence of unselfish love between man and woman in the individual, personal sphere is diminished by optimism in the political and ideological sphere. *Octaedro* is very different from that latest novel, for these short stories are laden with death, tears, fleeting love affairs and impossible explanations. The pessimism that prevails on the personal level of love between man and woman is but one element of the human destinies that are ultimately altered very little by exceptional events and discoveries glimpsed through dreams, obsessions, dangerous provocations and even chance. *Octaedro* is a continuation of the Cortázar that we know, but there is a difference: Julio is finally accustomed to viewing the other zone of reality. He knows it is there. He experiences it. He tries

to share it with us. But he finally must return from it to his everyday reality in despair. (pp. 588-89)

Evelyn Picon Garfield, "'Octaedro': Eight Phases of Despair," in Books Abroad *(copyright 1976 by the University of Oklahoma Press), Vol. 50, No. 3, Summer, 1976, pp. 576-89.*

JORGE H. VALDÉS

Cortázar's intention [in *A Manual for Manuel* is] to provide the reader with an understanding of the "apparently" confused and undeniably complex state of contemporary world affairs and, especially, the conflicts of Western society. To achieve this, he characterizes a group of revolutionary Frenchmen and Latin Americans in Paris fighting the oppression of bourgeois capitalist governments, including such destructive organizations as the CIA. The struggle, however, encompasses far more than politics; it is a quest for the total liberation of Man from the egotism, fears, and taboos brought about by a derailed historical course. . . .

Cortázar is very conscious of his literary technique. Capturing the reader's interest from the beginning, he makes him undergo the confusion and torment experienced by the protagonist. At the same time, Cortázar provides the reader with moments of joy, eroticism, and sheer humorous absurdity in the lives of his characters—all of which indicates an intention to evoke a rich and varied response. It is the range and complexity of *A Manual for Manuel* that will appeal particularly to the sophisticated reader and will attain for the novel, in Cortázar's own terms, permanent status as a true bridge. (p. 388)

Jorge H. Valdés, in Best Sellers *(copyright © 1979 Helen Dwight Reid Educational Foundation), February, 1979.*

D

DAVIDSON, Donald 1893-1968

Davidson was an American poet, critic, historian, and rhetorician. One of the original founders of the Fugitive school of poetry, Davidson created a verse marked by an uncompromising loyalty to the precepts of the Southern Agrarian movement. He explicated his artistic vision in poetry whose syntax and diction is drawn from the classical and biblical tradition. Of focal concern for Davidson are the problems of religion, tradition, and the fundamental integrity of man in the modern world. (See also *CLC*, Vol. 2, and *Contemporary Authors*, Vols. 5-8, rev. ed.; obituary, Vols. 25-28, rev. ed.)

RICHMOND C. BEATTY

The works of Mr. Davidson are of a piece and evoke a problem in every instance—the problem of belief. A man extremely fertile in ideas, he is rare among Southern authors in having been able to contemplate experience from a settled and definable point of view; he has kept his sensibility undissociated in this, perhaps the most distracted of all eras since the collapse of the Roman Empire. He has achieved this success at the cost of many repudiations, for value after value which the society of our own time has come to esteem or despairingly to accept he has submitted to searching examination. Always the examination has been made in the light of an attitude that is traditional to the author, who might be characterized as a highly intelligent and gifted Southerner, one who knows and cherishes his personal and cultural past, his country's history, and the intentions of the men who established its constitution. (p. 13)

[*Lee in the Mountains and Other Poems*] remains, nonetheless, by long odds his most ambitious work, one which reflects the effort of a contemporary mind to integrate itself with its own personal past and with the past of the early Tennessee settlers, the tall men. In addition, it is a commentary on the present, in terms of the past, rendered by turns autobiographically, dramatically, and lyrically. The poem is also in certain passages satiric, and the validity of its strictures on the artistic generation that flourished during the 1920's reads with undiminished conviction today, now that we are able to contemplate that generation in the light of a certain perspective. (p. 19)

[Mainly the] poems of this interesting book recount Civil War stories such as the "Running of Streight," a fragment of the saga of General Forrest, or the simple story of the "Deserter," a Christmas Eclogue regarding the misunderstanding of the Confederate government—it could be *any* government, *any* abstract organization—in recording this word against a man who left camp overnight to see how his people were getting along and to make some effort to protect them against the invader. It is a poem fully understandable only by defeated peoples whose family allegiance is stronger than their devotion to the idea of statehood. It is told in the language which Wordsworth preferred but did not always use—the language of everyday life.... The alert modern, or modernized, reader will probably find [these poems] tame, too colloquial, too unrelieved by the exciting contrasts of mood and diction which he has come to demand in contemporary poetry. In brief, it represents a kind of writing that is "provincial" in subject and character. But one should immediately add that in its overtones it is universal and that, in the judgment of the poet, every way of thinking about life is provincial, since it is limited necessarily by individual experience. (p. 26)

In suggesting the development Mr. Davidson's poetry has taken, it might be said that from the romantic, Blakean, and often successful qualities of the *Outland Piper* it has moved into a far more serious stage for a reason already indicated —namely that he prefers to write what in the deepest sense he believes about man's nature and place in society. Poetry is thus anything but a diversion or an escape for him. He is no experimentalist in metrics nor is he particularly rewarding to the reader who is fond of arresting images. A certain rhetorical eloquence of speech (again like Wordsworth) is the substitute for these devices; he is most interesting when considered in terms of the total context of a given performance. Moreover, insofar as I know, he is unique in modern times in having made the effort Wordsworth undertook in his *Prelude,* which was to understand himself first, if he would later dedicate himself to a literary career. *The Tall Men* is the result of that undertaking, and its limitations are soon forgotten by anybody willing to think of the difficulties that would be involved were he to try to work them out in a similar fashion for himself. (pp. 26-7)

[Davidson] is certainly in the deepest sense a moralist, as Thoreau and Carlyle were moralists, and his characteristic subject matter is identical with theirs. His writings are, moreover, Christian in the fundamental sense that they recommend a drastic curtailment of emphasis upon economic values and in the further implied argument of Thoreau that men are unique and inviolable individuals whose integrity ought to be respected despite whatever institutions they have collectively evolved, either through church or state. To argue that, because of such thinking, he should be labelled a modern Jeremiah is in no sense to divorce him from the major secular prophets who have attempted to awaken Western Man to an understanding of his oldest question—What is my nature, what should I truly value, and what is my destiny?—a question which Mr. Davidson (again like Thoreau) has posed in terms of specifically contemporary issues. To add further that, so constituted, he belongs rightly in the Church is to compel the melancholy reply that the Church, being an institution, is by its nature too confined to contain him, in much the same sense that it was unable to contain Emerson. (p. 27)

> *Richmond C. Beatty, "Donald Davidson as Fugitive-Agrarian," in* The Hopkins Review *(copyright, 1952, by* The Hopkins Review*), Winter, 1952, pp. 12-27.*

JOHN CROWE RANSOM

Of all the Fugitive poets who were writing and publishing verse from Nashville forty years ago, it is Donald Davidson who seems to have maintained continuity and development most steadily in his art. . . . It is Davidson who is most loyal to the old Southern way of life to which four of them [Tate, Ransom, Warren, and Davidson] gave allegiance in their Agrarian phase. His devotion is uncompromising; it is dangerously close to exclusive. . . .

The title of Davidson's book [*The Long Street*] seems to be a key phrase to denote the culture which he is fighting. The Long Street is his image of the Southern industrial development, which was not stayed by the Agrarian agitation. (p. 202)

Other fine poems here are available for the critic's notice. But at least two are of extraordinary originality. They are fantasies, and it will be to the reader's advantage to explore and ponder them for himself. One is in this second section, entitled "Old Sailor's Choice": the narrator suddenly becomes Ulysses, telling an up-to-date Circe how he ran the twinned and monstrous dangers of Scylla and Charybdis; the lines the poet has given him are of an English colloquial and racy like Homer's Greek. The other poem is "The Case of Motorman 17," which constitutes Section IV. The motorman's family name is Brown, but the Christian name is Orestes. Does that signify anything? Here too there is a felicity of language, this time based on the jargon language of the civil courts. But the reader had better not try to predict the speeches, or the verdict of the court. (pp. 206-07)

> *John Crowe Ransom, "The Most Southern Poet," in* Sewanee Review *(reprinted by permission of the editor; © 1962 by The University of the South), Spring, 1962, pp. 202-07.*

ALLEN TATE

What Mr. Davidson may want to restore, or not restore, or to destroy or create, is not the issue raised by a reading of [*The Long Street*]. What, in his poems, he is concerned with is the opposition of an heroic myth to the secularization of man in our age. Looked at from this point of view, his poetry is no more concerned with the restoration of the Old South than the *Aeneid* is with the restoration of Troy. . . . There is not one poem in the book to which I

cannot give entire assent; I should merely like to see more to assent to. These poems say something important about man in our time, even though they may be about a country fiddler or Mr. Davidson's patronymic ancestor, or about the mystery of time and motion in "At the Station." The gaze is into the past but the glance is at the present, and this glance is sharp and exact. (pp. 671-72)

[Mr. Davidson] is one of the best classical scholars I know; not a philologist, but a lover of *literae humaniores*. His lifelong reading of the Latin and Greek classics is more and more reflected in the simplicity and elegance of his diction, and in the unobtrusive formalism of his versification. *The Long Street* is one of the most impressive collections of American poetry since the first World War. It is all the more remarkable for its appearance late in Donald Davidson's career. To bring one's affection and admiration together, so that these emotions, rare even in isolation, are indistinguishable, is a privilege enjoyed not more than three or four times in one's life. (p. 673)

> *Allen Tate, "The Gaze Past, The Glance Present," in* Sewanee Review *(reprinted by permission of the editor; © 1962 by The University of the South), Autumn, 1962, pp. 671-73.*

M. E. BRADFORD

[Davidson's] poetic achievement has been continuous and considerable. Indeed it can reasonably be argued on the basis of his . . . collection of verse (1961), *The Long Street* (Davidson's favorite metaphor for his imaginative experience of life in this century), that his finest, most impressive poetry is coming at the end of his career; and what distinguishes and gives especial value to these productions of his artistic maturity is precisely what has set him off from his poetic contemporaries since the Fugitive days and the first publication of *The Tall Men* (1927)—a preference for and personal possession of a traditional idiom and sense of the metaphorical potential of the familiar. These he has drawn from the main streams of our Western cultural heritage, from Scripture, classics, and (as Louise Cowan has well described it) "a sacramental view of nature." That he seriously *means* this idiom and these metaphors gives to him what now fashionable critics might prefer to speak of as "a command of archetypes"—and (among the poets of this century) an almost unique relationship to his chosen role. (pp. 516-17)

An urgent concern for and anticipation of "the decline of the West" and the obliviousness with which we approach this dissolution Davidson has in common with a great many modern poets. We think immediately of his fellow Fugitive, Allen Tate; of Yeats ("The Second Coming" especially); of Auden, Eliot, and Pound. We have had no lack of apocalyptic oracles from contemporary English and American poets. However, Davidson's mature expression of his anxiety, well represented by the classical/Biblical idiom which is the flesh of this example of his most recent manner, has a quality of its own and is illustrative of a strategy itself worthy of attention. For Davidson is, in style, as indigenously American—*of* his particular heritage as a conservative Southerner, a product of classical education, orthodox religious orientation and experience of his times from the perspective which these, together, provide—as he is in theme. And the resolution of manner and vision in his recent verse . . . is as much high art as any of the now fashionable ingenious solipsisms whose example he has avoided. For reasons of history (i.e., origin, education, and open commitment to causes he could not and cannot but champion and still be himself), Davidson, as a poet and as a public man, has been denied the hearing he deserves. Too often has it been assumed that these commitments do themselves preclude any serious consideration of his art when in fact they are, insofar as they make "available" to him the language and perspective of our elder poets, a partial explanation of the merit of that art. (pp. 518-19)

The inveterate modern may cry out against a poetics such as that which operates in "A Touch of Snow," may object to the poet's scene. He may resent idiom, fable, and metaphorical texture when he perceives that all are seriously intended, that they are *meant;* for he is accustomed to structures which serve only as a platform for verbal displays. And he may miss the mannered "tension" of the pseudometaphysical in verse whose irony comes of the weighted application of a traditional language to homely materials. The aesthetic "shock" he anticipates is not the shock of recognition, the revival of memory. He expects . . . a clever "surprise," a reassurance of his membership in a self-designated elite whose only connection with the "funded wisdom" of his civilization is their rejection of it. But the poetry of earth is never dead. Like Antaeus, Davidson renews his vision wherever he looks; he has heard his own teaching and gives us more than "exhibitions." What he believes to be the true nature (and defense) of poetry makes him comfortable with and gives him authority in a language that to many of his contemporaries is (in the phrasing of Scott) "a clasped book and a sealed fountain." That they often do not perceive the world as he does he is willing to accept in the faith that they too shall hereafter be "encouraged." (pp. 522-23)

> *M. E. Bradford, "Meaning and Metaphor in Donald Davidson's 'A Touch of Snow'," in* The Southern Review *(copyright, 1966, by M. E. Bradford), Vol. II, No. 3, Summer, 1966, pp. 516-23.*

THOMAS DANIEL YOUNG and M. THOMAS INGE

Davidson's first poems were about lovers and dragons, tigers and tiger-women. This choice of subject may reveal the poet's inclination to avoid some of the unpleasant aspects of the materialistic world in which he lived and to escape into an imaginative realm where lovers, singers, and others of acute sensibilities could be shielded from the harsh realities of an unsympathetic society. (pp. 42-3)

"The Valley of the Dragon" . . . is typical. Filled with images of "colored flies on honeyed errands," "golden sunsets," "silver moons," "thatch so kind . . . against the cold and rain," and "Love's low breathing," it is a romantic tale of an idyllic love that flourished in a land where the lovers are shielded "from the serpent-thoughts of men." . . .

The Tiger poems follow the same pattern. (p. 43)

In these poems the poet's dissatisfaction with his predicament is evident, as is his desire to escape the restrictions of a materialistic world to find fulfillment in love and nature. "The curse, the hope, the beauty" can be found only outside the patterns of "civilized" living. (p. 44)

In addition to a crude kind of lyric symbolism, these first poems are seminal in that they introduce a basic theme found in much of the later poetry: a profound sense of loss in the modern world. The method, however changes: the

approach becomes more direct and expository; the style, less lyrical; the rhythm, less regular; and the imagery, less romantic. Certainly these poems do constitute more than "a symbolic flight" from reality . . . ; they are the first vague and incomplete statements of a theme which appears in much of Davidson's later poetry, the search for a rightful heritage, and which is fully developed for the first time in *The Tall Men.* (p. 46)

Again [in "Old Harp"] Davidson is expressing his longing for something which man once possessed but which now seems forever lost. This time, in rhythm appropriately elegiac, he laments the loss of the great songs, the passing of the lyric and folk tradition. (pp. 46-7)

An underlying theme in many of these early poems is the thinness of the present contrasted with the richness of the past. Here the poet laments the decline of poetry, its disappearance as a vital force in the lives of a people; later these views led him to pointed arguments in defense of traditionalism. (p. 47)

The best poetry in the second section of *An Outland Piper* contains what Davidson calls the "packed line." The poet is not striving in these poems for simplicity of execution: his approach is indirect; his intentions more deliberately modern; his tone more consciously ironical.

The best poems in the second section of the book are "Corymba," "Dryad," "Naiad," and "Avalon"—the ones Tate called "the Pan series." In all of these poems Davidson is attempting to combine a "certain satiric touch," a "hardness of texture" with "lyrical beauty." All of them are based on a theme of protest, and they employ an ironic and sometimes sarcastic tone. . . .

[Davidson's] poems about dragons, tigers, and tiger-ladies were attempts at [a] "mythologizing or quasi-mythological" treatment; but they did not "come off" because the basis of the myth was too personal and esoteric, the treatment too directly romantic. . . . (p. 48)

With the exception of the title poem and "Old Harp," the poems in the Pan series are the most successful in the book. . . .

Except for "The Wolf," the remaining poems in section two and those of section three are the least satisfying in the collection. Many of these poems treat various derogatory aspects of the American materialistic civilization, and they tend toward despair and cynicism. Their unity of tone is often disturbed by a pertness and by an attempt to shock.

The most successful of the poems concerned with the fallibilities of man is "The Wolf." Set in a country store, it employs the kind of material that Davidson later used; and, like "Corymba," it shows the poet experimenting with the theory of correspondences. According to this theory, "an idea out of one class of experience may be dressed up in the vocabulary of another." Using the language and imagery naturally associated with the country storekeeper in his usual surroundings, Davidson succeeds in presenting convincingly man's animalistic nature, his blood-sucking rapaciousness. In this context, the man becomes a wolf. The poem succeeds because of its language: simple and concrete, it appeals simultaneously to the senses and the intellect. Blending perfectly with the subject matter of the poem and its tone of high seriousness, the language succeeds in presenting, not stating, the poetic object. . . . (pp. 53-4)

Davidson's other satires on various aspects of twentieth-century life are much less successful than "The Wolf." They reveal an indecisiveness about poetic technique and, perhaps, a lack of conviction in what he is trying to do. (p. 54)

The fourth section of *An Outland Piper* is composed of a single poem—"The Man Who Would Not Die." The longest piece in the book, ... it, along with "The Swinging Bridge" and "Legend in Bronze," is most indicative of the subject matter and the manner of Davidson's mature poetry. The three poems anticipate Davidson's characteristic tone and mature style, first found in *The Tall Men.* The tone, particularly of "The Man Who Would Not Die," is sardonic rather than cynical. The blank verse, though conversational, is precisely phrased, looking toward the dignified, clear, and smooth, but not swinging, line of the mature poetry. His experimentation with the ballad stanza and with tetrameter and pentameter quatrains that is characteristic of much of his early verse is almost finished. He is moving toward the blank-verse line as the medium that gives greatest freedom to his narrative and descriptive abilities. (p. 56)

The period of experimentation ended ... as his personal convictions, his historical bias, and his intellectual views combined to persuade him that the South was more than an accidental locale for his artistic creations. As he became convinced that the section "still possessed remnants, maybe more than remnants, of a traditional society," his struggle to "unite the form" of his poetry "with the myth that ought to belong to it" was almost won; his search for subject was over. In the period immediately following, Davidson's poetic skill was challenged and his creative energy was consumed by the writing of his most ambitious poem—*The Tall Men.* (p. 58)

The Tall Men (1927) clarifies Davidson's development as a poet. ...

Although the poem may not be intentionally autobiographical, the *persona* from whose point of view the materials of the poem are presented has a background very much like Davidson's. His identity is clearly established in the Prologue "The Long Street": he is a modern Southerner examining his traditional heritage in an attempt to discover if he can continue to function as an integrated personality in a society that seems intent upon destroying the eternal verities upon which man has traditionally based his life. The metaphor of the Long Street is more than the old vague trope of life as a journey. Occurring many times in the nine sections of *The Tall Men,* and in much of Davidson's other poetry, the street isolates and identifies the most destructive characteristics of modern life. The figure suggests that the predicament of modern man has been caused by an enemy more definite and deadly than chance or circumstance. The endless, smoke-infested street, where only the steel thews of houses flourish, is so desolate and so sterile that the poet wonders "If anything in this vague inconceivable world / Can end, lie still, be set apart, be named."

Unwilling to submit to the anonymity of modern life, the *persona* indicates at the beginning of the poem that he is seeking self-identity. He recounts the past in an attempt to find the "permanent and vital stream behind history and behind all the cultural elements going into the making of modern man." (p. 65)

The Long Street, the route that the modern Southerner

takes in search of his identity, leads him from the time of the pioneers and the first settlers, the original tall men of his region, to another period of his past, that immediately preceding the Civil War. The tone of the opening section of "The Sod of Battle-Fields" blends perfectly with the closing lines of "The Tall Men." As "The Tall Men" concludes, men of the twentieth century are presented as they "glide home / Impatiently," "speeding with effort only of ankle and wrist." ... In this century, we are reminded, the Southerner is forbidden to remember his sectional heritage; for "The Union is saved. Lee has surrendered forever." ... One must not concern himself with the past; it is over and would best be forgotten. He cannot mourn for lost battles and for the virtues, either real or imaginary, of a civilization that has passed forever. If the Old South of moonshine and magnolias ever really existed, and there is real doubt that it did, it surely cannot be resurrected; consequently, one must concentrate on the problems of the present. (pp. 70-1)

As the streams of the past and present are continually brought together, [the modern Southerner] attempts to sift out the elements or influences that make him what he is, to get back to and restate deep sources of racial experiences. In emphasizing the heroic and romantic, the poet attempts "to arrive at some basis for an attitude of acceptance which, while resting on the past, would not wholly reject the present—a mood of positiveness rather than the gesture of defeat to be found, say in *The Waste Land.*" (p. 72)

Written out of a deep-seated dissatisfaction with the literary treatments of [World War I] available in the 1920's, the sections of "The Faring" dealing with the combat experiences of McCrory and his fellow soldiers are as good as any poetry Davidson wrote before "Lee in the Mountains." (p. 78)

In ["The Faring"] Davidson's blank verse functions well. The easy-flowing, run-on lines keep the fast-paced action constantly before the reader and create within him the impression of the horrors of modern warfare. Always the vision is limited to the minute—and perhaps inconsequential—sector of the battlefield in which McCrory and his comrades live, fight, and die. No editorial comments and no ironic overtones intrude as in other sections of the poem; there are no suggestions, subtle or otherwise, that modern man is entangled in some rather sorry institutions. The McCrory of World War I is, as was his ancestor in pioneer days, a well-trained, severely disciplined soldier. Although the modern soldier's actions are a little more mechanical than those of his courageous forebear, they are no less brave. Because the poet is content to present the action without comment, he avoids the taint of false sentimentality. (p. 79)

The Tall Men concludes with the plea that man must not forget his heritage; it must not be for naught that the tall men fought and died to beat back the Indians who would drive them out of the Tennessee hills. He must remember Hnaef and his sixty warriors "greedy for battle-joy." A careful reading of the poem reveals Davidson's "feeling of intense disgust with the spiritual disorder of modern life—its destruction of human integrity and its lack of purpose." But in one sense the journey down the Long Street, the current mind of his society, has been highly successful. The journey back through his experiences has not been easy; it has been painful because at almost every point there rose the inevitable comparisons between the heroism and common devotion of the previous age and the physical and spiritual softness of his own; it has been frustrating because the vagueness of the modern world prohibits even the simple act of naming objects. (p. 90)

Although *The Tall Men,* as Davidson has pointed out, is not intentionally autobiographical, it is obviously a very personal poem. In the recapitulation of the past, in the penetrating scrutiny of the present, and in the obvious contrasts between the two, the poet has discovered "that permanent and vital stream behind history and behind all the cultural elements going into the making of modern man." . . .

The artist had found his subject; from this time forward—in essay, poem, debate, and newspaper article—Davidson expressed his disgust with the spiritual disorder and lack of purpose of modern life. He had arrived, with *The Tall Men,* at a basis for an attitude of acceptance, which, while drawing on the past for its pattern, did not wholly reject the present. . . . His affirmation is embedded in his conviction that the present struggle must be to retain spiritual values "against the fiery gnawing of industrialism." He is no longer content to be a detached intellectual artist; and his future career can best be understood in terms of his attempt to "retire more deeply within the body of the [Southern] tradition to some point when he can utter himself with the greatest consciousness of his dignity as an artist." (p. 91)

Davidson's Agrarian views are everywhere present in [*Lee in the Mountains and Other Poems*]. In "The Tall Men" he had pictured the modern urban community as purposeless and as almost meaningless—as an existence without life. . . . In poem after poem in *Lee in the Mountains and Other Poems,* these convictions receive fuller and more forceful poetic expression. Davidson reiterated his impression of an urban wasteland; and in some poems—"Aunt Maria and the Gourds," "The Last Charge," and "Randall, My Son"—he utters a prophecy of doom for the modern industrial society. The emphasis is always on the necessity of preserving one's tradition, but the poems are often so declamatory and argumentative that the poet emerges as the injured prophet—as one who has foreseen and suffered. (pp. 98-9)

["Lee in the Mountains," the title poem of the volume,] succeeds because the poet is able to unite the form of the verse with the myth that ought to belong to it. In the tragic, final days of one of America's few truly great heroes, Davidson could see a profoundly moving example set by a man whose every act exemplified a life of principle and honor. Here with "the grandest face that ever looked / Victory to the conquered" was the noblest of the tall men—one whose greatness of soul compelled him to choose what he felt was the right even when another choice might have been of more immediate personal advantage.

The total purpose of the Agrarians, Davidson has said, was "to seek the image of the South which he could cherish with high conviction that to give it, wherever we could, the finality of art in those forms, fictional, poetical, or dramatic, that have the character of myth." (p. 101)

In technique, some of the latest poems are among Davidson's best. They demonstrate the master craftsmanship that one associates with the author of *The Tall Men* and "Lee in the Mountains": a sure ear for sound and rhythmic cadence; a simple, direct, straightforward, yet elegant, diction

that reflects the poet's lifelong interest in the Roman and Greek classics; and a stately, or dignified, line devoid of esoteric vocabulary and erudite references. The poetic forms vary considerably. "Old Sailor's Choice" is written in verse paragraphs of varying lengths, some rhymed and some unrhymed. "The Case of Motorman 17" is verse drama; "The Gradual of the Northern Summer," also in verse paragraphs, is composed of strongly rhymed couplets; "A Touch of Snow" has a carefully controlled stanza pattern and a regular rhyme scheme. "Meditation on Literary Fame" approximates the form of Pindar's Epinician odes. With their flavor of the folk ballad, some of the brief narratives—"Fiddler Dow," "Joe Clisby," and "The Old Man of Thorn"—demonstrate the poet's nearness to his folk heritage.

But even with these impressive technical qualities, these poems are in no way contrived. In the carefully molded lines there is always an intensity of feeling that comes from an inner integrity and from a strictly defined set of sincere convictions. The momentary lapses into near cynicism, apparent in some of the poems in the *Lee* volume, are gone; but the irony, grave and stern, remains. It is evident, too, in these poems that Davidson has avoided the "guarded style," against which he cautioned his fellow poets in "Poetry as Tradition." He not only has sincere convictions, but he employs his poems as vehicles to carry these beliefs. He had warned his readers of the dangers of the poet's isolating himself from his community—of writing esoteric and sophisticated poetry intended for the perusal of none except his fellow artists. This practice, he insisted, would assure the demise of poetry and the destruction of society. This verse, with its simplicity and elegance of diction and its direct, forceful assertiveness, is written in a most "unguarded" style. (pp. 110-11)

The later poems reveal a restraint and tolerance not always present in the earlier verse. Although Davidson is quick to suggest the error of man's deserting his traditional heritage, there is no bitterness; instead, the poet seems to hope that some of the foolish will yet see the way. (p. 111)

One of Davidson's favorite themes is modern man's dissociation, his alienation from his tradition, and his lack of concern about the dissolution of his society. . . . [Most] men are as complacent as the two painters in "A Touch of Snow" who disregard the natural signs indicating that summer is over and that the bad weather of winter is just ahead. . . . It is a man's nature, the poet suggests, to be oblivious to the future as long as things *seem* to be all right in the present. But the poet must warn them and lament that they are not wise enough to sense the impending danger facing the Western world. (p. 112)

One of [Davidson's] purposes is to restore to poetry its social function: to serve as "messenger" to his people and to "evoke / New praise and old remembrance." . . . At times in his role of bard and prophet, Davidson's argument becomes so obtrusive that the poem suffers. But, in the best of his verse, the totality of his vision, the range of his imagination, and the force and clarity of his presentation give him a place almost unique among his contemporaries. (p. 118)

Whether Davidson's reputation will rest primarily upon his achievements as a poet or as an essayist is not certain. While his best creative periods for poetry were occasional, prose was a dominant form of expression throughout his career as a literary critic and as a social and political philosopher, historian, scholar of native traditions, and rhetorician. One thing is certain—his prose, of a remarkably even quality, is distinguished by stylistic grace and persuasive logic. In one sense, poetry is easier to write because, as Davidson noted, "poetry is that form of statement which does not require or even imply proof." Convincing prose, on the other hand, demands cogent reasoning and demonstrated authority, both of which characterize his work. (p. 119)

It is difficult to say with any certainty what part Davidson will play in a future literary history of his era. He found himself among friends and colleagues, three of whom—John Crowe Ransom, Allen Tate, and Robert Penn Warren—left the South and attained national and international recognition for their creative achievement. Such a historical fact has made it difficult for Davidson's work to receive a fair and objective assessment as the inevitable comparison of his work with theirs is always misleading. As men of distinctive temperaments and talents, each deserves a separate hearing and this has seldom been accorded Davidson. Yet, as a prose stylist, Davidson has few peers in contemporary American literature. Neither Ransom, Tate, nor Warren has written essays with a precision, a grace, a force, or a conviction to match Davidson's. Because, however, modern society has not been entirely amenable to *what* Davidson had to say, it has little heeded or sought to appreciate *how* he said it. There is every reason to believe, when all is said and done, that Davidson will endure as a prose stylist of the first order in this century.

As a poet, Davidson's work has not been so sharply limited as Ransom's, so intellectually opaque as Tate's, or so undisciplined as Warren's but it is more reasonable to say that his work is distinctive and decidedly different rather than equal or superior to theirs. Actually, it is difficult to compare their achievements because each poet has created from a set of attitudes and poetic principles radically different from those of his fellows. In principle and practice, Davidson wanted to be a poet not of the academy but of the people, which is not to say that he descends to the democratically literal level of a Carl Sandburg. His mature work is closer to that of his Vermont friend and neighbor Robert Frost, in that a minimum of knowledge of poetic technique, and a genuine appreciation of the American language for its potential lyric beauty, enable the reader to yield to the power of his verse.

Like Frost, Davidson turned to the regional experience of his native soil rather than to Europe for his language and subject matter; and, through artistic intensity, he raised this material to a level of universal urgency. Every reading yields a meaning; and, the more often one reads his more successful poems, the fuller the complexity of meaning becomes. And seldom does one find in modern literature, as one does in *The Tall Men*, such a sustained, probing, disturbing poetic analysis of modern man—one that is aware of the influence of his traditional past and fearful of the destruction inherent in the technological path modern society has elected to follow. Because of the totality of Davidson's vision, the seriousness of his intent, and the integrity of his craftsmanship, he merits the attention of posterity. (pp. 148-49)

Thomas Daniel Young and M. Thomas Inge, in

their Donald Davidson (copyright 1971 by Twayne Publishers, Inc.; reprinted with the permission of Twayne Publishers, A Division of G. K. Hall & Co., Boston), Twayne, 1971.

* * *

DAVIES, Robertson 1913-

Davies is a Canadian novelist, playwright, critic, editor, and publisher. Both his fictional and critical work reflect his breadth of learning and are presented with wit and elegance. He is considered a central figure in Canadian letters. Davies has written under the pseudonym of Samuel Marchbanks. (See also *CLC*, Vols. 2, 7, and *Contemporary Authors*, Vols. 33-36, rev. ed.)

IVON OWEN

When it first appeared, *Tempest-Tost* struck one as a pure, delightful *jeu d'esprit*, quite what one would expect from the typewriter of Samuel Marchbanks. A funny book. In 1958, it stands as the first of three novels about the same Ontario town of Salterton, and this makes a difference. Novelists who return repeatedly, as Trollope did, to the same place or the same broad circle of characters, achieve in time a stereoscopic depth that can be attained in no other way. *Tempest-Tost* can now be seen through the stereoscope, and it is still a funny book, but it is a good deal more. (p. 56)

[The relationships between the characters] make for straight comedy in *Tempest-Tost*. In *Leaven of Malice* they dominate, and take on a darker hue. . . .

Essentially the book is about the efforts of the aged and unbalanced to fetter and cripple the sane and young. And though it is a very funny book there is genuine anger in it. It contains some of the author's best comedy: the ghastliest of his many ghastly parties, the Old Mess, and a fine discourse on Charles Heavysege would be enough to make it memorable. But the central story-line—who put in the announcement?—is too slight to bear the weight of incident and comment hung on it and yet too stressed to be considered a minor element.

The new novel, *A Mixture of Frailties*, is livelier, fuller, more imperfect, and more delightful. It has two plots, a Salterton and a London one. In the Salterton story, which forms the outer frame, the parent-child theme is carried to a yet higher pitch of indignation. (p. 58)

Set into this story is the history of Monica Gall, the soprano from the Heart and Hope Quartet of the Thirteenth Apostle Tabernacle who is chosen to benefit from [a] trust. . . .

Monica's training as artist and as human being takes place in Britain, and forms the heart of the novel. It is the largest thing Robertson Davies has attempted or done. This three-quarters of a novel is in fact, with all its faults, fuller and more interesting than the other two and a quarter novels put together. It is a rich mixture of attitudes (not frailties—it's a bad title), attitudes to art and to life in profusion.

Each of these novels expounds a professional topic of which the author has special knowledge. In *Tempest-Tost* it is how to direct a play (which he has done); in *Leaven of Malice*, the life of a daily editor (which he lives); in *A Mixture of Frailties* (and I *don't* know how he managed this one), how to be trained as a concert soprano. It is done in convincing and lively detail. (p. 59)

The difficulty of handling the art-and-life training themes is complicated further by the Canadian-in-England theme. So far as Monica is a provincial in London, she might just as well be from Leeds as from Salterton. There is nothing peculiarly Canadian about her situation. But since in fact she is from Canada, the situation does call for observations about the experience of being a Canadian in England, and the sensations—pleasant and miserable, physical and spiritual—of that experience are beautifully selected and described. However, the picture is put badly out of focus by the caricature of a Canadian couple in London. They are very funny but too far from any human reality to make a point.

Mr Davies will say—has already said—that he didn't write the novel to illustrate these themes. Of course not—good novels aren't written in that order. But it is the interplay of these themes and ideas that make the story; in a sense they *are* the story, a story of a mixture of attitudes.

In brief, it is a muddled, untidy novel. . . . But it is irresistible as entertainment. . . . Mr Davies, an actor and a playwright before he was a novelist, never forgets to be an entertainer. . . . His lively mind is host to a variety of interests, and he is always ready to stop and talk about them; just as he is ready to wrench the story about for a third-act effect. His plot-machinery, creaky at the best of times, makes an unpleasant grinding noise on these occasions.

His novels are frankly diffuse, and being novels they don't suffer from it. . . . But they are a playwright's novels: the story consists of well-defined scenes in which people advance the plot and reveal their characters almost entirely in talk. How they do talk. It is well-heard idiomatic talk; it is effortlessly readable and endlessly entertaining and often quite incredible. In a play, things that in real life are left unspoken are put into dialogue because that is the way the author has to tell the story; the characters talk with unfailing fluency in impossibly well-rounded sentences because they would soon empty the auditorium if they talked as we all do in our living rooms. This fluent volubility, this compulsion to put everything into words, is shared by nearly all Mr Davies's characters, and it comes directly from the stage. (pp. 61-3)

Ivon Owen, "The Salterton Novels," in The Tamarack Review, *Autumn, 1958, pp. 56-63.*

S. E. READ

[In *A Voice from the Attic* the] attic is "America's attic"—Canada—and the "voice" is that of Robertson Davies, critic, novelist, playwright, wit, humanist, actor, teacher, editor, publisher, and bibliophile, but above all passionate lover of literature, who stands firm in his belief that books are still a shaping power for good in this world of chaos and uncertainty. (p. 65)

"Clerisy" is a precious word, and, though Mr. Davies would have it otherwise, I doubt that it ever passed as common currency in the English language. But use it he must for it "has no familiar synonym" and is "little known because what it describes has disappeared".

But what does the word describe? What is it that has disappeared?

The clerisy are those who read for pleasure,

but not for idleness; who read for pastime but not to kill time; who love books, but do not live by books.

In years past, especially in the 19th century, the clerisy, he says, held "sovereignty in the world of letters". Through being united it wielded great power, but now, alas! if it exists at all, it is disunited, and "has been persuaded to abdicate its power by several groups . . . , which are part of the social and business organization of our time." Awake, then, oh Clerisy! Shake the slumber from your eyes; gird up your loins; and go forth once again, as your forebears did, to fight the battle for good books, good reading, and a better culture. Such is Mr. Davies' clarion call, and such the stated purpose of the book. But Mr. Davies is not really a pugnacious battalion commander, leading his Christian soldiers once again to war. Having uttered the call in his opening pages, he then gets down to his real purpose—to entertain the reader (with some Johnsonian instruction thrown in for good measure) through a series of brilliantly written essays on books and on reading. (pp. 65-6)

[The portions which show his love for the forgotten book] are brilliant fun, but to over-stress them is to do the book as a whole an injustice. For in nearly all cases the discussions of these works (and many others like them) are but prologues to deeply serious and sharp, razor-edge comments on some of the great and really significant writers of our own age, as well as on some writers who have achieved popularity without true greatness.

With a sure touch and with astonishing agility Mr. Davies moves rapidly from the works of Havelock Ellis, Freud, and Jung to the novels of Joyce Cary or the humour of Stephen Leacock. He discusses at some length the reading of drama and its relationship to live theatre. He looks at some of the problems that face the creative writer and briefly peers into those wells of inspiration from which writers take sustenance. He gives a cool appraisal of Maugham, the novelist (he "is a masterly conjurer, but we can only be deceived once"), and takes a close look at *The Robe* (that prime example of a best-seller by the "Lutheran Dumas", Lloyd Douglas) to probe the reasons why it achieved such phenomenal sales. He then compares it with Robert Graves' *King Jesus,* which, though a much greater work, was not a success at all. . . . And finally, after some despairing looks at the Romantic attitudes of North Americans and the role of the "Yahoo Hero" in modern fiction, he pleads with us to understand and to appreciate the role of literature in the modern world: . . .

[There] is nothing minor about it, and when it truly mirrors any part of the soul of the time, it is revelatory and prophetic as nothing else can be in quite the same way.

But no such summary as I have given can really indicate the flavour of the book, or its real values. To appreciate it at all fully one must read it at a leisurely pace so that the joy that is within it can be really tasted and its rich intellectual contents slowly digested. Certainly not many books of like value have appeared in the history of Canadian critical writing, and rarely does such a pleasant critical work appear anywhere. It will surely appeal to nearly all readers who can lay a claim to discrimination and taste in the world of books. They may be irritated (and rightly so) by Mr. Davies' occasional sweeping generalizations, they may take issue with some of his critical evaluations. But the irritations will be offset by the pleasures to be found on almost every page. For Mr. Davies is not only a man possessed of a daemon; he also has at his command an urbane wit, a sharp critical mind, and a vast store of learning, which he carries lightly and on which he draws without ostentation or pedantry. (pp. 67-8)

> *S. E. Read, "A Call to the Clerisy," in* Canadian
> Literature, *Winter, 1961, pp. 65-8.*

MARGARET WIMSATT

The Manticore is a funny, engaging, literate novel by a Canadian author who deserves to be better known in this country. It has the theatrical virtues of scene, set and design; it has the literary virtue of plot, incident and character. It is easy to read and hard to put down. It is almost unique in being a sequel-book that stands on its own. (p. 536)

The manticore does exist, as explained in the novel's pages and confirmed by my dictionary: a mythical beast with the head of a man, the body of a lion and the tail of a dragon or scorpion. It is one of the symbols that turn up in the course of an analysis undergone by the narrator. . . .

As a novelist, Mr. Davies has the great strength of invention. He thinks of things and people that make pale suburban novels look duller and paler yet. So it may sound like quibbling, with so much to be grateful for, to complain that Mr. Davies does not know how to end a book. (p. 537)

> *Margaret Wimsatt, in* America *(© America Press,*
> *1972; all rights reserved), December 16, 1972.*

JUDITH SKELTON GRANT

That there is a market in these days of tight publishing budgets for a bibliography of works by and on Robertson Davies, a study of his plays, and a collection of his "Pronouncements" is an index of Davies' current popularity. This popularity is based on his second trilogy—*Fifth Business, The Manticore,* and *World of Wonders*—for in these books Davies has created vivid and distinctive central characters whose eccentric interests have both popular appeal and a philosophic undercurrent. (p. 56)

[Davies'] childhood love of theater bore fruit in his excellent Oxford thesis, published under the title *Shakespeare's Boy Actors* (1939) and in a stream of plays from the mid-forties on. Fourteen of these have been published and some ten others produced. His early plays earned him a permanent place in the history of Canadian drama. (pp. 56, 58)

Some of [Davies'] witty and irascible comment on the passing scene published in the *Peterborough Examiner* under the pseudonym Samuel Marchbanks was collected in *The Diary of Samuel Marchbanks* (1947), *The Table Talk of Samuel Marchbanks* (1949), and *Marchbank's Almanack* (1967). Some of the *Saturday Night* book review articles constitute the core of *A Voice from the Attic* (1960). Here Davies first reveals the idiosyncrasy and breadth of his reading. His knowledgeable discussion of aspects of popular culture from Shakespeare's day to our own, ranging over subjects like joke books, sex manuals, popular science, health tracts, and melodrama is not only diverting reading but the first real hint of the resources Davies brings to his recent novels. The Marchbanks books and *A Voice* are the mere iceberg tip of Davies' writing for periodicals. (p. 58)

[His first trilogy: *Tempest-Tost* (1951), *Leaven of Malice* (1954), and *A Mixture of Frailties* (1958) is] in the mode of the satiric romance. Davies' long experience as critic, dramatist, and journalist gave them an astonishingly impressive finish. His dialogue rooted in comedy of manners is lively; his plots are tight and workmanlike. But these surface strengths cause problems. The plot of *Tempest-Tost* permits significant development for only one of the half dozen characters Davies brings convincingly to life. The frame devices of the first two novels, though interesting and lively, jar, because they differ in subject or tone from the rest of the books. And there are technical problems with the omniscient narrator. But Davies learns and develops as he moves from book to book. The third in the series, *A Mixture of Frailties,* is a very fine novel indeed. Here Davies holds satire to a minimum, keeps his narrative stance consistent, focuses attention on one developing central character, and tackles his theme, the value of culture, seriously and openly. (p. 59)

The three volumes of the Deptford trilogy—*Fifth Business, The Manticore,* and *World of Wonders* . . . were well worth waiting for. Davies had avoided first-person narration in his early novels because he felt uncomfortable with the self-revelation and direct communication he associated with the technique. Now he used it masterfully. The intertwined stories of Dunstan Ramsay, Boy Staunton, and Magnus Eisengrim are told by three distinctive and convincing first-person narrators who compel the reader's interest in the story that begins when the stone-laden snowball thrown at Dunstan by Boy hits Mrs. Dempster and causes the premature birth of Magnus.

Davies centers each story in a different kind of knowledge. In *Fifth Business* the consequences of the snowball lead Dunstan to saints and myth; in *The Manticore* they lead David Staunton (Boy's son) into Jungian analysis; in *World of Wonders* they lead Magnus to magic and stagecraft. These provide the thematic core of each book; but only in *Fifth Business,* the master work of the trilogy, does Davies create an organic whole from his disparate materials. All the lore on saints and myth is firmly connected to the central character, reflecting his interests, showing how he thinks, influencing his life, and playing a part in his interpretation of events. That this is not the case in *The Manticore* is partly intentional. David Staunton has held his life together by banishing some things from consciousness, acting in stereotyped patterns, and blunting his feelings with alcohol. When his father's suicide shatters his customary defenses, he needs outside help if he is to find a meaningful pattern in his life, and he finds this help at the Jung Institute in Zurich. There is thus an initial inevitable division between the narrated life and the Jungian theory supplied by his analyst. . . . *World of Wonders* likewise falls short of the standard set by *Fifth Business* and again the problem centers in Davies' handling of data which occupies long stretches of the book. (pp. 59-60)

Though flawed when compared with *Fifth Business, The Manticore* and *World of Wonders* are intriguing and challenging works. With *Fifth Business* they contain the self-revelation compelled by first-person narration that Davies had earlier avoided. What constitutes self-revelation is not autobiography but philosophy. The ideas that overarch the Deptford trilogy are of two kinds: the speculations about myth and psychology pertain to natural philosophy; those on saints and magic, good and evil, God and the Devil to moral philosophy. With the first Davies feels sure of his ground as he follows in the footsteps of such trail blazers as Frazer, Freud, and Jung; with the second he is tentative and suggestive.

Let us begin with his natural philosophy. In the first and third volumes, perceptive characters find in myth a tool for understanding character and for anticipating patterns of human behavior. In the middle volume, David's Jungian analyst explains why myth lays bare the core patterns of character and action as she tells David how he could dream of a manticore, a mythic creature unknown to him:

> People very often dream of things they don't know. They dream of minotaurs without ever having heard of a minotaur. Thoroughly respectable women who have never heard of Pasiphae dream that they are a queen who is enjoying sexual congress with a bull. It is because great myths are not invented stories but objectivizations of images and situations that lie very deep in the human spirit; a poet may make a great embodiment of a myth, but it is the mass of humanity that knows the myth to be a spiritual truth, and that is why they cherish his poem.

In other words, myth gives insight into human behavior because its ultimate source is the psyche. (p. 60)

Davies' use of this material goes far beyond the mythic interpretation of character and events and the revelation of the source of myth's interpretive power. It also influences the nature of the reality in each book. In *Fifth Business,* the world is that of every day reality; myth interprets but does not transform Dunstan's world. In *The Manticore,* David deserts the ordinary world. As he learns new ways of thinking about his life, he finds his dreams presenting glimpses of a myth-like psychic life, hitherto unimagined. In *World of Wonders,* Magnus' daily life in Wanless's World of Wonders, in the old-fashioned traveling troupe, and in the gothic house and household he joins at the end of his story, is mythic. The heroic world David is challenged to find in the depths of his own psyche at the end of *The Manticore* is the world in which Magnus lives, for he has the "Magian World View" where the archetype of the Magus and the myth of Merlin are one and the same, and exist in broad daylight.

About the relation of God and the Devil to the natural world, Davies is exploratory and tentative. . . .

[In] Davies' world, individuals continue to make meaningful choices, though always in the presence of absolute Good and Evil. (p. 61)

Where Dunstan moves toward God and Boy toward the Devil, Magnus experiences both. He seems to represent psychic wholeness, and the possibility of a rich middle ground where man, conscious of the vigor and omnipresence of the forces of good and evil, lives an heroic life.

And is this "wholeness" which seems to be Davies' ideal, a balancing of opposites? I think not. Rather it seems to be what a character in *Fifth Business* has in mind in saying that meeting the Devil is educational and what David's analyst in *The Manticore* means when she urges the value of reclaiming, examining and getting to know one's Shadow (the dark side of the self). For not everything that has been

labeled Evil proves to be so, nor all that has been repressed ought to remain so. And the genuinely evil and justifiably banished are weaker if faced and understood. Together with the vigorous, lively and eccentric narrators of the last trilogy, these moral and the earlier mythic and psychological ideas have given these books a place among the dozen significant works of fiction published in Canada during the seventies.

One Half of Robertson Davies (1977) is a selection of pieces read aloud on occasions ranging from convocation to All Hallow's Eve celebrations. It is not as fruitful a totality as *A Voice from the Attic* because it lacks the sustained argument of the earlier collection and because some of the selections are slight. Nonetheless, five lectures constituting the heart of the volume are compelling, meaty reading. "Jung and the Theatre" approaches the Jungian material in *The Manticore* from a different angle; the four lectures called "Masks of Satan" tackle evil and good. Idiosyncratically, Davies approaches the latter subject through the medium of melodramas and novels of the nineteenth century, ghost stories and novels of the twentieth. The main lines of his argument will surprise no thoughtful reader of his late fiction, but such a reader will find his grasp of Davies' religious beliefs enriched and broadened and will find himself ruminating about some of Davies' pronouncements. He talks illuminatingly about poetic justice (Magnus' Great Justice?). He declares that the greatest art is created by those who believe in the existence of absolute Good and Evil, in God and the Devil. He talks of the necessity of opposites. He talks with a vigor that persuades one to expect more books plumbing the riches of Jungian psychology and speculating about the impact of God and the Devil on man's life. (pp. 62-3)

> *Judith Skelton Grant, "Robertson Davies, God and the Devil," in* Book Forum *(copyright © 1978 by The Hudson River Press), Vol. IV, No. 1, 1978, pp. 56-63.*

* * *

DELBANCO, Nicholas   1942-

Delbanco is a British-born American author of novels, poems, and short stories. (See also *CLC*, Vol. 6, and *Contemporary Authors*, Vols. 17-20, rev. ed.)

Delbanco is one of those consistently highly acclaimed writers few readers have heard of, much less read. "Sherbrookes," his eighth novel, is also sure to be critically well received. A wonderful and strange book, written in lyrical yet spare prose, it contains insights few writers can claim. . . . Delbanco steers clear of grotesque or Gothic overtones; he keeps his story clean and taut. And although his characters and their lives are peculiar, if not unique, they are always credible, and their story is intriguing and compelling. (p. 64)

> Publishers Weekly *(reprinted from the November 6, 1978, issue of* Publishers Weekly, *published by R. R. Bowker Company, a Xerox company; copyright © 1978 by Xerox Corporation), November 6, 1978.*

GARRETT EPPS

[Nicholas Delbanco has depicted the] underside of family life in *Possession* (1977) and now *Sherbrookes,* the first two volumes of a trilogy about the waning days of a wealthy New England family. . . .

Besides the hovering ghost of Judah, *Sherbrookes* has many other elements of gothic romance: an ancient mansion, a family curse, an unbreakable will, a mysterious pregnancy, and a moonlight suicide. Certainly, it seems to me that *Sherbrookes* does not operate like a realistic novel—by means of character, incident, or plot. Many of the characters are blanks; this is particularly true of Ian Sherbrooke, who seems at first almost like an empty cell awaiting the entry of a new genetic core, the spirit of his dead father. The book's movement is more in the fashion of a long poem, or a series of vibrant images held in rigid frames. There is a moment late in the book when Maggie, whose lusty ways in youth had earned her the title of "old Sherbrooke's bare-naked wife," watches unobserved as her son's lover walks naked across a field, and recognizes the arrival of her own replacement, "a brown-haired image of herself when young, the same straight back, thin hips, and long-legged gait." It is not a likely moment, or even a plausible one, but it is not an image I will soon forget.

Delbanco's prose is consciously poetic as well—alliterative, allusive, determinedly elegant. He is at his best when rendering the Vermont landscape, or when detailing the steps of building a house. But in much of the rest of the book, the effort expended on fine prose makes the story tough going. Like a horse keeping an unfamiliar gait, Delbanco is prone to missteps which reduce him to a lumbering walk. . . .

In addition, he has chosen to tell novels in the narrative present. In the hands of a supple stylist . . . this device can give a story a seductive immediacy, narrowing the distance between reader and character. But, as used by Delbanco, it involves the reader in a confusion of tenses, and by the time he has finished sorting out "he is," "they would," "she had," and "he did," reader and narrative are barely within hailing distance. And, finally, Delbanco has a fatal weakness for clichés, balancing them in his characters' minds like teetering rocks: "Six of one, he argues, since he's in the neighborhood; half a dozen of the other," or "You take, Maggie knew, a stitch in time."

The result is a promising novel, rich in myth and allusion, gone stale, gray-toned, and ponderous. One can admire Delbanco's learning and respect his effort; but, when the encounter is over, we are left with a weary, disappointed feeling of loss.

> Garrett Epps, "New England Gothic," in Book World—The Washington Post (© 1978, The Washington Post), December 31, 1978, p. G9.

TIM MYERS

Delbanco's vision [in *Sherbrookes*] is fundamentally pessimistic in a time when this view has been criticized as being purely negative and unconstructive, threatening the future of fiction. Yet Delbanco deserves to be read precisely because in confronting his characters with the realities of death and isolation, he gives them compensating acts of love, will and endurance. (p. 41)

> Tim Myers, in The New Republic (reprinted by permission of The New Republic; © 1979 by The New Republic, Inc.), January 10, 1979.

*   *   *

DeLILLO, Don   1936-

DeLillo is an American novelist who writes satirically of con- temporary events. **Often compared to Thomas Pynchon and other metafictionists for his use of language, he has portrayed the chaos of society under the guises of football, science, rock music, and urban sophistication. The discrepancy between appearance and reality is a central concern in DeLillo's work. (See also *CLC*, Vols. 8, 10.)**

MICHAEL ORIARD

While Thoreau was able to shape his months on Walden Pond into an instructive lesson for his future life, and into a ritual rebirth as critics have named it, DeLillo's characters are invariably left at the end of the novels still groping, or, at best, tentatively embarking on a course of possible rebirth but uncertain outcome. (p. 5)

[DeLillo's] fifth novel, *Players* (1977), shares many of the major thematic and technical qualities of the first four, but in a most fundamental way it breaks the pattern. From *Americana* to *End Zone* to *Great Jones Street* to *Ratner's Star* DeLillo traces a single search for the source of life's meaning. By the end of *Ratner's Star* the quest has been literally turned inside out; the path from chaos to knowledge becomes a Moebius strip that brings the seeker back to chaos. The main characters in *Players* are not sustained by the illusion that answers to cosmic questions can be found; they seek meaning in their lives, but meaning of a tentative and minimal nature. The novels before *Players* create a quartet, a four-volume sequence that DeLillo's [next] novel does not directly extend.

DeLillo's first four novels, then, are segments of a single proto-novel. Certainly the casts of characters in all the novels share common traits. Whether they be media executives, college football players, rock musicians, or mathematicians, characters who populate DeLillo's fictional worlds speak as learned metaphysicians. (p. 6)

DeLillo is concerned less with creating verisimilitude than with allowing his characters' deepest being to speak directly to the reader. DeLillo's novels are also characterized by wacky off-beat humor, by verbal virtuosity that startles and delights and often puzzles, and by multiple digressions into realms of quirky erudition or profound wisdom. The novels are a little like jigsaw puzzles assembled on a card table that is bumped—the pieces are all there but they do not seem to fit neatly together. Such is their author's intention; in the concluding novel of the quartet, *Ratner's Star*, a character speaks about some imagined contemporary writers:

> There's a whole class of writers who don't want their books to be read. This to some extent explains their crazed prose. To express what is expressible isn't why you write if you're in this class of writers. To be understood is faintly embarrassing. What you want to express is the violence of your desire not to be read. The friction of audiences is what drives writers crazy. These people are going to read what you write. The more they understand, the crazier you get. You can't let them know what you're writing about. Once they know, you're finished. If you're in this class, what you have to do is either not publish or make absolutely sure your work leaves readers strewn along the margins.

DeLillo, of course, is teasing his audience here, but the reader, occasionally baffled by a particularly abstract excursion into seemingly irrelevant metaphysics, senses that the author is also at times purposely evasive—the center of the novels is not always clearly defined, but a lot of fun and wisdom is to be found along the margins. (pp. 6-7)

The quest of the soul for meaning that was begun in *Americana,* continued in *End Zone* and *Great Jones Street,* and seemingly concluded in *Ratner's Star* is not a once-only progression on a linear course from confusion to enlightenment, but one completion of the cycle of human seeking. DeLillo offers no final answers; the importance to him is not the completion of the cycle, but the vision of reality which the process reveals. (p. 10)

The basic plot in each of DeLillo's four books is simple and spare; it is in the tangential excursions that his main ideas emerge, and the novels show remarkable unanimity in their primary concerns. The settings of the four novels is their first similarity, typified by Gary Harkness's description of the landscape in *End Zone:*

> We were in the middle of the middle of nowhere, that terrain so flat and bare, suggestive of the end of recorded time, a splendid sense of remoteness firing my soul. It was easy to feel that back up there, where men spoke the name of civilization in wistful tones, I was wanted for some terrible crime. . . .

The "end zone" of [DeLillo's second novel] is thus the setting of the novel and of the other novels, too: not only the goal of the running back in a football game, but the human condition at the outer extremity of existence, a place where the world is on the verge of disintegration, and the characters teeter between genius and madness. (pp. 10-11)

In this region of end zones that DeLillo describes, characters struggle for order and meaning as their world moves inexorably toward chaos. DeLillo's men and women fight the natural law of entropy, while human violence hastens its inevitable consequences. (p. 11)

The characters in all four novels . . . perceive the world about them rushing toward oblivion, see order, rationality, and meaning increasingly elusive, and recognize their only hope to retard such disintegration in Thoreau's advice to simplify. David Bell observes that visionaries confront the "large madness" with purity of intention and simplicity; the rest face only complexity. But simplicity has its varieties: for the dropouts David encounters on the Indian reservation simplicity means conformity and obliteration of individual consciousness; for Americans, in general, it means the destruction of everything distinctive—forests, big red barns, colonial inns, snug little railroad depots—and their replacement with tasteless, identical structures. Even in a perverse drive toward uniformity, however, lies the possibility of regeneration, which DeLillo calls our American "asceticism," for asceticism too can be a ritual preparation for action. Gary Harkness embraces football because it is primitive, it harks back to "ancient warriorship," it is built on pain and discipline, and it epitomizes simplicity: "Existence without anxiety. Happiness. Know your body. Understanding the real needs of man." . . . His intention is not to obliterate uniqueness but to reestablish contact with the basic human values and virtues that are threatened by a vi-

olent and over-technologized society. Bucky Wunderlick's goal is similar when he says, "Least is best"; he attempts to "minimize," and to retreat to his room to test the depths of silence. Robert Pirsig observes that insight comes when monotony and boredom are accepted; this commitment Bucky makes as he awaits the inspiration to act. In *Ratner's Star,* too, Chester Greylag Dent chooses to live on the bottom of the ocean, in "the quietest place on earth," because, as he says, "True greatness always involves a period of complete withdrawal." . . . The appeal of mathematics itself is its simplicity; in a world of complexity, mathematics makes sense. . . . (p. 12)

The importance of mathematics is that it is a language without the ambiguities, imprecision, and distortions of verbal language, and it is thus considered in *Ratner's Star* as a possible solution to perhaps the most prominent issue in all four of the novels—the necessity of remaking language. The dislocation of characters from an ordered and meaningful center is consistently expressed in terms of the failure of language. (p. 13)

Final solutions, ultimate meanings are . . . not available to mankind, and the realization of this inescapable fact lies behind DeLillo's dominant attitude towards life. Life is a game, as Hemingway said, and writing fiction is a particular game within that larger game. "Game" is a broad category, and many kinds of games occur in DeLillo's fiction. Sexual play is described in *Americana* as "true public sport, a contest in which spectacle eclipsed outcome, winner gave nothing." . . . In the same novel "playing a game" is equated with consciously confusing others with teasing, unfathomable remarks. Games can also be profoundly serious: David Bell's father describes the advertising business as "a crap game in an alley for six million bucks"; the losers of the game can lose everything. David himself played dangerous sports in college—with sports cars, motorcycles, and motorboats—in which the closeness of death provided the satisfaction, and after college he plays tennis to assert his superiority over his opponents. (p. 14)

Besides the games characters play—for amusement, for domination, for self-fulfillment, or for their own sake—DeLillo's fiction is also suffused with a spirit of play itself or game-consciousness that similarly characterizes the fiction of John Barth and Robert Coover. In *Ratner's Star* Robert Softly introduces his colleagues to a game called halfball—similar to baseball except that runs, hits, and errors all count in the final score. A team can add to its total by committing errors, but those same errors can also contribute to the other team's score: "The errormaker must balance the gains he is making in his error column against the gains he is allowing the other player to make in the run column." . . . With slight alterations, the rules of halfball can describe DeLillo's fictional technique, for he tests limits and must weigh consequences, too. No errormaker, DeLillo challenges his readers with copious digressions and excursions along the tangents of his topics. The pleasures of his novels lie largely in those digressions, but if the reader becomes completely disoriented, the author has digressed too far, and the gain is negated by a greater loss. To risk nothing is unsatisfying—*Great Jones Street* is the least impressive of the novels, the least risky, and the least game-like. To risk too much is self-defeating, however—*Ratner's Star* occasionally leaves the reader grasping for a center that eludes his outstretched mind. The most successful of the novels is *End Zone,* for reasons closely tied to the subject of the book, football. (p. 15)

[*End Zone* is] representative of the [other novels] in its concerns for simplicity, language, and violence. To consider DeLillo's major themes and his skill in handling them, one must fully observe them in the context of a single novel. . . . [The characters] live their daily existence at the extreme limit of human experience, psychologically and intellectually as well as physically. In this end zone of the mind, life is simplified; the characters confront the basic determinants of their existence in an effort to prevent their own surrender to chaos. (p. 16)

End Zone is, above all else, a novel about language, the center of man's striving for, and deflection from, order and meaning.

That the novel is explicitly about language is hinted on the very first page when DeLillo playfully warns the reader, "double metaphor coming up." Like his contemporaries William Gass, Robert Coover, and John Barth, he may be termed a "metafictionist"; like these writers, he is strongly aware of the nature of language and makes language itself, and the process of using language, his themes. DeLillo's consciousness of the reality of words as things is obvious at every stage in the novel. . . .

A distinct play element is evident in DeLillo's use of language. Many words are spoken for their own sake, for their feel in the mouth of the speaker, for the harmony of their sounds, and for their originality. The book is filled with splendid vulgarity. . . . (p. 17)

But playfulness and the imaginative pleasures of language are not its only function in the novel. Words often bear great power in and of themselves. The name of the football team at Logos College is changed from Cactus Wrens to Screaming Eagles—to the obvious improvement of its hostile image. Players have their "private sounds," their "huh huh huh" or "awright, awright, awright," or "we hit, we hit" that become magic incantations producing high emotional intensity. Words like "queer," "relationship," and all "i-z-e words" are weighted with great significance for the characters, even when not specifically associated with any object or event. (p. 18)

DeLillo's primary intention, however, moves beyond his assertion of the creative power of the word to a judgment of language as an inadequate basis for our relationship to the objective world. Philosophers of language have taken two approaches to the limitations of language: some feel that language itself is inadequate by reason of its vagueness, unexplicitness, ambiguity, context-dependence, and misleadingness; and others hold that ordinary language is perfectly suitable, and that the mischief lies in deviating from ordinary language without providing any way of attaching sense to the deviation. DeLillo shares both skepticisms. The failure of ordinary language is manifested by the cliches that proliferate throughout the novel. The author's use of them is adroit and always with a purpose: he satirizes the cliche, exploits its meaninglessness, contrasts it to vital and significant language, revitalizes it with a skillful twist, or demonstrates how it cheapens experience and can lead to fraudulent action. The world of football is wonderfully appropriate as an arena for dissecting cliches, for no language is so fraught with them as sports jargon. DeLillo proves that even in sports reporting such overused termi-

nology can be avoided by a sufficiently fertile imagination. Part Two of the novel, for instance, contains a stunning description of a football game and has more vitality than any such account in other literature or journalism. In details throughout the rest of the novel the author is equally original; for example, when Gary says of one of his teammates, "He's the defensive captain. He captains the defense," he turns an innocuous but essentially unresonant phrase into a metaphor for the defensive team as ship or military unit. He does not change the connotations of "defensive captain" but rather restores its original meaning. DeLillo's comic touch is nearly perfect in his undercutting of cliches. When Gary, for example, complains of the "ambiguity of the whole business," he could not possibly be more ambiguous himself.

If language is desensitized by overuse, attempts to recreate language are often equally inadequate. The primary examples DeLillo uses for the abuse of language are the various jargons that dominate a technological society. The terminologies of business, electrical engineering, game theory, abstract philosophy, militarization, and space technology are no more intelligible to the mass of mankind than is the complex jargon of football. . . . One of the novel's characters includes in his list of barriers to communication "that of multiple definitions" and "that of terminologies which are untranslatable." Both of these failures are demonstrated on the football field where the players themselves do not understand the jargon, where one coach talks of "a planning procedures approach whereby we neutralize the defense," and another only screams, "I want you to bust ass out there today." Neither coach communicates to his players how the job is actually to be done. (pp. 18-19)

Many writers have emphasized the destructive violence of football; DeLillo has more insightfully recognized the truer meaning of the sport. Football celebrates the ability of men to transcend the essential violence of existence, to create beauty where none seems possible. . . . Football in *End Zone* is the metaphor for positive violence, the kind of "violence" needed to recreate language and thus a new perception of life. Such a regeneration is to be achieved by simplifying existence and harking back to primitive origins in order to recover the primal uses of language. The metaphor for the negative violence that overwhelms such possibility is war. (p. 20)

Football is an "illusion that order is possible," and language has sustained the same illusion. To change history and correct the illusion, one must first change language. DeLillo attempts to make the change on a small scale in his novel, but writers conscious of the need for a new language face a paradoxical problem. If language patterns inherited at birth dictate the patterns of a man's actions, how can a writer change those patterns through the medium of his inherited language? As Tony Tanner observes: "Any writer has to struggle with existing language which is perpetually tending to rigidify in old formulations and he must constantly assert his own patterning powers without at the same time becoming imprisoned in *them.* That DeLillo is conscious of the problem is clear in the novel's ambiguous conclusion. The final paragraph reads:

> In my room at five o'clock the next morning
> I drank half a cup of lukewarm water. It was
> the last of food or drink I would take for
> many days. High fevers burned a thin

straight channel through my brain. In the
end they had to carry me to the infirmary
and feed me through plastic tubes. . . .

The ending can be viewed as a vision of defeat—admission
that the course of history is impossible to alter because the
course of language is too firmly imbedded in our being. We
are doomed to remain "a nation devoted to human xerogra-
phy." The concluding incident can also be seen as a retreat
into the most extreme simplicity of existence, to a complete
voiding of old forms, to an asceticism from which Gary can
begin to generate something new. It can be a Phoenix image
of positive regenerative violence.

DeLillo does not attempt to solve the paradox with an easy
answer. . . . [His] failure to finish *his* story indicates his
own lack of clear solutions, but he has made the reader
aware throughout the novel of the primacy of language and
the need for using it in an original manner. His novel itself
is at least a tentative step toward reconstructing language
into a truer description of reality.

After *End Zone* DeLillo has continued the quest for a new
language and an ultimate understanding of life's meaning.
Although the ending of *Ratner's Star* brought the search to
confirmed inconclusion, if so paradoxical a term can be
used, it marked not a deadend for the writer but a culmination of one four-part exploration. *Players* does not so much
mark out new territoy as retrace some early side paths and
emphasize one in particular—the game-quality of life. The
novel's model protagonists, Lyle and Pammy Wynant, create at least the illusion of order in their lives by playing inconsequential solo games—from Pammy's tap dancing to
Lyle's arranging the contents of his pockets on his dresser
in a systematic manner. Their attempts to play more meaningful games with other people lead only to complications
and confusion, and to the eventual suicide of a sexually
troubled friend. At the end Pammy sees that despite her
efforts to live a contributive life, her fate (as well as that of
Lyle, last seen waiting forlornly in a motel room) is expressed in the single word on a flophouse marquee: TRAN-
SIENTS. The novel acknowledges no source nor even a
specific quest, but portrays only disengaged people attempting to make life more than random interactions—and
failing.

Players is as thoroughly game-centered as *End Zone* and is
DeLillo's most self-conscious fiction. The novel's two
parts, which recount first the Wynants' separate lives
viewed on a split screen and then their attempts to alter
them, are bracketed by a sort of Prologue and Epilogue that
explicitly establish the artificiality of DeLillo's fictional
creation. In his first four novels DeLillo chronicled the
modern American's futile search for the mystery of existence. In *Players* he observes the attempts of a representative couple to create minimal order and meaningfulness in a
world in which that mystery is hopelessly elusive. Whether
Players signals the game-filled mode and interest of De-
Lillo's novels to come is impossible to predict, but we can
say with certainty that his first five novels, though failing to
answer the riddles of the cosmos, honestly and wittily ask
the right questions, and in doing so establish Don DeLillo
as an important original voice in contemporary fiction. (pp.
22-3)

Michael Oriard, "Don DeLillo's Search for Walden Pond," in Critique: Studies in Modern Fiction
(copyright © by James Dean Young 1978), Vol.
XX, No. 1, 1978, pp. 5-24.

J. D. O'HARA

Don DeLillo is insufficiently known, although his last novel
[*Players*] got some media play. Like Shakespeare (how's
that for a start?) he is seldom sufficiently serious; only *End
Zone* displays his remarkable abilities with consistency. But
he admirably refuses to repeat himself: after surveying
America in *Americana* he considered a range of philosophic
and ethical complements in *End Zone*, worked out a fantasy
of drugs and rock in *Great Jones Street*, got into science
fiction with *Ratner's Star*, brooded about urban violence in
Players, and now has written an amusing and imaginative
send-up of the spy novel, with overtones [*The Running
Dog*]. The predictably violent crimes and creeps are here,
the mysterious overlords, the sexy women, the quaint settings, the spaghetti-structure plot, the absurd treasures (for
instance a porn movie made in Hitler's Berlin bunker), and
the obligatory paranoid chase—all reported in a remarkably
crisp, witty, and stylized English. . . . (p. 227)

J. D. O'Hara, in New England Review (copyright
© 1978 by Kenyon Hill Publications, Inc.), Vol. I,
No. 2, Winter, 1978.

ANTHONY BURGESS

As a European, I sometimes wonder whether the kind of
fiction that Don DeLillo and other Americans are writing
can be termed novels in the sense still current in Europe.
Here it is legitimate to fictionalize the breakdown of civilization, but only from the viewpoint of a protagonist who
holds to the values out of which the novel-form was begot-
ten. We need humanity to observe the death of humanity.
But in *Running Dog,* and in much contemporary American
fiction, we have no humanity at all—bodies, nerves, trigger-
fingers, money-lust, power-lust, but no (ah, ridiculous Dostoevskian archaism) soul. *Americana* is the title of De-
Lillo's first novel; Americana are still, in his sixth, his
theme. Americana is a neuter collective: American things.
His characters are all American things. . . .

In *Running Dog,* Radial Matrix, the ultimate intelligence
agency, and several underworld characters are fighting to
get hold of film mistakenly believed to be unedited *cinema
verité* of a final orgy in which the Fuehrer himself took part.
The pornmen want the film, and some of them are prepared
to kill to get it. It is, so to speak, the ultimate stimulus in a
sex-absorbed society that approaches impotence. The film,
however, turns out to be scenes of Hitler doing a Chaplin
act for Goebbels's children. . . .

The humanistic position, however black and white and
grainy, that Chaplin represents stands for something like a
moral absolute in DeLillo,s terrible contemporary America.
Elsewhere there is nothing but porn, corruption, death. . . .

To say that *Running Dog* has all the fascination of a plastic
formicary is to deny that it is a novel in the old sense. It
moves, scurries, is very much alive; it even reaches conclusions, but these conclusions are premises. If the innocence
of the content of the Hitler film is, after the slavering of the
pornmen, a shocking anticlimax, this dithering man doing a
Chaplin take-off is still the Great Dictator, and the Goebbels children are shortly to be killed by their own father.
There is no health anywhere. The term evil has no meaning,
since there is no definable good. The naiveté of this American picture, itself a symptom of post-Vietnam shock, is belied by the sophistication of DeLillo's verbal technique.
The cutting is as rapid as that found in Eisenstein's *October*

and often as confusing: With so little delineation of either character or *mise en scène*, things tend to run together, as in a dropped bag of rotten fruit. I came to *Running Dog* after a reread of Mann's *Doctor Faustus*—a more terrible picture of evil, since in that book evil corrupts the good—and found DeLillo's work a refresher course in the readjustment to contemporary literary values. There is something of Pynchon in it and a little of John Hawkes. DeLillo has his own voice, harsh, eroded, disturbingly eloquent.

> *Anthony Burgess, "No Health Anywhere," in* Saturday Review (© *1978 by Saturday Review Magazine Corp.; reprinted with permission), September 16, 1978, p. 38.*

THOMAS LeCLAIR

Plenitude and excess distinguish much of our best fiction: Pynchon's *Gravity's Rainbow*, Coover's *The Public Burning*, Gaddis's *JR*, McElroy's *Lookout Cartridge*. Don DeLillo has their exhaustive impulse, but his six novels, singly and together, are a reversed cornucopia. They spiral from the overripe riches of America toward a difficult silence. More than any other novelist to emerge in [the '70s], Don DeLillo knows the spoiled goods of America and knows as well that a novel made in the USA may be implicated in the waste and noise of its place. His tactics have been attack and withdrawal. . . .

"The beast is loose / Least is best" say the lyrics of Bucky Wunderlick in *Great Jones Street*. Minimalism has its great exemplars in Beckett and Borges, but it also has its attendant difficulty: "The less there is," says a character in *Running Dog*, "the more you're tested to find the things that do exist." It is a test for reader and writer alike, one that DeLillo does not manage well in this new novel. Narrowed, flattened and polished, *Running Dog* reads too much like some compacted version of the literary waste—the intrigue—from which DeLillo has presumably meant to separate it with artful reduction. But because *Running Dog* features the contractive method that worked in the earlier books, especially *Players*, it remains an interesting novel, an experimental coda to a major writer's career. (p. 33)

Running Dog is a world of behavior and use. People are points on a graph, points nearly obliterated by the plot lines that connect them. Violence and copulation are sudden, reactive, without what Selvy calls "moderating precepts." The dialogue is tough, short and brittle; the writing narrows to a succession of subjects, verbs, and objects, bodies in motion. I'd like to think DeLillo wanted the reduced manner of the novel—its emptiness and verbal impoverishment —to reflect the characters' reduced lives, the culture's reaching its most probable state; but instead he seems to be exploiting his material. Because they are figures from our public mythology, a flood of ready-made associations and connections fills the gaps created by DeLillo's subtraction. The novel's first line is "You won't find ordinary people here," but in fact its characters are as ordinary as dollar movies, prime-time television, and *People* magazine. The novel itself comes to be a stimulus-response machine, a transistorized potboiler.

Most of DeLillo's other novels could have been reduced to the outline that *Running Dog* is, but no matter how bleak the behavior in these books they have a gaiety of language, a cross-cutting of discourses. One understands why DeLillo has given up on people; but one hopes he hasn't given up

on words, of which fictional people are made. As Selvy travels toward his death, he lists what he has left behind: "All that incoherence. Selection, election, option, alternative. All behind him now. Codes and formats. Courses of action. Values, bias, predilection." The "incoherence" of multiple voices, the "codes and formats" of language itself, the "values" tested by silence—these are precisely what DeLillo leaves out of *Running Dog*, the qualities that make his other fiction so vital *and* lucid. DeLillo is too good, too verbally sophisticated a writer to knock off Jerzy Kosinski novels, which *Running Dog* resembles in its worst moments. A character in *End Zone* speaks of trying "to create degree of silence." That's DeLillo's gift, not zero degrees but degrees, fine gradients of something and nothing. (p. 34)

> *Thomas LeClair, in* The New Republic *(reprinted by permission of* The New Republic; © *1978 The New Republic, Inc.), October 7, 1978.*

RICHARD KUCZKOWSKI

[With] precision and order, *Running Dog* reveals pattern and network linking seemingly unrelated individuals and their rituals of distance, devotion, quest, connection, and separation enacted around a "pornographic" film. That film and the inability or unwillingness of the individuals involved to comprehend or transcend the true nature and full extent of their actions and relationships lend moral perspective to DeLillo's novel. . . .

Running Dog belongs to a special category of art, one that includes, say, Conrad's *Secret Agent*, Goddard's *Weekend*, and Tooker's paintings of petrified subway patrons. Works of this kind situate us precisely and concretely—if ironically —in recognizable contemporary reality slightly but purposefully heightened to exploit the ambiguous interfaces between system and chaos, the commerce between meaning and absurdity, perversion and normalcy. They show us society as an anti-anthill, a hive of grotesque conspiratorial cells, a dangerous maze of cross-purposes. But there is no preachment in *Running Dog*. DeLillo has reimagined the world of our recent and present history into a compact whole of speech and action in which the details of the present are perfected through careful craft into a metaphoric vision. The language of conspiracy, with its beginnings in self-repression and its "sexual sources and coordinates"; the stance of taut, impersonal reportage; a design full of disturbing parallels, odd echoes, abrupt disjunctions, and grim humor—DeLillo has fitted these elements together into a novel as meticulously constructed as Selvy's gun. (p. 27)

> *Richard Kuczkowski, in* New York Arts Journal *(copyright* © *1978 by Richard W. Burgin), #12, November-December, 1978.*

VALENTINE CUNNINGHAM

[A lesson] in how to compile a political thriller—smartly enigmatic, niftily cross-cut, bouncy with erotics, sudden deaths, and smartipants talk—is *Running Dog*, which wears its seriousness with fetching lightness. Cinematically, indeed fast-movingly done, it celebrates our cineastic age where only what moves is alluring: and where what allures its pawn-dealers, villains, journalists, and secret service operators most is a rumoured sex-orgy movie shot in Hitlers's bunker. Inevitably disappointing, the old footage has Hitler doing Chaplin impressions for Goering's kiddies. 'Could he tell them history is true?' a dealer wonders.

Hardly, the novel implies, in Kino America, where the real is merely a western reel. (p. 158)

Valentine Cunningham, in New Statesman (© 1979 The Statesman & Nation Publishing Co. Ltd.), February 2, 1979.

*   *   *

DU BOIS, W(illiam) E(dward) B(urghardt) 1868-1963

Du Bois was a black American essayist, novelist, biographer, poet, sociologist, and editor. He was one of the first black intellectuals to advocate a militant solution to racial problems, and in his best known work, *The Souls of Black Folk*, repudiated the accommodationist views of Booker T. Washington. In 1909 Du Bois helped found the National Association for the Advancement of Colored People, an organization from which he was asked to resign his membership in 1934. He was also a founder of the black literary journal *Phylon* and edited the NAACP journal *Crisis* for more than twenty years. (See also *CLC*, Vols. 1, 2.)

WILLIAM H. FERRIS

[Both Paul Laurence Dunbar and Charles Waddell Chesnutt] have artistically uncovered to our gaze the inner life of the Negro, but Du Bois has done this and something more. He has not only graphically pictured the Negro as he is, but he has brooded and reflected upon and critically surveyed the peculiar environment of the Negro, and with his soul on fire with a righteous indignation, has written with the fervid eloquence of a Carlyle. If one desires to see how it feels to be a Negro and a man at the same time, if one desires to see how a sensitive and refined Negro mentally and spiritually reacts against social, civil, and political ostracism, if one desires to see a Negro passing judgment upon his civil and political status, and critically dissecting American race prejudice as with a scalping knife, he must go to Du Bois. (pp. 88-9)

Du Bois' *Souls of Black Folk* came to me as a bolt from the blue. It was the rebellion of a fearless soul, the protest of a noble nature against the blighting American caste prejudice. It proclaimed in thunder tones and in words of magic beauty the worth and sacredness of human personality even when clothed in a black skin.

Du Bois is a literary artist who can clothe his thought in such forms of poetic beauty that we are captivated by the opulent splendor and richness of his diction, while our souls are being stirred by his burning eloquence. His style is not only graphic and picturesque, he can not only vividly describe a county, in his brilliant chapter upon the Black Belt, but there is a dreamy suggestiveness to his chapters "Upon our Spiritual Strivings," "The Wings of Atalanta," and "Alexander Crummell," a delicate literary touch, which entitles Du Bois to a place in the magic circle of prose poets. (p. 89)

What then does Du Bois lack? As Dunbar lacks a grasp of the problems that interest and perplex the modern mind, so Du Bois seems to ignore the unity of human history. He is the voice of one crying in the wilderness. . . . (pp. 89-90)

The Souls of Black Folk is the protest of Du Bois, the individual, and not the protest of the universe against caste prejudice.

But it may be that if the subjective and personal note was not so clear and strong in *The Souls of Black Folk;* if instead of having for its keynote a despairing wail, it had rung with the buoyant faith of a Browning, the book might not have caught the ear of the age in the way that it has. (p. 91)

That Du Bois' *Souls of Black Folk* has become the political bible of the Negro race, that he is regarded by the colored people as the long-looked-for political Messiah, the Moses that will lead them out of the Egypt of peonage, across the Red Sea of Jim Crow legislation, through the wilderness of disfranchisement and restricted opportunity, and into the promised land of liberty of opportunity and equality of rights, is shown by the recent Niagara Movement, which has crowned Du Bois as the Joshua before whom it is hoped the Jericho of American caste prejudice will fall down. (p. 92)

William H. Ferris, "The Emerging Leader: A Contemporary View" (originally published in his The African Abroad; Or His Evolution in Western Civilization, Tracing His Development under the Caucasian Milieu, Tuttle, Morehouse & Taylor Press, 1913), in W.E.B. Du Bois: A Profile, edited by Rayford W. Logan, Hill & Wang, 1971, pp. 86-121.

HERBERT APTHEKER

Dr. Du Bois was more a history-maker than an historian. The two were intertwined, however; what interested Du Bois as a maker of History helped determine what he wrote, and what he wrote helped make history. (p. 249)

As historian, dedicated to the most rigorous standards of integrity, he remained, nevertheless, agitator-prophet; present was another fundamental ingredient in the man, namely, the poet. (pp. 249-50)

Du Bois' extraordinary career manifests a remarkable continuity. From his 1890 Harvard Commencement address to his posthumously-published *Autobiography*, the *essential* theme is the beauty, rationality, and need of service and of equality, and the ugliness, irrationality, and threat of greed and elitism. Because of the especially oppressed condition of the colored peoples of the earth—and particularly of the African and African-derived peoples—Du Bois believed in their capacity for compassion and comradeship, or, as he put it in the 1890 speech, "for the cool, purposeful *Ich Dien* of the African." (p. 250)

For Du Bois, history-writing was *writing;* one who produces a book should try, thereby, to produce *literature.* He drove himself hard on this. All authors, I think, are anxious to see their work in print; crusading authors probably feel this anxiety more than others. . . . Yet, Du Bois wrote and re-wrote his massive *Black Reconstruction* three times; and after that, revised and revised and cut and cut. . . . (p. 251)

Du Bois was explicit in his belief that while living behind the Veil might carry the danger of provincialism, it had the great advantage of helping disclose truth or neglected aspects of reality exactly because its point of observation differed. There was something else, too; Du Bois not only held that a new vantage point offered new insights. He held also that a racist viewpoint was a blighted one; that it could not fail to distort reality and that an explicitly anti-racist viewpoint was not only different but better. Hence, he insisted that the view—or prejudice, if one wishes—which he brought to data would get closer to reality not only because it was fresh but also because it was egalitarian. (p. 252)

Du Bois in practice resolved the difficult problem of objectivity and partisanship, of truth and justice, of the moral and the scientific by affirming—perhaps assuming would be more exact, for the argument is never quite explicit—that separating morals from science caricatures the latter, that the just is the true, and that while objectivity in the sense of utter neutrality in any meaningful matter is absurd this does not rule out the describing of reality—of "telling it like it is"; that, rather, the solution to the apparent paradox has a paradoxical twist: it is intense partisanship—on the side of the exploited and therefore on the side of justice—that makes possible the grasping of truth. Or, at least, that such partisanship is the highway leading to that accumulation of knowledge which brings one closer and closer to the real but not reachable final truth. (pp. 254-55)

Du Bois had a towering sense of the Right, of the Just, a basic faith in reason and a passionate commitment toward achieving the just through the use of reason. Indeed, all this together is what Du Bois meant by that word which to him was most sacred: Science. And in his lifetime and in his experience the central lie was racism; this, therefore, received the brunt of his blows. (p. 256)

How shall we sum up Du Bois' conception of history? There is the facile technique of labels, normally unsatisfactory and in the case of a man as polemical, radical, and productive as Du Bois, bound to be, I suggest, especially unsatisfactory. (p. 259)

Having found Du Bois described as a confirmed Marxist, a plain Marxist, a quasi Marxist, and not a Marxist we have perhaps exhausted the possibilities.

Du Bois was a Du Boisite. His political affiliations or affinities varied as times changed, as programs altered, and as he changed. . . . (pp. 259-60)

While [*Black Reconstruction*] is weak insofar as it tends to ignore the former nonslaveholding whites who were landed —*i.e.,* the yeomanry—and who therefore had class as well as racist differences with the black millions, and is weak, too, insofar as it accepts the concept of a monolithic white South from the pre-Civil War period to Reconstruction, it pioneered in a related area, for it called attention very forcefully to the neglect, then, of the history of the poorer whites in the South.

The momentous impact upon the nature of U.S. society and therefore upon world history of the failure of the effort at democratizing the South—which is what the defeat of Reconstruction meant in Du Bois' view—is emphasized in *Black Reconstruction*. The consequent turn toward an imperial career, to which Woodrow Wilson pointed with delight, was a development which Du Bois denounced and concerning which he warned in prescient terms.

Du Bois also sought to make clear that Reconstruction was an episode in the entire—and worldwide—struggle of the rich versus the poor; in this connection he emphasized not only the specifics of the land question in the South but the whole matter of property rights; indeed, he called one of the most pregnant chapters in his volume, "Counter-Revolution of Property." He saw—as had Madison a century before him—that the right to and control of property was central to problems of the state and therefore of all forms of state, including that of democracy. Indeed, Du Bois—as Madison—emphasized the special connection between

democracy and property insofar as the principle of universal enfranchisement meant political power in the hands of the majority and that majority normally had been and was the nonpropertied.

In this sense, Du Bois saw the story of Reconstruction—especially as it concerned the millions of dispossessed blacks—as an essential feature of the story of labor; not labor in the sense of industrial and/or urban working people, but labor in the more generic sense of those who had to work—to labor—in order to make ends meet. I think, too, that Du Bois' use of the term proletariat was more classical than Marxian. . . . (pp. 265-66)

Certainly, in the Marxian sense, Radical Reconstruction represented an effort to bring a bourgeois-democratic order to the South and in this effort—given the formerly slave-based plantation economy—the idea of "land to the landless" was fundamental; this meant not the elimination of the private ownership of the means of production—a basic aim of the dictatorship of the proletariat—but rather its wider distribution. From this point of view Du Bois' choice of words and expressions was confusing—and erroneous; but his perception of the relationship of particularly exploited black masses to any effort at making democracy real and to any secure advance of the deprived of all colors—which is what he was bringing forward—was a profound one and remains a challenging one for today, not only in terms of history-writing but also in terms of history-making. (pp. 267-68)

It will be well . . . to allow Du Bois himself to state the basic theme of *Black Reconstruction;* presumably he is good authority for this. He stated this, in differing ways, several times; we shall for reasons of space, quote only one and that extremely brief:

> To me, these propositions, extreme as they may sound, seem clear and true:
>
> 1. The American Negro not only was the cause of the Civil War but a prime factor in enabling the North to win it.
>
> 2. The Negro was the only effective tool which could be used for the immediate restoration of the federal union after the war.
>
> 3. The enfranchisement of the freedmen after the war was one of the greatest steps toward democracy taken in the nineteenth century.
>
> 4. The attempts to retrace that step, disfranchising the Negro and reducing him to caste conditions, are the deeds which make the South today the nation's social problem Number One.
>
> (p. 269)

In the enormous body of Du Bois' writings, errors of fact will be found; almost always these are of a minor—even picayunish—nature. I think it is true that their occurrence is probably somewhat less uncommon than among historians of analogous scope. (p. 270)

Somewhat more serious was a kind of literary tendency on Du Bois' part which took the form of rather exaggerated assertions or a kind of symbolism that in the interest of effect might sacrifice precision. Professor Wesley in his . . .

review in *Opportunity* (1935) gave several examples of this tendency; he called it "a tendency to dismiss the explanation of some events with all too brief a wave of the hand." Exaggerations for effect would lead Du Bois to ascribe the Seminole Wars *purely* to the problem of fugitive slaves, or U.S. acquisition of the Louisiana Territory *solely* to the rebellion of Haitian slaves. A kind of poetic license would lead Du Bois to place John Brown's hopes as centering on the Blue Ridge Mountains—which was probably true—but he would add that it was in those same mountains "where Nat Turner had fought and died, [and] where Gabriel had sought refuge," which is simply not true; but probably this objection reflects the weaknesses of a pedestrian plodder before the canvases of an inspired poet-historian.

With such nitpicking I am reminded of Du Bois' "Forethought" to his immortal *Souls of Black Folk:* "I pray you, then, receive my little book in all charity, studying my words with me, forgiving mistake and foible for sake of the faith and passion that is in me, and seeking the grain of truth hidden there."

His grains accumulated to a vast monument and precious heritage. It was Du Bois who began the scientific study of the Negro's history, who saw that it constituted a test of the American experience and dream, that it was a basic constituent in the fabric of United States history, that it was part of the vaster pattern of the colored peoples who make up most of Mankind.

Even in detail, it was Du Bois who pioneered the study of the slave trade, who first offered new insights into the Freedmen's Bureau, who first pointed to the significance of the Negro in the Abolitionist movement, who contested the stereotype of the docile and contented slave, who helped illuminate the meaning of John Brown, who transformed approaches to the Civil War and Reconstruction, who pioneered in writing the history of African peoples, whose studies of Southern agriculture and of Northern cities—in particular Philadelphia—remain massive and—again—pioneering efforts in historiography. (pp. 270-71)

> Herbert Aptheker, "The Historian," in The Negro History Bulletin (reprinted by permission of The Association for the Study of Afro-American Life and History, Inc.), Vol. 32, No. 4, April, 1969 (and reprinted in W.E.B. DuBois: A Profile, edited by Rayford W. Logan, Hill & Wang, 1971, pp. 249-73).

WILSON J. MOSES

Du Bois's early work struggles to fuse two complementary but substantially different mythological traditions. The first of these is "Ethiopianism," a literary-religious tradition common to English-speaking Africans, regardless of nationality. The other is the European tradition of interpretive mythology, transplanted to America by its European colonizers. (p. 411)

Ethiopianism may be defined as the effort of the English-speaking Black or African person to view his past enslavement and present cultural dependency in terms of the broader history of civilization. It serves to remind him that this present scientific technological civilization, dominated by Western Europe for a scant four hundred years, will go under certainly—like all the empires of the past. It expresses the belief that the tragic racial experience has profound historical value, that it has endowed the African with

moral superiority and made him a seer. Du Bois's poetry, while highly original, is nonetheless a product of this tradition, and therefore traditional. T. S. Eliot's poetry, by way of comparison, works within the European tradition of interpretive mythology although it is clearly innovative.

European interpretive mythology is the second of the two traditions basic to Du Bois's mythmaking. . . . This tradition, once revived in the Middle Ages, endured throughout the Renaissance, and as Douglas Bush has shown, became a mode functional to English and American poetry.

How can it be known that Du Bois was aware of the tradition of interpretive mythology and that he consciously wrote in this tradition? In Chapter VIII of *The Souls of Black Folk,* in the section titled "Of the Quest of the Golden Fleece," Du Bois demonstrated his awareness of this kind of writing and his desire to experiment with it. . . . In an earlier chapter of the same book, "Of the Wings of Atalanta," Du Bois had demonstrated his skill at updating mythology and adapting it to the needs of his times. *The Quest of the Silver Fleece,* in 1911, brought to maturity the ideas briefly outlined in the parent essay. In this novel he created a universe in which the ideology of progressive socialism and the traditionalism of Christian black nationalism work harmoniously within the framework of a Greek myth. (pp. 416-17)

Can Du Bois the social scientist be reconciled with Du Bois the poet and prophet of race? How could a man so well trained in social science have allowed the Ethiopian tradition, rooted in nineteenth-century *Volksgeist* mythologies, to dominate his thought?

As a youth Du Bois was romantically involved with the idea of social science, which he naively believed might yield a science of racial advancement. He was infatuated, like many other young men of his generation with the notion of a "science of man." But Du Bois's theories of social change were not always consistent. Sociology became relatively less important with the passage of years until by 1910 it was no longer Du Bois's chief concern. Though he was capable of writing perfectly good sociology, it does not appear that he wanted to. He turned—and it would seem with more satisfactory results—to the power of imagination as his chief instrument for changing public morality. He became a crusading journalist, a novelist, and a poet of Ethiopianism, dedicated to embodying his view of history in mythical form. (pp. 425-26)

> Wilson J. Moses, "The Poetics of Ethiopianism: W.E.B. Du Bois and Literary Black Nationalism," in American Literature (reprinted by permission of the Publisher; copyright 1975 by Duke University Press, Durham, North Carolina), Vol. 47, No. 3, November, 1975, pp. 411-26.

*   *   *

DUBUS, Andre   1936-

An American novelist and short story writer, Dubus writes contemporary fiction concerning the relationship of the individual to society, focusing on loneliness, pettiness, and jealousy. (See also *Contemporary Authors,* Vols. 21-24, rev. ed.)

WALTER SULLIVAN

[Andre Dubus] is a southerner who almost never writes about the South. Most of the stories in *Separate Flights* take place in New England or the Middle West, and on a superficial level they have a great deal in common with the work of [Alan] Sillitoe, for they are filled with images and acts of sex. Dubus is good with quick strokes, slight details that bring whole sequences into focus. . . . Minor characters, people seen briefly in bars or at filling stations, give Dubus's work an enhanced sense of reality and an enriched texture.

What I do not like about Dubus's stories is the cumulative effect of the collection as a whole, the sameness of characterization from one piece to the next, the obsession with sexual congress and crumbling affections. For example, almost without exception the men, whatever their ages or morals or professions, are given to physical exercise. They run before breakfast; they work out at the gym. Men and women drink and smoke too much, so that one gets the feeling that Dubus cannot discover what business to put them to: when they are out of bed, they do not know what to do with their hands. This is a small matter, and one which a writer of Dubus's talent could easily rectify, but the obsession with sex gives me more serious concern. Sillitoe's people drink and fornicate because they are poor and bored and ignorant and desperate: such is the state of things in Nottingham. But has the whole world become an extension of this English hopelessness? Are the possibilities of literature reduced in our time to variations on a single theme? (pp. 544-45)

"Miranda over the Valley" . . . in my judgment shows Dubus at his best. . . . To get inside the mind of a woman and to portray her joy and her agony as Dubus has done here is accomplishment indeed. We have no right to ask him to do better. (pp. 545-46)

> *Walter Sullivan, in* Sewanee Review *(reprinted by permission of the editor;* © *1975 by The University of the South), Summer, 1975.*

MICHAEL HARRIS

It would not be inaccurate to call Andre Dubus an old-fashioned writer, for . . . he writes plotted stories about recognizable human beings in a language that, however highly polished, is nonetheless the English that you and I speak. Dubus is good at it—so good, in fact, that if the seven short stories and the novella that make up *Separate Flights* are your introduction to his work, as they were for me, you're apt to wonder where he's been hiding. He hasn't, of course —no more than any other purveyor of fictional subtleties in an age that prefers journalism and being kicked in the teeth.

But in another sense Dubus isn't old-fashioned at all. In the emotional weave of American literature, resignation is a minor strand, a barely visible warp in so much aspiration and struggle. One went down fighting, like Ahab, despairing, like Gatsby, or at least babbling, like Portnoy; but so long as life was alleged to promise Americans everything, resignation was a rarity. In the 1970s, this has changed. Significant numbers of us have turned our backs on the public life and brought to the private life a closer scrutiny than it can stand. The limitations of love become the dimensions of our cells. The resignation we have learned is not the stolid acceptance of the European peasant, but a painful awareness, by people who once expected better, that horizons are shrinking. Dubus is by no means a writer of tracts for the times, but he captures this mood as well as anyone today. . . .

There is nothing cheap or easy about these stories, nor is there anything dense about the characters. They look out through the gaps in their lives with remarkable clarity of vision, and with an equal clarity—wedded with compassion and insight—Dubus looks in on them, making their sorrows our own.

> *Michael Harris, "Love's Limitations," in* Book World—The Washington Post *(* © *1975, The Washington Post), July 20, 1975, p. 3.*

RICHARD TODD

I have a candidate [for "Most Underrated Writer of 1975"], a man who published a book this year to the merest flutter of applause, and deserved much more: Andre Dubus. . . . Dubus writes in an almost painfully unmodish way. He lacks tricks of style. He does not have a head full of helpful sociological constructs about his world. He is not a particularly close observer of trends in manners or speech. But he knows things. [The stories in *Separate Flights*] are mostly about spent and misspent love, and he knows how to dramatize love's counterfeit emotions: loneliness, jealousy, and pity. He's an imaginative writer, persuasive on the inner lives of women as well as of men. He can imagine his way, for instance, into the mind of a middle-aged woman so hungry to participate in her daughter's life that she incurs only her scorn. Debus is the sort of writer who instructs the heart, a phrase that ought to be redundant, but isn't. He ought to be discovered by any number of readers, but probably won't. (p. 96)

> *Richard Todd, in* The Atlantic Monthly *(copyright* © *1976 by The Atlantic Monthly Company, Boston, Mass.; reprinted with permission), January, 1976.*

JOYCE CAROL OATES

[*Separate Flights*] consists of a novella and seven short stories, each of which is a considerable achievement. Dubus's attentiveness to his craft and his deep commitment to his characters make the experience of reading these tales— which are almost without exception about lonely, pitiful people—a highly rewarding pleasure.

The author of a novel, *The Lieutenant*, published in 1967, Dubus writes in a vein that might be considered naturalistic, since he relies to a great extent upon charting his characters' experiences in a highly recognizable world, following them closely from one hour to the next, from one drink to the next, recording their unexceptional dialogues with one another, with great subtlety and tact pinpointing their rare moments of insight. All of his people are ordinary, though some have pretensions to being intellectual; many are trapped in stultifying marriages, though Dubus never suggests that they might have been capable of arranging other fates. Their arguments are familiar, even banal. Their defenses against the panic of dissolution are commonplace: drinking and adultery. But though Dubus's materials are naturalistic, and his style is never self-consciously lyric or poetic, one sees in the craftsmanship of the tales a rigorous paring-back, a concern for what is implied rather than stated, so that the stories as a whole—the eight "separate flights" of the collection—come to operate symbolically, to mean much more than they record. (p. 105)

The only complaint a reader might make about *Separate Flights* is Dubus's habit of characterizing his people by recording in detail the drinks they have: bourbon, Scotch, wine, martinis, gin, beer and ale. The possibilities are limited and it is here, perhaps, that the "naturalistic" technique is most troublesome. In general, however, Dubus's considerable skill transcends his material, and the collection is a fine one. (p. 106)

Joyce Carol Oates, in The Ontario Review *(copyright © 1976 by The Ontario Review), Fall-Winter, 1976-77.*

FRANCES TALIAFERRO

Andre Dubus is a skillful and temperate writer. [*Adultery and Other Stories*] takes some getting used to. As when a harpsichordist opens his recital with sounds that seem unbearably faint after the noise outside, Dubus invites us into a world of quiet melodies. Gradually the ear learns to hear them. When Dubus writes about growing up in Louisiana, he finds nothing of the Southern Gothic. These fine stories are the equivalent of Hopper landscapes, anywhere in small-town America. . . . People play golf, go to barbecues, have fights around the Coke machine at school. The mystery is out of all proportion to the events. "Contrition," the best story, is ostensibly about ten-year-old Paul and his brief involvement with the French horn. In fact it says all that ever need be said about the pain of family love. The title story, "Adultery," takes as its epigraph a quotation from Simone Weil: "Love is a direction and not a state of the soul." Dubus constructs a disturbing spiritual framework that mocks the accustomed tackiness of the subject. Less good are several rather trite stories set in the U.S. Marine community. This collection is uneven, but Dubus at his best can evoke thoughts that lie too deep for tears. (p. 87)

Frances Taliaferro, in Harper's *(copyright © 1977 by* Harper's Magazine; *all rights reserved; excerpted from the January, 1978 issue by special permission), January, 1978.*

*   *   *

DURRELL, Lawrence   1912-

Durrell is an English novelist, poet, short story writer, playwright, travel writer, editor, and translator. Though considered a masterful craftsman of several genres, his reputation rests mainly on the monumental *Alexandria Quartet*. In these four novels, Durrell experiments with an Einsteinian perspective of space and time, rejecting philosophical absolutes and exploring the elusive nature of truth. His style is rich and sensuous, often evoking place and character with the lyricism of poetry. Durrell's fiction has been strongly influenced by James Joyce, his poetry by Robert Browning and Walter Savage Landor. In its contempletiveness and spirituality, his poetry also reflects the influence of Eastern thought. Durrell has written under the pseudonyms of Charles Norden and Gaffer Peeslake. (See also *CLC*, Vols. 1, 4, 6, 8, and *Contemporary Authors*, Vols. 9-12, rev. ed.)

G. S. FRASER

The one *genre* of writing in which Durrell . . . has not achieved either popular or critical success, is the verse play. . . . Though full of beautiful passages of lyrical and meditative verse, [*Sappho,* his first play in this genre,] perhaps lacks the tensions and confrontations that are proper to drama; it is more like a versification of one of Landor's

Imaginary Conversations. In his next verse play, *Acte,* Durrell took this lesson to heart, and it is a melodrama in the style of Corneille, about honour and self-sacrifice, in which the language . . . is noticeably more rhetorical than is usual in Durrell's verse.

The best of Durrell's verse plays seems to me to be *An Irish Faustus,* a morality play in nine scenes, alternately farcical and frightening. His Faustus is somewhat reminiscent of Prospero, a magician who throws away his wand. . . . I think that Durrell's verse plays, like those of Wordsworth, Keats, Shelley, Browning, Tennyson, have suffered from his thinking of the verse play as primarily *literature:* he has never thought much of the problems of production, of timing, of the control of the audience, that 'great beast'. (p. 10)

In Durrell, fiction is consciously fictive; it is always transforming itself from the transcription of what life is like to an attempt to create the myth, myth rather than allegory, of what life is. Perhaps the home-keeping writer whom Durrell most resembles is Iris Murdoch, who, like Durrell, enjoys playing (almost as in a logical game with truth-tables) with the permutations and combinations of possible sexual relationships, who enjoys both the violent and the improbable, and who likes to show sexual and religious drives improbably and grotesquely fusing. [There] are those who would describe both of them as brilliant frauds. Both, perhaps, as prose-writers, are in the tradition of something that we might call romance or fantasy rather than in the tradition of the 'straight' novel. But this *genre* has its own distinction and validity. (pp. 13-14)

The poems are still, it seems to me, the part of his writings where Durrell is most his natural self. In the 1930s, a period of much polemical political verse, these poems did not harangue. Compared, also, with the prose of *The Black Book* . . . they did not strike me as too highly coloured, congested, over-spiced. Durrell's poems have from their beginnings been beautifully modulated; by the word 'modulation' I mean the way in which a really skilful poet can move gently from the expression of one mood at the beginning of a poem to that of a contrasting, contrary, or more fully inclusive mood at the end of a poem, without any effect like that of a motor-car abruptly and crashingly changing gears. (p. 16)

Durrell's tone in poetry I would call one of quiet amenity, of controlled poignancy. . . . The poetic personality that came across to me when I read those early poems which appeared so fugitively in the 1930s was one gentle, compassionate, temperamentally sad but quirkily humorous, essentially lonely. I thought these early poems also (as I think the later poems) the work of a religiously-minded man. (p. 17)

Durrell has never lost his freshness as a poet, but I do not think one can speak of his *development,* as one speaks of development in Eliot, Yeats, or Auden. As a writer both in prose and verse, I think Durrell acquired what educational psychologists call a 'set', a framework for perceiving the world, probably in mid-adolescence. All his writing from the age of nineteen or twenty onwards has been a feeding of experience into the 'set' rather than a use of experience fundamentally to change it. Clearly, it was a good or useful 'set', but one has always a sense, as it were, of Durrell durrellizing experience rather than of experience undurrellizing Durrell. I think this makes him a very good minor rather than a major poet. (p. 18)

From his earliest to his latest poems, Durrell has [a] concern with verbal texture, with sound-sense relationships. One way in which he has perhaps technically developed is in making this concern a little less obtrusive than in his earliest work, in achieving an impression of careless ease. Rather similarly, from *The Black Book* to *The Alexandria Quartet,* and from *The Alexandria Quartet* to *Tunc* and *Nunquam,* the prose is always rich and ornate, but *The Black Book* is congested and self-conscious in a way that *The Alexandria Quartet* is not, and *Tunc* and *Nunquam* move with a kind of ease, the style sometimes spoofing itself or 'sending itself up', in a way that is not typical of the great technicolour blocs, the magnificent set pieces, of *The Alexandria Quartet.* (p. 20)

The Black Book is perhaps less important as a novel than as an extraordinarily vivid, exact, and honest document for somebody who might want to write a latter-day version of William James's *The Varieties of Religious Experience.* Durrell did in it an extraordinarily cruel (clinically cruel, cruel to be kind) job of auto-analysis; explored Hell, and perhaps just got out of it; but taught himself, in his journey, compassion. . . .

Durrell can, in fact, and even in *The Black Book* sometimes does, write plain, direct, unornate prose. For all its spiciness and high colouring, *The Alexandria Quartet,* moves with a much bolder and more rapid rhythm, is nearer the speaking voice. *Tunc* and *Nunquam* are full of purple passages, but of purple passages that deliberately and jokily send themselves up; and the prose of these novels is still bolder, and still more rapid, than *The Alexandria Quartet.* (p. 31)

The current English case against Durrell's prose is that it is mannerist, too richly and consciously atmospheric and connotational. I am not sure that Durrell is as much a mannerist writer as, say, Hemingway or Gertrude Stein, writers who base their verbal art on a kind of de-connexion, a scrubbing out of traditional connotations, a decreation. . . . Compared to such writers, who, of course, were experimenting in this way thirty or forty years before him, Durrell is in a sense very old-fashioned. He never sets himself a schema or a project that will exclude spontaneity. He wants to tell a story that will attract a popular as well as a highbrow audience. He is not working in a word laboratory. We should perhaps not be excessively puritan in censuring a writer's under-the-sheet relationships with his main Muse, his crushingly rich maternal and paternal language.

If *The Black Book* has a special interest both as a kind of spiritual autobiography and as a young man's first finding of his real voice, it is on the four volumes of *The Alexandria Quartet, Justine* (1957), *Balthazar* (1958), *Mountolive* (1958), and *Clea* (1960) that Durrell's world-fame mainly rests. (pp. 32-3)

I find, in spite of the elements of Arabian night fantasy . . . , that I can believe both in the people and in what is happening to them in *The Alexandria Quartet.* . . . [In] one crude sense *The Alexandria Quartet* with its sudden revelations of hitherto unsuspected motivations and purposes at just the right moment to stir and surprise the reader is as neatly constructed as a novel by Simenon or Agatha Christie.

The structural mastery and the basic human plausibility are worth insisting on because *The Alexandria Quartet* has been a little too much regarded, at least in England, as a

triumph mainly of atmospheric bravura writing. For me, and I think for anybody who lived and served in Egypt during the war years, it has the flavour of truth about it: truth is not always drab and consistent and dun-coloured, but sometimes flaring and glaring, astonishing, incongruous. It may be true, nevertheless, that what we remember in the end is less the characters individually than the characters as functions of a landscape or townscape, characters as a function of the whole history of Alexandria, with its traditions of richness and sensuality . . . and of mysticism, magic, quarrelling theologies. . . . (pp. 37-8)

Durrell, [in *Aut Tunc Aut Nunquam*] as elsewhere always highly professional, knows exactly what he is doing, though what he is doing may disconcert many of his earlier admirers. Incidents and descriptions are deliberately garish and shocking, there is a lot of use of what one might describe as poster-colour: Durrell, in an age which is growingly non-literary, is deliberately competing for attention with, say, pop art and horror comics. If the passages one remembers most in *The Alexandria Quartet* are, so to say, erotic and lyrical, the typical note of *Aut Tunc Aut Nunquam* is macabre and grotesque. . . . (pp. 41-2)

The archetypal figures in [both] *Tunc* and *Nunquam,* like archetypal figures in dreams, both break many taboos and make us aware of primeval taboos we had forgotten. The double-decker story is much less visual than any previous work of fiction of Durrell's and makes more use—in its prose technique and, in a sense, even in its plot—of the auditory imagination, puns, ambiguous allusions, emblematic names, the idea of auditory hallucination. (pp. 42-3)

There is plenty of comedy in both works but the comedy in *Aut Tunc Aut Nunquam* is much nearer farce, or barrack-room bawdry, and has also an agreeable quality of self-parody. . . . If the deeper meaning of *The Alexandria Quartet* is a mystical or transcendental meaning, the deeper meaning of *Aut Tunc Aut Nunquam* is a social-philosophical one. . . . Durrell, I think, has never written more freshly and entertainingly than in these two books. (p. 43)

> *G. S. Fraser, in his* Lawrence Durrell *(© G. S. Fraser 1970; Longman Group Ltd., for the British Council), British Council, 1970.*

ROBERT MARTIN ADAMS

When Darley settles down with Clea to live happily ever after, the reader is more likely to sigh in disappointment than in satisfaction: we had thought there was more to [the *Alexandria Quartet*] than that, and indeed there was. The last volumes escape all too successfully from the baffling relativity which was the chief interest of the first two.

A mechanical but genuine source of power in the early books was multiple points of view. Quite apart from tacit transitions from one narrative eye to another, events were watched and recorded by three professional authors—Arnauti, Darley, and Pursewarden—in addition to diarists, letter-writers, and commentators, all of whose work was conveniently made available to the scribe. . . . In addition, we saw Darley at a variety of different stages in his career, and information was filtered into the novels from a number of different and competing intelligence agencies. All this made for an ingeniously interwoven fabric of times, places, and points of view, across which the reader's studious eye wandered in search of patterns and ever-deeper patterns. One part of the book called another into question; the various novelists circled around the problems of complex personalities in complex situations, throwing off ideas for novels which might or might not apply to the present one. All this uncertainty was more potent fictional stuff than any conceivable resolutions of it could be: especially since Durrell, though his characters are all erotically obsessed, and he himself proposes eros as an ultimate form of cognition, skimps actual erotic scenes and any definition of the knowledge gained from them as primly as any Victorian novelist. . . . (pp. 162-63)

Most of the romantic illusions in which the first text abounds are [in the second novel, *Balthazar,*] shattered by a more dispassionate and deeper-sighted observer—above all the romantic egotism with which Darley has experienced his affair with Justine. (In terms of prudential motivation, the question of why Justine, who's already involved in one massive intrigue, should jeopardize it by indulging in two others, with Darley and Pursewarden, never gets answered; but the novel's balance of forces is all the better for being precarious.) Balthazar, as invert, mystagogue, and medicine-man, is admirably suited to bring about these ironic counterpoints. Although this resource is not largely exploited, we sometimes see verbal tags familiar from one context given new resonance by being heard in another. (p. 163)

Alexandria usurps heavily on the Alexandrians; and Durrell, with a vivid pen for colors, smells, and popular oddities, can render a bazaar, a cheap cabaret, or a hunchbacked barber briefly and brilliantly. With profundities of thought or feeling he's less successful: the Cabala and the doctrines of the Gnostics remain bits of lifeless window-dressing, and the grand passions don't get much beyond the stage of cliché. Of course, that is one of the points of the tetralogy. With its gift for factoring people down to their common irreducible elements, it forms Nessim and Melissa, Darley and Justine into a crystalline quartet of compulsions and frustrations before which the explanations of time and history (whether personal or public) are relatively helpless. Racially and religiously the quartet is as balanced and unstable as the city itself, and its conflicts are quite as insoluble. But then solutions are not really in order; certainly the Joycean vision would not have encouraged Durrell to think that in *Mountolive* he could effectively lay out a political background along with an explanation of Pursewarden (so much better as an enigma than as a case history!) and in *Clea* score up a pseudo-Proustian ending-return. One senses that even though he carried it off, the romantic ending with Clea did not sit well on his artistic conscience, and in the desperate amputation of Clea's hand, he tried to set it off with a bit of strong stuff. But the redemption is very partial; and it's my own impression, having tried it both ways, that the tetralogy reads much more effectively backwards than forwards, which makes it wind up instead of winding down.

Among other things, the success of the first two novels is due to some consciously mosaic prose. Durrell is fond of writing what amount to epiphanies of Alexandria, though he never labels them as such. They are hard, brilliant, descriptive sketches, done with all the senses and nerves alight—really the finest pieces of writing in the sequence. It's an oddity that the man who writes so well can also fall into the weary, loose clichés of the romantic novelist. . . . Unfortunately, as the opportunity narrowed for the first sort of

prose (Alexandria having already been presented to us in all its sharp immediacy), the second sort came more and more to predominate. And there are still other veins that the author has tapped, in this eclectic sequence of actions—Scobie, for example, who flows forth like a Pickwickian eccentric given his head, indefatigably and to some extent irrelevantly. One can sympathize with Durrell in feeling that he is too good to waste, yet among the major themes of the novel he hardly fits at all, and apart from his own rich self-display serves no purpose except to demonstrate Clea's charity and the city's polymorphic religiosity. . . . (pp. 164-65)

[There's] a lot of uneven work in the *Quartet*—a splash of metaphysical prestidigitation mixed with a swatch of exotic Oriental sex, some menace after the manner of E. Phillips Oppenheim, with homely Malaprop humor at the Sarah Gamp level. The books are written to impress, to dazzle, to titillate, to enthrall; there are sustained passages where they do these various things, but there are also areas where the flats betray crude painting, the machinery creaks, and the characters stand about contriving stage-business to conceal the fact that they really don't know what to do with themselves. Durrell is a superior entertainer, who has found various elements of Joycean composition useful in putting together his kaleidescope. But he's a long way from the cold and distant perspective of Joyce even toward his own creation; one doesn't get any equivalent feel for the architecture of a fiction. Durrell in the Alexandria Quartet was evidently in a delayed Stephen-Dedalus stage of development—his books are built more in the loose form of theme-and-variations than after the strict mode of a quartet. (pp. 165-66)

> *Robert Martin Adams, in his* AfterJoyce: Studies in Fiction After "Ulysses" *(copyright © 1977 by Robert Martin Adams; used by permission of Oxford University Press, Inc.), Oxford University Press, New York, 1977.*

JANE LAGOUDIS PINCHIN

[In *The Alexandria Quartet* Durrell paints a] fevered city, a dying city, a prodigal, stranger-loving, leaf-veined city. A city of deep resignation, of spiritual lassitude and self-indulgence, of jealousy and retribution. . . .

How do all these divergent images add up? They are dramatic, erotic, anything but peaceful; they cannot be easily summarized, for Alexandria is like the recurring palms that appear in the mirrored walls of the ballroom at the Cecil, fractured and prismatic. She is to be discovered. (p. 163)

Alexandria is home of the medieval quest—a quest that, as John Unterecker suggests—lies at the core of most of Durrell's important work. The hero must take a ritual journey across water entering a sick land. There he seeks balms to cure his own wounds and those of his city: there he does battle with all the forces that would destroy.

But, ironically, the city that he would save, that he does save, is the dangerous power he must fight. . . . [For Durrell Alexandria is] dark femininity. We are not now dealing with Forsterian visions of a subtle mind, a unifying principle. The image moves closer to the chasm than the bridge. No, Durrell's city is like his women, passive and yet dangerously malevolent. She courts the Lord of Misrule and the many faces of Mephistopheles. She is reality, a force to be feared. (pp. 166-67)

Reading Durrell's translation of Cavafy's sad tribute "The City" brings to mind Durrell's letters and his own poems about Alexandria, about the loneliness and pain of men caught and held by war in that hybrid city of exiles. "The City" haunts *Justine,* where it sets the stage for Durrell's tales of Alexandria. (p. 168)

The poem becomes an emblem of despair. In the *Quartet* this is an early, temporary despair the hero-artist must go through before he can conquer the female, life, Alexandria, the city, before he can stand tall, take his glasses off, write, and reign. For Durrell's heroes the poem is a kind of lesson, not primarily that acceptance of failure is a part of living—an accent stronger in Cavafy than in Durrell—but that the battle must be fought now. . . . (pp. 168-69)

Durrell does not give us a chronological look at Alexandria and its surroundings down through the ages . . . but [he] does give us a *complete* picture. Because for Durrell the novel is a tale of quest, the hero must fight against all the dangers that are life, all its adventures extended through time and space. (pp. 169-70)

Durrell plays with history. In doing so he borrows from the best history and guidebook around. Justine's Gnosticism, Nessim's attraction to Plotinus, references to Petesouchos and the ankh—all find their origins in [Forster's] *Alexandria.* But it is *Pharos and Pharillon* from which Durrell the writer of historical fiction has really learned. . . . We hear echoes of "The Return from Siwa"—a note Durrell will pick up again in a march across the desert in *Monsieur*—and then, in a moment, the Cavafian irony of "Envoys from Alexandria." (pp. 170-71)

[All] of Durrell's women are Cleopatras, all of his men Antonys. . . . Durrell is interested in Cleopatra's story for the same reason he feels compelled to write about sexuality—"the root-knowledge" . . . —for it allows the artist to remove the codpiece, to discover himself. Homosexuality, infidelity, voyeurism, infant sexuality, prostitution, all help the lover to strip bare. But doubles and incestuous pairs hold a special fascination for Durrell; they throw mirrors back on the self, in a novel of mirrors, of splintered glass. (pp. 173-74)

Cleopatra was, for Durrell, the blackness that consumes, the earth, Alexandria, Justine—the feminine principle with which the artist must contend—and reality, the alternately passive and treacherous queen each Antony must love and fight to the death. The vision is of enemy and Adam's rib. Forster saw her as a rare flower opening before a simple Roman soldier; Cavafy focused on those around her, sons and lovers. How intriguing that only Durrell, the high priest of heterosexual love, finds her a terrifying creature whom man must ultimately conquer.

Like Forster's, Durrell's ancient Alexandria is a city of God as well as a city of love. Here too Durrell's quest requires that he cover the whole canvas, that he seek the healing balms wherever they may be found. (pp. 174-75)

[For] Durrell, extremes exemplify Alexandria, and life, his primary religious interests are with Gnosticism and the Cabal—*"indulge but refine"* . . . —and with figures like the sixteenth-century German Paracelsus who preach a magical and maniacal sympathy between the universe and the individual soul, who avoid the "tramlines of empirical fact." . . . The frequent images of incest in Durrell's work link

intensity of love with danger, and with evil. . . . In the *Quartet* Gnosticism engages readers and protagonists alike, as does the unrefined intensity of creatures who seem to have emerged from the desert in *Thais,* who may hold the answer to the question that is the quest, to the meaning of Alexandria. (pp. 175-76)

[In] his portrait of Memlik one can again see that Durrell, like Cavafy, could not leave history alone. (p. 178)

In the figure of Memlik we see an important way in which Durrell's attitude toward nineteenth- and twentieth-century Alexandrian history differs from Forster's, and get another glimpse of Durrell's vision of life, Alexandria, as battleground. Both Forster and Durrell wrote about the British presence in Egypt and about the conflict between a growing nationalism and the interests of a large foreign community. Both wrote about the ways in which the East can free the Englishman from a damning rigidity and complacency. (p. 179)

[Like] Forster [in *A Passage to India*] Durrell [In *The Alexandria Quartet*] writes about a friendship between Englishman and Oriental, that, for the former, defies race. He too knew the civil service and found himself drawn to those intrigues that entangle public and private selves, that involve all who have an historical imagination. (p. 180)

[Durrell's] talent is a large one, and in the *Quartet* the epic, historical sweep engulfs us in its magic, partly because it is so grand, partly because Durrell, a most un-Cavafian temperament, creates the old Greek poet as a presence in his work, a figure who adds a welcome tension to the quest, who can undercut pomposity and even the Passions of Justine. . . . History and landscape—reality itself—must be interpreted to be felt, to be understood. And for Durrell relativity is the key; there *seem,* at least, to be a thousand truths. (p. 184)

Durrell manipulates his readers just as Cavafy did—perhaps with more audacity, for he uses figures from our own recent past. D. H. Lawrence is Pursewarden's beloved friend! Rimbaud, Claudel, and Joyce are added to the tribe, but fittingly no historical personage, no artist—not even Lawrence—takes on the importance of C. P. Cavafy who, like the city herself, actually becomes a character in the novels. Durrell gives us more than a Cavafian character—although he does that too: he gives us Cavafy. Along with Cleopatra and Alexander the poet becomes an exemplar of the city. . . . His thoughts and even his voice frame and haunt the whole; his poems encompass it. (pp. 185-86)

[Durrell's Darley] is a character who bears witness and, only in the end, is able to leave and enter other worlds. He learns from foolish older men, . . . men who are privy to the wisdom of maturity and the Orient, and finally to the wisdom of death, who have accepted the chaos of violence and disorder with a measure of dignity—like Scobie and Pursewarden, like Cavafy and his friend Balthazar. (p. 186)

The use of the Cavafy poem ["The God Abandons Antony"] seems fitting, a leitmotif binding, lending a sort of homogeneity to, the *Quartet.* And in a way it is. As in Forster's vision, music holds together what relativity or even logic would pull apart. But Durrell has turned the poem on its head. Cavafy's poem is about endings, about the dignity that comes when we face loss without deception.

The leave-takings with which the *Quartet* closes do not

encompass loss; the war is over and all good lovers are united, almost as neatly as if "happily ever after" accompanied the "once upon a time" that Darley can finally write. (p. 198)

[Anthony] Burgess—and others like [D. J.] Enright and Bonamy Dobrée—strike a raw nerve when they complain of the violence in the *Quartet,* the sensationalism that, with the blink of an eye, does away with arms, noses, and eyes themselves. . . . We think of Pursewarden's nickname for Darley. But there of course is the final joke, the final irony. It is a touch that Cavafy would have thoroughly enjoyed. L.G.D. Old Lineaments of Gratified Desire knew his weakness all along—and made sure he would have the first chuckle. He even allows Pursewarden to parody Darley's prose—the prose of *Justine.* The *Quartet* becomes an ironic comment on itself, on its very style.

His readers get angry with Durrell—for overblown action, for a patronizing vision of the female and the oriental, for the need to write a masterpiece of size that would all but destroy the understated truth upon which poetry like Cavafy's is based. Then they hear echoes of another popular song that Durrell, the self-taught jazz pianist, brings into the *Quartet.* "Tiresias." Tiresias, master of masculine and feminine knowledge, with whom Cavafy has been aptly compared. Tiresias, who like Esmiss Esmoor becomes an oriental patron-saint, embodied as El Scob, at whose shrine men and women talk and laugh. Like Pursewarden's chuckle, here is a tune that encompasses loving-kindness and undercuts excess. . . . (pp. 198-200)

And if Durrell did not hear all the chords of "The God Abandons Antony," he does hear Cavafy in other poems and lets the old man's voice help him find the phrases of tenderness—and loss as well—that *are* in the *Quartet,* that become its magic, a magic of repetition as well as fragmentation. (p. 200)

[It] is the Cavafian love poem, hesitant and melancholy, that Durrell integrates into the *Quartet* so beautifully, adding much to the texture of his work. He does not use these poems in fictive relationships among homosexuals. . . . The homosexual in the *Quartet* is a loner, a wise old man, a Tiresias—an ironic observer of the scene.

Love relationships in the *Quartet* are not homosexual; they are heterosexual and in some ways strangely whole. By the end of *Clea* all those Alexandrians who have been in love are either linked with their perfect mates or, it would seem, equally neatly dead. (p. 204)

Two poems, "The Afternoon Sun" and "Far Away" (or "Long Ago"), are linked and used as a kind of refrain for the quiet and touching affection that binds Melissa to Darley, and for the loss of all precious moments. (p. 205)

In his notes Durrell-Darley gives us complete translations of both poems, but they appear and mingle in the text when, during the war, Darley once again enters the same flat to find old furniture and the Cavafian lines still knocking about in his mind. The servant Hamid gives him a crumpled photograph of Melissa and Darley walking arm in arm on a forgotten "winter afternoon around the hour of four." . . . "Yes, it was winter, at four o'clock. She was wearing her tatty sealskin. . . . 'Sometime in August—*was* it August?' I mentally quoted to myself again." (p. 206)

Like Durrell's portrait of Cavafy, Melissa is pieced together through images from the past. We remember what Durrell wrote about Cavafian "passionate actuality," when he was translating some of Cavafy's earliest poems. We see the poet allowing a simple, shop-worn object to reinfect his memory. But for Darley the experience is too wearying, and in a sense too real. Melissa had *"utterly vanished,"* could not be evoked—even "with that lying self-deception so natural to sentimentalists" . . . —for the poems will not allow the prose to exaggerate, to lie. It is fitting that Melissa is Greek and, although everyone's mistress, Darley's innocence.

Here is the sense of loss, of personal disappointment and ironic tenderness that Cavafy brings to the *Quartet.* At its best it is a small and subtle force, but like its poet, "standing at a slight angle to the universe," it does much to shape our vision of the whole. (pp. 206-07)

Jane Lagoudis Pinchin, "Durrell and a Masterpiece of Size," in her Alexandria Still: Forster, Durrell, and Cavafy (copyright © 1977 by Princeton University Press; reprinted by permission of Princeton University Press), Princeton University Press, 1977, pp. 159-207.

PETER STOTHARD

Over the years Durrell's mania for islands has spawned the pastoral optimism of his Corfu idyll, *Prospero's Cell,* pessimistic resignation in his portrait of Rhodes, *Reflections on a Marine Venus,* and an abject disillusion that dominates his Cypriot chronicle, *Bitter Lemons.* Now he has selected from his experiences of all the Greek islands. . . .

[On] the evidence of the text alone 'islomania', rather than overwhelming its victim in his old age, weakens and ages along with him.

The Greek Islands reveals Durrell as less now of an obsessive than a whimsical fanatic. . . .

Durrell claims to answer two questions to which his tourist-admirers might require answers: what would you have been glad to know when you were on the spot and what would you feel sorry to have missed? On the credit side it is difficult to read the book without feeling that one really is on a journey. The tone of Durrell's prose and comments stays steadily in tune with the changing scenery as he moves the reader from lush Corfu, through windswept Sporades and the dry sanctity of Delos, to Salamis, Spetsae and Aegina, islands that are little more than Athenian dormitory suburbs. As for telling the tourist what he'd want to know, the book has a cheerful carelessness for strict guidebookish facts. . . .

But after the first few chapters I have to admit that Durrell's ever-protean presence began to get on my nerves. Not only does he try to change his writer's voice as often as he changes ferries, there is also a hard core of Durrellness that remains equally irritatingly unchanged, for instance Durrell the travelling philologist, the chap who tells me that there is something especially indestructible about the Greek language because today's students of modern Greek begin by studying from an ancient attic grammar while it would be impossible for a Greek to learn English from Chaucer. Try learning modern Greek from Hesiod, one yearns to shout back.

An only slightly less disagreeable Durrell persona is that of the travelling mystic. . . .

It would be unfair, however, to leave *The Greek Islands* without mentioning the few exceptional descriptive passages for which alone this book deserves its present place in the best-seller lists. Durrell can still breathe the most extraordinary life into descriptions of the ordinary people of Greece, from the fatalistic sponge-fishers of Calymnos to Chios's camera-shy monks. And there are places, too, particularly some of the barer rock hunks of the Aegean, which, unlike the plane trees of Cos, benefit from every breath of imposed magic they can get. (p. 52)

> *Peter Stothard, in* Books and Bookmen *(© copyright Peter Stothard 1978; reprinted with permission), November, 1978.*

PETER KEMP

Mr Durrell's narrative [in *Livia*] is never impeded by qualms about verisimilitude.

Nor is it arranged into much shape. There are a few hieratic gestures intended to suggest that profoundly meaningful patterns are being unrolled. Durrell is writing about Blanford who is writing about Sutcliffe who is writing about. . . . And dark, devilish Livia is set against fair, wholesome Constance—her sister who goes to Vienna, not Munich; admires Freud, not Hitler; and, when war breaks out, heads for the Red Cross, not the Iron one. But these tired symbolic stand-bys fail to hold the story-line, which goes lurching round baroquely kinky tableaux like a drunk adrift in a Fellini film-set. Following its incoherent progress soon gets wearying. (p. 591)

> *Peter Kemp, in* The Listener *(© British Broadcasting Corp. 1978; reprinted by permission of Peter Kemp), November 2, 1978.*

PETER VANSITTART

Style, writes Proust, is in no way an embellishment . . . it is not even a question of technique; it is like colour with certain paintings, a revelation of a private universe which each one of us sees and which is not seen by others. The pleasure an artist gives is to make us know an additional universe.

This is handy for the heightened realities of *Livia,* successor to *Monsieur,* 'written in a highly eliptical quincunxial style invented for the occasion', set largely in the ominous late 'thirties. . . . The complex relationships of a group of young people are dramatized, occasionally blurred, by the fabled allusive atmospherics—the book is preceded by a Chinese proverb. 'Five colours mixed make people blind'—itself counterpointed by periodic intrusions of the squalid: an obsession with rancid armpits, a repulsive treatment of clap.

The evocations are dreamily persuasive. . . . Serious issues seem more explicit, the characters more fleshed, than in *Monsieur,* though their actual age seems speculative, time itself occasionally in abeyance. 'I am a writer who hovers over things' Durrell has said, elsewhere. The evil is more concrete as the Nazis reach full flourish. There is much silly, exuberant talk, absurd politics, and jet-set assertions. . . . Also a rankling nostalgia for lost domains, great wines, irreverent moonlit occasions, the elegiac courses of loves mislaid or doomed. (pp. 125-26)

> *Peter Vansittart, in* London Magazine *(© London Magazine 1978), December-January, 1978-79.*

ALASTAIR FORBES

Five years ago Lawrence Durrell announced in his envoi to "Monsieur" that it was to be the first novel in a quincunx—"five novels only dependent on one another as echoes might be." There he begat an alter ego, Blanford, with whom he shared the authorship of "Monsieur"; and Blanford begat another writer, Sutcliffe, whose commonplace book full of uncommonplace and conflicting thoughts supplies a sort of preposterously punning Greek chorus to the present volume ["Livia"]; Sutcliffe in turn begets another writer, Bloshford—and so on, one supposes, *ad finem quincunxis.* This "quincuncial style" may suit the author, but what one might call the Doppelgänger effect all too often leaves the reader in the lurch. "The writer Blanford suddenly felt like an enormously condensed version of a minor epic. Buried Alive!" Many readers may share that suffocating sensation as they worm their way through "Livia." . . .

The sense of place in Durrell's poetry and prose is always wonderfully strong and well-wrought. In "Livia," Avignon is given a connoisseur's celebration as his characters approach it by barge. Thereafter, every nook and cranny of the town is nocturnally explored, until on the last page Blanford, the narrator, contemplates a mechanical pump used to drain the primitive sanitation system and thinks to himself: "It is sucking out the intellectual excrement of the twentieth century in a town which was once Rome." . . .

Durrell, like his character, seems aware of the traps his self-indulgence can set for him ("He felt the lure of language stirring in him . . . a vomit of words linked by pure association"), and sometimes disarms his critics by preempting their criticisms. . . .

Still, even if he does give himself due warning ("Enough of the pornocratic-whimsical"), a sizable portion of "Livia" is taken up by a lamentable set piece in a brothel where demoiselles d'Avignon of varying shapes and ages above and below that of consent attempt to satisfy an elderly Egyptian prince stripped down to his Jermyn Street longjohns. Dwarves abound. Livia herself is a promiscuous lesbian with a special proclivity for gypsies, who are naturally thick on the ground between Avignon and the Camargue. It is all pure cinema and better left perhaps to Fellini, who has better mastered the genre.

One need not be angry with the good Durrell, poet-historian of the Mediterranean, when he nods. If in "Livia" he seems scarcely up to form, much of his writing—not least his jokes and puns, both good and bad—can still give its customary pleasure. I fear that many American readers of "Livia" may justifiably feel that anything Durrell once did, Updike can now do better. All the same, Durrell remains an irreplaceable master of English and European literature. Long may he continue to write.

> *Alastair Forbes, "Dwarves Abounding in Provence," in* The New York Times Book Review *(© 1979 by The New York Times Company; reprinted by permission), April 22, 1979, p. 14.*

E

EDSON, Russell 1935-

Edson is an American poet and playwright. He writes, typically, imaginative, often surrealistic prose poems in which word play and inventive metaphor reflect humor as well as pathos. (See also *Contemporary Authors*, Vols. 33-36, rev. ed.)

DENISE LEVERTOV

Russell Edson is one of those originals who appear out of the lonesomeness of a vast, thronged country to create a peculiar and defined world. Seen as through the wrong end of a spyglass, miniscule but singularly clear, this world within a world of his is one in which 'things'—chairs, cups, stones or houses—may be immobile but are not inanimate, and therefore experience solitude and suffering; where animals are unlikely to be dumb; and where man is often essentially immobilized by the failure to communicate. There is interaction but no interrelation. The inanimate before the animate, a child before his parents, man before woman, the eye before the world of appearance, each is alone. . . .

[While *The Very Thing That Happens*] can be opened anywhere it can also be read as a sequence that begins with marriage as a story of mutual destruction and leads through the deformation of offspring to the wanhope possible escape of the survivors. (p. v)

The themes sound grim, and they are; yet many of the stories are at the same time wildly funny. It's as if *King Lear* had been written and illustrated by Edward Lear. The violence in Lear's limericks, his persistent use of words like *bash* and *smash* to describe what happens to protagonists, surely expresses a desperation of similar quality to that pervasive desperation of Edson's world, in which the persons are rarely said to speak, but, quite casually, *scream* their conversation (their expressive non sequiturs seeming strangely kin to the virtuoso candor of the conversationalists created by Miss Compton-Burnett). Edson's mode is detached, oblique, austere. He is able to pass without loss of grace from the hilarious to a kind of dark gothic beauty, and sometimes to a tenderness that reveals him as no cruel puppetmaster but the anguished beholder of inexplicable cruelties. His art—its syntax, its elegant dryness, its bizarre condensed events—is the unique outgrowth of an eccentric imagination, the convoluted shell of the mind's hypersensitive, clairvoyant snail. (p. vi)

Denise Levertov, in her introduction to The Very Thing That Happens *by Russell Edson (copyright © 1964 by Russell Edson; reprinted by permission of New Directions Publishing Corporation), New Directions, 1964, pp. v-vi.*

DOROTHY NYREN

"What is right in the depths hardly obtains in the sunshine," Edson muses in [*The Childhood of an Equestrian,*] his volume of poems that hover between the depths and sunshine, shifting from strangeness to horror and back again, with only an occasional slip into silliness. . . . A poetry of images and sudden *aperçus*, good for a shudder or a smile. . . . (p. 3992)

Dorothy Nyren, in Library Journal *(reprinted from* Library Journal, *December 15, 1972; published by R. R. Bowker Co. (a Xerox company); copyright © 1973 by Xerox Corporation), December 15, 1972.*

GERRIT HENRY

Russell Edson's *The Clam Theater* is a volume of short prose poems, each of which very definitely has the quality of a "happy clam opening its shell" to reveal its delightfully hermetic inner workings. Edson's poems abound with puns, literary "sight gags", metaphors taken to their wildly illogical conclusions, and poem-within-a-poem architectures. . . . Every now and then, Edson's free-wheeling wit gets a little labored: "a funny thing happened to me on the way to the present." But at their best these prose poems are a happy marriage of French Surrealist techniques with a Marx Brothers-like insouciance and haplessness. . . . (pp. 295-96)

Gerrit Henry, in Poetry *(© 1974 by The Modern Poetry Association; reprinted by permission of the Editor of* Poetry), *August, 1974.*

Russell Edson has been shaking a bottle of cola some years now. With [*The Intuitive Journey and Other Works*] he lets the spray shoot out and cover the surrounding landscape, the consequences of his syntax active from the same source as Magritte's brush. The essential mystery of Edson's work is here so palpable, so tasty, there's no longer any hiding: his concerns, while idiosyncratic as ever, have increasingly become everyone's. Read this collection with delight and worry. (p. 58)

Virginia Quarterly Review *(copyright, 1977, by the Virginia Quarterly Review, The University of Virginia), Vol. 53, No. 2 (Spring, 1977).*

PETER SCHJELDAHL

Edson is a long-time practitioner of the "prose poem," that strange modern form or non-form favored by many writers for its ability to give matter-of-fact access to imaginary realms. Edson's are broad, small surrealistic fables and tales that deal in anthropomorphic animals and objects, metamorphoses, obscure acts of violence, cosmic anxieties enacted on miniature sets. Many have the sustained wackiness of old Warner Brothers cartoons. Their appeal is direct and obvious; they are precious in the good or in the bad sense, depending on one's taste or mood. (I've always liked coming across them in magazines; they please me less in bulk.) Edson comports himself a bit winsomely, perhaps, in his through-the-looking-glass world, but what happens there often has a ring of subjective truth. I can imagine his work reaching a wide audience not ordinarily interested in poetry. (p. 69)

> Peter Schjeldahl, *in* The New York Times Book Review *(© 1977 by The New York Times Company; reprinted by permission), May 1, 1977.*

Although the fifty-five short prose-fables of Russell Edson's *The Reason Why the Closet-Man is Never Sad* are presented in alphabetical order it is just possible that the work has an intended fictional unity, involving a number of dramatis personae who are made to undergo dreary and inconsequential non-experiences. . . .

Most of the pieces begin in a bright, buttonholing way, promising sometimes lyrical, sometimes fantastic or nightmare developments. . . . But the actual narrative developments are almost invariably flaccid bits of whimsy in which there is little of the sustained energy of art. . . .

Mr Edson's personae, their situations, and the nerveless language in which they are manipulated are so devoid of living characteristics that it is difficult for a reader to summon up sympathy enough to care. (p. 848)

> The Times Literary Supplement *(© Times Newspapers Ltd. (London), 1977; reproduced from* The Times Literary Supplement *by permission), July 15, 1977.*

DONALD HALL

Edson writes tiny short stories, which critics call prose poems mostly to let you know that they are crazy. (p. 100)

The typical Edson poem runs a page or a page and a half. It's fanciful, it's even funny—but this humor carries discomfort with it, like all serious humor. We may not *wish* to understand the fragility of our psychic borders, or that we partake of things outside ourselves, or that we may lose ourselves if we are not careful. Maybe we control nothing; if we control nothing with our egos, if we *let go,* perhaps we can recover an ancient self otherwise lost, or perceive a world never seen before.

Russell Edson's imagination is revolutionary. He explores a small territory, but it is unmapped land. He does adventurous spirit-work for all of us, recovering portions of the lost infant world for anyone who will follow him. (p. 102)

> Donald Hall, *in* The Atlantic Monthly *(copyright*

© *1977 by The Atlantic Monthly Company, Boston, Mass.; reprinted with permission), October, 1977.*

* * *

ELIOT, T(homas) S(tearns) 1888-1965

Born in the United States and later becoming a British subject, Eliot is considered by many to be the major poet and critic of our time. With *The Waste Land* came a radical, new poetry, filled with innovative rhythms and woven with foreign phrases and classical allusion. Eliot sought a union of intellect and feeling, frequently dealing with themes of time and disillusionment with the modern world. Initiating a new tradition in criticism as well as in poetry, Eliot wrote from a Christian, anti-romantic viewpoint, and gave new importance to such writers as Dante, Donne, and the French symbolists. As a playwright, he experimented with poetic drama, attempting a modern equivalent of Elizabethan blank verse. He was awarded the Nobel Prize for Literature in 1948. (See also *CLC*, Vols. 1, 2, 3, 6, 9, 10, and *Contemporary Authors*, Vols. 5-8, rev. ed.; obituary, Vols. 25-28, rev. ed.)

In a little short of 900 lines, [the] subtle, magnificent religious poems [in *Four Quartets*] contain more beauty and sense than any book within recent memory. They are capable of charming, and teaching, many thousands among the great general reading audience.

T. S. Eliot has never been an artist likely to please the bulk of that great audience. Simply as a rather solemn American-turned Englishman, he is personally unsympathetic to many. His work lacks commonness in the good sense of that word as well as the bad. It requires a patience of ear and of intellect which many readers lack; patience not merely in one reading but in many. For a long time, too, it was easy to misjudge Eliot, thanks to certain of his admirers, as the mere precious laureate of a Harvardian coterie. . . .

Eliot is, to be sure, not a poet in the grand antique sense of spontaneous and unprecedented song. But as a devoted artificer of words and as a distiller of experience, he has always been a poet, and a particularly fine one. Unlike many greater and lesser poets, moreover, he has constantly grown and changed. In his youth he was most notably a satirist; then a mosaic artist of exquisite sensibility, a man who used the perfected expression of past artists as frankly as he used his own, to arrange, fragment by fragment, edge by edge, an image of the desolation of his time. . . . (p. 120)

Of all his poems [the *Four Quartets*] are the most stripped, the least obviously allusive, the least ingratiating in image and in diction, the most direct. They are set in a matrix of subtly intensified, conversational style. To many readers they will look, and remain, flat and forbidding. But those who will give them the care they require will find, here, the finest work of a distinguished lifetime.

Readers familiar with the great "last quartets" of Beethoven will suspect that Eliot derived from them his title, much of his form, elements of his tone and content. They will almost certainly be right, for no other works in chamber music fit the parallel. Both Beethoven and Eliot are working with the most difficult and quintessential of all materials for art: the substance of mystical experience. Both, in the effort to translate it into art, have strained traditional forms and created new ones. Both use motif, refrain, counterpoint, contrasts both violent and subtle, the normal coinage of both arts, for purposes more profound and more intense than their normal coinage, for purposes more profound and more intense than their normal transactions.

Beethoven was a man of colossal genius, originality and definitiveness; Eliot is not. That might make all the difference in the world; it makes a good deal less than might be supposed. For Eliot, if he lacks major genius, is nevertheless a man of fine intellect, of profound spiritual intelligence, and of poetic talents which, if "minor," are nevertheless unmatched in his generation. And his subject is of a dignity which, if approached with these abilities, makes excellent poetry unavoidable and great poetry possible.

There is poetry of both kinds in *Four Quartets.*

The heart of Eliot's meditation is Time. Not time as that hypnosis of clocks and of history which holds all human existence captive—though this sort of time gets his attention too—but time as the mystic apprehends it, "at the still point of the turning world." (pp. 121-22)

There is an opposite pole to this stillness. It may be discerned behind "the strained time-ridden faces, distracted from distraction by distraction," of any great city, any "place of disaffection" . . . a darkening of the soul whose opposite and whose one cure is "the darkness of God." . . . (pp. 123-24)

Time, moreover, is our savior as well as our destroyer. It is the air we must breathe, the lens through which we perceive timelessness, through which we become conscious. . . .

Upon this theme, in poetry rich in paradox and reward, in mystery, in symbol, in despair and, ultimately, in hope, Eliot develops his great variations. . . . Each of the poems has not only its earthly-mystical locals but its season of the year and its Aristotelian element as well—which for which is not in every case clear. Of the first, the season seems to be spring, and the element air. Of the second: summer and earth. Of the third: fall and water. Of the fourth: "Winter spring" and fire. (p. 124)

> *"At the Still Point," in* Time *(reprinted by permission from* Time, The Weekly News Magazine; *copyright Time Inc. 1943), June 7, 1943 (and reprinted in* Parnassus: Poetry in Review, *Fall-Winter, 1976, pp. 120-25).*

GABRIEL PEARSON

'Gerontion' must be seen as central to Eliot's poetic practice; here he initiates and exhaustively explores permanent features of his basic idiom. Here also he enacts the logic—the social as well as verbal logic—of the conversion of words into the Word. Thereafter, the Word within the word is immanent as doctrinal justification for each poetic act. 'Gerontion' may well end in Eliot, as [Hugh] Kenner claims, one whole phase of Anglo-American linguistic practice; but emphatically it inaugurates that marriage of doctrine and poetic which determines our final sense of Eliot's career. (p. 83)

'Gerontion' by common agreement is a dramatic monologue in which the drama has collapsed into incoherence and the monologuist has disintegrated into fragments of his own

memory. So much is indicated by the epigraph, a quotation from the Duke's speech to Claudio in *Measure for Measure:*

> Thou hast nor youth nor age
> But as it were an after dinner sleep
> Dreaming of both.

This describes well enough the situation of Gerontion as a representative human figure, caught in time and shorn of grace. The epigraph serves to insist that Gerontion is not merely an emblem of modern man; his futility is the futility of all men at all times sundered from supernatural power by their refusal of faith. (p. 84)

Eliot's instinct in his choice of epigraph is unerring. If *Measure for Measure* is dramatically disintegrated in favour of its 'truth', then Eliot has pushed beyond every remaining coherence to recover his truth in the heart of the vortex of lost meaning, barely contained by the residual framework of dramatic monologue, a half-fractured shell merely:

> Here I am, an old man in a dry month,
> Being read to by a boy, waiting for rain. . . .
>   Tenants of the house,
> Thoughts of a dry brain in a dry season. . . .

The usefulness of calling 'Gerontion' a dramatic monologue practically disappears, since the major premise of the form —stable personality within an admittedly unstable order— has itself become one of the ghosts which Gerontion claims not to have. . . . (pp. 84-5)

If 'Gerontion' is not a dramatic monologue, then how do we read it? My sense is that 'Gerontion' is literally unreadable. What we 'read' are words, syntax, grammar, associations. Consider the line: 'Rocks, moss, stonecrop, iron, merds'. In an approximate way this could be an inventory of 'the field overhead', and, more generally, of the rubbish dump of memory. But for the reader the declarative import of the line is its least important. What he attends to is words as words, isolated in their strange completeness, as substantives, bonded, adjacent and yet discrete. . . . One thing is sure: though one gets images, a landscape of sorts, one hardly reads past and through the words to a world without.

Finally, we pause upon the word 'merds', sensing a complication—a social murmur almost—in the term's self-insistence. It is a stunned term for an explosive category: the silence of the word is noisy with what it names but does not say. One can attempt only the crudest translation. We find ourselves silently applauding the century or so's puritan urbanity that allows Eliot, by a dexterous deviation though his French culture, to render faeces as innocuous as tea-leaves. (p. 85)

The controlled good form that selects the term enacts an aristocratic repugnance and arrogance bred out of a loss of effective power in the face of bourgeois philistinism and democratic vulgarity. It becomes an exquisite mode of retaliation. As audience, we share, momentarily, in the values that permit the disdainful tact of its handling. Yet we are excluded, too: and before its audacious decorum we crouch as apenecked as Sweeney. The poet's skill and deftness are counters for a lightly carried superiority. There is insult, too, in the term: Eliot murmurs 'merds', and we are insulted and exult in the dexterity of insult. . . .

Eliot's words and cadences are memories, largely memories

of literature. Eliot's world is itself constructed as a huge, sounding memory in search of a contemporary identity to attach itself to. Such a condition arises when the present has lost its meaning. It represents an acute crisis of disinheritedness. Memory, and with it necessarily personal identity, ricochet back, as it were, off the blankness of the present. With no present to order and compose them, they have to form their own order, which often consists of construction and orchestration along associational filaments and zigzags. (p. 86)

Eliot, in *Four Quartets,* tries to cure this disease of autonomously active words with theology, but his real cure is more words, above all the beautiful cadence that suddenly harmonises the disorder, 'The loud lament of the disconsolate chimera', but which remains, after all, but words. One feels that throughout his career Eliot is shaking his bars, trying to get out, but his means of escape are through the very words that imprison him. The quest for 'the still point of the turning world' clearly goes deeper than theology.

One form of attempted escape is an implicating assault upon the reader. A crude large-scale version of this is the Knights' address to the audience at the end of *Murder in the Cathedral* or Becket's stab at the audience at the end of the first Act when he tells us

> . . . you, and you,
> And you, must all be punished. So must you.

Here, as with 'merds', the words seem calculated to detonate a series of small-scale explosions in the reader: the aim is to trap, arrest and implicate us. (p. 87)

[In] Eliot's case there is an unusual isolation of, and concentration on, language as direct enactment of social attitudes. Poetry has traditionally mediated social existence through conventions, genres, myths, symbols. For Eliot, this mediation has largely collapsed. Eliot is reputed a peculiarly learned and literary poet, and this is true. It is true also that a good deal of raw personal and social emotion is fed back into the action of the language; this need not involve contradiction. Traditional forms no longer compose an inherited order. Rather, they become themselves manifestations of despair and anxiety, because no longer credited and sanctioned. Hence the ultimate unfruitfulness of reading these poems as reworkings of traditional modes. These have become themselves objects of historical attention within a universe of relative values. They lie exposed on the surface of history like withered roots. When the poet self-consciously uses them and discriminates among them, he can no longer derive nutriment from them. Instead, he has to feed them out of the substance of his own life. From this derives the highly personal impersonality of much modern art, and the inevitably ironic uses of tradition. (p. 88)

[Burbank, the character from the poem of the same name,] is clearly close to Eliot himself. The poet, by encompassing Burbank and identifying and attacking the forces that make him a cultural eunuch, escapes becoming Burbank himself. (pp. 89-90)

The pieties of exegesis divert consideration from the poem's verbal behaviour which amounts to precisely 'execrable taste'. But that term is a little too bland. It is an odd procedure to devote minute attention to elucidating the most recondite allusions, and then sink the poem in a phrase. It is pointless merely to execrate because execration is precisely what the poem seeks to provoke. It is a hate poem, and when this is grasped its allusiveness . . . is understood as part of its central emotion, the wadding and buffering of raw places, disguises worn by the violence and despair enacted by stanza and syntax. This wadding becomes in turn an element of overcontrol or repression, which in turn generates further verbal violence.

Yet we must allow that the stanzaic poems of the 1920 volume represent an attempt to reconstitute what Eliot sees as a fragmented ruin. Meditation alone will not allow Burbank to put his fractured world together again. Eliot recognises that his poetry will never take form from a spontaneous unity of culture and consciousness. Unity has to be imposed by an act of willed juxtaposition of fragments. One cannot but feel that the epigraph to 'Burbank' is the doctrinal heart of the poem; the poem itself depending from it as an emotional *exemplum*. The epigraph's dashes both sunder and hyphenate their discrete materials. The order of language survives, at least partially, 'Time's ruins'.

'Burbank' and the other stanzaic poems of *Poems 1920,* are consciously clever, contrived and wilful. Their rage and social disgust have to be gathered by a kind of inductive leap behind their paraded façades. The poems of *Prufrock and Other Observations* are, by contrast, debile, fluctuating, helpless and self-ironic. . . . *Poems 1920* represents a deliberate hardening of the will. Fluctuating and self-ironic emotion is forcibly contained until it becomes explosive. (pp. 90-1)

'Gerontion' is haunted by the ghost of Henry Adams ('dogwood and chestnut, flowering judas' are quotations from *The Education*); Adams's view that the kinetic theory of gas proved that 'Chaos was the law of nature; Order was the dream of man' complicates my explanation. One has to say first that Adams's view of nature was the product of his view of history which in turn was, fairly avowedly, the product of his own experience as a disinherited political aristocrat. Eliot, inherits this disinheritance and 'Gerontion' shows its hold on his imagination. The 'flowering judas' of the quotation, however, alerts us to the degree of Eliot's distrust of Adams: he must have found his instinctive sympathy insidious. I interpret the presence of Adams in 'Gerontion' much as I interpret the figure of Burbank. He is there to be encompassed: the forces which caused his self-ironic despair are to be confronted, attacked and transcended. None the less, the kinetic theory of gas and Adams's view of history as a progressive complication and dissipation towards chaos doubtless excited Eliot's imagery of 'fractured atoms'. Eliot did believe Adams and only one thing could save him from his conclusion, the blind leap of faith in a providential divine agency. This explains why 'Gerontion' implicitly demands the Logos, and why, at the same time, the Logos does not naturally inhere in the ordering of the poem.

Eliot, by creating a self-substantive verbal universe, obviously continues the symbolist tradition into the twentieth century and into Anglo-American literature. Yet I would suggest that he is not so much in the tradition as using it and being used by it. Ultimately, his poetics cannot be made synonymous with his poetry. For Eliot, unlike Mallarmé, self-substantive verbal structure can never really hope to create 'un Livre explication de l'homme suffisante à nos plus beaux rêves . . .' [a book interpretation of man equal to our most beautiful dreams]. Such a creed is itself, for Eliot, a manifestation of a social and historical predicament, and this predicament becomes in turn a central issue of the poetry. The result is 'the intolerable wrestle with words' of *Four Quartets*. Verbal art fails to transcend and order social experience. Instead, social experience gets locked up in words and this imprisonment, too, becomes an issue of the poetry. The problem for Eliot was how to get them out again and so master the situation that necessitated symbolist aesthetic. Eliot's discursive writings, critical, social and theological, is one attempt to do this. In 'Gerontion' we see clearly for the first time the escape route that Eliot will use for the rest of his career.

Eliot took the logic of Symbolism to an extreme and then attempted to return it to experience by connecting the word with the Word. The Word, within its creative potency, must contain all experience. It is the Christ child who contains god and adult man and all creation; but paradoxically it is all these imprisoned in Eliot's own language, which, like the child, is dumb:

> The word within a word, unable to speak a word,
> Swaddled with darkness.

The indefinite article of 'a word' seems deliberately to reflect on the handling of words as discrete objects elsewhere in the poem. '*The* word', by contrast, is articled but uncapitalised. For light, maturity and the coronation of the capital, it has to wait until the fifth movement of *Ash-Wednesday*. . . . Eliot regards himself as living among 'an evil and adulterous generation'. As a poet he lives by the word and is afraid to die by the word. Moreover, the poet is peculiarly liable to mistake, as Mallarmé mistook, his signs for wonders. (pp. 92-4)

By converting the word into the Word, even though the Word remains a silent prisoner of words, Eliot seeks to be justified, even at the risk of damnation; for, as the later poetry insists, damnation is at least reality. 'And there shall be no sign given' amid a purely verbal world is the real despair. This despair is savagely vented by 'The tiger springs in the new year. Us he devours.' The syntax becomes suddenly almost over-coherent, particularly in contrast to the syntactical disembodiedness of

> In depraved May, dogwood and chestnut, flowering
> ̀ judas,
> To be eaten, to be divided, to be drunk
> Among whispers. . . .

a ghostly parody of the sacrament. The assertive 'Us' (typographically assertive, indeed) of 'Us he devours' sounds, amid such whispers and the sexual, historical and mental involutions that surround it, like a genuine tiger's roar. This may not be the roar of outer reality, but it shakes the inner walls of the poem's verbal system.

For Eliot, Symbolism is a poetic inheritance but also the manifestation of a predicament. The inheritance is complicated by the way that Symbolism is itself a formulated resistance against the debasements of bourgeois democratic mass society. This alone would explain Eliot's adoption of this tradition. (p. 94)

Yet Symbolism offered no way of confronting and mediating the social reality that created it. Inherently, it transforms experience into verbal metaphysic, an autonomous universe as against the autonomisms of society.

We have to say, then, that Eliot remained inside the Symbolist tradition and yet profoundly subverted it by translating it first into doctrine and then out of doctrine back into experience. It is that partial circuit which is the real shape of Eliot's career. I say partial, because the translation back into experience is so tentatively achieved. One senses both the logic and the failure of the logic most clearly within the clumsy schematisms of *The Rock*. . . . Obviously Eliot had a great time being the Rock. . . . But it does represent in its own way a return to the world. So indeed do the three plays written after *The Family Reunion*. They are messages to the world, societal in their concerns if always manipulated by doctrine. It is a matter of critical taste in the end, but my judgment on these plays is that while obviously products of an ingenious and subtle mind, they creak too loudly with the effort of unbending. Their human materials are coerced phantoms, delay is substituted for development and intervention for surprise. No one convinced of their value will be affected by these *ex cathedra* assertions. It is another argument. Yet, if I am right, one has to see their failure of dramatic life as a revenge of life itself. After so much denial of social experience, when Eliot seeks to return to it, all it offers are the shadowy stereotypes of the fictional worlds of Dorothy L. Sayers and Noel Coward. You cannot spend a career firmly informing your fellow men that 'The desert is squeezed in the tube-train next to you' without finding the world, when you want to return to it, a pretty dry terrain.

But there is the marvellous recovery of *Four Quartets*, achieved partly through splitting doctrine down into a core of mystical experience on the one hand, a romantic celebration of the mystery of childhood on the other, and relating these, in a formal pattern, to the experience of history and some guarded personal confession through a structure of musical analogies. *Four Quartets* comes as close as possible to producing a complete coincidence of poetics and poetry. Despite this, the four poems seem to me more flawed than criticism generally allows. One is aware of a good deal of management in the scrambling of the major symbols in the last movement of the poem. 'The Dry Salvages' in particular is full of some very ponderous commentary. The interspersed lyrics have a slightly surprised and ragged air, as though they had been torn out of the prose of the poem rather than naturally condensing it. The assertions of mystical experience remain assertions rather than being proved by the poetry.

These failures are in fact the seams opened up between verbal behaviour, doctrine and experience. This certainly accounts for wonderful moments within the poetry, and the delicate, almost ballet-stepping movement of argument over syntax that we find in, for example, the first section of 'Burnt Norton'. This should not obscure the degree to which the whole poem departs from the movement of experience itself and fails to unify it except as a complex of verbal echoes and associations. (pp. 95-6)

Eliot saw himself, and came to see his poetry, as essentially priestly. The poetry ends by moving between the confessional and the liturgical, uneasy where to settle. *Murder in the Cathedral* obviously gathers up all these tendencies; but Harry in *The Family Reunion* seems destined for the mission field, Celia in *The Cocktail Party* is actually martyred, while Colby in *The Confidential Clerk* is rather coyly permitted to remain artist as well as becoming priest:

> You'll be thinking of reading for orders.
> And you'll still have your music.

There is something very sad about the punctuation. This, then, is the final issue of the grandfilial recapitulation. It does not seem, as indeed it was not to prove, very fruitful. The real drama of Eliot's career lies in the initial repudiation of America and in the violence of repudiation that rocks and shatters the symbolist aesthetic that sought to contain it. Naturally, repudiation involves the reality that it excludes. We need now to read Eliot not so much for the truth he proffers as for the truth he cannot conceal. He is a seismograph from which, negatively, we can infer the force of the quake. And finally there remains the existential courage with which his absurd choices were assumed and then sustained.

It is, I believe, the violence of the initial motive that has launched Eliot into premature pre-eminence. He is so canonically installed in the landscape that we have lost the ability to imagine what it would look like without him. (p. 100)

> *Gabriel Pearson, "Eliot: An American Use of Symbolism," in* Eliot in Perspective: A Symposium, *edited by Graham Martin (© Macmillan and Co. Ltd. 1970; reprinted by permission of Macmillan, London and Basingstoke), Macmillan, 1970, pp. 83-101.*

ARNOLD P. HINCHLIFFE

The English verse dramatists sought to restore verse plays to their central place in the English theatre. T. S. Eliot began with certain advantages over poets like Claudel and Yeats because he had already brought back ordinary words and situations into poetry. Even so he experienced the inevitable difficulties of getting modern characters to speak verse convincingly. . . . Eliot saw his task as twofold: to overcome the prejudice against verse in the theatre and to prevent the enjoyment of verse for itself. Such enjoyment would distract the audience from the serious purpose of the plays, for Eliot had turned to the theatre to gain a wider audience for the ideas in his poetry.

Because of his great authority as poet and critic, Eliot strengthened the impression that the problem of verse drama was, simply, to find a type of verse that would work on the stage. It has always been a convention of verse drama that there was an agreed type of verse, as the Elizabethans used blank verse or French classicism the alexandrine. Given this basic premise and the dramatic quality of his poetry, Eliot's move into the theatre is extremely logical. *Murder in the Cathedral* (1935) was, in context, very successful but the context was not the world in which his audience lived and to which they returned at the end of the play. And Canterbury Cathedral was not the commercial theatre; it had a congregation rather than an audience. . . . Because he suspected that [a] wider audience would have a largely unthinking familiarity with theological matters he decided that such matters, which were the substance of his plays, would have to be presented in secular terms. He therefore modelled his plays on Greek myths which had provided the form for *Murder in the Cathedral* and now provided matter. He may have been influenced in this by the French dramatists although he works in a different way to them. Rather than rewriting the myth with modern characters he starts with modern characters and filters the myth through them and their actions. *The Family Reunion* (1939), as Eliot himself recognised, was not successful in adjusting Greek myth to a modern situation and ten years later he corrected this mistake in *The Cocktail Party* (1949). If the

opening of the play reminds us of Noel Coward the basis of the play is the *Alcestis* of Euripides. Eliot has also removed the exceptional person from the centre of the play, although she still makes her choice and accepts the consequences in a way that suggests existential drama. The verse is largely the poetry of statement and critics have already begun to object that the verse is very nearly prose. Eliot, writing on the poetry of Dr. Johnson, had suggested that the minimum requirement of good poetry is that it has the virtues of good prose. But it is not easy to create a verse which is flexible enough to cover making a telephone call and the crucifixion of Celia. At high moments the verse works. . . . (pp. 35-7)

Many critics feel that after *The Cocktail Party* there is a general loss in matter and verse. *The Confidential Clerk* (1953) showed Eliot moving towards comedy as a means of examining the choice between the ordinary routine and the dedicated life that leads to beatitude. [Denis] Donoghue loyally suggests that what Eliot has achieved here is not anaemia but *sostenuto* and by shifting the division between spiritual and secular to one between commerce and art Eliot has solved the division that threatens the unity of *The Cocktail Party*. But even his sympathetic critic D. E. Jones places this play 'just across the border from prose'. Eliot's last play *The Elder Statesman* (1958) shows a return to tragedy and a new version of *The Family Reunion*. The issues of guilt are reconsidered but contrition seems very easy and the pain is spoken about rather than made felt, while the verse is scarcely recognisable as verse.

Nevertheless T. S. Eliot made verse in the theatre a commercial proposition. He believed that 'the craving for poetic drama is permanent in human nature' but, as a poet, did not foresee that such drama might not have to be in verse. However secular his plays contrive to appear [they] all fulfil his maxim of religious usefulness. His plays were supposed to surprise people into the meanings and implications of Christianity but audiences could feel that they had not been to the theatre so much as tricked into attending church. Salvation presents the dramatist with difficulties as a theme since it is far less dramatic than damnation and does not lend itself to action, which, after all, is the mainspring of drama. . . . The theatre loves strong emotions and will ultimately reject him however noble his attempts to be serious, in verse, in a play. (pp. 38-9)

> *Arnold P. Hinchliffe, in his* British Theatre 1950-70 *(© Basil Blackwell 1974), Rowman and Littlefield, 1974.*

JOSEPH N. RIDDEL

Despite Eliot's professed historicism, and his concern with the tradition, the thing which characterizes the rhetoric of his criticism (and his poetry as well) is the absence of presence. To put it another way, history and art can only be an imperfect sign of the divine, an immanence available not to the will but only to an ascetic ecstasy. History and knowledge bear marks of guilt, as in "Gerontian," and only in the silence and innocence of the unspoken Word is the Word known in the world. As in the borrowing from the sermon of Lancelot Andrewes, the "sign" signifies an absence in itself in order to signify the "wonder" that it stands for—"The word within a word, unable to speak a word." The timeless monuments of history, of his early essay, "Tradition and the Individual Talent," are signs in time which signify an order that originates outside time and therefore seems to speak for the traditional idea of presence. But such signs in Eliot repeatedly become comments on themselves, and point to the silence of their own center. The sign is not of the center, but a mediation, a supplement. Eliot's symbolism is Episcopal, not Catholic, and thus a sign of history's lack, of language as a part of the universal problematic. Signs, and poems, become aesthetic objects . . . , each of which affirms its own center, its own silence, and not a creative origin outside itself. They are "symbols" of a lost significance. But by their own objective presence, their supplementation, they signify the Incarnation, itself a supplement that signifies the closure of history. These works, then, are evidence of man's desire to recover lost presence, and to redeem his original fault.

The enigmatic thing about Eliot's poetics, and the entire poetics of the New Criticism that derived from him, is the urgency with which it detached art from life into its own self-contained system, thus affirming the artifice of the center as the fiction of presence. The impersonality of art which Eliot asserts in "Tradition and the Individual Talent" cannot affirm a center or source outside the system of the work, except in some mysterious, lost origin. And those interpretations of Eliot's work which ascribe to him the faith in something like a Jungian universal unconscious, or which accept the fundamental structure of the Christian *logos* as an explanation of his ideal of the "autonomous" poem, do not honor the discourse of his method. For the Eliot who traveled to Spain or Southern France to stand in the presence of the prehistoric cave paintings, before he wrote "Tradition and the Individual Talent," and the one who derived his aesthetic from both the *Symboliste* and the Metaphysical poets, is a poet fully involved in the Modernist problematic.

What Eliot "interpreted" as the associated sensibility of the Metaphysical poets was the structure of the "self" as an aesthetic whole, a cosmos of centered elements in tension; or in other words, something different from the modern Bradleyan self, which is composed of those fragments of perception of which it is conscious. He aestheticized Renaissance philosophy, but in doing so, he brought into question the center which, because it is both within and without the "great chain of being" (both beginning and end), could hold otherwise irreconcilable opposites in tension. Eliot's metaphysical "conceit" becomes wholly an aestheic trope; his ideal of a reassociated self is the mark of contemporary dissociation. Poetry separates itself from life by feigning wholeness, by declaring itself a *sign* of wholeness. It is nostalgic for the old order. (pp. 265-67)

Eliot's poetry self-consciously separates itself from the world of sense experience, from life, from history, by the very acknowledgment of its centeredness and its artifice. Only by indulging the metaphors of religion as analogous to the metaphors of art can he bridge the distance between life and art. The metaphor of the Incarnation becomes his bridge, and selflessness (the state of innocence or will-lessness) his definition of recovered wholeness. But behind it all lies the problematic, what he called in the *Four Quartets* the "primitive terror" that confronts anyone looking backward "behind the assurance / Of recorded history" toward the lost origin. What he evidently saw in the depths of the prehistoric caves was the silence and darkness of the center, at once the terror it inspired and the potentiality for signification it admitted. What he saw in his poetry was the sadness of the absence of presence, and the guilt which

animated every effort toward its recovery. For him the poem becomes the supplement of an ideal of wholeness which is itself a sign of history's lack.

That Eliot chose, willfully, to substitute the metaphor of God for the "Something that is probably quite ineffable" which lay at the origin should not tempt one to define his poetics in terms of his professed orthodoxy. It is not historical cunning, or the "contrived corridors" of a history made up of multiple spars of Knowledge, that motivates Eliot's passiveness and impersonality or his orthodoxy. On the contrary, the admixture of innocence and intellectualism, emotion and knowledge, that bewilders his critics, discloses the kind of interpretion in which his poetry is involved. From beginning to end, from the dissociations of "Prufrock" to the "complete consort" of "Little Gidding," his effort is to reconstitute a lost whole, to recover a lost origin. His theme is fragmentation and guilt, the history of language and thus the history of history itself. His desire is to recover, if only in the game of art (so like the ritual of religion), the sign of the lost origin: the ineffable "still-point," the "silence" so fundamental to the structure of words and music.

The ideal of the "right" sentence in "Little Gidding," "where every word is at home, / Taking its place to support the others," tying end to beginning, is the ideal of "Every poem an epitaph." "Little Gidding," the last of the *Quartets,* those ritualized poems which attempt to evoke a figurative (still, silent) center within the brilliant articulations of their sounds, confesses to the endlessness of the search: "We shall not cease from exploration . . ." in search of a "condition of complete simplicity." That condition is of course the condition of unity, of the "fire and the rose" as "one." But it is only realizable in art, in the poem, in ritual, in those "signs" or "monuments" which are in history yet hint of the center which is outside it and known only by the slanted names. "History may be servitude, / History may be freedom"—thus a line in the third section of "Little Gidding," the section which introduces the metaphor of the hanged man (here, Christ) and leads to the figure of the Dove descending in section four. It is the figure of the "symbol perfected in death," and the perfect symbol of the problematic of language in Eliot. It links his poetry with Gnosticism in its attempt to transcend the paradox. Into the darkness at the center of the prehistoric caves, or into the silence at the center of words ("Words, after speech, reach / Into the silence"), the Word descends "With flame of incandescent terror / Of which the tongues declare, / The one discharge from sin and error." "Little Gidding" ends the *Quartets* by summing up the Eliot poetics. If history is either "servitude" or "freedom," history is the problematic; and therefore language is the universal problematic. The gesture of poetry's "exploration" is a gesture toward the recovery of what is lost. In Derrida's words, it "dreams of deciphering a truth or an origin which is free from freeplay," and thus free from the condition of the very medium, homeless words, to which it is condemned. (pp. 267-69)

Joseph N. Riddel, in his The Inverted Bell: Modernism and the Counterpoetics of William Carlos Williams *(copyright © 1974 by Louisiana State University Press), Louisiana State University Press, 1974.*

CALVIN BEDIENT

The Eliot of 'Gerontion' and 'The Hollow Men' . . . is a

quasi-Absentist, his protagonists the seeming victims of an incapacitated faith. The poems tempt us to share despair—at least they feel their way into it with a relish. At the same time they allow us to infer that not faith but the protagonists are to blame. They may be said to refer Christian belief to the reader and even to judge and as it were wait to receive the repentant speakers, who meanwhile enjoy their backwardness. So somehow the 'sightless' hollow men know that a holy plenitude is possible for others—others have crossed the tumid river with 'direct eyes, to death's other Kingdom'. Their desert Absentist realm, with its belatedness, its impotency, is not then the only kingdom, the only death. Now for the Absentist, absence is irremediable and insuperable; it pervades and limits everything; the 'broken jaw of our lost kingdoms' is all. By contrast, the hollow men torture themselves with knowledge of a numinous other realm—and please themselves by hanging back from it. 'Let me be no nearer', they pray as it were inversely, 'Let me also wear / deliberate disguises'. What is this if not self-willed? Their despair is disingenous.

Yet, spurious as spiritual destitution may be in his poems, Eliot provided models for Absentist forms. Introducing into English poetry an 'insidious' principle of disorientation, he dispersed the spatial and temporal closures of traditional verse. He exposed the medium itself to hesitations and reluctances, frustrations and panics. And he forced it to acknowledge the negative otherness of the world and the precipitate, arhythmic progress of mortality.

Thus beyond the suspended lines and through the unpunctuated breaks of 'The Hollow Men' gapes as you read it an alien space. 'Shape without form', the poem correlates visually with both the external and internal space of the hollow men. The poem *looks* like 'broken stone'. Asymmetrical in themselves, the verse paragraphs also fail to mirror one another in form.... [The poem] is not only visually but logically scattered, the isolated epithets being grammatically 'sightless', 'gesture without motion'. Then, too, the disconcerted rhythms send us forward unsatisfied, still on the surface. Absent is the repetition with variation that gives depth and life to rhythm; except for the nearly symmetrical quartet of epithets, with its treacherous paralysis, there is nothing here of the reservoir of duration formed by traditional metre. The unpredictable line length and (so to speak) rubbed-out punctuation also amplify despondency beyond the resources of traditional verse. Enigmatically fractured, simultaneously restive and paralysed, the poem is proto-Absentist. (pp. 18-19)

Calvin Bedient, in PN Review *(© PN Review 1976), Vol. 4, No. 1, 1976.*

JOHN BERRYMAN

To begin with Eliot's title, "The Love Song of J. Alfred Prufrock," is the second half quite what the first led us to expect? A man named J. Alfred Prufrock could hardly be expected to sing a love song; he sounds too well dressed. His name takes something away from the notion of a love song; the form of the title, that is to say, is reductive. How does he begin singing?

> Let us go then, you and I,
> When the evening is spread out against the sky . . .

That sounds very pretty—lyrical—he does seem, after all, in spite of his name, to be inviting her for an evening; there is a nice rhyme—it sounds like other dim romantic verse. Then comes the third line:

> Like a patient etherised upon a table . . .

With this line, modern poetry begins.

In the first place, the third line proves that the author of the first two lines did not mean them. They were a come-on, designed merely to get the reader off guard, so that he could be knocked down. The form, again, is reductive; an expectation has been created only to be diminished or destroyed.... And the word "then"—"Let us go *then*"—is really very unpromising; if he had only said, "Let us go," it would have sounded much more as if they were going to go; "Let us go then" sounds as if he had been giving it thought, and thought suggests hesitation. Of course he never goes at all: *the* visit, involving the "overwhelming question," the proposal of marriage, is never made. Here again we come on a reduction.

Also, the simile is not visual: it only pretends to be. No reader could possibly be assisted in seeing the evening spread out against the sky by having his attention suddenly and violently called to a patient laid out on an operating table. The device of simile is being put to a novel use, violating the ordinary logic of verse, just as the abrupt vision of a hospital violates the lyrical notion of an evening stroll.

What does the line mean? We are obliged to resort to suggestion, not to logic. The situation of a patient under ether is unenviable, risky: he is about to be cut into, soon he may be dead. This fear is basic to the poem: Prufrock finally says, in fact, "I was afraid." On the other hand, the situation of the patient can be regarded as desirable in that he *has* made a decision and now the result is out of his hands, he has no further responsibility, it is up to the surgeon to save him or not. This desire—to *have made* the proposal, and to have his fate left up to the woman—is also basic to the poem. We may think of that as quite a lot of work to get done in one line. Of course, the suggestion that Prufrock sees himself as *ill* is important also, and we will return to this.

Between the title, with its slight effect of double-take, and these opening lines, with their full effect of double-take, the poet has inserted an epigraph in Italian, six lines of it. A knowledge of Italian is of very little help. All the lines say is, "If I thought what I am going to tell you would ever get back to the world, you would hear nothing from me. But as it is," and so on. One has to know *who* is speaking in Dante's *Divine Comedy*. This is a lost soul, in Hell, damned in particular because he tried to purchase absolution *before* committing a crime. We are obliged to consider, that is, as of Prufrock with his dilemma of whether or not to propose marriage, whether the fundamental reason he does not do so—his sin—is his refusal to take the ordinary, inevitable human risks: he wants to know beforehand whether he will be accepted or not—in fact, he does *think* he knows already what will happen—but this belongs later for us.

Everything we have been saying paints a picture as different as possible from that of a writer sitting down to entertain, beguile, charm, and lull a reader or readers. Obstacles and surprise, of no pleasant kind, are this poet's stock-in-trade. The reader's expectation that *one* thing will happen is the first to be attacked. Several things are going to be happening simultaneously. One feels, even, a certain hostility on the part of the poet. The modern poet, characteristically, has *lost confidence* in his readers . . . , but so far from causing him to reduce his demands therefore, this loss of confidence has led to an *increase* in his demands. Good poetry has never been easy to read with any advanced understanding, but it has seldom been made so deliberately difficult.

Shall we . . . suggest that the poet's impatience is based on the fact that the reader's mind is full of vague and grandiose assumptions which seem to the poet contemptible? The poet sees himself as a warning voice, like a Hebrew prophet calling on the people to repent, to understand better themselves and the world. . . . Eliot had pretty certainly not read Freud when he wrote this poem. In some ways, however, their thought is parallel, for the "you" whom Prufrock invites to go with him for the visit must be another part of his own personality, whom he vainly invites to join him in the great task before them. . . . (pp. 270-72)

But the "you" is perhaps also the reader, addressed thus surprisingly in this dramatic monologue; and this device is French, part of the general air of elaborate sophistication adopted by Eliot in this poem. This tone is not original; it is borrowed from the French symbolist poet Jules Laforgue (1860-87), under whose influence Eliot first found his own voice. Some of the characteristic properties in "Prufrock" are Laforgue's, allusions to Hamlet and the sirens. But there is influence also from Elizabethan drama, in the speech rhythms (the poem is written in what is called "free verse," which only means that the laws it obeys are different from those of traditional stanza or blank verse); and there is influence from prose works, especially the expatriate American novelist Henry James's. In any event, Laforgue could never have conceived or written the poem. He only supplied the *manner,* and anyway his music—very beautiful sometimes—is hardly Eliot's.

Eliot's manner is highly sophisticated, but perhaps we ought not to call the poem sophisticated. Let us call it primitive. The poem pretends to be a love song. It is something much more practical. It is a study—a debate by Prufrock with himself—over the *business* of proposing marriage. . . . The first half of the poem looks forward to the proposal, the second half looks back on how it *would* have gone if it had gone at all. The poem is intensely anti-romantic, and its extremely serious subject, in a so-called Love Song, is another rebuke to the [reader]. . . . It is clear that the poet sympathizes with Prufrock. It is also clear that the poet damns Prufrock. Some of the basic emotions of the poem are primitive also—fear, malice—but lust is absent, and the prevailing surface tone is one of civilized, overcivilized anxiety. Prufrock's feelings are rather abstract; he never makes the woman real at all, except in one terrible respect, which let us reserve a little. He is concerned with himself. He is mentally ill, neurotic, incapable of love. But the problem that he faces is a primitive problem.

Eliot brings to bear on Prufrock's dilemma four figures out of the spiritual history of man: Michelangelo, John the Baptist, Lazarus, and Hamlet. (pp. 272-73)

The resort to these four analogues from artistic and sacred history suggests a man—desperate, in his ordeal—ransacking the past for help in the present, and *not finding it*—finding only ironic parallels, or real examples, of his predicament. The available tradition, the poet seems to be saying,

is of no use to us. It supplies only analogies and metaphors for our pain. (p. 275)

It must be obvious . . . that this extraordinarily ambitious poem, including as it does acrid sketches not only of man's spiritual but of his biological history, is not designed as entertainment, whatever the author may say to us (Eliot has defined poetry as "a superior amusement"), and whatever his mask *inside* the poem: the sophisticate, the disillusioned, the dandy with his particular social problem in Boston. . . . The poet has adopted the guise of light verse, but he writes as a prophet, without any trace of conciliation toward any possible audience. He does not write *directly.* He uses the mask of Prufrock—whose fate is like that of what are called the Vigliacchi in Dante. These sinners did neither good nor evil, and so they cannot be admitted even to Hell, lest the damned feel a certain superiority to them; they suffer eternally in what is called the vestibule of Hell. It is better, as Eliot says in one of his critical essays, to do evil than to do nothing. At least one exists in a relation to the moral world. Under this mask he sets up a ruinous antithesis to Victorian hope—in particular, to what must have seemed to him the vacuous optimism of the most recent master of dramatic monologue in English before him, Browning. Civilization is not condemned. The *results* of civilization are dramatized, that is all; above all, the destruction of the ability to love, and—in the well-meaning man—to be decisive. The poet speaks, in this poem, of a society sterile and suicidal. (pp. 277-78)

> *John Berryman, "Prufrock's Dilemma," in his*
> The Freedom of the Poet *(reprinted with permission of Farrar, Straus & Giroux, Inc.; copyright © 1949, 1960 by John Berryman; copyright © 1976 by Kate Berryman; renewed copyright © 1976 by Kate Berryman), Farrar, Straus, 1976, pp. 270-78.*

JACK BEHAR

The common observation of the coldly apocalyptic gesture in Eliot, the intoning of favored set phrases ("Unreal City"), the self-concealing reverie that proved a peculiarly satisfying mode, fit nonetheless with [Gabriel Pearson's account of the social situation of Eliot as an embattled aesthete]; but with the proviso that we take this in its spirit, since with slight alterations it could cover any symbolist retreat to language, any style enamored of obscure intensities of speech. Disinheritance being a general modernist theme, various social situations may lie behind it, not merely that of a poet who may have felt expelled from a world more sturdily composed than the one his poems would reflect. The tone of lament, or of disdainful surmise, implies some more hopeful relation to sources of health that the poems can only point to off-the-page. In certain of the early poems, some nicely turned pieces of grumbling are symptomatic of the banishment to an interior world or, more accurately, a composed and witty stage idiom, one incapable of offering any representation of the social world that is not immediately thrown into doubt by its own ironic self-regard, its appetite for appropriation and dissembling gestures.

It is of course understandably easy, and for polemical purposes useful, to allow Eliot's knowledge of certain intimate modern gestures to yield a large proposition about an entire way of life. Certainly "The Waste Land" sweeps up into one bold but under-articulated structure a great many intimations of decline and exhaustion, in this respect resembling other works written between the wars. . . . Eliot's intimations were bolstered by Frazer, and then were free to go their way, the common ritual that made the scaffolding of the poem being an immemorial fiction rather than a superior vision from whose standpoint behavior could be confidently judged. Part V solicits a vision that will not appear, and the composite figure it addresses disappears into the chaos that follows, the tottering capitals of Europe reduced to figures in a nightmare. This argues for Eliot's attraction to incantation as a way of resisting the temptation to transform indignant perceptions into a lawyer's brief, or overmoralized lament. . . . [One can, however,] point to what keeps the poem from being a half-hearted jeremiad or Spenglerian tract on the decline of the West; and this can only be its art, its chosen mode of language.

To take a minor instance of framing reverie, the somberly intoned "Unreal City," rather than leading us into the scene it frames, suspends a melancholy rhythm upon the mind; it leads to the marvelous lines, "A crowd flowed over London Bridge, so many, / I had not thought death had undone so many," lines chiming to inner lament and casting a pall ahead from which, as the poem goes along, there are to be moments of relief. The reflective, theatrical quality of such lines, at once self-interested and distressed, may spare the intellect's overstating its case. . . Eliot's anti-romanticism told against putting the social claims of poetry in any such exaggerated way. In the poetry itself, at least, the effect of theatrical idiom is to preclude the possibility of making social sense of who or where one is, or why one must be disguised in order to speak. Perhaps that was the province of prose, and more or less official proclamation. In "Prufrock," for example, the famous line "I should have been a pair of ragged claws / scuttling across the floors of silent seas" comes across as a comfortably poised conceit, too well turned in a Tennysonian way to be anything but an agreeable lament. It intones rather than articulates distress, and no account of its symbolic position in the poem will make it any more intelligible. Symbolism, in this sense, goes with the poetics of the Image, not with a composed, or superior, vision to which the Image tends, a presupposing belief that draws everything toward its center. (pp. 489-90)

Eliot was far from timid about enlisting poetry to the task of disencumbering the poet of certain violence-prone attitudes and feelings, some of these evidently odious to the man who contemplated them in the poems. Addicted to phantasmagoria, he was given to decomposing what, to the intellect, might have been overly familiar and overcomposed, as "Gerontion"—the most enticingly theatrical and hollowly exciting of the poems—shows. . . . [The] famous doctrine of impersonality in Eliot may simply endorse the need to pass beyond the limits of the old story, there to discover what might decompose or lighten or at least discomfort it, or perhaps just make it more monstrously entertaining than it already may be (pp. 490-91)

In "Gerontion" the obliqueness, the sense of high address followed by sudden decline, the broken or shifting accents may have followed from a belief about the "insubstantiality" of the self; the self as coterminous with its perceptions rather than a separated subject standing over against experience, assessing, explaining, organizing it. . . . [In] "Gerontion" at the start certain human actions are cited as though they offered autobiographical testimony, as though

they made real reference to a real past. But the poem offers little that allows for our moving confidently from brisk allusion to constituted figure, and thus discourages our taking its language as anything more than gestures erupting from a private, anonymous space. . . . The teasing obliqueness, however, may resemble that of earlier and simpler poems, where some resolving, if hesitant and ultimately canceled, moral commentary is offered to supply a drift of images with "meaning."

In "Preludes" (1909-1911) the poet-observer provides an urban landscape out of a series of seemingly flat notations; but not entirely flat or detached, since some gesture of the composing mind is inserted. . . . [The] poem solicits a vision that would make a moral meaning out of what it joins together. . . . [Eliot in the second poem of "Preludes"] appears perplexed by the gesture of sympathy he produces—it is transposed into a too agreeably romantic phrase—so that it is dismissed for another gesture that imputes to the scene an unfathomable and immemorial necessity. Something like acceptance, however embittered, appears then to be the final, but equivocal, poise in which the poem rests. But if we think of the poem as an action taken to compose bits of "data" into a whole meaning, then the poem would appear to be confessing the impossibility of there being such meaning. So it ends with a kind of metaphysical flourish—an embittered and despairing flourish—that is provoked by the poet's recognition of what he lacks.

"Preludes," of course, is to be sharply distinguished from "Gerontion"; its last embittered gesture arises to confess the defeat of moral statement; whereas "Gerontion" ends with a lame stab at closure, "Thoughts of a dry brain in a dry season," as though it were lamenting and, at the same time, apologizing for its incoherence. . . . The strategy of the poem, then, is to cast an ironical disclaimer in its midst, but one that functions as an all too easily decodable clue. . . . In "Gerontion" no logical, or structural, link exists to provide a context for the first triad of negatives in the poem, "neither . . . nor . . . nor," so that, correspondingly, no sense of a person living through, or recreating, an intimate memory can be forthcoming; the poem contrives a voice without a body, a purely mental universe. (pp. 491-93)

The declarative vigor of the start, with its pseudo-adverbial "placing" of the scene, gives way to a fudging together of literal and metaphorical, so that the innocuous and isolated phrase—"My house is a decayed house"—can suggest both a piece of oddly resonant information and a kind of disembodied whine. . . . What clues we get to the identity of the monologist are literary rather than narrative-autobiographical, and may be contrived to fit with a sad tale of undeserved cultural disgrace, a world passed over into "other" hands. "Dry month" grows by the addition of "dull" and "windy spaces" and "peevish gutter," and finally by "stiffen in a rented room," but it is really part of the apologia of the poem, suggesting that its gestures can only be self-reflecting, a play upon the nerves. (p. 493)

To be haunted by something means to be removed from it, and this covers what enters the poem with the Lancelot Andrewes bit from the Nativity Sermon, where the language plays ambiguously on Christ's simultaneous presence and absence, the annunciation and—as the lines mime this, act it out—the abandonment to history, Christ at our mercy. The speaker hesitates between being drawn to and drawing away from the thought of Christ, evidently being thrown into doubt by the memory of a pagan Nature in the midst of which the god stands:

> In the juvescence of the year
> Came Christ the tiger
> In depraved May, dogwood and chestnut, flowering judas

The doubt is registered in the words "In depraved May," and what follows enacts the abandonment of the figure of speech to the ghostly company who then emerge. . . . (p. 494)

The trouble comes when we think what to do with [the Christ-figure], obliterated but yet existing as a power for life, in connection with the meditation on history that follows. . . . [The] poem laments deceived or superannuated passions, while it can say nothing for the person as agent, as willing—rather than taking—what he gets. It is significant, of course, that the weak pronouns in the passage— "our" and "us"—barely figure as presences, and that it is the curse, in the Christian sense, visited upon action in which all the disappointments associated with history come to a rest. (pp. 494-95)

In Eliot's poem the speaker rises at the start of the last part to both entertain and resist the suspicion that, as poet, he may have been arranging an agreeable aesthetic spectacle, one allowing the image of his disgrace to father his eruptions. (p. 495)

The line "I would meet you upon this honestly," with its air of last-gasp urgency, introduces the passage lamenting the failure of some ideally full engagement of being, and what follows shows the major preoccupation of the poem: the speaker's subtilizing a familiar agony into familiarly theatrical gesture, these belonging to Jacobean dramatic verse. This puts us at a distance from him, as a man writing at a point where two nightmares cross, echoing the aftermath of some dissolution of sense, not just what can be imagined as some sustaining, life-giving contact. It is in this sense that the language of the poem becomes a language of gesture, since what it is "about" must not be other than dimly apprehended; this being the condition of its existing at all. Poems of whole vision came with "Ash-Wednesday" and *Four Quartets,* where the painfully affecting pass ages in a whole life, and in the memory of other lives, are raised into significance, illuminated, and self-transcendence works.

Starting with "What will the spider do" the poem may say something about the violence of history that descends upon everyone, but especially upon the disaffected; more immediately, however, it contrives a valedictory gesture out of its own exhaustion, declaring thereby both the impossibility of producing a structure that would contain its disparate gestures and what it finds most appealing about its own impulses: the "chilled delirium" that displaces "sense"; the pretending ignorance, the holding of ideas in abeyance, that allows it to become a poem; the exploration, in a language both self-condemning and self-exculpating, of some last wearied version of the familiarly complaining self—the self that elsewhere could become a writer of prose polemic addressed to the humanist ascendancy; and, finally, its way of refining nearly out of existence the grievance that first compelled it, by taking that to exist at a far remove from what it means to "take thought" about it, and by accepting

that it could only be reflected in a "delirium" from which all the heat had gone out—a "delirium," that is to say, that would make a motive for a poem. In Eliot's practice symbolist theory allowed for making the "delirium" both accessible and distant, a piece of excited reverie to correspond to what must be assumed to be a devastation but may have been only an invitation to the making of poems. (p. 496)

Jack Behar, "Eliot and the Language of Gesture: The Early Poems," in Twentieth Century Literature *(copyright 1978, Hofstra University Press), December, 1977, pp. 487-97.*

IRVIN EHRENPREIS

The strength of T. S. Eliot's poetry depends on insights that mediate between morality and psychology. Eliot understood the shifting, paradoxical nature of our deepest emotions and judgments, and tried to embody this quality in his style. "All that concerned my family," he once said, "was 'right and wrong,' what was 'done and not done.'" It became the poet's discovery that what is wrong when acted may be right when remembered, that today's gladness justifies yesterday's grief, and that religious serenity may be the upper side of skepticism.

Most of Eliot's innovations of poetic technique strive to disorientate the reader. They give one a literary experience that follows the contours of reversible emotions. Reading Eliot's lines sympathetically, one enters into a drama (often incomplete) of moral judgment imposing itself on a flux of contradictory moods. His ambitious effects are formal equivalents of the process by which insight interrupts experience.

The reason Eliot assigned such importance to ambiguous or paradoxical states is that he required high purpose to live by; and purpose involves choice. The eliciting of true decisions from evasive moods became for him a fundamental occupation. . . .

[Eliot conceived] of discipline rather than freedom as the first need of humanity. "At the bottom of man's heart," he said when he was twenty-eight—in a phrase that anticipates a line of "Gerontion"—"there is always the beast, resentful of restraints of civilized society, ready to spring out at the instant this restraint relaxes. . . . As a matter of fact, the human soul—*l'anima semplicetta*—is neither good nor bad; but in order to be good, to be human, requires *discipline*."

The relation between humility and discipline is obvious enough, and Eliot never lost sight of it. Years later, contrasting totalitarian government with his own idea of a Christian society, he said of the latter, "That prospect involves, at least, discipline, inconvenience and discomfort: but here as hereafter the alternative to hell is purgatory." . . .

In traditional literature (especially plays and novels), it is through the education of the affections that the soul achieves moral intelligence: famous examples are Tom Jones and Sophia, Darcy and Elizabeth Bennet. The pursuit of the beloved offers tests and challenges that dissolve impurities and clarify virtue. But Eliot distrusted the easy parallelism between courtship and illumination unless the lover's hopes were unsatisfied. In an early "Song" he yearns for significant passion but anticipates deprivation. This poignancy of revelations missed, of love evaded, was to stay with Eliot to the end of his course:

> The moonflower opens to the
> moth,
>   The mist crawls in from the
> sea;
> A great white bird, a snowy owl,
>   Slips from the alder tree.
>
> Whiter the flowers, Love, you hold,
>   Than the white mist on the sea;
> Have you no brighter tropic flowers
>   With scarlet life, for me? . . .

The economy, meticulous sound patterns, evocative imagery, and exact versification of this Tennysonian lyric all suggest the eagerness for self-denial that the poem expresses. Not only does one recognize the triple motif of humility, sacrifice, and barely attainable love. One also recognizes the poet's submission to an ascetic conception of art. It is in this spirit that an older Eliot was to say of unrhymed verse, "The rejection of rhyme is not a leap at facility; on the contrary it imposes a much severer strain upon the language."

Humility, I think, contributed to his habit of using other men's words rather than starting afresh with his own. Partly this is an acknowledgment of the older writers' excellence, a hint of the foolishness of making newborn speech do jobs that inherited language can do better. . . .

In discussing Eliot's deliberate allusions, our danger is to take them as referring to concrete persons or situations, particularly to conditions of life or heroic figures of the past, supposed to be offered as preferable to those of our own time. But it is always a poet's rendering that Eliot retrieves for us, rather than a fact or deed in its nakedness.

So he produces not the murder of Agamemnon but the tragic resonance of that crime for Aeschylus; not the routines of Italian monasteries under Boniface VIII, but Dante's idea of the contemplative life. (p. 3)

So also in finding out images, Eliot strove to be true to himself without celebrating his personality. He wanted images to be authentic, and therefore drawn from his own experience—if possible, from the deepest level of that experience. But they were also to belong to the archetypal sensibility of mankind, or at least be such as evoke strong, lingering associations in most men. He further preferred that they should have appeared in the work of earlier masters. Even for imagery as apparently original as the "Preludes"'

> Sitting along the bed's edge, where
> You curled the papers from your
>   hair,
> Or clasped the yellow soles of feet
> in the palms of both soiled hands . . .

he turned to a passage in a French novel he admired.

Yet again, the images were to suggest the paradoxical nature of moral judgment—that what seems meaningless now may be drenched in meaning later, that what seems like renunciation at dusk may be self-fulfillment at noon. Putting the elements together, one gets highly charged ambiguities in reverberating speech.

So it is that winter may represent both life and death, in words that echo the Victorian James Thomson (*Waste Land,* I). November may be confused with spring, in an image borrowed from Campion (*East Coker,* II). Fire may mean lust or purgation or divine love, in terms used by Buddha, St. Augustine, or Dante.

For the poet himself, the authority of his predecessors validated the images and their meaning. For the listener who picks up the reverberations (whether or not he identifies the source), they enrich the force of suggestion. But at the same time, as an expression of humility, such images diminish the personality of the poet. He hovers over the work without manifestly entering it.

Working within these limits, the poet makes himself something of a martyr. In a sense, he exchanges his identity for his poetry. But he wins a substantial reward; and this is the powerful, tenacious quality of verse that stirs us with its right rhythms, its mysterious overtones, and depth of meaning—verse that belongs to us like our early memories.

Yet on the opposite side, ambition constantly affirmed its claims. In his critical prose Eliot exhibited from the start a magisterial self-confidence that barely glanced at opposition. His assurance and assertiveness demolished an old orthodoxy and established a new one. They also served, I believe, to fence off Eliot's doubts about his poems.

But the style of the prose is not experimental. It was in verse that Eliot resolved to experiment, innovate, change. He wished to join his name to fundamental transformations of the technique of poetry: hence the variety in the small body of his *oeuvre.* Having mastered one set of devices, Eliot went restlessly on to another, bolder scheme—*Prufrock,* "Gerontion," *The Waste Land*—till he reached the audacities of *Ash-Wednesday.* Then he swerved on himself in a movement of conservation, from "Animula" to the five-part sequence of "Landscapes" (1933-1934). These embody the sense of place and the emotional trajectory of the final masterpiece, the *Quartets,* which came soon after.

We may estimate the height of Eliot's ambition from his aspiring to work not only with new metrical patterns but also with fundamental aspects of language itself: disruptions of syntax and meaning that startle the reader into attention while forcing him to reconsider the purpose and value of literary experience: proper names intruding with no reference to identify them, until we question the significance of identity; verb tenses slyly melting into one another, till we ponder the reality of time; third persons becoming second and first, till we stumble in the relativity of perception.

Eliot practiced confusing the literal and figurative sense of the same word; he gave intangible subjects to concrete verbs, and let the verbs themselves look like participles in one clause while serving as predicates in another. It becomes clear to attentive listeners that speech can separate men from each other, as well as join them; and the mystery of a divine Logos begins to seem not so different from the mystery of communication between self-contained persons.

Meanwhile, from "Prufrock" on, the experiments in versification were seducing and startling those who followed them. I think we may distinguish persistent modes related to changing themes. For example, the old poignancy of evasive moments and missed opportunities kept returning on the reader in patterned lines, incantatory and subtly regular: "She has a bowl of lilacs in her room" ("Portrait of a Lady," II); "Weave, weave the sunlight in your hair" ("La Figlia che Piange"); "He passed the stages of his age and youth" (*Waste Land,* IV).

The nostalgic moment recurs in passages of free verse, blank verse, and lyric stanzas: "Blown hair is sweet, brown hair over the mouth blown, / Lilac and brown hair" (*Ash-Wednesday*, III). It triumphs in Eliot's lament over the destruction wrought by the Second World War; and here the echoes of Tennyson are distinct. (The ash is dust settling after an air raid):

> Ash on an old man's sleeve
> Is all the ash the burnt roses leave.
> Dust in the air suspended
> Marks the place where a story
>   ended.
> Dust inbreathed was a house—
> The wall, the wainscot and the
>   mouse.
> The death of hope and despair,
>   This is the death of air.
>
>   (pp. 3-4)

Frail and transient are the things that feed such pathos—too fragile for a man to live by, although they tempt him to make the effort. As Eliot acknowledges and stands back from the temptation, he finds a second mode—irony, or his consciousness of the impotence of momentary yearnings to sustain high purpose. This consciousness may appear in the gentle mingling of pathos and irony, as in "Portrait of a Lady." It may also slip into satire—both self-satire and the ridicule of social types like oneself; or it may sink further, into loathing of oneself and others, as humility becomes a bottomless sense of unworthiness.

Here is the aspect of Eliot touched by Laforgue. We hear the satiric voice restrained, in free verse that tightens at points into blank verse; we also hear it bitter or even raging, in rhymed quatrains. The risk of such satire is that readers can ignore the poet's sense of degraded kinship with the figures he mocks; for his attitude is that of Baudelaire in "*Les Sept vieillards.*" If Eliot did not blame himself far more harshly, he would never stoop to injure someone like "Cousin Harriet."

Deeper yet is the risk of the spiteful rants against "Apeneck Sweeney" and "Bleistein—Chicago Semite Viennese." With these one must see that it is the squalor of the poet's own mind, the shallowness of his own culture, the lusts of his own eye, the passivity of his own will that he excoriates in the caricatures. (p. 4)

I have been suggesting a relation between Eliot's styles and his responses to the human condition. I would also suggest that the satiric impulse died after he wrote *The Waste Land* because to separate himself from any class of humanity, if only in appearance, became in his eyes an immoral act. So also the impulse to embody the various modes in dramatic speakers faded after *Ash-Wednesday* as the poet grew less covert about doctrine. The hidden springs of his poetic energy had always been didactic. With age he seemed to accept the fact and to let his unqualified voice be heard. Perhaps the writing of plays absorbed the imagination he had drawn on when assuming roles in verse.

The familiar images and motifs persist amazingly and in many forms, because the poet deliberately built his later work on the earlier. By a cunning irony the motto of *East Coker*, "In my beginning is my end," reminds one not only of Mary Stuart but also of the Lady in Eliot's "Portrait" saying, "But our beginnings never know our ends!" Thus the close of his career bows to the opening.

Yet the momentum of change continued. In technique the poet kept his instinct for matching form to meaning, but the experimental ambition dwindled. Instead, Eliot concentrated on refining and transforming his habitual modes. By gradations he arrived at the counterpoint of four modes in the *Quartets.* . . .

[It] is in the *Quartets* (1935-1942) that the great change of direction after *Ash-Wednesday* culminates. Here an unmasked poet gives voice to his reflections. He uses a four-fold mode of meditation derived from blank verse but freely expanding and contracting, turning inward and out on immediate thought and perception; rising to brief visions; interrupted by nostalgic memories; sinking to grim prospects of death in life.

Against the flow, the poet thrusts intensifications of the extreme modes: formal lyrics of purgatorial vision and prayer. And now he resolves the strain between humility and ambition by letting the theme of art emerge, and openly commenting on the labors of creation. In the brilliantly expressive versification of the last important poem he wrote (*Little Gidding*), the poet once more triumphs in paradox; for he reviews the disappointments of the creative imagination in a style of absolute mastery, and dramatizes his own personality in the voice of Dante. (p. 6)

> *Irvin Ehrenpreis, "Mr. Eliot's Martyrdom," in* The New York Review of Books *(reprinted with permission from* The New York Review of Books; *copyright © 1978 Nyrev, Inc.), February 9, 1978, pp. 3-4, 6-8.*

*   *   *

ELLISON, Harlan   1934-

Ellison, a short story writer, novelist, editor, and screenwriter, is one of America's foremost fantasists. His fiction most often depicts man in violent confrontation with the universe, a theme he presents in a prose rich in mythical allegory. An innovative craftsman, Ellison has forged a highly personal literary language. His work is both a critical and popular success, winning him many awards and prizes in the field of science fiction, including the Hugo and Edgar awards. (See also *CLC*, Vol. 1, and *Contemporary Authors*, Vols. 5-8, rev. ed.)

THEODORE STURGEON

Ellison's wild style, his unfinished sentences, his tumbling, driving pace, his mad, mixed metaphors and symbols and similes have exploded in all sorts of markets—mostly minor: girlie books, record-review columns, mystery and detective pulps, novels, radio and TV and the movies. But he began in and with science fiction; and his latest collection, *Paingod*, provides a fascinating study of what he was, and what he is becoming. What he is becoming is great. What he is having is a ball. He has now reached a point where the very worst he can become is the most sharply focused image-maker of contemporary *homo sap.* . . .

Ellison can be excruciatingly bad; . . . [but to dwell on examples] would be to commit a foolishness, for Ellison is a growing entity. One may recognize that a youth is not yet an adult; one does not, however, blame him for it. Buy *Paingod* and read it—and of it, especially the "non-introduction" and the rubrics between the stories. Then get hold of more Ellison titles—there are plenty. Watch him grow. Look, when the dazzle of his means fades from your reader's eye, at his ends: what he has to say, what he believes, believes in, and, clearly, is. (p. 690)

Theodore Sturgeon, in National Review (© *National Review, Inc., 1966; 150 East 35th St., New York, N.Y. 10016), July 12, 1966.*

GERALD JONAS

No one but Ellison could have written [the tales in "Deathbird Stories"]. No one but Ellison could have prefaced them with a box headed "CAVEAT LECTOR," containing the following words: "It is suggested that the reader not attempt to read this book at one sitting. The emotional content of these stories, taken without break, may be extremely upsetting. . . ." Like the prose in the box, the stories offer a mixture of overheated Hype and genuine concern for the human condition. It is Ellison's conceit that these stories form a "cycle" dealing with the death of mankind's old gods and the search for newer deities. A few stories, not necessarily the best, seem to fit into this framework; among them are the overrated "Paingod" and "Pretty Maggie Moneyeyes." A story about a highway duel in the near-future, "Along the Scenic Route," doesn't fit at all; stripped of pretensions, it is simply a standard S.F. nightmare of the machine age.

As a writer, Ellison has always specialized in excess. In this book, I lost count of the number of references to a piece of flesh being torn from someone's body. With enough repetitions, even this image loses its impact; then Ellison has to up the ante. . . .

There are times, however, when Ellison raises excess and pretension to a form of art. The last story in the book, "The Deathbird," is a compendium of every trick Ellison has ever pulled, every artistic sin he has ever committed; I found it genuinely moving. (p. 32)

Gerald Jonas, in The New York Times Book Review (© *1975 by The New York Times Company; reprinted by permission), March 23, 1975.*

ERIC KORN

The Americans do not need symposia; they have Harlan Ellison, not a one-man band but a symphony orchestra, complete with a thousand violins, shofar, and ordinance. I find it difficult to speak temperately about him. On one hand he is responsible for *Dangerous Visions*, and its successors, anthologies as cardinal as *New Signatures* or *des Imagistes;* on the other hand—a smaller, nipping and less important hand, like a crab's left claw—he exhibits all that is hateful about SF: the biographical and autobiographical logorrhoea, the cute titles, the steamy, cosy, encounter-group confessional tone, the intrusively private acknowledgments, the blurbs and afterwords. When I have read a good story I like to rest and smoke a fag; I do not want a writer rushing over and asking if the earth moved. . . .

Harlan Ellison has his own visions, some of a fine, universal menace, some dangerous only to the writer. . . . [The best thing in] *Approaching Oblivion* is another story of fascism with an American face, but the other stories are less uniformly minatory. There is one about new Orpheus—can anyone write about jazz without sickliness?—an involved and embarrassing Yiddish joke, and an introduction that takes it all back to being rejected by a gang of playground antisemites. Ellison has done a lot to drag SF out of the ghetto, but is building high, broken-glass-topped walls around his new Jerusalem. (p. 26)

Eric Korn, in The Times Literary Supplement (© *Times Newspapers Ltd. (London) 1977; reproduced from* The Times Literary Supplement *by permission), January 14, 1977.*

J. G. BALLARD

Exuberance, an attractive and abundant quality in science fiction, is comparatively rare among its writers, as anyone attending an sf convention soon notices. (p. 405)

The most notable exception among contemporary writers of sf is Harlan Ellison, an aggressive and restless extrovert who conducts his life at a shout and his fiction at a scream. Teenage gang-leader turned Hollywood screen-writer [and] polemicist . . . , Ellison is one of the most interesting and talented sf writers to appear since Ray Bradbury. (pp. 405-06)

[*Approaching Oblivion*] has all the visceral and paranoid obsessions that run through [his] anthologies. . . . However lurid, the stories have a relentless imaginative drive, suggesting that Ellison may be the first of a new kind of sf writer, completely uninterested in science but attracted to the medium by the ample opportunities which New Wave sf offers for exploiting the most sensational emotional mixes. (p. 406)

J. G. Ballard, in New Statesman (© *1977 The Statesman & Nation Publishing Co. Ltd.), March 25, 1977.*

JOHN CROW and RICHARD ERLICH

Harlan Ellison's *A Boy and His Dog* . . . is a cautionary fable employing satire and mythic patterns to define a future world that in some respects may already be with us. The "boy" is Vic . . . and the "dog" is Blood . . . ; their world is the American Southwest in 2024, shortly after World War IV and the near-total destruction of the human race. (p. 162)

In Blood, we have one of the variations in mythic patterns and folk motifs that make . . . [Ellison's novella] so fascinating and disturbing. At first glance, Blood seems much like the wise magic animal of folk and fairy tales who comes to the aid of the hero when the hero is at an impasse. But Blood goes beyond this role to become Vic's link to the lost pre-war civilization, teaching him reading, arithmetic, recent history, and "Edited English" grammar. He becomes the culture-bearer of the bombed-out wasteland, superior to Vic in everything but the necessary skills of animal survival. The normal relationship of human and animal is inverted.

This inversion and others that follow acquire significance when we see them against the structural pattern of the story. The pattern is the basic descent-containment-reascent pattern of initiation, which in primitive societies is usually a formalized ritual designed to bring a boy into manhood. It also appears in myths of the hero, where the hero undertakes the task of renewing the wasteland. Through the many variations of the pattern, the task confronting the protagonist remains the same: to maintain conscious "human" control over the unconscious "animal" instincts and responses, thereby overcoming fear, fatigue, inattention or disobedience, or the temptation to indulge appetites such as hunger or the sex drive. Since the sexual appetite presents such a powerful and persistent temptation to the hero, the feminine becomes a symbol of the danger of losing consciousness and regressing to instinctual, unconscious motivation. On the other hand, the feminine can function as mediatrix of the life force that brings renewal to the wasteland. In myth, the feminine has either positive or negative value according to whether she overwhelms the hero and renders him ineffectual by depriving him of human consciousness or joins him in the task of rejuvenating the wasteland.

All the elements of this mythic situation are present . . . : the bombed-out wasteland incapable of the renewal of life; the feminine sexual lure into the descent, represented by Quilla June Holmes . . . ; a hero divided between using good sense and pursuing his sexual desires; and the necessity for rebirth (the goal of initiation). (pp. 162-63)

Ellison's novella demands consideration of just how consciously our own society is proceeding into its technological future. It also has in its political implications a strong condemnation of any complacent "silent majority" who would deny time and change by a mechanistic application of outworn values. . . . [Ellison's story presents] a two-level world: on the surface we have "man in a state of nature," a la Thomas Hobbes, a life of "perpetual war of every man against his neighbor"; in the downunder we have a mechanized incarnation of Hobbes' Leviathan—a totalitarian society where people have renounced freedom, individuality, and, most of all, consciousness, for stability and order. This Hobbesian dichotomy presented in a mythic structure suggests the horror of a world not future, but present, a world where our surface struggles move in patterns dictated by our unconscious subservience to traditional forms. (pp. 165-66)

> *John Crow and Richard Erlich, "Mythic Patterns in Ellison's 'A Boy and His Dog',"* in Extrapolation *(copyright 1977 by Thomas D. and Alice S. Claveson), May, 1977, pp. 162-66.*

GEORGE EDGAR SLUSSER

It seems amazing that a writer like Harlan Ellison, with twenty years of work and many memorable stories behind him, has never been studied seriously and at any length before. This is surely because he writes fantasy, and fantasy as a genre is still more or less ignored, even today, when other, more specious "minorities" are having their day in the sun. I find particularly ironic the term "mainstream." Coined by writers of the 1930s to designate that other, better literature, it has helped drive into the ghetto what in fact has always been a dominant mode of literary expression in America. The kind of tale Ellison writes was done not only by Poe, but by Hawthorne, Melville, and Twain as well—mythical allegories which explore the mind and soul of a nation without a long cultural tradition or firm landmarks. Ellison belongs in this genuine mainstream. (p. 3)

A tireless experimenter with forms and techniques, Ellison has gradually worked toward an intricate, highly personal language of mythical expression. (p. 5)

What is Ellison's path as he moves from more traditional modes of fantasy to the highly original mythical allegories that have become his trademark? From the first, his stories reflect strong moral concern. . . . [But he] is not a didactic writer in the narrower sense. The journalist can comment and preach, but the storyteller's job is to explore deeper realms of experience. Much scientific fantasy simply trans-

poses contemporary society and its problems into the future; today's possibilities become actuality. For such tales, there is always an implicit moral: change our ways (or pursue them) before it is too late. Ellison, on the other hand, extrapolates downward and inward; his stage is man's primitive psyche, his basic urge for survival and revenge. It is not so much present and future time as mythic time. Increasingly, in his best stories of the Sixties and Seventies, Ellison makes bold use of the non-realistic conventions of fantasy to place his heroes on this timeless plane of action, to dig at the mythic underpinnings of basic human emotions, desires, and needs.

Ellison's man, unavoidably, is American man today, shaped by his particular ethos and landscape. The search for myth, for universal patterns, is necessarily a search for the meaning of modern life. Or is it rather an attempt to escape from it? At this point, Ellison's quest becomes perilous and paradoxical. (p. 6)

Since the Romantic writers, mythmaking has been discussed in terms of "concrete universals." The particular object or situation is rubbed, and archetypal patterns and primitive racial memories appear underneath; unusual and uncanny shapes are made to unfold in an unbroken line from the familiar thing, debased by too much use. This uniquely modern search for myth is a vital reaction to a world in which objects have become increasingly opaque, unresponsive to man's need to interact on deeper levels with his surroundings. Ellison's mythical imagination is impelled by the same wants. Oddly, though, in his earlier flights he tends to follow the logic of abandonment. In doing so, he runs two dangers. The lesser of these is the pitfall of private fantasy. (pp. 6-7)

A worse danger is the lure of myth itself. Instead of facing a difficult moral problem on its own ground, he bypasses it, transposing it to a plane beyond good and evil. . . . In thus trying to evade moral reality, one only magnifies it, and personifies it in the shadow. (p. 7)

Gradually, however, as his art evolves, Ellison not only discovers the danger, but puts it to creative use in his ongoing dialectic. The master myth of our time, he comes to realize, is escape, the transcendental pattern itself. His latest stories are quests of a new sort, neither withdrawal into self nor expansion outward. They are journeys backward and inward, in which an individual explores all avenues of communication between the moral and mythical levels of existence. In terms of form as well, the author is seeking new bridges across this empty center. Of these, the most interesting is his use of literary tradition itself, Eliot's "historical" link between the isolated case and totality. Ellison's formation as a writer was popular—he was weaned on the literature of fantasy and science fiction. Lately, though, he is turning more and more to the "classics," and to European tradition. The landscapes through which his heroes pass are no longer wholly timeless and faceless ones—naked urges, the eternal rhythms of survival or revenge. Now their journey is increasingly overlaid with references to other deeds, and other cultural heroes. A web of literary resonances surrounds the action that stood bare before, endowing it with a variety of potential moral meanings, at the very least.

Ellison today is a writer in ferment. The problems he is currently wrestling with are those of the American myth itself.

The outcome of this struggle is, perhaps, no less than the validity of such mythical fantasy as commentary on our times. To study Harlan Ellison from this perspective is not to study a "science fiction" writer. It is to examine, in a living, dynamic fashion, the art of mythmaking in America today.

Even the most casual reader of Ellison is struck by what appears to be two divergent, irreconcilable aspects to his writing. On one hand, there is the journalist, the public moralist, and commentator on our times. On the other, there is the rather private fantasist, whose tales disorient the reader, plunging him into an offbeat, intensely personal world. What relation is there between these two halves?

First of all, they are linked by the fact that both issue from a common source: they are equally the product of strong feeling. Ellison's journalism is not objective; rather, it is opiniated and impassioned. His stories too, he tells us, come from deep down inside. A more obvious bond is that the two halves complement each other in a functional sense: they form gloss and text. (pp. 7-8)

[What] kind of journalism is Ellison's? Measured against more recent reportorial standards, it seems rather old-fashioned. The tendency of the "new journalists" is to let the facts of American life speak for themselves.... [These] journalists pursue their object, listen and observe, record, and withhold overt judgment.

Ellison's eye is never on the object for long. Before the reader can even begin *The Glass Teat* (1969), the author sets him straight as to what he will find there: "I am not *really* talking about TV here. I am talking about dissidence, repression, censorship, the brutality and stupidity of much of our culture, the threat of the Common Man . . ." Nor is Ellison a listener. He is impatient with the endless patter of American life, and rudely cuts it off, passing to the attack. At once he sets himself forth as a moral spokesman, ready to root out folly and viciousness wherever they lurk. To find an equivalent voice, we must go back to someone like H. L. Mencken, whom Ellison resembles in certain ways.... Each of Ellison's essays is, to use Mencken's term, a "prejudice," opinion laid bluntly on the line in hopes of arousing violent response.

Ellison is less interested in facts than opinions. The vast majority of these, we soon discover, concern the writer's own existence. And they in turn gravitate around his works of fiction. (pp. 9-10)

[His] commentary can, of course, be both obtrusive and coercive, for Ellison is not above telling us how we should read his stories. One way . . . is to preface each tale with a note that describes its genesis, the mood it hopes to cast, and, on occasion, its meaning. Another way is to record group reactions to the story. (p. 11)

It is possible to dismiss [his commentary] . . . as Ellison's attempt to build a screen against criticism.... In this display of openness, Ellison actually cuts the ground from under the critic's feet. In doing so, he refuses to let literature be a two-way exchange. He would have his stories affect others, change their lives, but he refuses to allow criticism of his work to affect him.

There may be some truth in this view. And yet it completely ignores the ironic element present here. The "voice" is primarily a literary device, one that Ellison discovers and perfects as his style evolves. (pp. 12-13)

[There are three types of commentary:] the voice outside, with commentary detached from the texts; the voice inside, seeking to become the hero of a piece of non-fictional fiction; and the voice as mediator, or commentary engaged in dialogue with texts and reader. (p. 13)

In a very real sense, the speaker in the essays feels he is a voice crying in the wilderness. The "liberal" is a mask; the stand taken is fundamentally aristocratic and conservative.... Ellison does not (any more than Mencken) deny the American language. On the contrary, he uses its powers boldly, and flays those who debase it.... On occasion, however, his judgments, confronted with problems of a different order, show for all their apparent hardness of edge a sentimental underside. The rhapsody on poor and rich in Rio, for instance, is sadly ineffectual if held up to the complex social issues themselves. The mass of men now ask to be considered neither as dupes nor villains, but as people whose standard of living must be improved. Such pragmatism is out of phase with Ellison's static division of mankind into forces of dark and light, with the former inexorably spreading its dominion.

We can say, then, that the farther this voice gets from its own stories (Rio was too far), the closer it gets to sentimentality and empty ranting. On the other hand, it also seems true that if it gets too close, it loses its sense of balance. In *Memos from Purgatory* (1961), Ellison tried to move his *persona* completely inside the tale, to make himself its hero. If this experiment is less than successful, it is still interesting in many ways. (pp. 14-15)

This book is one of Ellison's worst. But the failure is instructive, for in it we discover the temperament of the writer, and the true nature of his *persona*. Ellison would make himself the hero of the story, but finds that to do so is only to make this "self" another character, and thus condemn him to choosing a single point of view. But the *persona*, like the personality it represents, is too mercurial to accept such strictures, or even the hegemony of an object. In both parts of *Memos*, the speaking voice, the "I," invariably draws attention away from the object toward this self. Is the book about prison and injustice, or the many masks of Harlan Ellison? Alternately, we have Cagney-style tough ("Get it straight now . . ."), Kafkaesque victim, Marx-Brother zany, ranting Jeremiah, average citizen who wants no trouble with the law. All these are fantasy roles, facets of the real man, to be sure, but magnified and projected. They and others form the sweep of this versatile voice. When held to some analytical or documentary task, this mimic virtuosity is fettered; if it bursts wholly out of control, as in the "Tombs" scene, chaos is the result.

Recently, however, this voice has made a new debut, in a series of long, elaborate "introductions" woven in and around various collections of stories. Here at last Ellison seems to have found the right field of activity for his *persona*—the literary process itself, the complex interplay between writer, work, and reader. Now, in this middle ground, moralist and hero, braggart and ironist, are at last free to trade off, to juggle masks at will. Because stories and writers are the stuffs of illusion, they form the perfect context for this illusion master, who stands beside and behind them, animating and provoking reactions on all sides. One is struck by the speaker's sheer delight in his art of masquerade.

In Ellison's latest books, the use of this *persona* has achieved new subtlety as the means of binding and unifying collections of his own stories. The author is now showing extreme concern for the groupings he gives his tales. *Deathbird Stories* (1976), for example, is an attempt to gather a number of works under a common thematic canopy. In doing so, Ellison not only acknowledges his preoccupation with god-myths over the years, but tries to arrange his experiments in some sort of logical order. The new edition of *Love Ain't Nothing But Sex Misspelled* (1976) is organized around the intruding *persona*. It is the most extraordinary example to date of a structural use of this device. (p. 20)

Surprisingly few of Ellison's fantasy stories are purely moral tales—illustrative of social doctrine, or condemnatory of society in parable. From the beginning, in fact, action takes place on a much more elementary level: it is the brutal struggle of an individual to survive in a hostile world. The battles Ellison portrays are, essentially, physical rather than moral. (p. 23)

Couched in the violent surface of these tales is a belief in the uniqueness of man, a faith in his ability to survive against the onslaught of any enemy—alien, machine, man himself as destroyer of nature and life. But is survival all he can achieve? Gradually, Ellison's stories have become more pessimistic: man's condition seems one of neverending strife. Progress is impossible; there is some primal blight or flaw at the heart of this cruel universe. In a series of tales of the late Sixties and early Seventies, the writer comes close to Calvinist gloom. These stories mark a crucial point in his career. If the human condition cannot be explained in social or moral terms, the writer must seek to do so in religious ones—we have dark forces, cruel gods, Fear personified. These, it turns out, are nothing more than projections, shadows of our plight on earth. They resolve nothing, and certainly take none of the blame; the finger points right back at the source. . . . The passage from center to circumference, the attempt at transcendence, is doomed to failure. If there is an answer, it must be sought in the other direction, backward and inward, down to the point, through the needle's eye of self. (p. 24)

[In his latest tales, "Silent in Gehenna," "Basilisk," and "Knox"], Ellison gives us, instead of geometry, a genuine ecology of darkness. From situation to situation, man is woven more and more inexorably into the fearful dynamics of nature. Social action is all but impossible. The institutions of this world are not only treacherous, claiming to bring light and actually serving darkness, but flimsy and inconsequential as well. Man can do little or nothing collectively to change his lot; laws and education can easily become instruments of tyranny in the wrong hands. The battle, for Ellison, remains an individual one; the true law is that of survival. . . . Man is on his own, and the strongest survives. There is more than a tinge of Calvinist gloom cast over man's collective efforts. This whole middle ground between the individual and his dark gods is without substance. (pp. 41-2)

To what extent is man to blame for his condition? In all these stories, he has made it worse by not accepting it. But how can he accept violence and suffering? Can he do anything? "Knox" ends on a note of bitter fatalism that could be a ray of hope. Ellison gives us a quote from Jung: "The only thing we have to fear on this planet is man." The cycle will begin all over again. Failure and suffering are part of the universal order. But if man cannot change things, per-

haps he can know more. The dark shapes are fed by our lies and hypocrisy; but must they always remain symbols of something incomprehensible? Must all our moments of recognition be as bewildered as that of Knox? In these stories, we have reached a "Job situation." Pain has become a fact of human existence, no more, no less. The "adversary" is neither wholly within nor wholly without. Nor is he a free agent. He is clearly recognized as part of a godhead whose real nature—like that of the leviathan—is beyond human understanding. The task of Ellison's mythical tales will be to rise to that superhuman plane, to explore the ways of these gods to man. (p. 42)

[Ellison's mythic tales] are of two basic kinds. First, there are the cosmologies, parables that explore the ways of the gods to man. What are the causes of man's condition? Is this natural order of pain and suffering part of some higher universal balance? Second, there are the tales of quest, individual man searching to define his role in the cosmic dynamic. Earlier heroes sought to conquer worlds; these seek to know self. (p. 43)

Only in "Paingod" (1964) do we first examine human suffering from the cosmic point of view. . . . The paingod has become dissatisfied with his job of dispensing pain: "It involved no feeling and no concern, only attention to duty. . . . How peculiar it was that he felt concern after all this time." But he is the highest authority, there is nowhere to go for answers but down. He goes all the way to the bottom of creation, skid row on the insignificant Sol III, a failed sculptor named Colin Marshack. Only when inside this minute human destiny can he feel the full, hot potency of this thing he so casually sprinkled over the universe. This in turn brings him to lift the man out of his shell, and whirl him through infinite space: "He poured him full of love and life and the staggering beauty of the cosmos." The sculptor returns to life to create a masterwork, and face even greater suffering because of it; the god goes back to come of age. But will he now spare the creatures of the universe this suffering? No, he will send more and more pain, for this is the most fortunate thing of all, without it there can be no happiness. The god was bored. Man too gives him a gift—in exchange for an instant of pain he receives an eternity of happiness. (pp. 44-5)

There is room then for both gods and men to grow, to change, but only within the fixed limits of this balance of forces. How human actions affect this balance—the possibility that man's desire to "better" his universe could ever change or alter the workings of this system—is the subject of one of Ellison's most interesting stories, "The Beast That Shouted Love at the Heart of the World" (1968). (p. 45)

Man then is not the center of the universe. But he is, necessarily, one of its poles. In both "Paingod" and "Beast" there is always that small point of contemporary American life, from which the cosmos expands, on which it contracts. Modern scientific man however would be not only center, but circumference as well, erect his systems and machines as absolutes, play god. These systems, we have seen in Ellison's fantasies, invariably absorb their builder, trap him in an inverted, perverted cosmos, a hell of his own making. In two other mythical allegories, "I Have No Mouth and I Must Scream" (1967), and "Pretty Maggie Moneyeyes" (1967), Ellison anatomizes man's relation to his machines, explores the outcome of our Faustian dreams. (p. 47)

In both these tales, the machine becomes man's other self, his "double," and this creature of his desires and urges literally swallows its creator. In expanding his ego, man succeeds only in turning it inside out; it becomes an inverted cosmos, and he is trapped in the world of self. There seem only two alternative ways in life: man can dream, pursue wealth, ideals, a false love of others which is really hate, love of self; or he can accept the raw, bloody struggle to survive. In past tales, neither has led to freedom. Maggie touches on both. She escapes to Heaven or Hell (which we are never told), seducing Kostner, the eternal loser, who is condemned by his own weaknesses to turn endlessly in an indifferent play of forces. But is man's fate always to be this prison of materiality, cold equations and laws of balance forever deaf to human aspirations? We hear Baudelaire's cry of despair—never to leave this world of things, quantities. Is there no spirit, no true peace anywhere? There is a third direction in Ellison, a way which grows stronger and stronger in the latter tales—the journey inward. These are strangely literal quests for self at the center of one's own being. . . . This too has its dangers, for the world inside may be no less a lie, a labyrinth, a prison. (pp. 50-1)

The quest for self, in Ellison, may be a conscious one however. . . . The hero of "One Life, Furnished in Early Poverty" (1969) seeks his identity by actually going back in time, meeting his past self. The protagonist's quest for love in "Catman" (1972) is in reality a search for self as member of a family that must quite literally be recreated. If these two works seem to say, in various ways, you can't go home again, the third story, "Adrift Just Off the Islets of Langerhans: Latitude 38 54′ N, Longitude 77 00′ 13″ W" (1975) is in its own strange way a successful quest. In this work Ellison achieves his most complex and moving mythical statement to date.

The hero of the curiously autobiographical "One Life" simply digs up his past. No time machines or magic, the road just leads back. He must find out "what turning point in my life it had been that had wrenched me from the course all little boys took to adulthood; that had set me on the road of loneliness and success ending here, back where I'd begun, in a backyard at now-twelve minutes to midnight." For a destiny that thinks itself so elliptical, this one is oddly circular. . . . The past is a gallery of mirrors, life a series of hopeless returns. He has brought about the very thing he would abolish. Love again turns to hate, he becomes a shadow in the process. . . . The devices of time travel are skillfully adapted here to Ellison's personal myths. (pp. 53-5)

"Adrift" is a story of affirmation, perhaps a turning point in Ellison's career. A new optimism is not simply pronounced; it is wrung with great struggle from the elements of the old, pessimistic view of man. And yet there is something frightening about this struggle, all the contraptions and ingenious twists. Why is it so hard to die in Ellison's world? He has created the only heaven a materialist society can conceive —the one inside self. Is this not the ultimate act of survival, to declare one's own body everything and always, so that one can die to live forever in one's own form undecaying? We are reminded here not of Emerson, but of Poe, with his nightmare fears of being buried, whose Ligeia's will to eternity raises her body from the dead, but as a corpse. Ellison's myth succeeds in countering these fears, but by

meeting Poe on the same ground, fails to break the circle of matter and quantity. His hero does not want death with all its terms, he desires "surcease," rest without decay. Ellison's tale is a masterpiece of wishful thinking. We are at point where myth becomes fantasy again.

This mood of reconciliation continues in Ellison's latest stories, tempered perhaps by irony. If "Adrift" is microcosm, then its companion tale, "The Deathbird" (1974), is macrocosm. In this retelling of *Prometheus Unbound*, quest for surcease passes through a mythic landscape, complete with snake-like nature force, and the tyrant god man has fashioned in the image of his unnatural aspirations. The hero is an American Adam, bearer of the human "spark." *Genesis* is reversed, and mankind's fall dates not from Eve, but from the earlier rupture with Lillith, the dark earth goddess. The hero, everyman, defeats God by withstanding despair; he ceases to believe, and the mind-forged chains fall. Rather than God, man should love fellow man, snake, animal—dog spelled backward is god. (pp. 59-60)

Other recent stories of this "optimistic pessimism" include "Croatoan" (1975), in which "dead dreams" are literally fetuses flushed down toilets, the aborted waste of perverted urban lives. (p. 60)

These late tales are all marked by new complexity of design and texture ("Deathbird" passes from high epic to a 'schoolboy' essay on the death of a dog). More and more, Ellison constructs not only the disparate voices of our modern world, but with its cultural bric-a-brac as well. Quotes, literary allusions are used increasingly; there seems a danger of overloading. . . . Yet this is done for reason. In the first work, man the dreamer assails nature; in the other, he suffers reversion to non-human form in the civilized nightmare he has created. Two juxtaposed visions form a new balance—the "monster" is man himself, his metamorphosis must be a return to nature. Like many American writers, Ellison is less intent on shoring up the ruins of tradition than in regrouping elements in flux, making them function as part of a new system. All these diverse cultural patterns are reduced to one basic polarity—man and universe.

Ellison's technical skill has grown, his vision of man shifted accents, but the underlying dynamic has not changed. This dynamic can be found in Emerson; it came to him as a fusion of Romantic science, native Calvinism, and Oriental philosophy. A century and a half later a modern fantasy writer is still shaping fiction in its matrix. Again it has proved flexible enough to unite the most disparate elements —social Darwinism, Old Testament ethic, Dionysian forces, modern ecology. Ellison's new "optimism" has not broken this balance; even though his heroes refute God, reestablishing primal bonds with family and nature, some price must still be paid. When love goes forward, hate goes backward. Ellison has not sought to strike a bridge from pole to pole, or offer a plan to replace the *Genesis* he casts aside. But how can the hater of systems make one himself? How can one who denies progress conceive human destiny in eschatological terms? We wonder where Ellison will go from here. Increasingly complex structures? More intricate, convoluted treatments of man's quandary? He has passed through the anger and violence, the grim despair at man's folly, to a mood of reconciliation. Still, the individual has not escaped the hateful contraries. Will Ellison suspend this iron law? Whatever the case, this genuinely mythic imagination will not stand still. Ellison has produced some of the finest, most provocative fantasy in America today; and more will surely follow. (pp. 60-1)

George Edgar Slusser, in his Harlan Ellison: Unrepentant Harlequin *(copyright © 1977 by George Edgar Slusser), The Borgo Press, 1977.*

MARK MANSELL

Let there be no doubt about it, a new Ellison collection is an *event*. Harlan Ellison is one of the best short fiction writers of our time, and [*Strange Wine*] gives ample evidence of his talent. Ellison writes with immense force and emotion. . . .

Ellison's books are more than just a group of his stories slapped between two covers. They capture his personality. Lest readers miss the meanings of the stories, he adds an introduction to the book, and a preface to each story. The Introduction—"Revealed at Last! What Killed the Dinosaurs! And You Don't Look So Terrific Yourself"—is a dangerous vision more frightening than anything Ellison put into his two anthologies of that name. You will never again feel complacent about watching the boob tube.

Unlike the prior Ellison collection *Deathbird Stories, Strange Wine* is compiled of not-previously-collected stories. There is no way to summarize an Ellison story—they're so tightly interwoven within themselves that no summary can do them justice. . . .

So well-known are Ellison's tales of the unpleasant inner morasses of mankind, that his lighter tales tend to be forgotten. That is a shame, since Ellison's lighter stories have a cutting, ironic touch. . . .

[They are] draughts of very strange wine, indeed. Through the years, Harlan Ellison continues to improve, never resting on his ample laurels. This book is a must-read. (p. 39)

Mark Mansell, in Science Fiction Review *(copyright © 1978 by Richard Geis; reprinted by permission of Richard Geis and Mark Mansell), September-October, 1978.*

*   *   *

EWART, Gavin   1916-

Ewart is a British poet who first gained recognition in the thirties with his collection *Poems and Songs*. Encouraged to begin writing again by *London Magazine* editor Alan Ross, Ewart published in 1966 what he considers some of his best poetry in *Pleasures of the Flesh*. Ewart acknowledges the influence of Auden evident in the light, witty, satirical quality of his verse.

PETER PORTER

[Ewart is] chiefly known to a wider audience as a light verse writer. Generations of students from Sydney to St Andrews have sung 'Miss Twye' to the National Anthem. But Ewart isn't just a light poet any more than Auden is. In fact, it could be argued that he is so obviously serious he sometimes spoils poems with liberal messages. While we can be glad that he is on the side of the angels, we may feel that he is often at his best when describing the works of the other side. *Pleasures of the Flesh* is echt Ewart, a remarkable flowering of a lyrical and satirical talent first revealed in 'Phallus in Wonderland', written when he was seventeen. . . .

In almost every respect these new poems are an advance on the brilliant early Ewart. . . . (p. 87)

[In] what is perhaps the most impressive poem in the book —'A Christmas Message'—he concludes:

> England is a Peloponnese
> and Father Christmas a poor old sod
> like any other, autochthonous. Who
>   believes
> in the beard and the benevolence?
>   Even in Greece
> or Rome there is only a bogus God
> for children under five. Those he
>   loves, he deceives.

Behind the kinky inventions and sexy observations of these poems, there is a reformer's zeal which hasn't turned to any closed system or religious orthodoxy. Ewart's emancipations are near-Groddeckian—if we let the sex in us grow straight we shall be saved. But he rarely lets his verse say this in any naïve way: he chooses instead to show it growing crooked or solacing itself with the fake achievements of status, money or kicks. One of the star turns of *Poems and Songs* was 'Audenesque for an Inititiation' in which he warns us:

> Don't forget that new proscriptions
>   are being posted now and then,
> Dr Johnson, Dr Leavis and the other
>   Grand Old Men—
> For, although they've often told us
>   that they try to do their best,
> Are they up to the Full Fruit
>   Standard, would they pass the
>   Spelling Test?

Pleasures of the Flesh lives up to the Full Fruit Standard all the way.

Ewart's originality lies in his use of sex, still the prime attention getter although we're saturated with it, as paradigm. (pp. 87-8)

Despite the raucous sexual imagery of ['After the Sex Bomb'], it is really about irrational fear. Ewart has performed the unlikely feat of reburying the Freudian bones in daylight. While anybody who once read a *Reader's Digest* article on psychoanalysis knows that hills remind us of women's breasts, Ewart is quietly turning the tables and pointing out that women's breasts may remind us of hills. Sex is ever present in his poems, because it is ever present in our minds. If we censor it or shut it out, we may lose touch with a lot of dependent things we're interested in. Not all the minds that write only about pure objects are themselves pure. Starting off from sex, often in one of its unhappier forms, Ewart comments on ambition, middle age, life in the suburbs, the boredom of wives, office politics, children, history etc. His scope is very wide, his world, London in the Sixties; his pleasures of the flesh include listening to music and watching the grotesques of our over-fed civilization. He is very good at the minatory, the unexpected, unexplained fear. . . . (p. 88)

[A] cryptic power makes 'Manifesto' one of the finest poems in the book. Here, though, there is no menace but an uncharacteristic note of prophecy. . . .

Pleasures of the Flesh is in two parts. Part 1, though inventive and audacious, is serious. Part 2 consists chiefly of lighter poems including the famous 'Eight Awful Animals'. I'm less fond of these than of most of the book's good unclean jokes. Not because they're too dirty or too undignified, but because the Ogden Nash long lines and facetious rhymes betray the poet into a more careless use of language than he would allow in any other kind of poem. Though he uses most of the plain words for sex, Ewart is usually an extremely fastidious writer. The Awful Animals are an exception. Nevertheless, they're full of good things. . . . (p. 89)

Part 1 has the main matter of the book. Through it moves the fore-suffering poet, a Tiresias with acute awareness of the pleasures, humiliations and, above all, the bafflements of life in the consumer's city. . . . Gavin Ewart's poems are heartening to anybody who believes, as I do, that *New Verse* is the best poetry magazine Britain has had and that Thirties' poetry, faults and all, had a liveliness and involvement (not commitment) we do not have today. *Pleasures of the Flesh* establishes Ewart as an important poet in the Sixties, one with something to say to us directly. The gestation which followed that early promise was a long one, but the results have been worth waiting for. (p. 90)

Peter Porter, in London Magazine © London
Magazine 1966), May, 1966.

DAVID HOWARTH

[Ewart] is a joker, taking the piss out of everyone and himself and doing it better than competently. In *Pleasures of the Flesh,* with a poem called 'Short Time', he manages to deflate even ''. . . the gentle hypocrite reader.'' He also analyses, very comically, certain sexual ''types''. The series 'Eight Awful Animals', describing fauna with names like ''Panteebra'' and ''Stuffalo'', is a wonderful classification of stereotypes, from the butch lesbian to the exclusive masturbator. In *The Deceptive Grin* . . . it is the advertising industry, the rat-racers and the slogan-mongers who come in for it. *The Gavin Ewart Show* is catholic. (p. 64)

[He] claims to be the inventor of the ''ewart'' (sic!) or count-down poem, where the unrhymed stanzas have a line length of 6, 5, 4, 3, 2, 1 (following John Cage into silence?) he is not so exclusive that he will not take a trick or two from O. Nash, W. Stevens and Wm. McGonagall. He is also the perpetrator of a very ugly-looking poem of three, eight-line stanzas in which every line, bar those at the ends of stanzas, ends with a split word. . . .

[This] is poetry for the masses and excellent too: a proof that the élite and the popular may be reconciled. I showed the book to a friend who ''. . . loves no plays . . . hears no music.'' and he enjoyed all that he was able to read in half-an-hour. (p. 66)

The book is in three parts (This being a show, why not ''acts''?) and the first division looks arbitrary. I see no unity of theme within sections one and two, nor do I see any significant differences in style or subject matter.

The poems of Part Three are united by form. These are 'The So-called Sonnets'. I like the title. Already Mr. Ewart has given us 'The Pseudo-Demetrius'. May we anticipate 'The Self-styled Epic'? the sonnets are all unrhymed octet/sestet. When I counted fourteen I began to suspect the anarchist of elaborate plotting, but I was wrong. This is not a ''cycle''. What a relief! . . . I began to count syllables

too, but soon gave it up as a worthless exercise. What's the point. Might as well write haiku.

Subjects treated in the sonnets (so-called) range from the simple scorn of 'A Sectarian View' . . . through the laconic 'Poetry is the Dustbin of the Emotions' [which notes] ''As invalids simply revel in invalid port / so we love our disabilities. They go well into verse'', to the satiric/polemic 'The Only Emperor is the Emperor of Ice Cream', an advertising copywriter's fantasy. He [wants] to be ''. . . a Verdi / of cornflakes or detergents consoling all'' but ''. . . Self-perpetuating markets / demand our sacrifice, my bending of the mind / I offer up to cans and aerosols and packs. / Surely someday those shining gods will speak?''

A ''fun time''? I'm not so sure. A lot of the work here is decidedly not frivolous. 'The Sentimental Education', for instance, recalls the intense bitterness of the ''Thirties Poets''. Its ending, especially, evokes MacNiece in its exasperation: ''All you learn—and from a lifetime—is that that's the way it goes. / That's the crumbling of the cookie, till the turning-up of toes.'' And talking of sentiment, I was affected by 'A Black Rabbit Dies for its Country', though I do not share Ewart's concern about using animals in experiments. What could easily have been sloppy and cheap is controlled; sensible. An object lesson for writers of tear-jerking documentaries.

Essentially, despite the seriousness of intent in many poems, *The Gavin Ewart Show* is, to use his own words: ''. . . sensual man's two-fingers-up to Culture.'' At all costs to be avoided by uncertain writers of theses. Much better to take Ewart's advice:

> Slup me rough and homely and I'll taste fine.
>
> (pp. 66-7)

David Howarth, ''Two-Fingers-Up,'' in Phoenix,
July, 1973, pp. 64-7.

DOUGLAS DUNN

Gavin Ewart's verse has sometimes been thought too close to doggerel for comfort, or too facile. These opinions ignore Ewart's poetic temperament. His varieties of comic verse are, like Enright's tones of voice, technical expressions of a seriously presented mischief. Given half a chance—a pension, say—Ewart could be a trouble-maker of the first water. The air of carelessness about his poems is nothing other than cheek, and, indeed, an ''air of'' rather than ''carelessness.'' In . . . *Be My Guest!,* ''The Larkin Automatic Car Wash'', for instance, imitates the stanza of ''The Whitsun Weddings'' with as tight a control of colloquial idiom as the original. Ewart, then, can be as metrically tight as he likes; that he doesn't always like is more to the point. He is fond of variety and the inane perspectives created by out-of-place metres like the limerick. . . .

Peculiarly English to the point of rating ''charm'' as an important poetic effect, Ewart is courageous in his reliance on *verse*. He is closer to Thomas Hood than any other poet I can think of, and in ''The Afterflu Afterlife'' he rhymes in the virtuoso manner of the Hood beloved by Auden. Each verse has the same five rhymes. The poem includes the deathless

> We heard the dead word ''troth'' once in Arbroath

which may well be intended as the most blatant line-for-the-sake-of-a-rhyme in English. But Ewart is that sort of poet—

209

gamey, exploiting what looks inconsiderable for the highly considerable purpose of verbal amusement, some of which is satirical. . . .

But the oddness of Ewart's poems is, in my opinion, more significant than showing an eccentricity for verse. His sonnets, for example, are called "The *So-Called* Sonnets", while his versions of four of Horace's Odes "were made on the principle that the word-order of the Latin should not on any account be changed." Inventiveness and disregard for what prevails as established definition or propriety are necessary subversions in any society. Ewart's rebellions are enacted through technique, and seem to me to embody a serious disgruntlement at the state of poetry and attitudes towards it. Ewart's chosen ways of writing may amount to a meaning, that any style is insecure, that—with the exception of elegy—an appropriate style is likely to be boring. There is certainly a feeling about his poems that suggests Ewart considers seriousness a wildly overrated expectation which can only lead to social diseases such as piles, pantheism, and under-arm bowling. (p. 78)

> *Douglas Dunn, in* Encounter *(© 1976 by Encounter Ltd.), February, 1976.*

JAMES FENTON

[Gavin Ewart] is a man who achieved a precocious fame in the '30s, and then went "silent." For the last decade or so he has been immensely productive in a way which very much goes against the contemporary grain. Here he is with his anthology, a pamphlet (*The First Eleven*), and a collection (*Or Where a Young Penguin Lies Screaming*). The anthology is good—far more varied and unusual than the Arts Council effort. The pamphlet is really nicely produced. The collection is excellent.

A particularly attractive quality of Mr. Ewart is his inventiveness, his genuine experimentalism. Much of the time he is out to amuse—with crackpot inventions like the "Semantic Limerick According to Doctor Johnson's Dictionary (Edition of 1765)." . . . (pp. 66-7)

At other times he can write at the opposite extreme, as in "The Gentle Sex", a cold and convincing exploration of the brutality of Ulster life. There are faults—in almost every poem there are faults, such as rich rhymes or whole lines which seem to have been put in for the sake of the form— but I have to say that I like Mr. Ewart's faults as much as his virtues. There is no sense that the stuff is being churned out. Rather, there is a hyperactive talent that *must write*. An enviable gift. (p. 67)

> *James Fenton, in* Encounter *(© 1978 by Encounter Ltd.), April, 1978.*

F

FIEDLER, Leslie A(aron)   1917-

Fiedler is an outspoken and controversial American critic, as well as novelist, short story writer, essayist, poet, and editor. Fiedler draws conclusions about a mythic, uniquely American consciousness from his study of literary figures. His criticism has been controversial both for this reasoning and for its psychosexual orientation. *Love and Death in the American Novel*, published in 1960, remains a provocative, highly individual landmark in literary criticism. (See also *CLC*, Vol. 4, and *Contemporary Authors*, Vols. 9-12, rev. ed.)

CHARLES R. LARSON

One cannot help asking just whom Fiedler was trying to put on when he wrote ["Come Back to the Raft Ag'in, Huck Honey"]—just as the same question needs to be asked with each ensuing volume of his studies in "literary anthropology," as Fiedler has frequently referred to his work. There has always been an element of absurdity or shock in Fiedler's work, and at times it is impossible not to wonder if Fiedler takes his own work seriously. (p. 133)

Reading over Fiedler's collected literary criticism, from *An End of Innocence* in 1955 to his . . . *The Return of the Vanishing American* in 1968, one cannot help being upset by the great number of generalizations, repetitions, and strained conclusions which so often have marred his frequently brilliant commentaries on American fiction. Yet, one cannot help thinking that Fiedler, as critic of the hip school of American criticism, and as guru of thousands of undergraduate English majors (and their younger instructors), deserves whatever following he has managed to build up for himself. It is not perhaps so much what Fiedler is saying that offends the other, shall I say, more traditional critic as much as his method: a frontal attack based on shock, entertainment (especially valuable it seems to me in a day when criticism takes itself far too seriously), and the destruction of shibboleths and prejudices we should have rid ourselves of years, if not generations, ago. The result has been that Fiedler's criticism remains for the most part highly readable and almost uniformly fresh—whether one agrees with what he says or not. One wonders if some critics have not even been a little jealous of Fiedler's quasi-underground fame. (pp. 133-34)

Clearly, Fiedler's criticism shows a number of obsessions, and he does use the word "myth" far too frequently. One hates to guess what a word count of Fiedler's collected writings would reveal about the use of this word. Much of this confusion is also due to two essays on the use of myth criticism itself included in *No! in Thunder* after their earlier publication in quarterlies, coupled with a much more generalized use of the word in the rest of his essays in this volume and the others. In the first of these, "In the Beginning Was the Word: *Logos* or *Mythos?*," Fiedler seems to be reacting more against the "a poem should not mean, but be!" school than actually attempting to set up viable criteria for myth criticism in poetry. The weakness of the essay is also due to the fact that Fiedler has shown himself essentially a critic of the novel rather than of poetry and poetics, and what he says of the use of myth in poetry frequently seems inconsistent with his mythological approach to fiction. (p. 135)

It is perhaps best to look at the end of Fiedler's essay first —it is here where a bridge can be built between poetry and and fiction. The last sentence reads, "In the beginning was *mythos,* and each new beginning must be drawn from that inexhaustible source." Fiedler believes that each generation, each age, will temper the myths of the past to meet its own needs, and each generation will create new myths relevant for its specific age. Fiedler is concerned with the element of distortion, getting too far away from the original myth. . . . The fault with our own age has been one of fear which has led to an emphasis not on *mythos* (poetry) but *logos* (philosophy and science.) This in turn has led to the critic who studies the poem in a scientific rather than in a mythological way. Poetry, Fiedler tells us, "is historically the mediator between *logos* and *mythos.*" The critic who uses depth psychology to interpret the myths of the past, and the ways in which they have been altered or profaned, is only doing as Freud who claimed "to translate out of Sophocles and Shakespeare what had always been there. . . ." (pp. 135-36)

"Archetype and Signature: A Study of the Relationship Between Biography and Poetry" is a remarkable essay for what it does—attempt to convince the critic that the biography of the poet may shed valuable information on the interpretation of a poem. The misunderstanding by the critics is simply their insistence on taking Fiedler at face value—in this case Fiedler's overemphasis to build a strong case for his thesis. (Fiedler's work so frequently approaches the superlative that one would think that by now the critics

211

would be catching on.) Then, too, the critic is put off by Fiedler's usual pompous opening. (p. 137)

Fiedler has learned the high art of literary charlatanism; in his criticism, he uses only those examples which will support his own theses, and all other facts are conveniently left out. (pp. 138-39)

Fiedler's definitions for archetype and signature . . . are fairly straightforward and, if left at that alone, would no doubt be acceptable to many critics. The confusion results, however, when Fiedler implies the need for an almost unique "signature" on the part of each poet—each writer. In short, he places too much emphasis on the poet's attempt to make his signature individually his own, i.e., by suggesting that the poet, once he has achieved fame, need not be concerned with poetry any longer at all but instead more concerned with making his own life into a myth. (pp. 139-40)

Ultimately—and I feel this is the crux of the problem with Fiedler—everything becomes a myth, and what started as a serious attempt to define *mythos* and its relationship to poetry . . . has grown into a gigantic tumor which Fiedler has used not as an appendage of literature but as literature itself —especially in his other writings. In his . . . *The Return of the Vanishing American* (1968), there is hardly a page, even a paragraph, where the word "myth" does not appear. The book itself is referred to as "an effort to define the myths which give special character to art and life in America, . . ." and Fiedler begins his analysis by such statements as: "the geography of the United States is mythological"; "a mythicized North, South, East, and West"; "it is the presence of the Indian which defines the mythological West"; and "Certainly the same myth that moved poets to verses moved Columbus to action." Nowhere in his entire career has Fiedler scraped so hard, searched so painstakingly to make us believe that the four myths he has found are, indeed, the actual myths that make up the American character. (p. 141)

One wonders what Fiedler would do if he did not upset his fellow critics—if no one paid any attention to him? That, of course, would not be easy to do, as Fiedler well realizes, yet one cannot help wondering if Fiedler, from the occasional asides he has made, isn't the prankster who is having the last word on his own books (and certainly the most fun) simply by the kinds of critical comments they draw. (p. 142)

It would be greatly oversimplifying the issue, however, to believe that Fiedler is simply playing the role of the American critics' bad boy. His recent run in with the law and the essay "On Being Busted at Fifty" show how sensitive he can be. Rather, I believe the explanation can be found in an essay called "My Credo." . . . In this essay Fiedler says that "the role of the critic resembles that of the poet"—that literary criticism is work which is just as serious as the work of the poet or the novelist. "The critic is least likely to be the victim of pride and more likely to be thought such a victim when he first opposes majority taste with a new claim." This sentence reads as a prophetic statement of what Fiedler was to become, once he had found his own signature and stamped it indelibly on his own critical works. (pp. 142-43)

Fiedler's critical writings have never been mere charts and tables. Rather, they are critical evaluations—often farfetched, often illogical, often strained, often brilliant—but

always marked indelibly with his own eccentric signature, a signature which tells us over and over again that just as the poet and the novelist has his own myths to live, so does the critic too; that just as the artist becomes the scapegoat of his society, so too the critic may become the scapegoat of his own fellow critics. In the beginning there was *mythos,* Fiedler wants us to believe, and myths are only, after all, the signature that the critic as artist gives to his work and his life. (p. 143)

Charles R. Larson, "Leslie Fiedler: The Critic and the Myth, the Critic As Myth," in The Literary Review *(copyright © 1970 by Fairleigh Dickinson University), Fall, 1970, pp. 133-43.*

ROBERT ALTER

Leslie Fiedler is, of course, better known as a critic than as a writer of fiction, and criticism has in fact been the more congenial medium for the exercise of his most engaging qualities of fictional invention. He is preeminently a novelist of ideas, using fiction to illustrate the ideas with a cartoon-like simplicity and, sometimes, vividness. The four volumes of fiction he published in the early and mid-1960's deal with the social, cultural and political issues that characteristically occupied intellectuals, and particularly Jewish intellectuals, during that period. Now, after a hiatus of eight years, Fiedler has written a new novel ["The Messengers Will Come No More"], once again reflecting the current preoccupation of the American "adversary culture"— which, now on the other side of the period of political activism and campus unrest, are very different from the questions that concerned Fiedler and his ambience a decade ago.

"The Messengers Will Come No More" might be described as a past-and-future fiction. It is set in the 25th century, on the site of ancient Palestine. . . .

For the first two or three chapters, I clung to the hope that [it] would prove to be a delightful spoof of science fiction, playing exuberantly with contemporary vogues and movements in the past-and-future settings. There are some incidental jokes, mostly invoking Yiddish colloquialisms or Jewish cuisine, that are amusing enough; but Fiedler, I fear, is bent on making most of his humor "pointed," which means that much of the novel deteriorates into a series of tediously sophomoric reversals of contemporary facts.

Thus, a good part of the globe is ruled by gynocracy, with black women at the top of the hierarchy, white males at the very bottom. Women, who have just grudgingly conceded the vote to men, callously joke about the frivolity, the sexual animality, of men—and so forth. The idea of a world ruled by women is an old science-fiction convention, but its deployment here is tendentious, unimaginative. The novel then proves to be a farrago of clichés, taken not only from science fiction but from sensationalistic popular history and history of religion, which somehow is meant to be read as a statement of profound spiritual issues. (p. 5)

"The Messengers Will Come No More" might well have been called "The Last Jew in the Cosmos": though monotheistic cults have been banned, Jacob, a lonely scribe in the wilderness, feels that somehow perhaps he is a Jew. . . . The theme of the last Jew, however, has only been impoverished by the temporal and spatial projection and the abstraction it has undergone. Jacob of the 1966 novella ["The Last Jew in America"] was a moving figure because he had the palpable weight of a particular life, a particular political and social background. Jacob of "The Messengers Will Come No More," thoroughly a creature of our own post-political moment, lured as it is by hazy vistas of myth and cult, is an abstract, insistently symbolic figure. . . .

The Jewish ground of Jacob's symbolic last stand comes to seem especially shaky because Fiedler regales the reader with an embarrassing wealth of misinformation flaunted as expertise: garbled Hebrew words, confusions about ritual practices, a polemic exegesis of biblical texts that pretends to comment on the original but betrays the writer's ignorance of the Hebrew words used in the texts discussed. . . .

The ultimate difficulty with this novel is that there is a heavily portentous vagueness at its core. Just before the end, Jacob in his cave reflects, "Every man must die, like me, deserted by all, yet ground down between the hammer and anvil of Male and Female, by which we are forged in the beginning." At least as far as I can determine, nothing more elucidating about the subject than this histrionic generality is ever conveyed through the action of the novel or the reflections of its two principal characters. . . . [The] fiction as it is concocted seems too often a theological joke without a point, or one that takes itself too seriously, or, still worse, a joke stitched together from threadbare materials, trying to simulate novelty chiefly through the aggressiveness of its bad taste. (p. 6)

> Robert Alter, in The New York Times Book Review (© 1974 by The New York Times Company; reprinted by permission), September 29, 1974.

JONATHAN YARDLEY

Middle aged, and having to his credit a substantial body of publications, Leslie Fiedler can no longer lay claim to the title of *enfant terrible* of American letters. After all as the dust jacket of his new novel somewhat smugly notes, *Love and Death in the American Novel* "is now being taught by the same people who were originally outraged by it." Yet even if he has moved perilously close to membership in the literary establishment Fiedler has shown little evidence of losing his refreshing talent for slaying dragons and tilting at windmills, his instinct for the jugular and the provocative.

So what is most surprising about *The Messengers Will Come No More* is that it is *not* provocative. It is dull. It works neither as fiction nor as polemic. As one of Fiedler's admirers who is occasionally vexed by him but usually pleased by his determined pugnacity, I cannot fathom his reasons for writing it, nor can I recommend reasons for reading it. (p. 42)

The setting of the novel is no less clichéd than the rhetoric. . . . Fielder merely pulls a convenient switch on contemporary realities and fantasies—a switch clearly designed to be a commentary as well, but a singularly facile one. (p. 43)

> Jonathan Yardley, in The New Republic (reprinted by permission of The New Republic; © 1974 by The New Republic, Inc.), November 9, 1974.

SAM BLUEFARB

Leslie Fiedler's *The Last Jew in America* (1966), the first [and title novella] of three novellas in a single collection, is set in the small Western college town of Lewis and Clark City, Montana. But the story, in the tradition of the oft-touted (and occasionally scorned) college novel goes beyond narrow academic concerns. It deals with the efforts of one Jacob Moscowitz . . . to bring together those Jews in the community . . . in order to reawaken whatever sense of Jewish identity still remains in their malnourished souls. (p. 412)

Jacob had originally moved West to convert the natives to socialism. But the effort had been a dismal failure; the Party could hardly have made a worse choice, either in Jacob Moscowitz the Old World Jew with the Yiddish accent, or the mythic "Western" ambience they have placed him into. The situation only serves to make more apparent the isolation Jacob finds himself in. . . . Years later Jacob will transform (or convert) this earlier mission into a more viable quest: to get together a *minyan,* or quorum, made up of half-or fully assimilated Jewish professors at the local university.

Under these conditions, the old socialist-agnostic seems to have found his way back to his own roots—i.e., to urge (or egg) on his fallen-away fellows-Jews into making their ritual calls on the dying Louis Himmelfarb on the holiest day of the Jewish year, the Day of Atonement. Thus Jacob creates for them, as well as for himself, an opportunity to come to terms with the ethical roots they seem to have lost in their search for the more secular "humanistic values." (p. 413)

Although Jacob's secular religion is (or perhaps was) socialism, his Jewishness runs deeper than the "humanist" commitments of his semi-Jewish acquaintances on campus and the sprinkling of Jews in the town's business community. Thus this story concerns itself far more with the change that has come over Jacob since his own early radicalism than the change he attempts—with some dubious success—to make among his fellow Jews. . . . The West, then, not only erodes plains, mountains, and canyons with its dry, singing winds, its brief but devastating thunderstorms, its flash floods; it also erodes identity; by its bigness it makes the individual, especially a Jew, smaller. But against this erosion of identity, Jacob, "the last Jew in America"—there is the illusion he *is* just that—will fight, in spite of his threadbare socialism. (pp. 414-15)

Irony of it all is that Jacob, the old (or former?) socialist-agnostic now looks upon his fellow Jews of the University community, those half-Jewish, not quite assimilated professors, as apostates.

In keeping with his ability for socialist (and American) adaptation, Jacob makes up his own version of the prayer for the Day of Atonement. What comes out is a mish-mash of socially conscious harangue and a plea for forgiveness for his fallen-away brothers on the faculty. (pp. 415-16)

Thus, we can say that Jacob has transformed his original mission from convert-maker to secular messianism to something which, if not conventionally religious, points to religious *directions.* How successful his efforts prove in making his academic co-religionists regain their religious conscience is not really of great moment; what matters is the effect on Jacob himself.

In the second story [*The Last Wasp in the World*], a poet named Vincent Hazelbaker, or Vin as he is called by close associates, has come *from* Lewis and Clark City to the East. Just as Jacob Moscowitz has moved West to fulfill a task of redemption, so Vin has gone East to do some re-deeming himself. He has not simply gone there to "make it" but to show the Eastern Jewish establishment—and perhaps himself—the "way." This creates a neat switch on the prototypal Christian missionary (or savior) to the Jews. But it will be *through his poetry* that Vin will attempt to redeem these materialists. What we get is an ironic turn-about, a characterological *volte-face*, with Jake Moscowitz turning into the last Jew in the spatially limitless West while Vin becomes the last WASP in the more hermetically lim-ited Eastern ambience of an urban Jewish wedding. (pp. 416-17)

Like Jacob in the first of the novellas, Vin is a stranger, cut off from his community. But where Jacob Moscowitz had attempted to exchange a more distant Jewish community for a later WASPy working class ghetto—and failed in the process—Vin is cut off from *his* community by his status as poet. (p. 418)

Toward the end of the story, Vin, in a memory flashback, returns to Lewis and Clark, only to find that most of the students at the University—even the married girl he'd once had an affair with—are now all Jewish. They have not even left him the whiff of the myth. And Vin finds himself yelling out of a motel window at passing cars with New York li-cense plates: "Leave us our West. . . . Goddamn it, leave us our dreams." . . . Sad to say, the dream is just that—a dream; except that Vin still believes in it. For even though, as he imagines, he is finally home again, he is not *at home.* WASP as he is, he is trapped in the role of "Jewish" poet who finds that even he cannot go home again. The world, the town, he himself—all have changed. The West has "moved East"—and neither the dream nor the myth which nourished it is left. (p. 419)

[In the third story, *The First Spade in the West,* black Ned York] runs a plush cocktail lounge in Lewis and Clark City, a form of integration, in spite of the alienation he shares with Jake Moscowitz, Jew, and Vincent Hazelbaker, WASP. While Ned may not be completely integrated into his community—it's doubtful whether he wants to be anyway—his bar is. (p. 420)

In spite of one weakness—the author's almost zealous ob-session with demythologizing the classic West—Fiedler does manage to establish his *donnée,* to show us the bond that binds the three main characters of the triptych to each other. That bond, paradoxically, involves separation rather than unity—separation from the larger white Protestant es-tablishment. For as Fiedler suggests, even such a WASP as Vin can himself be made to feel outside the pale. What of course draws Jake Moscowitz, Ned York, and Vincent Hazelbaker together in terms of their common "problem" —significantly WASP Vin, native of Lewis and Clark, is the only true exile from the town—is the town itself. Thus in this work Fiedler breaks through the stereotype to present us with a Jewish village philosopher in a Western town, a WASP poet acting more like a Jewish victim at a Jewish wedding; and a successful black entrepreneur of a bar in a not-so-Old West. All these conditions hold these three char-acters together; yet they also reveal a process of fragmenta-tion of the stereotype itself in American life. Indeed, Ned York turns out to be an *anti*-stereotype of the black man: he comes closer to the image of the Old West bartender we are accustomed to see in Western films than to any recog-nizable image of the black man as he is portrayed in count-

less novels, even by black writers. So that we end up with a fractured, but complexly true picture of a bar where the larger part of its clientele is white, but where the proprietor is black though hardly an Uncle Tom.

Fiedler thus breaks through the stereotype at three levels— the Jewish village philosopher in a movie-set Western town, a WASP poet who is more "Jewish" than WASP, and a black man who is the owner of a bar in the West patronized by white merchants and farmers. Each could well lend him-self to stereotyping—and certainly has in the past! Yet as Fiedler presents them (whether intentionally or not), they represent the very real break-up in recent years of the ster-otype in American life. Each of the characters is beginning to take on some of the features of his two other ethnic counterparts: they not only do not do the expected thing, but are displayed in action in unexpected ways. The image has been displaced. That Ned York is somehow more "in-tegrated" than some of the white misfits who frequent his bar does not necessarily say much for Ned's condition *as a black man.* Yet a positive point may be drawn from this mix-up: *people* are isolated or alienated; *people* are inte-grated or left out in the cold; *men* are the subject and object of man's inhumanity. *Men* are important rather than man in the abstract.

Finally, all three characters—the Jew, the WASP, the Black—have been placed in locations far from their "natu-ral" environs. Yet they still continue to search for a way home—to a geography, a way of life, a culture, which once might have existed for them, but which forever seems to elude them. (pp. 420-21)

                    Sam Bluefarb, "Pictures of the Anti-Stereotype:
                    Leslie Fiedler's Triptych, 'The Last Jew in Ameri-
                    ca'," in CLA Journal (copyright, 1975 by the Col-
                    lege Language Association), March, 1975, pp.
                    412-21.

DORIS GRUMBACH

Freaks: What a compendium! It is almost an encyclopedia. Fiedler admits that research assistants helped him gather this mountain of anecdote, fact, rumor, hearsay, literary allusion, and superstition, and I can well believe it. Produc-ing the book was a task beyond one man's industry. *Freaks* looks at everything, in every direction: into the mythic past, which supplies us with the monsters and dwarfs and giants of our childhood psychic terrors; into history; and into literature. . . .

[One] of the advantages of reading Fiedler's compilation is the opportunity to acquire some pretty exotic language. The study of Freaks is called teratology—freaks themselves are terata. As you read through the book (and it is hard to ima-gine anyone not following Fiedler's trail through the horror-laden chapters), you will pick up such words as achondro-plastics (dwarfs), ateliotics (incomplete persons), and epig-nathic parasites (parts of human beings growing out of whole bodies). . . .

[Though] the narrative and the illustrations are provocative, I· found myself wondering as I read: What is it all *for?* What's the point?

The answer is suggested by the book's subtitle: *Myths and Images of the Secret Self.* Fiedler explores "the supernat-ural terror, " the awe, and the natural sympathy that the sight of human monstrosities inspires in us. We look at them in carnivals, and we are reassured that our secret fears of our own freakishness are unfounded: "'*We* are the Freaks,' the human oddities are supposed to reassure us from their lofty perches. 'Not you. Not *you!*'"

Fiedler confesses to the same vertigo we experience in the presence of freaks: "In joined twins the confusion of self and other, substance and shadow, ego and other, is more terrifyingly confounded than it is when the child first perceives face-to-face in the mirror an image moving as he moves, though clearly in another world." These observations on the psychology of freaks and freakishness are among the most valuable comments in this volume, and we concur with Fiedler when he says, "The distinction between audience and exhibit, we and them, normal and Freak, is revealed as an illusion . . . defended, but untenable in the end."

Leslie Fiedler has always been an iconoclastic critic, writing about subjects no one else has even considered. In this new work he interests the reader consistently and falters noticeably only once: He leaves out of his literary survey the novelist Harry Crews, who has written two superb novels about freaks. . . . Readers will think, doubtless, of other omissions, but that will in no way diminish Fiedler's (and his researchers') achievement. In every way it's an absorbing book. (p. 54)

Doris Grumbach, in Saturday Review *(© 1978 by Saturday Review Magazine Corp.; reprinted with permission), March 18, 1978.*

*   *   *

FORSTER, E(dward) M(organ)   1879-1970

Forster was an English novelist, short story writer, essayist, and critic whose liberal humanism is evident in all his writing. He rejected the precepts of Christianity, and in his most famous work, *A Passage to India*, the central principle of Hinduism, total acceptance, is posited as the greatest unifying force for humanity. *A Passage to India*, published in 1924, was Forster's last major work, followed only by essays and minor pieces. Critics speculate that his inner struggle with his homosexuality, revealed only after his death, prevented Forster from adding to a collection of writing that marks him as a major twentieth-century author. (See also *CLC*, Vols. 1, 2, 3, 4, 9, 10, and *Contemporary Authors*, Vols. 13-14; obituary Vols. 25-28, rev. ed.; *Contemporary Authors Permanent Series*, Vol. 1.)

I. A. RICHARDS

Where another writer possessed of an unusual outlook on life would be careful to introduce it, gradually preparing the way by views from more ordinary standpoints, Mr. Forster does nothing of the kind. This very sentence tacitly assumes that the personal point of view is already occupied by the reader, who is left to orient himself as he can. This may lead to lamentable misunderstandings. For example, once we have picked up the author's position we see that the characters in his early books, Mrs. Herriton, Harriet, Gino, Mr. Eager, Old Mr. Emerson, are less to be regarded as social studies than as embodiments of moral forces. Hence the ease with which Miss Abbott, for example, turns momentarily into a goddess. *Where Angels Fear to Tread* is indeed far nearer in spirit to a mystery play than to a comedy of manners. This in spite of the astonishingly penetrating flashes of observation by which these figures are some-

times depicted. But to understand why, with all his equipment as an observer, Mr. Forster sometimes so wantonly disregards vivisimilitude we have to find his viewpoint and take up toward them the attitude of their creator. (pp. 15-16)

Mr. Forster never formulates his criticism of life in one of those principles which we can adhere to or discuss. He leaves it in the painful, concrete realm of practice, presenting it always and only in terms of actuality and never in the abstract. In other words, he has no doctrine but only an attitude. . . . (p. 16)

Mr. Forster is a peculiarly uncomfortable author for [those] who are not content merely to enjoy the surface graces of his writing and the delicacies of his wit, but make themselves sufficiently familiar with his temper to see life to some degree with his eyes. His real audience is youth, caught at that stage when rebellion against the comfortable conventions is easy because the cost of abandoning them has not been fully counted. (pp. 16-17)

It is Mr. Forster's peculiarity that he offers his discomforting vision with so urbane a manner. He is no "holy howlstorm upon the mountains." He has no thunders, no hoots, no grimaces, nor any of the airs of the denunciating prophet, yet at the heart of his work there is less satisfaction with human existence as he sees it than in the work of any other living writer I can call to mind. The earliest of his books, *The Longest Journey*, is perhaps an exception to what has just been remarked about his manner. It has the rawness and crudeness and violence we should expect in the work of a very young writer. Those who have not realized the intensity of the dissatisfaction behind Mr. Forster's work would do well to read it. There is much there, of course, which time has mellowed. But the essential standards, the primary demands from life, which still make unacceptable to him so much that ordinary people find sufficient, have not altered.

Mr. Forster's peculiar quality as a novelist is his fiercely critical sense of values. What was, in the days of *Longest Journey*, a revolt, has changed to a saddened and almost weary pessimism. He has, in his later writings, in *Pharos and Pharillon* and in *A Passage to India*, consoled himself to some degree by a cultivation of the less militant and more humorous forms of irony. He has stepped back to the position of the observer from which in his *Where Angels Fear to Tread* he was at such pains to eject his Philip. But his sense of values remains the same. He has the same terribly acute discernment of and the old insuperable distaste for what he once called "the canned variety of the milk of human kindness" and for all the other substitute products that in civilized communities so interfere between us and our fellows. . . . [To] Mr. Forster life does seem constantly vitiated by automatism, by official action, by insincerity, by organization when it touches charity, or any of the modes of human intercourse which once were governed, in small communities, by natural human feeling alone. (pp. 17-18)

We can trace to this horror of automatisms in human affairs, to this detestation of the non-spontaneous, very much that might seem unconnected and accidental in his books. The passion for the Italian character which animates *Where Angels Fear to Tread* and *A Room with a View*, the unfairness to the medical profession which crops up so markedly from time to time, as in *Howards End*, the exaggeration which mars his depiction of schoolmasters apart from Fielding, clergymen, and others in authority, his sentimentalization of Old England, and his peculiarly lively flair for social coercion in all its forms—all these spring from the same source. And I believe that the theme which more than any other haunts his work and most puzzles his attentive readers has the same origin.

A special preoccupation, almost an obsession, with the continuance of life, from parent to child, with the quality of life in the sense of blood or race, with the preservation of certain strains and the disappearance of others, such is the nearest description of this theme which I can contrive. In itself it eludes abstract presentation. Mr. Forster himself refrains from formulating it. He handles it in the concrete only, or through a symbol such as the house, *Howards End*. (Mrs. Wilcox, the most mysterious of his creations, was a Howard, it will be recalled.) This preoccupation is extremely far removed from that of the Eugenic Society— which would be, precisely, the canned variety; the speculations and calculations of the geneticist do not bear upon it, for it is to Mr. Forster plainly a more than half mystical affair, a vision of the ultimate drift or struggle of the universe and the refuge into which an original strong tendency to mysticism has retreated. The supreme importance to him of this idea appears again and again in his books and it is when automatisms such as social pressures and insincerities threaten to intervene here that he grows most concerned— witness *A Room with a View*. In *Longest Journey*, Rickie's mother appears to him in one of the most dreadful dreams in fiction. "Let them die out! Let them die out!" she says. His son has just been born a hopeless cripple. Gino in *Where Angels Fear to Tread* stands "with one foot resting on the little body, suddenly musing, filled with the desire that his son should be like him and should have sons like him to people the earth. It is the strongest desire that comes to a man—if it comes to him at all—stronger even than love or desire for personal immortality.... It is the exception who comprehends that physical and spiritual life may stream out of him for ever." Compare also the strange importance in *A Passage to India* of the fact that Mrs. Moore's children are Mrs. Moore's.

But the most fascinating example of the handling of this theme is in *Howards End,* the book that still best represents the several sides of Mr. Forster's worth, and in which its virtues and its occasional defects can best be studied. Two different aims are combined in *Howards End;* they have their interconnections, and the means by which they are severally pursued are very skilfully woven together; but it is true, I think, that the episodes which serve a double purpose are those which are usually regarded as the weakest in the book. One of these aims is the development of the half mystical, and inevitably vague, survival theme which we have been considering. The other is the presentation of a sociological thesis, a quite definite piece of observation of great interest and importance concerning the relations of certain prominent classes in Modern England. For that matter, they can be found without trouble in every present day community. To this second aim more than half the main figures of the book belong. A certain conflict between these aims is, I suggest, the source of that elusive weakness which, however, high and distinguished a place we may find for *Howards End*, disqualifies it as one of the world's greatest novels. (pp. 18-19)

I. A. Richards, "A Passage to Forster: Reflec-

tions on a Novelist," in The Forum *(reprinted by permission of the editors of* Current History *and the author), December, 1927 (and reprinted in* Forster: A Collection of Critical Essays, *edited by Malcolm Bradbury, Prentice-Hall, Inc., 1966, pp. 15-20).*

D. S. SAVAGE

[*The Longest Journey, Where Angels Fear to Tread*, and *A Room with a View*] are all] concerned with the dual theme of personal salvation and the conflict of good and evil. Of the three it is *The Longest Journey* which is the most emotionally intense and personal, the others being more objectively conceived novels of social comedy....

In each of these novels we have two opposed worlds or ways of life, and characters who oscillate between the two worlds. (p. 48)

In each of these novels, there is a spiritual conflict. In Forster's words, describing Lucy's inner struggle [in *A Room with a View*],

> The contest lay not between love and duty. Perhaps there never is such a contest. It lay between the real and the pretended....

The "real," however, seems to be associated with the natural; the "pretended," with the falsities of convention which deny and frustrate the natural impulses and passions. (p. 50)

In many respects the theme of *The Longest Journey* recapitulates that of *Where Angels Fear to Tread* and *A Room with a View:* but its development is more complex, and the spiritual drama more intense. It is, no doubt, this intensity which gives the book its overcharged emotional atmosphere and its consequent queer iridescence as of something faintly morbid or perverse.

For the intensity does not seem justified by the terms of the drama. Which means that the drama itself is emotionally worked up to a point at which it becomes false to the terms of reference within which the mind of the novelist is operating. Throughout all of Forster's writings there is to be seen an unfortunate tendency to lapse, at moments when the author feels the necessity to indicate something beyond the level of human relationships in their social setting (a level upon which alone he is perfectly at ease), into "poetical" vagueness of the most embarrassing kind. (p. 51)

Between the poles of conventionality and naturalness there is room for drama of a sort, but not a drama insufflated with the highly pitched emotional excitement of *The Longest Journey,* or even indeed that of the other two novels. This is not to say that the drama which is proposed is intrinsically unreal; only that it is made unreal by being set in such limited and lateral perspectives: the drama is too intense for the slight terms of reference. A spiritual conflict is imported into a naturalistic framework, and the effect is one, inevitably, of sentimentality and falsification.

This confusion of the spiritual and the natural runs throughout the earlier novels. As in D. H. Lawrence (who, however, avoided Forster's irrelevant sweetness and charm), spiritual attributes are conferred upon biological phenomena.... The importance which Forster confers upon sexual passion is shown both by the excessive excitement with which he approaches it, and the way in which he connects it with violent death—the finality of death being utilized to confer something of its own ultimate, absolute character upon the emotion stirred by sex.

To endow conventionality with all the attributes of the powers of darkness is, of course, grossly to overstate the matter. The world represented by the word "Sawston" has genuine undercurrents of evil which we are made to feel, but which are simply not explicable in the terms of Nature versus Convention which are proposed. (p. 54)

Not only in *The Longest Journey* is the question of salvation (raised in the action of the narrative and brought to an arbitrary conclusion there) left with a good many loose ends flying: the same is true of the other novels. What is to happen to Philip Herriton, now that his eyes have been opened to the wonder and beauty of life? What will happen to Lucy and George Emerson now that their difficulties are over and they are happily married? It is hard to see any more finality in their "saved" state than that implied in the insufficient and question-begging symbol, towards the end of *The Longest Journey,* of "Wiltshire"—the life of pastoral satisfactions.

The incompleteness and indeed the reversibility of Forster's moral symbolism is shown in his "realistic" confusion of the attributes of the "good" and "bad" types. . . . This confusion is true to life, no doubt, but it is not true to the symbolical pattern of the novels, and it is necessary to ask what are the reasons for this ambivalence.

The most plausible explanation of Forster's "realistic" confusion of good and bad types (a confusion which, it must be repeated, is out of place in a symbolical setting) lies in the very plain fact that the middle-class existence which Forster portrays . . . is false, because it is based upon social falsehood, and nothing can ever be made really right within it. Consequently, no stable system of moral symbolism can be erected upon it.

This is not to say that his characters are by that fact deprived of the possibility of spiritual struggle; only that such a struggle which takes place within a spiritual arena circumscribed by its reference to the framework of their false social order, and whose outcome does not result in an overthrowing or a repudiation of the limits set around their lives by their privileged social and economic position, is thereby rendered devoid of real and radical significance. . . . Their lives are lived in a watertight system abstracted from the larger life of society as a whole. They are out of touch with humanity, carefully, though for the most part unconsciously, preserving themselves, by means of their mental circumscriptions and social codes, from all encroachment of the painful and upsetting actualities which make their privileged existence possible. . . . [An] inner spiritual change which affects one's attitude to one or two other selected persons only, and does not extend itself to include every other human being irrespective of social distinction, is invalidated from the start. But at the point at which some attempt to deal with this question would seem necessary, Forster brings his stories to a close. (pp. 55-6)

[Forster], despite his perception of the reality of personal struggle towards salvation, is himself unable to transcend the pattern imposed on reality by the self-interest of the class to which he belongs, and instead, therefore, of permitting the drama with which he is concerned to break through the pattern and centre itself within the perspectives of reali-

ty, he curtails the perspectives themselves and attempts to persuade himself and his readers that the drama takes place between the poles of Nature and Convention, with Nature filling the place of God, or the Absolute. . . . The novelist's own awareness that this will not justify a real spiritual dynamism in his characters must eventually follow.

It is possibly the realization of something of this which led Forster to abandon the narrow personal drama and to embrace the social issues which are clearly displayed in his fourth novel, *Howards End* (1910). There is no doubt whatever as to the social orientation of this novel and its characterization, nor as to its bearing upon the logic of Forster's development. From the point reached in *The Longest Journey* there were two possible paths for one in Forster's situation: either to affirm the reality of the spiritual, and thus to justify the drama of personal salvation, by placing the individual (and thus by inference his social circumstances) in the ultimate perspectives of existence; or to affirm the primary reality of the social and to reduce the spiritual to an epiphenomenon dependent upon the social pattern. The first alternative would have made possible a continuation and development of the personal drama; and thus, conceivably, the transformation of Forster into a genuine creator: the second could only have necessitated a transition from the personal to the social level, a movement from the centre to the periphery; which was, in fact, the result.

Howards End must be interpreted from this point of view. Here is an evidently allegorical contrast between the inner world of personal existence, represented by the cultured sisters Helen and Margaret Schlegel, and the outer world of the practical organization of living. . . . (pp. 57-8)

[The] focal point is money. Hardly are the Schlegels introduced before the subject of their investments is touched upon. Money, indeed, is the *leit-motif* which accompanies the Schlegels throughout the book. And it is poverty, in the character of Leonard Bast, which underscores their wealth and culture. The significance of this bringing to the surface of what, in order to permit the strictly personal drama, had hitherto been kept in concealment, hardly needs to be emphasized. *Howards End* is in one of its aspects a justification of economic privilege; but the recognition of the individual's dependence upon social circumstances destroys the possibility of the drama of personal salvation, and substitutes the drama of social relationships. (p. 58)

Because he does not enjoy the financial advantages of the Schlegels, Leonard Bast's aspirations towards culture are made to appear pathetic in their hopelessness. But the character of Leonard Bast is not the result of authentic, disinterested observation of life; he is unconsciously falsified, in a manner which will be considered below, to fit within the preconceived interpretation of reality which underpins the structure of the novel. (pp. 58-9)

The argument of *Howards End,* at all times implicit and at times declared, is that culture and the good life depend upon economic security, which in the capitalistic world of the time means privilege. "To trust people is a luxury in which only the wealthy can indulge; the poor cannot afford it"—such statements as this are intermittent in the early parts of the book. (p. 59)

The respective positions of Leonard Bast and Henry Wilcox have an obvious symbolic importance, in that the leanings of the Schlegel sisters are divided between the two.

The impulsive and idealistic Helen reacts vehemently against Mr. Wilcox, and her reaction drives her towards Leonard Bast.... Margaret, on the other hand, wiser and more level-headed, so we are told, is drawn towards the Wilcox family and led to associate herself with the values they represent. (pp. 61-2)

The dramatic action of the book develops out of the schism which takes place between the Schlegel sisters as each moves further along her chosen path, Margaret towards the acceptance of the "outer life," expressed in her engagement to the widowed Mr. Wilcox, and Helen towards her pursuit of a somewhat vaguely conceived "ideal." The scales are, however, heavily weighted against Helen, who is used as a mere foil to her sister's maturer wisdom. (p. 62)

The morality of the story and the conclusion we are supposed to draw from it are plain. "Only connect ..." exhorts the book's epigraph; and Margaret it is, we are asked to believe, who accomplishes the connection.

In this novel, however, once again Forster's work suffers artistically as the result of the confusion between the symbolical and the realistic treatment of his subject....

The crucial falsification is not that of the characters of the Wilcoxes, who are presented honestly and objectively enough, but of the Schlegels and Leonard Bast. And it is here, perhaps, that we touch upon the psychological compulsion which inclined Forster's mind towards his admixture of the symbolical and the realistic—namely, in its effect in securing the falsification of symbolical truth necessary for the adaptation of the realities represented by the words "culture" and "poverty" to the far from disinterested preconceptions of the bourgeois liberal point of view. (p. 63)

What, indeed, is [the] "connection," but the bridging of the two worlds which were, in the earlier novels, held apart as spiritual antitheses: the world of falsity and convention and the world of the genuine and natural: the "pretended" and the "real"? Twists of presentation aside, in what essential respect can the Wilcoxes be said to differ from the Pembrokes of *The Longest Journey*? Yet while, in the earlier novel, for the sake of the personal drama which is enacted between those antitheses, the Pembrokes are represented as something at all costs to be eschewed and shunned, in the later book, where the personal drama gives place to the social, the same type, with a few changes, is represented as admirable and to be courted.

What is the reason for this change of attitude and the decision to compromise? The answer, it is not difficult to perceive, lies in the weakness and invalidity of the inner life, of "the real," as conceived by Forster, which, presented in naturalistic terms, has not sufficient inner vitality to maintain itself as a centre of spiritual energy in independence of the outer region of practical life. Forster's fundamental error consists of invoking the spiritual principle and then referring it for its ultimate sanction not to God, to the supernatural—a resort which would have had the effect of thoroughly disequilibrizing Forster's mental pattern and bringing it to a new and revolutionary centrality—but to Nature.... Forster's ethical naturalism will not bear the spiritual burdens which are placed upon it.... This inability to support the personal values represented by the Schlegels by an appeal to any higher order of being than that embodied in the mundanely "mysterious" figure of the first

Mrs. Wilcox with her tiresome wisp of hay (with the dew still on it) deprives the antithesis between Schlegels and Wilcoxes of its absolute character and therefore of all real value as a statement of the relationship between the inner and outer realms of existence—or the realm of subjectivity and that of objectivization. For neither can the Schlegel sisters really be accepted as adequately symbolizing the life of the spirit, nor can Leonard Bast be regarded as a truthful representation of the urge towards culture unsupported by economic privilege. The Schlegels are simply what they are "realistically" represented to be—two specimens of the leisured bourgeois parasite upon culture. And all that the book leaves us with is a statement of the real relations between "cultured, sensitive and democratic" liberalism and the capitalistic structure of Edwardian society which permits and guarantees its harmless, ineffectual and even charming existence. (pp. 64-5)

Forster's realistic presentation of the Schlegels enables him to get around the responsibility of declaring that his novel is an allegory of the inner life. Quite so. But if the Schlegels are only—the Schlegels, nothing more or less, then the book is deprived of inner significance. Forster's confused method enables him to retain the overtones of symbolical significance while presenting an apparently straightforward realistic narrative.... (p. 65)

Forster's evident determination that Leonard Bast should be made to fit the preconception that culture is secondary to economic security leads him to draw a portrait which is the least convincing fabrication in the book, and the one which most plainly calls into question the author's fundamental seriousness and responsibility as an artist. (p. 66)

With the resolution of the conflict between what is called, in *A Room with a View*, "the real and the pretended," signified by the union of the Schlegels with the Wilcoxes, the novelist's own inner thought-conflict, expressing the inner conflict which lies at the bottom of all the novels, comes to an end, and there is no longer any imperative urge towards fictional creation. Forster has exhausted his theme, and the dramatic materials are lacking. More, his interest has moved outward, peripherally, from the personal drama to a concern with the generalized problems of society, and it is now possible to speak of him (*vide* Burra) as "an artist on the fringe of social reform." The only way in which the novelist can finally exploit his basic situation is by transporting his mechanical dramatic apparatus to some external situation which it happens approximately and fortuitously to fit.... But the apparatus [of *A Passage to India*] hardly fits the drama, which, indeed, exiguous as it is, takes place, not in the battlefield of any individual soul, but on the plane of external action and political issues, where it is brought only to a precarious and inconclusive termination. The conflict is external to the author's mind. (p. 67)

[The most significant factor in *A Passage to India*] is the emotional background provided by the Marabar Caves, around which the action centres. It is the visit of Aziz, Mrs. Moore and Miss Quested to the caves which precipitates the drama, and throughout the novel the echoing "*Boumboum*" of the caves supplies an insistent undercurrent to the moods and thoughts of the characters.

The caves' horrible echo, is, however, a more elaborate repetition of something which has evidently lurked always at the edge of Forster's mind, for it has found expression in previous writings. It is indicated by the description of the infernal region in which a character in an early story finds himself after death, through his smug, unheroic life; and it is indicated also in the metaphor of the goblins "walking quietly over the universe" to describe the Beethoven Symphony in *Howards End*. ("Panic and emptiness," the message of the goblins, being the words which Helen has previously applied to the inner life of the Wilcoxes.) The caves reiterate the same message of meaninglessness and nullity, but more insistently and overpoweringly. The echo murmurs: "Pathos, piety, courage—they exist, but are identical, and so is filth. Everything exists, nothing has value." And the terror of the Marabar lay in the fact that it "robbed infinity and eternity of their vastness, the only quality that accommodates them to mankind." Not only does the echo of the caves prolong itself throughout the story to which it provides such a menacing undertone, but it has the effect of undermining and disintegrating Mrs. Moore's hold on life, and ultimately, of destroying her. When we recollect that Mrs. Moore is to *A Passage to India* what Mrs. Wilcox is to *Howards End*—that she is the "elemental character" who represents what appears to be the highest value to which Forster can appeal to sanction his interpretation of life, the metaphorical implications of her disintegration and its occasion are ominous, to say the very least. Nor is there anything in Forster's occasional and miscellaneous writings of the past twenty years to dispel the misgivings to which a consideration of the sequence of his novels, ending on this ominous note, gives rise. (pp. 68-9)

> D. S. Savage, "E. M. Forster," in his The Withered Branch: Six Studies in the Modern Novel, Eyre & Spottiswoode (Publishers) Ltd., 1950, pp. 44-69.

FREDERICK C. CREWS

The trouble with Rickie Elliot's short stories, and equally with Forster's own, is an overbalance of meaningfulness at the expense of represented life—a preponderance of "unearned" symbolism. That this imperfection is less conspicuous in Forster's novels is largely due, I think, to the operation of a contrary feeling, his sense of the comic. Comedy provides the counterweight to keep the symbolist from slipping too far toward allegory; it continually refreshes his awareness of the world's intractability to private patterns of meaning.

In saying this I do not mean that comedy and symbolism, taken as literary methods, are opposites. Forster's Italian novels [*Where Angels Fear to Tread* and *A Room with a View*], with their purposeful selectivity of detail and their almost geometrical structure, are also highly comic; the recurrent symbols or rhythms can appear with equal plausibility in scenes of tragedy and of farce. This is made possible, however, by the fact that Forster's sense of irony governs the world of these novels. To a great extent the meaning he wants to create is ironic meaning; the significant moments are usually the ones that confound our surface expectations and those of the comically wrong-headed characters. A fictional world of this kind is patently artificial, for its details are chosen for their usefulness to the author's practical jokes. There is no urgency here to the characters' task of extracting "symbolic moments" from the chaotic world, for the represented world is not chaotic at all; it has already been severely trimmed to suit the purpose of the plot.

The opposition between symbolism and comedy pertains rather to the author's own search for meaning.... The comic mode of vision is ... a helpful restraint upon the writer's zeal for meaning. (pp. 92-3)

This checks-and-balances notion of the writer's mind is the keynote of *Aspects of the Novel*. Forster's position on every question of theory is a middle one, involving a vital balance between extremes that threaten to "tyrannize" the novel. (p. 93)

Fantasy, we might say, is symbolism that has seized control of reality; it is the extreme luxury of self-indulgence which the true symbolist will try to avoid. In many of his tales Forster uses fantasy to manifest his belief in freedom and passion—in the typical situation a comically inhibited character is confronted with an ideally "free" world which he fails to comprehend—but the technique itself suggests an inflexible dogmatism of attitude. Since it undermines plausibility, we are not surprised to find that it plays only a minor part in Forster's relatively realistic longer fiction.

Forster's sense of muddle, his willingness to admit violations and absurdities into his moral universe, is really quite opposite in spirit to his use of fantasy. It is one thing to produce effects of muddle by thwarting the expectations of narrow-minded characters—fantasy is well suited for this—but something else again to allow one's own values to be softened or qualified by a feeling for comedy. As a creator of fantasy Forster aligns himself with the Swift of *Gulliver's Travels* and the Butler of *Erewhon:* that is, with contrivers of schematic machinery for satirizing attitudes that are opposite to their own. His writing is also distinguished, however, by comedy in the restraining, self-critical sense. Like the Butler of *The Way of All Flesh*, Forster usually manages to satirize intolerant people without losing his characteristic modesty and nonchalance; he does not fall into the tone of the saint or the misanthrope. (pp. 94-5)

We can best describe the operation of the comic spirit in Forster's novels if we place him beside Jane Austen, his favorite novelist. As in her works, Forster's comedy is usually generated by ironic contrasts between what is superficially "proper" and what is truly reasonable. . . .

Where Forster's comedy chiefly differs from Jane Austen's is in the acceleration of its witty reversals, the greater density of thematic irony, and the greater freedom with which Forster moves his focus from the world of his characters to that of general human nature. (p. 96)

However believable any one of Forster's coincidences of plot may be, the hand of the puppet-master is clearly in view above his "meaningful" scenes of comedy. The Italian novels are so rigidly governed by thematic irony that their plots give a total effect of fantasy; we find ourselves in a world where error is always punished with ironic appropriateness. (p. 99)

[The] idea of comic justice becomes progressively less relevant to our understanding of Forster's two final novels. Forster retains his satirical attitude toward egoists, of course, but his plots are not primarily concerned with exposing them. As moral questions become subordinate to questions about the ultimate meaning of human existence, the plot necessarily loses its function of superintending private morality. Indeed, the very possibility of a Meredithian comic plot diminishes as Forster's total attitude toward life becomes more conspicuous. That attitude . . . is one of extreme skepticism about the existence of a providential order. Such skepticism naturally precludes belief in a mechanical system of retribution against egoists; a novel based on such a system must be offered with a certain facetious flair. [But Forster's two last novels] resume the effort, gingerly undertaken in *The Longest Journey*, to reflect the real poignancy of man's isolation from meaning. Forster's plots remain comic in that the characters are handled ironically, but his comic distance from them begins to take on a sober philosophical import—until, in *A Passage to India*, the comic vision accurately conveys Forster's view of human pretensions in general. Forster remains comic, but in somewhat the same way that Chaucer is comic at the end of *Troilus and Criseyde*, where human tragedy is seen from the belittling perspective of divine indifference to our imperfect and undignified lives. (pp. 103-04)

> *Frederick C. Crews, "The Comic Spirit," in his* E. M. Forster: The Perils of Humanism *(copyright © 1962 by Princeton University Press; reprinted by permission of Princeton University Press), Princeton University Press, 1962, pp. 92-104.*

JANE LAGOUDIS PINCHIN

E. M. Forster arrived in Alexandria in 1915. He was thirty-six and already an established writer, with four novels and a collection of short stories behind him and a fifth novel written but unseen. Forster's was a unique voice, even from the start, large and marked by a generous humanism that has not found its equal in contemporary British fiction. He had already toured Greece, Italy, and India, and his early fiction reflects this contact with worlds that call into question the values of upper-middle-class England, the values of home, just as it reflects the special perception a homosexual brings to a heterosexual, and alien, world. (p. 82)

E. M. Forster's homosexuality shaped his writing—I'd venture to say, more than any other force did. And it influenced those works that do not explicitly deal with homosexuals every bit as much as it affected *Maurice* and the stories in *The Life to Come*. . . .

One can easily, and for the most part correctly, argue that even if the biographical pieces suffer from their lack of candor, we now have *Maurice* and *The Life to Come* and, what is more important, we have fiction in which Forster created masks, enabling him to talk about love as he felt it most deeply, producing a tension between the fictive and the real that resulted in fine novels. (p. 87)

Passion and truth sometimes seem sacrificed to convention in the early novels—in Ansell's reaction to Rickie's marriage or in Maurice's jealousy toward Ada—because of Forster's fear that if he really struck at the core of these relationships, he might not be able to come back to Sawston, or to Howards End. (p. 88)

Were the deep-seated forces that produced [Forster's] fiction in harmony with a critical faculty that called for the truth of separation and flux? (p. 89)

Forster's desire for continuity was incredibly strong. Before the First World War, before Alexandria, he could not look on his country's history—seen in its landscape and in its class structure—he could not look at art, without dwelling on permanence, on continuity. And when he turned to love, his desire for undying comradeship held his early fiction, not quite permitting it to tell a story of separation "not untrue to life."

In Forster's early novels history and art are always unifying forces. In *Howards End*, Forster writes: "Margaret realized the chaotic nature of our daily life, and its difference from the orderly sequence that has been fabricated by historians. Actual life is full of false clues and signposts that lead nowhere." . . . Even though he might wish it otherwise, history and art could not mirror chaos in Forster's work, because Forster could not yet accept what in *Room with a View* he called "the sadness of the incomplete—the sadness that is often life, but should never be Art." . . .

Perhaps this is why his early work is dominated by images of ancient Greece. . . . Greece and Greek art certainly symbolize the mythical and the sensual for Forster—"A Gothic statue implies celibacy, just as a Greek statue implies fruition." (pp. 89-90)

This connection between the Hellenic and the sensual is of extreme and lasting importance to Forster, but we should also note the link Forster makes in the early novels between his idea of Greece and his belief in the absolute necessity for continuity and unity. (p. 90)

[For] all his emphasis on marriage and manners, Forster's writing is not primarily about heterosexual love. In art, as in life, he was haunted by the image of undying affection between members of the same sex, which is precisely why comradeship, indeed the very word, was so important to Forster, almost permitting the unity of two irreconcilable forces: the respectability of home and the lawlessness of love. (p. 93)

Is comradeship sexual in Forster's fiction? It is, clearly, in the fiction published since his death, like the surprisingly similar works "Albergo Empedocle" and *Maurice*. But there are sexual dimensions to friendship and, especially, to sibling affection in Forster's other works as well. Forster wrote in a world in which he could not, and would not, speak directly about his own sexual life. Images of comrades and siblings gave him the necessary fictive mask through which he could deal with homosexuality, and often allowed him to dig to the roots of sexuality in familial and friendship relationships. They sometimes produced the tension we see in Cavafy's historical-love poems. I do not mean to suggest that the mask was always conscious. Nor do I feel that Forster was always courageous enough to face the sexuality he had created. But in the brotherhood of figures like Stephen Wonham and Rickie Elliot [in *The Longest Journey*], Forster found a permissible way of describing unpermissible impulses. The bond of flesh and blood serves well as a mirror for the bond of physical contact. Through it Forster could reach to some of the narcissistic links between lover and beloved and the patterns by which they reenact the roles of mother and child. (p. 95)

Forster's central characters are torn. Like Rickie, they are always faced with two beloveds, one spiritual and one physical, and in all cases their most successful relationship is with a Mediterranean man or British peasant, with an earthy mate. . . .

In *The Longest Journey* this division causes little pain—the fight with evil lies elsewhere and the two halves of Rickie's other self are happily united in the end. But in the raw, flamed, and honest *Maurice,* Forster ends with a scene in which author and protagonist seem out of control. The focus is wrong. When he should be loving Alec, Maurice is out chastising Clive. . . . The division should not have been necessary. But until Forster learned to love "better" and "differently," he and his heroes would have to live in this way.

No one who admires Forster's fiction can miss its sadnesses. . . . As in life, death is everywhere and a surprise. . . . There are also sadnesses more wearying than death. . . . About such things Forster tells his reader what Rickie tells Agnes, when her lover dies: "I did not come to comfort you. I came to see that you mind." . . . (pp. 96-7)

But Forster minded so much that he could not resist giving those fictive selves he loved eternal comfort. The contest is on in most of Forster's early novels. The prize is the direction of human destiny. The prize is England. The problem, a very poignant one for Forster and perhaps for most homosexuals, is that continuity and a type of unity are promised to most heterosexual couples. (p. 97)

Forster bears children in his fiction. They are never children of individual souls; they always carry with them the weight of history and human destiny. Stephen's child vies with Agnes' baby. The question is, who will inherit the earth? And the answer is plain. The good will inherit the earth. Time will stand still. Homosexual lovers will leave heirs. (p. 98)

[Forster] wrote with passionate concern about his people, as they lived on his beloved island and, chronicling their clash with others, as they moved in the world. At times the broad sweep fails—in the operatic conclusion to *Howards End* for example, where we feel the strain of an attempt to reconcile all the major forces in the English social structure —but at its best we hardly notice the immensity of Forster's scheme, perhaps because he, like Cavafy, wears the mask of a little man, certainly because he has the poet's uncanny ability to make larger historical and social pulls seem truly subordinate to the personal. (p. 104)

Those essays that Forster wished to reach a wider audience were collected as *Pharos and Pharillon.* The book—divided into two parts: *Pharos* ancient, and *Pharillon,* modern history—travels through Alexandria chronologically and, like Cavafy's poetry, although composed of autonomous sketches, forms a whole. (p. 121)

Forster, in his very best sketches, is closer to the poet Cavafy [than to Lytton Strachey and other biographical essayists], because both are interested in more than characterization. Both glimpse life through the very particular eyes of one human soul grounded in his own soil, at a peculiar—although not necessarily spectacular—moment in time. They see the irony that is the distance between that soul's vision and ours. A moment in time and space. History as fiction. (p. 126)

[*Alexandria: A History and a Guide* is not merely] an impressionistic account of character. Although grounded in generalized theories about human nature and the Alexandrian soul—"no impartial book but an Intelligent Tourist's Guide to Humanism"—it is also astoundingly thorough. Like Cavafy, who could tell you the probable cost of Kaisarion's pink silk, Forster combines the patience of the

"sticker" with the artist's love for the texture of detail. (p. 131)

Forster is thorough in still another odd way. One of the major concerns in this book, and indeed in all Forster's work, is with the question of what effect war and bureaucracy have upon civilizations and their art. . . . And yet Forster is fascinated by battles, describing them endlessly. . . . We learn every maneuver and think back to the battle of Magnesia, the Achaian League—the surprising importance of war in Cavafy's poetry.

Forster's Alexandria is characterized in many ways—it does not appreciate the pastoral, is not tragic, loves scientific toys and games—but amid the vivid detail one can see that, for Forster, Alexandria has three essential concerns: love; the theological question of how man and God are united; and the physical—and mystical—reality that makes the city a passage to India. The three are irrevocably bound. Emotionally, physically, and spiritually Forster's Alexandria is a bridge, a link.

The form of *Alexandria* is itself concerned with bridges.

> The "History" is written in short sections, and at the end of each section are references to the second part—the "Guide." On these references the chief utility of the book depends, so the reader is begged to take special note of them: they are to help him to link the present and the past. . . .

Past and present are bridged in yet another way in *Alexandria.* Just as in *Pharos and Pharillon,* Cavafy's "The God Abandons Antony" unites the two sections of this book.

The poem is particularly important here because the story of the lovers [Antony and Cleopatra] is central to *Alexandria.* Forster does not quite give us his own version of the tale, but Cleopatra interests him. . . . She becomes one of the ways he can show us that Alexandria has always been a city of love. (pp. 132-33)

Alexandria, like *Pharos and Pharillon* and *A Passage to India,* begins with geography. The sense of place is all-important. Early on, Forster tells us that ancient Alexandria "stood in the position of Port Said to-day; a maritime gateway to India and the remoter east." . . . The image is reinforced, not only with Plotinus, but with those who came to visit, or to conquer, as well. (p. 138)

[The] dream of passage is more important than its achievement, and in it Forster has created a chain of those who would follow Alexander in his "madness." The links include some, like Eliza Fay—that vicious but lively British woman—and Forster, who do not lead men (except the likes of poor Mr. Fay) but who are irrevocably touched by their own private passage to India—their glimpse of something great, if dangerous—and others, who have altered history—Antony, Napoleon, Mohammed Ali.

And this is primarily *why* Forster is fascinated by battles, by conquests. Cavafy saw in them the destruction of Magna Graecia, and used them as metaphors for individual defeat and hopeless hope. . . . [For Forster], conquest provides a form of knowledge, a strange kind of passage, the touch of two cultures. (pp. 139-40)

Forster focused his study of Alexandria on the metaphors of the bridge and the necklace: the link between man and

God; the love that binds men to one another; and geography, history, politics—the gateway between East and West. These links reappear in *A Passage,* touching Forster's last novel with a refracted light, with colors that are absent in his earlier works. (pp. 141-42)

Forster could almost be dismissed, or applauded, as a man concerned with a warm but not passionate unity of love. But in Alexandria unity of love was of necessity linked with passion *and* theology, underscoring mystical chords that had always existed in Forster's imaginative world. In going after a harmonizing spirit in the east, in attempting to understand death and life and capture the whole, Forster, like Alexander, like Mrs. Moore, had to confront madness and its echoes; he had to confront the prophetical. (p. 142)

The religious visions Forster confronts in *A Passage* are essentially the same as those in *Alexandria* and, as many have noted, the three-part structure of the novel moves us through Moslem, Christian, and finally Hindu answers to the nihilistic "Boum" of the caves. (p. 143)

It is [the] friendship between Aziz and Fielding, Easterner and Westerner, that stands at the center of [*A Passage*]. Here the beloved is no longer split into a sensual dark man or peasant and an intellectual friend. Forster now knew Easterners, knew them as poets, like Aziz and Cavafy, as lawyers, doctors, lovers, friends. (p. 151)

In the end [of *A Passage*] love has its grand moment. But as with spiritual triumph, it is a victory intertwined with loss. (p. 152)

Love was central to Forster's vision of Alexandria and India. But it was love grounded in geography and history. Like Cavafy, he was interested in the fates of peoples as they affect individual men, he would chronicle his race. Like Lawrence Durrell he understood how the land shapes people. Alexandria was a geographic as well as a spiritual gateway to India. . . .

It is not surprising that *A Passage to India* has such a strong sense of geography and often the flavor of a guide-book. Nor that it uses the metaphor of the guide that Aziz always fails to be and Ralph so easily becomes. The land, the weather veers toward chaos, only to be replenished by rain. But always there is a tension now, nothing so easy as the hayfields of Howard's End. (p. 153)

In Forster's earlier fiction the triumph of process had to be matched by the triumph of results. In *A Passage* Aziz and Fielding honor a moment of love, without illusion. Like the music surrounding Antony [in Cavafy's "The God Abandons Anthony"], "Here is something that does last—the note of permanence on which his soul was set. He has laboured sincerely, he has told a story not untrue to life." (p. 158)

> Jane Lagoudis Pinchin, "The Bridge: E. M. Forster in Alexandria," in her Alexandria Still: Forster, Durrell, and Cavafy (copyright © 1977 by Princeton University Press; reprinted by permission of Princeton University Press), Princeton University Press, 1977, pp. 82-158.

*   *   *

FROST, Robert   1874-1963

Frost is recognized as one of the foremost American poets of the twentieth century. The setting for his poems is predomi-nantly the rural landscapes of New England, his poetic language is the language of the common man. His work has often been criticized for its uneven quality, as well its simplistic philosophy and form. He embraced the problems of the common man, however, and because of the diversity and effective use of symbolism found in his poetry, enjoyed a wide appeal. Frost received the Pulitzer Prize in Poetry four times. (See also *CLC*, Vols. 1, 3, 4, 9, 10.)

AMY LOWELL

Mr. Frost is only expatriated in a physical sense. Living in England he is, nevertheless, saturated with New England. For not only is his work New England in subject, it is so in technique. No hint of European forms has crept into it. It is certainly the most American volume of poetry which has appeared for some time. I use the word American in the way it is constantly employed by contemporary reviewers, to mean work of a color so local as to be almost photographic. . . .

The thing which makes Mr. Frost's work remarkable is the fact that he has chosen to write it as verse. We have been flooded for twenty years with New England stories in prose. . . . [No hint of humor] appears in "North of Boston." And just because of the lack of it, just because its place is taken by an irony, sardonic and grim, Mr. Frost's book reveals a disease which is eating into the vitals of our New England life, at least in its rural communities. (p. 18)

[We cannot] explain the great numbers of people, sprung from old New England stock, but not themselves living in remote country places, who go insane.

It is a question for the psychiatrist to answer, and it would be interesting to ask it with "North of Boston" as a textbook to go by. . . . Mr. Frost's is not the kindly New England of Whittier, nor the humorous and sensible one of Lowell; it is a latter-day New England, where a civilization is decaying to give place to another and very different one. (pp. 18-19)

His people are left-overs of the old stock, morbid, pursued by phantoms, slowly sinking to insanity. (p. 19)

I have said that Mr. Frost's work is almost photographic. The qualification was unnecessary, it is photographic. The pictures, the characters, are reproduced directly from life, they are burnt into his mind as though it were a sensitive plate. He gives out what has been put in unchanged by any personal mental process. His imagination is bounded by what he has seen, he is confined within the limits of his experience (or at least what might have been his experience) and bent all one way like the wind-blown trees of New England hillsides. (p. 20)

He tells you what he has seen *exactly* as he has seen it. And in the word *exactly* lies the half of his talent. The other half is a great and beautiful simplicity of phrase, the inheritance of a race brought up on the English Bible. Mr. Frost's work is not in the least objective. He is not writing of people whom he has met in summer vacations, who strike him as interesting, and whose life he thinks worthy of perpetuation. Mr. Frost writes as a man under the spell of a fixed idea. He is as racial as his own puppets. One of the great interests of the book is the uncompromising New Englander it reveals. . . . Mr. Frost is as New England as Burns is Scotch, Synge Irish, or Mistral Provençal.

And Mr. Frost has chosen his medium with an unerring sense of fitness. As there is no rare and vivid imaginative force playing over his subjects, so there is no exotic music pulsing through his verse. He has not been seduced into subtleties of expression which would be painfully out of place. His words are simple, straightforward, direct, manly, and there is an elemental quality in all he does which would surely be lost if he chose to pursue niceties of phrase. He writes in classic metres in a way to set the teeth of all the poets of the older schools on edge; and he writes in classic metres, and uses inversions and *clichés* whenever he pleases, those devices so abhorred by the newest generation. He goes his own way, regardless of anyone else's rules, and the result is a book of unusual power and sincerity.

The poems are written for the most part in blank verse, blank verse which does not hesitate to leave out a syllable or put one in, whenever it feels like it. To the classicist such liberties would be unendurable. But the method has its advantages. It suggests the hardness and roughness of New England granite. It is halting and maimed, like the life it portrays, unyielding in substance, and broken in effect.

Mr. Frost has done that remarkable thing, caught a fleeting epoch and stamped it into print. He might have done it as well in prose, but I do not think so, and if the book is not great poetry, it is nevertheless a remarkable achievement. (pp. 20-1)

> *Amy Lowell, in* The New Republic *(reprinted by permission of* The New Republic; © *1915 The New Republic, Inc.), February 20, 1915 (and reprinted in* Robert Frost: The Critical Reception, *edited by Linda W. Wagner, Burt Franklin & Co., Inc., 1977).*

MARK VAN DOREN

At its worst [Mr. Frost's indirectness] is a mannerism, a tour de force of syntax; it puzzles with mere obscurity. At its best it is poetry of the subtlest sort, because it carries the conviction that there was no other way to communicate the reticence inherent both in the subject and in the poet. Out of "A Star in a Stone-Boat," for instance, an idea gradually emerges which Mr. Frost could not and should not have expressed directly. He has paced all the way around the idea, hinting of this or that aspect; the idea itself is left for the reader to get, and if he is the right kind of reader he will get it and rejoice. In a larger sense also the indirectness of Mr. Frost justifies itself. His love of the country is so profound that he will not say in so many words that he loves it. Indeed, one has the illusion that Mr. Frost would rather not talk at all. Now and then he has confessed to being moved by birches, or an occasional lonely house; but countless other things must wait their day, and most of them will wait in vain. To create such an illusion is to be one poet in ten thousand. (p. 61)

> *Mark Van Doren, in* The Nation *(copyright 1923 The Nation Associates), December 19, 1923 (and reprinted in* Robert Frost: The Critical Reception, *edited by Linda W. Wagner, Burt Franklin & Co., Inc., 1977).*

LOUIS UNTERMEYER

No contemporary poet has been more praised than Robert Frost, and no poet has ever been more praised for the wrong things. The early reviews of "West-Running Brook" have renewed the false emphasis. Most of the critics are surprised that the writer identified with the long monologues in "North of Boston" should turn to lyrics, forgetting that Frost's first volume (written in the 1890's and published twenty years later) was wholly and insistently lyrical. (p. 71)

Here, in his latest work, is a reflection and a restatement of his earliest. This is philosophy in terms of the lyric. But the first as well as the final appeal is neither to the brain nor to the ear; beneath the graceful image there speaks a greatness of soul.

It is this spiritual sustenance which has always strengthened Frost's passionate puritanism. . . . Frost, legend to the contrary, reveals himself, actually gives himself away with every raillery, every wisp of metaphor, every conversational aside. Avoiding the analytical, this poetry is a constant search; a search for absolutes. Better still, it is a search for the Absolute—in man, in poetry, in God. (p. 72)

["Bereft"] may be considered a key-note poem. It is, in a sense, a sequel to the extremely early "Trial by Existence"; here, at the end of independence, is only the last courage, the loneliness, the nothingness—"and where there is nothing, there is God." But "West-Running Brook" is not so much a sequel as it is a composite of the early and later Frost. What seems a mellowing and maturing turns out to be the fruit of intuition rather than experience. . . .

Frost's power of lifting the colloquial to the pitch of poetry has always been apparent (it raises even so broad a bucolic as "Something inspires the only cow of late"); in the new volume he maintains his rôle of half-earnest synecdochist. Here, again, offering the part for the whole, he reestablishes the force of suggestion and reaffirms his conviction: "All that an artist needs is samples." Parsimony is achieved in almost every one of the new poems. (p. 73)

A certain technical shift may be noticed here and there, a somewhat more rhythmic ease apparent in the slightest of his quatrains. The verse itself has more of the "sound" that Frost cherishes, a talk-flavored tone that has the common vitality of prose without ever ceasing to be poetry. . . .

Here, in ["West-Running Brook"] is the metaphysical lyric as no one but Robert Frost could write it. . . . The ripe repose, the banked emotion, the nicely blended tenderness and humor are everywhere. Growth? Change? A new note? The answers may be found in two lines of one of Frost's first poems, a premonitory couplet written before 1900:

> They would not find me changed from him they knew,
> Only more sure of all I thought was true.
>
> (p. 74)

> *Louis Untermeyer, "Still Robert Frost," in* Saturday Review of Literature *(copyright, 1928 by The Saturday Review Co., Inc.; reprinted with permission), December 22, 1928 (and reprinted in* Robert Frost: The Critical Reception, *edited by Linda W. Wagner, Burt Franklin & Co., Inc., 1977, pp. 71-4).*

JOHN CIARDI

Frost could not have known what a stunning effect his repetition of the last line [in "Stopping by Woods on a Snowy Evening"] was going to produce. He could not even know he was going to repeat the line. He simply found himself up against a difficulty he almost certainly had not foreseen and he had to improvise to meet it. . . .

It must have been in some such quandary that the final repetition suggested itself—a suggestion born of the very difficulties the poet had let himself in for. So there is that point beyond mere ease in handling a hard thing, the point at which the very difficulty offers the poet the opportunity to do better than he knew he could. What, aside from having that happen to oneself, could be more self-delighting than to participate in its happening by one's reader-identification with the poem? . . .

[The] human-insight of the poem and the technicalities of its poetic artifice are inseparable. Each feeds the other. That interplay is the poem's meaning, a matter not of WHAT DOES IT MEAN, for no one can ever say entirely what a good poem means, but of HOW DOES IT MEAN, a process one can come much closer to discussing. . . .

Once at Bread Loaf . . . I heard him add one very essential piece to the discussion of how ["Stopping by Woods"] "just came." One night, he said, he had sat down after supper to work at a long piece of blank verse. The piece never worked out, but Mr. Frost found himself so absorbed in it that, when next he looked up, dawn was at his window. He rose, crossed to the window, stood looking out for a few minutes, and *then* it was that "Stopping by Woods" suddenly "just came," so that all he had to do was cross the room and write it down.

Robert Frost is the sort of artist who hides his traces. I know of no Frost worksheets anywhere. If someone has raided his wastebasket in secret, it is possible that such worksheets exist somewhere, but Frost would not willingly allow anything but the finished product to leave him. Almost certainly, therefore, no one will ever know what was in that piece of unsuccessful blank verse he had been working at with such concentration, but I for one would stake my life that could that worksheet be uncovered, it would be found to contain the germinal stuff of "Stopping by Woods"; that what was a-simmer in him all night without finding its proper form, suddenly, when he let his still-occupied mind look away, came at him from a different direction, offered itself in a different form, and that finding that form exactly right the impulse proceeded to marry itself to the new shape in one of the most miraculous performances of English lyricism.

And that, too—whether or not one can accept so hypothetical a discussion—is part of HOW the poem means. It means that marriage to the perfect form, the poem's shapen declaration of itself, its moment's monument fixed beyond all possibility of change. And thus, finally, in every truly good poem, "How does it mean?" must always be answered, "Triumphantly." Whatever the poem "is about," *how* it means is always how Genesis means: the word become a form, and the form become a thing, and—when the becoming is true—the thing become a part of the knowledge and experience of the race forever. (p. 65)

> John Ciardi, "Robert Frost: The Way to the Poem," in Saturday Review (*Entire issue copyright 1958 by Saturday Review Associates, Inc.; reprinted with permission*), April 12, 1958, pp. 13-15, 65.

LAWRENCE THOMPSON

[Even] though Frost is extremely gifted in his ability to make even the least lyric poem dramatic, he is primarily a subjective lyric poet, at his best in his apparently contradic-tory moods of response to experience and in his figurative ways of defining differences. . . . [The] matrix-pattern of *A Boy's Will* foreshadows his persistent pleasure in employing the lyric mode as an expression of self-discovery, even of psychological self-education, concerning his own ties to his beloved, to strangers, to nature, to the universe, to God. If it might be argued that these are the familiar concerns of most lyric poets, one differentiation may be suggested. For Frost, the ultimate and ulterior preoccupation is with a poetic view of life which he can consider complete, in the sense that it encompasses and integrates all these relationships figuratively, and yet not systematically. His ulterior concern is always with psychic and spiritual salvation. Frost's awareness of his differences from conventional attitudes, in his defense of the unsystematic, is at least implied in such a confession as this:

> And were an epitaph to be my story
> I'd have a short one ready for my own.
> I would have written of me on my stone:
> I had a lover's quarrel with the world.

Once again, the contraries implicit in that phrase "lover's quarrel" do not imply either physical or metaphysical rebellion against the human condition. . . . His "lover's quarrel with the world" may have begun through his wanting and trying to discover or define his own sense of simultaneous separateness and integration. More than that, a large part of his poetic pleasure would seem to be derived from his finding verse not only an end in itself but also a means to the end of making each poem a "clarification of life," at least a clarification of his own attitude toward life. (pp. 15-16)

Repeatedly, in Frost's lyrics, the playful seriousness evokes ironies and ambiguities which imply that some of the poet's representations of his outward quarrels with the world may also be taken as either conscious or unconscious projections of inward conflicts. At times, some of his poems achieve an extra dimension of meaning if viewed as constructed around his conscious and yet unstated realization of his own divided awareness. His taunts and countertaunts thus pick up enrichments of meaning if the poem is viewed as contending, at one and the same time, with enemies inside and outside his own heart and mind. (p. 17)

Frost, who boasted of his Puritan descent, and who was decidedly puritanical in many of his sympathies, might be viewed as a nonconforming Puritan nonconformist.

For the sake of poetry, there would seem to be a kind of convenience or luxury or at least artistic usefulness in the very posture of heresy. It provides the artist not only with greater freedom to manipulate his raw materials but also with the added chance to indulge varying moods of belief and unbelief. He can say with Horatio, in *Hamlet,* "So have I heard and do in part believe it." But in Frost's case it would seem more accurate to suggest that his poetic flaunting of heresies largely stems from his inability to derive adequate intellectual-emotional-spiritual satisfaction from any systematic dogma which imposes intolerable limitations on a temperament which delights to seek truth through questions and dialogue. (p. 20)

For various and complicated reasons, his fluctuating and ambiguous viewpoint mocks, at times, any complacent notions concerning a benevolent design in nature. . . . For Frost, the attempt to see clearly, and from all sides, requires a willingness to confront the frightening and the appalling in even its darkest forms.

Any careful reader of Frost's poems notices how frequently "fear" provides different kinds of premises for him. If nature and human nature have the power to reduce man to a fearful sense of his own smallness, his own lostness, in a seemingly indifferent or even malicious universe, then one suggested way to confront such fear is to imagine life stripped down to a minimum; to decide whether enough is left to go on with; then to consider the question whether the possible gains are worth the necessary cost. . . . [Many of the later poems] closely represent the confrontations of fear, lostness, alienation, not so much for purposes of shuddering as for purposes of overcoming fright, first through individual and then through social ingenuity, courage, daring, and action. (pp. 20-2)

[Frost] mentioned Defoe's *Robinson Crusoe* and Thoreau's *Walden* as thematically rhyming for him: "*Robinson Crusoe* is never quite out of my mind. I never tire of being shown how the limited can make snug in the limitless. *Walden* has something of the same fascination. Crusoe was cast away; Thoreau was self-cast away. Both found themselves sufficient. No prose writer has ever been more fortunate in subject than these two." By implication, no subject matter has ever made stronger appeal to Frost, for poetry, than that same question as to how the limited man can make snug in the limitless. As it happens, many of his poems talk back and forth to each other as though calculated to answer something like Pascal's old-new observation, "When I consider the brief span of my life, swallowed up in the eternity before and behind me, the small space that I fill, or even see, engulfed in the infinite immensity of spaces which I know not, and which know not me, I am afraid." Understanding that kind of fear, Frost expresses much the same mood, with a twist, in his poem entitled "Desert Places." But he more often prefers to answer the existential problem of "what to make of a diminished thing" by representing characters who confront the excruciations by means of order-giving actions. For example, in the dramatic monologue entitled "An Empty Threat," the speaker is a fur trader who has chosen to work out his purposes almost alone, on the frozen shore of Hudson Bay. Although he recognizes all the symbols of defeat and death in the bleak landscape, the speaker is represented as uttering his flat rejoinder, "I stay," in the first line of the poem. . . . [The question of plan or design] obliquely raised suggests answers not so much in terms of the known or unknown but rather in terms of the possible. The poem concludes with the suggestion that if man is given his choice of succumbing to paralyzing doubts and fears or of translating even limited faith into possibly constructive action, then the choice ought to be made with ease. (pp. 22-3)

Even though he likes to indulge at least the posture of not-knowing, Frost sooner or later makes it clear that not too much is left in doubt, for him. If there are times when he seems to take particular pleasure in defining his beliefs in terms of his heresies, he cannot play metaphorical hide-and-seek too long without trailing clouds of puritanic certainty. For example, one of his most paradoxical and most metaphysical poems ["All Revelation"] begins by tantalizing the reader with ambiguities, and even continues with various forms of teasing provocation through the last line. . . . (p. 24)

The last line of "All Revelation" makes a use of hyperbole which ought to be challenged by any thoughtful reader.

"All revelation has been ours" is a very bold assertion. It might suggest that man endows nature with whatever order and meaning it has. But if that way of interpreting this last line may be attractive to some readers, it is not congenial to the controls provided by Frost's larger context of poetic utterances. . . . For Frost, whatever kind of revelation man here makes or achieves, through the uses of sense and skill, implies at least some kind of precedence of order and of design in nature. So the word "revelation," as poetically operative here, would seem to pick up its Frostian meaning only if it is viewed as representing a two-way process: an act of collaboration. . . . ([The] same theme, with its religious overtones of meaning, is developed further by Frost in *A Masque of Reason*.)

The counterbalancing of contrary attitudes or viewpoints, in "All Revelation," further suggests the poet's distaste for lingering too long in moods which merely accentuate the apparent design of darkness to appall, in the structure of the universe; his distaste for stressing too heavily the fright which can be and is derived from too much contemplation of inner and outer desert places. Yet he never lets us forget the limitations. At times, he editorializes or even preaches, poetically, with unabashed and strongly puritanical tones of warning and corrective, against the sin of indulging too much concern for the imponderables, in or beyond nature. (pp. 26-7)

Frost's recurrent elements of theme involving fear, isolation, lostness, not-knowing, and discontinuity . . . remain operative in the poems, side by side with these recurrent elements of faith and love and continuity. His juxtaposition of contrary and yet ultimately complementary images and themes finds its most elaborately paradoxical expression in those two masques which Frost chose to place in a significant summary position, at the conclusion to his volume which he also chose to entitle, with figurative overtones, *Complete Poems*.

As the titles suggest, *A Masque of Reason* and *A Masque of Mercy* explore contrary themes; yet once again they are contraries which permit us to view the two masques as complementary. More than that, they provide an epitome, or a gathering metaphor, of many major themes developed by Frost in the poems which precede and succeed them. Relationships are again explored in each of the masques; man's ultimate relationships to self, to society, to nature, to the universe, to God. Or, to say it another way, the two masques further extend themes involving man's perennial sense of isolation and communion, of fear and courage, of ignorance and knowledge, of discontinuity and continuity. (pp. 32-3)

In the initial action [of *A Masque of Reason*], Frost represents Job, his wife, and God as conducting an intimate post-mortem concerning the strengths and weaknesses of human reason in trying to understand the divine plan or design. Intimacy permits Job to ask his questions with all the ardor, boldness, even insolence of one participating in a family quarrel. If the orthodox reader should find himself offended by such apparent irreverence, or should find God represented in terms contrary to trite conventional concepts, the implicit mockery of accepted notions is again not accidental.

Because the action begins some two thousand years after the death of Job, all the characters have the advantage of encompassing modern knowledge and attitudes, so that the seeming anachronisms of reference suggest continuity in time and space. Job's concern is to ask God's "reason" for inflicting torture on innocent human beings. After preliminary hesitancy and sparring, God takes occasion to thank Job for his collaboration in an epoch-making action:

> I've had you on my mind a thousand years
> To thank you someday for the way you helped me
> Establish once for all the principle
> There's no connection man can reason out
> Between his just deserts and what he gets.

That phrase "the way you helped me" may recall notions advanced by William James and others concerning a suffering God, limited and thwarted in his plan to realize his divine purpose so long as man is indifferent and uncooperative. Also echoed throughout the masque is the related Bergsonian concept of a continuously creative process which develops the universe. But as Frost adapts these assumptions to his own sympathetic uses, he combines them with his favorite puritanic emphasis on the limitations of reason as it affects the relationship between man and God: "there's no connection man can *reason* out . . .". (pp. 33-4)

[God's] phrase "it was of the essence of the trial" may permit a further reminder here that Frost's earlier poems can be taken as notes and grace notes to these two masques. He had previously honored the conventional puritanic tendency to heap a heavy burden of meaning on the word "trial." . . . In *A Masque of Reason*, these various views are again invoked and now mingled with Jamesian-Bergsonian notions, as God reviews the changing or evolving attitude of man toward God, achieved with the help of Job and others. (pp. 34-5)

But Job, not yet satisfied with God's explanation of suffering, says at one point, "Such devilish ingenuity of torture / Did seem unlike You . . ." God has already admitted to Job that even as Job had been one of his helpers, so Satan had been another, with all his originality of sin. Job's wife helps by describing Satan as "God's best inspiration." In other words, good needs evil to complement it, else each would be meaningless. The conclusion of the masque represents God as confessing his motive had initially been that simple: "I was just showing off to the Devil, Job." (p. 36)

Considered as a work of art, *A Masque of Reason* is too largely composed of talk-talk, and too little dependent on action, to give it dramatic merit. But if considered as poetry, it can at least serve to clarify and unify many of the contrary meanings in the earlier and later poems. Notice that Frost's mockery of conventional religious concepts is here once again counterbalanced by sympathetic representations of theological views which, however fragmentary, are quite in accord with certain elements of Calvinistic Puritan doctrine. The masque thus provides further evidence that no matter how much Frost may have thought he rejected the received assumptions of his religious heritage, he indulged that posture of rejection, through his art and thought, to realize a difference which was never too pronounced. (pp. 36-7)

[The] dominant thematic concern of *A Masque of Mercy* may be said to pivot once again on the limitations of human knowledge as it involves different responses to various kinds of fear, starting and ending with the wisdom-unwis-

dom of man's fearing God. Indirectly, these notions are related to the convictions of Job, in the earlier masque, that no matter what "progress" may be, it cannot mean that the earth has become an easier place for man to save his soul; that unless earth can serve as a difficult trial-ground, the hardships of existence become meaningless. (p. 38)

Robert Frost did not bother to articulate more than fragments of his poetic theory, and yet certain essentials of it can be deduced from his poetic practice. If we remember that his wide acclaim has been earned during an era of artistic innovation and experiment, we may marvel at his having achieved such distinction merely by letting his idiom discover old ways to be new, within the traditional conventions of lyric and dramatic and thematic modes. While Yeats, Eliot, Pound, and others invoked or invented elaborate mythic frames of reference which have enriched and complicated artistic strategies, Frost would seem to have risked successfully the purification of poetic utterance, in complicating simple forms. As we have seen, however, he quite consciously assimilates to his own New England idiom such varieties of classical conventions as the relaxed modes of the Theocritan idylls, the terse epigrammatic brevity of Martial, the contemplative serenity of Horace, the sharply satirical intensity of Juvenal, the homely didacticism of Aesop. Yet his treasured firsthand familiarity with and admiration for the classics have not been displayed in ways which make his meanings depend on esoteric scholarship. Quite clearly, he has deliberately chosen to address himself to the common reader.

But if the majority of Frost's admirers would seem content to share the poet's delight in cherishing the humble beauties of nature, recorded by him with such precision of response to images of experience among New England fields, farms, roadsides, and forests, those readers have been willing to settle for too little, when so many other and deeper levels of meaning are available in his poems. It has frequently and correctly been pointed out that Frost's poetic concerns are akin to those which led Wordsworth to choose incidents and situations from common life and then to present them in a language actually used by the common man whose heartfelt passions are not restrained. Like Wordsworth, and like many poets before and after. Wordsworth, Frost has particularly emphasized his concern for catching within the lines of his poems the rhythms and cadences and tones of human speech. Among modern poets, he has been one of the many who have advocated a capturing of what he has repeatedly referred to as "the sound of sense" or "sound posturing" to provide a complicating enrichment of the underlying metrical rhythm. (pp. 40-1)

His primary artistic achievement, which is an enviable one, in spite of shortcomings, rests on his blending of thought and emotion and symbolic imagery within the confines of the lyric. It would seem to be an essential part of both his theory and practice to start with a single image, or to start with an image of an action, and then to endow either or both with a figurativeness of meaning, which is not fully understood by the reader until the extensions of meaning are found to transcend the physical.

While no one could correctly call Frost a transcendentalist, his kinship with Emerson goes deeper than might at first be noticed. (p. 41)

We have noticed in Frost's poetic theory and practice he

likes to endow images and actions with implicitly metaphorical and symbolic meanings until they repeatedly suggest a continuity between his vision of the human "fact" and the divine "fact." We have also noticed that he likes the tension between two ways of looking at such thought-felt moods; that his own moments of doubt, in these matters, seem to afford him the luxury of reaffirmation. In such a context, a poem like "Mowing" reveals further kinships between Frost and Emerson. In his essay on "The Poet" Emerson writes, "I find that the fascination resides in the symbol." Frost would agree. Emerson goes on to say that the response of the farmer to nature is a sympathetic form of worship. . . . Again Frost would agree, at least in part; but it must be pointed out that Frost's view of nature-as-symbol does not coincide with the Emersonian view. Neither does it coincide with the New England puritanical view of nature-as-symbol. Nevertheless, to those Puritan forefathers against whom both Emerson and Frost partially rebelled, self-reliance was God-reliance. Even those Puritan forefathers also insisted that *laborare est orare*. Whatever the differences in the three positions, the likenesses are significant.

"Prayer," says Emerson, with almost puritanical exultation, "is the contemplation of the facts of life from the highest point of view. It is the soliloquy of a beholding and jubilant soul." Frost would have been embarrassed to speak out that frankly in open meeting; but his poems obliquely imply his own assent to the notion. The core of his poetic theory, as of his poetic practice, is to be found in his uses of the sensuous responses of loving and cherishing, first as important poetic images of human actions; then, simultaneously, as even more important symbols of divine worship and even of prayer: "May my sacrifice be found acceptable in Heaven's sight."

In conclusion it should be said that the approach here used, in an attempt to increase our appreciation and understanding of Robert Frost's life and art, is only one of many possible approaches. It is calculated to suggest that many elements run counter to themselves, therein, without any ultimate contradictions. It also provides a means of noticing that Frost's entire work is deeply rooted in the American, even in the most vital Puritan, idiom. It is "native to the grain," and yet thoroughly original. (pp. 43-4)

> *Lawrence Thompson, in his* Robert Frost *(American Writers Pamphlet No. 2; © 1959, University of Minnesota), University of Minnesota Press, Minneapolis, 1959.*

RICHARD EBERHART

[The] personality of Robert Frost, the impact of his living presence, was known as inextricably bound up with his poetry. His mastery was also in what he would not do, in his recognition of what he could not do. (pp. 180-81)

If Poe showed a disintegrated personality, and if Emily Dickinson possessed one partly so, Robert Frost exhibited an integrated personality. He was integrated with the life of his times and his nation. He was integrated with nature because he began when man could feel a less urban sense of where man exists on the face of the earth and in relation to the universe. . . . Frost's poetry goes back to early American farm life, partaking of a pastoral feeling which, in turn, goes back to the Latin authors who formed his style. (p. 181)

While Frost was integrated with what might be termed the rural life of his times, and wrote a sort of elegant pastoral, there is a question whether in future his relevance to the whole of life will increase or diminish. (pp. 181-82)

[Perhaps] in the future Frost's vision will be pushed farther back in the past, in a sense, than would be expected, and he will be considered as dated and fixed to his times by the year 2000 as Longfellow is now for the most part only considered in relation to his times. This is a guess. A further guess is that a poet of comparable size in the near future, or in the far future, must be one who speaks not of country things, but holds a mirror up to the central doings, the goings and comings, the preoccupations and hazards of an almost totally urbanized population.

One reason why Frost is almost universally admired is that he believed in this world. He is skeptical of any other. He celebrates the possibilities of life as it is, its large and rich resources. In "Away!" (1958) he tells us, with a deeply reserved humor, that he'd like to come back to earth "from having died," if he doesn't like it over there. Earth's the best place for love.

This poem also shows his basic sense of will, the assumption that man should be able to control his own destiny. (p. 182)

While we are on this notion of death, it might be pointed out that in "A Soldier," written about the time of World War I, he goes as far toward spirituality as he ever does. He does not go as far as to embrace Christianity or any other religion, but his sensitivity for the dead soldier ends the poem as follows:

> But this we know, the obstacle that checked
> And tripped the body, shot the spirit on
> Further than target ever showed or shone.

It should be said that, although Frost's style and basic attitudes have not changed in a world of remarkable change, he was not paid attention to in the Thirties and part of the Forties as he was earlier and later. Having spoken of World War I in poetry, he left it to other poets to address and assess World War II. Having spoken for individualism, even optimism, and not being for any form of socialism, he was somewhat eclipsed for about two decades. It should also be said that the importance and religious convictions of T. S. Eliot cut down during this period on the interest in Frost's different kind of mind. Students of modern literature learn with amazement and joy of the great last period in the poetry of Yeats, wherein he perfected a new, austere style to express his mature convictions. In the late life of Frost there is no new style, rather, a consolidation of the old; there is a flowering of influence in the continuance of his old, excellent style which is almost without parallel. . . . Where Yeats at the last came to an "artifice of eternity," believing in mind alone, Frost offers a full humanity of head and heart. He also offers simplicity and understandability as essentials of poetry. And, as I said before, he believes in the world as it is, the visible and experiential world, showing it forth in rich terms. He comes to and stays in reality as men know it. His sometime sarcasm, even savagery are saved by a grace of wit which he knows well how to employ. It is not a withdrawn or a too fastidiously complex poet who maintained throughout his life a keen interest in the game of baseball. Poetry, the analogy is, must be a game too. While it is a matter of life and death to the poet, it must not be taken too seriously, in one sense. One must know how to manipulate it as a game or device. (pp. 183-84)

"The Silken Tent" has a more delicate feeling than we get in many of Frost's poems, an aesthetic feeling, wonderfully tender. It is one of the subtlest of his poems. It is a poetic triumph, a Shakespearean sonnet in one sustained sentence. The poem accords with Milton's specification for poetry that it should effect linked sweetness long drawn out. The subtlety of the poem is visual, as fine as the activations of the slightest breeze, yet the poem tantalizes beyond visual pleasure to induce, by "countless silken ties" of ideation, empathy with a natural world of harmony. Many of Frost's poems have a more prosaic feeling, and some have a dark fatalism about them. "Design" is also a sonnet. It is one of Frost's compelling poems, based on visual aesthetics, but, not suffusing the tranquil quality of "The Silken Tent," it disturbs the sense with a dark message although the colors shown are white. Yet the pleasure in reading the poem is so keen that the darkness of the message is masked as if by a withdrawal into undynamic aesthetics. (pp. 184-85)

[Design] shifts and holds off to a disinterested view the implacable workings of nature; then with a deft last stroke, as if not wishing to oppress the reader with dogma, it gives him an out or a leeway that maybe the vast design of the universe, however fixed, final, or fatal, may not be mirrored in a situation "so small" as that of the juxtaposition of spider, heal-all, and moth. This is a turn of Frost's nicest wit, a leaning back into the human as against the absolute confrontation of inhuman or superhuman forces. . . . (p. 187)

"Neither Out Far Nor In Deep" represents the humanistic nature of his thinking. He wishes never to go too far in any direction, but to keep his perceptions in the middle of his heart. He is thus able, in many poems as in this one, to speak for feelings that are universally valid. The situation is simple. People on land tend to look at the sea when they stand at the edge of the land. "They look at the sea all day." It is as if the sea might be or become a natural symbol of something beyond themselves. . . . The last stanza makes two broad generalizations out of the depths of Frost's feelings. These are based on strong restraint. "They cannot look out far. / They cannot look in deep." Behind these two sentences lies Frost's realization of the limitations of man. They suggest that there is something far and something deep to which man cannot get, but instead of erecting some new symbol for this farness, this depth, which a Romantic poet might do, Frost characteristically brings the matter home to a usable, natural consideration. When was the fact of our inability to perceive life as it may be a hindrance to our keeping watch on life as it is? Keeping watch on life as it is is what we have to do every day. It is this basic necessity which Frost celebrates in this poem.

The restraint of Frost's strongly balanced and Classical nature is shown again in "The Onset." With the beginning of winter, man may feel that he can do something about life or nature, but he knows that he cannot hold back winter. Frost says:

> I almost stumble looking up and round,
> As one who overtaken by the end
> Gives up his errand, and lets death descend
> Upon him where he is, with nothing done
> To evil, no important triumph won,

> More than if life had never been begun.

It is said as if in an aside, this hope of man to do something to evil. It is as if wit were the final motive for this, for any natural man knows that evil is ineradicable. The phrase is a kind of shadowboxing, a wish fulfillment, as if it were slipped in or allowed by the unconscious, not the conscious mind. It is a telling phrase; it tells us a great deal about Frost, driven by a demon of the will. Then the poem goes on in an arbitrary way to state that spring will overcome winter. He says: "Winter death has never tried / The earth but it has failed." We accept the end of the poem for what it is talking about; we warm to the poet's emphasis upon spring rather than winter. . . . The point of the poem is that it expresses man's universal wish for the death of winter.

Criticism of many of the poems is so easily available that it is not my purpose to adumbrate and elucidate many of his well-known poems. I would prefer to point up his powers of concentration in the shortest type of poem, the couplet or distich.

Frost has a group of couplets in which he can be arch and succinct. These are concentrated essences of meaning and suggestion.

"The Secret Sits" reads as follows:

> We dance around in a ring and suppose,
> But the Secret sits in the middle and knows.

This is an admirable closed statement. It admits the limits of man's knowledge. It is a truth-telling. Despite the frenzied actions of man, there is a still center. (pp. 191-92)

Frost unmasks himself in relation to God in "Not All There." It goes:

> I turned to speak to God
> About the world's despair,
> But to make bad matters worse
> I found God wasn't there.

> God turned to speak to me
> (Don't anybody laugh)
> God found I wasn't there—
> At least not over half.

The last line redeems the poem by some pity beyond derision. I assess it that Frost thinks God would want man to be whole. To make God find man only half there gives us a wry comment on life. This poem shows the artistic balance of Frost. The first four uncompromising lines are compromised in the second four. He allows the reader to have it both ways, an atheistical negation balanced by a dualistic system which can be read in terms of either God or man. (pp. 193-94)

When you read and make part of your consciousness and knowledge of life many of his poems, you may agree to a generalization that Frost stands firmly in this world and that his poems deal with an astute knowledge of others as well as of himself. He wants each of his poems to be in some way dramatic. He often told his audiences to note how different they are one from another. While he has deep personal lyrics, such as "Stopping by Woods on a Snowy Evening," Frost never lets himself go in a piercing, self-revelatory, Romantic way as Gerard Manley Hopkins did. (p. 194)

Frost is a different kind of poet. His self-revelations are

temporal and are embedded in poems showing human situations. He is not a confessional poet in the sense that Hopkins is a totally confessional one. Hopkins is committed to the Christian view. Frost is a secular poet, functioning and thriving in a Christian society. (p. 195)

Frost loved man as well as things. He does not turn away from mankind but speaks for it in some way in every poem. His great popularity is due in part to the love of life and of man, imperfect as they are. All readers can share in varying ways with this sympathy and this human understanding. (p. 196)

Frost was not a Platonist. He refused consciously throughout a lifetime to use the word "beauty" in his poetry. He was rooted in the here and now, the actual and the real, and it is easy to see that Frost belongs in the Aristotelian camp. He was not, of course, like Aristotle. Aristotle, while being almost everything else as a thinker, was not a poet. But Frost was also not at all like Shelley. It might be interesting for a moment to compare them. Shelley plucked poetry out of the air, as it were. He was protean, fertile, variable, quick, malleable. Frost is nothing like this. His poetry is rocklike, not ebullient; quiet, not wild; factual, not hallucinated; solid, not evanescent; relevant to things, not creating a dream world; rational, not irrational; well tempered, incapable of what the Greeks called divine frenzy; plausible, not an extremist; well grounded, not aerial; given to quatrains, couplets, and other set forms, not inventing new measures; recording man deep and sure, not strange and high. (p. 198)

The remarkable thing is that throughout his long, fruitful life Frost was able to write so many masterful poems, so consistently, and with so little deviation from the central excellence of his early work. He modestly said that he only wanted a few poems that men will not wish to get rid of; the few are, in fact, many. And no doubt men will be saying them "ages and ages hence." It may be that some of his attraction lies in the fact that urban man longs to remember a closer association he had with nature. . . . Certainly some of his attraction lies in the rare ability he has of appealing both to unsophisticated and to sophisticated readers of poetry. He cuts across all classes, is a classless poet. Children and young students can understand him; at the same time he appeals to the most learned men in many professions due to the subtlety of his thought. He is at once simple and profound. He has great range of interest and great breadth of technical resource. I have indicated repeatedly that his natural bias is in favor of this world; he engages us totally in what is commonly known and felt to be reality, and this may be his greatest gift. He is more of a realist than he is an idealist, as he is more a localist than an internationalist. But let me philosophize.

The brutal fact is that no man knows whether there is anything beyond death. This is a prime baffling fact of existence. Let us suppose that there is nothing to life but appearance, nothing to death but the appearance of death and therefore obviously no life after death. If this is the true state of things, then Robert Frost's poetry becomes more valuable than if this were not true. The fact that we do not know adds to the fascination of his ideas and to the potency of the poetical charge of his poems. For then we will have to admire him for his robust stronghearted resistance to any idea of life after death. We will have to salute him for persistent doubt. (pp. 199-200)

However, a deep idea in the world is that there is something beyond it; a deep look at appearance will see right through it that there is something behind or beyond the realm of appearance; an idea as ancient and persistent as man is that there are ultimate mysteries beyond our mortality, that God exists, that there may be life after death. One generation of men rules that there can be no life on any other planet, another generation holds that the mathematical probabilities are that there must be life beyond what we can see. There are notions of eternal recurrence in Oriental religions, the notion of Redemption in Christianity. If these ideas are true, if reality is not in appearances, but must include what does not appear, and if reason is not the highest faculty of man, but intuition is, then we are at liberty to adjust the value we set on Frost's poetry according to our own most intimate values.

Societies have a natural way of preserving their own images in literature. Frost is one of the vital poetic spokesmen of our time. Our society and our culture are sufficiently like his presentation of the meaning of life so that many Americans can read him with conviction.

Robert Frost is large in scope. He teaches us courage in the face of the enigmas of existence. We feel that he wears no mask and speaks the truth directly, and that his truth, if not the whole truth, is worthy of our serious, steadfast, and continuing love. (pp. 200-01)

> *Richard Eberhart, "Robert Frost: His Personality" (originally a speech delivered at the San Francisco Public Library on October 28, 1964), in* The Southern Review *(copyright, 1966, by Richard Eberhart), Vol. II, No. 4, Autumn, 1966 (and reprinted in his* Of Poetry and Poets, *University of Illinois Press, 1979, pp. 179-201.*

RANDOLPH PERAZZINI

Robert Frost was a man of many voices, the most elusive of which may be the lyric "I" of the New England poet-farmer. Believing that "the colloquial is the root of every good poem," and wanting as a corollary to bespeak American individualism and daring, he strove to be accessible without compromising his integrity as a serious, American poet. To do so he had to remain recalcitrantly local: "You can't be universal without being provincial, can you? It's like trying to embrace the wind," he said in a 1916 interview. Literally, of course, his locality is New England; figuratively, it is poetry's traditional themes—love, sorrow, death, nature, aloneness, art—and its traditional forms. It was a daring gamble to approach so near the mediocre and conventional, using them as a spacecraft uses gravitational fields to sling his poems at the last moment into striking newness that reveals what we have always known without seeing. A daring gamble, yes, but as he said, one could do worse. The burden is on him, therefore, to use not only the tension inherent in strict poetic form—the striking of "dramatic tones of meanings . . . across the rigidity of a limited meter"—but also the tension generated by the convergence of the poetic tradition, particularly the American and the modern and the highly individual talent. Tensions in his poetry redeem the miracle at the heart of the ordinary in any number of ways: in the masterly ear for rhythm and sound that is apparent not only in a *tour de force* like "Tree at My Window," but also in the spring of a line like "So was I once myself a swinger of birches"; in the imaginative brilliance of the controlling metaphors in poems like "West-

Running Brook'' and ''All Revelation''; in the challenges he sets himself in the organization of his books—the way pairs of poems play off each other in the ''Over Back'' section of *West-Running Brook,* or one metaphor develops another in the ''One or Two'' section of *A Witness Tree.* Most essentially, however, the poems create their tension by being dramatic. Even seemingly simple lyrics like ''The Road Not Taken'' and ''Stopping by Woods'' are dramatic monologues revolving around a concrete situation which the speaker shapes into instants of human meaning.

The drama of Frost's poetry also creates the second kind of tension mentioned above. Because of the modernist environment in which he worked, his traditionalism constantly tempts the reader to take him for granted. Frost took advantage of this tendency to nurture a public image which helped him stake out his poetic territory. By playing the role of the New England bard, he plays off the nineteenth century American tradition, not only to make it new, but to make it. This first encounter wins him the position from which he confronts living in the twentieth century. He can be read simply, and enjoyed (at least in his best work), and he would not dismiss the reader for whom ''The Death of the Hired Man'' is no more than a good sad story. But of the reader who seeks a richer understanding, he demands a willingness to sustain complex attitudes and perceptions, to keep hold of the earth even while straining toward the stars. I ''like the middle way,'' he said in a 1923 interview, ''as I like to talk to the man who walks the middle way with me.'' To balance oneself in the middle way is to be fully human. It helps to be versed in country things. In them we find not only the knowledge that the impersonal and irresistible workings of nature grind all human things back to the soil from which they came, but also the recognition that consciousness creates a condition which separates man from nature and demands a continuous effort to wrest ''a momentary stay'' against the process. So by keeping to the middle way, by insisting on the absolute necessity of making do with the limitations available, Frost paradoxically affirms from first to last the tragic dignity and heroism of everyday life. And that affirmation—all the stronger because it is made in the face of the same chaos that sent Yeats to the spirits and Eliot to church—sets Frost apart from the modern tradition out of which he springs. He is, as it were, the west-running brook of modern poetry. (pp. 332-33)

> *Randolph Perazzini, in* The Midwest Quarterly *(copyright, 1977, by The Midwest Quarterly, Kansas State College of Pittsburg), Spring, 1977.*

ROBERT B. THOMPSON

Coming in his final collection, *In the Clearing,* ''Accidentally on Purpose'' is a philosophical dispensation for the aged Frost. As such, it describes the fundamental uncertainty that underlies his post-romantic individuality. He admits the universe is ''but the Thing of things, / The things but balls all going round in rings,'' but attributes to ''They'' the belief that ''all was rolling blind / Till accidentally it hit on mind''; that, in fact, ''the Omnibus / Had no real purpose till it got to us.''

The fourth stanza indicates what appears, at first glance, to be Frost's denial of such a view: ''Never believe it. At the very worst / It must have had the purpose from the first / To produce purpose as the fitter bred: / We were just purpose coming to a head.'' Considered in light of the earlier poetry,

how are we to take this admonition to ''Never believe it''? Has the poet gleamed some producer of purpose outside himself, or is he only offsetting ''their'' theory with one of his own design? Does he mean never believe those who claim there is no real purpose because they are wrong, or is he in fact saying never believe such a truth because—to echo Eliot in ''Burnt Norton''—''human kind / Cannot bear very much reality''? At least two things favor this second view. First of all, being ''the very worst'' suggests that Frost's theory is merely one explanation among several possibilities. That he chooses the *worst* indicates not a willingness to believe its truthfulness, but only a crusty refusal to entertain the opposing view. Furthermore, his attitude in the next stanza implies an utter indifference towards the truth; he would leave to ''scientific wits'' to find out whose purpose it was, while asserting: ''Grant me intention, purpose, and design— / That's near enough for me to the Divine.''

The difference between this position which grants ''intention, purpose, and design'' and that which imagines ''all was rolling blind / Till accidentally it hit on mind'' is psychological rather than philosophical: Frost has compensated his realization of the accidental nature of the universe with a simple statement of disbelief. That disbelief represents a darkly romantic response to an ontological point of view which would, if sustained, elevate the individual to the role of creator, while at the same time destroying the essential meaning of his creation. More than this, the disbelief provides the basis for an uncertainty which signalizes the poet's move from romanticism towards existentialism.

> *Robert B. Thompson, ''Frost's 'Accidentally on Purpose','' in* The Explicator *(copyright © 1978 by Helen Dwight Reed Educational Foundation), Winter, 1978, p. 17.*

LAURENCE GOLDSTEIN

Frost considered ''Kitty Hawk'' the most important of his later poems, and on speaking engagements around the country often cited this passage as a culminating statement of his natural philosophy. It is a buoyant endorsement of the *via affirmativa,* reminiscent in principle of Whitman's progressive ideal, though Frost's clipped verse line discourages comparison with the bard of the pioneers. (p. 42)

Though Frost, true to type, recommends that his public hasten in ''getting thought expressed,'' he waited till the end of his career before writing the poem of Kitty Hawk. He tried once, in the 1930's, but after much whittling and revision, ''The Wrights' Biplane'' emerged as an undistinguished four line epigram. (p. 43)

Frost guides the reader of ''Kitty Hawk'' toward the awareness that he had reached by the time of composition. The authorial voice has the colloquial playfulness of Frost's lyrics, but it has also an insistent force of elevated diction unique even in the late work. A poem containing references to ''Alastor,'' ''Raleigh,'' ''Götterdämmerung,'' ''Lilliputians,'' ''Catullus,'' and the *''mens animi''* and which uses words like aliquid, nomenclature, apropos, and epithet seeks an audience accustomed to abstract thought and wide reading about matters of cultural significance. Frost's theme lies beyond the reach of untutored simplicity. Faced with the complexity of an historical imperative, Frost reaches deliberately for a higher order of word and thought, as Crane did in his long historical poem. (p. 45)

In "Kitty Hawk" Frost exchanges the spatial metaphors. The poet is depicted as inescapably egocentric. The range of his concern cannot easily extend beyond the immediate circumference of his beloved objects, whose compelling reality contains his vision and cinches it close. "The universe may or may not be very immense," Frost writes in "Skeptic,"

> As a matter of fact there are times when I am apt
> To feel it close in tight against my sense
> Like a caul in which I was born and still am wrapped.

The poet is the real skeptic, more often setting boundaries than transcending them. Metrical and rhyming patterns are examples of formal limitations he gladly imposes on himself, and though these are, in a sense, risks of spirit in substantiation, they contrast to the risks of the Understanding as it constructs mechanical wings for longer journeys deeper into the undefined.

"Kitty Hawk" is a kind of belated penance which Frost offers to share with his reading public. Poet and audience alike lack the true or prophetic understanding of historical events because both have been insufficiently trained in the quotidian coping ("Action is the word") of a frontier people. . . . Meditative it is not (Frost delights in the rhyme of meditation and stagnation); Americans more often seek to know the spiritual meaning of an event long after it has passed into history. History is an unending process, however, and even the poetic reconsideration remains of practical use. "Kitty Hawk" is also a warning to the nation which stands in 1953 upon the brink of penetration into the infinities. Frost of course endorses the aims of the space program. . . . (pp. 47-8)

Writing "Kitty Hawk" at the end of his career, Frost, his nation's unofficial Poet Laureate, aligned his vision with the orthodox American view of social evolution. Poets remain earthbound, yearning to penetrate out far and in deep. But in fact science, our greatness, can best play the heroic role which Fate has given the superior in spirit. . . . Those aptly named mechanics on Kill Devil Hill did win a race against the poet, and, in a larger sense, against poetry itself, but by saying so in 1953 Frost at least outran the astronauts, planting the Imagination's soiled flag in advance. (p. 49)

> Laurence Goldstein, "'Kitty Hawk' and the Question of American Destiny," in The Iowa Review (copyright © 1978, by The University of Iowa), Vol. 9, No. 1 (Winter, 1978), pp. 41-9.

* * *

FUENTES, Carlos   1928-

A Mexican novelist, playwright, short story writer, screenwriter, essayist, and critic, Fuentes creates prose noted for its innovative language and narrative technique. His concern for affirming a viable Mexican identity is revealed in his use of the history and legends of the Mexican past, from the myths of the Aztecs to the Mexican Revolution, which he uses allegorically and thematically in his narratives. (See also *CLC*, Vols. 3, 8, 10, and *Contemporary Authors*, Vols. 69-72.)

ALAN CHEUSE

Carlos Fuentes, Mexico's most versatile novelist, has looked the spy novel in the eye and produced a controversial world-class thriller. *The Hydra Head* reads as though it

has been freshly minted out of the turmoil and subterranean intrigue of current world affairs. . . .

[The] reader scarcely need suspend a single breath of willing disbelief. The CIA, the Israeli spy service, undercover Arab operatives and the ingenious but untested Mexican secret agents, sometimes in the person of the same (double or triple) operatives, clash violently in these intriguingly plotted pages. . . .

Fuentes skillfully conducts the reader through these wonderfully intricate narrative maneuvers, flying us from an intensely rendered Mexico City to Houston . . . , to Galveston, Coatzacoalcos, and back again to Mexico City in the company of the confused but credible Maldonado and a cast of menacing but attractive villains. Fuentes, however, is more than just the Ian Fleming of underdevelopment. In addition to creating the familiar atmosphere of compelling duplicity that characterizes the best of this variety of writing, he works another series of changes on the fictive motifs that have marked his literary career from the beginning: the ambiguous burden of social class among the Latin American bourgeoisie; the terrors of multiple personality and the masks of consciousness; and the struggle between conquerors and conquered in the dark night of the Mexican soul.

The Hydra Head is thus a tour de force, but unlike, say, Borges's detective fictions, beneath its impeccable surface lurks serious social content that adds incomparably to its intensity as narrative. Like Graham Greene in his "entertainments" and Gore Vidal in his science fiction, Fuentes has sounded his major obsessions in a minor key. The fence between fancy and imagination comes down while the charge that electrifies still remains in the air. (p. 39)

> Alan Cheuse, in The New Republic (reprinted by permission of The New Republic; © 1978 The New Republic, Inc.), December 23 & 30, 1978.

ANTHONY BURGESS

Early on in ["The Hydra Head"] an elevator attendant looks, as if for the first time, at the design on a Mexican peso—the eagle strangling the serpent. Toward the end, the narrator fantasticates the image in the service of explaining what the secret agent's trade is all about. The serpent is a hydra, and the agent is but one head of the hydra. Cut off that head and a thousand will replace it. The eagle is two-headed. "One head is called the CIA and the other the KGB. Two heads, but only one body. Almost the Holy Trinity of our age. . . . In serving one head we serve the other and vice-versa. There's no escape. The Hydra of our passions is trapped in the talons of the bicephalous eagle."

Or, put it another way, . . . the secret agent is trapped in a Manichean system in which there is an opposition of X and Y but not of good and evil. In dedicating his book to the memories of Conrad Veidt, Sydney Greenstreet, Peter Lorre and Claude Rains, Carlos Fuentes half lulls us into the expectation of a mere thriller, and the movie-buffery of the hero, Felix Maldonado, confirms that we ought not to expect much more than blood, the chase, the pedantic loquacity of Greenstreet villains. But the setting is a contemporary Mexico City drawn with the pencil of rage, and the issue is Mexican oil: "Like the Hydra, the oil is reborn, multiplied, from a single severed head. . . ."

Dr. Fuentes is a distinguished writer, and distinction resides even in the mandatory scenes of violence, the enforced plastic surgery that robs [the protagonist] Felix of his identity, the philosophical expatiations (complete with quotations from Gide and Kirkegaard) we now expect from our distinguished villains, the ridiculous coincidences, the Greene-type observations: "The Indians, so handsome in the lands of their origin, so slim and spotless and secret, in the city became ugly, filthy, and bloated by carbonated drinks."

Perhaps the true distinction of the novel resides in its having forever dispensed with the possibilities of the spy thriller as a serious form.

> Anthony Burgess, "Mexican Thriller," in The New York Times Book Review (© 1979 by The New York Times Company; reprinted by permission), January 7, 1979, p. 11.

DONALD A. YATES

Fuentes has a background in international politics and a political commitment that, traditionally, few North American writers bring to their work. Moreover, he is the author of the broad-canvas account of the Mexican experience, *Where the Air Is Clear* (1959), and the brilliant *Death of Artemio Cruz* (1962), one of the finest Mexican novels of our time. Possibly, there is no other writer who so accurately perceives the Mexican character, as well as the international role that the nation is likely to play in coming decades.

So when he undertakes to write a fictional account of the "first adventure of the Mexican secret service," one cannot fail to take note of his uncommon credentials. In fact, the great merit of *The Hydra Head* is that Fuentes has raised a popular literary form—the espionage novel—to the level of high art. He has done this through his inspired, always incisive evocation of Mexico on the point of emerging as one of the great oil-producing nations of the world.

The novel deals, quite simply, with a plot to keep the recently discovered and extensive Mexican oil reserves for the Mexicans—away from the encroaching demands of the U.S., and away from economic entanglements with Arab and Israeli oil interests. (pp. 1, 3)

A powerful reality occupies the center of *The Hydra Head*: the discovery of the Mexican petroleum fields at about the time of the Arab oil embargo is factual. . . .

But, as in most of Fuentes' work, there is also much artifice. He is a tireless experimenter with narrative techniques and points of view. We discover, for example, after some 100 pages that the seemingly omniscient narrator of Maldonado's story is, in fact, his chief, Timon, who has "reconstructed" the information reported to him by his agent. This tends to strain credibility, and the breaking point is approached when we are told that the last seven chapters are Timon's conjectures regarding what Maldonado will probably do when he finally realizes how he has been used. It really seems an unnecessary gimmick.

Also, I'm puzzled over one matter. Why does Maldonado return to play his role, under a new identity, in the planned presidential assassination on September 31? I am aware that Fuentes has stated that his narrators reserve the right to leave certain questions unanswered, certain ambiguities unresolved. Well, if that's a part of the game, so be it.

Characteristically there are many things "going on" in a

Fuentes novel. *The Hydra Head* is dedicated to the memory of four actors who specialized in espionage film roles—Conrad Veidt, Sidney Greenstreet, Peter Lorre and Claude Rains and we recognize all of them in characters Fuentes has created here. There are fond echoes of Chandler and Ambler, too, and what might be the first "hard-boiled" Mexican dialogue. . . .

All in all, it's a dazzling performance—one of the most successful books of Fuentes' 25-year career. (p. 3)

> Donald A. Yates, "Fuentes' First-Class Thriller," in Book World (© 1979, The Washington Post), January 14, 1979, pp. 1, 3.

REVEREND JAMES M. MURPHY

For a legion of reasons [*The Hydra Head*] was both difficult to read and hard to put down. Should it be raised to the cinema screen, only a Fellini or a Kubrick could direct it and for only an audience in a narcotized high. This reviewer neither enjoyed the book nor could find himself capable of a favorable review.

The problems are many: the writing style; the arrangement of the book; the constant, though not clever, shift of character from one charade to another and from one place to another. Kafkaesque, maybe, but should Kafka write a spy story for today's clientele? . . .

Things are never what they seem to be and why never makes sense. The text jumps not merely with "Alice in Wonderland" quotes but with the unreality of Alice's world itself. . . .

Though the book purports to be a spy story and an assassination thriller, it truly is a long nightmare, one experienced after a rich meal mixed with wine. Fuentes is no Le Carré, Graham Greene or Forsyth. As the title suggests, all is many headed and so will be the average espionage addict at the end!

Why did I write in the beginning that the book was hard to put aside? Because I could not wait to finish it! (p. 385)

> Reverend James M. Murphy, in Best Sellers (copyright © 1979 Helen Dwight Reid Educational Foundation), March, 1979.

VICTORIA NEUMARK

Fuentes's meta-thriller [*The Hydra Head*] takes the Arab-Israeli conflict as its paradigm of political dirty tricks; Mexican oil-fields, Mexican men and their passions are no more than the organisms on which violation and revenge feed. However many heads the human Hydra grows, 'the two-headed eagle laughs and devours' them.

This double-headed eagle—America/Russia—may be the final control on Felix, *The Hydra Head*'s 'unconscious hero', but it takes him a long, convoluted journey to find it out. A Mexican convert to Judaism, bearing an uncanny resemblance to Diego Velasquez, Felix one day steps out of a taxi full of hidden assignations and into a lost identity. No one in his office at the Ministry of Economic Affairs knows who he is. The parallel with Kafka, though, is fleeting: Fuentes shares something of the bite of K's narrative, but offers more fierce gusto—as well as more sex. (p. 334)

The Hydra Head is gripping, not least because of its sharply focused political discussions, whose dialectic is reminiscent of *The Magic Mountain*. (p. 335)

Victoria Neumark, in New Statesman *(© 1979
The Statesman & Nation Publishing Co. Ltd.),
March 9, 1979.*

G

GARNER, Hugh 1913-1979

Garner was a Canadian novelist, short story writer, and journalist. Urban life of the lower-middle classes is the background for such novels as *Cabbagetown* and *The Silence on the Shore*. His memoirs, *One Damn Thing after Another*, although flawed, do throw an interesting slant on his experiences and feelings as a proletarian writer. (See also *Contemporary Authors*, Vols. 69-72.)

CLAUDE T. BISSELL

[A] realistic novel that makes use of an accumulation of small, precise detail and concentrates on the plight of the little man is Hugh Garner's *Storm Below*. It is the account of the last four days of the voyage of a Canadian corvette, part of the escort force of a convoy proceeding from Londonderry to Newfoundland during the early spring of 1943. Although this is a war novel, Mr. Garner does not look outward to the big sensational facts of the conflict. . . . Rather, Mr. Garner wants to reveal to us the tiny, but intricate world of the corvette. To this end, he gives us an abundance of technical description and, more to the point, a full gallery of human portraits, embracing almost every naval rank and a wide assortment of Canadian types. In order to give movement and depth to what might have been an extended exercise in description, he has, first of all, devised a central situation that reaches out and touches the life of the entire ship. A young ordinary seaman is accidentally killed, and the captain decides to set aside the tradition of the sea and to keep the body on board for burial at St. Johns. The decision is an unfortunate one: ancient superstitions are aroused; the *esprit de corps* of the crew is endangered; and conflicts and antipathies long latent are brought with naked ugliness into the open. These conflicts and antipathies are not merely personal; they are entangled (here we have the second means of enriching the material) with the racial and political prejudices that are part of the society from which the men have come.

Storm Below, then, has its full quota of human misery and twisted passion. In one sense, the novel properly concludes with the burial of the lad whose death had threatened to turn the final days of the voyage into an ugly nightmare. The funeral service and burial, envisaged by the captain as a last tender gesture from the living to the dead, turns into meaningless protocol carried out in a make-shift manner. And yet *Storm Below* does not have a depressing effect.

The reason for this lies partially in the fact that Mr. Garner from time to time brings out the *camaraderie* and the warm sense of solidarity that come to men in a group under the stress of a simple, easily recognizable danger. More essentially it lies in Mr. Garner's considerable power to suggest the expansive quality of life. His characters are carefully selected so as to represent types and points of view; yet their uncensored speech, which is not without eloquence and cleansing wit, gives them a significance beyond the general and the representational.

Storm Below strikes me as so far the best Canadian novel based upon war experience. Its defect is primarily one of construction: there are too many points of interest that tend to pull away from the central situation. Still this is a minor blemish in a first novel that has so many shining virtues. (pp. 267-68)

> Claude T. Bissell, *in* University of Toronto Quarterly *(reprinted by permission of University of Toronto Press), April, 1950.*

MIRIAM WADDINGTON

Hugh Garner has often been praised for his good heart when it is really his good ear and sharp eye that deserve our admiration. It is no use to praise him for his compassion because it is a matter of grace whether a writer has it or not, and a matter of cultural conditioning whether a reader values it or not. But a good ear for dialogue, speech rhythms, and local semantic nuances cannot be brushed aside as easily as mere goodness of heart.

The way a novelist hears words and uses them, has to do with all the complex problems of language, and even of culture. Speech is a form of action, and in the area of dialogue —which is action between characters—Garner stands out among his Canadian contemporaries. (p. 72)

Garner also makes a completely selfconscious and natural use of local place names, brand names and celebrity names. Any Canadian reader will easily recognize, scattered through Garner's pages, his own favourite beer, political party and TV show; he'll even find his most familiar moral dilemmas. And if anyone is still searching for that elusive now-you-have-it-now-you-don't Canadian identity he need search no further. Canada may claim two or more identities, but Garner conveys at least one of them through the conversations, attitudes and secrets of the characters who inhabit his small town. He is also the only writer I know of who has managed to capture what E. K. Brown called the mysterious and obnoxious quality of Toronto, and he certainly catches the furtive suspiciousness of its outlying small towns. (pp. 72-3)

Garner's concern with truth places his work in the realm of social realism. The typicality and representativeness of his characters reinforces this literary position. I am defining realism according to George Lukacs, who suggests that in realist novels, man is portrayed as a social being and not an isolated one, as he appears to the modern existentialist view. Lukacs has pointed out that in the modern naturalist novel, social norms no longer exist, while collective values have been replaced by a myriad of individual ones. In addition, the modern novel more and more denies the existence of objective reality; it has moved the theatre of human action from the outside world to some inner stage. In such a world time cannot exist; there is no past, no history and there can therefore be no future, no hope. There is only the eternal static present in which nothing can change except the individual's states of consciousness.

In realist fiction, however, characters change as a result of their encounters with objective reality. The world acts on them, and dynamically they also act on the world. This happens in *A Nice Place to Visit,* even though it happens in a very odd and surreptitious way. (pp. 73-4)

> Miriam Waddington, "Garner's Good Ear," in Canadian Literature, *Autumn, 1971, pp. 72-5.*

DOUG FETHERLING

[Garner] has found the right title: *One Damn Thing After Another;* for [he] has spent his years stumbling day-to-day, like the rest of us, through the personal and public hells that make up most ordinary lives. The title also says something about the way in which the book has been put together. . . .

Aside from a frequent overlapping of subject matter, the thread that links his work . . . is a belief in the old freelancer's maxim, "Waste Nothing." While his stories and to a lesser extent his novels are spare in style, they are rich in small geographical and historical details that seem relevant because they help to create moods. His journalism is likewise littered with eccentric information (though often for its own sake) and tends as well to be repetitious. To the extent, then, that an autobiography should be the distillation of a whole career, this one serves its purpose: as he has wavered always between cheap work and good writing, as though unable to find his right level, so he does in this book, as though unable to decide if his past has been worth the trouble. Little here has been wasted and much has been included that should have been forgotten; and so much from both categories is needlessly repeated that *The Same Damn Things Again and Again* would have been an apt title, too.

Garner has written well here, but only in patches, and these invariably are the most revealing of his personality. There is a chunk about his childhood which in a few thousand words puts that period in sharper focus than the whole of the novel *Cabbagetown.* (p. 40)

A great deal of *One Damn Thing After Another* is taken up with his life as a salesman of what he has written rather than as creator of it. . . . He writes hardly at all about himself in artistic terms except to call himself a proletarian,

which I suppose he still is, and an anti-intellectual, which he is in the usual but not literal sense. Most of the remarks about his contemporaries are slurs or simple unopinionated anecdotes. . . . Anti-intellectual means dummy, which Garner never has been. He's just an intellectual misanthrope, which makes him fresh and rather appealing.

He has always been first of all a storyteller, in the simple sense, but in this book his own story is none too well related. The work contains all the things for which memoirs are enjoyable but not in the proper combinations or strengths. As for personal anecdotes, there are many good ones, most of them arising from his fondness for drink, which he says the navy instilled in him. . . . But one has the feeling throughout that there is much more he cannot or won't remember.

What is more disturbing, however, is that sometimes bitterness and venom spill from his pen and blot out whatever it was that actually happened. He writes about being interned during the war with so many veiled references and so much hatred that we know the place was hell. But that's all we know. Was there torture? Were there beatings? All Garner says of the guards is, "I hope God killed them all with cancer." The memories are obviously too painful to be given in detail, and perhaps a good deal of his life has not ripened enough yet for dispassionate retelling.

That what he really feels as a writer is also too private must be the reason why he speaks only of "this writing caper." . . . What he does tell, however, he tells with complete honesty; he has practically no *égoisme dans la fraternité,* only this running paradox about his professionalism as a writer. He points out several times, for instance, how clean his manuscripts are, in contrast with those of others he names and puts down for it. Yet *One Damn Thing After Another* is riddled with mistakes of fact and spelling as well as repetition. (pp. 41, 43)

The only time this tactic works at all well (and the only time it is defensible, because the material is nowhere else between covers) is with a series of three articles done in 1959 for the *Star Weekly* about returning to the battlefields of Spain. . . . This is good history, journalism and travel writing combined, though the ending suffers from appearing to have been stuck on carelessly.

At the end of the book, in the long segment about having sold reprint rights to this and a movie option on that, Garner does two curious things. First, he talks about how the writing of *One Damn Thing After Another* came about and progressed (it began as a file for McGraw-Hill's promotion department). Then he conducts an imaginary interview with himself in order to work in, before closing, anything he might have forgotten to say. These are fairly avant-garde things to do and, like many avant-garde things in writing, strangely boyish. But this is fitting conclusion to the work as a whole, since throughout Garner has been rather adolescent. He has been bitter and pouting, taking great offense at old affronts others would have dismissed years ago, and he has bubbled like the kids on television with no cavities about small and medium-sized successes which other writers of his reputation would have been embarrassed to put forward. (p. 43)

"In my sixtieth year," Garner writes, "I sometimes paused and wondered how I'd ever survived . . . " This is standard sentiment for survivors like Garner and particularly for those who are loners. Then he goes on and on about rights and permissions, editors' lunches, petty kindnesses and magnanimous insults and the apparent glee with which he barges into publishing houses demanding to see the president. Suddenly, the cumulative effect hitting you like delayed action vodka, it becomes clear. Hugh Garner, to some very real and very large extent not imagined before, has written eight novels, four books of stories and all the rest, including this autobiographical hodgepodge, because writing is the only surcease for loneliness, and loneliness simple and painful is what his life story has really been about. (p. 44)

> Doug Fetherling, "Memoirs of a Famous Survivor," in Saturday Night (copyright © 1973 by Saturday Night), *November, 1973, pp. 40-4.*

GEORGE WOODCOCK

The title—*One Damn Thing after Another*—says a great deal about the shape of the book, for, compared with Garner's novels and stories, it is unexpectedly loose and rambling. At first the apparent formlessness disconcerts one, but in one way it is a very natural way to write a book of memoirs, the thoughts and recollections put down as they come into the mind. It is, indeed, so much like a man talking that, as one reads, Garner's gravelly voice seems to sound in the ear and his compact cocky figure to take shape before the mind's eye.

One of the good things about this approach, from the viewpoint of any writer who will follow with a more formal biography of Garner, is the fact that he gives abundant detail on his publication record, even down to what happened to individual short stories. Another is that when he has written a good magazine piece about an episode in his life, Garner resurrects it instead of rewriting the incident from a later and vaguer perspective. (pp. 95-6)

An interesting aspect of Garner's present attitude is his retreat from the political engagement which led him to Spain; it is not the same thing as a repudiation of his past. (p. 96)

So here is Garner, warts and all, with no attempt to hide the bouts of drinking that alternate with long periods of severe and sober work . . . , with no attempt either to mitigate his vanity or to beautify his occasional fits of loud aggressiveness. All this goes with the refusal to give *One Damn Thing after Another* a form that would falsify the experiences. A professional writer's life, after all, *is* "one damn thing after another", since only those with independent means or university jobs can afford to turn down the hack work which the ordinary professional has to accept. The great thing in that life is never to let down your prose, and always to learn what you can in the way of facts and techniques which can be retained for better uses; these rules Garner has at most times followed, and so his periods of hack writing have hurt him no more than they hurt Defoe or Dickens. He emerges from *One Damn Thing after Another* as a writer dedicated and obsessed—and whenever I am asked to state in a word the secret of literary success, that word is "obsession". (pp. 96-7)

> George Woodcock, in Canadian Literature, *Winter, 1974.*

DOUG FETHERLING

Hugh Garner's 1950 novel, *Cabbagetown*, his second book, has dominated his reputation. It was a straight-forward nat-

uralistic story of a young man's progress, away from poverty and toward radicalism, in the 1930s. . . .

That Garner almost always writes about the present, that he writes about a social sensibility rather than a geographic or political stance, that half of his books have been published in the 1970s—all these facts run contrary to the accepted view that Garner has never quite managed to dispel. An important aspect of his new novel, *The Intruders*, is that he seems to say, "Oh, what the hell, there's no use arguing. I'll give them what they want." On the surface of it, *The Intruders* is a sort of *Cabbagetown Revisited*. (p. 60)

[In] *The Intruders*, he surveys what has become of the neighbourhood since his days there.

In the 1970s, TV unit managers, stained-glass artists, lawyers, CBC story editors, and other marginal types have purchased old Cabbagetown slums and sandblasted them, installing skylights and uncomfortable furniture. These are the people and the atmosphere Garner is attacking. Since Garner delights in making the middle class nervous, it's not illogical that he should let himself go and have some fun. And this he does. *The Intruders* at times harks back to the lesser works of Upton Sinclair. It is only slightly more a work of fiction than it is a letter-to-the-editor in the form of a novel. (pp. 60-1)

By now, people who care for Garner's work know who they are and those who don't care for it know that they don't and why. This, like all his other books, is a work of realism but not necessarily a realistic book. The writing is of a higher grade than that of the detective novels he's been publishing recently. . . . The real failure of the book, even within the province Garner has established for himself, is that the author deals scathingly and at length with people he does not understand. That's not to say that, if he did comprehend, he would treat them any differently or that he should treat them differently. It's only to say that he tries in *The Intruders*, as in most of his work, to paint a picture through masses of tiny detail but that, in this case, much of the detail is all wrong.

Garner is trying to show that, despite all its protestations to the contrary, Toronto is actually the most class-ridden city on the planet, with the possible exception of Bombay. . . . The way he shows this is not very subtle. He simply lashes out at all the middle class types and their institutions, as though such people *know* that others exist, as though they can be shocked into remembering. Alas, such is not the case in actuality. Toronto looks upon those who aren't middle class Torontonians not as persons apart but as performers hired to entertain them. Attacks always end in frustration, with the villains picking up the heroes' options for another thirteen weeks.

Where Garner really falls down is in dealing with the local political and cultural cabals. The way in which he does so is curious. At times he seems on the verge of turning the book into a *roman à clef*, but just as often he will use the names of actual public personalities. (pp. 61-2)

The Intruders is a grand idea for a Hugh Garner novel but doesn't quite live up to what it promises. The problem is simply that Garner knows more about one side of the tracks than the other. (p. 62)

> Doug Fetherling, "Hugh Garner in Trendy Cabbagetown," in Saturday Night (copyright © 1976 by Saturday Night), *July-August, 1976, pp. 60-2.*

SANDRA MARTIN

Garner is a comfortable writer. Invariably he tells a story that has both a beginning and an end and he uses a style that, while colourful, is devoid of artifice and pretentiousness. Often there is a narrator who speaks with a voice crackling with hard-earned experience. He is a regular guy, one who knows the way of the world. He may be soaked in cynicism and bitterness, nevertheless he is full of compassion for his fellow sufferers. Years ago he would have been in the thick of the story; now he is content to be a voyeur, watching as bullies and snobs get what's coming to them and the meek, bespectacled little guy over in the corner emerges as a hero.

Garner's world, which is almost exclusively urban, is filled with little people. Whether bartenders, clerks, mechanics; prostitutes, drunks, or murderers, the characters are diminished by the sordid pettiness of their lives; they respond physically, often brutally. As the author grows older, so do the characters, precipitating a new series of dilemmas about aging, unachieved goals, and loneliness.

The Legs of the Lame adheres to the ground rules, but with a surfeit of violence. Nine of the 14 stories in the collection deal with death and six are about murders. . . .

The title story is one of the more interesting ones. A rock promoter, Gordon Beaton, is abandoned by his group (named, ironically, "The Flack") with barely the price of a beer. Beaton meets a young faith healer, Clay Burridge, and talks himself into the job of business manager and advance man for the evangelist. All goes well until Burridge loses faith in himself as the interpreter and spokesman for Jesus Christ and quits the evangelical circuit. Garner manipulates our sympathies until we feel sorry for Beaton, the parasite who must find a new host. Beaton responds to his latest misfortune in typical style by getting drunk.

The title is taken from Proverbs: "The legs of the lame are not straight; so is a parable in the mouth of fools." It's a good summation of the characters and themes. Unfortunately, the problems (not to mention the solutions) presented in these stories are as axiomatic as the scripture quoted above. The results are predictable, sometimes trite. (p. 40)

> *Sandra Martin, in* Books in Canada, *March, 1977.*

MICHAEL SOTIRON

Writing a police procedural [*Death in Don Mills*] had its advantages as it allowed Garner to vent his authoritarian and oft-reactionary views on just about everything through the thoughts of his chief character.

The disadvantages, however, are that Garner's indulgences and interjections work to the detriment of his thriller and result in an overly long flaccid book, which too often strays from the central plot and resulted in a remarkably unthrilling book.

Far more insidious, however, than his frequent editorials are some of Garner's obvious assumptions. Throughout the book, Inspector McDumont commits some questionable and other plainly illegal acts, such as intimidation and threats of blackmail, in order "to get the facts". By having McDumont proven "right" (because he does solve the case) and by generally creating a favourable impression of McDumont, these police methods are thereby condoned

and supported. This evident bias in favour of police and their use of repressive methods becomes quite explicit when Garner has the gall to have his McDumont piously mouth the Metro Toronto Police force's slogan: "Yes, Ma'am, we're here to serve and protect." (p. 38)

> *Michael Sotiron, in* Canadian Dimension, *April, 1977.*

* * *

GILLIATT, Penelope 1932-

A British novelist, short story writer, and screenwriter, Gilliatt is perhaps best known as a film and drama critic. Her fiction is noted for its wit, its skillful dialogue, and its cast of clearly drawn and memorable characters. Gilliatt recently left her position as a film critic and writer for *The New Yorker*, a magazine with which she had been affiliated for many years. (See also *CLC*, Vols. 2, 10, and *Contemporary Authors*, Vols. 13-16, rev. ed.)

CATHERINE PETROSKI

Splendid Lives is generally unified by the advanced years of its stories' pivotal characters, who have led lives both very and not so splendid. Because many of these people lie at certain strata peculiar to English society, Americans reading the book will be reminded of how differently the English look upon society as a whole and their respective places in it. The tone of the stories is not entirely sympathetic or positive, though moments of laughter are to be found everywhere in Gilliatt's stories. Old age is anatomized, but held at arm's length, with the result that we have somewhat clinical appraisals of the characters' predicaments.

The predicaments found in *Splendid Lives* are often far from dire. . . . The title story depicts a cousin of Queen Victoria, a ninety-two-year-old retired bishop whose main concern is how to get his prize race horse back on feed. One notable detail about the collection is the appearance of equine images in nearly every story, and those images relate directly to the characters' social status.

But then we have "A Lovely Bit of Wood," with its somber picture of working-class retirement, and "Catering," rendering the tedium and hopelessness of lower-class family life. "Iron Larks" ought to become a definitive statement on how oblivious the academy can be. "Phone-In" is the collection's most adventurous story in terms of form, and in tone the most playful. (pp. 299-300)

In rhythm, idiom, and vocabulary, the language in *Splendid Lives* bears a distinctly British stamp. In voice, these stories emanate from a remote place, and the irony that permeates them results in most characters' being undercut. In scope, the stories imply more than the sum of their parts, for Gilliatt is a master of deceptively simple descriptions: "She was a beauty who lay now in bed wearing her pearls," she says of one of her dowagers. A reader can only marvel at the implications.

What one prefers and what one admires need not be identical, since preferences are questions of taste. The reader who seeks to be emotionally engaged by fiction's people or to be entertained by linguistic fireworks will need to look elsewhere. The reader whose tastes run to the refined, analytic, intellectual approach to fiction and who seeks a high sense of order, meticulous observation, and shrewd assessment of the human condition will find *Splendid Lives* a splendid place. (p. 300)

Catherine Petroski, "Splendour's Variorum," in Prairie Schooner (© 1978 by University of Nebraska Press; reprinted by permission from Prairie Schooner), Fall, 1978, pp. 299-300.

WILLIAM BOYD

[There's a] looseness, an almost decadent lack of direction, in Penelope Gilliatt's *The Cutting Edge*. The narrative hovers around the affection between two often-separated brothers—Benedick and Peregrine, a musician and a writer, respectively down and out in Istanbul and Positano—who are eventually reunited in the compliant arms of Benedick's ex-wife. There's an air of plundered notebooks about the desperately sparkling conversation and the redundant cast of eccentric minor characters, who look suspiciously like rejects from Miss Gilliatt's latest collection of short stories, *Splendid Lives*. At one point she says conversation is like 'the sound of souls buzzing in a glass prison of a world which they cannot escape but still try to understand'. This is all very well, but the chat has to be fairly remarkable if it's to continue to sustain our interest: 'We are the trustees of no culture but our own,' and so on. It's a shame, because Miss Gilliatt's laconic style occasionally creates moments of accurate poignancy which are worth pages of brittle dialogue and recycled *aperçus*. (p. 554)

William Boyd, in New Statesman (© 1978 The Statesman & Nation Publishing Co. Ltd.), October 27, 1978.

EVE ZIBART

Penelope Gilliatt, the acerbic British movie critic for the *New Yorker* . . . , has produced a "novel" [*The Cutting Edge*] by stringing together a series of just the sort of dry martini, upper-crust and stiff-upper-lip character sketches the *New Yorker* is famous for. And like a long bout with dry martinis, it may be fun, but ultimately there's very little nourishment in a handful of olives. . . .

The language of the book is determinedly literary, and often extremely effective; but it is most effective when most succinct. There are quick, glittering sentences ("He began to live in a chill delirium of work") and passages of extraordinary humor, as when Peregrine, who speaks little Italian, attempts to explain to his housekeeper in Positano that he is writing a play in poetry about a homosexual and instead informs her that he is composing a tragedy about spinach.

Gilliatt is keen to follow through with her investigation of "emotional links," etc. She loads the brothers down with a mirror image—another pair of siblings, these a set of twins, their illegitimate younger half-brothers. She then has Peregrine and Benedick change their hair and even their eye color (via contact lens) to more closely resemble one another. But three-quarters through the book having moved Benedick's ex-wife Joanna in with Peregrine, Gilliatt gives up. We know almost nothing about Joanna, little about why she left Benedick and even less about why she moves in with Peregrine. There is no ending and precious little ambiguous conclusion. When Peregrine says portentously, "I don't know whether you're in love with me because I'm like Benedick or because I'm not like Benedick," Joanna comes back with the one natural retort in the entire book—she tells him to shut up.

Eve Zibart, "Gilliatt's Glittering Surfaces," in Book World—The Washington Post (© 1979, The Washington Post), January 21, 1979, p. G3.

ANNE TYLER

[Ambiguity] is the subject of ["The Cutting Edge"]. There exist meaningful characters . . . who cannot be considered clearly right or clearly wrong, and meaningful events that will always be murky, ill organized and impossible to pigeonhole.

On occasion, "The Cutting Edge" appears to be narrated from the viewpoint of ambiguity personified. The two brothers, Peregrine and Benedick Corbett, start out as Brother A. and Brother B., owing to a delay in their christening, and they continue through life closer than most married couples, one dealing with what the other will not, so that there is a kind of interlocking of functions. . . . They are seldom even in the same country, but their fond, witty letters leap continents and they have the rare ability to resume their relationship instantly whenever they're brought together again. Inevitably, they both love the same woman. It's while attempting to sort out the triangle that Peregrine and Benedick learn that some things are not capable of being sorted out; their lives will forever contain a number of blurred boundaries.

Penelope Gilliatt's fiction has always been brisk and economical, but never as stripped-down as it is here. She circles a scene with a quick swath of words, cutting an empty shape in the air for the reader to fill in. It's not that there are no details, but that the details describe something slightly off-center—a side character, a spot on the canvas where we weren't even looking. There is a sense of speed. . . .

The brothers are described, on occasion, but so scantily that when they try to assume each other's physical characteristics, at a crucial stage in the plot, we almost fail to notice. Perhaps, therefore, the scantiness was deliberate—one more proof that, as Peregrine observes, truth comes and goes "as if it were mercury sliding about on a tray." But it seems a mistake when the reader loses great chunks of time flipping back and forth in the book, trying to recall who was originally stocky and who was thin, who wore glasses and who did not.

At any rate, once the adjustment is made and the rhythm has grown familiar, it begins to feel right. The nearly epigrammatic style suits the brothers, who view the world with a kind of distant amusement, and the style points up the abstractedness of their lives in comparison to those of the characters around them, each of whom is vividly described. . . . The brothers themselves—often lonely, at loose ends, wandering in foreign countries, dealing with various sorts of sorrow and bewilderment in their own wry manner—drift through their story like those fairytale heroes who go off to seek their fortunes and encounter any number of astounding sights along the way.

In fact, "The Cutting Edge," with its breathtaking spareness and its swoops through time, might very well be read as a particularly fascinating fairytale, which makes all the more wonderful the book's unfairytale-like thesis: "Who will ever know which brother she was angry with and which one she loved? Both, in both cases, it seemed, as is the way of things."

Anne Tyler, "Brother A and Brother B," in The New York Times Book Review (© 1979 by The New York Times Company; reprinted by permission), January 21, 1979, p. 14.

DAPHNE MERKIN

The Cutting Edge is, in a word, insufferable. It is self-congratulatory in the way of novels that presume shared allegiances with the reader, without bothering to establish them. It is not entirely clear to me, moreover, what Gilliatt had in mind with her portrayals of Peregrine and Benedick; perhaps she thought she was illuminating the fallacies of a populist age through the brothers' tetchy resistance to them. Unfortunately, the two are less rugged individualists than priggish separatists and Gilliatt's fatuous elitism is made to stand in for more valid protestations. Finally, she confuses issues of *taste* with issues of morality, and her confusion is indicative of the novel's ultimately shallow level of preoccupation: "Values can't be measured against each other. They're incommensurable. They allow no reduction below themselves. One may prefer Dante to Shakespeare, or claret to champagne, but that ends it." Except for those of us who drink Coke. (p. 15)

> Daphne Merkin, in The New Leader (© 1979 by the American Labor Conference on International Affairs, Inc.), January 29, 1979.

HELEN HARRIS

Much of the action [in *The Cutting Edge*] is narrated through letters. The characterization of the two brothers is often achieved by comparing them in a similar situation. This disciplined treatment and the fairly remote, privileged life-style of the gentle, intellectual characters . . . together produce a distinctly anachronistic impression. *The Cutting Edge* is endearingly reminiscent. It does not feel like the 1970s. (pp. 105-6)

This is partly because, as usual, Penelope Gilliatt provides a composite social and cultural background for her characters. As in many of the stories, the generations portrayed in *The Cutting Edge* are clearly the product of an education, the embodiment of a definite mentality. The two brothers, suitably named Peregrine and Benedick, reflect a caste of English society at odds with their time; the self-conscious sons of an eccentric, academic father. This heightens the historical aspect of the novel. So do stately sentences like 'In the guise they presented to the world, they were as different as in their gait.'

The Cutting Edge reaches beyond the self-imposed limits, however, because its author infuses them with her own sophistication. There are some meteoric diversions. Not only is her characters' behaviour unremittingly odd, they also grow progressively more enigmatic. Hints at possible homosexuality are discreetly introduced via the brothers' young half-brothers, Tom and Sam, and via a glancing reference to Oscar Wilde. Peregrine and Benedick's attempts to elucidate each other and themselves flounder.

Unfortuantely, the inevitable fusion of the two brothers in the bedroom, (if not actually in the bed), of their shared love, Joanna, seems forced. It does not resolve anything and it mars a novel of real quality. One of the book's many attractions is its neat symmetry and it is disappointing that at the very last this should override other considerations.

The Cutting Edge shares its predecessors' wit and polish. It is a pleasure to read. But Penelope Gilliatt seems to lay so much store by control and discretion that, despite her talent, there is something faintly brittle and glacial about the performance. (p. 106)

> Helen Harris, in London Magazine (© London Magazine 1979), February, 1979.

*   *   *

GINSBERG, Allen   1926-

Ginsberg is an American poet and the author of *Howl and Other Poems*, the little collection which Lawrence Ferlinghetti published at his City Lights press and successfully defended in court against obscenity charges. The book became the Beat Generation's "poetic manifesto" and Ginsberg its mentor, "the shaman and superstar of poetry readings and anarchic literary happenings all over the United States." Ginsberg has called himself "a fairy dope poet" and his poetic school "Beat-Hip-Gnostic-Imagist." Always at the disposal of those who want his help, Ginsberg established in 1966 the Committee on Poetry, the foundation dedicated to helping needy artists to which he still contributes most of his own income. (See also *CLC*, Vols. 1, 2, 3, 4, 6, and *Contemporary Authors*, Vols. 1-4, rev. ed.)

RICHARD EBERHART

The most remarkable poem of the young [Bay Region group,] written during the past year, is "Howl," by Allen Ginsberg. . . . [After] years of apprenticeship to usual forms, he developed his brave new medium. This poem has created a furor of praise or abuse whenever read or heard. It is a powerful work, cutting through to dynamic meaning. Ginsberg thinks he is going forward by going back to the methods of Whitman.

My first reaction was that it is based on destructive violence. It is profoundly Jewish in temper. It is biblical in its repetitive grammatical build-up. It is a howl against everything in our mechanistic civilization which kills the spirit, assuming that the louder you shout the more likely you are to be heard. It lays bare the nerves of suffering and spiritual struggle. Its positive force and energy come from a redemptive quality of love, although it destructively catalogs evils of our time, from physical deprivation to madness.

In other poems, Ginsberg shows a crucial sense of humor. It shows up principally in his poem "America," which has lines "Asia is rising against me. / I haven't got a Chinaman's chance." Humor is also present in "Supermarket in California." His "Sunflower Sutra" is a lyric poem marked by pathos. (pp. 145-46)

> Richard Eberhart, "West Coast Rhythms," in The New York Times Book Review (© 1956 by the New York Times Company; reprinted by permission), September 2, 1956 (and reprinted in his Of Poetry and Poets, University of Illinois Press, 1979, pp. 144-47).

KINGSLEY WIDMER

I think it should be granted from the start that [Allen Ginsberg] is not much of a poet in most usual literary senses, though he may well be an admirable and important practitioner of poetic saintliness. Carefully going again through his three volumes of published poetry covering the 50s (*Howl and Other Poems*, *Kaddish and Other Poems 1958-60*, and *Reality Sandwiches 1953-60*), I find three pieces that could well bear rereading as poems: "Howl," "America," and "Death to Van Gogh's Ear!" Other passages here and there give a curious surreal twist or are informative of matters most Ginsbergian, such as the bitter-bathetic physical description of his mad mother in the elegy-prayer "Kaddish," or maybe of some other non-literary interest. But most of it is poorly realized, pastiches of awkward language which many a poet could rewrite into more consistent style and apprehendable experience. The stuff of it seems more often unmade than crafted, and it is patent that Ginsberg never quite found a literary style of his own. Much of what he published as poems can better be considered pre-poems, fitting his own categories of "notes" and "nightmares" (including the drug "visions") and "musings." He is less writing poems than awkwardly adumbrating a personal and public "spiritual" mission. He adapts poetic methods to "widen the area of consciousness" and, while translating personal therapy as public revelation hopes that the reader will "taste my mouth in your ear."

Certainly Ginsberg displays considerable ambivalence about his poetic role, but finally degrades the writer to justify the seer. Though posing sometimes as a *naif* who wants a visceral poetry of direct screams and obscenities—a stance partly contradicted by his public as well as private acts of charm and intelligence and charity—he is also highly, probably excessively, literary, full of commemorative allusions to his whole tradition from Blake through Whitman to Apollinaire and his own contemporaries. In the provocative surrealist styled poem, "Death to Van Gogh's Ear!" he uses disparate images of the "mad" visionary poets, such as Mayakovsky and Crane, set against more truly insane public leaders and their order of "Money" and "Owners" and "vanishing Selfhood!" He suggests a government cabinet of mad poets, an anarchic cultural order in place of a repressive political one. With wry aptness, he comments within the poem on what he is doing: "History will make this poem prophetic and its awful silliness a hideous spiritual music."

Not so silly, with its vivacious disjunctures, wit, and (for once) meshing of syntax and sense, it sweepingly extends that most basic theme of modernist art, the culture against the society. This can also be said about the burlesque "America." Though ending with a comic pledge of allegiance ("America I'm putting my queer shoulder to the wheel."), he lashes out at an exploitatively false and insensitively technological civilization. "Your machinery is too much for me. / You made me want to be a saint." This conversion, though hardly realized as poetry, runs through all. Apparently central is that night in New York when he had a Blakean vision of eternity: "my eyes were opened for one hour / seeing in dreadful ecstacy / the motionless buildings of New York rotting / under the tides of Heaven." This intensity he desperately seeks to recapture in drugged and mythic and other gropings which don't quite translate into mere words.

The terms, the needs, of the conversion experience may be found in exacerbated awareness of loneliness, cruelty, madness and death. Their scene serves as equally important, the placement in the marginal ugliness of industrial-urban America and the indifferent skidrow human dumps of an aggrandizing society. The homely Jewish invert from the wastelands of New Jersey . . . wants to transcend his unsatisfactory self and world, transform all not only into "one moment of tenderness" but into that which will sustain it: "A MAGIC UNIVERSE." Of course he sees the absurdity of it, the grotesque effort to put "a flower in the ass." But "It's hard to eat shit, without having visions."

To love all, even one's ugly, perverted, inadequate self, requires the largest effort, beyond mere art, beyond the sophisticated whimper, then to the "Howl." (pp. 168-69)

"Howl" serves as one of the best known poems of our time. . . . Or perhaps it would be more accurate to say that its anguished view of contemporary life and yearning for tender poeticization of existence provide the most influential saintly gesture for a generation. Ginsberg's effort to spiritualize the self in a destructive order of commercial and technological domination—quite consciously a social-political as well as literary-religious rebellion—provides essential style for the underculture. It is poetry mostly because the poet is priest of the confession-conversion-protest. For this, it seems, the traditions of modernist poetic culture provide a better discipline than does theology and ritual, or ideology and politics. (p. 170)

Kingsley Widmer, in The Fifties: Fiction, Poetry, Drama, *edited by Warren French (copyright © 1970 by Warren French), Everett/Edwards, Inc., 1970.*

PAUL ZWEIG

It took half a dozen years, and more, for people to realise that Ginsberg, in *Howl*, had not merely invented a written equivalent of noise, but had opened language so wide, and made it so hungry, that nothing was safe any longer from poetry. Anything could be cut loose from its attachment to logical reality, and sent roaring into a sea of associations. Ginsberg's voice, in *Howl, Kaddish* and *Planet News* is omnivorous; its genius is to include and never to exclude. That is its connection to the surrealist practice of automatic writing which is also a method of radical inclusion, a way of putting a parenthesis around the will, while the contents of the psyche pour forth, unjudged. The poetry of *Howl* clarifies a profound implication of spontaneous language: it is an act of love. Not only noble images, but also the crippled children of the psyche will be loved, and the abortions and the terrors and the lonely ones. The surrealists argued that love was the essential revolutionary act. Love was the opposite of reason, because reason selects and judges, while love embraces. This was an argument that Whitman would have understood, and Ginsberg stands halfway between these two master-sources of his psyche, sometimes closer to one, sometimes to the other. . . . But there is an important difference between the spirit of his poetry and that of the French surrealists. Surrealism, in France, was attuned to psychic realities. It tended to view the outer world as a locus of repressions, a negative place to argue against or to destroy, not to embrace. But Ginsberg makes a further step. To embrace the rhythms of the unconscious mind, he felt that he also had to embrace the rhythms of the outer world. Ginsberg's poems turn crowded pads and bus stations and supermarkets and Warsaw cafes and his own aging body and his mother's insanity and crushed beercans and flowers and Wales hilltops, into moments of illumination. Unlike the surrealists, Ginsberg makes the language of unreason into an act of *amor fati*, an ultimate generosity which accepts to perceive the world even at its worst, unfiltered by habits or conventions or repressive judgements. Even Ginsberg's rage against the political falsity of America is a form of embracing; it is a warm, life-including anger. The surrealists were haunted by suicide. . . . This was because of an ambivalence in their attitude: unselective self-acceptance mingled dangerously with hatred of the ordinary world. The language of their texts verges on preciosity, as if their spontaneity retained an element of judgement resembling Baudelaire's longing to be "anywhere out of this world." Ginsberg, like Whitman, broadens the surrealist act, creating a poetry that evokes all the ranges of experience, a poetry anchored inside of life.

Although *Howl* almost singlehandedly dislocated the traditionalist poetry of the 1950's, its specifically literary influence has been negligible. Ginsberg made the experimental mode of the 1960's possible, but very few poets could approach the breadth of his surreal spontaneity. Self-indulgence on the grand scale is harder than it looks, as many liberated, anonymous poets discovered. (pp. 277-78)

> *Paul Zweig, in* Salmagundi *(copyright © 1973 by Skidmore College), Spring-Summer, 1973.*

LOUIS SIMPSON

[Ginsberg's] has been a spectacular career, and some of the thinking that went into making it is recorded in these "Journals"—but not enough. With all the traveling he did in these years, and the thinking he must have done to change the "shy" imitator of Williams into the astonishing poet of "Howl" and "Kaddish," Ginsberg's "Journals" do not yield episodes that reveal his development as a poet. There are trivial details and, at the other extreme, some mystic musings, but Ginsberg's strength as a writer is in neither of these: it lies in his ability to deal with the whole visible world, drawing sounds and images from it, so that we see things in a new way. Here and there in the "Journals" we come across a passage that has this quality, as in the description of roosters crowing in a village: "challenging in various cockly hoarse tones as if they existed in a world of pure intuitive sound communicating to anonymous hidden familiar chickensouls from hill to hill." But there is too little of this. Instead we have his dreams, acres of them—perhaps because he had been treated by psychiatrists and was undergoing psychoanalysis. (p. 46)

As a record of Ginsberg's formative years during which he produced many good poems, the "Journals" have some factual value and must be of interest to serious readers of poetry. Ginsberg has been one of the most influential poets in America in our time.

Robert Bly once said that people disliked Ginsberg's poetry because it expressed feeling. This strikes me wrong: it wasn't the feeling they disliked but the attitudes. Ginsberg had his own brand of morality, which consisted of views directly opposed to those held by the middle class, by businessmen and politicians. And he was given to promoting his views—for example, he often spoke about the beneficial results that could follow from the use of hallucinogens. (pp. 46-7)

Yet, though Ginsberg may take himself to be a prophet, in other moods he is warm and sympathetic, at times even humorous. His "America" is one of the few truly humorous poems in the language. And there are some entertaining "political ravings" in these "Journals," including insults to some people at Columbia who did not pay sufficient attention to his poems when they first came out. As I was one of those people, I am happy to have this opportunity to say that I was wrong—not merely wrong, obtuse. I still don't care for "Howl"—Lucien Carr and Neal Cassady were not my idea of "the best minds in America"—but other poems

in the volume are superb, and "Kaddish" is a masterpiece. Anything the author of these poems wrote deserves to be read, including his "Journals." (p. 47)

> *Louis Simpson, "Not Made for the World of Moloch," in* The New York Times Book Review *(© 1977 by The New York Times Company; reprinted by permission), October 23, 1977, pp. 9, 46-7.*

HAROLD BEAVER

Ginsberg's comic bravura, like Mailer marshalling armies of the night in his three-piece suit, is wholly Jewish and self-deprecatingly assured. Ginsberg neither attempts the Western role of urban gamecock nor indulges in camp comedy. Whitman manages both. . . in his endless saga of self-affirmation. Yet both share the need to leap for self-transcendence in a kind of cosmic love-affair that turns, as often as not, into a comic impasse of ecstasy foiled and rebuffed. . . .

Whitman, moreover, believed in his soul. He loafed and invited it, he said. Ginsberg does not:

> Let me say beginning I don't believe
> in Soul
> The heart, famous heart's a bag of
> shit I wrote 25 years ago.

Ginsberg prefers to be known as the man "Who saw Blake and abandoned God." *Mind Breaths* suggests spiritual afflatus and yoga exercises and consciousness-raising. . . . For what may seem, to the uninitiated, graffiti to decorate the walls of America are really "home made Blake hymns, mantras to raise the skull of America." . . .

The whole slim volume is no more than one filed catalogue among countless unfiled catalogues of awareness. . . . There are some fine new poems on old age, a New York mugging as well as a series of lilting pop lyrics fit for old-fashioned hurdy-gurdies. . . . But far more remarkable than any "Blakean Punk Epic with nirvanic Rune music" is the fact that the poet who entered howling in 1956 now exits shaking with laughter, like a great earth-bound Jewish-American Buddha: laughing with his jukebox prophecies; laughing with his pederast rhapsodies, even with his Dharma elegies; laughing on his own way to "Guru Death," singing the "Sickness Blues." . . . (p. 747)

> *Harold Beaver, in* The Times Literary Supplement *(© Times Newspapers Ltd. (London) 1978; reproduced from* The Times Literary Supplement *by permission), July 7, 1978.*

*   *   *

GORDON, Caroline   1895-

An American novelist, short story writer, and literary critic, Gordon writes about rural southern life, paralleling the decline of the family and its traditions with the disintegration of the South following the Civil War. Her novels are historically precise, painting a representative picture of her native Kentucky. (See also *CLC*, Vol. 6, and *Contemporary Authors*, Vols. 11-12; *Contemporary Authors Permanent Series*, Vol. 1.)

ASHLEY BROWN

[Miss Gordon] is a conscious heiress to what is probably the central tradition of modern fiction, which we can refer to, following some of its great practitioners, as the Impressionist novel. . . . Miss Gordon is more than the follower of a tradition; indeed, her innovations are bold and far-reaching. But she often works out her devices with an eye on the masters whom she honors. (pp. 279-80)

Her method, if we may call it that, consists in subtly adjusting her prose medium to her subject. If she were a Renaissance poet we would say that she obeys the ancient rhetorical principle of *decorum,* with the several styles adapted to the levels of subject. And indeed the old term is being revived today, notably by the most astute students of Joyce, who in *Ulysses* systematically exploits the possibilities of multiple style. Miss Gordon, however, does not plunge from one style to another; we might say she modulates the tone from a fixed position within each novel or story. (p. 281)

Penhally is a completely "rendered" novel, as [Ford Maddox Ford] would have said. Its method of presentation—the shifting post of observation in the line of succession among the Llewellyns—allows a remarkable degree of control for such a large subject. Its author has seldom written better. But she was not content with the perfection of a method, and her subsequent books have realized her subject by a variety of means. Her second novel, *Aleck Maury, Sportsman* (1934), for instance, is based on the convention of the old-fashioned memoir. Aleck Maury is the only one of her major characters whom Miss Gordon has granted the privilege of telling his own story, and she thus departs from what with her is a virtual principle. This, the most popular of her novels, can stand by itself, but it gains something from those written after it, as though it were cutting across a territory whose outlines are more fully revealed later on. Many readers are familiar with the Aleck Maury stories which group themselves round the novel ("Old Red" for instance frequently appears in anthologies) and so I shall point to only one leading feature of the book. Aleck Maury is of course the sportsman par excellence, and his book can be enjoyed simply as something pleasurable, like *The Compleat Angler.* But the author has deftly complicated things by introducing the image of Aeneas, fleeing the ruins of Troy with his decrepit father on his back. Aleck himself is a Virginian, the son of a Latinist who undertakes his boy's education by teaching him to read the *Aeneid.* The image is occasionally alluded to later in the book, but never insisted upon. . . . [It] suggests that Aleck himself is an Aeneas, who will leave the ruins of his father's house, but not under the aegis of any Venus who will guide him to another Troy. He has only the memory of a civilization to perpetuate. Dispossessed almost from the start, he is thrown back upon his sportsman's instincts for survival. (pp. 283-84)

[*None Shall Look Back* and *The Garden of Adonis*] complement each other in various ways. Both deal with the breakup of a family estate, and apparently the same family, the Allards, at different periods in their history. These are longer and more ambitious than her first two books, and they pose certain problems of structure and meaning. *None Shall Look Back* has for its model nothing less than *War and Peace.* In adapting her practice to the subject of some magnitude, she has had to use an economy of rendition in order to compose larger scenes than she tried to manage in her first books, and at times one can scarcely believe that *None Shall Look Back* was written by the same person who wrote *Penhally.* Like Tolstoy, she has written a novel of war and peace which has seemed to some readers to fall

into its component parts. She has, to start with, taken a Kentucky family, the Allards, with their various connections, through the vicissitudes of the Civil War. Under the impact of the war their fortunes undergo a decline; they are almost ruined; in the end we know they will somehow survive. But the novel is also about the war in its Western theater. We follow not only members of the Allard family, but the highest officers of the Confederate and Federal forces as they direct the operations. The war exists as something beyond any individual's comprehension of it, an enveloping action: everyone's destiny is shaped by it; no one escapes. The problem is to relate the two levels of action. Miss Gordon does this by having the young soldier Rives Allard, who now is in love with his adversary Death, shot from his horse. The author quickly takes the point of view from Rives to Bedford Forrest, a procedure which would ordinarily violate the structure of a scene. As Rives dies and falls to the ground, he becomes merely a "body" which the fleeing infantry must avoid in their rush. But Forrest sees the body, he recognizes it; then, as though there were a continuum of consciousness between the dead man and his commander, the focus moves entirely to Forrest, for the first and only time in the novel. Rives' tragedy is caught up in the larger action of which Forrest is the representative. This austere and remote figure participates in the pathos and is thus humanized. . . . The effect Miss Gordon gets is tragic, and it has been well prepared for. And this is the only one of her novels in which the tragic movement is complete.

The Garden of Adonis deals with four families, including the Allards, during the economic depression of the 1930's. This is Miss Gordon's "Agrarian" novel. Although the author solves the main structural problem by a shifting point of view, there is no true center of action as there is in *None Shall Look Back;* it is as though so much centrifugal energy proceeds from a source impossible to locate. The patriarch Mister Ben Allard is still the master of his property, but he is at the mercy of bankers, storekeepers, a falling tobacco market, and other forces almost beyond control. . . . This novel, though on occasion brilliant, suffers from long stretches of banality. Miss Gordon has been only too honest in presenting certain characters in their own idiom and at their own evaluation; ironically one of these is Mister Ben's daughter. The machine is at the center of her consciousness, and for pages at a time the effect is close to advertising copy. Her father, unlike the earlier patriarchs, is ineffectual, and his idiom no longer commands respect. Perhaps realizing this, Miss Gordon relies on the myth of Adonis—referred to in the title and derived from Sir James Frazer—to give depth to her situation. But this does not happen; the myth remains external to the action. (pp. 284-86)

The five novels which culminate in *Green Centuries* have much in common. With the exception of *Aleck Maury, Sportsman,* they exhibit a consistent movement towards tragedy, although only *None Shall Look Back* fulfills the movement. And the novels are conceived in a kind of grand design against the enveloping action of history. With these five books behind her, Miss Gordon had the choice of "filling out" her subject, perhaps using some of the characters she had already invented, or else of extending it by moving to another post of observation. Her second group of novels —*The Women on the Porch* (1944), *The Strange Children* (1951), and *The Malefactors* (1956)—does both. These books are set against the history of the South, like their predecessors, but only indirectly. And their mode is finally Christian comedy. About the time that she published *The Women on the Porch* Miss Gordon was beginning to doubt whether a "regional" literature in the South would continue much longer; it was her opinion that the renaissance in letters was coming to its end. Probably with some such feeling about her subject she has steadily widened its reference. (p. 287)

With the complexity of subject has come a new boldness of technique. These novels are more Jamesian than the earlier ones—the point of view is more strictly controlled—but they also draw extensively on the resources of poetry, such as *The Waste Land,* which lies back of *The Women on the Porch,* and Dante's *Purgatorio,* which informs *The Malefactors* to some extent. (pp. 287-88)

[We] should not assume that [Gordon] has been the virtuoso. On the contrary, her stylistic shifts are an index to the scale of her work. Her eight novels and her stories and even her critical essays compose a genuine *oeuvre.* Using the materials accessible to her (her own life, the history of her family, the history of her region), she has built up an impressive image of Western man and the crisis which his restlessness has created. We can see one instance of this restlessness in Rion Outlaw and his dream of infinite space. But there are scarcely any institutional forms to restrain him. Chapman, the sophisticated historian in *The Women on the Porch,* is the latest version of Rion Outlaw, and *his* dream of infinite space is a nightmare. Nearly all of Miss Gordon's heroes are aware of the general plight, but Chapman and Stephen Lewis and Tom Claiborne are intensely conscious of a failing in their lives, and their meditations take the form of an interior drama.

Most of Miss Gordon's heroes (and many of her heroines) are fleeing from some kind of historical ruin—the exceptions are old Nicholas Llewellyn and Fontaine Allard and even Mister Ben Allard in *The Garden of Adonis,* but even these patriarchs cannot check the forces of disruption very long. Miss Gordon seems to be saying that it was a mistake to make such an absolute commitment to the order of history. Aleck Maury perhaps understands this failure, and as classicist and sportsman he can still act the Aeneas who will never found another Troy. But even the sportsman's instinct for ritual as a barrier against the ruins of time cannot be counted on, and Jim Carter, a flawed sportsman-hero in *The Garden of Adonis,* hardly even makes the attempt. In *The Strange Children* we see the futility (or at least the irony) of the effort to perpetuate a history already ruined. Here and even more in *The Malefactors* Miss Gordon is saying that redemption must lie in another order of existence, and of course she finally makes no secret of her Christian emphasis. But the ruin is easier to dramatize than the act of redemption.

If the imagery of flight permeates her books, what is the counter-image, the emblem of stasis, even of fulfillment? That is a natural image which most frequently takes the form of a tree. (Like Yeats she seems to arrive at this image very easily.) Perhaps the most "typical" moments in Miss Gordon's fiction occur when her heroes step out of time, as it were, and contemplate the forest. There is the moment when young John Llewellyn, shot from his horse at Shiloh, watches a young maple leaf floating through the center of the destruction. Or there is Mister Ben Allard sitting under his favorite sugar tree and dreaming of his dead sweetheart. In *The Malefactors* the symbol of the natural order becomes more than that: Claiborne "stared at the copper beech tree as if he could find the answer there," and "he had felt that those dusky boughs harbored Presences." No other American writer has so patiently described the surfaces of trees, even the striations of leaves, or made so much of them. The tree as an image of "wholeness" yields a meaning to him who contemplates it lovingly, Miss Gordon seems to say, and the moment of stasis can perhaps be an intimation of something divine. The tragedy of historical ruin could be redeemed—so the movement from *Penhally* to *The Malefactors* suggests. (pp. 288-89)

[Miss Gordon] has tried to use the full resources of a tradition to create an enduring fictional illusion. She has been more conscious of her rôle than some other novelists. Did she choose wisely in associating herself with the masters of the Impressionist tradition? Their successes have been hard-won. The effort to achieve a fully realized illusion in the manner of Flaubert or James or Ford is always being threatened by the indifferent or the restless. (pp. 289-90)

Miss Gordon and several of her contemporaries carry on the tradition of the Impressionist masters, which still assumes that a public reality is accessible to a private vision. No one can say what this tradition will finally come to represent, but for the moment one can applaud Miss Gordon for her devotion to her chosen mission; her place in the line of succession should be secure, and one says this knowing that her career is not finished. Her desire for excellence has been an admirable thing. (p. 290)

> Ashley Brown, "The Achievement of Caroline Gordon," in The Southern Humanities Review (copyright 1968 by Auburn University), Summer, 1968, pp. 279-90.

LOUISE COWAN

Caroline Gordon's angle of vision—the vantage point from which she regards the moving configurations of human existence—is primarily epic. As an intrinsic structure, that is, as one of the fundamental generic patterns, the epic is concerned with the ongoing of history. Within its broad expanse everything is sacrificed to an essentially eschatological thrust; for nothing less than the outcome of the human enterprise hangs upon the success of its heroic quest. Domestic life must be set aside for epic endeavors, even though the feminine spirit encloses the action as guide and goal. (p. 7)

If Miss Gordon's characters hurtle into the abyss, they do so as epic and not tragic figures. Epic heroes do not struggle as tragic heroes do against the gods. Theirs is not a lonely battle within themselves, a striving to find interior dimensions of being; rather, epic heroes endeavor to maintain manliness and courage in a communal and cosmic realm, obeying whatever divine imperatives are given them, following a code of honor in a society that is in perpetual disorder.

But though the world about which an epic poet writes is frequently disunified and confused, and though the hero himself may be blinded into taking a fatal false step, it is nonetheless a requisite that the imaginative light by which the writer views his scene be clear. No moral ambiguities must cloud the poet's—the novelist's—mind if he is to depict the heroic. (pp. 7-8)

Miss Gordon's chief effort as an artist—like that of most other significant twentieth-century writers—has been to find a usable sacral system—a myth—in a society increasingly secular and consequently detached from the major symbols within its own cultural heritage. The Christian structure, which, for Western society, appropriated the mythic house of the gods and provided for centuries our major cultural figures, has gradually lost its imagistic concreteness and become associated in the modern mind with a set of moral principles by which one ought to live or with fossilized phrases and gestures. (p. 8)

No writer in our time has been more concerned with [the reconciliation of pagan myth and Christian faith] than Caroline Gordon. Her early novels deal overtly with neither pagan myth nor Christian mystery; but, concerned with the polarities of thinking and feeling, they dramatize the feminine and masculine principles in a devastated society that cannot surrender itself to love and integration, where death is the over-arching enemy. (p. 10)

One can only speculate on Miss Gordon's choice of title [for an early story, "One against Thebes"]; but since it speaks quite clearly of the life dedicated to following "an insistent voice" it seems possible to consider her story a parable of the artist, following a vocation in the path of the serpent, seeking the crystal palace, encountering undeserved suffering, and redeemed finally from the doomed city of Thebes to bless the fortunate and just city of Athens. It is the child herself who will become the "one against Thebes"; but at the same time her father, Aleck Maury, like the aging Oedipus, is also in a sense pitted against the forces of death and destruction. The child—in the earlier story Sally Maury, the daughter of Aleck—is here referred to simply as "the child." She is the young artist, called by an inner voice to a life of observation, of absorption, of re-mythologizing. Like the little girl in "A Narrow Heart: The Portrait of a Woman," . . . she is preoccupied with the qualities of things, with trying to know them as they are and as they establish themselves in consciousness. As an Antigone figure, she will have to guide and direct the humbled Oedipus and later take the part of the gods in struggle against the rationalistic edicts of Thebes. She will stand, like her father, as one against Thebes and will help to keep the city safe from the dragon's sons. But the artist is not, in Miss Gordon's view, the hero. The artist—the poet—is a seer, whose consciousness gives form to the total history of man. True, he observes the hero and appreciates him, understanding his courage and his mission because both have an inner voice to guide them, both are aware of dragons, both stand solitary over the abyss. Nevertheless, the artist has a different kind of toil: to construct an image of that essentially epic struggle. And though in this story Miss Gordon's referential imagination allies the child's father with the tragic figure of the old Oedipus, her view of him throughout the Aleck Maury stories has been cast in an epic, not a tragic, mold. (pp. 12-13)

One can speculate a bit further and conjecture that Miss Gordon's current novels, long under construction, depict these two basic realities to which contemporary man is related—the two supernatural dimensions in which he is enmeshed, with or without his awareness. The "lower pattern" of which she speaks is the primordial world of archetypes that, as she says, "lies at the bottom of every human consciousness." The "upper pattern" is no doubt a story of

Christian conversion and of the workings of grace in a particular life, located in a specific place and time—a Dantesque story which will preserve the "actuality of events." (pp. 13-14)

With its "upper" and "lower" stories, Miss Gordon's writing is epic in accord with the two symbolic structures of which I have been speaking. On the mythopoeic level, the epic journey symbolizes a quest for the integration of the component parts of man; it is a search for wholeness, for the union of earth and sky gods. It requires a descent into darkness; its obstacles are women and death. Its virtues are magnanimity and valor. In contrast, the Christian epic speaks allegorically of the progress of the soul; a glimpse of love and joy—what Jacques Maritain calls a "flash of reality"—impels it on its quest. The obstacle to be overcome is sin; the journey is toward grace, toward light out of darkness; but there is nevertheless a confrontation of the abyss. Woman is the mediatrix of grace in this journey, the Beatrice figure who impels and guides.

That Caroline Gordon's novels—her long fiction—possess an epic cast should not be difficult to demonstrate, since even a cursory reading of them uncovers a largeness of canvas that customarily goes with the heroic mold. But I should like to maintain that even her short stories are shaped by an epic vision, though one may be obliged to consider many of them fragments of that wide and majestic outlook. In all of her stories the man does what he "must"; he follows a code of honor that is fundamentally destructive to the feminine ancestral principle. Miss Gordon's early novels demonstrate his unvarying defeat; but as her works reflect more of the Christian eschatology, her epic vision changes its tone from tragic to comic.

In one group of short stories written early in her career, Aleck Maury is the central epic hero—a man who has found in his youth the "secret life" of joy and danger in the ritual of the hunt. He must ponder what it is in nature that wild creatures, dogs, and hunters sense—something which renders life incalculably precious. It is this search for the life abundant that pulls Maury away from home and family in a lifelong pursuit of hunting and fishing—in a lifelong flight, too, as it turns out, from his mortal enemy, death. Miss Gordon's later work demonstrates more openly her reconciliation of the pagan and Christian tropologies, but these short pieces contain in their depths the same twofold view of reality. (pp. 14-15)

Aleck Maury is the modern Odysseus—the comic epic hero who must live by his wits and come to terms with women. But Maury is the product of a land in which there is no longer any active faith, even in a desperate "lost cause"; for, though the South which he represents and loves has kept to a precious heritage of courtesy and hospitality, its essential deism contains within itself no principle of regeneration. . . . Aleck Maury is no grand epic figure; he has grown up after a devastating war which has virtually destroyed his people (he faces a land in desperate disorder), yet his concern is not to restore the patria so much as to find a separate peace. (pp. 15-16)

Aleck Maury [is] a man who, for all his gentleness and apparent traditionalism, is a romantic and a modern—a "superfluous man," as Turgenev characterized the figure. He turns away from society to the hunt, not for any shared ritual—for his is a solitary pursuit—but for a romantic quest to seek in nature what Wordsworth called the "visionary gleam." Like Rousseau's "solitary walker," he finds in society the chains that would bind him to routine, the forces that would corrupt his delight. He savors the Rousseauistic "sweet sentiment of his own existence" in field or stream; and his relationship to nature itself is not sacramental and submissive, but calculating and eventually cunning. (p. 26)

Unlike the narrator in *A Sportsman's Sketches* who does his solitary walking to gain the wisdom of the serfs, to observe the human community, Maury prefers to be alone or to have a single companion, with whom he has no relation, except on a limited basis. When he deals with the folk, it is to trick wisdom out of them. He alters nature, as in such instances as his placing pieces of iron in a pond to make trout breed. He constantly thinks that he can "figure out" the laws of nature and is continually in search of devices to make fish seek the hook more readily.

Further, in his attitude toward his own learning, the classics exist for him as a kind of enhancement of life; he does not make of his study an entrance into wisdom and love. He is a modern Cartesian man: split between mind and body and desperately seeking wholeness. He is a modern pantheist, repelled by the womanishness of religion, having to seek the sacred far apart from society and, as long as he has a pond or a stream, not needing a God. (pp. 26-7)

Two visual images have . . . made up the poles of Aleck Maury's life—the one of a possum blazing down at him, illuminating all of creation with an inner fire; and the other of an old woman looking up and beyond him toward something transcendent that is nevertheless a real "presence." Both visions are on the boundary of death, both are ultimate testimony to something in reality that lies behind the face of nature. The boy spends his entire life searching unconsciously for what his Aunt must have seen. But he seeks it on the lower level, by looking into the burning eyes of the natural world, rather than by construing it metaphysically, looking beyond nature into the heart of being. It is only when he himself stands on the borderline of death, in his old age, that he is ready to choose: he is at the *hour* (and Miss Gordon underlines this word) that is for the Christian the moment of choice. (p. 28)

> Louise Cowan, "Aleck Maury, Epic Hero and Pilgrim," in *The Short Fiction of Caroline Gordon: A Critical Symposium, edited by Thomas H. Landess (copyright 1972 The University of Dallas Press), The University of Dallas Press, 1972, pp. 7-31.*

ROBERT S. DUPREE

The twentieth century has been blessed with a number of excellent artists who have also been significant critics. The best of these have gone beyond the kind of activity which consists of mere apology or justification for their own work and have explored major questions of import to society as a whole in both their imaginative and discursive writings. Typical of this concern at its most intense among writers and critics of fiction is the work of Caroline Gordon, who has been emphatic in her insistence on the close unity between technique and vision, craft and moral implications in a work of art.

In an important study published in 1961, Wayne Booth takes Miss Gordon to task for arguing in favor of "show-ing" and against "telling." He is evidently an admirer of her stories; but he implies that her critical position is too narrow and arbitrary, too narrowly determined by certain vague principles to be an adequate account of the craft of fiction. Citing from her book *How to Read a Novel*, he notes that she insists on the necessity for certain "constants" to be found in "all good fiction, from Sophocles and Aeschylus down to a well-constructed nursery tale" and concludes that she remains on "the highest possible level of generality" when she contends that if "one is going to write or read fiction, it is of paramount importance to be able to recognize these 'constants' when one comes upon them, or, if they are not present in a work of fiction, to mark their absence." (p. 33)

Caroline Gordon obviously believes that the use of any given technique implies a moral position; she does not take the inhumanly "objective" stance that Booth attributes to the "realistic" movement in modern fiction. In *The House of Fiction*, for instance, she subscribes to the position that a "given technique is the result of a moral and philosophical attitude, a bias towards experience on the part of the author; and as the author begins to understand what it is in life that interests him most, he also becomes aware of the techniques which will enable him to create in language his fullest sense of that interest. Material and technique become in the end the same thing, the one discovering the other." . . . The subject of all great literature, she indicates, is the natural world; and the only attitude towards it which is possible in a truly great novelist is one of love. For this reason, the novel is often a tale of redemption or damnation. Even the damnation of a soul cannot be convincing if the writer has not provided us with the understanding that love and the world itself matter more than mere ideas about them. It is in this sense that Caroline Gordon is a "realist," but only in this sense. (p. 34)

In the light of this position, a piece like "Emmanuele! Emmanuele!" in *Old Red and Other Stories* takes on a peculiar significance. It is something more than a short story; it is perhaps a critical essay made flesh. . . . "Emmanuele! Emmanuele!" is hardly a short story of the same kind as most of her others; it is distinctly a "conte à clef," based on the life of André Gide. Indeed, the parallel is worked out in very great detail. "Emmanuele" was, in fact, the name that Gide used in his *Journal* and in *The Notebooks of André Walter* to refer to his wife, Madeleine Rondeaux. Moreover, the journal he kept, the letters he wrote to her which were burned, and the residence in Normandy are all aspects of the historical Gide's career. Raoul Pleyol, the poet-diplomat, is of course Paul Claudel; and the name itself would give away the identification even without the reference to the exchange of letters between the two men and certain actual passages, like "I grasp your hand," which are to be found in the correspondence. (pp. 34-5)

The central intelligence of the story is an American professor and poet, Robert Heyward, who is acting as secretary to the famous poet Guillaume Fäy [the Gide persona of the story]. In his adulation for the man he serves, he sees Fäy's every gesture and every word as great gifts to the world which he, as a near stranger, is privileged to witness at first hand. . . . Heyward is probably based on several young men who served as amanuensis to Gide during his career and this strategic use of a narrator allows Miss Gordon to pull together widely separated events in the life of the

French writer and to make of them a compact symbolic whole. (p. 35)

Why did Miss Gordon choose to write so blatantly about the Claudel-Gide relationship and the peculiar battle between them? . . . It is as a living myth that Caroline Gordon adopts the biography of Gide. Just as Dante uses real persons in his poem not for personal but for symbolic statements, so she takes Gide as part of the cultural myth of the artist in the modern world. Fäy is that aspect of Gide which is living allegory, and her critique of the French writer is as sympathetic, in its own way, as Dante's reluctant admission that even the greatest of poets cannot be saved from damnation if he does not adhere to the right forms of human behavior.

However, it is not for his homosexuality that Gide is condemned. (p. 37)

Fäy's contemplation of his own mirrored image is the real sodomy which condemns him. By putting his "real" self into the letters to his wife he had hoped to turn her into yet another mirror of himself, but he did not count upon the possibility that the mirror itself might be shattered and that the image it held would be dissipated forever. It is Gide's narcissism, on the one hand, and his technical timidity, his inability to write with conviction on the other, which condemn him in Miss Gordon's view. (p. 38)

"Emmanuele! Emmanuele!" is not at all [a schematic allegory of a wrong-headed modern artist]. It is a demonstration of Miss Gordon's ability to write about ideas without losing touch with the solidity of the real world or rejecting the critical principles of fiction which require a convincing image of the universe in which characters may move. A regular progression of images and details organizes the story in terms of particulars and acts in counterpoint to the obvious procession of ideas.

Heyward's point of view is important for the story . . . because it allows the figure of Fäy to be elevated. Through the young man's eyes the events take on the look of the tragic. The quest for the abyss is something an American like him cannot truly understand, but his foreign and sincere eyes allow him to seize the force of Fäy's destruction with full impact. (p. 40)

Fäy's tragedy is that he has indeed destroyed himself by feeding on his own substance. But he does not go into the abyss without a witness, the young man through whom we have viewed the consequences of his love of the abyss. He goes to Mme Fäy for the key to her secretary, expecting at last to receive the long-awaited revelation of Fäy's true character and that of his wife as well. Paradoxically, it is not in the letters that he comes to understand; it is in the final dramatic encounter between the forces of piety and the demonic. . . . The revelation that Fäy hoped to give in the letters was not his true self; the real image of Fäy is in the Gadarene swine, as Heyward witnesses in the plunge towards self-invited destruction. When the image of himself that Fäy has sought to create is shattered, he has no alternative self to turn to other than the demon enclosed in darkness.

The striking technique of this story is evident in the skilful way that Miss Gordon handles the physical reality of her settings. Without softening the impact of her ideas, she produces a version of her own *Counterfeiters* that is neither inconclusive nor unreal. Two strands of imagery, one containing fruit, trees, and blossoms, the other eyes, water, and light, organize the story into something much more complex than a mere fictional presentation of an intellectual and critical point of view. We see both North Africa and Normandy through the experiences of Robert Heyward, and the more we delve into the contrasts in imagery, the more there is to enrich the basic tragic experience of the plot. (pp. 42-3)

["The Olive Garden" illustrates] a final argument I wish to make about Miss Gordon's critical point of view, not because it is set in France, because it is like the other story concerned with a young American poet in Europe, nor even because its Proustian texture is an interesting contrast to the more intellectual surface of "Emmanuele! Emmanuele!" Rather its present merit is as an illustration of Miss Gordon's flexibility and of her central beliefs. Both stories are concerned with a young man who finds himself not in terms of his own actions but as a result of understanding the actions of another, whether it be Guillaume Fäy or Deucalion and Pyrrha. These, for the purposes of their stories, are equally mythological characters, though the myth of Gide is one that is within living memory. Heyward, whose name suggests "wayward" and hence a certain amount of aimlessness, is only half-hearted in his attempts to imitate Fäy directly. . . . In the other story, Dabney's wandering also appears to be aimless, a potentially self-indulgent and tearful attempt to search out times past. In the end, however, both men discover themselves by discovering meaning outside themselves. Miss Gordon, meanwhile, never resorts to aimlessness in exploring the random, or seemingly random, nature of their rich experiences. (p. 47)

The key to both the criticism and fiction of Miss Gordon is in illuminative detail. Though there is evident in her work the influence of Ford Madox Ford, who was also somewhat instrumental in developing the very similar imagist technique in poetry, we would be mistaken if we supposed that Miss Gordon's term "rendering" is part of a simple opposition to "telling." The Deucalion story at the end of "The Olive Garden" is "told" and not "shown." Nevertheless, it is an instance of the illuminative detail which makes sense of the whole. More than that, this single myth draws together a number of important points. Replanting the bones of his mother, Deucalion releases the energies of his own creativity by seizing part of his own past and acting upon it. It is in the conjunction of the masculine principle of action and the feminine principle of receptivity or pure being that a new race is formed. "Rendering" the bones of his dead mother to the earth was a better action than all the telling and spells and charms could ever accomplish. By moving out of the confines of being, which is static, inert, and lifeless, and into the realm of action, he puts into operation the energies of creation. What Mr. Booth has failed to see is that Caroline Gordon does not reject the novel of ideas, but she does insist that those ideas have to become alive through actions. Her "constants" are based upon that central notion, whether she speaks of plot, narrative technique, or the character of the hero. . . . (pp. 49-50)

Robert S. Dupree, "Caroline Gordon's 'Constants' of Fiction," in The Short Fiction of Caroline Gordon: A Critical Symposium, *edited by Thomas H. Landess (copyright 1972 The University of Dallas Press), The University of Dallas Press, 1972, pp. 33-51.*

THOMAS H. LANDESS

Miss Gordon's [early] stories rest on what were, at the time of their composition, relatively secure philosophical foundations, while her later works, including novels as well as short stories, are both structurally and texturally more complicated as a defense against those hostile armies which have appeared at the gates in ever-increasing numbers since the publication of *The Forest of the South*. . . .

The philosophical assumptions to which I refer are ontological and define man's place in the natural order of being. They are assumptions which informed the South of Miss Gordon's early years and indeed, for society at large, remained unquestioned in Western civilization from preclassical times until the nineteenth century. They might be summarized as follows: God, a transcendent Being, exists and orders all things; man, a natural being, is in some measure an imperfect analogue of God; man's soul, therefore, partakes of the divine as well as of the earthly; for this reason, man occupies a "middle position" in the hierarchical structure of being, and his noblest achievements involve the affirmation of the god-like portion of his nature at the expense of the merely animal, an affirmation realized most often through sacrifice or self-control. (p. 54)

Now a traditional society, whether medieval or Southern, is extremely complex in nature, but that complexity ultimately forms a whole; and while the society is still vital, it can be "taken in" by a wholeness of vision which renders elaborate explanation or argumentative definition unnecessary. Thus Miss Gordon's earlier stories are structurally and texturally simpler than her later works and are understandable in terms of modes of conduct which have their roots in an ontology which is pre-Christian as well as Christian, European as well as Southern. (p. 56)

[Selections] from *The Forest of the South* exemplify to a greater or lesser degree the same tissue of symbols supported by the same ontological assumptions. Yet each of these works—"Tom Rivers," "The Long Day," "Mr. Powers," and "Her Quaint Honor"—defines a different symbol of Southern ontology and does so in a way which suggests not only the presence of the *daimon* but also the mortal part as well. Thus life is imitated in the Aristotelian sense rather than ideologically falsified and the result is modern fiction in the distinctly classical mode.

The first of the stories, "Tom Rivers," is an account of two Kentucky cousins who meet in the western frontier town of Cisco, Texas, experience danger together, and then part forever. Although Tom Rivers, the older of the two, is clearly the heroic sacrificial figure, the full meaning of this heroism is apparent only after a careful examination of the story's structural elements. Part of this meaning, as Andrew Lytle [in an article entitled "The Forest of the South"] has pointed out, is to be found in the integrity of Tom's manhood as revealed in an early love affair. (pp. 56-7)

But Tom's masculine integrity, though by no means irrelevant to the story, is not its true subject. His refusal to submit to his demanding fiancee; his confrontation with a gun-wielding, frontier cardshard; his routing of a band of night riders: these dramatic gestures alone do not define the full measure of his *daimon* or explain the ultimate meaning of the narrative, a meaning which both contains the image of Tom's assertive manhood and effectively transcends it.

The action is presented in the form of a first-person reminiscence; and the narrator, Lew Allard, admits in his opening words that he does not understand the significance of his own recollections. The story he subsequently relates is long and anecdotal, but the key to its meaning lies in the second sentence of the narrative: "Still, in a large family connection such as ours every member, no matter how remotely related or unimportant, has his place and a sort of record in memory." (p. 57)

That Miss Gordon is primarily concerned with the proper attitude toward family seems evident from the way in which she continues to develop her story. . . .

Miss Gordon pauses to introduce a traditional symbol which gathers in the larger meaning of her narrative: the old spreading beech which, generation after generation, stands in the yard of the family place, filtering the light "always in the same pattern." . . . This image, that of the family tree itself, emphasizes the permanence of the collective memory which binds families together, those dead or absent as well as those living and present. (p. 58)

In his earlier renunciation of [his fiancee, Tom] chooses personal honor, the integrity of manhood which is more important to him than his desire for a woman. In his later departure from Cisco he is willing to sacrifice the glory of that manhood and the status and security it has bought him to reaffirm an ultimate commitment to family, the irrational ties of blood which symbolize the larger community of mankind. Thus a clear hierarchy emerges: the integrity of self belongs to a higher order of being than romantic love, but the submission of self to the welfare of family and all it represents is, in this story at least, existence on the highest level.

Like "Tom Rivers," Miss Gordon's story "The Long Day" is subtle and therefore open to misinterpretation, even by critics of some stature. One of several accounts in *The Forest of the South* which deal with Negroes, the narrative inevitably evokes reprisals from the ranks of twentieth-century secular Puritans. (p. 61)

Miss Gordon often invests her black characters with the same dignity and stature as does William Faulkner, though, like Faulkner, she presents them as credible human beings with the capacity for moral failure that one finds in her white characters. . . .

In the first place, Miss Gordon's better blacks, like her better whites, behave with a formal civility which derives from the ontology informing a traditional society. In such a world, manners serve not only as the necessary catalyst for social intercourse between members of disparate social orders, but also as a distinct mode of self-definition, as symbols for the *daimon*. (p. 62)

"The Long Day" is concerned with manners and their capacity to dignify and in some measure to redeem, though ostensibly the story is a particularly gruesome "initiation" —the exposure for the first time of a small boy named Henry to the shocking world of primitive passion and violence. And yet we cannot know the true nature of the boy's "epiphany" because the story ends abruptly with a vision of horror, and its impact on Henry is never rendered. What the vision essentially means, however, is obvious to the reader; and so one must conclude that the overall significance of the story is something more complex than simply what happens to the boy.

In order to understand more fully that significance it is first necessary to consider the nature of the central action. On the surface this action is concerned with Henry's attempt to cajole the Negro sharecropper Joe into taking him fishing, Joe's artful stalling and diversionary tactics, his mumbled apology and abrupt flight, and a final revelation to the boy that Joe's wife has died of razor wounds during the course of the day's seemingly trivial events. So we can see that two series of incidents compose the single action of the narrative: one series defines the apparent action, and the other series the hidden action. Thus one has only to juxtapose the two to understand the thematic implications of Miss Gordon's subtle story, implications which tell the reader a great deal about the nature and function of manners in society. For manners both *control* and *hide* the violence that perennially lies at the heart of the human community, and for this reason such modes of conduct are exercises in heroism. (p. 63)

[It] is the character of Joe that bears the dramatic burden of both actions; the overt and the hidden; and his conduct, while perhaps not perfect, reveals him to be a highly civilized individual who does not without a struggle surrender to "the violence of life and the lust of man." . . . Like Tom Rivers, he is a man who lives by a code which demands great personal sacrifice in a crucial situation where life and death hang in the balance. (p. 65)

"Mr. Powers" is a story specifically concerned with economics and its role in the hierarchy of traditional human values. Again the setting is the rural South of the early twentieth century, where sharecropping was a socially accepted arrangement between the haves and the have-nots. In this case both the landowners, Jack and Ellen Cromlie, and the tenant, Mr. Powers, are white: but their relationship is essentially the same as the one between whites and negroes like Joe. (pp. 65-6)

[The] arrangement with Mr. Powers becomes more complex when the Cromlies learn that he has been indicted for homicide, the accidental killing of his own son while in a jealous rage. The Cromlies discuss the matter, and Ellen is sympathetic. "We are going to let him stay," she asks. Jack, we *are* going to let him stay, aren't we?" (p. 66)

Miss Gordon is faced with a technical problem which tests to the utmost her skill as an artist. Had she chosen to depict Ellen as finally dominated by economic concerns the resolution of the story would have been simple: a dramatic confrontation with Mr. Powers rendered through dialogue and action. But the burden of her narrative, predictably enough, is the dominance of *caritas* over pride and self-interest, and the result of such a resolution is not action but inaction. Hence it is necessary for her to resolve the conflict within the consciousness of her central character.

She accomplishes this end through a subtle use of natural description which prepares the reader for Ellen's final decision to let Mr. Powers alone in his final ordeal before the bar of justice. (p. 67)

Faced with the prospect of confronting her "exploiter" she is suddenly moved by his tragic plight and begins to understand why Jack, a man and therefore more likely to identify with Mr. Powers's terrible predicament, has been unwilling to pursue the matter of [an] unpaid debt. The [atmospheric] light, which contains a number of traditional meanings, has struck her consciousness with all the power and certitude of

grace; and she is redeemed from the petty considerations which have prevented her from extending to the man her innately predominant charity. (p. 68)

"Her Quaint Honor" is perhaps the best story in this group of four, primarily because it reveals with the greatest subtlety and precision the essential complexity of human experience. It is easy to miss this complexity, however, if one views the action as mere social commentary; for once again the subject is the relationship in the South between the white man and the black, a relationship which Miss Gordon, like any sensible writer of fiction, views in human rather than in ideological terms.

On a cursory reading the meaning of the narrative seems to be obvious. Jim, the narrator, decides to sell his garage and to farm his grandmother's land, an occupation which is consistent with his own inclinations and with the traditions of his family. He asks Tom Doty, a Negro who has been connected with his family for years, to make the crop with him; and in, putting such a proposition to Tom, Jim incurs implicit obligations to the Negro; for in recent years Tom has prospered with Mr. Bannerman, a white landlord. Tom readily accepts Jim's offer, however, and things go well until their tobacco is picked and stored in the barn for curing. At this point Jim makes an error in judgment which leads to financial disaster: he hires Bud Asbury, a white man with a reputation for dissipation, to cure the tobacco. Asbury is attracted to Tom's light-skinned wife, Frankie; and when he makes advances to her, he incurs Jim's wrath, they fight, and Asbury is driven off the farm. But as a consequence the crop is ruined and brings no more than half of its potential value.

On the surface, then, the action is simple in its linear movement, a low-profile graph of tragedy. . . . Yet a closer examination of the motives which lie behind the action suggests that the story is more heroic than tragic in its implications, though the heroism defined, as in "The Long Day," is an imperfect one, tarnished to some degree by the nature of the fallen world in which all human action takes place.

In order to understand the meaning of Jim's sacrifice—for he is surely the hero, however flawed—we must examine Miss Gordon's use of the first person narrator, a point of view which provides the principal key to the inherently complex meaning of the action. For one thing, every first person narrator is, to some degree, fallible, for no one can view his own behavior or the operation of his own consciousness with complete understanding and objectivity. Even in retrospect, it is finally impossible for such a narrator to transcend the limitations of self, the ultimate barriers of individual experience; and some of the finest values in modern fiction have been realized by writers who use these limitations rather than struggle to minimize them. In "Her Quaint Honor" Miss Gordon has chosen to cut with the grain, and Jim in telling his story reveals an ignorance of the meaning of his own actions which creates not only an exquisite irony but also the subtle ambiguity of meaning which marks this work for special attention. (pp. 68-9)

The last two paragraphs [of the story] epitomize the greater dilemma both [Jim and Tom] have faced and suggest some of the subtler implications of that dilemma.

> Tom looked at the tobacco and then he
> looked at me. He poked his lip out. "That

Mister Bud Asbury," he said, "I don't care how good he can cure tobacco. He better stay away from my woman."

I didn't say anything. A man has to fight if somebody tries to take his woman. But I couldn't stand by and watch that nigger carve Bud up. It struck me as a funny business. Always has. . . .

(p. 71)

Tom's statement is simple enough in its meaning: he would rather retain his marital prerogatives than make a few hundred dollars more on his crop, though he still pays his respects to the code by referring to Asbury as "Mister." His manhood, then, is without its price, though it has been mitigated to some extent by his immediate surrender to Jim at the crucial moment of confrontation. Does this surrender proceed from his trust in Jim or does it proceed from the deficiency of a spirit broken by the code? These questions, I would suggest, are impossible to answer with any certitude. They contain within them the ambiguity of life itself, and there is evidence to support either contention—or both.

On the surface the case of Jim seems easier to deal with. For one thing, he is not faced with the same dilemma. Loyalty to his friend and loyalty to the social code demand of him exactly the same course of action, and the profanation of his family home is additional motivation for him to fight Bud Asbury. But the important thing to note is that Jim acts immediately and instinctively, with little or no concern for the economic consequences of his action. He regards neither Asbury nor Tom as merely a means to an economic end. Each is measured against a traditional code of conduct, and Asbury's misbehavior demands punishment.

Thus Jim acts out of "honor," as the title of the story suggests; but it is a "quaint" honor, extraordinary, perhaps even exotic, as foreign to outsiders as the practices of the aborigines. The reference here to Marvell is, I think, only obliquely important. Certainly the "honor" in both cases is related to sexual conduct; but the "Her" of Miss Gordon's title is more than a flesh-and-blood mistress, more than the Negro woman, Frankie, the only significant feminine character in the story. The "quaint honor" is also that of the South, the "lady" whose complex modes of behavior are so curious and frustrating to those who try to convert her to their own peculiar abstractions.

Jim's ultimate failure to understand his own conduct is typical of the traditional man, whose *daimon* is essentially intuitive because it feeds on a symbology of acts and anecdotes transmitted through the daily lives of men and women who have never thought deeply about the nature of their society. (pp. 71-2)

> *Thomas H. Landess, "Caroline Gordon's Ontological Stories," in* The Short Fiction of Caroline Gordon: A Critical Symposium, *edited by Thomas H. Landess (copyright 1972 The University of Dallas Press), The University of Dallas Press, 1972, pp. 53-73.*

*   *   *

GORDON, Mary   1949-

Gordon is an American novelist. Her first novel, *Final Payments*, chronicles a woman's attempt to escape the limits of a strict Catholic upbringing in her search for an independent self.

MAUREEN HOWARD

With the natural instincts of a good narrator, Mary Gordon [in "Final Payments"] has elected to keep to the single-minded voice of her heroine, for Isabel Moore is obsessed with her own story. . . . One of the great strengths of [the novel] is the suspense that Mary Gordon builds into her plot. What will her bright, untried heroine find beyond Queens and the great dominant passion of her past? Isabel Moore is an extremely complex figure: she is physically attractive, vulnerable, sensuous, self-centered, smug—and, above all, intelligent. Unfortunately, her sojourn in the big world is a lot less interesting than in her bondage. In contrast to the Moores' house, a forceful presence in the novel, Isabel's apartment in a town up the Hudson, and her adventures, might be found in any conventional fiction about the contemporary working girl and her problems.

In a series of accidents that have none of the mystery of true novelistic coincidence, Isabel is awarded a job and an adulterous love affair. There is such a precipitous falling off in the stylish center of "Final Payments" that it is easy to see why Isabel does not quite believe in the events of her life. It is curious, too, that between the serial installments of Isabel's romance, local political life, and the sexual vagaries of her two girlhood friends, the author, as though to keep us apprised of her larger sympathies and real capabilities, has written a series of splendid vignettes. In "Final Payments" Isabel's job is to interview old people who are cared for by foster families: if there was to be any hope for the late-blooming heroine, I felt it must be in Isabel's imaginative reading of the aged—their dignity, madness, continuing love and hostility—rather than in her girlish response to her cardboard lover.

Isabel Moore's freedom is illusory: she must punish herself for her success and for her sexual fulfillment, even for her advantages of good looks and intelligence. This novel confronts the strain in American life that is darkly puritanic, a theme that has haunted our literature from Hawthorne on. In the denial of pleasure Isabel seeks salvation. Once again, the novel takes on force when she atones for her sins by caring for the hideous Margaret Casey, a woman crippled in body and spirit. The reader will be tempted to hiss when Margaret comes on the scene, to cheer when Isabel, grown fat, idle and ugly, is saved by her own good sense. At its best, the novel has this sort of heightened drama and immediacy.

Along with her unmistakable talent Mary Gordon shows great respect for her craft: she cares about her diction, the rhythms of a sentence, the pacing of her paragraphs. . . . [Mary Gordon's cleverness] can be forced and somewhat parochial. She does not have anything like the easy wit and charm of Mary McCarthy about sex or politics; but what might prove infinitely more valuable to a writer of fiction is her fine fury with the false lessons of the past. We are made to care about Isabel Moore's arrested emotional development, her agony of guilt and pain—that is the genuine achievement of "Final Payments." (pp. 1, 32)

> *Maureen Howard, "Salvation in Queens," in* The New York Times Book Review *(© 1978 by The New York Times Company; reprinted by permission), April 16, 1978, pp. 1, 32.*

AMANDA HELLER

Mary Gordon is a young writer who obviously knows the

territory she writes about, semi-urban neighborhoods of houses "cared for with a fierce, unimaginative pride," in which education, social life, and daily transactions all revolve around the parish. When she writes of Isabel's Catholic upbringing, she does so with a charming combination of affection and cynical wit. Isabel and her friends are appealing if rather narrow characters. Unfortunately, the plot of the book takes a series of excessively contrived turns. An ungainly but very likable first novel. (p. 94)

> Amanda Heller, in The Atlantic Monthly (copyright © 1978 by The Atlantic Monthly Company, Boston, Mass.; reprinted with permission), May, 1978.

DAVID LODGE

Final Payments is a well-made, realistic novel of refined sensibility and moral scruple, informed by the values of orthodox Christianity—qualities one does not expect from the debut of a young American writer these days. . . . Anything more different from the school of Jong could hardly be imagined; but there is a perceptible affinity between *Final Payments* and, say, [Margaret Drabble's] *The Needle's Eye*. In both writers the primary source of interest and concern is the effort of an ironic and fastidious female sensibility to be good. . . .

Isabel Moore is a subtle, articulate, self-conscious narrator. She is well aware of the twists and turns of her own psyche —that she may have arranged to be caught in *flagrante delicto* to punish her father for taking her virtue for granted, and then punished herself by sacrificing her youth to his illness. . . . Indeed, the long illness of her father has been for her a kind of time-warp, from which she emerges, more frightened than exhilarated, to face the fact that she can make for herself any life she chooses. . . .

[The] novel, so firmly and freshly written at the outset, threatens to turn soft at the core, like a sleepy pear. The main trouble is the character of Hugh [Isabel's married lover], and it may be some measure of the author's inability to make anything of him that the heroine is peculiarly attracted by his back, so that he spends much of the novel with his face inscrutably averted from us.

Ms Gordon tries hard to compensate for this thinness of characterization by passages of discreetly erotic lyricism and anguished introspection by the heroine which only push the novel dangerously in the direction of superior women's magazine fiction. But it recovers its poise and power splendidly in the last eighty pages. . . . It says much for the power of Ms Gordon's writing that the reader feels a genuine sense of dismay at the spectacle of the heroine's physical and mental decline [after she renounces her lover and again reenters the Catholic ghetto of her youth], and a genuine sense of relief when she finally allows herself to be rescued from it.

In one sense *Final Payments* is a study in the power of traditional Catholicism over those who were indoctrinated in it at an impressionable age. The heroine's utter subservience to her father is obviously a microcosm of the power structure of the authoritarian, paternalistic pre-Conciliar Church; and her renunciation of her lover a desperate attempt to recover the assurance of personal salvation that she enjoyed as a result of her self-mortifying service. In the end the heroine breaks the suffocating grip of the Catholic ghetto, and opts for a more open and humanistic ethic. Yet the novel is steeped in nostalgia for, as well as nausea at, that kind of Catholicism, and the undoubted distinction of its writing owes much to the high-cultural equivalent of the Catholic ghetto—the "Catholic novel" of Greene, Mauriac, Bernanos, Bloy, with its characteristic fondness for aphorisms that are subversive of liberal, materialistic assumptions. "I was angry at myself", says the heroine at one point, "for making the equation, my father's equation, the Church's equation, between suffering and value", but the equation seems stronger than her anger, and ultimately impervious to it. . . .

I have emphasized the Catholic theme because it interests me particularly, but *Final Payments* is a rich, thoughtful, stylishly-written novel that should have a more than parochial appeal. The progress of its author will be worth watching.

> David Lodge, "The Arms of the Church," in The Times Literary Supplement (© Times Newspapers Ltd. (London) 1978; reproduced from The Times Literary Supplement by permission), September 1, 1978, p. 965.

BRUCE ALLEN

Mary Gordon's much-praised *Final Payments* may be the best American feminist novel yet, though its thematic emphases are skillfully concealed beneath its wry surface picturing of an Irish Catholic girl who "gives up her life" for her invalid father, nervously edges back into reality after his death, then chooses renunciation again (for "having put myself at the center of the universe")—in a drastic penitential act that is simply unbelievable in pure narrative terms (though it does deftly dramatize women's reluctance to claim all they're entitled to).

The overall shape of Gordon's story is itself an eloquent comment on the nature of woman's fate. The simple declarative style, with its emotion-charged repetitions, generates great intensity. And, not least of all, Gordon's spectacular verbal skill allows her heroine to express complex emotional and intellectual attitudes with great precision. *Final Payments* is, owing to the tactical error I have mentioned, not all it might have been—but is quite good enough to demonstrate that Mary Gordon is one of the most gifted writers of her generation. (p. 616)

> Bruce Allen, in Sewanee Review (reprinted by permission of the editor; © 1978 by The University of the South), Fall, 1978.

PAUL ABLEMAN

Final Payments is a work of casuistry concerned to examine the conflicting demands of morality, especially Catholic morality. Isabel Moore, the heroine, blunders about, discharging ruin and agonizing about whether she is behaving well. It would be reassuring to feel that Mary Gordon knew she had created a Pharisaic monster and would dissociate herself from sympathy with Isabel's lethal spiritual struggles. This is not made clear and I was left with the feeling that perhaps Isabel was intended by her creator to represent Heroic Virtue or something of the kind. . . .

[This] book invites judgement by moral, even more than by purely literary, criteria. (p. 23)

The characters in this book are static, in the sense that at the core of their being lies not a psychology but a morality.

They are almost 'humours'. Thus, although they interact they cannot change or evolve. Liz, the hard-bitten, but soft-hearted, girl-friend will grunt wise-cracks to the end of time. Judgement day will discover Margaret still reeking sourly and muttering envious complaint masked as devout solicitude. Isabel herself is essentially the idea of moral dilemma who will bounce indefinitely from socket to socket of the Catholic pin-ball machine with her shiny steel surface unscarred by earthly experience. The fundamental impulse behind *Final Payments,* adequately implied by the title, is eschatalogical rather than fictional.

This is matched by a curious feature of the writing: the image without real content. The offending lady at the bus terminal who 'laughed like an animal' is credited with patches in her hair 'the colour of egg yolks', 'eyes . . . the colour of a chemical', 'a face the colour of egg whites' and so on. Ignoring the obsessive egg comparisons, which might well haunt a childless woman, these similes seem to express a refusal to collaborate with mere matter and, although certain excellent passages reveal Mary Gordon's talent for description, generally speaking the novel is set in a kind of featureless limbo.

Readers will rightly suspect by now that I didn't much enjoy this book. It seemed to me to be theology posing as fiction, a hybrid form which compounds the tedium of the former with the imprecision of the latter to the advantage of neither. Nevertheless, a case, and even a strong one, can be made for the defence. Mary Gordon is a natural writer who has enough authority over language, imaginative strength and eye for character to furnish a splendid novel. The vignettes in which Isabel explores a variety of bewildered old folk lodged with sometimes negligent, sometimes caring hosts, struck me as excellent. There is no doubt that *Final Payments* is an auspicious debut . . . and little doubt that its author will speak to us again. My own hope is that next time her voice will be less that of the casuist than of the novelist. (p. 24)

Paul Ableman, "Last Things," in The Spectator *(© 1979 by The Spectator; reprinted by permission of* The Spectator*), January 13, 1979, pp. 23-4.*

*   *   *

GREEN, Henry (pseudonym of Henry Vincent Yorke) 1905-1974

Green was an English novelist. A man of original ideas and talents, Green possessed a unique style and approach to literature. Eschewing long passages of description, Green allowed his characters to reveal themselves through extensive dialogue, rendered in carefully wrought prose. Originally concerned with presenting a comic view of the life of the English upper class, Green expanded his artistic vision to include all strata of English society. Often the setting and background of his novels function symbolically, lending a mythic element to the lives and lifestyles delineated. The one-word titles of his novels, usually participles or gerunds (*Living, Loving, Concluding*), reflect the essence of Green's literary purpose: "to create 'life' which does not eat, procreate, or drink, but which can live in people who are alive." (See also *CLC,* Vol. 2, and *Contemporary Authors,* obituary, Vols. 49-52.)

MICHAEL DIRDA

More virtuoso performance than novel, *Blindness* remains beguiling for its prefiguration of the major themes and tech-

niques of Green's mature fiction: the exact rightness of the conversation of both landed gentry and servants, the machinations of people at cross-purposes, symbolism in nature and names, the young and old locked together in death-grip relations, and much humor and sadness. Significantly, the last sections of the novel are called "Finishing" and "Beginning Again"—participles that look forward to the titles of Green's later works. . . .

[Green] learned to write by listening to the workers around him [in his father's factory]: "Unlike literary men, factory workers are interested, passionately interested, in one subject above all—the lives and habits of other *people*. Get into conversation with any group of workmen—and *other people* is what they talk about."

In 1929 Green published *Living,* a novel very much about people. Like the other "ing" novels to follow, its title is exact: *Living* depicts daily life for a group of workers, a young girl, and an upper-class family that owns a foundry. The book received poor reviews, with the exception of one by the young Evelyn Waugh, who proclaimed it a "triumph." . . .

What most upset critics, and what makes the novel a bit foreboding, are the rapid scene shifts, loose grammar, and light punctuation—and the elimination of "a," "an," and "the" from much of the narration. "I wanted to make that book as taut and spare as possible," Green later explained, "to fit the proletarian life I was then leading. So I hit on leaving out the articles. . . . I suppose the more you leave out, the more you highlight what you leave in."

Especially "highlighted" was the realistic speech of the workers, a lingo that can be difficult to follow at first—especially for Americans. But it possesses such gritty authenticity that one is gradually sucked into the book's vision. (It would be easy, but wrong, to label this a naturalistic or leftist vision: There is absolutely no tendentiousness.) One gets to know the girl Lily Gates and the old moulder Craigan so well that one feels *with* them, never *for* them—they are living, and isolation from each other, small triumphs, and disillusionment make up the richness of their ordinary lives of work, love, and family. As Eudora Welty has said: "Here the world is always right up against our eyes." . . .

If *Living* seems to anticipate the novels of the 1930's, *Party Going* appears a holdover from the 20's, an echo of early Waugh and Huxley. Green worked on this "novel about my own circle in London" from 1931-1938. . . .

[This] novel transcribes bitchy upper-class speech as faithfully as *Living* replicated the talk of factory workers. However, Green's narration has changed: No longer does it lack articles; indeed, the prose becomes evocative and luxuriant in keeping with the character of decadent partygoers. A famous passage describes Amabel in her bath:

> As she went over herself with her towel it was plain that she loved her own shape and skin. When she dried her breasts she wiped them with as much care as she would puppies after she had given them their bath, smiling all the time. But her stomach she wiped unsmiling upwards to make it thin. When she came to dry her legs she hissed like grooms do. And as she got herself dry that steam began to go off the mirror walls

so that as she got white again more and more
of herself began to be reflected.

Such delicate and sensuous details . . . give the novel the
feel of a play, of a late Shakespearean romance with a hint
of doom just off stage. . . .

[In his Auxiliary Fire Service experience during the war]
Green rediscovered his "proletarian inspiration," out of
which emerged his next three novels—*Caught* (1943), *Loving* (1945), and *Back* (1946). *Caught* deals with firefighters
in London and *Back* is a highly symbolic novel about a returning veteran haunted by "rose"—the woman with this
name who is dead, the flower, and the color.

In *Loving* Green produced what many view as his most balanced achievement. Set in an Irish castle during the war,
Loving possesses more of the fairy-tale traits adumbrated in
Party Going (and which were to become an allegory of the
rose in *Back*).

The novel begins "Once upon a time" and ends with "and
they lived happily ever after." It is a love story between a
butler and a chamber maid, containing both satire and wonderfully human portraits of the cooks, nannies, and servants who have divided an estate into bailiwicks.

But above all, the action focuses on loving, its forms and
variations from the Platonic to the adulterous. . . . Around
them all, in this enchanted castle, come the rumors of war
and the I.R.A., but these are held off—for a while—by the
spell of Edith's "dazzled dazzling eyes."

After *Back,* Green brought forth in 1948 what he himself
called his best novel, *Concluding.* It is a rich, melancholy
work, offering all summer in a day, evoking the religious,
somber tone of a poem like "Four Quartets." (p. R11)

The few events of the novel take place in a single day when
two students disappear and one is found, while the remaining girls—whose names all begin with M—prepare for the
annual founder's day dance. Throughout, a sense of loneliness and age, of the animal need for love, and of the rivalry
between young and old, withered and blossoming, create a
trancelike feel to *Concluding*—from misty morning, to the
dizzy heat of day, to the romantic whirl of the dance, to the
overwhelming black of night.

Yet the conversation remains vivid. . . .

And Green's descriptions are never more provocative. . . .

If *Loving* is Green's fairy-tale Eden where all is lovely, then
Concluding is his autumnal world of romance after the Fall,
dominated by memory and nature and young girls swirling
in a dance to the music of time. . . .

In his last two books he once more changed his style and
returned to the milieu of the upper classes. *Nothing* (1950)
and *Doting* (1952) are written almost entirely in dialogue.
They are witty, but concentrate on shallow misalliances;
most readers feel Green denied himself too much by eliminating description. . . .

Green once described his artistic goals: "Prose is not to be
read aloud but to oneself at night, and it is not quick as poetry, but rather a gathering web of insinuations which go
further than names shared can ever go. Prose should be a
long intimacy between strangers with no direct appeal to
what both may have known. It should slowly appeal to feelings unexpressed, it should in the end draw tears out of the
stone."

In Henry Green's work, in his experimentation and rich
symbolism, in his masterful juxtaposition of scene, in his
musician's ear for speech and restrained sensuous detail, in
his focus on the ordinary activities of ordinary human
beings, above all, in his warmth and humor and absolute
inner integrity, the novel becomes vision, inescapable and
unforgettable. (p. R12)

Michael Dirda, "Rediscovering Henry Green," in
The Chronicle Review *(copyright © 1978 by The
Chronicle of Higher Education, Inc.), November
13, 1978, pp. R11-R12.*

IRVING HOWE

The fiction of Henry Green is utterly English in tone. A
disdain for used-up rhetoric, a nervous eccentricity of
voice, a liking for understatement now and again relieved
by shy outpouring of lyricism, a mild yielding to quirkiness
as the commonplace of existence—these make him seem an
English writer in the line often fecklessly called "minor."
. . .

Green's novels are comedies, but not often of the kind that
elicit bursts of laughter. Some of his books are shadowed
by fear and delusion, most speak of the usualness of the
unusual. Green keeps returning to the deceptions of the
self, in "Loving" to that complex kind of deception where
the charms of fantasy thicken into hallucination. He avoids
the large public themes favored by Victorian novelists; he
rarely indulges in ethical or social declamation. Psycholo-
gizing is also taboo: no hovering over the emotions of characters, no fussy probing into "depths." Green tries instead
to ambush experience, hoping to achieve freshness through
the oblique. . . .

Into each novel he fences a plot of English life. . . .
Through these miniature worlds, his brittle characters act
out private crises of friction and delusion. They act them
out against a lightly sketched background of English society
of the prewar years, that flittering, shaky scene of decline.
Green is especially good at noting "the half-tones of class."
Rarely sentimental and never pontifical, his novels still take
on large implications: "True life," he said, "has nothing to
do with sudden death and great tragedy." In his vision of
things, it has to do with wry vignette, clipped incident, sudden turns of feeling, bits of relationship falling into or out of
place. . . .

His greatest gift is for language. In the early novels he
yields to an irritating mannerism, so intent is he on "making it new," but later his prose becomes serene and supple.
Words are never used approximately, to induce clumsy
blotches of feeling. They point to objects, they take on
strength through particularity. From sentence to sentence
the flow of Green's prose is jumpy, as in some of Virginia
Woolf's novels, or, to venture a wilder comparison, as in
Seurat's Pointillist paintings, where the eye's unprepared
journey from dot to dot creates an effect of staccato flow, a
universe of perception no longer secure but nervous, insistent, renewed.

Not all of these traits are fully visible in "Blindness," [his
first and] perhaps the only Green novel that can be called
conventional. But as he goes along, one can see him sliding
into his own manner; indeed, a secondary pleasure in reading this book is watching a 20-year-old writer marshal his
gifts to become Henry Green. . . .

How is a novelist to represent the experience of blindness [suffered by Green's 17-year-old protagonist, John] which he himself has never known? How did Faulkner represent the experience of idiocy when creating Benjy in "The Sound and the Fury"? The answer is not a claim to be imitating a reality that by its very nature one cannot know, but to improvise a plausible simulacrum, an as-if version that can be accepted provisionally. Green doesn't convince us that he is protraying the actuality of a boy suffering blindness; he convinces us that, for the purpose of this novel, his fiction will serve as a kind of truth. (p. 11)

The novel concludes without high-minded fakery, asserted resolution. There is no cant about anything compensating for John's loss—what could? But we have been given a splendidly dry and controlled evocation of the boy's struggle to find his way in darkness.

Sometimes the book lags, sometimes its young author uses too much interior monologue. We know from the books to come that he will get better. Still, this is the real thing, the entry into literature of a writer who cares for exactness of looking. There ought to be some people willing to push past the mounds of rubbish that fill bookstores these days and find their way to the light of "Blindness." (p. 57)

Irving Howe, in The New York Times Book Review *(© 1978 by The New York Times Company; reprinted by permission), December 10, 1978.*

RICHARD HORN

Now that at least [*Loving, Living,* and *Party Going* by] Henry Green, most neglected of twentieth-century novelists, have been reissued (along with *Blindness,* his first novel . . .) after more than twenty years of out-of-print oblivion, any unfavorable criticism may seem like a badly timed kick in the face to an author who is just—posthumously—getting back on his feet. Still, though these four Green novels deserve to be welcomed back with praise, that praise should be qualified; writers are, after all, neglected for reasons.

For me, at least, *Loving/Living/Party Going* do not present Henry Green at his most accomplished. For that, one would have to pick up *Caught.* . . . With its weirdly incandescent setting in pre-Blitz London, its atmosphere of desperate sexuality, its awkwardly rounded-out characters and extremely peculiar construction that shifts almost imperceptibly from story to prose poem to slice-of-life dialogue to interior monologue, *Caught* may be one of the most convincing novels about daily life in wartime ever written. . . . Green wrote about people and how they got on with one another in the course of daily life, but where his contemporaries Elizabeth Bowen, Ivy Compton-Burnett, Virginia Woolf and E. M. Forster would tell all, Green is reticent. Unlike them, he says very little that is direct about his characters, and says it in a style given over to aimless conversations, bursts of dense metaphor and highly mannered description. Often the conversations have the ring and rhythm of real ones, and the prose itself can glow in places with an unexpected radiance. In *Caught* and *Concluding,* Green's concern is, as always, with the mundane incidents of everyday living, except that in both books life has assumed a dark, nightmarish quality, so that Green's characteristic reticence and the peculiar milieu of each meet halfway to create phantom worlds so bizarre that the meaning of what happens in them *can* only be guessed at.

In *Loving, Living,* and *Party Going,* Green's reticence keeps us in the dark, but this time in the midst of the talking, eating, working, hating and loving that all fall under the heading of daylit daily life. . . . Green stubbornly adheres to a set of rules that forbid his drawing us along with either story-line or psychological insight. Nothing happens—that's the point—and no one is explained. Because there is no pervasive rhythm of revelation or event to get caught up in, we are obliged to renew our interest in and revise our opinions of characters of whom we learn nothing with almost every line—a task that soon becomes impossible. We are left with an intentionally objective presentation of characters interspersed with precise descriptions wherein things take on a transcendent glow, and against these dreamlike backcloths the characters' actions are meant to become transcendent, too: mundane but glorious, an affirmation of life itself. Green's hope is that these scenes that never really "go" anywhere or build to anything will coalesce into what he calls in his "self-portrait" *Pack My Bag* "a gathering web of insinuations," whose accumulation will let flow the feelings we have searched for unsuccessfully on page after page. But when the glow of pure phenomena does not shine with the almost spiritual intensity Green counted on, the going can get pretty tedious. . . .

It is strange to spend two hundred pages with a group of characters who don't seem especially interesting without even knowing why the author bothered with them at all. . . . Green never tells us what *he* as author thinks about his characters, so all we as readers can do is keep guessing; are they idiots? are they sincere? are they pathetic? silly? malicious? and is this all "life itself"? . . .

Only at the end of *Loving* and *Party Going* does the uncertainty that has been thrown like a blanket over our heads provide a point/non-point-of-view of its own. We realize, perhaps too late, that the characters might have had depths we'd never suspected. Just as we close each book we feel that at last we know exactly what they were like, though we cannot say it. . . .

[The] author of the laconically-titled *Living, Loving, Party Going, Loving, Concluding, Nothing* and *Doing* is anything but giving. His determination to say nothing definite seems too coy, too calculated and too programmatic to be anything but a pose, and a rather cruel one at that. We read and read and read but it seems entirely up to us whether there is something there, or nothing at all—not an especially comfortable position to be placed in. . . . [To] be elusive *on purpose,* to avoid, out of reticence, committing oneself deeply to anything (even if it is something as transitory as a feeling) seems like a sneaky kind of sadism when it becomes the guiding principle for novels meant for others to read and presumably get something out of. We want to understand the author, he consistently defies our understanding. Like life itself, you say; like someone who refuses to make himself known, say I. . . . For those who like to see human interaction as one big riddle (or one big, million-faceted prism), *Loving, Living,* and *Party Going* will take the breath away. But those who ask fiction for something more sustaining and certain may accuse Henry Green of taking away the very air they breathe.

Richard Horn, "Breathless," in New York Arts Journal *(copyright © 1979 by Richard W. Burgin), #13, 1979, p. 16.*

BEN YAGODA

A host of conflicts animate Green's books—between the classes, between the generations, between expectation and reality—but none is so prevalent as that between what is said and what is understood. The ways Green's people manage to misconstrue each other constitute almost a catalogue of the hazards of language—solecism, lying, obfuscation, mumbling, on the part of the speaker; inattention, lack of interest, insufficient data, on the part of the listener. For Green, communication is so damnably difficult that when it is achieved—by sign language, shouting, or sheer luck—the appropriate response is rejoicing. . . .

[*Blindness*] is an accomplished novel, and all the more impressive in view of the author's age, but it offers little of the compelling originality of Green's later work. Still, *Blindness* sheds considerable light on this singular novelist. Its first twenty-five pages are from a diary John keeps at Noat before the accident [which leads to his blindness] and are easily the most rewarding section of the book. Here, as in the mature Green, drama and interest are found in the everyday and necessary, not in the catastrophic and contingent. . . .

Green's memoir, *Pack My Bag* (1938), reveals that he was secretary of the Eton Society of the Arts and was himself an aesthete ("that is a boy who consciously dressed to shock," he wrote later). One cannot help speculating on the relation between John Haye and Henry Vincent Yorke, or coming to the conclusion that the creator disapproved of his creation, and, by implication, himself. Although John is likeable enough, and almost touching in his enthusiasm . . . , Green clearly views the affliction as a deserved punishment. John had been living a useless, profligate life; only blindness, paradoxically, can make him "see." The fit and mysterious, redemptive vision he experiences in the final scene remind us of Dostoyevsky and *Crime and Punishment*, which he had described in the diary as "dreadful, awful, supremely great."

Was this book—and, in a way, his career—the punishment Green inflicted upon himself for his dandyism? One cannot say for sure; but this was certainly a young man who was very hard on himself. There is the simple fact that *Blindness* must have been an extraordinarily difficult book to write. After the diary, little real action transpires, with the bulk of the remainder being a mixture of dialogue and third-person exposition colored by any one of a half dozen characters' perceptions. The book had to have been *written*, in other words, not merely described. . . .

Living is correctly called a proletarian novel, but it is not didactic. . . . There is a fascinating dialectic—never resolved—conducted between optimism (images of birds, music, and children) and pessimism ("dully their lives went out onto the streets, promenaded dullness there. Ugly clothes, people, houses"). Green was only a little overambitious in choosing his title, for the novel is as noncommittal, various and full as life itself.

The unearthshaking events of *Living* are filtered through endless discussion by the characters, and here lies the novel's triumph. Whether or not Green's dialogue accurately reproduces "Brummagen," it is a marvel, for it does reproduce the redundancies, non sequiturs, inanities, profanity, deceptions, humor and eloquence of proletarian speech with a doggedness that must be unprecedented. *Living* is the first evidence of Green's belief in the supreme importance of dialogue, and a certain kind of dialogue. . . .

[From] *Living* on, Green decreases the proportion of third-person description, until his final novels, *Nothing* and *Doting* (1950 and 1952), which are almost all dialogue. Another paradox: only speech, which lies incessantly, does not lie.

But a good deal of *Living* is in Henry Green's voice and unlike *Blindness*, it could not have been written by anyone else. At times, in fact, we feel like echoing a character in a later novel who tells a companion, "Don't be so like yourself." Consider: "Dale wanted a knife, but, getting up from table, for himself fetched it." . . .

The style—marked by repetition; dropped articles, prepositions, and commas; archaic diction; inverted construction; run-on sentences; whatever the opposite of slickness is; and excessive literalness (Green will never write "he" when he can write "this man")—is influenced by Charles Doughty's 1888 *Travels in Arabia Deserta* and by the King James Bible, but really originates with Green. Indeed, its originality may have been more important than any particular characteristic. In [a] 1950 article, Green argued that novelists must use a "highly personal prose," because the "good English" and impersonal journalese that was prevalent deadened the reader's imagination. Nevertheless, Green's stylistic idiosyncrasy is not merely tactical: It can be most hauntingly musical, especially in the surprising bursts of lyricism that dot the early novels and contrast strikingly with the generally grim themes. (p. 23)

Party Going (1939) shows the other side of *Living*'s coin. The upper crust gets most of the space here, with the worker making only occasional appearances. Eight young socialites gather in a London railway station to leave for a holiday in the south of France, but the heavy fog forces them to spend four hours (the time span of the book) in a railway hotel. Physically, even less happens than in *Living*: what we learn about is the internal dynamics of the group, the shifting alliances, sexual games, and individual hobbyhorses that lurk not so far beneath the surface of their conventional, polite behavior.

Party Going introduces into the Green canon one of his major themes—sex. For the partygoers, sexuality is miles away from what it should be. Most of them are merely observers. . . . The real fight is for Max, who is footing the bill, and is waged between Amabel, his current companion and Julia, a comer. For them sex has nothing to do with love or even physicality: It is a transferable function of power. After having decided not to ask Amabel along, Max forgets his reasons and reverses himself. In the terminology of Green titles, these people are doting, not loving: Their bonds are ephemeral, and can be broken or altered on a whim.

The rhetoric of *Party Going* is a subtle irony achieved by montage and suggestion. In the first scene Miss Fellowes, an aunt of one of the party, finds a pigeon (the novel is as full of birds as *Living*) that, disturbed by the fog, "went flat into a balustrade, and slowly fell, dead, at her feet." She picks it up and walks into a tunnel with the word "Departures" over it. Immediately we are in an atmosphere of heightened significance. Green does not have to press his points: The job has been done, and we cannot help thinking about the "terminal" and the fog symbolically. (pp. 23-4)

The verdict on these parasites is guilty, guilty, guilty, but *Party Going* manages to be no more of an anticapitalist tract than *Living*. For one thing, Green spends so much time on his characters' words and thoughts that they cannot seem evil: They are simply there. And he is once again most interested in the way experience is refracted through the lens of talk. These people may speak more grammatically than ironworkers, but they misinterpret just as obsessively. That condition is here represented by one "Embassy" Richard, an absent member of their set who was recently involved in a minor scandal. His case is picked at to the point of absurdity, with people forgetting their arguments, changing sides and making pointless points, until talking about him appears as the ritual that it is. (On the third to last page, in a brilliant stroke on Green's part, Richard actually shows up; we had somehow assumed that he didn't really exist.) . . .

[The characters in *Loving,* perhaps Green's most conventional novel, are] on the whole, selfish, oblivious to the outside world, and ineffectual. It is a point of view that a reader of Green has come to be familiar with: Besides how bad he is at being bad, and an occasional burst of undeserved providence, man has precious little going for him.

In *Loving* Green is in complete control of the technique he had been developing. The method is familiar—the events of each day are turned over and over again by the servants' dinner table talk—but the touch is lighter, more effortless. It is left up to the reader, for example, to notice that Raunce, the butler, after berating a maid early on for wanting to quit without giving notice, takes the opposite tack when making elopement plans: "We shan't hand it in mate that's all. We'll flit." And Green here puts into practice for the first time what he had remarked on in *Party Going,* "how impossible it is to tell what others are thinking or what, in ordinary life, brings people to do what they are doing." *Loving* is filled with constructions like "she lied, it may have been to protect the lad"; "it must have been that she could not help herself"; and "it seemed that she was not thinking of the servants." Such circumspection strengthens Green's case: We never have to take him on his word. . . .

[*Living, Loving,* and *Party Going*] form a definite piece of the Green oeuvre. Each limns a world bounded by geography, viewpoint, and most important, language. The books are alike, too, in not really ending. Though a denouement of sorts is effected in each, the strong implication is that events will go on much as before. In *Loving*'s first scene the old butler Eldon, dying in his room, utters the name Ellen over and over (we never learn who she is). At the very end, Raunce, in "exactly that tone Mr. Eldon had employed when calling his Ellen," moans, "Edie." Life, love, and parties are circles.

In *Caught* and the later novels Green narrows his scope, but continues to experiment, with consistently impressive results. *Caught* . . . is unusual for presenting a character from the author's own social station who is sympathetic (albeit somewhat neurotic). *Back* (1946) is the story of a returning veteran's gradual recovery of emotional health; what distinguishes it from the comparable *Blindness* is the uncanny way Green makes the reader share in Charley Summers's delusions and discomfort. The extraordinary *Concluding* (1948) is set in a girls' boarding school in the future, when England is ruled by an authoritarian State. Published the same year as *1984,* it makes a stronger case: Totalitarianism is scarier when (as may be expected) the dictators are ineffectual and no one seems to know exactly

what's going on. *Nothing* and *Doting,* admittedly abstract novels, consist of spare set pieces in which the *Party Going* set, now middle-aged and suffering from the stringency of the postwar economy, comically reveal themselves to be as vacuous and sex-obsessed as ever.

What makes Henry Green a truly unusual writer . . . are his style and his pessimism, and these must be confronted by everyone who reads him. The former is not so difficult a proposition. Green felt the language available to him was lifeless, and he took it upon himself to make it new. After the initial testings of *Blindness* and the excesses of *Living,* he found his voice; it is "nonrepresentational," as he insisted in articles and interviews, and its stylization always reminds the reader that what's in front of him is more than a story. Green's prose takes some getting used to, but gradually his strange rhythms etch their way into the mind and become delightful.

His misanthropy is a little harder to swallow. . . . [There] is no room for a Henry Green in a Henry Green novel. His characters are above all limited, and live in a different world from their author's; if they end up happy or successful it is always in spite of themselves. He came down hardest on his peers. Virtually without exception, they lead lives in which doting replaces loving and party going replaces living: result, nothing. . . .

Whatever the reasons for Green's dim view of humanity in general and his class in particular, it consigns him to the position of comic novelist. For if people are deceived and ineffectual, and don't even know it, how can they enter the realm of tragedy? It is fortunate, then, that Green accepts the comic spirit so fully and so well. Unlike Waugh, who covered similar ground, he is never mean, and seems as pleased as his characters when their triumphs-in-spite-of-themselves transpire. He is genuinely grateful for small favors: "The mere fact that we talk to one another is man's greatest asset. That we talk to one another in novels . . . is nothing less than miraculous." Occasionally, in the midst of misunderstanding and deception, communication will actually be reached, or a wish will come true. . . . We can only marvel that the odds have been beaten, and thank Green for letting us know. (p. 24)

Ben Yagoda, "Hazards of Language," *in* New Boston Review *(copyright 1979 by Boston Critic, Inc.), February-March, 1979, pp. 23-4.*

*   *   *

GRIFFITHS, Trevor   1935-

Griffiths is a British author of juvenile fiction and plays for stage, radio, and television. Critics sometimes imply that style is sacrificed for his Marxist themes of revolution, socialism, the corruption of the bourgeois, and capitalistic failure. Griffiths is currently concentrating on television plays in order to reach the widest possible audience.

ALAN BRIEN

[Even] in these days of stage nudity and mimic intercourse, such an episode [as the one opening Griffiths's *The Party*] still requires some strong dramatic justification for its sensational presentation. Partly because it is one of only two flurries of actual action which occur throughout the oratorio of talk and argument that evening in 1968, in this London flat, during the Paris revolt of students and workers. Partly because it throws some background light on the central character which nevertheless fails to illuminate his psyche much better than his physique.

How is he so rich, for example? (pp. 39, 41)

What is his secret sorrow, evoked with such Chekhovian melancholy by Mr. Pickup, with the dented smile and neglected hair of an old paintbrush left behind by the decorators? . . . Nobody up there asks him, and so nobody down here is ever told. . . .

Such a subject [as the "Revolution" of May 1968] demands more than a Shavian rehash of what was said at the time by those who stayed in Britain wondering what hadn't hit them.

Either we need a multi-media, documentary post-mortem with first-hand evidence and all the stereoscopy of hindsight. Or we need to see how the event affected people here and then how *they* affected other people here.

The author, Trevor Griffiths, has said that 'nearly every major character in the play is me or is the scintilla of me'. It is an honest, and quite brave, admission of creative egoism. But I'm afraid it shows: for despite the dozen or so characters, and two outstanding performances, *The Party* remains a one-man show. (p. 41)

> *Alan Brien, in* Plays and Players *(© copyright Alan Brien 1974; reprinted with permission), February, 1974.*

J. W. LAMBERT

The Party is a truthful play; but it is also sadly muddled [and] theatrically ineffective. . . .

Essentially *The Party*—the title refers vaguely to political parties, specifically to a gathering of radicals called together by the TV producer—consists of three very long speeches. (p. 18)

Unfortunately the play in which Mr. Griffiths has framed these impressive diatribes is almost non-existent, and a notable step backward from his last full-length work, *Occupations*. . . .

The sum total, though intelligent and not really boring, is basically uninteresting, because there is no real conflict or development, psychological or otherwise, only a basically contemptuous summary of crippled progressives. And what induced Mr. Griffiths, even if he did not wish to complicate his picture by making much of the events of 1968 in Czechoslovakia, far more wretched than those in France, to throw in a mere flippant allusion to that unhappy country? A mildly comic au pair girl with a Czech flag on her back and a pet hamster named after a prominent Stalinist seems to me an exceptionally shoddy way to evade commenting on the fall of Dubchek. (p. 19)

> *J. W. Lambert, in* Drama, *Spring, 1974.*

PETER ANSORGE

The six young apprentice comics who attend the evening classes organised by one-time master comedian, Eddie Waters [in *Comedians*], are under no illusions about the state of their chosen profession. . . . [They are training for] TV-satiated audiences who have come to accept a whole new repertoire of outspoken radicalist and ugly, sexual jokes. 'It's not the jokes. It's what lies behind them,' insists

their teacher who is trying to maintain his humane standards against the increasing amorality of the business. At the end of the first act we meet the London agent, Challenor, who has come to judge the comics with the offer of contracts for the most successful. He tells the student comedians to forget the wisdom of their teacher. 'I'm not looking for philosophers. I'm looking for comics. . . . Any good comic can lead an audience by the nose. But only in the direction they're going. And that direction is quite simply . . . escape.'

The second act is taken up with the acts, observed by Challenor and the stoical Waters. It is an enthralling demonstration of how we can choose either to sell or to save ourselves on a stage. (p. 22)

The last scene is a moving epitaph to the comedian's art, an acknowledgement that jokes are, perhaps, a reflection of our worst rather than our best instincts. Reviews have criticised this moment as an instance of bad taste, excess and fantasy on the part of the writer. But the whole scene comes from a sense that the joking has ended, 'all the funny men have gone home'. Price [who is Waters' "favorite and most gifted pupil"] quotes from Robert Frost's poem about the world ending in ice rather than fire. He leaves the stage, but not, one imagines, to follow a career in comedy.

Griffiths has written a beautiful, multilayered and unforgettable account of the comic art. I hope that its very lucidity won't be taken as mere analytical dissection of something which remains, finally, undefinable—humour. . . .

There's a sense of staying power and parable about *Comedians*. . . . (p. 23)

> *Peter Ansorge, in* Plays and Players *(© copyright Peter Ansorge 1975; reprinted with permission), April, 1975.*

HAROLD CLURMAN

Trevor Griffiths's *Comedians* . . . is a distinctly worthwhile play, but there are some difficulties in the way of its full appreciation. The first arises from the American audience's unfamiliarity with its background. The second is a diffusion—perhaps more apparent than real—in the play's composition. Though *Comedians* is an altogether appropriate title, it tends to disorient the spectators because it sets up an expectation of continuous hilarity. The play is for the most part quite funny, but "fun" is not its point. . . .

There is a specifically British base to [*Comedians*]. Class differences and distinctions are crucial to every phase of English life. . . . The open battle of the classes in England began only lately on anything like a grand scale. The English drama of the past twenty years provides evidence of this. *Comedians* is a new and highly engaging variation on a theme that more and more preoccupies English society.

Griffiths's play is obliquely a correction, almost a rebuke, to much of recent English writing for the theatre. Too often, the playwright implies, it expresses mere resentment, disgust, cynicism, hopelessness. Such attitudes are not enough: they will not serve. . . .

The technical difficulty in the play is its seeming lack of continuity of intention from the first two acts to the transition of the last. What begins as a series of racy characterizations and gutter jokes ends in a sober, very nearly impassioned discussion of issues of which we are only faintly aware and scarcely involved. (p. 670)

Harold Clurman, in The Nation *(copyright 1976 The Nation Associates), December 18, 1976.*

JACK RICHARDSON

Starting from a premise that [*Comedians*] is novel and rich with antic possibility, the play manages to scuttle itself with perfunctory, self-righteous anger. Set in Manchester, *Comedians* begins with a group of young men who aspire to be nightclub comics, meeting in one of those dismal cubicles of adult education. . . .

There is one student . . . who we perceive has a genuine and personal comic imagination, whose humor, at least in the classroom, goes much deeper than that of his fellow students. Among those who are simply looking for a better way to earn a living, he stands out as a real artist. . . .

[We] wait for this prize pupil to perform in a manner that will send his provincial audience back to bingo and *Comedians*' audience into several levels of appreciative laughter.

While waiting, one is treated to a variety of ways in which a comedian can endure an agonizing death on stage, and in each of the bumbling performances, Griffiths manages to present not only the comedy of ineptitude, but also the true character of the performers. The failures are painful and funny, and one believes nothing can possibly go wrong in a work that seems so closely in tune with the lives and setting it depicts. But, alas, one's confidence is premature. The genius of the classroom comes on and proceeds to aspire to social significance. Wearing the make-up of a mime, he tries to make human contact with a pair of poshly dressed dummies that, naturally enough, remain indifferent to all his overtures of friendship and assumptions of common feeling. As he pushes his demands for some sort of acknowledgment from these upperclass effigies, his hostility mounts, and his crude cordiality changes into threatening anger. His act ends in harangue and homicide, a conclusion which, I suppose, informs one that comedy is a serious business.

After such a heavy intrusion of high purpose, it should be no surprise that the final act is mostly taken up with a fierce debate between pupil and teacher on the functions of comedy, a debate which manages to draw concentration camps and the problems of working-class solidarity into its arguments. It should also be no surprise that vitality and humor drain out of the play with each reference to the social obligations of comedy, and one can only remind oneself afterward how much of Griffith's drama deserved a fate better than this windy and hollow conclusion. (p. 74)

[Griffith] should have forgotten that when a comic must fall back on a "seriously-now-folks" plea to his audience, his act is in serious trouble. (p. 75)

Jack Richardson, in Commentary *(reprinted by permission; all rights reserved), April, 1977.*

*   *   *

GRUMBACH, Doris   1918-

An American novelist, critic, and biographer, Grumbach is the author of *Chamber Music*. This fictional memoir of a turn-of-the-century marriage juxtaposes the decorum of American puritanical manners against incest, homosexuality, and lesbianism in the elegantly archaic language of that time. Grumbach has also written a critical biography of Mary McCarthy, *The Company She Kept*. (See also *Contemporary Authors*, Vols. 5-8, rev. ed.)

PETER DAVISON

[*Chamber Music*] is relieved of anachronism or sensationalism by its historical similitude: the narrator's voice is slightly stilted, slightly vapid, of the genteel tradition. Caroline founds an artists' colony in Robert's memory. She and her new lover inhabit the estate; but, unlike its real-life counterparts at the MacDowell Colony and Yaddo, the Maclaren Community does not survive. Disease once again infests Caroline's destiny, but now she is the only one left to tell.

Artful, distinctive, provocative, compassionate, *Chamber Music* does not quite manage its tour de force. It is a failure less of nerve than of imagination. Caroline, despite the vitality of her narration, remains only a victim. Would not the publicly indomitable widow of Grumbach's imagined story have impinged, like her real predecessors . . . , more forcefully upon her surroundings than this pliant, pathetic slave to illusion who "lived an almost empty life into an overcrowded and hectic century"? (p. 134)

Peter Davison, in The Atlantic Monthly *(copyright © 1979 by The Atlantic Monthly Company, Mass.; reprinted with permission), March, 1979.*

NICHOLAS DELBANCO

Chamber Music owes its title and epigraph to James Joyce's first published collection of poems. The choice is apt. There's a certain lilting lyricism here and a prissy fin-de-siècle sense to the double entendre—the diseased male protagonist relieves himself in a chamber pot. More importantly, he is a composer and pianist, and music is present throughout. Most importantly perhaps, and as Carolyn Maclaren, the 90-year-old narrator, declares at novel's end: "Asked to write the history of a man and institution, I have managed to produce merely a sketch of the chamber of one heart. Like Robert, I see, I am a miniaturist."

This miniature, however, feels chockfull. . . .

Chamber Music is convincing indeed. The doughty dame who pens these lines, rejecting the offer of secretarial help, elects to write of "what seems real: disappointments, despairs, rare intense joys and even rarer loves. And finally, for us all, the omnipresent aloneness of our lives." . . .

Much of the shock value of the sexual revelations . . . seems coy. "Nowadays a relationship such as Anna and I had may be openly declared. Women who love as we loved are called freely by the name of the isle inhabited by the Greek poetess." And the clarion call rings hollow, or in a minor key. The dying Anna asks:

> . . . 'Carrie. Where is God?'
> 'God. What do you mean? The priest, do you mean the priest? Do you want me to call the priest?'
> 'Cold,' she said. 'God. Carrie.'
> And she died.

The problem with this voice is that it's at a third remove—remembered long after the fact by a nonagenarian not the author. So it's difficult to know with what degree of seriousness we're meant to receive such a message, and where to locate belief: is the juxtaposition of "god" and "Carrie" intentional, and on whose part? Similarly, are we meant to construe Caroline's ignorance of her husband's condition as foolish, innocent or syphiliphobic? She's telling us this tale, after all, a good 60 years after she found out the facts.

Yet such lapses are few and the accomplishments many. The novel never falters in its feel for period or place, and Ms. Grumbach writes with real tact. In scene after scene— an amateur soprano straining for an aria, an old man fashioning birdhouses for those birds that fail to migrate, a young woman planting horsehair to keep fruit trees from pests—she manages to make us hear the difficult music of grace. (p. 45)

> *Nicholas Delbanco, in* The New Republic *(reprinted by permission of* The New Republic; © *1979 The New Republic, Inc.), March 10, 1979.*

VICTORIA GLENDINNING

A novel from Doris Grumbach is an event, and *Chamber Music* does not disappoint. It is a book of originality and distinction. The change of key in the last movement, while it may seem self-defeating to some, will be central to the discussion that the novel is sure to provoke. *Chamber Music* is presented as the memoirs of an old woman born in the 1870s. . . .

[The] narrator, Caroline Maclaren, is the widow of a successful American composer; and the theme of the book is her experience of the wretched marriage that underpinned the public image: "History must be full of such alliances between famous men and their satellite, serving wives," Caroline says. "Their true persons and their inner lives are rarely known in the painful and almost faithless detail I have given here."

What gives the main part of this book its polish and flavor is the contrast between matter and manner. The matter is lurid. Young Caroline Newby marries Robert Glencoe Maclaren and soon learns that until her arrival Robert and his mother slept together in the mammoth four-poster, draped in yellowing lace, that she herself now shares with him. Later she discovers that her husband has a passionate relationship with another, male, musician. (p. E1)

His need of Caroline is minimal; all his "physical prowess" goes into his music. He becomes increasingly successful, and Caroline increasingly lonely and introverted, until a mysterious illness makes him totally dependent on her in their Saratoga Springs farmhouse. We are then treated to a horrific but masterly account of the symptoms and management of a man in the tertiary, terminal stage of syphilis.

Caroline relates the most intimate and appalling happenings in an archaic, elegant English that is full of echoes—Poe? Hawthorne? The vocabulary is on occasion esoteric ("haptic," "tristful"), sometimes needlessly so, as when Caroline describes herself tautologically as "mouselike, murine." The dialogue has an oddly wooden sound, as if in

translation. But the story up to Robert's death has an intensity that the arcane style seems only to reinforce. Grumbach can clothe the most modest perceptions in cultivated 18th-century prose rhythms which (and this is quite a feat) sound not at all pretentious, but graceful and musical.

But the upsetting thing is this: the book has a final third, titled "after-life," where in my opinion it falls on its nose and does not recover. After Robert's death Caroline discovers in herself a "profound love" for his young German nurse, Anna. (pp. E1, E6)

It is not, however, the accumulation of gothic catastrophe which is responsible for the to me disastrous loss of tone in this final movement. It is notoriously hard to write well about sexual happiness; and Caroline's accounts of bliss, and of Anna's "lissome, fine-boned, full-fleshed body" are soft unto pulpiness. . . .

The point about Anna seems to be that she answers the life of the educated mind with a countervailing instinctual, earthy wisdom. . . .

It is hard to believe that [Grumbach] conceived the book as a lesbian manifesto. For one thing, Anna comes so late that she shakes the structure. This may be "true to life," but it is risky in art. . . . The novel must rather be seen, much more simply and as Caroline herself describes it, as "a sketch of the chamber of one heart." But here reviewing ends, and argument begins: and one only argues over books that are provocative and worthwhile, as this one is. (p. E6)

> *Victoria Glendinning, in* Book World—The Washington Post *(© 1979, The Washington Post), March 18, 1979.*

GAIL GODWIN

[Doris Grumbach has given us in "Chamber Music"] a look into the chamber of one unassuming heart (a species of which there are undoubtedly many members); in being true to the character she has created in Caroline, she has forfeited robustness and humor. But that was her choice as a novelist. I myself suspect that, in sticking so close to the biographical data of the late composer Edward MacDowell . . . , she handicapped her own possibilities for creating a fictional hero who might have come to life more vividly. Readers will, no doubt, vary in their opinions as to whether Caroline or her creator should be credited for the memoir's occasionally stifled tone, and for its stolid preference for essayistic recollections over vividly dramatized scenes. (p. 115)

> *Gail Godwin, in* The New York Times Book Review *(© 1979 by The New York Times Company; reprinted by permission), March 25, 1979.*

H

HALL, Donald   1928-

Hall is an American poet, editor, biographer, critic, essayist, dramatist, and author of children's books. His poetry is characterized by a nostalgic yearning for lost virtues and values, coupled with respect for the cyclical processes of nature. (See also *CLC*, Vol. 1, and *Contemporary Authors*, Vols. 5-8, rev. ed.)

ROGER GARFITT

Donald Hall is another of the men-about-Parnassus . . . which makes it all the more surprising that in the central poems of *A Blue Wing Tilts at the Edge of the Sea,* four long sequences concerned with a love affair in middle age, he should show such calamitous lack of judgment. For every passage that rings true, is another that turns sickly, and a third that crassly exploits the delicate ironies of love in later years. Ingenuity outpaces feeling, except for a few opening poems and the last section of the book, where Mr Hall brings just the right degree of invention to bear on some quiet memories and observations. . . . (p. 960)

> *Roger Garfitt in* The Times Literary Supplement *(© Times Newspapers Ltd. (London) 1975; reproduced from* The Times Literary Supplement *by permission), August 29, 1975.*

RICHARD NALLEY

Donald Hall is a well-established figure on the contemporary American scene. [*Kicking the Leaves*] serves notice, however, that he is still willing to take a few risks. *Kicking the Leaves* is a strangely vulnerable work. It asks to be accepted on its own terms, as guileless, brooding and sentimental. Most of the poems were occasioned by Hall's taking possession of the farm in New Hampshire where his grandfather and great-grandfather had lived. Centered as it is around this experience, the book assumes a certain personal tenor. Its motive and concerns are very much Hall's own, and the reader who is unwilling or unable to interest himself in them will be disappointed.

Every poem in this collection deals overtly with the theme of death. There is not so much the evocation of anxiety, evanescence or nostalgia as there is the bold statement of their presence. The poet simply insists on it in every instance. . . . At its best, death is presented through amiable, though grotesque, conceits, as in the poet's identification with his slow-roasting dinner in "Eating the Pig," or in the homage to the Arctic survival yarn, "Wolf Knife." At its worst, Hall's preoccupation can come as close to banality as anything a poet of his calibre has written in recent memory. . . . (pp. 26-7)

Hall asks his readers to share not only his obsession with mortality, but also a sense of nostalgia for his own family. The poet's use of familial reminiscence in his present contemplation of himself and his world may put one in mind of other, similar works. Robert Lowell's *Life Studies* has become something of a standard for a poet's depiction of his family, but this comparison is useful here chiefly for its contrast. Hall is not, as Lowell was, rummaging through his past in order to come to grips with it through an uncompromising search for what it holds of value. Instead, there is a certain sentimentality and longing for the past in *Kicking the Leaves.* Hall wishes to make one feel an inclusive warmth and fine sadness. In this way, Hall's book bears much in common with Philip Levine's *1933.* In his book, however, Levine seeks to create tensions through the paradoxical working of vitality in the decayed or through the intense burning energy of what is dead and past. Hall's musings on his family and personal past do not crackle with this kind of ghostly electricity. *Kicking the Leaves* works rather with the distance between the poet's memory of his grandfather's home and his own present there. . . .

Perhaps the most illustrative poem in terms of Hall's obsession with death and his personal past is the beautiful title poem, "Kicking the Leaves." The poet remembers fall days of his youth, in college, as a teacher and up to the present. The poem, in seven segments, evinces a progression and the mortal tenderness of growth and change. Above all, it is a song of renewal, bespeaking the revitalization of Hall as a poet and as a man:

> This year the poems came back,
>   when the leaves fell.
> Kicking the leaves, I heard the
>   leaves tell stories,
> remembering, and therefore
>   looking ahead, and building
> the house of the dying. I looked
>   up into the maples
> and found them, the vowels of
>   bright desire.

I thought they had gone
forever . . .

"Kicking the Leaves" brings the circle around, showing the poet living in the house of his grandparents and great-grandparents. He feels that he has come to terms with the notion of death and has begun to live again himself. In this way, though the distance remains, the past provides the present with a perspective, renewing it with a sense of its fitness and continuity. (p. 27)

Richard Nalley, in The Harvard Advocate *(©
1978 by* The Harvard Advocate; *reprinted by permission), Vol. 112, No. 1, December, 1978.*

IRVIN EHRENPREIS

[Biography] is central to Donald Hall's *Remembering Poets.* His book is mainly a gathering of well-told anecdotes about the author's relations with Frost, Pound, Eliot, and Dylan Thomas. Hall deserves praise for the care he has taken to verify his information, to be accurate, to complete stories of which he knew only a part at first hand. The care is visible everywhere but most attractively in the author's frankness about himself. The refusal to cover up his blunders deepens the appeal and the humor of the narrative. His good nature and appreciativeness give it coherence. Readers in general, and young readers in particular, who hesitate to dip into poetry of any sort will find themselves reaching for the works of Hall's subjects as they yield to the charm of his voice.

That they will discover much about the poetry itself is less certain. Hall is aware of the limitations of his approach, and insists that one must not confuse the personality of a genius with his work. Yet for all his experience as a poet, Hall rarely shows much penetration or independent judgment when he acts as a critic. Biography is an efficient method of getting into the meaning and shape of works of art so long as the biographer is obsessed with the creative imagination of his subject.

Naturally, the characters of his four poets fascinate Hall and infuse drama into his accounts of them. . . . Some of the anecdotes move one deeply, like the report of Thomas planning to give up poetry for prose because he could make more money from prose. One also learns much from Hall about the career of a poet in our time—the mechanical, financial, and emotional problems of winning the attention of deafened ears.

But the paragraphs of comment on individual poems, of judgments about the *oeuvre* of a poet, or of generalization about the art of poetry are not incisive enough. The psychological and moral observations are more often honest than profound. Hall's notions about the relation of culture to society seldom enlighten one—for example, his speculation that if Thomas had lived in a society which "valued life over death," he might not have drunk himself into disaster.

For readers concerned with poetry itself, the most absorbing parts of the book will be the interviews with Eliot and Pound, which have been published before. But scrupulous as they are, these in turn remain less than they might appear to be. They bring us (as the whole book does) the speech of men at the end of their careers. Even the sympathy and intelligence of Mr. Hall cannot transform them into the young, creative innovators whom we yearn to know. (pp. 18-19)

Irvin Ehrenpreis, in The New York Review of Books *(reprinted with permission from* The New York Review of Books; *copyright © 1978 Nyrev, Inc.), December 7, 1978.*

GUY DAVENPORT

[All] the poems in *Kicking the Leaves* are about death, not food. Their persistent elegiac tone rises first of all from that roast pig, who—apple in mouth—in its anatomical wholeness touches the poet's sense of pity and starts him thinking about ancient modes of cooking when stoves were altars, slaughter was sacrifice, and ceremony attended both the death and the ingestion of animals. . . .

Food takes Donald Hall's heart back to his family's rhythms of seasons and deaths, back to his memories of his great-grandfather's farm in New Hampshire which is now his own.

So rich a theme has generated poems about roses, horses, oxcarts, black-faced sheep. Hall writes with clarity and honesty, enlisting none of the usual strategies of poetry such as rhyme, meter, or a heightened diction. His words are plain and right, and his manner is casual and alert. . . .

These poems are a celebration, as he makes clear, of the poet's middle age. They are a stock-taking, a sifting of values. The raw and unsettling evocations of death by violence (of wolves, pigs, people) are, it would seem, deliberate encounters with reality to be faced with a naked mind, without religion or philosophy. And, it must be added, without sentimentality or romantic coloring.

The taste these poems leave in the mind is the bitterness of life's brevity, the disgust we hide from ourselves at having to slaughter to live. Against the goodness of being alive runs the harshness of the bargains by which we live: the toil and death of other creatures both animal and human. This is a bleak way of looking at things. It is, in part, the way these poems look at the world. Such honesty has its reward. There are lights other than the worst to see things in, and, having insisted on the shadows, Hall feels free to exult in brightnesses.

Pity is an ambiguous emotion, part fear and part solicitude. Hall has purged fear from his pity (a purging that may be the theme that brings these poems into a unity), giving a kind of awe to his solicitude for the fragility and uncertainty of life.

Guy Davenport, "New Hampshire Elegies," in
National Review *(© National Review, Inc., 1979;
150 East 35th St., New York, N.Y. 10016), March
30, 1979, p. 430.*

*   *   *

HANLEY, James   1901-

An Irish novelist, essayist, and playwright now living in England, Hanley spent ten years at sea, and some of his best novels take place aboard ship. His is a bleak, sombre vision that bears comparison with Hardy as well as Dostoevsky. (See also *CLC,* **Vols. 3, 5, 8.)**

RUTH MATHEWSON

James Hanley has been discovered and rediscovered for almost half a century. When his last book came out in 1973, *Time* magazine, calling him "one of the most consistently praised and least-known novelists in the English-speaking world," echoed its judgment of 20 years before: "If critics' raves paid their way in royalties . . . Hanley might well be one of the richest authors alive." . . .

His earlier novels—more than 20—have been accorded a respectful neglect, not because he is particularly obscure or avant-garde, but because odd accidents of timing and shifts in public taste throughout his long career have resulted in such audiences as he has had being cut off from one another. In the case of his most ambitious undertakings, for example, a five-volume family saga of working-class life, many reviewers of the fifth book in 1958 were unaware that it was part of a cycle begun in 1935.

Much that Hanley has written is unavailable today, so it is difficult to get a clear sense of his growth. Moreover, those critics who could have kept the score have been less than helpful in their eagerness to claim him as another Joyce, Lawrence, Kafka, Dostoevsky, Strindberg; a new Melville, Bierce, Farrell or Faulkner; a second Balzac, Zola, Beckett or Pinter. Not all the comparisons are far-fetched, yet they tend to lose Hanley's special qualities in a welter of associations, to make him a kind of chameleon. To add to the confusion, there is little agreement about these qualities. Because he was born in Dublin, he is an Irish writer; since he has lived most of his adult life in Wales, he has been regarded as Welsh. But the Irish in his novels grew up, like the author, in Liverpool (for a long time he was so closely identified with that city that it belonged to him, one critic said, the same way London belonged to Dickens), and only a few of his works are set in Wales.

Hanley has also had a reputation as a writer of sea stories that Henry Green, among others, thinks superior to Conrad's. . . .

His stokers and seamen recall not Conrad, but the early O'Neill, Stephen Crane, Jack London, and B. Traven. Finally, for a time he was considered a proletarian novelist, raw and violent. He was not a social realist, though, and not much interested in politics. As he developed he became increasingly concerned with exploring self-imprisonment and spiritual deprivation in characters that have been compared with Henry Green's and Elizabeth Bowen's. Small wonder that the word "eccentric" constantly recurs in critical attempts to place Hanley in some tradition. (p. 17)

A Dream Journey is a good introduction to Hanley, combining as it does different layers of the author's career: the sailor, who confounds the glass shattered in the raids with the ice of the North Atlantic, is drawn from Hanley's close knowledge of the sea; the young model from Bermondsey is working class; the artist and his wife suffer the spiritual claustrophobia that became the writer's mature preoccupation. And in another respect—one I find almost as interesting as the story itself—the novel is a palimpsest of earlier Hanleys, for with very few changes its longest section, "Yesterday," is his old novella, *No Directions*, published in 1943. . . .

There is a wry joke in the possibility that in re-offering the wartime work as the major part of a "new" novel, Hanley is counting on the British public's past obliviousness to his existence. At the same time he may be testing the truth of the belief, expressed recently by Paul Theroux, that "his books live happily in the memory of a dozen good and well-known novelists." Surely some must still be around who in

1943 declared *No Directions* "a masterpiece . . . his greatest achievement." Presumably it has at least flourished in the memory of Henry Miller, who wrote an exuberant Introduction to the third edition in 1946. . . .

Despite the characteristic bravura, Miller has not exaggerated the power of this strange, unforgettable little book. One half wishes that it had been reissued just as it was, with the sequel to follow soon after. In its new positioning it becomes a new text, much as Pierre Menard's "modern version" of *Don Quixote* in Borges' story becomes utterly different although it is faithful word-for-word to Cervantes. . . .

When Henry Miller said in 1946 that at the end of *No Directions* we begin all over again, he was prescient about Hanley's need to return to the book. The author could not leave his characters standing at the foot of the stairs. He has described novel writing as "a series of blind gropings in a dark tunnel." In discussing his family saga he has said, "Once I actually did look back into it and something made me enter it again. . . . The people I had left there lying in a heap were not so limp as I thought so I gave each character an extra squeeze."

The people in *A Dream Journey* are obsessed, frightened, aging—but there is something permanent and passionate about them; they are not limp at all. We understand why their author could not forget them. (p. 18)

Ruth Mathewson, "Hanley's Palimpsest," in The New Leader *(© 1977 by the American Labor Conference on International Affairs, Inc.), January 3, 1977, pp. 17-18.*

MARY HOPE

'The worst thing is when nothing, absolutely nothing happens to a person in a whole lifetime. Just think of that.' Enduring, or escaping from such a nothing is what James Hanley's beautifully controlled, exquisitely written novel [*A Kingdom*] is all about. On the face of it, nothing much does happen. . . .

Death gives birth to links and significances previously slipped into the mind's back pockets, and this novel is not just about paternal dominance and filial acceptance . . . but about the recognition and acceptance of endurance. I cannot praise this book too highly. (p. 20)

Mary Hope, in The Spectator *(© 1978 by* The Spectator; *reprinted by permission of* The Spectator*), August 26, 1978.*

LAURA MATHEWS

The Welsh Sonata is a romantic, lyrical tale about a missing man, whose inexplicable departure from a tiny, locked-in village haunts the conscience of many and draws out the bardic talents of a few. The real subject of the book is a living and omnipresent network of private fantasies hoarded against the deprivations of a wilderness. Hanley conjures drama out of the seemingly endless inflections of a spare assortment of phrases and images that bring home "how far a word will go, how deep, or how high it can climb." (pp. 94-5)

Hanley's lulling, plainsong prose leads one gently but effectively into several unenviably bleak lives, redeemed by their private order and inner resourcefulness. (p. 95)

Laura Mathews, in The Atlantic Monthly *(copyright © 1978 by The Atlantic Monthly Company, Boston, Mass.; reprinted with permission), December, 1978.*

VICTORIA GLENDINNING

[The] idea of traveling—in the mind, over the mountains, or back in time—is central to ["The Welsh Sonata" and "A Kingdom"]. A day has its own elasticity—a morning "is beginning to stretch itself," and elsewhere, "to grow." The past of a man is never lost, but accumulates in the common memory: "Yesterday a man, today a tale." . . .

The writing in both books is sometimes laconic, sometimes poetic, sometimes graphically realistic. . . .

Mr. Hanley's solitary characters are mostly seen from the outside. The reader picks up clues about them, spurred on, like the policeman Goronwy Jones, by curiosity. In neither of these books is isolation examined minutely from the inside, as it is, for example, in Brian Moore's "The Lonely Passion of Judith Hearne." Yet solitude does not necessarily mean being invisible to others; indeed, the invisible ones are the conformists. . . . Mr. Hanley's solitaries are not unwatched. Their vagaries do not go unrecorded. Rhys the Cloud, and Cadi and her father are famous within their small communities. Their very unknowableness makes them mythical. Mr. Hanley, harping on the idea of man alone with—or against—nature, isolates him under a spotlight.

There is another, deeper, solitude that has no witnesses. James Hanley, for all his elusiveness, does not pursue it here. Uncompromising though he is as a novelist, and unconcerned with the literary "kings of tea," he is, by publishing his odd and to me absorbing books, staking his claim to stand in the world's spotlight. Although a lot of people may sneer away from Mr. Hanley's particular sort of Celtic Twilight, and he does not now have the recognition he deserves, he is the sort of figure to whom a cultish recognition will accrue, as it does within his books for his own characters. In his life and his work he lays the trail for his own myth. "Today a man, tomorrow a tale." (p. 11)

Victoria Glendinning, in The New York Times Book Review *(© 1978 by The New York Times Company; reprinted by permission), December 10, 1978.*

DESMOND GRAHAM

[James Hanley] is an example of a novelist who has often aimed at a poetic type of fiction, restricting the social range of his work in his quest for intensity and significant form. He has undoubtedly pursued his art with dedication and integrity, and although he has elicited few displays of enthusiastic acclaim he has rightly won a great deal of respect for his artistic purity. Of his two books recently published, the reissued *The Welsh Sonata* (1954) is much more conspicuously poetic than the less ambitious and less pretentious *A Kingdom*, but despite being more conventionally realistic this new novel also strives towards the poetic. Neither novel contains much in the way of narrative, but *The Welsh Sonata* is more extreme in this respect. . . . As the title indicates, the structure of the book is analogous to the three-movement form of the classical sonata, and the subtitle *Variations on a Theme* provides another clue to its quasi-musical organisation. Like Virginia Woolf in *The Waves*, for example, Hanley is attempting to do what Forster in *Aspects of the Novel* regarded as an impossibility—making the novel aspire to the condition of music. Different as [the village] Cilgyn is from Dylan Thomas's Llareggub in many ways, it resembles it in being a symbolic and non-naturalistic version of a Welsh village. Despite some twentieth-century features, Hanley's imaginary world possesses an air of timelessness like Llareggub and the locales of T. F. Powys's work; the action, unlike that of *A Kingdom*, cannot be located in time. If T. F. Powys is one possible influence on Hanley, the surrealist-tinged Welsh gothicism of some of Dylan Thomas's and Glyn Jones's stories is surely another. Yet Hanley's style is his own, and as is invariably the case with self-consciously poetic novels, it is the most distinctive feature of the book. There are passages in which the Old Testament rhythms of the King James Bible dominate, passages in which every sentence begins with 'And', and passages in which sentences are an accumulation of statements linked by 'and'. A very elliptical syntax is frequently employed so that normal sentence structures are avoided. Subordinate clauses, participial phrases or even single words form paragraphs, and some pages look like blank verse since every phrase is paragraphed separately. *The Welsh Sonata* is a stylistic *tour de force*, but Hanley's preoccupation with the poetry of fiction turns out, as it usually does, to be self-defeating. As in the case of some of Virginia Woolf's mature novels, so much has to be sacrificed for the "poetry" that the gains do not outweigh the losses. . . .

A Kingdom is less stylised and mannered than *The Welsh Sonata*, but again very little happens. The novel, set mainly in a remote Welsh smallholding, deals with the encounter between two sisters, Lucy and Cadi, in the days between their father's death and his funeral. . . . What interests [Hanley] are the psychological tensions, emotional nuances, and feelings of anxiety, hostility and guilt arising from the reunion of the sisters after many years of noncommunication, and the first meeting of Cadi and her brother-in-law. He explores the apparently undramatic lives of this trio, bringing out the delicate shifts of attitude and the growing understanding that occur in the days before the funeral. It is subtle, restrained, carefully shaded and Jamesian, and yet—there's the rub—it is not Jamesian enough. For many writers, the material of *A Kingdom* would have made a long short story, but not a novel. *Mutatis mutandis*, one can imagine Chekhov handling it as a story. In concentrating on a small family group in an isolated house during a short period of time, Hanley is relinquishing much of the traditional novelist's social territory (*pace* Richardson and Emily Brontë), and to expand the material at such length is therefore to take risks, especially as the lack of plot movement has to be compensated for by depth. Considering the scale of the book, there is insufficient depth, partly because the fairly conservative techniques Hanley uses do not permit him to unveil his characters all that thoroughly. It may seem inappropriate to invoke the yardstick of James, Joyce and Lawrence here, but it is a tribute to Hanley's seriousness as a novelist that he merits such comparison, even though he comes off badly by it. Ironically, if Hanley had expanded the book even more by building up the past through more flashbacks than he does, *A Kingdom* might have been considerably more distinguished than it is or than it would have been if compressed to novella length. It would have been a less tidy, formally pure work of art, but a humanly richer and more vital one. (pp. 50-2)

Desmond Graham, in Stand *(copyright © by Stand), Vol. 20, No. 1 (1978-79).*

*   *   *

HANSON, Kenneth O.   1922-

Hanson is an American poet and editor. (See also *Contemporary Authors*, Vols. 53-56.)

THOMAS LASK

The quality of being alive in his environment, with people around him, to the mood of a situation or scene marks every page of [Mr. Hanson's] work. It makes his poetry tangible, clear cut, full of presence.

[Mr. Hanson] is not one of those mystics who hugs himself for joy while uttering hymns to the creator. His poetry has bite and a harsh edge that come from a non-romantic approach to what he sees and experiences. . . .

He is open-eyed but not superior or patronizing. The pulse of life is enough for him. . . .

["The Distance Anywhere" is a] vigorous, hearty book, the work of a man fully engaged with the world and with God's creatures it it. (p. 29)

> *Thomas Lask, in* The New York Times *(© 1967 by The New York Times Company; reprinted by permission), September 9, 1967.*

JOHN N. MORRIS

Kenneth Hanson's *The Uncorrected World* is fifty-nine lucid pages of very quiet verse about being or not being in Greece, a book in which the author presents himself to us as a sort of tourist-in-residence. In his short, deliberately unpoetical lines we ride "out the good road / built by NATO" to discover, quite by chance, the birthplace of Hesiod; or, again pretty much by accident, we drink "from a spring / guaranteed to make you / immortal." . . . We accompany him to a bar in Athens, where we learn that the Colonels disapprove of "the breaking of plates for fun." We observe the sailors of the Sixth Fleet, how "They sparkle in their innocence / and whites." We go to a wedding or perhaps we visit a beach. . . . (pp. 112-13)

Thus described, Hanson's book may not sound very remarkable. And it's true that Hanson's poems, though easy to quote (being everywhere much the same in tone), are hard to quote from in a way that suggests the final character of the book, which is superior to the particular merits of the notations and anecdotes that are its parts. I think the whole enterprise comes into focus in the last four or five poems, where it becomes clear that the book is a meditation on the deep uses of travel, on the "distances we gaze into" of his last line. Hanson's Greece, however full it is of facts that he records, is in part an idea in his mind, his version or vision of The Other Place, that real fiction necessary to some of us if we are to have our home. The Other Place is the object of a quest: "It takes much looking / after which you must be lucky." (p. 113)

> *John N. Morris, in* The Hudson Review *(copyright © 1974 by The Hudson Review, Inc.; reprinted by permission), Vol. XXVII, No. 1, Spring, 1974.*

SALLY M. GALL

Hanson in *The Uncorrected World* depends heavily on literal situations for his poems' initial impetus. His descriptions, vignettes, and anecdotes of the passing Greek scene are . . . low keyed, however. His intensities are so tightly controlled by his flat, wry, self-ironic style that apparently passionate statements tend to be slightly cryptic, as in "Thermopylae," "Tsiganos," or "Desperate Moves." The desperate moves are those of a chameleon changing color as the background changes arbitrarily, apparently passive but endowed by the poet with some precious "split-second timing." The poem could be taken as a metaphor for Hanson's own poem making: an assertion that beneath a seemingly calm surface something vital, intense, and admirable is occurring. Hanson tends to understate both the historical and personal, while demanding the reader's sympathy for whatever psychological state he happens to be in. He seems to cultivate an air of rather weary detachment on the one hand while pleading for attachment on the other.

In "Flisvos Bus-stop" Hanson's objective note-taking style leaves a great deal up to the reader. We must make what we can of a meticulous description of a young wife serving her helpless husband. Are we to connect what might be deliberate mutilation with the junta's propensities for torture, or are we being asked to admire the young man's passive composure as all the ordinary motions of living go on around him? Hanson is noncommittal. He refers offhandedly to the junta's actions elsewhere, usually for lightly satirical purposes. . . . Rarely he allows himself a more savage bite, pointing up rather than playing down totalitarian fatuousness. (p. 57)

Perhaps we are expected to know the doings of the colonels intimately enough so that Hanson can rely on a subdued horror, a constant ironic undercurrent, to give his book some of the emotional force it lacks. One of his themes is changelessness despite change. Greece evidently exists apart from its current political realities, watching regimes come and go, forever presided over by the "hilarious face of god." With such a vision it is understandable why the real situation leaves Hanson untouched. His strongest personal relationship, with a young man named Evangelos, exhibits a similar strange detachment. . . . [The poet] believes in "the world of Evangelos" yet seems hopelessly outside it. Again, we don't know quite why, but are given a dream answer in "Next." . . .

Unrequited love, age, some incurable loneliness—Hanson is never forthcoming enough to tell us. This is confessional poetry without the confession; the book leaves a bitter taste of despair and self-irony and an odd sense that somehow Hanson has failed to discover where the emotional center of his poetry lies—or at least to convey it as fully as he might. (p. 58)

Hanson casts his poems adrift on a kind of cosmic sorrow, never quite pointing out what was *really* the "matter with last year." . . . (pp. 57-8)

> *Sally M. Gall, in* Shenandoah *(copyright 1974 by Washington and Lee University; reprinted from* Shenandoah: The Washington and Lee University Review *with the permission of the Editor), Fall, 1974.*

W. G. REGIER

If Kenneth O. Hanson's [*The Uncorrected World*] is like

anything else, it is like Kenneth Hanson's old book [*The Distance Anywhere*]. . . . The earlier book was full of weather, Greek geography, and lines the length and texture of blackboard chalk. *The Uncorrected World* is the same world, uninterrupted courses of weather, Greek geography, and lines that squeak like chalk. The book is as disappointing as too long a ride, and as annoying as a stutter. Mr. Hanson's [second] book may have interest for those who have not read his first. But the first remains more worthwhile, and the second seems painfully secondary. (p. 370)

W. G. Regier, in Prairie Schooner *(© 1976 by University of Nebraska Press; reprinted by permission from* Prairie Schooner*), Winter, 1975-76.*

*   *   *

HARDWICK, Elizabeth   1916-

Hardwick is an American novelist, short story writer, essayist, and editor. Although she is a noted writer of fiction, Hardwick was attracted to the essay early in her career, and has become a brilliant exponent of that form. Associated for many years with the *Partisan Review*, **Hardwick is also one of the founders of** *The New York Review of Books*. **(See also** *Contemporary Authors*, **Vols. 5-8, rev. ed.)**

THOMAS FITZSIMMONS

The Simple Truth, Elizabeth Hardwick's second novel, follows the trial of the boy, Rudy Peck, in order to describe and to judge the efforts of those trying to find out what happened that night, and why. The reader receives information as it is given the jury, which represents society. But he also is made privy to the speculations of two individual observers at the trial, a man, Joe Parks, and a woman, Anita Mitchell. The townspeople, who staff the jury, are, says Miss Hardwick, "utterly of this world," while Parks and Anita, who belong to the university, are in a sense "sophisticated." This double contrast between group and individual, simple and sophisticated is maintained throughout the story.

But beneath these contrasts is a common denominator: all these people, in the author's view, are pretentious fools. The jury, in its simple way, succumbs to sentiment and accepts an unsatisfactory explanation of the girl's death. Parks and Anita, rigorously analytical, project their private emotional disorders into the situation and pompously produce grotesque distortions of judgment.

So the author's statement comes to this: simple or sophisticated, neither the collective nor the single mind is equipped to distinguish reality from appearance; to pretend otherwise is absurd.

[*The Simple Truth*] is made or broken by its people, by the way the author sees and handles them rather than the plot. The plot is skillfully developed. Unfortunately, Parks, Anita, and the jury, all are caricatures. (pp. 325-26)

Poking fun at two dolls stuffed with clichés and at the stereotype of a jury is not an effective way, or even an interesting one, to comment on the delusions men may cling to in order easily to act without really knowing what is real and what is merely appearance. Elizabeth Hardwick has gone seriously wrong in *The Simple Truth*.

Yet there are things throughout the novel that are good, realized with an impressive economy of means: certain

quick scenes, an occasional mood, some of the people who appear briefly: the kinds of things that make for a good short story. Miss Hardwick has written good short stories. And the faults of this novel may only be the mistakes of a gifted writer struggling hard with a more complex form than usual and stretching too far for a subject. (p. 327)

Thomas Fitzsimmons, in The Sewanee Review *(reprinted by permission of the editor; © 1955 by The University of the South), Spring, 1955.*

ROSEMARY DINNAGE

[*Seduction & Betrayal: Women & Literature*] is so original, so sly and strange, but the pleasure is embedded in the style, in the way [Miss Hardwick] flicks the English language about like a whip. One is reluctant to start taking its epigrammatic charm to pieces and asking dull critical questions about its structure and intention. Yet the issues she raises are both complex and momentous. Her subject is not so much the seduction and betrayal of women *portrayed* in literature . . . , as seduction and betrayal itself, in literary contexts; the implicit axiom being that the arrangements made between men and women are never satisfactory. . . .

Miss Hardwick is best on women as characters rather than creators, both fictional characters and actual women whose importance is for what they were and felt rather than what they created—Dorothy Wordsworth, Jane Carlyle. Her critical approach is psychological and moral, not formal. . . . The literary devices that reproduce intangibilities, the feel of the moment and the structuring of time, are not things which engage her very deeply.

Her real concern is to present her own angry and witty view of the sexes, and for this she has more scope with the fictional beings and the companions of writers than with the great creative women, for these less easily align themselves with the victims. She writes sensibly of the Brontës, slyly of Bloomsbury, and compassionately of Sylvia Plath, but she is less at home with the ferocious *victories* of Plath, Emily Brontë, and Virginia Woolf than with stoic pathos. She stresses especially the financial helplessness of nineteenth-century woman, and sees the Brontës' greatest heroism as their willingness to turn their introverted talents outward to honest breadwinning account. . . .

Miss Hardwick is excellent on the women she dubs "amateurs", talented beings attached to men who overshadowed them. Towards Zelda Fitzgerald—on the basis of her novel, since Zelda herself is not actually included among the amateurs—she shows compassion and indignation for the way her writings were appropriated and her attempts to work and be independent consistently foiled. . . .

Of her third category, the fictional characters, this cannot be said—they seem fixed and defined by their creators; yet she has given them further authenticity by reinstating the literary portrait in a way that is quite free of its how-many-children-had-Lady-Macbeth associations. . . .

The final chapter on seduction and betrayal is a formidable analysis of the betrayed-woman theme in the novel. Every sentence resonates and surprises, glitters with a stoic contempt, and Miss Hardwick's method of contriving, obliquely, a simultaneous judgment on literature and life fully justifies itself. . . .

Miss Hardwick's book is in a different category from the usual works of feminist victimology, and simple arguments seem crude against its subtlety. One wants, however, at least to try to find one crucial, elusive piece that is missing from her pattern.

Rosemary Dinnage, "Men, Women and Books: The Rule of Heroism," in The Times Literary Supplement *(© Times Newspapers Ltd. (London) 1974; reproduced from* The Times Literary Supplement *by permission), November 29, 1974, p. 1333.*

JEAN STUBBS

[*Seduction and Betrayal: Women and Literature*] is a titillating title, and the contents bear it out—though not as some might think.

Miss Hardwick is no hand-wringer. She is a literary surgeon, admirably equipped to expose the nerves. The Brontës are her first patients and she sets to work on them with precision. Diagnoses: 'In the Brontë sisters there is a distinctly high tone and low spirit'. Charlotte 'underneath the correcting surface' is 'deeply romantic, full of dreams and visited by nightmares'. Emily has 'a spare inviolate centre, a harder resignation amounting finally to withdrawal'. Anne's 'religious earnestness' covers 'a secret suffering, a mute, hidden torment'. All three, quiet and repressed though they are, possess 'a disturbing undercurrent of intense sexual fantasy'. By the time Miss Hardwick has stitched them neatly up, and pronounced them heroic, we not only know the Brontës better, we also marvel. (p. 38)

One by one, the august literary bodies are wheeled into the theatre. Miss Hardwick selects another scalpel and reveals fresh aspects. . . . Her betrayed ladies emerge wonderfully changed under the inspection. Hester Prynne wearing her Scarlet Letter 'is an ideologue, making by way of her adulterous isolation a stand against Puritanism'. Hetty Sorrel 'is merely romantic in an ordinary way . . . we weep for her— but she is not a heroine'. Roberta in *An American Tragedy* 'We cannot quite forgive her the simplicity'. Clarissa 'seeks the net she flees from'. But Tess D'Urbeville 'is the most perfectly conceived of the modern betrayed heroines'. Miss Hardwick ends by reporting the death of sex as a tragic, exalted theme. We have, with the aid of contraception and a new attitude towards sexual morality, robbed it of drama. Venus, to quote Zola, is rotting! (pp. 38-9)

Elizabeth Hardwick's stringent perception, her elegant prose, her wit and commonsense, her objectivity, her knowledge of human nature, are enviable. I am prepared to swear that she would have survived somehow, as a feminine writer, anywhere and at any time in history. But I am grateful that she is writing now, when we can breathe more freely and appreciate her all the better. (p. 39)

Jean Stubbs, in Books and Bookmen *(© copyright Jean Stubbs 1976; reprinted with permission), January, 1976.*

JOAN DIDION

"I have always, all of my life, been looking for help from a man," we are told near the beginning of Elizabeth Hardwick's subtle and beautiful new book ["Sleepless Nights"]. "It has come many times and many more it has not. This began early." What follows eludes immediate summary or categorization. "Sleepless Nights" is a novel, but it is a novel in which the subject is memory and in which the "I" whose memories are in question is entirely and deliberately the author: we recognize the events and addresses of Elizabeth Hardwick's life not only from her own earlier work, but from the poems of her husband, the late Robert Lowell. . . . The result is less a "story about" or "of" a life than a shattered meditation on it, a work as evocative and difficult to place as Claude Lévi-Strauss's "Tristes Tropiques," which it oddly recalls. The author observes of her enigmatic narrative: "It certainly hasn't the drama of: I saw the old, white-bearded frigate master on the dock and signed up for the journey. But after all, 'I' am a woman."

This strikes an interesting note, a balance of Oriental diffidence and exquisite contempt, of irony and direct statement, that exactly expresses the sensibility at work in "Sleepless Nights." "But after all, 'I' am a woman." *Triste tropique* indeed. (pp. 1, 60)

In certain ways, the mysterious and somnambulistic "difference" of being a woman has been, over 35 years, Elizabeth Hardwick's great subject, the tropic to which she has returned incessantly: it colored both of her early novels, "The Ghostly Lover" in 1945 and "The Simple Truth" in 1955, as well as many of the essays collected in 1962 as "A View of My Own" and all of those published in 1974 as "Seduction and Betrayal: Women and Literature."

She has chronicled again and again the undertow of family life, the awesome torment of being a daughter—an observer in the household, a constant reader of the domestic text— the anarchy of sex. She has illuminated lives traditionally misrepresented as tragic instances of the way all women live. . . .

This is all very original and interesting, and so is Elizabeth Hardwick's radical distrust of romantic individualism, her passionate apprehension of the particular havoc that a corrupted individualism can play with the lives of women. Women adrift, in Elizabeth Hardwick's work, indulge a fatal preference for men of bad character. Women adrift take dancing lessons, and end up on missing-person reports.

Perhaps no one has written more acutely and poignantly about the ways in which women compensate for their relative physiological inferiority, about the poetic and practical implications of walking around the world deficient in hemoglobin, deficient in respiratory capacity, deficient in muscular strength and deficient in stability of the vascular and autonomic nervous systems. . . .

The ways in which "Sleepless Nights" recalls "Tristes Tropiques" are not only of tone. The method of the "I" in "Sleepless Nights" is in fact that of the anthropologist, of the traveler on watch for the revealing detail: we are provided precise observations of strangers met in the course of the journey, close studies of their rituals. These studies take the form of vignettes, recollections, stories that at first offer no sustaining thread. . . .

The meticulously transcribed histories begin to yield a terrible point, although not one that would astonish our mothers and grandmothers. In the culture under study, life ends badly. Disease is authentic. The freedom to live untied to others, however desired that freedom may be, is hard on men and hard on children and hardest of all on women. "Why is it that we cannot keep the note of irony, the jangle of carelessness at a distance?" the narrator of this extraordinary and haunting book asks toward the end of her reflections. "Sentences in which I have tried for a certain light tone—many of those have to do with events, upheavals, destructions that caused me to weep like a child." Oh yes. (p. 60)

Joan Didion, "Meditation on a Life," in The New York Times Book Review (© 1979 by The New York Times Company; reprinted by permission), April 29, 1979, pp. 1, 60.

LAURIE STONE

Sleepless Nights [is] a very beautiful and concise probe of the past told by a woman called Elizabeth.

I have almost nothing negative to say about this book: There are a few dead phrases, i.e., "moral unease hurt" and "I stepped into [the rooms] with the feeling of falling into a well of disgrace." Also, the second half of the book is a small letdown—stories of disappointment, despair, and the bittersweet ironies of aging—by comparison to the first half's extraordinarily powerful stories of promise, reckless extravagance, and determination.

But mostly Hardwick's sentences sing. By saying just enough, and never too much, she has perfected the art of making private meaning public. Hardwick passes the test autobiographical works always set: to write about passion, anger, and betrayal without blathering, sentimentalizing, or fuming. She sees the past with a clarity and a freedom from judgment that come not so much from remembering acutely —as forgetting acutely the feelings that blur.

Sleepless Nights is about a romance with memory, a habit of mind that defines the writer—at any given moment—by the way she "transmogrifies" the past. Hardwick seldom focuses directly on Elizabeth. She is revealed, instead, as she remembers and by what and whom she remembers. Unable to talk with her phantoms over a bottle of wine, as Elizabeth would prefer, she spins insomniac "letters" to the sleeping, the unreachable, and the dead. They are love letters without sap; her attraction is always compounded with a little awe, a little envy, a little irony. . . .

Written half in protest and half in acknowledgment, *Sleepless Nights* is the confession of a feminist who is also a heterosexual. "The break with human love remains somewhere inside, and at times, under rain clouds, it aches like an amputation," Hardwick wrote in *Seduction and Betrayal.* "I have always," Elizabeth says, "all my life, been looking for help from a man. It has come many times and many more it has not." She could have said the same of women, with whom her relationships are as varied and deep, but she does not: the "help" one woman gives another may be more critical to survival than sex and bonding, but once asserted, these needs, Hardwick shows, change the weight of everything. . . .

Propelled forward by the sheer energy of Hardwick's descriptions, only gradually did I observe the subtle connections and try to answer the question implicit in every portrait: What are so many strangers and partly-knowns to the writer that she should remember them so well?

What was Billie Holiday to Elizabeth Hardwick—Billie, followed nightly from club to club; Billie, quintessentially obsessed, talented, and isolated? She was a secret sharer for a period of time, the person—or animal—which expresses everything repressed, or feared or desired at that moment: "The creamy lips, the oily eyelids, the violent perfume," Elizabeth describes Billie, "and in her voice the

tropical l's and r's. Her presence, her singing created a large, swelling anxiety. . . . Onto the heaviest addiction to heroin, she piled up the rocks of her tomb with a prodigiousness of Scotch and brandy."

Hardly an addiction, failing or longing goes unmasked in *Sleepless Nights.* Hardwick is an artful and brainy moralist, never sententious, because Elizabeth's observations of others almost always imply, "me too." (p. 98)

This is what we know about Elizabeth: Life amounts to books and people; the face, the gesture, the memory are, for her, inseparable from the word. This is what we know of Hardwick's intention: Simply, it is "to lay out the evidence," as her character Alex says, and take pleasure in that. (p. 100)

Laurie Stone, "Hardwick's Way," in The Village Voice (reprinted by permission of The Village Voice; copyright © News Group Publications, Inc., 1979), May 7, 1979, pp. 98, 100.

*   *   *

HÉBERT, Anne   1916-

Hébert is a French-Canadian poet, novelist, short story writer, dramatist, and screenwriter. Her work is often religious in nature, for she sees the poet as a creative witness to God. (See also *CLC*, Vol. 4.)

JOHN WATT LENNOX

[In "Le Torrent" Anne Hébert deals with a protagonist who is] seeking the joy or freedom which . . . is, at the same time, apart from and part of [his] existence. . . . Hébert, through the image of the rapids, [articulates] the dilemma of a fragmented personality in search of some healing reconciliation, and in dealing with this search, the [work assumes a symbolic dimension which takes it] from the particulars of presentation into universal considerations of man's relationship to himself and others. . . .

["Le Torrent" deals] with attempts to come to necessary and violent terms with the past which is associated with the dominant figure of a mother who shuts off the protagonist from the community. [The world of "la grande Claudine"] is an oppressive, static world] whose very strength lies in unchangeability and in the maintenance of the rational status quo, and it is in the protagonist's violent challenge to the old established order that the [work finds its] full symbolic significance. . . .

François avoids knowledge, and in so doing he remains enclosed within the confines of his own personality. . . .

["Le Torrent" takes place in a closed environment which exists] apart from the larger outside world and which [suggests] the restricted psychological attitudes of the characters. . . . In "Le Torrent," François and his mother live on a plot of land which is isolated from the outside world by a forest. In this setting, the turbulent rapids at the bottom of the deep abyss come to suggest a masochism and morbidity which foretell violent dismemberment and death. (p. 70)

[François' world] is more psychological than physical, more description and suggestion than actual location, and . . . François is alienated from the world around him. He is alienated in two ways; through what his mother taught him and through his deafness. "La grande Claudine," his mother . . . , is someone marked more by her presence than her person. . . . [She really has no dimensions, but represents the past] and the force with which François must come to terms. She prevents him from establishing any contacts with people in the world around him and François in turn develops an unwillingness to move beyond the world his mother has created for him and to discover the world for himself. His act of revolt is not so much positive action toward a goal as simply an aimless, negative reaction against his mother. His mother strikes him with her large iron key ring . . . and in so doing, the doors to freedom and knowledge become locked forever. . . . To possess the world, one must have knowledge. Dispossessed psychologically and physically, François is doomed to ignorance, for instead of going out into the world, he is locked in.

The action of "Le Torrent" becomes more and more introspective as the story develops. It is with the advent of his deafness that the rapids become internalized within François. . . . Instead of possessing the world, he is eventually possessed by it. The story then shifts literally to the interior, to the mind, for just as the rapids have the power to dismember the body, they can devastate the psyche as well. . . .

[Allegorically], "la grand Claudine" might be seen as the repressive, religious conscience associated with fear. . . . Claudine can be seen as the expression of the rigid old order which depends implicitly upon the rationale of the status quo and which denies passion and spontaneity to the individual. In complete contrast to her is the horse, Perceval, which is marked by an explosive and passionate irrationality. The horse as the incarnation of brute force and passion is described through implicit comparison to the rapids. . . . And it is Perceval who destroys Claudine in a sudden and furious escape.

Once his mother has been murdered, one would suppose the new order would find expression in François. . . . But it is the horse which kills the mother. François has been only a witness. Because the beast has no guiding intelligence, the act is complete and final in itself. François . . . is an isolated world unto himself and consequently his involvement in Claudine's death is vicarious at best. His inturning consciousness is statically centred in the self and does not have the direction, however perverse, of "la grande Claudine." . . .

On another level, "Le Torrent" is a story about art and the artist. . . . In his introspection, [François] is linked more strongly to contemplation than to action, to art than to life. It is suggested in "Le Torrent" that turning inward leads to chaos resulting from a failure to look out upon the larger world, for François seems "to be haunted by the sterility of an overly ascetic order resulting from a complete withdrawal from life." (p. 71)

In "Le Torrent," there is no hope of community. Even the possibility of some healing emotional unity between man and woman is never realized. François buys his woman and she in turn steals from him. The irony of the name which François gives to her—Amica—shows how ignorant he is of the world outside his mute perception. Although François repudiates his mother, like her he rejects the irrational while being obsessed by it. He also attempts to enslave Amica just as his mother enslaved him. His essential inturning nature suggests qualities of obsessive self-interest which are destructive or individual, and by extension, on com-

munal levels. François, like the Narcissus figure which occurs elsewhere in French-Canadian literature, is destined to drown literally and figuratively in self-reflection. . . .

In "Le Torrent," François is the product of a negative and repressive spiritual code. His world is the world of unredeemed misery where the spiritual mood is one of fear and vengeance and where there is no father to legitimize his bastard physical and spiritual status. . . . Without redemption through community, he is left with a destructive self-perpetuating past which will eventually efface the present and leave him alone with darkness. . . . (p. 72)

John Watt Lennox, "The Past: Themes and Symbols of Confrontation in 'The Double Hook' and 'Le Torrent'," in Journal of Canadian Fiction (reprinted by permission from Journal of Canadian Fiction, 2050 Mackay St., Montreal, Quebec H3G 2J1, Canada), Vol. II, No. 1, Winter 1973, pp. 70-2.

PETER FRANCE

[Like much of québécois fiction "Le Torrent"] shows the distorting effect of a strict religious upbringing, in this case the stunting of the life of a child by a pious mother who is paying off an old debt to society. . . . The whole story is built round a series of polarities; the hero is held . . . between the attraction of a world of movement, smell, colour and danger . . . and the inculcated urge to call all this evil and master it. . . . There is no way out of this anguished state and the end can only be tragic. The tragic tone is created above all by an exalted simplicity of writing that reminds one of Camus's L'Etranger. "Le Torrent" is the work of a considerable poet.

Now, thirty years later, in Les infants du sabat, Anne Hébert is still caught in the same dilemmas, or at least she continues to make fiction of them. The hero of the earlier story managed to avoid becoming a priest; the heroine of this . . . novel is about to take monastic orders when (literally) all hell is let loose. She is invaded by images and desires which rise up from a childhood full of colours, smells, natural life, illicit alcohol, drugs, incest and witchcraft. . . .

In spite of its larger dimensions and more inflammatory subjects, Les infants du sabat is a less powerful piece of work than "Le Torrent". Instead of the obsessional first-person narration we have a shifting point of view which allows the author to make fun of many of her outwardly prim ecclesiastical characters.

Mother Church, dressed in black and white, is still an anti-life force, but her power is perhaps more easily subverted in the Québec of 1975. . . . Where the story was weightily tragic, the novel has a grotesque element strongly reminiscent of Bulgakov's The Master and Margarita. . . .

For all this irony, it is hard not to feel that black magic in the convent is a rather overplayed theme. It is not clear whether Anne Hébert wants us to believe that convents are like this, nor do the occasional historical references incline one to read the novel as a chronicle of Québec province. It seems more appropriate to see it in a dream-like projection of an old duality of "Le Torrent", again done in style, but perhaps too familiar to be really memorable.

Peter France, "The Rending of the Veil," in The Times Literary Supplement (© Times Newspapers Ltd. (London) 1975; reproduced from The

Times Literary Supplement *by permission), Octo-ber 10, 1975, p. 1208.*

DAVID WALKER

[Perhaps] no other Quebecois poet has so successfully pre-sented the long night of the French-Canadian soul as it seeks to exorcise its demons and escape from the small "chambre fermée" in which it finds itself imprisoned and exiled [than has Anne Hébert]. Although [her] poetry is deeply personal and highly original, it is difficult not to remark upon the similarities between the personal adven-ture of Anne Hébert and the general evolution of Quebec society in recent years. The two collections which make up *Poems—Tomb of the Kings* and *Mystery of the Verb*—were originally published in 1953 and 1960 respectively. The con-trast in style, tone and content between these two collec-tions reflects the development not only of Anne Hébert but of the collective Quebecois consciousness as well.

Tomb of the Kings is essentially a poetry of absence, an exploration of the pain and anguish which results from an awareness of one's solitude and of an all-consuming black-ness. Here the abundant water imagery promises, not fertil-ity, but rather loneliness and silence. . . . [In one sense] the poet chooses to continue to dwell in this world of silence and darkness, to perpetuate a situation in which she is a (willing?) victim. This apparent choice of a kind of death-in-life presents the fundamental conflict of *Poems*: the struggle between a pre-established state of inertia and isolation, and a yearning—present in the earliest poems—for activity and creation. . . .

The second collection, *Mystery of the Verb* . . . reflects, both in style and themes, a radical change in outlook. The short (rarely longer than six syllables), hammering line of *Tomb of the Kings* is replaced by long, luxuriant verses which express a new openness to reality, a refusal of closed spaces, and a desire to accept and name the physical world in all its variety. . . . *Mystery of the Verb* is not only a hymn to nature and to life; it is also a tribute to the ability of poetry to liberate both poet and reader by allowing them to rediscover and remake the world through the power of the "word." . . . The poetry of Anne Hébert, in its evolu-tion from a poetry of absence and death to one of rebirth and affirmation, corresponds in large part to the journey of the *âme québécoise*. The publication of *Mystery of the Verb* in 1960 corresponds in time to that collective breakaway from isolation and immobility known as the "Quiet Revolu-tion." The celebration and the naming of the physical world found in *Mystery of the Verb* will be continued in diverse modes by poets like Gatien Lapointe, Yves Préfontaine and Paul Chamberland, among others. Thus the poetic adven-ture of Anne Hébert, so profoundly personal, reveals itself, by its loyalty "to one's deepest truth, however dangerous it may be," to be an experience which resumes the deepest anxieties and aspirations of the collectivity. This is poetry which, despite its seemingly hermetic character, is ulti-mately open-ended and accessible. It is private and original poetry which nevertheless continuously transcends its spec-ificity and opens out upon the world. (p. 38)

> David Walker, "Exorcising Demons," in The
> Canadian Forum, *August, 1976, pp. 38-9.*

JOYCE CAROL OATES

In "Children of the Black Sabbath" [Anne Hébert] poses the timely question of whether a beautiful young girl from an impoverished rural community in Quebec can find happi-ness and contentment in the Sisterhood of the Precious Blood—whether she can take final vows as Sister Julie of the Trinity before her complicated, colorful past as the daughter of an alcoholic sorceress and a sado-masochistic father (in fact, the Devil himself) can cause mischief. She does not succeed.

Another dramatization of "possession." Another sequence of ostensibly inexplicable events, culminating in the actions (here thwarted) of a Grand Exorcist. One would think that Anne Hébert, or at the very least her publishers, would be hesitant about bringing out a novel that seeks to combine "The Exorcist" and "Rosemary's Baby." . . . Hébert might have turned the screw a bit more and made her nuns intentionally hilarious, or she might have slowed down and written a serious psychological sutdy of the delusions of "possession." . . . Where another Canadian writer, Marie-Claire Blais, strives to create bitter, elliptical poetry out of the economic and spiritual impoverishment of her region, Anne Hébert seems to have settled for dispirited pop fic-tion. And that it is so plainly derivative is both puzzling and embarrassing. (pp. 14-15)

> Joyce Carol Oates, in The New York Times Book
> Review (© 1977 by The New York Times Com-
> pany; reprinted by permission), July 24, 1977.

PAUL G. SOCKEN

[*Children of the Black Sabbath* is], simultaneously, the most traditional and the most unique [novel] on the Quebec literary scene. . . . Anne Hébert makes the point [that peo-ple are extensions of the land on which they live] unequivo-cally at several instances and readers acquainted with Quebec's literature will find the portrayal of the people suf-fering under the yoke of climate and clergy more than famil-iar. The worldliness and-hypocrisy of the Church, another theme "exposed" here, is also not without literary prece-dent. . . . In fact, an analysis of the thematic content will yield very little that is new or dynamic.

What, then, lends the book the awesome power discerned in it by various critics? Its strength, one might suggest, lies in its force of language, evident even in translation, its evocative imagery and its imaginative narrative technique.

Anne Hébert is, above all, a poet. The words spring to life, the images penetrate and reveal. . . .

[The] only "world" absent from the novel, and perhaps by inference from Quebec society according to Anne Hébert, is what we may call normalcy; that is, life not denied the right to act and react freely, not totally dominated by unful-filled and frustrated needs. That is what disturbs me most about the novel. It seems anachronistic after the Quiet Revolution . . . to continue painting a picture of Quebec that is one of unrelieved gloom and despair. . . . There is none of the guarded optimism of a Godbout, the painful humour of a Ferron, the tentative self-acceptance of a Ga-brielle Roy.

Anne Hébert is a great talent indelibly marked by her ex-periences of Quebec in the thirties, forties and fifties, but her communication of a mood of unmitigated futility and hopelessness, associated with that period, may date this work in spite of its technical mastery.

> Paul G. Socken, "Almost Anachronistic," in The
> Canadian Forum, *August, 1977, p. 39.*

HECHT, Anthony   1923-

A Pulitzer Prize-winning American poet, Hecht is a technically ingenious and accomplished craftsman who writes in an elegant, baroque style. A common theme of Hecht's—the ironic contrast between harsh reality and artistic (false) versions of reality—can be found in one of his frequently anthologized poems, the satirical "Dover Bitch." (See also *CLC*, Vol. 8, and *Contemporary Authors*, Vols. 9-12, rev. ed.)

HAROLD BLOOM

The high artistry of Anthony Hecht has been to nurture his own gift, and to work at it with the deliberateness and steadiness that it deserved from him. *A Summoning of Stones* (1954) and *The Hard Hours* (1967) have now been joined by *Millions of Strange Shadows*. . . . Emotional intensity and formal power were combined in Hecht from his beginnings; if there has been a deepening in so elegant and grave an art, it has been in the release of a humor gentler than the initial ironies of apprehension that Hecht once cultivated. The 30 poems in Hecht's new book are all fully *written*, but several truly are the best he has published and are very likely to endure. The very best is "Green: An Epistle," which is a lesson in profound, controlled subjectivity and self-revelation, an exact antithesis to the opaque squalors of "confessional" poets. Almost equally remarkable are "Coming Home," in which the poet John Clare receives a deeper interpretation than any critic has afforded him, and "Apprehensions," again a masterwork of dramatic introspection. (p. 25)

> *Harold Bloom, in* The New Republic *(reprinted by permission of* The New Republic; © *1977 by The New Republic, Inc.), November 26, 1977.*

G. E. MURRAY

Millions of Strange Shadows is only [Hecht's] third volume of original poetry in nearly three decades, the first since *The Hard Hours* (1967) was awarded the Pulitzer Prize. Anthony Hecht remains one of a shrinking handful of our most skilled poetic craftsmen. This is not to imply that his music overwhelms his substance, but the music *is* unforgettable. Listen, for instance, to one segment from "The Cost," a poem addressing the wages of war:

> Think how some excellent, lean torso hugs
>   The brink of weight and speed,
> Coasting the margins of those rival tugs
>   Down the thin path of friction,
> The athlete's dancing vectors, the spirit's need,
>   And muscle's cleanly diction.

It strikes me that this passage, pinched out of context, not only opens discussion on the standards and values of human conflict, but also is descriptive of the finest of Hecht's writing. Surely his messages conform to media that ride "the brink of weight and speed" and address "the spirit's need" as precisely and delightfully as sail on water. But the melody of language disposed in startling patterns of rhyme and meter is only one concern here.

In what is supposedly the heydey of the loose style and personal poem, Anthony Hecht admirably couples epic ambitions with an intense lyrical gift, laced with nerves of meaning. . . . (pp. 963-64)

Much of the grave perception and grey perspective that distinguished Hecht's two earlier collections, with "those neu-

ter, intermediary states / Of vacancy," are again present in [*Millions of Strange Shadows*], serving as "Reminder of a time, / An Aesopic Age when all the beasts were moral / And taught their ways to men." From not so innocent or grand a precipice, Hecht mourns our drab folly. . . .

There is often a long, hard sadness going through the poems in this volume, a sense of living at the end of a civilization cycle. More than ever before, however, love of wife and family and, most notably, humor, now infiltrate Anthony Hecht's vision. The addition is a blessing, particularly evidenced by the superb poem "The Ghost in the Martini," a wildly funny, yet bracing look at the hollow retreat into middle age. (p. 964)

> *G. E. Murray, in* The Georgia Review *(copyright, 1977, by the University of Georgia), Winter, 1977.*

IRVIN EHRENPREIS

Anthony Hecht certainly practices the poetry of limits. Yet he often handles obnoxious subjects: a description of the rotting corpse of a monkey ("Alceste in the Wilderness"), the horrors of war ("Christmas Is Coming," "Drinking Song," etc.), the destruction of the Jews ("Rites and Ceremonies"), the Lisbon earthquake. One of his least forgettable poems tells of the capture, humiliation, torture, and flaying of the Roman emperor Valerian ("Behold the Lilies of the Field"). But he manages the frightfulness within a perceptible design. . . .

When Hecht takes up quickening subjects—fatherhood, the praise of landscape, sexual tenderness—his sweet-and-sour tone gains force from hints that he also has in mind the death-bearing experiences. A knowledge of pain refines the edge of pleasure, as a knowledge of pleasure sharpens the acid of pain. It seems appropriate that Hecht likes to indulge in oxymoron: "dirge of birth" ("An Autumnal"), "awkward grace" ("Peripeteia"). . . .

In many poems Hecht gives the quickening experience an advantage. He does not imply that life, for any long period, is free from pain. On the contrary, he implies that pain and grief mix so homogeneously with the stuff of existence that we may assume their omnipresence. Love, beauty, and wisdom do not cancel them out and do not spring from them (alas!) but descend as a gift in spite of them. The graces of life barely compensate us for the omnipresence of grief or pain. This lowering truth is a reason for dwelling on the graces. . . .

Elaborate forms challenge Hecht's imagination. His most personal and tender poem of guilty love, "A Letter," is in a complicated, rhymed stanza that might have been used by his admired George Herbert.

[In] *Millions of Strange Shadows* (see Shakespeare, Sonnet 53), Hecht sounds more comfortable with the difficult forms and allows himself fewer archaisms than in his earlier work. But he still observes the fundamental human experiences through the settings and alternatives which oppose or threaten them: foregrounds seen through backgrounds, love through war, an impulse of vitality as a reminder of death. (p. 48)

> *Irvin Ehrenpreis, in* The New York Review of Books *(reprinted with permission from* The New York Review of Books; *copyright © 1978 Nyrev, Inc.), August 17, 1978.*

DESMOND GRAHAM

[It] is the ability to make poems, the command of a convention, which is so impressive about Anthony Hecht's *Millions of Strange Shadows*. . . . Hecht makes no bones about it: he is formal, immensely skilful, gives himself whatever room he needs for elaborate description, extended discourse, intricacies of reference and overlapping complexities of theme. Conscious art is Hecht's forte, and it is an art which can encompass—in the single poem ('The Cost')—a couple on a Vespa, the processes of history, the common soldier's fate, the fallibility of hope . . . my list is not exhaustive. Hecht's themes are moral, in both personal and public spheres; his imagination is philosophical; his art is as serious as it is authoritative. But. . . . And here the problem starts: his command of art filters experience (quite consciously so) to an extent which leaves me restless. I seek metaphors for what is wrong: the art is so finely inlaid, everything fits too well? It moves us through experience as if in a luxury car, observing the rough road, the changing weather? Somehow we *are* passengers in his poems. . . . Hecht does not strain, he opens his hand and images drop into it; cadence and balance and poise take their hold: but even granting that this is the opening—deceptively casual and leisurely—to an experience through which Hecht will take his time, something is slackened in our minds by such grace. Each epithet, descriptively perfect, is cushioned against discomforting weight. . . . (pp. 66-7)

[There] is nothing peripheral or trivial in Hecht's graceful art—but in so finely miming the false security which his words expose, his art is infected by this security. What the reader receives is not an art directing him outwards to the instances of suffering which are given, but an art closing in round its own beauty: ("elegance" would be too weak a word for these lines). (p. 67)

Not arch, not posed, not literary, [his poetry carries] a tenderness which is nonetheless impaired. We know too well where we are with this beautifully written book, and it is somewhere other than where we live. (p. 68)

Desmond Graham, in Stand *(copyright © by Stand), Vol. 20, No. 1 (1978-79).*

* * *

HEMINGWAY, Ernest   1899-1961

Hemingway was an American novelist, short story writer, and journalist. Numbered by many among the greatest American writers, Hemingway is master of the objective prose style which became his trademark. War and athletic competition often make up the subject matter of his works, allowing Hemingway to explore man's physical and metaphysical strivings. He was confounded by both the idea and the reality of death: indeed, an essential nihilism colors all of his work. Hemingway is noted for his superlative description of action, although some critics find the philosophy espoused in his later novels simplistic and pompous. He was awarded the Nobel Prize for Literature in 1954 and the Pulitzer Prize in Fiction in 1953. (See also *CLC*, Vols. 1, 3, 6, 8, 10, and *Contemporary Authors*, Vols. 77-80.)

MALCOLM COWLEY

When Hemingway's stories first appeared, they seemed to be a transcription of the real world, new because they were accurate and because the world in those days was also new. With his insistence on "presenting things truly," he seemed

to be a writer in the naturalistic tradition (for all his technical innovations). . . . Going back to his work [later], you perceive his kinship with a wholly different group of novelists, let us say with Poe and Hawthorne and Melville: the haunted and nocturnal writers, the men who dealt in images that were symbols of an inner world.

On the face of it, his method is not in the least like theirs. He doesn't lead us into castles ready to collapse with age, or into very old New England houses, or embark with us on the search for a whale that is also the white spirit of evil; instead he tells the stories he has lived or heard, against the background of countries he has seen. But, you reflect on reading his books again, these are curious stories that he has chosen from his wider experience, and these countries are presented in a strangely mortuary light. In no other writer of our time can you find such a profusion of corpses. . . . In no other writer can you find so many suffering animals. . . . And morally wounded people who also devour themselves . . .—here are visions as terrifying as those of "The Pit and the Pendulum," even though most of them are copied from life; here are nightmares at noonday, accurately described, pictured without blur, but having the nature of obsessions or hypnagogic visions between sleep and waking.

And, going back to them, you find a waking-dreamlike quality even in the stories that deal with pleasant or commonplace aspects of the world. (pp. 40-1)

Hemingway's stories are most of them continued, in the sense that he has a habit of returning to the same themes, each time making them a little clearer—to himself, I think, as well as to others. His work has an emotional consistency, as if all of it moved with the same current. (p. 41)

After reading [a later story, "Now I Lay Me,"] we have a somewhat different attitude toward the earlier ["Big Two-Hearted River."] . . . [We] now perceive what we probably missed at a first reading: that there are shadows in the background and that part of the story takes place in an inner world. We notice that Nick Adams regards his fishing trip as an escape, either from nightmare or from realities that have become a nightmare. . . . "Nick felt happy," the author says more than once. "He felt he had left everything behind, the need for thinking, the need to write, other needs. It was all back of him." He lives as if in an enchanted country. There is a faint suggestion of old legends: all the stories of boys with cruel stepmothers who wandered off into the forest where the big trees sheltered them and the birds brought them food. (p. 42)

[Fishing] is not the only activity of his heroes that Hemingway endows with a curious and almost supernatural value. They drink early and late; they consume enough beer, wine, anis, grappa, and Fundador to put them all into alcoholic wards, if they were ordinary mortals; but drinking seems to have the effect on them of a magic potion. (pp. 42-3)

[Hemingway tried in the] early days to state everything behavioristically, and it was not until later that he began to make a deliberate use of symbolism, together with other literary devices that he had avoided in the beginning, when he was teaching himself to write "commencing with the simplest things." . . .

Hemingway almost never makes the error that weakens the

effect of most symbolic fiction. Ordinarily we think of it as a type of writing in which the events in the foreground tend to become misty because the author has his eyes fixed on something else.... It is true that Maria, in *For Whom the Bell Tolls,* is almost more of a dream than she is a woman. When Frederic Henry dives into the flooded Tagliamento, in *A Farewell to Arms,* he is performing a rite of baptism that prepares us for the new life he is about to lead as a deserter from the Italian army; his act is emotionally significant, but it is a little unconvincing on the plane of action. These are perhaps the only two cases in which Hemingway seems to loosen his grip on reality. Elsewhere his eyes are fixed on the foreground; but he gives us a sense of other shadowy meanings that contribute to the force and complexity of his writing. (p. 46)

Hemingway's prose at its best gives a sense of depth and of moving forward on different levels that is lacking in even the best of his imitators, as it is in almost all the other novelists of our time. Moreover, I have at least a vague notion of how this quality in his work can be explained.

Considering his laborious apprenticeship and the masters with whom he chose to study; considering his theories of writing, which he has often discussed, and how they have developed with the years; considering their subtle and highly conscious application, as well as the very complicated personality they serve to express, it is a little surprising to find that Hemingway is almost always described as a primitive. Yet the word really applies to him, if it is used in what might be called its anthropological sense. The anthropologists tell us that many of the so-called primitive peoples have an extremely elaborate system of beliefs, calling for the almost continual performance of rites and ceremonies; even their drunken orgies are ruled by tradition. Some of the forest-dwelling tribes believe that every rock or tree or animal has its own indwelling spirit. When they kill an animal or chop down a tree, they must beg its forgiveness, repeating a formula of propitiation; otherwise its spirit would haunt them. Living briefly in a world of hostile forces, they preserve themselves—so they believe—only by the exercise of magic lore.

There is something of the same atmosphere in Hemingway's work. His heroes live in a world that is like a hostile forest, full of unseen dangers, not to mention the nightmares that haunt their sleep. Death spies on them from behind every tree. Their only chance of safety lies in the faithful observance of customs they invent for themselves. In an early story like "Big Two-Hearted River," you notice that Nick Adams does everything very slowly, not wishing "to rush his sensations any"; and he pays so much attention to the meaning and rightness of each gesture that his life in the wilderness becomes a series of little ceremonies.... The whole fishing trip, instead of being a mere escape, might be regarded as an incantation, a spell to banish evil spirits. And there are other rituals in Hemingway's work (besides drinking and writing . . .). [We] can recognize rites of animal sacrifice (as in *Death in the Afternoon*), of sexual union (in *For Whom the Bell Tolls*), of self-immolation (in "The Snows of Kilimanjaro"), of conversion (in *To Have and Have Not*), and of symbolic death and rebirth (in the Caporetto passage of *A Farewell to Arms*). When one of Hemingway's characters violates his own standards or the just laws of the tribe (as Ole Andreson has done in "The Killers"), he waits for death as stolidly as an Indian. (pp. 47-8)

[Hemingway] seems to have a feeling for half-forgotten sacraments; his cast of mind is pre-Christian and prelogical.

Sometimes his stories come close to being adaptations of ancient myths. His first novel, for example, deals in different terms with the same legend [that of the Fisher King] that T. S. Eliot was not so much presenting as concealing in *The Waste Land*. (p. 49)

And it is this instinct for legends, for sacraments, for rituals, for symbols appealing to buried hopes and fears, that helps to explain the power of Hemingway's work and his vast superiority over his imitators. The imitators have learned all his mannerisms as a writer, and in some cases they can tell a story even better than Hemingway himself; but they tell only the story; they communicate with the reader on only one level of experience. Hemingway does more than that. Most of us are also primitive in a sense, for all the machinery that surrounds our lives. We have our private rituals, our little superstitions, our symbols and fears and nightmares; and Hemingway reminds us unconsciously of the hidden worlds in which we live. (p. 50)

[Some of his] writing has gone bad, but surprisingly little of it. By now he has earned the right to be taken for what he is, with his great faults and greater virtues; with his narrowness, his power, his always open eyes, his stubborn, chip-on-the-shoulder honesty, his nightmares, his rituals for escaping them, and his sense of an inner and an outer world that for twenty years were moving together toward the same disaster. (p. 51)

> *Malcolm Cowley, "Introduction" (copyright 1944 by The Viking Press, Inc.; all rights reserved; reprinted by permission of Viking Penguin Inc.), in* The Portable Hemingway, *edited by Malcolm Cowley, Viking Penguin, 1944 (and reprinted as "Nightmare and Ritual in Hemingway," in* Hemingway: A Collection of Critical Essays, *edited by Robert P. Weeks, Prentice-Hall, Inc., 1962, pp. 40-51).*

ROBERT W. STALLMAN

Hemingway's narrator [in *The Sun Also Rises*] seemingly represents "the true moral norm of the book," but he appears as such only to the prejudiced reader, prejudiced by the bias of the narrator's authoritative voice....

Read the novel from Cohn's point-of-view, and you end obversely in bias against Jake Barnes and his sophomoric code and his friends who damn Cohn by it. Reversal of intention: that Hemingway consciously schemed it so is evidenced by the fact that his narrator is honest enough to include in his story the self-incriminating testimony of witnesses against him, namely Bill Gorton, Robert Cohn, and Jake Barnes himself. Jake confesses his defections from the code he seemingly exemplifies and from his role as historian of the pretenders to it. (p. 173)

Characteristically, what Jake says of his friends applies also to himself. Jake's portrait of Cohn reflects himself; it tells us as much about Jake as about Cohn.

On Jake's own admission, we cannot accept his portrait of Cohn with any certitude: "Somehow I feel that *I have not shown Robert Cohn clearly.*" ... Jake Barnes, New York *Herald* journalist, is not a trustworthy reporter. (pp. 176-77)

Cohn is [pictured as] awful because he is always merely nice. Niceness is discredited because it declares a weakness, an exposed flaw in the mask of mock sophistication which Jake and his friends subscribe to. The criterion is irony, and Cohn never once speaks ironically. . . .

In both *The Sun Also Rises* and *The Great Gatsby* the narrators default on the standards by which they measure and judge others. Duplicity characterizes both narrators. (p. 178)

Contra Carlos Baker's notion of "the moral vacuum in Cohn," Cohn stands out as exemplar of the Christian virtues. That *moral vacuum* is located—by my reading—in Jake, in Brett, and in Mike; also in Romero. (p. 180)

Hemingway's public has been brain-washed by the Hemingway Code.

The story narrated by Jake Barnes is the story of Robert Cohn, the betrayed tin Christ. Everyone in *The Sun Also Rises* regards himself as a little tin Christ—the exceptions are the Count and Montoya *and* Cohn. They crucify Cohn as though he were one. They hang a wreath of twisted garlics around his neck while he sleeps on some wine-casks. . . .

They blaspheme him. When Mike demands Cohn "Eat those garlics," . . . it is as though Cohn were Christ—Cohn crucified by Judas Mike. When Cohn awakes, it is as though Christ Cohn were resurrected from the dead. . . .

Says Judas Jake: "I'm not sorry for him. I hate him, myself." Says Brett: "I hate him, too. . . . I hate his damned suffering." . . . "Go away, for God's sake. Take that sad Jewish face away." So Mike speaks of Cohn as though Cohn were Christ. (p. 181)

Lady Brett Ashley has no sense of values *and* she has no sense of time: "I looked at the clock. It was half-past four. 'Had no idea what hour it was,' Brett said." . . . (p. 183)

Everything in *The Sun Also Rises* is rotten. Hemingway told Fitzgerald that *The Sun Also Rises* was "a hell of a sad story," whose only instruction was "how people go to hell." . . . (pp. 183-4)

Hemingway's narrator is crossed in identity with Cohn: "I put on a coat of Cohn's and went out on the balcony." . . . The surface reason for Jake's hatred of Cohn is envy that Cohn has possessed Brett, but the real reason stems from the subconscious recognition—rendered implicitly by his sharing Cohn's coat, for instance—that he, the outcast Jacob, shares identity with the outcast Robert Cohn and that in hating Cohn he is in effect expressing his own self-hatred.

That Jake shares identity with his antagonist, what does that spell out but the fact of a reversal of intention in *The Sun Also Rises*. How can Jake be represented by Hemingway critics as superior to Cohn if Jake is identified with Cohn? They thus switch places, and thereby I fashion my upside-down reading of the novel: Read it from Jake's side and he is right; read it from Cohn's side and he is right. But once you read it from Cohn's point of view, Jake is all wrong. Jake rebels against and disbelieves in that other side of his selfhood which Cohn represents. They are, as it were, the conflicting double selfhood of their creator—one side of Hemingway criticizing the other. (p. 188)

[Carlos Baker also] opines that Hemingway "early devised and subsequently developed a mythologizing tendency of

his own which does not depend on antecedent literatures, learned footnotes, or the recognition of spot passages," and he adds that Hemingway's esthetic opinions "carried him away from the literary kind of myth adaptation". . . ; but the fact is that Frazer's *The Golden Bough* is the well-spring source of Hemingway's mythologizing tendency in *The Sun Also Rises*. Any well-informed reading of the novel owes homage to *The Golden Bough*. It is loaded with "spot passages" and "learned footnotes" from Frazer, and—*contra* Baker—it exploits "the literary kind of myth adaptation." (pp. 189-90)

Ceremonies of haircutting, rituals and taboos of drinking and bathing and fishing—they are all recreated in *The Sun Also Rises* from *The Golden Bough*, a parallelism which has not been noticed (so far as I know). (p. 191)

Detached from Jake's claim—*that* is [Jew] Cohn's plight. If any remark by Cohn would detach him from Jake and his friends, it is his admission: "I'm not interested in bull-fighters. That's an abnormal life." . . . Cohn's values stand as the obverse of Jake's. Cohn's critique of the Narrator's Point-of-View provides the novel with its aesthetic antithesis. (p. 192)

> Robert W. Stallman, "'The Sun Also Rises'—But No Bells Ring" (a revision of a speech originally delivered at Centre Culturel Americain, Paris, in April 1959), in his The Houses That James Built and Other Literary Studies (copyright © 1961 by R. W. Stallman), Ohio University Press, 1961, pp. 173-93.

SEAN O'FAOLAIN

It is something of a joke, in view of the common belief that Hemingway is a tough, laconic writer, that the reason for the difficulty [in interpreting "A Clean, Well-Lighted Place"] is that this story by an acknowledged "realist" is as near, in its quality and its effect, to a poem as prose can be without ceasing to be honest prose. (p. 112)

Age, death, despair, love, the boredom of life, two elderly men seeking sleep and forgetfulness, and one still young enough to feel passion, cast into an hour and a place whose silence and emptiness, soon to become more silent and more empty still—it all creates in us, at first, a sad mood in which patience and futility feebly strive with one another, involve us, mesmerize us. Grimness is in the offing. Hemingway's kindness and tenderness save us from that. For Hemingway, deep down, is one of the kindest and most tender of writers. If our final feelings here are of pity and awe it is he who communicates them to us. I believe that Hemingway's "realism" is merely the carapace or shell that protects, grips, holds from overspilling a nature fundamentally emotional and tender. (pp. 112-13)

[With the waiter's confession, "I'm with all those who like to stay late at the café . . . With all those who need a *light* at night"] the meaning of the title becomes clear, and in the following references to light, as one of the defenses of man's sad soul against the Baudelaireian horror of Nothingness. As it becomes clear, the romantic notes darken. We realize that such notes as love, youth, the lighted leaves, the dew all carry dark shadows, that the silence is ominous and the night inimical. Youth implies age, love is an apple that must fall from its tree, the dew will dry, the light will go out. How unblatantly Hemingway does it! How subdued the irony of his title and his theme! And yet there is also a firm line and intention in it all. He has a strength that need never be confused with violence. He is a delicate sculptor of great muscle.

As for the craft by which Hemingway produces effects on us, transfers a somber yet soothing mood to us, this is so artfully contrived that the popular idea of the man is that he has no art at all—than which no art can be more successful. Yet his art is, in fact, a very clean, well-lighted place, practical, cool, sharp, colorless like an Italian café before the Italian decorators moved in, entirely functional and unobtrusive. His style is one of the most self-conscious, original, and personal styles ever invented, based on a proper respect for words such as a man might develop from the habit of sending cablegrams from battlefields at a high price per word. It is hard to describe an effect of simplicity originating in the silences and suppressions of a man of such deep feeling. (p. 113)

> *Sean O'Faolain, "'A Clean, Well-Lighted Place',"* in Short Stories: A Study in Pleasure, *edited by Sean O'Faolain (copyright © 1961, Sean O'Faolain; reprinted by permission of Little, Brown and Co.), Little, Brown, 1961 (and reprinted in* Hemingway: A Collection of Critical Essays, *edited by Robert P. Weeks, Prentice-Hall, Inc., 1962, pp. 112-13).*

PHILIP YOUNG

Very probably [Hemingway] intended [the title of *In Our Time*] as a sardonic allusion to a well-known phrase from the Church of England's Book of Common Prayer: "Give peace in our time, O Lord." At any rate the most striking thing about the volume is that there is no peace at all in the stories. The next most striking thing about them . . . is that half of the stories are devoted to the spotty but careful development of a crucial but long-ignored character—a boy, then a young man—named Nick Adams. These stories are arranged in the chronological order of Nick's boyhood and early manhood, and are intimately related, one to another. Indeed in this aspect the book is almost a "novel," for some of the stories are incomprehensible if one does not see the point, and it is often subtle, of some earlier piece. (pp. 5-6)

A careful reading of ["Indian Camp", the first story of *In Our Time*,] will show that Hemingway is not primarily interested . . . in [the] shocking events: he is interested in their effect on the little boy who witnessed them. For the moment the events do not seem to *have* any great effect on the boy. But it is very important that he is later on a badly scarred and nervous young man, and here Hemingway is relating to us the first reason he gives why that is so. (p. 6)

The six following stories from *In Our Time* concerning Nick Adams are not so violent as "Indian Camp," but each of them is unpleasant or upsetting in some way or other. (p. 7)

[An untitled sketch following the story "The Battler"] tells us that Nick is in World War I, that he has been wounded, and that he has made a "separate peace" with the enemy—is not fighting for his country, or any other, any more. It would be quite impossible to exaggerate the importance of this short scene in any understanding of Hemingway and his work. It will be duplicated at more length by another protagonist, named Frederic Henry, in *A Farewell to Arms,* and it will serve as a climax in the lives of all of Hemingway's heroes, in one way or another, for at least the next quarter-century.

The fact that Nick is seriously injured is significant in two important ways. First, the wound intensifies and epitomizes the wounds he has been getting as a boy growing up in the American Middle West. From here on the Hemingway hero will appear to us as a wounded man—wounded not only physically but, as soon becomes clear, psychologically as well. Second, the fact that Nick and his friend, also wounded, have made a "separate peace," are "Not patriots," marks the beginning of the long break with organized society as a whole that stays with Hemingway and his hero through several books to come. . . . Indeed the last story in this first volume, called "Big Two-Hearted River," is a kind of forecast of these things. It is obscure until one sees the point. . . . But it is really a very simple "story." It is a study of a young man who has been hurt in the war, who is all by himself on a fishing trip, escaping everyone. He is suffering from what used to be called "shell shock"; he is trying desperately to keep from going out of his mind. (pp. 8-9)

[The interest in "An Alpine Idyll"] focuses on the responses of Nick and others to a particularly shocking situation, as it did in the more famous "Killers." But whereas in the earlier story Nick was so upset by the thought of the man who was passively waiting to be murdered that he wanted to get clean out of the town where the violence impended, healthy tissue is now growing over his wounds, and the point of the story lies in the development of his defenses.

By now it is perfectly clear what kind of boy, then man, this Adams is. He is certainly not the simple primitive he is often mistaken for. He is honest, virile, but—clearest of all —very sensitive. He is an outdoor male, and he has a lot of nerve, but he is also very nervous. It is important to understand this Nick, for soon, under other names in other books, he is going to be known half the world over as the "Hemingway hero": every single one of these men has had, or has had the exact equivalent of, Nick's childhood, adolescence, and young manhood. This man will die a thousand times before his death, and although he would learn how to live with some of his troubles, and how to overcome others, he would never completely recover from his wounds as long as Hemingway lived and recorded his adventures.

Now it is also clear that something was needed to bind these wounds, and there is in Hemingway a consistent character who performs that function. This figure is not Hemingway himself in disguise (which to some hard-to-measure extent the Hemingway hero was). Indeed he is to be sharply distinguished from the hero, for he comes to balance the hero's deficiencies, to correct his stance. . . . [This man is generally called] the "code hero"—this because he represents a code according to which the hero, if he could attain it, would be able to live properly in the world of violence, disorder, and misery to which he has been introduced and which he inhabits. The code hero, then, offers up and exemplifies certain principles of honor, courage, and endurance which in a life of tension and pain make a man a man, as we say, and enable him to conduct himself well in the losing battle that is life. He shows, in the author's famous phrase for it, "grace under pressure." (pp. 10-11)

The finest and best known of these code heroes is old Santiago of *The Old Man and the Sea.* The chief point about him is that he behaves perfectly—honorably, with great courage and endurance—while losing to the sharks the giant fish he has caught. This, to epitomize the message the code hero always brings, is life: you lose, of course; what counts is how you conduct yourself while you are being destroyed. (p. 11)

The Sun Also Rises reintroduces us to the hero, here called Jake Barnes. His wound, again with both literal and symbolic meanings, is . . . to the genitals: Jake was, to speak loosely, emasculated in the war. His wound, then, has undergone a significant transformation, but he is still the hero, still the man who cannot sleep when his head starts to work, and who cries in the night. He has also parted with society and the usual middle-class ways; he lives in Paris with an international group of expatriates, a dissolute collection of amusing but aimless people—all of them, in one way or another, blown out of the paths of ordinary life by the war. (pp. 12-13)

Although it is not highly developed yet, Jake and the few people he likes have a code. There are certain things that are "done," and many that are "not done," and one of the characters distinguishes people as belonging or not belonging according to whether they understand or not. (p. 13)

Nothing leads anywhere in the book, and that is perhaps the real point of it. The action comes full circle—imitates, that is, the sun of the title, which also rises, only to hasten to the place where it arose (the title is, of course, a quotation from Ecclesiastes). For the most part the novel is a delightful one. The style is fresh and sparkling, the dialogue is fun to read, and the book is beautifully and meaningfully constructed. But its message is that for these people at least (and one gets the distinct impression that other people do not matter very much), life is futile.

It happens that this is not precisely the message Hemingway intended to give. . . . As far as he was concerned, he wrote his editor Maxwell Perkins, the point of his novel is, as the Biblical lines say in part, that "the earth abideth forever."

To be sure, some support for these contentions can be found in the novel itself. Not quite all the characters are "lost"—Romero is not—and the beauty of the eternal earth is now and again richly invoked. But most of the characters do seem lost indeed, a great deal of the time, and few readers have taken the passage from Ecclesiastes as Hemingway did. The strongest feeling in it is not that the earth abides forever, but that all motion is endless, circular, and unavailing. . . . (pp. 13-14)

[The hero of *A Farewell to Arms* comes to much the same conclusion.] Henry is left, at the end, with nothing. A man is trapped, Hemingway seems to be saying. He is trapped biologically and he is trapped socially; either way it can only end badly, and there are no other ways.

[*A Farewell to Arms*] is a beautifully written book. The prose is hard and clean, the people come to life instantly and ring true. The novel is built with scrupulous care. A short introductory scene at the very start presents an ominous conjunction of images—of rain, pregnancy, and death —which set the mood for, and prefigure, all that is to follow. Then the action is tied into a perfect and permanent knot by the skill with which the two themes are brought together. As the intentionally ambiguous title suggests, the two themes are of course love and war. (p. 15)

Despite the frequency of their appearance in the same books, love and war are—to judge from the frequency with which writers fail to wed them—an unlikely mixture. But in this novel their courses run exactly, though subtly, parallel, so that in the end we feel we have read one story, not two. In his affair with the war Henry goes through six phases: from desultory participation to serious action and a wound, and then through his recuperation in Milan to a retreat which leads to his desertion. Carefully interwoven with all this is his relationship with Catherine, which undergoes six precisely corresponding stages: from a trifling sexual affair to actual love and her conception, and then through her confinement in the Alps to a trip to the hospital which leads to her death. By the time the last farewell is taken, the stories are as one in the point, lest there be any sentimental doubt about it, that life, both personal and social, is a struggle in which the Loser Takes Nothing, either.

But like all of Hemingway's better books this one is bigger than any short account of it can indicate. For one thing there is the stature of Frederic Henry, and it is never more clear than here that he is the Hemingway "hero" in more senses than are suggested by the term "protagonist." Henry stands for many men; he stands for the experience of his country: in his evolution from complicity in the war to bitterness to escape, the whole of America could read its recent history in a crucial period, Wilson to Harding. When he expressed his disillusionment with the ideals the war claimed to promote, and jumped in a river and deserted, Henry's action epitomized the contemporary feeling of a whole nation. Not that the book is without positive values, however. . . . Henry progresses from the messiness represented by the brothel to the order that is love; he distinguishes sharply between the disciplined and competent people he has to do with and the disorderly and incompetent ones: the moral value of these virtues is not incidental to the action but a foundation on which the book is built. Despite such foundations, however, the final effect of this mixture of pessimism and ideals is one of tragedy and despair. (pp. 15-16)

[*To Have and Have Not* is not a good novel.] But it is one in which its author clearly showed that he had learned something that would become very important to him before he was done writing. As often before, and later too, it is the code hero, . . . Harry Morgan, who teaches the lesson. . . . In the end he is killed, but before he dies he has learned the lesson that . . . a man has no chance.

It is regrettable that this pronouncement, articulating a deathbed conversion, does not grow with any sense of inevitability out of the action of the book. A contrast between the Haves and the Have Nots of the story is meant to be structure and support for the novel and its message, but the whole affair is unconvincing. The superiority of the Nots is apparently based on the superiority of the sex life of the Morgans, on some savage disgust aimed at a successful writer in the book, and on some callow explanations of how the Haves got their money. Just how all these things lead to Harry's final pronouncement was Hemingway's business, and it was not skillfully transacted. (pp. 17-18)

The play [*The Fifth Column*] is distinguished by some excellent talk, and marred by a kind of cops-and-robbers action. The Hemingway hero, now called simply Philip, is immediately recognizable. . . . A kind of Scarlet Pimpernel dressed as an American reporter, Philip appears to be a charming but dissolute wastrel, a newsman who never files any stories. But actually, and unknown to his mistress, Dorothy, he is up to his neck in the Loyalist fight. The most striking thing about him, however, is the distance he has come from the hero, so like him in every other way, who decided in *A Farewell to Arms* that such faiths and causes were "obscene." (pp. 18-19)

[*For Whom the Bell Tolls*] is true to its controlling concept [as stated in the epigraph by John Donne "No man is an *Iland*, intire of itselfe. . . ."]. It deals with three days in the life of the Hemingway hero, now named Robert Jordan, who is fighting as an American volunteer in the Spanish civil war. He is sent to join a guerrilla band in the mountains near Segovia to blow up a strategic bridge, thus facilitating a Loyalist advance. . . . Jordan believes the attack will fail, but the generals will not cancel it until it is too late. He successfully destroys the bridge, is wounded in the retreat, and is left to die. But he has come to see the wisdom of such a sacrifice, and the book ends without bitterness.

This is not a flawless novel. For one thing the love story, if not sentimental, is at any rate idealized and very romantic; for another, there are a good many passages in which Jordan appears more to be struggling for the faith on which he acts than to have achieved it. The hero is still the wounded man, and new incidents from his past are supplied to explain why this is so; two of the characters remark pointedly that he was too young to experience the things he tells them of having experienced. But Jordan has learned a lot, since the old days, about how to live and function with his wounds, and he behaves well. (pp. 19-20)

The skill with which this novel was for the most part written demonstrated that Hemingway's talent was once again intact and formidable. None of his books had evoked more richly the life of the senses, had shown a surer sense of plotting, or provided more fully living secondary characters, or livelier dialogue (p. 20)

[*Across the River and into the Trees*] is a poor performance. . . . Again there is the "Hemingway heroine." . . . There are also many signs of the "code." But the code in this book has become a sort of joke; the hero [Richard Cantwell] has become a good deal of a bore, and the heroine has become a wispy dream. The distance that Hemingway once maintained between himself and his protagonist has disappeared, to leave us with a self-indulgent chronicling of the author's every opinion; he acts as though he were being interviewed. The novel reads like a parody of the earlier works.

But there is one interesting thing about it. Exactly one hundred years before the appearance of this novel Nathaniel Hawthorne published *The Scarlet Letter,* in which he wrote: "There is a fatality, a feeling so irresistible and inevitable that it has the force of doom, which almost invariably compels human beings to linger around and haunt, ghost-like, the spot where some great and marked event has given the color to their lifetime; and still the more irresistibly, the darker the tinge that saddens it." . . . [No] one in the history of American letters has demonstrated Hawthorne's insight with as much force and clarity as have Hemingway and his hero. And nowhere in Hemingway is the demonstration more clear than in *Across the River and into the Trees,* for it is here that Colonel Cantwell makes a sort of pilgrimage to the place where he . . . was first wounded. He

takes instruments, and locates by survey the exact place on the ground where he had been struck. Then, in an act of piercing, dazzling identification, he builds a very personal if ironic sort of monument to the spot, acknowledges and confronts the great, marked event that colored his lifetime, . . . and comes to the end of his journey (or the end so far), not at the place where he first lived, but where first he died. (pp. 20-2)

The thing that chiefly keeps *The Old Man and the Sea* from greatness is the sense one has that the author was imitating instead of creating the style that made him famous. But this reservation is almost made up for by the book's abundance of meaning. As always the code hero, here Santiago, comes with a message, and it is essentially that while a man may grow old, and be wholly down on his luck, he can still dare, stick to the rules, persist when he is licked, and thus by the manner of his losing win his victory. (p. 22)

To take the broadest view, however, the novel is a representation of life as a struggle against unconquerable natural forces in which a kind of victory is possible. It is an epic metaphor for life, a contest in which even the problem of right and wrong seems paltry before the great thing that is the struggle. It is also something like Greek tragedy, in that as the hero falls and fails, the audience may get a memorable glimpse of what stature a man may have. And it is Christian tragedy as well, especially in the several marked allusions to Christian symbolism, particularly of the crucifixion—a development in Hemingway's novels that begins, apparently without much importance, in the early ones, gathers strength in *Across the River and into the Trees,* and comes to a kind of climax in this book. (p. 23)

[*A Moveable Feast*] is easily the best nonfiction he ever wrote.

The achievement is chiefly stylistic; it is largely the shock of immediacy, the sense of our own presence on Paris streets and in Paris cafés, that makes the book. Some of the dialogue with the first Mrs. Hemingway is a little embarrassing, and occasionally the borders of sentimentality are at least skirted. But for the most part the prose glitters, warms, delights—or is witty, or hard-hitting as ever. It moves and evokes, as the author looks back on the time of innocence, poverty, and spring, so soon to pass. (pp. 24-5)

For the most part [Hemingway's prose style] is colloquial, characterized chiefly by a conscientious simplicity of diction and sentence structure. The words are normally short and common ones and there is a severe economy, and also a curious freshness, in their use. As Ford Madox Ford remarked some time ago, in a line that is often (and justifiably) quoted, the words "strike you, each one, as if they were pebbles fetched fresh from a brook." The typical sentence is a simple declarative one, or a couple of these joined by a conjunction. The effect is of crispness, cleanness, clarity, and a scrupulous care. (p. 37)

It is a remarkably unintellectual style. Events are described strictly in the sequence in which they occurred; no mind reorders or analyzes them, and perceptions come to the reader unmixed with comment from the author. The impression, therefore, is of intense objectivity; the writer provides nothing but stimuli. Since violence and pain are so often the subject matter, it follows that a characteristic effect is one of irony or understatement. The vision is narrow, and sharply focused.

The dialogue is equally striking, for Hemingway had an ear like a trap for the accents and mannerisms of human speech; this is chiefly why he was able to bring a character swiftly to life. The conversation is far from a simple transcription, however, of the way people talk. Instead the dialogue strips speech to an essential pattern of mannerisms and responses characteristic of the speaker, and gives an illusion of reality that reality itself would not give.

Nothing in this brief account of the "Hemingway style" should seem very surprising, but the purposes, implications, and ultimate meanings of this manner of writing are less well recognized. A style has its own content, and the manner of a distinctive prose style has its own meanings. The things that Hemingway's style most conveys are the very things he says outright. His style is as communicative of the content as the content itself, and is a large and inextricable part of the content. The strictly disciplined controls exerted over the hero and his nervous system are precise parallels to the strictly disciplined sentences. The "mindlessness" of the style is a reflection and expression of the need to "stop thinking" when thought means remembering the things that upset. The intense simplicity of the prose is a means of saying that things must be *made* simple, or the hero is lost, and in "a way you'll never be." The economy and narrow focus of the prose controls the little that can be absolutely mastered. The prose is tense because the atmosphere in which the struggle for control takes place is tense, and the tension in the style expresses that fact. (pp. 37-8)

[A near-perfect parallel can be made between Twain's Huck Finn and Hemingway's Nick Adams.] In both Huck and Nick . . . we have a sensitive, rather passive but courageous and masculine boy, solitary and out of doors, who is dissatisfied with respectability, chiefly as represented by a Bible-quoting woman of the house. Each runs away from home. "Home" in both cases . . . was a place of violence and pain, but though it was easy to flee the respectability, off on their own both boys came up against brutality harder than ever. Both were hurt by it and both ended by rebelling utterly against a society that sponsored, or permitted, such horror. Nick decides that he is not a patriot, and makes his own peace with the enemy; Huck decides that he will take up wickedness, and go to hell. He lights out for the territory, the hero for foreign lands. Huck and Nick are very nearly twins. Two of our most prominent heroes, Huck and the Hemingway hero, are casualties whom the "knowledge of evil," which Americans are commonly said to lack, has made sick.

This theme of the boy shattered by the world he grows up in is a variation on one of the most ancient of all stories, . . . the meeting of innocence and experience. (pp. 41-2)

The stories of Huck Finn and the Hemingway hero share this general theme, for they tell again what happens when innocence, or a spontaneous virtue, meets with something not at all itself. . . . [There] is nothing subtle about the force that confronts the natural goodness of Huck and Nick. It is violence, an essential experience of the frontier, and also in our time—which is a wartime—of the American in Europe. And there is nothing triumphant about the beating which innocence takes, or about what happens to it after it is beaten. (pp. 42-3)

[It is] a very limited world that we are exposed to through [Hemingway]. It is, ultimately, a world at war—war either literally as armed and calculated conflict, or figuratively as marked everywhere with violence, potential or present, and a general hostility. The people of this world operate under such conditions—of apprehension, emergency, stiff-lipped fear, and pleasure seized in haste—as are imposed by war. Restricted grimly by the urgencies of war, their pleasures are limited pretty much to those the senses can communicate, and their morality is a harshly pragmatic affair; what's moral is what you feel good after. Related to this is the code, summarizing the virtues of the soldier, the ethic of wartime. The activities of escape go according to the rules of sport, which make up the code of the armistice, the temporary, peacetime modification of the rules of war.

Hemingway's world is one in which things do not grow and bear fruit, but explode, break, decompose, or are eaten away. It is saved from total misery by visions of endurance, competence, and courage, by what happiness the body can give when it is not in pain, by interludes of love that cannot outlast the furlough, by a pleasure in the countries one can visit, or fish and hunt in, and the cafés one can sit in, and by very little else. Hemingway's characters do not "mature" in the ordinary sense, do not become "adult." It is impossible to picture them in a family circle, going to the polls to vote, or making out their income tax returns. It is a very narrow world. It is a world seen through a crack in the wall by a man pinned down by gunfire. The vision is obsessed by violence, and insists that we honor a stubborn preoccupation with the profound significance of violence in our time. (pp. 44-5)

> *Philip Young, in his* Ernest Hemingway *(American Writers Pamphlet No. 1; © 1959, 1964, University of Minnesota), University of Minnesota Press, Minneapolis, 1964.*

SCOTT DONALDSON

[Often] Hemingway's fictional women emerge as more admirable than his men: braver, more faithful and loving, more responsible. (p. 6)

[Hemingway expressed his view of the morality of compensation, in which nothing can be given or taken without an equivalent] in the metaphor of finance—a metaphor which runs through the fabric of [*The Sun Also Rises*] as a fine, essential thread. It is Jake Barnes who explicitly states the code of Hemingway's novel. . . . Jake reflects that in having Lady Brett Ashley for a friend, he "had been getting something for nothing" and that sooner or later he would have to pay the bill, which always came. . . . (p. 22)

Jake's philosophical musing is illustrated time and again in the profuse monetary transactions of *The Sun Also Rises*. . . . Between the beginning and the end, Hemingway specifically mentions sums of money, and what they have been able to purchase, a total of thirty times. (pp. 22-3)

Hemingway reveals much more about his characters' financial condition and spending habits than about their appearance. . . .

Hemingway had several good reasons to note with scrupulous detail the exact nature of financial transactions. Such a practice contributed to the verisimilitude of the novel, denoting the way it was; it fitted nicely with Jake's . . . obsession with the proper way of doing things; and mainly it illustrated in action the moral conviction that you must pay for what you get, that you must earn in order to be able to buy. . . . (p. 23)

Money and its uses form the metaphor by which the moral responsibility of Jake, Bill, and Pedro Romero is measured against the carelessness of Brett, Mike, and Robert. Financial soundness mirrors moral strength. (p. 26)

[Robert Cohn, a] romantic, . . . is understandably unable at first to conceive that his weekend with Brett at San Sebastian has meant nothing to her, but he forfeits any claim to sympathy by his subsequent stubborn and violent unwillingness to accept that obvious fact. Terribly insecure, he takes insult after insult from Frances and Mike without retaliation, though he is ready enough to fight with his "best friend" Jake over what he construes as insults to Brett and himself. A Jew in the company of gentiles, he is a bore who takes himself—and his illusions—far too seriously. Unlike Jake, he has not "learned about" things. He does not know how to eat or drink or love. (p. 27)

Still, it would be possible to pity Cohn for his dominant malady . . . were it not for his callous and opportunistic use of the money he has not earned. (pp. 27-8)

What comes too easily has a pernicious effect on him as a person. Having inherited a good deal of money, he wastes nearly all of it on a little magazine—and in purchasing the prestige that comes to him as its editor. But Cohn's most damning misuse of funds occurs when he attempts to buy his way out of obligations to women. . . . It is in his attempt to buy his way out of entanglements without expending anything of himself that Robert Cohn most viciously breaks the moral code of compensation. (pp. 28-9)

Both "The Short Happy Life of Francis Macomber" and, even more notably, "The Snows of Kilimanjaro" depict bad marriages held together by despicable financial binding. (p. 34)

In "The Snows of Kilimanjaro," the writer Harry [dies at the end, his demise] . . . brought about by a physical gangrene that parallels his moral rot. He has married Helen, an extremely wealthy woman, and let his talent go to seed. . . . Harry knows that what has happened is no one's fault but his own. After all, he had let himself be bought. . . . (p. 35)

[In his] fiction Ernest portrayed the rich as an entirely separate breed, more distasteful than the rest of mankind. Clearly, there was no doubt in his mind that an inverse relationship existed between money and morals. (pp. 53-4)

Marxist critics like Alvah Bessie had rightly complained that [For Whom the Bell Tolls] did not fulfill the promise of its title . . . by affirming the value of universal brotherhood. But For Whom the Bell Tolls does affirm the value of belonging to and sharing with a family (a word which Hemingway several times applies to Pablo's irregulars).

The point is emphasized through the metaphor of the gift. When Jordan first reaches the band, he jealously guards what is his. (p. 119)

After sharing danger and disappointment during his three days in the mountains, however, Jordan learns to put aside his selfishness and becomes "completely integrated" with the band. One of his teachers is the valiant El Sordo, whose generosity vividly contrasts with the American's possessiveness. (pp. 119-20)

[Jordan] remains behind to cover the retreat of Maria and the others at the end, and so makes the ultimate gift of self. "Each one does what he can," he thinks as he lies crippled.

"You can do nothing for yourself but perhaps you can do something for another."

Yet Jordan *does* do a good deal for himself in staying behind: he regains the dignity and self-respect which his own father had failed to bequeath to him. Visions of his brave grandfather and cowardly father course through his brain during his last hours, and it is only as one man alone that he can redeem the suicide of the father he cannot forgive. Like Anselmo, who, having been brought up in religion, misses God but realizes that "now a man must be responsible to himself," Jordan understands that the final test is within. (p. 120)

A Farewell to Arms supplies Hemingway's most extended fictional statement of [his disillusionment with war]. (p. 126)

The symbols of war—pistol, medal, helmet, salute—take on a shabbiness that parallels the quality of combat generalship. In Frederic's company, no one knows what is going on, though they all speak "with great positiveness and strategical knowledge," and it is no different at the top. . . .

Under the circumstances, patriotism seems out of place, and indeed most of the patriots whom Frederic meets are at considerable distance from the combat zone. (p. 128)

A Farewell to Arms has usually been interpreted as a tragic tale of two lovers, driven together by the war, who selflessly give themselves to each other in an affair that might have lasted in indefinite bliss had not fateful death unjustly intervened to snatch one away. . . . But to read *A Farewell to Arms* in this way drastically minimizes Hemingway's accomplishment. The construction of his 1929 book is far subtler and more complicated than that of the conventional sentimental novel, and the story it has to tell is anything but straightforward. (p. 151)

[The] character Frederic Henry, whom Rinaldi calls "the remorse boy," has a great deal to be remorseful about. In dealing with his own sins . . . , he tries to smooth them away, just as he had tried to brush the taste of harlotry away with toothpaste. The entire novel may reasonably be construed as his attempt to excuse himself from blame. But Hemingway does not let his storyteller off so easily. He makes it clear, between the lines, that we should take what Lieutenant Henry has to say with a grain of salt. The difficulty in grasping this point derives from the reader's tendency to identify with Frederic, who as first-person narrator serves as guide to what happens in the novel. He seems a trustworthy enough guide to the *action*. But as Hemingway warned, even when he wrote a novel in the first person, he could not be held responsible "for the *opinions* of the narrator."

People are always misspelling Frederic Henry's name, and no wonder: only once in the book does Hemingway supply it, in full, and those who know him best usually do not call him by any name at all. What is significant is what they do call him. . . . ["Baby" is] the term of affection which Rinaldi consistently and repeatedly uses in talking to Frederic. (pp. 152-53)

Whether they use "baby" or "boy," . . . the other characters in *A Farewell to Arms* clearly perceive Frederic Henry as young, inexperienced, and unaware. (p. 153)

A mere boy, Frederic Henry suffers at the beginning of the

novel from a pervasive lack of awareness. He does not know why he has enlisted in the Italian army, nor what he is fighting for. He lacks any perceptible ambition or purpose in life beyond the securing of his own pleasure. During the course of his war experiences he does to some degree grow in understanding. . . . The question at issue involves the extent of his education, how far Frederic Henry moved along the continuum from ignorant, self-centered youth to knowing, caring adulthood. (p. 154)

As the book progresses, [Frederic] becomes more loving and less selfish, but only as compared to an initial policy toward Catherine that can best be defined as exploitative. During their first meetings in Gorizia, Catherine poignantly reveals her vulnerability, but Frederic nonetheless treats her as he would any other potential conquest—as an opponent in the game of seduction he intends to win. (p. 156)

The love he feels is almost entirely sexual, however, and derives from the pleasure she gives him, pleasure far superior to that dispensed by the [prostitutes he has known]. . . . Since he is bedridden, she must come to him, a practice which symbolizes his role, then and later, as an accepter, not a giver, of services. (p. 157)

Throughout their affair, Frederic rarely displays honest and thoughtful concern for Catherine's feelings. Where she invariably thinks of him first, he often does not think of her at all. Only when she lies dying of childbirth in the Lausanne hospital does he finally begin to want to serve and to sacrifice for her. (p. 160)

The creator of Frederic Henry believed in retribution, in rewards and punishments, in actions producing consequences. . . . In an attempt to justify himself, he fixes all blame on a deterministic world. "The world" stands against the lovers; a vague "they" are at fault: "Now Catherine would die. That was what you did. You died. You did not know what it was about. You never had time to learn. They threw you in and told you the rules and the first time they caught you off base they killed you." Adopting the rhetorician's device of the second person "you," Frederic tries to gain his audience's assent to this philosophy. But there is a logical inconsistency in the terrible game of life-and-death he posits: though he is at least an equal partner in any mistakes that have been made, he survives and Catherine dies. (pp. 160-61)

[Frederic] attempts under cover of the doctrine of determinism to evade responsibility years after the fact of his affair with Catherine Barkley. Worse yet, he does not love Catherine as she deserves. He takes without giving. He withholds. By showing us these shortcomings in Frederic Henry and by implicitly repudiating his philosophical justifications, Hemingway distances himself from his protagonist, who is one of those first-person narrators whose opinions are not to be trusted. (p. 162)

Hemingway rarely again portrayed a woman as believable and sympathetic as the heroine of *A Farewell to Arms*. The bitches who populate his fiction of the 1930s, like Margot Macomber in "The Short Happy Life of Francis Macomber" and Helene Bradley in *To Have and Have Not,* yield in later novels to such Latinized child-women as Maria in *For Whom the Bell Tolls* and Renata in *Across the River and into the Trees*. . . . Dorothy Bridges in *The Fifth Column* . . . is satirically depicted as lacking in perception and understanding because of her foolish, knee-jerk liberalism. (p. 163)

More than half of the fifty-odd stories Ernest Hemingway wrote dealt with love in one form or another; but not one of them depicted a satisfactory, lasting, mutually shared love between a man and a woman. (p. 169)

Characteristically, Hemingway's fictional protagonists finish alone, a pattern which becomes increasingly dominant in his later writing. . . .

Most of Hemingway's love stories, which usually assume a dominant-submissive relationship, focus on [a symbiotic love, in which one partner assumes a passive, masochistic, inferior role to the other's active, sadistic superiority]. . . . Mature lovers, on the other hand, share equally: they give and gain by giving. (p. 173)

Among his fictional counterparts, Robert Jordan in *For Whom the Bell Tolls* comes closest to achieving the . . . state of mature love. Like Frederic Henry with Catherine, he resists Maria's desire to become exactly like him, to passively submerge herself in him. . . . Unlike Frederic, though, during his three days among the Spanish guerrillas, Jordan comes to understand the beauty of giving and the importance of selflessness to those in love. . . .

At least once in his fiction, then, Ernest Hemingway created a hero who loved maturely and selflessly without giving up his own integrity. (p. 174)

Driven to seek a substitute for the outmoded faith of their fathers, Hemingway's characters often turn to primitive rituals for comfort. They invest physical love-making with mystical import; they ritualize the mundane business of eating and drinking; they follow elaborate procedures derived from games. Such rituals, as they have always done, help to satisfy his characters' yearning for order and meaning in their lives. Sometimes they serve a therapeutic purpose as well. In this sense, [Malcolm] Cowley points out, Nick Adams' fishing trip in "Big Two-Hearted River" may be regarded "as an incantation, a spell to banish evil spirits" [see excerpt above]. (p. 234)

[*The Sun Also Rises*] is rather carefully organized around a contrast between paganism and Christianity. The initial scenes in Paris establish that cosmopolitan city as the home of paganism. Sexual aberrations proliferate there. . . . But as soon as Jake enters Spain, a far more devout Christian country, the references to churches multiply, and Jake goes to pray in them as he had not done in Paris. These two strains commingle during the fiesta of San Fermin ("also a religious festival") at Pamplona, where Brett is elevated to the status of a pagan idol by the drunken crowd. . . . She is forbidden entrance to one church because she has no head covering, and finds herself unable to pray for her lover Romero in another, because the experience makes her "nervy." She even asks to hear Jake's confession, but that, he tells her, is not allowed "and, besides, it would be in a language she did not know." (p. 235)

Hemingway used Christian symbolism in his fiction as it suited his artistic purposes, not so much out of calculation as instinctively. Thus, two very dissimilar protagonists, Colonel Richard Cantwell of *Across the River and into the Trees* and Santiago of *The Old Man and the Sea,* are both symbolically associated with Jesus Christ. . . . What [Cantwell and Christ] have most in common is suffering, and it is [Cantwell's] wounded places, especially his misshapen right hand, that Renata most loves. Cantwell acquired his wounded hand "Very honorably. On a rocky, bare-assed hill," like Calvary, which was surrounded by Christmas trees. (pp. 238-39)

Though he must die, he will not, the colonel decides, "run as a Christian" in the end. That would be hypocritical, since he resembles the Messiah closely only in the courage and endurance with which he faces suffering and death. Suffering was the natural condition of man and death his inevitable end, but each man could face these tyrants as he chose. Hemingway finds his heroes among those who, like Cantwell and Santiago, confront their fate with courage, endurance, and dignity.

Santiago is virtually inundated with religious imagery. . . . Despite all the religious imagery, however, *The Old Man and the Sea* is not a Christian fable. Hemingway nowhere suggests that we are all fallen with the persecutors of Christ or saved by His example. What he *is* celebrating is the capacity of one man to endure terrible suffering and pain with dignity. (pp. 239-40)

In exalting the value of the struggle itself, and in celebrating the endurance and bravery a man might summon in the face of suffering, Hemingway affirmed the grandeur of which the individual human being was capable. And there was one other article in Hemingway's private creed: a worship of the natural world around him. Santiago, for example, feels a powerful affinity for the sea which supports him. . . .

[Reverence] for the natural world, then, constitutes a kind of glory for Hemingway, but it is balanced—often overbalanced—by his concurrent sense of the blank, dark meaninglessness of our existence. In his feeling for nature, Hemingway stems from Emerson and Thoreau; in his consciousness of the blackness "ten times black," he derives from Hawthorne and Melville. His unsolved problem—a basic problem of modern faith—was to reconcile the two, the "glory and the blackness" both. (p. 240)

Hemingway used a memorable figure of speech to describe his most striking technique as storyteller: that of leaving out critical details. "I always try to write," he put it, "on the principle of the iceberg. There is seven eighths of it under water for every part that shows. Anything you know you can eliminate and it only strengthens your iceberg." . . . At its best, as in "Big Two-Hearted River," this device worked brilliantly. (p. 245)

As time wore on, the iceberg theory became less and less applicable to Hemingway's fiction. For one thing, he could seldom resist the opportunity to point his moral through irony. It is in terms of his use of irony that he may most accurately be called . . . a sentimentalist. His writing was not sentimental, of course, in the usual sense of calling for overblown emotional responses to trivial matters. In fact, if sentimentality is that error which exacts of the reader more emotion than the event calls for, Hemingway might be regarded as a sentimentalist in reverse, since in its understatement his writing apparently asks for less emotional expenditure than is warranted. Sometimes, though, he intrudes with irony to help make up for the unseen portions of his iceberg.

Hemingway's irony usually functions to separate the mechanical, unfeeling, unperceptive, and therefore immoral character from the one who feels deeply and sees well below the surface. Such distinctions abound in his fiction, and

occasionally—as at the end of *A Farewell to Arms* . . .—the irony seems to be tacked on gratuitously. In [that] novel, two nurses come hurrying along the hallway, laughing at the prospect of witnessing the Caesarean that will take Catherine's life. (pp. 245-46)

For Whom the Bell Tolls traces the painful education, telescoped into three short days, of its protagonist Robert Jordan. From Maria, he learns what it is to love. From Pilar and Anselmo, he learns what it is to belong to a family. Finally he learns in triumph how to die, the most difficult lesson of all and one which he must master on his own.

The novel stands as an in-depth study of death, a theme reflected not only in its title but in Hemingway's alternate title, "The Undiscovered Country" from whose bourn no traveler returns. Early in *For Whom the Bell Tolls*, Pilar "reads" Jordan's imminent death in his palm; after that, the issue becomes not whether Jordan will die, but how. (p. 299)

> *Scott Donaldson, in his* By Force of Will: The Life and Art of Ernest Hemingway *(copyright © 1977 by Scott Donaldson; all rights reserved; reprinted by permission of Viking Penguin Inc.), Viking Penguin, 1977.*

BEN STOLTZFUS

The themes that Hemingway weaves into *The Old Man and the Sea*, like counterpoint in a Bach fugue, explore the ideas of pride in killing and victory in conquest as opposed to humility in defeat and suffering in abnegation. Santiago is a pagan Catholic whose age, pride, honor, and courage force him to prove that pain is nothing to a man and that a fisherman can perform miracles. This Cuban protagonist of Spanish birth harpoons marlin like a matador and suffers pain like a Christ figure. Using Santiago as a symbolic namehead Hemingway fuses the themes into a moving experience of life and death. (p. 39)

C. N. Stavrou believes that in Hemingway's world human existence moves inexorably toward futility, vacancy, destruction, and waste; that the tug in the direction of death, nothingness, and despair is one of the most significant ingredients in his work. In *The Sun Also Rises* Jake characterizes Roman Catholicism as a "beautiful religion," but when he tries to pray and fails he concedes that prayer is "a futile gesture." In *The Old Man and the Sea* Santiago says a few perfunctory prayers, then goes about the more important and pressing business of catching the marlin and fighting sharks. There is also Hemingway's "memorable and excoriating travesty of the Lord's Prayer" in the short story "A Clean, Well-Lighted Place." . . . (p. 42)

[The saturation of Christian symbolism in *The Old Man and the Sea*] has prompted a number of commentators to see the novel as a Christian parable, though, in my opinion, the work should probably be classified as a pagan poem to existential man. (pp. 42-3)

[On] the conscious, verbalized, and symbolic levels the interpretations of the novel as parable rely on the fact that Hemingway gives it a prominent Christ motif. It should be noted that this motif has no bearing on Santiago's own evaluation of his experience. Santiago is a proud and not uncomplicated man, but his view of the world does not include the artistic dimension Hemingway structures for the reader. There is a fictional level . . . that carries beyond

Santiago's consciousness to include the Christian tradition. . . .

Is the comparison between [Christ and Santiago] important because in Hemingway's story "Today is Friday" one of the Roman soldiers admires the stoic way Christ took his suffering and that therefore Santiago's ordeal, like the Crucifixion, is the epitome of grace under stress? Such an answer, while relevant, is perhaps also too facile. Besides, it minimizes the artistry of the novel. The effect of the christological imagery on the reader, contrary to expectations generated by its use, is essentially non-Christian. (p. 43)

Santiago's ordeal through the stages of separation, vision, and return mirrors a heroic cycle of trial through endurance which, in spite of Hemingway's carefully structured parallel with Christianity, is more typical of the initiation rites of primitive societies than it is of the Crucifixion. On a cultural level the novel mirrors the cycle by which a moribund tradition must perhaps be slain and resurrected. The novel's Christian symbolism suggests that the tradition Hemingway is slaying is Christianity (the fish). Santiago's vision and message will be resurrected through Manolin (meaning Immanuel or the Messiah). When Santiago returns he ties the rope of his skiff to a rock. In Christian symbolism a ship represents the Church. God founded his Church upon the rock of St. Peter. Appropriately, Pedrico, Manolin's friend, gets the dead marlin's head. (p. 44)

The Christ motif in *The Old Man and the Sea* provides the imagery which the reader follows, but the idea that emerges is non-Christian. Why, for instance, does Pedrico get the marlin's head? (pp. 44-5)

Pedro, whose diminutive is Pedrico, is the Spanish for Peter. Saint Peter is known as the Great Fisherman and is the patron saint of fishermen. Peter is the leading Apostle of Christ. . . . Peter's name always *heads* the Twelve. . . . Peter was the *leader* of the apostolic church. . . . The Roman Catholic church considers Peter as its *first* pope. Peter is the *head* of the Christian church. . . .

Even though Pedrico's role is a minor one, the use of his name is consistent with the novel's Christ motif. Santiago's desire that Manolin give "the head" of the giant fish to Pedrico is given specific emphasis by being repeated twice. Manolin, the new Messiah, gets the marlin's spear. . . . This spear is also described as a rapier, which is a straight two-edged sword with a narrow pointed blade. In Christian symbolism the sword denotes spiritual warfare against the forces of evil. . . . Such biblical knowledge is extrinsic to the novel, yet it provides information, only hinted at in the narrative, which is essential for a correct reading of its intent. . . . The names Santiago, Manolin, and Pedrico, three very frequent and familiar Spanish names, work well in symbolic association with each other. (p. 45)

The reader is therefore perhaps justified in concluding that Santiago is the symbolic Father who teaches his symbolic Son and disciple, Manolin. After Santiago has once again proved his superiority as a fisherman by catching the largest marlin, Manolin, like Christ, will leave his parents in order to follow the teachings of his master, Santiago. . . . Manolin, the Messiah, gets the dead fish's spear which, in Christian terms, is also the sword of faith, and the reader infers that he, together with Pedrico, will spread the "good news" of Santiago's "victory." After his ordeal Santiago falls asleep in a cruciform position on his newspapers (good

news?). We have God, His Son, and Saint Peter—a trinity, the beginning of a new faith, the cell of a new religion, the founding rock of a new church. . . . Hemingway has used the archetypal quest not only as a structural device, but as a metaphor for the cultural quest to revitalize the dead God —that is, the cultural heritage—by resurrecting the Son. A myth is reborn and as though made new for an existential age. (pp. 45-6)

A number of commentators have mentioned the relevance of pride to the meaning of the novel, but none has given it central billing nor related it to Hemingway's attempt to substitute a naturalistic religion of man for an entire religious tradition. Astonishing perhaps is the fact that one of Hemingway's favorite themes, the solitude of man, should in this story have jelled into something beyond itself, be the catalyst for ideas affecting all men, and serve as an example and an ideal for man vis-à-vis himself and the world. . . . Repeatedly, Santiago's experience and physical suffering are compared to Christ's agony, yet Hemingway's message is one of pride rather than humility—an exaltation of man with only perfunctory obeisance to God. (pp. 46-7)

[Eyes are also a recurring motif.] While eyes are important in themselves, thematically . . . they serve to highlight the discrepancy between what the villagers see and what Santiago is—between appearance and reality, between what Santiago can still do and what others think he can, between past achievements and present failure. Santiago may seem to be on his last legs, but there is an inner, invisible strength of heroic proportions that will lead him to prove once more that he is still The Champion—*El Campeón*. Thus, one of the themes of *The Old Man and the Sea,* as it was the subject of "The Undefeated," is the gap between outward failure and inner pride, thereby suggesting that point of view is a relevant if not important issue. (p. 49)

While profoundly attuned to nature's rhythms Santiago is also in rebellion against nature. The fish and the stars are his brothers and while he says he "must kill" . . . the fish, he is glad he does "not have to try to kill the stars," or the moon, or the sun. . . . These are strange thoughts for an old man, thoughts which would seem to imply that if stars were as accessible as fish man would have to try to kill them too. Whatever for? . . . Man takes pleasure in giving death, says Hemingway, because in this way he can usurp one of the godlike attributes. The very need to assimilate such strength and dominion implies pride and pride in turn can lead to rebellion either against nature, or against God, or both. Santiago, for the sake of his pride, is rebelling against old age and death. . . . (pp. 49-50)

[Santiago's humility] is a humility of strength. The Christ motif is Hemingway's, not Santiago's (Santiago is blissfully oblivious of it all) and it is essential that we keep this dual point of view in mind. In fact, Hemingway sets Santiago up as a kind of superman rivaling the Deity. Santiago may be killing fish, but Hemingway is killing God. This is why Santiago is not tempted to cut the line and let the big fish go, as Norman Mailer says he should have been, because the despair and pride which drove him too far out in the first place also prompt him to hang on. He would rather die than lose the fish. (p. 52)

Santiago, from his boyhood onward, has always been self-reliant. He knows the ocean, he knows the weather, and he fishes with precision. The laws and moral code that he observes, except for the perfunctory and ritual use of prayer, are his own and those of the sea. The marlin will teach him dignity, nobility, and endurance, but the law of the sea, and this is the essential point, is survival. Furthermore, Hemingway's precise naturalistic descriptions of life in and on the Gulf Stream give us more than local color. Man-of-war birds . . . eat the flying fish, turtles eat the men-of-war. . . . Seahawks eat the little birds and so on and so forth. Santiago, as yet another manifestation of natural forces (and the survival in this case is of the most intelligent), catches and destroys a great sixteen-hundred pound marlin.

The laws of nature are a code in themselves, and man, like the marlin which swims for three days against the Gulf Stream, can, as long as he is alive, resist death and affirm his dignity by "swimming" against the current. . . . [There] is great symbolic value for Hemingway and existentialists alike in "swimming against the current." Santiago, like Sisyphus rolling his stone up the mountain, must affirm his identity as a fisherman (since that is what he was "born for") by fishing and proving it up to the very end. (pp. 52-3)

This is what it means to be a man cast adrift in a contingent universe, for who can be more alone than Santiago on the Gulf Stream with no relatives and nothing to return to but his shack in the village? Yet Santiago, the tenacious, precise, and intelligent fisherman shows what a man can endure, how he can behave, and how he can affirm his identity in the jaws of sharks, adversity, old age, and even death. . . .

Santiago's message is that "man can be destroyed but not defeated." . . . Santiago will die, but the example of his heroic struggle will live. To fight heroically is to affirm man's dignity. (p. 55)

Santiago kills fish, in part because he is a fisherman, but also because such acts tend to deny his mortal condition. This is metaphysical revolt, not Christian humility, because it questions the ultimate ends of Creation and protests conditions of mortality imposed on man. The rebel acknowledges yet challenges the power that forces him to live in that condition. Although he defies Creation, Santiago cannot deny it. He cannot suppress Creation, but he can challenge it. He must have the experience of Dominion which can only come through killing. He must continue killing sharks, up to the end, even though he knows it is hopeless, because only in this way can he redeem the initial act of going out "too far" or of "ruining" the marlin or himself. Such desperate heroism is of tragic proportions and relates the old man to Ahab [in Melville's *Moby Dick*]. . . . Santiago's quest, like Ahab's, is animated by a desire to conquer. (pp. 56-7)

Meeting death on his own terms is in part the reason behind Santiago's decision to venture out so far. . . . Too proud to be the laughing stock of the village or to accept his physical decline, Santiago will challenge nature and die, if necessary, rather than live rejected and humiliated by God, nature, and his fellow fishermen. Such feelings explain why he is never tempted to let go of the line, not even for one moment. (p. 59)

Hemingway's death roster includes people, bulls, big game, birds, fish, and ants. When Catherine Barkley and Robert Jordan die, it is tragic. But Hemingway also handles death with an ironic and even comic touch. In *Green Hills of Africa* bird and hyena shooting become a joke—a type of black humor. (p. 60)

Shooting animals is to consciously experience the acceleration of death. To kill an animal is to momentarily and vicariously become God—He who gives life and who takes it away. That is why, whenever Hemingway misses, the joke is on him, for he has claimed a power which he has not been able to deliver. His superior role has reversed itself and now the joke is on the would-be killer. He has tried to play God but his incompetence has transformed him into a clown. The same reasoning transforms the hyena into a superclown since we have a death scavenger in its death-throes devouring its own entrails. (pp. 60-1)

While animal death can have its comic asides, there is no humor in *The Old Man and the Sea*. This may be due to Santiago's play for the highest stakes—honor in life—but also to Hemingway's apparent desire to replace Christianity with his own brand of stoic humanism. In this novel, as in so much of Hemingway's work, the moment of death and the act of killing are central. (p. 61)

We have mentioned the Messianic aspect of the name Manolin—the diminutive for the Spanish Manuel which in English is Immanuel; "the true *God with us,* the Saviour, the Christ." Immanuel means "God is with" and that his message is true. (p. 62)

The Old Man and the Sea is a long prose poem that has to be read on several simultaneous levels: the realistic and the symbolic, the intrinsic and the extrinsic. Hemingway's writing produces a series of associations based on linguistic ambiguity and symbolic vibrations that give the reader a certain feeling about the work. These ineffable, undefinable, and intangible reactions to Santiago and the Christ motif combine to give an emotional impact that is a blend of the writer's skill, the reader's intuition, and his knowledge. The novel's realism constitutes one eighth of the iceberg. Seven eighths are underwater. Together they produce a "fourth" and "fifth dimension" which, according to Hemingway, come from a prose that has never before been written and which is more difficult than poetry. The combination reveals the inner, invisible dimension of the old man of the sea—his pride. . . . (pp. 78-9)

> *Ben Stoltzfus, in his* Gide and Hemingway: Rebels against God *(copyright © 1978 by Kennikat Press Corp.; reprinted by permission of Kennikat Press Corp.), Kennikat, 1978.*

*   *   *

HEYEN, William   1940-

Heyen is an American poet, essayist, and editor of German heritage. The experiences of his family during World War II form the subject of his most successful collection of poetry, *The Swastika Poems*. (See also *Contemporary Authors*, Vols. 33-36, rev. ed.)

JOHN T. IRWIN

William Heyen's *Depth of Field* is a brilliant first volume with a broad, coherent, and deeply moving design. The book is divided into two sections, *The Spirit of Wrath* and *The Dead from Their Dark*. Beginning in a confessional vein, Heyen confronts in separate poems the images of two uncles, one a German infantryman, the other a pilot of a Stuka, killed in the Second World War. The poet must face his personal heritage of the spirit of wrath, but he finds that it is the common heritage:

> Because the cause is never just,
> rest, my Nazi uncle, rest.
> All the oppressors are oppressed.
> The dog's heart is his only beast.
>
> . . . These are all your wars.
> Asia trembles. You are never dead. . . .

It is the characteristic confessional theme, the confrontation of man's animality and its consequences, which occupies in one way or another the rest of the poems in the first section. . . . For Heyen, the difference between man and animal is self-consciousness; animals have two-dimensional simple consciousness, while man has three-dimensional self-consciousness or "depth of field". Viewing man as a self-conscious animal, Heyen confronts the implications of this for the symbolic process in *Birds and Roses Are Birds and Roses* and *On the Thames*. In the latter poem the speaker, looking at flowers, thinks of what the "old masters" would have done with these blossoms, "But our generation can't do it, can't sing the mystic flames." In *I Move to Random Consolations* the speaker, watching a dying crane, faces the question of animal death as annihilation and says that "needing something to affirm" he "held to the knowledge that a bird's beak, / born of cells of bone, discourages the worm." Near the close of the volume, the speaker finds that "to end like the visible world is enough, is enough." And in the final sequence he comforts himself with two kinds of partial survival—that of the animal species and that of the work of art. It is impossible in a short space to do justice to the richness and variety of Heyen's volume; suffice it to say that this book is a "must" and that its author seems destined to be an important poet. (pp. 352-53)

> *John T. Irwin, in* Poetry *(© by The Modern Poetry Association; reprinted by permission of the Editor of* Poetry*), September, 1971.*

TOM MARSHALL

William Heyen's *Noise in the Trees* makes a new myth out of the circumstances of his own past and that of Long Island. Earlier American literature enters into this . . . but is less important in the creation of this poetic world than the personal and local history. Heyen presents again those classic American themes—the loss or corruption of youth, the idealized girl, the island, the wild, the animals. I have a sense of the presence of the Robert Lowell of *For the Union Dead,* and perhaps of *Life Studies* as well, though there are no shock tactics and less in the way of raw nerves displayed here. . . . [But] these echoes are peripheral, though highly relevant; at the centre of this world is the poet's own very appealing voice and personality. One hears a gentle, nostalgic man quietly and forcefully speaking of his anxieties, his old loves and obsessions, without any kind of sensationalism.

Heyen's obsessions, dreams, fantasies and memories are interesting in themselves as psychic autobiography; but they go farther out into the realm of cultural history, and deeper down into that underground area of our consciousness that . . . [is] ambivalent and potentially terrifying. The twenty-five prose-poem sections mix dreams and memories with a haunting sense that there is something underlying all this experience that is ultimately mysterious and indescribable. The thirty-eight poems are all good but have a less immediate evocative power than the "memoir;" one could

regard the memoir as a gloss on the poems, but it seems to me that, really, the poems are attendant, so to speak, upon the memoir. The prose is more fluid and suggestive, more "poetic," than the poetry. (p. 90)

Mr. Heyen's temperament is life-loving and life-affirming as well as elegiac, and this too is attractive in these apocalyptic times. Heyen does not deny the darkness, but he has retained an (American?) sense of wonder. Is he just a trifle innocent in this, or is that a Canadian prejudice? I suspect it may be true, as a reviewer of his first book apparently said [see excerpt above], that he is destined to be an important poet. (p. 91)

> *Tom Marshall, in* The Ontario Review *(copyright © 1975 by* The Ontario Review*), Spring-Summer, 1975.*

PETER STITT

In trying to make poetry out of such a subject as the Nazi atrocities, William Heyen has taken a tremendous artistic and emotional risk. That he has, on the whole, pulled it off is a testament to his large talent. Though he does not always avoid the pitfalls inherent in the attempt, he does mostly avoid them [in *The Swastika Poems*]. One is overwriting, which conspicuously appears in "Darkness," an emotionally-charged, dream monologue which reinforces its imagery through reiteration of the word "darker": ". . . darker. / Doctor, help me kill / the Goebbels children. Darker." The powerful nature of the subject demands an unusual restraint of the author; in this instance, Heyen has over-fueled his fire.

The book has, as we would expect, its learned dimension—Heyen has read many documents, both primary and secondary, in gathering his information. Occasionally he uses quotations in his poems, and this gives rise to a second artistic danger. Some of this material is so powerful that the poet's words turn pale and almost disappear beside it. How can Heyen compete with a passage such as this: "The bodies were tossed out, blue, wet with sweat and urine, the legs soiled with feces and menstrual blood. A couple of dozen workers checked the mouths of the dead, which they tore open with iron hooks." The reader may be sickened or he may be turned numb; in either case, the lines which follow can hardly be expected to register on his consciousness.

The other potential weakness here—again, one which Heyen mostly avoids—is a sentimental self-consciousness, something which critics have occasionally noticed in his earlier books. There are times when the poet's presence in his poems is felt as an intrusion, especially early in the book, before we are fully aware of why he is doing all this. (p. 957)

Heyen's fondest hope is that, through the ritual singing of his verse, he can somehow save himself and us from the heavy moral stain of our collective past. . . . (p. 958)

The book has a cumulative power—I have already spoken of the relative weakness of the first several poems; beyond them Heyen seems to get stronger and stronger. "Riddle" is based in form on the nursery rhyme, "Who Killed Cock Robin?" This is an ironic technique we have seen before, and seeing it here makes one wince at first because of the obvious poetic danger. But Heyen pulls it off, primarily because of the way in which he modulates his form. The first stanza sets the pattern and begins the questioning. . . . The second stanza consists of four negative answers, all having the same form: "Not I, cries the typist," then the engineer, Adolf Eichmann, Albert Speer. So far so familiar —but in the third and fourth stanzas, Heyen turns to examples of people who were actually killed. Another new rhetorical pattern appears at the end of the fourth stanza ("Some men signed their papers, / and some stood guard"), and is carried on for eight more lines. In his catalogue, Heyen moves from those most directly responsible, workers in the death camps themselves, to peripheral characters —farmers, steelworkers. The final two stanzas move further outward, giving a much enlarged meaning to Heyen's original question:

> Some smelled the smoke,
> some just heard the news.
> Were they Germans? Were they Nazis?
> Were they human? Who killed the Jews?
>
> The stars will remember the gold,
> the sun will remember the shoes,
> the moon will remember the skin.
> But who killed the Jews?

The poem doesn't just overcome our original reservations; it becomes a tremendously powerful statement, full of moral reverberations.

Elsewhere, Heyen's style is less rhetorically charged; the quality of his lyrical talent is, in fact, more clearly seen in quieter passages. . . . (pp. 958-59)

Heyen's book ultimately is as fine and important as it is courageous. These are not poems to be read and reread endlessly for the sheer pleasure of it; they are much too painful for that. I am sure there are many people, in fact, who will not be able to look these poems in the face. And how much harder must they have been to write? Such heavy moral labor must have cost the poet a great deal. But this book will not—cannot—be forgotten; it shows decency and human love triumphant over the darkest side of the human spirit, and we cannot ask for much more than that. (p. 959)

> *Peter Stitt, in* The Georgia Review *(copyright, 1977, by the University of Georgia), Winter, 1977.*

SANDRA McPHERSON

The significant. The love for humanity. These are Heyen's priorities. . . . And another one: to fight "this unfathomable oceanic ignorance of ourselves," the "arrogance, dogma, ignorance that did this." . . .

Along with feelings of guilt, grief, and responsibility, then, in *The Swastika Poems* there is life-giving benevolence and art. . . .

[*The Swastika Poems*] begins with a prosy description of Heyen's father on his 1928 immigration journey to America. It is not anti-poetry, may not perform the magic by which poetry identifies itself, but is clean-reading. Usually in Heyen this way of writing can suddenly take off into unexpected regions, as in "The Numinous," which nonetheless begins ordinarily:

> We are walking a sidewalk
> in a German city.
> We are watching gray smoke
> gutter along the roofs

> just as it must have
> from other terrible chimneys.
> We are walking our way
> almost into a trance.
> We are walking our way
> almost into a dream
> only those with blue
> numbers along their wrists
> can truly imagine.

I mention this artless way of writing first so we will not long dwell on weaknesses, the few passages where his language seems slow before his subject matter. . . .

When the details of Jewish martyrdom begin, they are "familiar":

> When the gas dropped in,
> scapegoat Jews scratched their appeals
> by bloody fingernails
> on their shower stalls.

They give up no new poetry. What do we want from them? Have they become "set" as part of a liturgy? Is it that they can't, musn't, be ignored? . . .

Poetry may seem to be helpless at times like these. Poetry appears weaker than grief. Grief is weaker than the historical atrocity. A bare prose account by any survivor of the death camps is so strong that a poet who wasn't there faces a very hard task indeed. . . .

Here Heyen begins to talk about the problem:

> Reader, all words are a dream.
> You have wandered into mine.

Words are his chosen and beloved medium whose limitations he knows. They are a dream for seeming insubstantial; but they are also the product of Heyen's obsessed subconscious—they have a validity of origin. He has adopted the responsibility of speaking in poetry the best he can. With this goal, or Dream . . . : to make the catastrophe as real, rememberable, for us as possible. The virtues he's after are . . . : truth, an outcome of saved lives, inspiration of wonder in that a poem exists at all. . . .

[Heyen himself] feels he doesn't "know how to talk to" his Nazi relatives but *has* to. Hitler's name was never mentioned in the Heyen home. Another reason perhaps why words must come out of hiding. Finally, he doesn't want to bear his burden *alone:* "We / will taste this history together, / my reader: take a deep breath."

The book has, then, a mature tone of responsibility. . . . And Heyen never sits back satisfied; he is relentless—the collection is intense with his own intensity of interest.

There begin to emerge in this book repetitions of Heyen's personal symbols. Most of these are original with the poet, at least I have not seen them used this way before. Many are very beautiful and they are stronger for his having discovered them than the universally cited gas showers and chimney smoke (yet even this hurts us afresh when Heyen terms it the "human haze").

He begins with a correlation of *the eye* with *darkness.* . . . History obscured with passing time and an individual's battle to *see.* How can he better see? Well, dreams fill his vision, books give him clear views (books provide information, epigraphs, inspiration, and actual lifted lines for many of *The Swastika Poems*), and television's *World at War* and *Ascent of Man* series see to it that he sees. "Darkness" is written in fragmented pulses, imagery frightening then vanishing as if the writer were trying to wake from a series of nightmares. Even Heyen's own motives torture him: could it be "that I am jealous of them,/the Nazi's hooked crosses, the Jews' stripes"? . . . If one wants to see in the darkness, one has to enter it and wait until the eyes get used to it. . . .

The last poem in the book tells how the "scarecrow, skeleton" swastika star that followed the Heyens metamorphosed into the softly radiant Star of David that young Heyen followed. (p. 31)

How Heyen writes about this strongest of all subjects, wrestles with it, exorcises it, or recreates it is an interesting study in itself. He tries everything and surrounds his subject with an army of approaches.

The most primitive approach is exemplified in "children no older than I were being put to death at Belsen" and "while I was playing in Woodhaven streets, six hundred people a day died at Belsen." The inconceivable is not rendered much more real by these equations, if only because this is what we tell ourselves each night after watching the news. . . .

Then he moves closer, describing photographs he sees on his visit to Belsen: "But this time these photographs are of the very place where you are standing; this is a dimension you have not entered before." The very fact that he has to tell us so, or tell himself so, means he still isn't satisfied he's found that vivid level of art that utterly convinces. But he's found the human nature of the way "You might say to yourself: *They are really here. I am at Belsen, and these are the graves of people who were murdered here. This is the camp at Belsen.*" . . .

Heyen's repetitive devices are a way of trying to convince, to feel, to talk himself into a stronger sensation of remembering. . . .

Although he infrequently uses startling language, sometimes he captures so many meanings within a single word that you feel for a moment as if you are inside a bell. . . .

[Concerning guilt,] Heyen says, "Reader, you have walked/into the smoke-streaked mirror/of my dream, but I can't,/or won't remember./Did my jackboots gleam?/Did I fill out quotas?/ . . . Did I close those doors."

If the guilty do not judge themselves, if guilt is spread out so thin it amounts to nothing more than "excessive attention to one's own business," Heyen sees that nonetheless people fell in two camps from which we have been spared only by luck and fortune (or, time and place): "this/fortune that you and I were not the victims, this/luck that you and I were not the murderers." And he concludes "we killed them all." Even God's complicity is not ignored. . . .

[If] *The Swastika Poems* contains any poems which don't work magic, they are, if not an addition to the art of poetry, an addition to the humanity of poetry.

The poems which perform miracles and do add to the art of poetry fulfill Heyen's goal to make us REMEMBER. The poems respond to Hitler's "Believe me, it is easy for me/to end my life. A brief moment/and I'm freed of everything." Often it is by the beautiful, the lyrical, in his poems that the reader is captured, made a captive: "I Dream of

Justice," "The Tree." There is the urgent "Lines to My Parents." In these and other poems he makes us feel the permanent alteration the world has endured, if words can say that. *The Swastika Poems* is in a way quiet as the stone of a monument and the monument's carved words. (p. 32)

Sandra McPherson, in The American Poetry Review *(copyright © 1977 by World Poetry, Inc.; reprinted by permission of Sandra McPherson), November-December, 1977.*

PAMELA S. RASSO

William Heyen's *The Swastika Poems* run the gamut of general to specific: they are mostly about war and the Nazi atrocities in World War II, but they are also about William Heyen and his family, who were divided and on different sides of the war. . . . It is apparent, throughout these poems, that William Heyen has spent a lifetime questioning the perplexities of Nazi Germany, and attempting to come to grips with his heritage.

This book is a study in psychology, a psychology that extends far beyond that of Nazi Germany. Heyen's poems are psychological in the same manner as the paintings and drawings of George Grosz: they do not constitute a formal psychological analysis of Nazi Germany, and from this standpoint they are indirect. However when considered in terms of emotional impact, vividness of imagery, and immediacy, they are very direct indeed. (pp. 158-59)

Many of Heyen's poems are exactly about group conformity and the loss of independence in judgment from social pressure. . . .

Heyen's prose poem "Noise In The Trees: A Memoir" in his second book is about the natural world of lyrical beauty and the pioneer spirit of growing up on Long Island. Throughout this piece however, there is a darker side, a haunting undercurrent that flows with undertows impossible to escape. This darker side of the prose poem is entirely different from the humorous themes that exist in the prose poems of Michael Benedikt and Robert Bly, and resembles the earlier efforts of Baudelaire, Rimbaud and other French Symbolist poets. In *The Swastika Poems*, there are three new prose poems, "The Spire," "Erika," and "The Tree," all of which continue the sense of the darker side, that release almost a Pandora's box of the grotesque. (p. 159)

In Heyen's poetry the conflict between the past, the present and the future is a battlefield, but there is an artistic advantage and even a kind of moral victory in acknowledging the conflict as a permanent condition of life. William Heyen realizes that Germany's winter's tale is all of our tale: it happened, it is happening now, and it will continue to happen until blindness bred of conformity becomes thought's independence. (p. 160)

Pamela S. Rasso, "A Winter's Tale," in Modern Poetry Studies *(copyright 1978, by Media Study, Inc.), Vol. IX, No. 2, 1978, pp. 158-60.*

*　　　*　　　*

HOCKING, Mary　1921-

Hocking is a British novelist.

JANET BURROWAY

Mary Hocking writes with very little of that verve that

makes [Alan] Sillitoe good company on a London-to-Nihilon Express, but *The Climbing Frame* wins hands down at linking socialism with nihilism. . . . *The Climbing Frame* is a meticulous book about the tedious tragedies of running a school system. An aggressively unwed mother draws drama to herself over a playground accident that doesn't merit a sticking plaster. A combination of circumstance, buckpassing, political in-fighting, personality clash and a dearth of news escalate the incident toward national press and television coverage. It is the sort of local crisis that brings out the worst in both individuals and the system. The novel contains a disastrous magazine-style romance, and the situation itself is of a kind that commends itself to television series. What lifts it above this level is Mary Hocking's sharp, forgiving focus on the minds and motives of the little politicians. No slaughter here, but this nonsense is truly menacing. (p. 370)

> Janet Burroway, in New Statesman (© 1971 The Statesman & Nation Publishing Co. Ltd.), September 17, 1971.

Before the psychiatrists made a fetish of it, novelists were quietly observing the tiny, crushing hypocrisies of family life and their effects. It would be a pity to say much about the actual plot of *Family Circle,* because it is unfolded through the subtlest of hints and revelations. It is the very best kind of middlebrow novel—and this is said with all respect. There are never enough of such books: readable, intelligent, observant, with no unmanageable pretensions, and styled as unobtrusively as the best gentleman's suiting. They pass the time more profitably and agreeably, nearly always, than the cinema or television; and sometimes they leave a scene, a character, an idea in the mind just as real literature does, to be thought about and used. (p. 1477)

> The Times Literary Supplement (© Times Newspapers Ltd. (London) 1972; reproduced from The Times Literary Supplement by permission), December 8, 1972.

[*Daniel Come to Judgement*] has clearly been sent out into the world as ladies' fiction, superior grade. This is as grossly deceptive an exterior as that of [Mary Hocking's] heroine, Dorothy, a sensible thirtyish lady, superior grade, "the sort of person who is always asked the way to the nearest public lavatory"—and who is also anarchic, compassionate, adulterous and sharp, and aware that she has a soul that is immortal, and quite amoral. The author's theme, as in her last book, is the contrast between those who have, and know they have, such a soul, and those who by various means succeed in disposing of it. . . .

If English novelists could be bought up for capital appreciation like equities or Victorian watercolours it would be a good idea to acquire some Hockings and their like and sell some of the showier names. Like watercolours, this is a genre we do well and its stock is sure to rise. When that happens, however, the reader will no longer have the almost *risqué* surprise of finding subtlety and strength in such a demure package.

> "Amoral Soul," in The Times Literary Supplement (© Times Newspapers Ltd. (London) 1974; reproduced from The Times Literary Supplement by permission), April 12, 1974, p. 396.

NEIL HEPBURN

Quite a lot of what Miss Hocking writes is over-specific and obvious, but in some important ways her touch is very delicate. The relationship developing between Hannah and the isolated figure of the local newspaper editor [in *The Bright Day*] is extremely well done, and what I take to be the key to the young MP's failure, his crypto-homosexuality, is almost too slyly hinted at. (p. 31)

> Neil Hepburn, in The Listener (© British Broadcasting Corp. 1975; reprinted by permission of Neil Hepburn), July 3, 1975.

NEIL HEPBURN

[In *The Mind Has Mountains,* Mary Hocking's story of] the breakdown of Tom Norris, Assistant Education Officer of a county about to be obliterated under the casual jackboot of a boundaries commission, there are no revenants, no demonic possessions, only the strangeness of human beings reacting to changes in themselves and their surroundings. Fortyish, Tom is distanced rather than estranged from his wife Isobel, worried by his dreams (in which the wolves return to his placid Sussex countryside), unsure of his identity, and near the end of the internal material from which he has successfully been fashioning children's stories for years. (pp. 486-87)

He does surprising, violent, mischievous things and at last, in the climax of a great snowstorm that obliterates all that is familiar to him, manages to break away from the dead shell of his past.

That he does so to retreat to a northern cottage, there to write the near-*Shardik* to follow his near-*Watership Down,* is something of an anti-climax; but then plain sanity after such crises of the spirit probably is anti-climactical. Miss Hocking's quiet, precise prose, anatomising this ordinary official's reconciliation with the extraordinariness of life, packs an astonishing emotional punch, and gives much satisfaction. (p. 487)

> Neil Hepburn, in The Listener (© British Broadcasting Corp. 1976; reprinted by permission of Neil Hepburn), October 14, 1976.

NICK TOTTON

Mary Hocking is acutely and probably permanently infected with truthfulness. *The Mind Has Mountains* explores the senses in which this condition is a matter of suffering, and those in which it is a matter for celebration. 'Some people manage to lose themselves forever out beyond the human stockade'; but others, like the protagonist and the author of this novel, accept the more difficult task of returning, and finding a way of communicating what they have seen. It isn't easy to tell: people are, quite reasonably, unwilling to be frightened, and it is necessary to be discreet; at the same time, it is only too easy to forget what one is talking about. Mary Hocking writes brilliantly on many levels at once, because she knows that the everyday contains another, stranger reality: it only takes attention, an at first casual intensification of vision, to open the crack between the worlds. . . .

The Mind Has Mountains is a funny, serious book, to be read and reread: the kind of book that bides its time, perhaps remaining an innocuous entertainment for years until a reader is opened to it by explosive experience—'so *that* was what it meant!' It is a *Steppenwolf* for our time; and, I think, the equal of Hesse's. (p. 22)

Nick Totton, in The Spectator *(© 1976 by* The Spectator; *reprinted by permission of* The Spectator*), October 16, 1976.*

*   *   *

HOFFMAN, Daniel   1923-

Hoffman, an American poet, critic, and editor, is a scholar concerned with exploring myth and folklore in his writing. (See also *CLC*, Vol. 6, and *Contemporary Authors*, Vols. 1-4, rev. ed.)

HOWARD NEMEROV

Mr. Hoffman's poetry [in *An Armada of Thirty Whales*] is extremely detailed in its observation of nature, and his clams and snails and pears and whales yield intricate parables by being so closely inspected. Perhaps not sentimentality so much as a diffidence about it, or fear of it, weakens so many of these poems just at the ending; his "Icarus, Icarus" moves with a goodly competence down to "what ecstasy of pride it was that shook / you loose from all that beeswax and those quills, / O how you soared," then drags in what I feel to be a plain irrelevance: "that instant before Breughel / showed human eyes unseeing at your fall." This or a similar fault diminished my pleasure in several other poems also, but I found one, "That the pear delights me now," whose ritual nature allows of a quiet, anticipated close, and which seems strong and fine throughout. (p. 66)

Howard Nemerov, in The Atlantic Monthly *(copyright © 1954 by The Atlantic Monthly Company, Boston, Mass.; reprinted with permission), September, 1954.*

ANTHONY HOLDEN

In [the] second paragraph [of *Poe Poe Poe Poe Poe Poe Poe*], Poe is 'complex, inspired, limited, pretentious, uncompromising, banal'; on page three his art is 'strange, haunted, tawdry, inexorable, remote yet inescapable'. And we've still got a long, long way to go. (p. 97)

Needless to say, Hoffman is a man obsessed, so much so that at times he apes his subject's manias: '. . . my chronicle of Poe's life and work and reputation and influence and how Edgarpoe wormed his way into my guts and gizzard and haunted my brain and laid a spell upon my soul which this long harangue is an attempt to exorcise'.

Now as Hoffman admits, a lot has been written about Poe. He is generous in his avowed indebtedness to fellow soulcritics such as Richard Wilbur, but crude in his dismissal of earlier biographers and analysts. Recounting Poe's marriage at 27 to his cousin Virginia, then 14, he condemns as 'an impertinence' the theory of two American psychoanalysts —based on Poe's poem *Annabel Lee*—that Virginia died a virgin because Poe was impotent. It's not our business, he declares, 'whether he could get it up or not'. What is our business? '*What he wrote*'—in screaming italics. Why, then, does Hoffman himself waste so much expendable space on idle biographical gossip, not least incredulity that his hero should lapse so far as to try for a military commission at West Point?

I suspect Hoffman is modelling himself on Charles Olson, especially his erratic study of Melville, *Call Me Ishmael*. There is the same wild, self-indulgent theorising, the same embarrassing attempt at a winningly colloquial prose style

(sentences beginning 'I mean, . . .', rhetorical questions to the reader: 'don't you think so?', two-word paragraphs, calling himself a 'dum-dum' for not having his blinding flashes of insight earlier *et al*). But where Olson is concise, Hoffman is diffuse; where Olson is original, Hoffman is simply inept. It is this hopeless attempt to be endearing that deprives his study of any vestige of seriousness or authority.

It's a great shame, really, because amid all the dross Hoffman serves his subject well. His review of the poetry rightly proves it underestimated; he affords proper status to often neglected works such as the *Narrative of Arthur Gordon Pym*, *Eureka* and the *Imp of the Perverse*. Above all, he demonstrates with remarkable effect the coherence of so diverse a body of work, so often taken as the random ravings of a mind half insane.

But the attempt is ruined by a failure that years of Poe involvement would understandably produce: overwriting. Mr Hoffman . . . sounds like a stimulating teacher. But the tone of his book, with its reckless enthusiasm, its unabashed egotism, its myopic sense of mission, is inexorably undergraduate. (pp. 97-8)

Anthony Holden, in Books and Bookmen *(© copyright Anthony Holden 1973; reprinted with permission), December, 1973.*

PETER COOLEY

Probably Daniel Hoffman writes as well as any poet in America today, but *The Center of Attention* . . . won't extend his reputation and it suffers from the same problems as its predecessor, *Broken Laws*. Hoffman is among those poets born in the 1920s (Wilbur, Simpson, Rich, and Dickey come to mind among others) who began as formalists and have gradually loosened their stanzas and rhythms to accommodate a wider range of experience and feeling than was possible in the autotelic structures they began with. What Hoffman lacks, however, is precisely what the title of the volume professes, a focus for his perception which can transcend the poem as exercise-on-a-topic (see both parts II and III for this tendency). The poems in Part I are strong, austere, varied in form and subject, and concerned with the dichotomy of private and public life: death is at the center of their vision. A poet as good as Hoffman could have written an entire book with the conviction one finds in "After God," "The Princess Casamassima," "Power," or the title poem. As it stands, *The Center of Attention* is two-thirds a collection, one-third a brilliant showcase for Hoffman's talents, certain of which he could push further. (p. 279)

Peter Cooley, in Prairie Schooner *(© 1976 by University of Nebraska Press; reprinted by permission from* Prairie Schooner*), Fall, 1976.*

ANDREW WATERMAN

The palindromic title given [*Able Was I Ere I Saw Elba*] intimates Hoffman's delight in verbal play; also perhaps a lack of stylistic "development" which, given his range, virtuosity and witty inventiveness, hardly matters. In "An armada of thirty whales" we read:

> The ceremonial motion
> of their ponderous race is
> given dandiacal graces
> in the ballet of their geysers.

Hoffman has dandiacal graces enough of his own: his zestful verbal flamboyance, supple use of rhyme and other sound-effects, linguistic quirks, while never so inordinate as to exasperate or baffle the reader, make the *processes* of his writing vital and interesting. . . . There is an early thematic shift from poems preoccupied with birds, beasts and flowers to wider human concerns. Hoffman shows a talent for symbolic fictions, in poems such as "The City of Satisfactions" where the reader is drawn into a fantasy-world made compelling by the recognizable dailiness of such appurtenances as "A Danish half-devoured by flies beneath specked glass, / Dirty cups on the counter."

Generally, though, Hoffman is a verbal "maker" rather than a poet driven by obsessions. I find no unifying vision at the heart of his work making everything cohere, as in the highest order of poets, into an organic imaginative world, but there are many very fine poems. . . .

[Crucially when something does well up from the depths, Hoffman possesses] a technique enabling its expression, as when, in "An Old Photo in an Old Life" he meditates on a picture of soldiers beside a river during the Boxer Rebellion. . . . Hoffman is a poet worth buying. (p. 936)

Andrew Waterman, in The Times Literary Supplement (© Times Newspapers Ltd. (London) 1977; reproduced from The Times Literary Supplement by permission), July 29, 1977.

JUDITH MOFFETT

Hoffman, like Winters, like the New Critics, like Berryman, Jarrell, Hollander, and a few others, is one of the minority of true writer/scholar/teacher hybrids whose intelligence turns as naturally to the crafting of creative scholarship as to poetry (if not perhaps with equal pleasure). . . .

If Hoffman is an academic professional, if he values, modifies, and uses easily the traditional forms of poetry in English, his own poetry would nevertheless be incorrectly characterized as "academic" if the term means drily bookish, bloodless, "dissociation from nature." Nor is it "intellectual," for all its intelligence; nor is it difficult of access, though the later work yields much of its potential quality and meaning after multiple readings. [*Able Was I Ere I Saw Elba: Selected Poems*] establishes Hoffman's as a poetry lovingly crafted, fine in its descriptions, haunting and strange in its myth-making, and increasingly memorable.

The pleasure of perusing this poet's work through the twenty years and half-dozen volumes represented in *Able Was I Ere I Saw Elba* is partly in seeing how the promise of the first two books—exuberant with experiments in form, sound, tone, the vocal exercising of a young singer whose voice is still changing—is fulfilled, thanks to all that practice, in a mature third book, and how it develops in range and grace through each of the three to fellow. (p. 171)

[Hoffman's first collection, *An Armada of Thirty Whales*, shows] him to be a person bemused and intrigued by nature, and by "natural" and "human" interactions; in them, natural things large as whales or small as mayflies often can be taken as metaphorical for human things—yet need not be. There is implicit in the closeness and care of his observations a love of clams for their courage, of snails for their concentration, the creatures rejoiced in fully as much for their own purposes as for any of ours. . . . That exuberance Hoffman brought to his early writing expresses itself in his

sound effects. . . . Slant rhymes and curious rhyme games (down / ground / by / died) abound.

The selections from the second book, *A Little Geste,* contain similarly self-conscious effects (the sun "wimples the wakeless water"; *truth* rhymes daringly with *sloops* on the pure strength of a vowel) but works also toward an easier and more colloquial idiom, and at the same time toward Hoffman's major thematic concerns. The impulse to play games with language, have fun with the sounds of words, led him later to call a critical study *Poe Poe Poe Poe Poe Poe Poe* and make the title of this selection under review a palindrome—though it doesn't read at all the same front to back! In both the first two books he tries by such means to achieve compression, to pack the skins of the poems full; and if there are stretch marks and signs of strain, the practice was crucial to the achievement of the mature style.

With *The City of Satisfactions*, his third book, the idiom of Hoffman's poetry has become, as it has remained, direct and informal. The skewing and convoluting of syntax is given up; those verses freed of formal conventions are surefooted and language, no longer forced into richness, attains its intensities by means more subtle. Several poems chosen from *A Little Geste*, and all eight from *The City of Satisfactions*, vary as they may in length, strategy, and form, tap the deep sources of myth, or assemble the landscapes of dream, or of surreality, or shape some combination of these; and the mood of each is vaguely or forthrightly ominous.

The selections from the last three books, *Striking the Stones, Broken Laws,* and *The Center of Attention,* can in terms of *voice* be grouped and thought of together; all of them are finished, mature poems. Hoffman's interests have broadened through his forties and early fifties, and his poetry has broken new ground: of history, of industrial cityscapes and agribusiness, of lawbreaking. But the territory staked out in the earlier work—nature and myth—has been no more abandoned than the technical possibilities of rhyme and meter were cast off when Hoffman discovered in himself a gift for a kind of free-verse lyric of short strong lines. (pp. 171-72)

The love of natural creatures that sweetens all the books, especially the first, is balanced neither there nor later by the sense of a matching love of people. Hoffman's family occasionally make an appearance; but the impression prevailing throughout *Able Was I Ere I Saw Elba* is that of a private voice, a private sensibility, observing and imagining and responding primarily in solitude. Early poems are mostly unpeopled, but for a persona who often seems to be only fractionally the poet. More recent work reveals an interest in crowds and rare characters; a group of poems in *The Center of Attention* features people known or imagined. . . . Hoffman's feelings sometimes seem less under wraps when he's writing about, for instance, the fidelity of mated eagles than when he presents human situations certainly chosen because they move him. In this he stands out against the group of poets called Confessional by M. L. Rosenthal and those called Autobiographical by David Kalstone, and indeed many contemporary poets seem more personal and open in their work. (p. 173)

Among the pure lyrics, emblems, narratives, and meditations in the last half of this collection are many more remarkable poems than I can discuss. . . . A chilling scheme

"To rid your barn of rats" (by floating a wooden chip, big enough to hold up one rat, in a barrel two-thirds filled with water, then sprinkling cornmeal over the water to make the barrel look full of meal) illustrates one of Hoffman's most highly-trained and gripping voices, the voice in which humor and horror are somehow successfully blended. (p. 174)

Able Was I Ere I Saw Elba identifies this poet as one who, choosing to sing after enduring his own journeys through the dark places, has come a pretty fair way along the road toward his admirable goals. (p. 175)

> *Judith Moffett, "A Wry Amaze of Attention," in* Poetry *(© 1978 by The Modern Poetry Association; reprinted by permission of the Editor of* Poetry*), June, 1978, pp. 170-75.*

JOHN ALEXANDER ALLEN

The title [of Hoffman's selected poems]—*Able Was I Ere I Saw Elba*—is appropriate in at least two ways. With its reference to Napoleon's enforced residence on Elba, the old palindrome suggests the principal theme of Hoffman's work —exile from "another country," one that he has known as though in a dream and to which he will one day return triumphantly. As for the fact that the title can be read both ways, Hoffman's work . . . not only can but should be read both in chronological and in anti-chronological order.

"Now why," asks Daniel Hoffman, "would a visitation from the Isles / Of the Blessed come to Swarthmore, Pa. 19081, a borough zoned / For single-family occupancy? No / Rocks of Renunciation on our / Assessors' rolls" ("A Visitation," *Striking the Stones*). These lines are typical of Hoffman's poetic product in a number of ways. The tone is conversational, the language colloquial. The mild wry humor co-exists naturally with a subject he takes very seriously indeed. Social satire is not his primary medium, but the jab at suburban complacency—the poet's own complacency— in the lines quoted typifies the habitual and endearing self-deprecation of this genuinely modest poet.

The experience so unpretentiously presented in "A Visitation" takes place as night gives way to dawn. This transitional hour, together with the time of gathering dusk, consistently provides the impulse for Hoffman's poems: the passing of dream into the waking day, and of the day back into dream again. As is likely to be true with all good poets, night, dream, death, the imagination and the possibility of rebirth are closely associated in Hoffman's mind. (p. 2)

Trees have a mantic role in Hoffman's poems; and, curiously, they are often sexual in what one might think of as an un-arboreal way: 'Between the thighs of trees old graves of sorrows / Open." But, also in connection with the trees, "a fresh wind stirs." Thus "A Visitation" ends on a positive note, though this note is well qualified by the evocation of death and deadliness that is inseparable from the old day's demise and from the prospects of the dawning sky, that "black widow," now about to take "her new lover," the rising sun.

Returning to the matter-of-fact specificity of Hoffman's opening, a visitation from the Isles of the Blessed did, after all, occur for the poet very early on the morning in question in Swarthmore, Pa. 19081. Hoffman, you will remember, begins his poem by asking why. It is perhaps obvious that there is no answer to that question. One can say, however, that Hoffman has reported such visitations throughout his

career of twenty years and more as a publishing poet. They are, I would infer, the most important experiences in his life, the lifeblood of his poems. Hoffman, who knows his limitations as well as he does his powers, does not make the mistake of trying to describe the visitation itself, here or elsewhere in his poems. All he gives us is "Somewhere, / A consecrated shore / Ringed by dolmens where the wind speaks." That may or may not evoke the Isles of the Blessèd for a given reader. If he wishes to find such a world described in detail, he must turn to another poet. What Hoffman gives us, in many of his poems, is not a guided tour of the Elysian Fields, but the longing of an exile to return there.

[A] sense of being exiled from another life has, from the beginning, been the keynote of Hoffman's poetry. . . . (p. 3)

[Hoffman's] ear for the sounds and rhythms of his own lines has always been as acute as his discriminating response to the corresponding phenomena in the natural world. In fact, his mastery of words, like every other aspect of his art, has undergone a striking refinement with the years, to excellent effect. One does not need to seek far in *An Armada* and *A Little Geste* to find him playing with sounds in a way that suggests the exuberance of an incompletely mastered talent. From "In a Cold Climate": . . . "Who would encumber / these huckleberryfields' sparse opulence with tropics' / richesse?"; and, from "The Everlasting," . . . "where the smith's sparks gonged in the deep shed's shade." Syntactically, there are snarls that rival Browning at his worst. . . . ["In the Beginning"] is one of Hoffman's best early poems. The subject is the magical use of language, observed in the poet's daughter Kate, who stands on the jetty and cries "Boat! Boat!," even when none is visible to the physical eye. Hoffman handles the incident with the warmth of feeling that will illuminate many of his more mature poems about imagination and the word. . . . But the poem suffers from a radical uncertainty of rhythmic effect. Its movement vacillates between that of actual speech, which is Hoffman's future métier ("Her passion / to name the nameless pulls her / from the syllabic sea / of incommunicate loneliness"), repetitive iambs ("the world without description / is vast and wild as death," and jouncing trisyllables ("But that makes no difference to Katy, / atingle with vision and word"). As a result, the little girl's excitement does not make itself adequately felt in the over-all tone of the poem.

For contrast, we can now usefully refer to the sounds, syntax and rhythms of a typical late poem from *The Center of Attention,* "The Wanderer":

> This body that has fastened
> Itself to the wanderer
>
> Who hastens with mysterious
> Balked purposes,
>
> These hands that answer,
> This face that turns
>
> At the calling
> Of the name
>
> That I am wearing
> Like one shoe
>
> —How did I come
> In all this gear
>
> Among so few

Clues to where I've come from

Or where
I am to go?

The syntax is crystal clear. The rhythm, which falls into no regular pattern, exactly reflects what is going on in the poet's head: a meditative examination of his problematic identity. Almost all of the important words in the poem (for example—fastened, face, few; body, balked; gear, go) are linked with others by alliteration, but always unobtrusively. The end rhymes are mostly slant and off-beat, producing an effect of order or continuity that remains elusive (wanderer, answer, gear, where; name, come, from; shoe, few, go). And the brief stanzas are all linked by inconspicuous assonance (fastened, hastens; purposes, turns; face, name; name, am; wearing, gear; gear, where; clues, go). All of this, in support of the poem's mood and theme, is the mark of the master craftsman. And Hoffman does it again and again, in poem after poem. (pp. 5-6)

A substantial number of Hoffman's poems deal with the big questions of his trade: What is the poet's purpose in writing, and How does a poem succeed in communicating what he wishes to say? Poems on these subjects can be tedious— mere shop talk or a kind of narcissism. On the other hand, such poems are always justified when the poet is not just taking you through his workshop but is pointing out that his problem as poet is everyman's problem: that of staying alive imaginatively and establishing the possibility of meaningful communication between the inner man (his emotions, his imaginative vision) and the world outside himself. Hoffman's poems about poetry are of this kind.

From various early poems by Hoffman, one gets the impression of an earnest, idealistic young man who tries to believe that the voice of the bard will collar passers-by and impose enlightenment upon them. . . . This is surely a sentiment that invites dissent. But time passes, with its attrition. Hoffman is not about to give up his faith in the imagination, but he finds that the spawn of unreason and power require that faculty, "great with rage," to

> Turn . . . and conceive
> On days like dragons' teeth.

to

> Retell, in the leaping of exultant breath,
> In the blood that sighs,
> What knowledge in the bone this side of death
> Death makes us prize.
> ("Reading the Times,"—*The City of Satisfactions*)

Hoffman's tone has again altered by the time that he faces "A New Notebook" in the last poem of *Broken Laws*. Here the emphasis is not on mantic authority nor on rage and imaginative frenzy but on redemptive vision and power analogous to that of love. He hopes to "incise" upon the empty pages "images / the soul has seized / out of confusion. . . ." . . . The case has altered once again in *The Center of Attention*, where the emphasis falls on waiting time out, paying attention, having patience: "What awaits us we / Can know only / By our deliverance" ("East"). Finally, in the last poem of the same volume ("The Poem"), Hoffman conceives of his art as itself an exile seeking deliverance. It remains faithful in adversity, and, with luck, may just have strength to deliver its message to the well-disposed reader. . . . (pp. 6-8)

It is apparent that Hoffman, from the beginning, has been blessed—or burdened—by a social conscience. He has written good poems against war, injustice, moral decay, destruction of the world's environment, the threat of computerized nonentity. Surely there have been few Phi Beta Kappa poems as humorous, eloquent and dignified as the one he delivered at Swarthmore College ("The Peaceable Kingdom" . . .) in 1964. After surveying the world's ills for the assembled youth who were about to be graduated into them, he asks, "are we ready to go forth?" If so, he sensibly advises, take with you "lists / of those Important Books as yet unread . . . and explications / of . . . the vertebrates / who, since the Good Duke dreamed a green world where the court / corrupts no man, agree upon hypotheses / that define the Good and tell the False from True." . . . There speaks Hoffman the humanist, man of literature and guide and guardian of youth.

But that is not, I think, where Hoffman really lives. In his poem "In Memory of Lewis Corey," . . . a former teacher whose message was reform, "It's fifteen years he's dead now," Hoffman reflects,

> yet the thought
> Of Corey makes my mind rehearse
> All that he taught,
> And this thought chides—
> How little else have I reformed, besides
> The diction of my verse;
> Should the commonwealth, like art, seek perfect forms
> What can it learn from my self-searching trade?

What, indeed! Hoffman knows the answer better than almost anyone. In "Filling the Forms," . . . he has his fun with a registrar who complains, "You've not filled in the subject of your course!"—

> My pencil lead turns golden, prints my calling:
> Donnez un sens plus pur aux mots—scratch that—
> REDEMPTION OF THIS GENERATION'S JARGON
> In conventional signs a Registrar can read.

Redemption of language from jargon is, of course, truly the subject taught by every English Professor, especially if he is a poet, and, above all, if he is Daniel Hoffman. Still more importantly, the purification of language is not only exemplified by Hoffman's poems but is also one of their most significant subject.

Every poet must sometimes wish that he could communicate without words. Hoffman . . . often finds birdsong at the center of his days. It is a language that seems to him more perfect than any he can marshal. . . . It is, however, characteristic of Hoffman's stance as exile from a more perfect world, a more perfect self, that he consistently represents himself as being unable properly to understand and communicate in the language of that world or self. The resultant frustration is, I believe, the source of a gentle but deep and persistent *weltchmerz* that contributes its notes to almost everything he writes. (p. 10)

Hoffman celebrates love in all of its aspects, from the physical through the intellectual to the spiritual. Like Yeats and Graves, whom he admires, he takes the Muse seriously and responds most readily, as poet, to the feminine sphere of existence (the Muse, growing things, the creatures of nature, night, water, the moon). His harshest criticism is reserved for such male-associated phenomena as war, intellectual pride, and, as mentioned above, the sun as emblem of egotism and the indifferent exercise of power. Although he has produced generous tributes to such fellow artists as Yeats, Williams, and Ives, he seldom celebrates male power. The notable exception is "'The Great Horse Strode Without a Rider.'" But even here the wonderful horse's destination is the sea into which he plunges. I cannot remember any poem in which Hoffman satirizes a woman or any womanly quality. On the other hand, his heroines abound. He gives us Maid Marian, [two portraits of Aphrodite, Thomas the Rhymer's dark lady, the Queen of Hearts, and the Muse herself]. . . . (pp. 12-13)

Hoffman's two most recent volumes, and, in particular, *The Center of Attention,* display a new emphasis by the mature poet on things that are mortal and, paradoxically, *therefore* permanent—what he calls "elementals." . . . The longing for an elusive world whose "vivid light" is "pure / Energy" ("This Life") persists, but it is increasingly balanced by an acute awareness of those natural phenomena that share with the poet what is mortal in himself. . . . *The Center of Attention* is full of poems that make such discoveries. The poet finds his own indestructible energy embodied in the elements ("Wind," "Fire," "Waves"), the points of the compass ("North," "East," "South," "West"), and sundry creatures ("Shrew," "Boar," "Dogfish"). The new emphasis, combined with an every-growing mastery of verse technique, permits a condensation so radical that some of the poems approach the absolute silence invoked in "A Gift of Tongues." (p. 14)

In an analogous way, Hoffman has found new, objective ways of communicating his frustration with the inadequacy of language, however finely honed, as a bridge between the inner conception and the poem, the poem and the reader. The would-be suicide in the title poem of *The Center of Attention* communicates with the crowd below him, and they with him, only so long as his life hangs in the balance and he therefore provides a diversion from the day's routine. The great Polish translator in "The Translators' Party" enjoys a few moments, among poets whose language is not his own, of warm reminiscence with Auden, but one reads in the *Times* soon afterward that "he was found / 'Apparently fallen' / From his high window, / That voice / Stilled now / On New York's alien ground." And the poet's ex-student, in "The Princess Casamassima," had listened to all that her teacher had to say in class and had then gone forth into the world possessed with the belief that there is meaning in blowing up buildings with dynamite.

Like most poets, Hoffman has been, and remains, dedicated to the faith that the best human qualities are incalculably precious, tending toward the divine. By the same token, he has staunchly attacked phenomena that seem to him to have a dehumanizing effect. Such phenomena are epitomized, for him, by the spread into every human activity of computer technology. The common belief that the heroes of our time are the technicians of space flight and those who operate their machines has appeared to him a dangerous illusion. (pp. 15-16)

When I first read *The Center of Attention* my admiration was tempered by disappointment. It seemed to me that Hoffman's technical skill had made still further strides, while in point of tone and subject he had drawn closer to the rather dreary guilt- and *angst*-ridden outlook that has become too familiar to us in contemporary poetry and fic-

tion. I now see that I was wrong. Hoffman's work has never been disfigured either by excessive egotism or by self-indulgent postures of despair. *The Center of Attention* represents, for Hoffman, a growth toward greater objectivity, a more inclusive realism. If some of his poems have been derivative (as what poet's are not?), they are mainly to be found in earlier volumes, not in this one. As I suggested in speaking of the earlier poems, they are valuable mainly as precursors of more fully realized work that followed them. Conversely, the most recent poems can best be read and can most fully be appreciated as the culmination of thought, feelings, visions, aspirations that the poet has long lived with and often before shaped into verse, but never before with such astonishing and beautiful success. . . .

To be sure, there has never been anything mean about Daniel Hoffman or about the poems he has given us. But every good person and good poet should be allowed his divine discontent. May the angelic Hoffman step from his split shell the just image of all he could wish to be, and may the exile live forever in the country of his choice. (p. 18)

> *John Alexander Allen, "Another Country: The Poetry of Daniel Hoffman," in* The Hollins Critic *(copyright 1978 by Hollins College), October, 1978, pp. 1-18.*

* * *

HRABAL, Bohumil   1914-

A Czech novelist, short story writer, and screenwriter, Hrabal uses elements of surrealism to present ordinary people surviving extraordinary events. His humor is frequently undercut by the undercurrent of impending tragedy. Hrabal collaborated with director Jiří Menzel on the screenplay for *Closely Watched Trains,* **which was adapted from his novel** *Ostře sledované vlaky.*

JOHN SIMON

[The film *Closely Watched Trains*] is a comic view of Czech resistance to the Nazis in which a bumbling youth tragicomically comes of age in sex and war. A dispatcher trainee at a puny railroad station, he has troubles with his work that stem from greater troubles with lovemaking, which terrifies him. The figures that surround him, notably the ambitious but inept stationmaster and a fly-specked Don Juan of a train dispatcher, are, like himself, drawn with a humor so sweeping that it would hurtle into satire or caricature were it not for the intense joviality and humaneness that inform it. Tenderness mitigates the farcical, a certain seriousness gives an edge to the laughter. . . . (p. 279)

I wish I had more space to expatiate about this superb film (I have not even mentioned as yet the fine screenplay by Bohumil Hrabal). . . . The best thing about *Closely Watched Trains* is that it impresses one as unique, indebted ultimately only to its individual genius. (p. 280)

> *John Simon, in his* Movies Into Film: Film Criticism 1967-1970 *(copyright © 1971 by John Simon; used by permission of The Dial Press), Dial, 1971.*

PHOEBE-LOU ADAMS

[In *The Death of Mr. Baltisberger*] short stories combine exuberant, exaggerated humor with an incongruous attention to realistic detail. The mixture is effective for the author's purpose, which is to draw attention to the ways in which ordinary people survive exasperating circumstances. Since Mr. Hrabal is a lively, intelligent, interesting writer, he remains largely unpublished in his native Czechoslovakia. (p. 122)

> *Phoebe-Lou Adams, in* The Atlantic Monthly *(copyright © 1975 by The Atlantic Monthly Company, Boston, Mass.; reprinted with permission), February, 1975.*

["The Death of Mr. Baltisberger" contains fourteen] harmless bagatelles from the Czech author of the novella for the film "Closely Watched Trains," all devoid of any compellingness, direction or humanity. Hrabal seems to share the Czech proclivity for simplistic political satire feebly expressed through surrealistically metaphorical plots—heavy-handed allegories on the insanity and incompetence of bureaucracy which get their entire motivation from the dialectic incongruity of pompousness and mediocrity. These are stories without compassion, without conviction, and unfortunately, because of the perpetual fog of fey symbolism, without meaning. (p. cxliv)

> Virginia Quarterly Review *(copyright, 1975, by the Virginia Quarterly Review, The University of Virginia), Vol. 51, No. 4 (Autumn, 1975).*

THOMAS LASK

Bohumil Hrabal . . . [has] a splendid ear for the trivia, the ephemera that make up so much of our discourse. The conversation at a bar, at a family picnic, even on a lover's walk reveals a design essentially patternless and, when juxtaposed to events of some weight or significance, results in a series of weird, grotesque tales. It is precisely the contrasts in ["The Death of Mr. Baltisberger," a] collection of stories, that hold the elements together. . . .

The key to Hrabal is that though the details are always realistic, the uses he puts them to are not.

The range, in these stories at least, is not wide, and a certain monotony begins to set in. But Hrabal shows an offbeat, original mind, a fey imagination and a sure hand in constructing his tales. I would be curious to see what the rest of his output is like. (p. 46)

> *Thomas Lask, in* The New York Times Book Review *(© 1975 by The New York Times Company; reprinted by permission), October 5, 1975.*

IGOR HÁJEK

Hrabal has his own particular way of looking at or reading the world, of exposing aspects of character or reality one hadn't thought of. It is a quasi-surrealist method, in which everything depends on an extraordinary angle of perception. It has its dangers: it consumes an inordinate amount of personal experience; its disjointed nature makes the development of a synthetic outlook or philosophy difficult (but it helps to avoid ideology); it generates an intoxication with words and images; and the inflexible originality it imposes, similar to that of a Sunday painter, may become too familiar for the reader and a self-perpetuating mould for the author.

A conventional strait-jacket does not suit Hrabal, however. Even *A Close Watch on the Trains,* his most conventional book, is really a series of picturesque episodes arranged in the shape of a novel. . . .

In *Postriziny,* too, he seems to have set himself a task not quite germane to his talent. The book, to which he refers only as "a text", is written in memory and celebration of his late mother, father and uncle: its eleven chapters describe the things they got up to while living in a brewery where his father was manager. The anecdotes dating from the 1920s and obviously handed down by family tradition rather than remembered were not quite zany enough by Hrabal's standards and needed embellishment. At the same time, respect for his parents has prevented the author from giving full rein to his prating. The result of the compromise is that the tone is tenderly evocative, as befits the occasion, although from time to time the strange juxtapositions seem to do no more than stretch a slight and static tale.

Perhaps we have been spoilt by Hrabal and it may be unfair to expect him to go on providing new sensations at a prodigious rate. The very fact that the book provokes argument and criticism places it high above the boring mediocrity of most contemporary Czech writing. . . .

The most authentic Hrabal available in English is contained in *The Death of Mr Baltisberger,* a book of short stories. . . . In this early collection . . . the weaknesses of Hrabal's method are avoided with bravura and its untamed originality is displayed to full advantage. Everyday drabness lights up into exceptional situations, beer talk is endowed with profound wisdom, and literature miraculously reintegrates neglected little eccentrics and outcasts into the mainstream of life. The concise form precludes spillage or thinning of content. In these stories Hrabal is as strong, sparkling and invigorating as Pilsner Urquell. *Postriziny* is just a very good local brew.

> *Igor Hájek, "Brewing Up," in* The Times Literary Supplement *(© Times Newspapers Ltd. (London) 1977; reproduced from* The Times Literary Supplement *by permission), May 20, 1977, p. 632.*

I

IRVING, John 1942-

**Irving, an American novelist, has created in his fourth novel,
The World According to Garp, a critical and popular success.
Irving's central concern in his fiction is human relationships,
particularly familial relationships. (See also *Contemporary
Authors*, Vols. 25-28, rev. ed.)**

HENRY S. RESNIK

Irving conceived a novel that would combine the horrors of
World War II with the far gentler troubles of a youth stumbling into self-awareness and manhood. *Setting Free the
Bears* is the result, and it represents a puzzling, often astonishing literary début.

The puzzling—and completely unresolved—aspect of the
book is its lack of identity with either the Jamesian tradition
or the American mainstream of the 1960s. *Setting Free the
Bears* simply isn't a contemporary American novel; the
language could almost be a European translation from an
original by a European writer.

There are no Americans in the book at all, and the few references to racial troubles in the United States, obviously
drawn in as parallels to the inhumanity of the war, seem
curiously out of place. The tone of the novel, in short, is
determinedly consistent with its setting—Vienna and the
Austrian countryside.

This would be no problem were it not for nagging reminders
throughout the book that something important—apparently
the author's American identity and sensibility—is missing.
More than half the narration is a first-person account of the
adventures of a young Austrian student, Hannes Graff, and
his wildly eccentric buddy, Siegfried. . . .

The first hundred pages, seen through the eyes of the shallow, humorless Graff, betray the novel's principal weakness so markedly that they nearly spoil the entire book.
Clearly Graff is an odd, distorted vision of Irving-in-Eu-
rope. . . .

But then the excitement starts. The long middle section of
the novel consists entirely of Graff's edited version of a
notebook Siggy has been keeping during a few days of lone
reconnoitering in the Hietzinger Zoo. "The Notebook" is a
skillful interweaving of two stories. First there is the struggle for survival of Siggy's parents and a band of Austrians
during the Hitler years, beginning with the fall of the repub-

lic in 1938 and ending after the war. Then there are the
"Zoo Watches," Siggy's nightly observations of the zoo's
activities while he is formulating his plan to free the animals. The night watchman at the zoo is a grotesque sadist
whom Siggy recalls in fantasies as a Nazi taking part in the
brutalization of Vienna. There are many moments within
this section when the symbolic and plot levels unite perfectly, when Irving creates tremendous suspense as well as an
absorbing comment on the brutality of man and beast.

After an unfortunate beginning, Irving proves in *Setting
Free the Bears* that he is a writer of uncommon imaginative
power. Moved by what must have been the awful reality of
Vienna's memories, he has transcended, though not without serious difficulties, the limbo of his European years. He
is back in America now, teaching at a small college in New
Hampshire; perhaps he will decide on an identity and produce an American novel. Whatever he writes, it will be
worth reading.

*Henry S. Resnik, "At Loose Ends in the Vienna
Woods," in* Saturday Review *(© 1969 by Saturday Review, Inc.; reprinted with permission), February 8, 1969, p. 26.*

JAN CAREW

Irving's first novel, "Setting Free the Bears" received the
kind of critical praise that makes one approach his second,
"The Water-Method Man" with a certain amount of caution. But the first few chapters of this new work dispel any
doubts about the sustained vigor of his talent. He quickly
reasserts his inventiveness, wit and obvious ability to devour new experiences, digest them rapidly and convert
them into imaginative symbols and lively literary episodes. . . .

"The Water-Method Man," a rambling, episodic novel, is
held together almost miraculously by the skill of an author
who is a born writer. The reader is bombarded with a surfeit of imaginative images, symbols and events. And after
putting down the novel and allowing some time to elapse,
the characters, the kaleidoscope of events assume a cohesive and even more meaningful form. (p. 46)

Jan Carew, in The New York Times Book Review
*(© 1972 by The New York Times Company; re-
printed by permission), September 10, 1972.*

S. K. OBERBECK

[*The 158-Pound Marriage*] is impressively flashy in episode and style, deceptively arch, and pocked all over with little depth charges of drama that rumble up with an aching, rueful but often hilarious humor. Irving fingers a human foible like a wary teenager feeling for incipient pimples: gingerly, gently, hoping against hope, but secretly stung by that sinking vision of victorious acne. . . .

Irving is an ambitious and clever writer who looks cunningly beyond the eye-catching gyrations of the mating dance to the morning-after implications. (p. 3)

> *S. K. Oberbeck, in* Book World—The Washington Post *(© 1974, The Washington Post), October 20, 1974.*

PEARL K. BELL

John Irving is a young, eccentrically talented novelist with a singular rage to instruct. His books—funny, cleverly written, sometimes oddly endearing—provide a wealth of information about subjects one hardly expects to encounter in works of fiction. . . . [In *The 158-Pound Marriage*] the title and many of the episodes derive from wrestling, a sport that, as far as I know, has been unnoticed by contemporary authors. From Irving's previous book, *The Water-Method Man,* one learned a great deal about a rare ailment of the male urinary tract, and that particular pain in the human condition has also been neglected by novelists in droves. In each case, of course, Irving's pedantic exposition is eventually linked to a subject that does indeed interest novelists—marriage, with all its devious sexual and emotional permutations—but one must wade through a lot of words about wrestling and urology before coming in sight of the human heart behind these awkward symbols. . . .

Like wrestling, marriage takes on the lineaments of metaphor, becoming a vehicle for Irving's concern with the differences between.Europeans and Americans. He is, in fact, highly romantic about his Europeans, who are consistently stronger, more earthy and solid, more attuned to life's mainstream, than his wan, attenuated, overintellectual, naïve Americans. . . . (p. 13)

But although he can graphically convey the special ambiance of a college gymnasium, his characters elude him; for all their sexual energy, they remain bloodless, ghostly lovers without bone and muscle. If, in the end, Irving seems to spell out his lesson . . . , along the way he has lost control of the affirmations his story is presumably meant to offer. Swathed in a tangle of irresolute hints and guesses, neither the wrestling nor the sex bestows sufficient substance or meaning to *The 158-Pound Marriage,* and one is left with a mood of shambling inconsequence. (p. 14)

> *Pearl K. Bell, in* The New Leader *(© 1974 by the American Labor Conference on International Affairs, Inc.), November 25, 1974.*

CHARLES NICOL

The title [*The 158-Pound Marriage*] comes from one of the characters who evaluates everything in terms of college wrestling weight classes; it indicates moderate approval. Although the novel is also middleweight in both size and subject, it is all muscle, all confidence and speed and sure grip. (p. 1187)

John Irving knows what he is doing, and his confidence is reflected in his decision to start his novel with two epi-

graphs, one from Ford Madox Ford's *The Good Soldier,* the other from John Hawkes's *The Blood Oranges*—two excellent novels with this same subject. Irving does not suffer in the comparison. He resembles Hawkes, however, in more than mere subject. His narrator, for instance, keeps the same distance between the reader and the story as a Hawkes narrator, neither directly taking charge of his story nor idly reminiscing but telling his experiences in bits and pieces, framing each event in impersonal analysis and personal asides, eventually coming up to the open present and its possibilities. Never totally able to assess the significance of what has happened but admiring its drama and offering interpretations, slightly lost but trying to be helpful, he still seems to hold something back—not because he is trying to conceal any secrets or mislead the reader, but because he is still within the story he tells at the present and hasn't yet completely formed his own opinion about its importance. Another resemblance is the way the characters keep returning to the college gymnasium with its womblike tunnel. . . . Like the obsessive, pregnant landscapes in a Hawkes novel, this gymnasium is an oversignificant inner mental construct held together more by psychic force than by the rules of architecture, an estranged dream in an alien world of consciousness, a lonely building placed under a spell. Overall, Irving is not quite as sensual, surreal, or mannered as Hawkes, but he has inclinations in all these directions. Both authors view comedy the same way, as a formal dance around the edge of a deep well. (p. 1188)

> *Charles Nicol, in* National Review *(© National Review, Inc., 1975; 150 East 35th St., New York, N.Y. 10016), October 24, 1975.*

JULIAN MOYNAHAN

"The World According to Garp" shows that John Irving is haunted by the high level of quotidian American violence and the vulnerability of American lives. He can't get the frequency of assassination as a method of settling our domestic political and social quarrels out of his mind; and he is tormentedly aware of something like a war on women going on in our society as women's struggle for real equality continues and intensifies. He has not, however, arrived at wisdom on any of these matters. Apart from Andrew Greeley and some other heavy-breathing pundits, who has? (p. 1)

Through its formal convolutions and sinuosities this novel is . . . a sort of treatise on how reality is processed by fiction; it takes a sophisticated view of the relations in art between the imaginary and the actual. For example, Garp writes as his fourth book "The World According to Bensenhaver." It has a lurid plot entailing rape, manslaughter and other violence, and represents Garp's idiosyncratic attempt to deal with the trauma of a terrible, ridiculous accident. . . . The Bensenhaver narrative, an entire chapter of which is included, is obviously a parody of the work containing it. So we are left to ponder the following question: What traumas suffered by John Irving elicited "The World According to Garp," as Garp's traumas elicited "The World According to Bensenhaver"? The fact that such questions are not really answerable, except in imagination, does not make them less interesting and important.

A bit more on this point of the relation of fiction and "reality." Jennie Fields's assassination while campaigning in a shopping plaza evokes the assassination attempt on George C. Wallace during the 1972 Presidential primaries. The woman gubernatorial candidate loses ground in her campaign when she bursts into tears during a public appearance, recalling the famous incident of Senator Edmund Muskie's "womanish" tears outside the newspaper office in Manchester, N.H. There is no doubt Mr. Irving wants us to make these connections. It's all part of his demonstration of how fiction, in creating a world of its own, remains tied by the lifeline of the writer's experience to the world we all share. . . .

[Is the tale told in "The World According to Garp"] implausible? Not nearly so implausible as the actual history we have been through in the time John Irving's fiction covers. . . . (p. 28)

All novelists, if they are any good, want to use their craft to tell the truth. But this aim was perhaps more difficult to keep in view during the last 10 or 15 years than at any comparable period in our literary history. There was the lurid and unending public melodrama, which seemed to put the merely private imagination into the shade unless it went out of its way to astonish and amaze. Academic modernists such as Robert Scholes and Tony Tanner plumped firmly for types of fictional "fabulation" that would outdo and ignore historical reality in the shaping of self-sufficient worlds. . . . No wonder then that a fairly typical young novelist of the late 1960's, Tom McHale, should have remarked . . . , "I am into exaggeration," and mentioned that several young writers in the University of Iowa Writing Program, when he was there, were into, or thinking of going into, the same racket.

The problem, of course, is to know when exaggeration becomes lying, emotional and mental lying, about the world one is struggling to discover and invent in one's fiction. This problem is not well handled in many fabulated works, and drastically limits their value. As for John Irving, who also did time at Iowa, I should say he was on the horns of the dilemma. That is, his new novel contains some febrile fabulations (the wrong sort of exaggeration) in its handling of the feminist theme, yet his instincts are so basically sound, his talent for storytelling so bright and strong, that he gets down to the truth of his time in the end. Especially in "The Pension Grillparzer," a touching work, as good as, and rather like the best of Buñuel, a work of love, realism and wild imagination that is both astonishing and true. (pp. 28-9)

Julian Moynahan, "Truths by Exaggeration," in The New York Times Book Review (© 1978 by The New York Times Company; reprinted by permission), April 23, 1978, pp. 1, 27-9.

ELIOT FREMONT-SMITH

The World According to Garp is a book of dimensions. It is entertainment on a grand, anyway stylish, scale. It is bravado transfigured into bravery—or maybe the other way around. In fact, I think quite often the other way around—which is not to damn, but to wonder. (p. 77)

Murder is a frequent occurrence in Garp (both Garp and his mother die in this fashion), but it isn't about murder really, it's about how to breathe life into life. Mayhem and mutilation are on every other page, but the theme of the book is addressed to making things whole. The Ellen Jamesians can't speak (and Garp himself smashes his jaw and must communicate by notes), yet the novel is concerned with articulation as perhaps the only saving grace. One of the most

unforgettable characters is a football tight end turned transsexual (there is homoerotic awareness everywhere), yet Garp is profoundly centered on heterosexual urges and itches and relationships and fulfillments, and, out of these and beyond them, on families and children. Garp is a true romantic hero: he wants the world safe, not for himself, but for them. . . .

One reads [the accident scene at the center of the book] transfixed in horror. Also with the lips quivering to smile. It's so awful, it's so funny. Perfect justice, and therefore farcical; its appropriateness (in New England yet) is raucous. . . .

Garp's world is so bizarrely and completely dangerous that while one nods how true, how true, one never quite suspends disbelief. Like the accident, everything awful could happen, but that it does is somehow too neat. Part of the manipulation is disarmament by irony—for an awareness of ironic possibility accompanies every disaster, every shock. . . . Garp's second son was conceived as, in a sense, a reserve—in case the first son became a victim of the unsafe world. It is the second who is killed.

So, the world (Garp's) is horrendous; yet his struggle to make it sensible—accountable, as it were, to a human sense of order—is strangely unnecessary. For the world (Irving's) works just fine: It is a marvelous invented contraption.

Another comparison comes to mind, The Wonderful Wizard of Oz. In Baum's tale, you will recall, Toto pulls aside a curtain in the Wizard's Emerald City palace to reveal the Wizard, not as he seemed to be to Dorothy and her companions, but as the former elixir salesman, now working his magic by manipulating a mechanical control board. Part of the lasting power of the Oz story is that while this magic is revealed, made rational, the greater magic (the cosmos of Oz) is left mysterious.

With Garp, however, it's the reader who pulls aside the curtain, and it is not Garp who is revealed at the controls, but John Irving. He is a master magician, and the show is great. But we see too much, and both Garp's dread and Irving's optimism fade away into what one too sharply realizes is an illusion. A grand illusion, very powerful; the book can freak you out. But, in the end, the interest of The World According to Garp lies not in that world, but in the wondrous mechanics of its invention and the deft manipulation—while the show goes on—of our awe and tears and laughter. (p. 78)

Eliot Fremont-Smith, "Blood and Ketchup on the Mat," in The Village Voice (reprinted by permission of The Village Voice; copyright © The Village Voice, Inc., 1978), May 22, 1978, pp. 77-8.

GREIL MARCUS

The most interesting book I've read in the last few months is John Irving's The World According to Garp. . . . Garp is both a family saga and the history of a marriage, and there's more than a little of Catch-22 at its heart; Irving's sense of humor is as wild and brutal as Joseph Heller's, and Garp's opening scenes, which involve the mating of an antisexual young nurse and a catatonic tail gunner, seem like an explicit wink at both Heller and his doomed Everyman, Snowden.

I've read Garp three times. I've liked it more with each reading, and I'm still damned if I know what to make of it.

The book's strengths and weaknesses are matters of real complexity; when the space I need to deal with them becomes available, I'll try to explain why this novel is a literary *Blood on the Tracks* [see excerpts below]. (p. 70)

Greil Marcus, in Rolling Stone *(by Straight Arrow Publishers, Inc.* © *1978; all rights reserved; reprinted by permission), Issue 270, June 27, 1978.*

MARGARET DRABBLE

[*The World According to Garp*] is not merely a book about writing a book: in the first chapters, [Irving's] defensive, distancing techniques strike more than the reality of the subject matter; it is only gradually that the meaning is released. This is just as well, for the book contains almost intolerable pain. It is a bloody package, and if he had flung this in front of us we would have backed away in horror. As it is, we read on, at first entertained, then puzzled, then trapped, wanting to look away, but by this time unable to avert our eyes . . . or at least, this is what happened to me. (p. 82)

It is a baffling book in many ways. Beneath the surface lies a solid, suburban, everyday life. . . . Garp's perceptions of his children, his anxious protective love, his rebellion against and acceptance of this deadly anxiety, are beautifully done: there is a fine scene where, worried about the fecklessness of the mother who has invited his son to stay for the night, he creeps around to spy at one o'clock in the morning, and sees through a window in the lethal rays of the television

> crammed against the sagging couch the casual bodies of Duncan and Ralph, half in their sleeping bags, asleep (of course), but looking as if the television has murdered them. In the sickly TV light their faces look drained of blood.

This sense of death round the corner grows in the novel, and finally dominates it: the Garp family calls it the Under Toad, after a misapprehension of Garp's baby Walt about warnings against the undertow in the ocean. Every anxious parent knows the Under Toad, and I am not sure if anxious parents should be recommended to read this book, for the way in which the Toad gets Walt is really too much to bear, even dressed up as it is in such a macabre array of horror.

The macabre elaboration is, I imagine, designed to diminish rather than to intensify the book's message about the violent insecurity of the world we are forced to inhabit. But Irving's fantasies are so near the bone that three-quarters of the way through the novel I began to wonder whether perhaps there really *was* an American feminist society called the Ellen Jamesians, named after a child rape victim named Ellen James whose tongue had been cut out by her attackers. Lost tongues, lost ears, severed penises, blinded eyes, broken bones, Gothic nightmares, Jacobean melodramas, tasteless jokes about disability: it all sounds like a self-indulgent fantasy, the kind of clever creative-writing-school trick writing that one would go a long way to avoid. But it isn't that, at all.

For one thing, it does have a good deal to say about feminist movements and the changing roles of husbands and wives. . . . More important, to me, was the novel's commentary on what I have to call the creative process, pretentious though those words always sound. Irving has some sharp comments on reviewers who look for autobiography in fiction, and the quarrels of Garp's biographers after his death ought to make one pause, but they don't. It is obvious that Garp/Irving is commenting in the novel on Irving's own literary career: his first novel, *Setting Free the Bears*, was set in Vienna and featured bears and the Vienna Zoo, as does Garp's first imaginative effort, "The Pension Grillparzer." . . . The worlds of Bensenhaver and Garp and Irving are the worlds of the mid-thirties, of mid-career, when a crushing awareness of an accumulating store of memory, most of it unpleasant, threatens to warp and inhibit the imagination. Irving's account of this process is particularly interesting. Unlike poets, most novelists seem to look forward to middle age, and to the fund of experience and observation upon which the older writer can draw: after all, many major writers didn't even start until they were older than Irving now is. Moreover, most novelists tend to look upon personal tragedy as something that can eventually be made useful, turned into grist for the mill; the more the writer suffers, the more he has to write about.

Irving challenges this assumption. His protagonist looks back to the days of visionary gleam, when he could write purely, happily, from out of the air, not from out of himself. These days have gone. Garp, struck down by the death of his son, for which he bears terrible responsibility, looks back to the first sentence of his first book, and says:

> Where had it come from? He tried to think of sentences like it. What he got was a sentence like this: "The boy was five years old; he had a cough that seemed deeper than his small, bony chest." What he got was memory, and that made muck. He had no pure imagination any more.

This is finely said, though luckily untrue, for the novel itself contains muck, memory, and imagination, and the muck gives it a weight that *Setting Free the Bears* lacked. The zaniness has been replaced by stoicism, and the jokes are now black. But there are also tenderness, respect, humanity. I particularly liked publisher John Wolf, surely one of the most appreciative portraits ever drawn by a writer; he smokes himself to death, for his "deep restlessness and unrelieved pessimism could only be numbed by smoking three packs of unfiltered cigarettes per day." Forget the bears: the wolves will do fine. (pp. 82-4)

Margaret Drabble, "Muck, Memory, and Imagination," in Harper's *(copyright* © *1978 by* Harper's *Magazine; all rights reserved; excerpted from the July, 1978 issue by special permission), July, 1978, pp. 82-4.*

GREIL MARCUS

People are dying almost from the first page [of *The World According to Garp*] but by the end the reader is neither bored with death nor hardened to it. Instead, an awful, beautiful aura of appropriateness settles over the novel. It's a strange, *Moby Dick*-like sense of completeness. One accepts what happens to Irving's characters, even though what happens may make one squirm, protest, or feel real grief. One accepts it because one has come to accept Irving's characters: as people, as friends, even though they too may be grotesque, perverse or sensational.

Irving blurs the line we tend to draw between "ordinary" and violent death, just as he erases the line that in fiction conventionally separates "normal" and perverse characters. In most novels we get one or the other, or we find the normal and the perverse in opposition, fighting over the definition of life. "The world according to Irving" might be a world in which the normal and the perverse coexist without ever considering that they shouldn't—or couldn't.

Take, for example, Irving's two most outrageous inventions, Roberta Muldoon and the Ellen Jamesians. Roberta Muldoon . . . is a transsexual. But not just any transsexual: she is the former Robert Muldoon, known all over America as Number Ninety, the vicious tight end for the Philadelphia Eagles. Such a setup gives Irving the opportunity for a lot of comedy, and he uses it: *Garp* is a comic novel suffused with menace and forgiveness. But when one has closed the book, it's clear that by taking the edge off his transsexual by making her transformation absurd—by pitching it on the most distant frontier of possibility—Irving makes us accept Roberta as anything but absurd.

Rejecting her genetic identity as a man, but never really rejecting her identity as the meanest body blocker in the NFL, Roberta comes to life as profoundly as any character in *Garp,* and the edge returns more sharply than ever, dulled neither by clichés nor cheap pathos. Like Jenny Fields, who takes Roberta under her wing in the hard days following her sex-change operation, Roberta becomes the rock the other characters in *Garp* can lean against: she seeks the role and lives up to it. (pp. 60, 62)

The Ellen Jamesians are the most disturbing and pathetic presence in the book. They are the adversaries of Garp, Helen and Roberta; the friends of Jenny Fields, who takes them in as she takes in all female strays who come to her.

[The] Ellen Jamesians seem condemned, by Irving's novel as well as by Garp, as mere crazies, or perhaps as one novelist's attempt to stay ahead of the craziness of American life. But as it happens, Irving sneaks in a scene in which an Ellen Jamesian takes on an undeniable dignity. . . . So the Ellen Jamesians, too, are given their claim on life. That means that none of the other characters in *Garp,* nor its readers, can escape them—and they have a lot more work to do before they finally fade away. (p. 62)

> Greil Marcus, "Garp: Death in the Family, I," in
> Rolling Stone *(by Straight Arrow Publishers, Inc.*
> © *1978; all rights reserved; reprinted by permission), Issue 272, August 24, 1978, pp. 60, 62.*

GREIL MARCUS

Garp is harder to take, and more exhilarating, than one has any right to expect. . . .

[In] *The World According to Garp* life is, more than anything else, intense . . . sharp-edged, and dangerous: the book is about the worst fears of its characters coming true. . . .

[Violence] and death in *Garp* hurt deeply because the lives Irving creates for his characters are full to bursting with humor, purpose, lust, revenge, love, eccentricity and the will to keep promises. The struggle defined in *Garp* is not the hopeless struggle of men and women to beat the Reaper (as "We are all terminal cases" seems to imply), but the struggle of certain men and women to keep faith with each other.

One becomes attuned to what is lost when these people die.

One understands just how their deaths will leave gaps—bleeding holes—in the lives of those who, for the time being, survive them. . . . Irving has written what, these days anyway, is the rarest sort of novel: a long, unsentimental, intricate, unfaked story about people who are basically good.

Garp is about the necessity and the limits of morals, which are seen as essential to a decent life, but which, no matter if you attach yourself to a moral system or draw morals out of yourself, can take you only so far; evil is identified with amorality (not the refusal of morals, but their absolute absence) and represented by rapists, only one of whom is given more than the thinnest presence. Some of Irving's principal characters are stupid, some are crazy, but none are corrupt—and Irving does not make the easy mistake of equating evil with stupidity or insanity. Evil, to Irving, is a fact of life. Good is much more interesting, much harder to get a fix on, much harder to bring off. (p. 76)

[To] say that these people are good doesn't mean good is what they create. They are honest, and intense, and without ever accepting the havoc they may wreak as the price one pays for refusing certain compromises—and such an acceptance underlies most serious fiction today—they try to push that honesty and that intensity to the limit, and to take those they care about with them. It works, too: Garp inherits that spirit from his mother, and his children inherit it from him. . . .

Garp is not sappy, and Garp's/Irving's "We are all terminal cases" to the contrary, it's neither woebegone nor banal. Irving deals with Freud—that is, with our suspicion of explicit motives—by writing as if, yes, motives are buried, mysterious, but no less real for all that: mystery is not a problem to be solved but an element of being. And he deals with mass murder—that is, with the political frame of reference of our lives—by personalizing and privatizing it. One of the most extraordinary things about *Garp* is that while most of the action is set during the time of the Vietnam War, the war is never mentioned, and yet is in the book anyway: the war is in the book the way the war was in *John Wesley Harding,* as a specter of uncertainty, fear, and death, as a specter to which one must respond by refusing to talk cheaply, or act casually. The lives of the characters in *Garp* are touched with violence not only because they produce it, but because violence is loose, appealing, pornographically exciting. As in a war, any act, any statement, can be lethal. But you can't look over your shoulder in every direction at once.

It is the violence in *Garp,* finally, that anchors the book. It anchors the action and the fate of the characters to a reality outside their own, and it anchors the characters to their own reality. Given what Irving has in store for them, Garp, Helen and Jenny could be sappy only if they were able to shrug off disaster, to trivialize it, and nothing could be farther from what they actually do. Rather, they live as if no moment could possibly be trivial. All things are opportunities for humor, dread, and good will, and so they make the most of them. (p. 79)

> Greil Marcus, "Garp: Death in the Family, II," in
> Rolling Stone *(by Straight Arrow Publishers, Inc.*
> © *1978; all rights reserved; reprinted by permission), Issue No. 274, September 21, 1978, pp. 76, 79.*

ANGELA HUTH

It must have been with a pretty desperate laugh that Irving thought up the plot for his richly nasty book [*The World According to Garp*]. Jenny Fields, a frigid American nurse, desires a child but no involvement with a man. She chooses Sergeant Garp, a ball-turret gunner shot down over France, capable only of muttering his name and squirting his aimless seed. His last shot is Nurse Fields's first—and last, too. 'She . . . felt Garp shoot up inside her generously as a hose in summer.' Thus she is impregnated; he dies.

Having accepted such a beginning—which is, indeed, highly acceptable in comparison with much richer parts of the book later on—one gets a brief spring of enjoyment. In the young Garp's childhood, as he is brought up by the resilient Jenny, who works as a nurse in a boys' school, there are some rewarding moments. . . .

When Garp is 19, he goes with his mother to Vienna. This is the Indian summer of the book, before the darkness of boredom and the thunder of repellent acts sets in. Mr Irving knows and evidently loves Vienna. He does not actually run to fine writing, but there are moments of pleasure. . . .

Back in America, Garp marries clever, colourless Helen and we are in for a long spell of a dull American marriage which, in hands less skilled than those of Updike or Heller, make tedious reading. . . . Inevitably, Helen has an affair, and here Mr Irving pulls out his 'funniest' trick. . . . Not content to leave it at that, we are then given a chapter of the novel that emerges as a result from the damaged Garp. It contains the nastiest, bloodiest rape-cum-murder scene I can ever recall in fact or fiction. . . .

The pity of it is that, beneath the commercial blood and lust that spews itself over the book with horrible inventiveness, something of a good writer is struggling to cleanse itself: Jenny Fields is a finely drawn and sensitive character. There are, too, signs of genuine dry humour—albeit blackish—as when Mr Irving has a go at a league of daft feminists who cut out their tongues in protest at the rape of an 11-year-old girl.

Perhaps now he has made his fortune, Mr Irving will consider replacing sensationalism with the more serious observation of which he is capable. Meantime, it would be wise to heed his ill-conceived hero's own words. 'I feel uneasy,' wrote Garp, 'that my life has come into contact with so much rape.' Let that be fair warning to all potential readers to whom the comic riches of that subject may not be apparent.

> *Angela Huth, "Rape Jape," in* The Listener (©
> *British Broadcasting Corp. 1978; reprinted by
> permission of Angela Huth), November 23, 1978,
> p. 690.*

BRYAN GRIFFIN

The World According to Garp was, of course, 1978's *Ragtime*, which is to say that it is the most recent manifestation of the greatest-novel-of-the-decade. (p. 50)

Mr. Irving's previous novels were much shorter than the *Garp* book, and they hadn't attracted a great deal of attention. True, the man was "one of the most imaginative writers of his generation" (Dutton), but then so was everybody else. Clearly it was going to take more than mere imagination to turn Mr. Irving into a major literary event. It was going to take greatness. Let's face it, it was going to take a little naked profundity. (pp. 50-1)

The World According to Garp does indeed have "extraordinary" qualities. Its plot, for one thing. Like so many extraordinary things, the story lacks, shall we say, credibility. That is not necessarily a criticism: John Irving has never been able to construct a believable plot, but he has always tried to make a virtue of this chronic deficiency. Which is to say that, like other formless novelists—Pynchon, Barth, Doctorow—he abandons any pretense at narrative (and therefore psychological) realism, and seeks instead to attract and maintain the reader's attention with random monstrosities and grotesque occurrences, chiefly sexual or violent in nature, frequently both. The idea, in other words, is to horrify or titillate the reader to such an extent that he or she will be compelled to continue reading, even without the promise of any realistic development of story or explication of character. (p. 51)

[Except] for numerous asides concerning art, genitalia, social diseases, and related subjects, it must be admitted that Mr. Irving writes mostly about (a) different ways of raping people and animals, and (b) different ways of killing people and animals. The novelist Garp is sometimes a participant, sometimes not.

Irving's talent is primarily comedic, and his purposes are best served by his dialogue, which is well done and often amusing. It is important to note at the outset that his style as a whole is *not* exhibitionistic, not even mildly tortured: it does not seek to function as a smokescreen for the author's views and perceptions. More than anything else, however, Irving's prose is the prose of a poorly educated man—his vocabulary is uninspiring, his knowledge of the grammatical proprieties is severely limited. He is a child of his time in his lack of respect for lucidity ("Garp was an excessive man," and "Garp felt a peculiar feeling of unfairness overwhelm him"). In Irving's case, however, the sporadic incoherence and the syntactical sloppiness seem to be simply the consequence of the author's unwillingness—or, perhaps, his inability—to polish his output, rather than a deliberate smog-policy. The carelessness, in other words, is in the expression, not in the sentiments which seek that expression. Like all other Major American Novelists, Irving says his ambition is to write "accessible" fiction, and he has done so. His style is simplistic, almost childlike—it is, in other words, what has come to be referred to as "readable." What *Garp* is, is a funny book. Or rather, it tries to be. But it is a low humor, based chiefly on the prepubescent assumption that conscientious vulgarity is by definition amusing.

The immature quality of John Irving's comedic sense is worth mentioning primarily because of its subsidiary effect, which is to conceal, or at least to disguise, the novel's more fundamental flaw. What we are talking about, of course, is Irving's obsession with kinky violence (or violent kinkiness, it is hard to say which), and what concerns us here is the perverse enthusiasm with which many American critics have embraced that eccentric quality. (pp. 51, 55)

The assumption of profundity extends . . . to the moral arena, so that many of us automatically accept John Irving's apparent bloodlust as something more than that, simply because the author's native intelligence is so obvious; whereas, in fact, the bloodlust may be merely . . . bloodlust. (p. 55)

> *Bryan Griffin, in* The Atlantic Monthly (© *1979 by
> The Atlantic Monthly Company, Boston, Mass.;
> reprinted with permission), June, 1979.*

J

JARRELL, Randall 1914-1965

Jarrell was an American poet whose extensive knowledge of American history, world literature, and the universal problems of war informed all of his poetry. John Crowe Ransom said that Jarrell had "an angel's velocity and range with language," and Robert Lowell called him the "most heartbreaking . . . poet of his generation." His best known work is "The Death of the Ball Turret Gunner." Jarrell also wrote penetrating and very readable literary criticism and a novel, *Pictures from an Institution*. (See also *CLC*, Vols. 1, 2, 6, 9, and *Contemporary Authors*, Vols. 5-8, rev. ed.; obituary, Vols. 25-28.)

ROBERT LOWELL

[Randall Jarrell is a poet] whose wit, pathos, and grace remind us more of Pope or Matthew Arnold than of any of his contemporaries. I don't know whether Jarrell is unappreciated or not—it's hard to imagine anyone taking him lightly. He is almost brutally serious about literature and so bewilderingly gifted that it is impossible to comment on him without the humiliating thought that he himself could do it better.

He is a man of letters in the European sense, with real verve, imagination, and uniqueness. Even his dogmatism is more wild and personal than we are accustomed to, completely unspoiled by the hedging "equanimity" that weakens the style and temperament of so many of our serious writers. His murderous intuitive phrases are famous; but at the same time his mind is essentially conservative and takes as much joy in rescuing the reputation of a sleeping good writer as in chloroforming a mediocre one.

Jarrell's prose intelligence—he seems to know *everything*—gives his poetry an extraordinary advantage over, for instance, a thunderbolt like Dylan Thomas, in dealing with the present; Jarrell is able to see our whole scientific, political, and spiritual situation directly and on its own terms. He is a tireless discoverer of new themes and resources, and a master technician, who moves easily from the little to the grand. Monstrously knowing and monstrously innocent—one does not know just where to find him . . . a Wordsworth with the obsessions of Lewis Carroll.

The Seven-League Crutches should best be read with Jarrell's three earlier volumes. *Blood for a Stranger* (1942) is a Parnassian tour-de-force in the manner of Auden; neverthe-

less, it has several fine poems, the beginnings of better, and enough of the author's personality for John Crowe Ransom to write in ironic astonishment that Jarrell had "the velocity of an angel." *Little Friend, Little Friend* (1945), however, contains some of the best poems on modern war, better, I think, and far more professional than those of Wilfred Owen. . . . The determined, passive, sacrificial lives of the pilots, inwardly so harmless and outwardly so destructive, are ideal subjects for Jarrell. In *Losses* (1948) and more rangingly in *The Seven League Crutches*, new subjects appear. Using himself, children, characters from fairy stories, history, and painting, he is still able to find beings that are determined, passive and sacrificial, but the experience is quiet, more complex, and probably more universal. It's an odd universe, where a bruised joy or a bruised sorrow is forever commenting on itself with the gruff animal common sense and sophistication of Fontaine. Jarrell has gone far enough to be compared with his peers, the best lyric poets of the past: he has the same finesse and originality that they have, and his faults, a certain idiosyncratic willfulness and eclectic timidity, are only faults in this context.

Among the new poems, "The Orient Express," a sequel, I think, to "Dover Beach," is a brilliantly expert combination of regular and irregular lines, buried rhymes, and sestinalike repeated rhymes, in which shifts in tone and rhythm are played off against the deadening roll of the train. "A Game at Salzburg" has the broken, charmed motion of someone thinking out loud. Both, in their different ways, are as skillful and lovely as any short poem I know of. "The Knight, Death, and the Devil" is a careful translation of Dürer's engraving. The description is dense; the generalizations are profound. It is one of the most remarkable word pictures in English verse or prose, and comparable to Auden's "Musée des Beaux Arts." (pp. 113-15)

Some of Jarrell's monologues are Robert Frost for "the man who reads Hamlet," or rather for a Hamlet who had been tutored by Jarrell. In "Seele im Raum," he masters Frost's methods and manages to make a simple half-mad woman speak in character, and yet with his own humor and terror.

My favorite is "A Girl in a Library," an apotheosis of the American girl, an immortal character piece, and the poem in which Jarrell perhaps best uses both his own qualities and his sense of popular culture. (p. 116)

"Belinda" [in Pope's "Rape of the Lock"] was once drawn with something of the same hesitating satire and sympathy. (p. 117)

Robert Lowell, "On 'The Seven-League Crutch-es'," in The New York Times Book Review *(© 1951 by The New York Times Company; reprinted by permission), October 7, 1951 (and reprinted in* Randall Jarrell: 1914-1965, *edited by Robert Lowell, Peter Taylor, & Robert Penn Warren, Farrar, Straus & Giroux, 1967, pp. 113-17.)*

JOHN BERRYMAN

[*Poetry and the Age*] is, I believe, the most original and best book on its subject since *The Double Agent* by R. P. Blackmur and *Primitivism and Decadence* by Yvor Winters. . . . It does not, indeed, contain [Jarrell's] most plunging criticism so far, which will be found in his articles and reviews and lectures on Auden, whose mind Jarrell understands better than anyone ought to be allowed to understand anyone else's, especially anyone so pleasant and destructive as Jarrell; these will make another volume. But it exhibits fully the qualities that made Jarrell the most powerful reviewer of poetry active in this country for the last decade; and in its chief triumphs, the second essay on Frost and the first review of Lowell (I mean the first of the two here preserved) it exhibits more.

William Empson I suppose was Jarrell's master. . . . His prose is not so manly as Empson's; it giggles on occasion, and nervous overemphasis abounds; but it sounds always like a human being talking to somebody—differing in this from nine-tenths of what other working American critics manufacture. It is cruel and amusing, undeniably well known for these qualities, which it developed so far beyond Empson's traces that that critic presents in comparison an icon of deadpan charity. But what really matter in Jarrell are a rare attention, devotion to and respect for poetry. These, with a natural taste in poetry hardly inferior to Tate's, restless incessant self-training, strong general intelligence, make up an equipment that would seem to be minimal but in fact is unique. (pp. 10-11)

Lord Weary's Castle was one of the stiffest books to review that has ever appeared. I have reason to know: Jarrell's was not only superior—far—to my own attempt: it is probably the most masterly initial review of an important poetic work, either here or in England, of this century so far. You have to compare it with wider-ranging reviews, like Eliot's of Grierson, of Dr. Johnson's of Soame Jenyns to feel its narrower but harder learning, its similar but submissive strength.

The studies of Ransom, Stevens, Marianne Moore (again especially the second piece on her), more conventional than those on Frost and Lowell, are nearly as good. A fine citation of Whitman, wittier even than usual, seems better now under a new, more modest title than it did originally, because it does not examine, as Jarrell usually does, substance or method or (save for a few remarks) style. This attention equally in him to matter and manner constitutes a development from what is called the New Criticism.

His general essays, on Obscurity and the Age of Criticism, which strike me as diffuse and making points rather familiar, will undoubtedly help many readers. At least the points made are right. A salient truth about Jarrell, for the present reader, is that he is seldom wrong. About William Carlos

Williams's poetry, some of which I love too, he does, I think, exaggerate, and these papers are his weakest; even here he says much that is true, gay, and useful. One of his shrewdest, most characteristic remarks is apropos of a poet one might suppose he would not appreciate at all, the author of the beautiful "Song of the Mad Prince": "It is easy to complain that de la Mare writes about unreality; but how *can* anybody write about unreality?" One cannot but remark the healthy breadth of Jarrell's taste. (pp. 11-13)

[Jarrell's] neglect to theorize about poetry, and to theorize above all about criticism, is one of the most agreeable features of a prepossessing and engaging book. . . . The point is to deal with the stuff itself, and Jarrell does, nobody better. Everybody interested in modern poetry ought to be grateful to him. (p. 13)

John Berryman, "On 'Poetry and the Age'," in Randall Jarrell: 1914-1965, *edited by Robert Lowell, Peter Taylor, and Robert Penn Warren (reprinted with the permission of Farrar, Straus & Giroux, Inc.; copyright 1953 by John Berryman), Farrar, Straus, 1967, pp. 10-13.*

M. L. ROSENTHAL

In [Jarrell's] poems there is at times a false current of sentimental condescension toward his subjects, especially when they are female. But more often another current carries us toward a realization of the ineradicable innocence and pity of the common life in all its alienating reality. This current did not really show itself, as a directive element in Jarrell's art, until the war poems of his second volume. In the first, *Blood for a Stranger*, some of his major themes were visible but neither voice nor tone was yet quite his own. One hears a sort of Auden-static everywhere, with other voices cutting in every so often. In the most accomplished poem of the book, "The Skaters," the voice seems a duet of Hart Crane and Edwin Muir. . . . (pp. 7-8)

Poetically, what is interesting in the relation of ["The Skaters" and "The Bad Music"] is the similarity of their *process*. Each starts in a state of passive melancholy and moves into active despair. Under surface differences of tone and theme, they share a configuration of feeling and imagery. The "mixed-up star" symbolism in both poems projects the speaker's relation to the elusive object of his love. Faces appear as part of a subjective constellation in which confusion reigns, and it is all but impossible to sort out lover from beloved (son from mother) or either one from the shifting mass of other people or, indeed, from the whole objective universe. The pattern of movement is characteristic of Jarrell: a static initial state of sadness; then a phase of confusion that lets deeper depression flood into the poem; and then a final bitter thrust. (pp. 9-10)

What Jarrell forces on our imaginations through his grotesque symbolism is the obscenity of war, its total subversion of human values. In highly compressed form, he has summoned up his subconscious preoccupations and the dynamics of poetic association they generate to make a poem that gets outside his own skin. The conversion process was not simple, though the result is emphatically clear in its narrative movement and in its succession of tones and intensities. Instead of the anapests that launch the first two lines, a suddenly lurching hovering-accent gets the third line off to a wobbling start that helps shake the poem open to let in wider ranges of felt meaning. (Effects of confusion and ambiguity, in rhythmic shifts as in the literal suggestions of language, often have this function in poems.) The brutal nastiness of the closing line refocuses the poem sharply, yet the final effect is not abrupt. The line is in hexameter, longer by a foot than any of the preceding lines. It has the impact of a final "proof" of war's nature as a mockery of all that is life-giving. (pp. 10-11)

The limitation in Jarrell's war poetry is not . . . political or intellectual. It is a matter of energy. He focuses on the literal data of war—their irreversible actuality, and the pity of the human predicament implicit in that actuality. The poems stop short of anger, of programs, of anything that would constitute a challenge to soldiers or to their commanders or to the statesmen who make policy. Letting the facts of war experience speak for themselves, Jarrell sank all his real poetic imagination into primary acts of empathy; ordinarily he resisted any obvious political rhetoric. In "Eighth Air Force" we have a rare instance of his swinging out of his usual orbit to deal with the moral issues of mass bombing. His failure to handle the problem poetically lay in inadequate resources of emotional complexity and intellectual power.

But within the narrower limits of its engagement, Jarrell's war poetry is often superb. In poems like "A Front," "A Pilot from the Carrier," "Pilots, Man Your Planes," and "The Dead Wingman"—the last of these a dream poem, but one that presents the essence of a familiar situation: a pilot searching for a sign of a shot-down wingman—the poet's entire effort is to project the sense of men and machines in action, from the viewpoint of a participant. In all the poems just named, Jarrell has a double aim. First, he wishes to get the technical and atmospheric details in coherent order. . . . And second, he desires to make the perspective that of a living, suffering man. (p. 18)

Both *Little Friend, Little Friend* and *Losses* contain many closeups and vignettes of soldiers: men being classified, a soldier whose leg has been amputated, prisoners, a soldier being visited in the hospital by his wife and baby, men being discharged from service, a field hospital. Politically and historically, the war may have been unavoidable, but for Jarrell this is more an existential than a moral reality. (p. 20)

That Jarrell wanted to suggest large historical and mythological considerations is clear from "The Wide Prospect," which comes just before "The Death of the Ball Turret Gunner" at the end of *Little Friend, Little Friend,* and from the two poems that close *Losses.* . . . (p. 22)

The poems at the end of *Losses* are superior in being free of the long, expository sections, with a forced liveliness of imagery but without driving energy, of "The Wide Prospect." "Orestes at Tauris," the closing poem, was according to Jarrell an early composition written before any of the poems from *Blood for a Stranger* included in the *Selected Poems.* Very different in character from anything else in the war books, it shows Orestes arriving in Tauris after being pursued relentlessly by the Furies. . . . The condition of Orestes and Iphigenia at the end then becomes a perfect mythic embodiment of Jarrell's vision of war as the sacrifice of driven innocents for the sake of a savage, mindless determinism inherent in our natures. . . . (p. 23)

["In the Ward: The Sacred Wood"] is perhaps Jarrell's most determined effort to give mythic dimensions to his theme of the sacrificed innocent in war. . . . [The] style of the poem, somewhat recall the symbolic distortions of thought and syntax of Lowell's early poems—

> Is the nurse damned who looked on my nakedness?
> The sheets stretch like the wilderness
> Up which my fingers wander, the sick tribes,
> To a match's flare, a rain or bush of fire. . . .

But Jarrell's movement does not rip free into Lowell's frenzied piling up of associations and allusions. In this poem, however, he surpasses Lowell in one important respect though he does not achieve that state of passionate intensity of speech which makes the whole language an electric field of highly charged, crackling movements of realization. At each point along the way, as the wounded soldier ponders the symbolic analogies with Christ implicit in his condition, he nevertheless at the same time maintains a basic simplicity and a distance from the mental game he is playing. Unlike "Eighth Air Force," this poem does not press an identity between the dying soldier and Christ. The dominant tone is one of a real man, without hope, letting go though aware of a dream of divinity incarnate—a tone corresponding to the progress of negative heroism in Read's "To a Conscript of 1940." Negation is accepted quietly; this is one of Jarrell's most touching and thoughtful poems. . . . (p. 24)

Jarrell's one novel, *Pictures from an Institution* . . . is an extremely clever work of satire as well as a humanely intelligent book. It is set in a progressive women's college not altogether unlike Sarah Lawrence College, and its pictures of the academic and personal life of all concerned remain extremely amusing. . . . It represents, I think, a completion of his attempt to assimilate his own frame of thought to that of cultivated and sensitive Europeans. The novel is written in the first person, from the viewpoint of a poet who has been teaching at Benton College for a number of years. The real hero, though, is an Austrian-Jewish composer named Gottfried Rosenbaum through whose eyes the provincialism, complacency, and emptiness of much of American education is made, somewhat lovingly, clear, while certain genuine American strengths and potentialities are seen as goods after all. (p. 38)

It is his most balanced work . . . and it helped him gain a precarious personal balance. It was also a self-deceptive balance, a standoff between barely repressed total revulsion and sentimental voting for the triumph, in any one person, of decency over stupidity and mean-spirited worldliness. A variety of sexual repression is involved as well. In the novel, as in Jarrell's poetry, sexuality in itself seems hardly present as a factor in his own thought and emotions or in those of his characters. His attitude toward women is a little like his attitude toward unhappy children and a little like Sophocles' toward "the Mothers": awe, mystification, and, sometimes, a cozy sympathy with a bitter edge nevertheless. The sense of a life ridden by despair that comes through in his last two books of poems is linked with that bitter sympathy. (p. 39)

Jarrell is in his own way as much an exotic as Lowell. The strains of his boyhood are as atypical as those of the privileged Bostonian, and the adult lives of both men have been atypical too. But often in these poems he summons up the world of plain-living, laboring souls and of the hardships and pleasures of ordinary life. The confusing images of his beloved grandmother wringing a chicken's neck, and of the already dead bird still running about in circles, recur, for instance, in a number of the poems. Each is an image of the brutal nature of existence and cannot be separated out from the meaning of love. (p. 41)

Where Jarrell differs from a true *naïf* . . . is in his superimposed notes of observation, themselves simple in tone but implying meditative and informed intelligence: "righteous love" (a note of psychological insight, for the woman's look is a gesture both of self-encouragement and of apology and self-justification); "away from Something" (a note to underline the presence of universal terror); "like a nun" (again, the note of reaffirmed innocence, which is yet "the center of each awful, anguished ring"); and at last the deliberate pointing up of the child's reactions. The easily colloquial iambic pentameter lines run on quite naturally; one hardly notices the alternating rhymes that help rock the movement into hysteria—that is, into the child's momentarily traumatized hypnosis by the impossible thing that is happening. Jarrell uses this pattern throughout the "Lost World" sequence. It makes for a slightly relaxed, anecdotal tone that drags boringly at times but provides a frame at others for effects such as this one. This weakness, in itself, is a reflection of Jarrell's desire to keep his form open to common speech and common psychology—something he much admired in Robert Frost's work. (pp. 42-3)

Our poetry—and it is Jarrell's *poetry* almost exclusively that we have been concerned with—is today struggling in a new way with the question of the role of an active, many-sided intellectuality in essential poetic structure. Jarrell might conceivably have contributed something of interest to his exploration. Meanwhile, he remains a force among us as a poet of defeat and loneliness who nevertheless does not allow himself to become less spirited. (p. 46)

M. L. Rosenthal, in his Randall Jarrell *(American Writers Pamphlet No. 103; © 1972, M. L. Rosenthal), University of Minnesota Press, Minneapolis, 1972.*

FRANCES FERGUSON

If we hope to avoid simple thematizing of Jarrell's work, and also to get beyond the respectable (and even appropriate) confusions of most readings, then a useful point of departure lies in Jarrell's own critical writings. His essay "Stories," perhaps the most interesting prose piece he ever wrote, is remarkable primarily for its unwillingness to yield to any of the dead-ended perplexities and simplifications that are ever-present dangers in the act of reading. "Stories," more a short story masquerading as a commentary on one man's anthology of great stories than a straight-forward critical essay, serves to remind us that Jarrell was not a poet with his left hand, and a critic with his right; like all of Jarrell's best critical essays—the two on Frost and the later one on Wallace Stevens in particular—"Stories" eschews the two basic approaches that criticism on Jarrell has followed. For him, "talking about" literature involves neither theme-hunting nor the discovery of a "tone," a way in which these words might be spoken. Jarrell's celebrated "authority" as a critic begins, on a close examination of "Stories," to participate in the same concern for "voice" that his poems reveal. (pp. 423-24)

In Jarrell's narrative, *everything* suddenly seems to be a story. From the inital use of a dictionary definition as an *objet trouvé* to [his subsequent gloss of that definition], the story about stories has expanded through reduction, so that the combination of logical-positivistic truth and aesthetic imitation which we all occasionally, primitively, appeal to appears instantly foolish. Stories, as Jarrell says, want to do as they please. And although he rehearses most of the traditional justifications for stories in terms of human needs, he keeps formulating his story as if stories had lives of their own. They are a part of us, but other. Even as Jarrell seems to ascribe the most simplistically biological causes possible to our love stories, the story again becomes the elusive agent of the piece. . . . (p. 425)

Yet if the essay "Stories" reads somewhat like a chant of other people's stories, we must keep in mind the fact that there are at least two dialogues here—Jarrell's dialogue with the storytellers whose stories he recounts, and (probably more importantly) the dialogue which emerges as the divided consciousness of the text itself. This latter dialogue may reveal some of the difficulties attached to the whole notion of "voice" for Jarrell's poetry, in which the apparent utility of voice is in expressing a sudden shock of recognition. (p. 426)

Throughout "Stories" we encounter a . . . conflation of third person and first person that makes it appear that the search for individual identity is somehow at issue. We start to wonder about a text which makes the Yeatsian concept of the "emotion of multitude" seem entirely reconcilable with distinct—even lonely—individuality. In this doubled version of things the voice does not make the self present to itself; instead, the voice seems to be performing two functions at once. The movement from the first to the third person registers the unease with which the self continues to be just that—a self; self-recognition, the implication is, is always best when it seems like the recognition of others (or at worst, of ourselves along with others). But the counter-movement, from the third to the first person, demonstrates the appropriateness of Jarrell's story about a sleeping baby's story: interpretation, like the existence of other people, forces an individual to discern the fact that others force existence upon him—a perception of him exists for others even when he does not exist for himself. (pp. 426-27)

Jarrell's examples throughout "Stories" involve "formal" or "structural" principles, of which repetition is only the most striking. Besides the obvious fact that repetition is essentially a temporal rather than a spatial concept, the repetitions within and between Jarrell's examples of stories—along with the essay's initial declaration that it will rehearse what has oft been thought and just so well expressed—create within the text the illusion that is multilingual—or at least bilingual. While writing has more temporal endurance simply because it can reread, the mythology of "voice" rests upon what can be re-said. But as Jarrell elaborates his version of "voice," it is not a concept that ultimately reveals a unique, individual selfhood to the speaker. Rather, the speakers in Jarrell's work have almost no individual character at all, precisely because the (at least) bilingual nature of his texts generates speakers which seem the spokesmen for a collective effort by dual or multiple characters.

It is, however, important to distinguish between such dual and multiple selves within the texts of Jarrell's poems and essays, on the one hand, and "representative characters," on the other. For if, as I have hinted, the awareness of the multiplicity of speakers in a voice involves primarily a recognition of the repetitions in disjunct temporal experience, then the foreshortening that is potential in focussing on a "representative man" may jeopardize the very perceptions on which the construction of voice is based. As Kierkegaard suggested when he insisted that a concern for the future rather than the past was the essence of true repetition, patience—the cherishing of manifestations in time—becomes an appropriate mental frame for this expansive movement of voice. And it seems precisely such patience that poems of "representative men" refuse, in their eagerness to make equations between men rather than to follow the processes through which individual selves seem to overlap in oscillating patterns of force. As a poem like "The Death of the Ball Turret Gunner" indicates, a collective consciousness can be projected beyond the figure of the individual speaker, but, ultimately, all of the members of the collective consciousness are rather undemocratically equal. . . . (pp. 430-31)

"The Death of the Ball Turret Gunner" has long been admired, and justly admired. Yet it does occupy a polar position in Jarrell's work, fixing the limit of omission. The poem so thoroughly manifests the lack of a middle between the gunner's birth and his death—in the life and in the brevity of the poetry—that the time between birth and death is lost. Because the poem presents a man who seems to have lived in order to die, we forget the fiction that he must have lived.

In this poem, Jarrell pays his shocked tribute to the indeterminate forces that produce mere circumstance, which in turn becomes a kind of grisly determinism as it overtakes the speaker, along with his counterparts, the nameless and faceless soldiers who died along with him. But the middling region between birth and death comes to occupy the central position in Jarrell's best and most characteristic poems—poems like "Eighth Air Force," "Cinderella," and "Jerome." In these poems, the initially individual speakers borrow from dream lives obliquely related to their own, and the speakers merge so thoroughly with their dream counterparts that they create new amplitude for themselves in the act of speaking. These Jarrell figures recognize their imaginary analogues primarily in terms of the limitations and burdens which they share. . . . Even though the likenesses emerge from a sense of shared limitation, no grim determinism constricts the speeches of these texts. Their beginnings and endings—their births and deaths—become insignificant as the overlappings of different selves begin to override the individual's concern with his own birth, his own death.

How Jarrell insinuates the dream voices into the speech of the apparently individual characters is really the question of how any one of his poems establishes his particular version of voice. "Jerome," a fine but rather neglected poem from *The Woman at the Washington Zoo,* stands as one of the finest examples of Jarrell's process of depicting an individual by dissolving the boundaries of his individuality. . . . (pp. 431-32)

"Jerome" becomes one of the most oxymoronic poems possible as it freely shuffles conjunctions and disjunctions, until we no longer know where the boundaries can be drawn between Jerome a modern psychiatrist and Jerome the learned saint—or where the boundaries can be drawn between the psychiatrist and the lion.

The physical image of the mirror recurs with great frequency in Jarrell's poems. "The Face," "The Player Piano," and "Next Day" explicitly dwell on the image, that becomes a vehicle forcing the characters who see themselves mirrored to recognize suddenly that they have changed irreversibly and that movement toward death is their fixed condition. The physical mirror denies their dreams of youth and beauty, and sternly locates the reality that they cannot escape from the limitations of their lives. In "Jerome," however, the mirroring is linguistic—a process rather than an image; the repetition of phrases, the substitution of one figure's dream for another's reality, and the cyclical movement of the poem establish an interpenetration of figures so that they reflect mutually in a release from individuality. Where Ego was, there Id shall be.

The verbal mirror in which Jerome reflects Jerome and in which both reflect the lion appears to develop from Jarrell's interpretation of Freud's observations on language; uttering one word may seem an arbitrary choice, but the arbitrary word begins to operate as a causal caprice; as soon as it is committed to consciousness, it infects the words which surround it. In comparing Jerome with Jerome, the poet initially seems to be giving himself up to the randomness of linguistic similarity. . . . Numerous hints of thoughts associate themselves in the speaker's mind, and linguistic contagion has overwhelmed ordinary logical distinctions: "As the sun sets, the last patient rises." Each phrase seems to call up a mirror phrase, but always with a difference; one never quite catches up with the meanings before they shift again in the process of association, so that a parallelism becomes a disappointed expectation. . . . No ego remains in place long enough for it to be fully constituted.

However much the parallelisms refuse to hold—or insist upon holding in an unpredictable fashion—the lines of the parallels perhaps create their most surprising effect when they turn out not to be dead ends. For the poem arrives at an ending which seems as premature as the psychiatrist's arrival at the zoo, in which "The old man walks placidly / To the grocer's; walks on, under leaves, in light, / To a lynx, a leopard—he has come." The alliterative movement from "leaves" to "light" shamelessly displays itself, conscious of its artifice and arbitrariness; but the arbitrary sequence of sound merges with an alliterative pattern that hovers around the object of the search. (pp. 433-34)

The sight may focus on the lion, but Jarrell's use of the lynx and the leopard in pointing to the lion diverts and blurs the focus. It is as if he could not individuate the lion, even in the act of moving toward him. And the reciprocal gestures of the psychiatrist and the lion at the ending . . . also avoid individuation even in the moment of recognition. The lion's motion perfectly fits with the man's, so perfectly that the two motions virtually constitute one continuous motion. In this unity, moreover, we return to the infinite regress of likenesses that shapes the earlier sections of the poem.

Because there are no precise boundaries to be drawn between individuals, the entire poem "Jerome" becomes a "middling" in which the beginning and the ending seems less to delimit the scope of the poem than to absorb themselves in infinitely self-repeating and self-extending association. Whereas "The Death of the Ball Turret Gunner" consists only of a beginning and an ending, "Jerome"—along with "Cinderella," "Eighth Air Force," and "Well Water" —erases its beginning and ending to put the entire poetic effort into the area of the included middle. Jarrell's "middling" becomes not only a process but a voice; it translates the determinism of the mediocre routines which Jarrell perceived in modern life into the possibility of escape from the term which can be limited, the self. As Jerome the saint, Jerome the psychiatrist, and the lion of their mutual unconscious merge into one another, the poem attaches less significance to the "I" than to the entreaty "Pass it on"—without defining and thus delimiting "it."

From looking at Jarrell's manuscripts of many of the poems, one begins to recognize that, for him, the language —even the very letters of the alphabet—seemed a supplemental consciousness, a partner in his enterprise of discovering the multiplicity of voice. Scratch sheets crawl with apparently random letters, traced over and over again until words came as the fuller form of the individual letters. . . . Jarrell's letter plays in his work sheets more radically reveal the Jarrellian-Freudian willingness to impute—and therefore to receive—significance from the smallest traces of forms. (pp. 434-35)

Although the concept of morality is, in some sense, the theme of "Eighth Air Force," one of Jarrell's most impressive war poems, the movement of the poem reveals that moral judgments have become inapplicable. (p. 436)

Because of the baleful implications that have been caught up in the dog-wolf imagery and because of the very vacillation of the moral argument from the "shall I say that man / Is not . . . a wolf to man"—a proposition waiting to be disclaimed—to the limp justification "Still, this is how it's done," one feels the logical security of the speech fall apart; the airman's arguments war with one another. . . . [Although the logical form remains, the fact that the speaker is an innocent, a murderer, and now a judge] erodes what once seemed like a logical appraisal into a moral limbo. (p. 437)

Although forces like the "State" apparently hold grim control over some of Jarrell's war poems, the voice of the airman finally evades all control, as the initially locatable speech becomes a voice constructed by the multiple participants in this unpathetic tragedy. While the woman at the Washington Zoo pleads, "Oh, bars of my own body, open, open!" the airman's body becomes less and less present, so that transcendence or de-incarnation seems irrelevant. What remains is the voice of a choric criminal-victim-saviour-spectator, whose incorporation of all of the possible stationings toward pain into himself is so thorough that moral scruples seem beside the point. On the one hand, it is as if the man destroys only himself; on the other, it is as if all the world would have to be punished if moral judgments were invoked against the untold, interlocking processes of inflicting and suffering pain. And in this poem, the possibility of apocalypse itself appears to be annihilated. The temporal patterning of the merged, multiple voice projects a future of repetition out of the infiltration of the poem's present by the imagined past of Pilate's speech.

Finally, in the poem "The Bird of Night," originally included in *The Bat Poet*, the traces of voice itself as a construct within the poem begin to dwindle away. If in "Jerome" and in "Eighth Air Force" the lion and puppy-wolf emerge as unconscious consciousnesses overlapping with the human, in "The Bird of Night" all vestiges of human selfhood seem to have diminished nearly to nothingness.

Voice becomes a register of the loss of all consciousness, all objects of consciousness and concern. . . . A nature that might be "red in tooth and claw" overturns its terror in being traced out of all apparent existence. The blank nothingness of death has already been appropriated into the being of the creatures, so that the death-bearing owl is a confirmation rather than a disruption of their state.

We are left with only the residue—the poet's written inscription on the page to remind us of the voice which once was written into the text. (pp. 438-39)

Through the course of Jarrell's work, the voice figures less as the presence of an aid to self-recollection than as an evanescent movement. The merger of selves with selves dissolves the boundaries of individual identity, thus freeing "voice" to represent a fictional temporal infinitude. "Voice" becomes the principle of learning how little will suffice, so that finally the text into which voice was written begins to reveal the disappearance of the voice itself, imitating the world which it drove away. (p. 439)

Frances Ferguson, "Randall Jarrell and the Flotations of Voice," in The Georgia Review *(copyright, 1974, by the University of Georgia), Fall, 1974, pp. 423-39.*

PATRICK J. HORNER

Most commentators on Randall Jarrell's "The Death of the Ball Turret Gunner" have identified the poem's theme as a condemnation of the insensitive, dehumanizing power of the "State," exhibited most graphically by the violence of war. Most have also agreed that the poem's effectiveness is due in large measure to its telescoping of time . . . and the paradoxical use of birth imagery, especially of the womb and the foetus, to describe death. In commenting on the poem's final line, however, critics have usually stressed the ironic use of water, with its traditional associations of rebirth, in these mechanized burial rites and praised the emotional power of the understated, matter-of-fact tone, while overlooking the continuing impact of the telescoping of time and the birth imagery. (p. 9)

The telescoping of time . . . omits the actual moment of the gunner's death. Just as the moment of physical birth became merely an anticlimactic transferral of the foetus from the mother's womb to the State's, so the finality of death is reduced to one more stage in the cycle of filling, emptying, and refilling the turret. The manipulation of time reveals the stunning brevity of the gunner's waking life and the State's total disregard for that phenomenon.

The birth imagery also emphasizes the State's uncaring efficiency. For example, using a hose . . . to remove the corpse indicates the body's badly mutilated condition. But since metaphorically the gunner is a foetus in a womb, the washing out of his remains by introducing a fluid under pressure clearly suggests one of the common procedures for ejecting a foetus after abortion. By implication then, the gunner, like an aborted foetus, was never allowed to achieve independent human life. Because of the telescoping of time and the imagery of birth the gunner's understated account of his life and death resonates with powerful feeling. (p. 10)

Patrick J. Horner, in, The Explicator *(copyright © 1978 by Helen Dwight Reid Educational Foundation), Summer, 1978.*

JILES, Paulette   1943-

Jiles is an American-born poet, short story writer, and screenwriter now residing in Canada. Her poetry is noted for its exuberant energy and vivid imagery.

DENNIS LEE

Paulette Jiles' *Waterloo Express* is made up of blues, shouts and meditations at the razor's edge. It's a sometimes electrifying fusion of folk and sophistication. The author is often presented in folk outline: she laments a string of busted love affairs, hits the road again and again to forget, and can talk as sardonic and lowdown as any blues momma. Yet the TNT and agony she drags around come crackling out in images of manic brilliance, controlled by a frequently superb ear. Jiles moves through the imaginative terrain of Plath, Atwood, perhaps Neruda, as naturally as through Bessie Smith, Kitty Wells, Joplin.

The poems go from hillbilly country in the United States to Toronto, then halfway round the world in an outside attempt to ditch the blues, then back to Canada. The round-the-world section is the least successful for me; too many poems consist of a series of knockout images but no poem. And the constant solipsism gets to be almost comical; it simply isn't true that every landscape on the planet is mined with Jiles' pain. Nevertheless, *Waterloo Express* is a gutsy, hard-edge book of real distinction. (p. 34)

Dennis Lee, in Saturday Night, *December, 1973.*

LINDA ROGERS

Paulette Jiles flashes words through train windows. Every poem in her first book, *Waterloo Express,* is a frame in a travelogue. The poems are points in the locus of a journey which takes the character everywhere in search of an author. . . .

The secrets of each new landscape are released with terrific energy as the poet tears through earth and air in the search for herself. She becomes the vehicle she rides, burning steel and cresting waves, learning and looking. In the process, she leaves the feminine stereotypes behind. She has taken over the traditional territory of the masculine romance figure, understanding earth and water, which have no dominion over her. She is always ahead of the seasons. . . .

Jiles is a lyric poet tumbling songs off the high wire where she skips alone. The dizzy music is checked only when she stumbles on the similies she has failed to heat into metaphor. The fantasy is aborted when we collide with "like", the clumsy reminder that we are only riders of the subway and not astronauts. There is no time in Jiles' fast ride for ordinary machinery. The images have a life of their own.

In visual terms, the poems are like the paints of Marc Chagall. Gorgeous disconnected figures float by on wisps of cloud and magic carpets of flowers. All the paraphernalia of life's circus is assembled in a giant mobile moving in the wind.

So much nervous energy is consumed in the effort to organize and move through the jumble of images. It is given off in the music of exposed nerves. The sounds of ordinary life, selected, become surreal, a neurotic accompaniment to the poetry. . . .

In the process of trying on countries, people and suits of clothes, Jiles has become a troubadour. Music is her real

author. It is the sound of the footsteps that keep her walking. . . .

Always she is listening, trying to find some meaning in strange voices; the scream of wheels on track, the noises of loving and dying, and the wise conversation of birds. (p. 122)

Linda Rogers, in Canadian Literature, *Summer, 1974.*

MARY JANE EDWARDS

Although Jiles·. . . uses time to organize *Waterloo Express* and comments on such aspects of it as "Clocks," images and motifs of place, space, and travel also provide some of the volume's most important patterns. Jiles' fascination for such images is indicated in the title and opening poem where the poet hops on the "Waterloo Express," rips up herself and her identity—"there they go—a toe, a finger, my coat"—as the train rips "up the dawn," pares herself down to "one white eye," and heads for whatever "Waterloo" may bring. As the rest of the poems reveal, Jiles' journeys to such places as "Brownsville," France, and Spain bring neither victory nor disaster. She concludes [in "Schooner Cove"]:

> We have travelled so far,
> from indifference to discovery.
> We have become larger and more desperate
> than the government itself. . . .

These lines with their prosaic structure, careful punctuation, ambiguity of meaning, and ironic undercutting both show some of Jiles' most effective techniques and suggest her feelings about her travels. The tone of "Schooner Cove," like that of many of the poems, is one of sadness and desperation. The sadness, however, is controlled and the desperation quiet. Thus, the reader leaves the volume with the feeling that Jiles is still much too interested in the world and her role in it, even in the "government itself," to drown in her desperation or to stay permanently in the cove. It is this sense of resiliency which makes Paulette Jiles' landscape in *Waterloo Express* appealing. (p. 42)

Mary Jane Edwards, in The Canadian Forum, *August, 1974.*

*   *   *

JOHNSON, Diane   1934-

An American novelist, Johnson is noted for her perceptive portraits of women caught in the conflict between individual desires and society's demands. *Lying Low* **is her latest novel and, like most of Johnson's fiction, is set in California. (See also** *CLC,* **Vol. 5, and** *Contemporary Authors,* **Vols. 41-44, rev. ed.)**

KARYL ROOSEVELT

"If you are going to have lovers and a life of freedom and intellect, you have to expect unwed pregnancies and divorces and malice and mistakes," [said N., the protagonist of *The Shadow Knows*]. But just a minute. Is that really what a life of intellect implies? It's hardly a foregone conclusion . . . [and] all this reductive reasoning is difficult to go along with.

We are never told what's responsible for N.'s incredible passivity, why she is so devoid of energy, always acted upon, a constant victim. The only explanation seems to be her overweening guilt, so enormous within her that she must be punished over and over and reminded in brutish ways of her own worthlessness. But the reasons for this masochistic personality are never brought out. We are not told, for instance, why she was incapable of taking care of her children during her marriage. Her husband points out that she couldn't even keep house, let alone take care of the children. She doesn't work . . . and she has no particular burning, thwarted ambition. So what is all this? Is she a psychotic, a paranoiac? Or just cranky and recalcitrant?

In this age of analysis, we have all become psychologists . . . , [but] if the reader [here] must now become an analyst, the author must not withhold information—it's not fair. In order to decide who is the lunatic, the murderer, the rapist, we must have some background, some histories, anecdotes, something to work with. And Diane Johnson doesn't give it to us. Her book conceals more than it reveals—I suspect because she doesn't know the necessary answers herself.

It's too bad, too, because she writes well. She has created a wonderful character in the mad Osella, who appears in the end as a performer in a surreal nightclub act, oiled, nude, immense, "superfemale" and "breathing up all the air in the room." She is able to make us believe in Ev, the baby-sitter, and she seems particularly adept in picking up the black dialogue of these women. She is obviously a careful listener: the conversations flow easily, without strain—we feel we're simply eavesdropping. She handles her difficult material smoothly too; that is, events and transitions are never jarring or unnatural, which is usually the case when violence is introduced. (pp. 6-7)

The attacker or murderer is never discovered, but it seems obvious that N. is her own destroyer. Her acceptance, even desire for abuse, is thoroughly rewarded. In the end she is raped by the unknown assailant . But amazingly, that seems to be all right with her. It wasn't *too* bad. In fact, "I felt happy. Anything bad can happen to the unwary, and when life sends you the *coup de grâce* you have a way of knowing . . . I feel better."

That may be impressive, but it's difficult to like or admire this woman. I think her lover saw his chance [to leave her] and took it. All of this grimy wallowing is not nice; it's tiresome and inevitably, as with some unexplained weakness of character that can't be changed, we grow impatient and simply don't want to deal with it anymore. (p. 7)

> *Karyl Roosevelt, in* The New York Times Book Review (© *1974 by The New York Times Company; reprinted by permission), December 22, 1974.*

A. S. BYATT

'No man knows what evil lurks in the secret heart of men. But the Shadow Knows.' So I am told by an American friend, a Valentine Dyall-like voice informed the Americans before every episode of a radio serial. The Shadow was a mastermind, a super-detective, anonymous, ubiquitous. The claim of the mystery-voice is, in itself, ambiguous. So, I take it, is Diane Johnson's novel, which is a cunning cross between the intensely articulate plaint of the under-extended intelligent woman and a conventional mystery, shading into a psychological horror-story. . . .

N. [the narrator], for all her sympathy with, and intermit-

tent admiration of, herself, is a chilly and rebarbative creature. A good feminist might say she was a typical product of a way of life she is feebly trying to rebut. Horrified by housework, blinded by smeary fingers of entirely uncharacterised children on her glasses, she takes to transformational grammar, about which she says nothing, and adultery, about which she says a lot. Her moments of vigour are those of the unliberated woman—bodily narcississm, a manipulative, masochistic helplessness before lover and reader. . . .

[N.'s] imagination can be seen as a self-referring, self-nourished, proliferating fantasy. All the other people in the book are two dimensional, mediated by her obsessive, self-castigating, self-justifying vision. The plot is in several ways *her* construct. . . . Psychoanalysed Bess claims glibly that the perils of the outer world are nothing compared to the dark abysses of the mind, 'strange powers which drive you into the arms of murderers'. . . .

Here, the dark American Gothic takes over. References are made to the Heart of Darkness. The blacks are at home in the world of Gothic and that of reality. . . . [N. undergoes] an easy, dream-like rape, in keeping with her fantasy-world of passion and violence; and claims, as a result, to have become 'a shadow, a creature of the dark', to have joined 'the spiritually sly'. Morality, as in so many American novels, slides into a dream of evil which underlies it.

> *A. S. Byatt, "American Gothic," in* New Statesman (© *1975 The Statesman & Nation Publishing Co. Ltd.), June 6, 1975, p. 760.*

Diane Johnson's account of the thoughts and deeds of her characters [in "Lying Low"] . . . is sensitive and subtle, but her descriptions of young folk sneaking around with noxious homemade "jelly and jam" (obviously explosives) are not, and the violent turn of events seems an awkward attempt to endow a cerebral narrative with the action of a thriller. (pp. 249-50)

> The New Yorker (© *1978 by The New Yorker Magazine, Inc.), November 13, 1978.*

ROBERT TOWERS

["The Shadow Knows" is an ambitious pseudo-suspense novel] notable for the psychological subtlety with which it traces the sliding of fear into paranoia and for its portrayal of two black women—one a born victim of great dignity, the other a madwoman of grotesque proportions—who are closely associated with the narrator. But for all its brilliance of insight and characterization, "The Shadow Knows" is significantly flawed by a basic irresolution, by the failure of [Diane Johnson] to track down a sufficiency of the hares she has let loose.

By contrast, "Lying Low" seems to me a nearly flawless performance—a beautifully constructed, elegantly written book, delicate in its perceptions, powerful in its impact. Set in the university town of Orris, Cal., it centers upon the four occupants of a Victorian house in a neighborhood that has seen better days. (p. 3)

The action occupies four days—Wednesday through Saturday—that begin with the killing of one of Theo's hens by a neighborhood dog and end with a catastrophe that is at once surprising and plausible. . . . [Many events occur] but they occur naturally, with none of the frantic piling on of incident typical of so much fiction of the hyperkinetic school. It is one of Diane Johnson's triumphs that she can capture and make interesting the sheer "dailiness" of existence within a framework that could so easily lend itself to melodrama. (pp. 3, 70)

"Lying Low" is composed of the mosaic-like juxtaposition of small paragraphs, each containing a short description, a bit of action, reflections of one of the principal characters, or a mixture of all three. . . .

Each paragraph is written in what might be called sharp focus, with almost no blurring or foreshortening of effect. But despite the lack of any headlong narrative rush, one's interest in the working out of the story is maintained at a high level by the skillful, unobtrusive distribution of plot fragments or suspense devices (to put it crudely) along the route of the reader's perceptions. The characters have premonitions: what is presumably the shadow of a vacuum cleaner cast momentarily upon the wall is perceived by Ouida as the shadow of death itself.

The grace, sensuousness and precision of Diane Johnson's prose is evident. . . . Skilled in rendering the perpetual flicker of thought and sensation, she can immerse herself in the consciousness of one of her characters and then draw back to comment crisply upon its limitations. A similar deftness distinguishes her use of dialogue, which weaves in and out of the play of consciousness, often with droll results.

Any reader of "The Shadow Knows" will expect Mrs. Johnson to excel in the characterization of women, and "Lying Low" will more than confirm that expectation. Theo, graceful at 60, bicycling through Orris in her black leotard, tights and a long black skirt with a ruffle at the bottom, is superbly drawn, so complex and so lifelike as almost to defeat analysis. . . . Marybeth is more journalistically conceived, perhaps, but nonetheless a vital and touching presence in the novel. . . . The characterization of Ouida is a tour de force—one that might daunt a less confident writer. Stumbling through the pages in her bewilderment, a compendium of every crackpot belief and superstition that has come her way, Ouida radiates an absurd but compelling charm. She also serves as a prism through which the racial and social anomalies of North American life are sometimes comically, often frighteningly, magnified and distorted.

It doesn't really matter that the leading male figures are less substantially rendered. . . . They function well enough for the purposes [Mrs. Johnson] has in mind. As does Ouida's friend, Mr. Griggs, whose passionate denunciation of the Bank of America and white folks' justice flashes like scarlet lightening across the smoky conclusion of this remarkable novel. (pp. 70, 72)

Robert Towers, "Four Days of Four Lives," in The New York Times Book Review *(© 1978 by The New York Times Company; reprinted by permission), November 19, 1978, pp. 3, 70, 72.*

THOMAS R. EDWARDS

Diane Johnson is uncannily alert to the subtleties of [her women characters' feelings in *Lying Low*], and she has no trouble in showing that the reality they inhabit is quite as dangerous as they think it is. (p. 34)

The book is less successful with, or maybe just less inter-

ested in, its male characters. Anton Wait's artistic and sexual complexities are mentioned rather than explored, and his marginal presence seems mainly designed to set off the quite different qualities of his sister. . . .

Chuck Sweet, Marybeth's beautiful football player from back home, is, as his name implies, virtually an allegorical character. . . . [When] Marybeth speculates that he may be "a designated agent of happiness," it sounds as if even she suspects that a puzzling authorial joke is being made.

But if Chuck himself seems a cartoon, Marybeth's reactions to him make sense. Men are good for incidental domestic pleasures, but they interfere with the serious business of a life like hers. . . .

At her best, with the women characters, Johnson does wonderfully what she can't or won't do with Chuck, which is to imagine the reality of other minds without forgetting their limitations. (p. 35)

Lying Low is an elegantly written and constructed novel, full of a talented writer's delight in her mastery of such things as multiple points of view and shifts in narrative verb tenses. And, though its subjects are somber enough, an equivalent delight comes through in Johnson's keen sense of the closeness of terror and comic absurdity. . . . Diane Johnson's picture of how a troubled past keeps reasserting itself by filling up an empty present with dire ideas of the future is a wholly serious one, but it makes living in such a present a little more fun. (pp. 35-6)

Thomas R. Edwards, in The New York Review of Books *(reprinted with permission from* The New York Review of Books; *copyright © 1978 Nyrev, Inc.), November 23, 1978.*

MARY GORDON

The pall of dread hangs over *Lying Low*—not terror, but something slower, vaguer, the nightmares of a summer afternoon before the thunder when the air is thick, and horror, yet unnameable, hints but does not reveal itself. The success of this novel rests almost entirely on its tone. Johnson speaks in the voice of the observer of the American condition whose data suggests that our only possible fate is to have our throats cut in our beds by unlikely strangers. . . .

Johnson is highly successful in depicting the inner life of this discriminating moralist [Theo] who is proud of her body's good condition as if her body were an animal she had reared, and romantic about Marybeth, the beautiful terrorist whom she vows to shelter even without knowing the specific nature of her crimes.

It may be the central flaw of this novel that even the reader does not know the specific nature of Marybeth's crimes. She floats through the novel, alternately longing for the peace of certain capture and trying to elude it by obtaining a false identity. . . . Johnson's description of the childless Marybeth's desperate attempt to keep [a] child entertained for a day . . . is a wonderfully observed and finely sustained episode. Marybeth's terror when she thinks the child is lost, her relief at finding him, her inept comprehension of his omnipresent physical needs are described with a finely paced precision that, alas, Johnson does not often achieve in *Lying Low*.

The end of the novel, which includes the disaster we have

all been waiting for, comes too fast. The details are blurred, and so is the terror. We ought to have been put through the horror of Theo's end with that same leisure of the postman surveying the neighborhood. I feel particularly cheated at not having had a slower look at Ouida's ruinous *festa*.

Johnson's conclusions are probably correct: disaster will come in precisely the place we forgot to fear it. *Lying Low* is full of ironic intelligence; the issues are right, but Johnson hasn't created characters fleshy enough to embody them. I cannot imagine Marybeth ever having had the wit or the rage to throw a bomb at anything: perhaps living underground for years has a bleaching effect, but this girl is almost lobotomized. And in a story so heavily dependent upon action, plotting is crucial. Johnson's timing is often off, particularly at the end when the shadowy Mr. Griggs tells a story of a Dostoevskian encounter with the Bank of America. It is precisely this kind of failure of justice that makes terrorism seem the only rational solution, but the connection is too oblique when we are waiting for the bomb to go off.

Lying Low is a deeply distressing novel. Jonson has a perfect sense of menace; her rough beast slouches, audible but nameless and he comes into our vision in his heavy danger. But the novel is a difficult form for dread and for terrorists; the kind of expansiveness that keeps it going may be inappropriate to dread, and the kind of detail about characters that connects the past to the characters' present is precisely the kind of detail that terrorists excise from their lives. But Johnson is impeccable at naming monsters; she approaches her nightmare subject with a solitary rigor, assuring us that everything we thought we saw is there, and turning on the lights.

> Mary Gordon, "*Hostages to Terror*," in Book World—The Washington Post (© 1978, The Washington Post), *November 26, 1978, p. E5.*

*   *   *

JONES, David   1895-1974

Jones was an Anglo-Welsh poet, novelist, essayist, painter, and engraver. His heritage plays a profound part in Jones's work, especially in his epic *In Parenthesis*, a unique blending of poetry and prose which draws upon Welsh legend and captures in verse the cadence and melodic quality of ancient Welsh prose. The sacramental aspect of Christianity provides a focal concern for his work, especially in the sense of the signification of an object as symbol in religious ritual, and further, in a work of art. (See also *CLC*, Vols. 2, 4, 7, and *Contemporary Authors*, Vols. 9-12, rev. ed.; obituary, Vols. 53-56.)

PETER LEVI, S.J.

[There] is no other modern English poet who raises such enthralling technical problems, or who (besides Eliot) seems to offer so deep an insight into what poetry is and can do [as David Jones]. . . . He is a unique, perhaps a difficult and certainly an original poet; the reward of his work is a gradual understanding of it which cannot be communicated. (pp. 80-1)

The special flavour of his poetry has continually become more intense, but it was already unmistakable in his long poem about the 1914 war. Since then his subject matter has ostensibly widened, he has become obsessed with the past,

with prehistory, with human tradition and with local *numina;* the 1914 war, the Roman empire and mediaeval Wales have each of them furnished the raw material of his poetry; these themes have been important to him because they are the most present to his understanding of history and of modern life; his poetry is in a way a struggle to talk about the history of the world. (p. 81)

What is special to David Jones is the extraordinary variety and particularity of his language. It can be looked at in two ways: as an expression of all those local and historic diversities which his intelligence sets out to comprehend, and which his poetry does against every convention express, or simply as language, as the construction of a moral context as demanding, as multiple and as strong as that of Jonson's theatre, a concern with the texture of words and their effect on each other like that of figures and colours on a painting in progress, so that it has not been by chance that probably no writer since the time of Shakespeare has brought to bear so wide a range of the English language and such different levels of it inside a few pages. (pp. 81-2)

In Parenthesis opens with exact and comprehensive description: the language is deadpan and empirical, the effect is of gathering tension. The tension increases against the ominous notes of the poet's voice *in propria persona,* to which the darkest and most compassionate themes are reserved, but at the same time the unity of language is broken by phrases of common speech like Shakespeare's and by actual Shakespearen and epic references. There is a certain distancing into an epic and more religious world, in fact into another conception of life, but the perspectives are broken, the language is in tatters, you are startled by the reality and particularity of everything. The consolations of poetry and of religion diversify the levels of thought and language, but they are identical with the tragic foreground. In this connection it is important that the principal religious thoughts and feelings in David Jones' writings have to do with the Roman Mass, which is itself in a profound sense poetic and historical. *The Anathemata* in which this emerges is not so sharp and terrible a book as *In Parenthesis* but there is a certain epic bleakness in it, and even its triumphant passages, like the closing passages in *In Parenthesis,* are orchestral from a vocabulary of dark sounds. (p. 82)

David Jones' feeling for language of this sort is rather like his passion for the proper and popular names of things, which extends from military equipment to the technical language of geology and archaeology. Fragments of dead and dying languages sometimes seem to him somehow magical, and in his use of them they become so. . . .

In his recent work the genuine snatches of remembered conversation which occur in *In Parenthesis* have given place to a compacted language, more economic but less urgently appealing, which is spoken by Roman soldiers and in which a mass of popular traditions is embedded. . . . Already in David Jones' poetry some of the common peoples' sentences are old-fashioned: like the diversities of place and cult that he so treasures, diversities of language are being ironed out. Of course such sentences as "Move them long York loins o'yorn" seem to be unkillable and are always cropping up, but we are committed to the end game of late capitalism, the progress of the world is irreversible, and the popular imagination and popular tradition that have guarded, nourished and recreated this diversity are perhaps beginning to dry up. This is at least a legitimate fear, and the fear conditions the way in which these beautiful scraps and tatters of speech are cherished and reused. (p. 83)

One of the lessons of David Jones' poetry is that with any less degree than his of fraternity and humanity, an epic impersonality becomes impossible. The strength of his poetry is its dealing directly with vast and serious themes; this poetry is very individual, but it should not be seen as eccentric; it was only through a fragmentation of language learnt from Joyce and intuitively applied to the ungovernable memory of the 1914 war, through obscure knowledge and extreme curiosity and particularity, that it was possible for him to speak of this kind of reality at all, to use this kind of word and phrase at all. . . .

[David Jones' poetry] is marked by an extreme, even a difficult precision. *The Anathemata* certainly needs several readings, and one can grasp the precise relations of words only after mastering the material in the notes. Fortunately the notes are most interesting even if there were no text, so this is not a painful process. Any poet who needs to be precise and particular over an enormous range of language as well as facts must necessarily make such a demand. (p. 85)

There are parts of *In Parenthesis* which I personally find it unbearable to read often and which I cannot read without tears. The context that is built up operates in the way of all poetry, resting its prolonged force on what had seemed simple phrases. A sentence that in its context takes on a frightful power is the ordinary military order 'And don't bunch on the left for Christ's sake.' It comes as a sudden and therefore startling piece of direct speech at a moment of tight tension, and the oath breaks the surface of the language in both a very dramatic and another way. (pp. 86-7)

There is an instructive contrast between David Jones and a very different writer, but one of the few certainly great modern poets, Constantine Cavafy. Cavafy's language is individual, and although he is a thousand miles from Joyce and had not, I suppose read Laforgue, he does (for different reasons) write on more than one level of language at a time. Also he writes about the late Roman world, his principal source being Gibbon's *Decline and Fall.* A seminal book for David Jones must I think have been Spengler's *Decline of the West,* which he has certainly not followed at a theoretic level, but the disturbed visions of which have perhaps haunted him. Cavafy writes with economy, and a rumbling, very strong irony, through which he breaks with direct and startling personal speech, and a sensuous power which in its way is without parallel. Each of these elements can exist only because of the others, and they strengthen and sharpen each other. . . . David Jones' Romans are old soldiers of the Boer War or 1914; their language is strong and strange; things are lightened or darkened not by the heroic past but by what is numinous, local and sweet, a reminiscence of a Welsh or British hill-cult; what they do is as terrible as what is done to them; it is the difference between Alexandria and North Wales: the contrast is not one of merit. (p. 87)

Peter Levi, S.J., "The Poetry of David Jones," in
Agenda, *Spring-Summer, 1967, pp. 80-9.*

DAVID BLAMIRES

[*The Anathemata*] is an attempt to create a kind of *summa* of poetic experience ranging through the world and time and has much in common with Pound's *Cantos.* The *Weltanschauung* of *The Anathemata* is one of a magnificent diversity, fundamentally optimistic and beautifully ordered. It is a coherent vision and one which—in contrast to much modern poetry—sees integration rather than disintegration as the chief characteristic of life.

The Anathemata is a work which defies attempts at classification. It shares the qualities of chronicle, epic, drama, incantation and lyric and is at the same time none of these and more than all put together. The poet himself defected in his own description of it as 'fragments of an attempted writing', and yet this does contain a necessary truth. He is right to call it an attempt—an attempt at a vision of Britain. . . . What distinguishes the *Cantos* or *Finnegans Wake* or *Ulysses* and *The Anathemata* is the fact that they are attempts to depict a *universum;* they represent a totality including the whole of history. This historical perspective, if the word is not too external in its connotations, is the animating force of *The Anathemata,* but it needs to be analysed before it can be properly understood. Wittgenstein said of philosophy that 'the problems are solved, not by giving new information, but by arranging what we have always known', and David Jones's 'attempted writing' can also be seen in these terms. He uses the data of history, the ever-accumulating fund of knowledge, and arranges them in such a way as to make them point to the dignity of labour in the diverse service of man and God. This last sentence puts brusquely and crudely one vital aspect of the poet's work, not only in *The Anathemata,* but also expressed in various essays, especially 'Art and Sacrament' and 'The Utile'. Nevertheless, it is important to be aware of this from the beginning, since the vision with which we are confronted is both strikingly positive and through and through Christian, two exceedingly unfashionable qualities for the mid-twentieth century. Perhaps only one firmly and deeply rooted in the Catholic tradition and with a keen awareness of what human creation demands could mould 'what we have always known' into a work of such subtle dimensions as David Jones has achieved. (pp. 101-02)

[In] his long preface to the book the poet quotes as shedding light on his own work a remark from the introduction to Nennius' *Historia Brittonum:* 'I have made a heap of all that I could find.' As regards the subject-matter, this is probably the most accurate summary, but St. Irenaeus provides the best antiphon—if I may use that ecclesiastical metaphor—on the techniques of organization of the subject-matter: '*Nihil vacuum neque sine signo apud Deum*'. This dictum of a second century saint marks above everything the continuity of the tradition in which David Jones stands. In the Christian scheme the signs are, of course, related to God and Christ but the *Correspondances* of Baudelaire in substituting nature shows the continuing attractiveness of the idea apart from its specifically Christian use. It needs no special insight to point out that the sign, under the more usual name of 'image', is the most widely known and used device of poetic technique, but there are few writers who have explored and almost systematized its use with such telling effects as the author, who would probably prefer to be called the maker, of *The Anathemata.* The very word chosen as the title, glossed with such loving care and at such length in the preface . . . is indicative of the many strands of thought running through the fabric of the poet's vision. . . . (p. 103)

There is no clearly conceived centre to the work, or rather ... the poem is a circle whose centre is everywhere and whose circumference is nowhere. For the important substance of the poem is to be found at every point in it. The direction and intention of the words are apparent from the start. The act of creation, the 'efficacious sign', is hymned in the very first words . . .:

> We already and first of all discern him making this thing other. His groping syntax, if we attend, already shapes:
>
> ADSCRIPTAM, RATAM, RATIONABI-LEM . . . and by pre-application and for *them,* under modes and patterns altogether theirs, the holy and venerable hands lift up an efficacious sign.

There is thus an extreme fluidity in the poem's structure of ideas. It is more like the sea with rivers running into it and islands than any building no matter how complicated; it is like the 'riverrun' of *Finnegans Wake.* And yet there are principles of construction about the work, as the division into eight named sections most clearly shows. (p. 107)

The Anathemata is concerned with both diversity and order, and it is intensely preoccupied with the particular. There is a precision and deliberateness about its language that exactly merits being called 'chiselled'. The details of observation, juxtaposition and association are, however, not there merely for themselves, but express beyond that an intuitive, even mystical knowledge of the oneness of life. The described object, the fragmentary quotation, the liturgical mood point beyond themselves; they are the signs and symbols of a fundamental harmony and unity. (p. 111)

> *David Blamires, "The Ordered World: 'The Anathemata' of David Jones," in* Agenda, *(Spring-Summer, 1967, pp. 101-11.*

SAMUEL REES

[David Jones's conversion to Catholicism in 1921] seems to have come about not through deep psychic struggle, not through pangs of conscience or intense sense of personal need, but through aesthetic theory. It was deep intellectual curiosity and critical investigation of the origins and continuing meaning of the arts, rather than concern for the soul or eternity, which brought Jones to his decision. . . . [His] Catholicism is secondary to his Welshness, though the two are mutually complementary and integrated wholly in his art. All of Jones's life and work was to be directed to the fulfilling of his vision of Catholic ideas in art; his poetry, particularly that following *In Parenthesis,* is a tenacious and dedicated affirmation of his Catholic subscription. (pp. 19-20)

[The essay "The Myth of Arthur" is a major piece] and displays erudition and scholarship of a uniquely imaginative variety. That is, Jones is concerned not merely to trace in chronological fashion the origins and various renditions of the story of Arthur, but more importantly to weave among those sources of "historical mythus" to see what significance the myth has had in Western history and if and how it can be seen to retain significance for moderns. He touches upon or reviews, as it were, the varied theories in scholarship as to the origins of Arthur, but his own contribution is not to quarrel with or quibble over details of "fact" or chronology or influence or literary "borrowing"; rather it is

to enquire and attempt to answer just "how came this ruling-class Romano-Briton . . . to be the focal point of medieval romance in Britain, France, Germany, indeed all the West?" . . .

Jones is concerned not to elevate Arthur in a narrow nationalistic way, but to see him in his many shapes. . . . (p. 37)

The Arthurian material is not for Jones of mere academic interest; it is one of his most important background sources and referents. But beyond even that it is central to his whole vision of man in twentieth-century civilization. . . . Jones proposes that in the figure of Arthur-Christ, "from the machine age the strayed machine-men may create a myth patient of baptism." . . . It is at least his hope. He does not consciously promote himself as a modern Malory or as the poet best qualified by ancestry or history to revitalize Arthur for his time, but the qualities he perceived in Malory are the standards he set for himself. . . . (p. 40)

Jones can be described as neither literary critic nor historian, though the prose writing in *Epoch and Artist* include a great deal of history, political and literary, and he does occasionally make judgments of the writings of other artists. He was not a social critic, nor was he a professional theologian or philosopher of aesthetics. He was a practicing artist, a practicing Roman Catholic; and while he enlisted the language of one subscription in support of the other and applied the language of both to the outer world, the war, specifically, and his "civilizational situation" in the world of technocracy, he did not invoke them on behalf of capitalized High Culture or political morality or action. He was both Welsh and British without being intense and chauvinist. Art for him is not to be seen as a trickle-down system; it is the one great equalizer, the one possession common to all men, the sole valid mediator between God and man. (p. 48)

In many places *In Parenthesis* reads like a traditional prose novel. That is, characters act and react in normal, realistic ways; they speak and are spoken to, command and obey; think of past, present, or future; muse, daydream, have the requisite bodies, souls, and spirits. Time passes apace as directed by the author; conventions of grammar and syntax prevail; and the controlling hand of an omniscient narrator is firmly in evidence. . . . There is, however, another style much in evidence: rapid-fire, idiomatic, unidentified by speaker, a confusion of voices all clamoring for attention. This, too, is a kind of "realism". . . .

And again there is a highly allusive, esoteric, and "scholastic" poetry, far removed (by the test of realism) from the idiom of private soldiers' speech in the trenches but carrying a special burden of mythic reference and meaning. . . . (p. 53)

[*In Parenthesis*] in some senses can be described in familiar, conventional terms. That is, it has purposeful movement in time and action, recognizable human characters and landscape, and a definable subject of man at war. It is arranged broadly in a linear, chronological sequence, and details the movement of a group of men in arms of all ranks from the staging grounds in England (Part 1) to their destiny seven months later in the trenches at the Somme (Part 7). . . . Jones uses, and uses with careful artistry, all the devices available to the modern poet and novelist: flashback and ahead, the "free association" of stream-of-consciousness writing, shifting point of view, abrupt juxtaposition and interpolations of speech, image, character, and scenes, which is to say nothing of his allusions to centuries distant persons and events and use of words and phrases from Latin, Welsh, French, and German.

Private 25201 Ball standing in, as it were, for Private David Jones in memory, is the central figure, but "protagonist" is too strong a word to describe his role, and he is certainly not a "hero" in any traditional sense of the word. . . . The point, and it is an important distinction, must be made that the relative "importance" of the characters lies not in their perceived relationships and dealings with each other but in the attention David Jones pays to them, the use he makes of them, as voices or recording sensibilities. They are made to bear a heavy load of referential mythic weight, and the problem Jones has posed for himself is to see that their immediate, recognizable humanity is not diminished or obscured by their other, more "poetic" uses. *In Parenthesis* bears no resemblance to a "fox-hole" novel in which characters learn to live, love, hate, fight, and perhaps die together and in which the reader is given characteristic or stereotypical "specimens." . . . "Archetypal" serves better to describe Jones's semifictional creations; the racial or mythic ancestry that Jones provides for them places them in the whole history of recorded time; they share the human psyche of the soldiers at Catraeth, at the Crucifixion, at Malplaquet, at Harfleur, wherever man has organized war against his own kind.

In Parenthesis is a poetic enactment of tradition and the individual in war in which today's action modifies our concepts and understanding of history and its wars, in which the actions and thoughts of David Jones's Private Ball modify our understanding of all the Privates Ball of the past, even as they of the recoverable past exert an inexorable influence on behavior today. David Jones is not a reporter, an admiring spectator, not a public-relations man for pacifism or for militarism. In chronicling the action of which he was a part, he does not seek to be an epic poet singing hymns of battle in which new heroes reenact the earth-shaking deeds of their ancestors. Without apology or special pleading, he details from intimate firsthand acquaintance with the present—and from affectionate intimacy with historical man —the minds and actions of those compelled, for whatever reason, whatever "accidents" of history and geography, to go "once more into the breach." *In Parenthesis* is not a poem either to provoke or to end a war . . . except as it adds to the accumulation of testimony to the stupidities and brutality of history that each age must learn from or, more likely, ignore. (pp. 54-6)

[In addition to the military chain of command, there is] another parallel institution, coexistent, and ultimately of a higher order, that is introduced in Part 1, and it is one which, by repeated reference throughout the poem, is to become unmistakable, all-pervasive. This is the liturgical or religious order of things, and is to be discerned first in the identification of "the silence peculiar to parade grounds and refectories" and in such language as "the liturgy of a regiment departing." (p. 57)

In Parenthesis is, as Jones intended, a "shape in words," the color, agony, humour, irony, tedium, violence, sacrament, the experience of the war "re-presented." Familiar, unfortunately, in its subject, it is unique in its telling. The art is grounded firmly in Jones's personal experience, and in language has that "necessary liaison with the concrete"

that Jones so admired in Malory. The result abides quibblings and demurrers about technique or "difficulty"; it is one of the most important pieces of writings to have come from the 1914-1918 War. (pp. 72-3)

The Anathemata does not have the confined narrative structure or the clear identification with classical epic of *In Parenthesis;* more ambitious, certainly, than that work, it attempts something approaching the whole cultural history of the British Isles. "What I have written has no plan, or at least is not planned," Jones writes; "if it has a shape it is chiefly that it returns to its beginning." . . . To read it is to engage, in a rare, esoteric way, from a most learned and demanding tutor, in a course in Western Civilization, which is something other than learning the sites of famous battles in Greece and being able to recite, in order, the rulers of Rome and the kings and queens of England. Ideally, it is to discover via surviving art and artifact and written word, and with application of all the modern insights and methods of literary study, anthropology, comparative religion, and linguistics, the essential human heritage that is ours. . . . The whole gesture of the poem, its whole rhetoric, is in the way of a question, or the putting, as it were, of a proposition, It lacks, deliberately, that purposeful grounding in experience, that kind of "necessary liaison with the concrete" that so informed *In Parenthesis;* in *The Anathemata* the intimate bodily apprehension of the trench experiences gives way to intellectual and spiritual musings and probings of the "Real Presence," as it were, of the Roman Mass.

Even with the aid of the preface and the "apparatus," *The Anathemata* remains for most a difficult poem. . . . Footnotes are lavish; they are prominently (if conveniently) displayed at the bottom of the page, where possible; in other instances they run to occupy a page and more in their own right. The thirty-four-page preface appears a little foreboding; seven of the nine illustrations are inscriptions in Latin. There is a total of 244 pages, which is a forbidding number for most twentieth-century readers of poetry. And there is the appearance of the poem on the page, seemingly the freest of free verse, with odd, irregular line length, and some prose narrative interspersed. The language is always demanding; not only are there words taken intact from Latin, Greek, German, Anglo-Saxon, and Welsh, but there are also words in English that are hardly commonplace. . . . The allusions, even when elucidated by footnote, are rare and esoteric. . . .

The poem is partially autobiographical in that it is composed of the meandering thoughts, the persistent, groping questions of a mind very much like and to be identified with David Jones's. . . . The progress of [the Mass] provides one of the poem's unities; each prescribed gesture and act performed by the priest stirs thoughts in both the conscious, and all levels of subconscious, states of the silent observer-worshiper. Another unity is provided by the chronology of events covered by this quasi-free associative method, the history of the world from the farthest reaches of pre-history to the local history of Britain—Wales, in particular—and the promise of a redeemed future first made possible for Britain by the coming of Christianity. These larger outlines enclose, define, and carry the poem, though there are other themes and subthemes which persist throughout. (p. 75)

The preface to *The Anathemata* is one of Jones's most important essays in its own right, to be included with "Art and Sacrament" and "The Myth of Arthur" as central to an understanding of his mind and work. Its importance lies far beyond its worth as an introduction to the poem, the "fragments of an attempted writing" that make up *The Anathemata*. For in the preface Jones gathers his crucial ideas . . . concerning the nature of all art and of his own intentions and practice as a poet. (pp. 76-7)

For Jones the word ["anathemata"] is nearly synonymous with the Welsh *"anoeth"* or the "deposits" of one's culture, which are not necessarily, though the term might include, archaeological findings or artifacts. In the larger sense, man's "anathemata" define all that legacy of man that is his, that is he. (p. 77)

The Anathemata is a devoutly religious poem, and the preface is intended finally as prologue to that poem and, by extension, to all of Jones's works, his artifacts, his deposits remade into things *sacra*, gathered and offered as the poet's Mass—not for the remission of sins but for art's sake, which is to say, for man's sake. (p. 81)

Clearly, it is the whole of human history and prehistory as perceived and experienced by Western man that is Jones's province in *The Anathemata*. In intention and performance the poem will withstand criticism's severest, most demanding tests of high seriousness and moral exactitude. In intention and performance it is governed, however, by the restrictions of its religious and national bias or authorial predispositions. To say this is not to use the word "restrictions" pejoratively; it is to isolate for further examination the conditioning forces working on, in, and through the poem that Jones, before anyone, would acknowledge. What makes *The Anathemata* significant, and significantly different, are two determining factors: first, it is informed and defined throughout by a Christian, or, more exclusively, a Roman Catholic point of view; and second, Jones is writing as a Welshman, a London Welshman.

The cross and the unnamed priest at the altar occupy the sacramental center of the poem; the island of Britain and the poet, David Jones himself, occupy the geographical center. Standing, as it were, with one foot in Wales, one in London, is the poet, who is celebrant, or at least silent and attentive observer, at the Mass. . . .

The Anathemata is a verse rendering of, a demonstration of, both a theory of poetry and a body of belief about the nature of man. . . . At its widest scope [its story] is the story of mankind on earth, his emergence from the reaches of prehistory, from rocks and caves that he decorated, as at Lascaux, adorning burial sites gratuitously, creating objects that are beautiful to an extrautile degree, and continuing, still an artmaker, to the wasted present, "at the sagging end and chapter's close." For David Jones, inextricably bound up with man's persistence as an art-making creature is the smaller story, that is potentially of infinitely wide, eternal scope, which is the "one tale to tell" of man's redemption by the gratuitous intercession of Christ on the Cross. At the center of *The Anathemata* is that cross, the "Axile Tree." . . . [Christ] validated the cross as man's artwork; Christ being lifted up made an efficacious sign, made "anathemata" of his own body. (pp. 95-6)

Jones's concern is to go beyond, if it is possible, the Mass as "merely" celebratory of the body and blood of Christ, and to see it as signifying the whole odyssey of the human experience on earth. Whether one believes that the events recorded in the Christian gospel actually happened or not,

or whether or not he believes that Christ was the Son of God, as He claimed to be, really matters little, for Western man's whole being, his history, his ancestry, his *"res,"* is wholly bound up in the myth. Jones establishes in *The Anathemata* that the art of the first Eucharist at the Last Supper redefines all preceding art, even as it was an act that with all its reverberations and implications transformed succeeding events and imparted a unique and new order to Western myth, legend, and history. The poem's last lines lead us from this present time . . . back again to the Creation, to the oreogenesis of foretime. While the final event referred to is the Crucifixion, that act is to be seen as the confirmed and eternally valid lifting up of a sign that actually resignifies events that preceded it. (pp. 96-7)

[If] man is distinguished from the angels and the beasts by his ability to create art, he is distinguished further by his lone passion for organized mass violence. *In Parenthesis* tested the military and liturgical forms of order and found them lacking, with neither efficacy for salvation nor effectiveness for survival. The Queen of the Woods, the great earth-goddess, the eternal female principle venerated by myth throughout the centuries, alone could restore order—but *post mortem*. In *The Anathemata* Jones renominates and celebrates the liturgy as the redemptive order for the living, as an art form. (p. 97)

In intention and scope Jones's poem is truly epic and might be said to rival in ambition Milton's attempt to "justify the ways of God to Men" for an age which urges art to be at the service of the ego, the State, or itself. In Jones's scheme of divine and universal things, "art for art's sake," were he to endorse Wilde's phrase, would reverberate with the utmost seriousness. In the Eucharist is central order, the ordering principle of art. . . . (pp. 97-8)

It is very difficult with David Jones to speak of sequential "progress" or "development" in his work. . . . Jones was past forty when his first written work was published, and he was by that time a mature artist, thinker, Catholic, man. Clearly there was a major step forward in *The Anathemata* (1952), but the fragments of *The Sleeping Lord* volume, variously dated from 1937 to the time of his death in 1974, do not submit to chronological discovery or ordering. The poems published in the twenty post-*Anathemata* years represent less an advance of theme or perspective than a backing and filling in of detail; each fragment has its place in the tapestry that is Jones's life-work. . . . [The] poetry is in the detail, often surprising, always precise in its concrete sign and evocation. The best of these fragments—"The Tutelar of the Place," "The Tribune's Visitation," "The Hunt" (happily one each from the mythic, Roman, and Arthurian groups)—succeed in that precision of frame, action, language, and perspective; it is not just that they are shorter or simpler than the epics. . . . [The] fragments of *The Sleeping Lord* point to, open up, and provide an access to *The Anathemata*. (p. 120)

Jones shares with Eliot and Pound a verse style characterized by its eschewal of clear narrative continuity, and by its use of esoteric allusions, abrupt juxtapositions, relative freedom in language(s), idioms, syntax, and verse forms. But with Pound the comparison stops quickly. "Cantos" is a term far more elevated than "fragments," and there is no shortage of them. In total conception they are perhaps a far more ambitious undertaking, though to what end they point or what solution they propose is far from clear. More documentary than doctrinal, Pound has no patience to try to rescue Western civilization, . . . and there is a world of difference between the poet who idealized Mussolini and David Jones, whose vision is of a resurrected King Arthur *cum* Christ. (p. 136)

Jones might well have admired Pound's techniques, though he did not read Pound until after publishing *The Anathemata* and did not write on him. He shares with Pound the practice of yoking violently together the idiom of the common man and the highly allusive esoterica of the scholar; but Jones's "low" idiom is never as low as Pound's, nor does he reach out to such diverse connections as [Pound's] . . . ; nor does he parade himself as did Pound. . . . The fundamental difference between Jones and Pound lies, I think, in their vision, which might start from the observation that the civilization lies in ruins but proceeds in radically different ways to establish what must be preserved. For Jones, the "answer" lies wholly within the Western tradition—of monarchy, Celtic matriarchy, deep-rootedness, and Christianity; and in that context his immediate mentor is T. S. Eliot. (pp. 136-37)

The "I" that might be the poetic voice of David Jones is scarcely ever discernible at all [in contrast with Eliot's voice throughout his poetry]; and there is scarcely a discernible public "I" of David Jones that would contend with or even be acknowledged in the same context as Eliot's—the voice of the editor, reviewer, essayist, and critical sage of the century. The interrogative voice and voices of *The Waste Land* have their equivalents in *The Anathemata,* but Jones's verse does not "testify" as does Eliot's to his conversion and its efficacy. . . . Jones is not concerned to exercise aloud the question, "What must I do to be saved?" . . . The *Four Quartets* are simultaneously personal and confessional and allusive and "historic," whereas Jones rigidly eschewed the personal pronoun "I." . . . [Surely] the "I" has a mediating function. It appears in Jones only in his prefaces and notes and occasional essays; Eliot learned to integrate it with his meditations on the past in the poetry. This is to point out the differences between the poets, in their most mature, sustained works, not to insist that Jones should have "imitated" Eliot; perhaps finally it is not the autobiographical "I" so much as a firm narrative stance or voice which serves as other than a masked exhibitor of historical deposits that is lacking in much of Jones's work. (pp. 137-38)

Joyce was both Catholic and Celtic, like Jones; also like Jones, his medium had to be English. . . . [For] Jones the perceived greatness of Joyce lay in his "proper understanding of the Catholic mind . . ." . . . . (p. 139)

Jones was by contrast far more self-critical and diffident, as the whole publishing history of his "fragments" in various stages of noncompletion testifies. Having once marked out the plot of ground he was to explore for further excavation and refining, Jones was the most patient and fastidious "propspector." He was that kind of loner or exile from the workaday concerns of the civilization he wished to reclaim. Both poets (the distinctions between poetry and prose being as blurred in Jones as in Joyce) were the products of those historical "accidents" which made them occupy "as it were junctional or terminal positions" in their time. (p. 140)

Jones lacks perhaps that truly radical energy that is so characteristic of Joyce's writings; he recognizes full well the

authentic *signa* of the past, presents and re-presents them, justifies them, pleads for them. The remaining critical question is whether or not he succeeded in reinvigorating them and charging them anew with "instress." There have been few writers of this or any age so resolutely uninterested in matters of public reputation or recognition. David Jones's life work is finally his testimony to this central credo: "We were then *homo faber, homo sapiens* before Lascaux and we shall be *homo faber, homo sapiens* after the last atomic bomb has fallen." . . . (pp. 140-41)

> *Samuel Rees, in his* David Jones *(copyright ©
> 1978 by G. K. Hall & Co.; reprinted with the permission of Twayne Publishers, A Division of G. K.
> Hall & Co., Boston), Twayne, 1978.*

STEPHEN SPENDER

David Jones, the author of "In Parenthesis," the most monumental work of poetic genius to come out of World War I, and of the greatly admired "Anathemata," left behind a mass of papers when he died in 1974. Collected here under the title "The Dying Gaul," they supplement the essays he published during his lifetime, "Epoch and Artist." His essays, like his poems and paintings, are the works of a visionary who seemed so rooted in his own life—separate from other lives yet inseparable from his work—that he did not belong to the literary world of his time. . . .

If Jones's geographical habitat is Celtic, his historical habitat is Wales before the Christian era and some centuries after it, the times of early Christianity. His connection with the past is neither nostalgic nor literary and antiquarian. It is archeological—established through contact with things. . . .

The very special charm of this book lies in the fascination of following an independent, original, utterly sincere, inquiring, erudite mind meditating on objects that attract him by their concentration of remote history and densely complex myth. Reading Jones on Wales, war, the Roland epic and "The Ancient Mariner," one feels oneself in contact with a highly personal, fanatically convinced (yet modest, courteous and unbullying) man and artist. Despite his deep seriousness, there is a childlike side of David Jones that makes him fun to read.

Running through all the essays (and indeed all his books) is an obsessive idea—a theme, if not a thesis—that civilization always threatens and often destroys cultures. Culture is local: the relationship of the people living in a given place to the religion they believe in, to the objects that surround them and to one another. Civilization is urban, central and centralizing, and much human history consists of the urban centralizing forces imposing themselves on the local ones and overwhelming them. David Jones thought that people living in a culture are able to unite the materialist and spiritual sides of their natures within creative, ritualistic, ceremonious acts and behavior—"making." This capacity, in his view, distinguishes the human from other forms of existence: "Man is the only maker, neither beast nor angel share this dignity with him."

The modern world is characterized by its worldwide civilization, whose values are "utile" and thus destructive of cultures. . . .

In the modern world, someone who feels as Jones did is an outcast from the culture of the past, consciously a member of a modern diaspora composed of those whose role is to remember what has been and is lost for good. The most he can attempt is to be a bridge between past and present. . . . (p. 9)

In various ways many writers, from the Romantics through the Victorians onward, have been saying this. . . . What is interesting about David Jones is that he did not speak merely from the standpoint of the artist—though he did believe that in a culture that unites the two sides of man's nature everyone is a "maker," an artist, and therefore the division between the artist and "the rest" does not, and should never, occur. (pp. 9, 26)

One must not expect consistency or lack of self-contradiction in a writer such as David Jones. He admired Virgil immensely, and the lettering on Roman monuments: Yet what was Rome except "civilizational" and thus the arch-destroyer of all local cultures. Jones was also perhaps a bit of a Baudelairean invalid, jaundiced by what he saw of the modern world. And as with every poet (perhaps everyone) who went through World War I, there is a sense in his work of some lesion from which he never recovered. All that is of little account beside the fact that he had something damning and terrible to say which admitted of no consolation, and that he said it persistently, disinterestedly and clearly. Like Thoreau, Melville and Hopkins, he was one of literature's saints who speak with an authority that comes more from religion than from the world of letters. (pp. 26-7)

> *Stephen Spender, "Civilization vs. Culture," in* The New York Times Book Review *(© 1979 by The New York Times Company; reprinted by permission), February 18, 1979, pp. 9, 26-7.*

K

KARAPÁNOU, Margaríta   1946-

Karapánou is a Greek novelist.

JEROME CHARYN

No retelling of "Kassandra and the Wolf" can explain its charm, or its riddles. A first novel by Margarita Karapanou, . . . "Kassandra and the Wolf" is one of those rare creations that come alive mysteriously, without any antecedents. The book is original, terrifying, complete. It invents its own history, eases in and out of nightmare as it mingles dream and fact.

"Kassandra and the Wolf" is a short, muscular novel with an absolute sense of craft. It is never sentimental, pretty or overblown. Margarita Karapanou understands that a story is nothing more than *detail, detail, detail;* we can howl about meaning, mutter little truths about character and development, but it is the *placement* of words in a particular order that makes a landscape credible, that forces us to believe in Kassandra, her grandmother, and Faní. . . . The language throughout is merciless and crisp. Wherever Margarita Karapanou has come from, wherever she goes, "Kassandra and the Wolf" remains a stunning achievement: a lovely, sinister book. (pp. 14, 18)

> *Jerome Charyn, in* The New York Times Book Review *(© 1976 by The New York Times Company; reprinted by permission), July 25, 1976.*

[In "Kassandra and the Wolf," the] adult world, or that part of it which is sexual and violent, [is] seen through the eyes of a precocious (to put it mildly) six-year-old girl named Kassandra. Miss Karapanou's first novel, which is fairly arresting at first because of the shock of reading about a small child's absorption with violence and sex, is really a collection of surreal vignettes about the child's relatives, servants, and playmates in Athens. All the vignettes are quite short—rarely longer than one or two pages—and all exemplify what the publisher calls Kassandra's "pristine sadomasochism." . . .

[It] all becomes terribly repetitive and boring, and even the violent sadomasochism takes on an unpleasant fashion-magazine chichi. (p. 79)

> The New Yorker *(© 1976 by The New Yorker Magazine, Inc.), August 2, 1976.*

MICHAEL G. COOKE

Karapanou [in *Kassandra and the Wolf*] exploits the frissón of the child-narrator vis-à-vis the harsh perversities of *soi-disant* adult sexuality, and with the license of a fairy tale she goes in heavily for metamorphosis. She alludes to Henry James's *The Turn of the Screw*, but she really pays homage to William Blatty's *The Exorcist*. Algolagnia, martyrdom, crucifixion, procrusteanism, suicide games, slaughterhouses, dementia crowd upon metamorphoses in this brief but repetitive book, which ranges in effect from fairly titillating to unfairly tedious. The staccato form—fifty-six sections and 115 pages—fragments instead of concentrating attention. It does not do violence to the work to cherish and regret the isolation of two sets of instruction concerning bedroom etiquette, from Fani the joyously sensual maid, and from Grandmother, that perpetual virgin of the mind. (p. 152)

> *Michael G. Cooke, in* The Yale Review *(© 1976 by Yale University; reprinted by permission of the editors), Autumn, 1976.*

KIMON FRIAR

Kassandra and the Wolf may technically be described as a series of loose, unchronological episodes pretending to be a novel, as told by a girl just beginning grade school. From the psychoanalytical point of view—the wrong one—it may be read partly as the polymorphous, perverse life of a little girl learning what in technical terms are perversions. But Katrapánou is too knowing in the ways of psychoanalysis to make of her book a case history. Those psychoanalytically or pornographically oriented will find ample ammunition for misinterpretation. . . .

Grandmother Sappho, when she is not reading *The Brothers Karamazov*, teaches Kassandra that well-bred girls who grow up to be ladies must never show they like the act of love. . . . But on the other hand, there are the servants. "My child," says Faní, the scullery maid, "learn the secrets under the sheet, open your legs, and let the little stars and hurricanes into your belly." It is no wonder that the little girl cannot sleep nights, as she broods: "I've got plenty of time before I become a nice Lady."

Karapánou's triumph is that she has transcended her technical insights and in this sublimated fiction has written a hilarious and moral indictment of the adult world. This is seen through the eyes of a child who is neither moral nor immoral but simply as amoral as a kitten; yet we must never forget that the insights are those of the mature woman who has created her. Through the child's amoral gaze peer the eyes of judgment that give to this book its moral depth. The little child becomes, in effect, the Kassandra of ancient Greek tragedy who, instead of being gobbled up by the Wolf, falls with him behind a settee in sexual delight. The Wolf is himself ambiguous: he is both the World-Wolf that eats up little children and the Wolf for whom Kassandra feels deep compassion when he has to digest as many as three little piglets.

Kassandra and the Wolf so combines hallucination and reality, fact and fiction, childhood and adult insight, that although ultimately grown-ups are savagely castigated for their hypocrisy in everything that matters—sexual, political, religious, social—they are nevertheless forgiven with great compassion. Denied the possession of a beloved kitten for more than a week, Kassandra slowly and lovingly tortures it, sticks needles in its eyes and drowns it in the bathtub. This, Karapánou implies, is what the adult world teaches children: love is either to be denied, destroyed, perverted or murdered. All this is done, of course, by professing the amenities, by elaborate pretense. But a child's clear-sighted gaze, as directed by a mature, knowing and fictitious mother such as Margaríta Karapánou, pierces the sham and shame and exposes the wolfish jaws hiding behind the polite masks of the upper bourgeoisie. To understand, it is said, is to forgive, but this book is pervaded by a forgiveness which does not fail to pass sentence on a depraved world. In her highly original first "novel" Karapánou has already shown a deep insight into the crooked ways of the world without relegating it either to heaven or to hell. Perhaps life is, in fact, purgatory. (p. 317)

Kimon Friar, in World Literature Today *(copyright 1977 by the University of Oklahoma Press), Vol. 51, No. 2, Spring, 1977.*

SUSANNAH CLAPP

[*Kassandra and the Wolf*] is admirably ambitious both in matter and manner. Short, unlinked episodes, headed like chapters in a child's primer—"The Lesson", "The Plasticine", "The Picnic"—mix probability and possibility, savagery and sweetness in unpredictable proportions. In short, determined sentences Kassandra explains that the local slaughterhouse is one of her favourite loitering-places, that she bites governesses, and is being read *The Turn of the Screw* at bedtime. But most of the information is more exotic and more slippery. . . .

Kassandra and the Wolf is best at showing a particular version of childhood; as a state where everything has significance and nothing has consequence. It is this which makes its fantasies persuasive. The ordinarily odd and the extravagant are nailed with the same amount of detail and the same lack of circumstantial proof: there is no immediate way of distinguishing fact from fantasy—only contradiction by subsequent stories. . . .

Of course, some fantasies are more interesting than others, and dud dreams stand out. Kassandra's more sweaty imaginings, involving bananas and beddings and father-figures racing along the sea-shore, are not particularly illuminating. But the moments at which the novel lashes itself into excitement are outweighed by a general steadiness of tone.

Miss Karapanou has perfected a style which does not sound weeny and does not sound arch, but which manages, by its jumbling together of the trivial and the enormous, and by a staccato manner of delivery which makes most observations into actions, to sound out of tune with adult life without sounding like a translation. It is a style which accommodates both realism and excess, and which enables Kassandra to chronicle striking states of emotion and moral disintegration in the shape of the grown-up figures who flit in and out of the scenes. In cataloguing the despairs of dypsomaniac aunts, masturbating governesses and MPs' mistresses, her coolness inevitably has on occasion some tinge of the cute, but she never appears merely as an emblem of childhood, nor as a particularly horrid little girl.

Susannah Clapp, "Nursery Notions," in The Times Literary Supplement *(© Times Newspapers Ltd. (London) 1978; reproduced from* The Times Literary Supplement *by permission), November 17, 1978, p. 1347.*

*   *   *

KAVAN, Anna (pseudonym of Helen Ferguson Woods)   1904-1968

Born in France, Kavan lived in the United States, Burma, Norway, New Zealand, and England. A novelist and short story writer, she is frequently compared to Anaïs Nin for the way in which she weaves the fabric of her exotic personal life into her fiction, for her landscape of dream life, and her nightmare imagery. (See also *CLC*, Vol. 5, and *Contemporary Authors*, Vols. 25-28.)

JOHN SPURLING

[In her foreword to *Sleep Has His House,* Kavan wrote:]

> If human life be taken as the result of tension between the two polarities night and day, night, the negative pole, must share equal importance with the positive day. At night, under the influence of cosmic radiations quite different from those of the day, human affairs are apt to come to a crisis. At night most human beings die and are born. *Sleep Has His House* describes in the night-time language certain stages in the development of one individual human being. . . .

The book is, in effect, a sort of autobiography of dreams, charting the stages of the subject's gradual withdrawal from all interest in and contact with the daylight world of received reality. Anna Kavan's 'night-time language' is in no way obscure; on the contrary, her dreams are as carefully notated, as lucid as paintings by Dali or De Chirico; the stages of withdrawal are separated by short 'day-time' passages of information—here the subject's mother dies, here the subject goes to school, here to university, etc.; the book's direction is clear and its episodes are in chronological order.

Yet in spite of all this clarity, in spite of the sometimes powerful, sometimes delicate imagery of the dreams, one never feels any desire to read on, or having read on, to read back. This is surely because Anna Kavan has given too much importance to the negative pole, and thereby destroyed the tension between night and day. The incessant actions of these dreams are as weightless as the incessant rapes and murders in a crude thriller. The reader is surfeited with images and retains no more of them than the vague impression of a coloured-light show or of his own dreams after waking. (p. 385)

John Spurling, in New Statesman (© *1973 The Statesman & Nation Publishing Co. Ltd.), March 16, 1973.*

ADRIANNE MARCUS

Anna Kavan is becoming known in this country at long last. Her death in 1968 deprived us of further stories, but the posthumous publication of her book *Julia and the Bozooka* brought her to the attention of reviewers, and hopefully, to a waiting public. Her *Ice* . . . is one of those rare books that has achieved an underground reputation. You may not find it in the s-f section, but in the "literary" section. Rightfully, it belongs in both.

It makes use of a standard science-fiction nightmare: the end of the world. But it becomes a study of impending catastrophe in human terms as two men (who may be the same man) pursue a passive, elusive woman. Kavan encloses them in a beautiful, deadly landscape: an encroaching glacial age. The woman, unable to free herself by passion or attachment from the two men who hope to haunt/save her is shown through the narrator's voice as his fantasies and cruelties center about her. She is the snow-queen, the elusive ice-woman. Past, present and future intermingle and the deliberate confusion of reality and imagination are chillingly present. Kavan's use of language has the heightened intensity of metaphor; passages, descriptions in the book make a surreal impact on the reader and the final beauty of the book is the beauty of ice: chilling, exquisite and deadly. (p. 4)

Adrianne Marcus, in Pacific Sun Literary Quarterly, *May 15, 1975.*

ELIZABETH TURNER POCHODA

Anna Kavan, like Anaïs Nin with whom she is often compared, is a cult writer. Her work is treasured by people who enjoy its sensitive probing of inner states and who do not require much in the way of narrative technique, imagination, or linguistic richness. The rawness of her personal experience in its rawest unworked state is apparently enough to satisfy. Like many cult figures, her life story is well known (nearly every one of her books contains an Introduction describing her lifelong addiction to heroin and her lonely death in her late sixties) and can be read into every line of her slim narratives. This is fine. But the extent to which this sort of writing has been identified as specifically female is something else again.

While Anna Kavan's work is an interesting example of a minor genre, it hardly makes sense to compare her, as Lawrence Durrell does on the book's dust jacket, to Djuna Barnes and Virginia Woolf. What separates writers such as Anaïs Nin and Anna Kavan from Barnes and Woolf is that in their exploration of subjective states they have only tunnel vision. Work so committed to subjectivity ends by being repetitive and inert. But in the hands of writers like Barnes, Woolf, or Proust, the subjective state still allows for peripheral vision so that the mind's interior is simply one more avenue for coming at the world and saying something new about it. Durrell, in his talk of the "subjective-feminist tradition," seems to forget that Woolf and Barnes are espe-

cially rich in wit (unlike Kavan or Nin, who never allow us a giggle) and that their wit arises from this interpenetration of interior and exterior worlds. . . . The total effect of [Kavan's] work is powerful, but for peculiar reasons: the reader is moved most by the sad fact that while the writer cared deeply about her art, she was at the same time in the grip of forces that prevented her from practicing it.

The final and most convincing statement of her madness lies not is the success of the stories, but in their failure. All her fiction, including her science-fiction novel *Ice* . . . , shows the writer spinning her wheels in the same groove: paranoid fantasies give way to a drugged numbness that in turn allows the heroine to inflict pain on others. Either she imagines herself hit by a car or she fantasizes that the onlookers are drowned in her blood. She is unreal; others are unreal.

None of this is especially new in the literature of madness, but what is fascinating is the strain of trying to bring it across when even, the demands of fiction must seem unreal. The imagination is so trapped that whenever the heart wishes to cry out about its pain, it cannot invent a name for it. Cliché must suffice when Kavan's enclosure prevents inventiveness. . . . Most painful of all is the realization that there is a literary world sentimental enough to encourage her limiting self-indulgence when it might have pushed her in the direction of art—an unwitting literary conspiracy on behalf of the "subjective-feminist tradition," which, if she'd thought of it that way, might have made paranoia seem justifiable.

Elizabeth Turner Pochoda, "Trapped Imagination," in Ms. (© *1975 Ms. Magazine Corp.), September, 1975, p. 42.*

DUNCAN FALLOWELL

On coming to what [*Eagle's Nest*] is about—plotwise—one has no option but to rely on the narrator himself, a distracted soul who never knows exactly what is going on either. For him the screen between real and imaginary actions was attacked by woodworm some good while before the novel began.

The narrator is first encountered behind a desk making Christmas angels out of papier mâché, loathing each one of them, and behind schedule to boot. From a successful career in business, redundancy has reduced him to the position of house artist to a departmental store. At first we presume him female. After a few pages he loses that and becomes indecipherable. But later on, when he is flirting with a hairdresser and exchanging psychotic reactions with a housekeeper called Penny, nothing jars. Kavan changes her sex with a fluency which suggests she must have transcended it, but impalpability is on her side as always and the cast not gregarious. There is hardly a conversation involving more than two persons in the entire book, unless one includes servants and at the house called Eagle's Nest one never does. Talk and action are at a minimum and the atmosphere is inebriating.

An extraordinary degree of suspense is achieved by imperceptible undertones never thrown away. Every sentence contains a mystery and as these accumulate so does the longing for at least one clear explanation. (p. 16)

A summary of *Eagle's Nest* cannot help but be vague whereas the book, funnily enough, is written precisely. It is set in a paranormal world, yet the picture is sharp in detail. Her vocabulary is not esoteric, her characters are disturbing rather than lunatic, nor are the events very improbable in an age of Charles Manson and Howard Hughes. The transforming element is of course in Kavan; and in her day the [National Health Service] guaranteed the supply of heroin. With emotions in silhouette, the attention momentarily unbugged, her hands were free to move through the endocrine swamps. Drabble, McCarthy, Murdoch, Spark: will they ever make it through the french windows? One cannot write properly with nappy pins in the mouth, however metaphorical they may be. One thing an authoress cannot afford to be is effeminate. Anna Kavan takes no chance, writing in the first person as a male. He is not very rectilinear, he flinches among nettles, but has nevertheless established a precarious *gite* in the outskirts of psychosis. (pp. 16-17)

> *Duncan Fallowell, "Anima and Enema," in* The Spectator *(© 1976 by* The Spectator; *reprinted by permission of* The Spectator), *January 31, 1976, pp. 16-17.*

BETTINA L. KNAPP

The dream encroached upon Anna Kavan's reality with such power as to submerge her ego. Yet, as Anaïs Nin has suggested in her introduction [to *Neige suivi de mal aimées*], Kavan's inner meanderings so unflinchingly delineated demonstrate an act of courage, even heroism.

Neige is an esthetic, psychological and metaphysical probing. In a series of exciting metaphors and disemboweled images the author reveals her own divided and tortured soul: iced, congealed, hard, brittle, white, as pure and as prismatic as crystal. The theme: a faceless and identity-less man longs for and is bedazzled by a beautiful, ethereal, silvery being, an anima figure, . . . whom he meets one summer evening in some spaceless area. She stands aloof and impervious in her icy frigidity to his inner cravings. His repeated attempts to liberate himself from this haunting being are to no avail. As he slowly succumbs to her impassible nature, so the snow-bound scenes increase in power and frequency, converging, smothering, freezing all in sight. Like the swan in Mallarmé's poem caught up in its own whiteness, immobility and impassibility, so the man is powerless in his attempt to possess the captivating being of his dream. As his fascination increases, so his horizons shrink; walled in by his phantasm, he is engulfed with tornado force in his own abyss, there to linger a while and finally diffuse into nothingness.

Mal aimées dramatizes the plight of Regina, a name perfectly suited to the protagonist, who commands the love of others but is herself cut off from the feeling principle. Tortured by her inability to experience but the most fleeting of relationships, by her compulsion to force men into submission, . . . she is a woman whose life becomes one long trial. Regina . . . always floats through existence incapable of responding authentically to others. (p. 102)

The constructs emerging as flesh-and-blood human beings in Anna Kavan's novels are captivating and terrorizing: captivating because of the evanescent and alluring beauty she invests in her descriptions; frightening because of the very real power they wield on the individuals involved. Both female protagonists are powerful *vagina dentata* types —possessive, domineering, death-dealing entities. The men are therefore impotent votaries. Anna Kavan's novels are

fascinating for the psychologist but captivating also as artistic documents. (p. 103)

> *Bettina L. Knapp, in* World Literature Today *(copyright 1977 by the University of Oklahoma Press), Vol. 51, No. 1, Winter, 1977.*

MAX EGREMONT

Anna Kavan's writing is inextricably tied up with the convolutions of her tragic life. Of course this is, to a greater or lesser extent, true of all writers. . . . Yet with Anna Kavan the stories and novels are so subjective in tone that it is as if she wishes, in reality, to write her own spiritual autobiography but, rather than do this, has dressed up her sufferings and longings in fictional terms. Often the short stories are little more than fragments illustrating individual paranoia or intense personal despair and, as such, are reminiscent more of pages from a psychiatrist's notebook than of works of imaginative fiction. These tales are maudlin, desperate in their evident knowledge that, for the narrator, escape from this hideous twilight world of hallucinatory imprisonment is impossible. (p. 43)

Anna Kavan possessed artistic integrity; of that there can be no doubt. Her stories are direct; there is no prostitution of contemporary trends or fads, no deviation from that extraordinary combination, peculiar to herself, of conversational ease and the loose, almost wild, imagery of some of the descriptive passages. But I am afraid, for me, there is in her work a dividing line on the one side of which she gives the best of her powers, leaving on the other a grim example of the truth of at least some of Baudelaire's warnings [of the negative implications of drug addiction]. This is unfashionable. . . . [I am] sure her disciples, with their customary passion for the lugubrious, the humourless, the portentous and the dull, admire her for her depressingly nihilistic snippets of self-pity, for the obtuse parabolic tilts at totalitarianism of her science fiction, rather than for her earlier, more conventional, for me more satisfying, work.

I am Lazarus conveniently shows a mixture of early and late Kavan. Some stories, echoing an earlier collection *Asylum Piece*, deal effectively and movingly with sanitorium life and mental derangement; others venture into the territory of the desperate sub-conscious, retiring from the world to cope wholly with inner fears, disturbances and threats. Here we are, inevitably, in the domain of Kafka; psychological turmoil, uncertainty, take the form of paranoiac terror, of fantasies woven around vast impersonal bureaucracies, forces shifting slowly but unavoidably against the unknowing individual unequipped to deal with them. Appointments are broken, orders given then mysteriously rescinded, soft voiced officials interrogate without reason, 'advisers' are sinister and unreliable; all this is familiar country, at times verging upon the imitative.

These visions were clearly, in Anna Kavan's case, founded upon a hideous reality, yet this reality was itself limited by being the product of individual fantasy. Here we should return to Baudelaire, to his strictures on the necessity of preserving some form of objective viewpoint and how a drug induced notion of terror, because it is an experience confined to a personal deranged imagination, is of little artistic value beyond its purely aesthetic appeal as a pattern of words, colours or sound. This for me, illustrates the limits of this side of Anna Kavan's work. (pp. 43-4)

Kafka's message was new; Anna Kavan's is not. Her fantasies of looming catastrophe and bureaucratic nightmare are occasionally vivid but rarely disturbing. Perhaps this is partly because they obviously represent a fevered artificial vision, partly also through their obvious debt to a great and original predecessor. Kafka's parables seem to speak for humanity; Miss Kavan's represent only an addict's personal despair. (p. 44)

> *Max Egremont, "The Twilight of Anna Kavan," in* Books and Bookmen *(© copyright Max Egremont 1978; reprinted with permission), June, 1978, pp. 43-4.*

*   *   *

KINNELL, Galway   1927-

Kinnell is an American poet, novelist, and translator. A writer of lyric free verse, he has gradually developed a personal and symbolic mythology to replace the natural imagery of his earlier poetry. His philosophy is perhaps best exemplified in a line from his *The Book of Nightmares*: "Living brings you to death, there is no other road." Many critics feel that this acceptance of mortality paradoxically enables him to place more value on life itself. (See also *CLC*, Vols. 1, 2, 3, 5, and *Contemporary Authors*, Vols. 9-12, rev. ed.)

RICHMOND LATTIMORE

Galway Kinnell does not dream into nightmares, he heads into them frontally. [*The Book of Nightmares*] strings on and on in non-metre; Kinnell's ear is good, but the lengths after a while cry out for more shape. We are exposed to repeated themes, such as dead hens full of eggs, bears eating flowers, babies being messily born. Kinnell can produce sufficiently revolting effects. . . . There is too much of this, and it becomes a weariness. I come out occasionally impressed, but never moved. (pp. 501-02)

> *Richmond Lattimore, in* The Hudson Review *(copyright © 1971 by The Hudson Review, Inc.; reprinted by permission), Vol. XXIV, No. 3, Autumn, 1971.*

JOHN HOBBS

In Galway Kinnell's poem "The Bear," a hunter stalks the bear to its death, falls asleep exhausted, dreams he becomes the bear, and then awakens somehow changed into a creature half-bear, half-man. The poem's strength and its problems hinge upon the hunter persona Kinnell adopts, attempting to fuse the consciousness of a modern man with that of a primitive Eskimo. This persona means that the poet must move through the technical realism of hunting to its metaphysical implications without spoiling one or the other, as he tries to illustrate man's sacred bond with nature by the simple, brutal hunting of the bear. . . .

Speaking of the origins of "The Bear" in an interview, Kinnell said,

> I guess I had just read Cummings' poem on Olaf, who says, "there is some shit I will not eat." It struck me that that rather implies that some of our diet, if not all, is shit. And then I remembered this bear story, how the bear's shit was infused with blood, so that the hunter by eating the bear's excrement was actually nourished by what the bear's wound infused into it.
>
> (p. 237)

Cummings' poem was . . . more an incidental stimulus than a source for "The Bear." Its moral is against killing while Kinnell's poem is about hunting, but its anal imagery and degrading torture do correspond to the agony first of the bear and then of the hunter in his dream.

Closer to "The Bear" is our next link between the metaphorical excrement of Cummings' poem and the actual excrement of the hunting story Kinnell recalled. Other versions of the action doubtless exist, but it appears likely that the story came from the first chapter of *Top of the World*, a popular adventure novel by Hans Ruesch. Ruesch fashions rudimentary characters and plots from the raw material of anthropological accounts of Eskimo life, emphasizing their most intriguing habits of diet, hygiene, and sex. (pp. 238-39)

The differences between Kinnell's hunter and [Ruesch's] two Eskimos are many. . . . These differences emphasize Kinnell's attempts to go beyond the realistic limits of his persona, the primitive Eskimo hunter.

This attempt can also be seen in the two crucial points at which poem and novel overlap—eating the bear's excrement, and preparing the coiled bone. Ruesch emphasizes how little hunger bothers the hunters, for "This was the Hunt—the very essence of life." . . . Contrast this matter-of-fact report with Kinnell's careful description:

> On the third day I begin to starve,
> at nightfall I bend down as I knew I would
> at a turd sopped in blood,
> and hesitate, and pick it up,
> and thrust it in my mouth, and gnash it down,
> and rise
> and go on running.

The verb sequence—"bend down," "hesitate," "pick it up," "thrust," "gnash it down"—extends and slows the action, showing the balance between disgust and fatalistic acceptance. If this act was the origin of the poem, it might explain the emphasis that otherwise violates by delicacy the account of a tough, native hunter.

No such delicacy intensifies the parallel descriptions of making the bait in Ruesch and Kinnell. . . . Kinnell condenses this preparation to the basic details:

> I take a wolf's rib and whittle
> it sharp at both ends
> and coil it up
> and freeze it in blubber and place it out
> on the fairway of the bears.

Again the verb sequence controls the description—"take," "whittle," "coil," "freeze," "place." Kinnell emphasizes the techniques of hunting in the first half of the poem. The weapon to kill the bear defines the relationship between hunter and prey. A gun would violate their bond while the device carved from bone and hidden in fat is part of the arctic world they share. Furthermore, only a slow death allows the long pursuit that makes an allegory of life out of the hunting trip. It is this Eskimo realism that Kinnell apparently borrows from Ruesch's account as the metaphorical basis for his metaphysical dream. (pp. 239-41)

The hunting technology in "The Bear" may be primitive, but the first half focuses steadily on the hunter's preparations—making the bait, and then stalking the wounded bear. As we have already seen in two sections,

Kinnell organizes the whole poem by verb sequences that sound almost like instructions. (p. 242)

The longer he hunts the bear, living by the end "on bear blood alone," the more he assumes the bear's identity, a process completed when he dreams inside the bear's carcass. (p. 243)

In another departure from realism, Kinnell rearranges time in "The Bear" to emphasize the hunter's techniques. . . . [In the dream] he returns in the bear's identity to the seven days of the hunt. Then the hunter half-awakens to resume the life represented by the bear when alive, moving toward its death once again when "one day I totter and fall." Even his dream moves by technique and sequence; first, how to escape the blood trail, and second, how the stomach tries to digest the bone. Time and description follow techniques until the dream doubles back to the past, yet even the dream follows a similar sequence of actions. (pp. 243-44)

Ruesch makes the reader see the bear in his last agony. Kinnell conveys its generalized despair but without animal details. (p. 244)

[The] transformation of man to animal remains incomplete —an animal body with a human consciousness. In "The Bear" his dream alters reality, so that "I awaken I think," uncertain about his return to everyday life. . . . Death coincides with birth; life begins for others as he nears by sure steps the end of his. In the spring natural processes resume, and "geese / come trailing again up the flyway." But his own life continues unchanged. Instead of progressing, this sequence repeats the first step, although his trudging carries with it a dream from the past, a question of life.

> And one
> hairy-soled trudge stuck out before me,
> the next groaned out,
> the next,
> the next,
> the next,
> the rest of my days I spend
> wandering: wondering
> what, anyway,
> was that sticky infusion, that rank flavor of blood, that
> poetry, by which I lived?

Half-bear with its "hairy-soled trudge," he is also the hunter "wandering" again as he wandered looking for the trail of blood before. . . . (p. 247)

Judging by the ending, then, should the whole poem be interpreted as an allegory of the poet? Kinnell sees this possibility but feels ambivalent about it.

> The idea that that poem was about the creative process never occurred to me until later, when I heard some people say that it might be. I don't really know what it's about. I guess it was Robert Bly who first suggested it, that the hunter was the mental person and the bear was the body and the unconscious, that when they came together then the poem was possible. He made it very persuasive to me, so that I see that it's one thing the poem must mean. But when I wrote "that poetry, by which I lived," I didn't have in mind at all the poetry which is written down on pages. I was thinking rather of poetry in another sense.

(p. 248)

Kinnell has his own ideas on the use of a persona, how it can either lead the poet deeper into himself, or let him evade the realities of his life by oversimplification.

> A persona has its uses, and also its dangers. In theory, it would be a way to get past the self, to dissolve the barrier between poet and reader. Writing in the voice of another, the poet would open himself to that person. All that would be required would be for the reader to make the same act of sympathetic identification, and, in the persona, poet and reader would meet as one.

The idea that poet and reader can merge in the persona may explain why Kinnell offers little in the way of characterization of his primitive hunter to distinguish him from modern men. Since the persona is not defined as one or the other, he can move at will between hunting and metaphysics. The reader may feel that Kinnell both complicates the hunter's problems and simplifies the poet's own view of life. For as Kinnell admits, it is hard to say just what "The Bear" is finally about. Many partial meanings enrich the text. Technique without dream is meaningless. Physicality is both man's pleasure and his ultimate agony. Man and animals are part of a single creation. The hunter can become the hunted. Etc. Yet no one of these meanings appears to dominate the others, because the hunter persona doesn't permit intellectual subordination and its resulting clarity. Like the many verbs connected by "and," everything exists on the same level for the hunter, despite Kinnell's attempts to suggest a significant hierarchy.

This intellectual confusion, however, may itself be part of the poem's theme. To the question of a conflict between the sacredness of all life and killing the bear, we can see that the hunter slowly becomes the bear, even after its death. Thus, he both causes and shares its agony as a fellow creature. In a sense, the hunter hunts and kills himself. He imitates the bear in stalking it, he climbs into its carcass to sleep, and dreams it back to life, a dream he cannot wake from completely. The bear has changed him forever, and it is not an easy change for him to accept. Half-bear, half-man, he must suffer for both kinds of being, must both kill and be killed. Kinnell, . . . quoting Gary Snyder, agrees that the "archaic and primitive ritual dramas, which acknowledged all sides of human nature, including the destructive, demonic, and ambivalent, were liberating and harmonizing." In its inclusion of life and death, hunting is surely one of these ritual dramas as Kinnell's hunter enacts it, a ritual of rules and careful preparations. For Kinnell's primitive hunter experiences his own death, yet goes beyond it. This experience also fits Kinnell's idea of poetry's highest achievement:

> The death of the self I seek, in poetry and out of poetry, is not a drying up or withering. It is a death, yes, but a death out of which one might hope to be reborn more giving, more alive, more open, more related to the natural life.

(pp. 248-50)

John Hobbs, "Galway Kinnell's 'The Bear': Dream and Technique," in Modern Poetry Studies *(copyright 1974, by Jerome Mazzaro), Winter, 1974, pp. 237-50.*

VERNON YOUNG

Galway Kinnell is a poet of astonishing incarnations, he never seems to be where you last met him and he's always secure in his new adaptation. [*The Avenue Bearing the Initial of Christ into the New World*] brings together poems from his first three books, covering the years between 1946 and 1964, many of the earliest [having] been returned to their pre-revised form which, upon rediscovery, the author himself preferred. . . . By turn and with level facility, Kinnell is a poet of the landscape, a poet of soliloquy, a poet of the city's underside and a poet who speaks for thieves, pushcart vendors and lumberjacks with an unforced simulation of their vernacular. New England woods, the Oregon coast, Calcutta, T'ang Dynasty China, Wales and Manhattan's ghetto: his geography is global and it reveals, when paid close attention, a perennial dialogue of death and resurrection. . . . (p. 599)

Hard to believe, as we turn the pages in admiration, that the same poet wrote "The Wolves" or "Where the Track Vanishes" or "Koisimi Buddhist of Altitudes" or, above all, "The Avenue Bearing the Initial of Christ into the New World" (I do think that title is a wounded snake), a masterwork of vocal effects, shared lamentation, unreserved closeups of ghetto characters who, after closing their junkshops and loading their pushcarts, withdraw into "chambers overhead". . . . . . and fluent panoramas that remind one of the swarming, funereal paragraphs of I. B. Singer. (p. 600)

> Vernon Young, in The Hudson Review (copyright © 1974 by The Hudson Review, Inc.; reprinted by permission), Vol. XXVII, No. 4, Winter, 1974-75.

JEROME McGANN

In [Galway Kinnell] we see that the idea of paradise gets reborn in the cultivation of waste places. (pp. 161-62)

Life is found in death, fountains in deserts, gain in loss, spring in winter, light in darkness. All these matters are the recurrent subjects of Kinnell's verse. He is a hero of the Absolute whose civilization exists in a burning mind which dreams forever upon itself, its first imagining. (p. 162)

The Avenue Bearing the Initial of Christ Into the New World, as the publisher's note in the book says, "will provide the opportunity to know the poems which were the preamble to the famous poems of [Kinnell's] later books," *Body Rags* and *The Book of Nightmares*. The collection in fact describes with terrible accuracy the career of a great poetic extremist, a self-confessed (or proclaimed?) "Damned nightmarer."

Here the sensible world is forever strangled in imagination. Nothing is sufficiently itself. A red kite appears along the Avenue and is instantly twisted to a symbol under the haunted gaze of Kinnell's evil eye: "A red kite wriggles like a tadpole / Into the sky beyond them, crosses / The sun, lays bare its own crossed skeleton." Skid row bums are themselves not sufficiently lost or degraded. Compared to the indigence which Kinnell can imagine, these men lead lives of leisure

> Southwards, towards Houston and Pitt
> Where Avenue C begins, the eastern ranges
> Of the wiped-out lives—punks, lushes,
> Panhandlers, pushers, rumsoaks, everyone
> Who took it easy when he should have been out failing
>   at something—

That failure which Kinnell demands merely expresses what he takes to be everyone's primal situation, however much they may seek to evade it. Kinnell's book comes from a mind which has not only not evaded this understanding:

> Each year I lived I watched the fissure
> Between what was and what I wished for
> Widen, until there was nothing left
> But the gulf of emptiness.

it has increasingly done everything in its power (which is considerable) to foster and nourish such an understanding. If Moses died of longing on the rim of a land flowing with milk and honey, Kinnell aims to die on an even more extreme verge of the same mountain. His life is bent, as the title of his poem says, "To the Wilderness."

> He puts the bead of his will on the peak
> And does not waver. He is dying:
> His plan is to look over the far side
> Of the hill on which Moses died looking this way,
> And to see the bitter land, and to die of desire.

The force which this myth exerts upon American poetry seems to me astonishing. Of course it is still producing some strong verse, yet surely one has to recognize, and deplore, the inhumanity of its programs. A poet like Kinnell would sooner lose the whole world than suffer the loss of his immortal soul. (pp. 163-64)

> Jerome McGann, in Chicago Review (reprinted by permission of Chicago Review; copyright © 1975 by Chicago Review), Vol. 27, No. 1, 1975.

J. T. LEDBETTER

Galway Kinnell's "The Bear" can be read as a graphic account of a hunter tracking and eating the totemic animal, thus insuring himself of future benefits from the gods as well as practical benefits of food and clothing here and now. The poem can also be seen as the record of a *shaman* whose job it is to infuse himself with the sacred animal and, by so doing, take unto himself the beast's wisdom, strength, cunning, or terror. Such readings seem to find little to impede them unless it be the final section . . . where the speaker awakens; even here the difficulty is slight, because the person seeming to wake could be the hunter or the shaman fantasizing about the ritual of the hunt. However, an alternate reading seems to represent itself: the poem may be about the writing of poetry. (pp. 3, 5)

[In the final section, there] is a surcease of both the transcendent joy in the writing and the feeling of loss of power immediately following the birth of the poem. The poet rests, thinks, sees the world as poetry. He is conscious of the inexhaustibility of the nature of art, of poetry.

And he already senses the footprint, the image to be seized, understood, described; the days to follow find him wondering about the power he has had, and whether and how soon he will find it (poem) again. The poet knows what has happened: he has written a poem. But he never fully comprehends the mystery, the terrible motion of the meaning of the experience. (p. 7)

> J. T. Ledbetter, in The Explicator (© copyright by The Explicator Literary Foundation, Inc.), April, 1975.

ALAN HELMS

With *The Avenue Bearing the Initial of Christ into the New World* and *The Book of Nightmares* we have a clear view of Galway Kinnell's work from the beginning to the present; what's immediately apparent is that the work, although occasionally excellent, is very uneven.

The Avenue contains Kinnell's first three books. *First Poems 1946-54* is the juvenilia its title augurs; except for a couple first-rate poems ("Indian Bread," "Walking Out Alone in Dead of Winter"), it's most remarkable for the unassimilated debts Kinnell incurs (Whitman, Frost, Williams, Eliot, Yeats, Roethke) and for the annunciation of an attitude [in "Conversation at Tea"] which will become the major theme of his later poetry:

> Most men have not seen the world divide,
> Or seen, it did not open wide,
> Or wide, they clung to the safer side
> But I have felt the sundering like a blade. . . .

In *What a Kingdom It Was* (1960) Kinnell pays off some of his debts; in *Flower Herding on Mount Monadnock* (1964) he's in the black, writing his own good poetry, especially in Part II of that book. And he's also aware of the postures and the limits of vision in his earlier work. . . . (pp. 288-89)

Kinnell's principal posture is that of representative post-Christian existential sufferer, but in *Flower Herding* the posture often becomes a calmly stated conviction: "I know I live half alive in the world, / I know half my life belongs to the wild darkness."

The Book of Nightmares explores that half of Kinnell's life which "belongs to the wild darkness." A single ambling meditation organized on the model of the *Duino Elegies* (ten long poems which in this version are divided into seven parts each), the book allows Kinnell to examine a variety of nightmares: the immanence of death, love's difficulties, the tortures of memory and doubt, the omnipresence of fear, etc. Kinnell's ambitions are clearly metaphysical.

The challenge of the book comes from the epigraph, the conclusion of Rilke's *Fourth Elegy:*

> But this, though: death,
> the whole of death,—even before life's begun,
> to hold it all so gently, and be good:
> this is beyond description!

Rilke is speaking here of his inability to describe the child's original grace, its unconsciousness of the death that grows within even as it grows. Kinnell revises Rilke's focus, staking claim to "the whole of death" as perceived by the adult who looks to his children with an agonized presentiment of their future.

When Kinnell is in fact looking to his children, speaking about or to the Maud and Fergus to whom the book is dedicated, his writing is often superb. (pp. 289-90)

When Kinnell's gaze wanders to the cosmos, however, he stumbles through a maze of muddled metaphysics: speculating on the nature of love, he opines:

> And yet I think
> it must be the wound, the wound itself,
> which lets us know and love,
> which forces us to reach out to our misfit
> and by a kind
> of poetry of the soul, accomplish,
> for a moment, the wholeness the drunk Greek
> extrapolated from his high
> or flagellated out of an empty heart,
>
> that purest,
> most tragic concumbence, strangers
> clasped into one, a moment, of their moment on earth.

"A kind of poetry of the soul"? Aristophanes drunk? extrapolating or flagellating (out of an empty heart?) a wholeness comprised of misfits? And considering that the passage starts with the assumption there is some virtue in being let "know and love," doesn't that "purest, most tragic concumbence" leave us a bit in the dark?

But then Kinnell's vision is dark. His book, after all, is *The Book of Nightmares,* and it carries a large freight of sorrow and despair, a psychological map of experience plotted by the profoundly pessimistic Freud of *Civilization and its Discontents,* a grisly view of a life. . . .

The vagueness of the passages I just quoted (and the dictionary English accompanying it) runs through much of the book. Rhythms are sometimes awkward, lines being arranged on the principle of keeping adjectives away from nouns, nouns from verbs—a capricious kind of syntactic rhyme which jerks us through the poetry. . . . (pp. 291-92)

Kinnell freely invents new symbols while ignoring the customary attributions of old ones (the apostle Peter becomes "he who crushed with his heel the brain out of the snake."). And when the cosmic yearning is most upon him, he reverts to his early habit of imitation: Book VI is modelled on Villon's *Testament;* an early description of mystical experience, on Whitman's famous passage in "Song of Myself." Kinnell suffers by both comparisons.

Taking into account these faults then, what does Kinnell's ledger look like on the basis of *The Book of Nightmares*? I think he's still, but barely, in the black. Since long poems invite failures, the central question is does the book hold together, does it work as an ensemble? For me it does. Though I'm annoyed by Kinnell's occasional poses and presumptions and his confused poetics, the best parts of his book continue to draw me in, persuading me over and over to participate in the nightmare of a possible, fully imagined and carefully registered fate. . . . (p. 292)

Kinnell's willed choice and his one necessity are to explore the confusion of a life beyond salvation, a death beyond redemption. The result is often compelling reading. Now that he has wandered among the darkest and worst his life holds, it should be exciting, given the quality of his best work, to see how he joins his nightmare vision with the other half of his life. (p. 293)

Alan Helms, in Partisan Review *(copyright © 1977 by Partisan Review, Inc.), Vol. XLIV, No. 2, 1977.*

ROBERT LANGBAUM

Galway Kinnell's *The Book of Nightmares* . . . emerges as one of the best long poems of recent years. It represents an unforeseeable leap forward for Kinnell. Although the earlier work prepares us for it through its imagery and concern with nature, there is nothing on this scale, nothing that extends man's spiritual dimensions so high and so low, nothing that extends the range of man's connections so far into biological and cosmic process—though such connections are made in the earlier poetry. . . . *The Book of Nightmares* is Kinnell's *Divine Comedy*, a *Divine Comedy* without God but with soul, a soul inseparable from body and from man's life in nature. Unlike Dante but like the romantic poets to whose tradition he belongs, Kinnell tries to pull an immortality out of our mortality.

The earlier poetry prepares us for *The Book of Nightmares* in that it shows Kinnell as one of our best nature poets. "Leaping Falls" is another version of Wordsworth's "Tintern Abbey." . . . Internal burning informs Kinnell's nature imagery; so does the murderousness of nature and the creative power of death. . . .

Kinnell's most ambitious poem prior to *The Book of Nightmares* is the title poem of his collected *Poems 1946-64*, "The Avenue Bearing the Initial of Christ into the New World." . . . The poem does not quite come off, because the subject matter is too external to Kinnell. Significantly, the best section is No. 11, on the killing and cleaning of a carp, where Kinnell can show the murderousness of our life in nature. The most spectacular example of this theme is "The Bear," the last poem in *Body Rags* (1968). . . . Poetry for Kinnell is regression, and he uses the nightmarish ingestion of animal life as an image of regression. The imagery of regression has since Wordsworth been a way of achieving intensity in nature poetry, and nature poetry has been a way of talking about the unconscious. That is how nature imagery turns surrealist in Kinnell . . . and the other so-called "new surrealist poets" of the late Sixties and the Seventies. Ingestion and the mixing of nightmare and reality are important themes in *The Book of Nightmares*. Of all Kinnell's earlier poems, only "The Bear" equals *The Book of Nightmares* in intensity.

Like all Kinnell's longer poems, *The Book of Nightmares* is a sequence. . . . [In] combining disparate lyrical passages, the sequence combines intensities without the need for slack transitions; and intensity is our main criterion of excellence. In all its seventy-five pages, *The Book of Nightmares* hardly ever declines from the highest pitch of intensity. Its few weak spots are the places where Kinnell strains after an intensity that does not come off—as in the lines, "inward-swirling / globes biopsied out of sunsets," which are spoiled by the failure of the adventurous word "biopsied."

The Book of Nightmares is, like so many recent poems, autobiographical and confessional. . . . Like most [of] his contemporaries, Kinnell uses free verse; but he universalizes his experience through an imagery that connects it with cosmic process. . . .

Poem I, about the birth and infancy of his daughter Maud, introduces three themes that run through the book—the road or journey; Maud, whose infancy is an event on the road; and nightmare. . . . Kinnell has a big voice. This is lyricism in the great tradition. (p. 30)

In "The Shoes of Wandering," Poem III, the poet continues his journey in old Salvation Army shoes with which he walks "on the steppingstones / of someone else's wandering." "The first step," he writes, echoing Eliot's *Four Quartets*, "shall be / to lose the way." Now he is attempting to make connections with other human beings rather than with nature. Like all nature poetry, *The Book of Nightmares* is about the attempt of the lonely soul, existing in a world where community has broken down, to reforge connections. . . . Poem III is tremendous in the way it magnifies man's spiritual dimensions by generating the highest spiritual intensity from the most sordid circumstances. The road becomes an icon. . . .

Poem V, "In the Hotel of Lost Light," returns to the poet lying on the hotel bed where he imagines a drunk died. . . . [This] poem, where the murderousness of nature is so sordid that nightmare overwhelms reality, is the book's nadir, its inferno. . . .

Poem VIII is remarkable in the way it ranges from the sexual to the spiritual, combining in the stately final section, which returns to the theme of the journey, the romantic and metaphysical styles. . . . Echoing Lawrence on tortoise calls and Eliot in *Ash Wednesday*, and *Four Quartets*, the poem discovers the rhythm that connects this world with the dim frontier of the next—the next conceived as, in Keat's phrase, our "happiness on Earth repeated in a finer tone." Poem VIII is the book's climax.

The last two poems are less intense. . . . In Poem X, "Lastness," the poet's son Sancho Fergus is born. The poet reiterates the book's central question: "Is it true / the earth is all there is, and the earth does not last?"; and the book's central point: "Living brings you to death, there is no other road." Stated so baldly, these seem rather banal observations. It is right, we are told, that "the tenth poem" should be "the last, that one / and zero" should

> walk off the end of these pages
>   together,
> one creature
> walking always side by side with
>   the emptiness.

This makes us realize that Kinnell's concern for connections stems from his loneliness. . . . The poet's inner division is reflected in the contradictory admonitions: "Sancho Fergus! Don't cry! / or else, cry"; and in the irony with which the poem ends: when the corpse is "laid out, see if you can find / the one flea which is laughing." The reference is probably to the statement in Poem VII that men should "feel as free on earth as fleas on the bodies of men," that we ought to enjoy our mortality as the fleas enjoy it. These last lines are ironical because only the flea is having a good time.

The irony makes a trivial ending after so long a stretch of passion and positive vision. Yet the irony, if it represents all Kinnell could come up with as a final statement, is at least honest; it is better than bombast. It seems anti-climactic just because Kinnell, at a time when so many poets are content to be skillful and trivial, speaks with a big voice about the whole of life—though society appears only as nightmare: the social filtered through the private nightmare. Even with its weak spots, its few lapses in intensity, *The Book of Nightmares* is major poetry. (p. 31)

Robert Langbaum, "Galway Kinnell's 'The Book of Nightmares'," in The American Poetry Review *(copyright © 1979 by World Poetry, Inc.; reprinted by permission of Robert Langbaum), March/April 1979, pp. 30-1.*

KOHOUT, Pavel   1928-

Kohout is a controversial Czech playwright, novelist, flimscript writer, essayist, and poet. His work is no longer published or produced in his own country as a consequence of his support for the 1968 "Spring in Prague." His provocative themes presented in highly original forms have gained him a wide audience. His satirical novels *From the Diary of a Counterrevolutionary* and *White Book in the Case of Adam Juráček* both attack the intractability of Marxism. (See also *Contemporary Authors*, Vols. 45-48.)

RONALD STEEL

Journal d'un contre-révolutionnaire, though completed in 1969, does not suffer from lack of perspective. It is a work of literature, perhaps the most brilliant and accomplished to come from Czechoslovakia since the intervention, and at the same time a triumph of clever political journalism. . . .

Kohout's book is not a self-justification, but an attempt to get the contradictions in his own life into some sort of coherent relationship. The *Journal* is made up three separate narratives, printed with rather obvious symbolism in three different typefaces, which advance in a sort of triple formation by installments. There is a journal which starts on August 21, which finds Kohout on holiday in Italy at a crisis in his relationship with the young girl Z. The second element is a refurbished journal covering the years between 1945 and late 1967, beginning with the Prague rising against the Germans and ending with a comic and memorable dramatization of the writers' congress on the eve of the reform. The third journal describes his own activities and reactions from January, 1968, until the last weeks before the [Soviet] invasion.

The three narratives are tightly pulled together by the presence of friends who appear in all of them in their own equally extraordinary transformations. . . . I know of no other book, apart from the novels of Kundera and Vaculik, that brings the foreigner closer to the personal realities of Czechoslovakia. (p. 24)

> *Ronald Steel, in* The New York Review of Books *(reprinted with permission from* The New York Review of Books; *copyright © 1971 Nyrev, Inc.),* September 2, 1971.

BRENDAN GILL

["Poor Murderer"] is highly accessible in its wit, in its unflagging energy, and in its nimble, crisscrossing cat's cradle of a plot, which throws off pleasing little surprises from first line to last. There are moments when it will put you in mind of Peter Weiss's "Marat/Sade," or of Tom Stoppard's "Rosencrantz and Guildenstern Are Dead," or possibly of one or another of Pirandello's darkly prankish pirouettes through time, but far from disowning these distinguished ancestors, "Poor Murderer" pays open tribute to them; [Pavel Kohout] also acknowledges his debt to Shakespeare, whose "Hamlet" forms portions of a play within the play, and to a short story by Leonid Andreyev called "Thought." For the thousandth time and with the usual delight, we observe how the artist, out of a past laboriously mastered, fashions with seeming ease something indisputably new. (p. 99)

> *Brendan Gill, in* The New Yorker *(© 1976 by The New Yorker Magazine, Inc.),* November 1, 1976.

JOHN SIMON

Pavel Kohout's *Poor Murderer* makes me doubly sorry for its author. Bad enough to be physically restrained in Czechoslovakia by refusal of a travel visa; how much worse to be intellectually sequestered from what goes on in the free world, so that you write as if Pirandello, Giraudoux and Anouilh were the reigning dramatists and concoct a pale pastiche of their manner.

The play (based on a story by the now passé Leonid Andreyev) concerns Kerzhentsev, an actor confined to a mental institution in turn-of-the-century St. Petersburg. . . .

We next are meant to wonder whether he is really mad, or merely, like Hamlet, feigning madness, but—since he is a garrulous, self-important dullard—it is unfortunately rather hard to care. As for the romantic triangle underlying the tale, it is so limply passionless as to make it sublimely unimportant who ends up with whom. Of course, it is also possible that the whole thing takes place in the hero's mind, that the entire thing is just a piece of phantasmagoria; but then there are things in the play that contradict even this—rather boring—possibility.

We are also meant to be in suspense about the outcome: Will the hero be declared sane and have to face [trial for murder]? Or insane, and remain confined to the asylum? Or somehow be set free? . . . I wouldn't give a kopek to know, even if the playwright had deigned to shed some of that ambiguity he wraps himself in. (p. 26)

> *John Simon, in* The New Leader *(© 1976 by the American Labor Conference on International Affairs, Inc.),* November 22, 1976.

MARKETA GOETZ STANKIEWICZ

"Pavel Kohout was given to our theater so that there would not be any peace and quiet." With these words a well-known Czech critic begins an essay on Kohout in which he commiserates with an imaginary scholar writing a book on contemporary Czechoslovak theatre. Faced with this *enfant terrible* of the Czech stage who has evoked more praise and more abuse than any other contemporary Czechoslovak writer, the hapless imaginary scholar would apparently feel himself "sliding down a curving ramp" which permitted neither foothold nor sense of direction. Appreciative of this unsolicited *a priori* description of the problematic nature of the task at hand, I shall try merely to suggest some areas of interest and value in Kohout's colourful body of work. (p. 251)

Kohout is an exciting writer. The very ease and nonchalance with which he manages to turn out one work after another—extremely varied in nature, each seeming to bear the imprint of a different type of creative genius—make his productions a cornucopia of surprises. (p. 252)

[The tremendous success of *Such a Love* (1957) is] surprising if we remind ourselves of the almost banal theme of the play: a two men/one woman situation that ends in the suicide of the girl. The main reason for the impact of this well-worn story was that Kohout had told it in a special form. Not that this form was particularly new; among others Brecht had used it and Pirandello before him. But Kohout seems to have found a particularly happy way of building the play around a courtroom scene and gradually illuminating the motivations of the characters involved. . . . As the past events of this seemingly simple story are brought to light, definite concepts of "guilt" and "innocence" fade, and it becomes less and less possible to use these absolute terms with regard to the characters' actions.

It is here perhaps that we find the essential reason for the great success of [his play]. . . . For the first time since the hiatus of the Second World War, an East European writer had written a play about an insoluble problem. The basic questions raised by the play—who is guilty of the tragedy? who is to judge where the borderline between guilt and innocence lies?—were new and provocative in a society where an unquestionable system had been providing unshakeable truths.

With this acute sense for the "hot topic"—a sense that has been called his glory as well as his downfall—Kohout had written a play that satisfied people's increasing need to think about those regions of life where relationships are multi-levelled, where the smooth road of predictable development turns out to be a delusion. (pp. 252-53)

Controversial in another way, Pavel Kohout, like Bertolt Brecht, has been variously chided for his willingness to use and adapt other writers' material. . . . [Kohout answers:] "I admit, I have more fun with adaptations for the stage than with my own plays. Writing is like a game of solitaire, the author plays against himself. An adaptation, on the other hand, is like a duel. You must force the picture to leave its frame and become alive. You must breathe life even into a collection of newspaper clippings." Without digressing into the question of the precision or fairness of this opinion, we can recognize Kohout's attitude that the main task of the playwright-adapter is to add "a third dimension" to a two-dimensional work of art. (pp. 253-54)

[The] artistic director of the Vinohrady Theatre in Prague asked Kohout to write a play for the 1962/63 season. . . . The result was the "Musical mystery" *War with the Newts* [an adaption of Karel Čapek's novel, *Válka s mloky*], conceived—and here again appear Kohout's sure dramatic intuition and flexibility—as a "live television coverage of the destruction of the world, with documentary photographs about the cause and the development of the apocalypse, relayed by the last yet unsubmerged television tower." The whole stage was conceived as one giant television screen. A chorus-like group of reporters propelled the action. Individually they would step out of the group in order to re-enact the most important incidents of Čapek's novel. Then they would merge again with the unified chorus, who recited in hexameter the terrible story of the rise of the Newts, thus giving the events the timeless awe-inspiring character of Greek tragedy. Čapek's *roman feuilleton* had been expanded into Kohout's "third dimension" and become something like a lightweight *Gesamtkunstwerk,* combining the explosive spectacle of a contemporary war film with the stark serenity of Greek tragedy.

The play was a huge success. Open to a variety of interpretations, Čapek's masterpiece of a utopian allegory about creatures initiated in methods of destructiveness by man himself radiated from the stage a variety of meanings that were electrifying to an audience who was eager to hear the opposite of a single-minded ideological message. Yet, ironically, Kohout's play was immune to political censorship, because long ago Čapek's novel had passed the censorship board with high marks. . . . [Paradoxically], Čapek's work found itself with just the right credentials to pass censorship

despite the fact that it consistently attacks non-democratic systems in any form as the prime enemies of all human culture and intellectual freedom. (pp. 254-55)

Kohout's three dramatic adaptations (the other two being Jules Verne's *Around the World in Eighty Days* and scenes from Jaroslav Hašek's *The Good Soldier Švejk*) have proved to be among the most highly demanded items of Czechoslovak literary export. The reason for this is threefold. First, part of the appeal results from the very choice of material, always a well-known work of literature that has been transferred to the stage. Second, the playwright-adapter has managed to preserve the particular genius and quality of the original work and at the same time to suggest in a highly imaginative way its meaning for the contemporary world. Third, but not last, Kohout and his team (whose good work he mentions at every opportunity) have created in each case excellent theatrical entertainment which, after all, has been the key to the best dramatic writing ever since the Ancient Greeks. (p. 256)

[In *August August august,* the] action consists of a circus performance with muscular trapeze artists; an elegant top-hatted Circus Manager using flowery language; a band which plays resolute marches, slow waltzes and fanfares according to the varying nature of the circus acts—and, of course, the inevitable clown who comes racing into the ring, asks awkward questions, believes anything anyone says, gets his face slapped, and delights the audience. (pp. 256-57)

Kohout's [clown] August in never shaken in his belief that his own great dream—to train eight white Lippizan horses for an exquisite dressage performance—is shared by the entire audience. (p. 257)

August is ready to accept any "condition" put to him to achieve his dream object, the horses. Perhaps we remember Samuel Beckett's clowns who also have to deal with a condition—that of waiting. Despite the fact that we might feel Kohout is overstating the case when he claims that "those conditions which my August is given by the Manager, become the basic condition of human life," we cannot fail to realize that the rising and ebbing waters of joy and disappointment, of hope and despair in the play are conceived on a much deeper level than a clown's bouts of laughter and tears. Kohout, as always writing not *for* the stage but *with* the stage, knew that heavy-handed symbolism was the enemy of the theatre. He had to avoid "letting the circus roof be crushed by the weight of the allegory, and turning the circus ring into a mere symbol." What was needed were all the trimmings of a real circus performance with its roars of laughter, its breathless tension, its gaudy colours and screeching sounds.

August August august is a work that has to be approached as one confronts a Russian doll which contains another doll which contains another doll. The play contains an idea within an idea within an idea. (p. 258)

There is nothing new about the literary figure of the dreamer; he has a long line of ancestry from Don Quixote onward. But there is a ring to Kohout's play which had an original and contemporary meaning for the Czechoslovak audience. The top brass of the circus never deny the possibility of August's dream coming true; in fact, they keep referring to it in a friendly manner. However, the dream material is carefully measured out, and when August overdoes his dreaming, he gets a lesson that causes a rude awakening. At a certain point, a man's dream becomes punishable. When August, with his clown-wife, Lulu, and their child as spectators, is given tails, a top hat and a whip, and is asked to perform his great dream-number, the horse dressage, we sense something sinister brewing. During the preparations, a huge cage is set up, beastly roars are heard from outside, and Lulu, who is asked to take a seat in the cage, expresses increasing anxiety. The Manager's last warning is ominous: "A dream should remain a dream, August. Otherwise you kill it. Do you understand that?" August's affirmative answer is, of course, meaningless. The only thing he understands about a dream is that "a dream is a dream if it is dreamt," and the only thing he wants is to perform his dressage with eight white Lippizan horses. August is incapable of understanding that this great wish, and the wisher too, will be destroyed once it becomes reality. Instead of the white dream horses, the audience catches a fleeting glimpse of the first ravenous tiger rushing toward August as the lights go out and a deafening drum-whirl fills the air. When, a few seconds later, the lights go on again, the performers take their bows from an empty circus ring. With flowery solemnity the Manager speaks the final words to the audience, wishing them "the very best for your way homeward and for our further common way into the future—." (pp. 258-59)

[Bad Luck under the Roof, Fire in the Basement, and War on the Fourth Floor, in Kohout's words,] "form a trilogy of one-act plays under the overall title Life in a Quiet House...." The three plays are variations on a theme that could be defined as a humorous version of a Kafka nightmare. State authorities of undefinable but obviously vast powers penetrate into the peaceful habitat of average couples and destroy their lives within the dramatic time at their disposal. In each case the powers' interference occurs in the same, seemingly inexplicable way. Servants of the state suddenly appear in the guise of postmen who have passkeys, firefighters sliding down a pole, masked guards emerging out of closets. Within a matter of seconds they have changed the quiet rooms—bedrooms in each case—into hectic scenes of uncannily military nature. They shout orders, telephone secret higher authorities, conduct cross-examinations of the stunned tenants, and thwart their questions with incomprehensible "official" language. In each case the victims are a couple—similarly surprised, harassed and driven to unforeseen extremities. Each time they are in bed—either in reality or, say, in spirit.... In all three plays, the privacy of a bed with all its connotations of the joys of intimacy, peace and safety from the world outside, is put in glaring contrast to the uniformed officiousness, punctilious legality, and omnipotence of the superior powers which, by the end of the play, have taken full possession of the scene. (pp. 259-60)

The author tells us that [Bad Luck under the Roof] explores the way in which "a constantly repeated lie or absurd claim, supported by all the means a modern power has at its disposal, becomes a reality." (p. 261)

Throughout Kohout's work we witness his particular characteristic—which is also a characteristic of Czechoslovak theatre—the constant fierce awareness that the actual text is only part of the whole structure of the play; that the word is only one of many possible ways an audience can be reached. Moreover, these other possibilities have a distinct advantage over the spoken word. They belong solely to the stage and have therefore a more immediate impact. It is here that we may find the hidden source of the strong bond between the social topicality and the circus-like quality of Kohout's work. . . . Kohout's theatre seems to have developed apart from general theatre repertory; in response to the general public's need to be offered topical entertainment, it draws its subject matter from their familiar contemporary scene. The author's somewhat uneven literary talent may lay itself open to criticism because of its very richness and many-sidedness. But one thing is certain: Kohout uses every aspect of the stage with unfailing intuition and to the delight of any audience. He is, one might say—entirely without irony—truly a playwright of the people. For the world outside watching the ups and downs of the rich theatre life of this small country. Pavel Kohout emerges as an outstanding, colourful sample of Czechoslovakia's dramatic culture and as a barometer of Czechoslovak theatre. (pp. 261-62)

Marketa Goetz Stankiewicz, "Pavel Kohout: The Barometer of Czechoslovakia's Theatre," in Modern Drama *(copyright © 1977, University of Toronto, Graduate Centre for Study of Drama; with the permission of* Modern Drama*), September, 1977, pp. 251-62.*

JOSEF ŠKVORECKÝ

In his personal story Pavel Kohout, known best as a playwright . . . , literally embodies the development of the intellectual core of the Czechoslovak Communist Party from the idealistic and sometimes downright idiotic acceptance of socialism reduced to Stalinist dogma in the fifties (his first poems and plays are an excellent example) to the sophistication of Czechoslovak Marxist thinking of the second half of the sixties (his latest plays amply demonstrate this). *White Book* is Kohout's first novel. . . .

The author's theatrical experience is clearly noticeable: the book uses techniques essentially similar to those employed by writers who, in the sixties, read their stories from the stages of the "small theatres" of Prague; these "text-appeal" stories too were predominantly satirical, and, more often than not, of an absurdist nature. But *White Book* is a fine novel, well shaped and absorbing, to which—as to the works of Kafka—history has added another dimension. . . .

White Book, written long before the latest Prague demonstrations of the "class concept" of legality, sheds a prophetic and wildly sarcastic light on the regime's present legal contradictions by having its hero break a natural law: contrary to Newton, Adam Juráček manages to levitate. There are numerous allusions to the events of 1968, but in the last analysis the entire grimly black joke can stand as a metaphorical judgment of a Marxism that can no longer cope with new facts, except in a (pseudo) legal and psychiatric fashion. . . .

White Book convincingly demonstrates that its author is one of those versatile writers who feel at home in all literary forms and in several genres. (p. 308)

Josef Škvorecký, in World Literature Today *(copyright 1978 by the University of Oklahoma Press), Vol. 52, No. 2, Spring, 1978.*

JEREMY TREGLOWN

Satire rarely translates well. It depends not only on common assumptions (no sweat in the particular case of Pavel Kohout's critique of Soviet oppression) but, more problematically, on a common shock-threshold. So *White Book* presents a dilemma. I wanted to find it a courageously funny act of protest by this Czech author against a regime whose response to such acts is (as the fiction reminds us) notably humourless. But after a few pages it reads predictably, a story that suffers in translation by comparison with the Western satiric fantasies it emulates (Pynchon, Vonnegut, Brautigan).

The first problem is that east of Berlin everyone needs something blunter than a rapier to get his ideas home. . . . We're in a particularly bad position to enjoy communist anti-establishment irony because the capitalist variety is— in proportion to the deviousness of its targets—so much subtler. Besides, in the Soviet case we don't really see the joke. The further an audience is from tragedy, the gloomier it wants to be made. What we ask from these chaps is a bit of pity and terror.

Kohout's absurdist story has a low surprise-quotient, too. It begins promisingly with a young PE teacher who, in defiance of socialist physics, learns to levitate. Every so often he just walks on the ceiling. What makes this idea in a damaging way more tragic than absurd is the inevitability of everything that follows. He becomes a folk hero but an official enemy; is involved in some bureaucratic confusions resulting from alternate attempts to exploit and obscure his achievement; is tried on various charges and sent to a psychiatric 'hospital' where, after prolonged resistance, he capitulates to gravity.

All this is presented as a sequence of heavily comic reconstructions of contemporary records, interspersed with accounts by people involved, transcripts of meetings, and so on, all annotated by anonymous officials. It's these *Dunciad*-like notes that pay off best, their plodding unimaginativeness a funny contrast with such freedom as the narrative manages. Historical 'errors' are corrected, jokes laboriously explained. In the end, though, it all seems underrealised: you need your own idiom—as provided in Stoppard's most recent plays—to bring the situation home in anything other than documentary terms. (p. 249)

> *Jeremy Treglown, in* New Statesman (© *1978 The Statesman & Nation Publishing Co. Ltd.), August 25, 1978.*

ARTHUR N. ATHANASON

New York Times critic Clive Barnes described *Poor Murderer* as "a strange, dazzling . . . intellectual play that zigzags across the stage and richochets across the mind."

The play's protagonist Anton Ignatyevich Kerzhentsev is a young turn-of-the-century Russian actor confined in the St. Elizabeth Institute for Nervous Disorders in St. Petersburg. . . .

[He] is granted permission to stage an autobiographical play in the great hall of the institute as a means of proving to the authorities and to himself that he is sane as well as guilty of a murderous act of passion. It becomes subtly apparent that Kerzhentsev's performance of the play-within-the-play is a desperate attempt to refute to himself and others his fear of being passionless; but the result is his realization that for his whole life, he, more than anyone else, has perpetrated his own emotional incarceration.

Poor Murderer is neither a great nor always dramatically satisfying play, for it attempts to deal with more awesome complexities of the human spirit than it can effectively handle in its two acts. But it is an ambitious, courageous and often passionate play about passionlessness and the enforced incarceration of the artist. (p. 654)

> *Arthur N. Athanason, in* World Literature Today *(copyright 1978 by the University of Oklahoma Press), Vol. 52, No. 4, Autumn, 1978.*

*   *   *

KUMIN, Maxine   1925-

Kumin, a Pulitzer Prize-winner, is an American poet, novelist, and writer for children. Her poetry is distinguished by sharp images of closely observed natural phenomena. (See also *CLC*, Vol. 5, and *Contemporary Authors*, Vols. 1-4, rev. ed.)

HELEN VENDLER

It's hard to know what to say about Maxine Kumin's new volume ["House, Bridge, Fountain, Gate"]. It suffers from a disease of similes: children "naked as almonds," kisses "like polka dots," a corset spread out "like a filleted fish," someone "patient as an animal," a visit "as important as summer," chromosomes "tight as a chain gang," and genes "like innocent porters" all inhabit one poem, and the disease (one shared with Anne Sexton) becomes mortal as the book continues. The poems talk about family, about living in Kentucky, about horses; and they have a cheerful will to make the best of things, to make things grow, to save things from frost, to take lessons from nature. There is something admirable about this as an attitude, but the whimsy in Kumin gets in my way, the spunkiness of "the survival artist" finally cloys. In "A Time for the Eating of Grasses" we progress through the seasons from spring to fall (and Kumin's poems are often predictable in their structure), watching grass being eaten by geese, then lambs, then cows, and finally by the goat. . . . There is no point in asking Kumin to be other than whimsical, because when she tries to be deadly serious she is speaking under strain and constraint. She dutifully describes, for instance, various hideous experiments performed by the Defense Department (sewing eyelids of rabbits open; giving shocks to dolphins, mice and monkeys; implanting electrodes into cats; substituting plastic hearts in calves) and then ends her poem— "Heaven as Anus"—with an embarrassing indictment of some invisible deity. . . . [There is, in this poem,] comic language presumably intending a Swiftian effect, with a side glance toward something dignified with the name of "excremental vision." But Swift would not have parodied the hymnal at the end; somehow the bitterness here can't find a proper language. Kumin's less ambitious poems, like the riddling "Song for Seven Parts of the Body," are closer to her competence; here she is plausible and light, if still too girlish for some tastes. (pp. 7-8)

> *Helen Vendler, in* The New York Times Book Review (© *1975 by the New York Times Company; reprinted by permission), September 7, 1975.*

BARBARA FIALKOWSKI

The fields of Maxine Kumin's new book of poems, *House, Bridge, Fountain, Gate*, are fusions of the external and internal worlds a poet must confront. They are her gardens and she as poet has been about naming their flora and fauna. Kumin has said that the poet must be "terribly specific about naming things . . . naming things that already exist, and making them new just because the names are so specific . . . bringing them back to the world's attention . . . dealing with names that are small and overlooked." (p. 108)

Kumin doesn't miss a speck. Her drive for detail and her compulsion to name recall Thoreau. Her poems speak to us of "wet burls of earthworms" ("Up From the Earth") and the "gaggle of gnats" ("Amanda Dreams She Has Died and Gone to the Elysian Fields") that "housekeeps in her" horse's "ears." . . .

Language is . . . swept up, as if uttered for the first time "bald as an onion." Kumin includes children's rhymes and games, imbuing them and thereby her poetry with surprises. (p. 109)

Kumin's poems happen in the present tense. Even history occurs now. In "The Death of Uncles" Kumin's metaphor for the presentness of the past is cinema. . . . There is no past in cinema. Events have the authority of Now.

Kumin speaks of this presence as if possessed by it, telling becomes her mission. In "Life's Work" she says,

> Well, the firm old fathers are dead
> and I didn't come to grief.
> I came to words instead
> to tell the little tale that's left. . . .

The past, things, these are possessors for which, as Kumin suggests in her epithet, the poet is merely voice. (pp. 109-10)

Yet though Kumin is the voice of her world, she is also its creator. The objective and subjective worlds come together as do the body and the spirit. . . . Kumin as poet is the voice of the spirit, the listening poet and the creator. (p. 110)

Her world is complete in that it incorporates change. She *is* change and does not regret giving herself up. . . . The violence of death is not frightening to Kumin. There is nothing of the romancer in her attitude toward nature. (pp. 110-11)

The poet has created herself, placed herself at the center of her poems. Kumin might well understand Alan Dugan's words in his poem, "Variation on a Theme by Stevens,"

> it is absolutely typical to say
> goodbye while saying hello.

The poems of *House, Bridge, Fountain, Gate,* are "absolutely typical." (p. 111)

> Barbara Fialkowski, in Shenandoah (copyright 1976 by Washington and Lee University; reprinted from Shenandoah: The Washington and Lee University Review with the permission of the Editor), Spring, 1976.

PHILIP BOOTH

[The maturity of Maxine Kumin's poems] is the uniquely lovely maturity of a woman who has never forgotten the girlhood she has long since outgrown.

The values *The Retrieval System* values . . . are primarily conservational. The book in no way presents itself as any kind of "breakthrough" experiment; it isn't *Life Studies* or

Ariel, nor does it want to be. It is, rather, prime Maxine Kumin, who has simply gotten better and better at what she has always been good at: a resonant language, an autobiographical immediacy, unsystematized intelligence, and radical compassion. One does not learn compassion without having suffered, but poems like "Splitting Wood at Six Above" amply show that suffering doesn't require confession to validate pain. Maxine Kumin's mode is memorial rather than confessional: in celebrating the past, and her own part in its passing, she celebrates in herself the very capacity to survive.

Recurrence and memory steady Maxine Kumin "against the wrong turn, / the closedward babel of anomie." Beyond her daily milk-runs between house and barn, she often makes the connection between present and past by way of dreams. But her dreams are dreams worked-through to poems: they shape and make a music of their meanings even as they explore and report them. Jerome Bruner says somewhere that the problem of information is "not storage but retrieval;" Maxine Kumin's poems are over and over informed, and lent depth by, the individuality of *The Retrieval System* which is this book's title and its introductory poem. She deeply sees . . .

> elderly aunts, wearing the heads of willful
> intelligent ponies, stand at the fence begging apples.
> The sister who died at three has my cat's faint chin,
> my cat's inscrutable squint, and cried catlike in pain.

> I remember the funeral. *The Lord is my shepherd,*
> we said. I don't want to brood. Fact: it is people who
>   fade,
> it is animals that retrieve them. . . .

What other poet (saving only, perhaps, Elizabeth Bishop or A. R. Ammons) would risk that "fact" with its colon? Few poets would chance *following* the flat statement of memory by the apparently equal flatness of "*The Lord is my shepherd,* / we said." But the flatness is redeemed by how "shepherd" is echoed by "said," "brood," "fade"; the irony of "we said" precisely derives from how the previous line is end-stopped. To miss as much, or as little, in reading Maxine Kumin is to miss—in this poem—how gently the ironies reverberate within its seeming facticity, until, in the unexcused absence of the Lord, it is animals that shepherd our most human remembering.

Maxine Kumin is, so to speak, as full of facts as either Bishop or Ammons, but her work is innately inclined toward less speculation about what she feels or how she sees. . . . Maxine Kumin's book most strongly of all calls to mind the charged facticity of Randall Jarrell's *The Lost World.* . . .

Nobody who has read her fiction, or "In April, In Princeton," here, can doubt her own urbanity. But the distinctive nature of Maxine Kumin's present poems derives from the primary fact that she lives in, and writes from a world where constant (if partial) recovery of what's "lost" is as sure as the procession of the equinoxes, or as familiar as mucking-out the horses' daily dung. (p. 18)

Such cyclical optimism isn't cheaply earned. When one reaches fifty, and beyond, regeneration of any kind is hard to come by. But the second essential fact of these poems is that Maxine Kumin has come to the time of her lifetime when, as poet and person, she finds it vitally necessary to

outlive the departed by surviving their present absence. . . .
[She] is familiar (in every sense) with how one's parents
depart toward death at nearly the same time one's children
leave to find lives of their own. Inevitable as such deser-
tions may be, their coincidence (multiplied by a close-in
suicide) is the shock which these seismographic poems record and try to recover from. . . .

Her compassion is never condescending; her emotions,
however complex, are always clear, even in those poems
which confront the suicide of her closest friend. *The Retrieval System* also deals strongly with the death of her
father; but Maxine Kumin is most of all moving when she
focuses on her daughters (to whom *Retrieval* is dedicated),
and the mutual "uncertainties" she shares with them in
what she wryly calls "this mothering business." . . .

Maxine Kumin knows that she and her lawschool daughter
"bulge toward the separate fates that await us," and that
her own fate is bearing the realization of mortality that accompanies maternity. . . . The poet says she is "afflicted"
with the immediacy of memory; but such memory is, as she
well knows, the sure vitality of these poems. Even in the
tense present of "Changing the Children," or "Parting," or
"Sunbathing . . ." or "Seeing the Bones," Maxine Kumin
sees both ways: *back* to her now very old mother . . . , and
forward to her hope (against death) that she may be "borne
onward" in her daughters' bellies

> like those old pear-shaped Russian dolls that open
> at the middle to reveal another and another, down
> to the pea-sized, irreductible minim . . .

Whether sensing the world *in utero* or *post partum*, Maxine
Kumin knows that we are all "locked up in our own story";
but she equally knows that to tell each story is part of the
poet's function. Whether she knows it or not, she is intuitively faithful to the sense of Isak Dinesen's "Be loyal to
the story" as Hannah Arendt interprets it: "Be loyal to life
. . . accept what life is giving you, show yourself worthy of
whatever it may be by recollecting and pondering over it,
thus repeating it in imagination; this is the way to remain
alive." These poems recollect in every sense; the story for
Maxine Kumin is most of all telling in how surely the laws
of conservation apply to family as well as to farmstead. . . .

But poems as human as these, by the very definition of
humanity, are bound to have some small failings. A line like
"when she was in the egg unconsidered" seems to me, in
context, rhythmically flat; I'm also stopped by some enjambed lines which look and sound (even within a single
poem) otherwise parallel to lines which are end-punctuated.
My reader's ear is repeatedly troubled that so aurally sophisticated a poet should add to modulated rhyming the si-
bilance that always derives from playing off what's singular
against plurals ("winter"/"manners" or "save"/"graves"
etc.). But these are mostly such minor flaws as one poet
often hears in another poet's work yet seldom notices in his
own. What is more surely worth notice in Maxine Kumin's
work is the extent to which she has individually outrun the
limitations of the generation which poetically came-of-age
twenty years ago. . . . One of Maxine Kumin's strengths
has always been the way in which her implied narratives
combine a Frostian delight in metaphor with Marianne
Moore's insistence on being a "literalist of the imagination." There are few poets who so clearly know the names
of things, or who value more deeply the eventful literalness

of our language. . . . Where being a "literalist" suffices,
Maxine Kumin can let language be; where she wants metaphor, her metaphors are deeply rooted in the facticity of
what Jarrell called "the dailiness of life."

Nobody's poems of that "dailiness" are, this side of Frost,
as strongly peopled as Jarrell's. Neither are anybody's peopled poems as strongly creaturely as those in *The Retrieval
System*. . . . [Maxine Kumin] has become the woman who
exorcises her demons by making a poetry of horses. And
not only horses, but the usual run of dogs, cats torturing
chipmunks, porcupines, raccoons, chickadees, deer,
fieldmice, frogs, woodchucks, pigs and lambs—the backyard familiars of rural life anywhere. . . . Reading *The Retrieval System,* I wonder if to refuse suicide, yet be able to
come to terms with a friend's killing herself, may not have
much to do with the dailiness of farm life and farm death,
with a poetry which comprehends how

> my pony
> filching apples, rears and catches
> his halter on a branch and hangs
> himself all afternoon. . . .

No, Maxine Kumin is not immune from anguish; but anguish becomes integrated in how the poems get written, in
how the book (or the life) is composed. *The Retrieval System* is brilliantly sectioned and ordered; its poems are so
much of a piece, so skilfully equal to the variety of their
concern, that each reinforces the other. An organic book, a
family of poems. It is not random that the book's second
from final poem is "How It Goes On," a poem which identifies, as Jarrell repeatedly did, with victimized innocence:

> O lambs! The whole wolf-world sits down to eat
> and cleans its muzzle after.

But it *does* go on, the dailiness of life, in spite of the ways
in which man is wolf to both lamb, wolf, and himself. . . . It
"goes on" every day. And every day has become for Maxine Kumin, as her final title tells, "A Mortal Day of No
Surprises." The poet rests in the marginal assurance that,
although "the mare's / in heat and miserable, / squirting,
rubbing her tail bare . . . ," the day is as predictable as the
song of a white-throat sparrow; the poet, too, will predictably pass:

> When I'm scooped out of here
> all things animal
> an unsurprised will carry on.

And there will even be, on that predictable land renewed by
another family, "someone else's mare to call / to the stallion."

As she lends "a rakish permanence to / the idea of going
on," Maxine Kumin's acceptance of death as "fact" (colon) in no way reduces her tough-minded will to survive, or
her capacities as surveyor of what's past but never done
with. Being gifted, she knows to give form to her recollection: in the full context they provide for their emotion, in
the generosity of their description, these poems clearly
make a present of the present. They honor the moment by
duly valuing the past that composes it; written from ground-
level, they are not above caring for horses as part of the
world's total poem. These poems retrieve our best instincts, our realizing that it is possible to survive grief: not
without pain, but also not without joy. (p. 19)

Philip Booth, "Maxine Kumin's Survival," in The

American Poetry Review *(copyright © 1978 by World Poetry, Inc.; reprinted by permission of Philip Booth), November/December, 1978, pp. 18-19.*

HARVEY CURTIS WEBSTER

Maxine Kumin thinks of Anne Sexton as her "best friend"; they lunched together cheerfully the day before Sexton killed herself. They shared a sense of woman's bondage by both nature and society. Though they have written occasionally of social matters . . . , neither has written poems of social protest comparable to Adrienne Rich's. Both have concentrated on their individual lives as subject matter. . . . [At] her worst (a rarity in her last two books), Kumin is too New Yorker-sophisticated. . . . Kumin uses similes more than Sexton, though sometimes her metaphors (the potatoes' "ten tentative erections") shock in the best sense of the word. . . . Kumin, who is [hard] to pin down, is represented rather well by her reluctant wearing of dead Sexton's clothes in "How It Is." Most of Kumin's poems turn from inside to outside. . . . Although Kumin can write a poem entitled "Heaven as Anus," and close one of her best poems with the line "I honor shit for saying: We go on," an appropriately startling conclusion to a poem that epitomizes *The Retrieval System,* usually it is her homely similes one remembers: cows wear "their flies like black tears"; she prays the Lord will raise her up each day "like bread." In their accurate specificity, Kumin's poems surpass Sexton's and rival [Peter] Davison's.

Kumin is almost consistently good as she diversifies her daily life into poems. Sometimes in *The Retrieval System*—a fine binding metaphor for all the poems in her current book—Kumin echoes Frost's rhythms and whimsy a shade too closely, as in "Extrapolations from Henry Manley's Pie Plant"; sometimes she is cutely obscure, as in "Song for Seven Parts of the Body." Usually she converts her own experience into anyone's experience without losing its particularity. (p. 232)

Harvey Curtis Webster, in Poetry *(© 1979 by The Modern Poetry Association; reprinted by permission of the Editor of* Poetry)*, January, 1979.*

L

LAGERKVIST, Pär   1891-1974

Lagerkvist was a Swedish poet, playwright, and novelist. Known as an expressionist in his early days, Lagerkvist is best known for his *Barabbas*, which was one of the first novels to deal with a biblical subject in a realistic manner. Known for his spare, haunting prose style, Lagerkvist won the 1951 Nobel Prize for Literature. (See also *CLC*, Vols. 7, 10, and *Contemporary Authors*, obituary, Vols. 49-52.)

GUNNEL MALMSTRÖM

"I constantly conduct a dialogue with myself," Pär Lagerkvist once said in a talk on his works, "one book answers the other".

Despite the constant varying of the answers, the dialogue is always concerned with the same thing, a search for the *meaning* of existence. Lagerkvist has experienced more intensely than most the central dilemma for twentieth-century man within the Christian sphere of influence: where can we find a foothold when we no longer believe in God?

The whole of Lagerkvist's creative work can be said to spring from a fundamentally divided experience of existence. We learn from the autobiographical description with the significant title "Gäst hos verkligheten" ("Guest of Reality") how the child and young man experienced two alternative worlds, the home, with the mother as its central support, and life outside. He himself stood apart from both, unable to commit himself fully to either.

His mother's world, illumined by Christian faith, represents meaningful coherence with a metaphysical superstructure and a firm system of values. Life implies a blind, biological, natural process in which man is merely an involuntary element with inescapable annihilation awaiting him. This is the meaning of the formula *"things as they are"* ("så som det är"), which recurs with minor variations throughout Lagerkvist's work, whereas the formula for his mother's world is *"that which does not exist"* ("det some inte finns").

These are the two poles in Lagerkvist's imaginative world, and he constantly swings between them. But it is always his mother's world that is the positive pattern. Most of the female figures in his work are formed in her image, and it is also from her world that he derives his two key words "light" and "peace". Even though Lagerkvist cannot by any means be said to have attained a firm faith in God, it is the two transcending forces in human life, the longing for spiritual reality and the longing for love, that always constitute the meaningful and controlling factors in his attempted solutions to the problem of life's significance. They are the very foundation pillars in "the world of the human heart" that he has mapped out for us.

The sense of alienation from existence is a major theme in twentieth-century literature, and as one of its interpreters Lagerkvist is akin to writers like Kafka and Camus. He belongs among those whose struggle against the dehumanization of mankind has led them to seek for *the hidden God*, a solution to the metaphysical riddles of life.

This has been particularly marked in the last two decades; from "Barabbas" onwards the magnetic power from the pole of "what does not exist" has been decisive in Lagerkvist's work. (pp. 57-8)

Lagerkvist's power to create images is perhaps his most characteristic gift as a writer. I do not think that Lagerkvist's books spring to mind primarily as quotations, but it is as pictures—of people and situations—that they remain in our memory. We need only think of figures like "the Hangman" and "the Dwarf", leading representatives of a one-dimensional world, "things as they are".

In his more recent phase Lagerkvist has given us a sequence of images for *man in relationship to the hidden God*. The pictures are taken in a peculiar twilight which often gives us plus and minus variants at one glance; it is the deep truth of paradox that they convey. (p. 58)

Lagerkvist's work from 1950 to 1964 constitutes a closely connected sequence, of which the five prose works, "Barabbas" (1950), "The Sibyl" (1956), "The Death of Ahasuerus" (1960), "Pilgrim at Sea" (1962) and "The Holy Land" (1964) are interlinked entities within a five-part picture, while "Aftonland" (1953) provides a lyrical background.

"Mariamne" (1967) . . . provides a more independent epilogue.

"Aftonland" is a fruitful place to begin our short survey precisely because the collection of poems acts as a sounding-board for the themes found separately in the novels.

The collection is divided into five sections, with varying themes, but the atmosphere is more or less the same throughout, and this gives the collection a powerful unity. The posing of the problems, or more accurately of the *questions* connected with man's relationship to God, also contributes to this effect.

After the first three sections have led us into "aftonlandet", the land of the preparation for death, and have emphasized man's eternal, unquenchable longing, we are confronted with the fourth and in every way the most powerful section. In twenty-four poems Lagerkvist here gives as many variations on the same theme, the relationship between mankind and the two powers, death and god.

It is also here that we find the most suggestive expression of the major dilemma, in the poem "En främling är min vän": "Vem är du som uppfyller mitt hjärta med din frånvaro? Som uppfyller hela världen med din frånvaro" ("Who are you who fills my heart with your absence? Who fills the whole world with your absence?"). This might be called the formula for man's relationship to the hidden God. (pp. 58-9)

The hidden God passes by, acting as it were absent-mindedly, without attention or consideration for the "victim" who is being overwhelmed, as is so often the case with Lagerkvist. (pp. 59-60)

The sense of alienation is dual: for the poet, God is alien, unattainable and incomprehensible, but at the same time the experience of him has such power that the poet is also a stranger in his surroundings. This is perhaps the heart of Lagerkvist's creative writing, most markedly so in his more recent period. It is a recurring theme in "Aftonland", and it distinguishes most of the characters in the prose works, especially Barabbas, the Sibyl and Ahasuerus. . . .

God's power over man is stressed in more aggressive, almost hostile images of man overwhelmed by God, *man in God's violent power,* another major theme in Lagerkvist's later work.

The main image in [the "Aftonland" collection], the *spear,* has been prepared for in a previous poem ("Säg mig du eviga stjärna"), where the hostility of the transcendent is clearly expressed in the image "the spearpoint from eternity". (p. 60)

The main stress can be laid on the *non-existence* of the spear-thrower God, while the spear-faith *does* exist irrespective of this: man's longing for the transcendent and his religious need are independent of the existence of God. . . .

The power which overwhelms man *from outside* is, however, so strongly stressed in the image of the spear, which must after all have been thrown by someone outside mankind, that it seems to me absurd not to place the greatest emphasis on this.

The paradoxical, and catastrophically devastating, power that the hidden God has over men even when they do not believe, is given expression in a number of poems. . . . (p. 61)

The final section in the collection is introduced by a poem in which Lagerkvist again approaches the language of the mystics. . . . The dark *spring* in this poem foreshadows a major symbol in the subsequent prose works and one particularly associated with Ahasuerus and Tobias.

It is also in this section that there appears the splendid sequence "Skapelsemorgon" ("The Morning of Creation") where nine poems give variations on the relationship between the Creator and creation and where loneliness and a sense of alienation are recurring motifs.

In the very last poem in the collection God's face has been reflected in "den stilla aftonfloden" but the wind in sorrow erases the reflection and the speaker of the poem sits abandoned in darkness. . . . The paradoxical bond between man and the hidden God provides the last chord of "Aftonland".

The most rewarding approach for the understanding of "Barabbas" is in my opinion to see the archetype in the protagonist's situation: that of *the redeemed in relation to the redeemer.* Who can illustrate man's relationship to the God of Christianity better than the convict in whose place (taken in a quite literal sense) Christ died?

The number of traits Lagerkvist has given him in common with his own *alter ego* Anders in "Guest of Reality" is, however, striking: a marked isolation within his own ego, an equally marked alienation from the world around him, an overmastering anguish at the thought of death, and an inability to believe, to name only the most important. One could even say that Lagerkvist has found in Barabbas his richest and fullest symbol for his own feelings about life, dominated as these are by the shadow of Christ on the cross, in whom he cannot believe and from whom he is unable completely to free himself.

The universally valid and archetypal is interwoven with the personal in the novel. This is true both of the main characters and the world in which they move. We find a similar interweaving in Lagerkvist's subsequent prose works, especially perhaps in "The Sibyl".

The ambivalence of irony is used as a creative device throughout "Barabbas" from the presentation of the man who was set free by Christ's death—and failed to recognize the hidden God!—right up to the scene of his death where, like Christ, he hangs on the cross and speaks into the darkness the words addressed by the redeemer to his Father. (pp. 61-2)

Barabbas is a man who really has met the hidden God, has indeed been given back his life by him, and the rest of his life is filled with God's absence. It is quite logical that *darkness,* the absence of light, should be a symbol for Barabbas throughout the book from the opening scene on Golgotha, where darkness is the only thing he experiences, to the death scene mentioned above. But the light is there, through its absence, just as the hidden God is. . . .

In "The Sibyl" man's experience of God is viewed in a richer and more complex perspective.

At the centre there are once again human beings who have actually met the hidden God, although their initial situation is quite unlike Barabbas's. The Sibyl is *chosen,* Ahasuerus is *condemned.* The result of their meeting with God is, however, the same as the result of Barabbas's. Each in his own degree illustrates the same formula from "Aftonland".

There is something akin to the fate-directed dramas of the Ancients in the Sibyl's life. She is presented as a human being utterly overmastered by the gods. But if the framework for the Sibyl's life is almost classical, the psychological portrait of her reveals a modern being who shares many important traits with the writer himself, not least his nature as writer and seer.

In the Sibyl Lagerkvist has described a human being who has not only been chosen and possessed by God, but who has known Him within herself, in the literal sense, by being raped—can one come nearer God than this?! And what is the result? First and foremost loneliness, and this despite the fact that the Sibyl's experience of God is one of the most complete ever described by Lagerkvist. The whole gamut of "Aftonland" chimes in with this.

The Sibyl has experienced God as a terrible, frightening, punishing power, but in ecstasy she is able to "dela guds lycka över att vara till"; she has experienced him as the *mysterium tremendum et fascinosum.* (pp. 62-3)

As opposed to the Sibyl Ahasuerus experiences only *the terrifying God,* akin to the spear-thrower in "Aftonland", the rejecting, annihilating God. . . .

They have in common an eternal unrest, these three who have in varying measure suffered the power of the hidden God: Barabbas, the Sibyl, and Ahasuerus.

They also share a deeply ironic fate. Barabbas has received a new life thanks to Christ, but what happiness has he gained by that? The Sibyl has come as near to God as is possible for a human, but what loneliness is greater than hers? And Ahasuerus with his anguish at the thought of death—he is condemned to eternal life and knows it to be a death sentence! The lives of all of them are marked by the dual sense of alienation which is the result of meeting the hidden God. . . .

In "Ahasverus död" Lagerkvist breaks the consistency of the legend and allows Ahasuerus to die. (p. 64)

Recognition is a moving force in the book, and the recognition of his fellowman (Tobias) as a brother and of Christ as a brother, accorded by Ahasuerus in his great monologue towards the end of the book, seem to be important steps on the road towards his final expiation and release in death. His great sin in the legend was precisely the elementary one of not recognizing God.

It is, however, indicative of Lagerkvist's ambiguity that in the final monologue he makes Ahasuerus arrive at another symbol for the experience of God which again stresses God's *hidden* nature: *the dark spring.* There is much to indicate that this symbol of the spring is nearly related to the one we noted in "Aftonland", and that it expresses a purely mystical longing for something that is truly "bortom gudarna", but which is *something other than* man. Lagerkvist calls it "det gudomliga".

In this book there appears a new character who "takes over" the wandering pilgrimage after Ahasuerus, and that is Tobias. He and Giovanni, who appears in the next book "Pilgrim på havet", represent new variants of man in relation to the hidden God: they have not themselves met him. (pp. 64-5)

Dream-illusion as opposed to reality-truth constitutes for me the innermost core of "Pilgrim på havet". Two symbols are central here, *the sea* and *the empty medallion* that Giovanni always wears.

The irresponsible, indifferent sea, which adopts no attitude to anything and has no aim, but is self-sufficient, as Giovanni puts it, represents blind life where uncertainty is the only certain thing. To give oneself up to it is to choose the truth devoid of illusions. . . . We are again faced by one of the most central of the problems formulated in Lagerkvist's work.

When Tobias realizes that the sea is, after all, not everything, that there is also a shore, an aim, this is especially caused by the medallion that Giovanni has shown him, the one that carries with it the power of love, even though it is empty.

These two symbols merge into each other as images for the strongest forces in human life, the longing for a meaning to believe in, an aim to strive for, and the longing for a human being to love, forces so strong that they are independent of whether the goal, the object, exists or not. They are two paradoxical symbols that say "yes" and "no" at the same time, and they belong to the same type as the spear that "no one" has thrown, as He who fills the world with his absence. . . .

In the last of the pilgrim novels, "Det heliga landet", Giovanni and Tobias also attain the same death in "peace" and "light" as Ahasuerus had done earlier.

Shortly after his arrival in the strange, barren, coastal country Tobias digs up an ancient image of a god, a carved stone face with a scornful smile. . . . This is Lagerkvist's well known, *averted god.*

The inhabitants of this country know nothing of God, but worship a little *child.* Giovanni states, somewhat drily, that there are also other divine children whose fate has been bound up with shepherds, a clear allusion to Christ. The child's mother is dead, and Tobias's meeting with the child primarily revives the memory of his own decisive betrayal of his beloved in his youth. At the end of the book Tobias meets the Virgin Mary in a vision and she tells him that she was unwittingly the mother of God's son. Later she merges with the beloved of Tobias's youth, who gives him freedom in death.

The hidden god is hinted at in this passage, most clearly in the reference to the unwitting mothers of God (compare the Sibyl).

It is striking throughout how much power *woman* gradually acquires in this land, which is otherwise only populated by old men. . . .

The mysterious woman with the poisonous snake is central here. She has several important functions, among others to give Giovanni freedom in death and to awaken Tobias's feelings of guilt, and she is clearly associated with the sacred, with higher powers. Is she perhaps a kind of intermediary—or substitute—for the hidden god?

Like Ahasuerus, Tobias reaches a spring at the end of his wanderings. It is not dark, . . . nor is it deep, but it slakes one's thirst for ever. It is giving and redeeming like Ahasuerus's spring.

The image of the empty medallion, taken over by Tobias from Giovanni, reoccurs in the last scene in the book. The woman from Tobias's youth, his Beatrice, takes from him the medallion, which she also sees is empty, and puts it on her own neck. . . . Love gives it significance and Tobias can die. (pp. 65-6)

Love also has the last word in "Mariamne".

The protagonist of the book is Herod, another dark figure in the drama of the Christian passion, like Barabbas and Ahasuerus. But Herod is not struck by God like these, he is *struck by love.* (pp. 66-7)

[It] is clear that Herod belongs to a different race from the eternally restless pilgrims fleeing from or seeking for the hidden God. He belongs rather to the race of the condottiere Boccarossa in "Dvärgen", the one-dimensional and earthbound.

It is thus not to be wondered at that his main symbol should be *the desert,* a recurring symbol in Lagerkvist's more recent work for a condition of separation from God (see, for example, "Barabbas", "Aftonland", "Det heliga landet"). Nor is it to be wondered at if *the star,* with its unmistakeably transcendent significance in Lagerkvist's writing, accompanies Herod as a kind of negative "counter-symbol". The "cold spear" of the stars recurs like a refrain in the descriptions of him, and we are reminded of the poem about the star as "spjutspets ur evigheten" in "Aftonland".

Herod does not recognize the hidden God either when he has the chance. The three wise men come and show him the star which tells them that a royal child has been born, but Herod cannot see anything remarkable in this star....

So far [Herod's] picture has been unambiguous and negative. *Self-contradiction, duality* come in with his building of the temple and his love for Mariamne, two motifs which recur throughout the narrative. It is really what is paradoxical and ambiguous in Herod's nature, his urge to build a temple for a god he does not believe in and his compulsion to love someone who does not love him, which make him "en bild av människan".

Seen in this way "Mariamne" is also a variation on the major themes of Lagerkvist's most recent work. (p. 67)

> *Gunnel Malmström, "The Hidden God," in* Scandinavica *(copyright © 1971 by Academic Press Inc. (London) Limited; reprinted with permission), Supplement to Vol. 10, May, 1971, pp. 57-67.*

EVERETT M. ELLESTAD

[The story *Det eviga leendet* is Lagerkvist's] first successful attempt at utilizing the architectonic principles of cubism. Instead of the parallel, static reflections found in his earlier works, we now find a "simultaneous dichotomy" of aspect, a process of "cubist dialectics" which is necessary for the total synthesis of perspective....

[Cubist perspective, according to Braque,] purposely perpetrates an ambiguity through the juxtaposition of two opposing aspects. (p. 38)

In *Det eviga leendet,* Lagerkvist has abandoned the expressionist influence of Strindberg, and has managed to construct the simplicity of narration and dialogue which he had called for in *Ordkonst och bildkonst.* (p. 39)

[In *Det eviga leendet,* the dead reminisce], and by doing so, they speak and "reflect" on their past lives. Each "reflection" is a different plane of reality and from a different time-continuum. It is as if Lagerkvist has "destructed" Stendhal's mirror and re-constructed the pieces in such a manner as to reflect different planes of reality simultaneously. A diffraction of the time-continuum as well as the

spatial "destruction" adds the fourth dimension: the "simultaneous perspective." We also find that Lagerkvist has included a *distorted* reflection of reality in the Kafkaesque tale of the young man at the flour mill. But it is not a discrete unity in itself—instead, the distance created by its grotesque nature enables one to apprehend yet another view of reality which, in turn, correlates with all of the other fragmented segments of life, all of the reaches of time past, into a new meaningful wholeness....

[Contradictions] of time, reality and illusion ... flow together in the solitary darkness that permeates the story to form and re-form in an ever shifting synthesis of new perspectives. It is the total synthesis in the reader's mind, of dimensionality and time (i.e., the "fourth dimension") which enables him to assimilate the "moment of truth" at the end of the story. (p. 40)

[Lagerkvist's writing became more elaborate and complex with the influence of the cubist perspective, revealed in] the painstaking attention given to the multiple interwoven but exactly wrought details which, through their correlative action create the phenomenon of the simultaneous perspective.... But man inherently demands that things be classified, arranged, or structured in some way. Even the cubist process of "destruction-construction" must be systematic and subservient to the intellect.... [As Lagerkvist's cubist style] developed and began to approach this complexity, he ... sensed the "psychedelic" panoptic impact that was to be gained through the exploitation of such contrasts in the fourth dimension of cubist perspective. This new cubist use of chiaroscuro emerges in Lagerkvist's works during the darkening politics of the thirties as the contrast between the forces of *good* and *evil.*

Bödeln (1933), Lagerkvist's attack against the ideology of Nazism, is a cubist study of the nature of this evil force constructed as a kind of "enthymeme." That is, although he concentrates on the forces of evil, one understands logically that evil is only relative—a counterpoint to it must exist—the reflected (and thereby reversed) image of evil is that which is good. Such a "cubist syllogism," therefore, is dialectical: the reader must first deduce the missing premise by reversing the images in his mind if he is to "see" the simultaneous perspective of the whole and thus construct the conclusion.... In *Bödeln,* however, as in *Dvärgen,* it is not enough to merely conclude that good is the logical opposite of evil, for as Lagerkvist explores the nature of evil, we must in turn explore the nature of the counterpoint. If this is done conscientiously, it will be found ... that Lagerkvist has chosen to re-define this dichotomy rather in the context of *love* and evil.... (pp. 41-2)

[Lagerkvist] does not change the simplicity of the whole nor the building blocks which he uses in his artistic expression.... [In his] development, his destruction-construction process undergoes change—becomes more elaborate, more complex—but his predilection for the older, simpler words ... still remains strong. (pp. 42-3)

Like *Det eviga leendet,* Lagerkvist's book *Bödeln* also reveals variegated planes of reality and a sudden leaping of the time-continuum. Furthermore, in *Bödeln,* the individual "pieces" of reality have been broken down into smaller and smaller fragments. What we learn of the executioner is derived more from the inter-woven, complex pattern of contradictory dialogue than from a series of short narrations.

The leap in time from the medieval tavern to a restaurant ostensibly somewhere in Germany divides the novella into almost equal parts. (pp. 44-5)

[The] various different views in the first part are synthesized into a new perspective; and then juxtaposed with similar amalgamations from the second part. Finally, the speech by the executioner serves as a catalyst to assist the reader in the synthesizing of all these discrete parts into the simultaneous perspective of the whole.

Lagerkvist's trend toward an increase in complexity in interweaving the myriad facets of reality appears evident in *Dvärgen* (1944) despite its outward simplicity.... Instead of an interaction of various contradictory statements and viewpoints from a series of different characters, we now have only the dwarf who continually clashes opposing views together within his own mind.... Each character in the book is constructed by ... a pattern of paradoxical contradictions in the mind of the dwarf. The reader is left to make the choice as to which is true and which is false. The answer ... is that none of them are, in fact, true or false. The answer lies outside, beyond them, in the "fourth dimension" of cubist perspective.

Another aspect of the increase in complexity is Lagerkvist's evolvement of a certain "cubist" vocabulary.... [He] manages to remove himself from the text (i.e., the ambiguity creates distance) and thus, "objectively" leaves the reader to make his own decisions. It is this process of intentional contradiction, ambiguity, and allusion which, in a continual chain-reaction synthesis, builds up the final unity in the reader's mind. (pp. 45-7)

In *Barabbas* and in the "Crucifixion Trilogy" of *Pilgrimen*, we find that Stendhal's mirror has undergone an almost total destruction and dissociation—that the views of reality have now become almost infinite—and that out of this "chaos," Lagerkvist, with his technique of total perspective in the simultaneity of the fourth dimension, has constructed for the reader a flawless unified structure. This effectiveness, I believe, is accomplished to a large degree through Lagerkvist's perfection of what I have chosen to call "cubist irony." (p. 48)

A vocabulary which he uses with cubist irony to create a kind of *Verfremdungseffekt*, i.e., the avoidance of straight "factual" description, etc. sets the reader at a "distance" and thus permits him to view the circumstances with an objective mind. (pp. 48-9)

[There are] at least four discrete narrators [employed by Lagerkvist in his fiction to present different narrative viewpoints]: (1) A "straight" narrator who simply tells the story in the third person. (2) A narrator who speaks (in third person) as though he were in the mind of the character. (3) A "dramatic" narrator (in first person) who speaks when an individual character is thinking or speaking. And, (4) a kind of omniscient, objective narrator who employs the interjection of ironically charged words and phrases. (p. 49)

Lagerkvist draws on all these elements of irony and intentional ambiguity to construct, on a larger scale, a triangular arrangement of points dealing directly with the final total wholeness.... One must remember that this triangular structure is an equilateral triangle: no individual point (or angle of perspective) is greater or lesser than any other. The result of this, we find, is once again—ambiguity. (p. 51)

Everett M. Ellestad, "Lagerkvist and Cubism: A Study of Theory and Practice," in Scandinavian Studies, *Winter, 1973, pp. 38-53.*

KENNETH REXROTH

One of Lagerkvist's earlier books was called *Angest, (Anguish)* and it might be thought from this that he was influenced by Kierkegaard. On the contrary, his dominant influence was Left Socialism....

Anguish was published in 1916 and its emotional and moral subject is the profound anguish that overwhelmed the revolutionary Socialist movement with the betrayal of the Second International and the participation of the Socialist Partys in the capitalist war they had unanimously vowed to prevent. It wasn't just political disillusionment, as with Lenin, but an awakening to the duplicity in the heart of man. The War taught Lagerkvist the truth of the "Socratic Dilemma"—when faced with a choice between a greater ultimate good and a lesser immediate good almost all men will choose the latter, and furthermore, in the face of reason many men will choose positive evil. It took Hitler to teach these self evident truths to the liberal and radical intellectuals of the world, who then, once the smoke of the gas ovens had blown away, almost immediately forgot.

The irrational corruption of mankind can be made much easier to bear if one believes in God and Original Sin. Lagerkvist believed in neither. Early on he referred to himself as a deeply religious atheist. Now the only large number of deeply religious atheists in the world are Buddhists, so it is not surprising that Lagerkvist's poetry and most especially the poems in *Evening Land* resemble certain of the most highly developed speculations of Mahayana Buddhism, just as the poems of Gunnar Ekelof owe so much to the great mystical poets of Persian Sufism. Ekelof consciously modeled himself on poets like Hafidh, and many of his poems read like translations. It is hard to tell just how much Lagerkvist was actually influenced by reading Mahayana Buddhist texts.... [There] is not the slightest echo of such terminology, not the slightest hint of exoticism. His "Doctrine of the Void" is not a doctrine at all, and the Void is there in Sweden, not in Kyoto. The transcendental Buddhas and Bodhisattvas of the immense pantheon of Buddhism are admittedly "conceptual entities," that is imaginary, part of the unreality of universal illusion behind them lies the Void known to Mind Only. In *Evening Land* Lagerkvist is continuously seeking identification with the Void behind an imaginary diety.

> Surrounded by a void
> as a constellation is by space
> with infinite distance between its luminous points,
> its timeless manifestations of itself.
>
> So in complete calm,
> in dead perfection,
> lives the Truth about the great Nothing.
> The soul of the void.
> Like a constellation
> named after an utterly forgotten divinity....

The religious experience itself is all the Reality there is, an idea not just theologically but emotionally unacceptable to Jews, Christians, and Muslims....

All the Buddhas and Bodhisattvas, like the deities of later Hinduism, have both beneficent and wrathful aspects—and yet they are "conceptual entities". So too is the divinity of Lagerkvist, even, or even more so, as revealed to the mind in his wrathful aspect.

All through the poems the narrator appears as "the Wanderer". The empiric ego, in the flux of time and space, in the crystal Swedish winter night under the immense geometrical winter constellations as fluxtuant as the Wanderer himself. "Shadows glide through my lands, quenched shapes of light . . . the mountains raise their desolate summits". "The combinations of the world are unstable by nature strive without ceasing." Nirvana.

It is extraordinary that a view of existence just now so extremely fashionable could be presented totally as the experience of one man in one place dealing only with the most objective poetic materials. . . . Lagerkvist's voice is a voice out of the far Northern forests like the Kalevala of Finland or like the darker and more cryptic poems of the Poetic Edda. He is one of the most sombre writers in modern literature. I am not particularly an admirer of Sibelius, but it is this quality that he sought in his music, the sound of a far away long wooden horn coming through the snow bound, low, sub-arctic forests, the cry of an unknown bird from the middle of a lake, white in the white night. Ibsen and Strindberg achieved moments of this. Lagerkvist didn't need to achieve it; it was there all the time, a habitude of soul.

> *Kenneth Rexroth, "On Lagerkvist's 'Evening Land'," in* The American Poetry Review *(copyright © 1978 by World Poetry, Inc.; reprinted by permission of Kenneth Rexroth), January//February, 1978, p. 46.*

*   *   *

LARKIN, Philip   1922-

Larkin is a British poet, novelist, and essayist. The subject of his poetry is his personal experience, the setting that of common provincial life. Larkin has consistently rejected what he feels to be the obscure symbolism of contemporary poetry and its focus on aesthetic problems. His concerns are humanistic, and a recurrent theme is man in his relationship to nature. (See also *CLC*, Vols. 3, 5, 8, 9, and *Contemporary Authors*, Vols. 5-8, rev. ed.)

ANTHONY THWAITE

The unanswerable perfection of [Larkin's] best poems, the inevitable finish which leaves nothing to be said, are so apparent that one has heard such comments as, 'Yes, marvellous—but minor', as if perfection implied diminution. Such ladder-ratings get one nowhere. Who is the greater—Mozart or Beethoven?

Innocence, the pathos and grim humour of experience, the poignancy of the past (whether one's own remembered past or the imagined past of another century), the change and renewal of nature, the dread of the future, death and all that leads up to it and away from it: such listing of the subject-matter of Larkin's recent poems quickly runs itself into flat abstractions, totally lacking the precise circumstantial figurativeness and sensitive cadences of the poems themselves. Larkin has said that a good poem is both 'sensitive' and 'efficient'—two more abstractions, but ones that are given flesh when one reads such poems as "Sad Steps", "The Explosion", "The Building", all published during the past few years. "The Building" opens with a typically dense and carefully selected proliferation of impressionist detail, so organised that it is only gradually one realises that the place being described is a hospital: as in the classic "Church-Going" and "The Whitsun Weddings", the detail is an embodiment of the poem, not the casual decoration its colloquial ease at first suggests. . . . (p. 59)

And in the end, relentlessly poised like the train in "The Whitsun Weddings", the realisation towards which the whole delicate structure has been aimed is achieved:

> All know they are going to die
> Not yet, perhaps not here, but in the end,
> And somewhere like this.
>
> (p. 60)

The stanzaic and rhymed structure of "The Building", typically, is so unobtrusive, draws so little superficial attention to itself, that only a closer look reveals how tightly organised it is. Each seven-line stanza is completely consistent in its rhyme scheme, but the first line of each stanza picks up the rhyme in the fifth line of the stanza preceding it, so that the whole poem can be seen to be made up of interlinked quatrains (ABCB:DCAD), the 'trailing' rhyme picking up the serpentine movement and running it on. To those who think such considerations trivial, mere fingering of an old-fashioned instrument, there are many possible answers: one is that it works.

Even Larkin's least elevated, most casually light poems have this refined technical skill, able to accommodate colloquial language and colloquial rhythms. . . . Both serious and light have the distinctive, subtle, sad and palpable flavour of an individual, with the loyalties, exasperations, illuminations and speaking voice of a distinctly irreducible character. Part of Larkin's breadth of appeal comes from the many kinds of poems this character can appear in: variety within unity. From the evocation of 19th-century emigrants (in "How Distant") to the lyrical naturalism of "The Trees", the breadth of sympathies is wide, the voice unmistakable. (pp. 60-1)

> *Anthony Thwaite, "Larkin's Recent Uncollected Poems," in* Phoenix, *Autumn & Winter, 1973-74, pp. 59-61.*

ALUN R. JONES

For the most part the poets of the 1950s, and particularly Philip Larkin, reject the traditions of their immediate past. Their poetry represents a revival of a tradition associated with Hardy and kept alive only through the vigour and persistence of poets like Robert Graves. Their distrust of political programmes or religious or philosophical ideas is profound; their hatred of the "old gang," whose faith in programmes and ideas led Europe into six years of slaughter, runs deep. In poetry they took pride in their craft, and in experience they felt themselves carefully forward taking nothing on trust—not even themselves. The poetry of Philip Larkin defines the mood of this post-war generation with great sensitivity. (p. 142)

The North Ship was generally regarded as promising but poetically immature and surprisingly Georgian in tone, and his reputation rests on the poems of *The Less Deceived* together with the few poems he has since published in journals and magazines. . . . [His novels] *Jill* and *A Girl in Winter,* both of which were written before 1946, . . . are bleak and pessimistic to the point almost of nihilism.

The strength of Philip Larkin's poetry lies in the sheer elegance of his craftsmanship, in the cool detachment of himself from his poetry, and in his tone. It is this sense of tone —in Larkin a delicate but precise irony continually undercutting the composure of the poem, largely self-directed but also used as a defensive intelligence through which to define the ambiguity of his attitude. Larkin is breaking new ground in English poetry; his poetry defines the attitudes of his time in his concern with the world of the individual unwilling to commit himself to ideas—philosophical, social, or even personal—and at the same time a world nonetheless concerned with these issues. He has managed to create a kind of poem in which he can set a space, a tension, between himself and the poem and within this space manipulate, mainly through irony (the holding of two or more often contradictory attitudes simultaneously), a considerable range of attitudes that he clarifies with subtle intelligence and vigour. The ambiguity is removed from image and metaphor . . . and is clearly suggested through texture and tone. He refuses—even in personal relationships—to commit himself through word and gesture, to lose his freedom by bringing himself to any statement or positive attitude, and his poetry reflects a world in which feeling and intelligence are actively engaged but in the manner of eighteenth-century scepticism. An intense sense of personal integrity, an urbane and sensitive intelligence, and a healthy, honest scepticism combining with a brilliantly polished control of poetic technique are the qualities admired and imitated by his contemporaries. (pp. 142-43)

Larkin's poetry is a direct expression of the sensitive and intelligent mind's refusal to be taken in [by causes]. As a writer he has avoided the literary, the metropolitan, the group label, and embraced the nonliterary, the provincial, and the purely personal. He embraces the uncertainties of life with all its contradictions and refuses illusions even where he would be most willing to accept them. His rejection of the past, the literary past and his own, is part of the pattern of his feeling that we can only honestly know the present, the now, and cannot honestly respond to this if we are at the same time committing ourselves to the future— "the past is past and the future neuter." . . . There is no self-pity in Larkin and he refuses sentimentality by withdrawing from experience at that point where it is necessary to make a choice, and no disillusion because he refuses all illusion—his ironic detachment is comprehensive. Even the intense beauty that his poetry creates is created by balancing on a keen ironic edge. His subjects in the end are the great commonplaces of life—time, suffering, love and death —and the final beauty is derived from a deep and moving source of melancholy—not pessimistic or cynical or bitter, but temperamental, and indigenous. (pp. 143-44)

["Toads" and "Reasons for Attendance" are] firstly an attack on the romantic illusion by the light of whose unreality so many are led into misery and disillusionment . . . — and secondly, an explicit statement as to the wholeness of separate worlds in which individuals live. In "Toads" he parodies the W. H. Davies super-tramp kind of romantic illusion. . . . The irony residing clearly in words like "folk" or "nippers" makes it quite clear that what is being parodied is the bourgeois, suburban dream of escape to some idea of the rustic, idyllic life of nature, and in the term "unspeakable wives" he allows the attitude he is parodying to reveal its own falsity. (pp. 144-45)

The metrical pattern is traditional and dextrously handled [in "Toads"]; the poem is organic and builds towards the last stanza gathering its meaning as it goes. The meaning is always quite lucid, and although with an occasional technical or archaic word or an unfamiliar idiom often suppressed in the line, the vocabulary is simple and informal. *The Less Deceived* is one of the most important volumes of verses to have been published since the war; "No Road" one of the finest personal love poems, and "Church Going" one of the richest and most intelligent statements of English post-war sensibility. . . .

"Next, Please" is a poem about *expectancy,* about the way in which we are all expecting the future to compensate for the deficiencies and disappointments of the present, about the way in which the present becomes, in a sense, merely a waiting, a marking time, until the future brings the riches we all hope for and half-expect. . . . (p. 146)

Characteristically, the abstract idea of expectancy in the first three lines is dramatised through conversation in the fourth, and the whole second stanza is a concrete, visual statement of the abstract idea—except that the idea has become enriched and the irony, detached and sardonic, has begun to play on the idea. In a most beautiful last stanza, Larkin makes clear that of this whole illusory armada only one ship—the ship of death—is really seeking us out. . . . There is an exactness of description here that minutely follows the accuracy of observation giving the poetry not only a concrete, visual quality of great clarity but also a subtle richness of texture as abstraction and metaphor are precisely overlayed. The poem achieves an immediacy of statement and an almost tactual quality rarely found in poetry—but somehow characteristic of Larkin's poetry. The image here is not mocking or satirical and the irony is completely submerged in this statement of man's tragic destiny.

"No Road" is characteristic of those poems in which he discusses personal relationships. With precision, with honesty, and without nostalgia, he discusses the present relationship existing between those who were once intimate but who now live, think, and feel apart. Time has gradually eroded the intimacy they once created and shared and which will never be restored to them. The poem is without sentimentality and yet suffused with a gentle persuasive melancholy. . . . [The] whole tone and phrasing is deliberately informal and designed to direct attention away from the poem as a poem towards the feeling for direct speech and intonation, towards almost casual utterance. And yet the poem itself is a very formal and tightly constructed piece of work and its effects could only have been achieved by a poet who is also a superb technician.

"Church Going" is altogether the most overt statement of Larkin's position in the volume, and is in itself a most moving and convincing summary of his intellectual scepticism. . . . His scepticism leads him to agnosticism, but his attraction towards the historical and religious past, to a time when thought led more easily to action, is weighted against a totally unbelieving future when religion will survive only in superstition and in church ruins. . . . (pp. 147-48)

The intellectual and emotional honesty necessary to sustain the balance of this courageous scepticism is the centre of Larkin's philosophical position.

In the poems of *The Less Deceived* he adds also a note of profound compassion for loneliness, for deprivation and for suffering. As a poet his output is small but each poem he has published since that time shows the same technical finish and high achievement of the earlier poems, but also a developing sense of compassion and a wider and more assured confidence in the value of his own personal experience.... Like his earlier poems, both ["The Whitsun Weddings" and "Ambulances"] are reflective, not participating in or even celebrating human experience, but commenting and reflecting upon life as it flows around him. Both poems move towards a larger area of experience than the purely personal and both are remarkable for a growing sense of compassion directed towards the lonely, the deprived, the suffering, and the tawdry.... His remarkable descriptive powers and astonishing acuteness of observation, together with the somewhat astringent tone, lead towards a general and compassionate statement about the human situation [in "The Whitsun Weddings"].... The irony and fastidiousness drop away in the conclusion as the train and its travellers take on a firm but delicate symbolism. Suggestions of arrival and death are balanced lightly against beginning and rebirth. The passengers, whether poet or newly-wed, are brought together by a 'frail travelling coincidence' and share for a short while their experience as they share the human predicament by virtue of their individual and distinct humanity.

This growing sense of relationships, however temporary or tentative, and his increasing willingness to accept the validity of his own personal world of experience marks a further stage in Larkin's development. He is certainly one of the most accomplished and influential poets now writing and the poems of *The Less Deceived* largely define the sensibility of English poetry in the 1950s. (pp. 149-51)

> *Alun R. Jones, "The Poetry of Philip Larkin: A Note on Transatlantic Culture," in* Phoenix, *Autumn & Winter, 1973-74, pp. 139-51.*

PEARL K. BELL

[In his third collection, *High Windows*], as in *The Less Deceived* and *The Whitsun Weddings* (one small and dazzling book every 10 years), [Larkin] writes with enormously concentrated, incandescent transparency about achingly intimate, precisely observed, familiar figures that fill him at once with parched despair and an affection so tainted with regret that it has all but been stifled....

Not for him the grand gestures of Robert Lowell and Dylan Thomas, the visionary ego of Yeats, the formal revolutions of Eliot and Pound. "Content alone interests me," he declares. "Content is everything." He fits with unresisting precision into traditional structures (and can also stand them hilariously on their heads), filling them with the melancholy truth of things in the shrunken, vulgarized and parochial England of the 1970s.

And what marvelous freshness and wit he bestows on the drab forms! ...

What sustains Larkin, this bleak and wintry spirit, is not the cozy backward glance to a better, smaller, greener England. He prefers the past, yet he is not sentimental. Rather, through his fanatically clear-eyed intelligence, refining and defining the shards of ancestral memory and contemporary fact, he offers an extraordinarily powerful, if wholly unaggressive, kind of resistance—the unworldly but perfect

triumph of imagination over the dry rot of despair. And because he writes with anguished lucidity, Larkin is not only admired by the critics of Great Britain, he is bought and read by the thousands. Since the death of Robert Frost, whose way of seeing was not unlike his own, Philip Larkin has had no American counterpart.

> *Pearl K. Bell, "Poets of Our Times," in* The New Leader *(© 1975 by the American Labor Conference on International Affairs, Inc.), May 26, 1975, p. 5.*

STANLEY POSS

The Librarian of Hull gives you recognizably the same product in his latest book [*High Windows*] as he did in his first, *The North Ship*, twenty years earlier. If you like that kind of thing, that's the kind of thing you like. I love it. Spare, evocative, heroically lucid, disabused, savage, understated, funny, brutal, subtle, the antithesis of Roethke's Open Houses and Rich's engagements, these are the supreme ordinary language poems, poems of desperate clarity and restraint and besieged common sense. And what they mostly say is, be beginning to despair, despair, despair. If Roethke is the poet of roots and shoots and sheath-wet beginnings, Larkin's the expert on ending up. (p. 398)

Twenty-four poems in ten years: that's a little better than one every six months. But as Virginia Woolf said of Milton, it's what's not written that counts too, it's the depth at which the options were taken, the commitments made, the decisions not to publish. What we do get in *High Windows* is much in little. These compressed, elegant, laconic poems are a little like the windfall apples Anderson described in *Winesburg*. Raunchy looking, they contain secret pockets of sweetness that do you more good than the shiny waxed stuff in the supermarkets. (p. 399)

Larkin is tough, even brutal, but also he's subtle and tender. Very much the poet of limitations, of wry, coerced common sense, he nonetheless turns on you frequently to reveal mystery, possibility, infinity. As John Bayley observes, "sun-comprehending glass" is as eloquent, as evocative as Yeats' "rook-delighting heaven," while "The Card-Players" starts as a genre piece—not that this is negligible in itself—but turns unexpectedly at the end from its Flemish interior to a choral comment that puts everything preceding it in a new context.... (p. 400)

When I think of England and English poets, it strikes me that the movement from Yeats to Auden to Larkin is rooted in realpolitik. Progressively more guarded, less willing to risk the grand style or to pronounce roundly on one's soul or others', the poets' very language recapitulates in little the whole anticolonial history of the country.... The energy of [Larkin's] language, the depth at which the decisions were made, the terror and despair and night fears checked by an intelligence that's consecutive and lucid up to the distant point at which being consecutive and lucid is irrelevant: these are virtues that dignify, even transform, the ostensible subjects. Art always affirms. (p. 402)

> *Stanley Poss, in* Western Humanities Review *(copyright, 1975, University of Utah), Autumn, 1975.*

MARTIN AMIS

[After "Jill" and "A Girl in Winter," Larkin's fiction] stopped dead. As Larkin has ruefully explained, he waited for more fiction to come—but it never did.

Why? Well, the two novels we have provide what clues there are. In this respect "Jill" (1946) is the less significant book. It is less significant because anyone could have written it—or, to put the point more exactly, it needn't have been written by Philip Larkin. Blending fantasy and self-absorption in the usual first-novel style, it recounts the gaucheries of a furtive, owlish working-class boy during his first term at Oxford: the hero's queasy sense of social inferiority, his emulation of a dissolute roommate, and his own graceless erotic yearnings combine to bring about his tragicomic humiliation. "Jill" is a funny, confused, likable and quite undisconcerting book.

"A Girl in Winter," published in England in 1947, is something else again: it is Larkinesque. At first it looks like a similar novel—indeed, the *same* novel, except that it is told from the woman's point of view. (p. 2)

It is a far more enigmatic book than "Jill"; and it is also, somehow, far less of a *novel*. Haltingly paced and erratically written, "Jill" is at least integrally thought out—its minor characters are assimilated, its questions resolved, its themes dispatched. In "A Girl in Winter" the fictional accessories are no more than listless toys in the glare of the heroine's solipsism. The minor figures are, strictly, mere walk-ons, liable to be shrugged off as soon as they cease to stimulate Katherine's introspection; and the moral appositions of the novel loom and flicker with similar caprice. But these aren't criticisms—they are clues. The answer is, of course, that Larkin is already becoming less of a novelist, and more of a poet.

The process of distillation, of reduction to essences, shows itself in a number of ways, some of them poignant, some of them effortful. Larkin is prepared, for instance, to write an impossibly flat sentence ("It was very solacing to be alone"; "The truth was, she had not been facing facts") if an abrupt mood-swing requires it. Then, too, he will fasten consecutive scenes on some tritely effusive image—there's a symbolic snail, a flock of symbolic pigeons, even a symbolic frog—and almost every other chapter fades out in a kind of neon wistfulness: "She dropped the dead flowers into the wastepaper basket," and the like. Correspondingly, though, "A Girl in Winter" gives us a unique insight into the origins of a remarkable talent. Here we see Larkin getting ready to use his special genius: his ability to make landscape and townscape answer to human emotion. The snow, the shopfronts, the rivers, the blacked-out streets—each gives its own expression to the intense seclusion at the heart of the book.

This is the larval Larkin, displayed more transparently here than in even his earliest verse. If you turn to "The North Ship" (1945) for some lines appropriate to "A Girl in Winter," you will find only a remote evocation:

> To pull the curtains back
> And see the clouds flying—
> How strange it is
> For the heart to be loveless, and as cold as these.

If you turn to "High Windows" (1974), however, you will find the essence of the same story, retold in poem after poem:

> The way the moon dashes through clouds that blow

> Loosely as cannon-smoke . . .
> Is a reminder of the strength and pain
> Of being young; that it can't come again,
> But is for others undiminished somewhere.
>
> (pp. 2, 16-17)

Martin Amis, in The New York Times Book Review *(© 1976 by The New York Times Company; reprinted by permission), December 26, 1976.*

BRUCE K. MARTIN

Never having felt quite comfortable with the various notions of poetry derived from others, [in the late 1940s Larkin] realized that he could depend on his own feelings for the appropriate manner in which to present such material. He learned from Thomas Hardy that his own life, with its often casual discoveries, could become poems, and that he could legitimately share such experience with his readers. From this lesson has come his belief that a poem is better based on something from "unsorted" experience than on another poem or other art.

The technical key to such poetry is, of course, clarity, while its bane is obscurity. (p. 27)

Larkin's views on art and literature match very closely the general attitudes attributed to a group of writers with which he has been associated, known as The Movement. While critics have debated whether Larkin's poetry is, in fact, "Movement" poetry, and while we can better determine that after examining his poems, there can be no question that his basic stance on the problems of modern poetry, the relationship of the poet to the reading public, and certain directions which British poetry ought to take, suggest a close alliance with the other so-called Movement writers.

The difficulty of determining his relationship to The Movement stems partly from the fact that the authors usually named in this connection never banded together, even informally, as any sort of literary school in the conventional sense. The Movement label, however useful for reference, is at best the invention of critics. . . . (p. 28)

[All of the authors considered Movement Writers] have called, implicitly in their poetry and fiction and explicitly in critical essays, for some sort of commonsense return to more traditional techniques. The rationale for this antimodernist, antiexperimental stance is their stated concern with clarity: with writing distinguished by precision rather than obscurity. . . . [They urged] not an abandonment of emotion, but a mixture of rationality with feeling, of objective control with subjective abandon. Their notion of what they felt the earlier generation of writers, particularly poets, lacked, centered around the ideas of honesty and realism about self and about the outside world. (p. 29)

Larkin's reputation as a leading contemporary poet rests mainly on *The Less Deceived* and *The Whitsun Weddings*. His earlier poetry and his prose writings are generally regarded as interesting backdrops to the richer and more characteristic work in those two collections of verse. And, though *High Windows* may signal a departure from those poems published in the 1950s and early 1960s, it probably will not alter the image of Larkin derived from them. . . . Clearly the kind of poems associated most often with Larkin reflect these two very popular collections.

One reason for the popularity of his poems is the apparent commonplaceness of their subjects. Larkin manages to project a very personal concern for the things which personally concern most people living in the modern world. . . . The world of his poems is a world to which most readers can readily respond. (p. 31)

Much of Philip Larkin's artistry rests in his ability to concretize—through setting, personality, and diction—many of the questions which have perplexed man almost since his beginning but which in modern times have become the province principally of academicians. In this he especially resembles Thomas Hardy. . . . [His poetry reflects] his faith in the common reader to recognize and respond to traditional philosophical concerns when stripped of undue abstractness and pretentious labels. (p. 46)

Larkin's concern with a human world caught up in time, desire, and disappointment connects him with the whole line of western philosophy dealing with the distinction between the ideal and the real. His peculiar emphasis upon this distinction has prompted one critic succinctly to label Larkin's viewpoint as "Platonism turned over or inside out," since the true Platonist reality, which is ulterior, becomes fantasy for the characters of Larkin's poems. However, the same critic, while noting Larkin's disbelief in any sort of Platonic Ideal, notes that such an ideal exists for Larkin in that he sees it as essential to the human state; we seem unable to live without positing impossible, unworkable ideals. Because Larkin, despite knowing better, presumably shares this proneness to idealize in the face of unpleasant or unrewarding reality, his attitude toward the idealizing tendency of his characters, or of mankind in general, can only be that of profound sympathy. Because Larkin's realism involves a hard look at life, because reality for him does not give cause for joy, he cannot deride the very natural bent toward escape-through-idealizing.

In fact, he can respond with wonder at the ingenuity with which men color reality. (p. 49)

One quality which both admirers and detractors of Philip Larkin have noticed is the sense of order which almost every one of his poems creates. Although many of his poems have aroused interpretive disputes and disagreement over precisely what happens in them or what is completed by their endings, each gives the impression that something indeed has been completed. As much as more specific technical elements or the operative assumptions of his poems, this sense of form has caused critics to link Larkin with the Augustan tradition in English verse. And, along with diction and syntax, this ready sense of structure has lured many readers into regarding his poetry as easily understood. As with Yeats or Auden, they are frequently surprised by disarmingly subtle implications in poems of seeming simplicty. (p. 63)

[Larkin's] is a style designed to hide itself behind the human situation and emotions revealed in the poems, a style founded on the assumption . . . that the poet's technique should never assert itself to complicate unnecessarily such understanding or enjoyment. . . .

The impossibility, or at least the folly, of separating style and content, which Larkin has suggested in his critical remarks, is . . . forcefully demonstrated through his own poetry. . . . (p. 91)

The speaking voice of his poems comes across as natural, encouraging the reader to believe that the style is indeed the man and that it represents a man with whom one can identify and from whom one can learn. This is not to suggest that Larkin's poetry is formally didactic . . . but that the reliable personae in many of his poems, as well as the implied authority behind his unreliable speakers, is not only a man speaking to men, but a sensitive and sympathetic sharer of life's pain and joy. . . . In a larger sense most of Larkin's poems remind us of the novel—and particularly the traditional English novel epitomized by George Eliot, Hardy, or Lawrence—in that their narrators and commentators exhibt both perspective and empathy with what they describe. (pp. 91-2)

One stylistic quality noted by many critics and indicative of the Larkin cast of mind is his tendency toward negative qualifiers, and especially his reliance on the prefix "un." In "Born Yesterday" he wishes the infant an "unemphasized" happiness, while elsewhere he speaks of someone being "untruthful" and "unfingermarked," and of things being "uncustomary," "unrecompensed," and "unclosing." Relatedly, in "The Importance of Elsewhere" he distinguishes between feeling "separate" and feeling "unworkable," citing the latter as his usual situation. Such avoidance of positives reflects a preference for whittling things down to their true dimensions and qualities, even at the risk of understatement. Because, as he implies in all of his poems, man tends to delusion about himself and life and thereby invites personal disaster, perhaps the most valuable service poetry can render as representer of truth is to remind us of this danger even in the very words used to describe the world of the poem. The poet thus teaches by example as much as by precept. (pp. 95-6)

Like his diction and syntax, imagery and figurative language in Larkin's poetry can go unnoticed as such, so much do they operate as natural parts of character and situation. Because of his disdain for the poetic extremes resulting from the modernist rubrics of Imagism and Symbolism, many of Larkin's more figurative poems seem strangely literal—literal because he generally avoids levels of meaning much divorced from the surface situation or problem, and strangely so because almost all of his poetry, even as it appears consistently literal, with equal consistency suggests a universality of reference. . . . Larkin's poems almost always have the effect of meaning more than they say, and of referring somehow to more than they mention.

The explanation for this subtle nonliteralism—or delusive literalism—lies partly in the subjects with which his poems and characters deal; they literally are a part of the lives of most readers. But even so, to them Larkin adds a measure of symbolic suggestiveness rising out of the very details in the poems themselves. Frequently objects and words take on an extraliteral meaning for the reader because they obviously do for the speaker. (pp. 97-8)

It is ironic to notice, therefore, that by many definitions of figurative or symbolic language such poems, for all of their quiet but intense emotion, are decidedly denotative and transparent. The images which the middle-aged man in "High Windows" carries in his mind as he finally turns his attention—the windows themselves, of "sun-comprehending glass," and the "deep blue air"—immediately represent for us the metaphysical dimension of human questing, the ultimate which religion seeks to embrace, because the character obviously sees them as such. . . . Having repeatedly insisted that a poet must, above all, be a man, Larkin seems to imply through such poems as these that a man, by virtue of his humanness, will be a poet, at least to himself. In a sense such poems involve the reader's eavesdropping on the unwitting poetic composition of characters. We see the speaker select what for him are satisfactorily representative details. The poem causes us to reconstruct that which they represent.

Equally impressive is Larkin's penchant for integrating conventionally figurative language into his poems. . . . [Slang metaphors] all appear the perfectly natural result, or indication, of the speaker's station and attitude, so natural that they are scarcely recognizable as metaphors.

Larkin's puns, usually of great significance in their contexts, are likewise camouflaged, so that they work on the reader without his being aware of anything so mechanical as word-play. (pp. 98-9)

Even when Larkin's skill with multiple meanings is more exposed, it operates naturally in the context of the particular poem. (p. 99)

Larkin's restraint in his use of figurative language makes it a telling if subtle tool. On occasion he does not hesitate to build a fairly elaborate metaphorical pattern. In such cases, though, the pattern becomes a self-characterizing device. Thus in "No Road" the speaker's embroidering the obvious metaphor of the unused road as the remnant of the once-thriving friendship, the homely references to bricking up gates and planting trees to enforce their parting, and the progress report of drifting leaves and creeping grass all mark the speaker himself as not only thoughtful, but as skillful in redeeming a potentially trite comparison into a very apt description of the relationship and the dilemma it poses. This kind of serious wit prepares the reader for the telling self-appraisal at the end of the poem. Perhaps exceptional among Larkin's poems in terms of its reliance on metaphor, "No Road" represents further evidence of his refusal to employ metaphor for any narrowly "poetic" effect, his determination to fuse poetic device and extrapoetic significance. (p. 100)

The final lines [of "The Whitsun Weddings"], in which the imminent setting-forth of the train's passengers is likened to "an arrow-shower / Sent out of sight, somewhere becoming rain," derive their profundity in part from the absence of such comparisons earlier in the poem. And, as is usual with Larkin, because the comparison is the speaker's and seems a natural result of his increasing emotion, the reader is made to feel that he has observed a plausible evolving of significance through scene and character, rather than the imposition of meaning by the poet.

The principle behind much of the prosodic element in Larkin's verse seems to be an unresolved tension between formal regularity and irregularity, and between subtlety and abrasiveness in the use of various devices. In this way technique parallels ideology, reminding us of various other basic tensions in the poems, such as that between the concern for security and the desire for excitement, or between the value placed on awareness and the need for sustaining illusions in life, or even between the urge to write and an underlying sense of the pointlessness of such activity. Larkin's greater commitment to traditional forms in comparison with other leading contemporary poets is misleading, since a close examination of his techniques reveals an insistent technical skepticism not unlike that with which he

treats the more explicit issues of his poetry. He cannot fully affirm a "free-verse" position in his poems because he cannot honestly affirm freedom as a realizable or even fully desirable style of life. Nevertheless he implies a questioning attitude toward traditional technical controls even as he uses them.

His use of the stanza to subdivide his poems exemplifies this principle. Because almost all of his poems are written in stanzas of some sort, to the casual observer they appear very old-fashioned. Yet, the type of stanza is almost never the same from poem to poem, and within a given poem usually there is marked irregularity, even from the beginning, in rhyme or meter. Such is the frequent complexity of the Larkin stanza that it appears to be a satire itself on the whole idea of the stanza. By setting up the stanzaic form and deviating from it in so many ways without abandoning it entirely, Larkin seems to turn the form upside-down, to question its validity even while maintaining a formal appearance. (pp. 102-03)

In many ways the poems in *The Whitsun Weddings* represent the full flowering of Larkin's poetic talents, the final casting off of his youthful misdirection. It was almost as if he had written a group of poems fully in line with his best writing in *The Less Deceived*. If not strikingly different from the immediately earlier collection, *The Whitsun Weddings* is notable in having a higher percentage of third-person poems, and of first-person poems with characters obviously not to be equated with Larkin himself. His bent toward realism, in characterization and setting, is evident in every one of these later poems, more so than in *The Less Deceived*.

For most readers, though, the poems of *The Less Deceived* blend into those of *The Whitsun Weddings;* we recognize these two books as Philip Larkin's central poetic achievement. His latest book, *High Windows,* clearly represents an extension of that achievement. With one or two exceptions, every one of these later poems recalls in some significant way an earlier poem by Larkin, which is why they fit so comfortably into a discussion of his characteristic attitudes and techniques. Nevertheless, some definite, if not surprising, trends away from *The Whitsun Weddings* period are evident here.

One of these is Larkin's greater bent in recent years toward contemporary topicality, both of subject and allusion. Perhaps this is a logical outcome of his steady development into realism. (p. 132)

A consequence or corollary to the older perspective in *High Windows* is Larkin's greater identification with the speaker in his poems, a reversal of his movement in the 1950s and early 1960s toward greater dramatization and irony even in first-person poems. Larkin comes closest to the self-deprecation of "Church Going." . . . Where the speaker achieves wisdom only at the end of those earlier poems, here he displays it from the beginning. (p. 134)

"High Windows" celebrates a stoic disavowal of simplistic envy for the young. . . . [Poems] like "To the Sea" and "Show Saturday" demonstrate his deep respect for those events and practices linking individuals and generations despite the onslaught of time, an onslaught perhaps presented most forcibly in the ephemera of fashion and commercialism separating us in death and threatening to isolate us in life. (pp. 134-35)

Perhaps the most startling thing about this last volume is its variety. Even though recalling others by him, each poem differs markedly from such predecessors, and in none of the earlier books has Larkin collected so many differing types of poems. (p. 135)

Larkin has extended the range of his wit to black humor, and revealed that element perhaps of despair, but certainly of cynicism, which may have lurked just behind his other humorous poems. As an interpretive allusion to all paintings with similar titles and subjects, ["The Card Players"] represents, for Larkin at least, a further means of weighing life, of showing the gap between reality and appearance, and perhaps of exploring the relationship between art and life. In projecting his viewpoint onto the stock materials of the genre painting, he has moved his poetry farther from concrete reality than before, and farther into the subconscious and nonrational. Perhaps more than any of his other recent poems, "The Card-Players" represents the kind of poem Larkin lately has wished to write, a kind not ordinarily associated with him. In this regard the whole of *High Windows* rewards his readers by reminding them of the range of his wit and talent sometimes forgotten by readers eager to praise or criticize his purely realistic writings. (p. 137)

> *Bruce K. Martin, in his* Philip Larkin *(copyright © 1978 by G. K. Hall & Co.; reprinted with the permission of Twayne Publishers, A Division of G. K. Hall & Co., Boston), Twayne Publishers, 1978.*

*   *   *

LAURENCE, (Jean) Margaret   1926-

A Canadian novelist, editor, and author of short stories, nonfiction, and books for children, Laurence bases her stories on her experiences in Africa and the rural Canadian town in which she was born. Rural Canada provides the setting for her Manawaka series, in which her characters struggle against both their inner conflicts and the strangely hypnotic influence of Manawaka on their lives. (See also *CLC*, Vols. 3, 6, and *Contemporary Authors*, Vols. 5-8, rev. ed.)

SANDRA DJWA

[Margaret Laurence] often casts a gently ironic eye upon the more fundamental absurdities of the human condition, particularly the discrepancy between the idealized and the actual. In . . . "The Merchant of Heaven," her wry humor is apparent in the contrast between the glorious mission field of Brother Lemon's apocalyptic imagination and the trying reality of his day-to-day existence as an apostle for the Angel of Philadelphia Mission. Yet, in the largest sense, "The Merchant of Heaven" also suggests a distinction between the literal Biblical word and the true spirit of Christian belief, a contrast which is developed through the distinction between the heavenly new Jerusalem of Brother Lemon's literal interpretation of Revelations, "where the walls are of jaspar and topaz and amethyst, and the city is of pure gold" and the new Jerusalem of the spirit implicit in the narrator Kitteridge's final vision. (p. 43)

The books of Jeremiah and Revelations as suggested by Margaret Laurence's African stories (*The Tomorrow-Tamer and Other Stories,* 1963) may appear at first glance to be a rather exotic locale . . . yet here, as in her prairie fiction, Laurence's affinities with Sinclair Ross are apparent. It is not just that there are often slight echoes of Ross through-

out Laurence's work. . . . [As] demonstrated by "The Merchant of Heaven," Laurence and Ross share a central vision—a sense of the ironic discrepancy between the spirit and the letter of the religious dispensation, a discrepancy which is often explored through an essentially psychological analysis of character (particularly through the interior monologue) with reference to Biblical myth. (p. 44)

[The characters of Margaret Laurence] all live in the same little "fundamentalist town" . . . and they all live their lives in stifling relation to the old gods of their fathers—gods which are dead and no longer viable for today's world yet nonetheless inescapable gods. Dominated by these gods which in some cases have been assimilated into a harsh and punishing super-ego, each character lives a child-like or inauthentic existence dominated by the dead parental voices of the past. (p. 45)

Laurence's interest in the growth of the human spirit into self-knowledge and freedom is suggested by her first collection of short stories, *The Tomorrow-Tamer and Other Stories* (1963). There is a sense in which all of these tales are parables of salvation or the failure to attain it, a failure which is always linked to personal bondage. (p. 46)

[Laurence] consistently invokes Biblical myth as archetypes of psychological man. Her characters are most often related mythically as are Abram-Hagar, Jacob and Ishmael in *The Stone Angel* or Rachel and Jacob in *A Jest of God* and often part of a controlling myth which verges on psychological allegory. It is not, of course, allegory, because Laurence in no sense sets up rigid levels of interpretation. Nonetheless, because Hagar refers to herself as "the Egyptian" and describes Marvin explicitly as "Jacob", it is impossible to read *The Stone Angel* without recognizing that Hagar sees and Laurence presents the human situation in terms of Biblical allegory. . . .

[Laurence] seems to write from a two-tiered world, ostensibly with God above and man below; a world in which there is always the ironic possibility of a reversal of man's plans by God. Although those two worlds are ostensibly parallel, they nonetheless appear to meet in the human spirit. Laurence, like Jung, seems to locate God in the human soul and to sometimes define religion in terms of the Jungian "numinous experience" which can lead to psychological change. For modern man, the old gods of the fathers are dead, or, if they still exist, they no longer manifest themselves in the old ways and must be re-defined by each person according to his own experience. (p. 49)

Further proof of Laurence's concern with the human condition is to be found in *A Jest of God* which suggests some aspects of existentialist thought as Rachel must choose between the nausea of bad faith and the anguish and despair of freedom. Laurence is also existential throughout her work in Sartre's primary sense in that her focus is on man's process of becoming, a process which reveals to him his essence or spirit. However, in distinction to existentialist thought and in accordance with the conventions of Christian belief, man discovers a preexisting spirit. . . . (pp. 49-50)

Looking back on Laurence's work, the primary impression is that the process of becoming is most often embodied in mythic metamorphosis. Hagar, the Egyptian, stone angel and imprisoned spirit, passes through these transitory forms in her spiritual metamorphosis. . . . Rachel, the virgin princess, Jerusalem, the shadow queen and finally the mother, undergoes a series of psychic metamorphoses which lead to a new state of being. (p. 50)

Sandra Djwa, in Journal of Canadian Fiction *(reprinted by permission from* Journal of Canadian Fiction, *2050 Mackay St., Montreal, Quebec H3G 2J1, Canada), Vol. I, No. 4, 1972.*

GLORIA WHELAN

Like Faulkner, who enabled his readers to experience the rural South in his novels of Yoknapatawpha County, Laurence has bestowed a kind of immortality on the small Canadian prairie town. Manawaka is not just a town from which one escapes as soon as possible; it has a further part to play in the lives of its emigrés. It cleaves to them just as its image stayed with Margaret Laurence in her years in England, a microcosm of her native country. (p. 95)

In *The Stone Angel,* the first novel of the Manawaka series, Hagar sees the world much as Sartre describes it in *Nausea:* "every existing thing is born without reason, prolongs itself out of weakness and dies by choice." In *The Diviners,* as in all the novels that have followed *The Stone Angel,* we see a more corrigible world. We have the impression of Laurence opening doors and rewarding struggle. She is the generous creator who endows her characters with the qualities that will save them.

Laurence's women are sensual, maternal, creative. They like men, are comfortable with their own bodies, see sex as a "conscious defiance of death." . . .

These are intelligent women with a good measure of self-awareness. They know what we know about them. They enjoy their own company. They are fiercely introspective and honest about their lives.

These are also self-serving women. They allow themselves to be used only to a point; then they take flight. . . .

If they can be selfish to save themselves, they also have a sense of accountability. They are able to live ethical lives in spite of the world around them. They are never malicious; they can hardly bring themselves to be rude; if hurt, they are apt to blame themselves, turning their anger and rage inward.

Their morality is a product of early religious training. In her first novel, *This Side Jordan,* Laurence was caught up in African mysticism. But mysticism was too exotic a flower to transfer to Manawaka. The God of the prairie is more utilitarian, a winter God. He is "the stern God of our fathers," consulted frequently by Rachel, Stacey, and Vanessa. It is through his eyes that they monitor their actions, anticipate their punishments, plead for mercy. (p. 96)

Few Canadian writers can match the scope of the Manawaka *oeuvre* or the quality of its writing, but Margaret Laurence is most effective when her symbols are life-sized. In [*The Diviners*] the individual seems submerged in the nation.

In *Survival,* Margaret Atwood draws on Laurence frequently to substantiate her theory that the central symbol for Canada is Survival, *la Survivance.* Laurence is the perfect example, for her heroines with their strengths, their tenacity, their firm roots in Canadian soil are somehow invulnerable (though they are not the haggard crones—Hagar—or frustrated spinsters—Rachel—that Atwood finds them

to be). They speak of the human condition as Laurence describes it in an early story from *The Tomorrow-Tamer,* "I have known the worst and the worst and the worst and yet I live. I fear and fear, and yet I live." (p. 97)

Gloria Whelan, in The Ontario Review *(copyright © 1975 by The Ontario Review), Spring-Summer, 1975.*

CLARA THOMAS

The Diviners is the most comprehensive [of all the Manawaka novels] in its quest and the most complicated in its structure. Morag's journey is epic in its striving and cosmological in its scope. She seeks to understand her relation to all life, all time and eternity, and the resolution she finally comes to has both sacred and secular meanings for her.

In all of her Manawaka novels, Margaret Laurence has worked with concepts of time. Hagar, Rachel, and Stacey are all enslaved by quantitative time, the man-made measurement of minutes, hours, and days that inexorably hastens Hagar towards her death, that wears away Rachel's life, . . . and that marks off Stacey's life in a grinding routine of household chores and family responsibilities. All these women are relentlessly in service to a schedule which is not self-determined but society-determined. In their heads, they also experience felt time, existential time, in memories and fantasies which are set in juxtaposition to the rigidly-measured minutes, hours and days of their experiential world. (pp. 402-03)

From the very beginning of *The Diviners,* Morag has one advantage over these other women. She is substantially free of the confines of man-measured time, and she is living largely in natural time, the flowing of day into night into day again, the changing of the seasons, spring into summer into autumn; and in her riverwatching she has the constant companionship and awareness of the water's ceaseless mixing flow. Specific signals like the ringing of the telephone recall her to man-measured time and return her to the anxieties that impel her to set out on her remembering journey. Morag herself, her very individuality, is threatened by her vulnerability to Pique's problems. Feelings of responsibility for Pique [Morag's illegitimate daughter] constantly move toward feelings of guilt that threaten to overwhelm her, and her consciousness of the inability to act threatens to debilitate and destroy her. She is also lonely—but her only defense against loneliness is to let all the past sweep back over her and, hopefully, to wrestle it into a supportive and not a destructive force for herself. (p. 403)

[While] Hagar's memories just seem to arrange themselves chronologically, Morag is always conscious of her own part in the process of remembering. Margaret Laurence has been conscious of the neat chronology of Hagar's memories as a possible flaw in *The Stone Angel's* technique. In *The Diviners* she makes Morag's part in the memory-process very clear. . . . Furthermore, the flow of time remembered does not stop with Morag. The memories flow together in her present consciousness and then flow out again into Pique's life and the next generation. It is the working out of this flow that gives her book a structural shape whose graphic image is also the Yoruba symbol of the continuum of time, the three interflowing circles of the serpent swallowing his tail. . . .

Pique is extremely important in *The Diviners.* At the center of Margaret Laurence's own consciousness is a strong feeling for the freedom of the individual personality, held in tension by an equally strong realization of the inevitable impinging, modification, damage, support, or enhancement of one personality by another. The mother-daughter relationship of *The Diviners* demonstrates this concern in a wide range of interplay and effect. (p. 404)

As Morag's past and present draw increasingly closer together through the "Rites of Passage," she can understand and integrate her past selves into her present: she can also increasingly accept the necessity of Pique's own "Rites of Passage." Her former anxiety for Pique had been compounded of both guilt and love—now she is increasingly able to rid herself of the self-destructive component of guilt. She can now recognize Pique as her own person, and she can relinquish Pique to her own life, her own journey. (p. 405)

The sense of place is very strong among the women of the Manawaka works, and in various ways the town of Manawaka has represented constraint and imprisonment to all of them. As a girl, Morag was desperately anxious to leave the town where she felt so much an outsider. Now, in her remembering, she realizes that she has always fled from one constraining place to another, always seeking freedom, but always isolating herself in the process. Isolation—the position of the outsider—is not freedom, but stasis. Now she knows that "islands aren't real," not in the sense of providing emotional safety, stability, and security. She also knows that she now neither needs nor wants to be isolated as the obstinately self-destined outsider.

Morag's relinquishing of the need for "island" moves her towards the recognition of "garden." This she voices in her last imaginary conversation with Catherine Parr Traill.

> I'll never till these blasted fields, but this place is some kind of a garden, nonetheless, even though it may be only a wild flower garden. It's needed, and not only by me. I'm about to quit worrying about not being either an old or new pioneer. . . .

To Morag Gunn, Catherine Traill, who had been a settler in her area, was the patron saint of all pioneer women. . . . In Morag's eyes, Mrs. Traill had actually tamed the wilderness, "drawing and naming wild flowers, writing a guide for settlers with one hand, whilst rearing a brace of young and working like a galley slave with the other". . . . Catherine Traill has seemed to her to be the perfect example of a woman who did it *all*, fulfilling her social *and* human responsibilities with apparent ease. And Morag, in her own eyes, has suffered in comparison. Now, however, Morag has come to a place of self-recognition and acceptance—she has "got herself together." As Catherine Traill had named the flowers and created her garden from the wilderness, so Morag now recognizes her own wild garden. She claims it, and she even recites a litany of weed names in celebration of her land. . . . This is her place, the space which she inhabits, and if she recognizes it as a garden, then for Morag it *is* one. She dismisses Mrs. Traill, "St. Catharine," for she no longer needs the inspiration or the intimidation of her example. Morag's recognition of her wild garden is not a claiming of territory as her exclusive right; it is a simple yet miraculous new "seeing" of the land, and in a real sense it frees her from the tyranny of place and the compulsion to seek "islands." (pp. 406-07)

When *The Diviners* was published, Margaret Laurence was widely quoted as saying that she might not write any more novels. . . . Not only had she closed the circle of the Manawaka works with a long, emotionally taxing, and technically complicated work, but in Morag's journey she had also written out the culmination of a spiritual journey of her own. The basic underlying theme of all Margaret Laurence's fiction, not only of the specifically Manawaka works, but of the African works as well, has been the search for home, the journey of a stranger in a strange land, the seeking of the outsider for his true place in the tribe of man. This quest has been signified overtly in the texts by the spiritual pilgrimages of her characters. It has also been based in, and reinforced by, the fabric of her language. (p. 409)

The garden-island pattern is one central mythological "signature" in Margaret Laurence's work; the concepts are related or paired; they are sometimes fused in their significance, and sometimes they are set up in a duality or dichotomy of meaning. Both can connote shelter and sanctuary. Island can be incorporated into the concept of garden, but more often, in Margaret Laurence's work, island connotes isolation, the "islanded" individual, shut away from other men and women, from a knowledge of self, and also from God. In "The Perfume Sea," for instance, a story written well before any of the Manawaka works, the garden pattern first occurred with a particular lexical density linked, as it is in *The Diviners*, with the island as a concept of isolation. Archipelago, the hairdresser, the "fat and frantic wizard," is true to his name, a cluster of islands. His past, his present, the gray fantasy-ladies he dreams of, and his tender and inarticulate love for Dorree are all isolated elements, guarded and defended by his urbane façade. Dorree, too, is an island, garrisoned within herself out of fear of any human contact. When these two leave their beauty shop at night, they go home to their "achieved and fragile quiet," their large green house and overgrown garden behind high green walls. The basic shelter-meaning of "house," "dwelling," and "veranda" in this passage of the story is extended by the words "domain," and "sanctuary." The concept of "garden" is also extended by a score or more of specific nouns, which name the plants that are Archipelago's delight and the birds and other creatures who live freely on Dorree's veranda. Theirs is in one sense a magic garden, made so for us and for them by its exotic flowers and birds, by its enclosure within the high green walls, and by its "peaceable kingdom" quality. . . . Like all magic worlds, however, this one is precarious, and its sanctuary is pitifully vulnerable. Archipelago and Dorree have been so hurt that they can only retain their emotional stability by living in isolation, even from each other. Their garden signifies beauty and safety, but it also signifies a retreat from life which is necessary for the survival of each one of them.

The Stone Angel begins with Hagar remembering the Manawaka Cemetery, an ironic garden of the dead, where the angel signifies the corporate pride of "aliens in an uncouth land" and the blindness of Hagar's own pride. Yet even here, the proper, man-made garden of the "planted peonies, dark crimson, wallpaper pink, the pompous blossoms hanging leadenly," is always challenged by the stubborn wild garden of couchgrass and cowslip. . . . Hagar takes refuge in a wild garden by the sea and finds sanctuary in the deserted fish cannery, but this garden is also her Gethsemane. (pp. 410-11)

The continuity of the garden metaphor is assured throughout all Margaret Laurence's work, not only by such major passages as these, but also by scores of flower references which form a part of the language-fabric of every text. Sometimes they are used simply and descriptively, sometimes symbolically as in the naming of Calla who was willing to extend her love for Rachel to an Easter sacrifice; or Flower, Stacey's speechless little girl, who finally talks and blooms; or Lilac Stonehouse, perilously and innocently wandering in a fallen world. Sometimes the stubborn vitality of the wild garden is reaffirmed and reasserted, as in *A Bird in the House,* where the helmeted snap-dragons stand in proper rows and the wild blue violets and creeping Charlie stubbornly grow again, even after each beheading by the guillotine lawnmower. . . .

The novels stand as unique and separate works of fiction, not autobiography; but they do contain a powerful and continuing spiritual autobiography. The reaching of equilibrium, of fluidity in time, as well as the profoundly religious acceptance of the mystery and the gift of grace are Margaret Laurence's as well as Morag Gunn's. (p. 411)

> *Clara Thomas, "The Wild Garden and the Manawaka World," in* Modern Fiction Studies *(© copyright 1976 by Purdue Research Foundation, West Lafayette, Indiana), Autumn, 1976, pp. 401-12.*

JOAN CALDWELL

Five of Margaret Laurence's books [*The Stone Angel, A Jest of God, The Fire-Dwellers, A Bird in the House,* and *The Diviners*] have Manawaka, a fictionalized re-creation of her hometown Neepawa, as their background if not their actual locale. But neither Manawaka nor Neepawa is "prairie" insofar as that word suggests endless plains where farmhouses sit solitary on the edge of their vast sections of the world's largest breadbasket. The essence of Manawaka is that it is small-town. . . . (p. 64)

This is not to deny, of course, that Margaret Laurence has a distinctively Canadian voice, nor that, though her concerns are of wider significance, they are deeply rooted in the local Canadian experience. (p. 65)

Before she could see her own place plainly, however, Laurence, like many other offspring of small towns, had to move away from home both physically and imaginatively. Born in 1926, she spent her first twenty-three years in Manitoba and then moved with her husband to live and work in Africa. On her experiences there, between 1950 and 1957, she has based five of her books. . . . *A Tree for Poverty* (1954) is a translation of Somali tales and poems. *The Tomorrow-Tamer* (1963) a collection of short stories, and *This Side of Jordan* (1960) a novel. Her travel-memoir *The Prophet's Camel Bell* (titled *New Wind in a Dry Land* in the American edition) appeared in 1963 and was followed in 1968 by a commentary on contemporary Nigerian writing entitled *Long Drums and Cannons.* Interesting though these books are as the fruit of seven years' observation of countries changing from colonialism to independence, they were, as their author says, "written by an outsider . . . who in the end had to remain in precisely that relationship, for it could never become the close involvement of family." (pp. 65-6)

It is on . . . the Manawaka books that Laurence's wide fame as a writer rests.

At first sight, the heroines of the Manawaka fiction seem an unprepossessing lot. . . . But heroine is the right word: each of these women is a fighter who suffers, weeps, errs, wounds, despairs, sometimes seems close to going under, but who, by learning to know herself a little better and by acknowledging an instinctive though far from orthodox faith, survives. "I am haunted by the women in Laurence's novels" wrote Joan Larkin in *Ms* Magazine, "as if they really were alive—and not as women I've known, but as women I've been." Laurence's power of characterization is formidable; her human beings are compelling under whatever unpleasant circumstances we find them. (So convincing and authentic is Hagar that *The Stone Angel* is a set text not only on scores of high school and college literature courses but also on nursing and medical courses dealing with old age and dying.) What keeps us steadily engaged with these women is more than just their reflection of feminine experience; it is the vigor of their speech, variations on first-person narratives which deftly experiment with flashback devices and screen-play interior monologues, their healthy sense of humor which is often courageously directed at themselves, and their fundamental will to survive.

Like Laurence herself, each of the women is occupied in trying to weave into an acceptable fabric the different strands of her own and her ancestral past, "partly in order to be freed from it, partly in order to try to understand myself and perhaps those of my generation through seeing where we had come from." . . . While the quest for lost or unknown parents has been a standard pattern in fiction since the eighteenth century, the particular nature of Laurence's search for ancestral roots is distinctively North American. Only in rare cases in European fiction does one find agonized searches for racial identity—the Jews know themselves to be Jews, the Irish are Irish, however much other peoples have imposed upon them and tried to destroy them.

Scottish Presbyterian and Protestant Irish grandparents proclaim themselves in Margaret Laurence's veins, and qualities both admirable and less than admirable in her characters reflect that mixed origin: stubborn pride, respectability, hard work, commonsense, uneasiness about the body, imaginative richness and the gift of the gab. Through Morag of *The Diviners,* the quest for racial identity is most fully explored. . . . [It] is Morag who actually goes back to Scotland in search of her roots, only to find that "it's not mine, except a long way back" and that Canada, where she was born and where her immediate ancestors forged a new society, is in fact her own place.

Morag's ancestors were particular kinds of emigrants, on one side the "famine Irish" and, on the other, Scots who were dispossessed by the Highland clearances. Not only then is Morag a kind of half-breed but she is descended from victims of greedy land-owners. This accounts for the importance of the Tonnerre family in the Manawaka novels and particularly in *The Diviners.* The Tonnerres are Métis, half-French, half-Indian people who were dispossessed of their lands, their horses and their proud heritage at the crushing of Louis Riel's rebellion in 1885. Morag is drawn to the pride, the language, the songs, the lost heritage of the Tonnerres, and Jules Tonnerre is clearly her spiritual and physical match from the beginning. The daughter Morag bears to Jules is named after his sister Piquette, whose fiery death is an emblem throughout the Manawaka books of the white man's failure to love.

Although this draws on obviously Canadian experience, the quest for identity widens also to universal implication. We have all in a sense been dispossessed at some time . . . and there lingers in the general memory the image of a lost Eden from which our common ancestors were expelled and to which we all seek return. The search for the lost Eden, for Jerusalem the Golden, for "the promised land of one's own inner freedom" is undertaken in one form or another by each of Laurence's heroines. Paradise is not attainable on earth, but each is led a little closer to it in moments of heightened self-knowledge and genuine reaching out to others. (pp. 66-7)

Joan Caldwell, "Margaret Laurence: In Search of Ancestors," in Book Forum (copyright © 1978 by The Hudson River Press), Vol. IV, No. 1, 1978, pp. 64-9.

* * *

LE GUIN, Ursula K(roeber)   1929-

Le Guin is an award-winning American writer of science fiction and fantasy whose primary genre is the novel. She has also published a compilation of short stories, *The Wind's Twelve Quarters*, and a volume of poetry, *Wild Angels*. Le Guin has likewise extended her creations of fantasy to the world of children's literature. *The Earthsea* trilogy is her most noted contribution in this field, and for the last volume of this set Le Guin won the National Book Award. Her work is noted for its clearly delineated portraits of alien worlds, often reflecting the author's own explorations into the philosophy of Taoism and the oriental view of history. Among her creations are the Hainish, an ancient people who claim to be the original human race and to have originally colonized Earth. The Hainish are central to five of Le Guin's novels. (See also *CLC*, Vol. 8, *Children's Literature Review*, Vol. 3, and *Contemporary Authors*, Vols. 21-24, rev. ed.)

GEORGE EDGAR SLUSSER

In terms of quality alone, it is difficult to speak of development in the fiction of Ursula K. Le Guin. Her writing has been good from the start. She has published short stories of high quality, selectively, over a period of thirteen years. Since 1966, she has written nine novels. Even the worst of these, *The Lathe of Heaven* is imaginative and ambitious, far superior to most SF being produced today. There is little doubt that Le Guin is one of the best writers currently working in the science fiction and fantasy genres. Apparently at the height of her powers, she promises much.

Nor has her world view changed or altered significantly since the beginning. . . . [Her best fiction] examines the possibility of balance between the individual and his world. Le Guin has always believed strongly in such balance, in the dynamics of polarity. Taoism is not an interlude; it is and has always been the strongest single force behind her work, the mold that shapes novel after novel, and binds them one to another in a coherent pattern of human history. Her use of oriental wisdom is highly personal, the creative adaptation of a philosophical system to a literary genre long dominated by a harshly western vision of evolution and technological progress. (p. 3)

To study Le Guin's novels is to study a complex organism that is growing and expanding harmoniously according to a central law of balance. This growth takes two forms. First, there is a shift in focus away from the celebration of balance and toward the problematics of balance, a shift which brings the individual closer to the center of this world, as maker and breaker of equilibrium. From novel to novel, man's relationship to the whole, and the nature and composition of that whole, become increasingly complex. Second, to render this complexity, there are important changes in form. Le Guin's later novels are much more elaborate, more concrete, more realistic. In place of vaguely stylized "worlds," we find carefully drawn societies; instead of "heroes," multifaceted, believable characters. Le Guin rapidly abandons the classic impersonal narrator, so dear to many old pseudo-epics and space operas, and begins to experiment with point of view. First a story is told from the limited perspective of one mind, and then through two or more centers of consciousness; diaries, interpolated tales, elaborate fictions of the editor, all have their place. Simple linear storytelling gives way to flashbacks, skillful juxtapositions of narrated time. Here, on this level, we may speak of synthesis. For what is happening, and will probably continue to happen in Le Guin's fiction, is an interesting merger of genres—the literature of speculation, science fiction and fantasy, with that of personal relationships and manners, the so-called "mainstream" novel.

From the start, Le Guin's writing is a fiction of ideas—or rather, of one idea: change in permanence, the dynamics of equilibrium. Her early novels are important because they lay the foundations of an historical vision from which she has not yet deviated. The two poles of that vision are, on one hand, celebration of balance and cosmic order, and on the other the difficulty of men to predict, to control the "way" this order will go. Even the best of intentions may go awry, bringing about the opposite result. Each of her novels presents a "problem," an inbalance to be stabilized, things apart that must be brought together. To do so takes effort; there must be will to order, and a hero. But if this is not to become a vicious circle, a comedy of errors where each new deed only wreaks more havoc, there must be some knowledge too. In Le Guin's universe man develops as he grows wiser.

The first novel, *Rocannon's World* (1966), and to some extent the second, *Planet of Exile* (1966), are exercises in paradox. What seems insignificant, misbegotten, hopeless, turns out in the end to yield unexpected riches. As individuals, the heroes play surprisingly little part in this process. They persevere, trust in things, but have little more than a token need to trust in others, and almost none to trust in themselves. In her third novel, *City of Illusions* (1967), a significant change occurs. The battlefield shifts from the external world of stock heroic adventure to the hero's mind itself. This internalization leads to new emphases; it increases the weight of personal responsibility, and with it the possibility of human evil arising from the burden of choice, the acceptance or rejection of the limits of existence. In these early novels what is called "evil" remains primarily an external factor, the fruit of ignorance, something to be converted or destroyed. But gradually, subtly, the spectre of self-delusion grows until, in her later novels, it turns things inside out. There, instead of demonstrating that untold "good" may come from the most insignificant act, Le

Guin warns that even the smallest deed, foolishly or maliciously done, can cause untold harm. (pp. 4-5)

Le Guin's saga does not follow the pathway of linear progression. No advance is permanent, no conquest stable. One thing brings about its opposite. The only certainties are balance and change. Two major themes in [the first three Hainish] novels indicate quite clearly the course of Le Guin's thought: telepathy, and the League of Worlds. (p. 7)

[In] the early Hainish novels, parochialism, cultural isolation, and xenophobia strike at the very heart of the League, despite its plans and laws. Without mutual understanding, fear and fanaticism take over. The Shing, the "alien," simply incarnate what is a human failing, and make it an absolute. They allow no physical contact with men; mentally they are cut off by the lie. Like Agat's colony, they too are dwindling in number; in spite of this, they would remain apart, willfully and perpetually. Their famous Law is, in reality, their means of cutting themselves off from life.... (p. 10)

Le Guin's "future history" differs greatly from the Heinleinian variety, where each episode is a decisive step in man's conquest of the universe. Here both man and technology are defeated; "survival of the fittest" is not a matter of guts or guile, but rather of adaptation, of knowing the limits of self and others, of reaching other minds, communicating with them but not coercing them. The rugged individuality so championed by other writers is never glorified by Le Guin. To be an individual in her universe is to be whole, and that can only happen when man accepts his responsibility as part of a balanced universe. The greater his role in that universe, the more urgent the need for understanding self and the limits of self.

Each of these three early novels celebrates balance—they are pearls on a string. In each of them two "principles" are at work—polar forces which generate and sustain their inner dynamic. The first could be called "elusiveness of control," its counterweight "fortunate paradox." What first seemed the right move, then turned out to be the wrong one, now by some unpredictable twist reveals itself to be correct after all, on another level altogether. The technique of dramatizing these intricacies of change in permanence is fully worked out in *Rocannon's World*—this is no "apprentice" piece. Later works will elaborate these techniques and explore their significance, but will not alter them in any fundamental way.

From novel to novel, mankind is growing up. As he does, more emphasis naturally falls on the individual. Balance becomes less a matter of the machine righting itself, and more a burden thrown on the hero. Rocannon is emmeshed in forces external to himself. Convention does not ask that he ponder self, but that he act. However, in *City* a shift has clearly occurred. Although this novel superficially relates a quest leading to the destruction of an unknown enemy, the difference in focus is striking. (pp. 10-11)

City of Illusions displays an even more elaborate, and nearly bewildering, profusion of binding symbols and paradoxes. However, the profusion of signs serves a precise thematic function. In a novel about illusion and reality, the hero's task, like ours, is to break through the shimmering surface to truth.

Paradox thrives in CI: The Shing are rulers ruled; reverence for life is really fear of death. And the patterns of imagery are even denser. Jewels and sun, reflected light and real light, patterning frames and the frame of heaven, illusion and reality, fill the novel from its first to last pages. All are shadows to one degree or another; the clear light of truth is never seen. (p. 15)

These early novels, however skillfully written, remain verbal skeletons, too stylized and bound by the conventions of the space adventure to be truly effective. In *The Left Hand of Darkness,* Le Guin takes a bold step, for here the Hainish saga is transposed into concrete terms—recognizable societies, with men instead of symbols.

The Left Hand of Darkness is far more complex than its predecessors; in terms of sheer technical skill, it is Le Guin's most satisfying work to date. A delicate balance of ideas and passions is maintained throughout. The storytelling process is intricate. Over all lies an editorial framework, intermingled with interpolated tales, documents, diaries, and constant shifts back and forth in narrative time. This richness of texture does not impede the forward movement of the story, or the sheer suspense of the main plot. The popularity of this novel ... is due at least partially to a striking central idea, a world whose people are androgynous. Also, this was the first time Le Guin dealt specifically with societies as such, and attempted explicit political commentary. This book is, however, more than a trick or a trend, but a well-crafted novel in its own right. It is also part of the Hainish cycle, continuing the League saga beyond the Great War into a time of consolidation; and can only be fully understood when read in this perspective. Once again, an ethnologist-observer, Genly Ai, comes to claim a planet for the organization of worlds. The basic pattern is the same, but what Le Guin does with it is profoundly different. (pp. 16-17)

Left Hand confronts men with viable, living societies. The vague, impersonal forces represented in the earlier books—nature in the raw or barbarian hordes—are still present, but play a secondary role before the precise social mechanisms of Winter. Some critics have spoken of a disparity between public and private "imperatives" in the novel: for the first time in Le Guin's work, union between men and the fixing of a bond of mutual trust are no longer automatically the basis for restored harmony in the public sphere. (p. 19)

Le Guin is not competing with Orwell or Hemingway. Her social analysis is acute, but its purpose is not indignation or reform. She has no social program, offers no panaceas. Nor does she, at the other extreme, give us characters who turn their backs on seemingly hopeless social chaos, and go off to the wilderness to carve some private relationship out of confrontation with the elements. Ai and Estraven are forced by society to cross the ice; there is no other way. They do not flee one society to return to another (both are inadequate), nor do they take refuge in each other. Paradoxically, they make their journey to renew society, but on a deeper level, at the roots. (p. 20)

The theme of roots and rootlessness is central to Le Guin's work. It has grown steadily in importance from novel to novel, culminating in the recent confluence of three favorite images—tree, root and dream.... This combined imagery lends a certain universality to her work that was never before present. From the start, her heroes have invariably been aliens of one sort or another, cut off from their roots....

At work in *Left Hand* is an intricate system of paradoxes: limits are freedom, freedom represents limits. To move in a circle is to progress; to progress is to return to move in a circle. Estraven seems to get nowhere in his political efforts, to be going in circles; but on another deeper path he is moving toward something of great public significance. His conservative return to the roots turns out to be the most revolutionary, far-seeing act in the novel. Circumstances in the social realm do not limit or prevent human contact between himself and Ai, they bring it about. (p. 21)

Things are not what they first seem. The wondrous balance of the earlier novels, which became almost an end in itself, has shifted. Individual man is placed squarely at the center of LHD [*Left Hand of Darkness*]; he must not only discover the fundamental rhythms of life, but commit himself to them and work toward equilibrium. Men are responsible for upsetting the balance; the visionary seeks to right it. Thus, Estraven sees, while Ai, the professional observer, is blind.

Vision is necessary to penetrate the complex patterns of imagery in this novel. Light and darkness, shadow and snow, are things of constantly shifting valence, ambiguous, inscrutable, and yet essential. They are not mere bindings—one follows Rocannon's jewel like a bouncing ball. This time they are interwoven solidly into the fabric of Gethen's institutions and culture. Ambiguity is no shimmering surface, a frame of illusion to be shattered; on the contrary, freedom lies, if anywhere, in embracing it. Nor is it a sign of nature's indifference to man. It is, rather, the ambiguity of a world order which, for man's ultimate salvation, defies that simple moral interpretation which would make white a "good" or an "evil." It is an order of primary substances which resist man's attempts to preempt or enclose them in systems, ideologies, or religious principles. In LHD, the heroes come in contact with the bases of things—cold, warmth, ice, visible darkness. (p. 22)

The ambiguity present in this book is the true state of things, according to Le Guin. Only in complexity does balance function; to simplify this process, or elevate one factor above all others, is to disturb the ongoing dynamic. Like the actions of the Shing, it is undoubtedly the result of profound misunderstanding. But here, in the world of real states and governments, ignorance is quickly perverted into a most tenacious evil. Meshe is not just blind; he also forces others to believe that he sees. The Ortoga are not merely incredulous; they show Ai a *will* to incredulity. In *Left Hand* man is put to the proof, and he shows us how serious his undoings can be. But if man takes things beyond the point where they can right themselves, then the only thing that can ever correct them is another man. The responsibility for order is henceforth in his hands. Estraven finds this task, his life's work, extraordinarily difficult. Where Rocannon simply followed his calling, Estraven must pass through a labyrinth of political intrigue. Wit is not enough to carry him forward; he must also have another guide, the muse Ai invokes at the beginning of his tale—imagination. (p. 25)

The earlier novels ended on a note of hope for the human race. Whatever losses were sustained were recoverable in the balance. *Left Hand* ends with a different mood. There is no "jewel of mourning," no epic funeral. What remains is a tale, and the imperfection of human friendship in the inconclusive world of man's affairs. (p. 30)

The *Earthsea Trilogy* has generally been ignored by commentators on Le Guin. Some may have been deterred by the silly publishing classification which designates the books as "children's literature." More likely, though, the trilogy has simply seemed a world apart, self-contained, obeying the laws of the high fantasy genre, and having little in common with the Hainish "mainstream." Such logic may apply to writers whose world view is incoherent or inconsistent, but not to Le Guin. *Earthsea* does stand apart to the extent that it forms a carefully balanced whole. But, more essentially, it creates a universe which is parallel to that of the Hainish novels, one in which major themes are not simply mirrored or reflected, but carried forward and developed in new ways. The problems of individual responsibility, of folly, evil and the search for selfhood, are examined throughout these books in all their purity. (p. 31)

The difference between the Earthsea novels and the others of the same period is, most fundamentally, one of style. In an essay written in 1973, "From Elfland to Poughkeepsie," Le Guin talks about writing fantasy stories: one's writing style, she says, should be neutral, with few modernisms or archaisms sprinkled in; it should attempt to create a world never before seen in the clearest, most direct language possible. . . . *Earthsea* is a work of high style and imagination. *The Farthest Shore* is a work of genuine epic vision.

Ged is a fully developed hero, and interestingly, one of a new sort. Le Guin's earlier heroes were scientists or statesmen. Ged is a "mage." In her essay, "Dreams Must Explain Themselves" (1973), Le Guin tells us her mage is an artist—the trilogy is an artist-novel. Traditionally, the artist is the most private of heroes; the struggle to create is primarily a struggle with self, with one's own powers and the need to control them and their consequences. The scientists and "observers" of earlier novels occupy an intermediate position between men of action and the artist. But in Le Guin the pull is always toward action. Both Rocannon and Genly Ai are drawn into an active role through contact with a man of action. Ged is a loner. (pp. 33-4)

In "Dreams Must Explain Themselves," Le Guin describes the thematic progression of the three Earthsea novels. *Wizard* deals with the hero's "coming of age." It is a novel of initiation and apprenticeship. The subject of *Tombs* is "sex"; it relates a "feminine coming of age." In broader terms, its theme is love. The third novel, *Farthest*, is about death, "a coming of age again," says Le Guin, "but in a larger context." This is the hero's last and greatest adventure. First an apprentice, then a master, Ged-grown-old now takes a new apprentice with him, thus completing the epic chain. (pp. 34-5)

The central theme of all these novels is the nature of human evil. The exploration takes place within the same limits as always: the universe is still a creative, dynamic balance, Yin and Yang, not a Manichean contention between light as good and darkness as evil. Evil is still explicable as a misunderstanding of the dynamics of life. What has become awesome, however, is the power one man, each man, wields, potentially and actually, to disrupt the balance. The setting in *Left Hand* is realistic; here it can only be called allegorical. (p. 35)

In a sense, Le Guin reaches her farthest shore in *Earthsea*. The geographic layout of this fantasy world is an exact parallel of her Hainish universe. In both, action has tended to take place, not at the center, but rather in the outlying reaches. . . . Three of the four earlier Hainish novels are situated on worlds at the fringe of the known universe (even the Earth of *City* is no center but a wasteland). *Left Hand* is the far point, both in terms of time and space; thereafter, Le Guin begins to work backward. Both *Word* and "Vaster" still take place on distant planets, and their time is pre-*Rocannon,* before the discovery of mindspeech. *The Dispossessed* represents a retreat in spatial terms as well, from the periphery of the Hainish universe to its core. The twin planets are the Cetian worlds, oft mentioned, but never before seen. In linear time, TD [*The Dispossessed*] represents the extreme point of retreat toward our present that Le Guin has yet explored. Terra has undergone eco-disaster, so we are definitely somewhere in the future. The event around which the novel revolves is the discovery of the theory of time which led to creation of the ansible, the faster-than-light communication device which first made the idea of a League possible. (p. 46)

[*The Dispossessed*] goes farthest of all Le Guin's novels in investigating the problem of evil in a fundamentally monistic universe. . . . [In] extending her world view into the realm of specific social speculation, Le Guin inherits certain problems as well. Goodman was troubled by the possibility of "unnatural" behavior: How can such a thing exist if nature is and always has been? Where could it have come from? Le Guin has, as we have seen, faced the same problem from the start in her Taoist universe. However tenacious and dangerous, evil has always been quantitative in nature—anti-natural actions, anti-kings. But is a qualitative evil possible; is there something in human nature itself which is unteachable, irremediable? Le Guin resists what Theodore Roszac calls the "satanic temptation." But in her strenuous, almost Puritanical probing of man's social conscience, she pushes her monist vision to new tensions and depths.

The problem in TD is not so much whether man can regulate himself; it is rather that he regulates himself naturally, and too much. The classic utopian question is asked here: What is the maximum personal freedom consistent with collective order? TD is less the story of social norms than that of the exceptional individual, Shevek. In any society, even the freest, his demands for freedom are excessive. Shevek's difficulties in realizing self are compounded; not only must he struggle against the self, but more fundamentally, against the walls men build around him. (p. 47)

Le Guin has called TD an "ambiguous utopia." The physical setting alone, as compared to that of *Left Hand,* reveals the complexity of the problem. We find little easy balance or fortunate paradox here. In LHD, there were two societies; surrounding both were the planet, a common nature, and a common culture in which men could seek their roots. Social reality may not be solid, but the base is. TD has two separate worlds, two distinct natures, two radically different societies. The only thing they have in common is that both are inhabited by men. Furthermore, Le Guin gives a twist to the simplistic utopian dream of the perfect society in a perfect setting. Urras, the world with the capitalist society, is lush, green, and bountiful. Anarres, the anarchist planet, is harsh, moonlike, and barren. (p. 48)

Where will Le Guin go from here? One can only speculate. A likely direction is inward, away from the collective drama, toward the individual which lies at its roots. The award-winning story "The Day Before the Revolution," written as a sequel to *The Dispossessed,* is perhaps symptomatic. Le Guin again goes back in time to relate the story of Odo, founder of the anarchist movement. Interestingly, the piece does not deal with her birth nor the revolutionary years, nor even with the writing of the *Principles* during her creative period. It recounts her death. . . .

The focus in this story is harshly realistic. Le Guin reaches behind the facade of ideals to reveal the basic drives that move humanity. Odo acknowledges sex and vanity; she acknowledges the private happiness sacrificed and lost. As a true anarchist, she refuses the static situation, and questions everything. In her old age, however, this has simply become testiness. Odo discovers the true limits of change—death. But there is no heroic rushing into it this time; her body just fails, and she is forced to accept. (p. 57)

The short story remains a short story, the perfect instrument for probing in depth within a larger framework. It tells nothing as to the nature of Le Guin's next large frame. But it does represent a far point. In the dynamic of change in permanence, the balance has come down hard on the side of human mutability. (p. 58)

> *George Edgar Slusser, in his* The Farthest Shores of Ursula Le Guin *(copyright © 1976 by George Edgar Slusser), The Borgo Press, 1976.*

ELIZABETH CUMMINS COGELL

Le Guin's books are characterized by a significant use of setting. . . . [Five of her Hainish stories, *Rocannon's World, Planet of Exile, City of Illusion, The Left Hand of Darkness,* and "The Word for World is Forest," demonstrate a] significant use to characterize native species on other worlds—a use which has become more complex in successive stories. It goes beyond the more obvious uses of setting to create atmosphere or to draw the reader into an alien environment and thus into the plot. The Hainish stories form a unit in which the theme and plot are dependent on the League or Ekumen contact with species which are native to—or at least have for a long time inhabited—that planet. Furthermore, these native species are shown in terms of the effect of environment on their lives, from straightforward geographical influence to influence on myth, ritual, and ways of perceiving the world. (p. 131)

Given [an] examination of Le Guin's use of setting, one initially concludes that it reveals her developing ability as a writer, ranging from her use of setting as a topographical and physiological influence to its mythological and psychological influence. Secondly, her total integration of setting and racial characterization leads to a re-examination of the concept of setting. Le Guin is not merely using it as a backdrop or atmosphere in the Hainish stories; she has intertwined it with the psychological nature of the Athsheans and with the mythological nature of the Gethenians. In these instances, it is nearly impossible to separate setting from characterization. Furthermore, Le Guin has integrated setting with two themes running through these stories. First, she has depicted each species' perception of reality as being dependent on its environment. Each of the species' vocabulary and metaphors are drawn from its encounters with the rhythms and processes of nature which are dynamic. An alien race or species may have a different perception of nature, and the native species will have to come to terms with that different reality; it will have to test it, evaluate it, and decide whether to accept it, reject it, or adapt it to its own view of reality. *Planet of Exile* is a clear example of this theme and here the conflict is also the novel's conflict. *The Left Hand of Darkness* and "The Word for World is Forest" demonstrate the same linking of conflict and setting.

Her second theme is that harmony of man and nature is necessary for racial survival and development. What frequently happens in her plots is a three-part encounter of Nature (setting), Self (the native species), and Other (the alien species). The encounter becomes the plot, and while in any individual novel a final synthesis is not detailed, synthesis does seem to be the prevailing pattern in this unit of five stories. It is an achievement which is not merely a compromise between competing species or the resignation of a species to the hardships of nature, but a dialectical relationship among the three. Stagnation occurs when any one is regarded as a static unity, separate from nature or other races, such as the tradition-bound Tevarans or the isolated species in *Rocannon's World*. This synthesis is best seen in the societies of *The Left Hand of Darkness*. Their mythology illustrates their adaptation to nature, the alien species jolts them into a changed perception of the universe, and what results is a realization that they live on an Ice Age planet in a changed universe. Le Guin's use of setting is as complex as the interlacing leaves, branches, roots, and lights in her forests. (pp. 139-40)

> *Elizabeth Cummins Cogell, "Setting As Analogue to Characterization in Ursula Le Guin," in* Extrapolation *(copyright 1977 by Thomas D. and Alice S. Clareson), May, 1977, pp. 131-41.*

BARBARA J. BUCKNALL

Le Guin insists that androgyny is not the main theme of [*The Left Hand of Darkness*], the main theme being rather that of fidelity and betrayal. But, quite apart from the instantaneous response that the idea of the androgyne evokes in the reader's imagination, there has to be a reason, and a reason that makes good sense in creative terms, for using the androgyne as a term of reference for the discussion of fidelity and betrayal. The androgyne, simply by being presented as existing, looks to the trusting and warm-hearted reader like the answer to a question, and that answer looms so large that the theme of fidelity and betrayal tends to get pushed a little to one side. If one thinks about the androgyne for a long time and investigates the full implications of *The Left Hand of Darkness*, the theme of fidelity and betrayal does, in fact, have importance. . . .

The androgyne looks to a lot of us like an answer. But, as the saying goes, "What is the question?" This whole issue of questions and answers is so important to Ursula Le Guin that she makes it a central feature of the Handdara, a mystical cult she has invented so that her androgynes can have a religion. . . . (p. 57)

By sending a conventional young man from Earth into a culture where there was no sexual differentiation, [as Le Guin did in *Left Hand of Darkness*] she made it possible for herself to imagine an area of humanity that would be shared by both sexes alike. (p. 58)

Le Guin, like any strong personality, has her dark side and recognizes it in other people, including the people she invents. Symbol of wholeness as her androgyne may be, the Gethenian is a human being, and consequently as subject to weakness, error, folly, and even crime as any other person. (p. 62)

[Incest] is a central theme in *The Left Hand of Darkness*, and it is largely in terms of incest that the idea of the androgyne is linked to the theme of fidelity and betrayal. Structurally, this is extremely important, because the basic situation on Gethen is somehow incestuous. At the beginning of the book, Estraven tosses off the epigram that "Karhide is not a nation but a family quarrel," and this turns out to be true. The basic social unit in Karhide is the Hearth, which is the home of the clan, and every social institution on Gethen is based in some form on the Hearth. . . . (pp. 63-4)

The sexual nature of the relationship between Genly and Estraven is blurred by the fact that Estraven is an androgyne who is neuter most of the time and Genly seldom has the opportunity to see him as a sexual being. But when he does, it is significant that he sees Estraven as a woman. As in *The Tombs of Atuan*, it is the "female" partner who contrives the male partner's escape. But Genly is very far from being the wise mage who serves the forces of light, and Estraven is by no means in the grip of the powers of darkness, but represents, in his own being, the reconciliation of darkness and light. Finally, there is no living happily ever after, for, in order to complete Genly's rescue, Estraven has to die, and in order to bring his mission to a successful conclusion, Genly has to break his promise to Estraven to clear his name. Love, although the one thing needful, is no longer a triumphant solution, but in itself, a source of grief and pain. And there is fidelity and betrayal on both sides.

The maturity of this conclusion to *The Left Hand of Darkness* chastens the reader somewhat, reducing the euphoria felt on first meeting the idea of the androgyne. The longing for a lost completeness, for, as Plato puts it, "the desire and pursuit of the whole," the nostalgia for a once-upon-a-time when all went well may, it seems, be a trap, a return to the incestuous bonds of childhood. But, since everything is double-natured (the Yin and the Yang again), this trap may be sprung and a way found out of it into greater harmony. As Estraven points out, duality is part of the androgyne, for there is always the Other. Recognition of the Other is the lesson of innocence and experience alike, and through this recognition we reach maturity.

In other words, Le Guin leaves us with an insight that is as classical as her way of presenting it is unorthodox. This is, basically, what makes *The Left Hand of Darkness* a work different in nature from other well-known thought-experiments in human sexuality. (p. 67)

> *Barbara J. Bucknall, "Androgynes in Outer Space," in* Critical Encounters: Writers and Themes in Science Fiction, *edited by Dick Riley (copyright © 1978 by Frederick Ungar Publishing Co., Inc.), Ungar, 1978, pp. 56-69.*

BARRY N. MALZBERG

[Le Guin is] perhaps the most successful and critically admired writer ever to produce a substantial body of work within the genre limits of science fiction. In terms of critical recognition, only Vonnegut and Bradbury come close, but Vonnegut's novels were published as literary, not genre, works, and the short stories that made Bradbury famous in the 1940s and 1950s appeared in mass circulation magazines. And neither has won a National Book Award as did Le Guin for juvenile literature. . . . (p. 5)

Le Guin's focus, from the outset, has been detailed and anthropological.... [*The Left Hand of Darkness*] in its careful documentation of a society whose mores superseded the individual choice of its members, was perhaps the most distinguished example since Hal Clement's *A Mission of Gravity,* in which the background became the main character of a science fiction novel. In ... *Lathe of Heaven* Le Guin backed off momentarily from these concerns into a kind of psychological, solipsistic subtext ..., but in 1974 *The Dispossessed,* considered a work even more successful than *LHD,* shifted into a novelistic modus operandi where not only was cultural background novel-foreground, but the nominal protagonist was merely a vessel through which the real conflict of the novel, that between cultures, could be enacted. It may be argued that *DIS* [*The Dispossessed*] is a metaphor; a kind of climactic East/West novel of the future or even a two-culture Vietnam novel, but I think that argument would be specious; *DIS* ... is about merely what it is about ... two invented, imaginary subcultures. It is a novel which could not have been done in any way other than as science fiction; it needs those devices in order to work and this, surely, is the central definition of a "good" science fiction novel. (p. 6)

We are, I believe, in a post-ideological time in science fiction and in the world: the great thrashings of the sixties have been overcome, and many of the nakedly dialectical or polemical approaches of the new writers of the last decade have almost entirely lost their audience.... The basic statement of the anthropologist is that the individual is essentially helpless, forced to enact in varying degrees the folkways and mores of his culture; the message of Le Guin is that culture predominates. No Ballardian wasteland here, no Dischian landscape of dread, no *Bug Jack Barron* in which the systems' interstices can be found and destroyed. In Le Guin the connection between individual and culture is seamless; and the character bears less responsibility for his acts than he does in the fiction of these other writers.

One does not want to push this point too far. Le Guin is a fine writer of decent range and sophistication; like all fine writers she would resent being categorized or used as a demonstration of anyone's theorem. Her work, like that of any important writer, must perversely resist labeling. Still, there are clues, consistencies, certain indications that Le Guin is reaching a large audience and is becoming science fiction's most successful writer both within and without the field because her work is centered around a point which a seventies American audience may need to consider: the individual responds only to the flux of culture; the individual no longer has ultimate responsibility for his/her acts.... What makes [Le Guin's novella "The Word for World is Forest"] particularly interesting is its direct (and I would claim, absolutely conscious) construction as a paradigm of Vietnam—the American occupation of Indochina taken to a science fictional context. Here ... is a clearly political work, but what renders it more interesting than most of this sort is not only its careful and patient crafting, its extensive limning of the alien subculture (Le Guin is nothing if not thorough), but the fact that its principals can take no action whatsoever to alter the system. The tragedy of cultural confrontation is the tragedy of history, Le Guin is saying, and the culture with weaker technology will always lose.

Beyond that bleak conclusion is little more; before it are only the thrashings of the principal as he first resists and then accepts this knowledge. *WWF* ["The Word for World is Forest"] is many things, and not the least of them is a distinguished and well-imagined work of fiction, but its ultimate point is even more horrid than that granted by Ballard's wasteland: no human impress can be left upon the social abstract. Nothing will change.... Le Guin sees "spirit" as merely another sociological folkway, inseparable from the cultural context in which it would arise.

LOH [*Lathe of Heaven*], by general agreement the least successful novel of Le Guin's mature period, fails, perhaps, because the vision is in the forefront and not to be subsumed by the detail. The dreamer, as in folklore, dreams real; he creates the world piece by piece. He seeks therapy and transfers his solipsism, ironically enough, to the psychiatrist. This novel, which seems in synopsis little more than a whimsy taken to extraordinary length, is at first puzzling and then frightening: the world and all its creatures seem merely to be a device, an incidental extension of the interrelation of the two characters (there are only two), but what is happening outside this single transaction cannot matter and eventually does not. The word for world in *LOH* is not forest. It is clutter. (pp. 6-8)

"The Ones Who Walk Away from Omelas," the Hugo winner, is a Borges pastiche which is very much fixated upon the single transaction as it describes an idealized society pivoting only on necessary brutalities to one child (echoes of Schwartz-Bart's thirty-six Just whose sufferings and witness make possible God's tolerance of existence). Some citizens can not accept such an unjust society and must leave it—although Le Guin does not say to where.... [And the Earthsea trilogy is] characteristically Le Guin and the style is consistent, but any understanding of these books must be accomplished outside the context of modern science fiction; they are linked to the far older tradition of fantasy.... (p. 8)

I would be almost sure that her next novel will not be science fiction or at least will not be published at all as science fiction; that eventually Le Guin will be writing complex fantasies ..., work having nothing to do with science fiction....

[I have] certain reservations about Le Guin and the eventual estimation of her work. She may be seen, some time from now, as less a perpetrator of visions than their mirror. Still, this does not take away from the essence: she is, as of the date of this essay, the most important contemporary writer of science fiction, and this field cannot be understood if she is not. No writer could ask for or receive better tribute. (p. 9)

Barry N. Malzberg, "Circumstance as Policy: The Decade of Ursula K. Le Guin," in Ursula K. Le Guin: Voyage to Inner Lands and Outer Space, *edited by Joe De Bolt (copyright © 1979 by Kennikat Press Corp.; reprinted by permission of Kennikat Press Corp.), Kennikat, 1979, pp. 5-9.*

KAREN SINCLAIR

Repeatedly in [Le Guin's] fiction we confront individuals who are of society and yet not quite a part of it. The outsider, the alien, the marginal man, adopts a vantage point with rather serious existential and philosophical implications. For Le Guin this marginality becomes a metaphor whose potency is fulfilled in a critical assessment of society. (p. 50)

The "chronic uprootedness," the disconnectedness, endows the protagonists with a vision that transcends that of the others around them, who see the world through culture-bound categories and characterizations. Yet theirs is not a happy plight. Their vision isolates them, while their attempts to promote understanding seem only to remove them further from their compatriots. Ultimately, despite her concern with utopias, Le Guin's view is not optimistic. It can be argued that her heroes' lack of success is due in fact to the failures of society—a failure to examine, to reappraise, and to change.

Le Guin squarely confronts the isolation and loneliness of her protagonists. Themes such as xenophobia, a suspicion and mistrust of all that is different, are developed in all her work, but reach a clear culmination in 1972 in ["The Word for World is Forest."] Here there is an explicit presentation of the heroes (Lyubov and Selver) as anthropologists in their roles as outsiders and translators. Consistently her portrayal is pessimistic. Such individuals suffer heartily. Abandoned, misread, and psychologically disoriented, they often sacrifice themselves or are sacrificed for their understanding. Yet often they represent the only hope.

Le Guin has, essentially, two modes for presenting her protagonists as outsiders: either they are true aliens (for example, Rocannon, Lyubov, Genly Ai, and Falk-Ramarren [*City of Illusions*]) or they are natives of a society, yet their perception of social life nevertheless sets them apart (for example, Shevek, Selver, Estraven [*The Left Hand of Darkness*], Jakob Agat [*Planet of Exile*], and George Orr [*The Lathe of Heaven*]). In either case, their problems, and more importantly their solutions, are of a similar nature. Their apartness precludes their complete membership in, or commitment to, any particular society. Yet their critical viewpoint gives them an insight into the nature of social relations that eludes their fellows.

[In *Rocannon's World*] we are presented with two important and consistent themes: the hero as observer and the tension, the mutual distrust, that so often prevails in intergroup relations. Here Rocannon is actually called an ethnographer, an investigator of *hilfs*, "high intelligence life forms." His approach and his dilemmas are distinctly anthropological in nature. It is apt that Rocannon is given a place, over his objections and disclaimers, in the local mythology. His name is "The Wanderer." He is no mere wanderer in geographical terms; he moves as well, and perhaps more fundamentally, in cultural space and time. His position is that of seeker, or questioner—an outsider, who, like all outsiders, sees two sides to all questions. Displaying the relativism, if not always the objectivity, that marks the discipline, he queries the motivations of the League, under those auspices his work is taking place. In pondering his affiliation with this organization, in the midst of strangers, his aloneness is only more evident. . . . (pp. 51-2)

[In *Rocannon's*] musings we see the true anthropological problem: he is a learner, not a teacher, and his acquired wisdom, whatever its bounds or limits, will be amassed, not applied. . . .

His inability to convince one group of the worth of the other underlines the impotence and powerlessness of the outsider whose perspective can bridge otherwise culture-bound characterizations. . . .

[In *City of Illusions*, Falk has] both to comprehend his surroundings and to overcome them. An amnesic interplanetary castaway, he is . . . dominated by the evil, mind-altering Shing. Although a true outsider, he is not a fearsome creature; rather, he is an individual whose insights force comprehension upon others. Unlike Rocannon, however, Falk has a self-awareness, a contemplativeness, and a scrutiny of personal motivations that we will see again in Shevek and Genly Ai. . . . Intensely aware of his solitariness, he realizes he is alone in the forest, alone on a planet where nothing is familiar to him and where he is familiar to no living being. (p. 53)

[Falk's] singularity is always emphasized. But intuitively he establishes relationships by seeking out commonalities, not by maintaining differences. . . . [For him] the difficulties of finding a dubious and elusive reality are paramount. He has to decide how his past experience colors his perceptions of his present condition. . . . [He] becomes a true participant observer. To survive, he must battle to separate two voices in his head. Falk, the identity achieved on this planet, resides simultaneously with his initial identity of Ramarren. His salvation lies in not forgetting either aspect of himself, while, at the same time, not permitting either personality to dominate or obliterate the other. (p. 54)

In *City of Illusions* and *Rocannon's World*, the theme of the outsider, who is both blessed and cursed in his attempts to understand the subtleties of social life, is presented. In addition, by offering the outsider as a contrast Le Guin challenges the parochialism and xenophobia so often characteristic of the insider's point of view. However, the inability to fit in, the unwillingness to accept the world as it is rather than as it might be, can be equally true for insiders. In [*The Left Hand of Darkness*] Le Guin explores alienation from both angles. Genly Ai is the alien ambassador to the planet Winter. Estraven, a native of Winter, has surmounted the ethnocentrism of his society. The extreme solitariness of both positions is mitigated as they come to discover a fellowship and camaraderie that exceeds, at least in intellectual force, the kind of bond that binds them to their own kind. . . .

[Genly Ai] has more to do than merely understand the multiple dimensions of the Gethenian adaptations: he has to confront the political and social disruption his presence occasions. He must examine his initial inability to accept their ambisexuality and, in doing so, he has the quite humbling experience of seeing himself through their eyes—a pervert. Le Guin thus illustrates the development of cultural relativism by permitting the reader to witness the maturing of the ethnographer. (p. 55)

[Ai's] pomposity at [the] early stage of the book contrasts with his later humanity, while his early ignorance becomes apparent only as his wisdom increases. . . .

Only when Ai transcends his own discomfort and looks about him, does he turn both inward to examine himself and outward to appreciate the hitherto unnoticed strength of Estraven. As much as xenophobia in all respects is a major subject of this novel, so too is the developing relationship between the two protagonists. (p. 56)

Shevek, the protagonist of *DIS* [*The Dispossessed*], finds, despite his anarchist ideals, the sameness of Anarres stultifying. In Shevek the insider's and the outsider's points of view are examined as we witness the development of his disenchantment with his native Anarres and his horror as he comes to understand Urras. Rather than presenting us with two individuals who view a similar situation differently, Le Guin now gives us two different situations as seen through the eyes of one individual. In both locales, however, Shevek remains a skeptical freethinker. In this instance, Le Guin examines another aspect of the problem that the individual faces in learning to come to terms with his society, namely, the moral responsibility of the citizen to the social order.... [Here, however,] the individual has a responsibility to himself and his ideals which often places him in a somewhat paradoxical situation if the two conflict. This is precisely the kind of conflict with which so many of Le Guin's heroes are confronted. They share commitments to at least two ideals and are often unable fully to realize either. Like so many of her other characters, Shevek is a powerful observer because he is an impotent participant. (pp. 60-1)

The theme of hero as translator and social commentator is more highly developed in *WWF*. But the pessimism evident in *DIS* is to be found here even more dramatically. For although the reader's sympathies are clearly with Lyubov and Selver, it is Davidson's view of the world which will prevail....

In Davidson, Lyubov, and Selver, Le Guin presents us with three different views of the same situation—the colonization and brutalization of the Athsheans and their world. Here too she explores in her most explicit manner the consequences of xenophobia. As in *LHD*, her heroes achieve a resolution: they have discovered that difference does not imply opposition, but leads, instead, to a new, more complex, relationship. Her point is more strongly made here, for the humanism of Lyubov is contrasted with the narrow, pedantic self-righteousness of Davidson. (pp. 62-3)

Selver and Lyubov strive to instruct one another in the ways of their respective cultures. Although each emerges with a new respect and understanding of the other, they, like Shevek, reach an impasse when they try to communicate this. The balance, a crucial theme in Le Guin's works, is irreparably damaged: Davidson and his cohorts distort and destroy the natural equilibrium, while the Athsheans, in learning to fathom and commit murder, are no longer in psychological harmony. (p. 63)

Lyubov is doomed: separated from his fellows, quarantined by the Athsheans, he ultimately is fatally wounded in the foray that results. Selver is transformed in a moral sense: the forest is returned to the Athsheans, but at a price that only Selver can realize. There has been no victory here. Though the humans retreat, we see barely a glimpse of redemption.

In the final analysis, however, Le Guin's anthropologist-outsiders have the edge over their fellows. For all their solitariness, their convictions are strengthened by their ordeals. They are no longer mystified by differences. They can grant humanity to others because they cease to glorify or stigmatize that which is not immediately comprehensible. The irony is that in their realization that opposition does not necessarily imply impenetrable boundaries, they erect barriers between themselves and their society. Because they recognize that the task of understanding is not impossible, they contribute to their own isolation. Their perception of balance is an appreciation of differences. And it is here that the paradox ultimately resides; for if there is

an aloneness in the chaos of social life, there is even greater solitariness once order is achieved. (pp. 64-5)

> Karen Sinclair, "Solitary Being: The Hero as Anthropologist," in Ursula K. Le Guin: Voyage to Inner Lands and Outer Space, *edited by Joe De Bolt (copyright © 1979 by Kennikat Press Corp.; reprinted by permission of Kennikat Press Corp.), Kennikat, 1979, pp. 50-65.*

* * *

LUZI, Mario   1914-

Luzi is an Italian poet, essayist, and playwright. (See also *Contemporary Authors*, Vols. 61-64.)

BRUCE MERRY

Mario Luzi is now one of the most fertile Italian poets.... He has gradually become the most discussed of the so-called 'second generation' of Italian hermetic poets, which includes Sereni, Bigongiari and Parronchi among others, and centred around the city of Florence in the late '30s and '40s. He has always been a difficult and esoteric author who seemed to write as much for himself as for any reader. His first six collections ... are now conveniently gathered in a single volume called *Il giusto della vita* (... 1960). Since that date there have been three more.... [The first of these, *Nel magma*,] is a harsh collection of reminiscences: quarrels, dialogue and meditation set in daringly free verse, suspended, like much of Luzi's thought, on a thin metaphorical wire in a hostile environment. The second is *Dal fondo delle campagne*, but these poems were written before the poetic break-through of *Nel magma*, and are better excluded from under the heading 'Luzi's recent poetry'. Third ... come the three short poems and three long poetic meditations of *Su fondamenti invisibili* (... 1971). Although Luzi hàd always been at the centre of modern Italian poetry, this most recent volume is so striking as to call for a re-evaluation of his poetics and an inquiry as to how the author of *Il giusto della vita* was metamorphosed into the poet of *Su fondamenti invisibili*. (p. 333)

Luzi is constantly tempted into a sumptuous use of metaphor, which is, after all, poetry's most drastic tool.... Some of these early metaphors verge on the gauche and inapposite.... His verbs are invariably set in the third person of the present tense, so they fall past the reader like a series of fixed photographs for him to observe.... But when we pause to make allowances for the precious word order and audacious metaphors, we are still faced by a poet drawing on all his resources of eloquence in an attempt to offer definitive statements about the world.... Often the definition is strong and decisive, but the conclusion that closes off the poem is weak in comparison with it.... The contrast of two possible attitudes to life—the cosmos-defining self-assured individual set against the speculative, self-questioning thinker—is actually made explicit in one of the closing poems of *Onore*. Two different types of passers-by are seen across wind and rain by a chosen 'just man', who is leaning against a pole, 'expiating the migrations of the world'.... It is not too bold to see this *tableau* as the first sign of real change in Luzi's poetics. One arm of the signpost is the fisher of eels who 'strides decisively through the quilt of damp'; it points backwards to the first six volumes from *La barca* to *Onore del vero*. In these Luzi has always been the principal citizen in a universe which is beautiful but basically familiar. His utterances have issued from a friendly Delphic oracle round the corner, invariably a Florentine street corner, with a spring or summer wind blowing up the road, roses and blossom dangling from the walls, and bright maidens chatting from first-floor balconies. But the other arm of the signpost points diffidently onward to *Fondamenti*, to the tentative, hesitant world of the 'uomo nuovo del posto'. This new Luzi is the inhabitant of a difficult and alienating world, a world where love affairs crumble into accusation and jealousy, where there are quarrels between old friends at the café and cars race across the polluted suburbs of a big city and stop on high river bridges while their driver contemplates the running water under the parapet.

Perhaps at this point one can borrow two terms from Barthes's *S/Z*, and say that the Luzi of this recent poetry is contemporary and essentially *scriptible*, in contrast with classical, *lisible* poetry, with its set modes and vocabulary, from which the reader is to draw limited permissible inferences. Luzi's recent work is *scriptible* (in the Barthesian sense) in that it tacitly invites the reader to collaborate in the arduous task of deciphering human experience on the page. The reader's own hesitations, his pauses to guess or interpret, if only to check a previous meaning or look ahead, are already paralleled in the writer's undogmatic presentation and informal technique. (pp. 334-36)

[His earlier poems] were varied and elegant, but ultimately bound by the author's fascination for saying the last word: by rich metaphorical declamation and the conflict of hard and fast categories such as youth/age, *dolore/speranza*, and life against death. They were eminently *lisible*, hermetic poems *par excellence*. Therefore to readers who knew this writer's work well there was a clear shock in, for example, the first four lines of 'Tra notte e giorno', the fifth poem in *Nel magma*. . . . Everything in these opening lines is an invitation to the reader to grasp an active role while the poet's own ego is presented as forlorn and insecure; this authorial *aporia* can be felt as it piles up in the swelling and contracting, concertina-like clauses of 'Ménage', the seventh poem in *Nel magma*, where the uneven progress of the lines effectively portrays the poet's intellectual grappling with an inscrutable adversary. . . . (pp. 336-37)

In *Fondamenti* . . . diffidence towards verbalization is turned into a positive asset of the poetry. (p. 337)

Yet this *afasia* invades the heart and the sleeping mind as well as the writer's intellect: it is not just an inability to coordinate tongue and brain. The supremely beautiful opening of the first long poem, 'Il pensiero fluttuante della felicità', brings this out clearly. . . . What is new is the relaxed syntax of the constructions. The lines and half-lines are put together with studied casualness, suggesting the free-associating characteristic of neurosis and the onslaught of fresh ideas couched as pangs of doubt. (pp. 337-38)

There is a kind of poetry which says what it means explicitly, and another which conveys its meaning by rhythm, structure and sound. The recent Luzi falls uncompromisingly into this latter category. Allied to his diffidence towards authority and definition, in *Fondamenti* there is displayed a profound distrust for semantic functions, a vote of no-confidence in the mere power of words as a repository for meanings. Thus when Luzi wishes to express the cas-

ualness of his love relationship, or rather its air of provisional openness, his frank *disponibilité* to any intellectual direction which may be imposed by a speculative mind, he keeps using what might be termed Eliot's 'specification' '*not* A etc., *but* B', a construction in which the air of speculative exploration is emphasized by the locking together of nouns without main verbs. . . . But the device will undergo an injection of intensity: in *Fondamenti* it has been transformed into a triumphant literary evasion, which colours all the phrases that are passed through it with the idea of alternativeness and hence renewed potentiality. Far from being an authority, the poet is a balancer of possibilities. He offers a *scriptible* verse, and it is the reader who discriminates and holds the scales. . . . (pp. 338-39)

[*Fondamenti*] is held in precarious tension, an effort to follow the golden thread and unravel the *matassa* of an equivocal world. His text lays no claim to any metaphysical jurisdiction over the direction and quality of this thread. Any sensitive human has an equal chance with the poet of achieving the balance between alternatives. Luzi's style in *Fondamenti*, with its brooding rhythms and fluctuating lines, with its unsyntactical or verbless constructions and Eliotesque 'specification', is a final renunciation of any oracular aspiration. The inclusive disjunction and recurring doublets (which are so far from being hendiadys) cast a wide net to contain a narrow truth. No word or experience is outside the poetic domain: harsh foreign terms . . . , inconclusive meditation and parenthetic exclamation are all drawn into the verse. . . . (p. 342)

Although the mystic thread is easily mislaid, India is diseased, the planet polluted, and all the while bazookas crash through the 'carbonized jungle' of Viet-Nam, although broken marriage, mental clinic and emotional chaos are the life expectation of twentieth-century Everyman, yet Luzi holds out one single consolation where the thread may be grasped and a vivifying meaning extrapolated from the surrounding uncertainty. This is the self-drowning, the Sartrean 'leap into the abyss', of momentary love. . . . Luzi's verse at last breaks into harmony and euphony at the point where the thread breaks into love. (p. 343)

> *Bruce Merry, "The Anti-Oracle in Mario Luzi's Recent Poetry," in* The Modern Language Review *(© Modern Humanities Research Association 1973), April, 1973, pp. 333-43.*

RADCLIFFE SQUIRES

Luzi's poems ought to make most contemporary American poets entirely ashamed. I refer to our habit, as X. J. Kennedy once put it, of using the public as our waste basket. Ninety percent of the poetry published today fails to make anything of experience for the simple reason that it makes everything of experience, so that experience becomes not tutor but a kind of trivial tyrant. For Luzi all experience alters, alters profoundly, yet the alteration alters only to lead the self into the self. Hence, like all major poets Luzi is freed from effect. When the publishers sent me the manuscript of this book last year, I wrote as follows (and see no risk in repeating myself now): "Mario Luzi is a wonderful poet, so sure of his truth that he has no use for glitter."

> *Radcliffe Squires, "Mario Luzi," in* Michigan Quarterly Review *(copyright © The University of Michigan, 1975), Winter, 1975, p. 118.*

GUIDO ALMANSI

[Mario Luzi's] *Su fondamenti invisibili* made us aware of a new, resolutely tragic tone in his voice. The *preciosite* characteristic of the Italian hermetic school had disappeared, and in its place we had heavy, slow-moving poems tending towards some negative revelation. Luzi has now produced a volume of critical essays, ranging in subject from Lucretius to Montale. [*Vicissitude e forma*] shows a remarkable advance on his previous critical work, if an increasing awareness of tragedy can be labelled as an advance. . . .

Every page of [*Vicissitude e forma*] turns out to be a desperate rather than a confident defence of poetry. Luzi seems to be making poetry into the legitimate expression of an inner world rather than a technique. But the battle for the preservation of this inner world is lost, and Luzi knows it.

> Guido Almansi, "Bearers of Ill-Luck," in The Times Literary Supplement (© Times Newspapers Ltd. (London) 1975; reproduced from The Times Literary Supplement by permission), January 24, 1975, p. 89.

ROBERT MAZZOCCO

Luzi is a meditative poet, conceives his themes generally against the coming of night, the break of day, silhouettes at noon; cherishes signs of Fate, Time, Woman, the Mother Church, of fire, smoke, dust, of rivers caught "between thunder and lightning," the exigencies of the Florentine flood; mythologizes the penalties of the day, spiritual and cultural unease. Politically, I suppose, he is a democrat and a humanist, would probably second Ortega's notion that "it is essential as Europeans adopt the point of view of life, of the Idea of Life, itself an advance over intellectualism, that they not let go of reason in the process."

But what really permeates his cool and somber world, I think, is a muted devotional air: the Catholic concepts of charity and grace, in particular, often being the fugitive accompaniment to many of the harsh settings. For Luzi's is a sort of skepticism that believes nonetheless, a resignation that does not imply despair. He's also something of a philosopher, which perhaps will not endear him to Americans.

Coleridge thought that "no man was ever yet a great poet, without being at the same time a profound philosopher." And while that's not at all true, I can't think of another American poet aside from Eliot (Stevens is an aesthetician —not the same thing) who would adequately fit the description, though of course there are many European or English poets who could. But Luzi goes somewhat wrong for me as a philosophical poet, in that, as never happens, say, in the works of Eliot or Montale or Rilke, his perceptions tend to turn into philosophical statuary, the owl of Minerva stuffed and on display at the end of the tour. (p. 25)

> Robert Mazzocco, "Between Thunder and Lightning," in The New York Review of Books (reprinted with permission from The New York Review of Books; © 1975 by Nyrev, Inc.), April 17, 1975, pp. 24-5.

M

MACDONALD, Cynthia

Macdonald is an American poet. She often employs grotesque imagery in her exploration of the pain and humor of life.

CHAD WALSH

Cynthia Macdonald in *Amputations* . . . writes like one who nightly explores the unconscious and comes up, in broad daylight, with bizarre reports which she expresses in elegant lines. Example: perhaps every mother has had times when the baby seemed to be devouring her alive, metaphorically and literally. But this poet pictures the baby, "At six months he grew big as six years . . . One day he swallowed / Her whole right breast . . ." And then—

> When he had ingested her entire, they built him
> A mesh form, towel-covered, with milk and music
> Piped in, so he could never stop: But
> The metal milk disagreed; both died,
> She inside him, curled like an embryo. . . .

Often fantastic, sometimes lucidly grotesque, these poems have a kind of inner authority that commands the reader's fascinated, if anxious, attention. (p. 6)

Chad Walsh, in Book World—The Washington Post *(copyright © 1972—The Washington Post Company), January 7, 1973.*

ROBERT PINSKY

The grotesque or distorted images of Cynthia Macdonald's poems are too directly significant—nearly allegorical—to be called "surreal", and her poetic method is based on the qualities of prose. But she uses prose forms as some writers use rhyme, ironically; which produces a deadpan effect that is sometimes funny or effective. (p. 243)

Unfortunately, the more of such writing one reads, the more the comic straight-face turns to plain slackness. [*Amputations*] is quite consistent in style, subject, procedure; what seems reasonably inventive in snatches becomes more and more heavily a "method". Finally, instead of seeming comic and simultaneously anguished, the poems seem to hedge evasively or uncertainly between two emotions. I suppose that one's response to *Amputations* depends in part upon how you feel about such compulsively protective irony. The fantasies or extended images or whatever you call them seem predictable to me. The wit often holds up best when the subject is literary. . . . (p. 244)

Robert Pinsky, in Poetry *(© 1974 by The Modern Poetry Association; reprinted by permission of the editor of* Poetry*), January, 1974.*

STANLEY POSS

[In *Transplants*] Macdonald is outrageous, both monstrously literal and filled with wild conceits. She's savage and demure, desperate and ladylike; . . . she balances pain and comedy, specializes in gallows humor and a tone of sardonic deadpan neutrality, as if, understanding all, she does in fact forgive, as if the comic vanity of her anguish is evident to her under the aspect of eternity. Many of her poems are narrative fables, sometimes with nursery rhyme sources. . . . She has a number of poems about her mother (and perhaps her father too, in the guise of the awful Dr. Dimity), about the "Innard Life" ("They slice me open and pull out my organs which / Play Bach fugues, alternating with skating rink selections"), about stained glass women ("'She has a cutting wit,' they say. / And I reply, 'To wit, to woo; cuckoo, cuckoo,' / Trying to make light, as a stained glass woman should"), about the world's biggest man, about detached retinas and bowls that took seven months to make, about her children and her men, and she always entertains, she's never dull, she's sprightly in her anguish, she doesn't insist too much, she's classical in her polish and wit and distance. She says not Behold my eloquent sorrow. How fortunate for you to witness the pain of so rare a one as myself but Listen to me and I'll help you digest your dinner in spite of my straits, which are as I hope we'll both admit funny as a crutch. (pp. 360-62)

Stanley Poss, in Western Humanities Review *(copyright, 1976, University of Utah), Autumn, 1976.*

ELIZABETH STONE

When I was a child, my first literary hero was the little boy who saw the naked emperor streaking in the streets and innocently said so. Even now, I am very grateful to those like Cynthia Macdonald who, without the armor of innocence, forswear Good Manners to tell the truth as they see it. Sometimes devastating truths, yes, but within them may lie delicate truths; perhaps how the hair tapers down the naked emperor's torso ever so softly.

Cynthia Macdonald's first mainly devastating book of poetry [*Amputations*] was about loss of life, limb, and love;

the poems were kept upright by the spine of pained humor and bitter wit that ran through them. . . . [Her second] book is *Transplants*—and eventually, it's about growth after loss.

Macdonald has recently compared herself as a poet to a circus juggler giving a performance. Her emphasis was on the fact of the audience and the performer's possible freakishness—she is not surprised when her work is compared with Diane Arbus's. But the mainly delicate truth is also that through the performance the performer can be transformed. In "Mistress Mary," she writes of a circus juggler who begins buried in snow juggling 16 inert silver bells. The juggling process itself abets her apotheosis. "Color flowed through her fingers like blood / Returning after freezing." At the end, the silver bells are changed, too, into colored living flowers.

Almost a quarter of the poems in *Transplants* are quite literally verbal juggling acts in which Cynthia sets in motion two or more voices or kinds of material. . . . [However] polished the juggling craft is, these poems start from somewhere—the plain old rag and bone shop of the heart.

For me, the most moving performance is "The Late Mother," the last and most climactic of several poems in which a daughter tries to come to terms with her mother's cancerous dying and death. The daughter has received a phone call telling her to rush to Boston because her mother "can't last long." But the buckle has come off her shoe. The poem moves in the spaces between the smooth sequential lines of the "Buckle My Shoe" nursery rhyme and the daughter's terse, angry, grieved recollections as she attempts—still cast as her mother's bumbling daughter—to sew the buckle on. The tinkle jingle innocence illuminates the daughter's vulnerability and, by contrast, her rage. . . . There's more anger still for a mother who was never a mother hen, never "a nest of softness," but a glimmer of understanding (maybe compassion to be retrieved later?) when the daughter says as an afterthought her mother "could not be."

By the poem's end what's been laid to rest is an old conviction that the women are opposites. Travelling the peculiar and elliptical logic of association, the poem discovers that *dead* means *late* means *not on time.* Her mother was often late; this time the daughter may be. And so by the closing lines, the two voices begin to transform in front of our eyes —not into a flower, but into a single adult voice planted in the present:

> The rhyme is over.
> We must leave the nursery
> But we are afraid.
> I hold her, eighty pounds in my arms,
> Becoming her mother and my own.

In this collection, Macdonald explores richer and more ambiguous emotional terrain—in the process giving life to a whole family (late of Winesburg, I think)—in a group of 10 sad and comic poems called "The Dr. Dimity Poems." The family includes the Doctor, his wife, Dorothy, and Daisy. Mrs. Dimity is in despair (her outlet being overeating and/or oversalting the soup), despite the fact that "Her bisque is so delicious / She was named bisque cook of the month." She is occasionally silly; her pain is very real. Dr. Dimity gets metaphysical migraines and ruminates about his one major (unnamed) flaw, which he says is what keeps his marriage together. But it doesn't, because eventually Mrs. D. leaves her husband and quits cooking soup. Who gets

custody of the kids? It's not clear, but probably Dr. Dimity because in the last poem, Dorothy sits in the drawing room trying to figure what to do about her father's fervent advances.

The Dimitys have the genes for cartoon grotesqueness shared by Cynthia Macdonald's earlier nameless characters. Yet there's new vigor here: This is the time of *Transplants* and not *Amputations*. All her people and all her voices are more substantial, more complicated—the targets of her wit, yes, but also the recipients of her compassion.

> *Elizabeth Stone, "Hearts in the Air," in* The Village Voice *(reprinted by permission of* The Village Voice; *copyright © The Village Voice, Inc., 1976), December 20, 1976, p. 106.*

ROBERT HOLLAND

Though she is no fool, and certainly nobody's fool, there is a kind of desperate fooling in Cynthia Macdonald's poetry. *Transplants*, like her first book, *Amputations* (1972), is a collection of grotesque and hard-edged allegories. . . . Macdonald maintains [an] allegorical method and tight-lipped, sardonic tone in most of the poems in this volume, and when it works it is one of her peculiar strengths, providing, in poems like *Severance Pay, In Preparation,* and *News of the Death of the World's Biggest Man,* a fresh if skewed (perhaps *because* skewed) perspective on human pain. And it is clear from the poems that Macdonald feels this pain, her own and other's, so acutely that it makes her bones ache; she succeeds as a poet when she makes the reader's bones ache as well.

But this exquisite sensitivity to pain is also at the base of the major problem in Macdonald's poetry. "I sing," she says, "to ward off danger", and this warding off forces her to wear very thick protective masks to shield her from the danger of her too-strong feelings. Sometimes this produces the large grotesque beauties mentioned above, but too often, as in a series called *The Doctor Dimity Poems,* her masks take on the small, pinched, and bitter contortions of an adolescent cynicism, a knowing sneer at the world's evil which reveals a deep sense of betrayal but fails to come to terms with it. And while this keeps her a distance from pain, it keeps her . . . a distance from love as well. The humor that saves *A Suspense Story* by making it generous fails to materialize in far too many poems.

Other poems, like *Getting to the End* and *Accomplishments,* fail because they are clichéd in their very conception, written out of tired and predictable formulae. . . . (pp. 289-90)

However, a more accomplished and subtle voice, a stronger, quieter, and less compulsive one, can be found in this book, in poems like *The Stained Glass Man* and, especially, *Direction.* The former is a dramatic monologue about a Dresden stained-glass artisan. Framed as a letter, it is constructed, appropriately, like a stained-glass window out of a mosaic of correspondence, conversation, and private meditation, and it reminds me of some of Richard Howard's best monologues. The latter poem, *Direction,* is spoken by a woman being led into the darkness and uncertainty of a love affair by a man seducing her with quail's eggs. Full of gentle wordplay and controlled yet full emotion, it shows what Macdonald is capable of when she loosens her grip on her mask. . . . If Macdonald would leave the cynicism and gimmicks behind and develop this voice, along with more masks for her grotesque gallery, she would be a wise fool indeed. (p. 290)

Robert Holland, in Poetry (© 1977 by The Modern Poetry Association; reprinted by permission of the Editor of Poetry), February, 1977.

*   *   *

MacEWEN, Gwendolyn   1941-

MacEwen is a Canadian poet, novelist, playwright, and short story writer. Exploring the ambiguous nature of time and reality, she seeks to uncover the patterns of myth that survive in contemporary culture. Irony and paradox are frequently among MacEwen's poetic tools, and all of her work is imbued with a sense of the magical and the mysterious. (See also *Contemporary Authors*, Vols. 9-12, rev. ed.)

ELLIOTT GOSE

The setting of [*Julian the Magician*] is vaguely post-Renaissance, but the language is poetic and ironic, slangy modern and analytic. The ingredients do not mix smoothly. There remains the story: Julian is imitating Christ, as indicated not only by chapter titles but by long italicized passages paraphrased from appropriate sections of the New Testament. Consequently, the reader who knows what happened to Christ knows what happens to Julian the Magician. (pp. 36-7)

The parallels with the life of Christ are there mainly because Julian forces them on himself and others. By the time we reach the end of the novel, we are even ready to believe that they are the natural manifestation of an archetypal pattern. I mention this possibility to indicate that Miss MacEwen is also self-conscious. Undigested references to little-read religious figures help attest to this: we are given quotations from Celsus, in his anti-Christian work; Origen, the early church father who answered him; Boehme and Paracelsus; the Zohar, the Kabalah and the *Pistis Sophia*. . . . (p. 37)

Miss MacEwen needs a greater mastery of the genre to make the image patterns work for her as naturally as they do in the [fairy] tale (where the impersonal form of repeated tellings is presumably substituted for the conscious form that a single individual must give). . . . [Yet] a great deal of effective patterning does exist in *Julian the Magician*. (pp. 40-1)

[By] allowing "the dead and disappeared life" to awaken in Julian and through him in other characters in the novel, Miss MacEwen has created patterns which may awaken her readers also. The only thing she lacks is enough control of the novel as a form, and by the time she gets into the diary, she has begun to develop that too. For the reader who can suspend his disbelief, *Julian the Magician* has a lot to offer. (p. 44)

Elliott Gose, "They Shall Have Arcana," in Canadian Literature, *Summer, 1964, pp. 36-45.*

GEORGE BOWERING

Gwendolyn MacEwen's poems are filled with the things she wants. And the language of the poems is a language of ambition, of wanting. It stands outside the mainstream of current Canadian poetry, which seems generally to belong to the post-Williams age. That is, Miss MacEwen's language is opposite to the language of . . . Raymond Souster. One is

aware of something like poetic diction, not the rhythmic arrangement of a prose line. In a poem like "All The Fine Young Horses", for instance, her "issues" if she claims any, are not of matter and the senses, but of a young, feminine, *personal* imagination. Anthology-makers or those who teach survey courses might call her a Romantic. . . .

[*The Rising Fire*] is the first major collection of Miss MacEwen's poetry. . . . [The] best poems are the later ones, and the book would be more enjoyable if the whole thing were made up of the later poems, like the musical "The Catalogues of Memory". (p. 70)

Miss MacEwen's usual unwillingness to be direct sets a distance at first. She is not an immediate poet in this time of immediacy. One may be put off by certain amateur tricks, such as the use of an adverb in place of an adjective ("like darkly trees"); or impatient with her effort to overcome the inertia of a heavy metaphor, as in the poem, "Eden, Eden". But in other poems such as "The Absolute Dance" and "The Dimensions of a Tiger", the voice *responds* as well as expressing, and the work becomes true . . . as well as lovely.

In other words, this is an important book. It contains within it the evidence that a young woman with a marvellous talent is beginning to take charge. (p. 71)

George Bowering, "A Complex Music," in Canadian Literature, *Summer, 1964, pp. 70-1.*

GEORGE JONAS

If Gwendolyn MacEwen's [*King of Egypt, King of Dreams*] were a landscape it would be a jungle of startling colours and strange sounds, dense vegetation and humid silence. If it were a fruit it would be over-ripe. If it were a dream it would be haunting and vivid and one would try to rouse oneself from it. As a woman it would be dramatic and demanding, with lips too pale and eye shadow too black, a soft voice and razor-sharp fingernails. A very impressive woman, but not everybody's type.

This is not to deny the novel beauty or significance. It is just to say that *King of Egypt, King of Dreams* is not an easy and comfortable book to read, and it should probably be taken over a period of time and in small doses. A sip could be delicious, a gulp nauseating. Enjoying Gwendolyn MacEwen's style may be an acquired rather than a natural taste. (pp. 37, 40)

Although *King of Egypt, King of Dreams* is based on historical characters and events, it has very little of the taint of reality. This is not because some licence is taken with facts or because where facts are not known they are replaced by invention. The exact manner in which Akhenaton met his death, or whether Ay was or was not the father of Nefertiti and the brother of Queen Tiy would not seem to affect much the essential reality of the novel. But when the young prince falls "flat on his face in sight of ten visiting ambassadors from Karaduniash" we enter the world and language of fairy tales. Ten ambassadors are nine too many even for the time and the place. Akhenaton in Egypt becomes Alice in Wonderland.

Not that this is displeasing; Egypt of the XVIIIth Dynasty is a pretty faraway place anyway and Gwendolyn MacEwen writes fairy tales delightfully. It is, in fact, precisely when it abandons itself to nonsense and non sequitur that the novel becomes highly witty and enjoyable. No one writing in Canada today handles the Lewis Carroll-type of description and dialogue with more ease and assurance, and to better effect, than Gwendolyn MacEwen. She is an absolute master of the genre; she does it subtly, and in a voice entirely her own.

Still, these are only minor-key effects in the stylistic orchestration of the novel. The main theme is a rich composition of words and images, overlaid with mystification and mystery. Fertile, in the way of a tropical pond, it is full of beautiful flowers and also things that creep and crawl on an altogether puzzling number of legs. One is fascinated by such a pond, without being sure if one ought to drink from it. It may be a work of nature but it resembles too closely a work of art. (p. 40)

> George Jonas, "MacEwen's Monarch: King of Myth, King of Magic," in Saturday Night (copyright © 1972 by Saturday Night), January, 1972, pp. 37, 40.

DOUGLAS BARBOUR

[Gwen MacEwen] is a wonder, a phenomenological mythicist, a poet of legendary process—how everyday *becomes* supernatural reality. *Magic Animals: Selected Poems Old and New* provides a welcome chance to become reacquainted with the best poems of her earlier books—for a change, I agree with almost all the selections—and to discover a group of new poems in which the poet explores the animal and vegetable kingdoms, and the somewhat ambiguous glory of god, providing, by the by, some witty and acute visions of man in the middle. . . .

[She] has a powerful command of tone, an ability to create mesmerizing patterns of sound and rhythm which make her best poems truly enchanting. What is not always mentioned, however, is her sly, feline sense of humour. Much of MacEwen's work is celebration, and celebration of her universe is a matter of cosmic laughter as often as not. (p. 757)

If you're missing any one of *A Breakfast for Barbarians, The Shadow Maker* or *The Armies of the Moon,* you should get this book. If you've somehow missed Gwen MacEwen's poems entirely, you have to get this book. If you can enjoy a poetry both sensual and sly, erotic and mythological, witty and occasionally savage in its assaults upon the human heart and mind, you'll *want* to get this book. *Magic Animals* is a rich and energetic testament to a career in full stride. We can look to read much more from MacEwen in the future. (p. 758)

> Douglas Barbour, in Dalhousie Review, Winter, 1975-76.

TOM MARSHALL

Gwendolyn MacEwan has always been a singer, one who sings forcefully of things exotic and mysterious. Readers and reviewers of [the 60's] responded immediately to her urgent and exuberant utterance even when—in some of the early poems—it approached incoherency. Indeed, a love of sheer sound, encouraged by her poetic idols Hart Crane and Dylan Thomas, sometimes ran away with the poem. But a myth was being unfolded in brief, sharp bursts of sound and imagery. One finds, for instance, from the beginning a desire for escape to other times and worlds (as in the poems of Michael Ondaatje) but also a passionate longing

for the integration of opposites or pairs—light and dark, male and female, Canada and the arcane mysteries, past and future. Hers is the alchemical search for the divine in the mundane; magic and myth abound but are expressed in terms of human emotion and an attractively colloquial and flexible voice. (pp. 100-01)

For MacEwen the individual discovery of the universe is also the creation of the universe. The swimmer, the astronaut, the dancer, the magician recur as images of the poet whose activity is mythmaking, the construction from experience of meaningful patterns, and thus of the larger self, the larger consciousness (a process that assumes overtly nationalist and feminist significances in the work of Margaret Atwood). In *A Breakfast For Barbarians,* MacEwen's first mature collection, the poet is by turns winemaker or magician or an escape artist who finds his way to a new heaven and earth. The poet's "intake" or swallowing of the world in metaphor makes a unity of self and world. . . .

The dangers of this stance and of MacEwen's markedly personal style were always evident, and they are evident in [*The Fire-Eaters*]. . . . [Her] poems have truly marvellous ease and energy but sometimes lack over-all shape. Again, one wonders if there is not something of an imbalance in the direction of inner experience here, an evasion of the overwhelming external challenge of Canadian space and society. On a vaster plane, one wonders (sometimes) if MacEwen has always been sufficiently aware of the trickiness, the humour, the *irony* of the God whom she engages.

To be fair, just such tensions and questions are at the heart of her best work; this is part of the reason for its dramatic effectiveness. In "The Discovery" and "Dark Pines Under Water" she sees . . . that Canada itself must be approached as exotic mystery. And she remarks early in her career:

> O baby, what Hell to be Greek in this country—
> without wings, but burning anyway. . . .
>
> (p. 101)

In *The Fire-Eaters* the poet still burns, but it would seem with the fires of perplexity. The book reads like a diary in which the reflections of the day (and the night) are set down. . . . [This book is] slighter than MacEwen's earlier collections, though it bears on every page the unmistakable stamp of her highly distinctive tone, but it suggests a transitional phase. It will be interesting to see where Canada's mystery-singer finds herself next. (pp. 101-02)

> Tom Marshall, in Canadian Literature, Summer, 1977.

JOAN McGRATH

Gwendolyn MacEwen has set a high standard against which her impressions of Greece must be measured: "Greece presents a very real challenge to whoever goes there—a challenge to do more, to be more, to better the present moment in whatever way is possible, to improvise, to expand. To get things *off the ground.*"

Unhappily, *Mermaids and Ikons* remains earthbound. The poet's ear, so dependable in her craft, plays her false when she turns to prose. This work suffers from a discordant flatness, frequent and abrupt descents into jargon that jolt and disturb. Mycenae "really cuts you down to size", its golden masks are "all flattened and funny", a notable poet she hoped to meet ". . . had died on me". Perhaps most glaring of all is "... how marvelously right on was her reaction ...". This prosaic style does not sort well with either mermaids or ikons.

However, there are memorable moments here too—glowing anecdotes such as that of the valiant Karaiskakis who, though under fire by the Turks, supplied his enemies with lead for their missiles rather than take the change that they should further damage the Acropolis. The story is simply told and is all the more effective when contrasted with the surfeit of whimsy reminiscent of the excesses of Richard Haliburton.

The author has fallen into a trap that gapes for every visitor abroad, that of dismissing the perceptions of other travellers as those of mere tourists "doing Diana", while reserving for oneself a finer, deeper, *exclusive* appreciation of truth and beauty. (p. 48)

> *Joan McGrath, in* Quill and Quive, *June, 1978.*

*   *   *

MacLEAN, Alistair   1922-

MacLean is an enormously popular Scots novelist, screenplay writer, and short story writer best known for *The Guns of Navarone* and *Ice Station Zebra*. Although he has been criticized for flat characterization and an occasional tendency to overwrite, MacLean is a master of the taut suspense novel, pitting man against an adverse environment and his own internal terrors. He has also written under the pseudonym Ian Stuart. (See also *CLC*, Vol. 3, and *Contemporary Authors*, Vols. 57-60.)

ROGER BAKER

I found [*Caravan to Vaccares*] childish schoolboy stuff. I can only think [Mr. MacLean] was having a slack moment, for *Bear Island* has all the tight construction, high adventure and excitement we really expect from [him]. But funnily enough, despite the setting—a charter ship with film crew on the Arctic seas and what must be the most inhospitable island of all time, and despite the tremendous violence of the action, Mr. MacLean and Miss [Agatha] Christie are siblings under the skin.

Quite simply it is who is doing what and why. The familiar formula is, like *The Mousetrap*, a collection of odd people in isolation. Murders happen (I lost count after a while) and gradually we understand that much mightier things are at stake than simple personal animosity. As always, Mr. MacLean's idea of women is fairly rudimentary, but the men are all fully developed and more than commonly tough. Technical knowledge—of ships and geography—is powerfully demonstrated, and overall *Bear Island* packs a great punch. (p. 46)

> *Roger Baker, in* Books and Bookmen (© *copyright Roger Baker, 1971; reprinted with permission*), *November, 1971.*

[*The Way to Dusty Death*] is a sad affair. Slackly written, uncompelling and uninventive, it lacks even the virtue of mere professionalism. The story concerns a formula-one driver who pretends to be a lush in order to trap those who are arranging fatal accidents on the track and causing him to be blamed. The narrative's passé jargon ("Will he sing?" "Like a linnet. If he talks, the police will forget that they ever saw his gun and knife ... " etc.) and other lapses ("li-

bel" rather than "slander" for spoken defamation) do nothing to assist a banal plot and pasteboard characters. The cars may be custom-built, but the book looks like just another assembly-line job. (p. 1045)

> *The* Times Literary Supplement (© *Times Newspapers Ltd. (London) 1973; reproduced from* The Times Literary Supplement *by permission*), *September 14, 1973.*

LINDA BRIDGES

Alistair MacLean is one of the best suspense writers around, and [*Breakheart Pass*]—in which, one by one, the passengers on an Army supply train in the Old West are found murdered—picks up speed rapidly and maintains it to the last page. In fact, it is such a good suspense novel that it's a pity it is not a better novel. The characters never do anything out of character, but they seem to be without thoughts, passions, even the little tics that can make a flat character come to life. Furthermore, the setting—the American West c. 1870—seems to have been chosen simply for the convenience of the plot: Mr. MacLean pretty well gives up the attempt at local color after the first chapter, and the characters speak with very English accents. A good book to read on a plane—or, more appropriately, a train—but not to read more than once. (p. 121)

> *Linda Bridges, in* National Review (© *National Review, Inc., 1975; 150 East 35th St., New York, N.Y. 10016), January 31, 1975.*

JULIAN BARNES

One of the manifestations of *encephalitis lethargica,* or sleepy sickness, is a condition known as akinesia. The sufferer presents a deceptive surface of passivity or inertia; but his difficulty in moving is in fact the product of an unceasing inner struggle.... It is a condition which can be simulated to a remarkable degree by reading Alistair MacLean. A coarsely thrustful plot impels you forward; a coarsely imprecise style retards you; and the result, even though you formally progress through the pages, is a frustrating state of tension, the slow downward psychological spiral of the encephalitic, and a craving for a gram of L-DOPA....

Mr. MacLean's style [in *The Golden Gate*], it must be said, does not normally pursue ... forthrightness. It is based on the British Tommy principle, namely that the best form of toughness is modest toughness, and also on the hyperbole of understatement and ironic negative. In this version of language, concepts like 'stupid' or 'unflappable' translate into 'could not be classed among the intellectually gifted', and 'not one much given to brow-mopping'. My favourite moment of all comes when the non-brow-mopping Revson is accused by smashing April Wednesday (a film part here for Tuesday Weld?) of being a cold fish. 'My eyes,' he retorts indignantly, 'are not those of a cod.' (p. 235)

> *Julian Barnes, in* New Statesman (© *1976 The Statesman & Nation Publishing Co. Ltd.), February 20, 1976.*

ROBERT A. LEE

MacLean's first novel, *H.M.S. Ulysses* [1955], though substantially different from his other books, does contain many elements typical of his later work. Certain aspects of structure reappear in all the books, and basic character types (such as the "rugged individualist") recur time and again in each of the novels. *Ulysses'* uniqueness lies in its semi-documentary nature. . . . Even in his first novel, MacLean has an acute sense of plot and structure, and it is clear that he understands quite well the consequences of action as defined by the necessities of story-telling.

This particular book is significant in other ways, too. The use of the sea as a character in itself is typical of Mac-Lean's best work. The Atlantic storm is as terrifying and destructive as the German submarines and bombers. Man must not only combat other men, but also the impersonal forces of nature. MacLean is obviously following the old dictum, "write about what you know." . . . The secret of MacLean's success as a suspense writer seems to lie in this juxtaposition of lone individual, enemy, and hostile natural forces. The resourceful man of action can triumph in the end, if his will and courage are strong enough; the rest will fall by the wayside. MacLean's heroes are strong men, who know themselves, and see the weaknesses in others; they survive because they want to.

This early apprentice piece differs from his later work in another respect. *Ulysses* has no central character or hero; the primary forces in the book are the ship, its crew, the enemy, and the sea/storm, all of which are impersonal to some degree. The point-of-view shifts back and forth among several figures, none of them more significant than the others. (pp. 5-6)

[A] brief rendition of the more prominent characters in the book delineates MacLean's difficulty in creating believable persons in his fiction. Too many of his characters are stereotypes: ship captains are strong and wise, able to unite their disgruntled sailors at a moment's notice; doctors are gentle, sage, and kind; brutal working-class sailors suddenly become noble patriots in the hour of need. And, since MacLean himself has popularized this particular kind of novel, it is easy to feel, as one reads through many of his books, that we've seen these people before, have experienced these scenes before, in a removed sort of *deja vu*. MacLean seems to have realized the samenesses in his books himself, for he has consciously tried to expand and diversify his fiction as his writing career has developed; unfortunately, his attempts to get away from the three basic settings of his novels, the sea, the war, and the Arctic, have generally proved to be failures, and in the end he always returns to the things he knows best.

Ulysses is also flawed in another sense. While the linear structure of the book is necessary to the plot, it also lends itself to cliched action; one by inevitable one, we meet nearly all the possible hazards, natural and man-made, of the typical sea story. . . .

What saves the novel from complete disaster is MacLean's ability to create memorable scenes, filled with extraordinary violence and bitterness. (p. 7)

The Guns of Navarone (1957) is MacLean's most famous and popular novel, and it was the first of his books to be made into a movie. In many ways, it stands as the prototype for all of his most successful work. Like *Ulysses,* the book is set during the second World War; however, Mac-Lean has abandoned the documentary trappings of the earlier book . . . , and has increased the emphasis on individual character, so obviously lacking in his first novel. (p. 9)

Because of its quick-moving, linear plot structure, and partially because it failed to focus on any one character, *Ulysses* contained little development of human emotion or motivation. The characters merely reacted to the stimuli around them. In *Navarone* . . . MacLean begins building complex pictures of human feelings, even though these are necessarily relegated to the demands of plot and action. Early in the book he develops a theme which will dominate much of his fiction. The scaling of the cliff of Navarone is the high point of the novel, and, in fact, one of the great scenes out of the entire corpus of his work. As usual, MacLean paints an extraordinary visual picture of the perils and danger accompanying the climb up Navarone's sheer rock walls. He does this not by focusing on Mallory or Andrea, both of whom are expert climbers, but by concentrating on Andy Stevens, who, though "a first-class" mountaineer, is young and inexperienced. The motive he stresses is fear. . . . The analysis of Stevens' fear is somewhat oversimplified. The cause, says MacLean, is Stevens' loss of self-respect, due to two acts of hesitation while fighting the enemy in actions prior to this climb. The inner battle of the man lies in the struggle between this loss of pride and the necessity to complete a mission on which 1200 lives depend. Thus Stevens climbs blindly upward. (pp. 10-11)

In this novel, the traitor is fairly obvious to the careful reader, but in later books MacLean will become adept at disguising the villain more carefully. In fact, as the novels grow more complex, the traitor-in-the-midst becomes the central mystery of many of the books: the adventure gives way to the puzzle story. In *Navarone,* however, Panayis is so sadistic and filled with hate, and so described in terms of evilness and viciousness that it comes as no surprise when he is found to be the double agent in Mallory's group. He meets, of course, a suitable fate.

[The crucial scene in the book, the ruining of the fortress] . . . does not seem to have quite the impact that the cliff-scaling had, perhaps because the focus in the earlier sections was on specific individuals, and their reactions to a tense and dangerous situation, while in the later parts, the action is on a grander scale, and seems to move ahead almost on its own accord. This is a key to MacLean's work. As he develops his writing skills, he becomes most effective in those scenes where the individual hero is either struggling with himself, struggling with others, or struggling with nature. The key battle is man against himself.

Although it is not his best book, *The Guns of Navarone,* MacLean's first real novel, is important in setting the stage for the later (and better) books. All the elements are present in this novel: the inner struggle of the heroes, the deception at the center of the plot structure, the gradual development of characters capable of feeling complex human emotions and motivations. The later books will simply elaborate on them. At the same time, it is also evident that MacLean is still learning his craft. For all of the book's driving action and grand suspense, it contains a certain artificiality that is almost inhuman. The dialogue often sounds like speeches staged between automatons, and we seldom feel that we are really seeing characters thinking their innermost thoughts. Everything is exaggerated: the guns are the biggest guns around; Mallory is the greatest mountaineer available; Andrea is the bravest and most indomitable of men, minor characters and situations suffer from excesses. . . . (pp. 12-13)

The characters [of *South by Java Head* (1958)] are more interesting than those in his two earlier books. John Nicolson, for example, has a human dimension rarely seen in *Navarone*. Similarly, the ancillary characters are just off-beat enough to move them out of the sterotypes that many adventure novelists, MacLean included, are always in danger of creating. The action is fast-paced, the descriptions of action well-handled. The most interesting facet of the book is the thread of deceit that runs throughout the novel. MacLean had used character deception before . . . , but this is the first time that he has consciously employed the technique to further the suspense of the book. At least four of the major characters in *Java* are eventually shown to be something other than what they pretended to be at the beginning of the book. This, coupled with the many twists and turns MacLean throws at his readers as the group runs from the Japanese, is captured and freed, recaptured and refreed, becomes MacLean's standard technique in most of his later books. He continually attempts to deceive the reader in an elaborate masquerade which is, when successful, a masterful way of maintaining the suspense of the story, and when unsuccessful, becomes mere trickery for its own sake. His best books are those which keep the reader guessing until the very end of the story.

MacLean's philosophy in these three early novels is conservative, nationalistic, and oriented towards an acceptance of authority. To some extent, this probably is due to the subject matter of the books; each takes place during the second World War, and military necessity demands the following of orders without question. In all three books, it is clear that the allies are the "good guys," and the Germans the "bad." MacLean does make some effort, though, to delineate certain levels of performance in each group: not all Germans are evil per se, and not all Britons are heroes. (pp. 17-18)

MacLean's emphasis has shifted significantly through the course of these three novels, from collective action to individual will. And while the essentially conservative values of society are not really questioned here—the allies are always right—the maintenance of these values is left in the hands of the individual working on the fringes of a society that really doesn't approve such actions. In short, MacLean is working towards and within a common literary tradition, the definition of literary heroism as the conflict between an uneasy accommodation of private action and the public good. (p. 18)

[In his next five novels] MacLean focuses very directly on either an indomitable secret agent (the hero of the novel), a first person narrator, or sometimes a combination of both. Character has superseded action per se. In addition, the war has been temporarily abandoned; evidently, MacLean felt he was getting into a rut, because he doesn't come back to the war milieu for quite some time. In the sequence of five novels beginning with *The Secret Ways* [1959], the scene shifts from Eastern Europe, and the smuggling of a scientist out of Hungary, to the Arctic, to a Pacific island, and finally, in *The Golden Rendezvous,* to a luxury liner on the Caribbean. These novels represent MacLean at the height of his powers. (p. 19)

[*The Secret Ways*] is a mediocre novel, but notable for its introduction of the secret agent into MacLean's fiction. . . . Other than one piece of daring-do on the top of a speeding railroad train, a scene which anticipates a more successful version in *Breakheart Pass* [1974], and an uninspiring bit of torture when Reynolds is captured, the action is rather tame for MacLean, and the novel is comparatively insipid. (pp. 19-20)

MacLean is also more loquacious than usual; several speeches go on for pages at a time, completely discarding the pretence of a normal conversation. They seem to have been inserted into the book merely to inform the reader of MacLean's version of history. (p. 20)

By any standard, *The Secret Ways* is one of MacLean's weaker efforts, and although it contains certain values that are interesting in their relationship to his other writings, they do not save the book from being over-written, over-long, and probably over-praised.

In sharp contrast, *Night Without End* (1960) is the first of MacLean's novels to use first person narration. And, excepting *Ulysses,* it is also the first of his books to be set in the Arctic, to which he has returned time and again in more recent works. For the first time, MacLean uses a physician as the central figure in the book, a technique he will employ most successfully in *Bear Island*. But *Night* ranks as one of MacLean's best books for other reasons: the combination of an exciting, imaginative plot, interesting characters, the antagonism of the Arctic climate, and the skillful masquerading of the real purposes of people left to their own devices. (pp. 21-2)

MacLean manages [descriptions of the harsh Arctic climate] in exceptional fashion. The hostile natural terrain is presented with a mixture of factual data and rhetorical dynamics that is credible, impressive, and inspiring. (p. 22)

The essence of MacLean's best work is found in the mixture of natural and human terrors. He throws together an extremely hostile climate with an equally malevolent group of people, and the result is fear, terror, a sense of impending death, and high suspense, all of which is communicated to the reader through his jumble of characters. This book is a particularly fine example of how MacLean meshes the two disparate elements to produce a unified whole. The characters are never allowed to sit still, except for dramatic effect, and by inference, neither is the reader. (pp. 22-3)

The Golden Rendezvous (1962) brings to a conclusion a period of writing which includes some of MacLean's most successful and effective books. . . . The specific mystery is kept well-hidden until midway through the book, although the suspense doesn't really approach that of *Fear* or *Night*. As he has done before, MacLean titles each chapter with sequential time frames, to stress the linear nature of the plot, and increase tension. (pp. 28-9)

The Golden Rendezvous is competent but redundant. Taken on its own terms, it works as a taut, suspenseful adventure story, good for a couple of hours reading, but no more. The feeling of self-jeopardy on the part of the hero is present, but not strongly stressed. The book merely continues the techniques and inventions that MacLean has developed in earlier fictions. (p. 29)

Strangely, the specific facts seem to matter very little in [*Ice Station Zebra* (1963)]. As the submarine makes its journey under the ice, and the details begin unfolding, the hazards of the mission are emphasized through a series of mishaps. The romantic lure of the Arctic, and the unique situation of a nuclear submarine crawling beneath the undersea mounds of ice hold the reader's attention longer than the plot might warrant in other circumstances. MacLean employs the natural forces of the cold climate to good advantage. The submarine surfaces close to the camp, and the race is on, through a blinding snow storm, to rescue the men of Ice Station Zebra. On the return voyage, a fire breaks out on the sub while it is still below the ice cap, and unable to surface; the threat of death is ever-present. While this is not MacLean's best fusion of natural hazards and man-made antagonism, certain scenes come close to his peak; the fire, for example, was set by a traitor as vulnerable to death as his potential victims. And once set, the flames are very difficult to control. The character of Dr. Carpenter shows the same judicious use of the first-person narrator that MacLean has developed in the past: Carpenter reveals just enough of the plot to entice the reader on, and at the same time maintains a sympathetic personality through whom we can view the perils as they're thrown at us. The fact that the villain of the book turns out to be another doctor is a minor fillip that MacLean no doubt finds delightful. The American sailors are discreetly drawn, and as far from the standard novel cliches as MacLean can manage. The surprises are kept at arm's length until just before the end of the book, maintaining the suspense throughout. Even when the book becomes tired and overlong, the basic situations are so competently handled that they carry the day. Alistair MacLean has obviously developed a certain measure of confidence as a writer; the only question remaining, both to him and to us, is continuity of performance. Can he keep coming up with new and exciting ideas? (pp. 32-3)

MacLean is always in jeopardy of writing the same story over and over again. The basic suspense plot involves some kind of secret quest, the submission of the hero and his allies to various kinds of peril, and the resolution of the mystery simultaneously with the safe dominance of the hero. In addition, MacLean uses as his own special trademarks the threat of impersonal climatic forces, and confusion in the identities of heroes, villains and purposes during the course of plot development. But there are only a finite number of variations on these basic themes, and therefore the author must keep striving to present them and rearrange them in such a way that they seem new to the reader, and at least give the semblance of novelty. At times, MacLean is quite successful, making the new developments both interesting and necessary to the plot; in [*When Eight Bells Toll* (1966)], however, the shark fishermen seem rather out-of-place, more forced than logical, more invented for their novelty than really necessary to the development of the story. (pp. 34-5)

Where Eagles Dare (1967) shows that MacLean has learned a great deal about the art of writing in his preceding novels; this book is no simple war story. It combines the war setting with the secret agent milieu, and uses the deceit and duplicity technique that has become one of his familiar trademarks. There are not only double agents, but triple agents and quadruple agents. No one is what he seems. . . . All of this duplicity is revealed piecemeal in the MacLean fashion; the solution doesn't arrive until the end of the book. The apparent roles of the actors are sketched out at the beginning of the book, and their reality revealed at the end, providing a neat circular plot. The middle section of the novel deals with the infiltration of the castle, and a later attack on its walls, a scene reminiscent of *The Guns of*

Navarone, and the assault on its impregnable fortress. In this book, the attack is accomplished more through disguise than outright assault, but the same basic theme is stressed in both. (pp. 35-6)

MacLean has carried his game of hide-and-seek about as far as it can be carried, and still remain explicable. The ploy works in this book: the repeated deceits and the large number of counter-agents build the tension to a high level, with constant twists and turns in the story line. The book is fast-paced, with plenty of action, and little opportunity for the casual reader to think too much about what he's reading. (p. 36)

Bear Island (1971) is quite possibly his finest achievement to date. The novel incorporates all the best elements of MacLean's standard themes and motifs. He returns to a first-person narrator, whose ostensible profession is that of a doctor. In reality, of course, he's a secret agent. MacLean seems to enjoy the physician character, having used it previously in several of his more successful novels, including *Night Without End* and *Ice Station Zebra*. And, once again, he returns to the Arctic settings that have done so well for him in the past. The first half of the novel deals with a journey on a boat, another situation MacLean always handles well. All of the elements are present, and they all combine beautifully into an organic whole.

Bear succeeds for other reasons as well, and the book reveals quite clearly how MacLean . . . manages to create dynamic scenes of suspense, tension, and mystery. The conversations and narrations balance each other out: each is just full enough to provide motivation for the characters, and the information necessary to keep the reader strung out, and not so long or rambling as to bore the reader, or make him lose the story line. The mystery is buried beneath a complex, twisting plot. As usual, the opening scene immediately grabs the reader's attention. We are suddenly on board a ship which is "coming apart at the seams" in an Arctic storm. The opening chapter introduces the characters in standard expository fashion. After the initial tensions of the storm have subsided, the Captain tells the passengers that the storm wasn't really that severe, although a number of the people have gotten seasick as a result. All of this is put into focus at the end of the first chapter, when the first death is discovered. MacLean also manages to drop hints that the first body won't be the last. (pp. 42-3)

MacLean's books work best when he allies evil and the natural forces of violence, when he makes the structure of his novels an undulation of tension, release, and tension, when he manages to twist his plots in such a way as to reveal parts of the mystery bit by bit, until a final stunning denouement at the end. When all these elements mesh together in one harmonious whole, the result is adventure writing at its best. No one understands these things better than MacLean himself, and his popularity is due completely to his total grasp of these techniques. Even his bad books read better than 99% of his competitors' works; at his best, no one else can touch him. His one serious problem has been and will continue to be lack of the right kind of novelty: as time goes on, he has obviously been making a serious effort to diversify his plots, and introduce new and exciting elements that will not give the reader a sense of *deja vu*. Ironically, the further he strays from what he knows, the sea, the Arctic wastes, the narrator-as-observor, the less successful his work has been; all of his best fiction have had one or more of these essential elements. . . . [His] latest books all represent attempts to break out of the mold, and all are more or less flawed. (pp. 46-7)

After *Bear Island,* MacLean made an obvious attempt to vary his standard formulas by introducing new locales, backgrounds, settings, and even characters. The four novels of this, his most recent period, are substantially different from anything else he has ever written, and are also, for the most part, less successful. There is a certain stiltedness to his recent work that makes it limp, rather than flow, along. In *The Golden Gate,* for example, he is obviously trying very hard to make his characters sound like real Americans; ultimately, however, the book doesn't work: you can research a locale, like the San Francisco setting of the book, but you can't really make it live unless you understand the people. The dialogue is off. The people in the novel stand out quite clearly as the creations of a middle-aged Briton; they neither sound nor act like Americans. This kind of problem turns up in each of the four books published since 1973. (p. 48)

Breakheart Pass, published in 1974, represents a unique departure for MacLean, his only work to date to be set in an historical framework (if we exclude his novels on the War). The action of the story takes place in the American West during the years following the Civil War, and has all the traditional trappings of the conventional western. Furthermore, MacLean attaches a cast of characters (with tongue-in-cheek descriptions of each) to the front of the book, enhancing its historical nature. (p. 50)

The style is curiously coy and forced, as if MacLean were trying to imitate historical American dialogue, but somehow had no real sense of how his characters should speak. Sometimes they sound like standard figures from sentimental Victorian fiction; on other occasions, the dialogue is indistinguishable from that in the rest of his work. In fact, the novel could equally well have been set in contemporary England as a nineteenth century America; there is nothing inherent in the plot, subject, or trappings of the novel that require it to be rendered in historical terms, unlike, for example, Michael Crichton's *The Great Train Robbery,* which could only exist in relationship to its insights to Victorian culture and society. (pp. 50-1)

This novel demonstrates MacLean's increasing contempt for society and its trappings, including societal leaders, laws, and civilization in general. The villains in these later books are invariably members of the power structure of the social groups they supposedly represent. The only thing that thwarts their nefarious schemes is the dauntless individual hero working on his own outside of official channels. Corruption, MacLean is saying, is inherent in bureaucratic structures, and the only way it can be cleaned out is by going around it, not through it. MacLean's philosophy has always tended towards right-wing radicalism, which is natural considering the themes of his books. But in the earlier novels, his heroes seemed to work with the officials representing the forces of good; now, it appears, one must go outside the law to accomplish the destruction of evil. Society can only be saved by purging it of the weak, the corrupt, and the stupid. MacLean's obvious contempt for bureaucracy is curious when matched against an equally obvious faith in the man on the white charger, who will somehow right every wrong, and lead society back to its proper course. (pp. 51-2)

MacLean's protagonists are so completely in charge in his later books, so confident, so aware of the villains' plans, so resourceful, that they hardly seem human anymore; the loss of their humanity is the loss of the suspense MacLean is trying so hard to achieve. . . . *Breakheart Pass,* although written with the usual MacLean competence, is no more than a minor adventure in his canon. (pp. 52-3)

[*Circus* (1975)] verges on science fiction in several respects: the formula is supposedly the key to the creation of anti-matter; also, MacLean seems to be obsessed with hidden listening devices of every kind, including counter-listening devices, and counter-counter listening devices.

The circus itself is an extraordinary world, peopled with unusual character types, somewhat more eccentric than those MacLean usually deals with. But even the eccentrics verge on stereotype. . . . MacLean has created a comic-strip hero; perhaps for the first time in his fiction, all of his characters lack credibility. (pp. 53-4)

For the first time, the word ludicrous can be applied to a MacLean novel. Earlier books have contained scenes that stretched the reader's credibility, but they were so marvelously constructed, and so imaginatively handled, that they could be enjoyed for their own sake, without apologies to anyone. In this book, however, the style is so wooden, the plot so contrived, the tone so uncertain (serious or light?), the threats so weak, that we can only come to the conclusion that MacLean had no coherent plan for the novel, and just allowed it to develop willy-nilly, as it would. Rather than the *tour de force* it might have been, *Circus* ranks as one of the worst books MacLean has written thus far, a labored and rather casual effort from a writer whose talents are much greater than this piece of froth would lead us to guess.

The sense of near-burlesque that permeates *Circus* continues in his most recent book, *The Golden Gate* [1976]. . . . The plot is one of his most bizarre. A master criminal attempts to hold hostage the President of the United States, and two visiting royalty from the oil-producing countries of the Middle East. The ambush takes place on the Golden Gate Bridge. (p. 55)

[The] action drags badly through the middle part of the novel. After the initial kidnapping scene, there is a long stretch where the kidnappers negotiate with the law enforcement officials surrounding the bridge, and this part of the book moves quite slowly. By setting the scene on the Golden Gate, MacLean has limited the possibilities for action and suspense; the fast movement of a journey, with its attendant opportunities for terror, is completely lacking. In addition, the plot is so far-fetched as to be virtually unbelievable, and believability lies at the heart of giving the reader a sense of fear. (p. 56)

The Golden Gate is just another in a string of novels that were better left unwritten. (p. 57)

Alistair has obviously reached a crossroads. On the one hand, he remains as popular as ever, selling millions of books annually to a solidly-established audience. Quite clearly, however, his latest efforts are second-rate when compared to *Bear Island* or *Night Without End,* and one wonders whether he will ever regain the magic formula that worked so well in in his earlier novels. MacLean seems to have grown weary of the whole game; his last few books lack the imaginative spark that kept his early fiction moving, even when the plots were less than his best. (p. 58)

Robert A. Lee, in his Alistair MacLean: The Key Is Fear *(copyright © 1976 by Robert A. Lee), The Borgo Press, 1976.*

NICK TOTTON

Alistair MacLean has . . . [little] emotional involvement in his tales. Many years and many books ago, he found a selling vein; and he has been opening it, bloodily, ever since. But Mr MacLean's violence has no real suggestion of pain; it is the 'Bang bang you're dead' violence of children's games. The impression is heightened by the constant reversals and counter-reversals of fortune, captures, escapes and recaptures, that keep the plot steaming along: either Mr MacLean's supermen are stunningly incompetent, or we are in the convention of Cowboys and Indians.

There is probably little point in running through the plot of *Seawitch:* those who read Alistair MacLean will read it, and those who do not need no encouragement. This time, it's about oil: the central protagonist, Lord Worth, is everyone's fantasy of a ruthless and arrogant billionaire (brought down a peg or two in the end, of course); and there is the usual cast of inhumanly skilful and talented villains and heroes, each with his identifying trait to minimise confusion. The only outstanding question is whether there may not be a sense in which fantasy violence is more vicious than violence which is at least conscious of suffering. (p. 23)

Nick Totton, in The Spectator *(© 1977 by The Spectator; reprinted by permission of* The Spectator*), January 22, 1977.*

HERBERT GOLD

A veteran of more than 20 novels, not all of them as bad as ["Goodbye California"], Mr. MacLean lectures us a bit about "Mankind's morbidly avid love of vicarious doom and disaster." I wish he wouldn't, because it is the source of his reknown. He has here dictated a script designed for those who do not treat the original "King Kong" as 30's camp. After California is saved, Ryder's wife, Susan, utters these words about the world-destroying villain: "Okay, he was a fiend. But he was a kindly fiend."

Most of us will prefer "'Twas beauty killed the beast." If this seems harsh judgment of a piece of mere merchandise, I can only defend myself by quoting what the author says about Professor Aachen, one of the victims in his book: "A broken spirit can take a long time to heal." (pp. 10, 39)

Herbert Gold, in The New York Times Book Review *(© 1978 by The New York Times Company; reprinted by permission), March 12, 1978.*

* * *

MALRAUX, (Georges-)André 1901-1976

A French novelist and critic, Malraux unceasingly pursued the possibility of the individual's transcendence of his mortal fate, his triumph over silence and death, and his subsequent ennoblement. He viewed Art as man's dynamic search for absolutes. His fiercely intelligent novels of ideas are considered among the world's most important contemporary works. (See also *CLC,* **Vols. 1, 4, 9, and** *Contemporary Authors,* **Vols. 21-22; obituary, Vols. 69-72;** *Contemporary Authors Permanent Series,* **Vol. 2.)**

LEON TROTSKY

Everything [in *The Conquerors*]—its dense and beautiful style, the keen eye of the artist, the original and daring observations—contributes to making this a novel of exceptional importance. If I speak of it at this time, it is not because the novel is filled with talent, though this is not a negligible fact, but because it is a most valuable source of political lessons. Do they stem from Malraux? No, they emerge from the story itself, unbeknown to the author, and testify against him, which does honor both to the observer and to the artist in him, but not to the revolutionary. However, we are justified in appreciating Malraux from this point of view: neither in his own name, nor, and above all, in the name of Garine his second self, is the author stingy with his judgments on the revolution.

The book is called a novel. What in fact we have before us is a fictionalized chronicle of the Chinese revolution during its first period, the Canton period. The chronicle is incomplete. It is in some cases deficient in its grasp of the social reality. By contrast, the reader sees not only luminous episodes of the revolution, but also clearly delineated silhouettes that engrave themselves in one's memory like social symbols.

By little touches of color, in the manner of the *pointillistes,* Malraux paints an unforgettable picture of the general strike, not, of course, as seen from below, as it is carried on, but as seen from above—the European colony is without luncheon, it suffocates from heat: the Chinese have stopped work in the kitchens and have ceased operating the ventilators. This is not by way of reproach to the author. The foreign artist could doubtlessly not have handled his themes otherwise. But another criticism can be made that is indeed important: the book lacks a natural affinity between the author, in spite of all he knows and understands, and his heroine, the Revolution.

The author's truly profound sympathy for insurrectionist China is undebatable. But it is corrupted by excesses of individualism and of esthetic caprice. In reading the book with sustained attention, one sometimes feels resentful when, from the tone of the writing, one perceives a note of patronizing irony toward these barbarians capable of enthusiasm. That China is backward, that certain of her political manifestations seem primitive, are not factors one asks be overlooked. But there should be a true perspective that puts everything in its proper place. The Chinese events that provide the backdrop for Malraux's novel are incomparably more significant for the future destiny of human culture than the vain and pathetic blustering of European parliaments and the mountains of literary products from stagnating civilizations. Malraux appears to be somewhat timid about recognizing this.

In the novel are pages, beautiful through their intensity, that demonstrate how revolutionary hate is born of imprisonment, ignorance, slavery, and how it tempers like steel. These pages might well have figured in the Anthology of Revolution had Malraux approached the masses with more freedom and daring, and had he not introduced into his story a little note of snobbish superiority. . . . (pp. 12-13)

Garine is not an official, is more original than Borodine, and perhaps closer to the type of a true revolutionary. But he is lacking in the necessary background. A dilettante and temporarily at center stage, he gets hopelessly embroiled in the great events, and this is constantly evident. Referring to the slogans of the Chinese revolution, he pronounces himself in this way: "... democratic gibberish, rights of man, et cetera." This has a radical ring to it, but it is a fake radicalism. The slogans of democracy are execrable gibberish in the mouths of Poincaré, Herriot, Léon Blum—fleecers of France, jailers of Indochina, Algeria, and Morocco. (pp. 14-15)

A solid inoculation of Marxism might have protected the author from fatal mistakes of this nature. But Garine, on the whole, considers revolutionary doctrine to be "doctrinal rubbish." He is, as we see, one of those for whom the Revolution is only an "established state of affairs." Is this not remarkable? It is precisely because the Revolution is a "state of affairs"—that is, a stage in the development of a society conditioned by objective causes and subject to established laws—that a scientific mind can foresee the general direction of the process.... The men who, without benefit of science, try to rectify the "state of affairs" known as sickness are called witch doctors or charlatans, and are prosecuted according to the law. Had there been a court to judge the charlatans of the Revolution, it is likely that Borodine, along with his Moscow inspirers, would have been severely condemned. Garine himself, I am afraid, would not have come off lightly. (p. 15)

Borodine and "all the Bolsheviks of his generation," attests Garine, "were marked by their fight with anarchists." This remark is essential to the author in order to prepare the reader for the battle between Borodine and Hong's partisans. Historically, this is false. Anarchy was unable to rear its head in Russia, not because the Bolsheviks successfully struggled against it, but because it had earlier dug its own grave. If anarchy does not remain within the four walls of intellectual cafes or editorial offices, but penetrates more deeply, it incarnates the psychology of despair among the masses, and represents the political punishment of the duperies of democracy and the betrayal of opportunism. The daring of Bolshevism in posing revolutionary problems and teaching their solutions left no room for the development of anarchy in Russia. However, even if Malraux's historic investigation is not precise, his story by compensation admirably shows how the political opportunism of Stalin-Borodine paved the way for anarchist terrorism in China....

The book is entitled *The Conquerors.* In the mind of the author, this double-edged title, concerning a revolution that takes the guise of imperialism, refers to Russian Bolsheviks, or more precisely, to a certain portion of them. The Conquerors? The Chinese masses arose for a revolutionary insurrection under the undeniable influence of the October *coup d'état* as their example, and of Bolshevism as their banner. But the "Conquerors" conquered nothing. On the contrary, they handed everything over to the enemy. If the Russian revolution produced the Chinese revolution, then the Russian epigones stifled it. Malraux does not make these deductions. He does not even seem to consider them. They only merge the more sharply from the depths of this remarkable novel. (p. 19)

> *Leon Trotsky, "La Révolution Etranglée," in* Nouvelle Revue Française, *April 1, 1931 (translated by Beth Archer and reprinted as "The Strangled Revolution" in* Malraux: A Collection of Critical Essays, *edited by R.W.B. Lewis, Prentice-Hall, Inc., 1964, pp. 12-19).*

EDMUND WILSON

[*La Condition Humaine (Man's Fate)*] develops in a more explicit way the ideas implicit in *Les Conquérants. La Condition Humaine* is a much more ambitious and a more remarkable book than *Les Conquérants.* In the latter, Garine pretty well holds the spotlight, and there is an "I" who plays the role of Dr. Watson, deeply agitated by his hero's every utterance and standing by, indefatigably wide-eyed, while Garine receives portentous telegrams. He also plays the role of Conrad's Marlow. He is, in fact, our old friend the fictional observer who, from a more or less conventional point of view, looks on at a mystery or a moral problem. In [*La Condition Humaine*], however, the novelist gets rid of his European observer and, meeting Trotsky's challenge [see excerpt above], attacks the revolution directly. Dealing with cultures the most diverse, moral systems the most irreconcilable, he establishes a position outside them which enables him to dispense with the formulas alike of the "academic mandarins" and of the orthodox Communists. I do not know of any modern book which dramatizes so successfully such varied national and social types. Beside it, even E. M. Forster's admirable *A Passage to India* appears a little provincial; you even—what rarely happens nowadays to the reader of a French novel—forget that author is French.... The personalities of Malraux's characters are organically created and thoroughly explored. We not only witness their acts and see them in relation to the forces of the social-political scene: we share their most intimate sensations. (p. 27)

The device of presenting in dramatic scenes the exposition of political events, to which we owe Garine and his eternal dispatches, here appears as a series of conversations so exhaustive and so perfectly to the point in their function of political analysis as—in spite of the author's efforts to particularize the characters—occasionally to lack plausibility. And we are sometimes thrown off the track when a thesis that deals with psychology comes butting into a paragraph devoted to explaining the "objective conditions" or when a description that had seemed as external as a colored picture postcard of Shanghai takes a sudden subjective turn.

Yet, on the whole, the author has met these problems with amazing originality and skill. He has a genius for effects of contrast. The opening of *La Condition Humaine,* which follows the activities of a Communist group—a Chinese, a half-breed Jap, a Belgian, and a Russian—the night before the insurrection, is a masterly dramatization. (pp. 27-8)

[Malraux was successful] in avoiding conventional formulas. Where, however, is his own center? What is his frame of reference? What he wants to show us, he says, is the human situation. What is his view of the human situation? What every human being wants, he makes his philosopher Gisors explain, is not the object of his ambition itself, but to escape from the conditions of life, to give oneself the illusion of being God. (p. 28)

There is, then, something else in the book besides the mere theme of escape from the human situation. The events described in *La Condition Humaine,* which occured in 1927, must still have been going on while *Les Conquérants* was being written. At the end of the earlier novel, the Chinese revolution—there presented as the work of Garine as well as of Chiang Kai-shek—is assumed to be already victorious; in the later, the Communists fail, sold out by Chiang Kai-shek to the interests of Western capital and paralyzed by the faulty policy of the Comintern itself. Malraux seems, in line with Trotsky's advice, to have made some progress in Marxism. His interpretation of recent events seems now essentially Marxist—though he never, as I have said, slips into the facile formulas; and though the criticism his characters make of the line of the Comintern is more or less that of Trotsky, he maintains in relation to Trotsky, too, an attitude of independence. Marxism, Gisors observes, is not a doctrine but a will; and it is simply that, in Malraux's world, the only men he respects are animated by the Marxist will. (p. 29)

> Edmund Wilson, "André Malraux" (1933), in his The Shores of Light *(reprinted with the permission of Farrar, Straus & Giroux, Inc.; copyright 1952 by Edmund Wilson), Farrar, Straus, 1952 (and reprinted in* Malraux: A Collection of Critical Essays, *edited by R. W. B. Lewis, Prentice-Hall, Inc., 1964, pp. 25-30).*

W. M. FROHOCK

[André Malraux] is often called a "tragic humanist," because in novels like *Man's Fate,* in particular, he was obsessed with the inherent tragedy of the human predicament. His characters were trapped by our common inability to transcend our human limitations, beginning with our mortality. But in later years his emphasis has changed somewhat: our metaphysical situation, as he sees it, remains tragic in essence, but his way of feeling it is less dramatic and he no longer writes tragic novels. He prefers to think of himself as a kind of "witness." (pp. 3-4)

The meaning of "witness" appropriate here emerges from a consideration of the *Anti-memoirs*. Nothing else explains the juxtaposition of brilliant passages from *The Walnut Trees* with accounts of interviews with Nehru, Mao, and de Gaulle, with a report of Malraux's own somewhat harebrained search for the lost capital of the Queen of Sheba. . . . (p. 4)

[In *Man's Fate*] Malraux uses an unidentified narrating voice that is free to assume various points of view as need arises. The action is concentrated in two spaces of time measurable in hours, with a lull separating them while the leaders go to Hangkow, so that the episodes take place either simultaneously or so nearly so that no single eye could plausibly observe them all. For a novel in which each character's "destiny" is equated with his particular *Angst,* Malraux's strategy permits him to avoid the two-dimensional, somewhat allegorical effect some readers find in the novels that preceded *Man's Fate.* Each tortured character, in other words, can be viewed through the eyes of various other, equally tortured ones, and made to appear more nearly in the round. (p. 18)

Man's Fate made Malraux an international figure, but is no more an orthodox Communist novel than *The Conquerors:* revolution again appears as an escape from personal anguish; the class struggle hardly figures in it; most of the characters are again alienated middle-class intellectuals—certainly not workers. And if a political lesson can be derived from the story, it is that the Internationale sets expediency above human values: the office in Hangkow is willing to let men like Malraux's heroes die rather than take a risk itself. (p. 21)

Days of Wrath is an excellent example of an essentially political emotion transmuted into an aesthetic object. It tells about a Communist imprisoned by the Nazis and his subsequent escape. (p. 22)

Malraux considers *Days of Wrath* "a botched job," quite possibly because it uses so much he had used before. He had tried to reduce his story to the ultimate essentials of tragedy—"one man and his destiny," as he has it in his introductory note—with the hero as a kind of Everyman, matching the resources of the human against the inhumanity represented by the Nazis. But stripped to its abstract schematic structure, *Days of Wrath* is strikingly like *The Royal Way:* each pits the human against the inhuman; the human wins, but the victory is temporary in each case. (pp. 22-3)

Uncharitable readers may feel that *Days of Wrath* suffers from incoherence. Or from putting too much meaning in too small a container. They will be better satisfied with *Man's Hope.*

This novel is unlike *Days of Wrath* in every conceivable way. It is the most populous of Malraux's fiction as well as the longest, full of action, interrupted by long and sometimes verbose conversations, and marked, according to most critics, by an epic rather than a tragic tone. Malraux does not share my belief that its value is somewhat impaired by a conflict between the needs of art and those of propaganda, and well-qualified critics, beginning with Joseph Frank, have agreed with him. It is clear, in any event, that Malraux was aware of the potential danger, as his foreward to *Days of Wrath* had already revealed. My feeling that by some emotional legerdemain he manages to substitute a victory for humanity for the defeat of the Spanish Loyalists is one that any reader is free to accept or reject. (p. 24)

It has always been conceded that Malraux's imagination is essentially visual. As early as *The Conquerors* his attention to the lighting of scenes, the planned play of light and shadow, has escaped few critics. In the crucial scene of *Man's Fate,* when Katow gives away his cyanide and is led out by his guards, the dominant effect is produced by following his shadow, which mounts the wall as he approaches the door until it is decapitated by the ceiling. By common consent, Malraux's eye is "cinematographic." (p. 26)

Man's Hope musters most of the themes exploited in the earlier novels, but it is now apparent that from novel to novel the emphasis has slowly changed. Concern about the absurdity of the human lot has largely disappeared. Death is too constantly present for the participants to brood about it much, and man's mortality becomes little more than a datum. Taking satisfaction in imposing one's will on others becomes less significant than imposing one's will on oneself. Sex is a casual diversion at most, and devoid of metaphysical implications. The characters are doubtless aware of fighting for their essential dignity and against the humiliation represented by Fascism, but most often leave the fact to be taken for granted. (p. 27)

No one questions the enormous extent of Malraux's knowledge, or the keenness of his vision. And some very gifted critics, beginning with Gaëton Picon, have also insisted that, whatever Malraux's standing with his expert colleagues, *The Voices of Silence* is a magnificent poem on the spiritual stature of Man. These are excellent reasons for honoring Malraux. But they are incidental to the primary purpose of his work, which is one of persuasion, and it is as a work of persuasion that his long monologue about the functions of art and of the artist does not succeed.

It fails, I believe, because by temperament he is indeed a poet and not a master of persuasive prose discourse. Any examination of his style reveals that it moves from idea to idea without much help of grammatical connectives, and, more particularly, is largely unaided by the conjunctions that link cause and effect. Each thought is a momentary flash of illumination, isolated from those that precede and follow by moments of darkness. (p. 34)

Malraux assumes that the readers of *Anti-memoirs* are familiar with all of his writing, including the essays on art, the novels he has been reluctant to reprint, and even the very early fantasy tales. His manner is elliptical as always, and he has grown no less elusive with the years: his disdain for transitions remains intact. But the pains he has taken in reworking the material from *The Walnut Trees,* and the prominent place he assigns it, suggest that the total meaning of the book is to be found in the relation of the other themes to those it contains. (p. 38)

In the final accounting the novels must stand as his major achievement. His friend Gaëtan Picon has written that for the generation just coming to literary maturity at the time, their impact was like "a slap in the face." Doubtless they do not have the same shock value for later readers, now that literary taste everywhere has turned resolutely away from the elevated style: Malraux's style is elevated to the point where seriousness borders on solemnity. Our current sensibility is not tragic, and few of us are tempted to write Man with a capital. . . . Yet for all this the novels do something that had not been done before, and that probably will not be done again. (p. 45)

> *W. M. Frohock, in his* André Malraux *(Columbia Essays on Modern Writers Pamphlet No. 71; copyright © 1974 Columbia University Press; reprinted by permission of the publisher), Columbia University Press, 1974.*

R. J. NORTH

[All Malraux's] novels, with the possible exception of *La Voie royale,* are set in contemporary history, telling of revolution and war. Malraux seems to rival the news reporter, indeed he uses reportage techniques. Incidents and scenes are dated: 5 June Shanghai, Madrid, Teruel, Guadalajara and so on. (p. 10)

The detail and the march of events may prove confusing at first reading—and this has been seen as a weakness in Malraux's narrative technique. He is not concerned with reporting or history; though some of the events happened, the actors are imagined and the testimony is not that of the eyewitness but of the analyst. While it has been said that Malraux's story offers the best account of the 'feel' of the Civil War, this can be true only for one side and for the early days of the campaign. In fact the matter of the novel is invention based on some personal experience.

The topical gives to character and situation in the novels a certain authenticity and a certain dramatic tension. The quality of lived experience is communicated and the realistic presentation seems to guarantee the reality of the problems, to make them real-life rather than philosophical issues. Action and situation reveal not only character but choice; it is not the factual which ultimately counts but the

meaning for the protagonists of the alternatives available to them or the forces which crush them. . . . Together with this reportage technique, Malraux uses the dramatic scene to powerful effect; at such moments the somewhat cryptic, nervous prose of narration, the clipped dialogue, the cut and thrust of debate, give way to a lyrical eloquence that heightens the tone and persuades the involved reader. The death-bed of Perken in *La Voie royale,* the assassination scene that opens *La Condition humaine,* the descent of the wounded aviators borne by the peasants in *L'Espoir,* the *Assaut de la pitié* in *Les Noyers* are splendid examples of Malraux's capacity to arouse emotion in the reader and to assert some simple but fundamental truth. . . . (pp. 10-11)

It is often alleged that Malraux's characters lack depth and complexity, that they are not like the rounded, fleshed-out creatures of Balzac or the self-conscious and self-analysing heroes of Stendhal. This is true, but for Malraux that is not a defect. He is not concerned with psychological analysis or complexity. His characters talk, think and act enough to appear human and individual but their reality for the reader comes from their reaction to situation and their weighing of issues. . . . [Like] Sartre, Malraux sets his characters in extreme situations, not perhaps so much to ensure that the attitudes adopted and the choices made should impress the reader as exemplary as to make clear in easily recognizable situations of great moment the anguish of choice and the importance of the issues. It is for this reason perhaps that the coolies, the masses, play only a background part. The issues are brought into focus in an individual experience.

These then are novels of ideas, not of reportage, not in the sense that ideas, philosophical propositions and moral precepts are debated and defined in abstract terms, though indeed the characters will from time to time argue their point of view, confront one another with opposing opinions. Each view arises from the character's own individual values and from his adaptation to the situation facing him. . . .

It is however essential to guard against identifying as Malraux's what any one of his characters may do or say in a given circumstance. A further temptation to be avoided is the collection of pithy sayings, the aphoristic utterances with which the novels are studded: these have all the appearance of moral maxims, of nuggets of wisdom, but often on closer examination turn out to be incisive, sometimes even cryptic, formulations of personal dilemmas. (p. 11)

Malraux sees men as weak, limited, doomed, yet able to rise above the fate that crushes them, able to transcend death and time. . . . That is to say Malraux sees it as the function of the writer, not only to give expression to the basic tragedy of the human condition but also to offer a means of transcendance. 'La fiction transforme le destin en conscience'—'On peut aimer que le sens du mot *art* soit tenter de donner conscience à des hommes de la grandeur qu'ils ignorent en eux'. An exploration and a questioning of man and the world, rather than a faithful representation of the actual and the quotidian, or the proclamation of a particular set of values didactically presented, the novels of Malraux correspond in intention to his view of art in general. (p. 14)

> *R. J. North, "The Novels of André Malraux (1901-1976): The Twentyman Lecture," in* Modern Languages, *March, 1977, pp. 7-14.*

WILLIAM CLOONAN

André Malraux wrote about men and places. The men were larger than life and the places distant. Women scarcely figured in his books, and when they did they functioned as backdrops which reflected and glorified their men. . . .

[For] Malraux, the novelist and the man, political controversies have always provided the pretext to confront larger, more metaphysical problems. The French title for *Man's Fate* is *La Condition humaine,* and this phrase, gleaned from Pascal, bespeaks a concern with broader issues than what political group would take over China. This novel's real theme is alienation; which Malraux highlights by having each character, no matter what his nationality, somehow bifurcated. . . . Like most novels that purport to be "philosophical" in nature, the political ramifications, if any, are profoundly conservative. At the end of *Man's Fate* the political situation has altered for the worse, but that is a detail. What has not changed is the human condition; man's fate remains one of alienation occasionally alleviated by the experience of fraternity.

The theme of *Man's Hope,* as well as that of *The Conquerors* and *The Royal Way,* is fraternity. Struggle, be it against men or nature, leads to the discovery of fraternity. Hence struggle is much sought after, and becomes at times an end in itself. . . .

Malraux claimed he discovered fraternity in Asia, and certainly *The Conquerors* and *The Royal Way* hinge on heroic friendships of men united against a common enemy. In *The Conquerors* Klein remarks that it is a rare thing to meet "ein Mensch, a real man," and what frequently makes these encounters possible is warfare.

What, then, is the substance of this fraternity? For Malraux fraternity, like art, is first and foremost an opposition to, and refusal of, death. It represents people banding together against all that is cruel and unjust in human existence. . . . *The Anti-Memoirs* contain a moving sentence which sums up the resistance of the incarcerated Jews in Nazi Germany: "Yet even among the dying there remained enough humanity to divine that the will to live was not animal, but obscurely sacred. The mystery of the human condition manifested itself there." It is the suffering and struggling together that engenders this "obscurely sacred" sentiment which is the essence of fraternity. Men united in heroic actions ultimately experience an apotheosis which moves them beyond the limits of the human condition and into a mystical realm where not even death can terrify them anymore because they have discovered that "it is not life alone which makes [man] a man."

Closely associated with fraternity is Malraux's concern with metamorphosis. This term is most often associated with Malraux's art criticism, but it is pertinent to his novels and his life as well. Generally speaking, metamorphosis refers to the transformation a work of art undergoes as it is perceived through the centuries, as it is placed in confrontation with newer works or with recently discovered ancient works unknown at the time of its creation. For Malraux and his heroes, metamorphosis is the experience of self-discovery and development which results from participation in the significant political and cultural events of the day. A life that is not constantly in the throes of metamorphosis is no life at all.

Malraux's fraternity and, to a lesser extent, his concept of metamorphosis when applied to fiction and life are at least as simplistic as they are noble. Fraternity-metamorphosis assumes life lived constantly at the highest possible tension and a world where Henry James's beast in the jungle is forever showing up; in short, the experience of fraternity-metamorphosis is impossible outside of an extreme situation. In *Man's Hope* a character states that fraternity is the opposite of being annoyed (*vexé*). And so it is. The fraternal feeling that Malraux describes moves one beyond life's petty problems and annoyances into a realm where the only issues are the great, "metaphysical" ones; it replaces doubts with certainties and clarifies all complexities.

An awareness of the simplification of human experience inherent in Malraux's guiding principles helps explain both the strengths and lacunae in his works. For instance, a possible reason for the relative absence of women in his novels is that emotional-sexual relationships are too difficult, too humanizing for the Malraux hero who needs must stand alone or united in male, asexual friendships against a larger than life foe. . . .

Another offshoot of Malraux's concern with fraternity-metamorphosis is his fascination with distant, exotic places. In his superb biography, *André Malraux,* Jean Lacouture points out that even at the height of Malraux's political activity in the thirties, his visits to Moscow and opposition to Nazism. Malraux appeared singularly disinterested in French politics. Lacouture goes on to explain that French politics were too well-known to Malraux, too real and banal to fire his imagination: "it was more exciting being a revolutionary d'Annunzio than laboriously trying to unite forces and people that the habits of a lifetime had made dull, touchy and jealous." (p. 3)

What is true of Malraux's politics is also true of his art. Once again it is Lacouture speaking: "It is as if, like the tragic poet of the French classical tradition, André Malraux considered worthy of his genius only a subject which, if not distant in time, was ennobled by distance in space." . . . Malraux's genius allows him to turn his lack of knowledge into an asset. He creates out of the half-known or imagined and thereby provides images that thrill and ideas that stimulate. (pp. 3-4)

A final ramification of Malraux's conception of fraternity-metamorphosis and the hero who experiences both concerns comedy. Malraux was famous as a dazzling conversationalist . . . and as a biting wit. . . . Yet comedy is totally absent from his writings. . . .

Malraux's heroes, like Hemingway's, can endure hardship, privations, mental anguish, and even a dose of philosophical speculation, but the one danger they are vulnerable to is laughter. . . . Malraux's books constantly border upon the edge of self-parody as he describes a world of extreme situations inhabited by men solemnly confident in the righteousness of their cause. In this context comedy is unthinkable since it would risk exposing the latent silliness behind some of his heroes' posturings. Also, for Malraux laughter would be as inappropriate in his novels as snickering at de Gaulle would be in real life, because the introduction of comedy can have the effect of making the greatest heroes as human as everyone else.

Heroic simplicities and exotic settings account in a large part for the appeal of Malraux's works. While he tells exciting stories he does not always tell them well. With the exception of *Man's Fate,* Malraux's novels, no matter how short, are too long; they are freighted down with philosophical ruminations and ideas masked as characters. Rather than being a novelist, Malraux at his best is a writer of purple passages, those thrilling scenes and descriptions that pop up continuously in his books.... The description in *Man's Fate* of the revolutionaries awaiting execution and the long narrative of the rescue of wounded flyers in *Man's Hope* are the best known examples of Malraux's gift for evocative and moving prose. Less celebrated, but perhaps the most powerful of all, occurs in Malraux's final, unfinished novel, *The Walnut Trees of Altenburg.* A French soldier, Vincent Berger (Malraux's name in the Resistance), captured by the Germans at the outbreak of World War II, recalls his father's role in the First, immodestly entitled Great, War. His father was an Alsatian and hence on the German side. A German gas attack against the Russians begins to destroy everything living, plants, animals, men. Berger wanders in stupor across a desiccated battlefield and then in a brilliant passage Malraux describes how Berger and the other German soldiers, mostly protected by masks, suddenly become so disgusted by what they see that, in a rush of fraternal sentiment, they drop their arms and hasten to aid the sickened and dying Russians....

Malraux's stature today reflects the triumph of fiction over reality. The fascination he possesses for so many people is only partly due to his distinguished accomplishments in a variety of fields. At the heart of the Malraux legend is its author's constant dramatization of himself, his suppression of the private, enigmatic André Malraux for a larger than life persona who stands at the center of twentieth-century history, both political and artistic, and exercises dynamic control over each. The fact that he was never completely successful in either sphere is a detail. Malraux made it seem as if he were. He had the uncanny knack of being able to transform (metamorphose, if you will) any situation or encounter into a mirror which reflected and heightened his own self-image. (p. 4)

André Malraux's greatest book is his *Anti-Memoirs,* and it is also his greatest novel. Here the artist is no longer encumbered by his heroic but imperfect personae, the Claudes, Garines, Kyos, Magnins, and Bergers—instead the true, flawless hero at last steps forth. This is not to say that in *Anti-Memoirs* Malraux finally takes off his various masks and shows his real self. The fact that I am terming this book a novel indicates the contrary. In *Anti-Memoirs* Malraux dons the mask which suits him best and portrays André Malraux playing André Malraux complete with maximum elusiveness and false trails. For instance, at the beginning of *Anti-Memoirs* the hero (I am applying this title to the André Malraux who appears in the book) ponders how to reduce the theatrical side of himself to a minimum. Had Malraux ever taken such a problem seriously, it would have called into question his entire life. A more illuminating comment is the assertion that: "I have never really learned to re-create myself, if to do so is to come to terms with that lonely halfway house which we call life." The issue, of course, is not that the hero should forego recreations, but that he must prevent life, rather than his own dramatic instincts, from dictating their nature and direction.

I mentioned earlier that Malraux is a gifted writer of purple passages. *Anti-Memoirs* is a collection of just such passages. The author jumps backward and forward through the

time and space of the twentieth century, but whatever the year and locale, the occasion is always momentous and the hero equal to it. (pp. 4-5)

Closely related to the purple passages, and perhaps a variation of the form, are the interviews the hero has with some of this century's greatest men. Invariably these meetings seem pregnant with importance if somewhat obscure in content, but what always emerges is that no matter how powerful his interlocutor, the hero is never relegated to a secondary position.... Ultimately what makes the hero one with the different leaders of the modern world is his knowledge that in some measure, however small, they are all reflections of himself....

Early on in his career a friend described André Malraux as "a great man, but doing his best to seem greater." Now that his life is done, it is a pleasure to report that he fully achieved his goal. (p. 5)

> *William Cloonan, "André Malraux: The Fictionalization of Self," in* New Boston Review *(copyright 1977 by Boston Critic, Inc.), Summer, 1977, pp. 3-5.*

*   *   *

McEWAN, Ian   1948-

McEwan is a British short story writer and novelist. He is a black humorist whose fiction is characterized by a unique blending of macabre plots, grotesque characters, and a lucid, almost pristine, prose style. (See also *Contemporary Authors,* Vols. 61-64.)

JONATHAN RABAN

First Love, Last Rites oozes with talent as wayward, original and firm in vision as anything since [Jean] Rhys's early novels about being alone and young in Paris and London.

McEwan's characters are adolescents; they bristle with the sudden violent consciousness of selfhood like hatching pupae. Or they are children, prematurely burdened with egos that give them the wizened gravity of infants in Renaissance paintings. Or they are men whose bodies have grown but whose minds have never broken free of the appalling second womb of puberty. Cruelty comes easily to them: they can wound or kill with the offhand grace of animals for whom the self is the only reality. They are profoundly disturbed by their own capacity to love another, which creeps up on them from behind like a pad-footed intruder on their barred and bolted rooms. They are endlessly curious about the world, but their curiosity has the roving neutrality of creatures in a zoo, unsure of what to focus on. They belong to no society. They are alarmingly in touch with blood and slime. (p. 81)

[The] great strength of McEwan's writing is that it is constitutionally incapable of being appalled. Taking nothing for granted, it is surprised by nothing and observant of everything. His style is wonderfully supple, open to experience, and certain in its movements. At its frequent best, it has a musical purity matched to music's deep indifference to the merely moral. McEwan's narrators are—in the world's terms—an unsavoury crew ... child-murderers, emotional cripples, brutally self-centred teenagers. Most of his characters are amply qualified for permanent residence in a prison or asylum. Yet they are all granted a Mozartian lucidity, a gift of clarity which turns them into angels despite the weight of the world's disapproval.

[In "Solid Geometry"] a man discovers how to make his wife disappear. Following a sequence of diagrams in his great-grandfather's diary, he persuades her that he has found a new love-making position, then folds up her naked body, turns the shape inside out, and she's gone. Just on the level of anecdote—the only level that most science fiction ever aspires to—the story is satisfyingly ingenious. What lifts it way above science fiction is the tone of the narration and its steady movement from inquisitive scientific cool to the wonder and joy of the experimenter at the moment of discovery. Yet Maisie, the wife, is such a thoroughly explored and observed character in her own right that the story has to win her disappearance by enlisting the reader as an accomplice to an outrageous act. It does so brilliantly, and in the process it teaches a dark truth about the abundant innocence of what is usually called evil.

McEwan does pay occasional penalties for being so confidently *sui generis*. Idiomatic writers are able to rely on the established standards of their idioms, but McEwan (and he shares this with Jean Rhys, too) sometimes lurches, apparently unconsciously, into stretches of bathos and carelessness. . . . But these are niggles. *First Love, Last Rites* is one of those rare books which strike out on a new direction in current English fiction. The most important question is what will McEwan do next? His abilities as a stylist and a storyteller are profuse, and these stories are only the first harvest. (p. 82)

Jonathan Raban, in Encounter *(© 1975 by Encounter Ltd.), June, 1975.*

JOHN MELLORS

In the black humour of McEwan's stories [in *First Love, Last Rites*] sometimes the blackness predominates, sometimes the humour. He can even be blackly Rabelaisian. . . . Always he is inventive, stylish and keenly observant of grotesque detail. He drives his plots logically to the most absurd or violent but, from his premises, inevitable ends. A brilliant and devastating début. (pp. 112-13)

John Mellors, in London Magazine *(© London Magazine 1975), August/September, 1975.*

It is likely that McEwan will be compared to other practitioners of the short story form, Roald Dahl in particular. There is about [*First Love, Last Rites*] the same juxtaposing of simple quirks and complex pathologies, and the same blurry distinctions between the normal and abnormal behavior of seemingly sane individuals that Dahl mastered in "Kiss Kiss" and "Someone Like You" a decade or so ago. At the same time, the comparison is perhaps unfair. McEwan is no mere emulator of the style of others as "Solid Geometry," perhaps the quintessential example of the genre, and contained herein, readily demonstrates. (p. cxlii)

Virginia Quarterly Review *(copyright, 1975, by the* Virginia Quarterly Review, *The University of Virginia), Vol. 51, No. 4 (Autumn, 1975).*

ANNE TYLER

["The Cement Garden"] is really a kind of extended dream, although there's nothing dreamy about the precision and clarity of the writing. Its narrator, Jack, is a 15-year-old English boy so sunk in self-loathing that there are long stretches when he can't even be bothered to bathe or brush his teeth. Jack's father is a crabbed, oppressive man . . .;

his mother is not much more than a shadow, and their neighborhood is a wasteland of abandoned prefabs. Life here seems smothered, flattened. For Jack, his two sisters and his little brother, the only pleasures are those that erupt beneath a rigid surface: some rather joyless sexual games and a few stolen moments of willful disobedience.

"The Cement Garden" describes the process that steadily isolates these four children, until they're so absolutely alone and so at odds with the rest of the world that there is no way of returning to normal life. First their father dies, and then their mother. The loss of their mother leaves them without relatives; so to avoid being separated they keep her death a secret and bury her in a trunkful of wet cement in the basement. From then on, it's all regression and decay. (p. 11)

In one sense, this is an easy novel to read. The story skims along, and the style is so direct that we have no trouble accepting the fact that it's a 15-year-old speaking. Jack is articulate but never precious; he succeeds all too well in letting us into his numbed, frozen world. "Except for the times I go down into the cellar," he says, "I feel like I'm asleep. Whole weeks go by without me noticing, and if you asked me what happened three days ago I wouldn't be able to tell you." . . .

But what makes the book difficult is that these children are not—we trust—real people at all. They are so consistently unpleasant, unlikable and bitter that we can't believe in them (even hardened criminals, after all, have some good points) and we certainly can't identify with them. Jack's eyes, through which we're viewing this story, have an uncanny ability to settle upon the one distasteful detail in every scene, and to dwell on it, and to allow only that detail to pierce the cotton wool that insulates him. . . . [This] is not the first book in which a pack of determined children bury their mother in secret, but it's almost certainly the first to cover, with such meticulous care, the putrefaction of her body. Nor is their reason for the burial a positive one; it's not love or loyalty that holds them together, but a hostility toward the rest of the world. Generally they're callous with one another, if not downright cruel.

It seems weak-stomached to criticize a novel on these grounds, but if what we read makes us avert our gaze entirely, isn't the purpose defeated? Jack, we're being told, has been so damaged and crippled that there's no hope for him. But if it's a foregone conclusion that there's no hope whatsoever, we tend to lose hope in the book as well. (pp. 11, 92)

Ian McEwan is a skillful writer, absolutely in control of his material, but in this first novel, at least, he could use a little more gleam. (p. 92)

Anne Tyler, "Damaged People," in The New York Times Book Review *(© 1978 by The New York Times Company; reprinted by permission), November 26, 1978, pp. 11, 92.*

TOM PAULIN

Privacy is one of the imaginative poles of a story [*The Cement Garden*] whose ambiguities tease and fascinate me the more I reflect on it. McEwan's imagination moves between extremes of *gemeinschaft* and *gesellschaft*, and he offers a series of charged phrases, images and atmospheres which give his story a mythic direction. Both domestic privacy and its opposite—society—are present in the young narrator's observation "I did not wish to be placed outside this intense community of work." They are present again in his father's wish to build "a high wall round his special world" in order to shield his garden from an urban landscape of demolished houses and "vacant sites . . . lush with weeds and their flowers." Some of the images have an extraordinary power: the derelict cement garden, the gardens of the abandoned prefabs, the fine black dust that blows "from the direction of the tower blocks", and the shovel lying in the centre of a round stain of dried cement "like the hour hand of a big broken clock." Jack thinks of all the "rooms that would one day collapse" and his description of this gutted prefab makes it resemble one of the "desolate places" in *Job*. . . . Obsessively, McEwan returns to images of dereliction, arbitrary living-spaces, family and the absence of family, guilt and its absence. In these burnt-out places there is no order—nature is dead, the city is dead, and the world is drained of meaning. What his fiction designs, I think, is a fable of a dead public world and an intensely private reality. . . . Using imagery drawn from the great waste places of the inner city he shows how the life of the emotions is like a weed flowering in a social desert.

In *The Cement Garden* we see a wish for an introverted independence cutting against a wish for dependence, a desire to live in a world without parents crossing a dream of a saving love. It's as though McEwan's imagination moves between images of public sterility and private sterility. He explores various tensions and strategies of meaning without offering a definite resolution. . . . (pp. 49-50)

McEwan has a strange notion of a sort of demonic or delinquent innocence which seeks to reflect itself in the blankness of a *tabula rasa*. It refuses experience and yet engages in sexual games that are part childish, part adult—the between state of early adolescence is his chosen territory. But what seems like a fixed state is in fact a stage in a natural process, and this is evident in the complicated situation at the end of the novel where Julie's boyfriend, Derek, is presented as an intruding stranger from the outside world. Julie says that he wants "to be one of the family . . . big smart daddy." In order to join the family he would have to share the guilty secret of the mother's grave in the cellar and turn his back on the outside world. This he refuses to do: he discovers the cement tomb and then fetches the police. To the children this seems like a betrayal. And yet the revolving blue light of the police car signals their difficult liberation into a world where a union may be possible between the public and private extremes which so occupy McEwan's imagination. . . .

McEwan's novel is a superb achievement: his prose has an intent lucid beauty and his narrative voice has a perfect poise and certainty. His account of deprivation and survival is marvellously sure, and the imaginative alignment of his story is exactly right. (p. 50)

Tom Paulin, in Encounter *(© 1979 by Encounter Ltd.), January, 1979.*

HELEN HARRIS

The events which take place in Ian McEwan's first novel, *The Cement Garden,* are as apparently unnatural, though less gratuitously so, as in most of the stories in *First Love, Last Rites* and *In Between the Sheets*. The ten tidy chapters are a chart of ugliness, death, rotting cadavers, incest and perversion. Most family taboos are briskly broken, but, on the part of the narrator at least, there is no relish. (p. 104)

It is the startling combination of everyday banality with the most horrendous acts that gives *The Cement Garden* its especial flavour.

As has been pointed out more than once, the plot bears a striking resemblance to that in a novel of the fifties by Julien Gloag—though McEwan claims not to have read it—and which was subsequently filmed, but the manner is rather different. The story is told in the first person by the elder boy, a sulkily resentful adolescent whose two conventional sisters seem to be growing up faster than he is. . . . [The] author maintains a passive stiffness, which is characterized by the grey cement of the title. No-one seems to react adequately in situations which amply provoke a reaction. Their world seems slightly anaesthetized, and it is the reader, whose emotions have not been dulled, who is most affected.

There is never much change inside *The Cement Garden*. Time passes. The climactic act of incest takes place. But the children twice describe their own situation as 'still and fixed'. At the end, their little brother is appropriately woken from a long sleep. Of course, there is development and dramatic irony, but, despite the grim secret in the cellar, the tension occasionally flags. This may be because the emotional deadness of the characters makes them impenetrable and the continuous physical details of their snot, pimples and masturbation tends to turn them into specimens, bodies rather than complete people.

The narrator appears detached, even though he participates. Once or twice, one is aware of a more sophisticated voice behind the teenage boy's; for instance, when he describes his dying mother's skin as 'dark and convoluted'. It might be a static, contrived world, with the characters under laboratory observation, but it remains a convincing one. The extraordinary distilled nastiness of the short stories cannot be as concentrated in a novel. However, McEwan knows instinctively how to disturb, without obvious effort, and his natural skill as a writer, if more patchily demonstrated in this novel, sustains the book. (pp. 104-05)

Helen Harris, in London Magazine *(© London Magazine 1979), February, 1979.*

ROBERT TOWERS

First Love, Last Rites [is] possibly the most brilliantly perverse and sinister batch of short stories to come out of England since Angus Wilson's *The Wrong Set* thirty years ago. Unlike Wilson, McEwan is not concerned with the teeth-baring of vicious little snobberies in an exhausted, class-ridden society; the England of his fiction is beyond all that —a flat, rubble-strewn wasteland, populated by freaks and reclusive monsters, most of them articulate enough to tell their own stories with mesmerizing narrative power and an unfaltering instinct for the perfect sickening detail. . . . With the exception of one piece ("Solid Geometry"), [the stories] are not really classifiable as examples of latter-day gothic; if nightmares, they are well-lit, *waking* nightmares, for there is nothing imprecise about them, no dislocations of time and space, no lapses in causality.

Much of the coloration and some of the preoccupations of *First Love, Last Rites* are to be found in [*The Cement Garden*]. . . .

The Cement Garden is in many ways a shocking book, morbid, full of repellent imagery—and irresistibly readable. It is also the work of a writer in full control of his materials. As in the short stories, the effect achieved by McEwan's quiet, precise, and sensuous touch is that of magic realism —a transfiguration of the ordinary that has a far stronger retinal and visceral impact than the flabby surrealism of so many "experimental" novels. The setting and events reinforce one another symbolically, but the symbolism never seems contrived or obtrusive. Along with his narrative and descriptive powers, McEwan possesses what seems to me a remarkable imaginative insight into the psychology of children who have never experienced a fully loving adult presence and are now set free from even a vestige of adult control. Though their collective pathology and deprivation are indeed extreme, the four children are made to seem entirely credible—in their avoidances as well as in their speech and overt behavior. Nor have sympathy and implicit pity been withheld.

It will be interesting to see what this gifted craftsman can do if his demons ever allow him to extend his range—to include, occasionally, a functioning adult or an unmaimed child. Presumably McEwan writes as he must—and his readers, however they respond to his subject matter, can be thankful that he writes so memorably and well. (p. 8)

> Robert Towers, in The New York Review of Books (reprinted with permission from The New York Review of Books; copyright © 1979 Nyrev, Inc.), March 8, 1979.

* * *

MEREDITH, William 1919-

Meredith is an American poet, playwright, editor, critic, and translator. In his verse he eschews a highly literary and intellectual expression in favor of a more natural, colloquial poetic style. His poems often deal with nature and the joys of the commonplace. Robert Frost is an acknowledged influence on both the style and content of Meredith's poetry. (See also *CLC*, **Vol. 4, and** *Contemporary Authors*, **Vols. 9-12, rev. ed.)**

PETER MEINKE

Moving gracefully with the years, William Meredith's poetry has modified its former formal elegance to a point where it can absorb casual conversation; observations of nature, human and otherwise; and meditations on art and society.... *Hazard, The Painter* moves gradually from [an] almost bathetic tone in the first poem to a tighter, still understated voice reminiscent of Philip Larkin's, though more optimistic, in the final poem.... *Hazard* is an intelligent, even charming book, full of liberal sense and sensibility. (p. 25)

> Peter Meinke, in The New Republic (reprinted by permission of The New Republic; © 1975 by The New Republic, Inc.), June 14, 1975.

JOHN MALCOLM BRINNIN

Read poet for painter [in "Hazard, The Painter"], and the changes that can be rung on identity quickly present themselves. The delicate social conscience of the man Meredith gives us is convincing, but his credibility as an artist is not. His one obsessive subject is more of a poet's concept than a painter's pictorial "fact," and the pictures registered in his memory are sometimes uneasily close to those of a

Norman Rockwell nudged by Social Realism. In poetic terms, Meredith takes us into a region recently charted by the knuckleboned asperities of Robert Lowell and by the vaudeville turns of conscience played out in the "Dream Songs" of John Berryman. If such influences pave his way, they do so without getting *in* his way. Meredith's language is often as lean as Lowell's and as rhythmically adroit as Berryman's. His tone has the consistency of an achieved mode and, true to the temper of his hero, he is modestly colloquial even when imagination strains for release into the upper air of rhetoric. What has allowed Meredith to take his bearings from these other poets without being driven off his own course is perhaps his wider tolerance for human inadequacy and his ability to dramatize personal dilemma without seeming to exploit it. (p. 39)

> John Malcolm Brinnin, in The New York Times Book Review (© 1975 by The New York Times Company; reprinted by permission), September 21, 1975.

RICHARD HOWARD

So skillful in his mild modernism . . . , so various in his errant annotations is Meredith [in *Hazard, the Painter*] that we do not know, even at the end, what hit us—a caress of ground glass and very finely honed feathery blades, most likely, so that hits just aren't in it. Mortality and the dimming senses are the apparent pretext of these ruminations.... But the real subject is *ressentiment*, even anger, and the real object throughout is America the Imperial, these States in their warring "decline" viewed from a perspective which has only darkened since Emerson unbosomed himself to his journal, 1847.... Meredith doesn't want to be a prophet, only an artist, a messenger, an angel maybe. But the observation, the organic detail plucked out and brooded upon until it yields up its sense, its significance—that is Emersonian (the ground-juniper), and it is Meredithian too:

> Near the big spruce, on the path that goes
> to the compost heap, broken members
> of a blue-jay have been assembled
> as if to determine the cause of
> a crash without survivors.
>   Walking
> with Hazard, the cat does not observe
> them. The cat will be disassembled
> in his own time by underground technicians.
> At this point Hazard's thought turns chicken.
> It is the first warm May day, the rich
> black compost heap is full of promise.

Promise! The decline which is the asseveration of mortality in a moribund democracy holds like a freeze in this little novel until winter sets in, the real freeze, and Hazard sets out again. And the book ends there, in a wonderful epitome of the two poets who have meant the most to Meredith's making, Frost and Auden—Frost for precisely that "beautiful condensation" not to be formed by our affluent drecky lives, Auden for the recognition of sacred sites, a commitment to Earth as transcendence.... I guess Hazard couldn't exist without Berryman's Henry, without Lowell's *History*, yet how much less posturing in this man—how much less is more! Maybe there *is* posturing ("devious in ways I still like better than plainspokenness" is Meredith's vaunt), but it is so attractive, so ingratiating that it seems, merely, how meaning turns in the mind's mouth, enjambment a way of walking, figuration a dead reckoning. I would not make overweening claims for the little suite which is mostly spoken under the breath, from a procumbent posture as it were, but the life is in it, unreconciled surds of identity, and I am grateful for the record of what it has been like, existing—if not exacting—in *my* hazardous time, too. (pp. 209-11)

Richard Howard, in The Georgia Review *(copyright, 1976, by the University of Georgia), Spring, 1976.*

ALAN HELMS

Since "Resemblances between the life and character of Hazard are not disclaimed but are much fewer than the author would like," we can take Hazard [of *Hazard, the Painter*] as Meredith's model of an admirable man as well as his opportunity to speak of himself in the third person—perhaps not such a surprising tactic in a poet so decorous and diffident, but a very surprising one in a poet who has spoken so beautifully for himself in his own person so often in the past.

In devising a persona through whom he will talk, Meredith places his voice at too far a remove from his experience (Hazard's experience is of course Meredith's, whether historically true or not); the voice becomes so elusive that Meredith is often in danger of vanishing from his own poetry.... [We] realize with acute discomfort that we're hearing Meredith talking about how Meredith talks about Hazard. Such convolution shows the seams of the art; the fiction evaporates and we're left with psychological history instead of poetry. What we finally hear is neither a whole characterization nor a whole poet, but a dispossessed consciousness shunting back and forth between the two.

Except for Hazard's equanimity in accepting age, it's hard to know why Meredith finds him admirable. (pp. 220-21)

Hazard seems out of touch with his own problems. His usual tactic, at Meredith's instigation, is to approach the boundary of a serious thought, perform a graceful manoeuvre of retreat (through wit or irony or grand sentiment or whatever), and withdraw—undefeated because unengaged. In fact, this is a remarkably unengaged book: though Meredith speaks in the final poem of Hazard's being "Gnawed by a vision of rightness / which no one else seems to see," we have no sense that Hazard is a tormented man. Dilemmas he has, but they are calm ones, presented in a measured decorous tone (a continuing hallmark of Meredith's style) which belies any real agitation. Hazard's most strenuous reflections have the casual cadences of a weekend stroll through the woods—Frost without pain, you might say. Skydiving one bright October day, Hazard "calls out to the sky, his voice / the voice of an animal that makes not words / but a happy, incorrigible noise, not / of this time" ("Hazard's Optimism"). Hazard is so good-humored that his most pessimistic thought is buoyed up by the "happy incorrigible noise" of his optimism. His most remarkable talent is his ability to frustrate thought about matters that frustrate him.... In "His Plans for Old Age," Hazard towels his aging body in front of the mirror: "He thinks about Titian and Renoir a lot / in this connection." It's easy to guess what he might think about Titian and Renoir; still, since Hazard is preoccupied with age it would be interesting to know. But Hazard doesn't tell us; Hazard's mind is on vacation.

"In all fairness," however, this is admittedly a kind of holiday book, one that issues from and describes a summer lull in the painter's life, a fallow period during which he is content to laze into early winter and the first snow whereupon he finally picks up his brush in earnest and gets down to work. The best expression of the book's prevailing mood, and one of its best poems, is "Rhode Island".... Quite a good poem, and reminiscent of Meredith at his quiet, cultivated best: the gentle wit; the graceful handling of a line which wonderfully replicates Hazard's lazy, random thought; that dextrously placed concluding joke whereby the enervated Hazard continues occupying a necessary space while the small frets of his life chatter on about him. But the charm of the poem derives from its inconsequentiality as much as from anything else.

That's a part of the hazard Meredith takes with his new book—the risk of making poetry out of slim occasions. But perhaps his largest risk lies in continuing to make poetry out of a sensibility which in its easy optimism, its insulating comforts, and its abiding concerns for custom and ceremony must seem to many quite at odds with the prevailing spirit of our times, not least to Meredith himself. (pp. 221-24)

Alan Helms, "Hazards," in Parnassus: Poetry in Review *(copyright © by Poetry in Review Foundation), Spring-Summer, 1976, pp. 220-24.*

HENRY TAYLOR

The Wreck of the Thresher, published in 1964, was the book which most firmly established the nature and strength of William Meredith's poetry. It seems now ... to have been the culmination of a development in certain directions from which the poet has since swerved, though not unrewardingly. *The Wreck of the Thresher* reveals unobtrusive mastery of craft traditionally conceived; it is not full of sonnets, villanelles, sestinas, or other insistent evidences that the poet is comfortable in formal cages; but beneath the steady, honest lines with their sometimes unpredictable rhyme schemes, there is a sense of assurance that for Meredith, form is a method, not a barrier. In its range of subject, tone and mode, the book consistently offers the voice of a civilized man, a man with good but not flashy manners, engaged in encounters with matters of inexhaustible interest.

This style did not come quickly to Meredith.... [In his first book, *Love Letter from an Impossible Land,* there] were a number of accomplished poems, including a few which spoke in the voice that would be so firmly Meredith's by the time *The Wreck of the Thresher* appeared twenty years later. Much of the book is apprentice work, but in the "impossible land" of the Aleutians, of the second World War, Meredith came to grips with strangenesses for which no borrowed voice could suffice. So the book falls into two parts, whose relation MacLeish describes as "the way in which the literary vehicle (for it is nothing else) of the Princeton undergraduate turns into the live idiom of a poet's speech reaching for poetry." What is there, one wonders, to like about "the literary vehicle of the Princeton undergraduate"? One possible answer is that the earlier poems show us a young poet diligently studying his craft. In the brief lyrics which acknowledge various masters, there is little room for the voice of Meredith, but there is in them a serious and intelligent setting-forth after the tools that will give the voice, when it speaks, the distinctiveness and force of the later poems. Craft matters to the young poet: of the thirty-three poems in *Love Letter,* eight are traditional sonnets, and seven others are near-sonnets of twelve to fourteen lines. If some of these are predictable or flat, or if others are too insistent upon their experimentation with formal expansion (as in the packed internal rhymes and slant end rhymes of "War Sonnet," for instance), practice has made nearly perfect by the time we come to "In Memoriam Stratton Christensen." . . . (pp. 1-2)

In "Notes for an Elegy," a longer poem whose ambition and achievement are larger than anything else in this book, Meredith sounds a note of modesty in the title, a note which he will sound again and again, even as his poems improve. This title, of course, means not to suggest that the poem is unfinished—it is quite brilliantly finished—but that in a time and place more distant from the war, it might have acquired more of the trappings of a formal elegy. Here, the first twenty-two lines, a meditation on flying and its relation to freedom, tyranny, and war, set the proper tone, verging toward an invocation to the muse. The death is that of an airman, but not one shot down in battle; for some mysterious reason, his plane has crashed in a wood. Having asked where the engine and the wings were at the crucial moment, the speaker concludes that

> the invitation
> Must have been sent to the aviator in person:
> Perhaps a sly suggestion of carelessness,
> A whispered invitation perhaps to death,
> Death.

The quietness of this passage, while it emphasizes the distance of the crash from any battle, belies the noisy violence of any plane's untimely coming down; it is as if the plane and its pilot had drifted silently to rest, like so many other things that fall in the forest when no one is there to hear them. This impression is confronted in the poem's remarkable conclusion, where the phrase "as it were in bed" lifts the tone out of solemnity toward something large enough to enclose great mystery. . . . (p. 3)

This ability to complicate tone by the subtle use of something close to humor has been important in much of Meredith's work, though it has been only recently that many of his serious poems have contained very wide streaks of humor. But fairly early, Meredith mastered an inclusiveness of tone which makes for greater strength than the owlish cultivation of high seriousness.

These qualities of strength and inclusiveness, however, are not much in evidence in Meredith's second book, *Ships and Other Figures,* which appeared in 1948, only four years after *Love Letter.* A note of acknowledgment states that "Most of these poems were written and all of them collected while the writer was a Woodrow Wilson Fellow of Princeton University," and one feels keenly the absence of peril in these poems, the safety of academe. Under the pressure of his credentials as a promising young poet, Meredith seems not to be the aviator inspired to struggle with his craft and its relation to puzzles of much magnitude; he seems instead to be a Wilson Fellow who would like to have enough poems for a book. Under such circumstances, he turns his hand to various exercises in tradition and occasion, and is sometimes successful with slight poems where, the pressure being momentarily off, he can indulge his excellent sense of play without fear of momentous failure. (p. 4)

This is not to suggest that, in his *New and Selected Poems* of 1970, Meredith saved from *Ships and Other Figures* all the wrong things; he saved the best six poems, but would not have tarnished his reputation by carrying forward a few more. The same could be said of his selection from *The Open Sea* (1958), a collection of nearly fifty poems, of considerable range and effectiveness. Here Meredith continues his exploration of difficult fixed forms, not merely in order to submit himself to complex rules, but also to see how some of these rules may be pushed around. Aside from the half-dozen or so sonnets which one might expect to find, there are also two sestinas and a dedicatory villanelle. The usefulness of these explorations is perhaps most apparent in the title poem, which fits the definition of none of the fixed forms mentioned above, but which clearly takes advantage of their existence. . . . (pp. 4-5)

The poem's debt to the formal repetitions of villanelle or sestina is clear enough; what is less clear is how the poet, in suggesting a form which already exists, walks the elusive line between failure to fulfill the contract and success in making something which is complete on its own terms. Here, the success is gained through a profound grasp of all the subtle tensions that arise between hypothetical form and human utterance. (p. 5)

Another fine example of what comes of serious play is "The Illiterate," a poem whose structure is that of a Petrarchan sonnet, but which uses repeated words at the ends of the lines, instead of rhymes. The octave begins by saying, "Touching your goodness, I am like a man / Who turns a letter over in his hand," and goes on to say that the man has never received a letter before, and is unable to read it, or to overcome his shame and ask someone to read it to him. The poem ends:

> His uncle could have left the farm to him,
> Or his parents died before he sent them word,
> Or the dark girl changed and want him for beloved.
> Afraid and letter-proud, he keeps it with him.
> What would you call his feeling for the words
> That keep him rich and orphaned and beloved?

The wit that chose recurring words instead of rhymes for a poem like this, and the craft that makes them work, have greatly matured since the early sonneteering experiments; this poem transcends its quite noticeable peculiarity, partly by drawing us away from the ends of the lines toward consideration of the subtle use of *your* and *you,* in the first and thirteenth lines respectively: these words and lines are just enough to keep the simile and the form from being self-conscious studies of themselves.

That such forms are, in some unself-conscious way, studies of themselves, almost goes without saying. Certainly by this time Meredith has wedded technique to meditation, so that they are harder to separate, even for convenience in discussion, than they were in his earlier work. Meredith finds several occasions in *The Open Sea* to be explicit about the value of art; there are several poems about music, painting, sculpture, architecture, the ballet, and so on, and in all of these one finds an admiration for formal restraint, especially when it is evident that there is something beneath the form that is worth restraining, whose power is worth conserving.

To this end, Meredith joins the urge to self-consciousness and a very light touch with meter, to strike a precise balance of tones in the pleasant but complicated "Thoughts on One's Head (IN PLASTER, WITH A BRONZE WASH)." In a delicate alternation of masculine and feminine rhymes, and in a meter of musical elasticity, these stanzas, like good heads, hold simultaneously a number of attitudes. . . . (pp. 5-6)

The Wreck of the Thresher is both larger and smaller than *The Open Sea.* It contains fewer poems, and there is less variety of form and subject; but several of these poems are considerably more ambitious than anything preceding them. In somewhat narrowing the range of his attention, Meredith deepens his focus, producing a few poems that can stand with the best poems of his generation. (p. 7)

The title poem is a bold achievement, one of Meredith's rare "public" poems; its occasion was the destruction at sea of the nuclear submarine *Thresher* on April 10, 1963. Much has happened since that date to make that disaster recede from the public consciousness; one of this poem's strengths is that it has not been diminished by a fifteen-year torrent of public catastrophes. The poem deserves closer attention than it has received. (p. 8)

In this poem, and in others in the collection, a quality of modesty asserts itself strongly; Meredith himself described it a few years later, in a foreword to *Earth Walks: New and Selected Poems;* he brought forward from earlier books, he says, "poems that try to say things I am still trying to find ways to say, poems that engage mysteries I still pluck at the hems of, poems that are devious in ways I still like better than plainspokenness." "The Wreck of the Thresher" only seems to be plainspoken; it engages and contains deep mystery, and makes it memorable.

Plucking at the hems of old mysteries sometimes requires a poet to go over ground he has visited before. "On Falling Asleep to Birdsong," the third poem in *The Wreck of the Thresher,* is reminiscent (in title only, it turns out) of "On Falling Asleep by Firelight," from *The Open Sea.* The earlier poem is perhaps too tidy to be convincing; the later poem is much better made, and goes beyond tidiness, drifting with the consciousness of a man falling asleep, who hears a whippoorwill and thinks of his parents' and his own death. Trying to dream of nightingales, he is led on to the story of Philomela, which appears gracefully in the poem. . . . (pp. 9-10)

This idea, that unwilled or semiconscious rumination leads on to meditation and sometimes to fable, is taken up several times in *The Wreck of the Thresher,* often in sequences or in poems separated into nearly self-contained sections. "Fables About Error," "Five Accounts of a Monogamous Man," and "Consequences" are all acts of a mind responding with attentive love to surfaces, but never being content with superficiality. (p. 10)

[An] attitude of hopefulness comes through these poems tentatively, free of the hectoring tone that often afflicts poems with something valuable to say. They are "all of a piece," and let themselves come gradually to those levels where they ring most truly. At such levels, they are beyond cleverness. . . .

[One] turns with greatest interest . . . to the fourteen new poems in *Earth Walk,* and one is struck first by the interesting variety of points of view. Poems spoken by fictional characters are not plentiful in Meredith's work, though on

some occasions, as in "Five Accounts of a Monogamous Man," he has adopted, as Yeats often did, the device of applying third-person titles to first-person poems. (p. 11)

[Delicacy sustains] "Effort at Speech," in which the speaker relates an encounter with a mugger. The speaker and the mugger wrestle briefly, the wallet parts "like a wishbone," the mugger flees with his ill-gotten half, and the speaker comes close to guilt at having retained the other half:

> Next time don't wrangle, give the boy the money,
> Call across chasms what the world you know is.
> Luckless and lied to, how can a child master
>   human decorum?
>
> Next time a switch-blade, *somewhere he is thinking,*
> I should have killed him and took the lousy wallet.
> *Reading my cards he feels a surge of anger*
>   *blind as my shame.*

The strength of the poet's control over these lines is felt in the prosody; this narrative of violence and guilt is cast in stanzas which come as close to Sapphics as idiomatic English can come. The classical echo puts a distance between the poet and the events described, but it also recalls the actual effort that real speech requires.

Colloquial language, contractions, and exclamations fall into regular stanzas in "Poem About Morning," a funny little lecture on waking up and facing the day. The suggestion of lecturing is made by casting the poem in the second person, though the "you" partakes of the speaker's experience, almost as if the speaker were addressing himself. And "Earth Walk" provides a final illustration of the experimentation with point of view which runs like a thread through these new poems. (pp. 12-13)

These new poems, with their restless personal pronouns, may now be seen as forerunners of Meredith's most recent book, *Hazard, the Painter* (1975). This collection of sixteen poems seems to have been designed to provoke a number of reactions, not all of them charitable, and not all of them familiar to readers of Meredith's previous books. . . . [There] are poems comprising a "characterization," as Meredith calls it in a cagey note; he adds, "Resemblances between the life and character of Hazard and those of the author are not disclaimed but are much fewer than the author would like." . . .

The style of *Hazard* appears to be more casual, less concentrated, than anything Meredith has written before. One notices, for instance, that there is not a semicolon anywhere in these poems; instead, the independent clauses tumble along over their commas, contributing to the feeling of interior life, as in the second half of this stanza from "Politics." . . . (p. 14)

Gradually, as one rereads these poems, the accumulation of anecdote and detail provides the density that is missing from the style, and there arises the illusion of a life, made difficult by a difficult time, but still enjoyable and cherished. . . .

The mask of Hazard gives Meredith, at least for the duration of this deceptively brief book, the freedom to work out of ways in which he might think he was becoming set. In the chattiness that contains more than it at first seems to, beneath the detailed surfaces, there is room here for satire as well as for a serious, loving exploration of a peculiar world.

But Hazard is not destined to take over Meredith's voice and life. He is an interesting character met along the way, and, having met him, Meredith is usefully diverted from his way. There are too few uncollected poems on which to base conclusions about apparent directions to come, except to note that in some recent "dialogue poems" responding to wittily chosen epigraphs, Meredith continues to find fresh ways of reminding us that there is joy in plucking at the hems of even the darkest mysteries. (p. 15)

> Henry Taylor, "In Charge of Morale in a Morbid Time: The Poetry of William Meredith," in The Hollins Critic (copyright 1979 by Hollins College), February, 1979, pp. 1-15.

*   *   *

MERRILL, James   1926-

Merrill is an American poet, novelist, and playwright. Throughout his distinguished career his poetry has grown more ambitious and his exploration of the human condition more intense. His exquisite, meditative poems have won for him both the Bollengen Prize and the National Book Award. (See also *CLC*, Vols. 2, 3, 6, and *Contemporary Authors*, Vols. 13-16, rev. ed.)

JUDITH MOFFETT

Divine Comedies is the watershed book of James Merrill's life as a poet. Characterized by resolution and reconciliation and by Proustian recall, it is his most important book. It displays Merrill at the peak of his lyrical and narrative powers; but it's a dense, strenuous book.... At the same time it is innocent of the charge of hermeticism, as his last two volumes were not. Difficult of access as these poems are, only a page or so is downright impossible; and for the first time Merrill has made available to readers, on the copyright page, sources of information outside his text.... Inevitably *The Book of Ephraim* overshadows [the] lesser Divine Comedies; but each of the long poems in Part I (and at least one of the three single-pagers that bracket and bisect them, a sweet-natured character sketch called *Manos Karastefanís*) is wonderful in its own way. All the long poems share a family resemblance as to form (loose pentameter, rhyme consistent or haphazard), ambition of scope, density of language, and intricacy of pattern.

To any reader familiar with Merrill's earlier work, held together by passion and problematical family relations at the vital center, the most inescapable resolutions of this new book are sexual and familial. (p. 40)

One of this poet's most remarkable and endearing qualities has always been his ability and willingness—save *in extremis*—to gather even the most dismal and disheartening situations of which his poems treat into a kind of unfaked, unforced "happy ending"; and in *Divine Comedies* too, in spite of his belief that the part of living he has cared about most is over for him, every poem resolves in the way of the pastoral elegy, and as *et vitam venturi saeculi* supersedes *crucifixus est*. (p. 41)

Though his *poems* never fake an affirmative conclusion, Merrill's first novel—*The Seraglio* (1957)—announced two resolutions prematurely, presenting as convictions what were in fact still wishful thinking. The novel's hero (and

Merrill's persona), Francis Tanning, is shown in the moments of reconciling himself both with his parents and to the world's reality; yet books published years after *The Seraglio* proved repeatedly how much unresolved Oedipal tension remained. Merrill's poem on the Psyche-Eros myth, *From the Cupola*, for instance—the most hauntingly memorable lyrical statement in *Nights and Days*—describes winged Eros in many guises and Aphrodite as a terrifyingly maternal coconut palm.... Now, twenty years after the false resolution of *The Seraglio* and a decade after *From the Cupola* appeared in *Poetry*, comes *Lost in Translation* with a natural, believable reconciliation. This poem, one of the most nearly flawless in *Divine Comedies*, retells and mythologizes the Proustian episode of Merrill, as a child, putting together a puzzle with his nanny during "A summer without parents"; and it mentions in passing some puzzle-pieces cut into recognizable shapes, each a symbol from Merrill's personal repertoire:

> Witch on broomstick, ostrich, hourglass,
> Even (surely not just in retrospect)
> An inchling, innocently branching palm.

This is a "palm" in two senses, one allied to Urania's "rosy-fingered flexings", tiny, harmless, and one which reappears as the poem ends—inconsequentially as it may seem—unless that towering moonstruck *other* palm tree has stayed in the mind.... The violence and terror of that earlier palm is brought to diminutive harmlessness as the poem is brought—by intensifying the poetic elements of its language—to symphonic resolution.

We know from *Braving the Elements* that the "S" referred to at the end of *Lost in Translation* is a young Greek named Strato, the epicenter of Merrill's love life for a number of years; and another reason to call *Divine Comedies* a watershed book is that for the first time Merrill takes the reader's awareness of his homosexuality for granted, so that no love poem of his need ever again be weakened by a nameless, faceless, genderless "you" at its heart.... *Yánnina* and *Lost in Translation*, both because they deal with Merrill's family history and because they are nearly perfect poems judged by the highest standards of style, compression, thematic integration, risk, and adequate accessibility, are the most "important" in Part I; and they do convey the sense that Merrill has really made his necessary peace with [his] problematical memories at last.... The four [other poems], as much as these, are worked together with complete attention to every descriptive and linguistic detail, and to the levels and layers behind every word and phrase with more than one meaning, like "palm", above. And every one of these six would stand out, some more and some less brilliantly but all brilliantly enough to deserve the word, in a less ambitious collection.

McKane's Falls is the only long poem in Part I of emphatically greater lyrical than narrative strength, and the only one seriously concerned with circumstances memorable from an earlier book (*Braving the Elements*). It's a stunning piece, displaying Merrill at his purely stylistic best, than which there is no better.... *McKane's Falls* expresses a different sort of reconciliation: an explicit breakaway—supported by lines in other *Divine Comedies* poems—from Merrill's career-long commitment to the integrity of masks and surfaces.... (pp. 42-4)

The relative nature of Truth is twice insisted on in *Divine*

Comedies, but never before has Merrill expressed a willingness to penetrate appearances in quest of any "inside story", since until this volume of passion's ebbing, truth was held to be the enemy of love. This is the first of his books in which *light* is viewed as a friendly force, or a companion asked to "See through me. See me through", or a woman seen as "Lovelier . . . without make-up", or full value given to the sort of love that transcends passion and outlasts it. The passage of time on a cosmic and/or personal scale occurs as a theme in every long poem. . . . Merrill is obviously preoccupied with the ravages of passing time, but his work has always been singularly free of self-pity. . . . (pp. 44-5)

The Will, a complex and fascinating surrealistic poem placed last in Part I, gathers together all the major themes explored in this first third of the book—family, time, passion and its lapse—withing the context of the great theme about to dominate the rest of it: Ephraim, Ouija, the Other World, the death which is sea-change and loss rather than annihilation. Is it possible, I wonder, for any reader unaware of Merrill's preference for saying serious things lightly to realize *how* serious he is about all this? . . . [No] poetry of Merrill's ever was less frivolous; for in it his marrow-deep mistrust of *our* world, the "real" world—with which both his novel and all his other books of verse were saturated—has finally given way. (p. 45)

Ephraim is no flimsy figment of Merrill's imagination, made up one dull day out of whole cloth; the poet has lived with the virtually unaltered idea of him for upwards of twenty years. A little simple collating shows how closely detail in *The Book of Ephraim* corresponds to detail in *The Seraglio,* where Francis and his Italian lover Marcello make contact with a spirit calling himself Mcno. Save for a bit of portentous 1950's censorship (incest is substituted for homosexuality as the "perversion" ascribed to the Emperor Caligula) and truncation of the story-line, the discrepancies in cosmology, physical and biographical details ascribed to Meno/Ephraim, even transcriptions of dialogue, are minor. (pp. 46-7)

This very long poem's major theme, as announced in Section A, was to have been "an old, exalted one: / The incarnation and withdrawal of / A god." In fact, it's hard to tell to what extent the "god", Ephraim, as representative of the spirit world, withdraws, and to what extent he is gradually abandoned, dismissed, as Merrill's preference for the earthly world increases. In Section X Ephraim is still featured as "the latest / Recurrent figure out of mythology / To lend his young beauty to a living grave / In order that Earth bloom another season"; but there's no evidence to show he does this voluntarily. He wants to keep in touch; it's his mediums who give him no chance to.

The Book of Ephraim is only the newest and most persuasive treatment of Merrill's choosing-the-world theme. . . . [As far back as *The Seraglio*] Francis accepts his unwilling loss of the spirit world and manages somehow to believe in this one. . . . (p. 47)

Section Z, finally, describes the carton of Ephraim's transcripts in Stonington which now might as well be burned, for surely no one will ever read them again. In fact, the wish to burn them accords with Tiberius's wish for his own manuscript buried in its bronze box "UNDER PORPHYRY", and with Auden's for *his* box of papers in Oxford

"that must QUICKLY BE/QUICKLY BURNED". . . . Ephraim's transcripts are spared, though a door is shut upon them with a sound of finality. Life, itself, the Real, intervenes to save them, demonstrating again the other world's dependency upon the real world; for while debate is underway the phone, becoming a metaphorical lifeline as well as a literal one, interrupts:

> So, do we burn the—Wait, the phone is ringing:
> Bad connection; babble of distant talk;
> No getting through. We must improve the line
> In every sense, for life. . . .

The reader is left believing that the affair with Ephraim, whether or not it has quite ended (that point is left unsettled), will never again seduce Merrill away from the life he means to improve the line—the telephone line, the line of verse—for. (pp. 50-1)

It is, finally, impossible to establish by the poem's own lights and terms whether or not the Other World is meant to be understood as objectively real. Its status is actually less important than this very ambiguity: the impossibility of proving that it is or isn't real, and the possibility that it *may* be just as real, or more real (as Merrill believed for a long time), than the world we live in. Merrill himself isn't sure. But "Ephraim, my dear, let's face it," he says. "If I fall / From a high building, its your name I'll call . . . / Let's face it: the Unconscious, after all . . .". The Unconscious, after all, just won't quite do. Merrill's choice for the world of "grim truths" must be understood not as a rational conclusion that Ephraim has been only a scion of his imagination and David Jackson's . . . or of their combined Unconsciouses . . ., but as an existential preference arrived at over many years without knowing even now whether the real world is any more real than the other world, without—finally—*needing* to know anything except that this world, our world, is the one he belongs to.

The recurrent command to BURN THE BOX—"demotic" for "*Children while you can, let some last flame / Coat these walls, the lives you lived, relive them*"— is the final consequence of Merrill's involvement with the other world. With *Divine Comedies* this command has been obeyed. In the long poem in which it is transcribed, as well as in all the lyrical narratives of Part I, the flame that burns is the flame not of passion but of memory. (p. 53)

> *Judith Moffett, "The Other World and the Real,"*
> *in* Poetry *(© 1976 by the Modern Poetry Association; reprinted by permission of the Editor of* Poetry*), October, 1976, pp. 40-53.*

CLARA CLAIBORNE PARK

[*Divine Comedies: Poems*] is a verse not orphaned but fully parented in the flesh and the spirit, suckled, if not by Woolf, by a crowd of others. Yeats and Stevens, Kafka, Proust, Auden, Izak Dinesen, Brünnhilde, Tadzio, Miss Malin Nat-og-Dag—past presences, real and fictional, pervade [Merrill's] poetry. Highly seasoned and anything but anonymous, it is in some important sense serene, with the serenity of those who can still experience history, personal and public, as properly occasioning love and honor. . . .

Fun, of course, is to be expected from comedies, but who today expects to realize expectations? Dante (the celestial mechanics of whose tour of the spheres Merrill will casually explain) certainly did not promise fun. Nevertheless the parallel Merrill's title asserts has more than the customary ironic validity. Dante is the most personal of poets, relying on those he had loved and honored to guide him through the universe, memorializing in rich human particularity the history, poetry, philosophy, the politics, the geography of his public and private world. Merrill's *Comedies* are similarly rooted. Like Dante, like Yeats too, Merrill makes his poetry out of events and people whose primary significance is that they have happened to him or that he has cared about them. It is a significance which, if the poet is good enough, is sufficient for us all. . . . Taking place over nearly twenty years (1955-74, Eisenhower to Watergate) the poem compasses the poet's own maturing and binds the generations. The huge cast of characters includes babies and adolescents as well as the youngish, the aging, the old, the dying, and the dead. Like Dante he secures his events in time. Dates are placed where we can find them, for it's by the calendar that we must grasp time's passage. . . . For Dante and Yeats personal experience leads beyond itself to, literally, another world, and Merrill's testimony, like theirs, is that that world is inherently personal. And for Merrill too the praise and interest of the other world is tempered by his unregenerate attachment to the things of this one. (p. 181)

[Merrill offers] persons and places and events perceived through the affections and rendered in orders and textures of language which affirm their value for the poet, and so for us. In this as in other ways Merrill has chosen to honor tradition. . . . Dante, like all the great narrative poets, lets us know clearly where he starts from, whom he proceeds with, what goes on—basic clarities which sustain us to attempt the incidental riddles and enjoy them. Merrill, though he's no more than Dante an easy poet, gives us all the clues we need to follow him through a poem of many riddles and many settings. Dante named every river in Italy. Merrill gives us Kandy, Kyoto, Kew, Geneva, Santa Fe, Venice, the papyrus swamps of the Nile, the South African veldt and, as exotic as any, Purgatory, Okla., where young Temerlin's educated chimp-child Miranda makes Merrill the sign for "happy" and charms him with a great open-jawed kiss. . . . Merrill, like Yeats and unlike Dante, has had to make his own myth. No wonder his narrative holds the attention; it's about reincarnation and communion with the cherished dead. (pp. 181-82)

Merrill's *Comedies* are well named. Where death is not accepted as final it is hard to sustain a sense of tragedy. But euphoria, too, passes. By the end of the poem Ephraim no longer comes, or the aging companions no longer summon him. *Tempora mutantur;* so do we. For all the frivolity, Merrill announced his theme at once in A: "the incarnation and withdrawal of a god."

> We've modulated. Keys ever remoter
> Lock our friend among the golden things that go
> Without saying, the loves no longer called up
> Or named.

Keys of music, keys that secure treasure—the play of language is for pleasure. But these persistent puns are more—they are the poet's testimony to an ancient faith, the faith in the profound significances handed us by the adventitious and the random. It is not merely incidental that Merrill reveals himself as a virtuoso of trope and form, blank verse his common speech, developing sonnets as casually as the rest of us stammer, sliding imperceptibly into couplets, "loose talk tightening into verse." He can toss off a whole

narrative section in sonnets; he casts his meeting with WENDELL P in supple terza rima, even ending, as Dante ended his canticles, with the word "stars." . . . But Merrill's faith is even more profoundly traditional: the faith that appearances and chance connections are upheld by correspondences no earthly poet has created. If our varied "languages"—his quotation marks—"bird-flight, // Hallucinogen, chorale, and horoscope" are all "facets of the universal gem," randomness is only apparent. Dante, whose terza rima mirrored the Trinity, would have found the idea wholly familiar; Renaissance cabalists would have seen nothing singular in making the letters of the alphabet an organizing principle. Merrill's virtuosity, while offering us all the traditional pleasures, remains a means, not an end. The end—even more profoundly traditional—is to mirror experienced truth. . . .

In Q, a prose section of personally significant Quotations, Merrill for once transmits Ephraim's message raw and unversified: & NOW ABOUT DEVOTION IT IS I AM FORCED TO BELIEVE THE MAIN IMPETUS Indeed; as Dante learned, it moves the sun and the other stars. Or in Merrill's own exquisite image, what ties us to the dust is "the tough tendril / Of unquestioning love alone." We owe him our gratitude for risking his credentials as a modernist to show us that poetry still offers its old-fashioned pleasures. These poems, in language we can remember and possess, are testimony to an achieved web of values both transcendent and human. (p. 183)

> *Clara Claiborne Park, "Dante on Water Street,"*
> *in* The Nation *(copyright 1977 The Nation Associates), February 12, 1977, pp. 181-83.*

DAVID KALSTONE

Merrill has absorbed into verse many of the resources of daily conversation and prose. Still, there is a special strangeness and sometimes strain to Merrill's colloquial style, a taut alertness to the meanings which lurk in apparently casual words and phrases. We may find this in all good poets, but Merrill raises it to a habit of vigilance, a quickened control and poise, sometimes bravado, which he clearly trusts as a source of power. When Merrill uses an idiom, he turns it over curiously, as if prospecting for ore. (pp. 79-80)

Merrill's absorption of prose rhythms and colloquial idioms has something of the structuralist's curiosity behind it, an interest in casual observations which both veil and betray buried feelings. In "Up and Down" Mother and son are alone in a bank vault to inspect her safe-deposit box: "She opens it. Security. Will. Deed." The puns are telling. The wit is there to reveal patterns that vein a life: a precarious and double use of ordinary speech much like the quality Merrill admires in the poetry of the contemporary Italian Montale, some of whose work he has translated. . . . (p. 81)

The figures who appear and re-appear in Merrill's poems have more substance than the legendary heroines who were muses to the sonneteers, but they also have the same mesmerizing force, as he considers and reconsiders their shaping impact on his life. To reread Merrill's books since *Water Street* is to discover him preparing a stage whose objects and cast of characters become increasingly luminous. They become charged with symbolic meaning and release symbolic reverberations from otherwise ordinary narrative event. (pp. 81-2)

Much of Merrill's interest in narrative and everyday experience has been aimed at discovering the charges with which certain objects have become invested for him. He seems in his developed poetry to be asking the Freudian or the Proustian question: what animates certain scenes—and not others—for us? Over the years Merrill's poems have used the objects and stages of daily life, the arrangements of civilized behavior, almost as if he expected to waken sleeping presences and take by surprise the myths he lives by. (p. 83)

The conviction that "life was fiction in disguise" charges his poetry from the very start. Yet *First Poems* (1951) and *The Country of a Thousand Years of Peace* (1959) stand apart. These are books in which Merrill is continually interrogating presences as if they were on the edge of eternity. *First Poems* is a lonely and tantalizing collection, whose characteristic speaker is a solitary, often a child, attempting to decipher or translate elusive natural emblems: a shell, periwinkles, a peacock. . . . Many of these poems take up the matter of going beyond appearances so earnestly as to make *First Poems* seem "last" poems as well. Still, behind the conversational ease and realism of Merrill's subsequent books is the feeling which animates the very first poem of this one, "The Black Swan": the child's yearning to see the world symbolically. It haunts, informs and strengthens everything he writes.

By the time of *The Country of a Thousand Years of Peace* . . . the solitary speaker had become a world traveller. Yet that worldly grounding only licenses and confirms his questions about the solidity of appearances. He is less interested in what the traveller sees and more in his distanced way of seeing things. Japan, India, Holland, Greece: the journey only confirms him in the feelings of exile and strangeness expressed in *First Poems*. (pp. 83-4)

It is in *Water Street* that Merrill commits himself to his brand of autobiography and, with a title as specific as his previous had been general, turns his poetry toward a "local habitation and a name." The occasion of the book is moving to a new house. The closing poem of the book, "A Tenancy," settles him in Stonington, Connecticut, on the village street of the title, in the house which is to be a central presence in his work. The move confirms him in poetic directions he had already begun to follow: "If I am host at last / It is of little more than my own past. / May others be at home in it." *Water Street* opens with "An Urban Convalescence," a poem which dismantles a life in New York City where life is continually dismantling itself. Merrill's move is inseparable from the desire to stabilize memory, to draw poetry closer to autobiography, to explore his life, writing out of "the dull need to make some kind of house / Out of the life lived, out of the love spent."

The domesticating impulse closes both "An Urban Convalescence" and "A Tenancy" and effectively frames the book. Imagined as dwelling places, the poems are at once new creations and dedications to what is durable, salvageable from the past. They emerge as signs of Merrill's deep and nourishing debt to Proust. . . . (pp. 84-5)

In his first two books Merrill had imagined the riddling objects and landscapes of nature and his travels as teasing him, just on the edge of releasing hidden meanings. They were stable, static, as if seen on a photographic negative or on an etcher's plate ("images of images . . . insights of the mind in sleep"). In *Water Street* the optical image is extended to motion-picture films and refined to accommodate mysteries interior and fleeting, stored in memory, only to be glimpsed in motion and discovered by activating the charged details of our own lives. (p. 86)

The particular houses Merrill writes about in later poems—however real, solidly located and furnished—are also imagined as vulnerable houses of the spirit. They are never mere settings. In the details he uses to conjure them up, there are always reminders of the particular kinds of exposure and emergency against which these domestic arrangements have been contrived. It is not simply that they displace confining dwellings of the past—the broken parental home, the narrow apartments of false starts. The very act of choosing what spaces, attributes, solid elements of the house to invoke *becomes* the action of the poem. A transparency of setting characterizes Merrill's writing, bleaching out distracting, merely accidental details and fixing most of his houses as improvised houses of survival and desire.

But in *Water Street,* the most powerful poems are those stressing the exposures against which Merrill's dwellings were to be devised. "An Urban Convalescence" is the best known of these poems, but "Childlessness" is probably the most important. "Childlessness" draws together narrative impulse and symbolic framework so violently that it seems not to fuse but confound them. Here, in a phantasmagoric landscape, houses "look blindly on"; the one glimmering light is not the poet's own. . . . No paraphrase could do justice to the uncomfortable marriage of poet and Nature which permeates this poem. Whether he is thinking of Nature as fostering the children he does not have or as infusing the visions of art, he remains battered between dream and nightmare. (pp. 89-90)

The transformations [in "Childlessness"] are hard to keep track of; the refusal to allow experience to settle is part of the poem's point. . . . The exotic colors of sunset, distilled from the storm, first *clothe* the poet, then *burst* along his limbs like *buds.* The image is meant to counter an earlier one: that nothing is planted in his garden (no natural blooms, like children). Then the *buds* become *bombs,* and the reward for being on target is a curious miniaturization of the world. A bombed metropolis is reassembled on sampans, a decimating version of the powers of art. The dream ends, as a *stained* dawn replaces the exotic dyes of sunset. Unlike those tropical shades, dawn's colors do not clothe him. For hours he cannot *stand* (both "bear" and "rise") to *own* the threadbare world—or to face its alternative: the cloak, a token for his parents who performed the expected service to nature. Their reward is also what devours them.

This is one of Merrill's most exposed poems, anticipated in the closing lines of "An Urban Convalescence." It offers rapid and conflicting perspectives against which to view the particulars of human feeling. Childlessness, guilt and suffering are set within the framework of nature's ample violence, its mysterious ecology, its occasionally exalting cyclical promise and power. Merrill has discovered a stage which will accommodate surrealistic effects released by a familiar domestic situation. The effect is like an opening out of space, a large corrective for moments of individual exposure. Merrill forces leaps from the "kitchen garden" to "really inhuman depths," the poetic gift he admired in Montale. But he also seems uncomfortable with these accesses of power. In "Childlessness" the technique is abrupt and insistent, a prey sometimes to strained self-justification or exaggerated guilt. It finds no way to separate the bareness and power of his own life from the punishment of his parents. And so the poem never really settles; at the close it comes to rest rather than resolution. Shuttling, adjusting perspectives constantly as we must to read this poem, we hear a mixture of self-accusation, self-delight and defiance. In the final lines the parents, consumed to the bone, are introduced with a baffling combination of bitterness, contrition and fierce confrontation with the way of the world. What happens violently in "Childlessness" happens with more meditative certainty later in his career. (pp. 92-3)

Nights and Days (1966), the next book, is the classic Merrill volume—jaunty, penetrating and secure. It contains some of his best poems, though later works were to be richer, more searching, high-flying, even shocking and relaxed. But several of the poems in *Nights and Days* are paradigms of how he was going to use autobiographical details in his poetry. Or to reverse it, in Merrill's own words, how the poet was to become a man "choosing the words he lives by." (p. 93)

From [the point of *Nights and Days* on] he seems entirely secure about the relation of his poems to autobiography and memory, to social surface and colloquial language. The security is reflected in pieces which begin or end with explicit references to writing. . . . The poet will be seen at his desk, looking back at an encounter or a crisis, or in the heat of events will glance forward to the time when he is alone and unpressured. [Merrill is committed] to capturing the immediate feel of experience, but often insistent that writing is part of that experience. (p. 96)

Merrill accepts the notions of poetic closure and the composed self—notions which many writers of autobiographical verse would suspect as artificial, false to the provisional nature of things. In many of Merrill's poems, the closing is also the point at which the poem opens out. . . .

Merrill prefers poems in the first-person present which begin "with a veil drawn" ("a sublimation of the active voice or the indicative mood . . . a ritual effacement of the ego"). That attitude helps explain the presence of a short poem as prologue to each of his later books. In particular, "Nightgown," "Log" and "Kimono" are small ritual prefaces, overheard, propitiatory, modest, veiled overtures of poet to Muse. (p. 97)

[Certainly] the repeated motifs of aroused flames and cooling attune us to an intensity of involvement seemingly at odds with the almost deadpan wit and surface detachment of many of the poems. As readers we have to be aware of the verbal "layers" of a Merrill poem: his way of shadowing plots beneath the narrative surface and suggesting the complex involvement of the ego in any given experience. While the civilized storyteller takes us into his confidence, adjustments of time, temperature, light and background call attention to his own emotional activity and psychic experience of the poem.

"The Broken Home" shows that double movement at its clearest. The home is the one he grew up in, but also one we are given to feel *he* breaks within the poem. We must watch two actions at the same time. In one, the poem seems like a series of slides of the past, each a sonnet long, presenting the characters of his Oedipal tale and encounters between them. In the other action, the present tense of the

poem, we watch the poet lighting his scenes. Behind these surfaces, changes of timing, brightness and scale render the scenes as transparencies. Or, to put it another way, the changes in his writing, the heightened temperature of involvement, coax out an inner experience. It is as if a poem required a kind of scrim among its resources, before or behind which action may be seen in new configurations as new beams of light are introduced. (pp. 99-100)

It may be a common—and mistrusted—device of poetic closure, Merrill's calling attention to the poet's role at the end of the poem. But in *Nights and Days*—and especially in the long major poems, "The Thousand and Second Night" and "From the Cupola"—attention to writing coincides with the notion of a house, a dwelling place, a point of repair at a particular moment, the desk, the typewriter. It is as if these poems fulfilled the promise of "An Urban Convalescence"—"To make some kind of house / Out of the life lived, out of the love spent." The conventional ending seems . . . newly discovered, a psychological necessity.

The very title of this volume refers to the interpenetration and inseparability of the days of raw experience and the nights of imaginative absorption and recall. It is in those late night moments that the poems discover the poet at his desk and perform the ritual separations of poet from his poem. Such episodes, though they occur elsewhere in Merrill's work, seem to have their authentic emotional center in *Nights and Days*. The close of "The Thousand and Second Night" was almost an emblem of what poetry had come to mean for Merrill. Scheherazade survives by telling her nightly tales, but yearns for "that cold fountain which the flesh / Knows not." The bondage and the pleasure of her stories are expressed in her marriage to the Sultan, the daytime spirit whose joys lie "along that stony path the senses pave." It is he to whom things happen, she who "embroiders" what they mean. In the tenderness of their addresses to one another, the book lays its true and inner counterpoise to the deadlocked male and female voices of "The Broken Home" and to the guilty son of "Childlessness." (pp. 103-04)

The almost eternal twinning of the Sultan and Scheherazade is one of the ways Merrill has of showing how memory and autobiography ("real life") serve poetry's power to reveal the myths we live by. (p. 104)

The Fire Screen is, among other things—and preeminently—the book of love. It reads like a sonnet sequence following the curve of a love affair to its close. Like important sonnet sequences, the implied narrative calls into play a range of anxieties not strictly connected to love, in Merrill's case challenging some of the balanced views of *Nights and Days*.

"The Friend of the Fourth Decade" is the launching point for this book—the poet at forty, setting one part of himself in dialogue with another. What is being tested here is the whole commitment to memory, to personal history, to a house and settling down—the very material to which Merrill entrusted himself after *Water Street*. The "friend" is an alter ego who comes to visit—really to confront—his poet-host, after a long absence. (p. 105)

"The Friend of the Fourth Decade" tests a dream of escape, a drama extended and detailed by the poems set in Greece which follow it in *The Fire Screen*. In some sense the book is . . . a deepening encounter with another language and a more elemental culture, in which the speaker becomes, from poem to poem, more identified with his new world, cleansed of the assumptions of the old. (p. 106)

It is hard to disentangle the impulses which contribute to ["Mornings in a New House"]—harder even because the poet has added a footnote taking some of it back, imagining passion as itself a defense, not a danger, like the screen of fire that protects Brünnhilde in Wagner's opera. But, in the poem proper, the fire screen is devised against the damages of love. It bears, in a sense, the whole retrospective power of his writing, the ability of memory and art to absorb and rearrange experience. What marks this off from earlier moments in Merrill's poetry is the long perspective which the poem opens up, receding past his immediate pain, past his own childhood of "The Broken Home," to his mother who stitched the screen as a device involving *her* mother.

After all the carefully noted impulses in *The Fire Screen* to leave the mother behind—the attempts to rinse away her handwriting in "Friend of the Fourth Decade"; even the efforts to be free of Latin languages, the "mother tongue" —the poet returns to her in a new way. The "new house" of this poem is interwoven with the house his mother had sewn, *her* mother's house, dwarfed by giant birds and flowery trees. The discovery of these entwined destinies "deep indoors" draws blood. There is something like the remorse of "Childlessness" in what happens. The resources of art are seen as self-protective, even vengeful, a miniaturization of human powers, like the moment in the earlier poem when the annihilated village—teeming generations in dwarfed versions—is loaded aboard sampans and set adrift. But in "Mornings in a New House" the experience is without guilt and is shared in its brittle complexity. Waves of warmth and anger carry him inward to an identification with the "tiny needlewoman" mother, to share the childish pleasure and fear which even then would shape her feelings for the child *she* would one day have. With "some faintest creaking shut of eyes" they both become toys in a larger pattern, at once foreshortened and part of their shared, terrifying but ungrudging humanity. I think what is most notable in this poem is that Merrill, however rueful and pained, has emerged from the erotic fire into a newly defined and felt natural perspective—one which becomes visible and palpable at length in many of the poems of his next book, *Braving the Elements*. (pp. 109-10)

We must pay special attention to [Merrill's] puns and . . . settings; they open alternative perspectives against which to read the time-bound and random incidents of daily life. In *Braving the Elements* (1972) and *Divine Comedies* (1976), he has become a master of this idiosyncratic method, something one might call—with apologies—symbolic autobiography, Merrill's way of making apparently ordinary detail transparent to deeper configurations. (p. 111)

[Merrill moves] toward larger and larger units of composition, not only long poems, but combinations of different forms, like the free juxtapositions of prose and more or less formal verse units in "The Thousand and Second Night" and "From the Cupola." The two sections of "Up and Down" limn out, together, an emotional landscape which neither of them could singly suggest.

On the surface it is a poem of contrasts: rising in a ski lift with a lover, descending into a bank vault with the mother; the ostensible freedom of one experience, while in the oth-

er, "palatial bronze gates shut like jaws." Yet the exhilaration of the ski lift—it begins in dramatic present tenses—is what is relegated finally to a cherished snapshot and to the past tense: "We gazed our little fills at boundlessness." The line almost bursts with its contradictions: unslaked appetite, or appetite only fulfilled and teased by "gazing our little fills." . . . "The Emerald," on the other hand, begins in brisk easy narrative pasts and moves toward a moment in the very present which the ski-lift section had forsaken. More important, whatever the surface contrasts between the two sections, there is an irresistible connection between the discoveries made by each. Or rather, the feelings of the opening poem enable the son to understand what happens to the mother in the closing poem. (pp. 113-14)

Some of the poems are pure ventriloquism. "The Black Mesa" speaks; so do "Banks of a Stream Where Creatures Bathe." They seem to embody a consensus of human voices, mythically inured to experience. History, the details of private lives—everything repeats itself in the long views these poems take. Hearing the poet take on these roles is like talking to survivors. (p. 116)

["The Book of Ephraim" is] full of the past, of luminous figures, the living and the dead, all of whom coexist in "The Book of Ephraim" by virtue of the attention Merrill has given them throughout his work and the value he has come to attach to them. The book includes figures resonant from other, earlier poems . . . as well as literary masters like Wallace Stevens and W. H. Auden. (p. 120)

[This] poem allows Merrill to think of the past as nourishing —and without the sense of elegy which marks Lowell's *History*. Ephraim speaks to the narrator (section Q) of a community "WITHIN SIGHT OF & ALL CONNECTED TO EACH OTHER DEAD OR ALIVE NOW DO U UNDERSTAND WHAT HEAVEN IS IT IS THE SURROUND OF THE LIVING". Of these figures he says "IT IS EASY TO CALL THEM BRING THEM AS FIRES WITHIN SIGHT OF EACH OTHER ON HILLS". Metaphorically speaking, it is the kind of writing Merrill has done which makes many of these figures, finally, so innocently available to him, part of a network of affinities. "The Book of Ephraim" bears witness to a lifetime of continuing attention to and care for figures who have become resonant in his memory.

This poem, for example, returns with feeling ease to the memories of his father and his father's death—all the more remarkable when one thinks of Merrill's gallery of reactions to his father, running the gamut from satire in "The Broken Home" and in his novel *The Seraglio* to the guilt reflected in "Childlessness." In "The Book of Ephraim" they are spunky affectionate equals in the plenum of birth and decay. The freedom that vision allows bears fruit in "Yánnina," one of the independent shorter poems in *Divine Comedies*. . . . After a visit to Yánnina, capital of the last Turkish potentate in Greece, Ali Pasha, Merrill draws a portrait of the old despot, of the two women most notably attached to him—one a spiritual, one a fleshly love—and of the conflated gore and charm of Ali's life. What comes to matter in the poem is the intricate interweaving of present and past. Toward the end he links Ali's dual nature with his (Merrill's) own father's. More important all along, in a dialogue with a younger companion, he has been testing contradictions in his own nature which subtly identify him with the two vanished "fathers" in the "brave old world" of the poem.

"Yánnina" is a tribute to the sifting, amassing and reconciling powers of memory. It shows how the attitudes behind "The Book of Ephraim" help to refigure individual experience under the elongating pressures of time. Within "The Book of Ephraim" Merrill was to acknowledge a new sense of his rapport with Proust. (pp. 120-21)

Writing the poem—making Ephraim's panorama his own—has brought Merrill to the point where he feels he has to withdraw. "Let's be downstairs, leave all this, put the light out." The end of the poem is deliberately muted, using neutral domestic gestures to cover a certain fear about the light his imagination has cast. The quoted sentence is meant to sound more like whistling in the dark than like a buried echo of a resolute Othello.

"The Book of Ephraim" is a compendium of voices—individual and social, emulated, sometimes feared and discarded. It suggests ways in which the apparently random material of our lives and reading, history, gossip—the rational and irrational bombardments—are somehow absorbed and selected for our experience. Echoes and re-echoes tease us with patterns whose existence we suspected but whose details were not yet clear. With its eddies and turns, its combination of tones, its range of high talk and low, "The Book of Ephraim" suggests how such patterns gather in a human life and assume the force of conviction. Merrill also suggests the price we pay for that knowledge. (pp. 124-25)

> David Kalstone, "James Merrill: Transparent Things," in his Five Temperaments: Elizabeth Bishop, Robert Lowell, James Merrill, Adrienne Rich, John Ashbery (copyright © 1977 by David Kalstone; used by permission of Oxford University Press, Inc.), Oxford University Press, 1977, pp. 77-128.

PHOEBE PETTINGELL

Ouija? Heavenly messengers? Their appearance will not surprise readers of Merrill's *Divine Comedies* (1976). In that work, the poet told of bizarre communications that he and his companion, David Jackson, had received over a 20-year period from "Ephraim"—a 1st-century Hellenistic Jew who claimed to have been a slave at the court of Tiberius. . . .

Through him, . . . JM and DJ were able to contact dead friends, in particular two quasi-parental figures: W. H. Auden, Merrill's poetic mentor, and Maria Mitsotáki, whom Merrill once addressed as "the Muse of my off-days" (*The Firescreen*, 1969). Such a high comic romp was rather startling after the previous "chronicles of love and loss." Still, it was undeniable that in shaking the burdens of nostalgia and regret, the poet's voice deepened with impressive authority.

Now it turns out that "The Book of Ephraim" was merely a curtain-raiser for *Mirabell*'s more solemn masque. Mysterious powers who "SPEAK FROM WITHIN THE ATOM" . . . have come to tell of the dangers of atomic energy. (p. 14)

[The] general movement of *Mirabell* manages to metamorphosize the ordinary, the trivial, the ridiculous into the sublime. Enter 741, a gentle bat, who conducts a seminar on the new religion of symbolic language. In the process, his four pupils—JM, DJ, Maria, and Wystan—teach him about

human manners, which elevate us above the animal world, and he is transformed into a peacock. JM names him "Mirabell," after the romantic hero of Congreve's *The Way of the World*. To celebrate the newfound faith, there is a picnic of words—a love feast or agape, introduced by Auden, whose much-missed voice Merrill resurrects with uncanny fidelity. . . .

Lest readers get the impression that *Mirabell* is chiefly devoted to the exposition of dubious metaphysics, I hasten to note that no summary can convey the variety or cohesion of its dramatic changes. A matter as frivolous as redecorating a room turns out to have cosmic significance. There are numberless subplots, each more delightful than the last. One involves the horrifying discovery by the late poet, Chester Kallman, that he is to be reborn as an African political leader; another relates how the spirit of Rimbaud ghostwrote *The Waste Land*. Akhnaton and his Queen Nefertiti, doomed by love and pride, provide what Merrill mockingly styles "*Nuits de Cleopatrè.*" Instruction in science, history and theology, Arabian Nights stories, arguments and debates are all interwoven with "set pieces"—lyrical poems of exquisite musicality, reminiscent of the songs in Goethe's *Faust*. There is something for everyone, yet it all forms a unity, bonded like those atoms the poem celebrates.

Perhaps the most powerful enchantment of the book is the vividness and charm of its characters. The angels are radiantly otherworldly; the bats frighteningly so, except for the humane Mirabell. . . .

What, then, of the "poems of science"? When his voices tell Merrill that "MAN'S TERMITE PALACE BEEHIVE ANTHILL PYRAMID JM IS LANGUAGE," they assume our ability to accept a metaphor that compares structures collectively built by social insects to human culture. . . .

Nevertheless, the Muses of most poets today parade like the Madwoman of Chaillot, dressed in outmoded fashions of thought, ready to do single-handed battle against modernism. *Mirabell*, by contrast, is not afraid to tackle the problem head-on. . . .

Merrill's celestial circus is a brilliant philosophy of metaphor—that "ritual of the new religion." At all times it is affirmed that there *are* no bats—spirits have no form. Maria explains that they are products of "the mind's eye," the imagination that must see an idea to conceive it. The poet's function is to translate the abstract into the vividly concrete. No reader of *Mirabell* will ever think of atoms quite the way he did before encountering the personifications of their forces. Yet after all the grotesques, arabesques, human interest, we become more sophisticated, and are prepared for the unadorned revelation of the angels.

James Merrill has created a poem as central to our generation as *The Waste Land* was to the one before us. (p. 15)

> Phoebe Pettingell, "Voices from the Atom, "in The New Leader (© 1978 by the American Labor Conference on International Affairs, Inc.), December 4, 1978, pp. 14-15.

*   *   *

MERWIN, W(illiam) S(tanley)   1927-

One of America's greatest living poets, Merwin is also a playwright, short story writer, and translator. He has written

poetry that has received much praise from critics, but relatively little attention from the reading public. He is a cerebral, often difficult poet, drawing his poetic imagery from the mythic past. He is the recipient of the Pulitzer Prize and the National Book Award. (See also *CLC*, Vols. 1, 2, 3, 5, 8, and *Contemporary Authors*, Vols. 13-16, rev. ed.)

THOM GUNN

I always find difficulty in adequately explaining my faint misgivings on reading the work of W. S. Merwin. For, though he doesn't have the range of Nemerov, he has an exceptional control over the resources of language and movement, an understanding of the relation between which enables him to perform, for instance, the audacities of documentary language in "Cape Dread" and "The *Portland Going Out*" in [*The Drunk in the Furnace*]. And each poem, moreover, has a beautiful self-sufficiency: part is linked to part firmly and cleanly.

Why, then, do his poems not interest more? In a sense, it may be that a poem by Merwin is *too* self-sufficient. It has reference *only* to the subject, which is not usually placed in a world larger than itself. . . . Merwin lacks that *absorption* in his subject matter which paradoxically ends by making a poem look outward, to the rest of the world. As it is, his poetry tells us something about a thing or an event with great accuracy, but is curiously barren of individual emotions or ideas. There is a sameness to it—both to a single poem and to the whole book—an evenness of texture, and a lack of any real contrast. (pp. 588-89)

> *Thom Gunn, in* The Yale Review (© *1961 by Yale University; reprinted by permission of the editors), Summer, 1961.*

CHERI COLBY DAVIS

Gifted with prophetic powers, Merwin has been aware, for longer than most, that our nation is headed on a course of environmental and economic self-destruction; and on a more metaphysical level, he has been more sensitive than most other poets to humanity's singular inability to perceive reality as intensely as they might, and thus to use time as effectively as they could. He has been preoccupied with both the public and private consequences of this lessening of time, and he renders the effects of its ineluctable passage poetically in his images. We are "The Last People." (pp. 226-27)

On a more positive note, Merwin can also effect a transcendence of time in his poetry: Certain poetic images or passages impart a sense of timelessness or suspension of time. He attempts to capture the absolute moment of time —a real time or stopped time—in his poetry. This "transcendence" of time is as important to an understanding of the poetry as are the images of end. (p. 227)

Merwin feels intensely his own blindness to the meaning of time, the significance of the present. He is painfully aware of his inability to seize the moment. In his poetry written during the sixties and in the poetry of *The Lice*, Merwin captures in frozen hysteria the horror of the constant running on and out of time—or the horror of the loss of the perfect moment. . . . (p. 229)

In Merwin's work, time participates in the syntactical order of the poem. The passage of time is rendered by shifts in verb tenses. The poem's temporal duration is expanded and thus poetic time is "created" by strategically placed line breaks. By these technical means he encourages an awareness of the plight of man caught in the flux of time and an awareness of the power of the poem to achieve the effect of timelessness, thereby conquering the flux of time.

One symbol the poet employs to create timelessness in the poem is the symbol of starlight, which moves simultaneously through immeasurable time and immeasurable space to reach us. In . . . "Under Black Leaves" Merwin effects a timelessness in and through the star symbol which temporally merges past and present and which physically combines movement through space and movement through time. This effect is furthered by frequent shifts in temporal frames of reference which ultimately create a sense of transcendence of time and thus force a recognition of absolute time. . . . (pp. 232-33)

The poem transcends time and space by fusing time with space and enters a new area of experience, sound. Through this fusion the poem reaches into the eternal; it achieves a timelessness or transcendence of time. Merwin's concept of the transmission of sound is purely poetic, since sound is not transmitted in outer space. The concept does, however, place his poetry squarely in the realm of myth rather than science where he seems to feel the important new discoveries are to be experienced.

Merwin's poems dealing with time are permeated by an eerie sense of unreality. He can envision time as sheer, ineluctable movement forward. His horror of losing time derives from a strong sense of his own inability to use time effectively: his realization of the proper use and meaning of the present comes only when it has past. For Merwin a voyager's arriving too late at a deserted port to tell the departed population the meaning of human life is an image of the tragic ineffectiveness of those who live in time and who try to do some good for humanity. (p. 235)

More and more in *Writings to an Unfinished Accompaniment*, however, Merwin appears to be exercising his skill at catching and fixing real time in the poem, and at effecting timelessness through symbols of transcendence of time. He seems to be leaving behind his old haunting awareness of time. (p. 236)

> *Cheri Colby Davis, "Time and Timelessness in the Poetry of W. S. Merwin," in* Modern Poetry Studies *(copyright 1975, by Jerome Mazzaro), Winter, 1975, pp. 224-36.*

LINDA W. WAGNER

As W. S. Merwin's work illustrates, the poet today wins his audience by involving it in his seemingly personal activity— or, as Merwin writes in "An Encampment at Morning," "I come that way in a breath cloud / learning my steps / . . . we are words on a journey / not the inscriptions of settled people." (p. 88)

The presence of the Merwin persona haunts all the poems of *The Compass Flower*. "I love voices not heard," "I consider life after life as treasures," "I have been younger in October," "I have watched your smile in your sleep"— whether or not the poem opens with the activity of the poet-persona, that activity, that recognition, is the heart of the poem. Meditative in both language and structure, Merwin's poems circle, angle, fuse: they do not aim for the normal chronological progression of story, of language caught in time. Merwin's language is caught in ontological necessity; it searches for repetition, pun, sound play, in its role of creating the semblance of matrix that the poem of process demands. The poem "Trees" illustrates some of the qualities that a Merwin poem often has.

> I am looking at trees
> they may be one of the things I will miss
> most from the earth
> though many of the ones that I have seen
> already I cannot remember
> and though I seldom embrace the ones I see
> and have never been able to speak
> with one
> I listen to them tenderly
> their names have never touched them
> they have stood round my sleep
> and when it was forbidden to climb them
> they have carried me in their branches

The random association from the poet's initial act, looking at trees, to the meditative, open process of re-creating a tree (the inevitable comparison with the Joyce Kilmer poem suggests the changes in poetry during the past fifty years—most noticeable, the complete lack of any moral, or of any physical description of the tree) takes the reader from the simple act of observing through the poignant discovery of the lack of individuation of the tree ("their names have never touched them") to the poet's stretch back into memory. The poem in its seemingly aimless structure thus links Merwin's suggestion of mortality in line 2 with his return to childhood in line 12: we have the complete human experience, yet unobtrusively.

Structurally, Merwin also works to create a deceptively artless mode for his poems. By using no punctuation or capitalization, he suggests that the poem is a thought, a stream-of-consciousness presentation whose chief structural device is a line pattern that helps to simultaneously create and control rhythm. Wonderfully readable, Merwin's poems contrive a spoken rhythm that lulls the reader into thinking that they are without contrivance. That the entire collection works in just this way, and that many of the poems are very effective—as is the sequence poem "Kore"—belies the easiness that some qualities of Merwin's work suggest. (pp. 88-90)

> Linda W. Wagner, in The Ontario Review (copyright © 1977 by The Ontario Review), Fall-Winter, 1977-78.

VERNON YOUNG

Collectively, [the verses of *The First Four Books of Poems*] echo and reaffirm a prolific anthology of tongues, testifying, of course, to Merwin as translator, one of the most authentic practitioners we have today. Imitations, in the best sense, accomplished exercises in an abundance of forms, their sources are variably the Biblical tales, Classical myth, love songs from the Age of Chivalry, Renaissance retellings; they comprise carols, roundels, odes, ballads, sestinas and they contrive golden equivalents of emblematic models: the masque, the Zodiac, The Dance of Death. Had Merwin never written any verse of his own save this, he would compel the ear of anyone decently educated to the liberal euphonies of the accumulated tradition. Were you to redistribute these poems, unsigned, among collections of translated material or of English Poetry Down the Ages, any but

the most erudite reader would heedlessly accept them as renderings of Theocritus, Catullus, Ronsard or, on a venture, as having been written by an anonymous Elizabethan, by George Herbert, by Thomas Campion, by Thomas Lovell Beddoes—or by Tennyson.

Critics are fond of pinpointing the moment at which a poet "finds his own voice." He finds it when he writes a successful poem: one that being heard gives pleasure, even if the immediate tune recalls that of a predecessor.... Merwin's great composite themes of seagoing and wreck, of the beast under the waters of consciousness announced by "Leviathan". in *Green With Beasts* (an essay in accentual verse that surpasses, to my ear, Pound's "The Seafarer"), were not suddenly ... torn from the void; they had already surfaced, occasional, played down but palpable, in the earlier context. At the outset ... "Anabasis" I and II, had introduced the maritime journey, and in line given to Proteus (in *The Dancing Bears*), attribution allowed for, "Odysseus" ... is recognizably prefigured....

One thing is certain. Before embarking on the narratives published in 1956 and after, Merwin was in secure formal command: shape and duration, melody, vocal inflection, were under superb control. No stanzaic model was alien to him; no line length was beyond his dexterity. Liberated from rhyme, if need be, having structured many of his poems into unrhymed units of 6 lines each—or 7, 9, 11, even 13 and 17—he was now prepared to launch into those lengthy, undivided blank-verse monologues, rhythmic without falter, solemn yet "conversational," which initiate *Green with Beasts* like organ voluntaries.... All these but "Leviathan" conjure the scenic ambience (and hints of Christian revelation) of a T. S. Eliot wasteland: dusty plains, olive trees, slack tents, "garden terraces / Vague through the afternoon, remembering rain; / But in the night green with beasts", and in "White Goat, White Ram" threads of Eliotic diction show conspicuously in the weave.... This is a rare instance, however, of almost completely opaque language; the general atmosphere of these poems is achieved visually and the effect is in every case slowly hair-raising. (p. 4)

> Vernon Young, "Same Sea, Same Dangers: W. S. Merwin," in The American Poetry Review (copyright © 1978 by World Poetry, Inc.; reprinted by permission of Vernon Young), January/February, 1978, pp. 4-5.

L. EDWIN FOLSOM

[Merwin's poetry] is not Whitmanesque, but, like Whitman, Merwin *has* been obsessed with the meaning of America. His poetry, especially *The Lice* and the American sequence in *The Carrier of Ladders*, often implicitly and sometimes explicitly responds to Whitman; his twentieth century sparsity and soberness—his doubts about the value of America—answer, temper, Whitman's nineteenth century expansiveness and exuberance—his enthusiasm over the American creation. In *The Lice* Merwin is interested in "what America *is*," and in *The Carrier of Ladders* he engages in a poetic search—a descent in time—to discover also what America *was*, to face and assume the guilt of the destructive American expansion across the continent, to invoke the vanished native and face the implications of his absence. (p. 57)

The Whitmanian self [is] a model of expanding America.... (p. 58)

With no regrets, Whitman/America goes about "Clearing the ground for broad humanity, the true America," and "These virgin lands" (the wilderness She) gladly give way "To the new culminating man" (the American He). . . . [The] still-uncreated West would always be, to the future-oriented Whitman, the "better" part of the American creation, for his concern was always with process, never with the finished product; hope was in the still unformed chaos, not in the already formed creation. . . . [He] claims that the natural never will really be lost, but instead will simply become part of the conquering white race: "To be in them absorb'd, assimilated."

In his American sequence in *The Carrier of Ladders*, Merwin offers a stark response to Whitman's claims of wilderness assimilation. In his ironically entitled poem, "The Free," he portrays the Indian dispossessed of his land. . . . The vast absurdity of claiming that we can "absorb" a race or a wilderness while we systematically exterminate them is one of Merwin's concerns in his American sequence; we play tricks with language that come back to destroy us. . . . In Whitman's system, the Indian was not killed, he was *absorbed*. Merwin answers such euphemistic claims, simply and beyond anger, "No." We have destroyed, not absorbed; killed, not evolved.

Merwin's answer to Whitman is begun in *The Lice*, an anti-song of the self. Here, instead of the Whitmanian self expanding and absorbing everything, naming it in an ecstasy of union, we find a self stripped of meaning, unable to expand, in a landscape that refuses to unite with the self, refuses to be assimilated, in a place alien and unnameable. . . . [This] self becomes voiceless, as the things he would use his voice to describe disappear; a barren landscape is all that remains, and the poet's stripped, barren words reflect it. Instead of expanding his senses, like Whitman, and intensifying his touch, sight, hearing, so that he could contain the multitudes around him, Merwin's senses, as in "Some Last Questions," crumble and fade, become useless. . . . All that is left is silence. . . . The self is dying, its head returning to "ash" in the withering flames of the twentieth century. (pp. 58-60)

Merwin wanders rootless in this land, searching for a new landscape that might reflect the self and be rendered in his language. . . . Unlike Whitman, whose song defined and named himself, whose expanding country reflected his expanding self, Merwin's self seems distantly apart from what he finds to name and from his words themselves: "my words are the garment of what I shall never be . . . ". . . . (p. 60)

Merwin faces a void and seeks a new language to describe it, but the void he encounters is not the "Western blank" that Whitman joyously entered into, not a hopeful place for future imposition of form, but instead it is the final void, the place where man can no longer impose any form. . . . (p. 61)

"The Last One" views America's westering creation as both a genesis and an apocalypse: a beginning followed by a quick end. The poem is filled with imagery of Genesis, but it describes an anti-creation, and of the books in the Bible, Revelation is "the last one." Here again we have the American Adam (and Eve) who blithely decide to begin to cut into the virgin wilderness; Whitman's grand ideals of a new race are reduced to an empty "why not?" . . . Suddenly the

whole American westering process, as it does in Whitman, comes to a halt at the Pacific Ocean. . . . In Merwin's vision the final tree, unlike Whitman's last, dying redwood, sings no praise to the axe-bearing men who chop it down. . . . The men come in the morning and cut the last tree down, but when "They took it away its shadow stayed on the water." Bothered by this turn of events, man tries all of his ingenious ways to rid himself of the shadow: shining a light on it, covering it up, exploding it, and sending smoke up between the shadow and the sun. But all of this is to no avail; the shadow remains, and then it begins growing. . . . [The] shadow (a dark, all-devouring blob) grows on and on, like some anti-Whitmanian force (reversing Whitman's American expansion into and absorption of nature), which now expands into and absorbs (or obliterates) man. . . . (pp. 61-3)

This poem, says Harvey Gross, "dramatizes nature's revenge against men. . . ." . . . But it is not nature gaining its revenge so much as nature's *shadow*—a hollow, dark force of non-nature, of obliterated nature, a dark, non-palpable reminder of what used to be. It is the *lack* of nature that creeps back over the continent, obliterating man. It is the *exhaustion* of natural resources that causes the machines to cease functioning and leads man back to a primitive state, forced once again to use sticks and his hands, because there is no energy left for his machines. As so often in *The Lice*, Merwin here personifies emptiness or nothing; the Nothing of destroyed nature is what will kill man, finally; Americans think they have conquered the wilderness, only to find that No-Wilderness will conquer them. This poem demonstrates the anti-creation of America; the movement here is from west to east as the poem of America is erased, the creation of America wiped out, and nothing is left, finally, but barren, empty, lifeless land. The virgin She was destroyed, and now her destroyer, the American He, is likewise demolished. Nothing remains. There is no sense of hope further West in the Far East (no "Passage to India" as there was for the later Whitman); the only (faint) hope is in the few chastened men who escape with their shadows, left to gnaw the crust of the earth in some remote corner of the ruined country.

Later in *The Lice*, Merwin looks at America's continued attempts to expand westward by going to Viet Nam. In "Asians Dying," the same process of de-creation is described as Americans destroy another wilderness further West in the Far East. . . . Even if Americans seek to complete Columbus' original goal to voyage to the Far East, suggests Merwin, they will only lay it to waste, too. The frontier, for Merwin, seems to be the meeting point not of "savagery and civilization" (as [Frederick Jackson] Turner defined it), but of pure nature and ash, the great walker. (pp. 63-4)

Throughout *The Lice*, Merwin's soul tries to fly, to transcend, to surge ahead like a Whitmanian soul, but the future is dead now; we are preparing "For a Coming Extinction," . . . and so Whitman's spirit is gone—"The tall spirit who lodged here has / Left already"—and the spirit of the new poet is wingless; it cannot fly or transcend; there is no future to soar into, nothing to expand into and name. . . . (pp. 64-5)

The self in these poems is infested with lice, with diseased things it cannot find and kill and so must carry with it. Whitman's self sought to contain all, to embody past, present, and future; Merwin's self seeks to contain nothing, to empty itself of a dead past . . . , a shattered present, and a dead and destructive future. . . . Memory is no virtue for Merwin, for he seeks to break off from a meaningless past. . . . Not to repossess the past, then, is to be in total darkness, but at least free; the need here—and it is opposite the need of Whitman—is to *empty* the self, to find a new void within, and then to listen and learn from the silence of a de-created history: "Now all my teachers are dead except silence." . . . (pp. 65-6)

[With Merwin's anti-song, the] American self/poem/country has ended its expansion and has entered its inevitable diminishment. The signs are on the pages themselves: Whitman's poems expand and flow, filling the void of the blank page with seemingly endless sentences; Merwin's poems, in stark contrast, are fragments, remnants: short, quiet markings that leave most of the page unfilled; the gaping void is creeping back in, threatening the very existence of speech. It is not a creative void that Merwin faces, not something he expands into and absorbs; rather, it is a destructive void which opens its dark abyss, ready to swallow the poet and all of life with him. It is the anti-creation of America, and the American poet—in contrast to his earlier, arrogant stance—retreats in quiet terror. "Song of Myself" ends confidently, sure of the self, looking outward toward ever-expanding journeys even in death: "If you want me again look for me under your boot-soles. . . . / Missing me one place search another, / I stop somewhere waiting for you." *The Lice* ends in a muted echo of these last words, with the Merwin-self divided, unsure, tentative: "Where else am I walking even now / Looking for me." . . . (p. 66)

Merwin, then, speaks from the void, from past all frontiers in a place where there is nothing but a no-land of no-hope. When Merwin arrives at the Pacific, there are no Whitman-like journeys on to the Far East for meditative knowledge. And in "Inscription Facing Western Sea," Merwin experiences a vision that relates to Whitman's "Facing West from California's Shores," one of the few poems in which Whitman expresses despair at what the great American creation, now reaching its continental fulfillment, was becoming. . . . [In this poem], Merwin places himself at the Pacific shore, where the "Lord of each wave comes in" and the American expansion is "finished ten thousand miles." Seeking (like Whitman) the meaning of the completed creation, the poet sees in the waves only "riderless horses no messages"; no hope is carried over from the Far East. So the expanding American lays empty claim to the land and leaves. . . . And the wars and destruction that brought America to the West coast simply continue on. . . . (pp. 66-7)

This poem is in *The Carrier of Ladders,* the book in which Merwin attempts an imaginative descent to the American past, to the native; such descents form a vital and familiar pattern for twentieth century American poets. For Whitman, the American direction was West and to the future; for twentieth century American poets, the direction has become, more and more, down—through the various layers of what America is and has been—and to the past. It is not an easy process for Merwin, because generally he seeks, as we have noted, to strip himself of memory, even though he knows he would not exist if it weren't for the past. . . . But the past is deceptive; it consists of fragments, half-remembered details, imagined (fictional) events. So the past is

false, and true wisdom can only be found in the present, where the future loss of detail has not yet occurred. . . . (p. 67)

In "The Lake," Merwin approaches his descent, which finally occurs in the American sequence of poems ("The Approaches" through "The Removal"). . . . [The] poet is on the surface layer of a continental palimpsest, on the flood of America that has covered (or perhaps obliterated) the native cultures; he looks far down, under, to the past. . . . (pp. 67-8)

In "The Approaches," the poet sets out on his imaginative journey to the past, and is deceived in his first glimpse of the Indian, but wanders aimlessly on, hoping to find signs of the past. . . . (p. 68)

[Moving] westward in his imagination, Merwin looks at "The Trail into Kansas"; he tries to merge with the westering settlers to get a glimpse of the virgin land, but "The early wagons left no sign." He does find a "line pressed in the grass *we were here*" (wagon wheel ruts tracing the American journey), and he begins to sense what it was like to enter the new land. . . . As they journey, they sense they are watched, but their movement is inexorable, and they have no fear; the natives are no threat now. . . . With no affection for the land or the natives they displace, [these settlers] dig in. . . . [The] natives will helplessly disappear as the white Americans approach. Merwin, in his merger with the frontier settler, then, senses the Indian watching, but still cannot find him, see him. . . . (pp. 69-70)

[In "Western Country," the] Indian has appeared, but only to disappear; Merwin finds no regeneration in his descent to the past; the Indian rises only to vanish, quickly, again. Merwin's chilled, exhausted voice rises in anger as he watches the dispossession. . . . In "The Removal," dedicated "to the endless tribe," Merwin sees the natives as "The Homeless"; they are "the echoes [that] move in files [one step ahead of the "long files" of the white settlers] / their faces have been lost / . . . tongues from lost languages." . . . And the American destroys not just the native, but the native's mother, the land itself; they ravage the wilderness She that had supported the Indian. . . . Toward the end of this sequence . . . Merwin's voice has merged with the Indian; . . . like [Gary] Snyder, he speaks ("we") from the Indian's perspective. But unlike Snyder's native perspective, Merwin's voice comes to us faintly, from a distant, irretrievable past, not from an angry present. (p. 70)

John Wesley Powell, the one-armed explorer, becomes the emblem for Merwin of the white man's movement into the wilderness. Powell, a geologist and geographer, led the Geologic Survey (1881-94) that mapped out the West, imposed American lines upon the wilderness. . . . All America, suggests Merwin, was a one-armed explorer. . . . Like the lines on Powell's many maps, the hand he kept on the eastern side of the frontier was familiar, known, lined, visible. But no white man knew the western side of the frontier; like an invisible hand, it was unlined, unmapped, unknown, unseen. . . . He touched the wilderness only to have it disappear, to have it become known at the very touch, to be fused to the American creation. The "virgin half," the half Powell could never really touch, could be sensed only with the missing hand, the hand of the imagination. So Merwin, in this sequence, tries to touch the virgin land, lost now in time and space, with the "missing hand" of his imagination, for no actual, real descent is possible. (pp. 71-2)

Only in "Huckleberry Woman" does Merwin finally fully merge, descend and touch the She with invisible hands. She (a native woman) emerges from the land itself (she cannot emerge from a sense of history, for he, like most Americans, was not taught the Indians' history), and the ground she emerges from is America before it was owned, before the white man imposed property upon it. . . . [The] poet is united with her for a moment, but is in pain at the realization of the vast loss she represents, the pain of the immeasurable and bloody distance between her past and the poet's present. . . . But at least, for a moment, they are united. . . . And at this point Merwin crosses the frontier; his attempted mergers with American explorers and settlers cease, and he assumes the perspective of the native, becomes "we" with them, but it is a fading perspective; he is grasping for the Indian as he slips from him and disappears, inexorably. Thus the sequence ends with another Indian woman, a widow, captured by the whites; she is stripped of her land and her compatriots; she is mingled in marriage with the white man so that "everywhere I leave / one white footprint." (pp. 72-3)

Merwin's descent ends here; the vacant rooms of the natives' death are vacant rooms in himself, too, as the Indian disappears from his imagination and he returns to the present. Unlike Gary Snyder in *Turtle Island*, Merwin does not return to the present replenished with the native ways: he returns only with an affirmation of American destructiveness, of man's stupidity and inhumanity, and of an irreplaceable emptiness lying beneath this continent. Having re-taken the Whitmanesque American journey, having relived the creation of the country via the medium of poetry, Merwin finds the American creation to be not a creation at all, but a destruction, an imposed obliteration that he believes will be repaid in kind. The emptiness he finds in himself is the emptiness he finds at the heart of American history; it is the same emptiness that his poems embody, as his words struggle to fill space, short epitaphs scratched on the encroaching void. (p. 73)

> *L. Edwin Folsom, "Approaches and Removals: W. S. Merwin's Encounter with Whitman's America," in* Shenandoah *(copyright 1978 by Washington and Lee University; reprinted from* Shenandoah: The Washington and Lee University Review *with the permission of the Editor), Spring, 1978, pp. 57-73.*

*   *   *

MIDDLETON, Christopher   1926-

Middleton is a British poet, editor, and translator now living in the United States. Avowedly modernist in his poetic theories, Middleton writes oblique, sometimes obscurely allusive poetry. A translator of recognized skill, he is especially well respected for his translations of German poetry. (See also *Contemporary Authors*, **Vols. 13-16, rev. ed.)**

JOHN SIMON

Individual poems by [Christopher Middleton] in magazines always gave me the feeling that a genuine sensibility was at work here, and that if only I were reading some other poem of his, it would surely satisfy me completely. Well, *Torse 3* ranges from obscurity to banality, and the two successful

poems, "Amigos de Corazon" and "At Porthcothan," are both of them narrative, which I consider the least interesting form of poetry. Nonetheless, some of "Alba After Six Years," the first stanza of "Waterloo Bridge," and parts of "Rhododendron Estranged in Twilight," for all its indebtedness to Rilke, hold out promise of better things to come. (p. 464)

> *John Simon, in* The Hudson Review *(copyright © 1962 by The Hudson Review, Inc.; reprinted by permission), Vol. XV, No. 3, Autumn, 1962.*

THOM GUNN

[Christopher Middleton's] epigraph, a dictionary definition of his title [*Torse 3*], runs: "A developable surface; a surface generated by a moving straight line which at every instant is turning, in some plane or other through it, about some point or other in its length." If I understand this correctly, it is a description—a very apt and ingenious one—of poetry as craft, and in fact the concern of his book is usually more with how he is writing than with what he is writing.

Mr. Middleton uses several clearly distinguishable styles, ranging from that of direct statement to that of impenetrable obliquity. . . . The quick changes from style to style may be partly explained by the fact that *Torse 3* is a collection of twelve years' work, but even so the effect is less of an evolution in the writing than of a man trying on different coats.

Mr. Middleton is at his best in "Ode, on Contemplating Clapham Junction," "Objects at Brampton Ash," "The Guest," and "The Thousand Things." The textures of style in these poems never seem superimposed on the meaning. The oddity and particularity of the imagery are not gratuitous, because the sense exists in terms of it. (pp. 135-36)

> *Thom Gunn, in* The Yale Review *(© 1963 by Yale University; reprinted by permission of the editors), Autumn, 1963.*

IAN HAMILTON

Just as it is hard . . . in *Torse 3* to pin down Middleton to any one poetic manner, to say—for instance—that surrealistic flights of fancy were better for what he had to say than Dylanesque labyrinths of rhetoric, or the optical exercises of Wallace Stevens, so in his . . . *Nonsequences* it is enormously difficult—and in spite of the sub- or joint-title, *Selfpoems*—to discover *him*. The style is more consistent, a chaste, neutral, rather laborious diction that can tighten up where it needs to but is mostly low-pressure and very humbly painstaking; he toys a bit with pregnant line-breaks and odd layouts but never takes the full experimentalist plunge —he is most easy, in fact, with longer lines and fairly formal stanzas. What mostly worries, though, throughout the book is this absence of any unifying personal pressure, an absence which one suspects to be deliberate. This is not to ask for autobiography or straight confession . . .—but somehow to miss the sense that all the words come naturally or necessarily from the one mouth, or are even weighed by the same imaginative measure. Middleton writes about his cat, his travels, his family and so on, and does so with an intent accuracy of detail but they all appear as features of a drama that is kept firmly distant from whatever the poet might feel about it; a drama in which the liberated, uninterfering eye, is allowed to call the tune. Never far from each of his situations there seems to be the attendant voice of theory pressing the poet to withhold himself, to stand back and not spoil the action. . . . The danger in refusing to infiltrate your facts with feeling is that you will be tempted to encircle them instead with abstract point-making; this is a danger that Middleton on the whole avoids but when he does intrude to argue, or just to fill in the background of whatever he is observing, he can get very tortuous. (pp. 81-2)

There are stretches of very fine descriptive writing in this book and perhaps only a neutral eye could have achieved them (though the best poem 'Sketch of the Old Graveyard at Col de Castillon' is far from neutral). It is significant that it is 'An Englishman in Texas' who yearns 'to be present, now, to drop character' and to 'move, once free of himself, into some few things', for it has surely been America—not just its landscapes but its current poetic fashions—that has persuaded Middleton to vanish from his poems. It is not only that we do not know what the ventriloquist poet feels about his dummies . . . ; there is nothing rooted or centrally worrying to which his imagery, once he has set it rolling, can be said to owe allegiance or promise illumination; the liberated eye, he seems to say, cannot hope to be reliably informed, it can only properly see what it does not seek and what it does see ought not anyway to be credited with more 'truthfulness' than what it might have seen. (pp. 82-3)

The sort of 'pure poetry' that Middleton seems broadly to be aiming at, a poetry that lives out its perceptive space on the white page and has no obligation to quicken back into actual life, to be instructive, consolatory, or metaphoric, can get to look very academic unless at some point it faces up to its own philosophical implications; there is a good chance that he knows this and will move on to do it—true to form and in spite of theory, he can still pull some fine surprises. . . . (p. 83)

> *Ian Hamilton, in* London Magazine *(© London Magazine 1966), February, 1966.*

DOUGLAS DUNN

Christopher Middleton's work shows [his] way of reflecting the self-conscious seriousness of art and poetry. His new book *The Lonely Suppers of W. V. Balloon* is his best yet. He has also been one of the most scrupulous of British poets involved in following the innovations of modernism. Indeed his work strikes me as having derived itself from modern painting as much as poetry. Imagination is used as an instrument for the precise measurement of observations and experience. Forms of writing are austerely devised to allow imagination its exits from mind and poem without distorting the accuracy of pictures and sensations as these are presented. His concentration is almost painterly in poems like "A Cart with Apples." . . . Middleton apparently considers it a moral responsibility to present sensations as much as possible in their own terms. He writes of nature as-it-is instead of as-it-is-significant. . . .

But while he is inventive, and, in his new book, productive . . . , [a sheer relish and exuberance of language] simply is not there. . . . Something constrictingly intellectual, I suggest, prevents that. Indeed, that is the hallmark of the deliberating, over-deliberating, modernist poet. . . .

"Le nu provençal" . . . begins

The wooden shutter hanging open,
sunlight commands the shapes around the room.
A jug has left its ovals on a flagstone,
and tilts a little, as if listening in
to a kneecap or a buttock

which illustrates what I meant earlier by accuracy through the use of imagination. The lines have their own tilt of surprise and charm. Middleton recreates the photograph on which the poem is based, specifying almost invisibly a sort of "point of view", a conclusion about what has been seen which is not *exactly* a conclusion but left open to our own experience. That Middleton is able to use objects in this way, cleverly, but with no obtrusive gimmickry, suggests that he is a poet of considerable importance—an avant-garde poet we can actually *read*. (p. 80)

> *Douglas Dunn, in* Encounter *(© 1975 by Encounter Ltd.), September, 1975.*

JAY PARINI

I took up *The Lonely Suppers of W. V. Balloon* with some excitement. I expected a little more, perhaps; but I can recommend this volume nonetheless. . . . (pp. 139-40)

[Middleton's] art is an elaborate personal mosaic of "fragments shored against our ruins." Middleton cares deeply for ". . . things / their mass & contour / & all beginnings" ("In Balthazar's Village"). Objects interest him in the same way they did Picasso, and the poems often remind one of Cubist paintings; the artist views the same thing from different angles, and the work becomes a dance around the object, an exercise in perspective. Wallace Stevens is a precursor in this vein, of course, and Middleton's "A Cart of Apples" resembles a poem like "Sea Surface Full of Clouds," in which each stanza shifts the scene slightly, juggling the same elements in search of a new perspective. . . . This is the poetry of process; in effect, the poet enacts before his reader the progress from what Coleridge termed the Primary to the Secondary Imagination. . . . The poet sees the object once, then breaks it up into constituent elements and reassembles it. In doing so, he imitates God; he restores the image to his reader in its original freshness. This theme links Middleton back to the Romantic poets, especially the English Romantics, who developed the heterocosmic analogue—the parallel between writing poetry and creating the universe anew.

Perhaps the most attractive of Middleton's poems on this theme is "A Drive in the Country / Henri Toulouse-Lautrec," which takes the process of re-creation one step further. Based on a painting by Toulouse-Lautrec, it represents not a diffusion of a scene offered up by the Primary Imagination, but a scene already once dissipated and re-created by another artist. It begins with the original figures "Drawn out of the bones of light / Definite figures, a few, ordinary." . . . Middleton proceeds, in true Romantic fashion, reassembling the picture from its own parts, getting down to underlying geometric shapes which are lost to the Primary Imagination in its original perception. We now see the "Interior oval, its yolk, / A yellow trap, the crystal sun chariot— / Across the emerald cone, an egg, tilted." Middleton forces us to reconsider the world we have observed too hastily and with too little imagination. He would have us internalize the world, to become like Toulouse-Lautrec who "scooped up this other universe / Out of the escaping bloody mucus." Interior and exterior reflect and define each other, thus unifying our divided consciousness. Again, I am reminded of Stevens and his unflagging attempt to reconcile inner and outer worlds.

Middleton has a fine sense of the absurd. "The Gloves" begins with this image: "A pair of gloves on the floor / of an empty spacious institutional john." A few couplets later, he comments: "it seems, you'd think, smothering a giggle, / someone has been sucked down the john." This is funny and eerie at the same time. . . . The gloves, the deep image at the center of this poem, point to a region of terror beyond themselves, being signs, not symbols.

Unlike [Charles] Causley, who affects a simplicity in keeping with his traditionalist mode, Middleton makes few concessions to the reader. His poems are doggedly "modernist," full of private allusions and the *disjecta membra* of a scholar's workshop. We are provided with a marvellous tongue-in-cheek appendix of explanatory notes rivalling Eliot's addendum to *The Waste Land*. . . . [Like] his modernist precursors, Middleton takes his inspiration not from native sources but from the Continent. (pp. 140-42)

Taken as a whole, *The Lonely Suppers of W. V. Balloon* is a daring and, largely, successful book. It [reminds] . . . us that the dialectic of tradition and experiment (or of traditionalist and modernist verse) remains as vital today as it was in the early days of this century in America when Frost and Eliot were pretending to dismiss or, at least, dislike each other. (p. 144)

Jay Parini, in Chicago Review *(reprinted by permission of* Chicago Review; *copyright © 1977 by* Chicago Review), *Vol. 29, No. 1, 1977.*

ALAN YOUNG

There is little doubt that of contemporary poets Christopher Middleton is in theory among the best equipped to lead an English team into post-modern Europe. Two important practical considerations stand in the way of his being selected. First, he is not naturally a team-player, preferring the accomplishment of dazzling but solitary runs and displays of pure skill. Second, and more alarming, he likes to make up new rules and does not really seem to care which way he is playing, being likely therefore to nod the ball with equal nonchalance into either team's net. *Pataxanadu and Other Prose* . . . exhibits more than ever before those cultivated eccentricities of Middleton's art which by turns fascinate, mystify and exasperate his readers.

Pataxanadu, the title-work, consists of twenty-one short pieces most of which seem to take their inspiration from European modernist sources, including Kafka at his most nightmarish and cruelly bleak, the zany nihilism of Dada, the bizarre anarchism of both 'Pataphysics (Jarry's "science of imaginary solutions") and Surrealism, as well as from some quirky prose minimalism in vogue just now in the United States. I say, "seem to take" because the final piece of *Pataxanadu* is a very learned and Germanic "review" by a Doctor Philden Smither of an even more learned German treatise, over a thousand pages in length, on the history of short prose. This unbearably portentous mock-review cites scores of formal literary parallels to the *Pataxanadu* pieces, but it is also genuinely informative and critical. Its effect, therefore, is to create uncertainty in the reader and to put any critic on the defensive. I suspect, however, that although this effect is deliberately engineered it mirrors Middleton's basic doubts and confusions not only

about scholarship and literary criticism but also about his own art. *Pataxanadu* is a work of art because it explores the borderlands of the imagination where art, anti-art and non-art overlap. But . . . it is not certain that Middleton has shown enough faith in either his creative or critical powers to sustain such a difficult artistic endeavour, and, consequently, his imaginative energies sometimes flag, leaving his material unfused and in a raw state.

That art is merely an amusing but inconsequential game seems to be a basic assumption underlying five of the *Pataxanadu* pieces which make use of a technique of vocabulary substitution originally employed to transform classical French texts by that well-known Satrap of the College of 'Pataphysics, Raymond Queneau. Middleton sets to work on texts in English by Malory, Melville, Urquhart (his version of Rabelais), Charles Doughty and Swift. . . .

The common theme of journeys through words, forms and styles and into places and their people which is glimpsed in these five amusing "pataxanadus" is developed in other sections of the work. Here the good humour is not so sustained. Some of these prose poems are journeys into the realms of paranoia, nightmare and near-madness. Several of them are gratuitously violent. At times *Pataxanadu* comes near to existential despair but everything seems to happen in a world beyond despair where horror and suffering have become accepted routine and can be observed with irresponsible detachment, completely without feeling.

Middleton's most successful vein is political satire. "The Great Duck" . . . is a superb prose-cartoon of de Gaulle, and "The Pocket Elephants" is worthy of Swift in its recreation of the blinkered logic and language of doctrinaire revolutionary politics. "The Spaniards Arrive in Shanghai" shows Middleton at his best, too—a serene eighteenth-century Chinese-eye-view written with the sort of austere clarity of word and image that would have delighted Ezra Pound. But "Adelaide's Dream", written in blank verse, is sexual fantasy which does not attain either the imaginative levels reached in the same genre by Joyce and Auden or the formally inventive levels of Joyce and Parker Tyler. . . .

Middleton tells us that the nine pieces which constitute the "other prose" in the title have their own unity, but they occupy much the same fanciful and shapeless territory as *Pataxanadu*. Some well-worn props such as Lautréamont's sewing-machine and a neo-Dada piano-smashing routine add to the sense of *déjà-vu*. There are two or three very successful pieces, particularly "Ignorance", which is a powerful contemplation of the known dead—especially the dead of our time—haunting the world of our dying selves. "A Certain Silence" is an effective parody in which our period of history is simplified and falsified much as we have treated the Dark Ages but from the viewpoint of a much more rigidly organized and less liberal society than ours. Such imaginative and prophetic pieces as these make us wish that Christopher Middleton would try to take the art-game rather less earnestly and much more seriously.

Alan Young, "Playing the Art-Game," in The Times Literary Supplement *(© Times Newspapers Ltd. (London) 1978; reproduced from* The Times Literary Supplement *by permission), January 13, 1978, p. 38.*

MONTAGUE, John   1929-

Montague is an Irish poet, short story writer, critic, playwright, journalist, editor, and translator. Regarding poetry as "an attempt to chart the secret progress of one's life," he fills his work with a sense of Ireland that is as much public as it is private, as full of the past as of the present. The landscape and legends of the Irish countryside color Montague's verse, and patterns of Gaelic poetry are frequently evident. Thematically, his work portrays death, change, and destruction, often against the backdrop of a rapidly vanishing rural life. Montague has cited William Carlos Williams and Ezra Pound as major influences on his style, and critics have praised his clarity of imagery and careful craftsmanship. (See also *Contemporary Authors*, Vols. 9-12, rev. ed.)

CHRISTOPHER HUDSON

[John Montague's] short, terse lines [in *Tides*] keep fervent Irish rhetoric at bay, and give the love poems an uncommon precision. The best of these bring something fresh to the worn theme of the transience of love and the nearness of death. In 'Tracks', the act of lovemaking is set against the morning after, in the hotel, where 'giggling maids push / a trolley of fresh / linen down the corridor'. And in 'Premonition', one of the most accomplished of the poems, the poet dreams in nightmare of the torture of his girl, while at the same time in the nearby hospital she survives a difficult birth. He sleeps, and then, 'released from dream, / I lie in a narrow room; / Low-ceilinged as a coffin / The dawn prises open.'

The last two sections are disappointing. When John Montague writes about the sea, he doesn't have anything more to say than most poets writing about the sea. But there is one outstanding ballad poem, taken from the ninth century Irish, called 'The Hag of Beare'. It rings with the implacability of a Norse saga, and is proof enough that John Montague has a wider scope than love poetry in which to write really well. (p. 733)

> *Christopher Hudson, in* The Spectator *(© 1970 by* The Spectator; *reprinted by permission of* The Spectator), *December 5, 1970.*

DEREK MAHON

[Although] *The Rough Field* appears, at first glance, to be a collection of poems of great formal variety, it soon reveals itself as a prolonged meditation on a single theme: the death of a culture. This is one of several themes that have preoccupied Montague in his previous books . . . and here finds its fullest expression. Now and then one comes across a section that previously appeared in an earlier volume; but where this happens one is conscious of a self-contained poem growing in stature in relation to its new context. One doesn't read at random. The poem must be read consecutively, for it has a cumulative effect, gathering momentum as it proceeds. There are seventy pages of it, a carefully planned structure, and one puts it down with the realization that this is something very unusual, on this (Eastern) side of the Atlantic at least, where the younger poets have for so long eschewed elaborate conceptions and formal complexities. Irish poets have been more adventurous in this respect than English ones; and, as an Irish poem, *The Rough Field* deserves at least the same status as [Patrick] Kavanagh's *The Great Hunger,* of which it is in some measure a contemporary updating.

The book is divided into ten sections, covering such areas as family life, religion, the lost language (Gaelic), the local society, and the present state of affairs in Ireland, North and South. These are very approximate, and perhaps rather fatuous headings to impose on a work whose movement is one of symbols, allusions, flashbacks, epiphanies; whose technical sophistication, indeed, makes Kavanagh look like a Victorian writer of sentimental songs. And yet there is, inevitably in a poem of this length, a substantial narrative and discursive content, a *prose* that is its own kind of poetry and on which the lyric bridge is built. Like [Hugh] MacDiarmid's *A Drunk Man Looks at the Thistle,* or the poems of Louis MacNeice, it is about real things, "the ordinary universe." . . . Montague is not a metaphysician: he is a historian and autobiographer, with the result that his finest flights—"Like Dolmens Round My Childhood," "The Wild Dog Rose"—take off from mundane, paraphrasable situations: the eccentricities of neighbours, a conversation with an aged spinster. The formal ingenuity sometimes looks like an attempt to solve the narrative problem, to break up material that would in the past have lent itself most naturally to Wordsworthian blank verse. This works, on the whole, as changes of tone and focus dictate changes of tempo. Where it fails the failure is generally extraneous to the text itself, being largely a matter of the marginal transcription of historical records, some well-chosen and commenting pointedly on the events described, but most, I fear, gratuitous and distracting.

I find four of the ten sections particularly interesting. Not necessarily because they are more successful than the others, but because they illustrate, in their different ways, significant strengths and weaknesses; because they have great *character;* and because they contain much that is new and unique in Irish poetry. . . . It is in these sections that Montague is at his liveliest and most inventive, forgoing elegy for satire, narrative for rhetoric, explanation for exclamation. (pp. 133-34)

Montague has been criticized for "using" the present crisis in Ulster as raw material for his poetry. (His critics do not, however, accuse Yeats of doing the same thing at an earlier period.) The criticism seems to me at best an injustice founded in misunderstanding—at worst a cheap jibe. The implication, an essentially philistine one, is that something as frivolous as poetry has no business concerning itself with something as serious as human suffering. . . . Ireland is central to Montague's myth, and has been since his first booklet, *Forms of Exile,* was published . . . in 1960. He would be dishonest if he didn't follow through the inner logic of his commitment. With that said, I must express my doubts about "A New Siege." . . . [It] seems to me to be marred by a certain stridency, by a willed determination to make cosmic significance out of a street-fight. . . . At the risk of appearing philistine, even callous, oneself, one is tempted to say, come now, is what happens in Derry really all *that* important? In this image drawn from physics, and in his invocation of the student uprisings in Paris and Berlin, he risks pretentiousness—because he tries to impose an intellectual order on something that simply will not be ordered in that way. The poetry is deafened by slogans. And then, superbly, he redeems himself in a quiet closing section, "The Wild Dog Rose." . . . [This is a rich and complex work by] the best Irish poet of his generation. The wealth of re-created history, the vivid flashes of autobiography, the dramatic visual sense, the anger and the wit, together with the subtly orchestrated music of the verse, will be sufficiently evident to the reader. This is John Montague's first peak. Others will follow. (pp. 136-37)

Derek Mahon, in The Malahat Review (© Derek Mahon, 1973), July, 1973.

BENEDICT KIELY

If I were . . . beginning a re-reading of John Montague, or if I were advising others where to begin reading him, I would go, and send those others to the heart of his collection, "Tides." . . . And to two works there, one of them a quite horrifying prose-poem entitled with a cold irony that is typical of Montague: "The Huntsman's Apology." (pp. 1-2)

The second work is brief, called "A Meeting," and is from the ninth-century Irish. . . . (p. 2)

The startling thing is that both are poems about varieties of love, or about love at different stages, of development or decay. They come at the heart of a book that holds other fine love-poems and in which the blurb, with perhaps an echo of the poet's voice, says with a great deal of justification that the directness and passion of Montague's love-poems have been admired, and his feeling for people and landscape, and claims that in this collection, "Tides," all these are seen as a part of a larger struggle where life and death are interwoven like the rhythms of the sea. (pp. 2-3)

Montague, lean and sharp and soft and sensible, as Berowne uses the word, sees his lovers absurdly balanced on the springs of a bed, shadows swooping, quarreling like winged bats, bodies turning like fish "in obedience to the pull and tug of your great tides." A wind-swept holiday resort on the shore of the North sea becomes a perfect setting for the monster of unhappiness, "an old horror movie come true," to crawl out of the moving deeps and threaten love. . . . It is a bitter sort of comedy.

It is scarcely then by accident that he places in the middle of all these love-poems the best rendering, from the Irish of the ninth-century, of the love-dirge, or bitter memory of past loves and bitter consciousness of bodily decay, of the *Cailleach Beara,* the Hag or Old Woman of Beare: which is the southwestern peninsula between Bantry Bay and Kenmare Bay, the land of the O'Sullivans. The Cailleach, a formidable ancient, overburdened with all knowledge and weariness and sometimes, all wickedness, is a recurring figure in Celtic mythologies and shows her face, on occasions and on various bodies, in Montague's poetry.

A one-eyed hag, she—or the poet who interpreted her, as Montague does eleven centuries later—reckons that her right eye has been taken as a down-payment on her claim to heaven; a ray in the left eye has been spared to her that she may grope her way to heaven's gate. Her life has come to be a retreating sea with no tidal return. Gaunt with poverty she, who once wore fine petticoats, now hunts for rags to cover her body. (p. 3)

In this collection, one of the . . . most striking poems is certainly: "Life Class." It opens calmly, clinically, a cool detailed survey of the body there to be studied, the hinge of the ankle-bone defining the flat space of a foot, the calf's heavy curve sweeping down against the bony shin, the arm cascading from shoulder-knob to knuckle, shapes as natural, as inanimate almost, as sea-worn caves, as pools, boulders, tree-trunks. This is the artist in the neolithic cavern

recording in wonderment the skeleton of the life he sees, an art that may have been as utilitarian as modern engineering. (p. 4)

There is much more in the collection, "Tides," than I have here indicated: more than love and lust, and woman, young and old, and ancient mythologies. There are, for instance, wise words to and about Beckett, and about Joyce, and a moving farewell to places and parents, and a seagull's view of his own town which misses only history and religion: which Montague is not to miss when later he takes a more-than-seagull's view of Garvaghey (Garbh Achaidh), "The Rough Field," where he comes from. The collection, too, is rich, as is his earlier poetry, with the preoccupations of a man who has known, and to the bone, the ways of three countries: Ireland, France and the USA. (p. 5)

[Generally throughout] "Poisoned Lands," and in the following collection, "A Chosen Light," [Montague] has hammered his thoughts, and his places, into unity, and, also, the past and present of his own country. The shape of his mind has been made clear and his style has a sinewy sort of seeming nonchalance on which he is steadily to work and rework giving "slight but memoried life" a deep, universal significance. He casts a careful eye even on an old-style country byre and sees the milking-machine at work, and the old ways changing. . . .

He walks among mythologies on the grassy mounds of the hill of Tara, that was the residence of the High Kings of pre-Christian Ireland, and wonders was it a Gaelic acropolis or a smoky hovel, and sees wolf-hounds "lean as models," follow at the heels of heroes out of the sagas: a sardonic bringing-together of the images of two ages. . . . The strangest variety of objects and people become symbols before his clear and wondering eye. . . . [His] is a rich and varied world. . . .

By the end of his second collection, "A Chosen Light," he has gathered together and arranged like ornaments his foreign experiences, he can cast a calm eye even if it is an eye of foreboding, on his own country: and the calmness and foreboding can burst into bawdy laughter. . . . (p. 9)

Utter assurance comes to Montague with the composition and arrangement of "The Rough Field," his most remarkable book and one of the most interesting statements made in this century about Ireland past and present. (p. 10)

It is a unity, a movement and sequence of poems as strong and steady as the mountain stream descending on the lowlands to define a world, taking with it the past and present of that one small backward place, but a place over-burdened with history: for it is part of the country of the great Hugh O'Neill who warred for nine years against Elizabeth the first of England. Montague glosses his text, indeed, with fragments of ancient history, with a clipping now and then from current news, even with a bigot's letter pushed through a letter-box and ranting against the Romish wafer. (pp. 10-11)

Family history and his own personal agony, and the history of the place over three and a half centuries, onward from the end of the great O'Neill to the calamities of the present, are all twisted together, strands in a strong rope. . . .

Nowhere in the book is the tight razor-edged discipline of his verse and his uncanny knack for gathering the ages together more on display than in the movement that deals with the present problems of Derry City! "A Second Siege." . . . An extra dimension is introduced from his experiences elsewhere and Irish troubles are seen as part of the world's experiences. He was in Berkeley, California, for the beginning of the campus tumults there, and bombs in the Bogside and napalm in Vietnam are all part of the human condition. . . . (p. 11)

[He] surveys a world that may, as because of the San Adreas fault, California may, fall apart any of these days. Although he can be agonized and terrified by memory it could still be that he is happiest with those old people who, like dolmens, surrounded his childhood: Jamie MacCrystal who sang to himself a broken song without tune: Maggie Owens who was "a well of gossip defiled." . . . (p. 12)

Since "The Rough Field" there have been two collections, "A Slow Dance" and "The Great Cloak." . . . [You] will find that they richly reward reading and re-reading, right through—so to speak, for the pace, arrangement and continuity are insistent, and they amply justify Robin Skelton's strong claim that Montague is: "clearly one of the most skilled and interesting poets alive, and one of the most original and disturbing." The poet . . . has the confidence and assurance, and for very good reasons, that the young man thirty years ago pretended to have. The pared-down lines are rich in irony, humanity, the sense of transience and mortality in love, in men and women, in nations and civilizations: a keen, exact expression.

That slow dance is a dance of life and death, of calm observation alternating with strange fantasy. . . . He sees a sawmill on the road to Geneva; sees life emerge, a calf licked clean by a cow, from the cave of an old limekiln in Ireland. . . . Sees an old French colonel in his final retreat in a Normandy chateau. Writes a lament "so total" that it mourns no one but the great globe itself.

"The Great Cloak" is an intensely personal poem-sequence about the death of love, and abandonment and betrayal, about the birth and growth of a new love. . . . The only poem I can compare it with, and it is very much a unity and no haphazard collection, is George Meredith's, "Modern Love": yet if it can, at times, be tense with agony and regret, it does not end as Meredith does in a sort of half-resigned despair, but rises to hope and renewal and a new life being born. No mortal who has realized that life is not a straight line can fail to be moved by this poem: happier people should cross themselves and thank whatever gods there be for something like good fortune. (pp. 12-13)

Benedict Kiely, "John Montague: Dancer in a Rough Field," in The Hollins Critic (copyright 1978 by Hollins College), December, 1978, pp. 1-14.

DESMOND GRAHAM

[*The Great Cloak* is] a record of a love relationship, shifting from the historical embedding of *The Rough Field* into a more personal key; but though Montague is a finely accomplished poet, I found this latest collection somewhat disappointing. . . . [It] fails to achieve an adequate subtlety of response; its language is on the whole . . . highly inflected, rhetorically resonant . . . , but there seems some subtle mismatching between that linguistic force and the relative uncomplexity of "content." . . . Montague's imagery seems too rhetorical, explicit and "head-on" for his emotions; so that when he ends a poem about the breakdown of a rela-

tionship with 'We shall never be / what we were, again. / Old love's refrain.' one feels like saying well, quite—that's about as far as it goes. In poem after poem, the craft is channelled into a web of imagery which, while officially *supporting* the dominant feeling, in fact tends to usurp it, leaving the emotional response itself fairly unremarkable. . . . (pp. 75-6)

Desmond Graham, in Stand (copyright © by Stand), Vol. 20, No. 1 (1978-79).

* * *

MOORE, Marianne 1887-1972

Moore was an American poet, translator, essayist, and editor. Her poetry is characterized by the technical and linguistic precision with which she reveals her acute observations of human character. Indeed, her role as "observer" is evident in the remarkable attention to detail found in her poetic descriptions, whether of an object, an animal, or the human condition. The later poems reflect a sense of moral judgment, in contrast to the objectivity of Moore's earlier work. Although her early poetry has often been connected to the Imagist school, her independence of style and vision have established her as a poet unique in her own right. (See also *CLC*, Vols. 1, 2, 4, 8, 10, and *Contemporary Authors*, Vols. 1-4, rev. ed.; obituary, Vols. 33-36, rev. ed.)

T. S. ELIOT

I have read Miss Moore's poems a good many times, and always with exactly the same pleasure, and satisfaction in something quite definite and solid. (p. 48)

Miss Moore's poems always read very well aloud. That quality is something which no system of scansion can define. It is not separable from the use of words, in Miss Moore's case the conscious and complete appreciation of every word, and in relation to every other word, as it goes by. I think that Those Various Scalpels is an excellent example for study. Here the rhythm depends partly upon the transformation-changes from one image to another, so that the second image is superposed before the first has quite faded, and upon the dexterity of change of vocabulary from one image to another. "Snow sown by tearing winds on the cordage of disabled ships:" has that Latin, epigrammatic succinctness, laconic austerity, which leaps out unexpectedly (altogether in Talisman).

> your raised hand
> an ambiguous signature:

is a distinct shift of manner; it is not an image, but the indication of a fulness of meaning which is unnecessary to pursue.

> blood on the stone floors of French châteaux, with
> regard to which guides are so affirmative:

is a satirical (consciously or unconsciously it does not matter) refinement of that pleasantry (not flippancy, which is something with a more definite purpose) of speech which characterizes the American language, that pleasantry, uneasy, solemn, or self-conscious, which inspires both the jargon of the laboratory and the slang of the comic strip. Miss Moore works this uneasy language of stereotypes—as of a whole people playing uncomfortably at clenches and clevelandisms—with impeccable skill into her pattern. . . . The merit consists in the combination, in the other point of view which Miss Moore possesses at the same time. What her imitators cannot get are the swift dissolving images.... (pp. 49-50)

Miss Moore's relation to the soil is not a simple one, or rather it is to various soils—to that of Latium and to that of Attica I believe (or at least to that of the Aegean littoral) as well as most positively to the soil (well top-dressed) of America. (p. 50)

And there is one final, and "magnificent" compliment: Miss Moore's poetry is as "feminine" as Christina Rossetti's, one forgets that it is written by a woman; but with both one never thinks of this particularly as anything but a positive virtue. (p. 51)

> T. S. Eliot, "Marianne Moore (1923)," (copyright 1923 by T. S. Eliot; reprinted by permission of Mrs. Valerie Eliot), in The Dial, December, 1923 (and reprinted in Marianne Moore: A Collection of Critical Essays, edited by Charles Tomlinson, Prentice-Hall, Inc., 1970, pp. 48-51).

R. P. BLACKMUR

In Miss Moore's work inverted commas are made to perform significantly and notably and with a fresh nicety which is part of her contribution to the language. Besides the normal uses to determine quotation or to indicate a special or ironic sense in the material enclosed or as a kind of minor italicization, they are used as boundaries for units of association which cannot be expressed by grammar and syntax. They are used sometimes to impale their contents for close examination, sometimes to take their contents as in a pair of tongs for gingerly or derisive inspection, sometimes to gain the isolation of superiority or vice versa—in short for all the values of setting matter off, whether in eulogy or denigration. As these are none of them arbitrary but are all extensions and refinements of the common uses, the reader will find himself carried along, as by rhyme, to full appreciation.... If it were a mere exercise of Miss Moore's and our own in punctuation, then as it depended on nothing it would have nothing to articulate. But Miss Moore's practice and our appreciation are analogous in scope and importance to the score in music. By a refinement of this notion Mr. Eliot observes in his Introduction [to Selected Poems] that "many of the poems are in exact, and sometimes complicated formal patterns, and move with the elegance of a minuet." It is more than that and the very meat of the music, and one need not tire of repeating it because it ought to be obvious. The pattern establishes, situates, and organizes material which without it would have no life, and as it enlivens it becomes inextricably a part of the material; it participates as well as sets off. (pp. 67-8)

[Miss Moore] couples external action and rhyme; and for her the expedient form is a pattern of elegant balances and compact understatement. It is part of the virtue of her attack upon the formless in life and art that the attack should show the courtesy and aloofness of formal grace. (p. 69)

Analysis cannot touch but only translate for preliminary purposes the poem the return to which every sign demands. What we do is simply to set up clues which we can name and handle and exchange whereby we can make available all that territory of the poem which we cannot name or handle but only envisage. We emphasize the technique, as the artist did in fact, in order to come at the substance which the technique employed. Naturally, we do not em-phasize all the aspects of the technique since that would involve discussion of more specific problems of language than there are words in the poem, and bring us, too, to all the problems of meaning which are not there. [Miss Moore commented in "Picking and Choosing": "We are not daft about the meaning but this familiarity with wrong meanings puzzles one."] We select, rather, those formal aspects which are most readily demonstrable: matters like rhyme and pattern and punctuation, which appear to control because they accompany a great deal else; and from these we reach necessarily, since the two cannot be detached except in the confusion of controversy, into the technical aspects, the conventional or general meanings of the words arranged by the form.... We show, by an analysis which always conveniently stops short, a selection of the ways in which the parts of a poem bear on each other; and we believe, by experience, that we thereby become familiar with what the various tensions produce: the poem itself. (pp. 69-70)

[We] find Miss Moore constantly presenting images ... most explicit but of a kind containing inexhaustibly the inexplicable—whether in gesture or sentiment. She gives what we know and do not know; she gives in ["Poetry"], for example, "elephants pushing, a wild horse taking a roll, a tireless wolf under a tree," and also "the baseball fan, the statistician." We can say that such apposites are full of reminding, or that they make her poem husky with unexhausted detail, and we are on safe ground; but we have not said the important thing, we have not named the way in which we are illuminated, nor shown any sign at all that we are aware of the major operation performed ... by such appositions. They are as they succeed the springboards—as when they fail they are the obliterating quicksands—of ecstasy. In their variety and their contrasts they force upon us two associated notions; first we are led to see the elephant, the horse, the wolf, the baseball fan, and the statistician, as a group or as two groups detached by their given idiosyncrasies from their practical contexts, we see them beside themselves, for themselves alone, like the lace in Velasquez or the water-lights in Monet; and secondly, I think, we come to be aware, whether consciously or not, that these animals and these men are themselves, in their special activities, obsessed, freed, and beside themselves. There is an exciting quality which the pushing elephant and the baseball fan have in common; and our excitement comes in feeling that quality, so integral to the apprehension of life, as it were beside and for itself, not in the elephant and the fan, but in terms of the apposition in the poem. (pp. 72-3)

[The] reader can measure for himself exactly how valuable this quality is; he can read the "same" poem with the quality dominant and again with the quality hardly in evidence. On page 31 in Observations the poem appears in thirteen lines; in Selected Poems it has either twenty-nine or thirty, depending on how you count the third stanza. For myself, there is the difference between the poem and no poem at all, since the later version delivers—where the earlier only announces—the letter of imagination.... [In] the earlier poem half the ornament and all the point are lacking. What is now clearly the dominant emphasis—on poets as literalists of the imagination—which here germinates the poem and gives it career, is not even implied in the earlier version. The poem did not get that far, did not, indeed, become a poem at all. What is now a serious poem on the nature of esthetic reality remained then a half-shrewd, half-pointless conceit against the willfully obscure. But it is not,

I think, this rise in level from the innocuous to the penetrating, due to any gain in the strength of Miss Moore's conception. The conception, the idea, now that we know what it is, may be as readily inferred in the earlier version as it is inescapably felt in the later, but it had not in the earlier version been articulated and composed, had no posture to speak of, had lacked both development and material to develop: an immature product. (pp. 73-4)

[The] earlier version shows a failure in the technique of making a thought, the very substantial failure to know when a thought is complete and when it merely adverts to itself and is literally insufficient. There is also—as perhaps there must always be in poetry that fails—an accompanying insufficiency of verbal technique, in this instance an insufficience of pattern and music as compared to the later version. Not knowing, or for the moment not caring, what she had to do, Miss Moore had no way of choosing and no reason for using the tools of her trade. Miss Moore is to an extent a typographic poet, like Cummings or Hopkins; she employs the effects of the appearance and arrangement of printed words as well as their effects sounding in the ear: her words are in the end far more *printed* words than the words of Yeats, for example, can ever be. And this is made clear by the earlier version which lacks the *printed* effect rather than by the later version which exhibits it. . . .

[The] later version looks better on the page, has architecture which springs and suggests deep interiors; we notice the rhymes and the stanza where they are missing and how they multiply heavily, *both to the ear and the eye,* in the last stanza; we notice how the phrasing is marked, how it is shaded, and how, in the nexus of the first and second stanzas, it is momentarily confused: we notice, in short, not how the poem was made—an operation intractable to any description—but what about it, now that it is made, will strike and be felt by the attentive examiner. Then turning back to the earlier version, knowing that it has pretty much the same heart, give as much occasion for ecstasy, we see indefeasibly why it runs unpersuasively through the mind, and why the later, matured version most persuasively invades us. . . .

[The] concept or idea or thought of the poem is not difficult, new or intense, but its presentation, in the later version, is all three. She found, as Yeats would say, the image to call out the whole idea; that was one half. The other half was finding how to dress out the image to its best advantage. . . . (p. 74)

[Miss Moore] resorts, or rises like a fish, continually to the said thing, captures it, sets it apart, points and polishes it to bring out just the special quality she heard in it. Much of her verse has the peculiar, unassignable, indestructible authority of speech overheard—which often means so much precisely because we do not know what was its limiting, and dulling, context. The quality in her verse that carries over the infinite possibilities of the overheard, is the source and agent of much of her power to give a sense of invading reality; and it does a good deal to explain what Mr. Eliot, in his Introduction, calls her authoritativeness of manner—which is a different thing from a sense of reality.

It does not matter that Miss Moore frequently works the other way round, abstracting her phrase from a guidebook, an advertisement, or a biography; what matters is that whatever her sources she treats her material as if it were

quoted, isolated speech, and uses it, not as it was written or said—which cannot be known—but for the purpose which, taken beside itself, seems in it paramount and most appropriate. . . . [She combines such phrases] in such a way that they declare themselves more fully, because isolated, emphasized. . . . The poet's labor in this respect is similar to that of a critical translation where, by selection, exclusion, and rearrangement a sense is emphasized which was found only on a lower level and diffusely in the original; only here there is no damage by infidelity but rather the reward of deep fidelity to what, as it turns out, was really there waiting for emphasis.

But besides the effect of heightened speech, Miss Moore relies also and as deeply upon the rhetorical device of understatement—by which she gains, as so many have before her, a compression of substance which amounts to the fact of form. (p. 77)

She is an expert in the visual field at compelling the incongruous association to deliver, almost startlingly to ejaculate, the congruous, completing image: e.g., in the poem about the pine tree called "The Monkey Puzzle,"—"It knows that if a nomad may have dignity, Gibraltar has had more." . . . (p. 79)

Although many of the poems are made on intricate schemes of paired and delayed rhymes—there being perhaps no poem entirely faithful to the simple quatrain, heroic, or couplet structure—I think of no poem which for its rhymes is so admirable and so alluring as "Nine Nectarines and Other Porcelain." Granting that the reader employs a more analytical pronunciation in certain instances, there is in the last distich of each stanza a rhyme half concealed and half overt. These as they are first noticed perhaps annoy and seem, like the sudden variations, trills, mordents and turns in a Bach fugue, to distract from the theme, and so, later, to the collected ear, seem all the more to enhance it, when the pleasure that may be taken in them for themselves is all the greater. More precisely, if there be any ears too dull, Miss Moore rhymes the penultimate syllable of one line with the ultimate syllable of the next. The effect is of course cumulative; but the cumulus is of delicacy not mass; it is cumulative, I mean, in that in certain stanzas there would be no rhyme did not the precedent pattern make it audible. If we did not have

> a bat is winging. It
> is a moonlight scene, bringing. . . .

we should probably not hear

> and sets of Precious Things
> dare to be conspicuous.

What must be remembered is that anyone can arrange syllables, the thing is to arrange syllables at the same time you write a poem, and to arrange them as Miss Moore does, on four or five different planes at once. Here we emphasize mastery on the plane of rhyme. But this mastery, this intricacy, would be worthless did the poem happen to be trash. (p. 81)

[There] is no meeting Miss Moore face to face in the forest of her poems and saying This is she, this is what she means and is: tautology is not the right snare for her or any part of her. The business of her poetry (which for us is herself) is to set things themselves delicately conceived in relations so fine and so accurate that their qualities, mutually stirred, will produce a new relation: an emotion. Her poems answer the question, What will happen in poetry, what emotion will transpire, when these things have been known or felt beside each other? (pp. 81-2)

With Miss Moore . . . there is less a freeing of emotions and images under the aegis of the title notion, than there is a deliberate delineation of specific poetic emotions with the title notion as a starting point or spur: a spur to develop, compare, entangle, and put beside the title notion a series of other notions, which may be seen partly for their own sakes in passing, but more for what the juxtapositions conspire to produce. . . . Miss Moore's emotions are special and specific, producing something almost a contraction of the given material, and so are themselves their own symbols. . . . It is not easy to say what one of Miss Moore's longer poems is about, either as a whole or in places. The difficulty is not because we do not know but precisely because we do know. . . . The parts stir each other up . . . and the aura of agitation resulting, profound or light as it may be, is what it is about. Naturally, then, in attempting to explain one of these poems you find yourself reading it through several times, so as not to be lost in it and so that the parts will not only follow one another as they must, being words, but will also be beside one another as their purpose requires them to be. This perhaps is why Miss Moore could write of literature as a phase of life: "If one is afraid of it, the situation is irremediable; if one approaches it familiarly what one says of it is worthless."

It is a method not a formula; it can be emulated not imitated; for it is the consequence of a radical leaning, of more than a leaning an essential trope of the mind: the forward stress to proceed, at any point, to proceed from one thing to another, crossing all gaps regardless, but keeping them all in mind. (pp. 82-3)

Miss Moore has a habit of installing her esthetics in her poems as she goes along. . . .

[Her method] is not only pervasive but integral to her work. It is integral to the degree that, with her sensibility being what it is, it imposes limits more profoundly than it liberates poetic energy. And here is one reason—for those who like reasons—for the astonishing fact that none of Miss Moore's poems attempt to be major poetry, why she is content with smallness in fact so long as it suggests the great by implication. Major themes are not susceptible of expression through a method of which it is the virtue to produce the idiosyncratic in the fine and strict sense of that word. Major themes, by definition of general and predominant interest, require for expression a method which produces the general in terms not of the idiosyncratic but the specific, and require, too, a form which seems to *contain* even more than to *imply* the wholeness beneath. The first poem in [*Selected Poems*], "Part of a Novel, Part of a Poem, Part of a Play," comes as near to major expression as her method makes possible; and it is notable that here both the method and the content are more nearly "normal" than we are used to find. Elsewhere, though the successful poems achieve their established purposes, her method and her sensibility, combined, transform her themes from the normal to the idiosyncratic plane. The poem "Marriage," an excellent poem, is never concerned with either love or lust, but with something else, perhaps no less valuable, but certainly, in a profound sense, less complete. (p. 84)

There is no sex anywhere in her poetry. No poet has been so chaste; but it is not the chastity that rises from an awareness—healthy or morbid—of the flesh, it is a special chastity aside from the flesh—a purity by birth and from the void. There is thus, by parallel, no contact by disgust in her work, but rather the expression of a cultivated distaste; and this is indeed appropriate, for within the context of purity disgust would be out of order. Following the same train, it may be observed that of all the hundreds of quotations and references in her poems none is in itself stirring, although some are about stirring things; and in this she is the opposite of Eliot, who as a rule quotes the thing in itself stirring; and here again her practice is correct. Since her effects are obtained partly by understatement, partly by ornament, and certainly largely by special emphasis on the quiet and the quotidian, it is clear that to use the thing obviously stirring would be to import a sore thumb, and the "great" line would merely put the poem off its track. . . . [Although] she refers eulogistically many times to the dazzling color, vivid strength, and torrential flow of Hebrew poetry, the tone of her references is quiet and conversational.

By another approach we reach the same conclusion, not yet named. Miss Moore writes about animals, large and small, with an intense detached intimacy others might use in writing of the entanglements of people. She writes about animals as if they were people minus the soilure of overweeningly human preoccupations, to find human qualities freed and uncommitted. Compare her animal poems with those of D. H. Lawrence. In Lawrence you feel you have touched the plasm; in Miss Moore you feel you have escaped and come on the idea. The other life is there, but it is round the corner, not so much taken for granted as obliviated, not allowed to transpire, or if so only in the light ease of conversation: as we talk about famine in the Orient in discounting words that know all the time that it *might* be met face to face. In Miss Moore life is remote (life as good *and* evil) and everything is done to keep it remote; it is reality removed, but it is nonetheless reality, because we *know* that it is removed. . . . Let us say that everything she gives is minutely precise, immediately accurate to the witnessing eye, but that both the reality under her poems and the reality produced by them have a nostalgic quality, a hauntedness, that cannot be reached, and perhaps could not be borne, by these poems, if it were.

Yet remembering that . . . her poems are expedient forms for ecstasies apprehended, and remembering, too, both the tradition of romantic reticence she observes and the fastidious thirst for detail, how could her poems be otherwise, or more? Her sensibility—the deeper it is the more persuaded it cannot give itself away—predicted her poetic method; and the defect of her method, in its turn, only represents the idiosyncrasy of her sensibility: that it, like its subject matter, constitutes the perfection of standing aside.

It is provisionally worth noting that Miss Moore is not alone but characteristic in American literature. Poe, Hawthorne, Melville (in *Pierre*), Emily Dickinson, and Henry James, all—like Miss Moore—shared an excessive sophistication of surfaces and a passionate predilection for the genuine—though Poe was perhaps not interested in too much of the genuine; and all contrived to present the conviction of reality best by making it, in most readers' eyes, remote. (pp. 85-6)

R. P. Blackmur, "The Method of Marianne

Moore" (1935), in Language as Gesture *(copyright 1952 by R. P. Blackmur; reprinted by permission of Harcourt Brace Jovanovich, Inc.), Harcourt, 1952 (and reprinted in* Marianne Moore: A Collection of Critical Essays, *edited by Charles Tomlinson, Prentice-Hall, Inc., 1970, pp. 66-86).*

LOUISE BOGAN

Impressionist critics, because they have attributed to Miss Moore many of their own manias and virtues, have left her actual virtue—her "secret"—untouched. She belongs to a lineage against which the impressionist and the "modernist" have for so long rebelled that by now they are forgetful that it ever existed. In Miss Moore two traditions that modernism tends to ignore, meet. She is, on the one hand, a nearly pure example of that inquisitive, receptive kind of civilized human being which flourished from the high Renaissance through the high Roccoco: the disciple of the "new" as opposed to the "old" learning, the connoisseur, the humane scholar—to whom nothing was alien, and for whom man was the measure of all. Her method, in her "observations," has been compared, and rightly, to that of Francis Bacon and Sir Thomas Browne. But we soon come upon in her work another, angularly intersecting, line. Miss Moore, child of Erasmus, cousin to Evelyn, and certainly close kin to the Mozart who refracted "Don Giovanni" as though from a dark crystal, does not develop, as we might expect, toward full Baroque exuberance. She shows—and not to her demerit—a definite influence derived from that Protestantism against whose vigor the vigor of the Baroque was actively opposed. Miss Moore is a descendant not of Swiss or Scotch, but of Irish presbyters. She is, therefore, a moralist (though a gentle one) and a stern—though flexible—technician.

It is a not infrequent American miracle, this combination of civilized European characteristics in one gifted nature. Miss Moore, American to her backbone, is a striking example of a reversion toward two distinct kinds of heritage; of an atavism which does not in any degree imply declension or degeneration of the original types involved. She does not write *à la maniére de* . . . She produces originals. She does not resemble certain seventeenth century writers; she might be one of them. She stands at the confluence of two great traditions, as they once existed, and as they no longer exist. "Sentiment" and the shams of the *pasticheur* cannot touch her, since she ends where they begin.

Examine her passion for miscellany: it is a seventeenth century passion. . . . Alive to the meaning of variation, Miss Moore can examine what the modern world displays, with an unmodern eye. This is her value to us. (pp. 198-99)

The tone of her poems often derives from her "other," Protestant inheritance. Are not many of her poems sermons in little, preached in the "plain style" but with overtones of a grander eloquence? Are not many of them discourses which are introduced, or subsumed, by a text? Note the frequent cool moral that she extracts from her poems' complexities; and the dexterity with which, from disparate and often heavy facts, she produces a synthesis as transparent and as inclusive as air. Her sensibilities are Counter-Reformation; her emotion and intellect Protestant.

She has immensely widened the field of modern poetry. She takes the museum piece out of its glass case, and sets it against the living flower. She produces living plants from the herbarium, and living animals from the bestiary. She relates the refreshing oddities of art to the shocking oddities of life. The ephemeral and the provincial become durable and civilized under her hands. She is a delayed product of long processes. (pp. 199-200)

Louise Bogan, "American Timeless," in Quarterly Review of Literature: Special Moore Issue, *Guest Editor, José Garcia Villa (copyright, 1948, by T. Weiss), Vol. IV, No. 2, 1948 (and reprinted in* Quarterly Review of Literature, *Special Issues Retrospective, edited by T. & R. Weiss, Vol. XX, Nos. 1-2, 1976, pp. 198-200).*

DAVID HSIN-FU WAND

Unlike Wallace Stevens who is known to have quoted lines of Chinese poetry in his writing . . . Marianne Moore never makes direct references to or gives quotations of classical Chinese poetry in her work. . . . But, while she is reticent about Chinese poetry, she alludes to Chinese *objets d'art* in many of her poems. . . . Miss Moore likens precision in writing to the skill of Chinese lacquer carving in her "Bowls." . . . With a "Chinese / 'passion for the particular,'" she talks about "Chinese carved glass," "landscape gardening twisted into permanence," and "the Chinese vermilion of / the poincianas" in "People's Surroundings." . . . [And] who but Miss Moore has the flashing wit and that "leap of the imagination" to confuse Mozart's "magic flute and harp" "with China's precious wentletrap" [as she does in "Logic and 'The Magic Flute'"]? . . . Here, in her own whimsical manner, Miss Moore contrasts the "precious wentletrap" of "The Magic Flute" with the "small audience-room" of Logic. In other words, she demonstrates that "The Magic Flute," the music that is as intricate as the "precious wentletrap" of life, cannot be confined in "the abalonean gloom" of our logical or rational mind. For life, like the water image . . . in Lao Tzu's *Tao Teh Ching,* overflows the boundary of words; it cannot be made to wear the straight-jacket of Logic. Here, Miss Moore's attitude reminds us of the anti-rationalism of the Zen masters. . . . A. Kingsley Weatherhead calls attention to the "wealth of contents" in her poetry and likens her unraveling of details to "what Ezra Pound called a 'periplum'." . . . [He] goes on to elaborate his theory by saying that, in Miss Moore's case, overcareful subordination of details to the whole "would defeat the poet's aim" because in some of her poems "discoveries are made by means of the fanciful relationships that are established." . . . [In] the act of composing her poetry, Miss Moore must have constantly astonished (and delighted) herself. (pp. 470-73)

Miss Moore's periplum technique, or her ability to make far-fetched associations, as demonstrated in her "Smooth Gnarled Crape Myrtle," is not unknown to the classical Chinese poets. And she herself is not unaware of the achievements of these poets when she mentions in her poem, "In Lieu of the Lyre," "the rime-prose revived by word-wizard Achilles—/ Dr. Fang." The "rime-prose"—better known to the Chinese as the *fu*—is a subgenre of Chinese literature. . . . Although Miss Moore's poems are never as extended and as full of particulars as [a virtuoso piece of rime prose such as] Ssu-ma Hsiang-ju's "Shang-lin Park," she is just as capable—if not more capable than the Chinese poet—of far-fetched associations. For instance, in her poem "Blue Bug," whose protagonist is a pony owned by "Dr. Raworth Williams," . . . she associates this "limber Bug" with a dancer, a dragonfly, "an ancient Chinese / melody," a "Yellow River- / scroll," the dubious etymology of "polo" as either "pelo" or "polos," a French painter, and a Chinese acrobat.... In this fantastic *tour de force*, Miss Moore's verbal agility (or *kinema*) is no less astounding than Ssu-ma Hsiang-ju's in his "Shang-lin Park," where flourish the dragons and the kylins (or Chinese unicorns), which equally delight Miss Moore in her own poems, "The Plumet Basilisk," "O To Be a Dragon," and "Nine Nectarines." (pp. 473-75)

The qualities of flexibility and versatility, the very qualities that Miss Moore has sought in the title poem, "O To Be a Dragon," are attained, like the "everchanging" dragon, in [that] volume. (p. 479)

Miss Moore has, through her assimilation of the Vital Spirit of the mythical Chinese beasts, managed to soar like the dragon and glide like the kylin from poem to poem. And as the dragon ranges from the sky to the seas and as the kylin sails the earth, they complement each other and dominate the universe. In inhaling the ch'i (breath or vital spirit) of the dragon and the kylin, Miss Moore has miraculously transported the essence of Cathay, or classical China, to the soil of American poetry. (p. 482)

> *David Hsin-Fu Wand, "The Dragon and the Kylin: The Use of Chinese Symbols and Myths in Marianne Moore's Poetry,"* in Literature East and West (© *Literature East and West Inc.*), Vol. XV, No. 3, 1971, pp. 470-84.

HUGH KENNER

Miss Moore's poems deal in many separate acts of attention, all close-up; optical puns, seen by snapshot, in a poetic normally governed by the eye, sometimes by the ears and fingers, ultimately by the moral sense. It is the poetic of the solitary observer, for whose situation the meaning of a word like "moral" needs redefining: her special move in the situation where [she is] . . . confronted by a world that does not speak and seems to want *describing*. Man confronted by brute nature: that is her situation.... Its etiology needs some looking into. (p. 92)

Her poems are not for the voice; she sensed this in reading them badly. In response to a question, she once said that she wrote them for people to look at. Moreover, one cannot imagine them handwritten.... Miss Moore's cats, her fish, her pangolins and ostriches exist on the page in tension between the mechanisms of print and the presence of a person behind those mechanisms. Handwriting flows with the voice, and here the voice is as synthetic as the cat, not something an elocutionist can modulate. The words on these pages are little regular blocks, set apart by spaces, and referrable less to the voice than to the click of the keys and the ratcheting of the carriage.

The stanzas lie on the page, one below another, in little intricate grids of visual symmetry, the left margin indented according to complex rules which govern the setting of tabulator stops. The lines obey no rhythmic system the ear can apprehend. We learn that there is a system not by listening but by counting syllables, and we find that the words are fixed within a grid of numerical rules. (pp. 98-9)

Marianne Moore's subjects—her fields of preoccupation, rather—have these two notable characteristics among others, that they are self-sufficient systems of energy, and that they can appropriate, without hostility, almost anything that comes near. They affirm, without saying anything, that "In This Age of Hard Trying, Nonchalance is Good," and that "There is a great amount of poetry in unconscious / fastidiousness." They are frequently animals; they feed and sleep and hunt and play; they are graceful without taking pride in their grace. They exemplify the qualities of the poems in which they are found.

Yes, they do; yes, it is striking, this pervasive singleness (though never obvious: nothing is *obvious* here). The singleness helps explain why she was able to make a revolutionary discovery, perhaps without ever knowing what it was. She resembles Columbus, whose mind was on something other than opening new worlds, and died supposing he had shown how to sail to China. For the language flattened, the language *exhibited*, the language staunchly condensing information while frisking in enjoyment of its release from the obligation to do no more than inform: these are the elements of a twentieth-century American poetic, a pivotal discovery of our age. And it seems to have been Marianne Moore's discovery, for [William Carlos] Williams, who also discovered it and extended it beyond the reach of her temperament, seems to have discovered it with the aid of her poems. A woman who was never convinced she was writing poems . . . ; she and a frantically busy physician who kept a typewriter screwed to a hinged leaf of his consulting-room desk, to be banged up into typing position between patients: not "poets," not professionals of the word, save for their passion: they were the inventors of an American poetry. The fact is instructive.

Extracting its instruction, we may begin with her avowed hostility to the poetic. We had better not dismiss this as whimsy; it was heuristic.

"I, too, dislike it," she wrote of something called "Poetry." ("I, too"? In alliance with whom? The public? Well, sensible people, presumably.) (pp. 105-06)

She did indeed dislike poetry, she used emphatically to insist. One time, citing

> No man may him hyde
> From Deth holow-eyed,

she made a little inventory of dislikes:

> I dislike the reversed order of words; don't
> like to be impeded by an unnecessary capital
> at the beginning of every line; I don't like,
> here, the meaning; the cadence coming close
> to being the sole reason for all that follows,
> the accent on "holow" rather than on
> "eyed," so firmly placed that the most will-
> ful reader cannot misplace it. . . .

This is to reject, well, very much. If more careful in its discriminations than Williams' shoving aside of "Europe—the past," it has a comparable thrust. Nevertheless, reading poetry without enchantment, "one discovers in it, after all, a place for the genuine": a place, as she went on to say in 1919, for "real toads." That's what poetry is, a place; not a deed but a location. "A kind of collection of flies in amber," Miss Moore was to call her own poetry, "if not a cabinet of fossils." (p. 108)

Miss Moore's modest effort was not to deflect "poetry" or to destroy it, but to ignore it: that is to say, ignore its rituals. She made up difficult rules of her own, some of which as they evolved remained in force (end-stopped lines for choice, and after 1929, rhyme), while others—the specific syllable grid, the density and audibility of the rhymes—hold good only for the duration of the poem in hand. It's a home-made art, like the sampler wrought in cross-stitch. Sometimes it will allow the conjunction between rule and theme to appear almost naïvely. . . . (pp. 109-10)

Like [Wallace] Stevens', hers is a poetry for one voice; like Stevens', it works by surface complication, with little variety of feeling. Unlike Stevens', it has no traffic—has never had any at all—with the cadences of the Grand Style, with Tradition, but works by a principle exclusively its own, the witty transit through minute predilections. Unlike Stevens' poetry, finally, hers deteriorates, as it were, through insufficient grasp of its own principles. Having been held together by a temperament, it grows dilute as the temperament grows more accommodating. And yet it is a turning point, as Stevens' is not. When American verse was looking for a way to cope with the perceived world's multifarious otherness, it was Marianne Moore's best work that was decisive.

Causing her best poems to enact with such rigor the moral virtues they celebrate, Miss Moore skirted the tradition of the dandy, whose life was a controlled thing and whose norms of conduct were stylistic. Dandyism's principal modern celebrant was Ernest Hemingway, whose bullfights and lion-hunts were aesthetic gestures and whose descriptions of clear water running over stones were moral achievements. (pp. 113-14)

But Hemingway's conception of style as the criterion of life contains one element totally alien to any poetic effect of Marianne Moore's: *self-appreciation*. To take satisfaction in one's achievements, and to undertake like achievements in quest of more of that satisfaction—this is the dual temptation by which such a poetic is beset; and the theme of many poems of Miss Moore is precisely the duty to resist it. (p. 114)

Some of the formal obstacles Marianne Moore laid across the assertions of her sentences were to help her avoid seeming to imply that a cat or a fish has never really been looked at before. Their presence raises, however, a further problem: how to avoid asserting that one has had the dexterity to overcome formal obstacles. It is here that her preoccupation with otherness helps.

For those autonomous envelopes of energy she so admired are *other*, as Nature for Wordsworth never was. Where Hemingway imitated bullfighters, she was content to admire ballplayers. Her cats, pangolins, jerboas, elephants are not beings she half-perceives and half-creates. Their accomplishments are wholly their own. It is not the poet who notes that the jerboa is sand-colored, but the jerboa that "honours the sand by assuming its colour." Similarly, it is the jerboa that has discovered a flute rhythm for itself, "by fifths and sevenths, / in leaps of two lengths," and to play the flageolet in its presence is not our ingenuity but our obligation. "Its leaps should be set / to the flageolet." So when, as normally, we find that the poem is itself enacting the virtues it discerns in its subject, we are not to say that it is commenting on its own aesthetic, as in Hemingway's celebrations of the way one works close to the bull; rather that its aesthetic is an offering to the virtuosity of the brisk little creature that changes pace so deftly, and direction so deft-

ly, and keeps intent, and keeps alert, and both offers and refrains from flaunting its agility.

This works best with animals, because they don't know their own virtuosity, and with athletes because at decisive moments they haven't time for self-appreciation, there being a ball to catch that won't wait. ("I could of caught it with a pair of pliers," said the exuberant outfielder, but that was afterward.) That is why Miss Moore's best poems are unpeopled save by glimpsed exemplars of verbal or synaptic dexterity. It is also why, as she admitted to her system other people's values, a poetic misfortune for which her sense of wartime obligations may be in part blamed, she relaxed and blurred her normal deftness and neatness, aware of the inappropriateness of seeming crisp. To be crisp even in praise of people's excellence is to make oneself a little the proprietor of their virtue; one senses that she sensed that to be improper.

At her best, she was other from us, and her subjects other from her, and saying with the elephant, "I do these / things which I do, which please / no one but myself," she was fulfilling a nature of her own. (pp. 116-17)

> Hugh Kenner, "Disliking It," in his *A Homemade World: The American Modernist Writers* (copyright © 1975 by Hugh Kenner; reprinted by permission of Alfred A. Knopf, Inc.), Knopf, 1975, pp. 91-118.

*   *   *

MROŻEK, Sławomir   1930-

Mrożek is a talented Polish playwright, novelist, and short story writer currently living in Italy whose work, although successful in many other countries, is not widely known in the United States. He writes in the Theater of the Absurd tradition about life behind the Iron Curtain. *Tango* is his best known play. (See also *CLC*, Vol. 3, and *Contemporary Authors*, Vols. 13-16, rev. ed.)

MARDI VALGEMAE

Put in very simple terms, the problem [facing the contemporary writer] involves the creation of an artistic language or structure that could describe the physical as well as the metaphysical anguish of man in post-atomic society. Complicated enough under ordinary circumstances, artistic communication becomes even more complex when subjected to ideological censorship. . . . [The] ruthless visual metaphors of contemporary absurdist drama have created an allegorical structure that expresses the agony of human guinea pigs better than could be achieved by ordinary verbal language. . . . The language of absurd visual images seems ideally suited for the construction of socialist allegories . . . for, as Martin Esslin has observed, absurd images enable East European playwrights to communicate their views on man and the totalitarian state without arousing the wrath of the censor. (p. 44)

[It] is to Poland that one must turn for the earliest—and the most widespread—flowering of East European drama that transcends the limitations of socialist realism. . . . [Sławomir Mrożek's] *Tango*, though much more "realistic" and rational than the dramas of Witkacy, Gombrowicz, or Różewicz, is the most widely known post-war Polish play in the idiom of the absurd. . . .

The couple in Mrożek's play have rebelled against Victorian social and moral conventions.... Mrożek's stage directions for Act I create a picture of chaotic freedom, suggesting a triumphant overthrow of the conventions of a time when it took great courage to dance the tango. Eleanor's and Stomil's son Arthur, however, endeavors to reinstate the old social and moral codes by ending what his granduncle calls fifty years of "jokes." ... Though Mrożek has not specified the time of the action of his play, it is clearly contemporary with the date of the initial production of the work in 1965. This places the beginning of "the joke" chronologically in the immediate vicinity of the Russian Revolution, and as Arthur's rebellion takes on added dimensions, *Tango* shifts from the realm of social comedy to that of political allegory. Approached from this point of view, Arthur's elders may be said to have overthrown a traditional political system in order to establish a revolutionary regime, the excesses of which more than equal the breach of social decorum committed by Eleanor and Stomil.... (p. 45)

[While political and allegorical elements of the play have been examined by other critics, it] remains to be shown how Mrożek conjures up a picture of totalitarianism by means of absurdist imagery.

When Arthur surprises the poker players in the opening scene, he disciplines his grandmother by forcing her to lie on a catafalque and punishes his granduncle by placing a bottomless birdcage over his head. To anyone familiar with Nazi or Soviet concentration camps and the brutal tactics of the secret police, these grotesque visual images of imprisonment and death speak with muted eloquence. Furthermore, the imaginative use of what may at first seem to be meaningless metaphors firmly establishes the allegorical texture of the play. Take, for example, Stomil's experimental theatricals. One of them features Adam and Eve in Paradise, whose brief colloquy is abruptly terminated by a shot from a revolver. The intrusion of naked power into the idyllic garden of Eden not only alludes to the recent (as well as the not-so-recent) history of Eastern Europe, but also anticipates the subsequent action of the play. First Arthur stages his counter-revolution with the aid of that revolver. Then Eddie re-establishes the dictatorship of the proletariat by using the same weapon to subdue Arthur. The play ends with the representatives of the old and the new order dancing a ritualistic tango over the dead body of the romantic intellectual. The social, moral, aesthetic, and political issues probed in this work have been fused into an absurdist allegorical finale, as Mrożek rephrases Hamlet's "to be or not to be?" in strikingly visual terms: is it possible to restore the old order, or must we go on dancing the tango? (pp. 45-6)

Mrożek's *Tango* ... [serves as an example] of a particular type of East European theatre of the absurd that differs somewhat from the French school of Beckett and his colleagues. For most French absurdists tend to concentrate on basic metaphysical issues, whereas many East European playwrights simply use absurd images in order to create social and political allegories. In the words of a Polish critic, the dramatic worlds of Beckett and Ionesco are microcosms, while the dramatic worlds of Mrożek ... are microsocieties. (p. 48)

Mardi Valgemae, in Comparative Drama (© copyright 1971, by the Editors of Comparative Drama), Spring, 1971.

HAROLD CLURMAN

Slaughterhouse is a satire on the destruction of artistic life —in this case music—in contemporary civilization. Musicians are enjoined, virtually compelled, to abandon their art for butchery! A violinist who cannot bring himself to do so commits suicide. (There is something of Ionesco's *Rhinoceros* in the notion.) (p. 93)

Harold Clurman, in The Nation (copyright 1975 The Nation Associates), August 2, 1975.

BENEDICT NIGHTINGALE

I confess to a mild prejudice against a play whose only two characters are called AA and XX. Such stuff tends to make me go ZZ. But after a longish, slowish start Mrożek's *Emigrés* turns out to be neither abstract nor boring.... [AA is a] political refugee, and XX ... is the sort of migrant wage-slave who may be found in many of the richer European nations, building tower blocks or digging sewers. Their somewhat unlikely cohabitation begins with bickering about food and rent, becomes a New Year's booze-up, and ends with the discussion about freedom and captivity that, given Mrożek's own status as an emigré from Poland, we should have expected all along. Both men, it emerges, feel more trapped in the liberal West than by any tyranny of secret police and one-party bureaucrats: the writer can't write, the labourer misses his family. A second and perhaps less persuasive conclusion is that it is bovine, lumpen XX who retains the more independence of soul in exile, and clever, contemptuous AA who is doomed to envy him from his intellectual icebox. At this point one might be inclined to accuse Mrożek of sentimentality, even self-pity; but there's a toughness, an unaffected humanity ... that sweeps away seven-eighths of the objection. (p. 59)

Benedict Nightingale, in New Stateman (© 1976 The Statesman & Nation Publishing Co. Ltd.), July 9, 1976.

*   *   *

MUELLER, Lisel   1924-

Mueller is a German-born poet now living in the United States.

STANLEY PLUMLY

Mueller is effective in direct proportion to the maintenance of high tension between herself and that thin membrane of material, the public world. She is a poet of deep moral conviction, whose private life is not only witness but watchboy. Poem after poem places the reader in a context of an "occupied country." ... The weaknesses in [*The Private Life*] ... have little to do with historical imperatives or possible anachronisms. It is when the tension between private passion and public concern breaks down that Mueller's poems begin to sound like speeches; it is when the urgency of experience (vicarious or direct) makes the language marketable that the poetry unravels into the discursiveness of prose. Cause or casuistry, the human voice in a poem is the one we hear from the back of the room, not the one on stage. "The Gift of Fire" ... is didactic, hardly the elegy it is intended to be to honor a suicide by fire. "Amazing Grace" ... is pick-up prose. And "Hope" ... is simply trite. All three of these poems would win us over by wit of their virtue. We need songs, not sermons, songs that Mueller, in her private life, sings so well. (p. 42)

Stanley Plumly, in The American Poetry Review *(copyright © 1976 by World Poetry, Inc.; reprinted by permission of Stanley Plumly), July, 1976.*

LOUIS MARTZ

[A] sense of wonder runs throughout [Lisel Mueller's] poetry: we may have thought it would never come again. She even dares to have a poem [in *The Private Life*] entitled "Hope": "the singular gift / we cannot destroy in ourselves." These are honest, open poems, a kind of verse that one is glad to have, because it runs so close to our own better responses. (p. 125)

Louis Martz, in The Yale Review *(© 1976 by Yale University; reprinted by permission of the editors), Autumn, 1976.*

PATRICIA BEER

Lisel Mueller is too fond of the word "small"—small poem, small mistake, small laugh, small hands; one gets to wait for it. And sometimes the accumulations of instance and example by which she conveys her ideas are not quite pointed enough, as in "Alive Together" and "Spell for a Traveller". But many of the poems in *The Private Life* are as precise and energetic as could be desired. (p. 1348)

Patricia Beer, in The Times Literary Supplement *(© Times Newspapers Ltd. (London) 1976; reproduced from* The Times Literary Supplement *by permission), October 29, 1976.*

DICK ALLEN

Lisel Mueller is one of those poets who has a genius for finding subjects. . . . [*A Private Life*] is thoroughly intelligent, the poems finding and holding onto subjects and feelings, images which occur to many but most often slip away unrecorded. Mueller can turn her attention almost anywhere and come up with a fine crafted poem. Her work is most characterized by its loving, responsive tone, her sympathy and awareness of how special it is to know you have a private life up to answering, with poems, things which delight or sadden you. (p. 346)

She goes after our secrets, this poet; often, she finds them. There are two or three too facile poems, set pieces; and sometimes Mueller falls into lilting amphibrachs which contrast in sound too drastically with the serious tone demanded by the poem's subject material. But these are minor flaws in the work of this most quotable poet. Mueller's poetry is satisfying, filled with love and knowledge of a species adrift. The only thing I miss is . . . the drive toward the core, the steady deepening. (p. 347)

Dick Allen, in Poetry *(© 1977 by The Modern Poetry Association; reprinted by permission of the Editor of* Poetry*), September, 1977.*

*   *   *

MUSGRAVE, Susan   1951-

A Canadian poet, Musgrave weaves images of death into her intense confessional poetry. She explains her use of death as a metaphor for separation, for relationships constantly frustrated. The elemental power of nature is evoked in one of her best poems, "Mackenzie River, North." Fantastic creatures created from a personal mythology haunt Musgrave's often bizarre landscapes. (See also *Contemporary Authors*, Vols. 69-72.)

MARYA FIAMENGO

Susan Musgrave is vibrantly self-engrossed. She is not careful; she is often careless, but spontaneously, valiantly, vividly so. Miss Musgrave is a young poet and [*Songs of the Sea-Witch*] is a young woman's book, but there is no mistaking the authentic voice of an emerging poet. Precision of observation, concreteness of language, vitality of imagery, imaginative power, all these Susan Musgrave abundantly displays.

> My ribs are torn
> like old whores' petticoats.

she writes in "Exposure"; and in "Jan. 6th":

> The long days mate with
> the nude on the calendar.
> I have packed time like a suitcase
> and now there is nothing left to do
> but organize my boredom.

Miss Musgrave's is a narrow canvas, but while highly personal it is no mere embroidery frame. She has the ability to evoke landscapes, but she is no nature pantheist. Her landscapes become a metaphor for a personal vision which mirrors an emotional, moral and intellectual state.

Not all Miss Musgrave's poems are equally successful. Parts of the title poem, "Songs of the Sea-Witch" are uneven. She might have been more selective; the confessional tone becomes occasionally repetitive; "North Sea Poem" repeats much of what "Mackenzie River, North" says. However, Miss Musgrave's is a young talent and I am inclined in her case to agree with Blake that this road of excess may yet lead to the palace of wisdom. (pp. 104-05)

Marya Fiamengo, in Canadian Literature, *Summer, 1972.*

Dreams, ghosts, magical presences and the whimsical-weird are the properties of Susan Musgrave's poems [in *Entrance of the Celebrant*]. They make up a bit of a witch's brew, in fact, in which the contents are arbitrary and the tone not as spell-binding (or bewitching) as it probably intends to be:

> I share you with beetles,
> I share you in my bones.
> Bite into me and
> open your mind to blood.
>
> (p. 10)

The Times Literary Supplement *(© Times Newspapers Ltd. (London) 1973; reproduced from* The Times Literary Supplement *by permission), January 5, 1973.*

LINDA ROGERS

Almost alone in the magic forest, Susan Musgrave blends her own weird voice with those of nature personified. Sounds of the rain forest echo poems in her skull, boiling with the witch's brew; moss and seaweed and trees twisted into toads. In her third book, *Grave-Dirt and Selected Strawberries*, nature, refracted off fairy lenses, assumes all the classic human disguises, goes through all the jigsaw possibilities of one living landscape. . . .

Musgrave's wilderness is magical and she is a character in her own fairy tale, the wizard of poems which spring from her intercourse with tides and seasons in the dark woods. . . . The magnifying glass she presses to the forest floor enlarges into grotesques the central issues of her own life as a woman in the macrocosmic world of humans who have shaped their own impulses into myth. Her landscape is burdened with the traditional struggle of things animal and vegetable for survival. Moss copulates under the glass and becomes metaphor. Humour is the leaven of these strange couplings. The poet is a woman bleeding through all the seasons of the moon, but managing to laugh at the crazy lunar mysteries. Grave dirt is fertilizer for the new generation. (p. 121)

Lest we take it all too seriously, the fragile transformation of event into ritual is finally parodied in "Selected Strawberries". Strawberry, everyone's splendour in the grass, threatens to become mouth and gobble her whole mythical world. Tired of the discipline of metaphor, the poet dumps the whole spice-box of words. (pp. 121-22)

> *Linda Rogers, in* Canadian Literature, *Summer, 1974.*

MARY JANE EDWARDS

Red, black, white, skulls, playing cards, and a strawberry decorate the cover of Susan Musgrave's *grave-dirt and selected strawberries* and introduce some themes and images which help shape each of the volume's three parts: "Gravedirt," "Kiskatinaw Songs," and "Selected Strawberries." The last is a collection of proverbs, definitions, poems, etc. about strawberries; under the heading "The genius, wit and spirit of a strawberry are discovered in its proverbs," for example, Musgrave alters Dollabella's comment in Dryden's *All for Love* that "Men are but children of a larger growth" to "Men are but strawberries of a larger growth." The effect of such changes is amusing and the idea is clever, but to me "Selected Strawberries" lacks the kind of wit that informs and illuminates as it amuses and surprises. The second part, "Kiskatinaw Songs," is a series of poems based on West Coast Indian lore, and the first part "Gravedirt," is a collection of poems which, like the Indian songs, use simple, strong rhythms and elemental images and explore such basic themes as love, sex, and death. The most moving poems in both parts are those that deal with sex and love, particularly from a woman's point of view. . . . [The] range of subject matter, form, and imagery in *grave-dirt and selected strawberries* creates an extremely varied landscape. The elemental power of some of these poems, furthermore, makes me think that . . . Susan Musgrave holds out the . . . promise of developing her landscape into a complete archetypal vision of men, women, and their world. (p. 43)

> *Mary Jane Edwards, in* The Canadian Forum, *August, 1974.*

STEPHEN MARTINEAU

[*The Impstone*] stimulates and disappoints at the same time. The stimulation comes from the four part structure of the book which leads progressively through the intricacies and failures of personal relationships to a spiritual world of Indian legend ("Only the dead / can lead you to the / / begi-

nning"); the disappointment comes from the stylistic limitations imposed on such far-ranging material. The style is certainly finely honed; in fact it shows a precision and sense of rhythm that is more confident and consistent than in any of her earlier work. But such an economic, polished effect often pulls against the reach towards the otherworldly, the spirit beyond the grave, and, as part IV begins, one feels the need for a change of pace and rhythm, for another perspective through which to breathe in the mysterious Indian lore and the abandoned villages of Kung and Yatza.

There is one poem in this last section, "Shadow-Shamans," that suggests the latent strength in a more varied approach: a simple, semi-prose narrative of an Indian legend is interwoven with short poetic stanzas as if the narrative provoked, insisted on a further reflection. In this way the poetic result is linked to and plays against its source, thus evoking stronger awareness of its mystic aura. But generally the style of this volume is more suited to immediate, personal situations. In this context the economy works in catching sharp moments, transfixing into stillness moments of action which leave people utterly stripped. . . .

The two strongest poems in the volume, however, break through to the other side of the personal through the invocation of a single, powerful image—invocation in the sense of casting a spell through rhythmic repetition of the key word. "Afterthought" is an urgent plea to "seed," a demand that the seed create no life within the body ("I don't want you swigging / my cool / statistical juices"). This demand for "emptiness" within herself, for "enormous darkness" is finely focussed because of its direct address to what is the sole creator of life; the poem goes directly to the source of life thus showing the desire for control and the fear at the very beginning of things. The same impulse and technique gives power to the title poem "The Impstone" which again invokes the "stone" through repetition and creates out of it a new version of *Genesis.* . . . [The stone is] continually transformed and acted upon, becomes fears and desires so as to incorporate a whole life cycle, only to return to the dream, to the urgency for articulation, to the failure to place or identify after all. When Susan Musgrave's images become central motifs in this way, they seem to expand effortlessly without losing their ground focus. But they return to the earth, more often than not to its association with death and the coldness of the grave. They return there, or rather the stylistic control turns them back, and I look forward to a style that can carry her through to the other side of the question at the end of "Invocation":

> I wait.
> I wonder.
>
> What secrets do you have
> to surrender;
> where do you go
> that it is
> for ever?

> *Stephen Martineau, "Catching Sharp Moments,"*
> *in* The Canadian Forum, *October, 1976, p. 30.*

N

NAIPAUL, V(idiadhar) S(urajprasad) 1932-

A novelist, essayist, short story writer, and author of travel books, Naipaul was born in Trinidad of Indian parents and has resided in England since 1950. His early works drew praise for their clear prose style and delicate sense of humor. Critics have lauded his ability to capture with wit and compassion the West Indian dialect and life style. (See also *CLC*, Vols. 4, 7, 9, and *Contemporary Authors*, Vols. 1-4, rev. ed.)

ROBERT D. HAMNER

Between *The Mystic Masseur* and publication of *In a Free State,* the structural organization of Naipaul's several novels has undergone a series of discernible changes. There is a marked difference between the early and late fiction, but the alterations in technique reveal a consistent development. Employing rather traditional plots and standard narrative exposition, he offers little that is innovative in the way of structure. In each book, whether the action is presented in simple, straight-forward narration or through a complex juxtaposition of episodes which assume significance accumulatively, Naipaul very carefully interrelates the various threads of his chosen plot.

Reduced to chronological outline, Naipaul's novels appear disarmingly simple. The basic framework does not rely for its effect on intricate complexity or on any "high seriousness" of action. Naipaul's primary focus is in his characters; all else depends upon them, and in recounting their experiences he is concerned that he tell their story well. Significantly, four of the published novels are presented through the eyes of a participating narrator. This contributes to the immediacy of these books, making the speaker's personality and the pattern of his emotional development an integral factor in the form of the works. At the same time, viewed from another perspective the narrator functions more as a device for continuity than as a fictional person; his point of view, his tone of voice, and his esthetic distance (not to be confused with that of the author) then assume importance as avenues through which the critic can view the work's basic structural arrangement. (p. 35)

First to be published, *The Mystic Masseur* sets the tone for the early novels. (p. 36)

Even though the anonymous narrator is hardly ever present in the body of the story, his occasional direct commentary is still in keeping with the overall fictional scheme of the book. From the outset the plot unfolds within a neatly constructed framework which is held together by the narrator. Chapter One, "The Struggling Masseur," not only gets the story off to a running start by opening *in medias res,* but in conjunction with the appended "Epilogue," it conveniently encloses Ganesh's entire rise and fall. (p. 37)

The surprise ending and some of the other devices used in *The Mystic Masseur* are standard tricks usually eschewed by sophisticated writers. Naipaul skillfully avoids sensationalism in this his first novel, but he is not above the use of mechanical ploys to create suspense, or, more properly, anticipation. (p. 38)

Had Naipaul been more skillful in conceptualizing the role of the narrator or otherwise less obviously dependent on plotting devices, the structure of the first novel would have been greatly strengthened. (p. 39)

Again [in *The Suffrage of Elvira*] Naipaul's straightforward narrative flows easily within the carefully restrictive limits he has set. A formal prologue and epilogue enclose the thirteen humorously engaging chapters. Internally, an episodic quality persists; transitional passages, a few marred perhaps by the author's overly explicit guiding hand, maintain progression at a quick rate. Naipaul has abandoned the first-person narrator and has assumed an outside position from which to supply necessary exposition. Unfortunately, his artistry is still slightly uneven; there are points, as there are in the first novel, where his technical machinery draws undue attention to itself. (p. 40)

Naipaul's propensity to stir expectation and cultivate suspense is intensified in his second novel. But here he has not the excuse of the narrator's fictional role; *The Suffrage of Elvira* is constructed on different terms. The action, rather than being presented as the reflections of a biographer, is more immediate; it continually develops from internal cause and effect. Through the emphasis on dramatic presentation, the reader is led to involve himself primarily with character and scene. The illusion is disrupted when extraneous incursions are made. (p. 41)

In *The Suffrage of Elvira* Naipaul is still experimenting with form. With the addition of minor subplots he has slightly increased the depth and complexity of his expression. Detrimental to his work up to this point, however, is his failure to maintain a consistent quality of internal control. Separate episodes are fairly well integrated into the structure, and the characters with which he succeeds—in most cases the more colorful the better—are well done. What problem exists with prolonged consistency is overshadowed by the effects of his felicitous handling, within carefully restricted limits, of such a variety of characters and actions.

Appearing next in order of publication is the book which is actually the first one written by Naipaul. Treatment of *Miguel Street* has been reserved until now because even though it was conceived first, it was withheld by the author until he was apparently satisfied as to its completeness. Even more than the second and third novels, this work reflects the color and texture of Caribbean life. (pp. 43-4)

Episodes in this novel are not bound together as self-consciously as they were in the earlier published works, but the underlying structure may be Naipaul's most consistent yet. He again resorts to an ingenuous speaker to shape the reader's response. In *Miguel Street*, unlike *The Mystic Masseur*, he goes one step farther and provides a second character to serve as a foil to the naïveté of the primary commentator. The result is a more evenly balanced perspective, and it effectively conceals the author's controlling hand. . . .

The importance of the narrator's expanding awareness is what makes *Miguel Street* fit the pattern of the *Bildungsroman*. Since the story is presented as past action, however, the process of thought development is not emphasized. Instead, the narrator provides an edited survey of his childhood. The youngster's growth is shown, but it is accomplished more by revealing his accumulated experiences than by tracing out a systematic development. (p. 46)

An intriguing study remains to be made of the original and the final manuscripts of this novel. If major changes are discovered—and if the first two published works are any indication of his early style—Naipaul's experimentation and practice in narrative techniques have been profitable. Either that, or all along Naipaul was creating in *Miguel Street* better than he knew. Advantageous to this novel is the consistent immediacy of the point of view from which the narrative is presented, and the substitution of less obtrusive double spacing for the editorial stars. At least for the present, he has foregone anticipatory devices, and his abrupt turns are made more palatable by his working them more integrally into the scenes in which they occur. His work is still episodic, and *Miguel Street* is more a collection of overlapping and interconnected sketches than a standard novel, but other considerations aside, with the noticeable refinements in his structural machinery, he has laid a solid foundation for his mature fiction.

With the appearance in 1961 of *A House for Mr Biswas*, Naipaul may have published his best fiction. It is even possible that this book is the best novel yet to emerge from the Caribbean. It is a vital embodiment of authentic West Indian life, but more than that, it transcends national boundaries and evokes universal human experiences. Mr. Biswas' desire to own his own house is essentially a struggle to assert personal identity and to attain security—thoroughly human needs. (p. 48)

As in *The Mystic Masseur* Naipaul reveals the end of the story before it begins, denying himself whatever superficial value might have resided in the temptation to keep the reader in suspense as to what would happen to his hero.

The first chapter and the epilogue . . . serve as "frames" for the plot, enclosing the shifting scenery of Mr. Biswas' world. From the early novels Naipaul retains anticipatory and summary passages, to a lesser degree minor unmarked breaks and mild shifts in narrative direction, and a few brief looks into the future; but these are now made so integral to the action of the story that they are unobtrusive, no longer drawing attention to themselves as plotting devices. As a matter of fact, on each level of the novel the structure is consistently molded more and more deeply into the texture of meaning. . . . [On] one level the framework is almost an outline, on a second it is a developing portrait, on a third it is an informing backdrop, and on another it is a fusion of motifs and themes.

Episodic as usual, the forthright plot of this finely wound novel does not separate easily into its several aspects, nor can the plot be divided from other aspects of the book. Even to its interspersed patterns of symbols and motifs, the narrative is connected with everything else. . . . As should be the case with the best fiction, to unfold the pattern of emotional development is essentially to analyze characterization, and to explore narrative technique is to investigate the texture of language throughout the work. Naipaul abandons narrative persona and simply concentrates on the presentation of an intriguing story. Technically, he employs the omniscient narrator, but the relation progresses with such unobtrusive ease that the reader's attention is seldom, if ever, distracted from the evolving action. (pp. 49-50)

Thus far, *A House for Mr Biswas* has been Naipaul's last exclusively West Indian novel. Those coming after it have shifted in locality and/or in the nationality of characters. *Mr Stone and the Knights Companion* is a complete break with the Caribbean. . . . This major change in setting is the most obvious, but not the only difference, between this and the last book: the "framing" technique disappears entirely; chapter titles are omitted; the field of action is severely restricted; and the tightly-knit story is told in less than 160 pages. (p. 52)

It is characteristic of Naipaul's later fiction that expectation and scope and intensity of action become more and more reduced. In *Mr Stone and the Knights Companion*, for example, even though an omniscient author presides over development, the central character is already mature and settled in his personality, and all that takes place is his painful adjustment to the inevitable problems (primarily emotional and mental) of old age. Naipaul has continually avoided sensationalism and melodramatic outbursts, but after *A House for Mr Biswas* the events he portrays are increasingly subdued in tone. In fact, a majority of the activity portrayed is internalized, given the form of mental reflection rather than of physical participation; and the shift in emphasis results in significant structural changes.

The Mimic Men is Naipaul's third novel on colonial politics, and it is by far his most complex and bitter treatment of the subject. The basic framework is, in fact, an improved replica of that employed in *The Mystic Masseur*. This time Naipaul's now familiar chronicle technique takes the form of a deposed officeholder's autobiography. Complicating the plot is the fact that events are not revealed in chronological order. Instead, it is up to the reader to arrange and fill in time slots as antecedent material is supplied during the course of the shifting narrative. (p. 55)

Unless the narrator is accepted along with his personal idiosyncrasies, the carefully sustained fabric of *The Mimic Men* will be misunderstood. He is egotistical, selfishly introverted and detached, and he seldom allows alternative concepts to enter into his narrative. Admittedly, this severely limits the scope of the book and sets it one remove from the type of dramatic tension which might normally be preferred, but the chosen method is exonerated by one overriding virtue—it consistently answers to the design of the novel. (pp. 58-9)

Naipaul is better able to sustain his own detachment and the point of view of his protagonist in *The Mimic Men* than he is in *The Mystic Masseur*. His advantage in the later novel is that the "framing" is less obtrusive, and the narrator's participation in the story proper is more conveniently explicable. . . . With hindsight, this development in Naipaul's technique might almost appear to be predictable. Each of his novels (with the qualified exception, perhaps, of *Mr Stone and the Knights Companion*) has been carefully placed within a frame which effectively separates it from outside reality. The frame is not necessarily artificial, but it reminds the reader more or less subconsciously of the presence of the artist-creator, until now in *The Mimic Men* the very presence of the narrator himself has developed into one of the primary focal points of the novel.

With these preliminary observations about the narrative voice in mind, the approach to the intricate structure of this novel is facilitated. . . . Not only episodes, but huge sections of *The Mimic Men* are taken out of chronological order and related according to the sequence imposed by the narrator's wandering memories. The manipulations of time are handled with such ease—what with moods and images carried back and forth—that continuity never falters; and the fluctuating dreaminess of the narrator's mental state only adds to the blending and mixing of realism and fantasy. (pp. 59-60)

A Flag on the Island is the title novelette in a collection of short stories and sketches. Though written as early as 1965 (two years before *The Mimic Men*), it was withheld from publication until 1967. . . . It is only eighty-seven pages in length, but its brevity belies the wealth of material that is concisely packed into those few pages. Naipaul returns in setting and in most of his characters to the islands of the Caribbean, but as is typical of his later novels, he continues to generate a more cosmopolitan atmosphere; this time he adopts a protagonist from the outside world, an American. The plot is not as involved as that in *The Mimic Men*, but the thin line between reality and unreality is maintained to such an extent that there is surprising complexity and depth in the simple narrative. (p. 61)

[Like other of Naipaul's novels, *A Flag on the Island*] runs full circle, beginning with an established mood, going back to the informing sources of the mood, carrying them through to the height of intensity, and then returning in the end to confirm the existing status. (p. 63)

The narrator's voice is so consistently in control that in this story the author's hand never appears. Unless an attempt is made to read Naipaul's direct statements from other works into the narrator's perspective, the fictional veil is not disturbed; there is certainly nothing in the text to disrupt the "suspension of disbelief." . . . The stream of consciousness freely intermingles inner and outer realities to produce a

variable perspective which one critic has described as jagged and hallucinatory in style. This fanciful element perhaps more than anything else accounts for the story's subtitle—*A Fantasy for a Small Screen*. Whether or not the script was really ever intended for a movie, as Naipaul contends in his preface, the fantasy is in a sense projected on the pages of his shortest novel. The screen is small, but the picture is in clear, vivid color.

The scenario of the title novella in *In a Free State* is similarly limited in scope. Narrative tone of voice and perspective never falter, and with a minimum of structural machinery the simple plot unfolds naturally. (pp. 63-4)

Both in emotional development and in structural arrangement, . . . the plot of *In a Free State* reflects the same kind of simple, straightforward method that Naipaul employs in his first five novels. In keeping with his typical manner, the emphasis is still on his characters—now, however, not so much showing any process of development, as disclosing personalities that have already been formed. He continues to delve into the intricacies of human relationships, bringing to the surface the frailty, the foolishness, and the cruelties of mankind. The conciseness of his expression is tighter in this novella than in any other of his books. This is both its strength and its weakness. It is unified and consistent, but so regular in shape that it lacks the passion and color of Naipaul's best work. (pp. 65-6)

There is considerable realism and constant attention to minute detail throughout Naipaul's fiction. Even in the humorously light-toned early novels with their surface appearance of farcical improbability, there are serious insights into the basic terms of existence for various levels of island society. (p. 70)

In *A House for Mr Biswas*, setting definitely becomes an integral aspect of the mental state of his leading character. Scenery has not existed simply for its own sake in earlier works, but with this book the impressions of environment become indispensable to the total literary experience—structure, character, and mood. (p. 73)

[*A House for Mr. Biswas*] signals a turning point, culminating one phase in Naipaul's artistic growth and commencing another. Faithfulness to the depth as well as to the surface color of his creation sets him well on the road to the intensive character studies typical of his later novels. Mr. Biswas is indentifiable with the background out of which he attempts desperately, despairingly to escape. . . . Mr. Biswas, more than the characters before him, utilizes his imagination to come to terms with reality; this is carried to such an extent that it is largely his personal conceptualization rather than perceived objects that occupies the central focus of the novel. (p. 75)

An immediate result of [the] developing process of introversion is the noticeable shift away from the prominence of local color and by degrees a discernible movement toward abstraction and less particularly identifiable localities. Dialect, for instance, diminishes in importance as the West Indianness of the fiction is deemphasized. In this respect, however, Naipaul's treatment of language has not undergone as much of a change as might be expected. There has been little reason for alteration because in the scenes in early books where carefully selective dialect occurs it has been standardized so that much of the strangeness is eliminated at the outset. The main features of the native language he preserves are the simplified grammar, limited vocabulary (very few completely foreign words of African and Indian origin), and slightly unique but plain syntactical structures, with normal spelling. (p. 77)

Naipaul's skill remains remarkably high as he smoothly alternates between levels of the language used by characters and the standard English of the ostensible author, whether the setting is West Indian, strictly the purest British, or, as with portions of the last three novels, a landscape predominantly of the mind. The steady restriction and normalization of dialect, then, help the smooth transition after *A House for Mr Biswas* into a more abstract atmosphere where the mental and emotional perception of the character takes precedence over outward manifestation of regional differences.

The change is one of emphasis. What happens is that episodes which might at first have been categorized as simply local color because of their superficial regional limitations or farcical because of their extravagance are toned down and handled more seriously. The trend is slightly noticeable in *A House for Mr Biswas* and marked in subsequent works in keeping with a maturing, increasingly complex style of writing. Following the pattern I have described above, elements of background and setting not only become significant because of the part they play in character revelation; they evolve into images and motifs which unify and integrate all phases of textual development. (p. 78)

Whatever the setting—the English middle-class drawing room, a metropolitan hotel, or the emerging Caribbean or African nation—Naipaul continually employs his sharp eye for telling detail and expressive gesture. The difference from earlier accuracy is in his not relying upon localized details. He selects those that are recognizable for their human rather than for their regional association. With the abatement of his earlier comic spirit he has turned more and more to the common elements in humanity for serious analysis and exposition. (p. 81)

Before the achievement of the classical Mohun Biswas and the meticulously executed psychological studies of the mature novels, Naipaul's characters are often delightfully lively and vividly dramatized, but they lend themselves too readily to the sort of typecasting that obscures individuality. (p. 82)

Naipaul employs a rather simple device to eliminate the possibility of his lightly sketched figures losing their personal individualities. For each of the minor and even most of the major characters he designates a peculiarity and by reiterating this "tag" in connection with the person at intervals throughout the story he effectively avoids confusion. (p. 84)

It is a mark of the brilliance in the creation of Mr. Biswas that he defies simple classification. Quite understandably, too, this character has drawn easily more critical attention than any other of Naipaul's protagonists. The designation "hero" is avoided at this point because in the minds of some critics there are reservations about his heroic proportions. (p. 88)

Mr. Biswas may be an archetypal "Everyman" but if so he is a modernized version, for in his confrontation with the vicissitudes of life he expresses an acute awareness of the absurd. (p. 89)

[In both *The Mimic Men* and *A Flag on the Island*] as in *Mr Stone and the Knights Companion,* an outstanding feature of Naipaul's characterization and style involves the subordination of all minor figures to the controlling influence of the heroes' personalities. (p. 100)

If the narrative tone [of *The Mimic Men*] is rather static, the protagonist cool and detached, the action described as often as it is portrayed, and the point of view restrictive, before these items may be leveled justly as criticism against the novel, the fictional situation created for its presentation must be carefully examined. More dramatic action and a broader, more varied perspective might be preferred by some, but the terms upon which the book is structured conform to a different pattern. In order to reveal the character of a man who is suspended without a meaningful existence between worlds to which he is unable to relate, Naipaul has chosen to allow the speaker to express himself in conformity with the type of person that he is. Ralph Singh is detached and philosophical, and he has arrived at this serene state only after exasperating years of fruitless involvement in pointless activity. (p. 102)

Turning from *The Mimic Men* to *A Flag on the Island,* it appears that character and style undergo little change. Local color is prominent here, but the controlling atmosphere of the story derives from the narrator's frame of mind. Frank is motivated by the same frenzied desire for order that drives Ralph. In Frank's case, however, his problem is not so much a lack of order as a rejection of the one that exists. (p. 103)

In *In a Free State,* as in the last two novels, the landscape tends to lose its distinctness at times. Place descriptions occur, but a sense of unreality enters Bobby's perception just as it has Ralph's and Frank's. Only slightly less self-consciously than Ralph, Bobby also experiences the feeling that he is performing a part, that he is involved in a drama. It becomes increasingly obvious that Naipaul's main concern is not with reality just as it might appear in a photograph but as it is perceived by his heroes. In depicting their introverted conceptualizations, he has certainly individualized each one, but he also concentrated on certain basic aspects that make them identical with mankind elsewhere.

It has been argued that in thus universalizing his presentation, Naipaul has damaged his sense of realism and has, in effect, gone the route of other self-exiled West Indian writers who critics say have lost essential contact with the most familiar source of their material. But in answer to this criticism I submit that there are valid grounds within the novels themselves to account at least partially for the "vagueness" and "distance" that critics have heretofore attributed to a fault in Naipaul's art. The protagonist's disengagement from the narrative strand can under certain circumstances be an asset rather than a liability. Ironic humor in the early novels and the detached, analytical tone of the later ones prevent the reader from becoming deeply involved in the stories, but at the same time they yield valuable insights into the personalities of the different protagonists. These devices may be viewed as defensive mechanisms which are just as much a part of character as any other trait. If it were a matter of the absence of concreteness and dramatic tension, then certainly the novels would be severely damaged; but this is not the case. Realism and verisimilitude are maintained at a high level of accuracy even when the view is of a mental landscape. There is truth in Frank's assertion, "all landscapes are in the end only in the imagination." (p. 104)

Naipaul's most prevalent attitude is satirical. Certain parts of his works fall into the category of satire under both of the usual definitions of the genre. His first four novels, especially with their colorful mixture and variety, make a "full plate, a medley"; and time after time throughout all his books, in action, character, setting and theme he employs his incisive wit to hold up to ridicule the foibles and follies of man and society. (p. 105)

In a sense, what Naipaul is asking for is the same kind of mature detachment [previously mentioned]. . . . Naipaul is usually successful in maintaining distance from his material, but . . . this does not necessarily mean that he is coldly detached or disdainful of that which he is depicting. Rather, his concerted effort to remove himself and his failure at times to keep his personal feelings hidden are evidence of his deeply rooted attachment to the people he criticizes. (p. 106)

There appear to be approximately three levels on which the humor functions. First are the jokes, pranks, and laughter-provoking incidents which occur among the characters. Second come eccentricities, language, and actions the humor of which is not always consciously felt by narrators and participants within the stories. On this level dramatic irony comes into prominence since the reader's position allows him fuller appreciation of meanings unavailable to the characters. Third is the sophisticated level on which the objects of satire come into sharper focus. Between these there are no gaps or boundaries; they are complementary, only gradations of emphasis marking them as closer to one end of the scale or the other.

The most literal phase, wherein the quality of humor is accommodated to the people who are joking and playing tricks on one another, has rather limited possibilities for use. It is a mark of Naipaul's comic style that his amusing comedy emerges through his character's individual dispositions and the thoughts they utter rather than through situation. (p. 107)

Naipaul holds up to ridicule several of the distasteful and irrational aspects of man and his institutions. More specifically (according to his own statements), he is concerned variously with "fantasy," "corruption," and "sickness." He begins with a recognition of the gross difference between the situation as he finds it and his conception of an ideal, and in order to draw attention to the discrepancy he selectively elaborates upon those things which he finds to be trivial, repellent, or otherwise contemptible. (p. 116)

Almost every topic Naipaul treats at any length, when reduced to its basic terms, ultimately resolves itself into the fundamental aspects of alienation. Though this necessarily entails a certain amount of repetition, there is no redundancy, due to the variety of forms in which the presentations are cast. . . . Naipaul's method of development might be called "incremental repetition," in the sense that the overall impression of his extant works appears to build cumulatively, each new expression of a previous concept modifying and illuminating what has gone before.

This is not to suggest that individual novels do not stand on their own merits, for they do. What it indicates is the pervasive unity of the fiction; and over a period of time it under-scores the consistency of Naipaul's progress as an author from the youthful comedies to his more seriously executed later works. (pp. 124-25)

Disorder and human frailty are underscored by the incompatibility between men and their surroundings. The difficulties these characters experience with the physical environment are only multiplied in societal relationships. (p. 127)

[It] is the transitoriness of accomplishment that stands out in Naipaul's fiction. The characters that he portrays—alienated, without exception—are motivated primarily by negative forces and they lack purposeful direction. . . . The transience, the dereliction they seek to escape lies within: they are wise to seek order and meaning and their authentic identities, but as Naipaul shows repeatedly they stand little chance of finding lasting answers to their needs in material gains. (p. 142)

> The social comedies I write can be fully appreciated only by someone who knows the region I write about. Without that knowledge it is easy for my books to be dismissed as farces and my characters as eccentrics. (Naipaul, 1958)

> All literatures are local. . . . The problems of Commonwealth writing are really no more than the problems of writing; and the problems of reading and comprehension are no more than the problems of reading literature of any strange society.   (Naipaul, 1965)

Just over seven years stand between these seemingly contradictory remarks, and in them may be observed evidence of the direction of Naipaul's development as a writer. At the time of his early complaint, *The Mystic Masseur, The Suffrage of Elvira,* and *Miguel Street* had been written. Added to these three books by the time of the second statement are *A House for Mr Biswas, The Middle Passage, Mr Stone and the Knights Companion,* and *An Area of Darkness.* His horizons have expanded, and his increased experience has provided a confidence allowing him to view what he had conceived to be a limited problem as one of much broader scope. (p. 147)

From the evidence gathered out of his scattered criticism it appears that Naipaul's most common concern is with the "socially redeeming" aspects of literature. The pattern of his thinking is noticeably consistent in this respect. In spite of his rather strong feelings about the need for an "informing spirit" in art, however, he seems to be careful in avoiding specific pronouncements. He is certainly a reformer, but when it comes to his fiction he always utilizes the method of indirection that is indispensable to artistic expression. (p. 156)

The mere fact of Naipaul's having expressed certain tenets, of course, does not guarantee their actual application in his own works. As it turns out, however, what he holds in theory does have a recognizable shaping influence on his fiction. Realizing the limitations of regionalism, after *Miguel Street* (1959) he deemphasizes local-color elements and brings out—as in *A House for Mr Biswas* (1961)—features of his characters and setting in such a way that they would have broader appeal. This is in keeping with his overt admission in *The Middle Passage* (1962) that the special situation of the West Indian writer deprives his work of universal appeal. (p. 157)

There is little real optimism in Naipaul's works, and he constantly adheres to the factual harshness of reality, but he also avoids overstressing the kind of fear "which only says 'This is life! Be afraid!'" That would be false, and he shows no inclination to elevate his characters beyond the level of ordinary experience. Indeed, the beauty and power of his accomplishment lie in his ability to capture and illuminate the deeper significance in even the least of man's actions. Herein he ultimately hits upon the most basic themes of the human spirit, transcending geographical and chronological barriers. Thus, ironically, in moving progressively away from nationalism, regionalism and in the strictest sense all but the most universal of "causes," he offers at last what the widest-ranging among his readers might well consider a greater contribution to his homeland than is possible from even the most devoted patriot. "In the end it is the writer and the writing that matter. The attempt to perfect Indian English or achieve Canadian-ness is the private endeavour of an irrelevant nationalism . . . a country is ennobled by its writers only if these writers are good." The larger consideration, then—that of art, that which is durable and most apt to be valuable to mankind in general—takes precedence over shortsighted aims. This makes of Naipaul's works, in turn, one of the strongest cultural links between Western Europe and the Americas. (pp. 158-59)

> *Robert D. Hamner, in his* V. S. Naipaul *(copyright 1973 by Twayne Publishers, Inc.; reprinted with the permission of Twayne Publishers, A Division of G. K. Hall & Co., Boston), Twayne, 1973.*

JOHN AYRE

[Naipaul] has become a kind of inspired commando parachuting into the underdeveloped world and writing about the color and people and distress that United Nations statistical reports can never convey. His collected essays, *The Overcrowded Barracoon,* represent probably the most direct image of the Third World we're ever going to receive. These essays are superior, I think, because Naipaul never loses his novelist's command of experience and detail.

This is precisely what disappoints me about his . . . *India: A Wounded Civilization,* a book more about ideas than people. . . . Instead of uncovering new material . . . [Naipaul] has largely gutted [another earlier book, *An Area of Darkness,*] of its central ideas and tightened them into a grand despairing condemnation of his Hindu ancestry. . . .

The Indian's idea of India, Naipaul believes, is a romantic retread of a glorious past which never really existed and has no magical power to solve the subcontinent's festering contemporary problems. . . .

Yet for the West as much as the country itself, India still often suggests benign Oriental Wisdom, Eternal Patience and the timeless pretty scenes of Roloff Beny photography. In *India* there is a rude but healthy destruction of that dangerous myth. More than images of backlit misty villages and meditation-zonked holy men, Naipual gives us the ultimate image of human uselessness. . . . (p. 33)

> *John Ayre, in* The Globe and Mail, *Toronto, July 16, 1977.*

JOHN UPDIKE

The so-called Third World has produced no more brilliant literary artist [than V. S. Naipaul]; but the propagandists and official spokesmen for the underdeveloped nations will find little to encourage them in Naipaul's cold-eyed fictional descriptions and journalistic reports. Where they would proclaim a decent hope and a revolutionary indignation, he sees stagnation, futility, and a sinister darkness as opaque as that which confounds Conrad's Mr. Kurtz and Greene's burnt-out case. His view of native possibilities in lands unregulated by white men seems no less dim than Evelyn Waugh's, though Naipaul's farce awakens fear sooner than laughter, and is informed not by a visitor's quizzical amusement but by a pained, partial identification. . . .

"A Bend in the River" struck me as an advance—broader, warmer, less jaded and kinky—over the much-praised "Guerrillas," though not quite as vivid and revelatory as the fiction of "In a Free State." There, in the two short stories "One Out of Many" and "Tell Me Who to Kill," the cataclysmic inner adjustments forced upon those of the world's poor who immigrate to Western metropolises are sketched with a fond accent and a gaiety of invention rare in Naipaul's rather stern later fiction. . . . Naipaul has written little that is better [than his "In a Free State"], and little better has been written about modern Africa. "A Bend in the River" is carved from the same territory—an Africa of withering colonial vestiges, terrifyingly murky politics, defeated pretensions, omnivorous rot, and the implacable undermining of all that would sustain reason and safety. (p. 141)

[The] author's embrace of his tangled and tragic African scene seems relatively hearty as well as immensely knowledgeable. Always a master of fictional landscape, Naipaul here shows, in his variety of human examples and in his search for underlying social causes, a Tolstoyan spirit, generous if not genial. "A Bend in the River" is the most genuinely exploratory novel about tropical Africa written by a non-African since Joyce Cary's "The African Witch." (p. 144)

> *John Updike, "Un Pé Pourrie," in* The New Yorker *(© 1979 by The New Yorker Magazine, Inc.), May 21, 1979, pp. 141-44.*

*   *   *

NEWBY, P(ercy) H(oward)   1918-

Newby is an English novelist, short story writer, playwright, editor, critic, and author of children's books. He often explores the clash of two cultures in his fiction, notably the English and Middle Eastern worlds. These cultures are seen through the eyes of a character who finds himself bewildered by the way of life in an alien world. Handled with Newby's characteristic wit and flair for satire, his characters never achieve any kind of mutual understanding. Even in his novels with English settings, Newby's main theme remains the difficulty of both self-discovery and communication with one's fellows in the fragmented and detached world of contemporary society. (See also *CLC,* **Vol. 2, and** *Contemporary Authors,* **Vols. 5-8, rev. ed.)**

V. S. NAIPAUL

Mr Newby writes with an ease which conceals the utmost care and economy. He is wonderfully and intelligently inventive, and organises his material so well that this complex story [*A Guest and His Going*], with its many layers of interest, never strains the reader. He manages continually to surprise, though on examination it is seen that he has left clues everywhere so quiet is his manner. Occasionally, however, a development seems imposed from without; and perhaps the element of fantasy is a little too strong. But this humane comedy is one of the best things Mr Newby has done. (p. 871)

V. S. Naipaul, in New Statesman (© 1959 The Statesman & Nation Publishing Co. Ltd.), June 20, 1959.

STEPHEN WALL

P. H. Newby's [*One of the Founders*] embraces limitation a little too willingly. *One of the Founders* has his flair for topicality: here, the world of the Robbins report, the material being the founding of a new university in a provincial town. . . . Assorted scenes from provincial life are briskly exhibited, and the two physical climaxes of the book are an absurd sort of seduction and a bungled sword-fight, both amusingly grotesque in the way that Mr Newby has long since mastered. The first half of the novel in particular is often very funny and is well-observed—though well-heard would be a better description, since the dialogue tells without revealing. . . . This is the sort of novel of which it is said that it works on more than one level, the truth being that it is far from clear which floor one is meant to be on at a given time; mezzanine fiction, perhaps.

Part of the trouble (if trouble it is and not obtuseness on the reviewer's part) is that Hedges [the novel's protagonist] resembles too closely for the novel's later good the over familiar device of handicapping the hero. . . . Hedges' generally unillumined state about his own motivation, his feeling that the vital clue lies just out of sight, is a dangerous one for the novelist to play, and one is inclined to suspect Mr Newby of souping up the action in order to stop the book coming to rest in a vacuum. But even if the more serious aspects of the book ought either to have added up to something more, or have been deducted in the interests of clarity, there is an extremely adroit and practised hand behind the comedy, and the characterization, though external, has its individual manner. . . . The final qualification, however, remains: whether [Mr Newby] ought not, with such gifts, to try to do more. The whole property has the air of being insured for more than it's worth. (pp. 99-100)

Stephen Wall, in London Magazine (© London Magazine 1965), *December, 1965.*

F. X. MATHEWS

For Newby's artistic development the placing of the trilogy [consisting of *The Picnic at Sakkara* (1955), *Revolution and Roses* (1957), and *A Guest and His Going* (1959)] is important. It follows immediately his attempt to come to terms with his memories of World War II in *A Step to Silence* (1952) and *The Retreat* (1953), novels in which the imagination becomes circumscribed, myth fragments, connections falter, and sanctuary is reached (if at all) only after violence, death, and mental peril. The comic trilogy provides a form of catharsis from the terrible new knowledge. Though its vision of the contemporary condition is essentially that of the war novels, the tone shifts radically. The comic, of course, is not a completely new departure for Newby; even his most serious novels contain an undercurrent of humor that threatens to subvert the tragic potential with what is now fashionably called dark comedy. But as a dominant tone the comic allows him to continue, without the stark conclusions of the war novels, his exploration of substantially the same political question: how does the individual,

locked in his own private fantasies, relate to events in an outer world that has gone mad? In a tragic reference he is driven to despair, insanity, or death. But the virtue of the comic answer is that it holds out the hope of survival. Freed from the desperate urgency to give his characters answers where answers may no longer be possible, Newby contents himself with exposing the complexity of illusion. None of the present novels is "pure" comedy: the laughter is both satiric and cathartic. (pp. 3-4)

[Satiric] comedy eliminates the demands on the hero. Set the hero on a desperate quest for identity in a hostile or indifferent universe and the outcome is the personal encounter with darkness and death of *Agents and Witnesses* and *The Retreat*. The hero is constrained to find salvation in terms of the novel, and either the novel contains that norm (as *The Retreat* very perilously does) or does not contain it (as in *Agents and Witnesses*), but in either case we search for the answer somewhere in the mysterious universe that the novelist has summoned up. But in Newby's trilogy, where there are no heroes, the norm lies outside the novel. It devolves upon the audience to supply it in an imaginative response broad enough to recognize the illusion and to extend charity to the comic characters.

Such disengagement does not imply an abnegation of authorial responsibility. In the present novels Newby sets up a twofold object of satiric attack. The first is the romantic illusion manifest in improbable heroism, misplaced idealism, the fantasy of innocence, or nostalgia for a past that never existed. The second is the illusion of theory: life, the novels maintain, is always larger than the ideas, theories, and sets of belief that are supposed to explain it. Beyond these general victims Newby's satire thrives in particular on a distinction between the English and the Egyptian character. I see the trilogy, then, as satiric comedy concerned with the exposure of illusion, both individual and cultural. Faced with issues urgently topical, the novelist retreats to a region of laughter where, with relative immunity, he may contemplate the clash of illusion against illusion. (p. 4)

Ultimately Newby sees no reconciliation between these separate worlds of illusion. Egypt remains Egypt and England adamantly England. To the last the Egyptian hopes to live out his contradictions and the Englishman fails to break out of his insular illusions. . . . Yet Newby maintains a balance between sympathy and detachment that avoids easy condescension. And mercifully he decides to make all the characters to some extent grotesque, so that the reader is spared the spectacle of grotesque Egyptians contrasted with pathetic Englishmen or (worse) pathetic suppressed Egyptians versus grotesque English warlords. (p. 5)

Consistently [*The Picnic at Sakkara*] is working toward [a] final ambiguity, made possible by the fact that Muawiya himself is intentionally contradictory. Though all Newby characters to some extent embody contradictions, what makes Muawiya distinctively Oriental in Newby's eyes is that he never suspects life might be otherwise. Whatever he feels or imagines at the moment is reality; consistency is irrelevant to truth. . . . To Muawiya there is no contradiction between loving Perry as a man and killing him as an Englishman. Endearing as this attitude may be, it is simply the comic extension of the tragic lesson of *A Step to Silence* and *The Retreat*: modern man cannot live simultaneously in antagonistic worlds of personal and political commitment. (p. 8)

The Picnic at Sakkara concludes with the ambiguity of the comic muddle. Yet from his vantage point outside the novel Newby gives life and color to the muddle. One suspects that Henry James would have understood. (p. 9)

Revolution and Roses is a slighter book than its predecessor. The prose is as controlled as ever, the humor even more outrightly funny, but Professor Perry is missed; in his place Newby supplies a gallery of humour characters manipulated into contrived situations.... Yet through these fantastics Newby is working toward a comment on social and political realities, or, to put it another way, the personal fantasies ironically reflect and satirize the public. (p. 10)

When in *Revolution and Roses* the illusion is defeated by the reality of Egyptian life, that reality itself becomes a form of illusion. Whatever the real Egypt is (presumably the Egypt one reads of in the newspapers) it is not the Egypt of this book. The bystanders' follies keep the political fact from coming into focus. There would seem to be an inherent ambiguity in Newby's concept of the political. On the one hand he affirms the necessity of coming to terms with the contemporary scene ("It is no longer possible for a Jane Austen to sit in a country parsonage writing novels of the first importance which ignore the wars and revolutions, for the wars and revolutions are so general that they cannot be ignored") and the necessity of reconciling the personal and the political (Thus Knight's discovery in *A Step to Silence:* "If he was to be adult at this moment in history he saw how each and every act must, in some way, however remotely, be a political act"). Yet Newby just as firmly takes his stand against the "political" novel—"that unhappy phase in English writing." The trilogy seeks to resolve the difficulty by a fiction in which the political is present by ironic implication in the individual gesture while the political *fact* is de-emphasized.... The novel asserts the impossibility of coming to direct terms with the political fact; by implication the fact of the revolution—filtered through the prism of each character's illusions—itself takes on the color of illusion.

In another novel these illusions might well have been tragic. But when Newby creates the outside vision, as with most of the characters in *The Picnic at Sakkara* and all the humour figures of *Revolution and Roses,* the result is comic conflict between a fantastic society and fantastic individuals. One value of the vision ... is satiric exposure—the devil bottom side up. Another might be called the value of cathartic laughter. Both find final fulfillment in the figures of the demon and the scapegoat in *A Guest and his Going.*

Reversing the pattern of the two preceding novels, *A Guest and his Going* brings the outsider from Egypt to England. (pp. 11-12)

[Beneath] the laughter is the same serious theme of the failure to connect [found in the two preceding novels]—of the individual to connect the contradictory sides of his nature, of the private to connect with the public, of two individuals or two nations to connect in friendship or in love....

For the most part, all that has changed since the first two books is the setting: characters, attitudes, and situations are substantially the same.... Newby neatly contrives to bring together his favorite characters from both earlier volumes. (p. 13)

In a sense the trilogy ends where it began—in absurdity. Though Perry's understanding has been enlarged, nothing has really changed. He has not only failed to communicate with Muawiya but also failed in his marriage.... He meets defeat. But he endures. And if he has been granted no positive vision, he has at least come to recognize his illusions for what they are....

Perhaps in a final evaluation Newby's trilogy is more important as exploration than destination. The satiric comedy, that pulls one society off the other's throat just at the throttling point, allows him a more detached contemplation of the contemporary scene. The hero has disappeared; in his place appear only the *eiron,* the *ingenu,* the scapegoat, the demon, the fool. Connections are thwarted. The character who rejects or is rejected by a fantastic society is himself the victim of illusions. At times the laughter is cruel; but ultimately it is also a laughter of deliverance, the contemplation of the gentlemanly Prince of Darkness bottom side up. (p. 15)

F. X. Mathews, *"Newby on the Nile: The Comic Trilogy," in* Twentieth Century Literature *(copyright 1968, Hofstra University Press), April, 1968, pp. 3-15.*

WILFRID SHEED

["Something to Answer For"] is in fact a rarity—a first-rate novel about a major political subject. And a close look at the problems it has to crawl around and under may help to show why such books *are* rare....

Newby has managed to combine the cartoon method with conventional storytelling in a sort of third force. Actually, he has been working on this method for some time, but in a series of miniatures, using small events to parallel large ones. In "Something to Answer For" he wheels out the large events themselves—a breakthrough that, like the juggler's sixth plate, might spell disaster.

Newby's text is the Suez snafu of a few years back. He is content to use a single consciousness, although he splits it with an introductory blow on the head. So we cannot, after the first chapter, be sure when his hero, Jack Townrow, is hallucinating and when he is seeing things straight. A sane head and a mad one—simple props. The mad head can be used as a recording device and an agent of illogic; it can get its owner into scenes that are barred to a sane man. The sane head must meanwhile plug through a sane plot that complements the crazy one, which complements Sir Anthony Eden and Suez. (p. 125)

[The] distinction of "Something to Answer For" does not lie in its being a psychologically plausible story that happens to contain symbols—a virtue that is commoner than one might suppose. Newby doesn't just want a story running alongside his politics, with gunfire in the distance; he wants it thrust right inside his politics. This means double duty for poor Townrow, who spends the book in a chronic state of fatigue. (p. 126)

To avoid the mere piling up of episodes, Newby has taken a large risk and allowed his hero to combine in himself the connecting overview of a reader with the particular confusions of a character. This sounds impossible, and it probably is.... But by conjoining hallucination, dream, sharp observation, and the ordinary newspaper reader's sense of fact, he concocts in Townrow's mind a montage of the Suez crisis that is both panoramic and specific, that sees all and yet is not the eye of God. This marshalling of all the resources of the human psyche to produce a universal historical consciousness is an enterprise worthy of Joyce. But although Newby does pick his way dexterously among Townrow's thoughts to find the stream of consciousness he needs, and although spends half the time thinking he might be an Irishman, the result is not really Joycean. Townrow's psyche is specifically devised for his situation, and exists only in relation to it. With Newby, the novel comes first.

What is interesting to us is never just Townrow but Townrow in Egypt. His hallucinations have a humdrum matter-of-factness, like the dreams in recent English movies, so they are not only hard to detect but the most informative hallucinations ever recorded; at his most farfetched, Townrow is always reporting. Newby's language has a small, persistent lilt, like the gently lapping sea that he uses as an image, and he is able to mesmerize the reader within seconds, or wake him, as need be. In short, he has mastered his particular method and can now juggle that sixth dish with ease.

The book is marred very slightly, as other Newby books have been marred, by a gruff, bashful moralizing at the end. . . . Newby has taken the chance of writing obscurely, but now he seems to feel he must make it up to the reader with a last flurry of explanation. The effect is weakening. "Some point he could call the heart" is the circumlocution of a public schoolboy afraid of sounding soppy. It is not right for Townrow or for Newby, who, besides being a highly gifted writer, is now, increasingly, an audacious one. (pp. 127-28)

Wilfrid Sheed, "Double Deal," in The New Yorker *(© 1969 by the New Yorker Magazine, Inc.), September 6, 1969, pp. 125-28.*

F. X. MATHEWS

[Out] of the tension between a disruptive reality seemingly antagonistic to art and a scrupulous devotion to the craft of fiction [P. H. Newby] creates his characteristic work. Willing on the one hand to agree with V. S. Pritchett that "the real subject of the best writing now being done is that impersonal shadow, 'the contemporary situation,'" he is confident that fidelity to the contemporary situation need not mean a dreary succession of "political" novels. . . . [When] "events" are no longer separable from the starkly unpoetic reality of a world at war, the unsettling doubts surface. In what terms can the transforming and shaping powers of the imagination be brought to bear on such insanity without falsifying? (pp. 121-22)

[In *A Step to Silence* and *The Retreat*] Newby poses most insistently the question of the responsibility of the private witness for a world of violence.

That question, and the particular approach of the war novels, Newby actually foreshadowed in his second novel, *Agents and Witnesses* (1947). . . . Three notes struck in *Agents and Witnesses* echo through the war novels. The first is an ironic perspective, an oblique approach to events that are "witnessed" by spectators unable to comprehend them. (pp. 122-23)

This relentless irony, which sets the hero's persistent belief that reality should have meaning against an intractable reality that refuses to impart it, leads to a second consideration:

the circumscribed imagination. . . . [But the] imagination is powerless against a world gone mad. . . .

Thirdly, Newby sees this frustrated quest as a religious one as well. Art, he once said, is "an act of faith," and I think he meant it quite literally. The artist's anguish in *Agents and Witnesses* is a spiritual anguish as well. (p. 123)

Death in *Agents and Witnesses* is absurd and gratuitous, the fate that rules the novel irrational. The individual and public worlds never come together. Indeed, the technique itself, which never allows the three strains of interest—the plague, the revolution, a love affair—to impinge except as ironic commentary on one another, bears this out. . . .

When Newby returned to the witness theme five years later in *A Step to Silence,* where the setting shifts to the more immediate reality of the outbreak of World War II, he had moved beyond the stance of *Agents and Witnesses.* Once again the theme is the individual passion for moral identity in a world of violence, and once again Newby poses the question: to what extent is the witness responsible for this violence? The answer that now comes is the protagonist's imaginative discovery that no witness can be simply innocent in the twentieth century, that even the personal gesture is of necessity political, and that the public nightmare is one with the private. The concept of an existential absurd gives way to a form of demonic vision: in their private hallucinations the characters mirror the obsession that is gripping Europe at large. Though this is hardly a comforting knowledge, it is, at least, an imaginative truth and marks a partial recovery of the imagination that was powerless in *Agents and Witnesses.* (p. 124)

Faced with [the] numbing "un-experience" [of the English soldier-writer writing for a British people who had experienced the war as both soldiers and civilians], Newby focuses not on the newspaper event, but on the psychic landscape—the personal hopes, fears, hallucinations, and obsessions that mirror the event. His approach is characteristically oblique, through the interior effect rather than the external fact. *A Step to Silence* begins with the obsession of the private world by public madness. The Mellingham Training College that Oliver Knight (whose name hints the familiar quest) attends may appear "as self-contained as a ship," but it reflects in its own grim way the fact that the year is 1937 and Munich is just around the corner. The college authorities, dedicated to the outdated fiction of a rationally ordered little world, fail to recognize the fascism in their midst, that [lies] beneath the traditional student ragging. . . . Knight, at eighteen, comes prepared to accept their reasoned fictions. His complacence is shattered by his involvement with a thirty-one-year-old romantic failure, Hesketh, who is the symbol of a dark, intuitive understanding and carries the novel.

Hesketh's tragedy is that, although he possesses the rare gift of imagination, he is a frail vessel for that gift. Intuitively he understands the college ragging because it springs from the same demonic impulse he contains within himself, but he fears the consequences of his understanding. He has the imaginative potential of a Hitler, a savior, or a victim, and in the course of the two novels [*A Step to Silence* and *The Retreat*] he plays all three roles. . . . The puppet becomes the central figure for characters who, often while recognizing the role, are manipulated by their own obsessions or by those of some larger system beyond them. Their lack of freedom is not simply an artistic contrivance, but, Newby would imply, a consequence of existence in 1937.

Hesketh marks one pole of Knight's awareness; the other is Jane Oliphant, a young schoolteacher staying with Knight's widowed mother. (pp. 124-25)

[The] argument of *A Step to Silence* is that no adult has a right to innocence in this moment of history, that innocence is an irresponsible sentimentality in the modern world. (p. 126)

[The] final chapter presents a scene whose terrible knowledge Knight cannot, at the time, go beyond; the most he can try to do is forget the vision. This last dramatic scene returns the image of puppet and puppet-master, which becomes, by implication, a symbol of the struggle for power in the world at large. For Hesketh, who here represents the subversive power of the demonic, now appears with the potential of a Hitler.... [The] hallucination, "the moment of hysteria" [Knight experiences as Kesketh portrays the role of Hitler]..., will pursue Knight through *The Retreat,* where he must work out his salvation *in* time. The conclusion of *A Step to Silence* is disturbingly inconclusive. Newby sends his protagonist out, with no other equipment than the knowledge that "no one ... was immune to innocence"..., into a world that has reverted to anarchy.

The Retreat opens with F/O Knight of the Nth Fighter Squadron making his way to Dieppe in the massive confusion of the retreat from Dunkirk in 1940. "A complicated organization had broken down." But this mass movement is only the overture to a subtler, more tortuous one: the retreat (more accurately, the many retreats) of the individual human being. Once again Newby isolates the individual atom as a commentary on the whole. Knight's overriding concern (even when he seems to be running from her) is to get back to Helen, a girl he married two weeks before leaving for war. "Helen was so much his wife that her absence gave curious drama to the landscape. Normandy was a stage, and every step he took was a step in an over-rehearsed play; the great, romantic play of war." ... The book explores the personal retreats that lie between this desire and the final reconciliation of husband and wife. A single image unites those two moments, a figure of calm amid the chaos of war. While retreating from Dunkirk, Knight comes upon a blue pond, where ducks float serenely, and beside it half a dozen nuns picnicking silently on the green grass. The image does not recur until the final pages. Till that moment Knight pursues a tangled journey illuminated by just such figures as this: external reality suddenly become personal, symbols that flare up mysteriously out of the landscape and just as mysteriously disappear, gestures suddenly frozen, as in a snapshot, out of the merciless press of time. This almost eucharistic transformation of the particular moment is characteristic of *The Retreat*. The method, of course, is not new with this novel; what is new is the weight it carries. In *A Journey to the Interior,* for instance, the moment was sustained by the myth, but in *The Retreat* whatever myth remains has been fragmented into discrete moments. Even in *A Step to Silence* these moments of vision were assimilated into conventional narrative elements: the interplay of characters through dialogue, the subtle analysis of complex emotions, the explanatory passages of self-discovery. In *The Retreat* these have all but vanished. There is no real dialogue, only the statements of one isolated individual to another individual. There are

no emotions to spare. There are no rationalized explanations of discovery but only mysterious signs along the dark road from Dunkirk to Helen. The language itself has undergone a change; a new, spare style, with almost all the clausal subordination reduced to a minimum, forces the images to yield up their meaning of themselves. It is a style peculiarly suited to the subject: the fragmentation, the neurasthenia, the loss of logical nexus, the collapse of complex systems in the face of war. (pp. 126-28)

[The] central image of retreat functions as a complex, multiple symbol: (1) on the most literal level, the retreat from Dunkirk, which forms the overture to the story; (2) the retreat from the system, the authorities who discover Knight has falsified his name and become a deserter; (3) the retreat from personal commitment, from Jane's husband Hesketh and Knight's wife Helen; (4) the retreat from the past and the self that existed in the past ... ; (5) the spiritual retreat underlying these ... ; (6) finally (and ironically the real ray of hope in the book), no retreat from retreat.... Whatever dark illusion their retreat leads them into, [Knight and Jane] cannot simply turn back—to Hesketh, Helen, God, the authorities—but must journey on until they find imaginative salvation. In this final sense the retreat is not a negative, but a positive symbol, the perilous journey of the imagination imposed on the characters with all the solemnity of a religious quest.

Newby never fails to contrast the integrity of this retreat/quest with the inadequacy of any systems (the rational illusions of order) to come to terms with it. (pp. 129-30)

If these characters were mere puppets of Newby's technical mastery, one might have just cause for complaint. But they are symbols of humanity at large, puppets in the grip not merely of their private illusions, but of the insanity that the external world has become. And even with their diminished freedom in this cruel puppet show, they are capable of human gestures. (pp. 130-31)

The escape into a timeless green world, which Knight flirted with at the end of *A Step to Silence,* is no longer possible: he must work out his salvation *in* time. But Newby's time is not a logical continuum. He manipulates his characters into patterns of flight and pursuit that underscore the anxiety of actual time, then liberates them through isolated moments of hallucinated vision in which reality becomes more than itself. The power of the imagination to transform reality into meaningful symbol in such chance and fragmented moments of vision is the only hope left in a Newby universe in which one can no longer look to rational systems to explain the meaning (or indeed even the existence) of external reality. (p. 131)

The process by which Knight reaches sanctuary while Hesketh and Jane are sacrificed along the way cannot be explained by any logical system (the systems, as Hesketh knows, only demand more victims). Possibly much of the outcome depends on the social dimension: the inhuman, random meting out of destiny in a world at war. But ultimately Newby seems to refer the outcome of his characters' confrontation with a hostile universe to the nonrational realm of religion. One would be tempted to use the word *grace* to explain Knight's salvation if that did not imply the totally gratuitous. For unfathomable though his deliverance ultimately is, it is also true that he has prepared for it, diligently pursuing the images of self till they finally take shape as a religious ritual leading to the "silence" promised in the preceding novel. . . . (p. 133)

Newby's approach to the war is perhaps best described in summary by the image of the witness. In an age of violence the witness is a mere spectator of, is blind to, reflects, or sees beyond irrational reality. The first is the concept of absurd existence to which *Agents and Witnesses* essentially limits itself. The irrational universe refuses to take shape under the artist's vision. (p. 134)

The theme of the blind witness dramatizes the inadequacy of the sentimental belief that in our time an individual or a system can be self-contained. . . . It is illusion characterized by the single word "innocence," to which Newby gives new meaning in *A Step to Silence*.

The third aspect of the witness theme is the compulsive: the violence of Hesketh, the madness of Jane, the obsessive retreat reflect an outer nightmare. Newby's image of puppet and puppet-master is not simply a description of the technical relation between the novelist and his characters, but a figure of modern man in the grip of a demonic possession.

Finally, the vision that sees beyond irrational reality is the imagination that interiorizes reality into a new truth. Hounded by time, Knight finds in moments of hallucinatory vision a means of engaging in time and transcending it. Such moments, present in all the novels, become almost the sole raison d'être in *The Retreat,* where a new cryptic style, characterized by fragmented myth, lack of logical nexus, dialogue interiorized and discovery unexplained, throws the weight on the individual image. Through the imagination reality becomes self-discovery and the discrete images a ritual that brings Knight, in time of political insanity, to a "silence" best described as religious. Variously I have referred to that final state, though in qualified terms, as salvation or deliverance. But Newby's own word "sanctuary" remains the most apt final description. For though the imagination carries Knight to the end of his quest, the terrible price exacted in an age of war dispels any simple illusions about victory. (pp. 134-35)

> *F. X. Mathews, "Witness to Violence: The War Novels of P. H. Newby,"* in Texas Studies in Literature and Language *(copyright © 1970 by the University of Texas Press), Vol. XII, No. 1, Spring, 1970, pp. 121-35.*

*   *   *

NGUGI, James
  See WA THIONG'O, Ngugi
*   *   *

NYE, Robert   1939-

Nye is a versatile British poet, playwright, short story writer, and author of novels for adults and children. His novels range from *Doubtfire* in the New Novel form to *Falstaff,* a fictional autobiography of Shakespeare's unscrupulous knight. His plays are sometimes based on medieval morality plays or Greek tragic myths. (See also *Contemporary Authors,* Vols. 33-36, rev. ed.)

GEORGE MacBETH

[The] specific tendency of Mr Nye's work can be seen as

interesting. He is the only poet I know now writing who seems to be directly influenced by the attitudes and the diction of the later nineteenth century: his book breathes the spirit of a queer Frenchified pre-Raphaelitism crossed with early Pound and Wallace Stevens. . . . Mr Nye is perhaps more like an even more recherché writer, the half-French neo-jongleur Theodore Julius Marzials, whose ninetyish farrago of the Gallic and the listless came out as early as 1873. Mr Nye has a taste for archaic language which he deploys mellifluously. In a love poem called 'Of A Jar You Are' he catalogues what I take to be a list of vessels (my dictionary baulked more than once at his vocabulary):

> Sendaument goodwill,
> Jorum and noggin,
> Come-cruse and shellsnail.
> Eve-spect manchyn

Now the point about this is that the precise meaning of the terms doesn't much matter: they're used for their sound and their mediaeval associations. . . . [This] is a protozoic sort of pleasure in poetry and Mr Nye as yet offers us little more. In another love poem called 'Other Times' he writes well about a bonfire night:

> The gloam rains slowly; fireworks kick with green,
> Attach all marigoldal to the hand.

Here both 'gloam' and 'marigoldal' are nice in themselves but they also work for their keep in the verse. If Mr Nye has more lines like these in his next book and less like

> Espy and wink of the impossibly moon

I shall applaud his progress. (p. 92)

> *George MacBeth, in* London Magazine *(© London Magazine 1962), January, 1962.*

GILLIAN FREEMAN

Alain Robbe-Grillet is, I suppose, the high-priest of the *roman nouveau.* I have never been an acolyte of the movement. . . . I confess I find Robbe-Grillet's flat prose style . . . excruciatingly tedious. . . . I felt much the same frustration as I read Robert Nye's *Doubtfire.* This is a ranging exploration of the mind of an adolescent boy who, developing towards sexual maturity, is unable to sort out reality from fantasy. The interaction of truth and fear and wish and memory, which ultimately leads him to attempt suicide, form a tightly interlocking narrative. . . . [With] the stylised names and speech one cannot tell where the characters are merely extensions of the boy's own personality, and where he has absorbed them from actuality. . . . (p. 176)

Robert Nye is funny, savage, witty, sharp and illuminatingly visual. I wanted to enter wholly into this disturbed boy's mind as the author had done, but I only achieved isolated moments of identification and comprehension. (p. 177)

> *Gillian Freeman, in* New Statesman *(© 1968 The Statesman & Nation Publishing Co. Ltd.), February 9, 1968.*

Robert Nye's poems in *Darker Ends* are so reticent they need to be hunted at night with an infra-red lamp. One called "Let It Go" will serve to demonstrate the poet's well-mannered whisper; unfortunately it is also typical of his attack:

Snow fell so quick
that snow was melt
before it lasted on the ground.
The fleering pane
of gloomy fire
turned steadfastness to water also.

It's the kind of thing you recite after trotting out from behind a screen with a paper flower in your hand. (p. 109)

> The Times Literary Supplement (© *Times Newspapers Ltd. (London) 1970; reproduced from* The Times Literary Supplement *by permission), January 29, 1970.*

DEREK STANFORD

One of those all round virtuosi, Robert Nye can be relied on to surprise, whether in verse or in prose. His two utterly different poems in the recently published *Scottish Poetry 7* . . . are examples of his power to create something new. Criticism—whatever its conclusions—is not usually prodigal in unexpected opening gambits, but Mr Nye can hang a whole essay on Donne upon the inaugural statement that the poet heartily detested milk. His mask in verse *The Seven Deadly Sins* . . . is a further manifestation of Mr Nye's extraordinary prestidigitation. . . .

Mr Nye's intention [is] to reflesh with modern speech the skeleton form of the mediaeval morality play. Indeed, it is indicative of his conjuror's imagination that he likes to think of his mask as replacing 'the earliest recorded morality play in English' which 'set forth the merits of the Lord's Prayer'. He tells us that his own work turns upon the prayer known to all Christians together with the Jesus Prayer of the Orthodox Church ('Lord Jesus Christ, Son of God, have mercy on me, a sinner').

For those who understand what Mr Nye is talking about when he refers to sin as 'so many little sips of the grave / Original and actual', here is a work to be read with profit as it is to be watched with pleasure. (p. 66)

> *Derek Stanford, in* Books and Bookmen (© *copyright Derek Stanford 1975; reprinted with permission), August, 1975.*

JOHN COLEBY

I do not know what to make of Robert Nye's version of *Penthesilea*, a Greek tragic myth written down, or up, by the late eighteenth century German, Heinrich von Kleist. . . . Wads of rather aerated imagery punctuated by artificial barracks-type slang leave one feeling that one might be watching *The Long, and the Short and the Tall* performed in period gear by the more intellectual members of a public school Combined Cadet Force. Apart that is from the Amazons whose Queen, Penthesilea, goes crazy about Achilles; in the end literally so. His death at her hands does messy violence to truth, both mythical and dramatic. (pp. 89-90)

> *John Coleby, in* Drama, *Summer, 1976.*

PAUL WEST

In the main, ["Falstaff" is] a fresco of groinwork, more monotonous than inventive, from a first-person Falstaff. He is worth hearing from because, as the Shakespearean scholar, John Dover Wilson puts it, we find it exhilarating to watch a being free of all conventions, codes and moral ties, who nonetheless wins us with "his superb wit, his moral effrontery, his intellectual agility, and his boundless physical vitality."

Well now, Nye's rampant loudmouth, while certainly a lord of misrule, a pastmaster of civil and military disobedience and a self-stroking hyperbole, isn't so much intellectually agile as ramshackle and offhand, and his wit is heartiness dolled-up. . . .

It's like being pounded at by an Ancient Mariner turned satyr. For all his procedural antics (portrait of the artist as a self-conscious tub of lard), his quotations from Shakespeare and his Tiresias S. Eliot pose, this Falstaff wears his welcome out. Talk of maypoles, bananas, Italian dildoes and Norfolk loaves cannot disguise his relentless empty-headedness over 452 pages. A Scotsman, Nye has written a novel of the type that British taste never seems to grow out of: Philistine knockabout, complete with cakes and ale, and not an idea in sight, its patron saint not Rabelais but Terry-Thomas. (p. 38)

> *Paul West, in* The New York Times Book Review (© *1976 by The New York Times Company; reprinted by permission), November 7, 1976.*

MICHAEL WOOD

[In a sense] the novel is flourishing, and always will be as long as we have an appetite for well-told lies of any length. Nye's *Falstaff*, the imaginary autobiography of Shakespeare's splendid old scoundrel, is an excellent representative of this continuing life, and a good example of what a talented writer can do with a string of shaggy dog stories and some fine lines.

The danger with Falstaff is that we shall lose him to melancholy, as Orson Welles does, albeit with some panache, in his lugubrious film *Chimes at Midnight*. Indeed, Shakespeare suggests that Falstaff dies of Hal's rejection of him. . . .

Nye's Falstaff is bawdy rather than melancholy, and often seems to have stepped out of Rabelais rather than Shakespeare. . . . The bawdy can seem tiresome—there is a predictable chapter on Falstaff's prick, and a lot of rogering and ramming whenever the pace threatens to slacken—but generally it takes on a rather attractive pathos, for we are rarely allowed to forget that Falstaff is not bragging, but *lying*, and that his "cunterbury tales," as he calls them, are a "requiem for a life he never lived." . . .

Shakespeare's Falstaff is a consummate liar, of course, counterfeiting death on the battlefield at Shrewsbury with such perfection that death itself, in the shape of the corpse of Hotspur, seems provisional ("how if he should counterfeit too and rise? . . . Why may he not rise as well as I?"). But here we have Shakespeare's fiction inside Nye's fiction inventing fictions, and the result is not self-consciousness or a contribution to literary theory but an exhilarating sense of a mind living its life again by making it up. "Lies about my whole life," Falstaff writes in a scribbled confession to his priest. "But try & explain: some *true* lies?"

Sometimes Nye has Falstaff sounding too much like your hearty British soldier, borrowed from Kipling and coarsened up . . . , and occasionally he resorts to the dubious expedient of *translating* Shakespeare. . . . [But] a Falstaff who not only borrows names from Shakespeare ("Now this Brokeanus was married to a lady called Goneril, or as some say it, Gladys'') but also craftily quotes Eliot, Joyce, Dylan Thomas, Coleridge, and maybe Hopkins is not a man to be trifled with. Falstaff's true lies point us past him to Robert Nye, who, like his much admired Rabelais, doesn't hide his sources and will not segregate his learning and his jokes. (p. 59)

> *Michael Wood, in* The New York Review of Books *(reprinted with permission from* The New York Review of Books; *copyright © 1977 Nyrev, Inc.), January 20, 1977.*

T. A. SHIPPEY

Three Red Ravagers of the Island of Britain: Arthur, and Run son of Beli, and Morgant the Wealthy. And Three Unfortunate Disclosures of the Island of Britain. And Three Fierce Handslaps. And Three Futile Battles. Everybody can do ancient Welsh triads once they've got the idea.

What turns up in Robert Nye's *Merlin* could be called "Three Enormous Spankings of the Court of King Arthur": first the birching of Vivien the virgin when she was with child with Merlin and no man had touched her. And second the whipping of Ygrayne the Countess by her husband's shape at the time her husband was alive and dead. And third the beating of Morgan le Fay by her half-brother that was King Arthur. But onto the loony taciturnity of the Red Book of Hergest have been grafted the finer details of the latest issue of *Flog* or *Lash:* "the eye pressed hard to the hole above grows colder and brighter as my mother's well whipped bottom grows red as a strawberry with the marks of the birch". And that's only after Dame Pudicity the abbess has given her brisk run-through of "naughty nights in

the convent". As Beelzebub observes to his brother Lucifuge, "You had her behaving at the end there almost like a parody of celibate sexuality gone mad."

The devils are the intellectuals of this book, adding a touch of dispassionate comment to the committed voyeurism which all the other characters go in for. They also betray a strong streak of *Fungus the Bogeyman* as they pour cognac over their maggots, tell each other stories about lazy incubuses, and dispute the reality of the witch's birds' nest full of male organs (and the finder couldn't steal the biggest for himself, because . . .). The novel fizzes along on a charge of multi-levelled inconsequential anecdote, very funny, very sexy, invariably rude, and quite often not as inconsequential as it looks. . . .

What it all has to do with poor King Arthur is another matter. *Merlin* takes off from the early rumour that its eponymous hero was born of a devil and a virgin, like a failed Antichrist, and goes on to consider the mechanics of this operation (the devil really prefers choirboys, you see), the results of the birth, the strange parallels with the conception of Arthur, and the sage's eventual imprisonment within the crystal cave of time, from which he becomes the ultimate voyeur or cosmospectator. If there's a moral in all that, it is that the world is a book and the devil writes it (unless it's Morgan le Fay)—an idea which all the great Arthurians of the past would, I'm sure, find repugnant.

> *T. A. Shippey, "Beat the Devil," in* The Times Literary Supplement *(© Times Newspapers Ltd. (London) 1978; reproduced from* The Times Literary Supplement *by permission), September 15, 1978, p. 1010.*

O

O'BRIEN, Edna   1932-

An Irish novelist, short story writer, playwright, and screen writer, O'Brien is considered a pioneer in exploring the condition of women in a society dominated by men. Coping with loneliness, repression, religious upbringing, and sexual needs, O'Brien's women are their own victims—passive and often ineffective because of emotional entanglements. Critics sometimes imply that her male characters are stereotypical puppets, serving only as props for their female counterparts. O'Brien's focus, however, is not romantic but realistic, confronting the key issues of feminism. Influenced by Joyce, her style is lucid, exhibiting a lyrical quality. Like the works of several of her fellow countrymen, O'Brien's novels have been banned in Ireland. (See also *CLC*, Vols. 3, 5, 8, and *Contemporary Authors*, Vols. 1-4, rev. ed.)

[*Johnny I Hardly Knew You*], while lapped in lyricism, is full of aggression: an aggression which is taken to its unnatural conclusion when Nora, the narrator, murders the young man she loves. . . . [Nora] is torn between hatred of the eternally defecting male and a longing for "a fruitful love". "Haven't I always been attending to a him, and dancing attendance upon a him, and being a slave to a him and being trampled on by a him?"

The final violence is not gratuitous: "Frankly, have I not always had a secret desire to kill?" When Hart has an epileptic fit in her bed she revenges herself on all men, especially on her father with his "long shins and his cuttlebone tongue", and knows "the gruesome power of the hand that strikes". . . . This vital link between fear and murderousness is well made; but the references on the jacket to *Crime and Punishment* and Camus's *Outsider* are ill advised. Edna O'Brien is not in that league.

Yet her writing fascinates. It flows with an undoubted authority, while always teetering on the brink of cliché and absurdity. She can, however, deflect with one effective word her own passionate flow: "I'm going to curse the womb that carried and bore me, and the bottle that gave me suck." It would have been so much more expected to have written "breasts" instead of "bottle". . . .

The artlessness of her art, and her recurring wryness, are Edna O'Brien's strengths. . . .

Artlessness, however artful, results in sudden flashes of truthfulness of a kind seldom expressed in more cerebral writing. . . . The novel is episodic, and several of the episodes—Nora seeing the Palio in Siena, Nora foiling an attempted rape, Nora as a green girl with other green girls visiting a newly married friend—could have stood on their own as short stories. Yet *Johnny I Hardly Knew You* is held together by what has always held Edna O'Brien's writing together: a fluency which celebrates the failure of love, and the belief that "even the blights of love have in them such radiance that they make other happiness pale indeed".

"Hymn to Him," in The Times Literary Supplement (© *Times Newspapers Ltd. (London) 1977; reproduced from* The Times Literary Supplement *by permission), July 15, 1977, p. 849.*

ANATOLE BROYARD

[In "Arabian Days"] Miss O'Brien picks her way through the debris of progress and the buildings that are like boxes waiting to be filled with the gifts of the future. She asks her shrewd and interested questions and few are willing to admit that there are, as yet, no answers. The women will not even tell her their dreams, which she asks for after every other inquiry has failed. Miss O'Brien is the only one of them who is not masked, but to anyone who knows her other books, it will seem that this is not a novel situation for her. (p. C9)

Anatole Broyard, in The New York Times (© *1978 by The New York Times Company; reprinted by permission), June 27, 1978.*

In her novels, O'Brien's mannered, almost curdled, passionate style is usually set off by meticulous honesty. But in [the dozen short stories in *The Rose in the Heart*] . . . she rarely has time to get real feelings fully wound up, and the style often oozes into self-parody. The sameness of theme doesn't help, either—mostly about middle-aged, lonely women making fleeting contacts that are never enough. . . . One story, "Starting," does seem fully warmed, not rushed: a divorcee meets a lovely, companionable, mature man, but can't stand to contemplate all the excitement and suspense of the *start* of a love affair; she'd rather come in somewhere in the middle, where it's already "as it was with her children, easy and silent and with an unutterable understanding." O'Brien, as anyone who knows her work will tell, is all heart—you can just about wring her out—but here that heart doesn't start pumping on such short notice; still, her fans will welcome this gathering of some previously uncollected favorites. (p. 1380)

Kirkus Reviews *(copyright © 1978 The Kirkus Service, Inc.), December 15, 1978.*

VICTORIA GLENDINNING

There is a body of opinion that has it that Edna O'Brien is overrated as a writer; that her success is due to the sex and Irish blarney in her work, and that any serious criticism of her books is out of place. . . .

If I am daft enough to put my head on the block again, it is because there really is something about the Edna O'Brien phenomenon that is worth defining.

With the passing of time, her settings have become more sophisticated. . . . In this collection of classic O'Brien stories . . . ["A Rose in the Heart"], there is an awareness of death not generally associated with this elegiac but most life-loving author. Graveyards are dwelt on, and the barriers between life and death are thin. In "Ways," the Vermont cemetery "seems integral to the town as if the living and the dead are wedded to one another." In "Baby Blue," the heroine grieves for "all those who were in boxes alone or together above or below ground, all those unable to accept their afflicted selves."

The "afflicted selves," however, who dominate these stories, find solace in earthly delights. Miss O'Brien is like Colette in her pleasured cataloguing of flowers, smells, landscapes, food and drink; these genderless sensualities heal and comfort the ladies whose love lives are awry.

Most of the stories spotlight particular phases in a sexual relationship; sometimes its consummation—"her body flooded open"—more often edgy beginnings or dismal endings. There is a wonderful resilience in the heroines, a readiness to expect Prince Charming. (p. 7)

There is also an unabashed acceptance of need, as in "Ways": "All she wants is for the man to come up and nuzzle her and hold her and temporarily squeeze all the solitude out of her." And yet in "Ways," as in two other of these stories, the woman runs out on the promising affair. Solitude, it seems, is often preferable to risking or inflicting pain.

The most powerful story here is not chiefly about sexual love at all. "A Rose in the Heart of New York" traces a daughter's relationship with her mother, from babyhood to her mother's death, with a high-pressure intensity and concentration. The least successful, for me, is "Clara," the narrator of which is a foreign entrepreneur in Ireland—a man. I never believed in him for a moment. Edna O'Brien's vision is preternaturally sharp for everything that grows—or wilts—in her own secret garden. Outside it, she is in the dark.

This singleness of focus is both her strength and her weakness. And by conventional standards she does not write "well." She writes, often, very badly. Her punctuation is all to hell, and she abuses both grammar and vocabulary. This is not because she has consciously decided to "remake" the language. Indeed, her unself-consciousness is the point. It is as if her fantasies, her elaborations of what happened, or what didn't happen, or what might have happened are projected in an undoctored tragicomic flow. It is

this authenticity that is the key to her quality and makes her a best seller.

It is also what irritates her critics. Because her fantasies are, necessarily, part of the common stock, people—especially women—say "Any of us could have written about *that.*" But we couldn't. What she has, and what many more highly educated, self-consciously literary writers would give their eyeteeth for, is a direct line between her own yeasty, mazy imaginings and her pen. And if some of what comes out is trite and second-rate, that is because human emotions *are* often commonplace. And if now, after years as a writer, she has learned consciously and professionally to harness this un-self-consciousness to her artful purposes, then more power to her elbow. (p. 22)

Victoria Glendinning, *"Elegiac and Life-loving,"* in The New York Times Book Review *(© 1979 by The New York Times Company; reprinted by permission), February 11, 1979, pp. 7, 22.*

MARY GORDON

When you call a book *A Rose in the Heart* you are taking a risk, perhaps a brave one; when you subtitle the same book "Love Stories," you may be approaching the territory of the sentimental with a foolhardy lack of regard. It is Edna O'Brien's particular genius to write about subjects which often fall to poor stylists or sloppy thinkers, because the best lack all conviction and the worst are full of passionate intensity. No one else writing today achieves what O'Brien does: the exploration of passionate subjects, and a deftness and precision of language accessible in our age most often to the chiefly cerebral, or to the detached.

Her real theme is loss and its effects: diminishment, revenge, reversal, cure. But she is never sentimental because she is never vague. Sentimentality is largely a failure of eyesight. . . . The lilt of her prose is an Irish legacy. . . . (p. 1)

Mary Gordon, *"Risks of Loving,"* in Book World —The Washington Post *(© 1979, The Washington Post), April 8, 1979, pp. 1, 4.*

*   *   *

O'CONNOR, (Mary) Flannery   1925-1964

O'Connor was an American short story writer, novelist, and essayist. A Roman Catholic from the Bible Belt, she liberally laced her fiction with material from each of these religious backgrounds to create a unique, highly personal vision. Her vision is a chilling one, reflected in a world characterized by sudden, bizarre violence and peopled with grotesques whom she sees as mirrors for men fallen from grace. O'Connor is considered one of the important figures of the Southern Renascence. (See also *CLC*, Vols. 1, 2, 3, 6, 10, and *Contemporary Authors*, Vols. 1-4, rev. ed.)

KENNETH FRIELING

Flannery O'Connor's themes are so traditional as to make her fiction seem unique within the context of the 50s. During a period in which regionalism was becoming suspect, O'Connor rooted her hilariously—often painfully—textured concrete reality in the regionalism of the Georgia sector of the Bible Belt. In a time whose literature still avoided absolutes in its various existential stances, she presents an anti-existential vision of a world offered the mystery of grace, the possibility of redemption through violent revelation. While always aware of being a practicing Catholic in the Protestant South, O'Connor is most fully aware of her challenge as an artist in a much broader area: "the business of fiction is to embody mystery through manners, and mystery is a great embarrassment to the modern mind."

A facile explanation of her reputation would be to ignore her fusion of Catholic mystery and Southern manners and point rather to the extraordinary verve of her brilliant style by which she presents grotesque characters experiencing horror coalesced with dark comedy. (pp. 111-12)

Much attraction lies in O'Connor's ability to depict her characters' shallowness in one adroit comment . . . , to expose their love of possessions as thoroughly alienated from what is natural . . . , and to present the characters' self-parodies through an outrageous image. . . .

Yet one cannot stop at this point, for her portraits of the physically grotesque reflect the spiritually distorted. (p. 112)

Just as her readers must recognize the grotesque as something other than horrific sensationalism, O'Connor's characters must recognize through violent revelation the grotesque as ugly, as unnatural distortion, and thus achieve the possibility of grace. (p. 113)

This recognition of the grotesque is accomplished through a violent displacement unleashing epiphanies with elemental religious force. The very violence of this epiphany and its accompanying potential of grace demands a vehicle which is brief, which is emphatically personal, which illuminates rather than explicates. Thus Flannery O'Connor most successfully presents mystery through manners within the structure of the short story.

This violence of revelation is artistically presented by O'Connor in her first collection of stories *A Good Man Is Hard to Find* through four interrealted techniques or "experiences," here artificially distinguished in order to discuss their function: (1) the recognition of an emblem's full significance, (2) the realization of a cliché's true implications, (3) the emerging epiphanic gesture indicating the recognition of humanity and the acceptance of grace, and (4) the violently catalytic effect of the presence of a prophet figure, typically an anti-prophet. Thus, the primary force of the title story, as mentioned above, emerges from the recognition of the emblematic significance of the name "Misfit" and the son's shirt, of the realization of the "good man" cliché's actual meaning, and of the gestures of the grandmother's touch and the Misfit's shot of recognition— all fused by the catalytic presence of the anti-prophet, the Misfit.

These artistic techniques—which are not merely extraneous stylistic tricks but the mode of revealing characters' interreacting experiences—are the basis for Flannery O'Connor's transcendence of the facile tags "religious writer" and "regionalist" in their pejorative sense, and further elucidate her success with the briefly illustrated (rather than novelistically resolved or explained) tableaux of the short story form. Nevertheless, the stories of *A Good Man* do comprise a related whole. This larger unity is not only one of a common thematic vision but also one of technique, as each story presents variation of the interrelationships of the four basic experiences which violently jolt the character into a realization of the possibility of grace. (p. 114)

The very sudden violence of the epiphanies—the strain of the interaction of the characters functioning as prophets; the revelation of the significance of an emblem; the cliché's explosion of meaning; and, the final gesture either of freedom from life (Bevel, General Sash), or the recognition of fellow humanity (the grandmother, Mr. Head, Ruby), or the revelation of the presence of God (Joy Hopewell, Mrs. Cope, the girl in "Temple")—necessitates a brief, terse form of presentation. Flannery O'Connor's ability to illustrate the presence of the Mystery of grace through the violent fusion of image and gesture into a concentrated revelatory illumination explains her success with the short story form as well as her success in presenting her religious vision, the "sense of Mystery," to a contemporary audience which would probably be offended or bored by a more expanded explanation or apology, more typical of the novel. Her characters' epiphanies must be illuminated as the extremely personal individual experiences they are; the tendency toward the more general in the novel form would possibly destroy this sense. (pp. 119-20)

Kenneth Frieling, "Flannery O'Connor's Vision: The Violence of Revelation," in The Fifties: Fiction, Poetry, Drama, *edited by Warren French (copyright © 1970 by Warren French), Everett/ Edwards, Inc., 1970, pp. 111-20.*

ROBERT MILDER

[What Miss O'Connor wrote] about might be comprehended by the word "mystery." "There are two qualities that make fiction," she was fond of saying: "One is the sense of mystery and the other is the sense of manners. You get the manners from the texture of experience that surrounds you"; the sense of mystery is the writer's own. [Mystery] for Miss O'Connor, a Roman Catholic, . . . centered upon the three basic theological doctrines of the Church: the Fall, the Redemption, and the Judgment. The South provided her with a language and a social fabric, a "texture of experience," but it was never more than the scene for a pageant universally enacted, the pageant of salvation through divine grace.

As an artist in the Jamesian tradition, profoundly convinced that a story "must carry its meaning inside it," Miss O'Connor was sensitive to the charge that Christian dogma inhibited a writer by imposing homiletic conclusions upon his work. . . . Belief, in her view, was an instrument for "penetrating reality," not for molding it, and the Catholic novel was nothing more or less than "one in which the truth as Christians know it has been used as a light to see the world by." "In the greatest fiction," she wrote, the artist's "moral sense" coincided with "his dramatic sense," with judgment so implicit in perception itself that the writer had no need to moralize. And here, she added, the Catholic writer enjoyed an inestimable advantage over the secular writer, who, skeptical of any absolute moral order, felt called upon to create one in his fiction. Secure in his faith "that the universe is meaningful," the Catholic writer was free to observe and reflect his world unburdened by the moral responsibilities of the unbeliever.

Had Miss O'Connor described her art as Christian rather than Catholic, the congruence between its theory and practice might have been almost complete. But she did not. The longest section in *Mystery and Manners* consists of four essays dealing with the Catholic writer and his audience, in each of which Miss O'Connor makes a strong case, implicitly or explicitly, for the Catholic nature of her fiction. She chooses "Catholic," she tells us, because "the word Christian is no longer reliable. It has come to mean anyone with a golden heart." And for Miss O'Connor a golden heart was not merely "a positive interference in the writing of fiction," but a symptom of everything that was wrong with modern religion—most notably, of the "tenderness" of the liberal reformer which she considered mawkish, "theoretical," and corrupt. By insisting upon "Catholic," Miss O'Connor sought to emphasize the literalness with which she took the traditional doctrines of the Church and to separate herself from "those politer elements for whom the supernatural is an embarrassment and for whom religion has become a department of sociology or culture or personality development." The paradox is that in repudiating what she regarded as the predominantly ethical mainstream of American Christianity, Flannery O'Connor was returning not to the Catholic tradition but to the evangelical Protestantism of the Reformation and the seventeenth century, a Protestantism whose lineal, if shrunken, descendants were the backwoods prophets of the modern South (pp. 802-04)

[When] a staunch Catholic writes of backwoods prophets, it would presumably be with a consciousness of the perils of private inspiration and, preferable as this may be to secularism or religious complacency, a strong sense that it is only a second best—the best lying within the tradition of the Church. This is the position Miss O'Connor develops in "The Catholic Novelist in the Protestant South," her most explicit treatment of the subject in *Mystery and Manners*. Elsewhere, however, Miss O'Connor has remarked of old Mason Tarwater, her prophet *par excellence*, that she is "right behind him 100 per cent," justifying this by distinguishing between the visible and the invisible church and making of her arch-Protestant what she calls "a natural Catholic": "When you leave a man alone with his Bible and the Holy Ghost inspires him, he's going to be a Catholic one way or another, even though he knows nothing about the visible church." The idea of an invisible church of devout believers, Catholic in spirit though not in form, is well within the pale of Catholic orthodoxy, provided such believers "are in good faith, and are simply and loyally seeking the truth without self-righteous obstinacy." Yet if old Tarwater is to be included among the census of Catholics, natural or otherwise, we are left with a Catholicism of an extremely latitudinarian sort, a Catholicism without Church or sacraments or priesthood, predicated solely upon the Bible and the individual's immediate confrontation with God—a Catholicism remarkably like Evangelical Protestantism.

Though Flannery O'Connor should not be identified with old Tarwater, whatever her sympathies for him, her particular brand of Catholicism would not have been averse to the old man. Like Protestantism, it elevated the Bible over those "legal and logical" aspects of Christianity which, according to Miss O'Connor, have been prominent in the Catholic tradition since the Counter-Reformation. More importantly, however, it reflected what one critic has called "a temperamental affinity with Jansenism," that tradition within the Catholic Church most akin to Calvinism in its ascetic spirit and its vision of Jesus "as a severe and inscrutable redeemer." . . . Miss O'Connor's vision of Christ [is of] "a stern and majestic Pantacrator, not . . . a smiling Jesus with a bleeding heart." (pp. 804-06)

[Two] of the "heresies" which aroused most opposition among the orthodox and caused the Jansenists to be labeled as Protestants in their own time are "heresies" which inform Miss O'Connor's vision and constitute the theological center of her work. The first is an insistence upon the absolute and irremediable corruption of the natural man, and consequently upon the necessity of divine grace for every good work; the second is an exaltation of private religious experience at the expense of the sacraments and the institutional Church. . . . [Both] are essential to the Protestantism of Flannery O'Connor's fiction. . . . (p. 806)

For the Protestant [specifically, the "Calvinist" or "Puritan"], the gulf between saint and sinner was absolute and unbridgeable; there was no middle way.

In this context Miss O'Connor's fiction belongs unmistakably to the Protestant tradition, for there is virtually nothing in her work to suggest an ethical alternative between her fanatical prophets and misfits at the one extreme and her motley assortment of worldlings, cynics, and "good country people" at the other. The rationalists Rayber (*The Violent Bear it Away*) and Sheppard ("The Lame Shall Enter First") represent the best hope for a middle way, if only because as social scientists they are closest to the modern liberal spirit. Yet it is precisely figures like Rayber, whom she regarded as "the typical modern man," that Miss O'Connor caricatures most savagely. If there is an unpardonable sin in Flannery O'Connor's fictional world, it is the pride of secular intelligence, the arrogant and self-deluded belief that man can be his own savior. . . . With their faith in the power of reason to understand and transform human life, Rayber and his analog, Sheppard, are embodiments of the melioristic spirit of sociology, and the failure and humiliation they both encounter are compelling evidence of the futility of secular works. (p. 807)

Theologically, what Miss O'Connor is insisting on through Sheppard and Rayber is the Protestant doctrine of the absolute corruption of all good works not founded upon divine grace. It is an uncompromising vision and, to the humanist, an appalling one. Because Rayber can offer him no middle way, young Tarwater is left to choose between the devil on the one hand and a half-crazed backwoods prophet on the other. . . . It is not merely that Tarwater's Christianity is uncongenial to the modern mind, it is unthinkable—a ludicrous anachronism in an age of behavioral psychologists and death-of-God theologians. Miss O'Connor herself was acutely aware of the problem, remarking, "When you write about backwoods prophets, it is very difficult to get across to the modern reader that you take these people seriously, that you are not making fun of them, but that their concerns are your own and, in your judgment, central to human life."

If Miss O'Connor's words seem explicit enough, they have not prevented readers from trying to mitigate what is essentially unmitigable in her vision: the absolute dichotomy between nature and grace. . . . Rayber's failure is not a failure of personality; it is the inevitable failure of the rationalist, the man of works, the unbeliever, who cannot offer love for the simple reason that (in Miss O'Connor's words) he is detached "from the source of love, the person of Jesus Christ." Grotesque as he seems, it is the old man who embodies the principle of divine love. . . . As readers we may be discomforted by the violence of old Tarwater's Christianity and search for an implied alternative, a gentler love which Rayber might have given but didn't. But this, Miss O'Connor would claim, is our own failure, not the story's: as modern men we have "the mistaken notion that a concern with grace is a concern with exalted human behavior." In Miss O'Connor's world the only alternative to violence is emptiness; and between Rayber and old Tarwater, Sheppard and the club-footed Rufus Johnson, Flannery O'Connor's own choice is unequivocal: the violent bear away the kingdom of heaven; the lame shall enter first. (pp. 808-09)

Perhaps Miss O'Connor's upbringing in the rural South made her more receptive to an evangelical, Bible-centered Christianity, in effect "Protestantizing" her Catholicism. Or perhaps a sense of the literary possibilities in the South —a Tarwater or a Hazel Motes—exercised a subtle but formative influence upon the shape of Miss O'Connor's vision, molding it to the exigencies of her art; so that being a writer (to paraphrase Blake), she came to belong to the Protestant party without knowing it. The result in either case was a dramatic ambivalence toward southern Fundamentalism: an awareness of the idiosyncracies of extreme Protestantism, yet an almost involuntary admiration for the intensity of its faith.

Miss O'Connor addressed herself to Fundamentalism in "The Catholic Novelist in the Protestant South," an extended apologia for her concern with Protestant culture and a eulogy on the religious heritage of the South. Chiding the Catholic for his condescension toward the Bible Belt, Miss O'Connor professed to see nothing unnatural in a Catholic's sympathy with southern Protestantism: the strenuousness of the Protestant reminded the Catholic of "the terrible loss to us in the Church of human faith and passion," while the waywardness of his "extreme individualism" revealed a need for tradition and authority which only the Church could fill. Though this seems a balanced estimate of both religions, the tenor of Miss O'Connor's essay is strangely laudatory of southern Protestantism. (pp. 809-10)

[What] made the Church unsatisfying to Miss O'Connor as an artist made it equally unsatisfying to her as a Christian. Far from lacking a culture, the Church in Miss O'Connor's view had too much of one—too much of a *social* culture, the very wealth and complexity of its communal life mitigating the force of its doctrines and insulating the believer from those spiritual discoveries often made by those in the invisible church. More than anything else, what Miss O'Connor sought in a culture was a universal sense of the immanence of the divine. And here she felt that the southern Protestant, with his dependence upon the Bible and the austerity of his religious life, possessed a more vitally Christian culture than did the Catholic and lived more immediately in the presence of God. (p. 811)

For Miss O'Connor the artist, this common scriptural heritage provided an ideal backdrop for a fiction concerned with the drama of salvation. Ultimately, however, Miss O'Connor's fascination with southern Protestantism derived less from its literary possibilities than from her temperamental response to its stark, unmediated version of Christianity.... In other circumstances Miss O'Connor's need for spiritual immediacy might have found expression in some form of neo-Jansenism or Pentecostal Catholicism. In the rural South it manifested itself in a compelling attraction toward southern Fundamentalism, a religion in which "the struggle against Satan is individual, continuous, and

desperate, and salvation is a personal problem, which comes not through ritual and sacrament, but in the gripping fervor of immediate confrontation with eternity." . . . For Miss O'Connor, as for the Protestant, the foundation of religious life lay not in the Church or the sacraments, but in the private and often terrifying experience of divine grace.

The effect of Flannery O'Connor's unmediated Christianity upon her fiction was an almost single-minded preoccupation with conversion experience—in her own words, with those moments "in which the presence of grace can be felt as it waits to be accepted or rejected." In dramatic terms, such moments arose during a moral crisis when a character was forced "to decide forever, betwixt two things" . . .—the two things generally consisting of God and Satan. What this type of art required of the novelist was a unique ability "to see different levels of reality in one image or situation," the eternal commitment as it revealed itself in the concrete choice—a way of seeing which Miss O'Connor, reviving the scholastic term, labeled the "anagogical vision." What it also required, however, was a belief that grace could be received directly through nature. In the Catholic tradition this idea is inherently suspect, for it threatens not only to bypass the sacraments but to dispense with the priesthood and the institutional Church.... For most Protestants, . . . and this would include the majority of English and American Puritans—grace was the culmination of a long process of "preparation" aimed at plowing up the stony ground of the heart in anticipation of the redeeming seed. Among the New England ministers of the seventeenth century the most articulate preparationists were Thomas Shepard and Thomas Hooker, who described the journey toward grace as a process of contrition and humiliation. . . . (pp. 811-13)

In bringing her characters to their own moments of potential grace, Miss O'Connor not only omits the orthodox Catholic means of sacrament and priest but leads them through a process of preparation remarkably similar to those defined by Shepard and Hooker, wrenching them from their self-satisfaction into a humiliating awareness of who and what they are—vain, selfish creatures blind to themselves, dead to others, and desperately in need of grace. It is so customary to speak of the "banality of evil" that the phrase itself has become banal, yet this is precisely what Miss O'Connor means by original sin: not the murderousness of a psychotic like the Misfit, but the complacency of Mrs. Turpin ("Revelation"), the bigotry of Mrs. Shortley ("The Displaced Person"), and the intellectual arrogance of Asbury Fox ("The Enduring Chill"). In a word, original sin is equivalent to "self," and before grace can be extended to a character that "self" must be annihilated.

For this reason, Flannery O'Connor's stories generally turn upon a moment of humiliation intended, like the Puritan's sermon, to prostrate the sinner and force upon him a sense of his helplessness. Sometimes, as in "Good Country People" and "Everything that Rises Must Converge," the moment of humiliation is just that: not an offer of grace but, through the discovery of spiritual emptiness, a realization of one's dire need for it. But often the moment of humiliation is a prelude to grace itself. In "The Artificial Nigger," to cite one example, Mr. Head's humiliation leads him through contrition and despair to his final regeneration through divine mercy. (pp. 813-14)

Although Mr. Head's moment of grace comes upon him unexpectedly, it has been amply prepared for through the spiritual process which began with his denial of Nelson. To the extent that this process takes place outside of the sacraments and culminates in an unmediated reception of divine mercy, it may be called Protestant rather than Catholic. But the resemblance is deeper and even more explicit, for in moving toward his moment of grace Mr. Head progresses through the four stages of evangelical conversion outlined by Thomas Shepard in a representative Puritan treatise on the subject: conviction of sin, compunction for sin, humiliation, and faith. . . . ["Conviction of sin"] was a vital, immediate, affective sense of one's own unworthiness, and this the Puritan minister sought to instill through the rhetoric of his sermon. . . . (p. 815)

Miss O'Connor's insistence on the free acceptance of grace is one of the few remaining doctrinal points which link her to the Catholic tradition. It is a position which she reiterates in several of the essays in *Mystery and Manners* and one which, in theory at least, is central to her anagogical vision. In some of her stories grace does seem to revolve upon a character's free choice, as in "A Good Man is Hard to Find" where the grandmother, in reaching out toward the Misfit, "does the right thing, she makes the right gesture." But these stories are more the exception than the rule. In "The Enduring Chill," for example, Asbury Fox not only fails to do "the right thing," he tries his best to keep from doing it: "A feeble cry, a last impossible protest escaped him. But the Holy Ghost, emblazoned in ice instead of fire, continued, implacable, to descend." Where the grandmother chooses grace, Asbury and Mrs. Turpin are chosen by it—"singled out," as Mrs. Turpin says, randomly and with no apparent regard for penitence or even for faith. Grace proceeds from the sovereign pleasure of an arbitrary, inscrutable God who saves whom He will, when He will, and whose offer of salvation can neither be declined nor withstood.

The issues of predestination and irresistible grace are particularly acute in Miss O'Connor's two novellas, *The Violent Bear it Away* and *Wise Blood,* whose heroes labor under an inescapable burden of prophecy. . . . [Miss O'Connor reconciles] freedom with religious calling through an appeal to mystery—a logic common enough in Protestant theology, where predestination coexists harmoniously with moral responsibility, but largely alien to Catholicism. On the questions of free will and spiritual election which have divided Catholics and Protestants since the Reformation, Miss O'Connor's fiction plants itself firmly on the Protestant side. (pp. 817-18)

[There] have been numerous attempts to mellow her Christianity, the Catholic critics seeking a more orthodox Catholicism, the secularists a liberal humanism. But the harsh, unrelenting core of Miss O'Connor's vision will not be tampered with. In its insistence on the corruption of all secular works and the divisiveness and irresistibility of grace, Miss O'Connor's Christianity is virtually indistinguishable from the Fundamentalist Protestantism of the South. Yet even more important for Miss O'Connor than what the Fundamentalist believed was how he believed it. Armed only with the Bible and his own invincible faith, the Fundamentalist went forward to a life of incessant battle against the temptations of the world. It was a strenuous but immensely exhilarating vision in which each moral decision became a contest between God and Satan and the smallest gesture assumed a profound anagogical significance. In

Mystery and Manners one finds Miss O'Connor struggling to preserve this same vital and immediate apprehension of Christian truth, defining herself successively as a southerner among Americans, a Catholic among southerners, and a dissident among Catholics—always separating herself from communal identities which would mitigate her fierce sense of the immanence of the divine.

To her own mind, Miss O'Connor was a theologically orthodox Catholic, never more so than when she was rebuking her fellow Catholics for what she considered their provincialism and spiritual sloth. Sharing the Church's distrust of "the merely extreme, the merely personal, the merely grotesque," she caught and reflected the extravagance of southern Protestants in a scathingly comic art. Having caricatured her backwoods prophets, however, Miss O'Connor was inexorably drawn back to them by the sheer intensity of their belief. Returning home "bedraggled and hungry" after days in the woods, Mason Tarwater, she wrote, "would look as if he had been wrestling with a wildcat, as if his head were still full of the visions he had seen in its eyes, wheels of light and strange beasts with giant wings of fire and four heads turned to the four points of the universe." At these times old Tarwater seemed every inch a prophet to his nephew—and, more subtly though with equal fascination, to the artist who created him. Behind Flannery O'Connor's vision, and informing it at all points, lay the Protestant's desire to wrestle with wildcats and gaze unobstructedly at God. (pp. 818-19)

Robert Milder, "The Protestantism of Flannery O'Connor," in The Southern Review *(copyright, 1975, by Robert Milder), Vol. XI, No. 4, Autumn, 1975, pp. 802-19.*

THOMAS LeCLAIR

Hazel's blinding [in *Wise Blood*] is neither gratuitous nor contrived, for his act is a consistent resolution of the Oedipal theme in the novel and of the pattern of vision imagery which O'Connor uses to reveal this theme. Because Flannery O'Connor often mocks intellectuals and their feeble constructs, one does not expect to find a psychological situation as potentially hackneyed as the Oedipal complex in her fiction, but the Oedipal situation works throughout *Wise Blood* to complicate Hazel Motes's religious problems. It should be emphasized that *Wise Blood* is not a psychological case study, a fictional dramatization of Freudian orthodoxies. Flannery O'Connor's primary interest, as she said, was "the action of grace in territory held largely by the devil." Part of that territory in *Wise Blood* is her hero's memory of Oedipal fixation. Because Hazel associates his lost religious faith with memories of Oedipal guilt and anxiety, his ultimate acceptance of religion is made difficult and meaningful. (p. 197)

As an adolescent Hazel tries to accept and avoid his mother and her religion at the same time. At twelve Hazel plans to be a preacher and follow his mother's belief and his grandfather's example, but Hazel is ambivalent about Jesus. Although he wants to avoid Jesus's omnipotent hold on his free will, Hazel also finds this devouring Jesus mixed up with an image of his all-seeing mother. . . . [His] mother becomes a temptation as well as a strict enforcer; the seductive Jesus . . . is Hazel's conflation of the two roles. Hazel's hope is to avoid sin, but he also avoids full belief in his mother's religion, for that would be an admission of her power and influence over him, as well as a reminder of his guilt. (pp. 199-200)

When Hazel arrives in the city, he has several strategies for establishing his independence from this dream of Oedipal experience and the religion which ties him to a guilty memory. Hazel does not articulate these strategies, but implicit in his actions are the following conditions and consequences. If Hazel can reject Christianity, he can break the hold his mother has upon his mind; if he can use other women as sexual objects, he can gain sexual autonomy. The test of these strategies, not surprisingly, is a series of maternal women who share some of the same traits and imagery. . . . Unable to prove himself completely, Hazel returns to preaching the Church Without Christ, a new way to reject his mother's influence on his life.

The religious ambivalence Hazel displayed as a boy is again evidenced in the city, for even while Hazel blasphemes in his preaching he is drawn to the blind preacher Asa Hawks, a man who bears some resemblance to Hazel's grandfather the preacher. In his relationship with Hawks, Hazel is attempting "to move forward and backward at the same time" . . . : forward to freedom through blasphemy, backward to his past and salvation. (p. 201)

The circumstances and meaning of his blinding and the ending need some clarification. Hazel's programs for sexual autonomy and religious independence have been frustrated, and his escape has been denied. Circumstances almost demand resignation, but the reader at this point should realize that resignation involves more than a return to a fanatical Christianity. Hazel's giving up his rebellion will mean accepting the inescapable dominance of his mother, will mean confessing his failure to liberate himself from her influence as well as Christ's. Because his movement to grace requires this kind of sacrifice of self, Hazel assumes heroic proportions in O'Connor's view. Once Hazel decides to accept his past despite his memories of guilt and fear, he needs some extreme act to signify his resolution and his complete abandonment of secular life. The fraudulent hero Hawks offers him an example. By blinding himself, Hazel expiates his guilt for blasphemy, for murder, and, if the parallel with Oedipus holds, for his incestuous fantasies. And through his self-sacrifice he proves his complete commitment to Christ. In full submission to the religion of his youth, Hazel mortifies himself as he did when he first fantasized about his mother and accepts his defeat as an independent man. (pp. 203-04)

Although some critics believe Enoch Emery's presence in *Wise Blood* disturbs its unity, I think Emery nicely, if somewhat obviously, sets off both the religious and sexual problems that plague Hazel Motes. Enoch's father has "traded" him to a Welfare woman, who sends him to the Rodemill Boy's Bible Academy. Enoch's solution to his distaste for religion and his "mother's" influence is much simpler than Hazel's: Enoch walks into her room and exposes himself. Enoch's life is not all success, though. As a lady's man he is as futile as, if less guilty than, Hazel, and Enoch also suffers under a religious compulsion he does not fully understand. Driven to desperation by his loneliness and compulsion, Enoch steals the mummy (the new Jesus) and, like Hazel, turns to violence. Again like Hazel, Enoch has a radical change of personality—he becomes Gonga the gorilla. His last scene has him, dressed as Gonga, looking over a vast expanse of space. When Hazel's car is pushed over the embankment, he too looks off into blank space, but O'Connor has him return from this moment of immobility to religious conversion. Enoch is left in his animalistic reversion. As secular man without religious tradition, Enoch moves on the dictates of his "wise blood," his intuition, but there is a wiser blood—that of Hazel's blinded eyes and that of the Christ crucified. Enoch's function is to demonstrate the secular man's answer to Hazel's problems, to set off that integrity Hazel achieves by accepting his psychological and religious past. (pp. 204-05)

Thomas LeClair, "Flannery O'Connor's 'Wise Blood': The Oedipal Theme," in The Mississippi Quarterly *(copyright 1976 Mississippi State University), Spring, 1976, pp. 197-205.*

JOSEPHINE HENDIN

[*The Habit of Being: Letters of Flannery O'Connor* offers] no striking literary theories, nor any statements inconsistent with what is already available in O'Connor's book of essays, *Mystery and Manners*. What [it reveals] is O'Connor's sensibility, shaped and hardened in the isolation of her life on her farm. (p. 34)

There has been no little sister in American letters to replace Flannery O'Connor. . . . [She] has emerged as one of the most gifted writers of recent decades. I am grateful to Sally Fitzgerald [editor] for bringing her back to speak to us again, as she spoke to her friends—as the Georgia hick, the witty writer, the Catholic, the southern lady—the woman of discipline whose many selves added up to genius. (p. 35)

Josephine Hendin, in The New Republic *(reprinted by permission of* The New Republic; © *1979 The New Republic, Inc.), March 10, 1979.*

J. O. TATE

[*The Habit of Being: Letters of Flannery O'Connor*] is more than an epistolary autobiography of a great American writer. It is also a "good read," and then some. Like everything O'Connor wrote, no matter how serious, it is very funny. The book intertwines the developing stories of her career, her many friendships, the progress of her omnivorous education, and her ordeal by disseminated lupus erythematosus, which ended her life at the age of 39. . . .

Flannery O'Connor was a master of paradox, as in her famous story "Good Country People." . . .

O'Connor's spreading wide of her narrow hands to unite the worlds of scholarly learning and ignorant truth is characteristic of her. So in her letters, O'Connor testifies over and over about such delectable items as Tube Rose Snuff commercials, religious aberrations, absurdities from the newspapers, etc., while at the same time commenting on her progress through Proust or her reading in theology. The catholicity of O'Connor's tastes and interests is staggering. (p. 364)

The power Flannery O'Connor displayed in her greatest works—the authority she achieved—was based on knowledge of the world, and a completely developed technique for conveying that knowledge. . . . Ichabod Crane and Brom Bones, the Confidence Man and his victims, and the Duke and the Dauphin would have felt right at home in the world limned by Flannery O'Connor. That world is a meretricious catalogue, "a shelf of false hands, imitation buck teeth, boxes of simulated dog dung to put on the rug, wooden plaques with cynical mottoes burnt on them . . .'' (*The Violent Bear It Away*). O'Connor was never over-refined.

The other side of the paradox, which springs at us from her books as from a box (and from the fictions as well as the letters) . . . is O'Connor's serious pursuit of art and learning. For her, this was finally and necessarily congruent with the theological underpinnings of her devout Roman Catholicism. Perhaps the most impressive strands in the letters are her accounts of her reading, sensitive literary advice to aspiring writers, and eloquent addresses on her faith composed for friends and correspondents. (pp. 364, 366)

Her best pieces defy second-guessing. Her greatness consists in the acuity of her eye, the accuracy of her ear, her perfect perceptions of the pitches of pride. Symbolist and satirist, she not only saw folly, but could judge it and deliver it whole, in the round, in a circumscribed perspective, the vanishing point of which rests at a profound depth. (p. 366)

> J. O. Tate, "The Village Theist," in National Review (© *National Review, Inc.*, 1979; 150 East 35th St., New York, N.Y. 10016), March 16, 1979, pp. 364-68.

MICHAEL TRUE

In *The Habit of Being*, selected letters superbly edited by O'Connor's friend and benefactor Sally Fitzgerald, the reader learns a great deal about the particular genius that enabled O'Connor to connect the visible and the invisible, the material and the spiritual in an original, powerful, and comic way. . . .

O'Connor's characters are backwoods prophets, itinerant farmers, and gossipy, simple people who talk in platitudes. It is the burden of her stories to prove, however, that their folksiness is often wise beyond words. In a typical O'Connor story, the logical positivist or existentialist and the Christ-haunted misfit confront one another in a life-and-death struggle, where logic and sophistication are no match for fundamentalist, even primitive, truth. . . .

Anyone who admires O'Connor's fiction, . . . would expect almost anything she wrote to be extraordinary; but I was unprepared for the splendor of these letters, the wit, the brilliance, the precision of statement, the deep intelligence. I laughed out loud at the tales O'Connor told, on others and on herself, to one of her many correspondents—the great and famous (Caroline Gordon, Robert Lowell), young apprentice writers (Maryat Lee, John Hawkes), as well as occasional and unknown questioners.

There is hardly a letter, in fact, that doesn't entertain, inform, or challenge the reader in a concrete way. . . .

The portriat of the artist that emerges from *The Habit of Being* is startling in its precision, clarity, and depth. It is a collage of critical comment on contemporary writers she admired (J. F. Powers, Bernard Malamud), on her reading (the Church fathers, Hannah Arendt), and on religious practice. O'Connor understood her strengths and weaknesses as a writer better than anyone. She wrote stories "because I write well," she told one questioner. Speaking admiringly of Faulkner, she said, "Probably the real reasons I don't read him is because he makes me feel that with my one-cylinder syntax I should quit writing and raise chickens altogether."

Yet O'Connor was not as simplistic in analysis and reflection as these statements perhaps make her appear. Her satire was most pointed in discussing people who pretended that complex problems have easy solutions. . . .

In addition to its many strengths as a cultural document, this book helps to establish O'Connor's place in the canon of American literature, to overcome the reservations harbored by some literary historians and critics because of her relatively small body of work. But her mastery of language and sureness of form are the marks of her craft, and her stories are more widely read and appreciated—and more necessary—than they were at the time of her death. . . .

The Habit of Being is one of the great collections of letters in American literature, equal in range and quality to those of Hawthorne and Melville and comparable, in what they tell us about the craft of fiction and writing, to the notebooks and prefaces of Henry James and the journals of Henry David Thoreau. With her occasional essays and prefaces, they are among the wisest reflections we have on art, on life in these United States, and on religion. They are, one might say, a university in themselves.

> Michael True, "The Luminous Letters of a Writer of Genius," in The Chronicle Review (*copyright* © 1979 by The Chronicle of Higher Education, Inc.), April 16, 1979, p. R6.

ROBERT TOWERS

Part of the fascination exerted by this thick volume of letters [*The Habit of Being*] has to do with their evocation of the period which they embrace; much more derives from their revelation of the personality and literary practice of a writer remarkable for the single-mindedness with which she developed and protected a talent that she regarded, quite literally, as God-given. The letters—the first sent from Yaddo to her future agent in 1948, the last a nearly illegible scrawl written six days before her death in 1964—cover her professional career as a writer almost as thoroughly as any biographer might wish. Regrettably, none of the letters written from the years (crucial to her development both as a writer and as a reader) spent at the School for Writers at Iowa State University could be included. Missing also are the letters (presumably of greater personal than literary interest) which she wrote every day to her mother during her year's stay with Sally and Robert Fitzgerald in Connecticut in 1949-1950. The only other gap that has come to my attention and that one might wish to be filled are the letters to Walker Percy, with whom she corresponded for several years; only a brief note of congratulations to him is included.

No doubt it is churlish to want more when nearly six hundred pages of letters have been provided, but I found myself tantalized and frustrated by the fact that the volume contains only Flannery O'Connor's letters; although much can be inferred from her replies, it would be nice to know not only the contents but the exact tone of the letters addressed to her by such literary correspondents as the Fitzgeralds, John Hawkes, Robert Lowell, Elizabeth Hardwick, Cecil Dawkins, Robert Giroux, Catharine Carver, and others. I would particularly like to see the often lengthy commentaries which Caroline Gordon enthusiastically wrote for each of Flannery O'Connor's stories and novels before they were finally revised and sent to the publisher. (p. 3)

Flannery O'Connor warns that "meaning cannot be captured in an interpretation'' and deplores the habit of approaching a story ''as if it were a research problem for which any answer is believable so long as it is not obvious,'' she indulges occasionally in some rather recondite interpretations of her own work. The publication of these letters, with all their explicit references to the fiction, is bound to produce a new and lively spate of interpretative activity in the academies and elsewhere.

Never mind. The stories are strong enough to survive any amount of exegetical excess—whether committed by the reader or the occasionally over-zealous author. As with the work of any profound artist, an element of the mysterious—of the unspoken, the unacknowledged—hangs like a shining mist over all that has been consciously intended and consciously achieved. (p. 5)

These droll, moving, intelligent letters are to be cherished not only for what they reveal of the life, mundane and spiritual, of an exceptionally afflicted young woman but also for what they have to say about a writer's intimate, almost daily, relationship with her vocation. While it would be excessive to place Flannery O'Connor's letters with those of Keats, D. H. Lawrence, or Virginia Woolf in their literary significance, they are certainly among the most valuable produced by any twentieth-century American writer.... (p. 6)

> Robert Towers, "Flannery O'Connor's Gifts," in *The New York Review of Books* (*reprinted with permission from* The New York Review of Books; *copyright © 1979 Nyrev, Inc.*), May 3, 1979, pp. 3-6.

*   *   *

O'HARA, Frank   1926-1966

O'Hara was an American poet, playwright, and critic. Although best known as a poet and prose writer, O'Hara was also drawn to the world of art, serving as assistant curator at the Museum of Modern Art as well as contributing to periodicals in the field of art criticism. His poetry is noted for its rather cluttered style, for O'Hara eschewed traditional meter and poetic diction in favor of a random outpouring of objects and imagery in his verse. The joyful profusion of visual detail in his poetry reflects the poet's exuberant vision of life, especially of the urban scene. (See also *CLC*, Vols. 2, 5, and *Contemporary Authors*, Vols. 9-12, rev. ed.; obituary, Vols. 25-28, rev. ed.)

THOMAS BYROM

Some poets should be allowed to wear their talents lightly. Frank O'Hara ... has been badly overdone by his friends and devotees, with their disfiguring puffs and silly elegies.... Devotion often makes a dull business of criticism.

But O'Hara is still bobbing. His gifts were for buoyancy, spontaneity and fun. Though he tried to write *de profundis*, his best poems stay closer to the surface and take their joy and verve from the gregarious life he led. He was, like Pound but in a smaller pond, the entrepreneur for a generation of artists....

He was especially the poet of the painters; he gave them a literacy, as their muse and critic, at a time when theory tended to precede paint and the word directed the image. But his touch was always personal; the public defending could be left to Clement Greenberg and Harold Rosen-

berg.... O'Hara was a smaller but not less commanding prominence. His art criticism, some of it collected in *Art Chronicles 1954-1966*, is light, fanciful and untheoretical. When he fashions himself after Apollinaire, who discovered the Cubists tucked away in Room 8 of the Salon d'Automne of 1911, we should not take him as seriously as his immortalizers have done. The emulation is a respectful bit of cheek, and a bit of chic too, playful and sassy. He was never so grave, never a campaigner. His manifesto *Personism* (1959) is a comic piece, speaking only for itself, and not, as has been claimed, with the voices of Rimbaud, Mayakovsky and Pasternak....

[O'Hara loved French poetry,] and his work is full of allusions to Baudelaire, Rimbaud, Verlaine, Apollinaire, Reverdy, Tzara, Péret. He identified in his life with the Symbolists, and in his writing with the Dadaists and Surrealists....

His Surrealist experiments of the late 1940s and early 1950s are really schoolboy productions. He liked to justify them by talk of ''all-over'' and ''push-and-pull'' and the other tags of Abstract Expressionism, but they are poetry of the surface only in being superficial. In all his early work, *Oranges, Memorial Day 1950, Second Avenue*, he spoils himself with chancy disjunctions and licentious associations....

As a Dada poet O'Hara does better. The love of horseplay and the solemn whimsies, the wit that refuses a programme, the uncritical spoofing, the fizziness of the gossip exactly suited him. He revives, for instance, the date poem—''It is 12.20 in New York a Friday''—which imitates ''At the Paul Guillaume Gallery'' by Pierre Albert-Birot....

He was not a radical poet but the conserver of an *avant-garde*, or just barely the latest of an *arrière-garde*. It is fitting that just before he died he was appointed a curator at the Museum of Modern Art. He was very much a caretaker and a presenter of exhibitions, rather than a historian or a forerunning poet.

His aesthetics are from a catalogue of late Victorian camp, a matter of excellent personal taste and of display.... His syntax has little of the crafty or inspired appositiveness of the Surrealist; it is an articulation of mental chatter and drift, and his style depends for its success wholly on his sensibility. Perhaps he is most like E. E. Cummings, the same soft verve, a sentimental eroticism, a certain heart.... Throughout his work there is an unwittingly incomplete parody of Romantic or Transcendentalist attitudes. He is, like Cummings, a cheating kid, he takes it all back, he plays safe. (p. 78)

There are too many moments in O'Hara when you can't tell if he means it, and you laugh anyway, only to have his irrepressible lack of dignity mock any judgment, even the most deserved. As the poet of New York he reflects uncritically and faithfully and with something of the maudlin gusto of Fitzgerald's ''My Lost City'' the brilliance, the vulgarity of the city. Starstruck, he is quite undone by the glamour in ''For James Dean''; but in ''Lana Turner Has Collapsed'' he recovers his wits and the surface glitters. His characteristic movement is from flat to fantasy, real to surreal, literal reference to comic reverie, and often he shifts up with panache.

The best of *Poems Retrieved* [are about friendships]....

His several reminiscences of Violet Lang—"To Violet Lang", "Le Boeuf Sur Le Toit", and a couple in *Selected Poems*—tell us a lot about the quality of his affection, and go deep by staying lovingly and respectfully slight.

His talent was social, and he was perhaps best in his collaborations, where he could count on his own gifts of sympathy and the nourishment of another sensibility to keep him free, high and quick. In the late 1950s he worked with Larry Rivers on a series of lithographs, *Stones*. Taking turns, O'Hara would scratch out a few lines of poetry, Rivers would draw something, until they had a clumsy, graceful and usually absurd bit of work and play: "US", "Rimbaud and Verlaine", "Love", "Melancholy Breakfast". The poorer stones illustrate precisely how O'Hara's craft could not survive his spontaneity. He was an improviser, a romancer of collage, a first-rate cut-and-paste poet. (p. 79)

> Thomas Byrom, "The Poet of the Painters," in The Times Literary Supplement (© Times Newspapers Ltd. (London) 1968; reproduced from The Times Literary Supplement by permission), January 27, 1968, pp. 78-9.

PAUL ZWEIG

1956-57 were good years for literary revolution. That is when *Meditations in an Emergency* and *Howl* appeared on opposite coasts, two of the most important first books of poetry to be published in America since the war. O'Hara like a violin, Ginsberg like a waterfall, let loose the flood of deep associations. They created a torrential rhetoric that literally washed away the poetry of the "silent generation." Certain texts in *Meditations in an Emergency* are clearly imitations of the French . . . , [when, for example, the] packaging of [a] poem into five line stanzas is not so much evidence of formal intention, as a joke about literary form. The language slips and leaps and interrupts itself with the limberness of the surreal countervoice. The text has no real subject matter; it is what it means: an incoherence of rhythms and images that is oddly seductive. Although passages like this are not the best part of *Meditations in an Emergency,* they form the bedrock of pure style from which the book emerges. O'Hara himself describes the paradox of his poetry: "I will my will, though I may become famous for a mysterious vacancy in that department . . ." The will that makes meanings struggles bravely with a flood of surreal associations, and the will loses; but the failure is a victory. The poem knocks down the retaining walls of form and meaning. Ordinary situations and rooms and streets become Rimbaudian voyages. . . . More than a decade later, *Meditations in an Emergency* remains a moving book, perhaps because O'Hara understood the risks, as well as the charms, caused by his "mysterious vacancy of the will." O'Hara was fascinated by the eternal youth of the psyche; but he was elegiac too, in mourning for the drabness of the "logical" world which would never be changed by literature. (pp. 275-76)

> Paul Zweig, in Salmagundi (copyright © 1973 by Skidmore College), Spring-Summer, 1973.

ARAM SAROYAN

O'Hara places himself most succinctly in his most famous essay, "Personism: A Manifesto," perhaps the closest thing to a definitive statement of the poetics of the New York School, when he worries if he isn't "sounding like the poor wealthy man's Allen Ginsberg . . .". . . . And yet, in his own way, Frank O'Hara was no less intent upon the liberation of American poetry from the clutches of the New Criticism of the forties and fifties, which, as he elaborates in an interview less than a year before his death, tended to look upon art as the raw material of criticism. . . .

He can talk about Jackson Pollack *and* Andy Warhol, about Gregory Corso *and* W. H. Auden. Throughout it all, he seems to be having a good time. More casual in tone than Allen Ginsberg, he is often equally as penetrating.

> Aram Saroyan, "Prose of a New York Poet," in The New York Times Book Review (© 1975 by The New York Times Company; reprinted by permission), December 14, 1975, p. 27.

FRED MORAMARCO

It is in the poetry of New York poets like O'Hara and Ashbery that the painterly esthetic of Abstract Expressionism manifests itself in literary art, though Olson's criticism provides for us its literary rationale. (p. 440)

O'Hara's connection with the New York art scene dates from about 1950, when he first worked at the Museum of Modern Art and became acquainted with many of the most innovative painters in the New York area at the time. But I am concerned here less with the biographical relationships between O'Hara . . . and the New York painters than with the esthetic relationship between [his] poetry and the canvases of the New York School. The "casual insight" that O'Hara finds at the center of Jackson Pollock's achievement, for example, is a description as well of his own poetic style. Writing about Pollock, O'Hara finds

> the ego totally absorbed in the work. By being "in" the specific painting, as he himself put it, he gave himself over to the cultural necessities which, in turn, freed him from the external encumbrances which surround art as an occasion of extreme cultural concern.

These external encumbrances are precisely what O'Hara liberates himself from in his own poetry. His is not a poetry of extreme cultural concern, but rather is one focused on the momentary and the transient, on the hundreds of minor details which make up all of our days. His poetry is concerned with movies he has seen, friends he has visited, stores he has shopped at, birthdays he has celebrated, meals he has eaten. The "action" of O'Hara's life is in his poetry in the same way that Pollock's creative life is directly captured in his paintings.

So many of O'Hara's poems are playful, "casually insightful" celebrations of the esthetic autonomy of the creative act. The last stanza of "Autobiographia Literaria" (the serious, Coleridge-inspired title, of course, totally at odds with the spirit of the poem) specifically celebrates this esthetic ego involvement:

> And here I am, the
> center of all beauty!
> writing these poems!
> Imagine!

The wonder here is a mock-wonder—whimsical rather than Whitmanic—but it is aimed at calling our attention to the "action" of making the poem. Here, as elsewhere in O'Hara's work, the mock-heroic posturing is only superficially satirical. Underlying the casual chronicles of everyday events in his work is a deep commitment to the transformative qualities of poetry—its ability to open our eyes, sharpen our perceptions, involve us more totally with the world around us. O'Hara's whimsy is, if I may be permitted an oxymoron, a serious whimsy. (pp. 440-41)

[O'Hara's work] has apparent affinities with Pop-Art: in poems like the one beginning "Lana Turner has collapsed" or the delightful poem called "the Lay of the Romance of the Associations" in which the Fifth and Park Avenue Associations in New York attempt to get together, only to be frustrated because "that bourgeois Madison Avenue continues to obstruct our free intercourse with each other." But the sense of playfulness and social satire O'Hara's poems share with Pop-Art seems to me less substantial than the "action" involvement of the writer within the poem and the relationship of that literary idea to the painterly esthetic of Abstract Expressionism. (pp. 442-43)

One gets the . . . sense of what I would like to call the "casual" total involvement in O'Hara's work in this statement by William Baziotes, the well-known painter of the New York School: "I work on many canvases at once. In the morning I line them up against the wall of my studio. Some speak; some do not. They are mirrors. They tell me what I am like at the moment." The last two sentences are pure O'Hara; the mimetic function of art is limited to an imitation of the artist's immediate sensibility—"what I am like at the moment"—not an external or objective scene or series of events, or enduring and universal human values.

The achievement of O'Hara and the Abstract Expressionists shows us that transient matters can be dealt with in an enduring way. The art of the moment does not always have to be propagandistic and tied to rapidly changing social issues. When the moment-to-moment reality of the individual becomes the focus, the art becomes made up of the very stuff of life itself. Art has always been preoccupied with the universal, these artists seem to be telling us, but life continues to serve up a steady diet of particulars. It is as a careful chronicler of those particulars that O'Hara has made his mark on literary history. (pp. 443-44)

"Poem for a Painter" makes specific O'Hara's painterly sympathies and his inclination to view the art of painting as more able to capture fleeting emotional moments than poetry. In lines reminiscent of Hart Crane, he writes, "The ice of your imagination lends / an anchor to the endless sea of pain." The painterly imagination is frozen; the event captured on the canvas is its own enduring record. O'Hara wrote a great deal about painters in his poetry as well as his prose, and there can be no question, I think, that he attempted to consolidate the achievement of Abstract Expressionism in literary art. (pp. 445-46)

Fred Moramarco, in Journal of Modern Literature
(© Temple University 1976), September, 1976.

MARJORIE PERLOFF

[It is] my growing conviction that O'Hara is one of the central poets of the postwar period, and that his influence will continue to grow in the years to come. He is also an important art critic, his improvisatory but incisive essays and reviews recalling those of an earlier poet-art critic whom he loved—Apollinaire. And his collaborations with painters, composers, playwrights, and film-makers have given us some of the most delightful mixed-media works of the fifties and sixties. (p. xii)

The notion of being "needed by things" . . . is a central feature of [O'Hara's] poetic. It derives, quite possibly, from Rilke, whose poetry O'Hara knew well and loved. . . . For both Rilke and O'Hara, it is the artist's "duty to be attentive" to the world of process in which he finds himself. And such attention requires a peculiar self-discipline, the ability to look at something and, paraphrasing Ezra Pound, to "See It New!" (pp. 19-20)

To be "influenced" by another artist . . . is to find new means of evading monotony, boredom, sameness—to force oneself to "see" in new ways, to *defamiliarize* the object. . . .

One way of avoiding boredom, of keeping oneself and one's reader "more keenly interested," is to create a poetic structure that is always changing, shifting, becoming. (p. 20)

Openness, quickening, immediacy—these are the qualities O'Hara wants to capture in his poetry. . . .

Photographs, monuments, static memories—"all things that don't change"—these have no place in the poet's world. We can now understand why O'Hara loves the *motion* picture, *action* painting, and all forms of dance—art forms that capture the *present* rather than the past, the present in all its chaotic splendor. And New York is therefore the very center of being, quite simply because it is the place where more is happening at once than anywhere else in the world. . . . (p. 21)

The *surface* of the painting, and by analogy the *surface* of the poem, must [for O'Hara] be regarded as a field upon which the physical energies of the artist can operate, without mediation of metaphor or symbol. The poet's images—for example, the "hum-colored / cabs," the "yellow helmets" worn by the laborers, or the "glass of papaya juice" in "A Step Away From Them" . . .—are not symbolic properties; there is nothing *behind* these surfaces. Rather, their positioning in the poet's field, their *push and pull* interaction, function metonymically to create a microcosm of the poet's New York world—a world verifiable on any city map yet also fictive in its fantastic configurations. . . . (p. 22)

[Distrust of symbolism is a central tenet of O'Hara's poetic and of his art criticism. For example, he praised Claes] Oldenburg's ability to make "the very objects and symbols themselves, with the help of papier-mâché, cloth, wood, glue, paint and whatever other mysterious materials are inside and on them, *into* art. . . . There is no hint of mysticism, no 'significance,' no commentary, in the work."

The aesthetic of *presence* rather than transcendence is formulated with particular force in O'Hara's first essay on David Smith. . . . Smith's sculptures, O'Hara argues, defy all our traditional notions of organic oneness and unity. "This is no longer the Constructivist intersection of colored planes, nor is the color used as a means of unifying the surface. Unification is approached by inviting the eye to travel over the complicated surface exhaustively, rather than inviting it to settle on the whole first and then explore details. It is the esthetic of culmination rather than examination."

The esthetic of culmination rather than examination—this

formulation applies nicely to O'Hara's own poetry. As in the case of Smith's sculptures, O'Hara's poems reject [a] dense network of symbolic images. . . . Rather, the reader's eye and ear must "travel over the complicated surface exhaustively," participating in the ongoing process of discovery and continually revising his sense of what the poem is "saying." The observer can no longer be detached. "The best of the current sculptures," says O'Hara, "didn't make me feel I wanted to *have* one, they made me feel I wanted to *be* one." . . . If the art work has *presence* and if the beholder is as *attentive* as possible, the process of identification thus becomes complete. (p. 35)

From the first, he accepted Williams as a master, no doubt because he identified with Williams's struggle against convention, pretentiousness, conformity—the "going thing." (p. 44)

O'Hara admires Williams's "liberation of language," his "attempt to find an honest, tough, hard, beautiful thing." He follows Williams in believing that "The objective in writing is to reveal." . . .

[His debt to Williams] is less to the complex epic poem *Paterson* than to the Dadesque prose poems of *Kora,* and especially to the early shorter poems, whose unrhymed tercets or quatrains are distinguished by their very short lines, broken at odd junctures, and their use of colloquial speech. (p. 45)

"Memorial Day 1950" [, one of O'Hara's first great poems, is his] version of Rimbaud's "Les Poètes de sept ans," part autobiographical memoir, part artistic manifesto—a portrait of the young artist escaping from the restrictions of his narrowly bourgeois childhood world. But whereas Rimbaud's poem still observes the unities of time (the terrible long Sundays) and place (the poet's stifling childhood home with its polished mahogany break fronts), and relates stimulus (the smell of latrines) to response (the longing for succulent grass) in what is still an essentially realistic mode, O'Hara's poem is the verbal equivalent of a Dada collage—a bright, colorful, exuberant poem that juxtaposes disparate images in dreamlike sequences.

Whereas O'Hara's first Surrealist experiments like *Oranges* are partial failures because they present a hothouse world under glass, a world cleverly organized around a particular set of images but too remote from the reader, "Memorial Day" succeeds because it fuses the colloquialism and natural speech rhythms of Williams with the dialectic of polarized images characteristic of Dada and Surrealism. It is a fusion O'Hara would not quite achieve again for some years to come.

The poem's language is dynamic and immediate: "Picasso made me tough and quick," "Once he got his axe going everyone was upset," . . . you must look things / in the belly, not in the eye," and so on. Such racy diction is very different from the frequently ornate style of *Oranges:* "My feet, tender with sight, wander the yellow grass in search of love." . . . (pp. 48-9)

But, more important, "Memorial Day 1950" is one of O'Hara's first poems to resemble film, with its dissolves, cuts, its images at once concrete and hallucinatory, bleeding into one another. (p. 49)

Of modern English and American poets, Williams, Pound, and Auden remained [O'Hara's] favorites, and certainly he never came to trust the school of Eliot, or to have much interest in Yeats, Hopkins, or Stevens. But despite his advocacy of the poetry of immediate experience, of concrete particulars and contemporary vernacular, his theory [as stated in 1951-52] remained ahead of his practice for another few years. . . . Auden, reading [his] Surrealist poems of the early fifties, wrote to O'Hara: "I think you . . . must watch what is always the great danger with any 'surrealistic' style, namely of confusing authentic non-logical relations which arouse wonder with accidental ones which arouse mere surprise and in the end fatigue."

This is an interesting observation. For curiously, the major poems of O'Hara's early New York period—"Chez Jane," "Easter," and "Second Avenue"—are not vernacular poems in the Pound-Williams-Auden tradition but Surrealist lyrics that carry the mode of the earlier *Oranges* to what is probably a point of no return. These are the poems of what John Ashbery has aptly called Frank's "French Zen period" . . .—fascinating, if not always successful, experiments. (pp. 62-3)

[In] a Surrealist poem like "Chez Jane," the dialectic of opposites has no "meaning" beyond itself. The "white chocolate jar" and tiger cat do not stand for any particular set of values; rather, the poet is interested in capturing the moment of metamorphosis itself, the moment when tiger piss turns into the sound of "Saint-Saëns." . . . O'Hara's [jar] is sometimes agent, sometimes acted upon. Everything is potentially something else, and the game is to record these changes.

In "Chez Jane," O'Hara was therefore doing something rather new in American poetry which was, despite the influx of French Surrealism during the war years, still essentially the poetry of Symbolism. Some readers may find O'Hara's poems excessively cold and intellectual; the poet himself is not yet present *in* the poem as mediator of polarities. But, taken on its own terms, "Chez Jane" has a kind of perfection and finish not yet found in the more prolix *Oranges,* written three years earlier. It is also quite free of the coyness—what we might call the "Dada giggle"—of such [earlier] poems as "Night Thoughts in Greenwich Village" or "Tarquin." . . . (p. 65)

[Kenneth Koch] quite rightly notes that O'Hara's technique [in "Easter"] is to detach beautiful words from traditional contexts, that the poem centers around a procession of bodily parts across a vast landscape, and that at the word "Easter," the tone and mood of the poem undergo a definite shift, death giving way to resurrection, separation to union. . . . Indeed, the poem ends on a note of joy. . . . Despite the references here to "cunts" and "shit," the poet is presenting a vision of new beauty. Sexual ecstasy is the keynote. . . . (p. 68)

[Contrary to some critical views] "Easter" does display a sense of form. Its consistent use of high-low polarities, its anaphoric "When the world . . ." clauses—clauses that are regularly left suspended but that nicely tie lines together—and the elaboration of its central Easter theme (here, of course, a secular, even a blasphemous Easter) make this a very exciting, innovative poem.

Yet the cataloguing technique of "Easter"—the endless piling up of polarized images in exclamatory phrases—is not without its dangers. Six months or so after he completed "Easter," O'Hara tried to carry its form one step further and the result is his most Byzantine and difficult poem, *Second Avenue.* . . . (pp. 68-9)

[*Second Avenue*] is perhaps too painterly a poem, O'Hara's most ambitious attempt to do with *words* ("you have to use words") what the Abstract Expressionists were doing with paint.

O'Hara does indeed include "everything" [in *Second Avenue*], and yet the question remains whether a poem, especially such a long poem, can "*be* the subject, not just about it," whether verbal structure can be so insistently nonmimetic. For the mode of *Second Avenue* seems to be one of intentional displacement and disorientation. (p. 70)

[One is] hard put to find any line of development in *Second Avenue;* individual sections appear in no particular sequence; scenes and images are juxtaposed without a view of their place in the larger scheme. Perhaps O'Hara wanted it that way, wanted to stun us by his insistent dislocations, . . . but such *vertige* ultimately cannot sustain the poem. . . . [The] poem's meanderings are less those of a diary than those of a catalogue of insufficiently related items.

Yet in many ways *Second Avenue* represents a real stylistic advance. (p. 72)

[There] are many lines and passages throughout *Second Avenue* that have the immediacy, excitement, and sense of *presence* that characterizes the later poetry. (p. 73)

[By late 1953] all the necessary ingredients were present: the passages of casual, colloquial diction capturing actual speech or actual events, the unique O'Hara syntax with its ambiguous verbal positioning, its odd line breaks and consistent enjambement—all working together to give the reader a sense of tautness and breakneck speed; the versions of painting rendered "poetically"; the vignettes of artists, friends, enemies, people in the street; the images of the city; the art world, the private world. But after *Second Avenue*, O'Hara learns to relate individual elements more intricately, to forge them into a coherent whole. And he now begins to put what we might call "straight Surrealism" behind him. In the poems of 1954-61, O'Hara's great period, we can no longer identify the echoes of Péret or Tzara or Desnos as readily; Surrealism has now been assimilated into an American idiom.

Nevertheless, when one looks at the *oeuvre* of these early years—years of testing—one is astonished by the poet's range, his daring, his willingness to experiment—and his frequent successes. If we replaced *A City Winter* with a more representative collection of early poems—a collection that would include "Autobiographia Literaria," "A Pleasant Thought from Whitehead," "The Critic," "An Image of Leda," "A Postcard from John Ashbery," "Les Etiquettes Jaunes," "Poem (I've got to tell you")," "Memorial Day 1950," "Easter," *Second Avenue*, and "Chez Jane"—O'Hara's central place in the literary scene of the early fifties would already be assured. (pp. 73-4)

[Painters] and painting provided O'Hara with one of his central subjects. (p. 77)

[One] strategy found in O'Hara's poems about art is to use an allusion to artists or works of art as a touchstone for grounding and authenticating a particular mood. (p. 80)

Another group of poems inspired by art can be classified as meditations on particular paintings with the intent of "translating" the tone of the painting into a verbal medium. These are poems that, unlike the passages from *Second Avenue* and "In Memory of My Feelings" . . . , treat the painting as an independent object, without reference to the artist. (p. 82)

[O'Hara] was really more at home with painting that retains at least some figuration than with pure abstraction. Pollock, Kline, and Motherwell may well have been O'Hara's Gods, but, practically speaking, it was difficult to carry over into poetry [total abstraction]. . . . Words, after all, have meanings, and thematic implications thus have a way of coming in by the back door. . . . [In] O'Hara's major poems, . . . he did, of course, make use of such major concepts of Abstract Expressionism as "push and pull," "all-over painting" (composition as continuum with no beginning or end), and Harold Rosenberg's famous observation that in Action Painting the canvas becomes an arena upon which to *act* rather than a space in which to reproduce. But as a poet, O'Hara displays a certain ambivalence to the great Abstract Expressionists, an ambivalence that creates interesting tensions in his art criticism. . . . (p. 85)

In O'Hara's art criticism, we find the very same qualities [found in the work of his life-long hero, Guillaume Apollinaire]: an absence of theoretical discourse and, except in rare cases, close technical analysis, counterbalanced by an astonishing ability to recognize greatness, to distinguish between the first-rate and the second-best. Like Apollinaire, O'Hara had the innate gift of entering a gallery in which a large group show was installed and immediately spotting *the* important painting or paintings. (pp. 86-7)

O'Hara is at his weakest when he tries to generalize about such abstractions as Art, Beauty, Reality, or Nature. (p. 89)

Few of the *Poem-Paintings* [done with painter Norman Bluhm] contain real poems. Number 3 boasts the single word *Bust;* number 6, the letters B-A-N-G in the four corners, surrounding a shape that looks like a comical furry phallus. Many are no more than in-jokes. . . . Number 5, which contains no visual images, is a more or less direct transcript of O'Hara's conversation: the words "I'm so tired of all the parties, it's like January and the hangovers on the beach" are scrawled across the surface of the picture.

Individually, these poem-paintings may be quite negligible —a stroke or two of paint, a few curved lines and drips, and a phrase like "reaping and sowing / sowing and reaping . . . Skylark," as in number 1. But John Perrault is surely right when he compares these collaborations to "footprints of a wild ballet." Like Chinese ink drawings, they have a lyric charm quite different from the more complex and subtle *Stones* [lithographs by O'Hara and Larry Rivers]. For one thing, O'Hara has a chance to display his beautiful handwriting which looks like calligraphy. The technique of making lithographs made this impossible in *Stones*, where the poet uses block print. The combination of O'Hara's rounded letters and Bluhm's curling horseshoe shapes, his thick white paint flecks, and suggestive, fleeting gestures, make *Poem-Paintings* real works of art even if their verbal messages hardly qualify as "poems." (p. 108)

Indeed, the twenty-six collaborations should be seen as an integral whole, a total event, rather than as separate paintings. Their inventiveness, wit, and charm become increasingly apparent as we study the relation of gesture to gesture, footmark to handprint, lyric phrase to four-letter word, proverb to sexy innuendo, white drop to black letter, and so on.

The "collaborations" of the sixties with such artists as Joe Brainard and Jasper Johns are no longer, strictly speaking, poem-paintings. (p. 109)

O'Hara used long lines frequently, evidently because he liked their appearance on the page—their ability to convey sensuality and strength. When spoken, however, these lines tend to break down into groups of twos or threes, as in the following example:

> Now the violets are all gone, / / the rhinoceroses, / / the cymbals. . . .

What is heard does not, then, reflect what is seen. (p. 116)

Poetry and life—O'Hara refused, at least consciously, to make a distinction between the two. He regarded both as part of the same vital process, living every moment as if it were his last, forcing himself to go without sleep so as not to miss anything. (p. 117)

"Music," the opening poem of *Lunch Poems,* written in 1954, contains most of the stylistic devices [which identify a particular lyric as a "Frank O'Hara poem"].

> If I rest for a moment near The Equestrian
> pausing for a liver sausage sandwich in the Mayflower
>   Shoppe,
> that angel seems to be leading the horse into Bergdorf's
> and I am naked as a table cloth, my nerves humming.
> Close to the fear of war and the stars which have
>   disappeared.
> I have in my hands only 35¢, it's so meaningless to eat!
> and gusts of water spray over the basins of leaves
> like the hammers of a glass pianoforte. If I seem to you
> to have lavender lips under the leaves of the world,
>   I must tighten my belt.
> It's like a locomotive on the march, the season
>   of distress and clarity
> and my door is open to the evenings of midwinter's
> lightly falling snow over the newspapers.
> Clasp me in your handkerchief like a tear, trumpet
> of early afternoon! in the foggy autumn.
> As they're putting up the Christmas trees on Park
>   Avenue
> I shall see my daydreams walking by with dogs in
>   blankets,
> put to some use before all those coloured lights come
>   on!
>   But no more fountains and no more rain,
>   and the stores stay open terribly late.

This is at once an "easier" and a "more difficult" poem than such earlier lyrics as "Chez Jane," "Easter," or "Memorial Day 1950." . . . [One's] first impression is that "Music" is no more than a record of daily trivia. . . .

But the real strategy of ["Music"] is to remove objects from what Viktor Shklovsky has called "the automatism of perception," by adapting the techniques of film and action painting to a verbal medium. For one thing, the poem is framed as a series of cuts and dissolves, whether spatial, temporal, or referential. Thus in line 3, the highly concrete setting—the Mayflower Shoppe on the Plaza—dissolves

into a comic fantasy scene, created by the optical illusion of staring into the Plaza fountain on a rainy day: "that angel seems to be leading the horse into Bergdorf's." Or again, the poem suddenly cuts from Fifth Avenue to Park. . . .

Temporal dissolves work the same way. (p. 121)

Time shifts are not, of course, anything new in poetry, but it is one of O'Hara's trademarks to maintain the present tense (or conditional present as in "If I rest . . .") regardless, and to supply no adverbial pointers (e.g., "when," "after," "before," "during") that signal a shift. The concept of person is similarly fluid. The "I"—a very familiar, intimate, *open* "I"—is omnipresent but whom is he addressing? . . . [A] close friend or lover, . . . [or] perhaps the Manhattan traffic, the rising moon, the sky, or indeed the whole universe as if to say, "You out there!" While the poet's self thus remains a constant center, anything or anyone that comes within its field of vision can be addressed or called by name. The repetition of definite articles and demonstratives reinforces this sense of intimate conversation and invites the reader's participation: "*The* Equestrian" (note the ellipsis of the noun here), "*the* Mayflower Shoppe," "*that* angel," "*the* Christmas trees on Park Avenue"—all these references suggest that the reader is familiar with the scene, indeed that he is part of it.

The syntax of "Music" may be described as a system of nonsequiturs. "If I rest for a moment . . ." the poet begins, but no "then" clause ever follows, and the conditional clause dissolves into the parenthesis of line 3. The second "If I seem to you" clause in line 8 is completed by "I must tighten my belt," a clause that follows grammatically but makes no sense. Appositives and parallel nouns similarly turn out to be pseudo-appositives and pseudo-parallels. . . . In what sense is a "season" a "locomotive on the march"? And why "distress *and* clarity," or "the fear of war *and* the stars"? The use of "and" to introduce coordinate clauses is similarly illogical. . . . (p. 122)

The syntactic dislocations of "Music" are by no means as radical as those found in such earlier poems as "Second Avenue," with its all but impenetrable verbal surface, its total ambiguity of reference. But the repeated nonsequiturs act to undercut the documentary realism of the poem's scene and introduce the opposing note: an element of fantasy, of imaginative transformation. . . . Nothing really *happens* to the poet; it is all potential, conditional, projected into a possible future ("I *shall see* my daydreams"). And individual images and metaphors are often comically or grotesquely far-fetched, reinforcing the fantasy note. . . . (pp. 122-23)

How do all these elements work together? Again, the title gives us a clue, for the poem is like a melodic graph of the poet's perceptions. The varied sound images—some documentary and realistic, some fanciful and surreal—fuse to create a pattern that brings to mind modern dance (another favorite O'Hara art form) rather than a "poem" in the traditional sense of the word. (p. 123)

"Music" thus captures the sense of magic, urgency, and confusion of the modern cityscape in its "season of distress and clarity." It presents an impression of total fluidity, conveyed by the repeated use of present participles. . . . And the deliberate indeterminacy of the long verse lines is offset and heightened by repetitive internal sound patterning. . . . The effect of all these devices is to create an aura of intense animation.

Like an action painting, "Music" presents the poet's act of coming to awareness rather than the results of that act. (pp. 123-24)

"Music" fuses realism and surrealism, the literal and the fanciful. In so doing, it marks a clear-cut rejection of the Symbolist mode that had dominated American poetry for the first half of the century. Unlike Prufrock's "sawdust restaurants with oyster shells," with their symbolic connotations of aridity, sterility, and decay, O'Hara's Mayflower Shoppe points to nothing beyond itself; it has no underlying significance that demands interpretation. The name "Mayflower," for example, does not, in this context, call to mind our Founding Fathers or the innocence of an Early America; the coffee shop is simply *there,* an authentic presence we can all locate and recognize. Or again, whereas Prufrock's fear of eating a peach reflects his fear of ripeness and fertility, O'Hara's "liver sausage sandwich" has no particular symbolic properties; it could, for that matter, be a salami or cheese sandwich just as easily. (pp. 124-25)

O'Hara's is thus what Charles Altieri has called a "landscape without depth," a presence stripped of its "ontological vestments." Aerial perspective, three-dimensionality give way to a world of surfaces. In poem after poem of this period, what looks like a flat literalism predominates. . . . (p. 125)

But whereas any number of minor poets can offer us such a *catalogue raisonné,* O'Hara's empiricism is deceptive for it modulates easily and surprisingly into fantasy and artifice. The lessons of Dada and Surrealism have, after all, been learned; even the most casual personal poems retain the witty modulations and sudden polarization of images found in the poetry of Tzara, Péret, and Breton, or, for that matter, in the poetry of Apollinaire, which is one of the dominant influences on O'Hara's poetry of this period. (pp. 125-26)

[Surprising] conjunctions of literal reference and comic fantasy are typical of O'Hara; he shifts from *real* to *surreal* and back again with astonishing speed. And this is why his poetry is ultimately so difficult to imitate. . . . (p. 127)

O'Hara's poetry is, as everyone has remarked, one of constant name-dropping. Interestingly, proper names are not used very frequently in the early work. . . .

By the late fifties, O'Hara had established an elaborate network of cross-references to close personal friends, artists, film stars, city streets, bars, exotic places, titles of books, movies, operas, and ballets—in short, the name of anyone or anything that happens to come across the poet's path. (pp. 127-28)

One's first response to these endless allusions is that they are part of a tiresome in-joke. Why should we know who [these people are]? And don't these very private allusions make excessive demands on readers, especially future readers who will need extensive annotation in order to understand a given O'Hara poem? (p. 128)

[In most cases] the referential quality of the names is purposely undercut. As Charles Altieri remarks:

> His [O'Hara's] texture of proper names gives each person and detail an identity, but in no way do the names help the reader understand anything about what has been

named. . . . [This] is rather a reminder for the reader that the specific details of another's life can appear only as momentary fragments, insisting through their particularity on his alienation from any inner reality they might possess.

This seems to me precisely the point. . . . O'Hara goes one step further than Pound, who still uses historical, literary, and mythological figures as touchstones. In O'Hara's poetry, such touchstones have largely disappeared; only the arts continue to be endowed with a certain value. His poetic world is thus one of immanence rather than transcendence; persons and places, books and films are named because they are central to O'Hara's particular consciousness, but they have no "inner reality." Compare O'Hara's treatment of, say, Jane Freilicher to Yeats's mythologizing portraits of Lionel Johnson or Lady Gregory, and the difference will become clear. (pp. 130-31)

When these syntactic and prosodic devices [shifting forms of pronouns, ambiguous references, pseudo-connectives, floating modifiers, spatial and temporal dissolves, ellipsis, absence of punctuation, and quirky line breaks] are used in conjunction, we get a poetry of great speed, openness, flexibility, and defiance of expectations. Like the "all-over" painting, an O'Hara lyric often seems intentionally deprived of a beginning, middle, and end; it is an instantaneous performance. Syntactic energy is thus equivalent to the painter's "push and pull"—the spatial tensions that keep a surface alive and moving. The rapid cuts from one spatial or temporal zone to another, moreover, give the poetry its peculiar sense of immediacy: everything is absorbed into the NOW. (p. 135)

[In O'Hara's major poems] the first person is ubiquitous. In "Music," the pronoun "I" and its cognates appear ten times in the space of twenty-one lines. Yet . . . "Music" does not explore the speaker's past so as to determine what has made him the person he is; it does not, for that matter, "confess" or "reveal" anything about his inner psychic life. The role of the "I" is to respond rather than to confess—to observe, to watch, to be attentive to things. The poet's ruminations are "Meditations in an Emergency" not *"on an Emergency"*—an important distinction for it suggests that the self, no longer able to detach itself from the objects it perceives, dissolves and becomes part of the external landscape. . . . [The] "I" fragments into the surfaces it contemplates. . . . [The poet] makes no attempt to reflect upon the larger human condition, to derive meaning from a series of past incidents, or to make judgments upon his former self, as Robert Lowell does in the *Life Studies* poems. Indeed, the past is often so immediate that it becomes the present. . . . It is a matter of reifying a feeling rather than remembering another person or a particular event; in so doing, that feeling becomes part of the poet's present.

Here the shift in pronouns . . . is relevant. When O'Hara switches from "I" to "one" in "A Step Away From Them," he enlarges the poem's horizons, making the seemingly personal situation . . . fictive, theatrical. . . . [The] confusing second-person references extend the range of the poem, drawing the reader into the situation. "Clasp me in your handkerchief like a tear!" the poet exclaims, and immediately we are drawn into the magic circle. We are *there.* (pp. 135-36)

O'Hara's poetry is characterized by a remarkable confluence of styles. Aside from the influence of painting . . . and the close bonds between O'Hara's lyric and the arts of film and music, the poems reflect an unusual combination of literary influences. Dada and Surrealism continue to stand behind O'Hara's distinctive imagery—an imagery inclining toward artifice and the landscape of dream. The colloquialism and celebration of ordinary experience recall Williams and, to a lesser extent, the later Auden; but the use of proper names and documentary "evidence" seems to derive from Pound rather than Williams. . . . O'Hara's syntactic structures were influenced by Apollinaire and Reverdy, while his peculiar brand of Personism can be traced back to Mayakovsky, Pasternak, and Rimbaud.

The *Collected Poems* is, in short, a very learned (detractors would say, an eclectic) book. O'Hara's reputation as casual improvisator, unschooled doodler, could hardly miss the mark more completely. (p. 138)

[O'Hara] reanimates traditional genres. Ode, elegy, pastoral, autobiographical poem, occasional verse, love song, litany—all these turn up in O'Hara's poetry, although his tendency is to parody the model or at least to subvert its "normal" conventions. (p. 139)

[The] enigmatic, elliptical "In Memory of My Feelings" (1956) [is] in my opinion not only O'Hara's best autobiographical poem, but one of the great poems of our time. Its central theme, the fragmentation and reintegration of the inner self—a self that threatens continually to dissipate under the assault of outer forces—is a familiar Romantic topos, but O'Hara turns the autobiographical convention inside out, fusing fantasy and realism in a painterly collage-poem, whose form is at one with its meaning. Grace Hartigan, to whom "In Memory" is dedicated, suggests that O'Hara's aim in this poem is to define "inner containment" —"how to be *open* but not violated, how *not to panic*." The structure of the poem embodies this theme; it is an extremely "open" lyric sequence that nevertheless never gives way to formlessness, never "panics."

O'Hara's actual biography plays a part in the poem, but it is subordinated to a series of hallucinatory visions and memories. The implication all along is that what matters is not what happened but how one felt or feels about it; the poet writes, after all, in memory of his "feelings." And evanescent as these feelings are, O'Hara unifies his kaleidoscopic visions by repeating certain key images. . . . (pp. 141-42)

Few poets of our time . . . could manage the difficult structural and textural modulations of ["In Memory of My Feelings"], its swift and sudden transitions from long flowing line to short choppy one, from romantic melody to jazz syncopation, from fact to fantasy, past to present, self to other, nightmare landscape to the direct presentation of things. The French influence is as important as ever, but it is now thoroughly domesticated, absorbed into the fabric of colloquial American idiom. . . . (p. 146)

[The odes] reveal a very different side of O'Hara from the one we have considered so far. Their tone is more oracular, impersonal, and exclamatory, their syntax insistently paratactic (the "and" clauses piling up to create an almost unbearable intensity), their prosody more formal and elaborate than is typical of O'Hara. "Ode to Joy" . . . , for example, has traces of the Greater or Pindaric Ode. Not that its three stanzas resemble the Pindaric model (strophe

—antistrophe—epode), but the subject is "elevated" (the triumph of love over time), the tone sublime, and the three "strophes" have an intricate and elaborate prosodic scheme. . . . [Although] O'Hara's strophes contain neither rhyme nor meter, and although enjambment is used so consistently that the integrity of the individual line is somewhat obscured, the overall pattern is [formal]. . . . Certainly, its visual appearance on the page is very tidy, the three strophes looking exactly alike. (p. 153)

Thematically, these odes are curious for their avoidance of Personism; they are perhaps closer to such earlier long poems as "Second Avenue" and "Easter." "Ode to Joy" is a celebration of erotic love, of sexual bliss as a way of defying death. This theme is insistently Romantic but O'Hara's imagery is often surrealistic. . . .

[Despite an] injection of parody, "Ode to Joy" is essentially quite serious about its theme. . . . (p. 154)

O'Hara's model is Shelley-cum-Dada, for the "Ode on Causality," like the "Ode to Joy," frequently injects comic burlesque elements. . . . But in ending his ode with the rhapsodic reference to the painter's apotheosis (he becomes a work of art), the poet recaptures his original ecstasy.

"Ode on Causality" [the finest of the 1957-58 odes] thus provides us with an interesting example of the fusion between disparate modes and conventions. . . . The total effect of the poem is that of a Brahms or Schumann *lied*, interrupted at certain junctures by "noise" passages in the vein of Satie or Cage. Such conjunctions are wholly characteristic of O'Hara's lyricism. (p. 156)

[The love poems written for Vincent Warren between 1959 and 1961,] forty-odd erotic lyrics, should be read in sequence, although they are not found that way in the chronologically arranged *Collected Poems*. The range of moods from sexual excitement, joy, and hope, to loneliness, delusion, despair, and cynicism, and finally to the stoical acceptance of the way things are is extraordinary. Even such seemingly trivial little songs [repay study]. . . .

The risk of the intimate erotic lyric is that the poet is too close to his own experience to objectify it; in O'Hara's words, "sentiment is always intruding on form." . . . And we do find cases in the Vincent Warren sequence where the sentiment is stated too flatly . . . [or] the poem may succumb to triviality . . . [or to] campy cuteness. . . . (p. 157)

But for the most part, the Vincent Warren poems do work because O'Hara defines his sexual longing or sexual pleasure in terms of witty and fantastic hyperbole. . . . [His] analogies are intentionally absurd. . . . (p. 158)

After the enormous productivity of the late fifties, a lull was perhaps inevitable, and, in any case, the Museum now took up much of his time and energy. Between 1961 and 1963, the poet seems to have suffered periodic bouts of depression. Emptiness, despair, and death now become frequent themes. . . . (p. 165)

A number of poems contain references to suicide, although O'Hara usually treats this subject with self-deprecatory humor. . . . (p. 166)

But one must be careful not to generalize about the later poems, for the same Frank O'Hara who wrote "The Clouds Go Soft" [a poignant and "dark" poem], also wrote the wonderfully droll "Poem (Lana Turner has collapsed!)." (p. 167)

[In the early sixties] he organized three major shows for the Musuem: *Motherwell, Nakian,* and *Smith.* The catalogues for these exhibitions are now collector's items, the poet's introductions reflecting, once again, his uncanny ability to make the important discriminations about the art of his day. At the time of his death, O'Hara was working on a major retrospective of Jackson Pollock and had begun to make plans for the first major exhibition of de Kooning's painting at the museum. (p. 168)

What is probably O'Hara's best play, *The General Returns from One Place to Another,* a parodistic fantasy about General MacArthur's return to the Pacific theater in peacetime—a general in search of a war—was produced . . . in 1964 and published the following year in *Art and Literature.* This comedy, evidently inspired by a production of Brecht's *In the Jungle of Cities,* exploits some wonderfully absurd devices. . . . Unlike some of the early plays like *Try! Try!,* which are merely silly, *The General Returns* has shrewd and funny things to say about East-West relations. (p. 169)

One concludes that O'Hara wrote fewer poems during the sixties than he had in preceding years primarily because he was too busy doing other things. Indeed, it is a particularly bitter irony that the very summer O'Hara died was a time of special promise, both personal and literary. (pp. 170-71)

Since the "For Your Information" poems were written . . . mostly for the poets' [O'Hara's and Bill Berkson's] own diversion, it may be unfair to judge them too stringently on aesthetic grounds. Nevertheless, I would argue that there *is* a falling off in the FYI poems, that "Lunch Hour" replaces the Personism of *Lunch Poems* with a somewhat self-conscious gamesmanship. Modulation now gives way to simple repetition ("Plank plank"); the language is usually that of ordinary talk ("roll OVER dammit") and simplistic sound imitation ("tappety-tap drrrrrrrrrrrp!"). These new lyrics are much more loosely articulated: words tend to be spread all over the page, the blank space becoming an important prosodic element as a sort of musical rest. The three-step (or modified two-step) line of Williams's late poems is used frequently as is the device of placing verse paragraphs alternately on the left and right sides of the page. . . . Often, as in the case of "Lunch Hour," one is hard put to find a *raison d'être* for the particular prosodic shape used; sheer randomness seems to be the rule. These are poems that can start or stop anywhere, that accommodate almost anything the poet happens to want to record. Their tone, moreover, is curiously detached; O'Hara's former emotional vibrancy . . . is absent.

But perhaps these "For Your Information" poems are best considered as bits of muscle flexing, exercises that prepare the way for that great Bill Berkson poem, "Biotherm." (pp. 172-73)

How much openness can a poem bear? This is a tricky question, of course, and for a long time I regarded "Biotherm" as just . . . a witty improvisation, a transcript of the charming if jumbled talk of a marvelous raconteur. Its endless puns, in-jokes, phonetic games, allusions, cataloguing, journalistic parodies, and irrelevant anecdotes may seem, on a first or even a later reading, merely tiresome. Interestingly, "Biotherm" also seems to have much less relationship to painting than do the earlier poems. Film is now the dominant sister art; the poem is full of references to movie

stars, Hollywood films, and invented scenarios, and its structure often resembles the film technique of crosscutting at accelerated speed, a technique particularly common in the silent film comedies of the twenties, for example those of Buster Keaton.

If we study O'Hara's crosscutting, we find that everything in this seemingly wild talk-poem relates to everything else. . . . Although the beach setting is never formally introduced or presented in realistic detail, sand, sea, and cloud images, as well as larger beach scenes, fade in and out at fairly regular intervals. . . . [The] brief flashes of real and fantastic beach locales provide a sense of continuity rather like that of a Godard film; they are brief reminders that the poem's variations radiate from a center which is the loving relationship between Frank and Bill. . . . What the poet preserves in "biotherm" in order to entertain his friend is a dazzling array of memories and inventions. (pp. 174-75)

Individually, [some] passages may seem to be pure slapstick, but the remarkable thing about "Biotherm" is that, as in a sophisticated orchestral composition, everything mentioned casually is picked up somewhere later in the poem in an altered context. (p. 177)

"Biotherm" consistently plays off the intensities of personal emotion against the vagaries of everyday conversation. It is an extremely difficult poem because the reader enters the "frame" only gradually, overhearing snatches of conversation . . . , and only gradually realizing that "Biotherm" is something of a rock opera, partly playful but also full of anxiety, alternating percussive passages with lyrical tunes, an extravaganza celebrating the poet's great love for his friend and memorializing their careless summer beach days. . . . Another way of putting it is that O'Hara's long lyric sequence is an elegy for "Biotherm," that magic potion that preserves roses—a potion interchangeable with "kickapoo joyjuice halvah Canton cheese / in thimbles" . . . or "marinated duck saddle with foot sauce and a tumbler of vodka." . . . Food and liquor images are especially prominent in this poem because the poet's imagination transforms them into *Plankton,* the "health-giving substance" that makes Biotherm so special. Thus when the poet says in one expansive moment:

> I am sitting on top of Mauna Loa seeing
> thinking feeling the breeze rustles through
> the mountains gently trusts me I am guard-
> ing it from mess and measure . . .

he is describing not only his guardianship of Mauna Loa but the creative act as well. "Biotherm" is a poem dangerous to imitate for it implies that anything goes, that all you have to do is "merely continue." But in fact O'Hara does succeed here in "guarding it from mess and measure"—that is, from total formlessness on one hand, and from a more traditional rhetorical and prosodic organization on the other. It is his last great poem and one of the important poems of the sixties. (p. 178)

> *Marjorie Perloff, in her* Frank O'Hara: Poet among Painters *(reprinted by permission of George Braziller, Inc., Publishers; copyright © 1977 by Marjorie Perloff), Braziller, 1977.*

*   *   *

OLSEN, Tillie   1913-

Olsen is a prize-winning American novelist and short story

writer. (See also *CLC*, Vol. 4, and *Contemporary Authors*, Vols. 1-4, rev. ed.)

In [*Yonnondio,*] a mercifully brief, emotionally charged narrative incorporating all imaginable horrors experienced by a destitute, ill, and starving family during the Depression in the early thirties, [Tillie Olsen] forcefully portrays their plight, not sparing the reader intrepid enough to endure so brutal an account of so much gloom and despair. Here is art of a kind for those who take vicarious delight in the contemplation of absolute human degradation. (p. cxx)

> Virginia Quarterly Review *(copyright, 1974, by the Virginia Quarterly Review,* The University of Virginia*), Vol. 50, No. 4 (Autumn, 1974).*

CATHARINE R. STIMPSON

Olsen's compelling gift is her ability to render lyrically the rhythms of consciousness of victims [in *Yonnondio: From the Thirties*]. Imaginative, affectionate, they are also alert to the sensual promise of their surroundings. Harsh familial, social, political and economic conditions first cramp, then maim, and then seek to destroy them. The fevers of poverty, dread and futility inflame their sensibilities. They risk reduction to defensive fantasy, pain, madness or cruelty. They remain, if in shadow, heroes and heroic.

Olsen assumes that such victims cannot often speak for themselves. Their dumbness is no fault of their own. Her self-imposed task is to become their voice as well as their witness, their text as well as their mourner. She signifies her respect for their dignity in the exactitude and scrupulous effort of her work. She sardonically tells her reader that the received categories of culture, such as classicism and romanticism, also fit the citizens of a Wyoming town as they wait to hear how many men have died in a mine explosion that official cowardice, incompetence and corruption have caused. If she were to take part in that theological quarrel over whether an artist's primary commitment is to craft or to social change, she might say that an artist can work for change through writing about the oppressed with all the craft and tools at hand. She also comments on the economic basis of high culture. She writes of an adolescent boy forced into the mines:

> Earth take your dreams that a few may languidly lie on couches and trill "How exquisite" to paid dreamers.

Olsen's politics and anger are a part of a particular decade: her subtitle, "From the Thirties," is seriously meant. She notes that *Yonnondio* "bespeaks the consciousness and roots of that decade, if not its events." An anachronism or two betrays the gap between narrative setting and actual reference. Despite her nostalgia for rural ritual, she refuses to offer an exclusive vision of bucolic joy. She wants unions and solidarity among all workers, no matter what their race or ethnic heritage. (p. 565)

> Catharine R. Stimpson, "Three Women Work It Out," in The Nation *(copyright 1974 The Nation Associates), November 30, 1974, pp. 565-66.*

PETER ACKROYD

[*Yonnondio*] is a conventional story, as stories go, but the plot is in fact the least important element of the novel. This is not because it is incomplete (the book has only recently been recovered in a less than perfect form), but because the narrative is consumed by the effects of Miss Olsen's prose. A pattern of images is cast over the writing from the opening chapters, and there is a characteristic attention to description rather than analysis—it is a matter of dialogue rather than character, of situations rather than incidents. *Yonnondio* is a romantic novel, in the sense that Man and Nature are seen in a close and often destructive relationship, and its language becomes the space between them—instinctive with life, both mortal and at the same time capable of expressing certain permanent truths.

It is out of the mouths of children that this will come most naturally and there are some marvellously childish moments in this book. (pp. 767-68)

Yonnondio is one of the most powerful statements to have emerged from the American 'thirties; a young woman has pulled out of that uneasy time a living document which is full of the wear and tear of the period, and she has done so without doctrinaire blues, and without falling into the trap of a sentimentality which is, at bottom, self-pity. (p. 768)

> Peter Ackroyd, in The Spectator *(© 1974 by The Spectator; reprinted by permission of* The Spectator*), December 14, 1974.*

ROBERT COLES

[Tillie Olsen] is, has been for decades, a feminist—unyielding and strong-minded, but never hysterical or shrill. Her essays reveal her to be brilliant, forceful and broadly educated. . . .

At times she has allowed herself, in a confessional vein not unlike that of "I Stand Here Ironing," a moment of regret, if not self-pity: if only there had been more time, an easier life—hence more stories, novels, essays written. . . . Everything she has written has become almost immediately a classic—the short stories especially, but also her two essays, her comment on the life and writing of Rebecca Harding Davis. . . . She has been spared celebrity, but hers is a singular talent that will not let go of one; a talent that prompts tears, offers the artist's compassion and forgiveness, but makes plain how fierce the various struggles must continue to be. (p. 30)

> Robert Coles, in The New Republic *(reprinted by permission of* The New Republic*; © 1975 The New Republic, Inc.), December 6, 1975.*

MARGARET ATWOOD

Tillie Olsen's is a unique voice. Few writers have gained such wide respect based on such a small body of published work. . . . Among women writers in the United States, "respect" is too pale a word: "reverence" is more like it. This is presumably because women writers, even more than their male counterparts, recognize what a heroic feat it is to have held down a job, raised four children and still somehow managed to become and to remain a writer. The exactions of this multiple identity cost Tillie Olsen 20 years of her writing life. The applause that greets her is not only for the quality of her artistic performance but, as at a grueling obstacle race, for the near miracle of her survival.

Tillie Olsen's third book, "Silences," is about this obstacle course, this ordeal, not only as she herself experienced it but as many writers have experienced it, in many forms. (p. 1)

Though Tillie Olsen begins with her own experience, she

rapidly proceeds to that of others. The second part of the book is a grab bag of excerpts from the diaries, journals, letters and concealed autobiographical work of a wide range of writers, past and present, male and female. They are used to demonstrate, first, the ideal conditions for creation as perceived by the writers themselves, and second, almost every imaginable impediment to that creation. . . . Reading this section may be hazardous if you are actually writing a book. It's like walking along a sidewalk only to be shown suddenly that your sidewalk isn't a sidewalk but a tightrope over Niagara Falls. How have you managed to do it at all? "Chancy luck," Tillie Olsen replies, and in view of the evidence she musters, she's probably—for all writers not white, male, rich and from a dominant culture—quite right.

Tillie Olsen's special concern is with how her general observations on silencings apply, more heavily and with additions, to women. Here, the obstacles may seem to be internal: the crippling effects of upbringing, the burdens of motherhood, the lack of confidence that may prevent women from writing at all; and, if they do write, their own male-determined view of women, the fear of competing, the fear of success. We've heard a lot of this before, but it's invigorating to see its first expressions by women coming new to the problems: Virginia Woolf worrying about her childlessness, Katherine Mansfield having to cope with all the domestic arrangements while John Middleton Murry nagged her about tea. And, in contrast, quotations from men whose wives dedicated their lives to sharpening pencils and filling the inkwell for them. As Tillie Olsen points out, almost all of the women in the 19th century who wrote were childless or had servants. . . .

In construction, "Silences" is a scrapbook, a patchwork quilt: bits and pieces joined to form a powerful whole. And, despite the condensed and fragmentary quality of this book, the whole is powerful. Even the stylistic breathlessness— the elliptical prose, the footnotes blooming on every page as if the author, reading her own manuscript, belatedly thought of a dozen other things too important to leave out— is reminiscent of a biblical messenger, sole survivor of a relentless and obliterating catastrophe, a witness: "I only am escaped alone to tell thee." The tone is right: The catastrophes do occur, daily, though they may not be seen as such. What Tillie Olsen has to say about them is of primary importance to those who want to understand how art is generated or subverted and to those trying to create it themselves. (p. 27)

> *Margaret Atwood, "Obstacle Course," in* The New York Times Book Review *(© 1978 by The New York Times Company; reprinted by permission), July 30, 1978, pp. 1, 27.*

PHOEBE-LOU ADAMS

In examining the failure of various talented writers (mostly women) to produce the amount or quality of work warranted by their apparent ability, Ms. Olsen blames, in *Silences,* everything except that standard ailment known as writer's block, while quoting the lamentations of a number of writers (mostly men) who suffered no other impediment. The result is a discussion with more eloquence than logic. (p. 96)

> *Phoebe-Lou Adams, in* The Atlantic Monthly *(copyright © 1978 by The Atlantic Monthly Company, Boston, Mass.; reprinted with permission), September, 1978.*

NOLAN MILLER

There is a good reason for [Tillie Olsen's] low production. For more than forty years she has been a wife and mother, a family wage-earner at dull and time-sapping menial jobs. She has been, like multitudes of other talents, frustratingly "silent"—silent because, most of all, of the necessities of earning a living and keeping a family together.

Silences, her third book, tells us all this—tells us why, and how arduous and obstructed her life, a woman's life, has been. She has not been alone. Her abundant quotations from others who have endured silently, both men and women, may seem abundant only to those unacquainted with or indifferent to society's waste of individual talents.

If categories are wanted, call this a highly personal commonplace book. Call it a case-book, a text. Above all, it bears the stamp of a passionate and reasonably angry voice. What is said here needed to be said, however it is said. Value the book as one values the person, the talent. One can only return to a reading of "Tell Me a Riddle" and "Hey Sailor, What Ship?" marveling the more. The experience of these stories can only be deepened by our knowledge of how they managed, eventually, to struggle into lasting significance. (p. 513)

> *Nolan Miller, in* The Antioch Review *(copyright © 1978 by the Antioch Press; reprinted by permission of the Editors), Vol. 36, No. 4, 1978.*

DAVID DILLON

[*Silences*] is a book about the relationships between literature and circumstances as well as a commentary on the mysterious workings of the creative imagination. . . .

Several of the essays in *Silences* were written in the early sixties, before the women's movement was really under way, and therefore seem a bit dated. What remains fresh and compelling is Tillie Olsen herself. Angry, sensitive, persistent, she has managed to create enduring literature under the most unpromising circumstances. Among women writers she is something of a saint, although she has done her best to avoid canonization. She makes it clear throughout this book that she is talking about a writer's problem, not just a woman's problem. (p. 105)

> *David Dillon, "Art and Daily Life in Conflict," in* Southwest Review *(© 1979 by Southern Methodist University Press), Winter, 1979, pp. 105-07.*

*   *   *

OPPEN, George   1908-

Oppen is an American poet associated with the Objectivist school. In poetry noted for its precision of language, he explores the traditional themes of love and death, history and human knowledge. He won the Pulitzer Prize in Poetry in 1969 for *Of Being Numerous*. (See also *CLC*, Vol. 7, and *Contemporary Authors*, Vols. 13-16, rev. ed.)

CID CORMAN

Oppen declared: "I'm really concerned with the substantive, with the subject of the sentence, with what we are talking about, and not rushing over the subject-matter in order to make a comment about it."

To make a thing of it—the poem—declaring itself:

The edge of the ocean,
The shore: here
Somebody's lawn,
By the water.

And here—if your breath bothers to shape the articulation as articulateness you will find—characteristic of this poet—each word loving itself—that sacrament of dancing together Eliot descried in *East Coker*. As if the ear perceived what the mind breathed.

You will say: But it's not profound. Yet love is revealed in just such quiet modulations, such excellence of attention, where the lover does not have to point to himself to exist. (pp. 85-6)

Oppen has a transparent faith—an active confidence—a loyalty to—his word—which is—as he realizes—ours too. "I was thinking about a justification of human life, eventually, in what I call the life of the mind." He joins Stevens at this point. But where Stevens—in his own version of the romantic—improvises and brings off remarkable cadenzas—Oppen prefers to try to see closer to find his leverage—as metaphysical Archimedes—towards spiritual community. . . . (pp. 86-7)

Oppen often repeats words—not for mere effect ever—but as if he were literally discovering the sense in them and he were startled by it. . . . *The shock is metaphysical.* (pp. 87-8)

Perhaps Oppen's most telling power is in his deceptively quiet—almost hidden—statements. Firm and yet requiring us to meet him in the words in order to come across—to reach their true depth. . . . (p. 89)

One fact only remains: Oppen is a poet—a maker of poems. And by that I mean in all simplicity and difficulty—one who has found through language a way to share what he has realized AS realization—AS experience. . . . You ask: What has happened through the years to the man's poetry? Has it developed—has it "grown"? You can see and hear the move beyond thing—beyond poem itself (not poetry)—into the plenum of what he is at—where a lifetime of feeling and intelligence brings him to be. "All that there is, is / Yours . . . " "We must talk now. Fear / Is fear. But we abandon one another." This is no longer a poetry of theoretics; it is one that can embrace its doubt. (pp. 90-1)

Cid Corman, "Together," in Parnassus: Poetry in Review (copyright © by Poetry in Review Foundation), Spring-Summer, 1976, pp. 85-91.

JONATHAN GALASSI

George Oppen's *Collected Poems* is . . . the record of a life-long confrontation between an unimpeachably free spirit's sense of order and "a world of things". . . . [His poems] are built out of words themselves. Oppen's lines move in fits and starts; they are slowly accrued "discrete series" of phrases, chains of associations which aim directly, often painfully, at an identifiable point. The lesson, the articulations of a meaning, is what matters. Words, imperfect and sometimes untrustworthy, are only the means to this end. . . . (p. 167)

The conception of the poet's role as that of the teacher accounts for the openly, even severely didactic tone of much of Oppen's work, though the sobriety and ponderousness are occasionally relieved by pure word-pictures, which

Oppen uses to beautiful effect. . . . I suppose he is most approachable through his imagery, though the rhythm can also be seductively real. But Oppen is probably destined never to be popular, for he demands too much of the reader. His fragmentary approach, his moral certitude, his conception of the poet's task in life (*To Make Much of Life*), hark back to the modernism we have been running away from for a generation. But his work resonates more and more profoundly the longer we spend with it. Oppen's deeply historical conception of himself as a Jew ("Neither Roman / nor barbarian") in an essentially alien culture is, by extension, a portrayal of the poet—and man himself—in the world; and his collected work, for all its scatteredness of exposition, presents a whole world-picture, embracing history, politics, race, society. Each of these slowly achieved, hard-won pieces of Oppen's thought is nothing less than an utterly authentic response to the grain of an idea which has irritated the poet into words, meant to be slowly taken. The poems often work together in groups; Oppen's best-known book, *Of Being Numerous*, which won the Pulitzer Prize in 1969, is a serial meditation on man's situation as a social animal, as the member of a tribe. Characteristically, it is highly dense, allusive, laden with historical reference. Many of the poems, predictably, deal with the nature of the poet's work and his role, in and out of society, as a user of language; i.e., as someone chosen—with all the responsibility and privilege the term implies—to speak for others. . . . (pp. 167-68)

Jonathan Galassi, in Poetry (© 1976 by The Modern Poetry Association; reprinted by permission of the Editor of Poetry), December, 1976.

MICHAEL HELLER

[While] the poems in "Primitive" are charged, as befits a man writing in his 70's, with the meaning of being a poet, they are also perhaps Mr. Oppen's most public and visionary poems. They are poems that . . . are a keeping of faith, an almost Whitmanesque faith, with the sources of his poetry:

> . . . I am
> of that people the grass
>
> blades touch
>
> and touch in their small
>
> distances the poem
> begins

They are at once celebratory and elegiac; even as they affirm kinship ("I dreamed myself of their people . . .") they probe loss, often speaking of something failed or incomplete, reminders of how much of Whitman's hopes remain unfulfilled. The lines intense, painful and declamatory have that unique tone that is Mr. Oppen's main contribtion to our poetry:

> . . . young workmen's
> loneliness on the structures has touched
> and   touched   the   heavy   tools   tools
> in our hands in the clamorous
> country birth-
> light savage
> light of the landscape

And suffused throughout is the presence of the companion he has lived with "fellow / me feminine / winds as you pass," of Mary Oppen as so much an essential part:

hat-brim fluttered in the air as she ran
forward and it seemed so beautiful so beautiful
the sun-lit air it was no dream all's wild
out there as we unlikely
image of love found the way
away from home

(pp. 9, 19)

Michael Heller, in The New York Times Book
Review *(© 1978 by The New York Times Company; reprinted by permission), December 31,
1978.*

* * *

ORTON, Joe   1933?-1967

**Orton was a British dramatist whose satires, with their formal language and intricate plots, "extend the style and savagery of Restoration comedy into twentieth century life,"
according to John Lahr. (See also *CLC*, Vol. 4, and *Contemporary Authors*, obituary, Vols. 25-28, rev. ed.)**

BENEDICT NIGHTINGALE

[The] Orton faithful claim that no play has been more viciously underrated than [*What the Butler Saw*]. . . . And yet, after seeing the piece twice fail to generate its quota of laughter, I have to ask if there isn't something intrinsically unfunny about it. . . . We can't easily laugh at someone's flouting of convention, or his furtive attempts to regain respectability, when no one onstage is remotely conventional, respectable or shockable. Farce simply won't breathe in an atmosphere of amorality and permissiveness. That's one trouble with the play: another is its peculiar blend of frenetic action with rotund aphorism. . . .

The problem is more acute in *The Butler* than in the earlier plays, because Orton's style grew progressively more mannered and farcical. In *Entertaining Mr Sloane*, the brother and sister have sensual designs on their psychopathic young lodger, but they tend to express themselves cautiously, obliquely, through euphemism, as one might expect in life. In *The Butler*, people genially flaunt their proclivities, blushing neither at social decorum nor at dramatic probability. . . . You get much the same openness in the middle play, *Loot*, which breezily presents a corrupt and violent policeman, a mass-murderess and two young bank-robbers, all equally unapologetic about their crimes. But there the characters are more strongly drawn, the lines sharper and more succinct, the plot better organised, the farce less random and frantic: which is why *Loot*, at least in its second and final version, seems to me the most successful of the three plays.

But Orton's defenders can reasonably reply that *The Butler* is more than a farce, and that their hero's reputation rests on something more solid than a knack for shaping plots and chiselling artful lines. He's important, not as a technician, but as an iconoclast, perhaps the most thoroughgoing in the history of British drama. *Entertaining Mr Sloane*—showing, as it does, two average citizens far less interested in their father's murder than in the sexual capture of his murderer—redefines love as greed and most of the other virtues as trumpery camouflage. *Loot* moves from the private world to the public, cocking a snook at the supposed hypocrisy of religion and corruption of authority. *The Butler* perpetuates the panning of officialdom, this time represented by an inspector-general whose obsession is certifying sane people. . . .

Comedy is often malicious, callous, cynical and negative, but rarely as unswervingly so as in Orton. . . . [Line after line cumulatively implies] an indiscriminate scorn for most things human, from institutions to affections. Altruism doesn't exist: nor does reason. And yet all this is shrugged off without regret or rancour, as a plain fact cheerfully contemplated somewhere between the brothel and the bedroom. It is this gleeful nihilism that characterises Orton—this that makes him fascinating and, to me, repellent and suspect. Could it be that, as a promiscuous homosexual and onetime jailbird, he found it necessary to prove that the world's judges, coppers, civil servants, psychiatrists and sturdily married heterosexuals were no better than himself? If everyone else is bad, it's easier to live with one's own excesses. If everyone else is telling lies about themselves, one can at least congratulate oneself on one's honesty.

Orton once called himself a 'puritan', whatever that means. I see more complacent hedonism than reformist zeal in his work. But there was perhaps a hint of something more serious and self-questioning at the end of *The Butler*. Inspector and nymphomaniac pull out guns and start to shoot. People are 'white with shock', 'screaming with terror'; a wound 'streams with blood', and blood 'pours' down someone else's leg. . . . [The] scene is sudden, unexpected, like nothing else in Orton's work, and therefore perhaps important. It is as if, right at the end of his writing career, he realised that his laissez-faire philosophy, as practised by moral morons, could result in injury, and that injury caused pain, and that pain actually *hurt*. Not long afterwards, he found out something of the sort the hard, personal way, from an axe that rained blows onto his sleeping head. He died, aged 34, and it is fruitless to guess at the sort of writer he might have become. As it was, he was a sparkling comedian and a smirking hooligan: enough there to keep us critics debating his posthumous reputation for some time.

Benedict Nightingale, "Orton Iconoclast," in
New Statesman *(© 1975 The Statesman & Nation
Publishing Co. Ltd.), July 18, 1975, p. 90.*

JOHN LAHR

Joe Orton's festival spirit scintillates through . . . *Loot*. In the anarchy of Orton's carnival, the sacred and the profane, good and evil, night and day are tumbled together. The boundaries of the everyday world are dissolved in order to be re-examined. A trickster, Orton put laughter back into sexuality and let its aggressiveness run riot. His jokes 'played for keeps' about serious issues. Comedy, like all play, is most thrilling when it is tense; and there was a whiff of danger in Orton's laughter. His plays were offensive, elegant, cruel, shocking, monstrous, hilarious and smart. In short, brilliant theatre.

Loot, whose original title was *Funeral Games*, sports with the culture's superstitions about death as well as life. 'It's a Freudian nightmare,' says the son, Hal, who is about to dump his mother's corpse from her coffin into the wardrobe in order to hide money he's stolen. And so it is. Comedy always acts out unconscious wishes which must be suppressed in daily life, and Orton seized this liberation with a vengeance. In *Loot*, viscera fly like brickbats around the room. . . . The shock of seeing 'human remains desecrated' is to realise that they are no longer human. Like gargoyles on a mediaeval cathedral, Orton's ghoulish spectacle is meant to scare people into life. Like all festivals, *Loot* revels in the gratifications of the moment. Hal, who is unrepentantly bisexual and who has no job, won't forestall pleasure at the threat of social 'death'. (pp. 30-1)

The trickster is an enemy to order. Orton sports with the police and the British public's uncritical acceptance of police authority. Truscott is an outlandish parody of the omniscient B-movie gumshoe.... Orton takes devastating potshots at authority and those, like the credulous Mr McLeavy, who surrender themselves completely to it....

In the end, greed conquers all. Truscott shares the money with the others; and the only innocent man on stage, McLeavy, is sent to prison.... [No] superstition, Orton is saying, can save us from the facts of life.

Loot is a major theatrical step forward from *Entertaining Mr Sloane,* but the style is caught between farce and satire....

Orton found his mature comic style in *Loot.* He couldn't resist writing his own review in Truscott's literary appraisal of Fay's confession: 'Your style is simple and direct. It's a theme which less skillfully handled could've given offence.' Orton still gave offence while pretending he wasn't. He called this tactic 'the British art of compromise'.... Orton's theatre world is irresistible. Orton expected to die young, but his plays were made to last. (p. 31)

John Lahr, in Plays and Players (© *copyright John Lahr 1975; reprinted with permission), August, 1975.*

JOHN LAHR

What the Butler Saw is [Joe Orton's] last and best piece of comic construction. Orton parodies farce in the play and makes use of it for his own serious and sublime comic ends. Farce is an act of literary aggression which Orton carried to its logical extreme—a battle of identity that makes a spectacle of disintegration. Orton saw in farce a way of making violence and frenzy into a resonant metaphor. As events spiral out of control, the characters become numbed victims of pace, moving too fast to notice the truth of their own destructiveness....

The phallus is the emblem of comedy's ruthless sexual mischievousness and amorality. Nobody came closer than Orton to reviving this spirit on the English stage and creating that purest (and rarest) of drama's by-products: joy. (p. 21)

In polite farce, characters keep their knickers on; but panic has another dimension in Orton's comedy and his laughter is never polite.

Orton's farce is a tremendous acting challenge. The epigrammatic style of his dialogue, which needs to be delivered standing still to get laughs, has to be synchronised with the play's frantic action.... The result is fascinating and hilarious. (pp. 21-2)

[In the second act] the fun machine turns into a replica of living hell. The psychiatrists declare each other mad at gunpoint, an alarm is pressed, and metal grilles fall over all the doors and windows ... with an impressive thud. The sound is terrifying and funny; the bars are a stunning image of spiritual stalemate. Orton's *coup de théâtre* elevates his farce onto an imaginative level unique in contemporary theatre.... [In] Orton's final and glorious image of transcendency, ... everyone leaves in one piece. 'Let us put on our clothes and face the world,' says Rance and the actors do just that. Each climbs up [a] ladder and out of sight.

The moment is a long but powerful one. As they clamber up, the daring and size of Orton's comic accomplishment sinks in. Laughter, he shows, is one way to move toward wisdom; but the mature Orton knew that the festival of fools must come to an end. (p. 23)

John Lahr, in Plays and Players (© *copyright John Lahr 1975; reprinted with permission), September, 1975.*

MANFRED DRAUDT

We do not expect that two plays [*Loot* and *Hamlet*] which at first sight seem to have nothing whatsoever in common should be based upon practically the same plot situation. Yet there are not only other surprising parallels and links between *Hamlet* and *Loot* but also illuminating affinities of Ortonian farce and Jacobean tragedy ... which are even more remarkable. (p. 202)

In *Hamlet* and *Loot* exactly the same issue is commented upon—the discrepancy between genuine, private emotions and feelings expressed publicly towards the deceased. As might be expected, the manner in which this idea is conveyed is very different. Whereas in *Hamlet* there is a straight-forward and serious statement, the social criticism of *Loot* is implied by the author's irony aiming at a different initial response from the audience: laughter. However, because Hamlet often resorts to irony and sarcasm, we may find a number of instances in which the two plays approximate to each other not merely in regard to the content but also in the tone of speech.

In *Loot,* Fay's lines are a mockery of the conventions that determine the period of mourning for a widower:

> You've been a widower for three days. Have
> you considered a second marriage yet? ...
> You must marry again after a decent interval
> of mourning. . . .· A fortnight would be long
> enough to indicate your grief. ...

This ridicule of propriety seems to echo Hamlet's ironic comments to Horatio and Ophelia:

> Thrift, thrift, Horatio. The funeral baked meats
> Did coldly furnish forth the marriage tables...
>
> ... look you how cheerfully my mother looks,
> and my father died within's two hours.—Nay,
> 'tis twice two months, my lord.—So long? ...

Although these passages from *Hamlet* and *Loot* are closely related as regards statement and technique, any interpretation which goes beyond the immediate contexts will reveal the difference in regard to function and meaning. In *Loot* the dialogue, appropriate to the world of farce, contributes very little to the description of character, whereas in *Hamlet* almost every single word and nuance adds to our understanding of the protagonist's mind and predicament. (p. 203)

Yet despite basic differences between the two plays which stem from the genres of tragedy and farce, there are a number of significant links between *Hamlet* and *Loot.* Particularly the treatment of death, which is a subject central to both plays, shows how many techniques Shakespeare and Orton have in common. *Loot* appears to be shocking for two reasons: firstly, because of the disrespectful handling of the deceased on stage, and secondly because of its abundance of macabre humour, which is the linguistic counterpart of the grotesque stage-business. (p. 204)

Regarding the theme of death, there are still other links between *Hamlet* and *Loot,* such as the figures of the grave-digger and the undertaker, whose attitude towards dying and corpses is 'professional' and therefore detached. In both plays death is also the subject of absurd humour that draws on commonplace or trite phrases taken literally. Hamlet's answer to Polonius's 'Will you walk out of the air, my lord?'—'Into my grave' . . . is echoed in *Loot* by Fay and Hal: 'What will you do when you are old?'—'I shall die.' . . .

The identification of parallels between an Elizabethan blank verse tragedy and a modern farce may lead to a reconsideration of the relationship of the genres and point to basic characteristics common to the 'tragic' and the 'comic'. Yet such an analysis may also contribute towards enhancing our awareness of the peculiar natures of Shakespeare's and Orton's plays respectively, because it directs our attention towards the differences in function and meaning of these common elements when viewed within the context of the individual play. Ironic, satiric, absurd, and macabre elements clearly dominate *Loot,* for they are the vehicles through which the author conveys his intention: the ridicule and parody of accepted mores and of various traditional norms and forms, including the thriller-form of the play itself. (pp. 205-06)

Whatever parallels and correspondences *Hamlet* and *Loot* possess, there remain fundamental differences between the plays, one of them being the fact that in Shakespeare's play it is always the dramatic character, Hamlet, who attacks and unmasks the hypocrisy of the court of Elsinore, whereas in *Loot* it is the author, Joe Orton, who levels his criticism at the audience and at the society outside and not within the world of the play. (p. 206)

Manfred Draudt, "Comic, Tragic, or Absurd? On Some Parallels between the Farces of Joe Orton and Seventeenth-Century Tragedy," in English Studies *(© 1978 by Swets & Zeitlinger B.V.), Vol. 59, No. 3, June, 1978, pp. 202-17.*

DAVID HARSENT

[*Daughters of Men* is] a very good example of Orton's black, farcical style. A neat flight of fancy puts authority, the family, class divisions and the church under one roof, as it were, at a holiday camp, where Peter Vaughan presides over the grotesqueries of chalet life with vicious paternalism. A raucous competition in the main hall gets badly out of hand and anarchy spreads as infuriated campers savage the redcoats, rape lady entertainers and finally march on the inner sanctum where Erpingham waits in morning-dress, flanked by the padre and a portrait of the Queen.

Apart from an overlong diversion—probably introduced in the re-write—when a camp entertainment is presented in a way that makes the audience become the punters, Orton's pacing is invariably effective. He always had a perfect ear for pompous circumlocution and for the strangled diction of received clichés. The spite is evident and vastly enjoyable, as is the way in which violent and ungovernable circumstance—serving violent and ungovernable motives—takes over by a series of small, cleverly promoted dramatic lesions. One thing, in Orton's work, invariably leads to two others, each more extreme than the other. By and large, the shifts are made verbally—it's the essence of his brand of farce, unique and delightfully unnerving. . . . (p. 124)

David Harsent, in New Statesman *(© 1979 The Statesman & Nation Publishing Co. Ltd.), January 26, 1979.*

P

PACK, Robert   1929-

Pack is an American poet, critic, editor, journalist, and author of children's books. Themes of time and mortality are important throughout his work, and frequently are found clothed in imagery of the natural world and the family. Pack skillfully uses symbol and repetition to create poetry that is tightly controlled, intense, and often formal. (See also *Contemporary Authors*, Vols. 1-4, rev. ed.)

X. J. KENNEDY

Pack knows the value of formal discipline and the art of drawing a character. In his range, anything is possible from a villanelle to an extended meditation in wide, Whitmanic, image-loaded lines ("The Last Will and Testament of Art Evergreen"). Another of his best is "Your Wound," which begins, "Your wound, like a stuck eye, why have you opened it?"—a poem with a definite cadence, but no pre-existing form that I can discover. . . .

Pack is less moralist or social critic than visionary incantor. His own form of protest, however, may be his vein of sinister humor, which comes through beautifully in "Burning the Laboratory," about a madman's plot for a little apocalypse.

At times, Pack hasn't discovered words simple enough to resolve his poems' inner complexities. Lines raise problems we don't feel challenged to solve:

> A son's parched mouse's springing tidal squeal
> Rides to a howling whale's vast sea decline.

That reads like Dylan Thomas on a bender. Pack can't resist sound effects. Bees *jabber*, crickets make *foot-screeps*. (Foot-screeps strikes me as accurate, jabber doesn't.) But when his reckless gambles succeed, the result can be wonderful. (p. 379)

> *X. J. Kennedy, in* The Nation *(copyright 1970 The Nation Associates), March 30, 1970.*

JASCHA KESSLER

Robert Pack's sixth volume of poems ["Nothing but Light"] continues in the line taken through the last decade: He is a householding poet, occupying the thoughtful middle way, domesticated, civil, intelligent and curious about the plain, diurnal world in which we live, and should live.

There are many who think otherwise, caught up in the fantastic realms our stony, or metallic, society creates: smoke whirling in the complex winds tearing over our cities. But Pack has settled down in the semirural where the seasons, their animals, their plants and human creatures have their times and proper modes of being.

He asks questions of life and death, and meditates not answers so much as possible responses of the grown man to the common matters of family, past and present, friends and lovers. His forms are longish, open and running sentences, variously musical in an agreeable way, and exact in diction and phrasing.

He has grown steadily over the years, and my use of the term householding is meant as praise for his sure and accomplished management of thought, feeling, language and closed and open formal structures. He can be read easily and with great pleasure.

> *Jascha Kessler, "Poetry of a Semirural Householder," in* The Los Angeles Times *(copyright, 1973, Los Angeles Times; reprinted by permission), January 21, 1973, p. 47.*

ARTHUR OBERG

In *Nothing but Light*, [Pack] continues to move amid dark and light, loss and praise. But what I see in this book that is new is an extension of Pack's lyrical-elegiac talent to the kind of quiet, careful attention that marks poems of William Carlos Williams like "The Descent" and "To Daphne and Virginia." Earlier, I would have put Pack in the line of very different, older American poets. But in poems from *Nothing but Light* like "My Daughter," "The Mountain Ash Tree," and "Now Full of Silences," I see the continuing of a tradition which would include W. C. Williams, and particularly the Williams of the poems I mentioned.

What I never seem able to forget in the poems from this new book of Robert Pack is that sense of the delight and pain of being alive, of having to hold on, of using poetry as that means of creating places and spaces (and, again, I think of Williams) for love. But even in the midst of trying to create a greater ease, of moving toward nothing but light, Pack returns to an older Pack, and for me a very essential Pack. It is not a backsliding or a regression, but rather a simultaneous, co-existent sense of something darker and other, perhaps the dark which poets like W. S. Merwin and

Mark Strand know and encounter when they, too, move toward light. But the dialectic in Pack never resolves the contraries as much as it tries to keep some of the Puritan tension of guilt and unease that has always marked his work.

Nothing but Light again establishes Pack as one of the best domestic, undomesticated poets we have around; over the years, his finest domestic pieces—poems of sons and fathers and daughters and mothers and wives—place him with poets as different as Robert Creeley and Tony Connor, and thereby indicate an existence for this major, important mode on both sides of the Atlantic. (pp. 89-90)

> *Arthur Oberg, in* Shenandoah *(copyright 1973 by Washington and Lee University; reprinted from* Shenandoah: The Washington and Lee University Review *with the permission of the Editor), Fall, 1973.*

VERNON YOUNG

In [*Nothing but Light*], the prevailing condition, intensifying to the last outcry, is an affirmed love of and faith in the near-at-hand, pierced by doubt or an engulfing hopelessness, the poet holding off despair tenaciously and always resolving it within the poem by a triumphant modulation of his initial metaphor. ("The Mountain Ash Tree" is a splendid example.) Indeed, were he not so constructively adept in the arts of poetic nuance and recovery, he would be subjectively unbearable to read; he is too vulnerable by far. His identification with the creatures he loves, those of the home, the garden or the wild, is passionate and jealously guarded; the thought of their extermination is the haunted premise of his poems. ("We love only that which we know will die," wrote Spengler.) Pack's empathy with birds, beasts, and flowers is an increasingly familiar and welcome element in the poetry of Americans. As he says, himself, of another faculty: "It is a trick of gathering oneself / into what one believes / And stepping forth." But not a *simple* trick! Over against James Dickey's impressive conjuring of the predator world, Pack has an equally intuitive gift for sensing the less spectacular lives of the hummingbird, the field mouse, and the pack rat. The latter, serving as subject for a quizzical and informed poem, may well be an intended pun, for although the rodent is described as an emblem of the symbiotic life which man has forsaken or abused, he could at the same time be taken as a rueful self-reflection of the poet: "moderate / Music maker with moderate powers, thumping / the drum of frightened ground . . ." Poem by poem, Pack is deceptively a child of the peaceable kingdom, yet to read his closing lines in this book with his opening lines in the memory is to recognize how much of the tragic sense he has overtaken within the span of 68 pages. . . . Pack is a poet of startling perceptions and uncomfortable reminders. (pp. 164-66)

> *Vernon Young, in* Parnassus: Poetry in Review *(copyright © by Poetry in Review Foundation), Spring/ Summer, 1974.*

HAROLD BLOOM

Robert Pack's *Keeping Watch* . . . has the quiet wisdom, sanity and good workmanship we rightly expect from him. *Maxims in Limbo* compares poorly to the Stevens of *Like Decorations*, which it invokes, but every other poem in the book is movingly closer to home. *Nothing but Light*, Pack's previous book, was better, but even this latest volume continues to show Pack's strength as an almost unique celebrant of married love and fatherhood, subjects by no means favorable to the poems of our climate. (p. 23)

> *Harold Bloom, in* The New Republic *reprinted by permission of* The New Republic; © *1976 by The New Republic, Inc.), November 20, 1976.*

G. E. MURRAY

Robert Pack's *Keeping Watch* reveals not only the presence of a gifted writer but a gifted man, steadfast and insightful. With this, his seventh book, Pack finally and fully unearths his truest resources in family and homestead, while channelling the currents of his warm and level voice into episodes as large as song. He has in the past spent the blood of many poems searching the nature of his bloodline, particularly the troublesome spectre of his father. But in his last book, *Nothing But Light* (1974), there was evidence of a swing in perspective from the poet-as-son to the poet-as-father. And with *Keeping Watch*, the movement is reinforced and elaborated. . . . This is the tough stuff of which Pack is recently about. It's a mood most strikingly revealed in "Pruning Fruit Trees," where the poet reconciles self with the sources of self. It is only incidentally about trimming trees, of course, as is illustrated by this advice: "The cut must be made close / to the parent limb / following the angle / of its growth":

> Don't be afraid to cut—that's it,
> cut more, it's good for the tree,
> lengthening life,
> making its fruit full.
> A farmer told me to talk
> to the trees. Tell them
> "this is good for you."
> Speak softly, thank them.

The question of fatherhood remains central to Robert Pack's verse, but this role is now marked by acumen rather than *angst*. The effect, I believe, is to move from the exclusivity of an interior world and to place concretely before us a world of empathy and understanding. This is especially so in "Elegy for a Warbler," where the poet sensitizes a brief moment with his daughter, against whose bedroom window "the warbler has broken / its small life," and for whom "All her immaculate dolls now weep." Pack resolves the bird's death in a fashion that avoids both sentimentality and overt didacticism. . . . (pp. 967-68)

Nearly one-fifth of Pack's collection is occupied by a work titled "Maxims in Limbo," a loosely-connected series of 101 epigram/ adages, not unlike the lyrical notes and sayings found in the *Adagia* section of Wallace Stevens' *Opus Posthumous*. (p. 968)

Pack's poetry develops through intricate, sometimes deceptively concrete, structures of language which attempt to comprehend the complex physical and emotional interweavings of his ideas. Now, after working carefully and steadily through a decade of revelatory changes in matter exposition, Robert Pack is proving to be an exhilarating and haunting poet. (p. 969)

> *G. E. Murray, in* The Georgia Review *(copyright, 1977, by the University of Georgia), Winter, 1977.*

RICHARD JACKSON

The direction of Robert Pack's *Keeping Watch* is a dialectic expansion outwards in which the poet's will appropriates the power of nature. In "A Spin Around the House," the opening poem, Pack describes how he rises from a table and, "starting to whirl, / nowhere to go," he "swirls" out to a "familiar pine / in its real place," and stops:

> Everything spins
> in its chosen space—I will it so,
>   a star's held silence
> pallors my cinnamon lips, and my arms,
>   each elbow galaxy,
> circle it all in. What shall I do with it?

The crucial point here is the definition of "will," what seems analogous to the Romantic poet's ability to actively participate in nature's processes. . . . Wordsworth and Pack share a threshold territory between reverence for and mastery of nature. "For a poet, to name/an object carefully, is to submit to its power" he says in one of his "Maxims in Limbo." . . . On the one hand, the poet "names" the world around him, participating like Adam in its creation, but on the other hand submits to the power that the given world has always possessed.

Pack's naming, his language, is his means of "keeping watch"—a keeping of his words, of his word as a bond of trust between himself and the world. . . . This language, founded upon conditional constructions and hypothetical questions, tends, under the pressure of Pack's incantatory rhythms, to become a language not of propositions but of willed theorems. . . . So finely has the world of imagination blended with reality that it is impossible to tell into which he rushes—which is the point: they are inseparable.

One of the best poems Pack has ever written, and this book is filled with excellent poems that will insure Pack's position among our best poets, is "October Prayer." It is a classic poem about the dialectic between the self and the world, creation and perception, and serves to summarize any discussion of his work. The poem begins as the poet remembers a vista, but a vista that has been acted upon by imagination ("the sun behind your eyes"). This memory is then modified by the overwhelming presence of the reality as it appears "again" at dawn. The synthesis is a newer, more imaginative vision. The poem is addressed to a "you" that includes the appropriated reader, who is in turn made part of the dialectic process. . . . [The] final lines gather key images from earlier in the poem—the frost and the sun, which suggest the end and the beginning—and let them redefine each other. The repetitions and "returns" here and throughout the book are not nostalgic glances toward the past, but ways of "remembering / what will come." This phrase is reminiscent of Kierkegaard's definition of repetition—"remembering forward"—the formula for what he and Pack call the "happy man," the man whose future is assured by his joyful participation in creation. (pp. 554-55)

> *Richard Jackson, in* Michigan Quarterly Review *(copyright © The University of Michigan, 1978), Fall, 1978.*

*   *   *

PICCOLO, Lucio   1901-1969

Piccolo was a Sicilian poet. Critics have admired his richly baroque imagery and his sensitively wrought regionalism.

ANTHONY BURGESS

Before we praise Piccolo the Sicilian poet, we ought to praise Piccolo the poetic Sicilian. However much we talk of the universality of art, an intense regionalism has never yet been a diminishing factor in literature, though a great regional writer will, in the paradox of art, exalt the province that has chosen him as its voice into a great metaphor of universal experience. A visitor to Faulkner's Mississippi or Joyce's Dublin has been schooled to an intense awareness of and relish in the qualities that make those regions what they are, but those qualities are sharpened, by the magic of literature, into archetypes or symbols of a validity that transcends time and space. In Piccolo's poems we meet a Sicily latent in the country of the tourist guides and the history books, but it was Piccolo far more than, say, Lampedusa who was destined to draw out the latencies, read the signatures, crack the code. On the most practical level, the moderately sensitive visitor to Sicily would do well to read Piccolo before buying his ticket.

His provincialism is limited to love of a particular place; there is nothing backward or bumpkinish about his sensibility or technique (again we think of Faulkner and Joyce). Piccolo is most original when he seems to remind us of other poets—D'Annunzio or Cardarelli or Campana—for the assumption of another voice is a deliberate act which serves to draw attention to an enigmatic personality lurking behind one mask or another. . . . (p. 74)

Piccolo is termed a baroque poet chiefly because of what, to the careless ear, sounds like rich encrustation, "conceit" in the English seventeenth-century sense, the pulling and twisting of imagery to impossible shapes. In reality he inhabits a territory between baroque and surrealism, but his aim is not to astonish or overwhelm. The complexities, in which he moves rapidly from the archaic to the colloquial, celebrate the vegetable world at one moment and the play of Caravaggian light and shadow the next, eventually part to reveal a traditional simplicity almost Theocritan. The verbal and imagistic proliferation force the reader into focusing on a path which leads to a clear patch of daylight.

Natale Tedesco, who sees Piccolo rightly as a *"scrittore di provincia (non della provincia)"*, draws attention to his adoration of the concrete world but immediately qualifies this by referring to his "existential melancholy", an orchestration of the physical world with the shifting colours of dream, a crepuscular aura. This describes his technique better than his overall effects, which are of a major-key clarity. As for the melancholy, it is not the particular brooding and somewhat sinister quality some have found in the Sicilian landscape but that universal transcience which resides, as Virgil saw, in all things. (pp. 74-5)

> *Anthony Burgess, "The Poetic Sicilian," in* Michigan Quarterly Review *(copyright © The University of Michigan, 1974), Winter, 1974, pp. 74-5.*

THOMAS G. BERGIN

If readers, confronting the verses now assembled in this appealing book [*Collected Poems of Lucio Piccolo*] are a little troubled about "placing" Piccolo's verse, they may console themselves with the thought that they are in good company, for Montale [author of the volume's "Afterword"] was somewhat uncertain as to the masters Piccolo may have learned from, groping among such native names as D'Annunzio, Campana and Pea, pondering such possible foreign paternities as Yeats and Hopkins. To this company Leonardo Sciascia, a shrewd critic, adds Jorge Guillén.

Had I the temerity to intrude my own impression, I would say that, reading Piccolo's lines, I am occasionally reminded of the sensitive lyrics of Giuseppe Villaroel, yet another Sicilian (and roughly contemporary), all but forgotten since his death in 1956. (pp. 228-29)

Piccolo is not always easy to understand . . . but I think, in substance, what we find in his verses is a contemplation of nature, richly embellished by personal association, observed religiously but with some skepticism, seen at once as unstable and eternal. Piccolo does not indulge to any great extent in the study of his fellow man, he has no "social message," nor does he (or so it seems to me) contemplate, save obliquely, his own *Angst* (wherein he differs from the hermetics). His report on what he sees is voiced in musical and artful cadences, in metrical and rhythmic patterns that can hardly be called revolutionary yet subtly vary from the conventional. In his letter to Montale . . . he said: "I want to speak of the world of baroque churches and old monasteries and of the persons who fit in with those places and have disappeared without leaving a trace. I have attempted not so much to call back this world as to interpret it on the basis of childhood memories." Hence he calls his lyrics "baroque" but he knew, I am sure, that the word has connotations beyond the architectural; it signifies ornament, restlessness, exuberance, other-wordliness, and, I think, also an all but arrogant elegance. Risking the histrionic, baroque reaches for the mystical. (p. 229)

Piccolo's music is highly original, full of seductive cadences, punctuated by rhymes—sometimes all but thrust on the reader, sometimes elusive and even furtive—and by tenuous echoes and assonances. . . . This somewhat self-conscious virtuosity has its dangers . . . and I confess that a few of the longer pieces seem to me a little over-elaborated and inflated. Perhaps a graver limitation is a kind of aloof solipsism that emerges from a reading of the poems. . . . Aside from "Sirocco" and "La meridiana" ("The sundial"), which are surely destined to find their places in anthologies of the future, this . . . book contains many lines that will delight and eventually haunt the reader. (p. 230)

> *Thomas G. Bergin, "Baroque, Sicilian Style," in* Parnassus: Poetry in Review *(copyright © by Poetry in Review Foundation), Spring/Summer, 1974, pp. 228-32.*

HELEN BAROLINI

Perhaps no poet of so scant acknowledgement in his lifetime and so little actual poetry has been so well served in the mere six years since his death as Lucio Piccolo with the appearance of his *Collected Poems*. . . . (p. 194)

Piccolo's poems . . . show time suspended, static, being held onto and re-evoked in resonances and touches—*l'ore sospese, l'ombre dei giorni*—these figures of time and substances held indefinitely in consciousness recur and recur. But everything about Piccolo is strange, mysterious, improbable, full of the turns and twists of chance. And irony. (pp. 195-96)

Piccolo's poetry carries the weight of . . . melancholy, [of] austerity of sentiment, [of the] seedy magnificence which is Sicily. (p. 200)

But still the Mediterranean sun shines through the poetry of the recluse. And in this constant counterpart of sun and night, light and dark, there is omnipresent the eternal Sicil-

ian theme. Piccolo's poetry is full of the melancholy of illusion, of loneliness and despair, and, at the same time, shot through with the language of light and sun . . . , and the enchantment of sea spaces and nature. (p. 201)

His poetry, at its finest and most moving, seems to tremble on the brink of discovery of another way of life, as if he were pushing at the shadows that separate him from it. . . . He speaks of revived echoes, the sob drawn from him, the voice which binds one to others, and, symbolically of his own painful life, "winters without hearth."

Piccolo's first published collection after San Pellegrino was *Canti Barocchi* and the descriptive adjective of the title, baroque, was taken to describe not only the florid, overcharged image-crammed, expansive, sumptuous mobility of the poetry but also the life style of Piccolo himself: his deliberate anachronisms, his cultivation of exclusiveness, his self-conscious insistence on forms. (pp. 201-02)

As his life was recondite so, often, is his poetry; not open. . . . It is heavy, sometimes, as the very sultriness of Sicily; and, like his land, superabundant, rich with images, figures, and allusions which are as exciting to the mind in their fluidity as the ceiling of a baroque church or the excesses of rococo fountains. It may have been a certain impatience with the facile categorizing of him as baroque that influenced Piccolo's last collection *Plumelia*, for though the subject matter is still his Sicily, the form in his new lyrics is much tighter, more concise. . . .

True. But still baroque. The adjective, like the attribute will, no matter what, stick to Lucio Piccolo; for it is, ineluctably, his essence, his heritage, his world, and his art. (p. 202)

> *Helen Barolini, "The Birth, Death, and Re-Life of a Poet: Lucio Piccolo," in* The Yale Review *(© 1975 by Yale University; reprinted by permission of the editors), Winter, 1976, pp. 194-202.*

*   *   *

PINGET, Robert   1919-

Pinget, a Swiss-French novelist, short story writer, playwright, and journalist, is also a painter. His work bears the influence of both the New Novel movement and the concepts of the theater of the absurd. Pinget's purpose is to expose the fragmented communication that characterizes contemporary life. This is reflected in prose lacking a coherent narrative structure, and in which language itself is fragmented. (See also *CLC*, Vol. 7.)

MARILYN GADDIS ROSE

Pinget's unillusioned tenderness towards the mixed creatures who inhabit his special French province makes him one of the most appealing of the *Nouveaux Romanciers*. Often compared to Beckett and Robbe-Grillet because of his stylistic demonstration of the inadequacy of language and the arbitrariness of narration, he departs from their examples by using anecdotes that are touching and unpretentious. Like Camus's Dr. Rieux, Pinget finds in man more to admire than condemn. (p. 182)

[*Le Libera* is an anti-novel,] set in the environs of Agapa like all his fiction and drama, including the fantasy pieces, and building on the same cast of characters. . . . The title, an echo from the Lord's Prayer ("*Deliver* us from evil") is introduced in the last five pages and modulates on the final page into the narrator's quasi-ironic prayer: "Libera me Domine . . . / De merda aeterna excusez le calembour." Resolute but alone, he faces his dilemma. . . . (pp. 182-83)

The conclusion, typographically like a Surrealist litany (and recalling the last lines of Beckett's *Malone meurt*), points to the emerging pattern of Pinget's fiction: a narrator, obsessed by an event, cannot get to the truth of it, but he is sufficiently playful, toughminded, and charitable to keep his subject from being unpleasant and his narration from being frustrating. (p. 183)

> *Marilyn Gaddis Rose, in* The French Review *(copyright 1970 by the American Association of Teachers of French), October, 1970.*

ALFRED CISMARU

Passacaille is a little novel, and we don't just mean in size. Completed in 1968, the same year that saw the publication of *Le Libera*, but published a year later, the book makes us wonder why an author who has such few things to say, and knows so poorly how to say them, believes it necessary to see himself in print so often.

Not that Robert Pinget was always so devoid of inspiration. In the 1950's we admired somewhat *Graal Flibuste, Le Fiston*, the play *La Manivelle*; and even as late as 1961 *Clope au dossier* revealed an intriguing writer who had learned a great deal from Ionesco and Beckett, and who could be, almost, as exciting. But *Autour de Mortin* in 1965, *Quelqu'un* in the same year (is he too concerned with quantity?) and the already mentioned *Le Libera*, offered nothing but tedious repetitions woven into storiless stories and presented with conscious, calculated and therefore artificial disregard to syntax.

Passacaille is no exception. . . . There is . . . in the book the slightly efficacious monotony of certain reappearing phrases: *le calme, le gris; des corbeaux ou des pies; quelque chose de cassé dans le mecanique; source d'information défaillante*. If these are supposed to remind us how miserable and uncomprehensible and inimical life is, what a bore. If they are simply used as a refrain to the unheard music of the *passacaille* (an ancient dance of Spanish origin), then these phrases play a passable role.

All in all, the worst in Ionesco and Beckett is better than the best in Pinget, and the worst in the latter is better than what we find in *Passacaille*. (p. 183)

> *Alfred Cismaru, in* The French Review *(copyright 1970 by the American Association of Teachers of French), October, 1970.*

STEVEN G. KELLMAN

Quelqu'un portrays and is itself a desperate attempt to create links between the narrator and the other characters and between the narrator and the reader, even if the universe which arises as a result is an infernal one. The title of the novel itself appears to demonstrate this awesome power of words. The word "quelqu'un" effectively emblematizes the major concerns of this work, as well as of Pinget's fiction in general. . . .

[Very] little specific information is advanced about the narrator, and we never even learn his name. Instead, the title of the novel suggests that he is simply "Quelqu'un," someone but no one in particular.

It is easy to see this Someone as a type of the alienated contemporary anti-hero plagued with the usual problems. As such, his anonymity is both descriptive and functional. It indicates his mediocrity; and, while denying him status as a rounded, independent personality, the narrator's anonymity also emphasizes his role as surrogate for the reader, making Quelqu'un, if not a contemporary Everyman, at least a type of contemporary man imprisoned within the suburban limbo between city and country and doomed never to meet Rivoire, his neighbor. (p. 138)

This someone who could be anyone is anxious throughout the novel to demonstrate the universality of his own petty experience. . . . [But] the narrator is uncertain about the existence of an external world and can only hope that he is not alone.

If the alienated Quelqu'un does succeed in functioning as a species of Everyman, then a paradox has been realized. As a representative for all of us, he must communicate the fact that we are all separate and incapable of converging and communicating. (p. 139)

"Quelqu'un," someone, also suggests some *one*, emphasizing the feeling of solitude pervading the novel. The narrator can never escape the fact that he is one person alone, and we readers are perpetually aware of the fact that we are confined to the first person narrative of one mind which can do nothing but circle around itself. The title *Quelqu'un* thus supports the intolerable sense of separation and imprisonment within the trivial existence of some one. (p. 140)

In *Quelqu'un*, although Rivoire's manuscript explains how to live happily alone, it is left as a legacy to someone else, and, although the narrator withdraws within himself, it is ironically in reaction to others and in the hope that by doing so he might possibly reach others.

Clearly, the narrator as "quelqu'un," some one, is not enough. He needs someone else. Within the fictional world, this explains his obsession with meeting and communicating with his neighbor, even if he has to talk about scarecrows, weather vanes, or garbage pails to do so. . . .

In addition, the narrative itself represents a desperate reaching out for "quelqu'un." The reference of the title thus shifts from the first person to the second person, from narrator to reader; we become the someone capable of breaking the circle of the writer's isolation. (p. 141)

Quelqu'un as direct address to "quelqu'un" is thus related to the epistolary nature of both *Baga* and *Graal Flibuste*. The king-narrator conceives of his narrative as, in effect, a series of letters to his nephews, thus placing it within the tradition of aids to the education of royal heirs. The sterile king, of course, has no children of his own and no prospects for any, but even the existence of any nephews soon becomes very questionable. . . . (pp. 141-42)

Like *Baga* and like *Quelqu'un*, *Graal Flibuste* is an attempt to recover a lost communion, an attempt which illuminates its own futility. It is the dry angel of letters with wings of paper who destroys the form of communication counted on by the drunkard. (p. 142)

Ultimately, the perfect reader, the final "quelqu'un," becomes God. There are some twenty occurrences of the word "Dieu" and many others of such words as "Seigneur" and "le ciel" in the ostensibly incongruous context of this novel. Yet, among others things, *Quelqu'un* is a novel of frustrated mysticism. (p. 143)

As the title *Baga* might emphasize, Pinget's narrators are and are concerned with "bagatelles." Through the power of their language, their "bagou," they must attempt to overcome this; those brief moments which present some glimmer of success have the mystical quality of genuine divine possession. . . . Pinget's narrators are in some sense vatic, transmitting through their words all of the power necessary to hold and convert us as someone else. But what their words do is essentially depict their pettiness. (pp. 143-44)

In a way, *Quelqu'un* is a solitary pilgrim, a devoted contemplative retreating to the suburbs from the sinfulness of the world, but the narrative also makes it clear that he is a terrified and isolated little man. He is some one cut off from someone; he inhabits a world irrevocably divorced from the divine and must cultivate a garden made barren by factory soot. Solitary, he can only begin, with no hope of consummation. . . . (p. 144)

Steven G. Kellman, in MOSAIC: A Journal for the Study of Literature and Ideas *(copyright © 1972 by the University of Manitoba Press; acknowledgment of previous publication is herewith made), Vol. V, No. 3 (Spring, 1972).*

ROBERT HENKELS, JR.

Words spill onto the white pages of *Passacaille* like the blood of a stricken animal staining the snow. Phrases and sentences flow from the pen of a narrator holed up behind the rough walls of a country house as winter winds cuff the building at nightfall. From outside press in on Mortin the fragments of a puzzle he has never managed to fit into a pattern he can understand: the hostility of his neighbors; the reasons for their comings and goings; the course of the seasons; the signs of approaching death. Something or someone is apparently bleeding to death out there in the dark, spilling life blood onto the manure pile. Meanwhile, the narrator slumps at his desk and stares vacantly from time to time at a clock whose hands he has torn off in despair. Mortin cannot put the cluttered house of his consciousness in order, unable as he is to sort out past and present, fact and fantasy. Pressures build up within the room and within the narrator. Loneliness, frustration, aggression drive him to the wall, to the window where he stands framed and pinned between alienation and disorder.

Mortin is a creature made of air. Breath rushing around his tongue and palate bring him into being. The Pingetian "I" discovers, creates and sustains its sense of identity by the hows and whats of saying. What we hear conditions who we are. We give ourselves away by speaking. The words which advance the line of print scanned by the reader's eye register the contours of pressures pushing at the chambers of Mortin's consciousness. The serpentine wall of letters marks the perimeter of the known and the unknown. It bends but never breaks. *Passacaille* grows from the kernel of the first sentence as page after page flows from the interplay of suggestion and association. The opening statement starts to set the tone. The tensions between syntax and sensibility, and reflection and observation fix the range and rhythm of the reactions of the speaking voice. (pp. 274-75)

Mortin seems to be telling a story at first, haltingly, sometimes incoherently, but doggedly. He speculates about the dead body, a broken-down tractor, the theft of change from a drawer, the movements around town of an outsider. . . . Mortin's words wall in nothing. The story lurches along like a child's Slinky Toy down a long stairway to nowhere. Each episode generates just enough momentum to keep it in motion. Pinget gives us not a plot but a "simulacre" or "sham" of one. *Le Simulacre* was his original idea for the title. The cadaver outside may be a scarecrow, the "simulacrum" of a man, a cow, the postman, a child, or none of the above. The repetition and movement of words replaces the things described at the center of our attention as in a Marx brothers' comic monologue.

Pinget relaxed while writing the récit by listening to music by Bach. He treats words in the novel like semi-plastic objects, repeating them in a fugal manner, whence the title *"Passacaille"* ("passacaglia"). The recurrence of "to fall", "descend", "cold", "gray", "night" evokes the chilling world of Mortin's mind on which Death is closing in. Longer phrases come back again and again as asides while Mortin groans about the difficulties of writing. The comments of the self-conscious author-protagonist appear more frequently or the straw stuffing shows through the scarecrow plot. They slowly reveal the novel's real subject, the frustration of the attempt to make order, in this case to write *Passacaille*. The reader must come to terms with what Pinget calls "the speaking voice" just as Mortin must struggle to explore mysteries outside and inside himself.

Mortin's voice calls out to an understanding listener in *Le Libéra*, the book which preceded *Passacaille*. He reaches out to caress a world of gossip and misunderstanding with playful diminutives. The earlier novel extends an invitation to enter the kitchen of the author's world and poke around, like a screen door left ajar in summer. The windows of the house in *Le Libéra* open onto Pinget's work. You can make out the towers of the Chateau de Broy and the steeple in Fantoine on the horizon. Mortin's voice changes in *Passacaille*. The words put barriers in the reader's way. Uncertainty dictates the novel's syntax. Repeated phrases show language turning upon itself. Mortin closes the windows and bolts the shutters against the wind. (pp. 275-76)

The voice in *Passacaille* says almost nothing to us we can "understand," if understanding means to extract its content and fit it into a logically consistent whole. It "simply burns," consuming anecdotal fragments like so many wood chips. Strangely enough, Mortin's strategic retreat does not put a frog into his throat. His voice rings out with increasing clarity. Pinget even pins down the spot from which Mortin writes at Sirancy, and he has quite obviously drawn its description from his farmhouse in Tourraine. He has woven Real and Imaginary, Development and Invention into the novel.

Nowhere does Pinget give us so sharp a sense of time and space. The depiction of winter's lifelessness chills the reader. The body or its "simulacre" lies bony and irreducible on the hard ground throughout the novel. Contradictory meanings and values attach themselves to it like the image of the drowned boy in Bergman's "Hour of the Wolf." Pinget walks around the corpse of spent desires, passions and dreams. He pokes at the embodiment of repressed sexuality, checked violence and strangled justifications talking to us as he goes. He stares at himself unblinkingly as dead, and sees his work mutilated and incomplete.

The "new novelists" avoid the furbelows of "beautiful"

prose. It would be difficult, however, to find a more movingly honest piece of contemporary writing than what the author gives us in *Passacaille*. The words describe the cadaver without and the loneliness within without overstatement, understatement or the slightest note of self-indulgence of any kind. The voice's very tremblings make it strong. Life and death embrace on the manure pile. The study of wintry death, and the breaking of silence gives life to the spirit, and to Pinget's expression of it. (p. 277)

Robert Henkels, Jr., "The New Novel: Self-Analysis," in Novel: A Forum on Fiction *(copyright © Novel Corp., 1972), Spring, 1972, pp. 274-77.*

ROBERT M. HENKELS, JR.

Although it is not directly derivative, *Cette Voix* bears the stamp of much that was creative in experimental, surrealist writing of the twenties. Pinget's prose abounds in hilarious malapropisms, expresses a delightful taste for the incongruous and the unexpected, and unfolds through a process of automatic writing, disciplined and focused by exhaustive reworking. There is no plot in the novel. Nor are there well-defined characters. Rather a voice or a series of voices rambles on about a variety of subjects with no apparent orderly progression. As in the theories of transformational grammarians, a small number of generative sentences evolve into an ever-changing verbal flow that follows rhythms and patterns of its own. . . . What could have been a dry, stylistic exercise is brought to life by weaving in strands of speech patterns and observations of small town life picked up "sur le vif." (pp. 641-42)

The goal of *Cette Voix* is an anamnesis to be achieved through the act of writing. . . . Pinget suggests that it is through words that man holds at bay disorder, disintegration and the final silence of death. Like the characters whose names vary, the story whose outlines blur, and the repeated phrases that echo through the text and disappear from the slate, language and its speakers are caught up in relentless change. . . . The attempt to achieve that anamnesis in *Cette Voix* is nevertheless engrossing, amusing, and deeply moving. . . . (p. 642)

Robert M. Henkels, Jr., in The French Review *(copyright 1976 by the American Association of Teachers of French), March, 1976.*

GRAHAM MARTIN

[*Recurrent Melody (Passacaille)*] has precisely the qualities of solemnity, of circular advance towards and withdrawal from a dark centre, of a stately and ominous dance, suggested by that musical term. Out of obsessive and sinister images, a marsh, a scarecrow, red rags of blood, hints of sorcery, a clock with its hands removed, the author struggles, it seems, to build a narrative which will hang together. Towards the end, assisted by some brief touches of gloomy humour, he almost succeeds; and the narrative then collapses once more into funeral shreds. Little enough to engage one's interest, one might think. But torn from any context, arranged in shifting patterns, linked explicitly in different and contradictory ways with one another, the novel's malignant images attract the full weight of our attention: they exercise, in fact, considerable poetic power. (pp. 104-05)

Graham Martin, in London Magazine *(© London Magazine 1976), June-July, 1976.*

POMERANCE, Bernard   1940-

An American playwright, Pomerance became known to Americans when *The Elephant Man*, his first play to be produced in New York, received a Tony Award and the New York Drama Critics Circle Award in 1979. Earlier plays had been written and produced in London.

RANDALL CRAIG

Bernard Pomerance's *Foco Novo* offered a three-cornered glimpse of the struggle between establishment (i.e. capitalist) forces and terrorists, with the United States intervening on the official side, in a South American state, not to say Brazil. Its circular plot actually demonstrated that guns solve no problems, but had been equipped with an epilogue hopefully suggesting that a hopeless and useless rising would after all act as an inspiration to the next wave. There was about the play a kind of undergraduate earnestness which rather swamped the dramatic moments. . . . (p. 39)

Randall Craig, in Drama, *Winter, 1972.*

RANDALL CRAIG

All too little has been heard of . . . Bernard Pomerance since his irritatingly titled *High in Vietnam Hot Damn*. Despite its almost equally irritating title, *Someone Else is Still Someone* is a thoroughly delightful play. . ., packing a great deal into just over an hour of welcomely interval-less action. . . . [Under] the hectic and hilarious comedy, which borders on farce, Pomerance is making a very serious point about depriving marital partners of the freedom they need and deserve. (p. 71)

Randall Craig, in Drama, *Autumn, 1974.*

RANDALL CRAIG

[*The Elephant Man*] is about charity and caring and the motives of those who are supposedly doing good works and indeed this is an important dramatic subject. But it seems to me that *The Elephant Man* badly misfires for two reasons. Commonsense and Jung tell us that all good drama is only another re-working of a universally held truth. But in this play Mr. Pomerance has stacked the cards against himself by focusing his play on a character/symbol, a total physical freak, which fortunately has always been a rarity. His leading character is John Merrick, 'The Elephant Man', who was born in the middle of Victoria's reign, grew to manhood in hideous deformity and died at an early age in a London hospital in 1890.

The other great fault of the play is the author's misanthropic view of mankind. He seems to believe that no-one gives charity for altruistic reasons. Every one of his characters (with the possible exception of Mrs. Kendal, the actress) is finally shown as motivated by pure selfishness. . . . I assume that Mr. Pomerance is not merely telling us that the Victorians were a materialistic and hypocritical society. After all many writers from Dickens through Samuel Butler to the last whimpers of Lytton Strachey have all told us that. Thus we must assume that the sad story of John Merrick is intended to be relevant *now*. But it is really impossible to make this leap. Pomerance locks us in a Victorian social framework with characters motivated by Victorian *mores*, while at the same time asking us to accept this as a microcosm of contemporary society. . . .

[There] is certainly an important play to be written about

caring for the unfortunate of the earth. But let the play be set *now,* instead of coyly sniping at our dubious motives from behind a Victorian barricade. Thus while I refuse to accept Mr. Pomerance's bleak view of humanity I might be more convinced if he were to come out into the open and write about a society of which we all have first hand knowledge. (p. 72)

Randall Craig, in Drama, *Winter, 1977/1978.*

MARTIN GOTTFRIED

The first of *The Elephant Man* is merely stunning. The second act does not fulfill all the promises, but enough answers to complete the play are there. As any artistic play must, it functions on the theatrical, emotional, literary, and metaphoric levels.

Set in Victorian London and presented in detached, formal, but stylized episodes, *The Elephant Man* is in fact about an elephant man—a freak. It has the audacity to depend upon a central character whose appearance is on the one hand crucial to the story while, on the other, theatrically impractical. It would be ludicrous to try to create this character, a hideously deformed young man named John Merrick, with putty and padding. The author's ingenuity, however, leads us to "see" this mutation in ghastly detail. . . .

John Merrick is kept at the hospital by Dr. Treves, who hopes that he can find a cure, and make him normal. The playwright knows as well as we that such massive bone deformities are not curable. But medicine was not so well informed in the 1880s, and this play never pretends to be naturalistic. . . .

Of course, Pomerance is using him metaphorically. He is all of us, deformed by our own individuality, an individuality that represents art. Dr. Treves, on the other hand, represents rules—conformity, if you like. Here is science versus art, reason versus spiritualism. Treves is trying to "normalize" Merrick by making him like himself. At the same time Merrick is an immensely believable and moving character, not just a symbol, and, capitalizing on the open speech patterns of an isolated human, Pomerance has given him poetic voice. "I don't know why I look like this," Merrick comments. "My mother was knocked down by an elephant when she was pregnant. . . . I think my head is so big because it is so full of dreams." . . .

Mrs. Kendal brings Merrick to the world. She takes him to the theater and to concerts. She brings her friends to meet him. With her as intermediary, they appreciate him. They see themselves in him. That, as Dr. Treves points out, is Merrick's peculiar quality. Still, though this elephant man begins to act like other people, his deformities do not diminish.

As the play progresses, its author's references grow diffuse. There are religious allusions, for instance. These are confusing, but they do not fatally mar the play, for what counts most is its overwhelming humanity; its tragedy and compassion; its soaring poetry; the theatrical beauty it makes of the contrast between innocence, deformity, and the stark Victorian staging.

Pomerance has not thought this play through clearly enough, but he can tackle the problem in his next play. The quivering power of *The Elephant Man* is much rarer, and more important to the theater. The play has the drama, poetry, humanity, and intensity that we go to the theater for. When Mrs. Kendal decides, as we know she will, to show her body to Merrick; when he sighs that it is the most beautiful thing he's ever seen; when Dr. Treves comes upon them and is horrified by the impropriety; when Mrs. Kendal explains that she and Merrick were merely in Paradise; when she is dismissed, and when Merrick commits suicide (by laying down his dream-filled head), we are much too moved—transported—to quarrel. (p. 60)

Martin Gottfried, in Saturday Review (© *1979 by Saturday Review Magazine Corp.; reprinted with permission), March 17, 1979.*

RICHARD EDER

"The Elephant Man," [is a] haunting parable about natural man trading his frail beauty and innocence for the protection and prison of society. . . .

Mr. Pomerance has used [the Elephant Man] figure to construct an image of the unspoiled natural man. . . . John Merrick has an uncomfortably pure sense of the good, an instinctive religious aspiration and a style of thought so unspoiled and direct that he is continually sabotaging the tutored assumptions of his protectors.

The deformity is used not for its own sake but to separate the protagonist from the society he encounters. . . .

His innocence manages to put in question all the assumptions, the order, the power of a society—the Victorian—that considered itself to have abolished once and for all the age-old dichotomy between doing good and doing well. And yet, like Lear's fool, he is helpless and terrified of being dispossessed from the protection that has been given him.

Treves . . . is a sincere moralist and a sincere success. He is a brilliant doctor and destined for big things. He shows total conviction as he, the Victorian missionary, gradually teaches the Elephant Man to conform to the habits and expectations of society.

But Mr. Pomerance has not given us a prig. Treves is gradually possessed by the magical innocence of his patient, even as the patient becomes attached to the comforts and social advantages of being a scientific celebrity. The doctor begins to realize what is being destroyed. At one point, he tells a colleague that the more "normal" the Elephant Man becomes, the more the illness that will kill him is advancing.

What he is saying by implication, and goes on to say more explicitly at the play's end, is that the free and boundless spirit of his patient has been gradually crushed. The Elephant Man gradually loses the questioning vitality he has at the start. He becomes an internal captive. His energy is channeled, as he sickens, into completing the model of a church. Art, for Mr. Pomerance, is a substitute for the natural grace that we lose in living. . . .

[The second act is] the weaker portion. In part it is inevitable: the opening up of the Elephant Man is more exciting than his decline. And furthermore, many of the themes that are dramatized at the beginning remain to be expounded at the end. They are expounded very well indeed, but some of the play's immediacy flags a bit.

This slowing down is perhaps less a defect than a trait. "The Elephant Man" is an enthralling and luminous play.

*Richard Eder, "Theatre: 'Elephant Man' Opens,"
in* The New York Times, *Section C (© 1979 by
The New York Times Company; reprinted by permission), April 20, 1979, p. 5.*

JOHN SIMON

[*The Elephant Man*'s first act is] terse, thoughtful, theatrical in the best sense, and devoid of spurious rhetoric—a
lesson from Brecht well learned, with an added touch of
humanity often lacking in the master. But what goes wrong
with Act II?

Some insufficiently developed marginalia . . . , some less
than revelatory speechifying. . ., some top-heavy irony with
a few minor characters reduced to overconvenient contrivances. Above all, too many, and conflicting, layers of symbolism. Thus the deformed Elephant Man becomes both the
noble savage destroyed by civilization and the artist co-
opted by society, both the monster in a Beauty-and-the-
Beast fable and an angelic intelligence that puts mere mankind to shame. Not only is this too much of a burden for
writing that is more decent than sublime; it is also, besides
being at odds with itself, in a clash with the simple historic
facts: It is hard to make death by disease pass also for
death from victimization, disenchantment, and unfulfilled
love.

Here lies another crucial weakness. Mrs. Kendal disrobes
for John Merrick, the freak whose sexual organs and appetites are quite normal, but without a real possibility of intercourse between them. . . . Thus an action supposed to be
generous and loving becomes, in truth, a piece of sexual
tantalizing, indeed cruelty. Yet even with these blemishes,
The Elephant Man is, clearly, the work of a serious and
gifted playwright. . . . (p. 85)

John Simon, in New York *Magazine (copyright ©
1979 by News Group Publications, Inc.; reprinted
with the permission of* New York *Magazine), May
7, 1979.*

STANLEY KAUFFMANN

A second viewing makes [*The Elephant Man*] at least as
enticing as before, a good work with great ambition. Its
assets now seem stronger: the large theme of the arbitrariness of existence, posed against a hunger for design—in
everyone but especially in Merrick. The weaknesses are
now a bit clearer too: the occasional soft patches in the
lean, evocative dialoque; the patness of such moments as
the doctor's entrance just when the actress bares her bosom
for Merrick; the fact that the play's metaphors don't sufficiently deepen.

This last defect—the major one—arises because Pomerance
hasn't fixed the *center* of the play. It begins as the drama of
Treves, the doctor who finds Merrick; then most of the action focuses on Merrick; and only near the end, by means
of a lengthy scene between Treves and the bishop, does
Pomerance try to move the focus back to the doctor. It's a
good scene, but it can't quite do that job. This split is what
makes the second act waver a bit and what keeps the metaphors visible, rather than ingested. Admittedly, it's difficult
to keep Treves at the center because Merrick is more theatrical. To cite a lofty analogy, it's the problem that Melville
faced in *Billy Budd,* in which Vere is the protagonist but
Billy takes the stage. The slight muzziness of that wonderful work comes from the attraction of the experience (Billy)

over the experiencer (Vere). The greater muzziness of this
lesser work comes from the same trouble.

But, . . . I can still maintain that this is the best new American play since 1972, the year of Shepard's *Tooth of Crime.*
(pp. 24-5)

Stanley Kauffmann, in The New Republic *(reprinted by permission of* The New Republic; ©
1979 The New Republic, Inc.), May 12, 1979.*

*   *   *

PORTER, Katherine Anne   1890-

**An American woman of letters, a master stylist, and the au-
thor of flawless, standard-setting short stories, Porter is
known to younger Americans primarily as the author of *Ship
of Fools,* a novel flawed but unremitting in its intensity. Porter instills her work with profound irony, and her thematic
considerations revolve around the workings of the heart and
emotions, the difference between appearance and reality, and
the consequences of self-deception. (See also *CLC,* Vols. 1, 3,
7, 10, and *Contemporary Authors,* Vols. 1-4, rev. ed.)**

CHRISTOPHER ISHERWOOD

Miss Porter has no genius but much talent. Her average
level is high, and she doesn't let you down. She is more
fundamentally serious than Katherine Mansfield, less neurotic, closer to the earth. She is dry-eyed, even in tragedy:
when she jokes, she does not smile. You feel you can trust
her. (p. 312)

I liked "Noon Wine" best of [the stories in *Pale Horse,
Pale Rider*]. It is an examination of "the nature of a
crime," a subtle, psychological theme handled so directly,
so concretely that one is reminded of de Maupassant. . . .
Only an exceedingly skilled writer could have presented the
. . . tragedy so vividly and with such absolute conviction.
The characterization is beautifully done, and the farm really
comes to life, with all its sounds and smells. . . .

The work of so important an artist as Miss Porter must be
judged by the lowest, as well as the highest standards—and,
curiously enough, it is by the lowest standards that she
fails. She is grave, she is delicate, she is just—but she lacks
altogether, for me personally, the vulgar appeal. I cannot
imagine that she would ever make me cry, or laugh aloud.
No doubt, she would reply that she doesn't want to. But
she should want to. I wish she would give herself a little
more freely to the reader. I wish she would paint with bolder, broader strokes. I wish she wouldn't be quite so cautious. (p. 313)

Christopher Isherwood, in The New Republic *(reprinted by permission of* The New Republic; ©
1939 The New Republic, Inc.), April 19, 1939.*

LODWICK HARTLEY

Katherine Anne Porter remains chiefly a writer's writer.
Such a circumstance is a pity, for in her short stories and
novelle she has a great deal to say to all intelligent readers;
and she says it with clarity and beauty. She is by no means
difficult to read; and, though her overzealous critics have
made a few of her short stories seem overwrought with
symbolism, there is actually little of the occult in her work.
She has always lacked patience with the literary faddists—
those people who affect newness of manner when they are
actually destitute of matter. She writes in the main stream

of English prose style and of English fiction without being imitative: a great achievement in itself. Her difficulty is an ironic one, though it involves no irony peculiar to her own time. In brief, she is a perfectionist, and perfectionists have rarely enjoyed popular success in any age. (p. 386)

Throughout her critical essays [in *The Days Before*] Miss Porter writes with such precision, compactness, and fine fluency that no perceptive reader can fail to be charmed by what she has to say. Whether everyone will want to accept her rigidly pure concept of the art of writing is another matter. Certainly, it will be easy to conclude that art is the nearest thing to a be-all and end-all in her existence. The bases of her position she has clearly marked out—so clearly, in fact, that the whole position may seem to approach rationalization. In short, one may be led to feel that her own peculiar experience has developed in her such a profound distrust of institutional religion and of human relationships that she has felt compelled to seek certainties elsewhere and that, consequently, her theory of art, beautiful and praiseworthy though it is, arises out of a peculiar personal necessity rather than out of a completely universal one. (pp. 386-87)

Miss Porter's pervading dislike of dogma and authoritarianism effectually prevents her acceptance of anything like neoclassical ideals in literature. Yet it leads her neither into a form of nineteenth-century Romanticism nor into sympathy with any of the various "revolutionary" schools of literature that have flourished so profusely in the twentieth century. The plain fact is that she wishes to be a classicist in the Greek tradition both in her practice and in her theory. . . .

For the floodtide of experimentalism that came in the twenties, Miss Porter has patent contempt. "Every day in the arts," she writes, "as in schemes of government and organized crime, there was, there had to be something new," a principle that operated in crass failure to recognize that in reality there is nothing new except that which conforms to the true classical ideal of being "outside of time and beyond the reach of change." (p. 388)

Naturally, it would be erroneous to feel that Miss Porter's fundamental quarrel has been with the spirit of experimentalism itself. Rather is it, indeed, with what she considers to be the superficiality and unreason of most innovators and with the use of "tricky techniques and disordered syntax" to disguise "poverty of feeling and idea." For the innovations of an artist like Edith Sitwell the matter is quite different. In Miss Sitwell's early work, for example, Miss Porter finds a "challenging note of natural arrogance" that is completely admirable, because it was "boldly experimental" and "inventive from a sense of adventure" rather than from a paucity of ideas.

But even in Miss Sitwell it is rather a classical quality than her experimentalism *qua* experimentalism that Miss Porter genuinely admires. . . . [It is the] classical quality of "realism" that Miss Porter seeks in both poetry and prose and that provides reason for her praise of the "objectivity" of Henry James or Willa Cather or Katherine Mansfield or Eudora Welty. It is always the concrete detail and the exact statement that matters. (p. 389)

Miss Porter's serene consistency in her philosophy and her tolerance of nothing less than the highest standards of performance for herself as well as for others deserve the high-

est admiration. It is true, however, that, beneath the almost perfect poise of her manner, her rigid purism and her championship of art as effectually comprehending both morality and religion may at times seem less like a confession of faith than an act of desperation. Moreover, like the brave generalization about truth and beauty made by Keats in the presence of physical disintegration, her solution has never been a universally satisfactory one. Though this philosophy, however explicitly stated in the critical essays, may appear only implicitly in Miss Porter's fiction, its limitation curiously suggests a possible restriction of her total appeal. "All the conscious and recollected years of my life," she writes in the 1940 Preface to *Flowering Judas,* "have been lived to this day under the heavy threat of world catastrophe, and most of the energies of my mind and spirit have been spent in the effort to grasp the meaning of these threats, to trace them to their sources and to understand the logic of this majestic and terrible failure of life in the Western World." But these efforts to understand the failure of life in the Western world, however important they may be in her heart and mind, could hardly be said to be the major subject of her art. Indeed, her writing—imaginative and critical—seems more nearly an attempt to escape from the central problem. Perhaps the reason that her work, for all its beauty, does not etch itself indelibly on our consciousness is that it ultimately does not illuminate the supreme tragedy of which she speaks. Thus, whatever may be the acuity, the vitality, and even the nicely calculated violence of some of her stories, and whatever may be the strength of her utterance in other fields, she may continue to be regarded essentially as a lovely, white-robed priestess of the shrine of Apollo—a role that she seems deliberately and expertly to have written for herself. (pp. 390-91)

> *Lodwick Hartley, "The Lady and the Temple: The Critical Theories of Katherine Anne Porter," in* College English *(copyright © 1953 by the National Council of Teachers of English), April, 1953, pp. 386-91.*

ROBERT PENN WARREN

Many of [Katherine Anne Porter's] stories are unsurpassed in modern fiction, and some are not often equaled. She belongs to the relatively small group of writers—extraordinarily small, when one considers the vast number of stories published every year in English and American magazines—who have done serious, consistent, original, and vital work in the form of short fiction—the group which would include James Joyce, Katherine Mansfield, Sherwood Anderson, and Ernest Hemingway. (p. 51)

In many instances, a story or novelette has not been composed straight off. Instead, a section here and a section there have been written—little germinal scenes explored and developed. Or scenes or sketches of character which were never intended to be incorporated in the finished work have been developed in the process of trying to understand the full potentiality of the material. One might guess at an approach something like this: a special, local excitement provoked by the material—character or incident; an attempt to define the nature of that local excitement, as local—to squeeze it and not lose a drop; an attempt to understand the relationships of the local excitements and to define the implications—to arrive at theme; the struggle to reduce theme to pattern. That would seem to be the natural history of the characteristic story. Certainly, it is a method which requires time, scrupulosity, and contemplation.

The method itself is an index to the characteristics of Miss Porter's fiction—the rich surface detail scattered with apparently casual profuseness and the close structure which makes such detail meaningful; the great compression and economy which one discovers upon analysis; the precision of psychology and observation, the texture of the style.

Most reviewers, commenting upon Miss Porter's distinction, refer to her "style"—struck, no doubt, by an exceptional felicity of phrase, a precision in the use of metaphor, and a subtlety of rhythm. It is not only the appreciation of the obviously poetical strain in Miss Porter's work that has tended to give her reputation some flavor of the special and exquisite, but also the appreciation of the exceptional precision of her language. (pp. 52-3)

It is, of course, just and proper for us to praise Miss Porter for her English and her artistry, but we should remind ourselves that we prize those things because she uses them to create vivid and significant images of life. . . . [We] remind ourselves of the vividness and significance in which Miss Porter's English and artistry eventuate, only because we would balance praise for the special with praise for the general, praise for subtlety with praise for strength, praise for sensibility with praise for intellect. (p. 54)

With all the enchanting glitter of style and all the purity of language and all the flow and flicker of feeling, Miss Porter's imagination . . . is best appreciated if we appreciate its essential austerity, its devotion to the fact drenched in God's direct daylight, its concern with the inwardness of character, and its delight in the rigorous and discriminating deployment of a theme. (pp. 56-7)

Miss Porter has the power of isolating common things, the power that Chekhov or Frost or Ibsen or, sometimes, Pound has, the power to make the common thing glow with an Eden-innocence by the mere fact of the isolation. It is a kind of indicative poetry.

Miss Porter's eye and ear, however, do not seize with merely random and innocent delight on the objects of the world, even though we may take that kind of delight in the objects she so lovingly places before us, transmuted in their ordinariness. If the fact drenched in daylight commands her unfaltering devotion, it is because such facts are in themselves a deep language, or can be made to utter a language of the deepest burden. (p. 57)

Is Mr. Thompson [protagonist of *Noon Wine*] innocent or guilty? He doesn't really know. Caught in the mysteriousness of himself, caught in all the impulses which he had never been able to face, caught in all the little lies which had really meant no harm, he can't know the truth about anything. He can't stand the moral uncertainty of this situation, but he does not know what it is that most deeply he can't stand. He can't stand not knowing what he himself really is. His pride can't stand that kind of nothingness. Not knowing what it is he can't stand, he is under the compulsion to go, day after day, around the countryside, explaining himself, explaining how he had not meant to do it, how it was defense of the Swede, how it was self-defense, all the while plunging deeper and deeper into the morass of his fate. Then he finds that his own family have, all along, thought him guilty. So the proud man has to kill himself to prove, in his last pride, that he is really innocent.

That, however, is the one thing that can never be proved,

for the story is about the difficult definition of guilt and innocence. Mr. Thompson, not able to trust his own innocence, or understand the nature of whatever guilt is his, has taken refuge in the lie, and the lie, in the end, kills him. The issue here, as in "Flowering Judas," is not to be decided simply. It is, in a sense, left suspended, the terms defined, but the argument left only at a provisional resolution. Poor Mr. Thompson—innocent and yet guilty, and in his pride unable to live by the provisional. (p. 60)

Old Mortality is relatively short, some twenty thousand words, but it gives an impression of the mass of a novel. One factor contributing to this effect is the length of the time span; ·the novelette falls into three sections, dated 1885-1902, 1904, and 1912. Another factor is the considerable number of the characters, who, despite the brevity of the story, are sketched in with great precision; we know little about them, but that little means much. Another, and not quite so obvious but perhaps more important, factor is the rich circumstantiality and easy discursiveness, especially in Part I, which sets the tone of the piece. The author lingers on anecdote, apparently just to relish the anecdote, to extract the humor or pathos—but in the end we discover that there has been no casual self-indulgence, or indulgence of the reader; the details of the easy anecdote, which seemed to exist at the moment for itself alone, have been working busily in the cellarage of our minds. (p. 61)

We see immediately that [*Old Mortality*] is a story about legend, and it is an easy extension to the symbol for tradition, the meaning of the past for the present. We gradually become acquainted with the particular legend through the little girls, but the little girls themselves, in their innocence, criticize the legend. Their father, speaking of Amy's slimness, for instance, says: "There were never any fat women in the family, thank God." But the little girls remember Aunt Keziah, in Kentucky, who was famous for her heft. (Such an anecdote is developed richly and humorously, with no obvious pointing to the theme, beyond the logic of the context.) Such details, in Part I, develop the first criticism of the legend, the criticism by innocent common sense. In Part II, the contrast between Gabriel as legend and Gabriel as real extends the same type of criticism, but more dramatically; but here another, a moral criticism, enters in, for we have the effect of Amy on other people's lives, on Gabriel and Miss Honey. This, however, is not specified it merely charges the scene of the meeting between Miranda and Cousin Eva on the way to Gabriel's funeral. Part III at first gives us, in Cousin Eva's words, the modern critical method applied to the legend—as if invoking Marx and Freud.

Up to this point, the line of the story has been developed fairly directly, though under a complicated surface. The story could end here, a story of repudiation, and some readers have interpreted it as such. But—and here comes the first reversal of the field—Miranda repudiates Cousin Eva's version, as romantic, too, in favor of the "reality" of her father, whom she is soon to see. But there is another shift. Miranda discovers that she is cut off from her father, who turns to Cousin Eva, whose "myth" contradicts his "myth," but whose world he can share. Miranda, cut off, determines to leave them to their own sterile pursuit of trying to understand the past. She will understand herself, the truth of what happens to her. This would provide another point of rest for the story—a story about the brave younger generation, their hope, courage, and honesty, and some readers have taken it thus. But—withheld cunningly until the end, until the last few words—there is a last reversal of the field. Miranda makes her promise to herself in "her hopefulness, her ignorance." And those two words, *hopefulness, ignorance,* suddenly echo throughout the story.

Miranda will find *a* truth, as it were, but it, too, will be a myth, for it will not be translatable, or, finally, communicable. But it will be the only truth she can win, and for better or worse she will have to live by it. She must live by her own myth. But she must earn her myth in the process of living. Her myth will be a new myth, different from the mutually competing myths of her father and Cousin Eva, but stemming from that antinomy. Those competing myths will simply provide the terms of her own dialectic of living.

We remember that the heroine's name is Miranda, and we may remember Miranda of Shakespeare's *Tempest,* who exclaims, "O brave new world, that has such people in it!" Perhaps the identity of the name is not an accident. Miranda of *Old Mortality* has passed a step beyond that moment of that exclamation, but she, too, has seen the pageant raised by Prospero's wand—the pageant evoked by her father, the pleasant everyday sort of father, who, however, is a Prospero, though lacking the other Prospero's irony. For *Old Mortality,* like *The Tempest,* is about illusion and reality, and comes to rest upon a perilous irony.

In *Old Mortality* Miss Porter has used very conventional materials; the conventional materials, however, are revitalized by the intellectual scope of the interpretation and the precision and subtlety of structure. But Miss Porter has not committed herself to one type of material. The world of balls and horsemanship and romance is exchanged in *Noon Wine* . . . for a poverty-ridden Texas farm; in *Pale Horse, Pale Rider,* for a newspaper office and a rooming house at the time of World War I; in "Hacienda," "Flowering Judas" and "María Concepción," for Mexico. We may ask, What is the common denominator of these stories, aside from the obvious similarities of style (though the style itself is very flexible)? What is the central "view," the central intuition?

In these stories, and, as I believe, in many others, there is the same paradoxical problem of definition, the same delicate balancing of rival considerations, the same scrupulous development of competing claims to attention and action, the same interplay of the humorous and the serious, the same refusal to take the straight line, the formula, through the material at hand. This has implied for some readers that the underlying attitude is one of skepticism, negation, refusal to confront the need for immediate, watertight, foolproof solutions. The skeptical and ironical bias is, I think, important in Miss Porter's work, and it is true that her work wears an air of detachment and contemplation. But, I should say, her irony is an irony with a center, never an irony for irony's sake. It simply implies, I think, a refusal to accept the formula, the ready-made solution, the hand-me-down morality, the word for the spirit. It affirms, rather, the constant need for exercising discrimination, the arduous obligation of the intellect in the face of conflicting dogmas, the need for a dialectical approach to matters of definition, the need for exercising as much of the human faculty as possible.

This basic attitude finds its correlation in her work, in the delicacy of phrase, the close structure, the counterpoint of incident and implication. That is, a story must test its thematic line at every point against its total circumstantiality; the thematic considerations must, as it were, be validated in terms of circumstance and experience, and never be resolved in the poverty of statement.

In one sense, it is the intellectual rigor and discrimination that gives Miss Porter's work its classic distinction and control—that is, if any one quality can be said to be uniquely responsible. No, no single quality can take that credit, but where many writers have achieved stories of perception, feeling, sensibility, strength, or charm, few have been able to achieve stories of a deep philosophic urgency in the narrow space, and fewer still have been able to achieve the kind of thematic integration of a body of stories, the mark of the masters, the thing that makes us think first of the central significance of a writer rather than of some incidental and individual triumph. For Miss Porter's bright indicative poetry is, at long last, a literally metaphysical poetry, too. The luminosity is from inward. (pp. 64-6)

> *Robert Penn Warren, "Irony with a Center: Katherine Anne Porter," in his* Selected Essays *(copyright 1941 and renewed 1969 by Robert Penn Warren; reprinted by permission of Random House, Inc.), Random House, 1958 (and reprinted in* Katherine Anne Porter: A Critical Symposium, *edited by Lodwick Hartley and George Core, University of Georgia Press, 1969, pp. 51-66).*

THOMAS F. WALSH

Katherine Anne Porter once wrote, "I have never known an uninteresting human being, and I have never known two alike; there are broad classifications and deep similarities, but I am interested in the thumbprint." No work could better illustrate her interest than "Noon Wine," whose four main characters, Mr. and Mrs. Thompson, Mr. Helton, and Mr. Hatch, are so clearly individuated through their actions, speech, and physical appearance that it is difficult to imagine how they could be more unlike each other. And yet their "broad classifications and deep similarities," attributable to their common parentage in the unifying and controlling imagination of their author, tell us more about the world which entraps them than their unique thumbprints. Miss Porter's own discussion of "Noon Wine" . . . proves the point: "Every one in this story contributes, one way or another directly, or indirectly, to murder, or death by violence," yet "every one concerned, yes, even Mr. Hatch, is trying to do right." Her generalizations clearly reveal the tragic dimensions of the story. (pp. 83-4)

First, we note that every character finds that his efforts to do right are thwarted by those in whom he has placed his trust. . . . This theme of undependability is found in Miss Porter's other works; for example, Miranda in "Old Mortality" loses faith in her parents and their contemporaries: "I will make my own mistakes, not yours; I cannot depend upon you beyond a certain point, why depend at all?"

It is true that characters in "Noon Wine" fail each other's trust, but it is also true that oftentimes they unreasonably place their trust where it is likely to fail. Mr. Hatch should not expect Mr. Thompson to help him capture Mr. Helton. And Mr. Thompson should not expect his wife to do all the chores which he considers unmanly. Although he attempts to reconcile himself to the reality of her frail health, he still feels that somehow he has been betrayed and so subconsciously blames her for the run-down condition of the farm when he should blame his own laziness. The shifting of blame from themselves to others is characteristic of the Thompsons and implicit in their discovery that others are not to be trusted.

This distrust and blame-shifting suggest that each character is ignorant of or unable to face his own weaknesses. Instead, he falsely bolsters his own self-esteem by detecting weaknesses in others. Thus his self-ignorance, compounded by his ignorance of others, never permits him to establish a firm foundation for mutual trust and understanding. (pp. 84-5)

The characters of "Noon Wine" do not so much share similarities as suffer from them. Ironically, their deepest similarity is their inability to recognize what makes them similar; if they could, they would not be what they are: well-meaning people who are victims of themselves, each other, and of a mysterious set of circumstances with which they are unable to cope.

It would be absurd to think that Miss Porter has mechanically forced her characters to illustrate a preconceived thesis; her own discussion of the story's sources and the inevitable way her plot unravels are proof against such a notion, if proof were needed. Nevertheless, when we view the story from the perspective of the author's tragic vision, we come to realize how thoroughly each character reflects it in their deep similarities to each other. Their invincible ignorance of themselves and of each other is the principal ingredient of that vision. (p. 85)

Appearing out of nowhere like the archetypal mysterious stranger, Helton and Hatch enter through the gate of Mr. Thompson's farm as if they were entering his innermost being. Although they are independent characters in their own right, whose actions precipitate their own deaths as well as Mr. Thompson's, they function as doubles of Mr. Thompson, symbolically representing hidden aspects of his personality which he does not comprehend. (pp. 85-6)

Because he operates only on the level of appearances, Mr. Thompson cannot comprehend the connection between his self image and his misfortune nor can he comprehend that his good fortune is his misfortune with a delayed reaction of nine years. Above all, he cannot even sense the psychological affinities between his character and that of the man who lives at the center of his misfortune. (p. 86)

Helton is a stranger, not just to Texas, but the world against which he holds a grudge and with which he refuses to communicate. His unhappy state almost literally resembles Miranda's in "Pale Horse Pale Rider": "Miranda looked about her with the covertly hostile eyes of an alien who does not like the country in which he finds himself, does not understand the language nor wish to learn it, does not mean to live there and yet is helpless to leave it at his will." The partial cause of Miranda's despair is her lost dream of a happy Edenic state, which makes the world seem so bitterly drab and empty by contrast. We can only conjecture that Helton has suffered the loss of a similar dream, symbolized by his song about drinking up all the wine before noon. . . . Helton's zombie-like existence on the farm is continually stressed. He moves about mechanically and with unseeing eyes. He is like a "disembodied spirit," whose voice comes "as from the tomb." It is only a

matter of time before his actual death will end his symbolic life-in-death. (pp. 86-7)

Only when Mr. Thompson's nine years of prosperity end in the deaths of Helton and Hatch do we realize that the "Noon Wine" song equally applies to him. At that point, Thompson's life more clearly follows the pattern of Helton's. . . . After Hatch's death, Thompson, unlike Helton, tries to communicate with others, but the results are the same since Thompson's neighbors do not understand him. (p. 87)

"Noon Wine" follows the pattern of other stories of the double in which the double's appearance does not begin a process, but symbolizes a psychic struggle already in process. (p. 88)

[To] understand Hatch's role as Thompson's double, we must see how all three men interrelate by comparing Thompson's interviews with Helton and Hatch, for the second interviewing a horrible parody of the first, with roles ironically reversed. In the first scene Mr. Thompson, displaying all the forced amiability of his public self confronts his secret, alienated, violent self; in the second scene Thompson confronts a parody of his public self of the first scene. (pp. 89-90)

Thompson's encounter with Hatch marks the point at which opposing elements of his character, represented by his two doubles, have grown so large that they can no longer be contained within him. Helton has seemingly fulfilled Thompson's desire to build a reputation in the eyes of the community as a successful, industrious, law-abiding, socially amiable family man. But ultimately Helton represents the price Thompson must pay for his prosperity because the industry that made it possible also includes an antisocial, foreign insularity, subversive to the community and the family, which threatens to break out in violence whenever it is threatened. Thus, as Helton "takes hold" on the farm, he creates Thompson's parasitic prosperity while at the same time undermining it. Hatch's appearance forces Thompson to confront a monstrously magnified image of his public self. Hatch is a parody of Thompson's stance as American-born solid citizen, upholding all the proclaimed standards of law and order. . . . [In] killing Hatch, he has most effectively killed "his dignity and his reputation that he cared about." His actual suicide is almost anticlimactic. (pp. 90-1)

Thomas F. Walsh, "Deep Similarities in 'Noon Wine'," in MOSAIC: A Journal for the Study of Literature and Ideas *(copyright © 1975 by the University of Manitoba Press; acknowledgment of previous publication is herewith made), Vol. IX, No. 1 (Fall, 1975), pp. 83-91.*

JOAN GIVNER

Because Katherine Anne Porter's fictional descriptions of the South of her childhood correspond so exactly to those in her factual accounts, her Miranda stories have been read as closely autobiographical. Although she has warned against such literal-mindedness, the author's own image as an aristocratic daughter of the Old South tends to confirm the authenticity of the background. The settings of "Old Mortality" and "The Old Order" seem entirely appropriate to Katherine Anne Porter. (p. 339)

In "Noon Wine: The Sources" she writes of the large

house, presided over by the grandmother, in which she grew up.... The description coincides with that of Miranda Gay's childhood home, which is given most fully in "The Journey" and is referred to in "Old Mortality" and in the first paragraph of "Pale Horse, Pale Rider." (p. 340)

There is ... in Porter's work a strong vein of actuality which argues against the fabrication of characters and settings out of thin air. She has said that she makes nothing up, that her fiction is really reportage, and that although she arranges it so that it becomes fiction, what she reports really happened.

She always made careful notes on her surroundings, and her correspondence over the years is studded with brilliant, detailed descriptions of her temporary homes.... All are meticulously described, and from her descriptions and from a variety of other circumstances the houses she attributes to her family can be identified with precision. They exist and can be seen today—not in the South as one might expect, but on the island of Bermuda [where Porter spent five months in almost complete seclusion]. (pp. 341-42)

Bermuda is more lush than the part of central Texas where Porter grew up, and the green and growing leafy landscape of the stories of *The Old Order* represents, like the scenes of family life, an idealized, heightened version of the author's early surroundings.

When Porter was writing the Miranda stories she was preoccupied with the relationship between actual and imaginary versions of the past. (p. 349)

The relationship between legend and memory is a central theme of "Old Mortality," a story which begins with Miranda's astonishment at her family's unreliability on matters of family history.... The very young Miranda tries to draw a clear line between what is true and what is not. At the end of the story she realizes the difficulty involved in such a distinction, but still, in her youthful ignorance and optimism, she determines to pursue the truth. In spite of her resolution, the effect of the story is to make Cousin Eva's realism seem shabby and destructive compared with the family's beautiful vision of its past. (pp. 349-50)

In Bermuda ... memories of the past came flooding back.... The past memories and the present surroundings harmonized so well that she combined the two scenes to create the fictional background of Miranda Gay. So successful was the grafting of Porter's own childhood into the Bermuda setting that the resulting fiction supplanted the actuality and yielded a vision of her own past which she never relinquished. (p. 350)

> *Joan Givner, "'The Plantation of This Isle': Katharine Anne Porter's Bermuda Base," in South-west Review (© 1978 by Southern Methodist University Press), Autumn, 1978, pp. 339-51.*

*   *   *

PORTER, Peter   1929-

Porter is an Australian poet now living in London. He has been praised for his ability to present traditional concerns in original forms and textures. (See also *CLC*, Vol. 5.)

MICHAEL WOOD

Peter Porter might be described, unkindly, as another, younger, quirkier, brighter Betjeman. Certainly his verse is marred by the same jocose, inapposite cleverness.... He is not always ... offensive [in *Preaching to the Converted*], he is often merely glib, and fancy: "I've never been on Ulysses' island / or on Isherwood's"; "God is a Super-Director / who's terribly good at crowd scenes, / but He has only one tense, the present." I take it there is a strategy here, rather than simple recklessness: hard, brittle jokes are an oblique (very oblique) mark of your sensibility. Of course, an open, sentimental concern for the issues of our time can look very fraudulent, and Porter nattily defends the old Poetry against the earnestness of the young.... But if you're defending the small, civilized life against the hordes of youth and socialism, if your line is the quiet human notations which make poetry precious under any historical conditions, you need to be rather more convincingly human yourself than Porter (or Betjeman) manages to be, you need to make civilization sound less like a club for you and your witty friends.

Porter's versions of Martial, apart from one or two over-cute anachronisms, come off very well, present a better picture of the poet Porter seems to want to be: urbane, ironic, funny, full of wisdom and common sense. "If I can't be famous till I'm dead," Porter has Martial say, "I'm in no great hurry to be read." ... But it would be unfair to leave Porter with this vicarious achievement. Every now and then one of his own poems will break through the brittleness into a very sharp, curious intensity, and [for example, his] vision of Hardy in London is tactful and subdued.... (pp. 46-7)

> *Michael Wood, in Parnassus: Poetry in Review (copyright © by Poetry in Review Foundation), Spring/Summer, 1974.*

PETER WASHINGTON

Porter is riotous, prolific. Fond of baroque, he is really a mannerist—that style which isn't a style but a near-chaos of old habits and new fashions fighting for life in an attempt at glory. He often refers to the period:

> Perhaps it did happen,
> the Renaissance, when even the maggots
> had humanist leanings.

It isn't that Porter sees the worm in every apple: for him having worms is all a part of being such fruit. In the same poem [in *Living in a Calm Country*] he calls it the "central unfairness." In others he takes this further: is it, he asks, essential to have an apple to be a respectable worm? Yes the two are inseparable: as unlikely the worm without edible home as the man without a world.

And a world is what he wants. Brilliant, sombre and always almost excessive, he wanders through gardens and dreams countries, the past, death and books, making each his own for a moment and looking for somewhere to stop.... Porter's quick intelligence, delighting in contrast, plays over the surfaces where "pain clings": resolving not into sureness but firm statements of doubt. Grotesque and Roman by turns, his style can now mock itself—as in 'Baroque Quatrains.' This is important: Porter must transcend his new Elizabethanism if he is to sustain his work at the high level it sometimes reaches in this book.

The blurb says that this is a book about landscapes. It is—not only of place and body, but even more crucially of time and books. A middle-aged man in a dying culture, Porter's "true and disciplined despair" takes fire from precision about date and place. The two become one:

> The heart of the storm is now.

as he puts it. And he ranges his various gods about him: literary—Eliot, Stevens, Auden and others are quoted and alluded to—and the other gods of antiquity. At first I was doubtful of them: like the creaking deities in the Augustan poetic machine they did their jobs, I thought, at the expense of all credibility. But re-reading brought illumination. In 'Good Vibes' the poet says that

> To have trod on ground in happiness
> Is to be shaken by the true immortals.

Here is a clue: another poet is coming to terms with his world—which is not bereft of gods; they simply demand a whole new language to capture them in and make their existence real to us. Without our perceptions, they do not live or care. They are ourselves. (p. 602)

Peter Washington, in The Spectator *(© 1975 by* The Spectator; *reprinted by permission of* The Spectator), *November 8, 1975.*

DOUGLAS DUNN

Peter Porter's poems have always represented the authority of the articulate and hallowed. A disturbing sanity has been at the centre of his work. Concern for cultural values and the dilemmas of metropolitan life has not led to whatever ossified styles "new geniuses" might have expected from him. Porter is a man of at least two artistic temperaments. Culturally he is conservative; artistically he is adventurous, and though his staple is simplified baroque, it has been seen capable of taking whatever weight of invention Porter would like it to carry. Though I have reservations about the extent to which Porter is willing to be a diehard in defence of his particular interpretation of "cultural values", there is no denying the conviction and strength of their expressions.

When Porter is self-effacing, or testing the state of mind of a persona against what it assumes to be ideal, there is a minimum of self and only the appearance of effacement. His "I" is seldom that of himself entirely; there is a strong fictional endeavour which gives his eager imagination its chance of freedom.... A necessary part of his moral schema is that the best that life offers is close to what life offers in its ordinary way. It is when Porter is concerned to make pronouncements on such subjects that his language loses poetic shape and becomes aphoristic in a no-man's land between prose and poetry....

Living in a Calm Country, though, has more examples of Porter avoiding that characteristic fault than ever before. Rhythmically, he is more assured; he is altogether closer to the mastery of idiom his ambitious work has been demanding. (p. 75)

Douglas Dunn, in Encounter *(© 1976 by Encounter Ltd.), February, 1976.*

RICHARD PEVEAR

[Porter's "Family Album"] is all too easy, too foreseeable, and too clever. Darkness, despair, and death are handed the victory without a struggle and apparently without cost to the poet, who passes off as insight or as truth what is merely the available, conventional resolution of the poem. Reading these things one trembles, as Kierkegaard said, "at the thought of what it is to be a man." (p. 310)

Richard Pevear, in The Hudson Review *(copyright © 1976 by The Hudson Review, Inc.; reprinted by permission), Vol. XXIX, No. 2, Summer, 1976.*

EMMA FISHER

Peter Porter's poems on the death of his wife, where the agonising minutiae—the appointment card from an optician, other mail after she's dead—are presented in all their nakedness [in *The Cost of Seriousness*]. He makes Gertrude Stein say:

> Nothing can be done in the face
> of ordinary unhappiness
> Above all, there is nothing to do in words
> I have written a dozen books
> to prove nothing can be done in words.

Porter does a lot in words but cannot do much about ordinary unhappiness, and this inability is a subject of many of the poems.

Despair and wit mingle uneasily. His cross—cultural jokes —as when Boccherini says:

> When I start an allegro
> it's planned like those washing
>   programmes
> right through to spin-dry

are typical of his rueful sense of himself as a responsive tourist of civilisation, celebrating other people's art and the absurdities of his own. But he keeps coming back from contemplation of some work of art—such as an angel at Blythburgh—to the fact of that death, as if by linking it in he could help heal the pain.

Often the message is 'they believed in God or an afterlife, but I don't and it's very hard'....

There is an irresistible pull in poems about death to come to some sort of resolution or acceptance, even if only a stoical one; but in Porter's poem the grief remains private and unbearable....

There is something tight-lipped about all this. Elsewhere, in *The Cost of Seriousness*, he says

> I have come no closer to my goal
> of doing without words, that
> pain may be notated some real way.

One suspects that he finds music a real way, although he says in 'The Lying Art' 'Music gets the better of it, since music is all lies'. It may seem unclear why he goes on writing at all; but in one of the best poems in the book, 'The Delegate', he has the answer:

> The artist . . . is being used despite
>   himself. The truth
> is a story forcing me to tell it. It is not
> my story or my truth. My misery
> is on a colour chart—even my death
> is a chord among the garden sounds.

He sees his unhappiness in perspective as only a part of a polychromatic, amoral, but inherently beautiful world, and this is his form of reconciliation. (p. 25)

Emma Fisher, in The Spectator *(© 1978 by* The Spectator; *reprinted by permission of* The Spectator), *July 8, 1978.*

ANNE STEVENSON

In Peter Porter's *The Cost of Seriousness*, language is not a vast element with which the poet contends, but a game rhetoric forces him to play. In this book it is also a faith that has failed. If the subject of Porter's poems is the death of his wife, their recurring theme is disillusionment with 'the lying art'. . . .

Porter has always been an erudite poet, and in this book (much his best) as in earlier ones, the safety net is expertly displayed—even when he attacks poetry as 'pointless'. . . . The poem ['An Exequy'] is a strange mixture of pastiche, doggerel and genuinely moving verse. It is as if Porter were unable to approach his grief without surrounding himself with intellectual paraphernalia. Yet he writes best when he writes humbly. (p. 62)

> *Anne Stevenson, in* The Listener (© *British Broadcasting Corp. 1978; reprinted by permission of Anne Stevenson), July 13, 1978.*

FLEUR ADCOCK

Peter Porter has always been, to put it mildly, interested in death: in his earlier collections he frequently reflected upon the deaths of others or contemplated his own, and even in his lighter poems death was always ready to sidle in among the lines of pointed social commentary and the mosaics of multi-cultural allusion. Now in this fine new collection [*The Cost of Seriousness*] death is at the centre. It is difficult to say it without sounding callous, but it needs somehow to be said: the death of his wife at the end of 1974 presented Mr Porter with a subject ideally suited to his gifts and temperament. The best of the poems about his loss have a poignant bleak simplicity, a sober concentration; without abandoning all his tricks of style he has refined out the baroque curlicues of his more playful works and achieved a flexible but direct eloquence. . . .

Not all of this collection broods upon death: there is a range of mood and of topic. Mr Porter's other chief subject has always been art (a word which crops up in these pages nearly as often as the word "hell"). (p. 88)

"Non Piangere, Liù" [is] one of the plainest and most piercingly immediate poems in the book. It begins:

> A card comes to tell you
> you should report
> to have your eyes tested.
>
> But your eyes melted in the fire.
> and the only tears, which soon dried,
> fell in the chapel.

and ends:

> The fire will come out of the sun
> and I shall look in the heart of it.

Writing like this he is totally convincing. (p. 89)

> *Fleur Adcock, in* Encounter (© *1978 by Encounter Ltd.), August, 1978.*

DESMOND GRAHAM

[*The Cost of Seriousness*] is important in what it attempts, and important for Porter, I should imagine—not just because of the more intimate and painful area of experience on which many poems draw, but because he has cut out so much of the clutter of cleverness which lumbered previous volumes.

The cost of seriousness is not, as Porter writes in his title poem, 'death', but emotional pain; and the pain in these poems extends beyond the poems directly mourning his wife, and reaches into the process of making art. Porter feels with force 'The Lying Art':

> . . . Real pain
> it aims for, but can only make gestures,
> the waste of selling-short, the 'glittering'. . . .

Art cannot reach the reality of pain. What does this leave Porter with, as artist? A combination of indirectness and statement: poems formally set, often offering open discourse or arguments with himself, which employ intimacies of tone, record intimate details, move through areas of privacy, all of this covered by both tact and the acknowledgement that this is not the whole truth.

The result, I find, is that the poems are at the mercy of the emotional state the reader brings to them. In different readings I have found them unbearably painful and been left cold by them. This, clearly, can happen with any poem: but trying again and again to reach these, I must conclude that Porter's attempted resolution has not worked. The problem is one of distance and control. . . . Porter does disrupt the surface of his art, but even when he does so, too much distance is retained. . . . (p. 68)

In one poem in this collection, 'The Delegate', Porter takes a minimum of distance, making the poem a direct address by the deceased. With this slackening of art's hold, the poem's acute understanding of the process of remembering the dead is allowed its freedom to move us. I make these comments on Porter, particularly aware that, in words I take from [Anthony] Hecht, they are 'provisionally true / As anything else one cares to think about.' (p. 69)

> *Desmond Graham, in* Stand (*copyright © by* Stand), *Vol. 20, No. 1, (1978-79).*

*   *   *

POUND, Ezra   1885-1972

American poet, translator, essayist, and critic, Pound is heralded as the initiator of modern twentieth-century poetry. Influenced by Whitman's *Leaves of Grass*, his own lifetime masterpiece, *Cantos*, was constantly revised and added to during the more than forty years of its construction. Literary allusions, foreign phrases and forms abound in this volume, which T. S. Eliot called "an inexhaustible reference book of verse form." His translations of Chinese poetry are often criticized as misrepresentative of their original structure, reading like Pound's own work; such experimentation, however, added new dimensions to the genre, later expounded upon by other twentieth-century poets. Pound's political sympathies at one time threatened to diminish his reputation as one of the most innovative and creative artists of his generation. Influencing poetry before, during, and after his career as a poet, Pound was a secretary to Yeats, playing an important part in transforming that great poet's artistic vision during his last period. He is responsible for editing *The Waste Land* into the form that won Eliot world-wide acclaim, and his tenacious support of Joyce during a period of financial distress allowed the novelist to finish *Ulysses*. (See also *CLC*, Vols. 1, 2, 3, 4, 5, 7, 10, and *Contemporary Authors*, Vols. 5-8, rev. ed.; obituary, Vols. 37-40, rev. ed.)

S. J. ADAMS

Surprisingly little has been written about Pound's translation of the Old English "Seafarer." (p. 127)

Truly, the scholar who possesses the original poem is in an awkward position, faced with two poems remarkably alike but different; his approach inevitably suffers from a psychological interference—something like hearing a new interpretation of a familiar song. He may prefer a bland Modern English substitute, that reminds him of the original, to a fully recreated poem. The scholar too will have his own understanding of the poem; Pound's, following a line of scholarship now in disfavor, will almost certainly differ. The reader without Old English, on the other hand, may find Pound's poem magnificent . . . , but he may be troubled by rumours of Pound's blunders. The question can only be settled by a line-by-line comparison of the two poems, with a mind alert to possible reasons for whatever divergences do exist—for it will be found that their number has been exaggerated. A simple check-list of Pound's "errors" is most misleading. But, before such a comparison is possible, some other points must be kept in mind.

Pound first published his "Seafarer" in . . . 1911. Except for a brief "philological note" it formed without comment the first of a series of twelve articles under the title "I Gather the Limbs of Osiris," which were said to illustrate a "new method" in scholarship. . . . His "new method" of scholarship is a deliberate reaction against the German philological tradition in which he was trained: he explains it as the method of the "luminous detail," the single relevant fact that crystallizes all the facts comprising the *Zeitgeist* more efficiently than the catalog-of-details method that he opposed. Like Pater before him, Pound took for his model Jacob Burckhardt's *Civilization of the Renaissance.* "The Seafarer," then, he offers as the "luminous detail" capturing the essence of pre-Christian Anglo-Saxon England. Such a method has less to do with scholarship, perhaps, than with imagism, which was the next step in Pound's development, and the method is sufficiently displayed in the *Cantos,* which combine both old and new in a veritable Germanic card-file of luminous details.

Thus the "Seafarer" has closer ties with Poundian imagism than first appears. The realism of the seafaring details in the original have impressed most of its readers (and they need not be less realistic even if we do accept the more recent allegorizing interpretations). And Old English poetry, like imagism, is a poetry of nouns. This is apparent even in the metric, which characteristically stresses nouns rather than verbs. The kennings, too, are strikingly reminiscent of the juxtaposed pictures, the "verb-nouns," that Pound was soon to discover in Fenollosa's notes on Chinese poetry. (pp. 128-29)

The appearance of the "Seafarer" . . . [points up Pound's desire] to show that translation is itself an act of criticism. The translator must not merely bring over the semantic meaning of his text, he must first determine the text itself and then try to recreate its indefinable poetic qualities within the conditions of another language. With a doubtful text, the translator must make editorial decisions for the reader. When matters of interpretation or nuance are doubtful, the translator must choose, while the reader of the original may suspend judgment. And when the original is remarkable for some one quality in particular, its sound for example, the translator is artful insofar as he captures it, even while sacrificing other more ordinary accuracies. Generally in translating Old English poetry there are two

special problems: to create a diction in which the kennings and double nouns seem natural, and to find an equivalent for a metric non-existent in Modern English.

Pound's solution for the diction of his poem has drawn criticism. . . . His diction is a vaguely archaic pastiche resembling no idiom ever spoken. Archaic language has been all but excluded from verse now for the past half century, and we commonly expect translations to pretend that they are poems written yesterday: for this Pound himself is partly responsible. But in 1911 not even Pound had shed the diction of Rossetti and the Nineties, and no contemporary poetic idiom was available. Contemporaneity had not yet emerged as a criterion. The archaic pastiche, with its "—eth" verbs and syntactic inversions, would have been more difficult to make convincing a few years later, but in 1911 it simply represented the first Georgian Anthology (1912) pushed to an extreme. This in itself would not save Pound's poem—it does not save William Morris's *Beowulf* or Gilbert Murray's *Euripides*—but Pound's diction proves itself capable of expressiveness, and I for one would not trade the passage beginning "Lordly men are to earth o'ergiven" for anything else in poetry. Pound, though, would not have made his seafarer speak like a contemporary in any circumstances. For one thing, Old English translates so readily into cognates and derivatives which tend to have a more archaic feeling than other types of words; yet Old English is comfortably translated so, while Latin poetry is insufferable in a Latinate vocabulary—a convincing demonstration that we still feel Old English as the root of the language. For another thing, Anglo-Saxon culture itself, like Provençal, has a remote and archaic feeling, while the culture of Latin poetry is closer to ours, decadent, urban, urbane. Accordingly, Pound's improvisations on Propertius are thoroughly modern, while his versions of Old English and Provençal are archaic, and those of Cavalcanti deliberately recall the idiom of Wyatt. (pp. 129-30)

The translator having dropped the pretense of contemporary diction, the alien constructions of Old English, the kennings, the double nouns, all fit naturally into a field of diction already remote in feeling. But this raises a further question: how metaphorical are the metaphors? The verb *wrecan* in the first line of the "Seafarer," for example—it means "to express," literally "to ex-press," to push out, and it is thus related metaphorically to the exile theme of the poem; but is the metaphor really felt, or has it been lost through overuse at the beginnings of poems? Some of the kennings, too, are doubtful. Is *hwaeles ebel* . . . really felt as "whale's home," or is it just another word for the sea, or is it more comparable to "scaly herd" for "fish" in a more recent poetic convention? . . . Pound, like most translators, assumes that such expressions ("song's truth," or "breast-cares") are truly metaphorical.

Pound's solution for the metric problem, unlike that for his diction, has been widely admired, and it is one of the best reasons for studying his "Seafarer." There is, or at least before Pound there was, no viable equivalent for the four-stress alliterative line; the translator must either use a metric already familiar (blank verse? fourteeners?) or else invent a form on the pattern of the original. (pp. 130-31)

Pound has always assumed that accurate translation includes an accurate equivalent for the sound and movement of the original, *if* the aural value is in some way remarkable. He had in these early days developed a mystique about word-rhythm, a belief in every rhythm as a unique *Ding an sich:* "I believe in an 'absolute rhythm,' a rhythm, that is, in poetry which corresponds exactly to the emotion or shade of emotion to be expressed." This belief stands behind some of the practices in his "Seafarer" translation just as it stands behind the *vers libre* of imagism. . . . Many times Pound sacrifices semantic meaning for a sound-effect. But is is amazing to see how Pound is able to reproduce the cadence and sound of so many lines with uncanny accuracy:

> hrim hrusan band,   haegl feoll on eorban. . . .
> Frost froze the land, hail fell on earth then. . . .

Obviously this sort of thing is not possible very often, but the frequency of Pound's successes suggests the direction of his effort.

While Pound attempts to reproduce the sound of the original line, sometimes slavishly, he does not, like some translators . . . , make his metric conform to the rules of Anglo-Saxon prosody. Most of Pound's lines alliterate, but not all, and some on patterns impossible in Old English ("*J*ourney's *j*argon, *h*ow I in *h*arsh days. . . .). A few stand as quasi-Virgilian half-lines. Pound most of the time tries to approximate the stress-pattern and the number of syllables found in the original, since variation in the number of slack syllables in the "drop" is the major resource for variety in a stress-metric. Pound's lines are tighter or looser, slower or faster, in accordance with the original; his divergences, though, are consistently in the direction of tightening the line, probably because in the new metre too many light syllables would create ambiguities about where the stress should fall. This results in a less free-flowing movement, a more gnomic quality than the original. In addition, Pound tends to break up longer sentences into shorter units, so that his style is somewhat more disjointed than some more recent critics might like.

Pound's most important metric practice, however, is a fairly simple one, yet it has been missed by every other translator I have seen. Old English verse rhythms are predominantly falling, and a majority of the lines drop away from a strong initial stress, presumably marked by the harp. Individual words, too, are regularly stressed on the first syllable (except for a few common prefixes). Consequently, Old English lines are marked as well by feminine endings, and individual words tend more toward feminine patterns than in Modern English (partly because of the inflections). This rhythmic phenomenon is perhaps a reason why the elegiac mood came so naturally to the Anglo-Saxon poet. But although falling rhythms are slightly unnatural in modern English verse, which is basically iambic, Pound takes great pains to preserve the falling patterns of the original. A glance at the beginnings of his lines will show how many have a strong initial stress—even more, in fact, than the original, as if to prove the point. I have looked too for single words with rising rhythm, but Pound seems to have avoided them entirely (again except for prefixes). And not surprisingly, Pound has taken equal care to make his line-endings overwhelmingly feminine. No other translation reproduces the falling rhythms of Old English poetry so successfully. (pp. 131-32)

Pound uses one device in his translations which has often been misrepresented as ignorance or carelessness, and this is the bilingual pun. An example is the translation of *wrecan*

as "reckon." Pound's rationale for this practice is connected with his effort to approximate sound-effects, even at the expense of semantic meaning. Nearly always, though, the meaning Pound substitutes is a fair paraphrase which would pass without comment were it not for the suspect pun. *Wrecan* means "to express," but the metaphorical weight is doubtful; Pound's word is another verb meaning roughly "to suppose," or even sometimes "to express," and it is a slightly overworn metaphor. . . . Pound's puns sometimes have little more defense than that he liked the sound. And it is no wonder that teachers of Old English raise their eyebrows, having watched so many students stumble into the same traps. But I think it is quite clear at least that Pound knew what he was doing—the device appears often enough in this and other translations, and Pound occasionally translates literally in one place and by pun in another. In nearly all cases the effect can be justified by sound, tone, or nuance.

I have stressed that translation is always a kind of interpretation, and the translator of the "Seafarer" is forced to make a number of editorial decisions. Much has happened in Old English scholarship since 1911 to date Pound's version of the poem. It is worth noting Pound's position on the two questions of interpretation that have occupied most of recent criticism. On the first of these it is enough to say that Pound agrees with Sweet and a majority of scholars that "the simplest view of the poem is that it is the monologue of an old sailor." (pp. 132-33)

The question of Pound's de-Christianization of the "Seafarer" is a more serious matter. The difference in tone between Pound's version and the current conception of the original as a Christian lament, or even a Christian allegory, is far more drastic for this reason than for all of Pound's local blunders taken together. Yet Pound was perfectly in line with the best scholarship of his day. This must be understood, or else Pound's suppression of the Christian elements in the poem will seem arbitrary. That it was clear in his own mind what he was doing is shown in the "philological note" appended to the *New Age* printing of the poem:

> The text of this poem is rather confused. I have rejected half of line 76, read "Angles" for angels in line 78, and stopped translating before the passage about the soul and the longer lines beginning, "Mickle is the fear of the Almighty," and ending in a dignified but platitudinous prayer to the Deity: "World's elder, eminent creator, in all ages, amen." There are many conjectures as to how the text came into its present form. It seems most likely that a fragment of the original poem, clear through about the first thirty lines, and thereafter increasingly illegible, fell into the hands of a monk with literary ambitions, who filled in the gaps with his own guesses and "improvements." The groundwork may have been a longer narrative poem, but the "lyric," as I have accepted it, divides fairly well into "The Trials of the Sea," its lure and the Lament for Age.
>
> (pp. 133-34)

Pound's purpose in including the "Seafarer" in his *New Age* series was . . . to represent the native, pagan Anglo-Saxon stock ready to receive influences from the south; he had by 1911, furthermore, developed his personal anti-Christian prejudices. Accordingly, and with the full sanction of scholarship, Pound attempted to recreate in his translation the original *Ur*-"Seafarer" systematically stripped of its Christian references. (p. 134)

S. J. Adams, "A Case for Pound's 'Seafarer'," in MOSAIC: A Journal for the Study of Literature and Ideas *(copyright © 1976 by the University of Manitoba Press; acknowledgement of previous publication is herewith made), Vol. IX, No. 2 (Winter, 1976), pp. 127-46.*

DONALD DAVIE

Because of [the] cavalier disregard of ascertainable facts and documents we can be offered, as a portrait of the youthful Pound, a figure who [according to George Quasha] "was seeking a radical redefinition of poetic possibilities and returning to the roots of civilization in order to show how much had been lost in the watery conventions handed over to us by the nineteenth century." The ascertainable records present us on the contrary with a man who admired Swinburne and Thomas Hardy and D. G. Rossetti, Beddoes and Landor and Browning, Gautier and Heine and Leopardi, Stendhal and Remy de Gourmont and Flaubert; a man who had virtually no views of American nineteenth-century literature, since he appears not to have read attentively (nor was he to read) Emily Dickinson or Melville or Hawthorne, Fenimore Cooper or Thoreau; who thought on the other hand that "there is more wisdom, perhaps more 'revolution' in Whistler's portrait of young Miss Alexander than in all the Judaic drawings of the 'prophetic' Blake", in short, a man who carried more nineteenth-century baggage than any comparably gifted contemporary among writers in English. If Pound is a master and founding father of twentieth-century modernism in the arts, it is certainly not by virtue of having exploded, and persuaded us to reject, nineteenth-century pretensions.

we may reach back further, and consider not the nineteenth century but the eighteenth.... As with nineteenth-century "romantic" culture, so with eighteenth-century "Enlightenment" culture, we find Pound cast in a role of iconoclast which an unprejudiced scrutiny of his recorded opinions simply will not support.

Accordingly, when we hear it happily declared of the United States in the 1970s, "Our scene is very different from the cultural vacuum at the turn of the century which drove Ezra Pound heroically to seek to 'resuscitate the dead art of poetry,'" we ought to be on our guard. And sure enough the documents make it clear that, for the young Ezra Pound, London between 1908 and 1912 was anything but a "cultural vacuum".... Moreover, many readers of Pound's *Hugh Selwyn Mauberley* take the line, "resuscitate the dead art of poetry," ironically, as a gibe at anyone who is damfool enough to think that the art of poetry is, or could be, "dead." In short, everywhere we turn, so long as we have some scruples about evidence, we encounter in the young Pound not a revolutionary or iconoclast but a sometimes militant conservative.

Indeed, it is possible to argue that Pound was at bottom an Edwardian man of letters ..., and that the provocative oddities of his later poetry and his later opinions reflect merely the increasingly desperate straits to which a man formed in that milieu was compelled, as political and social

developments destroyed any possibility of that kind of milieu being reconstituted. Certainly Pound's Edwardianism, if we may call it that, was something that he never wholly outgrew. And so when he died, there disappeared not only the last surviving specimen of one sort of twentieth-century modernist but also, odd as it must seem, the last survivor of a still older breed, formed by the century before. (pp. 7-9)

The European "confederation" that Pound thought he spoke for throughout his life was effectively a Europe that spoke Latin and its Romance derivatives, including English as the most remote and partial of those derivatives, and making special provision for classical Greek as in important ways the original source of them all, even of Latin. And the sanities and wisdoms that Pound conceived of himself as promoting against the evermore impudent barbarians were carried—so he thought, and was to think—pre-eminently in Latin and the Romance languages. . . . (p. 13)

But if the language trusted by the young Pound is Romance language in this respectable, technical, and well-defined sense, what's to be said of language like this?

> Aye, I am wistful for my kin of the spirit
> And have none about me save in the shadows
> When come they, surging of power, 'DAEMON'
> 'Quasi KALOUN'. S.T. says Beauty is most that, a
>   'calling to the soul.'
> Well then, so call they, the swirlers out of the mist of
>   my soul,
> They that come mewards, bearing old magic.

Here we have "Romance language" in an altogether less reputable sense, which has more to do with romanticism (and with Victorian late-romanticism) than with the harshly direct language of a genuine "Romance" poet like Villon. The lines above are from "In Durance" (1907), which appeared in Pound's third collection, *Personae* (. . . 1909); and what they are struggling to say is after a fashion in keeping with the language that Pound tries to say it in. "S.T." is Coleridge, and the Coleridge text appealed to is the essay "On the Principles of Genial Criticism," which advances a Platonic or neo-Platonic idea of the nature and function of poetry, as Pound's poem does also. Moreover, the neo-Platonic matter of these lines is something that persisted in Pound's thought. And if, as historians of ideas, we were to concentrate on the paraphrasable content of Pound's poetry, we could see such an early poem as saying things which he will still be saying at the end of his life. But it is precisely the radical difference in the manner of saying, early and late, which is crucial. For the experience of reading Pound's *Cantos* isn't remotely like the experience of reading neo-Platonic romantic poets like Shelley or D. G. Rossetti. . . . "Pseudo-archaic" is exact for "Aye, I am wistful," and "They that come mewards." . . . This is romance language in the sense that it is the language of historical romances written in late-Victorian and Edwardian England; it is not a medium in which anything can be communicated forcefully or crisply.

This is, however, only one component in the language of these lines. "Surging of power" belongs in some different idiom altogether, which is impossible to name; the notetaker's telegraphese of "S.T." belongs in another idiom again; and the Greek expressions, "DAEMON" and "Quasi KALOUN," belong in yet another. These last are syntactically quite without anchorage in what offers itself as a normal English sentence. And this abandonment of grammar mirrors accurately the desperation of the poet, who can manage no more than to have these disparate idioms jostle helplessly one against another, though he is possessed of a conviction that they could be articulated one with another, if only he could find the key. At this stage he cannot; and so all that is conveyed is the desperation of the effort and the need. The language is a chronically unstable mix of linguistic elements from the European past, held together by will, by nothing more than the urgency of the poet's need. Their coherence is something wished for and vehemently gestured at, certainly not demonstrated or achieved. The vehemence of the need is quite without parallel among poets writing and publishing in London in the first decade of this century. . . . (pp. 13-16)

[Pound's peculiar rashness and impetuosity] had everything to do with the fact that [he] was American; that is to say, a poet of the English tongue to whom it came naturally to regard English as just one of the princely dialects of Europe. An American like Pound came to *Europe;* and if he came to England, it was to one of the provinces of that larger cultural entity. No Edwardian Englishman thought of England that way. . . . [He] defined himself in his national identity as that which Continental Europe was not. But to a devoted American Europeanist like the young Pound, what was precious about England was not what marked her off from the Continent but what bound her to the Mediterranean heartlands. Hence the unconvincing impetuosity with which the poet of "In Durance" moves from mock-archaic English to Greek. . . . [Pound] wanted to create or re-create a *lingua franca* of Greco-Roman Christendom in which English would operate as a sister language with French and Spanish and Italian. The mere *mix* of "In Durance" was to become the compound language of *The Cantos*—a compound still perhaps unstable, but not so easily dissoluble:

The author of "In Durance" and of *The Spirit of Romance* was the author also of *Patria Mia* (1912), in which he wrote consciously and explicitly as a citizen of the United States, addressing himself specifically to the state of culture, and the prospects for culture, in his native land. (pp. 17-18)

It is in any case highly significant that [*Patria Mia*], Pound's most obviously and explicitly American book, should have a Latin title. He attempts to foresee a future for America according to paradigms he had learned about in Europe. Neither at this time nor afterward does Pound share the conviction and the hope which as a matter of historical record have fired the cultural achievements of the white man in North America ever since Plymouth Plantation—the hope and belief that the new continent offered a new start, a new Eden for a new Adam, liberated from the corruptions and errors of Europe and forewarned by European history of how to avoid European mistakes. On the contrary, Pound takes it for granted that if America is ever to produce or become a noble civilization, it can do so only by modeling itself on European precedents, precedents that are ultimately or originally Greek and Roman. (pp. 20-1)

Imagism (originally "imagisme," as if by French spelling to borrow the required Parisian *éclat*) was an exclusively literary movement, whereas the later vorticism claimed to comprehend all the arts and was strongest in painting and sculpture. Yet Pound himself seems to have thought of vorticism as only a prolongation and theoretical elaboration of what

he had fought for under the banner of imagism, until imagism was taken away from him, and trivialized, by Amy Lowell. If we ask for the theory of imagism, it is otherwise hard to find; though it can be put together out of certain speculations of T. E. Hulme as early as 1909, at which time the movement had had a sort of aborted birth. But the imagism of 1913, when Pound's energy and impudence made it a talking point in London and Chicago, was not theoretical at all but came across as two or three punchily expressed rules of thumb, as in the famous "A Few Don'ts for an Imagist":

> Use no superfluous word, no adjective, which does not reveal something.
>
> Don't use such an expression as "dim lands of *peace*." It dulls the image. It mixes an abstraction with the concrete. It comes from the writer's not realizing that the natural object is always the *adequate* symbol.
>
> Go in fear of abstractions. Don't retell in mediocre verse what has already been done in good prose. Don't think any intelligent person is going to be deceived when you try to shirk all the difficulties of the unspeakably difficult art of good prose by chopping your composition into line lengths. . . .
>
> Don't imagine that the art of poetry is any simpler than the art of music, or that you can please the expert before you have spent at least as much effort on the art of verse as the average piano teacher spends on the art of music.
>
> Be influenced by as many great artists as you can, but have the decency either to acknowledge the debt outright, or to try to conceal it.
>
> Don't allow "influence" to mean merely that you mop up the particular decorative vocabulary of some one or two poets whom you happen to admire. . . .
>
> Use either no ornament or good ornament.

This is a striking change from the "Romance language" of only a few months before. And with pronouncements in this impatient plain-man idiom there emerged the figure of Pound the iconoclast, a rhetorical illusion which still too often obscures the lineaments of the man who fabricated and deployed the rhetoric for certain short-term purposes; who chose for those temporary purposes to conceal the far from "plain-man" perspectives that he nonetheless had in mind. . . . In Pound's mind imagism was, perhaps centrally, a program [derived from convictions of Ford Madox Ford] for bringing into poetry the Flaubertian *mot juste*. In other words, it was, despite appearances, just one more program in, or out of, "Romance languages." (pp. 32-5)

The *mot juste* that Ford and Pound admired was to be found as readily in Catullus or Villon or indeed George Crabbe as in Flaubert. And a Catullus or a Villon was more instructive than Flaubert because, like any poet of any century, each had had to deny himself the cumulative effect with which a Flaubert could recreate a whole milieu by a multitude of exactly registered particulars. Upon the poet there was imposed the further task of selecting, from among the array of significant particulars, that one, or those one or two, which could be made, by judicious deployment of a specifically poetic resource like cadence, to stand for all the rest. And so there enters into Pound's thinking the principle of "the luminous detail," the single particular which, chosen with enough care and rendered with enough exactness, can impel the reader to summon up for himself all the other particulars implied by that salient one. It is a principle crucial to all poetic structures, as Pound realized. . . . In later life Pound was to suppose, perilously, that this principle which worked for poetic structures applied to intellectual structures also. . . . (pp. 35-6)

Pound was in trouble, in any case. For the valuable prosaicism which Ford had taught him to look for and demand is much more readily attainable, perhaps also more important, in poetry written for the speaking voice than in poetry that aspires to be sung. And yet Pound's natural bent and talent had always been for poetry that should be sung, rather than for such spoken *genres* as epigram, lampoon, epistle. Apart from anything else, these *genres* call for a sure grasp of social tone, whereas there is much evidence that Pound was socially maladroit. Accordingly, in the years of imagism and vorticism we find him painstakingly attempting, in epigram and lampoon, niceties of urbane insolence and Jamesian nuance such as he could not command. (pp. 36-7)

[There] is no question of making Pound out to be "classical" or a "classicist," as against "romantic" or "romanticist." . . . Pound was, despite appearances, *conservative;* and to be conservative in his generation meant prolonging some romantic attitudes as well as prolonging or reviving preromantic ones. (p. 38)

Pound had little patience with the central endeavor of *symbolisme,* which explored the analogy [of words] not with sculpture but with music. It is easy to get this wrong. Have I not just insisted that Pound wanted to write poems for singing rather more than poems for speaking? And do we not find him at every possible opportunity telling poets how much a study of music will do for them? Yes; but the music that Pound has in mind is real sounds in sequence, an actual melody, whereas the idea of music which fascinated Mallarmé and Valéry was precisely that—the *idea* of music, the idea of a poetic art that should be nonreferential or self-referential like the art of music. Pound seemingly had no interest in that. What Pound had in mind was a marriage of the two arts, not an analogy between them. . . . [The] momentousness of imagism as Pound conceived of it lies just in its being not a variant of *symbolisme* or a development out of it, but a radical alternative to it. . . . *Gaudier-Brzeska: A Memoir* (1916) is overtly concerned with vorticism, not imagism—which only shows how the two movements were, in Pound's sense of the matter, really one. *Gaudier-Brzeska* is a work of theory; and so the difference between *symbolisme* and imagism can there be presented as philosophical, epistemological. It should not by this time surprise us that in this perspective imagism is revealed as the conservative and traditional rejoinder to *symbolisme*'s dangerous innovations. The traditional authority that Pound appeals to is Aquinas. Like Aquinas, the imagist holds that a proposition—for instance, "the pine tree in mist upon the far hill looks like a fragment of Japanese armor"—is either true or false; true or false, not just to the state of mind or angle of vision of the perceiver but to the real appearance,

the real relations in real space, of what is perceived. Either what is reported of pine trees and plates of armor is a true account of the spatial and other relations asserted, or else it is not true, however honestly it may reproduce the impression produced upon a perceiver who may be abnormally situated or in an abnormal state of mind. The idea of "normality" is unphilosophical, in the sense that one takes on faith the existence of a norm in perceiving. But the imagist will make that act of faith, just as common sense does, and as the *symboliste* does not. Pound, like Gautier, is one of those *"pour qui le monde visible existe"*; and the best pages of *Gaudier-Brzeska* are those in which Pound most exultantly justifies that proclivity, and insists on the impoverishment that comes as soon as we begin to doubt that the perceivable world truly exists as something other than ourselves, bodied against us. On the other hand, we must not suppose that our organs of perception are limited to the five senses; Pound was sure—for some of us, excessively sure —that they were not. (pp. 39-41)

[*Hugh Selwyn Mauberley*] is, and has proved to be, the most accessible of Pound's longer poems, the one that it is easiest to start with. For just that reason it is a poem that one must grow through, and grow out of, though the literary world is full of people who got this far and no further— for whom, accordingly, this is Pound's best poem, or the only one of his poems that is "an assured achievement." Pound's word for it, when he sent it to Hardy, was "thin" —"the Mauberley is thin." And "thin" may well be the right word, which explains why thin and constricted and rancorously distrustful sensibilities can respond to this poem by Pound as to no other.

Hugh Selwyn Mauberley consists of two sequences, one of thirteen poems dated 1919, followed by one of five poems dated 1920. The appearance of intricate interlinkings and cross references between the sequences and between the poems is, I now think, largely illusory. But one that is not an illusion is the relationship between the poem that closes the second sequence, "Medallion," and the poem that closes the first, "Envoi." It has been proved that these two poems are companion pieces. . . . (p. 50)

[*Hugh Selwyn Mauberley*] is the elaborate culmination of Pound's attempts to be urbane, but urbanity did not come naturally to him; on the contrary, he rather often adopted the wrong strategems in social situations. Among such strategems was a range of expedients subsumed by Pound under the name of persona or mask. His protégé Eliot had made brilliant use of the strictly verbal *persona* J. Alfred Prufrock; and his Anglo-Irish mentor, Yeats, was to make brilliant histrionic use of masks called Michael Robartes and Owen Aherne and Crazy Jane. Pound seems to have intended Hugh Selwyn Mauberley to serve him in the same way. But his temperament was quite different from either Eliot's or Yeats's; his treatment of Villon in *The Spirit of Romance* reveals that he responded readily in his reading to a quality of robust self-exposure in poets, precisely what the doctrines of persona and mask were designed to obviate. Accordingly, Hugh Selwyn Mauberley is a mask that continually slips. . . . What is the mask for, if, as often as not, the poet throws it off and speaks vulnerably as and from himself? More distractingly still, since we are advised of the mask in the very title, how are we to know in which poems Pound speaks through the mask, in which he doesn't? *Hugh Selwyn Mauberley* remains a very important poem; apart from anything else, it has proved to be the most insidiously and aptly quotable of Pound's poems, and it has very great merit as an Englishing of Gautier. But it looks as if it will figure in Pound's *oeuvre* . . . as a relatively early piece which unsympathetic readers can use as a stick with which to beat later work that the poet set more store by. (pp. 53-4)

[The] language of *Homage to Sextus Propertius*, or . . . much of it, is "translatorese." . . . [It exemplifies] the English of the bored schoolboy lazily construing his Latin homework but, equally, the proudly pompous clerk (Pakistani, Cypriot, or whatever) using the language of those who were lately his imperial masters. The point is a crucial one, for *Homage to Sextus Propertius* is often presented as a model of how to translate, whereas much of the time it is a deliberate model of how not to! So far from being a model for translators to follow, it deliberately and consistently incorporates *mis*translation. . . . It is most often a case of unsuitably heightened diction; and this accounts for hilarious passages in an idiom which we have learned to call, since Pound's day, "camp." But sometimes . . . the comical oddity is not in the vocabulary so much as in word order and syntax. . . . (pp. 58-9)

Every [example] of mistranslation can be detected as such by an attentive and halfway sophisticated reader of the English. There is no need to check back to the Latin text of Propertius. But Pound, for good measure, deliberately planted ludicrous howlers, to amuse those who knew the Latin or chose to consult it. This was a miscalculation. . . . [All] the manifold ironies of *Homage to Sextus Propertius* are directed ultimately at the reader, who is convicted, line by line, of having only pompously imperial, [elaborately mistranslated] English, into which to render a poem that derides and deflates imperial pretensions. Thus it appears that by wholly transposing "imperialism" into language, into the texture of style, by forgetting his own existence "for the sake of the lines," Pound has effected a . . . wounding and penetrating critique of imperialism in general. . . . (pp. 60-1)

Those who know [*The Cantos*] by hearsay—and few know them any other way—will think they can declare at least some of the ideas of the poem. That usury is a vicious and desolating force in both public and private life; that it may be defined in such-and-such a way; that it has operated in recorded history after such-and-such a fashion; that international Jewry has played, and continues to play, such-and-such a crucial part in its operations; that Mussolini, unlike Roosevelt, had a grasp of what usury was and had a practicable plan for containing and disinfecting it—such, hearsay reports, are among the ideas which *The Cantos* incorporate, if indeed they are not the ideas which *The Cantos* were written to promote.

And yet these, it may be said, are not ideas at all, but opinions. For "opinions" read "convictions," and the case is not altered. . . . One may feel that in Pound's poem, when Roosevelt grapples with Mussolini, the bout is rigged; that one of the wrestlers is prevented from exerting his full strength; and accordingly that the fixity of the fixed opinion in favor of Mussolini lacks the vibrancy of the hard-earned fixities we esteem in other poems by other hands. (pp. 62-4)

What is crucial is that we should understand by "idea" in *The Cantos* the whole of [a] process of circling round and

throwing out. (An idea, we might say, is *thrown out*, whereas an opinion is *held by* or *held on to*.) The whole of this process, and indeed a little more; for [there is a] turning inside-out, [a] switch into [an] inverted spiral. . . . (p. 74)

What is fatal, though it is very common, is to regard the idea as having been stated in the initial proposition; and the verses which follow . . . as supplying no more than embroidery upon the idea, at best illustrations or elaborations of it. Read in that way, the *Cantos* are merely boring. They were found so by the late Yvor Winters, who, conceiving of an idea as that which could be stated in the form of a proposition, recorded his experience of reading *The Cantos* by saying, "We have no way of knowing whether we have had any ideas or not." Winters meant to be dismissive and disparaging; but in fact, if we take account of what he understood "idea" to be, Winters' remark is one of the few valuably exact formulations that we have, of what reading *The Cantos* amounts to, and feels like.

As we start to read *The Cantos*, we float out upon a sea where we must be on the lookout for waterspouts. These, when they occur, are ideas, the only sort that this poem is going to give us. And meanwhile we can forget about such much-debated nonquestions as whether this poem has a structure, and if so, what it is: or again, why the poem isn't finished, and whether it ever could have been. Does a sea have a *structure*? Does a sea *finish* anywhere? (pp. 74-5)

Though the *Cantos* are "epic," rather few of them display "the surge and sway of the epic music." (Canto I displays it, as does [part of] Canto 47; and so we respond to these without much trouble.) For the most part the rhythms of the *Cantos* . . . are the sung rhythms of Burns, not the intoned or chanted rhythms of Swinburne.

And so the verse lines of the *Cantos* have to be read *fast* for their meanings, but *slow* for their sounds. It is a miracle that they find any responsive readers at all. . . . (pp. 92-3)

In English there is no other poet of the twentieth century, and few of any century, with an ear fine enough to have managed [progressions as Pound has]. And in demonstrating it we've taken note only of those principles which our notation can register. The haunting musicality depends equally on other principles at work, which we detect at work but have no way of registering. (p. 98)

To Pound it seemed, as it has to others, that in Protestant cultures it was the Hebraic component which instilled fear and distrust of sensuous pleasure; and so he threw his weight always on the side of the Hellenic voice which called on sculptors to make images of the gods, as against the Hebraic iconoclasm which was set against "graven images." (p. 101)

[Poetry] composed so as to be spoken aloud, or to be chanted or sung to a suitably scrupulous accompaniment, *does* address itself directly to one of the senses. It addresses itself directly to the ear, by creating discernible and pleasurable audible rhythms. And this, as one might expect, is a dimension of literature with which Pound concerned himself very assiduously throughout his career. . . . Nothing marks Pound off so sharply from the avant-garde of the past thirty years, which tries to sail under his colors; for this avant-garde, if it does not explicitly abandon audible rhythms in poetry as a traditional indulgence which it will no longer tolerate, concerns itself with them not at all so as to give pleasure to reader or auditor but on the contrary only so as to stay purportedly more true to the mood, and the sensitive or even physical constitution, of the poet. It was not thus, nor on those grounds, that Pound declared: "To break the pentameter, that was the first heave." . . . [It] was because Pound knew himself capable of creating for his reader rhythmical pleasures which the expectation of the pentameter prevented both him and his reader from realizing. Many critics who would deny to Pound any other achievement have allowed him at least this one—that he had "an ear," that he truly could command a range of audible rhythms which only a liberation from the authority of the pentameter permitted him first, and his reader afterward, to recognize, positively *to hear.* (pp. 101-02)

> *Donald Davie, in his* Ezra Pound *(copyright © 1975 by Donald Davie; all rights reserved; reprinted by permission of Viking Penguin Inc.),* Viking Penguin, 1976.

JOHN BERRYMAN

The reader who is not a student of poetry has [a] ground for indifference [towards Pound]. Pound, he has always heard, has no "*matter.*" Granting the "importance" of his verse, granting the possibility that having been for poets fertile it might prove on acquaintance agreeable or beautiful, what has he to do with this sport, a matterless poetry? . . . "I confess," Eliot once wrote, "that I am seldom interested in what he is saying, but only in the way he says it"; and R. P. Blackmur, "He is all surface and articulation." We notice Eliot's qualification ("seldom") and we are puzzled by an ambiguity in Blackmur's "articulation" (is this jointing or merely uttering?); but on the whole they put authoritatively the established view. Now there can be no question of traversing such authorities directly. But it is a violent and remarkable charge; I think we are bound to look into it a little. (p. 256)

Pound's poetry treats of Provence, China, Rome, London, medieval living, modern living, human relationships, authors, young women, animals, money, games, government, war, poetry, love, and other things. This can be verified. What the critics must mean, then, is that they are aware of a *defect,* or defects, in the substance of the poetry. About one defect they have been explicit: the want of originality of substance. Pound has no matter *of his own.* Pound—who is even in the most surprising quarters conceded to be a "great" translator—is best as a translator. . . . I do not feel sure that time is bearing out . . . [this] judgment; the finest sections of Pound's postwar farewell to London, where the grotesquerie of Tristan Corbière is a new element in the complex style, naïve and wily, in which he celebrates the modern poet's difficulties and nostalgia, seem to me somewhat more brilliant, solid, and independent than the finest sections of the Roman poem [*Propertius*]. (p. 258)

Does any reader who is familiar with Pound's poetry really not see that its subject is the life of the modern poet? (p. 260)

It is everywhere (as well as in the Chinese work) in the more "original" poems and epigrams of *Lustra,* written 1913-16. (A lustrum is "an offering for the sins of the whole people, made by the censors at the expiration of their five years of office." It has not perhaps been sufficiently observed that Pound is one of the wittiest poets who ever wrote. Yet he is serious enough in this title. In certain

attitudes—his medieval nostalgia, literary anti-Semitism, others—he a good deal resembles Henry Adams; each spent his life, as it were, seeking an official post where he could be used, and their failure to find one produced both the freedom and the inconsequence that charm and annoy us in these authors.) (p. 261)

[Certain] themes in the life of the modern poet [are] indecision-decision and infidelity-fidelity. Pound has written much more love poetry than is generally realized, and when fidelity and decision lock in his imagination, we hear extraordinary effects, passionate, solemn. . . . If Pound is neither the poet apostrophized here nor the poet apostrophizing, not Milton or Wordsworth, his place will be high enough. These themes of decision and fidelity bear on much besides love in his poetry, and even—as one would expect with a subject of the poet-in-exile (Ovid, Dante, Villon, Browning, Henry James, Joyce, Pound, Eliot, as Mann, Brecht, Auden) whose allegiance is to an ideal state—upon politics:

> homage, fealty are to the person
> can not be to body politic . . .

Of course there are other themes, strong and weak, and multiplicity of topics, analogies to the life of the modern poet, with or without metaphor the *interests* of the poet. But this would appear to characterize any poet's work. I mean more definitely "Life and Contacts," as the subtitle of *Hugh Selwyn Mauberley* has it.

It is not quite Ezra Pound himself. . . . Pound is his own subject *qua* modern poet; it is the experience and fate of this writer "born / In a half savage country, out of date," a voluntary exile for over thirty years, that concern him. Another distinction is necessary. Wallace Stevens has presented us in recent years with a series of strange prose documents about "imagination" and "reality." If Stevens's poetry has for substance imagination, Pound's has for substance reality. A poem like "Villanelle: the Psychological Hour" . . . could have been made only by Pound, and the habit of mind involved has given us much truth that we could not otherwise have had. . . . The "distance" everywhere felt in the finest verse that treats his subject directly has, I think, two powerful sources, apart from the usual ones (versification and so on). First, there is the peculiar detachment of interest with which Pound seems to regard himself; no writer could be less revelatory of his passional life, and his friends have recorded—Dr Williams with annoyance—the same lifelong reticence in private. Second, his unfaltering, encyclopedic mastery of tone —a mastery that compensates for a comparative weakness of syntax. . . . Behind this mastery lies his ear. I scarcely know what to say of Pound's ear. Fifteen years of listening have not taught me that it is inferior to the ear of the author of *Twelfth Night.* The reader who heard the damage done, in my variation, to Pound's line—*So old Elkin had only one glory*—will be able to form his own opinion.

We write verse . . . with our ears, so this is important. Forming, animating, quelling his material, that ear is one of the main, weird facts of modern verse. It imposes upon the piteous stuff of the *Pisan Cantos* a "distance" as absolute as upon the dismissal of the epigram just cited. The poet has listened to his life, so to speak, and he tells us that which he hears.

Both the personality-as-subject and the expressive personality are nearly uniform, I think, once they have developed. In Yeats, in Eliot, we attend to re-formations of personality. Not really in Pound; he is unregenerate. "*Toutes mes pièces datent de quinze ans*," he quoted once with approval from a friend, and the contrast he draws between the life of the poet as it ought to be (or has been) and as it is, this contrast is perennial. But if this account of the poet's subject is correct, what can have concealed it from most even sympathetic and perceptive critics and readers? (pp. 262-64)

The reader is in one way more nearly right than the majority of critics. He is baffled by a heterogeneity of matter . . . , but he hears a personality in Pound's poetry. In fact, his hostility . . . is based upon this. The trouble is that he hears the personality he expected to hear, rather than the one that is essentially there. He hears Pound's well-known prose personality, bellicose, programmatic, positive, and he resents it. Pound is partly responsible. This personality does exist in him, it is what he has lived with, and he can even write poetry with it, as we see in "Sestina: Altaforte" and elsewhere early and late. A follower of Browning, he takes a keenly *active* view of poetry, and has, conceivably, a most imperfect idea both of just what his subject is and of what his expressive personality is like.

This personality is feline, supra-delicate, absorbed. If Browning made the fastest verse in English, Pound makes the slowest, the most discrete and suave. . . . There is restlessness; but the art of the poet places itself, above all, immediately and mysteriously at the service of the passive and elegiac, the nostalgic. The true ascendancy of this personality over the other is suggested by a singular fact: the degree in which the mantic character is absent from his poetry. He looks ahead indeed, looks ahead eagerly, but he does not *feel* ahead; he feels back. (p. 265)

The *Cantos* seem to be a metaphor. . . . I believe the critical view is that it is a "rag-bag" of the poet's interests, "a catalogue, his jewels of conversation." It can be read with delight and endless profit thus, if at any rate one understands that it is a work of versification, that is, a poem. The basal rhythm I hear is dactylic, as in the Swinburne and Ouang Chi passages and in the opening line, "And then went down to the ship,"—in this line we see the familiar tendency of English dactyls to resolve themselves into anapests with anacrusis, but the ambiguity seems to me to be progressively avoided as the poem advances. But the ragbag view depends for support upon lines that Pound cut out of the primitive printed versions of the earliest cantos; the form greatly developed, the form *for the subject*. For a ragbag, the poem sets out very oddly. (p. 266)

[The] interpenetration of life and art, in metaphor, is one of the poem's triumphs, a Coleridgean "fusing." (p. 267)

Reviewers of the *Pisan Cantos* have showed surprise that they were so "personal," and yet very fine,—it is the most brilliant sequence indeed since the original thirty. The *Cantos* have always been personal; only the persona increasingly adopted, as the Poet's fate clarifies, is Pound himself. The heterogeneity of material . . . seems to have three causes. The illusion of Pound's romanticism ("—if romanticism indeed be an illusion!" he exclaims in *Indiscretions*) has given him an inordinate passion for ages and places where the Poet's situation appears attractive, as in the Malatesta cantos, where Sigismondo is patron as much as ruler and lover . . . , and the Chinese cantos . . . ; here he is

sometimes wonderful but sometimes ungovernable. Then he is anxious to find out *what has gone wrong,* with money and government, that has produced our situation for the Poet; several of the money cantos . . . are brilliant, but most of the American historical cantos . . . are willed, numb, angry—the personae Jefferson and John Adams are not felt and so the material is uncontrolled. The rest of his heterogeneity is due to an immoderate desire, strong in some other modern artists also, for mere conservation—

> And lest it pass with the day's news
> Thrown out with the daily paper. . . .

Once the form, and these qualifications, are understood, Pound's work presents less difficulty than we are used to in ambitious modern poetry. Pieces like "A Song for the Degrees" (an anti-Psalm) and "Papyrus" (a joke, for that matter, a clear and good one) are rare. Occasionally you have to look things up if you don't wish to be puzzled; and it does no harm to use the index volume of Britannica 11th, and various dictionaries, and to be familiar with Pound's prose, when you read the *Cantos;* the labour is similar to that necessary for a serious understanding of *Ulysses,* and meditation is the core of it. To find out what a modern poet has done, we have often to ask *why* he did it.

The poet's own statements must be accepted with a certain reserve, which neither his admirers nor his detractors have always exercised. Thus the *Cantos* are said to be written in an equivalent for ideogram. We have recognized their relation to parts of Fenollosa. But Fenollosa's technical center is an attack on the copula; I observe that four of the lines about Ouang Chi successively employ the copula without loss to characteristic beauty, and I reason that we must inquire into these things for ourselves. More interesting, far, are the equivalents for musical form, and the versification. So with Pound's remark that the *Cantos* are "the tale of the tribe"; they seem to be only apparently a historical or philosophical epic, actually a personal epic—as he seems to understand himself elsewhere in *Culture* when he suggests that the work may show . . . the "defects inherent in a record of struggle." Pound, too, may really, like his critics, regard the work nearly plotless and heroless. . . . The Hell allusions in the first half of the work, with the allusions to Heaven in recent cantos, . . . strongly imply a major form. But all present discussion must be tentative. I have the impression that Pound allowed, in whatever his plan exactly is (if it exactly is, and if it is one plan), for the drift-of-life, the interference of fate, inevitable in a period of violent change; that this may give us something wholly unpredictable in the cantos to come, as it has given us already the marvellous pages of the *Pisan Cantos.* . . . It would be interesting, if the *Cantos* were complete, to compare the work with another poem, not more original in conception, exhibiting, if a smaller range of material and technical variety, greater steadiness, a similar substance, and a similar comprehensive mastery of expression, *The Prelude;* but the argument of my very limited essay is ended. Let us listen to this music. (pp. 267-69)

John Berryman, "The Poetry of Ezra Pound," in his The Freedom of the Poet *(reprinted with the permission of Farrar, Straus & Giroux, Inc.; copyright © 1949, 1960 by John Berryman; copyright © 1976 by Kate Berryman; renewed copyright © 1976 by Kate Berryman), Farrar, Straus, 1976, pp. 253-69.*

VINCENT MILLER

Joyce's and Eliot's concern for time certainly needs no emphasis. Everyone has spoken of it. But Pound's concern is probably less widely realized. And this despite the fact that his critics have written significantly about its importance. It is perhaps best, then, to begin with two of the finest of these, with Daniel Pearlman, who has stated Pound's interest strongly ("The *Cantos,* as I read the poem, is precisely an elaboration of this thesis—that the central problems in all spheres of human involvement must be referred ultimately to a consideration of the nature of time."—*The Barb of Time,* 1969), and with George Dekker, who finds in Pound's changing attitude toward "the tyranny of place and time" the *Cantos'* "formal principle of development" (*Sailing after Knowledge,* 1963).

These two critics must be consulted in detail by everyone interested in Pound's work. I refer to them primarily to single out a major point they both stress: that Pound found significance implicit in the very heart of this world and not in some ideal world set over against this one. This fact seems so important to Pearlman that he suggests a word for the view: "holism." And Dekker, who speaks of Pound's near pagan attachment to this world in many places, uses at one point a very enlightening metaphor. Speaking of the famous "Envoi" to the first section of *Hugh Selwyn Mauberley,* he says that in it timeless beauty suddenly breaks through that otherwise time-saturated poem "like Botticelli's Venus emerging from the flux of the sea." (pp. 194-95)

As George Dekker has said, the *Cantos* may be "the last great unqualified affirmation in English poetry of fertility and procreation—of the life force expressing itself through both man and nature, and, as such, harmonizing their wills." Thus the passage . . . from the celebration of fertility rites in Canto 47 is a very important one, central to the *Cantos* as a whole, as [many critics] have insisted. (p. 199)

Canto 47 is pagan. It celebrates life and death as aspects of one another. And it is in that pagan sense of unity that we approach what John Espey . . . and George Dekker have both called the Canto's "bedrock." . . . For Pound by the time he wrote Canto 47 there was no denying time's beauty or its most physical law, or their essential oneness:

> By this gate art thou measured
> Thy day is between a door and a door. . . .
> Thus was it in time.
>
> (p. 201)

In Canto 47 no final division can be made between those who experience the greatest fire and those who see the greatest light. The passage quoted above goes on immediately with [the lines central to the *Cantos* as a whole]:

> Hast thou found a nest softer than Cunnus
> Or hast thou found better rest
> Hast'ou a deeper planting, doth thy death year
> Bring swifter shoot?
> Hast thou entered more deeply the mountain?
>
> The light has entered the cave. Io! Io!
> The light has gone down into the cave,
> Splendour on splendour!
> By prong have I entered these hills. . . .

The interpenetration of the light and the fire to be observed here was crucially important to Pound, for it let him avoid a Western dichotomy he's been caught in. It helped him, that

is to say, to avoid an unbalanced emphasis upon either the light or the fire which he'd been led into one way with the troubadours (with their "lordship over the senses") and in another with Propertius (whose view [in *Homage*], as he clearly saw, was a lot more fire than light). But Canto 47 unified Pound's world only at a cost. A feeling for life based on pagan fertility rites and tied to the repeating cycles of the seasons could carry him just so far. He lived in a civilization whose defining characteristic was that it conceived of itself as moving through time in a linear and not a cyclical fashion; and a linear society's basic concern is that it sees itself involved in an ongoing course of things which asks more than the cyclical renewal of life as such. Neither sex nor fertility is in itself enough here for neither can give meaning to the wide range of individual and racial potentiality, or to the crucial problem of the individual's importance as an individual, which a linear view of time brings with it. (pp. 202-03)

[The] kind of awareness he found in [the troubadours] was of a highly esoteric order. They split his world in two: the fire of passion on the one hand, and on the other the light of an awareness that went so far beyond its Eleusinian base that the initial passion could only be seen as "an intellectual instigation" to the subsequent, highly refined intellectuality. As a result he had actually decided as early as 1917 that the troubadour way was fine for some but not widely applicable. As he wrote John Quinn in a letter I'll come to shortly, Provençe was "a special interest." It was China that was "fundamental."

What Pound found in China that he thought of use was of course the Chinese ideogram and Confucius. And what he found in both of these was that a single, evolving process flows through all things, even time itself. . . . [This process] does not lead away from the physical world or merely circle about within it. The process is infinitely perfectible, for the individual and the race. But it leads as it does only because desire and perception are clarified and perfected only by their mutual interaction in a continued, ever evolving relationship with the ongoing act of living in time. For Pound, the passage below and its ideogram became central to all he believed:

> This is the first chapter of the comment giving the gist (sorting out the grist) of the expressions: Make clear the intelligence by looking straight into the heart and then acting. Clarify the intelligence in straight action.

Pound had found what he wanted. And as a poet bent on writing an epic of man's achievement, he badly needed what he had found. For there just isn't any major Western philosophy or movement founded on the belief that a single process unites all things. . . . Pound's gloss upon the ideogram given with the passage above is therefore an important one:

> The sun and moon, the total light process, the radiation, reception and reflection of light; hence, the intelligence. Bright, brightness, shining. Refer to Scotus Erigena, Grosseteste and the notes on light in my *Cavalcanti.*

This passage shows us Pound's belief that what he found in Confucius echoed what he had found in the troubadours, in the medieval light philosophers, and in Dante and Caval-canti, thus bringing the West and East into relationship. And it did. But if the gloss seems to imply also that what Pound found in Confucius was not in any important way different, the gloss is misleading. For the difference is marked. First, though less important, Confucius was no mystic. He was indeed the most prosaic of philosophers, and his interest in the way a single light shines through all things was tied at every point to the everyday world. He therefore helped Pound about 1917—as did Propertius—to escape from the more neo-Platonic and cultish emphases that Pound had found in the troubadours about 1912 and at that time shared with them. (pp. 204-05)

But much more important, Confucius's concept of a single process uniting all orders of human activity gave Pound a way of grounding his thought in the process of nature which enabled him finally to escape from the typically Western separation of the enlightened spirit from the enlightening flesh which he had been forced to accept in one way with the troubadours and in another with Propertius, and to go on from the basic but limited way he had found the two at one in the fertility rites he celebrated in Canto 47. What Confucius taught Pound, then, was how to build a high civilization on the fact that (note the singular) "the celestial and earthly process pervades and is substantial; it is on high and gives light, it comprehends the light and is lucent, it extends without bounds and endures." (p. 205)

[In] the cantos Pound wrote in the late 'thirties, . . . he stopped—in George Dekker's phrase—"jumping about from epoch to epoch" and turned to writing of particular civilizations existing in fixed times and places, seeking to find in the prosaic facts of their histories "no end to the action" of the tensile light.

These two sets of cantos (the long history of China according to Confucian views and the "Confucian digest" of Charles Francis Adams's edition of his grandfather's works) are the longest and most "fact-ridden" in Pound's poem. In them Pound was putting his thesis to the test. For most critics the result is his least successful work. But writing these cantos on the eve of the Second World War Pound himself believed he had found his Tao. He had submitted to time and found its radiance. He was of course about to taste of a bitterness he could not have foreseen, a failure to succeed in time that was to cause him to deepen and revalue the view of the oneness of the celestial and earthly process (and of the unity of the sincere man with that process) which he had been working to clarify since he began to revise the first draft of his *Cantos* sometime after 1917. The *Pisan Cantos* initiate that deepening and revaluation: *Rock-Drill, Thrones,* and the final *Drafts and Fragments* carry it through to the *Cantos'* final lines:

> I have tried to write Paradise
> Do not move
>   Let the wind speak
>   that is paradise.
> Let the Gods forgive what I
>   have made
> Let those I love try to forgive
>   what I have made.

(pp. 207-08)

Vincent Miller, "Pound's Battle with Time," in The Yale Review (© *1976 by Yale University; reprinted by permission of the editors), Winter, 1977, pp. 193-208.*

*   *   *

PRICE, (Edward) Reynolds   1933-

Price, a southern American author of short stories, novels, essays, and poems, resists the inevitable comparisons with Faulkner, pointing out that southern writers may seem similar because they experienced a similar oral narrative tradition as well as a similar environment. Concerning that environment, Price comments that "complaining about its narrowness is like complaining that all the great Victorian novels were about England." (See also *CLC*, **Vols. 3, 6, and** *Contemporary Authors*, **Vols. 1-4, rev. ed.)**

ANNE HOBSON FREEMAN

When a work of fiction as compelling and original as [*The Surface of the Earth*] comes along, it deserves evaluation in its own terms. Why should the reader worry if, in its relatively straight forward narrative, its rich, rhythmical and rather formal language and its brooding obsession with family as a kind of fate which a child must come to terms with before he can be free "to walk clean away into his own life," it seems to be out of step with the march of most contemporary fiction?

More important is the fact that it meets what seems to me the supreme test of a novel: it manages to recreate a world and people it with characters as complex and stubbornly mysterious as those in life, and it draws the reader into that world—sensually, emotionally and intellectually—to the point that he experiences those lives and earns whatever insights may be gained from them.

In this, his longest and most ambitious novel, which took ten years of planning and three years of writing, Reynolds Price focuses on the harm that parents do, through the flawed choices, emotional failures and unsatisfied hungers they pass on to their children unto the third and fourth generation. (p. 637)

[A] curious deafness to the din of the world outside the family may be partially explained by the fact that Mr. Price presents his characters to us during periods of emotional crisis when they are forced to make, in minutes, choices that they and their children will spend decades, even lifetimes, living out. (p. 638)

Despite the book's length and what begins to seem toward the end a plethora of explanations and confessions from the characters themselves, the narrative remains, on the whole, surprisingly succinct, displaying Mr. Price's gift for catching whole landscapes in a few images, whole characters in a few telling gestures or fragments of talk. And what a luxury it is to be immersed in his majestic prose.

There is, however, a static quality to the novel as fragments of human experience are seized and held for microscopic observation, then analyzed at length from shifting points of view in dreams, in letters and in endless talk. This quality is suggested in the Blake-like image which the author has designed for the jacket of the book—a fixed sun face gazing with an intensity that threatens to burn through surfaces to the mysteries beneath them.

Admittedly, only a small patch of the surface of earth is under scrutiny here, . . . [but] this small area is evoked with such authority and examined so relentlessly that the reader feels, at times, perilously close to penetrating to that core which one character defines as "the heart of the world . . . the precious meaning of life and pain." (pp. 638-39)

Although this powerful novel seems in the end to be over-weighted with wordy explanations of the emotional demands, debts and failures that constrict the Mayfields' and the Kendalls' lives, it represents a leap forward by a gifted novelist into visionary territory which few of his contemporaries have the courage to explore, territory which, if conquered, can yield the hard-won wisdom of the human heart. (p. 641)

> *Anne Hobson Freeman, "Penetrating a Small Patch of the Surface of Earth," in* Virginia Quarterly Review *(copyright, 1975, by the* Virginia Quarterly Review, *The University of Virginia), Vol. 51, No. 4 (Autumn, 1975), pp. 637-41.*

WALTER SULLIVAN

[In *The Surface of the Earth*] Price works with a heavy hand. In almost every word he insists on his seriousness, the significance of the events as they unfold; and as if to underline the images that he wishes us to grasp, he repeats himself again and again through the course of the novel.

Miscegenation is rampant [in this forty-year chronicle of two families]. Children of mixed blood are born, one of whom, the son of a Mayfield, becomes a major character in the novel. Older generations interfere in the lives of the young; misunderstandings accrue; marriages are disrupted. . . . The men are weak, unreliable; the women are strong. Events, characters, gestures—males lying down on top of other males, not in sexual irregularity, but in mystic farewell—lead finally to a similarity of voice, a stylistic monotony that for a quarter of a million words is unrelieved. All the characters think in the same phrases, write the same letters, use the same diction when they speak.

I would suggest two things that have gone wrong in this novel. First, it appears to be a totally cerebral performance. One never gets the feeling that Price turned a corner and found a surprise, that events ever moved in a way he had not expected, or that the characters ever took over the dialogue and found their own words. Whatever the actual case may have been, the action has all the earmarks of having been given its final dimensions according to a procrustean plan. Second, I think Price has been injured by his determination to be southern above all else. I want to linger over this point only long enough to say that the southernness is studied and therefore stilted. The South Price writes about is not the South of his experience but the South he has learned about in books. Even in his rendition of the society he has drawn from a literary blueprint; he does not quite play straight. One of the reasons we do not believe in Grainger and Forrest and Rob and the others is that they are not really southerners of the first half of this century. Instead they are anachronisms, people enlightened by the later views and opinions of Reynolds Price. He has made them as he wishes they might have been, their morals reconstructed to suit the prejudices of the present, their social consciousness sharpened to fit a later time. This is romanticism in its destructive manifestation. (pp. 118-19)

> *Walter Sullivan, in* Sewanee Review *(reprinted by permission of the editor; © 1976 by The University of the South), Winter, 1977.*

JAY L. HALIO

The Surface of the Earth is a grim, Faulknerian story of three generations of middle-class southerners. . . . Covering a span of forty years and told largely through long letters or stylized speeches (sermons or lectures), the novel makes its stolid point: "People get what they need if they stand still and wait till the earth sends it up. . . . What they need, not want." This is the sum of Rob Mayfield's wisdom. . . . (p. 842)

The ideal is modest enough, as Rob describes it: "an ordinary home containing no more than an ordinary home. A decent grown man with clean work to push against ten hours a day that would leave him with the strength to come back at dark in courtesy and patience to the people who had waited—a woman he had chosen for their mutual want (who went on wanting and receiving as he did: courteous, patient) and the child they had made. . . ." Being so modest, why is it then so difficult to achieve? None of the characters in the book, for all of their articulateness and insight, attains the goal fully or for very long. The most they get is a little temporary easing of their pain or hunger, although several, like Rob's father, finally succeed with something stable but much more modest. . . . He attains what he does because he has at last learned to stand still and watch till the earth sends up what he needs, not wants. But most of the others either care or want too much, press for it, and lose. (p. 843)

> *Jay L. Halio, in* The Southern Review *(copyright, 1977, by Jay L. Halio), Vol. XIII, No. 4, Autumn, 1977.*

ANTHONY BURGESS

Reynolds Price is a considerable prose writer. "A Palpable God" must be taken as a serious testimony to a virtue rare among contemporary producers of fiction—the compulsion to examine at intervals the rationale of his craft. All we novelists forget too often that our job is not to spin words to the greater glory of the complex, book-drenched, allusion-loving, ambiguity-adoring civilized sensibility, but to tell tales. The telling of a plain tale is, however, as hard for the contemporary writer as plowing with a plank and a nail would be to the contemporary agricultural operative. Sometimes we have to get back to see how the ancients did it, and Mr. Price's mode of self-refreshment has been to examine the Bible. (p. 14)

[The 19th-century Roman poet Giuseppe] Belli, refreshing the dialect of the Roman streets through contact with the Bible, was, in his own way, on a quest that is perennial among writers. We have to get back to the beginning again, startle the dullness of our everyday language with a swipe from the exotic, and remember that "a need to tell and hear stories is essential to the species *Homo sapiens*—second in necessity apparently after nourishment and before love and shelter." That comes from Mr. Price's long introductory essay, which from now on must be required reading in creative-writing courses. (p. 22)

> *Anthony Burgess, in* The New York Times Book Review *(© 1978 by The New York Times Company; reprinted by permission), March 12, 1978.*

[*A Palpable God*] is a curious book. Reynolds Price begins with an interesting study of the origins of human narrative and concludes that the Bible offers us "a chance unique in our civilization for observing the rise and recording of primal sacred tales in close proximity to the events which generated them." Attempting to give the modern reader the same feeling of immediacy and freshness that the ancient listener experienced in the telling of these stories, Price then proceeds to translate thirty Biblical stories which he believes show "the core of sacred story—God's appearances to man, His withdrawals from him: presences and absences, our deepest hope and terror." All this is admirable and not uninteresting or untrue. But the key to the book —Price's translation and the Biblical excerpts chosen— doesn't really impress as fresh, strikingly different or particularly meaningful—results that would justify the big buildup. And, in the end, you might be forced to conclude that the book may be more rewarding for the writer than for the reader. (p. 91)

> The Critic (© The Critic 1978; reprinted with the permission of the Thomas More Association, Chicago, Illinois), Summer, 1978.

* * *

PRITCHETT, V(ictor) S(awden) 1900-

Pritchett is a British novelist, short story writer, literary critic, travel writer, autobiographer, and man of letters. In his beautifully written prose, Pritchett exhibits a Dickensian eye for detail and a fine sense of humor. Walter Allen, noting Pritchett's "unerring instinct for idiosyncrasy that reveals character," calls him "the complete master" of the short story form. (See also *CLC*, Vol. 5, and *Contemporary Authors*, Vols. 61-64.)

WALTER SULLIVAN

[V. S. Pritchett] . . . has been writing good short stories for many years. He is . . . no longer at the top of his form, but the leading story in *The Camberwell Beauty* is quite equal to work he did in his prime. One of Pritchett's great advantages as a writer—and one which is becoming rarer as our cultures become more fragmented—is his ability to create a variety of backgrounds: he is not tied, as so many writers are, to a single and usually restricted world. "The Camberwell Beauty" takes place among antique dealers, the best imaginable milieu for the development of its Jamesian theme. Pritchett convinces us that dealers are collectors before they are businessmen: each has his specialty, porcelain or silver or rare miniatures: buying and selling furniture is simply a means toward an avaricious end. The Camberwell Beauty is a girl, loved by a young man who wishes to marry her, but she is collected as an object, first by a disreputable dealer named August and later by the richer and more respectable Pliny, who never touches her sexually though she becomes his wife.

To put the story in such blunt terms is to rob it of its beauty but at the same time to demonstrate the dependence of the characters and the plot on the skill with which Pritchett makes his enclave of collectors come to life. Other stories in the volume have equally convincing backgrounds, but there is never quite the same perfect marriage of setting to myth. (pp. 540-41)

> Walter Sullivan, in Sewanee Review (reprinted by permission of the editor; © 1975 by The University of the South), Summer, 1975.

B. L. REID

V. S. Pritchett's first volume [of reminiscences] *A Cab at the Door*, takes its title from the family's habit of moving lodgings after each new failed enterprise: "A cabby and his horse would be coughing together outside the house and the next thing we knew we were driving to an underground station and to a new house in a new part of London, to the smell of new paint, new mice dirts, new cupboards." (p. 263)

The rootlessness of the Pritchetts' London life, coupled with a native hostility to rote learning, made a shambles of Victor's formal education. (p. 265)

When he is not yet sixteen the lad is abruptly removed from school and sent to work as an office boy in "the leather trade" at a large factor's in Bermondsey. Here he remained for four years. It is characteristic of Pritchett's sane realism not to treat the long interval as a waste nor to recall it with condescension or self-pity. (p. 266)

Pritchett is very frank and funny about adolescent sexuality, which torments him unbearably throughout these years. (p. 267)

It is a long serious illness in the postwar influenza epidemic that finally separates him from the leather trade and frees him to leave England and his family. His fortune consists of twenty pounds—enough, his father estimates, to keep him in Paris for a month. . . . On the train to Paris he tastes wine for the first time and finds it vinegary; but he is "committed" to liking it. The little transitional experiences are to be taken as premonitory.

So ends *A Cab at the Door*, about which one's feelings have been locally powerful but confused in sum, suspended. It is an effect, one supposes, of Pritchett's own feelings about the quality of his life in childhood and youth. The dominant impression is that of a hectic busyness, humming, hivelike, without clear direction or clear lines of emphasis: evidently the life was like that. The book like the boy is dominated by the family, and the family is dominated by the schizoid father, a small man driven by a need to be big: vain, unrealistic, tyrannical, totally undependable. The cab appears at the door too many times. It is a life without order or delicacy, in a family where, as Pritchett put the case in his second volume, "manners were unknown, where everyone shouted, and no one had any notion of taste, either good or bad. We lived without it." Yet the life has style of its own peculiar kind: the hive, especially young Victor, buzzes with energy and talent that seeks a vent and a way to work. The hive of the family is set inside the larger hive of lower-middle-class London, likewise elbowing, raucous, deprived, making do. One watches Victor defining his own nature and painfully, with heaves and lurches, pulling it free.

Pritchett writes of these matters in a style that is admirable for the level of feeling he means to allow expression. His mode is direct, clear, energetic, undecorated, dry: a sharpshooter's or perhaps a sniper's language. The vision at work is attentive and retentive, deprecatory—especially of the self, amused but sardonic, not particularly forgiving. What it sees is a comedy but not a jolly one, an ironical comedy that encloses a lot of suffering—yet the suffering is underplayed, by no means exploited. The language, the vision, one is tempted to call heartless, but that would be both uncharitable and inaccurate. Pritchett's manner is not heartless, but it is remarkably cool: call it emotionally underspecified.

The thing that is missing in the narrative is important: love. The word, or even the idea, is rarely mentioned in *A Cab at the Door,* and almost never in association with the family or any member of it. Like taste, love appears to be a thing the Pritchetts "lived without." It is only in middle life, and then with the help of another's insight, that Pritchett comes at last to see, for example, that his absurd vainglorious father had been a man tortured with affection and anxiety for his children. No doubt it is partly English reticence in personal narrative that makes Pritchett so wary of emotional commitment in his autobiography. But the matter seems more personal and peculiar than that; and one feels that the tendency is not only an effect of style but a fact of life, something in the man.

By ordinary literary-critical standards Pritchett's second volume, *Midnight Oil,* is a denser, finer, more "valuable" book than his first. Its essential subject is vocation: V. S. Pritchett making a beginning as a writer, finding direction by a mixture of purpose, accident, and necessity, reaching an established position. In all senses it is a professional book. It is full of matter and of wisdom. Within its set limits, it is actually more open, freer, warmer in expressed emotion than *A Cab at the Door.* Especially in its unpretentious way of presenting the self and its wise and straight way of talking about the craft of writing, it is a very winning book and an instructive one. Yet in turning professional Pritchett has become curiously less interesting. Perversely one finds oneself missing the very thing that had got on one's nerves in the first volume: the remorseless herky-jerky tension of the domestic comedy-drama. Pritchett by himself, turning literary, finding success, is a less involving figure than Pritchett beating his wings frantically in the hive of the family. The second book lacks the hectic vitality of the first, and the gain in serenity does not altogether compensate. (pp. 267-69)

Midnight Oil begins in a touching, gravely humorous way, with V. S. Pritchett at seventy years contemplating two photographs of himself. One is contemporary and shows a bald aging man writing on a pastry board . . . ; the other shows the same man as a youth of twenty sitting on a table in Paris: he looks vague, shapeless, cocky, histrionic. Pritchett says it is the "embarrassment" he feels at that early image that forms the subject of his book. He is trying to make peace with that image, and to make sense of it: to understand, so to speak, how he got from there to here. He writes, as he puts the matter movingly, out of the general mystification of age and experience: "One is less and less sure of who one is"; and from the point of view of the cumulative anonymity, the evacuated persona of the artist: "The professional writer who spends his time becoming other people and places, real or imaginary, finds he has written his life away and has become almost nothing." (p. 270)

The comedy of *Midnight Oil* extends and matures that of *A Cab at the Door:* it is gayer, more affirmative, less embarrassed and wounded. (p. 273)

The main impressions a reader takes away from his two volumes are those of courage, vitality, clarity, reserve. Those are properties of both subject and style; one need not labor to document them: they are audible everywhere in the

language. Both subject and style, furthermore, are properties of temperament. One is impressed both by what is there and by what is left out. Pritchett strikes me as a very tough and intelligent man who survived a long deep wounding. The wound and the bow: he has been to hell and come back to tell about it—up to a point. In his first thirty years Pritchett took on a great deal of scar tissue, and I suspect he chose to treat it as a protective second skin. (pp. 283-84)

[Few] writers can have been so utterly self-made. Pritchett learned to write by reading and writing. No master, no old boys, pulled him along. The whole process, in life and art, left him tight-lipped—in art: that we do not really learn how he is in life is precisely the problem. Pritchett's reticence is English but it is also profoundly personal, exceptional even for an Englishman. It strikes me not as stoicism but as a strongly developed instinct for privacy, not less prickly for being unstated. We hear, unstated, a gritty murmur: "Certain things are none of your damned business."

Revolted by the vanity and self-pity that make so much of current fiction, poetry, and even criticism unreadable, one is embarrassed to complain of reticence when it occurs. But the "laconic," the "definite," so rare and ordinarily so admirable, can turn into a dangerous virtue when the subject, inescapably, is the self. We don't need any more egos but we can use any number of lives, if they have been useful ones, like Pritchett's, and if we are allowed far enough inside to understand the working of motive and feeling. Pritchett does not allow us very far inside. His very reticence, when frankly applied to a permitted moment of emotion, such as the death of his mother, can create a stunning little point-blank effect: "She lay, a tiny figure, so white and frail that she looked no more than a cobweb. I stood there hard and unable to weep. Tears come to me only at the transition from unhappiness to happiness; now I was frozen at the thought of her life. She had been through so much and I had been so outside it." It bothers one, however, that the effect is in a significant degree an effect of style, a triumph of withheld climax allowed to shock an established reserve, taking much of its power from its rarity.

I do not think Pritchett is hostile or immune to strong feeling; but it is hard to be sure, and that is exactly the difficulty I have with the matter. Late in *Midnight Oil* he remarks almost in passing: "It is pretty certain that the effect of the violent quarrels in my childhood home was to close my heart for a long time." Perhaps these and other traumas in the hardship of his life really did freeze Pritchett's heart. I do not think so; I think his heart simply got so sore that he did not want to talk about it; but I do not know, and my uncertainty makes me uncomfortable. In another of his dense little throwaway lines he speaks of "the supreme pleasure of putting oneself in by leaving oneself out." One knows what he means, and honors it; but in autobiography it does make a problem. Pritchett trusts us too far to find the self in the understatement and the withholding. We come to know a personality but not really a whole person. I prefer Frank O'Connor's way of letting his heart hang out, so long as he does not caress it too much—as he does not.

None of this makes me think Pritchett's books less than superb. Nobody in years has talked so clearly and wisely about the craft of writing and what might be called the moral psychology of the writer. What he does choose to give us of his life is so rich in texture and so sharp in specification that we are glad to forgive him a willed reservation. (pp. 284-85)

*B. L. Reid, "Putting in the Self: V. S. Pritchett,"
in* Sewanee Review *(reprinted by permission of
the editor;* © *1977 by The University of the
South), Spring, 1977, pp. 262-85.*

IRVING HOWE

[In "The Gentle Barbarian"] V. S. Pritchett evokes the
characteristic Turgenev novel—that story of unfulfilled
affections, political disappointments, human wrenchings.
Delicate, short-breathed critic with delicate, short-breathed
author: a happy match. Nothing in this book is "heavy,"
nothing analyzed into the dust of boredom, nothing
stretched on the wrack of literary theory. Mr. Pritchett has
written a work of cameo refinement, yielding pleasure from
start to finish. (p. 1)

Mr. Pritchett has written a frail, elegant, loving book. It
lacks the solidity of Isaiah Berlin's study of Turgenev's intellectual background, "Fathers and Children"; it does not
have the magisterial completeness of Joseph Frank's recent
biography of the young Dostoyevsky. But as we read this
book we quickly realize that we are in the presence of an
artist in criticism, a virtuoso of lucid evocation and precise
judgment. For some four decades V. S. Pritchett has been
giving us pleasure with such criticism, and everyone who
loves the word will want to send him a salute of gratitude.
(p. 39)

Irving Howe, "A Happy Match," in The New
York Times Book Review *(©️ 1977 by The New
York Times Company; reprinted by permission),
May 22, 1977, pp. 1, 39.*

MICHAEL IRWIN

For all the praise [Pritchett] has won, his work has never
been fashionable in academic circles, and it is interesting to
speculate why.

In several respects his manner of writing harks back to an
earlier period. He has probably long been wearied by respectful comparisons with Dickens or Wells; but he recalls
these writers repeatedly in the vivid precision of his appeal
to the eye and ear. Each of his major characters is distinctly
visualized. . . .

To the fastidious critic, there may be something unnerving
in Pritchett's very gusto. His characters are a dubious
bunch, notably deficient in the conventional brands of dignity. In fact, many of them are seedy, tipsy, sly, raffish, or
randy. Yet quite clearly their creator likes and relishes
them all with cheerful impartiality. He writes like a fre-
quenter of pubs and clubs who finds ordinary people of any
class or condition endlessly entertaining.

To read this collection [*Selected Stories*] is to be reminded
that many of our best contemporary short story writers are
characteristically glum. They excel in chronicling small defeats. . . . A typical story by V. S. Pritchett, however, celebrates a victory. His characters are survivors. Somehow,
against the odds, an unlovable person finds love, an old
loyalty is rekindled, lost self-respect is retrieved. This implicit optimism may not lend itself to exegesis, but it is far
from facile. The tentative victories that Pritchett records
are a tribute to a great variety of human qualities: resilience, jauntiness, nerve, inventiveness, cheek. His tales
make life seem worth living because they repeatedly show
how interesting, how various, how resourceful, the most
mundane people can be.

If there is a weakness in his approach it is that his taste for
gamey personalities and high jinks makes some of the stories too highly flavoured, a little overripe. In this collection
the rather more sober narratives, "The Wheelbarrow",
"Blind Love", "The Skeleton", and "The Spree", seem to
come off best. There is in general a tendency for the predominant zest and sharpness both in description and in dialogue to crowd out the more subdued passages which the
narrative needs: "It was always quiet up at Heading.
Through the trees by the house you could see the stars, and
the grey stone was lit by them. There was a smell of cows
and woodsmoke, and there was a touch of frost in the air."
The reader who has attuned his ear to the broader, more
vigorous effects of the tale may miss such interludes, and
with them part of the complexity that the author is striving
for. Altogether these stories need suppler, more sensitive
reading than they seem at first glance to invite.

My only other reservation relates to the several stories that
are told in the first person. The narrator, gifted with all V.
S. Pritchett's narrative skills, tends to be difficult to place.
This is particularly true of "The Camberwell Beauty", perhaps the least assured work in the collection, where the
style of the opening sentences, and the narrative context
that they imply, are simply abandoned. But these are cav-
ils. Here is a volume full of energy, shrewdness, and good
humour. If Pritchett's stories have been academically un-
dervalued it may be merely because they are so straightforwardly and unfashionably enjoyable.

Michael Irwin, "Tentatively Victorious," in The
Times Literary Supplement *(©️ Times Newspapers Ltd. (London) 1978; reproduced from* The
Times Literary Supplement *by permission), May
12, 1978, p. 517.*

EUDORA WELTY

[Any] Pritchett story is all of it alight and busy at once, like
a well-going fire. Wasteless and at the same time well fed, it
shoots up in flame from its own spark like a poem or a
magic trick, self-consuming, with nothing left over. He is
one of the great pleasure-givers in our language.

Pritchett himself has said that the short story is his greatest
love because he finds it challenging. The new collection
["Selected Stories"] makes it clear that neither the love nor
the challenge has let him down.

As ever, the writing spouts with energy. Dialogue, in constant exchange, frisks like a school of dolphin. These are
social stories: Life goes on in them without flagging. The
characters that fill them—erratic, unsure, unsafe, devious,
stubborn, restless and desirous, absurd and passionate, all
peculiar unto themselves—hold a claim on us that is not to
be denied. They demand and get our rapt attention, for in
their revelation of their lives, the secrets of our own lives
come into view. How much the eccentric has to tell us of
what is central!

Once more, in the present volume, the characters are everything. Through a character Pritchett can trace a frail
thread of chivalry in the throatcutting trade of antique col-
lecting. Through a character he finds a great deal of intrigue
in old age. The whole burden of "The Spree" is grief and
what his character is ever to do with it. Paradox comes naturally to Pritchett, and he has always preferred, and ex-
celled in, the oblique approach; and I think all these varying
stories in today's book are love stories. (p. 1)

Of these 14 stories—chosen from four volumes published over the last nine years—"The Diver" is not the only one here to suggest that, in times of necessity or crisis, a conspiracy may form among the deep desires of our lives to substitute for one another, to masquerade sometimes as one another, to support, to save one another. These stories seem to find that human desire is really a *family* of emotions, a whole interconnection—not just the patriarch and matriarch, but all the children. All kin, and none of them born to give up. If anything happens to cut one off, they go on surviving in one another's skins. They become something new. In fact, they become storytellers.

In "Blind Love," when Mr. Armitage employs Mrs. Johnson, two people have been brought together who have been afflicted beyond ordinary rescue. . . . After they reach and survive a nearly fatal crisis of ambiguous revelation, the only possible kind, we see them contentedly traveling in tandem. "She has always had a secret. It still pleases Armitage to baffle people." But they are matched now in "blind love": They depend on each other altogether.

"The Marvelous Girl" is a double portrait. One side is blind love, love in the dark. The obverse side is a failed marriage in clear view. . . .

We read these stories, comic or tragic, with an elation that stems from their intensity. In "When My Girl Comes Home" Pritchett establishes a mood of intensification that spreads far around and above it like a brooding cloud, far-reaching, not promising us to go away. We are with a family in England 10 years after the last World War as they face the return of a daughter, gone all this time, who is thought to be a prisoner of the enemy. . . .

In the shock of reunion, the whole family—several generations and their connections—sees appearing, bit by bit, the evidence that all of them have been marred, too, have been driven, are still being driven and still being changed by the same war. Alone and collectively, they have become calloused as Hilda has been. . . .

None of the stories is livelier than these new stories of Pritchett's written of old age. Old bachelor clubman George is militant, astringent, biting, fearsomely grinning, in training with his cold baths, embattled behind his fossilized anecdotes, victoriously keeping alive ("he got up every day to win"). . . . (p. 39)

What wins out over George is not the East wind or the Arch Enemy but the warm arms of a large, drinking, 40-year-old woman with a kind disposition and a giggle for his indignation, who "drops in" ("What manners!") out of his past that he had thought safely sealed behind anecdotes. She was the woman the old man had admired once "for being so complete an example of everything that made women impossible."

It is thus that he faces "the affronting fact that he had not after all succeeded in owning his own life and closing it to others; that he existed in other people's minds and that all people dissolved in this way, becoming fragments of one another, and nothing in themselves. . . . He knew, too, that he had once lived, or nearly lived."

Of all the stories of desiring, and of all the stories in this collection, "The Camberwell Beauty" is the most marvelous. It is a story of desiring and also of possessing—we are in a world of antique-shop keepers—and of possessing that survives beyond the death of desiring. (pp. 39-40)

The young man is left "with a horror of the trade I had joined." He abhors "the stored up lust that seemed to pass between things and men like Pliny." It is not long before "the fever of the trade had come alive in me: Pliny had got something I wanted." The end is unescapable—for all, that is, who are connected with the trade.

"The Camberwell Beauty" is an extraordinary piece of work. Densely complex and unnervingly beautiful in its evocation of those secret, packed rooms, it seems to shimmer with the gleam of its unreliable treasures. There is the strange device of the bugle—which, blown by Isabel, actually kills desire. All the while the story is filled with longing, it remains savage and seething and crass and gives off the unhidable smell of handled money.

Most extraordinarily of all, it expresses, not the confusion of one human desire with another, not sexuality confused with greed, but rather the culmination of these desires in their *fusion*. . . .

Each story's truth is distilled by Pritchett through a pure concentration of human character. It is the essence of his art. And, of course, in plain fact, and just as in a story, it is inherent in the human being to create his own situation, his own plot. The paradoxes, the strategems, the escapes, the entanglements, the humors and dreams, are all projections of the individual human being, all by himself alone. In its essence, Pritchett's work, so close to fantasy, is deeply true to life. (p. 40)

Eudora Welty, "A Family of Emotions," in The New York Times Book Review *(© 1978 by The New York Times Company; reprinted by permission), June 25, 1978, pp. 1, 39-40.*

SARAH PRATT

Pritchett notes his debt to . . . other scholars at the outset [of *The Gentle Barbarian: The Life and Work of Turgenev*]. But he also brings two crucial gifts of his own to the work. First, he shows an unusual ability to draw the reader back into a world distant both in time and in space without allowing that world to deaden into a literary museum: *The Gentle Barbarian* is not only the kind of portrait with eyes that follow the viewer around the room, but a portrait so effective that its subject becomes a living part of the viewer's consciousness. Secondly, Pritchett, a writer by profession, shows himself to be a master of English prose style. This combination of fine portraiture and verbal mastery makes the book a great pleasure to read.

Much of the power of the portrait stems from Pritchett's skill at filling in the outlines of Turgenev's life with conjecture while avoiding lapses into the hazardous realm of fictionalized biography. . . .

Judicious conjecture also marks the narration of Turgenev's relation to Pauline Viardot. While he works his way to the inevitable conclusion that one cannot know the physical bounds of the relationship (Viardot seemed to be happily married and Turgenev was generally on good terms with her husband), Pritchett offers a lively portrayal of its waxing and waning and demonstrates its pervasive influence (often negative) on Turgenev's creative life.

The book's generalizations about Russian literature occasionally spill into the realm of overstatement. For example, the assertion that Turgenev was a "founder and innovator" because "there was no established tradition of story telling or novel writing in Russian literature,'' or that ''Pushkin sought to replace French influence by the influence of German and English—by Goethe and Shakespeare,'' can be bombarded with counter arguments. But at the same time, the book's generalizations about Turgenev's work without reference to Russian literary history are often full of insight. . . . (p. 295)

On one hand, it seems unfortunate that *The Gentle Barbarian* lacks the scholarly apparatus of footnotes, or at least an index. Statements about important figures like George Sand, Tolstoy, Bakunin, Belinsky, and an interesting story about a relationship Turgenev is said to have had with the wife of the poet Tyutchev all remain in an area of limited use because one can neither verify the original source of the information nor locate the relevant passage again without thumbing through the whole book. But on the other hand, Pritchett's refusal to admit the added weight of such scholarly baggage may well be one of the factors that has allowed him to create such a thoroughly life-like and, in its own way, informative portrait. (p. 296)

> *Sarah Pratt, in* Modern Fiction Studies *(© copyright 1978 by Purdue Research Foundation, West Lafayette, Indiana), Summer, 1978.*

*   *   *

PYM, Barbara   1913-

Pym, an English novelist and editor, writes wry comedies of manners. Thought by many to be underrated, her novels of the 1950s are currently being revived, while her present work is considered a fine combination of wit and irony. (See also *Contemporary Authors,* **Vols. 13-14, and** *Contemporary Authors Permanent Series,* **Vol. 1.)**

A. L. ROWSE

[Barbara Pym possesses] the advantages of a subtle writer where everything is toned down as against the appalling crudity and obviousness, the outrageous barrage (with its law of diminishing returns) of so much contemporary literature, if literature it can be called, as Miss Pym would say. . . .

[The] *piano* effects of Miss Pym's crisp comedy register; one cares for *her* characters and what happens to them, they are so real and truthfully rendered. Her books are a distillation of life; and if in watercolour, well, what better than the best English water-colours?

The novels are very lady-like—but so was Jane Austen—and what was wonderful about her is that, within the confines of a lady's view of the world, she understood everything about life: no illusions, knew perfectly what was what about people—rather better, in fact, than brute sensationalists.

The same is true of Miss Pym, for all the miniature scale on which she chooses to work: a very sharp eye, an occasionally tart comment on what she observes. . . .

Not many tears are brought to the eyes in Miss Pym's books—no room for sentimentality in her view of the world. . . .

There are particularly no illusions about Men. They don't notice much (Miss Pym notices *every*thing); they assume that the whole meal is for them; they will take the last chocolate biscuit on the plate; men are not nearly so good at

secrets as women; husbands will assume that their wives vote the same way as they do. (p. 732)

Miss Pym writes with the exquisite precision that is in keeping. As an old Oxford don, I can fault her only for omitting the accusative of the word ''who''—she doesn't say ''whom'' when she ought. But that is current usage (or misusage), and I daresay ''whom'' is going out (with much else). ''I wonder who we shall get as vicar?''—but one mustn't impute the grammar of the characters, any more than all the sentiments, to the author. . . .

[The 1950s] is her period—and how well she renders it! The war not long over, food still short, austerity still ruling in fuel, queues in shops; whole areas bombed, churches gutted—in one, three-quarters wrecked, the services held in the one aisle still roofed.

For it is the tail-end of a society that she is depicting; the gentlefolk, the ladies, are left-overs from a better world, not quite realising that theirs had gone for good. . . .

It is, of course, a society in deliquescence, only just emerging from the ruin and devastation of the war, on its way to the brave new social order (or disorder) of today. It is an authentic portrait of the transition: here are the signs and portents, the squalid cafeterias, the crowding and pushing, the scraps and litter on tables and floors. . . .

Though everything is toned down, in subtly sophisticated manner, Miss Pym cannot altogether hide her cleverness. (p. 733)

Everything is toned down, the comic effects obtained by underemphasis. But what would happen if Miss Pym were to tune up a bit and, instead of being so *piano,* wrote us a novel *con brio*?

I feel rather like the ridiculous clergyman—the Prince Regent's chaplain—who suggested to Miss Austen that she might try something on a larger scale, possibly an historical novel. Miss Austen replied that she would stick to her miniatures.

In fact, Jane Austen gives a real, not to say realist, portrait of the society of her time—if it is social realism that you want. And so does Miss Pym. . . .

It really is a shocker if this excellent writer has several unpublished novels in her drawers, when one thinks of the quantities of rubbish that get published. If Miss Compton-Burnet or Miss Murdoch is the Mrs Radcliffe *de nos jours,* with their Gothic fantasies and unreal horrors, with Miss Pym's quiet comedy, authentic and convincing, perhaps one may see something of a contemporary Jane Austen. (p. 734)

> *A. L. Rowse, ''Austen Mini?'' in* Punch *(© 1977 by Punch Publications Ltd.; all rights reserved; may not be reprinted without permission), October 19, 1977, pp. 732-34.*

TOM PAULIN

Barbara Pym is a neglected novelist who, after a long period of enforced silence, has recently published a bitterly amused account of decaying Englishness [*Quartet in Autumn*]. And although Lord David Cecil has called *Excellent Women* and *A Glass of Blessings* ''the finest examples of high comedy to have appeared in England during the past 75 years'', their comic vision is elegantly grey rather than "high"—unless that adjective refers to their type of Anglicanism. They define a spinsterly purgatory where characters with names like Rowena, Sir Denbigh Grote, Reresby-Hamilton, engage in politely meaningless conversations in a vanished world of trolley buses, Hillman Huskies and impoverished Anglo-Catholic gentlewomen. They attend moth-eaten jumble sales in draughty parish halls, sip weak China tea and read *The Church Times* and *Crockford's Clerical Gazette*. Meek spinsters imagine romance with an archdeacon among "chipped Della Robbia plaques, the hissing of gas fires and tea urns, and the smell of damp mackintoshes."

This sad aroma permeates *Quartet in Autumn* which is set in the 1970s, this unfinished decade of inflation, anxiety and soul-searching on a national scale. Barbara Pym neatly suggests such issues. . . .

Quartet in Autumn has an exact misery, and those "small poignancies and comedies of everyday life" which Philip Larkin has praised in Barbara Pym's work have now deepened into a formal protest against the conditions both of life itself and of certain sad civilities that no longer make even the limited sense they once acknowledged. (p. 72)

> *Tom Paulin, in* Encounter *(© 1978 by Encounter Ltd.), January, 1978.*

JEREMY TREGLOWN

After her brief charitable sortie into geriatric bedsitterdom in *Quartet In Autumn*, Barbara Pym [in *The Sweet Dove Died*] is back in Knightsbridge, exploring the romantic half-attachments of a new well-heeled heroine. It's as calculatedly thinblooded as her other novels but, like them, it achieves surprising pathos through the very limitedness of the expectations it sees in its characters and encourages in the reader. . . .

But it's the ironic control that gets the emotional saliva going. (Miss Pym is a very culinary novelist, in her finishing-school way) so that when she finally puts a small chop on your plate it can seem like the contents of half an abattoir. . . .

The danger is one of overstating Miss Pym's claims. What she does, after all, has been done in more substance before —not only by Jane Austen (a frequent, and inflated, source of comparison) but by Elizabeth Bowen. . . . (p. 27)

> *Jeremy Treglown, in* New Statesman *(© 1978 The Statesman & Nation Publishing Co. Ltd.), July 7, 1978.*

KARL MILLER

In London last year, the *Times Literary Supplement* asked a number of writers to draw up a list of overrated and underrated writers. By no means a thankless task, but among the sneers that leapt to the page were words of praise, from Philip Larkin and Lord David Cecil, which served to call attention to Barbara Pym. She had brought out six quiet novels in the Fifties, but had gone unsung, and even, during the eventful late Sixties and after, unpublished. Now she has been sung, and is "the in-thing to read," according to one British librarian. . . .

Philip Larkin has suggested that the men Miss Pym writes about behave worse than the women, and her novels could fairly be regarded as grist to the feminist mill. But [*Excellent Women*] makes much of . . . [Mildred,] a virgin

who is forever "venturing" or "faltering," sipping tea or sherry, catching the drone of music from a nearby church. . . .

Women like Mildred have been important to the England which has insulted them, which calls them, using the words that Lawrence used of Jane Austen, "narrow-gutted spinsters." . . .

It is said of Barbara Pym, as it has been said of other writers, that she is like Jane Austen, but this time at least the comparison needn't be resented. What is mostly meant by it is that she is a novelist of manners who writes about marriage and marriageability with the unromantic eye of a noticing, "positive" spinster. But the comparison can be taken further. There is a current reading of Jane Austen which holds that she is moved by the romantic attitudes with which she finds fault, and of Miss Pym, too, it can be claimed that she is both unromantic and romantic. The extent to which she is the second can be gauged by the extent to which the narrative, smilingly self-defined as that of a church-crawling "excellent woman," has in it the voice of the outcast. Mildred's authentic excellence is partly a matter of her ability to bear, and to take into constructive account, the responsibilities, sorrows, and incitements to self-pity, of such a plight.

Excellent Women made me think of *Mansfield Park*, in which the orphan Fanny lives, under insult, in the grand house of that name and is assailed by the blandishments of the talented but untrustworthy Crawfords. . . .

Mildred's progress is not very different from Fanny's. Here, too, Christian humility is assailed by the talented and untrustworthy, and rewarded with a good man, with whom she is to live happily if humbly ever after. . . . At the same time, there is more than a touch of the Gothic novel in *Excellent Women*: the grand names conferred on Everard and on Rockingham Napier suggest the Cavalier strain which is evident there, the heroine's faltering and venturing are Gothic acts and words, and Everard is the hostile male of the genre who grows into her lover and savior. He is Mildred's Rochester, just as the pseudo-orphan Allegra Gray is her vampire. . . . (p. 24)

In the same way, another of Mrs. Pym's books—like *Excellent Women,* one of her best—made me think of *Northanger Abbey*, whose heroine is bemused by a reading of Gothic novels, and which itself resembles the kind of novel it is laughing at. In *A Glass of Blessings*, published in 1958, Wilmet, a young woman with an unresponsive husband, lacks experience: "I had not had a lover before I married, I had no children, I wasn't even asked to clean the brasses or arrange the flowers in church." She yields to "wild imaginings." . . . "Perhaps," though, she finally wonders, her life has been a "glass of blessings," after all. The reference is to the very beautiful poem by Herbert, "The Pulley," which supplies the novel's title and epigraph:

> When God at first made man,
> Having a glass of blessings standing
> by;
> Let us (said he) pour on him all we
> can:
> Let the world's riches, which
> dispersed lie,
> Contract into a span.

(pp. 24-5)

Precious few rewards, desserts, or blessings await the four sufferers in Barbara Pym's new novel, *Quartet in Autumn.* Two men and two women, all near retirement, share an office in a huge firm whose business is too boring to mention. . . .

The blessings poured for the four are such as to make the Herbert poem seem like a painful satire: literature's poor things are very unfortunate if they prevent their authors, as often happens and as happens here, from conveying that they can ever have had a really good time.

Miss Pym's best books convey an impression altogether remote from this, however, and they are those of a very accomplished writer. Her favorites among contemporary English novelists are Ivy Compton-Burnett, Elizabeth Taylor, Anthony Powell, and Iris Murdoch, but she could rarely be mistaken for any one of these. She may be classed with Betjeman as a poet of High Church attendance. When incense is mentioned, it tends to be as a joke: some classes of the stuff are better bred than others, we are made aware. The odor of sanctity is missing from her books, except as a further joke, but a fragrance as of vegetables and salads, as of cresses, cucumbers, lettuce, Stilton, is not. Her interest in religion is anthropological, skeptical, sardonic; it may also be romantic; whether and in what way it is pious, I can't be sure. For all I can tell, she may be an "Anglican atheist": a term of Orwell's, which has been applied to Larkin.

Religion is treated as a comfort in her books, where shyness and reserve are treated as a strength. She has said in the *New Review* that she would "like to see more entertaining and and amusing works written and published," and she has not been too pious or too shy to write such works herself. Some readers have chosen to praise the "high comedy" generated by her High Churchgoers, and one might feel that the snobbish English language has helped to generate that emphasis: unlike much of the high comedy known to me, hers is funny. (p. 25)

> *Karl Miller, in* The New York Review of Books *(reprinted with permission from* The New York Review of Books; *copyright © 1978 Nyrev, Inc.), November 9, 1978.*

VICTORIA GLENDINNING

The narrator [of "Excellent Women"] is Mildred, a spinster in her 30's, self-effacing and dowdy, the daughter of an Anglican clergyman. Her outlets are going to church and her friendship with the vicar and his sister. She expects nothing much to happen to her, and indeed it does not; but she makes friends with people to whom things *do* happen, and is disturbed—just a little—by their emotions, and by the emotions they awaken in her. Miss Pym's technique for comic effect is to glide over the pain of big happenings and to make much of the disproportionate impact of tiny ones. . . .

[Mildred] is one of the "excellent women," the "rejected ones," always reliable in a crisis but never themselves part of the action. One's only doubt about Mildred is why she is so dim, when, like her creator, she is also so observant and critical. Miss Pym doesn't seem quite sure about this either. . . .

Apart from one charming cad, all the men in "Excellent Women" are sticks. The attitude toward marriage, though, is timorous but respectful; marriage is seen as "having a man to look after," and "surely wives shouldn't be too busy to cook for their husbands? I thought in astonishment." There is irony here, but not the steel jab of feminism, merely a mild, fine irony toward the ways of the world. It is the mildness of "Excellent Women" that gives it its charm, but this also, I think, keeps it from being "high comedy"—High Church comedy it certainly is, but that's another thing. . . .

[In "Quartet in Autumn" two] men and two women work in the same office. All live alone and none of them has much in the way of private life, but what there is of it each guards jealously and speculates upon in the other. Again, her women matter but not her men. . . . Letty is another Mildred, trim, controlled and devout; Marcia teeters on the edge of dottiness, using the public library shelves during the lunch hour as a place to dump her household rubbish. Both women reach retirement age and leave the office; deprived of the normalizing routine, they become more absolutely themselves. Inner chaos threatens both. Letty does not let down her defenses, and battles alone to preserve her sense of order and decency. Marcia, on the other hand, gives in entirely to her obsessions, hoarding plastic bags and old newspapers and milk bottles in her dirty house, eating nothing at all, and finally dying.

Miss Pym "comes out" in this novel as she did not in "Excellent Women." Marcia's craziness is what all solitary people fear, and it is tackled wittily but head-on. Even Letty's gallant keeping-up of appearances is scrutinized hard: Facing Christmas alone, she knows that it is not the solitude that she minds—she is used to that—but the fact that "people might find out that she had no invitation for the day and would pity her." Another question raised in a ghostly manner is this: If nothing happens between two people, no caress, no declaration, is it possible that there still was something? An unacknowledged meshing of hopes? A relationship, even?

The whole miniature Pym world of solitary women, "rejected ones," turns on this question. Letty, and all the other Lettys and Mildreds, are without experience in the world's terms; they are "emotionally deprived." "Yet she sometimes wondered, might not the experience of 'not having' be regarded as something with its own validity?" It is in the ironic exploration of "the experience of not having" that Barbara Pym's art and originality lie.

> *Victoria Glendinning, "The Best High Comedy," in* The New York Times Book Review *(© 1978 by The New York Times Company; reprinted by permission), December 24, 1978, p. 8.*

R

REANEY, James   1926-

Reaney is a Canadian playwright, poet, children's author, and editor. His drama effectively draws together elements of fantasy, melodrama, and ritual. The Donnellys Trilogy is his major dramatic work. (See also *Contemporary Authors*, Vols. 41-44, rev. ed.)

ALVIN LEE

Mr. Reaney's comedies demand of their audience, at least temporarily, a capacity to believe that the weapons of human consciousness—religion, art, thought, and love—can defeat all destructive powers. His plays are not for cynics, nor for those too sophisticated to let themselves play games if necessary to exorcise the black enchantments laid on them in childhood. The measure in which we feel these resolutions silly, or too far-fetched, is the measure of our own Malvolio-like nature. If the art of the comedy has done its work—and Mr. Reaney's plays have this art in abundant measure—our emotions of sympathy and ridicule have been raised and cast out. . . . (pp. 132-33)

> Alvin Lee, "A Turn to the Stage: Reaney's Dramatic Verse" (copyright by Alvin Lee; originally published in Canadian Literature, Winter, 1963), in Dramatists in Canada: Selected Essays, edited by William H. New, The University of British Columbia Press, 1972, pp. 114-33.

MICHAEL TAIT

As a playwright Reaney has tended to be a fine lyric poet. In certain respects the qualities of his verse enhance the plays. Genres, however, are not interchangeable and too often his early attempts at drama point up the defects of his strengths. The mode of theatre itself has sometimes seemed inhospitable to Reaney's genius. The public forum aspect of all stage production is not easily reconciled with the singular inwardness of his idiom. Certainly the conventional act and scene arrangement he adopts for *The Killdeer* or *The Easter Egg* serves him badly. This structure requires the shaping of materials over a sustained period, a long-range control of action, tone and climax. Reaney's, however, is a short term art of quick insights and volatile moods. *The Killdeer* breaks up into a collection of fragments, some of them brilliant. However, the effectiveness of one frequently weakens the impact of another and all suffer from the linear framework in which they are set. In a word, Reaney's prob-

lem as a dramatist has been to arrive at a form to suit his matter. In *Colours in the Dark* he finds it.

The play comprises some forty brief scenes, each one a self-contained minidrama. Each has its caption and, in a sense, its message. In most things Reaney is the antithesis of Brecht; what, however, he creates in this play is an epic theatre to the buried consciousness. The technique perfectly accommodates his quest for universal significance in a swirl of particulars. At the outset, he suggests we regard his drama not only as a play but as a play-box; that is, a structure which contains a miscellany of memory-objects. Having jettisoned linear plot, he is free to illuminate directly the rich chaos of darkest Canada: a national psyche shaped (and warped) by geology, history, weather, anonymous ancestors, King Billy, Queen Elizabeth, the Bible, the Devil, Little Orphan Annie and much besides. The range and variety of episodes make for instant entertainment. Reaney advertises a new play every two minutes, and he keeps his word. . . . (pp. 141-42)

Reaney's creation is *sui generis*, a luminous structure that invites but eludes classification. It is lyric in subjective intensity of mood; dramatic in the articulation of large conflicts; epic in its breadth of statement. Whatever the mode, the artist's transfiguring eye lights the scene and wrings a design from ignorant chaos.

"Everything is something." Indeed it is, and everything in *Colours in the Dark* is the common stuff of "uniquely Canadian" experience. A rich thing, and our own. (p. 144)

> Michael Tait, "Everything Is Something: James Reaney's 'Colours in the Dark'" (copyright by Michael Tait), in Dramatists in Canada: Selected Essays, edited by William H. New, The University of British Columbia Press, 1972, pp. 140-44.

MARGARET ATWOOD

Judging from a sampling of recent critical commentary on his collected *Poems*, Reaney's reputation is in [a slump] . . . ; which is a shame. Any poet who has created an original body of work, especially one of such uniqueness, power, peculiarity and, sometimes, unprecedented weirdness as Reaney's deserves better treatment. A critic might begin by attempting to actually *read* the poems, as opposed to reading into them various philosophies and literary theories which the poet is assumed to have. If you start this way, with the actual poems, one of your first reactions will almost certainly be that there is nothing else *like* them.

I'd never before read most of the uncollected single poems, . . . so I was most intrigued by sections I, III and V of this volume. I was especially struck by the early appearance of a number of Reaney images which crop up again and again, variously disguised, in his later work. The fascination with maps and diagrams ("Maps", 1945), the collections of objects ("The Antiquary", 1946), the sinister females, both mechanical ("Night Train", 1946) and biological ("Madame Moth", 1947), and that nightmare, the Orphanage, already present in "Playbox", 1945—all foreshadow later and more fully realized appearances.

But what became clear to me during a chronological reading of this book is that most commentators—including Reaney himself, and his editor and critics—are somewhat off-target about the much-discussed influence of Frye on his work. I have long entertained a private vision of Frye reading through Reaney while muttering "What have I wrought?" or "This is not what I meant, at all," and this collection confirms it. Reaney is to Frye as a Salem, Mass. 17th century tombstone is to an Italian Renaissance angel: Reaney and the tombstone may have been "influenced", but they are primitives (though later in time) and their models are sophisticates. The influence of Frye, however, was probably a catalyst for Reaney rather than a new ingredient; let me do a little deductive speculation.

The world presented to us in the early poems, up to and including *The Red Heart* (1949), does not "work" for the poet on any level. The people in them are bored and trivial, like "Mrs. Wentworth", or they are actual or potential orphans, loveless, lost or disinherited, like the speaker in "Playbox". . . . The reverse side of the melancholy state of being an orphan—hate for and disgust at the rest of the world and the desire for revenge—is explored in two other orphan poems, "The English Orphan's Monologue" and "The Orphanage". . . . In these "social" poems, Reaney does not analyze, he dramatizes; and, like a dramatist, he counterpoints. Thus to the smothered longing of the provincial in the "Canadian" poems he opposes the sneering of a cosmopolite who has escaped the Fathers of Confederation [and] is reading Tristram Shandy and Anais Nin. . . . If this poem had been written by anyone else but Reaney, everyone would have called it savage socialist satire; in fact it's a good deal more savage and socialist than much that passes by that name.

In these early poems the objects—and the poems bulge with objects—create the effect of a kind of rummage sale, partly because the objects are lacking in all but personal significance. . . . The speaker can rarely make "sense" of them by relating them to anything else; all he can do is record them, and the effect is a still-life, captured and rendered immobile. . . . (pp. 113-15)

In the early poems on "love"—and there are quite a few of them—the love is either unconsummated, as in "Platonic Love", or it turns into sex, which is as inextricably linked with death as it is in the poetry of Al Purdy. This is sex observed through a child's eyes, foreign and monstrous. At times Reaney manages a kind of queasy humour. . . . More often it is simple horror, mixed with revulsion, as in "The Orphanage". . . .

Reaney's early world, then, is an unredeemed one, popu-lated with orphans and spiritual exiles, littered with couples engaged in joyless, revolting and dangerous copulation, and crammed with objects devoid of significance. In it, babies are doomed as soon as conceived (as in "Dark Lagoon"), the "real world" is the one described at the end of "The School Globe", filled with "blood, pus, horror, stepmothers and lies", and the only escape is the temporary and unsatisfactory one of nostalgic daydreaming. If you believed you lived in such a world, you'd surely find the negative overwhelming. Anyone familiar with the techniques of brainwashing knows that all you have to do to convert almost anyone to almost anything is subject him to a nearly intolerable pressure, then offer him a way out. The intolerable pressures rendered with such verbal richness in the earlier poems are those of the traditional Christian version of this earth, but with Christ (and escape to Heaven) removed; sin with no possibility of redemption, a fallen world with no divine counterpart.

[Northrop] Frye's literary theories—this is a guess—would surely have offered Reaney his discredited childhood religion in a different, more sophisticated, acceptable form: the Bible might not be *literally* true, but under the aegis of Frye it could be seen as metaphorically, psychically true. Frye's "influence", then, is not a matter of the critic's hardedged mind cutting out the poet's soul in its own shapes, like cookie dough: "influence", for good poets, is surely in any case just a matter of taking what you need or, in reality, what you already have. (p. 115)

Horror remains and evil is still a presence, but a way past the world, the flesh and the devil is now possible. The redemptive agents are all invisible, internal: they are the imagination, the memory, verbal magic (Reaney has several poems about language, and many references to the magic tongue) and—I'm thinking here of the short story "The Bully"—dream. These elements are so important in Reaney's work because the hideousness of existence can be redeemed *by them alone:* it is the individual's inner vision, not the external social order, that must change if anything is to be salvaged.

It is this arrangement of priorities that surely accounts not only for some of Reaney's themes, but also for some of his characteristic structures, in the plays as well as the poems. The pattern I'm thinking of is that of the sudden conversion —a Protestant rather than a Catholic pattern. If you think of the Divine Comedy with the Purgatorio left out you'll see what I mean: we get the hellishness of the "earthly" situation and the quick turnabout followed by a transcendent vision, but we are never told how you get to the vision— what process you undergo, what brings it about. No indulgences sold here; it's Faith, not Works and you just somehow have to "see". (pp. 115-16)

In Reaney's work, the Songs of Innocence come *after* the Songs of Experience; in fact, you can take a number of figures or images from the earlier poems and follow them through the *corpus,* watching how the Lost Child gets found (most notably in *Night-Blooming Cereus*), how the sinister Orphan gets changed into the harmless comic-strip Little Orphan Annie, how the baby doomed from before birth is allowed more latitude . . . , and how the collection of random objects is permitted (or perhaps forced) to have universal significance. . . . (p. 116)

The problems I have with Reaney's work are both theoretical (I can't see certain pieces of evil, for instance Hitler and the Vietnam War, as angelic visitations or even unreal, no matter how hard I try; and I don't think that's a flaw in my vision) and practical—that is, some of the poems work admirably for me and others don't get off the ground at all. Reaney's best poems come from a fusion of "personal" and "mythic" or "universal"; when they lean too far towards either side, you get obscurity or straight nostalgia at one end or bloodless abstraction at the other. And at times, reading his work, I feel the stirrings of that old Romantic distinction between the Fancy and the Imagination, though I try hard to suppress it; I even hear a voice murmuring "Whimsy", and it murmurs loudest when I come across a concrete image linked arbitrarily and with violence to a "universal" meaning. If you can see a world in a grain of sand, well, good; but you shouldn't stick one on just because you think it ought to be there.

But this is a Collected rather than a Selected; it isn't supposed to be Reaney's best poems, it's all of his poems, and I can't think of any poet who produces uniformly splendid work. It's by his best, however, that a writer should ultimately be judged; and Reaney's best has an unmistakable quality, both stylistic and thematic, and a strength that is present only when a poet is touching on something fundamental. Certain of Reaney's poems do admirably what a number of his others attempt less successfully: they articulate the primitive forms of the human imagination, they flesh out the soul, they dramatize—like Blake's "Mental Traveller"—the stances of the self in relation to the universe. That sounds fairly heavy; what I mean is that Reaney gets down to the basics—love, hate, terror, joy—and gives them a shape that evokes them for the reader. This is conjuring, it's magic and spells rather than meditation, description or ruminating; Coleridge rather than Wordsworth, MacEwen rather than Souster. The trouble with being a magic poet is that when you fail, you fail more obviously than the meditative or descriptive poet: the rabbit simply refuses to emerge from the hat. But you take greater risks, and Reaney takes every risk in the bag, including a number of technical ones that few others would even consider attempting. (p. 117)

> *Margaret Atwood, "Reaney Collected," in* Canadian Literature, *Summer, 1973, pp. 113-17.*

LOUIS DUDEK

The plays of James Reaney . . . have a background of religious and philosophical concern behind them. The survey of philosophy in Reaney's "September Eclogue," in *A Suit of Nettles,* ends significantly with Heidegger and with games of magic taken from *The Golden Bough;* and Reaney's plays in general are shot through with a kind of religious-philosophical excitement that tells us there is much going on privately in that area. But he is a solitary exile in an empty land, almost unique in being troubled deeply and seriously with such questions; therefore his plays have a peculiar dislocation and feeling of unreality in the context of Canadian society. (p. 322)

[The] proposition that James Reaney's charming theatre is somehow a distant relation to, first, Bernard Shaw and, second, W. B. Yeats, may sound far-fetched, but I think it can help us to understand what is going on in the plays. In most of these plays of Reaney, . . . Canada has at last come in for sharp social satire. It was naturally made for it, from

the beginning, we suspect, but no playwright would have dared to undertake a full-scale satirical view of Canadian life before World War II. The soul has to be moved to satire by revulsion, and there must be a solid stone somewhere, on which the foot can lean while shaking off the muck. Reaney may be said to possess both these requirements: a major "criticism of life", and a strong intellectual conviction personally achieved. The satirical strain, however, is the lesser part of his purpose—I was going to say "lesser half", but it isn't anything like half—and the other part branches out rather discordantly from the first. This satirical part, however, is dramatically most reliable, and has the most dependable precedents, so that it tends to be theatrically more successful. The first act of several of his plays, as in *The Killdeer, The Sun and the Moon,* and *Three Desks* —the part of the play which is closest to social satire— comes off very well. (p. 323)

But the second and third acts of a Reaney play take a radical turn into strange territory. . . . In short, the play turns to the great romantic tradition, of transcendence, of magic, or religious implication, and here we are in the country of W. B. Yeats, Maurice Maeterlinck, J. M. Barrie and other visionaries of the "eternal return".

The satire itself springs from a very close personal response to provincial life: one has the impression of a very superior-minded young man cast by fate into a pathetic small-town environment and undergoing all the irritations of being forever trapped in a hen-house or a parsonage. (p. 324)

The strange infantilism of Reaney's poetry and plays is somehow related to this sense of the absurdity of life. The unkindest interpretation of this aspect of Reaney is that the painful prison of provincialism pressing on the mind of the gifted poet has produced a kind of "arrested development", in which the language and the fantasy-world of childhood remains the only imaginative and vital reality for him and the one to which he perpetually returns. A more sympathetic literary account would relate this infantile strain to Blake's theory of innocence and the general romantic idyllic myth of childhood.

William Blake was perhaps the first poet in history to offer infantile inanity and childish doggerel as serious poetry, and this to the eternal confusion of literature, since in his work abominable poetry is bound up with the most profound and far-reaching ideas. . . . The delusion that this sort of thing is high poetry . . . has led James Reaney to write pages of similar nonsense. . . . Who knows, some of [the] bathos in Reaney may derive from hymn-book quatrains, the bane of so much English poetry, even as Blake's namby-pamby style derived from the same source. . . . Also, it is one thing to write *for* children, as Edward Lear and Lewish Carroll have done—and as Reaney has in his specifically children's books—but quite another to be childish or stylistically insipid in a work written for adults. (pp. 324-25)

After all, one cannot put Reaney down as an idiot boy. The naive childlike style and childlike attitudes which are so recurrent in his plays are an affectation, perhaps with a secret self-indulgence, but nevertheless a conscious design aiming to simplify and to reach an indiscriminate audience. The plays could hardly occur on the stage in Paris or New York, though they might eventually get there. They could only originate in a country like Canada, a hinterland as far as drama is concerned, where an audience in church base-

ments and high schools must be gently prodded to participate in dramatics. The plays are conceived for a small parochial community—there is an aura of amateur theatre about
the whole thing—and the audience, one imagines, is composed of children, nice pleasant provincial ladies, and
placid hen-pecked husbands. (p. 326)

The ultimate aim of this simplified kind of play, a collage of
children's games (*Colours in the Dark*), or a fairy tale for
adults (*Nightblooming Cereus*), or a pastime for a sick boy
(*Listen to the Wind*), is anything but trivial and simple. By
means of would-be unpretentious play, purporting to gratify
the very simplest audience, Reaney intends to achieve the
widest possible scope of meaning, interpreting all life from
birth to death, all human history, and touching on the major
questions of religion and philosophy. His aim, in other
words, is epic, and his intentions are those of a major poet,
although this is concealed in the trappings of the nursery
and of childhood imagination. (p. 327)

Much of the *One-man Masque* and *Colours in the Dark*
reads like all the gists of *Finnegans Wake, Ulysses* and *The
Waste Land* rolled into a ball. The vast ambition of this
philosophical conception, as it stares through the child's
play of the surface, seems at odds with the quirky simplicity of the means adopted.

A little higher on the scale than the nursery or child's play I
would place Reaney's regressive attachment to melodrama
and the plot-patterns of the Victorian romance. Here at
least, we might say, we have a breakthrough—from infancy
to adolescence! (pp. 327-28)

I see James Reaney's plays as essentially poetic or lyrical
drama. The form of *One-man Masque,* which amounts to
little more than a stage setting for a reading of Reaney
poems—as does also a good deal of *Colours in the Dark*—
reveals the strong lyrical bent of this drama. The interpretation of the plays should be directed to the poetic subjectivity of their method, and they should be studied in conjuc-
tion with Reaney's poetry, . . . although the ultimate goal
will be a body of ideas, or a "vision", that will be objective
and significant for itself. (pp. 329-30)

The plays are a strange and wonderful experience—though
often an irritation—and they are a powerful contribution to
the possibility of theatre in Canada. Much as I may disagree, having my own way of searching through the creation, I want to stand up to applaud a fine achievement. For
my own taste, among the plays, I probably could do without *The Killdeer, The Sun and the Moon,* the *Three Desks,*
and *The Easter Egg*—much as there may be interesting
things in all of them—and I believe the best of Reaney's
theatre, pure Symbolism in the romantic vein of Maeterlinck and Yeats, is to be found in *Night-blooming Cereus,
One-man Masque,* and the moving and impressive later
plays, *Colours in the Dark* and *Listen to the Wind.* It is here
that he suggests vast meanings and haunting other-worldly
dimensions through the simplest verbal and theatrical techniques, namely through the symbolic interplay of action and
the incantation of poetry. (pp. 333-34)

The difficulty of the plays remains. It is a difficulty which is
both intellectual and sociological—hated words!—in that
the problem of these plays is to discover, with precision
and in detail (not always possible in such a case) what they
want to say, and at the same time to reach an audience
which is neither prepared for nor capable of any mental

exertion. And it all goes back to "vision"—the Greek
theoria—in which the divine was revealed in the epiphany
of the theatre: except that we today are not quite sure of
what we mean by the divine. In the meantime, the play—or
"play"—is the thing, if only as a childlike way to keep
things going. Reaney's emphasis is definitely on the play.
(p. 334)

> Louis Dudek, "A Problem of Meaning: The Plays
> of James Reaney" (originally published in a
> slightly different version in Canadian Literature,
> Winter, 1974), in his Selected Essays and Criti-
> cism (© 1978 Louis Dudek and The Tecumseh
> Press Limited; reprinted by permission of the au-
> thor), Tecumseh Press, 1978, pp. 320-35.

STEPHEN MARTINEAU

It was reassuring to find that the text [of *Sticks & Stones*]
does not lose the original spirit of live theatre. The secret
behind this is the way the directions for stage movement
have been so carefully integrated into the poetry of the
play; they are not merely instructions but a spur to the
imagination of the actor or director to discover the pattern
of movement best suited to the rhythm of the language and
the mood of the particular incident. This is most important
because Reaney's stage world is a simple open space scattered with everyday objects (sticks, stones, ropes, ladders)
and, through quick changes of rhythm and shape, this space
has to be transformed in the reader's imagination into whatever the situation demands of it. These transformations are
surely the key to Reaney's strengths as a playwright, for
they bring about an essential fusion of his poetic and his
theatrical imagination; the images draw from his language at
the same time as they become a part of the physical action
on stage. Two examples come to mind: the image of the
Donnellys hemmed in by concession lines and neighbours
expressed through patterns of rope or wood on the floor of
the stage as well as through the rhythmic chanting of the
roads of Biddulph and the names of the neighbours; and the
heroic journey of Mrs. Donnelly from Biddulph to Goderich
to appeal her husband's sentence, expressed physically
through the climbing of pyramids of ladders and verbally
through a "solo and choral response" that keeps rhythm
with the milestones of her journey. These are individual
examples, but in fact the overall design of the play is richer
still in its combinations of effects, reminding one of the intricacy of musical counterpoint as contrasting themes move
in and around each other, inseparable strands of action and
reaction reflecting in the process the suffocating closeness
of the world of Biddulph that does not look kindly on independent survival. (pp. 36-7)

The play sets itself up as a deliberate rebuttal of *The Black
Donnellys,* a violently anti-Donnelly version of the story. . . . Donnellys are allied firm and fast to Reaney's poetry throughout the play; they are the oppressed minority,
the fighters against all odds, and finally (in this play) the
heroic victors who refuse to be hounded from their land.
What this means is that the theatrical design of the play
minimizes as much as possible any act of hostility or violence on their part. For example, the central murder of Farrell by Donnelly is first presented by a travelling theatre
troupe in a way that brings out a barbarous brutality in
Donnelly. Immediately after, through Reaney's vision, we
are shown how the blow was more or less accidental and
that the blame should be laid on the liquor and the onlook-

ers who "sicced [him] on by their howls of encouragement."...

This unqualified support of the Donnellys has an interesting effect on the play and the reader. In the first place the reader is given no option but to side with the Donnellys.... A further consequence of this pro-Donnelly bias is that the play by immersing us in the history of one family and thereby closing the time gap, prevents more objective consideration of the period itself and its relevance to the present....

Sticks & Stones focuses on a woman as the imaginative and supporting centre of the action. It is a striking element in the design of Reaney's play that he should choose a woman to individualize a period in which the woman's role remains relatively unchronicled. It is Mrs. Donnelly, more than Donnelly himself, who is the constant bastion of defence against the surrounding hostility; it is she who relates proudly to her son her husband's refusal to do homage to the Whitefeet in Ireland; she who journeys to Goderich to appeal her husband's death sentence; she who keeps together land and children during his absence in prison; and she who rescues neighbour Donegan from brutal assault. It is this kind of heroic action, given double emphasis through Mr. and Mrs. Donnelly, that is the energy behind Reaney's play, an energy that exults in the staying-power of the individual under continuous harassment. And, whether we like it or not, the play demands that we be carried away by this energy. What we lose in the process is breathing-space and a little distance from which to reflect on a period of violence that is a fascinating part of our historical heritage; what we gain is an excitingly theatrical story of a family and an alliance with those who are unassailable and have the will, courage and strength to stand up against the villainy of the world.... (p. 37)

> *Stephen Martineau, "Canadian Myth Making,"*
> *in* The Canadian Forum, *October, 1975., pp. 36-7.*

DAVID JACKEL

[In] spite of the positive qualities one may find in this long overdue selection of Reaney's verse [*Selected Shorter Poems*], in spite of the evidence of growth, the poetry remains disturbingly eccentric—eccentric not in the sense of being merely odd or whimsical, but in the way it often seems removed from a common centre of human experience. Tarzan of the Apes, the Katzenjammer Kids, fantastic crows, choughs and woodpeckers, Spenser, Yeats, Blake, Isabella Valancy Crawford, the Brontës, Antichrist, Granny Crack—these are some of the figures who jostle in a private mythology which many readers are likely to find more perplexing than illuminating. The alternative vision which Reaney has substituted for the "great sad real" world may, after all, be only an evasion of that reality, not a transformation of it.

Doubts of this sort are likely to be provoked by *A Suit of Nettles*.... The poem is described by the author as, among many other things, a satire on "all the intellectual institutions of the age," but Reaney can deal with this overlarge subject only by oversimplifying the issues involved.... [His Canadian history, for example, is] seen from the limited perspective of Southern Ontario, perhaps not the best place for a satirist to be standing. Philosophy, too, is disposed of in a charmingly off-hand manner. We are given a merry-go-round ride through the history of the subject,

from Parmenides to Heidegger, and end where we began, having learned that the Aristotelean mean can be viewed as "a rather stocky Clydesdale with three saddles, three heads and three buttocks: one buttock is too hairy, the middle one is just right, and the left hand one has no hair at all."

When Reaney attempts to deal with literary criticism the result is not satire but travesty. A distinguished evaluative critic, whose characteristic method is badly misdescribed as "putting poems into order of merit," is allowed to defend his views by saying "Aooh! Bow wowwowwowwowwowwow." One does not need to be a disciple of Dr. Leavis to see that he is here being unfairly treated.... Germaine Warkentin claims [in her introduction] that *A Suit of Nettles* is the "toughest" and "most serious" long poem in English Canadian literature: "If there is one thing *A Suit of Nettles* makes you do, it is *think*." But when Reaney makes us think, he reveals his limitations, particularly his inclination to reduce complicated issues to a few phrases or images, and then to resolve all difficulties by dextrously juggling and patterning these fragments. This method, such as it is, will appeal only to readers seeking an easy escape from the demands of truly ordered thinking. Mr. Reaney's visions are much more appealing than his attempts to deal with the complexities of ordinary reality. (pp. 31-2)

> *David Jackel, "Easy Escapes," in* The Canadian
> Forum, *October, 1976, pp. 31-2.*

*   *   *

REED, Ishmael   1938-

Reed is a black American novelist, poet, and editor. A noted satirist, he creates a chaotic fictional world where dogma, whether scientific or religious, presents an ominous threat. Both black and white communities serve as targets for Reed's satire, for his purpose is to show the sacrifice of individuality inherent in accepting any rigid philosophical approach to life. (See also *CLC*, Vols. 2, 3, 5, 6, and *Contemporary Authors*, Vols. 21-24, rev. ed.)

BARBARA JOYE

Blacks and whites, avant-garde and mass culture, politics, even Reed's alma mater, the University of Buffalo, have their turn [in *The Free-Lance Pall Bearers*]. Features of the Gothic novel superimposed on an already flimsy plot do not help matters much.... The attempt to turn Bukka [Reed's anti-hero] into a revolutionary ten pages from the end ... seems tacked on and insignificant. I know that it was not a last-minute device to wrap up the story because I had the opportunity to read the last chapter and portions of others in manuscript. At that stage the book seemed tighter, more consistent in imagery and subject matter, and much more successful structurally. The printed version may represent misguided editing.

One flaw which must be blamed on the author is the failure of his experiments with dialect in the narrative portions of the book. His rendition of Negro and lower-class white accents (mostly New York-ish) sound all right from the mouths of the appropriate characters but they mingle uncomfortably together mixed in with the dominant Standard English of the narrative.... In considering the book's stylistic blunders, however, one cannot help but note that the direction of Reed's experiment deserves attention. Perhaps his next book will resemble a sort of third-person Huckleberry Finn, amalgamating many tongues of black and white

America. For the moment we have only a disorganized collection of excellent ideas and brilliant but isolated vignettes. (p. 411)

> Barbara Joye, in PHYLON: The Atlanta University Review of Race and Culture *(copyright, 1968, by Atlanta University; reprinted by permission of PHYLON), Vol. XXIX, No. 4, Fourth Quarter (December, 1968).*

MARTIN TUCKER

Ishmael Reed can hardly be called a camp follower. [*The Free-Lance Pall Bearers*] inverts conventional attitudes for sustained comic effect; his feints are brilliant and his punches swift. . . . [However], he is prone to rely on the in-joke, and to join in a growing army of writers who "grotest" too much. This army is losing some of its power to surprise. (p. 508)

> Martin Tucker, in Commonweal *(copyright © 1968 Commonweal Publishing Co., Inc.; reprinted by permission of Commonweal Publishing Co., Inc.), January 26, 1968.*

IRVING HOWE

Testimonials from weighty sources declare Mr. Reed a comic master; he himself announces his style to be "literary neohoodooism"; and I can only crustily say that I read him without a guffaw, without a laugh, without a cackle, without the shade of a smile. Packed with *Mad* Magazine silliness though his work is, Mr. Reed has one saving virtue: he is hopelessly good-natured. He may intend his books as a black variation of Jonathan Swift, but they emerge closer to the commercial cooings of Captain Kangaroo. (p. 141)

> Irving Howe, in Harper's *(copyright © by Harper's Magazine; all rights reserved; excerpted from the December, 1969 issue by special permission), December, 1969.*

GEORGE E. KENT

Among novelists writing today, Reed ranks in the top of those commanding a brilliant set of resources and techniques. The prose is flexible, easy in its shift of gears and capacity to move on a variety of levels. The techniques of the cartoon, the caricature, the vaudevillean burlesque, the straight narrative, the detective story, are summoned at will.

But his management of his resources in *The Last Days of Louisiana Red* fails to create a lasting or deep impression. The novel deals with areas which afford rich soil for the satirist, since rebellious and revolutionary movements are always harassed by paradox and baneful fruit no matter how necessary such movements reveal themselves to be. In the black movement: the attempt to transform criminal activity into political purpose aborting and now revealing a black community as the greatest victim of crime; the ideological shifts which threaten to swing around a circle; the romanticization of a jungle street world whose deadend "hipness" was often sold as true blackness, etc. What we get of such matters in the novel seems to come out of a simplicity which has not first felt the pressure of complexity. Except for an individual statement here and there, the center of values from which the attacks are to be made turn out to be rather vague suggestions about the artist, imagination, symbolic conjure. Or an uncritical and undisciplined endorsement of middleclass striving.

The imaging is a major problem. Approved images of black women are in the category of the vaguely drawn or conforming: Miss Better Weather and Sister. Powerful dramatization is conferred upon the betrayers, the "castrating," the crude. Coupled with statements by Papa LaBas, who makes a long accusatory speech regarding black women, the dramatic structure gives us conceptions of black women which could emerge from a peculiar and limited mix; the pimp code, Southern white apologists for plantation sexual relations, street corner raps, and school boy bull sessions. Perhaps the black women of the "silent black majority" are excepted from the mix. Unfortunately, they are both silent and unseen in this novel.

In the treatment of "militants" or "revolutionaries," the dramatic structure and comments seem designed to evoke pictures of the more spectacular and zany activities of the Panthers and street radicals in general. A number of their rituals . . . would certainly be irresistible to the satirist. But lingering in the shadows of one's consciousness is likely to be another sobering and terrifying image: that of men who soaked all their intentions and strivings in their own blood. Thus, despite wonderfully entertaining burlesque scenes, the reader's consciousness may still require that a satirist make his bold moves in a highly skilled stride through the after-rhythms and beats of pathos and tragedy. Perhaps a radicalism which could accomplish the task of bringing "down killers three times" its size, one that used ancient wisdom and techniques of "camouflage" and created silent and loyal workers, would be excepted from the simple, straight-line strictures of the novel. (pp. 192-93)

If we . . . try to put together the positive aspects of Reed's message, the results seem to be the following sum in addition: constructive builders, disciplined and undramatic workers, a draw upon the positive spirit available from aspiring blacks which makes possible construction and lethally destructive powers far beyond what numbers would imply, old virtues of self-reliance and individualism, necessitating acknowledgement of differences, and a rejection of destructive tendencies within the group. Unfortunately, much of the foregoing must be gained from statements and debates, rather than from imposing portraiture. Thus, if Reed wants to deliver the full force of his message, questions of adjustment of form may require his confrontation. (p. 193)

> George E. Kent, in PHYLON: The Atlanta University Review of Race and Culture *(copyright 1975, by Atlanta University; reprinted by permission of PHYLON), Vol. XXXVI, No. 2, Second Quarter (June, 1975).*

DARWIN TURNER

Who or what is the poet Ishmael? An intellectual anti-intellectual. A religious opponent of religion. A duelling pacifist. A black antagonist champion of blacks. A poet influenced by Yeats, Pound, Blake, and the Umbra poets. A Black Arts poet who attacks Black Arts critics and poets. A satirical creator of myths. An ideologue who derides ideologies. A poet who ranges in allusion from Nixon to Wotan and Osiris. A poet of the topical and the ancient. A poet ignored in Stephen Henderson's trenchant analysis of the blackness of contemporary black poetry (*Understanding The New Black Poetry*, 1973), but whose poetry offers a point-by-point illustration of Henderson's analysis. Stir these contradictions together in a vat of satire; whirl yourself wildly until dizzy; then pour slowly. The brew is the poetry of Ishmael Reed, to be sipped as delicately as one might sip a potion of 2 parts bourbon, 1 part vodka, and a dash of coke. There is no guarantee that every drinker will like the concoction. Occasionally, the sip is flat. Most often, however, it is quickly intoxicating. (pp. 209-10)

The great theme of black poetry, Henderson argues, is Liberation. For Reed, this term has double meaning: not only to get the white man's foot off his neck but also to escape the nets cast by his black brothers. (p. 210)

In addition to liberation, Reed explores black religion. Although Reed rejects the traditional Afro-American identification with Christianity and the current interest in the religion of Islam, he is no less devout in his desire to restore the black deities—Apis and Osiris. . . . "Neo-Hoodoo Manifesto" (*Conjure*) is his most explicit articulation of this religious creed.

Like other contemporary black poets, Reed draws his techniques from the black story-telling tradition to narrate the adventures of imaginary black characters. Reed actually uses the blues form itself, as in "Betty's Ball Blues." Or he hyperbolically describes a black character whose supernatural prowess derives from hoodoo power. . . . Often, however, Reed, writing in the first person, makes the narrator a hyperbolic character. . . . Reed infuses his narrative poems with a ribald humor, blending in allusions which demand a reader's knowledge of American history and black history (both in Africa and elsewhere).

For Stephen Henderson, the second element, structure, is the most difficult to isolate. Reed's experiments with typography are relatively conservative. He seems less concerned with the use of space on a page than with the capitalization of all letters in a line to indicate its stentorian quality, and the use of italics or lower-case type to give comic or didactic emphasis. He identifies the "prosey typography" not with black culture but with William Blake's "The Marriage of Heaven and Hell."

As Henderson explains, however, black poetry relies most on techniques taken from black speech and music, and he itemizes eight "obvious" forms of "black" linguistic elegance: virtuoso naming and enumerating, jazzy rhythmic effects, virtuoso free rhyming, hyperbolic imagery, metaphysical imagery, understatement, compressed and cryptic imagery, and worrying the line. Most of these are important in Reed's poetry.

Virtuoso naming and enumerating is a form of word play that demonstrates the poet's knowledge and/or wit. Virtuoso naming is not allusion, nor is it the Whitmanesque catalogue intended to identify the components of a whole. Virtuoso naming becomes an end in itself, the list limited only by the poet's imagination, interest, or suspicions about the reader's patience. . . . A variant of virtuoso naming gradually leads us from our startled response to meaningless coinages of interesting sounds to our perception of meaning, as in Reed's gaggle of monsters to avoid:

> The Gollygog
> The Bingbuffer
> The Moogie
> The Fillyloo
> The Behemoth
> The Snawfus
> The Gowrow
> The Spiro
> The Angew

(pp. 211-13)

Virtuoso naming is effective in oral poetry, for the poet appeals to the listener's curiosity and intensifies anticipation during the pauses between the items in the list. (In this he joins with the Black Arts poets.) Similarly, jazzy rhythmic effects may be more obvious to a listener than a reader. . . .

[In] virtuoso rhyming, . . . meaning counts less than the rhymed sounds.

Reed's hyperbolic imagery has already been [mentioned], but he also employs what Henderson describes as "metaphysical" imagery—the combination of hyperbole, precise intellectual statement, and witty comparison into a passionate and unified image. Reed's intellect, reading, and fascination with esoterica often blur the distinction between his hyperbolic and his "metaphysical" imagery. . . . (p. 214)

Other black "elegances" of language appear in Reed's poetry—in particular, Aesopian understatement:

> A crocidile [sic] dont hunt
> Him's victims
>
> . . .
> All he do is
> Open he jaws . . . .

and such cryptic and compressed images as "gunghoguru . . . from d heddahopper planet." But the verbal techniques of wit and blunt language—outrageous, hilarious, ribald— are the summit of Reed's talent. . . . (p. 215)

Like other black poets, Reed relates his poetry to black music—not merely by writing blues, but also by incorporating or alluding to contemporary songs or spirituals, song titles, contemporary musicians, or by using musical tones as poetic structure. . . .

Pulling lines or passages from context to demonstrate a particular technique fails to convey the verve or impact of the poem, in which Reed hurls the reader from one idea and device to another. An extended analysis can merely suggest the intellectual range, not the emotional effect. (p. 216)

[In "The Jackal-headed Cowboy from Ra"] Reed . . . conjures images of black power, and predicts that Blacks will crush a symbol of their economic oppression—the Wall Street moguls. Like Swift comparing writers with spiders spinning webs from their filth, Reed evokes the crushed stock-market bug whose "insides spill out like / reams of ticker tape," thus arousing emotional revulsion.

Reed vitriolically attacks the corrupt values and venal slogans slavishly venerated by "proper" Americans: pep pills (competitive drive), the artificially induced fetish for cleanliness and unblemished pale skin, antiseptic sexuality, etiquette, and other superficial paraphernalia of an "elegant" culture. His two-line insert of polite phrases is a mocking transition and prologue to the conversion of these values into a food that can be eaten only by indestructible people: an explosive stew "topped with kegs . . . of whipped dynamite and cheery smithereens." Evoking the images of blacks and black culture that whites have used pejoratively, the African-American god-narrator prophesies that blacks will pass through the baptism of fire and dance with the sun.

Reed's showmanship and conjuring can be spellbinding. Like T. S. Eliot, he demands that his readers comprehend his allusions; but unlike Eliot, he presumes that many who approach with child-like innocence will understand, or be fascinated by the sounds.

Reed fulfills Henderson's third category, "saturation," the communication of and fidelity to the truth of black experience—without continuously proclaiming his blackness. He carries no signs in protest marches, nor does he always write on black subjects. He decries popular white heroes while urging respect for black figures, summons black historical personages, encourages young black writers, and skillfully avoids European cultural entrapments. He compels by virtue of his effortlessly commanding black style. (pp. 217-18)

Darwin Turner, in Parnassus: Poetry in Review *(copyright © by Poetry in Review Foundation), Spring–Summer, 1976.*

LINDA SHELL BERGMANN

The American search for a usable past began with our first writers. American historians, cultural critics, and artists have repeatedly rewritten our history in response to evolving philosophies and social issues. And novelist, both serious and popular, have followed close behind, infusing fictional human relations with historical reality to cultivate—or to create—myths about our past. The old, tenacious forms of historical fiction either glamorize the past, reinforcing old myths of greatness, or revise history by exposing the lust, greed, despair, or irrationality of ages or men once considered stable, moral, and vital. But although contemporary novelists like Roth, Doctorow, Pynchon, Barth, and Ishmael Reed still mine and recast history, they have renewed and transformed the once-belittled historical novel. These novelists go beyond mere revisionism, questioning the possibility of historical understanding, rejecting the limits of historical reality and even of verisimilitude, exposing the irrelevance of both revering and rejecting the past.

The most recent example of this new kind of historical novel is Ishmael Reed's *Flight to Canada.* Through parody, exaggeration, anachronism, and the juxtaposition of literary myths, Reed transforms the experiences of slavery and the Civil War into comedy. Reed's two previous excursions into the American past, *Yellow Back Radio Broke-Down* and *Mumbo Jumbo,* exploit eras more easily transformed into comedy: the American West and the Twenties. But slavery, the Civil War, the assassination of Lincoln? Although they furnish material for the countless contradictory theses of historians, essayists, poets, and novelists, these aspects of our past have always been considered either tragic or epic. However Ishmael Reed has little use for the romanticism or social realism traditionally associated with the relations of slave and master. (p. 200)

Reed has made *Flight to Canada* a work of broadly comic

satire. And like the lampooned traders, Reed's slave masters expose their corruption in their own features and actions; they need no crushed and humiliated slaves to expose their guilt. Because Reed refuses to depict the abject misery and subjection of the slaves, *Flight to Canada* arouses neither sympathy and guilt nor pity and fear. Instead, Reed liberates the material of slave narratives from the form exploited and imposed by the likes of Harriet Beecher Stowe. He demands that his story be read as fiction rather than as bitter reality, and he demands that we consider him a novelist rather than a spokesman.

Reed's slaves are not liberated by the Civil War or the "Great Emancipator"; they liberate themselves. The novel begins with a poem, "Flight to Canada," by the ostensible writer of the story, Raven Quickskill. One line of plot traces the writer's emergence from slavery to self-mastery by showing his volatile relationship with his poem:

> Little did I know when I wrote the poem
> "Flight to Canada" that there were so many
> secrets locked inside its world. It was more
> of a reading than a writing. Everything it
> said seems to have caught up with me. Other
> things are running away. The black in my
> hair is running away. The bad spirits who
> were in me left a long time ago. The devil
> who was catching up with me is slipping behind and losing ground. What a war it was!
>
> (pp. 201-02)

Quickskill's growth is evident in the difference between the poem and the novel. He has liberated himself from the very kind of surliness, cynicism, and bitterness to the very kind of satirical humor that Reed described in *Mumbo Jumbo.* The poem is bitter, vengeful, murderous. In the poem, Quickskill robs Swille, seduces his favorite Quadroon, and poisons his Old Crow. The angry poet, still emotionally dominated by his master, flaunts his vengeance. In the novel, however, revenge would be a waste of energy. Swille is robbed and murdered by the decadence of his own way of life. No longer an object of fear and hatred, Swille loses his power, and thus he can become an object of comedy. Slavery, the South, and Canada are states of mind, no longer limited by time and space. (p. 203)

Even as Canada can be anywhere, so Southern masters are not restricted to plantations in Virginia. The slave catchers pursuing Quickskill—liberal racists—are also objects of satire. (p. 204)

Since Reed perceives slavery and the South as states of mind rather than spacial and historical entities, he can be liberal with his use of anachronism. Quickskill's characters are equipped with telephones, cars, xerox machines, airplanes, and Coffee Mate. Quickskill can watch *Our American Cousin* on educational television and see an instant replay of Lincoln's assassination. The historical era becomes irrelevant: slaves are slaves because they do not assert their freedom. And Southern masters—be they antebellum gentlemen, Oscar Wilde, or "blond beasts"—are Southern masters because they embrace the Arthurian ideal without realizing its implications. Reed insists that the underside of Tennyson is Poe: Camelot, needing whips and chains because it depends on slaves to do its work, is destroyed from both within and without by the inherent contradiction of grace depending on force. Arthur Swille, spokesman of the

Tennysonian ideal and third and last of his line, turns Camelot into the House of Usher. And Raven Quickskill, turning its fall into satiric comedy, insists "Nevermore."

Reed's *Flight to Canada* demolishes the stereotypes of countless historical novels, routing Uncle Tom, Scarlett O'Hara, Nat Turner. Since the sixties, historians have been reexamining slavery, seeking alternatives to the concept of the abjectly degraded slave deprived of heritage and will. Naturally, novelists followed them. But the brilliance of Reed's work rests in his translation of a new interpretation of our past into a new form of historical novel. Muses Quickskill: "Strange, history. Complicated, too. It will always be a mystery, history. New disclosures are as bizarre as the most bizarre fantasy." (pp. 204-05)

> *Linda Shell Bergmann, in* Chicago Review *(reprinted by permission of* Chicago Review; *copyright © 1976 by* Chicago Review*), Vol. 28, No. 2, 1976.*

ALLEN BELKIND

[Reed] has emerged as one of the more promising and prolific of the current young black writers in America. [*Shrovetide in Old New Orleans*] (articles, reviews, open letters, speeches and interviews) seems to represent everything that Reed has ever published. Such over-inclusion (some less worthy material) must relate to Reed's calling this collection "an autobiography of my mind starting in about 1970."

In his introduction Reed answers those critics who have called his fiction "muddled, crazy, incoherent" by explaining that his mind and method are multi-media oriented and by describing himself as a controversialist: "Stir things up a bit. Wake America from its easy chair and can of beer." Reed's aggressive polemical style, his attack upon American racism, his defense of a black esthetic and his opinions of white critics as bad judges of black writing have not endeared him to the white literary establishment. . . . Reed's often offensive tone is redeemed in part by his hip colloquial idiom, his penchant for self-dramatization and his passionate interest in everything that relates to African and Afro-American culture.

Especially interesting are Reed's travel-culture essays on the New Orleans Mardi Gras ("Shrovetide") and on post-Papa Doc Haiti ("I Hear You, Doc"). He is sensitive to cultural nuances and writes informatively about Haitian Vodoun, but his political opinions seem eccentric. He depicts Papa Doc Duvalier as a Houngan hero rather than a despot and feels that the Haitian poor (in their extreme squalor) are "happier" than poor American blacks because the Haitians have work and identity. Other pieces of interest include Reed's appreciative essay on Chester Himes, various interviews with black artists, a reassessment of Richard Wright and reviews about Josephine Baker and Charlie "Bird" Parker.

Despite father-destroying attacks on established writers—Ellison, Baldwin (very distasteful) and Mailer (excessively mauled)—Reed's collection offers many useful insights into current Afro-American culture. It is also a useful purgative for white complacency and an interesting self-portrait of a complex and talented black writer struggling for understanding and success on his own terms. (p. 635)

> *Allen Belkind, in* World Literature Today *(copy-*

right 1978 by the University of Oklahoma Press), Vol. 52, No. 4, Autumn, 1978.

STANLEY CROUCH

Tom-ing is such a normal thing, particularly in its urban capitol—New York—that one is sometimes shocked when a man, particularly a black man, decides not only to refuse to tom, but goes on the offensive, which, in the literary world, can mean muckraking. Ishmael Reed is such a man, and his most recent book *Shrovetide in Old New Orleans . . .*, is a collection of often bitter essays, reviews, and interviews that attack institutions and personages most black artists fume about in private and play the banjo for in public. . . .

Reed's own work draws strongly on popular culture, erudite information, and the technology of our time for a mixture and vindictive juxtaposition that, as in his novel *Mumbo Jumbo,* can hurl snowballs filled with stones at the heads of famous and brutal forces. Reed has never cared whether his targets were black or white, only if they tried to deprive him of what he considers his freedom of choice or aesthetic direction. He is always struggling for the right to be an individual.

He is also confusing. Not all of his ideas tie up, and he is caught more than once talking out of both sides of his mouth. . . . (p. 75)

Reed is arrogant, irascible, bitter, and quick to attack. His writing in this volume is full of incendiary barbs and barrages at opportunistic blacks who pimp tragedy for liberal tears and dollars, at a sullen and totalitarian black nationalism of the '60s that tried to trim all black artists to fit its own program (strangely, he never confronts LeRoi Jones head-on—Jones was responsible for much of that), at Marxists, liberals who leap from one "moral" fad to another, multinational corporations, what he considers the racist art establishment, and certain Jews in critical positions who uphold western culture as though it were sufficient to prevent a Hitler. Of course, he is prepared to take his lumps, to be called a tom, a reactionary, an anti-Semite, and "a part of the problem."

From the other side, there is an occasional tendency to glibness on Reed's part, and an odd sentimentality, as when in an otherwise well-written review of Chester Himes's *The Quality of Hurt* he quotes maudlin and self-congratulatory passages from the book which he says are *not* sentimental. Also, Reed sometimes seems much too busy himself with defending his work; he weakens his arguments by making it appear as though he were trying to gorilla white critics into accepting him, his aesthetic, the writers he likes. Nor am I sure that he is on very steady ground when he tries to equate folk art with that of sophisticated men like himself. . . .

Most of the interviews Reed includes suffer from unnecessary discursiveness. He seems to have difficulty developing the ideas that come up, or is too busy trying to draft his interviewees into his struggle against personal demons. As with the interview of since-deceased black conservative and novelist George Schuyler (then in his 70s) point after point is left dangling, and broad ranges of experience are overlooked, or fail to be clarified through precise questions. Yet Reed's interview with himself, however self-serving, shows the quality of his own ideas. . . . Conversely, as with the hysterically sexist *The Last Days of Louisiana Red,* what begins as a brilliant satire—on Angela Davis, Eldridge Cleaver, Marxism, Berkeley, and those who would dismiss the tradition of African-American culture in favor of a dull, slogan-laden, and obvious "revolutionary culture"—loses its force because the "written sculpture" takes on the shape of a clumsy club with which Reed doesn't so much beat the asses of his adversaries as bludgeon his own ideas to death. (p. 76)

Ishmael Reed is an important contemporary voice because he provokes ideas and realizes that the racial situation in America is now as much about ideas as anything else, and that the black writer who breaks with convention risks a very special castigation. If you disbelieve, read the reviews of Albert Murray's *Stomping the Blues* in much of the white jazz press (which is, incidentally, far more paternalistic and arrogant than the white literary establishment). For all the problems with this collection of essays, Reed's batting average is at least .450, which means he is right or illuminatingly suggestive four-and-one-half times out of 10. Human life being what it is—not to mention the insipidness of most racial commentary, black and white—seems pretty good to me. (p. 74)

> Stanley Crouch, "The Hoo Doo Wrath of Ishmael Reed," in The Village Voice (reprinted by permission of The Village Voice; copyright © The Village Voice, Inc., 1979), January 22, 1979, pp. 75-6, 74.

*   *   *

RICHLER, Mordecai   1931-

Richler is a Canadian novelist, screenwriter, essayist, short story writer, and children's book author who combines humor and satire with a strong moral and historical sense to create his interpretation of Jewish and Canadian experience; George Woodcock calls him "the essential Canadian." Richler is best known for *The Apprenticeship of Duddy Kravitz*, the story of a Montreal boy's attempt to outfox society. (See also *CLC*, Vols. 3, 5, 9, and *Contemporary Authors*, Vols. 65-68.)

[*Hunting Tigers Under Glass* is a collection of] a bundle of essays, reports and reviews on a variety of topics not immediately likely to fit together: Canada and sport, various forms of pop literature and art, Jewish-American writing, and Israel. The focus is Mordecai Richler himself. "After all, I'm a Jewish writer from Canada," he says. But so is Saul Bellow [sic]; and the book, on internal evidence alone, is not by him. The pieces, bitter-sweet and often very funny, form a kind of instant biography of reminiscence, observation and opinion: even when writing a fictional review of Malamud or Mailer, Mr. Richler usually turns the occasion into one for idiosyncrasy and recollection.

Moreover, they are written from a number of wry angles, some of them coming from Mr. Richler's intelligently common sense radical view of two forms of provincialism he knows very well indeed, the Jewish and the Canadian: and some from the fact that for a Jewish novelist he has taken the unpredictable tack of finding his cosmopolis not in New York but in London. More still come from the fact that the pieces address heterodox reading-publics. . . . (p. 117)

It all seems to go to show that it is, as they say, hard to know who one is nowadays: but actually Mr. Richler knows very well. He is a confessed product of the 1940s, when one was interested in pop not because it was camp but because

it was what there was, just as he says as a student he and his friends had sex in the afternoon not because they were radical or alienated but because they were horny. . . . [With] confident opinionation he cuts through the glossy romanticisms and belaboured intellectual worries in the interests of establishing the real feel of the thing.

The three essays on Canada and Canadianism here (while not as good as his brilliant treatment of the same thing in his novel *The Apprenticeship of Duddy Kravitz*) have some of the best insights into provincial cosmopolitanism, mainly because Mr. Richler observes, collects and remembers the essential data with at once an ironic and a sympathetic vision. The basic tactic of compassion and irony is very funny and it brings him right into the middle of the enclaves of *kitsch*. (p. 118)

The targets are never *too* easy since Mr. Richler is fully involved—as the Canadian-Jewish good-bad boy of the 1940s who himself went through both the bourgeois and the intellectual apprenticeship. . . . The kids on the block and what became of them through the past twenty years of complex history really form the theme that runs behind these pieces. The time is one in which it became easier to be a Jew (and Mr. Richler is excellent on the inept touchiness of hard-core Jewish culture, which he has constantly offended). (pp. 118-19)

But easier can be harder. Mr. Richler is a writer of ironies, detachment, and comic involvements rather than a voice of exile or anomaly; but one can see in his writings why the Jewish writer or intellectual might have gone a good deal deeper into self-doubt. In a critically sharp review of Malamud's *The Fixer*, he points out the way in which the Jewish writer tends, his modern experience being now pretty well on file in the Jewish-American efflorescence of the 1950s, to hark back to origins, to the *shtetl* or the archetypal pogrom. Mr. Richler himself holds to the fascination of ordinary origins, and comes out as a grand supra-provincial. . . .

This is a lively book, the more illuminating if you consider Mordecai Richler, and he goes on giving us more and more grounds for thinking so, an important novelist. And it is a usefully oblique insight into a body of experience that the Jewish-American novelists have gone through with more tension and bravura, but with a good deal less irony and humour. (p. 119)

> "On the Block," in The Times Literary Supplement (© Times Newspapers Ltd. (London) 1969; reproduced from The Times Literary Supplement by permission), January 23, 1969 (and reprinted in Mordecai Richler, edited by G. David Sheps, McGraw-Hill Company, 1971, pp. 117-19).

G. DAVID SHEPS

In their themes and motifs, Mordecai Richler's novels return regularly to a constant set of preoccupations. Despite this consistency, however, his career as a novelist has undergone some interesting alterations in terms of his moral attitudes towards his favourite preoccupations. This change of outlook has naturally been accompanied by a change in style and genre. It would have been difficult, on the basis of his early naturalistic novels, to anticipate the satirist and caricaturist who emerged with *The Incomparable Atuk* and *Cocksure*. . . . Occasional satirical elements are utilized by most novelists. It is another matter altogether to step from a dominant narrative mode of realistic characterization, verisimilitude of action and psychological plausibility to a dominant mode of conscious caricature in characterization, purposeful implausibility of action and fantasy in events. For a novelist to alter his style and narrative mode so decisively, a deliberate change in moral outlook must have occurred. . . . One of the theses of this interpretation is that, philosophically, Richler has moved from a tentative Romanticism to a kind of Classicism. (pp. ix-x)

In Richler's first novel, *The Acrobats,* we can already see most of the materials that recur in his later work: power, egoism, self-realization, struggle for survival, the conflict of generations and youthful rebelliousness, the need to escape from a confining environment, the sense of moral disillusionment and the fear of failure. The form of his first novel (and of all his naturalistic novels) is that most traditional of fictional structures: the attempted progress of the sensitive young man . . . in escaping the fetters of an inhibiting situation and in advancing towards a form of independence, realization of what he takes to be his inherent potentialities or worldly success and recognition. In other words Richler's theme is that of the attempted rise from rags to riches, on several moral and aesthetic levels. (p. x)

This configuration, of course, is not surprising in a novelist. It is a truism that the novel is *the* bourgeois literary form. Theorists of the novel, like Ian Watt, have emphasized that the novel is specifically the literary form which is structured by the sense of time and movement as progressive, qualitative change, i.e. the notion that time must not be wasted and that the measurement of time should also measure changes in the person's status or situation. . . . Naturally it reflects a society where social mobility and the idea of self-development are both possible and social and psychological imperatives. The novel, therefore, is the form which best expresses romantic individualism. . . . Richler's novels are located in bourgeois time. His young men in a hurry or on the make (whether the hustler, Duddy Kravitz; the impatient aesthete, André Bennett; or the mixture of the two, Noah Adler) are the distant cousins, not only of Paul Morel, Stephen Dedalus and Sammy Glick, but also of Raskolnikov, Julien Sorel, Emma Bovary and Hedda Gabler. Like these nineteenth century heroes and heroines, they are manic depressive (the characteristic bourgeois psychosis, if we can believe the evidence of Ibsen and Flaubert). They urgently need to succeed and are haunted by the fear of failure; they alternate between delusions of triumph and a suicidal sense of utter emptiness.

Richler's novels differ, however, in that they are obviously of the middle of the twentieth century and lack much of the partial optimism current in the previous century. His characters are acutely aware that they come after the disillusionment with several twentieth-century revolutions and causes. . . . Richler's characters, for all their ambition and energy, really know *from the beginning* that either they are defeated or their outcomes will be much drearier than their apparent victories might indicate. Duddy Kravitz, for example, appears successful in achieving his ambition. But there is every indication that he has been metamorphosed into something very like his antagonist, the odious Jerry Dingleman.

A further problem for Richler's protagonists (and it is a problem, often, with the novels themselves) is that they do not know what it is they are seeking. . . . They insist that salvation lies only in the adoption of personal values, but they are not sure which personal values to hold. The statement, in fact, becomes a mechanical formula with which they try to persuade themselves of something, rather than any passionately held and confident sense of personal identity. This becomes a problem for the reader as well as for the fictional character and represents the greatest weakness in Richler's writings. I don't mean to suggest that Richler ought to supply his characters with a facile affirmation. The problem is a genuine one. (This, I suppose, is why some people have referred to Richler's "existentialism." But this kind of comment, besides betraying a lack of understanding of existentialism as a philosophical standpoint, is itself a facile evasion of a problem and a retreat into a mechanistic formula.)

To be frank, it gets rather boring to be told repeatedly that all the good old causes are dead, that one knows what one dislikes but not what one likes, and then to be expected to be deeply concerned with the activities and fate of a very self-serving and self-pitying character. (pp. x-xii)

For myself, I am always rather puzzled by critics . . . who take at face value the moral posturings of many of Richler's main characters. After all, if we look at them with a cold eye, we often get a picture in which they appear something like this: they are egocentric and insensitive to others; they are ruthless and are basically indifferent even to those they sometimes claim to love; they will exploit or misuse their closest friends and relatives often on not much more than a whim; their claims to their own moral sensitivity and dilemmas are generally self-serving; they are usually contemptuous of the causes served by others at great personal risk; and they give little evidence of possessing either the kind of intelligence or knowledge which would be required to sustain the complexities and subtleties of the moral consciousness to which they pretend. Indeed, most of Richler's youthful rebels and idealistic questers share many characteristics with the hypocritical older generation, or the corrupt society, or the oppressors against whom they appear to be in revolt. (p. xiii)

[Nevertheless, Richler makes] claims on the reader to view with sympathy and concern the problems of his heroes. As many critics have pointed out, the author is often emotionally engaged himself with his heroes. This clear call for sympathy with these figures, many of whom objectively have unsympathetic or dull personalities, has divided Richler's readers. These are those who find the novels almost wholly objectionable because of the repugnant qualities of so many of the characters. Others are taken in by the postures adopted by his sensitive or lonely young men and thus uncritically proceed to sentimentalize these figures as courageous knights who assault the unrelieved evil of a corrupt society. . . . (p. xiv)

There is another possible approach to the reading of Richler's novels. One of the most interesting facts about these novels is that the ostensible heroes and the ostensible villains share many qualities. It is entirely possible to regard the apparent heroes unsympathetically and to respond even to the most malevolent figures, like the Nazi Kraus, Melech Adler, or Karp, sympathetically. Indeed, Richler's ability to make his characters sufficiently complex and humanly ambiguous, in a perfectly plausible manner, and to supply enough information so that we understand how they got to be the way they are is one of his most striking achievements. Some critics may fail to see the humanity in an apparently monstrous figure or naively may be taken in by a putatively sympathetic figure, but Richler the novelist does not make these mistakes.

Others have noted that Richler's characters are often "survivors" and that much of their energy is consumed by the strategies of survival in a competitive and hostile world. This is true enough. The Richler characters often have the wary, suspicious, necessarily egoistic psychology of the survivor. They move through life like tacticians, are survivors of concentration camps; various forms of persecution, war, or poverty; or simply painfully traumatic personal experiences and shattered dreams and ideals. They are frequently the floating debris of the wreckage of the modern period and this mental set conditions them to ruthlessness, emotional detachment and scepticism. Whatever hopes they have are tempered by an instinctive awareness of great odds against them. This often concludes in cynicism, barely suppressed hysteria, or submissive resignation. (p. xv)

This leads us to a consideration which is at the heart of Richler's books. The figures of the romantic individualist and the survivor merge. But not only in the obvious sense that the survivor is perforce an isolated individual. What I am suggesting is that the very concept of the romantic quest of the individual hero, either for worldly success or for self-realization, is itself treated in Richler's novels as a part of the debris that lingers after a cultural wreckage. Although Richler's heroes, from André Bennett to Duddy Kravitz, embrace this romantic concept, the concept itself is no longer wholly intact for these characters. There is something inauthentic, even spurious, about the quality of their hopes and quests. It is intimately related to their sense that they know what they oppose, but not what they positively want. And it is the reason they cannot formulate their ambitions with any more precision than that. There is the sense with several of Richler's more important characters that they *must*, even involuntarily, engage in individualistic, quixotic quests—although they can't say why and are sceptical if any reasons are proffered. Ironically, the young Richler hero has a culturally induced instinct—almost a blind instinct—to be rebellious, individualistic, iconoclastic. He must revolt against an Establishment and its values, whether that establishment be represented by a paternal figure, a teacher or professor, a philistine capitalist or a religious fanatic. They know they don't like these things, but will quickly admit that they can't suggest anything that is necessarily better. Significantly, collective actions like socialism are also spurned, but a bit more respectfully. (pp. xvi-xvii)

Characteristically, Richler's protagonists are those romantic, adolescent (of whatever age) "rebels without a cause" popularized by James Dean in the 1950s. This hero has no particular notions about the reconstruction of society or about the reconstruction of himself. His individualism is a matter of posture, a stance without content he adopts in opposition to his society. Hence, it is often expressed as a generational conflict between fathers (or grandfathers) and sons, as this is generally the most content-less of conflicts and the most readily articulated in terms of style of life—as only styles change drastically in a single generation. (pp. xvii-xviii)

I don't mean to pretend that some of Richler's figures do not suffer genuinely at the hands of their parents or communities. In many cases they clearly do and they are sometimes authentically shocked or repelled by hypocrisies they encounter. But frequently the degree of their contempt seems unwarranted by the objective quality of the putative cause. . . . Throughout the novels there are many instances where a younger man voluntarily assumes the psychological role of son to an older man or woman and then turns against them. The older person is usually childless, but wants children, and seeks out surrogate children who will betray them. If the youthful Richler hero may be described as simply wanting to "do his thing," his thing often enough seems to be devouring his parent figures. The surrogate father figures, like Norman Price and Theo Hall, pay their nostalgic respects to their own vanished youth by willingly presenting themselves for the feast, masochistically re-enacting themselves in their surrogate children.

Clearly defined motives and desires do not exist in relation to these figures, even for Duddy Kravitz and his ambition to acquire land. Rather, there are threads of various possible motives, often mutually contradictory, in the same person: escape from poverty and weakness, a search for economic security, the vague need to define one's own identity, a desire for a form of ecstasy, and others. To put it another way, their motives are a mixture of the varieties of motives that can be isolated in the heroes and heroines of nineteenth century literature. (pp. xviii-xix)

The repression and distortion of aesthetic values into their antitheses is one of the themes of Richler's writings. The more closely one examines the typical Richler character, the more evident it becomes that his actions are predicated on the idea of the expression of sensibility itself. It is not only the idea that the inner, private sensibility ought to remain inviolate . . . Richler's characters often aspire as well towards existing on a plane of pure, exquisite sensibility; a form of ecstasy. This, too, is in the Romantic tradition and is usually represented as the beatific side of the romantic individualist's medal. It is the reverse, yet the mirror image . . . of the individualist as robber baron or mercenary buccaneer. (pp. xix-xx)

As early as André Bennett in *The Acrobats,* Richler has figures who are partly driven by a sense of guilt or the memory of a dishonourable past of which they would like to purge themselves. Their striving for autonomy and the kind of fresh start which might release them from past generations and traditions is related to this. (p. xx)

The apparently inconsistent and confused motivations, the intransigent negativism, the moral attitudinizing, and the nebulously inarticulate anti-authoritarianism of Richler's heroes can be resolved and made articulate by the idea of sensibility. The characters usually will themselves into the attitude of the neo-Byronic hero. Thumbing their noses at an Establishment becomes the main expression and content of their rebellion, an act more of gesture than of coherent substance. A curious determinism, in fact, has molded them into the style and expression of "free spirits." Psychologically and historically they are the consequences of the romantic cult of self-expression, long after the substance has been drained out of the concept and all that remains are the involuntary reflexes of the old romantic revolution. As Marx said of historical repetition, the first time is tragedy and the second time is farce. History weighs heavily, if unconsciously, on these youths. But it is a specific history which has run its course and has left them only with the possibility of compulsively mechanical gestures which once, perhaps, had meaning.

These youths, after all, are the inheritors of the propaganda of the romantic era. Their imaginations have been nourished by the contemporary packaged versions of the dreams of that era: Byronism filtered through Hollywood films, the legends of heroically successful self-made men, and unreal images of a war in Spain ironically made seductively exotic through the songs of the losing side. In the synthetic myths of their popular culture, objective disparities and contradictions merge into a unitary image of glamour where capitalism's rugged individualist and the itinerant revolutionist present a single model to be imitated. Sensing also that this image presents a false model of reality, they nonetheless are fired by the romance they feel it ought to mirror. This accounts for their own mimicry of a posture they know to be anachronistic and their deep resentment of that history and those older generations which foisted such a dream upon them. (pp. xxi-xxii)

[It is] true that the older generation in Richler's work . . . have been sons to other fathers and have also been inspired and victimized by similar visions. This links the dilemmas of fathers and sons in an intergenerational iron chain of determinism where, with considerable irony, they are almost mechanically programmed to re-enact the ceremonies of "free spirits."

It is for this reason (although the process began in *A Choice of Enemies*) that in *Atuk* and *Cocksure* the most contemptuous satire is reserved for the information media—the world of film, TV, advertising, journalism and publishing—the pop culture industries which manipulate dreams and visions, determine the sensibilities of the populace, tamper with souls en masse. Star Maker (radically complete unto himself, the consummation of Romanticism), in *Cocksure*, is thus far Richler's most remarkably concentrated symbol for the destructively manipulative force of a spent historical romanticism. (p. xxii)

There is only so far an author can go with a historical and cultural situation which is trapped in a dead-end sensibility of burnt-out romanticism where the sensitive young men of the bourgeois epoch are fated to acting out illusions they can no longer believe. This, of course, is one of the fundamental problems of the novel today. The fact that the novel developed while formulating the ideology of that epoch is an important reason why so many contemporary novels are reduced to synthetically frenetic repetitions of the ethos of *Huckleberry Finn*. It is as if frenzied overstatement could resurrect the culturally dead the way Baroque art sought to restore the late medieval ethos through exaggeration of expression. An approach to Richler's writings like that of his earlier commentator Warren Tallman, who fundamentally misreads the import and direction of these novels, only sentimentalizes the hybrid Faustianism of a Duddy Kravitz. Reading through American ideological glasses, he sees Richler's themes as variants of the antihistorical innocence of American frontier ideology and manifest destiny at the very moment when Richler is beginning to satirize this romantic Faustianism almost as lucidly as Conrad does in *Heart of Darkness*. Such an approach cannot account for Richler's tactical shift from involvement to detachment and his adoption of satire as a formal mode (as opposed to satirical flashes in basically naturalistic novels) while maintaining his hold on the same set of cultural materials as subject matter.

After his first four novels, it would appear that Richler clearly realized a need to get away from characters attempting to live according to the measurements of bourgeois time. . . . As it was, his characters had strong doubts that [progress] was possible or significant even though they tried it. Comic forms, including satire, present one way out of this situation. In satires like *Atuk* and *Cocksure* we are no longer in the world of progressive and incremental mobility, even though men and women on the make still inhabit the world of these books. But the focus of interest here is no longer on their progress. . . . This particular shaping of our responses is assured because the author presents his characters as self-evident stereotypes. As soon as we see them, we know what they are like without waiting for their stories to unfold. We recognize them as caricatures of familiar attitudes and behaviour patterns, largely caricatures representing aspects of the world of contemporary popular culture. . . . The fictional time is relatively static as the characters do not grow and change. Rather, the reader simply sees layers being peeled away which reveal to him more information about the nature and meaning of the relationships and encounters among the various patterns of conduct of which the characters are emblems. The reader's response, therefore, is more cerebral than emotional. The satirical mode is closer to the purely intellectual.

One cannot, of course, assume that Richler will choose always to write in the same vein. As his perceptions of his materials change, so will his fictional techniques. But in these two latest books [*Atuk* and *Cocksure*,] he has begun to write comedy of manners and has revealed a spirit far closer to that of Congreve, Swift, and Shaw than one might have guessed from his earlier novels. (pp. xxiii-xxiv)

In my view, there is frequently an element of nihilism in the literary genre of comedy, particularly in its satirical side. . . . These elements of renewal and nihilism co-exist in a complex and fascinating tension. There is something about comedy that is not open-ended; that inflexibly closes off possibilities and is antipathetic to the idea of growth and change. It is not a form beloved by romantics and most of the great comic artists of English literature have not been romantics. (p. xxv)

An artist formulates and articulates the complex interactions of cultural experience. He does not prescribe for it. Richler makes no attempt at being a philosopher of history or a social visionary. Like many modern writers, he is aware that we are still wrestling with the problems bequeathed to us from the nineteenth century—that, indeed, twentieth century man is still intellectually and emotionally parasitic upon the concepts and dreams that both flourished and began to dissolve in the previous century. We still live with specific historical ghosts. The Romantic Revolution may be over, but its Faustianism is still operative in a thousand posthumous ways. Richler has no facile answers for this cultural situation and he eschews the posturings of prophecy. Proponents of a brave new world do not write comedies of manners. He is a writer devoted to his craft and the purpose of his craft is to articulate experience as it truly is. The immediate task of his craft is to discover fictional strategies for the accurate representation of reality. To represent the current dilemmas of the legacy of romanticism in the cold light of comedy is an illumination we require. (pp. xxv-xxvi)

G. David Sheps, in his introduction to Mordecai

Richler, *edited by G. David Sheps (copyright 1971; reprinted by permission of McGraw-Hill Ryerson Limited, Toronto), Ryerson Press, 1971, pp. ix-xxvi.*

F. M. BIRBALSINGH

[Canadianism and Jewishness] jointly form the main theme of [Richler's] fiction and the chief concern of all his writing. His novels deal, in general, with the large national problem of assimilating a Canadian identity out of disparate racial and cultural elements and, in particular, with the process of assimilating Jewish elements into an integrated Canadian culture.

Richler's first full-length work of fiction, *The Acrobats,* may be regarded as a beginner's novel. Its chief technique is to string together some of the author's most worrying dissatisfactions into a pastiche that is only mildly satirical. The satire is not completely effective because the writing is too derivative, relying more on the over-used jargon of literary idols like Hemingway and Dos Passos rather than on an individual style that bears the stamp of the author's own personality and conviction. Indeed, the most striking feature of this first novel is that the author has no firm or sincere convictions. His philosophical ideas are unstable and imprecise and represent a spontaneous overflow of merely personal grievances whose principal intention, it seems, is to afford the author psychological relief rather than express balanced or thoroughly digested opinions.

The Acrobats is greatly influenced by ideas and modes of thought which were fashionable during the decade of the 1950s; for it was the era of *Lucky Jim* and *On the Road,* of Colin Wilson and Allen Ginsberg, the Angry Young Men of England and the Beat Generation of America. Like the 1930s, it was a time when Gods had failed those who believed in them, when sensitive and intelligent young men, especially in England and America, experienced an acute sense of disillusionment because they felt there was a dearth of causes worth fighting for. They spurned traditional beliefs and could not commit themselves with any enthusiasm to such causes as were recognized by prevailing religious faiths and political allegiances. André Bennett, hero of *The Acrobats,* experiences the spiritual malaise of his contemporaries of the 1950s. . . . (pp. 72-3)

The Semitic aspect of Richler's theme is embodied in Chaim who represents the resilience of Jewishness, a faith and way of life that survives despite long and severe persecution. Neither this, however, nor the Canadian aspect of the theme is expressed with any coherence. One receives mere intimations of the author's passionate concern with Jewish-Canadianism; his attitude to his theme seems overwrought and confused. At the same time, the passion and intensity of Richler's concern are not missed. His rage and indignation are too over-powering for that. He rips into existing Canadian cultural standards and artistic achievement [with acid, searing fury]. . . . But this fury is not malice. . . . Richler's passion springs from devotion to his country, a patriotic desire to see the arts flourish in Canada, not through pretentious and insincere dilettantism or servile obsequiousness, but through the dissemination of a genuinely humane influence in a society marked by its own clearly-defined regional idiosyncrasies and cultural homogeneity. (p. 73)

Son of a Smaller Hero is set in Montreal and deals almost exclusively with Canadian subjects. The novel reproduces the local Jewish community in which the author himself grew up. The plot, such as it is, traces the career of Noah Adler, who rebels against the religious orthodoxy of his family, which he regards either as hypocritical or effete. Noah's perceptions and observations are frank and unsparing, and he holds nothing back, revealing to us with equal candour, the sneaking clannishness, inbred self-righteousness and internal squabblings of Jews, as well as the sordid anti-semitic prejudices, abandoned sexual promiscuity, and foul moral apathy of gentiles. (pp. 73-4)

To Noah [his family's] hypocrisy and duplicity are intolerable. . . . Noah's problem is that, as a Jewish-Canadian by birth, he feels neither wholly Jewish nor wholly Canadian. His lack of self-identity creates inner confusion and uncertainty, for it makes him spiritually rootless and places him in a moral chaos where there are no clear principles or standards by which he can regulate his thought and action. His rebellion and defiance therefore spring, not from malice or perversity, but from a vital longing for a clear identity which will free him from inner anxiety and doubt, and reconcile him to the two fundamental facts of his existence— born a Jew, and growing up in Canada.

Evidently disappointed by the result of his continuing experimentation in *Son of a Smaller Hero,* Richler returns to a European setting in his third novel, *A Choice of Enemies.* Like André Bennett, Ernst Haupt, the German hero of *A Choice of Enemies,* is worried by a dearth of causes worth fighting for. His sense of disillusionment is, however, less frenzied than André's, and his philosophical speculation more sophisticated. Ernst realizes that his problem is not simply to choose enemies, that is, to acknowledge loyalty to one side of the universal conflict between good and evil; firm loyalty to either side of this conflict can be equally menacing for 'the enemy was the hit and run driver on both sides'. Ernst's frustration is tempered, more balanced than André's. The change represents the author's own increasingly objective attitude toward his subject which is produced partly by the sobering effects of the McCarthy, anticommunist witch-hunt of the 1950s. The point was not lost on Richler that in the capitalist-communist conflict of those Cold War days, McCarthy was a hit and run driver on what Richler himself believes to be the good side of the conflict.

All three novels mentioned so far should be regarded as the training ground on which the author practises and sharpens the techniques that are later to convey, with greater success, his iconoclastic wit and satire. These three novels extend and develop his capacity for lively narrative and sparkling dialogue, while they also provide an opportunity for ideological experimentation. Richler's chief worry in the first novel is to find the right cause to support. By the third novel, however, he recognizes that even so-called good causes can become bad depending upon the people and circumstances involved. His philosophical outlook is therefore chastened, more stabilized. It is not that he is made less angry and bitter by the dissatisfaction embodied in his main theme; for extreme passion is the very substance of Richler's fiction, sustaining and promoting at all times the mordancy of his insights and the catholicity of his judgements. What he gains from the experiments in the first three novels is a more articulate voice and a more stable outlook, which together allow him to speak out his discontents with no less bitterness but with greater coherence and cogency and, ultimately, to better artistic purpose.

Fortified by all he has learnt from his first three books, Richler tackles his theme head-on in the fourth, with rare gusto, and an electric energy that is unparalleled in Canadian writing in English. . . . *The Apprenticeship of Duddy Kravitz* deals with the youth and early manhood of its Jewish hero, Duddy Kravitz, who lives in a Montreal slum: it is not only Richler's most impressive work, but the best satirical novel produced by a Canadian. . . . [The action is] exciting and flamboyant. . . . With shameless self-interest, Duddy eagerly plunges into one enterprise after the other, ruthlessly eliminating rivals along the way and showing not the slightest awareness of compassion. It is a savage portrait, bordering closely on caricature; Duddy comes close to being merely a neatly packaged capsule of energy, competence, and success; but the bracing vitality, electric energy, and pointed humour of the prose makes him thoroughly convincing as a human being. Duddy's fantastic career exposes to ridicule the contemptuous goy versus contemptible Jew relationship, pouring scorn on gentile and Jew alike for failings that are, in the end, not narrowly racial and cultural, but broadly human and universal. The point is not that Duddy is a nasty Jewish 'pusherke', for his behaviour is conditioned less by personal motives than by social pressures. His nastiness is his response to an existing social phenomenon, the antipathy between Jew and goy. Thus, Duddy is what he is because goys are what they are.

To Richler, racial discrimination is not a simple issue of good versus evil. Since hit and run drivers can appear on either side of racial conflict, Jews and gentiles alike (blacks and whites too) share a common, human guilt. Existing prejudices force both Jew and gentile, black and white, to adopt stereotyped attitudes that are mutually opposed. Solution does not lie in apportioning blame, but in erasing the stereotyped characteristics of either side. In Richler's view, Jewishness, like niggerness or untouchability, for that matter, is not so much a fact as an idea, a state of mind which confers a prescribed form of behaviour on groups of people whose main common feature is that they are social minorities. As Noah says in *Son of a Smaller Hero*:

> The important thing is not that they [the Nazis] burned Jews but that they burned men. . . .

Time and again, in his non-fictional writing, Richler underlines the point, that Jews are people first, and whatever else attaches to them as a minority only comes second. . . . (pp. 75-6)

If *The Apprenticeship of Duddy Kravitz* reveals the artificial qualities of Jewishness which he despises, Richler's fifth novel, *The Incomparable Atuk,* lays bare the synthetic aspects of Canadianism which he scorns. The hero, Atuk, is an Eskimo poet who is taken from his home in snow-bound Baffin Bay and placed in the Toronto metropolis. Slick promotion techniques soon turn him into a celebrity rubbing shoulders with the best of the urban 'soi-disant' intellectuals and sophisticates. Inevitably, he makes enemies, and is eliminated by means as slick as those which bring him wealth and fame. Atuk lacks the psychological depth of Duddy and so is more of a caricature. But this does not hinder the author's satirical method which is to give a broad and superficial exposé of those aspects of Canadian urban society of which he disapproves: its excessively commercialized habits, cultural hollowness, and moral fraudulence. These social weaknesses, in Richler's view, corrupt Canadianism and impair its natural qualities.

At one level, *The Incomparable Atuk* settles personal scores for the author by caricaturing certain well-known Torontonians. At another, it parodies Zionism by ridiculing the hero's views of reclaiming his Eskimo homeland. But the chief idea of the novel is not entirely limited by personal motives and polemical objectives; it is to prose an integrated Canadian identity within a comprehensive English-speaking culture that embraces the whole of North America. (pp. 76-7)

Arguments from preceding books are implicitly repeated [in *Cocksure*], while the author airs a few personal grievances against novelists he doesn't like or critics who accuse him of being anti-Semitic. Apart from all this, *Cocksure* is set in England, and contains English characters who do not strike us as completely successful. Richler fails to capture, with exact precision, English psychological niceties and mannerisms of speech. . . . The West Indian characters in *Cocksure,* also, are not fully convincing. The world of London is altogether too diverse and too unfamiliar to Richler, and his satire on such vaguely contemporary subjects as big business, sexual permissiveness, the communications industry, pop culture, and modern educational methods lacks sharpness and edge.

Richler's novels reveal original insights into the psychology of minorities. . . . (pp. 77-8)

Richler's work surpasses that of other Jewish-Canadians because it is less limited by its preoccupation with Jewishness. It falls short of American standards because he works within an unstable and debilitating national ethos that severely inhibits creativity. . . . Bellow's hero [Herzog] takes his Jewishness and Americanness for granted, and so can either ignore these aspects of himself, or subject them to a scrutiny whose objectivity would completely elude a Canadian hero such as Duddy Kravitz. Because of the vague and changeable national ethos in which they live, Richler's protagonists feel spiritually fragmented, and their chief concern is the desperate aim of achieving spiritual wholeness. They lack, totally, the moral equipoise that would enable them to examine their experience with the wide-ranging awareness and depth of a Moses Herzog. (pp. 79-80)

[It] is the whole substance of Richler's argument that Duddy is ridiculous because he is a bad Jew and a bad Canadian, not simply because he is Jewish-Canadian. In other words, Richler offers to his protagonists positive hope of salvation, namely, of being better Jewish-Canadians by following the true teachings of their religion and acknowledging the regional American character of their Canadian identity. (p. 81)

> *F. M. Birbalsingh, "Mordecai Richler and the Jewish-Canadian Novel," in* Journal of Commonwealth Literature *(copyright by F. M. Birbalsingh 1972; by permission of Hans Zell (Publishers) Limited), June, 1972, pp. 76-82.*

*   *   *

RITSOS, Yannis   1909-

Ritsos, a Greek poet, has worked in many forms: long narrative poems, dramatic monologues, and short lyrics. Because of his devotion to revolutionary socialism, and the expression of that love in poetry, Ritsos spent many years in political prisons. Capitulating to the demands of European intellectuals, the Greek government now allows Ritsos freedom to

live in Athens. (See also *CLC*, Vol. 6, and *Contemporary Authors*, Vols. 77-80.)

KOSTAS MYRSIADES

["Belfry"] passes through three movements: the first ambiguous and ephemeral, the second moving toward the concrete (a transition movement), and the third highly concrete and palpably immediate. "Belfry" is a work which, like *Romiosíni*, celebrates those who have fallen in the struggle for freedom; it is both a paean to the oppressed and a call to arms. . . . [The] poet speaks for the first time in many years in specific terms of the bitterness of his people, of the specters of the CIA, the B-52s and the Hilton beside the hovering headless Winged Victory and the lesson of Ché.

One hopes that "Belfry" can be considered a landmark of Ritsos's recent poetry. In much of his latest work he has launched his reader into a metaphysical realm of apparently solid obstacles occupying a fantasy landscape. His poems have appeared as incomplete statements sometimes without a clear object, the veiled expressions of a man who has learned to forbid himself any other mode. This ideological shadow-boxing is largely missing in "Belfry," much to the advantage of the wholeness and effect of this striking poem. "Belfry" displays a convincing force which others of Ritsos's recently published poems might have achieved, had the poet been able to publish freely without fear of reprisal from the ruling Junta.

Not to be compared with "Belfry," but deserving of note, is Ritsos's "Hymn and Lament for Cyprus." Dedicated to Makários, it is a brief testament to the Cypriots composed and published within a few months after the 1974 Turkish invasion of Cyprus. The work is made up of five short poems and is written in a Byzantine-style calligraphy in the poet's own hand (the only other work published in Ritsos's own hand is his *Eighteen Songs of a Bitter Country* . . .). The poems are rhymed lyrics written in the popular style of the demotic songs. (p. 826)

> *Kostas Myrsiades, in* Books Abroad *(copyright 1975 by the University of Oklahoma Press), Vol. 49, No. 4, Autumn, 1975.*

KOSTAS MYRSIADES

Yannis Ritsos's output since his first published book in 1934 has been almost exclusively poetic. His latest book, "Studies," a selection of six essays written between 1961 and 1963 and originally included as introductions to other works, is his only work of criticism. These essays—four on poets (Mayakovsky, Hikmet, Ehrenburg, Éluard) and two shorter ones on his own works. . . .—comprise the only theoretical writings published by Ritsos on his art. For this reason "Studies" is one of the most important works in Ritsos's oeuvre.

Ritsos finds the importance of the four leftist poets he is studying in the message of their poetry and not in their technique or style. Concerned that a poet may limit himself too strictly to his own times, Ritsos defends the need of his subjects to root among temporal materials for the very backbone of their work and finds in the immediate present and in material reality a springboard for crossing the gap to the realm of the universal. . . .

Reluctant to act as an intermediary between the reader and the poem, the poet refuses to comment at any length on his own work. . . . He reveals, nevertheless, that the intent of his later body of work, in particular *Martiríes*, has been to express gratitude toward human life and art, in all its trials, and toward death. He recognizes that his work has, over the years, tended more and more toward . . . an uplifting or positive poetry which depreciates and exploits the nightmare of death. (p. 217)

> *Kostas Myrsiades, in* Books Abroad *(copyright 1976 by the University of Oklahoma Press), Vol. 50, No. 1, Winter, 1976.*

MINAS SAVVAS

The poems in this exciting little collection [*Pétrinos hrónos*] are not among the best of Yannis Ritsos's fifty volumes. They are, however, among the most interesting and, in terms of the poet's own sufferings, among the most apocalyptic. They give us a good look at the poet-as-exile on the island of Makronisos, a concentration camp filled with rocks, lizards, thornbushes, barbed wire and sadistic guards. Written in 1949 while Ritsos and hundreds of other leftists endured hunger, humiliation and torture, the poems delineate an inhuman world in which the victims make noble efforts to sustain their ideas and dignity and to be sustained by them. . . . The promise that one day "we'll construct cities of greatness" allows Ritsos and his comrades to see their horrible ordeal as a Golgotha necessary for the Resurrection.

Then there is that nostalgia for the tranquil life, interwoven in these poems like a silken thread around barbed wire, which helps the mind. The red flags in Communist parades, the friendly dog running to greet its master, a cigarette enjoyed peacefully in a garden, "the voice of a child," "the shadow of a gentle hand," "the cat on the neighbor's roof" —such vignettes of secure consciousness riddle the nightmare, real as it may be, with pleasant memories of how life *could* be. But it is rocks, corpses and skeletal men at hard labor which emerge as the central symbols in *Pétrinos hrónos* (Rocky Time). (pp. 699-700)

Pétrinos hrónos indeed is a book worth reading, for, to quote Whitman: "Camerado, this is no book. Who touches this touches a man." (p. 700)

> *Minas Savvas, in* Books Abroad *(copyright 1976 by the University of Oklahoma Press), Vol. 50, No. 3, Summer, 1976.*

RACHEL HADAS

The career of Yannis Ritsos has been uncomfortably paradigmatic of the political fortunes of his native Greece. For much of this century Ritsos has been a major poetic spokesman of freedom; and for much of his life he has paid the penalty for his refusal to be silent. (p. 26)

Ritsos' strengths are also weaknesses because he writes so much and publishes so much of what he writes. . . . Clearly this is a poet for whom writing *all the time* has been both mode and symbol of survival under mostly adverse circumstances—a confirmation not merely of political steadfastness but of life itself.

The danger, of course, is that so unflagging an utterance will lose in precision, compression, and felicity what it gains in breadth and depth. Ritsos' work lacks the verbal inevitability that makes us memorize a poem without effort. He seldom treats a subject in such a way that we feel the last word has been said. His numerous short poems are the rapid preliminary sketches of an artist whose notice nothing escapes but who never puts his vignettes together in a single commanding composition. Symbols recur with increasingly ominous intensity: keys, sleepers, the moon, naked riders, abandoned houses. The obliquities imposed by the small, often skewed dimensions of the little poems give them an enigmatic menace often missing from the longer, looser pieces; but nowhere is the tension fully resolved. . . . *The Blackened Pot* (1949), a turgid rhetorical brew written in prison, is all fraternal solidarity but less musical and moving than *Epitaphios* (1936), another overtly political poem not included [in *The Fourth Dimension: Selected Poems of Yannis Ritsos*]. In another style, the many short poems . . . included show Ritsos' keen, elegiac sense of place tinged with surrealistic uneasiness. A carefully rendered landscape ends

> This land is much loved,
> with patience and pride. Each night, statues come out
> of the dry well cautiously and climb up the trees.
> ("Our Land")

Also well represented in *The Fourth Dimension* are the long dramatic monologues that wholly compose Ritsos' Greek volume of the same title. Uniquely Ritsos, these poems are nevertheless stuffed with resonances: Chekhov, Sartre's dramas, Eliot, and of course Greek mythology. The withered speakers in *Ismene* and *Beneath the Shadow of the Mountain* hail from the families of Oedipus and Agamemnon, while the protagonists of *Moonlight Sonata* and *The Window* are more or less contemporary. But "more or less" is crucial; all these poems deliberately and triumphantly elude location in a particular time. Characteristically the speaker surfaces from a murky pool of personal and dynastic decay and isolation, sinking back to silence or even death at the end. (pp. 27-8)

[Ritsos] is obsessively aware of the flaws and ironies that mar his country's past. The Greece of the long poems is a dead house inhabited by loquacious ghosts.

In *Twelve Poems to Cavafy* Ritsos again deals with past greatness in complex ways, but the mask donned is different. Sometimes the mode is simple mimesis, as if the speaker were huddled so close to his gigantic predecessor as to be all but invisible. In [the] evocation of twilight [in "Dusk"] the voice is nearly pure Cavafy. . . . But the relation between the older and younger poet is finally ambiguous, as the last poem of the sequence, "Legacy," spells out. . . . The Greek legacy can be a dangerous weapon. Mostly, though, Ritsos uses his heritage not to destroy but to probe, scan, above all ceaselessly to record. It is not his fault if the landscape he surveys is strewn with headless statues and dead houses. (pp. 28-9)

The poems in *The Fourth Dimension* set up haunting reverberations along the bleak dream landscape that Ritsos . . . [shares] with de Chirico. Whether or not all the poems are to one's taste, the book is a good introduction to an important voice. (p. 29)

Rachel Hadas, "Voice from an Empty House," in Parnassus: Poetry in Review *(copyright © Poetry in Review Foundation), Spring/Summer, 1978, pp. 26-9.*

KOSTAS MYRSIADES

Ritsos views modern man as the sum of the possibilities of his past. If those possibilities are less than evident in the present, then the task of modern man is to touch again in himself that heroic resource in his race to insure an influence over the future. Just as modern man in Ritsos' works must refuse the crushing weight of past myths that humiliate and diminish him, so must he have a say in determining his future fate, not, as in [George Seferis], in merely enduring it. Ritsos rejects Seferis' aristocratic and pessimistic view, a view reflecting a major strain in postwar poetry, which sees the past as a standard of greatness, a measure against which modern man can only be found wanting; he rejects Seferis' implication that there can be no thought of a future because modern man has none.

Yannis Ritsos' abiding interest is in the present and in its meaning for the future; consequently, he views the past as both a means of treating contemporary problems with historical detachment and as a burden which must be overcome. The historical identity of a people, Ritsos affirms, exists in the contemporary mind; modern man must explore his past as if it were the present—synchronous with the present—not as an ominous shadow. The present event is intensified by reference in name or memory to events in the past, infusing them with contemporaneity. Modern man, in this view, must either tune the past to present revelation and discover all time as one, thus liberating himself from the weight of his mythic past, or forever remain a slave to time and other men.

In such works as his classical cycle of eleven dramatic monologues (*The Dead House, Under the Mountain's Shadow, Ajax, Philoctetes, Agamemnon, Chrysothemis, Helen, Ismini, Persephone, Orestes,* and *The Return of Iphigenia*), Ritsos begins by stripping the classical myths of their antiquity. In *Philoctetes* the setting, we are told, is the island of Lemnos, "perhaps." . . . In *The Dead House,* recalling the mythic past through associations with events and objects whose place in time is not itself certain, the poet again keeps the reader suspended in time. . . . Vague references to the bath, to the mistress as a murderess, to the word "slaughtered," to the dead house of the title, evoke the Mycenean past and the myth of the House of Atreus. But the references are not specifically of one period or one myth. The mistress, the children, the bath could refer to Medea as well as Clytemnestra, to present as well as past horrors. Time and space are here dissolved so that the poet may extend through time the psychology and suffering of these figures. Ritsos can see himself in Clytemnestra or Medea because he is Clytemnestra, he is Medea; all Greeks participating in Greek history have experienced their agony. Far from imitating or repeating the splendor of the original (the past), the echo (the present) intensifies it, illuminating and extending the eternal cry of the human condition.

The dramatic monologue *Ajax,* representative of the attitude of the classical cycle as a whole, reveals that the eternal and essential nature of time has for Ritsos a spare and essential aspect. The poet reduces the characters used in the myth to a minimum. Only a voiceless and nameless figure (Ajax's wife Tecmessa) appears briefly as an audience for Ajax in the prose prologue and epilogue of the poem. The setting, once again, is anywhere in the essence of time. . . . This atmosphere of imprecision and synchronism in which historical incidents become one under different names establishes the poet's treatment of the past as continuously present history and not as isolated phenomena. At the same time, the past feeds the personal meaning of Ritsos' heroes, for the emotions which condition the inner man are caused by his interaction with other people, people who are basically the same in all ages. *Ajax* indicates how this process operates. Here action is suspended and the poet focuses on developing and revealing Ajax's emotional state. The poem is an outcry of a wronged and hurt man based on the famous speech in Sophocles' play. . . . [The] interest of the poem is focused on a man who, having served his country selflessly in his best years, now finds himself rejected by both man and god. . . . Ajax is but a mirror image of Ritsos himself, who rails at his own comrades for not recognizing his long struggle for the freedom of his country, a struggle which meant for Ritsos seven years of prison and torture and seven more of broken health in sanatoriums. *Ajax* becomes a cry of anguish against those friends who have now forsaken him in a moment of need. . . . (pp. 450-54)

Ajax serves, perhaps most importantly, as a mask behind which, protected from prying eyes, the poet is free to confess himself. Distanced from his own emotions, Ritsos can objectify them. He can be lucid, revealing, and yet safe from the government censors who sought him out. (p. 454)

Orestes serves as yet another mask for the poet, as Ritsos suggests in the prologue to the *Orestes* monologue. . . . Ritsos begins the monologue with the return of Orestes and Pylades to Argos as in Aeschylus' *The Libation Bearers*. But the place looks different, smaller, since these two men were last here many years ago. The major landmarks, however, are still in place . . . but into this supposedly Mycenean world private cars and tourist buses intrude, and we are plunged back into the present. It is Ritsos the modern Orestes who stands before present-day Mycenae, wrestling with questions of love, death, and freedom which once plagued the ancient figure. On the same spot on which Orestes stood stands modern man; time has stopped. The ancients are neither great models nor distant mysteries; they are themselves. (p. 455)

Thus in Ritsos' poetry the focus is on the ingestion of the past, anachronism gives way to synchronism, and all Greek history is understood to exist simultaneously. The ten-year-long Trojan struggle from which Ritsos draws most of his masks becomes the decade of war from 1912 to 1922, in which the Greeks fought the Turks; it becomes as well the decade of Greek resistance and the Greek Civil War between 1940 and 1950. To each era squabbling between comrades and factions is common; in each era the greed, self-interest, and self-aggrandisement of others cause the pain and suffering of an Ajax, of a Ritsos, of any man fighting for his ideals. . . . Christian myth becomes interchangeable with pagan myth. The two are woven into one uninterrupted thread, for both are part of the modern Greek experience. (p. 456)

The merging of past and present serves Ritsos' need to distance and objectify material too personal, too emotional, too close to the poet's own experience and suffering to be presented in its naked form. The mask of a classical persona and the framing of the present in the past are necessary to alienate events, to displace them elsewhere and to attribute them to someone else. As we see in his description of the rooms in *The Dead House,* the poet's objectivity allows him to look "at things from above / and at some dis-

tance, so as to feel / that we overlook and command our fate." . . . Only at a distance can he come out of himself, rendered whole enough to look at himself, in himself, to manipulate this experience, to command it, and thus to draw from it the lessons it offers. At dusk, as "all things bend towards the warm earth," . . . the poet is shed of his desires and shivering with the sharp, clean, healthy coldness of his objectivity, he is able to see all experience as one. From this distance one can see that things are as they always were, today's experiences the same as yesterday's. Distance, cold objectivity, in the dark void of life gives substance and meaning. . . . It is this alienation in the void that has led Ritsos in recent years to adopt more and more the third person point of view and to intersperse throughout his poetry phrases such as "he said," "they said," and "they used to say."

But in his distancing of events—his interlacing of present and past—Ritsos is not reversing his refusal to allow that which has already occurred and which can only be perceived through the imagination to take precedence over the sensibly felt immediate present. His displacement, his movement out of the realm of the painfully personal to that of the coldly analytical, is one of bitter immediate necessity. Because the displacement he feels is not that of the diplomat Seferis—a man isolated by choice or circumstance—but a displacement of imprisonment, torture, and suicidal impulses, he must view his world at a distance or risk insanity. The psychology of a prisoner of war or an inmate of a concentration camp applies here; one cannot be himself, suffer one's suffering, but must be removed, refusing to identify with the victim one has become, if one is to survive. For Ritsos that survival lies in finding his Greekness. As in his war poem *Romiosini,* composed during his partisan years of involvement, the future depends upon the continued existence of the past; Romiosini is the presence of continued Greekness. Necessary to the very being of the modern Greek, "romiosini" is that without which, by definition, "Greek" may not exist. Thus the contemporary sailor "drinks the bitter sea from the winecup of Odysseus" or the guerrillas meet "with Dighenis on those same threshing-floors." . . . (pp. 456-57)

In Ritsos' poetry, man refuses the past as a place in which he may hide or as a presence which overwhelms. The evocation of the past is achieved not to victimize the present but to define and celebrate it; and that celebration must occur not on universal and international terms, but in terms of the purely local and immediate national situation with an insistence on loci or popular attitudes and needs. Intermingling Christian myths with others, Ritsos is following a tradition established in the Greek folk song, in Byzantine iconography, and in folk art. . . .

Ritsos' preoccupation with the past is one in which his stance is always in the present. He does not intersect past and present to comment on the inadequacy of the present, as does Seferis; neither does he steer the past in the direction modern man would take were he set to live in that past, as does [Nikos Kazantzakis]; nor does he imbed himself in the past, using historical events and personages as ironic commentary on the present, as does [C. P. Cavafy]. Ritsos' personal world is still the everyday world of the peasant Greek in whose face and in whose constant struggle can be seen the sufferings and the dignity of all Greeks in that country's long history. It is that constant three-thousand-year striving for dignity, freedom, and the knowledge of self, which Ritsos sees in the myths of Greece, in its wars, and in its everyday peasant life, that leads him to see all time as present time. Unconcerned with searching for the continuity of past and present in order to transcend the contemporary world or to symbolically mediate between past and present, Ritsos takes on the past not as a gift but as a right, not as a limitation but as a possibility, not as a looming shadow which makes modern man appear puny by comparison, but as a tool, an instrument of liberation. (p. 458)

Kostas Myrsiades, "The Classical Past in Yannis Ritsos' Dramatic Monologues," in Papers on Language and Literature *(copyright © 1978 by the Board of Trustees, Southern Illinois University at Edwardsville), Fall, 1978, pp. 450-58.*

*   *   *

ROSS, (James) Sinclair   1908-

Ross, a Canadian novelist and short story writer, is best known for his realistic portraits of Canadian prairie life which are as vivid as they are bleak. His characters are sympathetically drawn from childhood memory: they are presented as victimized figures whose struggle with isolation and loneliness reflects Ross's own view of the human condition. (See also *Contemporary Authors*, Vols. 73-76.)

WARREN TALLMAN

The bleak assumption of this beautiful novel [*As For Me And My House*] is that Philip Bentley has no ground whatsoever upon which he might stand, no communion at all through which he might discover saving dimensions of self. The overwhelming desolation which rims Horizon around— the hostile wind, the suffocating dust and sand and the even more suffocating and claustrophobic heat—recurs on the pages of Mrs. Bentley's diary as outward manifestation of the inner desolation felt by her husband. All that Philip can claim or cling to is his maddeningly inarticulate impulse to create. The novel is less like a story than it is like a cumulative picture in which Ross, by a remarkable, almost *tour de force* repetition of detail, grains a central scene upon the reader's consciousness so that all other details and even the action of the novel achieve meaningful focus in relation to the one scene at the center, repeated some thirty times. It is of course that in which Philip is shown retreating to his study where he will sit interminable evening superimposed upon interminable evening, drawing or fiddling at drawing, or staring with baffled intensity at drawings he has in some other time and place tried to draw. Yet, "Even though the drawings are only torn up or put away to fill more boxes when we move, even though no one ever gets a glimpse of them . . . still they're for him the only part of life that's real or genuine." The novel is a projection through the medium of Mrs. Bentley's remarkably responsive consciousness of the despair in which her husband is caught. . . . And the town itself, with the dust "reeling in the streets", the heat "dry and deadly like a drill" . . ., is simply a place name for the limbo in which Bentley lives. . . . (pp. 14-15)

Philip's need to escape from this isolation drives him to art. But just as he can find no terms under which he may act as a self so he can find no terms under which he may act as an artist. His most characteristic drawing is a receding perspective in which a looming false-front building gives

way to a diminished next building, and a next, and a next, an endless progression which provides a portrait of the monotony of his own being. The novel is a study of a frustrated artist—actually, a non-artist—one unable to discover a subject which will release him from his oppressive incapacity to create. The excellence of the study traces to the remarkable resourcefulness with which Ross brings into place the day-to-day nuances of Mrs. Bentley's struggling consciousness as he builds up her account of an artist who cannot create because he cannot possess himself and who cannot possess himself because there is no self to possess. Certainly there are more deep-reaching portraits of the artist, for in this novel all is muffled within Philip's inarticulation, but none that I know represents with so steady a pressure of felt truth the pervasive undermining of all vital energies which occurs when the would-be artist's creativity is thwarted. No momentary exuberance survives. . . . Not once in the novel does Philip break through the torment of his constraint to utter a free sentence. Even when his wife confronts him with knowledge of his covert love affair with Judith West his response, beyond the endurance of even an Arthur Dimmesdale, is silence. But if the beauty is in the detailing, it does not trace to the dreariness which is portrayed. It traces to the constant presence in Mrs. Bentley's consciousness of an exuberance which flares up like matches in the wind and struggles to survive, a counter-impulse within her by which life attempts to defeat the defeated. This bravery loses out to the dreariness . . . but in the process of struggling it animates the novel. (pp. 15-16)

Warren Tallman, in Canadian Literature, *Summer, 1960.*

DONALD STEPHENS

Horizon, the town that is the setting for [*As For Me and My House*], could be any place on the prairie in the thirties; yet again, it can be anywhere at any time. It is bleak, it is tired, it is horribly true; and yet there is an element of the flower blooming on the desert, and the flying of feeling that transcends all, that gives to *As For Me and My House* a prominent position in Canadian letters. This is a novel which, despite its Puritanism, its grimness, its dustiness, gives to the reader many of the elements of optimism and romanticism so often found in Canadian literature. (p. 17)

[One] is first captured by the writing in the book. There is an exact vividness, pure diction choice, observation that is accurate, and a rhythm that is controlled. Everything seems to move at its own pace, and yet the tension of the characters renders vividly the actual setting. . . . (p. 18)

[The] simplicity of style and intricacy of mood create a prairie so immense that it virtually stuns the mind. The physical limitations of existence in Horizon pummelled by the visitations of a cruel God—though He is never blamed for what goes on—are clearly etched in the mind by the almost unbearable monotony of wind, sun, snow, and drought. It is a place with a past and a future, but with no real present. . . . Environment plays a strong rôle in the story, an environment that is at once uncluttered and cluttered. (pp. 18-19)

The sky and the earth fuse into a huge blur, a haze which envelopes the town and its people and stills all but the faintest murmur of hope for the future. There is a vivid immobility that lies stark against the dullness of the endlessly shifting dust. The theme is of the prairies during the thirties— the unrewarded, unremitting, sluggish labour of men coupled with the loneliness and nameless terror of the women —and is the only action upon the stage that Ross presents before his reader.... These people are not hard to imagine, but they are very difficult to understand, and consequently difficult to accept....

[Everywhere] there are the unmistakable signs of Puritanism: the standards are rigidly set; the struggles, the tenacity of people in so bleak a circumstance, the horror of hypocrisy and of sexual sin. Jealousy, failure, slow realization of forgiveness, possible redemption and reconciliation after anguish and torment, all take their places in the lives of these tenacious people. The problem of fighting versus flight, and the all powerful will of God remain in the foreground; the nerves of all the people of the town remain taut to the breaking point. (p. 19)

[Ross] does not immerse [his main characters] totally, but rather just dips them into this sheep-dip of futility and sets them into a corner to let the bitter juices seep into their absorbent beings. Perhaps he has not dipped them for long enough, or again, too much, for none of the characters seem to rise out of the story as individuals of total belief. They are at once types and individuals, yet never really discernable as one or the other. Despite this vagueness, the characters can be analyzed; unfortunately, with varying degrees of accuracy.

Ross chooses a woman's point of view for this novel, and obviously has tremendous insight into a woman's mind, and this particular woman's troubles.... [Mrs. Bentley] is the narrator, and if the reader takes her at her literal worth, then all the characters become exceptionally clear. But she is a paradox, and there becomes the necessity to probe beyond what she says superficially and to make conjectures as to her real meaning. (pp. 19-20)

She becomes through the novel an epitome of a type of woman; she displays intelligence, responds to situations with courage and sympathy, and displays a vague hope for better times (typical of prairie women of the period: clever, hard-working, hoping). Yet she is individualistic in that she rebels against the stifling pressures of propriety imposed by the town. Though she does not want impropriety, she scoffs at the pretentious airs that the citizens of Horizon so capably put on. She lives in a semi-vacuum, drawing from her stored-up intellectual resources what her husband and the other citizens fail to give her.

However, she is not as strong a person as she would have the reader believe. And this is Ross's point. Assailed by doubts she seems to hang on by sheer stubbornness. Everything she sees before her is thin, disheartening, dull and bare. There is an inert and chilly stillness to the life she leads, and it becomes evident in her thoughts. Yet, what kind of person is she? She seems to be strong, if what she says in her diary is to be taken literally. Her strength, however, comes from the knowledge of the falseness and the sham of the life that she and her husband lead. With this strength comes a certain smugness.... Though she abides by her husband, she is the one who makes the major decisions, she is the one who fights the internal battles for both of them, and it is because of her inner strength that they emerge triumphant.

She, like all the characters in the book, is hurt too easily, yet she is too enduring. She can see all things clearly and objectively because she is a stranger and cannot fit into the town and share its frustrations. This is her futility. Since she is outside of Horizon's influence, she can, for the most part, be cool, logical, and even somewhat caustic about its workings. (pp. 20-1)

She appears to be constantly saying—"Poor Philip", and by virtue of this negation, enhances her own virtuous qualities of wifehood. Her theme of "poor Philip" eventually grates sharply upon the reader's nerves. She protests too much his innocence, thereby attempting to absolve herself and him of blame for their torturous predicament. That she possesses an optimism for his future and hence her own is often negated by her emphasis on his moral and spiritual degradation.

She does not reveal enough to the reader for him to deduce anything other than what she wishes him to deduce....

She almost envisions herself as a goddess, all-seeing, but fearful to tell or show the reader lest he recognize yet another flaw in either herself or her husband. Ross's stylistic brevity does not make sufficient amends for Mrs. Bentley's brevity; the reader can make only his own hypothesis concerning their deeds, motives, and the subsequent results. (p. 21)

Philip never really emerges as a character, but then maybe that is his condition. He is contrived, far too mechanical to be other than fragmentary.... At first, sympathy and pity can be extended to Philip, but after a time irritation sets in with disbelief hard on its heels.

Is he the frustrated artist? Is he, rather, a weak, spineless hypocrite who cannot face what life puts before him? He is neurotic—far more than his wife—but do we know "why" he is? It is never solved. (p. 22)

Paul Kirby serves as a foil for both Bentleys. For a time a love interest seems to be developing, but it is foredoomed to oblivion and never gets under way.... He is perhaps the least faceted and least successful character in the story. He seems to have been brought in only for relief, when another page of Philip's sulkings and Mrs. Bentley's wanderings threaten a total suspension of belief.

Steve is opportunely introduced. He is the hope the Bentleys have been seeking; his exit almost extinguishes any hope that the reader and the Bentleys share.... His temporary importance to the plot cannot be overlooked....

Judith West is also shallowly drawn.... She displays the inner torments that also rack Philip, thus giving them their common ground on which to create. To Philip she is the rebel with whom he can identify. To Mrs. Bentley she is the potential and then the real "other woman" against whom she must pit her wiles. It is strange that Mrs. Bentley, with all her astuteness, cannot see the supposed power of attraction between Philip and Judith.

Sinclair Ross gives variety in character; not all the characters are those on the racks of internal torture beaten by the overwhelming powers of nature. (p. 23)

In general, the characters are made subservient to the environment of the story; the limitations of Ross's vehicle hamper the full realization of these characters. The only way the reader can realize the portent of all the characters is to let his imagination have full rein. Despite the shallowness of the characters, they are interesting, and at an intense, rather than a cursory, examination.

It is, then, the characters who make *As For Me and My House.* The place belongs to the history of Canada, the prairie town that is for the most part gone from our midst. . . . The time, too, belongs to history; the thirties, the depression, are only ugly dreams which man hopes will not become another reality. But the people remain the same. We are all typed in some way, and we all, too, hope that there is something individualistic about us that separates us from the crowd. But only rarely are we separated, and only rarely do Sinclair Ross's people separate from their world. And this is the way people are; this is why the reality of Ross's fictional world elevates his novel to a lasting and prominent position. (p. 24)

> *Donald Stephens, "Wind, Sun and Dust," in*
> Canadian Literature, *Winter, 1965, pp. 17-24.*

KEATH FRASER

The futile cycle of eking existence from an indifferent world predominates [*The Lamp at Noon and Other Stories*]—a kind of rural *Dubliners* in which the same adult impotence replaces a similar childish *Araby.* Overall, the book spawns variations on the theme of isolation and its haunting melody is unmistakable. The storm which creeps into Will's house [in "Not by Rain Alone"], killing his wife but undoubtedly allowing the child to relive the same empty cycle as its parents, also invades Martha's home in "A Field of Wheat," not as snow but hail. At the same time it crushes "the best crop of wheat John had ever grown." These prairie inhabitants own nothing that is inviolate; they can retreat nowhere that is not whirling vainly in an absurd seasonal cycle. . . . [The] storm motif recurs in sporadic and tragic fashion, proving a principal antagonist in each of the stories devoted exclusively to the adult (as opposed to the child) experience.

In "The Painted Door," . . . close to the finest [story] in Canadian literature, . . . [Ann's] husband wanders fatally into a blizzard after his discovery of her adultery (it is the only story which uses the adultery theme found in both Ross's novels). (pp. 77-8)

The story's conclusion does not appear gimmicky—rather a unique result of what Ross has established as part of the futility cycle. Ann decides that despite her affair with Stephen she does love her husband, and senses that any future lies with him. Yet she discovers him next day frozen to death, and on his palm a smear of white paint. Suddenly she realizes that John had indeed returned in the night, not merely in her dream, and had touched the freshly painted door of their bedroom as he watched the slumbering couple. In the husband's suicide the author intends us to discern an ending for a life that is less senseless, perhaps, than would have been his natural death: for Ross tells us earlier, "It was not what he actually accomplished that mattered, but the sacrifice itself, the gesture—something done for her sake." In future years John could offer her nothing anyway; to continue living with awareness of her deceit would have been disastrous, better for his wife to believe that he had never discovered her. But the smear of paint betrays him, and this image counterpoints in an uncanny coda Ann's own betrayal.

The illusion of the double wheel around the moon which had always warned Ann of an impending blizzard before they married, Ross picks up artistically in what his character imagines to be her husband standing over the bed that

final night when she dismisses him as an illusion—the first separation not realized because John always hiked through blizzards to see her in the past—but the second, fully accomplished, because it has divided them irrevocably for the future.

Not all Ross's couples part so dramatically. There are those who continue at the pump [Ross's recurrent symbol for their endless, futile labors], those who out of necessity restore shaky relationships when their quarrels subside. They are his rural Bentleys, saved from dependence upon the false-fronted town only by a candid consort—the land—from whom salvation remains uncertain. Sometimes it seems enough that the bad among them are punished (as is Luke Taylor in "The Runaway" when he dies in his burning barn, and the wife of the man he cheated calls up her Biblical clichés that justify his death). But when are the good rewarded? Not really ever; anyone who shows kindness, like the strange Arthur Vickers in "One's a Heifer," we see in a misunderstood, perverted light. Yet the reward for being good or bad does not interest Ross in his short stories so much as does the sweat of labour. When couples do not receive much from it (inevitably the case), he explores the attitude of their living, the consequences of their relentless—or disrupted—cycles. He writes with a lucidity characteristic of Joyce in the early years, while creating a prose music distinctly his own.

If his characters appear flat or two-dimensional at times it is because there are so many here the same. Yet that does not detract from their individual credibility. . . . (The fact that Ross can repeat his favourite adjective, "little," eighty-one times in nine stories without apparent repetition, attests to the freshness of each story.) When the totality of Ross's short fiction is recognized, then his characters emerge as a condition of it: that they appear similar in no manner decries their roundness. Because they meet isolation and futility at the pump, then "getting ahead" (the hope of man) becomes for them a particular obsession. But in their case the endurance continues even when that hope proves inescapably an illusion. And perhaps they are right—maybe Ross is saying that all the plateaux we climb toward are really part of a single prairie after all. But to give up is impossible because in the pumping we at least exist. (pp. 79-80)

> *Keath Fraser, "Futility at the Pump: The Short*
> *Stories of Sinclair Ross," in* Queen's Quarterly,
> *Spring, 1970, pp. 72-80.*

ROBERT D. CHAMBERS

A number of the stories [in *The Lamp At Noon and Other Stories*] are narrated from the viewpoint of a young boy between the ages of ten and fifteen. While he seldom felt inclined to use a distinctive idiom or dialect, such as Twain adopted for Huck Finn, Ross nonetheless wanted this youthful narrative voice to seem fresh and natural. He was also aware, from his own experience, that prairie farm boys in the 1930s entered early into the world of adult responsibility. The grim facts of the Depression required a maturity of outlook far beyond their years. Ross sought to combine the natural impulsiveness of youth with the tempered understanding and quiet acceptance of the adult world. Yet the meanings which the stories unfolded often demanded a kind of insight—and a phrasing of that insight—far beyond the limited powers of a young boy. . . . Twain would not have allowed Huck such big words as "august," "compliance," "inordinately proud" or "downright bigotry" [used by the boy in "Cornet at Night"]. (pp. 9-10)

Here and there, we may feel that the narrative voice grows slightly strained:

> I have always been tethered to reality, always compelled by an unfortunate kind of probity in my nature to prefer a bare-faced disappointment to the luxury of a future I have no just claims upon. . . .

A boy may well develop such an outlook on life, but no eleven year old could phrase it as perceptively. Ross overcomes this problem by consistent use of the past tense, and by such useful devices as the repetition in this passage of "always." The narrative voice takes on a retrospective quality, a distancing which makes us forget for a moment that we are listening to a youth. Ross adopted this rather complex narrative voice—youthful but also quietly sage—for several of his best stories. . . . (pp. 10-11)

A second distinctive narrative voice is that of the prairie farm woman. Two of Ross' finest stories, "A Field of Wheat" and "The Painted Door," employ this approach, thus allowing us to experience at first hand lives of terrible loneliness and isolation. Ross was particularly attracted to this narrative mode, and the novel *As for Me and My House* combines his two strongest forms of storytelling—the vivid intimacy of first-person narration combined with the prairie woman's point of view. (p. 11)

Ross is equally diverse and skilful when describing landscape, weather, and the seasons. The prairie writer is here faced with a special problem; to the outsider, the prairie appears empty, featureless, almost without character. It is thus a major triumph for Ross that the land comes to life so magnificently in these stories. But it is a particular kind of life. Here the landscape has a brooding, threatening quality, as though just beyond the horizon a malevolent God is preparing horrors of nature to hurl against an embattled people. Weather here is cursed, at first flattering human hopes, then mockingly dashing them asunder.

There is, of course, nothing made-up or fanciful about Ross' use in these stories of wind and storm, dust, hail, and snow.

During the time that he lived the experiences which became the raw material of his art, the Canadian prairies were a gigantic dust bowl for years on end. To the farmers it seemed that nature had turned against them forever, exacting a terrible price for some unknown crime. At the heart of the stories is an unequal, but nonetheless heroic, struggle between tenacious man and relentless nature.

Personification is of primary use in making nature seem hostile to his prairie farm characters. Wind doesn't merely blow in these stories; it pries into the very houses and lives of a people besieged. . . . But the personification works in two directions: we feel the savage attack of the wind but are never allowed to forget that a woman [as in "The Lamp At Noon,"] alone and tensely watching a clock listens to a predatory drama, which will go on and on and on . . . until she cracks. (pp. 11-12)

[In "The Painted Door," for example, the] powerful build-up to storm is described in no neutral way. Rather, some live but hostile force has selected this desolate farm house

as a target for its assault. With the outside world completely cut off, it begins to try its strength, and release its wrath, upon the lonely woman who stares unmoving through the frozen window.

Many of the finest moments in Ross' stories combine these few but simple elements: menacing nature, lonely humans, a tightening claustrophobia. The dominant mood is one of attrition, with a terrible harmony between the working of wind upon soil and snow and the slow undermining of human stamina and strength. (p. 13)

Ross' male characters, especially the farmers in the short stories, share with their creator [an] accumulated knowledge of prairie farm life. They can best be defined, not in relation to any society or to the universe, but simply in relation to nature. They think crop. They learn to read the skies. They are men who gauge and calculate, who play endlessly, as it were, a desperate game of chance with the weather and the seasons. (p. 15)

Ross records, with both power and compassion, the heroic lives of these simple but good men, and celebrates their intense loyalty to a land which had apparently gone bad forever.

The farm wives form a distant point of this impossible prairie triad: men, women, and land. A typical moment in a Ross story finds the wife alone in the farm house, straining for a glimpse through the window of her husband ploughing in far off fields or struggling through mountainous drifts of snow. These are the loneliest women in Canadian fiction, and Ross has an especial understanding of their unjust plight. They are basically good and faithful mates, with an instinctive awareness of the severe tensions under which their husbands labour. But the desolation and hopelessness of prairie farm life occasionally gets to them, often against their own wills and desires. . . . Sometimes the bleak face of despair leads to desperate acts. . . . It is the sense of being utterly cut off from the world . . . which vividly characterizes their lives. . . . Indeed, the overall testimony of these stories suggests only a single motivating force which keeps these prairie farm women struggling on—the hope that their children will one day enjoy a better way of life.

The children in the stories are a fascinating group. They share with their parents the discipline and hard work of prairie farm life, and their lives are likewise not without tensions. (pp. 15-17)

[The children] often find themselves caught between two different value systems. Fathers, needing help with the farm work, encourage the useful skills; mothers insist upon religion, good manners, and those dreary piano lessons! Somehow, between chores and cultural workouts, the youngsters find moments for exotic dreams or brave fantasies. The climactic moments of their young lives occur, however, when parental pressures subside, when both parents gladly hand over some adult sphere of responsibility to the proudly waiting child. And while we naturally welcome this initiation into the adult community, we also sense that this parental dream of a better future may never be realized for these children. We come away haunted by the thought that, as with their mothers and fathers before them, these children will in time yield to this lonely and harsh environment. (pp. 17-18)

["A Field of Wheat"] opens on a strong note of hope. After

years of blight and failure, a great crop of wheat is ripening for John. For his wife Martha, little dreams of the future begin to form, better schooling for the children, perhaps even something left over for herself and John. Ross creates in Martha's mind a quietly musing quality which parallels the outer scene of the great crop shimmering in the summer sun. This is one of the story's strong points—the subtle equation between the human world and the world of nature. Indeed, after sixteen years of marriage, Martha has come to see John almost in terms of the land—dried out and without hope. But this once, with the great crop coming on, she dreams that it (not herself) will restore John to his former self. This balanced tension between inner weather and outer weather is beautifully caught again in the symbol of the poppies, that most fragile of flowers, which the daughter Annabelle grows in the garden behind the house.... Ross thus establishes the terrible fragility of prairie farm life, the extraordinary beauty followed by sudden destruction and loss. And with this symbolic touch Ross begins the horrible prelude to storm.

The description of the hail storm—from Martha's first sensing it through its savage length—is one of the finest set pieces Ross has written, and takes its authority from his first-hand experience of prairie storms. This shows especially in Martha's frantic efforts at defence—throwing open the barn door for John and the horses, the children holding pillows against the exposed windows. And then the breaking ferocity of the storm, "like a weapon that has sunk deep into flesh," invading the house, smashing windows, lamps, dishes, and leaving the poor mutt Nipper beaten to death by the door. And after the storm has passed, they walk out into the [ruined] fields.... This is the farthest point of endurance, with the great promise of the season stretched dead before them. Both John and Martha are at the breaking point, but mask their agony before the children. It is only later, with anger and frustration and rage in her eyes and on her lips, that Martha seeks John in the barn, and finds him sobbing against the mane of a horse. Watching him cry is the most terrible moment of her life—a reaction which indicates the price exacted on these prairie farmers by the code of tough masculinity. Without letting him know that she has witnessed his agony, Martha creeps back to the house to clear up the mess left in the wake of the storm:

> Martha hurried inside. She started the fire again, then nailed a blanket over the broken window and lit the big brass parlour lamp— the only one the storm had spared. Her hands were quick and tense. John would need a good supper tonight. The biscuits were water soaked, but she still had the peas. He liked peas. Lucky that they had picked them when they did. This winter they wouldn't have so much as an onion or potato.

There is a fantastic strength of character in these final acts and thoughts of Martha (notice how the clipped rhythm of the sentences seems to keep the deeper emotions temporarily at bay), and the story's ending sees love and compassion wrenched from the potential chaos of human despair. The will to go on never completely dies in the world of Ross' fiction, and some of his finest moments show the little lights of hope burning bravely against the black and massive forces of negation. (pp. 18-20)

Ross handles the theme of ["Cornet at Night"] with great delicacy.... [We] see a process of growth—a developing awareness in Tommy [the young narrator] that farm values are not the only values. (The story of Tommy's later life is, in a sense, transferred to Sonny in *Whir of Gold.*) Moreover, the resolution of this story's tensions is supported throughout by a subtle deployment of diction. One notes, for example, how the word "lesson" threads through the story in a variety of contrasting contexts. There are the overt lessons—Tommy's music lessons.... And there are the hidden ones—the lesson which the Lord, so his mother claims, will teach Tommy's father for desecrating the Sabbath with work ...; the lesson which Tommy's parents sense from the beauty of cornet music by night; the lesson Tommy learns about the potential beauty of the world outside the farm.

Towards the end of the story, Ross plays with equally skilful effect on the word "golden." Its usual form is in such phrases as "golden harvest," but a rival connotation emerges in the beauty of the gleaming instrument which Philip raises to his lips. The quiet and subtle meaning of the story—an ironical probing into the value systems of prairie farm life—is superbly caught in the final sentence, where the different sets of values are brought together powerfully and established, once and for all, in their proper relationship: "A harvest, however lean, is certain every year; but a cornet at night is golden only once." ... (pp. 21-2)

The fictional characters Ross has created in his short stories are of a very special kind. Because of the power which the land exerts on them, they seem to have little of their own volition, little scope to choose the direction of their lives. There is about them a strongly deterministic quality.... [We] develop a deep sympathy for the situations life alloted to them; as fictional characters, however, we do not find them either very complex or very dramatic.

Ross' desire to go beyond the achievements of the stories— his desire to individualize and dramatize—led to *As for Me and My House* (1941). The book is comprised of a series of entries, covering slightly over a year, from the journal of Mrs. Bentley, the wife of a Protestant minister.... (pp. 25-6)

The world of the short stories is often grimly ironical, but none of its characters possesses an ironical cast of mind. Mrs. Bentley is not so simply constructed; not only is she more intelligent and cultured than the farm wives of the stories, but also she has the capacity to embrace both sides of a question. She can, for example, see the comic side of a gloomy situation, approve and disapprove simultaneously, acknowledging her honesty and her hypocrisy in the same breath. It is precisely these dimensions of character which make Mrs. Bentley such a memorable personality. But the complexity that issues from her irony and ambivalence has led to disagreement about her basic character. (pp. 26-7)

What we need to grasp ... is the real reason for Philip's dismissals in the past: his choice of the private relationship of marriage above the public life of his calling.

This public/private theme in the novel is complicated by the unique conditions in which ministers and their families live.... [The] constant invasion of privacy figures heavily in *As for Me and My House,* being at once a source of pressure upon the Bentleys—since, of course, hypocrisy is inevitably involved—but also a secret possibility of an intimacy that the townspeople can never touch.... (p. 28)

The resolution of [Philip's unhappiness] is the major business of the book, and becomes Mrs. Bentley's single aim in life. Her desire to free Philip (the irony of the saver-of-souls himself needing saving) consumes all her energies and transcends even the gravest threats to her marriage: the adoption of Steven, and Philip's adultery with Judith.

Saving Philip, however, involves Mrs. Bentley in a dilemma of her own. While she is prepared to abandon her own wishes for the sake of Philip's future, she nonetheless wants that future to include herself. She thus charts a precarious course which combines self-interest and self-sacrifice. Moreover, her drive to save Philip has her doing battle on two fronts—against the community and, paradoxically, against Philip himself. (p. 32)

Like so much of the book's texture, [the] final sentence poses precisely the complexity that Ross attaches throughout to Mrs. Bentley's character. Here, as elsewhere, the qualities of irony, paradox, and ambivalence characterize the writing. Mrs. Bentley's "I want it so" provides hostile critics with evidence of her continued desire to dominate Philip. They read the line "*I want it so*" in the sense of "I'm determined to have my own way." Mrs. Bentley's admirers find another meaning: "I *want* it *so*" / "I seek your happiness so very much." Perhaps it is both meanings at once, but the "it" of the sentence seems to me undeniably a recognition that Philip has at last emerged from his terrible isolation, and found a newness of being. It seems equally undeniable that Mrs. Bentley alone has brought that rebirth to pass.

This is the private side of the Bentleys' regeneration, but it also has its public consequences. Philip's decision to leave the church means overthrowing a profession which entailed a long apprenticeship and also assured a kind of livelihood. The economic aspect of the Bentleys' life needs further comment, since almost every page of the book raises the spectre of inadequate money. . . . Perhaps, then, the "want" of the final sentence has both an economic and personal connotation. Here, however, Ross leaves the future uncertain. Stability—whether private or public—remains tentative. . . . We cannot help but ask ourselves: Will they endure?

The answer to that question rests largely upon our assessment of Mrs. Bentley's character. Here, again, we notice a difference from the world of the short stories. Their endings often involve human tragedy or terrible loss, but in time the characters gradually readjust to the cycle of the seasons and the land. The close of *As for Me and My House* marks a significant difference. The Bentleys break with their environment; they leave Main Street and effect a change of direction in their lives. . . . We . . . experience a sense of personal triumph over externals. As Mrs. Bentley observes, possibly articulating Ross' own view: ". . . a man's tragedy is himself, not the events that overtake him." . . . No phrase more directly takes us to the heart of the book, or of Mrs. Bentley's character.

It is possible to view the Bentley's marriage as tragic. Even at times of deep despair, however, Mrs. Bentley does not view it so. She has much to lament, much to regret. . . . She is one of the loneliest women in all fiction—and one of the most remarkable. If there is any single value which Ross celebrates in this book it is Mrs. Bentley's incredible strength of character, her quietly creative determination to save her husband and her marriage. (pp. 35-7)

[The] contrasting worlds of past and present form part of Ross' strategy in [*The Well*]. Clearly, he wants us to question the human implications of the technological progress which transformed prairie life in the postwar period. . . . *The Well* is thus at one level a work of social criticism, a probing into some neglected side effects of that new prairie trinity: mechanization, mobility, and money.

Old Larson's life has straddled these two worlds. His hankering for the simple and heroic life of the Depression, despite its terrible hardships, is symbolized by the upkeep of the old well, whose waters he carefully guards and keeps perpetually clean. At times, the pressure of the past creates a traumatic tension in Larson which leads him to the borderline of insanity (there are affinities here in character with the crazed hermit of "One's a Heifer"). Ross brings this aspect of Larson's experience to a powerful climax in Chapter 26, as Larson kneels in the cold rain to tend the neglected grave of his son. His frantic rejection of his second wife Sylvia, striking wildly at her legs with a fistful of weeds, conveys a symbolic return on Larson's part to the simple mode of prairie life. Here, too, the elemental fidelity of Cora contrasts strongly with Sylvia's mercenary motives and sexual wanderings.

Sylvia functions in the novel primarily to emphasize the emergence of a new prairie mentality. . . .

Marriage is merely an escape [for her] from the endless drudgery of restaurant life. She wants fine clothes, a good time, exotic places. She finds old Larson both strange and repulsive; she lives for the day when his death will release her into wealth and freedom.

Nor has Sylvia any love for the land, nor any understanding of the deep, seasonal rhythms of the prairie farmer's life. Land is simply there to make money from; money is necessary to get you off the prairie and away to some romantic place. . . . (pp. 41-2)

Ross never resolves the question of Chris' possible guilt as a murderer, although the conclusion of the novel is designed to free him from the stereotype of the hardened and murderous personality. Chris' character is shaped to fit with great structural neatness into the polarities represented by Sylvia and Larson. The basic development of the book sees Chris vacillating between these two centres of contrasting values. He shares with Sylvia a desire for sudden wealth, ease, freedom: take what you can get from life today, at whatever cost—an attitude which Ross carefully plants in Chris' character with his original criminal act. But Chris is complex; there is in him a strain of goodness, sensitivity, and compassion which draws him, even against his will, towards old Larson. (p. 42)

[We] can see Ross gradually inching Chris towards regeneration. In this process, a variety of quietly humanizing forces come into play: the prairie land, with its subtle capacity to settle the restlessness of Chris' mind, to strip away all that hard glitter of city life and return him to the open and receptive nature of a child; the animals, whose quirks and oddities of behaviour begin to teach him a basic psychological insight denied by the crudely narrowing experiences of Boyle Street; and, finally, old Larson, who extends to Chris both the paternal anger and the tenderness which he had never known in his fatherless childhood. . . .

The central theme is the retrieval of Chris from alienation

as an outsider, from that ruthless pursuit of self which characterizes the loner in twentieth-century society. This theme, while typical of much modern literature, was especially popular in the angry books of the 1950s, and it is likely that Ross saw *The Well* as taking its place within a fashionable literary type. There is here, however, a rejection of the notion that the outsider is an especially attractive figure. Ross makes no attempt to glamourize an antihero. From the outset, Chris is sketched as raw and crudely self-centred, and it thus becomes Ross' major task to make us feel and believe that this shrewd opportunist with basically criminal instincts can be slowly, and at last completely, transformed. (p. 43)

Ross naturally uses the two basic modes of fictional development, external action and internal reflection. . . . [When he] blends these two approaches, we can see the process of regeneration at work. . . . (p. 44)

[The] narrative showdown, with a dying Larson providing evidence of Chris' innocence, ultimately fails to achieve real dramatic impact, although it suitably completes Chris' development in the novel. Nor does the sequence seem saved by the interesting structural device of the return journey to the old well (paralleling the earlier trip in Chapter 12). The final dumping of the dead Larson into the well's clean waters somehow fails to generate any clear symbolic meaning or evoke much emotional response—a failure which is compounded by the forced and unrealistic dialogue of the closing pages. The book ends with the flight of Sylvia, a fitting dispossession which leaves Chris, despite the hazards that lie ahead, successfully transplanted to a new life. The restless drifter from the eastern city has at last put down roots in prairie soil. (p. 45)

The world of the short stories and *As for Me and My House,* for all their rich ironies and ambiguities, is nonetheless a relatively homogeneous world made up of simple elements, as though Ross had deliberately set out to create a welding together of Old Testament and New World: arid land and a beleaguered people, evil visitations, inner struggle, acceptance and the will to go on.

Writers, however, do not stand still. Their experience changes and their art grows. . . . Once removed from his native prairie setting, and stimulated by the fresh experiences of war and life in a great metropolitan city, the focus of [Ross'] art begins to shift. His keen psychological insight, so obvious in the portrayal of Mrs. Bentley, continues to dominate his writing, but in the postwar period he starts to exercise it on rather different types of characters: outcasts, misfits, criminals. This shift is clear even before *The Well.* In characters such as Peter Dawson ("Barrack Room Fiddle Tune") and Private Coulter ("Jug and Bottle"), Ross reveals that he has moved on to delineate oddities and failures, people who simply do not belong, who cannot feel at home anywhere. (pp. 45-6)

Ross' next novel [*Whir of Gold*], published in 1970, is a slight affair, both in physical heft and literary quality. Its action is compressed into the span of a single week, and there are only a handful of characters. . . . Sonny McAlpine is familiar Ross material, sharing the psychological problems of Chris in *The Well.* His background, however, is very different. He might be one of the prairie lads from Ross' stories, now grown up and living away from home in a big eastern city. . . . Like the young farm boy of "Cornet

at Night," Sonny has become entranced with the strange power and beauty of music, and has followed it towards the bright lights of the eastern cities. Sonny has ranged from the piano to the clarinet but Ross' characterization of him as a musician lacks density. (p. 47)

The single glow of warm light which modifies the dark tones of Ross' canvas is the character called Mad. Sonny meets her in a bar on a dreary winter night and at first mistakes her friendliness for the overtures of a prostitute. Mad, however, is merely expressing her basic nature; she acts on impulse in singling out Sonny as "the right one" for her. Ross bows to the popular formula of getting them into bed as quickly as possible . . . , and at first sight we appear headed for another of those modern celebrations in which the delights of good old animal sexuality make us, at least momentarily, forget the dark world beyond the bedposts.

It turns out, however, that the book's central tension, apart from the conflict within Sonny himself, is a duel between Charlie [a racketeer] and Mad for possession of Sonny. (p. 48)

Although [Ross] again uses first-person narration (Sonny tells his own story as Mrs. Bentley had told hers), the style of *Whir of Gold* has a curiously clipped quality. There are few rounded sentences or paragraphs. Dialogue and descriptive passages take the form of broken phrases and fragments, a kind of cryptic shorthand whose meaning occasionally eludes the reader. Indeed, the writing often has the look and feel of a play script; . . . the jagged thoughts and notations of Sonny's mind seem stripped down to the bare economy of stage directions.

In much of the novel's content there exists what can only be called a desperate brand of naturalism. Ross' pages are covered with mundane and trivial things, as though the endless plates of bacon and eggs and all those nice hot cups of coffee will somehow cohere to underpin a work of art. But they utterly fail to do so. As a result, Sonny and Mad merely talk on in an uninteresting way about uninteresting things. By giving us a group of characters with so little scope (none of them has much traditional education or takes an imaginative or intellectual interest in the world around), Ross seriously restricts himself to the banalities of their limited existences—the movies, magazines and mindlessness of middle North America. Naturalism has always posed difficulties of representation for the writer, problems for which Ross finds no solutions within the course of this book.

With regard to other areas, however, the book merits a more positive comment. One interesting structural device that Ross develops is the use of the horse Isabel as both a transitional device between past and present and as a vantage point from which to view the relationship of Sonny and Mad. This high-spirited and quiet unpredictable mare (the same Isabel as in "The Outlaw") provides Ross with a useful way of conveying the quality of Sonny's youth. Isabel seems to have been the one thing which in the course of everyday prairie farm life eagerly excited his developing imagination and sense of beauty. . . . Ross skilfully parallels the Sonny/Isabel theme with the developing relationship between Sonny and Mad . . . , and this adds depth and clarity to material which otherwise rests too heavily on mere surface naturalism. (pp. 50-1)

Finally, it is of interest to note that the novel takes its title from what appears to be another of Ross' boyhood memories, one which captures the note of pessimism which permeates the book. In a remarkable piece of writing . . . , Ross describes how the lad Sonny, merely on impulse and without conscious evil intent, set a gopher trap near the nest of a brilliant prairie bird called the flicker, whose bright movements in the air dazzled the eyes as with a whir of gold. But the trap is soon enough sprung, and that bright glow, like the human warmth of Mad's presence or that once golden cornet at night, is soon stilled forever. . . . (p. 51)

This may seem a stark note on which to conclude a discussion of Sinclair Ross' writings, yet there is an appropriateness about the image. The idea of entrapment is a central aspect of Ross' vision, from the prairie farms of the short stories to Horizon's Main Street, and Sonny's slum boarding-house in Montreal. The limitations on human freedom are severe, and only a great effort of will, such as Mrs. Bentley's, can ease the fetters which environment fastens on human character. Despite their entrapment, Ross' characters nonetheless continue to hope, to plan, to dream. What makes this combination so moving and valuable is the sheer imbalance of its elements—the temptations of fatalism and despair greatly outweigh the likelihood of happiness or success, yet his characters face the world with a quiet determination that is truly impressive. The ultimate value of Ross' writings is his compassion for their plight. As harsh and destructive as the world may be, his characters are seldom touched by the same dark qualities. Our final impression of his world is not of the blackness that surrounds, but rather of the small gleam of beauty and humanity that bravely irradiates—like the after-image of a child's sparkler on the night air. (p. 52)

Robert D. Chambers, in his Sinclair Ross and Ernest Buckler *(© Robert D. Chambers; reprinted by permission of the publishers; distributed by Douglas & McIntyre Ltd.), Copp Clark Publishing, 1975, McGill-Queen's University Press, 1975.*

S

SARTRE, Jean-Paul   1905-

Sartre, a French playwright, essayist, philosopher, politician, and novelist, is considered by many to be the most influential thinker and writer of our time. The founder of existentialist philosophy, Sartre has examined virtually every aspect of human endeavor from the position of a search for total human freedom. Early in his career Sartre forged a philosophy of fiction revolving around the reader-author relationship which became a pivotal perspective of the New Novel school. Sartre called for the implication of the reader in fiction and the establishment of highly subjective points of view. He maintained that chronology could best be handled through a series of constantly unfolding and ongoing present moments. He received the Nobel Prize for Literature in 1964. (See also *CLC*, Vols. 1, 4, 7, 9, and *Contemporary Authors*, Vols. 9-12, rev. ed.)

DOROTHY McCALL

Sartre's plays, and especially *The Flies,* are generally considered to be vulgarizations of his previously elaborated philosophical positions. This assumption is misleading. *The Flies* is the first work in which Sartre presents what can be taken as an ethics of freedom. *Being and Nothingness* concerns not ethics but ontology, freedom not as value but as a structure of Being, that essential freedom which makes it possible and meaningful for man existentially to *make himself* free. In a footnote to the chapter of *Being and Nothingness,* "Concrete Relations with Others," Sartre indicates that his description of human reality does not exclude "the possibility of an ethics of deliverance and salvation." But, he continues, "this can be achieved only after a radical conversion." Such a radical conversion takes place . . . in Act II of *The Flies;* it involves a complete transformation in Orestes' understanding and use of his freedom. In committing murder, Orestes overthrows the moral and religious laws established by Jupiter. He kills Aegistheus and Clytemnestra in the name of his own liberation and that of the people of Argos. He has discovered that there are no *a priori* values, and that he must therefore bear the anguish of full responsibility for inventing values by his acts. (p. 12)

Clearly, Sartre intends Orestes to convey the idea that "existentialism is a humanism." The ethics of freedom embodied by Orestes involves a humanism that in certain historical situations must express itself in the form of violence. However, there is another aspect to Orestes which confuses his role as heroic liberator and points not to a dramatic richness in the character but to a confusion in Sartre's conception of him. Why does Orestes decide to leave Argos at the end of the play? Part of the reason is that Jupiter wants him to stay and to become ruler of Argos in place of the murdered Aegistheus. Here, as in committing the murder itself, Orestes' choice is defined in exact opposition to Jupiter's will. He says to the people of Argos: "I shall not sit on my victim's throne or take the scepter in my blood-stained hands. A god offered it to me, and I said no." On the other hand, he claims he has killed Aegistheus to liberate the people from their tyrant. . . . Orestes has freed the people from Aegistheus, but nothing indicates that he has freed them from the slave mentality which made Aegistheus' tyranny possible. . . . By some mysterious logic, Orestes seems to believe that by liberating himself, he is also liberating "his" people. (pp. 12-13)

In his fascination with the dark destiny he knows will be his, [Orestes] resembles more a romantic *force qui va,* gloriously doomed, than a *liberté en situation.* He acts, not with the fear and trembling of an individual who recognizes the risk inherent in every commitment, but with a kind of exalted joy. (p. 13)

The audience of *The Flies* in 1943 was less interested in the philosophical problems of the play than in its clear political meaning: satire of the Vichy puppets and praise of the Resistance. (p. 15)

The actual killing of Aegistheus and Clytemnestra, foreordained by the legend's tradition, is of secondary importance in Sartre's play. . . . The central question in the plot of *The Flies* is not whether Orestes will murder Aegistheus but how he will bear his act: will he take full responsibility for it, or will he abdicate his responsibility and disavow what he has done? The real murder of Aegistheus and Clytemnestra is meaningful only because of the symbolic murder of Jupiter that follows it. (pp. 16-17)

Orestes dramatizes in its most extreme form the power of freedom against tyranny. Sartre wrote his first play as a call to revolt; the freedom which inspires that revolt is meant as a passionate imperative. *The Flies* remains indispensable to any understanding of what Sartre is about. (p. 24)

Sartre has insisted that it was not his purpose in writing *The Devil and the Good Lord* to demonstrate that God does not exist. He stopped believing in God when he was twelve years old, he has asserted, and "the problem of God interests me very little." . . . Sartre deals in this play not so much with God as with all absolutes—Good and Evil, God and the Devil, Heaven and Hell—as evasions from the finitude of existence. (p. 32)

For Sartre freedom and solidarity are facts of human existence. They are also the basis for judgments of value. It is in the individual's awareness of his freedom and his solidarity with other men, in his will to assume responsibility for these facts and to work toward their realization as practical realities, that moral judgments are possible. In both *The Flies* and *The Devil and the Good Lord* the hero's conversion involves precisely this kind of awareness. (p. 33)

Like Orestes, Goetz is meant to serve as an example. The audience is supposed to identify with him, to learn from his mistakes and from his final heroic decision. (p. 36)

The evil with which Sartre is concerned in this play has no relation to the evil of which he has been able to speak so powerfully during and since the Occupation. It is a theological principle, by definition impossible to realize. Sartre explains his concept of "pure" evil in *Saint Genet:* "If he does not abhor Evil, if he does it out of passion, then, as Genet himself says, Evil becomes a Good. In actual fact, the person who *loves* blood and rape, like the butcher of Hamburg, is a criminal lunatic but not a true evildoer." The only "true evildoer," then, is Satan; no merely human creature is capable of pure evil. Even Faust, who sells his soul to the Devil, does not do evil for its own sake: he wants gold, women, power. It is because he is the Devil that Satan, through Faust, can be evil.

In another sense, too, Goetz's evil does not count as real. He pays no price for what he has done; his acts carry no consequences that limit his future possibilities. With Goetz's conversion, his past evil is erased. (p. 38)

[*The Flies* and *The Devil and the Good Lord* are Sartre's] spectacular plays; Orestes and Goetz are his two "heroic" heroes. In both cases, their conversions signify an absolute break with the past. Orestes' conversion, however, occurs early in the play. . . . For Orestes, the past involves no clearly definable self—that is, in Sartre's terms, no irrevocable action. Consequently, the past does not count heavily in that play's dramatic economy. Just before Orestes' conversion, his self is so light as to be almost nonexistent. This is not true in *The Devil and the Good Lord*. Goetz's conversion occurs in Act III, scene x; at this point his past should carry a good deal of weight. Man *is*, for Sartre, to the extent that he *has done*. Goetz has done many things, all of them with disastrous outcome. But the crimes of Goetz-Evil and the catastrophic mistakes of Goetz-Good never have any weight in themselves; they are simply lessons for Goetz and for the audience. With each metamorphosis Goetz is able to start again *tabula rasa*. (p. 39)

Goetz suddenly realizes that all his buffoonery has been in vain, that he cannot *be* anything in the eyes of God because there is no God for him to be for. Sartre would have us believe that this discovery makes of Goetz a completely changed man. This is difficult to believe, even on the basis of Sartre's own theories. His analysis of Genet draws extensively from Freud as well as from Marx; the conditions that define the situation within which Genet makes his choices are psychological as well as social. Sartre empha-

sizes the continuity underlying even the most radical of Genet's transformations. There is no such continuity in Goetz's conversion. (p. 40)

In *The Devil and the Good Lord* Sartre fails to create a language capable of embodying his hero's stated transformation. (p. 41)

Ideas in [*The Devil and the Good Lord*] do not arise from the confrontation of two wills in conflict; they exist as packaged goods compartmentalized within each character. . . . Goetz at the end of the play is like Faust saved instead of damned. Once he has seen the truth, he is able to take back his pact with the Devil and the Good Lord. (p. 42)

Although the theme of *The Victors* is heroism, the play has no hero. [There are no spectacular, exemplary individuals as in *The Flies* or *The Devil and the Good Lord* who] have the power to act, to change the world in which they find themselves. The five Resistance fighters in *The Victors* have no such power; things happen to them but they cannot make things happen. Evil in this play is not a metaphysical or theological idea as it is in *The Devil and the Good Lord*. The emphasis is on an extreme situation: torture. (p. 43)

Each of Sartre's Resistance fighters in *The Victors* is an exploration of one possible answer to the question: If they tortured me, what would I do? The *maquisards* are trapped in a closed situation in which action is no longer available to them. There is only suffering; all they can choose is the meaning of that suffering. They are defined not as personalities but in relation to their ordeal: to the threat of torture and to torture itself. In this situation, the problem of freedom is posed in a radical form. Each man must choose the attitude with which he will confront his torturers. Even under torture he is free since he must *decide* the exact moment he can no longer stand the pain, and what he will do at that moment. (p. 44)

One has to agree with Sartre that *The Victors* is less than successful. It fails for several reasons: the unsuitability of torture on the stage, the sketchy characterization of the torturers, the victims' failure to behave in such a way that the dramatic illusion is maintained. Its legitimate achievement is its presentation of the contest between torturer and tortured and its study of the fanatic pride that is part of heroism. (p. 52)

Although almost all critics of *Dirty Hands* have referred to [the protagonist] Hugo as a Hamlet-like character, the comparison does not take us very far, in spite of Hugo's long drunken tirade—"To be or not to be, eh? You see what I mean"—the worst speech in the play. Hamlet intellectually dominates every contest; Hugo always comes out a loser. He is bested by all the other characters. . . . Hugo is supposed to be lucid, but actually his lucidity operates only on his own inadequacies; he has little understanding of the events in which he wants to play a role.

As a psychological study . . . , Hugo is complex and interesting—one of the most fully realized characters in Sartre's plays. As spokesman for the moral position, however, he carries no weight at all. We are given psychological problems parading as legitimate moral dilemmas. (p. 59)

The real interest of *Dirty Hands* lies in the delineation of its three main characters: Hugo, Jessica, and Hoederer. None of them is reducible to an idea; in spite of the social issues involved, they communicate an immediacy and concreteness which makes us experience them also as private persons, a rare phenomenon in Sartre's plays. Sartre's portrait of Hugo, especially, involves an intimacy of understanding which Sartre does not usually give to his dramatic creations. He reveals Hugo from within, Hugo as he is for himself, with all the hesitations and blurs that such a portrait involves. . . . Hugo's wife Jessica, usually ignored or dismissed by critics, shows [a] kind of believable unpredictability of intelligence and emotion. . . . Hoederer, although an entirely admirable character, is neither stiff nor unconvincing. It is the three-way relationship between Hugo, Hoederer, and Jessica which finally makes the play interesting. (pp. 64-5)

In *Hugo*, Sartre explores many of the themes he deals with less successfully in *Orestes* and *Goetz*; Hugo stands as Sartre's modern humanized version of his two mythical heroes. Like them Hugo finds himself isolated, belonging to no collectivity he can experience as ''we'' instead of ''they'' and, as a result, suffers from a constant feeling of unreality. . . . In common with his larger, more heroic counterparts, Hugo is primarily concerned not with practical consequences, but with a justification for his existence: the salvation of his soul. All three characters need to be seen in order to be sure they exist: Orestes by the people of Argos, Hugo by his comrades in the Party, Goetz by God. They act not for ends, but for spectators. For this reason, the most extreme and irrevocable form of action—murder—becomes their chosen means of acceding to reality, of forcing ''them,'' Sartre's *Autrui*, to take their presence into account. (p. 66)

Hoederer is the one authentic hero of Sartre's plays, the one fully admirable character. His behavior has nothing in common with the flamboyant heroism of Orestes and Goetz, slaying their respective Gods; his concerns are practical objectives in a world of men. Orestes and Goetz must go through the ''baptism of blood'' before they can feel themselves free. Their ends, we are told, are noble; but we see only the means. Hoederer is more modest. Orestes and Goetz fight dragons; Hoederer simply gets work done. He represents Sartre's more sober ideal of political action. . . . (p. 73)

Although Sartre reveals Hugo from several points of view, giving the spectator the impression of complete familiarity, Hoederer remains elusive, constantly suggesting a complexity which never shows itself fully. It is significant that Hoederer is able to see Hugo, to understand what is going on inside Hugo's head, but for Hugo Hoederer always remains opaque, impenetrable. (p. 74)

It is Jessica who finally acts as catalyst of what we have known will be Hoederer's inevitable fate. Hugo kills Hoederer after Hoederer's one moment of weakness, the brief lapse in his will to stay away from Jessica and to ignore her insistent offer of herself. Hoederer's words to Slick and George after Hugo has shot him are characteristic: ''Don't hurt him. He was jealous. . . . I've been sleeping with his wife''. . . . Hoederer's final act of generosity is a lie.

Why does Hugo kill Hoederer? Hugo is his act; all that he has been, all his failures are synthesized in that one explosion. Whatever Hugo initially thought his intentions were, his real intentions are revealed by the fact of the murder itself. In *Being and Nothingness* Sartre makes a distinction

between the *motif* and the *mobile* of an action. He defines *motif* as the objective grasp of a situation, the understanding of how it can serve as a means for attaining a particular end. *Mobile*, on the other hand, refers to the psychological factors that motivate an act.

Hugo's initial *motif* was to assassinate Hoederer in order to eliminate a political enemy. This long-deliberated *motif*, however, has nothing to do with the crime as it actually happens. Hugo does not kill for political reasons or because his Party has ordered him to kill. In killing Hoederer, it is himself as a failure Hugo wants to kill. He hopes by a single act, a pistol shot, to inaugurate a future that signifies the destruction of his past. In fact he does just the opposite. Had he taken Hoederer's advice and accepted his help, Hugo's past would have become just a painful adolescent stage, the prelude to his manhood; with the act of murder, that past becomes a radical truth of his present and future. Each shot is the despairing confession of his complete alienation, his inability to escape from the prison of his childhood, his solitude, and his weakness. It is an admission that he cannot in any other way win the confidence of his comrades or respect from his wife. Only a dead body can make him feel that he has marked the world. (pp. 74-5)

Finally, after all the meanings of Hugo's crime have been explained into absurdity, all that remains is the act itself and its result—the dead body of Hoederer. Notwithstanding Hugo's long-planned intention, the crime as it takes place is unpremeditated. Hugo kills for no real reason; what happens is almost an accident, like Meursault's killing of the Arab because the sun was in his eyes. . . . He experiences what he has done as an act without an agent; for himself he is still only Hugo the actor, who happened to have real bullets in his play gun. (pp. 76-7)

Dirty Hands, like *The Victors*, is in a particular realistic tradition; it deals in a serious, nonmythical way with a contemporary crisis. . . . *Dirty Hands* avoids both the cerebralism and the sheer physical horror that weaken *The Victors*. Its intimate realism is entirely suited to the action of the play. Hugo's initial mission of assassinating an ideological adversary becomes the very different task of killing Hoederer; what begins for Hugo as an abstraction—the problem of ''red gloves''—changes into the terrible demand that he kill the one man who is willing to have confidence in him, who can help him, and whom he has grown to love in spite of himself. . . . *Dirty Hands* is less original than *No Exit* before it, less powerful than *The Condemned of Altona* after it. But it is the first play we have considered that escapes Sartre's great fault of sterilizing his drama with rhetoric; it inhabits a world to which we can give imaginative assent. (p. 78)

The defect of [*The Respectful Prostitute*] is that it vacillates uncertainly between realism and caricature. *The Respectful Prostitute* is meant to be an aggressive work, using ridicule as denunciation. Sartre, however, is unsure of his weapons. . . . We cannot recognize the characters as credible persons; nor is their distortion such that we can assent to it as functional caricature. (p. 85)

Both Sartre's satires, *The Respectful Prostitute* and *Nekrassov*, are weakened by the scene in which the play's action takes its crucial turn. In all Sartre's dramatic work the turning point occurs as a climactic confrontation between protagonist and antagonist. Only in *Kean*, whose plot

Sartre has taken from Dumas père, is there no such scene. Sartre's serious plays are constructed in such a way that this scene is a life-and-death contest between opposing wills. . . . In his two satires, Sartre keeps the climactic confrontation scene but, in both cases, uses it for edification rather than for comic effect. In *The Respectful Prostitute,* the awkward semirealism of Lizzie's contest with the Senator makes of her abdication a sentimental melodrama. In *Nekrassov,* too, Sartre cannot find the right tone for his scene of confrontation, primarily because he has used an irrelevant character to bring the turning point about; the contest to which *Nekrassov*'s structure has been leading us finally takes place not between Valéra and Palotin, but between Valéra and Veronique. (pp. 93-4)

When Sartre stays with his original intention of writing a satiric farce, he creates scenes of frequently brilliant comic technique. . . . Sartre does not want us puzzled by his comic types; he wants us to recognize them immediately so we can focus our interest on what happens to them. Except for Valéra and Veronique, who exist on a different level of reality, the characters in *Nekrassov* are deliberately simplified [and consistently successful]. . . . (p. 95)

The *pathétique* of Kean's situation as victim of society is of less interest to Sartre than the analysis of that situation [in *Kean*]. Kean, like Nekrassov, is a mystifier of society. Both protagonists, the actor and the adventurer, make their livelihood by pretending that they are what they are not. Each discovers that it is he who has been mystified, forced by society into a role which does not permit him to exist as a man. Kean has been created out of society's need for illusion; his function, simply, is to please. In carrying out that function, Kean has become an appearance of a reality. For himself he is only make-believe. Since the subjective sense of his reality eludes him, he must depend on the image he finds in the eyes of others. Both for himself and for others, he emerges as a reflection. Sartre describes Kean in the same terms as he earlier described Genet: "It was you who took an infant and turned him into a monster". (p. 102)

Kean, the drama of the actor, is a comic encapsulation of a theme present throughout Sartre's plays: the difference between gesture and act. Orestes, Goetz, Hugo, and Valéra, like Kean, all act for an audience, performing the role of an imaginary character. Their first concern is not to do, but to be seen, and they use a real or imagined audience as a means of acceding to the identity of hero. (p. 107)

Sartre allows himself the luxury of being comic in *Kean* because the play is not intended to be *engagé* in the same sense that *The Respectful Prostitute* and *Nekrassov* clearly are. In his two "serious" comedies Sartre is ultimately less concerned about comic coherence than about the clarity of his social message. But the world of the actor Kean—so like that of the actor-child of *The Words*—is one where politics "is not our line." (p. 109)

The most common accusation leveled against Sartre's novels and plays has been that they are too "philosophical," more concerned with ideas than with individuals. In this light, it is perhaps paradoxical that those two literary works generally considered Sartre's masterpieces [*Nausea* and *No Exit*] happen also to be those that proceed most directly from one of his major philosophical works, *Being and Nothingness*. . . . Sartre devotes large segments of *Being and Nothingness* to a close analysis of what is revealed

dramatically in *No Exit*. The section "Concrete Relations With Others" and, even more centrally, the chapter "The Look" serve as an ontological explanation of the play.

Yet *No Exit* is not a thesis play in the conventional sense, any more than *Nausea* is a conventional thesis novel. What makes *No Exit* a masterpiece is that Sartre is able to translate philosophy into dramatic form. *No Exit*—in contrast to Sartre's other plays—does not contain a lot of ideas; it is, in itself, a powerful literary idea. . . . Garcin, Estelle, and Inez are not independently interesting characters endowed, as the expression goes, with "a life of their own." What gives them interest is that they are incarcerated together. And it is their existence together, for eternity, that creates Sartre's idea and maintains it in dramatic action. (pp. 110-11)

Nausea is an individual confrontation with the world lived to such intensity as to be an obsession. Sartre's other fundamental obsession—his other philosophical myth—is expressed in its purest form in *No Exit:* the self petrified into an object by the Medusa-like look of other people.

For Sartre, "My original fall is the existence of the Other." The existence of the other is directly revealed to me by his look. The look that sees me endows me with an identity, a nature. . . . Sartre connects the fall . . . not with any particular sin but with my discovery in shame of a symbolic state of nakedness, of my defenseless state as an object in the eyes of the other. I experience his gaze as a form of possession and even of theft; he has me as I can never have myself. This fundamental alienation explains the lure of the mirror, which gives me the illusion of seeing myself as the other sees me, of becoming the other looking at me while still remaining myself. But in spite of my efforts, "The Other holds a secret—the secret of what I am." The self that I am for the other is in no way commensurate with my own experience of myself. My behavior has a particular meaning for me; seen by another it is defined, captured as by a photograph, given another meaning over which I have no control. (pp. 111-12)

The look becomes Hell when the other refuses the image of myself I want him to see. In *No Exit* this happens to each character in turn as he finds himself the one who looks and the one who is looked at, the torturer and the victim. As the play circles downward and inward to its conclusion, the three realize in horror their complete interdependence. (pp. 113-14)

Iris Murdoch reminds us that "Sartre, like Freud, finds in the abnormal the exaggerated forms of normality." Sartre's characters in *No Exit* express attitudes that are common enough in their basic form; Sartre takes those attitudes to their extreme possible consequences.

[We] see why Garcin, Inez, and Estelle have been damned in Hell. Even before their deaths, they were never completely alive. All three treated others as their possessions, objects to be used. Their punishment is appropriate to their sin. They existed through domination and sadism, taking pleasure in the suffering of their victims. Each one finds now that he himself is a victim, tortured unmercifully by his dependence on the others. . . .

It is because they are dead that Inez's retort to Garcin's last attempt to defend himself is a statement of horror: "You are—your life, and nothing else." For someone on the threshold of life, those same words could be exhilarating.

For Garcin, Estelle, and Inez, they are a final damnation. . . . If existence precedes essence, they have become their essence. . . . For all three of them, that essence is a form of failure. (pp. 121-22)

"Hell is—other people" is the central truth of *No Exit*. Within the play, it serves as a summing up of what has been dramatically revealed to us by the interaction of its three characters. It is important to remember, however, that within Sartre's philosophy that formula has a limited and specific meaning. Sartre has emphasized this point: "The only valid relationship is with other people. That can go even to hell. In order for it not to be hell, *praxis* must exist. The characters of *No Exit* are in a passive, changeless situation in which each of them is inevitably fixed in his essence by the others." Hell, then, is other people when they brand us with an image we cannot bear to accept as our own, and when we have no possibility to act so as to change that image. (p. 124)

In his "Forgers of Myth" speech, given in the United States in 1946, Sartre described as follows the new French plays born during the Occupation:

> Our plays are violent and brief, centered around one single event; there are few players and the story is compressed within a short space of time, sometimes only a few hours. As a result they obey a kind of "rule of the three unities," which has been only a little rejuvenated and modified. A single set, a few entrances, a few exits, intense arguments among the characters who defend their individual rights with passion.

No Exit entirely fits that characterization; it is the only one of Sartre's plays to do so. It is also the only Sartrean play to contend successfully with the problem of dramatic language, which Sartre has recognized as the fundamental problem of theatre. . . . In *No Exit* Sartre creates a language bare of extraneous rhetoric: the words act. Language can even be considered one of the themes of *No Exit*. (p. 125)

The terrible interdependence of man and his human prey, fixed by eternity in *No Exit*, dramatized in individual non-mythical terms in *Dirty Hands*, becomes in *The Condemned of Altona* the tragedy of history.

Most of Sartre's plays are concerned with man and history. *The Condemned*, however, is the first play in which man's struggle with history takes place in the claustrophobic world of Sartre's best early works. In Franz's room, enclosed behind the bolted door, history assumes a life and a tragic reality that is singularly absent from the open spaces of *The Flies* and *The Devil and the Good Lord*. (p. 150)

In contrast to so many of Sartre's heroes who are reduced to schematic formulas, Franz, in the best moments of the play, puts us in touch with that "infracassable noyau de nuit" [indestructible kernel of darkness] at the point where our individual and collective history meet. (p. 151)

It is worth noting that the much talked about "existentialist hero," considered a "positive" figure, does not appear at all in Sartre's novels or stories; he appears only in *The Flies* and *The Devil and the Good Lord*. Orestes and Goetz belong to no collectivity. Their past has left them only with a sense of what they are not. *Engagement* expressed in vio-

lence thus becomes their means of acceding to reality. In Sartre's heroic mythology, violence for a liberating cause is both a ritual of initiation into the human community and the exact price of his hero's salvation. (p. 152)

[It] is Sartre's *No Exit*, one of the two plays he might call a purely critical spectacle, that is also his most perfect: the only play in which Sartre fully realizes what he sets out to do. (pp. 152-53)

In his *What Is Literature?*, written in 1947, Sartre contrasts the prose writer with the poet or painter. He defines prose as essentially utilitarian, using words as signs that point to a particular meaning. The poet, on the other hand, like the artist with his paint, creates an object with words; as such it is opaque and self-contained. The context of Sartre's definitions implies a faith that prose literature can act in the real world.

This utilitarian conception of prose bears directly on Sartre's sense of literature as salvation. The connection lies in his position that "the 'engaged' writer knows that words are action. He knows that to reveal is to change and that one can reveal only by planning to change." In this definition Sartre does not distinguish between action and the image of action, or, as he so frequently puts it, between act and gesture. A magical leap has been made from the word to the world. (p. 157)

His central problem in the plays is one of language: his demand that words become action conflicts with their power as words.

No Exit is the only Sartrean play that triumphs completely over this problem. Its structure has [a] kind of mathematical purity. . . . The entire action is in the interaction of the three characters as they create their hell. Once the infernal machine is set in motion, it functions with its own automatic necessity. Nothing external intervenes to alter the initial situation; we simply watch the inevitable take place in a single dramatic movement that repeats itself again and again, each time with greater intensity until the final *prise de conscience* which is the play's climax.

The Condemned of Altona does not achieve the integration of form and content that gives *No Exit* its peculiarly classical beauty. The achievement of *The Condemned* is Franz. Earlier, in *Dirty Hands*, Sartre created in Hugo a character perhaps equally complex; as with Franz, we are given an intimate awareness of his public and private truths. Hugo, however, lacks the stature to embody those issues that the play requires him to embody. *Dirty Hands* nevertheless succeeds as effective drama because of the vitality of its central relationships. In *The Condemned*, a more ambitious and original effort than *Dirty Hands*, Sartre creates with Franz a character both fascinating in himself and large enough to support the themes with which the play contends. The scenes of Franz's madness, his attempts to find the words that will proclaim him innocent to the tribunal of crabs, are equal to the best in Sartre's writing.

Like *No Exit* and *The Condemned* Sartre's satiric comedies dramatize a negative image. *The Respectful Prostitute* and *Nekrassov* miss their mark, however, to the extent that Sartre distrusts the critical function of comedy. At crucial moments, he abandons his chosen weapon. . . . Rather than allowing his characters to speak as themselves, Sartre the political moralist, fearful of not being clear, periodically intrudes to explain what he really means.

Sartre often speaks of literature as an act of "disclosure," but the majority of his plays reach impatiently for a more concrete kind of action. In so doing, they rarely by indirections find directions out; instead, they rely on straightforward, didactic prose. . . . Sartre has always been fascinated by the absolute of literature and, at the same time, distrustful of its attraction. As a choice of the imaginary over the real, literature becomes suspect, since it is the real world that Sartre wants to change. (pp. 157-60)

Sartre sees the impasse of literature in general in its inability, at this point in history, to speak to all. His sense that literature must be *concretely* universal is particularly frustrated by the theatre as it exists institutionally. (p. 160)

[While] Sartre has complained of theatre as a bourgeois institution, his own plays do not attempt to change the old forms. The subject of all Sartrean plays is subversive; their end is to undermine the established system of values. Sartre sees the writer as a mediator who gives society a "bad conscience" by creating an awareness that contests its basic assumptions. But he presents this subversive content within a conventional form. Sartre has expressed great admiration for the dramas of Brecht, Genet, and Beckett; in his own plays, however, he has chosen to use traditional dramatic techniques rather than experiment with new ones. This traditionalism has often proved inadequate to sustain what he wants to say. (pp. 160-61)

For Sartre the idea of literature as an absolute is intimately connected with a faith in salvation. His most recent position, expressed in *The Words,* indicates that his loss of faith in one has meant loss of faith in both:

> For a long time, I took my pen for a sword; I now know we're powerless. No matter. I write and will keep writing books; they're needed; all the same, they do serve some purpose. Culture doesn't save anything or anyone, it doesn't justify. But it's a product of man: he projects himself into it, he recognizes himself in it; that critical mirror alone offers him his image.
>
> (pp. 161-62)

Sartre has constantly vacillated between the conviction that literature is everything and that literature is nothing, between the desire to capture in words a total reality and the frustration that that reality can be captured only in the imaginary. His autobiography relates his present disillusionment with literature; the words embody a power denied by their contents. (pp. 162-63)

> *Dorothy McCall, in her* The Theatre of Jean-Paul Sartre *(copyright © 1967, 1969 Columbia University Press; reprinted by permission of the publisher), Columbia University Press, 1969.*

CATHARINE SAVAGE BROSMAN

Although a number of scholars have noted the presence in Jean-Paul Sartre's fiction of images of insects and crabs, the role of numerous other animal images in *La Nausée* and their psychological and philosophical suggestiveness have not been fully explored. In the present essay I shall be concerned to study these in relation to its thematics and to draw some conclusions concerning Sartre's early view of nature. (p. 107)

In *La Nausée,* I count some 77 similes and metaphors in which an object or the human body—usually the latter—is compared in part or in whole to an animal or a part of an animal. . . . In addition, they are supported by at least 43 instances (excluding those in fixed locations) where names of animals or their characteristics occur in a non-comparative use. . . . There is thus a notable awareness of, and appeal to, the animal kingdom in this novel, set entirely within an urban setting, in which the main character expresses neither personal nor professional interest in animals. Considering that much of the language of the book is non-metaphoric, we can conclude that the use of animal imagery is noteworthy. The variety of animal forms and behavior offers the novelist a wide choice of metaphoric suggestions.

Since this is a first-person novel in the form of a journal, all the images can be taken to express the hero's own evaluation or reaction; they are supposed to derive immediately from his impressions. They reveal, moreover, a great deal about him—more than about the creatures themselves and often more than about their tenor (if it is not himself). To say that these images signify pure bestiality in the human world would be inadequate. What I should like to suggest, rather, is that the zoological realm contains in *La Nausée* a concentration of the negative characteristics of all "existants," as Roquentin terms them, especially of human existence, and therefore is particularly loathesome to him. Metaphors and similes derived from zoology are therefore consistently pejorative. At one end of the spectrum of material phenomena according to Roquentin's view is the mineral—that non-human area where hardness prevails and self-coincidence is most strikingly complete. . . . At the same end of the spectrum is that group of "existants" composed of the purely ideal—the circle, the jazz song, with their necessity, purity, and noncontingency. . . . Human existence . . . is on the contrary soft, empty, and lacking in self-coincidence or essence; it can reach neither mineral hardness nor the purity of a geometric figure. In Sartre's view, of course, consciousness is empty, free, and "néant," and the body of man or his facticity, although material and objective (part of the *En-soi*), is a constant reminder of consciousness's stickiness, softness, and emptiness, first by its distinction from consciousness—man's ineradicable distance from himself—and next by its relative flabbiness (or viscousness) compared with harder forms of existence. All that is physiological, then, is of negative valence to Roquentin. The zoological world represents existence at its most physiological: pure viscous flesh, without even the possibility of revolt against protoplasmic identity. Man's carnal existence is mirrored in animals; for this reason, Roquentin uses them repeatedly as illustrations of certain perceptions, and especially as a correlative for facticity.

Botanical phenomena raise a special problem in this connection. Differing radically, except at the lowest levels, from zoological forms, they seem at first less corrupt. . . . However, as soon as any plant is subjected to Roquentin's continued attention, it is assimilated to animal forms and processes. (pp. 107-09)

It is noteworthy, however, that Roquentin criticizes the anthropomorphism, or at least the animism, that all these comparisons presuppose. . . . What he accepts on an imaginative level he rejects on a philosophical level. . . . So the parallel between botanical and zoological existence is not ·really denied, and the effect of the various comparisons is to create a disquietingly animate nature, sometimes monstrous. . . . Moreover, this assimilation of plants to animals brings them close to human beings also by the metaphoric common denominator; we conclude that in Roquentin's imagination virtually all life approaches the animal, apparently the most loathesome manifestation of existence.

In short, animal imagery is used to convey a feeling of nausea inspired in part by the very existence of the organic, and the resulting philosophical pessimism that commentators have noted. Like many other objects in *La Nausée,* animals are not generally seen as having utilitarian value. Nor do they function in an ecological system. They are quite without the support of any economic framework or general embracing biological view. Any such view would be, for Sartre, artificial—imposed from without. This is consistent with Roquentin's final conclusion that nothing has necessity or justification and that all existence is an absurd excretion. It is also characteristic of his non-scientific view that the underlying question in his reflections on phenomena is not "how" but "why." This separates his view radically from that of the biologist and puts him closer to the theologian and the poet.

La Nausée contains a number of metaphoric references simply to animals, without indication of species. Some of these stress general features of animal life and reveal Roquentin's typical attitudes. . . . Imaginative transformation of inert objects into live animals foreshadows the gradual inclusion throughout the novel of many material phenomena in the category of animate existence, which the hero will find both upsetting and useless. It also identifies animation, or movement, as one of the things most threatening to his psyche. Another element of animal life is utilized in the metaphor "cette bête lymphatique" [that lymphatic beast], . . . representing humanism. This metaphor has the effect of reducing a major view on mankind to a rudimentary and unpleasant form, and also introduces in connection with animals as well as with a current in thought the category of the "visqueux" [viscous] and the implied reaction of nausea. Elsewhere, the heaviness of an unspecified animal is used to convey the awareness of existence, not quick and mobile in this case but crushing. . . . (pp. 109-10)

Another associated item is the frequent mention of blood, although blood is not used strictly as a metaphor. While he thinks in one instance of his own "beau sang rouge" [fine red blood] as opposed to "cette bête lymphatique" . . . , blood is generally repulsive in *La Nausée.* . . .

The choice of species most frequently mentioned by Roquentin is revealing. The small number of references to many of the higher mammals is noteworthy. Those that are named serve chiefly for characterization and seem not to interest Roquentin in themselves. There is no mention of wild herbivores such as deer, frequently representative in poetry of such qualities as freedom, purity, and the ideal. Farm animals appear rarely. . . . In these cases, as in a number of others, the animal comparison is essentially an ingredient of the caricature. During the museum scene [for example], sheep appear in a sarcastic reference to the parable of the lost sheep. (p. 111)

In two cases the import of a metaphor naming a higher mammal is more directly ontological rather than characterizing. In a metaphor underlining the difficulty of saving (the word is Sartre's) human existence even by a work of art,

Roquentin calls the composer of "Some of These Days" "un gros veau plein de sale bière et d'alcool" [a fat lout full of squalid beer and alcohol]. . . . The calf image as well as the dirty beer—not only a liquid, but a repugnant one—pulls the composer back to the level of facticity, in spite of his being "lavé du péché d'exister" [washed of the sin of existence]. . . . The donkey appears in a very important comparison during Roquentin's ride on the streetcar. . . . In fact the donkey, like the bench it is supposed to resemble, seems less an ordinary creature than a nameless, gross, disquieting transformation. It is significant that when Roquentin is face to face with brute, raw existence, . . . he should use this animal metaphor, among other types. . . . But though he cannot name them, they seem like grotesque, obscene creatures. This suggests that the animal is a common denominator of existence; it is crucial in Roquentin's imagination.

Among the animals used in some of the most striking passages are the crustaceans, insects, arachnids, larvae, centipedes, and other lower forms, commonly considered repellent, which are without powers of reflection or memory. Roquentin's predilection for these is striking. Indeed, he is quite fascinated by what is repulsive to him. First, I shall consider the long, slimy, or fuzzy forms—worms, larvae, and centipedes. The initial animal image of the novel is that of a "gros ver blanc" [huge white worm] which the Autodidact's hand resembles. . . . This comparison, which may suggest his sexual ambiguity (that is, lack of hardness and clear definition), also says something about the human hand. Ultimately, all existence is seen as "cette larve coulante" [this flowing larva] disgusting and without justification. . . . In his surrealistic vision, he imagines a tongue becoming a centipede which the person must try to tear out with his hands. . . . Such a vision denies all belief in the orderly processes of nature, since apparent pattern is merely the indolence of organic forms . . . or possibly of our induction. Moreover, as metamorphosis rather than simile, this vision plants right in the human body the unpleasant animal to which elsewhere the body is merely compared; it is in a sensitive organ—the mouth—where *two* senses operate and which also functions in speech, associated with what is distinctly human, as well as in feeding.

Crawling and flying insects and arachnids similarly convey both repulsiveness and a frightening vision of the possibilities of being, especially of absorption of consciousness by the *En-soi.* . . . The comparison with hands is particularly to be noted, since it figured in the first animal comparison and Roquentin subsequently studies his own hand as "une bête à la renverse" [an animal on its back]. . . . This image is modified in the crucial public garden passage into a view of all existence. . . . Here the insect suggests primarily not ugliness or repulsiveness or hostility, as with the spider web, but the awkwardness and futility of existence. Pathos does not attach to it, partly because few readers find pathetic the vicissitudes of an insect's existence, partly because of the adjective "maladroits" [awkward]. The image is thus a metaphoric support for the central plot line of the discovery of contingency.

While these are not strictly images in the technical sense, it is essential to recall in this connection the post-coital dream of a garden, foreshadowing the surrealistic revery and the episode in the public park. In addition to the hairy leaves . . . , Roquentin sees ants, centipedes, and moths running everywhere; then unnamed creatures. . . . He then imagines the Velleda of the public garden pointing to its sex; this brings together food, insects, and sexuality, themselves all associated elsewhere with existence at its most monstrous and repellent. (pp. 111-13)

In the category of insects, it is worthwhile noting a few additional items. In the public garden, the wind is compared to a large fly landing on the tree. . . . Here a gaseous (i.e., mineral) phenomenon is animated and thus included in the needless organic activity the hero is deploring. In comparison to traditional literary renderings of wind, which often suggest awesome natural force, or the movement of a natural or supernatural spirit, the image is pointedly unfavorable. . . .

Precisely because insects do inspire repugnance, they are used by Roquentin to convey protest against the reigning bourgeois values of Bouville. (p. 114)

While the crab metaphor has been examined by others, a short summary and further remarks can be useful. . . . In *La Force de l'âge,* Simone de Beauvoir relates Sartre's mescaline-induced hallucinations in the 1930's of octopuses and crabs and his subsequent visions of eyes and jaws, owls, and a lobster. The crab appears in a variety of Sartrean works, where Fields takes it to be chiefly a Freudian symbol signifying return to water and the pre-natal life, and also to stand for "l'idée de malfaisance" [the idea of evildoing]. . . . Boros, who takes issue with her, considers it "une transcription mythique du malaise profond qu'il était en train de vivre intensément" [a mythic transcription of the profound uneasiness that was living intensely]. She notes several instances, including two in *La Nausée,* of the crab seeming to symbolize enclosure and imprisonment, objectification by the look and also alienation from reality. More important for our purposes is that it suggests "une sorte de hantise de la chose figée, de l'homme devenu chose" [a sort of obsession with the fixed thing, with the man who had become a thing]. . . . Prince likewise takes the image to symbolize "la suppression de la liberté humaine, l'immobilisation de toute transcendance par autrui" [the suppression of human liberty, the immobilization of all transcendence through others]. . . . Crab-like qualities are connected [also] with solitude—a social aberration—but also with the processes of thought. Subsequently, Roquentin associates the crab with himself. . . . Doubtless Boros . . . is right to see it as symbolizing Sartrean fear of being engulfed by the *En-soi*. . . . Thus the crab has . . . been associated with both consciousness and body or facticity. (pp. 114-15)

One last crab image, not discussed by previous commentators on the question, is associated not with humankind but with nature in one of its most mysterious and awesome manifestations, the ocean. . . . Roquentin imagines the sea as inhabited by a monster of a vaguely crustacean nature. . . . The crustacean images lead us easily to those of other marine life: fish, polyps, mammals. Fish are not seen as food or in a marine system but are used rather as visual illustrations for human characteristics. (pp. 115-16)

Several other sea creatures furnish metaphorical vehicles in *La Nausée.* The chestnut root, for instance, has the hard and compact skin of a seal. (p. 116)

Although they do not receive the considerable imaginative value that some lower forms have, dogs and cats—which I

have chosen to treat separately from the other quadrupeds such as the donkey—are mentioned frequently by Roquentin. Their use is frequently humorous or sarcastic. As with many other animal comparisons, the effect is reductionist. . . .

The canine species is particularly associated with humanism, Roquentin's *bête noire* and, in most of its forms, his creator's. (p. 117)

Birds appear in several significant images. Swans and a white owl are mentioned, the latter as the dictation topic written on the muddy paper Roquentin cannot pick up . . . , the former as a simile for papers on the ground. . . . Here the whiteness and shine of the paper—which to some degree may represent consciousness (at least as it would wish itself to be), especially since paper can be connected with writing, thus with language and thought—are already subject to attack from the sticky earth; Roquentin's swans are not inviolate. . . . (p. 118)

Domestic fowl, used to convey physical features, as in "ce cou de poulet" for the Autodidact . . . and the young woman in the restaurant (object of the man's admiration) whose open mouth is like a "cul de poule" [backside of a fowl] . . . make the human beings unattractive, somewhat ludicrous. . . . The museum episode indicates that, for Roquentin, bourgeois leaders are really exploiters of the people whom they claim to protect; the eagle eye contributes to this impression by its suggestion of keen sight for the purpose of identifying and devouring victims. . . . Concerning humanism, Sartre makes what is perhaps an allusion to Baudelaire's L'Albatros when he says that the humanist's love for man expresses itself awkwardly. . . . In another passage, an obscene vision of the male genital organs, Roquentin sees birds flying around these and attacking them with their beaks to the bleeding point. . . . Such aggression turned against the organs of human reproduction . . . suggests on the thematic level hostility to physical life as well as a most unusual psychic makeup in Roquentin. Elsewhere, birds convey the quality of consciousness. . . . A reflection on seagulls similarly conveys an ontological meaning. Watching them fly over the seawall, he thinks of them not as birds but as *existing* phenomena. . . . The bird partakes here of the individual, non-categorized existence that Roquentin finds in nature. When he adds that the water of the garden fountain flows into his ears and makes a nest there . . . , the metaphor stresses the receptivity of consciousness, its obligation to be conscious of something exterior to itself.

Snakes appear in several comparisons in *La Nausée,* where their traditional symbolic value is less important than the graphic suggestiveness of their form and their threatening nature. . . . In the most clearly Cartesian passage of the novel—though perhaps a parody—the snake image has an entirely different value when the hero thinks of his awareness of his own existence as "le long serpentin, ce sentiment d'exister" [the long snake, this feeling of existence]. . . . The comparison between the length of the snake and human thought depends chiefly on its physical form; it may involve as a mediating factor the form of the intestines, since Sartrean awareness is in considerable part awareness of facticity. We may be reminded also of the Biblical serpent of knowledge, especially self-knowledge. Subsequently, the serpentine form is associated with the *En-soi* instead of the *Pour-soi* when Roquentin calls the chestnut tree root "ce long serpent mort à mes pieds, ce serpent de bois" [this long snake dead at my feet, this snake of wood]. . . . By this image which both animates ("serpent") and de-animates ("mort"), Sartre again draws botanical phenomena toward zoological ones, although ambiguously. Moreover, by virtue of the shared image, both Roquentin's thought and material existence are brought into the same category of phenomena—a crucial point in *La Nausée*, if Roquentin is to convince us that all existence is subject to the same contingency and lack of value, and thus strike down the Christian and humanistic views of mind as superior to matter. (pp. 119-20)

Animate nature viewed by Roquentin, with its general unpleasantness is far from that of the romantics. . . . Moreover, what we might call pattern, as well as fraternal meaning, is missing. The many heterogeneous forms and types of behavior seem to be without relationship to each other. But in these Roquentin sees an image of human features, thought, and action. And since this means complicity, he, and Sartre—to the degree that his hero spoke for him in the 1930s—reveal what is in some ways a romantic view of the world, which, like much Romanticism, is somber, pessimistic, tending toward the fantastic. By contextual implications, adjectives, and analogies, he projects onto animal forms the meanings he wishes to give them, and at the same time lets them retroact on him—a stance that Robbe-Grillet would call "tragic." This extends beyond the species themselves, for the animal world comes to taint other phenomena, in some degree—plants, human beings, wind, ocean.

Animals thus interest the Sartre of *La Nausée* not for themselves—a position that tends toward the scientific, and which Gide, for instance, had—but as reflections and symbols of men. General attitudes toward them are, however, discernable. By their near absence, such qualities as bravery, fidelity, and independence, which a certain humane view has tended to identify in some animals, are denied them. Indeed, most behavioral qualities and roles (though not aggression) are simply ignored. It would seem to be their forms, their physiology, and often their supposed closeness to the viscous (as well as men's attitudes in the case of canines) that lead Roquentin to mention them. Part of "cette ignoble marmelade" [this ignoble jelly] . . . , they represent existence—both human and inert—especially well to his imagination, since with that other race, *homo sapiens* whom they resemble, they are guilty, as he says at his most theological, of the unforgivable "péché d'exister" [sin of existence]. . . . (pp. 120-21)

> Catharine Savage Brosman, "Sartre's Nature: Animal Images in 'La Nausée'," in Symposium (copyright © 1977 by Syracuse University Press), Summer, 1977, pp. 107-25.

WALKER PERCY

[*Nausea* is] an onslaught on the "normal" or what is ordinarily taken for the normal. Unlike Sartre's later political novels, it is interesting because the attack is phenomenological, not political, an examination, that is, of the way things are.

What interests us about Roquentin, the protagonist of *Nausea*, in the present context is his conscious and deliberate alienation from those very aspects of French culture which by ordinary standards one would judge as eminently normal, for example, the apparently contented lives of the pro-

vincial bourgeoisie and the successful lives of the savants of the academy of science. (p. 368)

It is important to notice that *Nausea* is no ordinary free-thinking rationalistic-skeptical assault on the Catholic bourgeoisie. For Roquentin (and Sartre) have as little use for the opposition, the other triumphant sector of French society, the anti-clerical members of the academy, famous doctors, generals and politicians. (p. 369)

[What] are we to make of Sartre's and Roquentin's alienation? . . .

[Is] Sartre saying something of value about the condition of Western man in the twentieth century or perhaps about the human condition itself?

Or is Sartre's existentialism to be understood as only a way station in his transit from a bourgeois intellectual to a Marxist ideologue?

If Sartre is correct, then things have indeed been turned upsidedown. For in his novel the apparently well are sick and the apparently sick are onto the truth. But is the truth an unpleasant business we would do well to avoid? Roquentin thinks he knows something other people don't know, that he has made an unpleasant discovery which scarcely makes for happiness but allows him to *live* with an authenticity not attained by the happy bourgeoisie and the triumphant scientists. Anxiety, a sense of unreality, solitariness, loss of meaning, the very traits which we ordinarily think of as symptoms and signs of such and such a disorder are [in *Nausea*] set forth as appropriate responses to a revelation of the way things are and the way people really are. (p. 370)

> Walker Percy, in Michigan Quarterly Review (copyright © The University of Michigan, 1977), Fall, 1977.

*   *   *

SKELTON, Robin   1925-

Skelton is an English-born Canadian poet, essayist, and editor. The duality of his geographic background plus his wide-ranging interests in art, music, and poetry are reflected in the varied content and changing styles of his poetry. His influence on Canadian letters is felt through his editorship of the *Malahat Review*.

DOUG FETHERLING

Professor Skelton obviously learned to polish his verse into what . . . is now the "casual mastery" mentioned in one of the poems, but I am unable to find anything very new or interesting in what the poems stand for [in *Selected Poems*]. One of two examples exist where the conclusions are meant to be half understood by the readers. One is "At Walden Pond" where

> I stamp on the ice of a man a hundred years dead.
> My children scream half-laughters at the risk . . . (of
>   crossing the ice.)
> But I don't laugh.

The best poem in the collection is one about a prisoner of war released by the Japanese after World War Two who recalls having been marched through Nagasaki after the American atomic bombing:

"It looked like a flower
among the stones," he said,
"a cup and saucer
melted and hardened back
into folds of petals.
Lovely it was," he said,
"but I felt sick. . . ."

This poem and a much longer one about Vancouver Island make up for a lot. You've got to really go for Mr. Skelton's poetry to keep from wandering through the book, which also would have been better with the exclusion of his traditional ballads. (p. 30)

> *Doug Fetherling, in* The Canadian Forum, *December, 1968.*

DANIEL HOFFMAN

[Through] changes of venue and circumstance Mr. Skelton's verse retains its characteristic diction, stance, and rhythm. His normative mode works through short lines in strongly stressed dimeters or trimeters, conventional syntax, whether rhymed or no, and a vatic stance. (pp. 339-40)

These poems [in his retrospective *Selected Poems*] abound with such words as leaf, star, rock, love, breath, beast, death, the vocabulary of Celtic bards, of Yeats and Dylan Thomas and Vernon Watkins rather than the ironic, self-deprecatory domesticities of The (London) Movement and The Group. It is not surprising that Robin Skelton made anthologies of Irish verse and emigrated to British Columbia.

This Romantic amplitude of feeling and commitment to inherited meters is evident, too, in his ballads. I much prefer the Blakeian quatrains of *A Ballad of Johnnie Question* and *A Ballad of Despair* to the longer ballads in part three of the book. These swiftly grow monotonous, all in fourteeners broken into duple stanzas of eight lines, and based, not on the great ballads of old oral tradition, with their swift alternations between narrative and refrain, but on the tedious and circumstantial broadsides of the last century. (p. 340)

Other poems in other modes of Skelton's are admirable. *Begging the Dialect* beautifully dramatizes the tension between the transience of common speech, collected by a linguist in "crumpled villages", and the hoped-for permanence of verse, of language: "What is that? And that? And that? What did / your father call it? What his father? What?" . . . Two of the last poems are among the most memorable poems of the Second World War I have read. Both dramatize prisoners of war—in *Remembering Esquimalt*, a Canadian held by the Japanese; in *The Reliquary*, a German Skelton met in Africa, whose father and the poet's father had also fought on opposing sides of the same battle a generation before. In these poems sharp emotion is intensified by restraint. (pp. 340-41)

> *Daniel Hoffman, in* Poetry *(© 1969 by The Modern Poetry Association; reprinted by permission of the Editor of* Poetry*), August, 1969.*

NEIL RENNIE

If (as in Robin Skelton's first poem) 'the numbering disc' is the dial of a telephone, what etiolated banality cringes in the shadows of (his book's title) *The Hunting Dark*? Or in those of 'the rivering dark'? Or the 'vast unravelling dark'? The 'hunting dark' would seem to be the preying doubt to

which the middle-aged are particularly prone and Skelton, no exception, confirms his anxiety by haunting the scenes of his past. While the tone is well controlled and there are no histrionics, the information that places have changed, that people have died and that 'no dead awake' does not help to convince the reader of the necessity for these reminiscences.

His past accounted for, Skelton brings us up to date with the self-abnegating candour of the confessional poet who reports his lusts, his worries and the contents of his mirror: 'At forty sensual enough, no grey / at jaw or temple. . . .' And, at fifty: 'A plump dark man, / grey hair thick at the nape, bags under eyes . . .' etc. There are, too, the '. . . fragments . . . scattered, random, / fumbling scraps together'. 'Profound? or mad?' asks Skelton.

In the last pages of his book, the poems have been slimmed to a fashionable shape, an elegant brevity, and poetry supersedes autobiography with agreeable results. Some of these pieces are too fragmentary to be effective, but others are self-sufficient, laconic and focus the miniature image precisely realized:

> 'The earth is
> dark. I see
> owls in your
> palm. . . .'

I hope the poems in this volume are in a generally chronological order and that we can assume that Skelton has overcome his self-indulgence, written off the confessional poet (whose poems risk unflattering comparisons) and is developing an individual voice. For the variety of postures he adopts only serves to emphasize the absence from his writing of any definite personal style. (pp. 121-22)

> *Neil Rennie, in* London Magazine *(© London Magazine 1971), August-September, 1971.*

ROBIN MATTHEWS

Timelight, fittingly enough, is concerned with quest and travel—physical and psychological. A seven part series, it is the attempt of a battered and blunted and dulled ego to see itself in universal terms, principally by connecting (on a Canada Council travel grant) with foreign writers and scholars who have names. The unhappy speaker of the poems moves through time and travel deathwards, with metaphorical and real phlegm in his throat. Anguished, his "spirit enters waste / sargassoes of unreal / conformables and miles" ("The Fell of Dark"). He feels pain and frustration: "I beat upon the rock. / There is no answering voice" ("Lakeside Incident"). Finally, he can say: "I mingle memory / and desire / dream and dream / to hint a whole / beyond the vagaries / of its parts / . . . / turning my face / into the light" ("Timelight").

In his Preface, Skelton suggests the book has a major theme, which it is the reader's "duty . . . to identify". That's not too hard: Life is vanity; time steals away; look for the little light. But Skelton makes almost unconscious play upon the quest structure which is built from the Preface through to the appendix. The book becomes a comment upon its own apparent intentions. For the Preface is mock-humble. The poems have their life in a kind of strutting, hurting, black-country pretentiousness. The conclusion is almost a spoof on the scholarly appendix in which Skelton reveals his borrowings from (mostly) Pound and Eliot—and himself. The borrowings from the others are so obvious as to need no annotation. The borrowings from himself are lines only he could possibly remember.

"This is man's pretension", the book seems to say. "This is what life's about—always the scramble to belong." The speaker really meets Robert Graves and Ezra Pound. He connects with Yeats by writing about Yeats and himself in their forty-fifth years. The inveterate Kathleen Raine is also present, as are the other remnants and left-over people of a day that seemed to matter, there, once upon a time, long ago. . . .

But even while the speaker is building his house of cards (visiting cards?), he can't help communicating its sham: "This is the house I never meant to make" ("Things Past"). The cry is a cry of failure by one who doesn't know exactly where he went wrong. Neither Canada nor the city of Victoria ever enters the book. The alien mind travels and flails about to connect with something that matters, something from the culture he left behind, something to give him being. As a caricature of the great quests it is chilling. And it is chilling too, as a study of a certain kind of immigrant psyche.

The most painful thing about the book is that one cannot think of it being important to readers. The verse is rarely good or memorable. . . .

That is sad, because there is a yearning for significance in the book.

> *Robin Matthews, "Moonlighting in the Soul," in*
> The Canadian Forum, *April-May, 1975, p. 64.*

DAVID JACKEL

Here we have, as Skelton terms [*Because of Love*], "a more or less narrative sequence" (less rather than more, I think, since several of the poems were separately published before being gathered into this narrative), one which both depicts the course of a particular love affair and attempts to celebrate love as a vital force in human life. Technically the poetry is impressive in nearly every line. Skelton is a craftsman whose work shows that he has not merely studied but *absorbed* the major traditions of poetry in English, and can write with gracefully assured precision in a variety of tones and rhythmic forms.

His technical skill is expended, however, on delineating in this new book the nuances of feelings which are seldom clearly motivated. The sensitive speaker in the narrative is too much in love with love, and too self-consciously sensitive, to deal adequately with any person or quality outside himself; his beloved exists for the reader only as a set of gestures, detached phrases, and stray details of physical appearance. The speaker's response to her is vivid enough, but sexual attraction too often empties his mind of every other concern. Although he has much to say *about* love, the language he speaks is rarely the language *of* love, that language which shows desire and affection transforming the public and private aspects of a whole personality. (p. 38)

> *David Jackel, in* The Canadian Forum, *August, 1977.*

*   *   *

SNOW, C(harles) P(ercy)   1905-

A British novelist, statesman, physicist, and biographer,

Snow is noted for his ability to weave into his fiction realistic aspects of science, education, business, and government. He is best known for "Strangers and Brothers," a series of eleven novels that deals with questions of morality and power in contemporary England. Snow was knighted in 1957 and created Baron in 1964. (See also *CLC*, 1, 4, 6, 9, and *Contemporary Authors*, Vols. 5-8, rev. ed.)

BERNARD BERGONZI

[Future] social historians may find a lot to interest them in Snow's novels. But no literary work can be justified by its subject matter alone, though Snow's admirers sometimes seem to imply that he is such a good novelist simply because he writes about so many different aspects of our society. . . . Inevitably an author must be judged not merely on the variety of his materials, but on what he makes of it. (p. 215)

One of my initial difficulties in reading Snow at all is in coming to terms with his prose, which is at worst so arid as to be almost unreadable—*Strangers and Brothers* is particularly bad in this respect—and at best efficacious but banal. . . . I must emphasize that my objection to Snow's style is not primarily aesthetic; it is, rather, that I find it functionally disabling. Eliot's account of significant events is frequently so inexpressive that the reader has difficulty in being convinced of the emotional reality of what is described.

Snow himself has made it clear that though 'Strangers and Brothers' is meant to provide a variety of insights into contemporary society, the central interest of the work lies in Eliot himself. In a note to *The Conscience of the Rich* he writes that the inner design of the sequence 'consists of a resonance between what Lewis Eliot sees and what he feels. Some of the more important emotional themes he observes through others' experience, and then finds them enter into his own.' He instances the theme of possessive love, which appears in *The Conscience of the Rich* with Mr March's relation to his son, and which reappears in *The New Men* with Eliot's relation to his brother Martin, and again in *Homecomings* in his relations with Margaret. As a statement of intention this is of some interest, though it doesn't much modify my actual reading of 'Strangers and Brothers.' Yet it does indicate that Snow regards the sequence as a carefully planned whole. This being so, it is all the more surprising that he seems to have had no qualms about sticking throughout to the convention of the first-person narrator. There is no absolute reason why it shouldn't be used, provided the author understands its limitations. Snow, unfortunately, doesn't seem particularly aware of the inherent difficulties: here, in my opinion, lies the central flaw of 'Strangers and Brothers.'

In general, first-person narration falls into two kinds. In one the narrator is no more than a detached observer, a 'camera eye', who records the events taking place around him and keeps his own personality as unobtrusive as possible. The other is more avowedly autobiographic in form, where the narrator is actively involved in the tale, and may even be its central character. . . . Both these kinds have their characteristic dangers. . . . With the 'camera eye' method the narrator has to see and record everything important that happens: if he is describing a small and enclosed world this need not present any difficulties, but the larger and more varied the society, the greater the danger of manifest contrivance on the author's part in order to have his narrator in the right place at the right time. With the 'autobiographic' method, where the narrator is much more at one with what he writes about, this difficulty may not arise: but there is a corresponding one, which is that he will be unable to describe naturally and convincingly his own deepest emotional experiences: in such cases a note of embarrassment or strain nearly always obtrudes. In 'Strangers and Brothers' Snow uses both types of narration: in *Time of Hope* and *Homecomings* Lewis Eliot tells his personal history, and in the other novels he is an observer of the lives and actions of others.

In *Time of Hope* and *The Masters*, which I take to be his two most successful novels, Snow is largely able to avoid these inherent difficulties, though for very different reasons. *Time of Hope* was the third novel in the sequence to be published, but it takes first place chronologically, for it deals with Lewis Eliot's boyhood, youth and early manhood. . . . [The] first part of *Time of Hope*, which tells of Lewis Eliot's boyhood, and his ambiguous relations with his possessive and ambitious mother, seems to me to have an imaginative quality and emotional force that I don't find anywhere else in Snow's fiction. One is reminded, at times of the Lawrence of *Sons and Lovers*. The disabling quality of the style is less apparent here than in the other books, and the events of Eliot's boyhood are both intensely felt and given the kind of distancing that enables the author to describe them with imaginative freedom. There is an authenticity of feeling in the first part of *Time of Hope* which makes one aware, by contrast, of the thinness and shallowness of other parts of 'Strangers and Brothers.' In the later chapters we follow Eliot through his early struggles and successes, and his intense and hopeless passion for Sheila Knight. In his account of this relationship Snow's success is certainly less assured than in the boyhood chapters, but it must be recognized.

It is true that we don't really participate in Eliot's love for Sheila, and this is not surprising. For a first-person narrator to convey successfully and convincingly the quality of an over-mastering sexual love is so rare as to be almost unknown (the only work I can think of that comes anywhere near doing this is Hazlitt's *Liber Amoris*, though there may be others). Snow's attempts to do so result in vague emphatic gesturing, in a prose that is not just banal but positively and embarrassingly bad. . . . Yet despite this, we *are* made aware of the object of Eliot's love. The elusive personality of Sheila Knight, neurotic, destructive, pitiable, and yet oddly engaging, is caught and realized. She is almost the only one of Snow's female characters of whom this can be said. And though we can't share in Eliot's love for Sheila, we do sense the anguish that was an inescapable part of their relationship, both before and, still more, after their marriage.

In *Homecomings*, Snow's second sustained essay in the autobiographic mode, Eliot is further from his roots in early life and almost wholly absorbed in the world of affairs. In consequence the emotional texture of the novel seems very much thinner than that of *Time of Hope*. . . . Unlike Sheila, [Eliot's second wife] Margaret (for me, at least) doesn't begin to exist as a person: she is a mere cypher, adorned with various agreeable attributes. . . . [In] *Homecomings* [Snow] seems no longer interested in even attempting to present the quality of Eliot's love. (pp. 215-19)

In the other novels Eliot is not at the centre of affairs, but is, to a greater or lesser extent, an observer of other people. And here Snow falls foul of the danger that the 'camera eye' method of narration will make the story-teller seem overtly inquisitive, and even something of an eavesdropper and *voyeur*. Though Eliot's personality remains in many ways elusive, one does carry away the impression—which is probably irrelevant to Snow's intentions—that he is an indefatigable recipient of other people's confidences, and the kind of person who is much given to listening quietly and intently to private conversations. . . . [The] weakness is particularly apparent in *The Conscience of the Rich*, where we have to believe that Eliot, a Gentile and something of a social outsider, is so completely accepted by an aristocratic and clannish Jewish family that he is able to be present at their most intimate family discussions. . . . Few of us have the good fortune to be so invariably in the right place at the right time as Eliot does. Things might be more plausible if, just occasionally, Eliot missed some vital piece of information by *not* being on the spot when it was delivered. Again, in *The New Men*, one can believe that Eliot, as a wartime Civil Servant, is actively concerned with an atomic research project, but when we also have to accept that his brother is one of the scientists engaged on the project, so that Eliot has personal as well as official knowledge of the scheme one becomes a little incredulous. In the 'autobiographic' method the narrator is in some sense prior to the events he describes, they only happen at all because they happen to him; whereas with the 'camera eye' approach he is subservient to events, and is only there because they must be described. Snow has, I think, failed in the surely impossible task of effectively combining the two modes.

In some of the novels in 'Strangers and Brothers' Eliot is not so much concerned with a succession of events as with telling the story of some particular personality who is close to him. This, for instance, is the basis of *The Light and the Dark*, a work which I can only regard as a total failure. The central figure is Roy Calvert. . . . He is constantly before our eyes, and we are *told* a great deal about him. Nevertheless, he remains totally unrealized as a character: we simply don't *feel* that he was such a remarkable man as Snow tries to make us believe. In this failure of realization the limitations in Snow's narrative style become very apparent. . . . [His initial description] makes Calvert no more than a walking cliché from an old-fashioned novelette. (pp. 219-20)

Strangers and Brothers is another novel where the action is centred in a supposedly powerful and unusual personality. In fact, George Passant emerges much more fully as a character than Calvert, and within limits one can accept him for what he is: a solicitor's clerk in the provincial town where Eliot grew up, who is unusually able and intelligent, idealistic and at the same time somewhat boorish, with strong physical passions. Yet the whole intention of the novel is that we should see Passant as more than just this. We also have to believe that he was a man of such charm and personal magnetism that he could command the devotion and allegiance of a large circle of young people. And this is asking us to believe rather more than we are actually given: one isn't at all sure precisely what it was in George Passant's character that made him such a commanding person.

It is, then, to *The Masters* that we must turn if we wish to see Snow at his best in using Eliot as an observer. This story of Cambridge college politics has become deservedly popular, and has been aptly described by Lionel Trilling as 'a paradigm of the political life'. Though it lacks the imaginative depth of parts of *Time of Hope* it is certainly Snow's most successful piece of contrivance. Paradoxically, it suffers from a similar fault to *The Light and the Dark* in that though Jago, the favoured candidate for the Mastership of Eliot and his party, is frequently described as a man of admirable and unusual personal gifts, these are in no way made real to the reader. Yet in *The Masters* this is not a major fault, since the real interest is not centred in Jago but in the cross-currents of intrigue and bargaining that surround him in the small, jealous world of the senior common room. We are not concerned with exploring a single personality in depth, but in the interrelations between a group of characters, none of whom need be so fully realized. The peculiar structure of *The Masters* means that Snow's weaknesses are less apparent than usual, while at the same time his strength can be fully displayed. Thus, since Eliot is one of the dons most actively concerned in the election, he has an integral part in all the conversations that take place and which he reports: here he is in no sense an eavesdropper. Again, the subject of sexual love, which Snow usually has trouble with, is largely absent from the novel. . . . Most of the time we are in a wholly masculine society, given over to intrigue and a particular struggle for power. And it is in writing of intrigue and power-struggles that Snow excels. The other novels are most alive when dealing with similar subjects: as for instance in the trial of George Passant in *Strangers and Brothers*, the intrigues concerning the Communist news-letter in *The Conscience of the Rich*, and in the unmasking of the atomic spy Sawbridge in *The New Men*. Here, too, Snow has most scope for his special abilities in characterization. Usually unsuccessful in depicting attractive young men or women he can draw effective portraits of middle-aged or elderly men, especially those with eccentric tendencies. In *The Masters* there are the two elderly dons, Despard-Smith and Gay: elsewhere in the sequence one can think of Mr March, Martineau, Bevill, Austin Davidson, and above all, the shady but amiable barrister, Herbert Getliffe, perhaps Snow's most vividly realized single character.

Another element of interest in *The Masters* is Snow's constant use of certain motifs which occur elsewhere in the sequence and which are, on an imaginative level, the only genuine linking elements in it. These can be resolved to two basic images: the snug, enclosed room, usually with a bright fire burning in the grate and the curtains drawn; and the complementary image of lighted windows seen from outside. . . . It is significant that Snow should have associated Eliot with [the first of these images] when he first presented him to the reader, in the opening sentences of *Strangers and Brothers*: 'The fire in our habitual public-house spurted and fell. It was a comfortable fire of early autumn, and I basked beside it, not caring how long I waited.' This motif comes quite naturally in *The Masters*, since so many of the discussions inevitably take place in front of bright fires in curtained college rooms: at the same time, its recurrence gives an additional imaginative unity to the book.

The opposed image of the lighted window occurs more often in the other novels. It was first evident in *Time of Hope*, when the young Eliot spent long painful hours looking up at the lights of Sheila's house. . . . In fact, it is not difficult to associate these recurrent images with the per-

sonality of Eliot: the 'lighted windows' motif can be taken as standing for his sense of himself as an outsider, looking aspiringly at the symbols of power, riches, and sexual success. (pp. 221-23)

On the other hand the image of the snug, enclosed room can easily stand for Lewis's complementary sense of having 'arrived,' of now being a part of the world of high-powered discussions and well-conducted love-affairs. Yet there seems to be more to it than this: one does not have to be a very committed Freudian to catch the insistent suggestions of a womb-symbol in the recurring image of the warm, curtained room. . . . Not for nothing do we remember how Eliot's relationship with his mother had dominated the early chapters of *Time of Hope*. It is, I think, in these two motifs that we have the clue to the personality of Lewis Eliot, which is revealed as considerably more regressive than Snow would have us believe. Eliot, for all his ability and worldly success, has never really escaped from the obsessions of his early childhood and adolescence.

Beyond this, we really know very little about Eliot. 'You're not as nice as people think,' says Sheila to the young Lewis in *Time of Hope*. One is inclined to comment that one doesn't know how nice or how nasty Eliot in fact is. On the one hand he seems to have great charm, since so many people like him, and to be trustworthy, since so many of them confide in him. But on the other hand he is obsessed with power—'I had kept an interest in success and power which was, to many of my friends, forbiddingly intense' . . . —and he can act with extreme rughlessness. . . . All these characteristics could exist together in the same individual, admittedly, but he would be, to say the least of it, a morally complex personality who would need very careful realization to seem convincing. And this Snow is not capable of giving. Eliot remains a fragmentary collection of attributes.

There is an additional reason for this fragmentation, inherent in the form of the novel itself. 'Strangers and Brothers' proceeds by a method of simultaneous progression rather than a successive one. That is to say, two or three novels may cover the same period of time, and in each of them Eliot will be concerned with a different set of events. . . . Were Eliot really plausible these separate strands of experience would be co-existing in his consciousness and sensibility, modifying each other, and together forming new patterns. Instead of which they are separated into water-tight compartments. In each case, Eliot is less than the events he is describing, and there is no unifying principle to be detected.

Although Snow has claimed that the central interest of 'Strangers and Brothers' lies in 'a resonance between what Lewis Eliot sees and what he feels', this is scarcely possible: there is such a radical lack of balance between the two that one cannot conceive of a genuine 'resonance'. . . . If I have dealt somewhat exhaustively with flaws in characterization, it is because in the Trollopian mode that Snow favours solidity of character-drawing is of greater importance than it would be in a more formalized approach to fiction. I have deliberately said nothing about the moral assumptions underlying 'Strangers and Brothers', since they would require extended treatment of another sort. But they seem to me distinctly shallow: the book's underlying morality doesn't transcend the code of the good-chap-cum-man-of-the-world. Eliot, in fact, is too close to his world: he can describe it in fascinated detail, but he is not able to interpret it meaningfully. (pp. 223-25)

Bernard Bergonzi, "The World of Lewis Eliot," in The Twentieth Century (© The Twentieth Century, 1960), March, 1960, pp. 214-25.

PETER FISON

[To] blame Snow's style for lacking virtues which are not only irrelevant but would be completely out of place in the character of his work is ... inadequate. Lawrence Durrell can patch his pretentious productions with prose poetry to hide the joints, but for Snow the style is the work and his sparse prose has an organic function in the structure of the novels. He does not force his significances on us but lets them emerge naturally from the surrounding circumstances. The style is intentionally flat, recording every detail as the story proceeds through a level series of short chapters, each preoccupied with a single incident, some significant, others not. There is no emphasis on one more than another. As in real life, climaxes occur almost unrecognized in the steady procession of existence, and Snow never raises his voice. Each occasion is recorded in isolation so that casual relationship speaks for itself and emerges only when it is necessary for the story. (p. 568)

There is no reason to deny that certain books in the ['Strangers and Brothers' series] are weak. *Homecomings* for instance, is basically a brilliant novella, a study in inevitable schizophrenic despair; and the rest of the novel, tagged on after Sheila's suicide, is a let-down and acceptable only because of its structural importance in the progress of the series. None the less, one cannot help feeling it could have been done differently and much better. *Strangers and Brothers* too, is insufficiently taut: there is a tentativeness of approach about it, that its successors have overcome. But to ascribe this weakness to the characterization of George Passant seems perverse.

'One isn't at all sure,' Mr Bergonzi complains [see excerpt above], 'what it is in George Passant's character that made him such a commanding person', when the whole point of the book is spiritual poverty of the provinces in the 'twenties, where even a man like Passant, specious and full of the clichés of the metropolitan radical atmosphere, can because of his emotional warmth have a catalytic effect far beyond his spiritual calibre.

To find Snow's greatest success, as Mr Bergonzi does, in the earlier parts of *A Time of Hope,* is to impose the wrong criteria. Certainly Eliot's development among the lower middle classes of the Midland town, particularly his relationship with his mother, is well done; but this is all part of the Balzacian meticula that build the story, not the principal theme. To praise or condemn Snow's success in depicting such a relationship is equally incompetent. What contributes to Snow's purpose is not what he has in common with the inter-war novelists who recaptured their childhood for a reading public for whom this is exotic, nor even those (Lawrence springs to mind) who, much more profoundly than Snow, found their inspiration in these roots. This might lead to the sort of *Bildungsroman* more familiar to critics and therefore easier to judge, but it is irrelevant to Snow's intention, where the earlier development is a function of the society which, as a complex, is Snow's theme.... Mr Bergonzi himself has drawn attention to the persistence of certain images in Snow's work and their structural importance: it seems strange that he would ignore the symbolic value of the continually changing social setting. This is significant, not because of its variety but for the unity which can be found within this variety. For whatever world it reflects, the high politics of the Bevills, the professional world of the bar, the worlds of scholarship and research of literature or of human relationships, its preoccupation is the same: Power; and its manifestation in different circumstances is the theme of the whole series, a theme upon which unity is imposed by this variegated society itself, rather than by Lewis Eliot. (pp. 569-70)

Snow alone amongst post-war English novelists has come to terms with Hiroshima, has accepted that our whole civilization must bear its implications, as the whole German people must bear those of Auschwitz and Lidice. (p. 570)

The theme of *The New Men* is really a question. How is it, the scientists ask, that we have reached the abyss? Who is responsible? and this, by implication, is the subject of Snow's whole series. For 'Who is responsible' is merely another way of asking 'Where does power lie?'

It is a Stendhalian question, but the answer is very English: 'Usually it builds itself from a thousand small arrangements: ideas, compromises, bits of give and take'. The jockeying for position and prestige which takes up so much of official life is suddenly seen to be of vital importance: for only the right men in the right place could have stopped the unnecessary bomb, and this the scientists fail to achieve. It is committee politics, however petty, that determine momentous results and in face of them the individual is helpless. One committee is very mcuh like another, whether the local committee that opens *Strangers and Brothers* (a much more pervasive image this than the snug room, almost indeed a key signature) or the deliberations of the cabinet. That intricate study of personal politics, *The Masters,* is the essential clue to the events of *The New Men.* Through Eliot, the temporary civil servant's eyes, we see the final powerlessness even of the minister, even of the permanent head of a department like Hector Rose. Beginning, it would seem, from almost the same premises as the existentialists, Snow differs completely in his conclusions. In the end it would seem that not the Napoleonic figures, nor the oligarchies can be accepted as the genuine wielders of power; its true symbol is rather Arthur Brown, the comfortable, tenacious, conservative intriguer with a knowledge both of the limits of the possible and those minor human quirks whose myriad interactions underlie great events.

Here, surely, lies the explanation of Snow's attitude to human relations. Jago, Mr Bergonzi explains, is never made sympathetic enough to justify Eliot's insistence on his likeability. But the book is not an introspective study of Jago's character, but rather a dissection of its effects. Eliot's dryness is deliberate, for even in their private lives, ... Snow's characters seem perennially in committee; and life is made up of the apparently minute shifts of such relationships. Each novel is a study of some particular individual in what might be called his political capacity, his power-relationship to other people. For Snow all relationship is one of balance between individuals, of compromise and the maintenance of integrity. For Snow, but not necessarily for Eliot who is fallible and who, though frequently the witness and confidant in situations where he is not directly involved (a position incidentally that does not seem to me as contrived as it does to Mr. Bergonzi; one has after all known people who, not implicated themselves, seem always to be present in "inside" circumstances) is himself ineffective when his own life comes into play.

Public and private life interfuse, affecting each other only too sincerely; in Eliot's surroundings Snow finds a microcosm of the world. It is in the implications to Eliot of these surroundings, the resonance (if that unfortunate word must be used) between this and Eliot's own involvements, that is the purpose of Snow's series, and whether successful or not it is an attempt on a different scale from the cosy little introspective novel Mr Bergonzi seems to expect when he dismisses Eliot as 'a fragmentary collection of attributes'. (pp. 570-71)

> *Peter Fison, "A Reply to Bernard Bergonzi's 'World of Lewis Eliot,'" in* The Twentieth Century (© The Twentieth Century, 1960), June, 1960, pp. 568-71.

F. R. LEAVIS

[Not] only is [Sir Charles Snow] not a genius; he is intellectually as undistinguished as it is possible to be. If that were all, and Snow were merely negligible, there would be no need to say so in any insistent public way, and one wouldn't choose to do it. . . . Snow is a portent. He is a portent in that, being in himself negligible, he has become for a vast public on both sides of the Atlantic a master-mind and a sage. His significance is that he has been accepted— or perhaps the point is better made by saying 'created': he has been created an authoritative intellect by the cultural conditions manifested in his acceptance. Really distinguished minds, are themselves, of course, of their age; they are responsive at the deepest level to its peculiar strains and challenges: that is why they are able to be truly illuminating and prophetic and to influence the world positively and creatively. Snow's relation to the age is of a different kind; it is characterised not by insight and spiritual energy, but by blindness, unconsciousness and automatism. He doesn't know what he means, and doesn't know he doesn't know. That is what his intoxicating sense of a message and a public function, his inspiration, amounts to. It is not any challenge he thinks of himself as uttering, but the challenge he *is*, that demands our attention. (p. 297)

The Two Cultures exhibits an utter lack of intellectual distinction and an embarrassing vulgarity of style. The lecture, in fact, with its show of giving us the easily controlled spontaneity of the great man's talk, exemplifies kinds of bad writing in such richness and so significant a way that there would, I grant, be some point in the schoolmaster's using it as a text for elementary criticism: criticism of the style, here, becomes, as it follows down into analysis, criticism of the thought, the essence, the pretensions.

The intellectual nullity is what constitutes any difficulty there may be in dealing with Snow's panoptic pseudo-cogencies, his parade of a thesis: a mind to be argued with— that is not there; what we have is something other. Take that crucial term 'culture,' without which and the work he relies on it to do for him Snow would be deprived of his seer's profundity and his show of a message. His use of it focuses for us (if I may be permitted what seems to me an apt paradox) the intellectual nullity; it confronts us unmistakably with the absence of the thought that is capable of posing problems (let alone answering them). The general nature of his position and his claim to authority are well known: there are the two uncommunicating and mutually indifferent cultures, there is the need to bring them together, and there is C. P. Snow, whose place in history is that

he has them both, so that we have in him the paradigm of the desired and necessary union.

Snow is, of course, a—no, I can't say that; he isn't: Snow thinks of himself as a novelist. I don't want to discuss that aspect of him, but I can't avoid saying something. The widespread belief that he is a distinguished novelist (and that it should be widespread is significant of the conditions that produced him) has certainly its part in the success with which he has got himself accepted as a mind. The seriousness with which he takes himself as a novelist is complete— if seriousness can be so ineffably blank, so unaware. . . . [As] a novelist he doesn't exist; he doesn't begin to exist. He can't be said to know what a novel is. The nonentity is apparent on every page of his fictions—consistently manifested, whatever aspect of a novel one looks for. I am trying to remember where I heard (can I have dreamed it?) that they are composed for him by an electronic brain called Charlie, into which the instructions are fed in the form of the chapter-headings. However that may be, he—or the brain (if that's the explanation)—can't do any of the things the power to do which makes a novelist. He tells you what you are to take him as doing, but he can give you no more than the telling. When the characters are supposed to fall in love you are told they do, but he can't show it happening. Abundant dialogue assures you that this is the novelistic art, but never was dialogue more inept; to imagine it spoken is impossible. And Snow is helpless to suggest character in speech. He announces in his chapter-headings the themes and developments in which we are to see the significance of what follows, but what follows adds nothing to the effect of the announcement, and there is no more significance in the completed book than there is drama—or life. It is not merely that Snow can't make his characters live for us—that he lacks *that* creative power; the characters as he thinks of them are so impoverished in the interests they are supposed to have and to represent that even if they had been made to live, one would have asked of them, individually and in the lump: 'What of life is there here, and what significance capable of engaging an educated mind *could* be conveyed through such representatives of humanity?' (pp. 297, 299)

Among the most current novels of Snow's are those which offer to depict from the inside the senior academic world of Cambridge, and they suggest as characteristic of that world lives and dominant interests of such unrelieved and cultureless banality that, if one could credit Snow's art with any power of imaginative impact, one would say that he had done his university much harm. . . . Even when he makes a suspect piece of research central to his plot, as in that feeble exercise, *The Affair,* he does no more than a very incompetent manufacturer of whodunnits could do: no corresponding intellectual interest comes into the novel; science is a mere word, the vocation merely postulated. It didn't take a brilliant research scientist to deal with the alleged piece of research as Snow deals with it—or a scientist of any kind. . . .

What the novelist really believes in, the experience he identifies his profoundest ego with because it makes him feel himself a distinguished man and a lord of life, is given us in Lewis Eliot. Eliot has inhabited the Corridors of Power; that is what really matters; that is what qualifies him to look down upon these dons, the scientists as well as the literary intellectuals, with a genially 'placing' wisdom from above;

there we have the actual Snow, who, I repeat, is a portent of our civilisation; there we have the explanation of his confident sense of importance, which, in an extraordinary way, becomes where his writing is concerned a conviction of genius; he has known from inside the Corridors of Power. That he has really *been* a scientist, that science as such has ever, in any important inward way, existed for him, there is no evidence in his fiction. . . .

[In] *The Two Cultures and the Scientific Revolution* there is no evidence, either. The only presence science has is a matter of external reference, entailed in a show of knowledgeableness. Of qualities that one might set to the credit of a scientific training there are none. As far as the internal evidence goes, the lecture was conceived and written by someone who had not had the advantage of an intellectual discipline of any kind. . . . By way of enforcing his testimony that the scientists 'have their own culture,' he tells us: 'This culture contains a great deal of argument, usually much more rigorous, and almost always at a higher conceptual level, than literary persons' argument.' But the argument of Snow's Rede Lecture is at an immensely *lower* conceptual level, and incomparably more loose and inconsequent, than any I myself, a literary person, should permit in a group discussion I was conducting, let alone a pupil's essay. . . .

Snow's argument proceeds with so extreme a *naïveté* of unconsciousness and irresponsibility that to call it a movement of thought is to flatter it. . . .

He identifies 'the Literary Culture' with, to use his own phrase, the 'literary intellectual'—by which he means the modish literary world; his 'intellectual' is the intellectual of the *New Statesman* circle and the reviewing in the Sunday papers. Snow accepts this 'culture' implicitly as the *haute culture* of our time; he takes it as representing the age's finer consciousness so far as a culture ignorant of science can. He, we are to understand, has it, and at the same time the scientific culture; he unites the two. I can't help remarking that this suggested equivalence (equivalence at any rate in reality) must constitute for me, a literary person, the gravest suspicion regarding the scientific one of Snow's two cultures. For his 'literary culture' is something that those genuinely interested in literature can only regard with contempt and resolute hostility. Snow's 'literary intellectual' is the enemy of art and life.

Note with what sublime, comic and frightening ease (for this sage is after all a Cambridge man) Snow, without any sense of there having been a shift, slips from his 'literary culture' into 'the traditional culture.' The feat of innocent unawareness is striking and significant enough when he is talking of the contemporary scene. But when, with the same ease, he carries the matter-of-fact identification into the past—'the traditional culture,' he tells us, with reference to the Industrial Revolution, 'didn't notice: or when it did notice, didn't like what it saw'—the significance becomes so portentous as to be hardly credible. But Snow, we must remind ourselves, *is* frightening in his capacity of representative phenomenon. He knows nothing of history. He pronounces about it with as complete confidence as he pronounces about literature (French, Russian and American as well as English), but he is equally ignorant of both. He has no notion of the changes in civilisation that have produced his 'literary culture' and made it possible for C. P. Snow to enjoy a status of distinguished intellectual. . . . (p. 299)

Thinking is a difficult art and requires training and practice in any given field. It is a pathetic and comic—and menacing—illusion on Snow's part that he is capable of thoughts on the problems he offers to advise us on. If his lecture has any value for use in schools—or universities—it is as a document for the study of cliché. . . .

Snow not only hasn't in him the beginnings of a novelist; he is utterly without a glimmer of what creative literature is, or why it matters. That significant truth comes home to us, amusingly but finally, when, near his opening, he makes a point of impressing on us that, as himself a creative writer, he is humanly (shall I say?) supremely well qualified—that he emphatically *has* a soul. 'The individual condition of each of us,' he tells us, 'is tragic,' and, by way of explaining that statement, he adds, 'we die alone.' Once he says 'we live alone,' but in general—for he makes his point redundantly—he prefers to stress dying; it's more solemn. He is enforcing a superiority to be recognised in the scientists: they, he says, 'see no reason why, just because the individual condition is tragic, so must the social condition be.' For himself, with tragic stoicism, he says, 'we die alone: all right,' but—which is his message, the sum of his wisdom—'there is social hope.'

He is repetitious, but he develops no explanation further than this. It doesn't occur to him that there is any need. . . . What *is* the 'social condition' that has nothing to do with the 'individual condition'? What is the 'social hope' that transcends, cancels or makes indifferent the inescapable tragic condition of each individual? Where, if not in individuals, is what is hoped for—a *non*-tragic condition, one supposes—to be located? Or are we to find the reality of life in hoping for other people a kind of felicity about which as proposed for ourselves ('jam,' Snow calls it later—we die alone, but there's jam to be had first) we have no illusions. Snow's pompous phrases give us the central and supreme instance of what I have called 'basic cliché.' He takes over inertly—takes over as a self-evident simple clarity—the characteristic and disastrous confusion of the civilisation he is offering to instruct. (p. 300)

[What] primarily calls for emphasis is the poverty of Snow's own ostensible range of satisfactions—which is a poverty of his own canons, and of his sense of significance; a poverty in considering which one finds oneself considering the inadequacy of his sense of human nature and human need.

The significance of his blankness in the face of literature is immense. It is a significance the more damning (in relation to his pretensions) because of the conviction with which he offers himself as an authority on the literature of the present and the past. I didn't exaggerate when I said that he doesn't know what literature is. Every pronouncement he makes about it—and he makes a great many—enforces that truth. . . .

It is characteristic of Snow that 'believe' for him should be a very simple word. 'Statistically,' he says, 'I suppose slightly more scientists are in religious terms unbelievers, compared with the rest of the intellectual world. . . . Snow goes on at once: 'Statistically, I suppose slightly more scientists are on the Left in open politics.' The *naïveté* is complete; it is a *naïveté* indistinguishable from portentous ignorance. The ignorance is that which appears as historical ignorance in his account of the Industrial Revolution, and its consequences, in the nineteenth century. It manifests itself as a terrifying confidence of simplification—terrifying because of the distortions and falsifications it entails, and the part it plays in that spirit of practical wisdom about the human future of which Snow's Rede Lecture might be called a classic. . . . If one points out that the actual history has been, with significance for one's apprehension of the full human problem, incomparably and poignantly more complex than that, Snow dismisses one as a 'natural Luddite.' . . .

[Here] we have the gap—the gap that is the emptiness beneath Snow's ignorance—between Snow and not only Ruskin, but the great creative writers of the century before Snow; they don't exist for him; nor does civilisation. . . .

[His] is the world in which the vital inspiration, the creative drive, is 'Jam tomorrow' (if you haven't any today) or (if you have it today) '*More* jam tomorrow.' It is the world in which, even at the level of the intellectual weeklies, 'standard of living' is an ultimate criterion, its raising an ultimate aim, a matter of wages and salaries and what you can buy with them, reduced hours of work, and the technological resources that make your increasing leisure worth having; so that productivity—the supremely important thing—must be kept on the rise, at whatever cost to protecting conservative habit. . . .

I am not preaching that we should defy, or try to reverse, the accelerating movement of external civilisation (the phrase sufficiently explains itself, I hope) that is determined by advancing technology). Nor am I suggesting that Snow, in so far as he is advocating improvements in scientific education, is wrong (I suspect he isn't very original). What I *am* saying is that such a concern is not enough—disastrously not enough. Snow himself is proof of that, product as he is of the initial cultural consequences of the kind of rapid change he wants to see accelerated to the utmost and assimilating all the world, bringing (he is convinced), provided we are foresighted enough to perceive that no one now will long consent to be without abundant jam, salvation and lasting felicity to all mankind. (p. 302)

> *F. R. Leavis, "The Significance of C. P. Snow,"*
> *in* The Spectator *(© 1962 by* The Spectator; *reprinted by permission of* The Spectator*), March 9, 1962, pp. 297-303.*

["The Realists" is] wholly engaging: Lord Snow is a shrewd critic, alive to the imperfections of the masterpieces he discusses, as well as to the infirmities of character of their creators, and he never lets us forget that he is dealing with extraordinary human beings, all of whom, in one way or another, prevailed over circumstantial adversities. (p. 234)

> The New Yorker *(© 1978 by the New Yorker*
> *Magazine, Inc.), November 20, 1978.*

A. S. BYATT

[*The Realists*] is not a book about the nature, workings, values or preoccupations of realistic fiction. This is a pity, since, as critics like Rubin Rubinowitz have shown, C. P. Snow, as a reviewer in the early Fifties, wrote a series of attacks on 'experimental' writing and praise of socially responsible, 'neo-realist' novels which helped to influence both the writing and reading of fiction at that time. If his novels were then over-valued, I believe they are underrated now, because the realistic virtues they display have again

become unfashionable. The careful analysis of public behaviour, domestic affections and affiliations, ambition, movements of money, and organisations like the Law or the scientific hierarchy, are not what we are thought to want to read about, unless we are offered them with a touch of irreal nightmare mockery. Snow may, we suspect, not tell us exactly what we want to know about these things, and he may often be wrong, but very few novelists are telling us anything at all. There is room for a study of bureaucracy, or jobs, or heritage that is not presented only as a grotesque phantasmagoria.

So it would have been very interesting if Lord Snow, in treating of his eight chosen realists, had offered us an analysis of how they chose their subject-matter, how they found or created people, places, institutions, and where their techniques are better described by other critical words besides 'realist'. He does not really attempt any of this: his chapters are mannerly little biographical essays, containing judicial summings-up of plots and values of certain great works. . . . I found the essays interesting in proportion as I knew less about the writer concerned—which is to say that I only really enjoyed the chapter on Galdos, of whose work I was ignorant, and whom I now want to read. (p. 586)

His final conclusion is that his eight novelists have little in common except being nearly all short and fat and uncommonly bad at mathematics. Having studied their sexual force or timidity he does not . . . go on to wonder about Wordworth's definition of the Poet as a man 'possessed of more than usual organic sensibility, who has also thought long and deeply'. He concludes that realism flourishes in untidy, energetic, societies with small, appreciative reading publics and 'hope'—'both social and individual'. He feels that we possess the first two, but not the last—and indeed, absence of 'hope' is one possible explanation of nightmare mockery and wild humour as prevalent forms. At the end of his book I did feel some envy of his eight for their sense of hope, energy and possibility—but whether that was theirs, or that of their time and place, it is hard to tell. (p. 587)

> *A. S. Byatt, "Worldly Wise," in* New Statesman
> *(© 1978 The Statesman & Nation Publishing Co. Ltd.), November 30, 1978, pp. 586-87.*

HARVEY CURTIS WEBSTER

Snow's great merit as a critic is to make us think and feel and *not* compliment ourselves on how clever and complicated we are. . . . (p. 30)

> *Harvey Curtis Webster, in* The New Republic *(reprinted by permission of* The New Republic; *© 1978 The New Republic, Inc.), December 16, 1978.*

*   *   *

SONTAG, Susan   1933-

Sontag is an American novelist, short story writer, screenwriter, essayist, film director, and critic. She is better known as a critic of contemporary art forms than as a writer of fiction. In one of her best known and most controversial works, *Against Interpretation*, Sontag established her precepts for the evaluation of art. She wrote that art must be responded to with the sensory, not the intellectual, faculties, with greater emphasis given to the form rather than the content of a work. This philosophy is reflected in her novels, notably *The Benefactor* and *Death Kit*. Her concern is, in her words, "to show

how the work of art is what it is, even that it is what it is, rather than to show what it means." As a fiction writer and a filmmaker, her style is often experimental and surrealistic, involving the reader in a world that is dreamlike and ambiguous. (See also *CLC*, Vols. 1, 2, 10, and *Contemporary Authors*, Vols. 17-20, rev. ed.)

ALFRED KAZIN

Susan Sontag is a [grim] figure, for the idea of alternatives in every possible situation always replaces the bread of life. In her novels as in her essays, she is concerned with producing a startling esthetic which her words prolong. She is interested in advancing new positions to the point of making her clever, surprisingly sustained novels experiments in the trying-out of an idea. One respects these books, even their total intellectual solemnity, because they are entirely manifestations of Sontag's personal will over esthetic situations defined as those in which originality functions by asserting itself. (p. 180)

[What] makes Sontag's novels more than curiosities is her belief that fiction is a trying-out, an hypothesis which you carry out, not prove. The "world" is entirely plastic. Today we improvise, and tonight we shall improvise something else. Her books are films in the sense that there are shots of one idea after another. And they "work," they operate within their context (if hardly on our emotions), because Sontag is one of those provocative writers, like William Gass trained first in philosophy, for whom a narrative is a situation one "supposes" as philosophers do, in *illustration* of an argument—now just suppose that this table . . .—rather than a story the writer himself is the first to believe. (p. 181)

Sontag's two novels advance constructions of reality by the protagonists that *then* they try to live up to. In *The Benefactor* a nondescript young Frenchman, Hippolyte, has bizarre dreams and then tries to reproduce them in his life. The "dreams" are really scenarios, not dreams; Hippolyte's actual experiences are intellectually worked out footnotes to the dreams, and without the slightest touch of comedy. Surely a man trying to live by his dreams is naturally comic? But Sontag has no humor, for that would involve her in something like Kafka's whimsical identifications with "K." She is proud, but her hero is a ninny, a straw man. "*Now let us just imagine that this ninny, Hippolyte. . . .*"

But what is striking about *The Benefactor* especially is the fact that the author can sustain her hypothesis, her *fancy*, through a novel that takes place not in Paris, where the characters are living, but in Susan Sontag's will to keep this up. (p. 182)

The Benefactor works because its author really sees the world as a series of propositions *about* the world. Her theoreticalness consists of a loyalty not to certain ideas but to life as the improvisation of ideas. She is positive only about moving on from these ideas, and this makes her an interesting fantasist about a world conceived as nothing but someone thinking up new angles to it. Sontag writes about situations, is always figuring out alternatives to her existing ideas about them and thus works at situations in the way that a movie director works something out for an induced effect. But she is always in the book, visibly parallel to the scene she is writing. A book is a screen, as she is a mind visibly "projecting" her notion of things onto it. Screen and

mind are separated by Sontag's refusal to tell a story for its own sake.

Death-Kit—which improbably relates the effort of one "Diddy" to discover whether he did or did-he not commit a murder—also has a dummy for hero. His supposed plight is just an occasion for the author's ambitious critical intelligence to think ahead of the reader. Although Sontag admires the "new wave" French writers and movie directors, what excites her is not their hatred of all conventionality but a desire to astonish, to replace someone else's way of *looking* at things. The total abstractness of even the American setting in *Death-Kit* is striking. The book is a series of variations on the theme of perception, and just as Diddy is a pun on his need to find out whether he did or didn't kill a workman in a train tunnel, so the tunnel is obviously symbolic, as is the fact that Diddy writes advertising copy for a manufacturer of microscopes and that his girl Hester is blind. Exploring all sorts of interesting considerations about "sight," like exploring the fantasy gimmick of a man trying to make his life conform to his dreams, certainly keeps Sontag more interesting than her characters. Abstractness gives her total authority, and it would seem to be this total control that interests her in the writing of a book, and that interests us in the reading of it. We do not experience a novel; we experience her readiness to see what she can think of next. (pp. 183-84)

Alfred Kazin, in his Bright Book of Life: American Novelists & Storytellers from Hemingway to Mailer *(copyright © 1971, 1937 by Alfred Kazin; reprinted by permission of Little, Brown and Co. in association with The Atlantic Monthly Press), Atlantic-Little, Brown, 1973.*

ROBERT MELVILLE

[*On Photography*] is a surrealistic demonstration of the art of juxtaposition, a St Vitus's dance of modest, ambitious and absurd claims for photography interspersed with advertisements for cameras so simple to use that anyone can obtain instant results of high technical quality. The outcome is an effect of ironic neutrality. [Sontag's] essays on the other hand are analytical, paradoxical, controversial, always clever, often profound—and the outcome is an effect of ironic neutrality. (p. 69)

Sontag refers to a . . . sequence in *Blowup*. The photographer is sitting astride the thighs of a fashion model lying on the floor. He is madly clicking his camera at her face while she turns this way and that. The scene is a substitute for a paroxysmal rape. . . . Sontag cites this sequence from *Blowup* as evidence that the camera is a poor symbol for the penis, and finds the gun and the fast car more suitable analogies for the camera as a weapon. She quotes from a camera ad ("Just aim, focus and shoot") to prove that the camera is sold as a predatory weapon, but admits that it seems to be all bluff, "like a man's fantasy of having a gun, knife or tool between his legs", but since a man no more fantasises about having a car between his legs than having a camera there the symbolism gets a bit complicated. (pp. 69-70)

Placing her piece on [Diane] Arbus so that it would be immediately followed by her most provocative statement was good strategy by Sontag, and it is with evident glee that she announces that photography "has managed to carry out the grandiose, century-old threats of a Surrealist takeover of the modern sensibility, while most of the pedigreed candidates have dropped out of the race.''

I think we have to remember at this point that Sontag was growing up at a time when Abstract Expressionism was having its greatest triumphs. To a sensitive young American the ''revolt against calculation'' was what 20th-century painting was all about. The ''pedigreed candidates'' she mentions were the members of the Surrealist Group in Paris. The Surrealist painters had *their* great time in the 1930s and '40s. Almost all of them are dead, and it is a long while since any of them hoped to change the world. What Sontag has against them is that they were *figurative,* and she finds the idea of figurative painting in the 20th century so contemptible that she casts around for an insult and calls the paintings ''mostly wet dreams'', not a well-considered phrase from someone who admires Pollock's drip paintings. It must be quite confusing to have to argue, however cleverly, that nothing could be more surreal than a photograph ''which virtually produces itself and with a minimum of effort'', and at the same time be aware that André Breton's famous definition of Surrealism—''pure psychic automatism''—fits some of Pollock's paintings like a glove. (pp. 72-3)

> Robert Melville, ''Images of the Instant Past,'' in Encounter (© 1978 by Encounter Ltd.), November, 1978, pp. 69-73.

ANNE TYLER

The eight short stories in *I, etcetera* . . . reflect a vital and restless imagination cooking away in several directions. . . .

The typical Sontag character is intelligent, self-analytical, and suffering from a non-specific form of anxiety or discontent. He may be obsessed by thoughts of freedom, while continually fettering himself at every turn. He may long for change and space, but he's unwilling to give up the brittle shell he is accustomed to inhabiting. . . . Generally, he feels burdened by a body of fashionable knowledge that fails to solve any of his real problems. . . .

The drawback to stories written in an unself-aware state is . . . that at times they may turn too far inward, making no effort in the direction of the reader. Assuming that most writers are saying, ''I have something of myself that I want to express,'' we can't help feeling that on occasion Susan Sontag is adding, ''And don't you wish you knew what it was?'' Or (even greater insult) a brusque, ''But never mind.'' (p. 29)

Both [''Project for a Trip to China'' and ''Unguided Tour''] are more like notes for stories, and self-addressed notes at that. Paragraphs tend to consist of one short sentence—the length of easiest impact. Random observations are separated by weighty pauses. There is a scarcity of specific, human characters. None of these qualities are necessarily mistakes, of course. (Think what Donald Barthelme can accomplish with a clutch of offhand non-sequiturs apparently directed to himself alone.) And even here—especially in ''Project for a Trip to China''—there is an abundance of those startling ironies and wry, quirky jokes that make Susan Sontag so tempting to quote. . . . But ultimately, we feel cheated. We turn past the last page, looking for one more page that will make the story come together. Even the freest internal voice, listened to with the utmost lack of criticism, must in the final step be screened for readability.

But where these stories succeed, they succeed wonderfully. ''Debriefing'' is a friend's account of the slow descent of Julia, who starts out asking herself questions with no answers and ends up dead. . . . This is one story where the stray-observations approach works as it ought to. Everything seems to meander along, hit or miss, come what may, but the cumulative effect is staggering. Gradually, Julia emerges as absolutely specific and individual, even while she is suffering from what some people would probably call the disease of our times. ''Why you went under,'' her friend says, ''while others, equally absent from their lives, survive is a mystery to me.'' It's a mystery to all of us, and remains so, but ''Debriefing'' gives us a sense of a real person in real trouble and when she's gone we truly share the grief and bewilderment of her friend. (pp. 29-30)

I, etcetera is not always an easy book to read; it's not always a rewarding book, even. But it does possess its own kind of spirit and nerve, and it takes some magnificent chances. (p. 30)

> Anne Tyler, in The New Republic *(reprinted by permission of* The New Republic; © *1978 by The New Republic, Inc.), November 25, 1978.*

JOHN B. BRESLIN

Susan Sontag is best known as a critic who has insistently reminded American readers that a vast contemporary world of thought and imagination continues to evolve on the other side of the Atlantic. Whether she is discussing books or movies or philosophical concepts, Sontag finds her apt illustrations, if not her central theme, in the European tradition, especially in France. In this she bears a resemblance to Matthew Arnold whose love affair with Europe gave to his literary and cultural criticism a breadth of reference otherwise lacking in early Victorian England. Like Arnold, too, Sontag holds firmly to her belief in the saving power of reason . . . , but she never blinds herself to the sometimes dazzling light cast by the experience of the absurd. And so her collections of critical essays map the modern terrain from Camus to Camp, from Simone Weil's tormented life to Bergman's tortured and torturing characters.

It is in her criticism, as well, that we find a key to her fiction. An essay on ''The Pornographic Imagination'' leads Sontag to explore the diversities of prose narrative; in place of a simplified notion of ''realism,'' which would correspond roughly to representationalism in art, she offers as the writer's—and the critic's—principal focus ''the complexities of consciousness itself, as the medium through which a world exists at all and is constituted.'' With this more sophisticated point of view, ''exploring ideas'' becomes ''as authentic an aim of prose fiction'' as ''dramatic tension or three-dimensionality in the rendering of personal and social relations.'' Traditional character development gives way to the depiction of ''extreme states of human feeling and consciousness,'' where the links with concrete individuals may be no more than contingent.

In the essays, Sontag develops these points for a specific purpose—to argue that certain kinds of pornography, as the expression of just such an ''extreme state'' of consciousness, may be said to achieve the quality of art. But the same ideas apply equally well to her own—definitely non-pornographic—fictions. All of the stories in [*I, Etcetera*], with varying degrees of success, probe relentlessly at the thin membrane of our modern consciousness. Even the two "travel accounts" that bracket the collection, "Project for a Trip to China" and the splendidly lyrical finale, "Unguided Tour," have much more to do with the inner landscape of memory and imagination than with external geography. . . .

[What is striking about the stories in *I, Etcetera*] is the wide range of literary forms Sontag has chosen to exploit in presenting her various "extreme states of human feeling and consciousness." "The Dummy," for instance, her earliest effort, borrows a science-fiction prop—the perfect mechanical replica—to explore the desire to escape from one's role in life and yet continue to observe it. With a characteristic ironic twist, the dummy and his replica in turn prove to be much better at being human than their inventor, thus leaving the title suitably ambiguous. . . .

Whatever strategy she chooses in her quest for images of modern consciousness, Sontag deploys it with a sure sense of artistic form and ironic juxtaposition. Occasionally, however, her talent for appropriating and parodying the literary tradition overwhelms her own content and leaves the reader with the uneasy feeling that wit has triumphed over substance. But at her best, and this includes large chunks of even the less successful stories, Sontag illuminates our contemporary situation with the peculiar radiance that comes from the fusion of wide learning, precise thinking and deep feeling. Suddenly we see our own face in the mirror and hear our own voice with a shock of recognition all the greater for the restraint with which the revelation is made.

> *John B. Breslin, "Complexities of Consciousness," in* Book World—The Washington Post *(© 1978, The Washington Post), December 17, 1978, p. E3.*

MICHAEL WOOD

There is nothing ready-made about the eight stories in *I, etcetera*. Indeed the question of signature, of putting together an identity, is explicitly raised, and even when the characters worry about their facelessness, this preoccupation itself, and the writing which displays it, clearly wear the faces Sontag has chosen to give them. A man in one of the stories hands over his life to a dummy because he is "tired of being a person": "Not just tired of being the person I was, but any person at all." Simone Weil is quoted as saying that the only thing more hateful than a "we" is an "I"; and at another point this savage old question is fired off: "Who has the right to say 'I'?" The assertion of self is an ugly and dangerous habit, but the suppression of self is a feeble-hearted error. On this shifting terrain we have to learn to say "I" in the right tone of voice, and this, I take it, is the implication of the wry joke in the book's title. Once we have said "I" in the proper way, everything else we might say can be summarized as "etcetera."

In one sense this is a curiously American problem, individualism with a bad conscience. It is more American, even Jamesian, when it is linked to the theme of the unlived life—as if a life which is not aggressively asserted will simply not be there. Thus Dr. Jekyll, in Sontag's agile and funny rewriting of the famous tale, becomes a kind of cousin of the pale hero of James's "Beast in the Jungle": "Nothing is going to happen to me," he says. "I mean, I know what's going to happen to me. . . . I could already write my obituary." This Jekyll envies Hyde his freedom and his violence, what he sees as his *life*. Jekyll himself can only think of "all

the imaginary crimes he has committed, and of all the real crimes he has never imagined." In another story a sensible Mrs. Johnson, "proud wife and mother of three," "renowned for having the cleanest garbage on the block," sets out in search of a randy liberation and is counseled and bewitched by a variety of "American spirits," including those of Tom Paine, Betsy Ross, Ethel Rosenberg, Leland Stanford, Margaret Fuller, and Errol Flynn.

"Old Complaints Revisited" shows us a narrator who wishes to leave what he or she—nothing in the language or the names used indicates his or her sex—calls the movement or the organization, but can't. . . . "I accuse the organization of depriving me of my innocence. Of complicating my will." It is the opposite of liberty, it is a morbid loyalty to things beyond the self which means that the self is entirely starved. . . .

At other times this exile from immediate experience is seen as an advantage, a chance to unpack the clutter of the mind. "Perhaps I will write the book about my trip to China before I go," the narrator says at the end of the opening story, and it is a measure of Sontag's achievement here that this casual-seeming gag carries the weight of a whole perfect portrait. "China," a set of associations entertained by the narrator since childhood . . . becomes the ground of an eloquent meditation, a vision of the writer lapsing into the charmed guesswork of literature. . . .

[A] good deal of the book has the flavor of an articulate, affectionate inventory, with its lucid listings of "What is wrong," "What people are trying to do," "What relieves, soothes, helps," "What is upsetting," "What I'm doing," and its amused attention to the pathetic memories we tag onto words and phrases like *remember* and *last time* and *because,* murmured like magical spells that just might make our forlorn adventures come alive for us. . . . (p. 30)

Travel is the ideal metaphor for the unlived life, since all trips are overloaded with expectation, and visited places are scarcely ever quite real when they are actually seen. Experience is held off, sniffed at, toured. Or once in a while it is simply, overwhelmingly, suffered, and in either case it is missed, uncomprehended, over before we have grasped what it might have meant. This particular sense of exclusion remains American, I think. . . . I can't imagine an English writer being so preoccupied with the self; but then I can't think of another American writer with so delicate an awareness of the demands of others.

Sometimes the crackle of Sontag's epigrams gets in the way of the compassion which has prompted the writing: "Literature tells us what is happening to words"; "Don't take Mélisande to see *Pelléas et Mélisande*"; "No one is a devil if fully heard"; "Wisdom is a ruthless business"; "It's not Paradise that's lost." Grand as these glittering things are, they tend to short-circuit the writing, and keep us at arm's length, or even further away. In one or two of the stories, the determined execution doesn't quite catch up with the initial bright idea—I'm thinking especially of "Baby," which is the double monologue of two spoiled parents on the subject of their one spoiled child, as they tell a silent doctor their painful, self-excusing tales. The book in general, however, not only confronts and explores the life which is traveled rather than lived, it records a life fully lived in the face of all such doubts. No pain or horror is avoided, no occasion for despair is ducked. In "Debriefing," the most moving story in the book and surely a small masterpiece, a depressed friend wants to "talk sadness," and the narrator briskly responds like the sensible person she is:

> On cue, like an old vaudevillian, I go into my routines of secular ethical charm. They seem to work. She promises to try.

They don't work. Two days later the friend drowns herself in the Hudson. . . . Confronting this death, and a whole precisely realized panorama of the ills of New York and, by extension, of all sorts of other places, the narrator still refuses to give up, rolls her stone up the hill like a dogged Sisyphus. This is not simply a "positive" message, a mere assertion. It is something won, an earned survival. . . . "Only the greatest obstacle that can be contemplated without despair," Yeats wrote, "rouses the will to full intensity." And Susan Sontag, turning to yet another of those travelers' phrases she notes so acutely, crisply echoes the thought. . . .

> *The end of the world.* This is not the end of the world.

                                                        (pp. 30-1)

Michael Wood, in The New York Review of Books *(reprinted with permission from* The New York Review of Books; *copyright © 1979 Nyrev, Inc.), January 25, 1979.*

LIZ MEDNICK

Among the world's foremost equivalencers, Susan Sontag is a perpetual curiosity, especially noteworthy for her unequivocal promotion of unlikely equations whose virtues she apparently considers self-evident. In the title of her latest venture, *I, etcetera*, she manages a truly impressive equilibration. The reference to *I* is pretty clear, however, the *etcetera* could mean any number of things, as for instance: *I, me, myself and mine; I came, saw, conquered, think therefore etc.; I want-see-say-do-will-can-am;* or more probably, *I, everyone and everything else*. But no matter which you choose, etcetera has a way of equalizing whatever falls into its demesne; it renders further account or discrimination not only unnecessary but impossible. . . .

The first piece, "Project for a Trip to China," introduces what might be called Sontag's trademark—that is, her careful attention to the phenomenon of acquisitiveness. (p. 13)

The theme of travel as accumulation harks back to *On Photography*, where Sontag claims that "travel becomes a strategy for accumulating photographs." The strategy of "Project" is remarkably similar but it avoids the bothersome necessity of going anywhere. What Sontag accumulates and then presents as the material for this piece is a series of static images, like photographs, arranged in sequence but intended for further psychic rumination. . . . She relies on selective, discontinuous images of a photographic nature to provoke some kind of mental response. However, Sontag is careful to distinguish between literary and photographic imagery. . . . Since the act of photographing does not in fact materially disturb reality, the distinction she makes seems to rest more securely with the image itself than the process. Those images which are further from the appearance of reality are to Sontag less objectionable; conversely, as images approach reality she considers them parasitic. Sontag's preference for abstraction shows itself in the detached, two-dimensional quality of her characters. . . .

"Old Complaints Revisited" is about as exciting as the title might lead you to believe. . . . [The] story's protagonist refuses to commit itself to one sex or the other. . . .

Sontag's fascination with empirical gain and, in "The Dummy," the theme of the unlived life mark her a literary descendant of Henry James, but "Old Complaints" suggests a progenetrix of sorts as well; I mean Virginia Woolf. It is clearly paradoxical to speak of Woolf this way for several reasons, not the least of which is that the feature she shares with Sontag is a passion for androgyny. The same supposition that allows Woolf's Orlando to undergo a spontaneous change of sex without a commensurate shift in psychology gives Sontag license to regard sexual differentiation as an irrelevant and otherwise invisible part of her character's makeup, a mere hindrance to the reader's equity. Indeed, without being told, it would be hard to assign a sex confidently to any of her characters, and this may help account for their missing dimensions. Sontag and Woolf both intimate that male and female are mentally equivalent, emotionally the same—in other words, that the mind is an androgynous organ, a mere malevolent equisetum.

In a sense, androgyny works like etcetera and other less voluminous equivalences; it is a device for avoiding certain kinds of definition or differentiation. This sort of evasive tactic pervades Sontag's work, but it's easiest to observe in her critical rhetoric. (p. 14)

[There] are a few quirks in Sontag's critical methodology which are problematic in her fiction as well. Her work is constructed along predictable lines of defense and it aims to avoid certain distinctions as well as any vocabulary by which they might be implied. In her criticism, this evasiveness shows itself in a lack of rhetorical rigor, a dogged and shifty reliance on fashionable and abstruse authors with exotic surnames, a penchant for calling the particular absolute, for sapping terms like "aggression" of all significance except as a form of blind dodge, and a really irritating habit of withdrawing prematurely from a metaphor, generally one which is doomed in the end to be inconsistent.

As for her short stories, Sontag's problem is largely a formal one. For the most part *I, etc.* is a stilted fictional reiteration of her otherwise intractable *Weltanschauung*, but in the last three stories she begins to find a form capable of accommodating her ponderous cerebral equipage. . . .

Like the first piece, [the last,] "Unguided Tour" is about travel—a short dialogue between two women, one of whom recounts a trip to France, Italy and foreign places she has taken with an erstwhile lover—only this time a satirical eye is focused on the itinerant I, and apart from a brief lapse into sanctimony it remains constant throughout. The protagonist is not more or less attractive than the rest of Sontag's menagerie, in fact quite similar, only more tolerable for the satirical context. By its nature an admission of idiosyncracy, satire takes the categorical edge off of her private obsessions, leaving room in the world for the rest of us and at least tacitly allowing that if all things are equal, no two are exactly the same. (p. 15)

Liz Mednick, "Apres Moi, etcetera," in New York Arts Journal *(copyright © 1979 by Richard W. Burgin), #13, 1979, pp. 13-15.*

ANTHONY CLARE

The use of metaphors for illness and disease forms the subject of Susan Sontag's remarkable little book [*Illness as Metaphor*]. . . . (p. 294)

One can be critical of the process of converting illness into metaphor without having to fall back on a single-cause theory of disease. So why does Miss Sontag yoke them together so tightly? The answer, it seems to me, lies in her fear that any tendency to locate any responsibility for one's disease inside oneself may lead to a relentless scapegoating. . . . The desire not to add to the victim's terrible misfortune by identifying with any precision his actual responsibility provokes, in some people, the impulse to deny the evidence linking smoking and cancer. How much this impulse is strengthened by her single-cause theory of disease is unclear; yet it does seem that she believes that the only alternatives lie between absolving the individual of any responsibility, or blaming him totally for his predicament. Yet the answer to the cancer expert's, and indeed Miss Sontag's, dilemma is the realisation that smoking does not simply *cause* cancer any more than heavy drinking *causes* liver cirrhosis. It is a great pity that an otherwise scholarly, pungent and needle-sharp dissection of some of the woollier and moralistic notions that surround serious disease should be disfigured by a simplistic and excessively biological view of disease. It says a great deal for the power and persuasiveness of Susan Sontag's beautiful prose that the disfigurement is neither obvious nor lethal. (p. 295)

> *Anthony Clare, "The Guilty Sick," in* The Listener *(© British Broadcasting Corp. 1979; reprinted by permission of Anthony Clare), February 22, 1979, pp. 294-95.*

FRANK WILSON

Notes toward an evaluation of *I, etcetera*, a collection of stories by Susan Sontag:

Be objective. Note general characteristics. Eight stories, conventionally unconventional. Not much plot, not much action, not many incidents. Lots of wondering about things, though. And deadpan serious.

"Don't panic. Confession is nothing, knowledge is everything." That's a quote but I'm not going to tell who said it. Hints: —a writer —somebody wise —an Austrian (i.e., a Viennese Jew) —a refugee —he died in America in 1951.

"Confession is me, knowledge is everybody."

S. Quotes a lot. And hints a lot. . . .

In sum: pseudo-random selection of quasi or cyrpto-autobiographical details. Not much fun. Not very funny.

"No man"—or woman, for that matter—"ever lost money by underestimating the intelligence of the American people"—or by flattering the prejudices of self-styled cognoscenti. That's—in part—a quote too, but I'm not going to tell who said it (two can play this game).

Hints: —a journalist —a scourge of boobs and bunkum — he died in Baltimore in 1956.

Sontag. Sunday. Day of rest.

A good book to read in front of the fire. And nod off over. Or use as kindling. (p. 10)

> *Frank Wilson, in* Best Sellers *(copyright © 1979 Helen Dwight Reid Educational Foundation), April, 1979.*

SPARK, Muriel 1918-

Spark, a Scottish-born novelist, poet, short story writer, playwright, essayist, editor, biographer, and author of books for children, now resides in Rome. Critics note her masterful handling of dialogue and her witty, satiric characterizations. (See also *CLC*, Vols. 2, 3, 5, 8, and *Contemporary Authors*, Vols. 5-8, rev. ed.)

HAROLD W. SCHNEIDER

[Muriel Spark's short] stories represent a lesser achievement than her novels, particularly the pieces in . . . *Voices at Play*. On the surface this writer possesses all the writing virtues that should make her a master of the short story: she is able in the most crisp and economical prose quickly to develop believable characters and a situation in which the reader is immersed; she is skillful in developing personality through conversation and in finding exactly the right singularity of speech to make a character stand out as a type and as an individual at the same time . . . ; she is also able to handle point of view in any way that suits her, writing as omniscient author or in the character of a person in the story, either in the first person or as a consciousness described rather than describing; finally, she can construct her plots as tightly as her prose and bring them to their conclusions with no wasted effort. Because of these abilities there are no real failures among her stories, but one also feels there are not as many complete successes as there should be. . . . Perhaps what is at fault is Mrs. Spark's striking cleverness, her utter competence, and occasionally even her willingness to flirt with the supernatural and the incredible. Her stories entertain and sometimes enchant by the presence of a fantastic, strange, or unknown world or scene . . . , but while they please they are not always moving enough to be memorable.

Of the two volumes, *The Go-Away Bird and Other Stories* (1958) clearly has the most memorable pieces. "The Twins," a story about the rather diabolical influence of a very young boy and girl, develops chillingly to its climax as the young woman narrator becomes aware that between the ages of five and twelve these precocious and evil children have gained complete control over their parents and their parents' relations with other people. . . . This is a story of the triumph of evil over good—and the irony is that the evil comes from two beautiful and apparently guileless children. And there is a further irony: not only does the evil which triumphs over good come from the children; its triumph is largely good's own fault. Mrs. Spark surely means to show that such innocence as that of Jennie and Simon Reeves is not real goodness at all. Because they fail to recognize the evil in their children, they cannot cope with it and therefore do harm and injustice to themselves and their acquaintances. In order to combat evil, Mrs. Spark implies one must know it.

"The Twins" is fairly typical of Mrs. Spark's fiction, for it shows her concern with moral problems, sometimes even with unworldly "influences," her skill at quick characterizations, and her tight prose style. But the best and most compelling of the stories in this volume are the African tales. "The Pawnbroker's Wife," the least ambitious of these tales, is a realistic account of the triumph of a view of life over the real world. . . . [The] complication of the plot arises out of the stories the mother and daughters invent and force their lodgers to accept in silence to avoid expulsion from the house. "The Pawnbroker's Wife" is an amusing character study that succeeds at the same time in being a portrait edged in pathos. The second African tale, "The Seraph and the Zambesi," indulges Mrs. Spark's penchant for the fantastic. . . . [It] can be counted this writer's first considerable success. . . . This is an imaginative, wild and funny tale, quite different from either of the other African stories. In it Mrs. Spark plays with reality, creating her story out of her imagination and what must be scattered remnants of her African experience. (pp. 28-32)

["The Go-Away Bird"] seems to me the finest work of these two volumes of short stories—a haunting and deeply moving account, expressing the tragic loneliness of a human soul not sure of what it wants from life, not finding its kindred spirit or its proper end. . . . This story shows best the author's eye for the particular detail, her close concern for the events she describes, and her ability to place the reader in a situation and a scene essentially strange to him. . . . Her style is so spare it is almost flat, yet it serves her very well. (pp. 33-4)

[*The Comforters*] was admittedly a sort of therapy for Mrs. Spark: by it she was able to work herself out of her state of intellectual ferment and to find herself as a Catholic. She is clearly not on the side of those who accept their faith without retaining independence of thought. (p. 37)

Robinson (1958) is Mrs. Spark's least notable novel. Something of a cross between *Robinson Crusoe*, a mystery story, and *The Lord of the Flies*, it reflects the latter work's concern for the moral disintegration of people stranded on an island by an airplane crash, and at the same time it raises the question: who murdered Robinson, the owner of the island? In this novel alone Mrs. Spark uses a first-person narrator, the woman January Marlow, to tell her story. The technique does not work in this novel, for Jan is not merely the onlooker—she is at the center of the action. We are therefore diverted from our concern for the moral disintegration of the characters to concern for the heroine. Even the mystery is fairly transparent. The book's few distinct virtues are Mrs. Spark's competence in the sketching of characters and the presence of a reasonably good adventure plot, whatever the faults of the mystery. (pp. 37-8)

[In the superb *Memento Mori*] Mrs. Spark raises a serious question—how is one to face death?—and shows how it is answered by a number of very old people. The success of the novel results from two things: the way Mrs. Spark gets *inside* the minds of very different people, many of them on the verge of senility; and the way she maintains a consistent tone for the novel. The subject is one which could show lapses in taste or seem terribly macabre—death and senility are *not* pleasant things to consider—but in Mrs. Spark's pages even the unpleasant does not merely disturb, because it is true and it is right. (p. 38)

Memento Mori is surely a small masterpiece. In it for the first time Mrs. Spark has got her theme, her characters, all the techniques of her craft under her control. . . . The central question of the novel is an important one with universal significance; Mrs. Spark shows that the best way to answer it is with calmness. And, finally, in this rather unusual novel Mrs. Spark's method of presentation is simple and straightforward, and remarkable only in her special way: in this perfectly realistic story Death is a character, as though to emphasize the fact that allegory is not so far from life. (p. 39)

[If] there is anything that keeps one from pronouncing [*The Bachelors*] Mrs. Spark's finest work it is probably the kind of novel it is and the people in it. For the novel is concerned a good deal of the time with a kind of farcical social comedy . . . , some rather low people, and some fairly messy proceedings. While Mrs. Spark exhibits compassion for the actors in this drama, she packs her stage with rather a large number of God's most erring children. The novel's accounts of séances (though certainly funny) and the dreary doings of some of the characters may fill the reader with [distaste]. . . . If the novel is saved from the sordid, it is largely by the portrait of the epileptic Ronald, who sees life with a kind of saddened intensity. Prevented by his flaw from rising to a position for which he is mentally and emotionally fitted, he can only look about him and see a world in which others far more imperfect than he have less difficulty accomplishing their ends, however ignoble. . . . Ronald's vision of the world informs the novel and invests it with what is its essentially sad dignity. (pp. 41-2)

The Prime of Miss Jean Brodie (1962) is a nearly flawless work, to be ranked with or just behind *Memento Mori* and *The Bachelors*. What this novel exhibits is a remarkable technique and a rare polish in style. It also represents a departure for Mrs. Spark in being wholly free of the unworldly and the supernatural. In place of these the novel contains a kind of puzzle or problem, which each reader must solve for himself. (p. 42)

In many ways the reader finds Jean Brodie a wonderfully sympathetic person: she is intelligent, energetic, individualistic, personally attractive; a woman of taste and a challenge to the stuffiness and narrow-mindedness of the people around her. She encourages her girls to think and helps them to enjoy learning. But it gradually becomes clear, as we see her through Sandy's eyes, that she has flaws. . . . It is in the ambivalence of the portrait of Miss Brodie that Mrs. Spark's skill is best shown, for she emerges a many-sided creature, worthy of all of a reader's attention. (pp. 43-4)

The novel has many other things worth praising besides Miss Brodie's portrait. Particularly interesting is the technique of interweaving past and present time throughout the book. The story progresses in one line from the past, but at the same time bits of information are constantly being introduced to tell what happened later. These bits are like recurring motifs or clues to a mystery, for it is only at the end that their importance for an interpretation of what has happened is clear. (p. 44)

Harold W. Schneider, "A Writer in Her Prime: The Fiction of Muriel Spark," in Critique: Studies in Modern Fiction *(copyright © by* Critique *1962), Vol. V, No. 2, 1962, pp. 28-45.*

JOHN HAZARD WILDMAN

Muriel Spark, in a series of tightly organized, sharply pointed novels, has achieved, with an amazing degree of illumination, translations of vast abstractions into crisp, containing modern terms, never losing the necessary qualities of suggestiveness and humility.

For she has tackled the most difficult translation of all. . . . She has obviously set herself the task of bringing good and evil over into concrete objects of consideration and into explicit situations. It is a temptation to say that she is never didactic, but simply investigative, a sentiment of this sort usually being considered loftily complimentary. But actually she maintains firm stands: she is a translator of something objective (and in that sense foreign); she has the born translator's compulsion to make it accessible, and for the work which she loves, she entertains an undeviating conviction of the rightness of its terms.

Her frame of reference is the Catholic moral universe; her translations of its terms are into the language, actions, and above all, frames of mind of present-day England and derivative cultures. There must be an obstinate streak in her which insists upon the nearly impossible. . . . The achievements of Mrs. Spark are many, but surely the most striking is her totally successful air of unself-consciousness. She gives an impression of moving in an atmosphere rather than creating it. . . . [She] perceives effortlessly the real not only under the apparent, but permeating it. (pp. 129-30)

[In] her work the surfaces of life are both conductors to its depths and also—with the apparent inconsistency of existence—deceptive camouflage for its deeper reaches. In *Memento Mori,* she encompasses both extremes. Here, in a novel where almost all of the characters are belligerently old, she uses their apparent indestructibility as an ironic contrast with their frail tenure of mortality and also as a means of access to their fears. The stoutly barred door advertizes the terror within at the same time that it conceals it. And usually it includes the reason for the terror, for the murderer has entered long ago in the innocent glare of midday and lies happily hidden, waiting for his moment to come to him. (p. 131)

Mrs. Spark ticks off the types whose neat but adamantine self-sufficiency is the engine of their failure. In her method, there is a Kafka-like devotion to the point of contact between extremes. Possibly the chief note of distinction between the two, however, is that whereas Kafka uses disgust as the junction from which his many lines of meaning radiate, it is a sort of engagingness from which the trains go out in Mrs. Spark's interpretations. Alec Warner, in *Memento Mori,* is a far-from-lovable character, but there are in his composition those elements which cause a reader to warm to a character—which make the unregenerate Scrooge someone to collect in a way that no one ever wanted to collect a character from Theodore Dreiser. (p. 132)

[Within] the old minor poet Percy Mannering . . . smallness reaches large dimensions, and an epic pettiness is attained through lifelong unobstructed devotion. Here also the Kafka-like proneness of Mrs. Spark to convey large issues through familiar smallness comes to high achievement. . . . (pp. 132-33)

[Here] is no doomed universe. Mrs. Spark is as far from the authorized versions of predestination, newly revised, as she is from sentimental evasion. She would probably agree . . . that the action of a novel should ultimately rest on a realistic conception of existence. . . . (p. 133)

There is [in her work] a happy fusion of setting and people. As there is growth of personality and theme within her novels, so also as an integral part of this process, there is a progressive self-fulfillment of her setting. If there is none of the romantic proneness to treat the setting as opulent scenery before which the characters act, neither is there that self-consciously thematic treatment of setting which, in Thomas Hardy, makes the reader feel as though he were

being managed with the kindly condescension due to the slow-witted and having indicated to him, with a slow patient forefinger, the philosophical dimensions of the landscape. Mrs. Spark in this respect fits in admirably with Elizabeth Bowen's conception of setting brought to its ideal function: "Nothing can happen nowhere. The locale of the happening always colours the happening, and often, to a degree, shapes it." (pp. 133-34)

Possibly in *The Ballad of Peckham Rye* this admirable treatment of setting is most observable, although not any more skillfully used than in her other novels. Here, however, the devil walks in unlikely haunts. Why it should be unusual for him to circulate among the drab energetic ways of British middle-class to lower-middle-class existence is not clear, but somehow he is usually expected to function within greater ceremonial blaze. Nor is one definitely authorized by Mrs. Spark's treatment to call Dougal Douglas, the central figure of *The Ballad of Peckham Rye,* the devil; rather, one has suspicions in that direction. By the end of the novel, however, there is no doubt whatsoever as to the evil which he has so joyfully welcomed into himself and even more joyfully dispensed.

Yet Mrs. Spark has much of the mystery writer about her: she knows the importance of gathering effects. These she has invested with thematic significance far beyond the dimensions of the typical mystery; also, the truth progressively dawns rather than bursts at the end of things. But she knows the narrative importance of a growth of light, and the uses of tension in that respect. (p. 134)

[Mrs. Spark has the] cruel ability of certain ancient ballad writers to recognize marks and signs and to be shocked but not surprised when the diabolic eye grows drumly. There is an appropriate grimness with which she follows Dougal Douglas in his rise to clerkly importance and beyond, and retails his crescent ways. There is also a grim economy about her treatment of the bitterness, even to the point of death, which he causes.

Nor is one allowed the satisfaction of Dougal's failures; for when these occur, his manipulation of them is confident and authoritative, his transitions to something better easily within his own control. It is true that at the end when he is left writing successful autobiographical novels on the Riviera, all does not seem to be too entirely well with him, in the light of hints that previously he has slipped successfully out of so many fields of endeavor that almost no careers are any longer open to his talents. But nevertheless he remains a threat beyond the point of the novel's conclusion. (p. 135)

[In *Robinson*] evil moves more obliquely than it does in [Mrs. Spark's] other works. That is, its early ways are oblique; when it comes into direct attack, it becomes massively apparent, but always couched in human terms: when her effects come out of the foggy eeriness of adumbration, there is a sort of tropical glare lighting up their significance, the one exception being Robinson himself, the misanthrope. He stalks through the setting of his island, always alone, a trifle melodramatic in his lonely satisfactions, in his paradoxical pride that he has not allowed his three unwanted guests, sole survivors of the plane crash, to break through into the isolation of himself. His attitude is paradoxical, for there is a small note of surliness within it which contradicts his main point and which suggests that there has been an intrusion into his aloofness. But if his attitude is illogical in a minor way, it is even more impressively human. . . .

Robinson, like all of [Mrs. Spark's] major (and many minor) characters, is never imprisoned within a dominant trait. In his case, as in many others, it is a kind of central elusiveness—suggestive, but never admitting, of final definition, that provokes probing rather than cataloguing. And it is through the deserted island, over which Robinson nevertheless seems to rule so absolutely (and at least in the manner of crops, so inefficiently) that Mrs. Spark establishes his mysterious loneliness. (p. 136)

Roaming the landscape of the island, freed from both the restraints of life in England and from the presence of Robinson, are January's two fellow survivors of the plane crash, Jimmie Waterford and Tom Wells. In the case of each of them there is an ambiguity of intention in which evil may possibly have a full hold, as it most certainly does stand in part possession. Here, the probability of violence impinges; and there is a certain affinity with Graham Greene in the easy confluence of mystery suspense with theological conviction except that in Greene, mental action is matched with external movement; in Mrs. Spark, the second is emphatically subordinate to the first. In this respect, she is closer to the frame of mind of Joyce in *Ulysses* and Faulkner in *The Sound and the Fury* than she is to the Aristotelian conception of tragedy as an action. Suspense gathers mightily in her novel, but the approach is still more meditative than it is dramatic. The matter is, however, hierarchical, not competitive: psychological examination and spiritual examination have the upper hand.

Nevertheless, the obvious catalyst is the setting, the nature of the island. . . . [It] is the island whose oppressive rural charms lower upon [Tom] and compress secretiveness until its tightness must out. Nor can one evil fail in so obvious a situation to seek out another: the mysteriousness of Robinson demands a blackmailer's focused attention.

Jimmie also brings to the island a past that prefers wider places for freer circulation and that sort of concealment part of whose basic nature is circuitousness. His is a more amiable aptitude for perversity; his appetite for evil uses the pointed complaisance of the freeloader. It is a more pleasant brand than Tom's of the same general invention.

Her stay upon the island is both a revelation and a confirmation to January. As in all of Mrs. Spark's novels, examination reveals an interesting world in which grace wars with evil. The former is intrinsically invincible; but the latter flourishes where welcomed. . . . January has learned nothing new, but she has vastly extended the implications of a steady unsentimental Catholic view. (pp. 138-39)

Humor is the essential ingredient of a Muriel Spark novel, the pattern of mind which suffuses her translations. . . .

In *The Bachelors*, the humor flows easily into the word choice and the figures of speech, knowing where to stop and insinuate; for Mrs. Spark, like Lawrence Sterne and Lewis Carroll, knows that humor is never stronger than when it is suggestive. Her goal is not theirs, and the feeling of her humorous universe is quite different from theirs, but there is an identity of over-all control. (p. 139)

Mrs. Spark handles her most vital insinuations in the language, if not the century, of Lawrence Sterne.

In *The Bachelors*, the grimness of her humor enjoys special attention: she studies her bachelors when they are physically alone, and she watches them take this aloneness into

company. Often they compare, but they never share. They never give up this totally central possession. It is both their chief pleasure and their source of pathetic isolation. Above all, our own point of view remains investigative and even sympathetic, but we are denied an empathy that would confuse our critical faculties. (pp. 140-41)

What constitutes the prime of life? In British civilization it is certainly most accessible in those hearty, fortyish gentlemen from Charles Dickens or *Punch*, red-cheeked, joyous, and upright. Ideally, in their legend, there runs an insinuation of broad acres and constitutional goodness, but actually their real prototype is Hogarth's industrious apprentice grown rotund in belly and bank account, both swellings being virtue's behavior under active encouragement. . . .

The irony of *The Prime of Miss Jean Brodie* lies in superficial affinity with this legend, adapted to the terms and figure of an instructor in a successful girl's school, and in sharp inner distinction. One is tempted to see a commentary on the whole legend, but Mrs. Spark is primarily an analyzer of particular situations, not a satirist. The searching spotlight is very definitely on Miss Jean Brodie in particular, rather than on successfully domineering instructors in general. Indeed, so carefully is it focused on her ways and motives, shrewdly viewed, that the supernatural is relegated to the power behind an insinuated approach, in unawareness of which Miss Brodie moves, rather than something which touches down into the action. (p. 141)

Miss Brodie's pointed life left no room for fruitful bewilderment until it was too late. Like others in Mrs. Spark's works, she suffered from self-enclosure. Sandy Stranger, one of Miss Brodie's set of girls, now grown through the years into reminiscence and assessment, has thoughts on the subject: ". . . she began to sense what went to the makings of Miss Brodie who had elected herself to grace in so particular a way and with more exotic suicidal enchantment than if she had simply taken to drink like other spinsters who couldn't stand it any more." (p. 142)

[With] an objectivity that does not hesitate to lean cantingly from its own definition [Mrs. Spark] follows the trail of even-pulsed, practical evil, confident of its ways. In her short story "The Black Madonna" she records with a lively clinical exactitude the ruthless efficiency of a novena-faithful woman in giving away her embarrassingly dark child, who seems possibly to be the eventual result of many prayers to the Black Madonna.

Perhaps we have here the indication of whatever weakness Mrs. Spark bears as an artist. Like every other artist, she emphasizes—and in doing so, necessarily omits. There is kindness in here, a brisk sort of kindness, as in her approach to old Mrs. Jepp in *The Comforters*, but little sustained tenderness. There is also the penalty that has to be paid for that air of competence that surrounds all of her characters, but especially the wicked ones or the failures, who march so surely under their respective banners: their briskness lacks leisurely psychological curves. And perhaps even loneliness is too sure of its own nature and never gets lost in fearful informal curiosity about itself. (p. 143)

John Hazard Wildman, "Translated by Muriel Spark," in Nine Essays in Modern Literature, *edited by Donald E. Stanford (copyright 1965 by Louisiana State University Press), Louisiana State University Press, 1965, pp. 129-44.*

VICTOR KELLEHER

It is probably impossible to read several of Muriel Spark's novels without realizing that her Roman Catholicism is much more than an item of biographical interest: it is a potent force which has profoundly affected the shape of her art. For Miss Spark does not stop short at simply bringing the question of Catholicism into her work; she has chosen to place the traditionally Christian outlook at the very heart of everything she writes.

This "outlook" is perhaps best illustrated by one of her short stories, "A Playhouse Called Remarkable". In this, a character called Moon Biglow recounts how he and five other men descended from the moon shortly after the Flood. At that time mankind was a bored and dying race, with no conception of higher pursuits. Moon and his compatriots introduced the concept of art by opening a playhouse in which they enacted the "Changing Drama of the Moon", a myth-sequence relating to the eternal realities of the heavenly bodies. Such was the enthusiastic response to this drama that the people of the earth were rejuvenated, rediscovering the will to live. But this enthusiasm did not last. An opponent of Moon and his friends managed to suppress the drama, to expel most of the moon men, and to lure the people back to "pure and primitive passions". Nonetheless, the memory of the playhouse was not altogether stamped out. Earth-born artists gradually appeared, "attempting to express the lost moon drama". From that time on, Moon insists, the artist's task has been to "rise up and proclaim the virtue of the remarkable things that are missing from the earth".

The main point of the story is clear enough: all that is fine and good and creative in life comes from another, higher realm. . . . Translated into religious terms (and the reference to the Flood and such paradoxical phrases as "the uprising of my downfall" prompt us to do so), this simple tale is proclaiming the most basic of Christian truths: that all man's blessings emanate from God; that, in the absence of God, man is nothing more than a savage. (p. 79)

Significantly, this point of view is clearly enunciated in the very first of Miss Spark's novels, *The Comforters*. One of the characters, a woman called Georgina Hogg, possesses no spiritual insight; despite her nominal Catholicism, she is incapable of looking beyond her own small, mean world. As a result, she is a beast, a Hogg, a creature devoid of soul; and also a nothing, a vacuum, someone who ceases to exist when she is alone or unnoticed by others. . . . She is a subtle reminder in the novel that man, once dissociated from an eternal, cosmic plan, is a meaningless and therefore horrific phenomenon.

Yet this belief does not lead Miss Spark into despair. . . . [She] sees the passing parade of ephemeral life as something potentially vital, which can be transfigured and even partially redeemed by an expression of freedom and energy. . . .

But Muriel Spark's response to the expression of freedom and vitality, while it is sympathetic, is by no means uncritical. She is no admirer of mere libertarianism. And it is in this respect, above all, that she finds a place within the Christian tradition in literature. For her, as for Hopkins, the falcon, the Heraclitean fire, the energy inherent in man and in the rest of nature, is magnificent, but it is also tragically or foolishly wasted unless it is directed towards some higher end. (p. 80)

[The] Hopkins-like conflict between time and eternity, between the vital, ephemeral processes of nature and the unchanging sphere of God, is present in all of Miss Spark's work. However, it is not always resolved [neatly]. . . . On a number of occasions the conflict is evoked, but left intentionally unresolved; and it is in these instances, perhaps, that Miss Spark's work rises to its highest peak of perceptive and descriptive skill. (p. 81)

[For] Muriel Spark, as for all Christian thinkers, man is both contained by a stifling physical universe, and also possessed of a spirit which seeks to transcend that limited state; he is a creature of two conflicting worlds, a thing both of earth and of heaven. Which of these warring forces finally secures his soul, whether (in Biblical phrase) he is lost or found, is a question to which there is often no conclusive answer. And it is this question, together with the ambiguities and tensions arising from it, that dictates the form of what are probably Muriel Spark's two finest novels: *The Prime of Miss Jean Brodie* and *The Ballad of Peckham Rye*.

In *The Prime of Miss Jean Brodie* we can draw a sharp distinction between story and structure. As the broken time sequence suggests, the story is not wholly significant in itself: its main function is to illustrate and develop one of the most ancient of all mythical patterns—the struggle for a human soul between the forces of darkness and light. There are, of course, no angels or devils in the novel; yet the opposing extremes to which the soul is drawn are as present in this twentieth-century fable as they are in *Dr Faustus* or *Paradise Lost*. The only thing which is missing—and it is this, perhaps, which makes the novel a distinctly modern work—is the quality of anguish. Faustus and Lucifer are torn by their conflict, whereas Jean Brodie is completely unconscious of the disparate elements embattled within her. It is not she, but those with whom she comes into contact, who act out the Faustian role of indecision and suffering. (p. 83)

[We] are left with an ambiguous impression. Does Jean Brodie lighten or darken her world? Is she a spirit of freedom or of oppression? Does she redeem herself or damn herself eternally? *The Prime of Miss Jean Brodie* is specifically designed, not to answer, but simply to pose such questions. . . . Seen in her contradictory fulness, there is something almost archetypal about Jean Brodie. Neither wholly innocent nor completely guilty, trapped in a limited, physical environment yet forever seduced by a sense of something greater, she stands as a compelling representative of the Christian view of man. (p. 85)

When we turn to *The Ballad of Peckham Rye* the mood changes abruptly: tragi-comedy becomes farce; the grand commonplace of Edinburgh gives way to the down-at-heel, sinister, and comic commonplace of Peckham; and the dignified figure of Jean Brodie is replaced by the cavorting, irresponsible figure of the jester. Despite these changes, however, the challenge of the novel remains the same. Once again we are faced with the task of judging the central character. Who is he? Is he Dougal Douglas or Douglas Dougal? He answers to both names. What are we to make of his claim that he is growing horns? They may be a sign that he is the Devil incarnate; but it is just as likely, in context, that they are the horns of Moses, a proof of his superior knowledge. . . . At the heart of all such puzzling incidents and situations lies a single enigma—the way in which we are intended to interpret Douglas's devastating effect on the settled life of Peckham. . . . [Does] the disorder which follows in his wake emanate from him or from the people themselves, from their blind and frightened reaction to his exuberance? (p. 86)

[There are] two distinct ways of responding to Douglas. Ultimately, he is neither angel nor fiend, but rather a modern Proteus . . . in whom we may discern the complex interaction of conflicting attitudes. As with Jean Brodie, this fusion of opposing traits makes it impossible for us to pass a final judgment upon him. His is the vaunting humanist spirit which, following the example of Faustus, teeters perpetually between redemption and damnation.

Given Muriel Spark's religious beliefs there is only one possible way of escaping from this limbo—and that is for the Jean Brodies and Douglases of this world to dedicate their vitality and vision to the service of God. This solution (identical with Hopkins's "Golden Echo") is subtly referred to (though not developed) in both novels. . . .

Muriel Spark expands on this traditionally Christian solution to humanity's problems in several other novels. But in only one does she give equal weight both to the conflict inherent in such humanist characters as Jean Brodie, and also to the Christian method of resolving that conflict. This novel, *The Girls of Slender Means,* is particularly interesting, because it reveals clearly not only the source, but also the possible limitations of her artistic vision. Here, the ambiguous, contradictory role of Jean Brodie is played largely by the girls themselves. To some extent they represent the purity and vigour of youth, a facet of their natures that fascinates Nicholas. Seen in this light, the "slender means" of the title carry strong suggestions of an almost holy poverty. But their means are slender in another sense: beneath the youthful ebullience, there lurks a spiritual poverty, an unthinking animal self-centredness. (p. 87)

[Like Jean Brodie, the girls in this novel] are two things at once, a single composite image of both redeemed and fallen man. (p. 88)

The Girls of Slender Means embodies a full statement of Muriel Spark's religious philosophy. Moreover . . . , it works this statement into a complex symbolic pattern, pleasing in itself. Even if we feel no sympathy for the philosophy, we can still respond to the work of art—to its perfect shape and symmetry. In this respect it is typical of most of her work. But this point in itself raises a problem. Muriel Spark is doing more than simply construct aesthetically pleasing artefacts: she is also writing predominantly Christian novels in an age which is largely, if not increasingly, non-Christian. What significance can such work have for the atheist or agnostic reader? To appreciate it, must he tolerate the dogmatic viewpoint (for essentially her views are dogmatic) and respond to the perfection of form, admire the manipulation of ideas whilst ignoring the ideas themselves? (p. 90)

Muriel Spark does not, strictly speaking, belong to the past; she writes in a contemporary idiom about contemporary people. Even more to the point, she uses the medium of the novel; and it can be argued that our response to the novel differs in kind from, say, our response to lyric or narrative poetry. Because of its length, its ability to give us both detailed observation and breadth of view, it approaches more closely than any other *genre* to the processes of everyday life; it raises our expectations, prepares us for a direct critical re-enactment of the lives we lead. For this reason we cannot overlook the dogmatic content of a twentieth-century novel as easily as we might overlook the limited theology of *Paradise Lost.*

In *The Girls of Slender Means,* for example, post-war London is vividly evoked. The receding sounds of war, the shortages, the rationing, the comparative poverty, the possibility of an unexploded bomb buried in the heart of London, all these elements do more than symbolize the notion of man trapped in a temporal universe, besieged by uncertainty. They also revitalize our sense of a concrete situation, they create a recognizable image of the mid-twentieth century. Yet, disturbingly, the alternatives which the novel discusses do not altogether accord with that image. . . . [The central male character Nicholas] has to choose between order, which takes the form of the traditional, established truth of Christ, and the vigorous anarchy of animal life. But surely there are other choices open to him. As an inhabitant of post-war London, he should at least show some cognizance of current alternatives, of those modern attitudes of mind which could conceivably release him from the necessity of that choice. . . . (pp. 90-1)

In other words, there is a disturbing anomaly in *The Girls of Slender Means.* It purports to present us with a picture of modern life; yet when we look critically at the details of the picture, we discover not the restless, searching, often confused world of the present, nor even the quiet assurance of the eighteenth century, but rather the limiting, defensive Christianity of the middle- and late-nineteenth century. Like Hopkins, but in a less acceptable form, Miss Spark is constricting the universe, implying that man's choice is limited to order or anarchy, to the church or the cave. (p. 91)

[It] is both strange and disturbing that a novel which has all the trappings of modernity should fail to reflect the richness and challenge of its background. Yet the same point can be made about virtually all the other novels. In *The Public Image,* where we are faced with a dichotomy between the public and the private selves, it is as if Freud has never existed, as if we have been thrust back a hundred years, to an age which has not had to meet the challenge of levels of identity, facets of the self. Yet this simplified, traditional conception of the self is placed in the context of a modern movie set!

Unfortunately, there is no indication, even in her more recent work, that Muriel Spark intends coming to terms with this anomaly. In *The Driver's Seat, Not to Disturb,* and *The Hothouse by the East River,* she continues to narrow rather than to broaden her canvas: not just because she deals with such traditional problems as freedom of the will, predestination, and the illusory nature of reality; but because she succeeds in giving life and vitality to these problems only by impoverishing their apparently modern setting. . . . [In *The Hothouse by the East River* the] implication is that the twentieth century is bereft of ideas, of workable alternatives; and it is on the basis of this omission that the thesis of the novel is advanced—namely, the view that the lives we lead, the realms of history and fact, are mere insubstantial dreams compared with the cloud of unknowing, the one mystical reality that transcends time.

In itself, there is nothing inherently absurd in such a claim; Blake and Carlyle, it will be recalled, made similar assertions. They did so, however, not through a process of omission, but by the vigour of their opposition to the social, political, and intellectual realities of their time—realities which they faced squarely. One can only hope that in future novels Muriel Spark will follow their example, that she will add to her already considerable achievement, not by departing from her Catholic standpoint, but by showing us what happens to the Christian consciousness when it is genuinely pitched into the maelstrom of modern experience. (pp. 91-2)

> *Victor Kelleher, "The Religious Artistry of Muriel Spark," in* The Critical Review, *No. 18, 1976, pp. 79-92.*

DAVID LODGE

When a novelist embeds quotations from some fictitious novel in his/her own text [as Muriel Spark does in *Territorial Rights*], it is, of course, always with aesthetic intent, usually parodic. The glum kitchen-sink realism of Anthea's library book, its plodding record of banal thoughts and predictable emotions, is clearly intended to contrast with the sprightly narrative style, the glamorous local colour, the dazzlingly complex intrigue of *Territorial Rights,* and perhaps to underline the advantages enjoyed by a novelist residing in Italy. 'It may seem far-fetched to you, Anthea,' says Grace Gregory, reporting the latest developments to Anthea by telephone, 'But here everything is stark realism. This is Italy.'

We know from her previous novels that Muriel Spark is fascinated by the mixture of cynicism and passion, corruption and beauty in the Italian scene, finding in it (much as the Elizabethans found in Machiavelli's Italy) an image of contemporary decadence more to her purposes than dull old England. In *Territorial Rights* she has married this setting to a theme from her New York novel, *The Hothouse by the East River:* the resurrection of old ghosts and guilts from World War II. . . .

Territorial Rights has no central character, which makes for a diverting international comedy of manners, as the narrative perspective shifts from one character to another, observing them all observing each other, but at the same time leaves the reader sufficiently detached to reflect on how 'far-fetched' the plot is. Nor does the novel throw the reader off balance, as Mrs Spark's novels usually do, by exposing and undermining fictional conventions. . . . *Territorial Rights* is a highly entertaining novel: it tickles, it intrigues, it beguiles. If, in the end, it disappoints, that is because the author is one of our most gifted and original novelists. Even so, it's better by far than most of the novels in Anthea's library.

> *David Lodge, "Prime Cut," in* New Statesman *(copyright © 1979 The Statesman & Nation Publishing Co. Ltd.), April 27, 1979, p. 597.*

FRANCIS KING

From Thomas Mann to Patricia Highsmith and from Henry James to Daphne du Maurier, Venice has not merely exerted a potent fascination on novelists but has brought out the best in them. The beauty of mouldering palazzi reflected in water contaminated with garbage has represented spiritual deliquescence; secret courtyards, labyrinthine alley-ways and choked gardens have represented mystery, danger and intrigue.

The Venetian genius loci, corrupt and corrupting, broods over Muriel Spark's *Territorial Rights* like a miasma. It is evoked in a series of delicate, almost evanescent aquarelles. . . . (p. 28)

For this short novel, Miss Spark has taken over—not for the first time—the apparatus of the thriller and put it to her own idiosyncratic uses. . . . [The characters and coincidences characteristic of this form] are interwoven with the artificiality of a minor Restoration comedy or a lesser Feydeau farce. Obviously, Miss Spark does not intend this to be a realistic thriller in the Highsmith manner.

Since this is so, it would be pointless to object—as some readers may be tempted to do—that the fortuitous convergence of a number of interlinked lives not merely in Venice but in the same pensione at precisely the same time, strains the credulity. It would be no less pointless to object that the patterns of relationships keep changing with the arbitrariness of those within a constantly shaken kaleidoscope. (pp. 28-9)

From time to time the writing is less elegant than one has come to expect from this most elegant of novelists. . . .

As always, this author is remarkably economical in presenting the essential truth about a character or a situation in a mere half-a-dozen sentences. . . .

In this novel, the unease that underlies every Spark situation, however comic, is slightly more muted and muffled; the wit has a slightly less incisive edge; the fantasy is slightly less exuberant. One halts less often to exclaim in admiration at some passage of virtuoso writing. The final impression is one of larkish relaxation, as though the author were saying both to herself and to the reader: 'Oh, don't worry if this or that passage doesn't come off! Enjoy yourself!' Obviously she has enjoyed herself; and no less obviously the reader is going to find enjoyment. This may not be the vintage champagne of *Memento Mori* or *The Girls of Slender Means,* but it makes a refreshingly pétillant draught. (p. 29)

> *Francis King, "Venetian Lark," in* The Spectator *(© 1979 by* The Spectator; *reprinted by permission of* The Spectator), *April 28, 1979, pp. 28-9.*

*   *   *

SPILLANE, Mickey   1918-

An American writer of tough-guy mystery suspense novels, Spillane is one of the world's best-selling novelists. Although his fiction is attacked by critics for its gratuitous violence, and its demeaning portrayal of women, its fast-paced plots and uncomplicated philosophy have earned Spillane millions of readers. (See also *CLC*, Vol. 3, and *Contemporary Authors*, Vols. 25-28, rev. ed.)

KAY WEIBEL

No doubt one reason for the popularity of the early Spillane novels lies in their close mirroring of cultural attitudes of the 1950's. Spillane's treatment of women is particularly significant, moreover, since the hard-boiled detective formula, of which Spillane is the master seller, is the first fictional formula for men to focus explicitly on sexual relationships between men and women. In order to understand the importance of Spillane's definition of women, however, it is first necessary to view the novels as reflectors of fifties' attitudes in general.

Six of Spillane's first seven books have as their protagonist Private Eye Mike Hammer. Mike is a war hero who has re-channeled his violent energies into cleaning up criminal activities in New York City. As opposed to other detectives in the hard-boiled tradition, however, including Sam Spade, Philip Marlowe, Lew Archer and most television crime detectives, Mike Hammer does not actually solve his crimes. In fact, Spillane's Hammer novels are not really about crime detection; they are about war. Mike Hammer is a one-man war machine. He has the blind ideological faith in his cause that warring armies have. He is on the side of righteousness, and the city he is attacking, and by inference everyone in it, is evil. The perpetrators of the crime Mike is allegedly solving are always members of a large corrupt group or organization, and Mike merely maims or kills off everybody who is implicated in the group's activities. The last person left standing is presumed most guilty by Mike in the monologue he delivers before the final execution. Significantly, this last person is almost always female.

It is not surprising or unusual that popular fiction written in a postwar decade should be about war.... The Spillane version of war, however, is a highly glamorized one, in which the impossibility of the hero's defeat is always understood. Though the wartime ethic and wartime activities are retained, the wartime setting is altered. Mike Hammer's war is against inner city New York. (pp. 114-15)

In general, the imagery associated with the city is bleak. In *One Lonely Night,* Mike thinks after coming out of a Communist Party meeting, "The street was the same as before, dark, smelly, unaware of the tumor it was breeding in its belly."... Furthermore, much of the action in the novels takes place in inclement weather—usually rain or snow. Mike also makes constant reference to the congested crowds in the New York streets and to the constant din of street noises.

In his hatred of the big city, Mike reflects attitudes that cultural indicators show to be common in the 1950's. The fifties witnessed a massive movement out of large cities and into outlying suburban areas. (p. 115)

In Spillane, crime is always linked to another phenomenon of the fifties: fear of the large organization. Publicity of Communist and of Mafia activity stressed the corrupt and near-invulnerable power that a tight organization can wield. Mike, who frequently refers to himself as a one-man gang, fights the giant organization on his own, successfully bringing down major arms of the Communist Party of America (*One Lonely Night*), the Mafia (*Kiss Me, Deadly*), an international terrorist organization (*The Girl Hunters*), and three blackmailing rings (*I, The Jury, The Big Kill,* and *Vengeance Is Mine*). Johnny McBride, hero of *The Long Wait,* overthrows a small town gambling boss, his gang and the banker/embezzler they all take orders from.

Convinced of the evil of his enemies, Mike himself is full of the power of positive thinking. In his self-assurance, Mike reflects the belief of Americans in general in the post-war decade that God and justice were on the American side.... In his righteousness and his sense of superior justice, Mike considers himself above the law.... In each of the novels, Hammer thinks his mission puts him above the law. His justice is the Old Testament logic, "an eye for an eye and a tooth for a tooth," but his manner of proclamation is like an evangelical minister. Just before the final execution in each

of the novels, Mike delivers a sermon to the victims in which he outlines their sins. Mike is a minister of damnation only, though, who allows no opportunity for repentance.

As a man self-confidently at war in a just cause, then, Mike Hammer became the ideal role model for men in the 1950's. Here, between the pages of a paperback novel, was war the way it should have been fought—with the righteous army predestined to be victorious. But in addition, through Mike, the ex-GI could relive the wartime social code as well. Mike is a chain smoker who drinks heavily between skirmishes and who has "no strings" access to eager and aggressive woman. The reader in the fifties, however, while keeping his bottle and cigarettes, had left his Tiger Lily overseas and had married the girl next door. The wartime social code, then, had to be modified in the novels to accommodate both the wish and the reality. (pp. 115-17)

At the intersection of sex and motherhood, where sexual adventure meets redeeming social value, are located the novels of Mickey Spillane. On the one hand, Mike Hammer is a pious believer in the double standard and in the virtue of domesticity. Although the women in the Spillane novels are good looking and sexually aggressive, Mike is frequently most impressed by their alleged domesticity. Evil women even lull him into nonsuspicion by feigning love of children or of cooking....

Velda, Mike's girlfriend, secretary and second gun represents the ideal synthesis of mother and sexual toy in the novels. Velda comforts Mike after his close calls, cries whenever his good name or his life are in danger, and she asks no questions about his sexual escapades. (p. 119)

Mike Hammer feels perfectly free to engage in sexual relationships with all the women who make themselves available to him. Spillane hereby clearly endorses the double standard of sexual conduct. The implication is, moreover, that men should choose their sexual conquests from among the "lower classes" of women, since the women Mike has affairs with always have questionable pasts and frequently are suspects in the crime he is investigating. These women have something else in common. They exude sexuality—of the Marilyn Monroe, Jane Russell, Brigitte Bardot variety. Mike repeatedly avows his scorn for skinny women—the type that model clothes. He goes for the movie types, though naturally he doesn't put it that way. Despite their experience, furthermore, all of these women are sexually starved. They throw themselves at Mike not because of his good looks (he is careful to let it be known that he is *not* good looking) or because he has a strong line or a way with women; they throw themselves at him because he is violent. All these women know that Mike is a confessed killer, and it is this knowledge that kindles the fires of passion. The message is that the only way to satisfy a truly sexy woman is with violence. (pp. 120-21)

[In general] Mike's sexual episodes are immediately followed by an act of violent assault, usually murder. In addition, these episodes take place in dark, out-of-the-way places: stereotyped settings for rape.... In *One Lonely Night,* Mike meets a frightened woman being chased down a deserted bridge at night. He kills her pursuer and turns his attention to the woman, with his gun still in his hand. She takes one look at the "kill lust" in Mike's face and jumps over the bridge to her death.

It is no coincidence that the villains of Spillane's novels almost inevitably prove to be women. In his article "The Spillane Phenomenon," John Cawelti talks about the rhythm in Spillane's novels, stating that it reaches its final climax in "violence as orgasm." Since Mike is at war in the novels, a torturous rape would provide the natural climax. In that manner the sexual and violent tensions created by the action in the novels would be resolved simultaneously. Mike Hammer is not allowed this indulgence, however, since he is a believer in female purity and a righteous avenger serving the cause of justice, and atrocities, even in war, are always committed only by the enemy. Denied rape, Mike takes the next best alternative—pumping bullets from the gun that symbolizes his masculinity into the nude body of the villain.

The Spillane novels, then, attempt to resolve for men the two-way image of male/female roles provided by the popular media. On the one hand, men were being told to settle down and be the stable provider for the decade's heroine, Mother. The success of the supersex movie queens and of *Playboy* and its imitators, however, indicated that men had another and contradictory image of themselves as adventure-seeking bachelors. Mike Hammer's solution was simple: take the best of both worlds. Have handy an attractive mother/wife for emergencies and general support, but pursue the adventurous life, including violence and loose women, as well. The unworkability of this formula is revealed metaphorically, however, in the violent death of all the promiscuous women in the novels. Since the real wife/mother would not allow the intrusion of violence and other women in the life of her stable provider, the enjoyment of these adventures must be limited—to the span of time it takes to read a Mickey Spillane novel. (pp. 121-23)

> *Kay Weibel, "Mickey Spillane as a Fifties Phenomenon," in* Dimensions of Detective Fiction, *edited by Larry N. Landrum, Pat Browne, and Ray B. Browne (copyright © 1976 by Popular Press), Popular Press, 1976, pp. 114-23.*

R. JEFF BANKS

One only need remember that rebellion is not the exclusive property of the Left in this or any other country to feel no surprise that it is a strong feature of the works of the most popular fiction writer on the Right. Practically all of Mickey Spillane's heroes are anti-Establishment in sentiment, often outspoken in their views, and sometimes activist. The actions taken range from such petty harassment of a police officer as smashing his cigars by a carefully planned accident, through threatening bodily harm to a whole station house full of policemen, some of whom have been attempting to prove to the hero just how "tough" they are, to the actual killing of policemen in three of the stories. (pp. 124-25)

Through all the [Mike] Hammer books there are bad relations between the hero and successive District Attorneys, but generally the detective is on good terms with the New York City Police Department, especially as it is represented by his oldest and best friend Capt. Pat Chambers....

We may begin by assuming that the conflicts between Hammer and any District Attorney are little more than an observation by Spillane of one of the familiar conventions of the Hard-boiled detective story. Petty harassments on both sides and shouted exchanges of insults are entertaining

to Spillane's millions of readers, but with rare exceptions they are "gut issues" for neither Hammer nor Spillane.

When Pat Chambers has Hammer followed, as he does in *I, the Jury,* the detective makes a little game of making the police look ridiculous.... Whenever his activities bring him into contact with police who are merely doing their job and not infringing upon his rights, he performs as a docile good citizen. (p. 125)

Relations with federal officers are less easygoing. This is due in large part to the wholehearted acceptance by both Spillane and Hammer, along with Chambers and most of Hammer's other friends, of McCarthyism as a political philosophy. This is most apparent among the early works in *One Lonely Night.* However, McCarthyism permeates almost every novel and shorter story Spillane has published. (pp. 125-26)

Hammer's first description of the federal agents prominent in *Kiss Me, Deadly* shows respect for their organization and its reputation. Almost immediately, however, his attitude changes to jealous guardianship of his own rights, including the all-important one of revenge. He stops just short of threatening the F.B.I. men, but otherwise the exchange is not unlike those already mentioned with various District Attorneys. (p. 126)

In destroying one very serious Communist menace with both foreign and domestic agents ranged against him in *One Lonely Night,* Hammer uses characteristic violence. There is characteristic audacity too in his brief, spur-of-the-moment masquerade as an F.B.I. man in Chapter 10. A Spillanean kind of poetic justice appears in Hammer's mass execution of Reds with an F.B.I. tommygun. He even comments on the "cover-up" that this will eventually make necessary....

In Chapter 6 [of *Survival Zero*] Hammer's self-identification as someone the people "living on the perimeter of normalcy" (These are specifically enumerated as including prostitutes, the indigent aged and denizens of a Lower-Lower class bar, but presumably include all the picturesque types that writers of this genre have used to enliven their works since at least the early work of Hammett.) would be willing to talk to in preference to the police, because "I was one of them," opens a possible further insight to the relationship of Spillane's heroes to the Establishment. (p. 127)

[Hammer's] personal creed of being worse than the worst at their own game is present to some degree in most of the Hammer stories, indeed in most of Spillane, and along with actions designed to prove it, it provides a major objection on the part of the literati to Spillane's works. (p. 128)

The new and larger group of Spillane thrillers began in 1961 with one of his most peculiar books and (up to that time) heroes.

The title character of *The Deep* is a grown-up juvenile delinquent returning to his old territory after 25 years to claim control of the area segment of the underworld following the murder of a boyhood chum who had been the local crime czar. (pp. 128-29)

Motivated by knowledge of Deep's past and what he seems to be at present, ultra-tough police sergeant Hurd gives him the beginnings of a stereotyped "third degree" in Chapter 8, complete with a quick beating. However, the hero does well in the physical exchange, and in the surprise ending it is Hurd who first officially recognizes Deep as a superior in the New York City Police Department. Surely here we have the very type of Norman Mailer's hoodlum-policeman, who is just as surely represented by Hammer in the private detective role. (p. 129)

Shortly after the "rebirth" of Mike Hammer in *The Girl Hunters* in 1962, Spillane introduced a new series hero, Tiger Mann. He was intended to occupy the equivalent position in spy (actually counterspy) fiction to that of Hammer in detective fiction. As preparation for writing counterspy novels, Spillane had already done *One Lonely Night* and *The Girl Hunters* in the Hammer series. He has since had Hammer operating more-or-less as a counterspy in *The Body Lovers* and *Survival Zero*. Hammer is a private detective; Mann is a private counterspy (surely a unique figure in the crowded spy/counterspy field) on the payroll of oil super-billionaire Martin Grady, a somewhat less obviously insane version of the villain in Len Deighton's *Billion Dollar Brain*. Hammer competes with official law enforcement agencies (especially the New York City District Attorney's office); Mann competes primarily with federal counter-espionage agencies (especially the esoteric I.A.T.S.), although frequent mention is made of his part in Grady's overseas operations around the world. Hammer is the frequent target of gangland killers; Mann is near the top of the highest priority list of people to be assassinated by Communist agents. Over the years Hammer's tendency to kill the villains in his books has been one of the main things that most of his critics and competitors have objected to. Necessity has forced him to always make it possible to claim self-defense; Mann, benefitting from the years of conditioning reading audiences to James Bond's double-zero rating with its built-in "license to kill," kills more casually. Yet in the very nature of things, the reader finds him most frequently killing those who are out to kill him. Pat Chambers is Hammer's source of knowledge, protection and occasional special privilege in the official police camp; Col. (actually Gen., but Mann continues to call him "Colonel," out of World War II nostalgia) Charlie Corbinet, Mann's former commanding officer in the O.S.S., provides the same services for Mann from his high position in I.A.T.S. (pp. 129-30)

The very nature of Mann's work and his employer make clear the distrust of the Establishment—especially in the area of defense against Communism—which is the hallmark of this series. His first fictional encounter with I.A.T.S. is described succinctly. "They took turns interrogating me. For two hours I let them waste their time and told them nothing." Then when he was ready to terminate the interview, he showed knowledge of their supposedly secret telephone numbers and code words, plus a considerable degree of immunity from their interference. All this is obviously calculated by hero and author to show disrespect. (p. 130)

When Mann's activities are not illegal they are at least extra-legal, thus he is frequently brought into contact with local police forces—of New York City in the first three books and of a small town in Florida in *The By-Pass Control*—and expresses feelings regarding them. The attitude of his statement at the beginning of Chapter 5 in *The Death Dealers,* is more extravagantly worded than is usual, but the sentiments are typical:

> You take all your Federal agencies, your highly trained but obscure intelligence units,

your college degrees and your high IQ, hand-selected personnel working under bureau orders sure, you take them. When you want a job done, give me New York's finest in or out of uniform. Give me the beat cop, the plainclothesmen, the dedicated people so imbued with the city and its environs that they can do a character study of anybody in a half second.

(p. 131)

Then there are what might be termed the miscellaneous works. Ryan, the hero of "Me, Hood!" and "Return of the Hood" is a criminal by choice. We might take him as yet another fictional elaboration of Mailer's hoodlum policeman idea. He joyfully thumbs his nose at the police until forced to work with them and with federal agents in those two stories. At the end of "Return of the Hood," he realizes that he is a marked man, unable to return to his underworld friends and way of life. He accepts the new role of law abiding citizen with grace, if not with relish. (p. 132)

The title characters of *The Deep* and of "The Bastard Bannerman" . . . are, or seem to be, full-fledged gangster types. However, surprise endings in both stories have them turn out to be policemen. The Deep One is a New York City policeman detailed undercover to his old neighborhood to rid it of a long established criminal stranglehold. Bannerman is a West Coast policeman revisiting his Florida hometown to clean up a murder and a Mafia attempt to take over the town during a stopover while en route to pick up a prisoner being held by the New York Police.

Spillane skillfully builds in the reader an impression of disrespect for law and order in the part of the Deep One, but a careful reading shows that all the symptoms belong to his remembered juvenile delinquent days. He is very sentimental about "the old cop on the beat" whom he remembers fondly from his childhood. The one rebellious action that he does engage in is fisticuffs with a vicious policeman bent on giving him an old style "third degree." That device was originated by Mike Hammer in *Vengeance Is Mine* and repeated by George Weston-Johnny McBride in *The Long Wait*. Almost as much a Spillane trademark as the hero's being "taken for a ride" and managing to kill his captors (used more than a half-dozen times in the book length stories), it occurs again in two of the recent Hammer books, *The Girl Hunters* and *The Twisted Thing*. In every case the policeman is clearly in the wrong, and the hero's action is clearly justified as self defense. Following this incident in *The Deep,* the hero further puts the erring policeman in his place by informing him of his "downtown" connections and permission to operate freely in the precinct. (p. 134)

Perhaps the best known and most popular of the latter day Spillane works is *The Delta Factor*. . . . This is the story of Morgan the Raider, a modernday pirate who is pressed into government service. . . .

Certainly the hero's hostility towards authority pervades the entire story. Before it begins he has supposedly stolen $40 million, and at the end of it he escapes the spymasters who have used him to try to recover the loot. In the book he has ample opportunity to tell many authority figures what he thinks of them. (p. 136)

Still in the first chapter, like Hammer, Mann and others, Morgan brings up the threat of unfavorable publicity; he repeats it in Chapter 3. . . .

He exchanges gun threats with the regular United States agent who is assigned to him as combination guard and helper in Chapters 4, 5, 6, and 8. He threatens to rape this same agent, a girl who has married him as a part of their cover, in Chapters 3, 7, and 8. That he has a strong personal liking for the girl is apparent in the more sincere development of their relationship by the end of the book. However, that is not allowed to stand in the way of his dislike for her as a representative of the authority of the Establishment which he scorns. . . .

At the end of the book, in a final flaunting of our government's authority, he escapes three armed United States agents by parachuting from the airplane which is bringing him back to this country. That his escape is over the open sea and that he expects to be rescued by criminal associates in a motorboat adds the Spillane touch of flamboyance to the ending. (p. 137)

> *R. Jeff Banks, "Spillane's Anti-Establishmentarian Heroes," in* Dimensions of Detective Fiction, *edited by Larry N. Landrum, Pat Browne, and Ray B. Browne (copyright © 1976 by Popular Press), Popular Press, 1976, pp. 124-39.*

*   *   *

STEINBECK, John   1902-1968

Steinbeck was an American novelist, short story writer, dramatist, and essayist. He is best known for his realistic and vivid portrayal of the hardships of the Great Depression in *The Grapes of Wrath,* **which depicts a group of sharecroppers en route to California. While exposing the ordeal of their poverty, Steinbeck also seeks to affirm the sanctity of life and the unifying, clarifying forces inherent in human suffering. Although he was a popular success, Steinbeck has not enjoyed a consistently favorable critical reception. Critics note that his strong, sympathetic characterizations often lapse into sentimentality, although many find that the strength of his narrative line often compensates for this weakness. Steinbeck won the Pulitzer Prize in Fiction in 1940 and the Nobel Prize for Literature in 1962. (See also** *CLC,* **Vols. 1, 5, 9, and** *Contemporary Authors,* **Vols. 1-4, rev. ed.; obituary, Vols. 25-28, rev. ed.)**

EDMUND WILSON

[Mr. Steinbeck's] virtuosity in a purely technical way has tended to obscure his themes. He has published eight volumes of fiction, which represent a variety of forms and which have thereby produced an illusion of having been written from a variety of points of view. . . . [Attention] has been diverted from the content of Mr. Steinbeck's work by the fact that when his curtain goes up, he always puts on a different kind of show.

Yet there is in Mr. Steinbeck's fiction a substratum which remains constant and which gives it a certain weight. What is constant in Mr. Steinbeck is his preoccupation with biology. He is a biologist in the literal sense that he interests himself in biological research. The biological laboratory in the short story called *The Snake* is obviously something which he knows at first hand and for which he has a strong special feeling; and it is one of the peculiarities of his vocabulary that it runs to biological terms. But the laboratory described in *The Snake,* the tight little building above the water, where the scientist feeds white rats to rattlesnakes and fertilizes starfish ova, is also one of the key images of his

fiction. It is the symbol of Mr. Steinbeck's tendency to present human life in animal terms.

Mr. Steinbeck almost always in his fiction is dealing either with the lower animals or with humans so rudimentary that they are almost on the animal level; and the relations between animals and people are as intimate as those in the zoöphile fiction of David Garnett and D. H. Lawrence. . . . Mr. Steinbeck does not give the effect, as Lawrence or Kipling does [however], of romantically raising the animals to the stature of human beings, but rather of assimilating the human beings to animals. (pp. 35-7)

And Steinbeck does not . . . dwell much, as Lawrence likes to do, on the perfections of his various beasts each after its own kind. It is the habits and behavior of the animals, not the impression they make, that interests him.

The chief subject of Mr. Steinbeck's fiction has been thus not those aspects of humanity in which it is most thoughtful, imaginative, constructive, nor even those aspects of animals that seem most attractive to humans, but rather the processes of life itself. In the ordinary course of nature, living organisms are continually being destroyed, and among the principal things that destroy them are the predatory appetite and the competitive instinct that are necessary for the very survival of eating and breeding creatures. This impulse of the killer has been preserved in a simpleton like Lennie of *Of Mice and Men* in a form in which it is almost innocent; and yet Lennie has learned from his more highly developed friend that to yield to it is to do something "bad." In his struggle against the instinct, he loses. Is Lennie bad or good? He is betrayed as, the author implies, all our human intentions are, by the uncertainties of our animal nature. And it is only, as a rule, on this primitive level that Mr. Steinbeck deals with moral questions: the virtues like the crimes, for him, are still a part of these planless and almost aimless, of these almost unconscious, processes. The preacher in *The Grapes of Wrath* . . . evidently gives expression to Mr. Steinbeck's own point of view: "This here ol' man jus' lived a life an' jus' died out of it. I don't know whether he was good or bad, but that don't matter much. He was alive, an' that's what matters. An' now he's dead, an' that don't matter. . . ."

The subject of *The Grapes of Wrath,* which is supposed to deal with human society, is the same as the subject of *The Red Pony,* which is supposed to deal with horses: loyalty to life itself. The men who feel themselves responsible for having let the red pony die must make up for it by sacrificing the mare in order that a new pony may be brought into the world alive. And so Rose of Sharon Joad, with her undernourished baby born dead, must offer her milk . . . to another wretched victim of famine and flood, on the point of death from starvation. To what end should ponies and Oakies continue to live on the earth? "And I wouldn' pray for a ol' fella that's dead," the preacher goes on to say. "He's awright. He got a job to do, but it's all laid out for 'im an' there's on'y one way to do it. But us, we got a job to do, an' they's a thousan' ways, an' we don' know which one to take. An' if I was to pray, it'd be for the folks that don't know which way to turn." (pp. 38-9)

[What] differentiates Mr. Steinbeck's picture of a labor movement with radical leadership [in *In Dubious Battle*] from most treatments of such subjects of its period is again the biological point of view. The strike leaders, here, are

Communists, as they are in many labor novels, but *In Dubious Battle* is not really based on the formulas of Communist ideology. The kind of character produced by the Communist movement and the Communist strategy in strikes (of the Communism of the day before yesterday) is *described* by Mr. Steinbeck, and it is described with a certain amount of admiration; yet the party member of *In Dubious Battle* does not talk like a Marxist of even the Stalinist revision. The cruelty of these revolutionists, though they are working for a noble ideal and must immolate themselves in the struggle, is not palliated by the author any more than the cruelty of the half-witted Lennie; and we are made to feel all through the book that, impressive though the characters may be, they are presented primarily as examples of how life in our age behaves. There is developed in the course of the story. . . a whole philosophy of "group-man" as an "animal." (pp. 39-40)

[The] old pioneer of *The Leader of the People* describes a westward migration which he himself once led as "a whole bunch of people made into one big crawling beast. . . . Every man wanted something for himself, but the big beast that was all of them wanted only westering."

This tendency on Steinbeck's part to animalize humanity is evidently one of the causes of his relative unsuccess at creating individual humans. The *paisanos* of *Tortilla Flat* are not really quite human beings: they are cunning little living dolls that amuse us as we might be amused by pet guinea-pigs, squirrels or rabbits. They are presented through a special convention which is calculated to keep them cut off from any kinship with the author or the reader. In *The Grapes of Wrath*, on the other hand, Mr. Steinbeck has summoned all his resources to make the reader feel his human relationship with the family of dispossessed farmers; yet the result of this, too, is not quite real. The characters of *The Grapes of Wrath* are animated and put through their paces rather than brought to life; they are like excellent character actors giving very conscientious performances in a fairly well-written play. Their dialect is well managed, but they always sound a little stagy; and, in spite of Mr. Steinbeck's efforts to make them figure as heroic human symbols, one cannot help feeling that these Okies, too, do not exist for him quite seriously as people. It is as if human sentiments and speeches had been assigned to a flock of lemmings on their way to throw themselves into the sea. One remembers the short story called *Johnny Bear*. Johnny Bear is another of Steinbeck's idiots: he has exactly the physique of a bear and seems in almost every way subhuman; but he is endowed with an uncanny gift for reproducing with perfect mimicry the conversations he overhears, though he understands nothing of their human meaning.

It is illuminating to look back from *The Grapes of Wrath* to one of the earliest of Steinbeck's novels, *To a God Unknown*. In this book he is dealing frankly with the destructive and reproductive forces as the cardinal principles of nature. In one passage, the hero is described by one of the other characters as never having "known a person": "You aren't aware of persons, Joseph; only people. You can't see units, Joseph, only the whole." . . . This story . . . evidently represents, on the part of Steinbeck just turned thirty, an honorably sincere attempt to find expression for his view of the world and his conception of the powers that move it. When you husk away the mawkish verbiage from the people of his later novels, you get down to a similar

conception of a humanity not of "units" but lumped in a "whole," to a vision equally grim in its cycles of extinction and renewal.

Not, however, that John Steinbeck's picture of human beings as lemmings, as grass that is left to die, does not have its striking validity for the period in which we are living. . . . Many parts of the world are today being flooded with migrants like the Joads, deprived of the dignity of a human society, forbidden the dignity of human work, and made to flee from their houses like prairie-dogs driven before a prairie fire. (pp. 41-3)

The philosophy of Mr. Steinbeck is . . . not satisfactory in either its earlier or its later form. He has nothing to oppose to [the] vision of man's hating and destroying himself except an irreducible faith in life; and the very tracts he writes for the underdog let us see through to the biological realism which is his natural habit of mind. Yet I prefer his approach to the animal-man to the mysticism [for example] of Mr. Huxley; and I believe that we shall be more likely to find out something of value for the control and ennoblement of life by studying human behavior in this spirit than through the code of self-contemplation that seems to grow so rootlessly and palely in the decay of scientific tradition. (p. 44)

Mr. Steinbeck is equipped with resources of observation and invention which are exceptional and sometimes astonishing, and with color which is all his own but which does not, for some reason, possess what is called magic. It is hard to feel that any of his books, so far, is really first-rate. He has provided a panorama of California farm-life and California landscape which is unique in our literature; and there are passages in some ways so brilliant that we are troubled at being forced to recognize that there is something artistically bad about them. . . . [But we are often reminded] of the ever-present paradox of the mixture of seriousness and trashiness in the writing of Mr. Steinbeck. I am not sure that *Tortilla Flat*, by reason of the very limitations imposed by its folktale convention, is not artistically his most successful work.

Yet there remains behind the journalism, the theatricalism and the tricks of his other books a mind which does seem first-rate in its unpanicky scrutiny of life. (pp. 44-5)

Edmund Wilson, "John Steinbeck" (1940), in his Classics and Commercials: A Literary Chronicle of the Forties *(reprinted with the permission of Farrar, Straus & Giroux, Inc.; copyright © 1950 by Edmund Wilson; copyright renewed © 1978 by Elena Wilson), The Noonday Press, 1950, pp. 35-45.*

ALFRED KAZIN

Steinbeck's approach to the novel was interesting because he seemed to stand apart at a time when naturalism had divided writers into two mutually exclusive groups, since the negation of its starved and stunted spirit came more and more from writers who often had no sympathy with realism at all, and were being steadily pulled in the direction of surrealism and abstractionism. . . . (p. 393)

Steinbeck, standing apart from both the contemporary naturalists and the new novel of sensibility that one finds in Faulkner and Wolfe, brought a fresh note into contemporary fiction because he promised a realism less terror-ridden than the depression novel, yet one consciously responsible to society; a realism mindful of the terror and disorganization of contemporary life, but not submissive to the spiritual stupor of the time; a realism equal in some measure, if only in its aspiration, to the humanity, the gaiety, the wholeness, of realism in a more stable period.... Steinbeck is a greater humanist [than Farrell], and there is a poetry in some of his best work, particularly *The Long Valley* stories and *The Pastures of Heaven*, that naturalists of Farrell's stamp have never been able to conceive. But there is something imperfectly formed about Steinbeck's work; it has no creative character. For all his moral serenity, the sympathetic understanding of men under strain that makes a strike novel like *In Dubious Battle* so notable in the social fiction of the period, Steinbeck's people are always on the verge of becoming human, but never do. There is a persistent failure to realize human life fully in his books, where the characters in many American naturalistic novels have simply ceased to be human. After a dozen books Steinbeck still looks like a distinguished apprentice, and what is so striking in his work is its inconclusiveness, his moving approach to human life and yet his failure to be creative with it.

Steinbeck's moral advantage as a realist in the depression era was to be so different in his region—the Salinas Valley in California—his subject, as to seem different in kind. It was his famous "versatility" that first earned him his reputation . . . , but this was the least noteworthy thing about him and has come more and more to suggest not versatility but a need to feel his way. His great possession as a writer was not an interest in craft or an experimental spirit; it was an unusual and disinterested simplicity, a natural grace and tenderness and ease in his relation to his California world.... Steinbeck's gift was not so much a literary resource as a distinctively harmonious and pacific view of life. In a period when so many better writers exhausted themselves, he had welded himself into the life of the Salinas Valley and enjoyed a spiritual stability by reporting the life cycles of the valley gardeners and mystics and adventurers, by studying and steeping himself in its growth processes out of a close and affectionate interest in the biology of human affairs. Steinbeck's absorption in the life of his native valley gave him a sympathetic perspective on the animal nature of human life, a means of reconciliation with people as people. The depression naturalists saw life as one vast Chicago slaughterhouse, a guerrilla war, a perpetual bombing raid. Steinbeck had picked up a refreshing belief in human fellowship and courage; he had learned to accept the rhythm of life. (pp. 393-95)

People in Steinbeck's work, taken together, are often evil; a society moving on the principle of collective mass slowly poisons itself by corrupting its own members. But beyond his valley-bred conviction of the evil inherent in any society where men are at the mercy of each other's animalism, Steinbeck knew how to distinguish, in works like *The Long Valley, In Dubious Battle,* and *The Grapes of Wrath,* between the animal processes of life and social privation. Out of his slow curiosity, the strength of the agrarian tradition in him, Steinbeck was able to invest the migration of the Joads, if not his monochromatic characters, with a genuinely tragic quality precisely because he felt so deeply for them and had seen at first hand the gap between their simple belief in life and their degradation. He did not confuse the issue in *The Grapes of Wrath;* he was aroused by the man-made evil the Okies had to suffer, and he knew it as

something remediable by men. And where another social realist might have confused the dark corners he described with the whole of life, Steinbeck had the advantage of his Western training, its plain confidence in men. The old pioneer grandfather in *The Long Valley,* remembering the brutality of men on the great trek, also remembered [its glory].... (p. 396)

[This] contributed to the success of *The Grapes of Wrath* and made it the dominant social novel of the period.... [It was] the first novel of its kind to dramatize the inflictions of the crisis without mechanical violence and hatred. The bitterness was there, as it should have been, the sense of unspeakable human waste and privation and pain. But in the light of Steinbeck's strong sense of fellowship, his simple indignation at so much suffering, the Joads, while essentially symbolic marionettes, did illuminate something more than the desperation of the time: they became a living and challenging part of the forgotten American procession. Though the characters were essentially stage creations, the book brought the crisis that had severed Americans from their history back into it by recalling what they had lost through it. It gave them a design, a sense of control, where out of other depression novels they could get only the aimless maniacal bombardment of rage. The lesson of the crisis, so often repeated in the proletarian novel and yet so lifeless in it, was suddenly luminous: it was an event in history, to be understood by history, to be transformed and remembered and taught in history. It was as if Steinbeck, out of the simplicity of his indignation, had been just primitive enough to call men back to their humanity, to remind depression America that a culture is only the sum total of the human qualities that make it up, and that "life can give a periodical beating to death any time," as a contemporary poet put it, "if given a chance and some help."

It was this tonic sanity in a bad time, his understanding of the broad processes of human life, that gave Steinbeck his distinction among the depression realists. But no one can pretend, particularly after a book like *The Moon Is Down,* that it tells the whole story about him. For Steinbeck's primitivism is essentially uncreative, and for all his natural simplicity of spirit, there is a trickiness, a stage cunning, behind it that has become depressing. Though his interests have carried him squarely into certain central truths about the nature of life, he has not been able to establish them in human character. Nothing in his books is so dim, significantly enough, as the human beings who live in them, and few of them are intensely imagined as human beings at all. It is obvious that his mind moves happily in realms where he does not have to work in very complex types—the *paisanos* in *Tortilla Flat,* the ranch hands in *Of Mice and Men,* the Okies in *The Grapes of Wrath,* the strikers in *In Dubious Battle,* the farmers in *The Long Valley,* the symbolic protagonists of democratic struggle and Nazi power in *The Moon Is Down.* But what one sees in his handling of these types is not merely a natural affection for this simplicity, but a failure to interest himself too deeply in them as individuals.... Steinbeck's perspective on human life always gives him a sense of process, an understanding of the circuits through which the human animal can move; but he cannot suggest the density of human life, for his characters are not fully human.

It is in this light that one can understand why Steinbeck's moral serenity is yet so sterile and why it is so easy for him to slip into the calculated sentimentality of *Of Mice and Men* and *The Moon Is Down*. . . . He is a simple writer who has acquired facility, but though he is restive in his simplicity, his imagination cannot rise above it. And it is that simplicity and facility, working together, a tameness of imagination operating slickly, that give his work its surface paradox of simplicity and trickiness, of integrity of emotion and endless contrivance of means. This does not mean a lack of sincerity; it does mean that Steinbeck is not so simple that he does not know how to please; or to take, as it were, advantage of himself. (pp. 397-99)

What is really striking about [*The Moon Is Down*]—so openly written, like *Of Mice and Men*, for the stage—is how fantastically simple the whole anti-Fascist struggle appeared to Steinbeck even as an allegory, and yet how easy it was for him to transcribe his naïveté into the shabbiest theater emotions. There is credulity here, even an essential innocence of spirit, and the kind of slow curiosity about all these war-haunted creatures that has always made Steinbeck's interest in the animal nature of life the central thing in his work. He does not appeal to the hatred of Hitlerism, no; he has never appealed to any hatred. . . . We hear the affirmation of nobility Steinbeck wanted to make, as we hear it in all his work; but we cannot believe in it, for though it is intended to inspire us in the struggle against Hitlerism, there are no men and women here to fight it. . . . [These] are not Steinbeck's familiar primitives, only seeking to be human. No, they are not primitives at all. But Steinbeck's world is a kind of primitivism to the end—primitive, with a little cunning. (p. 399)

> *Alfred Kazin, in his* On Native Grounds: An Interpretation of Modern American Prose Literature *(copyright 1942, 1970, by Alfred Kazin; reprinted by permission of Harcourt Brace Jovanovich, Inc.), Reynal & Hitchcock, 1942.*

JOHN S. KENNEDY

[Steinbeck's] first nine works were markedly different one from another in matter and tone and style. He shifted sharply and with a show of ease from costume drama to fantasy at once earthy and lyric to knockabout farce to abrasive naturalism to argument none too successfully disguised as narrative, proving that he could do more or less creditably in a number of fictional forms, even if in none did he demonstrate the mastery and finesse of indisputable greatness.

But though his books might show contrast in form, pace and diction, they inevitably had certain things in common. For example, binding together the now rather extensive body of novels, short stories, sketches, plays, is the California setting, and specifically the Salinas Valley setting, of most of his productions. (p. 119)

Far more important than the common scene in Steinbeck is the common theme. Something of the sort is discernible, of course, in the output of any writer, however many-sided. In Steinbeck's case the common theme may be called "reverence for life." . . . Steinbeck's preoccupation with life and living is perhaps the main reason for his popularity and influence.

Dozens of his contemporaries write consistently better than he, with greater subtlety and polish, greater depth and force. He can produce pages of beauty and impact, preceded and followed by pages of sheer trash, the emptiness

of which is only accentuated by the pseudo-grandeur or pseudo-primitivism of the diction. He can be acutely sensitive and true for a chapter, then embarrassingly sentimental and cheaply trite. He can write dialog with authenticity and bite, and go on to more dialog which is reverberant rhetorical noise. He can juxtapose a penetrating analysis of human feeling, especially of sense impression, and painfully artificial fabrication. In short, he has at least as many faults as he has felicities in his talent; his books are by no means rigorously weeded.

Still, he has won both critical and popular acclaim, largely, it would appear, because he is, within limits, an affirmative writer. (p. 120)

He is no Pollyanna—far from it. He depicts human existence as conflict, unremitting and often savage battle. But he suggests that life is worth living, flagellant and baffling though it may be. When, as rarely happens, he produces a memorable character like Ma Joad, that character has an irrepressible will to live, even under heart-breakingly adverse conditions, is resourceful and indomitable before the hostility of a world apparently bent on his or her extermination. In a time when the prevalent note in creative literature is that of despondency and abandonment to malign fate, . . . Steinbeck's assertion of the resiliency and tough durability of life has set him off from the generality.

Moreover, his prepossession with life, rather than ideologies, has made it impossible to pigeonhole him politically, which is not true of many another novelist.

He did run afoul of the critical habit, prevalent in the 'thirties and early 'forties, that rated fiction principally, if not exclusively, according to [political bias]. . . . Thus *The Grapes of Wrath* (1939) was attacked by the politically conservative as out-and-out Communist propaganda. It was nothing of the sort. . . . (p. 121)

Steinbeck had written of Communists not unsympathetically and had hit at reactionary Red-baiters in earlier books, but had clearly demonstrated his critical awareness of the bad features of the Communist mentality and methods in the novel, *In Dubious Battle* (1936), dealing with an abortive strike by migrant fruit pickers of whom monolithically organized owners would take pitiless advantage. . . . Doc, the character who, it is manifest, speaks for Steinbeck, debunks the legend of the Communists' altruistic humanitarianism; and the Party's cold-blooded exploitation of misery, as well as its callous use of the most despicable means to its power-seeking ends, is graphically shown. Steinbeck evidently rejected communism because communism throttled life. (pp. 121-22)

[*The Grapes of Wrath*] said, at unconscionable length and with some resort to sensationalism and melodrama, something incontrovertibly true: namely, that thousands upon thousands of Americans were being cruelly victimized and heinously degraded by a system, crazily inept at least in part, which destroyed masses of ordinary people for the inordinate and socially unjust and detrimental enrichment of remote, impersonal corporations. Steinbeck, aroused over the trampling of human life, put this strongly in accents of burning anger and disgust. He did not have to be a Communist to do so, and indeed it was an appalling commentary on the inhumanity or stupidity of the comfortably circumstanced that his indictment of a reeking evil should be answered only by wholly irrelevant name-calling.

But it was not very long until Steinbeck was under fire for precisely the opposite reason and being styled a sort of crypto-Nazi. This happened when *The Moon Is Down* was published as a novel and produced as a play in 1942. . . . Steinbeck was writing of occupied Norway . . . , and his Nazi characters emerged as something like human beings, by no means admirable, but by no means demoniac either. For not making them intrinsically and uniformly monstrous, at a time when some of our most celebrated writers were trying to whip Americans up to a frenzy of indiscriminate hatred, Steinbeck was pilloried. (p. 122)

Communism and nazism have in common a commitment to collectivism, differing though they do as to the auspices under which it should be conducted. Was Steinbeck in favor of some sort of collectivism? It is plain from his books that he does not favor the familiar forms of economic or political collectivism, be they controlled by foreign dictators or native capitalists. For example, he writes scathingly of the monopolist who thwarts the poor Mexican in *The Pearl* (1947). He hits hard, for another example, at that centralization which would make of American agriculture no more than a mass-production scheme for the aggrandizement of urban shareholders, and this precisely because life is demeaned and quenched in the process. (pp. 122-23)

Steinbeck emphasizes the natural bond between life and productive property, the need that man has of a bit of earth to give him sustenance and dignity. (p. 123)

[In] *The Grapes of Wrath* Steinbeck seems to approve and recommend collectivism of a different sort, a collectivism which, according to him, would foster, rather than crush, life. The Okies have had their ramshackle but cherished homes and their small patches of earth snatched away from them by the insatiable behemoth of big-scale agriculture. What is wrong with this, it is suggested, is not the pooling of hundreds of family-size farms, but the fact of the alien ownership of the amalgam. . . . [He urges] a sort of popularly chosen and controlled socialism, which Steinbeck heatedly advocates without ever bothering to consider its pitfalls or its possible deleterious consequences.

This idea is not to be dismissed out of hand as absurd or pernicious. The social character of property, the legitimacy and desirability of social ownership of what is indispensable to the common good, the incomparable value and profoundly Christian character of voluntary cooperation and joint endeavor—these are not being called into question. But Steinbeck means something more, something different. Just here we are coming to grips with the central point in Steinbeck's concept of life: namely, that its fullness is found only in the group and never in the individual. While he regards with disfavor a superimposed collectivism, he believes ardently in the primacy of the collectivity. Permeating his works is this idea, which is the very heart of his philosophy of life: that the concrete person is in himself virtually nothing, whereas the abstraction ''humanity'' is all.

Consider some examples from books published over a span of years, and you will observe the persistency and growth of this attitude. In *To a God Unknown* (1933), Rama says:

> I tell you this man is not a man, unless he is
> all men. The strength, the resistance, the
> long and stumbling thinking of all men, and
> all the joys and suffering too, cancelling each
> other out and yet remaining in the contents.

He is all these, a repository for a little piece
of each man's soul, and more than that, a
symbol of the earth's soul.

In *In Dubious Battle*, Doc tells Mac, ''You might be an expression of group-man, a cell endowed with a special function, like an eye-cell, drawing your force from group-man . . .''. . . . Later, he asks another character, ''Can't a group of men be God?'' In *The Red Pony* (1937), the westward migration of the pioneers is described as ''a whole bunch of people made into one big crawling beast.'' In *The Grapes of Wrath* Tom Joad, quoting the ex-preacher Casy, declares:

> Says one time he went out into the wilderness to find his own soul, and he foun' he
> didn' have no soul that was his'n. Says he
> foun' he jus' got a little piece of a great big
> soul. Says a wilderness ain't no good, 'cause
> his little piece of soul wasn't no good 'less it
> was with the rest, an' was whole.
>
> (pp. 124-25)

[He] is ever more strongly affirming that, in the last analysis, man has no individual identity, that the human person as such, separately created and distinct from all others, does not in fact exist. Commitment to this idea may well be reaction against the unbridled, atomistic individualism which has wreaked havoc in society as a whole and in innumerable lives, and which, as his books indicate, Steinbeck recognizes as disastrous for mankind. But he has swung to and remains at the opposite extreme, that amalgamism which deprives the individual of initiative, responsibility, value, and even metaphysical being, and makes him no more than a cell in a supposititious monstrosity called ''group-man'' or an inextricable aspect of a pseudo-mystical entity called the ''great big soul.'' It is the ''great big soul'' which, for Steinbeck, is life.

Indeed, he goes further than blotting out the boundaries of personality which mark off one man from another. He declares that, for man to be whole, he must be indistinguishably at one with all that exists. Casy, in *The Grapes of Wrath*, says: ''There was the hills, an' there was me, an' we wasn't separate no more. We was one thing. An' that one thing was holy.'' Here again, one might dismiss objections, on the ground that all that exists, whether organic or inorganic, is interrelated and should be in harmony. There is an intimate interrelationship of all the levels of a universe made through, and bearing the mark of, the one Eternal Word. But Steinbeck is nowhere clear as to the essential, qualitative difference between man and the rest of created beings. (p. 125)

This can be plainly seen in what Edmund Wilson has called Steinbeck's ''animalizing tendency.'' Wilson says that ''constant in Mr. Steinbeck is his preoccupation with biology'' and points out ''his tendency in his stories to present life in animal terms'' [see excerpt above]. (p. 126)

[Habitually] and characteristically Steinbeck sets human conduct and animal conduct side by side, on the same plane, not simply as commentaries one on the other but as indications of the same nature in the two apparently disparate sorts of creature. (p. 127)

[He] incessantly presents man as a creature, indeed a captive, of instincts and appetites only, blindly desiring and striving, not reasoning, judging, choosing but automatically responding to impulses and attractions.

As for man's being moral, Doc (who, to repeat, is Steinbeck's spokesman in *In Dubious Battle*) says: "My senses aren't above reproach, but they're all I have . . . I don't want to put on the blinders of 'good' and 'bad,' and limit my vision." In *The Grapes of Wrath,* Casy says of sexual promiscuity: "Maybe it ain't a sin. Maybe it's just the way folks is . . . There ain't no sin and there ain't no virtue. There's just stuff people do. It's all part of the same thing." Pa Joad echoes this with, "A fella got to do what he got to do." And Ma Joad says, "What people does is right to do." (pp. 127-28)

And so in man, according to Steinbeck, what counts, what alone matters, is life, its preservation, its transmission. . . . [In *Burning Bright,* when his wife's child by another man] is born, Joe Saul greets it as his own, declaiming that every man is the father of every child and every child the off-spring of every man. Life is vindicated, life goes on, and whatever violence is done the moral code is of no moment alongside that fact.

The thoughtful reader is appalled by the complete sever-ance of man from morality which the book's argument rep-resents. He reflects that fundamentally what is amiss with these characters is failure or refusal to recognize and accept God's will and word: as regards physical defects, the exclu-siveness of marriage, the disposition of life. (p. 128)

[The] human collectivity, men *en masse,* may be all that is meant by the term "God." Several times in Steinbeck's works one finds the idea that a character has outgrown prayer because, with enlightenment, he no longer knows what or whom to pray to. . . . On the other hand, the igno-rant, superstitious people of whom Steinbeck is writing in *The Pearl* and *The Long Valley* (1938) pray because it is part of an immemorial behavior-pattern which, quite as uninformed as their forebears, they unquestioningly accept.

These benighted men and women, incidentally, are Catho-lic, and it is interesting to see how Steinbeck treats Catholi-cism. It is not understandingly or sympathetically. (pp. 128-29)

Nowhere does Steinbeck give evidence of adequate knowl-edge of the Catholicism on which he touches with evident disfavor in his various productions. He seems much more familiar with the cruder sort of evangelical Protestantism, and this is acidly treated in his books. (p. 130)

Steinbeck may justly be said to belong to that populous group of contemporary novelists who, rejecting as pro-crustean and unlivable a peculiar, diluted blend of Calvin-ism and Lutheranism, think that, in exposing such freakish-ness, they are refuting authentic Christianity. They look upon what is a caricature of authentic Christianity. . . . The privativism which Casy, Pat Humbert, and other Steinbeck characters find and disavow in what they take to be integral Christianity is actually a disease at the heart of a faint and fragmentary copy of genuine Christianity. (p. 131)

Steinbeck, therefore, nowhere comes to grips with the ba-sic, pristine Christian religion. Hence he never takes into account what it has to say about human nature, human life, human destiny. He is not conversant with its moral code as a whole. He is not familiar with its bearing upon the human predicament, the light it casts upon it and the resources it brings to mortals for managing and solving it.

His last book, *Burning Bright,* harshly highlights all that is weakest in Steinbeck as a philosopher and a writer of fic-tion. Even if one could do the impossible and agree that adultery is no more than an outdated word so long as life is propagated, there is the question of [the fate of Victor, the baby's father]. Friend Ed, goodness and wisdom personi-fied, recommends that Victor be used and then cooly kills the young man when convenience calls for that. There is no slightest hint that the murder is a wicked injustice. The bru-tality, the icy amorality of this is one of the most shocking things in all Steinbeck's output, the more shocking because it comes from a supposedly mature man and is surrounded with resounding generalities about the sacredness of life. Yet it is scarcely surprising in view of the sophistry in which, in his succession of works, Steinbeck has become ever more tightly entangled. And, by the way, one might here stress the fact that it is the sophistry, rather than the foul speech, which is most regrettable in Steinbeck's fic-tion. *Burning Bright* is almost entirely free of the vulgar, obscene, or blasphemous dialog which characterizes so many of Steinbeck's books. It is only the coarse Victor who recalls, and that but faintly and briefly, the profane and filthy language of the figures which dominate, and are con-stantly articulate in the idiom of lewdness, in several of the other novels. The rest of the principals use no offensive words, indeed their talk has an exalted ring to it, and yet the ideas they express are far worse than mere lurid utter-ance. To reproduce verbatim the gutter language of people who are virtually mute unless they resort to lascivious lingo is hardly to be compared with the communication of a phi-losophy of life which is totally fallacious. (pp. 131-32)

In *Burning Bright,* too, may be seen at its worst Steinbeck's failure with characters. He has written about fifteen vol-umes of fiction by now, yet given us almost no memorable characters. Ma Joad is a possible exception, but it is hard to name even half-a-dozen more. For the most part the men and women in Steinbeck's narratives are hazy, faceless, pithless. They are not sharply drawn, clearly projected, unmistakably themselves, or recognizable from one's ex-perience however catholic. They have no forms, in the phil-osophical sense, which is but another way of saying that they have no souls. There are about them certain superficial peculiarities which make for a measure of material individu-ation, but almost nothing making for personality. They are heavily documented types, not living people. Nor is this merely a deficiency in imagination or technique. It springs from Steinbeck's conviction that a man or woman is just "a little piece of a great big soul." It has been said of Stein-beck that he is not a creative artist; if this is true, it is to be attributed to his missing the point of God's several creation of humans, each a separate entity, each a microcosm and a mystery which cannot be wholly fused or confused with any other. There is not anything abstract about God's atti-tude toward men, but there is about Steinbeck's.

Also in *Burning Bright* there is on display Steinbeck's ten-dency to cause his characters to speak in bombast. This novel abounds in the most stilted, overblown, porous talk that a reader is likely to encounter anywhere. It is hardly more than an accumulation of big, empty words through which an aimless wind blows, making unintelligible noises. Here Steinbeck is manifesting his penchant for the amor-phous notion orotundly uttered. Imprecision in thinking is matched by imprecision in expression. The gutless abstrac-tion emerges as a vapor of speech.

This is the irony of John Steinbeck's work: that, in his concern for Manself and Life, he has dissolved both for want of exact and plenary knowledge of what they are. He who would affirm the dignity of man, deals that dignity a shattering blow by denying man the dimensions and the personality which alone confer a dignity that is intrinsic and not an accident of circumstance, the attributes of sovereign intellect and unforced free will which alone make man more than the beasts that perish. He who would extol Life and win its reverence, strips it of whatever differentiates it from mere biological existence. And yet, over and over again in Steinbeck's writing, there are crude intimations of something beyond what, when he is being definitive, he sets as the terms of man's being. One could wish that the novelist would rigorously examine these, for it is only from apprehension and appreciation of them that there can come the clarity and strength which his work lacks. (pp. 132-33)

The judgment one must pass on Steinbeck is this: that he is a sentimentalist. . . . [His sentimentality] is a way of regarding humanity, the way of feeling rather than of reason. "Steinbeck the realist" is a misnomer, for the flight from reason which, in common with so many of his contemporaries, he has indulged in, has prevented him from seeing reality as it is, in its entire fullness and proportioning and significance. (p. 134)

> *John S. Kennedy, "John Steinbeck: Life Affirmed and Dissolved," in* Fifty Years of the American Novel, *edited by Harold C. Gardiner, S.J. (abridged by permission of Charles Scribner's Sons; copyright © 1951 Charles Scribner's Sons), Scribner's, 1951 (and reprinted in* Steinbeck and His Critics: A Record of Twenty-five Years, *edited by E. W. Tedlock, Jr., and C. V. Wicker, University of New Mexico Press, 1957, pp. 119-34).*

T. A. SHIPPEY

It is when Steinbeck abandons caution [in *The Acts of King Arthur and His Noble Knights*] that he contributes most to the Arthurian tradition. In the early sections on Merlin, Balin and Balan, the feud with Morgan le Fay, he is often translating Malory closely. . . . As a result the modernisms show up.

The opening of the Arthurian story, though tidied and expounded, does not grip one's affections. When Malory starts to flag, however, Steinbeck takes over. The tale of Gawain, Ewain and Marhalt's involvement with the young, the old, and the middle-aged ladies is, in Malory, dull. Gawain shows the worst side of his character in philandering with Ettarde, Marhalt copes relaxedly with a giant, Ewain wins a two-against-one bout, and the ladies do nothing. To this Steinbeck adds suddenly and out of his own head the most compelling of twentieth-century thriller themes—professionalism, expertise, training. The elderly lady who takes Ewain over, it transpires, is the greatest coach there ever was, and she puts him through a crash course described in loving detail, wrinkle by wrinkle.

It is when his lady starts making remarks about weight and burst buttons that he sends for his questing gear. The effects are comic in detail, sombre in implication: distinctively of this century, and so in the spirit of all the other Arthurians who have, century by century, taken what significance they wanted from the matter they loved. It is only a pity that, having struck this vein, Steinbeck could take it no further than the end of "The Noble Tale of Sir Lancelot of the Lake." . . . Possibly the involved ironies and contending loyalties of the *Morte* would have defeated Steinbeck as they have other rehandlers. But the man who made George shoot Lenny might have coped even with Gawain's final letter to Lancelot. Or he might have left it out and told the story a new way.

> *T. A. Shippey, "East of Camelot," in* The Times Literary Supplement *(© Times Newspapers Ltd. (London) 1977; reproduced from* The Times Literary Supplement *by permission), April 29, 1977, p. 536.*

T

TENNANT, Emma   1937-

Tennant is a British novelist, critic, and editor. She has been involved in magazine publishing for a number of years, working on the editorial staff of such publications as *Queen*, *Vogue*, and *Bananas* (the literary magazine of the British Arts Council). (See also *Contemporary Authors*, Vols. 65-68.)

Perhaps [*The Time of the Crack*] isn't quite the short, sharp, entertaining novel we are all waiting for . . . , but it is certainly a step in the right direction. Short it certainly is, and rather amateurishly written . . . , but in a way this adds to its charm. Characterization is about on the level of *The Young Visitors*. Yet its merits far outweigh the minor faults.

A huge crack opens up in the bed of the Thames, separating London into two halves, leaving only the Playboy Club standing on the northern side; Lewis Carroll technique applied to H. G. Wells material. . . .

As a comic apocalypse this novel could hardly be bettered. It is very much a London book—a knowledge of the town and its geography helps a lot—but it does manage to say a few pertinent things about the society in which we live. As a first novel, too, it has a simplicity and enthusiasm that is often missing from the output of more professional writers of fiction. (p. 661)

> The Times Literary Supplement (© *Times Newspapers Ltd. (London), 1973; reproduced from* The Times Literary Supplement *by permission), June 15, 1973.*

YOLANTA MAY

With *The Last of the Country House Murders* we leave Life behind and begin to play the Tennant games. There is a strong Napoleonic streak in Miss Tennant, which first declared itself at the time of the crack and is now rampant once again: large armies sprout and march on; orders are expected and orders are issued; revolutions have taken place and others will follow. Whole galaxies have been swept off the skies with a few well-aimed sentences and now the Earth stands despondent and unaccompanied, but for the sun and the moon (a last-minute reprieve?), in the great chasm.

It is all, we look about apprehensively, a song of the Very Near Future. Persons like us, who only the other day were enjoying the twenties and the forties in the Orient Express, ornamental behind our famous Dorothy Lamour smiles, and resplendent underneath our Veronica Lake hair-styles, now shift our strangely diminished forms from one foot to the next, as we all jostle against others, similarly afflicted, on the great Salisbury plain. All of us, that is, except one Jules Tanner, a decadent whose head—red chignon piled high, Spanish comb—will roll shortly on the Aubusson carpet for the benefit of the dollar-bearing multitudes.

Miss Tennant has considerable, elegantly turned-out weapons at her disposal, only she will squander them on those armies. The visions of Borodino spring to the mind's eye. Also, the satirical possibilities of that central London group of equals have lost, we would have thought, their bloom some time ago. May they rest in peace! (p. 67)

> Yolanta May, in The New Review (© *TNR Publications, Ltd., London), March, 1975.*

VALENTINE CUNNINGHAM

Hotel de Dream is only hand-me-down Flann O'Brien, noticeably tireder than its master. The depressed gentlefolks of the grotty Westringham Hotel eagerly quit their pongy domicile . . . in rather obviously needful dreaming. The dreams' casts take to travelling from dream to dream and when a lady novelist arrives to complete her trilogy her characters pop in and out of both the real and dream life of the hotel. . . .

The only person Emma Tennant appears really to get into is a revolutionary whose Sixties career and politics she carefully describes but who is made to have precious little to do with the rest of the novel's doings. (p. 87)

> Valentine Cunningham, in New Statesman (© *1976 The Statesman & Nation Publishing Co. Ltd.), July 16, 1976.*

HARRIET WAUGH

In Emma Tennant's new novel, *Hotel de Dream*, the forces of reality and imagination are let loose on each other, and intermingle destructively; but then, just as the real world appears to be engulfed by the chaos of the overspilling dream world they are suddenly, and to my mind sadly, separated again into their component parts.

The centre of the action is a run-down boarding house, The

Westringham, presided over by a mean, decaying widow called Mrs Routledge who has fantasies of grandeur (she and the house could be said to represent England in her present parlous state). The house is inhabited by a collection of seedy, unhappy people who spend their nights and days in escaping reality by sleeping and dreaming. . . .

The skill of Miss Tennant's very enjoyable book, both in weaving . . . complex and different dimensional threads into one cohesive whole and in successfully making the reader part of this strange comic world, is enormous. My only niggling criticism, and that might well have more to do with my own rather prosaic and muddled mind than with the book, is that I failed to work out the different metaphysical interactions within the novel satisfactorily. The end seemed to imply a more simple structure than the middle and that I thought a pity. (p. 24)

> *Harriet Waugh, in* The Spectator (© *1976 by* The
> Spectator; *reprinted by permission of* The Specta-
> tor), *July 24, 1976.*

JAMES BROCKWAY

[Emma Tennant] has added another sample of her own brand of sci-fi fantasy to her first two, *The Time of the Crack* and *The Last of the Country House Murders*. Somewhere she has referred to her 'trilogy', so that *Hotel de Dream* may be intended as the last of her laughing-gas murders. Be that as it may, plenty of old English attitudes get murdered in this latest offering of hers and in her own wittily and elegantly lethal way too. Perhaps one needs to read the book more than once to catch the relevance of its satire on every point and to make up one's mind what it is really all about (apart from being a different way of writing a novel). On the surface at least, it is clear enough all the same.

Yet even if it weren't, the book's chief attractions would remain unimpaired: the agility and ebullience of the humour, the sense of the absurd in human beings—in most of us, at least, and in all the inmates of Mrs. Routledge's tatty boarding house in Kensington, her Hotel De Dream—and, best of all, the stylish verve of the writing.

Here the reader lives mainly in the dreams of the characters, but since this is a form of science fiction, dream life and waking life get muddled up, while the dreams of the various characters also start to invade one another. The opportunities this offers for satirical fun and fantasy are naturally as good as unlimited, but also the opportunities to build up fantastic scenes, settings and set pieces.

This Mrs Tennant achieves with great ease and gusto and especially with her chorus of giant female nudes caked with sand from the seashore—woman with a 'sense of collective will-power' which makes a mere male shudder—who at one point in her Miss Scranton's dream seem like nothing so much as all that pink flesh in Ingres's *Le bain turc* come to baleful, militant life.

There is imagination of a higher and subtler order in such scenes than in other more obvious, yet highly diverting, satirical dream situations. (pp. 40-1)

Mrs Tennant [also] invents another sort of dream—the novel as dream. For one of the occupants of the Westringham Hotel is a lady novelist (guess who?—your guess) who is having trouble with a couple of her characters. Indeed, *they* are having trouble with *her* and, impatient of her

arbitrary power over their movements and fate, plan to murder her.

This is really quite different satirical territory—less generalised—and it does not seem to fit in with the rest quite happily. I take this to be a fault, though a minor one, in a book which is otherwise written with the wit and expertise we have come to expect of Emma Tennant. I liked, too, the idea of the climax coming, as it should, before the end, although this may contribute to the novel's seeming a little less shapely than its forerunner and a little too long. For all that it is a mere 190 pages.

Does this novel amount to much more than an excellent example of contemporary cleverness? I don't think so. The fun here, however, is so intelligent and funny that one would be a fool to miss it. Mrs Tennant's book also contains reminders of modern man's and modern society's tendency to regress to infantility as did the two fantasies that went before it, and is accordingly a necessary warning. (p. 41)

> *James Brockway, in* Books and Bookmen (©
> *copyright James Brockway 1977; reprinted with
> permission), January, 1977.*

KARL MILLER

In Emma Tennant's *The Bad Sister*, gentlefolk are distressed when one of their number is put to death by his illegitimate daughter. Dependence on the fiction of the first Romantic period is in this case deliberate, explicit, and surprising. So far from shy is Emma Tennant that she has used as a model James Hogg's celebrated novel of 1824, *The Confessions of a Justified Sinner*. Hogg describes the ordeal of a fanatic, who, duped by antinomian Calvinism, by the teaching that those to whom God's grace has been given can do no wrong, anxiously aspires to a sense of infallibility, and falls into the "deep gulfs" reserved, in the poet Cowper's words, for God's castaway. . . . Emma Tennant writes about a modern fanaticism, a new infallibility. So far as execution or "finish" is concerned, objections can be pressed to what she does, but the strategy she has hit on for emulating the Ettrick Shepherd is ingenious and suggestive. (p. 25)

The Bad Sister resembles Hogg's novel in being, and in having to be, ideologically equivocal. Hogg, an admirer of the Covenanters, wrote, in the *Confessions*, what was taken to be an antipuritan work, an attack on the theology which had characterized, in later times, the sects who saw themselves as heirs to the Covenanters. As for Emma Tennant . . . ,she has written a book which could be taken to be an attack on feminist infallibility. . . . The *Confessions* can't have been liked by latterday Covenanters, the Wild, as they were eventually called, and Emma Tennant may have to justify herself before a court-martial of wild sisters. Her novel brings together romantic wildness and its opposites, and it is not the only novel . . . which does this. (p. 26)

> *Karl Miller, in* The New York Review of Books
> *(reprinted with permission from* The New York
> Review of Books; *copyright © 1978 Nyrev, Inc.),*
> *November 9, 1978.*

*   *   *

THOMAS, Audrey   1935-

An American-born Canadian novelist and short story writer,

Thomas has created psychologically complex feminine characters who have many biographical parallels with the author herself. Her narratives are kaleidoscopic and nonlinear but most critics agree that they maintain an artistic cohesiveness. Her latest novel is *Blown Figures*. (See also *CLC*, Vol. 7, and *Contemporary Authors*, Vols. 21-24, rev. ed.)

ANNE MONTAGNES

Audrey Thomas has made her bondage as daughter into an entire book [*Songs My Mother Taught Me*]. It is justifiable to describe it as Thomas' bondage, not that of a character: the heroine is called Isobel Cleary, but [the biographical details connect]. . . . (p. 46)

Warne, Isobel's father, an ardent Mason, a schoolteacher who puts on slang to gab with gas station attendants and the sellers of bait for the trout in his father-in-law's lake, is too improvident to look after his family without slipped twenties from his sister and an inherited house.

But it's more than Warne's improvidence that makes Clara Cleary, Isobel's mother, a screaming hysteric, a whiner, a fat eater of chocolates and reader of ladies' magazines on her bed. Clara depends on appearances. . . . Nonetheless, appearances don't retrieve for Clara the status she thinks she has lost in marriage with Warne. . . .

Clara despises Warne as a man, hints at unmentionable things he does in his handkerchiefs, says that Masons are all Mama's boys and perverts. Growing up between the two, the inadequate man and the compulsive angry woman —"Isobel, you're cold, your heart's a stone"—Isobel longs for love. What she finds, like so many of Atwood's women in fiction and poetry, . . . is sex. . . .

Thomas pulls back from a clear-cut message. Isobel is high on pain killers when she loses her virginity, and her final story, except for a summary reference to Alice and madness, is a sweet little memory of Harry [her grandfather]. It's as if she were trying to impose the shape of the conventional memoir over experience which proves that sex is the most important thing in life. Perhaps she looked for a new form because sex supreme was the message of two of her previous books. . . . She needn't have looked for a new form. A wiser, better balanced book would have come simply from measuring Clara's and Warne's accountability— the title points to Clara; daughters typically expect less from their fathers—to the one great good she found in life. (p. 47)

> Anne Montagnes, "The Bondage of the Daughter," in Saturday Night *(copyright © 1974 by Saturday Night), May, 1974, pp. 46-7.*

KAREN MULHALLEN

Songs My Mother Taught Me takes its title from a sentimental Victorian drawing room ballad. This seems appropriate for a portrait of a battered but charming adolescent girl who spends a great deal of time wallowing in selfish self-pity. There is, however, a courageousness about Isobel Cleary which engages the reader, in spite of the literary and nostalgic paraphernalia that surrounds her.

Occasionally one encounters a talented and evocative writer who does not trust her own talent. Audrey Thomas's fourth work is a novel marked by this kind of doubt. In a sense the novel is a regression for Mrs. Thomas. Each of her books flirts with the trendy, with the literary cliché. But

in the earlier books the use of Dante, Lewis Carroll, John Fowles, Shakespeare, Oscar Wilde, Borges, is integrated into the atmospheric conditions which prevail in the mind of the narrator. In *Songs My Mother Taught Me* an unacknowledged and inappropriate quotation from Yeats' *Lapis Lazuli* initiates the reader into the novel's two parts: Songs of Innocence and Songs of Experience. The novel neither portrays a journey from Innocence to Experience nor shows, as did Blake, two contrary states—unless a summer retreat in the mountains and a suburban madhouse be acceptable substitutes for interior landscapes.

Ostensibly the novel is a *bildungsroman* charting Isobel's growth to womanhood. Since Isobel herself remains fixed, the novel fails on its first premise. Moreover, the two direct addresses to the reader within the story and the splitting of the central persona between "I" and "Isobel" fail to convince us that the novel is an ironic exploration of the author's own childhood.

What *is* important about this novel is not only the superb rendering of the female consciousness which slides equally over people and objects alike but also the fleeting world of grotesques which passes before the heroine's eyes. In particular, the sister Jane, whom Isobel says she never knew but calls vulgar nonetheless, the worn and frantic mother, the mad old ladies in the asylum, rejects from a world less honest than their own, all have a vitality beyond their context. The men in the novel too threaten at any moment to become characters rather than caricatures who exist only as monolithic material for the heroine. . . . (pp. 18-19)

One would hope that Mrs. Thomas will bring us back to this world, hampered neither by the nostalgia of David Harum sundaes and strapless evening gowns, nor the deflections of Yeats and Blake. Her minute and introspective gifts bear watching. Perhaps the Canadian audience which Audrey Thomas desires will encourage her to present such characters again with a more mature persona and less fanfare. (p. 19)

> *Karen Mulhallen, in* The Canadian Forum, *May-June, 1974.*

GEORGE BOWERING

Stories written by Audrey Thomas tell about things happening to one, & the condition of that one, a person very much alone in the world. She is a child alone in an ugly & baffling world of adults, she is a North American woman alone in a bungalow in West Africa or in a museum in Mexico, she is a virgin far from home, bare naked in a college dorm on the North Sea. She is usually trapt alone in the self, resentful or fearful of failing at her role somewhere in society, an identity thrust at her out of the dark. If anything may be said to be Audrey Thomas' consistent theme, it is private fear. For Thomas it is in that context that events happen to the point-of-view character. . . .

In her writing Audrey Thomas has proceeded from an early portrayal thru psychological realism of her Alice [in Wonderland] character in herself baffled & angered by the outside world & its failure to accommodate her inside world, to either (1) a fiction that puts the reader in Alice's position (see *Blown Figures*), or (2) stories in which the point-of-view character gains a kind of strength by observing that other people too have their confusion, desperation & failures (see 'A Monday Dream at Alameda Park' or 'Initram'). (p. 29)

Audrey Thomas has publisht around twenty stories & I dont believe that she has ever publisht one that did not contain a discussion of private fears. The first two stories of *Ten Green Bottles* . . . cut time athwart as academy short stories are supposed to do, detailing the thoughts of a woman during two events at which time stands still & proves itself: a miscarried childbirth, & the funeral of a college friend & secret lover. . . .

['If One Green Bottle'] is presented as internal speech, between ellipses that represent birth contractions or catchings of breath, in one woman's present tense. No other characters arrive, save in memories recounted. We are privy to a free association of [the archetypal character] Isobel's isolation & her learning to be alone in childhood, a favorite time for the thoughts of Thomas characters. (p. 30)

In 'Still Life with Flowers' she feels a sinking to minus-one, the body & absence of the loved one, of course, & her own loneness among these others attending the funeral. Her secret & her secret detachment make her feel like an uninvited guest at a party. The others in the car she rides to the graveyard are school fellows, but are in this present become strangers.

We are given childhood memories again, playing of 'Dead Man's Body,' that scary game in the dark, where one is the isolated victim, of looking at sleeping parents & fearing that for this time they arent there. So she is afraid to look at the dead youth's body, embarrassed at her own presumptiveness should she spy on him who can not look back or even know that she is watching. This seems to me to be clear projection, & a good counterpiece to the terror of personal disappearance in the first story.

Stylistically, this second story seems more interesting than the first. It starts in the third person, but persists in falling more & more frequently into the first person, back inside where the panic can be contained or at least concentrated. The disappearance into the first person seems well to augment the sense of embarrassment & timidity in the fearful young woman. (We will see that in the later stories, of women moving with some courage into the external world, a greater reliance on the third-person narrative, or first-person account of another person's actions.) A third-person narrative allows a reader to stand beside the narrator, sharing the view. A first-person narrative makes the reader the second person, & thus creates a distance desired by the character who would protect her uncertainties from the world. (pp. 30-1)

Audrey Thomas & Africa have, of course, become associated in the minds of readers, not only of the novels, but also of her stories. In [a] *Capilano Review* interview Thomas said that she likes to tell her stories of Americans or Canadians set down in an alien culture so that their problems will appear more starkly. In 'Xanadu,' for instance, we get a somewhat sarcastic portrait of a wife & mother who feels those positions threatened by the male African housekeeper who does the jobs more efficiently than she does. (pp. 31-2)

The same woman is sorely tried in her role-confidence in a story called 'One is One and all Alone,' a number that can be worse, & perversely better, than the zero after the last bottle. Again we see the white wife in Africa, trapt alone in the self, insecure about her role in the family. She is presented as neurotically afraid of the responsibility laid upon

her when her husband goes up-country for several days. In this instance the fear is complicated by a particular kind of guilt. She sees that she inherited the habit of her timidity from her mother, who kept her 'always safe—and always afraid.' Now she fears also passing her habitual anxieties to her daughters. Even her fantasy of suicide is rejected because of her fear of shame (or embarrassment again) that would be laded onto her surviving family.

In the Thomas repertoire this story is perhaps the widest examination of the varieties of fear—we get a thunderstorm, a dentist's appointment, the embarrassment of falling to pieces in public—& a stream of symbols, such as ground-fogs, crackt sculptures, a safe Victorian doll's-house, & so on. But running thru the tests we become aware of another element that seems crucial. That is a hatred. The question is whether the hatred of her own fear will lead toward self-hatred or toward a strength that will defeat the neurosis. Correctly, this story does not so quickly resolve the question. At the end the woman faints in the dentist's office, thus becoming as uncomplicated as she believes the lives of others to be. It will be left to the later stories to see thru the right side of that one-way mirror. (p. 32)

'A Winter's Tale' is the strongest story in the collection. It is not so much a story as a history, really a departure toward the novels; it is a plunge into time, & a long space away from the first two stories. At the same time, it is the most interesting story in the book because what happens to the central figure is the passing of a door thru her; simply, she loses her girlhood & becomes a woman, joining the largest crowd of all. (p. 33)

['Salon des Refusés'] concerns life & death in a steel building for mentally defective old women. There is no central character at odds with the world & afraid of it. Everyone is in here together, the 'patients,' the trusties, the nurses, the orderlies. There is even some scary stuff for the reader, as for instance an undescribed amputation carried in a wrapper by an orderly at lunchtime. Everyone here is pictured as alone together, in a defensive community, handling fear with fantasy or with cruel humour, possible alternatives for Audrey Thomas the writer, too. We are told in various ways that this is the world, not simply imagined fears of the neurotic loner. Nurse Primrose says that a wife's job is just like hers. (p. 34)

The story acts as a nice comment upon the previous nine. It externalizes the terrible while showing it in terms of people who withdraw into their private paranoias. (pp. 34-5)

The stories publisht since *Ten Green Bottles* are clearly treatments of the private fears & associated neuroses felt by people no longer green. Experience & middle age require a treatment different from the narrative in the first book. Thomas the novelist is now no less autobiographical, but in her stories she has been shopping around for a variety of approaches. Two stories, 'Aquarius' & 'A Monday Dream at Alameda Park,' propose days in the lives of two university professors newly arrived at middle age, & married to women who are or seem to be much younger, physically more energetic, curious, sexy & strong. Most importantly, from the angle of the nervous academics, they seem to be without fear. . . .

Common to both stories is the male figure who had been for years out of touch with his body, until led out of sexual timidity by the young woman. Also common is the humiliation felt by the man whose body can not keep up with the curious energy of that woman figure. (p. 35)

Thomas has mentioned (in the *Capilano Review* interview) that she was first driven to write because she was 'small and shy and unconfident.' The writing was to make her 'large, non-shy and unconfident.' Then the words on the page were supposed to 'make some kind of order out of the chaos that my life was.' She also mentioned that one of her reasons for interest in the African experience is that Africans have ceremonies to get them thru times of fear, death, *etc.*; & because we dont, we become neurotic. So the ceremony becomes writing of stories. A common ceremonial procedure is to switch roles, poor become rich for a day, people become animals, animals become spirits. So those two stories in which the Thomas point-of-view character becomes older male looking at younger female. If it works it must be true, or at least of interest—one examines the important possibility of male insecurity, or one sees that the fear, while it may have just about everything to do with sex, has little to do with gender.

In any case, Thomas workt the vein longer than that, giving us one story of older woman & younger man ('Green Stakes for the Garden') & one story of older woman & younger woman ('Rapunzel'). (pp. 35-6)

'Kill Day on the Government Wharf' offers [a] variation on the [theme of the] mother & the young sexy man. This time she is pregnant, & proud of her ability to cope with the exigencies of survival in a cottage on a Gulf island, looking to her husband, simply 'strong and self-reliant and almost pretty.' Her child, she finds, is afraid of the dark, & she learns that her sturdy husband was afraid of the dark as a child, as was she. This is no longer the world of frightened Isobel *versus* self-assured family & neighbours. On visiting the wharf where the cod are being eviscerated, walking on the slippery wood, among still-beating heards & other gurry, **a** Mrs. surrounded by blood, she feels a little giddy, but presumptous rather than afraid, more thrilled than upset by the shiny ritual of death & food. Here the narration describes for us the change our Thomas woman has gone thru as she has learned to identify herself with the world:

> A year ago she felt, the whole scene would have sickened her—now, in a strange way, she understood and was part of it. Crab-like, she could feel a new self forming underneath the old, brittle, shell—could feel herself expanding, breaking free.

One is invited to draw comparisons with the frightened pregnant woman surrounded by blood & all alone, in the African hospital. (p. 37)

The mirror . . . is the frame of reference for 'Initram,' [a story] . . . somehow an opposite & development from the earliest stories. If the central character, she who is 'happened to,' of the first stories is Alice down the rabbit hole, this later one is Alice thru the looking glass. What she sees may be reverst & hence enough different to be seen with some objectivity, but it has to be in front of her eyes an image of herself, a picture to reflect upon. The title is 'Martini' written backward, & points to the ugly centre of the plot, simply enough for any reader to spell out.

The story begins as that other pivotal one, 'A Winter's Tale,' did, with a mature discussion of the story-teller's act, here a sly reference to the back yard story [of 'Green Stakes for the Garden'], hence gathering up the steps leading, story-by-story, to this one, or at least inviting us readers to do so. The writer says that the 'terrible' liar she is can convert a bothersome stranger into someone 'sinister, menacing, unpleasant.' But, she says, when moments of great archetypal truth appear (those moments when ceremony is appropriate to sanity, remember), the person simply wants to act as medium, let the world tell its true story thru her. So, perversely, she decided to tell her story to a fellow story-teller, a short-story writer who lives on a different island. (pp. 37-8)

There is . . . something brave about the obvious *conte-à-clef* quality of this story. The description of Lydia's career leaves no doubt as to the model. And while Thomas' earlier protagonist used to make literary allusions to her sophomore literature reading list, this one reports that upon arriving at her 'sister's' place she said, 'listen, I've got something I want to tell you,' only to be told, 'I've got something I want to tell you too.' Thomas is declaring a strength, a lack of fear in confronting the real, Alice is saying look, we have come thru. If one passes thru the looking glass perhaps things are no longer backward, & the once-backward girl is perhaps 'small and shy and unconfident' no longer. If I am playing with words, what the hell is Initram?

Audrey Thomas, in her stories as well as in her most recent novel, is saying that art does not mirror life. Perhaps life mirrors our life. The narrator of 'Initram' has broken thru into the real, no more dreams & nightmares. She says that she has an Indian wool spinner in her cottage, indigenous, not a 'fairytale spinner' (one of Thomas' inevitable puns), & now 'nothing for a Sleeping Beauty to prick her finger on.' (pp. 38-9)

> George Bowering, "Snow Red: The Short Stories
> of Audrey Thomas" (originally a speech delivered
> to the University of Ottawa conference on the
> Canadian short story in November, 1975), in Open
> Letter (copyright © 1976 by Frank Davey; re-
> printed by permission of the author), Summer,
> 1976, pp. 28-39.

B. GODARD

The ostensible subject matter of Audrey Thomas' book is familiar to her readers. Like many of her short stories, *Blown Figures* explores the blurred edges of sanity and madness; its protagonist Isobel, relives the experiences of Mrs. Blood, returning to Africa in search of the child she had miscarried there five years earlier. This journey into the past to face its horrors and bury its corpses is a familiar literary convention. But there is nothing reassuring about Thomas' handling of it just as there is nothing comforting in the landmarks of the story. Blown Figures, the title, refers as much to the effect on the reader as it does to the treatment of the subject and the structure of the book.

Rarely have I encountered a book which 'blew my mind' in quite this way. Most mothers will share Isobel's death obsessions as she remembers her miscarriage, its blood imagery adding to the cannibalistic images associated with the still-born child. But the disturbing quality of this book lies not in the narrative, but rather in what Thomas does not say. In her silences.

Let me explain. The most notable feature of the physical

book and the heart of its meaning lie in its blank pages. Sometimes a whole page is blank, others are only partly white. But as in music, these pauses are as important as the notes sounded. John Cage has explained that 'there is no such thing as silence. (; . . .) If we stop talking we will hear many sounds that you didn't intend. (. . .) The two sounds I hear are the functioning of the nervous system, and the sound of blood circulating; you don't hear the beat of your own heart, just the flow of the blood.' And in *Blown Figures* the blood flowing is not Isobel's, but ours spilling over the white pages, where the book really happens. Where Thomas' story stops and ours begins is hard to tell, for by the end, the reader, like Isobel, is working with more than two minds. . . . Just as we question the reality of Isobel's journey to Africa—is this dark continent a dream or a metaphor?—so too we reflect on our experience reading the book. Is it composed of our reverie, or is the blown figure a metaphor for chaos? Or is it all these at once. (p. 81)

There is no return to light, no spiritual growth as a result of this journey, only further fear and guilt and fragments. Is this voyage a purely psychic one made on the analyst's couch? This question eventually drifts to the surface.

Now, I think this is a possible answer. When I first read the novel, however, I was convinced that the narrative mode was similar to one used by Michel Butor in *La modification,* also written in the vocative. The 'Miss Miller' to whom Isobel's comments are addressed was just a name and seemed eventually to become merged with the reader in that intimate relationship with the author established as well through the white pages. Thomas' use of the cartoons, dictionary definitions, newspapers and letters seemed to create a leitmotiv of the act of reading making us aware that here too we are learning to read, to interpret, as we are in *La modification.* The greater openness of form of *Blown Figures* invites many more possible readings of the book. Here though, lies the true subject of the book, the creative act taking place in our minds. Michel Leiris' comment on *La modification* is true of *Blown Figures* as well: 'the baroque architecture of this book opens perspectives to infinity'. We must make the descent into hell along with Isobel. Like her we may well become lost in the labyrinth, changing our direction constantly as our expectations drift. The 'blown figures' may well be we, the readers.

This, as I suggested, was my original reading of the book, seeing the centre in the creative act of the reader induced by the appeal to us, stepping into Miss Miller's shoes. Now I believe the book is about the miscarriage of creation, a story of dispossession. Accidentally, I discovered that Jung in *Symbols of Transformation* wrote up the amnesiac fantasies of a 'Miss Miller,' an American who had travelled much through Europe and Africa, a person of unusual capacity for identification and empathy—a most suitable object for Isobel's address in her own disturbed state. Miss Miller, then, is something more than a name, something more than the 'you' with whom the reader identifies. Someone whose wanderings have been analyzed, she becomes a symbol of that analyzing and organizing force taking over Isobel's experience and turning it into narrative. . . .

Miss Miller is the one addressed, not the narrator. She is that aspect of Isobel most subject to control. Throughout the novel the reader is sent from one facet of Isobel to an opposing one, from order to chaos, in that 'baroque architecture' which refuses fixed points preferring dialectic, con-

tinually sending us back from Miss Miller to Isobel's fragments. *Blown Figures* marks a radical shift in Audrey Thomas' work away from the psychological explorations of her earlier fiction into the company of such surrealists as Butor, Leiris, Ferron, exploring through their fiction its basic elements, language and form. (p. 82)

> *B. Godard, "Dispossession," in* Open Letter *(copyright © 1976 by Frank Davey; reprinted by permission of the author), Summer, 1976, pp. 81-2.*

* * *

THOMAS, D(onald) M(ichael)   1935-

Thomas is a British poet, editor, critic, and translator who is known for his early science fiction poetry. He has broadened his range of topics, although he focuses on what he considers to be core subjects, sex and death. (See also *Contemporary Authors*, Vols. 61-64.)

MICHAEL MOTT

Two Voices by D. M. Thomas is at least two collections in one. The confusion is made the worse by the intrusive cover-photographs, clichés of the 1930's *avant garde,* which would be plain ugly in any period.

The long science-fiction poems in the early part of the book have a sort of ghost-written effect, but the interest comes and goes. Things improve with a number of shorter poems like *The Head-Rape,* a horror poem, but at least a convincing one, still in the science-fiction genre, and *Wolfbane,* which ends in a masterly fashion, with the mind of the witchgirl "under him / turned away / loping / into snowy / darkness".

But it is the *Requiem for Aberfan* that makes this collection memorable. (pp. 113-14)

D. M. Thomas is, on the whole, scrupulous in allowing us to draw our own dark questions from the way in which he describes the disaster. The detail is vividly rendered. The cruel shock waves run out in all directions from the main center of violence. (p. 114)

> *Michael Mott, in* Poetry *(© 1971 by The Modern Poetry Association; reprinted by permission of the Editor of* Poetry*), May, 1971.*

ALAN BROWNJOHN

Love and Other Deaths: you can take the choice. I don't feel that D. M. Thomas, a poet of ranging and fertile imagination, has yet settled for what he really wants, but at least [this] largish collection provides plenty to choose from. I'll take, not the sci-fi verse or mythological excursions which blend with it, but those compassionate, discerning, well-made poems 'of death and loss' which are closer to his personal concerns; especially 'Dream', and 'Reticent', about the gentle power of understatement on the lips of his dead parents. 'Dream' allows Thomas to use an experimental, disjointed form to excellent effect without dispersing the emotion in gimmickry; it is absolutely unforced, true and moving. (p. 60)

> *Alan Brownjohn, in* New Statesman *(© 1975 The Statesman & Nation Publishing Co. Ltd.), July 11, 1975.*

ALASDAIR MACLEAN

D. M. Thomas has divided [*Love and Other Deaths*] into

parts. The first contains more or less traditional poems dealing with family deaths. Often moving and sometimes quite good as well, they partly redeem the horror that comes after. Even here, . . . obligatory modishness creeps in with its spoiling hand. In "Dream", for example, we get a reference to "my woman", a phrase that has come to rank almost with the ampersand as a species marker. But "my woman" is phoney working-class realism, a doubtful memory of a vanished solidarity. And what follows shows the author in familiar vein, boldly going where fifty thousand little magazine contributors have gone before. British "experimental" poetry, in other words, with neither grace nor imagination nor humour nor skill to recommend it. It does not even shock. And it is about as experimental as the wheelbarrow. (p. 866)

Alasdair Maclean, in The Times Literary Supplement *(© Times Newspapers Ltd. (London) 1975; reproduced from* The Times Literary Supplement *by permission), August 1, 1975.*

JOHN MATTHIAS

There are always plenty of paramours in D. M. Thomas's work, and one must respect, if even at a certain hesitant distance, his nervous, experimental, and erotic muse. . . . Thomas is at it again [in *Love and Other Deaths*], what with three erotic sequences here, one based on the *I Ching*, another on the figure of Eve's apocryphal rival, Lilith, and the third on what he calls "a central contemporary myth: the kidnapping of a diplomat by extremists." I'm afraid I'm not very enthusiastic about any of them. It sometimes looks, especially in the case of poor Lil, as if Crazy Jane had been knocked up by Hughes's Crow, the unlikely issue having been midwifed by Nathaniel Tarn's Bride of God and Brother Antoninus working together. . . . Peter Porter has said, a propos of something else, "Nothing is worse than the man who pretends to be a ferocious Savonarola when really underneath he's just a fun-loving monk." Though we know there *is* something worse—namely, the Savonarola who pretends to be a fun-loving monk—any confusion of the two is distracting, and there is something of both in Thomas when he writes these erotic poems. Still, the first half of *Love and Other Deaths* has to do, not with the traditional erotic pun, but with the other deaths, and one can admire poems like *Cecie, The Journey, Rubble,* and *Dream* while not much liking some of the poems which follow. In general, I think Thomas is at his best both in this book and in his previous volume, *Logan Stone,* when he writes poems deriving from his family experience and his search for roots in Cornwall. (pp. 354-55)

John Matthias, in Poetry *(© 1977 by The Modern Poetry Association; reprinted by permission of the Editor of* Poetry*), March, 1977.*

PETER SCUPHAM

The mysterious privacy to be found in [the various landscapes of *The Honeymoon Voyage*] is one the poet shares with those divine and human presences who, whether rooted or in exile, define the numen of their homes and in collusion with their recorder allow the reader to participate in their own myths. In this sense Thomas is one of the least egocentric of writers, concerned to feel his way through self-effacements into the disturbing otherness of worlds where ancestral voices speak in their allusive tongues while he holds seance. . . .

The title poem sends the collection into a new direction, and possibly the least successful one. From our homes we make voyages into death and pain; the traverse is made through a dragging erotic sea, and the verse slips and sways towards its unconcluded ends. Syntax loosens; the cadences are held on light reins. Reason clouds, and the poems drift between sleep and wake, life and death. . . .

Thomas's concern is with the exchange of dreams, his work has the richness conferred by a temperament impatient of division and boundary. He works towards unity, towards removing the "perhaps" from the final stanza of "Stone":

> There is also the seventh book,
>   perhaps, the seventh,
> And called *The Seventh Book*
>   because it is not published.
> The one that a child thinks he
>   could have written,
> Made of the firmest stone and
>   clearest leaves,
> That a people keep alive by, keep
>   alive.

Peter Scupham, "Other Voices, Other Worlds," in The Times Literary Supplement *(© Times Newspapers Ltd. (London) 1978; reproduced from* The Times Literary Supplement *by permission), June 30, 1978, p. 728.*

*   *   *

THOMAS, R(onald) S(tuart)   1913-

A Welsh poet and a clergyman, Thomas writes in English of his rural parishioners and their somber homeland. The ordinary and bleak are made universal and tragic by his austere and passionate concern. (See also *CLC*, Vol. 6.)

W. MOELWYN MERCHANT

The poetry of R. S. Thomas conveys the prime impression of a single force directed to one carefully limited theme, the isolation of the natural rhythm of man's life ("Rhythm of the long scythe") in the natural order, seen with irony, occasional bitterness, with urbane control of word and metric, and a tautness of mind, the fruit of a particular urbanity. Indeed, there is especial irony in attributing this urbane quality to a poet who so passionately repudiates the urban.

For all the complexity of Thomas's tone and attitudes, it seemed that his craft had declared itself in full stature in the first volume, *The Stones of the Field,* in 1946, and then for nine years, through *An Acre of Land* (1952), the long broadcast poem, *The Minister* (1953) to the first collected edition, *Song at the Year's Turning* in 1955, had done no more than amplify the few original themes, turning them over, handling them with the deftness of a surgeon, revealing a few more strands of their texture but demonstrating no conspicuously new powers. And we should have been quite content with another thirty years of this detached compassion, united to a self-critical craftmanship as great as any shown in English verse to-day. But *Poetry for Supper,* published in 1958, and the few poems that have appeared in the journals since, are different in tone and range from the earlier works. The same subjects are treated and with the same attitudes, but the emotional range has greatly increased; the ironic comment has deepened (and with a lancing bitterness rarely heard before), while the compassion is wider. Above all R. S. Thomas has become more explicit in statement; while he forces no acceptable conclusion, makes no assumption of dogma, the credal implications always present in his work are now less allusive in statement. (p. 341)

No more than the rest of us who spoke two languages from our infancy has Thomas been able to escape the tensions of a minority culture; his integrity has always forced him to see the burden and to refrain from using the 'Welshness' as a saleable asset, but it has not before "A Welsh Testament" been expressed with such unsentimental clarity which sets aside both deprecation and pride:

> All right, I was Welsh; does it matter?
> I spoke the tongue that was passed on
> To me in the place I happened to be.

There are alienations within and without: within, of the stultifying Puritanism which crams God "Between the boards of a black book"; without, of the curious tourist gaze. . . . The alien demand, "You are Welsh, they said; Speak to us so," emphasises the exhibit status of the "rare portrait by a dead master" until the "museum" of his setting, the theatrical rôle. . . . Yet though the label has been repudiated, the fact has always been totally accepted, the dual ministry of parson-poet to a Welsh country community. (pp. 341-42)

The themes now expressed with such tautness have been present from the beginning. The titles of the first two volumes of his verse imply the most constant tension in his work, the gulf which separates the clerisy and the peasant. The first title (*The Stones of the Field*) adopts the core of Job's awareness, through his dereliction, of unity with subhuman creation: "for thou shalt be in league with the stones of the field", a community, even a complicity with the harshnesses which condition the life of his rural community. The second title quotes the sixteenth-century poet, Siôn Tudur [concerning] . . . dependence on that acre of land . . . which Thomas in his pastoral ministry knows to be the foundation (all too often the bed-rock) of his parishioners' lives. With few exceptions, this is the terrain to which he confines his poetry, an even sharper limitation than that self-imposed by Wordsworth or Robert Frost. Within this accepted limitation he works out the rhythms of the Church's sacraments and the dumb rejection by the peasant of all the grace and art with which the poet-priest confronts him.

It would be convenient—and absurd—to describe the relation between priest and peasant in these poems as 'ambivalent', absurd because there are no simple antitheses in these poems, of pastoral acceptance over against disgust and rejection. The poems would be dramatically interesting if this antithesis were their mainspring. But if an 'attitude' is to be defined here at all, it is of total acceptance, recording grace and shame in the lives of his parishioners, with the understanding, neutral charity and compassion of a confessor; yet more active than a confessor's, who channels grace, himself not necessarily more moved than a catalyst. (pp. 342-43)

The union of harsh understanding and ironic compassion in *The Stones of the Field* had, in *An Acre of Land*, crystallised out into separate components (perhaps the source of the second volume's success—the disparate elements were more comprehensible than the integrity of their jarring union). There is certainly a growing awareness of the nature

of his pastoral concern as an Anglican priest in the Welsh hill-country. His priest's vocation is never obtruded in the verse; there is rarely a theological statement in his writing, but I doubt if the verse would exist at all—it would certainly not have this ascetic spareness—but for his cure of souls. The essential document is the early poem, "A Priest to his People". . . . The relationship implied [in this poem] has room for neither sentimental hatred nor for facile admiration—nor even for the neutrality of tolerance. . . . [The] priest's condemnation of his "curt and graceless" people nonetheless acquiesces in the pagan substratum of their strength. . . . For all its complexity, this poem read in isolation is only a partial statement of his priestly concern. It has to be read with the later "Death of a Peasant":

> You remember Davies? He died, you know
> With his face to the wall, as the manner is
> Of the poor peasant in the stone croft
> On the Welsh hills

and with the two poems, "Country Church" and "In a Country Church", separated by many years of writing. The first church, Manafon, the place of his ministry at the writing of *The Stones of the Field*, is realised as a stone chalice or font:

> The church stands, built from the river stone,
> Brittle with light, so that a breath could shatter
> Its slender frame, or spill the limpid water,
> Quiet as sunlight, cupped within the bone.

The manner of this well-wrought conceit, admirable in its repose, is almost wholly lacking in the mature spirituality of the later poem. To the worshipper kneeling in this country church no word came in the presence of the "grave saints, rigid in glass"; but, wordless, this country worshipper has his dream of the rood:

> Was he balked by silence? He kneeled long
> And saw love in a dark crown
> Of thorns blazing, and a winter tree
> Golden with fruit of a man's body.

This is the same vision, but seen after the Deposition in the presence of the hills which "crowd the horizon" in the more recent poem "Pieta" (published in *The Listener* but not yet collected):

> And in the foreground
> The tall Cross,
> Sombre, untenanted,
> Aches for the Body
> That is back in the cradle
> Of a maid's arms,

a conjunction of moments compassed rarely, and, in painting rendered with this complexity only in Bellini's companion pieces of Nativity and Pieta. The hills of the poem's opening lines are, I suspect Welsh, not Palestinian in form, and the affirmations, even the revulsions, in Thomas's work become more than ever wedded to a passionate but unillusioned concern for Wales. . . . "The Welsh Hill Country" is no tourist's paradise . . . and there is sharp rejection of the nonconformist-druid romanticism, the Eisteddfod's bogus compensation for the loss of liturgy and rite, which is our inept reply to the tragedy which Thomas declares in *The Minister.* . . . (pp. 345-48)

Poetry for Supper gathers all the earlier speaking-tones in an authoritative maturity. The perspective is widened to take pride in "Athens, Florence"... . He is now relaxed enough to talk of his craft; in the earliest poems there was constant alertness and a disconcerting shift of reference and tone . . . , but his craftsmanship is now a matter of meditation, or moral choice, which can include condemnation of the poetaster as his only epitaph. . . . (p. 348)

R. S. Thomas is (always has been) classical, sophisticated, ironically aware of a European culture counter-posed against the peasant who is his pastoral care. Yet Iago Prytherch, all inarticulate, is seen as a possible companion for Kant. . . . The final relationship is reserved for one of the closing poems, "Absolution", in which the rôles of peasant and priest are reversed: "Prytherch, man, can you forgive?" The poet . . . , having experienced the peasant's endurance, receives his 'absolution',

> With the slow lifting up of your hand
> No welcome, only forgiveness. . . .

["The Country Clergy" reveals] an equal compassion for the priest in his spiritual isolation, and, taking death seriously, for the peasant and the sophisticate, tumbled into a common grave. The poem moves to a serene close, content with no immediate understanding of the priest's fulfilment, for

> . . . God in his time
> Or out of time will correct this.

The final concern of . . . *Poetry for Supper*, is not in fact for work and its results and rewards, but rather for direct affirmation. In the fragment of an allegory, "The Journey" there are encounters with those "whose eyes declare: There is no God" and with those of the same creed, "whose hands are waiting for your hand". The poem concludes not with any concern for doing, for consolation or attempt to convince.

> But do not linger,
> A smile is payment; the road runs on
> With many turnings towards the tall
> Tree to which the believer is nailed.

The strenuous intelligence of this parson-poet would appear to have a suitable point of rest in that closing identification of the believer with the crucified Christ; it would be dangerous in fact to expect any point of rest at this moment in the work of an exploratory mind which is as astringent in renouncing easy attitudes for itself as it is compassionately ruthless in analysing his neighbours. (pp. 348-51)

> *W. Moelwyn Merchant, "R. S. Thomas," in* Critical Quarterly, *Winter, 1960, pp. 341-51.*

PETER WASHINGTON

[*Laboratories of The Spirit*] has that rare combination of personal honesty and high artistic achievement which isn't so common: even the best "confessional" verse is, by its nature, often more than a little dishonest. And a poetry which consists so largely of statement refuses critical comment. Insofar as Thomas's book has a dominating theme it is formulated at once in the opening lines:

> Not as in the old days I pray,
> God. My life is not what it was.

The style says everything here, its sparseness allowing every nuance to register. The poet speaks of himself but he addresses his maker—and God the Creator plays the largest role in this book. When Thomas mentions a place explaining that:

> I often call there.
> There are no poems in it
> for me. . . .

The statement bears its weight of meaning exactly; in a brief poem we learn about a whole way of responding. Everything holds—evil is not outside, it is part:

> There is no meaning in life,
> Unless men can be found to reject love.

However we feel about Thomas's version of it, we recognise a central truth in his work: that life, however appalling is whole, is unified. . . . [This] is a marvellous book. (p. 602)

> *Peter Washington, in* The Spectator *(© 1975 by* The Spectator; *reprinted by permission of* The Spectator), *November 8, 1975.*

ANNE STEVENSON

R. S. Thomas is a religious poet, but what gives power to his writing is not his faith, but his fight to keep that faith alive. He is a modern puritan, with a gift for spiritual drama. He sees tragedy, not pathos, in the human condition, even now. He is one of the rare poets writing today who never asks for pity.

For these reasons, R. S. Thomas's poems have a flinty edge —an arrogance, even—that will not be popular with the sentimental. The evil that man has brought about on earth is part of the 'mixed things' of his making. 'I let you go,' God says in one poem, after having created the human hand, 'but without blessings.'

Thomas can be crabbedly ungenerous. Nevertheless, those contemporary poets Thomas unfairly mocks in his poem, 'Taste' [from *Laboratories of the Spirit*]—'the congestion at the turnstile of fame'—ought to be more in awe of him than they are. For R. S. Thomas has hammered strong poems out of granite while most of them have been experimenting with clay. (p. 484)

> *Anne Stevenson, in* The Listener *(© British Broadcasting Corp. 1976; reprinted by permission of Anne Stevenson), April 15, 1976.*

EMMA FISHER

R. S. Thomas's ['Frequencies'] continues to wrestle with the paradox of his need for God and the impossibility of knowing or accepting him. Or perhaps wrestling is the wrong word for poems as clear, steady and well made as these. 'Frequencies' suggests wave-bands, searching for a radio station through static; his images are often scientific, as cells and chromosomes and electrons represent both the anti-God advances of reason, and the perfection of design which implies God. One image constantly recurring is the mirror; in his last book, *Laboratories of the Spirit*, it sometimes reflected what he sought. . . . Through the poems we also see his seldom-full church, friends and parishioners, the stones and sea of Wales, history and a bleak future; Christ appears less than before. Thomas is not a poet who would . . . airily use 'bloodstream' in a poem mentioning Christ and mean nothing in particular by it. Every image counts, and he often manages to convey with amazing lucidity and strength the possibility of faith and honesty coexisting in a rational man. (p. 24)

Emma Fisher, in The Spectator (© *1978 by* The Spectator; *reprinted by permission of* The Spectator), *April 1, 1978.*

JOHN MOLE

The poems [in *Frequencies*] have become a cumulative succession of brief, intense engagements between need and silence; again and again they attempt an imaginative synthesis of "the interior / that calls", "the verbal hunger / for the thing in itself" and "untenanted space", "the darkness between stars".

As for Eliot, whose "vacant interstellar spaces" R. S. Thomas's universe recalls, "each venture is a new beginning" and a central theme of *Frequencies* is the inadequacy and failure of vocabularies. . . .

Frequencies is a profound collection with a beautiful gravity of utterance capable of absorbing its intermittent lapses into portentousness and abstraction. R. S. Thomas's strength has always been in his deployment of metaphor, and when he relies on plain statements of position he can teeter on the brink of the absurd. . . . As always there is a suspicion that some of the characteristic neat encapsulations come a trifle too easily ("time's face", "the mind's shelf", "the mind's tools", etc. though there are far fewer of them than in the earlier work), and there is also the sermonizing tendency to point up analogies. In "Fishing", for example, although there is some marvellous imagery ("the hook gleams / the smooth face creases in an obscene / grin") it is cramped by an explanatory framework: "Often it seems it is for more than fish / that we seek." But these are small faults to set beside R. S. Thomas's power, at his best, to involve his reader, passionately, in the riddle of existence. Despite his own use of the word "confrontation", and although he is sometimes ready to storm at God "as Job stormed, with the eloquence / of the abused heart", his debate with "ultimate reality", which could so easily flounder in abstraction, is infinitely more complex than that:

> Face to face? Ah, no
> God; such language falsifies
> the relation. Not side by side,
> nor near you, nor anywhere
> in time and space. . . .

and an apt emblem for the subtlety with which an unparaphrasable meaning penetrates the fabric of many of these poems is that of the human mind seen as "a spider spinning its web / from its entrails . . . swinging / to and fro over an abysm / of blankness". In fact it comes as no surprise to find that this image is a redeployment of one which appeared in a poem, "The Listener in the Corner", from R. S. Thomas's previous volume *The Way Of It.* Increasingly, without seeming repetitious in any slack way, his figures appear to be becoming counters manipulated in a passionate game of definition. It is almost as if he were attempting to crack God's code by restricting his own, and it gives those poems where abstractions are kept to a minimum a remarkable and immediate metaphysical intensity.

There remains, of course, the question "where next?", since, in essence, *Frequencies* does not (*cannot*) go beyond *Laboratories of the Spirit* and *The Way of It* except in the brilliance of its refinement. . . . [With] a poet as important

and exciting as R. S. Thomas there is always a particularly keen sense of anticipation. One knows that he will go on asking the same fundamental questions, because he is a writer incapable of trivia, but the shape they take as poetry may still—judging by his present power—hold even greater surprises than when Iago Prytherch vacated the stage for God.

John Mole, "Signals from the Periphery," *in* The Times Literary Supplement (© *Times Newspapers Ltd. (London) 1978; reproduced from* The Times Literary Supplement *by permission), June 2, 1978, p. 608.*

*   *   *

TOMLINSON, (Alfred) Charles   1927-

Tomlinson, a distinguished English poet, is said to be influenced by Pound, Marianne Moore, William Carlos Williams, and especially by Wallace Stevens. Calvin Bedient considers his most salient attribute originality, his chief theme "the fineness of relationships," noting that to read Tomlinson "is continually to *sound;* to meet with what lies outside the self in a simultaneous grace of vision and love." (See also *CLC,* Vols. 2, 4, 6, and *Contemporary Authors,* Vols. 5-8, rev.ed.)

MICHAEL MOTT

Charles Tomlinson has made the inquiry into craft almost the major subject of his poetry. His is an extremely self-conscious quest, yet, for all that, he has produced some finely achieved poems in his first three collections.

Before discussing what I believe to be Tomlinson's most important collection to date, *The Way of a World,* I want to share misgivings I had about his poetry, if only to shed a number of them now.

After reading and rereading *The Necklace, Seeing is Believing, A Peopled Landscape,* and *American Scenes and Other Poems,* one could be in no doubt about Tomlinson's accomplishment. The early, rather ornate, over-wordy poems had been replaced by poems which showed a rigorous and critical feeling for language. The careful study of a wide range of American poets is obvious enough. So is the influence of American landscape. Tomlinson is one of the few visiting poets to realize that parts of America are as much a "haunted landscape" as Europe.

The sensitive reader would soon discover from the poems themselves that Tomlinson is a painter. He shows an acute sense of color, certainly, but there is, above anything else, an overwhelming feeling that in so many of his earlier poems objects are being arranged for painting.

The world Tomlinson depicted in his early collections was never quite without sound; there are, for example, several overheard conversations effectively rendered in the Italian poems of appropriately enough, *A Peopled Landscape.* But the prevailing impression remains, of a poet with a predilection for ghost towns, or for cities imagined as ghost towns; for ruins, desert places, doors opening on nothing, for bone and shard; industrial *terraines vagues;* settings upon which human life had made some mark before leaving.

Tomlinson showed himself a master of the still-life then, perhaps of the "Vanitas" Still-Life Genre, or of the remarkably still landscape. He seemed a poet preoccupied with the painter's problems, allying himself with Cézanne, reluctantly rejecting Van Gogh. Indeed, he discusses the predilection himself most brilliantly in *A Garland for Thomas Eakins*, while the Negress in *Black Nude* is a painter's model, seen first in the room, then against the full light of the window.

Now there is nothing wrong with the still-life in painting or in poetry, but how still these were! How neutral the mind/eye that arranged and observed them! Above all, there was the coolly presented object in the center of *Head Hewn with an Axe*. Is it the critic's problem if the head does not fit into the middle of a still-life? (p. 105)

What makes *The Way of a World* so important is that Tomlinson has turned, in many of the poems in the collection, from his painter's preoccupation to a questioning of his craft as a poet. There is the same vigor, the same metaphysical bent, but with these, an even greater skill at making real experience and observation.

Tomlinson does not evade implications or raw statements of violence . . . , but he does challenge the response to violence in the work of many poets of extreme experience, confessional poets and others. . . .

[*Prometheus*] is the most *telling* of the poems in this collection. It is significant in every way that a poem that displays both Tomlinson's powers at their most effective and his reserves of power should make its point so well, since the whole theme of the poem is power and its abuse. (p. 106)

> *Michael Mott, in* Poetry (© *1971 by The Modern Poetry Association; reprinted by permission of the Editor of* Poetry), *May, 1971.*

EDWARD HIRSCH

Charles Tomlinson's poetry tempts one to adjectives like "restrained," "modest," "exquisite," "moral," "patient," and "attentive." He is the most fastidious and observant of poets, scrupulously probing into the world around him, continually noticing the fluctuations in that world's appearance. He has a physical and metaphysical concern with the shimmer and glamour of surfaces and for him, as for Ruskin and Stevens, "the greatest poverty is not to live in a physical world." . . . [He] brings to his poems a painter's sensitivity to the importance of exteriors. He shares with some of the painters he most admires . . . an attentiveness to physical detail, an objective concern with the shadings and shadows of landscape, a wonder before the natural object, a fidelity to the nuances of light and darkness. A moral sense informs Tomlinson's respect for the Other—both human and nonhuman—and much of his work investigates the complex relationship between the observer and the observed. The poems not only see, they are about the difficult and creative act of seeing. This in turn leads him to investigate the paradox of a dual allegiance to the shaping imagination and to the splendors of the unshaped natural world.

In the measure of his interests and in the measured way they are presented in the poetry. Tomlinson has some clear American prototypes and analogues. American connections are very much to the point since no other English poet has been more deeply influenced by, or attentive to, American poetry. Tomlinson's carefully noticed moral landscapes have much in common with the blocked observations of Marianne Moore . . . and the sharply focused 'machines' of William Carlos Williams. His concern with the shifting rela-

tionship between appearance and reality is reminiscent of Stevens, but the austerity of his presentation has more in common with the Objectivists. In fact, one of the paradoxes, indeed one of the pleasures of reading Tomlinson's work, involves watching how the extravagant painterly sensibility of, say, a Stevens can be tempered by and reflected through the stringent imaginings of, say, a Zukofsky. But although Tomlinson has deep affinities with Stevens and Moore, Pound, Williams, and Zukofsky, Bishop, Bronk, and Oppen, he is very much his own poet and has created his own singular body of work. . . . To my mind Charles Tomlinson is one of the most astute, disciplined, and lucent poets of his generation. He is one of the few English poets to have extended the inheritance of modernism and I suspect that his quiet meditative voice will reverberate on both sides of the Atlantic for a long time to come.

Tomlinson's first pamphlet, *Relations and Contraries* (1951), is weak and wholly derivative in uncharacteristic ways. The title resonates throughout Tomlinson's work, but only one poem from the book, somewhat chastely entitled "Poem," survives into the *Selected Poems*. It is with *The Necklace* (1955) that Tomlinson finds his characteristic subject and theme, although not quite his most natural manner, and it is here that any reading of the work must begin. Written under the elegant sign of Stevens . . . , *The Necklace* is a book of jewels and flutes, irised mornings and olive twilights. It does not quite escape its Stevensian echoes (Tomlinson's jewels are both more precious and more delicate than Stevens' wild diamonds) but the poems do sometimes swerve away from Stevens' influence and at such moments Italy becomes a plainer, barer, and altogether less Romantic and chimerical place. . . . His most decisive poems have edges and outlines, the sharp sculptural clarity of crystal. But most important is the fact that *The Necklace* declares the subject and the aesthetic of Tomlinson's work: the art and act of seeing, of noticing relations and contraries, of making space articulate. The poem "Aesthetic" is an early Ars Poetica.

> Reality is to be sought, not in concrete,
> But in space made articulate:
> The shore, for instance,
> Spreading between wall and wall;
> The sea-voice
> Tearing the silence from the silence.

Marking the voice between silence and silence, sighting the expanse of shore spreading between wall and wall; these are cognitive and creative acts, the way to search for and, hopefully, to discover reality. Tomlinson attends to the concrete in all its particularity, but the poems continually tell us that, for art, what matters is not the single object but the object in relationship to other objects, the tissue of relations that hold together the world.

The relationship between the voice (or in the case of the painter, the hand) and the eye is a complex one. . . .

> "Flute Music" relates that
> There is a moment for speech and for silence.
> Lost between possibilities
> But deploring a forced harmony,
> We elect the flute.

A season, defying gloss, may be the sum
Of blue water beneath green rain;
It may comprise comets, days, lakes
Yet still bear the exegesis of music.

The music's difficult job is to create a harmony (unforced), to gloss a season (which defies gloss), to govern "the ungovernable wave." It must translate the provisional world in all of its fullness (what we see) into the language of consonant forms (what we hear). . . . It is the supreme exegetical function of art to circumscribe the moonlight, to speak of the unspeakable, to embody in song the diversity and economy of the phenomenal world. The flute must move "with equal certainty" (and fidelity) "through a register of palm-greens and flesh-rose."

Such work demands a delicate balance: it eschews an extravagant Romanticism; it shuns "a brittle and false union." Tomlinson's aesthetic of quiet attentiveness stands in a calm Wordsworthian light; it also stands at the opposite end and indeed takes as its enemy—at the moment somewhat unfashionably so—the grandiloquent and frenzied propulsions of, say, a Shelley. It refuses the projection of the self onto a mute natural world. . . . [It] is not until he takes the lucid step into his first full scale collection, *Seeing Is Believing,* that Tomlinson's anti-Romanticism deepens into a profound mediative stance.

In *Seeing Is Believing* (1958) Tomlinson extends his subject and finds his characteristic voice. One has the impression of an exact and chaste mind registering the felicities of the thing seen, taking cognizance of the world's "spaces, patterns, textures." The poems begin with the visible, with the particular, but in the act of looking there is already what he will later call "a grasping for significance." From Ruskin he has learned that the work of art demands "First the felicities, then / The feelings to appraise them." So the particular radiates outwards, growing into meaning; the meaning inheres in the relationship between the thing seen and the eye seeing. And it is a very delicate human instrument that can translate the nuances of the visible into the rhythms of the spoken. There are any number of such correspondences between sight and sound in *Seeing Is Believing:* the slow, bulky movement of oxen in "Oxen: Ploughing at Fiesole," the clean, paring motion of "Paring The Apple," the momentary looming of clouds in "A Meditation on John Constable." (pp. 1-4)

[Tomlinson's work] is a celebration that hinges on the engagement of the eye, the contemplation of an object that, in the simple privileged status of its being, draws us into the pressures of a relationship and, in so doing, saves us from the false engagements of isolation. . . . [The] "labour of observation" is also the human labor of speaking to men. . . . Thus the poet's dual allegiance to the texture of the world and to the texture of the word.

Tomlinson's finest poems argue by arguing nothing; they illustrate by the simple example of their making. Certain visual artists . . . are for him exemplary presences; their formidable job is to detail the exterior world in all the manifestations of its complexity while, simultaneously, mapping the region of their own interiors. . . . Tomlinson's poems tell us again and again that we may only believe the artist when the work appears as an adequate gauge "of the passion and its object," with equal fidelity to both.

A Peopled Landscape (1963) and *American Scenes* (1966) develop and extend Tomlinson's central theme while adding a new dimension to his work. As the work progresses that theme finds its way closer and closer to a full articulation. Its announced intention is to save the appearances, to treat a landscape "where what appears, is." . . . The moral imperative of that theme is to approach the Other with a hard, contemplative eye, to caress and embody, to render and enact, always remembering the Stevensian proposition that "a fat woman / by Rubens / is not a fat / woman but a fiction." In a similar way William Carlos Williams categorically proposed "No ideas but in things" without forgetting that the writing is always of words. Tomlinson's finest poems, like Williams', are verbally rooted in a physical locality. His work proposes, as Marianne Moore's does, "a moral terrain where you must confront nature."

The references to Williams and Moore are appropriate since they are the guiding presences in much of Tomlinson's work. In *A Peopled Landscape* and *American Scenes* Tomlinson's flirtation with America (and with American poetry) is blown into a full scale love affair. (pp. 5-6)

These books illustrate Tomlinson's "dialogue with the spirit of the U.S." in a number of ways. On a personal level they recall his first visit to America and his subsequent year-long sojourn in New Mexico. Thus many of the poems are physically rooted in American territory, particularly in the southwest. Of greater significance is the fact that those poems which return to Tomlinson's own region do so with a new philosophical disposition to the local that in part derives from Williams and Moore. Many of the poems in *A Peopled Landscape* also employ the triadic stanza (staggered tercets) that are so readily associated with the poems of Williams' maturity. Poems like "Up at La Serra" and "The Picture of J. T. in a Prospect of Stone" are English in idiom . . . but are formally characteristic of American modernism. . . . To my mind Tomlinson never quite shapes the triadic stanza to his own hand . . . and after *A Peopled Landscape* few poems in tercets appear. But the experimentation with Williams' form introduced a new flexibility into Tomlinson's line, a new sense of ceremonious and sometimes hesitating motion and, consequently, his new found sense of rhythmic possibility infused and energized the major blank and free verse poems of the three volumes that follow *American Scenes.*

A Peopled Landscape and *American Scenes* also introduce a notable new element into the landscape of Tomlinson's poetry: people. Seashores and mountains are generally the major characters in a Tomlinson poem, but increasingly . . . he has turned his scrupulous eye to field hands and weeping women, Hopi Indians and desert motel owners. To be sure the task remains the same: "to obliterate mythology," to treat the human element with the same watchfulness, care, reticence, and respect that one accords to nature. . . . [The] introduction of people into Tomlinson's peopleless universe does bring with it a welcome note of lightness, warmth, wryness, and humor. . . . For Tomlinson, "pause and silence," and "a reticence of the blood," are essential virtues. The locale may be Taos, Fiascherino, or Bristol, but the qualities he admires remain the same. And of course the world remains "a presence which does not present itself" whether one engages the deserts of New Mexico, the pebble beaches of Italy, or the manscapes of England. It is also in the fortunate condition of things that men are as much a part of nature as mountains and seashores, that seashores may share their sliding surfaces with poems, that poems may share their modest insights with men.

The Way Of A World (1969) and *Written On Water* (1972) continue Tomlinson's delicate negotiations with the world. Negotiations (the title of the first section of *American Scenes*) involve interchange, balance, a healthy and sustaining respect for the Other. The chief negotiations of these two books are with water and time, each with its possibilities, recurrences, and contingencies, each with its merciful gifts and merciless denials. "Swimming Chenango Lake" is the major poem of Tomlinson's maturity, the central poem of his central theme; in it we see a mind of acute delicacy returning to its first concerns, asking and modifying its recurrent questions. (pp. 6-8)

Tomlinson's sense of courtesy, ritual, ceremony, and tradition sometimes leads him to political and anti-revolutionary poems ("Prometheus," "The Assassin") which are heavy-handed and moralizing in their pronouncements that "He who howls / with the whirlwind, with the whirlwind goes down." It is too often an unsympathetic set of opinions that keeps telling us how much a Genet missed of the world, how little a Van Gogh understood sequentiality. We are a little too often reminded that "The times / spoiled children threaten what they will do." And yet, perhaps I am mistaken, for Tomlinson's political notions sometimes root down to another layer of feeling. From its initial complaint, "Against Extremity" deepens like a coastal shell into a kind of prayer.

> Against extremity, let there be
>   Such treaties as only time itself
> Can ratify, a bond and test
>   Of sequential days, and like the full
> Moon slowly given to the night,
>   A possession that is not to be possessed.

There can be no doubt that these lines come from the same cautious hand that has also written, convincingly, "I have seen Eden." (pp. 10-11)

The Way In is a book of returns to the landscapes of England, to English elements and seasons. It is, in some ways, a more personal book than any of Tomlinson's others; in "The Marl Pits" the poet breathes "familiar, sedimented air"; in "At Stoke" he speaks of the first single landscape of his childhood. The poem also speaks (implicitly) of the journey to other landscapes (Italy, America) and of the gradual way home. . . . Most of *The Way In* speaks of a region tamed and handled, manmade, diminished. The poem "Foxes' Moon" presents "night over England's interrupted pastoral." And "After A Death" brings us to a place where "Verse . . . turns to retrace the path of its dissatisfactions." And yet this patched landscape has its own kind of fullness, its own "language of water, light and air." These churches, wards, midlands, and marl pits have their own kind of insistence; they call the meditating eye to a personal answering song.

The Way In is a gentle book of coming home, of witnessing and remembering, of negotiating with the regions of one's past. I feel certain that when these poems are stacked together with the new poems that will appear in a book to be called *The Shaft*, they will further demonstrate Tomlinson's unique moral imagination and deep reflective range. The poems in *The Shaft* continue to balance loss and metamorphosis, constancy and change, sunsets and dawn. They speak quietly of a singular past, but of even greater significance, they continue to encounter "the moment itself / abrupt in the pure surprise of seeing" ("The Gap"). No poem speaks more appropriately of Tomlinson's waving and graceful sense of the world than "Rhymes" which tells us

> Word and world rhyme
>   As the penstrokes might if you drew
> The spaciousness reaching down through a valley
>   view,
>   Gathering the lines into its distances
> As if they were streams, as if they were eye-beams:
>   Perfect, then, the eye's command in its riding,
> Perfect the coping hand, the hillslopes
>   Drawing it into such sight the sight would miss,
> Guiding the glance the way perfection is.

Charles Tomlinson's coping hand continues to probe into the surfaces around us, to guide us on a pleasurable and measured journey into the natural world. We may not ever arrive, but his life's work certainly helps us to glance, however imperfectly, "the way perfection is." (pp. 11-12)

Edward Hirsch, "The Meditative Eye of Charles Tomlinson," in The Hollins Critic *(copyright 1978 by Hollins College), April, 1978, pp. 1-12.*

ANNE STEVENSON

Tomlinson uses words like colours. Patterns of sounds either suggest themselves to him, or else he lays them on his verbal canvases with such professional ease that they seem to have grown there. His flowing, descriptive poems are uniquely delightful, leading from surface to surface in such a way as to suggest depths, or in some cases, to a dissolution of the surface altogether into pure sensation. Because the world Tomlinson observes is so accurately transformed into poetry, the world he imagines, in poems on Marat and Charlotte Corday [in *The Shaft*], comes as something of a surprise. The historical poems in *The Shaft* are less visual than Tomlinson's nature poems, and they suffer, slightly, from some heavy philosophising. . . . Poems like 'Casarola' and 'The Shaft', which slip an idea into an exquisitely embroidered texture of description, are perhaps the finest poems in this fine collection. (pp. 62-3)

Anne Stevenson, in The Listener *(© British Broadcasting Corp. 1978; reprinted by permission of Anne Stevenson), July 13, 1978.*

MICHAEL SCHMIDT

In "Small Action Poem" (1966) Charles Tomlinson introduces Chopin "shaking music from the fingers". Chopin's art was second nature to him. Tomlinson is not that sort of artist. He is to an unusual degree fastidious. In *The Shaft* . . . there are poems which he characterizes as "bagatelles" —a genre he has frequently exploited, most memorably in *American Scenes* (1966) which gives the lie to those critics who dismiss him as "humourless". Tomlinson's humour is broad, short on fashionable local wit but rich in human observation. Yet the bagatelles are marginal in Tomlinson's work. At the centre is not anecdote but an acute perception of a common world with a history, a world of movement and process—two of his favourite words. The poetry is as much about perception as about the things perceived. Variety of experience is reflected in a variety of forms, tones and techniques which must strike anyone who picks up . . . *Selected Poems 1951-1974* or *The Shaft*.

There is a unity of tone and theme throughout this diversity, but at the same time an impressive technical development from the flute tones of the first books to a more complex and rewarding orchestration. That development reaches its climax in poems of a directly civic character, especially the recent poems about the French Revolution which develop ideas first introduced in "The Ruin" and "Up at La Serra" (1963) and then, memorably, in "Prometheus" and "Assassin" (1969). . . .

Instead of irony, Tomlinson chose rhythmic modulation as his method of establishing due proportion and balance in his art. His was, and to a large extent still is, a phrased rather than a cadenced poetry. His rhythmic strategy meant that he retained the option of *vers libre*, the thematic resources of dream, and the technical resources of modernism. Tone and voice vary with the subject, and his entire effort is to "accord to objects their own existence", not to use objects or images in the service of a predetermined statement or form.

Yet the expression itself is precisely determined, each effect gauged to reveal some aspect of the object in its process of existing. Nowhere is this deliberateness more evident than in the rhythms themselves, always subtly managed. . . .

Such deliberate expression is no easy achievement, and the early poems are so carefully groomed that they occasionally achieve preciosity rather than a broader precision. . . . His early work was . . . distorted by an indignation which has never entirely left him. The distortion is towards a refinement which looks at times mannered, a scrupulous numbering of the streaks of the tulip. . . .

[His] work is a poetry of images which are paradoxically hard to visualize: they do not appear static but in process (those fluent clouds which traverse the sky of his imagination). Not only are they in movement: so, too, is the poet's perception of them. Synaesthesia is a common technique, even a theme, in his work. And the poems demand a quality of effort different from that which most modern work requires. They take some time to make themselves familiar to us. There is seldom conclusion, finality: they resolve on balance, on a taut clarity. They do not make statements but establish relationships. . . .

[Tomlinson] is at times inclined to borrow rather than assimilate and transform a compelling literary experience. In "John Maydew", an early poem in Williamsesque triplets, he seems to pour old wine into new bottles. The short, breathless free verse lines of Williams's unmediated observation become mannered in such passages as:

> He eyes the toad
> 　　beating
> 　　　　in the assuagement
> of his truth.

The deliberate diction is vitiated by an arbitrariness of lineation, with a rhythm all the more difficult to establish because of the elbowing enjambements. Objections to this mode are silenced by the success of such poems as "Up at La Serra" or the beguiling "Picture of J. T. in a Prospect of Stone", where the skipping triplet answers the necessary delicacy of thought in dialogue form. . . .

Rhythmic susceptibility has sometimes seriously betrayed him, and nowhere more so than in the "Seasons" section of *The Shaft*. There, and elsewhere in the collection, he follows not at a distance but almost mechanically the rhythmic patterns of Edward Thomas. This form of homage in Thomas's centenary year may have its point—but it worries me. Tomlinson's and Thomas's countrysides are very different worlds, and their poetries are fundamentally distinct. Thomas's images effortlessly carry a general and profound felt significance. Tomlinson's have the power of lucid particularity, but do not carry darkness or the conclusive charge which we experience in Thomas. Thomas wrote his poems because he must, but Tomlinson writes his Thomasesque poems because he wants to.

The tension in these ventriloquisms between Thomas's matter and rhythms and Tomlinson's processes leads to serious difficulties. Tomlinson is, in the best sense, a literary poet, while Thomas is anything but that. . . .

The continuity of concern in Tomlinson's work is of a kind we associate with Ruskin or Adrian Stokes. "The Ruin" (1960) and "Prometheus" (1969) complement each other across a decade. "At Holwell Farm" (1960) and "Movements (iv)" (1972) worry at the same, fundamentally Tomlinsonian theme of creative perception, in different terms but with distinct rhythmic affinities. In these poems, the civic theme emerges from a complex of particular perspectives and images, suggesting the quality of imagination which is discriminating and in a valid sense conservative. At every stage of the poetry the merely subjective is frustrated: there is no wilful distortion of the perceived or the historical world, rather an attempt to realize it in all its complexity: poetry as sculpture, the poet approaching now from one angle and now from another. As well as "Prometheus" and "Up at La Serra", "Assassin", "The Way In", and in the new book the formally rhetorical poems about Danton, Marat, Charlotte Corday and Jacques Louis David reveal an acute appreciation of human motive and consequence, the particular action and the general effect.

These poems seem to me to be part of Tomlinson's outstanding achievement, with a broad pertinence. These poems, and Tomlinson's philosophical ruminations on perception and imagination, such as "Movements" from *Written on Water* (1972), continue to strike me as his best. They achieve that sensuous thought he strives for in our recalcitrant English. The "In Arden" section of *The Shaft* comes closer to defining Tomlinson's Eden of civility and balance than any of his earlier work. His Eden is a distillation, not a fabrication.

The new *Selected Poems* ends abruptly in 1974. Readers will still need to possess *The Way In* (1974) and—if they can get it—*Written on Water*. In selecting his work, Tomlinson has destroyed some of his best sequences, including "Movements", which is a pity. One laments other absent friends: "The Impalpabilities", "Return in Hinton", "The Fox", "Processes," etc. Still, it is a generous selection—with about a hundred and fifty poems and a clutch of ten translations, and if one wishes that the publisher had extended himself to a *Collected*, that is only to pay tribute to a poet whose work is never less than engaging and—in its varied subjects and techniques—often illuminating to an unusual degree, visionary with precision.

Michael Schmidt, "In the Eden of Civility," in The Times Literary Supplement *(© Times Newspapers Ltd. (London) 1978; reproduced from* The Times Literary Supplement *by permission), December 1, 1978, p. 1406.*

R. W. FLINT

Is Mr. Tomlinson more touching than sustaining, more admirable than likable? Absolutely not. No truth whatever in the charge. But one does need to shove a little to get past his potent Praetorian Guard and into the presence of the living work. (p. 9)

Mr. Tomlinson is anything but apologetic about the bracing coolness, the receptive detachment, the intoxicating vigilance he brings to the task of survival in a country whose very indifference to poetry becomes an unlooked-for source of strength. A contemplative with a gift for the dramatic, he is as devoted as Wordsworth and Ruskin to the spirit of place. But he is enough a man of the world to know that it hardly matters whether or not he stays at home; thus he travels a lot, to Italy, Mexico and America. He knows, too, that it hardly matters whether or not he sticks to conventional forms and meters; so he experiments, brilliantly, with a versatile free-verse "rhetoric" adapted from . . . the objectivist-minimalist persuasion.

About Mr. Tomlinson critics are wont to use such words as "control" and "discipline" that are much too chilly for the purpose. Like the highly deliberate painter he also is, he manages to suspend himself, visibly, in the center of his enterprise; we never lose sight of the moving brush or the precarious scaffold. Those showy confidence-coercing poetic stances we know so well he succeeds in muting without ever abjuring them entirely. A contemplative is perforce something of a teacher, sometimes an aphorist, sage, or prophet. "His poems do not pale in the presence of ideas," as Denis Donoghue has accurately observed. But Mr. Tomlinson makes us constantly aware that some mysterious other thing, some functional *tertium quid,* lies between the poem and what it asks us to think or feel. That mystery is a quality of attention that he alone among the poets of his age and culture has learned to dramatize, that he alone has *wanted* to pull out of the obscurity in which it normally hides.

In taking up a chaste American prosody and marrying it to the "Augustan" instincts (his own word) he enjoys in the modern French from Baudelaire to Valéry, he throws his nets very wide, tempering his exquisitely fine sense of quantity and rhyme exactly to the occasion. Williams's onomatopoeia-of-movement, the "expressive form" that Yvor Winters used to rail against, is deployed against a powerful reflective counter-stress, creating a hybrid that miraculously works. . . . One positively enjoys the suspension between alternatives, each of which is suggested with almost the force of his apparent subject. The suspension, finally, *becomes* the subject—intricate secondary syncopations in pursuit of the simplest painterly harmonies.

Nor is this all. When the need arises, his scenes are more than adequately peopled. "John Maydew, or The Allotment" is an excellent point of entry. Or look at the three dramatic meditations (expansions of two earlier poems on Trotsky) that open "The Shaft": "Charlotte Corday," "Marat Dead" and "For Danton." Nothing in Winters or his disciples reveals a keener moral intelligence. Their massed effect is remarkably like the painting by David that inspired the second of the three. Maybe just a touch Parnassian, this kind of thing? Leconte de Lisle transplanted to the English Midlands? Possibly. But who can pretend to be sated with first-rate modern Parnassianism? If Mr. Tomlinson appears at the moment to bring more joy to profes-

sional critics than to everyday fans of Betjeman, Larkin, Hughes and Stevie Smith, it is because he has planned so broadly, looked so far ahead. The times will catch up. (pp. 9, 19)

"The Shaft" has 50 poems that oscillate between the monumentality of the opening sequence on the French Revolution, and a delightful versified cento of "Rumour and History compounded" on the life of the poet Sir John Denham, and two glistening witticisms, "A Night at the Opera" and "In Arden"—others more familiar. Will age, assurance and a growing capacity for being amused soften Mr. Tomlinson and lower his guard? Not likely. (p. 19)

> R. W. Flint, "Hard Way to Beauty," in The New
> York Times Book Review (© 1978 by The New
> York Times Company; reprinted by permission),
> December 31, 1978, pp. 9, 19.

*   *   *

TOOMER, Jean   1894-1967

Toomer, a black American novelist, short story writer, poet, and dramatist, was one of the most important writers of the Harlem Renaissance. His major work, *Cane,* is an extraordinary collection of prose and poetry combined in an experimental novel unlike anything that had appeared before in American letters. *Cane,* which blends rural folkways with urban avant-garde culture, is a lyrical celebration of the black experience. (See also *CLC,* Vols. 1, 4.)

ROBERT LITTELL

While Mr. Toomer often tries for puzzling and profound effects, he accomplishes fairly well what he sets out to do, and *Cane* is not seething . . . with great inexpressible things bursting to be said, and only occasionally arriving, like little bubbles to the surface of a sea of molten tar. . . .

Mr. Toomer shows a genuine gift for character portrayal and dialogue. In the sketches the poet is uppermost. Many of them begin with three or four lines of verse, and end with the same lines, slightly changed. The construction here is musical, too often a little artificially so. The body of the sketch tends to poetry, and to a pattern which begins to lose its effectiveness so soon as one guesses how it is coming out. . . .

[Once] we begin to regard Mr. Toomer's shorter sketches as poetry, many objections to the obscure symbolism and obliqueness of them disappear. There remains, however, a strong objection to their staccato beat. The sentences fall like small shot from a high tower. They pass from poetry into prose, and from there into Western Union.

"Kabnis," the longest piece in the book, is far the most direct and most living, perhaps because it seems to have grown so much more than been consciously made. There is no pattern in it, and very little effort at poetry. And Mr. Toomer makes his Negroes talk like very real people, almost, in spots, as if he had taken down their words as they came. A strange contrast to the lyric expressionism of the shorter pieces. A real peek into the mind of the South, which, like nearly all such genuinely intimate glimpses, leaves one puzzled, and—fortunately—unable to generalize.

Cane is an interesting, occasionally beautiful and often queer book of exploration into old country and new ways of writing. (p. 126)

Robert Littell, in The New Republic *(reprinted by permission of* The New Republic; © *1923 The New Republic, Inc.), December 23, 1923.*

DAVID LITTLEJOHN

Jean Toomer's career is still wrapped in foggy mystery: he wrote one esoteric work, difficult to grasp, define, and assess; he was associated with one of the more advanced white modernist cults, and adopted and taught Russian mysticism; and then he suddenly declared himself white, and disappeared.

His book, *Cane* (1923), is composed of fourteen prose pieces, ranging from two- and four-page sketches, to "Kabnis," an eighty-three-page *nouvelle;* and fifteen detached poems set in between. About half the "stories" have tiny lyric refrains tucked inside them as well.

The prose pieces in the first section of the book are detached vignettes of high female sexuality among the Negro peasants of the Dixie Pike. They are drawn with the new honest artfulness of the Stein-Anderson-Hemingway tradition, so crisp and icily succinct that the characters seem bloodless and ghostly, for all the fury of their indicated lives, all style and tone and suggestion. It is into this section that Toomer's finest poems are set—"Song of the Son," "Georgia Dusk," "Portrait in Georgia"—poems which reveal a great deal about his viewpoint and method. They are the most freely experimental Negro poems of the generation, far freer even than Langston Hughes' games with the rhythms of jazz and conversation. They view Southern Negro life with a chilling objectivity ("so objective he might not be a Negro," an early critic prophetically observed). Common things are seen as if through a strangely neurotic vision, transformed into his own kind of nightmare. (pp. 58-9)

In "Song of the Son" he tries to identify himself with the Georgia soil, but the very effort makes clear his distant view; the view of a sophisticated surrealist among an alien peasantry, a peasantry he transforms into something duskily primeval. (p. 59)

The prose pieces of the second section support this view, though now his bony surrealist's objectivity is transferred to Northern urban Negroes. In the two key stories, "Box Seat" and "Bona and Paul," he runs hot wires of anti-realism beneath a surface of realistic events, somewhat in the manner of Malcolm Lowry or John Hawkes, to imply a strange neurotic derangement in his characters. It is primarily a matter of imagery. . . .

The long story "Kabnis" that makes up the third part is crafted of nervous images and a strong sense of interior pain. The underground cellar symbolism is disturbing, as is, again, the utter objectivity of the narration. But the story drifts off into a hazy poetic incoherence, and—like most of the book, finally—is too insubstantial to be remembered. (p. 60)

David Littlejohn, in his Black on White: A Critical Survey of Writing by American Negroes *(copyright © 1966 by David Littlejohn; reprinted by permission of Viking Penguin Inc.), Viking Penguin, 1966.*

ARNA BONTEMPS

[The publication of *Cane* had an important effect on] practically an entire generation of young Negro writers then just beginning to emerge; their reaction to Toomer's *Cane* marked an awakening that soon thereafter began to be called a Negro Renaissance.

Cane's influence was by no means limited to the joyous band that included Langston Hughes, Countee Cullen, Eric Walrond, Zora Neale Hurston, Wallace Thurman, Rudolph Fisher and their contemporaries of the 'Twenties. Subsequent writing by Negroes in the United States, as well as in the West Indies and Africa, has continued to reflect its mood and often its method and, one feels, it has also influenced the writing about Negroes by others. Certainly no earlier volume of poetry or fiction or both had come close to expressing the ethos of the Negro in the Southern setting as *Cane* did. Even in today's ghettos astute readers are finding that its insights have anticipated and often exceeded their own.

There are many odd and provocative things about *Cane*, and not the least is its form. Reviewers who read it in 1923 were generally stumped. Poetry and prose were whipped together in a kind of frappé. Realism was mixed with what they called mysticism, and the result seemed to many of them confusing. (p. x)

The book by which we remember this writer is as hard to classify as is its author. At first glance it appears to consist of assorted sketches, stories, and a novelette, all interspersed with poems. Some of the prose is poetic, and often Toomer slips from one form into the other almost imperceptibly. The novelette is constructed like a play.

His characters, always evoked with effortless strength, are as recognizable as they are unexpected in the fiction of that period. (p. xii)

It does not take long to discover that *Cane* is not without design, however. A world of black peasantry in Georgia appears in the first section. The scene shifts, with almost prophetic insight, to the black ghetto of Washington, D.C. in the second. Rural Georgia comes up again in the third. Changes in the concerns of Toomer's folk are noted as the setting changes.

A young poet-observer moves through the book. . . . A native richness is here . . . and the poet embraced it with the passion of love. (pp. xii-xiii)

Arna Bontemps, "Introduction" (copyright © 1969 by Arna Bontemps; reprinted by permission of Harper & Row Publishers, Inc.), in Cane, *by Jean Toomer, Harper, 1969.*

DONALD B. GIBSON

[Although Jean Toomer] considered aesthetics as the proper end of poetry, he created in his poetry and prose a mythical black past to which he explored his connection. As Toomer seems to have sought the roots of race in mysticism and aestheticism, so his relation to blackness seems more of the imagination than of the blood. He translated imagined black experience into forms so idealized as to be little related to reality as commonly conceived. (p. 8)

Donald B. Gibson, in his introduction to Modern Black Poets: A Collection of Critical Essays, *edited by Donald B. Gibson (copyright © 1973 by Prentice-Hall, Inc.; reprinted by permission of Prentice-Hall, Inc., Englewood Cliffs, New Jersey), Prentice-Hall, 1973, pp. 1-17.*

FRITZ GYSIN

At first sight, *Cane* seems to be a collection of poems, sketches, stories, and dramatic passages.... The loose structure of the book has induced many critics to discuss the pieces that fit into one of the accepted genres and forget about their function within the whole. In a few cases the tendency to separate Toomer's prose from his poetry led to evaluations of the comparative merits of each, which in turn encouraged discussions whether Toomer should better become a poet or a novelist. In this way, the impression of the work as a whole was ignored, and with it the particular effect that the blending of the different genres produced.

A close reading of *Cane* reveals that Toomer's contribution to Negro literature is the experiment. His concern for language, his interest in creating a new idiom, which would allow him to express the complexities and intricacies of the modern experience, linked him with the writers of the *Lost Generation,* but it also prevented him from merely imitating his contemporaries and allowed him to find his own original style. The same is true of the imagery of *Cane.* The influence of Sherwood Anderson and Waldo Frank is obvious. Yet, Toomer's inventiveness helped him to go beyond these in boldly creating new images which are powerful enough to support the structure of the book.... [His] imagery performs the function that the plot performs in a novel or a play: it connects the various incidents, ... the poems, sketches, and episodes. In other words, the structural experiment of *Cane* consists in the organization of a series of emotions, situations, and actions by means of the 'inner form.' The blending of genres has the same result; in addition, it renders possible an experiment in point of view. This is obvious especially in the semi-dramatic passages of the second part. The characterization of *Cane* is dominated by a very sophisticated type of primitivism, which reveals the influence of Freud and makes Toomer one of the forerunners of the Harlem Renaissance. Finally, *Cane* is also an experiment in self-revelation, the expression of a quest for identity which does not shrink from facing the chaos at the bottom of the human soul. (pp. 38-9)

The book is divided into three parts of about equal length and equal importance. The first part, consisting of six prose pieces interspersed with ten poems, is an evocation of rural Georgia; the second part includes seven prose pieces and five poems, dealing mainly with Negro life in the cities; whereas the longer, semi-dramatic tale that constitutes the third part leads back to the rural Georgia town of Sempter.

In Part One the tales of six southern women, all victims of the caste system, are interwoven with short lyric poems to suggest the narrator's mystic unity with the Georgian soil and with his African heritage and to present a haunting vision of the 'parting soul of slavery.' (p. 39)

The second part of *Cane* exposes the Negro life in the city; the destructive influence of modern industrial society becomes evident in the spiritual emptiness and lack of vitality of near-white, bourgeois ('dicty') Negroes. (p. 42)

'Kabnis,' the third section of *Cane,* is a semi-dramatic story about a northern Negro in rural Georgia who is too weak to face his tradition. (p. 44)

[A wealth of grotesque material is revealed by a close reading of *Cane.* To discuss] the manifestations of the grotesque in *Cane,* we shall take the classification into figures, objects, and situations. We [define] the grotesque figure as a

human figure which is dehumanized by distortion to the point where it appears at the same time real and fantastic, beautiful and ugly, tragic and comic, human and inhuman, living and dead, or demonic and ludicrous. In *Cane* it is possible to distinguish between a first group containing characters that appear slightly grotesque for a short moment, a second group of characters endowed with a number of grotesque traits, and a third one which includes the actual grotesque figures. Needless to say, the borderlines are not very distinct, the three groups shade off into one another. (pp. 46-7)

In the characterization of Fern the grotesque traits prevail.... [At] the beginning of the story, her beautiful face appears distorted because of the weird quality of her eyes.... Her name alludes to a vegetable quality in her existence; the way she sits on her porch reminds us of a plant evading an obstacle while growing.... Unable to express her grief in normal language, she bursts out in a wailing song, her broken voice resembling that of a child or an old man. (pp. 48-9)

The grotesque *object* [can be defined] as a part of the mineral, vegetable, animal, or mechanical domain, which, by means of transformation or independent motion, assumes (or has assumed) traits of one or more of the other domains, including human traits, so that it appears to have become animated, to possess an unusual amount of energy, or to be the instrument of an ominous force. There are fewer grotesque objects in *Cane* than there are grotesque figures; their descriptions are usually a little shorter than those of the grotesque figures and situations, and most of them appear in a subordinated position. (p. 50)

The grotesque *situation* ... [is] a state of affairs in which the incongruence of various factors evokes the image of an estranged world: the violation of static laws, the disturbance of the perception of time and space, the presence or appearance of grotesque figures or objects may create a grotesque situation, but also the juxtaposition of incompatible actions, of incompatible elements of landscape, or of incompatible moods. (p. 52)

In 'Blood-Burning Moon' we might speak of a grotesque background, in 'Becky' of a grotesque atmosphere; in 'Esther,' however, there are two actual grotesque situations: the incident involving Barlo's vision and the second of Esther's two dreams. The first situation is a strange mixture of comic and tragic, real and unreal elements. King Barlo falls into a religious trance 'at a spot called the spittoon. White men, unaware of him, continue squirting tobacco juice in his direction. The saffron fluid splashes on his face.' ... The townspeople, eager for entertainment, gather round him—'a coffin-case is pressed into use,' ... while the sheriff hastily swears in three deputies. Motionless 'as an Indian fakir,' Barlo waits until the excitement has reached its climax, then he begins to describe his vision in the traditional manner of the Negro preacher, interrupted now and then by shouts from the congregation.... Christian and pagan, religious and political elements are condensed in a vision of the American Negroes' ancestor as a gigantic but helpless slave; the paradox suggests the hidden powers of the African soul. The sudden end of the sermon and the turbulent events following it remind us of the exaggerations of the tall tale.... (p. 54)

This description is followed by the account of Esther's two

dreams seven years later. In the first one, she imagines the windows of McGregor's notion shop—the place close to where Barlo had his vision—aflame, alarms the fire police and has them rescue a 'dimpled infant' whom she claims as her immaculately conceived child. Guilt feelings ('It is a sin to think of it immaculately') bring her back to reality. The second dream is a grotesque version of the first.... Whereas the first dream keeps within the limits of the rationally possible and breaks off at the moment of doubt, the second one moves on the border between reality and fantasy. (p. 55)

Like other elements of fiction, grotesque figures, objects, and situations consist first and foremost of words, and consequently the grotesque effect depends on the choice of words and of the way in which they are arranged.... [In literature] the juxtaposition or fusion of contrasting, paradoxical, or incompatible elements is achieved by means of language. Particular attention will have to be paid to the devices used in poetic language to connect contrasting elements; furthermore it will be interesting to find out how far Toomer makes use of the discrepancy between illusion and reality that is inherent in fiction to express the mixture of reality and fantasy, which is one trait of the grotesque....

Toomer presents grotesque material in four different ways: by direct comments, by reactions of the narrator or of other characters, by 'realistic' description in plain language, and by distorting description. Most of the grotesque passages are combinations of several methods.... (p. 56)

In the description of grotesque *figures* in *Cane,* the elements consist of human beings, parts of the human body, especially facial parts or extremities, or even spiritual qualities of man, whereas the images are drawn from the inorganic, the vegetable, and from the animal sphere, or from the world of objects (the mechanical sphere). Those taken from the human sphere generally signify illness and death. In the description of grotesque *objects,* the qualified elements are buildings or parts of buildings, pieces of furniture; in fewer cases plants, parts of language, processes, or conditions. Here almost all the images are taken from the animal and the human sphere. Two details are especially noteworthy: First, among the rather conventional images are a few very striking ones, which belong to a border-region between organic and inorganic material ('a murky wriggling water,' 'shredded life pulp,' 'sap,' 'amoeba,' etc.); second, only the use of imagery enables Toomer to draw abstract concepts like 'awakening,' 'life,' 'mind,' or 'soul' into the range of the grotesque. However, the single image does not contribute much to the explanation of the grotesque, unless it is discussed in connexion with the element it is supposed to qualify. This, in turn, cannot be done satisfactorily without studying the ways in which the images are connected with these elements.

In the grotesque passages of *Cane,* the most frequent means of connexion are simile and metaphor. As a form of comparison, the simile is by nature less radical than the metaphor, which functions predominantly as an equation or a substitution; thus the simile is less suited to distort, animate, or alienate than the metaphor. It is interesting to observe how, if it is too weak to perform the connexion between the two incompatible terms, or if it fails to convey the necessary intensity, the simile either gives way to a metaphor, or metaphorical elements are inserted into it. In the description of Father John in 'Kabnis,' e.g., the simile

is only effective as long as it is used to express the dead, static quality of the man: 'To the left, sitting in a high-backed chair which stands upon a low platform, the old man. He is like a bust in black walnut.' ... In the course of Kabnis's invective against him, a shift from simile to metaphor can be observed step by step: 'Your eyes are dull and watery, like fish eyes. Fish eyes are dead eyes. Youre an old man, a dead fish man, an black at that.' (pp. 59-60)

In the description of Esther's hair, the precision of the image helps to turn it into a grotesque trait: 'It looks like the dull silk on puny corn ears.' ... 'Silk' and 'ears' are dead metaphors designating parts of a corn-cob, but when applied to a rich girl's hair, they become functional again. The description continues: 'Her face pales until it is the color of the gray dust that dances with dead cotton leaves.' Having already become accustomed to the assumption of vegetable qualities by a part of the human body, we now have less difficulty in perceiving the implications of the death-metaphor: the face of the near-white child is distorted by the increase of her pallor; this in turn is achieved by the connexion with the dust that dances with *dead* plants. Again the comparison is intensified by means of a metaphor. (p. 60)

Among the metaphors occurring in the grotesque passages of *Cane,* we distinguish between those which link two concrete images and those which relate concrete images to (abstract) concepts.... [In the former group] the process consists in projecting a quality of the 'vehicle' (the second term, the image) onto the 'tenor' (the first term, the element to be qualified). Since this quality must be alien to the tenor, the intensity of the grotesque trait depends upon the emphasis laid on the *incompatible* features of the two terms. In the sentence: 'O Negro slaves, dark purple ripened plums / Squeezed and bursting in the pinewood air' ..., the image suggests color and ripeness (the qualities the two terms have in common), whereas the projection of a certain vegetable quality unto the 'Negro slaves' is a mere side effect.... A greater intensity of the grotesque is reached, if the tension between the incompatible features of the two terms predominates in strength over the element they have in common, so that the projected quality seems to be their actual connecting link. This is the case in the sentences: 'People come in slowly ... and fill vacant seats of Lincoln Theater. Each one is a bolt that shoots into a slot, and is locked there.' ... The metaphor is based on the assumption of a rather far-fetched similarity between two motions; it equates the agents, not the motions themselves, and thus emphasizes the incompatibility of the two terms. Consequently, the 'people' acquire the mechanic quality of the 'bolts' and appear dehumanized. (pp. 61-2)

The second group consists of metaphors that relate concrete images to abstract concepts. As in the above examples, the creation of the grotesque is based on the reduction to a minimum of the qualities the two terms have in common.... [The] more abstract the tenor becomes, the more radical the vehicle gets. 'Crimson Gardens,' though a mere name, still has some concrete connotations, but 'Seventh Street' lacks even those; this term is alienated by juxtaposition with an image so radical that it becomes grotesque itself: 'Seventh Street is a bastard of Prohibition and the War. A crude-boned, soft-skinned wedge of nigger life breathing its loafer air, jazz songs and love, thrusting unconscious rhythms, black reddish blood into the white and whitewashed wood of Washington.' . . . Spiritual faculties of man are distorted in this manner, too; Esther's inner confusion is made visible by a metaphor that equates her mind with a grotesque object: 'Her mind is a pink meshbag filled with baby toes.' . . . In this radical metaphor the only connexion is that of the copula; the two terms have nothing more in common, and what they suggest arises out of their incompatibility. No quality of the vehicle is projected onto the tenor; it is an instance of complete identification, by which we are forced to visualize the grotesque incarnation of Esther's mind. (In this context it is interesting that her desire for peace and steadiness is expressed in a *simile*: 'She wants her mind to be . . . solid, contained, and blank as a sheet of darkened ice.' (p. 63)

The tendency to shift from similes to metaphors or to insert metaphoric material into the similes in order to intensify the grotesque traits might lead to the question why Toomer does not simply rely upon metaphors to produce his grotesque figures and objects. The answer can be found, if we attempt to transform some of the similes quoted above into metaphors. In the few cases where this can be done successfully, we witness a change of character and intensity in the grotesque figure or object. Take e.g. Dan Moore's utterance: 'Give me your fingers and I will peel them as if they were ripe bananas.' Changed into a metaphor, this might read: 'Your fingers are ripe bananas, and I will peel them,' or 'Give me your banana fingers, and I will peel them.' The difference is evident. First, our own versions express an attempt to transform the fingers into bananas by means of a metaphor, so that the act of peeling is only a reinforcing image; in other words, the two incompatible elements would be the human flesh of the policemen's arms and the fruit pulp of the bananas grown to these arms. In Toomer's simile, however, the fingers are peeled before being compared to bananas, so that it is never quite clear whether they consist of a human or a vegetable substance. Secondly, since fingers and bananas are of a more or less similar shape, even an equation is not particularly striking; the metaphor lacks the intensity that is reached by the direct connexion of the fingers and the act of peeling in the simile. Similar tests could be made with other examples; e.g. in the sentence: 'The young trees that whinnied like colts impatient to be let free,' the grotesque object is the whinnying trees, whereas in a metaphorical version it might be a fusion of tree and colt. (pp. 63-4)

[We] infer that a mixture of simile and metaphor occurs, if the single trope (either a simile or a metaphor) is not radical enough to distort, animate, or alienate. Some of the most intense grotesque traits are achieved by means of such mixtures. All these tropes, however, whether pure or mixed, must be regarded merely as elements that are used in various ways to 'construct' grotesque figures, objects, or situations. (pp. 64-5)

[Toomer's] imagination is stimulated by figurative speech, . . . he takes the classical tropes only as points of departure, . . . he often uses them for purposes contrary to their original functions, and . . . he is prone to exploit the hidden potentialities of distortion, animation, and alienation inherent in language itself. (p. 65)

[Toomer prefers] *distortion and animation by figurative language* to the methods of *realistic description, comment,* and *description of reactions;* . . . this preference is apparent not only in single sentences describing grotesque traits but

also in the complete passages, even in whole stories, that instead of describing his grotesque figures, objects, or situations literally, Toomer likes to construct them almost synthetically by combining the four methods mentioned above while still laying great stress on imagery and figurative language. (p. 66)

[In 'Box Seat'] Toomer manages to create a series of overlapping grotesque situations, whose function is to express the protagonist's penetration of the superficial reality of life, his simultaneous participation in different kinds of existence. The strange mixture of nightmare and revelation exposes the intensity of Dan's imagination, which does not shrink from extremes, the pitilessness of his task to change mankind, but also the desolate condition of those who insist on living without the reality of love.

In 'Box Seat' Toomer envisages the rebirth of the Negro poet as a sophisticated primitive, as a paradoxical mixture of a sensitive dreamer and a merciless iconoclast, who will remain misunderstood while his grotesque counterpart, the stereotype of the Harlem Renaissance, will win the applause of an audience unaware of being ridiculed. The fact that he could not identify himself with this black Messiah in the long run is perhaps one of the main reasons for Toomer's tragic alienation from the Negro and from poetry. (pp. 76-7)

Without considerable changes, ['Kabnis'] could not possibly survive on the stage; the main reason lying . . . in the lack of dramatic intensity of the dialogue. Most of the dialogue remains static, whereas the 'stage directions' are often endowed with such dynamic power and depth of content as to make it impossible for them to serve their normal function in a stage production. On the other hand, the form has its merits, too. First, it is the ultimate result of Toomer's tendency towards the concentration of space and time; it allows him to focus on a few places of action and to condense the significant happenings into relatively short sequences. Secondly, much more actively than the use of the present tense, the semi-dramatic form helps to heighten the immediacy of the symbolic action. Thirdly, the extensive 'stage directions' justify the combination of two points of view, that of the omniscient author and that of the third person narrator. These three characteristics are closely related to Toomer's use of the grotesque. [In] *Cane* the concentration on essentials often results in a reduction to grotesque traits; that the intensity of a grotesque passage depends to a large degree on the immediacy of the presentation can also be deduced from the first two sections of the book. Finally, the combination of different points of view shows an affinity to the combination of the different methods Toomer uses to create a grotesque figure, object, or situation. More effective than a stage production would probably be the use of the story as a film script. The film, as a predominantly optical medium, might be able to give more accurate expression to the message contained in the 'stage directions' of 'Kabnis' than the theater.

Waldo Frank's charge of structural weakness can be refuted by a short analysis of the structure of the story. The distribution of day and night and the division of the six episodes into two groups, separated by the lapse of one month, help to create a symmetric structure, which maintains a certain balance in spite of the downward course of the action. The fact that the intermission between the third and the fourth episode, instead of disrupting the story, serves it as a kind of axis is another proof of the unity of 'Kabnis.' The downward movement of the linear action was observed very early by the critics. (pp. 77-8)

[Neither] the structure nor the atmosphere of the story loses its 'taut sustainedness'; as a matter of fact, the structure is supported by the atmosphere, and the tension increases parallel to the deterioration of the protagonist.

Waldo Frank's comment that Kabnis 'never altogether transcends inorganic life' contains an accurate observation, but it points in the wrong direction. The characterization of Kabnis is a combination of *realistic description* and *distortion;* the accumulation of grotesque traits accompanies the decline of his will-power and the increase of his morbid self-hatred. . . . [We] can observe the heightening of tension from the first to the third episode, a moment of relief, and the resumption of the same process in the remaining episodes. (p. 80)

Like the two other sections of *Cane,* ['Kabnis'] seems to be dominated by the racial theme. Throughout the story, color is used symbolically to indicate differences and nuances in the various characters' attitudes towards their existence as Negroes. (p. 85)

In accordance with the general tenor of *Cane,* 'Kabnis' concentrates on revealing interior conflicts of the Negro population and on presenting them as conflicts within the minds of individual characters. The racial theme is therefore limited to the Negro's struggle with his past and with his mixed origins. In *Cane* the term 'past' signifies two things: first, the tradition of slavery, a condition associated with shame, humiliation, and suffering, and second, the remote African heritage, a source of fear, mystery, and hidden power. A moral coward, Kabnis refuses to accept either of them; he insists that his ancestors were southern 'blue bloods,' he interprets his social status as a protection against violence, and he declines to acknowledge the old man as his spiritual forefather. His imagination, however, is constantly preoccupied with a 'pathological fear of being lynched,' with primitive superstition, and with a hidden fascination by Father John: the rock that is thrown through Halsey's window seems to possess a demonic power that sends him spinning like a top across the countryside, and the ghosts of the slave-hunters pursuing him in his fantasy resemble malevolent African demons. . . . Kabnis has no way of evading his tradition; if he runs away, he is pursued by its ghosts, if he tries to negate it by rational argument, it affirms its presence through his irrational fears. The more he tries to reject his past, the stronger he feels it, and finally, instead of mastering it, he becomes its helpless victim.

Kabnis's highly ambiguous attitude towards his past is directly related to his mixed origins. The importance of the bastard-theme in this story is stressed not only by direct comments (cf. e.g. the discussion in Halsey's parlor) and by the symbolical use of color, but also by hyperbolic statements that heighten Kabnis's bastardy to cosmic dimensions: 'look at me now. Earth's child. The earth my mother. God is a profligate red-nosed man about town. Bastardy; me. A bastard son has got the right to curse his maker. God . . .'. . . . Lacking the strength to keep all these contradicting forces in balance, Kabnis tends to accept an attitude closer to the white point of view. . . . (pp. 85-6)

From the very beginning of the story, Kabnis's rejection of his Negro-blood runs parallel to an ever increasing distur-

bance of identity. The image of the mask and the distinction between a real Kabnis and a dream-Kabnis point to an inner tension; the appearance of Lewis as a 'double' indicates the beginning of the split. . . . How deep the abyss is and how intensely Kabnis experiences his fall only becomes clear when we look at the passages in which he reveals himself as a frustrated poet.

In the exposition, Kabnis utters his wish to become a poet, so that he might be strong enough to face the south and sing of it. His frustrations become evident shortly afterwards, when he is unable to reconcile the extreme beauty of the southern night with the extreme ugliness of living conditions in Georgia and begins to curse and adore God simultaneously. . . . This combination of beauty and ugliness that confuses Kabnis in the south is one of the sources of the grotesque in this story. These thoughts recur in the fifth episode, but here the juxtaposition of beauty and ugliness, of imagination and reality assume existential significance. Kabnis claims to belong to a family of orators and tries to prove his superiority over Lewis and Halsey by telling them of the suffering his mission as a poet causes. Although these outcries of a tortured soul must be taken ironically with regard to Kabnis, Toomer here nevertheless makes some of his most profound statements about the condition of the poet in general, and it is these statements that carry the theme of the story beyond the problem of race and give it universal significance. . . . In this passage, poetry appears as a curse; the poet is stigmatized, but more than that: the ideal shape branded onto his soul materializes into a grotesque object, some kind of monster that emanates from a nightmare and feeds on twisted words. The only way to escape it is death, and a ritual death at that. . . . [Most] of the 'tortured words' Kabnis is compelled to utter in order to pacify the Moloch inside distort or alienate the person against whom they are directed. Distorting or alienating description, i.e. the use of grotesque elements in poetry, therefore seems to indicate that the poet is dominated and directed in his creative process by an unknown power.

The end of 'Kabnis' is ambiguous. Most critics recognize the redemptive power of Carrie Kate, the child of a new and healthy generation. Arna Bontemps even goes so far as to claim that Kabnis is 'finally redeemed from cynicism and dissipation by the discovery of underlying strength in his people.' Yet the desolate condition in which Kabnis climbs the steps at the end does not seem to support this interpretation. It will probably be safest to assume that Kabnis is lost, but that the new generation offers possibilities that go far beyond those attempted in this story. (pp. 87-8)

[In spite of Toomer's indebtedness to Sherwood Anderson], we must not disregard the basic difference between the manifestations of the grotesque in *Cane* and Anderson's definition of 'the grotesque' in the prologue to *Winesburg, Ohio.* According to the old man's theory in this prologue, a 'grotesque' is a person who has adopted one of the many truths in this world and lives with it, as if it were the whole truth, a person obsessed with an idée fixe, a spiritual failure as it were. In most cases such a person's incoherent behavior or strange looks originate from a particular humiliating experience, which is usually revealed as a flash-back in the sketch of the particular figure. Since Anderson's definition is based on content and meaning, it allows him to apply the term 'grotesque' to characters that are neither alienated nor distorted. In the few cases where actual grotesque features appear . . . , they are presented as results of extreme psychic deformation. The grotesque figures in *Cane*, however, are much more numerous, their distortion and alienation is not fully accounted for by their anamnesis, and in the few instances where hints are provided (e.g. in 'Esther'), the alienation originates much less from slavery than from light complexion or from the imitation of shallow white middle class behavior ('Rhobert'; Mrs. Pribby in 'Box Seat').

In order to understand the function and the meaning of the grotesque in Toomer's writing, we must . . . start from the formal and structural processes by which it is created, from the concretization and visualization of tropes in the specific details of a description as well as from the synthetic composition of such details to a new organism of words. These processes indicate that far from being elements of psychological realism, the grotesque figures, situations, and objects in *Cane* are indications of willful distortion, alienation, and animation by the author; their causes and meanings can only be found in the poetic intentions of Toomer himself. Thus the grotesque situations in this book suggest a blending of fascination by and revulsion from the racial landscapes of city and country, the simultaneous presence of a total involvement in the black experience and its critical appraisal from an extreme emotional distance. The grotesque figures reveal a combination of sophistication and primitivism that does not only reflect the artistic programme of the time but also the sensitive Negro's experience of cultural dualism.

The most striking peculiarity of the grotesque in Toomer's writing is its fusion of satire and mysticism. The dehumanized, ridiculous figures that assume divine qualities on the one hand (Fern, Barry), the vision of redemption and regeneration that suddenly turns into sarcastic bantering on the other (Barlo's sermon, Dan's disillusionment), show that without dulling the satirical sting of his social criticism, Toomer nevertheless changes its direction by emphasizing the spiritual regeneration that must precede any attempts at successful social change. It seems to be the function of the grotesque objects to emphasize moments of the mystic unity of soul and body, spirit and soil, stone and flesh, word and matter. . . . And yet, the ironic distance from which the narrator suddenly pokes fun at some of his transported grotesque sufferers prevents these portraits from becoming sentimental. . . .

Without resorting to amateur psychology, it seems to be fairly safe to assume that the ultimate reason for Jean Toomer's use of grotesque elements can be found in his complex and complicated relationship to his own racial identity. The necessity of having to qualify his experience from two points of view, either of which is modified by the other, must have asked for the conception of a mode of expression that would allow him to present his paradoxical truths in the most concrete manner possible. . . . [The] grotesque is able to meet such demands and, beyond that, to increase the compactness and the intensity of a work of art. . . . (pp. 89-90)

> *Fritz Gysin, "Jean Toomer," in his* The Grotesque in American Negro Literature: Jean Toomer, Richard Wright, and Ralph Ellison (© *A. Francke AG Verlag Bern, 1975), Francke Verlag Bern, 1975, pp. 36-90.*

CHARLES R. LARSON

Cane is not a typical novel. It is, in fact, *sui generis*—a unique piece of writing in American literature as well as in the entire scope of Third World writing. I suggest that *Cane* should be regarded as a lyrical novel—a narrative structured by images instead of the traditional unities. Its tripartite structure is developed from a series of thematic tensions: North/South; city/country (with the almost ubiquitous image of the land); past/present; black/white; male/female. Structured by these counterparts or tensions, *Cane* achieves a lyrical beauty and power which make it, for me, the most compelling novel ever written by a black American writer. (pp. 30-1)

The most fascinating aspect of Toomer's novel for me is . . . the narrator-observer who wanders throughout the book. This is the author's emotional center, for the fact is that *Cane* does have a central character—a figure who resembles Toomer himself, though cleverly disguised. In the course of the narrative he undergoes a number of metamorphoses, sometimes appearing as a first-person narrator (in 12 of the 28 sections of the first two parts), that is, as a participant in the activities described; or as an observer in a third-person narrative, like Conrad's Marlow. In two other main sections ("Bona and Paul" and "Kabnis") Toomer has disguised himself as the mulatto who cannot decide whether he should be black or white, thus introducing the theme of passing. *Cane*, then, may be regarded as the story of Jean Toomer's own vacillation between races—a rather common theme of American fiction during the 1920s. . . .

It is, of course, one of the great ironies of Toomer's life that his book fulfilled his artistic intentions though Toomer himself was unable to accept this heritage. One suspects that the publication of *Cane* must have acted as a kind of exorcism, bringing Toomer's own identity problems to a climax. . . . Toomer's personal vacillation between black and white damaged his own psyche beyond repair. Darwin T. Turner is correct when he says that in the end Toomer did not identify himself as a Caucasian any more than he did as an Afro-American, that he was "self-exiled from all races." *Cane* was his swan song, yet if Toomer in the long run was unable to accept his mixed heritage, there is little doubt that *Cane* has made it possible for others to find theirs. (The last scene in the novel—a symbolic sunburst surrounding Father John and Halsey's younger sister, Carrie Kate—is, in fact, a resounding affirmation of blackness.)

The novel, however, remains. Its influence on subsequent black writing cannot be denied—especially on the writers who wrote during the last years of the Harlem Renaissance, in the '20s and '30s. Yet its significance is much more than this, for *Cane* is one of the most innovative works of 20th-century American fiction—a landmark in American literature, foreshadowing the soon-to-follow experimental works of John Dos Passos and William Faulkner. The experimental novel in America begins not with those writers but with Jean Toomer's *Cane*. (p. 32)

> *Charles R. Larson, in* The New Republic *(reprinted by permission of* The New Republic; © *1976 by The New Republic, Inc.), June 19, 1976.*

U

UPDIKE, John   1932-

Updike is an American novelist, short story writer, poet, critic, essayist, and author of children's books. An acute observer of the human condition, Updike produces prose that is spare and rich in allegory. His characters, treated with sympathy and simplicity, are often depicted in hopeless marital and social situations. The way in which they grapple with love and, especially, lust represents Updike's central purpose: to explicate man's metaphysical strivings through an investigation of the strengths and limitations of his physical being. (See also *CLC,* **Vols. 1, 2, 3, 5, 7, 9, and** *Contemporary Authors,* **Vols. 1-4, rev. ed.)**

VICTOR STRANDBERG

Back in the second decade of this century, Herman Hesse remarked that "Human life is reduced to real suffering, to hell, only when two ages, two cultures and religions overlap." . . . In the figure of John Updike, Hesse's crisis of culture attains what we might call a culminating expression. Unwilling to exorcise the dilemma by making a game of it, in the mode of black humor widely prevalent among his contemporaries, Updike has confronted the problem of belief as directly as did Tolstoy and Tennyson a century earlier, but with the added authority of a mind keenly aware of twentieth-century science and theology. . . . Moving out from an intensely imagined vision of death as its starting point, this search for a belief that might provide a stay against death comprises the "figure in the carpet" that Henry James spoke of, the master theme that, threading from book to book, gives design to Updike's work as a whole and marks him as one of the leading religious writers of his age.

"Our fundamental anxiety is that we do not exist—or will cease to exist." That statement from Updike's essay on Denis de Rougemont's writings (*Assorted Prose* . . .) compresses within its narrow pith the most recurrent nightmare in Updike's work. . . . The dread of Death stalks softly through all of Updike's books. . . . (pp. 157-58)

[For example,] *Couples* (1968) notably places its erotic episodes against a background saturated with news of expiring flesh: the slow death of Pope John, the mysterious sinking of the submarine *Thresher,* the death of the Kennedy infant, the Diem assassinations, the murder of the President himself, the killing of Lee Oswald (which the Hanemas watch on television), two planes crashing in Turkey, a great Alaskan earthquake. The fictional world of *Couples* can hardly compete with such real life extinctions, but it does offer the slow dying of John Ong by cancer in counterpoint with the insomniac dread visited upon Piet Hanema ever since his parents died in a crash. . . .

Beyond this prospect of personal extinction lies that ultimate formulation of doom from the science of Physics, the theory of Entropy, which foresees the whole universe eventually burning out into a final icy darkness. This idea horrifies a good many Updike people, a typical instance being the tortured insomniac at the end of *Pigeon Feathers* who wakes his wife at last to share his terror: "I told her of the centuries coming when our names would be forgotten, of the millennia when our nation would be a myth and our continent an ocean, of the aeons when our earth would be vanished and the stars themselves diffused into a uniform and irreversible tepidity." . . . Worst of all is the eternally "forgotten" state in the above passage, a final and total extinction of the self that has haunted George Caldwell in *The Centaur* ever since he witnessed his father's death, though Caldwell accepts both death and entropy cheerfully enough otherwise. (p. 159)

Updike might as well have been speaking of himself when he described Conrad Aiken's stories as projecting a world whose "horror is not Hitlerian but Einsteinian," concerned not with crime and war but with the "interstellar gulfs" and "central nihil" of "the cosmic vacuity." . . . All of Updike's major work to date may be seen as some kind of response to this trauma; his people variously resist death through Christian faith (John Hook in *The Poorhouse Fair*), through the way of Eros (the Rabbit books, *Couples*), through Agape (George Caldwell), through art (Bech, Peter Caldwell), and through the metaphysical intuition that Updike himself calls "duality" (*A Month of Sundays* and elsewhere). . . . *The Centaur,* which gathers them all in its purview, remains Updike's most satisfactory treatment of his grand obsession.

To deal with the threat of non-existence, Updike has resorted largely to the oldest modes of immortality known to man—God and sex, more or less in that order, but sometimes meshed in a dubious combination. To judge from the bulk of Updike's writing, we might well surmise that Freddy Thorne, the high priest of *Couples,* speaks for his author when he says, "In the western world, there are only two comical things; the Christian church and naked women. . . . Everything else tells us we're dead." (pp. 159-60)

Back in his earliest novel, *The Poorhouse Fair,* where a head-on debate between a Christian and an atheist comprises the intellectual center of the work, it is ominously the atheist whose argument carries the weightiest evidence. . . . Perhaps Updike's most harrowing—and most brilliantly written—plunge into the abyss of religious skepticism occurs in "Lifeguard," whose divinity-student narrator skewers the whole line-up of Christian theologies like so much shish-ke-bob. (pp. 160-61)

When God goes, half-gods arrive; and in our post-Freudian age, what other god can stand before Eros, "the Genesis of All Things," as the Centaur teaches . . . , and the one surviving deity who delivers a kind of immortality people may yet live by. Perhaps it is natural that when faith fails, God and sex become blurred. . . . Some such subliminal transference seems to have worked itself out in Updike's fiction of the 1960's, whose tones have become steadily less Christian and more pagan, though without a clear victory on either side.

Updike's psychology of sex, as he himself has attested, owes a great deal to two books by Denis de Rougement, *Love in the Western World* and *Love Declared.* (p. 161)

Updike renders [the] connection between Eros, narcissism, and death metaphorically in his Erotic Epigram III . . . , which reads:

> Hoping to fashion a mirror, the lover
> doth polish the face of his beloved
> until he produces a skull.

So Eros becomes another mask for death, after all, rather than death's adversary; and the servant of Eros becomes "Mr. Death," as Ruth calls Rabbit—that proud lover—at the end. Presumably, the very reason Rabbit insisted on having sex with Ruth without contraceptives was to loosen his seed against death, affirming his being in reproduction. . . . Yet the final effect of Rabbit's erotic adventures is to inflict death by water upon his new-born daughter, death by fire upon his girl friend (in *Rabbit Redux*), death by abortion upon his unborn descendant, and spiritual death upon both his wife and his concubine: "I'm dead to you, and this baby of yours is dead too. Now; get out." (p. 162)

Couples is Updike's ultimate statement on the theme of Eros. Guided by Paul Tillich's headnote from *The Future of Religions* that our present world, like that of the Roman Empire, presents "a mood favorable for the resurgence of religion," we find in *Couples* just what that religion is likely to be: a worship of Eros complete with its high priest and prophet (Freddy Thorne), its sacrificial victims (Angela and Ken), and its lay communicants (the couples)—all under the purview of the town church with its "pricking steeple and flashing cock." . . .

In this book, Death is once again linked with Eros, in Foxy's abortion, for example. . . . More significant is the loss of personality, a kind of psychic death, that Eros exacts as its payment. Contrary to Freddy Thorne's sudden "vision" that "We're all put here to *humanize* each other," . . . Eros obviously dehumanizes his worshippers in this novel, not only—again—in victimizing the . . . "distressed

and neglected children," but with respect to the lovers themselves: "Frank and Harold had become paralyzed by the habit of lust; she and Marcia, between blowups, were as guarded and considerate with one another as two defaced patients in an accident ward." . . . Those critics and readers who complained of the lack of character development in *Couples*—the characters are mostly indistinguishable—have missed the point that it was meant that way. (p. 163)

Eros is in reality a living god of this world to whom all flesh must render service. And in that service may actually reside some measure of joy and hope and meaning, for here we encounter a strange paradox: the Christian hedonism of John Updike. He that lusteth after a woman in his heart hath defiled her already, according to Jesus Christ, but Updike's religious people seem marvelously at ease in their compliance with the laws of Eros. . . . Christ and Eros are not adversaries, he maintains, but collaborators, the asceticism of the Bible notwithstanding: "To desire a woman is to save her . . . Every seduction is a conversion." (p. 164)

The lifeguard's changing investment of belief, shifting from God to sex—that is, from a supernatural to a naturalistic mainstay against death—portends, I believe, a significant movement in Updike's larger career. . . . Certainly, his *Midpoint,* a collection of poems published in 1969 and narrated by Updike himself, would appear to verify a shift, though not a full break, away from Christianity towards hedonism in Updike's view of life. (pp. 164-65)

The "intelligent hedonism" of *Midpoint* and the "happy ending" of *Couples* . . . would appear to reflect an increasing commitment to the pleasure principle in Updike's thinking, as supernaturalism wanes and naturalism waxes. But Updike is nothing if he is not double-minded. *Rabbit Redux* (1971) gives us a revulsion against naturalism as powerful as T. S. Eliot's, where Eros is again the mad, cruel god, where all sexuality is joyless exploitation, and where drugs and the moon-landing (of 1969) prove empty substitutes for spiritual meaning. (pp. 165-66)

There is no subject, then, upon which Updike is so ambiguous in his judgments as the subject of Eros, doubtless because sex is so ambiguous a feature of actual life, almost evenly balanced between its pleasures and pains, its warmth and its cruelty, its powers to create and destroy. Looking at *The Centaur,* we find both attitudes locked in a typically dialectical configuration. (p. 166)

So the turn from Christ to Eros ends in paradox. On the one hand, in a time of failing belief Eros is at least one god that all men can believe in, one to whom bodies may be offered a living sacrifice and who may confer in return a provisional shelter against death and entropy and the protein acids ticking. On the other hand, the capture of civilization's inner citadel from its few rear-guard Christian defenders yields little joy to the army of neopagan victors, for the disappearance of Christianity in books like *Couples* and *Rabbit Redux* only displays the "central nihil" of the "cosmic vacuity" all the more intolerably. To find Updike's true refuge from death and its terrors we shall have to look to neither classical Eros nor orthodox Christian metaphysics but to a highly personal theology that sees Agape love and Erotic love as pointing toward "Duality," like two sides of a triangle or a Gothic arch whose base is Earth and whose tip pierces heaven. (p. 167)

The goodness Updike speaks of is what theologians call

agape, that love which St. Paul placed at the top of his famous triad in I Corinthians 13; and though we see very little faith and not much hope in *The Centaur,* we do see an abundance of love in George Caldwell, love which in the Pauline phrases "suffreth long, and is kind . . . seeketh not her own, is not easily provoked, thinketh no evil." Moving through a world that otherwise seems a throwback to the pagan hedonism of pre-Christian antiquity, Caldwell anachronistically dispenses agape-love in all directions.

Here perhaps a few words from Updike's religious mentor, Karl Barth, will focus Caldwell's role more clearly: "In *agape*-love a man gives himself to the other with no expectation of a return, in a pure venture, even at the risk of ingratitude." (p. 168)

Love—as *agape*—is a mighty ethical force, but matters of even greater moment hang by this tale. Ultimately, love implies that the physical universe has a spiritual counterpart, that metaphysical dimension of reality whose existence has been so much in question, and whose power is the only final recourse against death and entropy. Updike's word that encompasses this metaphysical dimension is "duality." . . . (p. 169)

By setting off *The Centaur* against Updike's erotic novels—*Couples, A Month of Sundays,* and *Marry Me*—we may observe how the author designates Agape and Eros as the two alternative pathways that connect the dualistic realms of reality. The way of Agape is surer but much more difficult, of course—straight is the path and few there be who find it. None do find it after Caldwell, who was not the last Christian for Updike (for his lovers are all Christians too), but who was the last Christian capable of a life of *agape* love. The noble centaur's exit thus leaves Eros as the major vehicle of dual consciousness in our ongoing twilight era.

Here Denis de Rougemont's thought makes its greatest impact on Updike's writing, for de Rougemont's connection between Eros and Duality makes possible a molecular fusion between Updike's sexual and religious psychology. Beyond the pleasure principle, that is to say, the Unattainable Lady of Updike/de Rougemont, provides a stay against death by opening to her lover a secret corridor for periodic visitations into the next world. . . .

Just such a system of thought pervades Updike's latest novel, *Marry Me* (1976). (p. 170)

At the end of [this] book, Updike affirms de Rougemont's system one last time by bringing into his text that classic movie archetype of the unattainable lady, Marlene Dietrich, whose most famous film, *The Blue Angel,* bears a title that happens to suit Updike's purpose to perfection.

In the end, then, the idea that poor Sally is asked to serve, at the risk of being called a whore, is that of Jerry's immortality. . . . (p. 171)

In *Couples,* Updike sometimes verges upon making a stilted morality play with de Rougemont's system, with Piet's name meaning "Hanema/Anima/Life" . . . and with Piet's wife Angela taking the role of the Angel not possessable in this world. (p. 172)

The ambiguity of Updike's erotic love, a life force harboring brutality, selfishness and a "mask of Death" quality, renders agape-love that much more efficacious by comparison. (p. 173)

Critics like Leslie Fiedler and Norman Podhoretz have sometimes disparaged Updike's work, calling it poor, mindless, and irrelevant, but those of us who find *The Centaur* a brilliant, moving book will agree that in his portrayal of George Caldwell, Peter/Updike has netted a splendid catch indeed, worthy of its epic analogies. In this apostle of agape-love, Updike has presented what still remains his surest answer to the problems of nihilism and the changing of the gods. As a side effect, he has also insured that his own name, while civilization lasts, is not likely to be forgotten. (p. 175)

Victor Strandberg, "John Updike and the Changing of the Gods," in MOSAIC: A Journal for the Study of Literature and Ideas *(copyright © 1978 by the University of Manitoba Press; acknowledgment of previous publication is herewith made), Vol. XII, No. 1 (Fall, 1978), pp. 157-75.*

DAPHNE MERKIN

[While] Updike is gifted at everything he puts his hand to, he is not equally gifted. Thus, although he is a first-rate miniaturist (his short stories are usually flawless, and his criticism can be truly remarkable . . .), he has failed to attain major status as a novelist. Perhaps his is a case of talent spread too thin to sustain the rigors of full-length fiction. Or perhaps something less tangible and more complicated is involved—a subtle clash between artistic ability and artistic inclination, between what John Updike is best equipped to write about and what he wants to write about. More specifically, he seeks to abandon his natural subjects—disgruntled marriages (*Couples, Marry Me*) and crumbling Wasp traditions (*A Month of Sundays*)—for darker, archetypal matters—alien accounts of wandering Jews (*Bech: A Book*) and militant blacks (*Rabbit Redux*). And these books of larger vision, despite not always being persuasive, are in fact the author's most interesting works. (p. 21)

The Coup is a very witty book about the merchandising of ideology. It is inventive in a Nabokovian way: nothing is too big—or small—to be poked fun at. The American scenes . . . have about them the pungency that last wafted through *Lolita.* It is almost as though Updike had to figuratively leave home—by impersonating the foreigner—in order to see most clearly into the frailties of home. . . . Flecked with sobriety and whimsy, *The Coup* counters a concern for *temps perdu* with a muscular sense of presentness. More important, here John Updike comes closer than he has ever come before to matching the intention to the act. (p. 22)

Daphne Merkin, "Updike in Africa," in The New Leader *(© 1978 by the American Labor Conference on International Affairs, Inc.), December 4, 1978, pp. 21-2.*

ROBERT TOWERS

"The Coup" is a comedy of racial and cultural incongruities; but whereas Waugh and Theroux use a white protagonist . . . to clear a path for us into the Dark Continent, Updike has the fictional audacity to project a black among blacks, a militant and culturally, though not sexually, puritanical Marxist-Muslim, the redoubtable Col. Hakim Félix Ellelloû, as the commanding figure and voice of his novel. (p. 1)

[Ellelloû] is an extraordinary tour-de-force of a character, an ideologue who reminds me of one of Nabokov's mad narrators, a Humbert Humbert or a Charles Kinbote; like them he is obsessed, self-destructive, nimble and often endearing. . . . The African wives, too, are distinctively fleshed-out and memorable, as are the old King and Ellelloû's elegant and treacherous associate, Michaelis Ezana. Oddly, the American characters are the least successful; in their case, Updike has contented himself with satirically outlined pinups.

Updike loves to show off his special areas of knowledge, whether Protestant theology or, in this case, the geography, geology and history of sub-Saharan Africa. . . . Whatever the effort involved, Updike's imagination has thoroughly assimilated his erudition, enabling him to render, with sublime authority, the look and and feel of this gritty, sunstruck region.

His stylistic virtuosity is more problematic. . . . Never was a writer so resolutely, so irrepressibly, metaphorical as he. . . . (pp. 1, 55)

Many of Updike's images are arresting, a delight to contemplate both for their ingenuity and accuracy; but too often he is tempted into glibness or excess, to a kind of overwriting that leaves the reader surfeited and slightly ill ("Directly overhead, an advance scout of the starry armies trembled like a pearl suspended in a gigantic goblet of heavenly nectar"). Updike's verbal exuberance is indeed "supermimetic." No one, I hope, will complain that Ellelloû's language cannot possibly be grounded in the background, education or psychology attributed to that character.

But the narcissistic, self-intoxicating element in Updike's style can also serve as a cover for certain defects of structure or narrative in his novel. Many aspects of Ellelloû's career remain improbable or unexplained in ways for which "creative license" is not an adequate excuse. . . . The premises of the novel are just realistic enough to make [certain] questions nag. Self-indulgence also accounts for the tedium that occurs in those passages where the characters make speeches at each other—brilliant speeches, to be sure, but speeches where the Updikean music leads *away* from the matter at hand.

Still, what a rich, surprising and often funny novel "The Coup" is. I had never thought of Updike as a particularly witty writer before, but "The Coup" displays an epigrammatic talent that again reminds me of Nabokov. . . .

This comedy of absurd cultural juxtaposition (which, like Waugh's, can sometimes bare a wonderfully menacing set of teeth) is sustained beautifully through much of Updike's fine novel. (p. 55)

> *Robert Towers, "Updike in Africa," in* The New York Times Book Review *(© 1978 by The New York Times Company; reprinted by permission), December 10, 1978, pp. 1, 55.*

JOHN THOMPSON

Updike was in Africa in 1973, one of the years of the great drought that reduced the always barren country around the Sahara to an absolute waste land. Out of what he saw, out of many books, and out of his own head he has made the nation of Kush [as the setting for his book, *The Coup*]. It is an audacious creation and there must have been some magic in it too because the entire nation is there in all its splendor, farce, and misery.

With much nerve and surely with some luck, Updike invented his Africa not the way other white novelists have done. He did not dispatch a Henderson or Lord Greystoke, some Francis Macomber or one of Paul Theroux's emissaries, or even a Basil Seal or a Marlowe to suffer his shock in the heart of darkness. Updike's book is written by the dictator himself, Colonel Hakim Félix Ellelloû. The Colonel is short, prim, and black. He is appealing and wicked, and to me at least he is like Africans I have known except that Updike knows him better than ever I knew an African and I knew them for years. The Colonel is frightening and I think he must have frightened Updike too, in a way that has done wonders for his writing.

In some twenty books of fiction, poetry, and criticism, Updike has tried to bring legend to his own America. He tried to give significance to the dumpy amours of housewives and dentists by lavishing on them many more metaphors than they knew what to do with. . . .

And the language was not just embroidery on nothing. Updike is a master of the techniques of modern fiction. His novels are solid with plot, character, and thought, as well as with melodious diction. He knows intimately the way the American middle class walks and talks, and knows every room in their "homes" and how they earn and spend money. He knows all too well how they fornicate. Why then should I say that I felt always something of the precocious in these substantial and skillful novels? It was as if some very clever boy with a great gift for language . . . , some clever boy was spying on the grownups with clairvoyant eyes for every gesture, every follicle and sebaceous cyst, but no real idea of why they are carrying on so disgustingly, or that to them it may not be ugly and evil to make love with another imperfect creature. That is why although it was right for Faulkner to use his Shakespearean powers on the ignoramuses of Mississippi, for Nabokov to give his murderer a fancy prose style—for that matter all right for Joyce—it has never seemed to me Updike quite got away with it. However it is not wrong to invoke these great names in the presence of John Updike's name.

In "Colonel Ellelloû"—"Félix"—"Hakim"—"Bini"— "Happy"—Updike has found his perfect spokesman. Overeducated in the French classics, overexperienced at Dien Bien Phu; overexposed to the dialects of the heartland of America at McCarthy College, Franchise, Wisconsin; oversold by Elijah Muhammad in the deviltries of whites and the glories of Islam: Félix is perfectly prepared to overwrite, and proud of it. . . .

The story jumps back and forth from farce to violence and from Kush to Franchise, Wisconsin. It is being told in his memoirs by the retired Colonel, where every detail of the story as plot appears most naturally and yet they are introduced, these details, even such little things as names, with the flair of a grand thriller. We learn early on that Félix has four wives; we are received by them, one by one, in the manner that only the best storytellers use in their invitations to meet people. Each is a brilliant surprise.

So, not at all to reproduce the manner of the telling, which is swift but intricate and never in serial chronology, sometimes in the first person and sometimes in Félix's view of himself in the third person—simply to give an idea of what it is about, it is about the ruler of a Waste Land. (p. 3)

Félix can speak out, as Updike never quite could, with

frankness what it is he hates and what he loves. Félix is very hard indeed on American blacks, American breakfast food, and on "Klipspringer," the all-knowing American global fixer. Félix is brilliantly hard on the Russians and on the slaveholding sheikdoms of Araby.

There is not a sentence in this book I will not gladly read again for instruction and delight. (pp. 3-4)

John Thompson, "Updike le Noir," in The New York Review of Books *(reprinted with permission from* The New York Review of Books; *copyright © 1978 Nyrev, Inc.), December 21, 1978, pp. 3-4.*

ALASTAIR REID

Kush, an imagined sub-Saharan country in Africa, a poor peanut-producing territory once ruled by the French under the name of Noire, is the improbable setting for John Updike's uncharacteristic new novel, "The Coup" . . . , and he has taken immense pains to make the territory tangible in some dazzling passages of physical description and re-creation. "The Coup" is really more fable than novel. At first reading, it seems to be a number of books in one, and veers abruptly from the lyrical to the intensely declarative to the hilarious, from character to caricature; but it has a high moral point of view, and some exotic set pieces, which contrive to move it toward the fabulous. Updike has become the most Nabokovian of writers—who else takes the trouble to make such beautifully modulated sentences, or gives prose in general the carefully observed attention more commonly given to poetry? "The Coup" purports to be the memoirs of Colonel Hakim Félix Ellelloû, . . . an account of the events leading to his fall, and sometimes a passionate, rueful tract on the post-revolutionary world. . . . (p. 65)

Updike most brilliantly contrives in language this struggle going on in Ellelloû, so that the reader is constantly aware of it. In his rather pompous piety, Ellelloû cites verses from the Koran, graceful and measured in their phrasing and wisdom. When a flat American cadence intrudes into the text, as it does increasingly, the effect is like a blow. It is, plainly, the language of the infidel. When Ellelloû goes to call on his second wife, Candace, whom he brought back to Kush from Franchise, and she greets him with the phrase "Holy Christ, look who it isn't," we wince. It is in language that Updike most clearly dramatizes his worlds in collision—the wild, untouchable natural world of Kush and the banal know-how of its ultimate colonizers—and it is in language, his true province, that the book is made to happen. It would do no service to "The Coup" to enumerate Updike's rich cast of minor characters, or the dramatic events he sets up to revel in, for the book ought to stay as an astonishment to his readers. Memorably, Kush lives. Call "The Coup" a caper, an indulgence, a tract, a chronicle, a fable—and it is all these things at different times—the fact is that Updike's sentences can be read with the pleasure that poetry can, and the fingers are more than enough to count the novelists of whom such a thing can be said. (pp. 66, 69)

Alastair Reid, "Updike Country," in The New Yorker (© *1978 by the New Yorker Magazine, Inc.), December 25, 1978, pp. 65-9.*

JOYCE CAROL OATES

What [Updike] has to say [in *The Coup*] is mordant, outrageous, and bitterly self-mocking, a lengthy monologue that really *is* a coup of sorts, constituting Updike's most experimental novel to date. Kush is Ellelloû's fiction just as *The Coup* is Updike's fastidiously circumscribed fiction, a country set in an "Africa" of words. And what a virtuoso display Updike gives us! Not even [Nabokov's] *Pale Fire,* another inspired work by another displaced "ruler," is more darkly comic, more abrasively surreal, than Updike's Ellelloû's testimony. . . .

Where Márquez's Faulknerian *The Autumn of the Patriarch* presented a bizarre dictator seen from without, filtered through the voices of a number of close observers, Updike's Nabokovian *The Coup* gives us the dictator in his own voice, as he sardonically and brokenly recounts the comic-opera events that led to his spiritual assassination. Nabokov's presence is felt throughout, but lightly and ingeniously, for Updike, unlike the self-indulgent Nabokov of *Ada,* that most relentlessly private of novels, has linked personal and authorial obsessions so gracefully with the outer chaos of Kush and the drama of the "super-paranoids" America and Russia that Ellelloû's story works quite satisfactorily as a story, without self-referential props. Updike's homage to Nabokov is clear enough, and rather touching: it is Ellelloû's "opposite number," the Soviet Colonel Sirin, who saves his life at a characteristically absurd moment—and Sirin, as we know, was Nabokov's early pseudonym. (p. 32)

Difficult as Kush's mountainous terrain is to navigate, by camel or Mercedes . . . the prose Updike has fashioned for him is even more difficult, and resembles nothing so much as an arabesque superimposed upon another arabesque. Motifs, phrases, "imagery," coarsely comic details from the "external world," Ellelloû's various and conflicting pasts, are rigorously interwoven into complex designs. The outer world, filling up slowly with American and Soviet junk, is a nightmare of vulgarity, and depressingly simple-minded; the inner world, the world of Ellelloû's ceaseless brooding, is correspondingly rich, elusive, teasing, ingenious. Updike has been accused in earlier, far more straightforward narratives like *Couples* and *The Centaur* (the novel that *The Coup* most resembles in its audacity and inspiration, if not in its tenderness) of writing self-indulgent, tortuous prose. That Updike has a painter's eye for detail, that he glories in what Joyce would call the suchness of a thing, and sees no reason, since it exists, *not* to describe it in detail, seems to me quite evident; but surely this is one of his strengths, one of the great virtues of his writing. By assigning the prose voice of *The Coup* to the defeated dictator Updike allows himself more freedom (or license) than he might ordinarily allow himself, and Ellelloû, plunging onward in his memoirs, as in his murky grotesque situation-comedy adventures, does the difficult work of characterizing himself. He remarks at one point that he knows his sentences are "maddeningly distended by seemingly imperative refinements and elaborations"; at another point—as he is about to execute the old king with a giant scimitar taken from its case in the People's Museum of Imperialist Atrocities—he thinks, "My mind in its exalted, distended condition had time to entertain many irrelevant images." Updike echoes or parodies earlier Updike, the earlier Updike (in the story "Wife-Wooing") paying homage to James Joyce of *The Sirens:* "Wide wadis remember ancient water, weird mesas have been shipped into shape by wicked, unwitnessed winds." (p. 33)

Beneath, behind, informing every scene of this inspired novel, which a superficial reading might judge as almost *too* inspired (a *tour de force* against readers' expectations, like Updike's very first novel *The Poorhouse Fair*, which was anything but a "young man's novel"), is a passionate and despairing cynicism which I take to be, for all its wit, Updike's considered view of where we are and where we are going. No moral uplift here; no gestures, like Bellow's, toward the essential "health" of the commonplace. (p. 34)

Judging from the stories in "another mode" in *Museums and Women*, and the highly self-conscious voice of *A Month of Sundays*, it might have seemed that Updike's genius was for fiction and not metafiction. (For why parody art if you can create it, why devise clever paste pearls if you own genuine pearls?) But *The Coup*, which makes only the most perfunctory gestures toward old-fashioned realism, let alone naturalism, is an immensely inspired and energetic work, striking, on page after page, the comic brilliancy that leaps from Joyce's *Ulysses*, in such chapters as *The Cyclops*, for instance, in which ferocious exaggeration becomes an art that is self-consuming; in its possibly more immediate relationship to Nabokov and Márquez, the novel sets down the improbable beside the probable, creating a "fictional" nation that is altogether convincing, and yet populating it with fools and knaves and tough-talking nagging wives who have the depth, if not the distinctiveness, of playing cards. *The Coup*'s coup is style. If entropy is capitalism's goal, just as it is "socialism's" goal, if life in our time has become so sterile . . . , there is all the more need for style, for art, for the unique, quirky, troubling visions that our finest artists force upon us.

Updike has grown amazingly cynical with the passage of time: how odd that the author of *Pigeon Feathers* should be evolving, before our eyes, into the Mark Twain of *The Mysterious Stranger*, or the Swift of Gulliver's final voyage, or the Samuel Beckett who says laconically that failure, not success, interests him! One would have not guessed the direction his novels might take, considering even the bitterly ironic ending of *Rabbit, Run* . . . , and the understated, unheroic conclusion of *Couples*, in which the hero and heroine, about whose emotions we know so very much, in such exhaustive detail, become, merely, in the end, just "another couple" in suburban America. Admirers of Updike's sardonic Bech stories, however, have sensed quite clearly the drift of Updike's mind, which finds its sharpest, least muffled, and least sentimental expression through the *persona* of Henry Bech, Updike's daimonic opposite (bachelor, Jew, perpetually blocked novelist who, at the conclusion of a recent story, finds that he cannot even sign his own name); Bech's view of the universe and of man's striving within it is as droll as Céline's, and he would, adroitly, with an allegorical instinct as habitual as Updike's, sketch in quick analogues between the drying-up of creative powers and the drying-up of fertile lands.

The world in which "Kush" is located is, after all, a "global village" in which individuals no longer exist, and tribes are relocated in a matter of days, to make way for multi-level parking garages, shopping malls, and McDonald's hamburger restaurants. Ellellou's prophetic zeal is commendable, but who among his people cares?—if "You will be Xed out by Exxon, ungulfed by Gulf, crushed by the US, disenfranchised by France, not only you but your entire loving nation of succulent wives, loyal brothers, right-

eous fathers, and aged but still amusing mothers. All inked out, absolutely. . . . In the vocabulary of profit there is no word for 'pity.'"

Is such cynicism soluble in art? Indeed yes. (pp. 34-5)

Joyce Carol Oates, in The New Republic *(reprinted by permission of* The New Republic; © *1979 by The New Republic, Inc.), January 6, 1979.*

GENE LYONS

The Coup attracted my interest because of its subject matter. Writing about the Sahel, I thought, might help transform the muffled glories of Updike's ornate prose into something leaner, or lend a gravity to his religious impulses that neither Skeeter nor the author's suburban adulterers had ever done. At times in *The Coup* that almost seems what Updike himself has in mind. . . .

Nobody would deny Updike's expository gifts, despite the occasional sentence that defies understanding. When it comes to such novelistic matters as plot, character and dialogue, however, his verbosity seems to overwhelm his judgment. Sentences and whole paragraphs detach themselves from the dramatic logic of the book until it can scarcely be said after a time to have one. Consider Kutunda, an illiterate, barefooted nomadic wench whom dictator Ellellou discovers on a tour of the drought-stricken northern part of the country while disguised as a beggar. . . . As an Updike character, of course, she . . . talks like this: "I'm sorry if I seemed preoccupied this morning, you caught me at a bad time, but I didn't fake my climax, I swear it. It was a beautiful climax, really. Only my President can lead me so utterly to forget myself. I am led to the brink of another world, and grow terrified lest I fall in and be annihilated. It's neat." Now astonishing cultural transformations are wrought everywhere in this electronic age of ours without the intervening stages of literacy, but *"It's neat"*? (p. 118)

Given that Updike cannot forbear making all of his characters sound like adulterous literature professors, it should not come as a surprise that the story line is a bit murky as well. In form the book is a memoir narrated by Ellellou from a Paris cafe table, where he has repaired in exile. Flashbacks to college days show the African student-in-exile in scenes more than a bit reminiscent of *Portnoy's Complaint* or *Annie Hall*. . . .

Outcroppings of thought-provoking eloquence decorate the text throughout, but are no sooner contemplated than they are followed by manifest absurdities. . . . For a time, indeed, I thought Updike's narrator had gone quite mad in the manner of Ellison's *Invisible Man*, particularly in the latter sections, and I have reread them carefully for clues. After a near fatal pilgrimage by foot and camel, Ellellou finds that the former King's head has been set up as a sort of tourist attraction with signs in several languages. Outside are concession stands "vending croissants and caviar, teriyaki and chili, kebab and hot dogs." Although the Russians are responsible, the King's head is pure Disneyland and speaks truth: "This man, while proclaiming hatred of the Americans, is in fact American at heart . . . and his political war, which causes him to burn gifts of food . . . is in truth a war within himself. . . ." In fact Updike goes to considerable lengths in his familiar fake-symbolic way, to insinuate that the desert nihilism that terrifies and attracts his hero, "the solitude, the monotony, the huge idiocy of this barren earth," is in fact, like the whiteness of Melville's whale, an essentially American form of dread. In the Portnoy-Annie Hall scenes, which are some of the best in the book and which Updike juxtaposes to the desert sequences, Wisconsin is full of snow, the enchanting but frightening nakedness of white women, and his future wife's living room, "the melting-iceberg shapes of its furniture, its whiteness and coldness and magnificent sterility; the emptiness, in short, of its lavish fullness. . . ." (p. 119)

That a symbolist reading of a long narrative can parse a Deep Hidden Meaning out of what is otherwise confused and even ridiculous is a symptom of a kind of cultural confusion about literary meaning that one can only point to in the space available. For all of his earnest erudition, Updike seems as incapable now of putting together a sustained and coherent novel without such foolishness as he was in *Rabbit Redux*. (p. 120)

> *Gene Lyons, "Cultural Deformations," in* The Nation *(copyright 1979 The Nation Associates), February 3, 1979, pp. 117-20.*

WILLIAM McPHERSON

The stories [in *Too Far to Go*] are consecutive, . . . and the same characters, Richard and Joan Maple, and the same themes—love, domesticity and infidelity, permanence and evanescence, blood and death—appear throughout. Together the stories form a single unit, rather like an Updike novel, rather like the Maples' marriage, a luxurious slow slide from grace, a 20-year trajectory from innocence to decadence.

The Maples begin, certainly, in innocence. . . . But they end, like the students in the butchers' school next to the church—two emblems that figure in the first story, "Snowing in Greenwich Village"—"all bloody and laughing." (p. E1)

Richard Maple is stubbornly determined to hold on to the aura of innocence while embracing the pleasures of decadence, rather like a spoiled child. . . .

Updike's protagonists always get the housewife up the street. It turns out she is much like the wife at home: intelligent, pretty, vaguely dissatisfied, compliant, ultimately mysterious. "They like one another," he writes in his foreword to the Maples stories, "and are mysteries to one another." Love and habit draw them together; time and boredom drive them apart. . . .

Updike writes in his foreword, "Though the Maples stories trace the decline and fall of a marriage, they also illumine a history in many ways happy, of growing children and a million mundane moments shared. That a marriage ends is less than ideal; but all things end under heaven, and if temporality is held to be invalidating, then nothing real succeeds."

These stories are real enough, as real as the toast crumbs on the breakfast table; the characters around it almost too familiar to inspire curiosity. The texture of the Maples' particular domestic life, the immediacy of their experience, is subtly, faithfully and rather wistfully rendered, perhaps because Updike's own experience seems to parallel that of Richard Maple. . . .

Fiction is not autobiography, yet all fiction, I am convinced, is in some sense rooted in autobiography though the connection to actual events may be tenuous indeed, even nonexistent. . . . It is the heightening of experience that I

miss in these stories, well-crafted and finely written as they are, and altogether unexceptional. They have the sweetness of almonds with a bitter one in the sack, and in a bitter almond there is a trace of cyanide, here masked as a charming but false innocence. The charm is seductive and ingratiating—winning in a child—but the innocence is meretricious. . . .

It seems to me [Updike] now faces a choice in his work: to recapitulate with another set of names the familiar story of peccadilloes in suburban paradises, of grace without pressure, or to go on to something else. He may already have done so. . . . [*The Coup*] seemed to point toward a tougher but wiser course. (p. E6)

> *William McPherson, in* Book World—The Washington Post *(© 1979, The Washington Post), March 18, 1979.*

PAUL THEROUX

So many of John Updike's characters seem to inhabit the suburbs of Splitsville and to toy with infidelity as soon as the shower presents are unwrapped that one things of them as naturally polygamous. . . . [It seems odd] that the gracenote of Updike's fiction should be optimism—a radiant box of corn flakes in the kitchen mess, a cascade of Calgonite offering an epiphany in the dishwasher, and so forth—because his people are not so much learning marriage as pondering a way out of it. . . .

Leaving aside the banality of this collection's title ["Too Far to Go"] (is it the "so long, so far" line of Donne's "The Extasie" hammered into Americanese?), there are several implausibilities in the stories. I am used to Updike's married men not having jobs, just as I am used to having him send his characters into the den to watch television so that he can make "Charlie's Angels" into a theology lesson, but Richard Maple looks so damnably unemployed that one begins to think this may be the cause of all the domestic uproar. "Domestic uproar" is a wild overstatement; indeed, that is my second suspicion of implausibility. . . . It strains one's credibility to read divorce stories in which none of the partners say "I could kill you!" or "You'll be sorry!"

But perhaps this is the very feature that distinguished them from the common run of howling, wound-licking, look-what-you-did-to-me fictions of recent years. They are the most civilized stories imaginable, and because of this the most tender. Updike, I thought when I read his novel "Marry Me," is the poet of the woe that is in marriage. It is rather to his credit that he conceives of marriage as something other than a Jabberwock; and because he avoids the pique and self-pity in that trap, his stories are celebrations rather than warnings. (p. 7)

If there is something seriously missing here, it is Joan's point of view. I think any married woman could quite justifiably accuse Updike of weighting his argument in favor of Richard; worse, he seems to want us to sympathize with and understand Richard, while at the same time pitying Joan. If the Maples were not being whirled apart—without a divorce they would hardly be worth writing about—this probably wouldn't matter; but it strikes me as special pleading to omit the other side of the story. We know too little about Joan and her analyst and her lovers and her panic.

"The moral of these stories is that all blessings are mixed,"

Updike writes in his foreword. "Also, that people are incorrigibly themselves." He might say as well that no one really belongs to anyone else and that marriage is an institution in which the exits are clearly marked. Updike is one of the few people around who has given subtle expression to what others have dismissed and cheapened by assuming it is a nightmare. The Maples are never closer than when they are performing their ceremony of divorce. (p. 34)

> Paul Theroux, "A Marriage of Mixed Blessings," *in* The New York Times Book Review (© *1979 by* The New York Times Company; reprinted by permission), April 8, 1979, pp. 7, 34.

W

WALKER, Ted (Edward Walker) 1934-

Walker is a British poet, editor, and translator. A nature poet frequently compared to Ted Hughes for his use of the natural world to comment upon human emotions, Walker is the cofounder of the literary magazine *Priapus*. (See also *Contemporary Authors*, Vols. 21-24, rev. ed.)

LAURENCE LIEBERMAN

In many of Ted Walker's poems, language facility works against the poet's eye; too many words with puzzling overtones, or connotations, pile up too fast, and the reader must strain to get past the impenetrable phrasing to anything behind it, beyond it. . . . Walker is more successful when a vividly pictured scene is kept sharply before the reader's eye until the finish, while meanings subtly add up to a forceful statement, inseparable from the persons or events which call them forth.

His best poems are the ones in which he dramatizes segments of being that have been crushed or suppressed by the conditions of civilized life, "wants kept caged on roofs / of the mind's tenements." Somehow, the dark neglected zones in the spirit hiddenly survive all the damages our indifference and half-aliveness can inflict. . . . In weaker poems, the shifts from description to message—statement of human analogy—are abrupt and unaccountable, and jar in the reader's ear. In the best poems, these two movements are carried on simultaneously, joined and jointed, seamlessly, in the poem's drama. The story movement—with animal protagonist in a setting that gradually shifts from a prescribed time and space to the stage of the human mind—is Walker's best mode. . . .

In Walker's vision, our suppressed animal impulses nearly always manifest themselves in our daily lives as mildly persistent fears, incipient edginess, emerging at odd moments from no detectable source, "some close, restless agency, half-detected." But if this queer nervousness often appears dimly to be at the mere periphery of our mental life, "the lurking spy / that snipes us from the wilderness / of dreams," it is because we have fallen so far from the essential core of our being, we don't guess the deeper vacuity of our inner life and its terrors. In these poems, we learn, self-defeatingly, to cope with our wasted inner life as mules, whose "withers twitch to flies." That is as far as Walker's first collection [*Fox on a Barn Door*] carried this drama—

the self exists in a stalemate with its terrors, half-crippled, conditioned to accept deadening compromises with loss.

But in *The Solitaries,* several poems deepen the vision, exploring psychic states in which the solitary human—or animal—soul, pushed or driven to harrowing extremity, finds a haunting beauty in the mere act of survival against powerful odds. (pp. 269-70)

> *Laurence Lieberman, in* The Yale Review (© *1968 by Yale University; reprinted by permission of the editors), Winter, 1968.*

The main reason [Ted Walker] does so much translating is probably that his own poems are limited, as well as fuelled, by his extraordinary penetration of nature, and the seed-catalogue specificity of terminology that seems to go with that cast of mind. Take this couple of stanzas from his poem "Bonfire" [in *The Night Bathers*]:

> All afternoon was the waft
> from blue fields, the stubble-scorch,
> prickling me to this. I crouch
> like an ancient to my craft,
> knowing this moment to lift
>
> dry leafage to little twigs
> and lean to a locked apex
> the slats of a smashed apple-box.
> Gripping broken ladder-legs,
> the blaze skips up to long logs
> of old, wasp-ruddled fruitwood. . . .

One relaxes in the safe hands of somebody who really knows his way around a garden. It's a quality of disciplined seeing that Richard Wilbur shares; the quality that Andrew Young used to exemplify. And over and above the quality of seeing there is the quality of the performance.

But *right* over and above both the seeing and the way the things seen are put together, the conclusions come pat: the poem's argument is all too plainly a vehicle for its particular images. As a consequence the satisfactions are many——gratifyingly many, and let there be no doubt that Mr. Walker is a good poet—but the surprises are few. . . .

From the make-up of this collection it's permissible to assume that Mr. Walker has sensed his danger and consequently stiffened his own work with translations of poems which attempt and achieve a greater amplitude of utterance

—poems which may start out from nature but which get something said without being dragged down into the concrete detail of chaffinch-husks and the precise pitch of a bloodwort's warble.

"The heart of Hialmar" is a case in point. The attentive reader may track down the original in Leconte de Lisle's *Poèmes barbares* and note how Mr. Walker has tried to meet the challenge of reproducing not only the movement of the quatrain (which pretty well means adding something of his own every four lines) but also the disturbingly familiar tone of Hialmar's address to the raven.

Unfortunately one can't successfully *tutoyer* in English by using the grammatically acceptable, but effectively counterproductive, *thou* and *thy,* so things go wrong: "Come, bold raven, eating men is thy art, Pick my breast open with thy iron beak", is not the same as "Viens par ici, Corbeau, mon brave mangeur d'hommes / Ouvre-moi la poitrine avec ton bec de fer". But at least the attempt to capture the purely human tone is there—and with all its nature-notes which may very well have attracted Mr. Walker's attention in the first place, *Le Coeur de Hialmar* is nevertheless primarily a poem about a man speaking. . . .

[The] translations should not be enough to mislead the reader into thinking that Mr. Walker, in his poetry as a whole, is easing up. On the contrary, he seems to be looking for a way out of the nature poetry he does to perfection and that comes to him with an ease which his artist's instinct is already teaching him to distrust.

> *"A Quality of Disciplined Seeing,"* in The Times Literary Supplement (© *Times Newspapers Ltd. (London) 1970; reproduced from* The Times Literary Supplement *by permission), June 18, 1970, p. 654.*

[Ted Walker] unites the compulsions of the natural world with the complexity of human energies. An elegant and sophisticated poet, despite the butch persona sometimes on view, he has consistently shown a rare delicacy in making the image that both precisely represents his natural subject and embodies psychological correspondences. He is as good at this in *Gloves to the Hangman* as in any of his previous collections; in "New Forest Ponies"

> I nudged them along the verge
> until their stallion came
> prancing a disremembered rage
>
> through the ice twilight. His strength
> was sapped, a softening thong
> of wash-leather.

It is Mr Walker's central gift that he is able to make that stallion, "a tame / elderly man in tweeds . . . all wildness shrunk", a superbly realized co-existent, as well as a symbol of sapped domestic man. . . . [*Gloves to the Hangman*] has many examples of this strength, "At Pentre Ifan", "Boy by a River" and "August" among them. There are two poems, however, that suggest new directions. One is "Letter to Marcel Proust", which is looser, more discursive and more humorous . . . than anything Mr Walker has [previously] published. The other is "Pig pig" in which the fourteenth-century hangman of the book's title tells in thirteen formally taut and physically gory sections why and how he executes his sow for killing a child. It is a poem of powerful narrative momentum, skilful characterization and

truly hideous, though in no way gratuitous, violence. In seeking and exposing the roots of cruelty, Mr Walker's savage drama is an exorcism, and his finest achievement. . . . (p. 646)

> The Times Literary Supplement (© *Times Newspaper Ltd. (London) 1973; reproduced from* The Times Literary Supplement *by permission), June 8, 1973.*

JULIAN GITZEN

[Ted Walker] conceives of living energy as the ultimate bulwark against mutability and death. Oppressed by man's cosmic isolation, Walker fittingly represents his human figures in spatial solitude. Those poems which concern his own experiences frequently portray him as a lonely figure silhouetted in dim light against a beach or moor. Sharing to an unusual degree the universal feeling that night is lonelier than day, Walker fittingly chooses dusk, darkness, or first light as backdrops for numerous poems, particularly those which find him brooding about death, to which he appears unable to reconcile himself. The vastness of the ocean, a regular presence in his verse, heightens the sense of loneliness, while his fascination with the tides reflects a preoccupation with mutability and death. For him change is more notable for what it destroys than for what it creates, and his sense of loss dictates his characteristic wistful or melancholy tone. He understands how time erodes our lives, as rain washes away the soil with terrifying steadiness, until at last all traces of our existence have been obliterated. . . . (pp. 329-30)

> *Julian Gitzen, in* The Midwest Quarterly *(copyright, 1974, by* The Midwest Quarterly, Kansas State College of Pittsburg), Summer, 1974.*

VERNON YOUNG

No poet writing in England today has a closer, more recondite knowledge of the secret life in the non-human universe than Ted Walker. In each of his four volumes to date . . . Walker has been contriving quiet, hair-raising (and musically precise) metaphors from his great gift for relating our inattentive senses to the cryptic features of animals, fish, birds—flowers, even—in which, if we paused to look (with *his* patience and his occult powers) we would see ourselves, or the wreck of ourselves, writ plain. A cautionary word. Walker does not on compulsion go hunting for similitudes; they arise naturally, or appear to, in the course of the poem, like a sudden tremor in tall grass as a fox shudders through before going to earth. . . . Walker is knowledgeably certain that life feeds on life; that our civil existence, for which he has a fully human respect, is purchased at the price of being witlessly outside the skin of things. He is nervously aware of blood under the fingernails, tyrannically, sensitive to the creep and push of seasons, something only a country-dwelling man would be alive to and suffer from or exult in—marvelling at our loss. (p. 599)

> *Vernon Young, in* The Hudson Review *(copyright © 1975 by The Hudson Review, Inc.; reprinted by permission), Vol. XXVIII, No. 4, Winter, 1975-76.*

CRAIG RAINE

Reading Ted Walker's well-made collection, *Burning the Ivy,* I was reminded of the joke about the man who invented television—in 1975. It worked but it wasn't sufficiently original. In order to praise Walker's animal poems, you'd have to forget that Ted Hughes invented animals in 1956. Naturally, there are good lines . . . but even the best have a remaindered feel about them. Moreover, Hughes isn't the only poltergeist throwing his weight around in these poems. . . . [Frost] is the main ghost in this cadence:

> Powdery mortar has begun to fall
> As fall it did our first winter here.

Throughout *Burning the Ivy,* one is aware of a white-haired figure guiding Ted Walker's elbow as he sagely moralises over his various agricultural tasks. But there are also touches of Betjeman . . . , Eliot's 'Burnt Norton' . . . , the awkwardly reverent Larkin . . . and Auden's 'Their Lonely Betters'. . . . In the end, you feel that literature itself is the really fatal influence. (p. 883)

Craig Raine, in New Statesman *(© 1978 The Statesman & Nation Publishing Co. Ltd.), December 22 & 29, 1978.*

ALAN BROWNJOHN

Burning the Ivy confirms [Ted Walker's] reputation rather than advancing it. What is by now a very familiar kind of animal poem (and Walker did a lot to make it familiar)—the one about the creature intensely observed when it suddenly intrudes on our over-civilised consciousness—gets shuffled towards the back of the book, where it is still very much alive in "Vipers" and "Wild bird in a living-room", and keeps company with a whole zodiac of others. Carefully crafted notations of domestic existence, of change, and mortality come forward, and most of them (including the poem providing the title) are honourably done, but solid instead of exciting. (p. 64)

Alan Brownjohn, in Encounter *(© 1979 by Encounter Ltd.), March, 1979.*

*   *   *

WALLACE, Irving   1916-

Wallace is a prolific American author of popular, topical novels, short stories, and screenplays. He has remarked that he tells his tales as if they were part of an oral tradition. (See also *CLC*, Vol. 7, and *Contemporary Authors*, Vols. 1-4, rev. ed.)

JOHN LEVERENCE

The flap about [*The Chapman Report*'s] overt sexuality was less than justified, especially when that novel is compared with *The Sins of Philip Fleming.* The earlier novel was much more sexually explicit, but no one bothered to attack it. The sexual controversy overlapped into the charges that Wallace had manufactured a bestseller by stringing together frantic sex with a scant story line. But if sex sold *Chapman,* then sex should have sold *Fleming.*

Wallace wrote *Chapman* because he wanted to write about married women and their problems—the sexual problems being minor compared to the insensitivity and stupidity of men. Thematically, *Chapman* is less about sexual matters than about the tensions of suburbia and how they are manifested in a variety of unhappy ways. If *Chapman* was bought and read for its sex, then many readers were disappointed. As Wallace told the Italian press after the novel was temporarily banned in Italy:

> I have not and cannot write obscenely or immorally. I have written of love and sex in

candid terms, and I shall again. In *The Chapman Report* I was writing not to stimulate, but to reflect an area of American society with which I am deeply acquainted. Too, I wished to explore certain aspects of female unhappiness and frustration in today's world. I wrote of American women I know—but perhaps I wrote of all women.

(p. 118)

Wallace's early mail came from middle-aged readers. By the late 1960's the majority of the fan mail was coming from high school and college students, and young people in their twenties or early thirties. "I couldn't fathom this at first, and finally I came to understand it. I had been, when I wrote *The Prize,* exactly where the maturing young people are today—suspicious of institutions, of bigness, of authority. In *The Prize* I had taken a sacred international institution, The Nobel Foundation, and I exposed the frailties of the institution, its politics, cynicism, pettiness. In search of truth I had traversed where our young would soon be marching. To have produced a work that would be respected and used by our young—well, that was truly gratifying." (pp. 124, 127)

What *The Chapman Report* owed to sex research was what *The Three Sirens* owed to anthropological forays into the South Seas, notably Margaret Mead's *The Coming of Age in Samoa.* Both novels were loosely based on a scientific activity that numerous people were involved in and some became famous for. No more, no less.

In *The Three Sirens* an American team of anthropologists and laymen descend upon a hidden Polynesian island to study a unique and hitherto undiscovered way of life. In the process they find that their own life styles need careful examination—perhaps more so than the lives of the natives. (p. 127)

If *The Three Sirens* dealt with anthropology, a subject not of general interest to the public, *The Man,* Wallace's next book, would touch two subjects that dominated our concerns from the early years of the 1960's until today—the death, or removal from office by impeachment, of a president, and the plight of Black America.

From the early 1950's Wallace had been eager to write a novel based on the situation of the Negro in contemporary America. He developed two novels and shelved both. He thought they added nothing to what had already been said well by Black authors. (p. 129)

Wallace's recurring interest in fact and fantasy has continuously dominated his writing, and the same fundamental questions have been raised again and again. Whatever the setting in whichever work, they are roughly these: What are the unique and shared problems of male and female in our society? How can an individual endure the social, psychological, physical and financial pressures of modern life and still be whole? Above all, where is the order and sense of it all?

In all of his novels Wallace has tried to tell readable, enjoyable stories, integrating plausible characters and thematic relevancies. In *The Sins of Philip Fleming* he tried to show how the pressures of career and marriage can render a man psychologically and physically impotent. In *The Chapman Report* he tried to reveal how the modern woman endures a multitude of indignities which leave her unfulfilled and un-happy, and how the modern means of learning the truth about her, as by sexual surveys, cannot reach the truth and can often do harm. In *The Prize* he investigated the mean-ing of success in contemporary society and sought to reveal the rickety facades of public honor and the latent strength within private failures. In *The Three Sirens* he wanted to show the restrictions and inhibitions imposed by artificial custom upon the lives of modern men and women, and to speculate on how they might learn from those they call un-civilized. In *The Man* he attacked the madness of racial prejudice and affirmed the intrinsic value as well as the human weaknesses beneath the skin of every individual. In *The Plot* he dealt with the central issue of our time, the possibility of nuclear destruction, and how men and women suffering our own sense of helplessness and fear can still affirm the worth of life. In *The Seven Minutes* he spoke out against moral prejudice and tried to show how censorship is a subtle form of the fear we ought to fear. In *The Word* he detailed modern man's lack of faith and his longing and need for that faith, and how our deepest personal problems are ineffable without a recognition of their spiritual roots. And in *The Fan Club* he described the sad and disturbing America that defines masculinity and femininity in terms of sex and power. (pp. 181-82)

> John Leverence, in his Irving Wallace: A Writer's
> Profile *(copyright © 1974 by The Popular Press),*
> *Popular Press, 1974.*

IRVING WALLACE

In beginning [research for a book], I'm always curious to investigate what psychological motives bring a certain per-son into his field or profession. Why is a surgeon a sur-geon? Why does he enjoy cutting flesh? Why is a psychia-trist a psychiatrist? Why does he like to tune in on patients' private lives? Why does that woman like to teach, and why does this man like to dig into the earth? And so—for *The Word*—why did this man choose to become a man of God? And, indeed, how much of a man of God is he truly? Is his motive spiritual, one of pure faith, and a desire to make life more bearable, and the certainty of death more acceptable to others? Or is his motive a desire for power and author-ity? Or is his motive more crass, a decision to promote be-lief in God in order to make a livelihood or gain wealth? (pp. 185, 187)

By the time I was ready to write, I was writing about a sub-ject as familiar to me as my own life. Indeed, the world of religion had become part of my life.

My earliest concept of *The Word* was to make it an inside story about the people who inhabit the world of Bible pub-lishing. . . . But as time passed, my approach to this novel began to change, and in the end I discarded most of this Bible publishing research and concentrated more on churchmen, theologians, and ordinary people seeking faith.

And, of course, as I wrote, I found I was writing more and more about myself. I mean, as much as you research new backgrounds or people, you still wind up writing about yourself in a novel. You have no choice. (p. 187)

[*The Prize*] is the novel that has the most of me in it. The protagonist is an author, Andrew Craig, and the great part of the inner Craig reflects the inner Irving Wallace, as well as many of the external facts about Craig which are drawn from my own history. In short, I'm saying an author can't

help but be a character in all of his books. The question is one of degree. . . . (p. 189)

My earliest books were nonfiction. But eventually I found this too restricting. The novel gave me a chance for more scope and variety. All of my novels, except my very first one, *The Sins of Philip Fleming,* and . . . [*The Fan Club*] have involved a good deal of research.

The Sins of Philip Fleming had no factual documentation and included no designed research whatsoever. The story, not the idea, simply was born out of my head, spontaneous-ly, from what I'd heard from other men. On this knowledge I superimposed my own experiences, feelings, and above all, my creative imaginings. From *The Chapman Report* to *The Word,* but much more in the latter than the former, I had wholly invented and imagined characters and situa-tions, but purposely set out to acquire factual information that seemed to belong in the narrative background and in dialogue. (p. 196)

This interspersing of fact with fiction gives most readers the feeling of absolute authenticity. I've had endless letters on *The Word* asking me if The Gospel According to James, which I had invented, really had been dug up by archeolo-gists, translated, and where copies might be purchased. Well, I suppose it seems real because I created the text par-tially out of my imagination and partially out of long neg-lected very real gospels that were passed over when the New Testament was assembled and sanctified. Further, while creating my gospel, I drew upon the best research, archeological discoveries, theories and speculations of the finest Biblical scholars. This gave my fiction an added un-derpinning of realism. (p. 197)

The reader has too much to cope with in daily life to spend spare time studying, learning. The reader wants to relax or escape. So the reader might buy a novel of mine and hope-fully become absorbed. In its pages he escapes, relaxes—but at the same time receives an almost subliminal input of off-beat, inside factual information. Education sugarcoated. Learning painlessly. . . .

There have always been documentary novels. But I've been credited with—or blamed for—starting the whole cycle again. (p. 199)

[My readers] are as curious about the world and its inhabit-ants as I am. . . . [They] want to know a truth that is truer than reality through fiction, but want that perceived truth supported by clearly factual evidence drawn from life and its histories around us. . . . [There] can no longer be una-dulterated fiction in the sense the purists would have it. The world is crowding us too much, flowing vats of information and experience into us at great speed. There are few earthly mysteries or wonders from afar. Unadulterated fiction can no longer compete with actuality. So fiction must absorb actuality, and then it must make an effort to exceed it to arrest and hold the weary through instinctive or carefully devised storytelling. (p. 201)

Perhaps the protagonists faintly resemble each other—but that is because each one, in part, reflects some part of my own character that is hidden. . . . [In] *The Fan Club,* there is no surrogate character representing me—there is no hero —there is only a heroine. And there is no research. I wanted to experiment, attempt a novel drawn entirely from my imagination, observation, experience, feelings—drawn out of my experience of years in this community—in Hollywood, in Los Angeles. In *The Fan Club,* I'm not dealing so much with my psyche as I am with my perceptions of persons I've been involved with or whose lives I've brushed against . . . , whose frustrations and yearnings have fascinated me. (p. 203)

[One] of the two things I'm interested in is people, yes—which translates into creating characters when writing. But the other thing I'm interested in . . . is ideas. I'm interested in the novel of ideas, the book that grows out of an unusual approach or notion, the book about something. (p. 206)

I like to have characters that I—and through me the reader—can identify with. Certainly, for the reader, a familiar character, one whose life resembles his life or the lives of others he knows, can be reassuring. You believe in a character who reacts to certain things the way you do, and it makes you feel better to read about a fictional character who secretly has your sexual hangups or perversions or who has your enthusiasms or doubts. The reader is very interested in such characters, and feels at home with them. And I attempt to create such characters because I feel at home with them.

There is one more point to be made about the value of familiar characters. . . . [The] reader may watch a small part of himself, or of someone close to him, perform—and know how it will come out, as he will seldom know how it will come out in real life.

On the other hand, I suspect most readers also like to read about characters they can't identify with, yet characters about whom they are very curious to know more.

You may choose to call such characters unique, but they are actually characters who are larger than life—certainly larger and far removed from the average person's life—the kind of characters the average person may read or hear about but will never come to meet or know intimately. (pp. 209-210)

[A] novel will be better and will last longer if it develops out of character. An idea can date, be wiped out fast by changing times and mores. But a book growing out of a memorable character—be it Robinson Crusoe or Emma Bovary or Sherlock Holmes—will be timeless and survive all change. (p. 214)

[Some] readers might avoid a novel about racism written by a black because they'd feel they were buying propaganda for the blacks, from a black. Those same readers, who know me as a storyteller with no single axe to grind, would more likely buy my novel on blacks [*The Man*] because they don't feel I'll be lecturing or propagandizing them. They know me, from the past, as a writer of suspense and entertainment, and they'll hope for more of the same, and indeed they'll get what they bargained for. But they'll get more. They'll get [a message, as well]. . . .

[My] mail from readers has been incredible—white readers admitting they'd been intolerant or bigoted but finding themselves caught up in *The Man,* well, it worked profound changes in their racial attitudes. That's been the most important thing of all to me, in terms of that novel and some of the others. The fact that what I've written has not only entertained people, but has actually changed them, educated them, made them better human beings by my standards. (p. 217)

I think writing for movies can be useful for most novelists. A remark like that is literary heresy, or at least it used to be. Years ago, the literati regarded movies as canned, contrived, glossy junk, the opposite of pure creativity. . . . Movies are no longer an anathema to the literati. With the death of the big studios, after television, movies became more freewheeling, creative, a burgeoning art form. So I guess it is less heretical for me, as a novelist, to say now that novelists have something to gain from movies other than money.

I'll tell you what a stint as a screenwriter can do for a novelist. For one thing, in working on screenplays, you learn to write a scene, to dramatize a confrontation, a conflict, or even a romantic meeting. You learn you can't have it happen off-stage, or condense it in exposition, or dust it off in past tense. (pp. 280-81)

Readers of my books often castigate me, in the mail, for allowing my stories to be changed in the film versions. They can't understand why I don't go along with the book, write the screenplay, and at least to see that the film is faithful to the book. They feel the movie is an extension of the book. I always write and tell them that it isn't, that the book is a separate thing, and my full and final statement. It would be too difficult for me to take materials I've lived with so many years in one medium, and attempt to condense and adapt them to another medium. Further, if I went along with each film, it would cost me, through loss of time, another book, and yet another. I prefer to stand on my book. The book represents me. The film is a different matter. I want the film to be good, of course, but if it is disappointing, it has nothing to do with me. The book is me. The film is them. (p. 327)

Irving Wallace, "Irving Wallace Speaking," in Irving Wallace: A Writer's Profile *by John Leverence (copyright © 1974 by The Popular Press), Popular Press, 1974, pp. 183-360.*

RAY B. BROWNE

In development, Wallace's novels start from a large and ranging base. Then they grow pyramidally, gradually concentrating the plot and shedding sub-plots and details as they rise until eventually the top is reached and the problem is solved. These plots are rich and complex, or they are overly complicated and confusing, depending on the reader's point of view. . . . [He] must have room and time to develop his novels in considerable detail to get across his message.

Once this message has been developed, however, after the puzzle has been solved, Wallace seems to lose most of his interest in the book. . . . [Wallace] is actually mostly gripped by the themes themselves. Little wonder then that after the questions and answers have been demonstrated and worked out, the author rushes to close the book, apparently content to erase the characters once they have illustrated his point. (p. 435)

Wallace assumes that after the problem raised in the novel has been settled, the world, which he does not see as having been really endangered, will rock on at about the same keel. Wallace's world is not as dark as those of many other writers. . . .

[Perhaps] it may seem absurd to say that Wallace can be embarrassed by sex and uses restraint in portraying it. But the statement holds. Wallace is the first to admit that sex sells books and that he wants to sell his works. But he also insists that sex is life and that he, if he would be true to life, must demonstrate that sex is a dominant force. (p. 437)

He is as explicit as he needs to be to demonstrate his point. But he is not salacious, not obscene, although he has been criticized for being so. Searchers for the pornographic need not look into his books. (p. 438)

Wallace has developed an effective style. It is direct, carefully chosen and clear. It is never tortured and egoistic. . . . If at times it appears wordy, this is because of Wallace's insistence that clarity of message is more important than brevity.

Both message and style have combined through the years to create works of considerable impact. *The Prize* set a kind of high-water mark in subject and accomplishment. Since that novel Wallace has continued to explore new areas of investigation and to provide rich entertainment. (pp. 438-39)

> *Ray B. Browne, "The Square Peg," in* Irving Wallace: A Writer's Profile *by John Leverence (copyright © 1974 by The Popular Press), Popular Press, 1974, pp. 431-42.*

TOM BUCKLEY

"The Two" is as much a curiosity as its subject [the life of Siamese twins]. The details of the collaboration between Irving Wallace, the novelist, and his daughter [Amy], a literary tyro, are not elucidated, but it seems unlikely that he spent much time on it. The lengthy list of acknowledgments includes Walter Kempthorne, whose "tireless correspondence and interviews, his initiative and persistence as a literary detective, truly made this book possible." Mr. Kempthorne's wife, Elizebethe, is thanked for "scholarship, fact checking and editing." Six other researchers here and abroad are cited by name.

Indeed, the book reads like a series of researchers' reports. The writing is flat, there is no point of view, and instead of a social context there are maddening irrelevancies. For example: The twins make a voyage, and the reader is treated to a minute description of the ship, its owner and his role in maritime commerce.

Chang and Eng, though, remain elusive. They were three-quarters Chinese, rather than Siamese. They spoke little, according to their families and friends, and seldom to each other. Proximity enforced mutual toleration. Their letters were formal in tone and content. Thus, their thoughts and emotions go largely unchronicled, and there are none of the imagined conversations that are an Irving Wallace hallmark.

Nor does "The Two" provide any information about Siamese twins in general. (pp. 46-7)

The most interesting material in "The Two," for that matter, has appeared before, in "Duet for a Lifetime" (1964) by Kay Hunter, a descendant of the discoverer of the twins, and in a third the space. (p. 47)

> *Tom Buckley, "The Siamese Connection," in* The New York Times Book Review *(© 1978 by The New York Times Company; reprinted by permission), March 19, 1978, pp. 14, 46-7.*

WARREN, Robert Penn   1905-

Warren is an American novelist, poet, critic, short story writer, playwright, essayist, and editor. His work is strongly regional in character, often drawing its inspiration from the land, the people, and the history of the South. The intense metaphysical nature of his poetry and the experimental style of his fiction have brought him critical acclaim. While he often incorporates elements of the past into his work and frequently bases his themes on specific historical events, Warren successfully transcends the local to comment in universal terms on the human condition. Warren has also achieved considerable status as a critic, and is generally regarded as a major exponent of the New Criticism. He has received Pulitzer Prizes for both fiction and poetry, and has won the National Book Award. (See also *CLC*, Vols. 1, 4, 6, 8, 10, and *Contemporary Authors*, Vols. 13-16, rev. ed.)

RICHARD LAW

Warren associated the acceptance of scientific determinism as a philosophy with the rise of totalitarianism—partly, one supposes, because that philosophy appears to be merely an expansion of the idea of cause and effect into a universal principle as applicable to human affairs as to the motion of billiard balls. Such a view *seems* scientific and therefore carries with it the implicit authority of science. . . . If, in an historical context, determinism tended to bolster non-ethical forms of authoritarianism, on the level of the individual life, Warren felt, with [John Crowe Ransom] and Allen Tate, that such a view of the world took man dangerously near the abyss. Warren's strategy in exploring that issue in *Night Rider* is to take a single catastrophic action (such as is imaged in the first scene in the novel) and to examine it in as many of its facets and implications as possible. The underlying question throughout is whether naturalism, as a frame of reference, is adequate to the "data" thus discovered: Does it encompass and account for all that we see? (pp. 43-4)

The issue of determinism is raised at several levels in the novel, most obviously in the political elements of the plot. Warren sets the action in a time of acute crisis analogous to the period in which he wrote, and the urgent and practical questions raised there translate very readily into more modern terms: is it possible to resist "outside" forces which threaten to plunge one's community into catastrophe? And if the community fights for certain idealistic values it holds dear, is it possible to preserve those values successfully on the battlefield? (p. 44)

[The bearing of] political events on the issue of naturalism seems clear: the antagonists seem unable to match the consequences of their actions with their intentions; they cannot control or predict the results of what they do, and they cannot act in the cause of "good" without committing "evil." There appear to be two worlds of experience which intersect only imperfectly in the action. The one, the external world, is deterministic, or largely so, and the other is subjective and internal. Human "will" in the latter does not translate simply or easily into action in the other. There is, in fact, as Warren has noted elsewhere, an "irony of success," something "inherent in the necessities of successful action which . . . [carries] with it the moral degradation of the idea."

At the political level, in fact, the evidence of the plot seems to point toward naturalism. Taken at face value, Munn's private fortunes also seem to confirm and illustrate the operation of deterministic forces. Initially, Munn's aims are partly idealistic. He shares with most of the other farmers in the association an ideal of economic justice. But as he is drawn deeper into the conflict, those ideals are among the first casualties of the war. Indeed, under the impact of what he feels forced to do, his very sense of identity becomes a casualty of the war. Munn's disintegration in turn calls into question the traditional, simplistic notion of will, for that conception presupposes a holistic entity or agent capable of volition. Warren's depiction of Munn's decline is a careful testing of our popular and largely unexamined mythology of self, especially as it relates to the larger issues of will and determinism. The calculated ironies between what Munn intends to do and what he achieves are illustrative of the problem. Munn becomes preoccupied with discovering or defining his own "real" nature, "a more than intermittent self." But in his search for self-identification, he kills a former client whom he had saved from hanging, rapes his own wife, helps lead a raid on tobacco warehouses, and betrays his best friend by committing adultery with his daughter. At the end, in an ironic inversion of "poetic justice," Munn is sought for a murder he did not commit, is betrayed because of an imagined offense he had not given, and—immediately after his first redeeming act—is ambushed and shot by soldiers sent to restore order to the community.

Like all the other events in his career, Munn's death is ambiguous, its actual nature an impenetrable mystery. It is impossible to determine whether it is a suicide "willed" by Munn himself or is rather the inevitable conclusion of a chain of events outside himself. (pp. 45-6)

The ambiguity of Munn's death-scene merely focuses the larger ambiguities which pervade the novel. If the outer world is a meaningless flux of forces as impersonal and amoral as the law of gravity, what of the human antagonists? There is the fact of their consciousness (the importance of which is continually emphasized through Warren's control of narrative perspective). But are the human actors in the drama nevertheless helpless atoms hurled this way and that in spite of their awareness? Warren raises several possibilities, ironically posing them for us in the consciousness of his baffled protagonist. (p. 46)

[Character and fate] are as symmetrically aligned in the novel as in Greek tragedy, and Warren seems to imply by that alignment yet another, and contrary, line of causation adequate to explain the action. What happens to most of the characters in the novel represents what they are at the deepest level. Their actions are a progressive and involuntary revelation of their inner natures, and death comes as a final epiphany of character. (p. 47)

Warren's intention in his first novel . . . is to pose these issues rather than resolve them. The most that one may properly claim is that, in spite of the artist's careful objectivity, there is some pressure exerted upon this "dialectical configuration" of "truths" to cohere in Truth. And the Truth which is being asserted is a definition of freedom of the will which transcends rather than denies the logic of naturalism.

Such a notion of truth, however, is so relative that it becomes nearly synonymous with "myth," as Warren has consistently used the word, and presages his later large af-

finities with the philosophy of William James. A myth is simply a version of reality, a construct by which the confusing welter of experience is reduced to order and significance. Warren, like James, seems to posit a "pluralistic" universe where no construct, however complex, is ever adequate to contain *all* of experience. (p. 51)

In *Night Rider,* the issue of naturalism obviously flows into the problem of defining the self, of discovering some entity capable of willing or of being acted upon by mechanistic forces. Controversy over the novel has centered from the first on Warren's characterization of Munn, but usually on other grounds. Most critics have judged Munn inadequate as a center of consciousness for the novel. It seems clear, however, that the obvious and severe limitations of Munn's awareness, rather than being the result of a defect in Warren's skill, are the point of the novel. . . . The characterization of Perse Munn is a brilliant device which involves the reader in a direct perception of that incongruity between intention and act, intellect and feeling, self and world, which so bewilders Munn. The reader's close-up view of Munn's disintegration is further calculated to dispel any predisposition toward a simplistic determinism or facile assignment of causes or motives in his decline, and should dissuade most readers from the view that the world is unitary and knowable.

Munn is indisputably an enigma, but he is an enigma to himself as well as to the reader, so the sources of his puzzlement are thematically significant. The narrative voice is limited, except in three or four instances, to a perspective approximately identical with Munn's, and those limitations seem expressly intended to convey the boundaries of Munn's vision. Munn, for instance, does not see very far into his own motives, and in nearly every case where he engages in baffled introspection, the narrative forces the reader to confront the same invisible barriers which encompass the protagonist. Through such means, the gradual crumbling of Munn's sense of identity is perceived directly by the reader, who is allowed, as it were, to participate in the very process of his disintegration.

In the first few scenes of *Night Rider,* Munn is established as a seemingly trustworthy center of consciousness and a ready object for the reader's sympathy. Warren then proceeds to undermine that too readily granted confidence until, by the end of the novel, the reader is largely alienated from what Munn has become. Precisely as alienated, in fact, as Munn is from himself. It is interesting to note that from the perspectives of most of the other characters in the novel . . . Munn seems an admirable, self-assured man. During the crisis in his community, he is selected as a leader almost as a matter of course. And it must be said in his behalf that he acts his part credibly.

The point is, however, that Munn's public behavior is a part which he acts, an unconscious role which both his community and he take for granted. Munn is the very figure of the Southern gentleman. . . . Outwardly, Munn represents his culture's version of the decent, enlightened gentleman.

Perse Munn is not the kind of man to engage frequently in deep soul-searching or introspection, but that, too, is part of his self-image as Southern gentleman. Munn's unexamined assumptions about his social identity unconsciously modify his every gesture and attitude. . . . Both the imperturbable reserve of [the] narrative voice and the consistent use of the appellation "Mr." before masculine proper names are echoes of Munn's own habits of address, and they suggest further how far he is imprisoned in a superficial public identity. Because he has no language—and no concepts, apparently—adequate to his inner life, Munn seems intolerably passive and emotionless. It is not that Munn lacks passions, but that he lacks a way to acknowledge and deal with them. (pp. 52, 54-6)

Why Munn's image of himself and his traditional role fail to provide him with a comprehensive mode of feeling and with values for dealing effectively with the world is left for the reader to infer. While he seems to embody important agrarian virtues and is the product of an agrarian culture, Munn is not immune to nihilistic doubt; he succumbs . . . to the forces of cultural change and upheaval. His social role and myth of himself become, under stress, a suffocating mask which distorts his vision and disguises him from himself. (p. 57)

The frequent need which Munn feels to discover the exact equivalent in language for some event in his experience is analogous to Warren's notion of the artist's task of rendering the world. To discover a language adequate to convey one's experience is to discover the meaning of that experience and to reduce it to coherence. But Munn finds in the constant disparity between word and event that same mysterious gap between conception and act which confronts him elsewhere. The "definition" of things on a page, he finds, is inevitably different from the things themselves. . . . And that difference produces in him a despairing lack of conviction in any construct or definition of reality. (pp. 57-8)

As Munn becomes detached from his own emotions, the language of the narrative becomes progressively detached and impersonal. There are provoking silences at crucial occasions in which both the reader and Munn are puzzled at Munn's inability to feel anything. (p. 59)

[By the end], whatever threads of continuity had existed among the confused and disparate elements of his being are irreparably snapped; the "seed of the future" has died in him, and he is numb to both the past and the future, able to exist imaginatively only in the present moment. . . . Toward the end Munn is startled by the unrecognizable face that stares at him from the mirror.

Munn's difficulty in sustaining his conviction of his own identity seems to imply the ultimate inadequacy of all such "myths," whether of self or of the world. The novel is thus not merely a depiction of the quest for "self-knowledge" that it is usually taken to be, but a depiction of the illusory and partial nature of all knowledge. The novel examines systematically the consequences of a loss of conviction in one's unconscious sense of self and all the unspoken, unexamined assumptions about the world which proceed from it. Toward the end, Munn cannot maintain the simplest connection among things in his mind: "the past . . . , which once seemed to have its meanings and its patterns, began to fall apart, act by act, incident by incident, thought by thought, each item into brutish separateness." . . . (pp. 59-60)

Munn's chief motive throughout the novel is the relatively modest hope of understanding what his life is about; it is the mainspring even of his atrocities. In this, and in his "restless appetite for definition," Munn is most typically human, most like ourselves, and like our conventional heroes. But everything Munn tries to grasp eludes him; for all his pain and effort, knowledge is not ultimately his. The naturalistic view of events at which he arrives late in the book clearly contributes to his problems rather than provides a solution. . . . To take the straight look at Nothing, at the abyss undisguised by our myths of order, is fatal. There is thus, finally, a pragmatic inadequacy in naturalism; it offers Munn nothing he can use, nothing he can live by. (pp. 60-1)

Richard Law, "Warren's 'Night Rider' and the Issue of Naturalism: The 'Nightmare' of Our Age," in The Southern Literary Journal *(copyright 1976 by the Department of English, University of North Carolina at Chapel Hill), Spring, 1976, pp. 41-61.*

DAVID BROMWICH

Mr. Warren's poetry has made itself felt, for some five decades, as a moral presence and a moral *pressure* of an unusual kind, and he is read by people who are genuinely interested in poetry. Since *Promises* (1956) the poems have grown steadily more impressive. He is not among the great originals of American poetry, yet, in their power to astonish, his poems resemble Melville's: there is the same tested and life-weary appeal to experience, with the sense of a fierce self-command maintained against all odds.

The modernism in Mr. Warren's poetry always seemed a displaced moralism. He refused to borrow, from Eliot or anyone else, new ways of organizing a poem: in this he was at several removes from the [Allen Tate] of "Ode to the Confederate Dead." What gave his early pieces the modern look was their use of such honorific abstractions as Time, and Hope, and Responsibility. Mr. Warren has become a better poet, to my mind, in proportion as he has learned to do without these. He is by temperament an observer of nature, a scholar of its morals, and an ironist when he is compelled to put nature side by side with morality. He can therefore be like Hardy, a little hard to take. But his vocabulary is more limited than Hardy's, and coaxes even more patiently, where decorum would lie in not coaxing at all. Mr. Warren sees, however, what few of us have seen. His poems draw their sustenance from a world of buzzards and swamps and forests almost unscarred; of iron loyalties and sudden betrayals; of the aimless talk of old men, interrupted by a rifle shot, and followed by silence. It is a world in which everything may depend on a rattlesnake heard scuttling for its hole, or a hawk seen obliquely among the shadows. (pp. 288-89)

The single lasting reservation one feels about this poet is that he cannot resist the big effect. There are times when it needs to be resisted, and a good poet ought to know those times: a phrase like "the delirious illusion of language" does not belong at the end of a genuine poem. Nevertheless, Mr. Warren has earned the name of poet several times over: a poet, after all, is a man who does what no one else, no other poet even, could do. (p. 289)

David Bromwich, in The Hudson Review *(copyright © 1977 by The Hudson Review, Inc.; reprinted by permission), Vol. XXX, No. 2, Summer, 1977.*

VICTOR H. STRANDBERG

A fundamental coherence unifies Warren's whole body of poetry, as though it constituted a single poem drawn out in a fugal pattern. . . . Ultimately, in fugal fashion, his three master themes interlock, so that at any point in the poet's career we are likely to see simultaneous traces of all three themes—and in at least one instance, "The Ballad of Billie Potts," they fuse into perfect harmony. But for the most part each theme has in its turn a period of predominance over the other two. (pp. 33-4)

By virtue of their dialectical interaction, Warren's grand themes of passage, the undiscovered self, and mysticism imparted continuous tension and growth. (p. 35)

In Warren's first published volume, *Thirty-six Poems* (1935), [the] theme of passage from innocence into a fallen state is apparent in a number of poem titles—"Man Coming of Age," "Problems of Knowledge," "So Frost Astounds," "Aged Man Surveys the Past Time," "The Garden"—and it not only permeates all the poems in the collection but also spills over into the subsequent *Eleven Poems on the Same Theme* (1942) and the new poems in *Selected Poems: 1923-1943*. As a whole, this latter collection (representing some twenty years of poetry-writing) divides itself fairly evenly between the two emotional poles that are naturally implicit in the lapsarian material: nostalgia and regret concerning paradise remembered; guilt, dread, and despair prevailing after the Fall. Often the two emotional states occur in the same poem, locked in dialectical conflict; but sometimes a whole poem is given over to one perspective or the other. (pp. 46-7)

[Considered as a whole], Warren's early poems constitute a rendering of the lapsarian experience and a weeding out of false responses to it. Following this weeding out process, the rudimentary elements of Warren's own response begin to appear in fragmentary passages. This response centers upon the poet's decision to accept his passage into the fallen world and to search for a sacrament, preferably in greater knowledge, whereby that world might compensate for its loss of meaning. As even Satan proclaimed while prostrate in Hell, all is still not lost so long as the unconquerable will endures. While hardly ready to emulate Milton's heroic rebel, Warren's persona does insist upon that small measure of existential freedom that even a fallen world cannot extinguish, and in that freedom some few embers of hope and courage may yet be nourished. (p. 62)

Of all the volumes of poetry Warren has published to date, *You, Emperors, and Others* remains the least satisfactorily understood and appreciated. Called "seventy-nine pages of poems largely about nothing in the world" by one critic, and "an exercise in metrical high jinks, . . . an artistic vacation" by another, the volume is best understood, I think, in the light of Warren's earlier poetry, particularly with reference to our three grand themes. . . . [The] poems of passage in *You, Emperors, and Others* properly begin with "Mortmain," the sequence on the death of the poet's father, an experience harrowing enough to set Time's reel moving backwards to both the poet's and his father's prelapsarian boyhood. (pp. 73-4)

Far removed from this family setting, the next victim of passage into the world's stew in *You, Emperors, and Others* is Achilles in "Fatal Interview: Penthesilea and Achilles," where Warren continues his longstanding practice of reinterpreting myth and history to suit his private system. [It is written] in the Homeric grand style, with admirably graphic details and vivid metaphors. . . . (p. 76)

In the final three sections of *You, Emperors, and Others* we find Warren's psychology of passage somewhat departmentalized according to life's major phases. "Autumnal Equinox on Mediterranean Beach" is an older man's mood poem, wherein gusty blasts of autumn wind are welcomed as a correlative of the speaker's disillusion with summer's phony paradise. . . . [The mood turns sourer] at the poem's conclusion, which observes that in this fallen world neither nature nor its God cares who suffers or who benefits in the turn of its seasons. The poem's cacophonous noises seem to objectify the speaker's black mood. . . . In form, content, theme, and setting, this poem sufficiently resembles Shelley's famous "Ode to the West Wind" to suggest possible parody: oh, wind, if autumn comes, can winter be far behind? (pp. 81-2)

During the six years between *You, Emperors, and Others* and the publication of *Tale of Time: New Poems, 1960-66*, several changes in the materials of the poet's art occur: a shift in geography with Vermont replacing Italy as a favored setting; and interest in biblical characters supplanting Achilles and the Roman emperors of classical antiquity; and the development of his children's minds providing a foil to his own melancholy meditations. In other respects, however, *Tale of Time* fastens upon the recurrently familiar, most importantly in the poems of passage situation. Of the six major poem sequences [in] the collection, five treat the Fall from a more innocent view of life as the predominant issue; the two poems that lie outside the sequence format also treat the theme of bitter knowledge. (One of these, "Shoes in the Rain Jungle," is an early protest poem that sees the Vietnam war as evidence of an ominous national innocence; and the other, "Fall Comes in Back-Country Vermont," exploits symbolically the poet's favorite seasonal setting.) (pp. 84-5)

[In *Can I See Arcturus from Where I Stand? Poems 1975*] we find the themes of his earlier volumes extended, modified, or otherwise "made new" through strikingly novel achievements in imagery, tone, and form. Concerning the theme of passage, the main event of these poems is a return to his motif of the bifurcated self—the unified prelapsarian psyche having been split, after the trauma of passage, between the fallen self in a ruined world and an alter ego or anima disappearing toward a higher realm of being. It was some forty years ago, in *Thirty-six Poems* (1935) and the first few of the *Eleven Poems on the Same Theme*, when Warren last addressed this subject so intensively. In these recent poems he extends the motif to what one must suppose is an ultimate level of intensity. There is also increasing use of the pronoun "you" to refer to the fallen self. (This "you" is sharply distinguished from the "you" of Warren's middle period, the 1940s and 1950s, when it referred to an idealized self-image.) (pp. 109-10)

[Through] what we have called Warren's poetry of passage, the configuration of his thought has assumed a pattern similar to that of poets like Wordsworth and Dylan Thomas in their regret over the loss of a prelapsarian self and in their poetic attempts to eulogize the lost self. Warren departs sharply from such companion spirits, however, in his next stage of development, wherein the psyche in its fallen state is at last compelled to cope with its new and terrible sense of reality. This new sense of reality, reaching both outward into the immensity of time and space and inward toward an innate depravity that Warren calls "Original Sin," typically imposes upon the Warren personae identities that they find unacceptable and seek to evade at all costs. Yet it is this mode of identity alone that can remedy the effects of passage on the Warren persona by reconciling the warring parts of the psyche and making possible redemptive mystic perceptions. Extending through *Eleven Poems on the Same Theme* (1942), "The Ballad of Billie Potts" (1943), and *Brother to Dragons* (1953), this psychological metamorphosis occupies the crucial center of Warren's poetic career, producing major changes in form and carrying his theme into that zone of the psyche which C. G. Jung denoted as "The Undiscovered Self." (p. 121)

As we proceed toward the center of Warren's poetic vision, we find that [the] vanishing of the prelapsarian self is prologue to a grander obsession in Warren's total canon—namely, the effort to find or construct some sense of identity that may fill what "The Ballad of Billie Potts" calls "the old shell of self," left behind in the fallen world like the cicada's cast-off casing, "thin, ghostly, translucent, light as air." This effort may never reach a satisfactory conclusion, for the experience of the Fall renders such genuine innocence and total wholeness of self irrecoverable. But the craving to recreate that original felicity is one of mankind's deepest obsessions, in Warren's judgment—it motivates the Happy Valley episode in *At Heaven's Gate* and Jack Burden's Great Sleep, Going West, and Back-to-the-Foetus psychology in *All the King's Men*, to mention two rather grotesque fictional examples.

Since the 1940s, when Warren's poetry first began to manifest such characteristics of short fiction as plot and character, this psychological dilemma has evoked narrative and dramatic elements to add to his already well-developed lyric mode of earlier decades. It is particularly through dramatic characterization—monologues, debates, parts of the self in conflict, dialectical confrontations—that Warren has developed his identity-psychology. At the same time he has relied on extended narratives or sequence-arrangements to effect dramatic development in a large number of shorter poems, several medium length ones ("The Ballad of Billie Potts" and *Audubon*), and one book-length masterpiece, *Brother to Dragons*. Among the diverse characters depicted —biblical, classical, legendary, or historical; and those drawn from personal reminiscence or imagination—the two types most important to Warren's identity-psychology are what we may call the Clean and the Dirty.

These two types, whose dialectical opposition provided much of the structure in *All the King's Men*, carry their warfare to the deepest psychological levels in Warren's poetry. Warren's Clean people—those who refuse passage into a polluted and compromised adult environment—range from mild and harmless eremites, victims perhaps of the fundamentalist Protestantism of the poet's native region, to murderous psychopaths like the prophet Elijah in *A Tale of Time* who "screams" in ecstasy at the spectacle of the Dirty people (the prophets of Baal) being butchered. As a poet of reality, Warren naturally tends to side with the Dirty people, partly because their apprehension of the world correlates more largely with the actual state of things, but most importantly because those who accept passage into the world's stew are empowered thereby to pro-

ceed to the subsequent stages of spiritual development represented in this discussion by the phrases "The Undiscovered Self" and "Mysticism."

If the poems of passage constitute, collectively, Warren's "Songs of Experience," we might call his small but fine group of poems on the Clean people his "Songs of Innocence"—with the concept of innocence, as we might expect in Warren's work, heavily drenched in irony. For in the "One Life" perspective there is no such thing as innocence, but only the delusion of one's separateness from the filth of the world or, even worse, the delusion that one must rise up and cleanse the fallen world of its putrid corruption. Warren's career as a prose writer began with his portrait of one such world-cleanser, the redoubtable John Brown, whose truth is lyrically still marching on but whose little known cleansing operations before Harper's Ferry included the deliberate slaughter of several whole families in the Kansas-Nebraska territory. Following the John Brown model, the Clean figure rising up in the holy purity of his ideal to rid the world of its putrefaction has been one of Warren's most recurrent fictional types.... Both the world-cleansers and those who merely retire from the world's stew into their private righteousness are making a cardinal error that precludes their glimpsing the one life or osmosis of being vision that is Warren's final answer to the quest for identity. After all, anyone might love the world after it has been purified and trasformed by the New Creation of religious prophecy or by its modern secular counterpart of political millennialism. But in Warren's opinion such love fails the first requirement of a realistic religious imagination, which is to love the world and its denizens just as they are, brimming with pain, injustice, and corruption.

Both of Warren's Clean types make their appearance at about the beginning of the middle phase of his poetic career in *Eleven Poems on the Same Theme* and the *Mexico Is a Foreign Country* sequence (in *Selected Poems: 1923-1943*); and both types have continued to figure in all of the subsequent volumes.... [In portraying the world-cleansers] what Warren objects to is the tendency of every ideology to interpret the world symbolically. When applied to human affairs this tendency has proved exceptionally catastrophic in our age, leading to terrorism, genocide, and military slaughter of unimaginable proportions. (pp. 122-24)

A willingness to shed other people's blood for the sake of an idea marks off these world-cleansers from Warren's other Clean people, whom he treats with a gentler irony that sometimes dissolves into empathy. (p. 126)

Warren's preference for the Dirty is not purely ironic or perverse. Like Hawthorne, Warren feels that in a fallen world some merit attaches even to sin, vice, and guilt. Whereas righteousness separates, guilt unifies the human community. To feel guilty towards someone is to have a genuine, if unhappy, relationship with the injured party; and to commit sin is to share a humiliation—an erosion of the ideal self-image—that exempts very few. Unbeknownst to the Clean in their aloofness, a sense of complicity is finally the true cement of the human bond, ultimately binding all creatures into Warren's "mystic Osmosis of Being." (p. 128)

So we come to the central subject of Warren's poetry and the most dramatic and original thing in it, to which the poems of passage form but an elaborate prelude. Culminating the motif of the Clean and the Dirty, Warren's long and crucial series of *you* poems forms the arena wherein guilt and innocence stage their epic battle for possession of the psyche—bringing us squarely into [Jungian territory]. . . . Beginning with *Eleven Poems on the Same Theme* and "The Ballad of Billie Potts" (1942, 1943), and continuing through *Brother to Dragons* (*you* being Thomas Jefferson), *Promises* (especially "Ballad of a Sweet Dream of Peace"), and *You, Emperors, and Others* (notably the "Garland for You" sequence), the *you* poems have been Warren's most obscure and for that reason least appreciated body of verse. But they are certainly his most distinctive and probably his most important poetic works.

In Warren's poems of passage, the trauma of passage typically involves recognition of the fallen world "out there," after a knowledge of naturalistic reality has cast the child-self out of his original worldly paradise and forced him irremediably into the realm of time and death and losses. But unlike such other poets of passage as Wordsworth, Housman, and Dylan Thomas, Warren proceeds beyond the self-consoling stance that normally obtains at this point . . . to deal with a trauma even greater than that of naturalistic loss and oblivion—namely, the humiliating sense of inward pollution that we might call the psyche's fall from the Clean to the Dirty. Beginning as a peripheral subject in *Thirty-six Poems*, this motif swelled to central importance in Warren's second volume, *Eleven Poems on the Same Theme*, and continued to dominate the poetry of the 1940s and 1950s. (pp. 130-31)

[*Eleven Poems on the Same Theme*] presents a psychological drama that defines the issues and equips us for understanding Warren's whole body of subsequent poetry. Its antagonists are the conscious against the unconscious self; its setting moves from the fallen naturalistic world of the poems of passage through the interior darkness in the house of the psyche (attic to cellar); and the issue at stake is the possible redemption of man, "the groping God-ward, though blind," through the uniting of self, of all selves, in the attainment of identity.

Above all, the development toward a Jamesian "Conversion" through the ministrations of a Jungian undiscovered self gives *Eleven Poems* a crucial place in the Warren canon, for its metaphor of a repressed shadow self that was slain and buried in the dank cellar of the house of the psyche (only to rise again) became a protean master metaphor in the later poems. . . . Although its central drama awaits resolution in Warren's later verse, *Eleven Poems on the Same Theme* may be considered a masterful achievement in its own right: original in its conception, significant in its import, and striking in its presentation. The emergence of a major new vision and voice in American poetry dates from this work.

In "The Ballad of Billie Potts" Warren's three ground themes of passage, the undiscovered self, and mysticism fuse for the first time into his single paramount theme of identity. (pp. 148-49)

[The] basic structure of "Billie Potts" follows the principle, common since Whitman's time, of patterning a poem after a musical composition. . . . Warren's "Ballad" unfolds in a fugue-like arrangement, its three ground themes interweaving throughout the poem until they converge to form a most extraordinary terminal crescendo. The theme of passage, to

begin, renders both setting and characters in such a way as to underscore appropriate mythical allusions. Although Warren sets his story in the frontier country of America, he evokes the image of a very ancient time through his setting "in the land between the rivers." Mesopotamia, which translated means "the land between the rivers," has long been regarded in Semitic myth, including the Garden of Eden story, as the birthplace of mankind. So Warren subtly implies as early as line 2 of this poem the origin and outcome of the myth he is recreating in the context of New World innocence and its Fall. The importance of this phrase ("the land between the rivers") is indicated by the fact that it becomes the recurrent refrain throughout the ballad, and it ties in with the water imagery that later emerges to predominant significance in the poem.

The characters also suggest Edenic analogies. In the first stanza Warren depicts Big Billie Potts as an American Adam—already fallen but not yet aware of the literal death his sin will entail for his posterity. . . . The resemblance between Big Billie's wife and Eve is seen [clearly]. . . . And Little Billie, if lacking Edenic dimensions, is at least a prime candidate for Warren's psychology of passage because of his rather vulnerable adolescent innocence. . . . (pp. 149-50)

[In the "Ballad"] the psychology of passage leads to Warren's second ground theme, the undiscovered self. Not the sought after innocence but a terrible knowledge has ended the quest for identity. Not the child-self but the Old Man has answered, in Mephistophelean perversity, the heart's deep summons, its yearning to complete its own definition. Allegorically, then, for Billie as for his Edenic prototypes, passage into the fallen world brings death and the Jungian shadow and subjects the seeker of identity mainly to knowledge of identity's limitations: naturalistic annihilation and inward depravity, twin gifts of the father, "the patrimony of your crime." With the hatchet's fall the theme of passage culminates; having fused sin and death in one sublime stroke, it can go no farther. The narrative part of the "Ballad" therefore unravels to its denouement quickly, with the conniving parents finding to their grief and horror just who was this stranger they have killed for his money.

With the narrative ballad finished and Little Billie dead, Warren is free to move his true subject and his true main character to center stage—namely, the *you* of the poem's parenthetical passages. For it is not Billie Potts, but *you* that he has been talking about all along, *you* being as always the Clean part of one's identity that William James called the ideal self and Freud called the superego. In fact, one of the subtlest and finest things in the poem is the shifting identity of *you*. Like Billie, *you* began the poem as a Clean fellow with primal innocence safely intact, as befits the conscious ego that is unaware of its connection to the Jungian shadow. To further bait the trap, Warren's narrator initially aligns *his* identity with *you*, both personae being mere innocent observers who scrutinize the scene of this crime of time past from the safely sanitized shelter of time present. . . . (p. 153)

[In] the seventh parenthetical passage, Little Billie vanishes from the text and leaves *you* fully to assume his quest and his identity, and so to carry them into the eighth and final parenthetical passage which concludes the poem. This passage—surely both one of the finest things Warren has written and one of the landmarks of modern poetry—resolves the theme of identity by dovetailing the undiscovered self with a pantheistic mysticism. So far as the undiscovered self is concerned, *you* now at last head back to the father figure whose fallen condition . . . represents the missing element of your identity: "And the father waits for the son." Bowing in humility to that loathsome figure and acknowledging consanguinity with him, *you* will thereby complete your knowledge of who you are. In *Eleven Poems* and later in *Brother to Dragons*, the theme of the undiscovered self is likewise resolved only when the Jamesian ideal self or Freudian superego submits in this fashion to acknowledge its id or animus or shadow. But it is doubtful whether Warren ever again captured that moment of fearsome though necessary psychic integration with such perfect clarity, economy, and power as he did at the end of "Billie Potts":

> And you, wanderer, back,
> After the striving and the wind's word,
> To kneel
> Here in the evening empty of wind or bird,
> To kneel in the sacramental silence of evening
> At the feet of the old man
> Who is evil and ignorant and old. . . .

This passage thus serves as the culmination for Warren's theme of the undiscovered self and also provides a convenient bridge to the poem's third ground theme of mysticism through religious diction and imagery. The devoutness of tone and setting ("in the sacramental silence of evening"), the hushed imminence of eternity ("evening empty of wind or bird"), the son's humble posture of genuflexion, the archetypal connotations of the father and son motif—echoes and allusions like these strike deeply into the Western religious consciousness. Above all in the tableau of Son bowing his head to the hatchet in the silence of evening we have overtones of Christ in Gethsemane. (pp. 156-57)

In "Billie Potts" [a wish for cosmic unity is] turned into reality, as Warren's earliest and perhaps most powerful version of his "osmosis of being" vision blooms suddenly vast as Dante's celestial rose. This irruption of what James and Freud called "cosmic consciousness" provides the poem's final resolution for Warren's ground theme of identity, a resolution that endures as the "One Flesh" idea—akin to Coleridge's "One Life" theme in *The Ancient Mariner*—throughout Warren's subsequent poetry. What binds the "One Life" into unity is precisely the intuition that, as Warren has said elsewhere, all life lifts towards its own definition. Ultimate identity comes from participation in that great quest shared alike by all creation. . . .

For its power of imagery, its remarkable richness of sound texture, and its profundity of theme, these closing stanzas of "Billie Potts" must rank as Warren's very finest achievement in verse. (p. 160)

"Billie Potts" is probably Warren's best poem, and almost certainly his most important. Its brilliant imagery, its wide-ranging command of sound texture, and its novel synthesis of Warren's three master themes—passage, the undiscovered self, and mysticism—render the "Ballad" analogous to *Tintern Abbey* as the crucial poem in its author's maturation as a poet. From this point on Warren would be a "finished" artist, capable of very substantial technical innovations in later decades, but having essentially completed his formation of a fully developed point of view. Perhaps it was

this sense of poetic self-completion that lay behind the ten year lapse between the "Ballad" and Warren's next publication in verse, *Brother to Dragons*. (p. 163)

[The] matter of communication between the conscious self and the unconscious is the crucial issue in *Brother to Dragons*, as it is in much of Warren's earlier verse. Here also, and with particular reference to *Eleven Poems on the Same Theme*, the initial overtures are made by the deeper self, the serpent-self which the conscious mind tries so hard to repudiate. In contrast to the aloof and prideful surface self, the deeper self appears not so monstrous after all. Instead, it comes forward in shy, sad humility, begging and giving forgiveness simultaneously, asking only to be reunited with its brother self, the conscious identity. (p. 180)

Warren's central themes and preoccupations have remained largely consistent. Questions of man's place in the total scheme of time and nature, of his relationship to the other beings with whom he shares existence, and of his guilt and complicity in the evils that surround him—those questions, in short, that make up the problem of the search for identity—recur from Warren's earliest work to his latest. Because the search for identity becomes, necessarily, an attempt to define reality, and because reality presents itself to us ambiguously—in men's heroism and depravity, in nature's beauty and horror—Warren's work most often assumes a dialectical configuration: the Clean versus the Dirty, the One versus the Many, Solipsism versus Synthesis of Being, Time versus no-Time, Consciousness versus Dream and Intuition. Given this dualistic perception of things, Warren's poetry must try to reconcile opposites. . . . (p. 191)

[His essay "Knowledge and the Image of Man"] advances two propositions: first, that the end or purpose of man's existence is knowledge, particularly self-knowledge; and second, that this knowledge—of one's ultimate identity, as it turns out—comes through a vision or experience of interrelationships that Warren calls "the osmosis of being": "[Man is] in the world with continual and intimate interpenetration, an inevitable osmosis of being, which in the end does not deny, but affirms, his identity."

In all his writings Warren's most negative characters are those who reject the osmosis of being, while his spiritual guides are those who accept it. . . . An awakening to this truth typically provides the structure for Warren's fiction and poetry alike. Osmosis of being affords the central vision of *Audubon: A Vision;* requires Jack Burden in *All the King's Men* to accept responsibility for history; causes Thomas Jefferson in *Brother to Dragons* to acknowledge complicity in murder; leads a long series of Warren characters in all his novels towards acceptance of a father figure, however shabby or tainted; and draws forth the theme of a reconciliation between conscious and unconscious zones of the psyche in Warren's poetry about the undiscovered self. And ultimately osmosis of being imparts whatever meaning the self may have within eternity, absorbing the self into the totality of time and nature with the consoling promise, often repeated in Warren's work, that "nothing is ever lost."

Hence, Warren's osmosis has moral, metaphysical, and psychological ramifications; it is his contribution to modern religious thought, having an ethical and a mystical dimension. Looking back over Warren's career, moreover, we may find that osmosis was there all the time, . . . implicit in the early works and explicit later on. (pp. 191-92)

Since he enunciated in *Promises* his central concept that "Time is a dream and we're all one Flesh, at last," Warren's subsequent volumes of poetry have been deeply affected by it. This concept has given coherence and direction to his work; it constitutes the "figure in the carpet" that Henry James talked about, "the primal plan" that "stretches from book to book." In *Tale of Time* (1966) and *Incarnations* (1968), Warren pursues the meanings of time and flesh somewhat separately, or at least with the stronger emphasis each title implies, although ultimately these meanings are inseparable. In these books, and in those that come before and after (*You, Emperors, and Others; Audubon: A Vision;* and *Or Else*), Warren's basic premise has been that the meaning of one's flesh is best perceived in the incarnation of other beings. Of paramount importance in this study is the recurrence in book after book of flesh which is dying or knows itself doomed to extinction. For the moment of extinction is when the dream of Time is about to end and the one Flesh concept is to become manifest. In *Promises* the snake propped high on a pitchfork tine and the men being hanged project this image, which the later books underscore increasingly. Some of the most moving poems in *You, Emperors, and Others* fall into this category. (p. 205)

[For] Warren, in Nature's grand eucharist, nothing is innocent and all are cannibals. . . . The meaning of one's flesh, therefore, can be understood, if at all, only in the light of an osmotic relationship that binds everything into unity and complicity together. (p. 209)

[For Warren himself], as for his various personae, a life as a conscious being is a tool to be used up in the service of the larger being that goes on eternally. But if the price of osmosis is high, meaning death for the conscious ego, its rewards are also high, meaning a kind of immortality through the ministrations of that shadow self so often shunned and loathed and locked out of the house of the psyche. For the shadow self, as made known in dream or animal intuition, is perfectly at ease in that infinitude of time and space which smites the conscious mind with the anxiety that man and his earth are bubbles in a cosmic ocean. The indestructibility of this deeper self was implied in its survival through *Eleven Poems,* despite murder and burial in the house of the psyche's cellar, and this immortality seems even clearer in *Brother to Dragons,* with particular reference to the serpent and catfish metaphors. In having "the face of the last torturer," the catfish is clearly associated with the "original sin" aspect of Warren's thought, but it also has redemptive possibilities not given to the conscious ego. Using ice to denote the separation between the world of light and time and consciousness above, and the timeless, totally dark world of unconsciousness below, Warren enviously describes the catfish as having "perfect adjustment" (or we might say osmosis) with its environment and thereby being "at one with God."

In its oneness with the total darkness under ice, the catfish need not fear, as the conscious ego must, the awesome infinitude of time and cosmos above the ice. . . . (pp. 214-15)

"Perfect adjustment," being "at one with God," and knowing at last who you are—such are the final rewards of Warren's osmosis, though its final price is the death of the conscious ego. "And the death of the self is the beginning of selfhood," R.P.W. had stated in *Brother to Dragons*. But the collective selfhood under the aegis of one flesh appears clearly superior to the separate ego, not only because of its

gift of immortality but also because of its access to redeeming knowledge. (p. 216)

[This is] the apex of Warren's mysticism: given the inability of even the most brilliant scientists, philosophers, and religious thinkers to encompass this most mysterious dimension of reality, Warren has permitted his intuitive powers to work freely in their stead, evolving thereby his conception of time as a dream.

The motif of the dream—a perception of reality arising from the unconscious, as the word dream implies—has probably been Warren's most important new theme in poetry since *Brother to Dragons. Promises* is full of this motif, relating its highest promise—"*All Time is a dream* and we're all one Flesh, at last"—to the whole of Nature. (pp. 217-18)

[In *Or Else*] the counterpoint between Warren's naturalistic poetry of passage and his mysticism gives the book's title its meaning. The mysticism, as always in Warren, implies fusion with this world rather than escape from it. (p. 224)

[The] longest and most ambitious entry in *Or Else,* is called "I Am Dreaming of a White Christmas: The Natural History of a Vision." The dream-vision of the title expands through the poem's dozen sections into one of Warren's grandest osmotic conceptions, rendering the oneness of time and flesh on a scale that binds together the living with the dead, family members with total strangers, densely compacted city-scape with vastly vacant countryside, summer heat and winter snow, past and present converging upon "the future tense / Of joy." (p. 225)

By implying a love of the world, joy is the surest mark of grace for the Warren persona; it is his sign of a religious redemption—redemption not in the sense of immortality, but in the sense that the world has come to seem permanently meaningful. This feeling of joy is the point at which Warren's two forms of mysticism converge—his osmosis of being and his epiphanies. And, repeatedly, joy affords the "moment of possibility" wherein the fallen persona may recapture his lost anima and dwell again, like the prelapsarian child-self, at least temporarily in paradise.

The turn to the animal kingdom or even to inanimate nature for osmotic wisdom appears to be culminating in Warren's latest poetry, which abounds with voices of nature striving to give utterance. As though reversing Freud's thesis about the inorganic hiding out within the organic, Warren in his "Arcturus" poems shows mountains, trees, and even the severed head of Mary, Queen of Scots, trying to say something. What they say, on one side, is that they share the human agony of limitations; and, on the other, that the human may share their perfect fullness of being. (p. 226)

Complementing his osmosis of being, [his] "unity with nature" that resembles "the unity of the lover with the beloved" is best seen in Warren's epiphanies, which carry his own love of the world to its ultimate expression. "We must try / To love so well the world that we may believe, in the end, in God," the speaker commented in "Masts at Dawn" (*Incarnations*). By providing "Joy," "Delight," and insight into "The True Nature of Time"—to quote Warren's designations—Warren's epiphanies convey a power that enables men, even after their trauma of passage into a fallen world, to "love the world" and so to love God, the world's otherwise unknowable sustainer. (p. 235)

Like his osmosis of being, Warren's epiphanies seem to

have come into play only after his "conversion" experience made them possible, and they have become a predominant note only in his recent volumes—flooding in as the undiscovered self theme was tailing off in the late 1950s. The early poems contain almost nothing of the epiphany experience. . . . [The] function of the epiphany as a final source of meaning in *Promises* constituted something new in Warren's poetry, an incursion of Pateresque thought set off in counterpoint against the long travail to wrest meaning from history in Warren's earlier writing. Jack Burden's venture into "history and the awful responsibility of Time" at the end of *All the King's Men* now yields to the ecstatic intensity of the moment. . . . (p. 236)

In the Rosanna sequence [of *Promises*] "The Flower" marks the major turning point in Warren's epiphanies. Through the earlier three poems the girl, in her prelapsarian state, had enjoyed a continuous paradisical condition, while the speaker slumped into postlapsarian despair. . . . In "The Flower," however, the absorption of the speaker into the girl's perspective permits not only a remembrance but a partial possession of paradise, and a way of transcending time's ruins after the Fall. . . . The essence of the epiphany is an intuition of Time's oneness that corresponds to the "One Flesh" doctrine developing elsewhere in Warren's poetry. . . . (p. 237)

If, over the half-century span of Warren's verse, there is one quality that most unmistakably lifts him to the first rank of American poets, then that quality would have to be the remarkable power, clarity, and originality of his imagery, flowing copiously into every part of his poetic canon from the first part of his career to the last. By imagery we refer to that verbal construct which, beginning with simple pictorial power, may ascend to metaphorical, symbolic, and even mythic significance as it implies larger dimensions of meaning. . . . [The] cumulative power of Warren's imagery in his eleven volumes is incalculable. (p. 273)

[As] prophet Warren has spoken movingly and meaningfully about some central issues of our time. But it is as art that his poetry must hope to survive. . . . How much of his poetry will ascend into the immortality of "poetry as art" remains to be seen. But his themes are likely to remain significant; and through a career that reaches back over a half century, encompassing schools of pre-Modern, Modern, and post-Modern aesthetics, he has displayed both growth and consistency in technical resources. With respect to the ageless elements of poetic technique—command of metaphor, control of tone and diction, powers of organization, mastery of sound effects, and the like—each phase of Warren's career has evinced a "morality of style" that is true to the classic standard. (p. 274)

Both as "prophecy" and as "art" the poetic canon of Robert Penn Warren evinces such significance, versatility, and excellence as to rank him among the finest and most fertile talents of his age. (p. 275)

> *Victor H. Strandberg, in his* The Poetic Vision of
> Robert Penn Warren *(copyright © 1977 by The
> University Press of Kentucky), University Press of
> Kentucky, 1977.*

RICHARD JACKSON

Typically, the voice in Robert Penn Warren's *Selected Poems, 1923-75* is situated in a moment, a boundary or threshold, where the meaning of time must be hazarded:

"the future is always unpredictable. / But so is the past, therefore / At Wood's edge I stand and, / Over the black horizon, heat lightning / Ripples the black sky" ("Tale of Time," IV). In this threshold moment (and it is usually a narrative one for Warren, not a lyric one as for Eberhart and Ammons), the speaker historicizes himself by extending the moment in time, by creating time. The "Tale of Time," for example, is based upon the expansion of an "interim" of consciousness that the speaker feels at his mother's death: "the time / Between the clod's *clunk* and / The full realization" (I). In the expanded moment that is the poem the speaker defines his historical relation to the world through the heritage he creates from his mother's life. In expanding or creating time the poet not only attempts to presence the past but to anticipate the future. . . . In manipulating time, the poet manipulates, creates his world. Warren's speakers are usually able to find a philosophical category, time, in which to order particulars, and this is perhaps his greatest advantage over a poet like Ammons. What the speaker of a Warren poem inevitably learns, like Saul, is that the difference between world and self is ambiguous. Like Audubon, the speaker discovers, "how thin is the membrane between himself and the world."

At the knife's edge, the poet anticipates a world he is in the process of creating through language: "Out of the silence, the saying. Into / The silence, the said. Thus / Silence, in timelessness, gives forth / Time." The process of language itself becomes history, and thus becomes the essence of the historical self: we are, says Heidegger, a "conversation," a progressive dialogue between subject and object, presence and absence. And yet language itself is simply one arbitrary system among systems for clarifying what we hope is "real." In moving from the isolated to the historical self, from interim to all of time, the principal tool is a language notorious for its ability to deceive. This problem is examined in several of the new poems in a section entitled "Can I See Arcturus From Where I Stand?" For example, in "Brotherhood in Pain" Warren exhorts the reader to focus "on any chance object" until it can be seen "in the obscene moment of birth." At this point, the object, the world really, so anthropomorphized by man's meditation on it, ironically turns to pity us who can "exist only in the delirious illusion of language." Our language fails us when we forget its essential temporality, when we forget it marks absence, not presence. When language fails us we become like the bodiless head of Mary of Scots rolling from our linguistic scaffolds: "The lips, / They were trying to say something very important" ("A Way To Love God.")

Warren, who may well turn out to be one of the two or three strongest poets of our age, finds a provisional solution in an idiom that is at once conversational and lyric, contemporary and historic, profane and sacred. It is a language in which he can slip easily from necessary precept to casual observation, cosmic vision to particular sighting. I quote from the end of the strongest of the new poems, "Evening Hawk." Under the hawk's eye, the speaker says, the day dissolves, "the world, unforgiven, swings / Into shadow." What we see from this point, as we replace the hawk's vision with our own, is half created and half perceived, half physical and half spiritual. . . . Warren's world is one that blends Plato's star and leaking pipes, the geology and history of the earth and the darkness of the cellar. It is a world whose reality, like the language of the bat that is written on air, is tentative, provisional. (pp. 549-51)

Richard Jackson, in Michigan Quarterly Review (copyright © The University of Michigan, 1978), Fall, 1978.

MARK ROYDEN WINCHELL

In *The American Adam* R.W.B. Lewis reminds us that during the nineteenth century many serious writers pictured America as a new Garden of Eden and saw the American as a new Adam, "a figure of heroic innocence and vast potentialities, poised at the start of a new history." The experience of the past century, however, has shattered the validity of such a myth. The serious American of today is more likely to see himself as a tainted anti-hero whose potentialities have been dissipated by imperialist expansion, racial discord, economic catastrophe, and a seemingly interminable series of wars.

If anything, our attitude today has swung too far in the direction of despair. The contemporary writer, rather than having to bridle excessive optimism, must seek a limited solution to the waste-land conditions of modern life. In *All the King's Men,* Robert Penn Warren forthrightly confronts such a bleak milieu. (p. 570)

Warren's vision in *All the King's Men* may well reflect a secularized form of one of the most pervasive motifs in ecclesiastical and literary history—the paradox of the Fortunate Fall. (p. 571)

Lewis finds the experience of a Fortunate Fall to be a key metaphor in early American literature. Those who saw the American as a new Adam, he argues, constituted a "party of hope," while those who viewed the new world as an absolute moral extension of the old were a "party of memory." Mediating between these two simplistic extremes was an infinitely more complex vision which affirmed both the reality of the Fall and the possibility of redemption. For, in the view of those whom Lewis calls the "Party of Irony," spiritual rebirth can occur only after one has discarded the illusion of innocence and has accepted the full burden of a fallen humanity. Indeed, Lewis contends that "as a metaphor in the area of human psychology, the notion of the fortunate fall has an immense potential. It points to the necessary transforming shocks and sufferings, the experiments and errors—in short, the experience—through which maturity and identity may be arrived at." And he concludes: "This was just the perception needed in a generation that projected as one of its major ideals the image of man as a fair unfallen Adam." . . .

Ironically enough, the *felix culpa* concept may also be a welcome corrective in an age whose paradigm figure is a totally fallen wastelander. (For even though the Fortunate Fall is most evident in such nineteenth-century works as Hawthorne's *The Marble Faun,* latter-day writers like Henry James and William Faulkner are also concerned with the fall from innocence and its psychological and moral consequences. . . .) . . . In *All the King's Men* [Warren] takes us to the underworld and back. Yet, his novel closes on a note of transcendent hopefulness. For in the midst of betrayal, suffering and death, there is still the movement of Grace. (p. 572)

To see Jack Burden's spiritual odyssey in terms of the Fortunate Fall is not to gainsay the consensus interpretation of Warren's novel. It is rather to restate that interpretation in a rich and allusive vocabulary. Warren does not impose an *artificially happy* resolution upon the contradictions in his characters' lives. Instead, he seems to view such contradictions as inherent to man's fallen condition. As such they can be resolved only if the effects of the Fall can be transcended. How this transcendence is achieved in the life of Jack Burden and fails fully to be achieved in the lives of Adam Stanton and Willie Stark is what *All the King's Men* is all about.

Adam, Willie, and Jack define a wide spectrum of human behavior and attitudes. In one significant respect, however, all three are similar. Each at significant points in his life must confront unexpected evil. And it is in such confrontations that each man, in effect, fails from innocence and begins to determine his own character and fate. Although the respective destinies of Adam and Willie are significant in their own right, they also function as foils to the more complete psychological evolution of Warren's moral norm—Jack Burden. (p. 573)

Surely Adam Stanton is the character in Warren's novel who fails most completely to make the [spiritual voyage that ends in rebirth]. As the author's name-typing would suggest, Stanton exists in a sort of psychic Eden. Although he may realize intellectually that evil exists in the world, he feels that that world must be different from the one he inhabits. He is an aristocrat and a Southern gentleman, unable to comprehend the corruption and vulgarity of a Willie Stark. Cut off from the creative ambiguity of human experience, Adam sees everything in scientific abstraction.

Dr. Stanton's inability to countenance any qualification of his world view leads to his eventual downfall. (p. 574)

If unfallen innocence involves an ignorance of good and evil, then it is a particularly wilful form of such innocence that incapacitates Adam Stanton. When confronted with the existential knowledge of good and evil, he falls and dies unredeemed.

If Adam Stanton is too innocent to live effectively in a fallen world, one suspects that Willie Stark is flawed by too much cynicism. When the Boss tells Jack to dig up some dirt on Judge Irwin and Jack suggests that this might not be possible, Willie replies: "'Man is conceived in sin and born in corruption and he passeth from the stink of the didie to the stench of the shroud. There is always something'." . . . We must remember, however, that Willie has not always been of this opinion. At the outset of his political career, Stark is the naive and idealistic "Cousin Willie," a public servant who wants to enlighten the populace and to govern honestly. It is only after such an approach fails that Willie decides to operate as a ruthless pragmatist. (pp. 574-75)

[Stark's] pragmatism is ultimately self-defeating. To understand evil does not mean that one must embrace it. And to seek to accomplish good through evil is to usurp the awful power of God without possessing His infinite wisdom. . . .

If Adam dies with little spiritual awareness and if Willie's enlightenment comes too late to be of any practical benefit to him, Jack's is a different story. He moves from innocence to experience, from flight to recognition, and finally to rebirth. The realization which Jack achieves at the end of the novel can only be understood in terms of the experience which leads up to it. As Jack himself observes: "all knowledge that is worth anything is maybe paid for by blood." . . . (p. 576)

Although he is in the thick of political action at the beginning of the novel, Jack performs his duties with the cool detachment of a hired hand. He cares little about the consequences of his deeds. Retreating from a knowledge of himself and of his past, Jack ignores the moral and spiritual dimensions of life and discounts any external reality with a glib Berkleyean idealism. Indeed, he describes himself as "a clammy, sad little foetus." . . . This foetal metaphor, coming early in the novel, suggests certain themes which are to recur. Jack tries for a long time to live like the sad, clammy little foetus, not knowing and not wanting to know: with knowledge comes the fall from innocence, and Jack wants to remain unfallen. He does not want to acknowledge his own sinfulness. But the end of man is to know (perhaps it is man's end in a double sense); and Jack's story is about his painful coming to knowledge.

Several times during his life Jack's lack of direction and his desire to remain inert reach pathological extremes. . . . During these periods [of the "Great Sleep"] he sleeps in excess of twelve hours a day, does nothing of consequence while he is awake, and returns longingly to the anonymity of sleep. Here, his characteristic lassitude has simply achieved an extreme manifestation.

If Jack sees himself as a foetus and if we can interpret the Great Sleep as an attempt to return to the womb, then we must look to his past to understand why Jack is so frightened of experience. Indeed, according to Louis D. Rubin [see *CLC*, Vol. 1], Jack's decision to work for Willie is "an attempt to deny the sense of futility, of aimlessness, of unreality that he had felt . . . as a child." Certainly, Jack's love-hate relationship with his mother and his lack of a strong father figure would account for certain psychological distress. One suspects, however, that the failure of his love affair with Anne Stanton has been the most profound influence on the picture of the world that Jack carries around in his head.

Viewed in this light, Jack's refusal to consummate his seduction of Anne Stanton is a significant evidence of his psychological malaise. Here, Jack refuses to violate a fixed ideal of innocence. (pp. 577-78)

[Jack] begins to be jarred out of his protective shell, though, when he learns of Anne Stanton's affair with Willie Stark. Fearing that he may somehow have driven Anne into Willie's arms, and disabused of his belief in her purity, Jack finds the actuality of evil impinging on his previously closed little universe. In reaction to this discovery, he flees to the West. (p. 580)

Structurally, it is significant that Warren gives us a chapter of flashbacks between Jack's flight and his decision to return home. Here, Jack's earlier relationship with Anne Stanton is painfully remembered. Here also, Jack concludes that in delivering to Anne the evidence of her father's crime, he has thereby delivered her to Willie Stark. Significantly, it is the belief that he has prompted his sister's affair with Stark that ultimately destroys Adam Stanton. . . . Thus, in returning home from the West, Jack achieves a greater level of maturity than Adam ever will. Yet that maturity is undercut by some glib rationalization: "There is no reason why you should not go back and face the fact which you have fled from," Jack tells us, "for any place to which you may flee will now be like the place from which you have fled . . . for things are always as they are." . . .

Adam and Eve flee from God in an attempt to avoid the consequences of their sin. When God confronts them with their disobedience, they seek to absolve themselves of blame—Adam blames Eve and Eve blames the serpent. Similarly, Jack Burden tries to discount his own complicity in evil by suggesting that reality is simply a mechanistic twitch. He calls it the "Great Twitch." No longer able to believe in Anne's unqualified innocence, he denies that guilt and innocence have any objective meaning. For him the Great Twitch is just another womb of not knowing. (p. 582)

It takes a series of traumatic events, however, for Jack's recognition and discovery to manifest themselves in a reversal of intention and action.

One of the most significant catalysts to Jack's rebirth is the death of Judge Irwin. Following instructions from Willie, Jack has tried to blackmail the judge into political subservience. Instead of succumbing to the blackmail, Irwin kills himself. Jack is then awakened by his mother's scream. She has just learned of the judge's death and is on the verge of hysteria. At this point she reveals that Judge Irwin was Jack's real father. Jack has suddenly and traumatically found and lost his true father. By learning the identity of his father, Jack is violently yoked to the past. And when he kills the father he has found, he is an Adamic innocent no more. . . .

Judge Irwin's death has made it impossible for Jack to discount his own moral culpability. By unwittingly bringing about the death of his father, Jack has brushed life's spider web, a distant vibration of which is his own rebirth. (Indeed, some readers hear Mrs. Burden's scream as a metaphorical cry of labor.) (p. 583)

From Judge Irwin's death on, the novel moves through several smaller crises to its climax in the assassination of Willie Stark. And in the final chapter Jack Burden reflects on what he has learned and on the sort of person he has become. Throughout, it is clear that events are changing the picture of the world that Jack carries around in his head. He is no longer a wet, clammy little foetus, warm in his not knowing. No longer is he an idealist, interpreting things solely in reference to his own perceptions; nor is he even part of a great mechanistic twitch.

The mature Jack Burden indicates that he had once believed in the Great Twitch "because it meant that he could not be called guilty of anything, not even of having squandered happiness or of having killed his father or of having delivered his two friends into each other's hands and death." . . . Jack Burden's suffering has changed his picture of the world into one in which men are free moral agents. Accepting this freedom and the responsibility it entails, he is able to forgive, love, and marry Anne Stanton. (p. 584)

Although Jack and Anne are not fortified by the vision which the Archangel Michael vouchsafed to Adam, Warren still seems to find the very possibility of happiness and hope to be grounded in certain eternal verities. And if his statement of these verities is neither as specific nor as orthodox as some might like, the novel's Christian allusions—particularly to the paradox of the Fortunate Fall—at least remind us that the modern *Slough of Despond* can claim none but the willing victim. (p. 585)

> *Mark Royden Winchell, "O Happy Sin! 'Felix Culpa' in 'All the King's Men'," in* The Missis-

sippi Quarterly *(copyright 1978 Mississippi State University), Fall, 1978, pp. 570-85.*

DENIS DONOGHUE

Lionel Trilling once wrote of E. M. Forster that he refused to be great—by contrast, presumably, with D. H. Lawrence, who insisted upon greatness. I am saying that those American poets who, under different circumstances, might make a leap toward greatness seem to have decided not to leap. It is not that present circumstances are in themselves desperately unpropitious. Who knows anything, in any case, about the circumstances that favor major work? It is that grandeur, especially of the bardic kind, is out of phase. Poets are more confident that something good may arise from the process of adding one fairly well-shaped brick to another. (pp. 9, 88)

Warren is exemplary in assessing the properties of his experience by appeal to whatever he thinks of as active beyond sense and mind: Sometimes he calls it History, sometimes Nature, sometimes Fate, without claiming to be on intimate terms with any of these gentlemen. It is agreed on all sides that Warren's recent volumes are his best: wise, wonderfully care-laden and yet not so care-laden as to let the spirit sink. His themes are the perennial ones, requiring an idiom of feeling, passion, speculation: Many of them are about the conditions in which a man meets, or fails to meet, his fate, the failure being then his direst fate.

I have implied that Warren's refusal to be great or major or whatever-we-call-it is not definitive; he could still be seized and driven beyond himself. (p. 88)

> *Denis Donoghue, in* The New York Times Book Review *(© 1978 by The New York Times Company; reprinted), December 3, 1978.*

DAVE SMITH

Warren has spoken often of Randall Jarrell's admonition that the true poet stays out in the rain and waits to be struck by the lightning. In poems that range from early iambic monotony to images of virulent, if disorderly power to a late and soaring architecture of the individual heart, Warren has submitted himself to that lightning. His character, his art, is the conduit of the violent and essential energy of the universe.

[Harold] Bloom, rightly, has said that Warren wants to be a hawk of life. As poet he is hawk-like, imperial and imperious, gliding over and holding in thrall everything that is. He rarely relaxes or clowns or indulges in the slighter uses of poetry. He has explored a continuous anatomy of ideas, a spectrum of recurrent images, with the doggedness of a prospector. . . . Warren has a vision: the unravelling tag ends of the world's body. We have no poet truer to a comprehensive, sustained evocation of the nature of existence; no one who grapples more with the nuances, the variations, the shadings of a core of thought. . . . In *Audubon: A Vision* (1969), that poem of few peers, Warren made everything he knew as clear as he could: the poems must define "the human filth, the human hope" and would be inextricable in filth and hope; must regard the human in his true humanity. The language became what it had been in fits and starts, a voice-instrument calibrated to final experience. Warren found what [John Crowe] Ransom had called for, a poetry of the right head, heart, and foot. Warren created a poetry which expressed and formed sacramental force as it flowed

through events of Love and Knowledge. Man, Warren says, must understand love is knowledge if he is to understand his fate and, moreover, to accept his fate. Audubon, the killer of birds and beauty, the creator of beauty and a possible joy, is Warren's deep analogue. (pp. 4-5)

If Warren's vision began with *Brother To Dragons*, his breakthrough came in *Promises* (1957), of which he has said, "Seeing a little gold-headed girl on that bloody spot of history [an Italian island-fortress which was both site and subject of the poems] was an event!" The image of beauty counterposed against the symbol of history's continuous and random grinding out of beauty suggests a medallion of Warren's art. It is at once the doubleness of reality, darkness and light, and though the mind must try to know multifoliate meaning, must rage for reconciliation, reconciliation fails; art witnesses and holds in tension the antinomies. All of Warren's poems are events rendered in a holding fabric of image, narrative, and meditative gloss; all attempt to do one thing:

> . . . what you are concerned with is a sense of contact with reality. And it's maybe a pinpoint touch or a whole palm of a hand laid, or something; but the important thing is the shock of this contact: a lot of current can come through a small wire.
>
> *Fugitives Return*

Touch, the laying on of the hand. What Warren has called a single, vital image. Contact. Always the figure of connection, the poem of reconnection, the failure of that ability to receive the energy, disruption, and the possibility of rejoining. For Warren, such poems function, the "poem does involve a potential action, it modifies our being in some way." That is, the poem is not a simple picture, but a picture with extended or exploded events ordered to demonstrate a right relationship, with moral and ethical resonances.

Now and Then: Poems 1976-1978, more physically objective than previous books, is a deeply moral vision, a continuation of Warren's long consideration of the "moral history of man." The book contains, looming like a granite cliff, one of the great poems of our language: "Red-Tail Hawk and Funeral Pyre of Youth." It stands with *Audubon* as emblematic of his full effort. . . . [It] is a mini-Mariner in plot, vision, and construction. (pp. 5-6)

[Two key questions posed by "Red-Tail Hawk . . ."], Nature's forgiveness and what one might do besides walk in the dark, remain unanswered. . . . [The poem] evolves from event to revelation to vision; moral history enacted, the imagination as alembic; the poem reveals itself as prayer for definition and responsibility, which is to say, failure: to act and to know the meaning as well as the cost of action. The poem is the story of human consciousness. It is dramatically and aesthetically and ethically true to experiential as well as emotional life. It is a grand, unfolded, unified, and felt experience.

Warren's *Now and Then* is divided into two sections, "Nostalgic" with ten poems and "Speculative" with twenty-six, these subtitles paralleling the temporal *now* and *then* in reverse. Typically, Warren takes a position, tests it emotionally and philosophically, then does the same test from an obverse position.

If "Red-Tail Hawk . . ." is the setpiece of both "Nostalgic" and the book, the initial poem, "American Portrait: Old Style," also looms grandly. It returns to home-ground and innocence, its event a visit with a boyhood friend who had won glory as an athlete and had been an early companion in invented stories. The visit occasions meditation on Warren's oldest subjects: Time, Self, Mutability, Love, and particularly Imagination. . . . In "Star-Fall" Warren writes:

> For what communication
> Is needed if each alone
> Is sunk and absorbed into
> The mass and matrix of Being that defines
> Identity of all?

That communication beyond speech, atavistic and premoral, is the oldest dream in Warren's poetry. But speech, art, is precisely necessary because we remain unconnected to the matrix. Art has been Warren's way back. Having spent more than fifty years to vivify and make whole this reality of interconnection, he has earned the right to rest and say: "I love the world even in my anger, / And love is a hard thing to outgrow." We expect the confirming, consolidating poems of "Nostalgic" at the end of a man's career, in his seventh decade, even should they sometimes recover old ground, even with glibness of glory.

But when we move into the poems of "Speculation" we discover once again that Warren has gone ahead of us. He surprises us with a darkly insistent mood in poems rooted in dying seasons, sunsets, autumn, gray light. . . . The collection radiates a *Tempest* tone while it hovers toward the few answers which might reveal at last "The possibility of joy in the world's tangled and hieroglyphic beauty." Has Warren, then, turned sour? No. But he has invoked the conceptions, and ideas, the imageries of his career only to question them again. In "Code Book Lost" he suggests he has failed the tenuous meaning he had worked for; the world isn't revealing anything. It is as if Warren has forced himself to start over entirely. He has, in fact, begun to speculate not simply on what death will be like, hence what value in any values, positions, hypotheses, but on what life is as *husk*. . . . All bodies of the world's body are husks, vehicles, containers, for that current which may pass through even small wires. Energy is life. Warren is recalling the totemic and hieratic images that fifty years have served toward defining the condition of joy: hawk, owl, beasts, lovers, landscapes of crag and sublimity. But he remembers another immediate truth: "So many things they say are true / but you / Can't always be sure you feel them. . . ." Have the images become a push-button reality? Are they only the furniture of the poems? For Warren, inevitably, the only things true are what survive the cauterizations of literal experience, its reflection and dissection.

And death, always Warren's main character, is nearer than ever. The figure of the hand's touch assumes a new context. Now it is the physician who stares into the patient's face "and you wish / He'd take his god-damn hand off your shoulder." In this poem, "Waiting," everything that has mattered seems stripped away. The woman a man has loved all his life says "she cannot / Remember when last she loved you, and had lived the lie only / For the children's sake." Is this what one comes to, is this reality? Is this the ease which comes to a man's seventh decade? You must wait to know. Warren, like everyone, must "pick the last alibi off, like a scab, and / Admire the inwardness. . . ." As

he says in *Democracy & Poetry* (1975), it is ever the poet's task to face the deep and dark inwardness of man's nature —to endeavor to be so much of the matrix that there will be no need to flinch before the hawk of reality. (pp. 6-7)

With "Sister Water" Warren evokes even the venerable "Original Sin: A Short Story," and an old man rattles the night-door as had the premoral monster who first announced the poet's idea that "nothing is ever lost," not even the will-corrupted and nightmare self. But in this new poem we cannot be sure time exists, much less continuity: "But is there a *now* or *then*?" Surely time is not of the matrix but of the human—or is it? Without definition, what human gesture is any good? Warren says, "You cannot pray. But / You can wash you face in cold water." How ironic and caustic. The story of these poems says you must do both to have a chance for reality through either act.

"Speculation" is a tragic and necessary movement which insists again that Warren, like Socrates, will not live the unexamined life but will ask, as he asked in *Audubon*, "what / Is man but his passion?" He had answered this ambiguously lineated question in a subsequent poem, saying, "Passion / Is all. Even / The sleaziest." The poems of "Speculation" reinforce this contention, but not without the stress test of experience. Of them, none is more blisteringly beautiful than the ouraboros-like "Identity And Argument For Prayer" and the book-ending "Heart of Autumn." . . . Warren still asks, in "Heat Wave Breaks," "For what should we pray to our God in the rumble and flare? / That the world stab anew in the lightning-stricken air?" The answer now is what Elizabeth Bishop calls "that peculiar / affirmative"—yes! For even if the promise of reality will be only the scalding of flesh and the not-knowing, passion is all. In this self-interrogation, Warren rejects an earlier *Tempest* tone and, like Lear, calls on the crack of winds. (pp. 7-8)

In perhaps his finest short lyric, "Tell Me A Story," the conclusion to *Audubon*, Warren became Audubon himself, went back to his boyhood and the dark flow before experience where he had heard "The great geese hoot northward."

> I could not see them, there being no moon
> And the stars sparse. I heard them.
>
> I did not know what was happening in my heart.

He prayed; the event of the poem became prayer: "Tell me a story of deep delight." That story is man's moral history that yields the full curve of specific individual experience which is not abstract but is archetypal. Warren asked to start with the world and to know how to live in its reality, to know the world's name and his own, to know love which would prove "all is only / All, and part of all." It is not, therefore, surprising that even in this ferociously eschatological re-examination of everything, Warren would return to those geese, to his lyrical yearning to know what was moving in the blind dark and to be of it. No one describes what he has been as poet better than he does when he says, "The palm of my hand was as / Wide as the world and the / Blaze of distance." With Warren, the love of the world is not cant, but reality itself. (p. 8)

Dave Smith, "He Prayeth Best Who Loveth Best," in The American Poetry Review *(copyright © 1979 by World Poetry, Inc.; reprinted by permission of Dave Smith), January/February, 1979, pp. 4-8.*

WA THIONG'O, Ngugi   1938-

Wa Thiong'o, formerly known as James Ngugi, is a Kenyan novelist, playwright, and short story writer, who, as Nadine Gordimer comments, succeeds in his fiction by placing the Mau Mau movement in the historical, political, and sociological context of the African continental revolution. (See also *CLC*, Vols. 3, 7.)

JOHN REED

[*Weep not, child* is] an autobiographical novel, and its weaknesses come from the need to make it at once a book about the Mau Mau Rebellion and yet also a book written out of immediate and personal experience. There are scenes when the author is trying to sum up or present the whole situation, for example the conversation between Njoroge and Stephen Howlands, the schoolboy son of the white farmer, at a football match between an African and a European school. This seems contrived and unconvincing. When Mr Ngugi brings the violence of Mau Mau directly upon the scene, as when he describes the murder of Mr Howlands by Njoroge's brother, there is a failure in the writing which is serious enough to damage the whole novel. He also runs into the problem of all autobiographical novels of childhood and youth—that of coming to a conclusion. The scene at the end of the book when Njoroge is prevented from hanging himself by the timely appearance of his mother is not a happy solution.

Weep not, child is at its best presenting the ordinary life and awareness of a young African as he achieves his formal and informal education. The attempts at more dramatic effect fail but do not ruin the book's muted everyday quality of conviction. The very simple and direct style used gives each scene actuality as we read but leaves nothing standing vividly out, and the novel lives on in the mind as an atmosphere and not as a series of sharply drawn incidents.

The River Between uses the same style and achieves the same kind of effect. But in this novel there is a need for more definition and sharpness. For this is a full historical novel—a novel, that is, about contemporary society which examines certain features of that society by exploring their origin and development in the past. The obvious comparison is with [Chinua Achebe's] two novels about the early contacts between Africans and Europeans in his own part of Eastern Nigeria, *Things Fall Apart* and *Arrow of God*. The comparison, I think, is fair and the reason why it is unfavourable to Ngugi is that the impressionistic and personal approach used in *Weep not, child* is insufficient in a novel attempting to explore the roots of a particular problem. Such a novel must show the characters acting in a social context and under social pressures and therefore must demonstrate to us convincingly that nature of their society. Achebe's novels do this. The tribal societies he shows us are completely articulated and comprehensible and his characters act out their destinies under social pressures that are made clear to us. In *The River Between* this is not so. Although like Achebe, Ngugi has set up certain connections between his two novels—for example the school at Siriana occurs in both of them—the exact historical period of the events in *The River Between* is never revealed, at least to the reader unversed in the details of European penetration into the various regions of Kenya. The social structure of the tribe and its political organization, although the plot turns on these matters, is never demonstrated to us in such

a way that we can understand their operation in the action of the novel. Hence the characters are seen in relationships only sketchily defined except in terms of emotion, and the real content of the social and political ends which they set themselves remains unspecified. (pp. 118-19)

What really interests Mr Ngugi is the inner life of his characters, their brooding on the nature of life as they stare at the falling rain or the water flowing in the river, their cloudy idealism, their religious ardours. In *Weep not, child* this inner life both contrasted with and also reflected apocalyptically the terrible passage of events as the emergency continued. But in *The River Between* the weakness of the writer's grasp on the details of social and political reality cripples the novel. For example, in the book, the growth of militantly anti-White feeling is attributed to an organization called the Kiama. Waiyaki is at first its secretary but later resigns. It is the Kiama that at the end of the book is responsible for the destruction of his influence. It is not that Mr Ngugi fails to explain or show how the Kiama works in the society he is describing. He makes no attempt to explain it. So the whole story turns on something of which we know only the name. (p. 120)

The tale of Muthoni is the most successful part of the novel. Her death falls into the situation, receiving different and I think developing interpretations among the other characters; to the Christians it confirms their belief in the barbarity of Gikuyu customs; to the tribalists it is a punishment because of the new faith. To Waiyaki and Muthoni's sister, Nyambura, it becomes almost a martyrdom suffered in the attempt to reconcile old and new ways and achieve a marriage between Christ and the ritual of the tribe. Perhaps a better novel could have been written with Muthoni instead of Waiyaki at the centre.

The novel Mr Ngugi has written is broken between his interest in the problem of the reconciliation of Christ with the tribe and his uneasy recognition that the real difficulties of the situation he is describing lie elsewhere. Thus he mentions several times the alienation of the tribal lands, yet almost in passing. He never demonstrates to us the concrete effects of European settlement, and I think the reason for this is that his characters do not live in any defined economic or political context at all. We hear nothing of their livelihood, the sources of their wealth or the causes of their poverty. Of course novels can be written about the personal and spiritual concerns of characters with their social context neglected. But *The River Between* I think makes a claim to be about a whole society at a critical moment without making the claim good. (p. 121)

John Reed, "James Ngugi and the African Novel," in Journal of Commonwealth Literature *(copyright by John Reed 1965; by permission of Hans Zell (Publishers) Limited), September, 1965, pp. 117-21.*

CHARLES R. LARSON

The weakness of Ngugi's ["Petals of Blood"] as a work of the creative imagination ultimately lies in the author's somewhat dated Marxism: revolt of the masses, elimination of the black bourgeois; capitalism to be replaced with African socialism. The author's didacticism weakens what would otherwise have been his finest work. (p. 22)

Charles R. Larson, in The New York Times Book Review *(© 1978 by The New York Times Com-*

pany; reprinted by permission), February 19, 1978.

CHARLES R. LARSON

[Though *Petals of Blood*] may not always fulfill the promise of [Ngugi's] earlier works, there is much to admire and ponder about it.

The narrative pattern is complex and at times difficult to follow, embracing a time sequence of twelve years with numerous flashbacks skipping back much earlier to develop important details in the lives of the four main characters. . . . Ngugi's narrative assumes the misleading appearance of a detective story, as the police begin to interrogate the main characters—all likely suspects . . . for the multiple murders. (p. 246)

Petals of Blood is a bold venture—perhaps a risky one—since it is obvious that the author's criticisms of his country's new ruling class will not go unnoticed. . . . Ngugi attacks neocolonialism manifested in the new materialism, as well as his nation's hasty and often shortsighted attempts at rapid industrialization. . . . If Ngugi at times becomes overly didactic and simplistic in his framing of capitalism versus African socialism, *Petals of Blood* is still a highly compelling work of fiction. There are scenes in this novel (especially those depicting the relationships between Wanja and her various lovers) that are as fine as anything I have read in years. Ngugi wa Thiong'o's novel always engages our attention and our admiration—no easy task for any novelist with a burning social conscience. (pp. 246-47)

> Charles R. Larson, in World Literature Today (copyright 1978 by the University of Oklahoma Press), Vol. 52, No. 2, Spring, 1978.

ANDREW SALKEY

[*Petals of Blood*] announces its radical political intention in the author's choices of sectional epigraphs: from Walt Whitman, William Blake and Amilcar Cabral, among other poets. It's a willfully diagrammatic and didactic novel which also succeeds artistically because of its resonant characterization and deadly irony. It satisfies both the novelist's political intent and the obligation I know he feels toward his art. . . .

[The novel shows] the workers at the overseas-owned Theng'eta Brewery in Ilmorog, a new town near the Trans-Africa Highway, . . . planning a militant strike, after the directors' meeting declared a no pay-raise decision; hours later three Theng'eta directors are found burnt to death; three townspeople are arrested. . . .

It becomes clear that the excoriating conflict of interests in Ilmorog is a microcosm of the larger national one in Kenya. (p. 681)

The novel closes with the people of Ilmorog not just sensing a mere illusory feeling of having experienced before their present revolutionary situation; it is *déjà vu* without the distance of illusion—with, in fact, the stark actuality of the approaching event of revolution. (p. 682)

> Andrew Salkey, in World Literature Today (copyright 1978 by the University of Oklahoma Press), Vol. 52, No. 4, Autumn, 1978.

WAUGH, Evelyn   1903-1966

A British novelist, short story writer, biographer, and writer of travel sketches, Waugh first gained renown for his satires on the "Bright Young People" of London between the wars. *Brideshead Revisited* was his most popular book in the United States and reflected his conversion to Catholicism. Waugh was a member of a distinguished literary family: his father was the critic and publisher Arthur Waugh, his brother novelist Alec Waugh, and his son, Auberon Waugh, is also a novelist. *The Ordeal of Gilbert Pinfold* is Waugh's moving self-portrait of a tormented writer. (See also *CLC*, Vols. 1, 3, 8, and *Contemporary Authors*, obituary, Vols. 25-28, rev. ed.)

EDMUND WILSON

Nothing can taste staler today than some of the stuff that seemed to mean something [at the end of the twenties], that gave us twinges of bitter romance and thrills of vertiginous drinking. But *The Great Gatsby* and *The Sun Also Rises* hold up; and my feeling is that [Waugh's novels of the period] are the only things written in England that are comparable to Fitzgerald and Hemingway. They are not so poetic; they are perhaps less intense; they belong to a more classical tradition. But I think that they are likely to last and that Waugh, in fact, is likely to figure as the only first-rate comic genius that has appeared in English since Bernard Shaw.

The great thing about *Decline and Fall,* written when the author was twenty-five, was its breath-taking spontaneity. The latter part of the book leans a little too heavily on Voltaire's *Candide,* but the early part, that hair-raising harlequinade in a brazenly bad boys' school, has an audacity that is altogether Waugh's and that was to prove the great principle of his art. This audacity is personified here by an hilarious character called Grimes. Though a schoolmaster and a "public-school man," Grimes is frankly and even exultantly everything that is most contrary to the British code of good behavior. . . . This audacity in Waugh's next book, *Vile Bodies,* is the property of the infantile young people who, at a time "in the near future, when existing social tendencies have become more marked," are shown drinking themselves into beggary, entangling themselves in absurd sexual relationships, and getting their heads cracked in motor accidents. The story has the same wild effect of reckless improvisation, which perfectly suits the spirit of the characters; but it is better sustained than *Decline and Fall,* and in one passage it sounds a motif which for the first time suggests a standard by which the behavior of these characters is judged: the picture of Anchorage House with its "grace and dignity and other-worldliness," and its memories of "people who had represented their country in foreign places and sent their sons to die for her in battle, people of decent and temperate life, uncultured, unaffected, unembarrassed, unassuming, unambitious people, of independent judgment and marked eccentricities."

In *Black Mischief* there is a more coherent story and a good deal of careful planning to bring off the surprises and shocks. . . . We note that with each successive book Evelyn Waugh is approaching closer to the conventions of ordinary fiction: with each one—and the process will continue —we are made to take the characters more seriously as recognizable human beings living in the world we know. Yet the author never reaches this norm: he keeps his grasp on the comic convention of which he is becoming a master

—the convention which makes it possible for him to combine the outrageous with the plausible without offending our sense of truth. . . . There are two important points to be noted in connection with *Black Mischief*. The theme of the decline of society is here not presented merely in terms of night-club London: it is symbolized by the submergence of the white man in the black savagery he is trying to exploit. The theme of audacity is incarnated here, not in a Philbrick or a Grimes, but in a bad-egg aristocrat, who steals his mother's emeralds to run away from England, manipulates the politics of Azania by talking modern ideas to the native king and, forced at last to flee the jungle, eats his sweetheart unawares at a cannibal feast.

A Handful of Dust, which followed, is, it seems to me, the author's masterpiece. Here he has perfected his method to a point which must command the admiration of another writer even more perhaps than that of the ordinary non-literary reader—for the latter may be carried from scene to scene of the swift and smooth-running story without being aware of the skill with which the author creates by implication an atmosphere and a set of relations upon which almost any other novelist would spend pages of description and analysis. The title comes from T. S. Eliot's line, "I will show you fear in a handful of dust," but, except on the title page, the author nowhere mentions this fear. Yet he manages to convey from beginning to end, from the comfortable country house to the clearing in the Brazilian jungle, the impression of a terror, of a feeling that the bottom is just about to drop out of things, which is the whole motivation of the book but of which the characters are not shown to be conscious and upon which one cannot put one's finger in any specific passage. . . . The audacity here is the wife's: her behavior has no justification from any accepted point of view, whether conventional or romantic. Nor does the author help out with a word of explicit illumination. He has himself made of audacity a literary technique. He exemplifies, like so many of his characters, the great precept of Benjamin Jowett to young Englishmen just starting their careers: "Never apologize, never explain."

The next novel *Scoop* is not quite so good as the ones just before and just after it, but it has in it some wonderful things. . . . The story is simpler than usual, and it brings very clearly to light a lineup of opposing forces which has always lurked in Evelyn Waugh's fiction and which is now even beginning to give it a certain melodramatic force. He has come to see English life as a conflict between, on the one hand, the qualities of the English upper classes, whether arrogant, bold and outrageous or stubborn, unassuming and eccentric, and, on the other, the qualities of the climbers, the careerists and the commercial millionaires who dominate contemporary society. (pp. 140-44)

Put Out More Flags, written during and about the war, has an even more positive moral. Basil Seal, the aristocratic scoundrel who has already figured in *Black Mischief*, exploits the war to his own advantage by informing against his friends and shaking down his sister's county neighbors with threats of making them take in objectionable refugees, but finally he enlists in the Commandos, who give him for the first time a legitimate field for the exercise of his resourcefulness and nerve. Evelyn Waugh's other well-born wastrels are already in the "corps d'élite," somewhat sobered after years of "having fun." (pp. 144-45)

We see now that not only has the spirit of audacity mi-

grated from the lower to the upper classes, but that the whole local emphasis has shifted. The hero of *Decline and Fall* was a poor student reading for the church, whose career at Oxford was wrecked by the brutality of a party of aristocratic drunks. . . . But it is now this young man, Percy Pastmaster, and Sir Alastair Digby-Vaine-Trumpington and the English county families generally who are the heroes of *Put Out More Flags*. Evelyn Waugh has completely come over to them, and the curious thing is that his snobbery carries us with it. In writing about Harold Nicolson, I remarked on his fatal inability to escape from the psychology of the governing class, which was imposed on him by birth and office. The case of Waugh is the opposite of this: he has evidently approached this class, like his first hero, from somewhere outside, and he has had to invent it for himself. The result is that everything is created in his work, nothing is taken for granted. The art of this last novel is marvellous. See the episode in which Basil Seal blackmails the young married woman: the attractiveness of the girl, which is to prompt him to try a conquest, and her softness, which will permit his success (Evelyn Waugh is perhaps the only male writer of his generation in England who is able to make his women attractive), are sketched in with a few physical details and a few brief passages of dialogue that produce an impression as clear and fresh as eighteenth-century painting.

Evelyn Waugh is today a declared Tory and a Roman Catholic convert; he believes in the permanence of the social classes and, presumably, in the permanence of evil. (pp. 144-46)

[But] his opinions do not damage his fiction. About this fiction there is nothing schematic and nothing doctrinaire; and, though the characters are often stock types—the silly ass, the vulgar parvenu, the old clubman, etc.—everything in it has grown out of experience and everything has emotional value. *Put Out More Flags* leaves you glowing over the products of public schools and country houses as examples of the English character; but it is not a piece of propaganda: it is the satisfying expression of an artist, whose personal pattern of feeling no formula will ever fit, whether political, social or moral. For the savagery he is afraid of is somehow the same thing as the audacity that so delights him. (p. 146)

> Edmund Wilson, "'Never Apologize, Never Explain': The Art of Evelyn Waugh," in his Classics and Commercials: A Literary Chronicle of the Forties *(reprinted with the permission of Farrar, Straus & Giroux, Inc.;* copyright © 1950 by Edmund Wilson; copyright renewed © 1978 by Elena Wilson), The Noonday Press, 1950, pp. 140-46.

STEPHEN JAY GREENBLATT

Evelyn Waugh, like Charles Ryder [the narrator of *Brideshead Revisited*], is an architectural painter who sees, with anger, horror, and a kind of fascination, the destruction of old homes, the decay of institutions, the death of meaningful values. But Waugh refuses to create a merely sentimental picture of the achievements of the past at the moment of extinction; he insists, rather, upon recording in scrupulous detail the actual process of demolition. In Waugh's satiric vision, seeming trivial events—the breaking up of a manor house, the redecoration of an old room with chromium plating, a drunken brawl in an Oxford courtyard—are symbols of a massive, irreversible, and terrifying victory of barbarism and the powers of darkness over civilization and light. Waugh's early novels, especially *Decline and Fall* (1928), *Vile Bodies* (1930), *Black Mischief* (1932), and *A Handful of Dust* (1934) are chronicles of that awful triumph. (p. 4)

The wholesale demolition of the value structures of the past and the creation in their place of a vile and absurd habitation is the central theme of Waugh's early novels. However, this theme does not always manifest itself in terms of a destroyed manor house. Man, in his fear and anxiety over the loss of values, unconsciously seeks dehumanization, but he may become a sort of animal as well as a machine. . . . [In Waugh's novels the] savage coexists perfectly with the streamlined man. . . . Against the technological skill of the machine and the voracity of the savage, culture, refinement, and tradition have little defense. The jungle is always threatening to overrun the city, the work crews are always tearing down a country estate, and hordes of howling aristocrats and gate-crashers are always sullying the sacred preserves of order and decency. (pp. 6-7)

Paul Pennyfeather, the young man so rudely thrust into the world [in *Decline and Fall*], is singularly unsuited for its trials, for Paul is a shadow-man, completely passive, completely innocent. One of Waugh's favorite satiric devices is suddenly to catapult a totally naïve individual into a grotesque and uncontrollable world, for, with this technique, he can expose both the corruption of society and the hopelessness of naïve goodness and simple-minded humanism. Since the essence of Waugh's criticism of Paul Pennyfeather's innocence is that it is too simple to cope with the complexities of the world, one cannot expect complex character delineation, and indeed Paul's flatness is very carefully and successfully pursued. "Paul Pennyfeather would never have made a hero," Waugh blandly observes in the middle of the novel, "and the only interest about him arises from the unusual series of events of which his shadow was witness." . . . (p. 8)

[The] laying of absurd religious doubt by equally absurd religious conviction, is the sort of hilarious and gruesome irony Waugh delights in. . . . [Gratuitous cruelty is] a quality of Waugh's work which many readers have found disturbing. The grotesque, the unreasonable, and the cruel are always asserting themselves in the satirist's world. . . . The amputation of Lord Tangent's gangrenous foot and his death, reported in widely separated and totally undramatic asides, are the source of great amusement in *Decline and Fall*. The deliberate accumulation of cruel details creates the atmosphere of [the novel's] world. . . . (p. 10)

[There is, however] a vital principle which has remained completely untouched by the change. This principle manifests itself in "the primitive promptings of humanity," epitomized by Captain Grimes. . . . Grimes is a powerful life-force existing outside the pale of conventional morality, and, audacious, elusive, outrageous, free, he represents the spirit of *Decline and Fall*. The growth of Waugh's pessimism is reflected in his treatment of Grimes spiritual heirs. Father Rothschild, S.J., in *Vile Bodies* and Krikor Youkoumian in *Black Mischief* are far less sympathetic, until, with Mrs. Beaver, in *A Handful of Dust,* the vital principle has become triumphant opportunism and moral blankness. (p. 11)

Decline and Fall was characterized by its wild audacity, but *Vile Bodies* is a comedy haunted by an inexplicable sad-

ness. . . . One of the curious qualities of *Vile Bodies* is the reader's inability to discriminate between guilt and innocence. In *Decline and Fall* Paul Pennyfeather was clearly an innocent suddenly thrown into a corrupt world, but the distinction is blurred in *Vile Bodies*. Adam sells his fiancée . . . and is an adulterer, but at the same time he exhibits an extraordinary naïveté and innocence, for he is conscious of breaking no moral norms.

Vile Bodies is an experimental novel. There is practically no plot and no continuity of narrative. The scenes shift wildly from the stormy English Channel to a party given for Mrs. Melrose Ape, the noted evangelist; from the intrigues of Father Rothschild, S.J., and the Prime Minister Walter Outrage to the small talk of two middle-class ladies on a train; from the drawing room of a huge mansion to the grease pit at the auto races. With this technique of disconnected and seemingly irrelevant scenes, Waugh is attempting to portray a world that is chaotic and out of joint. Readers have complained, with some justification, that the technique is all too successful, that the novel is disjointed and slights the affairs of Adam Fenwick-Symes and Nina Blount; but *Vile Bodies* is not a love story. Adam and Nina are significant only as representatives of the sickness of an entire generation, and their thwarted attempt to marry is meaningful and interesting only as a symbol of the frustrated search for values of all the Bright Young People. (pp. 12-14)

The fate of the old order with its decency, culture, and stability is represented by the fate of Anchorage House, the last survivor of the noble town houses of London. . . . A party at Anchorage House, "anchored" in custom and tradition, is juxtaposed with an orgy held by the Bright Young People in a dirigible, and the loss of the firm ground of the past is painfully obvious. (pp. 14-15)

Black Mischief is not a witty travelogue or, as some readers have felt, a vicious, racist attack on the African Negro. Rather, it treats precisely the themes of the earlier works— the shabbiness of Western culture, the decline and fall of institutions, the savagery underlying society.

Black Mischief chronicles the attempted modernization of a black nation by Seth, "Emperor of Azania, Chief of Chiefs of Sakuyu, Lord of Wanda and Tyrant of the Seas, Bachelor of the Arts of Oxford University." . . . As his title indicates, Seth's character is a paradoxical blend of savagery and civilization, the cannibal feast and the drawing room. He is unpredictable, cruel, naïve, insanely optimistic, lonely, terrified. . . . Seth's modernity . . . is not a meaningless label or a thin veneer of culture concealing the dominating violence of his black soul, for the meaning of *Black Mischief* is not the impossibility of civilizing the Negro. That the ideal of Progress in which Seth so fervently believes turns out to be a shabby concatenation of inane conventions is a condemnation far more of the cultivated Westerner than of the African. Seth serves the artistic purpose of a Paul Pennyfeather: he is a naïve outsider who, in his contact with an alien society, is the means of satirizing that society. (pp. 16-17)

The abortive attempt to modernize Azania is not a statement of the African nation's inability to share in the glories of civilization but a sly and satiric examination of modernity itself. The struggle which Seth envisages as a mortal combat between barbarism and Progress is a miserable sham, for Western culture itself is no longer meaningful. Those Western ideas which might have given Seth's project real significance have been abandoned. . . . The inspiring motto "Through Sterility to Culture" is the banner not merely of the participants in the birth-control pageant but of the entire European civilization. Western culture is sterile, totally isolated from the realities of human life and incapable of making man's existence more pleasant.

Waugh uses Africa as a lens which renders grotesque and revealing images of English institutions and social classes. The Bright Young People and their silly parents, scheming politicians and unscrupulous soldiers of fortune, crude peers and nouveau riche socialites are all represented in the Azanian court. (pp. 18-19)

As *Decline and Fall* was signalized by its comic audacity and *Vile Bodies* by its comic sadness, *Black Mischief* is characterized by its comic cruelty. Recurring references, quite hilarious in their context, to starving children, executed men, and mutilated bodies constantly remind the reader that as Seth's blind infatuation with Western culture grows, the savagery underlying the calm surface of the superimposed civilization becomes increasingly agitated until it explodes. . . . (p. 20)

Waugh's delight in architectural images does not diminish in *Black Mischief*. The tough old Anglican Cathedral . . . , that impractical and "shocking ugly building," is marked for demolition by Seth and the Ministry of Modernization to make way for the Place Marie Stopes. But the Cathedral, despite its many years of disuse, has a remarkable solidity. . . . The attempt to replace the worship of God with the worship of Progress is even more obvious in the site of the Ministry of Modernization, which occupies what had formerly been the old Empress' oratory.

Seth's palace compound, like the concept of progress it embodies, is a haphazard conglomeration of strange structures, refuse, and, occasionally, the flyblown carcase of a donkey or camel. Modernity and barbarism are linked in the grand work-projects of leveling and draining which are pursued without any success by gangs of prisoners chained neck to neck. (pp. 20-1)

The sense of desolation and decay is best conveyed, however, by another structure—a wrecked automobile, lying in the middle of the Avenue of Progress, its tires devoured by white ants, its motor removed by pilfering, its rusting body reinforced by rags, tin, mud, and grass and used as a home by a native family. The rotting car appears throughout *Black Mischief* as an impediment which Seth tries in vain to remove, and, at the end of the novel, when the British and French hold Azania as a joint protectorate, it is still blocking traffic, unmoved by the entire force of the League of Nations.

Seth's deposition and murder seems to be the laying of the ghost of madness and instability. The protectorate, with its pukka sahibs, police stations, snobbery, European clubs, polished brass, and Gilbert and Sullivan, promises to be a grand step forward in the onward March of Progress, but, like the reign of Seth, it is a ridiculous sham. . . . The history of Azania, like the dance of the witch doctors and the life of the Bright Young People, is a savage, futile, comic circle.

In *A Handful of Dust* Waugh returns to England to tell a seemingly simple story of the failure of a marriage. . . . What might have been a rather dull "bedroom farce," however, is transformed by Waugh into a terrifying and bitter examination of humanism and modern society, which is the culmination of his art. (pp. 21-2)

By the accumulation of a great many seemingly irrelevant details, Waugh evokes a whole world, a philosophy, and a way of life as well as an architecture and a landscape. Hetton [Tony's country home] is a lovely, sentimental, idealized world of the past and of childhood, at once silly and charming, hopelessly naïve and endearing. Far in the past Hetton had been an abbey, but, as religion receded, it became "one of the notable houses of the country" . . . , and, finally, in the nineteenth century, at the height of the Gothic revival, this structure was totally demolished and the present house was built as a monument to Victorian aesthetics. If the true significance and beauty of Hetton had been destroyed in 1864 or earlier when it ceased to shelter pious monks, at least the glazed brick and encaustic tile of the present structure have a character and sentimental worth completely lacking in the cold, oversize boxes being constructed in London. In the twentieth century, however, the huge building, with battlements and towers, a huge clock with maddeningly loud chimes, lancet windows of armorial stained glass, pitch-pine minstrels' gallery, Gothic bedrooms, moldy tapestries, and a fireplace resembling a thirteenth-century tomb, is rather impractical, mildly uncomfortable, and completely unfashionable.

Like the house itself, Hetton's proprietor, Tony Last, is a simple-minded creature of the past who has never quite grown up. . . . (pp. 23-4)

The infidelity and the disintegration of the marriage are not analyzed in terms of the characters' deep, personal drives or romantic love or even blind lust. Brenda cherishes no illusions about her chosen lover. . . . There are no soul-searchings, no tortured moments of guilt, no remorseful thoughts of home and family. Brenda's choice of John Beaver is completely thoughtless and completely appropriate, for they inhabit a world and share a set of values about which Tony Last, content at Hetton, can know nothing.

The complete absence of any emotional life in the characters of Waugh's satires has irritated certain critics. . . . But one must not ask Evelyn Waugh or any satirist for a deep psychological examination of his characters, for this would be inimical to the satire itself. Satire, like comedy, is bound to be directed at the nonpersonal and mechanistic, for it sees man as an automaton, swept up in the mad conventions of society. . . . Satiric detachment can only be maintained when characters are soulless actors in a social drama, when the author treats his creations not as individuals with private lives but as symbols of societal forces. Any single character taken out of this context and forced to stand naked before the critic will naturally seem flat and unreal, but this individual emptiness is not a symptom of . . . Waugh's "brilliant faking." Rather it is the result of an attempt to portray characters who have lost their inner beings, their complexity, their moral and intellectual independence. The satirist's careful and quite conscious shrinking of his characters' personalities does not mean, however, that satire must deal with trivialities, for, seen in his proper ambient, Tony Last transcends a shallow characterization of a sap and becomes the complex symbol of a dying value system at once hopelessly naïve and deeply sympathetic, unable to cope with society and yet the last spark of human decency in a vile world.

Waugh's brilliance and the source of his bitter pessimism is his remarkable ability to sustain an ironic double vision, to laugh uproariously at his posing, lying, stupid, carnal, vicious, and unhappy characters at the same time that he is leading them on to damnation through those very qualities. The plot of *A Handful of Dust* is very much that of a typical bedroom farce—the stupid country squire with the beautiful wife is cuckolded by a young man from the city—and Waugh does not hesitate to employ all the stock devices of such comedy. The husband, now called "old boy" by his friends, is the only person in the world who does not know of his wife's affair. The clever wife treats her husband outrageously and then makes him feel guilty for being such a suspicious old fool. Assignations are kept right under the husband's nose, to the delight of all informed onlookers. Old maids and matronly ladies get immense vicarious pleasure from the affair, which they treat as a marvelous fairy story of an imprisoned princess rescued by a shining hero. But the unrestrained laughter with which the reader is conditioned to greet such situations is never wholly fulfilled, for the reader is aware of the double vision, of the bitterly ironic and unforgiving theme underlying the surface gaiety and flamboyance. (pp. 24-6)

Waugh's world is one in which the worst possible events implicit in any situation can and do happen, a world where the savagery underlying a seemingly innocent remark is always fully realized.... *A Handful of Dust* is a novel filled with improbable events and grotesque characters, but nothing ever happens for which the reader is not thoroughly prepared by Waugh. Even the fantastic ending in the jungles of Brazil is foreshadowed in the Vicar's Christmas sermon, and, though the reader may never consciously make the connection, the logic of the finale has been established. If we characterize Waugh's first three novels as comic audacity, comic sadness, and comic cruelty respectively, *A Handful of Dust* may be understood as comic bitterness, the comedy of rigidity and misunderstanding, the bitterness of betrayed ideals and fallen dreams. (p. 28)

In his reaction to [his] child's death, Tony reveals the terrible price he has paid for his simple-minded humanism, for he has lost the ability to assert his identity even in the moment of greatest suffering. In complete abnegation, Tony worries about everyone's feelings but his own.... Tony, ignorant [and] self-deceived, ... is pitiable ..., but he is certainly not a tragic or even a wholly sympathetic figure. By constantly denying his own feelings, he has gradually reduced himself to a cipher. The fantasy world into which he had retreated to avoid the mechanical, dehumanized society has, ironically, robbed him of his humanity. (pp. 28-9)

[The] total disintegration [of Tony's life] recalls the mad banquet of Trimalchio in the *Satyricon* and the "universal Darkness" in the *Dunciad;* it is the vision of hell which has tormented every great satirist and which underlies all of Waugh's early work. (p. 30)

Tony's distant ancestors might have sought a hardheaded, human solution to the problems of unidealized existence, but the family line has gone sour and Tony is heir to the rottenness, imbecility, and sham of his nineteenth-century forebears who tore down a noble house to build a pretentious and fraudulent structure in its place. Faced with the

realities of human viciousness and supported by nothing but his useless humanism, Tony can only retreat into infantile fantasies.... The repeated juxtaposition of a scene in Brazil and a similar scene in London makes devastatingly clear Waugh's point that the foul, inhuman jungle in which Tony wanders feverishly is London transfigured. At the heart of darkness, the intricate and elaborate screen of lies with which modern man comforts himself is torn away, and the horror and savagery of society is laid bare. Here, in a world where the distinction between reality and nightmare has broken down, the inhabitants are avaricious, moronic, superstitious, insolent cannibals; reason can no longer control passion; nature is cruel and treacherous; exposed flesh is prey to the bloodsucking thirst of vampire bats and malarial mosquitoes.

Fever-ridden and raving, Tony at last grasps the whole of his life as a grotesque hallucination. In a remarkable and brilliant passage, all of the characters in the novel, ugly and distorted, dance around the sick man in a mad, fiendish circle. Rising from his hammock, Tony begins to plunge wildly through the jungle.... (p. 31)

[He reaches] a transfigured Hetton, but it is stripped of all the sentimental drivel. Instead of ceilings groined and painted in diapers of red and gold and supported by shafts of polished granite with carved capitals, there are palm thatch roofs and breast-high walls of mud and wattle; instead of a society of vicious sophisticates presided over by a cruel and unfaithful wife, there is a community of savages ruled by a cunning lunatic.... Tony Last, literally imprisoned now in a literal wasteland, has nothing left of his dream but a heap of broken images. The fulfillment of Tony's humanism, his selfless devotion, his abnegation is an endless self-sacrifice enforced by a madman in the midst of a jungle. There is no City. Mrs. Beaver has covered it with chromium plating and converted it into flats. (p. 32)

[Like Nina Blount in *Vile Bodies*, Waugh] regards what was once "a precious stone set in the silver sea" and is obsessed with an overwhelming sense of loss. His laughter at the masses of dirty, moronic, corrupt, and fornicating beings beneath him cannot conceal his bitter rage. For the glory, the beauty, the dignity, and the grace of England have been destroyed, and Waugh, like Nina, sees only straggling red suburb, nauseating filth, and appalling decay. (p. 33)

> *Stephen Jay Greenblatt, in his* Three Modern Satirists: Waugh, Orwell, and Huxley *(copyright © 1965 by Yale University), Yale University Press, 1965.*

MARTIN STANNARD

Work Suspended is the most enigmatic of Waugh's writings. Its mockery of socialism and philistinism is of course quite in keeping with his rôle as the right-wing Catholic apologist defending 'civilization' from the 'barbarians', but the emotional intensity of the work, expressed in a more conventional and committed prose style than that of the five early novels is surprising. Although unfinished, *Work Suspended* has an evasive cohesion, perhaps because the characterization appears to be based on values and assumptions which derive from a private world beyond the text. (p. 302)

Even when allowance is made for the narrating persona, Waugh appears to be laying his literary soul open in an entirely new fashion. It is true that the death of the old and the birth of a new, 'dark' age had been his subject since 1930 (*Vile Bodies* concludes with a scene set on 'the biggest battlefield in the history of the world') but this strange, incomplete tale alters his whole approach. What, then, is the significance of [the novel's] disparate figures? And why, when it is of such high quality, did he find himself unable to complete their history? (pp. 302-03)

[*Work Suspended*] seems simply a reaction to the war as a cultural watershed beyond which 'all our lives, as we had constructed them, quietly came to an end'. . . . The battlefield of *Vile Bodies* had been a [useful metaphor; but] the sirens of World War II represented an assault on civilization which necessitated a practical response from Waugh. In 1942 he was an enlisted soldier. It is therefore unremarkable, we might say, that he should have altered his lighter pre-war style to meet this challenge. (p. 303)

This explanation is only part of the story. A profound sense of spiritual exile . . . characterised Waugh's life during the early thirties. He poured his energy into travelling and (with great difficulty) into the conscious artistry of his novels. . . . His journalism . . . reveals a serious approach to aesthetics. . . . Clarity, concision, the use of the 'refrain' rather than statement, a sense of fantasy and of the self-supporting reality of a work of art beyond and above the 'issues' involved—these were the tenets of his aesthetic faith. The artist, in his view, should clarify and make exact those nebulous ideas thrown up by experience. His trade, like the priest's, was concerned with elucidation and communication, the formulation of order from chaos. (pp. 304-05)

His earlier writings, working within a humanist framework, described behaviour and asserted Catholic values by negative suggestion. But they seemed 'light' because they omitted 'the determining character' of the 'soul'. (He had described *Scoop* to his agents as 'light and excellent'.) They were [like the novels of *Work Suspended*'s central character, John Plant], subtle exercises in literary technique in which technical felicity had become an end in itself. (p. 308)

Work Suspended was the first of Waugh's novels to use first person narration and, although various aspects of his personality and attitudes are distributed between John Plant and his father, it is largely autobiographical. In John we find the practical, workmanlike approach to fiction, the growing consciousness of the evils of contemporary society, the older man with the young woman and the spiritual exile with a mild distrust of his contemporaries. In the father we see the immediate abandonment of popular causes, the aesthetic tradition of representational, communicative art, the abomination of the standards of his youth, the rejection of Clive Bell and Bloomsbury, and an almost perverse delight in formality: the 'huge grim and solitary jest' (of his 'Academy' teas) at the expense of his friends and the contemporary artistic establishment. (p. 311)

The paperback text we have today, however, is the result of a 1949 revision, transforming the work from a very personal document into a more soberly topical allegory. Revision generally took the form of omission. But it was at this stage that the 'Postscript' was added to move the story forward to 1939. The original text [of the novel] dealt in detail with John Plant's literary technique, emphasizing his relish in 'Gothic enrichments' and 'the masked buttresses, false domes, superfluous columns, all the subterfuges of literary architecture and the plaster and gilt of its decoration'. (p. 312)

The alterations, though, are 'cosmetic'; while increasing the topical relevance and toning down the invective of the story Waugh changed nothing of its essence as an autobiographical document. In the original text the war is not even mentioned. The technical literary discussion was probably omitted on aesthetic grounds for it represented material which might have been interesting in a magazine article but which bore no structural relevance to the plot (a critical point frequently reiterated in his reviews). Perhaps more importantly, it revealed too much of himself. Both Plant's and Waugh's aesthetic relied on the concept of art as artifice; it should have 'absolutely nothing of [himself] in it'. . . . This was the paradox at the heart of his 'climacteric'—the problem of describing the subjective objectively.

The novel is not, then, simply a reaction to the war but a discussion of deep-rooted personal aesthetic problems which the revisions attempt to disguise and objectify. (p. 313)

In altering and ironically inverting the titles of the two parts Waugh drew greater attention to the central theme of decay and regeneration. The birth is the birth of the new age; what has died with the father can never be replaced by the son. In the first section Waugh speaks of 'the hide and seek with one's own personality' and the exposing of 'the bare minimum of ourselves' as a characteristic of modern 'civilized' man. The violation of privacy becomes a subtle *leit-motif*. A high price is set on 'Modesty' and it is this which is raped by Atwater and the seedy world of pre-war Britain. (p. 314)

Work Suspended is essentially an exposition of John Plant's 'climacteric' as a writer. There is no direct correspondence between Plant's and Waugh's novels other than their mutual delight in craftsmanship; no hint is given as to the outcome of Plant's problem—a metaphor, surely, for Waugh's own. Like Plant, he had no idea where it would end. His second marriage (1937) and the certain prospect of socialist government represented an assault on his private world, the first willingly embraced, the second, he considered, attempting to subvert his individuality. He only knew that he needed 'new worlds to conquer' and feared that he might mechanically be 'turning out year after year the kind of book [he knew he could] write well', 'becoming purely a technical expert'. . . . (pp. 314-15)

The 'sense of homelessness' becomes a companion theme to that of the invasion of privacy. Plant is driven to the seclusion of the countryside; he no longer belongs to the London of his youth. This was amplified by Waugh in later works where refugees, numberless hordes of anonymous individuals are herded from place to place. The condition of 'homelessness' he saw as symptomatic of a society which condemned private property and discouraged individualism. (p. 315)

Doubtless Waugh felt that the first edition did not make his point strongly enough when in the 1949 revision, with the hindsight of the war, he added the 'Postscript'. In this the theme of the 'petrified egg' is reinforced by the image of the beavers in a concrete pool, which, with futile efforts, damn 'the ancestral stream'. Traditional values, bulwarks against chaos (controls on the flood) are now without point. In his dedication to Alexander Woollcott Waugh remarked: '. . .

even if I were again to have the leisure to finish it, the work would be vain, for the world in which and for which it was designed, has ceased to exist'. Plant's house is requisitioned, his father's house destroyed, Lucy lost forever. The novel, like Waugh's own, remains 'a heap of neglected foolscap at the back of a drawer'. (p. 318)

The discontinuation of the novel was symbolic. Its theme was, at least in part, an attempt to analyse why the civilized man's emotions must 'assume the livery of defence' before they can 'pass through the lines'. That shyness was now abandoned; an aggressive attitude was adopted after being so long submerged in an inability openly to wage war on the polite belief in the inevitability of 'progress'. The problem had been that there was no obvious enemy. . . .

Ultimately, we can only guess at the real reasons for Waugh's inability to complete *Work Suspended*. His explanatory dedication to Woollcott represents only one aspect of the truth. But perhaps it was simply because he felt that he had failed to resolve the aesthetic problem of rendering the subjective objectively. 'Objectivity' in his post-war work relies on the assumption of a higher reality ultimately governing the action, where the 'determining character of the human soul' is 'that of being God's creature with a defined purpose'. No such dimension had been built into *Work Suspended* and Waugh may have decided that to continue his normal, externalised analysis of behaviour was meaningless; the negative assertion of order through an evocation of the sordid, chaotic and sentimental now seemed inadequate. He had effected the stylistic but not the thematic transformation. (p. 319)

> Martin Stannard, "'Work Suspended': Waugh's Climacteric," in Essays in Criticism, *October, 1978, pp. 302-20 (revised by the author for this publication).*

*   *   *

WESCOTT, Glenway   1901-

Wescott is an American novelist, poet, short story writer, essayist, and editor. His work thematically reflects his native Wisconsin, as well as his period of European expatriation. Critics have admired his technical skill, his attention to rhythm, and his artfulness of construction. Wescott's fiction often deals with ideas of duty, the nature of freedom, and the perception of reality, both past and present. (See also *Contemporary Authors*, Vols. 13-16, rev. ed.)

KENNETH BURKE

[*The Apple of the Eye*] is a book almost exclusively of emotional propulsion. Indeed, it even becomes a drenching in emotions, those softer, readier emotions which we designate usually as "feminine," an experience purely of "delight and tears" . . . and is thus a kind of revival in letters, an atavism, albeit a revival which is done with such force, such conviction, that one is caught unawares, and before he knows it is deeply involved in these partings . . . , this girl like wilted flower left to perish, these stutterings of love, the sleep-walking in the moonlight, the call, or lure, of the city over the hills and plains. The machinery of pathos is well utilized—which, once again, fails to convey the quality of the story, for it is so obvious that the author did not think in terms of the "machinery" of pathos. [Mr Wescott's] book, if it makes few demands upon the intellectual equipment of the reader, is a profoundly appealing piece of

emotional writing, or one might better call it an emotional *experience,* for the reader's participation in the author's plot is intense enough to leave him in possession of the story's overtones much as one is left with the overtones of some dream or some actual event which has occurred in one's own life.

The principal objection I find to Mr Westcott's book is its failure to widen the field of our aesthetic perceptions. . . . In method, Mr Wescott's chief contribution is the bringing of a greater and more sensitive vitality to a type of book in which the typical novelist could feel very much at home. In subject-matter, the author has re-seen for us certain stock figures and situations of the contemporary story, re-seen with a keener eye, but no new angle of vision.

Yet this in itself becomes a kind of virtue. Our latent familiarity with the mould sets us for it so perfectly, that when Mr Wescott does his act with such vigour we are able to follow him without a wrench. There is a point whereat the average suddenly transcends into the natural, and at times Mr Wescott seems rewarded by precisely this illumination, so that his book becomes something of a racial experience, adjusting itself with sensitiveness to our desires for both satisfaction and frustration. The greatest book ever written will probably be so for the same reason. And it is here that Mr Wescott is rewarded for having kept the commandments, and the law as the apple of his eye.

There are certain writers who, in addition to the absolute values of their work, have for me a sort of barometric interest. . . . I feel this way also with reference to Wescott. Will his next book be a continuation of his present one . . . ; or will it, in some form or other, suffer that strange critical deflection . . . which has started so many modern artists through some personal migration parallel to Joyce's curve from Dubliners to Ulysses? (pp. 513-15)

Mr Wescott is of a much more highly critical temper than his first book would seem to indicate. He is, therefore, by no means immune from the Dubliners-to-Ulysses temptation. While on the other hand the brilliancy of his first book would certainly justify him in trying to develop in the avoidance of more specialized channels.

In any case, we may for the time being content ourselves with this opportunity to welcome a work of such keen emotional appeal and stylistic vigour as are displayed in *The Apple of the Eye.* (p. 515)

> Kenneth Burke, "Delight and Tears," in The Dial *(copyright, 1924, by the Dial Publishing Company, Inc.; reprinted by permission of J. S. Watson, Jr. and Scofield Thayer), December, 1924, pp. 513-15.*

GRANVILLE HICKS

[*The Apple of the Eye*] concerns the spiritual aspects of pioneering, especially the bleak, sterile attitude towards life that frontier hardships sometimes foster. Fundamentally it is the story of the conflict between two religions and of the effect of that struggle on a boy who wavers between them. On the one hand we find the narrow, rigid, utilitarian Protestantism of the frontier; on the other, a pagan acceptance of life and all its pleasures. (p. 279)

In *The Grandmothers* Wescott continued as he had begun, describing the frustration of three generations of pioneers. The pioneers, he suggests, were from the first unhappy men, and it was the absence of happiness that sent them westward. They struggled with the land, always in poverty. "God was poverty, but He was poverty which would become wealth." So they identified piety and prosperity, and bent their necks before the divinely-imposed yoke. In due course the continent revealed its riches and many became wealthy. "Nevertheless," Wescott goes on, "millions remained poor. Before their eyes lay the feast—they could not eat; and though there were millions of them, each felt alone in his poverty. They grieved, but stifled their grief, being ashamed of it; for if they had worked harder, if they had led purer lives, if they still worked harder. . . . Those who did not give up hated life secretly; those who did, despised themselves." Of the Towers, the family he is describing, he writes: "They said little, but this conviction took possession of all their minds: they were not born to be beasts of burden; they should not have to work as these others worked; they were not menials, but deserved a sweeter fate; life was unjust. This conviction was inherited by every Tower, from father to son; and in that inheritance younger son shared equally with elder. A grievance was their birthright."

Wescott himself, obviously, inherited this grievance, and in his novels and most of his short stories, he made it articulate. It was, for a novelist, not a bad inheritance: it protected him from the more obvious forms of sentimentality, and it sharpened his eyes to see the actual results of life on the much-romanticized frontier. He saw hardship and bitterness and sterility rather than the beauty and heroism Willa Cather saw. . . . [He felt no] desire to transform the conditions he detested. Instead, he felt from the first . . . the desire to escape. (pp. 279-80)

> *Granville Hicks, in his* The Great Tradition: An Interpretation of American Literature Since the Civil War *(copyright © 1933, 1935 by Macmillan Publishing Co., Inc.; originally published in 1933 by The Macmillan Company, New York; new material in the revised edition copyright © 1969 by Granville Hicks; reprinted by permission of Russell & Volkening, Inc., as agent for the author), revised edition, Macmillan, 1935, Quadrangle Books, 1969.*

MORTON DAUWEN ZABEL

[*The Pilgrim Hawk*] is less the "love story" its subtitle suggests than a fable, and it shows again, but more explicitly and with greater critical weight, [Wescott's] natural inclination toward symbolic and legendary values in narrative. Where once—in *The Apple of the Eye, The Grandmothers,* and *Goodbye, Wisconsin*—he elaborated the mythic clues of the pastoral and folk tale, the tribal ritual of the family photograph album or the local daemon that haunts the hearsay, superstitions, and country legends of his midwestern homeland, he here reverts to a time and place grown more fabulous than Wisconsin ever could—to the France of the expatriates after the First World War, a lost paradise removed to lunar distance by war and change, whose delusions of emancipation linger in the memory with the unreality of life on another planet. (p. 304)

Mr. Wescott's story is one of the remarkable works of its kind in recent American fiction. Its deft shaping, sensitive and disciplined insight, and hypnotic suggestive force show it to be the work of a scrupulous craftsman and fully conscious critical intelligence. It shows the studied effect and stylistic scruple that point to a serious effort in a classic tradition. Yet in spite of its distinction it must be said of it that the balance essential to its genre is never clearly defined or resolved. The dramatic substance of his scenes and characters does not succeed in sustaining the elaborate commentary and moral deliberation he has imposed upon it. The annotation of the situation becomes too elaborate, ingenious, and uncomfortably self-conscious. A tendency toward a worrying preciosity of inference and analysis is never genuinely subdued to the natural impulse of the events, the given qualities of the characters, and the result becomes something too urgently contrived and at times almost desperately *voulu*.

These effects certainly do not minimize the beauty of conception that declares itself in its pages, the great superiority of its style and feeling to the general ruck of fiction, or its always subtly considered, often brilliant observations. . . . [Repeatedly] Mr. Wescott condenses his insight into judgments that express his story's motive with admirable point and precision:

> Unrequited passion; romance put asunder by circumstances or mistakes; sexuality pretending to be love—all that is a matter of little consequence, a mere voluntary temporary uneasiness, compared with the long course of true love, especially marriage. In marriage, insult arises again and again and again; and pain has to be not only endured, but consented to; and the amount of forgiveness that it necessitates is incredible and exhausting. When love has given satisfaction, then you discover how large a part of the rest of life is only payment for it. . . . To see the cost of love before one has felt what it is worth, is a pity; one may never have the courage to begin.
>
> (pp. 306-07)

Such lucidity of scruple produces a valuable alertness in the conscience of a writer, but its insistence over and above the volition of his drama soon involves him in a radical difficulty: it leads not only to a serious enervation of the tone, force, and unity of his story and to the exaggerated preciosity which is the major weakness of this particular book, but to something more dangerous still—an enervation of his imaginative substance itself and of the impulse that must be counted on to project it as drama and reality. *The Pilgrim Hawk* is by way of being a serious assessment of talent and purpose, one of the most incisive examinations of the imaginative conscience recent American writing has produced. In what it does to sublimate the aesthetic inflation and self-regard of Wescott's earlier work it indicates a renewal of discipline that may recover the exquisite pastoral lyricism of *The Apple of the Eye* and direct it toward finer and more substantial uses. The tale leaves the question hanging in suspense. It marks a revival of courage and critical insight in its author, and it serves as a word of warning, an act of cautionary artistry and admirable dedication to the most serious purposes a writer of fiction can address himself to, for a new generation of American talents. But in itself the book tests and exercises, rather than masters, the faculties that have given us the finest examples of the modern fable. (pp. 307-08)

> *Morton Dauwen Zabel, "Readings in Fiction: The*

Whisper of the Devil'' (originally published in a slightly different version in The Nation, December 21, 1940), in his Craft and Character: Texts, Method, and Vocation in Modern Fiction (copyright © 1957 by Morton Dauwen Zabel; all rights reserved; reprinted by permission of Viking Penguin Inc.), Viking Penguin, 1957, pp. 304-08.

WALTER ALLEN

[Glenway Wescott's] main theme has been what might be called the Mid-Western version of the American's complex fate. For the greater part of the thirties Wescott was an expatriate, living in France, but, on the evidence of his fiction, still unable to escape from Wisconsin, his native state, which seems at times almost as much a state of mind as a place.... (p. 105)

Wescott's strength as a novelist lies in his very ambivalence towards his subject, and in his finest novel, *The Grandmothers* ..., it appears in depth and at length and with a nostalgia that is always controlled. The action flows between the present and the past; the novel is a discovery of the past, a coming to terms with it. It is in essence a young intellectual's imaginative reconstruction of the lives of his grandparents and their families and relations, pioneers in the opening up of Wisconsin in the middle years of last century. In a way, it is history become myth.... (p. 106)

Walter Allen, in his The Modern Novel in Britain and The United States (copyright © 1964 by Walter Allen; reprinted by permission of E. P. Dutton; in Canada by Harold Ober Associates Inc.), Dutton, 1965.

IRA D. JOHNSON

During the 1920's, Glenway Wescott ... was generally considered by critics and discriminating readers as one of America's most promising young writers. (p. 3)

In certain ways Wescott is [indeed] of his time and place and in the mainstream of American literature. His beginnings as an imagist poet, his early appearance as a critic-reviewer in the pages of *The New Republic, Poetry, The Dial*, and other little magazines, his themes and his experiments with form in his novels and short stories which appeared before he had turned thirty, his years as an expatriate—all have their parallels to the production and careers of other American writers of the twenties. Contemporary criticism, although appreciative and optimistic about his career, was with few exceptions brief and ephemeral, predominately placing him as a regionalist, a chronicler of pioneers, a recorder of frustrated and rebellious lives wasted away in remote middle-western towns. . . .

Despite the quality and the uniqueness of his sensibility ..., [Wescott] is not a major American writer.... [He] appeared to have just those qualities needed for major achievement and to have started early and fast in that direction, only to disappoint; by the time he was forty-four he had stopped writing fiction. (p. 4)

The Apple of the Eye [his first work of fiction (1924)] is characterized by many techniques in the modern tradition, but especially by a limited though powerful and rhetorical narrative voice. Two serious flaws are evident: the novel's didacticism, due to Wescott's conception of *image* and *truth*, and the disparity between the omniscient narrator and the rest of the work. Consideration of these two prob-

lems are necessary in measuring Wescott's intention and achievement. It soon becomes clear that it is only when he is able to resolve them that his fiction achieves the potential it at other times seems to promise.

The Grandmothers [1927] to a surprising degree does fulfill that promise, fusing secondary themes with what are always to be Wescott's major themes, love and the self. Here Wescott has found a form that is not only amenable to his subject, but perfectly suited to his strengths—and his failings—as an artist. His great technical achievement is the development of a participating narrator, identical to the author's second (artistic) self, inseparable from subject and form, and gifted with a voice able to exploit what is outstanding, the *lyrical* and *rhetorical* quality of his prose. Such a narrator nearly eliminates the disparity between voice and other elements, and it makes functional what in the first novel had been flaws—including the abstracting of *truths* from *images*, which now becomes essential to the narrator's rumination on the family of stories. Yet, rather than develop important techniques that would give him greater flexibility, Wescott was apparently, by means of the new participating narrator, able to make virtues of some of his rather pronounced artistic shortcomings. (pp. 5-6)

[The] theme of the self, the concept of *image* and *truth*, and the technique of the participating narrative voice are so fused in Wescott's creative imagination and, apparently, so closely related to the author's personal self, that this fusion results in his only consistently successful form of narration.

What Wescott sought was a greater distance between the personal self and the second, or artistic, self. In *The Babe's Bed* [1930], he attempts to put an end to the method of the participating narrator and to search out and destroy the psychological necessity behind it because he feels that the result is self-projection rather than what he calls *truth*. In this sense *The Pilgrim Hawk* [1940] is a rewriting of *The Babe's Bed*. Yet in neither work does Wescott recognize the contribution of his concept of *image* and *truth* to the very abstracting and generalizing he so deplores. A rationale that led to serious shortcomings in his other works, it is still retained in his attempt at an objective novel, *Apartment in Athens* [1945], and significantly contributes to its failure. Neither does Wescott succeed in eliminating the narrative voice; in its emasculated form it is the second major cause of that novel's failure, which suggests, along with evidence in the essays, *Images of Truth* (1962), that Wescott is still strongly drawn toward the form in which he achieved so much. Although the ultimate reasons are probably deeply personal, Wescott's long fictional silence [since *Apartment in Athens*] has been due to being drawn toward two opposing and irreconcilable concepts of narration and form, only to find himself immobilized between them. (p. 6)

The Apple of the Eye, The Grandmothers, Good-Bye, Wisconsin, a handful of uncollected short stories, and *The Babe's Bed*, more than half of Wescott's fiction and all of what is his first and largest period of production, make use of middle-western material. Yet to categorize Wescott as a regionalist, as some critics and reviewers have done, is to be short-sighted. (p. 8)

The Apple of the Eye is one of Wescott's minor works.... Characterization is certainly one of the novel's weaknesses. Of course, other qualities such as dialogue, dramatic realization and general conception, to name a few, are also pertinent to the characterization. But it is in the inadequacy of character in relation to the development of theme . . . that [the characters] fall most short of their function. Measuring them by the very moral framework that the novel insists upon reveals not only their lack of verisimilitude and realization, but the inadequacy and the moral confusion of the novel as a whole. (p. 11)

Dan Strane is, of course, the major character, and he is the most convincing and best-realized. The whole final third and much of the second section is directly concerned with his process of maturing, his growing break with his parents, family and home, "country" or region, and religion. It is here that Wescott's prose is able to serve its most sympathetic function; even though his character is not realized in very objective terms—it is hard to think of him except as a sensibility—what effectiveness there is in the final section depends on the successful rendering of the subjective life of Dan Strane. (p. 16)

The major symbol in the novel (barring Hannah) is the marsh. It is to some extent a cumulative symbol, taking on additional meaning with repeated usage, and it is a many-faceted or *revolving* symbol. That is, what it symbolizes depends on the context, but often on the character acting within the context as well, who may, or may not, be aware of its symbolic quality. As a symbol, the marsh is all-pervasive, and gives unity to the novel. As a part of the nature imagery it also aids the rhythmical structure. (pp. 18-19)

[In *The Apple of the Eye*] the use of imagery to create symbolic texture as an intrinsic quality of the prose, to build cumulative symbols which through their numerous facets of implication can be said to be revolving because they can be turned from one facet to another for meaning . . . form a major aspect of Wescott's art, a positive one, which even in this early novel is impressive, and which justifies serious attention to the work in spite of its shortcomings. . . .

Wescott's prose style is one of careful diction that achieves a finely-chiseled quality and a surface of meticulous finish imparted alike to landscape, animals, and human figures. It is the source of much of the regional quality of [*The Apple of the Eye*]. (p. 28)

The adjectives and adverbs, although profuse, are chosen with precision, the lushness often given by the modifying phrases and clauses. The sentences and paragraphs so carefully carved and fitted together, slow and even halt movement, giving a static effect, for there is a shift required from image to image. If action is involved it is nearly always slow, and the effect one of turgidity. (p. 30)

However, the lyric, disciplined, imagistic prose of sensibility—which is Wescott's notable achievement so early in this first novel—is markedly limited, inflexible and awkward when it comes to two important elements: creation of scene and dialogue. Except for Mike Byron, a sometimes garrulous mouthpiece of romantic sensibility, the other characters are not only awkward of speech but inarticulate. What is worse, the dialogue is strikingly unrealistic and often unauthentic—by forfeit, for the idioms common to region and time are remarkably few, and the result is a limp and emasculated standard American English. The dramatic potentialities of situations—for characterization, for thematic tension or clarification, and for other purposes —are rarely if ever imaginatively realized, especially in confrontations of character with character. (p. 31)

Wescott's use of point-of-view and narrator . . . is the most important key to both his powerful and impressive prose and to his fundamental failure in this novel. (p. 32)

The point-of-view . . . throughout the novel is omniscient, and the language and all its qualities (except for that of dialogue) are those of the omniscient narrator. [Sometimes] the point of observation is far outside, and, one may say, above that of the characters. The concern is with the matter of *distance,* the gap between the material viewed (countryside, people, or thoughts and feelings of character in isolation or dramatic action) and the means of viewing, which are here the omniscient narrator who quite deliberately colors with his vision everything seen, and what is very important, makes himself known in terms of *voice,* the accent or tone of the language which implies the attitude behind it.

Sometimes the narrator seems to lessen his distance to give us the thoughts of his characters. . . .

[When] the focus is on thought or attitude, exposition or analysis or generalization, the language is pithy and aphoristic, the *result* of insight—rather than the following of the flow of thought. (p. 34)

The omniscient narrator in this novel is all-pervasive. Armed with the impressive but nevertheless sometimes inflexible quality of Wescott's prose, making himself evident, making himself heard through the quality of voice, he is the very medium through which everything is experienced by the reader. Though the focus may vary, the voice always maintains a distinct distance. There is, of course, nothing wrong with such a technique in principle. But artistic success will then depend upon the success of the narrative voice. It is evident that characterization, realization of dramatic potentialities, and rendering of subjective states are often not successful. Yet the prose itself and the power of the voice is what makes the book more than the ordinary first novel. (pp. 36-7)

Nevertheless, there is a disparity between the narrator and other elements of the novel. The attention to the qualities which will make for spellbinding seems to be at the expense of "intellectual demands," particularly characterization, dramatic realization, and adequate confrontation of the two thematic polarities that should take on a form of believable life. It is at the expense of a moral vision complex enough, and realized enough, to justify what the narrator insists is the theme; for he does insist, in aphorism and generalized statement or through a substitute, didactic dialogue. It is this disparity that at the very beginning of his career is one of Wescott's fundamental artistic problems. By it his intention and achievement can be measured. It is only when he is able to overcome it that the result is fiction of the highest quality and significance. (pp. 39-40)

[It is] *The Grandmothers: A Family Portrait* upon which much of [Wescott's] literary reputation rests, fulfilling, essentially, the predictions of those who had seen him as a writer of great promise. . . . It is his greatest and most successful fictional exploitation of middle-western material. (p. 41)

The novel [is not] a regional work [, but rather] one of the reality and myth of the American past, of its meaning, in other words, to the modern pioneer, one who seeks to find and clarify the self—in this case, Alwyn Tower, expatriate and artist. His concern with the past is what sharply distinguishes Alwyn Tower from the expatriate protagonists of Hemingway, Fitzgerald, and others. (pp. 41-2)

It can hardly be overstressed that only in the larger, and hence metaphorical sense is pioneering the subject of the novel, and that its major themes are love and the self. Both of these are related to every other theme, it seems, intertwined, and sometimes indistinguishable. . . . (p. 58)

Two of the important motifs that are part of the general love theme are homosexuality and incest. . . . The novel delineates a sharp American polarity between the "masculine" and "feminine" traits. Sensibility (including artistic sensibility) is considered feminine, or at least effeminate, and insensibility, even brutishness, is considered masculine. (pp. 61-2)

Incest is of course a form of love, and what it emphasizes here is the claustrophobic nature of the Tower family relationships, their sensibility seeking love within the isolated family, a situation which is partly due to their idealism, pride and aristocratic pretensions. (p. 63)

The profuse generalizations throughout the novel lead to the broader generalizations developed in the conclusion. It is here, too, that the several themes find their synthesis in a broad family metaphor. They serve also as strands binding individual characters and chapters to each other, each character to the family, and the family and regional chronicle to the American past. The primary structural principle is that of the narrator. He is not only the primary structural principle but the primary formal one, the highly successful fusion of form and function in this novel rests on the successful use of the narrator and voice. . . .

[Each] of the dozen major characters upon which so much depends is adequately conceived for the purposes of the work. There is no sense here of the moral confusion, of the lack of verisimilitude, and faulty realization that so flawed *The Apple of the Eye*. . . . For one thing, no single character is meant to carry as heavy a thematic burden as Hannah Madoc, even though the characters in the second novel are generally more complex. No single character is intended to be a secular saint. Rather it is what may be learned from all of these lives, as they are made material for the investigating, ruminating, contemplating mind of Alwyn Tower. . . . (p. 65)

Wescott's fondness, even insistence, upon making generalities, upon carefully turning aphorisms and driving his "truths" home with specific statements is still with him. The difference, a great one, is that in his second novel the results of this fondness are in principle justified by the subject and form. Yet a question of degree is aesthetically important. . . . (p. 66)

Apparently, in Wescott's view, at least in his practice, *truths* are necessarily abstract and general. *Images* are concrete—an entire story may be an *image*—and *images* have to be, it seems, converted to *truths* before they can be mentally digested and then made use of, and it is the *use* of these *truths* that justified the creation of the *images*. This concept of *image* and *truth* applied in both of the first two novels is a curiously pragmatic and utilitarian view of art and human sensibilities, and one that would seem antithetical to Wescott's values generally in life and in art. It is a concept which works well enough in *The Grandmothers* and is central to the book's conception. The excess of gen-

erality is not enough to constitute a major flaw. But, in *The Apple of the Eye*, the concept is central to its failure, and it becomes a major aesthetic problem in Wescott's career.

Two related shortcomings in *The Apple of the Eye* which directly concerned unsuccessful characterization had to do with the inadequate quality of, and scarcity of, dramatic scenes and dramatic confrontations of character. Again there is a great gap between the two novels, at least in *effect*. Certainly a more mature and complex conception of character in the second novel makes a great difference. But what of the actual scenes and confrontations? True, there are many more of them, and they are certainly of higher quality. . . . [There] are numerous small incidents, lines of dialogue, shards of scenes, and summary references— sometimes a mere line or two of information—pertaining to one character but appearing in the story of others. These cross-connections of character are ligaments that help bind the individual to the family, as in a similar way the particular and abstract "truths" link them to the family also, and the family to the pioneers, and the whole work to the region and America.

The relation of this particular kind of structure to character is that the concentration, the focus, is upon one character at a time, even though the treatment may be broken into two or more pieces and separated. The character's sensibility is rendered through the narrator's sympathetic voice, and his character is structured in summary-narrative form. . . . Because of the album form, and the high degree of selection and concentration, it is possible for the author to avoid any but the most critically necessary confrontation of character and dramatic scene. This technique is . . . like that of *The Apple of the Eye*. . . . The narrative technique, the means of rendering character, however, is *essentially the same* [in the first two novels]. Even though Wescott has improved greatly in the execution of [his] technique, scene and confrontation are skimpy, and succeed mainly by virtue of being enclosed in the language of the commenting narrator. The successful narrative voice has the effect of making virtues of the author's shortcomings. (pp. 66-8)

The cumulative symbol and the revolving symbol are used throughout. Bird-imagery, an important pattern in the first novel, appears again, becoming the most important symbolic texture. (p. 69)

[Unlike the first novel, in *The Grandmothers*] prose descriptions with the quality of set-pieces are non-existent, and when landscape or images of nature appear, they are directly functional either to the narrative, scene, or evocation of character. . . . [The] prose is more immediately and directly functional and rather than lush, as in *The Apple of the Eye*, it is comparatively pruned and lean.

In creation of scene and dialogue discernable improvements are evident. In dialogue there is a general sense of improvement, but upon examination it is less than expected. (p. 74)

There is a remarkable lack of ear not only for vocabulary, but for the syntax of idiomatic speech. . . . The improvement in dialogue is mainly due to its unobtrusiveness. It is not typical, nor realistically accurate. It is ordinary. (p. 75)

The scenes have not the inflexibility, awkwardness and limitations which in *The Apple of the Eye* made themselves intrinsic to the very qualities of the prose. There is not the slackening of necessary thematic or dramatic tension that so often occurred in the first novel. If, as happens from time to time, it appears that some of the genuine dramatic possibilities in confrontation of character with character are avoided, the form ... allows for highly concentrated scenes, the narrative pace forces one to read on, the pace of course being in the control of the narrator. (p. 76)

The prose descriptions in some passages are, as in *The Apple of the Eye*, a substitute for the rendering of emotion. Often it is for purposes of establishing a tone with which the character's mood is in accord. But there is significant difference. With Alwyn as narrator recalling and recreating the character and his world, there is no longer the disparity between the language and tone of the description and that of which the character would be capable. (p. 78)

[Although] the omniscient narrator [of *The Apple of the Eye*] shifted *focus* on his material, including characters, his distance remained steady, relatively far above and outside his characters.... The same is found to be true in *The Grandmothers*. The great difference is that such steady distance, allied with other inadequacies of the narrator and prose, contributed to numerous flaws in the first novel. In *The Grandmothers*, such distance is quite justified and qualified by the characteristics of the narrator-character, who although all-powerful, must recreate from memory and imagination, which seems to necessitate a certain distance. (pp. 79-80)

Wescott still fails to render often the actual thought and emotion of his characters and is given to aphorism, paradoxical statement, image and metaphor, exposition, and summary—all about such feeling and thought. But the emotional *forte*, the spellbinding quality of the prose and the narrative voice, partly because of the vast aesthetic improvement of other elements and the superiority of the mind that it reveals in this second novel, and with the aid of a consistently effective nostalgic tone, is more spellbinding, more powerful than ever. Critics have again and again emphasized the lyric quality of the prose and narrator, attributing it to the predominant theme of the self, or even more often to the imagistic quality of the language, and finding its source sometimes in the emotion of the narrator....

[There are], with the advent of *The Grandmothers*, clearly two qualities of Wescott's prose (if we may lump characteristics around two terms) and his narrative strategy, both capable of spellbinding: the *lyrical*, with its imagistic, symbol-making, mood-creating quality, and the *rhetorical*, that of the ruminating, investigating, clarifying mind adept at aphorism, epigram, and organization of generality and abstraction. Both of these qualities were incipient in the first novel, the lyric quality particularly well-developed. But not until *The Grandmothers*, with the development of the narrative voice in control of the character in third-person, does Wescott find a technique so suited to his subject and artistic intentions. (p. 80)

[In *The Grandmothers* there] is no longer the disparity between the narrator and other elements of the novel. Rather than the narrator's qualities being at the expense of "intellectual demands," it is the primary means of satisfying them. Wescott's moral vision, his insight into the complexity of individuals has developed greatly too. Unquestionably, part of this difference, at least, is due to a narrator who is no longer separated from other elements in the novel, but

is the very dynamic principle on which its form relies. (p. 81)

Certain shortcomings and limitations remain, discernible under the surface of *The Grandmothers*. [Wescott] still has a weakness for the didactic, related intimately to his curious concept of the dichotomy of *images* and *truth* ..., and his insistence on separating the two is evident in both novels. In each, near the end of the book, the protagonists extract *truths* from the images of which the rest of the novel consists. In *The Apple of the Eye* the result alone would be enough to make the novel a failure. In *The Grandmothers*, however, such a method is intrinsic to the very subject and form. The danger is that Wescott takes the concept as therefore valid in principle, rather than appropriate for that particular work. (pp. 81-2)

["Good-Bye, Wisconsin," the title essay of his only collection of short stories,] is not a piece of objective social analysis, but an attack, which presents in terms of his personal vision the reasons why Wescott finds the Middle West and America a place that in countless ways prevents the development of the self....

The essay is pontifical, dogmatic, didactic, authoritative, and couched in a tone of nostalgia and lament. The prose style is dominated by aphorism, epigram, and paradoxical statement. In other words, this is the spellbinding narrative voice, the rhetorical voice so highly developed in *The Grandmothers*, which in fiction, after the first novel, has been the voice of the third-person participating narrator. Here first person is used, with no discernible difference in effect. Ruminating, yet persuasive, the voice is concerned with communicating *truth*. Relieved of most of the concerns necessary in fiction, the author indulges in a *tour de force* of the rhetorical voice. There are no symbols here, for instance, in the sense that they are successfully used in fiction; there is only rhetoric *about* symbols. Even the *images* which give rise to the generalities (the *truth*) or serve as examples are, as is so often the case when encompassed by the narrative voice, vague and general. (p. 103)

For the first half [of the long short story *The Babe's Bed*, the voice of the narrator] carries on its usual functions. The second half reveals the falsity of the symbolizing and generalities which are very characteristic of that voice, and layer by layer, it de-symbolizes and de-generalizes. Yet, incurably, and apparently without the awareness of either character or author, one of the greatest faults of this rhetorical narrator, his profuse capacity for generalizations, particularly in a *summing up* at the end of the story, is indulged in here to a degree beyond any aesthetic justification—an ironic, though unintentional, proof of the validity of the narrator's destructive analysis of himself.

What is especially significant about this story is that Wescott, having developed the participating third-person-narrator, capable of lyricism, but especially of rhetoric, and having failed with it in some stories, having utilized it brilliantly in one of his major works, *The Grandmothers*, now apparently is out to destroy his faith in this method and the psychological sources behind it.... It is one of Wescott's most inferior works. One can only assume that the nameless [narrator], since he is beset by the same problems of narrative art as Wescott himself, is, as artist, his duplicate, and that Wescott is determined to give up what was once his basic artistic method of narration, or even the writing of fiction itself. He nearly did just that. With the exception of three short stories, no fiction appeared from him until ten years later.

The short stories that were published after the collection in *Good-bye, Wisconsin* are few and inferior.... [In them, too,] Wescott's difficulties are to an important degree concerned with point-of-view and narration. (pp. 107-08)

[*The Pilgrim Hawk, Love Story*] is the culmination of his career as a fiction writer....

[In *The Pilgrim Hawk,* Alwyn Tower] is in a situation geographically the reverse of that in *The Grandmothers,* but essentially the narrative position is similar, for although Tower is now commenting on events that took place in Europe when he was an expatriate, he is, as in the earlier novel, commenting from time-present on events that took place in time-past. (p. 113)

[His] ruminations, meditations, and evaluations are, as in *The Grandmothers, The Babe's Bed,* and some of the stories, not only what hold the work together, but are, in the familiar pattern, the most important "events" taking place, for Alwyn Tower is the narrator and protagonist as well, and most important is what it all means to him. (p. 114)

[The] personal past, with which the main body of the narrative is concerned, is linked not only to the historical past of the twenties, but through the Cullens, the Duchesse, Europe itself, hunting and the four-thousand-year-old sport of falconry, to a broader historical past. The events are thus placed as remote and of another time, although only a decade away, and the events and characters take on a heightened quality, that of "a lost paradise."... It is in that exciting, optimistic time that the narrator has chosen to end his tale. The irony and nostalgic tone do not discredit that time; on the contrary, for the present of war-time is a chaos. In this sense, the novel might well have been subtitled *Good-bye, Europe.* (p. 116)

Wescott's main themes in *The Pilgrim Hawk* are as always related, and are the same as in earlier works, love and the self, the motifs of the artist and expatriatism being aspects of the theme of the self....

[In] *The Pilgrim Hawk,* the only sensibility rendered directly is that of the narrator himself. The other characters are observed by him, and it is his speculation and meditation on what he observes during one afternoon that characterizes them. The incorporation of the talents of the novelist of manners with his other gifts is appropriate to the difference in Wescott's material, and it is consistent with the worldly narrator who has been an expatriate.

One of the results is a new sharpness of focus on character confrontation, achieved with a greater subtlety.... (p. 129)

So concerned before with rendering the subjective sensibility of different characters, he now turns to rendering details of personality and dramatic action; there is a corresponding flexibility and precision of language in his prose that is new. (pp. 129-30)

In *The Pilgrim Hawk* there is a great improvement in dialogue. The authenticity is never in question, nor is it ever awkward or unlikely. There is no doubt that much of the improvement is due to the great difference in material. No longer dealing with the language of rural middle western Americans with whom he grew up, but with English-speaking expatriates from America and the British Isles, Wescott is much more at home. (p. 130)

Wescott's talent for the carefully turned aphorism and the memorably stated generality reaches a new level of achievement. There is not the faulty or strained expression or turn of phrase as is sometimes the case in previous work, nor the vague metaphor of excessive involution.... [Whether] or not one agrees as to the validity of the generalities, the quality of mind [is] calm, worldly-wise, sensitive, and disillusioned, capable of subtlety, paradox, and nuance. These qualities, of course, appear also as part of the flexibility and precision of language in rendering manners, and necessarily help characterize the narrator, as well as giving a new dimension to the narrative voice. (pp. 131-32)

The Pilgrim Hawk is the culmination of [the] symbolic methods which have appeared in all his novels and many of his short stories up to this time. The hawk is *cumulative* in taking on additional meaning with each reference, and it is *revolving* in that as the narrative progresses, the symbol is turned, so to speak, to reveal the many facets of meaning depending on the context. It is consistent with previous bird-symbology in that its implications are related to love or the inner life. But in this novel, the symbol as never before is in its revolving not only a primary principle upon which the structure depends, but the very turning of it for every aspect of meaning by the narrator is the action from which the themes of the self and the artist emerge. (p. 132)

The hawk is compared, and more often than once, to each of the four major characters, and the characters, of course, constantly illustrate and carry through the various themes that the hawk has suggested. The movement of the narrator's mind from hawk to speculation on symbolic meanings, or generalities, back to character, and often again to generalities carries the thread of first one theme, then another in repetition with variation. Thus spun from the revolving symbol of the hawk, the facets of meaning become motifs which are patterned through the work. (p. 135)

The negative qualities [of the narrator] are just what Tower calls attention to in the final parts of *The Pilgrim Hawk.* The narrator here despairs of his habit of abstracting, of his research for formula and moral. The habit is, of course, one with Wescott's concept ... [of] *images* being facts, or what passes for them in fiction, and *truth* being abstract, and as with Wescott previously, the very justification of fiction itself, hence his excess of generalities and his tendency to didacticism. In *The Pilgrim Hawk,* Wescott, through the narrator, seems to recognize by implication the fallacy of such an idea, and that the truth is in the image and not derived from it, yet there are strong indications that if he does he is like Alwyn Tower and "again and again" forgets it.

The recognition that is most important for him, however, is that his habit of mind seems incurable.... He destroys what he has created in *The Pilgrim Hawk* because the "whisper of the devil" tells him it is only a projection of the self.

The major theme of the work is that of the self, the self as artist, for the entire aesthetic construct is pointed toward self-examination, and the characteristic impulse of the mind of that self is the primary propulsion of the novel; it is the force that revolves the symbol and moves the narrative ...; it is the impulse of that mind that terminates in the conclusion that the mental effort is all lyricism and abstraction and must be rejected. Thus the very success of Alwyn Tower as narrator proves his failure as an artist, and the very success of *The Pilgrim Hawk* depends on Wescott convincing himself, apparently, of his failure as an artist. . . . It should be emphasized that the flaws that lead him to this destruction appear to be intrinsic characteristics of his most successful and important means of narration, the participating narrator, never to be used again.

One of the ironies is that *The Pilgrim Hawk* is one of the author's finest works of fiction, unique in form and finely wrought. (pp. 138-40)

If we are to accept Tower's judgment of himself as narrator (and Wescott's as writer), must we not accept the destruction of the very formal beauty we have enjoyed and the attributes of its parts? The judgment of Alwyn Tower on everything is then in doubt, his portrayal of people probably inaccurate, his generalities and aphorisms at best only half-truths. But even though there are clues here and there that such might be the case, the characters presented are among his most fascinating; never has Wescott's style been more admirable, his prose so satisfying to the ear and sense of phrasing; his generalities and aphorisms have the appearance, in context, of being true, and the continual accumulation of the symbolic layers around the hawk is exciting in its complexity and structure.

The point would seem to be that since this is after all fiction, an art form, it is possible to admire the beauty of the artistic object even if its theme denies that such beauty exists. The theme, after all, is one element, and, as Alwyn Tower himself might point out, an abstraction. The reality is the total form, not a statement that can be abstracted about what it means. (pp. 140-41)

Apartment in Athens can only be ranked as the least successful, artistically, of Wescott's novels. . . . [A major flaw] is its didacticism. Another concerns the prose, and still another the point-of-view and narrator and narrative voice. These flaws permeate every element of the novel, but it is particularly in characterization and structure in relation to theme that Wescott's insistence on getting across his "message," his *truth,* is most evident.

The major themes of love and the self which appear in all of Wescott's major work are here evident again, discernible, but flattened and distorted by the didactic intention. (pp. 148-49)

The characters in *Apartment in Athens* are on the whole the least compelling and interesting of any in Wescott's novels. (p. 151)

In attempting to present his concept of German temperament, character, and ideals, Wescott fails to present human temperament and character. There is no probing into the nature of man and his situation. . . . (p. 154)

[The dialogue is] generally of a quality that can only be called ordinary or, at best, adequate. As so often with Wescott, summary narration, rather than direct scenes, allows for a minimum of direct dialogue. (p. 156)

The qualities of technique in the modern tradition of fiction which have been Wescott's from the very first—a patterned, as distinguished from plotted, ordering of events, for design itself or mythic implications; a consistent arrangement of related images for symbolic texture; major symbols; a powerful narrative voice—all are either missing or attenuated and atrophied [in *Apartment in Athens*].

In the essay "Goodbye, Wisconsin," Wescott had expressed his desire for prose style "out of which myself, with my origins and my prejudices and my Wisconsin, will seem to have disappeared." In *The Babe's Bed* and in *The Pilgrim Hawk* he objectifies his complete distrust and rejection of the very lyrical and rhetorical qualities that were intrinsic to his most effective means of narration, the participating narrator with a powerful narrative voice. The quality of the prose and the means of the narration in *Apartment in Athens* are apparently the result of such desire and rejection. The participating narrator is abandoned for a third-person omniscient point-of-view much less lyrical or rhetorical than that of *The Apple of the Eye*. It is one of the major reasons for much that is inferior in the novel. (pp. 156-57)

[The] participating narrator was not only his greatest technical discovery, but, with the exception of a few short stories, his only successful means of narration. Having discarded such a narrator, Wescott in effect discarded for the most part the positive qualities of the voice that was inseparable from it: the *lyrical,* associated with the expression of self, the expression of the emotion of the narrator, the imagistic quality of the language, and the lyric creation of moods; and the *rhetorical,* which made itself evident in the tone and voice of the narrator by means of image and metaphor, by aphorism and generality, and which was the means to investigate, to communicate, and to persuade the reader of the actuality of events (*images*) and of *truths*. These qualities, of course, made possible an effective symbology. (p. 164)

What remains of the voice is simply incapable of the performance of the voice of the participating narrator. Nevertheless, although the voice is weak, and devoid of much of the lyrical and rhetorical qualities evident even in Wescott's first novel, it is, [in *Apartment in Athens*] as in *The Apple of the Eye* inescapable; and, as in that novel, the voice always maintains a distinct *distance* even though the *focus* may vary. The result is that, with such distance, artistic success will be impossible without the success of the narrative voice. . . . (pp. 164-65)

In *Apartment in Athens,* [Wescott's] work in an unfortunate way comes full circle and the novel repeats, fundamentally, the same aesthetic errors as the first. (p. 165)

The disparity between the narrative voice and other qualities of technique are discernible, in some form or another, in greater or lesser degree, throughout nearly all of Wescott's work. *The Pilgrim Hawk* is the noticeable exception. In *The Grandmothers* Wescott developed the participating narrator with his many capabilities, including an even more powerful and more flexible voice. Many of the flaws or shortcomings of technique that appeared in the first novel are, in the second, for the most part, justified by its distinctive form in which the narrator oversees all with his ruminating, involuting mind and colors it with the quality of his voice. Nevertheless, examination reveals that often, and significantly, technical flaws are not so much overcome by practice as circumnavigated, camouflaged, and avoided by the adoption of the participating narrator and the particular form intrinsic to him.

A major flaw in *The Apple of the Eye* was the detrimental

insistence upon certain *truths* as theme; it appears not only in the didactic dialogue but by means of the narrator. In this first novel the commitment to the idea of *images and truth* is already evident, and the means of abstracting *image* from *truth* is the narrative voice. In *The Grandmothers* the abstraction of *truths* from the *images* that are the family of stories is justified in principle because it is, to a high degree, functional; intrinsic to the very theme of the self and the form is the concluding rumination and analysis for a synthesis of what the narrator has learned. The lyrical and rhetorical voice with its symbol-making and abstracting and generalizing becomes inseparable from the overseeing mind that must draw conclusions, for that mind is the book's subject.

The technique of the participating narrator and his voice, the concept of *image and truth,* the theme of the self—each of these is in *The Grandmothers* dependent upon the others, and their interrelation is necessary. The dangers of slighting other techniques, by depending too much on the powers of the narrative voice, of over-generalizing and over-abstracting, of becoming didactic—these too are all perceivable in the novel in spite of its aesthetic success. The very fact that it does succeed as well as it does and seems perfectly suited in form to Wescott's talents and to his weaknesses and shortcomings powerfully suggest—in retrospect—that for the writer, the new narrator, the concept of *image and truth,* and the theme of the self are strongly fused in the crucible of the creative imagination; and what is more, the relationship of this particular form to the writer's personal self is very close. (pp. 169-70)

It appears likely that Wescott's long fictional silence is due to being immobilized between the pull of two opposing concepts of the novel form: one in which he has done his only significant fiction and which he rejects in spite of it having some deep personal appeal for him, and another which he admires and believes superior but in which he can do only the most inferior kind of work, or none at all, because it is a denial of all his talents and perfected techniques, as well as a denial of the self. (p. 176)

> Ira D. Johnson, in his Glenway Wescott: The Paradox of Voice *(copyright © 1971 by Ira Johnson; reprinted by permission of Kennikat Press Corp.), Kennikat, 1971.*

*   *   *

WILLIAMS, John A(lfred)   1925-

Williams is a black American novelist, journalist, short story writer, essayist, biographer, poet, and editor whose work concerns the effects of racism on individual identity and pride. Critics note that his changing personal opinions and literary style strengthen with each successive novel. *The Man Who Cried I Am* **is his best known work. (See also** *CLC,* **Vol. 5.)**

DAVID BOROFF

In his new work, *Sissie,* [John A. Williams] draws in part on his authoritative knowledge of [the jazz] world, but this novel is far richer and cuts deeper than most books about jazz. For *Sissie* is a chronicle of Negro life in transition, and it unites, as few novels do, the experience of the brutalized older generation of Negroes with that of the sophisticated young, who, one way or another, have made it in American life. As such, it is full of vivid contrasts, and it conveys memorably an image of the double war that Negroes wage—against their white oppressors on the one hand, and generation against generation on the other. In its portrayal of the conflict of generations, *Sissie* suggests the American-Jewish novel of a few decades ago in which the younger generation rebels against, but is emotionally wedded to, the experience of its parents.

Sissie is a proud, indomitable matriarch with two surviving children, Ralph and Iris. On one level the story is almost a sentimental saga of a Negro family that struggles against poverty and demoralization and finally achieves strenuous respectability. Here the book is akin to the traditional American "immigrant" novel. But *Sissie* is steadily redeemed from sentimentality by the grain of its sensibility and its implacable anger. There is none of the congratulatory tone of the usual up-from-the-slums story. The author is far too keenly attuned to the monstrous price of the victory. . . .

[Sissie] may well be the authoritative portrait of the Negro mother in America, that *Machtweib* who has given the beleaguered Negro family whatever strengh and stability it has. Williams depicts Sissie with stunning fidelity—her capacity to endure, her cunning, and her abiding strength, at once supportive and disabling. For what *Sissie* is really about is the effort of her children to emancipate themselves from this Big Mama who in nurturing them almost destroyed them. . . .

Inevitably, this novel invites comparison with James Baldwin's *Another Country. Sissie* is by far the better work. For all his platform polemics, Baldwin does not seem to possess the grasp of the Negro *milieu* that Williams displays. And where *Another Country* is shrill and noisy, *Sissie* is permeated by a quiet anger that builds and builds inexorably. John A. Williams may well be a front-runner in a new surge of Negro creativity.

> David A. Boroff, "Blue Note for Bigotry," in Saturday Review *(Entire issue copyright 1963 by Saturday Review Associates, Inc.; reprinted with permission), March 30, 1963, p. 49.*

BARBARA JOYE

In *The Man Who Cried I Am* John Williams uses conventional craftsmanship to induce readers to suspend their disbelief; then, at the end, he reveals a conspiracy theory of recent history which links a United States government blueprint for Negro genocide with [real events]. . . . Flashbacks intertwine this shocker with a great deal of more easily assimilable material. Williams' generally believable characterizations and constant references to painful aspects of modern American history will prepare most readers to accept the ending as at least symbolically true. It may be viewed as the logical extension of what we already know. Other readers less predisposed to Williams' point of view will regard the often stilted dialogue and the overambitious plot as defects that prevent the book from totally convincing. (p. 411)

Williams records his impressions of almost everything that has ever happened between World War II and 1964. His ability to work all this in depends mainly on his choice of a hero, Max Reddick, who is not only a successful Negro novelist, former officer of a segregated army unit during the invasion of Italy, resident of Harlem, the Midwest, and Paris, but also (like the author) a journalist with international experience. Williams does not present this subject matter for its own sake, however; Max can discover his individual identity only as he comes to understand the true history of Negroes in America. The book's ending builds upon the hero's earlier betrayals, which take place against a background of ineffectual white liberals and increasingly appealing Black Nationalists. (pp. 411-12)

In spite of his encyclopaedic tendencies, Williams manages to keep a good grip on two main characters and many minor ones. The hero maintains a nice balance between idealism and despair.... [He] is supplemented by the more cynical voice of the book's second major figure, Max Ames, who in many ways represents Richard Wright. Unfortunately, Williams gives Ames some sermons on the role of Negro artists which seriously impair the effect of the book's early scenes. Some of the minor characters seem even more artificial and stereotyped.

In spite of these faults, *The Man Who Cried I Am* grips the reader powerfully. Williams attempts to evoke many current moods and succeeds to an impressive degree. (p. 412)

> Barbara Joye, in PHYLON: The Atlanta University Review of Race and Culture *(copyright, 1968, by Atlanta University; reprinted by permission of* PHYLON*), Vol. XXIX, No. 4, Fourth Quarter (December, 1968), pp. 411-12.*

HUEL D. PERKINS

Mythic or not, *Mothersill and the Foxes* ... is yet another chapter in the long history of the Black man as lover, as phallic symbol.... Long live the myth! Long live copulation! Long live foxes (slang for fine chicks)! the author seems to be shouting at us in ear-shattering decibels....

Though the locale changes—hotel rooms, his apartment, the women's apartments, three continents—the setting is always the same, a bed. Professionally, Odell Mothersill is a social worker, but his talents lie in the direction of the "lay." ... Williams manages a skillful blending of the two consuming interests in the life of his main character with a deft manipulation of the plot culminating in a surprising denoument. He emerges as an arresting storyteller. (p. 89)

Odell Mothersill is a middle-class Black, escaping a prior generation of Pullman Car porters and maids, and ostensibly this raises the level of respectability of his amorous forays. He is college trained, professional, Ph.D., top management. He has fought his way to the top of the heap and is respected by Blacks and whites alike as a giant in his field. And with good cause, for he knows what he is doing and, despite his pleasurable sexual encounters, he comes through as a man of warmth and concern....

John A. Williams is never as effective when he is nice, gentle, soft as he is when he is brutal, intense, basic. His *The Man Who Cried I Am*, with the protagonist suffering from cancer of the rectum, is far more lucid than his *Sissie*, which deals with an indomitable matriarch and her two surviving children. Experience shapes the writer, and Williams has drained from his experiences every drop and distilled it into words for readers. In short, *Mothersill and the Foxes* is pure Williams—Williams doing the kind of writing he does with lusty aplomb.

The novel is in no way profound. It is gallantly entertaining. (p. 90)

That Williams is a gifted writer there can be no doubt.... That he is a prolific writer, there is hardly room for argument. There is no Black writer around who can match him for sheer quantitative output. There are few who can match him in ability.

What happens to myths? Some of them live on, and on in fictional characters like John Henry, like Joe the Grinder, like Odell Mothersill. (p. 91)

> Huel D. Perkins, in Black World *(reprinted by permission of* Black World *Magazine; copyright, 1975 by Johnson Publishing Company, Inc.), June, 1975.*

IVAN GOLD

John A. Williams is a black writer, the way the crocus is a spring flower. "The Junior Bachelor Society," his latest novel, is the story of nine middle-aged black men and what their lives have become in the more than three decades gone by since they played ball together, and grew up together, in Central City, in upstate New York. (p. 32)

[What] reunites them after all this time is a three-day testimonial to their former coach and character-builder Charles ("Chappie") Davis, now in his 70's. Sports, for all of them, was where it was. (pp. 32-3)

Along with the lives of the nine principals, rendered in loving detail, Williams also fleshes out their wives, and the marital relationships, as well as the intricate crosscurrents prevailing when they all get back together, for many of the women grew up in Central City as well....

Williams not only manages it all, combines and orchestrates it all, but gives the reader (as the best novelists have always done) the sense of still *more* interconnected life out there, still *more* books out there, already written and yet to come, than what is here so brilliantly encompassed....

Himself now in his early 50's, Williams is responsible, as author or editor, for some 18 books. Through sheer weight of craftsmanship, he should come crashing through one day soon to the kind of recognition he deserves. Until then ... between Frank Yerby and Eldridge Cleaver there are universes to explore, and it is good to know John A. Williams remains on the case. (p. 33)

> Ivan Gold, in The New York Times Book Review (© 1976 by The New York Times Company; reprinted by permission), July 11, 1976.

In writing ["The Junior Bachelor Society," a] novel about the thirtieth reunion of a group of upstate New York childhood friends and football teammates, Mr. Williams appears to have wanted to close the gap in literature about the black middle class single-handed. And he very nearly succeeds.... Many of [the] people are interesting, but Mr. Williams is in such haste to push on to the next character's life that it becomes increasingly difficult to remember which details belong with which character. The book is also rather awkwardly paced and has strange lacunae. One gets to know almost nothing, for example, about the old coach, Chappie, whom the men have come together to honor, and very little more about the man they all rally around in the novel's rather Hollywoodish ending—a pimp who recently murdered a policeman. For all its flaws, however, the book does tug one along, and it provides many evocative glimpses of people who wear American culture like a coat made of a material that they're allergic to but need for warmth. (p. 90)

The New Yorker (© 1976 by The New Yorker Magazine, Inc.), August 16, 1976.

*   *   *

WILLIAMS, Jonathan   1929-

Williams is an American poet and editor. Though often associated with the Black Mountain School and the beat poets, he feels his work is written "for those who long for the saving grace of language." A self-proclaimed ecologist of the word, he is admired for his sensitive chronicling of a rapidly changing language. His poetry mingles elements of word play with pieces of overheard dialogue, the rhythms and structures of music with the cadence of common speech. (See also *Contemporary Authors*, Vols. 9-12, rev. ed.)

RALPH J. MILLS, JR.

"I do / dig Everything Swinging," begins the *Credo* Jonathan Williams has placed at the outset of [*An Ear in Bartram's Tree: Selected Poems 1957-1967*, a] marvelous, handsome selection from his earlier, frequently scarce volumes, and indeed this witty, perceptive poet and printer manifests an individual enthusiasm for everything from Stan Musial, swinging his bat in Wrigley Field, in the first poem, to the jazz swinging of Miles Davis and Bud Powell; in between—or beyond—are Catullus, Tolkien, Edith Sitwell, Charles Ives, Mahler, and such living mentors as he names: Pound, Zukofsky, Creeley, Olson, Dahlberg, Buckminster Fuller. (p. 331)

Perhaps the most obviously striking quality in Williams's work, aside from the erudition and bookishness (which are of the delightful, never the pedantic variety), is the extraordinary acuteness of his ear. As a perpetual traveler, largely a hiker in America and England, he has attuned his sensitive powers of listening to every nuance of speech and sound, and given them back to his readers beautifully articulated. . . . His knowledge of herbs, flowers, trees everywhere 'pays off' poetically—in a musical catalogue: "a flame azalea, mayapple, maple, thornapple . . ." And there are other uses for this sharp ear, bawdy, comic, and satirical, in the pieces from *Lullabies Twisters Gibbers Drags* and *Jammin' the Greek Scene*. These elements of wit, criticism, and play easily recommend themselves in Williams's writing, and they are admirably polished and alive; but in passing I should like to call attention to his equally substantial gift for the descriptive and lyrical, . . . encountered throughout this book. Particularly moving are the poems of *In England's Green &* (which, remarkably, are about an *imagined* Britain, written before his visits there) and *Mahler*. . . . Observant, imaginative, learned, shrewd, these poems reveal the considerable range and strength of Williams's writing, to which the present selection offers a splendid introduction. (pp. 331-32)

Ralph J. Mills, Jr., in Poetry *(© 1971 by The Modern Poetry Association; reprinted by permission of the Editor of* Poetry*), February, 1971.*

HERBERT LEIBOWITZ

Williams's versatility and his labors at unearthing a kind of populist poetry in his backyard are on display in ["Blues & Roots/Rue & Bluets" and "A Garland for the Appalachians"]. They contribute to an unusual view of Appalachia.

"Blues & Roots/Rue & Bluets" is a sourcebook . . . of native forms, rhythms, sights and sounds. Williams listens to and transcribes the homespun sayings, the "vernal, verbal gift," of his mountain neighbors. One is startled by their unforced humor, self-delighting inventiveness, and lack of guile. Take "Aunt Creasy, On Work": "shucks / I make the livin / uncle / just makes the livin / worthwhile." Or "The Hermit Cackleberry Brown, On Human Vanity":

> caint call your name
> but your face is easy
>
> come sit
>
> now some folks figure
>   they're
> bettern
> cowflop they
> aint
>
> not a bit
>
> just good to hold the
>   world together
> like hooved up ground
> that's what

Dr. Johnson couldn't deliver a moral judgment with more confident finality. (pp. 56, 58)

Herbert Leibowitz, in The New York Times Book Review *(© 1971 by The New York Times Company; reprinted by permission), November 21, 1971.*

EDWARD F. GRIER

The Colonel is an adventurous experimenter. I confess to a prejudice against cut-ups, found poems, and concrete poetry, but the Colonel does them splendidly. See "A Mnemonic Wallpaper Pattern for Southern Two Seaters" or "A Chorale of Cherokee Night Music as Heard Through an Open Window Long Ago." Both lose by reduction to book-size format, and "A Chorale" also loses from the lack of its original color, but once they have been seen they are not forgotten.

He is also an ecologist before the letter. He is not, of course, concerned in his poetry about recycling or biodegradability, but with what is there. He knows his home terrain, the Appalachians, intimately, its contours, its flora and fauna, and its people. Although he has never really understood the Great Plains, which still await their poet, nor concerned himself with the Rockies, he has a most unusual sensibility to landscape, whether it is in Appalachia, Wales, or Yorkshire, where there are mountains or at least full-sized hills.

I have never understood the occasional complaint that his poetry is bookish. Of course it is, but bookishness is a hallmark of contemporary poetry. There are fashions in bookishness, however, and the Colonel's books are not modish. No Zen, no Tantrism, no Tarot, no astrology, no politics. Blake is recognizable, but not Samuel Palmer. . . . Among nature writers, although he knows Thoreau's Journals well he does not seem to be interested in *Natur-Philosophie*, but rather the simple and sensuous response of a field naturalist like Bartram or the mysticism of Palmer or John Clare. He uses quotations beautifully, for example the quotations from Thoreau, Clare and Palmer in "Symphony No. 3 in D Minor, II." In the third movement of the same poem he begins with a factual comment on the observations of the Georgia Ornithological Society. In a non-lyric mode he can give us "Common Words in Uncommon Orders"—perhaps a bit enriched, but not much. Their power comes not from the Li'l Abner setting or accent, nor even from the pungency of thought and feeling, but ultimately from the sound of sense. Words and rhythms are his art. Even nature must be transformed. There are two apposite quotations, one of which, from a place I can't put my finger on, in connection with hiking, is to the effect that words are ultimately more nutritious than raisins. The other is again from the Mahler "Symphony No. 3, II," (in response to John Clare's "The book I love is everywhere / And not in idle words"): "Muse in a meadow, compose in / a mind!" What the Colonel can do with books and nature can be seen in that very bookish sequence, *In England's Green &*, which comes to a climax with a hymn to the Appalachian rattlesnake. I fear and hate all snakes, but that poem is one of the great nature poems of the last twenty years.

He is also extraordinarily sensitive to music, verbal or tonal. . . . His sense of verbal music turns up, of course, often in the form of outrageous word-play. *Mahler Grooves* is a splendid example. . . . (pp. 100-01)

Several years ago I ventured to object to the Colonel about his found poems and concrete poems and asked for more Big Poems. I was firmly put down. Nevertheless *Mahler Grooves* is what I was asking for. (p. 101)

> Edward F. Grier, "A Health to Colonel Williams," in Vort, *Fall, 1973, pp. 99-102.*

ERIC MOTTRAM

Whatever the level of discourse a Williams poem will pun, pause and turn, combine invention with echo, autobiographical experience with literary information. Its sheer liveliness is exhilarating (and, rarely, self-indulgently buoyant, as if the poetic action shifted to formal abstraction only out of pleasure in virtuosity). Few other contemporary poets have his range of appreciation of rascality and corruption, his love of innocence and the ecstatic, and his intuitive and cultivated feeling for the visionary. He can finesse like Sahl or Bruce but he returns to a core of romantic vision for stability: Blake, Palmer, Vaughan in poetry and visual art, the voices of Thoreau and Clare, and the paintings of the Norwich watercolourists and "Mad Dick Dadd". (p. 106)

> Eric Mottram, "Jonathan Williams," in Vort, *Fall, 1973, pp. 102-11.*

JOHN JACOB

[*Untinears & antennae for Maurice Ravel*] displays Williams' range of abilities as a poet and commentator on contemporary life and culture. The poems acknowledge the talents of musicians from Ravel to Ellington and of performers in other fields, including Mean Joe Greene. The amalgam of stylistic turns is neither confusing nor difficult to accept. Some of the shorter pieces, whose seriousness is easily questioned if they stand alone, find completion among longer poems. Williams' free examination of the relationship—if any—between different types of artistic activity is pleasurable and intriguing. (p. 352)

> John Jacob, in Booklist (*reprinted by permission of the American Library Association; copyright 1977 by the American Library Association*), October 15, 1977.

WILLIAMS, William Carlos   1883-1963

One of the finest American poets of his generation, Williams was also a novelist, playwright, editor, essayist, and practicing physician. Rejecting the poetic style established by Eliot as overly academic, Williams sought a more natural poetic expression. He endeavored to replicate American speech forms and to capture the idiomatic cadence of both life and speech in America. Perhaps his greatest accomplishment is his collection *Paterson*, a poetic depiction of urban America. (See also *CLC*, Vols. 1, 2, 5, 9.)

MARIANNE MOORE

[In the main], Doctor Williams' topics are American—crowds at the movies

> with the closeness and
> universality of sand,

turkey nests, mushrooms among the fir trees, mist rising from the duck pond, the ball game:

> It is summer, it is the solstice
> the crowd is
>
> cheering, the crowd is laughing

or

> It is spring. Sunshine . . . dumped among factories
> . . . down a red dirt path to four goats. . . .
>
> (p. 214)

Essentially not a "repeater of things second-hand," Doctor Williams is in his manner of contemplating with new eyes, old things, shabby things, and other things, a poet. Metre he thinks of as an "essential of the work, one of its words." That which is to some imperceptible, is to him the "milligram of radium" that he values. He is rightly imaginative in not attempting to decide; or rather, in deciding not to attempt to say how wrong these readers are, who find his poems unbeautiful or "positively repellant." . . .

Facts presented to us by him in his prose account of The Destruction of Tenochtitlan, could not be said to be "new," but the experience ever, in encountering that which has been imaginatively assembled is exceedingly new. One recalls in reading these pages, the sense augmented, of "everything which the world affords," of "the drive upward, toward the sun and the stars"; and foremost as poetry, we have in a bewilderingly great, neatly ordered pageant of magnificence, Montezuma, "this American cacique," "so delicate," "so full of tinkling sounds and rhythms, so tireless of invention."

One sees nothing terrifying in what Doctor Williams calls a "modern traditionalism," but to say so is to quibble. Incuriousness, emptiness, a sleep of the faculties, are an end of beauty; and Doctor Williams is vivid. Perhaps he is modern. He addresses himself to the imagination. He is "keen" and "compact." "At the ship's prow" as he says the poet should be, he is glad to have his "imaginary" fellow-creatures with him. Unless we are very literal, this should be enough. (p. 215)

> Marianne Moore, "A Poet of the Quattrocento," in The Dial (*copyright, 1927, by The Dial Publishing Company, Inc.; reprinted by permission of J. S. Watson, Jr. and Scofield Thayer*), March, 1927, pp. 213-15.

EZRA POUND

The lack of celerity in [Williams'] process, the unfamiliarity with facile or with established solutions wd. account for the irritation his earlier prose, as I remember it, caused to sophisticated Britons. "How any man could go on talking about such things!" and so on. But the results of this sobriety of unhurried contemplation, when apparent in such a book as *In the American Grain,* equally account for the immediate appreciation of Williams by the small number of french critics whose culture is sufficiently wide to permit them to read any modern tongue save their own.

Here, at last, was an America treated with a seriousness and by a process comprehensible to an European.

One might say that Williams has but one fixed idea, as an author; i.e., he starts where an european wd. start if an european were about to write of America: sic: America is a subject of interest, one must inspect it, analyse it, and treat it as subject. There are plenty of people who think they "ought" to write "about" America. This is an wholly different kettle of fish. There are also numerous people who think that the given subject has an inherent interest simply because it is American and that this gives it ipso facto a dignity or value above all other possible subjects; Williams may even think he has, or may once have thought he had this angle of attack, but he hasn't.

After a number of years, and apropos of a given incident he has (first quarterly number of *transition*) given a perfectly clear verbal manifestation of his critical attitude. It is that of his most worthy european contemporaries, and of all good critics. It is also symptomatic of New York that his analysis of the so-called criticisms of Antheil's New York concert shd. appear in Paris, a year after the event, in an amateur periodical.

The main point of his article being that no single one of the critics had made the least attempt at analysis, or had in any way tried to tell the reader what the music consisted of, what were its modes or procedures. And that this was, of course, what the critics were, or would in any civilized country have been, there for. This article is perhaps Williams' most important piece of critical writing. . . . (pp. 398-99)

Very well, [Williams] does not "conclude"; his work has been "often formless," "incoherent," opaque, obscure, obfuscated, confused, truncated, etc.

I am not going to say: "form" is a non-literary component shoved onto literature by Aristotle or by some non-literatus who told Aristotle about it. Major form is not a non-literary component. But it can do us no harm to stop an hour or so and consider the number of very important chunks of world-literature in which form, major form, is remarkable mainly for absence. (p. 400)

The component of these great works and *the* indispensable component is texture; which Dr Williams indubitably has in the best, and in increasingly frequent, passages of his writing. . . .

Now in reading Williams, let us say this last book *A Voyage to Pagany* or almost anything else he has written, one may often feel: he is wrong. I don't mean wrong in idea, but: that is the wrong way to write it. He oughtn't to have said that. But there is a residue of effect. The work is always distinct from the writing that one finds merely hopeless and in strict sense irremediable. (p. 401)

If *Pagany* is not Williams' best book, if even on some counts, being his first long work, it is his worst, it indubitably contains pages and passages that are worth any one's while, and that provide mental cud for any ruminant tooth. . . .

A Voyage to Pagany has not very much to do with the "art of novel writing," whcih Dr Williams has fairly clearly abjured. Its plot-device is the primitive one of "a journey," frankly avowed. Entire pages cd. have found place in a simple autobiography of travel.

In the genealogy of writing it stems from *Ulysses.* . . .

As to subject or problem, the *Pagany* relates to the Jamesian problem of U.S.A. vs. Europe, the international relation etc. . . .

In the American Grain remains, I imagine Dr Williams' book having the greater interest for the European reader. (p. 403)

[The] best pages of Williams—at least for the present reviewer—are those where he has made the least effort to fit anything into either story, book, or (*In the American Grain*) into an essay. I wd. almost move from that isolated instance to the generalization that plot, major form, or outline shd. be left to authors who feel some inner need for the same; even let us say, a very strong, unusual, unescapable need for these things; and to books where the said form, plot, etc, springs naturally from the matter treated. (pp. 403-04)

As to the general value of Carlos Williams' poetry I have nothing to retract from the affirmation of its value that I made ten years ago, nor do I see any particular need of repeating that estimate; I shd. have to say the same things, and it wd. be with but a pretence or camouflage of novelty.

When an author preserves, by any means whatsoever, his integrality, I take it we ought to be thankful. We retain a liberty to speculate as to how he might have done better, what paths wd. conduce to, say progress in his next opus, etc. to ask whether for example Williams wd. have done better to read W. H. Hudson than to have been interested in Joyce. At least there is place for reflection as to whether the method of Hudson's *A Traveller in Little Things* wd. serve for an author so concerned with his own insides as is Williams; or whether Williams himself isn't at his best—retaining interest in the uncommunicable or the hidden roots of the consciousness of people he meets, but yet confining his statement to presentation of their objective manifests.

No one but a fanatic impressionist or a fanatic subjectivist or introversialist will try to answer such a question save in relation to a given specific work. (p. 404)

> *Ezra Pound, "Dr. Williams' Position," in* The Dial *(copyright, 1928, by The Dial Publishing Company, Inc.; reprinted by permission of J. S. Watson, Jr. and Scofield Thayer), November, 1928, pp. 395-404.*

JOHN CIARDI

["Paterson" is] epic in intent, if by "epic" one is willing to understand "the sustained handling of a society-enclosing subject matter." As such, "Paterson" is related to such poems as Pound's "Cantos," Eliot's "The Waste Land," and Crane's "The Bridge." If one may define traditional epic as "the celebration in narrative verse of great deeds performed by a single hero or set of heroes," this latter-day type of epic may be distinguished at once from the traditional by the fact that its development is not narrative but symphonic, and by the additional fact that time in this "modern" epic tends to become a continual present.

This modern epic is symphonic in its development because it does not tell a tale but, rather, orchestrates multiple themes of the human position. . . . [Its] subject is always in some sense what may be called "the racial memory"—the reflective conciousness in which past and future-anticipated blend at every moment with the present awareness of the poet-teller.

It may well be that in discarding so fundamental an attraction as narrative, these poems doom themselves to dullness. All of them can certainly be dull, and even impenetrable, at times. But partial failure does not preclude partial or even great success. . . .

[The] action-hero [of the heroic epic] is too grand and too simple a figure to express the scope of our times. And straight narrative is too single a method for the complexities of our world. . . .

"Paterson" is the process of an intellectual Ulysses, of the intellectual-hero rather than of the action-hero, of the reflective man seeking to evoke and to enter the meaning of the landscape of his life. (p. 37)

Paterson is more than the town built around the falls of the Passaic. At those falls a great stone outcropping causes a bend in the river and makes—if only in Williams's imagination—a natural shape that suggests the figure of a man lying on his side. That stone figure is also Paterson, the Sleeping Giant, the Genius of that Place. He is also the genius of time, for the falls changed that natural woodland into an industrial town. . . . And in so doing, Paterson converted Paterson into a dirty factory town. The very river (of time, of life, of beginnings) has been polluted and despoiled. Still another Paterson is William Carlos Williams himself—the man of that place, the man who walks that land with his memory and his mind open to what has been, to what is passing, and to what portends. . . . Like a theme in music, the Paterson-concept keeps developing and changing. (pp. 37-8)

The failure of communication between men is a constant theme of "Paterson." Another is the debasement of what was once good. "Paterson I" sets out to "trace the elemental character of the place." It ends, significantly, with a reference to the *choriambus* or "deformed" foot of the metric of Hipponax: "The choriambi are in poetry what the dwarf or cripple is in human nature. . . . Deformed verse was suited to deformed morality."

Of the various Patersons (Paterson-the-Sleeping-Giant, Paterson-New Jersey, and Paterson-Williams) I take "Paterson V" to be most intimately of Paterson-Williams. The first four books have about found the place. It is himself the poet must now find. Or rather, find again. (p. 38)

Here he introduces as another basic theme of "Paterson V" the Virgin and the Whore, the themes constantly changing and regrouping. They become Art and Morality. They become the Artist pursuing his Image. They become the aspiration of innocence and the pursuit of understanding. . . . And if I follow meaningfully the sequence of the thematic development, it is finally to that woman of the life-bearing virtues the poet comes, the virgin-and-whore, the whole woman with whom he has experienced that enduring human communication which is a lifetime of love. For unless that communication is achieved nothing can make meaning. . . . [The] "tragic foot" is not only the cleft foot of the satyr (a figure both of deformity and of sex) but a reference once more to the "deformed foot" of Hipponax.

And thus one may locate a third central characteristic of this sort of poetry: the statement is never complete at any one point. Like music it touches, develops, dissolves away from, returns to, puts into a new counterpoint, and finally brings to rest. But there is never any one statement on which one may put his finger and say "this is the meaning." The meaning is a constant process. And though there are times when I find myself baffled, Williams is still a master of this method, and still able to lure the reading on by the richness of the suggestion he does manage to release. (p. 39)

John Ciardi, "The Epic of a Place," in Saturday Review (*Entire issue copyright 1958 by Saturday Review Associates, Inc.; reprinted with permission*), October 11, 1958, pp. 37-9.

MIKE WEAVER

Having abandoned the borrowed nineteenth-century 'Composition' of his youth, Williams began with the 'Impression'. From 1913 to 1916 the portrait and the pastoral were his best media. If one were to turn for an analogy in painting for the poems in the collection *Al Que Quiere*, it would be to the Ashcan school of realism, in which the dignity of human life was rendered by impressionistic means. Williams' 'townspeople', although not products of the East Side slums, were similarly treated; for example, the old man who collects dog-lime from the gutter but whose walk is more majestic than that of the Episcopal minister. (p. 39)

The background of general revolt in art inspired . . . a sense of fellow-feeling in which Expressionist and Constructivist painters, the Blaue Reiter group and the Cubists, thought of themselves as one movement—the 'modern' movement. Williams, as it happened, was acquainted with a mixed group; mystical Cubists . . . , Dadaists . . . , and Expressionists. . . . In a period when he was producing improvisations, sedulously studying such a profoundly constructive, or 'synthetic', Cubist as Gris . . . , Williams' work was a composite plagiarism or generalised imitation of European innovations. While not being a painter himself he had joined the ranks of the painters who were poets 'on the side'; *Abseitigen* like Kurt Schwitters, Raoul Hausmann, Hans Arp, and Lajos Kassák.

The advantages in taking as an aesthetic point of reference the European modern movement in art rather than the English tradition in poetry were very great for an American bent on releasing the native ground to the imagination. Williams' well-known aversion for T. S. Eliot was not merely personal envy of the success of *The Waste Land*, but a rejection of the philosophy, including the philosophy of art, of a literary tradition in which he felt he could play no part. He was persuaded, furthermore, that no American faced with his local conditions and his own temperament could find a use for Eliot. A comparison between *The Waste Land* and Williams' lyric, 'By the road to the contagious hospital', published within months of each other, suggests how far apart in their sense of the ground Eliot and Williams really were. Eliot in London was abstracting spiritual values, or an absence of them, from the air; Williams, in the physical waste-land of his own part of New Jersey, detected an irrepressible force in the soil. (pp. 43-4)

Williams' analogies for invention in poetry in the late twenties were drawn from physics rather than from linguistics. While superficially sharing with the New Critics the principle of the autonomy of the poetic object, he did not share the preoccupations of Allen Tate and John Crowe Ransom with literary precedent. (p. 65)

The mechanical-plastic analogy of [Williams'] Objectivist phase resulted in a conception of the poem as an abstract design of inter-connected working parts, where the projective power of the verse was derived entirely from the organisation of those parts. But this analogy represented only one possibility to Williams. By 1944 . . . another analogy less consonant with the scientific age and more closely related to human capacity for projective power had presented itself again. It came from jazz. (pp. 70-1)

Rather like the jazz revivalists of the early forties . . . , Williams tried to find what American poetry had escaped the blight of *The Waste Land*. (p. 75)

Williams' notion of the variable foot bears a straightforward relation to the metrical organisation of jazz. The great rhythmic variety of the blues depends entirely upon the varying syllabic quantity compressed or expanded within the strictly temporal feet of its classic stanza. Its variety depends upon verbal improvisation, which in turn depends on performative flexibility within the vocal phrasing. . . . Where such easy rhythmic variability is present the poem may be said to swing, or in Williams' terms to possess the quality of measure. But swing or measure as a perceptual phenomenon depends entirely upon the relation between the phrasing and a steady beat, whether sounded or merely sensed. It defies notation, or scansion, because it is derived not from a time-signature but from performance.

What was merely 'hot' in manner was, as Williams knew, no substitute for swing, which requires not tension but relaxation in the performer. . . . Projective verse, [however] is the product not of a relaxed performer but a tense one. Like Abstract-Expressionist painting, its psychic content is more closely related to the aggression and anxiety of the Beat generation than to the primitive spontaneity of a late nineteenth-century Negro peasantry. (pp. 77-8)

In the company of Robert Duncan, Robert Creeley, and . . . Cid Corman, Williams was encouraged, while severely incapacitated by a series of cerebral strokes, to make explicit the tactic which he had pursued since 'Speech Rhythm' forty years before. The locomotor writing of this group is based essentially on the simple physiological functions of breathing and moving; man in general walks, the poet dances. Williams' own use of a description of the act of walking in *Paterson* catches the walker at the projective instant when the wave of energy breaks, and before the rhythmic recoil begins all over again. This was the simple conception of action which he wanted. But by the time his youthful followers had taken up his cause his own physical resources were checked.

Hugh Kenner, who edited Williams' final essay on 'Measure', has suggested that Williams' use of the three-part line

of the late poems stemmed from his inability to read after the brain damage of his strokes. . . . But, although this suggests a physical reason why Williams increasingly used the 'triadic foot' in the last years of his life, the evidence of the publication in *Paterson* in 1948 of 'The descent beckons' must be considered. The origin of the three-part line was probably in Pound's original printing of 'In a Station of the Metro'.

> The apparition   of these faces   in the crowd:
> Petals   on a wet, black   bough.

To re-arrange these groups of three in a step-down line was a natural, if unconscious, development of the idea of the musical phrase:

> The apparition
>   of these faces
>   in the crowd:
> Petals
>   on a wet, black
>   bough.

This use of a line with three feet or bars is, of course, neither accentual nor quantitative, but what Williams chose to call 'qualitative'. It answered the needs of the American idiom. . . . In 'The descent beckons' the changed tone falls on an apparently unimportant, but ambiguous 'even', which is in fact the pivot of the movement:

>   Memory is a kind
>   of accomplishment
>   a sort of renewal
>   even
>   an initiation, since the spaces it opens are new
> places
>   inhabited by hordes
>   heretofore unrealized

'Even' both refers back from renewal to memory and introduces an initiation to new places at the same instant. American intonation is what makes this possible, but the timing must also be exact if the point of balance is to be auditorily perceived. Straining towards the perfect 'image', Williams, like all the Imagists, endorsed the predominantly visual emphasis of the word. . . . Williams' 'measure' was inclusive; it embraced the theory of poetic structure, the perception of form, and man's objective and subjective role in the world; 'Measure is the only solidity we are permitted to know in our sensible world, to measure.'

The moral conviction that the language accurately used was objectively true to reality, and that the poet must be true to his materials, led Williams inevitably to political considerations. His belligerence towards British English was consistent with the surge of spirit that prompted him to write 'The Writers of the American Revolution', which asked for reconfirmation of 'a new world reconstituted on an abler pattern than had been known heretofore'. His attitude towards the English iambic line was expressed as an accusation of latent fascism when called it the 'medieval masterbeat'. The true government was 'the government of the words, since it is of all governments the archetype'. Language, prosody, and state rested on a single democratic idea. (pp. 85-8)

Zukofsky [after reading Williams' 'Democratic Party Poem'], chided him for his naivety in believing in a mythic democracy. Williams defended himself claiming that he had at one time considered an ironic ending for his poem, and had rejected it: 'I wanted to say "If this is all impossible, as you may see at once that it is, what then?"—.' (p. 91)

In Williams' understanding of the term, to be a revolutionary writer was to be an American writer. (p. 97)

In 1927 and 1928, in an extraordinarily violent piece of improvisation headed 'Rome', Williams poured out his radical thoughts on the value of the murderous and perverted element in American life. He suggested to himself that it was the degenerate element, the pure products of a country gone insane or syphilitic, which was the remnant of a heroic pioneer society. The wild, decayed, and doomed represented an aristocracy of the mind whose bodies obeyed impulses which if not socially beneficient showed a wholly admirable independence of conservative thought. No perversion, no matter how shocking, was worse than inversion. Inversion stemmed from an exaggerated respect for given forms; whether for woman, which resulted in homosexuality in men; or for the line in poetry, which resulted in inversion of the phrase. It was encouraged by the absurd prohibitions, by the forces opposed to change. An eruption like that of Mount Pelée was inevitable since 'the pleasure of motion to relief', whether in sex or poetry, was something which could not be averted, but only perverted in its outlet. It followed that the dignity of illegality was a value for Williams.... [His] attitude towards the place of the fantastic in life and in art was established earlier than the arrival of a literary movement like Surrealism in America. Mrs. Cumming, Marcia Nardi (the woman correspondent), and Alva Turner, are not represented in *Paterson* because they are neurotic, but because their veracity as thwarted human beings—their unimpaired though distorted vigour—finds expression in action. (pp. 132-33)

In deciding the value of Surrealism to himself Williams turned not to political or aesthetic politics but to the substantial facts of his landscape; now perceived as the straight representation of the photographer, now as the Surrealist symbol of the fantasist. To the extent that *Paterson* is a poem based on the three-personed figure of N. F. Paterson (Noah, Faitoute, and the Poet/City) related to a manifold experience of women (including the woman-mountain) it is an extended trope in which the elements, conscious and unconscious, representational and symbolic, collide and recoil continuously, compounded neither into a fixed level of awareness nor into a single mode of expression. (p. 144)

Williams' rationale in support of heterosexuality was based, of course, on his early ... sense of the dialectic between the sexes. Revolutionary potency depended upon the sexual relation, which the poet should carry through into his relation with the whole world. He opposed the domestication of the male element because, as he said, 'Man has been mother to woman so long that he has forgotten her function (and his own) in large measure. . . .' The significant conjunction of man and woman, city and mountain, before the cavern at Passaic Falls provides an alchemical setting for [*Paterson*]. . . . (pp. 151-52)

Mike Weaver, in his William Carlos Williams: The American Background *(© Cambridge University Press 1971), Cambridge University Press, 1971.*

HUGH KENNER

Williams was not, like Dickens or like Faulkner, an *impersonator*. But the habit of listening to voices extended to his own voice, so that he could write down the way he heard himself phrasing things:

THE POEM

It's all in
the sound. A song.
Seldom a song. It should

be a song—made of
particulars, wasps,
a gentian—something
immediate, open

      scissors, a lady's
      eyes—waking
      centrifugal, centripetal

You hear the staccato phrasing of a taut voice. You also hear things speech wouldn't know how to clarify: the auditory relationships . . . with the white space prolonging the tension after "should"; and "open" floating between "immediate," which it clarifies, and "scissors," which it specifies (the delay of the white space again withholding "scissors" till we've had time to take "open" with immediate"). "A lady's," similarly, seems to go with "scissors" till round the corner of the line we encounter "eyes," and the last two words—"centrifugal, centripetal"—seem to tell us how the lady's wakened attention turns outward then inward, until we remember the title and think to include "centrifugal, centripetal" among the specifications for "The Poem." It's not "oral," it's too quirky and tricky for orality, but one of its qualifications for anatomizing its theme is that it knows what a voice sounds like.

It's not only not "oral," this poem, it's not fully present, not even quite intelligible, in being read aloud, nor yet in being looked at on the page. It's an audio-visual counterpoint, and "the Imagination" Williams talked about is as good a name as any for the region where the complete poem can be said to exist.

This ability to move close to quite simple words, both hearing them spoken—not quite the same thing as hearing their sounds—and seeing them interact on a typewritten page, gave Williams the sense of constant discovery that saved him from feeling constantly responsible for weighty problems. He liked a poem he could spin round on one corner, and it freed him not to be encumbered with pronouncements. (pp. 85-7)

Process: growth and emergence: these were his themes: the effort of the new organism to define itself. They were comprised in what he meant by spring, by flowers and buds, by the "American idiom" (something *new*), by the effort at communal self-definition he discovered and re-enacted *In the American Grain*. (p. 88)

The struggle to get born, that was always Williams' plot; flowers fascinated him because they achieved it visibly, effortlessly. And then—the other half of his plot—the closure of the prison-house, as in Wordsworth and Blake, round the newborn potentiality. That prison-house—he is closer to Blake than to Wordsworth—is a communal failure, the lapsed Imagination. . . . [He] looked (like his classmate Pound) for a point of failure in history: no metaphysical wound . . . but a failure of vision, a lapsing of the Imagination. Hence his interest in the past of Paterson (which was never anything but a company town), and his singling out of the moment when "they saw birds with rusty breasts and called them robins."

> Thus, from the start, an America of which they could have had no inkling drove the first settlers upon their past. . . . For what they saw were not robins. They were thrushes only vaguely resembling the rosy, daintier English bird. . . .
>
> The example is slight but enough properly to incline the understanding. Strange and difficult, the new continent induced a torsion in the spirits of the first settlers, tearing them between the old and the new. And at once a split occurred in that impetus which should have carried them forward as one into the dangerous realities of the future. . . .

That is his myth of history, a birth rejected out of fear. His long career means that a poet needs no more ideas than that. . . . Chiefly a poet needs a passionate interest in the language, in the words people use, and the words they might use but do not. . . . What people say, what they do not say but might: that, related to a myth of history, was Williams' field of preoccupation. And the myth—remembering settlers who did not guess how much depended on what they should call the bird they chose to call "robin"— is written invisibly down the margins of his least pretentious poems, which affirm, again and again, no more than "how much depends": depends upon the act of finding a few dozen words, and upon their array once a poet has found them. (p. 90)

> *Hugh Kenner, in his* A Homemade World: The American Modernist Writers *(copyright © 1975 by Hugh Kenner; reprinted by permission of Alfred A. Knopf. Inc.), Knopf, 1975.*

WILLIAM BAKER

Note the urgency and immediacy of the opening paragraph [of *The Use of Force*]: "They were new patients to me, all I had was the name, Olson. Please come down as soon as you can, my daughter is very sick." The two sentences might have been punctuated as four, but William Carlos Williams, anxious to get to his point, uses commas to keep us flowing with him. Here and throughout he omits quotation marks for the direct address, another device to convey urgency. From the first rushing sentences Williams comes on like the Ancient Mariner, grabbing our lapels to tell of the doctor's compulsion. At first we think we might have a classic rescued-from-death tale, since early on we read, "As it happens we had been having a number of cases of diphtheria in the school to which this child went during the month." The last two thirds of the story, though, is not about death but about the strange problem of getting to see the girl's throat. (p. 7)

There are two conflicts: one within the girl and the other within the doctor. The girl feels, I believe, that if evil is not discovered it does not exist. As long as we keep evil to ourselves, it is containable and controllable. When others discover our secret, we are no longer in control and all is lost. Thus, the little girl hid her sore throat for the same reason that some of us avoid a dentist who will find cavities in our teeth. We know we are acting unreasonably, but we don't go to the same lengths, nor is our fear as strong as the girl's, for she fought with supreme effort, crying bitterly when she lost.

The second conflict, more interesting to Williams the writer rather than Williams the medical doctor, is about an adult's anger at himself when he is required to use force to accomplish his aim—even if the aim is noble in itself. Force is alien to a mature and cultivated mind, though learning about its psychological effect is part of growing up. When all else fails, reason tells us we must resort to force, but we are disgusted with ourselves when we give in. The anger and disgust rob the occasion of any sense of satisfaction: we win the physical battle but lose the war within our psyche.

A common-sense analysis would point out that it is natural to feel anger and disgust when using violent force, as in rape. The doctor says, "Perhaps I should have desisted and come back in an hour or more. No doubt it would have been better." The solution then is patience and a sensible and safe relief of frustration, but that's a story with a moral.

The power of the story is its sense of urgency and its brevity. The author doesn't have time to fill in the blanks. His intention is not character-development nor plot-exposition in the usual sense. His intention is to get in and get out quickly, focusing on what he has discovered about the use of force. (pp. 7-8)

> *William Baker, in* The Explicator *(copyright © 1978 by Helen Dwight Reid Educational Foundation), Fall, 1978.*

*   *   *

WILSON, Ethel Davis   1890-

A Canadian novelist, Wilson centers her novels in British Columbia. She uses a shifting point of view to examine the "equations of love" between people, particularly those of the working class. She also examines the role of memory as it plays upon the tension between changing time and static space.

HELEN W. SONTHOFF

The distinctive element in Ethel Wilson's fiction is its tone. It seems as if the centre of each book were not a main character, or a theme, or a plot, but an attitude toward the life of the tale. The subject matter with which Ethel Wilson deals varies considerably in event, character, setting. So does the form. But the tone, though not the same in each work, has certain recognizable characteristics.

It is, for one thing, quiet. It is persistently undramatic, allowing no sustained plot interest, no profound involvement with any character. Moments of wonder or sharp delight are followed by ordinary distractions; moments of concern or intense sympathy are commented on with wry humour. The tone is often funny, urbane, curious, inclusive. And what it primarily does is to render any subject matter in such a way that the reader's journey through it is very like his journey through any natural landscape, any ordinary day of his living. Meaning, in these novels as in living, comes upon him and fades. He encounters these characters as he might people in his own life, watching their surface, their manner and acts, knowing them, drifting away, doubting, hearing again, sometimes losing sight of them entirely. Should he for a moment lose himself in a scene or a gesture or mood, he will be brought back to his role as observer; he will have restored to him a perspective that persuades him to regard this fiction with a kind of equanimity.

Gertrude Stein says, "A long complicated sentence should force itself upon you, make you know yourself knowing it. . . ." These short complicated books make a similar requirement. . . . The sense of living given is that the way is the truth; it is the journey that matters, not the arrival points. (pp. 33-4)

To create this tone, this meaning, Ethel Wilson does extraordinary things with point of view and with narrative line. Not so much in her first novel, *Hetty Dorval*. Yet even here there is a pushing at the edges of the controlling voice. There is, in fact, nothing in the book, no reflection, no view that the narrator, Frankie Burnaby, might not have thought or said. But she does seem to shift her point of view in time. Sometimes she speaks as if she were, in imagination, very close to the experience she is recalling; sometimes it is as if she were taking a much more distant view of a scene wider and richer than the one actually being presented to us. . . . [The] knowledge that there are untold, unknown things and that other things are only guessed at informs *Hetty Dorval*. (p. 34)

There are also, in *Hetty Dorval*, scenes or events whose value seems not to depend on their relevance to this particular tale. . . . [Such] passages seem to have an absolute value, a vivid life outside the main line of the story. Each one could have seemed, to the narrator, relevant; she could have justified them. . . . But there is in them some force barely contained by the narrative.

That force is relaxed in *The Innocent Traveller*, an episodic book about a life which ". . . inscribes no sweeping curves upon the moving curtain of time . . . no significant design. Just small bright dots of colour, sparkling dabs of life." Here scenes occur or recur as if by chance, as if this event or that landscape had simply snagged the attention or the memory. (pp. 34-5)

The reader's attention is drawn away from then into now, from there to here, from small chaos to large, increasingly often as the book goes on.

There is a similar shifting round of point of view from one generation to another, from one member of this large family to another. The reader stays with no one view long enough to become ultimately acquainted with it. The effect is kaleidoscopic. There are relationships and patterns, but they seem temporary, transitory, as if made by chance. (p. 35)

Two chapters of *The Innocent Traveller* were published separately. Others could be, having a kind of enclosed life. But the tone of wonder, of mingled admiration and despair, grows only gradually through the whole book, through one episode simply "coming in beside" another in a grouping as accidental, a sequence as casual as any natural order. (p. 36)

The tone Ethel Wilson has created in *The Innocent Traveller* seems natural for a family tale. The combination of apparently exact and detailed accounts with frankly fanciful reconstructions implies a point of view like that of some younger member or friend of the family. The quiet, companionable voice which shares amusement, raises questions, and occasionally makes a fragmentary judgment precludes any final judgment. No pattern, no ultimate meaning in the life of Topaz Edgeworth could emerge from an author view which encompasses the many points of view of the family.

Tuesday and Wednesday, a novella published three years after *The Innocent Traveller*, is entirely concerned with the number of meanings that do not add up to one, the number of impulses and motives which are not links in a chain of purpose. Will and intention play some part in the lives of these characters, but not so much as accident and coincidence. The arrangement of episodes is loose, so that one becomes aware only gradually of a pairing which holds all things in balance: the intention acted upon and the intention deflected; the coincidence that alters a mood and the coincidence that doesn't; the accident that ends a life and the accident that is scarcely noticed.

The tone of this book, both more detached and more comic than that of *The Innocent Traveller*, is also more controlling. Each event and each character is made to seem as ordinary as can be. . . . Even when the apparently irrelevant assumes relevance, affecting mood and action, the tone of the passage makes the shift seem perfectly ordinary. (pp. 36-7)

Mood and motive shift about, on these ordinary days. . . . Like the balance of episodes, the balance of characters (not at first noticeable) makes it seem the oddest chance that two very different people should find themselves in similar or echoing circumstances. The effect one character has on another seems also accidental. One encounter may be a direct hit; another, a glancing blow; a third, abortive, so that neither character is really aware of the other at all. A missed connection is made to seem as fortuitous as a meeting which alters the course of a life. (p. 38)

In its quiet way, [*Tuesday and Wednesday*] is technically brilliant. The author voice, established in the opening paragraph, is sometimes omniscient, to show both the irrational connections and the many missed connections. It is sometimes an observing and commenting "I" who addresses the reader as "you." This device, moving toward conversation, makes observations seem natural, and thereby opens the small particular experiences of a few people into the daily life of anyone. (pp. 38-9)

The conversational author voice also allows the point of view to flow smoothly into one or another of the characters, whose experiences and responses are given largely through characteristic speech patterns. . . .

This novella is one of two published together, in a volume called *The Equations of Love*. The love Myrt and Mort have for each other is an extension of a self-love that is strong and inaccurate. What they and other characters in the story really love are the many images of themselves. In the second novella, *Lilly's Story*, Lilly's motivating love is also—in a way—self-love, but it turns very quickly from self-protection to the protection of her child. Her refrain, "A girl's gotta right to live," becomes "My kid's gotta right to have a chance."

The sharpest contrast between *Lilly's Story* and *Tuesday and Wednesday*, is that Lilly's is a story of single-minded purpose and ruthless perseverance. (p. 39)

Lilly's Story, like many of Ethel Wilson's tales, is about a triumph of the human spirit. (p. 40)

In *Swamp Angel* there is also a working out of a plan, but in a manner that is much more flexible. The narrative of this novel spreads out, flowing one way for a while, then bending round to follow another path, another character. The woman who carries out her plan, Maggie Lloyd, is as determined as Lilly, but where Lilly is slight, narrow, rigid with purpose, Maggie is ample, easy in her movements, intuitive. She too is reserved, not from fear but because she "did not require to talk, to divulge, to compare, to elicit." . . . Maggie, brought up from childhood by a man, with men, had never learned the peculiarly but not wholly feminine joys of communication. . . . (pp. 40-1)

The accidental or arbitrary encounter or event or vision in *Swamp Angel* is different from the accidental encounters of *Tuesday and Wednesday.* Maggie and Mrs. Severance have an awareness, a deliberateness that indicates some relationship between caprice and will, between the passive and the active. None of them is given as controlling his fate; each of them is in some way aware of it and consents to it. (p. 41)

The fantastic likelihood of coincidence does not function as strongly in *Swamp Angel* as in *Tuesday and Wednesday.* *Swamp Angel* is a more fluid work altogether, covering more ground. The movement of point of view and narrative line establishes an attitude or consciousness hard to define but pervasive enough so that no combination of motives and acts turns into an imposed pattern, a plot. Casual or symbolic connections do appear but are made to shift and finally dissolve.

In *Love and Salt Water,* the reader's attitude toward the life of the story is less clearly controlled. There is, on the one hand, some real power of plot in this novel. Whereas in *Swamp Angel,* Maggie's key decision has been made before the book opens so that her movements were those of relaxation and a natural return to her strongest self, in *Love and Salt Water* young Ellen Cuppy moves toward important decision. Her growth, over a period of fifteen years, gives a sense of motion toward some act, some knowledge or understanding. She is given a natural urgency and restless drive. On the other hand, there are the counter motions of such a passage as this:

> She did not at that moment think that there was somewhere some parallel of light and darkness, of illumination and blotting-out, and perhaps our whole existence, one with another, is a trick of light. That may be somewhere near the truth, which is often hard to determine because of the presence of the lights and shadows of look, word, thought which touch, glide, pass or remain.

In *Love and Salt Water,* there are not only comments in the distinctive author's voice but also divisions in the narrative, and several points of view. However, Ellen Cuppy's hesitations and actions, blunders and discoveries pull so strongly toward plot and character development that the counter weights cannot balance them. As soon as the balance tips, as soon as one hears the questions "Why does she do this?" "What does that mean?" one realizes how strongly Ethel Wilson has held, in many books, a difficult view. To see life as accidental, "a trick of light", "a series of combination of events", and to present it so with humour implies some balancing source of strength, some framework. In *Love and Salt Water,* the framework doesn't seem to hold. But in other works, especially in *Tuesday and Wednesday,* the balance is so fine that one gets the kind of impression one gets from a mobile: it moves of itself, by accident, by design. (pp. 41-2)

Helen W. Sonthoff, "The Novels of Ethel Wilson," in Canadian Literature, *Autumn, 1965, pp. 33-42.*

W. H. NEW

[*The Innocent Traveller*] explores innocence, independence, and order, and in presenting the character of Topaz it interprets both twentieth-century life and the necessary relationship that must exist between people in any society whose stability is, like this one, precariously founded in time.

Mrs. Wilson has in various places and in various ways been likened to Willa Cather, Jane Austen, Proust, Defoe, Blake, Butler, Trollope, and Bennett: an awesome group. . . . Mrs. Wilson's success in creating live people leads to one of the comparisons; her concern with time, her social consciousness, her irony, and her control of words lead to others. But the observation of likenesses only serves to clarify the nature of individual parts of a novel, and all those listed here exist in *The Innocent Traveller* not separately, like borrowings, but unified into a work of art. (pp. 22-3)

Hetty Dorval, the first of Ethel Wilson's works, studies the nebulous influence which the experienced title character has on a young girl. It is not just an opposition between youth and age, or between innocence and sophistication. What it explores, with reference to the whole question of morality and amorality, is the extent to which Hetty, though using the worlds through which she moves, can be an individual by exempting herself from ordinarily accepted codes of behaviour. The two novellas which make up *The Equations of Love* are also concerned with codes, but they observe "morality" from other angles, attempting to explore the nature of love by depicting generosity, narcissism, casual affairs, sacrifice, and many other subtleties of human response, in working-class settings. *Swamp Angel* and *Love and Salt Water* focus again on individual women: Maggie Lloyd, in the first book, finds she must escape suburban routine if she is to *be* the individual she knows she has the potential to be; and Ellen Cuppy, in the second, values her independence so much she flees marriage and, for a brief while, fancies she has escaped from time. But time, as *Love and Salt Water* also tells us, "is an agent", and the years of our life that seem irrelevant "stir, and take their unexpected vengeance in a variety of ingenious ways". . . . Time stirs even in *The Innocent Traveller,* where Topaz Edgeworth (with her own private morality and her protected world) moves gaily through life, but its "vengeance"here is felt in the world at large and only ironically, when at all, in relation to Topaz herself. (p. 23)

[Topaz's character] does not substantially change during her life; and Mrs. Wilson's novel gains its subtlety partly in language, partly in managing to create something significant out of an essentially plotless and insignificant life.

The Innocent Traveller is not a novel of plot and makes no pretence of being one. The very first chapters, depicting all the main characters of the book, immediately anticipate everyone's future, completely undercutting any "suspense." . . . What has happened [during the novel] except that a life was and then is not? Very little; just life itself. But can any life be insignificant? Or does insignificance only apply to the relationship between that life and the world around it? . . . [What] we see are "dots of life", the moments of vitality that seem to have created and to illustrate Topaz's personality. (p. 25)

Topaz's almost Blakean innocence—a harmony with the environment so complete that no sadness disturbs it, no disruption mars it, no experience is incapable of being absorbed into it all—depends, naturally, on a particular kind of environment surrounding her. . . . [She needs] a curious combination of confinement and freedom—or of freedom to do as she is inclined and freedom from all concern about the world around her. She depends heavily, that is, on the world being ordered and maintained for her, but she cannot survive in a society that observes rules above idiosyncrasies. Thus her departure from her brother John's Europe is a move to harmony. She finds *her* world in turn-of-the-century Vancouver, a frontier town that only a few years previously had been called Gastown and that was quickly disguising itself in propriety. Idiosyncrasy (at that time, at any rate—perhaps as in any Far West town) was a way of life, yet out of individuality was fashioned order.

In the irony created when we see this order in relationship with time lies yet another dimension to the novel. Topaz has an innate respect for the "spirit of History". . . . The trouble with history is that it does not exist just in the past; it is continually being made, and of this Topaz is ("innocently") unaware. The world her progenitors founded for her was the Victorian one. . . . But even the new world is influenced by time. Topaz's "open country" has "no time limit", but in 1914 the world around her knows that the Victorian sense of order and decorum is over. Time is continually operative within life, but in living their individual lives, people are often unconscious of it. They see only the spectacular event—Rose's becoming a woman goes unnoticed; her having become one therefore seems "sudden". The breakout of World War One and the concomitant end of the Victorian era seem comparably sudden, yet retrospectively they seem equally gradual in their development.

This novel, then, has at its base a kind of symbolic structure; by examining events in individual lives, it interprets a series of historical events that led to the twentieth century being what it is. . . . [Time's] effect is to make any social order or "absolute" code of morality that people establish seem a little ironic, for the only constant in such a life is change. Perhaps in time, then, is the only order we can know. . . . It is not a gloomy view, but it is a serious one, and its undercurrents stir in the depths of the novel, occasionally rising to remind readers that life, with all its frivolity, all its possible harmonies, is a mortal thing, and therefore, for most individuals, a Blakean Experience as well.

The two recurrent metaphors which Ethel Wilson uses to explore her subject both involve oppositions: peace and war, and surface and depth. Topaz's harmony is both peaceful and superficial; the world around her, by contrast, knows war and knows suffering. And so Topaz herself becomes a symbol of a certain kind of life. (pp. 26-8)

Her individuality is protected only because she lives in an environment that accepts it; in other words, for all the fact that it is individuals who create an ordered society, it is society that lets the individual survive, and any concept of individual "freedom" is ironic in its expectations if it does not take this into account.

Though Topaz lives for herself, she cannot even try to live on her own as Ethel Wilson's other characters Hetty Dorval and Maggie Lloyd do. . . . Neither of them, however, can isolate herself from the human race; their actions all touch others, and the books reiterate what the epigraph to *Hetty Dorval* borrows from Donne: no man is an island. In *The Innocent Traveller*, Topaz cannot isolate herself either, because she does not have either the wish to do so or the ability to survive should she have tried. In another sense, however, she is more isolated than Hetty Dorval or Maggie Lloyd could ever hope to be, for the fact that she lives a perfectly moral life that is not necessarily out of date but quite certainly out of touch with the present makes her influence upon her world negligible. . . . Ethel Wilson's book makes it quite clear that though Topaz delights, her particular life is, in time, of no importance. Why then write about her? Because her gaiety has value even if it is not useful, because her possibilities are those of Everyman, and because a comprehension of her life tells us something about life in general and about our own. (pp. 28-9)

The world is delightful, innocent, harmonious to Topaz precisely because she does not respond in depth to experience. She travels on, anticipating new scenery, even to the end—but reacting to it only in her own terms. . . . [Though] she by and large escapes sorrow, she also evades the extremes of joy, which others, responding sensitively and emotionally to the world, cannot do. (pp. 29-30)

Under [the novel's] surface lie deeps of emotional impact and intellectual perception which a careful reading will gradually reveal. It is a witty and sensitive book, too—stylistically apt, gently ironic, and quietly humane. (p. 30)

> W. H. New, "The Irony of Order: Ethel Wilson's 'The Innocent Traveller'," in Critique: Studies in Modern Fiction (copyright © by Critique 1969), Vol. X, No. 3, 1968, pp. 22-30.

C. M. McLAY

Ethel Wilson's short story "Mrs. Golightly and the First Convention" concerns a theme popular in these days of women's liberation, the initiation of an ordinary housewife with three children into her society, her movement, within certain defined limits, from innocence to experience, and her achievement of an individual identity. Mrs. Golightly's aim, expressed at a moment of recognition when it seems unattainable, is to be "a woman of the world." . . . The deliberate simplicity of the theme, the concentration of wish, recognition, and fulfilment within one or two days, the play of contrast and repetition and the surface naivety of the style all contribute to the total effect of a tale which, however slight it may at first appear, has a definite and continuing appeal and makes a serious statement about life.

The essential simplicity of theme and style conceals the sly sophistication of Mrs. Wilson's approach.

> In those days when a man said rather importantly, I am going to a convention, someone was quite liable to ask What is a Convention? Everyone seemed to think that they must be quite a good thing, which of course they are. . . .

The tone of the "historical note" and the choice of language in phrases such as "a very good thing" satirize both our desire for information and the vague flatness of our everyday diction. Moreover Mrs. Wilson cleverly turns the argument on us in "which of course they are"; again delightfully vague, the phrase appeals to our own sophistication. Indeed much of our delight in the story follows from our own implication of superiority, just as our enjoyment of Leacock's "My Financial Career" hinges on our dual sympathy with the protagonist as a representative of our own past experience, and our slight contempt for his innocence in the present. Mrs. Wilson shares with Leacock certain qualities of comic style: the apparent naivety, the use of exaggeration and repetition as major features of the structure, the technique of inverting the whole meaning of the sentence in the last two or three words, the surprise climax to the sentences, even perhaps the underlying social comment. But whereas "My Financial Career" and "The Excursion of the Mariposa Belle" may be enjoyed by children of ten or eleven, "Mrs. Golightly and the First Convention," depends for its success upon our knowledge of human relationships and of the complexity of man's experience in a social world. Although the viewpoint is third-person, the initiation of Mrs. Golightly is paralleled in the style by a movement from naivety to sophistication. (p. 52)

Though light in tone, even witty, the story is concerned with a serious theme, as Desmond Pacey notes, with individual isolation and the sense of being "out of place" among the members of one's society. Pacey's later comment on the tales as a whole, that the protagonists "mitigate their sense of loneliness . . . by firmly attaching themselves to a familiar and beloved environment" is also true to some extent of Mrs. Golightly who makes the world of the convention her place as it is the place of her husband. While Mrs. Wilson preserves her own sense of balance, suggesting the ultimate superficiality of such a society and of the convention mentality, the story is presented sympathetically and implies some level of achievement, the attainment of a real identity, however shallow.

The structure of the story is simple and controlled but not slavish or inflexible. The introduction provides a succinct but telling appraisal of the Golightly couple, and in particular of the character of Tommy as the measure of his wife's ideals. The simple plot of the journey provides a test for Mrs. Golightly's sense of identity; placed in the world of the convention, she is at first anonymous, but her development is swift. The third phase marks the turning-point; while Mrs. Golightly is partially defeated, she has begun to be aware of her potentialities, and in her delight in the scenery of the coast and the strong-bodied seals, she forgets her inhibitions and finds a contact with other members of this society. In the final stage, despite her social error in forgetting Mrs. Gampish, she achieves a certain presence and a tact in handling difficult situations, and ultimately she learns to accept herself as she is, and to enjoy that self. While this basic structure is linear, certain keys or symbols repeating at intervals through the story provide a cyclic rhythm which ties it together thematically, in particular the hat with the quill and the Old-Fashioneds which suggest social sophistication, and the mimosa tree with its counterpart, the seals, which represent the world of nature to which Mrs. Wilson's central characters always turn for rest and re-creation. The story then artfully resolves the disparate concerns of the writer: to capture the slippery essence, to make it "happen" while still disciplining and controlling the material, to appear artless while at the same time capturing with precision and economy the line and contour of life and character. (p. 53)

The story concludes with a moment of recognition. Mrs. Golightly has come to accept her own identity, not as a wife

or a mother or a friend: "Mr. Flanagan isn't a bit afraid to be him and Mrs. Gampish isn't a bit afraid to be her and now I'm not a bit afraid to be me . . . at least, not much." . . . She can dispense with the symbol, and she cuts off the damaged quill; she no longer needs its assurance, and she can accept its weaknesses, like her own, for what they are. And she recalls the whole day, the mysterious world of the convention, the beauty of the trees and the aid, the waves and the seals, Mrs. Finkel's loveliness and Mrs. Gampish's assurances, and looks ahead with "anticipation . . . a delicious fear . . . an unfamiliar pleasure." . . .

Yet Mrs. Wilson also implies the limitations of her dream, for her new world is a world of surface sophistication only, of busy-ness, of empty promises and social lies, of faceless names and anonymous numbers.

But the tale is not only a light comedy of manners. In the short stories as a whole, Pacey notes, Mrs. Wilson sees nature as both beautiful and menacing, and human beings as "lonely creatures who forever seek, and occasionally find, the comfort and sustaining power of mutual love." "Mrs. Golightly" provides a lighter statement, a counterpoint to this rather tragic vision of "loneliness and love, human vulnerability and tenacity." Here we find a nature beautiful without menace, a desire for release from alienation without the pain. The story provides a comic statement of integration, of the central theme of *The Swamp Angel* and *Hetty Dorval:* "No Man is an Island". It represents one pole of Wilson's view of the contemporary world, one possible reaction to this world in comic detachment where the defeats are temporary, almost unreal, and the protagonist triumphs over all obstacles to achieve her aim, limited though it may be. This is the world of Mrs. Golightly's initiation. (p. 55)

> *C. M. McLay, "The Initiation of Mrs. Golightly,"*
> *in* Journal of Canadian Fiction *(reprinted by permission from* Journal of Canadian Fiction, *2050 Mackay St., Montreal, Quebec H3G 2J1, Canada), Vol. 1, No. 3, 1972, pp. 53-5.*

P. M. HINCHCLIFFE

There is nothing provincial about Ethel Wilson's writing. Her novels and stories display a sensibility that is sophisticated and urbane. They are patently the work of an artist who has no patience with any kind of cultural or moral narrowness. Even if her characters are not always aware of their place in a larger world, Mrs. Wilson herself is, and she makes sure that her readers are aware of it too. But she has always been a determinedly regional writer. . . . A few of her stories are set outside British Columbia, but her home ground is Vancouver and the river valleys and mountain lakes that make up what dwellers on the British Columbia coast call "the Interior", and which they regard as their hinterland. Her novels and stories are filled with loving descriptions of Vancouver's streets and mountains and with favourite scenes from the Interior, like the marriage of the Fraser and Thompson Rivers and the flight of migrating geese, repeated again and again.

These scenes never take over the stories in which they appear because Ethel Wilson's centre of interest is not topography. It is the moral and effective lives of her characters, most of them women, who are all solitary persons to some degree, and who never merge with or are overcome by the landscapes in which they are placed. . . .

Just as her stories are set in the enclosed spatial region of British Columbia but with a constant awareness of the rest of the world outside it, so the time of her stories is a kind of enclosed area—the lives of two generations of British Columbians—in which she can move imaginatively backwards and forwards. . . . There is a difference between the two kinds of regionalism, of course. Space remains the same but time does not, and as time passes the perception of space, though not the space itself, changes.

One source of the astringent irony which is one of the delights of Ethel Wilson's fiction is her constant awareness of the tension between static space and changing time in her chosen regions. Her attitude to this tension can be described as elegiac, though never plaintive or nostalgic. This elegiac attitude gives a distinctive quality to her prose style, and because it is intimately connected with the exercise of memory, which is one of the major concerns of all her writing, it is an important structural element in her fiction as well. (p. 62)

Her position seems to be that here are people who have built a city and a province and given it a distinctive style of life. Most of these people are not aware that their way of life has been distinctive, and they do not care much about preserving their achievement. But it is an achievement and it ought to be preserved in spite of its creators' indifference. In her writing Ethel Wilson sees this act of preservation as one of her primary responsibilities, and I think that it is this sense of obligation that saves her style from coyness or self-indulgence in its repeated references to the scenic beauties of Vancouver and the British Columbia Interior. (pp. 62-3)

The culture that Ethel Wilson writes about is that of the colonists who peopled British Columbia during the sixty years between the completion of the Canadian Pacific Railway and the end of the Second World War. . . .

This culture has largely vanished during the past twenty-five years. Its old sense of a special British identity has been overtaken by the rush of post-war immigration, especially into Vancouver. . . .

Although Ethel Wilson began to write before these changes became apparent, she has always seen the culture of British Columbia as one in which change was inevitable. . . . Also, the reader should not assume that Mrs. Wilson's elegiac affection for British Columbia and its people implies uncritical admiration of the colonist culture that she depicts. Many of her characters who accept the values of this culture without question are narrowed or even destroyed by this acceptance. . . . (p. 63)

Furthermore, Ethel Wilson is aware that in some respects the culture of which she writes is shallow, almost a mushroom growth—or to use her own metaphor, the subsoil on which she stands has no continuity with the strata beneath it. . . . [The] lack of any sense of a collective past is characteristic of many of the people that Ethel Wilson writes about, and she regards it, rather wryly, as something that she must accept in her own characters. . . .

If the culture of British Columbia forgets its own past too easily, it is completely oblivious of the Indians' culture that the white colonists supplanted, and Ethel Wilson's fiction reflects this situation. The other culture with which her characters can interact is not Indian but Chinese, for the

Chinese also came to British Columbia with the railroad, and they too form a kind of cultural overlay on the native terrain. . . .

In a cultural situation like this, remembering the past becomes a deliberate action, not just an instinct or a reflex. Many authors are concerned with the operations of memory, but what distinguishes Ethel Wilson's writing is her insistence that we choose the memories that we carry with us and that we transmit to other people. The memories that we choose to remember (and those we choose to forget, as well) give our lives their characteristic shape, and collectively they give our culture its characteristic shape. For Ethel Wilson, choosing your memories properly is a moral responsibility. For herself as an author, recounting the past of British Columbia is part of her own duty to remember responsibly. (p. 64)

The book that maintains this elegiac quality most consistently is *The Innocent Traveller,* which as the Author's Note makes clear, is only partly fictional. Topaz Edgeworth is modelled in part upon Ethel Wilson's own great-aunt, and the Hastings family is in part her own family of English relatives settled in Vancouver. In a more sustained way than Ethel Wilson's other books *The Innocent Traveller* is concerned with death, or more precisely, with the impact that the deaths of the members of each generation and the passing of their way of life has on their survivors and descendants. In the course of her long life Topaz experiences intensely but without reflection deaths in her family and changes in the culture in which she lives. The reflection is left to us the readers, and in passage after passage the author's voice guides us in the performance of our task. We are also invited to reflect on the meaning of Topaz's life and death for our own lives as twentieth-century Canadians. (pp. 64-5)

The elegiac passages in Ethel Wilson's writing are almost always part of the narrator's comments, or if they are spoken by a character it is a minor one. . . . However, Mrs. Wilson's general principle, that the exercise of memory is a matter of responsible choice, applies to her major characters as well. The central situation in each of her novels, except *The Innocent Traveller,* and in several of her short stories can be fruitfully approached from this point of view. . . .

However, in order to be true, memories do not have to be factual, and this is one of the themes of *The Equations of Love.* As the epigraph from *Bleak House* indicates, the two novellas are concerned with the definition of truth "in a spirit of love", and of course both stories turn upon lies: Victoria May Tritt's account of how Mort Johnson died a hero's death trying to save a friend from drowning, and Lilly Waller's invention of the late Mr. Walter Hughes to explain the parentage of her daughter. Both lies are true "in a spirit of love" because they are enemies of the spirits of self-pity and moral laziness that Ethel Wilson perceives as deadly sins. (p. 65)

In *Swamp Angel* the responsible choice is to forget some memories—not all, of course: "I sit on top of my little mound of years," says Nell Severance, "and it is natural and reasonable that I should look back, and I look back and round and I see the miraculous interweaving of creation." But when Mrs. Severance realizes that her revolver and all its associations have become a moral danger to herself and her daughter, she sends it to Maggie Lloyd at her lake in the Interior. There, in a scene reminiscent of the ending of Tennyson's "Morte D'Arthur", Maggie throws the Swamp Angel into the lake, where it becomes "a memory, and then not even a memory." Maggie herself begins her part in the novel by leaving her impossible husband Edward Vardoe and making herself forget that she was ever married to him. She remembers herself only as the widow of her first husband Tom Lloyd. In the context of the novel this is not escapism or fantasy but a necessary and responsible choice. In forgetting Edward Vardoe Maggie is leaving behind what Ethel Wilson elsewhere calls the "years of elision", those years that provide only a "semblance of reality", and she is resuming her real life.

Ethel Wilson's last novel, *Love and Salt Water,* contains her most elaborate treatment of the uses of memory. In this novel all the situations that require moral judgment are posed in terms of remembering and forgetting. . . .

[The] action of *Love and Salt Water* sounds very complicated, and perhaps it is too complicated to be entirely effective. Nevertheless, this moral pattern is certainly present, and it is a logical extension of Ethel Wilson's concern with the nature of memory in her earlier novels. This last novel is also her most ambitious attempt to combine the world of private memory with the collective sense of British Columbia's past and to link them to a vision of the future which is both personal and social. Much more than the other novels, *Love and Salt Water* abounds in historical reminiscences and topographical vistas, and the sweeping journeys of all the major characters from west to east and back again are surely meant to provide a rhythm that will unify the reader's perception. If there is a fault here it comes from giving us too much, but even if *Love and Salt Water* does not achieve perfect symmetry of form it provides its own pleasures. Not the least of these is the communication of generous wisdom about ourselves and our past which this novel shares with the others and which makes all of Ethel Wilson's writing a source of continual delight. (p. 66)

> *P. M. Hinchcliffe, "'To Keep the Memory of So Worthy a Friend': Ethel Wilson as an Elegist'," in* Journal of Canadian Fiction *(reprinted by permission from* Journal of Canadian Fiction, *2050 Mackay St., Montreal, Quebec H3G 2J1, Canada), Vol. II, No. 2, 1973, pp. 62-6.*

*   *   *

WILSON, John Anthony Burgess
See BURGESS, Anthony

*   *   *

WOODS, Helen Ferguson
See KAVAN, Anna

*   *   *

WRIGHT, Charles   1935-

Wright is an American poet. His self-professed poetic concerns are with the "half-truths and fictions of the American Dream." His poetry is characterized by a catalogue-like rush of imagery, producing a dazzling kaleidoscopic effect. (See also *CLC*, Vol. 6, and *Contemporary Authors*, Vols. 29-32, rev. ed.)

JOHN N. MORRIS

Charles Wright's books seem to be coming fast now, per-

haps too fast: in 1973 *Hard Freight* and here, early in 1975, *Bloodlines*. I think it has to be said that *Bloodlines* is not quite so sustained a performance as *Hard Freight* was . . . , and perhaps the reader new to Wright should begin with that earlier elegy upon and qualified celebration of "The infinite rectitude / Of all that is past," that series of forward journeys backward "always into the earth." In *Bloodlines,* to be sure, much is much the same, as in the phrase "the clouds, those mansions of nothingness," which so clearly remembers "The clouds, great piles of oblivion." And I seem to recall from both *The Grave of the Right Hand* (his first book) and *Hard Freight* the largely mystifying private iconography of shoes, gloves, hats and hands that one encounters here. Indeed, not only in particular but in general, the manner here is much as before (and nothing wrong with that), a matter of making connections that are bizarre and appropriate at once.

Though I think that in *Bloodlines* Wright cares a little less than he used to do that that appropriateness be (however mysterious) immediately apparent. It seems sometimes that his devices leave us a little too much to our own. But this is quibbling. The pleasure this book affords has much to do with Wright's old clarities and graces. . . . (p. 453)

I confess that I was at first put off by both ["Skins" and "Tattoos," the principal] sequences. As they stand there on the page, the "Tattoos" group look a lot like Berryman "Dreamsongs"; and the "Skins" series not only looks like, but is, a set of loose, unrhymed, sort-of sonnets, as in Lowell's *Notebooks* or *History* or whatever it is next to be called. These appearances are appearances only: like skins, they are superficial, though maybe, like tattoos, they're intentional. But at first glance the resemblances suggested to me that here was nothing more than another mechanical effort, and a derivative one, to solve the problem that The Long Poem (or even the long*ish* poem) poses these days: if you can't build a building, try a picket fence (or a chain link fence, as in the title of a shorter sequence of Wright's that I'm not considering here). Not so—or not entirely so. But though those resemblances are chiefly external, "Tattoos" is full of dreams and visions and full, too, of autobiography and Experience, accounts of the infringements, the imprints of the world or worlds upon a self. And "Skins" makes a kind of reach after History, the history not of the autobiographical *I* of "Tattoos" but of *you*—i.e., Wright and us—who, having reached "that moment / When what you are is what you will be," must struggle on in the face of limitation and mortality.

Among the interesting things about these poems is how reluctantly they forego the consolations of Christianity. I take it that the difficulty and the necessity of doing so are the leading concerns of the "Skins" sequence and indeed of the book at large. This may seem, in so bald a statement of it, a desperately old-fashioned business. And the conclusion reached, a submission to the natural, is something we may have heard of before . . . (at moments in the book certain of Dylan Thomas' poems seem to be speaking again). But how many discoveries are there to be made in this department of life? In the process of attaining to [a sort of] religion of process—in, say, poem 15 through 19 of "Skins," a meditation on the four elements—Wright secures our acquiescence in his poetic procedures. Surely that's enough. (pp. 453-55)

> *John N. Morris, in* The Hudson Review *(copy-*

right © *1975 by The Hudson Review, Inc.; reprinted by permission), Vol. XXVIII, No. 3, Autumn, 1975.*

CAROL MUSKE

Wright himself is a contentious presence [in *Bloodlines*]. . . . He is on the move. His poems fairly explode from the page in hurly-burly refrain, elliptical syntax, and giddy shifts that recall Hopkins:

> Sucked in and sucked out, tidewash
> Hustles its razzamatazz across the cut lips
> of coral, the thousands of tiny punctures
> Spewing and disappearing. . . .
>
> (p. 117)

Wright is a sped-up silent flick, these poems are *ways out* of ourselves, ways to accomplish "the getaway by the light of yourself," ways to dream the page, then disappear. Wright invites comparison with the cinematic: some poems have a grainy, pointillist texture, particularly the "memory sequences"—flickering home movies with a hand-held camera. There is something "inhuman, something you can't know" in beauty and the poet does not want to *dwell* too long anywhere, or move too close to the mystery—home is "what you keep making." Wright's a perennial tenant—moves in and out of every temporary shelter he creates.

These poems are forward-looking, light-seeking, if not exactly optimistic. But the labor is away from dark and the poet does know the darkness. . . . (p. 118)

Close [to despair], but not close enough to succumb, he moves through the dilemma of the past, the debris of memory, sidestepping the ruins. (p. 119)

Begin again is his lesson—and regret becomes narrative, reminiscence, Wright flexing his muscles before tightening the spring and moving on again. He is already into the story, deeper into language itself, its changing promise and intelligence. He is sequestered in a fullblown and recognizable style. (pp. 119-20)

Wright's [genius] is to stand in the light till his words catch fire, acquire patina, then reflect the sun on their own. (p. 120)

> *Carol Muske, in* Parnassus: Poetry in Review *(copyright © by Poetry in Review Foundation), Spring-Summer, 1976.*

KATHLEEN AGENA

When Charles Wright's poems work, which is most of the time, the poetic energies seem to break the membrane of syntax, exploding the surface, reverberating in multiple directions simultaneously. It is not a linear progression one finds but rather a ricocheting, as if, at the impact of a single cue, all the words bounced into their pockets, rearranged, and displaced themselves in different directions all over again. And it seems to happen almost by accident, as if Wright simply sets the words in motion and they, playing a game according to their own rules, write the poem. Certainly Wright is aware of this strange power of words; all three of his books contain poems which, strictly speaking, refer only to words and their maneuverings. (pp. 625-26)

Oval, oval oval oval push pull push pull . . .
Words unroll from our fingers.
A splash of leaves through the windowpanes,
A smell of tar from the streets:
Apple, arrival, the railroad, shoe.

(p. 626)

One reads a poem like "Tattoos 12" and the first response is "that felt good!"; and only later . . . "what happened?" Of course Wright's poems are not without "sense," not without conceptual-symbolic dimensions, but it is the sense of primal consciousness, the sense of paradox and multiplicity almost, one might say, a syntax of eroticism—that binds these words and their meanings. Or, to use Lacan's terminology, it is "the letter in the unconscious," which, though it may oppose conscious purpose, is never arbitrary. . . . So in the afterglow of the initial reading one can go back and, unwinding the words from their embrace, realize, for example, that the reason "oval oval oval oval" works so well with "push, pull" is that an oval is a circle which has been squeezed, "pushed," or elongated, "pulled," at two points, that oval is the transcendent ease of the perfect equilibrium of the circle being subjected to pressure. The oval is also an egg, birth, the push and pull of form coming into existence. And what do "apple, arrival, the railroad, shoe" have to do with each other? Is this just perverse eroticism at work again? No, there is meaning in the apparent madness. All the words are related to movement—the "apple" to the movement toward knowledge, the expulsion from grace, the fall into the limits of temporal existence and guilt. With "apple" in the first slot and "arrival, the railroad, shoe" functioning as substitutions thereafter, the series together carries meanings of movement-knowledge-guilt-limit with a progressive emphasis on limitation: "apple" signifying a transcendental causal function; "arrival," because it is used nonspecifically, signifying an abstract goal of movement; "railroad" reducing the abstract movement to a finite vehicle of movement; and "shoe" further restricting movement and the vehicle of movement. The limit-restriction element is both a reverberation back to and an amplification of the first line—that is, it amplifies the sense of stress of "oval" and "push, pull" and it extends the notion of imperfectness implied there. The movement-knowledge-guilt-limit motif is also evident in the second, third, and fourth lines: "windowpanes," suggesting consciousness itself which receives the knowledge, immediately becomes contaminated with the "smell of tar," black, sticky, clinging guilt. Further, all of these motifs get connected with the "meaning" of words: after the first line, which simply establishes a process, comes the first subject in the poem ("words") and all the subsequent subjects which follow must be seen as substitutions, replacements, which serve to multiply the significations connected with that first subject. So, the first stanza as well as the entire poem is about words, about the way they come to carry meaning, the dynamic that exists between words as signifiers and the things they signify, the guilt of words as opposed to the purity of silence. (p. 627)

Wright's power as a poet lies in [his] ability to hook us, to intoxicate us with a language that radiates paradox—that is, the realm of symbol. To accomplish this demands, I think, a kind of surrender on the part of the poet, a loosening of intent, a trusting in the mad sense of language. And, in fact, Wright's poetry fails when he refuses to surrender enough, when he holds the reins on the words too tightly, when he seems too intent upon getting an idea across and, ironically, ends up writing poems less rich in meaning. But when the right balance between abandon and control is achieved, the nature of the tension is erotic. . . . (p. 628)

The connective threads, the concepts, that run through Wright's poems and make his collection read, as James Tate puts it, "like a book not a miscellany," have to do with Wright's insistence that the human is but one system, one way of ordering, one center exerting its force while simultaneously being permeated by the force of other systems, that progress in terms of any single system is an illusion; the center is always shifting. There is simply process, displacement, the perpetual turning of transformation. . . . In each of his books, Wright has moved closer and closer to this radical level ["where all is a true turning, and all is growth"]: in his latest book, he situates himself, metaphorically, in the flux itself. It is the numen of the blood that Wright explores in *Bloodlines*. In "Virgo Descending," the first poem in the collection, Wright draws us directly into a transformative dissolution and leads us to an archetypal image of the blood, the high priestess of the irrational, chthonic forces—the Great Mother. . . . (pp. 628-29)

Significantly, in "Virgo Descending" there is no directive agent, no subject which initiates the action. Instead, there is simply process itself and various stages in this process; the grandmother image does not signify an end stage of the process but rather its final opening-out. . . . Wright takes us into a place where there are no stable subjects, only momentary foci or centers of action, where the "I" itself is a "something else" that is, subjectively, nothing because it is perpetually subject to change. . . . The release from stable identity to process brings with it a "release" from security. It is a willingness to accept a subjectless play of forces similar to the Oriental concept of Tao and Wright's insight is that as long as one yearns for a permanently fixed center, an arbitrary pattern not found within the flux, within the blood (blood lines) there will, ironically, be only emptiness. . . . (pp. 629-30)

> *Kathleen Agena, "The Mad Sense of Language," in* Partisan Review *(copyright © 1976 by Partisan Review, Inc.), Vol. XLIII, No. 4, 1976, pp. 625-30.*

HAROLD BLOOM

Charles Wright's *China Trace* . . . is a book of apparently slight but actually firm and brilliant metaphysical lyrics. . . . I have not read this poet before and have missed therefore an admirable writer, whose diction is always precise and illuminating and who sustains his own poetics: *I write poems to untie myself, to do penance and disappear / Through the upper right-hand corner of things, to say grace.* (p. 26)

> *Harold Bloom, in* The New Republic *(reprinted by permission of* The New Republic; *© 1977 by The New Republic, Inc.), November 26, 1977.*

PETER STITT

Charles Wright is anything but a literalist in . . . *China Trace,* though such has not always been the case. Wright has progressed steadily away from clarity and directness in favor of an ever more personal, more private utterance. . . . The poems in Wright's first book, *The Grave of the Right Hand,* have the polished clarity one would expect from a

master of the plain style. They are obviously meant to speak to the reader, to communicate something he can share. Among the best is "To a Friend Who Wished Always to Be Alone." . . . This is beautifully written—the pacing and the pauses, the images and the sounds, everything contributes to the quiet, wry effectiveness of this elegy.

Lyricism is still present in *China Trace,* but the clarity is long since gone, having been finally put to rest in *Bloodlines.* Various areas of the . . . volume reveal certain obsessive concerns, and there seems to be a consistent spiritual quest throughout, but what the specific form or goal of this quest may be, I cannot say. . . . The primary concern of the first part is mortality, particularly the death and decay of the poet's own body. (pp. 478-79)

Wright is clearly seeking apotheosis throughout this book, longing to shed the restraints of mortal dross in favor of spiritual freedom. . . . We are told on the jacket of *China Trace* that Wright conceives of it as concluding a trilogy begun with *Hard Freight* and continued in *Bloodlines.* After rereading all three volumes in sequence, I confess to having only the vaguest notion of why they might constitute a trilogy; the conceptual basis of these books is too private, at least for now. (p. 479)

> *Peter Stitt, in* The Georgia Review *(copyright, 1978, by the University of Georgia), Summer, 1978.*

RICHARD JACKSON

Wright's epigraph for [*China Trace*], taken from T'u Lung, of the Ming dynasty, provides a key:

> I would like to house my spirit within my
> body, to nourish my virtue by mildness, and
> to travel in ether by becoming a void. But I
> cannot do it yet. . . . And so, being unable to
> find peace within myself, I made use of the
> external surroundings to calm my spirit, and
> being unable to find delight within my heart,
> I borrowed a landscape to please it.

In the context of an Idealistic Neo-Confucianism, Wright's world becomes one of presences that are inadequate substitutes for the absence he desires. As a result, the objects of his landscape aspire to the condition of language, our substitute, if we can trust our linguistic critics . . . for what we cannot fully possess, for what is missing. In a roundabout way, he hopes language will bring him the void, will allow him to become, as another epigraph suggests, "an emblem among emblems." The poet's trick is thus to "mimic the tongues of green flame in the grass" ("Where Moth and Dust Doth Corrupt"). The irony of such a procedure is that language itself becomes ineffable: "In some other language, / I walk by the same river, the same vowels in my throat. / I wish I could say them now" ("Wishes"). And when the poet can speak, when he does write, the language becomes one of numerous signifiers whose significance is enigmatic. Though the consequence is often a poem inexcusably vague, or inaccessibly solipsistic, in many cases the metaphysical reality of absence is powerfully evoked. . . . This book is the third in a trilogy, and it is far more abstract than its predecessors; however, the world it explores is more rich, more mysterious, and the reality it often earns is rewarding. It will be interesting to see where Wright goes from here. (pp. 555-56)

Richard Jackson, in Michigan Quarterly Review *(copyright © The University of Michigan, 1978), Fall, 1978.*

DAVID BROMWICH

Wright is . . . a thoroughly professional poet, and he writes the off-real journal entry, the shadowy song of rural experience, which is the characteristic magazine poem of our time. His technique, the over-all look and feel of his poems, come from Pound: the lines always hang nicely, and do their wire-walk quietly, without appearing to show off. The local texture, however, is *echt*-1970s. Here are middle-period Justice ("I open the phone book, and look for my adolescence. / How easy the past is—"), and Merwin ("The banked candles the color of fresh bone, / Smoke rising from the chimneys beyond the beyond, / Nightfires, your next address . . ."—which sounds *New Yorker*-ish, and when you look it up, it is), and James Wright's hammock poem ("Green apples, a stained quilt, / The black clock of the heavens reset in the future tense. / Salvation's a simple thing"). Charles Wright would be more intriguing if he found it not so fine a thing to relax into each inexpensive but portentous phrase as it rose to his mind and fell from his pen.

His reliance on phrases makes him seem, probably the last thing he wants to seem, *fluent:* "necktie of ice," "sleeves of bone"—these from different poems—and on a grander scale, "Daylight spoons out its cream-of-wheat," "God is the sleight-of-hand in the fireweed," "Heaven, that stray dog, eats on the run and keeps moving." . . . Wright some-times thinks of himself as a *Tiger* of Instruction. Let us wish him a swift recovery from the illusion that anything very edifying can be made of the paradox. In the meantime, faced with so ripe a specimen of our current poetic diction as

Each night, in its handful of sleep, the mimosa blooms.
Each night the future forgives.
Inside us, albino roots are starting to take hold,

the Socrato-Philistine who lurks in every reader will leap unembarrassed to the offensive, one sally for each line: (1) Why "handful," where the image is lost in the time it takes to think out the wit? (2) How do you know? (3) Oh, ick!

At his best, Wright deserves something better than the flippancy that is the healthy response to his easy jockeying for effect. [*China Trace*] has a few passages of tenderness and manly reserve, very close to Whitman in spirit and in sound. . . . The step-down to "enact" exhalation is mannered, and could simply have been a new line; but it is the Pound and not the Socrato-Philistine in every reader who says this. . . . And even when Wright is unforgivably slick, his cadences are measured and sure. Anyone who can imagine how this *might* be so, should inspect once again the emotionally ugly passages that have been quoted, and listen to the way they move. Wright's most impressive work has been appearing lately in the magazines and was evidently written after *China Trace*. We may come to regard him after all as a good poet who educated himself in public. (pp. 169-71)

David Bromwich, in Poetry *(© 1978 by The Modern Poetry Association; reprinted by permission of the Editor of* Poetry*), December, 1978.*

Y

YEHOSHUA, Abraham B.   1936-

An Israeli short story writer, playwright, and novelist, Yehoshua is gaining an increasingly wider reputation outside his country. The political and social realities of Israel form the background for much of his later work and particularly for his first full-length novel, *The Lover*. Many critics have praised his structural innovation. (See also *Contemporary Authors*, Vols. 33-36, rev. ed.)

ELI PFEFFERKORN

[Yehoshua] brings to his plays a knack for structural compactness, for manipulation of character and for creating a sense of an impending turning point. All these dramatic commodities are dynamically galvanized by a dialogue that rapidly alternates between poignant staccato utterances and a kind of lingering meditative lyricism. Using a dramatic strategy similar to that of Pinter in *The Birthday Party* and *The Homecoming*, Yehoshua gradually builds up a situation fraught with emotional tension that is abruptly discharged in a fierce dialogue by characters engaged in a series of interpersonal confrontations. Unlike Pinter's characters, however, who openly display an impulse toward wanton destructiveness, Yehoshua's dramatis personae often hide under the garb of urbane civility. Though not possessed by death, Yehoshua the playwright seems to enjoy depicting the emerging skull beneath the skin of his characters. Minutely exploring the tortuous contours of their psychic landscape, Yehoshua presents his characters as they abruptly vacillate between realism and fantasy. Out of joint with their immediate environment, they are either wearing an apocalyptic chip on their shoulders or else are hopelessly entangled in a psychological labyrinth. His [is a] predilection for the unique and the weird. . . . Yehoshua is at his best when engaging his characters in the game of psychological brinksmanship, pushing them to the extreme edge of their endurance. (pp. 198-99)

The compression of time and space [in "A Night in May"] functions as a catalyst to advance a series of sharp confrontations between the characters, whose latent conflicts are exposed in a nervous exchange of verbal fencing. . . . By the time the play has reached its climactic point in the middle of the third act, the emotionally wrought-up characters have spent themselves in a night of frenzied verbal combat. When the first rays of the Jerusalem dawn break through the window, the play makes its final movement, and the characters drift apart in the same casual manner in which they originally came together. Yehoshua seems to have steered his characters to the abyss of their existence only to leave them there at the end.

In "A Night in May" Yehoshua's narrative impulse still prevails over his dramatic craftsmanship. The play achieves a unity of atmosphere and being, but somewhat at the expense of a unity of action and doing. Or to put it in another way, Yehoshua enacts the dramatic events in a sequence of time not fully incorporated into the spatial form of the play. As a result of this, the language of the play is presented through dialogue that is not simultaneously embodied in the visual stage properties and images, or those elements that create a true theatrical experience.

Whereas in "A Night in May" the interaction between the verbal and visual components is rather loose, in "Last Treatments," written in 1973, word, image, gesture and stage props become orchestrated in a sequence of carefully timed events. Consequently, the characters presented are defined not in terms of their beings but in the way their beings manifest themselves in the process of action. Thus, the focal interest of the play shifts from a state of being to a dynamic situation of events.

As the plot unfolds, two opposing movements emerge: one strains toward severing the past from the future, and the other toward breaking away from the present into the past. The two movements form the fundamental conflict of the play, which materializes in the figures of Herman and Schatz. . . .

Yehoshua manages to establish a visual extension of the verbal constituencies. By means of an amazingly concise dialogue whose verbal images merge with the visual, the effect of total theatre is achieved. (p. 199)

Just as Schatz cannot escape from the realities of the present into the past, so too Herman is unable to escape from the past into the future. . . . .

Yehoshua pushes his characters to the very edge of the abyss in his relentless probing of their ability to endure moments of intense crisis. In the process, he leads his characters through an intricate maze in their search for meaning. Since their attempts to find meaning, according to the inner logic of the play, are doomed to failure, the characters move frenetically, in a vicious circle of trial and error, either unable or unwilling to achieve any real breakthrough. By using his dramatic powers to present man at the extreme edge of his existence, searching for meaning that constantly eludes him, Yehoshua has captured that mood or sensibility associated with the modern vision. Yehoshua's artistic vision inevitably turns, then, from a surface representation of Israeli reality in order to communicate an existential experience by means of spatial and temporal forms. In achieving this more profound sense of reality on stage, Yehoshua's work clearly signifies a landmark in the development of modern Hebrew dramaturgy. (p. 200)

> *Eli Pfefferkorn, "A Touch of Madness in the Plays of A. B. Yehoshua," in* Books Abroad *(copyright 1977 by the University of Oklahoma Press), Vol. 51, No. 2, Spring, 1977, pp. 198-200.*

DOV VARDI

It seems that the Israeli's relentless self-scrutiny since the Yom Kippur War has found [in *Ha-me'ahev (The Lover)*] a quarry for what is tormenting him: the sham of middle-class life, the inanity of success in enterprise, the infiltration of the economy by Arab hands, militant ultra-orthodoxy, unending reserve duty, the frantic search for missing Israelis, *yerida* (leaving the country) and, above all, "what happened to us since '48?"

Pirandello-like, the narrative develops through the monologues of six characters, each one like a persona in a morality play. . . .

Yehoshua cuts mercilessly into the Israeli dilemma—winner and loser. . . .

Underlining the Israeli scene, it is the political and social critic in Yehoshua which sets this work somewhere between journalism and complex art. The price he pays is to forgo a deeper search into human action and relationships through subtleties of character. This is only partly compensated for by the fascination of his theme and symbol. If one critic saw in this work "epic breadth," I must decline. "Breadth"—quite; "epic"—questionable. But wonderful reading. (p. 337)

> *Dov Vardi, in* World Literature Today *(copyright 1978 by the University of Oklahoma Press), Vol. 52, No. 2, Spring, 1978.*

WARREN BARGAD

In his fifteen-odd years of prose writing, Avraham B. Yehoshua has moved through three distinct phases. His first stories were brief, allegorical narratives, absurdist in tone and dramatization, and existential in import. Later, in the mid-sixties, he wrote longer stories, more psychologically focused and realistically framed, but still dependent upon strong doses of interpretation. And in the seventies, especially with his most recent Hebrew publication, *The Lover (haMe'ahev)*, Yehoshua has turned still further away from symbolism. Instead, his works have become rooted unambiguously in one, all-encompassing reality: war and its accompanying stresses on the human psyche.

The three stories collected in *Early in the Summer of 1970* span the three stages of A. B. Yehoshua's writing career. . . . "The Last Commander," collected in Yehoshua's first volume of stories (*The Death of the Old Man*, 1963), is a heavily symbolic work with socio-psychological implications. "Early in the Summer of 1970," first published in . . .

the spring of 1971, is structured along the lines of the French *nouveau roman*, blending reality and fantasy—the fall of a son and the father's wishful dream of his survival—with an abrogated sense of time. And "Missile Base 612," which appeared in . . . [1974], is a realistic but ironic work about ennui and futility in the life of an intellectual, both at home and at the front. The theme of war unites the three stories; but their particular chronology and varied modes of depiction and narration make the collection an interesting one indeed. (p. 76)

The dichotomous leadership [in "The Last Commander"] represents two diverse attitudes toward war and military achievement. [The commander] Yagnon—the name may be a pun on the Hebrew *yagon*, "sorrow" or "grief"—is the embodiment of indefatigable peacefulness, the antithesis of military action and efficiency. In contrast, the other commander symbolizes activity and accomplishment. He unfurls "the forgotten war flag," engages in constant war peptalks, and plans even more demanding exercises.

The contraposition of two seven-day periods bespeaks a dialectical scheme of things, a symbolic, dichotomous world of two extreme gods, one of total rest-peace and one of total action-war. . . . The "last commander," The Great God War, comes out of the sky to rescue [the] people from their useless lethargy; but he is rebuffed, banished by Yagnon, himself a symbolic victim of warfare. The men lie about in "a sleepy, paralyzed camp," watching sporadically for the helicopter's return. The Israelis are caught in constant limbo, says Yehoshua, between these two ambivalent modes of existence. (p. 77)

[The main character of "Missile Base 612"] ultimately becomes merely a conglomerate facsimile of a number of social and psychological problems. Enmeshed as he is in . . . a web of implications, he embodies a pastiche of motifs already familiar from other works by Yehoshua . . . and by other authors as well (especially A. Megged and A. Oz). Yehoshua has attempted to delve into the dilemmas confronting Israelis today, but the overdone characterization makes more for melodrama than for cogency.

By far the best selection in the volume is the title story. . . . [One day, an old Bible teacher is] told that his son has been killed in the Jordan Valley.

What follows is a mixed series of episodes and flashbacks. . . . The ordering of these flashbacks and scenes is not fixed chronologically. At one and the same time the reader is thrust into the past and impelled through the present. The abrogated time scheme—probably modelled after the French novelist Claude Mauriac's technique of the "immobilization of time"—provides the structure which allows Yehoshua to blend real and imagined occurrences. This deft blending of time elements results in a magnificently wrought study of shock and bereavement. Confronting a questionable present, the reader is all the more willing to suspend his disbelief; he accepts even entirely implausible situations. (pp. 77-8)

In this technically dazzling work it soon becomes clear that the entire action of the story has taken place in the mind of the bereaved father. The "time of narration" seems to encompass several days; but the story's "narrated time" is only of a few minute's duration. Informed of his son's sudden death, the old teacher faints dead away. The rest of the story is composed of a kind of dream sequence or inner depiction of the father's mind and feelings as he copes with the awesome truth. The story is a *tour de force* in structure and psychological portraiture. . . . "Early in the Summer of 1970" stands as one of A. B. Yehoshua's finest achievements to date. (p. 78)

Warren Bargad, "War, Allegory, and Psyche," in Midstream *(copyright © 1978 by The Theodor Herzl Foundation, Inc.), October, 1978, pp. 76-8.*

ROBERT ALTER

A vocal member of the disaffected Left in a country constantly straining under the pressures of political conflict, Mr. Yehoshua is acutely conscious of political issues in his work, but his deepest imaginative concerns lie elsewhere; and the delicate shifting tensions between political surface and what I would call elemental depths are a principal source of his fiction's piquancy, its elusive, haunting appeal.

The surface of "The Lover" would seem to justify describing it straightforwardly as a novel of the Yom Kippur War and its aftermath. The story, in a technique possibly suggested by Faulkner's "As I Lay Dying," is told through the alternating monologues of six central characters: Adam, a prosperous middle-aged Haifa garage-owner; Asya, his wife; Gabriel, her young lover, who has returned from a decade abroad to be swept up in the October war; Dafi, the teen-age daughter of Adam and Asya; Na'im, a young Arab worker at Adam's garage, who falls in love with Dafi; and Veducha, Gabriel's nonagenarian grandmother. When the war is over, Gabriel is missing in action, and the governing force of the plot is Adam's obsessive search for his wife's vanished lover.

As several Hebrew reviewers were quick to point out, Mr. Yehoshua's novel manages to touch most of the raw nerves of Israel's troubled national condition. . . . Mr. Yehoshua is keenly concerned about all [Israel's problems], but in his novel they are ultimately the means of dramatizing a more fundamental thematic interplay between youth and age, potency and impotence, living and dying, sleep and waking.

The addictive allure of sleep in fact has been an explicit theme of Mr. Yehoshua's since his earliest short stories, and in "The Lover" that theme is orchestrated through the various monologues with impressive resourcefulness. This is, indeed, a somnambulistic novel. One of the six protagonists, Asya, is actually always asleep when the narrative shifts to her point of view: All her monologues are reports of her dreams. Adam glides through the streets in his tow truck night after night, often in a daze of fatigue, searching for Gabriel, joined by his daughter Dafi, a precocious insomniac who snatches fragments of fitful sleep in her high-school classes during the day. And Veducha's first monologues, surely the most remarkable poetic achievement of the novel, are the asyntactical expression of the old lady's flickering consciousness in a coma as she imagines herself a stone, a root, a branch, a plant, something almost dead blindly clinging to life.

Even from this rapid summary of a novel rich in the ramification of incident and character, it should be apparent that Mr. Yehoshua is not in any conventional sense a realistic writer. His early stories were characterized by a certain self-consciousness about symbolic mechanisms and surrealistic effects. What he seems to have learned how to do adeptly from his second book onward was to make the famil-

iar world, rendered in realistic detail, imperceptibly merge with or suddenly collapse into the uncanny, and that is one of the chief strengths of "The Lover." The social types and settings, the political attitudes and conflicts, the public institutions represented in the novel often seem persuasively like those of Israel, 1973, but they obey their own spectral laws. The informing vision is grotesque and, often enough, grotesquely comic, because that matches the writer's sense of the fundamental bizarreness of living as a human being, hurtling from youth through age to death, spurred by lust and numbed by its fading away, trying to get a sight on reality, perhaps obscurely aspiring to something.

Thus, Gabriel's first entry into the arena of Adam's life is like a stage-farce transposition of a dream. (p. 15)

Other instances of Mr. Yehoshua's grotesque vision are less comic than deeply unsettling, like the moment when the hitherto sexually apathetic Adam, inflamed with sudden lust, makes love to a Lolita-like schoolchum of his daughter on the iron bed of an operating room in a geriatric hospital. It is hardly a pleasant moment and not, by any realistic standard, a likely one, but in its juxtaposition of child and man, the act of life in a place of the dying, carnal warmth and the chill of surgical steel, it perfectly expresses Mr. Yehoshua's vision of life as a tangle of weird contradictions. He is a writer who exhibits the rigorous fidelity to his own perceptions that produces real originality. (p. 46)

Robert Alter, in The New York Times Book Review *(© 1978 by The New York Times Company; reprinted by permission), November 19, 1978.*

ALFRED KAZIN

Missing connections, family anomie, and breakup inadmissible to Jewish piety and Israeli solidarity (but of course not exclusive of endless family discussions) are the favorite themes of the delicate and ironic young Israeli novelist Avraham Yehoshua. In two books of stories, *Three Days and a Child* and *Early in the Summer of 1970*, Yehoshua brought to his stories of alienation and antagonism within the Israeli family such fine political shading that I am not surprised to find in the comic situation of *The Lover*, his first novel, a parallel comedy of Arab-Jewish distrust that does not shirk the ferocity that grows every month. Through the eyes both of a fifteen-year-old Arab working in the husband's garage and of the lover's ninety-year-old grandmother . . . we see an Arab and an Israeli locked into a debate of proximity, alikeness, mental hatred, a debate that Yehoshua's superb ability to render *both* presences relieves of all sentimentality. . . .

What I value most in *The Lover*, and never get from discourse about Israel, is a gift for equidistance—between characters, even between the feelings on both sides—that reveals the strain of keeping in balance so many necessary contradictions. The story, mounting through the repetitive, circling, lightly touching personal monologues, ends up, like a circus performer balancing his body on one finger, on a harshly concentrated equipoise that cannot hold. There is no easy sleep in this land; insomnia and night prowling pervade the novel as among Israel's chief activities—along with endless meetings and military consciousness. . . .

Though the traditional "center" of Jewish existence, the family, does not hold, Yehoshua seems to suggest that the characters in their wandering and prowling and love-snatching find a perception in their isolated monologues, some imaginery volume of being, that makes a novel *possible*. All these lonelies, with their educational meetings, their many cars, make up a society. The characters in their isolation may not always seem real to themselves, but the country does. Hence the sense of danger that hovers over the book like the *hamsin*, the hot wind from the east. Although I detect some softness and old-style Zionist yearnings in the lovemaking between Arab and Jew, there is by the end of the book a steely stoicism and even an open fear on Yehoshua's part about the destructiveness that lies ahead. Politically a leading dove, Yehoshua as a novelist is most admirable in the courage he brings to his vision of what Israel *is* and of necessity will continue to be. . . .

> *Alfred Kazin, "Missing Connections," in* The New York Review of Books (*reprinted with permission from* The New York Review of Books; *copyright © 1978 Nyrev, Inc.), December 21, 1978, p. 25.*

*   *   *

YEVTUSHENKO, Yevgeni   1933-

Yevtushenko is a Russian poet known throughout the world for his superb dramatic readings of his own work. Although frequently critical of contemporary Soviet society, he remains essentially a regime poet. (See also *CLC*, Vols. 1, 3.)

J. M. COHEN

[Yevgeny Yevtushenko] writes about metaphysical overtones. The leading theme of his . . . sequence 'The Bratsk Station' is a dialogue between an Egyptian pyramid and this electrogenerating station in the Siberian tundra. The work Bratsk has a double meaning: it stands both for brotherhood and for the place. Yevtushenko's sequence hymns the Russian achievement and prophesies a spiritual future of vaster achievement, but not of faith; though his ideas are strictly Communist, his expression is individual. . . . This book contains Yevtushenko's best poetry till now: an individual restatement of a commonplace passionately accepted by his audience. It can and should be read in the West with suspension of disbelief, for it is fine poetry. . . . (p. 78)

> *J. M. Cohen, in* The Spectator (© *1967 by The* Spectator; *reprinted by permission of* The Spectator*), July 21, 1967.*

RIMA SHORE

The actors in Yevgeny Yevtushenko's *Under the Skin of the Statue of Liberty* wait onstage for the audience to enter. . . . Sitting casually against the large metal backdrop, eighteen youths talk in undertones, chew gum, smoke and stare indifferently or defiantly at the people who are joining them in the hall.

Cramped and restless, the actors are very close to the audience, practically within reach of the first row of seats. This first row is reserved. The audience, settling into place, has the time and proximity to absorb details of set and costume on the shallow stage. . . . This is American Youth as the Moscow audience might expect it to be, but the actors would probably strike the American viewer as middle-aged and dated, belonging more to the Beat Generation than to today's counter-culture. . . .

The main presence in the theatre is the metal backdrop, which replaces a curtain. All of the action of the performance takes place in front of this backdrop. Seamed together from sturdy sections of flat and corrugated metal, it creates a cold and urban setting. The last two words of a slogan, *the WAR,* painted in large, white English letters at the extreme left, leave to the imagination the beginning of the slogan and the extension of the metal curtain beyond the dimensions of the stage and theatre. (p. 138)

What we see and hear on stage is a series of enactments of political events or of events that are portrayed as central to the American Experience. (p. 139)

[Violence] alternates with less devastating skits. Some seem irrelevant, like a barker selling lottery tickets. Others strike the American viewer as on target, such as when a Gallup pollster, using the rope as a microphone, puts questions to Americans on the street who are handily portrayed by the four skulls. . . .

When the students play themselves, Yevtushenko's treatment is sympathetic, and the youth movement is depicted as a helpless, desperate attempt to reclaim innocence. Dr. Spock, "wiser than us all," emerges as a hero because he knows that *parents* should be treated for the diseases of childhood.

In the blending of old and new Yevtushenko verse, the male actors imitate the delivery style of Yevtushenko himself, whose image is present onstage in the form of a poster announcing the American concert tour of "Yevtushenko and Friends." To the American spectator, the declamation of poetry makes the character onstage impossible to identify with. The American viewer becomes acutely aware that the actor before him is a Soviet youth in American bluejeans.

The effect on the Soviet theatregoer is much different, and hard for an American to assess. The performance of poetry, a Soviet phenomenon, is central to the experience of Soviet youth. . . . Such performances have had an impact on Soviet youth culture that might be compared with that of rock festivals in America. Many lines of Yevtushenko poetry revived in *Under the Skin of the Statue of Liberty* are as familiar to the Moscow audience as lyrics of rock hits might be to a young American audience. This familiarity adds a note of nostalgia to the performance, for the height of Yevtushenko's popularity and visibility to the Soviet public passed with the sixties.

Some Western critics interpret the fact that Yevtushenko has chosen to portray Americans through a wholly Soviet art form as one more indication that the moral action of *Under the Skin of the Statue of Liberty* is not set in America at all. References to listening through walls, the recreation of Dostoevsky's character Raskalnikov, and even the presence onstage of a metal backdrop that could suggest an "Iron Curtain" might convince such critics that political innuendos of the play cut two ways, that there are anti-Soviet as well as anti-American elements. Some American viewers have concluded that *Under the Skin of the Statue of Liberty* is actually a thinly disguised anti-Soviet production. (p. 141)

The play *is* considered controversial, . . . [but Muscovites] seem to feel that its controversy stems from the play's anti-American implications at a time of official détente, not from anti-Soviet intentions.

Yevtushenko clearly does intend to reach beyond exclusively American experiences for more universal meaning, although his symbolism becomes ambiguous in the attempt. He blurs ideological lines with the token presence of non-American characters such as Raskalnikov and Pancho Villa, with the portrayal of positive American heroes such as Dr. Spock and President Kennedy, and with references to literary truisms, as Donne's "Ask not for whom the bell tolls . . ." America's various shames are actualized on the stage, but it is the Russian and fictional murderer Raskalnikov who smashes an ax into the symbolic skulls. All men kill that which they fear, all men murder that which causes them shame, Yevtushenko seems to be saying in his portrayal of American youth's search for innocence and redemption. (pp. 141-42)

> *Rima Shore, in* The Drama Review (© *1973 by* The Drama Review; *reprinted by permission; all rights reserved), No. 1, 1973.*

A. LAWTON

The general reader as well as the specialist in Russian literature will find [*Le betullenane*] extremely valuable. Although Yevtushenko is probably the Soviet poet best known abroad, several of the poems included in this collection are published for the first time outside of the Soviet Union. . . .

Yevtushenko, caught between [poles of eradicated traditions and anticipated phenomena], voices the "Soviet" anguish of the individual, whose ideological opposition to the old beliefs is frustrated by the absence of new positive values. In the search for new values, he alternately rejects and accepts official Soviet dogmatism and the pseudo-ideals of Western consumer society. This suffered uncertainty, far from being the reflection of a calculated compromise (as it has often been considered), reveals the full measure of his moral and artistic integrity. As a "dwarf birch" (the image which gives the title to the collection) tenaciously rooted in its inhospitable, frozen ground, he commits himself to life, even if its significance may forever remain a mystery. (p. 805)

> *A. Lawton, in* Books Abroad (*copyright 1975 by the University of Oklahoma Press), Vol. 49, No. 4, Autumn, 1975.*

VICKIE A. BABENKO

Many contemporary Soviet poets write about women . . . but Evtushenko's poems on the subject are somewhat different from those of other poets. While most of them present women in love this is a minor subject for Evtushenko. . . . His female characters have specific qualities; they are earthly creatures; their feelings are intense and real. Evtushenko does not distance them with abstract associations. At the same time his poetic "I" is less personally involved in the action than those of poets like Voznesenskii. Like Voznesenskii, however, he sees women as victims of a cruel fate who are to be pitied or admired. Yet each of them is an unique human being, and there is always a certain tragic tone about each one. Although his female characters are not the beauties that most poets present, Evtushenko dramatizes them in such a way that they appear more moving and attractive than the conventional love-goddesses.

Another feature of Evtushenko's poetry which distinguishes him from many poets who write about women is

that he is particularly fascinated by old women, those whose lives are filled with experience and on whom time has left its mark. He observes every reflection of their eyes, every movement of their hands, the color change of their faces. He is an astute psychologist in that he, like Gogol' and sometimes Tolstoi, uses outward signs to disclose the inner world of his characters. (pp. 320-21)

Love poems are relatively rare in Evtushenko's poetry. Most of them can be found in his earlier collections. In the 1959 edition of *Stikhi raznykh let* [*Poems of Various Years*] there are about a dozen poems dealing with love. The treatment of that theme seems artificial, however, the reader is not impressed. On the other hand, these poems do show the poet's maturing powers of observation and especially his attention to detail already being used as a means to penetrate more deeply into the nature of feelings and situations. (p. 322)

The colloquial speech used in all [Evtushenko's] poems and the carefully chosen detail of the scenes of Soviet life make the portrayal of the women come alive convincingly.

From his presentation of Russian women we deduce that they are no different from other women in the world, who all need love and care. But the different environment of the Russian women has certainly laid its mark on them. Evtushenko has caught the grotesque contrast between the theory and the reality, which has produced courageous and strong women, qualities that make them the "best men." According to Evtushenko, suffering, patience and loving hearts, which remain unhardened by everyday struggles, have ennobled these simple women. (pp. 332-33)

Although the tone of his lyrics is usually sad, when he is depicting these women's struggles against all kinds of misery, the sadness at times gives way to an optimistic, almost joyful mood, as is the case in "Po jagody," "Zhenshchina i more" and other poems. Suffering is a sign of life. That Russian women seem to master the impossible and survive enables Evtushenko to see them as superior human beings. (p. 333)

> *Vickie A. Babenko, "Women in Evtushenko's Poetry," in* The Russian Review (*copyright 1977 by The Russian Review, Inc.), July, 1977, pp. 320-33.*

L. B. CROFT

For the specialist, there is patently little point in acquiring [*From Desire to Desire*]. It is obviously intended for those romantic but uninitiated poetophiles who have somewhere heard of Yevtushenko and seek another name to drop in literary conversation. To this purpose it is well designed. (p. 642)

> *L. B. Croft, in* World Literature Today (*copyright 1977 by the University of Oklahoma Press), Vol. 51, No. 4, Autumn, 1977.*

BLAKE MORRISON

Love Poems cannot be regarded as one of [Yevtushenko's] major publications: only half a dozen poems have not appeared in translation before. . . . But it is part of the same venture to divert attention from public works such as "Babiy Yar" towards the more personal, though never hermetic, love lyrics. . . .

Recent poems suggest the development in Yevtushenko of

a dutiful and at times tiresomely moralistic persona— ''Where there is no love, how foul and disgusting / to copulate'', ''Oh bless the family, dear Lord, the crown of all mankind''—but it would be wrong to expect a complete, ''Dover Beach''-like withdrawal from public concerns. (p. 846)

> *Blake Morrison, in* The Times Literary Supplement *(© Times Newspapers Ltd. (London) 1978; reproduced from* The Times Literary Supplement *by permission), July 28, 1978.*

*   *   *

YORKE, Henry Vincent
    See GREEN, Henry

Appendix

THE EXCERPTS IN CLC, VOLUME 13, WERE REPRINTED FROM THE FOLLOWING PERIODICALS:

Agenda
America
American Literature
The American Poetry Review
The American Scholar
The Antioch Review
The Atlantic Monthly
Best Sellers
Black World
Book Forum
Book Week—The Chicago Sun-Times
Book World—The Washington Post
Booklist
Books Abroad
Books and Bookmen
Books in Canada
boundary 2
Bulletin of Hispanic Studies
Canadian Dimension
The Canadian Forum
Canadian Literature
Chicago Review
The Christian Science Monitor
The Chronicle Review
CLA Journal
College English
Commentary
Commonweal
Comparative Drama
The Critic
Critical Quarterly
The Critical Review
Critique: Studies in Modern Fiction
The Dalhousie Review
The Denver Quarterly
The Dial
Drama
The Drama Review
Drama Survey
Encounter
English Studies
Essays in Criticism
The Explicator
Extrapolation
The Forum
The French Review
The Georgia Review
The Globe and Mail
Harper's
The Harvard Advocate
The Hibbert Journal

Hispania
Hispanic Review
The Hollins Critic
The Hopkins Review
The Hudson Review
The International Fiction Review
The Iowa Review
The Jewish Quarterly
Journal of Commonwealth Literature
Journal of Modern Literature
Kirkus Reviews
Library Journal
The Listener
The Literary Review
Literature East and West
London Magazine
The Los Angeles Times
Malahat Review
Michigan Quarterly Review
Midstream
The Midwest Quarterly
The Minnesota Review
The Mississippi Quarterly
Modern Drama
Modern Fiction Studies
The Modern Language Review
Modern Languages
Modern Poetry Studies
MOSAIC: A Journal for the Study of
    Literature and Ideas
Ms.
The Nation
National Review
The Negro History Bulletin
New Boston Review
New England Review
The New Leader
The New Republic
The New Review
New Statesman
New York Arts Journal
New York Magazine
The New York Review of Books
The New York Times
The New York Times Book Review
The New Yorker
Nouvelle Revue Française
Novel: A Forum on Fiction
The Ontario Review
Open Letter
Pacific Sun Literary Quarterly

Papers on Language and Literature
Parnassus: Poetry in Review
Partisan Review
Phoenix
Phylon
Plays and Players
PN Review
Poetry
Prairie Schooner
Publishers Weekly
Punch
Quarterly Review of Literature
Queen's Quarterly
Quill and Quire
Review
Rolling Stone
Romance Notes
The Romanic Review
The Russian Review
Salmagundi
Saturday Night
Saturday Review
Scandinavian Studies
Scandinavica
Science Fiction Review
Sewanee Review
Shenandoah
The Southern Humanities Review
The Southern Literary Journal
The Southern Review
Southwest Review
The Spectator
Stand
Studies in Short Fiction
Symposium
The Tamarack Review
Texas Studies in Literature and Language
Time
The Times Literary Supplement
The Twentieth Century
Twentieth Century Literature
The University Bookman
University of Toronto Quarterly
The Village Voice
Virginia Quarterly Review
Vort
West Coast Review
Western Humanities Review
World Literature Today
The Yale Review

THE EXCERPTS IN CLC, VOLUME 13, WERE REPRINTED FROM THE FOLLOWING BOOKS:

Adams, Robert Martin, AfterJoyce: Studies in Fiction After "Ulysses," *Oxford University Press, 1977.*

Allen, Walter, The Modern Novel in Britain and the United States, *Dutton, 1965.*

Archer, Marguerite, Jean Anouilh, *Columbia University Press, 1971.*

Axthelm, Peter M., The Modern Confessional Novel, *Yale University Press, 1967.*

Berryman, John, The Freedom of the Poet, *Farrar, Straus, 1976.*

Bigsby, C.W.E., ed., Edward Albee: A Collection of Critical Essays, *Prentice-Hall, 1975.*

Blackmur, R. P., Language as Gesture, *Harcourt, 1952.*

Bradbury, Malcolm, ed., Forster: A Collection of Critical Essays, *Prentice-Hall, 1966.*

Brown, John Russell, and Harris, Bernard, eds., Contemporary Theatre, *Edward Arnold, 1962.*

Chambers, Robert D., Sinclair Ross and Ernest Buckler, *Copp Clark Publishing, 1975; McGill-Queen's University Press, 1975.*

Conarroe, Joel, John Berryman: An Introduction to the Poetry, *Columbia University Press, 1977.*

Cowley, Malcolm, ed., The Portable Hemingway, *Viking Penguin, 1944.*

Crews, Frederick C., E. M. Forster: The Perils of Humanism, *Princeton University Press, 1962.*

Davie, Donald, Ezra Pound, *Viking Penguin, 1976.*

De Bolt, Joe, ed., Ursula K. LeGuin: Voyage to Inner Lands and Outer Space, *Kennikat, 1979.*

Donaldson, Scott, By Force of Will: The Life and Art of Ernest Hemingway, *Viking Penguin, 1977.*

Dudek, Louis, Selected Essays and Criticism, *Tecumseh Press, 1978.*

Eberhart, Richard, Of Poetry and Poets, *University of Illinois Press, 1979.*

Esslin, Martin, Brief Chronicles: Essays on Modern Theatre, *Temple Smith, 1970.*

Ferris, William H., The African Abroad; Or His Evolution in Western Civilization, Tracing His Development under the Caucasian Milieu, *Tuttle, Morehouse & Taylor Press, 1913.*

Fraser, G. S., Lawrence Durrell, *British Council, 1970.*

French, Warren, ed., The Fifties: Fiction, Poetry Drama, *Everett/Edwards, 1970.*

Frohock, W. M., André Malraux, *Columbia University Press, 1974.*

Gardiner, Harold C., S.J., ed., Fifty Years of the American Novel, *Scribner's, 1951.*

Gibson, Donald B., ed., Modern Black Poets: A Collection of Critical Essays, *Prentice-Hall, 1973.*

Greenblatt, Stephen Hay, Three Modern Satirists: Waugh, Orwell, and Huxley, *Yale University Press, 1965.*

Gysin, Fritz, The Grotesque in American Negro Literature: Jean Toomer, Richard Wright, and Ralph Ellison, *Francke Verlag Bern, 1975.*

Hamner, Robert D., V. S. Naipaul, *Twayne, 1973.*

Hartley, Lodwick, and Core, George, eds., Katherine Anne Porter: A Critical Symposium, *University of Georgia Press, 1969.*

Hicks, Granville, The Great Tradition: An Interpretation of American Literature Since the Civil War, *Quadrangle Books, 1969.*

Hinchliffe, Arnold P., British Theatre 1950-70, *Rowman and Littlefield, 1974.*

Johnson, Ira D., Glenway Wescott: The Paradox of Voice, *Kennikat, 1971.*

Kalstone, David, Five Temperaments: Elizabeth Bishop, Robert Lowell, James Merrill, Adrienne Rich, John Ashbery, *Oxford University Press, 1977.*

Kazin, Alfred, Bright Book of Life: American Novelists & Storytellers from Hemingway to Mailer, *Atlantic-Little, Brown, 1973.*

Kazin, Alfred, On Native Grounds: An Interpretation of Modern American Prose Literature, *Reynal & Hitchcock, 1942.*

Kenner, Hugh, A Homemade World: The American Modernist Writers, *Knopf, 1975.*

Kinnamon, Keneth, ed., James Baldwin: A Collection of Critical Essays, *Prentice-Hall, 1974.*

Kitchin, Laurence, Drama in the Sixties: Form and Interpretation, *Faber and Faber, 1966.*

Landess, Thomas H., ed., The Short Fiction of Caroline Gordon: A Critical Symposium, *University of Dallas Press, 1972.*

Lee, Robert A., Alistair MacLean: The Key Is Fear, *Borgo Press, 1976.*

Lewis, R.W.B., ed., Malraux: A Collection of Critical Essays, *Prentice-Hall, 1964.*

Littlejohn, David, Black on White: A Critical Survey of Writing by American Negroes, *Viking Penguin, 1966.*

Logan, Rayford W., W.E.B. Du Bois: A Profile, *Hill & Wang, 1971.*

Lowell, Robert, Taylor, Peter, and Warren, Robert Penn, eds., Randall Jarrell: 1914-1965, *Farrar, Straus, 1967.*

Marowitz, Charles, Milne, Tom, and Hale, Owen, eds., The Encore Reader: A Chronicle of the New Drama, *Methuen, 1965.*

Martin, Bruce K., Philip Larkin, *Twayne, 1978.*

Martin, Graham, ed., Eliot in Perspective: A Symposium, *Macmillan, 1970.*

McCall, Dorothy, The Theatre of Jean-Paul Sartre, *Columbia University Press, 1969.*

Nance, William L., The Worlds of Truman Capote, *Stein and Day, 1970.*

New, William H., ed., Dramatists in Canada: Selected Essays, *University of British Columbia Press, 1972.*

O'Faolain, Sean, ed., Short Stories: A Study in Pleasure, *Prentice-Hall, 1962.*

Olander, Joseph D., and Greenberg, Martin Harry, eds., Arthur C. Clarke, *Taplinger, 1977.*

Perloff, Marjorie, Frank O'Hara: Poet among Painters, *Braziller, 1977.*

Picon, Gaëtan, Contemporary French Literature: 1945 and After, *Ungar, 1974.*

Pinchin, Jane Lagoudis, Alexandria Still: Forster, Durrell, and Cavafy, *Princeton University Press, 1977.*

Pronko, Leonard Cabell, The World of Jean Anouilh, *University of California Press, 1961.*

Rees, Samuel, David Jones, *Twayne, 1978.*

Riddel, Joseph N., The Inverted Bell: Modernism and the Counterpoetics of William Carlos Williams, *Louisiana State University Press, 1974.*

Riley, Dick, ed., Critical Encounters: Writers and Themes in Science Fiction, *Ungar, 1978.*

Rosenthal, M. L., Randall Jarrell, *University of Minnesota Press, 1972.*

Rovit, Earl, ed., Saul Bellow: A Collection of Critical Essays, *Prentice-Hall, 1975.*

Sheps, G. David, ed., Mordecai Richler, *Ryerson Press, McGraw-Hill, 1971.*

Simon, John, Movies into Film: Film Criticism 1967-1970, *Dial, 1971.*

Simon, John, Uneasy Stages: A Chronicle of The New York Theater, 1963-1973, *Random House, 1976.*

Slusser, George Edgar, The Farthest Shores of Ursula LeGuin, *Borgo Press, 1976.*

Slusser, George Edgar, Harlan Ellison: Unrepentant Harlequin, *Borgo Press, 1977.*

Slusser, George Edgar, The Space Odysseys of Arthur C. Clarke, *Borgo Press, 1978.*

Stallman, Robert W., The Houses That James Built and Other Literary Studies, *Ohio University Press, 1961.*

Stanford, Donald E., ed., Nine Essays in Modern Literature, *Louisiana State University Press, 1965.*

Stoltzfus, Ben, Gide and Hemingway: Rebels against God, *Kennikat, 1978.*

Strandberg, Victor, The Poetic Vision of Robert Penn Warren, *University Press of Kentucky, 1977.*

Sturrock, John, Paper Tigers: The Ideal Fictions of Jorge Luis Borges, *Oxford University Press, 1977.*

Tedlock, E. W., Jr., and Wicker, C. V., eds., Steinbeck and His Critics: A Record of Twenty-five Years, *University of New Mexico Press, 1957.*

Thompson, Lawrence, Robert Frost, *University of Minnesota Press, 1959.*

Tomlinson, Charles, ed., Marianne Moore: A Collection of Critical Essays, *Prentice-Hall, 1970.*

Vázquez Amaral, José, The Contemporary Latin American Narrative, *Las Americas Publishing, 1970.*

Wagner, Linda W., ed., Robert Frost: The Critical Reception, *Burt Franklin & Co., 1977.*

Warren, Robert Penn, Selected Essays, *Random House, 1958.*

Weaver, Mike, William Carlos Williams: The American Background, *Cambridge University Press, 1971.*

Weeks, Robert P., ed., Hemingway: A Collection of Critical Essays, *Prentice-Hall, 1962.*

West, Paul, The Modern Novel, Volume 2: The United States and Other Countries, *Hutchinson, 1965.*

Wilson, Edmund, Classics and Commercials: A Literary Chronicle of the Forties, *Noonday Press, 1950.*

Wilson, Edmund, The Shores of Light: A Literary Chronicle of the Twenties and Thirties, *Farrar, Straus, 1952.*

Worth, Katharine J., Revolutions in Modern English Drama, *Bell & Hyman, 1973.*

Young, Philip, Ernest Hemingway, *University of Minnesota Press, 1964.*

Young, Thomas Daniel, and Inge, M. Thomas, Donald Davidson, *Twayne, 1971.*

Zabel, Morton Dauwen, Craft and Character: Texts, Method, and Vocation in Modern Fiction, *Viking Penguin, 1957.*

Cumulative Index to Critics

Aaron, Jules
Jack Heifner **11**:264

Abbey, Edward
Robert M. Pirsig **6**:421

Abbott, John Lawrence
Isaac Bashevis Singer **9**:487
Sylvia Townsend Warner **7**:512

Abeel, Erica
Pamela Hansford Johnson
7:185

Abel, Lionel
Samuel Beckett **2**:45
Jack Gelber **6**:196
Jean Genet **2**:157

Abernethy, Peter L.
Thomas Pynchon **3**:410

Ableman, Paul
Mary Gordon **13**:250
Mervyn Jones **10**:295

Abrahams, William
Elizabeth Bowen **6**:95
Hortense Calisher **2**:97
Herbert Gold **4**:193
Joyce Carol Oates **2**:315
Harold Pinter **9**:418
V. S. Pritchett **5**:352

Abramson, Doris E.
Alice Childress **12**:105

Abramson, Jane
Peter Dickinson **12**:172
Christie Harris **12**:268
Rosemary Wells **12**:638

Ackroyd, Peter
Brian Aldiss **5**:16
Martin Amis **4**:19
Miguel Ángel Asturias **8**:27

Louis Auchincloss **6**:15
W. H. Auden **9**:56
Beryl Bainbridge **8**:36
James Baldwin **5**:43
John Barth **5**:51
Donald Barthelme **3**:44
Samuel Beckett **4**:52
John Berryman **3**:72
Richard Brautigan **5**:72
Charles Bukowski **5**:80
Anthony Burgess **5**:87
William S. Burroughs **5**:92
Italo Calvino **5**:100; **8**:132
Richard Condon **6**:115
Roald Dahl **6**:122
Ed Dorn **10**:155
Margaret Drabble **8**:183
Douglas Dunn **6**:148
Bruce Jay Friedman **5**:127
John Gardner **7**:116
Günter Grass **4**:207
MacDonald Harris **9**:261
Joseph Heller **5**:179
Mark Helprin **10**:261
Russell C. Hoban **7**:160
Elizabeth Jane Howard **7**:164
B. S. Johnson **6**:264
Pamela Hansford Johnson
7:184
G. Josipovici **6**:270
Thomas Keneally **10**:298
Jack Kerouac **5**:215
Francis King **8**:321
Jerzy Kosinski **10**:308
Doris Lessing **6**:300
Alison Lurie **4**:305
Thomas McGuane **7**:212
Stanley Middleton **7**:220
Michael Moorcock **5**:294

Penelope Mortimer **5**:298
Iris Murdoch **4**:368
Vladimir Nabokov **6**:358
V. S. Naipaul **7**:252
Joyce Carol Oates **6**:368
Tillie Olsen **13**:432
Grace Paley **6**:393
David Pownall **10**:418, 419
J. B. Priestley **9**:441
V. S. Pritchett **5**:352
Thomas Pynchon **3**:419
Peter Redgrove **6**:446
Judith Rossner **9**:458
May Sarton **4**:472
David Slavitt **5**:392
Wole Soyinka **5**:398
David Storey **4**:529
Paul Theroux **5**:428
Thomas Tryon **11**:548
John Updike **7**:488; **9**:540
Gore Vidal **8**:525
Harriet Waugh **6**:559
Jerome Weidman **7**:518
Arnold Wesker **5**:483
Patrick White **4**:587

Adamowski, T. H.
Simone de Beauvoir **4**:47

Adams, Alice
Lisa Alther **7**:14

Adams, James Truslow
Esther Forbes **12**:206

Adams, Laura
Norman Mailer **11**:340

Adams, Leonie
John Crowe Ransom **4**:428

Adams, M. Ian
Juan Carlos Onetti **10**:376

Adams, Percy
James Dickey **7**:81

Adams, Phoebe-Lou
Beryl Bainbridge **5**:40
Robert Cormier **12**:133
Dashiell Hammett **5**:161
James Herriot **12**:282
Jamake Highwater **12**:285
Bohumil Hrabal **13**:290
David Jones **7**:189
Jerzy Kosinski **6**:285
Harper Lee **12**:341
Yukio Mishima **9**:385
Berry Morgan **6**:340
Joyce Carol Oates **6**:374
Tillie Olsen **13**:433
Reynolds Price **6**:426
João Ubaldo Ribeiro **10**:436
Khushwant Singh **11**:504
Christina Stead **8**:500

Adams, Robert M.
Adolfo Bioy Casares **13**:87
Edward Dahlberg **7**:63
Peter Matthiessen **11**:361
Robert M. Pirsig **4**:404
Severo Sarduy **6**:485

Adams, Robert Martin
John Barth **10**:24
Jorge Luis Borges **10**:66
Richard Brautigan **12**:61
Anthony Burgess **10**:90
Lawrence Durrell **13**:185
T. S. Eliot **10**:171
William Faulkner **11**:201
Carlo Emilio Gadda **11**:215
William H. Gass **2**:154
José Lezama Lima **10**:321
Vladimir Nabokov **11**:393

Flann O'Brien 10:363
Thomas Pynchon 11:453
Alain Robbe-Grillet 10:437
J.R.R. Tolkien 12:586
Angus Wilson 2:472

Adams, Robin
Frank Herbert 12:279

Adams, S. J.
Ezra Pound 13:453

Adcock, Fleur
John Berryman 13:83
Robert Lowell 11:331
Peter Porter 13:453

Adelman, Clifford
John Berryman 3:71

Adler, Dick
Ross Macdonald 1:185

Adler, Renata
Mel Brooks 12:75

Adler, Thomas P.
Edward Albee 11:13

Agar, John
Jonathan Baumbach 6:32
Laurie Colwin 5:107

Agena, Kathleen
Charles Wright 13:613

Aggeler, Geoffrey
Anthony Burgess 2:86; 5:85
13:123

Agius, Ambrose, O.S.B.
Edward Dahlberg 7:64

Ahearn, Kerry
Wallace Stegner 9:509

Ahrold, Robbin
Kurt Vonnegut, Jr. 3:501

Aiken, Conrad
William Faulkner 8:206
St.-John Perse 11:433

Aiken, David
Flannery O'Connor 10:365

Aiken, William
David Kherdian 6:281

Alazraki, Jaime
Pablo Neruda 2:309; 7:261

Albertson, Chris
Stevie Wonder 12:662

Alderson, Brian W.
Leon Garfield 12:226
William Mayne 12:395, 401

Alderson, S. William
Andre Norton 12:464, 466, 470

Alderson, Sue Ann
Muriel Rukeyser 10:442

Alderson, Valerie
E. M. Almedingen 12:6

Aldiss, Brian
J. G. Ballard 3:33
Frank Herbert 12:272

Aldridge, John W.
James Baldwin 4:42
Donald Barthelme 2:39
Saul Bellow 2:49, 50
Louis-Ferdinand Céline 7:47
John Cheever 3:105
John Dos Passos 4:131

James T. Farrell 4:157
William Faulkner 3:150
William Gaddis 3:177; 6:193
Joseph Heller 5:177
Ernest Hemingway 3:231, 233
James Jones 3:261
Jerzy Kosinski 2:231
Alison Lurie 5:260
Norman Mailer 1:193; 2:258
Mary McCarthy 3:327, 328
Wright Morris 3:342
John O'Hara 2:323
Katherine Anne Porter 3:392
Philip Roth 4:459
Alan Sillitoe 3:447
William Styron 3:472
John Updike 2:439
Robert Penn Warren 1:356
Eudora Welty 2:461
Colin Wilson 3:536
Edmund Wilson 2:474
P. G. Wodehouse 2:478

Aldridge, Judith
Ruth M. Arthur 12:27

Alegria, Fernando
Jorge Luis Borges 2:71

Aletti, Vince
Stevie Wonder 12:656, 660

Alexander, Edward
Isaac Bashevis Singer 11:503

Alexander, John R.
Robinson Jeffers 2:215

Alexander, Michael
Donald Davie 5:113
Ezra Pound 7:336

Alexander, William
Carl Sandburg 4:463

Alexandrova, Vera
Mikhail Sholokhov 7:420

Algren, Nelson
Clancy Sigal 7:424

Ali, Tariq
Jules Archer 12:19

Allen, Bruce
Richard Adams 5:6
Julio Cortázar 5:110
Stanley Elkin 6:168
John Gardner 8:236
Mary Gordon 13:250
Thomas Keneally 5:212
Kenneth Koch 5:219
Peter Matthiessen 7:211
Iris Murdoch 6:347
Joyce Carol Oates 6:369
Manuel Puig 5:355
John Sayles 10:460
Isaac Bashevis Singer 6:509
Paul West 7:524
Patrick White 5:485

Allen, Carol J.
Susan Fromberg Schaeffer
11:491

Allen, Dick
Margaret Atwood 2:20
Wendell Berry 6:61
Hayden Carruth 7:40
Paul Goodman 2:169
Thom Gunn 6:221
Richard F. Hugo 6:245

Philip Levine 2:244
Lisel Mueller 13:400
George Oppen 7:281
Judith Johnson Sherwin 7:414

Allen, Gay Wilson
Carl Sandburg 10:447

Allen, Henry
Robert M. Pirsig 4:403

Allen, John Alexander
Daniel Hoffman 13:288

Allen, Merritt P.
Andre Norton 12:455

Allen, Tom S. C.
Mel Brooks 12:81

Allen, Walter
A. Alvarez 5:17
Kingsley Amis 1:5
Saul Bellow 1:30
Elizabeth Bowen 1:40
Paul Bowles 1:41
Truman Capote 1:55
Ivy Compton-Burnett 1:61
James Gould Cozzens 1:66
Edward Dahlberg 1:71
John Dos Passos 1:79; 8:181
Lawrence Durrell 1:85
James T. Farrell 1:98; 8:205
William Faulkner 1:101
E. M. Forster 1:104
John Fowles 4:170
William Golding 1:120
Henry Green 2:178
Graham Greene 1:132
L. P. Hartley 2:181
Ernest Hemingway 1:142
Richard Hughes 1:149
Aldous Huxley 1:150
Christopher Isherwood 1:155
Pamela Hansford Johnson
1:160
Doris Lessing 1:173
Richard Llewellyn 7:206
Bernard Malamud 1:197
John P. Marquand 2:271
Carson McCullers 1:208
Henry Miller 1:221
Wright Morris 1:231
Iris Murdoch 1:234
P. H. Newby 2:310
Flannery O'Connor 1:255
John O'Hara 1:260
William Plomer 4:406
Anthony Powell 1:277
Henry Roth 2:377; 11:487
J. D. Salinger 1:298
William Sansom 2:383
C. P. Snow 1:316
John Steinbeck 1:325
William Styron 1:330
Allen Tate 2:427
Robert Penn Warren 1:355
Evelyn Waugh 1:358
Glenway Wescott 13:592
Rebecca West 7:525
Angus Wilson 2:471

Allen, Ward
Donald Davidson 2:112

Allsop, Kenneth
J. P. Donleavy 6:139
Thomas Hinde 6:238

Alm, Richard S.
Betty Cavanna 12:99
Mary Stolz 12:548

Almansi, Guido
Mario Luzi 13:354

Alonso, J. M.
Rafael Alberti 7:11
Jorge Luis Borges 9:117

Alpert, Hollis
Vincent Canby 13:131
Daniel Fuchs 8:220
Budd Schulberg 7:402

Alter, Robert
S. Y. Agnon 4:11
Yehuda Amichai 9:23
John Barth 9:71
Donald Barthelme 8:49
Saul Bellow 3:48, 49
Jorge Luis Borges 2:76; 6:94
Leslie A. Fiedler 13:212
John Hollander 8:298
Jerzy Kosinski 2:232
Norman Mailer 3:312; 11:342
Bernard Malamud 3:320, 321
Claude Mauriac 9:366
Elsa Morante 8:402
Vladimir Nabokov 2:302; 8:414
Hugh Nissenson 4:380
Flann O'Brien 7:269
Manuel Puig 10:420
Thomas Pynchon 9:443
Raymond Queneau 10:429
Alain Robbe-Grillet 6:468
Earl Rovit 7:383
André Schwarz-Bart 4:480
Isaac Bashevis Singer 11:501
J.I.M. Stewart 7:465
John Updike 2:444
Kurt Vonnegut, Jr. 8:531
Elie Wiesel 3:526
Abraham B. Yehoshua 13:618

Alterman, Loraine
Jesse Jackson 12:291

Altieri, Charles
Robert Creeley 2:107

Altman, Billy
Brian Wilson 12:652

Alvarez, A.
John Berryman 2:58; 3:65
Albert Camus 4:89
E. M. Forster 1:109
Dashiell Hammett 3:218
Zbigniew Herbert 9:271
Miroslav Holub 4:233
Philip Larkin 3:275
Robert Lowell 3:300
Hugh MacDiarmid 4:309
Norman Mailer 3:312
Sylvia Plath 2:335; 3:388
Jean Rhys 4:445
Jean-Paul Sartre 4:475
Edith Sitwell 9:493
Aleksandr I. Solzhenitsyn 7:436
Patrick White 3:521
Elie Wiesel 3:527
Yvor Winters 4:589

Amacher, Richard E.
Edward Albee 1:5

Amado, Jorge
João Ubaldo Ribeiro 10:436

Ambrose, Stephen E.
Cornelius Ryan 7:385

Ambrosetti, Ronald
Eric Ambler 9:20

Ames, Evelyn
J. B. Priestley 5:351

Amis, Kingsley
Ray Bradbury 10:68
Arthur C. Clarke 13:155
Ivy Compton-Burnett 1:60
Leslie A. Fiedler 4:159
Philip Roth 1:293
Arnold Wesker 3:517

Amis, Martin
J. G. Ballard 6:27
Peter De Vries 7:77
Bruce Jay Friedman 5:127
Ernest J. Gaines 3:179
John Hawkes 7:141
Philip Larkin 13:337
Iris Murdoch 4:367
Vladimir Nabokov 8:412
Philip Roth 6:475
Fay Weldon 11:565

Amory, Cleveland
Rod McKuen 1:210

Anderson, David
Albert Camus 4:89,90
William Golding 3:197, 198
Jean-Paul Sartre 4:477

Anderson, David C.
L. E. Sissman 9:491

Anderson, Elliott
Vladimir Nabokov 3:354

Anderson, H. T.
Erich Segal 10:467

Anderson, Isaac
Agatha Christie 12:114
Joseph Krumgold 12:316

Anderson, Jack
Philip Levine 4:286
George MacBeth 2:252

Anderson, Jervis
James Baldwin 8:41

Anderson, Michael
Edward Bond 6:85
Tennessee Williams 11:577

Anderson, Patrick
Ward Just 4:266

Anderson, Quentin
Vladimir Nabokov 3:351

Anderson, Reed
Juan Goytisolo 10:244

André, Michael
Robert Creeley 2:107

Andrews, Peter
Michael Crichton 6:119
Arthur Hailey 5:157
Irving Stone 7:471

Andrews, Sheryl B.
Andre Norton 12:460

Angogo, R.
Chinua Achebe 11:2

Annan, Gabriele
Simone de Beauvoir 4:47
Heinrich Böll 9:111
Iris Murdoch 11:388

Annan, Noel
E. M. Forster 4:166

Ansorge, Peter
Trevor Griffiths 13:256
Sam Shepard 6:495

Appel, Alfred, Jr.
Vladimir Nabokov 1:240; 2:300

Apple, Max
John Gardner 10:222

Aptheker, Herbert
W.E.B. DuBois 13:180

Arbuthnot, May Hill
Frank Bonham 12:53
Julia W. Cunningham 12:164
Jesse Jackson 12:290
Joseph Krumgold 12:320, 321
Madeleine L'Engle 12:350
Emily Cheney Neville 12:452
Mary Stolz 12:553

Archer, Marguerite
Jean Anouilh 13:18

Arendt, Hannah
W. H. Auden 6:21

Arlen, Michael J.
Alex Haley 12:254

Armes, Roy
Alain Robbe-Grillet 4:449

Armstrong, William A.
Sean O'Casey 1:252; 9:407

Arnez, Nancy L.
Alex Haley 12:250

Aronowitz, Alfred G.
John Lennon and Paul
McCartney 12:364

Aronson, James
Donald Barthelme 1:18
Saul Bellow 1:33
James Dickey 1:73
John Fowles 1:109
John Knowles 1:169
John Updike 1:345
Eudora Welty 1:363

Arpin, Gary Q.
John Berryman 10:48

Arthos, John
E. E. Cummings 12:146

Arthur, George W.
Judy Blume 12:47

Asahina, Robert
Mel Brooks 12:80

Ascherson, Neal
György Konrád 10:304
Tadeusz Konwicki 8:327
Milan Kundera 4:278
Tadeusz Różewicz 9:465
Yevgeny Yevtushenko 1:382

Ashbery, John
A. R. Ammons 2:13
Elizabeth Bishop 9:89

Ashlin, John
William Mayne 12:390

Ashton, Dore
Octavio Paz 10:392

Ashton, Thomas L.
C. P. Snow 4:504

Asinof, Eliot
Pete Hamill 10:251

Aspler, Tony
William F. Buckley, Jr. 7:36
William Gaddis 8:226

Astrachan, Anthony
Vladimir Voinovich 10:509

Atchity, Kenneth John
Jorge Luis Borges 2:71
James Jones 3:261
Robert Penn Warren 4:581

Athanason, Arthur N.
Pavel Kohout 13:326

Atheling, William, Jr.
Isaac Asimov 3:17
Arthur C. Clarke 1:58
Harlan Ellison 1:93
Robert A. Heinlein 1:139; 3:227

Atherton, J. S.
Anaïs Nin 11:398

Atherton, Stan
Margaret Laurence 6:290

Atkins, John
L. P. Hartley 2:182

Atkinson, Brooks
Elmer Rice 7:361

Atkinson, Michael
Robert Bly 10:58

Atlas, Jacoba
Mel Brooks 12:78
Joni Mitchell 12:436

Atlas, James
Samuel Beckett 6:37
Marie-Claire Blais 6:82
J. V. Cunningham 3:122
Alan Dugan 6:144
Paul Goodman 4:198
Randall Jarrell 6:261
Galway Kinnell 5:217
W. S. Merwin 5:287
John O'Hara 6:386
Kenneth Rexroth 6:451
Laura Riding 7:375
Delmore Schwartz 4:478
L. E. Sissman 9:490
James Tate 2:431

Atwood, Margaret
Marie-Claire Blais 6:80
Susan B. Hill 4:227
Erica Jong 6:267
A. G. Mojtabai 5:293
Tillie Olsen 13:432
Sylvia Plath 11:451
James Reaney 13:472
Adrienne Rich 3:429; 11:478
Audrey Thomas 7:472

Auchincloss, Eve
R. K. Narayan 7:257

Auchincloss, Louis
Katherine Anne Porter 7:316

Aucouturier, Michel
Aleksandr I. Solzhenitsyn 7:432

Auden, W. H.
Joseph Brodsky 4:77
Loren Eiseley 7:90
Chester Kallman 2:221
J. R. R. Tolkien 1:336; 12:564
Andrei Voznesensky 1:349

Auster, Paul
John Ashbery 6:14
John Hollander 8:300
Laura Riding 7:375
Giuseppe Ungaretti 7:484

Avant, John Alfred
Eleanor Bergstein 4:55
Gail Godwin 5:142
Gayl Jones 6:266
José Lezama Lima 4:291
Carson McCullers 12:427
Joyce Carol Oates 6:371, 373
Tillie Olsen 4:386
Patrick White 5:486

Axelrod, George
Gore Vidal 4:556

Axelrod, Steven
Robert Lowell 2:249

Axelrod, Steven Gould
Saul Bellow 6:60

Axthelm, Peter M.
Saul Bellow 13:66
William Golding 10:232

Ayer, A. J.
Albert Camus 9:152

Ayling, Ronald
Sean O'Casey 11:409

Ayo, Nicholas
Edward Lewis Wallant 10:515

Ayre, John
Austin C. Clarke 8:143
Mavis Gallant 7:110
V. S. Naipaul 13:407
Mordecai Richler 5:378

B. D.
Sylvia Townsend Warner 7:511

Baar, Ron
Ezra Pound 1:276

Babbitt, Natalie
William Mayne 12:395
Katherine Paterson 12:403, 486

Babenko, Vickie A.
Yevgeny Yevtushenko 13:620

Backscheider, Nick
John Updike 5:452

Backscheider, Paula
John Updike 5:452

Bacon, Terry R.
Robert Creeley 11:137

Baer, Barbara L.
Harriette Arnow 7:16
Christina Stead 5:403

Bailey, Nancy I.
Roch Carrier 13:142

Bailey, O. L.
Eric Ambler 6:2
Dick Francis 2:142
George V. Higgins 4:223
Maj Sjöwall 7:501
Mickey Spillane 3:469
Per Wahlöö 7:501

Bailey, Paul
Gabriel García Márquez 3:180
Nadine Gordimer 10:239
Yasunari Kawabata 2:223
Brian Moore 3:341

CRITIC INDEX

Alberto Moravia **11**:384
James Purdy **2**:351
Philip Roth **3**:437
Muriel Spark **5**:400
David Storey **2**:426
Paul Theroux **11**:531
Gore Vidal **6**:550
Tennessee Williams **7**:544

Bailey, Peter
Nikki Giovanni **2**:165
Melvin Van Peebles **2**:447

Bair, Deirdre
Samuel Beckett **6**:43

Baird, James
Djuna Barnes **8**:49

Baker, A. T.
A. R. Ammons **5**:30

Baker, Carlos
Ernest Hemingway **6**:234

Baker, Donald W.
Edward Dahlberg **7**:63

Baker, Houston A., Jr.
James Baldwin **1**:16
Arna Bontemps **1**:37
Sterling Brown **1**:47
W. E. B. Du Bois **1**:80
Ralph Ellison **1**:95; **3**:145
Leon Forrest **4**:163
Langston Hughes **1**:149
LeRoi Jones **1**:163
Ann Petry **1**:266
Ishmael Reed **2**:369; **6**:449
Jean Toomer **1**:341
Richard Wright **1**:380

Baker, Howard
Caroline Gordon **6**:206
Katherine Anne Porter **1**:273

Baker, James R.
William Golding **3**:200

Baker, Nina Brown
Madeleine L'Engle **12**:344

Baker, Roger
Beryl Bainbridge **4**:39
John Buell **10**:81
Paula Fox **8**:217
Janet Frame **3**:164
John Hawkes **1**:139
Jerzy Kosinski **1**:172
Alistair MacLean **13**:359
Larry McMurtry **3**:333
Harold Robbins **5**:378
Herman Wouk **9**:580
Rudolph Wurlitzer **2**:483
Helen Yglesias **7**:558

Baker, William
William Carlos Williams **13**:606

Balakian, Anna
André Breton **9**:132
René Char **9**:164

Baldanza, Frank
Alberto Moravia **2**:293
Iris Murdoch **1**:235
James Purdy **2**:350; **4**:424;
10:421

Baldeshwiler, Eileen
Flannery O'Connor **1**:255

Balducci, Carolyn
M. E. Kerr **12**:297

Baldwin, James
Alex Haley **8**:259
Norman Mailer **8**:364

Bales, Kent
Richard Brautigan **5**:71

Ballard, J. G.
Philip K. Dick **10**:138
Harlan Ellison **13**:203
Robert Silverberg **7**:425

Balliett, Whitney
Richard Condon **4**:105
Clancy Sigal **7**:424

Ballif, Gene
Jorge Luis Borges **6**:87
Vladimir Nabokov **6**:351
Sylvia Plath **11**:449
Alain Robbe-Grillet **6**:464
Nathalie Sarraute **8**:469

Ballstadt, Carl
Earle Birney **6**:78

Bambara, Toni Cade
Gwendolyn Brooks **2**:81

Bander, Edward J.
Jules Archer **12**:16

Bandler, Michael J.
Elie Wiesel **11**:570

Bangs, Lester
John Lennon and Paul
McCartney **12**:381
Joni Mitchell **12**:437
Jimmy Page and Robert Plant
12:474, 476

Banks, Joyce
Ruth M. Arthur **12**:28

Banks, R. Jeff
Mickey Spillane **13**:527

Banning, Charles Leslie
William Gaddis **10**:210

Barber, Michael
Gore Vidal **4**:557

Barber, Raymond W.
Jean Lee Latham **12**:324

Barbera, Jack Vincent
John Berryman **8**:88

Barbour, Douglas
Louis Dudek **11**:160
Gwendolyn MacEwan **13**:358
Rudy Wiebe **6**:566

Barclay, Pat
Robertson Davies **7**:72

Bargad, Warren
Amos Oz **8**:436
Abraham B. Yehoshua **13**:617

Bargainnier, E. F.
Agatha Christie **12**:126

Barge, Laura
Samuel Beckett **10**:34; **11**:39

Barghoorn, Frederick C.
Aleksandr I. Solzhenitsyn **4**:508

Barker, A. L.
Edna O'Brien **5**:311

Barker, Frank Granville
Margaret Drabble **10**:163
J. B. Priestley **9**:442

Barker, George
Brian Aldiss **5**:14

Barksdale, Richard K.
Gwendolyn Brooks **5**:75

Barnes, Clive
John Bishop **10**:54
Alice Childress **12**:104, 105
Lawrence Ferlinghetti **2**:134
Simon Gray **9**:240
Jack Heifner **11**:264
Arthur Kopit **1**:170
Tom Stoppard **1**:328
Elizabeth Swados **12**:556
Michael Weller **10**:525
Lanford Wilson **7**:547

Barnes, Harper
James Tate **2**:431

Barnes, Julian
Richard Brautigan **5**:72; **9**:124
Vincent Canby **13**:131
Agatha Christie **12**:120
James Clavell **6**:114
Len Deighton **7**:76
B. S. Johnson **6**:264
Pamela Hansford Johnson
7:184
G. Josipovici **6**:270
Richard Llewellyn **7**:207
Alistair MacLean **13**:359
Vladimir Nabokov **6**:359
Joyce Carol Oates **9**:402
Richard Price **12**:490

Barnes, Regina
James T. Farrell **4**:158
Geoffrey Household **11**:277

Barnouw, Dagmar
Doris Lessing **6**:295

Barnstone, William
Jorge Luis Borges **6**:93

Barnstone, Willis
Jorge Luis Borges **9**:120

Baro, Gene
Auberon Waugh **7**:512

Barolini, Helen
Lucio Piccolo **13**:441

Baron, Alexander
Bernard Malamud **2**:268

Barrenechea, Ana María
Jorge Luis Borges **1**:38

Barrett, Gerald
Jerzy Kosinski **10**:305

Barrett, William
Samuel Beckett **2**:48
Albert Camus **2**:99
Arthur C. Clarke **4**:105
William Faulkner **3**:154
Ernest Hemingway **3**:238
Hermann Hesse **2**:191
Alain Robbe-Grillet **2**:377
Leon Uris **7**:491

Barrow, Craig Wallace
Madeleine L'Engle **12**:351

Barrow, Geoffrey R.
Blas de Otero **11**:425

Barry, John Brooks
T. S. Eliot **6**:165

Barry, Kevin
John Berryman **6**:65

Barthes, Roland
Raymond Queneau **5**:357

Bartholomay, Julia A.
Howard Nemerov **6**:360

Bartholomew, David
Larry McMurtry **11**:371

Barzun, Jacques
Lionel Trilling **11**:539

Bassoff, Bruce
William H. Gass **8**:244

Batchelor, John Calvin
Mark Helprin **10**:262

Batchelor, R.
Ardré Malraux **9**:353

Bates, Evaline
Ezra Pound **3**:397

Bates, Graham
Pär Lagerkvist **7**:198

Bates, Lewis
E. M. Almedingen **12**:2

Bateson, F. W.
W. H. Auden **6**:24
John Gardner **2**:151

Bauer, William
John Buell **10**:82

Bauke, J. P.
Jakov Lind **4**:292

Baumann, Michael L.
B. Traven **8**:520; **11**:535, 537

Baumbach, Jonathan
Truman Capote **8**:132
Ralph Ellison **1**:95
John Hawkes **4**:212
Norman Mailer **4**:318
Bernard Malamud **1**:197, 199
Mary McCarthy **5**:275
Wright Morris **1**:232
Flannery O'Connor **1**:256
Grace Paley **6**:393
J. D. Salinger **1**:299
William Styron **1**:330
Peter Taylor **1**:333
Edward Lewis Wallant **10**:511
Robert Penn Warren **1**:355

Bayley, John
Anna Akhmatova **11**:9
W. H. Auden **2**:27, 28
Anthony Burgess **4**:85
D. J. Enright **8**:203
Robert Lowell **4**:296
Amos Oz **11**:428
Anthony Powell **10**:417
Aleksandr I. Solzhenitsyn
4:511; **7**:444; **10**:479

Bazarov, Konstantin
Ivo Andrić **8**:20
Heinrich Böll **3**:76
James A. Michener **1**:214
Aleksandr I. Solzhenitsyn
2:411; **10**:483

Beacham, Walton
Erskine Caldwell **8**:124

Beagle, Peter S.
J.R.R. Tolkien **12**:567

Beards, Virginia K.
Margaret Drabble **3**:128

CRITIC INDEX

Beatie, Bruce A.
J. R. R. Tolkien 3:477

Beatty, Jerome, Jr.
Larry Kettelkamp 12:305

Beatty, Richmond C.
Donald Davidson 13:166

Beauchamp, Gorman
E. M. Forster 10:183

Beauchamp, William
Elizabeth Taylor 4:541

Beaufort, John
Elizabeth Swados 12:560

Beaver, Harold
Allen Ginsburg 13:241
Joyce Carol Oates 11:404

Bechtel, Louise S.
Margot Benary-Isbert 12:31, 32
Mary Stolz 12:546
John R. Tunis 12:596
Lenora Mattingly Weber 12:632

Beck, Marilyn
Rod McKuen 1:210

Beck, Warren
William Faulkner 11:197

Becker, Lucille
Michel Butor 11:80
Georges Simenon 2:398, 399;
8:488

Becker, Lucille F.
Louis Aragon 3:14

Becker, May Lamberton
Betty Cavanna 12:97, 98
Esther Forbes 12:207
Jesse Jackson 12:289
John R. Tunis 12:594, 595
Leonora Mattingly Weber
12:631, 632

Beckett, Samuel
Sean O'Casey 11:405

Bedient, Calvin
A. R. Ammons 8:13
W. H. Auden 2:27
Samuel Beckett 1:24
Leonard Cohen 3:110
Edward Dahlberg 7:67
Donald Davie 10:120
Richard Eberhart 11:178
T. S. Eliot 13:196
Louise Glück 7:119
John Hawkes 4:215
Joseph Heller 5:178
Geoffrey Hill 5:184
Daniel Hoffman 6:243
Ted Hughes 2:202; 4:235
David Ignatow 7:182
Thomas Kinsella 4:271
Philip Larkin 5:228
Robert Lowell 3:303
George MacBeth 5:264
James Merrill 8:381
Joyce Carol Oates 2:314; 3:362
Octavio Paz 4:398
Jon Silkin 6:498
R. S. Thomas 6:532
Charles Tomlinson 4:545, 547
Mona Van Duyn 7:499
Robert Penn Warren 10:523
Richard Wilbur 9:568
James Wright 5:520

Beer, Patricia
W. H. Auden 6:19
Eleanor Hibbert 7:156
Lisel Mueller 13:400
Alice Munro 10:357
Peter Redgrove 6:447

Beesley, Paddy
Horst Bienek 11:48

Begley, John
Oriana Fallaci 11:191

Behar, Jack
T. S. Eliot 13:198

Beichman, Arnold
Arthur Koestler 1:170
Anthony Powell 3:400

Beja, Morris
Lawrence Durrell 4:145
William Faulkner 3:153
Nathalie Sarraute 4:466

Belgion, Montgomery
André Malraux 4:334

Belitt, Ben
Jorge Luis Borges 2:75
Robert Lowell 4:297
Pablo Neruda 1:247

Belkind, Allen
Ishmael Reed 13:480

Bell, Bernard
William Styron 3:473

Bell, Bernard W.
Jean Toomer 4:550

Bell, Gene H.
Jorge Luis Borges 9:118
Alejo Carpentier 8:135
Vladimir Nabokov 6:360

Bell, Ian F. A.
Ezra Pound 10:404

Bell, Millicent
Margaret Atwood 2:19
Peter De Vries 2:113
Eugenio Montale 7:231
John O'Hara 2:325

Bell, Pearl K.
Martin Amis 4:20
John Ashbery 6:12
Beryl Bainbridge 4:39
James Baldwin 4:40
Saul Bellow 8:70
Marie-Claire Blais 6:81
Louise Bogan 4:69
William F. Buckley, Jr. 7:35
Eleanor Clark 5:106
Arthur A. Cohen 7:51
Len Deighton 7:76
William Faulkner 6:177
Paula Fox 2:140
Nadine Gordimer 5:146
Juan Goytisolo 5:149
Günter Grass 4:206
Graham Greene 3:214
Joseph Heller 5:180
George V. Higgins 7:157
Maureen Howard 5:189
John Irving 13:293
Ruth Prawer Jhabvala 8:311
Charles Johnson 7:183
Diane Johnson 5:199
Uwe Johnson 10:284
James Jones; 10:291

Milan Kundera 4:277
Philip Larkin 13:337
John Le Carré 5:232
Alison Lurie 4:307
Peter Matthiessen 5:275
John McGahern 5:281
A. G. Mojtabai 9:385
V. S. Naipaul 7:254
Amos Oz 5:335
Cynthia Ozick 7:288
Walker Percy 8:438
Anthony Powell 3:403
J. F. Powers 8:447
Ishmael Reed 6:448
Adrienne Rich 6:459
Jill Robinson 10:439
Anne Sexton 6:494
Alix Kates Shulman 10:475
Stephen Spender 5:402
Mario Vargas Llosa 6:546
Patrick White 3:523

Bell, Robert
Robert Cormier 12:137
Madeleine L'Engle 12:350
William Mayne 12:390, 399

Bell, Vereen M.
E. M. Forster 1:107
Ted Hughes 9:281

Bellamy, Joe David
Donald Barthelme 13:60
Sam Shepard 4:490
Kurt Vonnegut, Jr. 4:564

Bellman, Samuel Irving
Saul Bellow 8:81
Jorge Luis Borges 6:91
Jerome Charyn 5:103
Leonard Cohen 3:109
Stanley Elkin 6:169
William Faulkner 3:152
Leslie A. Fiedler 4:160, 161
Bruce Jay Friedman 3:165
Ernest Hemingway 3:234
Jack Kerouac 3:263, 264
Meyer Levin 7:205
Bernard Malamud 1:197; 3:320,
325
Saul Maloff 5:271
Wallace Markfield 8:380
James A. Michener 5:288
Harry Mark Petrakis 3:382
Philip Roth 3:435
John Updike 3:487
Elie Wiesel 5:490

Bellow, Saul
Camilo José Cela 13:144

Beloff, Max
Paul Scott 9:477

Beloof, Robert
Stanley J. Kunitz 6:285
Marianne Moore 4:360

Bender, Marylin
Alix Kates Shulman 2:395

Bender, Rose S.
Babbis Friis-Baastad 12:214

Bendow, Burton
Grace Paley 4:393

Benedikt, Michael
Galway Kinnell 2:230
Richard Wilbur 3:532

Benestad, Janet P.
M. E. Kerr 12:300

Benét, William Rose
Agatha Christie 12:111

Benham, G. F.
Friedrich Dürrenmatt 11:174

Benjamin, Cynthia
Madeleine L'Engle 12:351

Bennett, Joseph
Anthony Hecht 8:266

Bennett, Spencer C.
John Lennon and Paul
McCartney 12:365

Benson, Gerard
Leon Garfield 12:229

Benson, Jackson J.
Ernest Hemingway 6:232
John Steinbeck 9:517

Benstock, Bernard
William Gaddis 3:177
Flann O'Brien 7:270
Sean O'Casey 5:317

Benston, Alice N.
W. S. Merwin 2:276

Bentley, Allen
Morris L. West 6:564

Bentley, Eric
Robert Penn Warren 8:536
Herman Wouk 9:579

Bentley, Joseph
Aldous Huxley 1:152

Bentley, Phyllis
Pearl S. Buck 11:69

Berets, Ralph
John Fowles 3:163

Berger, Arthur Asa
Charles M. Schulz 12:529

Berger, Charles
Olga Broumas 10:77

Berger, Harold L.
Frank Herbert 12:278

Bergin, Thomas G.
Aldo Palazzeschi 11:432
Lucio Piccolo 13:440
Salvatore Quasimodo 10:429

Bergman, Andrew
Isaac Bashevis Singer 11:499

Bergman, Andrew C. J.
Peter Benchley 4:53
Guy Davenport, Jr. 6:124

Bergmann, Linda S.
Ronald Sukenick 4:531

Bergmann, Linda Shell
Ishmael Reed 13:479

Bergonzi, Bernard
Kingsley Amis 2:6, 9
W. H. Auden 6:22
John Barth 3:39
Paul Bowles 2:79
Anthony Burgess 2:85
Donald Davie 10:123
Nigel Dennis 8:173
Richard Fariña 9:195
John Fowles 2:138
Paula Fox 2:139
B. S. Johnson 6:262

CRITIC INDEX

Doris Lessing **3**:283
Iris Murdoch **2**:297
Flann O'Brien **4**:383
Anthony Powell **3**:400
Thomas Pynchon **3**:408
Alain Robbe-Grillet **4**:447
Andrew Sinclair **2**:401
C. P. Snow **4**:501; **13**:508
Evelyn Waugh **1**:357; **3**:510
Angus Wilson **2**:473

Berkson, Bill
Frank O'Hara **2**:320
Jerome Rothenberg **6**:477

Berkvist, Margaret
Babbis Friis-Baastad **12**:213

Berkvist, Robert
Earl Hamner, Jr. **12**:258
Andre Norton **12**:456, 457
Mary Rodgers **12**:493

Berlin, Isaiah
Aldous Huxley **3**:254

Berman, Paul
Isaac Bashevis Singer **11**:501

Berman, Susan K.
Fredrica Wagman **7**:500

Bermel, Albert
Ed Bullins **1**:47
Jean Genet **10**:227
Christopher Hampton **4**:211

Bernays, Anne
Alice Adams **6**:1
Adrienne Rich **11**:474

Berner, Robert L.
Alan Paton **10**:388

Bernetta (Quinn), Sister Mary, O.S.F.
Allen Tate **4**:539

Bernikow, Louise
Muriel Rukeyser **6**:479

Berns, Walter
Daniel J. Berrigan **4**:57

Bernstein, Burton
George P. Elliott **2**:131

Berrigan, Daniel
Horst Bienek **7**:28
Thomas Merton **11**:373

Berry, Wendell
Hayden Carruth **4**:94

Berryman, John
Saul Bellow **10**:37
T. S. Eliot **13**:197
Ernest Hemingway **10**:270
Randall Jarrell **13**:299
Ezra Pound **13**:460

Bersani, Leo
Julio Cortázar **2**:104
Jean Genet **2**:158
Norman Mailer **8**:364
Alain Robbe-Grillet **1**:288
Robert Wilson **7**:551

Berthoff, Warner
Alex Haley **12**:245
Norman Mailer **3**:313
Iris Murdoch **3**:345
Vladimir Nabokov **3**:352
Muriel Spark **3**:464
Edmund Wilson **2**:475; **3**:538

Bespaloff, Rachel
Albert Camus **9**:139

Bessai, Diane
Austin C. Clarke **8**:142

Besser, Gretchen R.
Julien Green **3**:205

Bessie, Alvah
Norman Mailer **3**:319

Bester, Alfred
Isaac Asimov **3**:16
Robert A. Heinlein **3**:227

Bester, John
Kenzaburo Oe **10**:372

Bethell, Nicholas
Aleksandr I. Solzhenitsyn **7**:441

Betsky, Celia
Max Apple **9**:32
Harriette Arnow **7**:15
Don DeLillo **10**:135
Doris Lessing **10**:315

Betsky, Celia B.
A. Alvarez **5**:19
Margaret Drabble **2**:119
John Hawkes **4**:217
Iris Murdoch **4**:370

Bevan, A. R.
Mordecai Richler **5**:377

Bevan, Jack
Arthur Gregor **9**:253

Bevington, Helen
Louis Simpson **4**:500

Bewley, Marius
A. R. Ammons **2**:11
John Berryman **2**:56
C. Day Lewis **6**:128
Thomas Kinsella **4**:270
Hugh MacDiarmid **2**:253
Sylvia Plath **2**:335
Herbert Read **4**:440
Charles Tomlinson **2**:436

Bezanker, Abraham
Saul Bellow **1**:32
Isaac Bashevis Singer **3**:454

Bianco, David
James Purdy **10**:426

Biasin, Gian-Paolo
Carlo Emilio Gadda **11**:211
Leonardo Sciascia **8**:473

Bick, Janice
Christie Harris **12**:269

Bickerton, Dorothy
Melvin Berger **12**:41

Bidart, Frank
Robert Lowell **9**:336

Bien, Peter
Yannis Ritsos **6**:462

Bienstock, Beverly Gray
John Barth **3**:41

Bier, Jesse
James Thurber **5**:434

Bierhaus, E. G., Jr.
John Osborne **11**:423

Bigger, Charles P.
Walker Percy **8**:440

Bigsby, C.W.E.
Edward Albee **9**:6, 9; **13**:4

Binns, Ronald
John Fowles **4**:171

Binyon, T. J.
Eric Ambler **9**:21
Peter Dickinson **12**:175, 176

Birbalsingh, F. M.
Mordecai Richler **13**:485

Birmingham, Mary Louise
Jesse Jackson **12**:289

Birnbaum, Milton
Aldous Huxley **3**:255; **4**:239

Birstein, Ann
Iris Murdoch **4**:370

Bishop, Claire Huchet
Joseph Krumgold **12**:316

Bishop, Ferman
Allen Tate **2**:428

Bishop, John Peale
E. E. Cummings **12**:142

Bishop, Lloyd
Henri Michaux **8**:390

Bishop, Tom
Jean Cocteau **8**:145
Julio Cortázar **2**:103
Raymond Queneau **5**:359
Claude Simon **9**:482

Bissell, Claude T.
Hugh Garner **13**:234

Black, Campbell
Isaac Bashevis Singer **6**:507

Black, Cyril E.
André Malraux **1**:203

Blackburn, Sara
R. V. Cassill **4**:95
Peter Dickinson **12**:169
Rosalyn Drexler **2**:120
Jim Harrison **6**:225
Maxine Hong Kingston **12**:313
Alan Lelchuk **5**:244
David Madden **5**:266
Michael McClure **6**:316
Toni Morrison **4**:365
Marge Piercy **3**:384
Alix Kates Shulman **2**:395
Gillian Tindall **7**:473
David Wagoner **5**:474
Fay Weldon **6**:562

Blackburn, Tom
Kingsley Amis **2**:6

Blackmur, Richard P.
E. E. Cummings **8**:154; **12**:140
Marianne Moore **13**:393
John Crowe Ransom **5**:363
Allen Tate **4**:536

Blaha, Franz G.
J. P. Donleavy **4**:125

Blais, Marie-Claire
Elizabeth Bishop **13**:88

Blake, George
John Cowper Powys **9**:439

Blake, Nicholas
Agatha Christie **12**:113

Blake, Patricia
Aleksandr I. Solzhenitsyn **1**:319; **7**:439
Andrei Voznesensky **1**:349

Blake, Percival
Leonardo Sciascia **8**:474

Blake, Richard A.
Norman Lear **12**:331

Blakeston, Oswell
Michael Ayrton **7**:19
Gabriel García Márquez **3**:180
P. G. Wodehouse **2**:480

Blamires, David
David Jones **2**:216, 217; **4**:260; **13**:308

Blassingame, Wyatt
Harriette Arnow **7**:15

Blaydes, Sophia B.
Simon Gray **9**:242

Blazek, Douglas
Robert Creeley **2**:107
W. S. Merwin **5**:286
Diane Wakoski **4**:573

Bleikasten, André
Flannery O'Connor **10**:366

Blindheim, Joan Tindale
John Arden **13**:26

Blish, James
John Brunner **10**:77

Blishen, Edward
William Mayne **12**:391, 394

Bliven, Naomi
Louis-Ferdinand Céline **4**:103
Agatha Christie **12**:125
Andrea Giovene **7**:117
Eugène Ionesco **6**:257
Anthony Powell **7**:343

Bloch, Adèle
Michel Butor **8**:120
Pär Lagerkvist **7**:200

Blodgett, E. D.
D. G. Jones **10**:285
Sylvia Plath **3**:388

Blodgett, Harriet
V. S. Naipaul **4**:375

Blonski, Jan
Czeslaw Milosz **11**:377

Bloom, Harold
A. R. Ammons **5**:25; **8**:14; **9**:26
John Ashbery **4**:23; **9**:41; **13**:30
W. H. Auden **6**:16
Saul Bellow **6**:50
Jorge Luis Borges **6**:87
James Dickey **10**:141
Allen Ginsberg **6**:199
Anthony Hecht **13**:269
John Hollander **8**:301, 302
Philip Levine **9**:332
Robert Lowell **8**:355
Archibald MacLeish **8**:363
James Merrill **8**:388
Howard Moss **7**:249
Robert Pack **13**:439
W. D. Snodgrass **10**:478
Robert Penn Warren **8**:539
Charles Wright **13**:614

Bloom, Robert
W. H. Auden **1**:10; **11**:13

CRITIC INDEX

Blotner, Joseph L.
J. D. Salinger **1**:295

Blow, Simon
Sylvia Plath **11**:451
Isaac Bashevis Singer **6**:510

Bluefarb, Sam
Leslie A. Fiedler **13**:213
Bernard Malamud **1**:196; **9**:350
John Steinbeck **5**:407
Richard Wright **3**:546

Bluestein, Gene
Bob Dylan **12**:189
Richard Fariña **9**:195

Bluestone, George
Nelson Algren **10**:5

Blumenfeld, Yorick
Yevgeny Yevtushenko **1**:382

Blundell, Janet Boyarin
Maya Angelou **12**:14

Bly, Robert
A. R. Ammons **5**:28
Carlos Castaneda **12**:94
Robert Lowell **4**:297

Blythe, Ronald
Erica Jong **6**:267
Alice Munro **6**:341
Joyce Carol Oates **6**:368
David Storey **8**:506

Boak, Denis
André Malraux **4**:330

Boardman, Gwenn R.
Yasunari Kawabata **2**:222
Yukio Mishima **2**:286

Boatwright, James
Paul Horgan **9**:278
James McCourt **5**:278
Gore Vidal **6**:549
Robert Penn Warren **1**:356

Boatwright, John
Walker Percy **8**:438

Boatwright, Taliaferro
Emily Cheney Neville **12**:450

Bobbie, Walter
Stephen King **12**:309

Bodart, Joni
Frank Herbert **12**:272
Rosemary Wells **12**:638

Bode, Carl
Katherine Anne Porter **7**:318

Bodo, Maureen
Gore Vidal **10**:504

Boe, Eugene
Christina Stead **2**:421

Boeth, Richard
John O'Hara **2**:324

Bogan, Louise
W. H. Auden **1**:9
Marianne Moore **13**:396
W. R. Rodgers **7**:377

Bohner, Charles H.
Robert Penn Warren **1**:354

Bok, Sissela
Vladimir Nabokov **1**:245

Boland, John
Brian Aldiss **5**:15

John Dickson Carr 3:101
Richard Condon **4**:106
Harry Kemelman **2**:225
Michael Moorcock **5**:293

Bold, Alan
Robert Graves **1**:130

Bolger, Eugenie
Hortense Calisher **8**:125
José Donoso **4**:130

Bollard, Margaret Lloyd
William Carlos Williams **9**:571

Bolling, Douglass
E. M. Forster **9**:206
Doris Lessing **3**:290
Rudolph Wurlitzer **4**:598

Bolton, Richard R.
Herman Wouk **9**:580

Bondy, François
Günter Grass **2**:173

Bone, Robert A.
James Baldwin **1**:15
Arna Bontemps **1**:37
W. E. B. Du Bois **1**:80
Ralph Ellison **1**:95; **3**:142
Langston Hughes **1**:147
Zora Neale Hurston **7**:171
Ann Petry **1**:266
Jean Toomer **1**:341
Richard Wright **1**:378
Frank G. Yerby **1**:381

Bongiorno, Robert
Carlo Emilio Gadda **11**:209

Boni, John
Kurt Vonnegut, Jr. **5**:465

Boniol, John Dawson, Jr.
Melvin Berger **12**:40, 41

Bontemps, Arna
Jean Toomer **13**:551

Booth, Martin
John Matthias **9**:361

Booth, Philip
Richard Eberhart **11**:176
Randall Jarrell **1**:159
Maxine Kumin **13**:327
Louis Simpson **7**:426

Borges, Jorge Luis
Adolfo Bioy Casares **4**:63

Borinsky, Alicia
Manuel Puig **5**:355

Borkat, Robert F. Sarfatt
Robert Frost **9**:222

Boroff, David
John A. Williams **13**:598

Borroff, Marie
John Hollander **2**:197
Denise Levertov **2**:243
William Meredith **4**:348
James Merrill **2**:274

Bosley, Keith
Eugenio Montale **7**:229

Bosmajian, Hamida
Louis-Ferdinand Céline **3**:103

Boston, Howard
Jean Lee Latham **12**:323

Bosworth, David
Kurt Vonnegut, Jr. **12**:629

Boucher, Anthony
Agatha Christie **12**:115, 116, 117
John Creasey **11**:134
C. Day Lewis **6**:128
Patricia Highsmith **2**:193
Harry Kemelman **2**:225
Mary Stewart **7**:467
Julian Symons **2**:426

Bouise, Oscar A.
Eleanor Hibbert **7**:155
Per Wahlöö **7**:501

Boulby, Mark
Hermann Hesse **11**:272

Boulton, James T.
Harold Pinter **6**:406

Bouraoui, H. A.
Nathalie Sarraute **2**:385

Bourjaily, Vance
Philip Roth **9**:460

Bourne, Mike
Jimmy Page and Robert Plant **12**:476

Boutelle, Ann E.
Hugh MacDiarmid **2**:253

Boutrous, Lawrence K.
John Hawkes **3**:223

Bowe, Clotilde Soave
Natalia Ginzburg **11**:228

Bowen, Barbara C.
P. G. Wodehouse **10**:538

Bowen, John
Arthur Kopit **1**:171

Bowering, George
Margaret Atwood **2**:19
Margaret Avison **2**:29
Earle Birney **4**:64
D. G. Jones **10**:288
Margaret Laurence **3**:278
Gwendolyn MacEwan **13**:357
A. W. Purdy **6**:428
Mordecai Richler **5**:374
Audrey Thomas **7**:472; **13**:538

Bowering, Peter
Aldous Huxley **4**:237

Bowers, A. Joan
Gore Vidal **8**:526

Bowers, Marvin
L. E. Sissman **9**:491

Bowie, Malcolm
Yves Bonnefoy **9**:114

Bowles, Gloria
Diane Wakoski **7**:505

Bowles, Jerry G.
Craig Nova **7**:267

Bowra, C. M.
Rafael Alberti **7**:7

Boyce, Burke
Esther Forbes **12**:205

Boyd, Blanche M.
Renata Adler **8**:5

Boyd, John D.
Theodore Roethke **11**:483

Boyd, Robert
James Purdy **2**:350

Boyd, William
Penelope Gilliatt **13**:238

Boyers, Robert
Saul Bellow **3**:57
Alan Dugan **6**:143
Witold Gombrowicz **7**:125; **11**:241
Robinson Jeffers **2**:214; **3**:258
Arthur Koestler **6**:281
Robert Lowell **8**:349; **9**:336
Sylvia Plath **11**:447
Adrienne Rich **7**:364
Theodore Roethke **8**:457
W. D. Snodgrass **2**:406
Gary Snyder **2**:406
Richard Wilbur **6**:569

Boyle, Kay
James Baldwin **1**:15
Tom Wicker **7**:534

Boyle, Ted E.
Kingsley Amis **2**:6
Brendan Behan **1**:26

Boylston, Helen Dore
Betty Cavanna **12**:97

Bracher, Frederick
James Gould Cozzens **11**:127

Bradbrook, M. C.
T. S. Eliot **1**:91; **2**:130

Bradbury, Malcolm
Ivy Compton-Burnett **10**:109
John Dos Passos **8**:181
E. M. Forster **4**:167; **10**:180
John Fowles **3**:162; **4**:172
William Gaddis **8**:227
Thomas Hinde **6**:240
Aldous Huxley **4**:244
Iris Murdoch **4**:367; **11**:388
John O'Hara **11**:413
C. P. Snow **4**:505
Muriel Spark **2**:418
Lionel Trilling **9**:531
Evelyn Waugh **8**:543
Angus Wilson **5**:513

Bradford, M. E.
Donald Davidson **2**:111, 112; **13**:167
William Faulkner **1**:102; **3**:155
Allen Tate **2**:429

Bradford, Melvin E.
Walker Percy **3**:381

Bradford, Richard
M. E. Kerr **12**:300
James Kirkwood **9**:319

Bradford, Tom
Ray Bradbury **10**:69

Bradley, Sculley
Robert Frost **3**:169

Brady, Charles A.
David Kherdian **6**:281

Brady, Patrick
Albert Camus **9**:147

Bragg, Melvyn
Kingsley Amis **13**:14
E. M. Forster **2**:136

Bragg, Pamela
Frank Bonham **12**:52

Braine, John
  Richard Llewellyn 7:207
  Fay Weldon 9:559

Brandriff, Welles T.
  William Styron 11:514

Brandt, G. W.
  John Arden 13:23

Brater, Enoch
  Samuel Beckett 6:42; 9:81

Braudy, Leo
  John Berger 2:54
  Thomas Berger 3:63
  Richard Condon 4:107
  Norman Mailer 1:193; 8:368

Braun, Julie
  Philip Roth 4:453

Braybrooke, Neville
  Graham Greene 1:130
  François Mauriac 4:337

Brée, Germaine
  Louis Aragon 3:12
  Marcel Aymé 11:21
  Samuel Beckett 10:27
  Stanley Burnshaw 13:128
  Albert Camus 1:54; 11:93
  Louis-Ferdinand Céline 1:57
  Jean Cocteau 1:59
  Georges Duhamel 8:186
  Jean Giono 4:183
  Julien Green 3:203
  André Malraux 1:202
  François Mauriac 4:337
  Raymond Queneau 2:359
  Jules Romains 7:381
  Jean-Paul Sartre 1:306; 7:397

Breit, Harvey
  James Baldwin 2:31

Brendon, Piers
  Donald Barthelme 5:53
  Rosalyn Drexler 2:119
  Daphne du Maurier 6:146
  Robert Penn Warren 4:582

Breslin, James E.
  T. S. Eliot 6:166

Breslin, Jimmy
  Gore Vidal 8:525

Breslin, John B.
  C. S. Lewis 6:308
  Tom McHale 5:281
  Wilfrid Sheed 10:474
  Susan Sontag 13:516

Breslin, Patrick
  Miguel Ángel Asturias 8:28

Bresnick, Paul
  James Purdy 10:425

Brew, Claude C.
  Tommaso Landolfi 11:321

Brewster, Dorothy
  Doris Lessing 1:173

Brickell, Herschel
  Harriette Arnow 7:15

Bricker, Karin K.
  Mavis Thorpe Clark 12:131

Brickner, Richard P.
  Anthony Burgess 2:86
  Jerome Charyn 8:136
  Frederick Exley 11:186

Bridges, Les
  Mickey Spillane 3:469

Bridges, Linda
  Donald Barthelme 5:55
  Alistair MacLean 13:359
  Georges Simenon 8:487

Brien, Alan
  Kingsley Amis 2:6
  Alan Ayckbourn 8:34
  Trevor Griffiths 13:255
  John Osborne 5:333
  Harold Pinter 6:418
  Tennessee Williams 8:547

Brigg, Peter
  Arthur C. Clarke 13:148

Briggs, Julia
  Leon Garfield 12:234

Brignano, Russell Carl
  Richard Wright 4:594

Brinnin, John Malcolm
  John Ashbery 6:12
  Allen Ginsberg 6:201
  Galway Kinnell 1:168
  William Meredith 13:372
  Sylvia Plath 1:269
  William Jay Smith 6:512

Bristol, Horace
  Pearl S. Buck 7:33

Brivic, Sheldon
  Richard Wright 9:585

Brockway, James
  Beryl Bainbridge 10:16
  Angela Carter 5:102
  J. P. Donleavy 4:126
  Mavis Gallant 7:111
  Penelope Gilliatt 10:230
  Julien Green 3:205
  Susan B. Hill 4:228
  Piers Paul Read 10:435
  Muriel Spark 5:399; 8:495
  Emma Tennant 13:537

Broderick, Dorothy M.
  Jesse Jackson 12:655

Brodin, Dorothy
  Marcel Aymé 11:22

Brodsky, Arnold
  Stevie Wonder 12:655

Brodsky, Joseph
  Czeslaw Milosz 11:376
  Eugenio Montale 9:388

Brogan, Hugh
  Mervyn Peake 7:301

Brombert, Victor
  St.-John Perse 4:398

Bromwich, David
  Conrad Aiken 5:10
  A. R. Ammons 9:28
  Hayden Carruth 10:100
  Robert Frost 9:266
  John Hawkes 4:216

Frederick Forsyth 2:137
  Herbert Gold 7:120
  Cormac McCarthy 4:341
  Vladimir Nabokov 3:355
  Harry Mark Petrakis 3:383
  Muriel Spark 3:465
  Richard B. Wright 6:581

  John Hollander 5:187
  Richard Howard 7:167
  Doris Lessing 3:288
  Penelope Mortimer 5:299
  Iris Murdoch 3:348; 6:347
  Howard Nemerov 9:394
  Robert Pinsky 9:416
  Anne Sexton 10:467
  Charles Simic 9:479
  Stevie Smith 8:492
  Muriel Spark 3:465
  Paul Theroux 5:427
  Robert Penn Warren 13:572
  Elie Wiesel 3:528
  Charles Wright 13:615

Bronowski, J.
  Kathleen Raine 7:352

Brooke, Jocelyn
  Elizabeth Bowen 1:39

Brooke, Nicholas
  Anne Stevenson 7:462

Brooke-Rose, Christine
  Ezra Pound 7:328

Brooks, Anne
  Mary Stolz 12:548

Brooks, Cleanth
  Randall Jarrell 1:159
  Marianne Moore 10:347
  Walker Percy 6:399
  Allen Tate 4:539; 11:522

Brooks, Ellen W.
  Doris Lessing 3:284

Brooks, Peter
  Alain Robbe-Grillet 1:287

Brooks, Rick
  Andre Norton 12:467

Broome, Peter
  Robert Pinget 7:306

Brophy, Brigid
  Kingsley Amis 2:5
  Simone de Beauvoir 2:42
  Hortense Calisher 2:95
  Ivy Compton-Burnett 3:111
  William Faulkner 1:102
  Jean Genet 2:157
  Patricia Highsmith 2:192
  W. Somerset Maugham 1:204
  Henry Miller 2:281
  Françoise Sagan 3:443; 6:482
  Georges Simenon 2:397
  Elizabeth Taylor 2:432
  Evelyn Waugh 3:509

Brophy, James D.
  W. H. Auden 11:15

Brose, Margaret
  Giuseppe Ungaretti 11:558

Brosman, Catharine Savage
  Jean-Paul Sartre 13:503

Broughton, Panthea Reid
  William Faulkner 6:175
  Carson McCullers 4:345

Brown, Ashley
  Caroline Gordon 6:204, 206;
    13:241
  Allen Tate 2:428

Brown, Calvin S.
  Conrad Aiken 3:4

Brown, Clarence
  Czeslaw Milosz 5:292
  Vladimir Nabokov 1:242

Brown, F. J.
  Arthur Koestler 3:271
  Alberto Moravia 2:293
  Mario Puzo 1:282
  Muriel Spark 2:417

Brown, Frederick
  Louis Aragon 3:13
  Jean Cocteau 1:60

Brown, Geoff
  Brian Wilson 12:648

Brown, Harry
  Hollis Summers 10:494

Brown, Ivor
  J. B. Priestley 2:346

Brown, John Russell
  John Arden 6:8
  John Osborne 5:332
  Harold Pinter 6:408, 413
  Arnold Wesker 5:482

Brown, Lloyd W.
  Imamu Amiri Baraka 3:35
  Langston Hughes 10:281

Brown, Margaret Warren
  Jean Lee Latham 12:323

Brown, Merle E.
  Kenneth Burke 2:88

Brown, Ralph Adams
  Andre Norton 12:455
  John R. Tunis 12:595

Brown, Robert McAfee
  Elie Wiesel 5:493

Brown, Rosellen
  Margaret Atwood 8:28
  Tim O'Brien 7:272
  May Sarton 4:471
  Judith Johnson Sherwin 7:414
  Diane Wakoski 4:572

Brown, Russell M.
  Robert Kroetsch 5:221

Brown, Ruth Leslie
  John Gardner 2:151

Brown, T.
  Louis MacNeice 10:323

Brown, Terence
  Kingsley Amis 2:6

Brown, William P.
  John Brunner 10:78

Browne, Ray B.
  Irving Wallace 13:569

Browne, Robert M.
  J. D. Salinger 12:511

Browning, Preston M., Jr.
  Flannery O'Connor 3:367

Brownjohn, Alan
  Dannie Abse 7:1
  Donald Davie 5:115
  C. Day Lewis 6:128
  Geoffrey Grigson 7:136
  Seamus Heaney 7:148
  Thomas Kinsella 4:270
  Philip Larkin 5:226
  George MacBeth 9:340
  Anthony Powell 7:341

Louis Simpson 7:428
D. M. Thomas 13:541
Ted Walker 13:567

Brownjohn, Elizabeth
Philip Larkin 5:227

Broyard, Anatole
Saul Bellow 2:52
Peter Dickinson 12:176
José Donoso 8:179
Jules Feiffer 8:217
Penelope Gilliatt 10:229
Günter Grass 2:172
Jerzy Kosinski 10:307
Bernard Malamud 2:266
Edna O'Brien 13:415
Philip Roth 3:436
Françoise Sagan 9:468
Nathalie Sarraute 8:473
Mark Schorer 9:473
Georges Simenon 8:488
Anne Tyler 11:553
John Updike 2:440; 9:539

Bruccoli, Matthew J.
James Gould Cozzens 11:131
John O'Hara 3:370

Brudnoy, David
James Baldwin 2:33

Bruell, Edwin
Harper Lee 12:342

Brukenfeld, Dick
Joyce Carol Oates 3:364

Brumberg, Abraham
Aleksandr I. Solzhenitsyn 4:514

Brummell, O. B.
Bob Dylan 12:183

Brustein, Robert
Edward Albee 3:6, 7
Jean Anouilh 1:6
James Baldwin 4:40
Brendan Behan 1:26
Jack Gelber 1:114
Jean Genet 1:115
Joseph Heller 3:228
Rolf Hochhuth 4:230
William Inge 1:153
Eugène Ionesco 1:154
Arthur Miller 6:330
John Osborne 5:332
Harold Pinter 1:266; 3:385, 386
Ronald Ribman 7:357
Jean-Paul Sartre 4:476
Murray Schisgal 6:489
Peter Shaffer 5:386
Tom Stoppard 3:470
Ronald Tavel 6:529
Jean-Claude Van Itallie 3:492
Gore Vidal 4:552, 553
Peter Weiss 3:514
Arnold Wesker 5:482

Bryan, C. D. B.
Julio Cortázar 2:103
Craig Nova 7:267

Bryant, J. A., Jr.
Eudora Welty 1:361; 5:480

Bryant, Jerry H.
James Baldwin 8:41
John Barth 2:36
Saul Bellow 2:52
William S. Burroughs 2:91

Joseph Heller 3:228
James Jones 3:261
Norman Mailer 2:260
Bernard Malamud 2:266
Carson McCullers 4:344
Toni Morrison 4:366
Flannery O'Connor 2:317
Walker Percy 2:333
Thomas Pynchon 2:353
Ayn Rand 3:423
John Updike 2:441
Kurt Vonnegut, Jr. 2:452
John A. Williams 5:497

Bryant, Nelson
James Herriot 12:282

Bryant, Rene Kuhn
Thomas Berger 8:83
Heinrich Böll 6:84
John Fowles 6:187
Paula Fox 8:219
John Hersey 7:154
Doris Lessing 10:316
James A. Michener 5:291

Bryden, Ronald
Peter Barnes 5:49
Doris Lessing 6:299
Peter Nichols 5:306
David Storey 4:529
Paul West 7:525

Buchanan, Cynthia
Norman Mailer 2:263

Buchen, Irving H.
Carson McCullers 10:334

Buchsbaum, Betty
David Kherdian 6:280

Buck, Philo M., Jr.
Jules Romains 7:378

Buck, Richard M.
Andre Norton 12:457

Buckle, Richard
John Betjeman 2:60

Buckler, Robert
Elia Kazan 6:274

Buckley, Priscilla L.
Eric Ambler 6:4

Buckley, Tom
Irving Wallace 13:570

Buckley, Vincent
T. S. Eliot 3:138

Buckley, Virginia
Katherine Paterson 12:487

Buckley, William F., Jr.
William F. Buckley, Jr. 7:35
Aleksandr I. Solzhenitsyn 4:511
Garry Trudeau 12:590
Tom Wolfe 2:481

Bucknall, Barbara J.
Ursula K. LeGuin 13:349

Buechner, Frederick
Annie Dillard 9:178

Buell, Ellen Lewis
E. M. Almedingen 12:3
Margot Benary-Isbert 12:31
Betty Cavanna 12:97, 98
Esther Forbes 12:207
Joseph Krumgold 12:317
Jean Lee Latham 12:323

Madeleine L'Engle 12:345
William Mayne 12:389
Andre Norton 12:456
Mary Stolz 12:545, 546, 547,
548, 549, 550, 551, 552
John R. Tunis 12:593, 594, 595,
596
Lenora Mattingly Weber 12:631

Buell, Frederick
A. R. Ammons 8:17

Buffington, Robert
Donald Davidson 2:112
John Crowe Ransom 4:430, 437

Bufithis, Philip H.
Norman Mailer 11:342

Bufkin, E. C.
Iris Murdoch 2:297
P. H. Newby 2:310

Buitenhuis, Peter
Harry Mathews 6:314
William Trevor 7:475

Bullins, Ed
Alice Childress 12:106

Bulman, Learned T.
Jean Lee Latham 12:323, 325
Andre Norton 12:456

Bunnell, Sterling
Michael McClure 6:321

Bunting, Basil
Hugh MacDiarmid 4:313

Burbank, Rex
Thornton Wilder 1:364

Burgess, Anthony
Kingsley Amis 1:6; 2:8
James Baldwin 1:16
Samuel Beckett 1:23; 3:44
Saul Bellow 1:31
Elizabeth Bowen 1:40; 3:82
Bridgid Brophy 6:99
William S. Burroughs 1:48
Albert Camus 1:54
Louis-Ferdinand Céline 7:46
Agatha Christie 1:58
Ivy Compton-Burnett 1:62
Don DeLillo 13:178
Lawrence Durrell 1:87
T. S. Eliot 3:139
E. M. Forster 1:107
Carlos Fuentes 13:231
Jean Genet 1:115
Penelope Gilliatt 2:160
William Golding 1:121
Günter Grass 1:125; 11:251
Henry Green 2:178
Graham Greene 3:207
Joseph Heller 1:140
Ernest Hemingway 1:143; 3:234
Aldous Huxley 1:151
Christopher Isherwood 1:156
Pamela Hansford Johnson
1:160
Arthur Koestler 1:169; 3:270
John Le Carré 9:326
Colin MacInnes 4:314
Norman Mailer 1:190
Bernard Malamud 1:199; 3:322
Mary McCarthy 1:206
Henry Miller 1:224
Iris Murdoch 1:235

Vladimir Nabokov 1:244; 3:352
Flann O'Brien 1:252
Lucio Piccolo 13:440
Reynolds Price 13:464
J. B. Priestley 2:347
Alain Robbe-Grillet 1:288
J. D. Salinger 1:299
William Sansom 2:383
Alan Sillitoe 1:307
C. P. Snow 1:317
Muriel Spark 2:416
Paul Theroux 11:528
John Wain 2:458
Evelyn Waugh 1:359; 3:510
Angus Wilson 2:472
Edmund Wilson 3:538

Burgess, Charles E.
William Inge 8:308

Burhans, Clinton S., Jr.
Joseph Heller 3:230
Ernest Hemingway 8:283
Kurt Vonnegut, Jr. 8:530

Burke, Jeffrey
Richard Price 12:492

Burke, Kenneth
Theodore Roethke 11:479
Glenway Wescott 13:590

Burke, William M.
John A. Williams 5:497

Burkom, Selma R.
Doris Lessing 1:174

Burnett, Michael
James Thurber 5:440

Burns, Alan
Ann Quin 6:442
C. P. Snow 1:317

Burns, Gerald
W. H. Auden 4:33
John Berryman 6:62, 63
Austin Clarke 9:169
Seamus Heaney 7:147
Robert Lowell 5:256
Frank O'Hara 5:324
Charles Olson 5:328
Ezra Pound 5:348
Gary Snyder 5:393
William Stafford 4:520
Diane Wakoski 11:564

Burns, Martin
Kurt Vonnegut, Jr. 12:608

Burns, Mary M.
Alice Childress 12:107
Peter Dickinson 12:171
Jamake Highwater 12:287
M. E. Kerr 12:297, 298
Jean Lee Latham 12:325
Nicholasa Mohr 12:445
Andre Norton 12:471

Burns, Stuart L.
Jean Stafford 4:517

Burns, Wayne
Alex Comfort 7:52, 53

Burnshaw, Stanley
James Dickey 10:141

Burroughs, Franklin G.
William Faulkner 3:157

Burrow, J. W.
Aldous Huxley 3:254
J. R. R. Tolkien 3:482

CRITIC INDEX

CRITIC INDEX

Burroway, Janet
James Leo Herlihy 6:235
Mary Hocking 13:284

Burton, Dwight L.
Betty Cavanna 12:99

Busch, Frederick
J. G. Farrell 6:173
John Hawkes 7:140
Alice Munro 10:356
Paul West 7:523

Bush, Roland E.
Ishmael Reed 3:424

Butler, Michael
Heinrich Böll 11:58

Butler, William Vivian
John Creasey 11:135

Butscher, Edward
John Berryman 3:67
John Gardner 3:185
Jerzy Kosinski 6:282
James Wright 5:519
Rudolph Wurlitzer 4:598

Butt, John
Carlos Fuentes 10:208

Butwin, Joseph
Richard Brautigan 12:62

Byatt, A. S.
Diane Johnson 13:305
Amos Oz 11:429
C. P. Snow 13:514

Byers, Margaret
Elizabeth Jennings 5:197

Byers, Nancy
Jean Lee Latham 12:324

Byrd, Max
Jorge Luis Borges 6:93
Peter DeVries 10:136

Byrd, Scott
John Barth 1:17

Byrom, Thomas
Frank O'Hara 13:423

Cadogan, Mary
William Mayne 12:404

Cahill, Daniel J.
Jerzy Kosinski 2:232

Cain, Joan
Camilo José Cela 13:147

Calas, Nicholas
André Breton 9:125

Calder, Angus
T. S. Eliot 2:128

Caldwell, Joan
Margaret Laurence 13:344
Audrey Thomas 7:472

Caldwell, Stephen
D. Keith Mano 2:270

Calisher, Hortense
Yukio Mishima 2:289
Vladimir Nabokov 1:246
Christina Stead 5:403

Callahan, John
Michael S. Harper 7:138

Callahan, John F.
Alice Walker 5:476

Callahan, Patrick J.
C. S. Lewis 3:297
George MacBeth 2:251
Alan Sillitoe 1:308
Stephen Spender 2:420

Callan, Edward
W. H. Auden 1:9, 11
Alan Paton 4:395

Callan, Richard J.
José Donoso 11:147

Callendar, Newgate
Eric Ambler 4:18
Isaac Asimov 9:49
William Peter Blatty 2:64
Robert Cormier 12:136
John Creasey 11:135
Peter Dickinson 12:170, 171, 177
Evan Hunter 11:279, 280
James Jones 3:262
Harry Kemelman 2:225
Emma Lathen 2:236
Ellery Queen 11:458
Georges Simenon 2:399
Mickey Spillane 3:469
Vassilis Vassilikos 8:524
Donald E. Westlake 7:528, 529

Callow, Philip
Andrew Sinclair 2:400

Cambon, Glauco
Robert Lowell 8:348
Eugenio Montale 7:224
Giuseppe Ungaretti 7:482;
11:555

Cameron, Ann
Tom Robbins 9:454

Cameron, Eleanor
Julia W. Cunningham 12:164
Leon Garfield 12:226
Joseph Krumgold 12:320
William Mayne 12:393
Emily Cheney Neville 12:452

Cameron, Elspeth
Margaret Atwood 13:44

Cameron, Julia
Judith Rossner 6:469

Camp, Richard
Leon Garfield 12:221

Campbell, Gregg M.
Bob Dylan 6:157

Canary, Robert H.
Robert Graves 11:256

Cannella, Anthony R.
Richard Condon 10:111

Cannon, JoAnn
Italo Calvino 11:92

Cansler, Ronald Lee
Robert A. Heinlein 3:227

Cantarella, Helene
Jules Archer 12:15

Cantor, Peter
Frederic Raphael 2:367

Capitanchik, Maurice
E. M. Forster 2:135
Yukio Mishima 6:338

Caplan, Lincoln
Frederick Buechner 6:103

Caplan, Ralph
Kingsley Amis 1:6

Capouya, Emile
Albert Camus 2:98
Camilo José Cela 13:145
Robert Coover 7:57
Paul Goodman 7:129
James Leo Herlihy 6:234
Ignazio Silone 4:493
Aleksandr I. Solzhenitsyn 1:320

Capp, Al
Mary McCarthy 5:276

Capps, Benjamin
Christie Harris 12:262

Caputo-Mayr, Maria Luise
Peter Handke 8:261

Caram, Richard
Anne Stevenson 7:463

Carew, Jan
John Irving 13:292
George Lamming 2:235

Carey, John
Lawrence Durrell 4:147
Richard Eberhart 3:135
William Empson 8:201
D. J. Enright 4:155
Doris Lessing 6:292
John Updike 7:489

Carey, Julian C.
Langston Hughes 10:278

Cargill, Oscar
Pearl S. Buck 7:32

Carlsen, G. Robert
Frank Herbert 12:273

Carlson, Dale
M. E. Kerr 12:296
Rosemary Wells 12:638

Carne-Ross, D. S.
John Gardner 3:185
Eugenio Montale 7:222

Carpenter, Bogdana
Zbigniew Herbert 9:274

Carpenter, Frederic I.
Robinson Jeffers 2:212; 11:311
Carson McCullers 12:417

Carpenter, John R.
Zbigniew Herbert 9:274
Greg Kuzma 7:196
John Logan 5:255
James Schevill 7:401
Gary Snyder 2:407
Diane Wakoski 2:459
Charles Wright 6:580

Carpio, Virginia
Andre Norton 12:464

Carr, John
George Garrett 3:190

Carr, Roy
John Lennon and Paul
McCartney 12:379

Carroll, David
Chinua Achebe 1:1
Jean Cayrol 11:107

Carroll, Paul
John Ashbery 2:16

Robert Creeley 2:106
James Dickey 2:116
Allen Ginsberg 2:163
Frank O'Hara 2:321
W. D. Snodgrass 2:405
Philip Whalen 6:565

Carruth, Hayden
A. R. Ammons 9:30
W. H. Auden 1:11
John Berryman 2:56
Earle Birney 6:75
Edward Brathwaite 11:67
Charles Bukowski 5:80
Cid Corman 9:170
Robert Creeley 8:153
J. V. Cunningham 3:121
Annie Dillard 9:177
Robert Duncan 2:122
Loren Eiseley 7:91
Clayton Eshleman 7:97, 98
Robert Frost 10:198
Jean Garrigue 8:239
Arthur Gregor 9:251
H. D. 8:256
Marilyn Hacker 9:257
John Hollander 8:301
Richard Howard 7:166
David Ignatow 7:174, 175, 177
June Jordan 11:312
Denise Levertov 8:346
Philip Levine 2:244
Robert Lowell 4:299; 9:338
W. S. Merwin 8:390
Josephine Miles 2:278
Howard Nemerov 2:306
Charles Olson 9:412
Robert Pinsky 9:417
J. F. Powers 1:280
Kenneth Rexroth 2:370
Reg Saner 9:468
Anne Sexton 2:390; 4:484
Gilbert Sorrentino 7:448
Diane Wakoski 2:459; 4:574
Theodore Weiss 8:545
Louis Zukofsky 2:487

Carson, Katharine W.
Claude Simon 9:485

Carson, Tom
Brian Wilson 12:653

Carter, Albert Howard, III
Italo Calvino 8:126
Thomas McGuane 7:213

Carter, Angela
Thomas Keneally 5:210

Carter, Lin
J. R. R. Tolkien 1:339

Carter, Paul
Eugenio Montale 9:387

Carter, Robert A.
Arthur Gregor 9:253

Cary, Joseph
Eugenio Montale 7:223; 9:386
Giuseppe Ungaretti 7:482

Casari, Laura E.
Adrienne Rich 11:479

Casebeer, Edwin F.
Hermann Hesse 3:245

Caserio, Robert L.
Gilbert Sorrentino 7:449

Casey, Carol K.
Eleanor Hibbert 7:156

Caspary, Sister Anita Marie
François Mauriac 4:337, 338

Casper, Leonard
Flannery O'Connor 6:375

Cassill, R. V.
Mavis Gallant 7:110
Thomas Hinde 6:241
Irwin Shaw 7:413
Wilfrid Sheed 2:393
Christina Stead 2:422

Castor, Gladys Crofoot
Betty Cavanna 12:98

Catinella, Joseph
Christopher Isherwood 1:157
Joel Lieber 6:311
Bernard Malamud 1:201

Causey, James Y.
Camilo José Cela 4:95

Caute, David
Jean Genet 5:137
Lionel Trilling 9:531

Cavan, Romilly
Derek Walcott 4:574

Caviglia, John
José Donoso 11:149

Cavitch, David
William Stafford 4:521

Cawelti, John G.
Mario Puzo 6:430
Mickey Spillane 3:468

Caws, Mary Ann
André Breton 2:81; 9:125
Yves Bonnefoy 9:113

Cecchetti, Giovanni
Eugenio Montale 7:221

Cecil, David
Aldous Huxley 3:252

Cerf, Bennett
John O'Hara 2:324

Chabot, C. Barry
Frederick Exley 11:187

Chace, William M.
Ezra Pound 4:415

Chaillet, Ned
Athol Fugard 9:232

Chamberlain, Ethel L.
E. M. Almedingen 12:8

Chamberlain, John
James Gould Cozzens 11:131
Mary McCarthy 3:326

Chamberlin, J. E.
Margaret Atwood 8:28
George MacBeth 5:265
W. S. Merwin 3:338
Charles Tomlinson 4:547;
  6:535, 536
David Wagoner 5:475

Chambers, Aidan
William Mayne 12:404

Chambers, Robert D.
Ernest Buckler 13:120
Sinclair Ross 13:492

Chambers, Ross
Samuel Beckett 9:77

Chametzky, Jules
Isaac Bashevis Singer 1:313

Champagne, Roland A.
Marguerite Duras 11:167

Chankin, Donald O.
B. Traven 8:517

Chapin, Katherine Garrison
Allen Tate 4:536

Chaplin, William H.
John Logan 5:253

Chapman, Raymond
Graham Greene 1:133

Chapman, Robert
Anthony Burgess 4:83
Ivy Compton-Burnett 3:112

Chappell, Fred
George Garrett 3:191
Richard Yates 7:554

Charnes, Ruth
M. E. Kerr 12:303

Charters, Ann
Charles Olson 5:326

Charters, Samuel
Robert Creeley 4:117
Robert Duncan 4:142
Larry Eigner 9:180
William Everson 5:121
Lawrence Ferlinghetti 6:182
Allen Ginsberg 4:181
Charles Olson 5:329
Gary Snyder 5:393
Jack Spicer 8:497

Charyn, Jerome
Kobo Abe 8:1
Martin Amis 9:26
R. H. W. Dillard 5:116
Elizabeth Jane Howard 7:165
Margaríta Karapánou 13:314
Richard Price 12:492
James Purdy 10:424
Judith Rossner 9:457
Jerome Weidman 7:518
Kate Wilhelm 7:538

Chase, Richard
Saul Bellow 1:27

Chasin, Helen
Alan Dugan 6:144
May Sarton 4:472

Chassler, Philip I.
Meyer Levin 7:205

Chazen, Leonard
Anthony Powell 3:402

Cheatwood, Kiarri T-H.
Ayi Kwei Armah 5:32

Cheever, John
Saul Bellow 10:43

Cheney, Brainard
Donald Davidson 2:112
Flannery O'Connor 1:254

Cherry, Kelly
John Betjeman 10:53

Cherry, Kenneth
Vladimir Nabokov 8:413

Cheshire, Ardner R., Jr.
William Styron 11:518

Chesnick, Eugene
John Cheever 7:48

Nadine Gordimer 7:133
Michael Mewshaw 9:376

Chester, Alfred
Terry Southern 7:454

Cheuse, Alan
Alejo Carpentier 11:100
Carlos Fuentes 13:231
John Gardner 5:132
André Schwarz-Bart 4:480
B. Traven 11:534

Chevigny, Bell Gale
Tillie Olsen 4:387

Chiari, Joseph
Jean Anouilh 8:23
Jean Cocteau 8:144

Chomsky, Noam
Saul Bellow 8:81

Christ, Ronald
Jorge Luis Borges 2:70, 73; 4:75
José Donoso 8:178
Gabriel García Márquez 3:179
Pablo Neruda 5:301; 7:260
Octavio Paz 3:375; 4:397; 6:398
Manuel Puig 5:354
Mario Vargas Llosa 9:542

Christgau, Robert
Richard Brautigan 9:124
John Lennon and Paul
  McCartney 12:358
Patti Smith 12:539
Stevie Wonder 12:658, 659

Churchill, David
Peter Dickinson 12:175

Churchill, R. C.
P. G. Wodehouse 10:537

Ciardi, John
Robert Frost 13:223
William Carlos Williams 13:602

Cifelli, Edward
John Ciardi 10:106

Ciplijauskaité, Biruté
Gabriel García Márquez 3:182

Cismaru, Alfred
Simone de Beauvoir 2:43
Albert Camus 11:95
Marguerite Duras 6:149; 11:164
Eugène Ionesco 9:289
Robert Pinget 13:442

Cixous, Helen
Severo Sarduy 6:485

Claire, Thomas
Albert Camus 9:150

Claire, William F.
Stanley Kunitz 11:319
Allen Tate 9:521
Mark Van Doren 6:541

Clancy, William P.
Carson McCullers 12:413
Brian Moore 7:235

Clapp, Susannah
Caroline Blackwood 9:101
Margaríta Karapánou 13:315
Seán O'Faoláin 7:274
George MacBeth 9:340
David Plante 7:308

Clare, Anthony
Susan Sontag 13:518

Clark, John R.
Doris Betts 6:69
Alan Sillitoe 1:308

Clarke, Gerald
Gore Vidal 2:449
P. G. Wodehouse 2:480

Clarke, Henry Leland
Melvin Berger 12:38

Clarke, Jane H.
Jesse Jackson 12:289

Clarke, Loretta
Paul Zindel 6:587

Claudel, Alice Moser
David Kherdian 9:317

Clausen, Christopher
T. S. Eliot 10:171

Clayton, John
Richard Brautigan 12:63

Clayton, John Jacob
Saul Bellow 6:50

Clements, Bruce
Robert Cormier 12:137

Clements, Robert J.
Pablo Neruda 2:308
Irving Stone 7:469
Vassilis Vassilikos 4:551

Clemons, Walter
Lisa Alther 7:12
James Baldwin 5:43
Saul Bellow 6:55
Peter Benchley 8:82
E. L. Doctorow 6:133
J. G. Farrell 6:173
Joseph Heller 5:176, 182
George V. Higgins 7:158
Maureen Howard 5:189
G. Cabrera Infante 5:96
Erica Jong 4:263
Milan Kundera 4:276
Doris Lessing 6:302
Alison Lurie 4:305
Ross Macdonald 1:185
James McCourt 5:278
Carson McCullers 1:210
Vladimir Nabokov 6:354
Donald Newlove 6:364
Joyce Carol Oates 2:316; 3:363
Flannery O'Connor 2:317
Grace Paley 4:391
Robert M. Pirsig 4:403
Manuel Puig 5:354
Adrienne Rich 6:458
Isaac Bashevis Singer 3:456
Raymond Sokolov 7:430
Tom Wicker 7:534
Richard B. Wright 6:582

Clifford, Gay
Stanley Middleton 7:221

Clifford, Paula M.
Claude Simon 9:485

Clinton, Farley
William Safire 10:447

Cloonan, William
André Malraux 13:368

Clucas, Humphrey
Philip Larkin 5:227

Clurman, Harold
Edward Albee 2:2; 5:14

CRITIC INDEX

Jean Anouilh **3**:12
Fernando Arrabal **2**:15; **9**:41
Alan Ayckbourn **5**:37; **8**:35
Samuel Beckett **2**:47; **6**:33
Ed Bullins **1**:47; **5**:83
Alice Childress **12**:106
D. L. Coburn **10**:108
E. E. Cummings **8**:160
Brian Friel **5**:129
Jean Genet **2**:158
Trevor Griffiths **13**:256
Bill Gunn **5**:153
Christopher Hampton **4**:211, 212
Rolf Hochhuth **4**:230
William Inge **8**:308
Eugène Ionesco **4**:250
Preston Jones **10**:296
Terrence McNally **4**:347; **7**:217, 218
Mark Medoff **6**:322
Arthur Miller **1**:218; **6**:335
Jason Miller **2**:284
Clifford Odets **2**:320
John Osborne **5**:330
Miguel Piñero **4**:402
Harold Pinter **6**:405, 410, 415, 419
David Rabe **4**:426; **8**:450, 451
Terence Rattigan **7**:355
Peter Shaffer **5**:388
Sam Shepard **6**:496, 497
Neil Simon **11**:496
Bernard Slade **11**:508
John Steinbeck **5**:408
Tom Stoppard **1**:327; **4**:526; **5**:411; **8**:501
David Storey **5**:417; **8**:505
Elizabeth Swados **12**:557
Gore Vidal **2**:450
Richard Wesley **7**:519
Thornton Wilder **6**:573
Tennessee Williams **2**:465; **5**:500, 504; **7**:545
Lanford Wilson **7**:549

Cluysenaar, Anne
László Nagy **7**:251
Jon Silkin **6**:498

Coale, Samuel
Jerzy Kosinski **3**:273; **6**:284
Alain Robbe-Grillet **6**:468

Cobb, Jane
Betty Cavanna **12**:97
Mary Stolz **12**:547

Cocks, Jay
Mel Brooks **12**:77
Harold Pinter **3**:388

Coe, Richard N.
Jean Genet **1**:117
Eugène Ionesco **6**:251

Coffey, Warren
Kurt Vonnegut, Jr. **3**:494

Cogell, Elizabeth Cummins
Ursula K. LeGuin **13**:348

Cogley, John
Dan Wakefield **7**:502

Cogswell, Fred
Earle Birney **1**:34

Cohen, Arthur A.
Joseph Brodsky **4**:77
Cynthia Ozick **3**:372

Cohen, Dean
J. P. Donleavy **1**:76

Cohen, J. M.
Yevgeny Yevtushenko **13**:619

Cohen, Larry
Jules Feiffer **2**:133

Cohen, Mitch
Brian Wilson **12**:652

Cohen, Nathan
Mordecai Richler **5**:371

Cohn, Dorrit
Alain Robbe-Grillet **1**:289

Cohn, Ruby
Edward Albee **1**:4; **2**:4
James Baldwin **2**:32
Imamu Amiri Baraka **2**:35
Djuna Barnes **4**:43
John Dos Passos **4**:133
Lawrence Ferlinghetti **2**:134
John Hawkes **4**:215
Robinson Jeffers **11**:310
Kenneth Koch **5**:219
Robert Lowell **11**:324
Arthur Miller **2**:279
Harold Pinter **6**:405
Kenneth Rexroth **11**:472
Tennessee Williams **2**:465

Colby, Rob
Olga Broumas **10**:76

Coldwell, Joan
Marie-Claire Blais **13**:96

Cole, Barry
Ann Quin **6**:442

Cole, Laurence
Jean Rhys **2**:372

Cole, Sheila R.
Julia W. Cunningham **12**:166

Cole, William
Charles Causley **7**:42
Alex Comfort **7**:54
Richard Condon **10**:111
Louis Simpson **7**:429
R. S. Thomas **6**:531

Coleby, John
Robert Nye **13**:413

Colegate, Isabel
Susan B. Hill **4**:227
Joyce Carol Oates **6**:369

Coleman, Alexander
Alejo Carpentier **11**:99
José Donoso **11**:145
Pablo Neruda **2**:309
Nicanor Parra **2**:331

Coleman, Sister Anne Gertrude
Paul Vincent Carroll **10**:95

Coleman, John
Mel Brooks **12**:79
Jack Kerouac **2**:227
Leon Uris **7**:490

Coles, Robert
Shirley Ann Grau **4**:208
Kenneth Koch **8**:324
Cormac McCarthy **4**:343
Tillie Olsen **13**:432
Muriel Rukeyser **10**:442
William Stafford **7**:461
William Styron **1**:331
James Wright **3**:544

Collier, Carmen P.
Pearl S. Buck **7**:32

Collier, Christopher
Esther Forbes **12**:212

Collier, Eugenia
James Baldwin **2**:33
Melvin Van Peebles **2**:447

Collier, Michael
Delmore Schwartz **10**:463

Collier, Peter
Earl Rovit **7**:383

Collings, Rex
Wole Soyinka **5**:397

Collins, Anne
Stephen King **12**:311

Collins, Harold R.
Amos Tutuola **5**:443

Collins, Ralph L.
Elmer Rice **7**:360

Columba, Sister Mary, P.B.V.M.
Rosemary Wells **12**:638

Commager, Henry Steele
Esther Forbes **12**:209
MacKinlay Kantor **7**:194

Compton, D. G.
Samuel Beckett **3**:47
Frederick Buechner **2**:84
John Gardner **2**:151
Bernard Kops **4**:274
Vladimir Nabokov **6**:352
Frederic Prokosch **4**:422

Conarroe, Joel
John Berryman **8**:91; **13**:76
Richard Howard **7**:167
Howard Nemerov **2**:307
Anne Sexton **2**:391
W. D. Snodgrass **2**:405

Condini, Nereo
Eugenio Montale **7**:230
Isaac Bashevis Singer **6**:511
Tom Wolfe **9**:579

Conley, Timothy K.
William Faulkner **9**:200

Conn, Stewart
Anne Stevenson **7**:463

Connell, Evan S., Jr.
Simone de Beauvoir **2**:43
James Dickey **2**:116
Wilfrid Sheed **2**:392

Connelly, Kenneth
John Berryman **1**:34

Conner, John W.
E. M. Almedingen **12**:5
Judy Blume **12**:44
Frank Bonham **12**:53
Nikki Giovanni **4**:189
Jesse Jackson **12**:290
Madeleine L'Engle **12**:348, 349, 350
Lenora Mattingly Weber **12**:635

Connolly, Cyril
Ernest Hemingway **6**:225
Louis MacNeice **4**:315
Ezra Pound **4**:408, 414

Conquest, Robert
Ezra Pound **7**:334

Collier, Carmen P.

Aleksandr I. Solzhenitsyn **2**:413; **4**:513

Conroy, Jack
Charles Bukowski **2**:84

Contoski, Victor
Robert Duncan **2**:123
David Ignatow **7**:175
David Kherdian **6**:281
Czeslaw Milosz **11**:376
Marge Piercy **6**:403
Charles Simic **9**:480

Conway, John D.
Paul Vincent Carroll **10**:98

Cook, Albert
Djuna Barnes **4**:43
André Malraux **4**:327

Cook, Bruce
Kingsley Amis **8**:11
James Baldwin **3**:32
Heinrich Böll **6**:84
William S. Burroughs **1**:49
Evan S. Connell, Jr. **4**:109
Gregory Corso **1**:64
Robert Duncan **1**:83
Allen Ginsberg **1**:118
Lillian Hellman **8**:281
Marjorie Kellogg **2**:224
Thomas Keneally **5**:211
Jack Kerouac **1**:166
Jerzy Kosinski **1**:171
Ross Macdonald **2**:256
Norman Mailer **1**:193
Brian Moore **7**:235
Charles Olson **1**:263
Ezra Pound **1**:276
Budd Schulberg **7**:403
Irwin Shaw **7**:413
Georges Simenon **2**:399
Gary Snyder **1**:318
Arnold Wesker **5**:484
William Carlos Williams **1**:372

Cook, David
Camara Laye **4**:283

Cook, Reginald L.
Robert Frost **1**:111

Cook, Richard M.
Carson McCullers **12**:429

Cook, Roderick
Harry Mathews **6**:314
Berry Morgan **6**:340

Cooke, Michael G.
Alex Haley **12**:246, 252
Gayl Jones **9**:308
Margaríta Karapánou **13**:314
George Lamming **4**:279
Joyce Carol Oates **9**:403
Jean Rhys **4**:445
William Styron **1**:331
John Updike **2**:443
Alice Walker **9**:558
Robert Penn Warren **4**:581

Cookson, William
David Jones **4**:260
Hugh MacDiarmid **4**:310

Cooley, Peter
Daniel Hoffman **13**:286
Ted Hughes **2**:201

Coombs, Orde
James Baldwin **8**:40

CRITIC INDEX

Cooper, Arthur
Richard Adams 5:5
Richard Condon 6:115
Michael Crichton 2:109
J. P. Donleavy 6:142
Ward Just 4:266
John Le Carré 3:281
James A. Michener 5:290
Wright Morris 7:245
Ishmael Reed 6:450
Philip Roth 2:378
Irwin Shaw 7:414
David Storey 5:417
Gore Vidal 6:549
Fay Weldon 6:563

Cooper, Philip
Robert Lowell 4:300

Cooperman, Stanley
W. S. Merwin 1:212
Philip Roth 3:438

Coover, Robert
José Donoso 4:127
Carlos Fuentes 8:224

Coppage, Noel
Joni Mitchell 12:439

Core, George
Edna O'Brien 8:429
Seán O'Faoláin 7:273
John Crowe Ransom 2:364;
  5:366
William Styron 1:331
Allen Tate 4:537
William Trevor 9:529

Corke, Hilary
John Cheever 3:106

Corman, Cid
George Oppen 13:433

Corn, Alfred
John Hollander 8:302
Boris Pasternak 7:300
Reg Saner 9:469

Cornwell, Ethel F.
Samuel Beckett 3:45
Nathalie Sarraute 8:471

Corodimas, Peter
Ira Levin 6:305

Corr, Patricia
Evelyn Waugh 1:356

Corrigan, M. A.
Tennessee Williams 11:571

Corrigan, Mary Ann
Tennessee Williams 11:575

Corrigan, Matthew
Charles Olson 5:328

Corrigan, Robert W.
Edward Albee 5:11
John Arden 6:9
Saul Bellow 6:51
Friedrich Dürrenmatt 8:196
Michel de Ghelderode 6:197
Arthur Miller 1:218
John Osborne 5:332
Harold Pinter 6:417
Thornton Wilder 5:494

Corrington, John William
James Dickey 1:73
Marion Montgomery 7:233

Cort, David
Jules Archer 12:16

Cortázar, Julio
Jorge Luis Borges 8:102

Cortínez, Carlos
Octavio Paz 10:393

Corwin, Phillip
Kay Boyle 5:67

Cosgrave, Mary Silva
Maya Angelou 12:13

Cosgrave, Patrick
Kingsley Amis 3:8
Robert Lowell 4:300
Georges Simenon 3:452

Cott, Jonathan
Bob Dylan 6:156
John Lennon and Paul
  McCartney 12:356
Patti Smith 12:542

Cotter, James Finn
Robert Bly 10:62
Mark Van Doren 6:542

Cottrell, Robert D.
Simone de Beauvoir 8:58

Coughlan, Margaret N.
E. M. Almedingen 12:4

Covatta, Anthony
Elio Vittorini 6:551

Coveney, Michael
Athol Fugard 5:130
Sam Shepard 6:496

Cowan, Louise
Caroline Gordon 13:243
John Crowe Ransom 5:363
Allen Tate 2:431
Robert Penn Warren 6:555

Cowan, Michael
Norman Mailer 8:371

Cowley, Malcolm
Conrad Aiken 10:3
Pearl S. Buck 7:31; 11:71
E. E. Cummings 3:118
John Dos Passos 4:135
William Faulkner 8:210
Robert Frost 4:173
Ernest Hemingway 13:270
Doris Lessing 6:303
John O'Hara 2:325
Ezra Pound 4:407
James Thurber 5:430

Cox, David
Wilfrid Sheed 4:489

Cox, Kenneth
Hugh MacDiarmid 4:311
Ezra Pound 4:413
C. H. Sisson 8:490
Louis Zukofsky 7:562; 11:582

Coxe, Louis
David Jones 2:217
Anne Sexton 2:391

Coyne, J. R., Jr.
Fredrick Forsyth 5:125
E. Howard Hunt 3:251

Coyne, John R., Jr.
Dick Francis 2:142
Ward Just 4:266
Donald E. Westlake 7:528
Tom Wolfe 2:481

Coyne, P. S.
Wilfrid Sheed 2:395

Coyne, Patricia S.
Kingsley Amis 3:10
Erica Jong 4:265
Joyce Carol Oates 9:402
Morris L. West 6:564

Craft, Robert
Aldous Huxley 5:193

Craft, Wallace
Eugenio Montale 7:230

Crago, Hugh
Andre Norton 12:460
J.R.R. Tolkien 12:573

Craib, Roderick
Bernard Malamud 3:322

Craig, Patricia
William Mayne 12:404
Edna O'Brien 8:429
Katherine Paterson 12:485

Craig, Randall
Jean Genet 2:160
Bernard Pomerance 13:444
Robert Shaw 5:390
Sam Shepard 4:489
E. A. Whitehead 5:489

Crain, Jane Larkin
Alice Adams 13:1
Caroline Blackwood 9:101
Sara Davidson 9:175
Lawrence Durrell 6:153
Bruce Jay Friedman 5:126
John Gardner 5:134
Gail Godwin 8:248
Shirley Ann Grau 9:240
Milan Kundera 4:276
Alan Lelchuk 5:244
Doris Lessing 6:299
Grace Paley 4:394
Walker Percy 6:401
Kathleen Raine 7:353
C. P. Snow 6:518
Muriel Spark 5:398
Mario Vargas Llosa 6:545
Gore Vidal 4:555
David Wagoner 5:474
Sol Yurick 6:583

Crankshaw, Edward
Aleksandr I. Solzhenitsyn 1:319

Creagh, Patrick
Giuseppe Ungaretti 7:484

Creeley, Robert
Robert Duncan 4:141
William Everson 5:121
Robert Graves 6:210
Charles Olson 5:326
Ezra Pound 3:395
William Stafford 4:519
William Carlos Williams 5:507
Louis Zukofsky 4:599

Crews, Frederick C.
E.M. Forster 13:219
Shirley Ann Grau 4:207
Philip Roth 2:379

Crews, Harry
Elliott Baker 8:39

Crichton, Michael
Frederick Forsyth 2:136
Kurt Vonnegut, Jr. 3:495

Crick, Francis
Michael McClure 6:319

Crick, Joyce
Michael Hamburger 5:159

Crider, Bill
Stephen King 12:310

Crinklaw, Don
John Gardner 3:186

Crinkley, Richmond
Edward Albee 2:3

Crist, Judith
Mel Brooks 12:81
Julia W. Cunningham 12:163
Harry Kemelman 2:225

Croft, L. B.
Yevgeny Yevtushenko 13:620

Cross, Michael S.
Frank Herbert 12:279

Crouch, Marcus
Ruth M. Arthur 12:28
Margot Benary-Isbert 12:34
Peter Dickinson 12:175
Leon Garfield 12:228
Andre Norton 12:464

Crouch, Stanley
Ishmael Reed 13:480

Crow, John
Harlan Ellison 13:203

Crowder, Richard
Carl Sandburg 1:300

Crowson, Lydia
Jean Cocteau 8:148

Crowther, Bosley
Norman Lear 12:326

Cruise O'Brien, Conor
Jimmy Breslin 4:76
Graham Greene 3:214
Seamus Heaney 7:149

Cruse, Harold W.
W. E. B. Du Bois 2:120

Cruttwell, Patrick
Adolfo Bioy Casares 4:64
Jerzy Kosinski 3:274
Iris Murdoch 2:296
Patrick White 7:529

Cuddon, J. A.
Peter De Vries 2:114
James Purdy 4:423
Frederic Raphael 2:367
Claude Simon 4:497

Culbertson, Diana
Alberto Moravia 7:243

Cullen, Elinor S.
Ruth M. Arthur 12:26

Culler, Jonathan
Walker Percy 8:439

Culpan, Norman
Andre Norton 12:470, 471

Cumare, Rosa
Flann O'Brien 5:317

Cunliffe, Marcus
Irving Stone 7:469

Cunliffe, W. G.
Heinrich Böll 11:57

CRITIC INDEX

CRITIC INDEX

Cunliffe, W. Gordon
Günter Grass 1:126
Uwe Johnson 10:283

Cunningham, Laura
Richard Price 6:427

Cunningham, Valentine
Louis Auchincloss 6:15
John Barth 5:51
Donald Barthelme 3:43
Richard Brautigan 12:70
Alejo Carpentier 8:134
Len Deighton 4:119
Don DeLillo 13:179
Shusaku Endo 7:96
Frederick Forsyth 5:125
Mervyn Jones 10:295
Anna Kavan 5:206
William Kotzwinkle 5:220
Mary Lavin 4:282
Colin MacInnes 4:314
Stanley Middleton 7:220
Yukio Mishima 4:358
Vladimir Nabokov 3:355
Hans Erich Nossack 6:364
David Plante 7:307
Françoise Sagan 9:468
William Sansom 6:484
Emma Tennant 13:536
Paul Theroux 8:513
Gillian Tindall 7:474
Ludvík Vaculík 7:495
Harriet Waugh 6:559
Arnold Wesker 5:483
Patrick White 4:587

Cuppy, Will
Agatha Christie 12:112, 113

Current-Garcia, Eugene
George Seferis 11:494

Currie, William
Kobo Abe 8:2

Curtis, Anthony
J. B. Priestley 5:351

Curtis, C. Michael
Sara Davidson 9:175
Annie Dillard 9:179

Curtis, Jerry L.
Jean Genet 10:224

Curtis, Penelope
Katherine Paterson 12:485

Curtis, Simon
Donald Davie 5:113
Seamus Heaney 7:151

Cushman, Jerome
Jascha Kessler 4:270

Cushman, Kathleen
Kurt Vonnegut, Jr. 12:610

Cushman, Keith
Mark Shorer 9:474

Cutler, Bruce
Louis Simpson 7:428

Cutter, William
S. Y. Agnon 4:15

Czajkowska, Magdalena
Tadeusz Rózewicz 9:463

Dabney, Lewis H.
William Faulkner 6:174

Dacey, Philip
Arthur Gregor 9:255

Daemmrich, Horst S.
Eugène Ionesco 11:289

Dahlie, Hallvard
Brian Moore 1:225; 7:237
Alice Munro 10:357

Daiches, David
W. H. Auden 1:8
Saul Bellow 3:55
Elizabeth Bowen 1:39
Ivy Compton-Burnett 1:60
C. Day Lewis 1:72
T. S. Eliot 1:89
William Empson 3:147
Christopher Fry 2:143
Robert Graves 1:126
Henry Green 2:178
Aldous Huxley 1:149
Hugh MacDiarmid 2:252
Louis MacNeice 1:186
Bernard Malamud 3:323
Henry Roth 6:473
Edith Sitwell 2:403
Stephen Spender 1:322
Evelyn Waugh 1:356

Daiker, Donald A.
Hugh Nissenson 4:381

Dale, Peter
John Berryman 2:58
Basil Bunting 10:84
Stanley Burnshaw 13:128,129

Daley, Robert
John R. Tunis 12:597

Dalgleish, Alice
Madeleine L'Engle 12:346, 347

Dallas, Karl
Joni Mitchell 12:435

Dalton, Elizabeth
Vladimir Nabokov 1:245
John Updike 1:344

Daly, Maureen
Mary Stolz 12:551

Dame, Enid
Chaim Potok 7:322

Dana, Robert
Yukio Mishima 2:286

Dangerfield, George
Rayner Heppenstall 10:272
Carson McCullers 12:410

Daniel, John
Ann Quin 6:441
Isaac Bashevis Singer 6:507

Daniel, Robert W.
W. D. Snodgrass 10:478

Daniels, Robert V.
Larry Woiwode 10:540

Danielson, J. David
Simone Schwarz-Bart 7:404

Danischewsky, Nina
Ruth M. Arthur 12:26
Peter Dickinson 12:167

d'Arazien, Steven
Hunter S. Thompson 9:528

Dardess, George
Jack Kerouac 5:213

Darrach, Brad
George V. Higgins 4:224

Joyce Carol Oates 2:313
Ezra Pound 7:336
Irving Stone 7:471

Datchery, Dick
Agatha Christie 12:120

Dauster, Frank
Gabriel García Márquez 3:182

Davenport, Basil
Daphne du Maurier 11:162
Carson McCullers 12:409

Davenport, G.
J. R. R. Tolkien 3:482

Davenport, Gary T.
Seán O'Faoláin 7:275
E. M. Almedingen 12:4

Davenport, Guy
E. M. Almedingen 12:4
Michael Ayrton 7:17
Beryl Bainbridge 8:36
Thomas Berger 8:82
Wendell Berry 8:85
Richard Brautigan 12:58
Frederick Buechner 2:82
Paul Celan 10:101
Louis-Ferdinand Céline 3:104
Evan S. Connell, Jr. 4:110
Joan Didion 1:75
J. P. Donleavy 4:124
Donald Hall 13:260
Miroslav Holub 4:233
Charles Olson 6:388; 9:412
Nicanor Parra 2:331
Chaim Potok 2:338
James Purdy 2:350
J.I.M. Stewart 7:466
Harriet Waugh 6:560
Richard Wilbur 6:569
Louis Zukofsky 2:487; 4:599;
  7:560

Davidon, Ann Morrissett
Simone de Beauvoir 8:57
Grace Paley 4:391
Gore Vidal 4:557

Davidson, Richard B.
Christie Harris 12:266

Davie, Donald
A. R. Ammons 5:30
John Berryman 8:87
Austin Clarke 6:112
Michael Hamburger 5:159
Anthony Hecht 8:267
John Hollander 8:299
Galway Kinnell 5:217
John Peck 3:377
Ezra Pound 13:456
Paul Theroux 11:529
J.R.R. Tolkien 12:572

Davies, R. R.
Joanne Greenberg 7:135
Diane Johnson 5:198
William Sansom 6:482

Davies, Russell
Richard Condon 8:150
Joan Didion 8:177
Thomas Hinde 11:273
Francis King 8:321
William Trevor 9:528

Davis, Charles T.
Robert Hayden 5:68

Davis, Cheri Colby
W. S. Merwin 13:383

Davis, Deborah
Julio Cortázar 5:109

Davis, Fath
Toni Morrison 4:366

Davis, George
George Lamming 2:235
Clarence Major 3:320

Davis, Hope Hale
John Cheever 8:140
Oriana Fallaci 11:190

Davis, L. J.
Richard Brautigan 12:71
Richard Condon 4:106
Peter De Vries 7:78
Stanley Elkin 4:153
Leon Forrest 4:163
Lois Gould 4:200
Hannah Green 3:202
John Hersey 2:188
Stanley Hoffman 5:184
James Jones 10:291
William Kennedy 6:274
Ira Levin 6:307
John O'Hara 2:324
J. F. Powers 8:448
Philip Roth 2:379
Françoise Sagan 6:481
Ronald Sukenick 4:531
J. R. R. Tolkien 8:516
Vassilis Vassilikos 8:524
Richard B. Wright 6:582

Davis, Lavinia
Margot Benary-Isbert 12:31

Davis, M. E.
José María Arguedas 10:10

Davis, Mary Gould
Betty Cavanna 12:98
Esther Forbes 12:207
John R. Tunis 12:595, 596

Davis, Paxton
Eric Ambler 9:18
George Garrett 3:189

Davis, Rick
Richard Brautigan 9:125
Richard Condon 10:111

Davis, Robert Gorham
Saul Bellow 2:49
John Dos Passos 1:78
William Styron 3:472

Davis, Robert Murray
Evelyn Waugh 1:359

Davis, Stephen
Jimmy Page and Robert Plant
  12:480
Brian Wilson 12:645

Davison, Peter
Robert Creeley 8:151
Robert Frost 4:175
Doris Grumbach 13:257
John Hollander 8:298
Galway Kinnell 2:229
Denise Levertov 8:345
Sylvia Plath 2:337
Anne Sexton 8:482
William Stafford 7:460

Davy, John
Arthur Koestler 1:169

Dawson, Helen
David Storey **4**:529

Day, A. Grove
James A. Michener **1**:214

Day, Douglas
Robert Graves **1**:127

Day, James M.
Paul Horgan **9**:278

Deane, Seamus
Seamus Heaney **7**:150

Debicki, Andrew P.
Claudio Rodríguez **10**:439

De Bolt, Joe
John Brunner **8**:110

deBuys, William
Paul Horgan **9**:279

Decancq, Roland
Lawrence Durrell **8**:191

de Charmant, Elizabeth
Giorgio Bassani **9**:74

Deck, John
Harry Crews **6**:17
Henry Dumas **6**:145
J. G. Farrell **6**:173
Michael Moorcock **5**:294
John Seelye **7**:406

Dector, Midge
Leon Uris **7**:491

Deedy, John
J. P. Donleavy **4**:123
Upton Sinclair **11**:498

Deemer, Charles
Renata Adler **8**:7
John Cheever **3**:108
Peter Handke **5**:165
Bernard Malamud **3**:324

Deen, Rosemary F.
Randall Jarrell **6**:259
Galway Kinnell **3**:268

De Feo, Ronald
Martin Amis **4**:21
Beryl Bainbridge **8**:37
Thomas Bernhard **3**:65
William S. Burroughs **2**:93
José Donoso **4**:128
Frederick Exley **11**:187
William Gaddis **6**:195
Gabriel García Márquez **2**:149;
  10:216
John Gardner **5**:131, 134
Graham Greene **6**:219
John Hawkes **1**:138
Richard Hughes **11**:278
Dan Jacobson **4**:255
Jerzy Kosinski **1**:172
Iris Murdoch **6**:345
Howard Nemerov **6**:360
Sylvia Plath **1**:270
Anthony Powell **3**:404
James Salter **7**:388
Gilbert Sorrentino **3**:461
William Trevor **7**:477
John Updike **5**:460
Angus Wilson **5**:514

Degenfelder, E. Pauline
Larry McMurtry **7**:213

Degnan, James P.
Kingsley Amis **2**:10

Roald Dahl **1**:71
Wilfrid Sheed **2**:394

de Jonge, Alex
Aleksandr I. Solzhenitsyn **9**:506

Dekker, George
Donald Davie **8**:166

Dekle, Bernard
Saul Bellow **1**:32
E. E. Cummings **1**:69
John Dos Passos **1**:80
William Faulkner **1**:102
Robert Frost **1**:111
Langston Hughes **1**:148
John P. Marquand **2**:271
Arthur Miller **1**:219
John O'Hara **1**:262
J. D. Salinger **1**:300
Upton Sinclair **1**:310
Thornton Wilder **1**:366
Tennessee Williams **1**:369
William Carlos Williams **1**:371

Delany, Paul
A. Alvarez **5**:19
Margaret Atwood **4**:24

Delattre, Genevieve
Françoise Mallet-Joris **11**:355

de Laurentis, Teresa
Italo Calvino **8**:127

Delbanco, Nicholas
Frederick Busch **10**:93
Graham Greene **9**:251
Doris Grumbach **13**:257

Deligiorgis, Stavros
David Kherdian **9**:318

Della Fazia, Alba
Jean Anouilh **1**:7

Delong-Tonelli, Beverly J.
Fernando Arrabal **9**:36

De Luca, Geraldine
J. D. Salinger **12**:517

DeMara, Nicholas A.
Italo Calvino **11**:87

Demarest, Michael
Michael Crichton **6**:119

DeMaria, Robert
Diane Wakoski **2**:459

Dembo, L. S.
Charles Olson **2**:327
George Oppen **7**:283
Louis Zukofsky **2**:488

de Mille, Richard
Carlos Castaneda **12**:95

Demos, E. Virginia
Larry Kettelkamp **12**:307

DeMott, Benjamin
Margaret Atwood **2**:20
James Baldwin **2**:32
Jorge Luis Borges **2**:70
Anthony Burgess **13**:126
Vincent Canby **13**:132
T. S. Eliot **2**:127
Russell C. Hoban **7**:162
Doris Lessing **2**:240
Henry Miller **2**:283
Philip Roth **9**:462
John Updike **5**:459
Kurt Vonnegut, Jr. **2**:453

Dempsey, David
Terry Southern **7**:454

Deneau, Daniel P.
Hermann Hesse **3**:249
Jakov Lind **1**:178
Alain Robbe-Grillet **4**:449

Denham, Paul
Louis Dudek **11**:159

Denne, Constance Ayers
Joyce Carol Oates **6**:372

Denney, Reuel
Conrad Aiken **1**:3

Dennis, Sr. M., R.S.M.
E. M. Almedingen **12**:1

Dennis, Nigel
Louis-Ferdinand Céline **1**:57
Günter Grass **11**:253
Robert Pinget **7**:305
E. B. White **10**:531

Dennison, George
Paul Goodman **4**:197

DeRamus, Betty
Joyce Carol Oates **3**:364

Deredita, John
Pablo Neruda **7**:257
Juan Carlos Onetti **7**:278

Der Hovanessian, Diana
David Kherdian **6**:280

Desmond, Harold F., Jr.
Melvin Berger **12**:38

Des Pres, Terrence
Peter Matthiessen **11**:360

Dessner, Lawrence Jay
Mario Puzo **6**:429

Detweiler, Robert
John Updike **2**:442

Deutsch, Babette
W. H. Auden **2**:21
Louise Bogan **4**:68
E. E. Cummings **3**:116
Richard Eberhart **11**:176
T. S. Eliot **2**:125
William Empson **8**:201
Robert Frost **3**:171
Jean Garrigue **8**:239
H. D. **3**:217
Stanley Kunitz **11**:319
Marianne Moore **2**:290
St.-John Perse **4**:398
Ezra Pound **2**:339
Kathleen Raine **7**:351
John Crowe Ransom **2**:361
Theodore Roethke **3**:432
Carl Sandburg **4**:463
Edith Sitwell **2**:402
Stephen Spender **2**:419
Allen Tate **2**:427
Richard Wilbur **9**:568
William Carlos Williams **2**:466
Marya Zaturenska **11**:579

DeVault, Joseph J.
Mark Van Doren **6**:541

Devert, Krystyna
Hermann Hesse **2**:189

DeVitis, A. A.
Graham Greene **1**:133

Devlin, John
Ramón Sender **8**:478

De Vries, Peter
James Thurber **5**:429

Devrnja, Zora
Charles Olson **9**:412
Charles Simic **9**:478

Dewsnap, Terence
Christopher Isherwood **1**:156

Dial, John E.
José María Gironella **11**:237

Díaz, Janet Winecoff
Ana María Matute **11**:363

Dick, Bernard F.
William Golding **1**:120
John Hersey **2**:188
Iris Murdoch **6**:342
Mary Renault **3**:426
Stevie Smith **8**:492
Gore Vidal **4**:558

Dick, Kay
Simone de Beauvoir **4**:48

Dickey, Chris
Kurt Vonnegut, Jr. **5**:470

Dickey, James
Conrad Aiken **1**:3
John Ashbery **2**:16
John Berryman **1**:33
Kenneth Burke **2**:87
Stanley Burnshaw **3**:91
Hayden Carruth **4**:93
E. E. Cummings **1**:68
J. V. Cunningham **3**:120
Robert Duncan **1**:82
Richard Eberhart **3**:133
William Everson **1**:96
Robert Frost **1**:111
Allen Ginsberg **1**:118
David Ignatow **4**:247
Robinson Jeffers **2**:214
Galway Kinnell **1**:167
James Kirkup **1**:169
John Logan **5**:252
Louis MacNeice **1**:186
William Meredith **4**:347
James Merrill **2**:272
W. S. Merwin **1**:211
Josephine Miles **1**:215
Marianne Moore **1**:226
Howard Nemerov **2**:305
Charles Olson **1**:262; **2**:327
Kenneth Patchen **1**:265
Sylvia Plath **2**:337
Herbert Read **4**:439
Theodore Roethke **1**:290
May Sarton **4**:470
Anne Sexton **2**:390
Louis Simpson **4**:497
William Jay Smith **6**:512
William Stafford **4**:519
Allen Tate **6**:527
Robert Penn Warren **1**:352
Theodore Weiss **3**:515
Reed Whittemore **4**:588
Richard Wilbur **3**:531
William Carlos Williams **1**:370
Yvor Winters **4**:590

Dickey, R. P.
Lawrence Ferlinghetti **6**:183
Robert Lowell **5**:258

Dickey, William
Daniel J. Berrigan **4**:56

CRITIC INDEX

CRITIC INDEX

John Berryman **13**:75
Hayden Carruth **7**:40
James Dickey **2**:115
William Everson **5**:121
W. S. Merwin **2**:277
George Oppen **7**:281

Dickins, Anthony
Vladimir Nabokov **2**:304

Dickinson, Hugh
Eugène Ionesco **6**:250

Dickinson-Brown, R.
Lewis Turco **11**:551

Dickstein, Lore
Gail Godwin **8**:247
Judith Guest **8**:254
Sue Kaufman **3**:263
Judith Rossner **6**:469
Isaac Bashevis Singer **3**:456

Dickstein, Morris
John Barth **7**:24
Donald Barthelme **6**:29
R. P. Blackmur **2**:61
Daniel Fuchs **8**:220
John Gardner **3**:184
Günter Grass **11**:252
Philip Roth **4**:454
Rudolph Wurlitzer **2**:484

Didion, Joan
John Cheever **8**:137
Elizabeth Hardwick **13**:265
Doris Lessing **2**:240
J. D. Salinger **12**:511

Diez, Luys A.
Juan Carlos Onetti **7**:280

Dillard, Annie
Evan S. Connell, Jr. **4**:109

Dillard, R. H. W.
W. S. Merwin **8**:389
Vladimir Nabokov **2**:304
Colin Wilson **3**:537

Diller, Edward
Friedrich Dürrenmatt **11**:171

Dillingham, Thomas
Susan Fromberg Schaeffer **6**:488

Dillon, David
John Hawkes **4**:218
Tillie Olsen **13**:433
Wallace Stegner **9**:509

Dillon, Michael
Thornton Wilder **6**:571

Dimeo, Steven
Ray Bradbury **3**:85

Di Napoli, Thomas
Günter Grass **11**:247

Dinnage, Rosemary
Isak Dinesen **10**:152
Elizabeth Hardwick **13**:264
Doris Lessing **6**:303

Di Piero, W. S.
John Ashbery **4**:22
John Hawkes **9**:269

Dirda, Michael
Henry Green **13**:251
John Knowles **10**:303

Ditsky, John
Richard Brautigan **12**:69

John Hawkes **2**:186
Erica Jong **8**:313
Joyce Carol Oates **2**:316

Dix, Carol
Martin Amis **4**:20

Dixon, John W., Jr.
Elie Wiesel **3**:527

DiZazzo, Raymond
Robert L. Peters **7**:303

Djilas, Milovan
Aleksandr I. Solzhenitsyn **2**:408

Djwa, Sandra
Margaret Lawrence **13**:341

Dobbs, Kildare
Margaret Laurence **3**:278
Alice Munro **6**:341

Dobie, Ann B.
Muriel Spark **2**:416

Dodd, Wayne
Madeleine L'Engle **12**:350

Dodsworth, Martin
Robert Bly **2**:65
Donald Davie **8**:163
James Dickey **2**:115
Marianne Moore **2**:291

Doerksen, Daniel W.
Margaret Avison **4**:36

Doerner, William R.
James Herriot **12**:282

Dohmann, Barbara
Jorge Luis Borges **2**:69
Julio Cortázar **2**:101
Gabriel García Márquez **2**:147
Juan Carlos Onetti **7**:276
Juan Rulfo **8**:461
Mario Vargas Llosa **3**:493

Dollen, Charles
William Peter Blatty **2**:64
Paul Gallico **2**:147
N. Scott Momaday **2**:289

Dombroski, Robert S.
Carlo Emilio Gadda **11**:208

Domowitz, Janet
Alice Adams **13**:3

Donadio, Stephen
John Ashbery **2**:19
Richard Fariña **9**:195
Sandra Hochman **3**:250

Donaghue, Denis
Donald Barthelme **13**:62

Donahue, Francis
Camilo José Cela **4**:97; **13**:147

Donahue, Walter
Sam Shepard **4**:491

Donald, David Herbert
Alex Haley **12**:246

Donaldson, Scott
Ernest Hemingway **13**:276
Philip Roth **1**:293

Donnard, Jean-Hervé
Eugène Ionesco **6**:249

Donnelly, Dorothy
Marge Piercy **3**:384

Donoghue, Denis
A. R. Ammons **9**:27
W. H. Auden **3**:24

Saul Bellow **2**:51
Elizabeth Bishop **13**:95
Marie-Claire Blais **2**:63
Kenneth Burke **2**:88
Austin Clarke **9**:167
C. Day Lewis **6**:129
Richard Eberhart **11**:175
T. S. Eliot **2**:126
John Fowles **10**:188
William H. Gass **11**:225
William Golding **3**:196
Shirley Ann Grau **4**:209
Graham Greene **9**:250
Anthony Hecht **8**:269
Paul Horgan **9**:278
Randall Jarrell **1**:160
Robert Lowell **4**:295
James Merrill **2**:274
W. S. Merwin **2**:277
Marianne Moore **2**:291
Ezra Pound **2**:340
Philip Roth **6**:476
Christina Stead **2**:422
Allen Tate **6**:527; **9**:521; **11**:526
Charles Tomlinson **2**:437
Lionel Trilling **9**:530; **11**:543
Derek Walcott **2**:460
Anne Waldman **7**:507
Robert Penn Warren **4**:579; **13**:581
Rebecca West **7**:525
William Carlos Williams **2**:467

Donoghue, Susan
Joni Mitchell **12**:435, 436

Donohue, John W.
Earl Hamner **12**:259

Donovan, Josephine
Sylvia Plath **3**:390

Dooley, D. J.
Earle Birney **6**:71

Dooley, Dennis M.
Robert Penn Warren **10**:517

Dorfman, Ariel
Miguel Ángel Asturias **13**:39

Dorsey, Margaret A.
Babbis Friis-Baastad **12**:214
Larry Kettelkamp **12**:305
Andre Norton **12**:458, 459

Dos Passos, John
E. E. Cummings **12**:139

Doubrovsky, J. S.
Eugène Ionesco **6**:247

Doubrovsky, Serge
Albert Camus **11**:93

Douglas, Ann
James T. Farrell **11**:196

Douglas, Ellen
Flannery O'Connor **6**:381
May Sarton **4**:471

Douglas, George H.
Edmund Wilson **2**:477

Dowling, Gordon Graham
Yukio Mishima **6**:337

Downer, Alan S.
Thornton Wilder **5**:495

Doxey, William S.
Ken Kesey **3**:267
Flannery O'Connor **3**:368

Doyle, Mike
Irving Layton **2**:236
A. W. Purdy **6**:428
Raymond Souster **5**:395, 396

Doyle, Paul A.
Pearl S. Buck **11**:71
Paul Vincent Carroll **10**:96
James T. Farrell **8**:205
MacKinlay Kantor **7**:195
Seán O'Faoláin **1**:259; **7**:273
Evelyn Waugh **1**:359

Drabble, Margaret
Michael Frayn **3**:164
John Irving **13**:295
Philip Larkin **8**:333; **9**:323
Iris Murdoch **4**:367
Muriel Spark **8**:494

Dragonwagon, C.
Stevie Wonder **12**:663

Drake, Robert
Carson McCullers **12**:426
Reynolds Price **3**:405
Eudora Welty **5**:478

Draper, Charlotte W.
Andre Norton **12**:471

Draudt, Manfred
Joe Orton **13**:436

Drew, Fraser
John Masefield **11**:356

Driver, Christopher
Yukio Mishima **4**:357

Driver, Sam N.
Anna Akhmatova **11**:6

Driver, Tom F.
Jean Genet **1**:115
Arthur Miller **1**:215; **2**:279

Druska, John
John Beecher **6**:49

Dryden, Edgar A.
John Barth **5**:52

Duberman, Martin
Ed Bullins **1**:47
Laura Z. Hobson **7**:163

Duberstein, Larry
Joel Lieber **6**:312

Dubois, Larry
William F. Buckley, Jr. **7**:34
Walker Percy **8**:445

Duddy, Thomas A.
Louis Zukofsky **11**:581

Dudek, Louis
James Reaney **13**:474

Duffey, Bernard
W. H. Auden **4**:35
Jack Kerouac **1**:66

Duffy, Martha
James Baldwin **4**:41
Jean Cocteau **1**:59
Joan Didion **1**:75
Nikki Giovanni **2**:164
Lillian Hellman **4**:221
D. Keith Mano **10**:328
Tom McHale **5**:281
Grace Paley **4**:393
Walker Percy **2**:334
Sylvia Plath **2**:336
Judith Rossner **6**:470
Patrick White **3**:523

Duhamel, P. Albert
Flannery O'Connor **1**:253
Paul Scott **9**:477

Dullea, Gerard J.
Gregory Corso **11**:123

Dumas, Bethany K.
E. E. Cummings **12**:159

Dunbar, Ernest
Jules Archer **12**:21

Duncan, Erika
William Goyen **8**:251
Anaïs Nin **8**:425

Duncan, Robert
John Wieners **7**:536

Dunlop, John B.
Vladimir Voinovich **10**:509

Dunn, Douglas
Giorgio Bassani **9**:77
John Berryman **4**:62
George Mackay Brown **5**:78
Donald Davie **5**:115
Lawrence Durrell **4**:147
D. J. Enright **4**:156; **8**:203
Gavin Ewart **13**:209
Geoffrey Grigson **7**:136
John Hawkes **7**:141
Seamus Heaney **7**:150
Erica Jong **6**:268
Christopher Middleton **13**:388
Sylvia Plath **5**:339
William Plomer **4**:407
Peter Porter **13**:452
Peter Redgrove **6**:446
Kenneth Rexroth **11**:473
Jon Silkin **6**:499
Anne Stevenson **7**:463
Charles Tomlinson **6**:534
Andrew Young **5**:525

Dupee, F. W.
Kenneth Koch **5**:218
Robert Lowell **3**:299
Norman Mailer **11**:339
Bernard Malamud **3**:321
W. S. Merwin **3**:338
John Osborne **5**:330
J. F. Powers **4**:418

Duplessis, Rachel Blau
Edward Albee **13**:6

Dupree, Robert
Allen Tate **6**:525

Dupree, Robert S.
Caroline Gordon **13**:245

Durbin, Karen
Eleanor Clark **5**:107

Duree, Barbara Joyce
Lenora Mattingly Weber **12**:633

Durgnat, Raymond
Ann Quin **6**:442

Durham, Frank
Elmer Rice **7**:363

Durham, Philip
Dashiell Hammett **3**:218

Durrant, Digby
Caroline Blackwood **6**:80
Julia O'Faolain **6**:383

Durrell, Lawrence
George Seferis **5**:385

Dust, Harvey
Jules Archer **12**:17

Duvall, E. S.
Ann Beattie **13**:66

Du Verlie, Claude
Claude Simon **4**:497

Dwyer, David J.
Mary Renault **3**:426

Dyson, A. E.
Sylvia Plath **11**:446

Dyson, William
Ezra Pound **1**:276

Dzwonkoski, F. Peter, Jr.
T. S. Eliot **6**:163

Eagle, Herbert
Aleksandr I. Solzhenitsyn **9**:504
Ludvík Vaculík **7**:495

Eagle, Robert
Thomas Hinde **11**:274
Alberto Moravia **7**:244
Flann O'Brien **4**:385

Eagleton, Terry
George Barker **8**:45
Donald Davie **8**:162
Thom Gunn **6**:221
Seamus Heaney **7**:150
Hermann Hesse **11**:272
William Plomer **8**:447
Stevie Smith **8**:491
Maura Stanton **9**:508
Charles Tomlinson **6**:535
John Wain **11**:561
Andrew Young **5**:525

Eakin, Mary K.
Mary Stolz **12**:553

Eastman, Fred
Marc Connelly **7**:55

Eaton, Anne T.
John R. Tunis **12**:593

Eaton, Charles Edward
Robert Frost **9**:225

Eberhart, Richard
Djuna Barnes **8**:48
Robert Frost **13**:227
Allen Ginsberg **13**:239
Archibald MacLeish **3**:310
Ezra Pound **7**:324
Kenneth Rexroth **2**:370

Echevarría, Roberto González
Alejo Carpentier **11**:101
Julio Cortázar **10**:114; **13**:158
Carlos Fuentes **10**:209
Severo Sarduy **6**:486

Eckley, Grace
Edna O'Brien **5**:312

Eddins, Dwight
John Fowles **10**:183

Edel, Leon
Lawrence Durrell **1**:85
William Faulkner **1**:100
Ernest Hemingway **10**:265
Alain Robbe-Grillet **1**:286
Nathalie Sarraute **1**:303

Edelheit, S. J.
Anthony Burgess **13**:126

Edelstein, Arthur
William Faulkner **1**:102

Janet Frame **6:190
Jean Stafford **7**:458
Angus Wilson **2**:472

Edelstein, J. M.
Patricia Highsmith **2**:193

Edelstein, Mark G.
Flannery O'Connor **6**:381

Edenbaum, Robert I.
Dashiell Hammett **3**:219
John Hawkes **2**:185

Eder, Richard
Edna O'Brien **8**:430
Bernard Pomerance **13**:445

Edinborough, Arnold
Earle Birney **6**:70

Edmiston, Susan
Maeve Brennan **5**:72

Edmonds, Walter D.
Esther Forbes **12**:204

Edwards, C. Hines, Jr.
James Dickey **4**:121

Edwards, Margaret A.
Betty Cavanna **12**:99
Mary Stolz **12**:546

Edwards, Mary Jane
Paulette Jiles **13**:304
Susan Musgrave **13**:401

Edwards, Michael
Donald Davie **5**:114
Charles Tomlinson **4**:547

Edwards, Sharon
Jessamyn West **7**:522

Edwards, Thomas R.
Lisa Alther **7**:14
Kingsley Amis **8**:12
James Baldwin **4**:41
Donald Barthelme **8**:49
Richard Brautigan **12**:73
Frederick Buechner **2**:83
Charles Bukowski **2**:84
Anthony Burgess **5**:88
John Cheever **7**:48
Evan S. Connell, Jr. **4**:108
Stanley Elkin **4**:153
Leslie A. Fiedler **4**:161
Paula Fox **2**:140
John Gardner **2**:151; **5**:133
Gail Godwin **8**:248
Herbert Gold **4**:193
James Hanley **8**:266
Diane Johnson **13**:306
James Jones **10**:293
Jerzy Kosinski **2**:233
George Lamming **2**:235
Norman Mailer **2**:264
Harry Mathews **6**:616
Peter Matthiessen **7**:211
Thomas McGuane **3**:330
Leonard Michaels **6**:324
Brian Moore **7**:237
Ishmael Reed **2**:368
Philip Roth **3**:437
André Schwarz-Bart **2**:389
Hubert Selby, Jr. **2**:390
Wilfrid Sheed **4**:488
John Updike **5**:460
Derek Walcott **4**:576
Tom Wolfe **1**:375

Edwards, William D.
Jules Archer **12**:18

Eggenschwiler, David
Flannery O'Connor **6**:378
William Styron **5**:419

Egoff, Sheila
Julia W. Cunningham **12**:165
Leon Garfield **12**:218
Christie Harris **12**:265

Egremont, Max
Anna Kavan **13**:317
Seán O'Faoláin **7**:276
Anthony Powell **7**:341; **9**:438
Gillian Tindall **7**:474
Ludvík Vaculík **7**:496

Ehre, Milton
Aleksandr I. Solzhenitsyn **2**:412

Ehrenpreis, Irvin
John Ashbery **6**:13
W. H. Auden **9**:58
T. S. Eliot **13**:200
Donald Hall **13**:260
Anthony Hecht **13**:269
Geoffrey Hill **8**:293
Donald Justice **6**:272
Robert Lowell **1**:180; **8**:353
George Oppen **7**:285
John Updike **5**:455

Eiseley, Loren
J.R.R. Tolkien **12**:566

Eiseman, Alberta
Betty Cavanna **12**:100
William Mayne **12**:390
Lenora Mattingly Weber **12**:633

Eisen, Dulcie
Ronald Tavel **6**:529

Eisenberg, J. A.
Isaac Bashevis Singer **1**:310

Eisinger, Chester E.
Arthur Miller **6**:331
Carson McCullers **12**:421

Eisinger, Erica M.
Marguerite Duras **11**:165

Elias, Robert H.
James Thurber **5**:431

Eliot, T. S.
Marianne Moore **13**:392

Elizondo, Salvador
Octavio Paz **3**:376

Elkin, Stanley
Frederick Forsyth **2**:136

Elleman, Barbara
Melvin Berger **12**:42
Madeleine L'Engle **12**:351
Katherine Paterson **12**:485

Elley, Derek
Mel Brooks **12**:79

Ellin, Stanley
Robert Cormier **12**:138

Ellestad, Everett M.
Pär Lagerkvist **13**:333

Elliott, George P.
Jean Giono **4**:187
Robert Graves **2**:176
Norman Mailer **3**:317
Susan Sontag **10**:485
David Wagoner **3**:507

CRITIC INDEX

Elliott, Janice
Patricia Highsmith 2:193
Aleksandr I. Solzhenitsyn 1:321

Elliott, Robert C.
Ursula K. LeGuin 8:341

Elliott, William I.
Shusaku Endo 7:95

Ellis, James
John Knowles 1:169

Ellison, Harlan
Barry N. Malzberg 7:208

Ellison, Ralph
Richard Wright 9:583

Ellmann, Mary
John Barth 2:39
Vladimir Nabokov 1:244
Joyce Carol Oates 3:364
Aleksandr I. Solzhenitsyn 1:321
J.R.R. Tolkien 12:571
Michel Tournier 6:538
Rebecca West 7:526
Vassily S. Yanovsky 2:485
Richard Price 12:490

Ellmann, Richard
W. H. Auden 9:55
Giorgio Bassani 9:76
Samuel Beckett 2:47

Elman, Richard
William Bronk 10:73
Frederick Busch 10:91
Richard Price 12:490

Elman, Richard M.
Charles Bukowski 9:137
Hannah Green 3:202
Jack Spicer 8:497
Hunter S. Thompson 9:526
Rudolf Wurlitzer 2:482

Elon, Amos
Yehuda Amichai 9:22

Elsom, John
Alan Ayckbourn 5:35
Samuel Beckett 6:43
Edward Bond 6:85
Michael Frayn 7:108
Sam Shepard 6:496
Tom Stoppard 5:412
E. A. Whitehead 5:488

Elstob, Peter
Len Deighton 4:119

Emanuel, James A.
Langston Hughes 1:147

Emblidge, David
E. L. Doctorow 11:143

Emerson, Donald
Carson McCullers 12:420

Emerson, Ken
Stevie Wonder 12:657

Emerson, O. B.
Marion Montgomery 7:232

Emerson, Sally
William Mayne 12:404

Emerson, Stephen
Gilbert Sorrentino 7:450

Emmons, Winfred S.
Katherine Anne Porter 1:273

Engel, Bernard F.
Marianne Moore 1:227

Engel, Marian
Penelope Gilliatt 2:160
Margaret Laurence 3:278
Françoise Mallet-Joris 11:356
Joyce Carol Oates 6:372
Françoise Sagan 6:481
Michel Tournier 6:537

Engle, Paul
Charles M. Schulz 12:531

Enright, D. J.
John Ashbery 9:49
Heinrich Böll 3:74; 11:52
Anthony Burgess 4:80
Stanley Burnshaw 3:90
James Clavell 6:114
Lawrence Durrell 6:151
Witold Gombrowicz 4:195
Günter Grass 2:271; 4:202
Robert Graves 2:175
Hermann Hesse 3:243
Randall Jarrell 9:296
Yasunari Kawabata 5:206;
  9:316
Milan Kundera 9:321
Philip Larkin 3:276
Doris Lessing 3:282
Czeslaw Milosz 5:291
Yukio Mishima 4:353
Vladimir Nabokov 3:352
V. S. Naipaul 4:371
Ezra Pound 3:395
Stevie Smith 3:460
C. P. Snow 9:496
Muriel Spark 3:463
John Updike 2:439

Enslin, Theodore
George Oppen 7:281

Eoff, Sherman H.
Jean-Paul Sartre 1:303
Ramón Sender 8:477

Ephron, Nora
Erich Segal 3:447
Garry Trudeau 12:589

Epps, Garrett
Thomas Berger 11:47
Nicholas Delbanco 13:174

Epstein, Joseph
E. M. Forster 4:165
Joseph Heller 5:174
Alan Lelchuk 5:241
Aleksandr I. Solzhenitsyn 2:409
Stephen Spender 5:402
Edmund Wilson 2:477; 8:551

Epstein, Lawrence J.
Elie Wiesel 5:493

Epstein, Seymour
Saul Bellow 13:72

Ericson, Edward, Jr.
Thornton Wilder 10:533

Ericson, Edward E., Jr.
C. S. Lewis 6:310
Aleksandr I. Solzhenitsyn 4:509

Erlich, Richard
Harlan Ellison 13:203

Erlich, Victor
Joseph Brodsky 6:96

Ernst, Margaret
Andre Norton 12:455

Eron, Carol
John Hawkes 4:218

Eskin, Stanley G.
Nicholas Delbanco 6:130

Esslin, Martin
Arthur Adamov 4:5
Edward Albee 2:4; 9:10
John Arden 6:5
Samuel Beckett 1:24; 4:52;
  6:33, 44
Edward Bond 13:98
Friedrich Dürrenmatt 4:139
Max Frisch 3:167
Jack Gelber 1:114
Jean Genet 1:117
Günter Grass 4:201
Graham Greene 9:250
Rolf Hochhuth 4:231
Eugène Ionesco 1:154; 4:252
Arthur Kopit 1:170
Slawomir Mrozek 3:344
Robert Pinget 7:306
Harold Pinter 1:268; 6:407, 414
Neil Simon 6:506
Peter Weiss 3:515

Estess, Sybil
Elizabeth Bishop 9:95

Estess, Ted L.
Samuel Beckett 11:41

Ettin, Andrew V.
James Merrill 2:273

Evans, Ann
Judy Blume 12:46

Evans, Don
Ed Bullins 5:82

Evans, Donald T.
Alice Childress 12:105

Evans, Eli N.
James Dickey 7:86

Evans, Fallon
J. F. Powers 1:279

Evans, Gareth Lloyd
Harold Pinter 11:444

Evans, Gwyneth F.
Christie Harris 12:267

Evans, Oliver
Paul Bowles 1:41
Carson McCullers 12:425

Evans, Robley
J. R. R. Tolkien 3:478

Evans, Timothy
Isaac Bashevis Singer 11:499

Evarts, Prescott, Jr.
John Fowles 2:138

Evett, Robert
Terrence McNally 7:219
Lanford Wilson 7:548

Ewart, Gavin
William Sansom 2:383

Ewers, John C.
Jamake Highwater 12:286

Eyre, Frank
Peter Dickinson 12:170
Leon Garfield 12:223
William Mayne 12:396

Eyster, Warren
James Dickey 1:74

Fabre, Michel
James Baldwin 3:31
Chester Himes 2:195

Faber, Nancy W.
Frank Bonham 12:50

Fadiman, Anne
Fran Lebowitz 11:322

Fadiman, Clifton
Carson McCullers 12:409

Fadiman, Edwin
Laura Z. Hobson 7:163

Faery, Rebecca B.
Richard Wilbur 9:570

Fager, Charles E.
Bob Dylan 12:185

Fahey, James
Evan S. Connell, Jr. 4:109

Faith, Rosamond
Rosemary Wells 12:638

Falck, Colin
A. Alvarez 5:16
John Berryman 2:55
William Empson 3:147
Geoffrey Grigson 7:136
Thom Gunn 6:220
Seamus Heaney 7:149
Ted Hughes 6:280
Philip Larkin 3:275, 276
Robert Lowell 2:245; 5:256
George MacBeth 9:340
Anne Sexton 8:483
Charles Tomlinson 2:436

Falk, Signi
Tennessee Williams 1:367

Falke, Wayne
Kenzaburo Oe 10:372
John Updike 5:453

Fallis, Laurence S.
Ruth Prawar Jhabvala 4:259

Fallowell, Duncan
Giorgio Bassani 9:77
John Berger 2:54
William Peter Blatty 2:64
Richard Brautigan 12:72
Robert Coover 3:114
Mark Helprin 7:152
Ruth Prawer Jhabvala 8:312
Anna Kavan 13:316
Jerzy Kosinski 3:274
Iris Murdoch 4:368
Tim O'Brien 7:272
Seán O'Faoláin 7:274
Mervyn Peake 7:303
David Plante 7:308
Françoise Sagan 9:468
James Salter 7:388
Hubert Selby, Jr. 2:390
Terry Southern 7:454
Muriel Spark 3:465; 8:493
Auberon Waugh 7:514

Fandel, John
E. E. Cummings 3:120

Fanger, Donald
Aleksandr I. Solzhenitsyn 1:319

Fantoni, Barry
Brian Wilson 12:640

Farmer, Betty Catherine Dobson
Donald Barthelme 13:58

Farmer, Penelope
William Mayne 12:401

Farrell, Diane
Andre Norton 12:459

Farrell, James T.
James M. Cain 11:84
Ben Hecht 8:269

Farrell, John P.
Richard Wilbur 3:532

Farwell, Harold
John Barth 5:50

Farwell, Ruth
George Mackay Brown 5:77

Farzan, Massud
Ahmad Shamlu 10:469

Faulks, Sebastian
Yasunari Kawabata 9:316

Fawcett, Graham
Anthony Burgess 8:111

Featherstone, Joseph
Katherine Anne Porter 3:392

Feaver, William
Michael Ayrton 7:19

Feder, Lillian
Conrad Aiken 5:8
W. H. Auden 4:33, 34, 35
George Barker 8:43
Samuel Beckett 6:37
T. S. Eliot 6:160
Robert Graves 6:210
Ted Hughes 9:281
Robert Lowell 4:301
Ezra Pound 3:396; 4:414

Federman, Raymond
Samuel Beckett 9:79

Feied, Frederick
John Dos Passos 1:80
Jack Kerouac 1:166

Feifer, George
Aleksandr I. Solzhenitsyn 7:444

Fein, Richard J.
Robert Lowell 3:304

Feingold, Michael
Dannie Abse 7:2
Athol Fugard 9:235
John Guare 8:252,253
Peter Handke 8:263
John Hopkins 4:234
Jim Jacobs and Warren Casey
12:294
Ira Levin 3:294
Miguel Piñero 4:401
Elizabeth Swados 12:557, 561
Tennessee Williams 7:544

Feinstein, Elaine
Gail Godwin 8:247
William Golding 2:169
Nadine Gordimer 3:202
George MacBeth 5:265
Mary McCarthy 3:329
Grace Paley 6:339
Christina Stead 5:403

Feirstein, Frederick
Robert Graves 2:177

Feld, Michael
Richard Brautigan 12:63
John Updike 2:445

Feld, Rose
Agatha Christie 12:114
Madeleine L'Engle 12:345
Jack Spicer 8:497

Feld, Ross
Paul Blackburn 9:98
Laurie Colwin 13:156
William H. Gass 11:225
Tom Wolfe 9:578

Feldman, Anita
Irwin Shaw 7:412

Feldman, Irma P.
Helen Yglesias 7:558

Feldman, Morton
Frank O'Hara 2:322

Felheim, Marvin
Ben Hecht 8:272
Carson McCullers 1:208
Eudora Welty 1:361

Felstiner, John
Pablo Neruda 1:247; 2:309;
5:302

Fender, Stephen
Richard Price 12:491
John Sayles 10:462

Fenton, James
W. H. Auden 6:18
Giorgio Bassani 9:76
Douglas Dunn 6:148
Gavin Ewart 13:210
Charles Tomlinson 6:534

Ferguson, Alan
Ivo Andrić 8:20

Ferguson, Frances
Randall Jarrell 13:301
Robert Lowell 4:302

Ferguson, Suzanne
Djuna Barnes 3:36
Randall Jarrell 2:209

Fernandez, Jaime
Jun'ichiro Tanizaki 8:511

Ferrari, Margaret
Marge Piercy 6:402

Ferrer, Olga Prjevalinskaya
Eugène Ionesco 6:256

Ferretti, Fred
Norman Lear 12:326

Ferrier, Carole
Diane Wakoski 7:505

Ferris, Ina
Rudy Wiebe 11:567

Ferris, William H.
W.E.B. DuBois 13:180

Ferry, David
Theodore Roethke 1:291

Fetherling, Doug
Hugh Garner 13:235,236
Mordecai Richler 3:431
Robin Skelton 13:506

Feuer, Kathryn B.
Aleksandr I. Solzhenitsyn 7:445

Feuser, Willfried F.
Chinua Achebe 7:6

Fialkowski, Barbara
Maxine Kumin 13:326

Fiamengo, Marya
Susan Musgrave 13:400

Fickert, Kurt J.
Friedrich Dürrenmatt 4:139

Fiedler, Leslie A.
John Barth 3:38
Saul Bellow 1:27, 31; 3:48
Leonard Cohen 3:109
Bob Dylan 3:130
William Faulkner 1:101; 3:149
Allen Ginsberg 2:162; 3:193
John Hawkes 3:221
Ernest Hemingway 1:143;
3:232, 233
John Hersey 7:153
Randall Jarrell 1:160
Robert Lowell 2:246
Norman Mailer 3:311
Bernard Malamud 9:341, 351
Henry Miller 2:282
Alberto Moravia 2:293
Wright Morris 1:232
Vladimir Nabokov 1:239
Ezra Pound 7:329
John Crowe Ransom 2:363
Mordecai Richler 5:375
Henry Roth 6:470
J. D. Salinger 12:512
Kurt Vonnegut, Jr. 12:603
Robert Penn Warren 4:579
Richard Wilbur 3:530
Herman Wouk 1:376

Field, Andrew
Vladimir Nabokov 1:242
Yevgeny Yevtushenko 1:382

Field, Colin
William Mayne 12:392

Field, George Wallis
Hermann Hesse 1:147

Field, Joyce
Bernard Malamud 9:348

Field, Leslie
Bernard Malamud 9:348

Field, Trevor
Julien Green 11:261

Fields, Beverly
Anne Sexton 2:391

Fields, Kenneth
J. V. Cunningham 3:121
Robert Lowell 4:299
N. Scott Momaday 2:290
Marya Zaturenska 6:585

Fifer, Elizabeth
Maxine Hong Kingston 12:314

Filer, Malva E.
Julio Cortázar 10:117

Finch, John
E. E. Cummings 12:144

Fincke, Gary
Ben Hecht 8:271

Finel-Honigman, Irène
Albert Camus 11:96

Finger, Louis
John Le Carré 9:326

Finholt, Richard
James Dickey 10:142
Ralph Ellison 11:184

Finkle, David
John Fowles 9:215

Finley, M. I.
Michael Ayrton 7:17

Finn, James
François Mauriac 4:339
P. G. Wodehouse 2:480

Firchow, Peter
Aldous Huxley 8:305

Firchow, Peter E.
W. H. Auden 11:17

Fireside, Harvey
Andrei Sinyavsky 8:489, 490

Firestone, Bruce M.
Anthony Burgess 10:89

First, Elsa
Carlos Castaneda 12:91

Fisch, Harold
Aharon Megged 9:374

Fischer, John Irwin
Brosman, Catharine Savage
9:135

Fischer, Marjorie
Margot Benary-Isbert 12:30
Joseph Krumgold 12:317

Fisher, Emma
John Berryman 10:47
Peter Porter 13:452
R. S. Thomas 13:544

Fisher, Margery
E. M. Almedingen 12:6
Ruth M. Arthur 12:25, 26
Judy Blume 12:47
Mavis Thorpe Clark 12:130,
131, 132
Robert Cormier 12:135, 137
Julia W. Cunningham 12:164,
165
Peter Dickinson 12:169, 174,
177
Esther Forbes 12:211
Leon Garfield 12:216, 217, 218,
223, 227, 231, 233, 234
William Mayne 12:389, 405
Emily Cheney Neville 12:450
Andre Norton 12:469, 470
Katherine Paterson 12:485
J.R.R. Tolkien 12:586
Rosemary Wells 12:638

Fisher, William J.
William Saroyan 8:466

Fison, Peter
C. P. Snow 13:511

Fitzgerald, Robert
Seamus Heaney 7:151
Robert Lowell 11:325

Fitzlyon, Kyril
Aleksandr I. Solzhenitsyn 1:321

Fitzsimmons, Thomas
Elizabeth Hardwick 13:264

Fiut, Aleksander
Czesław Miłosz 11:379

Fixler, Michael
Isaac Bashevis Singer 1:311

Flagg, Nancy
Jorge Amado 13:11

CRITIC·INDEX

CRITIC INDEX

Flaherty, Joe
Richard Brautigan 9:124

Flamm, Dudley
Robert M. Pirsig 4:404

Flanders, Jane
Katherine Anne Porter 10:396

Flanner, Janet
André Malraux 4:326

Fleckenstein, Joan S.
Edward Albee 11:13

Fleischer, Leonard
John A. Williams 5:496

Fleishman, Avrom
John Fowles 9:210

Fleming, Robert E.
John A. Williams 5:496

Fleming, Thomas J.
Emily Cheney Neville 12:450
Ira Levin 6:305

Fletcher, John
Uwe Johnson 5:201
Kamala Markandaya 8:377
Jean-Paul Sartre 7:398

Flexner, James Thomas
Esther Forbes 12:209

Flint, R. W.
A. R. Ammons 8:15; 9:29
Irving Feldman 7:102
Anthony Hecht 8:267
Randall Jarrell 1:159
Karl Shapiro 8:486
Charles Tomlinson 13:550

Floan, Howard R.
William Saroyan 1:301

Flood, Jeanne
Brian Moore 5:294

Flora, Joseph M.
Vardis Fisher 7:103
Günter Grass 6:209
J. E. Wideman 5:490
Nancy Willard 7:539

Flower, Dean
Hubert Selby, Jr. 8:477
Helen Yglesias 7:559

Flowers, Ann A.
Leon Garfield 12:239
Katherine Paterson 12:486

Flowers, Betty
Donald Barthelme 5:56

Fludas, John
Richard Price 12:491

Folsom, L. Edwin
W. S. Merwin 13:384

Fontenot, Chester J.
Alex Haley 8:260

Foote, Audrey C.
Anthony Burgess 4:81
Nathalie Sarraute 2:386
Christina Stead 5:404
Mary Stewart 7:468

Foote, Timothy
W. H. Auden 3:26; 6:24
Anthony Burgess 5:89
Peter De Vries 2:114
John Gardner 3:187

John Le Carré 5:232
V. S. Pritchett 5:352
Aleksandr I. Solzhenitsyn 4:516
Tom Stoppard 4:525
Tom Wolfe 2:481

Forbes, Alastair
Lawrence Durrell 13:189

Ford, Nick Aaron
Harper Lee 12:341

Ford, Richard J.
Hermann Hesse 2:189

Forman, Jack
Jules Archer 12:18, 20
Frank Bonham 12:51
Katherine Paterson 12:485, 486

Fornatale, Peter
Brian Wilson 12:646

Forrest, Alan
W. H. Auden 3:27
Mario Puzo 2:352

Forrey, Robert
Ken Kesey 11:316

Fortin, René E.
Boris Pasternak 7:296

Foster, David W.
Camilo José Cela 4:96

Foster, David William
Jorge Luis Borges 3:78; 6:89
Julio Cortázar 10:118
Ernesto Sábato 10:445

Foster, John Wilson
Seamus Heaney 5:170
Brian Moore 1:225

Foster, Richard
Norman Mailer 1:190; 8:365

Foster, Ruel E.
Jesse Stuart 1:328

Fotheringham, Hamish
William Mayne 12:388

Fowler, Alastair
Charles M. Schulz 12:532

Fowlie, Wallace
Michel Butor 8:119
René Char 9:158
Jean Genet 5:135
Julien Green 11:258
Henri Michaux 8:392
Anaïs Nin 4:378; 11:398
Jules Romains 7:379

Fox, Hugh
William Carlos Williams 5:509

Fox-Genovese, Elizabeth
William Gaddis 8:226

Frakes, James R.
Nelson Algren 4:17
Wendell Berry 4:59
Bruce Jay Friedman 5:127
Patricia Highsmith 2:194
Stanley Hoffman 5:185
Evan Hunter 11:280
Diane Johnson 5:198
Michael Mewshaw 9:376
Muriel Spark 2:418
Richard G. Stern 4:522

France, Peter
Anne Hébert 13:267

Francescato, Martha Paley
Julio Cortázar 10:116

Frank, Armin Paul
Kenneth Burke 2:89

Frank, Joseph
Djuna Barnes 8:47
André Malraux 4:327
Aleksandr I. Solzhenitsyn 7:443

Frank, Mike
Joseph Heller 11:266

Frank, Sheldon
Margaret Laurence 6:289
Hans Erich Nossack 6:365

Frankel, Bernice
Mary Stolz 12:547

Frankel, Haskel
Bruce Jay Friedman 3:165
Muriel Spark 2:417
Peter Ustinov 1:346
Charles Webb 7:514

Franklin, Allan
Jorge Luis Borges 9:116

Franklin, H. Bruce
J. G. Ballard 3:32

Fraser, G. S.
Basil Bunting 10:86
Robert Creeley 1:67
C. Day Lewis 6:127
Nigel Dennis 8:172
Lawrence Durrell 4:145;
  13:184
Jean Garrigue 2:153
Randall Jarrell 9:296
Robert Lowell 2:249; 11:325
Hugh MacDiarmid 11:337
W. S. Merwin 1:214
C. P. Snow 4:502
Gary Snyder 1:318
Louis Zukofsky 1:385

Fraser, John
Louis-Ferdinand Céline 1:56;
  4:102
Yvor Winters 4:592; 8:552

Fraser, Kathleen
Adrienne Rich 3:429

Fraser, Keath
Sinclair Ross 13:492

Frazer, Frances M.
Christie Harris 12:268

Fredeman, W. E.
Earle Birney 6:72

Freedman, Ralph
Saul Bellow 1:29
Hermann Hesse 1:146

Freedman, Richard
A. Alvarez 13:10
Hortense Calisher 2:96
Dick Francis 2:142
Lois Gould 4:199
S. J. Perelman 9:416
P. G. Wodehouse 5:517

Freedman, William
Henry Roth 11:487

Freeman, Anne Hobson
Reynolds Price 13:463

Freeman, Gillian
Robert Nye 13:412

Fremantle, Anne
W. H. Auden 1:10
Auberon Waugh 7:513

Fremont-Smith, Eliot
Richard Adams 4:6
Martin Amis 4:20
Max Apple 9:33
Louis Auchincloss 4:31
Laurie Colwin 13:156
E. L. Doctorow 6:132
Lawrence Durrell 6:152
Gael Greene 8:252
Joseph Heller 5:173; 11:268
Lillian Hellman 4:221
John Irving 13:294
Marjorie Kellogg 2:223
Jascha Kessler 4:269
Arthur Koestler 3:271
Jerzy Kosinski 1:172
John Le Carré 9:327
Alan Lelchuk 5:243
Norman Mailer 4:322
James A. Michener 5:289
Richard Price 6:426; 12:490
Philip Roth 4:453, 455
Alix Kates Shulman 10:476
Gore Vidal 6:54
Irving Wallace 7:510
Patrick White 3:524

French, Allen
Esther Forbes 12:206

French, Philip
Jorge Luis Borges 4:75
Truman Capote 8:132
Graham Greene 3:212; 6:220

French, Robert W.
Joyce Carol Oates 1:251

French, Warren
William Goldman 1:123
R. K. Narayan 7:254
James Purdy 2:349
J. D. Salinger 1:297; 12:514
John Steinbeck 1:324; 5:406
Thornton Wilder 1:366

Fretz, Sada
Julia W. Cunningham 12:165

Friar, Kimon
Margaríta Karapánou 13:314
Yannis Ritsos 6:463
Vassilis Vassilikos 8:524

Fried, Lewis
James T. Farrell 11:191

Friedberg, Maurice
Aleksandr I. Solzhenitsyn
  1:319; 7:435

Friedenberg, Edgar Z.
Hermann Hesse 2:190

Friedman, Alan
William S. Burroughs 5:93
John Gardner 7:112
Yukio Mishima 4:357
Amos Oz 8:435
Ishmael Reed 2:367
André Schwarz-Bart 2:389
Elie Wiesel 3:528

Friedman, Alan J.
Thomas Pynchon 6:434

Friedman, Alan Warren
Saul Bellow 8:69

Lawrence Durrell 1:87
Bernard Malamud 8:375

Friedman, Jack
Wendell Berry 4:59
José Lezama Lima 4:290

Friedman, John
William Eastlake 8:200

Friedman, Melvin J.
Bruce Jay Friedman 5:127
Eugène Ionesco 6:256
André Malraux 4:333
R. K. Narayan 7:255
Flannery O'Connor 1:253
Isaac Bashevis Singer 1:313

Friedman, Norman
E. E. Cummings 1:69; 12:149
David Ignatow 7:174

Frieling, Kenneth
Flannery O'Connor 13:416

Friesem, Roberta Ricky
Lenora Mattingly Weber 12:635

Frith, Simon
Patti Smith 12:543

Fritz, Jean
Ruth M. Arthur 12:24
Joseph Krumgold 12:318
Mary Stolz 12:553

Frohock, W. M.
James M. Cain 11:84
Erskine Caldwell 1:51
James Gould Cozzens 4:113
John Dos Passos 1:77
James T. Farrell 1:97
William Faulkner 1:99
Ernest Hemingway 1:141
André Malraux 4:324; 13:366
John Steinbeck 1:323
Robert Penn Warren 1:351

Frost, Lucy
John Hawkes 3:223

Fruchtbaum, Harold
Loren Eiseley 7:90

Frye, Northrop
Louis Dudek 11:158

Fryer, Jonathan H.
Christopher Isherwood 9:292

Fuchs, Daniel
Saul Bellow 3:62

Fuchs, Vivian
Thomas Keneally 10:299

Fuchs, Wolfgang
Charles M. Schulz 12:528

Fulford, Robert
Brian Moore 3:340
Mordecai Richler 3:429
Philip Roth 3:435

Fuller, Edmund
Paul Bowles 1:41
Frederick Buechner 4:80
James Gould Cozzens 1:65
James Jones 1:161
Jack Kerouac 1:165
Alan Paton 4:395
J. R. R. Tolkien 1:335
Herman Wouk 1:375

Fuller, Elizabeth Ely
Isak Dinesen 10:150

Fuller, John
Anna Akhmatova 11:9
Thom Gunn 3:215
Randall Jarrell 2:208
William Plomer 4:406
Ann Quin 6:441
Kathleen Raine 7:353
Jon Silkin 6:499
Andrew Young 5:523

Fuller, Roy
W. H. Auden 3:25
Aldous Huxley 5:192
Stephen Spender 2:420
Lionel Trilling 9:530

Fulton, Robin
Pär Lagerkvist 10:313

Furbank, P. N.
E. M. Forster 4:165, 168
Uwe Johnson 10:284
Gore Vidal 4:556

Fussell, B. H.
Peter Taylor 4:543

Fussell, Edwin
Wendell Berry 6:61
Hayden Carruth 7:40

Fussell, Paul
Thomas Keneally 8:318

Fussell, Paul, Jr.
Karl Shapiro 4:486

Fytton, Francis
Paul Bowles 2:78

Gabree, John
John Lennon and Paul
  McCartney 12:364

Gadney, Reg
George V. Higgins 7:158
Patricia Highsmith 2:194
Ross Macdonald 2:257
Alistair MacLean 3:309

Gagné, Sarah
Melvin Berger 12:42
Larry Kettelkamp 12:307

Gaines, Richard H.
Chester Himes 2:196

Gaiser, Carolyn
Gregory Corso 1:63

Gaither, Frances
Esther Forbes 12:210

Galassi, Jonathan
John Berryman 6:63
Robert Duncan 2:123
Robert Graves 6:212
Seamus Heaney 7:147
Randall Jarrell 9:297
Eugenio Montale 7:231
Howard Nemerov 9:396
George Oppen 13:434

Galbraith, John Kenneth
William Safire 10:446

Gall, Sally M.
Kenneth O. Hanson 13:263
Eleanor Lerman 9:329
Charles Wright 6:580

Gallagher, D. P.
Adolfo Bioy Casares 8:94;
  13:83
Jorge Luis Borges 6:88

Gabriel García Márquez 8:230
G. Cabrera Infante 5:96
Pablo Neruda 7:257
Octavio Paz 6:394
Manuel Puig 10:420
Mario Vargas Llosa 6:543

Gallagher, David
G. Cabrera Infante 5:95
Manuel Puig 3:407

Gallagher, Michael
Shusaku Endo 7:95

Gallant, Mavis
Simone de Beauvior 4:48
Louis-Ferdinand Céline 7:46
Günter Grass 4:205
Vladimir Nabokov 2:303

Galler, David
Ted Hughes 2:198
Howard Nemerov 2:307

Galligan, Edward L.
Georges Simenon 1:309

Galloway, David D.
Saul Bellow 3:51, 55
Stanley Elkin 4:152
Dan Jacobson 4:253
J. D. Salinger 3:445
William Styron 3:473
John Updike 3:486

Gannon, Edward, S.J.
André Malraux 4:326

Gant, Lisbeth
Ed Bullins 5:82

Ganz, Arthur
Harold Pinter 6:416

Ganz, Earl
John Hawkes 1:139
Flannery O'Connor 2:318

Garcia, Irma
Nicholasa Mohr 12:447

Gardiner, Harold C.
Robert Cormier 12:134

Gardner, Erle Stanley
Meyer Levin 7:203

Gardner, Harvey
Jimmy Breslin 4:76

Gardner, John
Saul Bellow 10:44
Anthony Burgess 2:84
Italo Calvino 8:129
John Fowles 9:215
William H. Gass 1:114
John Knowles 4:271
Brian Moore 8:395
Charles Newman 8:419
Walker Percy 8:442
Philip Roth 2:379
J.R.R. Tolkien 12:585
Patrick White 9:567
Larry Woiwode 6:578

Gardner, Marilyn
Mary Stolz 12:554

Gardner, Peter
John Hersey 9:277

Gardner, Philip
D. J. Enright 4:155
Philip Larkin 5:230

Garebian, Keith
Patrick White 9:563

Garfield, Evelyn Picon
Julio Cortázar 13:163

Garfield, Leon
William Mayne 12:395

Garfitt, Roger
George Barker 8:46
Martin Booth 13:103
Joseph Brodsky 6:96
Robert Creeley 4:118
Douglas Dunn 6:148
Geoffrey Grigson 7:136
Donald Hall 13:259
Anna Kavan 5:206
Reiner Kunze 10:310
Philip Larkin 8:332
George MacBeth 5:263
László Nagy 7:251
Julia O'Faolain 6:383
Peter Porter 5:346
Thomas Pynchon 3:418
Peter Redgrove 6:445
C. H. Sisson 8:490
Anne Stevenson 7:462
Derek Walcott 4:575

Garis, Leslie
Doris Lessing 6:302

Garis, Robert
Herbert Gold 4:191
Anthony Powell 3:400

Garner, Alan
Leon Garfield 12:219

Garnick, Vivian
Toni Morrison 10:355

Garrard, J. G.
Aleksandr I. Solzhenitsyn
  2:411; 9:503

Garrett, George
John Cheever 3:107
Sue Kaufman 8:317
Wright Morris 3:342

Garrigue, Jean
Marianne Moore 1:228

Garson, Helen S.
John Hawkes 9:268

Gasque, Thomas J.
J. R. R. Tolkien 1:337

Gass, William H.
Donald Barthelme 3:43
Jorge Luis Borges 3:76
Robert Coover 3:113
Vladimir Nabokov 3:351
J. F. Powers 1:281
Philip Roth 3:437
Isaac Bashevis Singer 3:454
Susan Sontag 10:484

Gassner, John
Edward Albee 3:6, 7
Jean Anouilh 3:11, 12
Samuel Beckett 3:44, 45
Brendan Behan 8:63
Lillian Hellman 4:220
William Inge 8:307
Eugène Ionesco 4:250
Archibald MacLeish 3:310
Arthur Miller 6:330
John Osborne 5:330

CRITIC INDEX

Harold Pinter 3:386
Thornton Wilder 5:495
Tennessee Williams 5:498, 500

Gates, David
Samuel Beckett 9:83

Gathercole, Patricia M.
Tommaso Landolfi 11:321

Gathorne-Hardy, J.
Vladimir Nabokov 3:354

Gatt-Rutter, John
Italo Calvino 11:89

Gaudon, Sheila
Julien Gracq 11:245

Gaull, Marilyn
E. E. Cummings 12:156

Gavin, William
Auberon Waugh 7:514

Gayle, Addison, Jr.
Gwendolyn Brooks 1:46

Geddes, Gary
Raymond Souster 5:395

Geering, R. G.
Christina Stead 2:423

Geherin, David J.
Joan Didion 8:173

Geis, Richard E.
Peter Dickinson 12:172

Geismar, Maxwell
Nelson Algren 4:16
John Beecher 6:48
Saul Bellow 1:27
Camilo José Cela 13:145
James Gould Cozzens 1:66
John Dos Passos 1:77
William Faulkner 1:100
Nadine Gordimer 5:146
Ernest Hemingway 1:142
John Hersey 1:144
Norman Mailer 1:187
Henry Miller 4:350
Henry Roth 6:471
J. D. Salinger 1:295
William Styron 1:329
Leon Uris 7:490
Herman Wouk 1:376

Gelb, Arthur
Alice Childress 12:104

Gelfant, Blanche H.
Yasunari Kawabata 9:316
Jack Kerouac 5:213
Jean Stafford 7:459

Gellatly, Peter
C. Day Lewis 6:128

Gelpi, Albert
Adrienne Rich 6:457

Geltman, Max
Arthur Koestler 8:325
Ezra Pound 5:349; 7:338

Geng, Veronica
Nadine Gordimer 5:148

George, Diana L.
Lionel Trilling 9:532

George, Michael
J. B. Priestley 5:350

Gerald, John Bart
Robert Lowell 3:302
Robert Stone 5:411

Gerhardt, Lillian N.
Betty Cavanna 12:101

Gerould, Daniel C.
Tadeusz Różewicz 9:463

Gerrard, Charlotte F.
Eugène Ionesco 9:286

Gerson, Ben
John Lennon and Paul
McCartney 12:366, 377

Gersoni-Stavn, Diane
See Stavn, Diane Gersoni

Gerstenberger, Donna
Iris Murdoch 6:348

Gertel, Zunilda
José Donoso 4:128
Juan Carlos Onetti 7:278

Giacoman, Helmy F.
Alejo Carpentier 11:97

Giannaris, George
Vassilis Vassilikos 8:524

Giannone, Richard
Kurt Vonnegut, Jr. 12:620

Gibbons, Boyd
James A. Michener 11:374

Gibbs, Beverly J.
Juan Carlos Onetti 10:374

Gibbs, Robert
Margaret Avison 2:29

Gibian, George
Aleksandr I. Solzhenitsyn 7:447

Gibson, Donald B.
James Baldwin 3:32
Imamu Amiri Baraka 5:46
Ralph Ellison 3:143
Langston Hughes 5:19
Jean Toomer 13:551

Gibson, Kenneth
Roch Carrier 13:143

Gibson, Margaret
Judith Wright 11:578

Giddings, Paula
Margaret Walker 1:351

Gide, André
Hermann Hesse 11:270
Pär Lagerkvist 7:199

Gidley, Mick
William Faulkner 3:156

Gifford, Henry
Joseph Brodsky 13:117
Marianne Moore 4:361

Gilbert, Sandra M.
Maya Angelou 12:13
Jean Garrigue 8:239
Sandra Hochman 8:297
Diane Johnson 5:200
Kenneth Koch 8:323
Eleanor Lerman 9:329
Anne Sexton 4:484
Kathleen Spivack 6:521
Diane Wakoski 9:554

Gilbert, W. Stephen
Peter Handke 5:163
J. B. Priestley 5:350
David Storey 5:416

Gilbert, Zack
Leon Forrest 4:164

Giles, Mary E.
Juan Goytisolo 10:243

Gill, Brendan
Edward Albee 5:12
Alan Ayckbourn 5:36; 8:34
John Bishop 10:54
Anne Burr 6:104
D. L. Coburn 10:107
Noel Coward 9:172, 173
James Gould Cozzens 11:126
Charles Gordone 1:125
Bill Gunn 5:152
John Hopkins 4:233
Preston Jones 10:296
James Kirkwood 9:319
Pavel Kohout 13:323
Ira Levin 6:306
David Mamet 9:360
Terrence McNally 7:219
Arthur Miller 6:334
Peter Nichols 5:307
Clifford Odets 2:319
John O'Hara 6:385
Ronald Ribman 7:358
William Saroyan 8:468
Murray Schisgal 6:490
Peter Shaffer 5:386
Neil Simon 6:505; 11:495
John Steinbeck 5:408
Tom Stoppard 4:526; 5:413;
8:504
David Storey 2:424
Gore Vidal 2:449
Tennessee Williams 5:503;
8:548
Lanford Wilson 7:547
Robert Wilson 7:550

Gillen, Francis
Donald Barthelme 2:40

Gillespie, John T.
Frank Bonham 12:51, 55
Alice Childress 12:107

Gillespie, Robert
Eric Ambler 6:2
Jorge Luis Borges 6:91
John Le Carré 9:326

Gilliatt, Penelope
Samuel Beckett 4:49
Noel Coward 9:172
Joe Orton 4:387

Gillis, William
Friedrich Dürrenmatt 11:170

Gilman, Harvey
Howard Nemerov 6:362

Gilman, Richard
Richard Adams 4:7
Edward Albee 5:10
John Arden 6:6
Imamu Amiri Baraka 5:44
Donald Barthelme 2:40
Saul Bellow 6:49
J. P. Donleavy 6:140
Bruce Jay Friedman 5:126
William H. Gass 2:154
Jack Gelber 1:114; 6:196
Graham Greene 6:214
Rolf Hochhuth 11:274
Eugène Ionesco 6:249
Kenneth Koch 5:218
Norman Mailer 2:260; 8:367
Michael McClure 10:331

Arthur Miller 6:326, 327
Sean O'Casey 5:319
Harold Pinter 6:405, 406, 410
Reynolds Price 6:424
John Rechy 7:356
Philip Roth 3:438
Robert Shaw 5:390
Neil Simon 6:502
John Updike 2:440
Tennessee Williams 5:499

Gilmore, Mikal
Stevie Wonder 12:660

Gilsdorf, Jeanette
Robert Creeley 4:118

Gindin, James
Kingsley Amis 2:4
Saul Bellow 3:54
Truman Capote 3:100
Margaret Drabble 10:165
E. M. Forster 3:160
John Fowles 10:189
William Golding 2:165; 3:198
Rosamond Lehmann 5:238
Doris Lessing 2:238
Iris Murdoch 2:295; 3:347
John Osborne 2:327
Philip Roth 3:436
Alan Sillitoe 3:447, 448
David Storey 2:423; 4:528
John Wain 2:457
Angus Wilson 2:470; 3:534

Gingher, Robert S.
John Updike 5:454

Gingrich, Arnold
Chester Himes 2:196

Ginsberg, Allen
Gregory Corso 11:123
Jack Kerouac 2:228

Giovanni, Nikki
Alice Walker 5:476

Gipson, Carolyn
W. E. B. Du Bois 2:120

Girson, Rochelle
Peter S. Beagle 7:25

Gitlin, Todd
James Baldwin 2:32
Robert Bly 2:66
Bob Dylan 4:150
Paul Goodman 7:130
Denise Levertov 2:243
Marge Piercy 3:383

Gitzen, Julian
Robert Bly 10:56
Seamus Heaney 5:172
Ted Hughes 4:237
Denise Levertov 5:250
Peter Redgrove 6:446
R. S. Thomas 6:531
Charles Tomlinson 2:437; 4:548
Ted Walker 13:566

Givner, Joan
Katherine Anne Porter 7:319;
10:398; 13:450
Eudora Welty 5:479

Glasser, William
J. D. Salinger 8:464

Glassman, Peter
Shirley Ann Grau 9:240

CRITIC INDEX

Glatstein, Jacob
Marianne Moore 4:358

Gleason, Judith Illsley
Chinua Achebe 7:3

Gleason, Ralph J.
Nelson Algren 10:7
Bob Dylan 6:156; 12:181

Gleicher, David
Margaret Atwood 3:19

Glen, Duncan
Hugh MacDiarmid 4:311

Glendinning, Victoria
Melvyn Bragg 10:72
Anthony Burgess 5:87
Angela Carter 5:101
Roald Dahl 6:122
Doris Grumbach 13:258
James Hanley 13:262
Chester Himes 7:159
Russell C. Hoban 7:160
Elizabeth Jane Howard 7:164
Joyce Carol Oates 11:404
Edna O'Brien 13:416
Barbara Pym 13:471
Françoise Sagan 9:468
Alan Sillitoe 6:500
J.I.M. Stewart 7:466
Fay Weldon 11:565

Glenn, Jerry
Paul Celan 10:102, 104

Glicksberg, Charles I.
Arthur Adamov 4:6
Albert Camus 1:52
Jean Genet 5:136
Hermann Hesse 3:244
Aldous Huxley 3:254
Eugène Ionesco 9:288; 11:290
Robinson Jeffers 3:260
André Malraux 1:201

Glimm, James York
Thomas Merton 3:337; 11:372

Glover, Al
Michael McClure 6:320

Glover, Elaine
John Fowles 6:188
Nadine Gordimer 7:131
Joseph Heller 8:279
Tim O'Brien 7:271

Glover, Tony
Patti Smith 12:534

Glover, Willis B.
J. R. R. Tolkien 1:340

Godard, B.
Audrey Thomas 13:540

Goddard, Donald
Lothar-Günther Buchheim 6:102

Godden, Rumer
Carson McCullers 12:418

Godshalk, William L.
Kurt Vonnegut, Jr. 3:500

Godwin, Gail
Beryl Bainbridge 5:39
Ann Beattie 13:64
Julien Green 3:205
Doris Grumbach 13:258

Goitein, Denise
Nathalie Sarraute 10:457

Gold, Herbert
Mel Brooks 12:78
Richard Condon 10:111
Alistair MacLean 13:364
John Dos Passos 4:136
Aleksandr I. Solzhenitsyn 2:409
Terry Southern 7:454
Gore Vidal 6:550

Gold, Ivan
George V. Higgins 10:273
Paul Horgan 9:279
John Updike 2:440
John A. Williams 13:599
Helen Yglesias 7:558

Goldberg, Steven
Bob Dylan 6:154

Goldberg, Vicki
Paul Theroux 11:530

Golden, Robert E.
Thomas Pynchon 3:409

Goldensohn, Lorrie
Ira Sadoff 9:466
Maura Stanton 9:508

Goldfarb, Clare R.
Aleksandr I. Solzhenitsyn 7:443

Goldknopf, David
Kurt Vonnegut, Jr. 12:600

Goldman, Albert
Bob Dylan 3:130; 12:186
John Lennon and Paul McCartney 12:367

Goldman, Mark
Bernard Malamud 1:197

Goldman, Merle
Jules Archer 12:19

Goldman, Michael
Joyce Carol Oates 3:361

Goldman, William
Ross Macdonald 1:185

Goldmann, Lucien
Witold Gombrowicz 11:239

Goldsmith, Arnold L.
John Steinbeck 9:515

Goldsmith, David H.
Kurt Vonnegut, Jr. 4:562

Goldstein, Laurence
Robert Frost 13:230
David Ignatow 4:248
Adrienne Rich 7:372
James Wright 3:541

Goldstein, Malcolm
Thornton Wilder 1:365

Goldstein, Richard
Bob Dylan 3:130 12:182
John Lennon and Paul McCartney 12:357

Goldstone, Richard H.
Thornton Wilder 6:574

Golffing, Francis
Salvatore Quasimodo 10:429

Gömöri, George
László Nagy 7:251

Goodheart, Eugene
Cynthia Ozick 3:372
Theodore Roethke 1:292
John Seelye 7:405
William Carlos Williams 5:510

Goodman, James
George Seferis 5:385

Goodman, Paul
Ernest Hemingway 1:144

Goodman, Robert L.
David Kherdian 6:280

Goodman, Walter
Thomas Berger 8:83

Goodrich, Norma L.
Jean Giono 4:187; 11:230

Goodsell, James Nelson
Jules Archer 12:18

Goodstein, Jack
Alain Robbe-Grillet 2:376

Goodwin, Michael
John Brunner 10:80

Goodwin, Polly
Emily Cheney Neville 12:450

Goodwin, Stephen
Walker Percy 2:335
Peter Taylor 1:334

Gordimer, Nadine
Chinua Achebe 3:2
V. S. Naipaul 4:372
James Ngugi 3:358

Gordon, Andrew
Ishmael Reed 2:368

Gordon, Cecelia
Ruth M. Arthur 12:27

Gordon, David J.
Herbert Gold 4:192
William Golding 1:122
Uwe Johnson 5:200
Brian Moore 1:225
Vladimir Nabokov 1:245
Tom Stoppard 1:328

Gordon, Jan B.
Richard Adams 5:4
John Braine 3:86
Doris Lessing 6:292
Iris Murdoch 3:349

Gordon, Mary
Diane Johnson 13:306
Edna O'Brien 13:416

Gornick, Vivian
Paula Fox 2:140
Lillian Hellman 8:282
Grace Paley 4:391

Gose Elliott
Marie-Claire Blais 13:96
Gwendolyn MacEwan 13:357

Gossett, Louise Y.
Flannery O'Connor 1:256

Gossman, Ann
Lawrence Durrell 1:87

Gott, Richard
Carlos Castaneda 12:86

Gottfried, Martin
Bernard Pomerance 13:445
Lanford Wilson 7:547

Gottlieb, Annie
Maya Angelou 12:11
Henry Bromell 5:74
Louis-Ferdinand Céline 4:104
Lois Gould 10:241
Charles Johnson 7:183
Tillie Olsen 4:386

Gottlieb, Elaine
Isaac Bashevis Singer 6:507

Gottlieb, Gerald
John R. Tunis 12:599

Gottschalk, Jane
Ralph Ellison 11:181

Gould, Jack
John Lennon and Paul McCartney 12:354

Gould, Jean
Elmer Rice 7:363

Goulianos, Joan Rodman
Lawrence Durrell 8:193

Goyen, William
Anaïs Nin 4:379

Goytisolo, Juan
Carlos Fuentes 10:204

Graff, Gerald
Donald Barthelme 6:30
Saul Bellow 6:54
Stanley Elkin 6:169
Norman Mailer 8:372

Graham, Desmond
Jorge Luis Borges 8:103
James Hanley 13:262
Anthony Hecht 13:269
Philip Larkin 5:229
Robert Lowell 11:329
John Montague 13:392
Eugenio Montale 9:388
Peter Porter 13:453

Graham, John
John Hawkes 3:221
Ernest Hemingway 3:236
Gibbons Ruark 3:441

Graham, Kenneth
Richard Adams 5:5
Laurens van der Post 5:463

Grande, Brother Luke M., F.S.C.
Marion Montgomery 7:232

Granetz, Marc
Donald Barthelme 13:61

Grange, Joseph
Carlos Castaneda 12:86

Grant, Annette
Shirley Ann Grau 4:209

Grant, Damian
W. H. Auden 6:17
Seamus Heaney 5:172
Sylvia Plath 2:337
Peter Porter 5:347

Grant, Judith Skelton
Robertson Davies 13:173

Grant, Patrick
Robert Graves 11:257

Grau, Shirley Ann
William Goyen 8:250
Marion Montgomery 7:233

Graver, Lawrence
Samuel Beckett 6:40
Doris Lessing 2:242
Carson McCullers 1:209
Iris Murdoch 3:347
Muriel Spark 2:417
Paul Theroux 8:513
William Trevor 7:475

CRITIC INDEX

Graves, Robert
Yevgeny Yevtushenko **1**:382

Gray, Francine du Plessix
Oriana Fallaci **11**:190

Gray, Mrs. Hildagarde
Katherine Paterson **12**:485

Gray, James
Pearl S. Buck **7**:32
Jules Romains **7**:381

Gray, John
Paul Bowles **2**:79

Gray, Mrs. John G.
Jules Archer **12**:20
M. E. Kerr **12**:298

Gray, Paul
Lisa Alther **7**:12
Samuel Beckett **6**:44
Adolfo Bioy Casares **8**:94
Vance Bourjaily **8**:104
Jimmy Breslin **4**:76
William F. Buckley, Jr. **7**:35
Alex Comfort **7**:54
Evan S. Connell, Jr. **6**:116
Peter De Vries **7**:78
Thomas M. Disch **7**:86
John Gardner **5**:132
William H. Gass **8**:246
Russell C. Hoban **7**:160
Maureen Howard **5**:189
Elia Kazan **6**:274
Maxine Hong Kingston **12**:312
Peter Matthiessen **5**:274
V. S. Naipaul **7**:253
Seán O'Faoláin **7**:274
Cynthia Ozick **7**:288
Reynolds Price **6**:425
Robert Stone **5**:409
John Updike **5**:457
James Welch **6**:561
Fay Weldon **6**:562

Gray, Paul Edward
John Fowles **1**:109
Iris Murdoch **1**:236
Joyce Carol Oates **1**:251
Eudora Welty **1**:363

Gray, Richard
William Faulkner **11**:202
Carson McCullers **12**:430
John Crowe Ransom **11**:469
William Styron **11**:520
Tennessee Williams **11**:577

Gray, Ronald
Heinrich Böll **9**:112

Greacen, Robert
W. H. Auden **3**:25
Samuel Beckett **4**:50
Margaret Drabble **2**:117
Bernard Kops **4**:274
Doris Lessing **3**:287
Harold Robbins **5**:378
Isaac Bashevis Singer **3**:457
Vassilis Vassilikos **4**:551

Grebanier, Bernard
Thornton Wilder **1**:365

Grebstein, Sheldon Norman
Ernest Hemingway **3**:235
Bernard Malamud **11**:348
John O'Hara **1**:261

Green, Alan
Peter De Vries **3**:126
Michael Frayn **3**:164

Green, Benny
John Fowles **6**:186
Brian Moore **7**:238
John O'Hara **6**:383
Charles M. Schulz **12**:533

Green, Gerald
Thomas Berger **3**:63

Green, Harris
Jim Jacobs and Warren Casey **12**:293

Green, Martin
E. L. Doctorow **6**:138
B. S. Johnson **6**:263
J. D. Salinger **1**:298

Green, Philip
E. E. Cummings **12**:147

Green, Randall
John Hawkes **4**:217
Aleksandr I. Solzhenitsyn **4**:512

Green, Robert J.
Roch Carrier **13**:141
Athol Fugard **9**:233

Greenberg, Martin
Reiner Kunze **10**:310

Greenblatt, Stephen Jay
Evelyn Waugh **13**:585

Greene, Daniel
Don L. Lee **2**:237

Greene, George
Paul West **7**:522

Greene, James
Eugenio Montale **9**:388

Greene, Robert W.
Raymond Queneau **10**:430

Greenfeld, Josh
Emily Cheney Neville **12**:451
Philip Roth **2**:378
Paul Zindel **6**:586

Greenfield, Jeff
John Lennon and Paul McCartney **12**:378
Dan Wakefield **7**:503

Greenman, Myron
Donald Barthelme **6**:29

Greenspan, Miriam
Maxine Hong Kingston **12**:313

Greenway, John
Norman Mailer **2**:262

Greenya, John
Budd Schulberg **7**:403

Gregor, Ian
Graham Greene **6**:214

Gregory, Helen
Betty Cavanna **12**:103

Gregory, Hilda
Joyce Carol Oates **1**:251; **2**:315
Mark Strand **6**:522
Nancy Willard **7**:540

Gregory, Horace
Laura Riding **7**:373

Greider, William
William Safire **10**:447

Greiner, Donald J.
Djuna Barnes **8**:48
Frederick Busch **10**:91
John Hawkes **1**:138; **4**:213; **7**:145
Kurt Vonnegut, Jr. **3**:499

Grella, George
Ian Fleming **3**:158

Grier, Edward F.
Jonathan Williams **13**:600

Griffin, Bryan
John Irving **13**:297

Griffin, Robert J.
Cid Corman **9**:169

Griffith, Albert J.
Carson McCullers **1**:209
Peter Taylor **1**:334; **4**:542
John Updike **5**:455

Grigsby, Gordon K.
Kenneth Rexroth **1**:284

Grigson, Geoffrey
Robert Lowell **3**:302
Kathleen Raine **7**:351

Griswold, Jerry
Ken Kesey **3**:268

Groden, Michael
William Faulkner **9**:198

Gropper, Esther C.
Hermann Hesse **2**:189; **3**:244

Gross, Barry
Arthur Miller **10**:344

Gross, Beverly
Jonathan Baumbach **6**:32
Saul Bellow **2**:52
B. H. Friedman **7**:109
Peter Spielberg **6**:514

Gross, Harvey
T. S. Eliot **6**:161
André Malraux **4**:335
Ezra Pound **4**:414

Gross, Theodore L.
J. D. Salinger **1**:300

Grosskurth, Phyllis
Margaret Atwood **2**:20

Grossman, Edward
Simone de Beauvoir **2**:44
Saul Bellow **8**:80
Thomas Berger **3**:63
Heinrich Böll **3**:75
Joseph Heller **5**:181
Doris Lessing **3**:287
Vladimir Nabokov **3**:355
Kurt Vonnegut, Jr. **5**:466

Grossman, Joel
Philip Roth **9**:459

Grossvogel, David I.
Agatha Christie **12**:127
Julio Cortázar **10**:112

Groth, Janet
John Cheever **8**:136

Groves, Margaret
Nathalie Sarraute **4**:470

Grumbach, Doris
Maya Angelou **12**:12
Simone de Beauvoir **4**:49
Kay Boyle **5**:66

Hortense Calisher **8**:124
Arthur A. Cohen **7**:50
Joan Didion **8**:175
E. L. Doctorow **6**:131
Daphne du Maurier **11**:164
Stanley Elkin **4**:154
Leslie A. Fiedler **13**:214
Susan B. Hill **4**:288
Maureen Howard **5**:188
Alison Lurie **4**:307
Cormac McCarthy **4**:342
Mary McCarthy **5**:276
A. G. Mojtabai **9**:385
Brian Moore **5**:297
Penelope Mortimer **5**:299
Julia O'Faolain **6**:383
Aldo Palazzeschi **11**:431
Judith Rossner **9**:457
J. R. Salamanca **4**:461
May Sarton **4**:471
Clancy Sigal **7**:425
Anne Tyler **7**:479
Nancy Willard **7**:538, 539
Sol Yurick **6**:584

Grunfeld, Frederick V.
John Lennon and Paul McCartney **12**:361

Gubbins, Bill
Brian Wilson **12**:648

Guerard, Albert J.
Donald Barthelme **5**:53
Jerome Charyn **5**:103
John Hawkes **2**:183; **3**:222

Guerrard, Philip
Mervyn Peake **7**:301

Guicharnaud, Jacques
Michel de Ghelderode **11**:226
Eugène Ionesco **6**:254
Jean-Paul Sartre **1**:304

Guicharnaud, June
Michel de Ghelderode **11**:226

Guild, Nicholas
Paul Theroux **11**:530

Guimond, James
Gilbert Sorrentino **3**:461

Guiton, Margaret Otis
Louis Aragon **3**:12
Marcel Aymé **11**:21
Albert Camus **1**:54
Louis-Ferdinand Céline **1**:57
Jean Cocteau **1**:59
Georges Duhamel **8**:186
Jean Giono **4**:183
Julien Green **3**:203
André Malraux **1**:202
François Mauriac **4**:337
Raymond Queneau **2**:359
Jules Romains **7**:381
Jean-Paul Sartre **1**:306

Gullason, Thomas A.
Carson McCullers **4**:344
Flannery O'Connor **1**:259

Gullon, Agnes
Pablo Neruda **7**:260

Gunn, Edward
Djuna Barnes **4**:44

Gunn, Thom
David Ignatow **7**:173
W. S. Merwin **13**:383

CRITIC INDEX

Christopher Middleton **13**:387
Howard Nemerov **9**:393
Charles Olson **11**:414
Louis Simpson **7**:426, 427

Gurewitsch, M. Anatole
William Gaddis **6**:195

Gurko, Leo
Ernest Hemingway **6**:226
John P. Marguand **10**:331
Edward Lewis Wallant **5**:477

Gussow, Mel
Ed Bullins **1**:47
Charles Gordone **1**:125
Elizabeth Swados **12**:558

Gustafson, Richard
Reg Saner **9**:469

Gustainis, J. Justin
Stephen King **12**:311
Amos Oz **11**:429

Gwynn, Frederick L.
J. D. Salinger **1**:295

Gysin, Fritz
Jean Toomer **13**:552

Gyurko, Lanin A.
Julio Cortázar **5**:108; **10**:112;
13:159

Haas, Diane
Judy Blume **12**:46

Haas, Joseph
Bob Dylan **12**:180
Jerome Weidman **7**:517

Haberl, Franz P.
Max Frisch **9**:218

Hack, Richard
Kenneth Patchen **2**:332
Colin Wilson **3**:537

Hadas, Pamela White
Marianne Moore **10**:348

Hadas, Rachel
Yannis Ritsos **13**:487

Haenicke, Diether H.
Heinrich Böll **6**:83
Paul Celan **10**:101
Friedrich Dürrenmatt **8**:194
Max Frisch **9**:217
Günter Grass **6**:207
Uwe Johnson **5**:201
Reiner Kunze **10**:310
Anna Seghers **7**:408

Haffenden, John
John Berryman **10**:45
Robert Lowell **11**:330

Haft, Cynthia
Aleksandr I. Solzhenitsyn **7**:435

Hagopian, John V.
James Baldwin **1**:15
William Faulkner **3**:157
J. F. Powers **1**:282

Hague, René
David Jones **7**:189

Hahn, Claire
William Everson **5**:122
Jean Garrigue **8**:239

Hainsworth, J. D.
John Arden **13**:24

Hájek, Igor
Bohumil Hrabal **13**:291

Halderman, Marjorie
Larry Kettelkamp **12**:304

Hale, Nancy
Jessamyn West **7**:522

Hales, David
Berry Morgan **6**:340

Halio, Jay L.
William Gaddis **10**:212
John Gardner **10**:220
Ernest Hemingway **6**:230
Mary McCarthy **5**:276
Reynolds Price **13**:464
Isaac Bashevis Singer **1**:314;
6:509
C. P. Snow **6**:517
Aleksandr I. Solzhenitsyn **7**:434
Alice Walker **5**:476

Hall, Donald
Russell Edson **13**:191
Allen Ginsberg **3**:195
Peter Matthiessen **11**:361
Rod McKuen **3**:333
Marianne Moore **4**:362

Hall, Elizabeth
Frank Herbert **12**:275
Stephen King **12**:309

Hall, James
Saul Bellow **3**:50
Elizabeth Bowen **3**:82
William Faulkner **3**:152
Graham Greene **3**:207
Iris Murdoch **2**:296
J. D. Salinger **3**:444
Robert Penn Warren **4**:577

Hall, James B.
Mario Puzo **1**:282

Hall, Joan Joffe
Wendell Berry **4**:59
Marie-Claire Blais **6**:81
Shirley Ann Grau **4**:210
Ursula K. LeGuin **8**:342
Robert Stone **5**:410
John Updike **5**:458

Hall, John
Gary Snyder **1**:318

Hall, Linda B.
Carlos Fuentes **8**:222
Maxine Hong Kingston **12**:314
Gabriel García Márquez **10**:214

Hall, Richard W.
Ezra Pound **5**:348

Hall, Stephen
R. H. W. Dillard **5**:116

Hall, Wade
Jesse Stuart **11**:511

Haller, Robert S.
Martin Booth **13**:104
Alan Sillitoe **6**:500

Halliday, Mark
Eleanor Lerman **9**:329

Halpern, Daniel
David Wagoner **5**:475

Hamill, Pete
Seán O'Faoláin **7**:272
Leon Uris **7**:492

Hamill, Sam
Greg Kuzma **7**:197

Hamilton, Alice
Samuel Beckett **10**:31
John Updike **2**:443; **5**:449

Hamilton, Daphne Ann
Melvin Berger **12**:41, 42

Hamilton, Ian
Kingsley Amis **2**:6
Robert Lowell **2**:246; **4**:303
Louis MacNeice **4**:317
Christopher Middleton **13**:387

Hamilton, Kenneth
Samuel Beckett **10**:31
John Updike **2**:443; **5**:449

Hamilton, Mary
Paul Vincent Carroll **10**:98

Hamilton, William
Albert Camus **1**:52
Paul Goodman **7**:128

Hammond, John G.
Robert Creeley **8**:151

Hammond, Jonathan
Athol Fugard **9**:229

Hamner, Robert D.
V. S. Naipaul **13**:402

Hampshire, Stuart
Christopher Isherwood **11**:296

Handa, Carolyn
Conrad Aiken **10**:1

Hanna, Thomas L.
Albert Camus **9**:143

Hannabuss, C. Stuart
Leon Garfield **12**:230, 234
Andre Norton **12**:463
J.R.R. Tolkien **12**:575

Hannah, Barry
William Eastlake **8**:200

Hanne, Michael
Elio Vittorini **9**:551

Hansen, Arlen J.
Richard Brautigan **3**:90

Hansen, Olaf
Peter Handke **10**:259

Harcourt, Joan
Roch Carrier **13**:141

Harder, Worth T.
Herbert Read **4**:443

Hardie, Alec M.
Edmund Blunden **2**:65

Hardin, Nancy S.
Margaret Drabble **3**:129

Hardin, Nancy Shields
Doris Lessing **6**:297

Harding, D. W.
Roy Fuller **4**:178

Hardison, O. B., Jr.
Larry McMurtry **7**:215

Hardwick, Elizabeth
Renata Adler **8**:6
Doris Lessing **3**:285
Marge Piercy **3**:383
Alexsandr I. Solzhenitsyn
10:480

Hardy, Barbara
A. Alvarez **5**:18

Hardy, Melody
Arthur C. Clarke **4**:105

Hare, David
Ngaio Marsh **7**:209

Hargrove, Nancy D.
T. S. Eliot **6**:165

Harmon, Elva
William Mayne **12**:392

Harold, Brent
William Faulkner **11**:199
Vladimir Nabokov **6**:356

Harper, Howard M., Jr.
John Barth **1**:18
Saul Bellow **1**:33
Jerzy Kosinski **1**:172
Vladimir Nabokov **1**:245
Philip Roth **1**:293

Harper, Michael S.
Robert Hayden **9**:269

Harper, Ralph
Eric Ambler **4**:18

Harper, Roy
Jimmy Page and Robert Plant
12:481

Harrington, Michael
Theodore Roethke **3**:433

Harrington, Stephanie
Norman Lear **12**:327, 334

Harris, Bruce
John Lennon and Paul
McCartney **12**:371
Jimmy Page and Robert Plant
12:475

Harris, Helen
Penelope Gilliatt **13**:239
Ian McEwan **13**:371

Harris, Jane Gary
Boris Pasternak **10**:382

Harris, Janet
June Jordan **11**:312

Harris, Leo
Ngaio Marsh **7**:209
Julian Symons **2**:426

Harris, Lis
Truman Capote **3**:100
Amos Oz **11**:429
Grace Paley **4**:392

Harris, Marie
Marge Piercy **6**:403

Harris, Michael
Thomas Berger **5**:60
Andre Dubus **13**:183
John Gardner **5**:133

Harris, Wilson
George Lamming **4**:279
V. S. Naipaul **4**:374

Harrison, Barbara Grizzuti
Ruth Prawer Jhabvala **4**:257
Iris Murdoch **6**:343

Harrison, Jim
Peter Matthiessen **11**:360
Larry McMurtry **2**:272

Harrison, Keith
Margot Benary-Isbert **12**:34
John Berryman **3**:69

Harrison, Tony
Lorine Niedecker 10:360

Harsent, David
Joe Orton 13:437

Harss, Luis
Jorge Luis Borges 2:69
Julio Cortázar 2:101
Gabriel García Márquez 2:147
Juan Carlos Onetti 7:276
Juan Rulfo 8:461
Mario Vargas Llosa 3:493

Hart, Jane
Carson McCullers 12:416

Hart, Jeffrey
E. L. Doctorow 6:136
Auberon Waugh 7:514

Hart, John E.
Jack Kerouac 3:264

Hart, Johnny
Charles M. Schulz 12:527

Hart-Davis, Rupert
Agatha Christie 12:114

Harte, Barbara
Janet Frame 3:164

Hartley, George
Philip Larkin 5:230

Hartley, Lodwick
Katherine Anne Porter 13:446

Hartman, Geoffrey
Ross Macdonald 2:257

Hartman, Geoffrey H.
A. R. Ammons 2:13
André Malraux 9:358

Hartt, Julian N.
Mary Renault 3:426

Hartung, Philip T.
Budd Schulberg 7:402

Harvey, David D.
Herbert Read 4:440

Harvey, G. M.
John Betjeman 10:52

Harvey, Lawrence E.
Samuel Beckett 9:80

Harvey, Robert D.
Howard Nemerov 2:306

Hasley, Louis
Peter De Vries 1:72
Joseph Heller 5:173
S. J. Perelman 3:381
James Thurber 11:532
E. B. White 10:526

Hass, Robert
Robert Lowell 9:336

Hassan, Ihab
John Barth 2:36
Samuel Beckett 1:23
Saul Bellow 1:29
André Breton 2:81
Frederick Buechner 4:79
William S. Burroughs 2:91
Truman Capote 1:55
J. P. Donleavy 1:75
Ralph Ellison 1:94
Jean Genet 2:159
Allen Ginsberg 2:164
Herbert Gold 4:190

Ernest Hemingway 3:237
Norman Mailer 1:188, 189; 4:319
Bernard Malamud 1:195, 196
Carson McCullers 1:207, 208
Henry Miller 1:222
Vladimir Nabokov 1:239
Alain Robbe-Grillet 2:375
J. D. Salinger 1:296; 3:446
Nathalie Sarraute 2:385
Jean Stafford 7:455
William Styron 1:330; 11:514
Kurt Vonnegut, Jr. 12:610

Hassett, John J.
José Donoso 4:129

Hatch, James V.
Alice Childress 12:106

Hatch, Robert
Anne Burr 6:104

Hatfield, Henry
Günter Grass 2:173

Hauck, Richard Boyd
Kurt Vonnegut, Jr. 5:465

Haugaard, Kay
Betty Cavanna 12:102

Haugh, Robert
John Updike 7:489

Hauptman, Ira
John Buell 10:81

Hausermann, H. W.
Herbert Read 4:438, 439

Havard, Robert G.
Jorge Guillén 11:262

Haverstick, S. Alexander
John Knowles 4:271

Haviland, Virginia
E. M. Almedingen 12:5
Ruth M. Arthur 12:25
Margot Benary-Isbert 12:30
Betty Cavanna 12:100
Mavis Thorpe Clark 12:130, 131
Julia W. Cunningham 12:165
Leon Garfield 12:218
Christie Harris 12:264
Jamake Highwater 12:287
Larry Kettelkamp 12:304
Joseph Krumgold 12:317
Jean Lee Latham 12:323
Andre Norton 12:456, 466
Mary Rodgers 12:494
Mary Stolz 12:546, 550, 555

Hawkes, John
John Barth 10:21
Flannery O'Connor 1:254

Haworth, David
Morris L. West 6:563

Hay, Samuel A.
Ed Bullins 5:83

Hayakawa, S. I.
E. E. Cummings 12:144

Haycraft, Howard
Agatha Christie 12:118

Hayden, Brad
Richard Brautigan 12:72

Hayes, Brian P.
Joyce Carol Oates 1:252

Hayes, E. Nelson
J. R. Salamanca 4:461

Hayes, Noreen
J. R. R. Tolkien 1:336

Hayman, David
Samuel Beckett 11:34
Louis-Ferdinand Céline 7:42

Hayman, Ronald
Robert Duncan 7:88
Robert Frost 4:174
Allen Ginsberg 6:198
Arthur Miller 6:331
Charles Olson 5:327
Anne Sexton 4:482
David Storey 5:414
Charles Tomlinson 4:544

Haynes, Elizabeth
Andre Norton 12:459

Haynes, Muriel
Shirley Ann Grau 4:208
Lillian Hellman 4:222
Thomas Keneally 5:210

Hays, Peter L.
Henry Miller 9:379

Hayward, Max
Andrei Voznesensky 1:349

Hazo, Samuel
John Berryman 2:57

Hazzard, Shirley
Jean Rhys 2:371
Patrick White 3:522

Headings, Philip R.
T. S. Eliot 1:91

Healey, James
Catharine Savage Brosman 9:135
Michael Casey 2:100
Leonard Cohen 3:110

Heaney, Seamus
David Jones 7:187

Hearron, Thomas
Richard Brautigan 5:68

Heath, Jeffrey M.
Evelyn Waugh 8:543

Heath, Susan
Martin Amis 9:25
John Hersey 7:154
Yasunari Kawabata 5:208
John Knowles 4:272
Yukio Mishima 6:337
Anaïs Nin 4:379
Richard Price 12:489
V. S. Pritchett 5:353
Kurt Vonnegut, Jr. 3:503

Heath, William
Paul Blackburn 9:100

Hecht, Anthony
W. H. Auden 2:22
Ted Hughes 2:198
James Merrill 2:273
Marianne Moore 2:291
Howard Nemerov 2:306
L. E. Sissman 9:489
Richard Wilbur 9:570

Heck, Francis S.
Marguerite Duras 11:166

Heckard, Margaret
William H. Gass 8:244

Heckman, Don
John Lennon and Paul McCartney 12:358

Hector, Mary Louise
Margot Benary-Isbert 12:32, 33
Mary Stolz 12:552

Heffernan, Michael
Albert Goldbarth 5:143
Gibbons Ruark 3:441

Heidenry, John
Agatha Christie 6:110
Robert M. Pirsig 4:405

Heilbut, Anthony
Stanley Elkin 9:191

Heilman, Robert B.
Edward Albee 5:11
Max Frisch 3:168
Harold Pinter 3:386

Heims, Neil
Paul Goodman 4:198

Heiney, Donald
Jean Anouilh 8:22
Natalia Ginzburg 11:227
Alberto Moravia 2:294
Elio Vittorini 9:546, 548

Heins, Ethel L.
Ruth M. Arthur 12:24
Julia W. Cunningham 12:166
Peter Dickinson 12:177
Leon Garfield 12:231
Joseph Krumgold 12:318
Emily Cheney Neville 12:451
Katherine Paterson 12:487

Heins, Paul
Frank Bonham 12:50
Robert Cormier 12:136
Julia Cunningham 12:164, 166
Peter Dickinson 12:171
Madeleine L'Engle 12:347
William Mayne 12:398, 402
Nicholasa Mohr 12:446

Heiserman, Arthur
J. D. Salinger 12:496

Heller, Amanda
Max Apple 9:32
John Cheever 8:138
Don DeLillo 8:171
Joan Didion 8:175
William Gaddis 6:194
Mary Gordon 13:249
Mark Helprin 7:152
Leonard Michaels 6:325
Fay Weldon 11:566
Larry Woiwode 6:579

Heller, Michael
William Bronk 10:75
Cid Corman 9:170
George Oppen 9:284; 13:434
Charles Reznikoff 9:449

Helms, Alan
John Ashbery 2:18
Robert Bly 10:61
Galway Kinnell 13:321
Philip Levine 4:287
William Meredith 13:373

Helms, Randel
J.R.R. Tolkien 12:578

Hemenway, Leone R.
Melvin Berger 12:39

Hemenway, Robert
Zora Neale Hurston 7:170

Hemmings, F.W.J.
Mary Stewart 7:467

Henault, Marie
Peter Viereck 4:559

Henderson, Tony
Patricia Highsmith 4:226

Hendin, Josephine
John Barth 3:42
Donald Barthelme 6:28
Richard Brautigan 1:45
William S. Burroughs 5:92
Janet Frame 2:142
John Hersey 2:188
Marjorie Kellogg 2:224
Robert Kotlowitz 4:275
Doris Lessing 3:286
Michael McClure 6:316
Joyce Carol Oates 6:371; 9:404
Flannery O'Connor 6:375;
13:421
Thomas Pynchon 6:436
Hubert Selby, Jr. 1:307; 4:482
Paul Theroux 5:427
John Updike 9:536
Kurt Vonnegut, Jr. 4:569

Hendrick, George
Jack Kerouac 2:227
Katherine Anne Porter 1:273

Hendricks, Sharon
Melvin Berger 12:42

Henighan, T. J.
Richard Hughes 1:149

Henkel, Wayne J.
John Knowles 4:272

Henkels, Robert M., Jr.
Robert Pinget 13:443, 444
Raymond Queneau 10:430

Henninger, Francis J.
Albert Camus 4:93

Henry, Avril
William Golding 10:237

Henry, Gerrit
Russell Edson 13:190
W. S. Merwin 5:287

Hentoff, Margaret
Paul Zindel 6:586

Hentoff, Margot
Joan Didion 8:174

Hentoff, Nat
Bob Dylan 12:180
Paul Goodman 4:197
Alex Haley 12:243
Colin MacInnes 4:314

Hepburn, Neil
Rayner Heppenstall 10:273
Mary Hocking 13:285
Thomas Keneally 5:211; 10:299
Tim O'Brien 7:272
David Plante 7:308
William Sansom 6:484
William Trevor 7:477
John Updike 7:489
Fay Weldon 9:559

Hepner, Arthur
John R. Tunis 12:594

Herbold, Tony
Dannie Abse 7:2
Michael Hamburger 5:159

Hermann, John
J. D. Salinger 12:510

Hernández, Ana María
Julio Cortázar 13:162

Hernlund, Patricia
Richard Brautigan 5:67

Herr, Paul
James Purdy 2:347

Herrera, Philip
Daphne du Maurier 6:147

Hertzel, Leo J.
J. F. Powers 1:281

Hesse, Eva
Ezra Pound 7:329

Hesseltine, William B.
MacKinlay Kantor 7:194

Hewes, Henry
Edward Albee 2:2; 13:3
Ed Bullins:5
84 Günter Grass:2
173 Jim Jacobs and Warren
Casey 12:293
Terrence McNally 7:216
David Rabe 4:425
Peter Shaffer 5:388
Tom Stoppard 4:524
Melvin Van Peebles 2:447
Gore Vidal 2:450
Tennessee Williams 2:465

Heyen, William
Robert Bly 5:61
Louise Bogan 4:68
John Cheever 3:106
E. E. Cummings 3:118
James Dickey 2:117
Richmond Lattimore 3:278
Denise Levertov 1:177
Hugh MacDiarmid 2:253
Arthur Miller 6:336
Theodore Roethke 3:433
Anne Sexton 6:491
Neil Simon 6:503
W. D. Snodgrass 6:513
William Stafford 4:520
Lewis Turco 11:550
John Updike 3:485
Richard Wilbur 3:533
William Carlos Williams 2:468

Heymann, Hans G.
Horst Bienek 7:29

Heywood, Christopher
Peter Abrahams 4:1

Hibberd, Dominic
William Mayne 12:406

Hickey, Dave
B. H. Friedman 7:108

Hicks, Granville
Louis Auchincloss 4:28, 30;
9:52, 53
James Baldwin 2:31
Peter S. Beagle 7:25
James Gould Cozzens 1:66
Herbert Gold 4:189
Shirley Ann Grau 4:207
Elia Kazan 6:273

Ken Kesey 6:277
Meyer Levin 7:204
Bernard Malamud 1:200; 11:345
Harry Mathews 6:314
Flannery O'Connor 1:258
Katherine Anne Porter 7:312
Reynolds Price 3:404, 405
Ann Quin 6:442
J. D. Salinger 12:502
Kurt Vonnegut, Jr. 2:451;
12:602
Auberon Waugh 7:514
Glenway Wescott 13:590
Herman Wouk 1:376

Hiesberger, Jean Marie
Charles M. Schulz 12:533

Highet, Gilbert
Henry Miller 1:224
Ezra Pound 1:276

Highsmith, Patricia
Georges Simenon 2:398

Hildick, Wallace
William Mayne 12:390

Hill, Donald L.
Richard Wilbur 3:530

Hill, Helen G.
Norman Mailer 4:321

Hill, Susan
Daphne du Maurier 6:146

Hill, William B.
Peter De Vries 10:137

Hill, William B., S.J.
Robert Cormier 12:133
Paul Gallico 2:147
Bernard Malamud 5:269
Anthony Powell 10:417
Muriel Spark 2:418

Hilliard, Stephen S.
Philip Larkin 9:323

Himmelblau, Jack
Miguel Ángel Asturias 8:25

Hinchcliffe, P. M.
Ethel Davis Wilson 13:610

Hinchliffe, Arnold P.
John Arden 13:28
Edward Bond 6:86
T. S. Eliot 13:195
Harold Pinter 1:267

Hinden, Michael
John Barth 3:41

Hindus, Milton
Louis-Ferdinand Céline 1:56

Hingley, Ronald
Aleksandr I. Solzhenitsyn
1:319; 4:515; 7:445
Andrei Voznesensky 1:349

Hinz, Evelyn J.
Doris Lessing 6:293
Anaïs Nin 1:248; 4:377

Hipkiss, Robert A.
Ernest Hemingway 3:242

Hippisley, Anthony
Yuri Olesha 8:433

Hirsch, Edward
Geoffrey Hill 8:296
Isaac Bashevis Singer 11:499
Charles Tomlinson 13:546

Hirsch, Foster
Ernest Hemingway 1:144
Mary McCarthy 3:328
Tennessee Williams 5:505

Hirt, Andrew J.
Rod McKuen 3:332

Hislop, Alan
Jerzy Kosinski 2:233
Wright Morris 3:344
Frederic Prokosch 4:422

Hiss, Tony
Patti Smith 12:536

Hitchcock, George
Diane Wakoski 7:503

Hitrec, Joseph
Ivo Andrić 8:19

Hjortsberg, William
Angela Carter 5:101
Rosalyn Drexler 2:120

Hoag, David G.
Melvin Berger 12:40

Hoagland, Edward
Erskine Caldwell 8:123
Peter Matthiessen 11:359
William Saroyan 8:468; 10:454

Hoban, Russell
Leon Garfield 12:232
William Mayne 12:403

Hobbs, John
Galway Kinnell 13:318

Hobson, Laura Z.
Norman Lear 12:327

Hochman, Baruch
S. Y. Agnon 4:12
Isaac Bashevis Singer 1:312

Hodgart, Matthew
Kingsley Amis 5:23
V. S. Pritchett 5:353
J.R.R. Tolkien 12:568

Hodgart, Patricia
Paul Bowles 2:78

Hoeksema, Thomas
Ishmael Reed 3:424

Hoerchner, Susan
Denise Levertov 5:247

Hoffa, William Walter
Ezra Pound 2:343

Hoffman, Daniel
A. R. Ammons 2:11
W. H. Auden 2:25
Richard Eberhart 3:133, 134
Ted Hughes 2:198
Robert Lowell 2:247
Robin Skelton 13:507

Hoffman, Frederick J.
Conrad Aiken 1:2
James Baldwin 1:15
Samuel Beckett 1:21
Saul Bellow 1:30
John Dos Passos 1:79
James T. Farrell 4:157
William Faulkner 1:100
John Hawkes 4:212
Ernest Hemingway 1:142
Aldous Huxley 11:281
Katherine Anne Porter 1:272

Theodore Roethke 3:434
Philip Roth 4:451
John Steinbeck 1:325
Robert Penn Warren 1:353

Hoffman, Michael J.
Henry Miller 1:224

Hoffman, Nancy Y.
Anaïs Nin 4:380
Flannery O'Connor 3:369

Hogan, Randolph
Larry Kettelkamp 12:305

Hogan, Robert
Paul Vincent Carroll 10:97
Arthur Miller 1:216
Elmer Rice 7:361

Hoggart, Richard
W. H. Auden 1:9
Graham Greene 6:217

Hokenson, Jan
Louis-Ferdinand Céline 9:152

Holahan, Susan
Frank O'Hara 5:324

Holbert, Cornelia
Kenzaburo Ōe 10:373

Holden, Anthony
Rayner Heppenstall 10:272
Daniel Hoffman 13:286

Holden, David
Piers Paul Read 4:445

Holden, Jonathan
Nancy Willard 7:540

Holden, Stephen
Bob Dylan 12:191
John Lennon and Paul
McCartney 12:372
Joni Mitchell 12:438
Patti Smith 12:535
Elizabeth Swados 12:561

Holder, Alan
Robert Lowell 5:256

Holder, Stephen C.
John Brunner 8:107

Holland, Bette
Eleanor Clark 5:106

Holland, Philip
Leon Garfield 12:236

Holland, Robert
Elizabeth Bishop 13:95
Marilyn Hacker 9:258
Cynthia Macdonald 13:356

Hollander, John
A. R. Ammons 2:12
Howard Moss 7:247

Hollington, Michael
Günter Grass 11:250

Hollingworth, Roy
Jim Jacobs and Warren Casey
12:295

Hollis, James R.
Harold Pinter 11:439

Holman, C. Hugh
John P. Marquand 10:328
Robert Penn Warren 4:576

Holmes, Carol
Joseph McElroy 5:279

Holmes, Charles M.
Aldous Huxley 11:283

Holmes, Charles S.
James Thurber 5:439, 441

Holmes, John Clellon
Jack Kerouac 2:227

Holmes, H. H.
Andre Norton 12:456

Holmes, Kay
Emma Lathen 2:236

Holroyd, Michael
William Gerhardie 5:139

Holsaert, Eunice
Madeleine L'Engle 12:344

Holzinger, Walter
Pablo Neruda 9:396

Hood, Robert
Emily Cheney Neville 12:449

Hood, Stuart
Aleksandr I. Solzhenitsyn 1:319

Hope, Christopher
Nadine Gordimer 5:147
Louis Simpson 9:486
Derek Walcott 9:556

Hope, Mary
Richard Brautigan 12:74
Brigid Brophy 11:68
James Hanley 13:261
Fay Weldon 11:566

Hopkins, Crale D.
Lawrence Ferlinghetti 10:174

Hopkinson, Shirley L.
E. M. Almedingen 12:3

Horn, Carole
Caroline Blackwood 6:80

Horn, Richard
Henry Green 13:253

Horner, Patrick J.
Randall Jarrell 13:303

Horovitz, Carolyn
Esther Forbes 12:210
Joseph Krumgold 12:318
Madeleine L'Engle 12:347

Horowitz, Michael
Jack Kerouac 5:214

Horowitz, Susan
Ann Beattie 8:54

Horton, Andrew S.
Ken Kesey 6:278
John Updike 7:487

Horvath, Violet M.
André Malraux 4:332

Hosking, Geoffrey
Vladimir Voinovich 10:507

Howard, Ben
Loren Eiseley 7:92
Marilyn Hacker 5:155
Anne Sexton 6:494

Howard, Jane
Maxine Kumin 5:222

Howard, Leon
Wright Morris 1:232

Howard, Maureen
Donald Barthelme 8:50
Samuel Beckett 11:43

Jorge Luis Borges 1:38
Paul Bowles 2:79
Isak Dinesen 10:150
Margaret Drabble 2:117;
10:163, 165
Mary Gordon 13:249
Peter Handke 8:261
Lillian Hellman 8:281
Doris Lessing 6:301
Toni Morrison 10:356
Philip Roth 1:292
Isaac Bashevis Singer 11:502
John Updike 9:537
Kurt Vonnegut, Jr. 1:347
Tennessee Williams 1:369

Howard, Richard
A. R. Ammons 2:12; 5:24
John Ashbery 2:17, 18; 13:30
W. H. Auden 2:26; 3:23
Imamu Amiri Baraka 10:18
Donald Barthelme 13:61
Marvin Bell 8:67
Robert Bly 5:61
Millen Brand 7:29
Gregory Corso 1:63
James Dickey 7:79
Irving Feldman 7:102
Paul Goodman 7:128
Daniel Hoffman 6:244
John Hollander 5:185
Uwe Johnson 5:201
Galway Kinnell 5:215
Kenneth Koch 5:219
Denise Levertov 5:245
Philip Levine 5:251
John Logan 5:252, 254
William Meredith 4:348; 13:372
James Merrill 2:274
W. S. Merwin 2:277; 5:284
Howard Moss 7:249
Frank O'Hara 5:323
Sylvia Plath 5:338
Adrienne Rich 3:428
Raphael Rudnik 7:384
Gary Snyder 5:393
William Stafford 7:460
Allen Tate 4:538
Mona Van Duyn 3:491
David Wagoner 5:473
Robert Penn Warren 6:557
Theodore Weiss 3:516
James Wright 5:518; 10:547
Vassily S. Yanovsky 2:485

Howard, Thomas
Frederick Buechner 2:82

Howarth, David
Gavin Ewart 13:209

Howe, Irving
James Baldwin 3:31
Saul Bellow 3:49, 60; 8:79
Louis-Ferdinand Céline 3:101
James Gould Cozzens 4:111
Ralph Ellison 3:141
William Faulkner 3:151
Paula Fox 2:139
Robert Frost 3:170
Daniel Fuchs 8:221
Henry Green 13:252
James Hanley 8:265
Ernest Hemingway 3:232
György Konrád 4:273
Jerzy Kosinski 1:171

Norman Mailer 3:311
Bernard Malamud 8:376
Octavio Paz 3:377
Sylvia Plath 1:270; 3:391
Ezra Pound 2:344
V. S. Pritchett 13:467
Ishmael Reed 13:477
Philip Roth 2:380; 3:440
Delmore Schwartz 10:466
Ignazio Silone 4:492, 494
Isaac Bashevis Singer 1:311
Lionel Trilling 9:533
Edmund Wilson 3:538
Richard Wright 3:545; 9:585

Howe, Russell Warren
Alex Haley 12:247

Howell, Elmo
Flannery O'Connor 3:369

Howlett, Ivan
John Osborne 5:333

Hoyem, Andrew
Larry Eigner 9:180

Hoyenga, Betty
Kay Boyle 1:42

Hoyt, Charles Alva
Bernard Malamud 1:196
Muriel Spark 2:414
Edward Lewis Wallant 5:477

Hubert, Renée Riese
André Breton 2:80
Alain Robbe-Grillet 4:449
Nathalie Sarraute 4:470

Hubin, Allen J.
Michael Crichton 6:119
Peter Dickinson 12:168, 169
Harry Kemelman 2:225

Huck, Charlotte S.
Julia W. Cunningham 12:164
Joseph Krumgold 12:320

Hudson, Christopher
John Montague 13:390

Hudson, Peggy
Earl Hamner, Jr. 12:259
Norman Lear 12:330

Huebner, Theodore
Anna Seghers 7:408

Hughes, Carl Milton
Chester Himes 4:229
Ann Petry 1:266
Richard Wright 1:377
Frank G. Yerby 1:381

Hughes, Catharine
Edward Albee 2:3; 9:6
Samuel Beckett 2:47
Daniel J. Berrigan 4:57
Ed Bullins 5:82
D. L. Coburn 10:108
Allen Ginsberg 2:164
Charles Gordone 4:199
Rolf Hochhuth 4:232
James Kirkwood 9:320
Carson McCullers 12:419
Mark Medoff 6:323
David Rabe 4:427
Robert Shaw 5:391
Neil Simon 11:496
Michael Weller 10:526
Tennessee Williams 2:466;
5:502

Hughes, Daniel
John Berryman 3:70

Hughes, Dorothy B.
Donald E. Westlake 7:528

Hughes, James
Louis Auchincloss 9:53

Hughes, John W.
Dannie Abse 7:1
John Ashbery 2:17
W. H. Auden 2:26
John Ciardi 10:106

Hughes, Olga R.
Boris Pasternak 7:297

Hughes, R. E.
Graham Greene 1:131

Hughes, Riley
Robert Cormier 12:133

Hughes, Ted
Leon Garfield 12:219
Sylvia Plath 1:270
Clancy Sigal 7:423

Hughes-Hallett, Lucy
Bernard Slade 11:508

Humes, Walter M.
Robert Cormier 12:137

Hughson, Lois
John Dos Passos 4:136

Hugo, Richard
Theodore Roethke 8:458

Hulbert, Ann
Ann Beattie 13:65

Hulbert, Debra
Diane Wakoski 4:572

Hume, Kathryn
C. S. Lewis 6:308

Humphrey, Robert
William Faulkner 1:98

Humphreys, Hubert
Jules Archer 12:19

Hunt, Albert
John Arden 6:5

Hunt, Peter
Peter Dickinson 12:176
Leon Garfield 12:233
William Mayne 12:406

Hunter, Jim
Anne Tyler 11:552

Hunter, Kristin
Ann Beattie 8:55

Hurren, Kenneth
Samuel Beckett 6:43
Christopher Fry 2:144
John Hopkins 4:234
Peter Nichols 5:306
Harold Pinter 6:418
Peter Shaffer 5:388
Neil Simon 6:505
Tom Stoppard 4:527
David Storey 5:415
James Thurber 11:534

Hush, Michele
Brian Wilson 12:645

Hussain, Riaz
Philip K. Dick 10:138

Hutchens, John K.
P. G. Wodehouse 2:481

Hutchings, W.
Kingsley Amis 13:12

Hutchison, Joanna
Peter Dickinson 12:172

Huth, Angela
John Irving 13:297

Hux, Samuel
John Dos Passos 8:182

Huxley, Julian
Aldous Huxley 3:253

Hyde, Lewis
Vicente Aleixandre 9:18

Hyde, Virginia M.
W. H. Auden 3:23

Hyman, Stanley Edgar
W. H. Auden 2:22
James Baldwin 2:32
Djuna Barnes 3:36
John Barth 2:35
Truman Capote 3:99
James Gould Cozzens 11:124
E. E. Cummings 3:117
T. S. Eliot 6:159
William Faulkner 3:152
Janet Frame 2:141
Bruce Jay Friedman 3:165
William Golding 2:168
Ernest Hemingway 3:234
Norman Mailer 2:258
Bernard Malamud 2:265
Wallace Markfield 8:378
Henry Miller 2:283
Marianne Moore 2:291
Vladimir Nabokov 2:299
Flannery O'Connor 1:257
Seán O'Faoláin 7:273
J. F. Powers 4:419
James Purdy 2:348
Thomas Pynchon 2:353
John Crowe Ransom 2:363
Alain Robbe-Grillet 2:374
J. D. Salinger 3:444
Isaac Bashevis Singer 3:452
John Steinbeck 5:405
Jun'ichiro Tanizaki 8:510
John Updike 2:440
Yvor Winters 4:589
Herman Wouk 9:579

Hynes, Joseph
Graham Greene 9:244
Evelyn Waugh 3:511

Hynes, Samuel
W. H. Auden 1:11; 3:24
C. Day Lewis 10:130, 131
T. S. Eliot 10:172
E. M. Forster 3:161
William Golding 1:122
Graham Greene 6:219
Louis MacNeice 4:317; 10:326
Stephen Spender 5:401; 10:488
J.I.M. Stewart 7:464

Ianni, L. A.
Lawrence Ferlinghetti 2:133

Idol, John
Flannery O'Connor 3:366

Ignatow, David
Denise Levertov 8:347
George Oppen 7:282
Diane Wakoski 7:506

Inge, M. Thomas
Donald Davidson 13:168

Ingram, Phyllis
Betty Cavanna 12:102

Innis, Doris
Jesse Jackson 12:289

Irele, Abiola
Chinua Achebe 7:3

Irving, John
John Cheever 11:121

Irwin, John T.
George P. Elliott 2:131
William Heyen 13:281
David Ignatow 7:177
Louis MacNeice 1:187
Thomas Merton 3:336
William Jay Smith 6:512
David Wagoner 3:508
Theodore Weiss 3:517

Irwin, Michael
Isak Dinesen 10:149
V. S. Pritchett 13:467
Paul Theroux 11:528
John Updike 9:539

Isaac, Dan
Isaac Bashevis Singer 3:453
Elie Wiesel 5:493

Isbell, Harold
John Logan 5:253

Isherwood, Christopher
Katherine Anne Porter 13:446

Ishiguro, Hidé
Yukio Mishima 9:384

Italia, Paul G.
James Dickey 10:139

Itzin, Catherine
Jack Gelber 6:197

Iverson, Lucille
Judith Leet 11:323

Iwamoto, Yoshio
Yukio Mishima 9:381

Izard, Anne
Babbis Friis-Baastad 12:213
John R. Tunis 12:597

Jackel, David
James Reaney 13:476
Robin Skelton 13:508

Jackson, Al
Andre Norton 12:463

Jackson, Angela
Henry Dumas 6:145

Jackson, Blyden
Gwendolyn Brooks 5:75
Robert Hayden 5:169
Langston Hughes 5:191
Margaret Walker 6:554

Jackson, Ester Merle
Tennessee Williams 7:540

Jackson, Joseph Henry
Irving Stone 7:468

Jackson, Richard
Robert Pack 13:439
Robert Penn Warren 13:578
Charles Wright 13:614

Jackson, Richard L.
Ramón Gómez de la Serna 9:239

Jackson, Robert Louis
Aleksandr I. Solzhenitsyn 7:446

Jacob, John
Jonathan Williams 13:601

Jacobs, Nicolas
David Jones 4:261

Jacobs, Rita D.
Saul Bellow 10:42

Jacobs, Ronald M.
Samuel R. Delany 8:168

Jacobs, William Jay
John R. Tunis 12:598

Jacobsen, Josephine
Arthur Gregor 9:256
Daniel Hoffman 6:242
David Ignatow 4:249
Denise Levertov 3:293
James Schevill 7:401
Mona Van Duyn 7:498

Jacobson, Dan
D. J. Enright 4:155
Andrei Sinyavsky 8:490

Jacobson, Irving
Arthur Miller 6:333; 10:345

Jacobus, John
Charles M. Schulz 12:531

Jacobus, Lee A.
Imamu Amiri Baraka 5:46

Jaffee, Cyrisse
Betty Cavanna 12:102

Jaffe, Dan
A. R. Ammons 2:12
John Berryman 2:57
Gary Snyder 2:406
Hollis Summers 10:493

Jaffe, Harold
Peter S. Beagle 7:26
Kenneth Rexroth 2:369

Jahiel, Edwin
Marguerite Duras 6:150
Antonis Samarakis 5:381
Vassilis Vassilikos 4:552

Jahn, Janheing
Camara Laye 4:282

Jamal, Zahir
Alberto Moravia 11:384

James, Clive
W. H. Auden 3:28
John Betjeman 6:66
Lillian Hellman 8:280
Philip Larkin 5:225, 229
John Le Carré 9:327
Norman Mailer 3:317
Aleksandr I. Solzhenitsyn 7:436
Yvor Winters 8:553

James, Kathryn C.
Christie Harris 12:263

James, Stuart
James A. Michener 5:290

Jameson, Fredric
Larry Niven 8:426

Janeway, Elizabeth
Pamela Hansford Johnson 7:184
Jessamyn West 7:519

CRITIC INDEX

Janeway, Michael
Anne Tyler 7:479
Tom Wicker 7:533

Janiera, Armando Martins
Kobo Abe 8:1
Jun'ichiro Tanizaki 8:510

Jarrell, Randall
Conrad Aiken 3:3
W. H. Auden 2:21
John Berryman 13:75
Elizabeth Bishop 1:34; 4:65
R. P. Blackmur 2:61
Alex Comfort 7:54
E. E. Cummings 3:116
Robert Frost 1:109; 3:169
Robert Graves 1:126; 2:174
David Ignatow 7:173
Robinson Jeffers 2:213
Robert Lowell 1:178; 2:246
Josephine Miles 1:215
Marianne Moore 1:226; 2:290
Ezra Pound 2:340
John Crowe Ransom 2:361
Theodore Roethke 3:432
Muriel Rukeyser 6:478
Carl Sandburg 4:462
Karl Shapiro 4:485
Christina Stead 2:420
Richard Wilbur 3:530
William Carlos Williams 1:369;
2:467

Jeanneret, F.
Adolfo Bioy Casares 13:87

Jebb, Julian
Alison Lurie 5:259

Jefferson, Margo
Beryl Bainbridge 5:39
Rosalyn Drexler 6:142
Nadine Gordimer 7:133
Jack Heifner 11:264
Elizabeth Jane Howard 7:164
Gayl Jones 6:265
V. S. Naipaul 7:253
Juan Carlos Onetti 7:280

Jelenski, K. A.
Witold Gombrowicz 7:123

Jellinck, Frank
Rex Stout 3:472

Jenkins, Cecil
André Malraux 4:336

Jenkins, David
A. R. Ammons 5:28

Jennings, Elizabeth
Robert Frost 3:171

Jervis, Steven A.
Evelyn Waugh 1:359

Jochmans, Betty
Agatha Christie 8:142

John, Roland
Stanley J. Kunitz 6:287

Johnson, Abby Ann Arthur
Penelope Gilliatt 10:229

Johnson, Ann S.
David Garnett 3:188

Johnson, Colton
Anthony Kerrigan 6:276

Johnson, Curtis
Guy Davenport, Jr. 6:125

Johnson, Diane
Donald Barthelme 13:59
Don DeLillo 8:172
Joan Didion 8:176
Nadine Gordimer 5:147
Erica Jong 8:315
Maxine Hong Kingston 12:313
Doris Lessing 3:286; 10:316
Toni Morrison 10:355
Joyce Carol Oates 3:361
Jean Rhys 6:453
Muriel Spark 3:465
Gore Vidal 10:502
Paul West 7:524

Johnson, Douglas
Louis-Ferdinand Céline 7:45
Claude Mauriac 9:367

Johnson, Greg
John Updike 9:538

Johnson, Halvard
Gary Snyder 1:318

Johnson, Ira D.
Glenway Wescott 13:592

Johnson, James William
Katherine Anne Porter 7:311

Johnson, Kenneth
Richard Wilbur 6:570

Johnson, Marigold
Bernard Malamud 3:324

Johnson, Nora
Darcy O'Brien 11:405

Johnson, Richard
W. H. Auden 2:26

Johnson, Richard A.
Turner Cassity 6:107
Anthony Hecht 8:268
Delmore Schwartz 2:387

Johnson, Rosemary
John Ashbery 13:35

Johnson, Thomas S.
Bob Dylan 12:194

Johnston, Albert H.
Patti Smith 12:541

Johnston, Arnold
William Golding 3:198

Johnston, Dillon
Austin Clarke 6:111
Albert Goldbarth 5:143
Seamus Heaney 7:147

Johnston, Kenneth G.
William Faulkner 11:199

Johnstone, J. K.
E. M. Forster 3:160

Jonas, George
Margaret Atwood 3:19
Gwendolyn MacEwan 13:357

Jonas, Gerald
Isaac Asimov 9:49
Arthur C. Clarke 13:155
Samuel R. Delany 8:168, 169
Harlan Ellison 13:203
Frank Herbert 12:278, 279
Ursula K. LeGuin 8:343
Barry N. Malzberg 7:209
Larry Niven 8:426
Andre Norton 12:470
Kate Wilhelm 7:538

Jones, A. R.
Sylvia Plath 9:430

Jones, Alun R.
Philip Larkin 13:335
Eudora Welty 1:362; 2:460

Jones, Bernard
John Cowper Powys 9:441

Jones, Brian
Howard Nemerov 2:306

Jones, D. A. N.
Ed Bullins 1:47
John Fowles 6:184
Mervyn Jones 10:295
John Wain 11:564
Fay Weldon 11:565

Jones, D. Allan
John Barth 5:52

Jones, D. G.
Earle Birney 6:76; 11:49
Anne Hébert 4:219
Irving Layton 2:237

Jones, David R.
Saul Bellow 13:69

Jones, Edward T.
John Updike 3:487

Jones, Ernest
Aldo Palazzeschi 11:431
Budd Schulberg 7:403

Jones, Granville H.
Jack Kerouac 2:226

Jones, John Bush
Harold Pinter 9:418

Jones, Louisa E.
Raymond Queneau 10:431

Jones, Margaret E. W.
Ana María Matute 11:362, 365

Jones, Rhodri
Leon Garfield 12:227, 235

Jones, Richard
L. P. Hartley 2:182
Anthony Powell 7:346

Jones, Robert F.
James Jones 3:262

Jones, Roger
Saul Bellow 10:39

Jong, Erica
Sara Davidson 9:174
Doris Lessing 3:287
Anne Sexton 4:483; 8:484
Eleanor Ross Taylor 5:425

Joost, Nicholas
T. S. Eliot 9:190

Jordan, Alice M.
Esther Forbes 12:207
Andre Norton 12:455
John R. Tunis 12:593

Jordan, Clive
Martin Amis 4:19
Dan Jacobson 4:253
G. Josipovici 6:271
Yukio Mishima 4:356
Thomas Pynchon 6:432
Gillian Tindall 7:473
Ludvík Vaculík 7:494
Kurt Vonnegut, Jr. 4:567

Jordan, Francis X.
Gore Vidal 10:501

Jordan, June
Maya Angelou 12:13
Millen Brand 7:30
Nikki Giovanni 2:165
Zora Neale Hurston 7:171
Gayl Jones 9:306
Marge Piercy 6:402

Joseph, Gerhard
John Barth 1:17

Josipovici, Gabriel
Saul Bellow 3:54
Vladimir Nabokov 3:353

Joye, Barbara
Ishmael Reed 13:476
John A. Williams 13:598

Judson, Jerome
John Ciardi 10:105

Jumper, Will C.
Robert Lowell 1:178

Justus, James H.
John Berryman 4:60
John Crowe Ransom 4:431
Karl Shapiro 4:487
Robert Penn Warren 4:578, 582

Kabakoff, Jacob
Aharon Megged 9:375

Kabatchnik, Amnon
William F. Buckley, Jr. 7:36

Kael, Pauline
Mel Brooks 12:76
Norman Mailer 3:315

Kahn, Lothar
Arthur Koestler 3:271
Jakov Lind 4:293
André Schwarz-Bart 4:479
Peter Weiss 3:515
Elie Wiesel 3:527

Kaiser, Walter
George Seferis 11:493

Kakish, William
Peter Hundke 10:260

Kalem, T. E.
Edward Albee 2:2; 5:12
Kingsley Amis 3:8
Samuel Beckett 2:47
Ed Bullins 5:84
Anne Burr 6:104
Friedrich Dürrenmatt 4:141
Jules Feiffer 8:216
Robert Graves 2:177
Bill Gunn 5:152
John Hopkins 4:234
Ira Levin 3:294
Terrence McNally 7:217
Jason Miller 2:284
Peter Nichols 5:307
Sean O'Casey 5:319
Murray Schisgal 6:490
Neil Simon 6:506
Isaac Bashevis Singer 6:511
Aleksandr I. Solzhenitsyn 1:321
Tom Stoppard 4:526
David Storey 2:424, 425; 4:530
Thornton Wilder 6:572
Tennessee Williams 7:545
Robert Wilson 7:550

Kalstone, David
A. R. Ammons 2:12
John Ashbery 2:17; 13:31

John Berryman **3**:69
Elizabeth Bishop **13**:95
A. D. Hope **3**:250
Philip Levine **5**:250
Robert Lowell **11**:326
James Merrill **2**:273, 275; **13**:378
Adrienne Rich **11**:475
James Schuyler **5**:383

Kameen, Paul
Daniel J. Berrigan **4**:57
Robert Lowell **3**:303

Kamin, Ira
Charles Bukowski **9**:137

Kane, Patricia
Chester Himes **7**:159

Kanfer, Stefan
Jerzy Kosinski **6**:285
Terrence McNally **7**:218
Brian Moore **7**:237
Isaac Bashevis Singer **3**:453;
6:510
John Steinbeck **5**:408

Kanon, Joseph
Louis Auchincloss **4**:29
Carlos Castaneda **12**:88
Daphne du Maurier **6**:147
Penelope Gilliatt **2**:160
Jacqueline Susann **3**:475
John Updike **2**:444

Kantra, Robert A.
Samuel Beckett **3**:46

Kaplan, Johanna
Dan Jacobson **4**:254
Cynthia Ozick **7**:287

Kaplan, Sydney Janet
Doris Lessing **6**:296

Kapp, Isa
John Cheever **11**:120
Oriana Fallaci **11**:189
Jascha Kessler **4**:269
Grace Paley **4**:394
Philip Roth **4**:459

Karimi-Hakkak, Ahmad
Ahmad Shamlu **10**:470

Karl, Frederick R.
Samuel Beckett **1**:20
Elizabeth Bowen **1**:40
John Braine **1**:43
Ivy Compton-Burnett **1**:60
Lawrence Durrell **1**:83
E. M. Forster **1**:103
William Golding **1**:119
Henry Green **2**:178
Graham Greene **1**:132
L. P. Hartley **2**:181
Joseph Heller **1**:140
Aldous Huxley **1**:150
Christopher Isherwood **1**:155
Pamela Hansford Johnson
1:160
Doris Lessing **1**:173, 175
Iris Murdoch **1**:233
P. H. Newby **2**:310
Anthony Powell **1**:277
William Sansom **2**:383
C. P. Snow **1**:314, 315, 316
Muriel Spark **2**:414
Evelyn Waugh **1**:357
Angus Wilson **2**:471

Karlen, Arno
Edward Dahlberg **7**:62

Karlinsky, Simon
Vladimir Nabokov **1**:241; **2**:305
John Rechy **7**:357
Aleksandr I. Solzhenitsyn **2**:408
Yevgeny Yevtushenko **1**:382

Karp, David
Meyer Levin **7**:203

Kasack, Wolfgang
Aleksandr I. Solzhenitsyn **7**:434

Kasindorf, Martin
Christopher Hampton **4**:212
Norman Lear **12**:335

Kattan, Naim
Mordecai Richler **5**:373

Katz, Claire
Flannery O'Connor **6**:379, 380

Katz, Jonathan
Albert Goldbarth **5**:144

Kauffmann, Stanley
Edward Albee **2**:3; **5**:11, 14
Fernando Arrabal **2**:15; **9**:41
Alan Ayckbourn **5**:37
John Berryman **3**:69
Mel Brooks **12**:80
Ed Bullins **7**:36
Anthony Burgess **2**:86
D. L. Coburn **10**:108
E. L. Doctorow **6**:133
Athol Fugard **5**:130; **9**:230
Peter Handke **5**:164
James Leo Herlihy **6**:234
James Kirkwood **9**:319
Jerzy Kosinski **1**:171; **2**:233
Arthur Miller **2**:280
Henry Miller **4**:350
Peter Nichols **5**:307
Hugh Nissenson **9**:399
Edna O'Brien **3**:365
John O'Hara **2**:325
Miguel Piñero **4**:402
Harold Pinter **3**:386, 387; **6**:417
Bernard Pomerance **13**:446
David Rabe **4**:425, 426; **8**:450
Terence Rattigan **7**:356
James Salter **7**:387
André Schwarz-Bart **2**:388
Irwin Shaw **7**:412
John Steinbeck **5**:408
Tom Stoppard **4**:527
Elizabeth Swados **12**:560
Gore Vidal **2**:450
Kurt Vonnegut, Jr. **2**:452
Tennessee Williams **5**:504;
7:545
Robert Wilson **9**:576

Kaufman, Donald L.
Norman Mailer **2**:263

Kaye, Howard
Yvor Winters **4**:593

Kaye, Lenny
Jimmy Page and Robert Plant
12:475
Stevie Wonder **12**:656

Kaysen, Xana
Jerzy Kosinski **10**:309

Kazin, Alfred
Renata Adler **8**:7

James Baldwin **1**:13; **13**:52
Donald Barthelme **13**:54
Brendan Behan **1**:25
Saul Bellow **1**:28; **3**:61
Jane Bowles **3**:84
Paul Bowles **1**:41
William S. Burroughs **5**:91
Albert Camus **2**:97
Louis-Ferdinand Céline **9**:158
John Cheever **3**:108
James Gould Cozzens **4**:116
E. E. Cummings **8**:155
Joan Didion **3**:127
Lawrence Durrell **1**:83
Ralph Ellison **1**:93; **3**:146
Frederick Exley **6**:170
Gabriel García Márquez **2**:149
William H. Gass **8**:240
Paul Goodman **4**:195
Graham Greene **1**:131
Joseph Heller **11**:265
Ernest Hemingway **3**:242
David Ignatow **4**:249
Jack Kerouac **1**:165
Alan Lelchuk **5**:241
Robert Lowell **1**:179
Norman Mailer **1**:187
Bernard Malamud **1**:194; **3**:326
Wallace Markfield **8**:379
John P. Marquand **2**:271
Mary McCarthy **3**:329
Carson McCullers **4**:345
Vladimir Nabokov **3**:356; **8**:418
V. S. Naipaul **4**:373; **9**:393
Joyce Carol Oates **2**:313; **3**:363
Flannery O'Connor **1**:259;
3:370
John O'Hara **1**:260; **3**:371
Walker Percy **2**:334
Ann Petry **1**:266
Thomas Pynchon **3**:419
Kenneth Rexroth **1**:284
Philip Roth **1**:292
J. D. Salinger **1**:295, 296; **3**:446,
458
Karl Shapiro **4**:484
Isaac Bashevis Singer **1**:310;
3:457; **9**:487
C. P. Snow **1**:314
Aleksandr I. Solzhenitsyn
2:410; **4**:515
Susan Sontag **13**:515
John Steinbeck **13**:530
Peter Taylor **4**:543
Paul Theroux **8**:514
John Updike **3**:488; **9**:538
Kurt Vonnegut, Jr. **3**:505
Robert Penn Warren **1**:352;
4:582
Edmund Wilson **2**:475
Abraham B. Yehoshua
13:618

Keane, Patrick
Galway Kinnell **5**:216

Kearns, Edward
Richard Wright **1**:379

Kearns, Lionel
Earle Birney **6**:77

Keates, Jonathan
Jorge Luis Borges **6**:94
John Fowles **10**:187
John Hersey **7**:155

Keating, Peter
Erica Jong **8**:315

Kee, Robert
Agatha Christie **12**:115

Keefe, Joan
Flann O'Brien **10**:362

Keeley, Edmund
George Seferis **11**:492

Keen, Sam
Carlos Castaneda **12**:93

Keenan, Hugh T.
J. R. R. Tolkien **1**:336

Keene, Donald
Yukio Mishima **2**:287; **4**:354
Jun'ichirō Tanizaki **8**:509

Keeney, Willard
Eudora Welty **1**:361

Keils, R. M.
Vladimir Nabokov **11**:391

Keith, Philip
J. E. Wideman **5**:489

Kelleher, Victor
Muriel Spark **13**:523

Keller, Jane Carter
Flannery O'Connor **3**:365

Keller, Marcia
Agatha Christie **12**:117

Kellman, Steven G.
Aharon Megged **9**:374
Robert Pinget **13**:442

Kellogg, Gene
Graham Greene **3**:208
François Mauriac **4**:339
Flannery O'Connor **3**:365
J. F. Powers **4**:419
Evelyn Waugh **3**:511

Kelly, Ernece B.
Maya Angelou **12**:9

Kelly, James
Irwin Shaw **7**:411

Kemball-Cook, Jessica
Andre Norton **12**:465

Kemp, Peter
Lawrence Durrell **13**:189

Kempton, Murray
Gore Vidal **4**:554

Keneas, Alex
Ira Levin **6**:305

Kenefick, Madeleine
Gayl Jones **6**:265
Cynthia Ozick **7**:290

Kennard, Jean E.
Anthony Burgess **10**:86
William Golding **10**:233
Joseph Heller **8**:275
James Purdy **10**:421
Kurt Vonnegut, Jr. **12**:611

Kennebeck, Edwin
Terry Southern **7**:453

Kennedy, Andrew K.
John Arden **6**:10
Samuel Beckett **6**:46
T. S. Eliot **6**:166
John Osborne **11**:422
Harold Pinter **6**:419

CRITIC INDEX

Kennedy, Dorothy Mintzlaff
Raymond Federman **6**:181
Howard Nemerov **6**:363

Kennedy, Eileen
Penelope Gilliatt **10**:230

Kennedy, John S.
John Steinbeck **1**:323; **13**:532

Kennedy, Ray
Joseph Wambaugh **3**:509

Kennedy, William
Jorge Amado **13**:11
Thomas Bernhard **3**:64
Carlos Castaneda **12**:92
Robertson Davies **2**:113
Don DeLillo **10**:134
Gabriel García Márquez **8**:232
John Gardner **7**:111
Joseph Heller **5**:179
Elia Kazan **6**:273
William Kotzwinkle **5**:219
Peter Matthiessen **7**:211
Mordecai Richler **5**:378

Kennedy, X. J.
A. R. Ammons **2**:13
Edward Dahlberg **7**:62
Eleanor Lerman **9**:328
James Merrill **2**:275
Robert Pack **13**:438

Kenner, Hugh
W. H. Auden **2**:29
Samuel Beckett **11**:43
Robert Bly **10**:62
John Dos Passos **8**:182
Ernest Hemingway **8**:285
Marianne Moore **4**:360; **13**:397
Vladimir Nabokov **6**:357
George Oppen **7**:283, 285
Ezra Pound **2**:345; **4**:412; **7**:325
Mary Renault **11**:472
Richard G. Stern **4**:522
William Carlos Williams **2**:469;
  13:605
James Wright **10**:546
Louis Zukofsky **7**:561, 562

Kenney, Edwin J., Jr.
Elizabeth Bowen **11**:61
Iris Murdoch **6**:345

Kent, Cerrulia
Laura Z. Hobson **7**:164

Kent, George E.
James Baldwin **1**:15
Gwendolyn Brooks **1**:46
Chester Himes **4**:229
Ishmael Reed **13**:477

Kermode, Frank
W. H. Auden **2**:25
Beryl Bainbridge **8**:37
Samuel Beckett **2**:46
T. S. Eliot **2**:126, 128
E. M. Forster **10**:178
William Golding **2**:167, 169
Nadine Gordimer **10**:240
Graham Greene **6**:215
Peter Handke **5**:165
Christopher Isherwood **11**:296
Henry Miller **2**:282
Iris Murdoch **2**:298
Philip Roth **3**:440
J. D. Salinger **12**:497
Muriel Spark **2**:414, 415, 418

Kern, Edith
Samuel Beckett **2**:47

Kern, Robert
Richard Brautigan **12**:71
Gary Snyder **9**:500

Kernan, Alvin B.
Philip Roth **4**:453
Evelyn Waugh **1**:358

Kerr, John Austin, Jr.
José Rodrigues Miguéis **10**:341

Kerr, Walter
Alice Childress **12**:106
Charles Gordone **1**:124
Jim Jacobs and Warren Casey
  12:292
Harold Pinter **1**:267
Neil Simon **6**:503
Kurt Vonnegut, Jr. **12**:605
Michael Weller **10**:526

Kerrane, Kevin
Robert Coover **7**:59

Kerrigan, Anthony
Jorge Luis Borges **4**:74; **9**:115;
  13:109
Camilo José Cela **13**:145

Kerr-Jarrett, Peter
Octavio Paz **6**:397

Kessler, Edward
Daniel Hoffman **6**:242
Charles Wright **6**:580

Kessler, Jascha
A. R. Ammons **5**:28
Imamu Amiri Baraka **2**:34
Charles Bukowski **5**:79
James Dickey **7**:79
Loren Eiseley **7**:91
Irving Feldman **7**:101
Lawrence Ferlinghetti **10**:174
Robert Graves **2**:176
Sandra Hochman **8**:297
Ted Hughes **2**:201
June Jordan **5**:203
Anthony Kerrigan **4**:269
György Konrád **10**:304
Don L. Lee **2**:238
Thomas Merton **3**:335
Robert Pack **13**:438
Octavio Paz **10**:388
John Crowe Ransom **11**:467
Karl Shapiro **8**:485
Muriel Spark **8**:492
John Wain **11**:561, 563
Robert Penn Warren **4**:578
Louis Zukofsky **7**:560

Kettle, Arnold
John Berger **2**:55
Ivy Compton-Burnett **3**:111
E. M. Forster **3**:159
Graham Greene **3**:206
Aldous Huxley **3**:252

Keyser, Barbara Y.
Muriel Spark **8**:494

Kherdian, David
Philip Whalen **6**:565

Kibler, Louis
Alberto Moravia **11**:382

Kidder, Rushworth M.
E. E. Cummings **8**:161

Kidel, Mark
Bob Dylan **12**:198

Kieffer, Eduardo Gudiño
Jorge Luis Borges **9**:117

Kieley, Benedict
Brendan Behan **11**:44
John Montague **13**:391

Kiely, Robert
Maeve Brennan **5**:73
Hortense Calisher **2**:96
Michael Frayn **7**:106
Gabriel García Márquez **2**:148
William H. Gass **2**:155
Bernard Malamud **3**:323

Kieran, Margaret Ford
Mary Stolz **12**:547

Kiernan, Robert F.
John Barth **3**:42

Killam, G. D.
Chinua Achebe **1**:1

Killinger, John
Fernando Arrabal **9**:37

Kilroy, Thomas
Samuel Beckett **3**:45

Kimball, Arthur G.
Yasunari Kawabata **9**:309

Kimmel, Eric A.
Emily Cheney Neville **12**:452

Kindilien, Glenn A.
Saul Bellow **10**:44

King, Bruce
Nadine Gordimer **10**:240
Ruth Prawer Jhabvala **8**:312
V. S. Naipaul **9**:392

King, Charles L.
Ramón Sender **8**:479

King, Edmund L.
Jorge Guillén **11**:263

King, Francis
Aldous Huxley **5**:193
Iris Murdoch **11**:388
Muriel Spark **13**:525

King, Larry L.
Kurt Vonnegut, Jr. **12**:602

King, Thomas M.
Jean-Paul Sartre **7**:394

Kingsbury, Mary
M. E. Kerr **12**:298

Kingston, Carolyn T.
Margot Benary-Isbert **12**:35
Emily Cheney Neville **12**:453

Kinkead, Gwen
Penelope Gilliatt **2**:161

Kinnamon, Keneth
James Baldwin **13**:52

Kinney, Jeanne
Carson McCullers **4**:344; **12**:427

Kinsella, Anna M.
Alberto Moravia **7**:242

Kinsella, Thomas
Austin Clarke **6**:111

Kinsey, Helen E.
Margot Benary-Isbert **12**:33

Kinzie, Mary
Jorge Luis Borges **2**:73

Kirby, Emma
Lenora Mattingly Weber **12**:633

Kirby, Martin
Walker Percy **8**:440

Kirby-Smith, H. T., Jr.
Elizabeth Bishop **4**:66
Arthur Gregor **9**:254

Kirk, Elizabeth D.
J. R. R. Tolkien **1**:341

Kirk, Russell
Ray Bradbury **10**:68

Kirkham, Michael
Charles Tomlinson **4**:543

Kirsch, Robert
Jascha Kessler **4**:270

Kitchin, Laurence
John Arden **13**:24
Arnold Wesker **5**:481

Kitching, Jessie B.
E. M. Almedingen **12**:3

Kizer, Carolyn
Ted Hughes **2**:201

Klaidman, Stephen
Juan Goytisolo **5**:150

Klappert, Peter
Daniel Mark Epstein **7**:97
Kathleen Spivack **6**:520

Klarmann, Adolf D.
Friedrich Dürrenmatt **11**:168

Klein, Marcus
Saul Bellow **1**:29
Ralph Ellison **1**:94

Klein, Theodore
Albert Camus **11**:95

Kleinberg, Seymour
Isaac Bashevis Singer **3**:458

Klemtner, Susan Strehle
William Gaddis **10**:212

Kliman, Bernice W.
Philip Roth **3**:438

Klinkowitz, Jerome
Imamu Amiri Baraka **5**:45
Donald Barthelme **3**:43; **5**:52;
  6:29; **13**:60
Jonathan Baumbach **6**:32
Erica Jong **6**:269
Jerzy Kosinski **3**:272
Flann O'Brien **7**:269
Gilbert Sorrentino **3**:462
Ronald Sukenick **3**:475; **4**:530
Kurt Vonnegut, Jr. **1**:348;
  3:500; **4**:563

Klockner, Karen M.
Madeleine L'Engle **12**:352

Kmetz, Gail Kessler
Muriel Spark **8**:493

Knapp, B. L.
Marguerite Duras **6**:151

Knapp, Bettina Liebowitz
Jean Anouilh **8**:24
Jean Cocteau **8**:145
Georges Duhamel **8**:187
Jean Genet **1**:116
Anna Kavan **13**:317
Robert Pinget **7**:305
Nathalie Sarraute **8**:469

Knapp, James F.
T. S. Eliot **6**:163
Ken Kesey **11**:317
Delmore Schwartz **2**:387

Knapp, John V.
John Hawkes **7**:145

Knelman, Martin
W. Somerset Maugham **11**:370
Harold Pinter **9**:421
Mordecai Richler **5**:377

Knieger, Bernard
S. Y. Agnon **8**:8

Knight, Damon
Isaac Asimov **3**:16
Ray Bradbury **3**:84
Robert A. Heinlein **3**:224

Knight, G. Wilson
Sean O'Casey **11**:406
John Cowper Powys **7**:347

Knight, Karl F.
John Crowe Ransom **4**:428

Knight, Susan
Frederick Busch **7**:38
John Gardner **3**:186
József Lengyel **7**:202

Knobler, Peter
Bob Dylan **12**:189

Knoll, Robert E.
Ezra Pound **3**:398

Knopp, Josephine
Elie Wiesel **5**:491

Knorr, Walter L.
E. L. Doctorow **11**:142

Knowles, A. Sidney, Jr.
Marie-Claire Blais **2**:63
Frederic Prokosch **4**:421

Knowles, Dorothy
Eugène Ionesco **11**:290

Knowles, George W.
Marie-Claire Blais **13**:96

Knudsen, Erika
Elisaveta Bagryana **10**:11

Kobler, Turner S.
Rebecca West **7**:526

Koch, Kenneth
Frank O'Hara **2**:322

Koch, Stephen
Hermann Hesse **3**:243
Reynolds Price **6**:425
Nathalie Sarraute **8**:472
Christina Stead **5**:404
Gore Vidal **4**:554

Koenig, Peter William
William Gaddis **10**:209

Koethe, John
John Ashbery **2**:17; **3**:15
Sandra Hochman **3**:250
Theodore Weiss **3**:517

Kogan, Rick
Richard Price **12**:489

Kohler, Dayton
Carson McCullers **12**:413

Kohn, Hans
E. M. Almedingen **12**:2

Kolodny, Annette
Thomas Pynchon **3**:412

Kolonosky, Walter F.
Vladimir Voinovich **10**:508

Koltz, Newton
Wright Morris **3**:343
Patrick White **3**:524

Korg, Jacob
Bernard Malamud **2**:269

Korges, James
Erskine Caldwell **1**:51

Korn, Eric
Philip K. Dick **10**:138
Harlan Ellison **13**:203
Rayner Heppenstall **10**:272
Judith Rossner **9**:457
Claude Simon **9**:482
Gore Vidal **10**:502
Fay Weldon **11**:566

Kornfeld, Melvin
Jurek Becker **7**:27

Kosek, Steven
Kurt Vonnegut, Jr. **4**:569

Kostach, Myrna
Rudy Wiebe **6**:566

Kostelanetz, Richard
R. P. Blackmur **2**:61
Ralph Ellison **3**:141
Ezra Pound **2**:344

Kostis, Nicholas
Julien Green **11**:259

Kotin, Armine
Jean Arp **5**:33

Kott, Jan
Andrei Sinyavsky **8**:488

Kountz, Peter
Thomas Merton **11**:372

Kovar, Helen M.
Christie Harris **12**:261

Kozol, Jonathan
Marjorie Kellogg **2**:223

Kramer, Aaron
Stanley J. Kunitz **6**:287

Kramer, Hilton
Donald Barthelme **8**:50
E. L. Doctorow **6**:137
Robert Lowell **8**:357
Archibald MacLeish **8**:362
Mary McCarthy **5**:276
L. E. Sissman **9**:492
Allen Tate **11**:527
Robert Penn Warren **8**:538

Kramer, Jane
Maxine Hong Kingston **12**:312

Kramer, Nora
Betty Cavanna **12**:99

Kramer, Peter G.
William Goyen **5**:149

Krance, Charles
Louis-Ferdinand Céline **9**:153

Kraus, Elisabeth
John Hawkes **7**:146

Krensky, Stephen
Frank Bonham **12**:55

Krickel, Edward
James Gould Cozzens **1**:67
William Saroyan **1**:302

Kriegel, Leonard
T. S. Eliot **6**:166
James T. Farrell **11**:193
Günter Grass **2**:172
James Jones **10**:293
Iris Murdoch **1**:234
Ezra Pound **7**:333
Harvey Swados **5**:423
Edmund Wilson **2**:475

Krim
James Jones **10**:290

Kroll, Ernest
Peter Viereck **4**:559

Kroll, Jack
Edward Albee **2**:1
Jean Anouilh **3**:12
W. H. Auden **3**:27
Alan Ayckbourn **5**:36
Saul Bellow **6**:55
Mel Brooks **12**:80
Ed Bullins **1**:47
Anne Burr **6**:103, 104
Rosalyn Drexler **2**:119
Frederick Exley **6**:171
Jules Feiffer **8**:216
Jean Genet **2**:158
John Guare **8**:253
Bill Gunn **5**:152
Ted Hughes **2**:200
Stanley J. Kunitz **6**:286
Ira Levin **6**:306
David Mamet **9**:360
Terrence McNally **7**:218
Mark Medoff **6**:322
Arthur Miller **2**:280; **6**:334
Jason Miller **2**:284
Rochelle Owens **8**:434
Miguel Piñero **4**:402
Terence Rattigan **7**:355
Jonathan Reynolds **6**:451
Ronald Ribman **7**:358
Murray Schisgal **6**:490
Neil Simon **6**:504
Tom Stoppard **5**:414
David Storey **2**:424, 426
Elizabeth Swados **12**:559
Kurt Vonnegut, Jr. **2**:452
Lanford Wilson **7**:548

Kroll, Steven
Irvin Faust **8**:215
Thomas McGuane **3**:330
Dan Wakefield **7**:503
Irving Wallace **7**:510

Krouse, Agate Nesaule
Agatha Christie **12**:119

Krumgold, Joseph
Joseph Krumgold **12**:319

Krupka, Mary Lee
Margot Benary-Isbert **12**:33, 34

Krutch, Joseph Wood
Brigid Brophy **11**:67
Erskine Caldwell **8**:122
Elmer Rice **7**:360

Krzyzanowski, Jerzy R.
Tadeusz Konwicki **8**:325

Kuczkowski, Richard
Anthony Burgess **13**:125
Don DeLillo **13**:179
Susan Sontag **10**:485

Kuehl, Linda
Doris Lessing **3**:282
Iris Murdoch **3**:345
Marge Piercy **3**:384
Muriel Spark **2**:417
Eudora Welty **5**:479

Kuehn, Robert E.
Aldous Huxley **11**:284

Kuhn, Doris Young
Julia W. Cunningham **12**:164
Joseph Krumgold **12**:320

Kunitz, Stanley
John Berryman **8**:86
Robert Creeley **8**:152
Robert Frost **9**:223
Jean Garrigue **8**:240
H.D. **8**:255
Robert Lowell **9**:334
Marianne Moore **8**:397; **10**:346
John Crowe Ransom **11**:467
Theodore Roethke **8**:458

Kustow, Michael
Arnold Wesker **3**:519

Kyle, Carol A.
John Barth **9**:65

LaBarre, Weston
Carlos Castaneda **12**:88

Laber, Jeri
Aleksandr I. Solzhenitsyn
2:411; **4**:514

Labrie, Ross
Thomas Merton **11**:373

La Charite, Virginia
René Char **9**:167; **11**:113

Lafore, Lawrence
Irving Wallace **7**:509

LaFrance, Marston
Evelyn Waugh **1**:358

Lahr, John
Edward Bond **13**:103
Arthur Kopit **1**:171
Darcy O'Brien **11**:405
Joe Orton **4**:388; **13**:435, 436
John Osborne **11**:422
Harold Pinter **6**:411
Richard Price **12**:489
Sam Shepard **4**:491

Laidlaw, Marc
Stephen King **12**:311

Laing, Alexander
Esther Forbes **12**:208

Lake, Steve
Patti Smith **12**:536

Lally, Michael
Charles Bukowski **9**:138
Larry Eigner **9**:182
Kenneth Koch **8**:323
Howard Moss **7**:249
Anne Sexton **6**:493

Lambert, Gavin
Agatha Christie **8**:142
John O'Hara **6**:384

Lambert, J. W.
Edward Albee **2**:4
Alan Ayckbourn **5**:35
Peter Barnes **5**:50
Edward Bond **4**:70; **6**:84

CRITIC INDEX

A. E. Ellis 7:95
Michael Frayn 7:108
Athol Fugard 5:130
Trevor Griffiths 13:256
John Osborne 2:328
Sam Shepard 6:496
Bernard Slade 11:508
Tom Stoppard 3:470; 5:413
David Storey 2:425; 4:530
Arnold Wesker 3:518

Lamie, Edward L.
John Brunner 8:110

Lamming, George
Ishmael Reed 3:424
Derek Walcott 4:574

Lamont, Rosette C.
Fernando Arrabal 9:35
Eugène Ionesco 1:155; 6:252,
256; 9:287

Lamport, Felicia
S. J. Perelman 5:337

Landau, Jon
Bob Dylan 12:190
John Lennon and Paul
McCartney 12:377
Joni Mitchell 12:438
Jimmy Page and Robert Plant
12:475
Stevie Wonder 12:655, 657

Landess, Thomas
Thomas Merton 1:211

Landess, Thomas H.
John Berryman 2:60
Caroline Gordon 6:205; 13:247
William Meredith 4:349
Marion Montgomery 7:234
William Jay Smith 6:512
Allen Tate 4:540
Mona Van Duyn 3:491
Eudora Welty 1:363
James Wright 3:541

Landy, Francis
A. Alvarez 13:9

Lane, James B.
Harold Robbins 5:379

Lanes, Selma G.
Richard Adams 4:9

Langbaum, Robert
Samuel Beckett 9:85
E. M. Forster 1:107
Galway Kinnell 13:321

Langford, Paul
Leon Garfield 12:233

Langlois, Walter
André Malraux 9:355

Langton, Jane
William Mayne 12:402
Mary Rodgers 12:493
Rosemary Wells 12:637

Lardner, John
Irwin Shaw 7:409

Lardner, Susan
György Konrád 10:305
Joyce Carol Oates 9:404
Wilfrid Sheed 2:393

Larkin, Joan
Hortense Calisher 4:88

LaRocque, Geraldine E.
Madeleine L'Engle 12:348

Larrabee, Eric
Cornelius Ryan 7:385

Larrieu, Kay
Larry Woiwode 10:542

Larsen, Anne
Lisa Alther 7:11
Leonard Michaels 6:325

Larsen, Eric
Charles Newman 8:419

Larson, Charles
Hyemeyohsts Storm 3:470

Larson, Charles R.
Peter Abrahams 4:2
Chinua Achebe 5:1
Ayi Kwei Armah 5:31
Leslie A. Fiedler 4:163; 13:211
Camara Laye 4:284
Kamala Markandaya 8:377
Peter Matthiessen 7:210
V. S. Naipaul 7:253
R. K. Narayan 7:255
James Ngugi 7:263
Simone Schwarz-Bart 7:404
Raymond Sokolov 7:430
Wole Soyinka 5:396
Jean Toomer 13:556
Amos Tutuola 5:445
Ngugi Wa Thiong'o 13:583, 584
James Welch 6:561

Lasagna, Louis, M.D.
Michael Crichton 2:108

LaSalle, Peter
J. F. Powers 8:448

Lask, I. M.
S. Y. Agnon 4:10

Lask, Thomas
Richard Brautigan 12:60
Kenneth O. Hanson 13:263
Bohumil Hrabal 13:291
David Ignatow 7:177
Ross Macdonald 1:185
Georges Simenon 8:486
W. D. Snodgrass 2:405

Laska, P. J.
Imamu Amiri Baraka 10:21

Lassell, Michael
Tennessee Williams 11:573

Lasson, Robert
Mario Puzo 2:352

Latham, Aaron
Jack Kerouac 2:228

Lathen, Emma
Agatha Christie 12:123

Latiak, Dorothy S.
Jules Archer 12:17

Latshaw, Jessica
Christie Harris 12:268

Latrell, Craig
Harold Pinter 9:421

Lattimore, Richmond
John Berryman 2:59
Jorge Luis Borges 2:73
Edgar Bowers 9:121
Joseph Brodsky 6:97

Michael Casey 2:100
Alan Dugan 6:144
Daniel Hoffman 6:243
Galway Kinnell 13:318
Vladimir Nabokov 8:407
Adrienne Rich 7:364
L. E. Sissman 9:491

Laughlin, Rosemary M.
John Fowles 2:138

Laurence, Margaret
Chinua Achebe 7:3

Laut, Stephen J., S.J.
John Gardner 10:220

Lavers, Annette
Sylvia Plath 9:425

Lavers, Norman
John Hawkes 2:186

Lavine, Stephen David
Philip Larkin 8:336

Law, Richard
Robert Penn Warren 13:570

Lawall, Sarah
Yves Bonnefoy 9:113

Lawler, Daniel F., S.J.
Eleanor Hibbert 7:156

Lawler, James R.
René Char 11:117

Lawless, Ken
J. P. Donleavy 10:155

Lawrence, D. H.
Edward Dahlberg 7:61
Ernest Hemingway 10:263

Lawrence, Peter C.
Jean Lee Latham 12:324

Lawson, Lewis A.
William Faulkner 3:153
Flannery O'Connor 1:255

Lawton, A.
Yevgeny Yevtushenko 13:620

Lazarus, H. P.
Budd Schulberg 7:401

Leach, Edmund
Carlos Castaneda 12:85

Leaf, David
Brian Wilson 12:652

Leahy, Jack
David Wagoner 5:474

Leal, Luis
Juan Rulfo 8:462

Lear, Norman
Norman Lear 12:328

Learmont, Lavinia Marina
Hermann Hesse 2:191

Leary, Lewis
Lionel Trilling 9:534

Leary, Timothy
Bob Dylan 12:193

Leavis, F. R.
John Dos Passos 11:152
C. P. Snow 13:512

Leavitt, Harvey
Richard Brautigan 5:67

Lebowitz, Alan
Ernest Hemingway 1:144

Lebowitz, Naomi
Stanley Elkin 4:152
E. M. Forster 4:166
J. F. Powers 1:279

LeClair, Thomas
John Barth 7:23
Saul Bellow 6:53
Anthony Burgess 1:48
Carlos Castaneda 12:95
Jerome Charyn 5:103; 8:135
Don DeLillo 10:135; 13:179
J. P. Donleavy 1:76; 4:124;
6:141; 10:154
Stanley Elkin 6:170; 9:190
John Gardner 8:236
John Hawkes 7:141, 144
Joseph Heller 8:278
Flannery O'Connor 13:420
Walker Percy 8:400
David Plante 7:307
Thomas Pynchon 6:435
Tom Robbins 9:454
Ronald Sukenick 6:523
Harvey Swados 5:420

LeClercq, Diane
Patricia Highsmith 2:194
Susan B. Hill 4:226
William Sansom 6:483

Ledbetter, J. T.
Mark Van Doren 6:542
Galway Kinnell 13:320

Lee, Alvin
James Reaney 13:472

Lee, Charles
Earl Hamner, Jr. 12:257

Lee, Dennis
Paulette Giles 13:304
A. W. Purdy 6:428

Lee, Don L.
Nikki Giovanni 4:189
Conrad Kent Rivers 1:285

Lee, Hermione
Elizabeth Bowen 11:65

Lee, James W.
John Braine 1:43

Lee, Robert A.
Alistair MacLean 13:359

Leech, Margaret
Esther Forbes 12:206

Leeds, Barry H.
Ken Kesey 6:278
Norman Mailer 1:191
D. Keith Mano 2:270

Leeming, Glenda
John Arden 6:9

Leer, Norman
Bernard Malamud 8:374

Lees, Gene
John Lennon and Paul
McCartney 12:358

Leffland, Ella
Lois Gould 10:242

Legates, Charlotte
Aldous Huxley 11:287

Lehan, Richard
Walker Percy 2:332
Wilfrid Sheed 2:392
Susan Sontag 1:322

Lehman, David
  W. H. Auden **11**:20
  David Ignatow **7**:182
  Charles Reznikoff **9**:449
  Ira Sadoff **9**:466

Lehmann, John
  W. Somerset Maugham **11**:370
  Edith Sitwell **2**:403

Lehmann-Haupt, Christopher
  Michael Crichton **2**:109
  Rosalyn Drexler **2**:119
  Pete Hamill **10**:251
  Charles Newman **2**:311
  Richard Price **12**:488

Leib, Mark
  Sylvia Plath **3**:389

Leibowitz, Herbert
  Elizabeth Bishop **13**:91
  Robert Bly **2**:66
  Jean Garrigue **2**:153
  Robert Lowell **4**:297
  Josephine Miles **2**:278
  Kenneth Rexroth **6**:451
  Theodore Roethke **3**:434
  Delmore Schwartz **2**:388
  Isaac Bashevis Singer **3**:453
  W. D. Snodgrass **2**:405
  Gary Snyder **5**:395
  Mona Van Duyn **3**:492
  Jonathan Williams **13**:600
  William Carlos Williams **9**:574
  Edmund Wilson **3**:540

Leibowitz, Herbert A.
  Frank O'Hara **2**:321

Leigh, David J., S.J.
  Ernest Hemingway **6**:233

Leiter, Robert
  Janet Frame **6**:190
  Nadine Gordimer **7**:132
  Cormac McCarthy **4**:342
  Jean Rhys **6**:453
  Clancy Sigal **7**:424
  Larry Woiwode **10**:541

Lejeune, Anthony
  Agatha Christie **12**:117
  Paul Gallico **2**:147
  Anthony Powell **7**:345
  P. G. Wodehouse **2**:480

Lelchuk, Alan
  Isaac Bashevis Singer **11**:500

LeMaster, J. R.
  Jesse Stuart **8**:507; **11**:509

Lemay, Harding
  J. R. Salamanca **4**:461

Lemmons, Philip
  Brian Moore **8**:396
  William Trevor **7**:478

Lemon, Lee T.
  Kenneth Burke **2**:87, 89
  Louis-Ferdinand Céline **3**:105
  Guy Davenport, Jr. **6**:124
  Judith Guest **8**:254
  Jack Kerouac **5**:213
  Jerzy Kosinski **10**:306
  Joyce Carol Oates **6**:369
  John Rechy **1**:283
  C. P. Snow **4**:503
  Patrick White **5**:485
  Yvor Winters **4**:591

L'Engle, Madeleine
  Mary Stolz **12**:552

Lennox, John Watt
  Anne Hébert **13**:266

Lensing, George
  James Dickey **4**:120
  Robert Lowell **1**:183
  Louis Simpson **4**:498
  Louis Zukofsky **1**:385

Lenski, Branko
  Miroslav Krleža **8**:329

Lent, Henry B.
  John R. Tunis **12**:596

Lentfoehr, Sister Therese
  David Kherdian **6**:281

Leonard, John
  Lisa Alther **7**:12
  Saul Bellow **6**:56
  John Cheever **3**:107; **8**:139
  Joan Didion **1**:74
  Doris Lessing **3**:285
  Alison Lurie **4**:306
  Larry McMurtry **2**:271
  Thomas Pynchon **3**:414
  Wilfrid Sheed **2**:393

Lernoux, Penny
  Mario Vargas Llosa **9**:544

LeSage, Laurent
  Robert Pinget **7**:305

Leslie, Omolara
  Chinua Achebe **3**:2

Lessing, Doris
  Kurt Vonnegut, Jr. **2**:456

Lester, Julius
  Henry Dumas **6**:146

Lester, Margot
  Dan Jacobson **4**:256
  Hugh Nissenson **9**:400

Le Stourgeon, Diana E.
  Rosamond Lehmann **5**:235

Levensohn, Alan
  Christina Stead **2**:422

Levenson, J. C.
  Saul Bellow **1**:29

Levenson, Michael
  Herbert Gold **7**:121
  Tom McHale **5**:282
  John Updike **5**:460

Leventhal, A. J.
  Samuel Beckett **11**:32

Leverence, John
  Irving Wallace **13**:567

Levertov, Denise
  Russell Edson **13**:190
  David Ignatow **7**:173
  John Wieners **7**:535

Levey, Michael
  William Faulkner **1**:102
  W. Somerset Maugham **1**:204

Levi, Peter
  David Jones **4**:261; **13**:307
  George Seferis **5**:384
  Yevgeny Yevtushenko **1**:381

Leviant, Curt
  S. Y. Agnon **4**:12

Jakov Lind **4**:292
Isaac Bashevis Singer **3**:453
Elie Wiesel **3**:530

Levin, Bernard
  Aleksandr I. Solzhenitsyn **7**:436

Levin, Dan
  Yasunari Kawabata **2**:223

Levin, Elena
  Yevgeny Yevtushenko **1**:382

Levin, Irene S.
  Elizabeth Swados **12**:558

Levin, Martin
  Brian Aldiss **5**:14
  Taylor Caldwell **2**:95
  Austin C. Clarke **8**:143
  Robert Cormier **12**:134
  George MacDonald Fraser **7**:106
  Paul Gallico **2**:147
  Natalia Ginzburg **5**:141
  Earl Hamner, Jr. **12**:258
  William Kotzwinkle **5**:220
  Richard Llewellyn **7**:207
  John McGahern **5**:280
  Alice Munro **6**:341
  Craig Nova **7**:267
  J. B. Priestley **2**:347
  Ann Quin **6**:441
  Jean Rhys **2**:371
  Judith Rossner **6**:468
  Terry Southern **7**:452
  David Storey **4**:530
  Jesse Stuart **8**:507
  Hollis Summers **10**:493
  Elizabeth Taylor **4**:541
  Fredrica Wagman **7**:500
  P. G. Wodehouse **2**:479; **5**:516
  Louis Zukofsky **2**:487

Levin, Meyer
  Elmer Rice **7**:358
  Henry Roth **6**:472

Levin, Milton
  Noel Coward **1**:64

Levine, George
  John Gardner **7**:113
  Paul Goodman **2**:171
  Juan Carlos Onetti **7**:279
  Thomas Pynchon **3**:414

Levine, June Perry
  Vladimir Nabokov **6**:352; **11**:396

Levine, Paul
  Truman Capote **1**:55; **3**:99
  J. D. Salinger **12**:498

Levine, Suzanne Jill
  Severo Sarduy **6**:486
  Mario Vargas Llosa **6**:547

Levitas, Gloria
  Frank Bonham **12**:54

Levitin, Alexis
  J.R.R. Tolkien **12**:574

Levitt, Morton P.
  Michel Butor **3**:92
  Claude Simon **4**:495

Levitt, Paul M.
  Brendan Behan **11**:45
  Jorge Luis Borges **9**:116
  Michel de Ghelderode **11**:226

Levitzky, Sergei
  Aleksandr I. Solzhenitsyn **4**:507

Levy, Francis
  Thomas Berger **3**:64
  Ruth Prawer Jhabvala **4**:257

Levy, Frank
  Norman Lear **12**:330

Levy, Paul
  Kingsley Amis **13**:14
  Roald Dahl **6**:122
  E. L. Doctorow **11**:141
  Doris Lessing **6**:301

Lewald, H. Ernest
  Ernesto Sábato **10**:446

Lewis, C. S.
  J. R. R. Tolkien **1**:336; **12**:563

Lewis, Janet
  Caroline Gordon **6**:206

Lewis, Naomi
  Leon Garfield **12**:217

Lewis, Paula Gilbert
  Gabrielle Roy **10**:440

Lewis, Peter
  Horst Bienek **11**:48

Lewis, Peter Elfed
  Marvin Bell **8**:65
  Ruth Prawer Jhabvala **8**:313

Lewis, R. W. B.
  Graham Greene **1**:131
  André Malraux **4**:328
  John Steinbeck **9**:512

Lewis, Robert W.
  Edward Lewis Wallant **10**:516

Lewis, Robert W., Jr.
  Ernest Hemingway **1**:142

Lewis, Stuart
  Bruce Jay Friedman **3**:166

Lewis, Theophilus
  Neil Simon **6**:502, 503

Lewis, Tom J.
  Stanislaw Lem **8**:344

Lewis, Wyndham
  Ezra Pound **7**:322

Ley, Charles David
  Vicente Aleixandre **9**:10

Lhamon, W. T., Jr.
  Anthony Burgess **5**:89
  Bob Dylan **6**:158; **12**:192
  John Gardner **3**:187
  William Kennedy **6**:275
  Joseph McElroy **5**:280
  Robert M. Pirsig **4**:405
  Thomas Pynchon **3**:412
  Kurt Vonnegut, Jr. **4**:568

Libby, Anthony
  Theodore Roethke **11**:484
  William Carlos Williams **2**:470

Libby, Margaret Sherwood
  Margot Benary-Isbert **12**:33
  Betty Cavanna **12**:100
  Leon Garfield **12**:215
  Christie Harris **12**:261
  Jean Lee Latham **12**:323

Libby, Marion Vlastos
  Margaret Drabble **5**:117

CRITIC INDEX

Liberman, M. M.
Katherine Anne Porter 1:274; 7:318
Jean Stafford 4:517

Libhart, Byron R.
Julien Green 11:260

Lieber, Joel
Lois Gould 4:199

Lieber, Todd M.
Ralph Ellison 3:144
Robert Frost 9:221
John Steinbeck 5:406

Lieberman, Laurence
Rafael Alberti 7:10
A. R. Ammons 2:11
John Ashbery 9:44
W. H. Auden 2:28
John Berryman 1:33
Edward Brathwaite 11:67
James Dickey 1:73; 2:115
Arthur Gregor 9:252
Anthony Hecht 8:268
Zbigniew Herbert 9:271
Richard Howard 7:165
Galway Kinnell 1:168
Stanley J. Kunitz 6:286
W. S. Merwin 1:212; 3:338
Howard Moss 7:248
Howard Nemerov 2:307
John Peck 3:378
Kenneth Rexroth 2:371
W. D. Snodgrass 2:405
William Stafford 4:520, 521
Mark Strand 6:521
Ted Walker 13:565
Theodore Weiss 3:517
Reed Whittemore 4:588

Lifton, Robert Jay
Albert Camus 2:99
Kurt Vonnegut, Jr. 2:455

Light, Carolyn M.
Madeleine L'Engle 12:347

Lima, Robert
Jorge Luis Borges 6:88
Ira Levin 6:306
Colin Wilson 3:538

Lindberg-Seyersted, Brita
Bernard Malamud 9:343

Lindborg, Henry J.
Doris Lessing 6:299

Lindfors, Bernth
Chinua Achebe 7:4

Lindner, Carl M.
Robert Frost 3:175
James Thurber 5:440

Lindop, Grevel
John Berryman 3:66
Bob Dylan 4:148

Lindquist, Jennie D.
Margot Benary-Isbert 12:32
William Mayne 12:387
Mary Stolz 12:546, 550
Lenora Mattingly Weber 12:633

Lindsey, Byron
Joseph Brodsky 13:116

Lindsey, David A.
Jules Archer 12:22

Lindstrom, Naomi
Bob Dylan 12:191

Linehan, Eugene J., S.J.
Taylor Caldwell 2:95
James Herriot 12:283
Irving Wallace 7:509

Lingeman, Richard R.
James Herriot 12:283
Charles M. Schulz 12:531
Erich Segal 10:466
Garry Trudeau 12:590

Lipsius, Frank
Herbert Gold 7:121
Bernard Malamud 2:268
Henry Miller 2:283
Thomas Pynchon 6:434

Listri, Pier Francesco
Allen Tate 6:525

Litsinger, Kathryn A.
Andre Norton 12:465

Littell, Robert
Jean Toomer 13:550

Little, Roger
St.-John Perse 4:400; 11:433, 436

Littlejohn, David
James Baldwin 5:40
Imamu Amiri Baraka 5:44
Samuel Beckett 2:45
Jorge Luis Borges 2:68
Gwendolyn Brooks 5:75
Lawrence Durrell 4:144
Ralph Ellison 11:179
Jean Genet 2:157
John Hawkes 2:183
Robert Hayden 5:168
Joseph Heller 3:229
Chester Himes 7:159
Langston Hughes 5:190
Robinson Jeffers 2:214
John Oliver Killens 10:300
Henry Miller 2:281, 283
Ann Petry 7:304
Jean Toomer 13:551
J. E. Wideman 5:489
Richard Wright 9:583

Littler, Frank
Nigel Dennis 8:173

Livesay, Dorothy
Louis Dudek 11:159

Livingstone, Leon
Azorín 11:25

Lloyd, Peter
Leonardo Sciascia 9:476

Locke, Richard
Donald Barthelme 8:52
Thomas Berger 8:83
Heinrich Böll 3:73
John Cheever 8:139
Joan Didion 8:175
Joseph Heller 11:268
John Le Carré 5:233
Vladimir Nabokov 2:303; 8:418
Thomas Pynchon 2:356
John Updike 1:345; 9:540

Lockerbie, D. Bruce
C. S. Lewis 1:177

Locklin, Gerald
Richard Brautigan 12:67

Lockwood, William J.
Ed Dorn 10:159

Lodge, David
Kingsley Amis 2:10
William S. Burroughs 2:92
Mary Gordon 13:250
Graham Greene 1:134; 3:206
Ted Hughes 2:199
Norman Mailer 4:321
Alain Robbe-Grillet 4:447
Wilfrid Sheed 2:394
Muriel Spark 13:525

Loewinsohn, Ron
Richard Brautigan 12:59

Logan, John
E. E. Cummings 3:117

Lomas, Herbert
Roy Fuller 4:179
John Gardner 7:115
Paul Goodman 4:196
John Hawkes 7:143
Robert M. Pirsig 6:421
Ezra Pound 3:398

Long, Robert Emmet
Ernest Hemingway 3:237
Edmund Wilson 8:550

Longley, Edna
Douglas Dunn 6:147
Seamus Heaney 5:170

Longley, John Lewis, Jr.
Robert Penn Warren 1:355

Longstreth, T. Morris
Jean Lee Latham 12:322

Longsworth, Polly
Madeleine L'Engle 12:349

Loprete, Nicholas J.
William Saroyan 10:457

Lorch, Thomas M.
Edward Lewis Wallant 10:512

Lorich, Bruce
Samuel Beckett 6:34

Losinski, Julie
Christie Harris 12:263

Lothian, Helen M.
Christie Harris 12:262

Lourie, Richard
Joseph Brodsky 13:114

Lowell, Amy
Robert Frost 13:222

Lowell, Robert
W. H. Auden 1:9
John Berryman 2:57
Randall Jarrell 2:207; 13:298
Stanley J. Kunitz 6:285
Allen Tate 4:535

Lowenkron, David Henry
Samuel Beckett 6:40

Lubbers, Klaus
Carson McCullers 12:423

Lucas, John
Ezra Pound 7:332

Lucey, Beatus T., O.S.B.
Daphne du Maurier 6:146

Luchting, Wolfgang A.
José María Arguedas 10:9
José Donoso 4:126, 127
Gabriel García Márquez 2:150
Mario Vargas Llosa 10:496

Lucid, Luellen
Alexsandr I. Solzhenitsyn 10:480

Lucid, Robert F.
Ernest Hemingway 6:232
Norman Mailer 4:323

Lucie-Smith, Edward
Sylvia Plath 9:424

Luckett, Richard
Anthony Powell 7:339
Robert Penn Warren 6:555
Edmund Wilson 3:540

Ludwig, Jack
Bernard Malamud 2:269

Ludwig, Linda
Doris Lessing 6:301

Lueders, Edward
Jorge Luis Borges 2:72
George MacBeth 2:252

Lukacs, John
Aleksandr I. Solzhenitsyn 7:438

Lukacs, Paul
Anthony Burgess 13:125

Lukens, Rebecca J.
Mavis Thorpe Clark 12:132
Madeleine L'Engle 12:351

Lumley, Frederick
Terence Rattigan 7:354

Lumport, Felicia
Jessamyn West 7:520

Lundquist, James
J. D. Salinger 12:518
Kurt Vonnegut, Jr. 12:615

Lupoff, Richard
Kurt Vonnegut, Jr. 12:629

Lurie, Alison
Richard Adams 5:7
Iris Murdoch 3:348

Luschei, Martin
Walker Percy 3:378

Lustig, Irma S.
Sean O'Casey 9:411

Luttwak, Edward
Bernard Malamud 3:325

Lydenberg, Robin
Jorge Luis Borges 13:111, 113

Lydon, Susan
John Lennon and Paul McCartney 12:362

Lyell, Frank H.
Harper Lee 12:340

Lyles, W. H.
Stephen King 12:310

Lynch, Dennis Daley
William Stafford 7:462

Lynch, Michael
Richard Howard 7:168
Michael McClure 10:332

Lyne, Oliver
Ted Hughes 9:282

Lynen, John F.
Robert Frost 1:110

Lyon, George W., Jr.
Allen Ginsberg 3:194

Lyon, Melvin
  Edward Dahlberg 1:72

Lyons, Bonnie
  Margaret Atwood 8:33
  Henry Roth 2:378; 6:473
  Delmore Schwartz 10:463

Lyons, Eugene
  Walker Percy 6:399
  John Updike 3:486

Lyons, Gene
  Peter Benchley 8:82
  Len Deighton 7:75
  John Hersey 9:277
  Elia Kazan 6:274
  George MacBeth 9:340
  John Updike 13:562
  Irving Wallace 7:510
  Robert Penn Warren 8:540
  Richard Yates 7:555

Lyons, John O.
  Vladimir Nabokov 1:241

Lytle, Andrew
  Allen Tate 4:535

MacAdam, Alfred
  Thomas Pynchon 11:455

MacAndrew, Andrew R.
  Yuri Olesha 8:430

Macaulay, Jeannette
  Camara Laye 4:285

Macauley, Robie
  R. P. Blackmur 2:61
  Patrick White 9:566

MacBeth, George
  Robert Nye 13:412

MacBrudnoy, David
  George MacDonald Fraser
  7:106

MacDiarmid, Hugh
  Ezra Pound 4:413

Macdonald, Dwight
  James Gould Cozzens 4:111
  Philip Roth 1:293

MacDonald, John D.
  James M. Cain 11:87

Macdonald, Rae McCarthy
  Alice Munro 10:357

Macdonald, Ross
  Nelson Algren 10:8
  Dashiell Hammett 5:160

MacDonald, S. Yvonne
  Christie Harris 12:266

MacInnes, Colin
  James Baldwin 1:14
  Alex Haley 12:244

MacIntyre, Alasdair
  Arthur Koestler 1:170

Maciuszko, George J.
  Czeslaw Milosz 5:292

Mackay, Barbara
  Imamu Amiri Baraka 10:19
  Ed Bullins 7:37
  James Kirkwood 9:319

MacKenzie, Robert
  Norman Lear 12:337

MacKinnon, Alex
  Earle Birney 6:79

Macklin, F. Anthony
  Gore Vidal 2:449

Maclean, Alasdair
  D. M. Thomas 13:541

MacLeish, Archibald
  Ezra Pound 3:399

MacLeish, Roderick
  Eric Ambler 6:3
  Richard Condon 8:150
  Len Deighton 7:74
  George V. Higgins 4:224

Macnaughton, W. R.
  Ernest Hemingway 8:286

MacQuown, Vivian J.
  Mary Stolz 12:552

MacShane, Frank
  Jorge Luis Borges 2:76
  Edward Dahlberg 1:71
  W. S. Merwin 1:212
  Pablo Neruda 9:399

MacSween, R. J.
  Ivy Compton-Burnett 10:110

Madden, David
  James M. Cain 3:96; 11:86
  William Gaddis 1:113
  Wright Morris 1:230; 3:343

Maddocks, Melvin
  Richard Adams 4:7
  Kingsley Amis 2:7, 8
  John Beecher 6:48
  Heinrich Böll 3:75
  Paul Bowles 2:78
  J. P. Donleavy 6:142
  Ernest J. Gaines 3:179
  John Gardner 2:152
  Joseph Heller 5:176
  Thomas Keneally 5:209, 212
  Doris Lessing 2:239; 6:298, 303
  Bernard Malamud 2:267
  Thomas Pynchon 2:354
  Piers Paul Read 4:444
  Philip Roth 4:456
  Cornelius Ryan 7:385
  Angus Wilson 3:536

Madsen, Alan
  Andre Norton 12:457

Magalaner, Marvin
  E. M. Forster 1:103
  Aldous Huxley 1:150

Magid, Nora L.
  Mordecai Richler 9:450

Magliola, Robert
  Jorge Luis Borges 10:68

Magner, James E., Jr.
  John Crowe Ransom 4:431

Mahlendorf, Ursula
  Horst Bienek 7:28

Mahon, Derek
  Austin Clarke 9:168
  Donald Davie 10:125
  Frederick Exley 11:186
  John Le Carré 5:233
  József Lengyel 7:202
  John Montague 13:390
  Brian Moore 8:394
  Edna O'Brien 8:429

Maida, Patricia D.
  Flannery O'Connor 10:364

Mairowitz, David Zane
  Edward Bond 6:86

Maitland, Jeffrey
  William H. Gass 11:224

Maitland, Sara
  Flann O'Brien 5:314

Majdiak, Daniel
  John Barth 1:17

Majeski, Jane
  Arthur Koestler 8:324

Majkut, Denise R.
  Bob Dylan 4:148

Major, Clarence
  Ralph Ellison 3:146

Malanga, Gerard
  Anne Waldman 7:508

Malin, Irving
  Saul Bellow 13:70
  Frederick Busch 7:39
  Hortense Calisher 4:87
  Eleanor Clark 5:105
  B. H. Friedman 7:109
  John Hawkes 4:217
  Joseph Heller 5:182
  Ken Kesey 6:278
  Carson McCullers 4:344
  Flannery O'Connor 2:317
  Walker Percy 8:445
  James Purdy 2:347
  Muriel Spark 5:398; 8:496
  Peter Spielberg 6:519
  Harvey Swados 5:421
  Elie Wiesel 5:490

Malkin, Lawrence
  Harold Pinter 6:418

Malko, George
  Frederick Buechner 4:80

Malkoff, Karl
  Kenneth Rexroth 1:284
  Theodore Roethke 1:291
  May Swenson 4:533

Mallalieu, H. B.
  John Gardner 7:116
  Pablo Neruda 7:261
  David Pownall 10:419

Mallet, Gina
  Iris Murdoch 1:237
  Tennessee Williams 7:545

Malley, Terrence
  Richard Brautigan 3:88

Malmström, Gunnel
  Pär Lagerkvist 13:330

Maloff, Saul
  Nelson Algren 4:18
  Louis Auchincloss 4:30
  Heinrich Böll 9:110
  Frederick Busch 7:38
  Edward Dahlberg 7:68
  Ernest Hemingway 3:236
  Milan Kundera 9:321
  Norman Mailer 2:264
  Vladimir Nabokov 6:356
  Flannery O'Connor 3:365
  Clifford Odets 2:319
  Sylvia Plath 2:336
  Philip Roth 3:435; 4:455
  Alan Sillitoe 1:307
  Calder Willingham 5:512

Maloney, Douglas J.
  Frederick Exley 6:171

Malzberg, Barry N.
  Ursula K. LeGuin 13:349

Mandel, Siegfried
  Uwe Johnson 5:200

Mandelbaum, Allen
  Giuseppe Ungaretti 7:481

Mandelbaum, Bernard
  Elie Wiesel 11:570

Mander, John
  Günter Grass 6:208

Mangelsdorff, Rich
  Michael McClure 6:318

Mangione, Jerry
  Andrea Giovene 7:116

Manlove, C. N.
  J.R.R. Tolkien 12:580

Mann, Elizabeth C.
  Mary Stolz 12:551

Mann, Golo
  W. H. Auden 3:29

Mann, Jeanette W.
  Jean Stafford 7:458

Mann, Thomas
  Hermann Hesse 11:270

Manning, Olivia
  Sylvia Townsend Warner 7:511

Mano, D. Keith
  Richard Adams 4:9
  J. G. Ballard 3:34
  Thomas Berger 5:60
  Daniel J. Berrigan 4:58
  Jorge Luis Borges 2:71
  John Cheever 3:108
  Evan S. Connell, Jr. 6:117
  Peter DeVries 10:136
  J. P. Donleavy 4:125
  Irvin Faust 8:214
  William Gerhardie 5:140
  James Hanley 3:221
  Joseph Heller 5:180
  George V. Higgins 4:224
  B. S. Johnson 6:263, 264
  Erica Jong 8:315
  James A. Michener 11:376
  Vladimir Nabokov 2:301
  Hugh Nissenson 9:400
  John O'Hara 2:325
  Philip Roth 4:458
  William Saroyan 10:456
  Alexander Theroux 2:433
  John Updike 2:444; 5:456
  Patrick White 3:525
  Tennessee Williams 7:546

Mansell, Mark
  Harlan Ellison 13:208

Manso, Susan
  Anaïs Nin 8:424

Manthorne, Jane
  Frank Bonham 12:50, 51
  Mavis Thorpe Clark 12:130
  James Herriot 12:283
  Andre Norton 12:457

Maples, Houston L.
  Joseph Krumgold 12:318
  William Mayne 12:392

Marcello, J. J. Armas
Mario Vargas Llosa 10:499

Marciniak, Ed
Frank Bonham 12:50

Marcotte, Edward
Alain Robbe-Grillet 6:467

Marcus, Adrianne
Anna Kavan 13:316
Jon Silkin 2:395
William Stafford 4:520

Marcus, Greil
Wendell Berry 8:85
E. L. Doctorow 6:134
Bob Dylan 12:197
John Irving 13:294, 295, 296
John Lennon and Paul
  McCartney 12:382
Richard Price 12:490
John Sayles 10:460
Patti Smith 12:535
Raymond Sokolov 7:431
Robert Wilson 9:576

Marcus, Mordecai
William Everson 1:96
Robert Frost 9:224
Ted Hughes 2:203
Bernard Malamud 1:199

Marcus, Steven
William Golding 2:165
Dashiell Hammett 10:252
Bernard Malamud 2:265
Irving Stone 7:470

Marguerite, Sister M., R.S.M.
Eleanor Hibbert 7:155

Mariani, John
Aleksandr I. Solzhenitsyn 7:440

Mariani, Paul
Robert Penn Warren 8:536
William Carlos Williams 9:572

Marill-Albérès, René
Jean-Paul Sartre 1:304

Marius, Richard
Frederick Buechner 4:79

Markmann, Charles Lam
Julien Green 3:205
Joyce Carol Oates 2:313

Markos, Donald
Hannah Green 3:202

Markos, Donald W.
James Dickey 1:74

Markow, Alice Bradley
Doris Lessing 6:297

Marks, Mitchell
Frederick Busch 7:38

Marowitz, Charles
John Arden 13:23
Ed Bullins 1:47
John Osborne 5:331
Tom Stoppard 1:327
Tennessee Williams 11:576

Marranca, Bonnie
Peter Handke 8:261; 10:256

Marsh, Dave
Bob Dylan 12:192
Jimmy Page and Robert Plant
  12:480
Patti Smith 12:539
Brian Wilson 12:654

Marsh, Fred T.
Carson McCullers 12:409

Marsh, Irving T.
Jean Lee Latham 12:323

Marsh, Pamela
Agatha Christie 1:58
Joseph Krumgold 12:317
Mary Stolz 12:552

Marshall, Donald
Stanislaw Lem 8:343

Marshall, Tom
Margaret Atwood 8:29
William Heyen 13:282
Gwendolyn MacEwen 13:358
P. K. Page 7:292

Martin, Bruce K.
Philip Larkin 13:338

Martin, Gerald
Miguel Ángel Asturias 13:37

Martin, Graham
Roy Fuller 4:177
Robert Pinget 13:444

Martin, Jay
Robert Lowell 1:181

Martin, Robert A.
Arthur Miller 10:346

Martin, Robert K.
Richard Howard 10:274

Martin, Sandra
Hugh Garner 13:237

Martin, Terence
Ken Kesey 11:314

Martin, Wallace
D. J. Enright 8:204

Martineau, Stephen
Susan Musgrave 13:401
James Reaney 13:475

Martinez, Z. Nelly
José Donoso 8:178

Martz, Louis L.
Robert Creeley 1:67
X. J. Kennedy 8:320
Robert Lowell 1:181
Lisel Mueller 13:400
Joyce Carol Oates 9:403
Robert Pinsky 9:417
Ezra Pound 1:276
Reg Saner 9:469
Jon Silkin 2:396
William Stafford 4:521
John Wain 2:458

Martz, William J.
John Berryman 1:34

Marwell, Patricia McCue
Jules Archer 12:22

Masinton, Charles G.
J. P. Donleavy 10:153

Maskell, Duke
E. M. Forster 1:108; 9:203

Maslin, Janet
Alex Haley 12:254
Joni Mitchell 12:440, 443
Mary Rodgers 12:495

Mason, Ann L.
Günter Grass 4:204; 11:247

Mason, Michael
Donald Barthelme 8:53
George V. Higgins 10:273

Massingham, Harold
George Mackay Brown 5:76

Mathews, F. X.
P. H. Newby 13:408, 410

Mathews, Laura
James Hanley 13:261
Richard Price 12:491

Mathewson, Joseph
J.R.R. Tolkien 12:566

Mathewson, Rufus W., Jr.
Boris Pasternak 7:299
Mikhail Sholokhov 7:421
Aleksandr I. Solzhenitsyn 7:441

Mathewson, Ruth
Alejo Carpentier 8:134
Joan Didion 8:176
J. P. Donleavy 10:154
Margaret Drabble 8:184
Paula Fox 8:219
James Hanley 13:260
Christina Stead 8:500
Robert Penn Warren 8:540

Matlaw, Myron
Alan Paton 10:387

Matthews, Charles
John Hawkes 2:183

Matthews, Dorothy
J.R.R. Tolkien 12:583

Matthews, J. H.
André Breton 2:80

Matthews, Robin
Robin Skelton 13:507

Matthews, T. S.
Edmund Wilson 8:551

Matthews, Virginia H.
Betty Cavanna 12:98

Matthias, John
Elizabeth Daryush 6:123
Michael Hamburger 5:158
David Jones 7:189
Anne Stevenson 7:463
D. M. Thomas 13:542
R. S. Thomas 6:530

Maunder, Gabrielle
Ruth M. Arthur 12:27

Maurer, Robert
A. Alvarez 5:17
Robertson Davies 7:73
José Donoso 8:180
MacDonald Harris 9:258
Pablo Neruda 9:398
Clancy Sigal 7:425

Maurer, Robert E.
E. E. Cummings 8:155

Mauriac, Claude
Samuel Beckett 2:44
Albert Camus 2:97
Henry Miller 2:281
Alain Robbe-Grillet 2:373
Nathalie Sarraute 2:383
Georges Simenon 2:396

Maurois, André
Aldous Huxley 3:253
Jules Romains 7:381

Maury, Lucien
Pär Lagerkvist 7:198

Maxwell, D. E. S.
Brian Friel 5:128

May, Derwent
Nadine Gordimer 5:145
Alison Lurie 4:305
Tadeusz Rózewicz 9:463
Louis Simpson 9:485

May, John R.
Kurt Vonnegut, Jr. 2:455

May, Keith M.
Aldous Huxley 4:242

May, Yolanta
Emma Tennant 13:536

Mayer, Hans
Friedrich Dürrenmatt 4:140
Witold Gombrowicz 4:193
Günter Grass 4:202
Jean-Paul Sartre 4:473

Mayhew, Alice
Graham Greene 1:134
Claude Mauriac 9:363

Maynard, Robert C.
Alex Haley 8:259
Garry Trudeau 12:588

Mayne, Richard
Saul Bellow 8:70
J.I.M. Stewart 7:465

Mayo, Clark
Kurt Vonnegut, Jr. 12:617

Mazrui, Ali A.
Alex Haley 12:249

Mazzaro, Jerome
Elizabeth Bishop 9:88
David Ignatow 7:175, 178
Randall Jarrell 6:259
Robert Lowell 4:295, 298
Joyce Carol Oates 3:359
Ezra Pound 4:417
John Crowe Ransom 2:366
W. D. Snodgrass 6:514
William Carlos Williams 5:508

Mazzocco, Robert
John Ashbery 3:15
Chester Kallman 2:221
Philip Levine 5:251
Mario Luzi 13:354
William Meredith 4:348
Anne Sexton 6:492
Eleanor Ross Taylor 5:426
Gore Vidal 6:548

McAleer, John J.
MacKinlay Kantor 7:195
Alain Robbe-Grillet 10:438

McAllister, H. S.
Carlos Castaneda 12:92

McAllister, Mick
Michael McClure 6:319

McAuley, Gay
Jean Genet 10:225
Peter Handke 10:254

McBride, James
Frank Bonham 12:49

McCabe, Bernard
Wilfrid Sheed 10:474

McCaffery, Larry
Donald Barthelme **5**:55
William H. Gass **8**:242

McCahill, Alice
Elizabeth Taylor **2**:432

McCall, Dorothy
Jean-Paul Sartre **7**:388; **13**:498

McCarthy, Colman
P. G. Wodehouse **5**:516

McCarthy, Harold T.
Henry Miller **9**:377
Richard Wright **3**:545

McCarthy, Mary
William S. Burroughs **2**:90
Ivy Compton-Burnett **3**:112
Vladimir Nabokov **2**:301
J. D. Salinger **3**:444
Nathalie Sarraute **2**:384

McClain, Ruth Rambo
Toni Morrison **4**:365

McClanahan, Ed
Richard Brautigan **12**:64

McClatchy, J. D.
A. R. Ammons **5**:31
Louise Glück **7**:119
Richard Howard **7**:167
Robert Lowell **8**:355
James Merrill **6**:324
Robert Pinsky **9**:417
Sylvia Plath **5**:346
Ira Sadoff **9**:466
Maura Stanton **9**:507
Diane Wakoski **7**:504
Robert Penn Warren **6**:557
Theodore Weiss **8**:546
Charles Wright **6**:581

McClellan, Edwin
Yukio Mishima **6**:338

McClelland, David
Flann O'Brien **5**:315
Patti Smith **12**:536

McComas, J. Frances
Frank Herbert **12**:270

McConnell, Frank
John Barth **7**:25
Saul Bellow **6**:54
John Gardner **7**:115

McConnell-Mammarella, Joan
Carlo Emilio Gadda **11**:210

McConville, Edward
John Sayles **10**:461

McCullers, Carson
Carson McCullers **12**:417

McCullough, Frank
George Garrett **3**:189

McDaniel, Richard Bryan
Chinua Achebe **7**:6

McDiarmid, Matthew P.
Hugh MacDiarmid **11**:334

McDonald, James L.
John Barth **2**:38

McDonald, Susan S.
Harriet Waugh **6**:560

McDonnell, Jane Taylor
Galway Kinnell **2**:230

McDowell, Frederick P. W.
John Braine **1**:43

Lawrence Durrell **1**:87
E. M. Forster **1**:107; **10**:181
Doris Lessing **1**:175
Iris Murdoch **1**:236
Frederic Raphael **2**:366
Muriel Spark **2**:416

McDowell, Myles
Leon Garfield **12**:228
William Mayne **12**:404

McDowell, Robert
Thomas Merton **11**:374

McDowell, Robert E.
Thomas Keneally **10**:298

McElroy, Joseph
Samuel Beckett **2**:48
Italo Calvino **5**:99
Vladimir Nabokov **2**:304

McElroy, Wendy
Gabriel García Márquez **10**:217

McEvilly, Wayne
Anaïs Nin **1**:248

McFadden, George
Robert Lowell **9**:333

McFerran, Douglas
Carlos Castaneda **12**:93

McGann, Jerome
Robert Creeley **2**:106; **8**:151
David Jones **7**:188
X. J. Kennedy **8**:320
Eleanor Lerman **9**:331

McGann, Jerome J.
Turner Cassity **6**:107
Daniel Mark Epstein **7**:97
A. D. Hope **3**:251
Donald Justice **6**:272
Galway Kinnell **13**:320
Muriel Rukeyser **6**:479
Judith Johnson Sherwin **7**:415

McGhan, Barry
Andre Norton **12**:459

McGilchrist, Iain
W. H. Auden **9**:57

McGinnis, Wayne D.
Kurt Vonnegut, Jr. **8**:529

McGinniss, Joe
George V. Higgins **4**:222

McGrath, Joan
Gwendolyn MacEwen **13**:358

McGregor, Craig
Bob Dylan **4**:148

McGuane, Thomas
Richard Brautigan **1**:44
John Hawkes **2**:185

McGuinness, Frank
Kingsley Amis **1**:6
Andrew Sinclair **2**:400

McGuire, Alice Brooks
Betty Cavanna **12**:98
Jean Lee Latham **12**:322

McHale, Tom
Diane Johnson **5**:198
D. Keith Mano **2**:270
J. F. Powers **8**:447

McHargue, Georgess
Nicholasa Mohr **12**:447

McInerney, John
John Knowles **10**:303

McInerny, Ralph
Anthony Burgess **4**:80

McKenzie, Alan T.
John Updike **5**:452

McKinley, Hugh
Anthony Kerrigan **6**:275

McKinnon, William T.
Louis MacNeice **10**:324

McLaughlin, Pat
Charles M. Schulz **12**:533

McLay, C. M.
Margaret Laurence **3**:278
Ethel Davis Wilson **13**:609

McLean, David G.
Lewis Turco **11**:551

McLellan, Joseph
Donald Barthelme **8**:52
John Berryman **8**:90
Arthur Hailey **5**:156
Robert Heinlein **8**:275
George V. Higgins **10**:274
John Sayles **7**:399
J.R.R. Tolkien **8**:515

McLeod, A. L.
Patrick White **7**:531

McLuhan, Herbert Marshall
John Dos Passos **11**:154

McMahon, Joseph H.
Jean-Paul Sartre **7**:389

McMahon-Hill, Gillian
Russell C. Hoban **7**:161

McMichael, James
May Sarton **4**:471

McMullen, Roy
Nathalie Sarraute **2**:385

McMurtry, Larry
Vardis Fisher **7**:103
Ernest J. Gaines **11**:217
Ward Just **4**:265

McNally, John
Carson McCullers **12**:429

McNeil, Nicholas J., S.J.
Eleanor Hibbert **7**:156

McNeill, William H.
Charles M. Schulz **12**:524

McNelly, Willis E.
Ray Bradbury **10**:70
Robert Heinlein **8**:274
Frank Herbert **12**:277
Kurt Vonnegut, Jr. **2**:452

McPheeters, D. W.
Camilo José Cela **4**:98

McPheron, Judith
Jamake Highwater **12**:287

McPherson, Hugo
Mordecai Richler **5**:374

McPherson, Sandra
William Heyen **13**:283

McPherson, William
Margaret Atwood **8**:30
Paula Fox **8**:218
John Gardner **8**:235
Günter Grass **11**:252
Maxine Hong Kingston **12**:312
Maxine Kumin **5**:222
John Updike **5**:457; **13**:563

McSweeney, Kerry
V. S. Naipul **9**:391
Anthony Powell **9**:435

McWilliams, Dean
Michel Butor **3**:94
Marguerite Duras **3**:129

McWilliams, Nancy R.
John Steinbeck **5**:405

McWilliams, W. C.
Mary Renault **11**:472

McWilliams, Wilson C.
John Steinbeck **5**:405

Meades, Jonathan
Simone de Beauvoir **2**:43
Jorge Luis Borges **1**:39; **3**:77;
4:74
Louis-Ferdinand Céline **3**:105
Iris Murdoch **2**:297
Vladimir Nabokov **2**:302; **3**:354
Alain Robbe-Grillet **1**:289;
2:376; **4**:448
Kurt Vonnegut, Jr. **2**:455

Meckier, Jerome
Aldous Huxley **11**:285
Evelyn Waugh **3**:512

Medawar, Peter
Arthur Koestler **6**:281; **8**:324

Mednick, Liz
Susan Sontag **13**:518

Meehan, Thomas
Bob Dylan **12**:180

Meek, Margaret
Peter Dickinson **12**:175
William Mayne **12**:391, 394,
399, 405

Meeter, Glenn
Kurt Vonnegut, Jr. **4**:566

Megaw, Moira
W. H. Auden **6**:24

Megged, Aharon
S. Y. Agnon **4**:14

Meiners, R. K.
James Dickey **7**:81
Robert Lowell **1**:182
Delmore Schwartz **2**:387
Allen Tate **4**:536

Meinke, Peter
W. H. Auden **6**:20
John Beecher **6**:48
John Dos Passos **4**:136
H. D. **8**:256
Marilyn Hacker **5**:155
Ted Hughes **4**:236
Philip Levine **5**:250
William Meredith **13**:372
Howard Nemerov **2**:307
Muriel Rukeyser **6**:478
Anne Sexton **4**:483
Diane Wakoski **7**:504
Robert Penn Warren **6**:555
Charles Wright **6**:579

Meisel, Perry
Joni Mitchell **12**:440

Mellard, James M.
Bernard Malamud **1**:198
François Mauriac **9**:367
Kurt Vonnegut, Jr. **3**:504; **4**:565

CRITIC INDEX

Mellers, Wilfrid
Bob Dylan **12**:187
John Lennon and Paul
McCartney **12**:374

Mellor, Isha
Sol Yurick **6**:583

Mellors, John
Martin Amis **4**:20
Louis Auchincloss **6**:15
Beryl Bainbridge **10**:17
Thomas Berger **5**:60
Caroline Blackwood **9**:101
Melvyn Bragg **10**:72
Angela Carter **5**:102
Peter De Vries **7**:77
Shusaku Endo **7**:96
John Fowles **6**:188
John Hawkes **7**:141
Mark Helprin **10**:260
Dan Jacobson **4**:253
Ruth Prawer Jhabvala **8**:312
G. Josipovici **6**:270
Bernard Malamud **5**:269
Ian McEwan **13**:370
Stanley Middleton **7**:219
Yukio Mishima **4**:357
Alberto Moravia **7**:244
Iris Murdoch **4**:369
Julia O'Faolain **6**:382
V. S. Pritchett **5**:353
Piers Paul Read **4**:444; **10**:435
William Sansom **6**:484
Nathalie Sarraute **10**:460
Penelope Shuttle **7**:422
Alan Sillitoe **6**:499
Wole Soyinka **5**:398
Richard G. Stern **4**:523
David Storey **8**:504
Ludvík Vaculík **7**:495
Charles Webb **7**:516
Patrick White **5**:485

Mellown, Elgin W.
Jean Rhys **2**:373
John Wain **2**:458

Melly, George
Jean Arp **5**:33

Meltzer, R.
John Lennon and Paul
McCartney **12**:382
Patti Smith **12**:538

Melville, Robert
Herbert Read **4**:438
Susan Sontag **13**:515

Mendelsohn, John
Jimmy Page and Robert Plant
12:473, 474

Mendelson, David
Eugène Ionesco **6**:255

Mendelson, Edward
John Berryman **4**:61
Thomas Pynchon **3**:415; **6**:439

Mengeling, Marvin E.
Ray Bradbury **1**:42

Mercer, Peter
John Barth **9**:61

Merchant, W. Moelwyn
R. S. Thomas **13**:542

Mercier, Jean F.
Ruth M. Arthur **12**:27

Melvin Berger **12**:42
Betty Cavanna **12**:103
Jamake Highwater **12**:288
M. E. Kerr **12**:300
Madeleine L'Engle **12**:352
Katherine Paterson **12**:484, 486
Rosemary Wells **12**:637

Mercier, Vivian
Samuel Beckett **6**:38
Michel Butor **11**:78
Harry Crews **6**:118
J. P. Donleavy **4**:125
E. M. Forster **2**:135
George V. Higgins **4**:222
Aldous Huxley **5**:193
Iris Murdoch **4**:368
Raymond Queneau **5**:360
Alain Robbe-Grillet **6**:465
Nathalie Sarraute **4**:466
Claude Simon **4**:496

Meredith, William
John Berryman **2**:59; **3**:68
Anthony Hecht **8**:268
Robert Lowell **2**:248
Muriel Rukeyser **10**:442

Merideth, Robert
Norman Mailer **1**:192

Meritt, Carole
Alex Haley **12**:250

Merivale, Patricia
Vladimir Nabokov **1**:242

Merkin, Daphne
Ann Beattie **13**:65
Vincent Canby **13**:132
Penelope Gilliatt **13**:239
Chaim Potok **7**:321
John Updike **13**:559

Merrill, Reed B.
William H. Gass **8**:245

Merrill, Robert
Kurt Vonnegut, Jr. **8**:534

Merrill, Thomas F.
Allen Ginsberg **1**:118
Charles Olson **11**:417

Merry, Bruce
Mario Luzi **13**:352

Mersand, Joseph
Elmer Rice **7**:359

Mersmann, James F.
Robert Bly **5**:62
Robert Duncan **4**:142
Allen Ginsberg **4**:182
Denise Levertov **5**:247
Diane Wakoski **7**:507

Merton, Thomas
Albert Camus **1**:52
J. F. Powers **1**:281

Mesher, David R.
Bernard Malamud **9**:346; **11**:353

Mesic, Michael
James Dickey **4**:121
Chester Kallman **2**:221

Mesnet, Marie-Béatrice
Graham Greene **3**:210

Messer, Bill
Peter Dickinson **12**:171

Metcalf, Paul
Charles Olson **9**:413

Metzger, C. R.
Lawrence Ferlinghetti **10**:176

Mewshaw, Michael
Jonathan Baumbach **6**:31
Doris Betts **3**:73
Robertson Davies **7**:74
William Eastlake **8**:200
B. H. Friedman **7**:108
Robert F. Jones **7**:192
Stephen King **12**:310
David Slavitt **5**:391
Raymond Sokolov **7**:430
Peter Spielberg **6**:519
Paul Theroux **5**:427

Meyer, Ellen Hope
Erica Jong **4**:264
Joyce Carol Oates **2**:315

Meyer, Thomas
Lorine Niedecker **10**:360

Meyers, Jeffrey
E. M. Forster **3**:162; **4**:169
Doris Lessing **2**:241
André Malraux **4**:333

Mezey, Robert
Jerome Rothenberg **6**:478
Gary Snyder **9**:498

Michaels, Leonard
John Barth **2**:37
Samuel Beckett **11**:43
Thomas Berger **11**:46
Jorge Luis Borges **2**:77
Dashiell Hammett **5**:160
Peter Handke **8**:264
Joseph Heller **11**:269
Erica Jong **8**:314
Bernard Malamud **3**:324
Peter Matthiessen **11**:361
Vladimir Nabokov **8**:417

Michener, Charles T.
Anthony Powell **3**:402; **7**:343

Middlebrook, Diane
Allen Ginsberg **6**:199

Mihailovich, Vasa D.
Miroslav Krleža **8**:330

Milch, Robert J.
Chaim Potok **2**:338

Milder, Robert
Flannery O'Connor **13**:417

Miles, William
Langston Hughes **1**:148

Milford, Nancy
Louise Bogan **4**:69

Millar, Margaret
Daphne du Maurier **6**:146

Miller, Adam David
Alex Haley **12**:249

Miller, Alice
Rosemary Wells **12**:637

Miller, Baxter
Langston Hughes **10**:282

Miller, David
Michael Hamburger **5**:158

Miller, James E., Jr.
William Faulkner **6**:180
J. D. Salinger **1**:298; **12**:496

Miller, Jane
Simone Schwarz-Bart **7**:404

Miller, Jeanne-Marie A.
Imamu Amiri Baraka **2**:35
Gwendolyn Brooks **1**:46; **4**:78
Charles Gordone **4**:198

Miller, Jim
Jimmy Page and Robert Plant
12:477
Brian Wilson **12**:644, 648

Miller, Jim Wayne
Jesse Stuart **11**:513

Miller, Karl
Kingsley Amis **13**:14
Martin Amis **4**:21
Paula Fox **8**:218
Ted Hughes **4**:236
Dan Jacobson **4**:256
Hugh MacDiarmid **2**:254
Flann O'Brien **5**:316
Barbara Pym **13**:470
Anne Roiphe **9**:456
Emma Tennant **13**:537
Paul Theroux **11**:530
Michel Tournier **6**:538

Miller, Neil
Julio Cortázar **2**:103

Miller, Nolan
Henry Bromell **5**:73
Tillie Olsen **13**:433

Miller, Stephen
Zbigniew Herbert **9**:272

Miller, Tom P.
William Stafford **4**:521

Miller, Vincent
T. S. Eliot **9**:182
Ezra Pound **13**:462

Millgate, Michael
James Gould Cozzens **4**:114
John Dos Passos **4**:133

Millichap, Joseph R.
Carson McCullers **12**:428

Mills, James
George V. Higgins **4**:222

Mills, John
John Arden **13**:26

Mills, Ralph J., Jr.
Yves Bonnefoy **9**:112
René Char **9**:160
Richard Eberhart **3**:134, 135
David Ignatow **7**:174, 179
Maxine Kumin **5**:222
Denise Levertov **2**:243; **3**:293
Philip Levine **4**:287
Kathleen Raine **7**:351
Theodore Roethke **1**:291
Anne Stevenson **7**:462
Jonathan Williams **13**:600

Millstein, Gilbert
Irvin Faust **8**:215
John R. Tunis **12**:598

Milne, Tom
Mel Brooks **12**:79
John Osborne **5**:330

Milne, W. Gordon
John Dos Passos **4**:134

Milner-Gulland, Robin
Andrei Voznesensky **1**:349
Yevgeny Yevtushenko **1**:381

CRITIC INDEX

Milosh, Joseph
John Gardner **10**:220

Milton, Edith
Beryl Bainbridge **10**:17
Frederick Buechner **9**:136
Alan Sillitoe **10**:477

Milton, John R.
Vardis Fisher **7**:105
N. Scott Momaday **2**:290

Milton, Joyce
Jules Feiffer **8**:217

Milun, Richard A.
William Faulkner **6**:177

Mindlin, M.
Yehuda Amichai **9**:22

Miner, Robert G., Jr.
Charles M. Schulz **12**:529

Minogue, Valerie
Michel Butor **11**:82
Alain Robbe-Grillet **10**:437
Nathalie Sarraute **10**:458

Mirsky, Mark J.
John Hawkes **7**:145

Mirsky, Mark Jay
Samuel Beckett **6**:38
Anthony Burgess **4**:83
Günter Grass **4**:205
Flann O'Brien **5**:314
Manuel Puig **3**:407

Mitchell, Julian
Ivy Compton-Burnett **10**:110

Mitchell, Juliet
Norman Mailer **1**:192

Mitchell, Loften
Alice Childress **12**:104

Mitchell, Marilyn L.
John Steinbeck **9**:516

Mitchell, Penelope M.
Christie Harris **12**:263

Mitchell, W.J.T.
Hubert Selby, Jr. **4**:481

Mitchison, Naomi
W. H. Auden **9**:57

Mitgang, Herbert
Giorgio Bassani **9**:75
Leonardo Sciascia **9**:475

Mittleman, Leslie B.
Kingsley Amis **8**:11

Mitton, Pat
Christie Harris **12**:265

Miyoshi, Masao
Yasunari Kawabata **9**:311

Mizener, Arthur
James Gould Cozzens **4**:115
John Dos Passos **4**:133
Anthony Hecht **8**:266
Anthony Powell **10**:408
J. D. Salinger **12**:501
James Thurber **5**:439
Edmund Wilson **2**:475

Mo, Timothy
Jennifer Johnston **7**:186
John Le Carré **5**:234
Colin MacInnes **4**:315
Wilfrid Sheed **4**:489
Harriet Waugh **6**:559

Moers, Ellen
Lillian Hellman **2**:187

Moffett, Judith
Daniel Hoffman **13**:287
James Merrill **13**:376

Mojtabai, A. G.
Yasunari Kawabata **5**:208
Thomas Keneally **5**:211
Richard Yates **8**:555

Mok, Michael
Aleksandr I. Solzhenitsyn **2**:409

Mole, John
Louis Simpson **7**:428
R. S. Thomas **6**:530; **13**:545

Molesworth, Charles
John Berryman **2**:56; **8**:89
Ted Hughes **4**:236
Galway Kinnell **3**:269
Anne Sexton **8**:483
Charles Tomlinson **4**:548

Molloy, F. C.
John McGahern **9**:370

Moloney, Michael F.
François Mauriac **4**:337

Momaday, N. Scott
Jamake Highwater **12**:288

Momberger, Philip
William Faulkner **6**:179

Monagan, John S.
Anthony Powell **7**:342

Monas, Sidney
Aleksandr I. Solzhenitsyn **4**:511

Monegal, Emir Rodríguez-
See **Rodríguez-Monegal, Emir**

Monet, Christina
Mark Medoff **6**:323

Monguió, Luis
Rafael Alberti **7**:8

Monogue, Valerie
Harold Pinter **6**:404

Monsman, Gerald
J. R. R. Tolkien **1**:339

Montagnes, Anne
Brian Moore **5**:297
Audrey Thomas **13**:538

Montague, John
Hugh MacDiarmid **11**:333

Monteiro, George
Bob Dylan **4**:149
Robert Frost **4**:174; **10**:199
Ernest Hemingway **6**:231

Montgomery, Marion
T. S. Eliot **6**:163
Robert Frost **10**:195
Flannery O'Connor **1**:258

Montgomery, Niall
Flann O'Brien **7**:269

Moody, Michael
Mario Vargas Llosa **9**:544

Moorcock, Michael
Angus Wilson **3**:535

Moore, Anne Carroll
Margot Benary-Isbert **12**:30

Moore, Brian
Robertson Davies **2**:113

Moore, D. B.
Louis MacNeice **4**:316

Moore, Gerald
Chinua Achebe **11**:1

Moore, Harry T.
Arthur Adamov **4**:5
Kay Boyle **5**:65
John Dos Passos **4**:132
E. M. Forster **1**:106
Herbert Gold **4**:190
Eugène Ionesco **4**:252
James Jones **3**:262
Meyer Levin **7**:204
Henry Miller **4**:350
Alain Robbe-Grillet **2**:374
Nathalie Sarraute **2**:384
Georges Simenon **2**:397
Claude Simon **4**:494
John Steinbeck **5**:405

Moore, Honor
Marilyn Hacker **5**:156
June Jordan **5**:203

Moore, Hugo
Hugh MacDiarmid **4**:311

Moore, Jack B.
Carson McCullers **12**:425
Frank Yerby **7**:556

Moore, John Rees
James Baldwin **2**:31
Samuel Beckett **10**:29
J. P. Donleavy **1**:76; **4**:124
Robert Penn Warren **6**:558

Moore, Marianne
E. E. Cummings **12**:141
Ezra Pound **7**:322
Edith Sitwell **9**:493
William Carlos Williams **13**:601

Moore, Maxine
Isaac Asimov **9**:49

Moore, Richard
George Garrett **3**:192

Moore, Stephen C.
John Cheever **7**:49
Robert Lowell **3**:301

Moorman, Charles
J. R. R. Tolkien **1**:337

Moramarco, Fred
John Ashbery **4**:22; **9**:42
Robert Creeley **1**:67
David Ignatow **7**:181
Galway Kinnell **2**:229
W. S. Merwin **1**:213
Frank O'Hara **13**:424
James Schevill **7**:401

Moran, Ronald
Wendell Berry **4**:59
Robert Creeley **4**:117
David Ignatow **4**:248
Marge Piercy **6**:402
Louis Simpson **4**:498
James Tate **6**:528

Moravia, Alberto
Truman Capote **13**:132

Mordas, Phyllis G.
Melvin Berger **12**:40

Morello-Frosch, Marta
Julio Cortázar **2**:104
Gabriel García Márquez **3**:183

Morgan, Edwin
John Berryman **10**:47
Hugh MacDiarmid **11**:338
Eugenio Montale **9**:387

Morgan, Ellen
Doris Lessing **3**:288

Morgan, John
Günter Grass **6**:209

Morgan, Robert
Geoffrey Hill **8**:294

Morgan, Speer
Dan Jacobson **4**:256

Morley, Patricia A.
Margaret Atwood **13**:41
Patrick White **7**:529

Morley, Sheridan
Terence Rattigan **7**:354

Morris, Alice
Christina Stead **2**:422

Morris, C. B.
Rafael Alberti **7**:9
Vicente Aleixandre **9**:12

Morris, Christopher D.
John Barth **7**:23

Morris, H. H.
Dashiell Hammett **10**:253

Morris, Harry
Louise Bogan **4**:68
James Dickey **1**:73
Jean Garrigue **2**:154
John Hollander **2**:197
George MacBeth **2**:251
Louis Simpson **4**:498

Morris, Ivan
Yasunari Kawabata **2**:222

Morris, Jan
Laurens van der Post **5**:464

Morris, John N.
Kenneth O. Hanson **13**:263
Donald Justice **6**:271
Adrienne Rich **7**:370
Mark Strand **6**:521
Nancy Willard **7**:539
Charles Wright **6**:580; **13**:612

Morris, Robert K.
Anthony Burgess **4**:81; **5**:86
Lawrence Durrell **4**:146
John Fowles **6**:189
James Hanley **5**:167
Doris Lessing **6**:290
Olivia Manning **5**:271
Anthony Powell **1**:278; **3**:404;
 7:345
V. S. Pritchett **5**:354
C. P. Snow **6**:515
Thornton Wilder **6**:578

Morris, Wesley
John Crowe Ransom **4**:433

Morris, Wright
Ernest Hemingway **1**:141

Morrison, Blake
Donald Davie **10**:124
Yevgeny Yevtushenko **13**:620

Morrison, Harriet
Frank Bonham **12**:53

Morrison, J. Allan
Leon Garfield **12**:226, 234

CRITIC INDEX

Morrison, J. M.
Hugh MacDiarmid 2:254

Morrison, John W.
Jun'ichirō Tanizaki 8:509

Morrison, Lillian
Mary Stolz 12:549, 551

Morrison, Philip
Christie Harris 12:262
Larry Kettelkamp 12:304

Morrison, Phylis
Christie Harris 12:262
Larry Kettelkamp 12:304

Morrison, Theodore
Robert Frost 1:111

Morrissette, Bruce
Alain Robbe-Grillet 1:287

Morrissey, Daniel
John Updike 7:488

Morrow, Lance
John Fowles 6:187
Erica Jong 8:314
Yasunari Kawabata 5:208
James A. Michener 5:290
Yukio Mishima 4:356, 358

Morse, J. Mitchell
Kingsley Amis 2:6
James Baldwin 2:32
Bruce Jay Friedman 3:165
Joanne Greenberg 7:134
Jakov Lind 2:245
Mary McCarthy 1:207
Vladimir Nabokov 2:299
Peter Weiss 3:514

Morse, Jonathan
John Dos Passos 11:156

Morse, Samuel French
W. H. Auden 6:18
Margaret Avison 2:29
John Berryman 3:65
Robert Lowell 3:301
Louis Zukofsky 1:385

Mortimer, John
James Thurber 5:433

Mortimer, Penelope
Elizabeth Bishop 9:89
Nadine Gordimer 7:132
Fay Weldon 6:562

Moscoso-Gongora, Peter
José Lezama Lima 10:319

Moser, Gerald M.
José Rodrigues Miguéis 10:340

Moses, Edwin
Albert Camus 9:148

Moses, Joseph
E. L. Doctorow 11:140

Moses, Robbie Odom
Edward Albee 11:12

Moses, Wilson J.
W. E. B. DuBois 13:182

Moskowitz, Moshe
Chaim Grade 10:248

Mosley, Nicholas
J. P. Donleavy 10:155

Moss, Elaine
Madeleine L'Engle 12:347

Moss, Howard
W. H. Auden 6:20
Elizabeth Bishop 1:35; 9:91
Elizabeth Bowen 1:41; 3:84
Graham Greene 6:217
Flann O'Brien 1:252
Katherine Anne Porter 1:272
Jean Rhys 6:454
Nathalie Sarraute 1:302
Eudora Welty 2:463

Moss, Leonard
Arthur Miller 1:217

Moss, Robert F.
John Berryman 13:76
Lawrence Durrell 6:153
John O'Hara 6:384

Moss, Stanley
Stanley J. Kunitz 6:286

Mossman, Elliott
Boris Pasternak 10:382

Motley, Joel
Leon Forrest 4:164

Mott, Michael
A. R. Ammons 8:15
Geoffrey Grigson 7:135
David Jones 7:186
D. M. Thomas 13:541
Charles Tomlinson 13:545

Mottram, Eric
Fielding Dawson 6:126
Michael McClure 6:317
Arthur Miller 1:218
Gilbert Sorrentino 7:449
Diane Wakoski 4:572
Jonathan Williams 13:601

Moulton, Priscilla L.
E. M. Almedingen 12:1
Christie Harris 12:262

Mount, Ferdinand
Peter Handke 10:257

Movius, Geoffrey H.
William Carlos Williams 9:575

Moynahan, Julian
Louis Auchincloss 9:54
Frederick Buechner 9:137
Anthony Burgess 8:113
J. P. Donleavy 4:126
Ernest J. Gaines 11:218
John Irving 13:293
Jack Kerouac 2:228
Ken Kesey 6:277
Tom McHale 3:331
Brian Moore 3:341; 8:394
Seán O'Faoláin 7:274
Anne Roiphe 9:455
Wilfrid Sheed 10:472
James Tate 2:431

Moynihan, Julian
James Thurber 11:532

Mozejko, Edward
Elisaveta Bagryana 10:13

Muchnic, Helen
Mikhail Sholokhov 7:418, 421
Aleksandr I. Solzhenitsyn 9:507

Mudrick, Marvin
Donald Barthelme 2:39
William S. Burroughs 2:90
E. M. Forster 2:135

John Fowles 2:137
Jerzy Kosinski 2:231
Doris Lessing 2:239
Norman Mailer 1:192
Bernard Malamud 1:200
Vladimir Nabokov 3:355
Joyce Carol Oates 2:314
Nathalie Sarraute 2:384; 4:468
David Wagoner 3:508

Mudrovic, Mike
Claudio Rodríguez 10:440

Mueller, Lisel
Robert Bly 1:37
Louise Glück 7:118
Michael S. Harper 7:138
Jim Harrison 6:223
Anthony Hecht 8:268
W. S. Merwin 1:212
Marge Piercy 6:401
Peter Viereck 4:559
Alice Walker 6:553
Reed Whittemore 4:588

Muggeridge, Malcolm
Paul Scott 9:478

Mulhallen, Karen
Audrey Thomas 13:538

Mullen, Patrick B.
E. E. Cummings 12:157

Muller, Gilbert H.
William Faulkner 8:212

Müller-Bergh, Klaus
José Lezama Lima 4:288

Mumford, Olive
Larry Kettelkamp 12:304

Munk, Erika
Martin Duberman 8:185
Elizabeth Swados 12:560, 561

Murchison, John C.
Jorge Luis Borges 2:71, 75

Murchison, W., Jr.
John Dickson Carr 3:101

Murchland, Bernard
Albert Camus 2:97
Jean-Paul Sartre 7:396

Murdoch, Charles
John Glassco 9:236

Murdock, Kenneth B.
Esther Forbes 12:203

Murillo, L. A.
Jorge Luis Borges 4:70

Murphy, Reverend James M.
Carlos Fuentes 13:232

Murphy, Richard
Philip Larkin 5:231

Murr, Judy Smith
John Gardner 10:219

Murray, Atholl C.C.
David Jones 7:188

Murray, Donald C.
James Baldwin 13:53

Murray, Edward
Samuel Beckett 6:35
William Faulkner 6:176
Ernest Hemingway 6:229
Eugène Ionesco 6:251
Arthur Miller 6:327, 332

Alain Robbe-Grillet 6:466
Tennessee Williams 5:501

Murray, G. E.
Anthony Hecht 13:269
Robert Pack 13:439

Murray, Jack
Alain Robbe-Grillet 1:287

Murray, John J.
Robert Penn Warren 4:579

Murray, Michael
Edward Albee 2:3

Murray, Michele
Robert Cormier 12:134
Paula Fox 2:140
Susan B. Hill 4:227
Robert Kotlowitz 4:275
Pär Lagerkvist 7:200
Mary Lavin 4:282
William Mayne 12:399
Grace Paley 4:392

Murray, Philip
Aldous Huxley 3:256

Murray, William J.
Melvin Berger 12:38

Murtaugh, Daniel M.
Marie-Claire Blais 4:67
Wilfrid Sheed 2:393

Mus, David
T. S. Eliot 2:129

Musher, Andrea
Diane Wakoski 7:505

Muske, Carol
Jon Anderson 9:31
Charles Wright 13:613

Myers, Robert J.
Lothar-Günther Buchheim 6:100

Myers, Tim
Nicholas Delbanco 13:175

Myrsiades, Kostas
Yannis Ritsos 6:463; 13:487, 488

Nadeau, Maurice
Louis Aragon 3:13
Simone de Beauvoir 1:19
Samuel Beckett 1:22
Michel Butor 1:49
Albert Camus 1:54
Louis-Ferdinand Céline 1:56
Jean Genet 1:115
Jean Giono 4:185
Raymond Queneau 2:359
Alain Robbe-Grillet 1:288
Françoise Sagan 3:444
Nathalie Sarraute 1:303
Jean-Paul Sartre 1:305
Claude Simon 4:495

Nadeau, Robert L.
Djuna Barnes 11:29

Naiden, James
Lorine Niedecker 10:360

Naipaul, Shiva
Miguel Ángel Asturias 8:27
José Donoso 4:130

Naipaul, V. S.
Jorge Luis Borges 2:77
P. H. Newby 13:407
Jean Rhys 2:372

Nalley, Richard
Donald Hall **13**:259

Nance, William L.
Truman Capote **13**:133

Nance, William L., S.M.
Katherine Anne Porter **7**:314

Nardin, Jane
Evelyn Waugh **8**:544

Naremore, James
Philip Larkin **5**:226

Nassar, Eugene Paul
Ezra Pound **7**:335

Nathan, George Jean
Noel Coward **9**:171
Terence Rattigan **7**:353
Elmer Rice **7**:359

Natov, Roni
Leon Garfield **12**:239

Naughton, John
A. Alvarez **13**:9

Navarro, Carlos
Jorge Luis Borges **3**:79

Navasky, Victor S.
Jules Archer **12**:21
Meyer Levin **7**:204

Nazareth, Peter
James Ngugi **7**:266

Nebecker, Helen E.
Shirley Jackson **11**:302

Needleman, Ruth
Octavio Paz **3**:375

Neimark, Paul G.
Agatha Christie **1**:58

Neiswender, Rosemary
E. M. Almedingen **12**:4

Nelson, Alix
Mary Rodgers **12**:494

Nelson, Dorothy H.
Esther Forbes **12**:211

Nelson, Howard
Robert Bly **10**:54

Nelson, Hugh
Harold Pinter **6**:413

Nelson, Joyce
Kurt Vonnegut, Jr. **4**:562

Nelson, Paul
John Lennon and Paul
McCartney **12**:378
Patti Smith **12**:538

Nelson, Raymond
Chester Himes **2**:196

Nemerov, Howard
Conrad Aiken **3**:4
Kingsley Amis **2**:5
Djuna Barnes **3**:36
Kenneth Burke **2**:89
James Dickey **4**:120
Daniel Hoffman **13**:286
Harry Mathews **6**:315
Marianne Moore **4**:359
Howard Moss **7**:247
Kathleen Raine **7**:353

Nesbitt, Bruce
Earle Birney **11**:49

Nettelbeck, Colin W.
Louis-Ferdinand Céline **3**:103

Neumark, Victoria
Carlos Fuentes **13**:232

Nevins, Francis M., Jr.
Ellery Queen **3**:421; **11**:458
Rex Stout **3**:471

Nevius, Blake
Ivy Compton-Burnett **1**:62

New, W. H.
Ethel Davis Wilson **13**:608

New, William H.
Margaret Avison **4**:36
Robertson Davies **7**:73
Simon Gray **9**:241

Newberry, Wilma
Ramón Gómez de la Serna
9:237

Newfield, Jack
Bob Dylan **12**:183

Newlin, Margaret
Sylvia Plath **3**:389

Newlove, Donald
Peter Benchley **4**:53
Joseph Brodsky **4**:78
Thomas Kinsella **4**:271
W. S. Merwin **5**:287
J. D. Salinger **8**:463

Newman, Barbara
Jamake Highwater **12**:288

Newman, Charles
James Baldwin **13**:48
Saul Bellow **6**:59
Sylvia Plath **9**:421
Philip Roth **4**:457

Newman, Christina
Brian Moore **8**:395

Newman, Michael
W. H. Auden **6**:25

Newton, Francis
John Lennon and Paul
McCartney **12**:353

Nichol, B. P.
Earle Birney **6**:76

Nicholas, Brian
Graham Greene **6**:214

Nichols, Stephen G., Jr.
John Hawkes **3**:221

Nicholson, C. E.
Theodore Roethke **11**:486

Nicol, Charles
Kingsley Amis **5**:22
Brigid Brophy **6**:100
Anthony Burgess **5**:90
John Cheever **11**:121
Peter De Vries **7**:77
Dashiell Hammett **5**:162
John Hawkes **4**:218; **7**:144
John Irving **13**:293
Milan Kundera **9**:320
Norman Mailer **4**:323
Vladimir Nabokov **1**:244
Kurt Vonnegut, Jr. **3**:504;
8:534; **12**:602

Niemeyer, Gerhart
Aleksandr I. Solzhenitsyn **7**:439

Nightingale, Benedict
Alan Ayckbourn **5**:35
Edward Bond **4**:70
A. E. Ellis **7**:93
Michael Frayn **7**:107
John Hopkins **4**:234
David Mercer **5**:284
Sławomir Mrożek **13**:399
Peter Nichols **5**:305, 306
Joe Orton **13**:435
John Osborne **5**:333
J. B. Priestley **5**:350
Neil Simon **6**:504
Tom Stoppard **5**:412
David Storey **5**:415
E. A. Whitehead **5**:488

Nilsen, Alleen Pace
Maya Angelou **12**:14
Judy Blume **12**:44
M. E. Kerr **12**:300
Nicholasa Mohr **12**:447
John R. Tunis **12**:599

Nimmo, Dorothy
Judy Blume **12**:45

Nissenson, Hugh
Chaim Potok **2**:338; **7**:321

Nitchie, George W.
Robert Lowell **8**:350
George MacBeth **2**:251
Marianne Moore **8**:397

Noble, David W.
James Baldwin **4**:40

Nokes, David
Michael Mewshaw **9**:377

Nolan, Paul T.
Marc Connelly **7**:55

Noland, W. Richard
Elliott Baker **8**:38

Nomad, Max
Ignazio Silone **4**:493

Norman, Albert H.
Richard Brautigan **12**:58

Norman, Gurney
Richard Brautigan **12**:64

Norris, Leslie
Andrew Young **5**:525

Norsworthy, James A.
Jamake Highwater **12**:286

North, R. J.
André Malraux **13**:367

Norton, Dale
Alex Haley **12**:248

Norwood, Gilbert
Agatha Christie **12**:113

Norwood, W. D., Jr.
C. S. Lewis **1**:177

Noth, Dominique Paul
Garry Trudeau **12**:589

Novak, Michael
Norman Lear **12**:338

Novak, Michael Paul
Robert Hayden **5**:169

Novak, William
Grace Paley **6**:391
Susan Fromberg Schaeffer
6:488

Novick, Julius
Edward Albee **9**:10
John Bishop **10**:54
Simon Gray **9**:242
David Mamet **9**:360
Sean O'Casey **11**:411
David Rabe **4**:425
Neil Simon **11**:496
Tom Stoppard **4**:525; **8**:504
David Storey **8**:505
Tennessee Williams **8**:548

Nugent, Robert
René Char **11**:111

Nyabongo, V. S.
Alice Walker **6**:554

Nye, Robert
Brigid Brophy **6**:98
E. M. Forster **3**:162
David Garnett **3**:189
Graham Greene **3**:214
Bernard Malamud **5**:269
Anthony Powell **3**:402
John Cowper Powys **7**:349
William Sansom **6**:483
Penelope Shuttle **7**:422

Nye, Russel
John Lennon and Paul
McCartney **12**:366

Nyren, D.
Marie-Claire Blais **13**:97

Nyren, Dorothy
Russell Edson **13**:190

Oakley, Helen
Lenora Mattingly Weber **12**:633

Oates, Joyce Carol
Harriette Arnow **2**:14
James Baldwin **5**:42
Frederick Busch **7**:38
James M. Cain **3**:95
Carlos Castaneda **12**:88
John Cheever **11**:120
Robert Coover **7**:58
Robert Creeley **8**:152
Roald Dahl **1**:177
James Dickey **7**:83
Joan Didion **8**:175
Margaret Drabble **2**:118; **5**:117
Andre Dubus **13**:183
James T. Farrell **4**:158
Janet Frame **2**:141
Gail Godwin **5**:142
William Goyen **8**:250
Jim Harrison **6**:224
Anne Hébert **13**:268
Maxine Kumin **5**:222
Philip Larkin **8**:337
Mary Lavin **4**:282
Doris Lessing **2**:241
Philip Levine **4**:286, 288
Norman Mailer **11**:341
Bernard Malamud **3**:323
Berry Morgan **6**:339
Alice Munro **6**:342
Iris Murdoch **1**:237; **11**:389
Vladimir Nabokov **2**:304
Charles Newman **2**:312; **8**:419
Flannery O'Connor **1**:258
Sylvia Plath **2**:338; **5**:340
Philip Roth **4**:454
Anne Sexton **6**:492

CRITIC INDEX

Elizabeth Taylor 2:433
Peter Taylor 1:335
Paul Theroux 8:512
William Trevor 9:529
John Updike 2:441; 13:561
Kurt Vonnegut, Jr. 12:603
Fay Weldon 9:559
Eudora Welty 1:363
Richard Yates 7:554

Oberbeck, S. K.
Kingsley Amis 2:7
Frederick Forsyth 5:125
John Hawkes 1:137
John Hersey 7:154
John Irving 13:293
Norman Mailer 2:264
Joyce Carol Oates 2:315
Georges Simenon 2:398
Kurt Vonnegut, Jr. 3:502
Stevie Wonder 12:655

Oberg, Arthur
John Berryman 4:66
Galway Kinnell 3:270
Greg Kuzma 7:197
Philip Levine 2:244
John Matthias 9:362
Joyce Carol Oates 6:367
Robert Pack 13:438
Anne Sexton 4:482
Mona Van Duyn 7:498
Derek Walcott 9:556

Oberhelman, Harley D.
José Donoso 11:146

O'Brien, James H.
Liam O'Flaherty 5:321

O'Brien, John
Gilbert Sorrentino 7:450

Obuchowski, Chester W.
Pierre Gascar 11:220

Obuchowski, Mary Dejong
Yasunari Kawabata 9:316

O'Connell, Shaun
Marjorie Kellogg 2:224
Gilbert Sorrentino 7:447

O'Connor, Garry
Jean Anouilh 8:24

O'Connor, Gerald
J.R.R. Tolkien 12:576

O'Connor, John J.
Earl Hamner, Jr. 12:258
Norman Lear 12:333, 334, 337
Lanford Wilson 7:547

O'Connor, Mary
Caroline Gordon 6:203

O'Connor, William Van
Kingsley Amis 1:5
Donald Davie 5:113
D. J. Enright 4:154
Elizabeth Jennings 5:197
Philip Larkin 3:275
Iris Murdoch 1:234
Ezra Pound 1:275
John Wain 2:458

O'Daniel, Therman B.
Ralph Ellison 1:95

O'Doherty, Brian
Flann O'Brien 5:314

O'Donnell, Thomas D.
Michel Butor 11:81

O'Faolain, Julia
Beryl Bainbridge 10:15
Mark Helprin 10:260
Edna O'Brien 5:311
Isaac Bashevis Singer 9:489

O'Faoláin, Seán
Daphne du Maurier 11:162
Ernest Hemingway 13:272

Oglesby, Leora
Frank Bonham 12:50

Ogunyemi, Chikwenye Okonjo
Toni Morrison 10:354

O'Hara, J. D.
Kingsley Amis 8:11
Donald Barthelme 5:54
Ann Beattie 8:54
Samuel Beckett 6:39
Jorge Luis Borges 2:77
Kay Boyle 5:66
Richard Brautigan 12:58
Anthony Burgess 5:86, 88
Louis-Ferdinand Céline 4:103
Laurie Colwin 13:156
Roald Dahl 6:121
Edward Dahlberg 7:71
Don DeLillo 13:178
Lawrence Durrell 6:152
George V. Higgins 4:223
José Lezama Lima 4:288
Vladimir Nabokov 1:246
Judith Rossner 6:469
C. P. Snow 9:498
Kurt Vonnegut, Jr. 12:608

O'Hara, T.
Derek Walcott 4:575

O'Hara, Tim
Ronald Sukenick 4:531

Ohmann, Carol B.
Alex Haley 12:244
J. D. Salinger 12:516
Muriel Spark 2:414

Ohmann, Richard M.
Pär Lagerkvist 7:199
J. D. Salinger 12:516

O'Keeffe, Timothy
Patrick White 3:521

Olderman, Raymond M.
John Barth 3:40
Peter S. Beagle 7:26
Stanley Elkin 4:153
John Hawkes 3:222
Joseph Heller 3:229
Ken Kesey 3:266
Thomas Pynchon 3:411
Kurt Vonnegut, Jr. 3:505

Oldfield, Michael
Jimmy Page and Robert Plant 12:477

Oldham, Andrew
Brian Wilson 12:640

Oldsey, Bernard S.
William Golding 2:167

Oliphant, Dave
Albert Goldbarth 5:143

Oliver, Edith
Ed Bullins 5:83; 7:36
Anne Burr 6:103
Alice Childress 12:105

John Guare 8:253
Christopher Hampton 4:211
Jim Jacobs and Warren Casey 12:292
Mark Medoff 6:322
Rochelle Owens 8:434
Terence Rattigan 7:355
Jonathan Reynolds 6:451
Sam Shepard 6:497
Tom Stoppard 3:470; 4:525
Elizabeth Swados 12:557, 559
Kurt Vonnegut, Jr. 12:605
Derek Walcott 2:460
Richard Wesley 7:518

Oliver, Raymond
Arthur Gregor 9:255

Oliver, Roy
Arthur A. Cohen 7:51

Olivier, Edith
Esther Forbes 12:203

Olmert, Michael
Philip Roth 4:452

Olney, James
Chinua Achebe 1:2
Loren Eiseley 7:92

Olsen, Gary R.
Hermann Hesse 6:238

Olshen, Barry N.
John Fowles 9:210

Olson, David B.
Robert Penn Warren 10:518

Olson, Lawrence
Yukio Mishima 2:288

Olson, Toby
Diane Wakoski 7:505

O'Neill, Kathleen
Michel Butor 11:80

O'Neill, Tom
Giuseppe Ungaretti 11:557

Onley, Gloria
Margaret Atwood 4:25; 13:42

Onyeama, Dillibe
Alex Haley 12:252

Opdahl, Keith
Saul Bellow 3:51

Oppenheim, Shulamith
Leon Garfield 12:230

Oppenheimer, Joel
Philip Roth 4:457
William Saroyan 10:456

Ordóñez, Elizabeth
Ana María Matute 11:366

O'Reilly, Timothy
Frank Herbert 12:279

Orgel, Doris
Emily Cheney Neville 12:453

Oriard, Michael
Don DeLillo 13:175

Ormerod, Beverley
Édouard Glissant 10:230

Ormerod, David
V. S. Naipaul 4:371

Ornstein, Jacob
Camilo José Cela 4:95

O'Rourke, William
Rosalyn Drexler 2:120
Craig Nova 7:267

Orr, Leonard
Richard Condon 4:107

Orth, Maureen
Bob Dylan 3:130
Stevie Wonder 12:657

Ortiz, Gloria M.
Pablo Neruda 7:260

Ortiz, Miguel A.
Alice Childress 12:108
Nicholasa Mohr 12:448

Orwell, George
Alex Comfort 7:52
Graham Greene 6:216

Osborn, Neal J.
Kenneth Burke 2:87

Osborne, Charles
William Faulkner 1:102
W. Somerset Maugham 1:204

Osborne, David
Albert Camus 2:99

Osborne, Trudie
Madeleine L'Engle 12:345

Osgood, Eugenia V.
Julien Gracq 11:244

Ostriker, Alicia
Ai 4:16
Cid Corman 9:170
Alan Dugan 2:121
Paul Goodman 7:131
Anne Waldman 7:508

Ostroff, Anthony
Donald Justice 6:271
Kathleen Spivack 6:520
Mark Van Doren 6:542

Ostrom, Alan
William Carlos Williams 1:370

Ostrovsky, Erika
Louis-Ferdinand Céline 4:98

Otten, Anna
Heinrich Böll 2:66
Michel Butor 8:120
Alain Robbe-Grillet 6:467; 8:453
Nathalie Sarraute 2:386
Claude Simon 4:497

Oviedo, José Miguel
Mario Vargas Llosa 10:497, 500

Owen, Carys T.
Louis-Ferdinand Céline 9:155

Owen, I. M.
Robertson Davies 7:72

Owen, Ivon
Robertson Davies 13:171

Owens, Iris
Lois Gould 4:200

Owens, Rochelle
Diane Wakoski 7:505

Ower, John
Frank Herbert 12:273
Mordecai Richler 9:451
Edith Sitwell 9:494

Ower, John B.
Edith Sitwell 2:404

Ownbey, Steve
George V. Higgins 10:273
Georges Simenon 8:486

Owomoyela, Oyekan
Chester Himes 7:159

Ozick, Cynthia
Saul Bellow 10:43
Frederick Buechner 2:83
Bernard Malamud 11:346
Hugh Nissenson 4:380

Pace, Eric
Joseph Wambaugh 3:508

Pacernick, Gary
Millen Brand 7:30

Pachter, Henry
Paul Goodman 7:129

Pachter, Henry M.
Hermann Hesse 6:236

Pack, Robert
James Schevill 7:400

Packard, Nancy H.
Grace Paley 6:393

Page, James A.
James Baldwin 3:32
Ralph Ellison 3:145
Richard Wright 3:546

Page, Malcolm
John Arden 13:25

Palevsky, Joan
Isak Dinesen 10:148

Palley, Julian
Azorín 11:25

Palmer, Eustace
Chinua Achebe 7:5
James Ngugi 7:265

Palmer, Penelope
Charles Tomlinson 6:536

Palmer, R. Roderick
Haki R. Madhubuti 6:313
Sonia Sanchez 5:382

Palmer, Tony
Bob Dylan 12:196
Jimmy Page and Robert Plant
12:481

Panshin, Alexei
Robert A. Heinlein 3:224

Panter-Downes, Mollie
John Le Carré 9:327

Papatzonis, Takis
Giuseppe Ungaretti 11:557

Parachini, Allan
Garry Trudeau 12:589

Parameswaran, Uma
Derek Walcott 9:557

Pareles, Jon
Bob Dylan 12:197
Joni Mitchell 12:443

Parente, Diane A.
James Dickey 10:142

Parente, William J.
Alexsandr I. Solzhenitsyn
10:479

Parini, Jay
Christopher Middleton 13:388

Parisi, Joseph
X. J. Kennedy 8:320
Susan Fromberg Schaeffer
11:491
Mark Van Doren 6:543

Park, Clara Claiborne
Brigid Brophy 6:99
James Merrill 13:377
Richard Wilbur 9:568

Park, John G.
Shirley Jackson 11:302

Park, Sue Simpson
Joyce Carol Oates 11:400

Parke, Andrea
Mary Stolz 12:548

Parkhill-Rathbone, James
C. P. Snow 1:317; 6:518

Parkinson, Robert C.
Frank Herbert 12:271

Parkinson, Thomas
Robert Lowell 1:179, 180
Gary Snyder 1:317

Parr, J. L.
Calder Willingham 5:510

Parrinder, Patrick
Philip K. Dick 10:138
B. S. Johnson 9:302

Parrish, Anne
Esther Forbes 12:202

Parrish, Paul A.
Elizabeth Bowen 11:59

Parsons, Ann
William Carlos Williams 2:469

Parsons, Gordon
Ruth M. Arthur 12:27
Leon Garfield 12:231, 241

Parsons, I. M.
Agatha Christie 12:112

Parsons, Thornton H.
John Crowe Ransom 2:364

Partridge, Marianne
Patti Smith 12:538

Partridge, Ralph
Agatha Christie 12:113, 114

Paschall, Douglas
Theodore Roethke 3:434

Paterson, Katherine
Rosemary Wells 12:639

Patten, Brian
Isaac Asimov 3:17
Kurt Vonnegut, Jr. 3:504

Patten, Frederick
Stephen King 12:310
Andre Norton 12:471

Patten, Karl
Graham Greene 1:131

Paul, Sherman
Paul Goodman 1:123
Charles Olson 11:420
Boris Pasternak 7:295
Edmund Wilson 1:373

Paulin, Tom
Kingsley Amis 13:15
John Fowles 10:189
Jerzy Kosinski 10:308

Ian McEwan 13:370
Barbara Pym 13:469

Pauly, Rebecca M.
Kurt Vonnegut, Jr. 12:609

Pawel, Ernst
Heinrich Böll 2:67; 9:109
Hermann Hesse 2:192
Jakov Lind 2:245

Payne, Robert
Yuri Olesha 8:432
Boris Pasternak 7:292

Paz, Octavio
Elizabeth Bishop 9:89
André Breton 9:129
Alexsandr I. Solzhenitsyn
10:478
William Carlos Williams 5:508

Pearce, Richard
Saul Bellow 8:72
John Dos Passos 8:181
John Hawkes 9:266
Henry Roth 6:473
William Styron 11:515

Pearson, Carol
Joseph Heller 11:265

Pearson, Gabriel
John Berryman 2:55
T. S. Eliot 13:192

Pearson, Norman Holmes
Ezra Pound 2:340

Pease, Howard
John R. Tunis 12:596

Peavy, Charles D.
Hubert Selby, Jr. 1:306

Peck, Richard
Robert Cormier 12:135
Katherine Paterson 12:485

Peden, William
James Baldwin 8:40
Doris Betts 6:70
Ed Bullins 7:37
John Cheever 7:49
Laurie Colwin 5:108
James T. Farrell 8:205
Ernest J. Gaines 11:217
Shirley Ann Grau 9:240
Chester Himes 7:159
Langston Hughes 10:281
Grace Paley 6:392
Ann Petry 7:305
William Saroyan 8:468
Irwin Shaw 7:411
Isaac Bashevis Singer 6:509
Jesse Stuart 8:507
Tennessee Williams 5:502

Peel, Marie
John Osborne 2:329
Peter Redgrove 6:445, 446
Penelope Shuttle 7:423
Alan Sillitoe 3:448
David Storey 2:425
R. S. Thomas 6:531

Pelli, Moshe
S. Y. Agnon 8:8

Pelorus
Judy Blume 12:45
Robert Cormier 12:135

Pemberton, Clive
Leon Garfield 12:219

Penner, Allen R.
Alan Sillitoe 1:308

Pennington, Lee
Jesse Stuart 11:508

Peppard, Murray B.
Friedrich Dürrenmatt 1:81

Pepper, Nancy
Anaïs Nin 11:399

Perazzini, Randolph
Robert Frost 13:229

Percy, Walker
Walter M. Miller, Jr. 4:352
Marion Montgomery 7:232
Jean-Paul Sartre 13:506
Eudora Welty 1:362

Perera, Victor
Miguel Ángel Asturias 3:18

Perez, Gilberto
Beryl Bainbridge 10:16
Alan Sillitoe 10:477
Anne Tyler 11:553

Pérez Firmat, Gustavo
José Lezama Lima 10:319

Perkins, David
W. H. Auden 11:19
Richard Eberhart 11:179
Ezra Pound 3:397
Carl Sandburg 10:449

Perkins, Huel D.
John A. Williams 13:599

Perlberg, Mark
Larry Eigner 9:181
Michael S. Harper 7:138
George Oppen 7:285

Perloff, Marjorie G.
John Berryman 2:59
Ed Dorn 10:156
Clayton Eshleman 7:99
Thom Gunn 3:216
Ted Hughes 2:204; 4:235
Richard F. Hugo 6:244
Erica Jong 6:270
Galway Kinnell 2:230
Denise Levertov 2:243
Robert Lowell 1:181
Frank O'Hara 2:322; 5:325;
13:425
Charles Olson 11:415
Sylvia Plath 9:432
Ezra Pound 10:400
Adrienne Rich 7:369
Françoise Sagan 6:482
Mark Van Doren 10:496
Mona Van Duyn 3:492
Diane Wakoski 7:504
John Wieners 7:537
James Wright 3:542, 544

Perrick, Eve
Ira Levin 3:294

Perrin, Noel
James Gould Cozzens 11:132

Perrine, Laurence
John Ciardi 10:105

Perry, R. C.
Rolf Hochhuth 11:276

Peter, John
Edward Bond 13:102

CRITIC INDEX

CRITIC INDEX

Peterkiewicz, Jerzy
Witold Gombrowicz **4**:195
Alain Robbe-Grillet **4**:447

Peters, Daniel James
Thomas Pynchon **3**:412

Peters, Margot
Agatha Christie **12**:119

Peters, Robert
Charles Bukowski **5**:80
Clayton Eshleman **7**:99
Michael McClure **6**:316
Anne Waldman **7**:508

Peters, Robert L.
Hollis Summers **10**:493

Petersen, Clarence
Charles M. Schulz **12**:527

Peterson, Clarence
Wilfrid Sheed **2**:392

Petrie, Paul
A. Alvarez **5**:16

Petroski, Catherine
Penelope Gilliatt **13**:237

Petticoffer, Dennis
Richard Brautigan **12**:73

Pettingell, Phoebe
Donald Hall **1**:137
Philip Levine **9**:332
Robert Lowell **8**:353
James Merrill **13**:382
John Wain **11**:563

Pettit, Philip
J. R. R. Tolkien **3**:483

Pevear, Richard
A. R. Ammons **3**:10
Charles Causley **7**:42
Richmond Lattimore **3**:277
Denise Levertov **3**:292
Hugh MacDiarmid **4**:313
James Merrill **3**:334
Pablo Neruda **5**:301
George Oppen **7**:286
Peter Porter **13**:452
Ezra Pound **2**:343
Louis Zukofsky **7**:563

Peyre, Henri
Marcel Aymé **11**:21
Simone de Beauvoir **1**:19
Albert Camus **1**:53
Louis-Ferdinand Céline **1**:57
René Char **9**:162
Georges Duhamel **8**:186
Jean Giono **4**:185
Julien Green **3**:203
André Malraux **1**:201
François Mauriac **4**:338
Raymond Queneau **5**:358
Alain Robbe-Grillet **4**:446
Jules Romains **7**:383
Nathalie Sarraute **4**:464
Jean-Paul Sartre **1**:305
Claude Simon **4**:494

Pfeffercorn, Eli
Abraham B. Yehoshua **13**:616

Pfeiffer, John R.
John Brunner **8**:105

Phelps, Donald
Fielding Dawson **6**:125
Gilbert Sorrentino **7**:451

Phelps, Robert
Dan Wakefield **7**:502

Phillips, Allen W.
Octavio Paz **3**:376

Phillips, Delbert
Yevgeny Yevtushenko **3**:547

Phillips, Frank Lamont
Maya Angelou **12**:12

Phillips, Norma
Alan Sillitoe **6**:501

Phillips, Robert
Hortense Calisher **8**:125
Arthur A. Cohen **7**:52
James T. Farrell **4**:158
Allen Ginsberg **6**:199
William Goyen **5**:148, 149
Richard Howard **10**:275
Robert Lowell **4**:303
Bernard Malamud **3**:325
Carson McCullers **4**:345; **12**:432
Brian Moore **7**:239
Joyce Carol Oates **11**:404
Patrick White **4**:586
Marya Zaturenska **11**:579

Phillips, Steven R.
Ernest Hemingway **3**:241

Pichaske, David R.
John Lennon and Paul
McCartney **12**:373

Pick, Robert
Frank Yerby **7**:556

Pickering, Sam, Jr.
Anthony Powell **7**:338
P. G. Wodehouse **5**:517

Pickering, Samuel F., Jr.
Joyce Carol Oates **6**:369

Pickrel, Paul
Aldo Palazzeschi **11**:431
Sylvia Townsend Warner **7**:511

Picon, Gaëtan
Jean Anouilh **13**:21
Michel Butor **8**:119
Albert Camus **9**:144
Henri Michaux **8**:392

Piercy, Marge
Margaret Atwood **3**:20
Margaret Laurence **6**:289
Alice Walker **9**:557

Pigaga, Thom
John Hollander **2**:197

Piggott, Stuart
David Jones **4**:261

Pinchin, Jane Lagoudis
Lawrence Durrell **13**:186
E. M. Forster **13**:220

Pinckney, Darryl
Gayl Jones **9**:307
Richard Wright **9**:585

Pinkerton, Jan
Peter Taylor **1**:333

Pinsker, Sanford
Bernard Malamud **3**:322
Joyce Carol Oates **11**:402
Isaac Bashevis Singer **3**:454
John Updike **7**:489

Pinsky, Robert
John Berryman **8**:93

Ted Hughes **9**:282
Philip Levine **9**:332
Cynthia Macdonald **13**:355
Theodore Roethke **8**:461
Raphael Rudnik **7**:384

Pippett, Aileen
Julia W. Cunningham **12**:163

Pitou, Spire
Jean Cayrol **11**:110

Pittock, Malcolm
Ivy Compton-Burnett **10**:108

Planchart, Alejandro Enrique
John Lennon and Paul
McCartney **12**:359

Plumly, Stanley
Lisel Mueller **13**:399

Plummer, William
Jerzy Kosinski **10**:306

Poague, Leland A.
Bob Dylan **6**:156

Pochoda, Elizabeth
Djuna Barnes **11**:30

Pochoda, Elizabeth Turner
Anna Kavan **13**:316
Tadeusz Konwicki **8**:327
Alan Lelchuk **5**:245
Joyce Carol Oates **6**:373

Podhoretz, Norman
James Baldwin **1**:13, 14
Saul Bellow **1**:28
Albert Camus **1**:52
J. P. Donleavy **1**:75
George P. Elliott **2**:130
William Faulkner **1**:98
Paul Goodman **1**:123
Joseph Heller **1**:139
Thomas Hinde **6**:239
Jack Kerouac **1**:165
Norman Mailer **1**:188
Bernard Malamud **1**:194
Mary McCarthy **1**:205
John O'Hara **1**:260
Philip Roth **1**:292
Nathalie Sarraute **1**:302
John Updike **1**:343
Edmund Wilson **1**:372, 373

Poggioli, Renato
Eugenio Montale **7**:221

Poirier, Richard
John Barth **3**:40
Saul Bellow **8**:74
Jorge Luis Borges **3**:77
T. S. Eliot **3**:140
Robert Frost **4**:176; **9**:226
Lillian Hellman **4**:221
John Lennon and Paul
McCartney **12**:368
Norman Mailer **2**:263, 265;
3:314; **4**:322
Vladimir Nabokov **6**:354
Thomas Pynchon **2**:355; **3**:409
William Styron **3**:474
Gore Vidal **4**:553
Rudolph Wurlitzer **2**:482; **4**:597

Polacheck, Janet G.
Jules Archer **12**:18

Poland, Nancy
Margaret Drabble **5**:118

Pollitt, Katha
Alice Adams **13**:1, 2
Margaret Atwood **8**:30
Sandra Hochman **8**:298
James Purdy **10**:425
Anne Tyler **7**:479

Ponnuthurai, Charles Sarvan
Chinua Achebe **5**:3

Pontac, Perry
Miguel Piñero **4**:401

Pool, Gail
Anne Sexton **10**:468

Poore, Charles
Wilfrid Sheed **2**:392

Popkin, Henry
Albert Camus **9**:145

Porter, Katherine Anne
Ezra Pound **7**:325

Porter, M. Gilbert
Saul Bellow **2**:54; **8**:72

Porter, Michael
Horst Bienek **11**:48

Porter, Peter
Gavin Ewart **13**:208
Stevie Smith **3**:460
Judith Wright **11**:578

Porter, Raymond J.
Brendan Behan **8**:64

Porter, Robert
Milan Kundera **4**:276

Porterfield, Christopher
Kingsley Amis **2**:8
Christopher Fry **2**:143
Ted Hughes **2**:199
Donald E. Westlake **7**:528

Poss, Stanley
John Hollander **8**:301
Philip Larkin **13**:337
Cynthia Macdonald **13**:355
P. H. Newby **2**:310
Adrienne Rich **7**:370
Theodore Roethke **8**:460
Nancy Willard **7**:539

Postell, Frances
Christie Harris **12**:263

Potok, Chaim
Paul West **7**:523

Potoker, Edward Martin
Judith Rossner **9**:456
Ronald Sukenick **6**:524

Potts, Paul
George Barker **8**:43

Pouillon, Jean
William Faulkner **8**:208

Pound, Ezra
William Carlos Williams **13**:602

Povey, John F.
Chinua Achebe **1**:1; **7**:6
Cyprian Ekwensi **4**:151

Powell, Anthony
Evelyn Waugh **3**:513

Powell, Neil
Thom Gunn **3**:216

Power, K. C.
Michael McClure **6**:321

Pratt, Annis
Doris Lessing **3**:288; **6**:292

Pratt, John Clark
John Steinbeck **1**:326

Pratt, Linda Ray
Sylvia Plath **3**:390

Pratt, Sarah
V. S. Pritchett **13**:468

Pratt, William
John Berryman **10**:45
Joseph Brodsky **6**:97

Prescott, Orville
Michael Ayrton **7**:17
Earl Hamner, Jr. **12**:257
J.I.M. Stewart **7**:466
Robert Penn Warren **8**:543

Prescott, Peter S.
Alice Adams **6**:1
Richard Adams **4**:7
Eric Ambler **6**:3
Kingsley Amis **3**:8
Martin Amis **4**:20
Donald Barthelme **5**:54
William Peter Blatty **2**:64
Vance Bourjaily **8**:104
Kay Boyle **5**:65
Richard Brautigan **5**:71
Lothar-Günther Buchheim **6**:101
Anthony Burgess **5**:85
Agatha Christie **12**:120
Michael Crichton **6**:119
Robertson Davies **7**:73
Len Deighton **7**:75
Don DeLillo **8**:171
Peter De Vries **7**:78
John Dos Passos **4**:137
Lawrence Durrell **6**:151
Leslie A. Fiedler **4**:161
John Fowles **6**:186
Michael Frayn **3**:165
Nadine Gordimer **5**:146
Graham Greene **3**:213
Lillian Hellman **4**:221
George V. Higgins **4**:223
Russell C. Hoban **7**:161
Geoffrey Household **11**:277
Dan Jacobson **4**:254
Diane Johnson **5**:198
Robert F. Jones **7**:193
Thomas Keneally **8**:318
William Kennedy **6**:275
Jerzy Kosinski **6**:285
John Le Carré **5**:232, 234
Doris Lessing **2**:241
Peter Matthiessen **5**:274
Cormac McCarthy **4**:341
John McGahern **5**:280
A. G. Mojtabai **9**:385
Brian Moore **7**:236
Toni Morrison **4**:365
Penelope Mortimer **5**:299
Joyce Carol Oates **6**:374
Flann O'Brien **5**:314
Reynolds Price **6**:425
Philip Roth **2**:378; **4**:455; **6**:475
Isaac Bashevis Singer **3**:458
Aleksandr I. Solzhenitsyn **4**:516
Muriel Spark **5**:399
Robert Stone **5**:409
Harvey Swados **5**:422
Paul Theroux **5**:428
Michel Tournier **6**:537
William Trevor **7**:478
John Updike **5**:455, 458
Gore Vidal **4**:554
Jessamyn West **7**:521
Patrick White **3**:524
P. G. Wodehouse **5**:515
Larry Woiwode **6**:579
Richard Yates **7**:555

Presley, Delma Eugene
John Fowles **3**:163
Carson McCullers **4**:346

Press, John
John Betjeman **6**:67
Philip Larkin **8**:339
Louis MacNeice **4**:316

Price, Derek de Solla
John Brunner **10**:80
Ursula K. LeGuin **8**:343

Price, James
Martin Amis **9**:26
Beryl Bainbridge **8**:37
Caroline Blackwood **9**:101
Margaret Drabble **8**:184

Price, John D.
St.-John Perse **11**:434

Price, Martin
Marjorie Kellogg **2**:224
Iris Murdoch **1**:236; **3**:349
Joyce Carol Oates **1**:251
Nathalie Sarraute **4**:469
C. P. Snow **1**:317
David Storey **4**:530
Angus Wilson **5**:514

Price, R. G. G.
Kingsley Amis **2**:7
Paul Bowles **2**:78
L. P. Hartley **2**:182
Elizabeth Taylor **2**:432

Price, Reynolds
William Faulkner **1**:102; **3**:151
Graham Greene **3**:212
Toni Morrison **10**:355
Walker Percy **8**:442
James Welch **6**:560
Eudora Welty **2**:463

Priebe, Richard
Wole Soyinka **3**:463

Priestley, J. B.
T. S. Eliot **3**:135
William Faulkner **3**:150
Ernest Hemingway **3**:232
Ezra Pound **3**:394

Prigozy, Ruth
Larry McMurtry **3**:333

Primeau, Ronald
John Brunner **8**:109

Prince, Peter
Martin Amis **4**:19
Charles Bukowski **5**:80
Anthony Burgess **4**:84
John Fowles **6**:184
Thomas Hinde **11**:273
Thomas Keneally **5**:210
Alice Munro **6**:341
David Pownall **10**:419
Piers Paul Read **4**:444
Philip Roth **3**:439

Pringle, John Douglas
Hugh MacDiarmid **4**:312

Pritchard, William
John Berryman **3**:72
Anthony Burgess **4**:84
Thomas Pynchon **3**:418
Richard G. Stern **4**:523

Pritchard, William H.
Dannie Abse **7**:1
Margaret Atwood **3**:19
Wendell Berry **8**:85
John Berryman **8**:90
Henry Bromell **5**:74
Anthony Burgess **1**:48
Donald Davie **8**:162, 163
John Fowles **9**:214; **10**:189
Allen Ginsberg **3**:195
Robert Graves **2**:177
Marilyn Hacker **9**:257
John Hollander **5**:187
Ted Hughes **9**:281
Richard F. Hugo **6**:244
Alan Lelchuk **5**:245
Denise Levertov **2**:242
Philip Levine **2**:244
Robert Lowell **1**:184
Louis MacNeice **4**:316
Iris Murdoch **8**:406
Vladimir Nabokov **3**:353
Howard Nemerov **6**:363
Anthony Powell **7**:339
Kenneth Rexroth **2**:369
Adrienne Rich **3**:427; **6**:459
Susan Fromberg Schaeffer **6**:489
Aleksandr I. Solzhenitsyn **4**:510
Kathleen Spivack **6**:520
Robert Stone **5**:410
May Swenson **4**:532
Elizabeth Taylor **2**:433
Paul Theroux **11**:531
John Updike **3**:487
Richard Wilbur **6**:571
James Wright **3**:544
Rudolph Wurlitzer **4**:597
Richard Yates **7**:556

Pritchett, V. S.
Kingsley Amis **13**:15
Simone de Beauvoir **4**:48
Samuel Beckett **4**:50
William Golding **2**:168
Juan Goytisolo **5**:151; **10**:245
Norman Mailer **2**:262
Carson McCullers **12**:415
Vladimir Nabokov **6**:356
Flann O'Brien **10**:364
Aleksandr I. Solzhenitsyn **1**:320
Paul Theroux **8**:513
James Thurber **5**:433
Gore Vidal **8**:529

Procopiow, Norma
Marilyn Hacker **5**:155
Eleanor Lerman **9**:329
Anne Sexton **4**:483

Proffer, Carl R.
Aleksandr I. Solzhenitsyn **9**:506

Pronko, Leonard C.
Eugène Ionesco **1**:154

Pronko, Leonard Cabell
Jean Anouilh **13**:16

Proteus
Agatha Christie **12**:112

Pryce-Jones, Alan
Michael Ayrton **7**:16
John Betjeman **6**:69
Italo Calvino **5**:98
Vladimir Nabokov **1**:246

Pryse, Marjorie
Helen Yglesias **7**:558

Puckett, Harry
T. S. Eliot **10**:167

Puetz, Manfred
John Barth **9**:72
Thomas Pynchon **6**:434

Pugh, Anthony R.
Alain Robbe-Grillet **4**:450

Purcell, H. D.
George MacDonald Fraser **7**:106

Purdy, A. W.
Earle Birney **6**:73

Purtill, Richard
J.R.R. Tolkien **12**:577

Pyros, J.
Michael McClure **6**:320

Quennell, Peter
Robert Graves **6**:210

Quigly, Isabel
Natalia Ginzburg **11**:230
Pamela Hansford Johnson **1**:160

Quinn, Sister Bernetta, O.S.F.
Alan Dugan **2**:121
David Jones **4**:259
Ezra Pound **4**:416; **7**:326
William Stafford **7**:460
Allen Tate **4**:539
Derek Walcott **2**:460
See also Bernetta (Quinn), Sister Mary, O.S.F.

Quinn, James P.
Edward Albee **5**:11

R
David Jones **4**:259
Arthur Koestler **6**:281
Aleksandr I. Solzhenitsyn **4**:506

Raban, Jonathan
A. Alvarez **5**:18
Kingsley Amis **8**:11
Beryl Bainbridge **5**:40
John Barth **1**:17
Saul Bellow **1**:32
E. L. Doctorow **11**:141
Stanley Elkin **6**:169
Nadine Gordimer **5**:145
Erica Jong **4**:265
Mary McCarthy **1**:207
Ian McEwan **13**:369
John McGahern **9**:369
Stanley Middleton **7**:220
Brian Moore **1**:225
Iris Murdoch **4**:369
Vladimir Nabokov **6**:359
Jean Rhys **6**:456
Richard G. Stern **4**:523
William Trevor **7**:476

Rabassa, Gregory
Alejo Carpentier **11**:99
Gabriel García Márquez **3**:180

CRITIC INDEX

Rabinovitz, Rubin
Kingsley Amis **5**:20
Samuel Beckett **6**:40, 41
Norman Mailer **5**:267
Iris Murdoch **1**:235; **2**:297
C. P. Snow **4**:500
Angus Wilson **5**:512

Rabinowitz, Dorothy
Beryl Bainbridge **8**:36
Elliott Baker **8**:40
Giorgio Bassani **9**:77
Maeve Brennan **5**:72
Anthony Burgess **5**:88
Hortense Calisher **4**:87; **8**:124
John Cheever **3**:107
Lois Gould **4**:201
Peter Handke **5**:165
Mark Helprin **7**:152
Dan Jacobson **4**:254
Ruth Prawer Jhabvala **4**:256, 257; **8**:311
Robert Kotlowitz **4**:275
Mary Lavin **4**:281
Doris Lessing **2**:241
Meyer Levin **7**:205
Larry McMurtry **11**:371
Brian Moore **7**:237
Wright Morris **3**:344
Edna O'Brien **5**:312
John O'Hara **6**:384
Grace Paley **4**:392
S. J. Perelman **5**:337
Philip Roth **3**:437
Anne Sexton **10**:468
John Updike **2**:445
Gore Vidal **4**:553
Dan Wakefield **7**:503
Joseph Wambaugh **3**:509
Harriet Waugh **6**:560
Arnold Wesker **5**:482

Rabkin, Eric S.
Donald Barthelme **13**:58

Rabkin, Gerald
Derek Walcott **9**:556

Rachewiltz, Boris de
Ezra Pound **7**:331

Rackham, Jeff
John Fowles **2**:138

Radcliff-Umstead, Douglas
Alberto Moravia **11**:381

Rader, Dotson
Hubert Selby, Jr. **4**:481
Yevgeny Yevtushenko **3**:547

Radford, C. B.
Simone de Beauvoir **4**:45, 46

Radin, Victoria
Sara Davidson **9**:175

Radke, Judith J.
Pierre Gascar **11**:221

Radner, Rebecca
Lenora Mattingly Weber **12**:635

Radu, Kenneth
Christie Harris **12**:264

Rae, Bruce
John R. Tunis **12**:593

Rafalko, Robert
Eric Ambler **9**:22

Rafalko, Robert J.
Philip K. Dick **10**:138

Raffel, Burton
J. R. R. Tolkien **1**:337
Louis Zukofsky **11**:580

Ragusa, Olga
Alberto Moravia **2**:292

Rahv, Betty T.
Albert Camus **9**:148
Alain Robbe-Grillet **8**:451
Nathalie Sarraute **8**:469
Jean-Paul Sartre **7**:395

Rahv, Philip
Saul Bellow **2**:50
Richard Brautigan **12**:57
T. S. Eliot **2**:126
Ernest Hemingway **3**:231
Arthur Miller **2**:278
Delmore Schwartz **10**:462
Aleksandr I. Solzhenitsyn **2**:411

Raine, Craig
Harold Pinter **6**:419
Ted Walker **13**:566

Raine, Kathleen
David Jones **2**:216; **7**:191
St.-John Perse **4**:399
Herbert Read **4**:440

Rainer, Dachine
Rebecca West **7**:525

Rama Rau, Santha
Khushwant Singh **11**:504

Rampersad, Arnold
Alex Haley **12**:247

Ramras-Rauch, Gila
S. Y. Agnon **4**:14

Ramsey, Paul
Robert Bly **5**:62
Edgar Bowers **9**:121
Hayden Carruth **10**:100
Larry Eigner **9**:181
Eleanor Lerman **9**:328
W. S. Merwin **5**:286
Howard Nemerov **9**:394

Ramsey, Roger
Friedrich Dürrenmatt **4**:140
Pär Lagerkvist **10**:311

Rand, Richard A.
John Hollander **5**:187

Randall, Dudley
Robert Hayden **5**:168
Margaret Walker **6**:554

Randall, Julia
Howard Nemerov **2**:308
Gabrielle Roy **10**:441

Ranjbaran, Esmaeel
Ahmad Shamlu **10**:469

Ranly, Ernest W.
Kurt Vonnegut, Jr. **2**:453

Ransom, John Crowe
Donald Davidson **13**:167
Randall Jarrell **1**:159
Allen Tate **4**:535

Ransom, W. M.
Galway Kinnell **3**:268

Raphael, Frederic
Michael Frayn **7**:107
Jakov Lind **4**:293

Rascoe, Judith
Laurie Colwin **5**:107

Rasi, Humberto M.
Jorge Luis Borges **2**:74

Rasso, Pamela S.
William Heyen **13**:284

Rathburn, Norma
Margot Benary-Isbert **12**:32

Ratner, Marc L.
William Styron **5**:418

Ratner, Rochelle
Clayton Eshleman **7**:100
Patti Smith **12**:541

Ravenscroft, Arthur
Chinua Achebe **11**:1

Rawley, James
Donald Barthelme **13**:63

Ray, David
E. E. Cummings **12**:151

Ray, Robert
James Baldwin **2**:34
J. I. M. Stewart **7**:466

Ray, Sheila G.
E. M. Almedingen **12**:7

Rayme, Anne C.
Larry Kettelkamp **12**:307

Raymond, John
Daphne du Maurier **11**:163
Georges Simenon **3**:449

Raynor, Vivien
Evan S. Connell, Jr. **6**:115
Iris Murdoch **3**:348
Edna O'Brien **3**:364

Rea, Dorothy
Auberon Waugh **7**:514

Read, Esther H.
Melvin Berger **12**:40

Read, Forrest, Jr.
Ezra Pound **7**:327

Read, Herbert
Allen Tate **4**:535

Read, S. E.
Robertson Davies **13**:172

Real, Jere
Peter Shaffer **5**:388

Rebay, Luciano
Alberto Moravia **7**:239

Rechnitz, Robert M.
Carson McCullers **1**:209

Reck, Rima Drell
Louis-Ferdinand Céline **7**:44
Françoise Mallet-Joris **11**:355

Redding, Saunders
Shirley Ann Grau **4**:208
Richard Wright **1**:377

Redfern, W. D.
Jean Giono **4**:186

Redmon, Anne
Judy Blume **12**:45

Reed, Diana
J. G. Ballard **6**:28

Reed, Ishmael
Chester Himes **2**:195

Reed, John
Arthur Hailey **5**:156
Ngugi Wa Thiong'o **13**:583

Reed, John R.
William Dickey **3**:127
D. J. Enright **4**:155
Daniel Hoffman **6**:243
John Hollander **8**:302
Richard Howard **7**:169; **10**:276
Judith Leet **11**:323
James Merrill **8**:388
Charles Reznikoff **9**:450
David Wagoner **3**:508
Philip Whalen **6**:566

Reed, Peter J.
Kurt Vonnegut, Jr. **3**:495; **12**:626

Reed, Rex
Tennessee Williams **2**:464

Reedy, Gerard
C. S. Lewis **6**:308

Reedy, Gerard C.
Richard Price **12**:490

Rees, Goronwy
Richard Hughes **11**:278

Rees, Samuel
David Jones **13**:309

Reeve, Benjamin
Grace Paley **4**:393

Reeve, F. D.
Joseph Brodsky **6**:98
Aleksandr I. Solzhenitsyn **1**:319

Regan, Robert Alton
John Updike **5**:454

Regier, W. G.
W. H. Auden **3**:22
Michael Benedikt **4**:54
Kenneth O. Hanson **13**:263
Howard Nemerov **9**:395
Pablo Neruda **5**:305
Francis Ponge **6**:423

Reibetanz, John
Philip Larkin **8**:334

Reichek, Morton A.
Chaim Grade **10**:249

Reid, Alastair
Jorge Luis Borges **2**:73
Pablo Neruda **5**:302
John Updike **13**:561

Reid, B. L.
V. S. Pritchett **13**:465

Reilly, John M.
B. Traven **11**:538

Reilly, Peter
Joni Mitchell **12**:436

Reilly, Robert J.
C. S. Lewis **3**:298
J. R. R. Tolkien **1**:337; **3**:477

Reitberger, Reinhold
Charles M. Schulz **12**:528

Reiter, Seymour
Sean O'Casey **5**:319

Remini, Robert V.
Gore Vidal **8**:526

Rendle, Adrian
Tom Stoppard **3**:470

Renek, Morris
Erskine Caldwell **8**:123

Rennie, Neil
　Robin Skelton **13**:507

Renshaw, Robert
　J. R. R. Tolkien **1**:336

Resnik, Henry S.
　Richard Fariña **9**:195
　John Irving **13**:292
　Wilfrid Sheed **2**:392
　J.R.R. Tolkien **12**:566

Rexine, John E.
　Vassilis Vassilikos **4**:552

Rexroth, Kenneth
　Robert Creeley **4**:116
　Robert Duncan **1**:82; **2**:123
　T. S. Eliot **2**:127
　William Everson **1**:96
　Allen Ginsberg **2**:164; **3**:193, 194
　William Golding **3**:196
　Paul Goodman **2**:169
　Robinson Jeffers **2**:211
　Pär Lagerkvist **13**:334
　Denise Levertov **1**:175; **2**:243; **3**:292
　W. S. Merwin **2**:278; **3**:338
　Henry Miller **1**:219
　Marianne Moore **2**:292
　Kenneth Patchen **2**:332
　Laura Riding **3**:432
　Muriel Rukeyser **6**:478
　Carl Sandburg **1**:300; **4**:463
　Isaac Bashevis Singer **3**:452
　Edith Sitwell **2**:403
　Gary Snyder **2**:407
　Jean Toomer **4**:548
　Philip Whalen **6**:565
　William Carlos Williams **1**:371; **2**:469
　Yvor Winters **4**:594

Reynolds, R. C.
　Larry McMurtry **7**:215

Reynolds, Stanley
　Frederick Exley **11**:186
　Anna Kavan **5**:205
　Robert Penn Warren **4**:582

Rhoads, Kenneth W.
　William Saroyan **10**:455

Rhodes, Joseph, Jr.
　W. E. B. Du Bois **2**:120

Rhodes, Richard
　Chester Himes **2**:194
　MacKinlay Kantor **7**:196
　Wilfrid Sheed **2**:394

Ribalow, Harold U.
　Meyer Levin **7**:205
　Henry Roth **6**:471
　Arnold Wesker **3**:518

Ribalow, Menachem
　S. Y. Agnon **4**:10

Rice, Edward
　Thomas Merton **3**:337

Rice, Julian C.
　LeRoi Jones **1**:163

Rich, Adrienne
　Jean Garrigue **8**:239
　Paul Goodman **2**:170
　Robert Lowell **3**:304
　Robin Morgan **2**:294
　Eleanor Ross Taylor **5**:425

Rich, Alan
　Alan Ayckbourn **8**:34
　Jules Feiffer **8**:216
　Simon Gray **9**:241
　John Guare **8**:253
　Preston Jones **10**:297
　Tom Stoppard **8**:501, 503
　Elizabeth Swados **12**:558
　Tennessee Williams **7**:545
　Lanford Wilson **7**:549

Rich, Nancy B.
　Carson McCullers **10**:336

Richards, I. A.
　E. M. Forster **13**:215

Richards, Lewis A.
　William Faulkner **3**:153

Richardson, D. E.
　Catharine Savage Brosman **9**:135

Richardson, Jack
　John Barth **3**:39
　Saul Bellow **8**:71
　T. S. Eliot **9**:182
　Trevor Griffiths **13**:257
　Jack Kerouac **2**:227
　Arthur Miller **2**:280
　Vladimir Nabokov **2**:300
　Peter Shaffer **5**:389
　Tom Stoppard **4**:527

Richardson, Maurice
　J.R.R. Tolkien **12**:565

Richie, Donald
　Yukio Mishima **2**:288; **4**:357

Richie, Mary
　Penelope Mortimer **5**:300

Richler, Mordecai
　Ken Kesey **3**:267
　Bernard Malamud **2**:267
　Alexander Theroux **2**:433

Richman, Sidney
　Bernard Malamud **1**:198

Richmond, Jane
　E. L. Doctorow **6**:131
　Thomas McGuane **3**:329

Richmond, Velma Bourgeois
　Muriel Spark **3**:464

Richter, David H.
　Jerzy Kosinski **6**:283

Richter, Frederick
　Kenzaburo Oe **10**:373

Ricks, Christopher
　Giorgio Bassani **9**:75
　Samuel Beckett **2**:48
　Charles Causley **7**:41
　Robert Creeley **2**:108
　Nadine Gordimer **7**:131
　Marilyn Hacker **5**:155
　Geoffrey Hill **8**:293
　Richard Howard **7**:167
　Galway Kinnell **5**:217
　Robert Lowell **1**:181; **9**:335
　Louis MacNeice **1**:186
　Reynolds Price **6**:423
　Christina Stead **8**:499
　John Updike **1**:346
　Robert Penn Warren **6**:556
　Patrick White **4**:586

Riddel, Joseph N.
　C. Day Lewis **10**:125
　T. S. Eliot **13**:195

Rideout, Walter B.
　John Dos Passos **4**:131
　Randall Jarrell **2**:207
　Norman Mailer **4**:318
　Henry Roth **2**:377
　Upton Sinclair **11**:497

Ridley, Clifford A.
　Julian Symons **2**:426

Rieff, David
　Anthony Burgess **13**:124

Riemer, Jack
　Elie Wiesel **11**:570

Ries, Lawrence R.
　William Golding **10**:239
　Ted Hughes **9**:283
　John Osborne **11**:424
　Anthony Powell **9**:439
　Alan Sillitoe **10**:476
　John Wain **11**:561

Riesman, Paul
　Carlos Castaneda **12**:87

Righter, William
　André Malraux **4**:329

Riley, Clayton
　Charles Gordone **1**:124

Rinzler, Alan
　Bob Dylan **12**:198

Rinzler, Carol Eisen
　Judith Rossner **6**:469

Risdon, Ann
　T. S. Eliot **9**:190

Ritter, Jess
　Kurt Vonnegut, Jr. **4**:563

Ritterman, Pamela
　Richard Brautigan **12**:57

Riva, Raymond T.
　Samuel Beckett **1**:25

Rivera, Francisco
　José Donoso **4**:129

Rizza, Peggy
　Elizabeth Bishop **4**:66

Rizzardi, Alfredo
　Allen Tate **4**:538

Robbe-Grillet, Alain
　Samuel Beckett **10**:25

Robbins, Jack Alan
　Louis Auchincloss **4**:28
　Herbert Gold **4**:189
　Bernard Malamud **1**:200
　Flannery O'Connor **1**:258

Roberts, Cecil
　W. Somerset Maugham **11**:370

Roberts, David
　R. V. Cassill **4**:94

Roberts, Thomas J.
　Italo Calvino **8**:129

Robins, Wayne
　Joni Mitchell **12**:438

Robinson, Beryl
　Andre Norton **12**:462
　Mary Rodgers **12**:494

Robinson, Jill
　Alice Adams **6**:2
　Anna Kavan **5**:206
　Fran Lebowitz **11**:322
　Larry McMurtry **11**:371

Robinson, Louie
　Norman Lear **12**:332

Robinson, Robert
　Saul Bellow **6**:54

Robinson, W. R.
　George Garrett **3**:190

Robson, Jeremy
　W. H. Auden **4**:33
　Leonard Cohen **3**:110

Rockwell, John
　Peter Handke **5**:164
　Patti Smith **12**:537
　Stevie Wonder **12**:661

Rodgers, Audrey T.
　T. S. Eliot **6**:162, 166

Rodman, Selden
　Carlos Fuentes **10**:207

Rodrigues, Eusebio L.
　Saul Bellow **3**:56; **6**:52

Rodríguez-Monegal, Emir
　Jorge Luis Borges **2**:72; **3**:80
　Adolfo Bioy Casares **13**:84
　Gabriel García Márquez **3**:183
　Juan Carlos Onetti **7**:276, 279

Rodriguez-Peralta, Phyllis
　José María Arguedas **10**:8

Rodway, Allan
　Samuel Beckett **4**:51
　Tom Stoppard **8**:502

Rogan, Helen
　Maeve Brennan **5**:73
　John Gardner **5**:134
　Jennifer Johnston **7**:186
　Irving Wallace **7**:510

Rogers, Deborah C.
　J.R.R. Tolkien **12**:584

Rogers, Del Marie
　Reynolds Price **6**:423

Rogers, Linda
　Margaret Atwood **4**:27
　Paulette Jiles **13**:304
　Susan Musgrave **13**:400
　Angus Wilson **5**:515

Rogers, Michael
　Peter Benchley **4**:54
　Richard Brautigan **12**:70
　Bob Dylan **12**:187
　John Gardner **3**:188
　Richard Price **4**:489
　Piers Paul Read **4**:445

Rogers, Norma
　Alice Childress **12**:106

Rogers, Pat
　Daphne du Maurier **11**:163

Rogers, Philip
　Chinua Achebe **11**:3

Rogers, Thomas
　Vladimir Nabokov **6**:358
　Tom Stoppard **1**:328

Rogers, W. G.
　Pearl S. Buck **7**:33
　Joanne Greenberg **7**:134

CRITIC INDEX

Rogoff, Gordon
David Mamet 9:361

Rohlehr, Gordon
V. S. Naipaul 4:372

Rohter, Larry
Carlos Fuentes 8:223

Roiphe, Anne
Earl Hamner, Jr. 12:259

Rollins, Ronald G.
Sean O'Casey 9:409

Rolo, Charles
Marcel Aymé 11:21

Rolo, Charles J.
Pär Lagerkvist 7:198
Irwin Shaw 7:411

Roman, Diane
Paul Vincent Carroll 10:98

Romano, John
Ann Beattie 8:56
Thomas Berger 11:47
Frederick Busch 10:92
Laurie Colwin 13:156
Joyce Carol Oates 9:406
Sylvia Plath 5:342
Gore Vidal 10:501

Rome, Florence
Muriel Spark 3:465

Ronge, Peter
Eugène Ionesco 6:249

Roosevelt, Karyl
Diane Johnson 13:304

Root, William Pitt
Sonia Sanchez 5:382
Anne Sexton 4:483

Rorem, Ned
Paul Bowles 2:79
Tennessee Williams 5:502

Rose, Ellen Cronan
Doris Lessing 6:300

Rose, Ernst
Hermann Hesse 1:145

Rose, Kate
Richard Brautigan 12:59

Rose, Lois
J. G. Ballard 3:33
Arthur C. Clarke 4:104
Robert A. Heinlein 3:226
C. S. Lewis 3:297
Walter M. Miller, Jr. 4:352

Rose, Marilyn
Julien Green 3:204

Rose, Marilyn Gaddis
Robert Pinget 13:441

Rose, Stephen
J. G. Ballard 3:33
Arthur C. Clarke 4:104
Robert A. Heinlein 3:226
C. S. Lewis 3:297
Walter M. Miller, Jr. 4:352

Rose, Willie Lee
Alex Haley 8:260

Rosen, Norma
Paula Fox 8:218

Rosen, R. D.
James Tate 6:528

Rosenbaum, Ron
Richard Condon 4:106

Rosenberg, Harold
André Malraux 4:334
Anna Seghers 7:407

Rosenberger, Coleman
Carson McCullers 12:412

Rosenblatt, Roger
Renata Adler 8:5
Norman Lear 12:332
Ludvík Vaculík 7:496
Thornton Wilder 6:572

Rosenfeld, Alvin H.
Herbert Gold 7:122
Jakov Lind 4:293

Rosengarten, Herbert
Margaret Atwood 8:33

Rosenthal, David H.
Louis-Ferdinand Céline 7:45
Austin C. Clarke 8:143
Nicanor Parra 2:331

Rosenthal, Lucy
Hortense Calisher 2:96
Richard Llewellyn 7:207
Sylvia Plath 2:336
Alix Kates Shulman 2:395

Rosenthal, M. L.
Yehuda Amichai 9:25
A. R. Ammons 2:13
Imamu Amiri Baraka 2:34;
10:19
John Berryman 2:56
John Betjeman 2:60
Kay Boyle 1:42
John Ciardi 10:105
Austin Clarke 6:110
Robert Creeley 2:105
E. E. Cummings 1:68
James Dickey 2:115; 7:81
Robert Duncan 2:122
Richard Eberhart 11:178
T. S. Eliot 2:125
D. J. Enright 4:155
Robert Frost 1:110
Allen Ginsberg 1:118; 2:162
Paul Goodman 1:124; 4:196
Jim Harrison 6:223
Ted Hughes 2:197; 9:280
Randall Jarrell 13:299
X. J. Kennedy 8:320
Galway Kinnell 1:168
Thomas Kinsella 4:270
Philip Larkin 3:275, 277
Denise Levertov 2:242
Robert Lowell 1:179; 2:247
George MacBeth 2:251
Hugh MacDiarmid 2:253
W. S. Merwin 1:211
Marianne Moore 1:226
Charles Olson 2:326
Robert L. Peters 7:304
Sylvia Plath 2:335
Ezra Pound 1:274; 7:332
Kenneth Rexroth 1:283
Theodore Roethke 3:432
Delmore Schwartz 2:387
Anne Sexton 2:391
Karl Shapiro 4:484
Charles Tomlinson 2:436
Reed Whittemore 4:588
William Carlos Williams 1:370

Rosenthal, R.
Paula Fox 2:139

Rosenthal, Raymond
Edward Dahlberg 7:66
Tennessee Williams 8:547

Rosenthal, T. G.
Michael Ayrton 7:20

Rosenzweig, A. L.
Peter Dickinson 12:169

Roshwald, Miriam
S. Y. Agnon 8:9

Ross, Alan
Kingsley Amis 2:7
Alberto Moravia 7:244

Ross, Gary
Margaret Atwood 4:27

Ross, James
Reynolds Price 6:426

Ross, Mary
Madeleine L'Engle 12:344

Ross, Morton L.
Norman Mailer 1:192

Rossi, Louis R.
Salvatore Quasimodo 10:427

Rosten, Norman
James Tate 2:431

Roszak, Theodore
Paul Goodman 2:170

Roth, Philip
Edward Albee 9:1
Saul Bellow 6:52
Norman Mailer 5:268
Bernard Malamud 5:269; 8:376
J. D. Salinger 8:464
Fredrica Wagman 7:500

Rothberg, Abraham
Graham Greene 3:211
Gary Snyder 9:499
Aleksandr I. Solzhenitsyn
4:507; 7:437

Rother, James
Vladimir Nabokov 11:391
Thomas Pynchon 11:453

Rothman, Nathan L.
Frank Yerby 7:556

Rothstein, Edward
Agatha Christie 8:141

Roudiez, Leon
Michel Butor 8:114
Claude Mauriac 9:363

Routh, Michael
Graham Greene 9:246

Rovit, Earl H.
Saul Bellow 1:31; 8:71; 13:71
Ralph Ellison 1:93
John Hawkes 2:184
Norman Mailer 8:372
Bernard Malamud 1:195

Rowan, Diana
Heinrich Böll 11:58

Rowan, Louis
Diane Wakoski 7:506

Rowan, Thomas
J. F. Powers 1:281

Rowley, Peter
Paula Fox 2:139
John Knowles 4:272

Rowse, A. L.
Flannery O'Connor 2:318
Barbara Pym 13:469

Roy, Joy K.
James Herriot 12:284

Ruark, Gibbons
Andrei Voznesensky 1:349

Ruben, Elaine
Maureen Howard 5:189

Rubenstein, Roberta
Margaret Atwood 8:31
Doris Lessing 6:303; 10:316

Rubin, Louis D., Jr.
William Faulkner 1:101
Carson McCullers 10:338
John Crowe Ransom 4:428;
5:365
Carl Sandburg 10:450
Susan Sontag 10:484
William Styron 3:473
Allen Tate 9:523
Robert Penn Warren 1:353;
4:577
Eudora Welty 1:361

Rubins, Josh
Brigid Brophy 11:69
Agatha Christie 6:108

Ruby, Michael
Charles M. Schulz 12:528

Rudin, Ellen
Emily Cheney Neville 12:449

Rueckert, William
Wright Morris 7:245

Rukeyser, Muriel
John Crowe Ransom 11:466

Rupp, Richard H.
John Updike 1:343

Ruskamp, Judith S.
Henri Michaux 8:392

Russ, Joanna
Robert Silverberg 7:425
Kate Wilhelm 7:537

Russ, Lavinia
Ruth M. Arthur 12:25
Judy Blume 12:44
M. E. Kerr 12:298

Russell, Charles
John Barth 7:22
Richard Brautigan 9:123
Jerzy Kosinski 6:284
Vladimir Nabokov 6:353
Ronald Sukenick 6:523

Russell, John
André Malraux 9:357
Anthony Powell 3:402

Ryan, Frank L.
Daniel J. Berrigan 4:56
Anne Hébert 4:220

Ryan, Marjorie
Diane Johnson 5:198

Ryf, Robert S.
Henry Green 2:179
B. S. Johnson 9:299
Doris Lessing 10:313
Vladimir Nabokov 6:353
Flann O'Brien 7:268

Ryle, John
Mark Helprin **10**:261

Rysten, Felix
Jean Giono **11**:232

Saal, Hubert
Irwin Shaw **7**:411

Sabin, Edwin L.
Lenora Mattingly Weber **12**:631

Sabiston, Elizabeth
Philip Roth **6**:475
Ludvík Vaculík **7**:497

Sabri, M. Arjamand
Thomas Pynchon **3**:417

Sacharoff, Mark
Elias Canetti **3**:98

Sachs, Marilyn
Nicholasa Mohr **12**:445, 446

Sadoff, Dianne F.
Gail Godwin **8**:247

Säez, Richard
James Merrill **6**:323

Sagar, Keith
Ted Hughes **2**:203

Sage, Lorna
Olga Broumas **10**:76
Erica Jong **6**:267
Iris Murdoch **11**:384
Vladimir Nabokov **8**:412
Sylvia Plath **11**:450

Sage, Victor
David Storey **8**:505

Said, Edward W.
R. P. Blackmur **2**:61
Paul Goodman **2**:169

Sainer, Arthur
Martin Duberman **8**:185
Simon Gray **9**:242
Michael McClure **6**:317
Miguel Piñero **4**:401

St. John-Stevas, Norman
C. S. Lewis **6**:308

St. Martin, Hardie
Blas de Otero **11**:424

Sakurai, Emiko
Kenzaburo Oe **10**:374
Kenneth Rexroth **11**:474

Sale, Roger
E. M. Almedingen **12**:3
A. Alvarez **13**:10
Kingsley Amis **5**:22
Saul Bellow **6**:61
Thomas Berger **8**:84
Richard Brautigan **12**:70
Frederick Buechner **2**:83; **6**:103
Anthony Burgess **5**:87
Frederick Busch **10**:94
Agatha Christie **8**:141
Richard Condon **8**:150
Robertson Davies **7**:72
E. L. Doctorow **6**:135
Margaret Drabble **2**:118, 119;
  8:183
George P. Elliott **2**:131
Frederick Exley **6**:172
Leslie A. Fiedler **4**:162
B. H. Friedman **7**:109
Paula Fox **2**:141
Herbert Gold **7**:121

Witold Gombrowicz **7**:122
Dashiell Hammett **5**:161
John Hawkes **4**:214
Mark Helprin **10**:261
Maureen Howard **5**:188
Ken Kesey **6**:278
John Le Carré **5**:234
Alan Lelchuk **5**:240
Doris Lessing **2**:239, 242; **6**:299,
  304
Alison Lurie **4**:306
Ross Macdonald **2**:255
David Madden **5**:266
Norman Mailer **2**:261; **4**:319
Peter Matthiessen **7**:212
Iris Murdoch **8**:404
Tim O'Brien **7**:271
Grace Paley **6**:392
J. F. Powers **8**:447
Richard Price **6**:427
Judith Rossner **6**:470
Philip Roth **2**:381; **6**:476
Andrew Sinclair **2**:400
Isaac Bashevis Singer **9**:487
Robert Stone **5**:410
Paul Theroux **5**:428
J. R. R. Tolkien **1**:338
Anne Tyler **11**:553
Mario Vargas Llosa **6**:547
Kurt Vonnegut, Jr. **8**:532
David Wagoner **5**:475
Larry Woiwode **10**:541

Salisbury, Harrison E.
Aleksandr I. Solzhenitsyn **4**:511

Salkey, Andrew
Ngugi Wa Thiong'o **13**:584

Salomon, I. L.
Robert Duncan **4**:142

Salomon, Louis B.
Carson McCullers **12**:408

Salter, D. P. M.
Saul Bellow **2**:53

Salway, Lance
Robert Cormier **12**:136
Peter Dickinson **12**:168

Salzman, Jack
John Dos Passos **4**:138
Jack Kerouac **2**:229
Tillie Olsen **4**:386

Samet, Tom
Henry Roth **11**:488

Sammons, Jeffrey L.
Hermann Hesse **11**:271

Sampley, Arthur M.
Robert Frost **1**:112

Sampson, Edward C.
E. B. White **10**:529

Samuels, Charles Thomas
Richard Adams **4**:7
Donald Barthelme **3**:43
Lillian Hellman **2**:187
Christina Stead **2**:421
John Updike **1**:344; **2**:442
Kurt Vonnegut, Jr. **2**:454

Sanborn, Sara
Anthony Burgess **4**:84
Rosalyn Drexler **6**:143
Alison Lurie **4**:305
Joyce Carol Oates **3**:363

Sandars, N. K.
David Jones **4**:260

Sandeen, Ernest
R. P. Blackmur **2**:62

Sander, Ellen
John Lennon and Paul
  McCartney **12**:364
Joni Mitchell **12**:435

Sanders, Charles L.
Norman Lear **12**:330

Sanders, David
John Hersey **1**:144; **7**:153

Sanders, Ed
Allen Ginsberg **4**:181

Sanders, Frederick L.
Conrad Aiken **3**:5

Sanders, Ivan
György Konrád **4**:273; **10**:304
Milan Kundera **4**:278
József Lengyel **7**:202
Amos Oz **8**:436

Sanders, Peter L.
Robert Graves **2**:176

Sandler, Linda
Margaret Atwood **8**:29, 30
Ernest Buckler **13**:123

Sandrof, Ivan
Jean Lee Latham **12**:324

Sanfield, Steve
Michael McClure **6**:320

Sargent, David
Robert Wilson **9**:576

Sarland, Charles
William Mayne **12**:402

Saroyan, Aram
Kenneth Koch **8**:323
Frank O'Hara **13**:424
Anne Waldman **7**:508

Saroyan, William
Flann O'Brien **10**:362

Sarris, Andrew
Mel Brooks **12**:75
Norman Mailer **3**:315
Wilfrid Sheed **4**:487

Sartre, Jean-Paul
John Dos Passos **11**:153
William Faulkner **9**:197
Jean Genet **2**:155

Savage, D. S.
E. M. Forster **13**:216

Savvas, Minas
Yannis Ritsos **13**:487

Sayre, Nora
Iris Murdoch **1**:236
Anne Roiphe **3**:434
Elizabeth Taylor **2**:432
Kurt Vonnegut, Jr. **3**:502

Sayre, Robert F.
James Baldwin **1**:15

Scaduto, Anthony
Bob Dylan **4**:148

Scannell, Vernon
Martin Booth **13**:103
Randall Jarrell **9**:298
George MacBeth **9**:341

Scarbrough, George
James Schevill **7**:400

Scarf, Maggie
Susan Sontag **10**:487

Schaap, Dick
Mario Puzo **2**:351

Schaefer, J. O'Brien
Margaret Drabble **5**:119

Schafer, William J.
David Wagoner **3**:507

Schaffner, Nicholas
John Lennon and Paul
  McCartney **12**:385

Schapiro, Leonard
Aleksandr I. Solzhenitsyn **7**:440

Schatt, Stanley
Langston Hughes **10**:279
Isaac Bashevis Singer **3**:459
Kurt Vonnegut, Jr. **1**:348;
  4:560; **12**:614

Schechner, Mark
Lionel Trilling **11**:540

Schechner, Richard
Edward Albee **11**:10
Eugène Ionesco **6**:253

Scheerer, Constance
Sylvia Plath **9**:432

Schickel, Richard
Louis Auchincloss **9**:54
Joan Didion **1**:75
Norman Lear **12**:333
Alan Lelchuk **5**:242
Ross Macdonald **1**:185
Thomas Pynchon **2**:358
Peter Shaffer **5**:387

Schickele, Peter
John Lennon and Paul
  McCartney **12**:355

Schier, Donald
André Breton **2**:81

Schiller, Barbara
Brigid Brophy **11**:68

Schjeldahl, Peter
Paul Blackburn **9**:100
André Breton **2**:80; **9**:129
Russell Edson **13**:191
James Schevill **7**:400
Diane Wakoski **11**:564

Schlueter, June
Arthur Miller **10**:346

Schlueter, Paul
Pär Lagerkvist **7**:201
Doris Lessing **1**:174; **3**:283
Mary McCarthy **1**:205

Schmerl, Rudolf B.
Aldous Huxley **3**:255

Schmidt, Arthur
Joni Mitchell **12**:437
Brian Wilson **12**:641, 645

Schmidt, Michael
Donald Davie **8**:165
George MacBeth **2**:252
Jon Silkin **2**:396
Charles Tomlinson **13**:548

Schmidt, Pilar
Lenora Mattingly Weber **12**:634

Schmitz, Neil
Donald Barthelme 1:19
Richard Brautigan 3:90
Robert Coover 3:113; 7:58
Thomas Pynchon 6:435
Ishmael Reed 5:368; 6:448

Schneck, Stephen
Richard Brautigan 1:44
LeRoi Jones 1:162

Schneidau, Herbert N.
Ezra Pound 4:408

Schneider, Alan
Edward Albee 11:10

Schneider, Duane
Anaïs Nin 1:248; 11:396

Schneider, Elisabeth
T. S. Eliot 3:140

Schneider, Harold W.
Muriel Spark 13:519

Schneider, Richard J.
William H. Gass 8:240

Schoenbrun, David
Cornelius Ryan 7:385

Schoenstein, Ralph
Garry Trudeau 12:590

Scholes, Robert
Jorge Luis Borges 10:63
Lawrence Durrell 8:190
John Hawkes 9:262
Frank Herbert 12:276
Ishmael Reed 5:370
Kurt Vonnegut, Jr. 2:451; 4:561

Schorer, Mark
Truman Capote 3:98
Lillian Hellman 4:221
Carson McCullers 4:344
Katherine Anne Porter 7:312

Schott, Webster
Richard Adams 5:6
Louis Auchincloss 4:31
W. H. Auden 2:25
Donald Barthelme 2:41
Saul Bellow 8:69
William Peter Blatty 2:63
Vance Bourjaily 8:103
Vincent Canby 13:131
James Clavell 6:113
Robert Coover 7:57
Michael Crichton 2:108
John Gardner 10:223
Ira Levin 6:305
Larry McMurtry 2:272
Sylvia Plath 2:338
Raymond Queneau 10:432
Philip Roth 3:436
Susan Fromberg Schaeffer
11:492
Georges Simenon 2:398
Harvey Swados 5:421
Thomas Tryon 11:548
Elio Vittorini 6:551
Jessamyn West 7:520
Tennessee Williams 5:506

Schow, H. Wayne
Günter Grass 11:248

Schraepen, Edmond
William Carlos Williams 9:575

Schramm, Richard
Philip Levine 2:244
Howard Moss 7:248

Schrank, Bernice
Sean O'Casey 11:411

Schreiber, Jan
Elizabeth Daryush 6:122

Schreiber, LeAnne
Jerome Charyn 8:135

Schroth, Raymond A.
Norman Mailer 2:261; 3:312

Schulder, Diane
Marge Piercy 3:385

Schuler, Barbara
Peter Taylor 1:333

Schulman, Grace
Jorge Luis Borges 13:110
Richard Eberhart 3:134
Pablo Neruda 5:302
Octavio Paz 6:395
Adrienne Rich 3:427
Mark Van Doren 6:541
Richard Wilbur 9:569

Schulz, Charles M.
Charles M. Schulz 12:527

Schulz, Max F.
John Barth 9:68
Norman Mailer 1:190
Bernard Malamud 1:199
Kurt Vonnegut, Jr. 1:347

Schuster, Arian
Richard Brautigan 12:74

Schuster, Edgar H.
Harper Lee 12:341

Schwaber, Paul
Robert Lowell 1:184

Schwartz, Delmore
Randall Jarrell 1:159
Robinson Jeffers 11:304

Schwartz, Edward
Katherine Anne Porter 7:309

Schwartz, Howard
David Ignatow 7:178

Schwartz, Kessel
Vicente Aleixandre 9:15
Adolfo Bioy Casares 8:94
Gabriel García Márquez 10:215
Juan Rulfo 8:462

Schwartz, Lloyd
Elizabeth Bishop 9:93, 97

Schwartz, Lynne Sharon
Beryl Bainbridge 5:40
Natalia Ginzburg 5:141
Susan Fromberg Schaeffer
11:491
Alix Kates Shulman 10:475
Anne Tyler 11:552
Fay Weldon 9:560

Schwartz, Nancy Lynn
Jill Robinson 10:438

Schwartz, Paul J.
Samuel Beckett 6:41
Alain Robbe-Grillet 8:453

Schwartz, Ronald
Miguel Delibes 8:169
José María Gironella 11:234

Schwarzbach, F. S.
Thomas Pynchon 9:443

Schwarzchild, Bettina
James Purdy 2:349

Schwerner, Armand
Diane Wakoski 7:506

Scobbie, Irene
Pär Lagerkvist 10:312

Scobie, Stephen
John Glassco 9:237

Scobie, W. I.
Melvin Van Peebles 2:448
Derek Walcott 2:459

Scofield, Martin
T. S. Eliot 9:186

Scoggin, Margaret C.
Mary Stolz 12:547, 549, 550,
552
John R. Tunis 12:594

Scoppa, Bud
John Lennon and Paul
McCartney 12:366
Jimmy Page and Robert Plant
12:479

Scott, Alexander
Hugh MacDiarmid 4:310

Scott, Carolyn D.
Graham Greene 1:130

Scott, J. D.
Andrew Sinclair 2:400

Scott, Lael
Mary Stolz 12:554

Scott, Malcolm
Jean Giono 11:232

Scott, Nathan A., Jr.
Charles M. Schulz 12:522
Richard Wright 1:378

Scott, Peter Dale
Mordecai Richler 5:372

Scott, Tom
Hugh MacDiarmid 4:309
Ezra Pound 4:413

Scott, Winfield Townley
David Ignatow 7:173
Louis Simpson 7:426

Scott-James, R. A.
Edith Sitwell 9:493

Scouffas, George
J. F. Powers 1:280

Scruggs, Charles W.
Jean Toomer 4:549

Scruton, Roger
Sylvia Plath 5:340

Sculatti, Gene
Brian Wilson 12:642

Scupham, Peter
W. H. Auden 6:16
Robert Graves 6:211
H. D. 8:257
David Jones 4:262
D. M. Thomas 13:542

Searle, Leroy
Dannie Abse 7:2
Erica Jong 4:264

Searles, Baird
Anna Kavan 5:205
Andre Norton 12:459

Searles, George J.
Joseph Heller 8:279

Seaver, Richard
Louis-Ferdinand Céline 1:57

Seay, James
James Wright 3:543

Sedgwick, Ellery
Esther Forbes 12:208

Seebohm, Caroline
Kamala Markandaya 8:377

Seed, David
Isaac Bashevis Singer 9:487

Seelye, John
Donald Barthelme 2:41
Norman Mailer 3:316
Marge Piercy 3:383
Charles M. Schulz 12:531
James Thurber 5:439
David Wagoner 5:474

Segal, Lore
Joan Didion 1:75

Segovia, Tomás
Octavio Paz 3:376

Seib, Kenneth
Richard Brautigan 1:44

Seiden, Melvin
Vladimir Nabokov 2:302

Selby, Herbert, Jr.
Richard Price 6:427

Seligson, Tom
Hunter S. Thompson 9:527

Sellin, Eric
Samuel Beckett 2:47

Selzer, David
Peter Porter 5:346

Sena, Vinad
T. S. Eliot 6:159

Servodidio, Mirella D'Ambrosio
Azorín 11:24

Seybolt, Cynthia T.
Jules Archer 12:21, 22

Seymour-Smith, Martin
Robert Graves 1:128

Shadoian, Jack
Donald Barthelme 1:18

Shaffer, Dallas Y.
Jules Archer 12:16
Frank Bonham 12:53

Shahane, Vasant Anant
Khushwant Singh 11:504

Shands, Annette Oliver
Gwendolyn Brooks 4:78, 79
Don L. Lee 2:238

Shannon, James P.
J. F. Powers 1:279

Shapcott, Thomas
Frank O'Hara 2:323
W. R. Rodgers 7:377

Shapiro, Charles
Meyer Levin 7:203
David Madden 5:265
Joyce Carol Oates 3:363
Anthony Powell 1:277
Harvey Swados 5:420
Jerome Weidman 7:517

Shapiro, David
Hayden Carruth 10:100
X. J. Kennedy 8:320

Shapiro, Jane
Rosalyn Drexler 6:143

Shapiro, Karl
W. H. Auden 1:8; 3:21
T. S. Eliot 3:136
Rod McKuen 1:210
Henry Miller 4:349
Ezra Pound 3:394
William Carlos Williams 5:506

Shapiro, Laura
Elizabeth Swados 12:560

Shapiro, Paula Meinetz
Alice Walker 6:553

Sharpe, Patricia
Margaret Drabble 10:162

Shattan, Joseph
Saul Bellow 8:80

Shattuck, Roger
Jean Arp 5:32
Saul Bellow 6:57
Alain Robbe-Grillet 2:376

Shaw, Evelyn
Melvin Berger 12:37

Shaw, Greg
Brian Wilson 12:647

Shaw, Irwin
James Jones 10:290

Shaw, Peter
Robert Lowell 8:351
Hugh Nissenson 9:400

Shaw, Robert B.
A. R. Ammons 3:11
W. H. Auden 2:26
Wendell Berry 8:85
Stanley Burnshaw 3:91
James Dickey 2:117
Robert Duncan 7:88
Allen Ginsberg 6:201
John Glassco 9:236
Richard Howard 7:166
David Ignatow 4:248
Philip Larkin 8:338
William Meredith 4:348
Adrienne Rich 6:457
Raphael Rudnik 7:384
Charles Simic 6:501; 9:479
Allen Tate 2:430
Mark Van Doren 6:541
Marya Zaturenska 6:585

Shayon, Robert Lewis
Norman Lear 12:329

Shea, Robert J.
Budd Schulberg 7:403

Shear, Walter
Bernard Malamud 1:197

Shechner, Mark
Tadeusz Konwicki 8:328

Sheed, Wilfrid
Edward Albee 1:4
James Baldwin 1:16; 8:42
Robert Coover 7:58
Robert Frost 1:110
William Golding 1:121
Joseph Heller 5:182
James Jones 1:162
Norman Mailer 1:193; 4:320
Terrence McNally 7:216
Arthur Miller 1:217

Alberto Moravia 2:292
Iris Murdoch 1:236
P. H. Newby 13:409
John Osborne 1:263
Walker Percy 2:332
Neil Simon 6:503
William Styron 1:330
John Updike 1:343
Kurt Vonnegut, Jr. 1:347
Evelyn Waugh 3:512
Arnold Wesker 3:518
Tennessee Williams 1:369
Tom Wolfe 2:481

Sheehan, Donald
John Berryman 1:34
Richard Howard 7:166
Robert Lowell 1:181

Sheehan, Ethna
E. M. Almedingen 12:1
Christie Harris 12:261

Shelton, Austin J.
Chinua Achebe 7:4

Shelton, Frank W.
Robert Coover 7:60
Ernest Hemingway 10:269

Shelton, Robert
Bob Dylan 12:179

Shepard, Paul
Peter Matthiessen 5:273

Shepard, Ray Anthony
Alice Childress 12:107
Nicholasa Mohr 12:446

Shepherd, Allen
Reynolds Price 3:405, 406
Robert Penn Warren 1:355

Sheppard, R. Z.
Louis Auchincloss 4:30
Saul Bellow 6:55
William Peter Blatty 2:64
Lothar-Günther Buchheim 6:101
Anthony Burgess 5:85
Peter De Vries 2:114
E. L. Doctorow 6:133
Alex Haley 8:260
Frank Herbert 12:270
James Leo Herlihy 6:235
Dan Jacobson 4:254
Bernard Malamud 2:266
S. J. Perelman 5:338
Ishmael Reed 5:370
Harvey Swados 5:422
Michel Tournier 6:537
Mario Vargas Llosa 6:545
Gore Vidal 6:548
Paul West 7:523

Sheps, G. David
Mordecai Richler 13:481

Sherwood, Terry G.
Ken Kesey 1:167

Shinn, Thelma J.
Flannery O'Connor 6:375
Ann Petry 7:304
William Saroyan 10:452

Shippey, T. A.
Robert Nye 13:414
John Steinbeck 13:535

Shippey, Thomas
Lothar-Günther Buchheim 6:100

Shivers, Alfred S.
Jessamyn West 7:520

Shore, Rima
Yevgeny Yevtushenko 13:619

Shorris, Earl
Donald Barthelme 2:42
John Gardner 3:184
William H. Gass 2:155
Thomas Pynchon 3:414

Short, Robert L.
Charles M. Schulz 12:522, 525

Shorter, Eric
Alan Ayckbourn 5:36
Agatha Christie 12:118

Shoukri, Doris Enright-Clark
Marguerite Duras 3:129

Showalter, Elaine
Mary McCarthy 3:329

Showers, Paul
Peter De Vries 2:114
James Herriot 12:283
John Seelye 7:407

Shuman, R. Baird
William Inge 1:153
Clifford Odets 2:318, 320

Shuttleworth, Martin
Christina Stead 2:421

Shuttleworth, Paul
Leon Uris 7:492

Sibbald, K. M.
Jorge Guillén 11:263

Sicherman, Carol M.
Saul Bellow 10:37

Siegal, R. A.
Judy Blume 12:47

Siegel, Ben
Saul Bellow 8:78
Bernard Malamud 1:195
Isaac Bashevis Singer 1:313

Siegel, Paul N.
Norman Mailer 5:266

Siemens, William L.
Julio Cortázar 5:110

Sigal, Clancy
Kingsley Amis 3:9; 5:22
Melvyn Bragg 10:72
Alan Sillitoe 3:448

Sigerson, Davitt
Brian Wilson 12:653

Siggins, Clara M.
Taylor Caldwell 2:95
Lillian Hellman 4:221
Saul Maloff 5:270

Silbajoris, Rimvydas
Boris Pasternak 10:387

Silber, Irwin
Bob Dylan 12:181

Silenieks, Juris
Édouard Glissant 10:231

Silet, Charles L. P.
David Kherdian 9:317, 318

Silkin, Jon
Geoffrey Hill 5:183

Silverman, Malcolm
Jorge Amado 13:11

Silverstein, Norman
James Dickey 7:81

Silvert, Conrad
Peter Matthiessen 7:210

Simels, Steve
Jimmy Page and Robert Plant 12:476
Patti Smith 12:537
Brian Wilson 12:651

Simenon, Georges
Georges Simenon 3:451

Simmons, Ernest J.
Mikhail Sholokhov 7:416, 420

Simon, John
Edward Albee 2:1; 5:13; 11:11; 13:3, 4
Jean Anouilh 13:22
Alan Ayckbourn 8:34
Peter Barnes 5:49
Samuel Beckett 3:47
Mel Brooks 12:80
Ed Bullins 5:84; 7:36
Anne Burr 6:104
Martin Duberman 8:185
Jules Feiffer 2:133
Lawrence Ferlinghetti 2:134
Athol Fugard 9:230
Frank D. Gilroy 2:161
Charles Gordone 1:124
Günter Grass 11:252
Bill Gunn 5:153
Christopher Hampton 4:211
Joseph Heller 11:265
Lillian Hellman 8:281
Rolf Hochhuth 11:275
Bohumil Hrabal 13:290
William Inge 8:308
Pavel Kohout 13:323
Arthur Kopit 1:171
Ira Levin 3:294
Robert Lowell 4:299; 11:324
Norman Mailer 2:259; 3:316
Terrence McNally 4:347; 7:217, 218, 219
Mark Medoff 6:321, 322
Christopher Middleton 13:387
Arthur Miller 2:279, 280; 6:335
Jason Miller 2:284, 285
Joyce Carol Oates 11:400
Joe Orton 4:387
John Osborne 2:328; 11:421
Rochelle Owens 8:434
S. J. Perelman 5:337
Harold Pinter 3:386, 387; 11:443
Bernard Pomerance 13:446
David Rabe 8:449, 451
Jonathan Reynolds 6:452
Murray Schisgal 6:490
Peter Shaffer 5:387, 389
Ntozake Shange 8:484
Sam Shepard 6:497
Neil Simon 6:506; 11:495, 496
Bernard Slade 11:507
John Steinbeck 5:408
Tom Stoppard 3:470; 4:525, 526; 5:412; 8:504
David Storey 4:528; 5:415, 417
Elizabeth Swados 12:559, 562
Ronald Tavel 6:529
Melvin Van Peebles 2:448
Gore Vidal 2:450; 4:554; 10:503

CRITIC INDEX

CRITIC INDEX

Derek Walcott 2:460
Peter Weiss 3:513
Michael Weller 10:526
Thornton Wilder 10:535
Tennessee Williams 2:464;
   5:501; 7:544; 8:549; 11:571
Robert Wilson 7:550, 551

Simonds, C. H.
Joan Didion 1:74

Simpson, Allen
Albert Camus 11:96

Simpson, Elaine
Andre Norton 12:456

Simpson, Louis
Robert Bly 2:65
Allen Ginsberg 13:241
James Merrill 8:380
Kenneth Rexroth 2:370
W. D. Snodgrass 2:405

Sinclair, Dorothy
Erich Segal 10:467

Sinclair, Karen
Ursula K. LeGuin 13:350

Singer, Marilyn
Frank Bonham 12:54

Singh, G.
Eugenio Montale 7:223, 226
Ezra Pound 2:342, 344; 7:334

Sinyavsky, Andrei
Robert Frost 4:174

Sire, James W.
C. S. Lewis 1:177

Sisco, Ellen
Jamake Highwater 12:286

Sisk, John P.
J. F. Powers 1:280

Sissman, L. E.
Kingsley Amis 2:7; 5:22
Martin Amis 4:21
Jimmy Breslin 4:76
Michael Crichton 6:119
J. P. Donleavy 4:126
J. G. Farrell 6:174
Natalia Ginzburg 5:141
Joseph Heller 8:278
Dan Jacobson 4:255
Thomas McGuane 3:329
Tom McHale 3:332; 5:282
Brian Moore 7:237
Anne Roiphe 3:434
John Updike 2:441
Evelyn Waugh 3:513
Fay Weldon 6:563
Edmund Wilson 2:478

Sisson, C. H.
H. D. 8:257

Skau, Michael
Lawrence Ferlinghetti 10:177

Skelton, Robin
Anthony Kerrigan 6:276
Dorothy Livesay 4:294

Skerrett, Joseph T., Jr.
Ralph Ellison 11:182

Sklar, Robert
J.R.R. Tolkien 12:568

Skodnick, Roy
Gilbert Sorrentino 7:448

Skow, Jack
John Gardner 5:132
Robert Graves 2:176

Skow, John
Richard Adams 5:5
Richard Brautigan 3:86
Arthur A. Cohen 7:52
Richard Condon 4:107; 6:115
Julio Cortázar 5:109
Robertson Davies 2:113
Lawrence Durrell 6:152
Charles Johnson 7:183
Robert F. Jones 7:193
Sue Kaufman 3:263
Yasunari Kawabata 5:208
Milan Kundera 4:277
John D. MacDonald 3:307
Iris Murdoch 4:370
Vladimir Nabokov 6:354
Harold Robbins 5:379
Susan Fromberg Schaeffer
   6:488
Irving Stone 7:471
Kurt Vonnegut, Jr. 4:568
Morris L. West 6:564
Patrick White 3:525

Škvorecky, Josef
Pavel Kohout 13:325

Slade, Joseph W.
James T. Farrell 11:192

Slater, Candace
Elizabeth Bishop 13:88
Salvatore Espriu 9:193

Slater, Jack
Stevie Wonder 12:662

Slaughter, Frank G.
Millen Brand 7:29

Slavitt, David R.
George Garrett 11:220
Ann Quin 6:441

Slethaug, Gordon E.
John Barth 2:38

Slonim, Marc
Mikhail Sholokhov 7:415, 418
Aleksandr I. Solzhenitsyn 1:320

Sloss, Henry
Richard Howard 10:276
James Merrill 8:381, 384
Reynolds Price 3:406
Philip Roth 1:293

Slusser, George Edgar
Arthur C. Clarke 13:151
Harlan Ellison 13:204
Ursula K. LeGuin 13:345

Smeltzer, Sister Mary Etheldra
Larry Kettelkamp 12:306

Smith, A.J.M.
Earle Birney 6:74
P. K. Page 7:291

Smith, Barbara
Ishmael Reed 6:447
Alice Walker 6:553

Smith, C.E.J.
Mavis Thorpe Clark 12:130
Leon Garfield 12:231

Smith, Dave
Harry Crews 6:118
Albert Goldbarth 5:144

Louis Simpson 7:429
Robert Penn Warren 13:581

Smith, David E.
E. E. Cummings 8:158

Smith, Grover
Archibald MacLeish 8:359

Smith, H. Allen
Jacqueline Susann 3:476

Smith, Harrison
Madeleine L'Engle 12:345

Smith, Iain Crichton
Hugh MacDiarmid 11:336

Smith, Janet Adam
Richard Adams 4:8
J. R. R. Tolkien 2:435

Smith, Liz
Truman Capote 8:133

Smith, Mason
Richard Brautigan 12:60

Smith, Maxwell A.
Jean Giono 4:184
François Mauriac 4:340

Smith, Michael
Rosalyn Drexler 2:119
Anthony Kerrigan 6:275
Tom Stoppard 1:327
Robert Wilson 7:549

Smith, Phillip E., II
Charles Olson 11:420

Smith, Raymond J.
James Dickey 10:141

Smith, Robert
Jimmy Page and Robert Plant
   12:481

Smith, Roger H.
John D. MacDonald 3:307

Smith, Sherwin D.
Charles M. Schulz 12:530

Smith, Sidonie Ann
Maya Angelou 12:10

Smith, William James
Kurt Vonnegut, Jr. 12:601

Smith, William Jay
Elizabeth Bishop 13:89
Louis MacNeice 4:315

Smyth, Pat
William Mayne 12:395

Smyth, Paul
Derek Walcott 4:575

Sniderman, Stephen L.
Joseph Heller 3:230

Snodgrass, W. D.
Theodore Roethke 8:455

Snow, C. P.
Norman Mailer 4:322

Snow, George E.
Aleksandr I. Solzhenitsyn 4:507

Snow, Helen F.
Pearl S. Buck 7:33

Snowden, J. A.
Sean O'Casey 9:406

Sobran, M. J., Jr.
Norman Lear 12:338

Socken, Paul G.
Anne Hébert 13:268

Soderbergh, Peter A.
Upton Sinclair 11:497

Soile, Sola
Chinua Achebe 11:4

Sokel, Walter Herbert
Heinrich Böll 9:102

Sokolov, Raymond A.
E. L. Doctorow 6:132
Dan Jacobson 4:254
Gayl Jones 6:265
Thomas Keneally 8:319
József Lengyel 7:202
John Sayles 7:400

Solecki, Sam
Earle Birney 11:50

Solnick, Bruce B.
George Garrett 11:220

Solomon, Barbara Probst
Juan Goytisolo 5:151
João Ubaldo Ribeiro 10:436
Mario Vargas Llosa 10:500

Solotaroff, Theodore
Saul Bellow 1:33
Paul Bowles 1:41
Anthony Burgess 1:48
William S. Burroughs 1:48
Albert Camus 9:146
Alex Comfort 7:54
George P. Elliott 2:130
John Fowles 6:185
Herbert Gold 7:120
Paul Goodman 1:123
Günter Grass 1:125
Stanislaw Lem 8:344
Bernard Malamud 1:196, 200
Henry Miller 1:219
Flannery O'Connor 1:256
Katherine Anne Porter 1:271
V. S. Pritchett 5:352
James Purdy 2:348
Philip Roth 4:451
Jean-Paul Sartre 1:304
Hubert Selby, Jr. 8:474
Susan Sontag 1:322
Vladimir Voinovich 10:508
Richard Wright 1:377
Richard Yates 7:553

Somer, John
Kurt Vonnegut, Jr. 4:566

Somers, Paul P., Jr.
Ernest Hemingway 8:283

Sommer, Sally R.
Alice Childress 12:108

Sommers, Joseph
Miguel Ángel Asturias 13:39

Sonkiss, Lois
Jamake Highwater 12:286

Sonnenfeld, Albert
Heinrich Böll 9:107

Sonntag, Jacob
Amos Oz 8:435
Isaac Bashevis Singer 3:456
Arnold Wesker 3:519

Sontag, Susan
James Baldwin 4:40
Albert Camus 4:88
Paul Goodman 2:170
Rolf Hochhuth 4:230

Eugène Ionesco 4:251
Nathalie Sarraute 4:465
Jean-Paul Sartre 4:475
Sonthoff, Helen W.
Ethel Davis Wilson 13:606
Sorrentino, Gilbert
Paul Blackburn 9:99
Richard Brautigan 12:57
Robert Creeley 2:106
Robert Duncan 2:122
William Gaddis 8:227
Charles Olson 2:327
John Wieners 7:535, 536
Louis Zukofsky 7:563
Soskin, William
Esther Forbes 12:204
Sotiron, Michael
Hugh Garner 13:237
Soul, Amoral
Mary Hocking 13:285
Soule, Stephen W.
Anthony Burgess 5:90
Sourian, Peter
Albert Camus 2:98
Eleanor Clark 5:105
Jack Kerouac 2:227
Norman Lear 12:336
William Saroyan 8:468
Vassilis Vassilikos 4:552
Southerland, Ellease
Zora Neale Hurston 7:171
Southern, David
Michael McClure 6:320
Southern, Terry
John Rechy 1:283
Kurt Vonnegut, Jr. 12:601
Southworth, James G.
E. E. Cummings 3:115
Robert Frost 3:168
Robinson Jeffers 3:257
Archibald MacLeish 3:309
Laura Riding 7:373
Souza, Raymond D.
Octavio Paz 10:392
Ernesto Sábato 10:444
Spacks, Patricia Meyer
Kingsley Amis 5:24
Nicholas Delbanco 6:130
Hannah Green 3:202
Joseph Heller 5:183
Jennifer Johnston 7:186
D. Keith Mano 10:328
Alberto Moravia 2:294
Iris Murdoch 6:347
Anne Sexton 8:483
Andrew Sinclair 2:402
Muriel Spark 2:419; 5:400
Peter Spielberg 6:520
J.R.R. Tolkien 1:336
Elio Vittorini 6:551
Eudora Welty 2:464
Paul West 7:524
Patrick White 4:587
Spain, Francis Lander
Margot Benary-Isbert 12:31
Spann, Marcella
Ezra Pound 4:413
Spanos, William V.
Yannis Ritsos 6:460

Spaulding, Martha
Laurie Colwin 13:156
Kamala Markandaya 8:377
J.R.R. Tolkien 8:516
Spears, Monroe K.
W. H. Auden 2:22
John Berryman 2:57
James Dickey 2:116
T. S. Eliot 2:127
Robert Graves 11:254
Ted Hughes 2:199
David Jones 2:217
Madison Jones 4:263
Robert Lowell 2:248
Ezra Pound 2:342
John Crowe Ransom 2:366
Karl Shapiro 4:487
Allen Tate 2:430
Robert Penn Warren 1:355;
4:579
Spector, Ivar
Mikhail Sholokhov 7:420
Spector, Robert D.
William Bronk 10:73
Robert Duncan 7:87
D. J. Enright 4:156
David Ignatow 7:174
Kenneth Rexroth 2:371
Speer, Diane Parkin
Robert Heinlein 8:275
Spence, Jon
Katherine Anne Porter 7:320
Spencer, Benjamin T.
Edward Dahlberg 7:70
Spencer, Jack
André Schwarz-Bart 2:388
Spencer, Sharon
Djuna Barnes 3:38
Jorge Luis Borges 3:77
Julio Cortázar 3:114
Carlos Fuentes 3:175
Anaïs Nin 4:376
Alain Robbe-Grillet 4:448
Spendal, R. J.
James Wright 10:546
Spender, Stephen
A. R. Ammons 2:12
W. H. Auden 3:25, 27
Robert Graves 2:177
Thom Gunn 3:216
Ted Hughes 2:200
Aldous Huxley 3:253; 5:192;
8:304
David Jones 13:312
Philip Levine 4:287
James Merrill 3:335
W. S. Merwin 3:340
Eugenio Montale 7:225
Elsa Morante 8:403
Sylvia Plath 9:429
William Plomer 4:406
James Schuyler 5:383
Gore Vidal 2:450; 8:527
James Wright 3:541
Spicer, Edward H.
Carlos Castaneda 12:85
Spiegel, Alan
Jean-Paul Sartre 7:398
Spiegelman, Willard
John Betjeman 10:53

Richard Howard 7:169
James Merrill 8:384
Adrienne Rich 7:370
Spieler, F. Joseph
Robert Wilson 9:577
Spilka, Mark
Ernest Hemingway 10:263
Doris Lessing 6:300
Erich Segal 3:446
Spina, James
Jimmy Page and Robert Plant
12:482
Spitz, Robert Stephen
Pete Hamill 10:251
Spivack, Kathleen
Robert Lowell 2:248
Spivey, Herman E.
William Faulkner 6:176
Spivey, Ted R.
Conrad Aiken 5:9
Flannery O'Connor 1:255
Sprague, Rosemary
Marianne Moore 4:362
Sprague, Susan
Mavis Thorpe Clark 12:132
Spurling, Hilary
Anthony Powell 10:417
Spurling, John
Peter Barnes 5:50
Samuel Beckett 6:42
Peter Benchley 4:54
Anna Kavan 13:315
Francis King 8:322
David Mercer 5:284
Yukio Mishima 9:384
Peter Nichols 5:308
David Plante 7:307
Peter Shaffer 5:388
Elie Wiesel 5:491
Squires, Radcliffe
Caroline Gordon 6:204
Randall Jarrell 6:260
Robinson Jeffers 11:305
Mario Luzi 13:353
Frederic Prokosch 4:420
Allen Tate 2:429; 4:540; 11:524
Stabb, Martin S.
José Donoso 11:149
Stade, George
Kingsley Amis 8:10
E. E. Cummings 3:119
E. L. Doctorow 6:132
John Gardner 3:186
Robert Graves 1:129
Jerzy Kosinski 3:272
Alan Lelchuk 5:243
Joseph McElroy 5:279
Jean Rhys 6:452
Wilfrid Sheed 4:488
Muriel Spark 2:416
John Updike 5:458
Kurt Vonnegut, Jr. 3:501
Stafford, Jean
M. E. Kerr 12:296, 298
James A. Michener 5:289
Paul West 7:523
Stafford, William
Millen Brand 7:29

Loren Eiseley 7:93
David Kherdian 6:280
Kenneth Rexroth 2:370
Louis Simpson 7:427
Theodore Weiss 8:546
Stallknecht, Newton P.
Amos Tutuola 5:445
Stallman, Robert W.
Ernest Hemingway 13:271
Stambolian, George
Sam Shepard 4:490
Stampfer, Judah
Saul Bellow 6:60
Philip Roth 6:476
Stanford, Ann
May Swenson 4:533
Stanford, Derek
A. Alvarez 13:9
Earle Birney 4:64
Robert Creeley 2:106
C. Day Lewis 1:72
Lawrence Durrell 4:147
Aldous Huxley 5:192
Elizabeth Jennings 5:197
Hugh MacDiarmid 4:313
Louis MacNeice 1:187
Robert Nye 13:413
William Plomer 4:406
Stephen Spender 1:322; 2:419
Yevgeny Yevtushenko 3:547
Stanford, Donald E.
Caroline Gordon 6:202
Marianne Moore 4:364
Ezra Pound 10:407
Allen Tate 2:430
Yvor Winters 4:591
Stange, Maren
Susan Sontag 10:486
Stankiewicz, Marketa Goetz
Pavel Kohout 13:323
Sławomir Mrożek 3:345
Stanlis, Peter L.
Robert Frost 3:174
Stannard, Martin
Evelyn Waugh 13:588
Staples, Hugh B.
Randall Jarrell 6:261
Robert Lowell 2:246
Stark, John
Jorge Luis Borges 8:94
E. L. Doctorow 6:131
William Gaddis 8:228
Vladimir Nabokov 8:407
Stark, John O.
John Barth 7:22
Stark, Myra
Adrienne Rich 11:477
Starr, Kevin
E. L. Doctorow 6:136
John Dos Passos 8:181
Starr, Roger
Anthony Powell 3:403
Stasio, Marilyn
Anne Burr 6:105
John Hopkins 4:234
Terrence McNally 4:346, 347
Jason Miller 2:284

David Rabe 4:426
Melvin Van Peebles 2:448
Murray Schisgal 6:491

States, Bert O.
Harold Pinter 6:412

Stavn, Diane Gersoni
Frank Bonham 12:51
M. E. Kerr 12:297
Joseph Krumgold 12:320
Emily Cheney Neville 12:451

Stavrou, C. N.
Edward Albee 5:12

Steck, Henry J.
Jules Archer 12:20

Steel, Ronald
Pavel Kohout 13:323

Stefanile, Felix
William Bronk 10:73
Lewis Turco 11:552

Stegner, Page
Vladimir Nabokov 1:239

Stein, Benjamin
Joan Didion 8:177

Stein, Charles
Jerome Rothenberg 6:477

Stein, Howard F.
Alex Haley 12:251

Stein, Robert A.
J. V. Cunningham 3:122

Stein, Ruth M.
Jamake Highwater 12:287

Steinberg, M. W.
Robertson Davies 7:72
Arthur Miller 1:215

Steiner, Carlo
Giuseppe Ungaretti 7:483

Steiner, George
Jorge Luis Borges 2:70
C. Day Lewis 6:126
Lawrence Durrell 4:144
Paul Goodman 7:127
Graham Greene 6:220
Aldous Huxley 5:194
Thomas Keneally 8:318; 10:298
Robert M. Pirsig 4:403
Sylvia Plath 11:445
Jean-Paul Sartre 7:397
Aleksandr I. Solzhenitsyn 4:516
John Updike 5:459
Patrick White 4:583

Stepanchev, Stephen
John Ashbery 2:16
Imamu Amiri Baraka 2:34
Elizabeth Bishop 4:65
Robert Bly 2:65
Robert Creeley 2:105
James Dickey 2:115
Alan Dugan 2:121
Robert Duncan 2:122
Jean Garrigue 2:153
Allen Ginsberg 2:162
Randall Jarrell 2:208
Robert Lowell 2:247
W. S. Merwin 2:276
Charles Olson 2:325
Kenneth Rexroth 2:369
Karl Shapiro 4:485
Louis Simpson 4:498

William Stafford 4:519
May Swenson 4:532
Richard Wilbur 6:568

Stephens, Donald
Dorothy Livesay 4:294
Sinclair Ross 13:490
Rudy Wiebe 6:567

Stephens, Martha
Richard Wright 1:379

Stephens, Robert O.
Ernest Hemingway 3:239

Stephenson, William
James Dickey 4:122

Stepto, Robert B.
Michael S. Harper 7:139

Stern, Daniel
Paul Bowles 2:79
Joanne Greenberg 7:134
Marjorie Kellogg 2:223
Jakov Lind 4:292
Bernard Malamud 3:324
Chaim Potok 2:339
Ann Quin 6:441
Paul West 7:523
Elie Wiesel 3:529

Stern, David
Robert Kotlowitz 4:275
Amos Oz 5:334

Sterne, Richard C.
Octavio Paz 10:391

Sterne, Richard Clark
Jerome Weidman 7:517

Stetler, Charles
Richard Brautigan 12:67
James Purdy 4:423

Stevens, Peter
A. R. Ammons 8:14
Margaret Atwood 4:24
A. W. Purdy 3:408

Stevens, Shane
John Rechy 7:356

Stevens, Wallace
Marianne Moore 10:347

Stevenson, Anne
Elizabeth Bishop 1:35
Peter Porter 13:453
R. S. Thomas 13:544
Charles Tomlinson 13:548

Stevenson, David L.
James Jones 3:260
Jack Kerouac 2:226
William Styron 1:329

Stevenson, Patrick
W. R. Rodgers 7:377

Stevick, Philip
Donald Barthelme 8:53
William S. Burroughs 5:93
William H. Gass 8:247
Jerzy Kosinski 6:283
Jean Stafford 4:518
Kurt Vonnegut, Jr. 5:465

Stewart, Corbet
Paul Celan 10:102

Stewart, Harry E.
Jean Genet 10:225

Stewart, John L.
John Crowe Ransom 2:362

Stewart, Robert Sussman
Heinrich Böll 2:67

Stewart, Ruth Weeden
William Mayne 12:387

Stiller, Nikki
Louis Simpson 9:486

Stilwell, Robert L.
A. R. Ammons 3:10
Sylvia Plath 1:269
Jon Silkin 2:395
James Wright 3:540

Stimpson, Catherine R.
Tillie Olsen 13:432
Marge Piercy 6:403
J. R. R. Tolkien 1:338

Stineback, David C.
Allen Tate 9:525

Stinson, John J.
Anthony Burgess 4:82

Stitt, Peter A.
John Ashbery 13:34
John Berryman 10:46
William Heyen 13:282
Louis Simpson 7:429
Robert Penn Warren 10:519
Charles Wright 13:614
James Wright 10:542

Stock, Irvin
Saul Bellow 2:50
Mary McCarthy 1:206

Stocking, Marion Kingston
Galway Kinnell 1:168
Gary Snyder 1:318

Stokes, Eric
Kamala Markandaya 8:378

Stoltzfus, Ben F.
Ernest Hemingway 13:279
Alain Robbe-Grillet 1:285

Stolz, Herbert J.
Larry Kettelkamp 12:307

Stone, Chuck
Garry Trudeau 12:590

Stone, Elizabeth
John Fowles 9:213
John Gardner 8:234
Cynthia Macdonald 13:355

Stone, Laurie
Max Frisch 9:217
Elizabeth Hardwick 13:266
Anaïs Nin 8:423
Anne Roiphe 9:455

Stone, Robert
Peter Matthiessen 5:274

Stoneback, H. R.
William Faulkner 8:213

Storch, R. F.
Harold Pinter 6:409

Storr, Catherine
Leon Garfield 12:221

Story, Jack Trevor
C. P. Snow 6:517

Stothard, Peter
Lawrence Durrell 13:188

Stouck, David
Marie-Claire Blais 2:63
Hugh MacLennan 2:257

Stover, Leon E.
Frank Herbert 12:276

Stowers, Bonnie
Hortense Calisher 4:88
Saul Maloff 5:271

Strandberg, Victor H.
John Updike 13:557
Robert Penn Warren 13:573

Stratford, Philip
Graham Greene 6:212

Straub, Peter
Michael Ayrton 7:19
Beryl Bainbridge 8:36
James Baldwin 4:43
J. G. Ballard 3:35
Donald Barthelme 3:44
Brian Glanville 6:202
Hermann Hesse 6:237
Jack Kerouac 3:266
Francis King 8:321
Margaret Laurence 6:290
Olivia Manning 5:273
Thomas McGuane 7:213
Michael Mewshaw 9:376
James A. Michener 5:291
Anaïs Nin 8:419
Joyce Carol Oates 9:402
Flann O'Brien 4:385
Simone Schwarz-Bart 7:404
Isaac Bashevis Singer 6:509
Richard G. Stern 4:523
John Updike 5:457
Morris L. West 6:563

Strauch, Carl F.
J. D. Salinger 12:505

Street, Douglas O.
Lawrence Ferlinghetti 6:183

Strehle, Susan
John Gardner 10:218

Strong, L.A.G.
John Masefield 11:356

Stroupe, John H.
Jean Anouilh 13:22

Strouse, Jean
Bob Dylan 12:185

Strout, Cushing
William Styron 5:420

Strozier, Robert M.
Peter De Vries 7:78
S. J. Perelman 5:337
P. G. Wodehouse 5:517

Struve, Gleb
Vladimir Nabokov 1:241

Struve, Nikita
Aleksandr I. Solzhenitsyn 7:433

Stuart, Dabney
Ted Hughes 2:201

Stubblefield, Charles
Sylvia Plath 1:270

Stubbs, Harry C.
Melvin Berger 12:38

Stubbs, Helen
William Mayne 12:399

Stubbs, Jean
Julio Cortázar 2:102
Daphne du Maurier 6:147
George Garrett 3:193

Elizabeth Hardwick **13**:265
Eleanor Hibbert **7**:155
Anaïs Nin **8**:421

Stubbs, John C.
John Hawkes **1**:138

Stubbs, Patricia
Muriel Spark **3**:466

Stumpf, Thomas
Hayden Carruth **7**:41
Daniel Mark Epstein **7**:97
Ishmael Reed **5**:368
Muriel Rukeyser **6**:479

Stupple, A. James
Ray Bradbury **10**:69

Sturgeon, Ray
Joni Mitchell **12**:443

Sturgeon, Theodore
Isaac Asimov **3**:16
Michael Crichton **2**:108
Harlan Ellison **13**:202
Frank Herbert **12**:276
Barry N. Malzberg **7**:208

Sturrock, John
Jorge Amado **13**:12
Jorge Luis Borges **13**:105
Peter De Vries **3**:125
Gabriel García Márquez **8**:233
10:217
Alain Robbe-Grillet **8**:454

Styron, William
Terry Southern **7**:453

Suczek, Barbara
John Lennon and Paul
McCartney **12**:369

Suderman, Elmer F.
John Updike **2**:443; **3**:488

Sukenick, Lynn
Maya Angelou **12**:12
Doris Lessing **3**:288
Anaïs Nin **8**:421
Robert L. Peters **7**:303

Sukenick, Ronald
Carlos Castaneda **12**:89
Rudolph Wurlitzer **2**:483

Sullivan, Anita T.
Ray Bradbury **3**:85

Sullivan, Jack
Richard Condon **8**:150
Paul Horgan **9**:279
Stephen King **12**:309
J. B. Priestley **9**:442

Sullivan, Kevin
Flann O'Brien **5**:316
Sean O'Casey **5**:320

Sullivan, Mary
B. S. Johnson **6**:262
William Sansom **6**:483
Fay Weldon **6**:562

Sullivan, Nancy
May Swenson **4**:534

Sullivan, Richard
Harper Lee **12**:340
Mary Stolz **12**:547

Sullivan, Rosemary
Marie-Claire Blais **6**:81

Sullivan, Ruth
Ken Kesey **6**:278

Sullivan, Tom R.
William Golding **8**:249
Michel Tournier **6**:538

Sullivan, Victoria
Saul Bellow **8**:76

Sullivan, Walter
Donald Barthelme **1**:19
Saul Bellow **8**:81
Elizabeth Bowen **11**:64
Guy Davenport, Jr. **6**:124
Margaret Drabble **8**:184
Andre Dubus **13**:182
George Garnett **11**:219
William Golding **2**:166, 168
Graham Greene **6**:219
Richard Hughes **11**:278
Bernard Malamud **1**:200
Joyce Carol Oates **6**:368; **9**:405
Flannery O'Connor **2**:317
John O'Hara **6**:385
Reynolds Price **13**:464
V. S. Pritchett **13**:465
Jean Rhys **6**:456
Alan Sillitoe **6**:501
Anne Tyler **11**:553

Sullivan, Wilson
Irving Stone **7**:470

Sullivan, Zohreh T.
Iris Murdoch **11**:386

Sullivan, Zohreh Tawakuli
Iris Murdoch **6**:346

Sultan, Stanley
Ezra Pound **7**:331

Suplee, Curt
Thomas Berger **11**:46

Suter, Anthony
Basil Bunting **10**:83, 84

Suther, Judith D.
Eugène Ionesco **11**:292

Sutherland, Donald
Rafael Alberti **7**:10
Octavio Paz **10**:389
St.-John Perse **4**:399
Francis Ponge **6**:422

Sutherland, Ronald
Roch Carrier **13**:140

Sutherland, Stuart
A. Alvarez **13**:8
Peter De Vries **10**:137

Sutherland, Zena
E. M. Almedingen **12**:3, 4, 7
Melvin Berger **12**:39, 40, 41
Judy Blume **12**:44
Frank Bonham **12**:49, 50, 51,
52, 53, 54, 55
Betty Cavanna **12**:102
Alice Childress **12**:107
Mavis Thorpe Clark **12**:132
Babbis Friis-Baastad **12**:214
Jesse Jackson **12**:290, 291
M. E. Kerr **12**:298
Larry Kettelkamp **12**:305, 306,
307
Joseph Krumgold **12**:318, 321
Madeleine L'Engle **12**:350
Nicholasa Mohr **12**:447
Emily Cheney Neville **12**:450,
451, 452
Katherine Paterson **12**:484, 486

Mary Stolz **12**:551, 553, 554,
555
John R. Tunis **12**:599
Lenora Mattingly Weber **12**:634
Rosemary Wells **12**:639

Sutton, Graham
W. Somerset Maugham **11**:367

Sutton, Walter
Allen Ginsberg **4**:181
Robert Lowell **4**:303
Thomas Merton **3**:336
Marianne Moore **4**:364
Ezra Pound **3**:395

Swados, Harvey
David Ignatow **4**:249

Swartley, Ariel
Joni Mitchell **12**:442

Swartney, Joyce
Charles M. Schulz **12**:533

Sweeney, Patricia Runk
M. E. Kerr **12**:301

Swenson, May
Robin Morgan **2**:294
Anne Sexton **2**:392
W. D. Snodgrass **2**:406

Swift, Pat
George Barker **8**:44

Swigg, Richard
E. M. Forster **9**:209
Philip Larkin **9**:324

Swigger, Ronald T.
Raymond Queneau **2**:359

Swinden, Patrick
C. P. Snow **4**:503

Swing, Raymond
John R. Tunis **12**:596

Swink, Helen
William Faulkner **3**:154

Sykes, Christopher
Aldous Huxley **4**:244; **8**:303

Sykes, S. W.
Claude Simon **9**:483

Sylvester, R. D.
Joseph Brodsky **13**:114

Symons, Julian
Eric Ambler **4**:18
W. H. Auden **2**:28
John Berryman **2**:59
Edward Brathwaite **11**:66
John Dickson Carr **3**:101
John Cheever **8**:140
Agatha Christie **6**:107; **8**:140;
12:121, 126
John Creasey **11**:134
C. Day Lewis **6**:129
Len Deighton **4**:119
Friedrich Dürrenmatt **4**:141
Ian Fleming **3**:159
Roy Fuller **4**:178
Dashiell Hammett **3**:219
Lillian Hellman **4**:222
Patricia Highsmith **2**:193; **4**:225
Chester Himes **4**:229
Evan Hunter **11**:279
John Le Carré **3**:282
John D. MacDonald **3**:307
Ross Macdonald **3**:307
Mary McCarthy **3**:326

Henry Miller **2**:281
Ellery Queen **3**:421
Kenneth Rexroth **11**:473
Laura Riding **3**:431
Georges Simenon **3**:451; **8**:487
Louis Simpson **4**:498
Maj Sjöwall **7**:501
C. P. Snow **4**:500
Mickey Spillane **3**:469
Rex Stout **3**:471
Per Wahlöö **7**:501
Robert Penn Warren **4**:577
Patrick White **3**:523
Angus Wilson **3**:536

Syrkin, Marie
Henry Roth **6**:472

Szanto, George H.
Alain Robbe-Grillet **1**:288

Szogyi, Alex
Lillian Hellman **2**:187
Isaac Bashevis Singer **11**:501

Szporluk, Mary Ann
Vladimir Voinovich **10**:504

Tabachnick, Stephen E.
Conrad Aiken **5**:9

Tait, Michael
James Reaney **13**:472

Talbot, Emile J.
Roch Carrier **13**:144

Talbott, Strobe
Aleksandr I. Solzhenitsyn **4**:516

Taliaferro, Frances
Laurie Colwin **13**:157
Andre Dubus **13**:184
Nadine Gordimer **5**:147
Tom McHale **5**:283

Tallman, Warren
Earle Birney **11**:50
Ernest Buckler **13**:118
Robert Creeley **11**:135
Mordecai Richler **3**:430
Sinclair Ross **13**:490

Tanner, Stephen L.
Ernest Hemingway **8**:288

Tanner, Tony
John Barth **1**:17; **2**:37
Donald Barthelme **2**:40
Richard Brautigan **12**:66
William S. Burroughs **2**:92
William Gaddis **3**:177
John Gardner **2**:152
John Hawkes **2**:185; **7**:143
Ernest Hemingway **10**:266
Norman Mailer **1**:189
Bernard Malamud **2**:267
James Purdy **2**:351; **4**:422
Thomas Pynchon **6**:430, 432
Susan Sontag **1**:322
John Updike **2**:445
Kurt Vonnegut, Jr. **12**:606

Tapscott, Stephen
Friedrich Dürrenmatt **11**:173

Tarn, Nathaniel
William H. Gass **1**:114

Tarshis, Jerome
J. G. Ballard **3**:34

Tate, Allen
Donald Davidson **13**:167

John Crowe Ransom 2:363;
  5:364
Eudora Welty 1:362

Tate, J. O.
  Flannery O'Connor 13:421

Tate, Robert S., Jr.
  Albert Camus 1:54

Tatham, Campbell
  John Barth 1:18
  Raymond Federman 6:181
  Thomas Pynchon 2:354

Tatum, Charles M.
  José Donoso 11:146

Taubman, Robert
  Cynthia Ozick 7:287

Tavris, Carol
  Kate Wilhelm 7:538

Taylor, Clyde
  Imamu Amiri Baraka 5:47

Taylor, F. H. Griffin
  George Garrett 3:192; 11:219
  Robert Lowell 1:181
  Theodore Weiss 3:516

Taylor, Henry
  Marvin Bell 8:64
  Irving Feldman 7:103
  X. J. Kennedy 8:319
  William Meredith 13:373
  Howard Nemerov 6:363
  Flannery O'Connor 1:258
  James Wright 5:521

Taylor, Jane
  Galway Kinnell 1:168

Taylor, John Russell
  John Arden 6:4
  Alan Ayckbourn 5:34
  Brendan Behan 11:44
  Edward Bond 4:69
  Mel Brooks 12:78
  David Mercer 5:283
  Peter Nichols 5:305
  Joe Orton 4:388
  Harold Pinter 11:436
  Terence Rattigan 7:354
  Robert Shaw 5:390
  Tom Stoppard 4:524
  David Storey 4:528
  E. A. Whitehead 5:488

Taylor, Lewis Jerome, Jr.
  Walker Percy 6:399

Taylor, Mark
  W. H. Auden 3:27
  John Berryman 3:72
  Tom McHale 5:282
  Walker Percy 3:378
  Earl Rovit 7:383
  Edmund Wilson 8:550
  Richard Yates 8:555

Taylor, Michael
  Gillian Tindall 7:474

Taylor, William L.
  J.R.R. Tolkien 12:569

Tebbel, John
  Charles M. Schulz 12:527

Temple, Joanne
  John Berryman 3:72

Temple, Ruth Z.
  Nathalie Sarraute 1:303; 2:386

Templeton, Joan
  Sean O'Casey 11:406

Tenenbaum, Louis
  Italo Calvino 5:97

Tennant, Emma
  J. G. Ballard 6:28
  Italo Calvino 5:100
  Thomas Hinde 6:242
  Penelope Mortimer 5:298

Terbille, Charles I.
  Saul Bellow 6:52
  Joyce Carol Oates 6:371

Teresa, Vincent
  Mario Puzo 2:352

Terrien, Samuel
  Fernando Arrabal 2:15

Terris, Susan
  Rosemary Wells 12:639

Terry, Arthur
  Vicente Aleixandre 9:17
  Salvador Espriu 9:192
  Octavio Paz 10:393

Teunissen, John T.
  Doris Lessing 6:293

Therese, Sister M.
  Marianne Moore 1:229

Theroux, Paul
  Frederick Buechner 2:83
  Anthony Burgess 5:89
  John Cheever 7:48
  Peter De Vries 3:126; 7:76
  Lawrence Durrell 6:151
  George MacDonald Fraser
    7:106
  Nadine Gordimer 5:147
  Shirley Ann Grau 4:209
  Graham Greene 3:213
  Ernest Hemingway 6:229
  Susan B. Hill 4:226
  Erica Jong 4:264
  John Knowles 4:272
  Milan Kundera 4:276
  Mary McCarthy 5:277
  Yukio Mishima 4:356
  Brian Moore 3:341; 7:236
  V. S. Naipaul 4:373, 374; 7:252
  Cynthia Ozick 7:288
  S. J. Perelman 9:415
  Jean Rhys 2:372
  David Storey 4:529
  Peter Taylor 4:542
  John Updike 13:563
  Kurt Vonnegut, Jr. 5:470

Thiher, Allen
  Fernando Arrabal 9:33
  Louis-Ferdinand Céline 4:101

Thody, Philip
  Albert Camus 4:91
  Jean-Paul Sartre 4:476

Thomas, Carolyn
  David Jones 7:191

Thomas, Clara
  Margaret Laurence 3:281;
    13:342

Thomas, D. M.
  Martin Booth 13:103
  John Matthias 9:362

Thomas, David
  James Baldwin 5:43

Thomas, David P.
  Christopher Isherwood 1:157

Thomas, M. Wynn
  Katherine Anne Porter 10:394

Thomas, Peter
  John Betjeman 6:65
  Robert Kroetsch 5:220

Thomas, S. L.
  John R. Tunis 12:592

Thompson, Eric
  T. S. Eliot 2:125

Thompson, John
  John Berryman 3:71
  Irving Feldman 7:102
  Natalia Ginzburg 5:141
  Joseph Heller 5:176
  Robert Lowell 9:338
  Amos Oz 5:335
  John Updike 13:560

Thompson, Lawrence
  Robert Frost 13:224

Thompson, Leslie M.
  Stephen Spender 10:487

Thompson, R. J.
  John Hawkes 4:214
  Mary Lavin 4:282

Thompson, Robert B.
  Robert Frost 13:230

Thompson, Toby
  Bruce Jay Friedman 5:126

Thomson, George H.
  J. R. R. Tolkien 1:335

Thomson, Jean C.
  Leon Garfield 12:216
  Madeleine L'Engle 12:347

Thorburn, David
  Renata Adler 8:7
  Ann Beattie 8:57
  Judith Guest 8:254
  Norman Mailer 3:315
  Thomas Pynchon 3:416

Thorp, Willard
  W. D. Snodgrass 2:404

Thorpe, Michael
  Doris Lessing 3:291

Thurman, Judith
  Joyce Carol Oates 6:374
  Jean Rhys 6:456
  Laura Riding 7:374

Thwaite, Ann
  E. M. Almedingen 12:5

Thwaite, Anthony
  W. H. Auden 6:24
  Charles Causley 7:41
  Douglas Dunn 6:148
  Geoffrey Grigson 7:136
  Seamus Heaney 7:147
  David Jones 7:187
  Philip Larkin 13:335
  R. K. Narayan 7:256
  Darcy O'Brien 11:405
  C. P. Snow 4:503

Tillinghast, Richard
  James Merrill 2:274
  Adrienne Rich 3:427

Tilton, John W.
  Kurt Vonnegut, Jr. 12:614

Timms, David
  Philip Larkin 5:223

Tindall, Gillian
  Louis-Ferdinand Céline 7:45
  Leon Garfield 12:227

Tindall, William York
  Samuel Beckett 1:22

Tinkle, Lon
  Jean Lee Latham 12:324
  Hollis Summers 10:493

Tisdale, Bob
  John Hawkes 4:215

Tobias, Richard C.
  James Thurber 5:435

Tobin, Patricia
  William Faulkner 3:155

Tobin, Richard L.
  Lothar-Günther Buchheim
    6:101

Todd, Richard
  Renata Adler 8:4
  Louis Auchincloss 9:54
  Donald Barthelme 8:49
  Saul Bellow 6:55, 61
  Thomas Berger 3:64
  Eleanor Bergstein 4:55
  Vance Bourjaily 8:104
  E. L. Doctorow 6:138
  Andre Dubus 13:183
  Bruce Jay Friedman 5:126
  John Hawkes 4:216
  Sue Kaufman 8:317
  William Kotzwinkle 5:220
  Cormac McCarthy 4:343
  Walker Percy 8:443
  Marge Piercy 6:402
  Robert M. Pirsig 6:420
  Judith Rossner 6:470
  John Updike 7:489
  Kurt Vonnegut, Jr. 3:501
  Richard Yates 7:555

Toliver, Harold E.
  Robert Frost 4:175

Tomalin, Claire
  Beryl Bainbridge 10:15
  Charles Newman 2:311
  Paul Theroux 5:427

Tonks, Rosemary
  Adrienne Rich 3:428

Toolan, David S.
  Tom Wicker 7:535

Torchiana, Donald T.
  W. D. Snodgrass 2:404

Totton, Nick
  Beryl Bainbridge 8:37
  Heinrich Böll 9:111
  Gail Godwin 8:249
  James Hanley 8:265
  Mary Hocking 13:285
  Francis King 8:322
  Alistair MacLean 13:364
  Iris Murdoch 8:405
  Vladimir Nabokov 8:417
  David Pownall 10:419
  Piers Paul Read 10:434

Towers, Robert
  Renata Adler 8:4
  Donald Barthelme 13:59

John Cheever 8:138; 11:122
Stanley Elkin 9:191
John Gardner 8:233
Diane Johnson 13:305
Ian McEwan 13:371
Larry McMurtry 7:214
Flannery O'Connor 13:422
Walker Percy 8:444
Anthony Powell 9:435
Philip Roth 9:461
James Salter 7:387
Wilfrid Sheed 10:473
Paul Theroux 8:512
John Updike 13:559
Kurt Vonnegut, Jr. 8:533
Rebecca West 9:562

Townsend, John Rowe
Peter Dickinson 12:172
Esther Forbes 12:211
Leon Garfield 12:222, 224
Jesse Jackson 12:291
Madeleine L'Engle 12:350
William Mayne 12:397
Andre Norton 12:460

Toynbee, Philip
Arthur Koestler 1:170
Mordecai Richler 5:375

Trachtenberg, Alan
Henry Miller 4:351
Tom Wolfe 9:578

Tracy, Honor
Graham Greene 3:206

Tracy, Phil
Kingsley Amis 3:9

Traschen, Isadore
William Faulkner 9:201

Trease, Geoffrey
Leon Garfield 12:216, 217
William Mayne 12:390

Treece, Henry
Herbert Read 4:437

Treglown, Jeremy
Brigid Brophy 11:68
Parel Kohout 13:325
Joyce Carol Oates 11:403
Barbara Pym 13:470
Tom Robbins 9:454

Trewin, J. C.
Agatha Christie 12:125

Trickett, Rachel
James Purdy 2:349
Andrew Sinclair 2:401
Wallace Stegner 9:508
Angus Wilson 2:473

Trilling, Diana
Esther Forbes 12:209
Aldous Huxley 8:304
Irwin Shaw 7:410

Trilling, Lionel
E. M. Forster 1:104
Robert Graves 2:174

Trimpi, Helen P.
Edgar Bowers 9:121, 122

Trodd, Kenith
Andrew Sinclair 2:400

Trotsky, Leon
André Malraux 13:364

Trotter, Stewart
Jean Genet 5:137
Graham Greene 6:220

Trowbridge, Clinton
John Updike 2:442

True, Michael
Daniel J. Berrigan 4:58
Paul Goodman 2:169
Flannery O'Connor 13:422

Trueblood, Valerie
Margaret Atwood 13:43

Truscott, Lucian K.
Bob Dylan 3:131

Tsuruta, Kinya
Shusaku Endo 7:96

Tucker, Carll
Imamu Amiri Baraka 10:19
Ed Bullins 7:37
Jules Feiffer 8:216
Richard Howard 7:169
Robert Lowell 9:338
Archibald MacLeish 8:363

Tucker, James
Anthony Powell 7:338; 10:409

Tucker, Ken
Patti Smith 12:543

Tucker, Martin
Chinua Achebe 3:1
Cyprian Ekwensi 4:152
Nadine Gordimer 3:201
Ernest Hemingway 3:234
Jerzy Kosinski 1:172
Bernard Malamud 3:322
James Ngugi 3:357
Cynthia Ozick 7:287
Alan Paton 4:395
William Plomer 4:406
Ishmael Reed 13:477
Wole Soyinka 3:462
Amos Tutuola 5:443
Laurens van der Post 5:463

Tucker, Nicholas
Judy Blume 12:45

Tunney, Gene
Budd Schulberg 7:402

Turan, Kenneth
Elie Wiesel 11:570

Turco, Lewis
Edward Brathwaite 11:67
Robert Hayden 9:270

Turin, Michele
Alix Kates Shulman 10:476

Turnbull, Colin M.
Christie Harris 12:262

Turnbull, Martin
François Mauriac 4:340

Turnell, Martin
Graham Greene 1:134

Turner, Alice K.
Jamake Highwater 12:285

Turner, Darwin
Ishmael Reed 13:477
Alice Walker 9:558

Turner, E. S.
Daphne du Maurier 11:164

Turner, Gil
Bob Dylan 12:179

Tuttleton, James W.
Louis Auchincloss 4:29

Tyler, Anne
John Cheever 11:121
Marilyn French 10:191
Penelope Gilliatt 13:238
Lois Gould 10:241
Sue Kaufman 8:317
Thomas Keneally 10:299
Ian McEwan 13:370
Alix Kates Shulman 10:475
Susan Sontag 13:516
Paul Theroux 11:529
William Trevor 7:478

Tyler, Ralph
Richard Adams 5:5
Agatha Christie 6:109
S. J. Perelman 9:416
Jean Rhys 6:455

Tyler, Tony
John Lennon and Paul
  McCartney 12:379

Tyms, James D.
Langston Hughes 5:191

Tyrmand, Leopold
Witold Gombrowicz 7:124

Tytell, John
Jack Kerouac 3:264

Uhelski, Jaan
Jimmy Page and Robert Plant
  12:478

Ulam, Adam
Agatha Christie 12:120

Ullman, Montague
Melvin Berger 12:42
Larry Kettelkamp 12:308

Unger, Arthur
Alex Haley 12:253

Unger, Leonard
T. S. Eliot 1:90

Unsworth, Robert
Mavis Thorpe Clark 12:131

Unterecker, John
Lawrence Durrell 1:84
Ezra Pound 4:415
Kenneth Rexroth 2:370

Untermeyer, Louis
Robert Frost 13:223

Updike, John
Michael Ayrton 7:20
Ann Beattie 8:55
Samuel Beckett 6:45
Saul Bellow 6:56
Jorge Luis Borges 8:100
Italo Calvino 5:101; 8:130
Albert Camus 9:149
John Cheever 7:50
Julio Cortázar 5:109
Don DeLillo 10:135
Margaret Drabble 8:183
Daniel Fuchs 8:221
Witold Gombrowicz 7:124
Günter Grass 2:172; 4:206
Ernest Hemingway 8:285
Ruth Prawer Jhabvala 8:312
Gayl Jones 6:266; 9:307
Erica Jong 4:263
Jerzy Kosinski 6:282

Alberto Moravia 7:243
Wright Morris 7:245
Iris Murdoch 6:344
Vladimir Nabokov 2:301; 3:351;
  6:355; 8:414, 415, 416, 417;
  11:395
V. S. Naipaul 13:407
R. K. Narayan 7:256
Flann O'Brien 7:269, 270
John O'Hara 11:414
Robert Pinget 7:306
Raymond Queneau 5:359, 362
Alain Robbe-Grillet 8:452
Françoise Sagan 6:481
J. D. Salinger 12:513
Simone Schwarz-Bart 7:405
Muriel Spark 5:400
Christina Stead 8:499, 500
James Thurber 5:433
Anne Tyler 7:479
Sylvia Townsend Warner 7:512
Edmund Wilson 8:551

Uphaus, Robert W.
Kurt Vonnegut, Jr. 5:469

Urang, Gunnar
C. S. Lewis 3:298
J. R. R. Tolkien 2:434

Urbanski, Marie Mitchell Oleson
Joyce Carol Oates 11:402

Uroff, Margaret D.
Sylvia Plath 3:391

Ury, Claude
Jules Archer 12:17

Usborne, Richard
MacDonald Harris 9:261

Usmiani, Renate
Friedrich Dürrenmatt 8:194

Vaizey, John
Kingsley Amis 5:22

Valdéz, Jorge H.
Julio Cortázar 13:165

Valgemae, Mardi
Sławomir Mrożek 13:398
Jean-Claude Van Itallie 3:493

Valley, John A.
Alberto Moravia 7:243

Vallis, Val
Judith Wright 11:578

Van Brunt, H. L.
Jim Harrison 6:224

van Buren, Alice
Janet Frame 2:142

Vande Kieft, Ruth M.
Flannery O'Connor 1:258
Eudora Welty 1:360

Vandenbroucke, Russell
Athol Fugard 9:230

van den Haag, Ernest
William F. Buckley, Jr. 7:34

van den Heuvel, Cor
James Wright 10:545

Vanderbilt, Kermit
Norman Mailer 3:319
William Styron 3:474

Vanderwerken, David L.
Richard Brautigan 5:69

CRITIC INDEX

Van Doren, Carl
  Esther Forbes **12**:205, 208

Van Doren, Mark
  E. E. Cummings **12**:139
  Robert Frost **13**:223
  Robinson Jeffers **11**:304
  John Cowper Powys **7**:346

Van Duyn, Mona
  Margaret Atwood **2**:19
  Adrienne Rich **3**:427
  Anne Sexton **2**:391

Vansittart, Peter
  Lawrence Durrell **13**:189
  Piers Paul Read **10**:436

Vardi, Dov
  Abraham B. Yehoshua **13**:617

Vargas Llosa, Mario
  Gabriel García Márquez **3**:181

Vargo, Edward P.
  John Updike **7**:486

Vázquez Amaral, José
  Julio Cortázar **13**:157

Vendler, Helen
  A. R. Ammons **2**:14
  Margaret Atwood **8**:29
  John Berryman **3**:68; **10**:46
  Elizabeth Bishop **9**:90
  Olga Broumas **10**:77
  Hayden Carruth **7**:41
  E. E. Cummings **3**:119
  D. J. Enright **8**:203
  Allen Ginsberg **2**:163; **3**:195
  Louise Glück **7**:118
  Seamus Heaney **7**:152
  John Hollander **5**:187
  Richard F. Hugo **6**:245
  Randall Jarrell **9**:295
  Erica Jong **4**:263
  Maxine Kumin **13**:326
  Haki R. Madhubuti **6**:313
  Mary McCarthy **3**:328
  James Merrill **2**:275
  Howard Moss **7**:250
  Joyce Carol Oates **3**:361
  Frank O'Hara **5**:323
  Octavio Paz **4**:397
  Adrienne Rich **7**:367
  Irwin Shaw **7**:414
  Allen Tate **2**:429
  Charles Tomlinson **6**:535
  Diane Wakoski **7**:504
  Robert Penn Warren **10**:525
  Charles Wright **6**:581

Verani, Hugo J.
  Juan Carlos Onetti **7**:277

Vernon, John
  Michael Benedikt **4**:54
  James Dickey **7**:82
  David Ignatow **4**:247
  James Merrill **3**:334
  W. S. Merwin **1**:213
  Thomas Pynchon **11**:452

Verschoyle, Derek
  Rayner Heppenstall **10**:271

Vickery, John B.
  John Updike **5**:451

Vickery, Olga W.
  John Hawkes **4**:213

Vickery, R. C.
  Jules Archer **12**:23

Vidal, Gore
  Louis Auchincloss **4**:31
  Italo Calvino **5**:98
  John Dos Passos **4**:132
  William H. Gass **11**:224
  E. Howard Hunt **3**:251
  Norman Mailer **2**:265
  Carson McCullers **12**:418
  Henry Miller **2**:282
  Yukio Mishima **2**:287
  Anaïs Nin **4**:376
  John O'Hara **2**:323
  Thomas Pynchon **11**:452
  Alain Robbe-Grillet **2**:375
  Aleksandr I. Solzhenitsyn **4**:510
  Susan Sontag **2**:414
  Tennessee Williams **7**:546

Vidal-Hall, Judith
  Leon Garfield **12**:230

Viguers, Ruth Hill
  E. M. Almedingen **12**:2
  Ruth M. Arthur **12**:24
  Margot Benary-Isbert **12**:33
  Betty Cavanna **12**:100
  Leon Garfield **12**:218
  Christie Harris **12**:261, 262
  Joseph Krumgold **12**:320
  Madeleine L'Engle **12**:345, 346
  William Mayne **12**:393
  Emily Cheney Neville **12**:450,
    451
  Mary Stolz **12**:553
  Lenora Mattingly Weber **12**:632

Vilhjalmsson, Thor
  Gabriel García Márquez **2**:150

Vine, Richard
  Stanley Kunitz **11**:319

Vintcent, Brian
  Marie-Claire Blais **4**:67
  Roch Carrier **13**:143
  Anne Hébert **4**:220

Viorst, Judith
  Lois Gould **10**:243

Vogel, Dan
  William Faulkner **6**:177, 178
  Arthur Miller **6**:333
  Robert Penn Warren **6**:556
  Tennessee Williams **5**:504

Volpe, Edmond L.
  James Jones **1**:162

Vonalt, Larry P.
  John Berryman **3**:66; **4**:60
  Marianne Moore **1**:230

Von Hallberg, Robert
  Charles Olson **6**:386

Vonnegut, Kurt, Jr.
  Joseph Heller **5**:175

Voorhees, Richard J.
  P. G. Wodehouse **1**:374

Vopat, Carole Gottlieb
  Jack Kerouac **3**:265

Voss, Arthur
  James T. Farrell **11**:191
  John O'Hara **11**:413

Waddington, Miriam
  Hugh Garner **13**:234

Wade, David
  J. R. R. Tolkien **2**:434

Wade, Michael
  Peter Abrahams **4**:2

Waggoner, Diana
  William Mayne **12**:406

Waggoner, Hyatt H.
  E. E. Cummings **3**:117
  Robert Duncan **2**:122
  T. S. Eliot **2**:127
  Robert Frost **3**:173
  H. D. **3**:217
  Robinson Jeffers **2**:214
  Robert Lowell **3**:300
  Archibald MacLeish **3**:310
  Marianne Moore **2**:292
  Ezra Pound **2**:341
  John Crowe Ransom **2**:363
  Theodore Roethke **3**:432
  Carl Sandburg **4**:463
  Karl Shapiro **4**:485
  Lewis Turco **11**:549
  Richard Wilbur **3**:532
  William Carlos Williams **2**:468

Wagner, Dave
  Robert L. Peters **7**:303

Wagner, Dick
  Yukio Mishima **9**:381

Wagner, Geoffrey
  R. P. Blackmur **2**:61

Wagner, Linda
  Diane Wakoski **9**:554

Wagner, Linda Welshimer
  William Faulkner **1**:103
  Ernest Hemingway **6**:231
  Denise Levertov **1**:176; **5**:247
  Philip Levine **9**:332
  W. S. Merwin **13**:383
  Diane Wakoski **9**:555

Waidson, H. M.
  Heinrich Böll **11**:55

Wain, John
  William S. Burroughs **5**:91
  Edward Dahlberg **7**:66
  C. Day Lewis **6**:127
  Günter Grass **2**:173; **4**:202
  Michael Hamburger **5**:158
  Ben Hecht **8**:270
  Ernest Hemingway **3**:233
  Aldous Huxley **5**:192
  Flann O'Brien **4**:383
  C. P. Snow **4**:500

Wainwright, Andy
  Earle Birney **6**:77

Wainwright, Jeffrey
  Ezra Pound **7**:332

Wakefield, Dan
  J. D. Salinger **12**:500
  Harvey Swados **5**:422
  John R. Tunis **12**:597
  Leon Uris **7**:490

Wakoski, Diane
  Clayton Eshleman **7**:98
  David Ignatow **4**:248
  John Logan **5**:255
  Robert Lowell **4**:304
  Anaïs Nin **4**:377
  Jerome Rothenberg **6**:477

Walcott, Ronald
  Hal Bennett **5**:57, 59
  Charles Gordone **4**:199

Walcutt, Charles Child
  James Gould Cozzens **4**:114
  John O'Hara **1**:262

Waldemar, Carla
  Anaïs Nin **11**:399

Waldmeir, Joseph
  John Updike **5**:450

Waldron, Randall H.
  Norman Mailer **3**:314

Waldrop, Rosemary
  Hans Erich Nossack **6**:365

Walkarput, W.
  Vladimir Nabokov **11**:392

Walker, Alice
  Ai **4**:16
  Flannery O'Connor **6**:381
  Derek Walcott **4**:576

Walker, Carolyn
  Joyce Carol Oates **3**:360

Walker, Cheryl
  Richard Brautigan **12**:68
  Adrienne Rich **3**:428
  Robert Penn Warren **6**:558

Walker, David
  Anne Hébert **13**:268

Walker, Greta
  Babbis Friis-Baastad **12**:214

Walker, Robert G.
  Ernest Hemingway **8**:287

Walker, Ted
  Andrew Young **5**:523

Wall, Stephen
  P. H. Newby **13**:408

Wallace, Irving
  Irving Wallace **13**:568

Wallace, Michele
  Ntozake Shange **8**:485

Wallenstein, Barry
  James T. Farrell **11**:195
  Ted Hughes **2**:200

Waller, Claudia Joan
  José Lezama Lima **10**:317

Waller, G. F.
  Paul Theroux **8**:514

Walsh, Chad
  Robert Bly **2**:66
  Stanley Burnshaw **13**:129
  Robert Graves **6**:212
  Ted Hughes **2**:197
  Philip Larkin **5**:228
  Cynthia Macdonald **13**:355
  Archibald MacLeish **3**:311
  Howard Nemerov **2**:306
  Jerome Weidman **7**:517

Walsh, Thomas F.
  Katherine Anne Porter **13**:449

Walsh, William
  Earle Birney **6**:78
  R. K. Narayan **7**:254
  Thomas Tryon **11**:548
  Patrick White **3**:521; **4**:583, 584;
    7:532; **9**:567

CRITIC INDEX

Walsten, David M.
Yukio Mishima **2**:286

Walt, James
Jean Cayrol **11**:110
Ward Just **4**:266
John O'Hara **6**:385
J. R. Salamanca **4**:462

Walter, James F.
John Barth **10**:22

Walters, Jennifer R.
Michel Butor **3**:93

Walters, Margaret
Brigid Brophy **6**:99

Walton, Alan Hull
Colin Wilson **3**:537

Walton, Edith H.
Esther Forbes **12**:204

Walton, Richard J.
Jules Archer **12**:20

Walzer, Michael
J. D. Salinger **12**:503

Wand, David Hsin-Fu
Marianne Moore **13**:396

Ward, A. C.
W. H. Auden **1**:8
Samuel Beckett **1**:21
Edmund Blunden **2**:65
Ivy Compton-Burnett **1**:62
Noel Coward **1**:64
T. S. Eliot **1**:90
E. M. Forster **1**:104
Christopher Fry **2**:143
Robert Graves **1**:128
Graham Greene **1**:132
Aldous Huxley **1**:150
W. Somerset Maugham **1**:204
Iris Murdoch **1**:234
J. B. Priestley **2**:346
Edith Sitwell **2**:403
C. P. Snow **1**:316
Evelyn Waugh **1**:358
Arnold Wesker **3**:518
P. G. Wodehouse **1**:374

Ward, Andrew
Bob Dylan **12**:197

Ward, David E.
Ezra Pound **1**:275

Ward, J. A.
S. J. Perelman **9**:414

Ward, Leo
Harper Lee **12**:341

Ward, Margaret Joan
Morley Callahan **3**:97

Warkentin, Germaine
A. W. Purdy **3**:408

Warner, Edwin
Jorge Luis Borges **2**:71

Warner, John M.
John Hawkes **3**:223

Warner, Jon M.
George MacBeth **5**:263

Warner, Rex
E. M. Forster **1**:105

Warnke, F. J.
Richard Yates **7**:553

Warnock, Mary
Brigid Brophy **6**:98
Iris Murdoch **8**:404

Warren, Robert Penn
James Dickey **10**:140
Alex Haley **12**:243
Katherine Anne Porter **13**:447
Eudora Welty **1**:362

Warsh, Lewis
Richard Brautigan **3**:86

Warshow, Robert
Arthur Miller **1**:215

Washburn, Martin
Richard Adams **4**:7
Anthony Burgess **4**:84
Nicholas Delbanco **6**:129
John Gardner **3**:187
Lois Gould **4**:200
Juan Goytisolo **5**:150
Günter Grass **4**:206
Dan Jacobson **4**:255
György Konrád **4**:273
Denise Levertov **3**:293
Alison Lurie **4**:306

Washington, Mary Helen
Alice Walker **6**:554

Washington, Peter
Seamus Heaney **7**:149
Peter Porter **13**:451
Stevie Smith **8**:491
R. S. Thomas **13**:544

Wasilewski, W. H.
Theodore Roethke **11**:486

Wasserman, Debbi
Murray Schisgal **6**:490
Sam Shepard **4**:489
Tom Stoppard **4**:525
Richard Wesley **7**:519

Waterhouse, Keith
Harper Lee **12**:341

Waterman, Andrew
Daniel Hoffman **13**:286
John Matthias **9**:361

Waterman, Arthur
Conrad Aiken **3**:5

Waters, Chris
Tim O'Brien **7**:271

Waters, Harry F.
Norman Lear **12**:335, 338

Waterston, Elizabeth
Irving Layton **2**:236

Watkins, Floyd C.
Robert Frost **9**:219
Ernest Hemingway **3**:239

Watkins, Mel
James Baldwin **2**:33
Ernest J. Gaines **11**:218
Simone Schwarz-Bart **7**:404
Alice Walker **5**:476

Watson, J. P.
J. R. R. Tolkien **2**:434

Watt, Ian
John Fowles **2**:137

Watts, Harold H.
Aldous Huxley **1**:151
Ezra Pound **7**:323

Watts, Richard
Lanford Wilson **7**:548

Waugh, Auberon
Michael Ayrton **7**:18
James Leo Herlihy **6**:235
Elizabeth Jane Howard **7**:164
Tom Robbins **9**:453
Gillian Tindall **7**:474
William Trevor **7**:476
P. G. Wodehouse **5**:516

Waugh, Evelyn
Aldous Huxley **11**:281

Waugh, Harriet
Emma Tennant **13**:536

Way, Brian
Edward Albee **9**:2

Weales, Gerald
Edward Albee **9**:4
Beryl Bainbridge **4**:39
Elizabeth Bowen **6**:95
Ivy Compton-Burnett **1**:63
J. P. Donleavy **4**:123
John Hawkes **1**:139; **4**:213
Robert Lowell **4**:299
Norman Mailer **3**:319; **4**:319
Bernard Malamud **1**:201
Mark Medoff **6**:322
Arthur Miller **1**:218
Harold Pinter **9**:420
James Purdy **2**:348; **4**:422
David Rabe **4**:427
Ronald Ribman **7**:357
Peter Shaffer **5**:390
Sam Shepard **4**:489
Wole Soyinka **3**:463
Tom Stoppard **1**:327; **8**:502
David Storey **2**:424
James Thurber **5**:430
Robert Penn Warren **1**:356
Thornton Wilder **10**:536
Tennessee Williams **1**:368;
2:466

Weatherhead, A. Kingsley
Robert Duncan **1**:82; **7**:88
Marianne Moore **4**:360
Charles Olson **1**:263
Stephen Spender **1**:323
William Carlos Williams **1**:371

Weathers, Winston
Par Lägerkvist **7**:200

Weaver, Mike
William Carlos Williams **13**:603

Webb, Phyllis
D. G. Jones **10**:285

Weber, Brom
Thomas Berger **5**:60
Edward Dahlberg **7**:69
Bernard Kops **4**:274
C. P. Snow **4**:503
John Updike **2**:442

Weber, Ronald
Saul Bellow **1**:32

Webster, Grant
Allen Tate **2**:427

Webster, Harvey Curtis
Maxine Kumin **13**:329
C. P. Snow **13**:514

Webster, Ivan
James Baldwin **4**:43
Gayl Jones **6**:266

Weeks, Brigitte
Judy Blume **12**:46
Marilyn French **10**:191
M. E. Kerr **12**:301
Iris Murdoch **8**:405

Weeks, Edward
Margaret Atwood **4**:25
Jorge Luis Borges **1**:39
Lothar-Günther Buchheim
6:102
Pearl S. Buck **7**:33
Daphne du Maurier **6**:147;
11:163
Loren Eiseley **7**:91
Esther Forbes **12**:208
James Herriot **12**:283
Yasunari Kawabata **5**:208
Madeleine L'Engle **12**:344
Peter Matthiessen **5**:273, 275
Iris Murdoch **6**:344
Vladimir Nabokov **6**:357
André Schwarz-Bart **4**:480
Irwin Shaw **7**:413
Mikhail Sholokhov **7**:418
Joseph Wambaugh **3**:509
Jessamyn West **7**:519
Herman Wouk **1**:377

Weesner, Theodore
Robert Cormier **12**:134

Wegner, Robert E.
E. E. Cummings **12**:153

Weibel, Kay
Mickey Spillane **13**:525

Weigel, John A.
Lawrence Durrell **1**:86

Weightman, John
Alan Ayckbourn **5**:37
Simone de Beauvoir **4**:49
Albert Camus **2**:98
Louis-Ferdinand Céline **4**:100
Marguerite Duras **6**:149
A. E. Ellis **7**:94
Jean Genet **5**:136, 139
André Malraux **9**:359
Peter Nichols **5**:308
Francis Ponge **6**:422
Alain Robbe-Grillet **2**:377
Nathalie Sarraute **4**:468, 469
Jean-Paul Sartre **9**:473
Tom Stoppard **5**:412
David Storey **5**:416
Gore Vidal **4**:555

Weinberg, Helen
Saul Bellow **2**:53
Ralph Ellison **11**:180
Herbert Gold **4**:192
Norman Mailer **2**:261
Philip Roth **4**:452

Weinberger, Deborah
Adolfo Bioy Casares **13**:86

Weinberger, G. J.
E. E. Cummings **8**:160

Weinfield, Henry
Gilbert Sorrentino **7**:448, 449

Weintraub, Stanley
William Golding **2**:167
C. P. Snow **9**:497, 498

CRITIC INDEX

Weisberg, Robert
Stanley Burnshaw 3:92
Randall Jarrell 2:211
Richmond Lattimore 3:277

Weisman, Kathryn
Larry Kettelkamp 12:308

Weiss, Theodore
Donald Davie 5:115
Ezra Pound 10:405

Weiss, Victoria L.
Marguerite Duras 6:150

Welburn, Ron
Imamu Amiri Baraka 2:35
Don L. Lee 2:237
Dudley Randall 1:283

Welch, Chris
Jimmy Page and Robert Plant 12:476, 478

Welch, Elizabeth H.
Jules Archer 12:19

Wellek, Rene
R. P. Blackmur 2:62
Kenneth Burke 2:89

Weller, Sheila
Ann Beattie 8:55
Gael Greene 8:252
Diane Wakoski 7:507

Wells, John
Bob Dylan 12:200

Wellwarth, George
Arthur Adamov 4:5
Edward Albee 2:1
John Arden 6:8
Samuel Beckett 2:46
Brendan Behan 8:63
Friedrich Dürrenmatt 4:138
Max Frisch 3:166
Jean Genet 2:157
Michel de Ghelderode 6:197
Eugène Ionesco 4:251
Bernard Kops 4:274
John Osborne 2:327
Harold Pinter 3:385
Arnold Wesker 3:518

Welty, Eudora
Elizabeth Bowen 6:94
Annie Dillard 9:175
E. M. Forster 3:161
Ross Macdonald 2:255
V. S. Pritchett 13:467
Patrick White 5:485

Welz, Becky
Betty Cavanna 12:101

Wernick, Robert
Wright Morris 3:343

Wersba, Barbara
Julia W. Cunningham 12:164, 165, 166
Leon Garfield 12:222

Wertime, Richard A.
Hubert Selby, Jr. 8:475

Weschler, Lawrence
Mel Brooks 12:82

Wescott, Glenway
Katherine Anne Porter 7:313

Wesling, Donald
Ed Dorn 10:157

Wesolek, George
E. E. Cummings 12:152

West, Anthony
Jorge Amado 13:11
Yehuda Amichai 9:22
Leonardo Sciascia 9:474
Sylvia Townsend Warner 7:512

West, Paul
Miguel Ángel Asturias 3:18
Michael Ayrton 7:18
Samuel Beckett 2:48
Earle Birney 6:72
Heinrich Böll 3:74
Michel Butor 8:113
Alejo Carpentier 11:99
Camilo José Cela 13:146
Louis-Ferdinand Céline 1:57
Evan S. Connell, Jr. 4:108
Julio Cortázar 2:103
Guy Davenport, Jr. 6:123
José Donoso 4:127
Gabriel García Márquez 10:215
John Gardner 2:150
William H. Gass 11:224
William Golding 1:122
Peter Handke 5:166
MacDonald Harris 9:261
Uwe Johnson 5:202
Jakov Lind 2:245
Charles Newman 2:311
Robert Nye 13:413
Sylvia Plath 1:271
André Schwarz-Bart 2:389
Allen Tate 11:526
Robert Penn Warren 1:353

West, Ray B.
Katherine Ann Porter 1:272

Westbrook, Max
Saul Bellow 1:30
William Faulkner 1:101
Ernest Hemingway 1:143
J. D. Salinger 1:299
John Steinbeck 1:326
Robert Penn Warren 1:355

Westbrook, Perry D.
Mary Ellen Chase 2:100

Westbrook, Wayne W.
Louis Auchincloss 4:30

Westburg, Faith
Adolfo Bioy Casares 4:64
Jerzy Kosinski 3:274

Westerbeck, Colin L., Jr.
Mel Brooks 12:76, 77

Westlake, Donald E.
Gael Greene 8:252

Weston, John
Paul Zindel 6:586

Weston, John C.
Hugh MacDiarmid 11:335

Wetzsteon, Ross
Charles Gordone 1:124
May Sarton 4:472

Whedon, Julia
Judy Blume 12:46
Penelope Gilliatt 2:160

Wheeler, Charles
William Safire 10:447

Wheelock, Carter
Jorge Luis Borges 2:76; 3:81; 4:72; 6:90; 13:104
Julio Cortázar 5:109

Wheelock, John Hall
Allen Tate 4:536

Whelan, Gloria
Margaret Laurence 13:342

Whichard, Nancy Winegardner
Patrick White 4:583

Whicher, Stephen E.
E. E. Cummings 3:116

Whissen, Thomas R.
Isak Dinesen 10:144, 149

Whitaker, Jennifer Seymour
Alberto Moravia 7:243

Whitaker, Thomas R.
Conrad Aiken 3:3

White, E. B.
James Thurber 5:432

White, Edmund
John Ashbery 6:11
Edward Dahlberg 7:65
Thomas M. Disch 7:87
Lawrence Durrell 6:153
Jean Genet 5:138
Russell C. Hoban 7:161
Eugène Ionesco 11:290
Yasunari Kawabata 5:207
Marjorie Kellogg 2:224
Fran Lebowitz 11:322
José Lezama Lima 4:290
Harry Mathews 6:315
Yukio Mishima 4:355
Howard Moss 7:248
Vladimir Nabokov 2:304
James Schuyler 5:383
Gore Vidal 8:527
Tennessee Williams 5:503

White, Gertrude M.
W. D. Snodgrass 10:477

White, Jean M.
Dick Francis 2:143
Ross Macdonald 3:308
George Simenon 2:398
Maj Sjöwall 7:502
Per Wahlöö 7:502
Donald E. Westlake 7:529

White, John
Michael Ayrton 7:18

White, John J.
MacDonald Harris 9:259

White, Patricia O.
Samuel Beckett 1:25

White, Ray Lewis
Gore Vidal 2:448

White, Victor
Thornton Wilder 10:536

White, William Luther
C. S. Lewis 3:295

Whitehead, James
Jim Harrison 6:224
Stanley J. Kunitz 6:287
Adrienne Rich 3:427
Gibbons Ruark 3:441

Whitehead, John
Louis MacNeice 1:186

Whitman, Ruth
Adrienne Rich 6:459
Anne Sexton 6:494

Whitney, Phyllis A.
Mary Stolz 12:551

Whittemore, Reed
Allen Ginsberg 2:163
James Kirkwood 9:320
Charles Olson 2:326
Tom Robbins 9:453

Whittington-Egan, Richard
Truman Capote 8:133
Rayner Heppenstall 10:272

Whitty, John
Tennessee Williams 11:575

Wickenden, Dan
Brigid Brophy 11:68

Wickes, George
Henry Miller 1:221
Anaïs Nin 1:247

Widmer, Kingsley
John Dos Passos 4:133
Leslie A. Fiedler 4:160
Allen Ginsberg 13:239
Herbert Gold 4:191
Henry Miller 1:220

Wiegand, William
J. D. Salinger 1:295
Jerome Weidman 7:516

Wiegner, Kathleen
Judith Leet 11:323
Diane Wakoski 9:555

Wiersma, Stanley M.
Christopher Fry 2:144; 10:202

Wiesel, Elie
Chaim Grade 10:246

Wieseltier, Leon
Yehuda Amichai 9:24
Isaac Bashevis Singer 11:502
Elie Wiesel 3:529

Wiggins, William H., Jr.
John Oliver Killens 10:300

Wilcher, Robert
Samuel Beckett 11:35

Wilcox, Thomas W.
Anthony Powell 7:341

Wilde, Alan
Donald Barthelme 13:55
Christopher Isherwood 1:156; 9:290

Wilder, Virginia
M. E. Kerr 12:301

Wildgen, Kathryn E.
François Mauriac 9:368

Wilding, Michael
L. P. Hartley 2:182
Jack Kerouac 5:215
Christina Stead 2:422, 423

Wildman, John Hazard
Mary Lavin 4:281
Joyce Carol Oates 6:367
Reynolds Price 6:423
Muriel Spark 13:520

Wilhelm, James J.
Ezra Pound 4:418

Wilkinson, Doris Y.
Chester Himes **7**:159

Willard, Nancy
Pierre Gascar **11**:222
Pablo Neruda **1**:246
J.R.R. Tolkien **8**:515

Willett, Ralph
Clifford Odets **2**:319

Williams, David
Christina Stead **2**:423

Williams, Gladys
Leon Garfield **12**:226

Williams, Hugo
Horst Bienek **7**:29
Richard Brautigan **12**:60
William S. Burroughs **5**:92

Williams, John
Henry Miller **1**:223

Williams, Jonathan
Richard Brautigan **3**:87
Rod McKuen **3**:333
Anne Sexton **4**:482

Williams, Lloyd
James Ngugi **7**:262

Williams, Miller
Donald Davidson **2**:111
John Crowe Ransom **4**:434
Hollis Summers **10**:493
Andrei Voznesensky **1**:349

Williams, Paul
Brian Wilson **12**:641

Williams, Raymond
Aleksandr I. Solzhenitsyn **2**:407

Williams, Richard
Allen Ginsberg **6**:201
Richard Wilbur **6**:568
Brian Wilson **12**:644, 646, 650

Williams, Sherley Anne
James Baldwin **3**:32
Imamu Amiri Baraka **3**:35;
   10:20
Ralph Ellison **3**:144
Haki R. Madhubuti **6**:313

Williams, Tennessee
William Inge **8**:307
Carson McCullers **12**:412

Williams, William Carlos
Marianne Moore **10**:348

Williamson, Alan
Jon Anderson **9**:31
Robert Bly **5**:65
Galway Kinnell **5**:216
Robert Lowell **4**:304
Gary Snyder **5**:394
James Wright **3**:541; **5**:519, 521

Williamson, Chilton, Jr.
Norman Lear **12**:331

Willis, Ellen
Bob Dylan **3**:131; **12**:183, 186
Stevie Wonder **12**:658

Willis, J. H., Jr.
William Empson **3**:147

Wills, Garry
Thomas Keneally **5**:210
James A. Michener **11**:375
Vladimir Nabokov **3**:356

Wilms, Denise Murko
Jules Archer **12**:23
Frank Bonham **12**:55
Betty Cavanna **12**:103
Larry Kettelkamp **12**:306

Wilner, Eleanor
Adrienne Rich **7**:369

Wilson, Angus
Kingsley Amis **3**:9
L. P. Hartley **2**:181
Christopher Isherwood **11**:294

Wilson, Bryan
Kenneth Rexroth **11**:473

Wilson, Colin
Jorge Luis Borges **3**:78
Christopher Isherwood **11**:297

Wilson, Douglas
Ernest Hemingway **3**:241

Wilson, Edmund
W. H. Auden **2**:21; **4**:33
Marie-Claire Blais **2**:62; **4**:66
Morley Callaghan **3**:97
Agatha Christie **12**:114
John Dos Passos **4**:130
Anne Hébert **4**:219
Hugh MacLennan **2**:257
André Malraux **13**:365
Carson McCullers **12**:410
Katherine Anne Porter **7**:309
Aleksandr I. Solzhenitsyn **2**:407
John Steinbeck **13**:529
J. R. R. Tolkien **2**:433
Evelyn Waugh **13**:584
Angus Wilson **2**:470

Wilson, Frank
Susan Sontag **13**:519

Wilson, J. C.
Wright Morris **7**:246

Wilson, Jane
Andrew Sinclair **2**:401

Wilson, Keith
David Kherdian **6**:280

Wilson, Milton
Earle Birney **6**:74, 75

Wilson, Reuel K.
Tadeusz Konwicki **8**:328

Wilson, Robley, Jr.
Daniel J. Berrigan **4**:56
Richard Howard **7**:165
Philip Levine **4**:285

Wimsatt, Margaret
Margaret Atwood **3**:19
Robertson Davies **13**:173
Graham Greene **3**:208

Winch, Terence
Ann Beattie **13**:64
W. S. Merwin **8**:388, 390
Flann O'Brien **10**:363

Winchell, Mark Royden
Robert Penn Warren **13**:579

Windsor, Philip
Aleksandr I. Solzhenitsyn **7**:441

Winegarten, Renee
Ruth Prawer Jhabvala **4**:258
Bernard Malamud **3**:324; **8**:375
André Malraux **1**:203
Grace Paley **6**:392

Winehouse, Bernard
Conrad Aiken **10**:2

Wing, George Gordon
Octavio Paz **3**:376

Winks, Robin W.
Len Deighton **7**:75

Winter, Thomas
Anthony Burgess **4**:81

Winters, Yvor
Robert Frost **10**:192

Wintz, Cary D.
Langston Hughes **10**:279

Wirth-Nesher, Hana
Amos Oz **11**:427

Wisse, Ruth R.
Saul Bellow **8**:68
Chaim Grade **10**:246
Cynthia Ozick **7**:289

Wistrich, Robert
A. E. Ellis **7**:93

Witherington, Paul
Bernard Malamud **11**:352

Witt, Harold
Conrad Aiken **1**:4

Wixson, Douglas Charles, Jr.
Thornton Wilder **10**:531

Wohlers, H. C.
Melvin Berger **12**:40

Woiwode, L.
John Cheever **3**:107

Wolcott, James
William F. Buckley, Jr. **7**:35
Alex Haley **12**:253
Peter Handke **10**:255
Norman Lear **12**:333, 337, 338
Jimmy Page and Robert Plant
   12:480
Wilfrid Sheed **10**:472
Gore Vidal **8**:528

Wolf, Barbara
Yukio Mishima **2**:288; **6**:338

Wolf, Manfred
Brigid Brophy **11**:68

Wolf, William
Gordon Parks **1**:265

Wolfe, G. K.
Kurt Vonnegut, Jr. **3**:495

Wolfe, George H.
William Faulkner **9**:203

Wolfe, H. Leslie
Laurence Lieberman **4**:291

Wolfe, Peter
Richard Adams **5**:6
A. Alvarez **5**:20
Maeve Brennan **5**:72
Laurie Colwin **5**:108
Jakov Lind **1**:177
Walker Percy **2**:333
Mary Renault **3**:425
Charles Webb **7**:515
Patrick White **3**:522

Wolfe, Tom
John Lennon and Paul
   McCartney **12**:355, 363

Wolff, Geoffrey
Frederick Buechner **2**:83

Arthur A. Cohen **7**:52
Julio Cortázar **3**:115
J. P. Donleavy **6**:140
George P. Elliott **2**:131
Paula Fox **8**:217
John Gardner **2**:152
James Jones **3**:261
Jerzy Kosinski **1**:171; **3**:272;
   6:282
D. Keith Mano **2**:270
Peter Matthiessen **5**:273
Wright Morris **7**:247
Donald Newlove **6**:363
Ezra Pound **2**:342
Thomas Pynchon **2**:356
Isaac Bashevis Singer **3**:456

Wolfley, Lawrence C.
Thomas Pynchon **9**:444

Wolitzer, Hilma
Richard Yates **8**:556

Wolkenfeld, J. S.
Isaac Bashevis Singer **1**:311

Wollheim, Donald A.
Isaac Asimov **1**:8
Ray Bradbury **1**:42
Arthur C. Clarke **1**:59
Harlan Ellison **1**:93
Philip Jose Farmer **1**:97
Edmond Hamilton **1**:137
Robert A. Heinlein **1**:139
Andre Norton **12**:466
Clifford D. Simak **1**:309
A. E. Van Vogt **1**:347
Kurt Vonnegut, Jr. **1**:348

Wood, Anne
Leon Garfield **12**:232

Wood, Charles
Kurt Vonnegut, Jr. **4**:565

Wood, Karen
Kurt Vonnegut, Jr. **4**:565

Wood, Michael
Miguel Angel Asturias **3**:18
John Barth **2**:37
Donald Barthelme **2**:41
John Betjeman **6**:66
Adolfo Bioy Casares **4**:63
Elizabeth Bishop **9**:95
Jorge Luis Borges **2**:72
Anthony Burgess **8**:112
Italo Calvino **8**:131
Alejo Carpentier **11**:101
Evan S. Connell, Jr. **6**:116
Julio Cortázar **2**:105
Lawrence Durrell **6**:153
T. S. Eliot **10**:169
Stanley Elkin **4**:154
William Empson **8**:201
Carlos Fuentes **8**:225
John Gardner **5**:131; **8**:235
Juan Goytisolo **5**:150
Judith Guest **8**:253
John Hawkes **4**:219
Seamus Heaney **7**:147
Erica Jong **4**:264
Stanislaw Lem **8**:345
John Lennon and Paul
   McCartney **12**:365
José Lezama Lima **4**:289
Norman Mailer **3**:316
Thomas McGuane **3**:330

CRITIC INDEX

A. G. Mojtabai 9:385
Brian Moore 8:395
Berry Morgan 6:340
Vladimir Nabokov 2:303
Pablo Neruda 5:303
Hans Erich Nossack 6:365
Robert Nye 13:413
Joyce Carol Oates 2:316
Grace Paley 4:392
Octavio Paz 4:396
Peter Porter 13:451
Ezra Pound 2:345
Anthony Powell 3:403
Manuel Puig 3:407
Thomas Pynchon 2:357
Raymond Queneau 10:432
Philip Roth 4:456
Severo Sarduy 6:487
Isaac Bashevis Singer 3:459
Susan Sontag 13:517
Muriel Spark 5:399; 8:495
J.R.R. Tolkien 12:570
Charles Tomlinson 6:534
John Updike 2:445
Mario Vargas Llosa 6:546
Gore Vidal 8:525
Kurt Vonnegut, Jr. 3:503
Eudora Welty 2:463
Angus Wilson 3:535
Rudolph Wurlitzer 2:483

Wood, Peter
Peter De Vries 2:114
Alberto Moravia 2:293

Wood, Susan
Alice Adams 13:2
Penelope Gilliatt 10:230
John Wain 11:564

Wood, William C.
Wallace Markfield 8:380

Woodbery, W. Potter
John Crowe Ransom 11:467

Woodcock, George
Earle Birney 6:71, 75; 11:51
Camilo José Cela 13:145
Louis-Ferdinand Céline 9:158
Hugh Garner 13:236
Jean Genet 5:138
Denise Levertov 5:246
Hugh MacDiarmid 2:255
Brian Moore 1:225; 3:341
Herbert Read 4:441
Kenneth Rexroth 2:370, 371
Mordecai Richler 5:375
Rudy Wiebe 11:569

Woodfield, J.
Christopher Fry 10:200

Woodruff, Stuart C.
Shirley Jackson 11:301

Woods, Crawford
Ross Macdonald 3:308
Isaac Bashevis Singer 3:457
Hunter S. Thompson 9:526

Woods, William C.
Lisa Alther 7:13
Leon Uris 7:492

Woods, William Crawford
Jim Harrison 6:225

Woodward, C. Vann
William Styron 3:473

Wooten, Anna
Louise Glück 7:119

Worsley, T. C.
Stephen Spender 10:488

Worth, Katharine J.
Edward Bond 13:99

Worton, Michael J.
René Char 11:115

Wrenn, John H.
John Dos Passos 1:77

Wright, David
C. Day Lewis 6:126

Wright, George T.
W. H. Auden 1:10
T. S. Eliot 3:137

Wright, James
Richard F. Hugo 6:244

Wright, Richard
Carson McCullers 12:408

Wunderlich, Lawrence
Fernando Arrabal 2:16

Wyatt, David M.
Ernest Hemingway 8:288
Robert Penn Warren 8:541

Wylder, Delbert E.
William Eastlake 8:198

Wylie, Andrew
Giuseppe Ungaretti 11:556

Wylie, John Cook
Earl Hamner, Jr. 12:257

Wymard, Eleanor B.
Annie Dillard 9:177

Wyndham, Francis
Caroline Blackwood 6:79
Agatha Christie 12:120

Yagoda, Ben
Margaret Drabble 10:164
Henry Green 13:254

Yamashita Sumi
Agatha Christie 12:117

Yannella, Philip R.
Pablo Neruda 5:301

Yardley, Jonathan
Chinua Achebe 3:2
Kingsley Amis 2:8
Hal Bennett 5:59
Wendell Berry 4:59; 6:62
Doris Betts 3:73
Frederick Buechner 6:102
Harry Crews 6:117, 118
Peter De Vries 7:77
James Dickey 2:116
Frederick Exley 6:171
William Faulkner 3:158
Leslie A. Fiedler 13:213
Brian Glanville 6:202
James Hanley 5:167, 168
Jim Harrison 6:224
John Hersey 9:277
George V. Higgins 7:157
Diane Johnson 5:199
Madison Jones 4:263
Ward Just 4:266
Thomas Keneally 8:319; 10:299
John Knowles 4:271; 10:303
Bernard Malamud 2:267
Saul Maloff 5:271

Cormac McCarthy 4:342
James A. Michener 11:375
A. G. Mojtabai 5:293
Toni Morrison 4:365
Walker Percy 3:381
Piers Paul Read 4:444
J. R. Salamanca 4:462
John Seelye 7:406
Wilfrid Sheed 2:394; 4:488
Thomas Tryon 3:483
Jerome Weidman 7:518
Eudora Welty 2:462
Tom Wicker 7:533
Calder Willingham 5:511, 512

ya Salaam, Kalumu
Nikki Giovanni 4:189

Yates, Donald A.
Jorge Amado 13:11
John Dickson Carr 3:100
Carlos Fuentes 13:232

Yates, Norris W.
Günter Grass 4:203
James Thurber 5:433

Yenser, Stephen
Robert Lowell 3:305
James Merrill 3:335
Adrienne Rich 11:479
Robert Penn Warren 8:537, 540

Yglesias, Helen
Ludvík Vaculík 7:494

Yglesias, Jose
Christina Stead 2:421
Mario Vargas Llosa 6:547

Yglesias, Luis E.
Pablo Neruda 7:262; 9:398

Yoder, Edwin M.
MacKinlay Kantor 7:195

Yohalem, John
Richard Brautigan 5:70
James McCourt 5:277
Charles Webb 7:516

Yolen, Jane
Jamake Highwater 12:287

Young, Alan
Christopher Middleton 13:389

Young, Alan R.
Ernest Buckler 13:118, 119

Young, Charles M.
Mel Brooks 12:83
Patti Smith 12:543

Young, Dora Jean
Katherine Paterson 12:484

Young, Dudley
Carlos Castaneda 12:84

Young, Israel G.
Bob Dylan 12:180

Young, Marguerite
Carson McCullers 12:411
Mark Van Doren 10:495

Young, Peter
Andrei Voznesensky 1:348

Young, Philip
Ernest Hemingway 13:273

Young, Thomas Daniel
Donald Davidson 13:168
John Crowe Ransom 4:433, 436

Young, Vernon
W. H. Auden 2:28
George Mackay Brown 5:77
J. V. Cunningham 3:121
William Dickey 3:126
Lawrence Ferlinghetti 6:183
John Hollander 2:197
Richard F. Hugo 6:245
Galway Kinnell 13:320
Laurence Lieberman 4:291
Robert Lowell 5:258
W. S. Merwin 13:384
Pablo Neruda 1:247
Robert Pack 13:439
Nicanor Parra 2:331
Yannis Ritsos 6:464
Jon Silkin 2:396
Maura Stanton 9:508
James Tate 2:432
Diane Wakoski 2:459; 4:573
Ted Walker 13:566

Youree, Beverly B.
Melvin Berger 12:41

Yuill, W. E.
Heinrich Böll 11:52

Zabel, Morton Dauwen
Glenway Wescott 13:591

Zacharias, Lee
Truman Capote 13:139

Zak, Michele Wender
Doris Lessing 6:294

Zaller, Robert
Anaïs Nin 4:377

Zatlin, Linda G.
Isaac Bashevis Singer 1:312

Zaturenska, Marya
Laura Riding 7:373

Zavatsky, Bill
Ed Dorn 10:157

Zehr, David E.
Ernest Hemingway 8:286

Zeik, Michael
Thomas Merton 3:337

Zeller, Bernhard
Hermann Hesse 2:190

Zibart, Eve
Penelope Gilliatt 13:238

Zilkha, Michael
Mark Medoff 6:323

Zimbardo, Rose A.
Edward Albee 13:3

Zimmerman, Eugenia N.
Jean-Paul Sartre 9:472

Zimmerman, Paul
R. K. Narayan 7:256

Zimmerman, Paul D.
E. M. Forster 2:135
Lois Gould 4:199

Ziner, Feenie
Frank Bonham 12:53

Zinnes, Harriet
Robert Bly 1:37
Robert Duncan 1:83
Anaïs Nin 4:379; 8:425
Ezra Pound 3:399
May Swenson 4:533, 534
Mona Van Duyn 7:499

CRITIC INDEX

Ziolkowski, Theodore
  Heinrich Böll 2:67; 6:83
  Hermann Hesse 1:145, 146;
    3:248
  Hans Erich Nossack 6:364

Zivanovic, Judith
  Jean-Paul Sartre 9:470

Zivkovic, Peter D.
  W. H. Auden 3:23

Zivley, Sherry Lutz
  Sylvia Plath 9:431

Zolf, Larry
  Mordecai Richler 5:376

Zoss, Betty
  Jesse Jackson 12:290

Zucker, David
  Delmore Schwartz 10:464

Zuckerman, Albert J.
  Vassilis Vassilikos 4:551

Zuger, David
  Adrienne Rich 7:372

Zweig, Paul
  Richard Adams 5:6
  A. R. Ammons 5:29
  John Ashbery 2:18
  William Dickey 3:126
  Clayton Eshleman 7:100
  Allen Ginsberg 13:240
  Günter Grass 11:254
  John Hollander 5:186
  David Ignatow 7:181
  Kenneth Koch 8:322
  Philip Levine 4:286

  Peter Matthiessen 11:358
  Leonard Michaels 6:325
  Czeslaw Milosz 5:292
  Vladimir Nabokov 3:354
  Pablo Neruda 5:303
  Frank O'Hara 13:424
  George Oppen 7:284
  Charles Simic 6:502
  William Stafford 7:461
  Diane Wakoski 4:571
  James Wright 3:542

CRITIC INDEX

Cumulative Index to Authors

Abe, Kōbō 8
Abrahams, Peter 4
Abse, Dannie 7
Achebe, Chinua 1, 3, 5, 7, 11
Adamov, Arthur 4
Adams, Alice 6, 13
Adams, Richard 4, 5
Adler, Renata 8
Agnon, S(hmuel) Y(osef) 4, 8
Ai 4
Aiken, Conrad 1, 3, 5, 10
Akhmatova, Anna 11
Albee, Edward 1, 2, 3, 5, 9, 11, 13
Alberti, Rafael 7
Aldiss, Brian 5
Aleixandre, Vicente 9
Algren, Nelson 4, 10
Almedingen, E. M. 12
Alther, Lisa 7
Alvarez, A(lfred) 5, 13
Amado, Jorge 13
Ambler, Eric 4, 6, 9
Amichai, Yehuda 9
Amis, Kingsley 1, 2, 3, 5, 8, 13
Amis, Martin 4, 9
Ammons, A(rchie) R(andolph) 2, 3, 5, 8, 9
Anderson, Jon 9
Anderson, Roberta Joan
  See Mitchell, Joni 12
Andrews, Cecily Fairfield
  See West, Rebecca 7, 9
Andrić, Ivo 8
Angelou, Maya 12
Anouilh, Jean 1, 3, 8, 13
Antschel, Paul
  See Celan, Paul 10

Anthony, Florence
  See Ai 4
Antoninus, Brother
  See Everson, William 1, 5
Apple, Max 9
Aragon, Louis 3
Archer, Jules 12
Arden, John 6, 13
Arguedas, José María 10
Armah, Ayi Kwei 5
Arnow, Harriette 2, 7
Arp, Jean 5
Arrabal, Fernando 2, 9
Arthur, Ruth M(abel) 12
Ashbery, John 2, 3, 4, 6, 9, 13
Asimov, Isaac 1, 3, 9
Asturias, Miguel Ángel 3, 8, 13
Atwood, Margaret 2, 3, 4, 8, 13
Auchincloss, Louis 4, 6, 9
Auden, W(ystan) H(ugh) 1, 2, 3, 4, 6, 9, 11
Avison, Margaret 2, 4
Ayckbourn, Alan 5, 8
Aymé, Marcel 11
Ayrton, Michael 7
Azorín 11
Bagryana, Elisaveta 10
Bainbridge, Beryl 4, 5, 8, 10
Baker, Elliott 8
Baldwin, James 1, 2, 3, 4, 5, 8, 13
Ballard, J(ames) G(raham) 3, 6
Baraka, Imamu Amiri 2, 3, 5, 10
  See also Jones, (Everett) LeRoi 1
Barker, George 8
Barnes, Djuna 3, 4, 8, 11
Barnes, Peter 5

Barondess, Sue Kaufman
  See Kaufman, Sue 3, 8
Barth, John 1, 2, 3, 5, 7, 9, 10
Barthelme, Donald 1, 2, 3, 5, 6, 8, 13
Bassani, Giorgio 9
Baumbach, Jonathan 6
Beagle, Peter S(oyer) 7
Beattie, Ann 8, 13
Beauvoir, Simone de 1, 2, 4, 8
Becker, Jurek 7
Beckett, Samuel 1, 2, 3, 4, 6, 9, 10, 11
Beecher, John 6
Behan, Brendan 1, 8, 11
Belcheva, Elisaveta
  See Bagryana, Elisaveta 10
Bell, Marvin 8
Bellow, Saul 1, 2, 3, 6, 8, 10, 13
Benary-Isbert, Margot 12
Benchley, Peter 4, 8
Benedikt, Michael 4
Bennett, Hal 5
Berger, John 2
Berger, Melvin 12
Berger, Thomas 3, 5, 8, 11
Bergstein, Eleanor 4
Bernhard, Thomas 3
Berrigan, Daniel J. 4
Berry, Wendell 4, 6, 8
Berryman, John 1, 2, 3, 4, 6, 8, 10, 13
Betjeman, John 2, 6, 10
Betts, Doris 3, 6
Bienek, Horst 7, 11
Bioy Casares, Adolfo 4, 8, 13
Birney, (Alfred) Earle 1, 4, 6, 11
Bishop, Elizabeth 1, 4, 9, 13

Bishop, John 10
Blackburn, Paul 9
Blackmur, R(ichard) P(almer) 2
Blackwood, Caroline 6, 9
Blais, Marie-Claire 2, 4, 6, 13
Blake, Nicholas
  See Day Lewis, C(ecil) 1, 6
Blatty, William Peter 2
Blixen, Karen
  See Dinesen, Isak 10
Blume, Judy 12
Blunden, Edmund 2
Bly, Robert 1, 2, 5, 10
Bogan, Louise 4
Böll, Heinrich 2, 3, 6, 9, 11
Bond, Edward 4, 6, 13
Bonham, Frank 12
Bonnefoy, Yves 9
Bontemps, Arna 1
Booth, Martin 13
Borges, Jorge Luis 1, 2, 3, 4, 6, 8, 9, 10, 13
Bourjaily, Vance 8
Bowen, Elizabeth 1, 3, 6, 11
Bowers, Edgar 9
Bowles, Jane 3
Bowles, Paul 1, 2
Boyle, Kay 1, 5
Bradbury, Ray 1, 3, 10
Bragg, Melvyn 10
Braine, John 1, 3
Brand, Millen 7
Brathwaite, Edward 11
Brautigan, Richard 1, 3, 5, 9, 12
Brennan, Maeve 5
Breslin, Jimmy 4
Breton, André 2, 9
Brodsky, Joseph 4, 6, 13

Bromell, Henry 5
Bronk, William 10
Brooks, Gwendolyn 1, 2, 4, 5
Brooks, Mel 12
Brophy, Brigid 6, 11
Brosman, Catharine Savage 9
Broumas, Olga 10
Brown, George Mackay 5
Brown, Sterling 1
Brunner, John 8, 10
Buchheim, Lothar-Günther 6
Buck, Pearl S(ydenstricker) 7, 11
Buckler, Ernest 13
Buckley, William F(rank), Jr. 7
Buechner, (Carl) Frederick 2, 4, 6, 9
Buell, John 10
Bukowski, Charles 2, 5, 9
Bullins, Ed 1, 5, 7
Bunting, Basil 10
Burgess, Anthony 1, 2, 4, 5, 8, 10, 13
Burke, Kenneth 2
Burnshaw, Stanley 3, 13
Burr, Anne 6
Burroughs, William S(eward) 1, 2, 5
Busch, Frederick 7, 10
Butor, Michel 1, 3, 8, 11
Cabrera Infante, G(uillermo) 5
Cain, James M(allahan) 3, 11
Caldwell, Erskine 1, 8
Caldwell, Taylor 2
Calisher, Hortense 2, 4, 8
Callaghan, Morley 3
Calvino, Italo 5, 8, 11
Camus, Albert 1, 2, 4, 9, 11
Canby, Vincent 13
Canetti, Elias 3
Capote, Truman 1, 3, 8, 13
Carpentier, Alejo 8, 11
Carr, John Dickson 3
Carrier, Roch 13
Carroll, Paul Vincent 10
Carruth, Hayden 4, 7, 10
Carter, Angela 5
Casares, Adolfo Bioy
  See Bioy Casares, Adolfo 4
Casey, Michael 2
Casey, Warren 12
Cassill, R(onald) V(erlin) 4
Cassity, (Allen) Turner 6
Castaneda, Carlos 12
Causley, Charles 7
Cavanna, Betty 12
Cayrol, Jean 11
Cela, Camilo José 4, 13
Celan, Paul 10
Céline, Louis-Ferdinand 1, 3, 4, 7, 9
Char, René 9, 11
Charyn, Jerome 5, 8
Chase, Mary Ellen 2
Cheever, John 3, 7, 8, 11
Childress, Alice 12
Chitty, Sir Thomas Willes
  See Hinde, Thomas 11
Christie, Agatha 1, 6, 8, 12
Ciardi, John 10
Clark, Eleanor 5
Clark, Mavis Thorpe 12
Clarke, Arthur C(harles) 1, 4, 13

Clarke, Austin 6, 9
Clarke, Austin C(hesterfield) 8
Clavell, James 6
Coburn, D(onald) L(ee) 10
Cocteau, Jean 1, 8
Cohen, Arthur A(llen) 7
Cohen, Leonard 3
Colwin, Laurie 5, 13
Comfort, Alex(ander) 7
Compton-Burnett, Ivy 1, 3, 10
Condon, Richard 4, 6, 8, 10
Connell, Evan S(helby), Jr. 4, 6
Connelly, Marc(us) 7
Coover, Robert 3, 7
Corman, Cid (Sidney Corman) 9
Cormier, Robert 12
Cornwell, David
  See Le Carré, John 3, 5, 9
Corso, (Nunzio) Gregory 1, 11
Cortázar, Julio 2, 3, 5, 10, 13
Coward, Noel 1, 9
Cox, William Trevor
  See Trevor, William 7, 9
Cozzens, James Gould 1, 4, 11
Creasey, John 11
Creeley, Robert 1, 2, 4, 8, 11
Crews, Harry 6
Crichton, (John) Michael 2, 6
Cummings, E(dward) E(stlin) 1, 3, 8, 12
Cunningham, J(ames) V(incent) 3
Cunningham, Julia 12
Dahl, Roald 1, 6
Dahlberg, Edward 1, 7
Dannay, Frederick
  See Queen, Ellery 3, 11
Daryush, Elizabeth 6
Davenport, Guy, Jr. 6
Davidson, Donald 2, 13
Davidson, Sara 9
Davie, Donald 5, 8, 10
Davies, (William) Robertson 2, 7, 13
Dawson, Fielding 6
Day Lewis, C(ecil) 1, 6, 10
Deighton, Len 4, 7
Delany, Samuel R. 8
Delbanco, Nicholas 6, 13
Delibes, Miguel 8
DeLillo, Don 8, 10, 13
Dennis, Nigel 8
Destouches, Louis-Ferdinand
  See Céline, Louis-Ferdinand 1, 3, 4, 7, 9
De Vries, Peter 1, 2, 3, 7, 10
Dick, Philip K(indred) 10
Dickey, James 1, 2, 4, 7, 10
Dickey, William 3
Dickinson, Peter 12
Didion, Joan 1, 3, 8
Dillard, Annie 9
Dillard, R(ichard) H(enry) W(ilde) 5
Dinesen, Isak 10
Disch, Thomas M(ichael) 7
Doctorow, E(dgar) L(awrence) 6, 11
Donleavy, J(ames) P(atrick) 1, 4, 6, 10
Donoso, José 4, 8, 11
Doolittle, Hilda
  See H(ilda) D(oolittle) 3, 8

Dorn, Ed(ward) 10
Dos Passos, John 1, 4, 8, 11
Drabble, Margaret 2, 3, 5, 8, 10
Drexler, Rosalyn 2, 6
Duberman, Martin 8
Du Bois, W(illiam) E(dward) B(urghardt) 1, 2, 13
Dubus, Andre 13
Dudek, Louis 11
Dugan, Alan 2, 6
Duhamel, Georges 8
Dumas, Henry 6
du Maurier, Daphne 6, 11
Duncan, Robert 1, 2, 4, 7
Dunn, Douglas 6
Duras, Marguerite 3, 6, 11
Durrell, Lawrence 1, 4, 6, 8, 13
Dürrenmatt, Friedrich 1, 4, 8, 11
Dylan, Bob 3, 4, 6, 12
Eastlake, William 8
Eberhart, Richard 3, 11
Edson, Russell 13
Eigner, Larry (Laurence Eigner) 9
Eiseley, Loren 7
Ekwensi, Cyprian 4
Eliot, T(homas) S(tearns) 1, 2, 3, 6, 9, 10, 13
Elkin, Stanley 4, 6, 9
Elliott, George P(aul) 2
Ellis, A. E. 7
Ellison, Harlan 1, 13
Ellison, Ralph 1, 3, 11
Empson, William 3, 8
Endo Shusaku 7
Enright, D(ennis) J(oseph) 4, 8
Epstein, Daniel Mark 7
Eshleman, Clayton 7
Espriu, Salvador 9
Everson, William 1, 5
Evtushenko, Evgeni
  See Yevtushenko, Yevgeny 1, 3, 13
Ewart, Gavin 13
Exley, Frederick 6, 11
Fallaci, Oriana 11
Farigoule, Louis
  See Romains, Jules 7
Fariña, Richard 9
Farmer, Philip Jose 1
Farrell, J(ames) G(ordon) 6
Farrell, James T(homas) 1, 4, 8, 11
Faulkner, William 1, 3, 6, 8, 9, 11
Faust, Irvin 8
Federman, Raymond 6
Feiffer, Jules 2, 8
Feldman, Irving 7
Ferguson, Helen
  See Kavan, Anna 5, 13
Ferlinghetti, Lawrence 2, 6, 10
Fiedler, Leslie A(aron) 4, 13
Fisher, Vardis 7
Fleming, Ian 3
Forbes, Esther 12
Forrest, Leon 4
Forster, E(dward) M(organ) 1, 2, 3, 4, 9, 10, 13
Forsyth, Frederick 2, 5
Fournier, Pierre
  See Gascar, Pierre 11
Fowles, John 1, 2, 3, 4, 6, 9, 10

Fox, Paula 2, 8
Frame, Janet 2, 3, 6
Francis, Dick 2
Fraser, George MacDonald 7
Frayn, Michael 3, 7
French, Marilyn 10
Friedman, B(ernard) H(arper) 7
Friedman, Bruce Jay 3, 5
Friel, Brian 5
Friis-Baastad, Babbis 12
Frisch, Max 3, 9
Frost, Robert 1, 3, 4, 9, 10, 13
Fry, Christopher 2, 10
Fuchs, Daniel 8
Fuentes, Carlos 3, 8, 10, 13
Fugard, Athol 5, 9
Fuller, Roy 4
Gadda, Carlo Emilio 11
Gaddis, William 1, 3, 6, 8, 10
Gaines, Ernest J. 3, 11
Gallant, Mavis 7
Gallico, Paul 2
García Márquez, Gabriel 2, 3, 8, 10
Gardner, John 2, 3, 5, 7, 8, 10
Garfield, Leon 12
Garner, Hugh 13
Garnett, David 3
Garrett, George 3, 11
Garrigue, Jean 2, 8
Gascar, Pierre 11
Gass, William H(oward) 1, 2, 8, 11
Gelber, Jack 1, 6
Genet, Jean 1, 2, 5, 10
Gerhardi, William
  See Gerhardie, William 5
Gerhardie, William 5
Ghelderode, Michel de 6, 11
Gilliatt, Penelope 2, 10, 13
Gilroy, Frank D(aniel) 2
Ginsberg, Allen 1, 2, 3, 4, 6, 13
Ginzburg, Natalia 5, 11
Giono, Jean 4, 11
Giovanni, Nikki 2, 4
Giovene, Andrea 7
Gironella, José María 11
Glanville, Brian 6
Glassco, John 9
Glissant, Édouard 10
Glück, Louise 7
Godwin, Gail 5, 8
Gold, Herbert 4, 7
Goldbarth, Albert 5
Golding, William 1, 2, 3, 8, 10
Goldman, William 1
Gombrowicz, Witold 4, 7, 11
Gómez, de la Serna, Ramón 9
Goodman, Paul 1, 2, 4, 7
Gordimer, Nadine 3, 5, 7, 10
Gordon, Caroline 6, 13
Gordon, Mary 13
Gordone, Charles 1, 4
Gorenko, Anna Andreyevna
  See Akhmatova, Anna 11
Gould, Lois 4, 10
Goyen, (Charles) William 5, 8
Goytisolo, Juan 5, 10
Gracq, Julien 11
Grade, Chaim 10
Grass, Günter 1, 2, 4, 6, 11
Grau, Shirley Ann 4, 9
Graves, Robert 1, 2, 6, 11

Gray, Simon 9
Green, Hannah 3
    See also Greenberg, Joanne 7
Green, Henry 2, 13
Green, Julien 3, 11
Greenberg, Joanne 7
    See also Green, Hannah 3
Greene, Gael 8
Greene, Graham 1, 3, 6, 9
Gregor, Arthur 9
Grieve, C(hristopher) M(urray)
    See MacDiarmid, Hugh 2, 4,
    11
Griffiths, Trevor 13
Grigson, Geoffrey 7
Grumbach, Doris 13
Guare, John 8
Guest, Judith 8
Guillén, Jorge 11
Gunn, Bill 5
Gunn, Thom(son) 3, 6
H(ilda) D(oolittle) 3, 8
Hacker, Marilyn 5, 9
Hailey, Arthur 5
Haley, Alex 8, 12
Hall, Donald 1, 13
Hamburger, Michael 5
Hamill, Pete 10
Hamilton, Edmond 1
Hammett, (Samuel) Dashiell 3,
    5, 10
Hamner, Earl, Jr. 12
Hampton, Christopher 4
Handke, Peter 5, 8, 10
Hanley, James 3, 5, 8, 13
Hanson, Kenneth O. 13
Hardwick, Elizabeth 13
Harper, Michael S(teven) 7
Harris, Christie 12
Harris, MacDonald 9
Harrison, Jim 6
Hartley, L(eslie) P(oles) 2
Hawkes, John 1, 2, 3, 4, 7, 9
Hayden, Robert 5, 9
Heaney, Seamus 5, 7
Hébert, Anne 4, 13
Hecht, Anthony 8, 13
Hecht, Ben 8
Heifner, Jack 11
Heiney, Donald
    See Harris, MacDonald 9
Heinlein, Robert A(nson) 1, 3, 8
Heller, Joseph 1, 3, 5, 8, 11
Hellman, Lillian 2, 4, 8
Helprin, Mark 7, 10
Hemingway, Ernest 1, 3, 6, 8,
    10, 13
Heppenstall, (John) Rayner 10
Herbert, Frank 12
Herbert, Zbigniew 9
Herlihy, James Leo 6
Herriot, James 12
Hersey, John 1, 2, 7, 9
Hesse, Hermann 1, 2, 3, 6, 11
Heyen, William 13
Hibbert, Eleanor 7
Higgins, George V(incent) 4, 7,
    10
Highsmith, (Mary) Patricia 2, 4
Highwater, Jamake 12
Hill, Geoffrey 5, 8
Hill, Susan B. 4
Himes, Chester 2, 4, 7

Hinde, Thomas 6, 11
Hiraoka, Kimitake
    See Mishima, Yukio 2, 4, 6, 9
Hoban, Russell C(onwell) 7
Hobson, Laura Z(ametkin) 7
Hochhuth, Rolf 4, 11
Hochman, Sandra 3, 8
Hocking, Mary 13
Hoffman, Daniel 6, 13
Hoffman, Stanley 5
Hollander, John 2, 5, 8
Holt, Victoria
    See Hibbert, Eleanor 7
Holub, Miroslav 4
Hope, A(lec) D(erwent) 3
Hopkins, John 4
Horgan, Paul 9
Household, Geoffrey 11
Howard, Elizabeth Jane 7
Howard, Maureen 5
Howard, Richard 7, 10, 11
Hrabal, Bohumil 13
Hughes, (James) Langston 1, 5,
    10
Hughes, Richard 1, 11
Hughes, Ted 2, 4, 9
Hugo, Richard F(ranklin) 6
Hunt, E(verette) Howard 3
Hunter, Evan 11
Hurston, Zora Neale 7
Huxley, Aldous 1, 3, 4, 5, 8, 11
Ignatow, David 4, 7
Inge, William 1, 8
Innes, Michael
    See Stewart, J(ohn) I(nnes)
    M(ackintosh) 7
Ionesco, Eugène 1, 4, 6, 9, 11
Irving, John 13
Isherwood, Christopher 1, 9, 11
Jackson, Jesse 12
Jackson, Laura Riding
    See Riding, Laura 3, 7
Jackson, Shirley 11
Jacobs, Jim 12
Jacobson, Dan 4
Jarrell, Randall 1, 2, 6, 9, 13
Jeffers, Robinson 2, 3, 11
Jennings, Elizabeth 5
Jhabvala, Ruth Prawer 4, 8
Jiles, Paulette 13
Johnson, B(ryan) S(tanley) 6, 9
Johnson, Charles 7
Johnson, Diane 5, 13
Johnson, Marguerita
    See Angelou, Maya 12
Johnson, Pamela Hansford 1, 7
Johnson, Uwe 5, 10
Johnston, Jennifer 7
Jones, D(ouglas) G(ordon) 10
Jones, David 2, 4, 7, 13
Jones, Gayl 6, 9
Jones, James 1, 3, 10
Jones, (Everett) LeRoi 1
    See also Baraka, Imamu
    Amiri 2, 3, 5, 10
Jones, Madison 4
Jones, Mervyn 10
Jones, Preston 10
Jones, Robert F(rancis) 7
Jong, Erica 4, 6, 8
Jordan, June 5, 11
Josipovici, G(abriel) 6
Just, Ward 4

Justice, Donald 6
Kallman, Chester 2
Kaminsky, Melvin
    See Brooks, Mel 12
Kantor, MacKinlay 7
Karapánou, Margaríta 13
Kaufman, Sue 3, 8
Kavan, Anna 5, 13
Kawabata, Yasunari 2, 5, 9
Kazan, Elia 6
Kellogg, Marjorie 2
Kemelman, Harry 2
Keneally, Thomas 5, 8, 10
Kennedy, Joseph Charles
    See Kennedy, X. J. 8
Kennedy, William 6
Kennedy, X. J. 8
Kerouac, Jack 1, 2, 3, 5
Kerr, M. E. 12
Kerrigan, (Thomas) Anthony 4,
    6
Kesey, Ken 1, 3, 6, 11
Kessler, Jascha 4
Kettelkamp, Larry 12
Kherdian, David 6, 9
Killens, John Oliver 10
King, Francis 8
King, Stephen 12
Kingston, Maxine Hong 12
Kinnell, Galway 1, 2, 3, 5, 13
Kinsella, Thomas 4
Kirkup, James 1
Kirkwood, James 9
Knowles, John 1, 4, 10
Koch, Kenneth 5, 8
Koestler, Arthur 1, 3, 6, 8
Kohout, Pavel 13
Konrád, György 4, 10
Konwicki, Tadeusz 8
Kopit, Arthur 1
Kops, Bernard 4
Kosinski, Jerzy 1, 2, 3, 6, 10
Kotlowitz, Robert 4
Kotzwinkle, William 5
Krleža, Miroslav 8
Kroetsch, Robert 5
Krumgold, Joseph 12
Kumin, Maxine 5, 13
Kundera, Milan 4, 9
Kunitz, Stanley J(asspon) 6, 11
Kunze, Reiner 10
Kuzma, Greg 7
Lagerkvist, Pär 7, 10, 13
Lamming, George 2, 4
Landolfi, Tommaso 11
Larkin, Philip 3, 5, 8, 9, 13
Latham, Jean Lee 12
Lathen, Emma 2
Lattimore, Richmond 3
Laurence, (Jean) Margaret 3, 6,
    13
Lavin, Mary 4
Laye, Camara 4
Layton, Irving 2
Lear, Norman 12
Lebowitz, Fran 11
Le Carré, John 3, 5, 9
Lee, Don L. 2
    See also Madhubuti, Haki
    R. 6
Lee, Harper 12
Lee, Manfred B(ennington)
    See Queen, Ellery 3, 11

Leet, Judith 11
Léger, Alexis Saint-Léger
    See Perse, St.-John 11
LeGuin, Ursula K(roeber) 8, 13
Lehmann, Rosamond 5
Lelchuk, Alan 5
Lem, Stanislaw 8
L'Engle, Madeleine 12
Lengyel, József 7
Lennon, John 12
Lerman, Eleanor 9
Lessing, Doris 1, 2, 3, 6, 10
Levertov, Denise 1, 2, 3, 5, 8
Levin, Ira 3, 6
Levin, Meyer 7
Levine, Philip 2, 4, 5, 9
Lewis, C(ecil) Day
    See Day Lewis, C(ecil) 1, 6
Lewis, C(live) S(taples) 1, 3, 6
Lezama Lima, José 4, 10
Lieber, Joel 6
Lieberman, Laurence 4
Lima, José Lezama
    See Lezama Lima, José 4
Lind, Jakov 1, 2, 4
Livesay, Dorothy 4
Llewellyn, Richard 7
Llosa, Mario Vargas
    See Vargas Llosa, Mario 3, 6
Lloyd, Richard Llewellyn
    See Llewellyn, Richard 7
Logan, John 5
Lowell, Robert 1, 2, 3, 4, 5, 8, 9,
    11
Lurie, Alison 4, 5
Luzi, Mario 13
MacBeth, George 2, 5, 9
MacDiarmid, Hugh 2, 4, 11
Macdonald, Cynthia 13
MacDonald, John D(ann) 3
Macdonald, (John) Ross 1, 2, 3
MacEwen, Gwendolyn 13
MacInnes, Colin 4
MacLean, Alistair 3, 13
MacLeish, Archibald 3, 8
MacLennan, (John) Hugh 2
MacNeice, Louis 1, 4, 10
Madden, David 5
Madhubuti, Haki R. 6
    See also Lee, Don L. 2
Mailer, Norman 1, 2, 3, 4, 5, 8,
    11
Major, Clarence 3
Malamud, Bernard 1, 2, 3, 5, 8,
    9, 11
Mallet-Joris, Françoise 11
Maloff, Saul 5
Malraux, (Georges-) André 1, 4,
    9, 13
Malzberg, Barry N. 7
Mamet, David 9
Manning, Olivia 5
Mano, D. Keith 2, 10
Markandaya, Kamala
    (Purnalya) 8
Markfield, Wallace 8
Markham, Robert
    See Amis, Kingsley 1, 2, 3, 5,
    8
Marquand, John P(hillips) 2, 10
Márquez, Gabriel García
    See García Márquez,
    Gabriel 2, 3, 8, 10

Marsh, (Edith) Ngaio 7
Masefield, John 11
Mathews, Harry 6
Matthias, John 9
Matthiessen, Peter 5, 7, 11
Matute, Ana María 11
Maugham, W(illiam)
    Somerset 1, 11
Mauriac, Claude 9
Mauriac, François 4, 9
Mayne, William 12
McBain, Ed
    See Hunter, Evan 11
McCarthy, Cormac 4
McCarthy, Mary 1, 3, 5
McCartney, Paul 12
McClure, Michael 6, 10
McCourt, James 5
McCullers, (Lula) Carson 1, 4,
    10, 12
McElroy, Joseph 5
McEwan, Ian 13
McGahern, John 5, 9
McGuane, Thomas 3, 7
McHale, Tom 3, 5
McKuen, Rod 1, 3
McMurtry, Larry 2, 3, 7, 11
McNally, Terrence 4, 7
Meaker, Marijane
    See Kerr, M. E. 12
Medoff, Mark 6
Megged, Aharon 9
Mercer, David 5
Meredith, William 4, 13
Merrill, James 2, 3, 6, 8, 13
Merton, Thomas 1, 3, 11
Merwin, W(illiam)
    S(tanley) 1, 2, 3, 5, 8, 13
Mewshaw, Michael 9
Michaels, Leonard 6
Michaux, Henri 8
Michener, James A(lbert) 1, 5,
    11
Middleton, Christopher 13
Middleton, Stanley 7
Miguéis, José Rodrigues 10
Miles, Josephine 1, 2
Miller, Arthur 1, 2, 6, 10
Miller, Henry 1, 2, 4, 9
Miller, Jason 2
Miller, Walter M., Jr. 4
Milosz, Czeslow 5, 11
Mishima, Yukio 2, 4, 6, 9
Mitchell, Joni 12
Mohr, Nicholasa 12
Mojtabai, A(nn) G(race) 5, 9
Momaday, N(avarre) Scott 2
Montague, John 13
Montale, Eugenio 7, 9
Montgomery, Marion 7
Montherlant, Henri de 8
Moorcock, Michael 5
Moore, Brian 1, 3, 5, 7, 8
Moore, Marianne 1, 2, 4, 8, 10,
    13
Morante, Elsa 8
Moravia, Alberto 2, 7, 11
Morgan, Berry 6
Morgan, Robin 2
Morris, Steveland Judkins
    See Wonder, Stevie 12
Morris, Wright 1, 3, 7
Morrison, Toni 4, 10

Mortimer, Penelope 5
Moss, Howard 7
Mrożek, Sławomir 3, 13
Mueller, Lisel 13
Munro, Alice 6, 10
Murdoch, (Jean) Iris 1, 2, 3, 4,
    6, 8, 11
Musgrave, Susan 13
Nabokov, Vladimir 1, 2, 3, 6, 8,
    11
Nagy, László 7
Naipaul, V(idiadhar)
    S(urajprasad) 4, 7, 9, 13
Narayan, R(asipuram)
    K(rishnaswami) 7
Nemerov, Howard 2, 6, 9
Neruda, Pablo 1, 2, 5, 7, 9
Neville, Emily Cheney 12
Newby, P(ercy) H(oward) 2, 13
Newlove, Donald 6
Newman, Charles 2, 8
Ngugi, James 3, 7
    See also Wa Thiong'o, Ngugi 13
Nichols, Peter 5
Niedecker, Lorine 10
Nin, Anaïs 1, 4, 8, 11
Nissenson, Hugh 4, 9
Niven, Larry 8
Norton, Alice Mary
    See Norton, Andre 12
Norton, Andre 12
Nossack, Hans Erich 6
Nova, Craig 7
Nye, Robert 13
Oates, Joyce Carol 1, 2, 3, 6, 9,
    11
O'Brien, Darcy 11
O'Brien, Edna 3, 5, 8, 13
O'Brien, Flann 1, 4, 5, 7, 10
O'Brien, Tim 7
O'Casey, Sean 1, 5, 9, 11
O'Connor, (Mary) Flannery 1,
    2, 3, 6, 10, 13
Odets, Clifford 2
Ōe, Kenzaburō 10
O'Faolain, Julia 6
O'Faoláin, Seán 1, 7
O'Flaherty, Liam 5
O'Hara, Frank 2, 5, 13
O'Hara, John 1, 2, 3, 6, 11
Olesha, Yuri 8
Olsen, Tillie 4, 13
Olson, Charles 1, 2, 5, 6, 9, 11
Onetti, Juan Carlos 7, 10
O'Nolan, Brian
    See O'Brien, Flann 1, 4, 5, 7,
    10
Oppen, George 7, 13
Orton, Joe 4, 13
Osborne, John 1, 2, 5, 11
Otero, Blas de 11
Owens, Rochelle 8
Oz, Amos 5, 8, 11
Ozick, Cynthia 3, 7
Pack, Robert 13
Page, Jimmy 12
Page, P(atricia) K(athleen) 7
Palazzeschi, Aldo 11
Paley, Grace 4, 6
Parks, Gordon 1
Parra, Nicanor 2
Pasternak, Boris 7, 10

Patchen, Kenneth 1, 2
Paterson, Katherine 12
Paton, Alan 4, 10
Paz, Octavio 3, 4, 6, 10
Peake, Mervyn 7
Peck, John 3
Percy, Walker 2, 3, 6, 8
Perelman, S(idney) J(oseph) 3,
    5, 9
Perse, St.-John 4, 11
Peters, Robert L(ouis) 7
Petrakis, Harry Mark 3
Petry, Ann 1, 7
Piccolo, Lucio 13
Piercy, Marge 3, 6
Pincherle, Alberto
    See Moravia, Alberto 11
Piñero, Miguel 4
Pinget, Robert 7, 13
Pinsky, Robert 9
Pinter, Harold 1, 3, 6, 9, 11
Pirsig, Robert M(aynard) 4, 6
Plaidy, Jean
    See Hibbert, Eleanor 7
Plant, Robert 12
Plante, David 7
Plath, Sylvia 1, 2, 3, 5, 9, 11
Plomer, William 4, 8
Poirier, Louis
    See Gracq, Julien 11
Pomerance, Bernard 13
Ponge, Francis 6
Porter, Katherine Anne 1, 3, 7,
    10, 13
Porter, Peter 5, 13
Potok, Chaim 2, 7
Pound, Ezra 1, 2, 3, 4, 5, 7, 10,
    13
Powell, Anthony 1, 3, 7, 9, 10
Powers, J(ames) F(arl) 1, 4, 8
Pownall, David 10
Powys, John Cowper 7, 9
Price, (Edward) Reynolds 3, 6,
    13
Price, Richard 6, 12
Priestley, J(ohn) B(oynton) 2, 5,
    9
Pritchett, V(ictor) S(awden) 5,
    13
Prokosch, Frederic 4
Puig, Manuel 3, 5, 10
Purdy, A(lfred) W(ellington) 3, 6
Purdy, James 2, 4, 10
Puzo, Mario 1, 2, 6
Pym, Barbara 13
Pynchon, Thomas 2, 3, 6, 9, 11
Quasimodo, Salvatore 10
Queen, Ellery 3, 11
Queneau, Raymond 2, 5, 10
Quin, Ann 6
Quoirez, Françoise
    See Sagan, Françoise 3, 6, 9
Rabe, David 4, 8
Radvanyi, Netty Reiling
    See Seghers, Anna 7
Raine, Kathleen 7
Rand, Ayn 3
Randall, Dudley 1
Ransom, John Crowe 2, 4, 5, 11
Raphael, Frederic 2
Rattigan, Terence 7
Read, Herbert 4
Read, Piers Paul 4, 10

Reaney, James 13
Rechy, John 1, 7
Redgrove, Peter 6
Reed, Ishmael 2, 3, 5, 6, 13
Renault, Mary 3, 11
Rexroth, Kenneth 1, 2, 6, 11
Reyes y Basoalto, Ricardo
    Eliecer Neftali
    See Neruda, Pablo 1, 2, 5, 7, 9
Reynolds, Jonathan 6
Reznikoff, Charles 9
Rhys, Jean 2, 4, 6
Ribeiro, João Ubaldo 10
Ribman, Ronald 7
Rice, Elmer 7
Rich, Adrienne 3, 6, 7, 11
Richler, Mordecai 3, 5, 9, 13
Riding, Laura 3, 7
Ritsos, Yannis 6, 13
Rivers, Conrad Kent 1
Robbe-Grillet, Alain 1, 2, 4, 6,
    8, 10
Robbins, Harold 5
Robbins, Tom 9
Robinson, Jill 10
Rodgers, Mary 12
Rodgers, W(illiam) R(obert) 7
Rodríguez, Claudio 10
Roethke, Theodore 1, 3, 8, 11
Roiphe, Anne 3, 9
Romains, Jules 7
Ross, (James) Sinclair 13
Rossner, Judith 6, 9
Roth, Henry 2, 6, 11
Roth, Philip 1, 2, 3, 4, 6, 9
Rothenberg, Jerome 6
Rovit, Earl 7
Roy, Gabrielle 10
Rózewicz, Tadeusz 9
Ruark, Gibbons 3
Rudnik, Raphael 7
Ruiz, José Martínez
    See Azorín 11
Rukeyser, Muriel 6, 10
Rulfo, Juan 8
Ryan, Cornelius 7
Sábato, Ernesto 10
Sadoff, Ira 9
Safire, William 10
Sagan, Françoise 3, 6, 9
Salamanca, J(ack) R(ichard) 4
Salinger, J(erome) D(avid) 1, 3,
    8, 12
Salter, James 7
Samarakis, Antonis 5
Sanchez, Sonia 5
Sandburg, Carl 1, 4, 10
Saner, Reg(inald) 9
Sansom, William 2, 6
Sarduy, Severo 6
Saroyan, William 1, 8, 10
Sarraute, Nathalie 1, 2, 4, 8, 10
Sarton, (Eleanor) May 4
Sartre, Jean-Paul 1, 4, 7, 9, 13
Sayles, John 7, 10
Schaeffer, Susan Fromberg 6,
    11
Schevill, James 7
Schisgal, Murray 6
Schorer, Mark 9
Schulberg, Budd 7
Schulz, Charles M(onroe) 12
Schuyler, James 5

Schwartz, Delmore 2, 4, 10
Schwarz-Bart, André 2, 4
Schwarz-Bart, Simone 7
Sciascia, Leonardo 8, 9
Scott, Paul 9
Seelye, John 7
Seferiades, Giorgos Stylianou
    See Seferis, George 5, 11
Seferis, George 5, 11
Segal, Erich 3, 10
Seghers, Anna 7
Selby, Hubert, Jr. 1, 2, 4, 8
Sender, Ramón 8
Sexton, Anne 2, 4, 6, 8, 10
Shaffer, Peter 5
Shamlu, Ahmad 10
Shange, Ntozake 8
Shapiro, Karl 4, 8
Shaw, Irwin 7
Shaw, Robert 5
Sheed, Wilfrid 2, 4, 10
Shepard, Sam 4, 6
Sherwin, Judith Johnson 7
Sholokhov, Mikhail 7
Shulman, Alix Kates 2, 10
Shuttle, Penelope 7
Sigal, Clancy 7
Silkin, Jon 2, 6
Sillitoe, Alan 1, 3, 6, 10
Silone, Ignazio 4
Silverberg, Robert 7
Simak, Clifford D(onald) 1
Simenon, Georges 1, 2, 3, 8
Simic, Charles 6, 9
Simon, Claude 4, 9
Simon, (Marvin) Neil 6, 11
Simpson, Louis 4, 7, 9
Sinclair, Andrew 2
Sinclair, Upton 1, 11
Singer, Isaac Bashevis 1, 3, 6, 9,
    11
Singh, Khushwant 11
Sinyavsky, Andrei 8
Sissman, L(ouis) E(dward) 9
Sisson, C(harles) H(ubert) 8
Sitwell, Edith 2, 9
Sjöwall, Maj
    See Wahlöö, Per 7
Skelton, Robin 13
Slade, Bernard 11
Slavitt, David 5
Smith, Florence Margaret
    See Smith, Stevie 3, 8
Smith, Patti 12
Smith, Stevie 3, 8
Smith, William Jay 6
Snodgrass, W(illiam)
    D(eWitt) 2, 6, 10
Snow, C(harles) P(ercy) 1, 4, 6,
    9, 13
Snyder, Gary 1, 2, 5, 9
Sokolov, Raymond 7
Solwoska, Mara
    See French, Marilyn 10
Solzhenitsyn, Aleksandr
    I(sayevich) 1, 2, 4, 7, 9, 10

Sontag, Susan 1, 2, 10, 13
Sorrentino, Gilbert 3, 7
Souster, (Holmes) Raymond 5
Southern, Terry 7
Soyinka, Wole 3, 5
Spark, Muriel 2, 3, 5, 8, 13
Spender, Stephen 1, 2, 5, 10
Spicer, Jack 8
Spielberg, Peter 6
Spillane, Mickey 3, 13
Spivack, Kathleen 6
Stafford, Jean 4, 7
Stafford, William 4, 7
Stanton, Maura 9
Stead, Christina 2, 5, 8
Stegner, Wallace 9
Steinbeck, John 1, 5, 9, 13
Stern, Richard G(ustave) 4
Stevenson, Anne 7
Stewart, J(ohn) I(nnes)
    M(ackintosh) 7
Stewart, Mary 7
Stolz, Mary 12
Stone, Irving 7
Stone, Robert 5
Stoppard, Tom 1, 3, 4, 5, 8
Storey, David 2, 4, 5, 8
Storm, Hyemeyohsts 3
Stout, Rex 3
Strand, Mark 6
Stuart, Jesse 1, 8, 11
Styron, William 1, 3, 5, 11
Sukenick, Ronald 3, 4, 6
Summers, Hollis 10
Susann, Jacqueline 3
Sutton, Henry
    See Slavitt, David 5
Swados, Elizabeth 12
Swados, Harvey 5
Swenson, May 4
Symons, Julian 2
Tanizaki, Jun'ichiro 8
Tate, (John Orley) Allen 2, 4, 6,
    9, 11
Tate, James 2, 6
Tavel, Ronald 6
Taylor, Eleanor Ross 5
Taylor, Elizabeth 2, 4
Taylor, Peter 1, 4
Tennant, Emma 13
Tertz, Abram
    See Sinyavsky, Andrei 8
Theroux, Alexander 2
Theroux, Paul 5, 8, 11
Thomas, Audrey 7, 13
Thomas, D(onald) M(ichael) 13
Thomas, R(onald) S(tuart) 6, 13
Thompson, Hunter S(tockton) 9
Thurber, James 5, 11
Tindall, Gillian 7
Tolkien, J(ohn) R(onald)
    R(euel) 1, 2, 3, 8, 12
Tomlinson, (Alfred) Charles 2,
    4, 6, 13
Toomer, Jean 1, 4, 13
Tournier, Michel 6

Traven, B. 8, 11
Trevor, William 7, 9
Trilling, Lionel 9, 11
Trudeau, Garry 12
Tryon, Thomas 3, 11
Tunis, John R. 12
Turco, Lewis 11
Tutuola, Amos 5
Tyler, Anne 7, 11
Ungaretti, Giuseppe 7, 11
Updike, John 1, 2, 3, 5, 7, 9, 13
Uris, Leon 7
Ustinov, Peter 1
Vaculík, Ludvík 7
van der Post, Laurens 5
Van Doren, Mark 6, 10
Van Duyn, Mona 3, 7
Van Itallie, Jean-Claude 3
Van Peebles, Melvin 2
Van Vogt, A(lfred) E(lton) 1
Vargas Llosa, Mario 3, 6, 9, 10
Vassilikos, Vassilis 4, 8
Vidal, Gore 2, 4, 6, 8, 10
Viereck, Peter 4
Vittorini, Elio 6, 9
Voinovich, Vladimir 10
Vonnegut, Kurt, Jr. 1, 2, 3, 4, 5,
    8, 12
Voznesensky, Andrei 1
Wagman, Fredrica 7
Wagoner, David 3, 5
Wahlöö, Per 7
Wain, John 2, 11
Wakefield, Dan 7
Wakoski, Diane 2, 4, 7, 9, 11
Walcott, Derek 2, 4, 9
Waldman, Anne 7
Walker, Alice 5, 6, 9
Walker, Margaret 1, 6
Walker, Ted 13
Wallace, Irving 7, 13
Wallant, Edward Lewis 5, 10
Wambaugh, Joseph 3
Warner, Sylvia Townsend 7
Warren, Robert Penn 1, 4, 6, 8,
    10, 13
Wa Thiong'o, Ngugi 13
    See also Ngugi, James 3, 7
Waugh, Auberon 7
Waugh, Evelyn 1, 3, 8, 13
Waugh, Harriet 6
Webb, Charles 7
Weber, Lenora Mattingly 12
Weidman, Jerome 7
Weiss, Peter 3
Weiss, Theodore 3, 8
Welch, James 6
Weldon, Fay 6, 9, 11
Weller, Michael 10
Wells, Rosemary 12
Welty, Eudora 1, 2, 5
Wescott, Glenway 13
Wesker, Arnold 3, 5
Wesley, Richard 7
West, Jessamyn 7
West, Morris L(anglo) 6
West, Paul 7

West, Rebecca 7, 9
Westlake, Donald E(dwin) 7
Whalen, Philip 6
White, E(lwyn) B(rooks) 10
White, Patrick 3, 4, 5, 7, 9
Whitehead, E. A. 5
Whittemore, (Edward) Reed 4
Wicker, Tom 7
Wideman, J(ohn) E(dgar) 5
Wiebe, Rudy 6, 11
Wieners, John 7
Wiesel, Elie(zer) 3, 5, 11
Wight, James Alfred
    See Herriot, James 12
Wilbur, Richard 3, 6, 9
Wilder, Thornton 1, 5, 6, 10
Wilhelm, Kate 7
Willard, Nancy 7
Williams, John A(lfred) 5, 13
Williams, Jonathan 13
Williams, Tennessee 1, 2, 5, 7,
    8, 11
Williams, William Carlos 1, 2, 5,
    9, 13
Willingham, Calder 5
Wilson, Angus 2, 3, 5
Wilson, Brian 12
Wilson, Colin 3
Wilson, Edmund 1, 2, 3, 8
Wilson, Ethel Davis 13
Wilson, John Anthony Burgess
    See Burgess, Anthony 1, 2, 4,
    5, 8, 10
Wilson, Lanford 7
Wilson, Robert 7, 9
Winters, Yvor 4, 8
Wodehouse, P(elham)
    G(renville) 1, 2, 5, 10
Woiwode, Larry 6, 10
Wolfe, Tom 1, 2, 9
Wonder, Stevie 12
Woods, Helen Ferguson
    See Kavan, Anna 5, 13
Wouk, Herman 1, 9
Wright, Charles 6, 13
Wright, James 3, 5, 10
Wright, Judith 11
Wright, Richard 1, 3, 4, 9
Wright, Richard B(ruce) 6
Wurlitzer, Rudolph 2, 4
Yanovsky, Vassily
    S(emenovich) 2
Yates, Richard 7, 8
Yehoshua, Abraham B. 13
Yerby, Frank G(arvin) 1, 7
Yevtushenko, Yevgeny 1, 3, 13
Yglesias, Helen 7
Yorke, Henry Vincent
    See Green, Henry 2, 13
Young, Andrew 5
Yurick, Sol 6
Zaturenska, Marya 6, 11
Zimmerman, Robert
    See Dylan, Bob 12
Zindel, Paul 6
Zukofsky, Louis 1, 2, 4, 7, 11